standard catalog of

CHRYSLER

1914-2000

D1476928

Second Edition

Edited by James T. Lenzke

Published by

**krause
publications**

700 E. State Street • Iola, WI 54990-0001
Telephone: 715/445-2214

Please call or write for our free catalog.
Our toll-free number to place an order or obtain a free catalog is 800-258-0929
or please use our regular business telephone 715-445-2214
for editorial comment and further information.

Library of Congress Catalog Number: 90-60577
ISBN: 0-87341-882-4

Printed in the United States of America

CONTENTS

CATALOG STAFF

EDITOR: James T. Lenzke
COVER DESIGN: Kim Schierl
COLOR GALLERY DESIGN: Donna Mummery
PAGE DESIGN: Jeannie Altenburg
                             Patsy Howell
                             Shelly Johnson
                             Kay Sommerfeld
                             Wendy Wendt

FOREWORD

The concept behind Krause Publications' *Standard Catalog of American Cars* series has been to compile massive amounts of information about motor vehicles and present it in a standard format that the hobbyist, historian, collector, or professional dealer can use to answer some commonly asked questions.

These questions include: What year, make, and model is the vehicle? What did it sell for new? How rare is it? What is special about it? Some answers are provided by photos and others by the fact-filled text.

Chester L. Krause, founder of Krause Publications, is responsible for the concept of creating the *Standard Catalog* series covering American automobiles. David V. Brownell undertook preliminary work on the project while serving as editor of *Old Cars Weekly* during the 1970s. Then-editor John A. Gunnell assumed the project in 1978. The first *Standard Catalog*, covering post-World War II models (1946-1975), was originally published in 1982 and is now in its fourth (1997) edition. Beverly Raye Kimes researched and wrote *Standard Catalog of American Cars 1805-1942*, which was first published in 1985 and is now in its third (1996) printing. Edited by Gunnell and first published in 1987, *Standard Catalog of American Light-Duty Trucks 1896-1986* was reprinted in 1993. Further spin-offs in the *Standard Catalog* series have subsequently included *American Motors 1902-1987, Imported Cars 1946-1990, Independents,* and marque-specific *Catalogs* covering all Chevrolet and Ford products, as well as Buick, Cadillac, Oldsmobile, and Pontiac.

Currently, the *Standard Catalog* series enjoys excellent sales (as evidenced by the frequent reprintings of its individual titles) in the old-vehicle hobby and provides a wealth of detailed information that car and truck collectors, hobbyists, restorers, and investors will not find offered by any other publishing house.

The scope of these *Catalogs* has been to cover the major manufacturers that have survived to the end of the millennium—DaimlerChrysler, Ford, General Motors, BMW, and others—as well as companies that they have absorbed and companies no longer with us today. Independent carmakers such as Checker, Hudson, Kaiser-Frazer, Nash, Packard, Studebaker, and Willys are included in the earlier *Catalogs*, as well as more than 200 producers of low-volume nameplates from Airscoot to Yenko. In each case, the information compiled encompasses a physical description, list of known equipment and original specifications, technical data, historical footnotes, and—in most cases—an indication of the car's current "ballpark" value.

For each *Catalog*, compilations were made by an experienced editorial team consisting of the automotive staff of Krause Publications and numerous other contributors who are recognized experts on various marques or specific areas of automotive history. A major benefit of combining teamwork with expertise has been the gathering of many siginificant facts about each model.

No claims are made that these *Catalogs* are history textbooks or encyclopedias. Nor are they repair manuals. They are, rather, intended as contributions to the pursuit of knowledge about many of the wonderful cars and trucks that have been produced by the primary industrialized nations of the world since 1805. They are much larger in size, broader in scope, and more deluxe in format than any previously published collectors' guides, buyers' digests, or pricing guides.

The long-range goal of Krause Publications is to make all of these *Catalogs* as nearly perfect as possible. At the same time, we expect such reference works will always raise new questions and bring forth new facts that were not previously unearthed in the countless hours of research by our team. All contributors are requested to maintain an ongoing file of new research, corrections, and additional photos that can be used to refine and expand future editions.

We thank the editors and contributors to the three-volume *Standard Catalog of American Cars* series for providing much of the material contained herein. Special thanks are extended to Sherwood Kahlenberg, John R. Smith, and Charles Webb for their particular expertise regarding Chrysler products. For it is through the research and editing efforts of all of these that we produce this *Standard Catalog of Chrysler 1914-2000* with the assurance that the great bulk of information from those three *Catalogs* combined here is accurate and well-researched.

1955 Chrysler C-300 two-door hardtop (OCW)

Should you have access to expanded information that you wish to share, please don't hesitate to contact the editors, in care of Krause Publications, *Standard Catalog of Chrysler 1914-2000*, 700 E. State St., Iola, WI 54990-0001.

Other *Catalogs* currently available include: *Standard Catalog of American Cars 1805-1942, Standard Catalog of American Cars 1946-1975, Standard Catalog of American Cars 1976-1999, Standard Catalog of American Light-Duty Trucks 1896-1986, Standard Catalog of 4x4s 1945-1993, Standard Catalog of Chevrolet 1912-1998, Standard Catalog of Ford 1903-1998, Standard Catalog of American Motors 1902-1987, Standard Catalog of Independents,* and *Catalogs* dealing specifically with Buick (1903-1999), Cadillac (1903-1990), Oldsmobile (1897-1997), and Pontiac (1926-1995).

For ordering information and current prices, please call 1-800-258-0929, Code AUBR, or write to Krause Publications, Automotive Books Dept. AUBR, 700 E. State St., Iola, WI 54990-0001.

ABBREVIATIONS

A/C . . . . Air conditioning
A.L.A.M. . . . Assoc. of Licensed Automobile Mfgs.
Adj . . . . Adjustable
Aero . . . . Fastback
AM, FM, AM/FM . . . Radio types
Amp. . . . . Ampere
Approx . . . . Approximate
Auto. . . . . Automatic
Auxil. . . . . Auxiliary
Avail. . . . . Available
Avg. . . . . Average
BxS . . . . Bore x Stroke
Base . . . . Base (usually lowest-priced) model
Bbl. . . . . . . Barrel (carburetor)
B.H.P. . . . . . Brake horsepower
BSW . . . . Black sidewall (tire)
Bdrcl. . . . . Broadcloth
Bus. . . . . Business (i.e. Business Coupe)
C.C. . . . . Close-coupled
Cabr. . . . . Cabriolet
Carb. . . . . Carburetor
Cass. . . . Cassette (tape player)
CB . . . . Citizens Band (radio)
CEO . . . Chief Executive Officer
C.I.D. Cubic inch displacement
Clb. . . . . . . Club (Club Coupe)
Clth. . . . . . . Cloth-covered roof
Col. . . . . Colonnade (coupe body style)
Col. . . . . Column (shift)
Conv/Conv. . . . . . . Convertible
Conv. Sed . . Convertible Sedan
Corp Limo Corporate Limousine
Cpe . . . . Coupe
C.R. . . . . . . Compression ratio
Cu. In. . . . . Cubic Inch (displacement)
Cust. . . . . Custom
Cyl. . . . . Cylinder
DeL. . . . . DeLuxe
DFRS . . Dual facing rear seats
Dia . . . . Diameter
Disp . . . . Displacement
Dr. . . . . Door

Ea . . . . Each
E.D. . . . . Enclosed Drive
E.F.I. . Electronic Fuel Injection
E.W.B. . . . Extended Wheelbase
Eight . . . . Eight-cylinder engine
8-tr . . . . Eight-track
Encl. . . . . Enclosed
EPA . Environmental Protection Agency
Equip. . . . . Equipment
Exc. . . . . Except
Exec. . . . . Executive
F . . . . Forward (3f - 3 forward speeds)
F.W.D. . . . . . Four-wheel drive
Fam. . . . . Family
Fml . . . . Formal
"Four" . . . Four-cylinder engine
4WD . . . . . Four-wheel drive
4-dr. . . . . Four-door
4-spd. . . . . Four-speed (transmission)
4V . . . . Four-barrel carburetor
FP . . . . Factory Price
Frsm . . . . Foursome
Frt . . . . Front
FsBk . . . . Fastback
Ft. . . . . Foot/feet
FWD . . . . . Front-wheel drive
GBR . . . . Glass-belt radial (tire)
Gal. . . . . Gallon
GT . . . . Gran Turismo
G.R. . . . . Gear Ratio
H . . . . Height
H.B. . . . . Hatchback
H.D. . . . . Heavy Duty
HEI . . . . High Energy Ignition
H.O. . . . . High-output
H.P. . . . . Horsepower
HT/HT Hdtp. . . . . . . Hardtop
Hr . . . . Hour
Hwg . . . . Highway
I . . . . Inline
I.D. . . . . Identification
In . . . . Inches
Incl. . . . Included or Including
Int. . . . . Interior

Lan . Landau (coupe body style)
Lb. or Lbs. . Pound-feet (torque)
LH . . . . Left hand
Lift. . . . . Liftback
Limo . . . . Limousine
LPO . Limited production option
Ltd. . . . . Limited
Lthr. Trm. . . . . . Leather Trim
L.W.B. . . . . Long Wheelbase
Mag. . . . . Wheel style
Mast. or Mstr. . . . . Master
Max. . . . . Maximum
MFI . . . . . Multi-port Injection
M.M. . . . . Millimeters
MPG . . . . . . Miles per gallon
MPH . . . . Miles per hour
N/A . . . . Not Available (or not applicable)
NC . . . . No charge
N.H.P. . . . . Net horsepower
No. . . . . Number
Notch or N.B. . . . . Notchback
OHC . . Overhead cam (engine)
OHV . . Overhead valve (engine)
O.L. . . . . Overall length
OPEC . . . . Organization of Petroleum Exporting Countries
Opt . . . . Optional
OSRV . . . . . Outside rear view
O.W. or O/W . . Opera Window
OWL . Outline White Letter (tire)
Oz. . . . . Ounce
P . . . . Passenger
PFI . . . . . . Port fuel injection
Phae . . . . Phaeton
Pkg. . . . . Package
Prod. . . . . Production
Pwr. . . . . Power
R . . . . Reverse
RBL . . . Raised black letter (tire)
Rbt. . . . . Runabout
Rds . . . . Roadster
Reg . . . . Regular
Remote . . . . . Remote control
Req. . . . . Requires
RH . . . . Right hand drive
Roch. . . Rochester (carburetor)

R.P.M. . Revolutions per minute
RPO . Regular production option
R.S. or R/S . . . . . . Rumbleseat
RV . . . . . . Recreational vehicle
RWL . . Raised white letter (tire)
S.A.E. . . . Society of Automobile Engineers
SBR . . . . . . Steel-belted radials
Sed . . . . Sedan
SFI . . . Sequential fuel injection
"Six" . . . . . Six-cylinder engine
S.M. . . . . Side Mount
Spd . . . . Speed
Spec . . . . Special
Spt. . . . . Sport
Sq. In. . . . . Square inch
SR . . . . Sunroof
Sta. Wag. . . . . Station Wagon
Std. . . . . Standard
Sub. . . . . Suburban
S.W.B. . . . . Short Wheelbase
Tach . . . . Tachometer
Tax. . . . . Taxable (horsepower)
TBI Throttle body (fuel) injection
Temp. . . . . Temperature
3S . . . . Three-seat
Trans. . . . . Transmission
Trk. . . . . Trunk
2-Dr. . . . . Two-door
2 V . . . Two-barrel (carburetor)
2WD . . . . . Two-wheel drive
Univ . . . . Universal
Utl. . . . . Utility
V. . . . . Venturi (carburetor)
V-6, V-8 . . . . . Vee-type engine
VIN . . . . Vehicle Identification Number
W . . . . With
W/O . . . . Without
Wag. . . . . Wagon
w (2w) . Window (two window)
W.B. . . . . Wheelbase
Woodie . . Wood-bodied car
WLT . . . . White-letter tire
WSW . . . . White sidewall (tire)
W.W. . . . . Whitewalls
W. Whl. . . . . Wire wheel

PHOTO CREDITS

Whenever possible, throughout this Catalog, we have striven to illustrate all cars with photographs that show them in their most original form. Each photo caption ends in an alphabetical code that identifies the photo source. These codes are interpreted below.

(AA) Applegate & Applegate
(FR) Fred Roe
(HAC) Henry Austin Clark, Jr.
(IMS) Indianapolis Motor Speedway
(JAC) John A. Conde

The editor wishes to extend special thanks to the editors of all previous editions of Krause Publications' *Standard Catalog of American Cars* series for their original research and for obtaining many of these photos of Chrysler products over the years.

(JB) Jim Benjaminson
(JL) John Lee
(OCW) Old Cars Weekly
(PH) Phil Hall
(TVB) Terry V. Boyce

HOW TO USE THIS CATALOG

APPEARANCE AND EQUIPMENT: Word descriptions identify cars by styling features, trim and (to a lesser extent) interior appointments. Most standard equipment lists begin with the lowest-priced model, then enumerate items added by upgrade models and option packages. Most lists reflect equipment available at model introductions.

I.D. DATA: Information is given about the Vehicle Identification Number (VIN) found on the dashboard. VIN codes show model or series, body style, engine size, model year and place built. Beginning in 1981, a standardized 17 symbol VIN is used. Earlier VINs are shorter. Locations of other coded information on the body and/or engine block may be supplied. Deciphering those codes is beyond the scope of this catalog.

SPECIFICATIONS CHART: The first column gives series or model numbers. The second gives body style numbers revealing body type and trim. Not all cars use two separate numbers. Some sources combine the two. Column three tells number of doors body style and passenger capacity ('4-dr Sed-6P' means four door sedan, six-passenger). Passenger capacity is normally the maximum. Cars with bucket seats hold fewer. Column four gives suggested retail l price of the car when new, on or near its introduction date, not including freight or other charges. Column five gives you the original shipping weight. The sixth column provides model year production totals or refers to notes below the chart. In cases where the same car came with different engines, a slash is used to separate factory prices and shipping weights for each version. Unless noted, the amount on the left of the slash is for the smallest, least expensive engine. The amount on the right is for the least costly engine with additional cylinders. 'N/A' means data not available.

ENGINE DATA: Engines are normally listed in size order with smallest displacement first. A 'base' engine is the basic one offered in each model at the lowest price. 'Optional' describes all alternate engines, including those that have a price listed in the specifications chart. (Cars that came with either a six or V-8, for instance, list the six as 'base' and V-8 'optional'). Introductory specifications are used, where possible.

CHASSIS DATA: Major dimensions (wheelbase, overall length, height, width and front/rear tread) are given for each model, along with standard tire size. Dimensions sometimes varied and could change during a model year.

TECHNICAL DATA: This section indicates transmissions standard on each model, usually including gear ratios; the standard final drive axle ratio (which may differ by engine or transmission); steering and brake system type; front and rear suspension description; body construction; and fuel tank capacity.

OPTIONAL EQUIPMENT LISTS: Most listings begin with drivetrain options (engines, transmissions, steering/suspension and mechanical components) applying to all models. Convenience/appearance items are listed separately for each model except where several related models are combined into a single listing. Option packages are listed first, followed by individual items in categories: comfort/convenience, lighting/mirrors entertainment, exterior, interior, then wheels/tires. Contents of some option packages are listed prior to the price: others are described in the Appearance/Equipment text. Prices are suggested retail, usually effective early in the model year. ('N/A' indicates prices are unavailable.) Most items are Regular Production Options (RPO), rather than limited-production (LPO), special-order or dealer-installed equipment. Many options were available only on certain series or body types or in conjunction with other items. Space does not permit including every detail.

HISTORY: This block lists introduction dates, total sales and production amounts for the model year and calendar year. Production totals supplied by auto-makers do not always coincide with those from other sources. Some reflect shipments from the factories rather than actual production or define the model year a different way.

HISTORICAL FOOTNOTES: In addition to notes on the rise and fall of sales and production, this block includes significant statistics, performance milestones, major personnel changes, important dates and places and facts that add flavor to this segment of America's automotive heritage.

1959 DODGE

CORONET SERIES — (6-CYL/V-8) — The new Dodges were easily recognizable as Dodges, even though the styling of the 1957-1958 models was simply exaggerated. The fins were more rakish, the brows over the headlights were much larger and the entire car was longer, lower and wider than in previous years. The grille was a modification of the split bumper grille bar theme backed by an aluminum mesh. The great horsepower race of the 1950s was over, but Dodge continued to build high-performance cars. This year's offering in the high horsepower category was the first of the famous 383-cid V-8 engines, which Chrysler used for more than a decade. The 383 boasted 345 hp in its Super D-500 format. Also new for 1959 was the Swivel-Seat option. A simple motion of the lever, at the side of the seat, and the unit swung out to meet the occupant. Dodge experimented with self-leveling rear air suspension, called LevelFlite, as an option. The Coronet continued to be the base trim level and included chrome windshield and rear window moldings, a single horizontal chrome strip along the bodyside and chrome trim at the lower edge of the fender fin. The Dodge name, in block letters, appeared on the trunk lid (directly below a combination Dodge crest and trunk handle). The Coronet name, in script, appeared on the front fender. At midyear, a "Silver Challenger" option was available on the two-door sedan.

CORONET I.D. DATA: Six-cylinder-powered Coronets assembled in Detroit were numbered M302100001 and up. Those assembled in Newark were numbered M305100001 and up. V-8-powered models assembled in Detroit were numbered M312100001 and up. Those assembled in Newark were numbered M315100001 and up. V-8 models assembled in California were numbered M314100001 and up.

CORONET SERIES

Model No.	Body/ Style No.	Body Type & Seating	Factory Price	Shipping Weight	Prod. Total
MD1/2L	41	4-dr Sed-6P	2537/2657	3425/3615	8,103
MD1/2L	21	2-dr Clb Sed-6P	2466/2586	3375/3565	5,432
MD1/2L	23	2-dr Lancer HT-6P	2594/2714	3395/3590	2,151
MD2L	43	4-dr Lancer HT-6P	2792	3620	8,946
MD2L	27	2-dr Conv-6P	3039	3775	1,840

Note 1: A total of 96,782 Coronet models were produced during calendar year 1959. Exactly 151,851 Dodges were built for the 1959 model year. In slightly rounded off figures, the model year output of Coronets was counted at 96,900 units.

Note 2: Prices and weights to left of slash marks are for sixes, to right for V-8s.

ENGINES:

(Six) L-head. Inline. Cast iron block. Displacement: 230 cid. Bore and stroke: 3.25 x 4.38 inches. Compression ratio: 8.0:1. Brake hp: 135 at 3600 rpm. Four main bearings. Solid valve lifters. Carburetor: Stromberg one-barrel.

(Red Ram V-8) Overhead valve. Cast iron block. Displacement: 326 cid. Bore and stroke: 3.95 x 3.31 inches. Compression ratio: 9.2:1. Brake hp: 255 at 4400 rpm. Five main bearings. Hydraulic valve lifters. Carburetor: Carter two-barrel.

(Ram Fire V-8) Overhead valve. Cast iron block. Displacement: 361 cid. Bore and stroke: 4.12 x 3.38 inches. Compression ratio: 10.1:1. Brake hp: 295 at 4600 rpm on Royal and Sierra models, 305 at 4600 rpm on Custom Royal and Custom Sierra models. Five main bearings. Hydraulic valve lifters. Carburetor: (295 hp) Carter two-barrel; (305 hp) Carter four-barrel.

(D-500 V-8) Overhead valve. Cast iron block. Displacement: 383 cid. Bore and stroke: 4.25 x 3.38 inches. Compression ratio: 10.1:1. Brake hp: 320 at 4600 rpm. Five main bearings. Hydraulic valve lifters. Carburetor: Carter four-barrel.

(Super D-500 V-8) Overhead valve. Cast iron block. Displacement: 383 cid. Bore and stroke: 4.25 x 3.38 inches. Compression ratio: 10.0:1. Brake hp: 345 at 5000 rpm. Five main bearings. Hydraulic valve lifters. Carburetor: Two Carter four-barrel.

CHASSIS FEATURES: Wheelbase: 122 inches. Overall length: 217.4 inches (216.4 inches on station wagons). Tires: (Coronet) 7.50 x 14; (all others) 8.00 x 14 tubeless black sidewalls.

CONVENIENCE OPTIONS: TorqueFlite transmission, all V-8 models ($226.90). PowerFlite transmission, Coronet and Royal ($189.10). Power steering, V-8 only ($92.15). Power brakes ($42.60). Power window lifts ($102.30). Power tailgate window, two-seat wagons ($34.10). Six-Way power seat ($95.70). Dual exhaust ($30.90). Push-button radio ($86.50). Rear speaker ($14.95). Radio with dual antenna ($14.05). Heater and defroster ($93.55). Tires: white sidewall 7.50 x 14, Coronet except convertible ($33.35); 8.00 x 14, other models ($41.75). Two-tone paint standard colors ($18.55); Deluxe colors ($34.10). Solex glass ($42.60); windshield only ($18.55). Back-up lights ($10.70). Wheel covers ($14.30); Deluxe ($30.50). Electric clock ($15.95). Windshield washer ($11.80). Variable speed windshield wipers ($6.60). Windshield washer and Vari-speed wipers ($18.25). Front and rear Air Foam seat ($10.70). Undercoating ($12.85). Air conditioning with heater, V-8s only ($468.55); wagons ($662.95). Carpets ($11.80). Rear window defroster ($20.60). Sure-Grip differential, all except convertible ($49.70). Padded instrument panel ($20.00). Padded sun visors ($8.00). Automatic headlight beam changer ($49.70). Heavy-duty 70-amp battery ($8.60). Custom trim package, Coronet except convertible ($56.00). D-500 383 cid/320 hp four-barrel carb engine with dual exhaust and TorqueFlite transmission, Coronet convertible ($368.00); Coronet V-8 except convertible ($398.90); Royal and Sierra station wagons ($328.10); Custom Royal convertible ($273.35); Custom Royal and Custom station wagons ($304.15); Super D-500 345 hp engine, Coronet V-8 except convertible ($540.45); Coronet convertible ($509.60); Royal and Sierra station wagons ($469.65); Custom Royal convertible ($414.95); Custom Royal and Custom station wagons ($445.75). LevelFlite, V-8s only ($127.55). Outside rearview mirror ($6.45). Remote control left outside rearview mirror ($17.75); right ($8.60). Co-Pilot speed warning device ($12.85). Storage compartment with lock, two-seat station wagons ($28.20). Swivel seat ($70.95).

HISTORICAL FOOTNOTES: The 1959 Dodges were introduced on Oct. 10, 1958. Model year production peaked at 151,851 units, of which approximately 15,600 were sixes and 136,200 were V-8 powered. Dodge assembled 13,515 two-door sedans; 65,752 four-door sedans; 29,610 two-door hardtops; 16,704 four-door hardtops; 2,733 convertibles; 13,515 four-door station wagons and 10,022 four-door three-seat station wagons in the 1959 model year. Dodge Division's calendar year output was 192,798 units this year, accounting for a 3.44 percent share of the total market. M.C. Patterson continued as president and general manager of Dodge Division this season. For the model run, about 94 percent of all Dodges had automatic transmissions; 68.9 percent had power steering; 27.4 percent had power brakes; 23.2 percent had windshield washers; 84.7 percent had back-up lights. 4.5 percent had air conditioning and only 0.7 percent had the rare air suspension, an option that did not last long.

BODY STYLES

Body style designations describe the shape and character of an automobile. In earlier years automakers exhibited great imagination in coining words to name their products. This led to names that were not totally accurate. Many of those **"car words"** were taken from other fields: mythology, carriage building, architecture, railroading and so on. Therefore, there was no "correct" automotive meaning other than that brought about through actual use. Inconsistencies have persisted into the recent period, though some of the imaginative terms of past eras have faded away. One manufacturer's "sedan" might resemble another's "coupe." Some automakers have persisted in describing a model by a word different from common usage, such as Ford's label for Mustang as a "sedan." Following the demise of the true pillarless hardtop (two- and four-door) in the mid-1970s, various manufacturers continued to use the term "hardtop" to describe their offerings, even though a "B" pillar was part of the newer car's structure and the front door glass may not always have been frameless. Some took on the description "pillared hardtop" or "thin pillar hardtop" to define what observers might otherwise consider, essentially, a sedan. Descriptions in this catalog generally follow the manufacturers' choice of words, except when they conflict strongly with accepted usage.

One specific example of inconsistency is worth noting: the description of many hatchback models as "three-door" and "five-door," even though that extra "door" is not an entryway for people. While the 1976-1999 domestic era offered no real phaetons or roadsters in the earlier senses of the words, those designations continue to turn up now and then, too.

TWO-DOOR (CLUB) COUPE: The Club Coupe designation seems to come from club car, describing the lounge (or parlor car) in a railroad train. The early postwar club coupe combined a shorter-than-sedan body structure with the convenience of a full back seat, unlike the single- seat business coupe. That name has been used less frequently in the 1976-99 period, as most notchback two-door models (with trunk rather than hatch) have been referred to as just "coupes." Moreover, the distinction between two-door coupes and two-door sedans has grown fuzzy.

TWO-DOOR SEDAN: The term sedan originally described a conveyance seen only in movies today: a wheeless vehicle for one person, borne on poles by two men, one ahead and one behind. Automakers pirated the word and applied it to cars with a permanent top, seating four to seven (including driver) in a single compartment. The two-door sedan of recent times has sometimes been called a pillared coupe, or plain coupe, depending on the manufacturer's whim. On the other hand, some cars commonly referred to as coupes carry the sedan designation on factory documents.

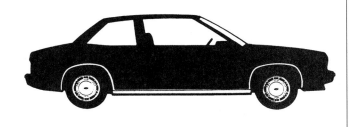

TWO- DOOR (THREE-DOOR) HATCHBACK COUPE: Originally a small opening in the deck of a sailing ship, the term "hatch" was later applied to airplane doors and to passenger cars with rear liftgates. Various models appeared in the early 1950s. but weather-tightness was a problem. The concept emerged again in the early 1970s, when fuel economy factors began to signal the trend toward compact cars. Technology had remedied the sealing difficulties. By the 1980s, most manufacturers produced one or more hatchback models, though the question of whether to call them "two-door" or "three-door" never was resolved. Their main common feature was the lack of a separate trunk "Liftback" coupes may have had a different rear-end shape, but the two terms often described essentially the same vehicle.

TWO-DOOR FASTBACK: By definition, a fastback is any automobile with a long, moderately curving, downward slope to the rear of the roof. This body style relates to an interest in streamlining and aerodynamics and has gone in and out of fashion at various times. Some (Mustangs for one) have grown quite popular. Others have tended to turn customers off. Certain fastbacks are, technically, two-door sedans or pillared coupes. Four-door fastbacks have also been produced. Many of these (such as Buick's late 1970s four-door Century sedan) lacked sales appeal. Fastbacks may or may not have a rear-opening hatch.

TWO-DOOR HARDTOP: The term hardtop, as used for postwar cars up to the mid-1970s, describes an automobile styled to resemble a convertible, but with a rigid metal (or fiberglass) top. In a production sense, this body style evolved after World War II, first called "hardtop convertible." Other generic names have included sports coupe, hardtop coupe or pillarless coupe. In the face of proposed rollover standards, nearly all automakers turned away from the pillarless design to a pillared version by 1976-77.

COLONNADE HARDTOP: In architecture, the term colonnade describes a series of columns, set at regular intervals, usually supporting an entablature, roof or series of arches. To meet federal rollover standards in 1974 (standards that never emerged), General Motors introduced two- and four-door pillared body types with arch-like quarter windows and sandwich type roof construction. They looked like a cross between true hardtops and miniature limousines. Both styles proved popular (especially the coupe with louvered coach windows and canopy top) and the term colonnade was applied. As their "true" hardtops disappeared, other manufacturers produced similar bodies with a variety of quarter-window shapes and sizes. These were known by such terms as hardtop coupe, pillared hardtop or opera-window coupe.

FORMAL HARDTOP: The hardtop roofline was a long-lasting fashion hit of the postwar car era. The word "formal" can be applied to things that are stiffly conservative and follow the established rule. The limousine, being the popular choice of conservative buyers who belonged to the Establishment, was looked upon as a formal motorcar. So when designers combined the lines of these two body styles, the result was the Formal Hardtop. This style has been marketed with two or four doors, canopy and vinyl roofs (full or partial) and conventional or opera-type windows, under various trade names. The distinction between a formal hardtop and plain pillared-hardtop coupe (see above) hasn't always followed a strict rule.

CONVERTIBLE: To Depression-era buyers, a convertible was a car with a fixed-position windshield and folding top that, when raised, displayed the lines of a coupe. Buyers in the postwar period expected a convertible to have roll-up windows, too. Yet the definition of the word includes no such qualifications. It states only that such a car should have a lowerable or removable top. American convertibles became extinct by 1976, except for Cadillac's Eldorado, then in its final season. In 1982, though, Chrysler brought out a LeBaron ragtop; Dodge a 400, and several other companies followed it a year or two later.

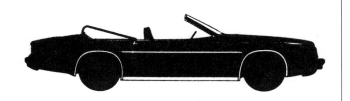

ROADSTER: This term derives from equestrian vocabulary where it was applied to a horse used for riding on the roads. Old dictionaries define the roadster as an open-type car designed for use on *ordinary* roads, with a single seat for two persons and, often, a rumbleseat as well. Hobbyists associate folding windshields and side curtains (rather than roll-up windows) with roadsters, although such qualifications stem from usage, not definition of term. Most recent roadsters are either sports cars, small alternative-type vehicles or replicas of early models.

RUNABOUT: By definition, a runabout is the equivalent of a roadster. The term was used by carriage makers and has been applied in the past to light, open cars on which a top is unavailable or totally an add-on option. None of this explains its use by Ford on certain Pinto models. Other than this inaccurate usage, recent runabouts are found mainly in the alternative vehicle field, including certain electric-powered models.

FOUR-DOOR SEDAN: If you took the wheels off a car, mounted it on poles and hired two weightlifters (one in front and one in back) to carry you around in it, you'd have a true sedan. Since this idea isn't very practical, it's better to use the term for an automobile with a permanent top (affixed by solid pillars) that seats four or more persons, including the driver, on two full-width seats.

FOUR-DOOR HARDTOP: This is a four-door car styled to resemble a convertible, but having a rigid top of metal or fiberglass. Buick introduced a totally pillarless design in 1955. A year later most automakers offered equivalent bodies. Four-door hardtops have also been labeled sports sedans and hardtop sedans. By 1976, potential rollover standards and waning popularity had taken their toll. Only a few makes still produced a four-door hardtop and those disappeared soon thereafter.

FOUR-DOOR PILLARED HARDTOP: Once the "true" four-door hardtop began to fade away, manufacturers needed another name for their luxury four-doors. Many were styled to look almost like the former pillarless models, with thin or unobtrusive pillars between the doors. Some, in fact, were called "thin-pillar hardtops." The distinction between certain pillared hartops and ordinary (presumably humdrum) sedans occasionally grew hazy.

FOUR-DOOR (FIVE-DOOR) HATCHBACK: Essentially unknown among domestic models in the mid-1970s, the four-door hatchback became a popular model as cars grew smaller and front-wheel-drive versions appeared. Styling was similar to the original two-door hatchback, except for — obviously — two more doors. Luggage was carried in the back of the car itself, loaded through the hatch opening, not in a separate trunk.

LIMOUSINE: This word's literal meaning is "a cloak." In France, limousine means any passenger vehicle. An early dictionary defined limousine as an auto with a permanently enclosed compartment for 3-5, with a roof projecting over a front driver's seat. However, modern dictionaries drop the separate compartment idea and refer to limousines as large luxury autos, often chauffeur-driven. Some have a movable division window between the driver and passenger compartments, but that isn't a requirement.

TWO-DOOR STATION WAGON: Originally defined as a car with an enclosed wooden body of paneled design (with several rows of folding or removable seats behind the driver), the station wagon became a different and much more popular type of vehicle in the postwar years. A recent dictionary states that such models have a larger interior than sedans of the line and seats that can be readily lifted out, or folded down, to facilitate light trucking. In addition, there's usually a tailgate, but no separate luggage compartment. The two-door wagon often has sliding or flip-out rear side windows.

FOUR-DOOR STATION WAGON: Since functionality and adaptability are advantages of station wagons, four-door versions have traditionally been sales leaders. At least they were until cars began to grow smaller. This style usually has lowerable windows in all four doors and fixed rear side glass. The term "suburban" was almost synonymous with station wagon at one time, but is now more commonly applied to light trucks with similar styling. Station wagons have had many trade names, such as Country Squire (Ford) and Sport Suburban (Plymouth). Quite a few have retained simulated wood paneling, keeping alive the wagon's origin as a wood-bodied vehicle.

LIFTBACK STATION WAGON: Small cars came in station wagon form too. The idea was the same as bigger versions, but the conventional tailgate was replaced by a single lift-up hatch. For obvious reasons, compact and subcompact wagons had only two seats instead of the three that had been available in many full-size models.

DIMENSIONS

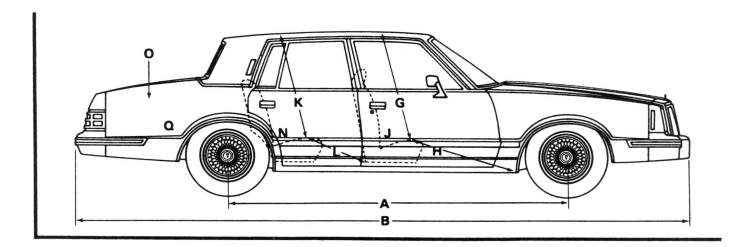

Exterior:
A Wheelbase
B Overall length
C Width
D Overall height
E Tread, front
F Tread, rear

Interior — front:
G Headroom
H Legroom
I Shoulder room
J Hip room

Interior — rear:
K Headroom
L Legroom
M Shoulder room
N Hip room
O Trunk capacity (liters/cu. ft.)
P Cargo index volume (liters/cu. ft.)
Q Fuel tank capacity (liters/gallons)

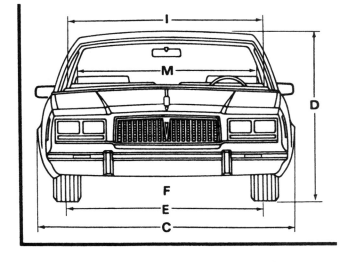

Chrysler

CHRYSLER
1924-2000

The evolution of the Chrysler represents one of the more stirring sagas in the history of the American automobile. First, there is the fact that no other individual since has managed to do what Walter Percy Chrysler was the last to accomplish in the mid-1920s—and that is, simply to start a new automobile company and to make it survive. But second, there is the marvelous tale about how he managed to do it. From an early career as a farm hand, grocery boy, silverware salesman, and round house sweeper for the Union Pacific, Walter Chrysler had moved up to Pittsburgh plant manager of the American Locomotive Company when his talents first came to the attention of the automobile industry and he was brought to Flint, Michigan as the works manager for Buick in 1910. In 1919, when he slammed the door on his way out of General Motors, he was Buick's president. Though he had liked the job, he found working with William C. Durant taxed his patience beyond the endurable. He left Buick a wealthy man, Durant later commenting that he had paid Chrysler $10 million for his stock, enough to provide a comfortable kitty with which to start his own automobile company. One suspects Walter Chrysler had that in mind all along. But first, another job from Chase National Bank beckoned that promised to be both challenging (taking over management of the faltering automotive business of John North Willys) and lucrative (Chrysler's fee was a cool million dollars a year). At this point, mid-1919, the Willys lineup was focused on three cars: an Overland to compete with the Model T Ford, a line of Willys-Knight fours, and a Willys Six then under development and under wraps in the former Duesenberg plant in Elizabeth, New Jersey. Working on the last-named car for Willys Corporation (the holding company for all John North Willys' interests, and separate from Willys-Overland) were three former Studebaker engineers named Fred Zeder, Owen Skelton, and Carl Breer. Neither the low-priced field nor sleeve-valve engines piqued Chrysler's interest much, which meant he didn't care particularly about the Overland or the Willys-Knight. But that Willys Six prototype in the Elizabeth plant intrigued him. Indeed, during 1920, rumors floated that the car would be introduced as the Chrysler Six, and at least one published ad alluded to that effect as late as January 1921, which provides an idea of the power Chrysler was exerting at the time over Willys affairs.

1924 Chrysler Six Model B-70 touring (OCW)

But Chrysler remained with Willys for only two years, and then left ostensibly because his job of streamlining the organization was finished, or conceivably because he thought Willys was. From banker friends he immediately launched himself into a similar salvage operation with another faltering automobile company, the Maxwell Motor Corporation, which had recently been merged, none too happily, with Chalmers. Meanwhile, the Willys Six prototype had not yet been marketed because John North Willys remained in a fight to wrest control of Willys from the banks, which he deftly accomplished by maneuvering Willys-Overland stock and moving his Willys Corporation holding company into receivership. This resulted in the Elizabeth plant and the prototype inside being sent to the auction block.

1931 Chrysler Imperial LeBaron roadster (OCW)

And there, ironically, Walter Chrysler (now Maxwell's president) was outbid by his old boss William C. Durant, who had meanwhile been kicked out of General Motors and was beginning his second empire. Fortunately for Chrysler, Durant wanted a car that was bigger and more expensive than the Willys Six that he had bought with the Elizabeth factory, and consequently that prototype was extensively revamped to become the new Flint. This left Zeder, Skelton, and Breer free to develop their original design further, which they did at the enthusiastic urging of Walter Chrysler. By mid-1923 they were installed in the Chalmers plant in Detroit, where the Chalmers car was by now being phased out of production. In January 1924, at the Commodore Hotel in New York City, the new Chrysler was introduced. By the end of December, 32,000 had been sold, a new first-year sales record in the industry. What the Chrysler represented was something new in America. Its six-cylinder L-head engine displaced only 201.5 cubic inches, but with a 4.7:1 compression ratio (the industry norm was 4.0:1) developed 68 bhp at 3,200 rpm. And the Chrysler could be had for $1,395. It was America's first medium-priced car with a high-compression engine. Nor was that all; the specification also included four-wheel hydraulic brakes, aluminum pistons, full-pressure lubrication, and tubular front axle among other features never before combined on a volume-produced car. Seventy miles an hour was the Chrysler's comfortable top speed. As Fortune magazine noted a few years later, here was a car perfectly suited to the '20s, "a period when desires had supplanted needs . . . an era when a car which could give for $1,500 the 'thrills' of a car of $5,000 was precisely what the people who could buy it would most wish to buy." In competition the Chrysler fared nicely. On July 16, 1924, Ralph De Palma drove one of the cars to the top of Mt. Wilson, not only winning the event and bettering the previous stock car record by over two minutes, but faster by more than a minute than the previous race car record, too. At the Culver City Board Speedway in 1925, De Palma and the Chrysler won a 1,000-mile stock car race at a 76.3-mph average. The Chrysler was the first American car to

contest Le Mans, competing there four times, finishing third and fourth in 1928. But the contest of most interest to Walter P. Chrysler was within the industry itself. In mid-1925 he took his first step, with the organization of Chrysler Corporation, succeeding Maxwell. By year's end, "in response to a public demand for another car bearing the Chrysler name," as the press release put it, a four-cylinder Chrysler was introduced. It was really just an updated Maxwell, a fact that went unmentioned, of course. Also introduced for 1926 were two more Chrysler sixes, one a price echelon below the original, the other the Imperial, a 92-hp car designed to compete with Lincolns and the like. By 1927, in three short years, Walter Chrysler had moved up from the bottom rung (32nd place) in the industry to fourth. In 1928 he purchased Dodge, introduced the Plymouth and the DeSoto, and slipped neatly into third. In 1929, Chryslers were styled longer, lower, and with a thin-profile radiator that would be widely copied in Europe—and on the now lengthened Imperial chassis. Chrysler entered the custom field with limited production series of designs by LeBaron, Locke, and Dietrich. By 1931, most Chrysler models were straight-eights. In 1934 the Airflow arrived. It was perhaps Chrysler's first mistake. A revolutionary car, and a most interesting one, the Airflow had begun in a miniature wind tunnel with Chrysler's engineering triumvirate—or the Three Musketeers, as Zeder, Breer, and Skelton were now known—determining that a zeppelin-like oval tapering to the rear was the automobile's optimum shape. From this followed an engine placed over the axle, not behind it, and a welded chassis/body construction with the passenger compartment cradled between the axles. Body styling was the province of Oliver Clark (who had designed the first Chrysler), though aerodynamic considerations really styled the Airflow. Its hood cascaded into a grille that looked like a waterfall with flush-mounted headlamps (designed by Breer and consulting engineer C. Harold Wills) on each side. A curved, one-piece windshield was an innovation on the Custom Imperial model.

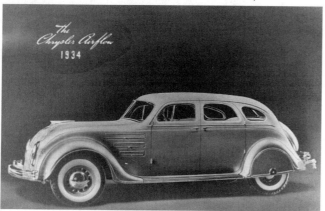

1934 Chrysler Airflow four-door sedan (OCW)

"The beauty of nature itself" was the way Chrysler described the Airflow's appearance; "breathlessly different-looking" was the assessment of a Harper's Bazaar fashion artist. Unfortunately, the vast majority of the public found it bizarre, or just plain ugly. Combined with this were production delays occasioned by the necessity for retooling, which resulted in rumors spreading that the cars were faulty. The Airflow was a disaster in the marketplace. In 1934, only 11,292 of them were sold in three model lines, 2-1/2 times less than the single conventional Chrysler in the model lineup that year. Attempts to make the Airflow more palatable in appearance followed, plus the addition of more comely Airstream models, though it was 1937 before all Chryslers became conventionally styled again. By then Ray Dietrich had been brought in as chief body designer, with Oliver Clark moving up to executive rank. In 1940-'41, Ralph Roberts of LeBaron designed two gorgeous idea cars—the Thunderbolt (a retractable hardtop coupe) and the Newport (a dual cowl pha-

eton)—of which six examples each were built and displayed around the country. On August 18, 1940, Walter P. Chrysler died. Five years earlier he had relinquished the presidency of his corporation to right-hand-man Kaufman Thuma Keller. It would be K.T. Keller who would lead Chrysler into the postwar era.

1939 Chrysler New Yorker four-door sedan (OCW)

Chrysler Corporation was heavily involved with war production even prior to the curtailment of automobile manufacturing in February 1942. As the war drew to a close, both in Europe and the Pacific, plans were put into effect to resume the production of automobiles, based mainly on the designs of 1942.

Chrysler's start-up time for retooling, plus nationwide materials shortages, delayed the onset of the manufacturing until the end of 1945. The 1946 models were carried forward, virtually unchanged, through 1948. This was due to the unparalleled demand for vehicles in the immediate postwar period. This demand, coupled with the long lead time for complete model changeovers, prevented major styling advances until the 1949 model year.

1948 Chrysler Windsor Traveler four-door sedan (OCW)

The new Town & Country series showed one marked departure from earlier, prewar patterns. Formerly relegated only to station wagon models, the unique, wood-bodied line now adopted four-door sedan and convertible styles in place of station wagons. In addition, a small number of two-door hardtops were built off the convertible's body and one prototype two-door Brougham was built. A roadster design was contemplated, but never left the drawing board.

The 1949 Chryslers, while all-new, did not move as far ahead, stylingwise, as the rest of the industry. As a result, Chrysler remained 12th ranked in sales standings for the model year.

The same basic "25th Anniversary"-type body was carried through 1954. The major advance, during 1949-'54, was introduction of the Firepower V-8 with hemispherical combustion chambers. The same year, 1951, the corporation pioneered popular acceptance of power steering. A minor face-lift occurred in 1953, when the one-piece curved windshield was reintroduced. In midyear 1953, the fully-automatic PowerFlite transmission was introduced.

1951 Chrysler New Yorker convertible (OCW)

In 1955, Chrysler registered its Imperial as a separate division. Even so, the acceptance of a brand new, "100-Million-Dollar Look," rendered by designer Virgil Exner, moved Chrysler Division to ninth rank on the industry's sales charts. The year 1955 also brought another important advance, introduction of the mighty Chrysler 300 "Letter Car" series, which was immediately embraced by enthusiastic buyers. The Chrysler 300 earned championship titles in both NASCAR Grand National and AAA stock car racing.

In 1956, a turnabout took place and Chrysler sales plummeted to their lowest level in a decade. This happened in spite of slightly revised styling that brought with it a new, more tasteful finned look. The second Chrysler Letter Car, dubbed the 300B, was offered in two horsepower ratings. This helped it bring more fame to the company through repeated achievements on the nation's stock car racing tracks. The 300B broke the world's passenger car speed record in competition at Daytona Beach, Fla., with an average of nearly 140 mph.

By 1957, a new direction in styling was unleashed by Exner and his talented staff. This new "Forward Look," with its graceful tail fins, took numerous styling awards. The major chassis development, which was to remain a Chrysler forte into the 1980s (on some models), was a torsion bar front suspension. Motor Trend magazine awarded the 1957 Chrysler its highest honor—the "Car of the Year" title. Its superb handling qualities and engineering characteristics were the main reasons for the award.

Model year 1958 brought a minor face-lifting, from the standpoint of styling. At this time, the first-generation hemispherical (Hemi) engine was in its last year. An electronic fuel-injection system, designed by Bendix, was briefly made available as an option on the latest 300D Letter Car. For the following season, 1959 styling was given another period of exposure, before another new look was introduced. There was, however, a brand-new Chrysler engine introduced this year, called the "Golden Lion" V-8. It was larger in displacement than its predecessor and used a wedge-shaped combustion chamber design.

1958 Chrysler New Yorker convertible (OCW)

A new era for Chrysler began in 1960, as a switch to building unitized bodies was made. These "Uni-Body" cars were styled with the customary tail fins, although they were more rakish in overall design. A major engineering feat was the introduction of ram-induction manifolding. On the corporate level, Lester L. Colbert replaced William C. Newberg as president of Chrysler around midyear.

The 1961 models were again slightly face-lifted. The major degree of change was reflected in frontal appearance and at the rear, with alterations to the headlights and taillamps. Sales improved sufficiently to boost Chrysler Division to 11th position on industry sales charts.

By 1962, tail fins were no longer the order of the day. A new, mid-priced 300 series was offered, along with the luxurious, high-performance Letter Car 300 series.

Styling in 1963 was totally revamped. A clean, slab-sided look evolved. To the dismay of management, sales dropped and Chrysler remained America's 11th largest automaker. A five-year or 50,000-mile warranty on all drivetrain components became a marketing tool to boost confidence and spur extra sales. A slight styling revision was seen for 1964 and sales climbed over 30 percent. Unfortunately, the company remained at the number 11 slot.

Freshly styled 1965 models helped set a blistering, all-time sales record. National economic gains, combined with the extended warranty program, established an excellent business climate and generated a 65-percent sales gain. But, thereafter, styling stayed basically unchanged until the 1969 model year. And why not, since Chrysler had continued to break records, reaching more and more buyers every season. For the 1966 to 1968 period, the company placed ninth or 10th in sales each year.

1966 Chrysler New Yorker four-door hardtop (OCW)

The 1969 model year debuted with a popular, new "fuselage look" and yet Chrysler dropped back to 11th position. A slight economic recession, in conjunction with only minor 1970 changes, caused Chrysler deliveries to nosedive 30 percent. For the first time since the 1964 model year, the division marketed fewer than 200,000 cars.

John J. Riccardo was installed as Chrysler president in early 1970. The so-called fuselage look remained in vogue. It lasted until the announcement of 1974 models. Prior to its disappearance, a 1973 production model became the one-millionth car ever to bear the Chrysler nameplate.

1970 Chrysler Newport Custom four-door hardtop (OCW)

A total redesign highlighted the introduction of the 1974 Chryslers. The new cars were shorter, wider, and lower. Sales, however, fell off drastically, mainly as a result of the Arab oil embargo against the United States. From that point on, all manufacturers de-emphasized styling changes, and Chrysler's designs remained somewhat static until 1975. According to reports of the day, the changing expectations caused by economic and political turmoil were soon to bring a major revamping of the Chrysler Corporation.

While all American-built cars shrunk in size and power over the 1976-'86 decade, none changed more than Chrysler. Riding a 124-inch wheelbase, on a platform introduced two years earlier, the '76 Chrysler Newport and New Yorker Brougham carried on the long tradition of luxury (and excess). Both continued the pillarless four-door hardtop a little longer, while Town & Country wagons displayed their own brand of deluxe styling. Imperial, the poshest of all, had been dropped after 1975; but New Yorker slipped neatly into its niche with an increase in luxury extras. New Yorker's engine was the huge 440-cid V-8, producing 205 hp. Chryslers, then, were big and expensive. With one exception, that is, the Canadian-built Cordoba coupe, introduced in 1975. It cost as much as a Newport, but sat on a 115-inch wheelbase. Engine choices reached up to a high-performance 400-cid V-8, rated at 240 hp, and Cordoba sold better than all other Chryslers put together. Strong promotion by actor Ricardo Montalban didn't hurt. Still, overall sales slipped downward, as they had in 1975.

The following year brought another surprise; the luxury mid-size LeBaron, smallest Chrysler ever, was added as a 1977-1/2 model. Designed as a rival to Cadillac's Seville and Lincoln's new Versailles (as well as Mercedes-Benz), LeBaron was actually a derivative of the Dodge Aspen/Plymouth Volare duo. No matter, though; Seville and Versailles had origins in "lesser" models, too. LeBaron offered one unique mechanical change, turning the familiar Chrysler torsion bars from their customary position to transverse mounting. While Cordoba sales sagged a bit, both the new LeBaron and carryover full-size models performed well in the marketplace.

1977 Chrysler New Yorker Brougham four-door hardtop (OCW)

Full-size Chryslers kept their ample dimensions for 1978, even though General Motors models had been downsized a year earlier. The big Town & Country station wagon was dropped, but its name continued on a smaller LeBaron version. New Yorker Broughams could have a Salon decor package with silver paint and vinyl roof, while TorqueFlite transmissions added a lockup torque converter. Strong LeBaron sales couldn't keep the corporate total from slipping downward.

All-new Newport/New Yorker four-doors emerged for 1979, reduced to 118.5 inches in wheelbase. Both the 400- and 440-cid V-8s disappeared, leaving a 360 as the biggest engine. Newport actually came with a standard Slant Six. Both models still managed to look big, even though they lost over 800 pounds. New Yorkers featured hidden headlamps and could be had with a Fifth Avenue Edition option highlighted by cream/beige body paint. Cordoba brought the "300" nameplate

back to life temporarily on an option package with a 195-hp engine, but it was a pale imitation of past 300 glories. While the smaller full-size models sold better than their predecessors, Cordoba slipped again.

A revised 1980 Cordoba dropped down to a 112.7-inch wheelbase—same as LeBaron—and carried a standard six-cylinder engine. The most desirable example might be the Corinthian Edition, especially with a high-output V-8 under the hood. LeBaron adopted a luxurious Fifth Avenue package similar to New Yorker's, with formal roofline and carriage roof, but only 654 were installed. This was a tough year for the industry as a whole, but worse yet for Chrysler, whose financial troubles were beginning to get plenty of publicity. Sales fell by one-third. Among other troubles, Chrysler just wasn't responding to the public demand for greater fuel efficiency. Lee Iacocca was now in charge, though. As just about everyone in the world became aware over the next few years, his administration managed to turn things around for Chrysler, with the help of government-guaranteed loans that were paid back in full much sooner than many had predicted.

Another Canadian-built model appeared the next year, reviving a familiar name. The ultra-luxurious "bustleback" Imperial carried a modest engine, though, a fuel-injected 318-cid V-8. In fact, that was now the biggest engine in the Chrysler lineup. In an attempt to attract a few younger customers, Cordoba turned to a more sporty "LS" model with 300-style cross-bar grille and "soft" front end. Most prospects seemed to resist the temptation. At the upper end of the scale was the latest Fifth Avenue version of the New Yorker, with just about every extra on its equipment list.

New Yorkers turned to a smaller platform for 1982 (LeBaron's old one, actually, as that model took a new form). The Newport name was gone. LeBaron was now front-wheel-drive, with a four-cylinder engine under the hood, a trend that would continue through the coming years. Most tempting was the new LeBaron convertible, the first American to return to drop-top production after the demise of Cadillac's Eldorado convertible in '76. A fair number of the posh Imperials had been sold in 1981, but the total slipped close to 2,300 this year. An "FS" package (named for Frank Sinatra) might make a rather rare collectible one day, but didn't do much for Imperial sales at the time.

Traditionalists might be forgiven for failing to recognize Chryslers as the 1980s continued. LeBaron got a standard five-speed gearbox for 1983, though its new Town & Country convertible evoked memories of T&C convertibles of the 1940s. In a shuffling of nameplates, the rear-drive model was now called New Yorker Fifth Avenue. How come? Because there was another New Yorker, now front-drive, along with a related E Class model. Attracting considerable publicity, not all of it favorable, was the new Voice Alert system, the car that talked. Some observers felt it talked too much, or about the wrong things. The next year, a shutoff switch was added. Even the new Executive sedan and limousine turned to front-wheel drive and four-cylinder power, vastly removed from the last previous limos in 1970.

Imperial did not return for 1984, but a sporty new Laser hatchback coupe appeared, a near twin to Dodge's Daytona and a far cry from past Chryslers. Adding further surprise, a turbocharged four-cylinder engine became available, not only on Laser, but under LeBaron, E Class, and New Yorker hoods as well. Fifth Avenue was the last remaining rear-driver, with the old 318-cid V-8 engine.

Yet another model joined the lineup the following year, the LeBaron GTS performance-oriented sedan, also available with turbo power. Model year sales rose again, just as they had in '84. Both the new GTS and old rear-drive Fifth Avenue found surprising numbers of customers. That rear-drive had to pay a gas guzzler tax in 1986, but remained a strong contender for sales. Limousines had standard turbocharged four-cylinder en-

gines, and what a shock that must have been to potential customers who'd not followed Chrysler's changes over the past few years.

Which Chryslers might collectors find worth a glance? Cordobas had their fans and foes when new, but the 1980 and later models, in particular, seem to look better all the time. Corinthian Editions and special roofs may be the best bets. Early LeBaron convertibles probably are worth hanging onto. The slow-selling 1981-'83 Imperial didn't appeal to everyone's tastes, but could easily become collectible. A "Sinatra" edition would be the rarest. Lasers? Maybe not yet, but a turbocharged XT wouldn't be the worst example to keep in a garage for a while. Then too, holding onto one of those final big guzzlers of 1976-'78 might not be a bad idea.

For Chrysler Corp., 1987 was a profitable year, highlighted by the acquisition of American Motors Corp. for $1.5 billion on August 5th. Chrysler-Plymouth and Dodge M-cars were built in AMC's Kenosha, Wisconsin plant for the 1987 model year. The Chrysler Division of Chrysler Motors Corp., headquartered in the Walter P. Chrysler Building in Detroit, Michigan, was headed by E. Thomas Pappert, Chrysler Group VP for sales at the time.

Retail car sales for Chrysler-Plymouth rose three percent in 1986; Chrysler's 1987 price tags went up two percent above comparably priced '86 models.

Chrysler and Plymouth became separate divisions for the '87 model year, further distinguishing Chrysler, Plymouth, and Dodge nameplates. The "truck" division stayed with Dodge, but Chrysler and Plymouth held onto the Voyager minivan, including a stretch version and an optional Mitsubishi-built three-liter V-6 engine for 1987.

In 1987, at Chrysler-Plymouth, there was an upscale subcompact waiting to be announced—the Sundance—which was built alongside the H-cars at Chrysler Corp.'s Sterling Heights, Michigan, assembly plant. Another important entry was the Chrysler-Maserati luxury two-seater scheduled for 1987.

Referred to as the biggest news at Chrysler in 1987 was the start of production of its new front-drive C-car sedans in July 1987 at Belvidere, Illinois. The new cars, the Chrysler New Yorker and New Yorker Landau, were powered by a three-liter V-6 engine built by Mitsubishi Motor Corp. in Japan. During this year, Chrysler surrendered its Laser model, but got rights to the new LeBaron J-body coupe and convertible.

Despite these two new entries, Chrysler-Plymouth Division saw '88 model year sales of only 581,220 units vs. 600,020 for '87. However, the J-body LeBaron coupe and New Yorker C-car, including the Landau version, combined for a respectable 171,674 sales in 1988.

Chrysler's E-body New Yorker was dubbed the New Yorker Turbo in '88 to differentiate it from the C-car New Yorker, but the car was short-lived. It ceased production in September 1987.

Continuing a sales decline that originated in 1987, Chrysler-Plymouth Division sales in model year '89 decreased to their lowest point in seven years. From an '88 mark of 581,220 units sold, the follow-up year's mark slumped to 527,817. This resulted in a 6.6 percent U.S. market share for Chrysler-Plymouth Division compared with 7.9 percent in 1988. An overall decline in the market was partly to blame for lagging sales, but the fact that Chrysler-Plymouth Division was undergoing a transition period also contributed to the downturn.

The transition included the phasing out of several car lines in favor of new ones. Ended in '89 was the Chrysler K-car era. Aries/Reliant production ceased at both the Jefferson Avenue plant in Detroit and the Toluca facility in Mexico. Also purged from the Chrysler product line was the LeBaron GTS. The J-body coupe and convertible remained to continue the LeBaron name. The end of production also came for the rear-drive M-body Chrysler Fifth Avenue, which tallied sales of 49,547 in 1988.

Launched in the '89 model year was Chrysler's two-seat convertible Italian luxury model, the TC (turbocharged coupe) by Maserati. With a base price of $35,000, the front-drive TC featured a 2.2-liter, 220-hp engine and had a curb weight of 3,274 pounds. The limited-production model was built in Milan, Italy, by Officine Alfieri Maserati SpA and sold in the United States by Chrysler-Plymouth dealers.

Also debuting in the Chrysler-Plymouth lineup in July 1989 was the Chrysler Town and Country minivan, kin to the Plymouth Voyager. The front-drive, seven-passenger luxury minivan was assembled in St. Louis, Missouri, and was powered by a 3.3-liter V-6 engine. Sales of the $23,500 minivan in its initial year of production reached 1,812 units.

In September 1989, Chrysler began production of the '90 model LeBaron sedan. Created on an A-body, this LeBaron was produced at Chrysler's Newark, Delaware, plant. Under Chrysler-Plymouth Division General Manager Michael V. Howe, the Imperial name returned once again to the lineup in model year '90 as Chrysler's longest, heaviest, most luxurious model for the marque. Starting at $26,045, the reborn Imperial featured anti-lock brakes and fabricated aluminum wheels as standard equipment.

1989 Chrysler LeBaron convertible (OCW)

The Imperial and the new New Yorker Fifth Avenue were assembled on the Y-platform (a stretched C-car) in Belvidere, Illinois. Both front-drive models were powered by the 3.3-liter V-6 mated to a four-speed automatic transmission. The 3.3-liter V-6, produced in Chrysler's Trenton, Michigan, plant, was standard equipment for the Y-platform, but an option for the C-car-based New Yorker Landau and New Yorker Salon (new for the '90 model year as a replacement for the New Yorker sedan).

Production of Chrysler's TC by Maserati was discontinued in May 1990 after 7,300 units were assembled. Sales of the luxury two-seater reached 2,924 units in 1989. Another discontinued item was the Chrysler headquarters building in Highland Park, Michigan. The new year found a new headquarters building completed down the road in Auburn Hills.

The TC by Maserati got a one-year reprieve in that after its 7,300 production goal was met in 1990, enough of the luxury convertibles were left over that they were sold as 1991 models. That year's LeBaron drop-top—the only domestic example designed and built as a convertible at the time—was the world's best-selling convertible, meaning a plentiful supply (and affordable prices?) for collectors in the future.

In 1992, the big news at Chrysler was not about its vehicles, but instead about the retirement of the legendary Lee Iacocca, the man who spearheaded Chrysler Corp.'s return from "the dead." He was replaced by Robert Eaton.

The following year, with Eaton at the helm, Chrysler embarked on its new direction of producing "cab forward"-designed automobiles. The Concorde was the first, as one-by-one, the "old" names (Imperial, New Yorker, etc.) dropped out of production to be replaced by the aerodynamic LH-platform "wunderkinds." In 1994, the LH-based "new" New Yorker and LHS sedans joined the Concorde in the cab forward ranks.

1993 Chrysler Concorde four-door sedan (OCW)

The last of Chrysler's non-cab forward cars, the LeBaron GTC convertible, was in its final year in 1995, to be replaced by the 1996 Sebring convertible, another cab forward member. Also new to the 1995 lineup was the Sebring coupe and Cirrus sedan.

The New Yorker sedan lasted only three model years before the plug was pulled in 1996, the victim of getting "lost" between the Concorde and LHS sedans. Not sold in large numbers during its brief availability, the cab forward New Yorker was extremely well appointed and well powered (3.5-liter V-6) and both its vaunted name and low production should mark it as a "recommended" car for collectors to seek in the future. Also in 1996, the Chrysler Corp. consolidated its Chrysler-Plymouth and Jeep-Eagle divisions.

Chrysler's new "winged" logo debuted on a 1997 Sebring coupe, while that model's convertible introduced AutoShift, a shiftable four-speed automatic transmission. Production of the LHS sedan was suspended that year, awaiting arrival of the new-design 1999 version (based on the LHX concept car) launched early in mid-1998. The second-generation cab forward Concorde also came on line in 1998.

It was part of the rumor mill for months prior, but the announcement was akin to a nuclear explosion when Chrysler Corp. made known that it would merge with German auto manufacturer Daimler-Benz. From 1999 on, the new entity would be known as DaimlerChrysler (one word), and it effectively ended the era of the "Big Three" (Chrysler Corp., Ford Motor Co., and General Motors). At the same time, in a move that probably helped to calm longtime Mopar enthusiasts who felt Chrysler products would never be the same after the merger, the letter series 300 model was revived after an absence of almost 35 years. Leaving off in 1965 with the 300L, the 300M debuted in 1999 as a performance sedan powered by a High-Output 3.5-liter V-6 rated at 253 hp. This "M" car may carry equal weight in the future with collectors of the previous Letter cars, and it will be interesting to see if Chrysler—make that DaimlerChrysler—ever makes it all the way to "Z."

Chrysler's millennium-ending 2000 lineup remained unchanged from 1999, with the exception of the re-introduction of a four-cylinder Cirrus LX, absent since 1997. Much anticipated, however, was the introduction—scheduled for spring of 2000—of Chrysler's next "retro-style" offering, the PT Cruiser, a Neon-based wagon reminiscent in appearance of a late-'30s Ford sedan, but classified as a minivan by the EPA.

Chrysler Town & Country sedans of the 1946-'49 (first series) era on the assembly line (OCW)

1924 CHRYSLER

1925 CHRYSLER

1924 Chrysler, Six, Model B-70, touring (OCW)

1925 Chrysler, Model B-70, four-door sedan (OCW)

CHRYSLER — MODEL B-70 — SIX: The Chrysler was introduced at the New York Auto Show in the city's Hotel Commodore. There was a full range of nine different body styles. Styling features included step-type fenders, drum headlights, vertical hood louvers, and a prominent double belt line molding on closed cars. The distinctive Chrysler radiator had a thick, rounded shell and a double winged radiator cap with the Chrysler Viking helmet logo located at the upper center. Split windshields were used on early production open cars.

I.D. DATA: Serial numbers stamped on a plate attached to front of dash and on left frame side member at rear spring horn. Starting: 1001. Ending: 32813. Engine numbers were stamped on a boss on top of chain case. Engine number information not available.

Model No.	Body Type & Seating	Price	Weight	Prod. Total
B-70	2-dr. Rds.-4P	1525	2805	Note 1
B-70	4-dr. Tr.-5P	1335	2730	Note 1
B-70	4-dr. Phae.-5P	1395	2785	Note 1
B-70	4-dr. Sed.-5P	1625	3060	Note 1
B-70	4-dr. Imp. Sed.-5P	1895	3085	Note 1
B-70	2-dr. Brgm.-5P	1795	2995	Note 1
B-70	4-dr. Crw. Imp. Sed.-5P	2195	3090	Note 1
B-70	2-dr. Cpe.-4P	1195	2935	Note 1
B-70	4-dr. Twn. Car-5P	3725	3225	Note 1

Note 1: Total calendar year production of Chryslers and Maxwells combined was 79,144.

ENGINE: Inline. L-head. Six. Cast iron block. B & S: 3 x 4-3/4 in. Disp.: 201 cu. in. C.R.: 4.7:1. Brake H.P.: 68 @ 3000 R.P.M. N.A.C.C. H.P.: 21.60. Main bearings: seven. Valve lifters: solid. Carb.: Ball & Ball.

CHASSIS: W.B.: 112-3/4 in. O.L.: 160 in. Tires: 30 x 5.75 or 29 x 4.5 on demountable, six-lug rims.

TECHNICAL: Manual transmission. Speeds: 3F/1R. Floor shift controls. Conventional clutch. Shaft drive. Four-wheel hydraulic brakes. Steel disc wheels on touring. Wood-spoke wheels on other models.

OPTIONS: Double bar front bumpers. Double bar rear fender guards. Wind wings. Step plates. Trunk rack. Spare tire. Sidemounted spare tires. Accessory radiator cap. Whitewall tires. Sidemount covers (leather). Side curtains. Outside rear view mirror. Touring trunk.

HISTORICAL: Introduced in January 1924. High compression engine used Ricardo type cylinder head. With a top speed of 70-75 mph, the new Chryslers were only five mph slower than the Packard Eight. The Chrysler replaced the Maxwell and calendar year production figures include both marques. More than 32,000 of these cars were Chryslers. A total of 19,960 Chryslers were registered during the calendar year. Ralph De Palma used a Chrysler to win the famous Mt. Wilson hill climb. He then drove the same car 1,000 miles in 1,007 hours at the Fresno, California, board racing track setting numerous stock car racing records.

CHRYSLER — MODEL B-70 — SIX: There were relatively few changes in the 1925 Chryslers. Open cars now used a one-piece windshield that was hinged at the top instead of a horizontally split two-piece type. After November 1924, Chrysler bodies were built by Fisher Body Co. At the middle of the year, Chrysler purchased the Kercheval Body factory in Detroit, and started producing its own bodies. A longer gearshift lever was used for 1925 models and there were a number of technical refinements including the addition of a vibration damper and the use of rubber engine mounts. There was a Chrysler Four, introduced in a *Saturday Evening Post* ad on June 27, 1925, that became the F-58 in 1926.

I.D. DATA: Serial numbers were in the same locations. Starting: B-32813. Ending: B-81000. Engine numbers were in the same location. Engine numbers not available.

Model No.	Body Type & Seating	Price	Weight	Prod. Total
B-70	2-dr. Rds.-4P	1625	2805	Note 1
B-70	4-dr. Tr.-5P	1395	2730	Note 1
B-70	4-dr. Phae.-5P	1495	2785	Note 1
B-70	4-dr. Sed.-5P	1825	3060	Note 1
B-70	4-dr. Imp. Sed.-5P	2065	3085	Note 1
B-70	2-dr. Brgm.-5P	1965	2995	Note 1
B-70	2-dr. Coach-5P	1545	2895	Note 1
B-70	2-dr. Roy. Cpe.-4P	1895	2935	Note 1
B-70	4-dr. Crw. Imp. Sed.-5P	2195	3090	Note 1
B-70	4-dr. Twn. Car-5P	3725	3225	Note 1

Note 1: Total 1925 calendar year production of Chryslers and Maxwells combined was 132,343.

ENGINE: Inline. L-head. Six. Cast iron block. B & S: 3 x 4-3/4 in. Disp.: 201 cu. in. C.R.: 4.7:1. Brake H.P.: 68 @ 3000 R.P.M. N.A.C.C. H.P.: 21.60. Main bearings: seven. Valve lifters: solid. Carb.: Ball & Ball.

CHASSIS: W.B.: 112-3/4 in. O.L.: 160 in. Tires: 30 x 5.75 on demountable, six-lug rims.

TECHNICAL: Manual transmission. Speeds: 3F/1R. Floor shift controls. Conventional clutch. Shaft drive. Four-wheel hydraulic brakes. Wood-spoke wheels.

OPTIONS: Double bar front bumper. Double bar rear guards. Wind wings. Step plates. Trunk rack. Spare tire. Sidemount spares. Accessory radiator cap. White sidewall tires. Sidemount covers (leather). Side curtains. Outside rear view mirror. Special Duco paint colors. Wire-spoke wheels.

HISTORICAL: Introduced January 1925. Chrysler calendar year production was approximately 76,600. New car registrations for Chrysler were 68,793. On June 26, 1925, Maxwell was reorganized and incorporated in the state of Delaware as Chrysler Corporation. Lawyer Nicholas Kelley was president of the new company for two weeks, after which Walter P. Chrysler became president. Chrysler of Canada, Ltd. was also formed this year. Ralph De Palma set more new stock car records at Culver City, California, by driving a stripped down touring car 1,000 miles in 786 minutes on January 5, 1925. In England, Sir Malcom Campbell drove a streamlined Chrysler to a new lap record of 100 mph at Brooklands race track. Another Chrysler was raced at the French Grand Prix at Le Mans.

1925 Chrysler, Model B-70, roadster (JAC)

1926 CHRYSLER

CHRYSLER — MODEL F-58 — FOUR: The four-cylinder Chrysler was a continuance of the Maxwell with a new, rounded radiator shear. The design was thinner than that used on Chrysler sixes, but had a family resemblance. Also, belt line moldings of the Chrysler type were used along with new "cadet" type visors on closed cars. These bodies were designed and built by Budd Manufacturing Co. of Philadelphia. Closed cars had one-piece windshields; open cars had two-piece types of the swing out style. The winged Viking hood ornament identified the cars.

CHRYSLER — MODEL G-70 — SIX: The Chrysler G-70 was a refinement of the previous B-70 and had basically the same styling except that the door openings were raised a bit higher off the body sills. Minor variations in headlamp design were seen as running changes between early and late production units. The early cars of 1925-26 manufacture had drum headlamps with hooded rings. The early 1926 series had plain drum headlights. The later 1926 models had bullet-shaped headlamps.

1926 Chrysler, Model G-70, roadster (OCW)

CHRYSLER — SERIES E-80 — SIX: The Chrysler Imperial E-80 was a luxury series with distinctive styling, longer wheelbases, and a larger and more powerful engine. A styling innovation was a scalloped hood and radiator design. The Imperials also used bullet-shaped headlamps. Standard equipment was on the rich end of the scale including many fancy trim features not offered with other Chryslers.

I.D. DATA: [Model F-58] Serial numbers were in the same locations. Numbers for the 1925-1/2 F series were WW100P to WY560W; those for the 1926 F-58 series were YC200P to YRO56S. Engine numbers were F-25000 to F-110000. [Model G-70] Serial numbers were in the same locations. G-70 numbers for the 1925-26 series were WY580W to WD999D; G-70 numbers for the first 1926 series were PP580P to PP454R and G-70 numbers for the late 1926 series were PP930S to PS287D. Engine numbers were G-81001 to G-142300. [Series E-80] Serial numbers were in the same locations. Serial numbers were ED000W to EW655S. Engine numbers were also in the same locations. Engine numbers unavailable.

1926 Chrysler Imperial, Series E-80, touring (OCW)

Model No.	Body Type & Seating	Price	Weight	Prod. Total
F-58	2-dr. Rds.-2P	890	2375	Note 1
F-58	4-dr. Tr.-5P	895	2390	Note 1
F-58	2-dr. Cpe.-2P	995	2495	Note 1
F-58	2-dr. Coach-5P	1045	2590	Note 1
F-58	4-dr. Sedan-5P	1095	2680	Note 1

Note 1: Approximately 81,089 Series F-58 Chryslers were built to the 1926 specifications.

Model No.	Body Type & Seating	Price	Weight	Prod. Total
G-70	2-dr. Rds.-2/4P	1625	2805	Note 2
G-70	2-dr. Roy. Cpe.-2/4P	1795	2935	Note 2
G-70	4-dr. Tr.-5P	1395	2785	Note 2
G-70	2-dr. Coach-5P	1445	2895	Note 2
G-70	2-dr. Brgm.-5P	1865	2995	Note 2
G-70	4-dr. Sed.-5P	1695	3060	Note 2
G-70	4-dr. Crw. Sed.-5P	2095	3090	Note 2

Note 2: Total G-70 production was 72,039 cars.

Note 3: The brougham is also called a "leather trimmed touring sedan" and the Crown sedan is also called a "landau sedan."

Model No.	Body Type & Seating	Price	Weight	Prod. Total
E-80	2-dr. Rds.-2/4P	2885	3730	Note 4
E-80	4-dr. Phae.-5P	2645	3775	Note 4
E-80	2-dr. Cpe.-4P	3195	4015	Note 4
E-80	4-dr. Sed.-5P	3395	4104	Note 4
E-80	4-dr. Imp. Sed.-7P	3595	4225	Note 4
E-80	4-dr. Ber. Limo.-7P	3695	4260	Note 4

Custom Bodies

Model No.	Body Type & Seating	Price	Weight	Prod. Total
E-80	4-dr. L'let.-7P	NA	NA	Note 4
E-80	4-dr. Twn. Car-7P	NA	NA	Note 4

Note 4: Total E-80 production was 9,114 cars.

Note 5: The custom body models were designed for the 127-inch extended wheelbase. It's possible other custom body Imperials were built on a special 133-inch wheelbase available for special order coachwork.

1926 Chrysler, Model G-70, Crown sedan (JAC)

ENGINE: [Model F-58] L-head. Inline. Four. Cast iron block. B & S: 3-5/8 x 4-1/2 in. Disp.: 185.8 cu. in. Brake H.P.: 38 @ 2200 R.P.M. N.A.C.C. H.P.: 21.03. Valve lifters: solid. Carb.: Stewart. [Model G-70] Inline. L-head. Six. Cast iron block. B & S: 3-1/8 x 4-3/4 in. Disp.: 218.6 cu. in. C.R.: 4.7:1. Brake H.P.: 68 @ 3000 R.P.M. N.A.C.C. H.P.: 21.60. Main bearings: seven. Valve lifters: solid. Carb.: Ball & Ball. [Series E-80] Inline. L-head. Six. Cast iron block. B & S: 3-1/2 x 5 in. Disp.: 288 cu. in. C.R.: 4.7:1. Brake H.P.: 92 @ 3000 R.P.M. N.A.C.C. H.P.: 29.4. Main bearings: seven. Valve lifters: solid. Carb.: Ball & Ball.

CHASSIS: [Model F-58] W.B.: 109 in. Tires: 30 x 5.25. [Model G-70] W.B.: 112-3/4 in. O.L.: 160 in. Tires: 30 x 5.77. [Series E-80] Standard W.B.: 120 in.; Seven-passenger wheelbase: 127 inches; Special order wheelbase: 133 in. Tires: 32 x 6.25.

TECHNICAL: Manual transmission. Speeds: 3F/1R. Conventional clutch. Shaft drive. Mechanical rear wheel brakes on early F-58s. Hydraulic rear wheel brakes on late F-58s. Four-wheel hydraulic brakes on other models. Wood-spoke wheels on all models.

OPTIONS: Double bar front bumpers. Double bar rear guards. Wind wings. Step plates. Trunk rack. Spare tire. Sidemount spares. Accessory radiator cap. Touring trunks. White sidewall tires. Side curtains. Outside rear view mirrors. Pedestal mirrors for sidemounts. Special paint. Wire-spoke wheels.

HISTORICAL: Introduced at various points throughout the year. Calendar year production: 162,242. Calendar year registrations: 129,565. An Imperial roadster was the Indy 500 pace car. The Fleetwood Body Corp. cataloged several custom body designs for the 127-inch wheelbase Chrysler Imperial chassis. Chrysler was America's seventh ranked automaker this year. Walter P. Chrysler remained as president of the company bearing his name. The Fedco serial numbering system was adopted for the 1926 season and was used through 1930 by Chrysler.

1927 CHRYSLER

1927 Chrysler, Series 50, sedan (JAC)

CHRYSLER — SERIES 50 — FOUR: The wheelbase on the four-cylinder Chryslers was reduced by three inches, although the basic styling was carried over from the previous year. The number of models was expanded to eight with the addition of a rumbleseat roadster, a leather-trimmed sedan, and a landau sedan that had the rear quarters upholstered with rubberized fabric and decorated with dummy landau irons.

1927 Chrysler, Series 60, roadster (JAC)

CHRYSLER — SERIES 60 — SIX: The Chrysler 60 was an all-new car that was introduced as a mid-1926 model. It was carried over, with minor changes, through the 1927 model year. These cars had typical Chrysler styling with bullet-shaped headlights. The wheelbase was 109 inches, the same formerly used on the four-cylinder models, but the engine was an improved type six. Early 60 series cars had 30 x 5.25 tires and five lug wheels. Later versions had smaller tires, four lug wheels, and an illuminated instrument panel that was finished in white.

1927 Chrysler, Series 70, roadster (JAC)

CHRYSLER — SERIES 70 — SIX: This was a carryover of the 1926 G-70 series with several new models including "sport" and "custom sport" versions of the phaeton, a rumbleseat cabriolet, rumbleseat coupe, and a landau brougham. New bullet-shaped headlights were used on the open-bodied models only, while the closed cars continued to feature drum-type headlights. Standard equipment included Delco Remy ignition, hydraulic brakes, and one-piece windshields. A new equipment feature was a coincidental transmission lock. Early 1927 Series 70 models had five lug wheels and 30 x 5.75 tires, while later versions had four lug wheels with 30 x 6 tires. These cars were known as Chrysler's "Finer 70s."

1927 Chrysler Imperial, Series 80, roadster (OCW)

IMPERIAL — SERIES 80 — SIX: This was Chrysler's prestige car line. It was marketed as a 1927-28 series. Features included lower, longer bodies, hydraulic brakes, Delco Remy ignition, and Chrysler's high-compression "Red Head" engine. Standard equipment on open styles included wind wings and leather exterior door trim panels. Bullet-shaped headlights were featured. The scalloped hood and radiator shell design was used for Imperials and many of the cars had two-tone finish. Chrysler's first true convertible, with functional landau irons, was offered in this line. A richly appointed town car was available on special order. Custom body builders offered coachcraft designs for the long wheelbase Imperials.

I.D. DATA: [Series 50] Serial numbers were in the same locations. Starting: FW000P. Ending: HW000W. Engine numbers were in the same locations. Engine numbers are not available. [Series 60] Serial numbers were in the same locations. (1926-1/2) Starting: YR500W. Ending: YYD242D. (1927) Starting: YD243W. Ending: LW000W. Engine numbers were in the same locations. Starting: H-21001. Ending: H-72800. [Series 70] Serial numbers were in the same locations. (1926-1/2) Starting: PP930S. Ending: PS287D. (1927) Starting: PP454Y. Ending: CW000W. Engine numbers were in the same locations. Starting: G-142301. Ending: G-151600. [Series 80] Serial numbers were in the same locations. Starting: EW655L. Ending: EP000R. Engine numbers were also in the same locations. Engine numbers are not available.

Model No.	Body Type & Seating	Price	Weight	Prod. Total
50	2-dr. Rds.-2P	750	2025	Note 1
50	2-dr. R/S. Rds.-2/4P	795	2130	Note 1
50	4-dr. Tr.-5P	750	2125	Note 1
50	2-dr. Cpe.-2P	750	2230	Note 1

Model No.	Body Type & Seating	Price	Weight	Prod. Total
50	2-dr. Coach-5P	780	2335	Note 1
50	2-dr. Lthr. Trim Sed.-5P	795	2410	Note 1
50	4-dr. Sed.-5P	830	2410	Note 1
50	4-dr. Lan.-5P	855	2410	Note 1

Note 1: Total series production was 82,412.

Model No.	Body Type & Seating	Price	Weight	Prod. Total
60	2-dr. Rds.-2P	1145	2545	Note 1
60	2-dr. R/S Rds.-2/4P	1175	2615	Note 1
60	4-dr Tr.-5P	1075	2575	Note 1
60	2-dr. Cpe.-2P	1125	2585	Note 1
60	2-dr. R/S Cpe.-2/4P	1245	2685	Note 1
60	2-dr. Coach-5P	1195	2780	Note 1
60	2-dr. Lthr. Trim Sed.-5P	1225	2780	Note 1
60	4-dr. Sed.-5P	1295	2840	Note 1

Note 1: Total series production is not available.

Model No.	Body Type & Seating	Price	Weight	Prod. Total
70	2-dr. R/S Rds.-2/4P	1495	2845	Note 1
70	4-dr. Phae.-5P	1395	2905	Note 1
70	4-dr. Spt. Phae.-5P	1495	2905	Note 1
70	4-dr. Cus. Spt. Phae.-5P	1650	2950	Note 1
70	2-dr. R/S Cabr.-2/4P	1745	2935	Note 1
70	2-dr. Cpe.-2P	1545	2850	Note 1
70	2-dr. R/S Cpe.-2/4P	1595	2950	Note 1
70	2-dr. Clb. Cpe.-4P	1565	2905	Note 1
70	2-dr. Brgm.-5P	1525	3090	Note 1
70	2-dr. Lan. Brgm.-5P	1550	—	Note 1
70	4-dr. Roy. Sed.-5P	1595	3150	Note 1
70	4-dr. Crw. Sed.-5P	1795	3160	Note 1

Note 1: Total series production was 48,254.

Model No.	Body Type & Seating	Price	Weight	Prod. Total
80	2-dr. R/S Rds.-2/4P	2595	3805	Note 1
80	2-dr. Spt. Rds.-2/4P	2795	3850	Note 1
80	4-dr. Phae.-5P	2495	3925	Note 1
80	4-dr. Spt. Phae.-5P	2895	4240	Note 1
80	4-dr. Phae.-7P	2645	4115	Note 1
80	2-dr. Bus. Cpe.-2P	2895	4220	Note 1
80	2-dr. Clb. Cpe.-4P	2895	4090	Note 1
80	2-dr. Clb. Cpe.-5P	3095	4220	Note 1
80	4-dr. Std. Sed.-5P	2695	4055	Note 1
80	4-dr. Sed.-5P	3195	4260	Note 1
80	4-dr. Lan Sed.-5P	3295	4215	Note 1
80	4-dr. LWB Sed.-7P	3295	4450	Note 1
80	4-dr. Limo.-7P	3595	4370	Note 1
80	4-dr. Twn. Car-7P	5495	4265	Note 1

Note 1: Total series production is not available.

1927 Chrysler, Series 80, Imperial phaeton (JAC)

ENGINE: [Series 50] Inline. L-head. Four. Cast iron block. B & S: 3-5/8 x 4-1/8 in. Disp.: 170.3 cu. in. Brake H.P.: 38 @ 2200 R.P.M. N.A.C.C. H.P.: 21.03. Main bearings: three. Valve lifters: solid. Carb.: Ball & Ball. [Series 60] Inline. L-head. Six. Cast iron block. B & S: 3 x 4-1/4 in. Disp.: 180.2 cu. in. Brake H.P.: 54 @ 3000 R.P.M. N.A.C.C. H.P.: 21.6. Valve lifters: solid. Carb.: Stromberg. [Series 70] Inline. L-head. Six. Cast iron block. B & S: 3-1/8 x 4-3/4 in. Disp.: 218.6 cu. in. Brake H.P.: 68 @ 3000 R.P.M. N.A.C.C. H.P.: 23.44. Valve lifters: solid. Carb.: Stromberg. [Series 80] Inline. L-head. Six. Cast iron block. B & S: 3-1/2 x 5 in. Disp.: 288.6 cu. in. Brake H.P.: 92 @ 3200 R.P.M. N.A.C.C. H.P.: 29.40. Main bearings: seven. Valve lifters: solid. Carb.: Stromberg.

CHASSIS: [Series 50] W.B.: 106 in. Tires: 29 x 4.75. [Series 60] W.B.: 109 in. Tires: (early) 30 x 5.25; (late) 28 x 5.25. [Series 70] W.B.: 112-3/4 in. Tires: (early) 30 x 5.75; (late) 30 x 6. [Series 80] W.B.: (standard) 120 in.; (custom) 127 in.; (special order) 133 in. Tires: 30 x 6.75.

DRIVETRAIN: Manual transmission. Speeds: 3F/1R. Floor shift controls. Conventional clutch. Shaft drive. Overall gear ratios: [Series 50] 4.7:1; [Series 60] 4.6:1; [Series 70] 4.3:1; [Series 80] 4.82:1. Mechanical rear wheel brakes standard on Series 50. Hydraulic rear wheel brakes available at extra cost on Series 50. Four wheel hydraulic brakes available on other series. Wood-spoke wheels standard. Starting in August 1926, Budd-Michelin steel disc wheels were available on all 1927 series Chryslers.

OPTIONS: Double bar front bumper. Double bar rear fender guards. Sidemount spare tires. Leather sidemount covers. Heater. Clock. Cigar lighter. Wind wings. Step plates. Rear mount spare. Rumbleseat windshield. Rumbleseat wind wings. Outside rear view mirror. Trunk rack. Touring trunk. Dual wipers. Dual taillights. Steel disc wheels. Wire-spoke wheels on sport models. Side curtains. Custom coachwork bodies.

HISTORICAL: Early series introduced August 1926. Late series introduced January 1927. Calendar year production: 182,195. Calendar year new car registrations: 154,234. An Imperial made a high-speed, non-stop run of 6,726 miles from San Francisco to New York to Los Angeles. The car's average speed was 40.2 mph. Walter P. Chrysler was again president of the company. Chrysler ranked seventh in U.S. auto sales.

1928 CHRYSLER

CHRYSLER — SERIES 52 — FOUR: The Series 52 was basically a continuation of the Chrysler 50. Styling differences included bullet-shaped headlights and a new kind of visor on closed cars. The visor was narrower and had a greater slope; it did not jut out quite as far when viewed in profile. A new instrument panel featured indirect illumination and had the gauges and controls housed in a rectangular panel, instead of an oval one. Standard equipment included an adjustable steering wheel and I-beam front axle. Hydraulic brakes were available at extra cost. This series became the Plymouth in 1929.

CHRYSLER — SERIES 62 — SIX: Chrysler's "small" six had a higher radiator. These cars returned to the use of drum type headlights and cowl lights were eliminated. Standard equipment included an electric gas gauge, hydraulic brakes, rubber engine mounts, ignition lock on dash, ventilating type windshield, and light control on steering wheel. The design of the instrument board was changed from an oval to rectangular panel, as on the Chrysler 50. The new cadet sun visor design was used on the 62 also.

CHRYSLER — SERIES 72 — SIX: A higher radiator and cowl were used on the Chrysler 72. Headlight posts were now firmly attached to the frame of the cars. Standard equipment included hydraulic brakes, tubular front axle, rubber shock insulators on springs, and a new oblong instrument panel. Throttle and headlight controls were repositioned on a thinner new steering wheel.

1928 Chrysler, Series 72, four-door sedan (JAC)

IMPERIAL — SERIES 80 — SIX: Early 1928 Chrysler Imperials were a carryover of the 1927 Series 80. These cars had Fedco serial numbers EW853S through EW911R and engine numbers E9709 through E10248. There were no important changes in styling or specifications. Refer to 1927 specifications for these cars.

IMPERIAL — SERIES 80L — SIX: The "new" 1928 Imperials were on a 136-inch wheelbase. They retained the scalloped type radiator and hood design. There was a line of factory bodied models, a second line

of semi-custom LeBaron-bodied models, a third line of Dietrich-bodied semi-custom models and one design from Locke. These were all richly appointed cars intended for prestige class buyers. Styling traits included the removal of the monogram from the radiator and the use of large, plated, bullet-shaped headlights.

I.D. DATA: [Series 52] Fedco numbering system used 1926-1929. Serial number symbol plate built into instrument panel above and to left of the instruments or in center of panel over instrument board. Starting: HW000P. Ending: HL685L. Engine numbers were on upper left side of block, between first and second cylinders, just below head. Starting: 1-83074. Ending: 1-166185. [Series 62] Fedco serial numbers were in the same location. Starting: LW000P. Ending: LS101C. Engine numbers were in the same location. Starting: M-72641. Ending: M-135784. [Series 72] Fedco serial numbers were in the same location. Starting: CW000P. Ending: CR838L. Engine numbers were in the same location. Starting: J192950. Ending: J242900. [Series 80 & 80L] Fedco serial numbers were in the same location. Starting: EP000P. Ending: EP315C. Engine numbers were stamped on top of the timing gear chain case. Starting: L1201. Ending: L4069.

Model No.	Body Type & Seating	Price	Weight	Prod. Total
52	2-dr. Rds.-2/4P	670	2075	Note 1
52	4-dr. Tr.-5P	695	2130	Note 1
52	2-dr. Cpe.-2P	670	2180	Note 1
52	2-dr. Del. Cpe.-2/4P	720	2240	Note 1
52	2-dr. Coach-5P	670	2300	Note 1
52	4-dr. Sed.-5P	720	2375	Note 1
52	4-dr. Del. Sed.-5P	790	2375	Note 1

Note 1: Total series production was 76,857.

62	2-dr. Rds.-2/4P	1075	2705	Note 1
62	4-dr. Tr.-5P	1095	2740	Note 1
62	2-dr. Bus. Cpe.-2P	1065	2780	Note 1
62	2-dr. Cpe.-2/4P	1145	2855	Note 1
62	2-dr. Coach-5P	1095	2855	Note 1
62	4-dr. Sed.-5P	1175	2905	Note 1
62	4-dr. Lan. Sed.-5P	1235	2940	Note 1

Note 1: Total series production was 64,136.

72	2-dr. Rds.-2/4P	1495	3005	6416
72	2-dr. Spt. Rds.-2/4P	1595	3005	Note 1
72	2-dr. Cpe.-4P	1595	3160	6869
72	2-dr. RS Cpe.-2/4P	1545	3130	Note 2
72	2-dr. Conv. Cpe.-2/4P	1745	3100	1729
72	4-dr. Twn. Sed.-5P	1695	3270	4977
72	4-dr. Roy. Sed.-5P	1595	3235	3266
72	4-dr. Crw. Sed.-5P	1795	3235	Note 3
72	4-dr. C.C. Sed.-5P	1595	3240	Note 4
72	4-dr. Imp. Twn. Cabr.-5P	3595	3485	36

Note 1: Production of the standard roadster and sport roadster was a single total with no breakouts available.

Note 2: Production of the standard coupe and rumbleseat coupe was a single total with no breakouts available.

Note 3: Production of the Crown sedan and Royal sedan was a single total with no breakouts available.

Note 4: Production of the closed-coupled sedan and the town sedan was a single total with no breakouts available.

Model No.	Body Type & Seating	Price	Weight	Prod. Total
80L	2-dr. Rds.-2/4P	2795	3870	281
80L	4-dr. Sed.-5P	2945	4125	790
80L	4-dr. Twn. Sed.-5P	2995	4140	431
80L	4-dr. Sed.-7P	3075	4250	374
80L	4-dr. Limo.-7P	3495	4285	86
(LeBaron Bodies)				
80L	4-dr. Trav. D.C. Phae.-4P	4185	4200	31
80L	2-dr. Clb. Cpe.-2/4P	3995	4150	25
80L	2-dr. Twn. Cpe.-4P	3995	4150	21
80L	2-dr. Conv. Cpe.-2/4P	3995	4150	39
80L	4-dr. C.C. Conv. Sed.-4P	6485	4250	4
80L	4-dr. Twn. Car.-7P	3595	NA	1
(Dietrich Bodies)				
80L	4-dr. D.C. Phae.-7P	6795	4300	5
80L	4-dr. Imp. Conv. Sed.-5P	6795	4300	10
80L	4-dr. Sed.-4P	5795	4300	4
(Locke Bodies)				
80L	2-dr. Imp. Trav'let-4P	4485	4165	21

Note 1: Total 80L series production included 1,962 factory bodied cars and 161 custom-bodied cars. Grand total: 2,123.

ENGINE: [Series 52] Inline. L-head. Four. Cast iron block. B & S: 3-5/8 x 4-1/8 in. Disp.: 170.3 cu. in. C.R.: 4.7:1. Brake H.P.: 38-45 @ 2600 R.P.M. N.A.C.C. H.P.: 21.03. Valve lifters: Solid. Carb.: Carter. [Series 62] Inline. L-head. Six. Cast iron block. B & S: 3 x 4-1/2 in. Disp.: 180.2 cu. in. C.R.: 5.2:1. Brake H.P.: 54 @ 3000 R.P.M. N.A.C.C. H.P.: 21.60. Main bearings: seven. Valve lifters: solid. Carb.: Stromberg (Note:

Above specifications for engine with standard "Silver Dome" head. The high-compression "Red Head" with 6.2:1 compression and 60 bhp was optional). [Series 72] Inline. L-head. Six. Cast iron block. B & S: 3-1/4 x 5 in. Disp.: 248.9 cu. in. C.R.: (std.) 5.1:1; (opt.) 6.2:1. Brake H.P.: (std.) 75 @ 3200 R.P.M.; (opt.) 85 @ 3200 R.P.M. N.A.C.C. H.P.: 25.36. Main bearings: seven. Valve lifters: solid. Carb.: Ball & Ball. [Series 80 & Series 80L] Inline. L-head. Six. Cast iron block. B & S: 3-5/8 x 5 in. Disp.: 309.3 cu. in. C.R.: (std.) 4.75:1; (opt.) 6.0:1. Brake H.P.: 100 @ 3200 (std. head); 112 @ 3300 ("Red Head"). Invarstrut pistons. Valve lifters: solid. Carb.: Stromberg.

1928 Chrysler Imperial, Locke, dual cowl phaeton (OCW)

CHASSIS: [Series 52] W.B.: 106 in. Tires: 29 x 4.75. [Series 62] W.B.: 108-3/4 in. Tires: 28 x 5.25. [Series 72] W.B.: 118-3/4 in. Tires: 30 x 6. [Series 80] W.B.: (std.) 120 in.; (Custom) 127 in.; (Special) 133 in. Tires: 30 x 6.75. [Series 80L] W.B.: 136 in. O.L.: 203 in. Tires: 30 x 6.75.

TECHNICAL: Manual transmission. Speeds: 3F/1R. Floor shift controls. Conventional clutch. Shaft drive. Overall gear ratio: [Series 52] 4.7:1; [Series 62] 4.6:1; [Series 72] 4.3:1; [Series 80] 4.83:1; and [Series 80L] 4.08:1. Two-wheel mechanical brakes standard on Series 52. Four-wheel hydraulic brakes standard on other series. Wood-spoke wheels were standard equipment on factory bodied cars.

OPTIONS: Front bumper. Rear bumper. Sidemount tire(s). Leather side-mount covers. Trunk rack. Touring trunk. Wind wings. Rear mount spare tire. Rear fender guards. Rear covered spare. Outside rear view mirror. Accessory radiator cap. Pedestal mirrors for sidemounts. Trippe lights. Radiator guard. Spotlight(s). Disc wheels. Wire wheels. Rear windshield on dual cowl phaetons. Special paint. Special order custom coachwork.

HISTORICAL: All series, except for the 80L, were introduced in July 1927. The 80L series was introduced in November 1927. Calendar year production: 160,670. Calendar year registrations: 142,024. This was Chrysler's all-time highest production year for the prewar era and also the highest until 1950. Chrysler entered four Imperial roadsters in the 24 Hours of Le Mans. The Chrysler team placed third and fourth in class. The winning car averaged 64.5 mph for the race. Another Imperial placed second in the Belgian 24-hour grand prix and two Series 72 Chryslers took third and fourth in the same race. Chrysler purchased Dodge Brothers this year.

1929 CHRYSLER

CHRYSLER — SERIES 65 — SIX: The four-cylinder Chryslers were renamed Plymouths this year. The company's basic line was now a six called the Series 65. These cars featured narrow profile radiators and higher cowls. A longer wheelbase was used. An ignition keyhole replaced the old switch type. Other styling features included bowl-shaped headlights, full crown "Air Wing" fenders, and a new silver and black finished instrument panel. Arched windows were another advance in design for closed cars. Standard equipment included Lockheed internal hydraulic brakes and hydraulic shock absorbers.

CHRYSLER — SERIES 75 — SIX: The 75 series Chryslers had about the same appearance changes as the Chrysler 65. They included narrow profile radiators, full crown fenders, arched windows on closed cars (a more rounded sun visor was also used), bowl-shaped headlights, dual cowl ventilators, vertical hood louvers and a lengthened wheelbase. Standard equipment included Lockheed hydraulic brakes and Lovejoy shock absorbers. The Chrysler 75 instrument panel was done in black and gold. These were the first Chryslers to feature built-in radiator shutters.

1929 Chrysler, Series 75, roadster (OCW)

IMPERIAL "L" — SERIES IMPERIAL — SIX: A narrow profile radiator, automatic radiator shutter, slender front body pillars, shatterproof glass, arched windows, dual cowl ventilators, fuel gauge on dash, and arched vertical hood louvers were features of 1929 Imperials. Eight factory body styles were listed by the National Automobile Dealers Association and a few custom bodies were available, too. Standard equipment included hydraulic brakes and Houdaille shock absorbers. The factory semi-custom bodies were by Locke.

1929 Chrysler, Series 75, four-passenger coupe (JAC)

I.D. DATA: [Series 65] Fedco serial numbers were in the same locations. Starting: LS400P and DW000W. Ending: LD999D and DC507D. Engine numbers were on the upper left side of block in same location. Starting: P175001. Ending: P241336. [Series 75] Fedco serial numbers were in the same locations. Starting: CY050P and ZW000P. Ending: CD999D and ZW672L. Motor numbers were in the same location as on 65s. Starting: R250001. Ending: R309150. [Series IMPERIAL] Fedco serial numbers were in the same locations. Starting: EP320P. Ending: EP542P. Engine numbers were located on the top of timing gear chain case. Starting: L4070. Ending: L6358.

1929 Chrysler, Imperial seven-passenger sedan (JAC)

Model No.	Body Type & Seating	Price	Weight	Prod. Total
65	2-dr. Rds.-2/4P	1065	2730	4953
65	4-dr. Tr.-5P	1075	2770	65472
65	2-dr. Bus. Cpe.-2P	1040	2780	4655
65	2-dr. 5W Cpe.-2/4P	1145	2875	7603
65	2-dr. Sed.-5P	1065	2905	8846
65	4-dr. Sed.-5P	1145	2960	24958

Note 1: Total series production was 116,487.

Model No.	Body Type & Seating	Price	Weight	Prod. Total
75	2-dr. Rds.-2/4P	1550	3190	6414
75	4-dr. Phae.-5P	1795	3110	248

Model No.	Body Type & Seating	Price	Weight	Prod. Total
75	4-dr. Phae.-7P	1865	3235	11
75	4-dr. Ton. Phae.-4P	1835	3290	227
75	2-dr. 3W Cpe.-2P	1535	3235	9488
75	2-dr. Conv. Cpe.-2/4P	1795	3320	1430
75	2-dr. 5W Cpe.-4P	1655	3335	1016
75	4-dr. Roy. Sed.-5P	1535	3280	22456
75	4-dr. Twn. Sed.-5P	1655	3360	3408
75	4-dr. Crw. Sed.-5P	1655	3365	3814
75	4-dr. Conv. Sed.-5P	2345	3430	337
75	2-dr. Jan. Tr. Cabr.-2P	NA	NA	1

Note 1: Total series production was 48,850 (approximate).

Note 2: The custom-bodied touring cabriolet was built by French coachmaker Carrosserie Janssen of Paris. Other custom bodies may have been sold on the Series 75 chassis.

Model No.	Body Type & Seating	Price	Weight	Prod. Total
L	2-dr. Rds.-2/4P	2675	3955	41
L	4-dr. Phae.-7P	3095	3925	15
L	2-dr. Cpe.-2P	2895	4020	149
L	2-dr. Conv. Cpe.-2/4P	2995	4035	142
L	4-dr. Sed.-5P	2975	4335	838
L	4-dr. Twn. Sed.-5P	2975	4310	379
L	4-dr. Sed.-7P	3095	4460	442
L	4-dr. Limo. Sed.-7P	3475	4510	99
L	2-dr. Locke Cus. Rds.-2/4P	NA	NA	NA
L	2-dr. Imp. Rds.-2/4P	2895	NA	401
L	4-dr. Locke Conv. Sed.-5P	NA	NA	NA
L	2-dr. Dtrch Cpe.-2/4P	NA	NA	NA

Note 1: Total series production for 1929-1930 was 2,506 cars, excluding an unknown amount of custom body jobs.

Note 2: This series was carried over as a 1930 series. The 1930 Imperials were those with serial numbers EP542C to EP608R and engine numbers L6359 to L6998. The 1930 prices increased $100-$200, but other specifications were basically the same except that a four-speed "Multi-Range" transmission was used in 1930 production units along with smooth, non-corrugated bumpers.

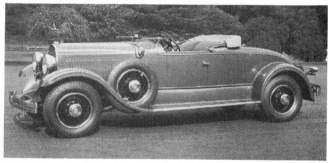

1929 Chrysler, Imperial roadster, Locke (JAC)

ENGINE: [Series 65] Inline. L-head. Six. Cast iron block. B & S: 3-1/8 x 4-1/4 in. C.R.: (std.) 5.2:1; (opt.) 6.0:1. Brake H.P.: (std.) 65 @ 3000 R.P.M.; (opt.) 70 @ 3200 R.P.M. N.A.C.C. H.P.: 23.44. Valve lifters: solid. Carb.: Stromberg. [Series 75] Inline. L-head. Six. Cast iron block. B & S: 3-1/4 x 5 in. Disp.: 248.9 cu. in. C.R.: (std.) 5.2:1; (opt.) 6.0:1. Brake H.P.: (std.) 75 @ 3200 R.P.M.: (opt.) 84 @ 3400 R.P.M. N.A.C.C. H.P. 25.35. Main bearings: seven. Valve lifters: solid. Carb.: Ball & Ball. [Series Imperial L] Inline. L-head. Six. Cast iron block. B & S: 3-5/8 x 5 in. Disp.: 309.3 cu. in. C.R.: (std.) 5.2:1; (opt.) 6.0:1. Brake H.P.: (std.) 110 @ 3200 R.P.M.; (opt.) 112 @ 3300 R.P.M.N.A.C.C. H.P.: 31.54. Valve lifters: solid. Carb.: Stromberg

CHASSIS: [Series 65] W.B.: 112-3/4 in. Tires: 5.50 x 18. [Series 75] W.B.: 121 in. Tires: 6.00 x 18. [Series 80L] W.B.: 136 in. O.L.: 203 in. Tires: 17 x 7.00.

TECHNICAL: Manual transmission. Speeds: 3F/1R. Floor shift controls. Conventional clutch. Shaft drive. Overall ratio: [Series 65] 4.9:1; [Series 75] 4.3:1; [Series 80L] 3.77:1 to 4.45:1. Four wheel hydraulic brakes on all models. Wood spoke wheels or wire wheels as standard equipment.

OPTIONS: See 1928 options.

HISTORICAL: The 65 and 75 series were introduced June 1928. The Imperial 80L series was introduced in October 1928. Calendar year production: 92,034. Calendar year new car registrations: 84,520. A team of two stripped down Imperial roadsters and two Series 75 roadsters competed at Le Mans in 1928, placing sixth and seventh in their class. The same cars took part in other European grands prix, but did not do well. A Series 65 Chrysler ran 53,170 non-stop miles to set a World Class endurance record in Germany.

1930 CHRYSLER

CHRYSLER — SERIES 66 — SIX: A number of styling changes on the 1930 Chrysler 66 included heavier fenders, bowl-shaped headlights, slender profile radiators, and pennon-type hood louvers. Standard equipment consisted of Delco Remy ignition, hydraulic brakes, rubber spring shackles and a new three-spoke steering wheel. Cars with serial numbers above H143EY and engine numbers above C16440 had larger more powerful engines and vertical hood louvers. On some cars split vertical louvers, located inside an arch-shaped panel, were used.

1930 Chrysler, Series 70, coupe (AA)

CHRYSLER — SERIES 70 — SIX: Styling features of the Chrysler 70 included narrow profile radiator, bowl-shaped headlights, and pennon-type hood louvers on early year cars. Standard equipment included Delco Remy ignition, hydraulic brakes, four-speed transmission, mechanical fuel pump, downdraft carburetor, and new "paraflex" springs. Late year cars with serial numbers above P-116SS and engine numbers above V-13595 had a larger engine, vertical hood louvers, new type instrument panel, and thermostatic radiator shutters.

CHRYSLER — SERIES 77 — SIX: The Chrysler 77 featured hydraulic internal brakes, four-speed transmission, double-drop frame, parking lamps on the front upper corner pillars, and distinctive concave moldings on the open cars. Pennon-type hood louvers were used on early production units, while later cars switched to a vertical louver design.

1930 Chrysler, Series 77, roadster (AA)

IMPERIAL — SERIES IMPERIAL — SIX: The 1930 Imperial was a carryover of the 1929 Imperial 80L. New features were automatic radiator shutters, vertical hood louvers, and four-speed transmission. The only specifications changes from 1930 were the prices. The roadster was $2,995; the phaeton was $3,195; the coupe was $3,095; the sedan was $3,075; the town sedan was $3,075; the seven-passenger sedan was $3,195; and the limousine was $3,575. Consult 1930 specifications chart for additional information.

CHRYSLER — SERIES CJ — SIX: The Series CJ was a line of all-new, downsized models bearing the Chrysler name. This series was actually a 1930-1/2 series and was introduced in February 1930. Features included a new, low-slung chassis, hydraulic internal brakes, fuel pump, rubber spring shackles, hydraulic shock absorbers, and rubber engine mounting system. Like other Chryslers, they had bowl-shaped headlights, narrow profile radiators, and standard wood-spoke wheels. Three groupings of vertical hood louvers were carried in an arched-shaped panel on the sides of the hood. This was the first Chrysler built since 1925 that did not carry a model designation indicating the top speed of the car.

I.D. DATA: [Series 66] Serial numbers were in the same locations. Starting: H001WP. Ending: H252SY. Engine numbers on upper left side of block, between cylinders one and two, just below cylinder head. Starting: C1001 to C28055. [Series 70] Serial numbers were in the same locations. Starting: P001WP. Ending: P180YE. Engine numbers were in the same locations. Starting: V1001. Ending: V27181. [Series 77] Serial numbers were in the same locations. Starting: C001WP. Ending: C187DH. Engine numbers were in the same locations. Starting: W1001. Ending: W26976. [Series CJ] Fedco serial numbers were in the same locations. Starting: H400WP. Ending: H471CS. Engine numbers were in the same locations. Starting: CJ1001. Ending: CJ24494. (Note: When the Fedco numbering system was dropped in late 1930, some CJ-6s carried conventional type serial numbers. Starting: 6500001. Ending: 6514919).

Model No.	Body Type & Seating	Price	Weight	Prod. Total
66	2-dr. Rds.-2/4P	1025	2625	1213
66	4-dr. Phae.-5P	1025	2695	26
66	2-dr. Bus. Cpe.-2P	995	2750	2014
66	2-dr. Roy. Cpe.-2/4P	1075	2850	3257
66	2-dr. Brgm. Sed.-5P	1000	2850	2343
66	4-dr. Roy. Sed.-5P	1095	2930	13753

Note 1: Total series production was 22,606.

70	2-dr. Rds.-2/4P	1345	3205	1431
70	4-dr. Phae.-5P	1295	3315	279
70	2-dr. Bus. Cpe.-2P	1345	3410	766
70	2-dr. Roy. Cpe.-2/4P	1395	3490	3135
70	2-dr. Conv. Cpe.-2/4P	1545	3450	705
70	2-dr. Brgm. Sed.-5P	1345	3490	1204
70	4-dr. Roy. Sed.-5P	1445	3590	11213

Note 1: Total series production was 18,733.

77	2-dr. Rds.-2/4P	1665	3370	1729
77	4-dr. Phae.-5P	1795	3495	173
77	2-dr. Bus. Cpe.-2P	1625	3560	230
77	2-dr. Roy. Cpe.-2/4P	1725	3615	2954
77	2-dr. Crw. Cpe.-4P	1795	3580	883
77	2-dr. Conv. Cpe.-2/4P	1825	3580	418
77	4-dr. Roy. Sed.-5P	1725	3750	436
77	4-dr. Crw. Sed.-5P	1795	3760	2654
77	4-dr. Twn. Sed.-5P	1795	3720	436

Note 1: Total series production was 9,913.

CJ	2-dr. Rds.-2/4P	835	2390	1616
CJ	4-dr. Tr.-5P	835	2455	22
CJ	2-dr. Bus. Cpe.-2P	795	2560	2267
CJ	2-dr. Conv. Cpe.-2/4P	925	2540	579
CJ	4-dr. Roy. Sed.-5P	845	2695	20748

Note 1: Total series production was 10,915.

1930 Chrysler, Series 66, four-door sedan (JAC)

ENGINE: [Series 66] (Early): Inline. L-head. Six. Cast iron block. B & S: 3-1/8 x 4-1/2 in. Disp.: 195.6 cu. in. Brake H.P.: 65 @ 3200 R.P.M. N.A.C.C. H.P.: 23.44. Carb.: Stromberg. (Late): Inline. L-head. Six. Cast iron block. B & S: 3-1/8 x 4-3/4 in. Disp.: 218.6 cu. in. Brake H.P.: 68 @ 3000 R.P.M. N.A.C.C. H.P.: 23.44. Carb.: Stromberg. [Series 70] (Early): Inline. L-head. Six. Cast iron block. B & S: 3-1/8 x 4-3/4 in. Disp.: 218.6. cu. in. Brake H.P.: 75 @ 3200 R.P.M. N.A.C.C. H.P.: 23.44. Carb.: Stromberg. (Late): Inline. L-head. Six. Cast iron block. B & S: 3-3/8 x 5 in. Disp.: 268.4. Brake H.P.: 93 @ 3200 R.P.M. N.A.C.C. H.P.: 27.34. Carb.: Stromberg. [Series 77] Inline. L-head. Six. Cast iron block. B & S: 3-3/8 x 5 in. Disp.: 268.4 cu. in. Brake H.P.: 93 @ 3200 R.P.M. N.A.C.C. H.P.: 27.34. Carb.: Stromberg. [Series CJ] Inline.

L-head. Six. Cast iron block. B & S: 3-1/8 x 4-1/4 in. Disp.: 195.6 cu. in. Brake H.P.: 62 @ 3200 R.P.M. N.A.C.C. H.P.: 23.44. Carb.: Carter.

CHASSIS: [Series CJ-6] W.B.: 109 in. Tires: 19 x 5.00. [Series 66] W.B.: 112-3/4 in. Tires: 18 x 5.50. [Series 70] W.B.: 116-1/2 in. Tires: 18 x 5.50. [Series 77] W.B.: 124 in. Tires: 18 x 6.00. [Imperial Series] W.B.: 136 in. Tires: 18 x 7.00.

TECHNICAL: Three-speed manual transmission on Series CJ-6 and Series 66 models. Four-speed "multi-range" manual transmission on other series. Speeds: 3F/1R and 4F/1R. Floor shift controls. Conventional clutch. Shaft drive. Overall ratio: [Series CJ-6] 4.7:1; [Series 66] 4.7:1; [Series 70] 4.1:1; [Series 77] 3.58:1 on open cars and 3.82:1 on closed cars. [Imperial Series] 3.77:1 to 4.45:1. Wood-spoke wheels standard on all models. Hydraulic brakes standard on all models.

OPTIONS: Front bumper. Rear bumper. Rear fender guards. Spare tire. Sidemounted spare tire(s). Wire-spoke wheels. Outside rear view mirror. Pedestal sidemount mirror(s). Cowl lights. Cigar lighter. Trunk rack. Touring trunk. Special solid paint. Two-tone sweep panel finish on Series 77 roadsters and phaetons. Leather sidemount covers. Metal sidemount covers. Metal sidemount cover trim moldings. Spotlight(s). Trippe lights. Wind wings. Imperial custom bodies.

HISTORICAL: The CJ Series six was introduced in February 1930. All other series introduced in July 1929. Calendar year production: 60,199. Calendar year new car registrations: 60,908. Innovations: Four-speed transmission. Fuel pump. "Futura" design instrument panels on 70/77. CJ six-cylinder engine was first Chrysler six to have four main bearings instead of seven. A Chrysler-powered racing car owned by Julius Slade qualified for the Indianapolis 500 and was driven by Roland Free for 69 laps until the clutch burned out. The Chrysler Building in New York City was completed this year.

1930 Chrysler, Series 77, four-door sedan (JAC)

1931 CHRYSLER

1931 Chrysler, Series CG, Imperial town car, LeBaron (AA)

CHRYSLER — SERIES CJ — SIX: The Series Six Chrysler was carried over as a 1931 model with little change, except that cowl lamps were

now mounted on the surcingle and new special type spring shackles were introduced.

CHRYSLER — SERIES 66 — SIX: This was another carryover series. A new feature was a curved headlamp tie-bar with "66" in center. Serial numbers for the 1931 series were H252SS to H262ER. Engine numbers for the 1931 series were C28056 to C28968. Specifications were the same as for late 1930 Series 66 models. Prices were unchanged. Weights increased by five pounds. Consult 1930 listings for further information.

CHRYSLER — SERIES 70 — SIX: This was another carryover series. A styling change was seen in the use of a new, low, flat, vee-type radiator. Serial numbers for the 1931 series were P180YD to P188DW for early year cars with Fedco type numbers and 79970001 to 7998712 for later in the year cars. Engine numbers for the 1931 series were V27182 to V29413. Specifications were the same, except that prices and weights on closed cars changed as follows: business coupe was $1,245 and 3,425 pounds; Royal coupe was $1,295 and 3,520 pounds; brougham was $1,245 and 3,530 pounds; and Royal sedan was $1,295 and 3,590 pounds. Consult 1930 listing for additional information.

1931 Chrysler, Series CD, convertible coupe (OCW)

CHRYSLER — SERIES CD — EIGHT: Chrysler's first eight had a wide profile vee-type radiator that somewhat resembled the radiator of the L-29 front-wheel drive Cord. Other styling features included two cowl ventilators, vertical louver hoods, sloping windshields, and cowl lamps. The first series CD (80 hp) was built from July 1930 to about January 1931. It was succeeded by a second series CD (88 hp) built from approximately January 1931 to April 1931. Body styling for these two lines was virtually identical.

IMPERIAL — SERIES CG — EIGHT: A totally new Imperial was seen for 1931. With its vee-type radiator, long hood, broad sweeping fenders, and slanting split windshield, it took Chrysler's new "L-29 look" one step further than the smaller cars. Features included interior sun visors, adjustable front seats and steering columns, hydraulic brakes, four-speed transmission, hydraulic shocks, rubber spring shackles, and a new instrument panel. Standard factory bodies were by Briggs. Semi-custom bodies were by LeBaron. Waterhouse, Locke, Derham, and Murphy also produced individual custom bodies on the Imperial chassis.

1931 Chrysler, Series CG, Imperial dual-cowl phaeton, LeBaron (JAC)

CHRYSLER — SERIES CM — SIX: This so-called "New Series Six" for 1931 was introduced in January 1931 as a mid-year model, probably at the New York salon. It featured a new, wide profile, vee-type radiator, vertical hood louvers, cowl lamps and two cowl ventilators. A new double-drop frame design gave extremely low-slung, sporty lines that followed Chrysler's "L-29 look" theme. Early closed cars were even built without external sun visors. Most likely, this change proved unpopular as later editions had small, rounded visors. Sport models were highlighted by including several accessories - such as sidemounts and wire wheels - as regular equipment.

1931 Chrysler, Series CD, roadster (JAC)

CHRYSLER — DELUXE CD SERIES — EIGHT: The Deluxe CD series replaced the second series CD line in May 1931. It was a fancier more powerful version of this sporty looking 1931 Chrysler eight. Identification features included dual (split) windshields, screened vee-type radiators, and winged radiator caps. Standard equipment included hydraulic brakes, four-speed transmission, four-point engine mounting, and rubber spring shackles.

I.D. DATA: [Series CJ] Serial numbers were now on the right front door hinge pillar. Starting: 6514920. Ending: 6520171. Engine numbers remained in the previous location. Starting: CJ24495. Ending: CJ30292. [Series CD] Serial numbers were in the same location. (First Series) Starting: 7500001. Ending: 7510538. (Second Series) Starting: 7510539. Ending: 7514222. Engine numbers were in the same location. (First Series) Starting: CD-11531. (Second Series) Starting: CD-11532. Ending: CD-15671. Note: The use of the first and second series designations is believed to be relatively modern and both were probably considered a single line when new. Production figures for both seem to be lumped together. The CD series should not be confused with the CD Deluxe Eight line introduced in May 1931, which had a more powerful 100 hp engine. [Series CG] Serial numbers were in the same locations. Starting: 7800001. Ending: 7802915. Engine numbers were stamped on top of the timing gear chain cover. Starting: CG1001. Ending: CG3924. [Series CM] Serial numbers were in the same location. Starting: 6520501. Ending: 6548433. Engine numbers were in the same location as on other Chrysler engines (but not Imperial engines). Starting: CM1001. Ending: CM30828. [Series CD] Serial numbers were in the same locations. Starting: 7514601. Ending: 7519758. Engine numbers were in the same locations. Starting: CD16001. Ending: CD21140.

Model No.	Body Type & Seating	Price	Weight	Prod. Total
CJ	2-dr. Rds.-2/4P	785	2390	1616
CJ	4-dr. Tr.-5P	785	2455	279
CJ	2-dr. Cpe.-2P	745	2560	2267
CJ	2-dr. Roy. Cpe.-2/4P	785	2590	3593
CJ	2-dr. Conv. Cpe.-2/4P	875	2550	705
CJ	4-dr. Roy. Sed.-5P	795	2695	20748

Note 1: Total production was 29,239.
Note 2: Bold face indicates 1930-31 combined total.

CD	2-dr. RS Rds.-2/4P	1495	3100	1462
CD	2-dr. Spt. Rds.-2/4P	1595	3270	Note 2
CD	4-dr. D.W. Phae.-5P	1970	3490	85
CD	2-dr. Std. Roy. Cpe.-2/4P	1495	3290	3000
CD	2-dr. Spl. Roy. Cpe.-2/4P	1535	3290	Note 3
CD	2-dr. Spl. Conv. Cpe.-2/4P	1665	3195	700
CD	4-dr. Std. Roy. Sed.-5P	1525	3405	9000
CD	4-dr. Spl. Roy. Sed.-5P	1565	3405	Note 4

Note 1: Total Series CD production was 14,355. This includes all first and second series cars including 108 chassis only supplied to custom coachbuilders.
Note 2: Production totals of the roadster and sports roadster is combined.
Note 3: Production of the standard and special Royal coupes is combined.
Note 4: Production of the standard and special Royal sedans is combined.

(Semi-Custom)

CG	2-dr. LeB. Rds.-2/4P	3220	4530	100
CG	4-dr. LeB. D.C. Phae.-5P	3575	4645	85
CG	2-dr. LeB. Cpe.-2/4P	3150	4605	135
CG	2-dr. LeB. Conv. Cpe.-2/4P	3320	4570	10

Model No.	Body Type & Seating	Price	Weight	Prod. Total
(Standard Factory)				
CG	4-dr. Sed.-5P	2745	4705	909
CG	4-dr. C.C. Sed.-5P	2845	4685	1195
CG	4-dr. Sed.-7P	2945	4825	403
CG	4-dr. Limo. Sed.-7/8P	3145	4915	271
(Individual Custom)				
CG	2-dr. Waterhouse Conv. Vic.-5P	—	—	6
CG	2-dr. LeBaron Spdstr. Conv.-2P	—	—	1
CG	2-dr. Drauz (German) Conv. Sed-5P	—	—	1
CG	2-dr. LeBaron Conv. Sed.-5P	—	—	1
CG	4-dr. LeBaron Twn. Car-7P	—	—	unknown

Note: Total Imperial Series CG production was 3,228 cars of all types. This includes 99 chassis supplied to custom coachbuilders on which individual custom models were constructed. The above list of individual customs illustrates some models known to have been made. It does not represent a complete list and the production totals provided are strictly estimates.

CM	2-dr. RS Rds.-2/4P	885	2565	2281
CM	2-dr. Bus. Cpe.-2P	865	2730	802
CM	2-dr. RS Cpe.-2/4P	885	2775	5327
CM	2-dr. Conv. Cpe.-2/4P	970	2870	1492
CM	4-dr. Sed.-5P	895	2850	28620
CM	4-dr. DW Phae.-5P	915	2740	196
CM	Chassis Only	NA	NA	99

Note 1: Total Series CM production was 38,817.

Del CD	2-dr. RS Rds.-2/4P	1545	3330	511
Del CD	4-dr. Phae.-5P	1970	3545	113
Del CD	2-dr. RS Cpe.-2/4P	1525	3525	1506
Del CD	2-dr. Bus. Cpe.-2/4P	1565	3575	500
Del CD	2-dr. Conv. Cpe.-2/4P	1585	3445	501
Del CD	4-dr. Sed.-5P	1565	3640	5843
Del CD	Chassis Only	NA	NA	126

Note 1: Total DeLuxe CD series production was 9,106.

ENGINE: [Series CJ] Inline. L-head. Six. Cast iron block. B & S: 3-1/8 x 4-1/2 in. Disp.: 195.6 cu. in. C.R.: 5.2:1. Main bearings: four. Valve lifters: solid. Carb.: Carter 1V. [Series CD] (First Series): Inline. L-head. Eight. Cast iron block. B & S: 3 x 4-1/4 in. Disp.: 240.33 cu. in. C.R.: 5.2:1. Brake H.P.: 80 @ 3400 R.P.M. N.A.C.C. H.P.: 28.8. Valve lifters: solid. Carb.: Stromberg Model BXV-2. (Second Series): Inline. L-head. Eight. Cast iron block. B & S: 3-1/8 x 4-1/4 in. Disp.: 260.8 cu. in. C.R.: 5.2:1. Brake H.P.: 88 @ 3400 R.P.M. N.A.C.C. H.P.: 31.25. Valve lifters: solid. Carb.: Stromberg. [Series CG] Inline. L-head. Eight. Cast iron block. B & S: 3-1/2 x 5 in. Disp.: 384.84 cu. in. C.R.: 5.2:1. Brake H.P.: 125 @ 3200 R.P.M. N.A.C.C. H.P.: 39.2. Main bearings: nine. Valve lifters: solid. Carb.: Stromberg Model DD-3. [Series CM] Inline. L-head. Six. Cast iron block. B & S: 3-1/4 x 4-3/8 in. Disp.: 217.8 cu. in. C.R.: 5.35:1. Brake H.P.: 78 @ 3400 R.P.M. N.A.C.C. H.P.: 25.35. Main bearings: seven. Valve lifters: solid. Carb.: Stromberg UR-2. [Deluxe CD Series] Inline. L-head. Eight. Cast iron block. B & S: 3-1/4 x 4-1/4 in. Disp.: 282.1 cu. in. C.R.: 5.2:1. Brake H.P.: 100 @ 3400 R.P.M. N.A.C.C. H.P.: 33.8. Valve lifters: solid. Carb.: Stromberg Model DXC-3.

CHASSIS: [Series CJ] W.B.: 109 in. Gas tank: 15.5 gal. Tires: 19 x 5.00. [Series 66] W.B.: 112-3/4 in. Gas tank: 11 gal. Tires: 18 x 5.50. [Series 70] W.B.: 116-1/2 in. Gas tank: 19.5 gal. Tires: 18 x 5.50. [Series CD] W.B.: 124 in. O.L.: 186 in. Gas tank: 19.5 gal. Tires: 18 x 5.50. [Series CG/Imperial] W.B.: 145 in. Gas tank: 21.5 gal. Tires: 18 x 7.00 or 18 x 7.50. [Series CM] W.B.: 116 in. Gas tank: 15.5 gal. Tires: 19 x 5.00 or 19 x 5.25. [Series DeL. CD] W.B.: 124 in. Gas tank: 19.5 gal. Tires: 17 x 6.50.

TECHNICAL: Three-speed manual transmission in CJ and CM sixes. Speeds: 3F/1R. Four-speed manual "multi-range" transmission in other series. Speeds: 4F/1R. Floor shift controls. Conventional clutch. Shaft drive. Overall ratio: [Series CJ] 4.7:1; [Series 66] 4.7:1; [Series 70] 3.82:1; [Series CD] 4.10:1; [Series CG] 4.1:1; [Series CM] 4.66:1; and [Series DeL. CD] 4.3:1. Hydraulic brakes standard on all Chryslers and Imperials. Wire wheels standard on CD/CG; wood-spoke wheels standard on other series.

OPTIONS: Front bumper. Rear bumper. Rear fender guards. Spare tire. Sidemounted spare tire(s). Wire-spoke wheels. Outside rear view mirror. Pedestal sidemount mirror(s). Cowl lights. Cigar lighter. Trunk rack. Touring trunk. Special solid paint. Two-tone sweep panel finish on Series 77 roadsters and phaetons. Leather sidemount covers. Metal sidemount covers. Metal sidemount cover trim moldings. Spotlight(s). Trippe lights. Wind wings. Imperial custom bodies.

1931 Chrysler, Series CD, four-door sedan (JAC)

HISTORICAL: The CM series was introduced in January 1931. The De-Luxe CD series was introduced in May 1931. All other series introduced in July 1930. Calendar year production: 52,819. Calendar year new car registrations: 52,650. The 1931 Imperial CG is often considered the most beautiful Imperial ever built. Chrysler appeared in the Indy 500 and European Grand Prix racing again this year. Stock car driver Harry Hartz set numerous speed records with an Imperial sedan at Daytona Beach, Florida. Mayor Al Smith, of New York City, drove an Imperial LeBaron Phaeton.

1931-32 CHRYSLER

CHRYSLER — CM SERIES — SIX: After July 1931 the Chrysler CM Six was sold as a first series 1932 model. This was basically a carryover series, with only small changes in the cars. The changes included a narrow profile radiator, cowl lights mounted on the body surcingle, and the introduction of freewheeling as an option. Horsepower ratings increased slightly.

CHRYSLER — 70 SERIES — SIX: This series was also sold as a carryover line during the first part of the 1932 model year, which began in July 1931. Styling features included a new narrow profile radiator with the pennon-type hood design. Standard equipment included four-speed transmission, downdraft carburetor, rubber spring shackles and fuel pump.

CHRYSLER — CD SERIES — EIGHT: The Deluxe Eight series was also carried over into the early part of the 1932 model year. Features were unchanged.

IMPERIAL — CG SERIES — EIGHT: In July 1931, the Chrysler Imperial CG series was also carried over into the first part of the 1932 model year. Features included dual sloping windshields, interior sun visors, vertical hood louvers, and a streamlined vee-type radiator. Standard equipment included four-speed transmission, hydraulic brakes, and four point engine mounting.

I.D. DATA: [CM Series] Serial numbers were in the same location. Starting: 6548434. Ending: 6557326. Engine numbers were also in the same location. Starting: CM30829. Ending: CM39467. [70 Series] Serial numbers were in the same location. Starting: 7998713. Ending: 7999974. Engine numbers were also in the same location. Starting: V29414. Ending: V30378. [CD Series] Serial numbers were in the same locations. Starting: 7519759. Ending: 7523531. Engine numbers were also in the same locations. Starting: CD21141. Ending: CD25182. [CG Series] Serial numbers were in the same location. Starting: 7802916. Ending: 7803273. Engine numbers were in the same location. Starting: CG3925. Ending: CG4268.

Model No.	Body Type & Seating	Price	Weight	Prod. Total
CM	2-dr. Rds.-2/4P	885	2615	Note 1
CM	4-dr. Phae.-5P	915	2740	Note 1
CM	2-dr. Bus. Cpe.-2P	865	2765	Note 1
CM	2-dr. RS Cpe.-2/4P	885	2830	Note 1
CM	2-dr. Conv. Cpe.-2/4P	935	2785	Note 1
CM	4-dr. Sed.-5P	895	2935	Note 1

Note 1: See 1931 Chrysler CM Series production totals.

SPECIFICATIONS: [70 Series] Only four body styles in the Chrysler 70 series were carried over as 1932 model year offerings. They were the business coupe, Royal coupe, brougham and Royal sedan. Prices and weights for the four models were unchanged. Refer to the 1931 specifications for details. [CD Series] There were no changes in available body styles, prices, or weights. Refer to the 1931 specifications for details. [CG Series] There was now a total of nine models. Eight were the same ones offered in 1931. The descriptions, prices, weights, and production totals were unchanged except that the former Custom Phaeton was now called a Custom sport phaeton. There was also one new model:

Model No.	Body Type & Seating	Price	Weight	Prod. Total
CG	4-dr. Cus. Conv. Sed.-5P	3995	4825	25

ENGINE: [CM Series] Inline. L-head. Six. Cast iron block. B & S: 3-1/4 x 4-3/8 in. Disp.: 217.8 cu. in. C.R.: 5.35:1. Brake H.P.: 78 @ 3400 R.P.M. N.A.C.C. H.P.: 25.35. Carb.: Schebler model UR-2. (70 Series) The Chrysler 70 series engine was unchanged. Refer to the 1931 engine specifications for details. [CD Series] The Chrysler CD Deluxe Eight engine was unchanged. Refer to the 1931 engine specifications for details. [CG Series] The Imperial CG engine was unchanged. Refer to the 1931 engine specifications for details.

CHASSIS: Chassis specifications for all models were the same as 1931 specifications except: 1932 CM sixes used 19 x 5.25 tires and 1932 Imperial CGs used 17 x 7.50 tires.

TECHNICAL: Same as 1931 models.

OPTIONS: Same as 1931 models.

HISTORICAL: Same as 1931 models. While these cars were sold as 1932 models, their production was included in 1931 Chrysler production records.

PRICING: Consult 1931 price listings.

1932 CHRYSLER

1932 Chrysler, Series CI, roadster (OCW)

CHRYSLER — SERIES CI — SIX: The second series 1932 Chrysler sixes were extensively updated. Styling changes included a new oval instrument board, new dual (split) vee-type windshields on closed cars (one-piece on open cars), dual cowl ventilators, and larger hubcaps that covered the wheel lugs. Standard equipment included Delco Remy ignition, hydraulic brakes, flexible "Floating Power" type engine suspension system, double drop frame, dash-controlled freewheeling, and hydraulic shock absorbers. New optional features included an automatic vacuum-controlled clutch and silent gear selector. Six wire wheels were standard equipment on the convertible sedan. For the English market, these cars were sold as the Richmond and Kingston, a third six-cylinder car was called the Mortlake but it was based on the DeSoto SC.

CHRYSLER — SERIES CP — EIGHT: This new second series 1932 series featured all steel bodies, a new double drop "girder truss" frame, narrow vee-type radiator, split vee-type windshields on closed cars, interior sun visors, cowl lamps, and twin trumpet-type horns. Standard equipment included Delco Remy ignition, hydraulic brakes, Floating Power, four-speed transmission, dash button controlled freewheeling, rubber spring shackles, and six wire wheels on the convertible sedan and limited edition LeBaron town car. Automatic vacuum controlled clutch was optional. Following the practice of naming models after suburbs of London, this model was sold in England as the Hurlingham.

1932 Chrysler, Series CP, convertible coupe (JAC)

IMPERIAL — SERIES CH — EIGHT: This new second series 1932 line featured dual vee-type windshields, cowl lamps, twin inside sun visors, twin trumpet horns, an indirectly lighted oval instrument panel, and luxury appointments. Standard equipment included Delco Remy ignition, hydraulic brakes, Floating Power, double drop frame, freewheeling, four-speed transmission, downdraft carburetor, rubber spring shackles, wire wheels, and rear-mounted spare (on most body types). Six wire wheel equipment was standard on the convertible sedan. The optional automatic vacuum operated clutch feature was available.

CUSTOM IMPERIAL — SERIES CL — EIGHT: The 1932 Custom Imperial CL models had a special lengthened hood with door-type hood ventilators instead of vertical louvers. Differences from the Imperial CH models included a longer wheelbase, larger overall size, bigger tires, a walnut dashboard with machine tooled instrument cluster, and twin glove boxes and custom bodies. Most of the cars had LeBaron semi-custom coachwork, but five chassis were supplied for individual custom bodies, of which two were done for the Walter P. Chrysler family.

1932 Chrysler, Series CL, Imperial convertible sedan, LeBaron (AA)

I.D. DATA: [Series CI] Serial numbers were again found on a plate located on the right front door hinge pillar post. Starting: 6557401. Ending: 6575639. Engine numbers were again located on the upper left side of the cylinder block between one and two cylinders, just below the cylinder head. Engine Nos. Starting: C11001. Ending: C119425. [Series CP] Serial numbers were in the same location. Starting: 7523601. Ending: 7528546. Engine numbers were in the same location. Engine Nos. Starting: CP10001. Ending: CP6171. [Series CH] Serial numbers were in the same location. Starting: 7900001. Ending: 7901362. Engine numbers were in the same location. Engine Nos. Starting: CH1001. Ending: CH2416. [CL Series] Serial numbers were in the same location. Starting: 7803301. Ending: 7803527. Engine numbers were in the same location. Engine Nos. Starting: CL1001. Ending: CL1247.

Model No.	Body Type & Seating	Price	Weight	Prod. Total
CI	2-dr. Rds.-2/4P	885	2830	474
CI	4-dr. Phae.-5P	915	2905	59
CI	2-dr. Bus. Cpe.-2P	865	2915	345
CI	2-dr. R/S Cpe.-2/4P	885	3040	2913
CI	2-dr. Conv. Cpe.-2/4P	935	2970	1000
CI	4-dr. Sed.-5P	895	3135	13,772
CI	2-dr. Conv. Sed.-5P	1125	3160	322
CI	Chassis only	NA	NA	70

Note 1: Total series production was 18,964.

Note 2: A limited amount of custom bodied cars were built on the Chrysler CI six chassis. They are eligible for full Classic status upon individual application.

CP	2-dr. R/S Cpe.-2/4P	1435	3735	718
CP	2-dr. Cpe.-5P	1475	3810	396
CP	2-dr. Conv. Cpe.-2/4P	1495	3705	502
CP	4-dr. Sed.-5P	1475	3885	3198
CP	4-dr. Conv. Sed.-5P	1695	4090	251
CP	Chassis only	NA	NA	48
CP	4-dr. LeB. Twn. Car-5P	3975	4320	(-12)

Note 1: Total series production was 5,113.

Note 2: A limited amount of custom bodies were built on the Chrysler CP eight chassis. Of the 48 chassis supplied to custom coachbuilders, it is believed that less than one dozen had the semi-factory LeBaron town car body for which the price and weight are listed above. Specifications for other individual customs are not available.

CH	2-dr. R/S Cpe.-2/4P	1925	4480	239
CH	4-dr. Sed.-5P	1945	4645	1002
CH	4-dr. Conv. Sed.-5P	2195	4890	152
CH	Chassis only	NA	NA	9

Note 1: Total series production was 1,402.

Note 2: Nine custom bodies were built on the 1932 Imperial CH chassis.

Note 3: All Imperial CH models are considered full Classics.

CL	4-dr. LeB. D.C. Phae.-5P	3395	5065	14
CL	2-dr. LeB. Conv. Rds.-2/4P	3295	4930	28
CL	4-dr. LeB. C.C. Sed.-5P	2895	5150	57
CL	4-dr. LeB. Conv. Sed.-5P	3595	5125	49
CL	4-dr. LeB. Sed.-7P	2995	5295	35
CL	4-dr. LeB. Sed. Limo.-7/8P	3295	5330	32

Individual Customs

CL	2-dr. LeB. Rds./Spds.-2P	NA	NA	1
CL	4-dr. LeB. Land. Limo.-7P	NA	NA	1
CL	Others	NA	NA	3

Note 1: Total series production was 220.

Note 2: Five chassis were supplied to coachbuilders for individual custom bodies. The LeBaron landau limousine was built for Walter P. Chrysler. It was fitted with early bowl-type headlights and a special fabric-covered hard top. The LeBaron roadster-speedster was built for one of Walter P. Chrysler's sons.

1932 Chrysler, Series CI, convertible coupe (OCW)

ENGINE: [Series CI] Inline. L-head. Six. Cast iron block. B & S: 3-1/4 x 4-1/2 in. Disp.: 223.98 cu. in. C.R.: 5.35:1. Brake H.P.: 82 @ 3400 R.P.M. N.A.C.C. H.P.: 25.35. Valve lifters: solid. Carb.: Ball & Ball model 6A1. [Series CP] Inline. L-head. Eight. Cast iron block. B & S: 3-1/4 x 4-1/2 in. Disp.: 298.6 cu. in. C.R.: 5.2:1. Brake H.P.: 100 @ 3400 R.P.M. N.A.C.C. H.P.: 33.80. Valve lifters: solid. Carb.: Stromberg model DXR-3. [Series CH] Inline. L-head. Eight. Cast iron block. B & S: 3-1/2 x 5 in. Disp.: 384.84 cu. in. C.R.: 5.2:1. Brake H.P.: 125 @ 3200 R.P.M. N.A.C.C. H.P.: 39.20. Valve lifters: solid. Carb.: Stromberg model DD-3. [Series CL] See 1932 Imperial CH series engine specifications.

CHASSIS: [Series CI] W.B: 116 in. Tires: 18 x 5.50. Gas tank: 15.5 gal. [Series CP] W.B.: 125 in. Tires: 17 x 6.50. Gas tank: 19.5 gal. [Series CH] W.B.: 135 in. Tires: 17 x 7.00. Gas tank: 21.5 gal. [Series CL] W.B.: 146 in. Tires: 17 x 7.50. Gas tank: 21.5 gal.

1932 Chrysler, Series CL, Imperial coupe (JAC)

TECHNICAL: Three-speed manual transmission in Series CI Chrysler Six. Speeds: 3F/1R. Four-speed manual transmission in all other series. Speeds: 4F/1R. Floor shift controls. Conventional clutch. Shaft drive. Overall gear ratios: [CI] 4.6:1; [CP] 4.3:1; [CH/CL] 4.1:1. Four-wheel hydraulic brakes on all series. Wood-spoke wheels standard on Chryslers; wire-spoke wheels standard on Imperials.

OPTIONS: Front bumper. Rear bumper. Rear fender guards. Rare spare (on Chryslers). Sidemounted spares. Leather sidemount covers. Metal sidemount covers. Chrome plated sidemount covers. Outside rear view mirror. Pedestal type outside rear view mirrors with sidemounts. Jumbo type Goodyear "Air Wheel" tires. Steel spoke wheels on Chrysler sixes and eights. Trunk rack. Touring trunk. Leather rear tire cover. Wire wheels (on Chrysler sixes and eights). Cigar lighter. Radio. Radio antenna. Wind wings. Heater. Clock. Spotlight(s). Trippe lights. Rear windshield (phaeton). Automatic vacuum-operated clutch. Silent gear transmission.

HISTORICAL: The second series 1932 models were introduced in January 1932. Calendar year production: 25,291. Calendar year registrations: 26,016. Model year production: 25,699. Innovations: Freewheeling. Automatic vacuum clutch. Silent gear transmission. "Floating Power" flexible engine mounts. Chrysler was 10th in U.S. model year sales and 11th in calendar year output. The Chrysler-powered George Howie Special qualified for the Indy 500, but was bumped from the field before the race started. The Chrysler-powered Golden Seal Special started 36th in the Indy 500 and went out with a burned clutch on lap 17. Two "Trifon Special" prototypes for the Chrysler Airflow were built.

1933 CHRYSLER

1933 Chrysler, convertible coupe (OCW)

CHRYSLER — CO SERIES — SIX: The Chrysler sixes were the company's best selling cars for 1933. They had more massive streamlined fenders that swept lower in the front. Other styling changes included a long, cowl-less hood with door-type ventilators, single bar bumpers, "suicide" rear hinged doors, sloping vee-type radiators, slanting vee-type windshields and more rakish, slanted door openings. Standard equipment included Delco Remy ignition, hydraulic brakes, "Floating Power," automatic vacuum clutch, freewheeling, silent helical gear transmission,

Oilite springs, and a new coincidental starter/accelerator pedal. The sixes came with single windshield wipers and without external trumpet horns. Six wire wheel equipment was standard on convertible sedans.

1933 Chrysler, Series CT, Royal convertible coupe (JAC)

CHRYSLER ROYAL — CT SERIES — EIGHT: The Royal eights for 1933 also had the new sweeping fenders, single bar bumpers, "suicide" doors, sloping vee-type radiator, slanting vee-type windshield, door-type hood vents, and more streamlined looks. Distinctive features of the Royal eights included all-steel body construction, dual windshield wipers, dual tail-lights, and dual chrome trumpet horns. Standard equipment included Delco Remy ignition, Lockheed hydraulic brakes, "Floating Power," co-incidental starter, automatic vacuum clutch, adjustable front seats, automatic-control shock absorbers, and six wire wheel equipment on the convertible sedan. A high horsepower engine option was available.

IMPERIAL — SERIES CQ — EIGHT: The Imperial CQ was an all-new, smaller car that was downsized about nine inches from comparable 1932 models. It shared the annual styling theme of sweeping fenders, sloping vee-type radiators, a cowl-less hood with door type ventilators, single bumpers, and slanting vee-type windshields. Rear hinged "suicide" doors were, however, found only on the Imperial CQ convertible sedan. Standard equipment included dual wipers, taillights and external chrome trumpet horns, a covered rear spare, Delco Remy ignition, Lockheed hydraulic brakes, "Floating Power," automatic vacuum clutch, and freewheeling. Six wire wheel equipment, landau irons, and a touring trunk were standard on convertible sedans. In a new twist, Imperial buyers were offered a *lower* horsepower engine option.

CUSTOM IMPERIAL — CL SERIES — EIGHT: This richest of all Chrysler series also had sweeping fenders, sloping vee-radiators, sloping dual windshields (on open and closed cars), a cowl-less hood with door-type ventilators, single bar bumper, and chrome external trumpet horns. Rear hinged "suicide" doors were used on all Custom Imperials, except the limousine. As usual, the factory cataloged semi-custom bodies were by LeBaron. Only six chassis and cowls were supplied to custom coach-builders and at least two of them were bodied in Switzerland by the shops of Lagenthawl and Jean Oygaz. Standard Custom Imperial features included Delco Remy ignition, Lockheed hydraulic brakes, "Floating Power," automatic vacuum clutch, coincidental starter, and freewheeling. The Custom Imperials also had rust-proofed fenders, automatic heat control, downdraft carburetion, and safety glass throughout. Wire wheels were standard on all models, but could be deleted upon owner request. Six wire wheels and a trunk were standard on phaetons and convertible sedans.

1933 Chrysler, Series CO, business coupe (JAC)

CHRYSLER — WIMBLEDON — SIX: Following its practice of selling a smaller or less expensive car in overseas markets, Chrysler marketed what was in reality the model SD DeSoto in Great Britain. Although fitted with a small-bore export engine, the Chrysler Wimbledon was generally equipped with deluxe appointments such as dual fender-mounted spare tires.

CHRYSLER — KEW — SIX: The smallest and least expensive Chrysler sold in the United Kingdom was in reality a rebadged Plymouth Six. The Chrysler Kew appears to have made its English debut in 1931 and would survive until England's entry into World War II in 1939.

I.D. DATA: [CO Series] Serial numbers were again found on a plate located on the right front door hinge pillar post. Starting: 6576001. Ending: 6592816. Engine numbers were again located on the upper left side of the cylinder block between the one and two cylinders, just below the cylinder head. Starting: C01001. Ending: C018608. [CT Series] Serial numbers were in the same location. Starting: 7000001. Ending: 7010035. Engine numbers were in the same location. Starting: CT10001. Ending: CT11396. [Series CQ] Serial numbers were in the same location. Starting: 7529001. Ending: 7532779. Engine numbers were in the same location. Starting: CQ1001. Ending: CQ4864. [CL Series] Serial numbers were in the same location. Starting: 7803551. Ending: 7803705. Engine numbers were in the same location. Starting: CL1251. Ending: CL1408.

Model No.	Body Type & Seating	Price	Weight	Prod. Total
CO	2-dr. Bus. Cpe.-2P	745	2968	587
CO	2-dr. RS Cpe.-2/4P	775	3018	1454
CO	2-dr. Conv. Cpe.-2/4P	795	3013	677
CO	2-dr. Brgm.-5P	745	3078	1207
CO	4-dr. Sed.-5P	785	3143	13264
CO	4-dr. Spl. Int. Sed.-7P	825	3160	51
CO	2-dr. Conv. Sed.-7P	945	3212	207
CO	4-dr. Sed.-7P	NA	NA	151
CO	Chassis & Cowl	NA	NA	267

Note 1: Total series production was 17,814.

(120" wb)

CT	2-dr. Bus. Cpe.-2P	895	3303	226
CT	2-dr. RS Cpe.-2/4P	915	3343	1033
CT	2-dr. Conv. Cpe.-2/4P	945	3363	539
CT	4-dr. Sed.-5P	925	3483	7993
CT	2-dr. Conv. Sed.-5P	1085	3617	257

(128" wb)

CT	4-dr. Sed.-7/8P	1125	3658	246
CT	Chassis & Cowl	NA	NA	95

Note 1: Total series production was 10,389.

Note 2: Custom-bodied cars built on the 128 in. wheelbase CT Series chassis may be accepted by the Classic Car Club of America on an individual application basis.

CQ	2-dr. RS Cpe.-2/4P	1275	3734	364
CQ	2-dr. Vic. Cpe.-5P	1295	3754	267
CQ	2-dr. Conv. Cpe.-2/4P	1325	3754	243
CQ	4-dr. Sed.-5P	1295	3864	2584
CQ	4-dr. Conv. Sed.-5P	1495	4144	364
CQ	Chassis & Cowl	NA	NA	16

Note 1: Total series production was 3,838.

(LeBaron semi-custom)

CL	4-dr. Phae.-5P	3395	4890	36
CL	2-dr. Rds. Conv.-2/4P	3295	4910	9
CL	4-dr. C.C. Sed.-5P	2895	5045	43
CL	4-dr. Sed.-8P	2995	5240	21
CL	4-dr. Limo.-8P	3295	5245	22
CL	4-dr. Conv. Sed.-5P	3395	5135	11

(Individual Customs)

CL	2-dr. Stationary Cpe.	NA	NA	3
CL	Chassis & Cowl	NA	NA	6

Note 1: Total series production was 151.

ENGINE: [CO Series] Inline. L-head. Six. Cast iron block. B & S: 3-1/4 x 4-1/2 in. Disp.: 223.98 cu. in. C.R.: 5.35:1. Brake H.P.: 83 @ 3400 R.P.M. N.A.C.C. H.P.: 25.35. Main bearings: four. Valve lifters: solid. Carb.: Stromberg IV. (Note: Optional engine with 6.2:1 high compression "Red Head" and 89 BHP @ 3400 R.P.M. available). [CT Series] Inline. L-head. Eight. Cast iron block. B & S: 3-1/4 x 3-1/8 in. Disp.: 273.7 cu. in. C.R.: (Std.) 5.4:1. (Opt.) 6.2:1. Brake H.P.: (Std.) 90 @ 3400 R.P.M.; (Opt.) 98 @ 3400 R.P.M. N.A.C.C. H.P.: 25.35. Main bearings: five. Valve lifters: solid. Carb.: Stromberg IV model EX-32. [Series CQ] Inline. L-head. Eight. Cast iron block. B & S: 3-1/4 x 4-1/2 in. Disp.: 298.65 cu. in. C.R.: (Std.) 6.2:1; (Opt.) 5.2:1. Brake H.P.: (Std.) 108 @ 3400 R.P.M.; (Opt.) 100 @ 3400 R.P.M. N.A.C.C. H.P.: 33.80. Main bearings: nine. Valve lifters: solid. Carb.: Stromberg IV model EX-32. [CL Series] Inline. L-head. Eight. Cast iron block. B & S: 3-1/2 x 5 in. Disp.: 384.84 cu. in. C.R.: (Std.) 5.8:1; (Opt.) 5.2:1. Brake H.P.: (Std.) 135 @ 3200 R.P.M.; (Opt.) 125 @ 3200 R.P.M. N.A.C.C. H.P.: 39.20. Main bearings: nine. Valve lifters: solid. Carb.: Stromberg 2V model EE-3.

CHASSIS: [Series CO] W.B.: 117 in. Tires: 17 x 5.50. Gas tank: 15.5 gal. [Series CT] W.B.: 120/128.5 in. Tires: 17 x 6.00. Gas tank: 16 gal. [Series CQ] W.B.: 126 in. Tires: 17 x 6.50. Gas tank: 19.5 gal. [Series CL] W.B.: 146 in. Tires: 17 x 7.50. Gas tank: 21.5 gal.

TECHNICAL: Manual transmission. Speeds: 3F/1R. (Note: The four-speed transmission with four speeds forward and one reverse was still used on Imperials.) Floor shift controls. Conventional clutch. Overall ratios: (CO) 4.37:1. (CT/CQ) 4.3:1. (CL) 4.10:1. Wire wheels were standard equipment on all Chryslers. Lockheed four-wheel brakes used on all series.

OPTIONS: Front bumper. Rear bumper. Rear spare (Chryslers). Side-mounted spares. Leather sidemount covers. Metal sidemount covers. Chrome sidemount covers. Outside rear view mirror. Pedestal outside rear view sidemount mirrors. Special Goodrich spoke wheels with General Jumbo tires. Trunk rack. Touring trunk. Leather rear tire cover. Wire wheels (chrome plated). Cigar lighter. Radio. Antenna. Wind wings. Heater. Clock. Spotlight(s). Trippe lights. Rear windshield (phaeton). Demountable wood-spoke wheels. Chrome steel spoked wheels. Chrome-plated hood ventilator doors. Retractable tonneau windshield (Custom Imperial phaeton).

1933 Chrysler, Imperial dual cowl phaeton, LeBaron (AA)

HISTORICAL: Introduced: The CL series was introduced at mid-model year in February 1933. Other series introduced in December 1932. Calendar year production: 30,220. Model year production: 32,241. Calendar year new car registrations: 28,677. Chrysler was America's ninth largest auto manufacturer on a model year basis and tenth ranked automaker on a calendar year sales basis. Innovations: new three-speed silent helical gear transmission on Chryslers. Improved steel alloy exhaust valve seats. New type oil filter. Automatic choke. Finishing fourteenth at the Indy 500, the Golden Seal Special was the last Chrysler-powered car to compete at Indianapolis in the prewar years. Development work on the Airflow design continued in 1933. This was also the last year that Chrysler produced a roadster.

1934 CHRYSLER

CHRYSLER — SERIES CA/CB — SIX: The Chrysler sixes for 1934 were the company's only conventional cars, as Chrysler and Imperial Eights took the new Airflow styling. New features included valanced front and rear fenders, horizontal hood louvers, body color radiator shells, and one-piece windshields. "Suicide" doors were used on all models in the short wheelbase CA line and on all models, except the convertible sedan, in the long wheelbase CB line. Standard equipment included Delco Remy ignition, independent front suspension, "Floating Power," front vent windows, dual windshield wipers, and steel spoke wheels.

1934 Chrysler, Series CA, sedan (JAC)

CHRYSLER AIRFLOW — SERIES CY — SIX: Following a confusing corporate policy of building special models for the export or Canadian markets, the CY Airflow fits neatly into this category. The CY was actually a DeSoto Airflow fitted with Chrysler trim. The CY sold for about $60 more than the SE DeSoto upon which it was based. Based on serial number sequence, only 444 were built.

1934 Chrysler, Series CU Airflow, four-door sedan (OCW)

CHRYSLER AIRFLOW — SERIES CU — EIGHT: The Chrysler eight used the new, ultra streamlined Airflow design with unit body construction. Features included an alligator hood, recessed headlights mounted in teardrop-shaped housings that incorporated the parking lights, triple bar bumpers, valanced fenders with full shroud rear fender skirts, a waterfall grille with multiple vertical blades, sloping vee-type windshield, front and rear vent windows (most models), and six vertical hood louvers arranged in groups of two with each pair of descending size. Standard equipment included Delco Remy ignition, Lockheed hydraulic brakes, cross flow radiator, automatic vacuum operated clutch, and "Floating Power." The town sedan had a blind rear quarter styling treatment.

IMPERIAL AIRFLOW — SERIES CV — EIGHT: This was a larger version of the new Airflow with more luxurious equipment and appointments. Features included a split windshield and triple bar bumpers. Standard equipment was the same as on the Chrysler CU Airflow eights, plus downdraft carburetor and vacuum assisted "power" brakes.

CUSTOM IMPERIAL AIRFLOW — SERIES CX — EIGHT: This was a new intermediate-sized series in the Airflow line. It was actually a long wheelbase version of the Imperial Airflow CV and used the same styling and equipment features. Even the engine had the same specifications. Although four body styles were cataloged, it appears that only two town limousines and one prototype version of the town sedan were built.

CUSTOM IMPERIAL AIRFLOW — SERIES CW — EIGHT: These were special models built in limited production quantities. They included the largest and heaviest models ever made by Chrysler Corporation. Special features included the first ever curved one-piece windshield, dual "step plate" runningboards with chrome trim moldings, an extended length cowl with longer trim moldings, and four bar bumpers. They had rounded radiator grilles and headlamps and parking lights that were integral with the hood. Full chrome wheel disks were available only on this series. Standard equipment included everything found on lower priced Airflows, plus automatic overdrive and ride stabilizer bars.

CHRYSLER — KEW — SIX: Again the smallest and least expensive Chrysler model sold in Great Britain, the Kew was in reality a rebadged Plymouth, fitted with the small-bore export engine of 170 cubic inches.

1934 Chrysler, Kew, two-door sedan (JB)

CHRYSLER — WIMBLEDON — SIX: Based on the Plymouth this year, the Wimbledon differed in appointments and had the regular bore Plymouth engine. Among the items special to England was a sliding roof

panel. The Plymouth was shipped as a CKD (completely knocked down) unit to Chrysler Kew assembly plant for final trim and finish.

CHRYSLER — CROYDON — SIX: This Chrysler model was in reality a DeSoto Airflow SE sold in the English market.

1934 Chrysler, Series CA, coupe (OCW)

I.D. DATA: [Series CA/CB] Serial numbers were again found on a plate on the right front door hinge pillar post. Starting: 6650001. Ending: 6672665. Engine numbers were again located on the upper left side of the cylinder block between the one and two cylinders, just below the cylinder head. Starting: CA1001 and CB1001. [Series CU] Serial numbers were in the same location. Starting: 6593001. Ending: 6601154. Engine numbers were in the same location. Starting: CU1001 (& up). [Series CV] Serial numbers were in the same location. Starting: 7010101. Ending: 7012191. Engine numbers were in the same location. Starting: CV1001 (& up). [Series CX] Serial numbers were in the same location. Starting: 7901401. Ending: 7901528. Engine numbers: See CV series engine codes. [Series CW] Serial numbers were located in the same location. Starting: 7803751. Ending: 7803798. Engine numbers were in the same location. Starting: CW1001. Ending: CW1071. CY serial numbers (Canada): Starting: 9820676. Ending: 9821120.

Model No.	Body Type & Seating	Price	Weight	Prod. Total
(CA Series)				
CA	2-dr. Bus. Cpe.-2p	775	2879	1650
CA	2-dr. Del. Cpe.-2/4P	830	2903	1875
CA	2-dr. Conv. Cpe.-2/4P	865	2889	700
CA	2-dr. Brgm.-5P	795	3019	1575
CA	4-dr. Sed.-5P	845	3123	17,617
CA	Chassis & Cowl	NA	NA	385
(CB Series)				
CB	4-dr. C.C. Sed.-5P	935	3094	980
CB	4-dr. Conv. Sed.-5P	985	3069	450
CB	Chassis & Cowl	NA	NA	20

Note 1: Total CA series production was 23,802.

Note 2: Total CB series production was 1,450.

CU	2-dr. Cpe.-5P	1345	3736	732
CU	2-dr. Brgm.-5P	1345	3741	306
CU	4-dr. Twn. Sed.-6P	1345	3716	125
CU	4-dr. Sed.-6P	1345	3760	7226

Note 1: Total series production was 8,389.

CV	2-dr. Cpe.-5P	1625	3929	212
CV	4-dr. Sed.-6P	1625	3974	1997
CV	4-dr. Twn. Sed.-6P	1625	3969	67
CV	Chassis & Cowl	NA	NA	1

Note 1: Total series production was 2,277.

CX	4-dr. Sed.-6P	2245	4154	25
CX	4-dr. Twn. Sed.-6P	2245	4160	1
CX	4-dr. Limo.-8P	2345	4299	78
CX	4-dr. Twn. Limo.-8P	2345	4304	2

Note 1: Total series production was 106.

CW	4-dr. Sed.-8P	5000	5780	17
CW	4-dr. Twn. Sed.-8P	5000	5815	28
CW	4-dr. Cus. Limo.-8P	5145	5900	20
CW	4-dr. Twn. Limo.-8P	5145	5935	2

Note 1: Total series production was 67.

ENGINE: [Series CA/CB] Inline. L-head. Six. Cast iron block. B & S: 3-3/8 x 4-1/2 in. Disp.: 241.6 cu. in. C.R.: (Std.) 5.4:1 (Opt.) 6.2:1. Brake H.P.: (Std.) 93 @ 3400 R.P.M.; (Opt.) 100 @ 3400 R.P.M. N.A.C.C. H.P.: 27.34. Main bearings: four. Valve lifters: solid. Carb.: Ball & Ball IV. [Series CU] Inline. L-head. Eight. Cast iron block. B & S: 3-1/4 x 4-1/2 in. Disp.: 299 cu. in. C.R.: 6.5:1. Brake H.P.: 122 @ 3400 R.P.M. N.A.C.C. H.P.: 33.80. Valve lifters: solid. Carb.: Stromberg model EX-32. [Series CV] Inline. L-head. Eight. Cast iron block. B & S: 3-1/4 x 4-7/8 in. Disp.: 323.5 cu. in. C.R.: 6.5:1. Brake H.P.:

130 @ 3400 R.P.M. N.A.C.C. H.P.: 33.80. Valve lifters: solid. Carb.: Stromberg IV model EE-22. [Series CX] See Imperial Airflow CV engine data. [Series CW] Inline. L-head. Eight. Cast iron block. B & S: 3-1/2 x 5 in. Disp.: 384.84 cu. in. C.R.: 6.5:1. Brake H.P.: 145 @ 3200 R.P.M. N.A.C.C. H.P.: 39.20. Valve lifters: solid. Carb.: Stromberg 2V model EE-3.

1934 Chrysler Imperial, Airflow, limousine (OCW)

CHASSIS: [Series CA] W.B.: 117 in. Tires: 16 x 6.50. Gas tank: 15 gal. [Series CB] W.B.: 121 in. Tires: 16 x 6.50. Gas tank: 15 gal. [Series CU] W.B.: 122.8 in. Tires: 16 x 7.00. Gas tank: 21 gal. [Series CV] W.B.: 128 in. Tires: 16 x 7.50. Gas tank: 21 gal. [Series CX] W.B.: 137.5 in. Tires: 16 x 7.50. Gas tank: 21 gal. [Series CW] W.B.: 146 in. Tires: 17 x 7.50. Gas tank: 30 gal.

TECHNICAL: [Custom Imperial Airflow CW] Manual transmission. Speeds: 4F/1R. [Other Series] Manual transmission. Speeds: 3F/1R. Floor shift. Conventional clutch. Shaft drive. Overall ratios: (CA/CB) 4.11:1; (CU/CV/CX) 4.10:1; (CW) 4.14:1. Steel spoke wheels standard on all series. Lockheed hydraulic four wheel brake standard on all series (vacuum assisted on CW).

OPTIONS: Front bumper. Rear bumper. Sidemount(s) on series CA/CB six. Leather sidemount cover. Steel sidemount cover. Chrome sidemount cover. Spotlight(s). Trippe lights. Rear spare (Chrysler sixes). Rear spare cover. Pedestal mirrors (with sidemounts). Outside rear view mirror(s). Clock. Cigar lighter. Radio. Antenna. Electric horns. Trunk rack. Touring trunk. Chrome wheel trim rings. Fender skirts (Airflow). Full wheel disks (Custom Imperial CW).

HISTORICAL: Introduced January 1934. Calendar year production: 36,929. Model year production: 36,091. Calendar year new car registrations: 28,052. Chrysler was America's 10th ranked automaker on a model year production basis and 11th ranked automaker on a calendar year sales basis. Innovations: five-degree tip to Airflow engine. Airflow steering gear in front of axle. Power brakes on Imperial CW Airflows. First curved one-piece windshield. Softer Airflow springs. Ten-inch wider seats in Airflows. Driver Harry Hartz established 72 stock car speed and endurance records at Daytona Beach, Florida, with a 1934 Airflow CU coupe. Hartz also averaged 18.1 mpg while driving a similar car coast-to-coast from Los Angeles to New York City.

1935 CHRYSLER

CHRYSLER AIRSTREAM — C-6 — SIX: Chrysler's conventional cars were now called Airstream models. They had new, all-steel unit bodies, slightly convex grilles, horizontal hood louvers and sloping rear panels with built-in luggage compartments. Standard equipment included Autolite ignition, hydraulic brakes, "Floating Power," synchromesh transmission, and a ventilated clutch. Sixes had single windshield wipers and taillights as standard equipment. There was also only one interior sun visor.

CHRYSLER AIRSTREAM — SERIES CZ — EIGHT: Chrysler's CZ Airstream Eight had a three-inch longer wheelbase than the Airstream Six. The cars in both lines looked basically the same otherwise, but the Eights had dual sun visors, wipers, and taillights added to the standard equipment list. They also had slightly larger tires.

CHRYSLER DELUXE AIRSTREAM — CZ (DELUXE) — EIGHT: DeLuxe Airstream Eights could be readily identified by their dual chrome trumpet horns, fender mounted parking lights, twin bullet-shaped taillights and winged "8" emblem on the front sides of the hood. Runningboards on the DeLuxe models had chrome trim moldings. These cars were actually a CZ subseries, but had specific serial numbers. Two body styles were offered with a longer than normal wheelbase. It's likely that most if not all of the bare chassis sold were also long wheelbase units.

CHRYSLER AIRFLOW — SERIES C-1 — EIGHT: The 1935 Airflow had a new hood that extended forward in a vee-shape. Single broad bumpers were used and the louvers on the hood were decorative, rather than functional. The new grille had a greater slope from top to bottom and ended squarely at the top of the radiator instead of tapering over the center. Standard equipment included Autolite ignition, hydraulic brakes, "Floating Power," automatic choke, and a stabilizer in back of the front axle.

1935 Chrysler, Series CZ, Airstream Deluxe, four-door sedan (AA)

IMPERIAL AIRFLOW — SERIES C-2 — EIGHT: The front fender valances, cowl sides, and decorative hood louvers on Imperial Airflows were longer than on the Chrysler Airflows. Tire sizes were larger, too. Interior appointments were correspondingly richer. An aluminum cylinder head and overdrive transmission were standard equipment for Imperials. Another feature was a Stromberg two-barrel carburetor. The Imperial Airflows also had vacuum-assisted power brakes.

IMPERIAL CUSTOM AIRFLOW — SERIES C-3 — EIGHT: The C-3 Imperial Custom Airflow was a big car with a wheelbase nearly 10 inches longer than the regular Imperial Airflow. Most of this extra room was evident in the car's longer front doors and side windows. There were four body styles in this series but two were built in extremely limited quantities and had a mixture of 1934 and 1935 features. For example, one town sedan limousine had triple bar bumpers and 1934 type hood doors combined with the new 1935 style grille and hood.

1935 Chrysler, Airflow, four-door sedan (OCW)

CUSTOM IMPERIAL AIRFLOW — SERIES CW* — EIGHT: In 1935, the CW Custom Imperial was replaced with the CW* with one-piece front and rear bumpers and decorative louvers instead of hood doors. These cars again had a distinctive, one-piece curved windshield. The interior featured rich upholstery and trim. A disappearing partition window was used in the limousines. Available records show 32 production units sold in 1935. However, it seems likely that additional cars were assembled this year and, later updated for sale in subsequent years.

I.D. DATA: [Series C-6] Serial numbers were on a plate on the front door hinge pillar post. Starting: 6800001. Ending: 6823250. Engine numbers were on the left side of cylinder block, between one and two cylin-

ders, just below cylinder head. Starting: C6-1001. Ending: C6-25519. [Series CZ] Serial numbers were in the same locations. Starting: 6701501. Ending: 6707676. Engine numbers were in the same locations. Starting: CZ-1001. Ending: CZ-10341. [Series CZ (DeLuxe)] Serial numbers were in the same location. Starting: 6707677. Ending: 6710401. Engine numbers were in the same location. Starting: CZ-1001. Ending: CZ-10341. [Series C-1] Serial numbers were in the same location. Starting: 6601201. Ending: 6606200. Engine numbers were in the same location. Starting: C1-1001. Ending: C1-6037. [Series C-2] Serial numbers were in the same location. Starting: 7012301. Ending: 7014900. Engine numbers were in the same location. Starting: C2-1001. Ending: C2-3632. [Series C-3] Serial numbers were in the same locations. Starting: 7528551. Ending: 7528675. Engine numbers were in the same location. Starting: C3-1001. Ending: C3-1135. [Series CW] Serial numbers were in the same locations. Starting: 7803799. Ending: 7803835. Engine numbers were in the same locations. Starting: CW-1049. Ending: CW-1080.

Model No.	Body Type & Seating	Price	Weight	Prod. Total
C6	2-dr. Bus. Cpe.-2P	745	2863	1975
C6	2-dr. RS Cpe.-2/4P	810	2953	861
C6	2-dr. Conv. Cpe.-2/4P	870	3053	Note 2
C6	2-dr. Tr. Brgm.-5P	820	2988	1901
C6	4-dr. Sed.-5P	830	3013	6055

Model No.	Body Type & Seating	Price	Weight	Prod. Total
C6	4-dr. Tr. Sed.-5P	860	3048	12,790
C6	Chassis	NA	NA	476
C6	2-dr. Fs. Bk. Sed.-5P	820	2990	400

Note 1: Total series production was 24,458.

Note 2: There is no available record of production of the C6 convertible coupe.

CZ	2-dr. Bus. Cpe.-2P	910	3103	Note 1
CZ	2-dr. RS Cpe.-2/4P	935	3138	Note 1
CZ	2-dr. Tr. Brgm.-5P	960	3203	Note 1
CZ	4-dr. Sed.-5P	975	3213	Note 1
CZ	4-dr. Tr. Sed.-5P	995	3263	Note 1

Note 1: Production of the Airstream Eights and DeLuxe Airstream Eights was recorded as a single, combined total. See figures listed below for DeLuxe Airstream Eight.

CZ	2-dr. Bus. Cpe.-2P	930	3138	100
CZ	2-dr. RS Cpe.-2/4P	955	3233	550
CZ	2-dr. Conv. Cpe.-2/4P	1015	3298	101
CZ	2-dr. Tr. Brgm.-5P	980	3293	500
CZ	4-dr. Sed.-5P	985	3333	2958
CZ	4-dr. Tr. Sed.-5P	1015	3338	4394
CZ	4-dr. LWB Trav. Sed.-5P	1235	3513	245
CZ	4-dr. LWB Sed.-7P	1235	3538	212
CZ	Chassis	—	—	237

Note 1: Total production of CZ Airstream Eights and CZ Deluxe Airstream Eights together was 9,297.

Note 2: The designation LWB means long wheelbase.

C-1	2-dr. Bus. Cpe.-2P	1245	3823	72
C-1	2-dr. Cpe.-6P	1245	3883	307
C-1	4-dr. Sed.-6P	1245	3828	4617

Note: Total series production was 4,996.

C-2	2-dr. Cpe.-6P	1475	4003	200
C-2	4-dr. Sed.-6P	1475	3998	2398

Note 1: Total series production was 2,598.

C-3	4-dr. Sed.-6P	2245	4208	69
C-3	4-dr. Twn. Sed.-6P	2245	4308	1
C-3	4-dr. Sed. Limo.-8P	2345	4378	53
C-3	4-dr. Twn. Sed. Limo.-8P	2345	4478	2

Note 1: Total series production was 125.

CW*	4-dr. Sed.-8P	5000	5785	15
CW*	4-dr. Twn. Sed.-8P	5000	5885	0
CW*	4-dr. Sed. Limo.-8P	5145	5990	15
CW*	4-dr. Twn. Sed. Limo.-8P	5145	6090	2

Note 1: Total series production (per available records) was 32.

Note 2: Some sources show production of non-Custom Imperial CW Airflows as follows: four-door sedan (17); four-door limousine (28); and four-door town sedan (2). These figures cannot be substantiated by contemporary historical sources that show no listings for a non-Custom series. It's likely that the figures could apply to cars sold in later years with updated sheet metal.

ENGINE: [Series C-6] Inline. L-head. Six. Cast iron block. B & S: 3-3/8 x 4-1/2 in. Disp.: 241.5 cu. in. C.R.: (std.) 6.0:1; (opt.) 6.5:1. Brake H.P.: (std.) 93 @ 3400 R.P.M.; (opt.) 100 @ 3400 R.P.M. N.A.C.C. H.P.: 27.34. Main bearings: four. Valve lifters: solid. Carb.: Carter 1V model E6F2. Torque: (std.) 180 lb.-ft. @ 1200 R.P.M.; (opt.) 185 lb.-ft. @ 1200 R.P.M. [Series CZ] Inline. L-head. Eight. Cast iron block. B

& S: 3-1/4 x 4-1/8 in. Disp.: 273.8 cu. in. C.R.: (std.) 6.2:1; (opt.) 7.0:1. Brake H.P.: (std.) 105 @ 3400 R.P.M.; (Opt.) 110 @ 3400 R.P.M. N.A.C.C. H.P.: 33.8. Main bearings: five. Valve lifters: solid. Carb.: Stromberg 1V model EX-32. Torque: (std.) 200 lb.-ft. @ 1200 R.P.M.; (opt.) 206 lb.-ft. @ 1200 R.P.M. [Series CZ (DeLuxe)] The DeLuxe Airstream Eights used the same engines as the standard Airstream Eights. See specifications above. [Series C-1] Inline. L-head. Eight. Cast iron block. B & S: 3-1/4 x 4-7/8 in. Disp.: 323.5 cu. in. C.R.: (std.) 6.2:1; (opt.) 6.5:1. Brake H.P.: (std.) 115 @ 3400 R.P.M.; (opt.) 120 @ 3400 R.P.M. N.A.C.C. H.P.: 33.8. Main bearings: five. Valve lifters: solid. Carb.: Stromberg 1V model EX-32. Torque: (std.) 240 lb.-ft. @ 1200 R.P.M.; (opt.) 250 lb.-ft. @ 1200 R.P.M. [Series C-2] Inline. L-head. Eight. Cast iron block. B & S: 3-1/4 x 4-7/8 in. Disp.: 323.5 cu. in. C.R.: (std.) 6.5:1; (opt.) 7.45:1. Brake H.P.: (std.) 130 @ 3400 R.P.M.; (opt.) 138 @ 3400 R.P.M. N.A.C.C. H.P.: 33.8. Main bearings: five. Valve lifters: solid. Carb.: Stromberg 2V model EE-22. Torque: (std.) 250 lb.-ft. @ 1600 R.P.M.; (opt.) 265 lb.-ft. @ 1600 R.P.M. [Series C-3] The Custom Imperial Eights (C-3) used the same engines as the Imperial Eights (C-2). See specifications above. [Series CW*] Inline. L-head. Eight. Cast iron block. B & S: 3-1/2 x 5 in. Disp.: 384.8 cu. in. C.R.: 6.5:1. Brake H.P.: 150 @ 3200 R.P.M. N.A.C.C. H.P.: 39.2. Main bearings: five. Valve lifters: solid. Carb.: Stromberg 2V model EE-3.

CHASSIS: [Series C6] W.B.: 118 in. Tires: 16 x 6.25. [Series CZ] W.B.: 121 in. Tires: 16 x 6.50. [Series CZ (DeLuxe)] W.B.: 121 in. Tires: 16 x 6.50. [Series CZ (DeLuxe/LWB)] W.B.: 133 in. Tires: 16 x 6.50. [Series C-1] W.B.: 123 in. Tires: 16 x 7.00. [Series C-2] W.B.: 128 in. Tires: 16 x 7.50. [Series C-3] W.B.: 130 in. Tires: 16 x 7.50. [Series CW*] W.B.: 146-1/2 in. Tires: 17 x 7.50.

TECHNICAL: Manual transmission (with automatic overdrive in Imperial Airflows). Speeds: 3F/1R (Imperials have overdrive fourth). Floor shift controls. Conventional clutch. Shaft drive. Overall ratios: (C6) 4.11:1; (C2) 3.95:1; (C1) 4.1:1; (C2/C3 & CW) 4.3:1. Lockheed four wheel brakes. Steel-spoke wheels.

OPTIONS: Front bumper. Rear bumper. Trumpet horns. Dual sidemounts. Sidemount cover(s). Fender skirts (std. on Airflows). Bumper guards. Radio. Heater. Clock. Cigar lighter. Radio antenna. Seat covers. Spotlight(s). Outside rear view mirror. Full wheel disks. Chrome wheel trim rings. Trunk rack (Airstream). Touring trunk (Airstream). Division window. Overdrive (C-1 Series). Power brakes (C-1 Series).

1935 Chrysler, Wimbledon, four-door sedan (JB)

HISTORICAL: Date of introduction: (DeLuxe Airstream) May 1, 1935; (others) January 2, 1935. Innovations: (Airstream) All-steel body. Balanced weight distribution. New Autolite ignition. New eight-cylinder engine. Engine repositioned six inches forward. More sloping windshield. Synchromesh transmission. Independent front suspension. (Airflow) New grille. Automatic overdrive and aluminum head on Imperials. Calendar year production: 50,010. Model year production: 38,533. In 1935, Chrysler was America's 10th ranked automaker in both model year and calendar year production. Walter P. Chrysler was elected chairman of the corporation bearing his name. K.T. Keller took his place as Chrysler's new president. Chrysler experimented with the concept of a compact car during 1935. The Custom Imperial CW models are full Classics.

1936 CHRYSLER

1936 Chrysler, Series C-8, Airstream four-door sedan (AA)

CHRYSLER AIRSTREAM — SERIES C-7 — SIX: Changes to Chrysler's 1936 Airstream models were minor ones. The new die-cast grille was oval shaped when viewed head-on. It consisted of multiple vertical blades that swept over the nose of the car in waterfall style. The center vertical molding was thicker. A molding on the sides of the hood continued, horizontally, across the nose. Horizontal, dart-shaped hood louvers were used. The headlights were again torpedo-shaped and torpedo-shaped parking lamps were mounted on the front-fender catwalks. Open cars had flat one-piece windshields. Closed cars had split two-piece windshields. Standard equipment included Autolite ignition, Lockheed hydraulic brakes, dual sun visors, wipers and taillights, no draft ventilation and safety glass all around. The convertible sedan made its return this season.

CHRYSLER DELUXE AIRSTREAM — SERIES C-8 — EIGHT: DeLuxe Airstream styling changes were similar to those on 1936 Airstream Sixes. The Eights featured special trim such as bright metal runningboard moldings and a winged "8" badge on the hoodside louvers. Both regular 121-inch and extended 133-inch chassis were available. Standard equipment included Autolite ignition, hydraulic brakes, and the small Chrysler Straight-Eight with a downdraft Stromberg carburetor.

CHRYSLER AIRFLOW — SERIES C-9 — EIGHT: Slight modifications to the basic Airflow design included a hump-back style built-in luggage compartment, all-steel top construction, new grille similar in design to the Airstream type, and egg-crate style hood ventilators. "Life Guard" tire tubes and vertically adjustable front seats were new innovations. Only one coupe was available.

1936 Chrysler Imperial, Airflow Custom, seven-passenger four-door sedan (AA)

IMPERIAL AIRFLOW — SERIES C-10 — EIGHT: The front fender valance panels, cowl side panels, and hood ventilators were longer on Imperial Airflows. An aluminum cylinder head and automatic overdrive transmission were standard, as was a two-barrel carburetor. Imperials continued to offer power brakes at regular price.

CUSTOM IMPERIAL AIRFLOW — C-11 — EIGHT: The C-11 Custom Imperial Airflow used the new grille, egg-crate hood trim, all-steel top construction and hump-back luggage compartment introduced on 1936 Airflows. The longer chassis length was consumed with lengthened front

doors having larger door windows. Single bar bumpers with guards, split vee-type windshields, and larger tires were other features of these rare cars.

CUSTOM IMPERIAL AIRFLOW — SERIES CW — EIGHT:** Ten long wheelbase CW** type Custom Imperial Airflows were sold this year. These cars may have been 1934 chassis with updated sheet metal and trim parts. They were not regular production models and exact specifications are not available. Prices and weights were about the same as in 1935. Engine specifications were unchanged. These cars featured one-piece curved windshields. Body style breakouts of the 10 cars are not available.

1936 Chrysler, Series C-8, Airstream convertible sedan (JAC)

I.D. DATA: [Series C-7] Serial numbers were on a plate on the front door hinge pillar post. Starting: 6823301. Ending: 6865003. Engine numbers were on the left side of cylinder block, between one and two cylinders, just below cylinder head. Starting: C7-1001. Ending: C7-44530. [Series C-8] Serial numbers were in the same locations. Starting: 6710501. Ending: 6719499. Engine numbers were in the same location. Starting: C8-1001. Ending: C8-10554. [Series C-9] Serial numbers were in the same locations. Starting: 6606201. Ending: 6607879. Engine numbers were in the same locations. Starting: C9-1001. Ending: C9-2852. [Series C-10] Serial numbers were in the same locations. Starting: 7014901. Ending: 7019398. Engine numbers were in the same locations. Starting: C10-1001. Ending: C10-5536. [Series C-11] Serial numbers were in the same locations. Starting: 7803851. Ending: 7803925. Engine numbers were in the same locations. Starting: C11-1001. Ending: C11-1075.

Model No.	Body Type & Seating	Price	Weight	Prod. Total
C-7	2-dr. Bus. Cpe.-2P	760	2962	3703
C-7	2-dr. Conv. Cpe.-2/4P	925	3053	650
C-7	2-dr. R/S Cpe.-2/4P	825	3037	759
C-7	2-dr. Tr. Brgm.-5P	825	3082	3177
C-7	4-dr. Conv. Sed.-5P	1125	3282	497
C-7	4-dr. Tr. Sed.-5P	875	3137	34099
C-7	Chassis	NA	NA	586

Note 1: Total production was 43,471.

(121" wb)

C-8	2-dr. Bus. Cpe.-2P	925	3155	520
C-8	2-dr. R/S Cpe.-2/4P	995	3220	325
C-8	2-dr. Conv. Cpe.-2/4P	1075	3350	240
C-8	2-dr. Tr. Brgm.-5P	995	3330	268
C-8	4-dr. Conv. Sed.-5P	1265	3495	362
C-8	4-dr. Tr. Sed.-5P	1045	3345	6547

(133" wb)

C-8	4-dr. Trav. Sed.-5P	1245	3500	350
C-8	4-dr. Sed.-7P	1245	3550	619
C-8	4-dr. Sed. Limo.-7P	1865	NA	67
C-8	4-dr. Leb. Twn. Car-7P	4995	NA	8
C-8	Chassis	NA	NA	196

Note 1: Total series production was 9,502.

Note 2: The long wheelbase LeBaron town sedan, a true town car, was built only on special order.

C-9	2-dr. Cpe.-6P	1345	3997	110
C-9	4-dr. Sed.-6P	1345	4102	1590

Note 1: Total series production was 1,700.

C-10	2-dr. Cpe.-6P	1475	4105	240
C-10	4-dr. Sed.-6P	1475	4175	4259
C-10	Chassis	NA	NA	1

Note 1: Total series production was 4,500.

C-11	4-dr. Sed.-5P	2475	NA	38
C-11	4-dr. Sed. Limo.-7P	2575	NA	37

Note 1: Total series production was 75 cars.

ENGINE: [Series C-7] Inline. L-head. Six. Cast iron block B & S: 3-3/8 x 4-1/2 in. Disp.: 241.5 cu. in. C.R.: (std.) 6.0:1 (opt.) 6.5:1. Brake H.P.: (std.) 93 @ 3400 R.P.M. (opt.) 100 @ 3400 R.P.M. N.A.C.C.

H.P.: 27.34. Main bearings: four. Valve lifters: solid. Carb.: Carter 1V model EGG1 (BB). Torque: (std.) 180 lb.-ft. @ 1200 R.P.M.; (opt.) 185 lb.-ft. @ 1200 R.P.M. [Series C-8] Inline. L-head. Eight. Cast iron block. B & S: 3-1/4 x 4-1/8 in. Disp.: 273.8 cu. in. C.R.: (std.) 6.2:1; (opt.) 7.0:1. Brake H.P.: (std.) 105 @ 3400 R.P.M.; (opt.) 110 @ 3400 R.P.M. N.A.C.C. H.P.: 33.8. Main bearings: five. Valve lifters: solid. Carb.: Stromberg 1V model EXV-3. Torque: (std.) 200 lb.-ft. @ 1200 R.P.M.; (opt.) 206 lb.-ft. @ 1200 R.P.M. [Series C-9] Inline. L-head. Eight. Cast iron block. B & S: 3-1/4 x 4-7/8 in. Disp.: 323.5 cu. in. C.R.: (std.) 6.2:1; (opt.) 6.5:1. Brake H.P.: (std.) 115 @ 3400 R.P.M.; (opt.) 120 @ 3400 R.P.M. N.A.C.C. H.P.: 33.8. Main bearings: five. Valve lifters: solid. Carb.: Stromberg 1V model EXV-3. Torque: (std.) 240 lb.-ft. @ 1200 R.P.M.; (opt.) 250 lb.-ft. @ 1200 R.P.M. [Series C-10] Inline. L-head. Eight. Cast iron block. B & S: 3-1/4 x 4-7/8 in. C.R.: (std.) 6.5:1; (opt.) 7.45:1. Brake H.P.: (std.) 130 @ 3400 R.P.M.; (opt.) 138 @ 3400 R.P.M. N.A.C.C. H.P.: 33.8. Main bearings: five. Valve lifters: solid. Carb.: Stromberg 2V model EE-22. Torque: (std.) 250 lb.-ft. @ 1600 R.P.M.; (opt.) 265 lb.-ft. @ 1600 R.P.M. [Series C-11] The Custom Imperial C-11 engines were the same as those used on Imperial C-10. See specifications above.

1936 Chrysler, Kew "Airglide," Carlton (JB)

CHASSIS: [Series C-7] W.B.: 118 in. Tires: 16 x 6.25. [Series C-8] W.B.: 121 or 133 in. Tires: 16 x 6.50. [Series C-9] W.B.: 123 in. Tires: 16 x 7.00. [Series C-10] W.B.: 128 in. Tires: 16 x 7.50. [Series C-11] W.B.: 137 in. Tires: 16 x 7.50. [Series CW**] W.B.: 146.5 in. Tires: 17 x 7.50.

TECHNICAL: Same as 1935.

OPTIONS: Same as 1935.

HISTORICAL: Date of introduction: (C-11) February 5, 1936; (others) November 2, 1935. Innovations: (Airstream) New rear axle with silent hypoid gears. New automatic overdrive option ($37.00). Redesigned rear fenders. (Airflow) "Life Guard" tire tubes. Vertically adjustable front seat. All-steel top. Calendar year registrations: 58,698. Calendar year production: 71,295. Model year production: 59,248. The president of Chrysler was K.T. Keller.

The 1936 season was Chrysler's best year since 1929. Still, the company fell to 11th position on the U.S. sales charts. A prototype small car with front-wheel drive and a five-cylinder radial engine was the company's experimental project this year. The CW Imperial Custom Airflows are recognized CCCA Classic cars.

1937 CHRYSLER

CHRYSLER ROYAL — SERIES C-16 — SIX: Chrysler's six-cylinder line was named Royal this season. These cars had all-new styling combined with a shorter chassis. The grille consisted of multiple horizontal bars that were longer at the top and shorter towards the bottom. Horizontal moldings decorated the sides of the hood and swept around the nose, but did not quite touch at the center. Bullet-shaped headlights were mounted high on the front fenders. New features included built-in windshield defroster vents, fully insulated body mountings and safety padding on the back of the front seats. A long-wheelbase Royal sub-series featured two body styles.

IMPERIAL — SERIES C-14 — EIGHT: The true 1937 Imperial was no longer an Airflow. These cars had the same basic styling as the new Royal six with a longer hood and cowl. The Imperial name appeared on the nose between the grille and the wraparound hood louvers. Imperials had a longer wheelbase, larger tires and more luxurious interior appointments than the sixes. They also had the new, built-in defroster vents, insulated body mountings, and seat safety padding. The Imperial engine continued to use an aluminum cylinder head in both its low and optional high-compression forms.

1937 Chrysler, Series C-17, Imperial sedan (JAC)

CHRYSLER AIRFLOW — SERIES C-17 — EIGHT: The only true 1937 Airflows were a Chrysler series. They had new, safety instrument panels with no protruding knobs. There was a concealed crank for raising the windshield. The hood was hinged at the cowl and opened from the front; side hood panels were released by catches on the inside. Other features included built-in defroster vents, padded front seat backs, safety-type controls and hardware, soft armrests, and a flat floorboard. Standard equipment included hydraulic brakes, double acting hydraulic telescoping shock absorbers, fully insulated engine mountings, and a hypoid rear axle. The 1937 models had horizontal hood louvers and chrome-plated beads, headlamps mounted on the front hood sides, and license plate lamps and brackets mounted in the center of the body. The grille was similar to that used on conventional models. The name "Chrysler Airflow" appeared, in chrome scripts, on the body color panel between the grille and the wraparound hood louvers.

1937 Chrysler, Series C-15, Imperial touring sedan (AA)

IMPERIAL CUSTOM — SERIES C-15 — EIGHT: The Custom Imperial had basically the same styling and equipment features as the Imperial C-14s. A longer wheelbase was used and body and door panels were stretched accordingly. The Custom Imperial town sedan limousine, with blind rear quarter panels, was available on special order. Custom coach-built bodies ranging from a fastback town car to a beautiful Derham convertible victoria were produced on the 16 Custom Imperial chassis supplied by Chrysler. The Custom Imperials, whether factory built or custom bodied, had extra-rich upholstery and trim.

1937 Chrysler, Series C-16, Royal four-door sedan (AA)

CUSTOM IMPERIAL — SERIES CW — EIGHT: Although no Custom Imperial CW models were actually built in 1937, three such cars were updated with 1937 style bumpers, grilles, and trim and sold as 1937 automobiles. One was built for the Hershey family of candy bar and antique car fame. A second one was built for Manuel L. Querzon, President of the Philippines. A third car was delivered to radio personality Major Edward Bowes. The Querzon and Major Bowes cars survive today. One is owned by the Government of the Philippines; the other by collector Frank Kleptz of Terre Haute, Indiana. All of the cars seem to have been specially equipped, by Chrysler and LeBaron, with numerous features not found in other CWs. A 1940 *Life* magazine article put the value of the Major Bowes car at $25,000.

CHRYSLER — KEW — SIX: For the English motorist who wanted a small Chrysler, this badge-converted Plymouth was just the ticket. Fitted with the small-bore 170-cubic-inch engine, the Kew was rated at a tax-beating 19.8 horsepower.

CHRYSLER — WIMBLEDON — SIX: A slightly more upscale version of the Kew Six, the Wimbledon utilized Plymouth's 201-cubic-inch six-cylinder engine and featured such amenities as a sliding roof panel and overdrive transmission. The Wimbledon was rated at 23.4 horsepower for Great Britain's taxation purposes. Shipped as CKD units from Detroit to the Chrysler works at Kew, Surrey, even chassis and engines were shipped in knocked-down form for 1937.

CHRYSLER — RICHMOND — SIX: For the wise English motorist who preferred something more than a disguised Plymouth but who couldn't afford a "real" Chrysler, there was always the Richmond, which was based on the U.S. S-3 DeSoto Airstream.

I.D. DATA: [Series C-16] Serial numbers were on a plate on the front door hinge pillar. Starting: 6865101. Ending: 6948225. Engine numbers were on the left side of the block, between cylinders no. 1 and no. 2, just below the cylinder head. Starting: C16-1001. Ending: C16-88640. [Series C-14] Serial numbers were in the same location. Starting: 6719601. Ending: 6733606. Engine numbers were in the same location. Starting: C14-1001. Ending: C14-15572. [Series C-17] Serial numbers were in the same location. Starting: 7019401. Ending: 7024000. Engine numbers were in the same location. Starting: C17-1001. Ending: C17-5618. [Series C-15] Serial numbers were located in the same positions. Starting: 7804001. Ending: 7805201. Engine numbers were in the same positions. Starting: C15-1001. Ending: C15-2237. [Series CW] Serial numbers were in the same location. These cars were numbered in the years they were built and do not have 1937 serial numbers. Serial and engine numbers are not available.

Model No.	Body Type & Seating	Price	Weight	Prod. Total
(116" wb)				
C-16	2-dr. Bus. Cpe.-2P	810	3049	9830
C-16	2-dr. Conv. Cpe.-2/4P	1020	3274	767
C-16	2-dr. R/S Cpe.-2/4P	860	3099	1050
C-16	2-dr. Brgm.-5P	870	3114	750
C-16	2-dr. Tr. Brgm.-5P	880	3094	7835
C-16	4-dr. Sed.-5P	910	3124	1200
C-16	4-dr. Tr. Sed.-5P	920	3134	62,408
C-16	4-dr. Conv. Sed.-5P	1355	3484	642
(133" wb)				
C-16	4-dr. Tr. Sed.-7P	1145	3544	856
C-16	4-dr. Sed. Limo.-7P	1245	3550	138
C-16	Chassis	NA	NA	524

Note 1: Total series production was 86,000.

C-14	2-dr. Bus. Cpe.-2P	1030	3374	1075
C-14	2-dr. R/S Cpe.-2/4P	1070	3449	225
C-14	2-dr. Conv. Cpe.-2/4P	1170	3609	351
C-14	2-dr. Tr. Brgm.-5P	1070	3544	430
C-14	4-dr. Tr. Sed.-5P	1100	3564	11,976
C-14	4-dr. Conv. Sed.-5P	1500	3824	325
C-14	Chassis	NA	NA	118

Note 1: Total series production was 14,500.

C-17	2-dr. Cpe.-6P	1610	4225	230
C-17	2-dr. Tr. Sed.-6P	1610	4300	4370

Note 1: Total series production was 4,600.

(Factory Semi-Customs)				
C-15	4-dr. Tr. Sed.-5P	2060	4500	187
C-15	4-dr. Tr. Sed.-7P	2060	4522	721
C-15	4-dr. Sed. Limo.-7P	2160	4644	276
(Individual Customs)				
C-15	4-dr. LeB. FsBk. Twn. Car-7P	NA	NA	1
C-15	2-dr. Der. Conv. Vic.-5P	NA	NA	1
C-15	4-dr. Der. Conv. Sed.-7P	NA	NA	1
C-15	4-dr. Der. Conv. Twn. Car-5P	NA	NA	1
C-15	2-dr. Der. Vic. Twn. Car-5P	NA	NA	—
C-15	4-dr. LeB. Twn. Sed. Limo.-7P	NA	NA	—

Note 1: Total series production was 1,200 including 16 chassis supplied to custom coachbuilders. The individual customs listed above represent some body styles known to have been produced on the 16 chassis. The production totals given are estimates.

CW	4-dr. Sed. Limo.-7P	NA	NA	3

Note 1: The figure of three cars built with 1937 trim and appointments is a rough estimate based on known facts. It's possible that others of these cars were made.

ENGINE: [Series C-16] Inline. L-head. Six. Cast iron block. B & S: 3-3/8 x 4-1/4 in. Disp.: 228.1 cu. in. C.R.: (std.) 6.5:1; (opt.) 7.0:1. Brake H.P.: (std.) 93 @ 3600 R.P.M.; (opt.) 100 @ 3600 R.P.M. N.A.C.C. H.P.: 27.34. Main bearings: four. Valve lifters: solid. Carb.: Carter 1V model E6KI-4 (BB). Torque: (std.) 168 lb.-ft. @ 1200 R.P.M.; (opt.) 176 lb.-ft. @ 1200 R.P.M. [Series C-14] Inline. L-head. Eight. Cast iron block. B & S: 3-1/4 x 4-1/8 in. Disp.: 273.8 cu. in. C.R.: (std.) 6.7:1; (opt.) 7.4:1. Brake H.P.: (std.) 110 @ 3600 R.P.M.; (opt.) 115 @ 3600 R.P.M. N.A.C.C. H.P.: 33.80. Main bearings: five. Valve lifters: solid. Carb.: Stromberg 2V model EE-22. Torque: (std.) 212 lb.-ft. @ 1600 R.P.M.; (opt.) 220 lb.-ft. @ 1600 R.P.M. [Series C-17] Inline. L-head. Eight. Cast iron block. B & S: 3-1/4 x 47/8 in. Disp.: 323.5 cu. in. C.R.: (std.) 6.2:1; (opt.) 6.5:1. Brake H.P.: (std.) 130 @ 3400 R.P.M.; (opt.) 138 @ 3400 R.P.M. N.A.C.C. H.P.: 33.80. Main bearings: five. Valve lifters: solid. Carb.: Stromberg 2V model AAOV-1. Torque: (std.) 250 lb.-ft. @ 1600 R.P.M.; (opt.) 265 lb.-ft. @ 1600 R.P.M. [Series C-15] The Custom Imperial engine was the same as the Airflow engine. See specifications in chart above. [Series CW] Inline. L-head. Eight. Cast iron block. B & S: 3-1/2 x 5 in. Disp.: 384.4 cu. in. C.R.: (std.) 5.8:1; (opt.) 5.2:1. Brake H.P.: 150 @ 3200 R.P.M. N.A.C.C. H.P.: 39.2. Main bearings: five. Valve lifters: solid. Carb.: Stromberg 2V model EE-3. Torque: 260 lb.-ft. @ 1200 R.P.M.

CHASSIS: [Series C-16] W.B.: 116 in. Tires: 16 x 6.25. [Series C-16 (LWB)] W.B.: 133 in. Tires: 16 x 6.25. [Series C-14] W.B.: 121 in. Tires: 16 x 6.50. [Series C-17] W.B.: 128 in. Tires: 16 x 7.50. [Series C-15] W.B.: 140 in. Tires: 16 x 7.50. [Series CW] W.B.: 146.5 in. Tires: 17 x 7.50.

TECHNICAL: Manual synchromesh transmission. Speeds: 3F/1R. Floor shift controls. Conventional clutch. Shaft drive. Hypoid rear axle. Overall ratios: (C-16/C-14) 4.10:1; (C-17) 4.30:1; (C-15) 4.27:1; (CW) 4.30:1. Four wheel hydraulic brakes. Steel-spoke wheels.

OPTIONS: Front bumper. Rear bumper. Single sidemount (Airstream). Dual sidemount (Airstream). Sidemount cover(s). Fender skirts. Bumper guards. Radio. Heater. Clock. Cigar lighter. Radio antenna. Seat covers. Outside rear view mirror. Spotlight(s). Trippe lights. Whitewall tires. Special paint. Special upholstery.

HISTORICAL: Introduced October 1936. Innovations: Built-in defroster vents. Safety type interior hardware and seat back padding. Fully insulated engine mountings. Improved six-cylinder engine. Increased horsepower on eight. Calendar year registrations: 91,622. Calendar year production: 107,872. Model year production: 106,120.

1937 Chrysler, Series C-16, Royal coupe (JAC)

Chrysler was America's ninth largest automaker on a model year basis and the tenth largest automaker on a calendar year basis. A Custom Imperial convertible sedan was used as AAA Official Car at the Indy 500. The car was painted silver and black to commemorate the speedway's 25th anniversary. K.T. Keller was president of Chrysler Motors.

1938 CHRYSLER

1938 Chrysler, Wimbledon, seven-passenger limousine (JB)

CHRYSLER ROYAL — SERIES C-18 — SIX: The Airflow disappeared in 1938, but the Chrysler Royal was back for its second year. There were obvious styling changes to the grille, headlights, and hood trim. The new grille consisted of horizontal bars filling a shield-shaped opening that tapered towards the bottom. There was a vertical center molding and chrome chevron trim below the grille. Scripts on the nose of the car read "Chrysler Royal." The torpedo-shaped headlights now sat on top of the fenders, instead of alongside the grille. The hood was of the side-opening type with removable side panels. The hood louvers were a long, narrow casting with three openings at the rear. All Chryslers used a deluxe steering wheel on which a narrow inner rim acted as the horn button. The emergency brake lever was mounted under the cowl, at its center. Standard equipment included hydraulic brakes, Autolite ignition, and a larger, more powerful engine. The standard wheelbase was increased by three inches and the two long wheelbase models were stretched accordingly. At least one Derham Custom town car was constructed on the Chrysler Royal Six chassis, although most of the units built were probably ambulances and funeral cars.

1938 Chrysler, Series C-19, New York Special sedan (JAC)

IMPERIAL AND NEW YORK SPECIAL — SERIES C-19 — EIGHT: Imperials had the same basic styling changes as Royals for 1938. They could be identified by the addition of chrome chevrons on the front of each front fender and the model scripts on the hubcaps and above the grille. Naturally, the Imperials had richer interior upholstery and trim. A longer hood was used, too. A brand new Imperial sub-series was the New York Special line. Interestingly, the New York Specials were considered Chryslers, although they were built on the Imperial chassis and used the Custom Imperial engine. As listed in contemporary reference sources, the New York Special line consisted of a business coupe and touring sedan. However, no coupes are known to have been built. The New York Special used a distinctive grille with wider horizontal openings. Special broadcloth upholstery was available only in this model. It came in two single color and four two-tone combinations. The New York Special model later grew into the Chrysler New Yorker series. Instrument panels in the Imperials had highly polished woodgrain finish; New York Special instrument panels were finished to harmonize with the upholstery colors.

CUSTOM IMPERIAL — SERIES C-20 — EIGHT: The Custom Imperials were larger, fancier versions of the Imperials on a longer wheelbase chassis. Their longer length required larger front doors and rear doors with correspondingly longer window openings. The seven-passenger sedan had two auxiliary folding seats in the front seat back. The five-passenger sedan had storage compartments in the same space. The limousine had folding seats and a division window between the front and rear compartments. Eleven individual customs were built on chassis supplied to coachmakers. Most, if not all, of these units carried special Derham bodies. Instrument panels on Custom Imperials were finished to harmonize with the upholstery colors.

CHRYSLER — KEW/WIMBLEDON — SIX: Buyers in Great Britain had their choice of two Chrysler models this year, both based on the Plymouth body shell and drivetrain. There is some confusion as to whether the 201-cubic inch engine-equipped car was sold as a Wimbledon as had been practice in previous years, some references noting only "two models" of the Kew, a standard and a deluxe. Previously all Kew models were fitted with the 170-cubic inch export Plymouth engine. Deluxe Kew models featured 12-volt electrics (which U.S. Plymouths would not see until 1956), leather upholstery, sunshine roof, twin wipers and a rear-seat center armrest.

I.D. DATA: [Series C-18] Serial numbers were located on the right front door hinge pillar post. Starting: 7532801. Ending: 7573257. Engine numbers were located on the left side of block, between cylinders one and two, just below the cylinder head. Starting: C18-1001. Ending: C18-43001. [Series C-19] Serial numbers were in the same location. Starting: 6734001. Ending: 6742105. Serial numbers for the New York Special were 6607901 to 6609802. Engine numbers were in the same location. Starting: C19-1001. Ending: C19-9172. Engine numbers for the New York Special were C20-1001 to C20-3525. [Series C-20] Serial numbers were in the same location. Starting: 7805501. Ending: 7806033. Engine numbers were in the same location. Numbers were the same as those given above for New York Specials.

Model No.	Body Type & Seating	Price	Weight	Prod. Total
(Standard wheelbase)				
C-18	2-dr. Bus. Cpe.-2P	918	3090	4840
C-18	2-dr. R/S Cpe.-2/4P	963	3135	363
C-18	2-dr. Conv. Cpe.-2/4P	1085	3250	480
C-18	2-dr. FsBk. Brgm.-5P	963	3160	88
C-18	2-dr. Tr. Brgm.-5P	975	3165	3802
C-18	4-dr. Tr. Sed.-5P	1010	3180	31,991
C-18	4-dr. FsBk. Sed.-5P	998	3170	112
C-18	4-dr. Conv. Sed.-5P	1425	3450	177
(Long wheelbase)				
C-18	4-dr. Tr. Sed.-7P	1235	3450	722
C-18	4-dr. Sed. Limo.-7P	1325	3545	161
C-18	Chassis	NA	NA	564

Note 1: Total series production was 43,300.

(Imperial Eight)				
C-19	2-dr. Bus. Cpe.-2P	1123	3450	766
C-19	2-dr. R/S Cpe.-2/4P	1160	3515	80
C-19	2-dr. Conv. Cpe.-2/4P	1275	3630	189
C-19	2-dr. Tr. Brgm.-5P	1165	3560	245
C-19	4-dr. Tr. Sed.-5P	1198	3565	8554
C-19	4-dr. Conv. Sed.-5P	1595	3835	113
C-19	Chassis	NA	NA	55
(New York Special)				
C-19	2-dr. Bus. Cpe.-2P	1255	3475	Note 2
C-19	4-dr. Tr. Sed.-5P	1370	3600	Note 3

Note 1: Total series production was 10,002.

Note 2: Records indicate that no New York Special business coupes were built.

Note 3: Production of the New York Special touring sedan included in Imperial Eight touring sedan total.

(Factory Models)				
C-20	4-dr. Tr. Sed.-5P	2295	4495	252
C-20	4-dr. Tr. Sed.-7P	2295	4510	122
C-20	4-dr. Sed. Limo.-7P	2395	NA	145
(Individual Customs)				
C-20	2-dr. Der. Conv. Vic.-5P	NA	NA	Note 2
C-20	4-dr. Der. Twn. Sed.-5P	NA	NA	Note 2
C-20	4-dr. Der. Conv. Sed.-5P	NA	NA	Note 2
C-20	4-dr. Der. Twn. Limo.-7P	NA	NA	Note 2
C-20	Chassis	NA	NA	Note 2

Note 1: Total production of factory models was 519.

Note 2: A total of 11 Custom Imperial chassis were built. The four cars listed are among those known to have been made on these chassis.

ENGINE: [Series C-18] Inline. L-head. Six. Cast iron block. B & S: 3-3/8 x 4-1/2 in. Disp.: 241.5 cu. in. C.R.: (std.) 6.2:1; (opt.) 7.0:1. Brake

H.P.: (std.) 95 @ 3600 R.P.M.; (opt.) 102 @ 3600 R.P.M. N.A.C.C. H.P.: 27.34. Main bearings: four. Valve lifters: solid. Carb.: Carter 1V model E6MI. Torque: (std.) 180 lb.-ft. @ 1200 R.P.M.; (opt.) 190 lb.-ft. @ 1200 R.P.M. [Series C-19] Imperial Engine: Inline. L-head. Eight. Cast iron block. B & S: 3-1/4 x 4-1/2 in. Disp.: 298.7 cu. in. C.R.: (std.) 6.2:1; (opt.) 7.4:1. Brake H.P.: (std.) 110 @ 3400 R.P.M.; (opt.) 122 @ 3400 R.P.M. N.A.C.C. H.P.: 33.80. Main bearings: six. Valve lifters: solid. Torque: (std.) 214 lb.ft. @ 1600 R.P.M.; (opt.) 238 lb.-ft. @ 1600 R.P.M.; New York Special Engine: Inline. L-head. Eight. Cast iron block. B & S: 3-1/4 x 4-1/2 in. Disp.: 298.7 cu. in. C.R.: (std.) 6.5:1; (opt.) 7.4:1. Brake H.P.: (std.) 115 @ 3400 R.P.M.; (opt.) 122 @ 3400 R.P.M. N.A.C.C. H.P.: 33.80. Main bearings: six. Valve lifters: solid. Torque: (std.) 225 lb.-ft. @ 1600 R.P.M.; (opt.) 238 lb.-ft. @ 1600 R.P.M. [Series C-20] Engine specifications were the same as those given above for New York Specials.

1938 Chrysler, Series C-18, Royal four-door sedan (OCW)

CHASSIS: [Series Royal (std.)] W.B.: 119 in. Tires: 16 x 6.25 [Series Royal (LWB)] L.W.B.: 136 in. Tires: 16 x 6.25. [Series Imperial] W.B.: 125 in. Tires: 16 x 6.50. [Series New York Special] W.B.: 125 in. Tires: 16 x 6.50. [Series Custom Imperial] W.B.: 130 in. Tires: 16 x 7.50.

1938 Chrysler, Series C-18, Royal convertible sedan (JAC)

TECHNICAL: Three-speed manual synchromesh transmission. Speeds: 3F/1R. Floor shift controls. Conventional clutch. Shaft drive. Hypoid rear axle. Overall ratios: (C-18) 4.1:1; (C-19) 3.91:1; (C-20) 4.55:1. Four wheel hydraulic brakes. Steel-spoke wheels.

1938 Chrysler, Series C-19, Imperial touring sedan (AA)

OPTIONS: Whitewall tires. Wheel trim rings. Full wheel disks. Dual sidemounts. Sidemount cover(s). Fender skirts. Bumper guards. Radio. Heater. Clock. Cigar lighter. Radio antenna. Seat covers. Trippe lights. Spotlight(s). Fog lamps. Outside rear view mirror. Special paint. Special upholstery. Custom coachbuilt bodies. License plate frame.

HISTORICAL: Introduced October 1937. Innovations: New side opening hood. Repositioned emergency brake. New steering wheel with chrome horn ring. Introduced rubber insulated steering gear, an industry first. Front and rear sway bars in all Imperials. Calendar year registrations: 46,184. Calendar year production: 41,496. Model year production: 52,949. Chrysler was America's ninth largest automaker in terms of model year production and 11th largest in terms of calendar year output. Major Bowes "Original Amateur Hour" radio show was sponsored by Chrysler and the Major continued to drive his $25,000 Airflow CW limousine. George Dammann's book *70 Years of Chrysler* suggests that some Custom Imperials built late in 1938 may have had Fluid Drive semi-automatic transmissions.

1939 CHRYSLER

CHRYSLER ROYAL — SERIES C-22 — SIX: For 1939, Chrysler brought out new body styling with narrower runningboards and the headlamps recessed into the fenders. The grilles on the various series were similar, but differed in details. A chrome strip ran vertically up the prow-shaped nose of the cars, with horizontal moldings on either side running a short distance back. Multiple vertical moldings ran down the fender aprons and front panel in "waterfall" style. Royal sixes had five of the horizontal moldings on either side and 19 bars in the waterfall. A long molding traveled along the side of the hoods and was underscored by three horizontal slashes near the cowl. An upper belt molding began at the cowl and continued to the rear of the body. The word Chrysler appeared, in script, on either side of the nose. Other new styling features included a vee-shaped windshield, concealed rear luggage compartment, and an attractive front bumper with a dip in its center and a twin bar guard arrangement. Cars in the Windsor sub-series had this model name spelled out with a small chrome signature behind three vertical bars on the front hood sides. Standard equipment included Solar Spark ignition, hydraulic brakes, steering wheel mounted gear selector, and an illuminated speedometer. Royal Windsors had fancier interior appointments. Two long wheelbase models were found in the Standard Royal line only.

1939 Chrysler, Series C-22, Royal sedan (JAC)

1939 Chrysler, Series C-23, New Yorker, four-door sedan (OCW)

IMPERIAL/NEW YORKER/SARATOGA — SERIES C-23 — EIGHT: Imperials, New Yorkers, and Saratogas were all built on the same chassis

and shared the same powerplants. These cars were styled similarly to other Chryslers but had fewer horizontal and vertical grille bars on the two new sub-series. There were three horizontal bars on either side of the nose and only 11 bars in the lower "waterfall" grille on New Yorkers and Saratogas. Imperials had five horizontal bars (like Royals) but had 23 bars in their wider waterfall lower grilles. Each series also had small chrome signatures bearing the model name incorporated into the decorative trim on the front of the hood sides. New Yorkers were the "luxury" line and had two-tone upholstery and rich appointments. Saratogas were "sports luxury" cars with their leather and Bedford cord upholstery selections. Both lines included a special victoria coupe built in limited production by the Hayes Body Co. of Grand Rapids, Michigan. They had a rounded top, fastback rear deck, and split rear window treatment. A sun roof was optional on New Yorker and Saratoga sedans. Solar Spark ignition, hydraulic brakes, a new eight-cylinder engine and larger tires were standard equipment on cars in each of the three lines. The optional high-compression engine available in these cars had the aluminum cylinder head.

1939 Chrysler, Series C-24, Imperial sedan (OCW)

CUSTOM IMPERIAL — SERIES C-24 — EIGHT: Custom Imperials had basically the same trim features as C-23 Imperials combined with a longer wheelbase, correspondingly longer body panels, richer interior appointments and standard full wheel discs. A new "Cruise and Climb" overdrive transmission was standard in cars of this line and optional in other 1939 models. The Custom Imperials also had larger tires and the standard engine, while having the same compression ratio as the C-23 engine, and were slightly more powerful because the aluminum "Silver Dome" cylinder head was standard. The optional Custom Imperial engine was, however, the same as the optional C-23 engine. Several individual customs were built on C-24 running gear.

CHRYSLER — PLYMOUTH — SIX: For the first time since the early 1930s Chrysler of Great Britain used the word Plymouth in selling its smaller line of Chryslers. This car was a badge-engineered Plymouth P-7 Roadking replete down to its standard floor shift transmission. The Chrysler Plymouth was available only in a five-passenger "touring saloon" body style. The only engine offered was the 170-cubic inch Plymouth export unit.

CHRYSLER — KEW — SIX: Now the middle series, the Kew was badge engineered from the U.S. P-8 Deluxe Plymouth, which included column-mounted transmission controls and the choice of either the small-bore export engine or the regular Plymouth 201-cubic inch engine, as well as the choice of cloth or leather upholstery. Standard equipment included a single fog lamp. The Kew could be had as either a five-passenger sedan or a two-passenger convertible coupe.

CHRYSLER — WIMBLEDON — SIX: The 1939 Wimbledon would prove to be the last badge engineered Plymouth sold overseas as a Chrysler. The only engine offered in the Wimbledon was the Plymouth 201-cubic inch version. Buyers could specify cloth or "English trim" (leather) upholstery. Body styles included a five-passenger saloon, a long wheelbase eight-passenger sedan or eight-passenger limousine, a convertible coupe, and a Carlton-bodied four-place convertible victoria. Standard equipment included a single fog lamp and "dual power" overdrive transmission; all eight-passenger models were fitted with fender skirts. "Real" Chryslers could also be had in Royal, Imperial, or Custom Imperial models.

I.D. DATA: [Series C-22] Serial numbers were located on the right front door hinge pillar post. Starting: (Royal) 7574001; (Royal Windsor) 6948301. Ending: (Royal) 7624876; (Royal Windsor) 6954947. Engine numbers were located on the left side of the block, between cylinders one and two, just below the cylinder head. Starting: (All) C22-1001. Ending: (All) C22-5874. [Series C-23] Serial numbers were in the same location. Starting: (Imperial) 6742201; (New Yorker) 6609901; (Saratoga) 6672701. Ending: (Imperial) 6750055; (New Yorker) 6613333; (Saratoga) 6673414. Engine numbers were in the same locations. Starting: C23-1001. Ending: C23-13107. [Series C-24] Serial numbers were in the same locations. Starting: 7806201. Ending:

7806507. Engine numbers were in the same locations. Starting: C24-1001. Ending: C24-1322.

Model No.	Body Type & Seating	Price	Weight	Prod. Total
(Royal)				
C-22	2-dr. Cpe.-2P	918	3120	(4780)
C-22	2-dr. Vic. Cpe.-4P	970	3160	(239)
C-22	2-dr. Brgm.-5P	975	3200	4838
C-22	4-dr. Sed.-5P	1010	3265	(45,955)
(LWB Royal)				
C-22	4-dr. Sed.-7P	1235	3520	621
C-22	4-dr. Limo.-7P	1325	3625	191
(Royal Windsor)				
C-22	2-dr. Cpe.-2P	983	3130	(4780)
C-22	2-dr. Vic. Cpe.-4P	1035	3165	(239)
C-22	2-dr. Clb. Cpe.-5P	1185	3245	2983
C-22	4-dr. Sed.-5P	1075	3275	(45,955)
C-22	Chassis	NA	NA	394

Note 1: Total series production was 60,001.

Note 2: The figures in brackets indicate where the production of Royal and Royal Windsor models is a combined total. No breakouts for either sub-series are available.

(Imperial)				
C-23	2-dr. Cpe.-2P	1123	3520	492
C-23	2-dr. Vic. Cpe.-4P	1160	3555	35
C-23	2-dr. Brgm.-5P	1165	3610	185
C-23	4-dr. Sed.-5P	1198	3640	(10,536)
(New Yorker)				
C-23	2-dr. Cpe.-2P	1223	3540	(606)
C-23	2-dr. Vic. Cpe.-4P	1260	3580	99
C-23	2-dr. Clb. Cpe.-5P	1395	3665	(606)
C-23	4-dr. Sed.-5P	1298	3695	(10,536)
(Saratoga)				
C-23	2-dr. Clb. Cpe.-5P	1495	3665	134
C-23	4-dr. Sed.-5P	1443	3720	(10,536)
C-23	Chassis	NA	NA	48

Note 1: Total series production was 12,001.

Note 2: Combined production of Imperial, New Yorker, and Saratoga sedans was 10,536 (as shown in parenthesis). No further series breakouts are available.

Note 3: Combined production of the New Yorker business coupe and club coupe was 606 (as shown in parenthesis).

C-24	4-dr. Sed.-5P	2595	4590	88
C-24	4-dr. Sed.-7P	2595	4620	95
C-24	4-dr. Limo. Sed.-7P	2695	4665	117
C-24	4-dr. Der. Conv. Twn. Car	NA	NA	1
C-24	4-dr. Der. Conv. Sed.	NA	NA	1
C-24	4-dr. Der. Tr. Phae.-7P	NA	NA	1
C-24	Chassis	NA	NA	(7)

Note 1: Total series production was 307.

Note 2: The three individual customs listed above were among special models built on the seven (total shown in parenthesis) Custom Imperial chassis delivered to coachbuilders this year. The convertible town car by Derham was built for the visit of England's King George VI and Queen Elizabeth to the United States. This car was later donated to a Detroit American Legion post.

ENGINE: [Series C-22] Inline. L-head. Six. Cast iron block. B & S: 3-3/8 x 4-1/2 in. Disp.: 241.5 cu. in. C.R.: (std.) 6.5:1; (opt.) 7.0:1. Brake H.P.: (std.) 100 @ 3600 R.P.M.; (opt.) 107 @ 3600 R.P.M. N.A.C.C. H.P.: 27.34. Main bearings: four. Valve lifters: solid. Carb.: Carter 1V model E6N1. Torque: (std.) 184 lb.-ft. @ 1200 R.P.M.; (opt.) 190 lb.-ft. @ 1200 R.P.M. [Series C-23] Inline. L-head. Six. Cast iron block. B & S: 3-1/4 x 4-7/8 in. Disp.: 323.5 cu. in. C.R.: (std.) 6.8:1; (opt.) 7.45:1. Brake H.P.: (std.) 130 @ 3400 R.P.M.; (opt.) 138 @ 3400 R.P.M. N.A.C.C. H.P.: 33.80. Main bearings: five. Valve lifters: solid. Carb.: Stromberg 2V model AAV-Z. Torque: (std.) 250 lb.-ft. @ 1600 R.P.M.; (opt.) 265 lb.-ft. @ 1600 R.P.M. [Series C-24] Inline. L-head. Eight. Cast iron block. B & S: 3-1/4 x 4-7/8 in. Disp.: 323.5 cu. in. C.R.: (std.) 6.8:1; (opt.) 7.45:1. Brake H.P.: (std.) 132 @ 3400 R.P.M.; (opt.) 138 @ 3400 R.P.M. N.A.C.C. H.P.: 33.80. Main bearings: five. Valve lifters: solid. Carb.: Stromberg 2V model AAV-Z. Torque: (std.) 254 lb.-ft. @ 1600 R.P.M.; (opt.) 265 lb.-ft. @ 1600 R.P.M.

CHASSIS: [Series C-22 (SWB)] W.B.: 119 in. Tires: 16 x 6.25. [Series C-22 (LWB)] W.B.: 136 in. Tires: 16 x 6.50. [Series C-23] W.B.: 125 in. Tires: 16 x 7.00. [Series C-24] W.B.: 144 in. Tires: 16 x 7.50.

TECHNICAL: (Chrysler): Synchromesh transmission (Imperial) Fluid Drive. Speeds: 3F/1R (overdrive standard on Custom Imperial). Steering column gear selector. Conventional clutch. Shaft drive. Hypoid rear axle.

Overall ratios: (C-22) 4.1:1 or 4.3:1; (C-23) 3.91:1; (C-24) 4.9:1. Lockheed four-wheel hydraulic brakes. Steel-spoke wheels.

1939 Chrysler, two-door brougham (OCW)

OPTIONS: Whitewall tires. Wheel trim rings. Full wheel discs (standard Saratoga and Custom Imperial). Dual sidemounts (Imperials-last year). Metal sidemount cover(s). Fender skirts. Bumper guards. Radio. Heater. Clock. Cigar lighter. Radio antenna. Seat covers. External sun shade. Spotlight(s). Trippe lights. Ski rack. Rooftop "Tour Rack." Sun roof (used on 239 New Yorker and Saratoga sedans). Runningboard courtesy lamps. Fog light(s). Exhaust pipe extension. License plate frames. Individual custom bodies (special order). Signal lights. Padded roof (Customs). Oversized tires. Special paint. Special upholstery. Fluid Drive transmission (standard in Custom Imperial/optional in all other eights).

HISTORICAL: Introduced October 1938. Innovations: Fluid Drive on Custom Imperials. Improved eight-cylinder engine. "Super finish" paint jobs. Column-mounted gearshift. New sun roof option. Calendar year registrations: 63,956. Calendar year production: 67,749. Model year production: 72,443. In terms of model year output, Chrysler was America's 11th largest automaker this season. The company slipped to 12th place in calendar year sales. Radio personality Major Bowes drove a new 1939 Custom Imperial limousine. Derham also created a number of individual customs on the smaller chassis and produced a one-off Saratoga sedan with a padded leather roof treatment.

1940 CHRYSLER

1940 Chrysler, Series C-25, Royal coupe (JAC)

CHRYSLER — SERIES 25 — SIX: The Chrysler Six came in five sub-series this year: Royal; long wheelbase Royal; Windsor; long wheelbase Windsor; and Windsor Highlander. All were basically similar in appearance. New styling features included more massive fenders with recessed headlamps, sealed beam headlights, longer wheelbases, wider front and rear seats, longer hoods and "Airfoam" seat cushions. Horizontal grille bars extended across the lower half of the radiator and fender aprons. The model name appeared spelled out on each side of the hood at the forward end. Highlanders had authentic Scotch plaid and moleskin leather upholstery. Convertibles were re-introduced and two-tone paint jobs were made available again. Standard equipment included Solar Spark

ignition, hydraulic brakes, dual sun visors, dual taillights and dual windshield wipers. Buyers had the option of ordering their cars with conventional runningboards or more streamlined chrome trimmed rocker panels. The Chrysler Six was available with an optional high-compression engine utilizing the "Silver Dome" aluminum head.

1940 Chrysler, Series C-26, New Yorker convertible coupe (JAC)

CHRYSLER — SERIES 26 — EIGHT: The Chrysler Eight came in four sub-series: Traveler; New Yorker; New Yorker Highlander; and Saratoga. All were on the same 128-1/2 inch wheelbase. Styling features were like those on Chrysler Sixes except for the slightly longer sheet metal and the addition of front fender parking lights. Model names appeared on each side of the hood near the front end. The Traveler was the economy eight with the plainest interior and standard transmission. The New Yorker had upgraded interior appointments and Fluid Drive was optional. The Saratoga was available only as a four-door sedan in two interior configurations: sport or formal. The sport sedan had leatherette trimmed seats and door panels. The formal sedan had a lowerable division window. Standard equipment included Solar Spark ignition, hydraulic brakes, dual sun visors, dual taillights, dual wipers, an improved six main bearing engine, and two-barrel carburetor. The Chrysler Eight was available with an optional high-compression engine utilizing the "Silver Dome" aluminum head.

1940 Chrysler, Series C-27, Crown Imperial, limousine (AA)

CROWN IMPERIAL — C-27 — EIGHT: There were only three Imperials in 1940 and all were Crown models on a stretched wheelbase. Basic styling was similar to that of other Chryslers with larger doors and sheet metal. The Crown Imperials featured front fender parking lights and came only with conventional runningboards. In six-passenger cars the front seatback incorporated storage compartments and there were foot rests on the rear floor. Eight-passenger models had jump seats in place of storage compartments and no foot rest. The limousine had a division window and could be ordered with leather upholstery in the driver's compartment. Fluid drive, automatic overdrive, and vacuum-operated power brakes continued to be standard equipment on this line. Both low- and high-compression versions of the Crown Imperial engine used the aluminum cylinder head. The engine was the updated 323.5-cubic inch job with six main bearings. Only one individual custom - a parade phaeton by Derham - was made on the Crown Imperial chassis.

I.D. DATA: [Series 25] Serial numbers were located on the right front door hinge pillar post. Starting: (Royal) 7625001; (Windsor) 6955201. Ending: (Royal) 7657487; (Windsor) 6993727. Engine numbers were on the left side of block, between one and two cylinders, just below cylinder head. Starting: (Royal) C25-1001; (Windsor) C25-70147. Ending: (Royal) C25-1001; (Windsor) C25-72067. [Series 26] Serial numbers were in the same location. Starting: (Traveler) 6750101; (New Yorker) 6613401; (Saratoga) 6673501. Ending: (Traveler) 6756417; (New Yorker) 6624087; (Saratoga) 6674100. Engine numbers were in

the same location. Starting: (Traveler) C26-1001; (New Yorker) C26-1001; (Saratoga) C261001. Ending: (Traveler) C26-18753; (New Yorker) C26-18761; (Saratoga) C26-18700. [Series C-27] Serial numbers were in the same location. Starting: 7806551. Ending: 7807401. Engine numbers were in the same location. Starting: C27-1001. Ending: C27-1875.

Model No.	Body Type & Seating	Price	Weight	Prod. Total
(Royal)				
C-25	2-dr. Cpe.-3P	895	3075	Note 2
C-25	2-dr. Cpe.-6P	960	3110	Note 3
C-25	2-dr. Vic. Sed.-6P	960	3150	Note 4
C-25	4-dr. Sed.-6P	995	3175	23,274
(LWB Royal)				
C-25	4-dr. Sed.-8P	1235	3550	Note 5
C-25	4-dr. Limo.-8P	1310	3640	Note 6
C-25	Chassis	NA	NA	152
(Windsor)				
C-25	2-dr. Cpe.-3P	935	3095	Note 2
C-25	2-dr. Cpe.-6P	995	3135	Note 3
C-25	2-dr. Vic. Sed.-6P	995	3175	Note 4
C-25	2-dr. Conv. Cpe.-6P	1160	3360	Note 7
C-25	4-dr. Sed.-6P	1025	3210	Note 8
(LWB Windsor)				
C-25	4-dr. Sed.-8P	1275	3575	Note 5
C-25	4-dr. Limo.-8P	1350	3660	Note 6
(Highlander)				
C-25	2-dr. Cpe.-6P	1020	3135	Note 3
C-25	2-dr. Conv. Cpe.-6P	1185	3360	Note 7
C-25	4-dr. Sed.-6P	1050	3210	Note 8

Note 1: Total series production was 73,998.
Note 2: Combined production was 5,117.
Note 3: Combined production was 4,315.
Note 4: Combined production was 9,851.
Note 5: Combined production was 439.
Note 6: Combined production was 98.
Note 7: Combined production was 2,275.
Note 8: Combined production was 28,477.

(Traveler)				
C-26	2-dr. Cpe.-3P	1095	3475	Note 2
C-26	2-dr. Cpe.-6P	1150	3525	Note 3
C-26	2-dr. Vic. Sed.-6P	1150	3555	Note 4
C-26	4-dr. Sed.-6P	1180	3590	Note 5
(New Yorker)				
C-26	2-dr. Cpe.-3P	1175	3490	Note 2
C-26	2-dr. Cpe.-6P	1230	3570	Note 3
C-26	2-dr. Conv. Cpe.-6P	1375	3775	Note 6
C-26	2-dr. Vic. Sed.-6P	1230	3610	Note 4
C-26	4-dr. Sed.-6P	1260	3635	Note 5
C-26	4-dr. Fml. Sed.-6P	1335	NA	Note 5
(Highlander)				
C-26	2-dr. Cpe.-6P	1255	3570	Note 3
C-26	2-dr. Conv. Cpe.-6P	1400	3775	Note 6
C-26	4-dr. Sed.-6P	1285	3635	Note 5
(Saratoga)				
C-26	4-dr. Sed.-6P	1375	3790	Note 5
C-26	4-dr. Fml. Sed.-6P	1450	NA	Note 5
C-26	Chassis	NA	NA	29

Note 1: Total series production was 17,600.
Note 2: Combined production was 711.
Note 3: Combined production was 1,117.
Note 4: Combined production was 275.
Note 5: Combined production was 14,603.

(Crown Imperial)				
C-27	4-dr. Sed.-6P	2245	4340	355
C-27	4-dr. Sed.-8P	2345	4330	284
C-27	4-dr. Limo.-8P	2445	4365	210
C-27	4-dr. Parade Phae.-6P	NA	NA	1

Note 1: Total series production was 850.

ENGINE: [Series 25] Inline. L-head. Six. Cast iron block. B & S: 3-3/8 x 4-1/2 in. Disp.: 241.5 cu. in. C.R.: (std.) 6.5:1; (opt.) 7.0:1. Brake H.P.: (std.) 108 @ 3600 R.P.M.; (opt.) 112 @ 3600 R.P.M. N.A.C.C. H.P.: 27.34. Main bearings: four. Valve lifters: solid. Carb.: Carter 1V model BB-E6S1. Torque: (std.) 188 lb.-ft. @ 1200 R.P.M.; (opt.) 194 lb.-ft. @ 1200 R.P.M. [Series 26] Inline. L-head. Eight. Cast iron block. B & S: 3-1/4 x 4-7/8 in. Disp.: 323.5 cu. in. C.R.: (std.) 6.8:1; (opt.) 7.45:1. Brake H.P.: (std.) 132 @ 3400 R.P.M.; (opt.) 143 @ 3400 R.P.M. N.A.C.C. H.P.: 33.80. Main bearings: six. Valve lifters: solid. Carb.: Stromberg 2V model AAV-2. Torque: (std.) 255 lb.-ft. @ 1600

R.P.M.; (opt.) 270 lbs.-ft. @ 1600 R.P.M. [Series C-27] Inline. L-head. Eight. Cast iron block. B & S: 3-1/4 x 4-7/8 in. Disp.: 323.5 cu. in. C.R.: (std.) 6.8:1; (opt.) 7.45:1. Brake H.P.: (std.) 132 @ 3400 R.P.M.; (opt.) 143 @ 3400 R.P.M. N.A.C.C. H.P.: 33.80. Main bearings: six. Valve lifters: solid. Carb.: Stromberg 2V model AAV-2. Torque: (std.) 260 lb.-ft. @ 1600 R.P.M.; (opt.) 270 lb.-ft. @ 1600 R.P.M.

1940 Chrysler, Series C-26, Traveler sedan (JAC)

CHASSIS: [Series C-25] W.B.: 122.5 in. Tires: 16 x 6.25. [Series C-25 (LWB)] W.B.: 139.5 in. Tires: 16 x 6.50. [Series C-26] W.B.: 128.5 in. Tires: 16 x 6.50 or 16 x 7.00. [Series C-27] W.B.: 143 in. Tires: 15 x 7.50.

TECHNICAL: (C-27) Fluid Drive transmission; (Others) synchromesh manual. Speeds: 3F/1R (overdrive standard on C-27). Column-mount gearshift. Multiple dry disc clutch. Shaft drive. Hypoid rear axle. Overall ratio: (C-25) 4.1:1; (C-26) 3.9:1; (C-27) 4.55:1. Lockheed four-wheel hydraulic brakes. Steel-spoke wheels.

OPTIONS: Whitewalls. Full wheel discs. Wheel trim rings. Two-tone paint. Outside rear view mirror. Fender skirts. Bumper guards. Radio. Heater. Clock. Cigar lighter. Radio antenna. Seat covers. External sun shade. Spotlight(s). Fog light(s). Front fender parking lights (six). Rear fender gravel guards. Chrome trimmed rocker panels. Leather driver's seat (limousine). Bumper crash bars. Wind wings (convertible).

HISTORICAL: Introduced September 1939. Innovations: Sealed beam headlights. Six main bearing eight-cylinder engine. "Airfoam" seat cushions. Calendar year registrations: 100,117. Calendar year production: 115,824. Model year production: 92,419. Chrysler held 10th place in U.S. model year production. The company was ninth in calendar year output. The Derham Crown Imperial parade phaeton survives in the Henry Ford Museum. Derham also produced a special order Crown Imperial town limousine, a Royal Six town car, a Saratoga town car. Six Newport prototype parade phaetons and six Thunderbolt prototype sport roadster-hardtops designed by LeBaron were also built. One of the Newports was the Indianapolis 500 pace car in 1940. Walter P. Chrysler died on August 18, 1940.

1941 CHRYSLER

1941 Chrysler, Town & Country, station wagon (OCW)

CHRYSLER — SERIES 28 — SIX: The 1941 Chrysler Six came in the same five sub-series. Styling was basically the same as in 1940, except

the bodies were slightly wider and lower and had increased glass area in the front and rear. The number of horizontal grille bars was reduced from nine to six, with wider spaces between them. The Chrysler script nameplate appeared directly on the nose and trim louvers were not used on the hood sides. Decorations on the trunk were redesigned as were the bumper guards, which had three horizontal ribs. All models came with or without runningboards. Fluid Drive was standard and a new "Vacamatic" semi-automatic transmission was available at extra cost. Innovations included a new "Spitfire" engine, Automatic Safety control gearshift, inside hood lock and a steering wheel with no spokes in the upper half. An important new model was the Windsor Six Town & Country wagon, a "barrel-back" suburban type vehicle designed by Chrysler President David A. Wallace. It had a steel top, but the body was covered with white ash wood framing and genuine mahogany veneer panels.

CHRYSLER — SERIES 30 — EIGHT: The Traveler economy series was deleted. Remaining were the Saratoga, New Yorker, and New Yorker Highlander sub-series. General styling features were like those on Chrysler Sixes except for slightly longer sheet metal. Small signature scripts placed on the trailing edge of the hood supplied model identification. In the middle of the year, the New Yorker line was made Chrysler's top sub-series. Standard equipment included Solar Spark ignition, hydraulic brakes, dual sun visors, dual taillights, dual wipers, a "Spitfire" eight-cylinder engine with a two-barrel carburetor and Fluid Drive. One Town & Country wagon was constructed, upon special order, on the Saratoga chassis.

1941 Chrysler, New Yorker, convertible coupe (OCW)

CROWN IMPERIAL — SERIES C-33 — EIGHT: There was one new hybrid in the 1940 Imperial line. Called the Special town sedan, it used the New Yorker chassis, but had a Crown Imperial nameplate. New Crown Imperial features included Laidlaw interior fabrics, safety rim wheels, Double Eagle tires, and optional, hydroelectric power windows. The master control unit for the power windows was mounted on top of the instrument panel. Crown Imperials had the general styling of other models, with body panels "stretched" to fit the longer wheelbase. Custom Imperial chrome signatures appeared on the rear of the hood sides, below the beltline trim. Fluid Drive was among the Crown Imperial's standard equipment.

1941 Chrysler, Crown Imperial, landau limousine (TVB)

I.D. DATA: [Series 28] Serial numbers were located on the right front door hinge pillar post. Starting: (Royal) 7657501; (Windsor) 7901601. Ending: (Royal) 7736429; (Windsor) 7957099. Engine numbers were located on the upper left side of the block, between cylinders one and two, just below the cylinder head. Starting: (All) C28-1001. Ending: (All) C28-135725. [Series 30] Serial numbers were in the same location. Starting: (Saratoga) 6756501; (New Yorker) 6624101. Ending: (Saratoga) 6762251; (New Yorker) 6642655. Engine numbers were in the

same location. Starting: (All) C30-1001. Ending: (All) C30-25734. [Series C-33] Serial numbers were in the same location. Starting: 7807501. Ending: 7808214. Note: The Special town sedans had New Yorker serial numbers. Engine numbers were in the same location. Starting: C33-1001. Ending: C33-1735. Note: The Special town sedans had New Yorker engine numbers.

1941 Chrysler LeBaron Custom Town Limousine

Model No.	Body Type & Seating	Price	Weight	Prod. Total
(Royal)				
C-28	2-dr. Cpe.-3P	995	3170	6846
C-28	2-dr. Clb. Cpe.-6P	1085	3260	10,830
C-28	2-dr. Lux. Brgm.-6P	1066	3270	8006
C-28	4-dr. Sed.-6P	1091	3300	51,378
C-28	4-dr. Twn. Sed.-6P	1136	3320	1277
(LWB Royal)				
C-28	4-dr. Sed.-8P	1345	3650	297
C-28	4-dr. Limo.-8P	1415	3740	31
C-28	Chassis	NA	NA	3
(Windsor)				
C-28	2-dr. Cpe.-3P	1045	3170	1921
C-28	2-dr. Clb. Cpe.-6P	1142	3260	8513
C-28	2-dr. Conv. Cpe.-6P	1315	3470	4432
C-28	2-dr. Lux. Brgm.-6P	1128	3270	2898
C-28	4-dr. Sed.-6P	1165	3300	36,396
C-28	4-dr. Twn. Sed.-6P	1198	3315	2704
(LWB Windsor)				
C-28	5-dr. T&C Sta. Wag.-6P	1412	3540	200
C-28	5-dr. T&C Sta. Wag.-9P	1492	3595	797
C-28	4-dr. Sed.-8P	1410	3650	116
C-28	4-dr. Limo.-8P	1487	3740	54
(Highlander)				
C-28	2-dr. Cpe.-3P	1065	3170	Note 2
C-28	2-dr. Clb. Cpe.-6P	1162	3260	Note 2
C-28	2-dr. Conv. Cpe.-6P	1335	3470	Note 2
C-28	2-dr. Lux. Brgm.-6P	1148	3270	Note 2
C-28	4-dr. Sed.-6P	1185	3300	Note 2
C-28	4-dr. Twn. Sed.-6P	1218	3315	Note 2
(LWB Highlander)				
C-28	4-dr. Sed.-8P	1430	3650	Note 2
C-28	4-dr. Limo.-8P	1507	3740	Note 2

Note 1: Total series production was 136,701.

Note 2: Production of cars with the plaid "Highlander" interior was lumped together with Windsor production. No breakout is available.

(Saratoga)				
C-30	2-dr. Cpe.-3P	1245	3600	Note 2
C-30	2-dr. Clb. Cpe.-6P	1299	3685	Note 3
C-30	2-dr. Lux. Brgm.-6P	1293	3715	Note 4
C-30	4-dr. Sed.-6P	1320	3755	Note 6
C-30	4-dr. Twn. Sed.-6P	1350	3750	Note 7
C-30	5-dr. T&C Sta. Wag.-9P	NA	NA	1
C-30	Chassis	NA	NA	9
(New Yorker)				
C-30	2-dr. Cpe.-3P	1325	3635	Note 2
C-30	2-dr. Clb. Cpe.-6P	1369	3690	Note 3
C-30	2-dr. Conv. Cpe.-6P	1548	3945	Note 5
C-30	2-dr. Lux. Brgm.-6P	1369	3745	Note 4
C-30	4-dr. Sed.-6P	1389	3775	Note 6
C-30	4-dr. Twn. Sed.-6P	1399	3785	Note 7
(New Yorker Highlander)				
C-30	2-dr. Cpe.-3P	1345	3635	Note 2
C-30	2-dr. Clb. Cpe.-6P	1389	3690	Note 3
C-30	2-dr. Conv. Cpe.-6P	1568	3945	Note 5
C-30	2-dr. Lux. Brgm.-6P	1389	3745	Note 4

Model No.	Body Type & Seating	Price	Weight	Prod. Total
C-30	4-dr. Sed.-6P	1409	3775	Note 6
C-30	4-dr. Twn. Sed.-6P	1419	3785	Note 7

Note 1: Total series production was 24,301.
Note 2: Combined production was 771.
Note 3: Combined production was 2,845.
Note 4: Combined production was 293.
Note 5: Combined production was 1,295.
Note 6: Combined production was 15,868.
Note 7: Combined production was 2,326.

(C-30 Crown Imperial Line)

C-30	4-dr. Spl. Twn. Sed.-6P	1760	3900	894

(C-33 Crown Imperial Line)

C-33	4-dr. Sed.-6P	2595	4435	179
C-33	4-dr. Sed.-8P	2695	4495	205
C-33	4-dr. Limo.-8P	2795	4560	316
C-33	Chassis	NA	NA	1

Note 1: Total C-33 series production was 701. (This does not include the Special town sedan that is totaled as part of the New Yorker series above.)

Note 2: The limousine production total includes an undetermined number of LeBaron Custom town limousines, a limited edition model built only on special order.

Note 3: The single Crown Imperial chassis was used for a Custom landaulet limousine built for Chrysler president Walter O. Briggs.

1941 Chrysler, Royal, coupe (JAC)

ENGINE: [Series 28] Inline. L-head. Six. Cast iron block. B & S: 3-3/8 x 4-1/2 in. Disp.: 241.5 cu. in. C.R.: (std.) 6.5:1 or 6.8:1; (opt.) 7.2:1. Brake H.P.: (std.) 108 @ 3600 R.P.M. or 112 @ 3600 R.P.M.; (opt.) 115 @ 3600 R.P.M. N.A.C.C. H.P.: 27.34. Main bearings: four. Valve lifters: solid. Carb.: Carter 1V model BB-E6W1. Torque: (std.) 188/190 lb.-ft. @ 1200 R.P.M.; (opt.) 196 lb.-ft. @ 1200 R.P.M. (Note: Cars built early in the year had the 6.5:1 low-compression engine. Cars built later in the year had the 6.8:1 low-compression engine.) [Series 30] Inline. L-head. Eight. Cast iron block. B & S: 3-1/4 x 4-7/8 in. Disp.: 323.5 cu. in. C.R.: (std.) 6.8:1; (opt.) 6.8:1 w/aluminum head. Brake H.P.: (std.) 137 @ 3400 R.P.M.; (opt.) 140 @ 3400 R.P.M. N.A.C.C. H.P.: 33.80. Main bearings: six. Valve lifters: solid. Carb.: Stromberg 2V model AAV-2. Torque: (std.) 225 lb.-ft. @ 1600 R.P.M.; (opt.) 260 lb.-ft. @ 1600 R.P.M. [Series C-33] Inline. L-head. Eight. Cast iron block. B & S: 3-1/4 x 4-7/8 in. Disp.: 323.5 cu. in. C.R.: 6.8:1 (with aluminum head). Brake H.P.: 140 @ 3400 R.P.M. N.A.C.C. H.P.: 33.80. Main bearings: six. Valve lifters: solid. Carb.: Stromberg 2V model AAV-2. Torque: 260 lb.-ft. @ 1600 R.P.M.

1941 Chrysler, Thunderbolt, convertible show car (FR)

CHASSIS: [Series C-28] W.B.: 121.5 in. Tires: 16 x 6.25. [Series C-28 (LWB)] W.B.: 139.5 in. Tires: 16 x 6.50. [Series C-30] W.B.: 127.5 in. Tires: 15 x 7.00. [Series C-33] W.B.: 145.5 in. Tires: 15 x 7.50.

TECHNICAL: Fluid Drive transmission. Speeds: 3F/1R. Column-mounted gearshift. Conventional clutch. Shaft drive. Hypoid rear axle. Overall ratio: (C-28) 3.9:1; (C-30) 3.91:1; (C-33) 4.55:1. Four wheel hydraulic brakes. Steel disc wheels.

1941 Chrysler, Windsor, sedan (JAC)

OPTIONS: Whitewalls. Full wheel disks. Wheel trim beauty rings. Two-tone paint. Outside rear view mirror(s). Fender skirts. Bumper guards. Radio. Heater. Clock. Cigar lighter. Radio antenna. Seat covers. External sun shade. Spotlight(s). Fog lamps. Vacamatic transmission. Conventional runningboards (on C-30s). Leather driver's seat (limousine). Bumper crash bars. Master grille guard. Chrome exhaust extension. Hydro-electric power windows (Imperial). Highlander plaid upholstery (Windsor & New Yorker). Navajo style interior. Saran trim package. Rear fender gravel guards.

1941 Chrysler, Newport, dual cowl phaeton show car (FR)

HISTORICAL: Production started August 1940. Production ended July 1941. Introduced September 1940. Innovations: New "Spitfire" engines. Automatic safety control. Power windows optional on Crown Imperial. Town & Country introduced. Vacamatic four-speed transmission. Convertible has rear quarter windows. Calendar year registrations: 143,025. Calendar year production: 141,522. Model year production: 161,704. Company president was Walter O. Briggs. Chrysler was America's 10th ranked automaker in model year 1941. On a calendar year basis, the company was the eighth largest carmaker. Chrysler buyers had a choice of 13 color combinations and 27 interior trim combinations. Chrysler showrooms enjoyed increased traffic as crowds thronged to view the exciting Newport and Thunderbolt "dream" cars. Six of each were built and exhibited until the U.S. entry in World War II. Walter Chrysler, Jr., kept one of the Newports; the other 11 cars were sold.

1941 Chrysler, Crown Imperial, town sedan (TVB)

1942 CHRYSLER

CHRYSLER — SERIES C-34 — SIX: The 1942 Chrysler grille consisted of five chrome horizontal bars that ran across the front end and part of the fenders. Horizontal parking lamps were recessed into the grille. The one-piece alligator hood was unlocked by a knob in the driver's compartment. There were also five chrome bars on the rear fenders. Runningboards were concealed for a streamlined appearance. Standard equipment for all sixes included Solar Spark ignition, hydraulic brakes, full circle horn rings, and dual visors, wipers, and horns. Windsor models also had "Air Foam" seat cushions, broadcloth upholstery, electric clock, whitewall wheel rims, mirror hubcaps, and front carpets. The Windsor sedan and brougham had folding armrests in the rear seat. Cars built late in the year had painted "blackout" trim instead of chrome parts. The available car lines included the Royal and Windsor and each had a long wheelbase sub-series consisting of two models. Highlander plaid interiors were optional on Windsors at $20 extra.

1942 Chrysler, Windsor, convertible (TVB)

CHRYSLER — SERIES C-36 — EIGHT: The Chrysler Eights had the same general styling as sixes, with slightly longer front end sheet metal. Small chrome signatures on the rear sides of the hood, under the beltline trim, identifed the cars as Saratogas or New Yorkers. New Yorkers had upscale interiors with front carpets, clocks, and folding rear seat armrests. Highlander plaid or Indian style "Thunderbird" upholstery was optional in New Yorkers at $20 extra. Derham converted at least one New Yorker convertible into a sports model with cut-down doors, sweep spear side moldings, and fender skirts. Its production is included with that of the regular convertible.

1942 Chrysler, Crown Imperial, limousine (OCW)

CROWN IMPERIAL — SERIES C-37 — EIGHT: The Crown Imperial was on Chrysler's longest wheelbase and had larger hoods, fenders and doors to eat up the extra space. Interiors were richly upholstered and appointed with folding auxiliary seats in eight-passenger cars. The limousine had a leather front seat and division window. Chrysler built two C-37 chassis, but Derham made at least three special Crown Imperials. The first was a semi-custom blind-rear-quarter open town car — actually a converted limousine. The two real customs were a four-door convertible sedan and a distinctive-looking formal open town car.

I.D. DATA: [Series C-34] Serial numbers were located on the right front door hinge pillar. Starting: (Royal) 70001001; (Windsor) 70010179. Ending (Royal) 70010179; (Windsor) 70514481. Engine numbers were located on the left side of the block just below the cylinder head. Starting: (All) C34-1001. Ending: (Royal) C34-2392; (Windsor) C34-23922. [Series C-36] Serial numbers were in the same location. Starting: (Saratoga) 6762501; (New Yorker) 6674201. Ending: (Saratoga) 6764094; (New Yorker) 6684754. Engine numbers were in the same location. Starting: (Saratoga) C36-1001; (New Yorker) C36-1001. Ending: (Saratoga) C36-13516; (New Yorker) C36-13526.

1942 Chrysler, Royal, two-door brougham (TVB)

Model No.	Body Type & Seating	Price	Weight	Prod. Total
(Royal)				
C-34	2-dr. Cpe.-3P	1075	3331	479
C-34	2-dr. Clb. Cpe.-6P	1168	3406	779
C-34	2-dr. Brgm.-6P	1154	3431	709
C-34	4-dr. Sed.-6P	1177	3476	7424
C-34	4-dr. Twn. Sed.-6P	1222	3481	73
(LWB Royal)				
C-34	4-dr. Sed.-8P	1535	3854	79
C-34	4-dr. Limo.-8P	1605	3944	21
(Windsor)				
C-34	2-dr. Cpe.-3P	1140	3351	250
C-34	2-dr. Clb. Cpe.-6P	1228	3426	1713
C-34	2-dr. Conv. Cpe.-6P	1420	3661	574
C-34	2-dr. Brgm.-6P	1220	3441	317
C-34	4-dr. Sed.-6P	1255	3496	10,054
C-34	4-dr. Twn. Sed.-6P	1295	3506	479
C-34	4-dr. T&C Wag.-6P	1595	3614	150
C-34	4-dr. T&C Wag.-9P	1685	3699	849
(LWB Windsor)				
C-34	4-dr. Sed.-8P	1605	3879	29
C-34	4-dr. Limo.-8P	1685	3954	12

Note 1: Total series production was 23,991.

Model No.	Body Type & Seating	Price	Weight	Prod. Total
(Saratoga)				
C-36	2-dr. Cpe.-3P	1325	3703	80
C-36	2-dr. Clb. Cpe.-6P	1380	3788	193
C-36	2-dr. Brgm.-6P	1365	3798	36
C-36	4-dr. Sed.-6P	1405	3833	1239
C-36	4-dr. Twn. Sed.-6P	1450	3843	46
C-36	Chassis	NA	NA	2
(New Yorker)				
C-36	2-dr. Cpe.-3P	1385	3728	158
C-36	2-dr. Clb. Cpe.-6P	1450	3783	1234
C-36	2-dr. Conv. Cpe.-6P	1640	4033	401
C-36	2-dr. Brgm.-6P	1440	3798	62
C-36	4-dr. Sed.-6P	1475	3873	7045
C-36	4-dr. Twn. Sed.-6P	1520	3893	1648
C-36	4-dr. T&C Wag.-9P	NA	NA	1

Note 1: Total series production was 12,145.

Model No.	Body Type & Seating	Price	Weight	Prod. Total
C-37	4-dr. Sed.-6P	2815	4565	—
C-37	4-dr. Sed.-8P	2915	4620	—
C-37	4-dr. Limo.-SP	3065	4685	—
(Derham Semi-Custom)				
C-37	4-dr. Twn. Car-8P	NA	NA	NA
(Derham Custom)				
C-37	4-dr. Conv. Sed.-6P	NA	NA	1
C-37	4-dr. Fml. Twn. Car-6P	NA	NA	1

Note 1: Total series production was 450.

ENGINE: [Series C-34] Inline. L-head. Six. Cast iron block. B & S: 3-7/16 x 4-1/2 in. Disp.: 250.6 cu. in. C.R.: 6.6:1. Brake H.P.: 120 @ 3800 R.P.M. N.A.C.C. H.P.: 27.34. Main bearings: four. Valve lifters: solid. Carb.: Carter IV model EE-1. Torque: 200 lb.-ft. @ 1600 R.P.M. [Series C-36] Inline. L-head. Eight. Cast iron block. B & S: 3-1/4 x 4-7/8 in. Disp.: 323.5 cu. in. C.R.: 6.8:1. Brake H.P.: 140 @ 3600 R.P.M. N.A.C.C. H.P.: 33.80. Main bearings: six. Valve lifters: solid. Carb.: Stromberg 2V

model AAV-2. Torque: 260 lb.-ft. @ 1800 R.P.M. [Series C-37] The Crown Imperial used the Saratoga/New Yorker engine.

1942 Chrysler, Town & Country, station wagon

CHASSIS: [Series C-34] W.B.: 121-1/2 in. Tires: 16 x 6.25. [Series C-34 (LWB)] W.B.: 139-1/2 in. Tires: 16 x 6.50. [Series C-36] W.B.: 127-1/2 in. Tires: 15 x 7.00.

TECHNICAL: Transmission: (six) manual; (eight) Fluid Drive. Speeds: 3F/1R. Column shift controls. Multiple disc clutch. Shaft drive. Hypoid rear axle. Overall ratio: (C-34) 3.9:1; (C-36) 3.9:1; (C-37) 3.58:1. Four wheel hydraulic brakes. Steel-disc wheels.

OPTIONS: Whitewall wheel discs. Mirror hubcaps. Outside rear view mirror(s). License plate frame. Chrome exhaust extension. Fender skirts. Bumper guards. Radio. Heater. Clock. Cigar lighter. Radio antenna. Seat covers. External sun shade. Spotlight(s). Fog lamps. Highlander plaid upholstery ($20.00). Thunderbird American Indian upholstery (20.00). Two-tone paint. Special paint colors. Fluid drive (standard on Town & Country wagon and eights). Vacamatic transmission. Fender skirt medallions.

1942 Chrysler, New Yorker, convertible coupe, (JAC)

HISTORICAL: Production started August 1941. Production ended January 1942. Introduced September 1941. Innovations: Dash controlled alligator hood. Larger more powerful six-cylinder engine. Blackout trim on cars built after December 1941. Concealed runningboards on all models. Thunderbird interior. Calendar year registrations: none. Calendar year production: 5,292. Model year production: 36,586. Chrysler was 12th in calendar year sales for 1942. The company's model year ranking was 10th. A unique semi-custom built this season was the "Laura A.," a Town & Country wagon converted into an open, four-door touring car. It appeared in Hollywood films and is believed to have been built by the shop of Bohman & Schwartz in Pasadena, California.

1946 CHRYSLER

ROYAL SERIES — (6-CYL) — The Royal was the least expensive car of the postwar Chrysler family. Design was based on the 1942 models. Refinements and advances included front fenders that flowed smoothly into newly-skinned front doors, beautifully detailed die-cast eggcrate style grille, new front and rear bumpers and different fender trim. Some year-to-year running changes occurred. The body structure was all steel, a

longtime Chrysler hallmark. Separate chassis/frame construction was used. Body insulation included the interior structure of the body, roof, side panels, floor, cowl and trunk. Postwar developments were Safe Guard hydraulic brakes and a permanent Oilite fuel tank filter. Rust-proofing protected the interior body structure. Series identification was provided by nameplates found on the hood sides. Standard equipment included armrests on both front doors; directional signal; entrance light; brake warning light; cigar lighter with illuminated ashtray; rubber floor covering in front compartment (except club coupe and eight-passenger sedans, which are carpeted); dual outside front door locks; glovebox light and lock; pile fabric or broadcloth upholstery; luggage compartment light; assist straps and robe cords on sedans and broughams; dual two-speed electric wipers; plastic steering wheel; automatic dome light; white wheel-trim rings and interior door locks.

1946 Chrysler, Royal four-door sedan, 6-cyl (AA)

CHRYSLER I.D. NUMBERS: Serial numbers are found on the left front door hinge post. Engine numbers were located on the left side of the block below the cylinder head between the first and second cylinders. Serial numbers 70011001 to 70023022 appeared on Royals and Royal engine numbers ran from C38-1001 and up. Serial numbers 70515001 to 70564428 appeared on Windsors and 71000001 to 71000127 appeared on Windsor Town & Countrys. Windsor engine numbers ran from C800-1001 and up. Serial numbers 6765001 to 67665545 appeared on Saratogas and Saratoga engine numbers ran from C39-1001 and up. Serial numbers 7025001 to 7037248 appeared on New Yorkers. New Yorker Town & Country serial numbers ran from 7400001 to 7402036. New Yorker engine numbers ran from C39-1001 and up.

ROYAL SERIES

Model No.	Body/ Style No.	Body Type & Seating	Factory Price	Shipping Weight	Prod. Total
(STANDARD WHEELBASE)					
C38S	N/A	2-dr Cpe-3P	1415	3373	Note 1
C38S	N/A	2-dr Clb Cpe-6P	1535	3443	Note 1
C38S	N/A	2-dr Sed-6P	1510	3458	Note 1
C38S	N/A	4-dr Sed-6P	1545	3523	Note 1
(LONG WHEELBASE)					
C38S	N/A	4-dr Sed-8P	1925	3977	Note 1
C38S	N/A	4-dr Limo-8P	2045	4022	Note 1

Note 1: 1946-1949 first-series production recorded as a single total, with no model year breakouts available. See the 1948 Chrysler section for these totals.

1946 Chrysler, Windsor two-door three-passenger coupe, 6-cyl

WINDSOR SERIES — (6-CYL) — This upgraded version of the Royal included all Royal features, plus two-tone wool broadcloth upholstery, carpeted front compartment, electric clock, rear seat folding armrest on sedans and exterior 'goose neck' mirror on convertibles only. The Windsor offered luxury on par with the New Yorker line, but was powered by the L-head six-cylinder engine. Windsors were identified by nameplates on both sides of the hood. An optional Highlander interior was available on both open and closed models. Wood-bodied Town & Countrys were considered an integral part of the Windsor series, though serial numbers were not integrated. All Town & Country sedans, except for 100 eight-cylinder

sedans built in late 1946, were powered by the six-cylinder L-head engine offered on all Windsors.

WINDSOR SERIES

Model No.	Body/ Style No.	Body Type & Seating	Factory Price	Shipping Weight	Prod. Total
(STANDARD WHEELBASE)					
C38W	N/A	2-dr Cpe-3P	1465	3383	Note 1
C38W	N/A	2-dr Clb Cpe-6P	1585	3448	Note 1
C38W	N/A	2-dr Conv-6P	1845	3693	Note 1
C38W	N/A	2-dr Sed-6P	1575	3468	Note 1
C38W	N/A	4-dr Sed-6P	1595	3528	Note 1
C38W	N/A	4-dr T&C-6P	2366	3917	Note 1
(LONG WHEELBASE)					
C38W	N/A	4-dr Sed-8P	1975	3977	Note 1
C38W	N/A	4-dr Sed-8P	2095	4052	Note 1

Note 1: 1946-1949 first-series production was recorded as a single total, with no model year breakouts available. See the 1948 Chrysler section for these totals.

SARATOGA SERIES — (8-CYL) — The Saratoga was an eight-cylinder equivalent to the six-cylinder Royal in appointments. The wheelbase was lengthened six inches, forward of the cowl, to accommodate the longer engine. Fluid Drive was standard, as well as hydraulic rear sway strut; electric clock; rear fold down armrests in sedan and two-door sedan (Brougham); wax-impregnated springs and gray pile fabric or broadcloth upholstery. Four choices of optional color leather upholstery were available at extra cost. Only the Club Coupe was offered with a carpeted front compartment. Only the three-passenger coupe used a rubber rear mat instead of carpeting. Saratoga nameplates were located on hood sides.

SARATOGA SERIES

Model No.	Body/ Style No.	Body Type & Seating	Factory Price	Shipping Weight	Prod. Total
C39K	N/A	2-dr Cpe-3P	1735	3785	Note 1
C39K	N/A	2-dr Clb Cpe-6P	1830	3892	Note 1
C39K	N/A	2-dr Sed-6P	1838	3875	Note 1
C39K	N/A	4-dr Sed-6P	1845	3972	Note 1

Note 1: 1946-1949 first-series production recorded as a single total, with no model year breakouts available. See the 1948 Chrysler section for these totals.

NEW YORKER SERIES — (6-CYL) — The high-line New Yorker models included all of the standard equipment found on the Saratoga and added such features as two-tone wool broadcloth upholstery, a carpeted front compartment and, on convertibles, a 'goose neck' style mirror. New Yorker production began in January 1946. Model identification was found on nameplates mounted on the side of the hood near the cowl. Highlander plaid upholstery was an option available on the New Yorker. The cars so-equipped wore a "Highlander" nameplate. Town & Country models were mounted on the New Yorker chassis and are included in New Yorker series. All engine numbers used the same C39 prefix.

1946 Chrysler, Town & Country two-door convertible, 8-cyl

NEW YORKER SERIES

Model No.	Body/ Style No.	Body Type & Seating	Factory Price	Shipping Weight	Prod. Total
C39N	N/A	2-dr Cpe-3P	1825	3805	Note 1
C39N	N/A	2-dr Clb Cpe-6P	1930	3897	Note 1
C39N	N/A	2-dr Conv-6P	2175	4132	Note 1
C39N	N/A	2-dr Sed-6P	1920	3932	Note 1
C39N	N/A	4-dr Sed-6P	1945	3987	Note 1
C39N	N/A	4-dr Sed T&C-6P	2718	4344	(100)
C39N	N/A	2-dr Conv T&C-6P	2725	4332	Note 1

Note 1: 1946-1949 first-series production recorded as a single total, with no model year breakouts available. See the 1948 Chrysler section for these totals.

ROYAL/WINDSOR ENGINE: L-head six-cylinder. Cast iron block. Displacement: 250.6 cid. Bore and stroke: 3.438 x 4.50 inches. Compression ratio: 6.6:1. Brake hp: 114 at 3600 rpm. Four main bearings. Solid lifters. Carburetors: (Fluid Drive and Vacumatic) B-B EV1-EV2 or E7L4; (Standard transmission) B-B EX1, EX2, EX3.

SARATOGA/NEW YORKER ENGINE: L-head eight-cylinder. Cast iron block. Displacement: 323.5 cid. Bore and stroke: 3.25 x 4.875 inches. Compression ratio: 6.7:1. Brake hp: 135 at 3400 rpm. Five main bearings. Solid lifters. Carburetor: B-B E7A1.

CHASSIS FEATURES: (ROYAL/WINDSOR) Wheelbase: (long wheelbase models) 139-1/2 inches; (all others) 121-1/2 inches. Three-speed manual transmission standard with Fluid Drive and hydraulically operated M-5 transmission optional. Whitewalls not available in 1946. Tires: Short wheelbase cars used 6.50 x 15 and long wheelbase cars used 7.00 x 16. (SARATOGA/NEW YORKER): Wheelbase: 127-1/2 inches. Fluid Drive and hydraulically operated M-5 transmission standard.

OPTIONS: Highlander upholstery. All-Weather Air control system. Twin heaters with heat, defroster and fan control. Comfort Master Heater. Right-hand unit for All-Weather Air control system (fresh air intake optional). Deluxe heater mounted on dash with fan and defroster controls. Radios: Model 602 with six tubes and automatic tuning, Model 802 with eight tubes and automatic tuning. Three types of radio antennas, including a concealed cowl-mounted unit. Central bumper guard. Electric clock (Royal). Lifeguard tubes. Six-ply tires. Top luggage rack on eight-passenger models. Mopar locking gas cap. Spare tire valve extension. Refrigeration unit. Weatherproof ignition. Mopar Auto Compass. Exhaust extension. Underhood light. Spotlamp. Windshield washer and sun visor. Fog lamps. Spotlight(s).

1947 CHRYSLER

1947 Chrysler, Royal two-door Club Coupe, 6-cyl

ROYAL SERIES — (6-CYL) — There were virtually no changes in the 1947 Chrysler models. Whitewall tires became available after April 1, 1947, which necessitated a change to rear fenders with larger wheelhouse openings. The high-beam indicator was moved from above the speedometer on the 1946 model to the speedometer dial, replacing the left turn signal arrow light. The right arrow now became a signal flashing indicator light. Red taillamp buttons replaced the white buttons used on 1946 Chryslers. Also, door locks and lock covers were changed in design from earlier models. Prices were slightly changed and a small weight increase was noted in specification charts over the earlier model. Standard equipment remained as before.

1947 Chrysler, Town & Country four-door sedan, 6-cyl (AA)

CHRYSLER I.D. NUMBERS: Serial numbers are found on the left front door hinge post. Engine numbers were located on the left side of the block below the cylinder head between first and second cylinders. Serial numbers 70023023 to 70029673 appeared on Royals and Royal engine numbers ran from C38-1001 and up. Serial numbers 70584429 to 70633016 appeared on Windsors and 71000128 to 71002879 appeared on Windsor Town & Countrys. Windsor engine numbers ran from C38-1001 and up. Serial numbers 6766546 to 6768485 appeared on

Saratogas and Saratoga engine numbers ran from C33-1001 and up. Serial numbers 7037249 to 7062597 appeared on New Yorkers. New Yorker Town & Country serial numbers ran from 7402037 to 7405173. New Yorker engine numbers ran from C39-1001 and up.

ROYAL SERIES

Model No.	Body/ Style No.	Body Type & Seating	Factory Price	Shipping Weight	Prod. Total
(STANDARD WHEELBASE)					
C38S	N/A	2-dr Cpe-3P	1431	3378	Note 1
C38S	N/A	2-dr Clb Cpe-6P	1551	3448	Note 1
C38S	N/A	2-dr Sed-6P	1526	3458	Note 1
C38S	N/A	4-dr Sed-6P	1561	3573	Note 1
(LONG WHEELBASE)					
C38S	N/A	4-dr Sed-8P	1943	3917	Note 1
C38S	N/A	4-dr Limo-8P	2063	4022	Note 1

Note 1: 1946-1949 first-series production recorded as a single total, with no model year breakouts available. See the 1948 Chrysler section for these totals.

1947 Chrysler, Windsor Traveler four-door sedan, 6-cyl

WINDSOR SERIES — (6-CYL) — This upgraded version of the Royal included all Royal updates and features plus two-tone wool broadcloth upholstery; carpeted front compartment; electric clock; rear seat folding armrest on sedans and exterior 'goose neck' mirrors on convertibles only. The Windsor offered luxury on par with the New Yorker line. The Windsors were nearly indistinguishable from their 1946 counterparts, except as noted in the Royal series updates. Town & Country sedans were now produced with six-cylinder engines only. This policy lasted until the end of production of the first series 1949 models.

1947 Chrysler, Windsor two-door convertible, 6-cyl

WINDSOR SERIES

Model No.	Body/ Style No.	Body Type & Seating	Factory Price	Shipping Weight	Prod. Total
(STANDARD WHEELBASE)					
C38W	N/A	2-dr Cpe-3P	1481	3383	Note 1
C38W	N/A	2-dr Clb Cpe-6P	1601	3448	Note 1
C38W	N/A	2-dr Conv-8P	1861	3693	Note 1
C38W	N/A	2-dr Sed-6P	1591	3468	Note 1
C38W	N/A	4-dr Sed-6P	1611	3523	Note 1
C38W	N/A	4-dr Trav-6P	1846	3610	Note 1
C38W	N/A	4-dr T&C-6P	2366	3917	Note 1
(LONG WHEELBASE)					
C38W	N/A	4-dr Sed-8P	1993	3977	Note 1
C38W	N/A	4-dr Limo-8P	2113	4052	Note 1

Note 1: 1946-1949 first-series production recorded as a single total, with no model year breakouts available. See the 1948 Chrysler section for these totals.

SARATOGA SERIES — (8-CYL) — There were virtually no changes in the 1947 Saratoga, except as outlined in the Royal series for 1947. Prices were up slightly from 1946 models and published specification

charts indicate a slight weight increase (less than one percent). As noted earlier, whitewall tires were made available after April 1947 as an option. Standard equipment remained unchanged.

1947 Chrysler, Windsor eight-passenger limousine, 6-cyl (JL)

SARATOGA SERIES

Model No.	Body/ Style No.	Body Type & Seating	Factory Price	Shipping Weight	Prod. Total
C39K	N/A	2-dr Cpe-3P	1753	3817	Note 1
C39K	N/A	2-dr Clb Cpe-6P	1848	3892	Note 1
C39K	N/A	2-dr Sed-6P	1838	3907	Note 1
C39K	N/A	4-dr Sed-6P	1863	3972	Note 1

Note 1: 1946-1949 first-series production recorded as a single total, with no model year breakouts available. See the 1948 Chrysler section for these totals.

NEW YORKER SERIES — (8-CYL) — There were virtually no changes in the 1947 New Yorker series, except as outlined in the 1947 Royal series. Prices were up slightly from 1946 models and published specification charts indicate a slight weight increase over the previous model. As noted earlier, whitewall tires became an option after April 1947. Standard equipment remained unchanged. Town & Country models were now all built on the New Yorker chassis and all were convertibles.

NEW YORKER SERIES

Model No.	Body/ Style No.	Body Type & Seating	Factory Price	Shipping Weight	Prod. Total
C39N	N/A	2-dr Cpe-3P	1853	3837	Note 1
C39N	N/A	2-dr Clb Cpe-6P	1948	3897	Note 1
C39N	N/A	2-dr Conv-6P	2193	4132	Note 1
C39N	N/A	2-dr Sed-6P	1938	3932	Note 1
C39N	N/A	4-dr Sed-6P	1963	3987	Note 1
C39N	N/A	2-dr Conv T&C-6P	2998	4332	Note 1

Note 1: 1946-1949 first-series production recorded as a single total, with no model year breakouts available. See the 1948 Chrysler section for these totals.

ROYAL/WINDSOR ENGINE: L-head six-cylinder. Cast iron block. Displacement: 250.6 cid. Bore and stroke: 3.438 x 4.50 inches. Compression ratio: 6.6:1. Brake hp: 114 at 3600 rpm. Four main bearings. Solid lifters. Carburetors: (Fluid Drive and Vacumatic) B-B EV1, EV2 or E7L4; (Standard transmission) B-B EX1, EX2, EX3.

SARATOGA/NEW YORKER ENGINE: L-head eight-cylinder. Cast iron block. Displacement: 323.5 cid. Bore and stroke: 3.25 x 4.875 inches. Compression ratio: 6.7:1. Brake hp: 135 at 3400 rpm. Five main bearings. Solid lifters. Carburetor: B-B E7A1.

ROYAL/WINDSOR CHASSIS FEATURES: Wheelbase: (long wheelbase models) 139-1/2 inches; (all others) 121-1/2 inches. Fluid Drive and hydraulically operated M-5 transmission optional. Whitewalls available after April 1947. During model year, tire size changed from 6.50 x 15 to 7.60 x 15 on Royal and Windsor short wheelbase cars.

NEW YORKER/SARATOGA CHASSIS FEATURES: Wheelbase: 127-1/2 inches. Fluid drive and hydraulically operated M-5 transmission standard. Whitewall tires available after April 1947. Tire size changed during the model year to 8.20 x 15.

OPTIONS: Highlander upholstery. All-Weather Air control system. Twin heaters with heat, defroster and fan control. Comfort Master Heater. Right-hand unit for All-Weather Air control system (fresh-air intake optional). Deluxe Heater, mounted on dash with fan and defroster control. Radios: Model 602 with six tubes and automatic tuning; Model 802 with eight tubes and automatic tuning. Three types of antennas, including a concealed cowl mounted unit. Center bumper guard. Electric clock (Royal). Lifeguard tire tubes. Six-ply tires. Top luggage rack on eight-passenger models (Traveler rack standard). Mopar locking gas cap. Refrigeration unit. Weatherproof ignition. Mopar Auto Compass. Exhaust extension. Underhood light. Spotlamp. Windshield washer. Sun visor. Fog lamps.

1948 Chrysler, Windsor two-door convertible, 6-cyl

ROYAL SERIES — (6-CYL) — Minimal physical changes marked the Royal models built in the final production run, although rather steep price increases were recorded. Some additional colors became available during the model year. The larger, low pressure tires adopted in 1947 became standard fare in 1948. Stainless steel trim rings became more common once whitewall tires were made optional again. Cars built after Dec. 1, 1948, were officially considered as First Series 1949 models.

CHRYSLER I.D. NUMBERS: Serial numbers are found on the left front door hinge post. Engine numbers were located on the left side of the block below the cylinder head between first and second cylinders. Serial numbers 70029674 to 70037180 appeared on Royals. Effective Dec. 1, 1948, Royals with serial number 70037181 to 70038791; were considered 1949 models for purposes of registration only. Royal engine numbers ran from C38-1001 and up. Windsor serial numbers ranged from 70663017 to 70702442 and 70702443 to 70717748 for first-series 1949 models of Detroit manufacture. Los Angeles-built cars had numbers 67001001 to 67001920 and 67001921 to 67003000 for first-series 1949s. Windsor Town & Countrys were all built in Detroit and were numbered 71002880 to 71004055. Saratoga serial numbers ran from 6768486 to 6770180 for 1948 designated models and from 6770181 to 6770612 for first-series 1949s. Saratoga engine numbers ran from C39-1001 and up. New Yorker serial numbers ran from 7062598 to 7085469 for the 1948 series. First-series 1949 numbers ran from 7085470 to 7092068. Engine numbers began with the C39 prefix and were located as on the Saratoga series. New Yorker Town & Country serial numbers ranged from 7405174 to 7408109 for 1948 and their first-series 1949 numbers ran from 7408110 to 7408483. New Yorker engine numbers ran from C39-1001 and up.

1948 Chrysler, Windsor Traveler four-door sedan, 6-cyl

ROYAL SERIES

Model No.	Body/ Style No.	Body Type & Seating	Factory Price	Shipping Weight	Prod. Total
(STANDARD WHEELBASE)					
C38S	N/A	2-dr Cpe-3P	1839	3395	1,221
C38S	N/A	2-dr Cpe-6P	1954	3473	4,318
C38S	N/A	2-dr Sed-6P	1928	3498	1,117
C38S	N/A	4-dr Sed-6P	1975	3533	24,279
C38S	N/A	Chassis	—	—	1
(LONG WHEELBASE)					
C38S	N/A	4-dr Sed-8P	2400	392	626
C38S	N/A	4-dr Limo-8P	2526	4022	169

Note 1: Production totals above cover all 1946-1949 Chrysler C38 and C39 models.

WINDSOR SERIES — (6-CYL) — This upgraded version of the Royal had virtually no changes. There was little to distinguish 1946-1947 Chrysler Windsor models from their 1948 and first-series 1949 counterparts. Low pressure tires were now standard for short wheelbase cars.

1948 Chrysler, Town & Country two-door convertible, 8-cyl

WINDSOR SERIES

Model No.	Body/ Style No.	Body Type & Seating	Factory Price	Shipping Weight	Prod. Total
(STANDARD WHEELBASE)					
C38W	N/A	2-dr Cpe-3P	1906	3393	1,980
C38W	N/A	2-dr Clb Cpe-6P	2020	3463	26,482
C38W	N/A	2-dr Conv-6P	2434	3693	11,200
C38W	N/A	2-dr Sed-6P	2009	3508	4,034
C38W	N/A	4-dr Sed-6P	2041	3528	161,139
C38W	N/A	4-dr Trav-6P	2183	3610	4,182
C38W	N/A	4-dr T&C-6P	2880	3957	3,994
C38W	N/A	Chassis	—	—	1
(LONG WHEELBASE)					
C38W	N/A	4-dr Sed-8P	2454	3935	4,390
C38W	N/A	4-dr Sed Limo-8P	2581	4035	1,496

Note 1: Production totals above cover all 1946-1949 Chrysler C38 and C39 models.

Note 2: One chassis-only was built. It was apparently used to build a prototype two-door Town & Country Brougham.

SARATOGA SERIES — (8-CYL) — There were virtually no changes in the 1948 Saratoga as compared to the 1947 model. Prices were up substantially over earlier years.

SARATOGA SERIES

Model No.	Body/ Style No.	Body Type & Seating	Factory Price	Shipping Weight	Prod. Totals
C39K	N/A	2-dr Cpe-3P	2190	3817	74
C39K	N/A	2-dr Clb Cpe-6P	2290	3930	765
C39K	N/A	2-dr Sed-6P	2279	3900	155
C39K	N/A	4-dr Sed-6P	2316	3972	4,611

Note 1: Production totals above cover all 1946-1949 Chrysler C38 and C39 models.

NEW YORKER SERIES — (8-CYL) — There were virtually no differences between the 1948 New Yorker and its 1947 counterpart. The change to larger, low-pressure tires and a change in rear fender design were the only significant revisions.

NEW YORKER SERIES

Model No.	Body/ Style No.	Body Type & Seating	Factory Price	Shipping Weight	Prod. Total
C39N	N/A	2-dr Cpe-3P	2068	3837	699
C39N	N/A	2-dr Clb Cpe-6P	2410	4037	10,735
C39N	N/A	2-dr Conv-6P	2840	4132	3,000
C39N	N/A	2-dr Sed-6P	2153	3932	545
C39N	N/A	4-dr Sed-6P	2436	3987	52,036
C39N	N/A	Chassis	—	—	2
C39N	N/A	2-dr T&C HT			7
C39N	N/A	2-dr T&C Conv-6P	3420	4332	8,368

Note 1: Production totals above cover all 1946-1949 Chrysler C38 and C39 models.

ROYAL/WINDSOR ENGINE: L-head six-cylinder. Cast iron block. Displacement: 250.6 cid. Bore and stroke: 3.438 x 4.50 inches. Compression ratio: 6.6:1. Brake hp: 114 at 3600 rpm. Four main bearings. Solid lifters. Carburetors: (Fluid Drive and Vacumatic) B-B EV1, EV2 or E7L4; (Standard transmission) B-B EX1, EX2, EX3.

SARATOGA/NEW YORKER ENGINE: L-head eight-cylinder. Cast iron block. Displacement: 323.5 cid. Bore and stroke: 3.25 x 4.875 inches. Compression ratio: 6.7:1. Brake hp: 135 at 3400 rpm. Five main bearings. Solid lifters. Carburetor: B-B E7A1. Stromberg AAUS-2 also used.

ROYAL/WINDSOR CHASSIS FEATURES: Wheelbase: (long wheelbase models) 139-1/2 inches; (all others) 121-1/2 inches. Short wheelbase cars used 7.60 x 15 tires. Fluid Drive and M-5 hydraulically operated transmission optional.

SARATOGA/NEW YORKER CHASSIS FEATURES: Wheelbase: 127-1/2 inches. Fluid Drive and hydraulically operated M-5 transmission standard. Tire size: 8.20 x 15. Separate body and frame. Box-type frame with coil springs front and leaf springs at rear. Sway eliminator standard on all models.

OPTIONS: Highlander upholstery. All-Weather Air control system. Twin heaters with heat, defroster and fan control. Comfort Master Heater. Right-hand unit for All-Weather Air control system (fresh air intake optional). Deluxe heater, mounted on dash with fan and defroster controls. Radios: Model 620 with six tubes and automatic tuning; Model 802 with eight tubes and automatic tuning. Three types of antennas, including a concealed cowl mounted unit. Center bumper guard. Electric clock (Royal). Lifeguard tire tubes. Six-ply tires. Top luggage rack on eight-passenger models. Mopar locking gas cap. Spare tire valve extension. Refrigeration unit. Weatherproof ignition. Mopar Auto Compass. Exhaust extension. Underhood light. Spotlamp. Windshield washer. Sun visor. Fog lamps.

1949 CHRYSLER

1949 Chrysler, Royal station wagon, 6-cyl

ROYAL SERIES — (6-CYL) — The first postwar all-new styling change welcomed Chrysler's 25th Anniversary model to the motoring public. The well-known eggcrate grille was simplified. Chair-high seats were a strong selling point and bodies appeared taller and boxier than previous models. Front and rear overhangs were shortened. Coupled with the bustle back rear styling, this gave the car a stubby look similar to the same year DeSoto, which shared the same body. A station wagon, the first for Chrysler since 1942, appeared in this series. It was given a look reminiscent of the wood-bodied Town & Country. The spare tire was mounted on the tailgate this year only. Wheelbase was stretched four inches, with all the increase due to moving the rear axle housing further aft. Price increases continued into the 1949 model year as a result of labor settlements of 1948.

CHRYSLER I.D. NUMBERS: Serial numbers were located on the left front door hinge post. Cars built in Detroit used number 70041001 to 70572284. Cars built in Los Angeles used number 65002001 to 65003000. Engine numbers were in the same position as on earlier models and began with C45-1001 and ended with C45-93419. Windsor serial numbers were 70725001 to 70793638 on Detroit-built cars. Los Angeles numbers were 67005001 to 67010795. Windsor engine numbers were C45-1001 to C45-93419. Saratoga serial numbers ranged from 6772001 to 6774475. Saratoga engine numbers ranged from C46-1001 to C46-28838. No code numbers were provided for positive identification of body/style type. New Yorker serial numbers ranged from 7094001 to 7118581. Town & Country models used serial numbers beginning with 7410001 and ending with 7411001. New Yorker Town & Country engine numbers ran from C46-1001 to C46-28838.

ROYAL SERIES

Model No.	Body/Style No.	Body Type & Seating	Factory Price	Shipping Weight	Prod. Total
(STANDARD WHEELBASE)					
C45S	N/A	2-dr Clb Cpe-6P	2002	3531	4,849
C45S	N/A	4-dr Sed-6P	2021	3571	13,192
C45S	N/A	4-dr Sta Wag-9P	2968	4060	850

Model No.	Body/Style No.	Body Type & Seating	Factory Price	Shipping Weight	Prod. Total
(LONG WHEELBASE)					
C45S	N/A	4-dr Sed-8P	2843	4200	185

1949 Chrysler, Windsor Highlander two-door convertible, 6-cyl

WINDSOR SERIES — (6-CYL) — This upgraded version of the Royal included Fluid Drive and Presto-matic transmission as standard fare. All 1949 dashboards were padded for safety. Key starting was now available across the board on all Chryslers. Windsor nomenclature was found on the rear part of the front fender, above the trim strip. Highlander plaid upholstery was an option. The gas filler was now located on the left rear fender. Production began late, due to a strike affecting tooling in 1948. Front and rear exterior door locks were standard on all eight-passenger sedans. Three-passenger coupes were dropped at end of the 1948 run.

1949 Chrysler, Windsor four-door sedan, 6-cyl

WINDSOR SERIES

Model No.	Body/Style No.	Body Type & Seating	Factory Price	Shipping Weight	Prod. Total
(STANDARD WHEELBASE)					
C45W	N/A	2-dr Clb Cpe-6P	2186	3631	17,732
C45W	N/A	4-dr Sed-6P	2206	3681	55,879
C45W	N/A	2-dr Conv-6P	2598	3845	3,234
(LONG WHEELBASE)					
C45W	N/A	4-dr Sed-8P	3037	4290	373
C45W	N/A	4-dr Sed Limo-8P	3164	4430	73

SARATOGA — (8-CYL) — This low-line eight was available in only two body styles: Club Coupe and four-door sedan. Fluid Drive and Presto-matic transmission were standard. The Saratoga nameplate was located on the rear portion of the front fender, just above the horizontal trim molding. The chassis was lengthened four inches in the same manner as the six-cylinder cars of 1949. A padded dash was featured, with all gauges arranged in a round housing located directly in front of the driver. The dash chrome trim below the padding had a horizontal "combed" look. The radio was offset to the left of center for driver convenience. The heater controls were placed directly below the radio.

SARATOGA SERIES

Model No.	Body/Style No.	Body Type & Seating	Factory Price	Shipping Weight	Prod. Total
C46K	N/A	2-dr Clb Cpe-6P	2448	4115	465
C46K	N/A	4-dr Sed-6P	2473	4187	1,810

1949 Chrysler, New Yorker two-door Club Coupe, 8-cyl

NEW YORKER SERIES — (8-CYL) — This high-line version of the Saratoga had the same mechanical features, while interior appointments surpassed those offered in the low-line eights. The Town & Country was offered as a convertible only this year, although one prototype Town & Country hardtop was built and listed as available in some sales literature. The Town & Country was a part of the New Yorker series and was offered in eight-cylinder form only. Ash woodwork was used over an all-steel body. Dinoc inserts replaced the real mahogany panels used on early Town & Country models. Late production cars deleted the Dinoc and used body color painted panels. A weight increase on the T&C was more related to the across-the-board increases on all 1949s rather than to the heaviness of wood itself, as on the previous T&Cs. The advertising theme was, "Bigger on the inside, smaller on the outside." An interesting styling note was the wraparound rear bumper, which fit into a recess in the rear fender.

NEW YORKER SERIES

Model No.	Body/ Style No.	Body Type & Seating	Factory Price	Shipping Weight	Prod. Total
C46N	N/A	2-dr Clb Cpe-6P	2558	4115	4,524
C46N	N/A	4-dr Sed-6P	2583	4187	18,779
C46N	N/A	2-dr Conv-6P	3039	4277	1,137
C46N	N/A	2-dr T&C Conv	3765	4610	993
C46N	N/A	Chassis	—	—	1

ROYAL/WINDSOR ENGINE: L-head six-cylinder. Cast iron block. Displacement: 250.6 cid. Bore and stroke: 3.438 x 4.50 inches. Compression ratio: 7.0:1. Brake hp: 116 at 3600 rpm. Four main bearings. Solid lifters. Carburetors: (standard shift) Ball and Ball Model B-B EX1R or B-B EX2R; (Fluid Drive and M-6 transmission) Ball and Ball model B-B E7L1, L2.

SARATOGA/NEW YORKER ENGINE: L-head eight-cylinder. Cast iron block. Displacement: 323.5 cid. Bore and stroke: 3.25 x 4.875 inches. Compression ratio: 7.25:1. Brake hp: 135 at 3200 rpm. Torque: 270 lb.-ft. at 1600 rpm.

CHASSIS FEATURES: [Royal and Windsor] Wheelbase: (long wheelbase models) 139.5 inches; (all others) 125.5 inches. Tires: 7.60 x 15 and 8.20 x 15 for long wheelbase models and station wagon. Three-speed manual standard on Royals. Fluid Drive and M-6 optional on Royals and standard on Windsors. [Saratoga and New Yorker] Wheelbase: 131.5 inches. Tire size: 8.20 x 15 for all eight-cylinder models. Presto-matic semi-automatic transmission standard on all eight-cylinder models. Chrysler Safe-Guard hydraulic brakes.

OPTIONS: White sidewall tires. Wing vent wind deflectors. Middle rear bumper guard. Exhaust deflector. Fog lights. Grille guard (dealer installed). Highlander plaid upholstery. Radio. Heater. Locking gas cap. Weatherproof ignition. Mopar Auto Compass. Underhood light. Spotlamp. Windshield washer. Spare tire valve extension.

1950 CHRYSLER

ROYAL SERIES — (6-CYL) — This was the last year for the Royal nameplate. A minor face lift of the shortlived 1949 series centered around a bolder, heavier looking eggcrate grille treatment. Blade-like front and rear bumpers appeared. License plate location changed from the deck lid to the center of the rear bumper. The "Town & Country" station wagon was not a part of the Town & Country series, which was built on the New Yorker chassis. This wagon carried over 1949 styling, except for offering a different configuration for the rear spare tire embossed tailgate. No longer was the embossment visible from the exterior. Also continued was ash paneled trim, bolted onto the steel body. Later, a new all-steel station wagon body was introduced as a running addition to the line. A three-piece rear window was common on all sedans and Club Coupes. Royal nameplates were found on the front fender, behind the wheelhouse opening and below the horizontal trim molding.

1950 Chrysler, Royal station wagon, 6-cyl

CHRYSLER I.D. NUMBERS: Serial numbers were located, as in previous models, on the left door hinge post. Engine numbers were found on the left side of the block below the cylinder head between the first and second cylinders. [Royal] Detroit-built serial numbers ran 70058001 to 70079351. Los Angeles-built Royals used serial number 65004001 to 65063318. Engine numbers ran from C48-1001 to C48-133824. [Windsor] Detroit production numbers ran from 70794001 to 70889370. Los Angeles serial numbers ran from 67011001 to 67024682. Engine numbers for all six-cylinder cars started at C48-1001 and ended with C48-133824. [Saratoga] Saratogas were built only in Detroit. Serial numbers were 6774501 to 6775800. Engine numbers on the eights ranged upward from C49-1001 to C49-43041. [New Yorker] Serial numbers ranged from 7119001 to 7159341. Town & Country numbers ran from 7411501 to 7412201. Engine numbers were C49-1001 to C49-43041.

ROYAL SERIES

Model No.	Body/ Style No.	Body Type & Seating	Factory Price	Shipping Weight	Prod. Total
C48S	N/A	2-dr Clb Cpe-6P	2114	3540	5,900
C48S	N/A	4-dr Sed-6P	2154	3610	17,713
(LONG WHEELBASE)					
C48S	N/A	4-dr Sed-8P	2855	4190	375
C48S	N/A	4-dr T&C Sta Wag-6P	2735	3964	599
C48S	N/A	4-dr Sta Wag-6P	3163	4055	100

1950 Chrysler, Windsor two-door Club Coupe, 6-cyl

WINDSOR SERIES — (6-CYL) — Traditionally an upgraded Royal, the Windsor line now had a different selection of body styles to offer. No station wagon was available. A Traveler sedan melded sedan styling with the utility of a station wagon. The floor extended from rear deck lid to the back of the front seat when the rear seat was folded forward. The Traveler, while not popular, included a Town & Country-style roof rack. Big news this year was the Newport two-door hardtop, which featured a new roofline and wraparound three-piece rear window. Taillamps were small and rectangular and set mid-height in the back portion of the rear fenders. Separate back-up lights were inset from the taillamps, on the main body panel, beside the rear deck lid. Presto-matic transmission was standard. Windsor nameplates were located on the front fender.

WINDSOR SERIES

Model No.	Body/ Style No.	Body Type & Seating	Factory Price	Shipping Weight	Prod. Total
(STANDARD WHEELBASE)					
C48W	N/A	2-dr Clb Cpe-6P	2306	3670	20,050
C48W	N/A	4-dr Sed-6P	2329	3765	78,199
C48W	N/A	2-dr Conv-6P	2741	3905	2,201
C48W	N/A	2-dr Newport-6P	2637	3875	9,925
C48W	N/A	4-dr Trav-6P	2560	3830	900
(LONG WHEELBASE)					
C48W	N/A	4-dr Sed-8P	3050	4295	763
C48W	N/A	4-dr Limo-8P	3176	4400	174

SARATOGA SERIES — (8-CYL) — The Saratoga followed the path of the other 1950 models with a minor face lifting of 1949 lines. Styling touches used to distinguish the Saratoga from its six-cylinder brethren included the longer hood and front fenders, necessitated by the longer

eight-cylinder engine, and stainless steel facia, surrounding the parking lamps beside the grille. Only two body styles were offered in this low-line eight series.

SARATOGA SERIES

C49K	N/A	2-dr Clb Cpe-6P	2616	4110	300
C49K	N/A	4-dr Sed-6P	2642	4170	1,000

1950 Chrysler, Town & Country two-door hardtop, 8-cyl

NEW YORKER SERIES — (8-CYL) — This became the last year for the Chrysler inline eight that began production (in 1930) on the 1931 Series CD-8. The high-line New Yorker used all wool carpeting and offered a larger selection of interior fabrics and colors than the comparable Saratoga. The Newport two-door hardtop was another first for Chrysler, although seven hardtops had been manufactured as Town & Country semi-customs in 1946. Body shells of the Newport were shared with the convertible. The Town & Country was now produced as a Newport only and 1950 was to be the last year of wood-trimmed cars from Chrysler. Bodies were all-steel with wood trim added as in 1949. Tail-lamps were unlike other 1950 series Chryslers, but were more closely akin to the 1949 Town & Country. The rear bumper no longer wrapped around the rear fender as in 1949. The back-up light was now placed on Town & Country's rear deck and the license plate frame was now mounted to the rear bumper, as on other 1950 Chryslers. Rear fender trim was also mounted in a higher position than on other 1950 Chryslers. Panels between the ash-wood structure were painted body color.

NEW YORKER SERIES

Model No.	Body/ Style No.	Body Type & Seating	Prod. Price	Shipping Weight	Prod. Total
C49N	N/A	2-dr Clb Cpe-6P	2732	4110	3,000
C49N	N/A	4-dr Sed-6P	2756	4190	22,633
C49N	N/A	2-dr Conv-6P	3236	4360	899
C49N	N/A	2-dr Newport-6P	3133	4370	2,800
C49N	N/A	4-dr Wood Wagon	—	—	1
C49N	N/A	Chassis	—	—	2
C49N	N/A	2-dr T&C Newport	4003	4670	700

ROYAL/WINDSOR ENGINE: L-head six-cylinder. Cast iron block. Displacement: 250.6 cid. Bore and stroke: 3.438 x 4.50 inches. Compression ratio: 7.0:1. Brake hp: 116 at 3600 rpm. Five main bearings.

SARATOGA/NEW YORKER ENGINE: L-head eight-cylinder. Cast iron block. Displacement: 323.5 cid. Bore and stroke: 3.25 x 4.875 inches. Compression ratio: 7.25:1. Five main bearings. Brake hp: 135 at 3200 rpm.

CHASSIS FEATURES: Wheelbase: (New Yorker/Saratoga) 131.5 inches; (Royal/Windsor) 125.5 inches; (long wheelbase models) 139.5 inches. Overall length: (New Yorker/Saratoga) 214-1/8 inches; (station wagons) 214-1/8 inches; (long wheelbase models) 222-1/4 inches; (standard Royal/Windsor) 208-1/2 inches. Tires: (station wagons and long wheelbase models) 8.20 x 15; (all other models) 7.60 x 15.

CONVENIENCE OPTIONS: White sidewall tires. Wing vent wind deflectors. Exhaust deflector. Radio. Heater. Locking gas cap. Weatherproof ignition. Mopar Auto Compass. Windshield washer. Spare tire valve extension. A brand new option, for eights only, was electrically operated power window lifts.

HISTORICAL FOOTNOTES: Dealer introduction for 1950 Chrysler was Jan. 5, 1950. The Town & Country Newport hardtop was added to the line May 23, 1950.

1951 CHRYSLER

WINDSOR SERIES — (6-CYL) — The Royal line was dropped from the Chrysler fold and the Windsor became the low-priced series. A major

sheet metal revision of the 1950 Chrysler line was accomplished with relative ease. The grille lost the costly eggcrate styling look. Parking lamps were now located directly below the headlamps within the top grille molding. The top grille molding also wrapped completely around the front end and ran rearward to the middle of the front door. The three-piece rear window now wrapped around the rear roof area, emulating the style and theme of the 1950 Newport hardtop. Production of this series ran for two model years (18 months). Production figures are combined as a two-year total in the same fashion as the 1946-1948 Chrysler totals. Rear styling essentially duplicated the 1950 Chrysler, with the exception of a new bumper design. Windsor nameplates were located on the front fenders, above the trim moldings. Town & Country station wagons were a part of the Windsor series.

1951 Chrysler, Windsor Deluxe two-door Club Coupe, 6-cyl.

CHRYSLER I.D. NUMBERS: Serial numbers located on the left front door hinge post. Engine numbers were located on the left side of the block below the cylinder head, between the first and second cylinders. Only serial numbers were used for identification purposes. [Windsor] Detroit-built cars used numbers 70081001 to 70094148. Los Angeles-built cars used numbers 65007001 to 65008808. Engine numbers ranged from C51-1001 to C51-84487. [Windsor Deluxe] Detroit-built cars were numbered 70891001 to 70952163. Los Angeles-built cars were numbered 67026001 to 67033209. Engine numbers used the same prefix as on Windsors. [Saratoga] Detroit-built cars had numbers 76500001 to 76511983. Los Angeles-built cars had numbers 66500001 to 66501672. Engine numbers began with C51-8-1001 and up. [New Yorker] Serial numbers for the New Yorkers ranged from 7165001 to 7199806. Engine numbers used the C51-8 prefix. New Yorkers were manufactured in Detroit only.

1951 Chrysler, Windsor two-door convertible, 6-cyl

WINDSOR SERIES

Model No.	Body/ Style No.	Body Type & Seating	Factory Price	Shipping Weight	Prod. Total
(STANDARD WHEELBASE)					
C51	N/A	2-dr Clb Cpe-6P	2368	3570	Note 1
C51	N/A	4-dr Sed-6P	2390	3627	Note 1
C51	N/A	4-dr Sta Wag-6P	3063	3965	Note 1
C51	N/A	4-dr Ambulance	—	—	(153)
(LONG WHEELBASE)					
C51	N/A	4-dr Sed-8P	3197	4145	Note 1

Note 1: Production totals for 1951-1952 combined; see 1952 chart.

WINDSOR DELUXE SERIES — (6-CYL) — This top-of-the-line six was identified externally by the use of a Windsor Deluxe nameplate on the front fender, above the wheelhouse opening. Presto-matic transmission was standard on this model. This was the final year for the 250.6-cid six-cylinder engine. The Traveler model was continued in this series, with the same features as the 1950 Traveler. However, the luggage rack now became an optional feature.

1951 Chrysler, Saratoga four-door sedan, V-8

WINDSOR DELUXE SERIES

Model No.	Body/ Style No.	Body Type & Seating	Factory Price	Shipping Weight	Prod. Total
(STANDARD WHEELBASE)					
C51-2	N/A	2-dr Clb Cpe-6P	2585	3700	(8,365)
C51-2	N/A	4-dr Sed-6P	2608	3775	Note 1
C51-2	N/A	4-dr Trav-6P	2867	3890	(850)
C51-2	N/A	2-dr Conv-6P	3071	3845	Note 1
C51-2	N/A	2-dr Newport-6P	2953	3855	Note 1
(LONG WHEELBASE)					
C51-2	N/A	4-dr Sed-8P	3416	4295	(720)
C51-2	N/A	4-dr Limo-8P	3537	4415	(152)

Note 1: Production totals for 1951-1952 combined; see 1952 chart.

1951 Chrysler, New Yorker Newport two-door hardtop, V-8

SARATOGA SERIES — (8-CYL) — The big news for 1951 was the introduction of the new Hemi engine. Combining a Windsor series chassis with the new V-8 engine resulted in an upgraded Saratoga. Its wheelbase was a full six inches shorter than the Hemi-engined New Yorker, while weight was about 250 pounds less than for the longer series. The Saratoga was a late addition to the line and was introduced to the public more than three months after other 1951 Chryslers. Saratoga nameplates were located on the front fenders and a new 'V' ornament graced the hood and deck lid. Presto-matic semi-automatic transmission was standard equipment. A Town & Country station wagon was a part of this series and was the first of this nameplate with a V-8 engine.

SARATOGA SERIES

Model No.	Body/ Style No.	Body Type & Seating	Factory Price	Shipping Weight	Prod. Total
(STANDARD WHEELBASE)					
C55	N/A	2-dr Clb Cpe-6P	2989	3948	Note 1
C55	N/A	4-dr Sed-8P	3016	4018	Note 1
C55	N/A	4-dr T&C Wag-6P	3681	4310	Note 1
(LONG WHEELBASE)					
C55	N/A	4-dr Sed-8P	3912	4465	Note 1
C55	N/A	4-dr Limo-8P	4240	—	Note 2

Note 1: Production totals for 1951-1952 combined; see 1952 chart.

Note 2: Special order.

NEW YORKER SERIES — (8-CYL) — This top-of-the-line Chrysler was the first New Yorker to use a V-8 engine. Wheelbase was longer than the Windsor or Saratoga models by six inches. Cars with V-8 power in the Chrysler lines were identified by large 'V' ornaments on the hood and deck lid. New Yorker nameplates were placed on the front fenders. The V-8 was called the 'Firepower' engine. Power steering was an industry first and Oriflow shock absorbers were now available. Styling changes were basically limited to the area in front of the cowl. Grille changes consisted of a heavily chromed look with a chromed centerpiece. There was a new location for the parking lights, below the headlamps and a chrome panel separated the two grille bars on each fender. Side trim on the rear fender began above the stone shield, then dipped abruptly before

continuing, horizontally to the rear. Town & Country rear fenders matched those of the Windsor and Saratoga in design. The dash panel continued its padded design and remained similar to the 1949 type.

1951 Chrysler, New Yorker four-door sedan, V-8

NEW YORKER SERIES

Model No.	Body/ Style No.	Body Type & Seating	Factory Price	Shipping Weight	Prod. Total
C52	N/A	2-dr Clb Cpe-6P	3348	4145	(3,533)
C52	N/A	4-dr Sed-6P	3378	4260	Note 1
Cs2	N/A	2-dr Conv-6P	3916	4460	Note 1
C52	N/A	2-dr Newport-6P	3798	4330	Note 1
C52	N/A	4-dr T&C Wag-6P	4026	4455	(251)

Note 1: Production totals for 1951 and 1952 models were recorded as a single total, with no model year breakout available except as shown for some 1951 models.

SIX-CYLINDER ENGINES: L-head. Cast iron block. Displacement: 250.6 cid. Bore and stroke: 3.438 x 4.50 inches. Compression ratio: 7.0:1. Brake hp: 116 at 3600 rpm. Five main bearings. Solid lifters. Carburetor: B-B E9A1 with Fluid Drive and M-6 transmission.

HEMI V-8 ENGINE: Overhead valve. Displacement: 331.1 cid. Bore and stroke: 3.81 x 3.63 inches. Brake hp: 180 at 4000 rpm. Five main bearings. Hydraulic valve lifters. Compression ratio: 7.5:1. Carburetors: Early cars used Carter WCD 830S, 830SA, 830SB or 931 SC. Later cars used Carter WCD 931 S, 931 SA, 931 SB or 931 SC.

CHASSIS FEATURES: Wheelbase: (New Yorker) 131.5 inches; (Windsor/Windsor Deluxe/Saratoga) 125.5 inches. Long wheelbase models measured 139.5 inches. Tire size: 7.60 x 15 for Windsor and Windsor Deluxe short wheelbase and 8.20 x 15 for long wheelbase. Saratoga used 8.00 x 15 and 8.20 x 15 for long wheelbase. New Yorkers used 8.20 x 15. Windsor and Windsor Deluxe were 202.5 inches overall. Saratogas were 207.8 inches in overall length.

CONVENIENCE OPTIONS: White sidewall tires. Electric window lifts. Sun visor. Radio. Heater. Power steering. Fluid-Torque Drive. Exhaust deflector. Locking gas cap. Windshield washer. Fog lamps. Outside rear-view mirror. Vanity mirror.

HISTORICAL FOOTNOTES: Dealer introduction of 1951 Chryslers was scheduled for Feb. 9, 1951. On a calendar year basis, total 1951 production was 165,000 units of which 78,000 were six-cylinder powered and 87,000 had the new Firepower V-8 installed. Also on a calendar year basis for 1951, Chrysler manufactured approximately 4,000 convertibles, 14,460 two-door hardtops and 1,950 station wagons. (Note: It should be pointed out that calendar and model years were nearly concurrent at this time, as opposed to the system in use today).

1952 CHRYSLER

WINDSOR SERIES — (6-CYL) — A continuation of the 1951 Windsor series carried forward with only a minor change in taillamp design. Back-up lamps were now integrated into the taillamp itself. The engine was modified with a longer stroke giving more torque and horsepower.

CHRYSLER I.D. NUMBERS: Serial numbers were located on the left front door hinge post. Engine numbers were located on the left side of the block below the cylinder head, between the first and second cylinders. Only serial numbers were used for identification purposes. [Windsor] Detroit-built cars had numbers from 70094301 to 70103232. Los An-

geles-built cars had numbers 65008901 to 65009895. Engine numbers continued with the C52 prefix. [Windsor Deluxe] Detroit-built cars used numbers 70952301 to 70936308 and Los Angeles-built cars used numbers 67033301 to 67036059. [Saratoga] Detroit-built cars used numbers 76512101 to 76593089 and Los Angeles-built cars used 66501801 to 66505363. Engine number prefix was C52-8. [New Yorker] 1952 production runs began with car number 7199901 and ended with car number 7217301. Engine number prefix was C52-8.

1952 Chrysler, Windsor four-door sedan, 6-cyl

WINDSOR SERIES

Model No.	Body/ Style No.	Body Type & Seating	Factory Price	Shipping Weight	Prod. Total
(STANDARD WHEELBASE)					
C51-1	N/A	2-dr Clb Cpe-6P	2475	3550	6,735
C51-1	N/A	4-dr Sed-6P	2498	3640	16,112
C51-1	N/A	4-dr T&C Wag-6P	3200	4015	1,967
(LONG WHEELBASE)					
C51-1	N/A	4-dr Sed-8P	3342	4145	633

Note 1: Production totals are combined 1951-1952 output, with no breakouts, except as shown in 1951 Windsor section.

WINDSOR DELUXE SERIES — (6-CYL) — The use of the larger six-cylinder engine and taillamp change paralleled the low-line 1952 Windsor series. For the 1952 model year, the Club Coupe was dropped as well as the Traveler and eight-passenger models in this series. Interior appointments were slightly upgraded over the Windsor series.

WINDSOR DELUXE SERIES

Model No.	Body/ Style No.	Body Type & Seating	Factory Price	Shipping Weight	Prod. Total
C51-2	N/A	4-dr Sed-6P	2727	3775	75,513
C51-2	N/A	2-dr Cpe-6P	3210	3990	4,200
C51-2	N/A	2-dr Newport-6P	3087	3855	10,200
C51-2	N/A	2-dr Conv-6P	3230	3945	4,200

Note 1: Production totals are combined 1951-1952 output, with no breakouts, except as shown in 1951 Windsor Deluxe section.

SARATOGA SERIES — (8-CYL) — This series continued with virtually no changes from the 1951 model. The taillamp design with integral back-up lamp was the major styling change.

SARATOGA SERIES

(STANDARD WHEELBASE)					
C55	N/A	2-dr Clb Cpe-6P	3187	3948	8,501
C55	N/A	4-dr Sed-6P	3215	4010	35,516
C55	N/A	4-dr T&C Wag-6P	3925	4345	1,299
C55	N/A	4-dr Ambulance	—	—	1
(LONG WHEELBASE)					
C55	N/A	4-dr Sed-6P	4172	4570	183

Note 1: Production totals are combined 1951-1952 output, with no breakouts, except as shown in 1951 Saratoga section.

Note 2: One hardtop with New Yorker body is included in the total for Club Coupe.

NEW YORKER SERIES — (8-CYL) — New Yorker design was a continuation of the 1951 model with the only styling change paralleling other 1951-1952 changes in the taillamps. The Club Coupe and Town & Country bodies were dropped with the onset of 1952 production.

NEW YORKER SERIES

C52	N/A	4-dr Sed-6P	3530	4260	40,415
C52	N/A	2-dr Conv-6P	4033	4460	2,200
C52	N/A	2-dr Newport-6P	3969	4325	5,800
C52	N/A	Chassis	—	—	1

Note 1: Production totals are combined 1951-1952 output, with no breakouts, except as shown in 1951 New Yorker section.

SIX-CYLINDER ENGINE: L-head. Cast iron block. Displacement: 264.5 cid. Bore and stroke: 3.438 x 4.75 inches. Compression ratio: 7.0:1. Brake hp: 119 at 3600 rpm. Five main bearings. Carburetors: (with Fluid Drive and M-6 transmission) B-B E9A1 Carter or Stromberg 380349.

HEMI V-8 ENGINE: Overhead valve with hemispherical combustion chamber. Displacement: 331.1 cid. Bore and stroke: 3.81 x 3.63 inches. Brake hp: 180 at 4000 rpm. Five main bearings. Hydraulic valve lifters. Compression ratio: 7.5:1. Carburetors: Carter WCD 931 S, 931 SA, 931 SB or 931 SC.

CHASSIS FEATURES: Wheelbase: (New Yorker) 131.5 inches; (Windsor/Windsor Deluxe/Saratoga standard wheelbase) 125.5 inches, (long wheelbase models) 139.5 inches. Tire size: (Windsor/Windsor Deluxe) 7.60 x 15 and 8.20 x 15 for long wheelbase; (Saratoga) 8.00 x 15 standard wheelbase and 8.20 x 15 for long wheelbase; (New Yorker) 8.20 x 15.

CONVENIENCE OPTIONS: White sidewall tires. Electric window lifts. Sun visor. Radio. Heater. Power steering. Fluid-Torque Drive. Exhaust deflector. Spare tire valve extension. Locking gas cap. Windshield washer. Fog lamps. Outside rearview mirror. Vanity mirror. Solex glass (1952 only). Power brakes.

HISTORICAL FOOTNOTES: The 1952 Chrysler line was introduced in dealer showrooms on Dec. 14, 1951. Chrysler received OPS (Office of Price Stability) permission to raise prices on Feb. 11, 1952, as was necessary in the Korean War era. Calendar year production was registered at 120,678 units. Model year production or sales totals for 1952 Chryslers were not reported as single year figures, but only as a combined total with cars sold as 1951 models. On a calendar year basis, Chrysler was estimated to have turned out 8,337 two-door hardtops; 2,793 convertibles; and 1,942 station wagons built to 1952 model specifications. (Note: Model years and calendar years were nearly concurrent at this time). On a calendar year basis, Chrysler manufactured approximately 46,491 six-cylinder 1952 models and 70,206 cars carrying the new Firepower V-8 engine. (All figures above include Imperials, which are covered in the Imperial section of this catalog). Power steering was available on sixes this year.

1953 CHRYSLER

1953 Chrysler, Windsor Deluxe two-door convertible, 6-cyl

WINDSOR SERIES — (6-CYL) — A major change in most sheet metal panels carried forward the styling of 1951-1952. The major changes were in the new sloping roofline, one-piece curved windshield (the first since the Series CW Airflow of 1934-1937), taillamps and the grille. The Club Coupe now became more sedan-like in style and all station wagons and eight-passenger cars continued to use the 1951-1952 rear fenders including trim and taillamps. The gas filler was now located below the deck lid on the left side, except on those models using the earlier style fender. PowerFlite, a fully automatic two-speed transmission, debuted near the end of the model year. Chromed wire wheels made their debut after a hiatus of 20 years. The Windsor remained the low-price Chrysler offering.

CHRYSLER I.D. NUMBERS: The serial number was found on the left door hinge post and the six-cylinder engine number was on the left side of the block below the head between the first and second cylinders. Engine numbers on the V-8 were positioned on top of the engine block between the heads and under the water outlet elbow. [Windsor] Detroit-built cars had numbers 70110001 to 70140156. Los Angeles cars

had numbers 65011001 to 6013020. Engine numbers ranged from C53-1001 to C53-82918. [Windsor Deluxe] Detroit-built cars used serial numbers 71005001 to 71050372 and Los Angeles-built cars used numbers 67040001 to 67043434. Engine numbers used the C53 prefix. [New Yorker] Serial numbers for Detroit-built cars were from 76540001 to 76585872. Serial numbers for Los Angeles-built cars were 66506001 to 66509462. Engine numbers were from C53-8-1001 to C53-8-86292. [New Yorker Deluxe] Detroit numbers were 7222001 to 7245465. Los Angeles numbers were 69001001 to 69003868. Engine numbers used the C53-8 prefix as on the New Yorker.

WINDSOR SERIES

Model No.	Body/ Style No.	Body Type & Seating	Factory Price	Shipping Weight	Prod. Total
(STANDARD WHEELBASE)					
C60-1	N/A	2-dr Clb Cpe-6P	2555	3595	11,646
C60-1	N/A	4-dr Sed-6P	2577	3655	18,879
C60-1	N/A	4-dr T&C Wag-6P	3279	3955	1,242
(LONG WHEELBASE)					
C60-1	N/A	4-dr Sed-8P	3279	3955	425

WINDSOR DELUXE SERIES — (6-CYL) — An upgraded version of the Windsor featured only three body styles. Styling was identical to the Windsor series. Parking lamps were located on a separate pod below the headlamps and between the upper and lower wraparound grille bars. Chrysler added a third grille bar to the New Yorker, which encompassed the parking lamps. Windsor rear fender stone shields were noted for their stylized horizontal bumps. Rear taillamps used an integrated back-up lens with the upper red lens divided vertically.

WINDSOR DELUXE SERIES

Model No.	Body/ Style No.	Body Type & Seating	Factory Price	Shipping Weight	Prod. Total
C60-2	N/A	4-dr Sed-6P	2806	3770	45,385
C60-2	N/A	2-dr Conv-6P	3290	4000	1,250
C60-2	N/A	2-dr Newport-6P	3166	3770	5,642

1953 Chrysler, New Yorker Deluxe Newport two-door hardtop, V-8

NEW YORKER SERIES — (8-CYL) — The third year for the Hemi engine continued with the same configuration of 331.1 cid and 180 bhp. Even the Buick surpassed the mighty Chrysler in the horsepower department. Major styling changes paralleled the Windsor changes, although there were additional model definition, grille, and rear fender splash shield differences. The Saratoga series was dropped and replaced by the New Yorker on the Windsor wheelbase of 125.5 inches. This was the first attempt by Chrysler to downsize during the postwar period. A reduction in weight of five percent was noted in the V-8 Chryslers for 1953. A common option was two-tone paint. The 'V' insignia was affixed to the hood and rear deck lid and denoted the Hemi engine. The eight-passenger and Town & Country models used the 1951-1952 style rear fenders and trim.

NEW YORKER SERIES

Model No.	Body/ Style No.	Body Type & Seating	Factory Price	Shipping Weight	Prod. Total
(STANDARD BASE)					
C56-1	N/A	2-dr Clb Cpe-6P	3336	3920	7,749
C56-1	N/A	4-dr Sed-6P	3365	4000	37,540
C56-1	N/A	2-dr Newport-6P	3782	4015	2,252
C56-1	N/A	4-dr T&C Wag-6P	4077	4260	1,399
(LONG WHEELBASE)					
C56-1	N/A	4-dr Sed-8P	4363	4510	100

NEW YORKER DELUXE SERIES — (8-CYL) — The top-of-the-line Chrysler used the same wheelbase as all other Chrysler series in 1953. The Deluxe offered an additional body style, the convertible coupe and deleted the eight-passenger sedan and Town & Country station wagon. The upholstery was upgraded notably. Air conditioning and wire wheels were the big option news in 1953. PowerFlite automatic transmission became standard equipment late in the model year replacing Fluid Drive or Fluid-Torque Drive transmissions. Nameplates were located on the front fender above the wheelhouse opening.

NEW YORKER DELUXE SERIES

Model No.	Body/ Style No.	Body Type & Seating	Factory Price	Shipping Weight	Prod. Total
C56-2	N/A	2-dr Clb Cpe-6P	3470	3920	1,934
C56-2	N/A	4-dr Sed-6P	3526	4020	20,585
C56-2	N/A	2-dr Conv-6P	4025	4290	950
C56-2	N/A	2-dr Newport-6P	3493	4020	3,715
C56-2	N/A	Chassis	—	—	1

WINDSOR SERIES ENGINES: L-head six-cylinder. Cast iron block. Displacement: 264.5 cid. Bore and stroke: 3.438 x 4.75 inches. Compression ratio: 7.0:1. Brake hp: 119 at 3600 rpm. Five main bearings. Carburetors: (Fluid Drive and M-6 transmission) Carter Ball and Ball E9A1; (standard transmission) B-B E9C, E9C1.

NEW YORKER ENGINE: V-8. Overhead valve with hemispherical combustion chamber. Displacement: 331.1 cid. Bore and stroke: 3.81 x 3.63 inches. Brake hp: 180 at 4000 rpm. Five main bearings. Hydraulic valve lifters. Compression ratio: 7.5:1. Carburetors: Carter WCD 935 S, 935 SA.

CHASSIS FEATURES: All standard wheelbase cars used a 125.5-inch wheelbase. Long wheelbase cars used the 139.5-inch wheelbase. Six-cylinder cars used 7.60 x 15 tires. New Yorker V-8s used 8.00 x 15 tires. The long wheelbase cars used 8.20 x 15 tires. Overall length for standard wheelbase cars was 211 inches.

CONVENIENCE OPTIONS: Air conditioning. Power steering. Power brakes. Power windows. Radio. Heater. Outside rearview mirrors. Two-tone paint. Wire wheels. Continental wheel kit. Locking gas cap. Fog lamps. Fluid-Torque Drive. PowerFlite (late in model year). Windshield washer. Solex glass. Exhaust deflector. Spare tire valve extension. Sun visor.

HISTORICAL FOOTNOTES: The 1953 Chrysler line was introduced in dealer showrooms on Oct. 30, 1952. A new Chrysler Custom Imperial Newport was added to the line March 18, 1953. Prices on most Chrysler models were lowered on March 25, 1953, by $27-$274. Model year production was counted at 182,187 cars. Calendar year production totals included 78,814 sixes and 83,373 V-8s. PowerFlite transmission was introduced in June and over 35,000 had been installed in Chryslers by the end of the model year.

1954 CHRYSLER

WINDSOR DELUXE SERIES — (6-CYL) — A minor face lift of the relatively popular Windsor series of 1953 personified the single series six-cylinder offering of 1954. Gone now was the low-line Windsor series, which was combined in 1954, with a Windsor Deluxe series. Only one Windsor was available in 1954 (the Windsor Deluxe). The face-lifting consisted of changes to the grille, trim and taillamps. The dash while showing a resemblance to the earlier 1949-1953 Chryslers, was restyled. The front grille trim no longer wrapped around the fenders ala previous Imperial style. The Windsor Deluxe grille center bar was abbreviated at both ends, which helped to differentiate it from the upscale New Yorker's. The flat six-cylinder was now in its last year in a Chrysler. The Club Coupe was also in its last year as a Chrysler body style.

1954 Chrysler, Windsor Deluxe two-door convertible, 6-cyl

CHRYSLER I.D. NUMBERS: Serial numbers were found on the left front hinge post. Engine numbers were located on the block behind the water

pump. Only serial numbers were meant to be used for identification purposes. Cars built in Detroit were numbered 70141001 to 70181908. Los Angeles-built cars were numbered from 65014001 to 65015185. Engine numbers used a C54 prefix. [New Yorker] Cars built in Detroit used numbers 76591001 to 76610490. Los Angeles-built cars used numbers 66510001 to 66510937. Engine numbers began with C541-8-1001 and up. [New Yorker Deluxe] Cars built in Detroit were numbered 7249001 to 7279807. Los Angeles-built cars used numbers 69005001 to 69007248. Engine numbers began with C542-8-1001 and up.

WINDSOR DELUXE SERIES

Model No.	Body/ Style No.	Body Type & Seating	Factory Price	Shipping Weight	Prod. Total
(STANDARD WHEELBASE)					
C62	Note 1	2-dr Club Cpe-6P	2541	3565	5,659
C62	Note 1	4-dr Sed-6P	2562	3655	33,563
C62	Note 1	2-dr Conv-6P	3046	3915	500
C62	Note 1	2-dr Newport-6P	2831	3685	3,655
C62	Note 1	4-dr T&C Wag-6P	3321	3955	650
(LONG WHEELBASE)					
C62	Note 1	4-dr Sed-8P	3492	4186	500

Note 1: Code numbers identifying body style were not used.

1954 Chrysler, New Yorker two-door Club Coupe, V-8

NEW YORKER SERIES — (8-CYL) — A slight face lift of the 1953 model paralleled the changes in the Windsor Deluxe series as far as body and trim. Only New Yorker nameplates were seen on the rear fenders and the 'V' insignia on the hood and deck lid were means of outwardly identifying this Hemi-engined model. It was the last year for the long wheelbase 139.5-inch chassis. One-piece rear windows were now used on all body styles.

NEW YORKER SERIES

(STANDARD WHEELBASE)					
C63-1	Note 1	2-dr Clb Cpe-6P	3202	3910	2,079
C63-1	Note 1	4-dr Sed-6P	3229	3970	15,788
C63-1	Note 1	2-dr Newport-6P	3503	4005	1,312
C63-1	Note 1	4-dr T&C Wag-6P	4023	4245	1,100
(LONG WHEELBASE)					
C63-1	Note 1	4-dr Sed-8P	4368	4450	140

Note 1: Code numbers identifying body style were not used.

NEW YORKER DELUXE — (8-CYL) — This top-of-the-line Chrysler used more trim than other series in 1954. The grille center bar was bow shaped and dipped at both ends to parallel the upper grille design. The front fender stone shield was unique to the New Yorker Deluxe. The rear fender stone shield had a horizontal trim piece in the middle, matching the trim on the front fender shield. Hubcap design was unique to the New Yorker Deluxe and consisted of a flat spinner-like design in gold color that matched the exterior insignia. The big news this year was the beginning of the horsepower race, as Chrysler raised the ante with new heads, four-barrel carburetors and dual exhaust. The division capped the top spot in the performance race with a rating of 235 hp. The 1954 Chrysler was advertised as "Anything less ... Yesterday's Car!" Styling, however, was essentially six years old and sales plummeted more than 40 percent on all Chryslers, although the New Yorker Deluxe outsold its 1953 counterpart by nearly 25 percent. Performance, it seems, did sell cars in 1954.

NEW YORKER DELUXE SERIES

Model No.	Body/ Style No.	Body Type & Seating	Factory Price	Shipping Weight	Prod. Total
C63-2	Note 1	2-dr Clb Cpe-6P	3406	4005	1,816
C63-2	Note 1	4-dr Sed-6P	3433	4065	26,907
C63-2	Note 1	2-dr Conv-6P	3938	4265	724
C63-2	Note 1	2-dr Newport-6P	3707	4095	4,814
C63-2	Note 1	Chassis	—	—	17

Note 1: Code numbers identifying body style were not be not used.

1954 Chrysler, New Yorker Deluxe four-door sedan, V-8

WINDSOR DELUXE ENGINE: L-head six cylinder. Cast iron block. Displacement: 264.5 cid. Bore and stroke: 3.438 x 4.75 inches. Compression ratio: 7.0:1. Brake hp: 119 at 3600 rpm. Five main bearings. Carburetors: (PowerFlite transmission) Carter, Ball and Ball, Model B-B E9B1; (standard transmission) B-B E9C, E9C1.

NEW YORKER ENGINE: V-8. Overhead valve with hemispherical-segment combustion chambers. Displacement: 331.1 cid. Compression ratio: 7.5:1. Bore and stroke: 3.81 x 3.63 inches. Brake hp: 195 at 4400 rpm. Five main bearings. Hydraulic valve lifters. Carburetor: Carter WCD 2039S, 2039SA.

NEW YORKER DELUXE ENGINE: V-8. Overhead valve with hemispherical combustion chamber. Displacement: 331.1 cid. Compression ratio: 7.5:1. Bore and stroke: 3.81 x 3.63 inches. Brake hp: 235 at 4400 rpm. Five main bearings. Hydraulic valve lifters. Dual exhaust system. Carburetor: WCFB Carter 2041S.

CHASSIS FEATURES: A 125.5-inch wheelbase was used with all models, except for eight-passenger sedans. Tire size: 7.60 x 15 Windsor Deluxe; 8.00 x 15 New Yorker and New Yorker Deluxe; 8.20 x 15 long wheelbase cars. Coil springs, front; leaf springs, rear. Length: 215.5 inches for New Yorker and New Yorker Deluxe.

OPTIONS: PowerFlite on Windsor ($175). Power steering ($130). White sidewall tires. Power brakes. Radio ($101). Heater ($79). Air Temp air conditioning ($595). Solex tinted glass ($20). Fog lights. Wire wheels ($260). Continental kit. Rear seat radio speaker. Windshield washers. Spot lamps. Outside rearview mirror. Two-tone paint. Highlander trim ($63). New Yorker leather trim ($121). Power windows ($125).

HISTORICAL FOOTNOTES: Chrysler opened its Chelsea Proving Grounds in 1954 and Chrysler test drivers teamed with Tony Bettenhausen to complete a 24-hour endurance run of 2,836 miles averaging 118.18 mph.

1955 CHRYSLER

WINDSOR DELUXE SERIES — (8-CYL) — The "100 Million Dollar Look" designed by Virgil Exner brought Chrysler fans an all-new car from stem to stern. The six-cylinder engine was no longer available in any Chrysler series. The new powerplant was a 301-cid V-8. A pair of two-door hardtops were offered in the Windsor series. The low-line version was named the Nassau and the high-line was named the Newport. Later in the model year another Newport was offered, with slightly modified trim borrowed from the New Yorker St. Regis. Depending upon the color ordered the late versions were named 'Green Falcon' or 'Blue Heron.' In addition, the sedan used the same trim package as the later Newports. Windsor Deluxe grilles were identical with the upgraded New Yorker, except the Windsor used round parking lamps while the New Yorker parking lamps were a part of the upper bumper guard. Lower grille areas behind the bumper were also different on the Windsor Deluxe. Windshields were now of the wraparound style, as were the rear windows on the hardtop and sedan. Taillamps were integrated into a housing that began at the top of the rear fender and dropped toward the bumper. Back-up lamps were affixed to the panel beneath the deck lid. A new, highly touted feature was the dash-mounted shift lever for the PowerFlite automatic transmission.

CHRYSLER I.D. NUMBERS: Serial numbers were found on the left front hinge post. Engine numbers were located on the block behind the water pump. [Windsor Deluxe] Detroit-built cars were numbered W55-1001 to W55-99194. Los Angeles-built cars were numbered WSSL-1001 to WSSL-4777. Engine numbers were WE55-1001 and up. [New Yorker Deluxe] Detroit numbers were N55-1001 to N55-49395 and Los An-

geles-built cars had numbers NSSL-1001 to NSSL-3560. Engine numbers began with NE55-1001 and up. [Chrysler 300] Detroit-built cars numbered 3N55-1001 to 3N55-2724. Engine numbers ranged from 3NE55-1001 and up.

1955 Chrysler, Windsor Deluxe four-door sedan, V-8

WINDSOR DELUXE SERIES

Model No.	Body/ Style No.	Body Type & Seating	Factory Price	Shipping Weight	Prod. Total
C67	Note 1	4-dr Sed-6P	2660	3915	63,896
C67	Note 1	2-dr Nassau-6P	2703	3920	18,474
C67	Note 1	2-dr Newport-6P	2818	3915	13,126
C67	Note 1	2-dr Conv-6P	3090	4075	1,395
C67	Note 1	4-dr T&C Wag-6P	3331	4295	1,983

Note 1: Code numbers to provide positive identification of body type were not provided.
Note 2: Production totals for special hardtops and sedans are included in totals for standard offerings.

1955 Chrysler, Windsor Deluxe station wagon, V-8

NEW YORKER DELUXE SERIES — (8-CYL) — This top-drawer Chrysler continued the use of the 331.1-cid Hemi engine, although horsepower increased. The two-door hardtop came as a standard Newport and an upgraded St. Regis, the latter noted for its unique two-tone styling. Later, a summer sales special used the St. Regis curved upper bodyside trim on the standard New Yorker Deluxe Newport, providing a rather unusual two-toning effect. The 'Forward Look' made a successful debut with new styling and engineering changes. Minor lower grille and bumper alterations were seen in the front and a different rear bumper treatment set the New Yorker apart from its Windsor brethren. Insignia was placed at the rear of the bodyside color sweep on standard cars and to the rear, below the horizontal molding, on the St. Regis.

1955 Chrysler, New Yorker Deluxe St. Regis two-door hardtop, V-8

NEW YORKER DELUXE SERIES

Model No.	Body/ Style No.	Body Type & Seating	Factory Price	Shipping Weight	Prod. Total
C68	Note 1	4-dr Sed-6P	3494	4160	33,342
C68	Note 1	2-dr Newport-6P	3652	4140	5,777
C68	Note 1	2-dr St Reg-6P	3690	4125	11,076
C68	Note 1	2-dr Conv-6P	3924	4255	946
C68	Note 1	4-dr T&C Wag-6P	4208	4430	1,036
C68	Note 1	Chassis	—	—	1

Note 1: Code numbers to provide positive identification of body type were not provided.
Note 2: Production totals for midyear additions to the line are included in the totals for standard offerings.

1955 Chrysler, New Yorker Deluxe four-door sedan, V-8

CHRYSLER 300 SERIES — (8-CYL) — The most powerful automobile of the year sported a much modified Hemi engine of 331.1 cid developing 300 brake horsepower. Two four-barrel carburetors, a full race camshaft and heavy-duty suspension, coupled with an Imperial grille and full leather interior, marked this car as something special. Performance and styling, combined in one package of such magnitude, created an aura that was to last for more than a decade.

300 SERIES

Model No.	Body/ Style No.	Body Type & Seating	Factory Price	Shipping Weight	Prod. Total
C68-300	Note 1	2-dr HT Cpe	4109	4005	1,725

Note 1: Code numbers to provide positive identification of body type were not provided.

WINDSOR DELUXE ENGINE: V-8. Overhead valve. Cast iron block. Displacement: 301 cid. Bore and stroke: 3.625 x 3.625 inches. Compression ratio: 8.0:1. Brake hp: 188 at 4400 rpm. Hydraulic valve lifters. Carburetors: (standard shift) Carter BBD 2180S, 2180SA, 2180SB. (PowerFlite) BBD 2162S, 2162SA, 2162SB.

1955 Chrysler, C-300 two-door hardtop, V-8

NEW YORKER DELUXE ENGINE: V-8. Overhead valve with hemispherical combustion chambers. Displacement: 331.1 cid. Bore and stroke: 3.81 x 3.63 inches. Brake hp: 250 at 4600 rpm. Five main bearings. Hydraulic valve lifters. Dual exhaust system. Compression ratio: 8.5:1. Carburetor: Carter WCFB 2126S.

CHRYSLER 300 ENGINE: V-8. Overhead valve with hemispherical combustion chambers. Cast iron block. Displacement: 331.1 cid. Bore and stroke: 3.81 x 3.63 inches. Brake hp: 300 at 5200 rpm. Compression ratio: 8.5:1. Solid lifters with full-race camshaft. Two four-barrel carburetors.

CHASSIS FEATURES: Wheelbase: (all) 126 inches. Overall length: (Windsor Deluxe) 218.6 inches; (all other models) 218.8 inches. Tires: (Windsor) 7.60 x 15; (New Yorker) 8.00 x 15; (New Yorker and Town & Country with wire wheels) 8.20 x 15. Six-volt positive ground electrical system.

OPTIONS: PowerFlite transmission on Windsor Deluxe. Power steering. White sidewall tires. Chrome wire wheels. Air Temp air conditioning. Power brakes. Radio. Heater. Solex glass. Fog lights. Spotlamps. Rear seat radio speaker. Windshield washers. Outside rearview mirror. Two-tone paint. Power windows. Power front seat.

HISTORICAL FOOTNOTES: The Chrysler and Imperial lines for 1955 (including Nassau and St. Regis hardtops) were introduced Nov. 17, 1954. Chrysler Town & Country station wagons were added to the line

Jan. 5, 1955. The Chrysler 300 was added to the line Feb. 10, 1955. Chrysler took second place in the high-priced sales field this season.

1956 CHRYSLER

WINDSOR SERIES — (8-CYL) — The "100 Million Dollar Look" was carried forward with a tasteful face lift centered around grille changes and integrated taillamps. The two-piece grille of 1955 was redesigned with a look reminiscent of the FliteSweep I show car. Three horizontal grille bars floated within a chrome surround. The new taillamps formed a natural extension of the uplifted outer rear bumper ends. The Windsor line had some further subseries that covered all body styles. A pillarless four-door hardtop was introduced and 12-volt electrical systems were adopted for all Chrysler models. Standard features included Oriflow shock absorbers, new safety door latches, independent parking brake, safety rim wheels and center plane brakes.

1956 Chrysler, Windsor two-door convertible, V-8 (AA)

CHRYSLER I.D. NUMBERS: Serial numbers were found on the left front hinge post. Engine numbers were located on the block behind the water pump. [Windsor] Detroit-built cars were numbered W56-1001 to W56-75206. Los Angeles-built cars were numbered W56L-1001 to W56L-7091. Engine numbers ranged from WE56-1001 to WE56-81623. [New Yorker] Detroit-built cars were numbered N56-1001 to N56-36162. Los Angeles-built cars were numbered N56L-1001 to N56L-5197. Engine numbers ranged from NE56-1001 to NE56-40609. [300B] Production of Chrysler 300 Letter Cars took place exclusively in Detroit, with numbers ranging from 3N56-1001 to 3N56-2150. Engine numbers were 3NE56-1001 to 3NE56-2174.

WINDSOR SERIES

Model No.	Body/ Style No.	Body Type & Seating	Factory Price	Shipping Weight	Prod. Total
C71	Note 1	4-dr Sed-6P	2770	3900	53,119
C71	Note 1	2-dr Conv-6P	3235	4100	1,011
C71	Note 1	4-dr T&C Wag-6P	3498	4290	2,700
C71-1	Note 1	2-dr Nassau-6P	2804	3910	11,400
C71-2	Note 1	2-dr Newport-6P	2941	3920	10,800
C71-2	Note 1	4-dr Newport-6P	3028	3990	7,050

Note 1: Code numbers to provide positive identification of body type were not used.

NEW YORKER SERIES — (8-CYL) — Tastefully restyled, the New Yorker used a finer detailed grille and different bumpers to set it apart from the Windsor. Additional moldings created unique two-tone paint combinations and a tri-tone combination in the St. Regis series. Big news this year was the first size increase for the Hemi engine, to 354 cid. This increased brake horsepower, in standard form, by more than 10 percent. A distinctive New Yorker styling touch was the appearance of eight chromed teeth on the rear fender, above the horizontal molding. This feature was to become a New Yorker hallmark for many years. Push-buttons at the left edge of the dash controlled all Chrysler automatic transmissions.

NEW YORKER SERIES

Model No.	Body/ Style No.	Body Type & Seating	Factory Price	Shipping Weight	Prod. Total
C72	Note 1	4-dr Sed-6P	3673	4110	24,749
C72	Note 1	2-dr Conv-6P	4136	4360	921
C72	Note 1	4-dr T&C Wag-6P	4417	4460	1,070
C72-1	Note 1	2-dr Newport-6P	3845	4175	4,115
C72-1	Note 1	4-dr Newport-6P	3995	4220	3,599
C72-2	Note 1	2-dr St Reg-6P	3889	4175	6,686

1956 Chrysler, New Yorker four-door sedan, V-8 (AA)

300B SERIES — (8-CYL) — The 300B's styling reflected the same unique flavor of the first Chrysler Letter Car introduced in 1955. Changes were essentially limited to taillamp alterations, in line with those appearing on other Chryslers. The push-button control for the PowerFlite cars (later cars had TorqueFlite transmission) was positioned to the left side of the dashboard. Technically a subseries of the New Yorker, the 300B was available with automatic or standard shift transmissions and two high-performance Hemi engines. Leather upholstery was standard fare.

300B SERIES

Model No.	Body/ Style No.	Body Type & Seating	Factory Price	Shipping Weight	Prod. Total
C72-300	Note 1	2-dr HT Cpe-6P	4242	4360	1,102

Note 1: Code numbers to provide positive identification of body type were not used.

WINDSOR ENGINE: V-8. Overhead valve. Cast iron block. Displacement: 331.1 cid. Bore and stroke: 3.81 x 3.63 inches. Compression ratio: 8.5:1. Brake hp: 225 at 4400 rpm. (Optional engine with dual exhaust and single four-barrel carburetor produced 250 brake horsepower.) Hydraulic valve lifters. Carburetors: (standard shift) Carter BBD 2312S; (PowerFlite) Carter 2313S; (Power package, with all transmissions) Carter WCFB 2367S or 2367SA.

NEW YORKER ENGINE: V-8. Overhead valve. Cast iron block. Displacement: 354 cid. Bore and stroke: 3.94 x 3.63 inches. Brake hp: 280 at 4600 rpm. Compression ratio: 9.0:1. Five main bearings. Hydraulic valve lifters. Carburetor: Carter WCFB 2314S or 2314SA.

300B ENGINE: V-8. Overhead valve. High-lift camshaft. Extra stiff valve springs. Cast iron block. Displacement: 354 cid. Bore and stroke: 3.94 x 3.63 inches. Brake hp: 340 at 5200 rpm (with optional 10.0:1 compression ratio, brake horsepower became 355 at 5200 rpm).

CHASSIS FEATURES: Three-speed column-mounted transmission standard on the Windsor (available on special order on 300B). PowerFlite transmission standard on New Yorker and 300B. Late 300Bs used three-speed TorqueFlite transmissions. Wheelbase: (all models) 126 inches. Overall length: (Windsor) 220.5 inches; (New Yorker) 221 inches; (New Yorker Town & Country) 221.2 inches; (Windsor Town & Country) 220.4 inches. Last year for front coil springs combined with rear leaf springs.

1956 Chrysler, 300B two-door hardtop, V-8 (AA)

OPTIONS: Power steering. Power brakes. Power front seat. Highway Hi-Fi record player. Air Temp air conditioning. Electric window lifts. Power radio antenna. Hot water heater. Instant gas heater. Solex safety glass. Whitewall tires. Steering wheel mounted clock. Power package on Windsor (included dual exhaust and four-barrel carburetor).

1957 CHRYSLER

WINDSOR — (8-CYL) — The second edition of Chrysler's 'Forward Look' was widely acclaimed. Drawing the most attention were the sweeping rear fender fins. Dual headlamps became standard equipment shortly after production commenced. The 1957 Chryslers had new bodies as well as new chassis features. Torsion bar suspension was one innovation this year. The longstanding Newport name was no longer used for the pillarless body styles. Hardtop models had optional 'Flight Sweep' color panels on the rear fenders. Dual rear aerials were an interesting option.

1957 Chrysler, Windsor four-door hardtop, V-8

CHRYSLER I.D. NUMBERS: Serial numbers were found on the left front door hinge post. Engine numbers were located on the block behind the water pump. [Windsor] Detroit-built cars were numbered W57-1001 and up. Los Angeles-built cars were numbered W57L-1001 and up. Engine numbers ranged from WE57-1001 to WE57-48864. [Saratoga] Detroit-built cars were numbered L57-1001 and up. Los Angeles-built cars were numbered L57L-1001 and up. Engine numbers ranged from LE57-1001 and up. [New Yorker] Detroit-built cars were numbered N57-1001 and up. Los Angeles-built cars were numbered N57L-1001 and up. Engine numbers ranged from NE57-1001 to NE57-35552. [300] Serial numbers were 3N57-1001 and up. Engine numbers ranged from 3NE57-1001 to 3NE57-3338. All production of Chrysler 300s was quartered in Detroit.

WINDSOR SERIES

Model No.	Body/ Style No.	Body Type & Seating	Factory Price	Shipping Weight	Prod. Total
C75-1	145	4-dr Sed-6P	3088	3995	17,639
C75-1	146	2-dr HT-6P	3153	3925	14,027
C75-1	149	4-dr HT-6P	3217	4030	14,354
C75-1	148	4-dr T&C Wag-6P	3574	4210	2,035

SARATOGA SERIES — (8-CYL) — The Saratoga name returned after an absence of five years. This mid-line Chrysler, based on Windsor components, featured upgraded upholstery, a higher horsepower engine with dual exhaust, back-up lamps and brake warning signals. TorqueFlite transmission, stainless steel wheel covers and power steering were standard equipment. A single horizontal trim molding ran from front to rear, giving the car a long sweeping look that reflected Virgil Exner's design inspiration. Two-tone finish was optional and popular. The Saratoga insignia was located below the horizontal trim line, just left of the front wheelhouse opening. The grille used a broad, horizontal motif. Early cars had single headlamps, with a dual system optionally available.

SARATOGA SERIES

Model No.	Body/ Style No.	Body Type & Seating	Factory Price	Shipping Weight	Prod. Total
C75-2	255	4-dr Sed-6P	3718	4165	14,977
C75-2	256	2-dr HT-6P	3754	4075	10,633
C75-2	259	4-dr HT-6P	3832	4195	11,586

NEW YORKER SERIES — (8-CYL) — This top-of-the-line model featured the largest production car engine available in 1957. The Hemi engine's bore and stroke were increased. Displacement was raised nearly 10 percent. A narrow, dart-like color sweep distinguished the sides of the New Yorker. Cars with two-tone finish had the roof color added to the side trim area. Advertised as, "The most glamorous cars in a generation," all body styles were included in this series. Dual rear antennas were a popular option that emphasized the sweep of the tailfins. Chrysler 'firsts' for 1957 included Torsion-Aire ride, completely concealed tailpipes, spool-like engine mounts and optional Captive-Aire tires on the New Yorker Town & Country station wagon (a spare tire was not provided on this model).

NEW YORKER SERIES

Model No.	Body/ Style No.	Body Type & Seating	Factory Price	Shipping Weight	Prod. Total
C76	165	4-dr Sed-6P	4173	4315	12,369
C76	166	2-dr HT-6P	4202	4220	8,863
C76	169	4-dr HT-6P	4259	4330	10,948
C76	163	2-dr Conv-6P	4638	4365	1,049
C76	168	4-dr T&C Wag-6P	4746	4490	1,391

1957 Chrysler, New Yorker two-door hardtop, V-8

300C SERIES — (8-CYL) — The third version of the 300 continued as the fastest and most powerful production car in the country. The 300 featured full leather interior trims and a new masculine grille that was unlike any seen on previous Chrysler offerings. Exterior ornamentation was kept to a minimum with single spear-like moldings on the lower rear quarter panels. The round 300 medallion, with a red-white-blue background and model numbers and lettering made its debut. Medallions were placed on the side spears, one on each hubcap, one each on the hood, deck lid, glovebox and another within the steering wheel center hub. Only the two on the spears carried both numbers and letters. The others had only the '300' designation. The colors of the emblem were claimed to be representative of the high-performance nature of the American car-buying public. With smaller, 14-inch wheels being used, it was found necessary to provide for additional brake cooling on the Chrysler 300. This was accomplished by adding a rectangular opening below the headlamps that admitted air and guided it, via a duct, to the front brakes. Monotone colors were used exclusively on the 300 and the front did not have the short, narrow vertical bumper guards found on other 1957 Chryslers. The 300s were considered a part of the New Yorker series, but were actually a world apart from most other U.S. production automobiles of the day.

300C SERIES

Model No.	Body/ Style No.	Body Type & Seating	Factory Price	Shipping Weight	Prod. Total
C76-300	566	2-dr HT-6P	4929	4235	1,918
C76-300	563	2-dr Conv-6P	5359	4390	484

WINDSOR ENGINE: V-8. Overhead valve. Cast iron block. Displacement: 354 cid. Bore and stroke: 3.94 x 3.63 inches. Compression ratio: 9.25:1. Brake hp: 285 at 4800 rpm. Five main bearings. Hydraulic valve lifters. Carburetor: Carter two-barrel, Type BBD Model 2527S.

1957 Chrysler, 300C two-door hardtop, V-8

SARATOGA ENGINE: V-8. Overhead valve. Cast iron block. Displacement: 354 cid. Bore and stroke: 3.94 x 3.63 inches. Compression ratio: 9.25:1. Brake hp: 295 at 4600 rpm. Five main bearings. Hydraulic valve lifters. Carburetor: Carter WCFB2589S four-barrel (dual exhaust).

NEW YORKER ENGINE: V-8. Cast iron block. Overhead valve with hemispherical combustion chambers. Displacement: 392 cid. Bore and stroke: 4.00 x 3.90 inches. Compression ratio: 9.25:1. Brake hp: 325 at 4600 rpm. Five main bearings. Solid valve lifters. Carburetor: Carter WCFB Model 2590S four-barrel (dual exhaust).

300C ENGINE: V-8. Cast iron block. Overhead valve with hemispherical combustion chambers. Displacement: 392 cid. Bore and stroke: 4.00 x 3.90 inches. Compression ratio: 9.25:1. Brake hp: 375 at 5200 rpm. Five main bearings. Carburetor: Two Carter Model WCFB 2334S four-barrel.

OPTIONAL 300C ENGINE: V-8. Cast iron block. Overhead valve with hemispherical combustion chambers. Displacement: 392 cid. Bore and stroke: 4.00 x 3.90 inches. Compression ratio: 9.25:1. Brake hp: 390 at 5400 rpm. Five main bearings. Carburetor: Two Carter Model WCFB 2334S four-barrel. This extra-cost solid lifter competition engine was intended mainly for acceleration trials and stock racing cars. It was available only with stickshift (adapted from a Dodge column-mounted three-speed) and no power options. It had a 10.0:1 compression ratio, four-bolt cast iron exhaust headers and a 2-1/2-inch low back-pressure exhaust system. Solid valve lifters and twin four-barrel carburetors were used.

CHASSIS FEATURES: Standard shift standard on Windsor. TorqueFlite optional on Windsor; standard on Saratoga, New Yorker and 300C. Wheelbase: 126 inches. Separate body and frame construction. Hotchkiss drive. Hypoid rear axle. Total-Contact brakes. Overall length: (Windsor, Saratoga, New Yorker and 300C) 219.2 inches; (Town & Country wagon) 218.9 inches. Safety wheel rims. Tires: (Windsor and Saratoga) 8.50 x 14; (New Yorker and 300C) 9.00 x 14. Front tread: (Windsor and Saratoga) 61 inches; (New Yorker) 61.2 inches. Rear tread: (Windsor and Saratoga) 59.7 inches; (New Yorker) 60 inches. Width: (all models) 78.8 inches. Torsion bar front suspension.

OPTIONS: Power steering on Windsor (standard on other series). Handbrake warning signal option on Windsor. Back-up lights optional on Windsor. Dual headlamps (became standard on all lines shortly after production commenced). Air-Temp air conditioning. Power brakes. Power window lifts. Six-Way power seat. Whitewall tires. Nylon tires. Chrome stainless steel wheel covers on Windsor. Radio with Music Master or Electro-Touch tuner. Dual rear antennas. Power front antenna. Rear seat speaker. Fresh air heater. Instant Air heater. Two-tone finish. Tinted glass. Rear window defroster. Windshield washer. Undercoating. Non-slip differential. Outside mirrors. Full-flow oil filter on Windsor. Captive-Aire tires on Town & Country station wagon. Hi-Way Hi-Fi phonograph.

HISTORICAL FOOTNOTES: The 1957 Chrysler models were introduced on Oct. 29, 1956. Output in 1957 was 156,679 cars of which 118,733 were Chryslers and 37,946 Imperials. Since 1926, when the first one was produced, Imperials had been built in the corporation's East Jefferson plant at Detroit, along with Chryslers. Beginning in 1955, the Imperial was given a distinctively different styling treatment and, by 1957, there no longer were any body parts interchangeable with Chrysler.

1958 CHRYSLER

1958 Chrysler, Windsor Dartline two-door hardtop, V-8

WINDSOR SERIES — (8-CYL) — A Dodge chassis was now used under the Windsor's sheet metal. The car had typical Chrysler styling motifs, with the major change being that the front end sheet metal was capped-

off with a chrome eyebrow running from side-to-side above the headlamps. The 1958 style grille was tastefully adapted to the Dodge-like front end. Side trim on the standard offering was a single molding, at mid-level, running horizontally from the rear to just aft of the front wheelhouse opening. In the spring, a Dartline package was introduced, which added some flair to the Windsor's styling. The Dartline package was an addition to the hardtop line. Besides additional trim on the front fender and a metal insert, this option included bright sill moldings, special roof trim and three slim moldings on each side of the rear deck license plate housing. The standard two-door hardtop used a sweep of color similar to the 1957 version with the major difference being the sharper pointed front part of the sweep on the 1958 model. Introduced this year was Auto-Pilot speed control and a new three-seat nine-passenger station wagon. The third seat faced to the rear.

1958 Chrysler, Saratoga two-door hardtop, V-8

CHRYSLER I.D. NUMBERS: Serial numbers were found on the left front hinge post. Engine numbers were located on the block behind the water pump. [Windsor] Detroit-built cars were numbered LC1-1001 and up. Los Angeles-built cars were numbered LC1L-1001 and up. Engine numbers ranged from 58W-1001 and up. [Saratoga] Detroit-built cars used numbers LC2-1001 and up. Los Angeles-built cars used numbers LC2L-1001 and up. Engine numbers ranged from SAS-1001 and up. [New Yorker] Detroit-built cars were numbered LC3-1001 and up. Los Angeles-built cars were numbered LC3L-1001 and up. Engine numbers ranged from 58N-1001 and up. [300D] All 300s were built in Detroit and serial numbers began with LC4-1001 and up. Engine numbers started at 58N3-1001 and up.

WINDSOR SERIES

Model No.	Body/ Style No.	Body Type & Seating	Factory Price	Shipping Weight	Prod. Total
LC1-L	513	4-dr Sed-6P	3129	3895	12,861
LC1-L	512	2-dr HT-6P	3214	3860	6,205
LC1-L	514	4-dr HT-6P	3279	3915	6,254
LC1-L	571	4-dr T&C Wag-6P	3616	4155	862
LC1-L	572	4-dr T&C Wag-9P	3803	4245	791
LC1-L	515	2-dr Conv-6P	—	—	2

SARATOGA SERIES — (8-CYL) — This series continued almost unchanged from 1957. Instrument panel background color changed, as did the metal background of the radio and heater control panels. The side trim began at the forward edge of the front door and continued rearward to the taillamp bezel. The Saratoga nameplate was placed to the rear of the front fender, directly in line with the side trim molding. A color spear was available at extra cost. On cars with this option the extra trim began at the middle of the front door and rose slightly, in a gentle line, as it ran rearward. The taillamps were similar to the previous type, except that the lenses rose to a point only two-thirds the way up rather than running full height, as in 1957. The lenses were also narrower and revealed more of the housing itself. The grille continued its horizontal flair with the topmost part of the bumper horizontally dividing the opening. Dual headlamps were a standard feature. The rearview mirror, as in all 1957 and 1958 models, was mounted on the dash rather than the windshield header.

SARATOGA SERIES

Model No.	Body/ Style No.	Body Type & Seating	Factory Price	Shipping Weight	Prod. Total
LC2-M	533	4-dr Sed-6P	3818	4120	8,698
LC2-M	532	2-dr HT-6P	3878	4045	4,456
LC2-M	534	4-dr HT-6P	3955	4145	5,322

NEW YORKER SERIES — (8-CYL) — Little changed from 1957 as far as New Yorkers went. A face lift paralleled changes seen in the less expensive Chrysler models. The Saratoga-style mid-line body trim molding was seen but a unique emblem, placed just rearward of the front door, set New Yorkers apart. A color spear of anodized aluminum graced the area between the two trim pieces and covered the rear portion of the car. While not as substantial or as long as the color sweep of 1957, it helped distinguish this model from its brethren. Auto-Pilot and remote-control outside rearview mirrors were new options. Interior fabric was

'Fountainebleu' Jacquard and metallic vinyl and was slightly richer than the 'Chainmail' fabric and metallic vinyl used on the Saratoga (Windsors used 'Bahama' Jacquard and metallic vinyl trim combinations). The Town & Country station wagon now had a third seat option, with the seat facing the rear of the car. All hardtops sported the new domed windshield introduced on 1957 convertibles.

NEW YORKER SERIES

Model No.	Body/ Style No.	Body Type & Seating	Factory Price	Shipping Weight	Prod. Total
LC3-H	553	4-dr Sed-6P	4295	4195	7,110
LC3-H	552	2-dr HT-6P	4347	4205	3,205
LC3-H	554	4-dr HT-6P	4404	4240	5,227
LC3-H	555	2-dr Conv Cpe-6P	4761	4350	666
LC3-H	575	4-dr T&C Wag-6P	4868	4435	775
LC3-H	576	4-dr T&C Wag-9P	5083	4445	428

1958 Chrysler, New Yorker four-door hardtop, V-8

300D SERIES — (8-CYL) — This super high-performance car was again a subseries of the New Yorker. It carried forward the design motifs of 1957 with only minor alterations. The windshield on hardtops now conformed to the windshield style (domed) of the convertible. Hubcaps now had red finish, painted in the depressed outer areas of the wheel covers. Instrument face backgrounds were identical to those of other 1958 Chryslers. Large red-white-blue rear quarter panel medallions returned for the second year, but the letter 'D' replaced the 'C' used in 1957. In all, there were 10 locations for the various size 300 medallions on the car: glovebox, grille, deck lid, steering hub, hubcaps and the aforementioned rear quarters. A limited number of 300Ds were built with an electronic fuel injection system called the Bendix Electrojector. This marked the first use of a computer in a Chrysler product. A recall program was instituted, in late summer 1958, and most of the EFI units were replaced by conventional carburetors in the dual four-barrel configuration that was standard on all 300s. It was also the last year for the 'Firepower' Hemi engine.

300D SERIES

Model No.	Body/ Style No.	Body Type & Seating	Factory Price	Shipping Weight	Prod. Total
LC3-S	592	2-dr HT-6P	5173	4305	618
LC3-S	595	2-dr Conv Cpe-6P	5603	4475	191

WINDSOR ENGINE: V-8. Overhead valve. Cast iron block. Displacement: 354 cid. Bore and stroke: 3.94 x 3.63 inches. Compression ratio: 10.0:1. Brake hp: 290 at 4600 rpm. Five main bearings. Hydraulic valve lifters. Carburetor: Carter Type BBD Model 2733S two-barrel.

SARATOGA ENGINE: V-8. Overhead valve. Cast iron block. Displacement: 354 cid. Bore and stroke: 3.94 x 3.63 inches. Compression ratio: 10.0:1. Brake hp: 310 at 4600 rpm. Five main bearings. Hydraulic valve lifters. Carburetor: Carter four-barrel.

NEW YORKER ENGINE: V-8. Cast iron block. Overhead valve with hemispherical combustion chambers. Displacement: 392 cid. Bore and stroke: 4.00 x 3.90 inches. Compression ratio: 10.0:1. Brake hp: 345 at 4600 rpm. Five main bearings. Hydraulic valve lifters. Carburetor: Carter Type AFB four-barrel Model 2651S. Dual exhaust.

300D ENGINE: V-8. Cast iron block. Overhead valve with hemispherical combustion chambers. Adjustable valve lifters. Displacement: 392 cid. Bore and stroke: 4.00 x 3.90 inches. Compression ratio: 10.0:1. Brake hp: 380 at 5200 rpm. Dual Carter WCFB four-barrel carburetors.

EFI ENGINE: Optional fuel injected engine produced 390 brake horsepower at 5200 rpm. Low back pressure exhaust system available.

CHASSIS FEATURES: Standard shift standard on Windsor. TorqueFlite optional on Windsor and standard on Saratoga, New Yorker and 300D. Wheelbase: 122 inches on Windsor; 126 inches on all other series. Constant control power steering optional on Windsor and standard on other series. Torsion-Aire front suspension sway bar and Oriflow shock absorbers standard on all models. 300D used larger diameter torsion bars. Windsor length was 218 inches (217.7 inches on Town & Country). Saratoga was 220 inches in length. New Yorkers were 220.2 inches (Town & Country was 219.9 inches). Tire size: 8.00 x 14 for Windsor;

8.50 x 14 for Saratoga and 9.00 x 14 for New Yorkers and 300D. Safety rim wheels were standard on all models.

OPTIONS: Power steering on Windsor. TorqueFlite on Windsor. Power brakes. Power windows. Power seat. Air-Temp air conditioning. White sidewall rayon tires (nylon tubeless super soft cushion tires in black and white optional). Stainless wheel covers on Windsor. Remote control mirror. Radios. Antennas including power antenna. Two-tone finish. Tinted glass. Heaters. Rear window defroster. Windshield washer. Undercoating. Non-slip differential. Hi-Fi Phonograph. Auto-Pilot.

HISTORICAL FOOTNOTES: Dealer introductions of 1958 Chryslers were held on Nov. 1, 1957. Production included 26,500 Windsors; 18,300 New Yorkers and 15,700 Saratogas. Emphasizing the Imperial as a separate line was a major step in the division's 1958 activities. Passenger car production for calendar year 1958 was 63,186 units, including Imperial's share of 13,673 or 21.6 percent of the total. Installation rates of the leading equipment items continued high on 1958 models. Such accessories as automatic transmission, power steering, heater and windshield washer, neared 100 percent for Chrysler. Auto-Pilot was Chrysler's unique driver assist option. First introduced in 1958, the device permits the driver to dial his speed and remove his foot from the accelerator while cruising.

1959 CHRYSLER

1959 Chrysler, Windsor two-door hardtop, V-8

WINDSOR — (8-CYL) — The low-line Windsor used the same basic body structure of the earlier finned versions, but the sheet metal was craftily changed. Although continuing the dartlike shape of Virgil Exner's famous design theme, a new look was achieved. The grille carried forward its horizontal flair, but the lower section now wrapped around the fender and ran back to near the wheelhouse opening. Bumpers, front and rear, were noticeably different and the rear license plate was no longer embedded in the deck lid. It was now positioned at the center inset of the rear bumper. Taillamps were placed in a notched housing totally unlike previous designs. A unique feature was the 'outlined roof' treatment that, as an option, could be ordered in colors that matched the bodyside sweep inserts. A new, wedge-like combustion chamber "Golden Lion" V-8 engine was used on all 1959 Chryslers. This engine was a derivative of the B-block introduced in 1958 for DeSoto, Dodge and Plymouth. The Town & Country name continued to identify the station wagons. All hardtops and convertibles used the dome-like windshield pioneered on 1957 convertibles. Interior upholstery came in 14 color and fabric choices using 'Times Square' metallic threaded cloth with pleated vinyl inserts. Swivel seats were available on all body styles, except the station wagon, and were standard on Chrysler 300Es. The Windsor continued to be built on the Dodge chassis.

CHRYSLER I.D. NUMBERS: Serial numbers were found on the left front hinge post. Engine numbers were located on the boss behind the water pump. Chrysler instituted a new serial number coding system that consisted of 10 symbols. [Windsor] First symbol 'M' indicated 1959. The second digit '5' indicated Chrysler. The third digit '1' indicated Windsor and the fourth digit indicated the assembly plant, as follows: 1=Detroit; 4=Los Angeles. The last six symbols represented the production sequence number, beginning with 100001. Detroit-built cars were numbered M511-100001 and up. Los Angeles-built cars were numbered M514-100001 and up. Detroit-built station wagons were numbered M571-100001 and up. Los Angeles-built station wagons were numbered M574-100001 and up. [Saratoga] Detroit-built cars used numbers M531-100001 and up. Los Angeles-built cars used numbers M534-100001 and up. The coding system was the same used on all Chryslers.

The third symbol '2' indicated Saratoga. [New Yorker] Detroit-built cars used numbers M551-100001 and up. Los Angeles-built cars used numbers M554-100001 and up. Detroit-built station wagons used serial numbers M571-100001. Los Angeles-built station wagons used numbers M574-100001 and up. The third symbol '3' indicated New Yorker/300E. [300E] All cars were built in Detroit and were numbered M591-100001 and up.

WINDSOR SERIES

Model No.	Body/ Style No.	Body Type & Seating	Factory Price	Shipping Weight	Prod. Total
MC1-L	513	4-dr Sed-6P	3204	3800	19,910
MC1-L	512	2-dr HT Cpe-6P	3289	3735	6,775
MC1-L	514	4-dr HT Sed-6P	3353	3830	6,084
MC1-L	515	2-dr Conv-6P	3620	3950	961
MC1-L	576	4-dr T&C Wag-6P	3691	4045	992
MC1-L	577	4-dr T&C Wag-9P	3878	4070	751

1959 Chrysler, Saratoga four-door hardtop, V-8

SARATOGA SERIES — (8-CYL) — The Saratoga used the long wheelbase chassis (126 inches). From the cowl area back, the sheet metal was identical to that of the Windsor. However, the front end sheet metal was four inches longer. A new color sweep began at the lower rear quarter panel and arched upward, in a graceful manner, to a mid-body location. It then ran forward to the tip of the front fender. Standard two-tone color combinations had the body and roof panel insert in the same color and contrasting finish on the color sweep, roof outline and C-pillar. A Saratoga nameplate was located just forward of the taillamp housing. A Golden Lion medallion was used in Chrysler's new promotional theme, "Chrysler 1959 — presenting the Lion-hearted Car that's every inch a New Adventure." An array of options included the unique swivel seat. Interiors were all vinyl. Optional were seat inserts made of Jacquard material called 'Mayfair.'

SARATOGA SERIES

Model No.	Body/ Style No.	Body Type & Seating	Factory Price	Shipping Weight	Prod. Total
MC2-M	533	4-dr Sed-6P	3966	4010	8,783
MC2-M	532	2-dr HT Cpe-6P	4026	3970	3,753
MC2-M	534	4-dr HT Sed-6P	4104	4035	4,943

NEW YORKER SERIES — (8-CYL) — The B-series engine was used for the first time in a New Yorker. The Hemi engine was no longer available. Horsepower was up slightly, as was displacement. Engine weight, simplicity of design and lower manufacturing costs were the principal reasons for the change in powerplant. The New Yorker used a spear-like color sweep with horizontal top trim. The lower trim molding dipped and broadened, at the rear, running to bumper level height. An anodized insert ran from front to rear, within the color spear, and seven slash-type strips were added at the rear. They continued the same pattern used on previous New Yorkers. The Golden Lion insignia was placed below the New Yorker script at the rear portion of the front fender. Upholstery options consisted of 22 combinations of vinyl and Jacquard fabric. The instrument panel and dashboard were relatively unchanged from the two previous years.

NEW YORKER SERIES

Model No.	Body/ Style No.	Body Type & Seating	Factory Price	Shipping Weight	Prod. Total
MC3-H	553	4-dr Sed-6P	4424	4120	7,792
MC3-H	552	2-dr HT Cpe-6P	4476	4080	2,435
MC3-H	554	4-dr HT Sed-6P	4533	4165	4,805
MC3-H	555	2-dr Conv-6P	4890	4270	286
MC3-H	578	4-dr T&C Wag-6P	4997	4295	444
MC3-H	579	4-dr T&C Wag-9P	5212	4360	564
MC3-H	—	Chassis	—	—	2

300E SERIES — (8-CYL) — Considered a part of the New Yorker series, the "Beautiful Brute" continued the tradition of luxurious, high-performance driving pleasure. Minor styling revisions and the use of a wedge-shaped combustion chamber engine were changes. The new engine was

said to have performance equal to or slightly better than the Hemi engine, which left no doubt as to the car's heritage. A revised grille, on the familiar theme, eliminated the vertical bar look. A 300 insignia was placed on the driver's side of the hood, in line with the headlamps. Swivel bucket seats were available and the red-white-blue medallion was positioned in its usual place. The letter 'E' was added to the medallion to signify the new model as the 300E. This was the last year for separate body and frame design.

300E SERIES

Model No.	Body/ Style No.	Body Type & Seating	Factory Price	Shipping Weight	Prod. Total
MC3-H	592	2-dr HT-6P	5319	4290	550
MC3-H	595	2-dr Conv-6P	5749	4350	140

1959 Chrysler, 300E two-door hardtop, V-8

WINDSOR ENGINE: V-8. Cast iron block. Displacement: 383 cid. Bore and stroke: 4.03 x 3.75 inches. Compression ratio: 10.1:1. Brake hp: 305 at 4800 rpm. Five main bearings. Hydraulic valve lifters. Carburetor: Carter Type BBD two-barrel Model 2872S.

SARATOGA ENGINE: V-8. Cast iron block. Displacement: 383 cid. Bore and stroke: 4.03 x 3.75 inches. Compression ratio: 10.1:1. Brake hp: 325 at 4600 rpm. Five main bearings. Hydraulic valve lifters. Carburetor: Carter Type AFB four-barrel Model 2797S.

NEW YORKER ENGINE: V-8. Cast iron block. Displacement: 413 cid. Bore and stroke: 4.18 x 3.75 inches. Compression ratio: 10.0:1. Brake hp: 350 at 4600 rpm. Five main bearings. Hydraulic valve lifters. Carburetor: Carter Type AFB four-barrel.

300E ENGINE: V-8. Cast iron block. Displacement: 413 cid. Bore and stroke: 4.18 x 3.75 inches. Compression ratio: 10.1:1. Brake hp: 380 at 5000 rpm. Five main bearings. Hydraulic valve lifters. Carburetors: Two Carter four-barrel Type AFB Model 2798S.

CHASSIS FEATURES: Wheelbase: (Windsor) 122 inches; (Saratoga) 126 inches; (New Yorker) 126 inches; (300E) 126 inches. Overall length: (Windsor) 216.6 inches; (Saratoga) 220.6 inches; (New Yorker) 220.9 inches; (300E) 220.9 inches. Front tread: (Windsor) 60.9 inches; (Saratoga) 60.9 inches; (New Yorker) 61.2 inches; (300E) 61.2 inches. Rear tread: (Windsor) 59.8 inches; (Saratoga) 59.8 inches; (New Yorker) 60.0 inches; (300E) 60.0 inches. Tires: (Windsor) 8.00 x 14; (Saratoga) 8.50 x 14; (New Yorker) 9.00 x 14; (300E) 9.00 x 14.

OPTIONS: Power steering (Windsor). TorqueFlite (Windsor). Power brakes (Windsor). Power seat. Swivel seats. Air-Temp air conditioning. Custom super-soft cushion rayon tires. White sidewall tires. Nylon and Captive-Aire tires. Stainless steel wheel covers on Windsor (standard on Windsor Town & Country). Remote control mirror. Radios. Antennas (including power antenna). Two-tone finish. Solex glass. Heater. Rear window defroster. Auto-Pilot. Windshield washer. Undercoating. Non-slip differential. Handbrake warning lights. Back-up light (Windsor). Sill moldings (Windsor).

HISTORICAL FOOTNOTES: First year for 'B' block engines. Last year for separate body and frame construction. Golden Lion was new advertising theme. The 1959 models were introduced Oct. 24, 1958.

1960 CHRYSLER

WINDSOR SERIES — (8-CYL) — An all new body style featured a 300-type grille and a modified fin look. The big news this year was unibody

construction. The Windsor series was again on the short wheelbase platform and was the least expensive Chrysler. The grille insert was a mesh-like affair with a golden lion medallion affixed to the center. Fins were rakish and set at an angle. They were emphasized by deep, rounded indentations at mid-body height. Station wagons used a pillarless design giving a hardtop-style look. Taillamps were set into a sharply arched housing mounted at the extreme end of the tailfin. Dual headlamps were standard fare. An optional Flitesweep deck lid was available at modest cost. Stone shields and sill moldings were a Windsor option.

1960 Chrysler, Windsor two-door hardtop, V-8

CHRYSLER I.D. NUMBERS: Serial numbers were found on the left front hinge post. Engine numbers were located on the boss behind the water pump. [Windsor] Detroit-built cars were numbered 8103-100001 and up. Los Angeles-built cars were numbered 8105-100001 and up. Windsor station wagons were numbered 8503-100001 and up. [Saratoga] Detroit-built cars were numbered 8203-100001 and up. [New Yorker] Detroit-built cars were numbered 8303-100001 and up. [300F] Serial numbers began with 8403-100001 and up. Engine numbers were identical to the New Yorker series. All 300s were built in Detroit. A new engine numbering system deciphered as follows: First symbol indicated year/series: PR=1960 Windsor; second symbol indicated displacement: 38=383 cid; third symbol indicated month (7=July) and day (1=first day of month, etc.). Thus, the code PR-387-5 indicates a Chrysler Windsor/Saratoga 383 V-8 built on July 5. The code for a New Yorker/300 engine built the same day would be: P-41-7-5, as P=1960 model year; 41=413-cid V-8; 7-5=date of manufacture (July 5).

WINDSOR SERIES

Model No.	Body/ Style No.	Body Type & Seating	Factory Price	Shipping Weight	Prod. Total
PC1-L	813	4-dr Sed-6P	3194	3815	25,152
PC1-L	812	2-dr HT Cpe-6P	3279	3850	6,496
PC1-L	814	4-dr HT Sed-6P	3343	3855	5,897
PC1-L	815	2-dr Conv-6P	3623	3855	1,467
PC1-L	858	4-dr Sta Wag-6P	3733	4235	1,120
PC1-L	859	4 dr Sta Wag-9P	3814	4390	1,026

SARATOGA SERIES — (8-CYL) — The Saratoga was built on the long wheelbase chassis and included, as standard equipment, many features not found on the less expensive Windsor series. Front fender script was the basic means of identification, although the longer front sheet metal was readily apparent to a sharp-eyed enthusiast. Interior fabrics were of better quality than in the Windsor series. Standard equipment included: TorqueFlite transmission; power steering and brakes; rear foam seats; electric clock; wheel covers; Deluxe steering wheel; windshield washers; padded dash; back-up lights; parking brake lights; map lights; luggage lights; stone shields and sill moldings.

1960 Chrysler, Saratoga two-door hardtop, V-8

SARATOGA SERIES

Model No.	Body/ Style No.	Body Type & Seating	Factory Price	Shipping Weight	Prod. Total
PC2-M	823	4-dr Sed-6P	3929	4010	8,463
PC2-M	822	2-dr HT Cpe-6P	3989	4030	2,963
PC2-M	824	4-dr HT Sed-6P	4067	4035	4,099

1960 Chrysler, New Yorker two-door hardtop, V-8

NEW YORKER SERIES — (8-CYL) — The New Yorker was built on the long wheelbase chassis. The masculine 300-type grille was 'trenched'. A fine horizontal bar motif inset appeared within the grille outline. New Yorkers continued to use rear fender trim bars for the fifth consecutive year. For 1960, the number of bars was increased to nine. Exterior brightwork was kept to a minimum with stone shields and sill moldings standard. The front bumper dipped in the center to match the lower contour of the grille opening.

NEW YORKER SERIES

Model No.	Body/ Style No.	Body Type & Seating	Factory Price	Shipping Weight	Prod. Total
PC3-H	833	4-dr Sed-6P	4409	4145	9,079
PC3-H	832	2-dr HT Cpe-6P	4461	4175	2,835
PC3-H	834	4-dr HT Sed-6P	4518	4175	5,625
PC3-H	835	2-dr Conv-6P	4875	4185	556
PC3-H	878	4-dr Sta Wag-6P	5022	4515	624
PC3-H	879	4-dr Sta Wag-9P	5131	4535	671

1960 Chrysler, 300F two-door convertible, V-8

300F SERIES — (8-CYL) — The sixth edition of the letter series 300 continued its tradition as a high-performance vehicle. Besides the all-new styling and unibody construction, big improvements in engineering were evident with the unveiling of a Ram-Tuned induction manifold option. Ram-tuning had long been a means of raising torque and horsepower for drag racing. Chrysler engineers adapted this idea with cross-over ram induction manifolds, which placed one bank of cylinder's carburetor on the far side of the opposing bank of cylinder's carburetor. No longer were the carburetors placed inline, between the cylinder heads, as on previous dual carbureted 300s. Two horsepower versions were available in 1960, and a few cars (seven to 10, including at least one convertible) were built with the French Pont-A-Mousson four-speed gearbox. All New Yorker standard features were included on the 300F, plus power swivel seats. White sidewall nylon tires were standard.

300F SERIES

Model No.	Body/ Style No.	Body Type & Seating	Factory Price	Shipping Weight	Prod. Total
PC3-300	842	2-dr HT Cpe-5P	5411	4270	964
PC3-300	845	2-dr Conv-5P	5841	4310	248

WINDSOR ENGINE: V-8. Cast iron block. Displacement: 383 cid. Bore and stroke: 4.03 x 3.75 inches. Compression ratio: 10.0:1. Brake hp: 305 at 4800 rpm. Five main bearings. Hydraulic valve lifters. Carburetor: Carter Type BBD two-barrel.

SARATOGA ENGINE: V-8. Cast iron block. Displacement: 383 cid. Bore and stroke: 4.03 x 3.75 inches. Compression ratio: 10.0:1. Brake hp: 325 at 4600 rpm. Five main bearings. Hydraulic valve lifters. Carburetor: Carter AFB-2927S four-barrel.

NEW YORKER ENGINE: V-8. Cast iron block. Displacement: 413 cid. Bore and stroke: 4.188 x 3.75 inches. Compression ratio: 10.0:1. Brake

hp: 350 at 4600 rpm. Five main bearings. Hydraulic valve lifters. Carburetor: Carter AFB-2903S four-barrel.

300F ENGINE: V-8. Cast iron block. Overhead valve. Displacement: 413 cid. Bore and stroke: 4.188 x 3.75 inches. Brake hp: 375 at 5000 rpm. (Optional engine: 400 at 5200 rpm.) Compression ratio: 10.1:1. Hydraulic valve lifters. (Optional engine: solid valve lifters.) Dual carburetion with 30-inch Ram Induction manifold. (Optional engine: dual carburetion with 15-inch Ram Induction manifold.)

CHASSIS FEATURES: Wheelbase: (Windsor) 122 inches; (Saratoga) 126 inches; (New Yorker and 300F) 126 inches. Overall length: (Windsor) 215.5 inches; (Windsor station wagon) 216 inches; (Saratoga) 219.4 inches; (New Yorker) 219.6 inches; (New Yorker station wagon) 220 inches. Front tread: (Windsor and Saratoga) 61 inches; (New Yorker) 61.2 inches. Rear tread: (Windsor and Saratoga) 59.7 inches; (New Yorker) 60 inches. Tires: (Windsor) 8.00 x 14; (Windsor station wagon and Saratoga) 8.50 x 14; (New Yorker and 300F) 9.00 x 14.

OPTIONS: Power steering, on Windsor ($108). TorqueFlite, on Windsor ($227). Power brakes on Windsor ($44). Power windows on Windsor and Saratoga ($108). Power seat ($102). Swivel seats, except two-seat station wagons and 300F. Air conditioning ($510). Dual air conditioning, all except convertible and 300F ($714). Heater ($102). Golden tone radio ($100). Golden tone with touch tuner ($124). Rear seat speaker ($17). Power antenna ($26). Auto-Pilot ($486). Automatic beam changer ($44). Flitesweep deck lid, all but 300F and station wagons ($43). Windsor fender ornament ($9). Rear window defogger ($21). Sure Grip differential ($52). Remote-control left outside mirror, standard in New Yorker ($18). Solex glass ($43). Two-tone paint, on New Yorker ($20); on Windsor and Saratoga ($40). Windshield washer on Windsor ($14). White sidewall tires: size 8.00 x 14 rayon, on Windsor ($42); nylon ($60); Size 8.50 x 14 rayon, on Windsor station wagon and Saratoga ($46); nylon ($66). Size 9.00 x 14 rayon, on New Yorkers ($51); nylon ($72); Captive-Aire, on station wagons; on Windsor ($89); on New Yorker ($94). Vacuum door locks, on two-doors ($37); on four-doors ($56).

HISTORICAL FOOTNOTES: The 300F continued traditions by winning the first six places in Flying Mile competition at Daytona with a top speed of nearly 145 mph. William C. Newberg ascended to the presidency of Chrysler Corp., but was forced to resign within months when conflict of interest with suppliers came to light. Lester L. (Tex) Colbert became president after Newberg's resignation. Chrysler sales improved more than 25 percent over 1959, but the division remained in 12th place in industry standings.

1961 CHRYSLER

1961 Chrysler, Newport four-door hardtop, V-8

NEWPORT SERIES — (8-CYL) — In an attempt to offer Chrysler automobiles to a larger segment of the marketplace, Chrysler management reintroduced the Newport name (formerly applied to a hardtop body style) to create a low-line series. Using the previous year's Windsor wheelbase, Chrysler was able to slash its entry level prices by nearly seven percent. The same number of total series was retained, by discontinuing the Saratoga nameplate. The result was a tremendous price gap between the top and bottom priced Chryslers. Minor face-lifting of the 1961s centered on the grille. It now had a fine horizontal bar motif, a straight bumper and slanted headlamps. Taillamps were relocated into the deck lid latch panel and the tailfins ended in chromed inserts with tiny back-up lamps. The rear fins looked similar to the 1960 style, although there were changes from the middle of the front door forward. This was the last year for Virgil Exner's fins. Lighter weights, coupled with the smallest

engine offered in a Chrysler, helped the Newport win the 1961 Mobil Oil economy run.

CHRYSLER I.D. NUMBERS: Serial numbers were found on the left front hinge post. Engine numbers were located on the boss behind the water pump. [NEWPORT] Serial numbers began with 8113-100001 and up. Station wagons used numbers 8513-100001 and up. Engine numbers indicated the year, cubic inch displacement and date of manufacture only. They were not used for identification purposes. [WINDSOR] Windsor series serial numbers began with 8213-100001 and up. [NEW YORKER] Serial numbers began with 8313-100001 and up. Station wagons began with 8713-100001 and up. [300G] Serial numbers for Detroit-built cars began with 8413-100001 and up.

NEWPORT SERIES

Model No.	Body/ Style No.	Body Type & Seating	Factory Price	Shipping Weight	Prod. Total
RC1-L	813	4-dr Sed-6P	2964	3710	34,370
RC1-L	812	2-dr HT Cpe-6P	3025	3690	9,405
RC1-L	814	4-dr HT Sed-6P	3104	3730	7,789
RC1-L	815	2-dr Conv-6P	3442	3760	2,135
RC1-L	858	4-dr Sta Wag-6P	3541	4070	1,832
RC1-L	859	4-dr Sta Wag-9P	3622	4155	1,571

WINDSOR SERIES — (8-CYL) — The Windsor was upgraded in status in comparison to the 1960 version. It shared the same three body styles used on the longer wheelbase Saratoga series, which it effectively replaced. Styling features paralleled those found on the Newport, although additional standard features were available. They included a larger displacement engine, chrome drip rail moldings, seat side shields, full wheel covers and chrome upper door covers on the sedan.

WINDSOR SERIES

Model No.	Body/ Style No.	Body Type & Seating	Factory Price	Shipping Weight	Prod. Total
RC2-M	832	4-dr Sed-6P	3218	3730	10,239
RC2-M	822	2-dr HT Cpe-6P	3303	3710	2,941
RC2-M	824	4-dr HT Sed-6P	3367	3765	4,156

NEW YORKER SERIES — (8-CYL) — Minor face-lifting on the New Yorker followed the same pattern as changes in the shorter wheelbase Newports and Windsors. Side trim was kept to a minimum. The rear fender trim bars were now divided into two groups of five bars each. Side trim consisted of sill and wheelhouse moldings. Station wagons used the 1960 style rear quarter panels and taillamp design. The horizontal grille bars were divided by seven fine vertical bars in an unobtrusive manner. Many features were standard equipment on the New Yorker. Dual exhaust were optional except on the station wagons.

1961 Chrysler, New Yorker four-door hardtop station wagon, V-8

NEW YORKER SERIES

Model No.	Body/ Style No.	Body Type & Seating	Factory Price	Shipping Weight	Prod. Total
RC3-H	833	4-dr Sed-6P	4133	4055	9,984
RC3-H	832	2-dr HT Cpe-6P	4175	4065	2,541
RC3-H	834	4-dr HT Sed-6P	4261	4100	5,862
RC3-H	835	2-dr Conv-6P	4592	4070	576
RC3-H	878	4-dr Sta Wag-6P	4764	4425	676
RC3-H	879	4-dr Sta Wag-9P	4871	4455	760

300G SERIES — (8-CYL) — The 300G was still considered a part of the high-performance market by those who appreciated brute horsepower in a luxury automobile. Its styling mirrored the minor styling changes found in the other 1961 Chryslers. The grille insert was 300 through-and-through and the lower rear quarter panel molding and red-white-blue medallion remained for the fifth continuous model year. Ram manifolding (long-type) continued as standard fare. A few cars were built with three-speed standard shift. Some cars were built with a special "short-ram" high-output engine. These short rams look virtually identical to long rams on the outside, as the shortening was done to the effective length of the inside of the tubes.

300G SERIES

Model No.	Body/ Style No.	Body Type & Seating	Factory Price	Shipping Weight	Prod. Total
RC4-P	842	2-dr HT Cpe-5P	5411	4260	1,280
RC4-P	845	2-dr Conv-5P	5841	4315	337

1961 Chrysler, 300G two-door hardtop, V-8

NEWPORT ENGINE: V-8. Cast iron block. Overhead valve. Displacement: 361 cid. Bore and stroke: 4.125 x 3.375 inches. Brake hp: 265 at 4400 rpm. Compression ratio: 9.0:1. Five main bearings. Hydraulic valve lifters. Carburetor: Stromberg WWC-3188 two-barrel.

WINDSOR ENGINE: V-8. Cast iron block. Overhead valve. Displacement: 383 cid. Bore and stroke: 4.25 x 3.375 inches. Compression ratio: 10.0:1. Brake hp: 305 at 4800 rpm. Five main bearings. Hydraulic valve lifters. Carburetor: Carter BBD 2923SA two-barrel.

NEW YORKER ENGINE: V-8. Cast iron block. Overhead valve. Displacement: 413 cid. Bore and stroke: 4.188 x 3.75 inches. Brake hp: 350 at 4600 rpm. Compression ratio: 10.1:1. Carburetor: Carter AFB-3108S four-barrel.

300G ENGINE: V-8. Cast iron block. Overhead valve. Displacement: 413 cid. Bore and stroke: 4.188 x 3.75 inches. Brake hp: 375 at 5000 rpm. (400 at 5200 rpm optional.) Compression ratio: 10.1:1. Five main bearings. Hydraulic valve lifters. (Solid valve lifters on optional V-8.) Carburetors: Two Carter Type AFB Model 2903S four-barrel.

CHASSIS FEATURES: Wheelbase: (Newport and Windsor) 122 inches; (New Yorker and 300G) 126 inches. Overall length: (Newport and Windsor) 215 inches; (Newport station wagon) 216.1 inches; (New Yorker and 300G) 219.8 inches; (New Yorker station wagon) 220.1 inches. Tires: (Newport and Windsor) 8.00 x 14; (Newport station wagon) 8.50 x 14; (New Yorker) 8.50 x 14; (New Yorker station wagon) 9.00 x 14; (300G) 8.00 x 15.

OPTIONS: Power steering on Newport and Windsor ($108). TorqueFlite in Newport and Windsor ($227). Power brakes in Newport and Windsor ($44). Power windows, except standard in 300G ($108). Power seat ($102). Swivel seat in Newport convertible and New Yorkers except station wagons ($87). Heater ($102). Air conditioner, all except station wagons ($510). Air conditioner, in station wagons ($714). Golden Tone radio ($100). Golden Touch Tuner radio ($124). Power antenna ($26). Auto-Pilot, except in 300G ($86). Flitesweep deck lid, except station wagons and 300G ($43). Rear window defogger ($21). Sure Grip differential ($52). Left-hand outside remote mirror, in all except New Yorker ($18). Tinted glass ($43). Undercoating, standard on 300G ($18). Dual exhaust, New Yorkers except station wagons ($27). Closed crankcase vent system ($5).

HISTORICAL FOOTNOTES: Last year for Virgil Exner's finned look. Newport wins Mobil Gas Economy Run with an average just below 20 mpg. Lester L. Colbert resumed position as chairman of the board and Lynn Townsend became Chrysler president. Elwood Engel, former Ford design chief, was appointed to replace fired Exner as Chrysler chief designer. First year for the low-block 383-cid engine in a Chrysler.

1962 CHRYSLER

NEWPORT SERIES — (V-8) — The volume low-priced Chrysler continued with the same body styles found in 1961. While mechanical details were similar to its predecessor a minor face lift gave the car a distinctly different look. Gone forever were the Exner-inspired tailfins and the indented side body styling. The grille, headlamps, front bumper and parking lamps were essentially unchanged from their 1961 counterparts. The grille mesh was reminiscent of the 1960 Windsor and Saratoga series. Taillamps now wrapped over the de-finned, flattened rear fenders and a stainless steel trim piece ran from the front to the rear at mid-body height. A new aluminum-cased TorqueFlite transmission was the last to use a parking brake at the rear of the case. Lighter weight and improved engine efficiency accounted for an increase of seven percent in claimed fuel economy. All 1962 models, except for the New Yorker, used the 122-inch wheelbase.

1962 Chrysler, Newport four-door sedan, V-8

CHRYSLER I.D. NUMBERS: Serial numbers were found on the left front hinge post. Engine numbers were located on the boss behind the water pump. [NEWPORT] Newport serial numbers began with 8123-100001 and up while station wagon numbers began with 8523-10001 and up. [300 SPORT SERIES] Serial numbers for the Detroit-built cars began with 8223-100001 and up. The engine code began with the 'S' prefix, plus the two digit code signifying displacement and the date. [NEW YORKER] Detroit-built serial numbers began with 8323-100001 and up. Station wagons began with 8723-100001 and up. [300H SERIES] Serial numbers began with 8423-100001 and up. Chrysler engine numbers were stamped with a letter denoting the year code, plus two numbers denoting cid: [Newport/Sport 300] 38=383 and additional symbols signify month/day. [New Yorker] The engine prefix was S41. [300H] The engine code began with S41, then the date, plus a horsepower code. The date was given in numerical form, such as 11-12 = November 12. Chrysler engines no longer had a true serial identification number.

NEWPORT SERIES

Model No.	Body/ Style No.	Body Type & Seating	Factory Price	Shipping Weight	Prod. Total
SC1-L	813	4-dr Sed-6P	2964	3720	54,813
SC1-L	812	2-dr HT Cpe-6P	3027	3705	11,910
SC1-L	814	4-dr HT Sed-6P	3106	3735	8,712
SC1-L	815	2-dr Conv-6P	3399	3780	2,051
SC1-L	858	4-dr Sta Wag-6P	3478	4125	3,271
SC1-L	859	4-dr Sta Wag-9P	3586	4185	2,363

1962 Chrysler, 300 Sport Series two-door hardtop, V-8

300 SPORT SERIES — (V-8) — The Windsor name was dropped to make room for a Sport Series 300 line. Confusion resulted from this marketing move as buyers associated the 300 name with high-performance and high-cost. The exterior appearance of the hardtop (two-door) and the convertible were identical to the 300H Letter Car, except for hubcaps and the lack of a tiny 'H' on the rear deck. A four-door hardtop had never been offered in the Chrysler 300 Letter Car line. Even the grille, medallions and side trim were indistinguishable, at first glance, from the higher-priced, performance-oriented 300H. The Sport Series 300 interiors were upgraded versions of the low-line Newport series.

300 SPORT SERIES

Model No.	Body/ Style No.	Body Type & Seating	Factory Price	Shipping Weight	Prod. Total
SC2-M	823	4-dr Sed-6P	3258	3780	1,801
SC2-M	822	2-dr HT Cpe-6P	3323	3765	11,776
SC2-M	824	4-dr HT Sed-6P	3400	3610	10,030
SC2-M	825	2-dr Conv-6P	3883	3880	1,971

NEW YORKER SERIES — (8-CYL) — The New Yorker continued to use the long wheelbase chassis although it was available only in three body types, all with four doors. The New Yorker nameplate was found at the same location (near the parking lamp) as in 1961. The 10 bar rear fender trim continued on the rear quarters of New Yorkers, except the station wagon. The rear quarter panel on the station wagon was styled differently than sedan or hardtop models. The grille used the crossbar look, formerly found only on the 300 series.

1962 Chrysler, New Yorker four-door hardtop, V-8

NEW YORKER SERIES

Model No.	Body/Style No.	Body Type & Seating	Factory Price	Shipping Weight	Prod. Total
SC3-H	833	4-dr Sed-6P	4125	3950	12,056
SC3-H	834	4-dr HT Sed-6P	4263	3970	6,646
SC3-H	878	4-dr Sta Wag-6P	4766	4325	728
SC3-H	879	4-dr Sta Wag-9P	4873	4385	793

300H SERIES — (V-8) — The true high-performance 300 used the same series designation as the Sport Series 300, but serial number identification was different. Tan leather upholstery was standard, although special order colors were available. Both interiors and exteriors came with special colors in earlier years. A variety of high-performance engine options were available, although the inline, dual carbureted engine was standard. The 300H chassis was no longer shared with the New Yorker series, as with past models. Sales dropped dramatically for the Letter Cars this year, due mainly to the competition of the Sport Series 300, which offered nearly everything found on the 300H as standard or optional equipment.

1962 Chrysler, 300H two-door convertible, V-8

300H SERIES

Model No.	Body/Style No.	Body Type & Seating	Factory Price	Shipping Weight	Prod. Total
SC2-M	842	2-dr HT Cpe-5P	5090	4050	435
SC2-M	845	2-dr Conv-5P	5461	4105	123

NEWPORT ENGINE: V-8. Overhead valve. Cast iron block. Displacement: 361.8 cid. Bore and stroke: 4.125 x 3.375 inches. Compression ratio: 9.0:1. Brake hp: 265 at 4400 rpm. Five main bearings. Hydraulic valve lifters. Carburetor: Stromberg Type WWC3 two-barrel Model 201A.

300 SPORT ENGINE: V-8. Overhead valve. Cast iron block. Displacement: 383 cid. Bore and stroke: 4.25 x 3.375 inches. Compression ratio: 10.0:1. Brake hp: 305 at 4600 rpm. Five main bearings. Hydraulic valve lifters. Carburetor: Carter Type BBD two-barrel Model 3244S.

NEW YORKER ENGINE: V-8. Overhead valve. Cast iron block. Displacement: 413.3 cid. Bore and stroke: 4.188 x 3.75 inches. Compression ratio: 10.1:1. Brake hp: 340 at 4600 rpm. Five main bearings. Hydraulic valve lifters. Carburetor: Carter Type AFB four-barrel Model 3251S.

300H ENGINE: V-8. Overhead valve. Cast iron block. Displacement: 413.3 cid. Bore and stroke: 4.188 x 3.75 inches. Compression ratio: 10.1:1. Brake hp: 380 at 5200 rpm. Five main bearings. Solid valve lifters. Carburetor: Two Carter Type AFB four-barrel Model 3258S.

CHASSIS FEATURES: Wheelbase: (Newport/300 Sport Series/300H) 122 inches; (New Yorker) 126 inches. Overall length: (Newport/300 Sport Series/300H) 214.9 inches; (Newport station wagon) 216.4 inches; (New Yorker) 219.3 inches; (New Yorker station wagon) 220.4 inch-

es. Tires: (Newport and Sport Series 300) 8.00 x 14; (Newport station wagon) 8.50 x 14; (New Yorker) 8.50 x 14; (New Yorker station wagon) 9.00 x 14; (300H) 7.60 x 15.

OPTIONS: Power brakes ($48). Power steering ($108). Air conditioning ($510); same with groups 304 or 306 ($409). Dual Deluxe air conditioning ($714). Power radio antenna ($26). Auto-Pilot ($86). Rear window defogger ($21). Vacuum door locks ($56). Custom Conditionaire heater ($102). Left outside remote control mirror ($18). Power door locks ($56). Front power seat ($102). Rear shelf radio speaker ($17). Golden Tone radio ($93). Golden Touch Tone radio ($129). Tinted windshield ($29). Tinted glass, all windows ($43). Shaded backlight ($74). Newport full wheel covers ($19). Newport windshield washer ($14). Leather front bucket seats ($201). Vinyl trim in Newport ($121). Vinyl trim in New Yorker ($86). Vinyl trim in New Yorker four-door hardtop ($65). Variable speed windshield wipers ($6). Tailgate assist handle ($17). Padded steering wheel in Newport ($16). Electric clock in Newport and Sport 300 ($19). Undercoating ($18). Three-speed manual transmission with non-synchro first and floor shift was standard on Newport and Sport Series 300. Automatic transmission was standard with New Yorker and 300H. Optional automatic transmission ($227). V-8 413 cid/340 hp four-barrel carb engine ($162). V-8 413 cid/380 hp dual four-barrel carb engine ($486). V-8 413 cid/405 hp ram-induction engine. Positive traction rear axle ($52). Available rear axle gear ratios: 2.93:1; 3.23:1.

HISTORICAL FOOTNOTES: A 1962 Chrysler New Yorker won luxury class in the Mobil Gas Economy Run with slightly more than 18 mpg. No two-door model was offered in the Chrysler New Yorker series for the first time since the New York Special of 1938. Chrysler sales rose slightly more than 10 percent, but industry position remained unchanged (11th place).

1963 CHRYSLER

NEWPORT SERIES — (V-8) — A major, tasteful restyling of the entire 1963 Chrysler line used a semi-slab side look with a minimal use of trim. Hood, fenders and rear deck had a flat, broad look that contributed to the overall integrated styling theme. For the first time since its inception in the 1961 model year, the closed crankcase venting system became standard equipment across the board. The Newport was built on the 122-inch wheelbase, as were all other Chryslers this year. Headlamps reverted back to a more normal horizontal style. The grille theme continued the 300 crossbar look pioneered in 1957. Thin horizontal bright bars were placed in front of a blacked-out thin vertical bar background giving the car a broader, lower frontal appearance. Rear taillamps were mounted on pods on each side of the rear end. Chrysler included a five-year/50,000-mile warranty on all drivetrain parts. This policy helped Chrysler improve market penetration approximately 50 percent in a short period of time.

1963 Chrysler, Newport four-door sedan, V-8 (MC)

CHRYSLER I.D. NUMBERS: Serial numbers were found on the left front hinge post. Engine numbers were located on the boss behind the water pump. [NEWPORT SERIES] Serial numbers began with 813-100001 and up. Station wagons began with 8533-100001 and up. [300 SPORT SERIES] Detroit-built cars began with serial number 8233-100001 and up. Engine prefix was the letter 'T' [NEW YORKER SERIES] Detroit-built cars began with serial number 8333-100001 and up. Station wagons used serial numbers 8733-100001 and up. Engine prefix began with T-41 and then the date code as on previous series engines. [300J SERIES] Numbers began with 8433-100001 and up. Engine prefix was C300J and then a month, day, year code (i.e.: 11-10-62 denoted November 10, 1962, build date).

NEWPORT SERIES

Model No.	Body/ Style No.	Body Type & Seating	Factory Price	Shipping Weight	Prod. Total
TC1-L	813	4-dr Sed-6P	2964	3745	49,067
TC1-L	812	2-dr HT Cpe-6P	3027	3735	9,809
TC1-L	814	4-dr HT Sed-6P	3106	3775	8,437
TC1-L	815	2-dr Conv-6P	3399	3800	2,093
TC1-L	858	4-dr Sta Wag-6P	3478	4175	3,618
TC1-L	859	4-dr Sta Wag-9P	3586	4190	2,948

300 SPORT SERIES — (V-8) — The 300 Sport Series continued with the same body types as used in 1962. A later addition to the 300 lineup was the Pace Setter Series, introduced to commemorate the use of a 300 as the Pace Car for the Indianapolis 500 mile race. Pace Setter editions were identified by special interiors and a small checkered flag placed below the front fender 300 emblem. They had a square-shaped steering wheel, as opposed to the round steering wheel used in other Sport 300s. An option was full leather in cars with a bucket seat interior.

1963 Chrysler, 300 Sport Series two-door convertible, V-8 (IMS)

300 SPORT SERIES

Model No.	Body/ Style No.	Body Type & Seating	Factory Price	Shipping Weight	Prod. Total
TC2-M	822	2-dr HT Cpe-6P	3430	3765	9,423
TC2-M	823	4-dr Sed-6P	3765	3785	1,625
TC2-M	824	4-dr HT Sed-6P	3400	3790	9,915
TC2-M	825	2-dr Conv-6P	3790	3820	1,535
TC2-M	802	2-dr Pace Car HT	3769	3790	306
TC2-M	805	2-dr Pace Car Conv	4129	3840	1,861

Note 1: The four-door sedan referred to above was built as a Saratoga for the Canadian market, but counted in the plant as a 300.

NEW YORKER SERIES — (V-8) — The New Yorker displayed the crisp, new custom look emphasized in 1963 advertising. A thin beltline molding ran from front to rear and the unusual New Yorker trim bars were now found on the front fender, behind the wheel opening and below the New Yorker nameplate. The number of trim bars was reduced to six. Interiors featured deeply quilted, luxurious Jacquard fabrics and soft durable vinyl trim. The grille was divided into two halves and eggcrate style inserts, reminiscent of the earlier 1955 and 1956 Imperials, added to the custom look. Wheelbase this year matched the other less expensive lines wearing the Chrysler nameplates. A four-door hardtop Salon option was offered with a luxurious interior, vinyl roof and special side trim plus 'Salon' nameplates.

NEW YORKER SERIES

Model No.	Body/ Style No.	Body Type & Seating	Factory Price	Shipping Weight	Prod. Total
TC3-H	833	4-dr Sed-6P	3981	3910	14,884
TC3-H	834	4-dr HT Sed-6P	4118	3950	10,289
TC3-H	884	4-dr Salon-6P	5344	4290	593
TC3-H	878	4-dr Sta Wag-6P	4708	4350	950
TC3-H	879	4-dr Sta Wag-9P	4815	4370	1,244

300J SERIES — (V-8) — Available in two-door hardtop form only, the 300J continued Chrysler's image of providing the motoring public with a high-performance luxury automobile so synonymous with previous 300s. Leather interiors were standard and special 'J' medallions distinguished this car from the more common 300 Sport Series models. Heavy-duty torsion bars, shocks and springs, plus Ram-Tube induction manifolds were the main backbone of the 300J's image.

300J SERIES

Model No.	Body/ Style No.	Body Type & Seating	Factory Price	Shipping Weight	Prod. Total
TC2-M	842	2-dr HT Cpe-6P	5260	4000	400

NEWPORT ENGINE: V-8. Overhead valve. Cast iron block. Displacement: 361 cid. Bore and stroke: 4.12 x 3.38 inches. Compression ratio: 9.0:1. Brake hp: 265 at 4400 rpm. Five main bearings. Hydraulic valve lifters. Carburetor: Stromberg Type WWC-3 two-barrel Model 221.

300 SPORT ENGINE: V-8. Overhead valve. Cast iron block. Displacement: 383 cid. Bore and stroke: 4.25 x 3.375 inches. Compression ratio: 10.0:1. Brake hp: 305 at 4600 rpm. Five main bearings. Hydraulic valve lifters. Carburetor: Carter Type BBD two-barrel Model 3476S.

NEW YORKER ENGINE: V-8. Overhead valve. Cast iron block. Displacement: 413.8 cid. Bore and stroke: 4.188 x 3.75 inches. Compression ratio: 10.0:1. Brake hp: 340 at 4600 rpm. Five main bearings. Hydraulic valve lifters. Carburetor: Carter Type AFB four-barrel Model 3256S.

300J ENGINE: V-8. Overhead valve. Cast iron block. Displacement: 413.8 cid. Bore and stroke: 4.188 x 3.75 inches. Compression ratio: 10.0:1. Brake hp: 390 at 4800 rpm. Five main bearings. Solid valve lifters. Carburetor: Two Carter Type AFB four-barrel Model 3505S.

CHASSIS FEATURES: Wheelbase: (all) 122 inches. Overall length: (Newport station wagon) 219.4 inches; (New Yorker station wagon) 219.7 inches; (all other models) 215.3 inches. Front tread: (Newport and 300) 61 inches; (New Yorker) 59.7 inches. Rear tread: (Newport and 300) 59.7 inches; (New Yorker) 59.9 inches. Tires: (Newport and 300 Sport Series) 8.00 x 14; (New Yorker) 8.50 x 14; (300J) 7.60 x 15.

OPTIONS: Power brakes in Newport and Sport 300 ($48). Power steering in Newport and Sport 300 ($108). Dual air conditioning in Newport and Sport 300 ($612). Air conditioning with heater ($150). Power antenna, except station wagons ($26). Auto-Pilot ($86). Front console in 300 ($165). Rear window defogger ($21). Custom Conditionaire heater ($102). Left outside remote control mirror ($18). Station wagon two-tone paint ($20). Left or right power bucket seat ($93). Power door locks in four-door ($56). Power front bench seat ($102). Power windows ($108). Golden Tone radio ($93). Golden Touch Tune radio ($13). Rear speaker, except convertible and station wagon ($17). Pair of front seat belts ($24). Tailgate assist handle ($17). Tinted windshield ($29). All tinted glass ($43). Leather trim in 300 hardtop and convertible ($93). Undercoating ($18). Leather front bucket seats in 300 four-door hardtop ($201). Vinyl bucket seats in 300 four-door hardtop ($108). Vinyl bucket seats in New Yorker ($86). A three-speed manual transmission with non-synchro first and floor shift was standard on Newport and Sport 300s. Automatic transmission was standard on New Yorkers and 300Js. V-8 413 cid/360 hp twin four-barrel carb engine ($162). V-8 413 cid/365 hp twin four-barrel carb engine. V-8 426 cid/373 hp twin four-barrel carb engine. V-8 426 cid/415 hp short ram engine. V-8 426 cid/425 hp short ram engine. Positive traction rear axle ($52).

HISTORICAL FOOTNOTES: The 1963 Chryslers were introduced Sept. 26, 1962. Model year production peaked at 118,800 units. Calendar year sales of 116,040 cars was recorded. P.N. Buckminster was chief executive officer of the company this year. Chrysler held 11th rank in the auto industry this season. A Chrysler 300 'Pace Setter' convertible paced the 1963 Indianapolis 500 mile race.

1964 CHRYSLER

1964 Chrysler, Newport Town & Country four-door hardtop station wagon, V-8

NEWPORT SERIES — (V-8) — A minor face lift greeted 1964 Chrysler buyers on new model announcement day. The grille now had brightwork with an emblem centered on each of three cross-bars. Side trim had a wider look with a gentle thickening towards the rear. Taillamps were located at the extreme side of the rear end, but were rectangular in nature, versus the round 1963 housings. Station wagons continued to use the four-door pillarless body style introduced in 1960. Prices remained relatively constant with prior years.

1964 Chrysler, 300 two-door hardtop, V-8

CHRYSLER I.D. NUMBERS: Serial numbers were found on the left front hinge post. Engine numbers were located on the boss behind the water pump. [NEWPORT SERIES] Engine numbers used a V36 prefix plus the date of build. Serial numbers began with 8143-100001 and up. Station wagons used 8543-100001 and up. [300 SERIES] Serial numbers began with 8243-100001 and up. Prefix for the 300 began with V38 for the standard engines and V41 for the optional 413-cid engine. [NEW YORKER] Engine prefix was V41. Serial numbers began with 8343-100001 and up. Salons began with 8843-100001 and up while Town & Country station wagons used 8743-100001 and up. [300K SERIES] Serial numbers began with 8443-100001 and up. Engine numbers began with V41 and then the date code as before. 11-12 referred to November 12 production date. The letters HP were also stamped on the non-Ram-Tuned 300Ks. Ram-Tune inducted cars used a slightly different system. The prefix was C300K followed by the complete date (i.e.: 11-12-63).

NEWPORT SERIES

Model No.	Body/Style No.	Body Type & Seating	Factory Price	Shipping Weight	Prod. Total
VC1-L	813	4-dr Sed-6P	2901	3790	55,957
VC1-L	812	2-dr HT Cpe-6P	2962	3770	10,579
VC1-L	814	4-dr HT Sed-6P	3042	3810	9,710
VC1-L	815	2-dr Conv-6P	3334	3830	2,176
VC1-L	858	4-dr T&C Wag-6P	3414	4165	3,720
VC1-L	859	4-dr T&C Wag-9P	3521	4200	3,041

CHRYSLER 300 SERIES — (V-8) — This series dropped the 'Sport' designation used in earlier years. Silver anodized side trim was unique to the 300. A special 300 was introduced as a spring option. It included a silver exterior finish and black vinyl roof with black leather/vinyl interior. A star-shaped insignia was placed at the C-pillar on hardtops and the rear part of the front fender on convertibles. The insignia matched the style of the grille insert used on all 300s.

300 SERIES

Model No.	Body/Style No.	Body Type & Seating	Factory Price	Shipping Weight	Prod. Total
VC2-M	822	2-dr HT Cpe-6P	3443	3850	13,401
VC2-M	824	4-dr HT Sed-6P	3521	3865	11,460
VC2-M	825	2-dr Conv-6P	3803	4120	2,026
VC2-M	823	4-dr Sed-6P	3371	3875	N/A

1964 Chrysler, New Yorker four-door sedan, V-8

NEW YORKER SERIES — (V-8) — The New Yorker face lift paralleled changes seen throughout the 1964 Chrysler lineup. The eggcrate grille halves were dropped and a fine horizontal bar ensemble was placed within the cavity. The New Yorker Town & Country station wagon used the same side trim as the Newport Town & Country. The New Yorker Salon's base price made it the most expensive regular Chrysler model of the year. It carried virtually every available option, except dual unit air conditioning, adjustable steering wheel, Sure Grip differential and leather trim. The New Yorker script was placed low on the rear portion of the

front fender, except on the Salon, where a Salon script was set slightly higher on the fender.

1964 Chrysler, New Yorker four-door hardtop, V-8

NEW YORKER SERIES

Model No.	Body/Style No.	Body Type & Seating	Factory Price	Shipping Weight	Prod. Total
VC3-H	832	2-dr HT Cpe-6P	N/A	N/A	300
VC3-H	833	4-dr Sed-6P	3994	4015	15,443
VC3-H	834	4-dr HT Sed-6P	4131	4030	10,887
VC3-H	878	4-dr T&C Wag-6P	4721	4385	1,190
VC3-H	879	4-dr T&C Wag-9P	4828	4395	1,603
VC3-H	884	4-dr Salon-6P	5860	4280	1,621

Note 1: Some sources list production of four-door hardtop Salon as 1,748.

300K SERIES — (V-8) — The convertible returned to the Chrysler 300 Letter Car series lineup after a one year hiatus. Styling paralleled the regular 300 series, although interiors were more luxuriously detailed. A between-the-seat console was standard and leather trim was optional. A Ram-Tuned induction manifold setup was available as an option.

300K SERIES

Model No.	Body/Style No.	Body Type & Seating	Factory Price	Shipping Weight	Prod. Total
VC2-M	300842	2-dr HT Cpe-4P	4056	3965	3,022
VC2-M	300845	2-dr Conv-4P	4522	3990	625

NEWPORT ENGINE: V-8. Overhead valve. Cast iron block. Displacement: 360.8 cid. Bore and stroke: 4.125 x 3.375 inches. Compression ratio: 9.0:1. Brake hp: 265 at 4400 rpm. Five main bearings. Hydraulic valve lifters. Carburetor: Stromberg Type WWC-3 two-barrel Model 244.

1964 Chrysler, 300K two-door convertible, V-8

300 ENGINE: V-8. Overhead valve. Cast iron block. Displacement: 383 cid. Bore and stroke: 4.25 x 3.375 inches. Compression ratio: 10.0:1. Brake hp: 305 at 4600 rpm. Five main bearings. Hydraulic valve lifters. Carburetor: Carter Type BBD two-barrel Model 3685S.

NEW YORKER ENGINE: V-8. Overhead valve. Cast iron block. Displacement: 413.8 cid. Bore and stroke: 4.188 x 3.75 inches. Compression ratio: 10.0:1. Brake hp: 340 at 4600 rpm. Five main bearings. Hydraulic valve lifters. Carburetor: Carter Type AFB four-barrel Model 36155.

300K ENGINE: V-8. Overhead valve. Cast iron block. Displacement: 413.8 cid. Bore and stroke: 4.188 x 3.75 inches. Compression ratio: 10.1:1. Brake hp: 390 at 4800 rpm. Five main bearings. Solid valve lifters. Carburetor: Dual Carter Type AFB four-barrel Model 3614S.

CHASSIS FEATURES: Wheelbase (all series) 122 inches. Overall length: (Newport and 300) 215.3 inches; (Newport station wagon) 219.4 inches; (300J and New Yorker) 215.5 inches; (New Yorker station wagon) 219.7 inches. Tires: (Newport, 300, 300K) 8.00 x 14; (New Yorker) 8.50 x 14.

OPTIONS: Power steering in Newport and 300, standard in other ($108). Power brakes in Newport and 300 standard in others ($48). Power

windows, all models ($108). Six-Way power seat in Newport and New Yorker ($102). Power door locks in four-door styles ($56). Heater and defroster all models ($102). Air conditioning, all models ($510). Deluxe dual air conditioning, all except convertibles ($714). Golden Tone radio, all models ($93). AM/FM radio, all models ($157). Golden Touch Tuner radio, all models ($129). Center Console in all 300 models ($129). Leather trim in 300 and 300K ($94). Leather trim in New Yorker Salon ($72). Seat belts, all models ($7). Heavy-duty springs, shocks, sway bar and brakes ($36). Adjustable steering wheel, all models ($47). Undercoating, all models ($18). Tinted glass, all windows ($43). Three-speed manual floor mounted transmission with non-synchro first gear was standard on Newport and non-Letter Series Chrysler 300s. Automatic transmission was standard on New Yorker and 300K. Automatic transmission was optional on Newport and non-Letter 300 ($227). Close-ratio four-speed manual floor shift was optional ($227). V-8 413 cid/360 hp four-barrel carb engine on 300 and 300 J. ($43). V-8 413 cid/390 hp dual four-barrel Ram-Tuned induction engine ($375). Positive traction rear axle ($52). Available rear axle gear ratios: 3.23:1; 3.91:1; 2.76:1.

HISTORICAL FOOTNOTES: The 1964 Chryslers were introduced Sept. 20, 1963. Model year production peaked at 145,192 units. Calendar year production of 145,338 cars was recorded. This was the last year for the optional availability of the Ram-Tuned induction V-8. Chrysler sales rebounded by 11 percent, although the division remained the 11th ranked American automaker. Fifty experimental Chrysler gas turbine cars were provided to selected individuals for test driving and field evaluations under normal operating conditions. The majority of these unique automobiles were later destroyed, although several survive in private collections, museums and the Chrysler Historical Collection.

1965 CHRYSLER

1965 Chrysler, Newport four-door hardtop, V-8

NEWPORT SERIES — (V-8) — A major retooling effort coupled with a base price of less than $3,000 helped Chrysler achieve a banner year with sales rising about 55 percent over those of the previous year. Nearly half of all Chrysler sales were in the Newport series. Newports featured a boldly sculptured side panel that was outlined with stainless steel at the top beltline and again at a level slightly above wheel hub height. Both headlamps and taillights were inset from the outer edges of the fender line. The taillamps were set in a horizontally outlined panel above the rear bumper and below the deck lid. The dual headlamps were nestled within the grille area, which carried the same broad outlined look of the side panels. The grille insert was a fine, horizontal bar motif with a rectangular medallion set upright in the center. The new chassis used a two-inch longer wheelbase than previous Newports. A new, larger displacement engine was now featured as was a six-window sedan, which complemented the standard sedan. The common sedan outsold the new style by five-to-one.

CHRYSLER I.D. NUMBERS: [NEWPORT SERIES] A new serial number format was introduced. The location of the serial numbers and engine numbers was unchanged from previous series. Detroit-built cars used serial numbers with C153-100001 and up. Delaware-built cars used serial numbers C156-100001 and up. Newport station wagons built in Detroit used numbers C553-100001 and up and those built in Delaware used serial numbers beginning with C556-100001 and up. The engine prefix was 'A' for 1965 models. The engine displacement code followed and preceeded codes depicting month and date. A-383-9-12 can be identified as a 1965 Newport with a 383-cid engine built on Sept. 12 (of 1964). [300 SERIES] Serial numbers for Detroit-built cars began with C253-100001 and up. Delaware-built cars began with C256-100001 and up. Chrysler 300s with the standard 383-cid V-8 had

engine numbers with an A-383 prefix located on the front, right-hand side of the engine block. Chrysler 300s with the optional 413-cid V-8 had engine numbers with an A-413 prefix located on the top of the block, to the left of the water pump. [NEW YORKER] Detroit-built cars began with serial number C353-100001 and up and Delaware-built cars began with C356-100001 and up. Station wagons built in Detroit used C753-100001 and up and those built in Delaware used C756-100001 and up. Engine prefix was A-413. [300L SERIES] Detroit-built units began with C453-100001 and up while Delaware-built cars began with C456-100001 and up. Engine prefix began with A-413 and then the date code. 300L's also had an 'HP' stamped on the block, alongside the date code.

NEWPORT SERIES

Model No.	Body/ Style No.	Body Type & Seating	Factory Price	Shipping Weight	Prod. Total
AC1-L	C13	4-dr Sed-6P	2968	4025	61,054
AC1-L	C18	4-dr Twn Sed-6P	3100	4040	12,411
AC1-L	C12	2-dr HT Cpe-6P	3028	3985	23,655
AC1-L	C14	4-dr HT Sed-6P	3582	4040	17,062
AC1-L	C15	2-dr Conv-6P	3192	4070	3,192
AC1-L	C56	4-dr T&C Sta Wag-6P	3470	4400	4,683
AC1-L	C57	4-dr T&C Sta Wag-9P	3576	4465	3,738

1965 Chrysler, 300 two-door hardtop, V-8

300 SERIES — (V-8) — A star-shaped emblem continued to be used on the blacked-out grille bars as on the previous Chrysler 300 series. Headlamps were set within the outlined grille and were covered by a unique glass shield. Lower body trim differed from the Letter Car series 300. It had three uniquely stamped imprints at the forward edge of the trim, behind the wheelhouse opening. The interiors of the non-Letter Car 300s were upgraded over the Newport versions. The four-door sedan found in the 300 series was the six-window version.

300 SERIES

Model No.	Body/ Style No.	Body Type & Seating	Factory Price	Shipping Weight	Prod. Total
AC2-M	C22	2-dr HT Cpe-5P	3500	4115	11,621
AC2-M	C24	4-dr HT Sed-5P	3575	4210	12,452
AC2-M	C25	2-dr Conv-5P	3852	4185	1,418
AC2-M	C28	4-dr Sed-6P	3570	4160	2,187

1965 Chrysler, New Yorker two-door hardtop, V-8

NEW YORKER SERIES — (V-8) — The all-new New Yorker featured glass-covered headlamps like the 300 models. The grille had bold vertical and horizontal divisions, which gave the effect of rectangular spaces filled with finer bars. The grille was worthy of the New Yorker's status at the top-of-the-line. The station wagons now featured a center pillar like the sedans. The hardtop look in the station wagon was no longer available. Fender skirts were standard on all models in 1965. The New Yorker script was placed on the rear quarter panel. The New Yorker sedan was of the six-window Town Sedan-type.

NEW YORKER SERIES

Model No.	Body/ Style No.	Body Type & Seating	Factory Price	Shipping Weight	Prod. Total
AC3-H	C38	4-dr Sed-6P	4173	4245	16,339
AC3-H	C32	2-dr HT Cpe-6P	4098	4190	9,357
AC3-H	C34	4-dr HT Sed-6P	4173	4245	21,110
AC3-H	C76	4-dr T&C Wag-6P	4751	4645	1,368
AC3-H	C77	4-dr T&C Wag-9P	4856	4710	1,697

1965 Chrysler, 300L two-door hardtop, V-8

300L SERIES — (V-8) — This was the last year for the Letter Series high-performance specialty car. It closely resembled the standard 300. The letter 'L' in the center of the grille cross-bar lit-up when the lights were turned on. The 300L used high-performance tires and suspension. Coupled with a high-output 413-cid single carb engine, this set it apart from the regular 300. Styling touches used to distinguish the Chrysler 300L were a painted insert in the upper body molding and a damascened insert between the rear taillamps. There were also special interior appointments and appropriate Letter Series medallions.

300L SERIES

Model No.	Body/ Style No.	Body Type & Seating	Factory Price	Shipping Weight	Prod. Total
AC2-P	C42	2-dr HT Cpe-5P	4090	4225	2,405
AC2-P	C45	2-dr Conv-5P	4545	4155	440

NEWPORT ENGINE: V-8. Overhead valve. Cast iron block. Displacement: 383 cid. Bore and stroke: 4.25 x 3.375 inches. Compression ratio: 9.2:1. Brake hp: 270 at 4400 rpm. Five main bearings. Hydraulic valve lifters. Carburetor: Carter Type BBD two-barrel Model 3849S.

300 ENGINE: V-8. Overhead valve. Cast iron block. Displacement: 383 cid. Bore and stroke: 4.25 x 3.375 inches. Compression ratio: 10.0:1. Brake hp: 315 at 4400 rpm. Five main bearings. Hydraulic valve lifters. Carburetor: Carter Type AFB four-barrel Model 3855S.

NEW YORKER ENGINE: V-8. Overhead valve. Cast iron block. Displacement: 413.8 cid. Bore and stroke: 4.188 x 3.75 inches. Compression ratio: 10.0:1. Brake hp: 340 at 4600 rpm. Five main bearings. Hydraulic valve lifters. Carburetor: Carter Type AFB four-barrel Model 3858S.

300L ENGINE: V-8. Overhead valve. Cast iron block. Displacement: 413.8 cid. Bore and stroke: 4.188 x 3.75 inches. Compression ratio: 10.0:1. Brake hp: 360 at 4800 rpm. Five main bearings. Hydraulic valve lifters. Carburetor: Carter Type AFB four-barrel Model 3880S.

CHASSIS FEATURES: Wheelbase: (Newport, 300, New Yorker) 124 inches; (Town & Country station wagon) 121 inches. Overall length: (Newport, 300, New Yorker) 218.2 inches; (Town & Country station wagon) 218.4 inches. Tires: (Newport, 300) 8.25 x 14; (New Yorker, 300L, Town & Country) 8.55 x 14.

OPTIONS: Power steering (Newport, 300). Power brakes (Newport, 300). Power windows. Power seat. Reclining bucket seats. Power door locks. Heater and defroster. Air conditioner (dual air conditioning on all except convertible). Golden Tone radio. AM/FM radio. Golden Touch tuner. Rear seat speaker. Console (300). Seat belts. Heavy-duty springs, shocks, sway bar and brakes (300). Adjustable steering wheel. Undercoating. Tinted glass. Day/Night rearview mirror. Remote control mirror. Three-speed manual transmission was standard in Newport and non-letter 300. Automatic transmission was standard in New Yorker and 300L models. Automatic transmission was optional in Newport and non-letter 300s. Automatic transmission column shift controls replaced push-buttons this year. Four-speed manual floor shift transmission was optional in Newports, 300s and 300Ls. V-8 383 cid/315 hp four-barrel carb engine in Newports. V-8 413 cid/360 hp four-barrel carb engine in 300s and New Yorkers. Positive traction rear axle was optional in all models at extra cost.

HISTORICAL FOOTNOTES: Last year for Letter Series 300s. Chrysler built more than 200,000 cars for the first time ever. Last year for the 413-cid engine.

1966 CHRYSLER

1966 Chrysler, Newport two-door convertible, V-8

NEWPORT — (V-8) — The Newport, for 1966, continued as the Chrysler price leader with minimal styling changes. There were the usual cosmetic touches to the grille and rear deck area. The lower trim molding had a painted insert, which ran forward from the rear bumper to just ahead of the front door hinge post. From there a solid, non-painted trim piece continued further forward. Fender skirts were a standard item on all body styles. Nameplates were placed on the rear quarter panels. The six-window sedan was in its second and last year of production, as sales slid nearly 25 percent from 1965. The station wagon continued with its sedan look but used a shorter chassis. Overall, Chrysler sales rose more than 14 percent. A Cleaner Air Package was available for emission control and a shoulder harness was a new safety option.

CHRYSLER I.D. NUMBERS: Serial numbers and engine numbers were located in the usual positions. Serial numbers now included a code that revealed the body styles, as follows: 23=two-door hardtop; 41=four-door sedan; 42=six-window four-door sedan; 27=convertible; 45=six-passenger station wagon and 46=nine-passenger station wagon. The type of engine was designated by an alphabetical code as follows: 'G' = 383-cid V-8; 'J' = 440-cid V-8. A '6' was the next symbol and designated the 1966 model year. Numerical codes designated the assembly plant, as follows: '3' = Detroit and '6' = Delaware. The last six symbols were the sequential manufacturing number. Engine numbers had a 'B' prefix and then three numbers designating displacement as in previous years. [NEWPORT SERIES] Newports built in Detroit used serial numbers CL23G63-100001 and up and Delaware-built cars used serial numbers CL23G66-100001 and up. [300 SERIES] 300 serial numbers were assigned in a similar fashion to the Newport series except that the prefix was 'CM' rather than 'CL'. CM23J66-100001 and up would identify a 1966 Chrysler 300 two-door hardtop with the 440-cid engine built in Delaware. [NEW YORKER] Detroit-built serial numbers for sedans were CH42J63-100001 and up while Delaware-built sedans began with CH42J66-100001 and up. Engine prefix was B-440 and then the date code as in previous years.

NEWPORT SERIES

Model No.	Body/ Style No.	Body Type & Seating	Factory Price	Shipping Weight	Prod. Total
BC1-L	CL41	4-dr Sed-6P	3474	3875	74,964
BC1-L	CL42	4-dr Twn Sed-6P	3605	3910	9,432
BC1-L	CL23	2-dr HT Cpe-6P	3534	3845	37,622
BC1-L	CL43	4-dr HT Sed-6P	3612	4010	24,966
BC1-L	CL27	2-dr Conv-6P	3898	4020	3,085
BC1-L	CL45	4-dr T&C Wag-6P	4177	4370	9,035
BC1-L	CL46	4-dr T&C Wag-9P	4283	4550	8,567

300 SERIES — (V-8) — The face lift of the design introduced in 1965 was limited to trim alterations, plus minor changes to the front and rear facades. The glass covered headlamps and the cross-bar grille motif were dropped in favor of a more contemporary look. Two decorative trim pieces were added to each front fender, behind the wheelhouse opening, as a styling flair. Bucket seats were standard on this model. The 300 offered an optional engine for the performance enthusiast.

1966 Chrysler, 300 two-door hardtop, V-8

300 SERIES

Model No.	Body/ Style No.	Body Type & Seating	Factory Price	Shipping Weight	Prod. Total
BC2-M	CM23	2-dr HT Cpe-5P	4005	3940	24,103
BC2-M	CM43	4-dr HT Sed-5P	4081	4000	20,642
BC2-M	CM27	2-dr Conv-5P	4358	4015	2,500
BC2-M	CM41	4-dr Sed-6P	N/A	N/A	2,353

Note: Style CM41 was probably built for Canadian market and called a Saratoga.

NEW YORKER SERIES

Model No.	Body/ Style No.	Body Type & Seating	Factory Price	Shipping Weight	Prod. Total
BC3-H	CH42	4-dr Sed-6P	4192	4110	13,025
BC3-H	CH23	2-dr HT Cpe-6P	4248	4095	7,955
BC3-H	CH43	4-dr HT Sed-6P	4324	4140	26,599

NEW YORKER SERIES — (V-8) — The New Yorker continued as the high-line Chrysler series. An optional high-performance engine was available. New Yorker styling was a gentle face lift of 1965 Chrysler styling. New Yorker medallions were located just behind the front wheelhouse opening and above the lower trim molding. Headlamps were located at the outer edge of the grille cavity within a chromed, recessed bezel. This was the last year for the six-window Town Sedan.

1966 Chrysler, New Yorker four-door hardtop, V-8

NEWPORT ENGINE: V-8. Overhead valve. Cast iron block. Displacement: 383 cid. Bore and stroke: 4.25 x 3.375 inches. Compression: 9.2:1. Brake hp: 270 at 4400 rpm. Five main bearings. Hydraulic valve lifters. Carburetion: Canter Type BBD two-barrel Model 4125S.

300 ENGINE: V-8. Overhead valve. Cast iron block. Displacement: 383 cid. Bore and stroke: 4.25 x 3.375 inches. Compression ratio: 10.1:1. Brake hp: 325 at 4800 rpm. Five main bearings. Hydraulic valve lifters. Carburetor: Carter Type AFB four-barrel Model 4130S.

NEW YORKER ENGINE: V-8. Overhead valve. Cast iron block. Displacement: 440 cid. Bore and stroke: 4.326 x 3.75 inches. Compression ratio: 10.1:1. Brake hp: 350 at 4400 rpm. Five main bearings. Hydraulic valve lifters. Carburetor: Carter Type AFB four-barrel Model 4131S.

CHASSIS FEATURES: Wheelbase: (passenger cars) 124 inches; (station wagons) 121 inches. Overall length: (passenger cars) 219 inches; (station wagons) 219.6 inches. Tires: (Newport) 8.25 x 14; (300, New Yorker, station wagons) 8.55 x 14.

OPTIONS: Power steering. Power brakes. Power windows. Power seat. Power door locks. Heater and defroster. Air conditioner (dual air conditioning on all except convertible). Golden Tone radio. AM/FM radio. Golden Touch Tuner. Rear seat speaker. Console (300). Seat belts. Heavy-duty springs, shocks, sway bar and brakes. Adjustable steering wheel. Undercoating. Tinted glass. Day/night mirror. Remote control mirror.

White sidewall tires. Front disc brakes. Three-speed manual transmission was standard in the Newport and 300 models. Automatic transmission was standard in New Yorker models. Automatic transmission was optional in the Newport and 300 models. Four-speed manual floor shift transmission was optional in 300 models. V-8 383 cid/325 hp four-barrel carb engine in Newport. V-8 440 cid/365 hp four-barrel carb engine in all models. Positive traction rear axle was optional in all models.

HISTORICAL FOOTNOTES: The variety of Chrysler offerings was reduced from the 1965 model lineup. Sales rose more than 12 percent. Cleaner Air Package offered for emission control. Six-window sedan was the only sedan available in the New Yorker series. This was the first year for the 440-cid engine.

1967 CHRYSLER

1967 Chrysler, Newport Custom two-door hardtop, V-8

NEWPORT SERIES — (V-8) — In 1967, the Newport series was marketed in standard and slightly upgraded Custom trim. The low-line Newport had a major face lift consisting of the customary changes to the grille, rear deck and side body panels. The six-window Town Sedan was no longer provided. The two-door hardtop had a redesigned roof with a convertible-like look. Lower sill moldings were the only trim on the base Newport. This model had an exclusive taillamp treatment with a tiered effect. A thin, horizontal bar on the rear deck lid was the only vestigial indication of the side-to-side taillamp ensemble seen in previous years. Standard equipment included all federal safety features plus carpeting; front and rear ashtrays; three-speed wipers; electric windshield washers; trip odometer; cigar lighter; glovebox with three-cup tray; secret compartment; center panel convenience drawer; brake warning system; front foam cushion with center folding armrest; heater and defroster; and 383-cid two-barrel V-8. The convertible had front and rear foam seat cushion and a glass rear window. Hardtop styles featured Flow-Thru ventilation and rear pillar interior courtesy lamps.

1967 Chrysler, 300 two-door hardtop, V-8

CHRYSLER I.D. NUMBERS: [Newport] The numbering system and code locations were the same as for previous models. The first four symbols designated the Body/Style Number using the codes reflected in the second column of the charts below. The first symbol designated the engine and was 'G' for the 383-cid V-8. The sixth symbol designated the model year and was a '7' for 1967. The seventh symbol designated manufacturing plant: '3' = Detroit; '6' = Delaware. The following group of six symbols was the sequential unit production number beginning with 100001 at each assembly plant. [Newport Custom] The first two symbols were 'CL' to indicate Chrysler Newport Custom series. Additional coding was the same as on base Newports. The letter 'H' as the fifth symbol indicated the attachment of the optional high-performance 383-cid V-8 engine. [300] The first two symbols were 'CM' to indicate Chrysler 300 series. Additional coding followed the same system utilized on Newports and Newport Customs. The letter 'K' as the fifth symbol indicated the attachment of the standard 440 cid/350 hp V-8; the letter 'L' indicated attachment of the optional 440 cid/375 hp V-8. [New Yorker] The first two symbols were 'CH' to indicate Chrysler New Yorker series. Additional

coding followed the same system utilized on other series. The letter 'K' as the fifth symbol indicated attachment of the standard 440 cid/350 hp V-8; the letter 'E' indicated attachment of the optional 440 cid/375 hp V-8.

NEWPORT SERIES

Model No.	Body/ Style No.	Body Type & Seating	Factory Price	Shipping Weight	Prod. Total
CC1-E	CE41	4-dr Sed-6P	3579	3950	48,945
CC1-E	CD23	2-dr HT Cpe-6P	3639	3925	26,583
CC1-E	CD43	4-dr HT Sed-6P	3716	3985	14,247
CC1-E	CE27	2-dr Conv-6P	4003	3975	2,891
CC1-E	CE45	4-dr T&C Wag-6P	4286	4500	7,183
CC1-E	CE46	4-dr T&C Wag-9P	4390	4555	7,520

NEWPORT CUSTOM SERIES — (V-8) — Upgraded upholstery options and a change in lower body moldings set the Newport Custom apart from its lower priced brethren. Fender skirts were standard equipment on the Newport Custom, as on all 1967 Chryslers. Only three body styles were offered in this series. Newport Customs came with all features found on or in base Newports, plus front bumper reveal moldings; front and rear foam seat cushions; closed crankcase ventilation system and, on the four-door sedan, bright upper door moldings and seat side shields.

NEWPORT CUSTOM SERIES

Model No.	Body/ Style No.	Body Type & Seating	Factory Price	Shipping Weight	Prod. Total
CC1-L	CL41	4-dr Sed-6P	3767	3980	23,101
CC1-L	CL23	2-dr HT Cpe-6P	3827	3940	14,193
CC1-L	CL43	4-dr HT Sed-6P	3905	4000	12,728

300 SERIES — (V-8) — The Chrysler 300 series was further upgraded in comparison to the Newport Custom. Unique to the 300 was the rear end assembly, including deck lid, rear fender quarter panels and rear bumper. Taillamps were located at the extreme end of the rear fender and sloped from deck level down to bumper height. The back-up lamps were set into the bumper, below the taillamps, in a similar form. The effect was pleasing and smooth. The front grille was in the style of previous 300 series models, with the usual cross-bar division within the grille cavity. Hubcaps with small spinners were an added touch. Standard equipment on 300 models included all features found on Newport Custom, plus bright interior garnish moldings; TorqueFlite automatic transmission; bucket seats with center armrest; lower door trim carpet panels; carpeted bucket seatbacks; left-hand ashtray; Deluxe spinner wheel covers (as described above); 8.55 x 14 black sidewall tires and 440-cid four-barrel V-8 powerplant.

CHRYSLER 300 SERIES

Model No.	Body/ Style No.	Body Type & Seating	Factory Price	Shipping Weight	Prod. Total
CC2-M	CM23	2-dr HT Cpe-5P	4134	4075	11,556
CC2-M	CM43	4-dr HT Sed-5P	4210	4140	8,744
CC2-M	CM27	2-dr Conv-5P	4487	4110	1,594

1967 Chrysler, New Yorker four-door hardtop, V-8

NEW YORKER SERIES — (V-8) — New Yorker series bodies differed from Newports and 300s in the style of the rear taillamps and rear quarter panels. Safety features included reduced glare windshield wiper arms and blades, double ball joint mirror mount and cushioned instrument panels and visors. The instrument panel was symmetrical and anchored by air conditioner vents at the extreme ends. Lights, to indicate low brake hydraulic pressure, turn signals, coolant temperature, high beam operation, and oil pressure, were placed on a horizontal plane above the speedometer assembly and below the cushioned upper dash. The front fenders differed from the other series by using parking lamp housings, in line with the grille, at the extreme forward position. The rear taillamps wrapped around the rear fenders. Standard equipment included all items found on Chrysler 300s, plus power brakes; undercoating; hood pad; light package; clock; bright upper door and front bumper reveal moldings; walnut appliques; power steering; wraparound taillights; front and rear center armrests; cloth and vinyl bench seats; glovebox, twin ashtray, map, courtesy and trunk lights; carpeted trunk; fender mounted turn signals; and Deluxe steering wheel.

NEW YORKER SERIES

Model No.	Body/ Style No.	Body Type & Seating	Factory Price	Shipping Weight	Prod. Total
CC3-H	CH41	4-dr Sed-6P	4299	4190	10,907
CC3-H	CH23	2-dr HT Cpe-6P	4355	4175	6,885
CC3-H	CH43	4-dr HT Sed-6P	4430	4245	21,665

NEWPORT/NEWPORT CUSTOM ENGINE: V-8. Overhead valve. Cast iron block. Displacement: 383 cid. Bore and stroke: 4.25 x 3.375 inches. Compression ratio: 9.2:1. Brake hp: 270 at 4400 rpm. Five main bearings. Hydraulic valve lifters. Carburetor: Carter Type BBD two-barrel Model 4296S.

CHRYSLER 300/NEW YORKER ENGINE: V-8. Overhead valve. Cast iron block. Displacement: 440.7 cid. Bore and stroke: 4.326 x 3.75 inches. Compression ratio: 10.1:1. Brake hp: 350 at 4400 rpm. Five main bearings. Hydraulic valve lifters. Carburetor: Holley four-barrel Model R-3667A.

CHASSIS FEATURES: Wheelbase: (passenger cars) 124 inches; (station wagons) 122 inches. Overall length: (Newport, Newport Custom, New Yorker) 219.3 inches; (Chrysler 300) 223.5 inches; (Town & Country) 220.3 inches. Tires: (Newport) 8.25 x 14; (Town & Country) 8.85 x 14; (Chrysler 300 and New Yorker) 8.55 x 14.

OPTIONS: Power brakes ($47). Power steering ($107). Air conditioning ($406). Dual Unit air conditioning ($605). Auto-Pilot ($84). Automatic headlamp dimmer ($45). Credit for vinyl bench seats in Chrysler 300 ($82). Disc brakes ($70). Leather bucket seats in Chrysler 300 ($129). Electric clock ($19). Rear window defogger ($21). Single head rests ($21). Town & Country roof luggage rack ($97). Two-tone paint ($26). Power antenna ($25). Power door locks, two-doors ($37). Power door locks, four-doors ($55). Six-Way power bench seat ($100). Six-Way left-hand bucket or split-type seats ($91). Six-Way bucket or split-type seats, pair ($183). Power trunk release ($11). Power vent windows ($53). Power windows ($106). Golden Tone AM/FM radio ($154). Golden Tone radio ($91). Golden Touch Tuner AM/FM radio ($186). Rear reverberator speaker ($32). Right-hand recliner seat in Newport and 300 ($32). All glass tinted ($42). Three-speed manual transmission was standard on Newport and Newport Custom. Automatic transmission was standard on other Chrysler models. Automatic transmission was optional on Newport and Newport Custom ($222). Newport V-8 383 cid/325 hp four-barrel carb engine ($34.50). Newport V-8 440 cid/375 hp four-barrel carb 'TNT' engine ($198.35). Town & Country V-8 440 cid/375 hp four-barrel carb 'TNT' engine ($164). New Yorker/300 V-8 440 cid/375 hp four-barrel carb 'TNT' engine ($79.40). Positive traction rear axle ($50.70). Heavy-duty positive traction rear axle for Chrysler 300 only ($140.65). Heavy-duty air cleaner ($25).

HISTORICAL FOOTNOTES: The 1967 Chryslers were introduced Sept. 29, 1966. Model year production peaked at 218,716 units. Calendar year sales of 206,974 cars was recorded. G.E. White was the chief executive officer of the company this year. Virgil Boyd was promoted to the presidency of Chrysler Corp. effective Jan. 1, 1967. Sales of Chrysler Division models, excluding Imperial, slipped by 10.9 percent during calendar year 1967. Options and accessories with low installation rates included: movable-type steering column (4.8 percent); disc brakes (6.2 percent); power side windows (19.8 percent); power tailgate window (7.4 percent); dual exhaust (2 8 percent); limited slip differential (11.4 percent) and Auto-Pilot (5.0 percent). Bucket seats were installed in 13.2 percent of all 1967 Chryslers.

1968 CHRYSLER

1968 Chrysler, Newport two-door hardtop (with Sports Grain option), V-8

NEWPORT SERIES — (V-8)

Front bumpers, grilles and rear end treatments were restyled for 1968. The Newport had a V-shaped, mesh-type grille insert with horizontal highlight moldings running between the four beam headlights. A vertical Chrysler badge was set into its center and Chrysler block lettering appeared at the edge of the hood. An indented, horizontal panel at the rear of the car stretched full-width, above the bumper, and housed a large taillamp at each end. Small, square, side marker lamps on the rear fenders were an all-new 1968 feature required by federal law. Standard equipment on base Newports included all Chrysler safety features; carpeting; dual front and rear ashtrays; trip odometer; cigar lighter; glovebox with three-cup tray and secret compartment; center panel convenience drawer with coin sorter; heater and defroster; cleaner air systems; exhaust emission controls; torsion air suspension; 8.55 x 14 blackwall tires; and a 383-cid two-barrel V-8. Hardtops had rear pillar lamps and convertibles had all-vinyl bench seats with a front center armrest. Town & Country station wagons had all these features plus lighting group; bright upper door moldings and seat side shields; power brakes; power steering; foam seat cushions; three-speed wipers; Deluxe wheel covers; TorqueFlite transmission; time delay ignition light switch; power tailgate window; all-vinyl bench seats with front center armrests; and simulated woodgrained exterior body paneling. Three-seat station wagons had a rear step/pad bumper guard. Two-seat station wagons had lockable hidden storage compartments. Buyers were offered a choice of 8.85 x 14 or 8.85 x 15 black sidewall tires. All Newports came with rear wheel opening skirts. Controls for the Auto-Pilot speed control option were now integral with the turn signal lever, on cars so-equipped. An attractive option, made available in the spring, was woodgrained exterior side body paneling for Newport convertibles and two-door hardtops. Chrysler's new styling was well received and sales climbed by nearly 10 percent over 1967.

CHRYSLER I.D. NUMBERS: Serial numbers were now located on a plate attached to the left side of the instrument panel and visible through the windshield. Serial numbers consisted of a seven symbol prefix, plus production sequence code. The first symbol 'C' = Chrysler Division. [NEWPORT] The second symbol indicated series and was an 'E' for base Newports. The third and fourth symbols indicated a Body/Style code that corresponded to the numerical portion of the codes in the second column of the chart below. The fifth symbol was an engine code as follows: 'G' = 383-cid V-8; 'H' = high-performance 383-cid V-8; 'K' = 440-cid V-8; 'L' = high-performance 440-cid V-8 and 'M' = special order V-8. The sixth symbol was a '8' indicating 1968 model year. The seventh symbol indicated the assembly plant, as follows: 'C' = Detroit and 'F' = Newark. (All station wagons and convertibles were assembled in Detroit at the Jefferson Avenue plant.) The production sequence code followed and began with 100001 at each factory. Engine numbers were now stamped on the left rear portion of the block near the oil pump flange. They took the form PT44021870002 with this specific code designating a Trenton (engine) plant 440-cid V-8 built on July 24, 1967, and second sequentially. The symbols 'PT' are the factory code; the symbols '440' indicate 440-cid V-8 and the symbols 2187 are the day production code. [NEWPORT CUSTOM] The numbering system and code locations were the same as for base Newport models with the second symbol changed to an 'L' to indicate a Newport Custom model. The code 'G' 383-cid two-barrel V-8 was the standard engine for 1968 Chrysler Newport Customs. [CHRYSLER 300] The numbering system and code locations were the same as for previous models with the second symbol changed to an 'M' to indicate a Chrysler 300 model. The code 'K' 440-cid V-8 was the standard engine for 1968 Chrysler 300s. [NEW YORKER] The numbering system and code locations were the same as for previous models with the second symbol changed to an 'H' to indicate a Chrysler New Yorker. The code 'K' 440-cid V-8 was the base engine for 1968 New Yorkers.

NEWPORT SERIES

Model No.	Body/ Style No.	Body Type & Seating	Factory Price	Shipping Weight	Prod. Total
DC1-E	CE41	4-dr Sed-6P	3727	3850	61,436
DC1-E	CE23	2-dr HT Cpe-6P	3787	3840	36,768
DC1-E	CE43	4-dr HT Sed-6P	3865	3865	20,191
DC1-E	CE27	2-dr Conv-6P	4125	3910	2,847
DC1-E	CE45	4-dr T&C Wag-6P	4286	4500	9,908
DC1-E	CE46	4-dr T&C Wag-9P	4390	4555	12,233

NEWPORT CUSTOM SERIES — (V-8) — The Newport Custom models were dressed-up versions of the base Newport offerings, available in a more limited range of body styles. Standard equipment included all items found on base Newports, plus bright seat side shields; front and rear foam seat cushions; bench seats with front center armrest; and bright, upper door moldings on the Custom four-door sedan. As on base Newport models, the center section of the redesigned grille met the forward edge of the hood and then faded inward, as it approached the deeply inset four-beam headlamps. The rear deck lid panel ensemble for 1968 had the same styling motifs found on the front of the car. The horizontal, rectangular taillamps pointed towards the outer edge of the fenders, with a raised section of the taillamp outline continuing towards the center of the panel. Whereas the base models carried their identification script at

the rear of the back fenders, the Custom editions wore script nameplates high on the front fenders, near the sides of the cowl. Newport Customs also had the federally required side marker lamps this season.

NEWPORT CUSTOM SERIES

Model No.	Body/ Style No.	Body Type & Seating	Factory Price	Shipping Weight	Prod. Total
DC1-L	CL41	4-dr Sed-6P	3914	3865	16,915
DC1-L	CL23	2-dr HT Cpe-6P	3973	3860	10,341
DC1-L	CL43	4-dr HT Sed-6P	4052	3890	11,460

CHRYSLER 300 SERIES — (V-8) — The Chrysler 300 models were distinguished by special grille, front bumper and body decoration treatments. The grille featured a blacked-out finish highlighted by a full-width horizontal bar design and incorporated hidden headlights. The front bumper had long, horizontal air slots on either side of the center license plate indentation. Bright body underscores ran between the wheel openings and had long, rear extensions. Five short, slanting slashes of chrome were placed behind the front wheel openings. Three-Hundred lettering appeared on the trailing sides of the rear fender, directly in front of circular side marker lamps. New, cast metal 'road wheels' were an option introduced for Chrysler 300s this season. Standard equipment included all items found on Newport Customs, plus a 70-amp battery; TorqueFlite automatic transmission; Deluxe wheel covers; all-vinyl bucket seats with center cushion armrest; bright metal horn blow ring; and the previously mentioned hidden headlights. The base powerplant for Chrysler 300s was a 440-cid four-barrel carb V-8. The word Chrysler was placed on the right-hand front edge of the hood on 300 models, instead of at the center.

1968 Chrysler, 300 two-door hardtop, V-8

CHRYSLER 300 SERIES

Model No.	Body/ Style No.	Body Type & Seating	Factory Price	Shipping Weight	Prod. Total
DC2-M	CM23	2-dr HT Cpe-5P	4209	3985	16,953
DC2-M	CM43	4-dr HT Sed-5P	4285	4015	15,507
DC2-M	CM27	2-dr Conv-5P	4536	4050	2,161

NEW YORKER SERIES — (V-8) — The New Yorker featured a third style of frontal design. The grille insert was V-shaped and had a grid-type pattern highlighted by a horizontal center blade stretching between quad headlamps. New Yorker headlights, however, were housed in distinctive square bezels. The front bumper and hood lettering treatments were similar to the Newport style. Wide, bright metal panels underscored the rocker sill and extended to the fender skirts and lower rear quarter panels. The deck lid latch panel was beautified with a grid pattern rear grille that covered the recessed taillights. On the sedan, a New Yorker script was placed low on the front fenders, behind the wheel opening. Similar signatures appeared on the rear roof pillars of hardtops in place of the front fender script. Standard equipment was of the Chrysler 300 level, with the following additions or variations: light group; electric clock; remote control left-hand outside rearview mirror; power brakes; power steering; Deluxe steering wheel with horn bars; undercoating; hood insulation pad; three-speed wipers; time delay ignition switch light; pleated cloth and vinyl bench seats with center armrest; body accent stripes; fendertop turn indicator lamps; textured vinyl roof pillar appliques on four-door hardtops; and bright upper door moldings on four-door sedans.

NEW YORKER SERIES

Model No.	Body/ Style No.	Body Type & Seating	Factory Price	Shipping Weight	Prod. Total
DC3-H	CH41	4-dr Sed-6P	4459	4055	13,092
DC3-H	CH23	2-dr HT Cpe-6P	4516	4060	8,060
DC3-H	CH43	4-dr HT Sed-6P	4592	4090	26,991

NEWPORT/NEWPORT CUSTOM ENGINE: V-8. Overhead valve. Cast iron block. Displacement: 383 cid. Bore and stroke: 4.25 x 3.375 inches. Compression ratio: 9.2:1. Brake hp: 290 at 4400 rpm. Five main bearings. Hydraulic valve lifters. Carburetor: Carter Type BBD two-barrel Model 4422S.

1968 Chrysler, New Yorker two-door hardtop, V-8

CHRYSLER 300/NEW YORKER ENGINE: V-8. Overhead valve. Cast iron block. Displacement: 440 cid. Bore and stroke: 4.326 x 3.75 inches. Compression ratio: 10.1:1. Brake hp: 350 at 4400 rpm. Five main bearings. Hydraulic four-barrel Model R-3918A)

CHASSIS FEATURES: Wheelbase (station wagons) 122 inches; (passenger cars) 124 inches. Overall length: (nine-passenger station wagons) 220.3 inches; (six-passenger station wagons) 219.5 inches; (passenger cars) 219.2 inches. Front tread: (all models) 62 inches. Rear tread: (all models) 60 inches. Tires: (station wagons) 8.85 x 14; (station wagons) 8.85 x 15; (passenger cars) 8.55 x 14.

OPTIONS: Power brakes ($47). Power steering ($107). Air conditioning ($406). Dual air conditioning ($636). Automatic speed control. Torque-Flight and power brakes required ($67). Front and rear bumper guards ($34). Electric clock ($19). Console, on models with bucket seats ($127). Rear window defogger ($22). Tinted glass, all windows and windshield ($42). Left and right front head restraints ($44). Automatic headlamp dimmer ($47). Safeguard sentinel ($34). Station wagon rooftop luggage rack ($97). Two-tone paint on specific models ($28). Special buffed paint, all models ($22). Power radio antenna ($27). Remote control trunk release ($13). Power vent windows ($53). Power side windows ($108). Golden Tone AM radio with tape deck ($222). Golden Tone AM radio ($92). Golden Tone AM/FM Touch Tuner radio ($187). Golden Tone AM/FM Multiplex radio ($247). Three-in-one vinyl bench seat ($106). Three-in-one cloth and vinyl bench seat ($70). Vinyl bucket seats in Newports ($99-$158). Leather bucket seats in New Yorker/300 ($129-$189). Tilt-A-Scope steering wheel ($88). Vinyl roof, except station wagon ($109). Styled 14-inch road wheels for Newports ($99). Styled 14-inch road wheels for 300/New Yorker ($80). Deluxe 14-inch wheel covers, Newports ($18). Deluxe 15-inch wheel covers, Newports ($25). Sport wheel covers, Chrysler 300 ($19). Deep dish 14-inch wheel covers, Newports ($54). Deep dish 14-inch wheel covers, other models ($35). Three-speed windshield wipers ($5). Station wagon window wiper and washer for tailgate ($39). Basic accessory group package ($211). Light group package ($23). Heavy-duty suspension package ($13). Disc brakes ($74). Rear seat heater, except station wagon ($62). Cornering lights ($36). Remote control left-hand outside rearview mirror ($10). License plate frames ($7). Six-Way power bench seat ($100). Left and right power bucket or three-in-one seats ($183). Rear seat radio speaker ($17). Pair of shoulder belts ($27). Passenger side reclining front seat ($32). Vinyl bench seats in Chrysler 300, credit ($82). Cloth and vinyl bench seat in Chrysler 300, credit ($82). Sports Grain woodgrain applique side trim on Newport two-door hardtop, convertible and T&C station wagons. Three-speed manual transmission was standard in Newport/Newport Custom. Automatic transmission was optional in Newport/Newport Custom, with the four-barrel 383-cid engine ($227); with the four-barrel 440-cid engine ($227); and with the two-barrel 383-cid engine ($222). Automatic transmission was standard in Chrysler 300s, Town & Country and New Yorker. The 330 hp four-barrel high-performance 383-cid engine was optional in Newport/Newport Custom and Town & Country ($68). The 440 cid/350 hp four-barrel carb V-8 with dual exhaust was optional in Town & Countrys ($164). The 440 cid/375 hp four-barrel carb 'TNT' engine was optional in Newport/Newport Custom with TorqueFlite automatic transmission ($198) and optional in all Chrysler 300s and New Yorkers ($79). Sure-Grip differential was optional in all models ($51). A 46-amp alternator was optional in all models ($11) and standard on cars with air conditioning. Numerous tire options also available.

HISTORICAL FOOTNOTES: The 1968 Chryslers were introduced in September 1967. Model year production peaked at 264,863 units. Calendar year sales of 263,266 cars was recorded. Robert Anderson was the chief executive officer of the Chrysler-Plymouth Division this year. The intro-

duction of the Newport two-door hardtop coupe and convertible with woodgrained exterior paneling took place at the 1968 Chicago Automobile Show in February. A limited number of cars with this particular option were sold. Chrysler was America's 10th ranked auto manufacturer this season.

1969 CHRYSLER

NEWPORT SERIES — (V-8) — All-new styling greeted Newport buyers this year. It used smoother, arched side panels creating an airplane fuselage look. A massive front bumper structure housed a wide grille formed of many fine horizontal blades. The V-shaped look was continued, but was toned down with a flattened center section decorated with three, stacked star-type Chrysler emblems. Newports carried a Chrysler signature on the right-hand side of the grille insert. A molding ran from the front bumper to the rear bumper ends, angling slightly downward so that it passed through the front wheel opening, but above the unskirted rear wheel cutout. Standard Newport equipment included all Chrysler safety features; cleaner air system; odometer; tripometer; heater and defroster; carpeting; dual rear seat ashtrays; 8.55 x 15 black sidewall tires; the two-barrel 383-cid V-8; and, on convertibles, all-vinyl bench seats with a front center armrest. The Town & Country station wagons were no longer grouped with Newport models. Base Newport models carried a chrome signature-type nameplate on the rear fender, above the rear tip of the side trim molding.

CHRYSLER I.D. NUMBERS: Serial numbers were now located on a plate attached to the left side of the instrument panel and visible through the windshield. Serial numbers consisted of a seven symbol prefix, plus production sequence code. The first symbol 'C' = Chrysler Division. The second symbol indicated series and was an 'E' for base Newports. The third and fourth symbols indicated a Body/Style code that corresponded to the numerical portion of the codes in the second column of the chart below. The fifth symbol was an engine code as follows: 'G' = 383-cid V-8; 'H' = high-performance 383-cid V-8; 'K' = 440-cid V-8; 'L' = high-performance 440-cid V-8 and 'M' = special order V-8. The sixth symbol was a '9' indicating 1969 model year. The seventh symbol indicated the assembly plant, as follows: 'C' = Detroit and 'F' = Newark. (All station wagons and convertibles were assembled in Detroit at the Jefferson Avenue plant.) [NEWPORT] Production sequence code followed the same format and began with first two symbols 'CE.' The code 'G' engine was again the base powerplant. [NEWPORT CUSTOM] The numbering system and code locations were the same as for previous models with the second symbol changed to an 'L' to indicate Newport Custom. The code 'G' engine was standard equipment. [CHRYSLER 300] The numbering system and code locations were the same as for previous models with the second symbol changed to an 'M' to indicate Chrysler 300. The Code 'K' engine was standard equipment. [NEW YORKER] The numbering system and code locations were the same as for previous models with the second symbol changed to an 'H' to indicate Chrysler New Yorker. The code 'K' engine was standard equipment. [TOWN & COUNTRY] The numbering system and code locations were the same as for previous models with the second symbol changed to a 'P' to indicate Town & Country. The code 'G' engine was standard equipment.

NEWPORT SERIES

Model No.	Body/ Style No.	Body Type & Seating	Factory Price	Shipping Weight	Prod. Total
EC-E	CE41	4-dr Sed-6P	4252	4001	55,083
EC-E	CE23	2-dr HT Cpe-6P	4323	3991	33,639
EC-E	CE43	4-dr HT Sed-6P	4387	4016	20,608
EC-E	CE27	2-dr Conv-6P	4661	4061	2,169

1969 Chrysler, Newport Custom four-door hardtop, V-8

CHRYSLER 300 SERIES

Model No.	Body/ Style No.	Body Type & Seating	Factory Price	Shipping Weight	Prod. Total
FC-M	CM23	2-dr HT Cpe-5P	4849	4125	9,589
FC-M	CM43	4-dr HT Sed-6P	4625	4005	9,846
FC-M	CM27	2-dr Conv-5P	5195	4225	1,077
FC-M	CM23	2-dr Hurst-5P	5842	N/A	485

CHRYSLER/HURST 300-H SERIES ENGINE: V-8. Overhead valve. Cast iron block. Displacement: 440 cid. Bore and stroke: 4.326 x 3.75 inches. Compression ratio: 9.7:1. Brake hp: 375 at 4600 rpm. Five main bearings. Hydraulic valve lifters. Carburetor: four-barrel.

NEW YORKER SERIES — (V-8) — Three body styles were offered in this series. They had a slight face lift of the fuselage shape design. The grille used the characteristic horizontal and vertical bars with fine horizontal bars placed within the outline. A broad trim molding ran from front to rear at a level even with the lower portion of the bumpers. The rear taillamp ensemble had a horizontal bar look. The center section of the rear latch panel 'grille' was shaped like the front grille. Standard equipment included power brakes; carpeted trunk; electric clock; light group; left-hand outside rearview remote control mirror; power steering; undercoating; hood insulation; three-speed windshield washers; dome light; time delay ignition switch; fresh air heater and defroster; simulated walnut instrument panel applique; pleated cloth and vinyl bench seats with folding center armrests (front only in two-doors); rear cigar lighters; fender mounted turn signals; exhaust emission controls; J78-15 tires (black sidewall); and the 440 cid/350 hp code 'T' V-8 engine. New Yorker signature script appeared on the lower front fenders, behind the wheelhousings, and on the right-hand corner of the trunk lid.

NEW YORKER SERIES

Model No.	Body/ Style No.	Body Type & Seating	Factory Price	Shipping Weight	Prod. Total
FC-H	CH41	4-dr Sed-6P	5241	4230	9,389
FC-H	CH23	2-dr HT Cpe-6P	5292	4155	4,917
FC-H	CH43	4-dr HT Sed-6P	5372	4265	19,903

TOWN & COUNTRY SERIES — (V-8) — Chrysler's Town & Country station wagon line was a separate series again this year. Advertised as a "Luxury Car Made Into a Wagon," the Town & Country was designed for work, for comfort and for pleasure. Simulated Brazilian Rosewood bodyside and tailgate appliques were standard. There was 109.2 cubic feet of storage space, including a lockable storage compartment, plus room for a 4 x 8-foot piece of plywood. Carrying capacity was a selling feature of the full-size wagons. Front power disc brakes were standard equipment. Other features provided at base cost to all Chrysler station wagon buyers included cleaner air system; exhaust emission control; TorqueFlite automatic transmission; 59-amp/hour battery; power steering; light group package; time delay ignition switch; glovebox and dashboard simulated walnut appliques; vinyl bench seats with front center armrest; foam padded cushions; carpeting; carpeted lower door trim panels and cargo deck; wind deflector; stainless steel wheel covers; dual action tailgate; fender mounted turn signals; J78-15 black sidewall tires; and 383 cid/290 hp V-8.

TOWN & COUNTRY SERIES

Model No.	Body/ Style No.	Body Type & Seating	Factory Price	Shipping Weight	Prod. Total
FC-P	CP45	4-dr T&C Wag-6P	5349	4445	5,686
FC-P	CP46	4-dr T&C Wag-9P	5435	4505	9,583

NEWPORT/NEWPORT CUSTOM/T&C ENGINE: V-8. Overhead valve. Cast iron block. Displacement: 383 cid. Bore and stroke: 4.25 x 3.375 inches. Compression ratio: 8.7:1. Brake hp: 290 at 4400 rpm. Five main bearings. Hydraulic valve lifters. Carburetor: Carter Type BBD two-barrel Model 4894S.

CHRYSLER 300/NEW YORKER SERIES ENGINE: V-8. Overhead valve. Cast iron block. Displacement: 440 cid. Bore and stroke: 4.326 x 3.75 inches. Compression ratio: 9.7:1. Brake hp: 350 at 4400 rpm. Five main bearings. Hydraulic valve lifters. Carburetor: four-barrel.

CHASSIS FEATURES: Wheelbase (station wagon) 122 inches; (passenger cars) 124 inches. Overall length: (station wagon) 224.8 inches; (passenger car) 224.7 inches. Front tread: (all models) 62.1 inches. Rear tread: (all models) 62 inches. Tires (Newport/Custom/300) H78-15; (New Yorker/station wagon) J78-15.

OPTIONS: Power brakes in Newport, Custom and 300 ($46.85). Door locks in two-door ($45.55); in four-door ($69.50). Power Six-Way bench seat ($102.80). Power buckets or three-in-one left and right seats ($188.05). Power steering in Newport, Custom, 300 ($117.20). Power vent windows ($54.25). Heavy-duty suspension ($17.50). Remote trunk release ($14.75). Power side windows ($111.55). Front disc brakes ($46.85). Electric clock ($19.05). Console ($67.95). Sure-Grip differential ($50.70). Tinted glass, all windows ($44.80). Automatic headlight beam changer ($48.70). Cornering lights ($36.50). Time delay headlights ($18.40). Air conditioning ($405.85), with Auto Temp ($481.20). Dual air conditioning in station wagons ($635.80), with Auto Temp ($712.40). Luggage rack ($63.95). Two-tone paint ($43.05). Golden Tone AM radio ($92.30). Golden Tone AM radio with Stereo Tape Player and speakers ($222.25). Golden Tone AM/FM radio Search Tuner ($186.90). Multiplex AM/FM radio with Stereo Type Player and speakers ($353.95). Rear seat speaker ($17.00). Vinyl roof covering ($124.55). Automatic speed control ($66.50). Tilt and Telescope wheel with rim blow ($90.50). Undercoating and hood insulator pad ($20.50). Chrome-styled road wheels, except station wagon and Cordoba ($98.50). Three-speed manual transmission was standard in Newport and Newport Custom. Automatic transmission was standard in all other series. Automatic transmission in Newport/Custom with '383' ($229); with '440' ($234). V-8 383 cid/335 hp four-barrel carb engine ($68). V-8 440 cid/350 hp station wagon engine ($164). V-8 440 cid/375 hp 'TNT' engine in Newport Custom ($198); in New Yorker/300 ($79). Positive traction rear axle ($51).

HISTORICAL FOOTNOTES: This was the last year for the Chrysler convertible. Sales declined more than 30 percent for the year, but industry sales position climbed to 10th place. John J. Riccardo became Chrysler president.

1971 CHRYSLER

NEWPORT ROYAL SERIES — (V-8) — The Newport Royal was considered a subseries of the Newport. The Royal nameplate returned after an absence of more than 20 years and signified, as before, the low end of the price spectrum. The fuselage shape, introduced in 1969, was retained with minimal changes to the grille and rear taillamp assembly. The 360-cid V-8 Chrysler engine made its debut in the Newport Royal series. The 360 engine was not available in any other 1970 Chrysler series. Optional engines, however, were available. Unique cloth and vinyl upholstery identified Royal interiors.

1971 Chrysler, Newport two-door hardtop, V-8

CHRYSLER I.D. NUMBERS: Serial numbers were now located on a plate attached to the left side of the instrument panel and visible through the windshield. Serial numbers consisted of a seven symbol prefix, plus production sequence code. The sixth symbol changed to '1' to indicate the 1971 model year. [NEWPORT ROYAL] Serial numbers began with

the Body/Style Number. CE41K1C-100001 could be deciphered as a Series CE Chrysler Newport Royal Body/Style Number 41 four-door sedan with standard 360 engine (K) made in Detroit (C) as the first car built sequentially (100001). [NEWPORT] Serial numbers and engine numbers were the same as for Newport Royal series, except the engine code for the standard 383 engine was L. [NEWPORT CUSTOM] CL23U1C-100001 could be deciphered as a Series CLL Newport Custom Body/Style Number 23 two-door hardtop with optional high output 440 engine (U) for 1971 (1), made in Detroit (C) as the first car built sequentially (100001). [CHRYSLER 300] CS23T1C-100001 could be deciphered as a Series CS Chrysler 300 Body/Style Number 23 two-door hardtop with the standard 440 engine (T) for 1971 (1), made in Detroit as the first car built sequentially. [NEW YORKER] CH43U1C-100001 could be deciphered as a Series CH New Yorker Body/Style Number 43 four-door hardtop with optional 440 'TNT' engine (U) for 1971 (1), made in Detroit (C) as the first car built sequentially (100001). [Town & Country] CP46U1C-100001 could be deciphered as a Series CP nine-passenger Chrysler Town & Country Body/Style Number 46 station wagon with optional 440 'TNT' engine (U) for 1971 (1), made in Detroit (C) as the first car built sequentially (100001). Engine serial numbers contained a plant code PM (Mount Rd.), displacement code 360 (360 cid) and a four-digit calendar date/correlated number 3444 (Jan. 1, 1971) followed by a four digit sequential number for each day's production.

NEWPORT ROYAL SERIES

Model No.	Body/ Style No.	Body Type & Seating	Factory Price	Shipping Weight	Prod. Total
GC-E	CE41	4-dr Sed-6P	4597	4060	19,662
GC-E	CE23	2-dr HT Cpe-6P	4672	4010	8,500
GC-E	CE43	4-dr HT Sed-6P	4735	4080	5,188

NEWPORT SERIES — (V-8) — The Newport was identical to the Royal subseries except for the addition of body side moldings; its own cloth and vinyl seat trim and a larger displacement base powerplant. The TNT optional engine was no longer available in the Newport series as the performance era was waning. Newport side body trim ran from front to rear, unlike the Royal trim, which ran from rear to just forward of the front door.

NEWPORT SERIES

Model No.	Body/ Style No.	Body Type & Seating	Factory Price	Shipping Weight	Prod. Total
GC-E	CE41	4-dr Sed-6P	4709	4120	24,834
GC-E	CE23	2-dr HT Cpe-6P	4784	4070	15,549
GC-E	CE43	4-dr HT Sed-6P	4847	4140	10,800

NEWPORT CUSTOM SERIES — (V-8) — The Newport Custom models included a number of features not found in the two lower priced Newports. A single front seat folding armrest; front and rear armrests; bodyside moldings with vinyl inserts; bright upper door frames on the sedan; front seat foam cushions; and upgraded cloth and vinyl upholstery were standard on this slightly restyled series. The Newport Custom grille matched that of the lower series Chrysler in design.

NEWPORT CUSTOM SERIES

Model No.	Body/ Style No.	Body Type & Seating	Factory Price	Shipping Weight	Prod. Total
GC-L	CL41	4-dr Sed-6P	4838	4130	11,254
GC-L	CL23	2-dr HT Cpe-6P	4910	4075	5,527
GC-L	CL43	4-dr HT Sed-6P	4990	4160	10,207

300 SERIES — (V-8) — The Chrysler 300 series used its own distinctive grille (with hidden headlights) and full-width taillamps. Color-coordinated vinyl side rub strips and unique hubcaps helped to distinguish the 300 from the other series. Only two body styles were offered this season as the 300 nameplate was in its last year.

300 SERIES

Model No.	Body/ Style No.	Body Type & Seating	Factory Price	Shipping Weight	Prod. Total
GC-S	CS23	2-dr HT Cpe-6P	5126	4195	7,256
GC-S	CS43	4-dr HT Sed-6P	5205	4270	6,683

NEW YORKER SERIES — (V-8) — The New Yorker styling changes paralleled those of the other 1971 Chryslers. The grille texture was more detailed than that found on the Newport. Cairo cloth and vinyl upholstery was a standard New Yorker feature as was full carpeting (including trunk); cigarette lighters; electric clock; light group; left-hand remote control mirror; rear fender skirts; wide lower side body moldings; front fender peak strips; paint accent stripes; wheelhouse opening moldings; undercoating; hood insulation; and three-speed windshield wipers.

NEW YORKER SERIES

Model No.	Body/ Style No.	Body Type & Seating	Factory Price	Shipping Weight	Prod. Total
GC-H	CH41	4-dr Sed-6P	5555	4335	9,850
GC-H	CH23	2-dr HT Cpe-6P	5606	4250	4,485
GC-H	CH43	4-dr HT Sed-6P	5686	4355	20,633

TOWN & COUNTRY SERIES — (V-8) — The Town & Country had a minor face lift from 1970. The station wagons continued to use the Brazilian wood applique on the side and rear panels although this type of trim could be deleted without credit. Town & Country offered all New Yorker features, except the electric clock, mirror and undercoating. Standard features included luggage compartment lock; all-vinyl front bench seat with center armrest; dual action tailgate; and aerodynamic rear roof wind deflector. Station wagon sales rose nearly 10 percent over 1970 totals.

TOWN & COUNTRY SERIES

Model No.	Body/ Style No.	Body Type & Seating	Factory Price	Shipping Weight	Prod. Total
GC-P	CP45	4-dr Sta Wag-6P	5596	4525	5,697
GC-P	CP46	4-dr Sta Wag-9P	5682	4580	10,993

NEWPORT ROYAL ENGINE: V-8. Cast iron block. Displacement: 360 cid. Bore and stroke: 3.91 x 3.58 inches. Brake hp: 255. Compression ratio: 8.7:1. Five main bearings. Hydraulic valve lifters. Carburetion: two-barrel.

NEWPORT/NEWPORT CUSTOM/T&C ENGINE: V-8. Cast iron block. Displacement: 383 cid. Bore and stroke: 4.25 x 3.375 inches. Brake hp: 275. Compression ratio: 8.5:1. Five main bearings. Carburetion: two-barrel.

300/NEW YORKER ENGINE: V-8. Cast iron block. Displacement: 440 cid. Bore and stroke: 4.326 x 3.75 inches. Brake hp: 335. Compression ratio: 8.8:1. Five main bearings. Hydraulic valve lifters. Carburetion: four-barrel.

CHASSIS FEATURES: Wheelbase: (passenger cars) 124 inches; (station wagon) 122 inches. Overall length: (passenger cars) 224.6 inches; (station wagon) 224.8 inches. Tires: (Newport Royal) G78-15; (300) H78-15; (New Yorker) J78-15; (Town & Country) L84-15.

OPTIONS: Power brakes in Newport ($76). Power steering in Newport ($125). Air conditioning ($426); with Automatic Temperature control ($501). Power door locks, in two-doors ($48). Power door locks, in four-doors ($73). Six-Way power bench seat ($106). Pair of Six-Way power bucket or 50/50 seats ($198). Power vent windows, New Yorker four-door hardtop ($67). Power windows ($133). Heavy-duty suspension ($18). Remote trunk release ($16). Electric clock, standard in New Yorker ($19). Center console ($71). All tinted glass ($54). Automatic headlamp dimmer ($51). Cornering lights ($38). Safeguard Sentinel ($37). Dual air conditioning, Town & Country ($656). Town & Country luggage rack ($69). Two-tone paint ($45). High-impact paint ($15). AM radio ($92). AM radio with stereo tape ($224). AM/FM Search-Tuner radio ($196). AM/FM stereo system ($243). AM/FM stereo with cassette tape ($407). Rear seat speaker ($19). Automatic speed control ($69). Tilt and Telescope steering ($91). Vinyl roof ($128). Sun roof ($598). Strato Ventilation, without air conditioning ($18). Road wheels ($102). Undercoating and hood insulation ($27). Three-speed manual transmission was standard on all early Newport models. Automatic transmission was optional on all early Newports ($241). It was made standard equipment, on these cars, later in the year. Newport Royal V-8 383 cid/275 hp two-barrel carb engine ($27). Newport Royal V-8 383 cid/300 hp four-barrel carb engine ($98). Newport V-8 383 cid/300 hp four-barrel carb engine ($71). Newport Custom V-8 383 cid/300 hp four-barrel carb engine ($71). Town & Country V-8 383 cid/300 hp four barrel carb engine ($71). Town & Country V-8 440 cid/355 hp four-barrel carb engine ($125). Newport V-8 440 cid/335 hp four-barrel carb engine ($208). Newport Custom 440 cid/335 hp four-barrel carb engine ($208). Chrysler 300 V-8 440 cid/370 hp four-barrel 'TNT' engine ($83). Positive traction rear axle ($51).

HISTORICAL FOOTNOTES: Chrysler sales declined only three-percent from 1970 figures. It was the last year for the Chrysler 300 series. Convertibles were no longer available in any Chrysler line. Around May 1971, automatic transmission became standard equipment on all Chryslers and prices were increased to reflect the change.

1972 CHRYSLER

NEWPORT ROYAL SERIES — (V-8) — The Newport Royal series in 1972 combined the two low-end models (Newport Royal/Newport) of 1971. The basic fuselage shape was retained but a clever restyling of all sheet metal bodyside panels plus front and rear ends including the hood and deck, provided a fresh look. The heavily chromed front bumper/grille combination was retained but was now divided in the center providing two grille inserts. The rear taillamps were located at the outer

ends of the rear bumper, with the lower half inset to the bumper and the upper half inset to the fender. The taillamps were unique to the Newport Royal series. Newport Royals now included many standard features such as: power front disc brakes; color-keyed carpeting; electronic ignition; power steering; and automatic transmission.

1972 Chrysler, Newport Royal two-door hardtop, V-8

CHRYSLER I.D. NUMBERS: Serial numbers and engine numbers were located in the usual positions. Serial numbers began with the Body/Style code. [NEWPORT ROYAL] CL41K2C-100001 could be deciphered as a Newport Royal four-door sedan (CL41) with standard 360 engine (K) for 1972 (2), made in Detroit (C) as the first car built sequentially (100001). Engines were built at the Trenton plant and used the prefix PT. Codes revealed the displacement (360) and a four-digit calendar date/correlated code (3809 denoting Jan. 1, 1972, for example). A four-digit sequential number indicated each day's production. The code for the optional 440-cid Newport engine was 'T.' [NEWPORT CUSTOM] CM23M2C-100001 could be deciphered as a Chrysler Newport Custom two-door hardtop (CM23) with standard 400 engine (M) for 1972 (2), made in Detroit (C) as the first car built sequentially. Engines were identified as on the Newport Royal series. [NEW YORKER] Serial numbers and engine numbers were located in the usual position. Serial numbers began with the usual Body/Style code. CH43T2C- 100001 could be deciphered as a New Yorker four-door hardtop [CH43] with 440 standard engine (T) for 1972 (2), made in Detroit (C) as the first car built sequentially. Engine Numbers were assigned as on the Newport Royal series. [NEW YORKER BROUGHAM] CS41T2C-100001 could be deciphered as a Chrysler New Yorker Brougham four-door sedan (CS41) with 440 engine (T) for 1972 (2), made in Detroit (C) as the first car built sequentially (100001). Engine numbers were assigned as on previous series. [TOWN & COUNTRY] CP45T2C-100001 could be deciphered as a six-passenger Town & Country station wagon (CP45) with 440 engine (T) for 1972 (2), made in Detroit (C) as the first car built sequentially (100001). Engine numbers were assigned as on previous models.

NEWPORT ROYAL SERIES

Model No.	Body/ Style No.	Body Type & Seating	Factory Price	Shipping Weight	Prod. Total
HC-L	CL41	4-dr Sed-6P	4557	4197	47,437
HC-L	CL23	2-dr HT Cpe-6P	4630	4132	22,622
HC-L	CL43	4-dr HT Sed-6P	4692	4202	15,185

NEWPORT CUSTOM SERIES — (V-8) — The Newport Custom series was identical in style to the Newport Royal, but had an enriched interior with foam seat cushions; cloth and vinyl bench seat; front folding center armrest; and bright finished bases on the door armrests. The four-door sedan had bright upper door frames as standard equipment. The base engine for the Newport Custom was the all-new 400-cid V-8. All two-door hardtops used a new roof structure this year, in keeping with the other sheet metal changes outlined in the Newport Royal series.

NEWPORT CUSTOM SERIES

Model No.	Body/ Style No.	Body Type & Seating	Factory Price	Shipping Weight	Prod. Total
HC-M	CM41	4-dr HT-6P	4793	4287	19,278
HC-M	CM23	2-dr HT Cpe-6P	4863	4232	10,326
HC-M	CM43	4-dr HT Sed-6P	4941	4297	15,457

NEW YORKER SERIES — (V-8) — The New Yorker series was split into two distinct parts this year to replace the 300 series, which was no longer offered. The New Yorker had an interior that was considerably upgraded from the Newport Custom. It featured unique cloth and vinyl seats, with front and rear center folding armrests and an electric clock. Trunk carpeting was also standard along with the light group package; left-hand remote control outside rearview mirror; lower bodyside moldings; undercoating; hood insulation pad; and rear fender skirts. The same front bumper/grille combination used on Newports was seen but the grille insert had a horizontal flair. The rear taillamp assembly was inset into the bumper, in narrow rectangular fashion, and was divided, in the center, by the back-up lamps.

NEW YORKER SERIES

Model No.	Body/ Style No.	Body Type & Seating	Factory Price	Shipping Weight	Prod. Total
HC-H	CH41	4-dr Sed-6P	5502	4437	7,296
HC-H	CH23	2-dr HT Cpe-6P	5552	4372	5,567
HC-H	CH43	4-dr HT Sed-6P	5630	4467	10,013

1972 Chrysler, New Yorker Brougham four-door hardtop, V-8

NEW YORKER BROUGHAM SERIES — (V-8) — The Brougham was the top-of-the-line Chrysler and included, as standard equipment, many features that were optional on other models. Console-style front and rear armrests with woodgrained trim; fender mounted directional light indicators; front fender peak moldings; automatic seatback release (on two-door hardtops); special two-spoke steering wheel; and power windows were just a few of the Brougham's standard extras. Unique chrome 'Brougham' emblems graced the C-pillar and the rear deck lid.

NEW YORKER BROUGHAM SERIES

Model No.	Body/ Style No.	Body Type & Seating	Factory Price	Shipping Weight	Prod. Total
HC-S	CS41	4-dr Sed-6P	5728	4437	5,971
HC-S	CS23	2-dr HT Cpe-6P	5777	4372	4,635
HC-S	CS43	4-dr HT Sed-6P	5856	4467	20,328

1972 Chrysler, Town & Country station wagon, V-8

TOWN & COUNTRY SERIES — (V-8) — Styling changes seen on the Town & Country followed those of sedans and hardtops this year. The grille was identical to the New Yorker type. The loop-style front bumper had a center bar that split the grille. The simulated woodgrain applique was placed lower on the side body panels than in 1971. Sales increased more than 20 percent over the previous station wagons, with the nine-passenger model showing a substantial improvement. Standard equipment included electric clock; lockable luggage compartment; all-vinyl bench seats with folding center armrest; automatic locking tailgate; dual action tailgate; power-operated tailgate window; aerodynamic rear roof wind deflector; and bodyside and rear panel woodgrain appliques.

TOWN & COUNTRY SERIES

Model No.	Body/ Style No.	Body Type & Seating	Factory Price	Shipping Weight	Prod. Total
HC-P	CP45	4-dr T&C Wag-6P	5692	4712	6,473
HC-P	CP46	4-dr T&C Wag-9P	5576	4767	14,116

NEWPORT ROYAL ENGINE: V-8. Cast iron block. Displacement: 380 cid. Bore and stroke: 4.00 x 3.58 inches. SAE Net hp: 175. Compression ratio: 8.8:1. Five main bearings. Hydraulic valve lifters. Carburetor: two-barrel.

NEWPORT CUSTOM/NEW YORKER BROUGHAM/T&C ENGINE: V-8. Cast iron block. Displacement: 400 cid. Bore and stroke: 4.34 x 3.375 inches. SAE Net hp: 190. Compression ratio: 8.2:1. Five main bearings. Hydraulic valve lifters. Carburetor: two-barrel.

NEW YORKER ENGINE: V-8. Cast iron block. Displacement: 440 cid. Bore and stroke: 4.326 x 3.75 inches. SAE Net hp: 225 (245 with

optional dual exhaust). Compression ratio: 8.2:1. Five main bearings. Hydraulic valve lifters. Carburetor: four-barrel.

CHASSIS FEATURES: Wheelbase: (passenger cars) 124 inches; (station wagons) 122 inches. Overall length: (passenger cars) 224.1 inches; (station wagons) 224.8 inches. Tires: (Newport Royal and Custom) H78-15; (New Yorker and Brougham) J78-15; (station wagons) L84-15.

OPTIONS: Air conditioning ($416), with Automatic Temperature control ($490). Dual air conditioning ($640), with Auto-Temp ($714). Power door locks, two-door ($47). Power door locks, four-door ($72). Six-Way power bench seat ($104). Six-Way power buckets or 50/50 seat ($193). Power vent windows, New Yorker four-door hardtop ($65). Power windows ($131). Remote trunk release ($15). Electric clock ($19). All tinted glass ($42). Cornering lights ($38). Luggage rack and assist handles ($86). Two-tone paint ($44). New Yorker/Brougham paint stripe ($16). AM radio ($90). AM radio with 8-track stereo tape ($219). AM/FM Search Tuner radio ($192). AM/FM stereo ($237). AM/FM stereo with cassette ($398). Vinyl roof cover ($125). Station wagon vinyl roof cover ($141). Automatic speed control ($68). Chrome styled road wheels ($100). Sun roof ($585). Heavy-duty shock absorbers ($5). Automatic transmission was standard on all 1972 Chryslers. Dual exhaust were optional on all models combined with the 440-cid V-8 ($35). A 70-amp battery was optional on all models, except standard with New Yorkers ($15). An engine block heater was optional on all models ($15). Electronic ignition was optional on all models ($34). An optional exhaust emission control system was available for all, mandatory with California sale ($28). V-8 440 cid/225 hp four barrel carb engine, except standard in New Yorker ($122). Positive traction rear axle. Optional rear axle gear ratios included: 2.76:1 ($13) and 3.23:1 ($13).

HISTORICAL FOOTNOTES: This was the last year for the Royal nameplate after a brief revival. Chrysler sales rose more than 16 percent over one-year-earlier totals, reflecting the popularity of the new sheet metal restyling. A new 400-cid engine made its debut. Horsepower ratings for 1972 were expressed in SAE net horsepower and seemed much lower than before.

1973 CHRYSLER

NEWPORT SERIES — (V-8) — The Royal portion of the name was dropped this year and the low-line Chrysler was the Newport. A Newport sedan became the millionth car to bear the Chrysler nameplate. Styling refinements centered around the front bumper and grille area. The loop-type bumper was changed to a more conventional type, with the dual headlights and rectangular grille outlined in chrome above the bumper. The grille had a fine vertical/horizontal bar motif. The rear taillamps had a slight cosmetic change. An electronic ignition system became standard equipment along with power disc brakes; front and rear bumper guards; inside hood release; wheelhouse moldings; pedal dress-up kit; and trip odometer. A special 'Navajo' package was offered. It featured Navajo copper metallic paint; orange paint stripes; vinyl roof; and white bench seats with unique Navajo (Indian blanket) cloth inserts.

1973 Chrysler, Newport Royal four-door hardtop, V-8

CHRYSLER I.D. NUMBERS: Serial numbers and engine numbers were located in the usual positions. Serial numbers began with the Body/Style code. [NEWPORT] CL41M3C-100001 could be deciphered as a Newport four-door sedan (CL41) with standard 400-cid engine (M) for 1973 (3), made in Detroit (C) as the first car built sequentially. [NEWPORT CUSTOM] CM23T3C-100001 could be deciphered as a Newport Custom two-door hardtop (CM23) with optional 440 engine (T) for 1973 (3), made in Detroit (C) as the first car built sequentially (100001). [NEW YORKER] CH41U3C-100001 could be deciphered as a New York-

er four-door sedan (CH41) with optional 440 engine (U) for 1973 (3), made in Detroit (C) as the first car built sequentially (100001). [NEW YORKER BROUGHAM] CS43T3C-100001 could be deciphered as a New Yorker Brougham four-door hardtop (CS43) with standard 440 engine (T) for 1973 (3), made in Detroit (C) as the first car built sequentially (100001). [TOWN & COUNTRY] CP46T3C-100001 could be deciphered as a nine-passenger station wagon (CP46) with standard 440 engine (T) for 1973 (3), made in Detroit (C) as the first car built sequentially (100001). Engine numbers were found on the right-hand side of the 400-cid V-8 and the left bank of cylinders, adjacent to the tappet rail, on the 440-cid V-8. Engine numbers were assigned as on previous models.

NEWPORT SERIES

Model No.	Body/ Style No.	Body Type & Seating	Factory Price	Shipping Weight	Prod. Total
3C-L	CL41	4-dr Sed-6P	4693	4305	54,147
3C-L	CL23	2-dr HT Cpe-6P	4766	4265	27,456
3C-L	CL43	4-dr HT Sed-6P	4828	4315	20,175

NEWPORT CUSTOM SERIES — (V-8) — This was an upgraded version of the Newport. Newport Custom nameplates were placed on the C-pillar, rather than on the front fender behind the wheelhouse molding. This series offered enriched interiors, with unique cloth and vinyl bench seats; bodyside moldings with vinyl inserts; bright upper door moldings on the sedan; single center folding front armrests; and bright finished bases on the front and rear door armrests.

NEWPORT CUSTOM SERIES

Model No.	Body/ Style No.	Body Type & Seating	Factory Price	Shipping Weight	Prod. Total
3C-M	CM41	4-dr Sed-6P	4931	4305	20,092
3C-M	CM23	2-dr HT Cpe-6P	4996	4250	12,293
3C-M	CM43	4-dr HT Sed-6P	5079	4330	20,050

1973 Chrysler, New Yorker four-door sedan, V-8

NEW YORKER SERIES — (V-8) — The New Yorker was offered in only two body styles this year. They had a unique grille insert with a horizontal flair and a thinner upper grille surround. Taillamps were also unique to the New Yorker. They used a horizontal layout structured within the rear bumper. The New Yorker's standard features included a larger battery; full carpeting (including trunk); electric clock; left-hand remote-control outside rearview mirror; wheelhouse opening moldings; rear fender skirts; undercoating; hood insulation; three-speed windshield wipers; and upgraded cloth and vinyl seats.

NEW YORKER SERIES

Model No.	Body/ Style No.	Body Type & Seating	Factory Price	Shipping Weight	Prod. Total
3C-H	CH41	4-dr Sed-6P	5641	4460	7,991
3C-H	CH43	4-dr HT Sed-6P	5769	4480	7,619

NEW YORKER BROUGHAM SERIES — (V-8) — The New Yorker Brougham was the top-of-the-line Chrysler with many features as standard equipment. They included: rear folding armrests; bucket seats or three-in-one bench seat with folding armrests; light package; fender mounted directional signal indicators; front fender peak moldings; automatic seatback release (two-door hardtop); two-spoke rim-blow steering wheel; power windows and concealed three-speed windshield wipers with coordinated washers. With the new styling, sales of this series increased more than 40 percent.

NEW YORKER BROUGHAM SERIES

Model No.	Body/ Style No.	Body Type & Seating	Factory Price	Shipping Weight	Prod. Total
3C-S	CS41	4-dr Sed-6P	5876	4530	8,541
3C-S	CS23	2-dr HT Cpe-6P	5925	4440	9,190
3C-S	CS43	4-dr HT Sed-6P	6004	4545	26,635

TOWN & COUNTRY SERIES — (V-8) — Styling of the Town & Countrys reflected the changes of the other 1973 Chryslers. The New Yorker grille

was seen and the woodgrain side and rear body panels continued to be used. Other standard features included an electric clock; luggage compartment lock; all-vinyl bench seats with front center armrest; automatic tailgate lock; dual action tailgate; power-operated tailgate window; and aerodynamic rear roof wind deflector. Station wagon sales, even with the new styling, fell 2.5 percent over the banner year of 1972.

TOWN & COUNTRY SERIES

Model No.	Body/ Style No.	Body Type & Seating	Factory Price	Shipping Weight	Prod. Total
3C-P	CP45	4-dr T&C Wag-6P	5885	4775	5,353
3C-P	CP46	4-dr T&C Wag-9P	6010	4838	14,687

NEWPORT/NEWPORT CUSTOM ENGINE: V-8. Cast iron block. Displacement: 400 cid. Bore and stroke: 4.34 x 3.375 inches. SAE Net hp: 185. Compression ratio: 8.2:1. Five main bearings. Hydraulic valve lifters. Carburetor: four-barrel.

NEW YORKER/NEW YORKER BROUGHAM/T&C ENGINE: V-8. Cast iron block. Displacement: 440 cid. Bore and stroke: 4.326 x 3.75 inches. SAE Net hp: 215. Compression ratio: 8.2:1. Five main bearings. Hydraulic valve lifters. Carburetor: four-barrel.

CHASSIS FEATURES: Wheelbase: (passenger cars) 124 inches; (station wagons) 122 inches. Overall length: (passenger cars) 230.1 inches; (station wagons) 229.6 inches; (New Yorker) 230.8 inches. Front tread: 62.1 inches. Rear tread: 63.4 inches. Tires: (Newport and Newport Custom) H78-15; (New Yorker and New Yorker Brougham) J78-15; (station wagons) L84-15.

OPTIONS: Door locks, two-door ($47.40); door locks, four-door ($72.75). Power Six-Way bench seat ($105.30). Power Six-Way buckets or 50-50 seat ($195.75). Power vent windows in New Yorker/New Yorker Brougham ($66.00). Power windows, standard in Brougham ($132.20). Remote control trunk release ($15.15). Electronic digital clock ($39.40). Electric clock ($19.15). Tinted glass ($53.00). Cornering lights ($38.00). Air conditioning ($420.85); with Auto-Temp ($495.15). Dual air conditioning on wagons ($648 00); with Auto-Temp ($722.60). Luggage rack and assist handles ($87.35). Two-tone paint ($44.40). Paint stripe (New Yorker and Brougham $15.90). AM radio ($91.40). AM radio with Stereo Tape eight track ($221.55). AM/FM Search Tuner ($194.55). AM/FM Stereo ($240.35). AM/FM with Stereo Tape cassette ($402.80). AM/FM Stereo with eight track Stereo Tape ($376.80). Vinyl roof cover ($126.60). Automatic speed control ($68.70). Chromed styled road wheels ($101.35). Premier wheel covers ($40.30). Sun roof ($592.00). Heavy-duty suspension ($39.90). Security alarm system ($101.20). 440 engine, Newport and Custom ($123.10). Sure-Grip differential ($50.30).

HISTORICAL FOOTNOTES: The one-millionth Chrysler was produced this year. It was also the last year for the fuselage body design introduced in 1969. Sales increased 15 percent over 1972 totals.

1974 CHRYSLER

1974 Chrysler, Newport two-door hardtop, V-8

NEWPORT SERIES — (V-8) — An all-new Newport was introduced this year. It was distinctively sized: one inch lower, one inch wider, and five inches shorter than the 1973 model. The front grille had a heavy chrome outline and the grille insert was a richly designed affair with three tiers of squares, outlined with bold horizontal and vertical bars. The squares were filled in with smaller vertical and horizontal bars giving a true luxury appearance. Sales declined drastically, because of the Arab oil embargo. Chrysler, for the first time ever, offered a small displacement engine option at no extra cost (360-cid V-8 instead of 400-cid V-8).

CHRYSLER I.D. NUMBERS: Serial numbers and engine numbers were located as on previous models. Serial numbers began with the Body/Style code. [NEWPORT] CL41J4C-100001 could be deciphered as a Newport four-door sedan (CL41) with optional 360 engine (J) for 1974 (4), made in Detroit (C) as the first car built sequentially (100001). [NEWPORT CUSTOM] CM23M4C-100001 could be deciphered as a Newport Custom two-door hardtop (CM23) with standard 400 engine (M) for 1974 (4), made In Detroit (C) as the first car built sequentially (100001). [NEW YORKER] CH43U4C-100001 could be deciphered as a New Yorker four-door hardtop (CH43) with optional 440 engine (U) for 1974 (4), made in Detroit (C) as the first car built sequentially (100001). [NEW YORKER BROUGHAM] CS43T4C-100001 could be deciphered as a New Yorker Brougham four-door hardtop (CS43) with standard 440 engine (T) for 1974 (4), made in Detroit (C) as the first car built sequentially (100001). [TOWN & COUNTRY] CP45T4D-100001 could be deciphered as a Town & Country six-passenger station wagon (CP45) with standard 440 engine (T) for 1974 (4), made in Belvidere (D) as the first car built sequentially. The 360-cid engine had the serial number on the left front of the block, below the cylinder head. 4M360R0910-0001 could be deciphered as 1974 Mound Road-built powerplant (4M) of 360-cid displacement (360), designed for regular fuel and manufactured on September 10 (0910) as the first engine built that day (0001). Serial numbers on 400-cid engines were located on the right-hand side of the block, adjacent to the distributor. Serial numbers on 440-cid engines were located on the left-hand bank of cylinders, adjacent to the front tappet rail. The 400/440 cid engines used the following method of identification: 4T440R8222, which could be deciphered as 1974 Trenton plant (4T), 440 displacement, regular fuel engine (R), built on August 22 (822) during the second shift (2).

NEWPORT SERIES

Model No.	Body/ Style No.	Body Type & Seating	Factory Price	Shipping Weight	Prod. Total
4C-L	CL41	4-dr Sed-6P	5225	4530	26,944
4C-L	CL23	2-dr HT Cpe-6P	5300	4480	13,784
4C-L	CL43	4-dr HT Sed-6P	5364	4540	8,968

NEWPORT CUSTOM SERIES — (V-8) — The Newport Custom used the same distinctive grille and taillamps as the Newport. The Custom, however, added its own 50/50 bench front seat with folding center armrest and cloth and vinyl trim. Also included, as in previous years, were front and rear door armrests; vinyl bodyside inserts; and bright upper door moldings on the sedan. Like Newports, Customs offered, as standard equipment, electronic ignition; automatic transmission; inside hood release; power front disc brakes; wheelhouse moldings; and inside day/night mirrors. Newport Custom sales fell more than 45 percent, owing to the Arab oil embargo.

NEWPORT CUSTOM SERIES

Model No.	Body/ Style No.	Body Type & Seating	Factory Price	Shipping Weight	Prod. Total
4C-M	CM41	4-dr Sed-6P	5586	4580	10,569
4C-M	CM23	2-dr HT Cpe-6P	5653	4530	7,206
4C-M	CM43	4-dr HT Sed-6P	5738	4600	9,892

NEW YORKER SERIES — (V-8) — The New Yorker shared the styling changes of the Newport, except the grille insert retained its horizontal flair of previous years. The rear bumper and taillamp assembly was totally unique to the New Yorker. Taillamps retained the narrow, across-the-width look of previous years and the rear license plate was mounted in the center of the bumper just above the lower edge. Only two four-door styles were available in this series. Sales fell more than 60 percent in comparison to the totals a year previous, owing to the Arab oil embargo.

CHRYSLER NEW YORKER SERIES

Model No.	Body/ Style No.	Body Type & Seating	Factory Price	Shipping Weight	Prod. Total
4C-H	CH41	4-dr Sed-6P	5554	4560	3,072
4C-H	CH43	4-dr HT Sed-6P	5686	4595	3,066

NEW YORKER BROUGHAM — (V-8) — The New Yorker Brougham was an upgraded version of the New Yorker and included such additional items as automatic seatback release; two-spoke rim-blow horn; power

windows; light package; 50/50 divided bench seat; unique cloth and vinyl upholstery; and woodgrained console style front and rear door armrests. A special St. Regis package was available and included fixed formal open windows, body paint accent stripes and forward half-covered vinyl roof.

NEW YORKER BROUGHAM SERIES

Model No.	Body/ Style No.	Body Type & Seating	Factory Price	Shipping Weight	Prod. Total
4C-S	CS41	4-dr Sed-6P	6479	4740	4,533
4C-S	CS23	2-dr HT Cpe-6P	6530	4640	7,980
4C-S	CS43	4-dr HT Sed-6P	6611	4755	13,165

1974 Chrysler, New Yorker four-door hardtop, V-8

TOWN & COUNTRY SERIES — (V-8) — Styling of the Town & Country followed the pattern of the New Yorker series. Woodgrain appliques were standard on the body side and rear panels. Taillamps were unique to the wagon as they were placed horizontally on the tailgate and wrapped around the sides. A new hood ornament sat atop the broad, chromed hood outline as on the New Yorker series. The emblem featured a mythological animal, the griffin, in profile. As in previous years, the Town & Country had, as standard equipment, an electric clock; luggage compartment lock; all-vinyl 50/50 bench seats with front center armrest; automatic locking tailgate; three-way action tailgate (with power-operated window); and rear aerodynamic wind deflector. Town & Country sales declined more than 55 percent. All were built at the Belvidere assembly plant.

TOWN & COUNTRY SERIES

Model No.	Body/ Style No.	Body Type & Seating	Factory Price	Shipping Weight	Prod. Total
4C-P	CP45	4-dr T&C Wag-6P	5767	4915	2,236
4C-P	CP46	4-dr T&C Wag-9P	5896	4970	5,958

NEWPORT/NEWPORT CUSTOM ENGINE: V-8. Cast iron block. Displacement: 400 cid. Bore and stroke: 4.34 x 3.375 inches. Brake hp: 185. Compression ratio: 8.2:1. Five main bearings. Hydraulic valve lifters. Carburetor: two-barrel.

NEW YORKER/NEW YORKER BROUGHAM/T&C ENGINE: V-8. Cast iron block. Displacement: 440 cid. Bore and stroke: 4.326 x 3.75 inches. Brake hp: 230. Compression ratio: 8.2:1. Five main bearings. Hydraulic valve lifters. Carburetor: four-barrel.

CHASSIS FEATURES: Wheelbase: 124 inches. Overall length (passenger cars) 225.1 inches; (station wagons) 224.7 inches. Tires: (Newport and Newport Custom) HR78-15; (New Yorker and New Yorker Brougham) JR78-15; (Town & Country) LR78-15.

OPTIONS: Door locks on two-door ($50.65), on four-door ($77.80). Power Six-Way bench seat ($112.60). Power Six-Way 50/50 seat ($209.35). Power vent windows ($141.35). Remote control release ($16.60). Electronic digital clock ($42.10). Tinted glass ($56.65). Cornering lights ($40.60). Engine block heater ($16.60). Air conditioning ($50.20); with Auto-Temp ($129.70). Locking gas cap ($455). AM radio ($97.75). AM/FM radio ($156.90). AM/FM Stereo Search Tune ($313.80). AM/FM Stereo with eight track stereo tape ($305.30). Vinyl roof cover ($135.40). Automatic speed control ($73.40). Heavy-duty suspension ($19.40). Manual vent windows on four-door models ($36.10). Chrome styled road wheels ($108.40). Premier wheel covers ($43 10). Security alarm system ($108.20). 400-cid four-barrel carb V-8 in Newport and Newport Custom ($39.75). 440-cid four-barrel carb V-8 in Newport and Newport Custom ($131.65). Sure-Grip differential ($53.80). Automatic transmission, power steering and power disc brakes were standard. The 360-cid engine was a no-cost option for Newports.

HISTORICAL FOOTNOTES: The Arab oil embargo played havoc with the sale of large-size automobiles. Chrysler sales fell almost 50 percent

when compared to the 1973 model year totals. R.K. Brown was group vice-president of Chrysler-Plymouth Division this year. Model year sales peaked at 107,059 units.

1975 CHRYSLER

NEWPORT — (V-8) — The Newport remained relatively unchanged from its 1974 counterpart. A new front bumper with openings, plus a new grille insert accentuated with horizontal ribs, were styling highlights. A molded fiberglass headliner was standard, as were front and rear bumper guards and steel-belted radial tires. A fuel pacer with fender-mounted light (using the same indicator as turn signal lights) was optional. Electronic ignition; power front disc brakes; power steering and automatic transmission continued as standard equipment.

CHRYSLER I.D. NUMBERS: Serial numbers and engine numbers were located in the same positions as on previous models. Serial numbers began with the Body/Style code. [NEWPORT] CL41K5-100001 could be deciphered as a Newport four-door sedan (CL41) with 360-cid standard engine (K) for 1975 (5), made in Detroit (D) as the first car built sequentially (100001). [NEWPORT CUSTOM] CM23J5C-100001 could be deciphered as a Newport Custom two-door hardtop (CM23) with optional 360-cid four-barrel engine (J) for 1975 (5), made in Detroit (C) as the first car built sequentially (100001). [NEW YORKER BROUGHAM] CS43T5C-10001 could be deciphered as a New Yorker Brougham four-door hardtop (CS43) with standard 440 engine (T) for 1975 (5), made in Detroit (C) as the first car built sequentially (100001). [TOWN & COUNTRY] CP46N5D-10001 could be deciphered as a nine-passenger Town & Country wagon (CP46) with optional 400-cid engine (N) for 1975 (5), made in Belvidere (D) as the first car built sequentially. [CORDOBA] 5522G5R-100001 could be deciphered as: a Cordoba specialty hardtop (5522) with standard 318-cid engine (G) for 1975 (5), made in Windsor, Canada (R) as the first car built sequentially (100001). Engine numbers were assigned as on previous series.

NEWPORT SERIES

Model No.	Body/ Style No.	Body Type & Seating	Factory Price	Shipping Weight	Prod. Total
5C-L	CL41	4-dr Sed-6P	5428	4450	24,339
5C-L	CL23	2-dr HT Cpe-6P	5511	4405	10,485
5C-L	CL43	4-dr HT Sed-6P	5582	4485	6,846

NEWPORT CUSTOM SERIES — (V-8) — The Custom series was identical to the Newport, except for the usual upgraded interior appointments. Special cloth and vinyl upholstery and 50/50 bench seats with folding front center armrests; bright upper door moldings on the sedan; front and rear door armrests; and bodyside vinyl insert moldings were standard items on the Newport Custom.

NEWPORT CUSTOM SERIES

Model No.	Body/ Style No.	Body Type & Seating	Factory Price	Shipping Weight	Prod. Total
5C-M	CM41	4-dr Sed-6P	5828	4405	9,623
5C-M	CM23	2-dr HT Cpe-6P	5903	4455	5,831
5C-M	CM43	4-dr HT Sed-6P	5997	4525	11,626

NEW YORKER BROUGHAM SERIES — (V-8) — The New Yorker Brougham was the only New Yorker offered in 1975. A new grille insert (divided into six rectangular sections by chrome moldings) was the major styling change. The 400-cid V-8 could be had in the Brougham, at no extra cost, as an economy option. The St. Regis package was available as an extra cost item. Broughams featured power windows; automatic seatback release (in two-doors); three-speed coordinated windshield wipers and washers; folding rear armrest on rear seats; and a light package as standard equipment.

NEW YORKER BROUGHAM SERIES

Model No.	Body/ Style No.	Body Type & Seating	Factory Price	Shipping Weight	Prod. Total
5C-S	CS41	4-dr Sed-6P	7818	4660	5,698
5C-S	CS23	2-dr HT Cpe-6P	7875	4680	7,567
5C-S	CS43	4-dr HT Sed-6P	7965	4785	12,774

TOWN & COUNTRY SERIES — (V-8) — The Town & Country styling changes followed those of the New Yorker Brougham. A molded fiberglass headliner was standard and a new electrically heated rear tailgate window

was available. Another option was the automatic vehicle ride height control system. The 400-cid engine was a no charge option, in lieu of the standard 440-cid powerplant.

TOWN & COUNTRY SERIES

Model No.	Body/ Style No.	Body Type & Seating	Factory Price	Shipping Weight	Prod. Total
5C-P	CP45	4-dr T&C Wag-6P	7954	5080	1,891
5C-P	CP46	4-dr T&C Wag-9P	8099	5119	4,764

1975 Chrysler, New Yorker Brougham four-door hardtop, V-8

CORDOBA SERIES — (V-8) — A new specialty hardtop, the Cordoba, was built with luxury trim and appointments on a wheelbase of 115 inches. The front grille was mostly similar in appearance to the other Chryslers of 1975. However, there were two horizontal bars, which divided numerous fine vertical bars. Single headlamps were located in pods and smaller pods contained the parking lamps. The hood and deck lids were highly sculptured and vertical rectangular taillamps were suggestive of the Newport-type. A Cordoba nameplate graced the front fenders and distinctive medallions were set into the taillamps and the stand-up hood ornament. Cordoba seats were upholstered in brocade trim. One optional interior was a combination of leather and vinyl. Opera windows were seen in the rear quarter roof pillars. The Cordoba sales picture was the only bright spot in the Chrysler line for all of 1975.

CORDOBA SERIES

Model No.	Body/ Style No.	Body Type & Seating	Factory Price	Shipping Weight	Prod. Total
5S-S	SS22	2-dr HT Cpe-6P	5581	4035	150,105

NEWPORT/NEWPORT CUSTOM ENGINE: V-8. Overhead valve. Cast iron block. Displacement: 400 cid. Bore and stroke: 4.34 x 3.38 inches. Compression ratio: 8.2:1. SAE Net hp: 175 at 4000 rpm. Five main bearings. Hydraulic valve lifters. Carburetor: two-barrel.

NEW YORKER BROUGHAM/T&C ENGINE: V-8. Cast iron block. Displacement: 440 cid. Bore and stroke: 4.326 x 3.75 inches. Brake hp: 215 at 4000 rpm. Compression ratio: 8.2:1. Five main bearings. Hydraulic valve lifters. Carburetor: four-barrel.

CORDOBA ENGINE: V-8. Cast iron block. Displacement: 318 cid. Bore and stroke: 3.91 x 3.31 inches. Brake hp: 150 at 4000 rpm. Compression ratio: 8.5:1. Five main bearings. Hydraulic valve lifters. Carburetor: two-barrel.

CHASSIS FEATURES: Wheelbase: (Chryslers) 124 inches; (Cordoba) 115 inches. Overall length: (Town & Country) 227.2 inches; (Newport Custom) 227.1 inches; (New Yorker/Brougham) 226.6 inches; (Cordoba) 215.3 inches. Front track: (Chrysler) 64 inches. (Cordoba) 61.9 inches. Rear track: (Chrysler) 63.4 inches. (Cordoba) 62 inches. Tires: (Newport/Newport Custom) HR78-15; (New Yorker/Brougham) JR78-15; (Town & Country) LR78-15; (Cordoba) GR78-15.

OPTIONS: Door locks, two-door ($60.70), Cordoba ($59.90). Door locks, four-door ($88.35). Power bench seat, Newport ($121.35). Power Six-Way 50/50 seat, right and left ($242.70). Power bench, Cordoba ($117.15). Power bucket, left-Cordoba ($117.15). Remote trunk release ($18.70). Remote trunk release, Cordoba ($18.45). Sure-Grip differential ($54.55). Sure-Grip differential, Cordoba ($49.95). Tinted glass, ($63.35). Tinted glass, Cordoba ($50.70). Air conditioning ($475.15), add $76.60 for Auto-Temp. Air conditioning, Cordoba ($436.90). Locking gas cap ($6.00). Locking gas cap, Cordoba ($5.95). AM Radio ($99.10), standard on Cordoba. AM/FM Radio ($159.05). AM/FM Radio, Cordoba ($76.85). Heavy-duty suspension ($26.70). Heavy-duty suspension, Cordoba ($23.70). Sun roof ($781.20). Sun roof-manual, Cordoba ($296.10).

POWERTRAIN OPTIONS: 400-cid V-8 in Newport/Newport Custom ($40.30), 440-cid V-8 in Newport/Newport Custom ($164.65), 400-cid V-8 in Cordoba ($73). Sure-Grip differential, in Cordoba ($49.95); in other Chryslers ($54.55).

HISTORICAL FOOTNOTES: Sales of large body cars such as Newport and New Yorkers fell another 12 percent in 1975. The only bright spot was the Cordoba, which had 60 percent of all Chrysler sales. Chrysler sales were the best showing for the division since 1969's banner year.

1976 CHRYSLER

1976 Chrysler, Cordoba hardtop (OCW)

None of the Chrysler models displayed notable change in appearance for 1976. The luxury Imperial had been dropped at the end of the '75 model year, but New Yorker and, to a lesser extent, Newport were upgraded to take over its niche in the market. Both Newport and New Yorker still offered a real (pillarless) four-door hardtop, along with some big V-8 engines. Late in the 1976 model year an Electronic Lean Burn System was introduced on all 400 and 440 cu. in. V-8s. A miniature computer absorbed data from sensors on throttle position, engine rpm, manifold vacuum and coolant temperature, then continually adjusted spark timing for the leanest (most economical) mixture. Lean Burn engines were available everywhere except California. An optional trailer towing package included large side mirrors.

CORDOBA — SERIES SS — V-8 — Chrysler's personal-luxury coupe, billed as "the small Chrysler," appeared for 1975. This year it gained a new fine-line vertical grille texture, along with new standard full-length bodyside and Decklid tape stripes with filigree inserts. The grille was made up of thin vertical bars, with pattern continued in bumper slots below. Separate 'Chrysler' letters stood on its upper header molding while front fenders held a 'Cordoba' nameplate and medallion. The standup hood ornament displayed a Cordoba crest. Round park/signal lamps were between the grille and headlamps. At the sides were small three-section front and rear side marker lenses. Vertical rectangular taillamps each were split by a vertical divider bar with emblem. Backup lamps were mounted in the back bumper. The rear license plate housing was recessed. Cordoba script was on the decklid; Cordoba medallions on wheel covers. Cordoba had standard opera windows and opera lamps, full wheel opening moldings, bright aluminum windshield moldings, bright roof drip and window moldings, bright belt and hood rear moldings, bright sill moldings, plus bumper guards and rub strips. Seven new body colors were new: Saddle Tan, plus metallic Jamaican Blue, Jade Green, Caramel Tan, Light Chestnut, Vintage Red Sunfire, and Deep Sherwood Sunfire. Also available were (metallic) Silver Cloud, Platinum, Astral Blue, Starlight Blue, Bittersweet, Inca Gold, and Spanish Gold; plus Rallye Red, Yellow Blaze, Golden Fawn, Spinnaker White, and Formal Black. Interior colors were blue, red, green, black and gold, along with tan (new this year). Base engine was a 400 cu. in. V-8. Either a 360 or 318 V-8 was available at no extra cost. Standard equipment included power steering and brakes, three-speed TorqueFlite automatic, GR78 x 15 SBR WSW tires, digital clock, dual horns, and front/rear sway bars. New Brazilian Rosewood woodtone trim arrived on instrument panel and door panels. The dash held gauges for alternator, temperature, oil pressure and fuel, plus an LED low-fuel warning. Dials had new graphics, metric readings, and bright bezels. A new three-spoke deep-dish steering wheel held a Cordoba medallion and horn switches on spokes. Optional: a new two-spoke tilt wheel. A new 60/40 front seat had dual seatback recliners and folding center armrest. Other options included power front seats and door locks, electric decklid release, manual sunroof, automatic speed control, tachometer, and space-saving spare tire.

1976 Chrysler, Newport hardtop (OCW)

NEWPORT — SERIES CL/CM — V-8 — Three body styles were offered in the Newport line: hardtop coupe, hardtop sedan, and four-door sedan. Newport Custom had some distinctive styling features, extra equipment, and a price tag about $400 higher. All full-size models rode on a 124-inch wheelbase. Newport had a chrome-plated grille with an undivided crosshatch pattern and a medallion on the driver's side. 'Chrysler' lettering was on its upper header molding. Side-by-side round quad headlamps sat in squarish bright housings. Fender tips held wraparound park/marker lenses, outboard of the headlamps. 'Chrysler' script was also on the decklid; Newport nameplates on front fenders. Recessed vertical taillamps were made up of two side-by-side segments that extended down into a notch in the bumper, with small backup lamps directly below (inset into bumper). Newport had bright headlamp bezels and hood rear edge molding, bright windshield and back window moldings, bright roof drip rail and pillar moldings, plus bright wheel opening moldings with black paint-fill. Front bumper guards were standard (rear optional). Deluxe wheel covers highlighted standard HR78 x 15 SBR blackwall tires. Seats had a standard front folding center armrest. Base engine was a 400 cu. in. V-8 with two-barrel carburetor (four-barrel in California). Both 360 and 440 cu. in. V-8s were available. Newport Custom's new grille had a fine crosshatch pattern divided by one vertical and two horizontal bars into six sections with bright upper header containing 'CHRYSLER' letters. The bumper had two small slots, alongside a center license plate housing. A Griffin medallion was on the stand-up hood ornament and the fuel filler door. 'Newport Custom' nameplates were on front fenders. Bodysides displayed full-length dual paint stripes. New wide horizontal taillamps each were split by a horizontal divider bar. Standard Custom features included bright sill, decklid and quarter extension moldings, plus bright door upper frame moldings on the four-door sedan. Base Newports had wheel lip moldings only. Customs had both sill transition and wheel lip moldings. Standard Custom 50/50 split-bench front seats had front/rear folding center armrests. A three-spoke steering wheel was new this year. Among the optional items were rear wheel-opening skirts. Body colors were: Powder Blue, Sahara Beige, Saddle Tan, Golden Fawn, Spinnaker White, and Formal Black; plus metallic Silver Cloud, Platinum, Astral Blue, Starlight Blue, Vintage Red, Bittersweet, Jade Green, Tropic Green, Deep Sherwood, Moondust, Dark Chestnut, Inca Gold, and Spanish Gold.

1976 Chrysler, Newport Custom hardtop with optional chrome-styled wheels (OCW)

TOWN & COUNTRY WAGON — SERIES CP — V-8 — Front end appearance of the full-size station wagon was the same as Newport Custom. The grille was divided into six rectangular sections by chrome moldings, with the pattern continued in openings in the bumper. A new two-spoke steering wheel had woodtone accents. Molded fiberglass formed the headliner. Wiper-arm mounted windshield washer jets were standard. Options included a heated doorgate window defroster, lighted passenger vanity mirror, and an automatic height control system that adjusted rear shock absorbers using air pressure. Base engine was a 400 cu. in. V-8; optional, a 400 V-8. Standard tires were LR78 x 15 steel-belted radials.

NEW YORKER BROUGHAM — SERIES CS — V-8 — In taking over the role of the departed Imperial, the New Yorker Brougham got a luxury

front end with concealed headlamps, plus unique rear end styling. The tour-door sedan was dropped, but New Yorker came in two-door or four-door hardtop form. The Imperial-like "waterfall" grille had a pattern of thin vertical bars that wrapped over the top (and was repeated within twin bumper slots below), divided into two sections by a body-color vertical element. Clear park/signal lamps rode the fender tips. The front license plate was bumper-mounted, below the left headlamp cover. Large horizontal front side marker lenses sat low in fenders. On the hood was a stand-up medallion. Vertical taillamps extended down into bumper tips. 'Chrysler' lettering was on the driver's side headlamp door; 'New Yorker' on front fenders; 'Chrysler New Yorker' on the decklid. Rear roof pillars displayed a 'Brougham' medallion. Broughams had rear wheel skirts with bright lower moldings, bright front wheel opening moldings, dual full-length bodyside accent stripes, and unique wheel covers. The driver's mirror was remote controlled. Standard engine was a four-barrel 440 cu. in. V-8; standard tires JR78 x 15 steel-belted radial whitewalls. Wheelbase was the same as Newport's: 124 inches. Standard fittings included a digital clock, 65-amp alternator, color-keyed shag carpeting, rear reading lamps and lavaliere straps. Cornering lamps were among the many options.

1976 Chrysler, Town & Country station wagon (OCW)

I.D. DATA: Chrysler's 13-symbol Vehicle Identification Number (VIN) was on the upper left corner of the instrument panel between the wiper pivot and 'A' post, visible through the windshield. Symbol one indicates Car Line: 'S' Cordoba; 'C' other Chryslers. Symbol two is Price Class: 'S' Special; 'L' Low; 'M' Medium; 'P' Premium. The next two symbols denote body type: '22' 2-dr. pillared hardtop coupe; '23' 2-dr. hardtop coupe; '41' 4-dr. sedan; '43' 4-dr. hardtop; '45' two-seat station wagon; '46' three-seat wagon. Symbol five is the engine code: 'G' V8318 2Bbl.; 'K' V8360 2Bbl.; 'M' V8400 2Bbl.; 'N' V8400 4Bbl.; 'P' Hi-perf V8400 4Bbl.; 'T' V8440 4Bbl. Next is the model year code: '6' 1976. Symbol seven indicates assembly plant: 'A' Lynch Road (Detroit); 'D' Belvidere, Illinois; 'R' Windsor, Ontario. The last six digits make up the sequential serial number. An abbreviated version of the VIN is also stamped on the engine block (on a pad to rear of right engine mount) and on the transmission housing. Serial numbers for 318 and 360 cu. in. engines are coded as follows: first letter series (model year); second assembly plant; next three digits indicate displacement (cu. in.); next one or two letters denote model; next four digits show the build date; and final four digits are the engine sequence number. Coding of 400 and 440 cu. in. engines is: first letter series (model year); next three digits are displacement; next one or two letters indicate model; next four digits show the build date; and the final digit reveals the shift on which the engine was built. Information on over/undersized parts is stamped on 318/360 engines at the left front of the block, just below the head; on 400 V-8, just ahead of the No. 2 cylinder, next to the distributor; and on left bank pad of 440 V-8 adjacent to front tappet rail. A Vehicle Safety Certification Label that shows (among other data) the date of manufacture is attached to the rear facing of the driver's door.

CORDOBA (V-8)

Model No.	Body/ Style No.	Body Type & Seating	Factory Price	Shipping Weight	Prod. Total
SS	22	2-dr. HT Cpe-6P	5392	3957	167,618

Production Note: All Cordobas were built in Canada.

NEWPORT (V-8)

CL	23	2-dr. HT Cpe-6P	5076	4431	2,916
CL	41	4-dr. Sed-6P	4993	4415	12,926
CL	43	4-dr. HT Sed-6P	5147	4500	3,448

NEWPORT CUSTOM (V-8)

CM	23	2-dr. HT Cpe-6P	5479	4483	3,855
CM	41	4-dr. Sed-6P	5407	4457	9,448
CM	43	4-dr. HT Sed-6P	5576	4547	6,497

TOWN & COUNTRY STATION WAGON (V-8)

Model No.	Body/ Style No.	Body Type & Seating	Factory Price	Shipping Weight	Prod. Total
CP	45	4-dr. 2S Wag-6P	6084	4982	1,271
CP	46	4-dr. 3S Wag-8P	6244	5002	3,227

NEW YORKER BROUGHAM (V-8)

| CS | 23 | 2-dr. HT Cpe-6P | 6641 | 4752 | 9,748 |
| CS | 43 | 4-dr. HT Sed-6P | 6737 | 4832 | 23,984 |

1976 Chrysler, New Yorker Brougham hardtop sedan (OCW)

ENGINE DATA: OPTIONAL V-8 (Cordoba): 90-degree, overhead valve V-8. Cast iron block and head. Displacement: 318 cu. in. (5.2 liters). Bore & stroke: 3.91 x 3.31 in. Compression ratio: 8.5:1. Brake horsepower: 150 at 4000 R.P.M. Torque: 255 lb.-ft. at 1600 R.P.M. Five main bearings. Hydraulic valve lifters. Carburetor: 2Bbl. Carter BBD80695 (or BBD80995). VIN Code: G. OPTIONAL V-8 (Cordoba, Newport): 90-degree, overhead valve V-8. Cast iron block and head. Displacement: 360 cu. in. (5.9 liters). Bore & stroke: 4.00 x 3.58 in. Compression ratio: 8.4:1. Brake horsepower: 170 at 4000 R.P.M. Torque: 280 lb.-ft. at 2400 R.P.M. Five main bearings. Hydraulic valve lifters. Carburetor: 2Bbl. Holley R7364A (Carter TQ90555 in Calif.). VIN Code: K. BASE V-8 (Cordoba, Newport): OPTIONAL (N.Y., Brougham): 90-degree, overhead valve V-8. Cast iron block and head. Displacement: 400 cu. in. (6.6 liters). Bore & stroke: 4.34 x 3.38 in. Compression ratio: 8.2:1. Brake horsepower: 175 at 4000 R.P.M. Torque: 300 lb.-ft. at 2400 R.P.M. Five main bearings. Hydraulic valve lifters. Carburetor: 2Bbl. Holley R7366A. VIN Code: M. OPTIONAL HIGH-PERFORMANCE V-8 (Cordoba): Same as 400 cu. in. V-8 above, except with Carter TQ9054S 4Bbl. carburetor. B.H.P.: 240 at 4400 R.P.M. Torque: 325 lb.-ft. at 3200 R.P.M. VIN Code: P. OPTIONAL LEAN BURN V-8 (all models): Same as 400 cu. in. V-8 above, except with Electronic Lean Burn System and 4Bbl. Carter TQ9064S or TQ9097S carburetor. B.H.P.: 210 at 4400 R.P.M. Torque: 305 lb.-ft. at 3200 R.P.M. VIN Code: N. BASE V-8 (Town & Country, N.Y. Brougham): OPTIONAL (Newport): 90-degree, overhead valve V-8. Cast iron block and head. Displacement: 440 cu. in. (7.2 liters). Bore & stroke: 4.32 x 3.75 in. Compression ratio: 8.2:1. Brake horsepower: 205 at 3600 R.P.M. Torque: 320 lb.-ft. at 2000 R.P.M. Five main bearings. Hydraulic valve lifters. Carburetor: 4Bbl. Carter TQ9058S (TQ9059S in Calif.). VIN Code: T.

CHASSIS DATA: Wheelbase: (Cordoba) 115.0 in.; (others) 124.0 in. Overall length: (Cordoba) 215.3 in.; (Newport) 227.1 in.; (Newport Cust) 226.6 in.; (T&C wag) 227.7 in.; (N.Y. Brghm) 232.7 in. Height: (Cord.) 52.6 in.; (Newpt HT cpe/sed) 54.4 in.; (Newpt sed) 55.2 in.; (T&C) 57.6 in.; (N.Y. Brghm) 54.5 in. Width: (Cord.) 77.1 in.; (Newpt cpe) 79.7 in.; (Newpt 4-dr.) 79.5 in.; (T&C) 79.4 in.; (N.Y. Brghm cpe) 79.7 in.; (N.Y. Brghm sed) 79.5 in. Front Tread: (Cord.) 61.9 in.; (others) 64.0 in. Rear Tread: (Cord.) 62.0 in.; (others) 63.4 in. Wheel size: 15 x 5.5 in. exc. (T&C, N.Y. Brghm) 15 x 6.5 in. Standard Tires: (Cord.) GR78 x 15 WSW; (Newpt) HR78 x 15; (T&C) LR78 x 15; (N.Y. Brghm) JR78 x 15.

TECHNICAL: Transmission: TorqueFlite three-speed automatic standard. Gear ratios: (1st) 2.45:1; (2nd) 1.45:1; (3rd) 1.00:1; (Rev) 2.22:1. Standard final drive ratio: 2.71:1. Steering: recirculating ball, power-assisted. Suspension: (Cordoba) front torsion bars, rear asymmetrical leaf springs and front/rear sway bars; (others) front torsion bars, sway bar and lower trailing links, and rear asymmetrical leaf springs. Brakes: Front disc, rear drum (power-assisted). Ignition: Electronic. Body construction: Unibody. Fuel tank: (Cordoba) 25.5 gal.; (Newpt/N.Y. sed) 26.5 gal.; (T&C wag) 24.0 gal.

DRIVETRAIN OPTIONS: Engines: 400 cu. in., 4Bbl. V-8 w/single exhaust: Cordoba ($45): Newpt/Cust ($45): N.Y., T&C (NC). 400 cu. in., 4Bbl. V-8 w/dual exhaust: Cordoba ($96). 440 cu. in., 4Bbl. V-8: Newpt ($184). Transmission/Differential: Sure-grip differential: Cordoba ($54); others ($58). Optional axle ratio ($15). Suspension: Heavy-duty susp. ($20-$27). H.D. shock absorbers ($7) exc. Cordoba. Automatic height

control ($100) exc. Cordoba. Other: Light trailer towing pkg.: Cord. ($74): Heavy trailer towing pkg.: Cord. ($298).

CORDOBA CONVENIENCE/APPEARANCE OPTIONS: Option Packages: Easy-order pkg. ($856). Comfort/Convenience: Air conditioning ($490). Strato ventilation ($20). Rear defroster ($81). Automatic speed control ($77). Power bench seat ($130). Power driver's bucket or 60/40 seat ($130). Power windows ($104). Power door locks ($65). Power decklid release ($19). Tilt steering wheel ($59). Tinted glass ($52). Tinted windshield ($38). Tachometer ($62). Lighting and Mirrors: Remote-control left mirror ($15). Dual remote chrome mirrors ($29-$44). Dual sport remote mirrors: painted or chrome ($37-$52). Entertainment: AM radio ($79). w/8track stereo tape player ($119-$220). AM/FM radio ($71-$149). AM/FM stereo radio ($153-$254): w/8track stereo tape player ($256-$357). Search tune AM/FM stereo radio ($213-$314). Rear speaker ($22); w/radio. Exterior Trim: Sunroof, manual ($311). Full vinyl roof ($115) exc. ($15) w/easy-order pkg. Landau vinyl roof ($100). Vinyl side molding ($40). Door edge guards ($7). Undercoating ($30). Interior Trim/Upholstery: Console ($18). Castilian velour cloth/vinyl bench seat w/armrest ($18). Velour cloth/vinyl 60/40 split bench seat w/dual recliners ($124). Leather bucket seats ($196). Wheels and Tires: Wire wheel covers ($62). Styled wheels ($113). HR78 x 15 SBR WSW tires ($25). GR70 x 15 SBR RWL ($37). Space-saver spare (NC).

NEWPORT/NEW YORKER/T&C CONVENIENCE/APPEARANCE OPTIONS: Option Packages: St. Regis pkg. (padded canopy boar-grain vinyl roof w/formal opera windows): Newpt Cust., N.Y. ($455-$598). Light pkg.: Newpt ($75): T&C ($37). Basic group: Newpt ($894): T&C ($950): N.Y. ($698). Easy order pkg.: Newpt ($1245-$1268), T&C ($1370), N.Y. ($1327). Town & Country pkg.: T&C ($122). Deluxe sound insulation pkg. ($41). Comfort/Convenience: Air cond. ($533). Auto-temp air cond. ($618) exc. ($85) w/option pkg. Rear defroster ($82) exc. T&C. Auto. speed control ($83). Power six-way bench seat: Newpt ($132). Power six-way 50/50 driver's seat ($132) exc. base Newpt. Power six-way 50/50 driver/passenger seat ($132-$264) exc. Newpt. Power windows ($167). Power door locks ($66-$95). Luxury steering wheel ($17). Tilt/telescope steering wheel ($83-$100). Tinted glass ($66). Electric clock: Newpt ($21). Digital clock ($24-$45). Lighting and mirrors: Cornering lamps ($43). Remote-control driver's mirror ($15). Remote passenger mirror: N.Y. ($30). Dual remote mirrors ($45) exc. N.Y. Lighted vanity mirror ($43). Entertainment: AM radio ($99). AM/FM radio ($62-$161). Search tune AM/FM stereo radio ($197-$318). AM/FM stereo w/8track tape player ($57-$375). Rear speaker ($22). Power antenna ($42) w/radio. Exterior Trim: Power sunroof ($754-$897). Vinyl roof ($143). Vinyl side molding ($47). Door edge protectors ($8-$13). Upper door frame moldings: Newpt sed ($29). Interior Trim/Upholstery: Vinyl bench seat trim: Newpt ($31). Castilian velour cloth/vinyl seat trim: Newpt ($84). Highlander cloth/vinyl 50/50 bench seat trim: Newpt Cust ($49). Leather 50/50 bench seat: N.Y. ($210). Wheels and Tires: Chrome styled wheels ($147); N/A T&C. Premier wheel covers ($45). HR78 x 15 WSW ($43). JR78 x 15 WSW ($31-$74). LR78 x 15 WSW ($36-$110).

HISTORY: Introduced: October 16, 1975. Model year production: Chrysler reported total shipments of 244,938 units (incl. Canadian-built Cordobas). Calendar year production: (U.S.) 127,466; (Canadian Cordoba) 200,986. Calendar year sales by U.S. dealers: 277,809 (incl. 175,456 Cordobas) for a 3.2 percent share of the market. Model year sales by U.S. dealers: 278,233 (incl.180,938 Cordobas).

HISTORICAL FOOTNOTES: Sales slipped this year, just as they had in 1975. Cordoba had sold well that year, however, and continued to find a lot of buyers in '76. In fact, more Cordobas were sold than all other Chryslers put together, and the personal-luxury coupe ranked second only to Chevrolet's Monte Carlo in that league. Movie stars pushing Chrysler products helped Cordoba at its debut and later. Also on the promotional scene, Chrysler produced a TV commercial with Jack Jones singing "What a beautiful New Yorker." That may have helped almost 40,000 Broughams find buyers for the 1976 model year, well above the 1975 total. In mid-year 1975, Chrysler-Plymouth Division had added the imported Arrow, built by Mitsubishi in Japan.

1977 CHRYSLER

Most Chrysler V-8s now had a Lean Burn engine using a computer-controlled electronic spark advanced forerunner of the fully computerized controls that soon would become standard in the industry. Introduced first on the 400 cu. in. V-8 during 1976, Lean Burn was offered this year on the 360, 400 and 440 V-8s; and later in the season, also the 318. For the first time, a Lean Burn (440 cu. in.) was announced for California

Chryslers. One goal was to meet emissions standards without a catalytic converter. But because of stricter standards, Lean Burn engines had to add a catalytic converter anyway. Also new this year was a more powerful version of the reliable 225 slant six, dubbed the "Super Six."

1977 Chrysler, LeBaron Medallion coupe with optional wire wheel covers and landau vinyl roof (OCW)

LEBARON — SERIES FH/FP — V-8 — As part of its attempt to recapture a greater share of the luxury market, Chrysler introduced the M-body LeBaron luxury mid-size as a 1977-1/2 model. The Medallion, in particular, emphasized luxury interior detailing. LeBaron was intended to rival Cadillac Seville, Lincoln Versailles and Mercedes-Benz. Dodge Diplomat was its mate. Arriving at Chrysler-Plymouth dealers in May 1977, it was called a "new-size" Chrysler; a "leaner, lighter Chrysler" for the modern era; and "the beginning of a totally new class of automobiles." Wheelbase (112.7 inches) was identical to Plymouth Volare, and Le-Baron even shared some Volare components. LeBaron, in fact, was the smallest (and lightest) Chrysler ever produced. The suspension used transverse torsion bars in front, with leaf-spring (live axle) rear. LeBaron's profile was highlighted by a long hood and sleek deck. Up front, its grille was made up of thin horizontal bars, split into an 8 x 4 pattern of wide rectangular holes by three vertical and two horizontal divider bars. Amber quad parking lamps stood directly above the quad rectangular headlamps, and both continued around the sides to meet two-section side marker lenses. The solid round stand-up hood ornament held a crest. Two-door (fixed-pillar) coupe and four-door sedan bodies were offered. LeBaron's coupe had longer door windows than Plymouth Volare, but smaller rear quarter windows. The back window showed a slight "vee" peak at center. Inside was a standard 60/40 split-bench front seat in choices of trim that ranged up to soft Corinthian leather. Medallion sedans had a padded vinyl roof, three overhead assist handles, rear vanity lamps with mirrors, and velour/vinyl or leather upholstery with fold-down center armrest. A curved left-hand dashboard section put radio and heat controls near the driver. Fuel, alternator and temperature gauges were included. Standard equipment included a 318 cu. in. V-8 with Electronic Lean Burn system, TorqueFlite automatic transmission, power brakes and steering, radial tires, and such extras as overhead reading lamps. Options included a Landau roof, 15-inch forged aluminum wheels, lighted vanity mirror, air conditioning, vinyl roof, cruise control, electric rear defroster, tilt steering, power seats, power windows, power door locks and a sliding steel sunroof.

1977 Chrysler, Cordoba hardtop with optional vinyl roof (OCW)

1977 Chrysler, Cordoba hardtop with optional landau vinyl roof (OCW)

1977 Chrysler, Cordoba hardtop with optional T-bar roof (OCW)

CORDOBA — SERIES S — V-8 — New front and rear styling arrived on Cordoba, which was called "the most successful car ever to carry the Chrysler nameplate." A new formal-look grille had a fine crosshatch pattern dominated by vertical bars, with 'Chrysler' lettering in its header. As before, the pattern repeated in bumper slots. Otherwise, the front end (and overall) appearance didn't change drastically. Opera windows had a more rectangular shape. New taillamps were similar to 1976 but were now recessed, with a different crest. Backup lamps again were inset in bumper slots, close to bumper guards. Interiors held five lights and standard plush Verdi velour cloth/vinyl split-bench seating with center armrest. Standard engine was the Lean Burn 400 cu. in. V-8 with four-barrel carburetor; optional, a 318 V-8. California and high-altitude Cordobas could have a 360 V-8. GR78 x 15 glass-belted radial blackwall tires rode 5.5-inch wheels. Cordoba colors were Claret Red, Golden Fawn, Jasmine Yellow and Spinnaker White, plus metallic Silver Cloud, Cadet Blue, Starlight Blue Sunfire, Vintage Red Sunfire, Jade Green, Forest Green Sunfire, Burnished Copper, Russet Sunfire, Caramel Tan, Light Chestnut, Coffee Sunfire, Inca Gold, Spanish Gold or Formal Black Sunfire. Joining the option list were two new roof styles. The Crown landau roof in padded elk-grain vinyl had unique opera windows and back window lighted by a slender band across the top. A new T-bar roof had lift-out tinted glass panels. Also available: a manual sunroof, plus Halo or Landau vinyl roof with opera windows and slim opera lamps. Interior options included an all-vinyl bench seat or Corinthian leather buckets, along with 60/40 reclining seats in Checkmate cloth or Verdi velour. New this year was a tilt steering wheel with hand-stitched Corinthian leather-covered rim.

1977 Chrysler, Newport hardtop sedan (OCW)

NEWPORT — SERIES CL — V-8 — Moderate front and rear restyling hit Chrysler's lower-rung full-size, while its Custom model was discontinued. Upgrading of the base Newport put it closer to the Custom's trim level. Newport's new classic-style grille (borrowed from the former Custom) had wide, bright surround moldings. The new wide horizontal taillamps also came from Custom, and the hood ornament was new. Otherwise, appearance was largely unchanged. Newport's rear bumpers had rubber-covered steel corner guards. A four-door pillarless hardtop remained available. The two-door hardtop could have a St. Regis decor package with padded Seneca grain vinyl canopy roof (forward half), formal opera windows, and color-keyed moldings for roof and opera windows. Base engine was the 400 cu. in. Lean Burn V-8. Standard inside was a cloth/vinyl split-back bench seat with folding center armrest. An optional 50/50 Williamsburg cloth bench seat had vinyl accents. Full-size body colors were: Wedgewood Blue, Mojave Beige, Golden Fawn, Jasmine Yellow, and Spinnaker White plus metallic Silver Cloud, Cadet Blue, Starlight Blue Sunfire, Vintage Red Sunfire, Jade Green, Forest Green Sunfire, Burnished Copper, Russet Sunfire, Coffee Sunfire, Moondust, Inca Gold, Spanish Gold, and Formal Black Sunfire.

TOWN & COUNTRY WAGON — SERIES CP — V-8 — Station wagons duplicated Newport's front end styling and wraparound taillamps, but came with standard 440 cu. in. Lean Burn V-8. The three-way doorgate had a power window and automatic lock. A roof air deflector was standard. Inside was all-vinyl 50/50 bench seating. Wagons rode standard blackwall

LR78 x 15 steel-belted radial tires, but weren't available in California or high-altitude areas. Options included wheelhouse opening skirts.

NEW YORKER BROUGHAM — SERIES CS — V-8 — The luxury Brougham continued its "classic" appearance and "Torsion-Quiet" ride with little change. Both two-door and four-door hardtop styles were still available. 50/50 seating came in Cortez ribbed cord and crushed velour. Instrument panels displayed simulated rosewood accents, while interiors held front and rear armrests. Standard equipment included a digital clock, remote-control left mirror, reading lamps, built-in pillows on rear pillars, and lavaliere straps (on four-door). Options included a power sunroof, electric rear defroster, new vent windows (four-door), and lighted vanity mirror. The optional St. Regis group consisted of a formal Seneca grain padded vinyl canopy (forward-half) roof, opera windows, and color-keyed molding trim for roof and opera windows. Only the St. Regis could have Burnished Silver metallic paint.

1977 Chrysler, New Yorker Brougham hardtop sedan (OCW)

I.D. DATA: Chrysler's 13-symbol Vehicle Identification Number (VIN) was on the upper left corner of the instrument panel, between the wiper pivot and 'A' post, visible through the windshield. Symbol one indicates Car Line: 'F' LeBaron; 'S' Cordoba; 'C' other Chrysler. Symbol two is Price Class: 'S' Special; 'L' Low; 'H' High; 'P' Premium. The next two symbols denote body type: '22' 2-dr. pillared hardtop coupe; '23' 2-dr. hardtop coupe; '41' 4-dr. sedan; '43' 4-dr. hardtop; '45' two-seat station wagon; '46' three-seat wagon. Symbol five is the engine code: 'G' V8318 2Bbl.; 'K' V8360 2Bbl.; 'N' V8400 4Bbl.; 'T' V8440 4Bbl. Next is the model year code: '7' 1977. Symbol seven indicates assembly plant: 'D' Belvidere, Illinois; 'R' Windsor Ontario. The last six digits make up the sequential serial number. Engine number coding and locations are the same as 1976.

LEBARON (V-8)

Model No.	Body/Style No.	Body Type & Seating	Factory Price	Shipping Weight	Prod. Total
FH	22	2-dr. Cpe-6P	5066	3510	7,280
FH	41	4-dr. Sed-6P	5224	3555	12,600

LEBARON MEDALLION (V-8)

FP	22	2-dr. Cpe-6P	5436	3591	14,444
FP	41	4-dr. Sed-6P	5594	3645	11,776

CORDOBA (V-8)

SP	22	2-dr. HT Cpe-6P	5368	N/A	Note 1
SS	22	2-dr. HT Cpe-6P	5418	4004	163,138

Note 1: Figure shown includes all Cordobas, which were built in Canada.

NEWPORT (V-8)

CL	23	2-dr. HT Cpe-6P	5374	4354	10,566
CL	41	4-dr. Sed-6P	5280	4372	32,506
CL	43	4-dr. HT Sed-6P	5433	4410	14,808

TOWN & COUNTRY STATION WAGON (V-8)

CP	45	4-dr. 2S Wag-6P	6461	4935	1,930
CP	46	4-dr. 3S Wag-8P	6647	4961	5,345

NEW YORKER BROUGHAM (V-8)

CS	23	2-dr. HT Cpe-6P	7090	4676	16,875
CS	43	4-dr. HT Sed-6P	7215	4739	45,252

ENGINE DATA: BASE V-8 (LeBaron): OPTIONAL (Cordoba): 90-degree, overhead valve V-8. Cast iron block and head. Displacement: 318 cu. in. (5.2 liters). Bore & stroke: 3.91 x 3.31 in. Compression ratio: 8.5:1. Brake horsepower: 145 at 4000 R.P.M. Torque: 245 lb.-ft. at 1600 R.P.M. Five main bearings. Hydraulic valve lifters. Carburetor: 2Bbl. Carter BBD81335 (Cordoba); BBD81425 or R7990A (LeBaron). VIN Code: G. OPTIONAL V-8 (Cordoba, Newport): 90-degree overhead valve V-8. Cast iron block and head. Displacement: 360 cu. in. (5.9 liters). Bore & stroke: 4.00 x 3.58 in. Compression ratio: 8.4:1. Brake horsepower: 155 at 3600 R.P.M. Torque: 275 lb.-ft. at 2000 R.P.M. Five

main bearings. Hydraulic valve lifters. Carburetor: 2Bbl. Holley 2245. VIN Code: K.

Note: A 4Bbl. V8360 was available in California and high-altitude areas, rated 170 horsepower. BASE V-8 (Cordoba, Newport); OPTIONAL (N.Y. Brougham, T&C): 90-degree, overhead valve V-8. Cast iron block and head. Displacement: 400 cu. in. (6.6 liters). Bore & stroke: 4.34 x 3.38 in. Compression ratio: 8.2:1. Brake horsepower: 190 at 3600 R.P.M. Torque: 305 lb.-ft. at 3200 R.P.M. Five main bearings. Hydraulic valve lifters. Carburetor: 4Bbl. Carter TQ91025. Electronic Lean Burn System. VIN Code: N. BASE V-8 (Town & Country, N.Y. Brougham); OPTIONAL (Newport) 90-degree, overhead valve V-8. Cast iron block and head. Displacement: 440 cu. in. (7.2 liters). Bore & stroke: 4.32 x 3.75 in. Compression ratio: 8.2:1. Brake horsepower: 195 at 3600 R.P.M. Torque: 320 lb.-ft. at 2000 R.P.M. Five main bearings. Hydraulic valve lifters. Carburetor: 4Bbl. Carter TQ9078S. Electronic Lean Burn System. VIN Code: T.

CHASSIS DATA: Wheelbase: (LeBaron) 112.7 in.; (Cordoba) 115.0 in.; (others) 124.0 in. Overall length: (LeB cpe) 204.1 in.; (LeB sed) 206.1 in.; (Cord.) 215.3 in.; (Newport) 226.6 in.; (T&C wag) 227.7 in.; (N.Y. Brghm) 231.0 in. Height: (LeB cpe) 53.3 in.; (LeB sed) 55.3 in.; (Cord.) 52.6 in.; (Newpt 2-dr. HT) 54.3 in.; (Newpt sed) 55.1 in.; (Newpt 4-dr HT) 54.4 in.; (T&C) 57.0 in.; (N.Y. Brghm) 54.5 in. Width: (LeB cpe) 73.5 in.; (LeB sed) 72.8 in.; (Cord.) 77.1 in.; (Newpt/N.Y. cpe) 79.7 in.; (Newpt/N.Y. sed) 79.5 in.; (T&C) 79.4 in. Front Tread: (LeB) 60.0 in.; (Cord.) 61.9 in.; (others) 64.0 in. Rear Tread: (LeB) 58.5 in.; (Cord.) 62.0 in.; (others) 63.4 in. Wheel Size: 15 x 5.5 in. exc. (N.Y. Brghm) 15 x 6.0 in.; (T&C) 15 x 6.5 in. Standard Tires: (LeB) FR78 x 15 polysteel (Cord.) GR78 x 15 GBR BSW; (Newpt) HR78 x 15 SBR BSW; (T&C) LR78 x 15 SBR WSW; (N.Y. Brghm) JR78 x 15 SBR WSW.

TECHNICAL: Transmission: TorqueFlite three-speed automatic standard. Gear ratios: (1st) 2.45:1; (2nd) 1.45:1; (3rd) 1.00:1; (Rev) 2.22:1. Standard final drive ratio: 2.71:1 exc. (LeB) 2.76:1; (Cord. V8318) 2.45:1; (N.Y. Brghm) 3.23:1. Steering: recirculating ball, power-assisted. Suspension: (Cordoba) front torsion bars, rear asymmetrical leaf springs and front/rear sway bars; (others) front torsion bars and sway bar, rear asymmetrical leaf springs. Brakes: Front disc, rear drum (power-assisted). Ignition: Electronic. Body construction: Unibody. Fuel tank: (LeB) 19.5 gal.; (Cordoba) 25.5 gal.; (Newpt/N.Y. sed) 26.5 gal.; (T&C wag) 24.0 gal.

DRIVETRAIN OPTIONS: Engines: 318 or 360 cu. in. V-8: Cordoba (NC). 360 or 400 cu. in. V-8: Newpt/N.Y. (NC). 440 cu. in., 4Bbl. V-8: Newpt ($196). Transmission/Differential: Sure-grip differential: Cordoba ($57); others ($61). Optional axle ratio ($16). Suspension: Heavy-duty susp. ($20-$27). H.D. shock absorbers ($7) exc. T&C. Automatic height control ($109) exc. Cordoba. Other: Light trailer towing pkg.: Cord. ($79); Newpt, T&C ($80). Heavy trailer towing pkg.: Cord. ($316); Newpt/N.Y./T&C ($321). Fuel pacer system ($22). Long-life battery: Cord. ($31); N.Y., T&C ($32). Engine block heater ($18) exc. Cordoba. California emission system ($74-$95). High-altitude emission system ($23-$24).

CORDOBA CONVENIENCE/APPEARANCE OPTIONS: Option Packages: Easy-order pkg. ($1110). Light pkg. ($26). Comfort/Convenience: Air cond. ($518). Rear defroster ($86). Automatic speed control ($84). Power bench seat ($143). Power driver's bucket or 60/40 seat ($143). Power windows ($113). Power door locks ($71). Power decklid release ($21). Leather steering wheel ($36). Tilt steering wheel ($59). Tinted glass ($57). Tinted windshield ($40). Tachometer ($66). Digital clock ($47). Locking gas cap ($7). Lighting and Mirrors: Remote-control left mirror ($16). Dual remote chrome mirrors ($31-$47). Dual sport remote mirrors: painted or chrome ($39-$55). Lighted vanity mirror ($45). Entertainment: AM radio ($76). AM/FM radio ($74-$149). AM/FM stereo radio ($134-$234): w/8track stereo tape player ($232-$332). Search tune AM/FM stereo radio ($214-$314). Rear speaker ($24). Exterior Trim: T-Bar roof w/lift-out panels ($605). Crown landau elk-grain vinyl roof w/over-the-top illuminated lamp band ($579-$733). Sunroof, manual ($330). Full vinyl roof ($116) exc. ($5) w/easy-order pkg. Landau vinyl roof ($112). Vinyl side molding ($42). Door edge guards ($8). Bumper rub strips ($32). Bodyside tape stripes ($42). Decklid tape stripe ($21). Undercoating ($32). Interior Trim/Upholstery: Console ($18). Vinyl bench seat ($29). Velour/vinyl 60/40 bench seat w/armrest and recliners ($132). Cloth/vinyl 60/40 bench seat w/Checkmate trim, armrest and recliners ($152). Leather bucket seats ($208). Color-keyed floor mats ($18). Pedal dress-up ($9). Trunk dress-up ($45). Wheels and Tires: Wire wheel covers ($73). Styled wheels ($120). GR78 x 15 GBR WSW (NC to $43). GR78 x 15 SBR WSW ($50-$93). HR78 x 15 SBR WSW tires ($77-$120). GR70 x 15 fiber-belt RWL ($40-$82). Conventional spare tire (NC).

NEWPORT/NEW YORKER/T&C CONVENIENCE/APPEARANCE OPTIONS: Option Packages: St. Regis pkg. (padded canopy Seneca-grain vinyl roof w/formal opera windows): Newpt, N.Y. ($455-$600). Light pkg.: Newpt ($80); T&C ($39). Basic group: Newpt ($939); T&C

($999); N.Y. ($730). Easy order pkg.: Newpt ($1305); T&C ($1429); N.Y. ($1384). Town & Country pkg.: T&C ($128). Deluxe sound insulation pkg.: Newpt ($43). Comfort/Convenience: Air cond. ($560). Auto-temp air cond. ($645) exc. ($85) w/option pkg. Rear defroster ($87). Auto. speed control ($88). Power six-way bench seat: Newpt ($145). Power six-way 50/50 driver's seat ($145). Power six-way 50/50 driver/passenger seat ($145-$290). Power windows ($179) exc. N.Y. Power door locks ($72-$102). Power decklid release ($21). Luxury steering wheel ($18) exc. N.Y. Tilt/telescope steering wheel ($88-$106). Tinted glass ($72). Electric clock: Newpt ($22). Digital clock ($26-$48). Deluxe wiper/washer pkg.: Newpt ($17). Locking gas cap ($8). Lighting and Mirrors: Cornering lamps ($46). Remote-control driver's mirror ($16) exc. N.Y. Remote passenger mirror: N.Y. ($31). Dual remote mirrors ($32-$48) exc. N.Y. Lighted vanity mirror ($46). Entertainment: AM radio ($99). AM/FM radio ($62-$161). Search tune AM/FM stereo radio ($195-$318): std. on N.Y. AM/FM stereo w/8track tape player ($31-$349). Rear speaker ($25). Power antenna ($44). Exterior Trim: Power sunroof w/vinyl roof ($764-$908). Vinyl roof ($145). Manual vent windows: 4-dr. ($43). Vinyl side moldings ($48). Wheelhouse opening skirts: Newpt ($46). Door edge protectors ($9-$14). Upper door frame moldings: Newpt 4-dr. ($31). Rear bumper guards: T&C ($24). Undercoating ($37) exc. N.Y. Interior Trim/Upholstery: Vinyl bench seat trim: Newpt ($33). Cloth 50/50 bench seat: Newpt ($127). Vinyl 50/50 bench seat: Newpt ($141). Leather 50/50 bench seat: N.Y. ($223). Color-keyed floor mats ($20). Trunk dress-up ($24-$45). Wheels and Tires: Chrome styled wheels ($156): N/A T&C. Premier wheel covers ($48). HR78 x 15 WSW (NC to $48). JR78 x 15 WSW ($32-$80). LR78 x 15 WSW ($38-$118). Conventional spare tire (NC).

LEBARON OPTIONS: LeBaron arrived late in the model year. Options were similar to those offered during the complete 1978 model year; see that listing.

HISTORY: Introduced: October 1, 1976. Model year production: 336,520 (incl. Canadian-built Cordobas). Calendar year production (U.S.): 247,063. Calendar year sales by U.S. dealers: 317,012 for a 3.5 percent share of the market. Model year sales by U.S. dealers: 302,629 (incl. 147,814 Cordobas).

HISTORICAL FOOTNOTES: Impressive model year sales were led by a strong start for the new LeBaron. Newport/New Yorker sales also rose, unlike those of the full-size Plymouth. Cordoba declined, however. Sales for the Chrysler-Plymouth Division enjoyed only a slight increase, even though production jumped by some 22 percent. The LeBaron name had enjoyed a long, if sporadic history at Chrysler, stretching back to 1933 when the company took over the Briggs body company. But LeBaron-bodied Chryslers had been built even before that time.

1978 CHRYSLER

1978 Chrysler, LeBaron Medallion coupe with optional wire wheel covers and landau vinyl roof (OCW)

Major technical news for 1978 was the arrival of a new lockup torque converter for the TorqueFlite automatic transmission. Direct drive cut in at about 27-31 miles per hour. All V-8 engines now had Electronic Lean Burn, including the California four-barrel 318. The newest electronic sound system was an AM/FM stereo with foot-operated floor switch search-tune capability. Also new: a 40-channel CB transceiver built into AM or AM/FM stereo radios. Chrysler and Plymouth were trimmed in weight to boost fuel economy. Many parts were redesigned with aircraft-type lightening holes in steel panels. Models weighed an average 300 pounds less than their predecessors of 1977. Corrosion protection included the use of one-side galvanized sheet steel for front fenders and door

outer panels of compacts and mid-sizes; also in door outer panels of standard-size cars. Big Chrysler station wagons dropped out of the lineup, but LeBaron added a new wagon to carry on the Town & Country name.

1978 Chrysler, LeBaron Medallion coupe with optional T-bar roof (OCW)

1978 Chrysler, LeBaron Medallion sedan with optional wire wheel covers (OCW)

LEBARON — SERIES F — SIX/V-8 — A Town & Country station wagon joined the two-door coupe and four-door sedan that had been introduced in spring 1977, on the same 112.7-inch wheelbase. LeBaron had first appeared with a standard 318 cu. in. V-8; but for full year 1978 the 225 cu. in. Super Six became standard, with either a 318 or 360 V-8 optional. Overdrive-4 manual transmission was standard with both the six and 318 V-8. A new low-budget 'S' series was priced about $200 lower than base LeBarons. LeBaron's grille had bold rectangular openings framing fine horizontal chromed bars. 'Chrysler' lettering was on the bright upper grille molding. Quad side-by-side rectangular headlamps sat directly below rectangular parking lamps. Chromed headlamp/parking lamp framing wrapped around to car sides to frame amber marker lamps and cornering lamp lenses. On the hood was a stand-up eagle ornament. Opera lamps were standard on two-doors; padded full vinyl roof on four-doors. Wraparound taillamps held eagle medallions. Door pull straps were standard, as were power brakes and steering. The step-up Medallion added center-pillar assist handles (two-door), door courtesy lights, rear pillar vanity mirrors with lamps (four-door), and a map reading lamp. LeBaron tires were FR78 x 15 glass-belted radial blackwalls. Marine teakwood woodtone bodyside and liftgate trim on the new Town & Country wagon was framed with simulated white ash moldings. Authentic grain patterns and simulated finger-locking joints enhanced its effect. Wide sill moldings and wheel opening moldings were available if the "wood" exterior was deleted. The carpeted cargo compartment held stainless-steel skid strips. 'LeBaron' script was on front fenders and tailgate, 'Chrysler' block letters on the liftgate, a Chrysler eagle on cornering lamp lenses. A Town & Country nameplate stood on quarter panels and a LeBaron medallion on 'C' pillars. Rear bumper guards held protective inserts. Bright moldings went on the windshield, quarter windows, liftgate window, roof drip rail, belt, and door upper frame. New 60/40 thin front seats with center armrests were standard on wagon and Medallion.

CORDOBA — SERIES SS — V-8 — The personal-luxury Cordoba coupe featured a new front end look, highlighted by vertically-stacked rectangular headlamps that replaced the former round units. The plainer square crosshatch pattern of the new finely meshed, forward-jutting chrome grille continued in twin bumper slots below. 'Chrysler' lettering again appeared in the grille header. At the corners of front-fender end panels

were combined park/signal/marker lamps (clear/amber/clear). 'Cordoba' script stood just ahead of the door, accompanied by a round emblem. The see-through stand-up hood ornament consisted of a round insignia inside a five-sided frame. This year's decklid showed a sharper character line. Taillamps with round Cordoba crest were larger, and the back bumper was new. The license plate no longer extended down into the back bumper notch. Rear side marker lamps consisted of two side-by-side elements instead of one tri-section unit. Cordoba also had new wide full-length sill moldings, plus front and rear bumper guards. Nine new colors were offered. The full list included: Dove Gray, Classic Cream, Spinnaker White and Formal Black plus metallic Pewter Gray, Charcoal Gray Sunfire, Cadet Blue, Starlight Blue Sunfire, Tapestry Red Sunfire, Mint Green, Augusta Green Sunfire, Caramel Tan, and Sable Tan Sunfire. Inside was a new thin split-back bench seat with folding center armrest. Standard upholstery choices were Cortez ribbed velour and Whittier cloth. Two new interior trim colors were offered: Dove Gray and Canyon Red. Instrument panel inserts were simulated Brazilian rosewood, with circular dials and miles/kilometers speedometer display. New to Cordoba was an optional 318 cu. in. V-8 with Lean Burn. Standard engine was the Lean Burn 400 cu. in. V-8, with the 360 cu. in. V-8 also optional. A new 'S' model, priced $200 lower than the base Cordoba, amounted to 7.7 percent of total production. New options included cornering lamps and a factory-installed power sunroof. Also available: the Crown and T-bar roofs introduced in 1977, a cream-colored vinyl roof, three-spoke steering wheel with Corinthian leather-wrapped rim, forged aluminum wheels, and premium wheel covers with classic hex-nut hub and Cordoba crest. New optional low-back bucket seats came in Corinthian leather or Cortez cloth. An all-vinyl bench seat and cloth/vinyl 60/40 split-bench seats also were available.

1978 Chrysler, LeBaron Town & Country station wagon with optional air deflector (OCW)

NEWPORT — SERIES CL — V-8 — Both the Newport sedan and Town & Country station wagon were dropped for 1978, but the T & C name emerged on the new LeBaron wagon. Newport's appearance changed little. The Lean Burn 400 cu. in. V-8 with four-barrel was now standard on both Newport and New Yorker Brougham. Newports could also have a 360 V-8. Both full-size Chryslers had six new body colors. The complete list included: Formal Black, Jasmine Yellow, Golden Fawn, Dove Gray, and Spinnaker White plus metallic Starlight Blue Sunfire, Cadet Blue, Spanish Gold, Charcoal Gray Sunfire, Pewter Gray, Tapestry Red Sunfire, Mint Green and Augusta Green Sunfire. The new lock-up torque converter in third gear was standard with 400 cu. in. V-8s (and 360 cu. in. V-8s in California), but not available with trailer-assist option, or for high altitudes. The standard Cambridge cloth/vinyl split-back bench seat had a fold-down center armrest; all-vinyl was available. New optional sill moldings enhanced the body lines. Also joining the option list was geometric-design Tuscany textured velour fabric with Newport's 50/50 optional front seat, premium wheel covers, a digital clock, and two new vinyl roof colors (red and silver). A St. Regis padded formal roof and trim was available for the Newport coupe.

1978 Chrysler, Cordoba hardtop with optional landau vinyl roof (OCW)

NEW YORKER BROUGHAM — SERIES CS — V-8 — Luxury Broughams got a new segmented grille and modified bodyside styling, along with the six new body colors and two new optional vinyl roofs offered on both full-size models. Once again, the grille held concealed headlamps. The new divided grille, similar to the 1977 design, held a broadband top and wide center divider; but vertical bars on each side of the divider separated the tighter pattern into four sections. Along Brougham bodysides, new double tape stripes followed the lower body character lines; and at the rear, a dual tape stripe accented the decklid and matched the new side stripes. Bright vertical accent lines appeared on lens centers of the dual-element taillamps. Rearview mirrors and door handles had color-keyed accents, while the driver's mirror displayed Chrysler script. Intermittent wipers and a digital clock were now standard. Power windows continued as standard. Floating-pillow 50/50 seats were upholstered in Verdi crushed velour, with fold-down armrests. Four-doors had lavaliere straps in back and a reclining passenger seat. Rear pillars held integral pillows. The 400 cu. in. V-8 replaced the Brougham's previous 440, which was still an option this year. For $631, four-door Broughams could get an optional Salon decor package with special high-gloss silver crystal metallic paint, silver vinyl roof, formal back window, body and deck stripes, leather-covered steering wheel, and aluminum fascia road wheels. Nearly six percent of New Yorkers carried the Salon package. New optional wheel covers displayed brushed-finish centers and simulated hex nuts.

1978 Chrysler, Newport hardtop with optional chrome-styled wheels (OCW)

I.D. DATA: Chrysler's 13-symbol Vehicle Identification Number (VIN) again was on the upper left corner of the instrument panel, between the wiper pivot and 'A' post, visible through the windshield. Symbol one indicates Car Line: 'F' LeBaron; 'S' Cordoba; 'C' Newport/New Yorker. Symbol two is Price Class: 'S' Special; 'L' Low; 'M' Medium; 'H' High; 'P' Premium. The next two symbols denote body type: '22' 2-dr. pillared hardtop coupe; '23' 2-dr. hardtop coupe; '41' 4-dr. sedan; '43' 4-dr. hardtop; '45' two-seat station wagon. Symbol five is the engine code: 'D' L6225 2Bbl.; 'C' L6225 1Bbl. (Calif.); 'G' V8318 2Bbl.; 'K' V8360 2Bbl.; 'J' V8360 4Bbl. (Calif.); 'L' H.O. V8360 4Bbl.; 'N' V8400 4Bbl.; 'T' V8440 4Bbl. Next is the model year code: '8' 1978. Symbol seven indicates assembly plant: 'C' Jefferson; 'G' St. Louis; 'R' Windsor, Ontario. The last six digits make up the sequential serial number. Engine number coding is similar to 1976-77.

LEBARON (SIX/V-8)

Model No.	Body/ Style No.	Body Type & Seating	Factory Price	Shipping Weight	Prod. Total
FH	22	2-dr. Cpe-6P	5114/5290	3420/3505	15,999
FH	41	4-dr. Sed-6P	5270/5446	3465/3550	22,215

LEBARON 'S' (SIX/V-8)

| FM | 22 | 2-dr. Cpe-6P | 4894/5080 | 3335/3415 | 2,101 |
| FM | 41 | 4-dr. Sed-6P | 5060/5246 | 3400/3485 | 2,101 |

LEBARON MEDALLION (SIX/V-8)

| FP | 22 | 2-dr. Cpe-6P | 5484/5660 | 3495/3580 | 29,213 |
| FP | 41 | 4-dr. Sed-6P | 5640/5816 | 3550/3635 | 35,259 |

LEBARON TOWN & COUNTRY (SIX/V-8)

| FH | 45 | 4-dr. Sta Wag-6P | 5672/5848 | 3600/3685 | 21,504 |

LeBaron Price & Weight Note: Figures before the slash are for six-cylinder engine, after the slash for lowest-priced V-8 engine.

CORDOBA (V-8)

| SS | 22 | 2-dr. HT Cpe-6P | 5750 | 4021 | 108,054 |

CORDOBA 'S' (V-8)

| SS | 22 | 2-dr. HT Cpe-6P | 5550 | N/A | Note 1 |

Note 1: Figure shown above includes both base and 'S' Cordobas, all of which were built in Canada.

NEWPORT (V-8)

| CL | 23 | 2-dr. HT Cpe-6P | 5727 | 4394 | 5,987 |
| CL | 43 | 4-dr. HT Sed-6P | 5802 | 4460 | 24,089 |

NEW YORKER BROUGHAM (V-8)

| CS | 23 | 2-dr. HT Cpe-6P | 7591 | 4619 | 9,624 |
| CS | 43 | 4-dr. Pill. HT-6P | 7715 | 4669 | 26,873 |

ENGINE DATA: BASE SIX (LeBaron): Inline, overhead valve six-cylinder. Cast iron block and head. Displacement: 225 cu. in. (3.7 liters). Bore & stroke: 3.40 x 4.12 in. Compression ratio: 8.4:1. Brake horsepower: 110 at 3600 R.P.M. Torque: 180 lb.-ft. at 2000 R.P.M. Four main bearings. Solid valve lifters. Carburetor: 2Bbl. Carter BBD. VIN Code: D.

Note: California and high-altitude LeBarons had a 1Bbl. six-cylinder engine, rated 90 horsepower. OPTIONAL V-8 (LeBaron, Cordoba): 90-degree, overhead valve V-8. Cast iron block and head. Displacement: 318 cu. in. (5.2 liters). Bore & stroke: 3.91 x 3.31 in. Compression ratio: 8.5:1. Brake horsepower: 140 at 4000 R.P.M. Torque: 245 lb.-ft. at 1600 R.P.M. Five main bearings. Hydraulic valve lifters. Carburetor: 2Bbl. Carter BBD or Holley. Electronic Lean Burn. VIN Code: G. BASE V-8 (Cordoba 'S'); OPTIONAL (other models): 90-degree, overhead valve V-8. Cast iron block and head. Displacement: 360 cu. in. (5.9 liters). Bore & stroke: 4.00 x 3.58 in. Compression ratio: 8.4:1. Brake horsepower: 155 at 3600 R.P.M. Torque: 270 lb.-ft. at 2400 R.P.M. Five main bearings. Hydraulic valve lifters. Carburetor: 2Bbl. Holley. Electronic Lean Burn. VIN Code: K.

Note: A 4Bbl. V8360 was available in California and high-altitude areas, rated 170 horsepower. A heavy-duty 4Bbl. was also available, without Lean Burn, rated 175 horsepower. BASE V-8 (Cordoba, Newport, New Yorker); OPTIONAL (Cordoba 'S'): 90-degree, overhead valve V-8. Cast iron block and head. Displacement: 400 cu. in. (6.6 liters). Bore & stroke: 4.34 x 3.38 in. Compression ratio: 8.2:1. Brake horsepower: 190 at 3600 R.P.M. Torque: 305 lb.-ft. at 3200 R.P.M. Five main bearings. Hydraulic valve lifters. Carburetor: 4Bbl. Carter TQ. Electronic Lean Burn System. VIN Code: N. OPTIONAL V-8 (Newport, New Yorker): 90-degree, overhead valve V-8. Cast iron block and head. Displacement: 440 cu. in. (7.2 liters). Bore & stroke: 4.32 x 3.75 in. Compression ratio: 8.2:1. Brake horsepower: 195 at 3600 R.P.M. Torque: 320 lb.-ft. at 2000 R.P.M. Five main bearings. Hydraulic valve lifters. Carburetor: 4Bbl. Carter TQ. Electronic Lean Burn System. VIN Code: T.

1978 Chrysler, New Yorker hardtop sedan (OCW)

CHASSIS DATA: Wheelbase: (LeBaron) 112.7 in.; (Cordoba) 114.9 in.; (others) 123.9 in. Overall length: (LeB cpe) 204.1 in.; (LeB sed) 206.1 in.; (LeB wag) 202.8 in.; (Cord.) 215.8 in.; (Newport) 227.1 in.; (N.Y.) 231.0 in. Height: (LeB cpe) 53.3 in.; (LeB sed) 55.3 in.; (LeB wag) 55.7 in.; (Cord.) 53.1 in.; (Newpt/N.Y.) 54.7 in. Width: (LeB cpe) 73.5 in.; (LeB sed/wag) 73.3 in.; (Cord.) 77.1 in.; (Newpt/N.Y.) 79.7 in.; (Newpt/N.Y. sed) 79.5 in. Front Tread: (LeB) 60.0 in.; (Cord.) 61.9 in.; (others) 64.0 in. Rear Tread: (LeB) 58.5 in.; (Cord.) 62.0 in.; (others) 63.4 in. Wheel size: 15 x 5.5 in. Standard Tires: (LeB) FR78 x 15 GBR BSW; (Cord.) FR78 x 15 GBR BSW; (Newpt) GR78 x 15 BSW; (N.Y.) HR78 x 15 SBR WSW.

TECHNICAL: Transmission: Overdrive-4 manual trans. standard on LeBaron cpe/sed. Gear ratios: (1st) 3.09:1; (2nd) 1.67:1; (3rd) 1.00:1; (4th) 0.71:1; (Rev) 3.00:1. TorqueFlite three-speed automatic standard (optional on LeBaron): (1st) 2.45:1; (2nd) 1.45:1; (3rd) 1.00:1; (Rev) 2.22:1. Standard final drive ratio: (LeB) 3.23:1, 2.94:1 or 2.45:1; (Cord.) 2.45:1; (Newpt/N.Y.) 2.71:1. Steering: recirculating ball, power-assisted. Suspension: (LeBaron) front transverse torsion bars with control arms and anti-sway bar, rigid rear axle with semi-elliptic leaf springs; (Cordoba) front torsion bars, rear asymmetrical leaf springs and front/rear sway bars; (Newport/N.Y.) front torsion bars and sway bar, rear asymmetrical leaf springs. Brakes: Front disc, rear drum (power-assisted). Ignition: Electronic. Body construction: Unibody. Fuel tank: (LeB) 19.5 gal.; (Cordoba) 25.5 gal.; (Newpt/N.Y. sed) 26.5 gal.

DRIVETRAIN OPTIONS: Engines: 318 cu. in., 2Bbl. V-8: LeBaron ($176); Cordoba (NC). 318 cu. in., 4Bbl. V-8: LeB ($221). 360 cu. in., 2Bbl. V-8: LeB ($285). H.D. 360 cu. in., 2Bbl. V-8: LeB ($345). 360 cu. in., 4Bbl. V-8: LeB ($330); Cordoba (NC); Cordoba 'S' ($45); Newpt/N.Y. (NC). H.D. 360 cu. in., 4Bbl. V-8: LeB ($481); Cordoba ($102); Cordoba 'S' ($195). 400 cu. in. V-8: Cordoba 'S' ($94). H.D.

400 cu. in. V-8: Cordoba ($128); Cordoba 'S' ($222). 440 cu. in., 4Bbl. V-8: Newpt ($207). Transmission/Differential: Automatic trans.: LeB ($165). Sure-grip differential: LeB/Cord. ($62); others ($68). Suspension: H.D. susp. ($26-$28). H.D. shock absorbers ($7) exc. LeB. Automatic height control: Newpt/N.Y. ($122). Other: Heavy-duty trailer assist pkg.: LeB ($154); Cord. ($183); Newpt/N.Y. ($184). Long-life battery ($33-$34). Engine block heater: Newpt/N.Y. ($19). California emission system ($79-$80). High-altitude emission system ($34-$35).

LEBARON CONVENIENCE/APPEARANCE OPTIONS: Option Packages: Basic equipment pkg. ($1055-$1219). Light pkg. ($69-$80). Deluxe wiper/washer pkg. ($41). Deluxe insulation pkg. ($9-$80). Comfort/Convenience: Air cond. ($563). Rear defroster ($91). Automatic speed control ($94). Power seat ($155). Power windows ($129-$179). Power door locks ($83-$116). Power decklid or tailgate release ($22-$23). Luxury steering wheel ($19). Leather-wrapped steering wheel ($57). Tilt steering wheel ($71). Tinted glass ($65). Digital clock ($50). Locking gas cap ($7). Lighting and Mirrors: Cornering lamps ($48). Remote-control left mirror ($17), right ($33). Dual remote chrome mirrors ($33-$56). Lighted vanity mirror ($48). Entertainment: AM radio ($81). AM/CB radio ($333-$414). AM/FM radio ($81-$161). AM/FM stereo radio ($157-$237), w/CB ($490-$570). AM/FM stereo w/8track player ($256-$336). Search tune AM/FM stereo radio ($284-$365). Rear speaker ($25). Power antenna ($46). Exterior Trim: T-Bar roof w/lift-out panels ($643). Power sunroof: metal ($626); glass ($788). Landau vinyl roof ($137). Vinyl bodyside molding ($44). Front bumper guards ($21). Door edge guards ($11-$20). Decklid tape stripe ($23). Luggage rack: wag ($89). Air deflector: wag ($29). Undercoating ($24). Interior Trim/Upholstery: Vinyl bench seat ($48). Cloth 60/40 seat: wag ($140). Leather 60/40 seat ($270-$410). Color-keyed floor mats ($22). Color-keyed seatbelts ($16). Pedal dress-up ($10). Wheels and Tires: Wire wheel covers ($58-$99). Premier wheel covers ($41). Forged aluminum wheels ($208-$248). FR78 x 15 GBR WSW ($48). FR78 x 15 SBR WSW ($57-$106). Conventional spare tire (NC).

CORDOBA CONVENIENCE/APPEARANCE OPTIONS: Option Packages: Basic equipment pkg. ($1053). Light pkg. ($28). Comfort/Convenience: Air cond. ($563). Rear defroster ($91). Automatic speed control ($94). Power seat ($155). Power windows ($129). Power door locks ($83). Power decklid release ($24). Leather-wrapped steering wheel ($38). Tilt steering wheel ($71). Tinted glass ($65). Tinted windshield ($42). Tachometer ($70). Digital clock ($50). Deluxe wipers ($34). Locking gas cap ($7). Lighting and Mirrors: Cornering lamps ($48). Remote-control left mirror ($17). Dual remote chrome mirrors ($33-$50). Dual sport remote mirrors painted or chrome ($41-$58). Lighted vanity mirror ($48). Entertainment: Same as LeBaron. Exterior Trim: T-Bar roof w/lift-out panels ($643). Crown landau elk-grain vinyl roof w/over-the-top illuminated lamp band ($668-$785). Power sunroof ($516). Full vinyl roof ($121) exc. ($5) w/easy-order pkg. Landau vinyl roof ($117). Vinyl bodyside molding ($44). Door edge guards ($11). Bumper rub strips ($35). Bodyside tape stripes ($45). Decklid tape stripe ($23). Undercoating ($34). Interior Trim/Upholstery: Console ($58). Vinyl bench seat ($31). Velour/vinyl 60/40 bench seat w/armrest and recliner ($140). Velour/vinyl bucket seats w/armrest and dual recliners ($70). Leather bucket seats ($270). Color-keyed floor mats ($22). Color-keyed seatbelts ($16). Pedal dress-up ($10). Trunk dress-up ($47). Wheels and Tires: Wire wheel covers ($99). Premium wheel covers ($41). Styled wheels ($248). GR78 x 15 GBR BSW ($21). GR78 x 15 GBR WSW (NC to $48). GR78 x 15 SBR WSW ($57-$106). HR78 x 15 SBR WSW tires ($83-$131). GR60 x 15 Aramid-belt RWL ($219-$267). Conventional spare tire (NC).

NEWPORT/NEW YORKER CONVENIENCE/APPEARANCE OPTIONS: Option Packages: New Yorker Salon pkg.: 4-dr. ($631). St. Regis pkg.: padded canopy Seneca-grain vinyl roof w/formal opera windows and trim-off moldings ($493-$642). Light pkg., Newpt ($85). Basic group: Newpt ($1222); N.Y. ($1084). Deluxe sound insulation pkg., Newpt ($46). Comfort/Convenience: Air cond. ($602). Auto-temp air cond. ($693) exc. ($91) w/option pkg. Rear defroster ($98). Auto. speed control ($99). Power driver's seat ($157); both ($314). Power windows: Newpt ($198). Power door locks ($84-$118). Power decklid release ($24). Luxury steering wheel: Newpt ($19). Tilt/telescope steering wheel ($100-$119). Tinted glass ($79). Electric clock: Newpt ($23). Digital clock: Newpt ($51). Deluxe wiper/washer pkg.: Newpt ($42). Locking gas cap ($9). Lighting and Mirrors: Cornering lamps ($49). Remote-control driver's mirror: Newpt ($17). Remote passenger mirror: N.Y. ($33). Dual remote mirrors: Newpt ($33-$51). Lighted vanity mirror ($49). Entertainment: AM radio ($103). AM/CB radio ($337-$440). AM/FM radio ($70-$173). AM/FM stereo radio w/CB ($484-$587). AM/FM stereo w/8track tape player ($197-$353). Search tune AM/FM stereo radio ($181-$369). Rear speaker ($26). Power antenna ($47). Exterior Trim: Power sunroof w/vinyl roof ($763-$912). Vinyl roof ($149). Manual vent windows: 4-dr. ($46). Vinyl side moldings ($50). Sill moldings ($29). Wheelhouse opening skirts ($49). Door edge protectors ($12-$20). Bodyside tape stripe: Newpt ($46). Undercoating: Newpt ($40). Interior Trim/Upholstery: Vinyl bench seat trim: Newpt

($35). Cloth 50/50 bench seat: Newpt ($135). Vinyl 50/50 bench seat: Newpt ($150). Leather 50/50 bench seat: N.Y. ($274). Color-keyed floor mats ($24). Color-keyed seatbelts: Newpt ($17). Trunk dress-up ($27-$48). Wheels and Tires: Chrome styled wheels ($140). Premier wheel covers ($50). HR78 x 15 BSW ($25). HR78 x 15 WSW (NC to $51). JR78 x 15 WSW ($52-$103). Conventional spare tire (NC).

HISTORY: Introduced: October 7, 1977. Model year production: 303,019 (incl. Canadian-built Cordobas). Calendar year production (U.S.): 236,504. Calendar year sales by U.S. dealers: 298,892. Model year sales by U.S. dealers: 304,608 (incl. 112,560 Cordobas).

HISTORICAL FOOTNOTES: Chrysler-Plymouth model year sales slumped by 10 percent for 1978. Sales of full-size Chryslers slipped by 35 percent. Only LeBaron made a good showing, with sales up handsomely: from just 41,536 in a short 1977 model year to 118,583 in full-year '78. This was the final year for big Chryslers, which would be replaced for 1979 by new R-body versions.

1979 CHRYSLER

1979 Chrysler, LeBaron Medallion coupe with optional landau vinyl roof and sunroof (OCW)

1979 Chrysler, LeBaron sedan (OCW)

Full-size Chryslers finally departed, their place taken over by the new R-body versions. These downsized Newport/New Yorker four-door pillared hardtops riding on a 118.5-inch wheelbase still carried six passengers and were "engineered to provide big-car ride and handling while incorporating many new weight-saving materials for fuel efficiency." Efficiency, in fact, was this year's Chrysler/Plymouth byword. The 400 and 440 cu. in. V-8s were dropped, while the 318 and 360 cu. in. V-8s were lightened. More models now came with slant six-cylinder engines (which had a new two-piece aluminum intake manifold). Newport/New Yorker were the first domestic Chrysler cars to use chrome-plated stamped aluminum bumpers, which saved 50-60 pounds. All models had aluminum and plastic master cylinders. Engines had lightweight radiators. All domestic Chrysler products had a diagnostic connector this year, on the left wheelhouse. That was to be used in conjunction with Chrysler's electronic engine performance analyzer. The 360 cu. in. V-8 included a new 430-amp maintenance-free battery. Improved anti-corrosion protection included many more body panels of galvanized steel.

LEBARON — SERIES F — SIX/V-8 — LeBaron's lineup was revised to include base, high-line Salon and premium Medallion models. A new chrome-plated grille had bold, rectangular openings formed by one vertical and two horizontal divider bars enclosing a pattern of fine vertical chromed bars. Quad rectangular parking lamps again stood directly over quad rectangular headlamps. Framing for headlamps and parking lamps wrapped around fenders to contain the amber marker lamps and cornering lamp lenses. A distinctive round eagle ornament stood on the hood.

Medallion 'C' pillars held a new opera lamp. New wide wraparound three-segment taillamps held bright eagle medallions in the center squares. Backup lamps were set into the bumper, while large 'Chrysler' block letters went on the panel between the taillamps. Sculptured-look quarter panels on two-doors curved downward just to the rear of the door. Rectangular opera windows with two-door vinyl roofs followed the body slope at their base. Salon models had new standard bodyside accent tape stripes. Medallions added deck lower panel accent striping. Salon/Medallion four-doors had a full padded vinyl roof with brushed stainless center pillar moldings. Town & Country station wagons again had teakwood-grain woodtone appliqués with simulated white ash moldings (woodtone could be deleted). Base engine was the one-barrel 225 cu. in. slant six; two-barrel Super Six optional (except in California). Both 318 and 360 cu. in. V-8s were available. Overdrive-4 manual transmission was standard with the one-barrel six. TorqueFlite with lock-up torque converter came with normal-duty V-8s (and 225 2Bbl. without air conditioning). Power brakes and steering were standard, as was a compact spare tire (except on wagons). All models had woodtone trim on instrument cluster and glovebox door. All but the base model had door-pull straps. Door courtesy lights were standard on Medallion; center-pillar assist handles on Medallion two-doors. Salon and Medallion two-doors had windshield header reading lamps; Medallion added map-reading lamps. Added to LeBaron's option list were halogen headlamps and new wire wheel covers. Two- and four-door Salons could have cloth/vinyl bucket seats with center cushion and folding center armrest. A new Landau vinyl roof with rectangular opera windows was available on two-doors. A total of 1,936 LeBarons had the Sport appearance package installed. That package included a three-spoke steering wheel, color-keyed remote sport mirrors, and sport wheels. LeBaron body colors were: Dove Gray, Chianti Red, Spinnaker White, Formal Black and Light Cashmere; plus metallic Cadet Blue, Ensign Blue, Teal Frost, Regent Red Sunfire, Teal Green Sunfire, and Sable Tan Sunfire. Wagons could also get Medium Cashmere Metallic.

1979 Chrysler, LeBaron Town & Country station wagon with optional luggage rack and forged aluminum wheels (OCW)

1979 Chrysler, Cordoba hardtop (prototype with non-vinyl roof and two-tone paint treatment) (OCW)

CORDOBA — SERIES SS — V-8 — A bold new vertically-textured grille, with thin vertical strips and heavy frame surround, repeated its pattern in twin bumper slots of Cordoba, billed as "the contemporary classic." Stacked quad rectangular headlamps appeared again, along with combined parking/turn signal/side marker lights mounted at corners of the front end panel. 'Chrysler' letters were recessed into the grille header. Front fenders held Cordoba nameplates and medallions. On the hood was a stand-up ornament. Chrysler script and a Cordoba nameplate also went on the decklid. Large taillamps displayed a distinctive crest. In addition to opera windows and lamps, Cordobas held an ample array of brightwork, including full wheel opening moldings and wide lower sill moldings (plus fender and quarter extensions). Seven body colors were new. The list included: Dove Gray, Nightwatch Blue, Chianti Red, Light Cashmere, Spinnaker White and Formal Black; plus metallic Frost Blue, Teal Frost, Teal Green Sunfire, Regent Red Sunfire, and Sable Tan Sunfire. Three new trim colors were available: Midnight Blue, Teal Green, and Cashmere. The standard split-back bench seat had a folding center

armrest. Woodtone trimmed the instrument panel, and there was a new standard High-Low heater/defroster. Joining the option list were semi-automatic temperature-control air conditioning, two new aluminum wheel styles, and a Roadability package (including rear sway bar and 15 x 7 inch wheels). New two-tone paint treatments could be ordered with Crown and Landau vinyl roofs. Halogen headlamps and wire wheel covers also were available. A new $527 Special Appearance package included two-tone paint, accept stripes, square-cornered opera windows, black nerf stripes, dual remote sport mirrors (color-keyed to lower body), leather-wrapped three-spoke steering wheel, and Aramid-belted radial tires with gold/white sidewalls. (Sill molding extensions were deleted.) Only 693 Cordobas came with the Crown roof. One noteworthy late addition to the option list was a Cordoba "300" package (RPO Code A74) that included bucket seats, blacked-out crossbar grille with medallion, special trim, and the 195-horsepower 360 cu. in. V-8 engine. A total of 3,811 Cordobas had that package installed, for a price of $2,040. This was the first use of the 300 nameplate since 1971, though the new version hardly rivaled the performance of its predecessors. Available only with Spinnaker white body paint, the package included red/white/blue bodyside and decklid striping, white sport remote mirrors, front fender louvers, '300' quarter-window decals with decorative bar below, and white bumper guards and rub strips. Inside were red leather bucket seats, an engine-turned dash appliqué, tachometer, and leather-wrapped steering wheel. The 300 had a special handling suspension, plus GR60 x 15 OWL Aramid-belted radial tires on aluminum wheels with a '300' medallion in each hub.

1979 Chrysler, Newport pillared hardtop with optional Premier wheel covers (OCW)

NEWPORT — SERIES TH — SIX/V-8 — Both Newport and the posher New Yorker shrunk considerably in size with their new R-bodies. Like the related Dodge St. Regis, they rode on a 118.5 inch wheelbase and lost over 800 pounds, but both kept much of their 'heavy' appearance. No two-door models remained in the new size. Newport's angled-back front end held a distinctive grille and exposed quad rectangular headlamps. The grille contained tight (3 x 3) crosshatching within larger crosshatch sections, in an overall 8 x 4 hole pattern. The grille molding was curved at the lower corners, but square at the top. Small amber side markers aligned with parking lamps, back just slightly on fenders; clear lenses were farther down, just ahead of each wheel. Wide wraparound taillamps were split by horizontal divider bars. Widely-spaced 'Chrysler' letters stood on the decklid. Newport had a chromed square stand-up hood ornament. Large "contemporary" windows held tinted glass. Interior trim came in three new colors (Midnight Blue, Teal Green and Cashmere), plus carryover Canyon Red and Dove Gray. Newport's split-back bench seat held Riviera cloth-and-vinyl trim and a folding center armrest. All-vinyl was available, as were 60/40 seats. A multi-function control lever on the steering column handled turn signals, dimmer, and wiper/washer. The two-spoke steering wheel had woodtone trim. There was a new high-low heater/defroster. In the trunk was a compact spare tire. Base engine (except in California) was the 225 cu. in. slant six, with optional 318 or 360 cu. in. V-8. An Open Road handling package was optional. Seven new body colors were offered: five metallics and two solids. Colors were: Dove Gray, Formal Black, Nightwatch Blue, Spinnaker White, Light Cashmere, plus metallic Teal Frost, Regent Red Sunfire, Sable Tan Sunfire, Medium Cashmere, Frost Blue, and Teal Green Sunfire.

NEW YORKER — SERIES TP — V-8 — Concealed headlamps were the most noticeable difference between the downsized New Yorker and its less expensive Newport mate. Though 9.5 inches shorter than before, New Yorker had a long, flat hood and distinctive grille with massive chrome header, plus a limousine-like rear area with fixed quarter windows. A Landau vinyl roof was standard (including rear-door opera windows and lamps). So were body-color door handle inserts chromed aluminum bumper guards with protective pads, and a jeweled square hood ornament (Newport's was chrome). Headlamp bezels and front-fender end caps were made of soft urethane. Front fenders held louvers, just ahead of the door. The vertical-look grille used a pattern of many vertical bars that made up 16 sections across, with two subdued horizontal dividers. A heavy bright grille header wrapped over the top reaching back to the hood opening. The new taillamp design reached all the way across the rear end in five sections, with 'New Yorker' block lettering in

the center. Flag-type outside mirrors were standard. Colors were the same as Newport except for Light Cashmere. Inside was a standard 60/40 split bench seat with Richton cloth-and-vinyl trim and folding center armrest. Leather was available. Rear seats had a folding center armrest, plus assist straps and reading lamps. A digital clock was standard. So was a three-spoke luxury steering wheel with woodtone rim insert. A far cry from the old 440 cu. in. V-8 versions, the contemporary New Yorker had a standard 360 (or optional 318) cu. in. V-8. TorqueFlite was standard. A total of 16,113 New Yorkers came with the optional Fifth Avenue Edition package, with two-tone Designer's Cream-on-Beige paint treatment and medium beige accent stripes. Called "the most exclusive Chrysler you can own," Fifth Avenue displayed a unique pentastar hood ornament, wire wheel covers, whitewall radials with gold accent stripes, and color-keyed Laredo-grain vinyl landau roof. Special edge-lighted quarter windows had 'Fifth Avenue' nomenclature instead of the standard New Yorker opera lamps. The color-coordinated theme extended to driftwood appliqués on instrument and door trim panels. The leather-wrapped steering wheel had an inlaid pentastar emblem. Fifth Avenue's unique Champagne interior included garnish moldings, instrument panel, crash pad, package shelf, headlining, and 'C' pillar trim; plus light Champagne leather 60/40 split bench seat. All this added as much as $1,500 to New Yorker's price tag.

1979 Chrysler, New Yorker pillared hardtop with optional Premier wheel covers (OCW)

I.D. DATA: Chrysler's 13-symbol Vehicle Identification Number (VIN) again was on the upper left corner of the instrument panel, between the wiper pivot and 'A' post, visible through the windshield. Symbol one indicates Car Line: 'F' LeBaron; 'S' Cordoba; 'T' Newport/New Yorker. Symbol two is Price Class: 'S' Special; 'L' Low; 'M' Medium; 'H' High; 'P' Premium. The next two symbols denote body type: '22' 2-dr. pillared hardtop coupe; '41' 4-dr. sedan; '42' 4-dr. pillared hardtop; '45' two-seat station wagon. Symbol five is the engine code: 'C' L6225 1Bbl.; 'D' L6225 2Bbl.; 'G' V8318 2Bbl.; 'K' V8360 2Bbl.; 'L' V8360 4Bbl. Next is the model year code: '9' 1979. Symbol seven indicates assembly plant: 'A' Lynch Road; 'F' Newark; 'G' St. Louis; 'R' Windsor, Ontario. The last six digits make up the sequential serial number. An abbreviated version of the VIN is also stamped on the engine block, on a pad below No. 6 spark plug (six-cylinder) or to rear of right engine mount (V-8). Six-cylinder engine numbers are at right front of block, below cylinder head. V-8, at left of block below head. Six-cylinder coding is: first letter series; next three digits are displacement; next one or two letters indicate model; next four digits show the build date; and the final digit reveals the shift on which the engine was built. Serial numbers for V-8 engines are coded as follows: first letter series (model year); second assembly plant; next three digits indicate displacement (cu. in.); next one or two letters denote model; next four digits show the build date; and final four digits are the engine sequence number.

1979 Chrysler, New Yorker pillared hardtop with optional Fifth Avenue Edition package (OCW)

LEBARON (SIX/V-8)

Model No.	Body/ Style No.	Body Type & Seating	Factory Price	Shipping Weight	Prod. Total
FM	22	2-dr. Cpe-6P	5024/5260	3270/3365	Note 1
FM	41	4-dr. Sed-6P	5122/5358	3330/3425	Note 1

Note 1: Total coupe/sedan production, 25,019.

LEBARON SALON (SIX/V-8)

FH	22	2-dr. Cpe-6P	5261/5497	3285/3385	Note 2
FH	41	4-dr. Sed-6P	5489/5725	3350/3450	Note 2

Note 2: Total coupe/sedan production, 35,906.

LEBARON MEDALLION (SIX/V-8)

FP	22	2-dr. Cpe-6P	5735/5971	3345/3440	Note 3
FP	41	4-dr. Sed-6P	5963/6199	3425/3520	Note 3

Note 3: Total coupe/sedan production, 35,475.

LEBARON TOWN & COUNTRY (SIX/V-8)

FH	45	4-dr. Sta Wag-6P	5955/6191	3585/3675	17,463

CORDOBA (V-8)

SS	22	2-dr. HT Cpe-6P	5995	3680	73,195

CORDOBA 300 (V-8)

SP	22	2-dr. HT Cpe-6P	7666	N/A	Note 4

Note 4: Cordoba 300 was actually an option package, installed on 3,811 Cordobas. Figure shown above includes both standard and 300 Cordobas, all of which were built in Canada.

NEWPORT (SIX/V-8)

TH	42	4-dr. Pill HT-6P	6089/6328	3484/3573	60,904

NEW YORKER (V-8)

TP	42	4-dr. Pill HT-6P	8631	3727	43,636

Factory Price & Weight Note: Figures to left of slash are for six-cylinder engine, to right of slash for the least expensive V-8.

ENGINE DATA: BASE SIX (LeBaron): Inline, overhead valve six-cylinder. Cast iron block and head. Displacement: 225 cu. in. (3.7 liters). Bore & stroke: 3.40 x 4.12 in. Compression ratio: 8.4:1. Brake horsepower: 100 at 3600 R.P.M. Torque: 165 lb.-ft. at 1600 R.P.M. Four main bearings. Solid valve lifters. Carburetor: 1Bbl. Holley 1945 (R8917A). VIN Code: C. **BASE SIX (Newport); OPTIONAL (LeBaron):** Same as above, but with Carter BBD 2Bbl. carburetor. Brake horsepower: 110 at 3600 R.P.M. Torque: 180 lb.-ft. at 2000 R.P.M. VIN Code: D. **OPTIONAL V-8 (all models):** 90-degree, overhead valve V-8. Cast iron block and head. Displacement: 318 cu. in. (5.2 liters). Bore & stroke: 3.91 x 3.31 in. Compression ratio: 8.5:1. Brake horsepower: 135 at 4000 R.P.M. Torque: 250 lb.-ft. at 1600 R.P.M. Five main bearings. Hydraulic valve lifters. Carburetor: 2Bbl. Holley 2280 (R8448A). VIN Code: G. **BASE V-8 (New Yorker); OPTIONAL (other models):** 90-degree, overhead valve V-8. Cast iron block and head. Displacement: 360 cu. in. (5.9 liters). Bore & stroke: 4.00 x 3.58 in. Compression ratio: 8.4:1. Brake horsepower: 150 at 3600 R.P.M. Torque: 265 lb.-ft. at 2400 R.P.M. Five main bearings. Hydraulic valve lifters. Carburetor: 2Bbl. Holley 2245. VIN Code: K. **HIGH-OUTPUT V-8; OPTIONAL (all models):** Same as 360 cu. in. V-8 above, but with 4Bbl. Carter TQ carburetor. Compression ratio: 8.0:1. Brake horsepower: 195 at 4000 R.P.M. Torque: 280 lb.-ft. at 2400 R.P.M. VIN Code: L.

CHASSIS DATA: Wheelbase: (LeBaron) 112.7 in.; (Cordoba) 114.9 in.; (Newport/N.Y.) 118.5 in. Overall length: (LeB cpe) 204.1 in.; (LeB sed) 206.1 in.; (LeB wag) 202.8 in.; (Cord.) 215.8 in.; (Newport) 220.2 in.; (N.Y.) 221.5 in. Height: (LeB cpe) 53.0 in.; (LeB sed) 55.3 in.; (LeB wag) 55.7 in.; (Cord.) 52.1 in.; (Newpt/N.Y.) 54.5 in. Width: (LeB cpe) 73.5 in.; (LeB sed/wag) 72.8 in.; (Cord./Newpt/N.Y.) 77.1 in. Front Tread: (LeB) 60.0 in.; (others) 61.9 in. Rear Tread: (LeB) 58.5 in.; (others) 62.0 in. Standard Tires: (LeB) FR78 x 15 GBR BSW; (Cord.) FR78 x 15 GBR BSW; (Newpt) P195/75R15 GBR BSW; (N.Y.) P205/75R15 GBR WSW.

TECHNICAL: Transmission: Overdrive-4 manual trans. (floor shift) standard on LeBaron cpe/sed (exc. in Calif.). Gear ratios: (1st) 3.09:1; (2nd) 1.67:1; (3rd) 1.00:1; (4th) 0.71:1; (Rev) 3.00:1. TorqueFlite three-speed automatic standard (optional on LeBaron): (1st) 2.45:1; (2nd) 1.45:1; (3rd) 1.00:1; (Rev) 2.22:1. Standard final drive ratio: (LeB six) 3.23:1 or 2.94:1 exc. 2.76:1 or 2.71:1 w/auto.; (LeB V-8) 2.47:1, 2.45:1 or 3.21:1; (Cord. V8318) 2.71:1; (Cord. V8360) 2.45:1 or 3.21:1; (Newpt six) 2.94:1; (Newpt V-8) 2.45:1 or 3.21:1; (N.Y.) 2.45:1 exc. (H.D. V8360) 3.21:1. Steering: recirculating ball power-assisted. Suspension: (LeBaron) front transverse torsion bars with control arms and anti-sway bar, rigid rear axle with semi-elliptic leaf springs; (others) longitudinal front torsion bars and anti-sway bar, rear asymmetrical leaf springs. Brakes: Front disc, rear drum (power-assisted). Ignition: Electronic. Body construction: Unibody. Fuel tank: (LeB) 19.5 gal.; (others) 21.0 gal.

DRIVETRAIN OPTIONS: Engines: 225 cu. in., 2Bbl. six: LeB (NC). 318 cu. in., 2Bbl. V-8: LeB ($236); Newpt ($239). 318 cu. in., 4Bbl. V-8: LeB ($296); Cord. ($61); Newpt ($300). 360 cu. in. 2Bbl. V-8: LeB ($426); Cord. ($191); Newpt ($432). 360 cu. in. 4Bbl. V-8: LeB ($487); Cord. ($251); Newpt ($493-$664); N.Y. ($61-$232). H.D. 360 cu. in., 4Bbl. V-8: LeB ($655); Cord. ($420); Newpt ($664); N.Y. ($232). Transmission/Differential: Automatic trans.: LeB ($193). Sure-grip differential: LeB/Cord. ($67); others ($72). Optional axle ratio ($20). Suspension: H.D. susp. ($28). H.D. shock absorbers ($8) exc. LeB. Other: Heavy-duty trailer assist pkg.: LeB ($170); Cord. ($150); Newpt/N.Y. ($152). Long-life battery ($35). California emission system ($87).

LEBARON CONVENIENCE/APPEARANCE OPTIONS: Option Packages: Basic group ($1130-$1355). Sport appearance pkg. ($110-$219). Spring sport special pkg. (landau roof, cloth/vinyl bucket seats, sport wheels/mirrors): Salon cpe ($261). Light pkg. ($72-$84). Deluxe wiper/washer pkg. ($47). Deluxe insulation pkg. ($10-$93). Comfort/Convenience: Air cond. ($584). Rear defroster ($98). Automatic speed control ($107). Power seat ($167). Power windows ($137-$194). Power door locks ($89-$124). Power decklid or tailgate release ($25). Luxury steering wheel ($20). Leather-covered steering wheel ($40-$60). Tilt steering wheel ($58-$77). Tinted glass ($73). Digital clock ($56). Locking gas cap ($7). Lighting, Horns and Mirrors: Halogen headlamps ($26). Cornering lamps ($51). Dual horns ($9). Remote-control left mirror ($19). Remote right mirror: Medallion ($35). Dual remote chrome mirrors ($35-$54). Dual remote sport mirrors ($48-$67). Lighted vanity mirror ($50). Day/night mirror: base ($12). Entertainment: AM radio ($87). AM/CB radio ($287-$373). AM/FM radio ($80-$167). AM/FM stereo radio ($154-$240) w/CB ($440-$527). AM/FM stereo w/8track player ($256-$343). Search tune AM/FM stereo radio ($281-$368). Rear speaker ($26). Power antenna ($48). Exterior Trim: T-Bar roof: cpe ($675). Power glass sunroof ($827). Landau vinyl roof: cpe ($148). Full vinyl roof: base sed ($165). Vinyl bodyside molding ($45). Front bumper guards ($24). Bumper rub strips ($37). Door edge guards ($13-$22). Luggage rack: wag ($94). Air deflector: wag ($30). Undercoating ($25-$36). Interior Trim/Upholstery: Vinyl bench seat ($50-$67). Cloth 60/40 seat ($175). Leather 60/40 seat ($283-$430). Cloth/vinyl bucket seats: Salon ($110). Color-keyed floor mats ($25). Color-keyed seatbelts ($20). Pedal dress-up ($10). Wheels and Tires: Wire wheel covers ($111-$300). Deluxe wheel covers: base ($45). Premium wheel covers ($45-$90). Forged aluminum wheels ($116-$305). FR78 x 15 WSW ($50-$110). Conventional spare tire (NC).

CORDOBA CONVENIENCE/APPEARANCE OPTIONS: Option Packages: '300' pkg. ($2040). Basic group ($1089-$1125). Crown roof two-tone paint pkg. ($777-$971). Special appearance pkg. ($527). Two-tone paint pkg. ($158). Roadability pkg. ($29). Light pkg. ($29). Comfort/Convenience: Air cond. ($584). Auto-temp air cond. ($628) exc. w/option pkg. ($44). Rear defroster ($98). Automatic speed control ($107). Power seat ($167). Power windows ($137). Power door locks ($89). Power decklid release ($26). Leather-wrapped steering wheel: two-spoke ($77); three-spoke ($40). Tilt steering wheel ($77). Tinted glass ($73). Tinted windshield ($47). Tachometer ($73). Digital clock ($56). Deluxe wipers ($40). Locking gas cap ($7). Lighting and Mirrors: Halogen headlamps ($26). Cornering lamps ($51). Remote-control left mirror ($19). Dual remote chrome mirrors ($35-$54). Dual sport remote mirrors: painted or chrome ($48-$67). Lighted vanity mirror ($50). Entertainment: Same as LeBaron, plus: AM radio w/8track player ($166-$252). Exterior Trim: T-Bar roof w/lift-out panels ($675). Crown landau Laredo-grain vinyl roof w/illuminated lamp band and "frenched" windows ($691-$823). Power sunroof ($546). Landau vinyl roof ($132). Vinyl bodyside molding ($45). Door edge guards ($13). Bumper rub strips ($37). Bodyside tape stripes ($47). Decklid tape stripe ($24). Undercoating ($36). Interior Trim/Upholstery: Console ($60). Vinyl bench seat ($32). Velour/vinyl 60/40 bench seat w/armrest and recliner ($147). Leather bucket seats ($283). Color-keyed floor mats ($25). Color-keyed seatbelts ($20). Pedal dress-up ($10). Trunk dress-up ($47). Wheels and Tires: Wire wheel covers ($211-$255). Premium wheel covers ($45). Aluminum wheels w/trim rings ($213). Forged aluminum wheels ($260). Aluminum fascia wheels ($164). FR78 x 15 WSW ($50). GR78 x 15 BSW ($22). GR78 x 15 WSW ($22-$72). HR78 x 15 WSW ($87-$160). GR60 x 15 RWL ($230-$302). Conventional spare tire (NC).

NEWPORT/NEW YORKER CONVENIENCE/APPEARANCE OPTIONS: Option Packages: Fifth Avenue Edition N.Y. ($1307-$1500). Basic group: Newpt ($1176): N.Y. ($1098). Open road handling pkg. ($194-$216). Two-tone paint pkg. ($160). Light pkg. ($91-$96). Comfort/Convenience: Air cond. ($628). Automatic air cond. ($673) exc. ($45) w/option pkg. Rear defroster ($105). Auto speed control ($112). Power seat ($170). Power windows ($212). Power door locks ($126). Power decklid release ($27-$35). Luxury steering wheel: Newpt ($20); N.Y. ($60). Leather-covered steering wheel ($41-$60). Digital clock: Newpt ($57). Locking gas cap ($9). Lighting and Mirrors: Halogen headlamps ($27). Cornering lamps ($57). Remote control driver's mirror: Newpt ($20). Remote passenger mirror: N.Y. ($24). Dual remote mirrors: Newpt ($24-$44). Lighted vanity mirror ($50). Entertainment: AM radio ($106). AM/CB radio ($215-$396). AM/FM radio ($76-$182). AM/FM stereo radio ($71-$253); w/CB ($361-$543). AM/FM stereo w/8track tape player ($179-$360). Search tune AM/FM stereo radio ($191-$372).

Rear speaker ($28). Power antenna ($50). Exterior Trim: Power glass sunroof ($993). Vinyl roof: Newpt ($152). Vinyl side moldings ($51). Bumper guards: Newpt ($60). Door edge protectors ($23). Bodyside/tail-lamp tape stripes: Newpt ($72). Undercoating ($30). Interior Trim/Upholstery: Vinyl split-back bench seat: Newpt ($33). Cloth 60/40 bench seat: Newpt ($149). Vinyl 60/40 bench seat: Newpt ($181). Leather 60/40 bench seat: N.Y. ($287). Color-keyed floor mats ($26). Color-keyed seatbelts: Newpt ($21). Pedal dress-up ($10). Trunk dress-up ($67). Litter container ($8). Wheels and Tires: Wire wheel covers ($259). Premier wheel covers ($54). Aluminum wheels ($175) w/trim rings ($216). P195/75R15 WSW ($51). P205/75R15 WSW ($23-$134). P225/70R15 WSW ($24-$75). Conventional spare tire (NC).

HISTORY: Introduced: October 5, 1978. Model year production: 291,598 (incl. Canadian-built Cordobas). Calendar year production (U.S.): 181,427. Calendar year sales by U.S. dealers: 248,840. Model year sales by U.S. dealers: 277,749 (incl. 70,970 Cordobas).

HISTORICAL FOOTNOTES: Division sales fell for the 1979 model year by more than eight percent (including the three Plymouth-badged imports). Cordoba sales slipped by 37 percent, but full-size Chryslers rose nearly 24 percent. Production for the model year dropped 12 percent. Weight-cutting had become a major theme. The heaviest Chrysler product weighed less than 3,900 pounds at the curb. As part of modernizing the old Lynch Road assembly plant, the use of lead solder was curtailed, thus eliminating the risk of lead poisoning. Synthetic solder was used instead. Many Chrysler, Dodge and Plymouth models had become quite alike in recent years, often differing from each other in little other than nameplate. Dodge's Magnum XE, for instance, was a near twin to Chrysler's Cordoba, but sold far fewer copies. Lee Iacocca was determined, as one of his many goals, to give Dodge Division back its separate identity, in an attempt to tweak sales of each brand.

1980 CHRYSLER

Cordoba got a fresh restyle this year and new model designations, while other models were largely carried over or given modest styling changes. LeBaron added a base station wagon and lower-priced Special sedan. New Yorker's Fifth Avenue edition was offered again this year, while Cordoba's 300 faded away after a short rebirth.

1980 Chrysler, LeBaron station wagon with optional air deflector (OCW)

LEBARON — SERIES F — SIX/V-8 — A new grille made up of thin, close-together vertical strips was split in two by a wide vertical divider between the sections. Distinctive quad parking/signal lamps sat directly above quad rectangular headlamps and wrapped over fender tops. Above the grille was an eagle hood ornament. Amber-over-clear side marker lenses stood just ahead of each front wheel opening angled to follow its shape. A 'LeBaron' nameplate was just ahead of the door. Narrow vertical red lenses sat above backup lamps at quarter panel tips, while wide taillamps with center emblems reached the license plate opening. LeBaron had sharper fenderline creases this year, as well as a revised, more squared-off roofline. Two-door models shrunk in length, now riding on a 108.7 inch wheelbase rather than the 112.7 inch platform used by sedans and wagons. Base two-doors included bright windshield, back window, roof drip, belt, center pillar, quarter window, wheel opening, and wide sill moldings. Woodtoning adorned the instrument panel, two-spoke steering wheel, and door trim panels. Standard equipment included front bumper guards, hubcaps, TorqueFlite transmission, power steering and brakes, two-speed wipers, and trip odometer. Salon added a day/night mirror, dual horns, deluxe wheel covers, and bodyside accent stripes. The top-of-the-line Medallion added a landau or full padded vinyl roof with opera lamps, and sill molding extensions, plus warning chimes and left remote mirror. New to the option list was the illuminated entry

system with halo lamps around door locks. Auto-temp air conditioning also was available. Station wagons came with or without the simulated white ash moldings and teakwood appliqué. The new non-wood base wagon was available for a lower price. LeBaron colors were: Baron Red, Light Cashmere, Spinnaker White, Nightwatch Blue, Formal Black, Light Heather Gray, Natural Suede Tan, plus metallic Burnished Silver, Mocha Brown, Light Heather Gray, Frost Blue, Teal Frost, Teal Tropic Green, and Crimson Red. An LS Limited package was offered on the two-door coupe only, with unique classic diamond-mesh wire grille texture and integral eagle medallion in the upper center of the grille frame (protruding into each section). Quarter window glass showed LS ornamentation. Unique two-tone paint made hood, roof front and a narrow band surrounding front windows the same color as that on lower bodyside, while the rest of the car was a second color. Quarter and back window moldings were painted. Instead of a nameplate, a set of vertical (non-functional) fender louvers was mounted just ahead of the door. Inside were high back cloth bucket seats. Wire wheel covers, dual remote mirrors, three-spoke steering wheel, P205/75R15 steel-belted radial whitewalls, and a brushed-finish instrument cluster bezel were among many LS Limited extras. An LS package was similar, but without the two-tone. A total of 948 LeBarons had the LS Coupe package. while 2,257 carried the LS Limited Coupe option. Chrysler also borrowed from New Yorker to produce a luxury Fifth Avenue package for LeBaron, which debuted at mid-year. A total of 654 were installed. Fifth Avenues had a different formal-look roofline with padded carriage roof and blanked rear quarter windows in the back doors, thin opera lamps in a wrapover roof band at the front of the vinyl portion, and a smaller "frenched" back window. The package also included wire wheel covers.

1980 Chrysler, LeBaron Salon coupe (OCW)

CORDOBA — SERIES S — SIX/V-8 — The restyled second-generation personal-luxury coupe actually became a close relative to LeBaron, riding the same 112.7 inch wheelbase. Though shaped similar to the prior version, the new Cordoba had a more formal appearance. It was also smaller - six inches shorter and over four inches narrower. For the first time, Cordoba came with a standard six-cylinder engine, with V-8 optional. Notable among the changes was a switch to single recessed rectangular headlamps. Cordoba's vertical style grille had seven primary ribs, plus many vertical strips in between. 'Chrysler' block letters were inset in the grille header molding. Horizontally-ribbed clear parking lamps stood between grille and headlamps. The stand-up hood ornament held a Cordoba replica "coin" (Franklin Minted). Amber/clear side marker lenses sat low, just ahead of wheels. A grooved bodyside accent stretched from front to rear, up and over the wheel openings. A deeply sculptured lower accent line reached from front to rear bumper tips. 'Cordoba' script and minted medallion were on each front fender, ahead of the door. Full-length striping was higher up, above the door handle. Sill moldings were standard. Tri-lens taillamps consisted of three wide elements on each side, trimmed with a pair of horizontal strips. Backup lamps were alongside the license plate. 'Chrysler' block lettering was on decklid center; 'Cordoba' script on passenger side. Rear quarter extensions had a pointy (razor-edge) look. Slim opera lamps were angled to match the pillar angle. Standard equipment included TorqueFlite automatic, power brakes and included two-spoke steering wheel with woodtone insert, front/rear bumper guards and rub strips, coat hooks, tinted glass, bi-level heater/defroster, AM radio, dual horns, keyless door locking, and day/night mirror. Also standard: a chrome driver's outside mirror, opera windows, compact spare tire, two-speed wiper/washers, and deluxe wheel covers with P195/75R15 GBR WSW tires. Colors were White, Natural Suede Tan, Light Cashmere, Baron Red, Formal Black, Nightwatch Blue, and Light Heather Gray, plus metallic Light Heather Gray, Burnished Silver, Frost Blue, Crimson Red, and Mocha Brown. A Cabriolet roof option gave a convertible look, with fabric-like canvas that even covered the triangular quarter windows. New optional leather/vinyl bucket seats had a center cushion and folding center armrest. Cordoba Crown added a padded landau vinyl roof; brushed finish up-and-over roof molding; color-keyed vinyl roof termination and opera window moldings; opera lamps; "Frenched" back windows with no exposed moldings; wide sill moldings with rear extensions; and Premier wheel covers. The Crown Corinthian Edition had Black Walnut metallic or Designer's Cream-on-Beige paint treatment. The black version had gold accent stripes and black walnut reptile-grain padded landau vinyl roof. Cream/beige Corin-

thians showed medium beige accent stripes and light beige Laredo-grain padded landau vinyl roof. Inside was cashmere 60/40 leather/vinyl seating and a leather-wrapped tilt steering wheel. Also included: 'Corinthian Edition' identification; dual chrome remote mirrors; intermittent wipers; wire wheel covers and wide whitewall P205/75R15 Goodyear tires. A total of 305 Cordobas came with the Crown special edition package, while 2,069 were Corinthian Editions.

1980 Chrysler, New Yorker pillared hardtop (OCW)

NEWPORT — SERIES TH — SIX/V-8 — Following its 1979 downsizing, Chrysler's "friend of the family" showed no significant change this year beyond a new pentastar stand-up hood ornament. Optional this year were an illuminated entry system and forged aluminum wheels. An Open Road Handling package included Firm-Feel suspension (heavy-duty sway bars front/rear, heavy-duty torsion bars and springs, heavy-duty shocks); special Firm-Feel power steering and P225/70R15 wide whitewall SBR tires on wide rims. Solid colors for 1980 were: Light Heather Gray, Nightwatch Blue, Baron Red, Light Cashmere, Natural Suede Tan, Formal Black and Spinnaker White plus metallic Light Heather Gray, Frost Blue, Teal Frost, Teal Tropic Green, Crimson Red, and Mocha Brown. Newport had five two-tones available.

NEW YORKER — SERIES TP — V-8 — No major changes went on New Yorker in its year-old downsized form. 'Chrysler' block letters again were on the driver's side headlamp cover. Clear wide parking lamps were inset into the bumper. New Yorker had a pentastar hood ornament. Full-width taillamps had their outer segments recessed. Colors were the same as Newport, except for Light Cashmere. Six two-tones were offered Fifth Avenue, promoted as "The One and Only," had new small tri-sectioned amber marker lenses near front fender tips, plus larger horizontal lenses farther down. The Fifth Avenue Edition package included Black Walnut metallic or Designer's Cream/Beige paint; leather-and-vinyl trimmed 60/40 split-back bench seat in Champagne color; beige/cashmere bodyside accent tape stripes (gold stripes with black walnut body); and padded landau beige Bancroft-grain vinyl roof (black walnut reptile-grain with black body). Edge-lighted quarter windows displayed 'Fifth Avenue' script. Also included: simulated front fender louvers; color-keyed bumper guards and protective strips; P205/75R15 SBR wide WSW tires; wire wheel covers; light package; tilt steering; intermittent wipers; leather-covered steering wheel; Driftwood appliqués on instrument panel and trim; and Champagne interior trim. A total of 3,608 Fifth Avenue packages were installed, along with 386 Fifth Avenue Special Editions.

I.D. DATA: For the last time, Chrysler had a 13-symbol Vehicle Identification Number (VIN) on the upper left corner of the instrument panel, between the wiper pivot and 'A' post, visible through the windshield. Coding was similar to 1979. Engine code 'D' for 2Bbl. six was dropped. Model year code changed to 'A' for 1980. The Newark assembly plant (code 'F') switched to Aspen/Volare production. Engine number codes again were stamped on the block.

LEBARON (SIX/V-8)

Model No.	Body/Style No.	Body Type & Seating	Factory Price	Shipping Weight	Prod. Total
FM	22	2-dr. Cpe-6P	5948/6178	3220/3300	8,000
FM	41	4-dr. Sed-6P	6103/6333	3300/3385	8,391
FM	45	4-dr. Sta Wag-6P	6305/6535	3455/3535	1,865

LEBARON SPECIAL (SIX)

Model No.	Body/Style No.	Body Type & Seating	Factory Price	Shipping Weight	Prod. Total
FL	41	4-dr. Sed-6P	5995/----	3260/----	3,139

LEBARON SALON (SIX/V-8)

Model No.	Body/Style No.	Body Type & Seating	Factory Price	Shipping Weight	Prod. Total
FH	22	2-dr. Cpe-6P	6229/6459	3230/3310	10,575
FH	41	4-dr. Sed-6P	6348/6578	3325/3405	10,980

LEBARON MEDALLION (SIX/V-8)

Model No.	Body/Style No.	Body Type & Seating	Factory Price	Shipping Weight	Prod. Total
FP	22	2-dr. Cpe-6P	6783/6888	3285/3360	5,955
FP	41	4-dr. Sed-6P	6888/7118	3400/3485	8,500

LEBARON TOWN & COUNTRY (SIX/V-8)

Model No.	Body/Style No.	Body Type & Seating	Factory Price	Shipping Weight	Prod. Total
FH	45	4-dr. Sta Wag-6P	6894/7124	3525/3610	6,074

CORDOBA (SIX/V-8)

Model No.	Body/Style No.	Body Type & Seating	Factory Price	Shipping Weight	Prod. Total
SH	22	2-dr. HT Cpe-6P	6601/6831	3270/3355	26,333

CORDOBA 'LS' (SIX/V-8)

Model No.	Body/Style No.	Body Type & Seating	Factory Price	Shipping Weight	Prod. Total
SS	22	2-dr. HT Cpe-6P	6745/6840	3270/3365	3,252

CORDOBA CROWN (SIX/V-8)

Model No.	Body/Style No.	Body Type & Seating	Factory Price	Shipping Weight	Prod. Total
SP	22	2-dr. HT Cpe-6P	7051/7281	3320/3400	16,821

NEWPORT (SIX/V-8)

Model No.	Body/Style No.	Body Type & Seating	Factory Price	Shipping Weight	Prod. Total
TH	42	4-dr. Pill. HT-6P	6849/7082	3545/3630	10,872

NEW YORKER (V-8)

Model No.	Body/Style No.	Body Type & Seating	Factory Price	Shipping Weight	Prod. Total
TP	42	4-dr. Pill. HT-6P	10459	3810	10,166

Factory Price & Weight Note: Figures to left of slash are for six-cylinder engine, to right of slash for the least expensive V-8. All models had a series of price increases during the model year.

1980 Chrysler, Newport pillared hardtop with optional sunroof and forged aluminum wheels (OCW)

ENGINE DATA: BASE SIX (LeBaron, Cordoba, Newport): Inline, overhead valve six-cylinder. Cast iron block and head. Displacement: 225 cu. in. (3.7 liters). Bore & stroke: 3.40 x 4.12 in. Compression ratio: 8.4:1. Brake horsepower: 90 at 3600 R.P.M. Torque: 160 lb.-ft. at 1600 R.P.M. Four main bearings. Solid valve lifters. Carburetor: 1Bbl. Holley 1945 (R8831A). VIN Code: C. **BASE V-8** (New Yorker); OPTIONAL (all models): 90-degree, overhead valve V-8. Cast iron block and head. Displacement: 318 cu. in. (5.2 liters). Bore & stroke: 3.91 x 3.31 in. Compression ratio: 8.5:1. Brake horsepower: 120 at 3600 R.P.M. Torque: 245 lb.-ft. at 1600 R.P.M. Five main bearings. Hydraulic valve lifters. Carburetor: 2Bbl. Carter BBD. VIN Code: G. Note: A 4Bbl. 318 rated 155 horsepower was available in California. **OPTIONAL V-8** (Newport, New Yorker): 90-degree, overhead valve V-8. Cast iron block and head. Displacement: 360 cu. in. (5.9 liters). Bore & stroke: 4.00 x 3.58 in. Compression ratio: 8.4:1. Brake horsepower: 130 at 3200 R.P.M. Torque: 255 lb.-ft. at 2000 R.P.M. Five main bearings. Hydraulic valve lifters. Carburetor: 2Bbl. Carter BBD. VIN Code: K. **HIGH OUTPUT V-8** (Cordoba): Same as 360 cu. in. V-8 above, but with 4Bbl. Carter TQ92445 carburetor. Compression ratio: 8.0:1. Brake horsepower: 185 at 4000 R.P.M. Torque: 275 lb.-ft. at 2000 R.P.M. VIN Code: L.

CHASSIS DATA: Wheelbase: (LeBaron cpe) 108.7 in.; (LeB sed/wag) 112.7 in.; (Cordoba) 112.7 in.; (Newport/N.Y.) 118.5 in. Overall length: (LeB cpe) 201.2 in.; (LeB sed) 205.2 in.; (LeB wag) 205.5 in.; (Cord.) 209.8 in.; (Cord. LS) 209.5 in.; (Newport) 220.2 in.; (N.Y.) 221.5 in. Height: (LeB cpe) 53.4 in.; (LeB sed) 55.3 in.; (LeB wag) 55.5 in.; (Cord.) 53.3 in.; (Newpt/N.Y.) 54.5 in. Width: (LeB) 74.2 in.; (Cord.) 72.7 in.; (Newpt/N.Y.) 77.6 in. Front Tread: (LeB/Cord.) 60.0 in.; (Newpt/N.Y.) 61.9 in. Rear Tread: (LeB/Cord.) 59.5 in.; (Newpt/N.Y.) 62.0 in. Standard Tires: (LeB/Cord./Newpt) P195/75R15 GBR WSW; (N.Y.) P205/75R15 SBR WSW.

TECHNICAL: Transmission: TorqueFlite three-speed automatic standard. Six-cylinder gear ratios: (1st) 2.74:1; (2nd) 1.54:1; (3rd) 1.00:1; (Rev) 2.22:1. V-8 ratios: (1st) 2.45:1; (2nd) 1.45:1; (3rd) 1.00:1; (Rev) 2.22:1. Standard final drive ratio: (LeB/Cord. six) 2.76:1; (LeB/Cord. V-8) 2.17:1; (Newpt six) 2.94:1; (Newpt/N.Y. V-8) 2.45:1. Steering: recirculating ball, power-assisted. Suspension: (LeBaron/Cordoba) front transverse torsion bars with control arms and anti-sway bar, rigid rear axle with semi-elliptic leaf springs; (others) longitudinal front torsion bars and anti-sway bar, rear leaf springs. Brakes: Front disc, rear drum (power-assisted). Ignition: Electronic. Body construction: Unibody. Fuel tank: (LeB/Cord.) 18 gal.; (Newpt/N.Y.) 21 gal.

DRIVETRAIN OPTIONS: Engines: 318 cu. in., 2Bbl. V-8: LeBaron/Cord ($230). Newpt ($233). 318 cu. in., 4Bbl. V-8: LeB/Cord. ($291); Newpt ($295); N.Y. (NC). 360 cu. in., 2Bbl. V-8: Newpt ($457); N.Y. (NC). Axle/Suspension: Sure-grip differential ($71-$77). Heavy-duty susp. ($28-$30). H.D. shock absorbers ($8) exc. LeB. Other: Heavy-duty trailer assist pkg.: Newpt/N.Y. ($258). Max. cooling: LeB/Cord. ($37-$63); Newpt/N.Y. ($77-$104). Long-life battery ($36). California emission system ($254).

1980 Chrysler, LeBaron Salon LS Limited coupe (OCW)

LEBARON CONVENIENCE/APPEARANCE OPTIONS: Option Packages: Fifth Avenue pkg. (N/A). LS coupe pkg.: Salon ($353-$421). LS Limited coupe pkg.: Salon ($954-$974). Sport appearance pkg. ($166-$290). Two-tone paint pkg. ($162). Handling pkg. ($151). Protection group ($61-$70). Deluxe insulation pkg. ($10-$110). Comfort/Convenience: Air cond. ($623). Auto-temp air cond. ($673) exc. w/option pkg. ($50). Rear defroster ($106). Automatic speed control ($116). Power seat ($179). Power windows ($148-$209). Power door locks ($96-$136). Power decklid or tailgate release ($27). Illuminated entry system ($58). Luxury steering wheel ($20). Leather-covered steering wheel ($41-$61). Tilt steering wheel ($63-$83). Tuff steering wheel ($36-$56). Tinted glass ($78). Liftgate wiper/washer: wag ($69). Digital clock ($60). Locking gas cap ($8). Lighting, Horns and Mirrors: Halogen headlamps ($41). Cornering lamps ($55). Dual horns ($10). Remote-control left mirror ($20). Remote right mirror: Medallion ($41). Dual remote chrome mirrors ($41-$61). Dual remote sport mirrors ($56-$76). Lighted vanity mirror ($51). Day/night mirror: base ($12). Entertainment: AM radio ($99). AM/FM radio ($63-$162). AM/FM stereo radio ($101-$200); w/CB ($383-$482). AM/FM stereo w/8track player ($181-$280); w/cassette ($240-$339). Search tune AM/FM stereo radio ($227-$326). Rear speaker ($21). Power antenna ($52). Exterior Trim: T-Bar roof: cpe ($715). Power glass sunroof ($871). Upper door frame moldings: base wag ($10). Rear bumper guards ($36). Door edge guards ($14-$23). Luggage rack: wag ($100). Air deflector: wag ($32). Undercoating ($25). Interior Trim/Upholstery: Console: Salon cpe ($109). Vinyl split-back bench seat ($51-$69). Cloth/vinyl 60/40 seating: Salon ($230). Vinyl 60/40 seat: Salon/wag ($212-$281). Cloth 60/40 seat: Salon/wag ($160-$281). Leather 60/40 seat ($37-$619). Cloth/vinyl bucket seats: Salon cpe ($103). Color-keyed floor mats: front ($26); rear ($21). Color-keyed seatbelts ($27). Pedal dress-up ($10). Trunk dress-up ($49). Cargo area carpet: base wag ($75); w/stowage bins ($101). Cargo security cover: wag ($61). Wheels and Tires: Wire wheel covers ($114-$308). Deluxe wheel covers: base ($48). Premium wheel covers ($45-$138). Premier wheel covers ($45-$93). Styled wheels ($101-$194). Forged aluminum wheels ($72-$380). P205/75R15 SBR WSW ($89). P205/75R15 Aramid-belted white/gold sidewall ($86-$135). Conventional spare tire ($27).

CORDOBA CONVENIENCE/APPEARANCE OPTIONS: Option Packages: Corinthian Edition: Crown ($1203-$1818). Basic group ($889-$1082). Cabriolet roof pkg. ($624-$950). Cabriolet roof two-tone pkg. ($745-$1071). Sport appearance pkg. ($171-$191). Two-tone paint pkg. ($73-$172). Sport handling pkg. ($192). Roadability pkg. ($29). Protection pkg. ($61). Light pkg. ($104). Comfort/Convenience: Air cond. ($623). Auto-temp air cond. ($675) exc. w/option pkg. ($52). Rear defroster ($106). Automatic speed control ($116). Power seat ($179). Power windows ($148). Power door locks ($96). Power decklid release ($28-$44). Illuminated entry system ($58). Luxury steering wheel ($22). Leather-wrapped steering wheel ($39-$61). Tilt steering wheel ($61-$83). Tuff steering wheel ($34-$56). Digital clock ($60). Intermittent wipers ($43). Locking gas cap ($8). Lighting Horns and Mirrors: Halogen headlamps ($41). Cornering lamps ($55). Reading lamp ($21). Triad horns ($22). Remote-control left mirror ($20). Dual remote mirrors ($57-$77). Lighted vanity mirror ($51). Entertainment: AM/FM radio ($63). AM radio w/8track ($156). AM/FM stereo ($101); w/CB ($383); w/8track ($181); w/cassette ($240). Search tune AM/FM stereo radio ($227). Rear speaker ($21). Power antenna ($52). Radio delete ($56 credit). Exterior Trim: T-Bar roof ($715). Power sunroof ($787). Landau vinyl roof ($141). Vinyl bodyside molding ($48). Door edge guards ($14). Bodyside/decklid tape stripes ($74). Hood tape stripe ($25). Undercoating ($25). Interior Trim/Upholstery: Console ($66). Vinyl bucket seats ($103). Leather bucket seats: Crown ($455). Color-keyed floor mats: front ($26); rear ($21). Color-keyed seatbelts ($27). Pedal dress-up

($10). Trunk dress-up ($49). Wheels and Tires: Wire wheel covers ($170-$262). Premium wheel covers ($46-$92). Forged aluminum wheels ($216-$334). P205/75R15 GBR WSW ($22). P205/75R15 SBR WSW ($89). P205/75R15 Aramid-belted gold-band WSW ($175). P215/70R15 RWL SBR ($114). Conventional spare tire ($27).

NEWPORT/NEW YORKER CONVENIENCE/APPEARANCE OPTIONS: Option Packages: Fifth Avenue Edition pkg.: N.Y. ($1120-$1300). Fifth Avenue Special Edition ($1881-$2092). Basic group: Newpt ($1203); N.Y. ($242). Open Road Handling pkg.: Newpt ($269); N.Y. ($177). Two-tone paint pkg. ($168). Light pkg. ($81-$87). Comfort/Convenience: Air cond. ($670). Auto temp air cond.: Newpt ($720); N.Y. ($50). Rear defroster ($113). Auto. speed control ($122). Power seat ($183). Power windows: Newpt ($228). Power door locks ($139). Power decklid release ($30-$46). Illuminated entry system ($62). Luxury steering wheel: Newpt ($20). Leather-covered steering wheel: Newpt ($62); N.Y. ($42). Tilt steering: Newpt ($85); N.Y. ($65). Digital clock: Newpt ($61). Locking gas cap ($9). Lighting, Horns and Mirrors: Halogen headlamps ($42). Cornering lamps ($55). Triad horns ($22). Remote-control driver's mirror: Newpt ($21). Remote passenger mirror: N.Y. ($31). Dual remote mirrors: Newpt ($31-$52). Lighted vanity mirror ($53). Entertainment: AM radio: Newpt ($106). AM/FM radio: Newpt ($58-$164). AM/FM stereo radio: Newpt ($103-$209). AM/FM stereo w/8track tape player: Newpt ($181-$287); N.Y. ($78). AM/FM stereo w/cassette: Newpt ($241-$347); N.Y. ($138). AM/FM stereo w/CB: Newpt ($389-$495); N.Y. ($286). Search tune AM/FM stereo radio: Newpt ($224-$330); N.Y. ($121). Rear speaker ($22). Power antenna ($54). Exterior Trim: Power glass sunroof ($1053). Full vinyl roof: Newpt ($162). Vinyl side moldings ($55). Bumper guards: Newpt ($62). Door edge protectors ($24). Bodyside/taillamp tape stripes: Newpt ($74). Undercoating ($31). Interior Trim/Upholstery: Vinyl split-back bench seat: Newpt ($34). Cloth/vinyl 60/40 bench seat: Newpt ($152). Vinyl 60/40 bench seat: Newpt ($186). Leather 60/40 bench seat: N.Y. ($432). Color-keyed floor mats: front ($26); rear ($21). Color-keyed seatbelts: Newpt ($27). Pedal dress-up ($10). Trunk dress-up: Newpt ($70). Litter container ($9). Wheels and Tires: Wire wheel covers ($266). Premier wheel covers: Newpt ($44). Premium wheel covers ($91). Forged aluminum wheels ($336). P205/75R15 SBR WSW ($92). P205/75R15 white/gold Aramid-belted ($87-$179). P225/70R15 SBR WSW ($93-$186). Conventional spare tire ($27).

HISTORY: Introduced: October 1, 1979. Model year production: 130,923 (incl. Canadian-built Cordobas). Calendar year production (U.S.): 82,463. Calendar year sales by U.S. dealers: 142,245. Model year sales by U.S. dealers: 151,752 (incl. 50,580 Cordobas).

HISTORICAL FOOTNOTES: The newly restyled Cordoba lost some 350 pounds and over 2 inches of wheelbase, but wasn't exactly a hot seller in its modestly shrunken form. Even LeBaron, so popular at first and newly restyled, dropped by 43 percent in sales for the 1980 model year. Chrysler's financial troubles had become all too well-known by the public, which doubtless had an impact on sales this year, especially since some fresh models were expected for 1981. Apart from Omni and Horizon and the captive imports, Chrysler Corp. wasn't capitalizing on the rising public clamor for fuel efficiency either. Thus, sales for model year 1980 dropped by one-third from the 1979 figure. Full-size Chryslers fared worse yet, slipping by some 61 percent. Production for the model year fell by 38 percent for the CP Division. Starting this year, the Plymouth Voyager passenger van was considered a truck for statistical purposes, thus affecting sales/production figures. Early in 1980, the Hamtramck (Michigan) assembly plant shut down.

1981 CHRYSLER

1981 Chrysler, LeBaron Medallion sedan with optional wire wheel covers (OCW)

Changes were minimal for 1981, as Chrysler fans awaited the arrival of a front-drive model for '82. This year, the renowned Imperial name returned on a new "bustleback" luxury model, built in Windsor, Ontario. Under Chrysler hoods, the Slant Six engine added hydraulic valve lifters. Actually, the biggest change may have been the disappearance of the 360 cu. in. V-8, leaving the 318 as the largest powerplant offered by Chrysler. That one came in two- and four-barrel versions.

1981 Chrysler, LeBaron Town & Country station wagon with optional roof rack, air deflector and wire wheel covers (OCW)

LEBARON — SERIES F — SIX/V-8 — Interior modifications and some new body colors were the extent of appearance change for LeBaron, which was promoted as a mid-size vehicle. A two-door coupe was added to the low-budget Special line. LeBaron also came in base, Salon, and Medallion trim, along with the fake wood Town & Country station wagon. Thicker primer, more (one-side) galvanized and precoated steel increased corrosion resistance. Full and landau vinyl roof options were added. Standard equipment included TorqueFlite automatic transmission, power brakes and steering, P195/75R15 glass-belted radial whitewall tires, cigarette lighter, locking glove compartment, belt and drip rail moldings, wheel lip moldings, driver's side remote-control mirror, deluxe wheel covers, sill moldings, front bumper guards, and courtesy lamps. LeBaron Salon added dual horns, day/night inside mirror, and upper door frame moldings (four-doors). Medallion added premier wheel covers, a padded vinyl roof, luxury steering wheel, and trunk dress-up items.

1981 Chrysler, Cordoba coupe with optional Crown Special Edition landau vinyl roof (OCW)

1981 Chrysler, Cordoba coupe with optional Corinthian Edition package and Cabriolet roof package (OCW)

CORDOBA — SERIES S — SIX/V-8 — After its 1980 restyle, Cordoba was carried over with little change. The shift pattern of the wide-ratio automatic transmission was modified for smoother acceleration in city driving. Cordobas had a transverse torsion bar front suspension (like LeBaron) and rear leaf springs. High-strength steel bumpers were new this year. Standard cloth/vinyl 60/40 seats had a folding center armrest. Leather/vinyl buckets were optional. Cordoba solid colors were: Light Heather Gray, Nightwatch Blue, Mahogany Starmist, Graphic Red, Spice Tan Starmist, Baron Red, Pearl White, Formal Black and Light Cashmere, plus metallic Daystar Blue or Burnished Silver. Three two-tones were offered. The Corinthian came in Mahogany Starmist or Formal Black, or three two-tones. A sporty new 'LS' model with 'soft' front end was aimed at the youth market. It carried a crossbar blackout grille like that formerly used on the 300; just a body-colored horizontal/vertical crossbar with round 'LS' emblem in the center. Below the bumper rub strips were two thin slots. Unlike standard Cordobas, 'LS' had both headlamps and adjoining parking lamps set in a recessed housing. At the rear were body-colored taillamp bezels instead of the customary chrome. High-back vinyl bucket seats were standard, along with dual painted remote-control mirrors. Trim included thin red/white/blue bodyside and decklid accent stripes. In addition to a Special Edition padded vinyl landau roof, Cordoba's Corinthian Edition had a leather-wrapped rim two-spoke steering wheel with Cordoba "coin" insert. Also included: Corinthian Edition rear pillar identification, color-keyed bumper guards and rub strips, color-keyed door handle tape inserts, remote chrome mirrors, wire wheel covers, P205/75R15 SBR wide WSW tires, plus bodyside and decklid accent stripes. A total of 1,957 Cordobas had the Corinthian Edition package installed. A total of 998 had the simulated convertible top package, while 334 had that package with two-tone paint. A new vinyl roof featured covered-over opera windows and a small back window.

NEWPORT — SERIES TH — SIX/V-8 — Newport didn't look much different from 1980, but its grille now showed a simple tight crosshatch pattern with vertical elements dominant; no more pattern within a pattern. A 430-amp maintenance-free battery was now standard. Base engine remained the 225 cu. in. slant six, now with hydraulic lifters, with the 318 cu. in. V-8 optional. This year's colors were: Nightwatch Blue, Light Heather Gray, Pearl White, Baron Red, Light Cashmere, Formal Black, plus metallic Daystar Blue, Heather Mist, or Coffee Brown. Mahogany Starmist cost extra.

1981 Chrysler, Newport pillared hardtop (OCW)

NEW YORKER — SERIES TP — V-8 — Like its less expensive full-size mate, New Yorker got a new grille; this one made up of all thin vertical bars of identical width. Otherwise, little was new or different. Base engine was the 318 cu. in. V-8. Options included Heavy-Duty and Open Road Handling packages. A total of 3,747 New Yorkers are reported to have had the Fifth Avenue package installed, while 347 are listed with an S/E version. Fifth Avenues included nearly all available optional equipment and came in three two-tone combinations, as well as solid Nightwatch Blue. An optional Carriage Roof package included a sunroof, aluminum wheels, four-barrel 318 cu. in. V-8, and Sure-grip axle. In fact, those were the only options available on the Fifth Avenue, either individually or in package form. Chrysler called it a "completely equipped luxury car."

1981 Chrysler, New Yorker S/E pillared hardtop with optional wire wheel covers (OCW)

IMPERIAL — SERIES YS — V-8 — Striking in design and fully loaded with equipment, the new limited-production 'bustleback' Imperial weighed nearly two tons, even though it was close to two feet shorter than the last previous (1975) Imperial. With no options available apart from a $1,044 power moonroof, the two-door pillared hardtop coupe carried a price tag of $18,311. Buyers had several no-extra-cost choices though: clearcoat paint; Mark Cross leather (or cloth) upholstery; digital electronic instruments; and a selection of AM/FM stereo systems. A "classic" vertical grille was accompanied by hidden headlamps. The bustle trunk, begging comparison with Cadillac's Seville, looked huge almost like it was tacked on. Powerplant was a new fuel-injected 318 cu. in. V-8 with 8.5:1 compression, rated 140 horsepower at 4000 rpm. The suspension consisted of transverse torsion bars in front and leaf springs (live axle) in back. The basic platform was based on Cordoba's, but special chassis design and acoustics created what was described as "the quietest car in Chrysler history." Imperials wore the new Goodyear Arriva tires with low rolling resistance. The lengthy standard equipment list included TorqueFlite, semi-automatic air conditioning, automatic speed control, accent stripes, chimes, crystal hood ornament, digital clock (with date), electronic instrumentation, leather-wrapped steering wheel, tinted glass, tilt steering, and much more. A total of 148 Imperials came with

a "Sinatra" package. Its availability wasn't surprising, since Frank Sinatra did a TV commercial for the car. Top-notch quality control was used in Imperial's assembly process, including a 5-1/2 mile road test.

1981 Chrysler, Imperial coupe (OCW)

I.D. DATA: Chrysler had a new 17-symbol Vehicle Identification Number (VIN) on the upper left corner of the instrument panel, again visible through the windshield. The first digit indicates Country: '1' U.S.A.; '2' Canada. The second symbol is Make: 'C' Chrysler; 'A' Imperial. Third is Vehicle Type: '3' passenger car. The next symbol ('B') indicates manual seatbelts. Symbol five is Car Line: 'M' LeBaron; 'J' Cordoba; 'R' Newport/New Yorker; 'Y' Imperial. Symbol six is Series: '2' Low; '3' Medium; '4' High; '5' Premium; '6' Special. Symbol seven is Body Style: '2' 2-dr. coupe or hardtop coupe; '6' 4-dr. sedan; '7' 4-dr. pillared hardtop; '9' 4-dr. station wagon. Eighth is the Engine Code: 'E' L6225 1Bbl.; 'K' V8318 2Bbl.; 'M' V8318 4Bbl.; 'J' V8318 EFI. Next comes a check digit: 0 through 9 (or X). Symbol ten indicates Model Year: 'B' 1981. Symbol eleven is Assembly Plant: 'A' Lynch Road; 'G' St. Louis; 'R' Windsor, Ontario. The last six digits make up the sequential serial number, starting with 100001. An engine identification number is stamped on a pad at the right of the block on six-cylinder engines, below No. 6 spark plug. On V-8s, that pad is on the right of the block to the rear of the engine mount. An engine serial number is on the right of the block below No. 1 spark plug on six-cylinder engines, and on the left front corner of the block below the cylinder head on V-8s. A Body Code Plate is on the upper radiator support, left front fender shield, or wheel housing.

LEBARON (SIX/V-8)

Model No.	Body/ Style No.	Body Type & Seating	Factory Price	Shipping Weight	Prod. Total
FM	45	4-dr. Sta Wag-6P	7346/7408	3470/3590	2,136

LEBARON SPECIAL (SIX/V-8)

FL	22	2-dr. Cpe-6P	6672/6734	N/A/N/A	Note 1
FL	41	4-dr. Sed-6P	6495/6557	3275/----	Note 1

Note 1: Total Special production, 11,890.

LEBARON SALON (SIX/V-8)

FH	22	2-dr. Cpe-6P	7263/7325	3200/3325	Note 2
FH	41	4-dr. Sed-6P	7413/7475	3305/3430	Note 2

Note 2: Total Salon production, 17,485.

LEBARON MEDALLION (SIX/V-8)

FP	22	2-dr. Cpe-6P	7768/7830	3255/3380	Note 3
FP	41	4-dr. Sed-6P	7917/7979	3355/3490	Note 3

Note 3: Total Medallion production, 7,635.

LEBARON TOWN & COUNTRY (SIX/V-8)

FH	45	4-dr. Sta Wag-6P	8008/8070	3545/3665	3,987

CORDOBA (SIX/V-8)

SP	22	2-dr. HT Cpe-6P	7969/8033	3355/3495	12,978

CORDOBA 'LS' (SIX/V-8)

SS	22	2-dr. HT Cpe-6P	7199/7263	3300/3420	7,315

NEWPORT (SIX/V-8)

TH	42	4-dr. Pill. HT-6P	7805/7869	3515/3635	3,622

NEW YORKER (V-8)

TP	42	4-dr. Pill. HT-6P	10463	3805	6,548

IMPERIAL (V-8)

YS	22	2-dr HT Cpe-6P	18311	3870	7,225

Factory Price & Weight Note: Figures to left of slash are for six-cylinder engine, to right of slash for the least expensive V-8.

Model Number Note: Some sources identify models using the new VIN data to indicate Car Line, Price Class and Body Style. Example: LeBaron station wagon (FM45) has the equivalent number CM39, which translates to LeBaron line, Medium price class, and station wagon body. See I.D. Data section for breakdown.

ENGINE DATA: BASE SIX (LeBaron, Cordoba, Newport): Inline, over-head valve six-cylinder. Cast iron block and head. Displacement: 225 cu. in. (3.7-liters). Bore & stroke: 3.40 x 4.12 in. Compression ratio: 8.4:1. Brake horsepower: 85 at 3600 R.P.M. Torque: 165 lb.-ft. at 1600 R.P.M. Four main bearings. Hydraulic valve lifters. Carburetor: 1Bbl. Holley 1945 (R9253A). VIN Code: E. BASE V-8 (New Yorker); OPTIONAL (all models): 90-degree, overhead valve V-8. Cast iron block and head. Displacement: 318 cu. in. (5.2-liters). Bore & stroke: 3.91 x 3.31 in. Compression ratio: 8.5:1. Brake horsepower: 130 at 4000 R.P.M. Torque: 230 lb.-ft. at 2000 R.P.M. Five main bearings. Hydraulic valve lifters. Carburetor: 2Bbl. Carter BBD 8291S. VIN Code: K. OPTIONAL V-8 (Newport, New Yorker and California LeBaron/Cordoba): Same as 318 cu. in. V-8 above, but with Carter TQ9283S 4Bbl. carburetor. Brake horsepower: 165 at 4000 R.P.M. Torque: 240 lb.-ft. at 2000 R.P.M. VIN Code: M. IMPERIAL V-8: Same as 318 cu. in. V-8 above, but with electronic fuel injection. Brake horsepower: 140 at 4000 R.P.M. Torque: 240 lb.-ft. at 2000 R.P.M. VIN Code: J.

CHASSIS DATA: Wheelbase: (LeBaron cpe) 108.7 in.; (LeB sed/wag) 112.7 in.; (Cordoba/Imperial) 112.7 in.; (Newport/N.Y.) 118.5 in. Overall length: (LeB cpe) 201.7 in.; (LeB sed) 205.7 in.; (LeB wag) 206.0 in.; (Cord.) 210.1 in.; (Cord. LS) 209.5 in.; (Newport) 220.2 in.; (N.Y.) 221.5 in.; (Imperial) 213.3 in. Height: (LeB cpe) 53.3 in.; (LeB sed) 55.3 in.; (LeB wag) 55.5 in.; (Cord./Imp.) 53.2 in.; (Newpt/N.Y.) 54.5 in. Width: (LeB) 74.2 in.; (Cord./Imp.) 72.7 in.; (Newpt/N.Y.) 77.6 in. Front Tread: (LeB/Cord./Imp.) 60.0 in.; (Newpt/N.Y.) 61.9 in. Rear Tread: (LeB/Cord./Imp.) 59.5 in.; (Newpt/N.Y.) 62.0 in. Standard Tires: (LeB/Cord./Newpt) P195/75R15 GBR WSW; (N.Y./Imp.) P205/75R15 SBR WSW.

TECHNICAL: Transmission: TorqueFlite three-speed automatic standard. Gear ratios: (1st) 2.74:1; (2nd) 1.54:1 or 1.55:1; (3rd) 1.00:1; (Rev) 2.22:1. Standard final drive ratio: (LeB) 2.76:1, 2.26:1 or 2.45:1; (Cord.) 2.76:1; (Newpt six) 2.94:1; (Newpt/N.Y./Imp. V-8) 2.24:1; (Newpt/N.Y. V-8 4Bbl.) 2.45:1. Steering: recirculating ball, power-assisted. Suspension: (LeBaron/Cordoba/Imperial) front transverse torsion bars with control arms and anti-sway bar, rigid rear axle with semi-elliptic leaf springs; (Newport/New Yorker) longitudinal front torsion bars with lower trailing links and anti-sway bar, rear leaf springs. Brakes: Front disc, rear drum (power-assisted). Ignition: Electronic. Body construction: Unibody. Fuel tank: (LeB/Cord./Imp.) 18 gal.; (Newpt/N.Y.) 21 gal.

DRIVETRAIN OPTIONS: Engines: 318 cu. in., 2Bbl. V-8: LeB/Cord./Newpt ($62). 318 cu. in., 4Bbl. V-8: LeB/Cord./Newpt ($62); N.Y. (NC). Axle/Suspension: Sure-grip differential ($75-$114) exc. LeB wag ($70). Heavy-duty susp. ($27-$29). H.D. shock absorbers ($8) exc. LeB. Other: Heavy-duty trailer assist pkg.: Newpt/N.Y. ($246). H.D. cooling: LeB/Cord./Newpt ($127). Long-life battery ($35-$39). California emission system ($46).

LEBARON CONVENIENCE/APPEARANCE OPTIONS: Option Packages: Basic group ($937-$1125). Sport appearance pkg. ($154-$258). Two-tone paint pkg. ($158). Handling pkg. ($163). Protection group ($58-$67). Light pkg. ($85-$99). Deluxe insulation pkg. ($10-$109). Comfort/Convenience: Air cond. ($606). Auto-temp air cond. ($656) exc. w/option pkg. ($50). Rear defroster ($107). Automatic speed control ($136). Power seat ($177). Power windows ($145-$202). Power door locks ($96-$136). Power decklid or tailgate release ($29). Illuminated entry system ($57). Luxury steering wheel ($39). Leather-covered steering wheel ($21-$60). Tilt steering wheel ($83). Sport steering wheel ($16-$55). Tinted glass ($78). Deluxe wiper/washer ($51). Liftgate wiper/washer: wag ($82). Digital clock ($56). Locking gas cap ($8). Lighting, Horns and Mirrors: Halogen headlamps ($40). Cornering lamps ($54). Dual horns ($10). Remote-control left mirror ($20). Remote right mirror ($41). Dual remote chrome mirrors ($41-$61). Dual remote sport mirrors ($56-$76). Lighted vanity mirror ($50). Day/night mirror ($13). Entertainment: AM radio ($92). AM/FM radio ($59-$151). AM/FM stereo radio ($94-$186); w/CB ($355-$447). AM/FM stereo w/8-track

player ($169-$261); w/cassette ($223-$315). Search tune AM/FM stereo radio ($211-$303). Rear speaker ($21). Radio upgrade w/dual speakers ($26). Premium speaker pkg. ($93). Power antenna ($49). Exterior Trim: T-Bar roof: cpe ($695). Power glass sunroof ($865). Full vinyl roof: sed ($131). Padded landau vinyl roof: Salon cpe ($173). Starmist paint ($55). Vinyl bodyside moldings ($43). Upper door frame moldings ($38). Rear bumper guards ($25). Door edge guards ($13-$22). Bodyside tape stripe: base wag ($50). Hood tape stripe ($24). Luggage rack: wag ($98). Air deflector: wag ($31). Undercoating ($25). Interior Trim/Upholstery: Console: Salon cpe ($108). Center cushion: Salon cpe ($42). Vinyl split-back bench seat ($50-$68). Vinyl 60/40 split bench seat w/recliner ($208-$276). Cloth 60/40 seat: wag ($208-$276). Cloth/vinyl 60/40 seat: Salon ($226). Leather 60/40 seat ($364-$608). Cloth/vinyl bucket seats: Salon cpe ($101). Color-keyed floor mats: front ($25); rear ($20). Pedal dress-up ($10). Trunk dress-up ($47). Cargo area carpet: base wag ($74); w/stowage bins ($25-$99). Cargo security cover: wag ($60). Wheels and Tires: Wire wheel covers ($106-$249). Premium wheel covers: Medallion ($43-$88). Premier wheel covers ($45). Styled wheels ($98-$143). Forged aluminum wheels ($183-$326). P205/75R15 SBR WSW ($101). Conventional spare tire ($39).

CORDOBA CONVENIENCE/APPEARANCE OPTIONS: Option Packages: Corinthian Edition ($765-$888). Basic group ($791-$908). Cabriolet roof pkg. ($517-$634). Cabriolet roof two-tone pkg. ($615-$732). LS Decor pkg. ($450). Two-tone paint pkg. ($73-$170). Sport handling pkg. ($139-$240). Roadability pkg. ($31). Protection pkg. ($68). Light pkg. ($117). Comfort/Convenience: Air cond. ($606). Auto-temp air cond. ($654) exc. w/option pkg. ($48). Rear defroster ($107). Automatic speed control ($136). Power seat ($177). Power windows ($145). Power door locks ($96). Power decklid release ($28-$43). Illuminated entry system ($57). Luxury steering wheel (NC). Leather-covered steering wheel ($39) exc. LS (NC). Tilt steering wheel ($83). Sport steering wheel ($34); std. on LS. Digital clock ($59). Intermittent wipers ($43). Locking gas cap ($8). Lighting, Horns and Mirrors: Halogen headlamps ($40). Cornering lamps ($54). Reading lamp ($20). Triad horns ($22). Remote-control left mirror ($20). Dual remote mirrors ($57-$77). Lighted vanity mirror ($50). Entertainment: AM/FM radio ($59). AM/FM stereo ($95); w/CB ($355); w/8-track ($169); w/cassette ($223). Search tune AM/FM stereo radio ($211). Rear speaker ($20). Radio upgrade w/dual speakers ($26). Premium speaker pkg. ($93). Power antenna ($49). Radio delete ($85 credit). Exterior Trim: T-Bar roof ($695). Power sunroof ($758). Crown Special Edition landau vinyl roof ($268). Landau vinyl roof ($131). Premium paint ($68). Vinyl bodyside molding ($45). Sill moldings: LS ($30). Wheel lip moldings: LS ($26). Door edge guards ($13). Deluxe rear bumper guards: LS ($25). Bodyside/decklid tape stripes ($72). Hood tape stripe ($25). Undercoating ($25). Interior Trim/Upholstery: Console ($66-$108). Center cushion w/armrest ($42). Cloth/vinyl bucket seats: LS ($91). Leather bucket seats ($447-$540). Color-keyed floor mats: front ($25); rear ($20). Pedal dress-up ($11). Trunk dress-up ($47). Litter container ($10). Wheels and Tires: Wire wheel covers ($160-$206). Premium wheel covers ($46). Forged aluminum wheels ($237-$283). P205/75R15 GBR WSW ($27). P205/75R15 SBR WSW ($101). P215/70R15 SBR WSW ($60-$161). P215/70R15 RWL SBR: LS (NC to $157). Conventional spare tire ($39).

NEWPORT/NEW YORKER CONVENIENCE/APPEARANCE OPTIONS: Option Packages: Fifth Avenue Edition pkg.: N.Y. ($1822). Basic group: Newpt ($993); N.Y. ($156). Open Road Handling pkg.: Newpt ($281); N.Y. ($180). Carriage roof pkg.: N.Y. ($854). Light pkg.: Newpt ($103). Comfort/Convenience: Air cond.: Newpt ($646). Auto-temp air cond.: Newpt ($692) exc. w/option pkg. ($46). Rear defroster ($112). Auto. speed control ($139). Power seat ($179). Power windows: Newpt ($218). Power door locks ($138). Power decklid release ($30-$45). Illuminated entry system ($60). Luxury steering wheel ($39). Leather-covered steering wheel: Newpt ($60); N.Y. ($41). Tilt steering ($84). Digital clock: Newpt ($62). Intermittent wipers ($44). Locking gas cap ($9). Lighting, Horns and Mirrors: Halogen headlamps ($41). Cornering lamps ($54). Triad horns ($22). Remote-control driver's mirror: Newpt ($21). Remote passenger mirror: N.Y. ($30). Dual remote mirrors: Newpt ($30-$51). Lighted vanity mirror ($52). Entertainment: AM radio: Newpt ($97). AM/FM radio: Newpt ($54-$151). AM/FM stereo radio: Newpt ($95-$192). AM/FM stereo w/8track tape player: Newpt ($166-$263); N.Y. ($71); Fifth Ave. (NC). AM/FM stereo w/cassette: Newpt ($221-$318); N.Y. ($126); Fifth Ave. (NC). AM/FM stereo w/CB: Newpt ($356-$453); N.Y. ($261); Fifth Ave. (NC). Search tune AM/FM stereo radio: Newpt ($206-$303); N.Y. ($111); Fifth Ave. (NC). Rear speaker ($21). Radio upgrade w/dual speakers ($26). Premium speaker pkg. ($95). Power antenna ($50). Exterior Trim: Power glass sunroof ($934). Special paint ($68). Vinyl side moldings ($54). Bumper guards: Newpt ($60). Door edge protectors ($23). Undercoating ($31). Interior Trim/Upholstery: Vinyl split-back bench seat: Newpt ($34). Cloth/vinyl 60/40 bench seat: Newpt ($148). Leather 60/40 bench seat: N.Y. ($376). Color-keyed floor mats: front ($25); rear ($20). Pedal dress-up ($11). Trunk dress-up: Newpt ($65). Litter container ($10). Wheels and Tires: Wire wheel covers ($251). Premium turbine wheel covers ($86).

Forged aluminum wheels ($321) exc. Fifth Ave. ($70). P205/75R15 SBR WSW ($101). P225/70R15 SBR WSW ($91-$192). Conventional spare tire ($39).

IMPERIAL OPTIONS: Imperial had only one extra-cost option, the Moonroof ($1044).

HISTORY: Introduced: October 13, 1980. Model year production: 80,821 (incl. Canadian-built Cordobas and Imperials). Calendar year production (U.S.): 57,315. Calendar year sales by U.S. dealers: 90,616. Model year sales by U.S. dealers: 105,584.

HISTORICAL FOOTNOTES: Chrysler's model year sales shrunk considerably, though sales for the Chrysler-Plymouth Division rose nine percent. But since 1980 was such a terrible year, even that increase wasn't so impressive. At the end of 1980, LeBaron production ceased as the Lynch Road plant in Detroit shut down. For 1982, the LeBaron name would return in front-drive form. Ads claimed that "It's Time for Imperial," yet only 6,368 of the new luxury coupes found buyers for the model year, which was more limited production than the "new Chrysler Corporation" had in mind.

1982 CHRYSLER

1982 Chrysler, LeBaron coupe (OCW)

Newport left the lineup this year, while New Yorker went to a smaller platform. LeBaron emerged in an all-new form, with front-wheel drive. In addition to the coupe sedan and Town & Country station wagon, that series added a convertible, the first domestic-built ragtop since the '76 Cadillac Eldorado.

1982 Chrysler, Cordoba hardtop with optional wire wheel covers (OCW)

LEBARON — SERIES C — FOUR — Chrysler's first front-drives came in standard and Medallion trim, in two-door coupe or four-door sedan body styles. Though nearly two feet shorter and 800 pounds lighter, the new versions still carried six passengers, but managed up to 26 miles per gallon city (40 highway) in EPA gas mileage ratings. Wheelbase was now 99.9 inches. An overhead-cam 135 cu. in. (2.2-liter) Trans-4 engine was standard with four-speed manual transaxle. The single powerplant option was a Mitsubishi-built Silent Shaft 156 cu. in. (2.6-liter) overhead-cam four. An automatic transaxle was also available. Front suspension used MacPherson Iso-Struts with linkless sway bar, while the rear held a flex arm beam axle with trailing links and coil springs. Power rack-

and-pinion steering was standard. Related to the Dodge 400, the CV-bodied mid-size LeBaron was based on the recently introduced K-car but more posh. Dimensions, drivetrains and dash were the same as Dodge Aries/Plymouth Reliant. LeBaron's sharply-angled, formal-look grille (similar to Imperial's) consisted of thin vertical bars with an upper header that wrapped over the top and held a pentastar hood ornament. The grille pattern continued in a wide slot below the bumper rub strip. Quad rectangular recessed headlamps were used. Small parking lamps sat down in the bumper. Amber and red side marker lenses were in the front and rear bumper strip extensions. Clear cornering lamps (optional) went below the amber lenses. Overall, LeBaron displayed a rather angular, upright profile devoid of curves, but sharply angled at the front fender tips and with protruding bumper. Wide taillamps reached from license plate opening to decklid edge, with bright molding and backup lamps above. The decklid held a pentastar emblem in its center, plus 'Chrysler' and 'LeBaron' lettering. Two-door coupes had opera windows while back doors of four-door sedans had blanked (covered) windows at the rear. LeBaron standard equipment included power brakes and steering, four-speed manual transaxle, a padded vinyl roof, digital clock, bumper rub strips, lighter, chimes, electric cooling fan, pentastar hood ornament, dual horns, and day/night inside mirror. Also standard: dual chrome outside mirrors, AM radio, P185/70R14 SBR WSW tires, and deluxe wheel covers. Medallion added halogen headlamps, a light/gauge alert group, dual mirrors, bodyside stripes, premium color-keyed wheel covers, and trunk dress-up items. LeBaron colors were: Formal Black, Morocco Red, Light Blue Crystal, Sterling Silver Crystal, Nightwatch Blue, Goldenrod Tan Crystal, Manila Cream, Spice Tan metallic, Pearl White, Charcoal Gray metallic, and Mahogany metallic; plus four two-tones. Two notable additions arrived at mid-year. LeBaron's Town & Country station wagon had simulated wood (plastic) trim on bodysides and liftgate, similar to prior T&C wagons. Its standard engine was the 2.6-liter four with automatic transmission. Also standard: a crystal hood ornament, plus vinyl front bucket seats with folding center armrest. Also appearing was a LeBaron convertible (and matching Dodge 400). Both were converted from two-door coupe bodies by Cars & Concepts in Brighton, Michigan. Ragtops had a small back window and wide rear quarters. Equipment included vinyl bucket seats, standard automatic transaxle, center console, color-keyed remote-control mirrors, and power top with tailored boot. For extra dollars, buyers could have a Mark Cross convertible whose many standard features included the 2.6-liter engine, distinctive Mark Cross leather/vinyl bucket seats and rear bench seat, plus air conditioning, automatic transmission, power windows and door locks, and remote decklid release. Not every body color was available on convertibles or Town & Country wagons.

CORDOBA — SERIES S — SIX/V-8 — This year's Cordoba appeared much like the 1981 edition, but without 'Cordoba' script and medallion on front fenders. A new standard padded vinyl landau roof came in nine colors, highlighted by an up-and-over molding with brushed finish. Standard 60/40 seating had new cloth/vinyl trim, with folding center armrest and passenger seatback recliner. Optional: a seek/scan AM/FM stereo radio. Halogen headlamps and dual remote mirrors were now standard. Galvanized steel was used extensively for body panels. Base engine again was the 225 cu. in. (3.7-liter) slant six, with 318 cu. in. V-8 optional. A wide-ratio automatic transmission with lockup torque converter was standard. The sporty LS, called the "very affordable" Cordoba, also looked much the same. Priced nearly $1,000 lower, the LS was said to have "more youthful styling" rather then "upscale sophistication," with a "wickedly slanted grille." Inside were high-back vinyl bucket seats. Options included the convertible-like cabriolet roof, plus cloth/vinyl bucket seats with folding center armrest. Standard Cordoba colors were: Royal Red Crystal, Goldenrod Crystal, Light Auburn Crystal, Pearl White, Sterling Silver Crystal, Formal Black, Glacier Blue Crystal, Nightwatch Blue, and Manila Cream; plus metallic Charcoal Gray, Mahogany, or Spice Tan. Cordoba LS came in Morocco Red, Nightwatch Blue, Formal Black, Pearl White or Burnished Silver metallic. A total of 1,612 Cordobas had the cabriolet roof.

1982 Chrysler, Cordoba LS hardtop with optional cabriolet roof package (OCW)

1982 Chrysler, New Yorker sedan with optional Fifth Avenue Edition package and wire wheel covers (OCW)

NEW YORKER — SERIES FS — SIX/V-8 — While retaining rear-wheel drive, a revised New Yorker four-door rode a new smaller platform with 112.7 inch wheelbase (eight inches shorter than before). It was actually LeBaron's old M-body, viewed as mid- rather than full-size. The former R-body versions (including Newport) had been dropped early in 1981. Plymouth's Gran Fury was a close relative. Base engine now was the 225 cu. in. (3.7-liter) slant six, with 318 cu. in. V-8 optional. Standard equipment included semi-automatic air conditioning, bumper guards and rub strips, lighter, digital clock, automatic transmission, power brakes/steering, tinted glass, dual horns, halogen headlamps, AM radio, twin remote-control mirrors, decklid and bodyside striping, and a trip odometer. Wide parking lamps stood directly over quad rectangular headlamps. The upright rectangular grille was made up of thin vertical bars with a heavier center bar, plus two subdued horizontal dividers. The grille surround molding extended outward at the base, to fender tips. Above the grille and parking lamps was a heavy bright horizontal molding, just ahead of the hood (which held a pentastar hood ornament). New Yorkers no longer had concealed headlamps. Vertical front fender louvers were just ahead of the door; small horizontal amber marker lenses just ahead of front wheels. At the rear were wide wraparound taillamps, while the padded vinyl landau roof held a small formal 'trenched' back window. 'New Yorker' script appeared in the portion of the padded top that extended in to the backs of the rear doors. Standard cloth/vinyl 60/40 individually adjustable seats had a folding center armrest and passenger seatback recliner. New Yorker's rather modest option list included an electronic-tuning AM/FM stereo radio, leather-covered steering wheel, and forged aluminum wheels. Body colors were: Goldenrod Crystal Coat, Nightwatch Blue, Charcoal Gray metallic, Formal Black, Morocco Red, Sterling Silver Crystal, Mahogany metallic, and Pearl White. Nearly four-fifths of the New Yorkers shipped were Fifth Avenue Edition. That $1,647 option package included loose-pillow 60/40 seats in Corinthian leather or velvet cloth, with folding center armrest and passenger seatback recliner; plus power seat, windows, door locks, and decklid release. The standard tilt steering column held a leather-wrapped wheel. Also standard: 'Fifth Avenue' identification on rear door plug, 318 cu. in. V-8 engine, illuminated entry system, lighted vanity visor mirror, power antenna, AM/FM stereo radio, automatic speed control, hood stripe, and intermittent wipers.

1982 Chrysler, Imperial "Frank Sinatra" Edition coupe (OCW)

IMPERIAL — SERIES YS — V-8 — Suffering a shortage of sales, the mid-size luxury Imperial coupe changed little for 1982. Now priced at $20,988, it had a vast list of standard equipment and virtually no options. Customers could select body color, seat covering, sound system, and wheel type. Standard engine again was the 318 cu. in. (5.2-liter) V-8 with electronic fuel injection. New interiors held Kimberley velvet cloth upholstery in a choice of six colors. Crystal Coat paint came in three new colors: Sterling Silver, Golden Tan, and Light Blue. Only 2,329 Imperials were built in the model year, 279 of which had the "FS" Sinatra package.

That one had special paint and emblems and included a set of 8-track tapes, with Frank's top hits, in a special console.

I.D. DATA: Chrysler again had a 17-symbol Vehicle Identification Number (VIN) on the upper left corner of the instrument panel, visible through the windshield. Coding changed somewhat with the revised model lineup. The first digit indicates Country: '1' U.S.A.; '2' Canada. The second symbol is Make: 'C' Chrysler; 'A' Imperial. Third is Vehicle Type: '3' passenger car. The next symbol ('B') indicates manual seatbelts. Symbol five is Car Line: 'C' LeBaron; 'S' Cordoba; 'F' New Yorker; 'Y' Imperial. Symbol six is Series: '4' High; '5' Premium; '6' Special. Symbol seven is Body Style: '2' 2-dr. coupe or hardtop coupe; '5' 2-dr. convertible coupe; '6' 4-dr. sedan; '9' 4-dr. station wagon. Eighth is the Engine Code: 'B' L4135 2Bbl.; 'D' L4156 2Bbl.; 'E' L6225 1Bbl.; 'K' V8318 2Bbl.; 'M' V8318 4Bbl.; 'J' V8318 EFI. Next comes a check digit: 0 through 9 (or X). Symbol ten indicates Model Year: 'C' 1982. Symbol eleven is Assembly Plant: 'C' Detroit; 'G' St. Louis; 'F' Newark; 'R' Windsor, Ontario. The last six digits make up the sequential serial number, starting with 100001. An engine identification number is stamped on the rear face of the block of the 2.2-liter four, directly beneath the cylinder head (left side of car). On the 2.6-liter four, that number is on the left side of the block, between the core plug and the rear face of the block (radiator side). Six-cylinder identification numbers, as before, are on the right of the block, below No. 6 spark plug; V-8s, on right of block to rear of engine mount. An engine serial number with parts replacement data is just below the identification number on the 2.2 engine; and on right front of the 2.6 block, adjacent to exhaust manifold stud. Serial numbers are on the right of the block below No. 1 spark plug on six-cylinder engines, and on the left front corner of the block below the cylinder head on V-8s. A Body Code Plate is on the upper radiator support, left front fender shield, or wheelhousing.

1982 Chrysler, LeBaron Medallion sedan (OCW)

LEBARON (FOUR)

Model No.	Body/ Style No.	Body Type & Seating	Factory Price	Shipping Weight	Prod. Total
CH	22	2-dr. Cpe-6P	8143	2470	14,295
CH	41	4-dr. Sed-6P	8237	2455	19,619
CH	27	2-dr. Conv-4P	11698	2565	3,045

LEBARON MEDALLION (FOUR)

CP	22	2-dr. Cpe-6P	8408	2475	12,856
CP	41	4-dr. Sed-6P	8502	2465	22,915
CP	27	2-dr. Conv-4P	13998	2615	9,780

LEBARON TOWN & COUNTRY (FOUR)

CP	45	4-dr. Sta Wag-5P	9425	2660	7,809

CORDOBA (SIX/V-8)

SP	22	2-dr. HT Cpe-6P	9197/9267	3370/3520	11,762

CORDOBA 'LS' (SIX/V-8)

SS	22	2-dr. HT Cpe-6P	8258/8328	3315/3465	3,136

NEW YORKER (SIX/V-8)

FS	41	4-dr. Sed-6P	10781/10851	3510/3655	50,509

IMPERIAL (V-8)

YS	22	2-dr. HT Cpe-6P	20988	3945	2,329

Factory Price & Weight Note: Figures to left of slash are for six-cylinder engine, to right of slash for 318 cu. in. V-8.

Model Number Note: Some sources identify models using the new VIN data to indicate Car Line, Price Class and Body Style. Example: LeBaron coupe (CH22) has the equivalent number CC42, which translates to LeBaron line, High price class, and coupe body. See I.D. Data section for breakdown.

ENGINE DATA: BASE FOUR (LeBaron): Inline, overhead cam four-cylinder. Cast iron block; aluminum head. Displacement: 135 cu. in. (2.2-liters). Bore & stroke: 3.44 x 3.62 in. Compression ratio: 8.5:1. Brake horsepower: 84 at 4800 R.P.M. Torque: 111 lb.-ft. at 2400 R.P.M. Five main bearings. Hydraulic valve lifters. Carburetor: 2Bbl. Holley 6520 or 5220. VIN Code: B. **BASE FOUR (LeBaron Town & Country); OPTIONAL (other LeBarons):** Inline, overhead cam four-cylinder. Cast iron block; aluminum head. Displacement: 156 cu. in. (2.6-liters). Bore & stroke: 3.59 x 3.86 in. Compression ratio: 8.2:1. Brake horsepower: 92 at 4500 R.P.M. Torque: 131 lb.-ft. at 2500 R.P.M. Five main bearings. Solid valve lifters. Carburetor: 2Bbl. Mikuni. VIN Code: D. **BASE SIX (Cordoba, New Yorker):** Inline, overhead valve six-cylinder. Cast iron block and head. Displacement: 225 cu. in. (3.7-liters). Bore & stroke: 3.40 x 4.12 in. Compression ratio: 8.4:1. Brake horsepower: 90 at 3600 R.P.M. Torque: 160 lb.-ft. at 1600 R.P.M. Four main bearings. Hydraulic valve lifters. Carburetor: 1Bbl. Holley 1945 or 6145. VIN Code: E. **OPTIONAL V-8 (Cordoba, New Yorker):** 90-degree, overhead valve V-8. Cast iron block and head. Displacement: 318 cu. in. (5.2-liters). Bore & stroke: 3.91 x 3.31 in. Compression ratio: 8.5:1. Brake horsepower: 130 at 4000 R.P.M. Torque: 230 lb.-ft. at 2000 R.P.M. Five main bearings. Hydraulic valve lifters. Carburetor: 2Bbl. Carter BBD. VIN Code: K. **CALIFORNIA V-8 (Cordoba, New Yorker):** Same as 318 cu. in. V-8 above, but with Carter TQ 4Bbl. carburetor. Brake horsepower: 165 at 4000 R.P.M. Torque: 240 lb.-ft. at 2000 R.P.M. VIN Code: M. **IMPERIAL V-8:** Same as 318 cu. in. V-8 above, but with electronic fuel injection. Brake horsepower: 140 at 4000 R.P.M. Torque: 245 lb.-ft. at 2000 R.P.M. VIN Code: J.

CHASSIS DATA: Wheelbase: (LeBaron) 99.9 in.; (Cordoba/New Yorker/Imperial) 112.7 in. Overall length: (LeB) 179.7 in.; (LeB wag) 179.8 in.; (Cord.) 210.1 in.; (Cord. LS) 209.6 in.; (N.Y.) 206.7 in.; (Imperial) 213.4 in. Height: (LeB cpe) 52.6 in.; (LeB sed) 53.0 in.; (LeB wag) 52.7 in.; (LeB conv.) 54.1 in.; (Cord./Imp.) 53.2 in.; (N.Y.) 55.3 in. Width: (LeB) 68.5 in.; (Cord./Imp.) 72.7 in.; (N.Y.) 74.2 in. Front Tread: (LeB) 57.6 in.; (Cord./N.Y./Imp.) 60.0 in. Rear Tread: (LeB) 57.0 in.; (Cord./N.Y./Imp.) 59.5 in. Standard Tires: (LeB) P185/70R14 SBR WSW; (Cord.) P195/75R15 GBR WSW; (N.Y./Imp.) P205/75R15 SBR WSW.

TECHNICAL: Transmission: Four-speed manual trans. standard on LeBaron. Gear ratios: (1st) 3.29:1; (2nd) 1.89:1; (3rd) 1.21:1; (4th) 0.88:1; (Rev) 3.14:1. TorqueFlite three-speed automatic optional on LeBaron: (1st) 2.69:1; (2nd) 1.55:1; (3rd) 1.00:1; (Rev) 2.10:1. TorqueFlite standard on other models: (1st) 2.74:1; (2nd) 1.54:1 or 1.55:1; (3rd) 1.00:1; (Rev) 2.22:1. Standard final drive ratio: (LeB) 2.69:1 exc. 2.78:1 w/auto.; (Cord.) 2.94:1; (N.Y. six) 2.94:1; (N.Y. V-8) 2.2:1; (Imp.) 2.20:1. Steering: (LeBaron) rack-and-pinion; (others) recirculating ball, power-assisted. Suspension: (LeBaron) MacPherson Iso-Struts and linkless sway bar in front, flex arm beam axle with trailing links and coil springs at the rear; (others) front torsion bars and anti-sway bar, rear leaf springs; stabilizer bar on Imperial. Brakes: Front disc, rear drum (power-assisted). Ignition: Electronic. Body construction: Unibody. Fuel tank: (LeB) 13 gal.; (Cord./N.Y./Imp.) 18 gal.

DRIVETRAIN OPTIONS: Engines: 2.6-liter four: LeBaron ($171). 318 cu. in. V-8: Cord./N.Y. ($70). Transmission/Suspension: Auto. trans. LeB ($396). Heavy-duty cooling: ($26-$31). Rear sway bar: Cord. ($34). Other: H.D. cooling: LeB/Cord. ($141). H.D. 500-amp battery ($43). California emission system ($65).

LEBARON CONVENIENCE/APPEARANCE OPTIONS: Option Packages: Easy-order packages (N/A). Mark Cross pkg. ($861). Two-tone paint ($170-$269). Light/gauge alert group ($79). Comfort/Convenience: Air cond. ($676). Rear defroster ($125). Automatic speed control ($155). Power seat ($197). Power windows ($165-$235). Power door locks ($106-$152). Power decklid release ($32). Leather-wrapped or sport steering wheel ($50). Tilt steering wheel ($95). Tinted glass ($88). Deluxe wipers ($47). Lighting and Mirrors: Halogen headlamps ($15). Cornering lamps ($57). Reading lamp ($24). Dual remote mirrors: base ($55). Lighted vanity mirror ($50). Entertainment: AM/FM stereo radio ($106); w/CB ($364); w/8-track player ($192). Electronic-tuning AM/FM stereo radio ($250); w/cassette ($455). Radio upgrade w/dual speakers ($27). Premium speaker pkg. ($126). Radio delete ($56 credit). Exterior Trim: Glass sunroof ($99). Crystal coat paint ($99). Front or rear bumper guards ($23). Sill moldings ($23). Door edge guards ($15-$25). Bodyside tape stripe: base ($48). Undercoating ($39). Vinyl lower body protection ($39). Interior Trim/Upholstery: Console ($100). Center armrest ($59). Vinyl bucket seats: base ($92). Cloth/vinyl bucket seats: Medallion ($151). Leather bucket seats: Medallion ($414). Color-keyed floor mats: front ($25); rear ($20). Trunk dress-up ($51). Cargo area tonneau cover: wag ($64). Wheels and Tires: Wire wheel covers ($244-$257). Cast aluminum wheels ($344-$357). Conventional spare tire ($51).

CORDOBA CONVENIENCE/APPEARANCE OPTIONS: Option Packages: Basic group ($552-$1205). Cabriolet roof pkg. ($554). Protection pkg. ($107-$137). Light pkg. ($137-$159). Comfort/Convenience: Air

cond. ($731). Rear defroster ($125). Automatic speed control ($155). Power seat ($197). Power windows ($165). Power door locks ($106). Power decklid release ($32-$49). Illuminated entry system ($72). Leather-wrapped steering wheel ($50). Tilt steering wheel ($95). Sport steering wheel ($50). Digital clock ($61). Intermittent wipers ($47). Lighting, Horns and Mirrors: Cornering lamps ($57). Triad horns ($25). Lighted vanity mirror ($58). Entertainment: AM/FM radio ($106). AM/FM stereo w/CB ($364); w/8-track ($192). Electronic-tuning AM/FM stereo w/cassette ($455). Search-tune AM/FM stereo radio ($239). Radio upgrade w/dual speakers ($28). Premium speaker pkg. ($126). Power antenna ($55). Radio delete ($56 credit). Exterior Trim: T-Bar roof ($790). Landau vinyl roof: LS ($157). Crystal coat paint ($99). Sill moldings: LS ($34). Wheel lip moldings: LS ($30). Bodyside/decklid tape stripes: LS ($72). Bodyside/decklid/hood tape stripes ($96). Undercoating ($39). Interior Trim/Upholstery: Console ($75-$124). Center armrest ($49). Cloth/vinyl bucket seats: LS ($103). Leather bucket seats ($499). Trunk dress-up ($60). Wheels and Tires: Wire wheel covers ($216). Premium wheel covers ($53). Forged aluminum wheels ($323). P205/75R15 SBR WSW ($116). P215/70R15 SBR RWL ($182). Conventional spare tire ($51).

1982 Chrysler, LeBaron convertible with optional Mark Cross leather interior (OCW)

NEW YORKER CONVENIENCE/APPEARANCE OPTIONS: Option Packages: Fifth Avenue Edition ($1647). Protection group ($66). Comfort/Convenience: Auto. speed control ($155). Power seat ($197). Power door locks ($152). Power decklid release ($32). Illuminated entry system ($72). Leather-covered steering wheel ($50). Tilt steering ($95). Intermittent wipers ($47). Lighted vanity mirror ($58). Entertainment: AM/FM stereo radio ($106); w/CB ($258-$364); w/8-track ($86-$192). Electronic-tuning AM/FM stereo w/cassette ($349-$455). Search-tune AM/FM stereo radio ($133-$239). Radio upgrade w/dual speakers ($28). Premium speaker pkg. ($126). Power antenna ($55). Exterior Trim: Power glass sunroof ($982). Crystal coat paint ($99). Hood tape stripe ($27). Undercoating ($39). Interior Trim/Upholstery: Cloth 60/40 bench seat (NC). Leather 60/40 bench seat ($306). Wheels and Tires: Wire wheel covers ($170). Forged aluminum wheels ($101-$271). Conventional spare tire ($51).

IMPERIAL OPTIONS: Imperial had only one extra-cost option, the Sinatra Edition ($1078). Customers could choose among several no-cost options: cloth/vinyl or leather split bench seat; AM/FM stereo w/CB, 8-track or cassette; and wire wheel covers or cast aluminum wheels.

HISTORY: Introduced: October 14, 1981, except LeBaron, October 29, 1981, and LeBaron convertible, April 1982. Model year production: 158,055 (incl. Canadian-built Cordobas, Imperials and New Yorkers). Calendar year production (U.S.): 114,443. Calendar year sales by U.S. dealers: 178,970. Model year sales by U.S. dealers: 152,436.

HISTORICAL FOOTNOTES: Although the Chrysler-Plymouth Division gained in market share this year, model year sales declined. The new front-drive LeBaron sold considerably better than its rear-drive predecessor of 1981, partly as a result of interest in the new convertible. Cordoba sales fell by nearly half, but New Yorker made a strong showing in its shrunken form. At the modernized St. Louis assembly plant, selected LeBaron two-doors were subjected to a special Quality Assurance Program. One in three cars was given a three-mile road test, then underwent a thorough inspection.

1983 CHRYSLER

After a year in service, Chrysler's own Trans-4 2.2-liter four-cylinder engine added 10 horsepower by means of reworked manifolds and recalibrated fuel/spark control. Compression also got a boost, to 9.0:1. Le-

Baron got a new standard five-speed manual gearbox. In a slightly confusing shuffle of nameplates, the rear-drive M-body was called New Yorker Fifth Avenue this year, while the new E-body got the plain New Yorker (and E Class) badge. Electronic Voice Alert became optional on LeBaron and E Class/New Yorker. "Message Center" lights warned of such maladies as an open door or low fuel level, on a car diagram. The EVA system added audio warnings for the 11 monitored functions. Not everyone appreciated the intrusive voice, which would be modified for 1984. LeBaron added a Town & Country convertible with fake wood paneling like the T&C station wagon, similar to the simulated wood convertibles of the same name three decades earlier. The wood-look ragtop, in fact, was advertised as "Re-introducing an American classic." An Executive sedan and limousine became available, stretched out from front-drive LeBaron coupes. The five-seat Executive sedan rode a 124.3 inch wheelbase. A seven-passenger limousine with jump seats and electric division window had a 131.3 inch wheelbase. These were the first limos since the Imperials of 1970. Chrysler production totals show that only two LeBarons were produced with the A89 limo package.

1983 Chrysler, LeBaron sedan (OCW)

1983 Chrysler, LeBaron Town & Country station wagon with optional roof rack and wire wheel covers (OCW)

1983 Chrysler, LeBaron Town & Country "Mark Cross" Edition convertible (OCW)

LEBARON — SERIES C — FOUR — Only one trim level was offered by the front-drive LeBaron in its second year, as the upper-level Medallion was dropped. LeBaron was essentially a posher version of the K-car (Dodge Aries and Plymouth Reliant). New standard equipment included halogen headlamps, a tethered gas cap, and 'ram air' heater/vent system with outlets on the dashboard. Brake rotors grew this year, and rear drum brakes became self-adjusting. The manual transaxle (standard only on coupes) gained a gear, offering five forward speeds instead of four. The convertible came in base, luxury Mark Cross, and (a little later) Town & Country form, with fake wood trim. Electronic Voice Alert was standard on the Mark Cross ragtop and T&C station wagon. Door latches were made quieter, with sound-deadening materials. Appearance changed little for 1983. LeBaron had a formal-looking sloped grille with thin vertical bars and slightly wider center vertical bar, plus a pentastar hood ornament. Clear rectangular parking lights set into the bumper, where the grille pattern repeated in a grille-width center slot. Bright bodyside moldings with vinyl inserts extended into partial (upper half) wheel opening moldings. Low-back vinyl bucket seats with adjustable head restraints and dual recliners were standard in coupe and convertible. They came in silver, red, beige, brown or (convertible only) red/white. Standard in four-doors and Town & Country was a cloth bench seat with center armrests, in blue,

silver, red, beige, or brown. Body colors were: Black, Crimson Red, Glacier Blue Crystal Coat, Silver Crystal Coat, Nightwatch Blue, Beige Crystal Coat, Pearl White, Charcoal Gray Metallic, and Sable Brown. Black and Crimson Red were not available with the Mark Cross package on convertibles. Glacier Blue, Silver, Nightwatch Blue and Charcoal Gray were not available on any convertible. Glacier Blue and Nightwatch Blue were unavailable on Town & Country. LeBaron's standard equipment also included an AM radio, digital clock, roll-resistant SBR whitewalls, luxury wheel covers, carpeted trunk floor, luxury two-spoke color-keyed steering wheel, power brakes, power rack-and-pinion steering, electronic digital clock, cloth-covered headliner, and inside hood release. Two-door coupes also had a padded vinyl landau roof. All models except the coupe had standard TorqueFlite automatic transmission. Convertibles had a center console, color-keyed dual remote mirrors, power top with zip-down window and weather-seal sides, plus tailored top boot. The standard 2.2-liter OHC four had chrome valve stems, alloy valve seats, and moly-faced compression rings. A new optional electronic travel computer displayed fuel used, trip mileage, average speed, and cruising range. The Mark Cross convertible added a host of extras: air conditioning, Mitsubishi-built Silent Shaft 2.6 OHC four, special low-back Corinthian leather bucket seats with console and freestanding center armrest, leather-wrapped steering wheel, vinyl door trim inserts and Mark Cross medallions, front/rear bumper guards, cornering lamps, upper body accent stripes, and wire wheel covers. Electronic Voice Alert, electronic-tuning AM/FM stereo radio, tilt steering column, power windows and door locks, power decklid release, automatic speed control, deluxe wipers, and Travel Computer also were Mark Cross standards. A Mark Cross package on other models included a 50/50 leather bench seat with dual armrests and recliners; vinyl door trim panels with leather inserts and medallions; leather-wrapped steering wheel; Electronic Voice Alert; and Travel Computer cluster.

1983 Chrysler, E Class sedan (OCW)

E CLASS/NEW YORKER — SERIES T — FOUR — Chrysler's new front-drive, mid-size E-body came with a new and an old name: E Class (first called Gran LeBaron) and arriving a bit later, the upper level New Yorker. A three-inch stretch of the K-car wheelbase provided the platform. To avoid confusion with the former rear-drive, that one was now called New Yorker Fifth Avenue. Both new models were six-window four-door sedans. New Yorker seated five; E Class, six. E Class featured a vertical-bar grille like that used on LeBaron and Imperial. New Yorkers carried a similar "waterfall" grille with larger header molding. New Yorker also had a formal, limousine-like roofline with wide rear quarters, heavily padded at the rear in landau style, covering the narrow windows. A brushed-finish wrapover roof band held opera lamps, while front fenders had small louvers and cornering lamps. Standard were bright moldings around sills, lower doors and wheel openings. Base engine on both models was the Trans-4 2.2-liter four. Three-speed TorqueFlite had wide-ratio gearing (high-ratio first and second for improved pickup and economy). Optional was the Mitsubishi-built 2.6-liter four. Both had an Iso-Strut front suspension with integral linkless anti-sway bar, rubber-isolated from the body. At the rear was a beam axle with trailing arm, coil springs, track bar, and torsion-tube anti-roll control. Electronic Voice Alert was standard on both models; a Travel Computer on New Yorker. E Class standard equipment included: power brakes and steering, AM radio, dual horns, lighter, color-keyed wheel covers, halogen headlamps, power decklid release, digital lock, and dual chrome mirrors. Cloth bench seats had a center armrest and adjustable headrests. The fuel filler door opened from inside the car. In addition to a padded landau roof, New Yorker added tinted glass, cornering and opera lamps, remote-control mirrors, bright sill and quarter-window moldings, bodyside and deck tape stripes, intermittent wipers, and locking wire wheel covers. New Yorkers had cloth-upholstered 50/50 reclining bench seating with storage pockets in back and separate armrests. A crystalline pentastar hood ornament was standard. E Class rode on P185/70R14 steel-belted radial whitewall tires, while New Yorker's were P185/75R14. New Yorker body colors were: Charcoal Metallic, Nightwatch Blue, Bright Silver Crystal Coat, Beige Crystal Coat, Glacier Blue Crystal Coat, Crimson Red, Sable Brown, Black, and Pearl White. A $696 Mark Cross package included plush leather-and-vinyl seats in four-color choices, plus unique door trim panels with piped inserts; leather-wrapped luxury steering wheel; and special identification.

CORDOBA — SERIES S — SIX/V-8 — For its final year, Cordoba enjoyed little change beyond a switch from amber/clear to amber front side marker

lenses and a new crystalline pentastar hood ornament. The low-budget LS model was dropped, leaving just one coupe choice. A new standard 60/40 split-bench seat had a passenger seatback recliner. Optional again was the Cabriolet simulated convertible roof, but only 899 Cordobas had one installed. Premium wheel covers were revised. Wide taillamps each were arranged in three rows, with vertical backup lamps between taillamps and license plate. Colors this year were: Nightwatch Blue, Glacier Blue, Crystal Coat, Black, Silver, or Beige Crystal Coat, Crimson Red, Sable Brown, Pearl White, and Charcoal Gray metallic. Cordoba's ample standard equipment list included the 225 cu. in. (3.7-liter) slant six engine, power brakes and steering, wide-ratio TorqueFlite automatic transmission, and Special Edition padded landau vinyl roof with brushed-finish roof band and opera lamps. Also standard: a cigarette lighter, digital clock, bumper guards and rub strips, tinted glass, dual horns, halogen headlamps, dual remote-control chrome mirrors, sill moldings with rear extensions, and sport wheel covers. The standard AM radio could still be deleted. As before, the 318 cu. in. (5.2-liter) V-8 was optional.

1983 Chrysler, Cordoba hardtop with optional wire wheel covers (OCW)

NEW YORKER FIFTH AVENUE — SERIES FS — SIX/V-8 — What had for several years been a luxury option now became a full-length model, as the Fifth Avenue name was added to the rear-drive New Yorker. Chrysler described it as "a car with charisma" with an "aristocratic grille." Unchanged this year, that upright grille consisted of narrow vertical bars with somewhat thicker center bar, plus two horizontal divider bars. Simulated vertical front fender louvers appeared again. The formal padded vinyl landau roof had a unique backlight. 'Fifth Avenue Edition' script went on the rear-door portion of the padded vinyl top, just behind the bright brushed-finish wrapover roof molding. That molding held optional electro-luminescent opera lamps. Up front was a new pentastar hood ornament, inside, a two-spoke steering wheel. Premium wheel covers were standard; wire covers optional. Once again, a 225 cu. in. (3.7-liter) slant six was the base engine, with the 318 cu. in. V-8 the sole option. Standard equipment included three-speed automatic transmission, air conditioning, power windows, power steering/brakes, digital clock, dual remote mirrors, bodyside and decklid accent stripes, and tinted glass. Fifth Avenue colors were: Beige Crystal Coat, Nightwatch Blue, Charcoal Gray metallic, Formal Black, Crimson Red, Silver Crystal Coat, Sable Brown, and Pearl White. An $1,870 Luxury Equipment package added a heavy-duty battery, V-8 engine, illuminated entry system, lighted right visor vanity mirror, electro-luminescent opera lamps, power door locks and decklid release, power driver's seat, AM/FM stereo radio, 60/40 leather seats, automatic speed control, intermittent wipers, and wire wheel covers.

1983 Chrysler, New Yorker Fifth Avenue sedan (OCW)

IMPERIAL — SERIES YS — V-8 — "A singular statement of car and driver." That's how the factory catalog described the luxury Imperial coupe, now in its third (and last) year. Changes were minimal to the sculptured-look bustleback body, apart from new colors. The Sinatra edition was abandoned. Price was cut by $2,300 down to $18,688 and Imperials offered an extended warranty; yet only 1,427 were produced this year. Concealed headlamps stood above wide parking lamps in Imperial's angled front end. The forward-peaked grille had a bright upper header molding. Upholstery came in Mark Cross 60/40 Corinthian leather or Kimberley velvet. As before, the fuel-injected 318 cu. in. (5.2-liter) V-8 was standard.

1983 Chrysler, Imperial coupe (OCW)

I.D. DATA: Chrysler again had a 17-symbol Vehicle Identification Number (VIN) on the upper left corner of the instrument panel, visible through the windshield. Coding changed somewhat with the revised model lineup. The first digit indicates Country: '1' U.S.A.; '2' Canada. The second symbol is Make: 'C' Chrysler; 'A' Imperial. Third is Vehicle Type: '3' passenger car. The next symbol ('B') indicates manual seatbelts. Symbol five is Car Line: 'C' LeBaron; 'T' E Class and New Yorker (front-drive); 'S' Cordoba; 'F' New Yorker Fifth Avenue (rear-drive); 'Y' Imperial. Symbol six is Series: '4' High; '5' Premium; '6' Special. Symbol seven is Body Style: '1' 2-dr. sedan; '2' 2-dr. hardtop coupe; 'S' 2-dr. convertible coupe; '6' 4-dr. sedan; '9' 4-dr. station wagon. Eighth is the Engine Code: 'C' L4135 2Bbl.; 'G' L4156 2Bbl.; 'H' L6225 1Bbl.; 'P' V8318 2Bbl.; 'N' V8318 EFI. Next comes a check digit. Symbol ten indicates Model Year: 'D' 1983. Symbol eleven is Assembly Plant: 'C' Detroit; 'F' Newark; 'G' St. Louis; 'R' Windsor, Ontario. The last six digits make up the sequential serial number, starting with 100001. Engine number coding is similar to 1982.

LEBARON (FOUR)

Model No.	Body/Style No.	Body Type & Seating	Factory Price	Shipping Weight	Prod. Total
CP	22	2-dr. Cpe-6P	8514	2430	18,331
CP	41	4-dr. Sed-6P	8790	2480	30,869
CP	27	2-dr. Conv-4P	12800	2470	9,891

LEBARON TOWN & COUNTRY (FOUR)

Model No.	Body/Style No.	Body Type & Seating	Factory Price	Shipping Weight	Prod. Total
CP	45	4-dr. Sta Wag-5P	9731	2600	10,994

LEBARON MARK CROSS CONVERTIBLE (FOUR)

Model No.	Body/Style No.	Body Type & Seating	Factory Price	Shipping Weight	Prod. Total
CP	27	2-dr. Conv-4P	14595	N/A	Note 1
CP	27	2-dr. T&C Conv-4P	15595	N/A	Note 1

Note 1: Mark Cross and Mark Cross Town & Country convertibles are included in base convertible total above. A total of 1,520 T&C convertible packages were installed, plus 5,441 Mark Cross convertible packages.

E CLASS (FOUR)

Model No.	Body/Style No.	Body Type & Seating	Factory Price	Shipping Weight	Prod. Total
TH	41	4-dr. Sed-6P	9341	2525	39,258

NEW YORKER (FOUR)

Model No.	Body/Style No.	Body Type & Seating	Factory Price	Shipping Weight	Prod. Total
TP	41	4-dr Sed-5P	10950	2580	33,832

CORDOBA (SIX/V-8)

Model No.	Body/Style No.	Body Type & Seating	Factory Price	Shipping Weight	Prod. Total
SP	22	2-dr. HT Cpe-6P	9580/9805	3380/3515	13,471

NEW YORKER FIFTH AVENUE (SIX/V-8)

Model No.	Body/Style No.	Body Type & Seating	Factory Price	Shipping Weight	Prod. Total
FS	41	4-dr. Sed-6P	12487/12712	3540/3690	83,501

IMPERIAL (V-8)

Model No.	Body/Style No.	Body Type & Seating	Factory Price	Shipping Weight	Prod. Total
YS	22	2-dr. HT Cpe-6P	18688	3910	1,427

EXECUTIVE (FOUR)

Model No.	Body/Style No.	Body Type & Seating	Factory Price	Shipping Weight	Prod. Total
CP	48	4-dr. Sed-5P	18900	N/A	N/A
CP	49	4-dr. Limo-7P	21900	N/A	N/A

Factory Price & Weight Note: Figures to left of slash are for six-cylinder engine, to right of slash for 318 cu. in. V-8.

Model Number Note: Some sources identify models using the new VIN data to indicate Car Line, Price Class and Body Style. Example: LeBaron coupe (CP22) has the equivalent number CC51, which translates to LeBaron line, Premium price class, and two-door body. See I.D. Data section for breakdown.

ENGINE DATA: BASE FOUR (LeBaron, E Class, New Yorker): Inline, overhead cam four-cylinder. Cast iron block; aluminum head. Displacement: 135 cu. in. (2.2-liters). Bore & stroke: 3.44 x 3.62 in. Compression ratio: 9.0:1. Brake horsepower: 94 at 5200 R.P.M. Torque: 117 lb.-ft. at 3200 R.P.M. Five main bearings. Hydraulic valve lifters. Carburetor: 2Bbl. Holley 6520. OPTIONAL FOUR (LeBaron, E Class, New Yorker): Inline, overhead cam four-cylinder. Cast iron block; aluminum head. Displacement: 156 cu. in. (2.6-liters). Bore & stroke: 3.59 x 3.86 in. Compression ratio: 8.2:1. Brake horsepower: 93 at 4500 R.P.M. Torque: 132 lb.-ft. at 2500 R.P.M. Five main bearings. Solid valve lifters. Carburetor: 2Bbl. Mikuni. BASE SIX (Cordoba, Fifth Ave.): Inline, overhead valve six-cylinder. Cast iron block and head. Displacement: 225 cu. in. (3.7-liters). Bore & stroke: 3.40 x 4.12 in. Compression ratio: 8.4:1. Brake horsepower: 90 at 3600 R.P.M. Torque: 165 lb.-ft. at 1600 R.P.M. Four main bearings. Hydraulic valve lifters. Carburetor: 1Bbl. Holley 1945. OPTIONAL V-8 (Cordoba, Fifth Ave.): 90-degree, overhead valve V-8. Cast iron block and head. Displacement: 318 cu. in. (5.2-liters). Bore & stroke: 3.91 x 3.31 in. Compression ratio: 8.5:1. Brake horsepower: 130 at 4000 R.P.M. Torque: 230 lb.-ft. at 1600 R.P.M. Five main bearings. Hydraulic valve lifters. Carburetor: 2Bbl. Carter BBD. IMPERIAL V-8: Same as 318 cu. in. V-8 above, but with electronic fuel injection. Brake horsepower: 140 at 4000 R.P.M. Torque: 245 lb.-ft. at 2000 R.P.M.

CHASSIS DATA: Wheelbase: (LeBaron) 100.3 in.; (E Class/N.Y.) 103.3 in.; (Cordoba/Fifth Ave./Imperial) 112.7 in. Overall length: (LeB) 179.6 in.; (LeB wag) 179.8 in.; (E Class/N.Y.) 185 7 in.; (Cord.) 210.1 in.; (Fifth Ave.) 206.7 in.; (Imperial) 213.3 in. Height: (LeB cpe) 52.6 in.; (LeB sed) 53.0 in.; (LeB wag) 52.7 in.; (LeB conv.) 54.1 in.; (Cord./Imp.) 53.2 in.; (E Class/N.Y.) 53.9 in.; (Fifth Ave.) 55.3 in. Width: (LeB) 68.5 in.; (E Class/N.Y.) 68.0 in.; (Cord./Imp.) 72.7 in.; (Fifth Ave.) 74.2 in. Front Tread: (LeB/E Class/N.Y.) 57.6 in.; (Cord./Fifth Ave./Imp.) 60.0 in. Rear Tread: (LeB/E Class/N.Y.) 57.0 in.; (Cord./Fifth Ave./Imp.) 59.5 in. Standard Tires: (LeB/E Class) P185/70R14 SBR WSW; (N.Y.) P185/75R14 SBR WSW; (Cord.) P195/75R15 GBR WSW; (Fifth Ave./Imp.) P205/75R15 SBR WSW.

1983 Chrysler, Executive Sedan (OCW)

TECHNICAL: Transmission: Five-speed manual trans standard on LeBaron. Gear ratios: (1st) 3.29:1; (2nd) 1.89:1; (3rd) 1.21:1; (4th) 0.88:1; (5th) 0.72:1; (Rev) 3.14:1. TorqueFlite three-speed automatic optional on LeBaron, standard on E Class and New Yorker: (1st) 2.69:1; (2nd) 1.55:1; (3rd) 1.00:1; (Rev) 2.10:1. TorqueFlite standard on other models: (1st) 2.74:1; (2nd) 1.54:1; (3rd) 1.00:1; (Rev) 2.22:1. Standard final drive ratio: (LeB) 2.57:1 exc. 2.78:1 w/auto.; (LeB conv.) 3.02:1; (E Class) 3.02:1; (New Yorker) 2.78:1 or 3.02:1; (Cord./Fifth Ave. six) 2.94:1; (Fifth Ave. V-8) 2.26:1; (Imp.) 2.24:1. Steering: (LeB/E Class/N.Y.) rack-and-pinion; (others) recirculating ball, power-assisted. Suspension: (LeB/E Class/N.Y.) MacPherson Iso-Struts and linkless sway bar in front, flex arm beam axle with trailing links and coil springs at the rear; (others) front torsion bars and anti-sway bar, rear leaf springs. Brakes: Front disc, rear drum (power-assisted). Ignition: Electronic. Body construction: Unibody. Fuel tank: (LeB/E Class/N.Y.) 13 gal.; (Cord./Fifth Ave./Imp.) 18 gal.

DRIVETRAIN OPTIONS: Engines: 2.6-liter four: LeB/E Class/N.Y. ($259). 318 cu. in. V-8: Cord./Fifth Ave. ($225). Transmission/Suspension: Auto. trans.; LeB ($439). Heavy-duty susp.: Cord. ($36); Fifth Ave. ($26). Sport suspension: LeB/E Class/N.Y. ($55). Rear sway bar: Cord. ($36). Other: H.D. cooling: LeB/E Class/N.Y. ($141). H.D. 500-amp battery ($43). California emission system ($75).

LEBARON CONVENIENCE/APPEARANCE OPTIONS: Option Packages: Mark Cross A61 pkg. ($963-$1232). Easy-order package A91 ($577-$645); A92 ($2022-$2147). Two-tone paint ($176). Comfort/Convenience: Air cond. ($732). Rear defroster ($137). Automatic speed control ($174). Travel computer ($206). Audible message center ($63). Power seat ($210). Power windows ($180-$255). Power door locks ($120-$170). Power decklid or liftgate release ($40). Leather-wrapped or sport steering wheel ($50). Tilt steering wheel ($105). Tinted glass ($105). Intermittent wipers ($52). Lighting and Mirrors: Cornering lamps ($60). Reading lamp ($24). Dual remote mirrors ($57). Dual power remote mirrors ($47-$104). Lighted vanity mirror ($50). Entertainment: AM/FM stereo radio ($109). Electronic-tuning AM/FM stereo radio ($263); w/cassette ($402) exc. Mark Cross conv. (NC). Premium speaker pkg. ($126). Radio delete ($56 credit). Exterior Trim: Front or rear bumper guards ($23). Sill moldings (NC to $24). Door edge protectors ($15-$25). Luggage rack: wag ($106). Bodyside tape stripe ($42). Undercoating ($41). Vinyl lower body protection (NC to $39). Interior Trim/Upholstery: Console

($100). Center armrest ($59). Cloth/vinyl bucket seats: cpe/conv. ($160). Color-keyed floor mats: front ($25), rear ($20). Trunk dress-up ($51). Wheels and Tires: Wire wheel covers ($257). Cast aluminum wheels ($357) but (NC) w/Mark Cross conv.

E CLASS AND NEW YORKER CONVENIENCE/APPEARANCE OPTIONS: Option Packages: Protection group: E Class ($64-$120). Easy-order pkg.: E Class ($676 or $2196). Mark Cross pkg. ($696). California/Hawaii Advantage: E Class ($1409). Comfort/Convenience: Air cond. ($732). Rear defroster ($138). Auto. speed control ($174). Travel computer: E Class ($206). Power windows ($255). Power door locks ($170). Power seat ($210). Tinted glass ($104). Leather-wrapped steering wheel ($50). Tilt steering ($105). Intermittent wipers: E Class ($52). Lighting and Mirrors: Cornering lamps: E Class ($60). Dual remote mirrors: E Class ($57). Dual power remote mirrors: E Class ($107). Lighted vanity mirror ($58). Entertainment: Same as LeBaron. Exterior: Two-tone paint: E Class ($170). Bodyside and deck stripe: E Class ($63). Sill moldings: E Class ($23). Front or rear bumper guards ($28). Door edge protectors ($25). Vinyl lower body protection: E Class ($39). Undercoating ($41). Interior: Vinyl split bench seat: E Class (NC). Cloth 50/50 bench seat: E Class ($267). Color-keyed mats: front ($25); rear ($20). Trunk dress-up: E Class ($51). Wheels and Tires: Wire wheel covers: E Class ($244). Cast aluminum wheels: E Class ($363). N.Y. ($119). Conventional spare ($63).

CORDOBA CONVENIENCE/APPEARANCE OPTIONS: Option Packages: Basic group ($1121). Premium equipment ($2471). Cabriolet roof pkg. ($587). Protection group ($114). Light pkg. ($143). Comfort/Convenience: Air cond. ($787). Rear defroster ($138). Automatic speed control ($174). Power seat ($199). Power windows ($180). Power door locks ($120). Power decklid release ($40). Illuminated entry system ($75). Leather-wrapped steering wheel ($53). Tilt steering wheel ($99). Intermittent wipers ($52). Lighting, Horns and Mirrors: Cornering lamps ($60). Triad horns ($27). Lighted vanity mirror ($61). Entertainment: AM/FM radio ($109). Electronic-tuning AM/FM stereo ($154-$263); w/cassette ($293-$402). Radio upgrade w/dual speakers ($28). Premium speaker pkg. ($126). Power antenna ($60). Radio decklid ($56 credit). Exterior: Bodyside/decklid/hood tape stripe ($98). Undercoating ($41). Interior: Console ($75). Leather bucket seats ($529). Trunk dress-up ($48). Wheels and Tires: Wire wheel covers ($244). Premium wheel covers ($57). Forged aluminum wheels ($107). P205/75R15 SBR WSW ($116). P215/70R15 SBR RWL ($66-$182). Conventional spare tire ($63).

NEW YORKER FIFTH AVENUE CONVENIENCE/APPEARANCE OPTIONS: Option Packages: Luxury equipment ($1870). Protection group ($70). Comfort/Convenience Auto. speed-control ($170). Power seat ($199). Power door locks ($159). Power decklid release ($40). Illuminated entry system ($75). Leather-covered steering wheel ($53). Tilt steering ($99). Intermittent wipers ($49). Lighted vanity mirror ($61). Entertainment: Same as Cordoba. AM/FM stereo radio ($109). Electronic-tuning AM/FM stereo ($154-$263); w/cassette ($293-$402). Radio upgrade w/dual speakers ($28). Premium speaker pkg. ($126). Power antenna ($60). Exterior: Power glass sunroof ($1041). Hood tape stripe ($29). Undercoating ($41). Interior: Cloth 60/40 bench seat (NC). Leather 60/40 bench seat ($356). Wheels and Tires: Wire wheel covers ($170). Michelin WSW tires (NC). Conventional spare tire ($63).

IMPERIAL OPTIONS: Apart from the California emission system ($75), Imperial had no extra-cost options. Customers could choose among several no-cost options: cloth/vinyl or leather 60/40 split bench seat; electronic-tuning AM/FM stereo w/cassette; and wire wheel covers or cast aluminum wheels.

HISTORY: Introduced: October 1, 1982. Model year production: 241,574 (incl. Canadian-built Cordobas, Fifth Avenues and Imperials). Calendar year production (U.S.): 234,203. Calendar year sales by U.S. dealers: 262,037. Model year sales by U.S. dealers: 243,664.

HISTORICAL FOOTNOTES: Chrysler-Plymouth sales went up 20.2 percent for the 1983 model year, due largely to success of the new E-cars. Fifth Avenue (formerly New Yorker) sales jumped over 50 percent, to 77,700. Cordoba sales fell prompting its dismissal from the line, despite a resurgence of interest in cars of that league. Imperial was dropped too, never having found enough buyers even for a limited-production model. Production of rear-drive intermediates (including Fifth Avenue) moved from Windsor, Ontario to St. Louis during 1983. LeBaron's base convertible price was cut in January, from $12,800 down to just $10,995. Late in 1982, Kenyon & Eckhardt Inc. was appointed the exclusive Chrysler-Plymouth ad agency. Vice-President of Marketing Joseph A. Campana wanted to promote an "image of engineered-in value with Chryslers for "luxury and class," Plymouth for economy. Chrysler Corp. was in better financial shape, reaching a market share of over 10 percent again for 1982 and paying back its highly-publicized loan. At year's end, NHTSA was investigating alleged carburetor defects on 1.8 million Chrysler Corp. vehicles with 1.7- and 2.2-liter engines. Up to this point, Chrysler had an impressively low record of mandated recalls.

Both Cordoba and Imperial left the lineup this year, while a new Laser hatchback sport coupe was added. The 2.2-liter four-cylinder engine switched from carburetion to single-point, throttle-body electronic fuel injection, though early models still carried carburetors. All radios had electronic tuning. Laser XE offered Chrysler's LCD electronic dashboard. Electronic Voice Alert was improved to make more useful audio comments - and added a shutoff switch in the glove compartment. In the performance department, a turbocharged version of the 2.2 engine, rated at 140 horsepower, became available on Laser, LeBaron and E Class/New Yorker. Front-drive fuel tanks grew from 13 to 14 gallons.

1984 Chrysler, Laser hatchback with turbocharged engine (OCW)

LASER — SERIES GC — FOUR — Chrysler described its new front-drive hatchback Laser coupe as "a definitive statement of motion technology." The all-new aerodynamic design featured a front air dam, plus flush windshield and glass for reduced drag. Dodge's Daytona was nearly identical. Four-passenger Laser bodies held recessed quad headlamps, with recessed parking lamps below the bumper rub strips. The minimalist grille consisted of one large slot that occupied half the angled upper panel, with two additional slots below (inboard of the parking lamps). Above was a laydown pentastar hood ornament. Louvers appeared atop the hood, on a modest bulge between its side creases. Small horizontal side marker lenses were just below the bodyside moldings. A 'Laser' decal went below the outside mirror, along the bodyside stripe. 'Turbo' identification (if applicable) was at the base of the window, just above the door handle. A 'Chrysler' nameplate was on the left side of the hatch; 'Lasers' on the right side. A red Electronic Fuel Injection decal went on the door window frame. A new "dual path" upper Iso-Strut mount in the front suspension was designed to send shock absorber loads in one direction, spring loads in another. The rear suspension used gas-charged shock absorbers, plus a large-diameter tubular sway bar inside the rear axle. A track bar was mounted alongside. Power brakes and quick-ratio rack-and-pinion steering were standard. The five-speed close-ratio manual transaxle featured a reworked linkage. Laser equipment also included a console, digital clock built into AM radio, leather-wrapped steering wheel, lighter side window demisters, halogen headlamps, optical horn (pass/flash), dual horns, dual mirrors (left remote), rear spoiler, intermittent wipers, and premium wheel covers. Low-back cloth bucket seats had dual recliners. Turbocharging of the 2.2-liter engine was available on both the base Laser and the performance Laser XE. Developed from a Garrett AiResearch unit, the turbocharger delivered 7.5 psi maximum boost. Multi-point fuel injection used Bosch injectors at each cylinder. Turbos had a water-cooled turbine end-shaft bearing, hotter cam, bigger oil pump, low-restriction exhaust, plus tighter piston rings and seals. Dished-top pistons cut compression down to 8.1:1. The turbo was rated 142 horsepower at 5600 rpm. A total of 32,538 Lasers had the AGT Turbo package. Laser XE also included a standard cloth/vinyl "enthusiast" driver's seat with air-filled bladders for adjustable (inflatable) thigh/lumbar support, plus tilt steering wheel. Other XE extras were an 11-function Electronic Navigator illuminated entry system, electronic instrument cluster, dual electric remote mirrors, and AM/FM radio. Standard Laser tires were P185/70R14 blackwall steel-belted radials on 5.5 inch wheels. XE had the same size raised black-letter tires on cast aluminum wheels. A Special Handling Suspension available on XE included higher-rate springs and control arm rear bushings, gas-charged front shocks and Iso-Struts. Laser colors were: Beige Crystal Coat, Gunmetal Blue Pearl Coat, Black, and Radiant Silver Crystal Coat (plus Garnet Red or Mink Brown Pearl Coat at extra cost). XE came in black. Six two-tone combinations were offered.

1984 Chrysler, LeBaron coupe (OCW)

LEBARON — SERIES KC — FOUR — Unchanged up front, LeBaron carried a revised rear end with wraparound taillamps that were taller than before, with horizontal trim strips. Vertical backup lamps were inboard, next to the license plate opening. Full wheel-opening moldings and body sill moldings also were new this year. The full padded vinyl roof again extended into upper rear doors. T&C station wagons had a new standard roof rack. Under the hood, the new turbocharged engine was available, while the base 2.2-liter version added fuel injection. Once again, the Mitsubishi-built 2.6-liter four was optional, making three choices in all. Inside was a new luxury two-spoke steering wheel and instrument cluster with dark butterfly walnut woodtone accents, plus a new padded top for the instrument panel. Digital clocks were built into all the new electronic-tuning radios, including the standard AM version (which could be deleted for credit). Wide-ratio TorqueFlite was the standard transmission. Coupes had cloth high-back bucket seats; four-doors and the T&C wagon, a cloth/vinyl front bench seat with folding center armrest. Body colors were: Crimson Red, Garnet Red Pearl, Mink Brown Pearl, Beige Crystal, Gunmetal Blue Pearl, Black, Charcoal Pearl, Radiant Silver Crystal, and White. Two two-tone combinations were offered. Convertibles had larger (full-width) back seats, glass back windows (formerly plastic), power rear-quarter windows, and a new roof latch mechanism. The T&C version with fake wood trim was offered again, as was the Mark Cross Edition. The Mark Cross convertible added an electronic instrument cluster with electronic speedometer and odometer, analog fuel/voltage/oil/temp gauges, and graphic message center, along with low-back leather bucket seats, power driver's seat, and an illuminated entry system. A total of 5,401 nonconvertible LeBarons carried a Mark Cross option package (code AFC). That one included a leather/vinyl 50/50 front seat with dual armrests, center consolettes, and seatback recliners; plus door trim panels with leather-like inserts and Mark Cross medallions, and leather-wrapped steering wheel.

1984 Chrysler, LeBaron Town & Country station wagon with optional wire wheel covers (OCW)

E CLASS/NEW YORKER — SERIES ET — FOUR — New Yorker's appearance was similar to 1983, but new wraparound taillamps had five thick, bright horizontal trim strips that stretched all the way from license plates around the quarter panel. The new "waterfall" grille also was similar to the 1983 version, but its bright surrounding molding now extended outward beneath the headlamps. Saddle-type belt moldings and full wheel opening moldings were new. New Yorker's padded vinyl landau roof held coach lamps and a bright roof band. Standard wire wheel covers had integral locks. Suspension improvements included recalibrated spring rates, redesigned spring seats, new jounce bumpers, and new dual path bushings; plus new standard all-weather P185/75R14 SBR tires with wide whitewalls. New pillow-style 50/50 front seats in luxury cloth featured driver/passenger recliners, dual armrests, storage consolettes, seatback and cushion pockets. Leather/vinyl seating was optional. New Yorkers had roof-mounted passenger assist handles and C-pillar courtesy/reading lamps. Power windows became standard this year. Door panels and dash had dark butterfly walnut woodtone accents and bright trim. A new electronic instrument cluster displayed oil pressure, voltage, fuel, and temperature, plus a digital speedometer. A Visual Message Center was standard on New Yorker, while a new optional Electronic Navigator showed miles per gallon, driving range and such at the touch of a button. The standard electronic-tuning AM radio held a digital clock. Body colors were: Crimson Red, Garnet Red Pearl, Mink Brown Pearl, Beige Crystal, Nightwatch Blue, Gunmetal Blue Pearl, Black, Charcoal Metallic Pearl, Radiant Blue Crystal, and White. E Class was the stepdown version of the front-drive E body, priced $2,600 lower and carrying less equipment (but an extra passenger). Its sharply-angled grille was made up of many evenly-spaced vertical bars topped by a heavy bright header that wrapped over the top, toward the hood. The grille pattern continued in a wide slot below the bumper rub strip. E Class had a stand-up crystalline pentastar hood ornament recessed quad rectangular headlamps and small horizontal parking lamps set into the bumper (below the rub strip). Appearance was similar to New Yorker, but in six-window design rather than four. New Yorker-style full-width wraparound taillamps had thinner bright horizontal trim strips. Backup lamps were a continuation of the taillamps, alongside the license plate opening. Standard equipment included power brakes and steering, three-speed automatic transaxle, graphic message center, halogen headlamps, and concealed two-speed wipers. Also standard: door armrests, bumper rub strips, lighter, AM radio with digital clock, coat hooks, power fuel filler door release, dual horns, day/night mirror, dual mirrors (left remote), and premium wheel covers. E Class came in: Crimson Red, Garnet Red Pearl, Mink Brown Pearl, Beige Crystal, Nightwatch Blue, Black, Charcoal Gray Clear, Radiant Silver Crystal, White, and Gunmetal Blue Pearl. Two two-tones were available. Standard interior was a cloth bench seat with center armrest in blue, silver, red or beige. Base engine for both front-drive models remained the Trans-4 2.2-liter, now with fuel injection; but a turbocharged version also was offered. So was the Mitsubishi 2.6-liter four. Cast aluminum wheels were available on both, as was an illuminated entry system.

1984 Chrysler, E Class sedan (OCW)

1984 Chrysler, Fifth Avenue sedan with optional wire wheel covers (OCW)

FIFTH AVENUE — SERIES MFS — V-8 — The last rear-drive Chrysler dropped the New Yorker name completely this year. Appearance changes were modest. Its grille now consisted of vertical bars with no horizontal dividers. Full-width wraparound taillamps weren't as tall as New Yorker's, with subtle trim and small horizontal backup lenses. As in 1983, between the taillamps was a separate rectangular panel with Chrysler block-letter nameplate. The license plate again was down in the back bumper. Fifth Avenue front fenders again displayed non-functional louvers. 'Chrysler' identification went on the driver's side mirror. The padded vinyl formal landau roof had its unique backlight and brushed-finish transverse roof molding. Sill moldings had front and rear extensions. Bodyside and decklid accent stripes were standard. After several years with six-cylinder power (which most buyers ignored), the 318 cu. in. V-8 became the sole engine. Chrysler touted Fifth Avenue as having "45 luxury features as standard equipment." The new standard AM radio had a digital readout and digital clock. Silver sputter chrome treatment went on instrument panel overlays. Cloth/vinyl 60/40 front seats with individual adjustments came in silver, dark blue, red or beige. Halogen headlamps came with time delay switches. Trunk and map/dome reading lamps were standard. Options included a power glass sunroof and new cast aluminum wheels. A Luxury Equipment Package included such extras as illuminated entry, automatic speed control, tilt steering, opera lamps, and power driver's seat. Fifth Avenue colors were: Radiant Silver Crystal Coat, Beige Crystal Coat, Crimson Red, Sable Brown, Charcoal Gray Pearl Coat, Nightwatch Blue, Black, or White.

1984 Chrysler, New Yorker sedan (OCW)

EXECUTIVE — SERIES KCP — FOUR — An Executive sedan and limousine, announced earlier, were now official parts of the Chrysler lineup and listed in production totals. Conversions were done by ASC Corporation, near Chrysler's St. Louis assembly plant, adding 13 to 24 inches to a K-body platform. Roof, floorpan, sill and roof rail sections were added, along with a B-pillar. Sill areas were reinforced; front suspension strengthened; brakes enlarged. This produced what Chrysler called "Traditional limousine characteristics in a modern, efficient size." Seven-passenger limos rode on a 131 inch wheelbase and were 220.5 inches long (much smaller and lighter than a Cadillac). Wheelbase of the five-passenger Executive Sedan was 124 inches. Both Executives carried the Mitsubishi-built 2.6-liter four and automatic transaxle.

I.D. DATA: Chrysler again had a 17-symbol Vehicle Identification Number (VIN) on the upper left corner of the instrument panel, visible through the windshield. Coding changed somewhat with the revised model lineup. The first digit indicates Country: '1' U.S.A.; '2' Canada. The second symbol is Make: 'C' Chrysler. Third is Vehicle Type: '3' passenger car. The next symbol ('B') indicates manual seatbelts. Symbol five is Car Line: 'A' Laser; 'C' LeBaron (and Executive); 'T' E Class and New Yorker (front-drive); 'F' Fifth Avenue. Symbol six is Series: '4' High; '5' Premium; '6' Special. Symbol seven is Body Style: '1' 2-dr. coupe; '3' 2-dr. sedan; '4' 2-dr. hatchback; '5' 2-dr convertible coupe; '6' 4-dr sedan; '7' 4-dr. limousine; '9' 4-dr. station wagon. Eighth is the Engine Code: 'D' L4135 EFI; 'E' Turbo L4135 EFI; 'G' L4156 2Bbl.; 'P' V8318 2Bbl. Next comes a check digit. Symbol ten indicates Model Year: 'E' 1984. Symbol eleven is Assembly Plant: 'C' Detroit; 'F' Newark; 'G' or 'X' St. Louis. The last six digits make up the sequential serial number, starting with 100001. Engine number coding is similar to 1982-83.

LASER (FOUR)

Model No.	Body/ Style No.	Body Type & Seating	Factory Price	Shipping Weight	Prod. Total
GCH	24	2-dr. Hatch-4P	8648	2525	33,976

LASER XE (FOUR)

Model No.	Body/ Style No.	Body Type & Seating	Factory Price	Shipping Weight	Prod. Total
GCP	24	2-dr. Hatch-4P	10546	2545	25,882

LEBARON (FOUR)

Model No.	Body/ Style No.	Body Type & Seating	Factory Price	Shipping Weight	Prod. Total
KCP	22	2-dr. Cpe-6P	8783	2445	24,963
KCP	41	4-dr. Sed-6P	9067	2495	47,664
KCP	27	2-dr. Conv-4P	11595	2530	16,208

LEBARON TOWN & COUNTRY (FOUR)

Model No.	Body/ Style No.	Body Type & Seating	Factory Price	Shipping Weight	Prod. Total
KCP	45	4-dr. Sta Wag-5P	9856	2610	11,578

LEBANON MARK CROSS CONVERTIBLE (FOUR)

Model No.	Body/ Style No.	Body Type & Seating	Factory Price	Shipping Weight	Prod. Total
KCP	27	2-dr. Conv-4P	15495	N/A	Note 1
KCP	27	2-dr. T&C Conv-4P	16495	N/A	Note 1

Note 1: Mark Cross and Mark Cross Town & Country convertibles are included in base convertible total above. A total of 1,105 T&C convertible packages (code AFG) were installed, plus 8,275 Mark Cross convertible packages (code AFD).

E CLASS (FOUR)

Model No.	Body/ Style No.	Body Type & Seating	Factory Price	Shipping Weight	Prod. Total
ETH	41	4-dr. Sed-6P	9565	2530	32,237

NEW YORKER (FOUR)

Model No.	Body/ Style No.	Body Type & Seating	Factory Price	Shipping Weight	Prod. Total
ETP	41	4-dr. Sed-5P	12179	2675	60,501

FIFTH AVENUE (V-8)

Model No.	Body/ Style No.	Body Type & Seating	Factory Price	Shipping Weight	Prod. Total
MFS	41	4-dr. Sed-5P	13990	3660	79,441

EXECUTIVE (FOUR)

Model No.	Body/ Style No.	Body Type & Seating	Factory Price	Shipping Weight	Prod. Total
KCP	48	4-dr. Sed-5P	18975	2945	196
KCP	49	4-dr. Limo-7P	21975	N/A	594

Model Number Note: Some sources identify models using the new VIN data to indicate Car Line, Price Class and Body Style. Example: base Laser (GCH24) has the equivalent number

CA44, which translates to Laser line, High price class, and hatchback body. See I.D. Data section for breakdown.

ENGINE DATA: BASE FOUR (Laser, LeB, E Class, N.Y.): Inline, overhead cam four-cylinder. Cast iron block; aluminum head. Displacement: 135 cu. in. (2.2-liters). Bore & stroke: 3.44 x 3.62 in. Compression ratio: 9.0:1. Brake horsepower: 99 at 5600 R.P.M. Torque: 121 lb.-ft. at 3200 R.P.M. Five main bearings. Hydraulic valve lifters. Electronic fuel injection. **TURBOCHARGED FOUR** (Laser, LeB, E Class, N.Y.): Same as 135 cu. in. four above, but with turbocharger. Compression ratio: 8.1:1. Brake horsepower: 140 at 5200 R.P.M. (142 at 5600 w/manual shift). Torque: 160 lb.-ft. at 3600 R.P.M. **BASE FOUR** (Executive); **OPTIONAL** (LeB, E Class, N.Y.): Inline, overhead cam four-cylinder. Cast iron block; aluminum head. Displacement: 156 cu. in. (2.6-liters). Bore & stroke: 3.59 x 3.86 in. Compression ratio: 8.7:1. Brake horsepower: 101 at 4800 R.P.M. Torque: 140 lb.-ft. at 2800 R.P.M. Five main bearings. Solid valve lifters. Carburetor: 2Bbl. Mikuni. Built by Mitsubishi. **BASE V-8** (Fifth Avenue): 90-degree, overhead valve V-8. Cast iron block and head. Displacement: 318 cu. in. (5.2-liters). Bore & stroke: 3.91 x 3.31 in. Compression ratio: 8.7:1. Brake horsepower: 130 at 4000 R.P.M. Torque: 235 lb.-ft. at 1600 R.P.M. Five main bearings. Hydraulic valve lifters. Carburetor: 2Bbl Carter BBD.

CHASSIS DATA: Wheelbase: (Laser) 97.0 in.; (LeBaron) 100.3 in.; (E Class/N.Y.) 103.3 in.; (Fifth Ave.) 112.7 in.; (Executive) 124.0 in.; (Limo) 131 in. Overall length: (Laser) 175.0 in.; (LeB) 179.8 in.; (LeB wag) 179.9 in.; (E Class) 187.2 in.; (N.Y.) 185.7 in.; (Fifth Ave.) 206.7 in.; (Exec.) 203.4 in.; (Limo) 220.5 in. Height: (Laser) 50.3 in.; (LeB cpe) 52.6 in.; (LeB sed) 53.0 in.; (LeB wag) 52.7 in.; (LeB conv.) 54.1 in.; (E Class/N.Y.) 52.9 in.; (Fifth Ave.) 55.3 in.; (Exec.) 53.0 in. Width: (Laser) 69.3 in.; (LeB/Exec.) 68.5 in.; (E Class/N.Y.) 68.3 in.; (Fifth Ave.) 74.2 in. Front Tread: (Laser/LeB/E Class/N.Y./Exec.) 57.6 in.; (Fifth Ave.) 60.0 in. Rear Tread: (Laser/Exec.) 57.2 in.; (LeB/E Class/N.Y.) 57.0 in.; (Fifth Ave.) 59.5 in. Standard Tires: (Laser/LeB/E Class) P185/70R14 SBR WSW; (Laser XE) P185/70R14 SBR RWL; (N.Y./Exec.) P185/75R14 SBR WSW; (Fifth Ave.) P205/75R15 SBR WSW.

TECHNICAL: Transmission: Five-speed manual trans. standard on Laser/LeBaron. Gear ratios: (1st) 3.29:1; (2nd) 2.08:1; (3rd) 1.45:1; (4th) 1.04:1; (5th) 0.72:1; (Rev) 3.14:1. TorqueFlite three-speed automatic optional on Laser/LeBaron, standard on E Class and New Yorker: (1st) 2.69:1; (2nd) 1.55:1; (3rd) 1.00:1; (Rev) 2.10:1. TorqueFlite standard on Fifth Ave.: (1st) 2.74:1; (2nd) 1.54:1; (3rd) 1.00:1; (Rev) 2.22:1. Standard final drive ratio: (Laser) 2.57:1 exc. 3.22:1 w/auto.; (LeB) 2.57:1 exc. 3.02:1 w/auto.; (E Class/N.Y.) 3.02:1; (Fifth Ave.) 2.94:1; (Exec.) 3.02:1. Steering: (Laser/LeB/E Class/N.Y.) rack-and-pinion; (others) recirculating ball, power-assisted. Suspension: (Laser) dual-path Iso-Strut front with anti-sway bar, trailing arm rear with tubular sway bar inside rear axle and track bar alongside, plus gas-charged shock absorbers; (LeB/E Class/N.Y.) MacPherson Iso-Struts and linkless sway bar in front, flex arm beam axle with trailing links and coil springs at the rear; (Fifth Ave.) front torsion bars and anti-sway bar, rear leaf springs. Brakes: Front disc, rear drum (power-assisted). Ignition: Electronic. Body construction: Unibody. Fuel tank: (Laser/LeB/E Class/N.Y.) 14 gal.; (Fifth Ave.) 18 gal.

DRIVETRAIN OPTIONS: Engines: 2.6-liter four: LeB/E Class/N.Y. ($271). Turbo 2.2-liter four: LeB/E Class/N.Y. ($610). Transmission/Suspension: Auto. trans.: Laser/LeB ($439). Heavy-duty susp.: Fifth Ave. ($27). Sport susp.: E Class/N.Y. ($57). Handling susp.: Laser XE ($102). European handling pkg.: LeB ($57). Other: H.D. cooling: LeB/E Class/N.Y. ($141). H.D. 500-amp battery ($44). California emission system ($99).

LASER CONVENIENCE/APPEARANCE OPTIONS: Option Packages: Turbo pkg.: base ($934); XE ($872). Basic group ($1194-$1319). Cargo trim/quiet sound: base ($154). Light group: base ($97). Comfort/Convenience: Air cond. ($737). Rear defroster ($143-$168). Automatic speed control ($179). Electronic navigator: base ($272). Electronic voice alert: base ($66). Power seat ($215). Power windows ($185). Power door locks ($125). Tinted glass ($110). Illuminated entry system ($75). Tilt steering wheel: base ($110). Dual power remote mirrors: base ($48). Entertainment: AM/FM stereo radio: base ($125). Premium electronic-tuning seek/scan AM/FM stereo ($160-$285); w/cassette ($299-$424). Premium speaker pkg. ($126). Radio delete ($56 credit). Exterior: Removable glass sunroof ($322). Pearl coat paint: base ($40). Interior: Low-back vinyl bucket seats: base (NC). Low-back cloth/vinyl bucket seats ($362). Low-back leather bucket seats: base ($929); XE ($567). Front/rear mats ($45). Wheels: 15 in. aluminum wheels: XE (NC). 14 in. aluminum wheels: base ($316).

1984 Chrysler, LeBaron convertible (OCW)

LEBARON CONVENIENCE/APPEARANCE OPTIONS: Option Packages: Mark Cross A61 pkg. ($833-$1000). Easy order package: AAA ($476-$631); AAB ($1827-$1982). Two-tone paint ($232). Comfort/Convenience: Air cond. ($737). Rear defroster ($143). Automatic speed control ($179). Electronic voice alert ($66). Power seat ($215). Power windows ($185-$260). Power door locks ($125-$175). Power decklid or liftgate release ($40). Illuminated entry ($75). Leather-wrapped steering wheel ($50). Tilt steering wheel ($110). Tinted glass ($110). Intermittent wipers ($53). Lighting and Mirrors: Cornering lamps ($60). Dual remote mirrors ($59). Dual power remote mirrors ($48-$107). Lighted vanity mirror ($58). Entertainment: Electronic-tuning AM/FM stereo radio ($125); w/cassette and seek/scan ($424) exc. Mark Cross conv. (NC). Premium seek/scan AM/FM stereo radio ($285). Premium speaker pkg. ($126). Radio delete ($56 credit). Exterior Trim: Front and rear bumper guards ($56). Pearl coat paint ($40). Vinyl bodyside moldings ($55). Bodyside tape stripe ($45). Undercoating ($43). Interior Trim/Upholstery: Console ($105). Center armrest ($61). Cloth/vinyl bench seat: cpe (NC). Vinyl bucket seats: wag (NC) Cloth/vinyl bucket seats: sed ($166).Color-keyed floor mats: cpe front ($25); both ($45). Trunk dress-up ($51). Wheels and Tires: Wire wheel covers ($215). Cast aluminum wheels ($322) but (NC) w/Mark Cross conv. Conventional spare tire ($83).

E CLASS AND NEW YORKER CONVENIENCE/APPEARANCE OPTIONS: Option Packages: Luxury equipment: N.Y. ($2622). Protection group: E Class ($81). Easy-order pkg.: E Class ($710 or $1965); N.Y. ($1143). Comfort/Convenience: Air cond. ($737). Rear defroster ($143). Auto. speed control ($179). Electronic navigator: N.Y. ($272). Electronic voice alert: E Class ($66). Power windows ($260). Power door locks ($175). Power seat ($215). Tinted glass: E Class ($110). Illuminated entry ($75). Leather-wrapped steering wheel ($50). Tilt steering ($110). Intermittent wipers: E Class ($53). Lighting and Mirrors: Cornering lamps: E Class ($60). Dual power remote mirrors: E Class ($82). Lighted vanity mirror ($58). Entertainment: Same as LeBaron Exterior: Two-tone paint: E Class ($232). Pearl coat paint ($40). Bodyside stripe: E Class ($45). Bodyside molding ($55). Front and rear bumper guards ($56). Door edge protectors ($25). Undercoating ($45). Interior: Vinyl bench seat: E Class (NC). Cloth 50/50 bench seat: E Class ($278). Leather 50/50 seats: N.Y. ($395). Color-keyed mats ($45). Trunk dress-up: E Class ($51). Wheels and Tires: Wire wheel covers: E Class ($215). Cast aluminum wheels: E Class ($322); N.Y. ($107). Conventional spare ($83).

FIFTH AVENUE CONVENIENCE/APPEARANCE OPTIONS: Option Packages: Luxury equipment ($1915). Protection group ($70). Comfort/Convenience: Auto. speed control ($179). Power seat ($175-$215); dual ($430). Power door locks ($175). Power decklid release ($40). Illuminated entry system ($75). Leather-wrapped steering wheel ($60). Tilt steering ($110). Intermittent wipers ($53). Lighted vanity mirror ($58). Entertainment: AM/FM stereo radio ($125). Premium seek/scan AM/FM stereo ($125-$250); w/cassette ($264-$389). Premium speaker pkg. ($126). Power antenna ($60). Exterior Trim: Power glass sunroof ($1041). Hood tape stripe ($29). Undercoating ($43). Interior Trim/Upholstery: Cloth 60/40 bench seat (NC). Leather 60/40 bench seat ($379). Wheels and Tires: Wire wheel covers ($197). Cast aluminum wheels ($47-$244). Conventional spare tire ($93).

EXECUTIVE SEDAN/LIMOUSINE OPTIONS: AM/FM stereo radio w/cassette: sed ($139). Leather bucket seats: sed ($950-$1075). Wire wheel covers: sed ($263). Cast aluminum wheels: sed ($370).

HISTORY: Introduced: October 2, 1983. Model year production: 333,240. Calendar year production: 403,699. Calendar year sales by U.S. dealers: 328,499. Model year sales by U.S. dealers: 314,438 (incl. a few leftover Cordobas and Imperials).

HISTORICAL FOOTNOTES: Lasers were built at St. Louis, on the same line as LeBaron and Reliant. Chrysler-Plymouth model year sales (including imports) rose 15 percent, due largely to initially strong Laser sales (52,073 for the model year). The front-drive New Yorker saw a sales increase of 67 percent; LeBaron a less dramatic 20 percent. Calendar year production for the division rose by 38 percent over 1983,

reaching 1,247,826. Workers put in considerable overtime to keep pace. Chrysler's sixth U.S. passenger car plant opened near year's end at Sterling Heights, Michigan, to produce the new LeBaron GTS and Dodge Lancer. The five-year, 50,000-mile warranty was extended late in the year to include light-duty trucks. Turbos were most in demand on Lasers (and Dodge Daytonas), making Chrysler No. 1 in turbo production. Chrysler claimed that Laser outperformed "the vast majority of sports cars sold in the U.S." The car was marketed against Firebird and Nissan 280ZX. This was Chrysler's 60th anniversary year.

1985 CHRYSLER

Chrysler's turbocharged 2.2-liter engine added an electronic wastegate control that varied maximum boost from 7.2 to 9.0 psi. More notable than that was the arrival of yet another new model: the LeBaron GTS four-door liftback performance sedan. Billed as "new midsize," GTS was intended to combine European look and feel with American-style roominess.

1985 Chrysler, LeBaron sedan with optional wire wheel covers (OCW)

LASER — SERIES GC — FOUR — After reasonably good sales in its first year, Laser returned with only modest revisions. They included the improved turbo engine option (now rated at 146 horsepower), new undercoating, and two new body colors. The close-ratio five-speed gearbox had a new 'dual rail' shift linkage. Laser XE now had standard cast aluminum wheels with 205/60HR15 tires. Fuel and hatch door releases moved from the console glovebox to outside the driver's seat. Laser's suspension included nitrogen-charged rear shock absorbers. A European handling suspension (optional on XE) added front gas shocks. Standard engine was the 2.2-liter Trans-4 with EFI. Cloth/vinyl low-back bucket seats had dual recliners and inertia latches. All-vinyl upholstery was available on the base Laser; Mark Cross Corinthian leather optional on both base and XE. An 'enthusiast' seat was optional (standard on XE). Base Lasers had a Rallye cluster of analog gauges, including tachometer, plus a Graphic Message Center. Non-turbo models included an upshift indicator light. XE again had an electronic cluster with quick-read digital speedometer, odometer, and trip odometer; plus an analog tachometer and gauge set. XE's standard Electronic Monitor displayed a two-line message on-screen, reporting on up to 21 functions and conditions, both visually and by 'voice.' Electronic Navigator was another XE standard. AM radio was standard on Laser; AM/FM stereo on XE. Turbo versions had functional hood louvers to release turbocharger heat, plus equal-length driveshafts to help reduce 'torque steer.' Both models had a functional front air dam and rear spoiler. Standard equipment also included a center console, driver's side footrest, digital clock, black remote-control mirrors, side window demisters, and inside hood release. Base Lasers came in six solid colors (Crystal or Pearl Coat); XE either in black or a choice of six two-tones. A total of 3,452 Lasers are reported to have added an XT performance package (code AGB), which wasn't available early in the year.

LEBARON — SERIES KC — FOUR — No more five-speed LeBarons could be ordered, as TorqueFlite automatic became the standard transmission. Appearance was similar to 1984, except for a new grille. It had the same overall shape but now was split into eight side-by-side sections (each made up of vertical strips), divided in half by a center bar. The grille pattern repeated in a wide slot below the bumper rub strip. As before, the full padded vinyl roof extended to the rear section of the back door on four-doors, which made for a narrow door window and private back seat area. Coupes, sedans and convertibles had new bodyside stripes. LeBaron's lineup was unchanged: four-door sedan, two-door coupe, convertible (standard or Town & Country), and T&C station wagon. Standard engine was the Trans-4 2.2-liter with fuel injection. Mitsubishi's

MCA-JET Silent Shaft 2.6-liter four was standard on T&C, optional on others. Also optional on all body styles including (for the first time) the Town & Country wagon: the turbo 2.2, with new electronic wastegate control. Front suspension consisted of dual-path Iso-Struts with linkless anti-sway bar. The rear beam axle used trailing arms and coil springs. Sport/handling suspension was recommended with the turbo four. Coupes had a new full-length console between the high-back cloth bucket seats, with storage for coins and cups (or tape cassettes). Sedans had a cloth bench seat. Convertibles had sporty low-back vinyl bucket seats with fixed center armrest/console. New heat (and air conditioning) controls allowed more precise settings. Intermittent wipers were now standard. Body colors were: Garnet Red, Mink Brown, Gold Dust, Cream, Gunmetal Blue, Ice Blue, Black, Radiant Silver, White, or Nightwatch Blue (all either Crystal or Pearl coat). Two two-tones were available. LeBaron's Mark Cross package added leather bucket seats and vinyl door trim panels with designer medallions, plus a leather-wrapped steering wheel, electronic instrument cluster, Ultimate Sound system radio, and locking wire wheel covers (or cast aluminum wheels). A total of 4,817 AFC Mark Cross packages were installed. Popular Equipment and Luxury Equipment Discount packages delivered a load of options without having to pay full price for each one.

1985 Chrysler, LeBaron GTS sports sedan with turbocharged engine and optional cast aluminum wheels (OCW)

LEBARON GTS — SERIES HC — FOUR — Chrysler's new H-bodied five-passenger hatchback sport sedan, with a drag coefficient of only 0.37, might be viewed almost as a four-door Laser. Dodge's Lancer was its near twin. The aero-styled six-window design featured a low profile front end and "delicately sloped" hood, aero-wrap flush-mounted windshield, and short deck. That hood, whose slope actually appeared somewhat sharp, led into a squat grille made up of evenly-spaced vertical bars, with center pentastar badge. Grille sides were slightly angled to match the housings for the quad rectangular headlamps. Wide parking lamps were inset into the bumper, below the rub strip. Full-width horizontally-ribbed wraparound taillamps had backup lamps at the inner ends, adjoining the license plate opening. On the decklid was the 'Chrysler' and 'LeBaron GTS' lettering, plus a center pentastar emblem. Aircraft-style doors protruded slightly into the roof and held semi-flush side windows. GTS also had bright-edged black bodyside moldings and tape striping. 'Turbo' lettering (if applicable) went on front fenders. Gas-charged dual path front Iso-Struts and rear shocks were part of the standard GTS road-touring suspension, which had large-diameter solid front and tubular rear anti-sway bars. Quick-ratio power steering and power brakes in a diagonally-split system were standard. Base engine was the 2.2-liter four with electronic fuel injection. The turbocharged 2.2 was optional. A close-ratio five-speed manual transaxle was standard, with upshift light on the non-turbo engine. High Line (base) models included a mechanical instrument cluster with analog gauges. Premium (LS) models featured an electronic cluster with digital speedometer/odometer and trip odometer, plus electronic analog display of engine speed, voltage, oil pressure, temperature and fuel level. Standard equipment on the base model included an AM/FM stereo electronic-tuning radio with digital clock, side window demisters, halogen headlamps, map pockets in front doors, remote control driver's mirror, bodyside moldings, low-back cloth/vinyl bucket seats with recliners and one-piece rear folding seatback. P185/70R14 SBR tires, and two-speed wiper/washer. The Premium (LS) model added an intermittent wiper/washer, liftback and rear fascia striping, wheel opening and door frame surround striping, low-back cloth/vinyl front bucket seats with recliners and 60/40 split rear folding seatbacks, time delay headlamp switch, driver's left footrest, and armrest console with storage bin and rear seat courtesy light. Low-back

bucket seats had recliners and adjustable headrests. Both models had a fold-down rear seatback, but the LS version was split. Remote controls opened the liftback and fuel filler door. LeBaron GTS colors were: Black Crystal Coat, Gunmetal Blue Pearl Coat, Ice Blue Crystal Coat, Nightwatch Blue Crystal Coat, Desert Bronze Pearl Coat, Mink Brown Pearl Coat, Cream Crystal Coat, Gold Dust Crystal Coat, Garnet Red Pearl Coat, and Radiant Silver Crystal Coat. (Some colors cost extra.) Two special price packages were offered: Popular Equipment and Luxury Equipment. Also optional were two Sport Handling Suspension packages. The standard one, installed on 3,143 cars, included P195/70R14 RBL performance tires. The Sport II package came with P205/60HR15 RBL tires on cast aluminum 15 inch wheels. That one went on 12,436 GTS models. A total of 11,779 cars had the AGT Turbo Sport I package, which included the turbocharged engine and 14 inch aluminum wheels.

NEW YORKER — SERIES ET — FOUR — Only the New Yorker name remained on the front-drive E body, which changed little except for three new body colors. The E Class sedan of 1983-84 joined the Plymouth stable as a new Caravelle. Standard engine switched from the 2.2-liter Trans-4 to the MCA-Jet Silent Shaft 2.6-liter four with three-speed automatic. A turbocharged 2.2-liter was optional. Appearance was just about identical to 1984, but with three new body colors. A new cloth-covered overhead storage console held reading/courtesy lamps and two storage compartments. Rear seat headrests were new. So were cornering lamps, a 400-amp maintenance-free battery, and remote-control fuel filler door and decklid releases. Body colors were: Black, Ice Blue, Nightwatch Blue, Cream, Gold Dust, Radiant Silver or White Crystal Coat, and Gunmetal Blue, Mink Brown or Garnet Red Pearl Coat. New Yorker had an aerodynamically slanted hood, "classic" grille, quad halogen headlamps, decorative (non-functional) front fender louvers, and bodyside/decklid accent stripes. Locking wire wheel covers and steel-belted radial whitewalls were standard. New heater/air conditioner controls offered more choices for directing heated/cooled air. New Yorkers had a standard electronic instrument cluster and graphic message center, plus AM radio with digital clock. Power seats were now available for both passenger and driver. Other options: Electronic Navigator, and a new AM stereo/FM stereo Ultimate Sound radio with graphic equalizer. A Luxury Equipment Discount Package included such extras as the turbo engine, air conditioning, electric rear defroster, Electronic Navigator, and leather 50/50 power seats; plus a compass and outside temperature digital readout for the overhead console.

1985 Chrysler, New Yorker sedan with turbocharged engine (OCW)

1985 Chrysler, Fifth Avenue sedan with optional wire wheel covers (OCW)

FIFTH AVENUE — SERIES MFS — V-8 — Chrysler's last rear-drive model looked just about identical to the 1984 version, except that this year's rear end trim panel between the taillamps appeared darker. Fifth Avenue's distinctive formal roofline continued with a revised landau padded vinyl roof that again extended into the rear of the back door, plus familiar up-and-over roof molding ahead of the vinyl. Inside were velvet cloth 60/40 pillow front seats, with leather/vinyl optional. Standard equipment included auto-temp control air conditioning, rear defroster, power windows, tinted glass, AM radio, and dual chrome remote mirrors. A Luxury Equipment Package included power door locks and decklid

release, illuminated entry, AM/FM stereo radio with power antenna, intermittent wipers, and other extras. Colors this year were Crimson Red, Gold Dust, Nightwatch Blue, Radiant Silver, White or Black Crystal Coat and Mink Brown or Gunmetal Blue Pearl Coat. Sole powertrain was the 318 cu. in. (5.2-liter) V-8 and TorqueFlite transmission. That engine now had roller tappets and higher compression (9.0:1) for a boost of 10 horsepower. Fifth Avenue's suspension consisted of transverse front torsion bars and anti-sway bar, plus rear leaf springs. New standard equipment included a 400-amp battery and tethered gas filler cap. Joining the option list: Ultimate Sound stereo and, later, a trim package with two-tone paint and vinyl roof.

EXECUTIVE — SERIES KCP — FOUR — Only the long-wheelbase (131 inch) front-drive limousine remained in the Executive series; the five-passenger sedan was dropped. This limo measured "only" 210.8 inches in length and carried a standard Mitsubishi-built MCA-Jet 2.6-liter engine and automatic transaxle. New this year: an Ultimate Sound AM stereo/FM stereo system with graphic equalizer and cassette player. Separate illuminated entry systems worked with front and rear compartments. Under the hood was a new 500-amp maintenance-free battery. Front seatbacks held new storage pockets. Limos had two rear-facing jump seats, plus a standard divider window with power-operated sliding glass. Two colors were new: Gunmetal Blue and Black Crystal Coat.

1985 Chrysler, Executive Limousine (OCW)

I.D. DATA: Chrysler again had a 17-symbol Vehicle Identification Number (VIN) on the upper left corner of the instrument panel, visible through the windshield. Coding changed somewhat with the revised model lineup. The first digit indicates Country: '1' U.S.A.; '2' Canada. The second symbol is Make: 'C' Chrysler. Third is Vehicle Type: '3' passenger car. The next symbol ('B') indicates manual seatbelts. Symbol five is Car Line: 'A' Laser; 'C' LeBaron (and Executive limo); 'H' LeBaron GTS; 'T' New Yorker; 'F' Fifth Avenue. Symbol six is Series: '4' High; '5' Premium; '6' Special. Symbol seven is Body Style: '1' 2-dr. coupe; '2' 4-dr. limousine; '4' 2-dr. hatchback; '5' 2-dr. convertible coupe; '6' 4-dr. sedan; '8' 4-dr. hatchback; '9' 4-dr. wagon. Eighth is the Engine Code: 'D' L4135 EFI; 'E' Turbo L4135 EFI; 'G' L4156 2Bbl.; 'P' V8318 2Bbl. Next comes a check digit. Symbol ten indicates Model Year: 'F' 1985. Symbol eleven is Assembly Plant: 'C' Detroit; 'F' Newark; 'G' or 'X' St. Louis; 'N' Sterling Heights. The last six digits make up the sequential serial number, starting with 100001. Engine number coding is similar to 1982-84.

LASER (FOUR)

Model No.	Body/Style No.	Body Type & Seating	Factory Price	Shipping Weight	Prod. Total
GCH	24	2-dr. Hatch-4P	8854	2525	32,673

LASER XE (FOUR)

Model No.	Body/Style No.	Body Type & Seating	Factory Price	Shipping Weight	Prod. Total
GCP	24	2-dr. Hatch-4P	10776	2545	18,193

LEBARON (FOUR)

Model No.	Body/Style No.	Body Type & Seating	Factory Price	Shipping Weight	Prod. Total
KCP	22	2-dr. Cpe-5P	9460	2445	24,970
KCP	41	4-dr. Sed-6P	9309	2495	43,659
KCP	27	2-dr. Conv-4P	11889	2530	16,475

LEBARON TOWN & COUNTRY (FOUR)

Model No.	Body/Style No.	Body Type & Seating	Factory Price	Shipping Weight	Prod. Total
KCP	45	4-dr. Sta Wag-5P	10363	2610	7,711

LEBARON MARK CROSS CONVERTIBLE (FOUR)

Model No.	Body/Style No.	Body Type & Seating	Factory Price	Shipping Weight	Prod. Total
KCP	27	2-dr. Conv-4P	15994	N/A	Note 1
KCP	27	2-dr. T&C Conv-4P	16994	N/A	Note 1

Note 1: Mark Cross and Mark Cross Town & Country convertibles are included in base convertible total above. A total of 595 T&C convertible packages (code AFG) were installed, plus 6,684 Mark Cross convertible packages (code AFD).

LEBARON GTS (FOUR)

Model No.	Body/Style No.	Body Type & Seating	Factory Price	Shipping Weight	Prod. Total
HCH	44	4-dr. Spt Sed-5P	9024	N/A	33,176
HCP	44	4-dr. LS Sed-5P	9970	N/A	27,607

NEW YORKER (FOUR)

Model No.	Body/Style No.	Body Type & Seating	Factory Price	Shipping Weight	Prod. Total
ETP	41	4-dr. Sed-5P	12865	N/A	60,700

FIFTH AVENUE (V-8)

Model No.	Body/Style No.	Body Type & Seating	Factory Price	Shipping Weight	Prod. Total
MFS	41	4-dr. Sed-6P	13978	3660	109,971

EXECUTIVE (FOUR)

Model No.	Body/Style No.	Body Type & Seating	Factory Price	Shipping Weight	Prod. Total
KCP	49	4-dr. Limo-7P	26318	N/A	759

Model Number Note: Some sources identify models using the new VIN data to indicate Car Line, Price Class and Body Style. Example: Base Laser (GCH24) has the equivalent number CA44, which translates to Laser line, High price class, and hatchback body. See I.D. Data section for breakdown.

ENGINE DATA: BASE FOUR (Laser, LeBaron, LeBaron GTS): Inline, overhead cam four-cylinder. Cast iron block; aluminum head. Displacement: 135 cu. in. (2.2-liters). Bore & stroke: 3.44 x 3.62 in. Compression ratio: 9.0:1. Brake horsepower: 99 at 5600 R.P.M. Torque: 121 lb.-ft. at 3200 R.P.M. Five main bearings. Hydraulic valve lifters. Electronic fuel injection. TURBOCHARGED FOUR (Laser, LeBaron, LeBaron GTS, New Yorker): Same as 135 cu. in. four above, but with turbocharger. Compression ratio: 8.1:1. Brake horsepower: 146 at 5200 R.P.M. Torque: 168 lb.-ft. at 3600 R.P.M. BASE FOUR (New Yorker, Executive Limousine); OPTIONAL (LeBaron): Inline, overhead cam four-cylinder. Cast iron block; aluminum head. Displacement: 156 cu. in. (2.6-liters). Bore & stroke: 3.59 x 3.86 in. Compression ratio: 8.7:1. Brake horsepower: 101 at 4800 R.P.M. Torque: 140 lb.-ft. at 2800 R.P.M. Five main bearings. Solid valve lifters. Carburetor: 2Bbl. Mikuni. BASE V-8 (Fifth Avenue): 90-degree, overhead valve V-8. Cast iron block and head. Displacement: 318 cu. in. (5.2-liters). Bore & stroke: 3.91 x 3.31 in. Compression ratio: 9.0:1. Brake horsepower: 140 at 3600 R.P.M. Torque: 265 lb.-ft. at 1600 R.P.M. Five main bearings. Hydraulic valve lifters. Carburetor: 2Bbl.

1985 Chrysler, Laser XE hatchback with turbocharged engine (OCW)

CHASSIS DATA: Wheelbase: (Laser) 97.0 in.; (LeBaron) 100.3 in.; (LeB T&C) 100.4 in.; (LeBaron TS) 103.1 in.; (N.Y.) 103.3 in.; (Fifth Ave.) 112.7 in.; (Executive) 131.3 in. Overall length: (Laser) 175.0 in.; (LeB) 179.1 in.; (LeB conv.) 180.7 in.; (GTS) 180.4 in.; (N.Y.) 185.1 in.; (Fifth Ave.) 206.7 in.; (Exec.) 210.8 in. Height: (Laser) 50.3 in.; (LeB cpe) 52.7 in.; (LeB sed) 52.9 in.; (LeB wag) 53.2 in.; (LeB conv.) 53.7 in.; (GTS) 53.0 in.; (N.Y.) 53.1 in.; (Fifth Ave.) 55.3 in.; (Exec.) 53.6 in. Width: (Laser) 69.3 in.; (LeB/N.Y.) 68.0 in.; (GTS) 68.3 in.; (Fifth Ave.) 74.2 in.; (Exec.) 67.9 in. Front Tread: (Laser/LeB/GTS/N.Y./Exec.) 57.6 in.; (Fifth Ave.) 60.0 in. Rear Tread: (Laser/LeB/GTS/N.Y./Exec.) 57.2 in.; (Fifth Ave.) 59.5 in. Standard Tires: (Laser/LeB) P185/70R14 SBR WSW; (Laser XE) P205/60HR15 SBR RBL; (GTS) P185/70R14 SBR BSW; (N.Y./Exec.) P185/75R14 SBR WSW; (Fifth Ave.) P205/75R15 SBR WSW.

TECHNICAL: Transmission: Five-speed manual trans. standard on Laser/GTS. Gear ratios: (1st) 3.29:1; (2nd) 2.08:1; (3rd) 1.45:1; (4th) 1.04:1; (5th) 0.72:1; (Rev) 3.14:1. TorqueFlite three-speed automatic optional on Laser/GTS, standard on LeBaron and New Yorker: (1st) 2.69:1; (2nd) 1.55:1; (3rd) 1.00:1; (Rev) 2.10:1. TorqueFlite standard on Fifth Ave.: (1st) 2.74:1; (2nd) 1.54:1; (3rd) 1.00:1; (Rev) 2.22:1. Standard final drive ratio: (Laser/GTS) 2.57:1 exc. 3.01:1 w/auto; (LeB/N.Y./Exec.) 3.02:1; (Fifth Ave.) 2.26:1. Steering: (Laser/LeB/GTS/N.Y.) rack and pinion; (others) recirculating ball, power-assisted. Suspension: (Laser/GTS) Dual-path Iso-Strut front, trailing arm rear with front/rear sway bars and gas-charged rear shock absorbers; (LeBaron/New Yorker) Dual-path Iso-Struts and linkless sway bar in front, beam axle with trailing arms and coil springs at the rear; (Fifth Ave.) transverse front torsion bars and anti-sway bar, rear leaf springs. Brakes: Front disc, rear drum (power-assisted). Ignition: Electronic. Body con-

struction: Unibody. Fuel tank: (Laser/LeB/GTS/N.Y.) 14 gal.; (Fifth Ave.) 18 gal.

DRIVETRAIN OPTIONS: Engines: 2.6-liter four: LeB/N.Y. ($282). Turbo 2.2-liter four: LeB/GTS/N.Y. ($634). Turbo pkg.: Laser ($1002); Laser XE ($907); GTS ($1141); GTS LS ($1091). Transmission/Suspension: Auto. trans.: Laser/GTS ($457). Heavy-duty susp.: Fifth Ave. ($27). Euro handling susp.: Laser XE ($106); LeB/N.Y. ($59). Sport handling pkg.: GTS ($122). Sport II handling pkg.: GTS ($644-$694) exc. ($187) w/turbo pkg. Other: H.D. cooling: Fifth Ave. ($156). H.D. 500-amp battery ($46). California emission system ($103).

LASER CONVENIENCE/APPEARANCE OPTIONS: Option Packages: Luxury equipment: base ($1186). Popular equipment: base ($793). Cargo trim/quiet sound: base ($72-$180). Light group: base ($138). Protection pkg. ($92). Comfort/Convenience: Air cond. ($766). Rear defroster ($149-$175). Automatic speed control ($186). Electronic Voice Alert and navigator: ($377). Power seat ($224). Power windows ($192). Power door locks ($130). Tinted glass ($114). Illuminated entry system ($78). Tilt steering wheel: base ($114). Liftgate wiper/washer ($125). Dual power remote mirrors: base ($50). Entertainment: AM/FM stereo radio: base ($166). AM/FM stereo w/cassette ($274-$440). Premium memory scan AM/FM stereo w/cassette ($465-$631). Radio delete ($56 credit). Exterior: Removable glass sunroof ($335). Pearl coat paint: base ($42). Interior: Low-back vinyl bucket seats: base ($25). Low-back cloth/vinyl bucket seats: base ($376). Low-back leather/vinyl bucket seats: base ($966); XE ($590). Wheels/Tires: 14 in. aluminum wheels: base ($335). P195/70R14 SBR RBL: base ($95). Conventional spare: base ($86-97).

LEBARON CONVENIENCE/APPEARANCE OPTIONS: Option Packages: Mark Cross AFC pkg. ($866-$1040). Luxury pkg. ($1227-$1496). Popular equipment ($646-$1104). Comfort/Convenience. Air cond. ($766). Rear defroster ($149). Automatic speed control ($186). Power seat ($224). Power windows ($192-$270). Power door locks ($130-$182). Power decklid or liftgate release ($42). Illuminated entry ($78). Leather-wrapped steering wheel ($52). Tilt steering wheel ($114.). Tinted glass ($114). Lighting and Mirrors: Cornering lamps ($62). Dual remote mirrors ($59). Dual power remote mirrors ($85). Lighted vanity mirror ($60). Entertainment: Electronic-tuning AM/FM stereo radio ($130); w/cassette and seek/scan ($310-$440). Premium seek/scan AM/FM stereo radio ($501-$631). Radio delete ($56 credit). Exterior: Front/rear bumper guards ($58). Pearl coat paint ($42). Two-tone paint ($194). Bodyside moldings ($57). Undercoating ($45). Interior: Console ($145). Center armrest ($63). Cloth/vinyl bench seat: cpe (NC). Vinyl bucket seats: wag (NC). Cloth/vinyl bucket seats: sed ($173). Color-keyed floor mats: conv. front ($26); other front/rear ($47). Trunk dress-up ($53). Wheels and Tires: Wire wheel covers ($225). Cast aluminum wheels ($110-$335) but (NC) w/Mark Cross conv. Conventional spare ($86).

LEBARON GTS CONVENIENCE/APPEARANCE OPTIONS: Option Packages: Electronic feature pkg. (voice alert/navigator); LS ($398); w/illuminated entry ($536). Luxury equipment ($1101-$1314). Popular equipment ($480-$693). Light pkg. ($76). Comfort/Convenience: Air cond. ($766). Rear defroster ($149). Auto. speed control ($186). Power seat ($224). Power windows ($270). Power door locks ($182). Illuminated entry: LS ($78). Tinted glass ($114). Leather-wrapped steering wheel ($52-$95). Tilt steering ($114). Gauge set: LS (NC). Premium sound insulation: base ($45). Intermittent wipers: base ($55). Liftgate wiper/washer ($125). Lighting and Mirrors: Dual remote mirrors ($67). Dual power remote mirrors ($48-$115). Lighted visor vanity mirror ($60). Entertainment: Seek/scan AM/FM stereo w/cassette ($316). Memory scan AM/FM stereo w/cassette ($507). Radio delete: base ($152 credit). Exterior: Removable glass sunroof ($335). Pearl coat paint ($42). Undercoating ($45). Interior: Console: base ($82). Folding center armrest ($45). Leather/vinyl bucket seats: LS ($590). Color-keyed floor mats ($47). Wheels/Tires: Cast aluminum wheels, 14 or 15 in. ($335-$385). Styled steel wheels ($12-$62). P185/70R14 SBR WSW ($60). P195/70R14 SBR RBL ($95). P205/60HR15 SBR RBL ($187-$282).

NEW YORKER CONVENIENCE/APPEARANCE OPTIONS: Option Packages: Luxury equipment ($3220). Comfort/Convenience: Air cond. ($766). Rear defroster ($149). Auto. speed control ($186). Electronic navigator ($283). Power door locks ($182). Power seat ($224). Illuminated entry ($78). Leather-wrapped steering wheel ($52). Tilt steering ($114). Lighted vanity mirror ($60). Entertainment: Same as LeBaron, plus: Premium speakers ($131). Exterior: Pearl coat paint ($42). Bodyside molding ($57). Door edge protectors ($26). Undercoating ($45). Interior: Leather/vinyl 50/50 seats ($411). Color-keyed mats ($47). Wheels/Tires: Cast aluminum wheels ($110). Conventional spare ($86).

FIFTH AVENUE CONVENIENCE/APPEARANCE OPTIONS: Option Packages: Luxury equipment ($1782-$1915). Protection group ($132). Comfort/Convenience: Auto. speed control ($186). Power seat ($224). Power door locks ($182). Power decklid release ($42). Illuminated entry

system ($78). Leather-wrapped steering wheel ($62). Tilt steering ($114). Intermittent wipers ($55). Underhood light ($16). Lighted vanity mirror ($60). Entertainment: AM/FM stereo radio ($130). AM/FM stereo w/cassette ($274-$404). Memory scan AM/FM stereo w/cassette ($465-$595). Power antenna ($62). Exterior: Power glass sunroof ($1083). Hood tape stripes ($30). Undercoating ($45). Interior: Cloth 60/40 bench seat (NC). Leather/vinyl 60/40 bench seat ($394). Wheels/Tires: Wire wheel covers ($205). Cast aluminum wheels ($49-$254). Conventional spare tire ($97).

EXECUTIVE LIMOUSINE OPTIONS: Clearcoat paint ($42). Leather bucket seats ($1118).

HISTORY: Introduced: October 2, 1984, except LeBaron GTS, January 2, 1985. Model year production: Chrysler reported total factory shipments of 375,894 units. Calendar year production: 414,193. Calendar year sales by U.S. dealers: 375,880. Model year sales by U.S. dealers: 373,088.

HISTORICAL FOOTNOTES: Strongest model year sales in eight years was good news for the Chrysler-Plymouth Division. The total came to 752,203, which was 18 percent over 1984 and not so far from the 828,315 cars sold in 1977. This was the third year in-a-row to produce a sales increase. The rear-drive Fifth Avenue sold nicely, at 112,137 units (up by 43 percent and well over corporate predictions). V-8 engines attracted quite a few buyers. LeBaron GTS also sold beyond expectations, finding 55,740 customers. GTS production began in late '84 at the new Sterling Heights, Michigan, plant, which Chrysler had bought from Volkswagen. A Laser turbo turned in a 0-50 mph time of 5.8 seconds, as recorded by USAC (United States Auto Club). That same organization claimed that LeBaron GTS surpassed BMW 528e and Mercedes 190E in their tests. Chrysler was an official sponsor of the U.S. Equestrian Team, which accounted for a focus on horses in the LeBaron catalog.

1986 CHRYSLER

A new 153 cu. in. (2.5-liter) Chrysler-built overhead-cam four-cylinder engine replaced the Mitsubishi 2.6 in most front-drive models. Rated 100 horsepower at 4800 rpm, the new four had fuel injection and a longer stroke than the 2.2. Twin nodular iron balance shafts counter-rotated at twice crankshaft speed. The 2.5 was standard on New Yorker, Laser XE, and T&C wagon; optional on Laser, LeBaron and GTS. New single-point fuel injection with a low-pressure (15 psi) fuel regulator arrived on all fours, with a new speed compensating feature for smoother idling. Its Electronic Control Unit not only adjusted the air/fuel mixture and spark timing, but kept a record of engine operations to spot malfunctions. A new air cleaner housing on four-cylinder engines was easier to remove, while a labyrinth distributor was smaller in size with fewer parts. The "fast-burn" cylinder head on 2.2 and 2.5 fours was modified to speed combustion and improve idling. On-board diagnostics was part of all 2.2-liter engines. New Electronic Vehicle Height Control that adjusted the rear suspension to keep the car at proper height regardless of load was standard on LeBaron Town & Country, optional in New Yorker's Luxury Equipment package. New child safety rear door locks were standard on LeBaron GTS; intermittent rear wipers optional on Laser and LeBaron GTS. A microcomputer regulated incoming air temperature on New Yorker's optional Automatic Temperature Control. Four-way adjustable head restraints were available on New Yorker, Laser and GTS. All models had a new center high-mounted stop lamp, and all front-drives had "Precision-feel" power steering that was introduced in 1985.

1986 Chrysler, Laser XT hatchback with turbocharged engine and optional T-bar roof and rear window louvers (OCW)

LASER — SERIES GC — FOUR — Three Laser price classes were offered this year: base, XE and a new XT. The base model had 14 inch all-season SBR tires and sport wheel covers; XE rode on P205/60HR15 special-handling raised-black letter tires on 15 inch cast aluminum wheels. Also

on XE: an adjustable steering column, electronic instrumentation, 21-feature electronic monitor, Electronic Navigator, and "enthusiast" performance bucket seats with new four-way head restraints. XE's electronic instrumentation featured multicolor graphics including quick-read digital speedometer, odometer and trip odometer, plus analog tach and engine readouts. A five-speed manual transaxle was standard. The new 2.5-liter four was standard on XE, while base Lasers came with the 2.2 four. Laser XT, which was actually a performance option package, added aerodynamic components, new P225/50VR15 uni-directional tires, turbo engine and boost gauge, and performance suspension. Its dash displayed gauges and a graphic message center, but not the Navigator. The turbocharged four had multi-point fuel injection and produced 146 horsepower, with boost beginning at just 1200 rpm. XT's close-ratio five-speed transaxle with overdrive fifth gear had a higher-capacity clutch. A total of 6,989 Lasers had the XT package installed. Laser's grille was a simple 4 x 2 pattern of wide holes set in a slot at the lower portion of the grille panel, flanked by quad rectangular headlamps. Parking lamps were below, well outside the twin air slots. Except for bodyside moldings with inserts, rather than the ribbed look of 1985, this year's Laser didn't change too much in appearance. Lasers had a rear spoiler and full-wrap lower front fascia with low-profile air dam; XE added lower bodyside sill spoilers. Colors were: Garnet Red Pearl Coat, Golden Bronze Pearl Coat, Ice Blue, White, Black, Radiant Silver, Gold Dust, and Gunmetal Blue Pearl Coat. Laser XT also came in Flash Red. A total of 4,966 Lasers carried the new T-bar roof that included two removable tinted glass panels with keyed locks, offered in a package with power windows and larger aero-look power mirrors. A "Sun, Sound & Shade" package included sunroof, AM stereo/FM stereo radio with cassette, and black rear window louvers.

1986 Chrysler, LeBaron GTS sports sedan with turbocharged engine and optional cast aluminum wheels (OCW)

LEBARON — SERIES KC — FOUR — Changes focused on LeBaron's front end, which was moderately restyled with a new grille texture and header. The grille now consisted of thin vertical bars separated by a wider center bar. Large wraparound marker lamps now flanked the quad rectangular headlamps. Front bumper and soft fascia were new. So were the taillamps, rear end caps, and decklid. LeBarons had a new electromechanical instrument cluster and message center, plus a new AM stereo/FM stereo radio. Standard wheel covers were new. So were the padded landau roof on four-door sedans, as well as low-travel power window and door lock switches. Base engine remained the 2.2-liter four, with standard automatic transaxle. Optional: either the turbocharged 2.2- or new 2.5-liter four. Three convertibles were offered: base, Mark Cross Edition, and Town & Country (with decklid luggage rack). A total of 3,941 non-convertible LeBarons had the Mark Cross package. Standard equipment included a dual-note horn, locking glove box, power rack-and-pinion steering, two-spoke luxury steering wheel, upper bodyside accent stripes, P185/70R14 SBR whitewall tires, intermittent wipers, tinted glass, and day/night inside mirror. Town & Country wagons included automatic load leveling, roof luggage rack, front anti-sway bar, and simulated woodgrain bodyside paneling. Convertibles had dual remote-control mirrors.

LEBARON GTS — SERIES HC — FOUR — Little change was evident on Chrysler's sport performance sedan in its second year. Air conditioning was not standard on the Premium (HCP44) model, while both had tinted glass. New this year were rear-door child safety locks, an electro-mechanical 125 mph speedometer, and four-way adjustable front head restraints. Power door lock and window switches also were new. A modified "fast-burn" cylinder head went on the standard 2.2-liter four-cylinder engine. Both the turbo 2.2- and new 2.5-liter four were optional. The manual five-speed transaxle remained standard. GTS showed a steeply raked windshield (58 degrees), rounded contours, and high decklid. The six-window design had flush windshield and liftback glass and semi-flush side glass, plus snug-fit "aircraft" doors. Body colors were: Garnet Red, Dark Cordovan, Light Rosewood Mist, Golden Bronze or Gunmetal

Blue Pearl Coat, Light Cream, Ice Blue, Black, Radiant Silver, or Gold Dust. Three two-tone options were offered on base models only. An electromechanical instrument cluster with analog gauges was standard on the High Line (base) model; full electronic cluster on Premium model, with digital speedometer/odometer and trip odometer readouts plus an analog tachometer and gauge set. Both had an incandescent message center that displayed a car outline with warning lights for such maladies as door/liftback ajar and low washer fluid. The standard AM stereo/FM stereo radio had a built-in digital clock and electronic tuning. Options included a 10-function Electronic Navigator and 10-function Electronic Voice Alert system. An optional center folding armrest and cushion package added space for a sixth passenger. Base models had low-back cloth/vinyl bucket seats; LS had upgraded cloth or optional leather. Standard suspension included dual-path upper Iso-Strut mounts, constant camber trailing arm-beam rear axle, large-diameter tubular rear sway bar, plus gas front struts and rear shocks. Two Sport Handling packages were available. Package I included Goodyear Eagle GT P195/70R14 blackwalls, higher-control struts/shocks, performance-tuned spring rates, and higher-capacity compact spare tire. Sport Handling Package II added P205/60R15 Eagle GT tires on 15 inch aluminum wheels.

1986 Chrysler, New Yorker sedan with turbocharged engine (OCW)

NEW YORKER — SERIES ET — FOUR — Only a few changes were evident from the front of the front-drive New Yorker. Opera lamps moved from the vinyl roof to the up-and-over trim molding, while side marker lenses were absent from rear quarter panels. New rear styling included decklid panels, moldings, and full-width taillamps that combined side marker lamps and reflectors. Also new: a soft bumper fascia, bumper guards with license plate lamps, accent stripes, electro-luminescent opera lamps, and vinyl roof moldings. Narrower wraparound taillamps now had only two thin horizontal trim strips that stretched across the full width of the rear end, as there was no longer a recessed license plate housing between them. Front fenders still held louvers, and a pair of louver sets sat on the hood, at either side of the center crease. Colors were: Dark Cordovan, Light Rosewood Mist, Golden Bronze or Gunmetal Blue Pearl Coat; plus Light Cream, Ice Blue, Black, Radiant Silver, or White. New electronic instrumentation included a cluster containing a digital speedometer and odometer, vertical-bar gauges with red warning segments for oil/voltage/temp/fuel, warning lamps, and diagnostics. A trip computer revealed trip miles, trip fuel efficiency, instant fuel efficiency, distance to empty tank, and elapsed time. New plush velvet cloth 50/50 pillow front seats had dual armrests and recliners, plus four-way head restraints. The forward console was new. Electronic automatic temperature control was new, while electronic load leveling became optional. Standard engine was the new 2.5-liter four with balance shafts, while a turbocharged 2.2 was optional.

1986 Chrysler, Fifth Avenue sedan (OCW)

FIFTH AVENUE — SERIES MFS — V-8 — New body colors were offered on the rear-drive Fifth Avenue, including three two-tones. But that was about the extent of the changes for 1986. Standard equipment included the 318 cu. in. (5.2-liter) V-8 engine, TorqueFlite transmission, power brakes and steering, air conditioning, P205/75R15 steel-belted radial whitewalls, hood ornament, tinted glass, fender louvers, and AM radio with digital clock. Also standard: electric rear window defroster, tethered fuel filler cap, dual-note horn, courtesy lights, wheel opening and belt moldings, vinyl padded landau roof, bodyside/decklid tape stripes, and premium wheel covers. Colors were: White, Radiant Silver, Crimson Red, Gold Dust, and Nightwatch Blue; plus Gunmetal Blue or Mink Brown

Pearl Coat. Three two-tone combinations were available at extra cost. Standard 60/40 seats were velvet cloth; Corinthian leather with vinyl trim optional. A new Luxury Equipment Discount package included power 60/40 Corinthian leather seats, power door locks, power antenna, digital AM/FM stereo radio, power decklid release, illuminated entry, automatic speed control, and tilt steering column.

1986 Chrysler, LeBaron Town & Country station wagon with turbocharged engine and optional wire wheel covers (OCW)

EXECUTIVE — SERIES KCP — FOUR — Chrysler's front-drive limousine, measuring under 211 inches overall, had a standard turbocharged 2.2-liter four-cylinder engine and the same front-end appearance as New Yorker. This year it got new decklid panels, rear bumper fascia, and end caps. The plush cloth interior had a pillowed back seat with center armrest (leather front seats optional). Air conditioning had five rear vents. Standard equipment included heavy-duty suspension, electro-luminescent opera lamps, rear compartment console, and glamour light module.

I.D. DATA: As before, Chrysler's 17-symbol Vehicle Identification Number (VIN) was on the upper left corner of the instrument panel, visible through the windshield. Coding was similar to 1985. Engine code 'G' was dropped; code 'K' (L4153 FI) added. Model year code changed to 'G' for 1986. Engine number coding was similar to 1982-85.

LASER (FOUR)

Model No.	Body/ Style No.	Body Type & Seating	Factory Price	Shipping Weight	Prod. Total
GCH	24	2-dr. Hatch-4P	9364	2560	21,123

LASER XE (FOUR)

GCP	24	2-dr. Hatch-4P	11501	2665	15,549

LASER XT (FOUR)

GCP	24/AGB	2-dr. Hatch-4P	11854	2695	Note 1

Note 1: A total of 6,989 Lasers had the XT package (RPO code AGB).

LEBARON (FOUR)

KCP	22	2-dr. Cpe-5P	9977	2475	24,761
KCP	41	4-dr. Sed-6P	10127	2500	40,116
KCP	27	2-dr. Conv.-4P	12695	2565	19,684

LEBARON TOWN & COUNTRY (FOUR)

KCP	45	4-dr. Sta. Wag-5P	11370	2660	6,493

LEBARON MARK CROSS CONVERTIBLE (FOUR)

KCP	27	2-dr. Conv.-4P	16595	N/A	Note 1
KCP	27	2-dr. T&C Conv.-4P	17595	N/A	Note 1

Note 1: Mark Cross and Mark Cross Town & Country convertibles are included in base convertible total above. A total of 501 T&C convertible packages (RPO code AFG) were installed, plus 6,905 Mark Cross convertible packages (code AFD).

LEBARON GTS (FOUR)

HCH	44	4-dr. Spt Sed-5P	9754	2605	42,841

LEBARON GTS PREMIUM (FOUR)

HCP	44	4-dr. Spt Sed-5P	11437	2695	30,716

NEW YORKER (FOUR)

ETP	41	4-dr. Sed-5P	13409	2655	51,099

FIFTH AVENUE (V-8)

MFS	41	4-dr. Sed-6P	14910	3655	104,744

EXECUTIVE (FOUR)

KCP	49	4-dr. Limo-7P	27495	3155	138

Model Number Note: Some sources identify models using the new VIN data to indicate Car Line, Price Class and Body Style. Example: base Laser (GCH24) has the equivalent number CA44, which translates to Laser line, High price class, and hatchback body. See I.D. Data section for breakdown.

ENGINE DATA: BASE FOUR (Laser, LeBaron FTS); Inline, overhead cam four-cylinder. Cast iron block; aluminum head. Displacement: 135 cu. in. (2.2 liters). Bore & stroke: 3.44 x 3.62 in. Compression ratio: 9.5:1. Brake horsepower: 97 at 5200 RPM. Torque: 122 lb.-ft. at 3200 RPM. Five main bearings. Hydraulic valve lifters. Electronic fuel injection. TURBOCHARGED FOUR: BASE (Limousine); OPTIONAL (Laser, LeBaron, LeBaron GTS, New Yorker): Same as 135 cu. in. four above, but with turbocharger. Compression ratio: 8.1:1. Brake horsepower: 146 at 5200 RPM. Torque: 170 lb.-ft. at 3600 RPM. BASE FOUR (Laser XE, LeBaron T&C/wagon, New Yorker): OPTIONAL (Laser, LeBaron, LeBaron GTS): Inline, overhead cam four-cylinder. Cast iron block; aluminum head. Displacement: 153 cu. in. (2.5 liters). Bore & stroke: 3.44 x 4.09 in. Compression ratio: 9.0:1. Brake horsepower: 100 at 4800 RPM. Torque: 136 lb.-ft. at 2800 RPM. Five main bearings. Hydraulic valve lifters. Electronic fuel injection. BASE V-8 (Fifth Avenue): 90-degree, overhead valve V-8. Cast iron block and head. Displacement: 318 cu. in. (5.2 liters). Bore & stroke: 3.91 x 3.31 in. Compression ratio: 9.0:1. Brake horsepower: 140 at 3600 RPM. Torque: 265 lb.-ft. at 1600 RPM. Five ain bearings. Hydraulic valve lifters. Carburetor: 2 Bbl.

1986 Chrysler, LeBaron coupe (OCW)

CHASSIS DATA: Wheelbase: (Laser) 97.0 in.; (LeBaron) 100.3 in.; (LeB conv.) 100.4 in.; (LeBaron GTS) 103.1 in.; (N.Y.) 103.3 in.; (Fifth Ave.) 112.6 in.; (Limousine) 131.3 in. Overall length: (Laser) 175.0 in.; (LeB) 179.2 in.; (GTS) 180.4 in.; (N.Y.) 187.2 in.; (Fifth Ave.) 206.7 in.; (Limo) 210.7 in. Height: (Laser) 50.4 in.; (LeB cpe) 52.5 in.; (LeB sed/conv.) 52.9 in.; (LeB wag) 53.2 in.; (GTS) 53.0 in.; (N.Y.) 53.1 in.; (Fifth Ave.) 55.1 in.; (Limo) 53.6 in. Width: (Laser) 69.3 in.; (LeB/N.Y.) 68.0 in.; (GTS) 68.3 in.; (Fifth Ave.) 72.4 in.; (Limo) 68.0 in. Front Tread: (Laser/LeB/GTS/N.Y./Limo) 57.6 in.; (Fifth Ave.) 60.5 in. Rear Tread: (Laser) 57.6 in.; (LeB/GTS/N.Y./Exec.) 57.2 in.; (Fifth Ave.) 60.0 in. Standard Tires: (Laser/LeB) P185/70R14 SBR WSW; (Laser XE) P205/60HR15 SBR RBL; (GTS) P185/70R14 SBR BSW; (N.Y./Exec.) P185/75R14 SBR SW; (Fifth Ave.) P205/75R15 SBR WSW.

TECHNICAL: Specifications same as 1985.

DRIVETRAIN OPTIONS: Engines: 2.5-liter four: LeBaron/GTS ($279). Turbo 2.2-liter four: LeB/GTS/N.Y. ($628). Turbo pkg.: Laser ($993); Laser XE ($733). Transmission/Suspension: Auto. trans.: Laser/GTS ($478). Heavy-duty susp.: Fifth Ave. ($27). Euro handling susp.: LeB/N.Y. ($58). Sport Handling pkg.: GTS ($580-$642). Sport Handling pkg. II: GTS ($27-$688). Other: Maintenance-free 500-alp battery ($45). California emission system ($102).

LASER CONVENIENCE/APPEARANCE OPTIONS: Option Packages: Luxury equipment: XE ($1572-$1583). Popular equipment ($332-$436); w/air cond. ($937-$1066). Sun/sound/shade pkg. ($639). Protection pkg. ($90). Comfort/Convenience: Air cond. ($780). Rear defroster ($152-$188). Automatic speed control ($184). Electronic navigator: base ($280). Power driver's seat ($232). Power windows ($201). Power door locks ($134). Tilt steering wheel ($118). Liftgate wiper/washer ($129). Dual power remote mirrors: base ($58). Entertainment: AM stereo/FM stereo w/cassette ($251). Ultimate sound radio w/cassette ($216-$467). Exterior: Removable glass sunroof ($342). Pearl coat paint: base ($41). Interior: Low-back cloth/vinyl bucket seats: base ($404). Low-back leather/vinyl bucket seats: base ($988); XE ($584). Wheels/Tires: 14 in. aluminum wheels: base ($332). P195/70R14 SBR RBL: base ($95). Conventional spare ($85).

1986 Chrysler, LeBaron convertible with turbocharged engine (OCW)

LEBARON CONVENIENCE/APPEARANCE OPTIONS: Option Packages: Mark Cross AFC pkg. ($1040). Luxury pkg. ($1087-$1278). Popular equipment: cpe/sed ($1087). Deluxe convenience ($302). Power convenience ($335-$463). Center console pkg. ($206). Interior light pkg.: cpe/sed ($137). Protection pkg. ($115). Cold weather pkg.: cpe/sed ($197). Comfort/Convenience: Air cond. ($780). Power seat ($232). Power decklid or liftgate release ($41). Illuminated entry ($77). Leather-wrapped steering wheel ($52). Dual power remote mirrors ($88). Lighted vanity mirror ($60). Entertainment: Seek/scan AM stereo/FM stereo radio w/cassette ($436). Ultimate sound AM stereo/FM stereo w/cassette ($652). Exterior: Front/rear bumper guards: wag ($58). Pearl coat paint ($41). Two-tone paint: cpe ($193). Interior: Vinyl bucket seats: conv. (NC). Cloth/vinyl bucket seats: cpe/sed ($171). Color-keyed floor mats: conv. front ($26); other front/rear ($46). Trunk dress-up ($53). Wheels/Tires: Wire wheel covers ($180). Cast aluminum wheels ($101-$281) but (NC) w/Mark Cross conv. Conventional spare ($85).

LEBARON GTS CONVENIENCE/APPEARANCE OPTIONS: Option Packages: Electronic feature pkg. incl. voice alert/navigator ($348-$393). Luxury equipment ($688-$1078). Popular equipment ($667-$1503). Deluxe convenience pkg. ($118-$302). Power convenience ($463). Highline upgrade: base ($125). Protection pkg. ($90). Cold weather pkg. ($197). Comfort/Convenience: Air cond. ($780). Power driver's seat ($232). Leather-wrapped steering wheel ($52-$94). Liftgate wiper/washer ($129). Lighting and Mirrors: Dual remote mirrors ($66). Dual power remote mirrors ($115). Lighted visor vanity mirror ($60). Entertainment: Premium AM stereo/FM stereo w/cassette ($293). Ultimate sound AM stereo/FM stereo w/cassette ($509). Exterior: Removable glass sunroof ($342). Pearl coat paint ($41). Two-tone paint: base ($233). Interior: Console and armrest: base ($81). Folding center armrest ($44). Leather low-back bucket seats: Premium ($583). Wheels/Tires: Cast aluminum wheels: 14 in. ($333-$381); 15 in. ($580-$642). Styled steel wheels ($14-$62). P185/70R14 SBR WSW ($60). P195/70R14 SBR RBL ($95). Conventional spare ($85).

NEW YORKER CONVENIENCE/APPEARANCE OPTIONS: Option Packages: Luxury equipment ($3413). Deluxe convenience pkg. ($302). Comfort/Convenience: Automatic air cond. ($927). Rear defroster ($152). Power door locks ($185). Power seat ($232). Illuminated entry ($77). Leather-wrapped steering wheel ($52). Twin lighted vanity mirrors ($120). Entertainment: AM stereo/FM stereo w/cassette ($287). Ultimate sound radio w/cassette ($503). Power antenna ($67). Exterior: Pearl coat paint ($41). Bodyside molding ($57). Undercoating ($44). Interior: Cloth 50/50 bench seat (NC). Leather 50/50 seats ($407). Color-keyed mats ($46). Wheels/Tires: Wire wheel covers ($181). Cast aluminum wheels ($110-$291). Conventional spare ($85).

FIFTH AVENUE CONVENIENCE/APPEARANCE OPTIONS: Option Packages: Luxury equipment ($1817-$1947). Two-tone paint pkg. ($153-$474). Protection group ($131). Comfort/Convenience: Auto. speed control ($184). Power seat ($232); dual ($232-$464). Power door locks ($185). Power decklid release ($41). Illuminated entry system ($77). Leather-wrapped steering wheel ($62). Tilt steering ($118). Intermittent wipers ($55). Lighted vanity mirror ($60). Entertainment: AM stereo/FM stereo radio ($149); w/seek, scan and cassette ($251-$400). Ultimate sound AM stereo/FM stereo w/cassette ($497-$616). Power antenna ($67). Exterior: Power glass sunroof ($1108). Pearl coat paint ($41). Hood tape stripes ($30). Undercoating ($44). Interior: Cloth 60/40 bench seat (NC). Leather/vinyl 60/40 bench seat ($390). Wheels/Tires: Wire wheel covers (NC or $212). Cast aluminum wheels ($39-$251). Conventional spare tire ($96).

HISTORY: Introduced: October 1, 1985. Model year production: 357,264. Calendar year production: 368,638. Calendar year sales by U.S. dealers: 353,888. Model year sales by U.S. dealers: 370,544.

HISTORICAL FOOTNOTES: Chrysler retained one note of notoriety, offering the only domestic cars that had to pay a gas guzzler penalty of $500 apiece. The V-8 Fifth Avenue couldn't manage the required 22.5 miles per gallon minimum this year. This was especially ironic since Chrysler had been the only member of the Big Three to meet the original CAFE standards for 1986. Plymouth's Gran Fury also failed the test. Laser sales fell considerably for 1986 (down to 31,458 from a healthy 54,758 in model year 1985). Dodge's Daytona did better. LeBaron GTS, on the other hand, sold almost 16,000 more copies this model year than in its first season. Fifth Avenues sold rather well, even with their gas guzzler reputation (and penalty). Overall Chrysler-Plymouth sales rose three percent, to 775,025 units (including 69,402 imports). Incentives were big news this year. Chrysler and Plymouth would become separate divisions for the 1987 model year. A Maserati-built two-seat sport coupe was shown at auto shows during 1986, scheduled for 1987 release as a Chrysler product (but not actually available until 1988).

1987-1/2 Chrysler, LeBaron coupe with turbocharged engine (OCW)

Laser left the lineup this year, while LeBaron coupes and convertibles took a brand-new form, far more curvy than before. Otherwise, this was a year of minimal change.

1987 Chrysler, LeBaron convertible with turbocharged engine (OCW)

LEBARON — SERIES J/K — FOUR — Two completely different LeBarons appeared this year: a four-door sedan and station wagon carrying on the same style as before, on the K-car platform; plus a dramatically new two-door coupe and convertible. The curvaceous two-doors, long in hood and with a short decklid, featured hidden headlamps, a vertical-bar grille, and what some called a "Coke bottle" profile. Both rode on a lengthened Daytona platform with P185/70R14 tires and came with a standard five-speed manual gearbox. Bigger tires were available. Sedans carried a 2.2-liter four-cylinder engine; all other LeBarons came with the 2.5-liter version, which had a balance shaft. All models had the turbocharged engine option. A three-speed automatic was standard on the sedan/wagon, optional on the coupe/convertible.

1987 Chrysler, LeBaron GTS sports sedan with turbocharged engine (OCW)

LEBARON GTS — SERIES H — FOUR — Except for the addition of a stainless steel exhaust system, little changed on Chrysler's mid-size four-door hatchback. Models with the optional 2.5-liter engine and automatic transmission got a new lockup torque converter to boost gas mileage. Standard engine was again the 2.2-liter four, with a 146-horsepower turbo four optional. Joining the option list this year: an overhead console with compass and thermometer, and an Infinity six-speaker sound system.

NEW YORKER — SERIES E — FOUR — Not much was new in the front-drive luxury Chrysler, except for the addition of a lockup torque converter to the automatic transmission, and that only in models with the base 2.5-liter four-cylinder engine. Electronic speed control joined the option list. So did a new six-speaker sound system.

FIFTH AVENUE — SERIES M — V-8 — Chrysler's luxurious rear-drive model continued with little change. Sole powertrain was the familiar 318 cu. in. (5.2-liter) V-8 with three-speed automatic.

1987 Chrysler, Fifth Avenue sedan (OCW)

I.D. DATA: Chrysler's 17-symbol Vehicle Identification Number (VIN) was on the upper left corner of the instrument panel, visible through the windshield. Coding was similar to 1986. Model year code changed to 'H' for 1987. Engine number coding was similar to 1982-86.

LEBARON (FOUR)

Model No.	Body/ Style No.	Body Type & Seating	Factory Price	Shipping Weight	Prod. Total
JCH	21	2-dr. Cpe-5P	11295	2690	44,124
JCP	21	2-dr. Prem Cpe-5P	12288	2731	31,291
JCP	27	2-dr. Conv.-5P	13974	2786	8,025
KCP	41	4-dr. Sed-6P	10707	2582	54,678

LEBARON TOWN & COUNTRY (FOUR)

KCP	45	4-dr. Sta. Wag-6P	12019	2759	5,880

LEBARON GTS (FOUR)

HCH	44	4-dr Spt Sed-5P	9774	2641	23,772

LEBARON GTS PREMIUM (FOUR)

HCP	44	4-dr. Spt Sed-5P	11389	2709	15,278

NEW YORKER (FOUR)

ETP	41	4-dr. Sed-6P	14193	2757	68,279

FIFTH AVENUE (V-8)

MFS	41	4-dr. Sed-6P	15422	3741	70,579

ENGINE DATA: BASE FOUR (LeBaron sed, LeBaron GTS): Inline, overhead cam four-cylinder. Cast iron block; aluminum head. Displacement: 135 cu. in. (2.2 liters). Bore & stroke: 3.44 x 3.62 in. Compression ratio: 9.5:1. Brake horsepower: 97 at 5200 RPM. Torque: 122 lb.-ft. at 3200 RPM. Five main bearings. Hydraulic valve lifters. Electronic fuel injection. TURBOCHARGED FOUR; OPTIONAL (LeBaron, LeBaron GTS, New Yorker): Same as 135 cu. in. four above, but with turbocharger. Compression ratio: 8.1:1. Brake horsepower: 146 at 5200 RPM. Torque: 170 lb.-ft. at 3600 RPM. BASE FOUR (LeBaron cpe/conv/wag, New Yorker); OPTIONAL (LeBaron GTS): Inline, overhead cam four-cylinder. Cast iron block; aluminum head. Displacement: 153 cu. in. (2.5 liters). Bore & stroke: 3.44 x 4.09 in. Compression ratio: 9.0:1. Brake horsepower: 100 at 4800 RPM. Torque: 133 lb.-ft. at 2800 RPM. Five main bearings. Hydraulic valve lifters. Electronic fuel injection. BASE V-8 (Fifth Avenue): 90-degree, overhead valve V-8. Cast iron block and head. Displacement: 318 cu. in. (5.2 liters). Bore & stroke: 3.91 x 3.31 in. Compression ratio: 9.0:1. Brake horsepower: 140 at 3600 RPM. Torque: 265 lb.-ft. at 1600 RPM. Five main bearings. Hydraulic valve lifters. Carburetor: 2 Bbl.

CHASSIS DATA: Wheelbase: (LeBaron) 100.3 in.; (LeBaron GTS) 103.1 in.; (N.Y.) 103.3 in.; (Fifth Ave.) 112.6 in. Overall length: (LeB cpe/conv) 184.9 in.; (LeB sed) 179.2 in.; (LeB wag) 179.0 in.; (GTS) 180.4 in.; (N.Y.) 187.2 in.; (Fifth Ave.) 206.7 in. Height: (LeB cpe) 50.9 in.; (LeB conv) 52.9 in.; (LeB sed) 52.9 in.; (LeB wag) 53.2 in.; (GTS) 53.0 in.; (N.Y.) 53.1 in.; (Fifth Ave.) 55.0 in. Width: (LeB cpe/conv) 68.4 in.; (LeB sed/wag) 68.0 in.; (GTS) 68.3 in.; (N.Y.) 68.0 in.; (Fifth Ave.) 72.4 in. Front Tread: (LeB/GTS/N.Y.) 57.5-57.6 in.; (Fifth Ave.) 60.5 in. Rear Tread: (LeB cpe/conv) 57.6 in.; (LeB sed/wag) 57.2 in.; (GTS/N.Y.) 57.2 in.; (Fifth Ave.) 60.0 in. Standard Tires: (LeB) P185/70R14; (GTS) P185/70R14 SBR BSW; (N.Y./ Exec.) P185/75R14 SBR SW; (Fifth Ave.) P205/75R15 WSW.

TECHNICAL: Transmission: Five-speed manual trans. standard on LeB cpe/conv and GTS. Three-speed TorqueFlite standard on LeB sed/wag, New Yorker, Fifth Avenue; optional on GTS and LeB cpe/conv. Steering:

(LeBaron/GTS/New Yorker) rack and pinion; (Fifth Ave.) recirculating ball, power-assisted. Suspension (front): (LeBaron/GTS/N.Y.) MacPherson struts with lower control arms, coil springs and stabilizer bar; (Fifth Ave.) transverse front torsion bars and anti-sway bar. Suspension (rear): (LeBaron/GTS/N.Y.) beam flex axle with trailing arms, coil springs and stabilizer bar; (Fifth Ave.) semi-elliptic leaf springs. Brakes: Front disc, rear drum. Body construction: Unibody. Fuel tank: (LeB/GTS/N.Y.) 14 gal.; (Fifth Ave.) 18 gal.

1987 Chrysler, New Yorker sedan with turbocharged engine (OCW)

DRIVETRAIN OPTIONS: Engines: Turbocharged 2.2-liter four: LeB ($685); GTS/N.Y. ($685). 2.5-liter four: GTS ($287). Transmission/Differential: Three-speed auto. trans.: LB GTS ($534).

LEBARON SEDAN/WAGON CONVENIENCE/APPEARANCE OPTIONS: Popular Equipment Discount Pkg. (Rear defogger, tinted glass, AM/FM stereo ET radio, trunk dress-up, cruise control, tilt steering column): sed ($1157); wag ($1434). Luxury Equipment Discount Pkg. (Popular Equipment plus power windows, wire wheel covers, power door locks, power seats, power remote mirrors, power liftgate release on wagon): sed ($2197); wag ($2067). Mark Cross Pkg. (50/50 reclining leather seats w/dual armrests, seatback pockets, vinyl door panels, leather-wrapped steering wheel) ($1049). Protection Pkg.; sed ($209); wag ($148). Rear Defogger Pkg. ($148). Deluxe Convenience Pkg. (cruise control, tilt steering) ($310). Pearl coat paint ($41). High-back bucket seats w/center armrest, console & dual recliners, sed ($377). Low-back vinyl bucket seats w/center armrest, console & dual recliners, wag ($206). Air cond. ($790). California emissions system ($102). Power Convenience Discount Pkg. ($437). Power decklid release ($51). Power seat, left or bench ($242). AM & FM stereo cassette ($292). Leather-wrapped steering wheel ($61). Sport handling suspension ($59). Trunk dress-up ($53). Conventional spare tire ($85). Locking wire wheel covers ($181).

LEBARON COUPE/CONVERTIBLE CONVENIENCE/APPEARANCE OPTIONS: Similar to 1988: see that listing.

1987 Chrysler, LeBaron sedan with optional wire wheel covers (OCW)

LEBARON GTS CONVENIENCE/APPEARANCE OPTIONS: Leather seats & steering wheel rim, Premium ($644). Popular Equipment Discount Pkg. (air cond., light package, floormats, cruise control, tilt steering column, undercoating): Highline w/5-speed ($901). Highline including automatic ($1245). Premium w/5-speed (2.2-liter turbo engine, cruise control, floormats, tilt steering column, undercoating, luxury wheel covers, P205/60R15 tires) ($1011). Premium w/automatic ($1305). Console/Lights Convenience Pkg.(Light package, dual illuminated visor mirrors, console/armrest, overhead console with compass and outside temperature thermometer): Highline ($236). Highline w/Popular Equipment ($166). Premium ($279). Deluxe Convenience Pkg.(tilt steering column, cruise control, floor mats, undercoating) ($401). Electronic Features Pkg. (Electronic Voice Alert, 500-amp battery, Electronic Navigator): Premium ($393). Premium w/rear defogger ($348). Air cond.: Highline ($790). Rear defogger ($198). Power Convenience Discount Pkg. ($481). Power driver's seat ($242). AM/FM stereo cassette ($298). AM/FM stereo cassette w/graphic equalizer (Ultimate Sound) ($510). Removable glass sunroof ($376). w/Console/Lights Convenience Pkg. ($201). Sport handling suspension ($27). Cast aluminum 14 in. road wheels ($332). Cast aluminum road wheels w/15 in. tires ($617). Rear wiper/washer ($130). P195/70R14 handling tires ($102).

NEW YORKER CONVENIENCE/APPEARANCE OPTIONS: Luxury Equipment Discount Pkg. (2.2-liter turbo engine, rear defogger, 500-amp battery, power antenna, dual illuminated visor mirrors, bodyside molding, power door locks, dual power seats, cruise control, leather-wrapped steering wheel, tilt steering column, undercoating, illuminated entry system, 50/50 leather seats, automatic air cond., compass and outside temperature readouts, floormats, automatic rear load leveling, wire wheel covers) ($3703). Deluxe Convenience Pkg. (cruise control, tilt steering) ($310). Protection Pkg. ($151). Rear defroster pkg. ($197). Auto temp. control air cond. ($934). Pearl coat paint ($41). Bodyside protective moldings ($61). California emissions pkg. ($102). Power door locks ($197). Power driver's seat ($242). AM/FM stereo cassette ($292). AM/FM stereo cassette w/graphic equalizer (Ultimate Sound) ($504). Conventional spare tire ($85). Leather-wrapped steering wheel ($61). Sport handling suspension ($59). Wire wheel covers ($181). Cast aluminum 14 in. wheels ($291); w/Luxury Equipment ($110).

FIFTH AVENUE CONVENIENCE/APPEARANCE OPTIONS: Luxury Equipment Discount Pkg.: (heavy-duty battery, AM/FM stereo radio with power amplifier and power antenna, illuminated entry system, illuminated right visor mirror, remote decklid release, power door locks, power front seats, 60/40 leather front seat with passenger recliner, cruise control, tilt steering column, leather-wrapped steering wheel, hood stripe, wire wheel covers, electro-luminescent opera lights in door appliqué, intermittent wipers, Protection Group) w/o Ultimate Sound ($2251); w/Ultimate Sound ($2113). Heavy-duty suspension ($26). Power door locks ($195). Power seat, left ($240); left & right ($480). Cruise control ($179). Intermittent wipers ($58). Tilt steering column ($125). Leather-wrapped steering wheel ($60). AM/FM stereo ($155). AM/FM stereo cassette ($399); w/Luxury Equipment ($254). AM/FM stereo cassette w/graphic equalizer (Ultimate Sound) ($609); w/Luxury Equipment ($464). Electric sliding glass sunroof ($1076). Heavy-duty battery ($44). California emissions package ($99). Illuminated entry system ($75). Illuminated visor mirror, right ($58). Leather upholstery (60/40 split bench) ($395). Pearl coat paint ($40). Two-tone paint ($485); w/Luxury Equipment ($148). Conventional spare tire ($93). Undercoating ($43). Power decklid release ($50). Wire wheel covers ($206). Cast aluminum wheels ($244); w/Luxury Equipment ($38). Protection Group ($132).

HISTORY: Model year production: 360,613. Calendar year production: 357,148. Calendar year sales: 295,125. A turbocharged LeBaron convertible paced the 1987 Indianapolis 500 with Carroll Shelby selected as the driver.

1988 CHRYSLER

A completely different New Yorker joined the Chrysler lineup this year, powered by a V-6 engine. The former New Yorker carried on for only part of the season, now powered only by a turbocharged four. Otherwise, Chrysler models changed mainly in their equipment and option lists. Driver's side airbags began their phase-in on the Fifth Avenue at mid-year.

1988 Chrysler, LeBaron Town & Country station wagon with turbocharged engine and optional wire wheel covers (OCW)

LEBARON — SERIES J/K — FOUR — Two versions of the curvy convertible were available this year: base (Highline) and Premium. LeBaron standard equipment now included an electric rear-window defogger. Base models had the five-speed manual as standard. Premium coupes and convertibles added an automatic transmission plus power heated mirrors, power door locks, and automatic temperature control. The Premium coupe came with an overhead console that contained a digital thermometer and compass. Premium convertibles included a tilt steering wheel, cruise control, power antenna, cassette player, and two-tone paint. Base coupe/convertible engine remained the 2.5-liter four, with turbo four optional. That engine had a new turbocharger unit this year,

built by Mitsubishi. Though also front-drive and with similar overall dimensions, the LeBaron sedan and station wagon were built on a completely different platform, related to the Dodge Aries/Plymouth Reliant. The wagon had a standard 2.5-liter four, while the sedan used the 2.2-liter version, with 2.5 optional. Both four-door models could get the 146-horsepower turbo four.

1988 Chrysler, LeBaron GTS sports sedan with turbocharged engine (OCW)

LEBARON GTS — SERIES H — FOUR — Changes in standard equipment were the only modifications to Chrysler's four-door hatchback sedans. The base model switched from a solid rear seatback to a 60/40 split, with a back that folded down. A rear defogger also became standard. The Premium GTS moved up to a standard 2.5-liter four, while the base model kept the 2.2-liter. Also added to the Premium standard equipment list: larger P195/70R14 tires, twin power heated mirrors, lighted visor vanity mirrors, carpeted floormats, and power door locks. A five-speed manual gearbox was again standard on both models, with three-speed automatic optional. Joining the option list was a power slide/tilt sunroof. Air conditioning was standard on the Premium model, optional on the base unit.

NEW YORKER TURBO — SERIES E — FOUR — For only a portion of the 1988 model year, Chrysler turned out a final stock of the old E-body New Yorkers, all powered by the 146-horsepower turbo four. Standard equipment now included cruise control, a rear defogger and tilt steering. After these were produced, the New Yorker name resided only on the completely different C-body version.

1988 Chrysler, New Yorker sedan (Series C) (OCW)

NEW YORKER — SERIES C — V-6 — The name was old, but the car was new. The New Yorker designation now went on a front-drive, mid-size sedan, riding the same C-body platform as the new Dodge Dynasty. Longer than the former New Yorker (which continued in the Turbo model), it carried a standard Mitsubishi-built 3.0-liter V-6 with three-speed lock-up automatic transmission. Anti-lock four-wheel disc brakes were optional. This revised New Yorker had concealed headlamps and came in base or Landau trim.

1988 Chrysler, Fifth Avenue sedan with optional wire wheel covers (OCW)

FIFTH AVENUE — SERIES M — V-8 — Still rear-drive and V-8 powered, the biggest Chrysler continued as before except for a new padded vinyl roof design. A new two-tone paint scheme also became available.

I.D. DATA: As before, Chrysler's 17-symbol Vehicle Identification Number (VIN) was on the upper left corner of the instrument panel, visible through the windshield. Coding was similar to 1986-87. The model year code changed to 'J' for 1988. Engine number coding was similar to 1982-87.

LEBARON (FOUR)

Model No.	Body/ Style No.	Body Type & Seating	Factory Price	Shipping Weight	Prod. Total
JCH	21	2-dr. Cpe-5P	11473	2769	38,733
JCP	21	2-dr. Prem Cpe-5P	13830	2875	9,938
JCH	27	2-dr. Conv-5P	13959	2860	23,160
JCP	27	2-dr. Prem Conv-5P	18079	2964	15,037
KCP	41	2-dr. Sed-6P	11286	2559	24,452

LEBARON TOWN & COUNTRY (FOUR)

KCP	45	4-dr. Sta Wag-6P	12889	2702	2,136

LEBARON GTS (FOUR)

HCH	44	4-dr. Spt Sed-5P	10798	2641	9,607

LEBARON GTS PREMIUM (FOUR)

HCP	44	4-dr. Spt Sed-5P	12971	2709	4,604

NEW YORKER TURBO (FOUR)

ETP	41	4-dr. Sed-6P	17373	2826	8,805

NEW YORKER (V-6)

CCH	41	4-dr. Sed-6P	17416	3214	23,568
CCS	41	4-dr. Lan Sed-6P	19509	3276	47,400

FIFTH AVENUE (V-8)

MFS	41	4-dr. Sed-6P	17243	3759	43,486

ENGINE DATA: BASE FOUR (LeBaron sed, LeBaron GTS): Inline, overhead cam four-cylinder. Cast iron block; aluminum head. Displacement: 135 cu. in. (2.2 liters). Bore & stroke: 3.44 x 3.62 in. Compression ratio: 9.5:1. Brake horsepower: 93-100 at 4400-5200 RPM. Torque: 122/133 lb.-ft. at 2800-3200 RPM. Five main bearings. Hydraulic valve lifters. Electronic fuel injection. TURBOCHARGED FOUR: BASE (NY Turbo); OPTIONAL (LeBaron, LeBaron GTS): Same as 135 cu. in. four above, but with turbocharger. Compression ratio: 8.0:1. Brake horsepower: 146 at 5200 RPM. Torque: 170 lb.-ft. at 2400-3600 RPM. BASE FOUR (LeBaron cpe/conv/wag, GTS Premium): Inline, overhead cam four-cylinder. Cast iron block; aluminum head. Displacement: 153 cu. in. (2.5 liters). Bore & stroke: 3.44 x 4.09 in. Compression ratio: 9.0:1. Brake horsepower: 100 at 4800 RPM (GTS, 96 at 4400). Torque: 133 lb.-ft. at 2800 RPM. Five main bearings. Hydraulic valve lifters. Electronic fuel injection. BASE V-6 (New Yorker): Overhead cam V-6. Displacement: 181 cu. in. (3.0 liters). Bore & stroke: 3.59 x 3.99 in. Compression ratio: 8.9:1. Brake horsepower: 136 at 4800 RPM. Torque: 168 lb.-ft. at 2800 RPM. Hydraulic valve lifters. Port fuel injection. BASE V-8 (Fifth Avenue): 90-degree, overhead valve V-8. Cast iron block and head. Displacement: 318 cu. in. (5.2 liters). Bore & stroke: 3.91 x 3.31 in. Compression ratio: 9.1:1. Brake horsepower: 140 at 3600 RPM. Torque: 265 lb.-ft. at 2000 RPM. Five main bearings. Hydraulic valve lifters. Carburetor: 2 Bbl.

1988 Chrysler, New Yorker Landau sedan (Series C) (OCW)

CHASSIS DATA: Wheelbase: (LeBaron) 100.3 in.; (LeBaron GTS) 103.1 in.; (N.Y. Turbo) 103.3 in.; (N.Y.) 104.3 in.; (Fifth Ave.) 112.6 in. Overall length: (LeB cpe/conv) 184.9 in.; (LeB sed) 179.2 in.; (LeB wag) 179.0 in.; (GTS) 180.4 in.; (N.Y. Turbo) 187.2 in.; (N.Y.) 193.6 in.; (Fifth Ave.) 206.7 in. Height: (LeB cpe) 50.9 in.; (LeB conv) 52.2 in.; (LeB sed) 52.9 in.; (LeB wag) 53.2 in.; (GTS) 53.0 in.; (N.Y. Turbo) 55.7 in.; (N.Y.) 55.0 in.; (Fifth Ave.) 55.0 in. Width: (LeB cpe/conv) 68.4 in.; (LeB sed) 68.0 in.; (GTS) 68.3 in.; (N.Y. Turbo) 68.0 in.; (N.Y.) 68.5 in.; (Fifth Ave.) 72.4 in. Front Tread: (LeB/GTS) 57.5-57.6 in.; (N.Y.) 57.6 in.; (Fifth Ave.) 60.5 in. Rear Tread: (LeB cpe/conv) 57.6 in.; (LeB sed/wag) 57.2 in.; (GTS) 57.2 in.; (N.Y. Turbo) 57.2 in.; (N.Y.) 57.6 in.; (Fifth Ave.) 60.0 in. Standard Tires: (LeB sed/wag)

P185/70R14 SBR WSW; (LeB cpe/conv) P195/70R14; (GTS) P185/70R14; (GTS Premium) P195/70R14; (N.Y. Turbo) P185/75R14 SBR WSW; (N.Y.) P195/75R14 SBR WSW; (Fifth Ave.) P205/75R15 SBR WSW.

TECHNICAL: Transmission: Five-speed manual trans. standard on LeBaron cpe/conv and GTS. TorqueFlite three-speed automatic standard on LeBaron sed/wag, New Yorker and Fifth Ave.; optional on others. Steering: (LeBaron/GTS/N.Y.) rack and pinion; (Fifth Ave.) recirculating ball, power-assisted. Suspension: Same as 1987. Brakes: Front disc, rear drum (power-assisted). Body construction: Unibody. Fuel tank: (LeB/GTS) 14 gal.; (N.Y. Turbo) 14 gal.; (N.Y.) 16 gal.; (Fifth Ave.) 18 gal.

DRIVETRAIN OPTIONS: Engines: Turbocharged four: LeB/GTS ($700). 2.5-liter four: LeB sed/base GTS ($288). Transmission/Differential: Automatic trans.: LeB cpe/conv, GTS ($546). Brakes: Anti-lock four-wheel disc brakes: N.Y. ($956).

LEBARON COUPE/CONVERTIBLE CONVENIENCE/APPEARANCE OPTIONS: Overhead Console, GTC Cpe ($360). Popular Equip. Discount Pkg.: JCH21 ($963). JCH27 ($1322). Lux. Equip. Discount Pkg.: JCH21 ($1806). JCH27 ($643). Light Pkg. ($198). Dlx. Convenience Pkg. ($300). Electronic Features Pkg. ($477). Turbo Coupe Pkg.: JCH21 ($4000). JCH27 ($3848). Air Cond. ($775). Electronic Navigator ($272). Calif. Emissions Control System & Testing ($99). Pwr. Convenience I Pkg. ($446). Pwr. Convenience II Pkg. ($236). Power Driver's Seat ($240). Pwr. Windows ($210). Pearl Coat Paint ($40). Two-Tone ($226). Perm. Leather Low Back Bucket Seats ($627). Incl. (JPS) on JCP27 ($1080). Leather Trim, Incl. Pwr Seat; JCH21 w/ALJ Pkg. ($867). JCH27 w/ALJ Pkg. ($1080). Compact Disc Player ($400). Prem. AM Stereo/FM Stereo w/Cass. Incl. Seek & Scan plus 6 spkrs.: JCH21, JCH27 ($289). JCP21 ($557). AM Stereo/FM Stereo w/Cass., Ultimate Sound, Seek & Scan, plus 6 spkrs, Graphic Equalizer & Pwr. Ant.: JCP21 ($767). JCH21 w/(AAM) or (AFF) ($767). JCH27 w/(AAM) or (AFF) ($737). JCP27 ($210). JCH21, JCH27 w/(AGT) ($210). Glass Sun Roof: JCH21 ($372). JCH21 w/(AGT) ($197). JCP21 ($197). P195/70R14 SBR BSW Touring Tires (NC). P185/75R14 SBR WSW tires ($72). 14-in. Cast Alum. Wheels ($322). Road Hdlg. Suspension ($57). 15-in. Handling Tire/Suspension ($201/$523).

LEBARON SEDAN/WAGON CONVENIENCE/APPEARANCE OPTIONS: Popular Equip. Discount Pkg.: KCP41 ($1153). KCP45 ($1127). Lux. Equip. Discount Pkg.: KCP41 ($2163). KCP45 ($2073). Mark Cross Pkg.: KCP45 ($1019). Protection Group Pkg.: ($148). KCP45 ($88). Air Cond. ($775). Frt. Lic. Plate Bracket (NC). Rr. Window Defroster ($145). Calif. Emissions Cntrl. System & Testing ($99). Illum. Entry System ($76). Power Driver's Seat (or Bench) ($240). Prem. AM Stereo/FM Stereo ETR, w/Cass. Incl. Seek & Scan plus 6 spkrs. ($289). Conventional Spare Tire ($83). Wire Wheel Covers ($176). Pearl Coat Paint: KCP41 ($40). Cloth Bucket Seats, Hi-back w/Arm Rest, Console & Dual Recliners: KCP41 ($366). Vinyl Bucket Seats, Low-back w/Arm Rest, Console & Dual Recliners: KCP45 ($200).

LEBARON GTS CONVENIENCE/APPEARANCE OPTIONS: Pearl Coat Paint ($40). Two-Tone Paint ($266). Leather Low Back Prem Pwr Bucket Seats incl. Leather-wrapped Strg Wheel ($625). Basic Equip. Discount Pkg. ($984). Popular Equip. Discount Pkg., w/Manual Trans, HCH44 ($1361). W/Auto. Trans. HCH44 ($1797). Luxury Equip. Discount Pkg.; HCH44 w/Manual Trans. ($1888). W/Auto. Trans ($2324). HCP44 w/Manual Trans ($903). W/Auto. Trans. ($1339). Turbo Sport Discount Pkg.; HCP44 ($1822). Dlx. Convenience Pkg. ($300). Electronic Features Pkg.; HCP44 ($272). Air Cond. ($775). Frt. License Plate Bracket (NC). Calif. Emission Cntrl. System & Testing ($99). Pwr. Dr. Locks ($195). Pwr. Convenience Discount Pkg., HCH44 ($514). Pwr. Driver's Seat ($240). Pwr. Windows ($285). Prem. AM Stereo/FM Stereo w/Cass., incl. 6 spkrs. ($463). Ultimate Sound, AM Stereo/FM Stereo ETR w/Cass., Infinity Spkrs. & Graphic Equalizer ($673). Removable Sunroof: HCH44 & HCP44 ($774). W/(AFF), HCP44 ($599). Sport Hdlg Suspension ($85). P185/70R14 Steel Radial WSW Tires ($68). P195/70R14 SBR BSW All Season Performance tires ($112). 15-in. Wheel Covers/Tires ($290). 15-in. Wheel/Tires ($500). Liftgate Wiper/Washer ($126).

NEW YORKER CONVENIENCE/APPEARANCE OPTIONS: Pearl Coat Paint ($40). Lux. Equip. Discount Pkg.: CCH41 ($1584). CCS41 ($1276). Mark Cross Pkg.: CCH41 ($2374). CCS41 ($2066). Dlx. Convenience Pkg. ($300). Interior Illum., ($192). Frt. Lic. Plate Bracket (NC). Overhead Console ($670). Pwr. Deck Lid, Pull-Down ($80). Pwr. Dr. Locks ($285). Calif. Emissions ($99). AM/FM Stereo Cass. Radio: CCS41 w/(AFF) or (AFC) ($487). Others ($557). AM/FM Stereo Cass. w/5-Band Graphic Equalizer: CCS41 w/o (AFF) or (AFC) ($697). Others ($767). AM/FM Stereo Cass. Radio ($254). Pwr. 6-Way Driver's Seat ($240). Pwr. 6-Way Pass. Seat ($240). Pwr. Sun Roof ($776). Road Handling Suspension ($57). Auto Rr. Load Leveling ($180). Conventional Spare Tire ($83). Wire Wheel Covers ($224). Cast Alum Wheels: CCH41 or CCS41 ($273). CCH41 or CCS41 w/(AFC) ($49).

NEW YORKER TURBO CONVENIENCE/APPEARANCE OPTIONS: Lux. Equip. Discount Pkg. ($2052). Protection Pkg. ($152). Pearl Coat Paint ($41). Frt. Lic. Plate Bracket (NC). Calif. Emission Cntrl. System & Testing ($102). Pwr. Driver's Seat ($248). AM Stereo/FM Stereo w/Cass. Player w/6 Infinity Spkrs. ($426). AM Stereo/FM Stereo w/Cass. Player, 5-Band Graphic Equalizer & 6 Infinity Spkrs ($218). Road Touring Suspension ($59). Conventional Spare Tire ($86). Wire Wheel Covers ($182). Cast Alum. 14-in. Wheels ($292). W/(AFF) ($110).

FIFTH AVENUE CONVENIENCE/APPEARANCE OPTIONS: Pwr. Convenience Pkg. ($785). Lux. Equip. Discount Pkg. ($2039). Pearl Coat Paint ($40). 60/40 Split Bench (NC). Frt. License Plate Bracket (NC). Calif. Emission Cntrl. System & Testing ($99). AM Stereo/FM Stereo Radio w/Cass Player ($254). Conventional Spare Tire ($93). Pwr. Sun Roof ($901). H.D. Suspension ($26). Undercoating ($43). Wire Wheel Covers ($206).

HISTORY: Model year production: 278,287. Calendar year production: 248,012. Calendar year sales by U.S. dealers: 269,254.

1989 CHRYSLER

The GTS badge left this year (except as a high-performance submodel), but the hatchback car remained, now called, simply, LeBaron sedan. LeBaron added some high-performance versions to its coupe and convertible lineup, with standard 174-horsepower intercooled turbo engine.

1989 Chrysler, LeBaron GTC coupe with turbocharged engine (OCW)

LEBARON — SERIES J/K — FOUR — Both the station wagon and the notchback sedan departed from LeBaron's lineup. The curvaceous coupe and convertible continued in their 1987 form, adding four-wheel disc brakes and a driver's airbag, while the hatchback four-door sedan was essentially the same as the former LeBaron GTS sedan. Two turbocharged engines were offered this year: either 2.2 liters (174 horsepower) with an intercooler, or 2.5 liters with a 150-horsepower rating. High-performance GTC/GTS models had the more potent turbo as standard, offered only with five-speed manual shift. The less-powerful turbo was offered as a credit option on the GTC/GTS, or at extra cost on other models.

1989 Chrysler, LeBaron GTC convertible with turbocharged engine (OCW)

NEW YORKER — SERIES C — V-6 — For its second season in the lineup, the front-drive sedan added a little horsepower to its 3.0-liter V-6 engine and got a new four-speed overdrive automatic transmission with electronic control. New options included an eight-way power driver's seat with memory, and a new anti-theft system. The Landau model had

---

a vinyl landau roof, automatic power door locks, cruise control, leather-wrapped tilt steering wheel, and six-way power driver's seat. Anti-lock disc brakes were optional again.

1989 Chrysler, Fifth Avenue sedan with optional wire wheel covers (OCW)

FIFTH AVENUE — SERIES M — V-8 — Nearing its final days in the Chrysler lineup, the traditional rear-drive V-8 model continued with little change except for minor revisions in the option list. A driver's side airbag had become standard during the 1988 model year.

I.D. DATA: As before, Chrysler's 17-symbol Vehicle Identification Number (VIN) was on the upper left corner of the instrument panel, visible through the windshield. Coding was similar to 1986-88. The model year code changed to 'K' for 1989.

LEBARON (FOUR)

Model No.	Body/ Style No.	Body Type & Seating	Factory Price	Shipping Weight	Prod. Total
JCH	21	2-dr. Cpe-5P	11495	2810	Note 1
JCP	21	2-dr. Prem Cpe-5P	14695	2495	Note 1
JCH	21	2-dr. GTC Cpe-5P	17435	N/A	Note 1
JCH	27	2-dr. Conv-4P	13995	2929	Note 1
JCP	27	2-dr. Prem Conv-4P	18195	3038	Note 1
JCH	27	2-dr. GT Conv-4P	14795	N/A	Note 1
JCH	27	2-dr. GTC Conv-4P	19666	N/A	Note 1

Note 1: LeBaron two-door production totaled 90,993 (53,504 coupes and 37,489 convertibles) with no further breakdown available.

LEBARON SEDAN (FOUR)

HCH	44	4-dr. Spt Sed-5P	11495	2714	Note 1
HCP	44	4-dr. Prem Sed-5P	13495	2827	Note 1
HCX	44	4-dr. GTS Sed-5P	17095	2926	Note 1

Note 1: LeBaron four-door production totaled 5,436 with no further breakdown available.

1989 Chrysler, New Yorker sedan (OCW)

NEW YORKER (V-6)

CCH	41	4-dr. Sed-6P	17416	3214	34,811
CCS	41	4-dr. Lan Sed-6P	19509	3276	56,751

FIFTH AVENUE (V-8)

MFS	41	4-dr. Sed-6P	18345	3741	14,534

ENGINE DATA: BASE FOUR (LeBaron sed): Inline, overhead cam four-cylinder. Cast iron block; aluminum head. Displacement: 135 cu. in. (2.2 liters). Bore & stroke: 3.44 x 3.62. Compression ratio: 9.5:1. Brake horsepower: 93 at 4800 RPM. Torque: 122 lb.-ft. at 3200 RPM. Five main bearings. Hydraulic valve lifters. Throttle-body fuel injection. **BASE TURBOCHARGED FOUR** (LeBaron GTC/GTS): Same as 2.2-liter four above, except turbocharged. Brake horsepower: 174 at 5200 RPM. Torque: 200 lb.-ft. at 2400 RPM. **BASE FOUR** (LeBaron cpe/conv, Prem sed): Inline, overhead cam four-cylinder. Cast iron block; aluminum head. Displacement: 153 cu. in. (2.5 liters). Bore & stroke: 3.44 x 4.09 in. Compression ratio: 9.0:1. Brake horsepower: 100 at 4800 RPM. Torque: 135 lb.-ft. at 2800 RPM. Five main bearings. Hydraulic valve lifters. Throttle-body fuel injection. **OPTIONAL TURBOCHARGED FOUR** (LeBaron): Same as 2.5-liter four above, except tur-

bocharged. Brake horsepower: 150 at 4800 RPM. Torque: 180 lb.-ft. at 2000 RPM. BASE V-6 (New Yorker): Overhead cam V-6. Displacement: 181 cu. in. (3.0 liters). Bore & stroke: 3.59 x 3.99 in. Compression ratio: 8.9:1. Brake horsepower: 141 at 5000 RPM. Torque: 171 lb.-ft. at 2800 RPM. Hydraulic valve lifters. Port fuel injection. BASE V-8 (Fifth Avenue): 90-degree, overhead valve V-8. Cast iron block and head. Displacement: 318 cu. in. (5.2 liters). Bore & stroke: 3.91 x 3.31 in. Compression ratio: 9.1:1. Brake horsepower: 140 at 3600 RPM. Torque: 265 lb.-ft. at 2000 RPM. Five main bearings. Hydraulic valve lifters. Carburetor: 2Bbl.

1989 Chrysler, New Yorker Landau sedan (OCW)

CHASSIS DATA: Wheelbase: (LeBaron) 100.3 in.; (LeBaron sed) 103.1 in.; (N.Y.) 104.3 in.; (Fifth Ave.) 112.6 in. Overall length: (LeB cpe/conv) 184.9 in.; (LeB sed) 180.4 in.; (N.Y.) 193.6 in.; (Fifth Ave.) 206.7 in. Height: (LeB cpe) 50.9 in.; (LeB conv) 52.2 in.; (LeB sed) 53.0 in.; (N.Y.) 55.7 in.; (Fifth Ave.) 55.0 in. Width: (LeB cpe/conv) 68.4 in.; (LeB sed) 68.3 in.; (N.Y.) 68.5 in.; (Fifth Ave.) 72.4 in. Front Tread: (LeB) 57.5-57.6 in.; (N.Y.) 57.6 in.; (Fifth Ave.) 60.5 in. Rear Tread: (LeB cpe/conv) 57.6 in.; (LeB sed) 57.2 in.; (N.Y.) 57.6 in.; (Fifth Ave.) 60.0 in. Standard Tires: (LeB) P195/70R14; (N.Y.) P195/75R14 SBR WSW; (Fifth Ave.) P205/75R15 SBR WSW.

TECHNICAL: Transmission: Five-speed manual trans. standard on LeBaron. TorqueFlite three-speed automatic standard on LeBaron Premium and Fifth Ave.; optional on others except LeB GTS. Four-speed automatic standard on New Yorker. Steering: (LeB/N.Y.) rack and pinion; (Fifth Ave.) recirculating ball; power-assisted. Brakes: Front disc, rear drum (power assisted) except (LeB cpe/conv) four-wheel disc. Body construction: Uni-body. Fuel tank: (LeB) 14 gal.; (N.Y.) 16 gal.; (Fifth Ave.) 18 gal.

DRIVETRAIN OPTIONS: Engines: Turbocharged four: LeB ($698). Transmission/Differential: Automatic trans.: LeB ($552). Brakes: Anti-lock four-wheel disc brakes: N.Y. ($954).

1989 Chrysler, LeBaron GTS sedan with turbocharged engine (OCW)

LEBARON COUPE/CONVERTIBLE CONVENIENCE/APPEARANCE OPTIONS: Deluxe Convenience Pkg.; Incl. Electronic Spd Cntrl, Tilt Strg Col, Highline cpe ($310). Light Pkg.; Incl. Headlights w/Time Delay, Illum. Entry, Illum. Vanity Mirrors, Highline cpe ($198). Power Convenience II Pkg.; Incl. Pwr. Dr. Locks, Pwr. Remote Heated Mirrors, Pwr. Windows, Highline cpe ($456). Power Convenience I Pkg.; Incl. Pwr. Dr. Locks, Pwr. Remote Heated Mirrors, Highline cpe ($241). Popular Equip. Discount Pkg.; Incl. Air Cond, Floormats, Electronic Spd Cntrl, Tilt Strg, Undercoating ($1053). Luxury Equip. Discount Pkg.; Incl. Air Cond, Floormats, Headlights w/Time Delay, Illum. Entry, Illum. Vanity Mirrors, Pwr. Dr. Locks, Pwr. Remote Heated Mirrors, Pwr. 6-Way Driver's Seat, Pwr. Windows, Electronic Spd Cntrl, Tilt Strg Col, Undercoating, Leather-Wrapped Strg Wheel, Overhead Console ($2166). Deluxe Convenience Pkg.; Incl. Electronic Spd Cntrl, Tilt Strg Wheel, Highline Conv ($310). Light Pkg.; Incl. Headlights w/Time Delay, Illum. Entry, Illum. Vanity Mirrors, Highline Conv. ($198). Power Convenience I Pkg.; Incl. Pwr. Dr. Locks, Pwr. Remote Heated Mirrors, Highline Conv ($241). Popular Equip. Discount Pkg.; Incl. Air Cond, Floormats, Headlights w/Time Delay, Illum. Entry, Illum. Vanity Mirrors, Pwr. Dr. Locks, Pwr. Remote Heated Mirrors, Electronic Spd Cntrl, Tilt Strg Col, Undercoating, Highline Conv ($1387). Electronic Discount Pkg.; Incl. Electronic Mon-

itor, Electronic Navigator, Premium Conv ($477). Dlx Convenience Pkg.; Incl. Spd Control, Tilt Strg Col, Premium Cpe ($310). Light Pkg.; Incl. Headlights w/Time Delay, Illum. Entry, Illum. Vanity Mirrors, Premium Cpe ($198). Electronic Discount Pkg.; Incl. Electronic Monitor, Electronic Navigator, Premium Cpe ($477). Lux. Equip. Discount Pkg.; Incl. Air Cond, Floormats, Pwr. Dr. Locks, Pwr. Remote Heated Mirrors, Pwr. Driver's 6-Way Seat, Pwr. Windows, Spd Control, Tilt Strg Col, Leather-Wrapped Strg Wheel, Undercoating, Premium cpe ($738). Pearl Coat Paint ($40). Two-Tone Paint ($226). Leather Bucket Seats ($627). Premium Bucket Seats ($1080). Air Cond ($775). Calif. Emissions System & Testing ($100). Frt. Lic. Bracket (NC). Electronic Navigator ($272). Pwr. Driver's Seat ($240). Pwr. Windows ($215). AM/FM Radio Cass w/4 Spkrs ($152). Compact Disc Player ($400). AM/FM Stereo Cass/Seek & Scan, Incl. 6 Infinity Spkrs, Pwr. Antenna, P21, GTC H21 ($552). AM/FM Stereo Cass/Seek/Scan/Graphic Equalizer, Incl. Power Antenna, 6 Infinity Spkrs ($732). AM/FM Stereo Cass/Seek/Scan/Graphic Equalizer, Incl. Pwr. Antenna, 6 Infty Spkrs, Premium Cpe ($762). AM/FM Stereo Cass/Seek/Scan/Graphic Equalizer, Incl. Pwr. Antenna, 6 Infinity Spkrs, Premium Conv ($210). Removable Sunroof ($397); w/o Overhead Console ($222). Overhead Console, H21 ($260). P195/75R14 WSW Touring tires ($72). 14-in. Cast Alum wheels ($322). GTC Body Model Spt. Handling Suspension, Qck Ratio Pwr. Strng, Upgraded Sway Bars ($57). Performance Hdlg Suspension (NC). Handling Wheel Cover 15-in., Incl. P205/60R15 BSW Perf tires ($319). Handling Alum Wheel 15-in., incl. P205/60R15 BSW Perf tires, Cast Alum Whls ($641). Pearl Coat Paint (NC). Two-Tone Paint (NC). Cloth Premium Bckt Seat, GT (NC). Leather-Prem. Bckt Seats, Incl. Pwr Seat, GT cpe w/ALJ ($867); GT conv w/ALJ ($1080). Leather-Pwr. Enthusiast Bucket Seats, Incl. Driver Side Manual Recliner, Electric Lumbar & Thigh Inflator, GTC w/AGT only ($627). Emissions System & Testing ($100). Frt. License Bracket (NC). Power Driver's Seat ($240). Pwr. Windows ($215). Compact Disc Player ($400). AM/FM Stereo Cass/Seek/Scan/Graphic Equalizer, Incl. Pwr Antenna, 6 Spkrs, GTC ($210). Removable Sunroof, GTC w/AGT ($222); GT w/ALJ ($397). Overhead Console ($260). Electronic Navigator ($272).

NEW YORKER CONVENIENCE/APPEARANCE OPTIONS: Luxury Equip. Pkg.; Incl. Auto. Pwr. Dr. Locks, Bodyside Mldg, Elect. Instrument Cluster, Electronic Spd Control, Floor Mats, Illum. Entry, Illum. Vanity Mirrors, Leather-Wrapped Strg Wheel, Load-Leveling Suspension, Pwr. 6-Way Driver & Pass Seats, Tilt Strng Col, Trip Computer, Undercoating, Wire Wheel Covers, ACCH41 ($1503). Mark Cross Edition; incl. Auto. Pwr. Dr. Locks, Bodyside Mldg, Elect. Instrument Cluster, Electronic Spd. Cntrl, Floor Mats, Illum. Entry, Illum. Vanity Mirrors, Leather 50/50 Bench Seats w/Vinyl, Leather-Wrapped Strg Wheel, Load-Leveling Suspension, Pwr. 6-Way Driver & Pass Seats, Tilt Strg Col, Trip Computer, Undercoating, Unique Door Trim Panels, Wire Wheel Covers, CCH41 ($2069). Interior Illumination; Incl. Illum. Entry, Dual Illum. Vanity Mirrors ($192). Dlx. Convenience Pkg.; Incl. Electronic Spd Cntrl, Tilt Strg Col, CCH41 ($310). Luxury Equipment Pkg.; incl. Bodyside Mldg, Floor Mats, Illum. Entry, Illum. Vanity Mirrors, Overhead Console w/Elect. Info Center, Pwr. Antenna, Pwr. 8-Way Driver & Pass Seats, Undercoating, Wire Wheel Covers, Leather-Wrapped Strg Wheel, Landau ($1901). Mark Cross Edition; incl. Bodyside Mldg, Floor Mats, Illum. Entry, Illum. Vanity Mirrors, Leather 50/50 Bench Seats w/Vinyl, Overhead Console w/Elect. Info Center, Pwr. Antenna, Pwr. 8-Way Driver & Pass Seats, Undercoating, Unique Door Trim Panels, Wire Wheel Covers, Leather-Wrapped Strg Wheel, Landau ($2467). Interior Illumination: Illum. Entry, Illum. Vanity Mirrors, Landau ($192). Pearl Coat Paint ($40). Frt. Lic. Plate Bracket (NC). Overhead Console w/Elect. Info Center ($746). Pwr Door Locks ($290). Calif. Emissions ($100). AM/FM Stereo/Cass Radio w/Seek & Scan ($254). AM/FM Stereo/Cass. Pkg.; Incl. AM/FM Stereo Cass, 6 Infinity Spkrs, Pwr. Antenna, Digital Clock, w/AFF ($482); w/o AFF ($552). AM/FM Stereo/Cass w/5 Band Graphic Equalizer Sound Pkg., Landau ($692); N.Y. ($762). Security Alarm ($146). Pwr. 6-Way Driver's Seat ($240). Pwr. 8-Way Driver & Pass Seat w/Memory & Power Recliner ($341). Pwr. Sunroof incl. Sunshade & Wind Deflector ($776). Road Handling Suspension ($57). Rr Auto Load-Leveling Suspension ($180). Conventional Spare Tire ($83). Wire Wheel Covers ($224). Cast Alum Wheels ($49); w/o AFF or AFC ($273).

FIFTH AVENUE CONVENIENCE/APPEARANCE OPTIONS: Power Convenience Pkg.; Incl. Auto Spd Control, Pwr. Deck Lid Release, Pwr. Dr Locks, Pwr. Driver's Seat ($680). Luxury Equip. Discount Pkg.; Incl. Auto Spd Cntrl, Color-Keyed Bodyside Vinyl Mldg, Floor Mats, Illum. Entry Syst., Leather Seats w/Vinyl (or cloth). Leather-Wrapped Lux. Strg Wheel, overhead Console w/Compass & Temp Readout, Pwr. Antenna, Pwr. Deck Lid Release, Pwr. Dr Locks, Pwr. Driver's Seat, Dual Visor Vanity Mirrors, Wire Wheel Covers ($1921). Pearl Paint ($41). Frt. Lic. Plate Bracket (NC). Calif. Emissions ($100). Pwr. Pass. Seat ($247). AM/FM Stereo/Cass ($262). Conventional Spare Tire ($96). Pwr. Sunroof ($928). Undercoating ($44). Wire Wheel Covers ($212).

HISTORY: Model year production: 224,097. Calendar year production: 197,898.

1990 CHRYSLER

1990-1/2 Chrysler, LeBaron sedan (OCW)

1990 Chrysler, New Yorker Fifth Avenue sedan (OCW)

1990 Chrysler, Imperial sedan (OCW)

Finally, the traditional rear-drive Fifth Avenue was gone, leaving Chrysler with nothing other than front-drive models in its luxury lineup. For the first time since 1983, the Imperial badge was used, adorning the top-of-the-line sedan. Chrysler also introduced a Town & Country minivan this year, comparable to the Dodge Grand Caravan/Plymouth Grand Voyager. LeBaron's ragtop was the best-selling convertible in the world, adding the prospect of V-6 power this year. Chrysler's own new V-6 replaced the former Mitsubishi powerplant under New Yorker hoods, as well as in the new Imperial.

LEBARON — SERIES J (coupe and convertible)/SERIES A (sedan) — FOUR/V-6 — Four powerplants were available in the LeBaron line, including a new Mitsubishi-built 3.0-liter V-6 rated 141 horsepower. The V-6 was standard in the Premium and GT coupe and convertible, as well as in the sedan. This sedan was different from the former one, which had evolved from the earlier LeBaron GTS. Instead, it was closely related to the Dodge Spirit and Plymouth Acclaim. The high-performance LeBaron GTC had a standard 174-horsepower intercooled VNT (Variable Nozzle Turbo) Turbo IV engine and five-speed manual gearbox, while the base sedan ran with the basic 100-horsepower, 2.5-liter four. An electronically variable suspension now allowed the driver of a GTC to change shock-absorber damping characteristics. A four-speed overdrive automatic transmission was available for the first time on LeBaron, standard on the sedan. Also standard on the sedan: digital instruments, air conditioning, a landau roof, cruise control, and a cassette player. Coupes and convertibles also got a revised dashboard layout this year, with a more rounded appearance.

1990 Chrysler, New Yorker Salon sedan (OCW)

NEW YORKER — SERIES C — V-6 — What had been the base New Yorker was called "Salon" this year, while the Landau continued as top-drawer model. Under both hoods, a Chrysler-built 147-horsepower, 3.3-liter V-6 engine replaced the former standard Mitsubishi-built V-6. Standard equipment on the Landau included a one-touch power window, air conditioning, landau vinyl roof, and automatic rear load leveling. Salon carried less equipment for its lower price, but that included a four-speed overdrive automatic transmission, rear defogger, remote mirrors, and tinted glass. Options for both included antilock brakes, a power sunroof, and power memory driver's seat. Salon buyers could also get a road/handling suspension.

NEW YORKER FIFTH AVENUE — SERIES Y — V-6 — The front-drive New Yorker's platform got a five-inch stretch to produce a modern version of the Fifth Avenue, only slightly less posh than the new Imperial. Powerplant was Chrysler's new 3.3-liter V-6, rated at 147 horsepower and hooked to a four-speed overdrive automatic transmission. Standard equipment included highline trim, power windows and door locks, automatic rear load leveling, and automatic climate control. Options included a power sunroof.

IMPERIAL — SERIES Y — V-6 — Revising an old Chrysler nameplate, the new Imperial went on the same front-drive platform as the revised New Yorker, but the Imperial measured four inches longer overall. Imperial carried more standard equipment than the New Yorker, including four-wheel anti-lock disc brakes, power memory seatback recliners, and leather upholstery. An air suspension system was optional.

I.D. DATA: As before, Chrysler's 17-symbol Vehicle Identification Number (VIN) was on the upper left corner of the instrument panel, visible through the windshield. Coding was similar to 1986-89. Model year code changed to 'L' for 1990.

LEBARON (FOUR/V-6)

Model No.	Body/ Style No.	Body Type & Seating	Factory Price	Shipping Weight	Prod. Total
JCH	21	2-dr. Cpe-5P	12495	2684	Note 1
JCP	21	2-dr. Prem Cpe-5P	16415	2684	Note 1
JCH	21	2-dr. GT Cpe-5P	15725	2714	Note 1
JCH	21	2-dr. GTC Cpe-5P	18238	2684	Note 1
JCH	27	2-dr. Conv-4P	14995	2775	Note 1
JCP	27	2-dr. Prem Conv-4P	19595	2775	Note 1
JCH	27	2-dr. GT Conv-4P	17799	2775	Note 1
JCH	27	2-dr. GTC Conv-4P	20406	2775	Note 1
ACP	41	4-dr. Sedan-6P	15995	2854	27,312

Note 1: LeBaron two-door production totaled 59,034 (20,106 coupes and 38,928 convertibles) with no further breakout available.

NEW YORKER SALON (V-6)

CCH	41	4-dr. Sed-6P	16395	2977	Note 1

NEW YORKER LANDAU (V-6)

CCS	41	4-dr. Sed-6P	18795	3212	Note 1

Note 1: New Yorker production (both Salon and Landau) totaled 39,089 with no further breakout available.

NEW YORKER FIFTH AVENUE (V-6)

YCS	41	4-dr. Sed-6P	21395	3363	40,623

IMPERIAL (V-6)

YCP	41	4-dr. Sed-6P	24995	3481	13,882

ENGINE DATA: BASE TURBOCHARGED FOUR (LeBaron GTC): Inline, overhead cam four-cylinder. Cast iron block; aluminum head. Displacement: 135 cu. in. (2.2 liters). Bore & stroke: 3.44 x 3.62 in. Compression ratio: 8.0:1. Brake horsepower: 174 at 5200 RPM. Torque: 210 lb.-ft. at 2400 RPM. Five main bearings. Hydraulic valve lifters. Port fuel injection. BASE FOUR (LeBaron highline): Inline, overhead cam four-cylinder. Cast iron block; aluminum head. Displacement: 153 cu. in. (2.5 liters). Bore & stroke: 3.44 x 4.09 in. Compression ratio: 8.9:1. Brake horsepower: 100 at 4800 RPM. Torque: 135 lb.-ft. at 2800 RPM. Five main bearings. Hydraulic valve lifters. Throttle-body fuel injection. OPTIONAL TURBOCHARGED FOUR (LeBaron): Same as 2.5-liter four above, except turbocharged. Compression ratio: 7.8:1. Brake horsepower: 150 at 4000 RPM. Torque: 180 lb.-ft. at 2060 RPM. BASE V-6 (LeBaron sedan); OPTIONAL (LeBaron): Overhead cam V-6. Displacement: 181 cu. in. (3.0 liters). Bore & stroke: 3.59 x 3.99 in. Compression ratio: 8.9:1. Brake horsepower: 141 at 5000 RPM. Torque: 171 lb.-ft.

at 2800 RPM. Hydraulic valve lifters. Port fuel injection. BASE V-6 (New Yorker, Imperial): Overhead valve V-6. Displacement: 201 cu. in. (3.3 liters). Bore & stroke: 3.66 x 3.19 in. Compression ratio: 8.9:1. Brake horsepower: 147 at 4800 RPM. Torque: 183 lb.-ft. at 3600 RPM. Hydraulic valve lifters. Port fuel injection.

CHASSIS DATA: Wheelbase: (LeB) 100.3 in.; (LeB sed) 103.3 in.; (N.Y.) 104.3 in.; (Imperial/Fifth Ave.) 109.3 in. Overall length: (LeB cpe/conv) 184.9 in.; (LeB sed) 182.7in.; (N.Y.) 193.6 in.; (Fifth Ave.) 198.6 in.; (Imperial) 203.0 in. Height: (LeB cpe) 51.0 in.; (LeB conv) 52.3 in.; (LeB sed) 53.7 in.; (N.Y.) 54.8 in.; (Fifth Ave.) 55.9 in.; (Imperial) 56.3 in. Width: (LeB cpe/conv) 68.5 in.; (LeB sed) 68.1 in.; (N.Y.) 68.5 in.; (Fifth Ave./Imperial) 68.9 in. Standard Tires: (LeB) P195/70R14; (LeB Premium) P205/60R15; (LeB GTC) P205/55R16; (N.Y./Fifth Ave./Imperial) P195/75R14 WSW.

TECHNICAL: Transmission: Five-speed manual trans. standard on Le-Baron. Three-speed automatic standard on LeBaron Premium. Four-speed automatic standard on New Yorker, Imperial, and LeBaron sedan. Brakes: Front disc, rear drum (power-assisted) except (LeB cpe/conv) four-wheel disc; (Imperial) anti-lock four-wheel disc. Body construction: Unibody. Fuel tank: (LeB) 14 gal.; (N.Y./Imperial) 16 gal.

DRIVETRAIN OPTIONS: Engines: Turbocharged four: LeB ($700). 3.0 liter V-6: LeB highline ($700). Transmission/Differential: Three-speed automatic trans.: LeB GT ($552). Four-speed automatic trans.: LeB GT V-6 ($646); LeB highline V-6 ($94). Brakes: Anti-lock four-wheel disc brakes: N.Y./Fifth Ave. ($954).

1990 Chrysler, LeBaron GTC coupe with turbocharged engine (OCW)

LEBARON COUPE CONVENIENCE/APPEARANCE OPTIONS: Popular Equip. Discount Pkg.; Incl. Air Cond, Rr. Window Defroster, Floor Mats, Spd Control, Tilt Strg Column, Undercoating, CH21 ($1269). CH21 w/AJK; Incl. Air Cond, Rr. Window Electric Defroster, Floor Mats, Undercoating ($914). Luxury Equip Discount Pkg.; Incl. all in Popular Equipment Pkg. Plus Illum. Entry, Illum. Vanity Mirrors, Overhead Console, Power Dr Locks, Dual Pwr. Heated Remote Control Mirrors, Pwr. 6-Way Driver's Seat on CH21, 8-Way on CP21, Leather-Wrapped Strg Wheel ($2278). CH21 w/AJW; does not incl. Power Dr Locks & Mirrors ($2008). CP21; same as above ($815). Deluxe Convenience Pkg.; Incl. Electric Spd Control, Tilt Strg Col, CH21 & CP21 ($325). Light Pkg.; Incl. Illum. Entry, Illum. Vanity Mirrors, CH21 & CP21 ($197). Power Convenience Pkg.; Incl. Pwr. Dr Locks, Dual Pwr. Heated Remote Control Mirrors, CH21 ($300). Air conditioning ($819). Frt License Plate Bracket (NC). Overhead Console ($268). Rr Window Electric Defroster ($155). Calif. Emissions ($103). Electronic Instrument Cluster ($308). Delete Electronic Instrument Cluster (replaced w/Mechanical Cluster) (NC). Electronic Vehicle Info Center ($698); AFF req'd on P21 ($544). Two-Tone Paint ($233). Pearl Coat/Clear Coat Paint ($75). Leather Pwr. 8-way Driver's Seat ($970). Leather, Pwr. Enthusiast Seat ($1227). Compact Disc Audio System ($453). AM Stereo/FM Stereo Cass w/4 Spkrs ($157). AM Stereo/FM Stereo incl. 6 Infinity Spkrs & Pwr. Antenna, CP21 ($569). AM Stereo/FM Stereo Cass, Seek & Scan, 5-Band Graphic Equalizer, Pwr. Antenna & 6 Infinity Spkrs ($785); CH21 w/AGT ($216). Pwr. 6-Way Driver's Seat ($258). Pwr. 8-Way Driver's Seat ($324). Security Alarm ($150). Removable Sunroof, CH21 & CH21 w/ALJ ($408); CP21 & CH21 w/AGT ($229). Spt Handling Suspension, CH21 ($59). P195/70R14 Whitewall Touring Tires, CP21 ($74). P205/60R15 Whitewall Touring Tires, CP27 ($78). Handling Wheels, 15-in. Cast Alum., Incl. Spt Handling Suspension, 205/60R15 Performance Tires ($646); CP21 ($547). Cast Alum 14-in. Wheels ($332).

LEBARON CONVERTIBLE CONVENIENCE/APPEARANCE OPTIONS: Popular Equip. Discount Pkg.; Incl. Air Cond, Floor Mats, Elect. Spd Control, Tilt Strg Col, Undercoating, CH27 ($1084). Deluxe Convenience Pkg.; Incl. Elect. Spd Control, Tilt Strg Col, CH27 ($325). Light Pkg.; Incl. Illum. Entry, Illum. Vanity Mirrors, CH27 ($197). Power Convenience Pkg., Incl. Power Dr Locks, Dual Pwr. Heated Remote Control Mirrors, CH27 ($300). Air Conditioning, CH27 ($819). Frt License Plate Bracket (NC). Calif. Emission ($103). Electronic Instrument Cluster ($308). Delete Electronic Instrument Cluster (replaced w/Mechanical Cluster), CP27 (NC). Electronic Vehicle Info Center, CP27 & CH27 w/AGT ($698). Compact Disc Audio System, CP27, CH27 w/ALJ & w/AGT

($453). AM Stereo/FM Stereo with Cass and w/4 Spkrs, CH27 ($157). AM Stereo/FM Stereo, Incl. 6 Infinity Spkrs & Pwr. Antenna, CP27 (NC). AM Stereo/FM Stereo Cass, Seek & Scan, 5-Band Graphic Equalizer, Pwr. Antenna & 6 Infinity Spkrs, CH27 ($785); w/AGT ($216). Pearl Coat/Clear Coat Paint ($75). Pwr. 6-Way Driver's Seat ($258). Pwr. 8-Way Driver's Seat ($324). Leather & Pwr 8-Way Driver's Seat, CP27 & CH27 w/ALJ ($1227); Vinyl, CH27 & CH27 w/ALJ ($103). Security Alarm, CP27 & CH27 w/AGT ($150). Spt Handling Suspension, CH27 ($59). P195/70R14 Whitewall Touring tires, CP27 ($74). P205/60R15 Whitewall Touring tires, CP27 ($78). Cast Alum 15-in. Wheels, Incl. Spt Handling Suspension, P205/60R15 Performance Tires, CH27 ($646); CP27 ($547). Cast Alum Wheels, 14-in. ($332).

1990 Chrysler, LeBaron GTC convertible with turbocharged engine (OCW)

NEW YORKER SALON CONVENIENCE/APPEARANCE OPTIONS: Popular Equip. Discount Pkg.; Incl. Dlx Convenience, Air Cond, Pwr. Dr Locks, Flr Mats, Dual Pwr. Remote Control Heated Mirrors, Elect. Spd Control, Tilt Strg Col, Undercoating, Pwr. Windows ($1560). Luxury Equip. Discount Pkg.; Incl. Popular Equip. & Interior Illumination, Day/Night Rr View Auto Adjustment Mirror, Leather-Wrapped Strg Wheel, Pwr. 6-Way Driver & Pass Seats, Security Alarm, Wire Wheel Covers ($2756). Interior Illumination; Incl. Illum. Entry, Illum. Visor Vanity Mirrors ($197). Deluxe Convenience Pkg.; Incl. Spd Control, Tilt Strg Col ($325). Power Accessories: Incl. Auto Decklid Pulldown, Power Antenna ($154). Air Conditioning ($819). Frt License Plate Bracket (NC). Pwr. Door Locks ($304). Calif. Emissions ($103). Pearl Coat/Clear Coat Paint ($75). AM/FM Stereo Cass, 4 Spkrs ($157). Infinity I, Premium AM Stereo/FM Stereo Cass Radio w/Seek & Scan plus 6 Infinity Spkrs ($497). Infinity II, Premium AM Stereo/FM Stereo Cass w/Graphic Equalizer w/Seek & Scan plus 6 Infinity Spkrs ($713). Security Alarm ($150). Pwr. 6-Way Driver's Seat ($258). Pwr. 8-Way Driver & Pass Seat w/Memory & Pwr Recliners, Incl. 2 Position Memory Mirrors ($372). Pwr. Sunroof ($799). Road Handling Suspension ($59). Auto Rear Load Leveling ($185). Conventional Spare Tire ($85). Wire Wheel Covers ($231). Cast Alum Wheels ($281); w/AFF ($50).

1990 Chrysler, New Yorker Landau sedan (OCW)

NEW YORKER LANDAU CONVENIENCE/APPEARANCE OPTIONS: Luxury Equip. Discount Pkg.; Incl. Dlx Convenience, Pwr. Dr Locks, Flr Mats, Auto Headlamp Delay System, Illum. Entry, Illum. Visor Vanity Mirrors, Bodyside Mldg, Pwr. 6-Way Driver & Pass Seats, Spd Control, Tilt Strg Col, Undercoating, Wire Wheel Covers ($1671). Mark Cross Edition Discount Pkg.; all equipment above Plus: Leather 50/50 Bench Seats, Leather-Wrapped Strg Wheel ($2315). Deluxe Convenience Pkg.; Incl. Spd Control, Tilt Strg Col ($325). Electronic Features Pkg.; Incl. Overhead Console, Electronic Vehicle Information Center, Day/Night Rearview Auto Adjustment Mirror, Electronic Instrument Panel ($1252). Power Accessories Pkg.; Incl. Decklid Pulldown, Pwr. Antenna ($154). Frt License Plate Bracket (NC). Power Door Locks ($304). Calif. Emissions ($103). Pearl Coat/Clear Coat Paint ($75). AM Stereo/FM Stereo Cass w/Seek & Scan, 4 Spkrs ($262). Infinity I, Prem AM Stereo/FM Stereo Cass w/Seek & Scan plus 6 Infinity Spkrs ($497). Infinity II, Prem AM Stereo/FM Stereo Cass w/Graphic Equalizer w/Seek & Scan plus 6 Infinity Spkrs ($713). Security Alarm ($150). Pwr. Driver Seat ($258). Pwr. 8-Way, Driver/Pass Seat w/Memory & Pwr Recliners, Incl. 2-Position Memory Mirrors ($372). Power Sunroof ($799). Conventional Spare Tire ($85). Wire Wheel Covers ($231). Cast Aluminum Wheels ($281); w/AFF or AFC ($50).

NEW YORKER FIFTH AVENUE CONVENIENCE/APPEARANCE OPTIONS: Luxury Equip. Discount Pkg.; Incl. Int. Illumination, Body-color Bodyside Mldg, Illum Entry, Flr Mats, Headlamp Delay System, Illum. Visor Vanity Mirrors, Pwr Antenna, Decklid Pulldown, Dual O/S Heated Mirrors w/2-Position Memory, Driver & Pass 8-Way Seats w/Recliner & 2-Position Memory, Security Alarm w/Panel Warning Light, Undercoating, Wire Wheel Covers ($1550). Mark Cross Edition; Incl. Lux Equip & Int Illum., Mark Cross Leather Interior, 50/50 Frt Bench ($2133). Interior Illumination Pkg.: Incl. Illum. Entry, Illum. Visor Vanity Mirrors ($197). Electronic Features Pkg.; Incl. Overhead Console Electronic, Vehicle Information Center, Electronic Instrumentation Cluster, Rr View Mirror w/Auto Day/Night Adjustment ($1252). Frt License Plate Bracket (NC). Calif. Emissions ($103). Pearl Coat/Clear Coat Paint ($75). Pull down Power Deck Lid ($82). AM Stereo/FM Stereo, Prem Cass, 8 Infinity Spkrs, Seek/Scan, Digital Clock ($497). AM Stereo/FM Stereo, Prem Cass, 8 Infinity Spkrs, Seek/Scan, Digital Clock 5-Band Graphic Equalizer ($713). Security Alarm w/Panel Warning Light ($150). Conventional Spare Tire ($85). Cast Aluminum Wheels ($50). Wire Wheel Covers ($231).

IMPERIAL CONVENIENCE/APPEARANCE OPTIONS: Electronically Controlled Air Suspension ($628). Electronic Features Pkg., Incl. Overhead Console, Electronic Vehicle Information Center, Electronic Instrument Cluster, Rr View Mirror w/Auto Day/Night Adjustment, Infinity II Premium AM Stereo/FM Stereo Radio Cass w/Seek & Scan & Graphic Equalizer, Security Alarm w/Panel Warning Light ($1618). Frt License Plate Bracket (NC). Calif. Emissions (NC). Pearl Coat/Clear Coat Paint ($75). Security Alarm ($150). Conventional Spare Tire (NC). Mark Cross Leather Interior ($365).

HISTORY: Model year production: 174,266. After years of red ink, Chrysler posted a $68 million profit in 1990. Chrysler Corp. Chairman Lee Iacocca's ambitious cost-cutting measures were cited as the reason for the automaker's ledger's black ink.

1991 CHRYSLER

All Chrysler models in 1991 received improved front suspension and steering components. Also, as either standard or optional equipment all Chryslers were offered with anti-lock brakes. The Imperial now was powered by a new 3.8-liter V-6 while the LeBaron GTC was available with the new 2.5-liter High Torque Turbo I four-cylinder engine. The previously offered LeBaron Premium coupe and convertible models gained an LX designation. The formerly available New Yorker Landau sedan was discontinued. While not covered in this catalog, production of the imported Chrysler TC by Maserati, launched in 1989, was ceased in spring 1990 after the limited edition production goal of 7,300 was met. Enough of the luxury convertibles (with detachable hardtop) were left over that these were sold as 1991 models, powered by the previously optional 3.0-liter V-6 rated at 141 horsepower.

1991 Chrysler, LeBaron coupe with optional sunroof (OCW)

LEBARON — SERIES J (coupe and convertible)/SERIES A (sedan) — FOUR/V-6 — The Series J LeBarons, offered in coupe and convertible body styles, were available in three trim levels: base, LX and GTC. The lone offering in the Series A LeBaron lineup was the six-passenger sedan. Four-wheel disc anti-lock braking was offered as an option on all LeBarons in 1991. Coupe and convertible models received a suspension upgrade including realigned steering arms and revalved shock absorbers to improve steering response and increase straight line stability. The LeBaron sedan's standard fare included a touring suspension package with front gas-charged position-sensitive struts and front and rear sway bars. Base LeBarons were powered by the 2.5-liter electronically fuel-injected four-cylinder engine linked to a three-speed automatic transmission. A 3.0-liter V-6 came standard with the LX, GTC and sedan models; optional on the base LeBarons. Chrysler's Ultradrive four-speed automatic was

standard on the LX models and sedan while the GTC used the five-speed manual transmission. A 2.5-liter High Torque Turbo I four-cylinder engine was optional on base and GTC models; the base also could be ordered with a five-speed manual or Ultradrive four-speed automatic transmission. GTC's option transmissions were either the three-speed or Ultradrive automatics. Standard features of the coupe and convertible LeBarons included two-way manual seat adjuster, console storage box, power rack and pinion steering, tinted glass, power windows, airfoil wiper system, electric rear window defroster and concealed quad halogen headlights. The LX models added air conditioning, tilt steering column, speed control, wide bodyside moldings, two-tone bodyside accent stripes and luxury wheel covers. Unique to the LX convertible was a Highland grain leather interior with eight-way power adjustable driver's seat. The GTC models additional standard fare included new bodyside molding graphics, monochromatic finish, color-keyed cast aluminum wheels and leather-wrapped steering wheel and shift knob. The LeBaron sedan featured Chrysler's trademark waterfall grille, a padded landau roof, full-width taillights, woodgrain-finish instrument panel, intermittent wipers, 50/50 reclining cloth seats and premium wheel covers. New-for-1991 was the standard electronic analog speedometer with secondary metric scale, tach, odometer and gauge readings. Optional on the sedan were leather seats, wire wheel covers, power six-way driver's seat and leather-wrapped steering wheel. New options included an overhead console with compass and outside temperature gauge and portable cell phone.

1991 Chrysler, New Yorker Salon sedan (OCW)

NEW YORKER — SERIES C — V-6 — The ranks of the New Yorker series were thinner in 1991 as the previously offered Landau sedan was discontinued, leaving the Salon and Fifth Avenue sedans available to buyers. Standard powertrain in New Yorkers again was the 3.3-liter multiport fuel-injected V-6 paired with the Ultradrive electronic four-speed automatic transmission. Chrysler's new 3.8-liter multi-port fuel-injected V-6 was optional in both sedans. The front suspension and steering of New Yorkers was refined in 1991 to reduce body roll and improve handling. New Yorker's standard equipment included power rack and pinion steering, driver's side airbag, tinted glass, concealed quad halogen headlights, air conditioning, power windows, graphic message center, electromechanical instrument cluster, improved ergonomic climate controls and rear window defroster. Additionally, the upscale Fifth Avenue featured power six-way adjustable front 50/50 bench seats, speed-actuated power door locks, automatic speed control and automatic load-leveling rear suspension. Optional equipment on Salon sedans included remote keyless entry, security alarm, electronic speed control, tilt steering, cell phone, wire wheel covers, leather-wrapped steering wheel, automatic day/night rearview mirror, headlight delay and speed-activated power door locks. Uniquely optional to the Fifth Avenue were an automatic air suspension system, Mark Cross leather seats, eight-way power driver's seat with two-position memory and a sunroof.

IMPERIAL — SERIES Y — V-6 — Known as the corporate "flagship," the six-passenger Imperial sedan received the new 3.8-liter V-6 as its standard engine, replacing the previously used 3.3-liter V-6. The new V-6 was mated to the Ultradrive electronic four-speed automatic transmission. Among Imperial's standard features were road touring suspension with automatic rear load-leveling, power rack and pinion steering, power four-wheel disc brakes with anti-lock, driver's side airbag, padded landau roof, eight-way adjustable driver's seat with two-position memory, tinted glass, speed-actuated power door locks, electronic vehicle information center, automatic headlight delay, tilt steering, intermittent wipers, rear window defroster, electronic speed control, leather-wrapped steering wheel, power windows with one-touch down driver's window, electro-mechanical instrument cluster, graphic message center, waterfall grille and wire wheel covers. Optional equipment included remote keyless entry, security system, cell phone and automatic air suspension.

I.D. DATA: As before, Chrysler's 17-symbol Vehicle Identification Number (VIN) was on the upper left corner of the instrument panel, visible through the windshield. Coding was similar to 1986-90. The model year code changed to 'M' for 1991.

LEBARON (FOUR/V-6)

Model No.	Body/ Style No.	Body Type & Seating	Factory Price	Shipping Weight	Prod. Total
JCH	21	2-dr. Cpe-5P	13160/13854	2853/3000	Note 1
JCP	21	2-dr. LX Cpe-5P	15685	3015	Note 1

Model No.	Body/ Style No.	Body Type & Seating	Factory Price	Shipping Weight	Prod. Total
JCH	21	2-dr. GTC Cpe-5P	15788	2853	Note 1
JCH	27	2-dr. Conv-4P	15705/16399	2991/3133	Note 1
JCP	27	2-dr. LX Conv-4P	18955	3166	Note 1
JCH	27	2-dr. GTC Conv-4P	18176	2991	Note 1
ACP	41	4-dr. Sedan-6P	16699	3064	17,752

Note: Base LeBaron prices and weights to left of slash for four-cylinder engine, to right for V-6.

Note 1: LeBaron two-door production totaled 39,854 (10,771 coupes and 29,074 convertibles) with no further breakout available.

NEW YORKER (V-6)

CCS	41	4-dr. Salon Sed-6P	17899	3348	14,348
YCS	41	4-dr. Fifth Ave. Sed-6P	20875	3452	40,918

IMPERIAL (V-6)

YCP	41	4-dr. Sed-6P	26705	3570	10,155

ENGINE DATA: BASE FOUR (LeB cpe/conv): Inline, overhead cam four-cylinder. Cast iron block; aluminum head. Displacement: 153 cu. in. (2.5 liters). Bore & stroke: 3.44 x 4.09 in. Compression ratio: 8.9:1. Brake horsepower: 100 at 4800 RPM. Torque: 135 lb.-ft. at 2800 RPM. Five main bearings. Hydraulic valve lifters. Throttle-body fuel injection. OPTIONAL TURBOCHARGED FOUR (LeB cpe/conv, LeB GTC): Same as 2.5-liter four above, except turbocharged. Compression ratio: 7.8:1. Brake horsepower: 152 at 4800 RPM. Torque: 210 lb.-ft. at 2400 RPM. BASE V-6 (LeB LX, LeB GTC, LeB sed); OPTIONAL (LeB cpe/conv): Overhead cam V-6. Displacement: 181 cu. in. (3.0 liters). Bore & stroke: 3.59 x 2.99 in. Compression ratio: 8.9:1. Brake horsepower: 141 at 5000 RPM. Torque: 171 lb.-ft. at 2800 RPM. Hydraulic valve lifters. Multi-Port fuel injection. BASE V-6 (N.Y.): Overhead valve V-6. Displacement: 201 cu. in. (3.3 liters). Bore & stroke: 3.66 x 3.19 in. Compression ratio: 8.9:1. Brake horsepower: 147 at 4800 RPM. Torque: 183 lb.-ft. at 3600 RPM. Hydraulic valve lifters. Multi-Port fuel injection. BASE V-6 (Imperial); OPTIONAL (N.Y. Fifth Ave.): Overhead valve V-6. Displacement: 230 cu. in. (3.8 liters). Bore & stroke: 3.78 x 3.42 in. Compression ratio: 9.0:1. Brake horsepower: 150 at 4400 RPM. Torque: 203 lb.-ft. at 3200 RPM. Hydraulic valve lifters. Multi-Port fuel injection.

1991 Chrysler, LeBaron convertible (OCW)

CHASSIS DATA: Wheelbase: (LeB cpe/conv) 100.3 in.; (LeB sed) 103.3 in.; (N.Y. Salon) 104.3 in.; (N.Y. Fifth Ave., Imperial) 109.3 in. Overall length: (LeB cpe/conv) 184.9 in.; (LeB sed) 181.2 in.; (N.Y. Salon) 193.6 in.; (N.Y. Fifth Ave.) 198.6 in.; (Imperial) 203.0 in. Height: (LeB cpe) 51.0 in.; (LeB conv) 52.3 in.; (LeB sed) 53.7 in.; (N.Y. Salon) 53.5 in.; (N.Y. Fifth Ave.) 55.1 in.; (Imperial) 55.3 in. Width: (LeB cpe/conv) 68.5 in.; (LeB sed) 67.3 in.; (N.Y., Imperial) 68.9 in. Front tread: (LeB conv/sed) 57.6 in.; (LeB cpe) 57.5 in.; (N.Y.) 57.6 in.; (Imperial) 57.6 in. Rear tread: (LeB conv/cpe) 57.6 in.; (LeB sed) 57.2 in.; (N.Y.) 57.6 in.; (Imperial) 57.6 in. Standard Tires: (LeB) P195/70R14; (LeB GTC) P205/55R16; (N.Y., Imperial) P195/75R14.

TECHNICAL: Transmission: Five-speed manual standard on LeB GTC. Three-speed automatic standard on LeBaron cpe/conv. Four-speed automatic standard on LeB LX, LeB sed, N.Y., and Imperial. Steering: (all) Power rack and pinion. Front Suspension: (LeB) Iso-Strut w/coil springs, gas-charged hydraulic shock absorbers and stabilizer bar; (N.Y., Imperial) Iso-Strut w/coil springs and stabilizer bar. Rear Suspension: (LeB, N.Y., Imperial) Trailing flex-arm w/track bar, coil springs, gas-charged hydraulic shock absorbers and stabilizer bar. Brakes: Front disc, rear drum (power-assisted) except (Imperial) anti-lock four-wheel disc. Body construction: Unibody. Fuel tank: (LeB cpe/conv) 14 gal.; (LeB sed, N.Y., Imperial) 16 gal.

DRIVETRAIN OPTIONS: Engines: Turbocharged four: LeB cpe/conv ($694); LeB GTC (NC). 3.0-liter V-6: LeB cpe/conv ($694). 3.8-liter V-6: N.Y. Fifth Ave. ($262). Transmission/Differential: H.D. five-speed manual trans.: LeB GTC (NC). Three-speed automatic trans.: LeB GTC ($392). Four-speed automatic trans.: LeB cpe/conv ($93). LeB GTC

w/V-6 ($640). Brakes: Hi-Perf four-wheel disc: LeB cpe/conv ($183). Anti-lock four-wheel disc: LeB sed ($899); N.Y. ($899). Suspension: Rear automatic load-leveling: N.Y. Salon ($225). Elect. Controlled Air Susp.: N.Y. Fifth Ave. ($650); Imperial ($650).

LEBARON COUPE/CONVERTIBLE CONVENIENCE/APPEARANCE OPTIONS: (AAM) Popular Equip. Discount Pkg.; Incl. Air Cond, Floor Mats, Elect. Spd Control, Tilt Strg Column: cpe ($580); conv ($1148). (AAF) Luxury Equip. Discount Pkg. (N/A conv); Incl. all in Popular Equipment Pkg. Plus Illum. Entry, Illum. Vanity Mirrors, Overhead Console, Power Dr Locks, Dual Pwr. Heated Remote Control Mirrors, Pwr. 6-Way Driver's Seat on CH21, 8-Way on CP21, Leather-Wrapped Strg Wheel, Bodyside Stripe ($1784). (AJK) Deluxe Convenience Pkg.: Incl. Elect. Spd Control, Tilt Strg Col ($372). (ADA) Light Pkg.: Incl. Illum. Entry, Illum. Vanity Mirrors ($196). (AJW) Power Convenience Pkg.: Incl. Pwr. Dr Locks, Dual Pwr. Heated Remote Control Mirrors, CH21 ($338). (AGT) GTC Performance Pkg.: Incl. Turbo I 2.5-liter Four-Cylinder Engine, H.D. 5-spd Manual Trans., Enthusiast Sport Bucket Seats, Hi-Perf 4-wheel Disc Brakes, Turbo Boost Gauge, Perf Handling Suspension, P205/55R16 Tires and Cast Alum Wheels: cpe ($1052); conv ($1823). (ADS) Sport Coupe Pkg. (N/A conv): Body Color Grille, Fascias and Bodyside Moldings; Dark Quarter Windows, Lace Wheel Covers (NC). Air cond ($831). Frt License Plate Bracket (NC). Overhead Console, cpe only ($265). Calif. Emissions ($102). Elect. Instrument Cluster ($305). Elect. Vehicle Info Center ($690). Extra Cost Paint ($77). Vinyl Seat Trim, conv only ($102). Pwr. 6-way Driver's Seat ($296). Pwr. 8-way Driver's Seat ($367). Leather Pwr. 8-way Driver's Seat: cpe ($1006); conv ($1223). Leather, Pwr. Enthusiast and 12-Way Driver's Seat ($639). Compact Disc Audio System ($449). AM Stereo/FM Stereo Cass w/4 Spkrs ($155). AM Stereo/FM Stereo incl. 6 Infinity Spkrs & Pwr. Antenna ($569). AM Stereo/FM Stereo Cass, Seek & Scan, 5-Band Graphic Equalizer, Pwr. Antenna & 6 Infinity Spkrs ($785). Security Alarm ($150). Removable Sunroof, cpe only ($230-$405). Trip Computer ($93). (AY3) Handling Pkg.: Incl. 15-in. Cast Alum Wheels, Sport Handling Suspension, P205/60R16 Tires ($532-$647). P195/70R14 WSW ($74). P205/60R15 WSW, CP21 ($78). Cast Alum 14-in. Wheels ($328).

LEBARON SEDAN CONVENIENCE/APPEARANCE OPTIONS: (AFF) Luxury Equip. Discount Pkg.: Incl. Overhead Console w/F&R Reading Lamps/Outside Temp Readout/Compass/Storage for Garage Opener, Dual Illum. Visor Vanity Mirrors, Pwr Dr Locks/Mirrors/Windows/Seat, Leather-wrapped Stng Whl and Wire Whl Covers ($878). (AJP) Pwr Equip. Discount Pkg.: Incl. Pwr Dr Locks/Mirrors/Windows (NC). (AFH) Overhead Convenience Pkg.: Incl. Overhead Console w/F&R Reading Lamps/Outside Temp Readout/Compass/Storage for Garage Opener and Dual Illum. Visor Vanity Mirrors ($383). (ADM) Elect. Display Pkg.: Incl. Elect. Instrument Panel Cluster w/125 mph Speedometer/Trip Computer/Graph Display ($317). Frt License Plate Bracket (NC). Pwr Door Locks w/Ignition Interlock ($250). Calif. Emissions ($102). Extra Cost Paint ($77). Infinity I AM/FM Stereo Radio w/Cass, Seek & Scan, Digital Clock & 4 Spkrs ($306). Infinity II AM/FM Stereo Radio w/Cass, Graphic Equal., Seek & Scan, Digital Clock & 4 Spkrs ($520). Pwr Driver's Seat ($296). Leather-Wrapped Strg Whl ($60). Conventional 14-in. Spare Tire ($95). Wire Whl Covers ($228). Leather Seats ($668).

1991 Chrysler, LeBaron sedan with optional wire wheel covers (OCW)

NEW YORKER SALON CONVENIENCE/APPEARANCE OPTIONS: (AAB) Popular Equip. Discount Pkg.: Incl. AJK Dlx Convenience Pkg., Pwr. Dr Locks, Flr Mats, Elect. Spd Control, Tilt Strg Col, Undercoating ($393). (AFF) Luxury Equip. Discount Pkg.: Incl. AAB Popular Equip., Auto. Headlamp Delay Syst., Interior Illumination, Day/Night Rr View Auto Adjustment Mirror, Leather-Wrapped Strg Wheel, Pwr. 6-Way Driver & Pass Seats, Bodyside Mldg., Cell Phone Prewire Wire Wheel Covers ($1739). (AJK) Deluxe Convenience Pkg.: Incl. AAB Popular Equip., AFF Luxury Equip., Elect. Spd Control, Tilt Strg Col. ($372). (AJB) Security Pkg.: Incl. AAB Popular Equip., Security Alarm, Remote Keyless Entry, Remote Dr Lock Activation, Decklid Release ($277-$473). (AJW) Pwr Accessories Pkg.: Incl. AFF Luxury Equip., Decklid Pulldown, Pwr Antenna ($159). Frt License Plate Bracket (NC). Pwr. Door Locks ($331). Calif. Emissions ($102). Pearl Coat/Clear Coat Paint ($77). AM/FM Stereo Radio w/Cass, 4 Spkrs ($155). AM/FM Stereo Radio w/Cass, Seek & Scan, Graphic Equal., 4 Spkrs ($428). Infinity Syst.,

w/10 Spkrs & Trunk-Mounted Amp ($812). Leather Seat Trim ($590). Pwr. 6-Way Driver's Seat ($296). Pwr. 8-Way Driver & Pass Seat w/Memory & Pwr Recliners, Incl. 2 Position Memory ($396). Pwr. Sunroof ($792). Conventional Spare Tire ($85). Wire Wheel Covers ($228). Cast Alum Wheels, AFF req'd ($50).

1991 Chrysler, New Yorker Fifth Avenue sedan (OCW)

NEW YORKER FIFTH AVENUE CONVENIENCE/APPEARANCE OPTIONS: (AFF) Luxury Equip. Discount Pkg.: Incl. Interior Illumination, Body-color Bodyside Mldg, Illum Entry, Flr Mats, Illum. Visor Vanity Mirrors, Dual O/S Heated Mirrors w/2-Position Memory, Driver & Pass 8-Way Seats w/Recliner & 2-Position Memory, Leather-Wrapped Strg Whl, Cell Phone Prewire, Undercoating, Wire Wheel Covers ($1512). (AFC) Mark Cross Edition: Incl. AFF Luxury Equip., Mark Cross Leather Interior, 50/50 Frt Bench Seat ($2089). (AJB) Security Pkg.: Incl. Alarm w/Panel Warning Light, Remote Keyless Entry, Remote Dr Lock Activation, Decklid Release ($277-$473). (AJW) Pwr Accessories Pkg.: Incl. AFF Luxury Equip., Pwr Antenna, Pwr Decklid Pulldown ($159). (ADM) Elect. Features Pkg.: Incl. Overhead Console w/Elect. Vehicle Info Center, Elect. Instrument Cluster, Rr View Mirror w/Auto Day/Night Adjustment ($1241). Auto Temp Control Air Cond ($152). Frt License Plate Bracket (NC). Calif. Emissions ($102). Pearl Coat/Clear Coat Paint ($77). AM/FM Stereo Radio w/Cass, Seek & Scan, Graphic Equal., 4 Spkrs ($428). Infinity Syst. w/10 Spkrs & Trunk-Mounted Amp ($812). Pwr Sunroof ($792). Conventional Spare Tire ($85). Cast Aluminum Wheels, AAF req'd ($50). Wire Wheel Covers ($228).

IMPERIAL CONVENIENCE/APPEARANCE OPTIONS: (AFC) Mark Cross Leather Int. w/50/50 Bench Seat ($649). (AJB) Security Pkg.: Incl. Alarm w/Panel Warning Light, Remote Keyless Entry, Remote Dr Lock Activation, Decklid Release ($277). (ADN) Elect. Features Pkg.: Incl. Overhead Console w/Elect. Vehicle Info Center, Elect. Instrument Cluster, Rr View Mirror w/Auto Day/Night Adjustment, Infinity Syst. w/10 Spkrs & Trunk-Mounted Amp, Cell Phone Prewire ($1689). Frt License Plate Bracket (NC). Calif. Emissions ($102). Pearl Coat/Clear Coat Paint ($77). Conventional Spare Tire ($85).

1991 Chrysler, Imperial sedan (OCW)

HISTORY: Model year production: 123,018. Calendar year sales: 126,383 (including 1,077 imported TC by Maserati two-seaters). By 1991, the LeBaron convertible was, at that time, the world's best-selling ragtop as well as the only domestic ragtop designed and built from the ground up as a convertible.

1992 CHRYSLER

The LeBaron sedan lineup was expanded in 1992 with the addition of LX and Landau trim levels joining the existing base sedan. The LeBaron convertible was offered with an optional Sport Appearance Package. Both the 3.0-liter V-6 and 3.8-liter V-6 powering Chryslers received sequential fuel injection, replacing the multi-port setup previously employed.

LEBARON — SERIES J (coupe and convertible)/SERIES A (sedan) — FOUR/V-6 — Adding balance to the LeBaron series, buyers now had three choices each of coupe, convertible and sedan. Returning in coupe and convertible form were the base, LX and GTC trim levels. Joining the previously available base sedan were LX and Landau trim levels. Also new-for-1992 was an optional Sport Appearance Package available only on the LeBaron convertible. Base LeBarons as well as the new Landau sedan were powered by the electronically fuel-injected 2.5-liter four-cylinder engine mated to a three-speed automatic transmission. All LX and GTC models used the 3.0-liter V-6, now with sequential fuel injection, which was an option engine for base LeBarons. The LX models employed a four-speed automatic transmission as standard, while the GTC models used a five-speed manual transmission. The base coupe/convertible and GTC LeBarons could be ordered with the optional Turbo I 2.5-liter turbocharged four-cylinder engine. Transmission options were four-speed automatic for all base models and five-speed manual for coupe/convertible, heavy-duty five-speed manual, three- and four-speed automatics for GTC and four-speed automatic for the Landau sedan. LeBaron's new features for 1992 included a clutch/ignition interlock system for models with manual transmissions, and a park/ignition interlock system for models equipped with automatics. Coupes and convertibles featured a new cast aluminum 14-inch wheel while 16-inch aluminum wheels and tires were optional. LeBarons were offered in several new exterior colors including Teal and Bright Silver Quartz on the sedan. Sedans also now were equipped with illuminated entry with illuminated door lock.

1992 Chrysler, LeBaron convertible (OCW)

NEW YORKER — SERIES C — V-6 — The New Yorker's overall appearance was "freshened" for 1992 with front and rear treatments and exterior ornamentation updated, with the most apparent change being the reshaping of the decklid. The lineup again consisted of Salon and Fifth Avenue sedans. Powertrain was again the 3.3-liter multi-port fuel-injected V-6 paired with the Ultradrive electronic four-speed automatic transmission. Again the 3.8-liter V-6 was optional on the Fifth Avenue. New features for New Yorker included an overhead lamp module with storage pocket and several new interior and exterior colors. The Salon offered a vinyl landau roof cap in four colors. The New Yorker's option list added an electrochromatic rearview mirror with headlamp-automatic with time delay feature and floor console.

1992 Chrysler, New Yorker Salon sedan (OCW)

IMPERIAL — SERIES Y — V-6 — The traditionally styled Imperial returned with minor changes including both two new exterior and interior colors offered. The 3.8-liter V-6 powering the Imperial was now sequentially fuel injected. This V-6 again was paired with the Ultradrive electronic four-speed automatic transmission. Two additional options offered in 1992 were an electrochromatic rearview mirror with headlamp-automatic with time delay feature and floor console.

I.D. DATA: As before, Chrysler's 17-symbol Vehicle Identification Number (VIN) was on the upper left corner of the instrument panel, visible through the windshield. Coding was similar to 1986-91. The model year code changed to 'N' for 1992.

LEBARON (FOUR/V-6)

Model No.	Body/ Style No.	Body Type & Seating	Factory Price	Shipping Weight	Prod. Total
JCH	21	2-dr. Cpe-5P	13488/14182	2863/2882	Note 1
JCP	21	2-dr. LX Cpe-5P	16094	3019	Note 1

Model No.	Body/ Style No.	Body Type & Seating	Factory Price	Shipping Weight	Prod. Total
JCH	21	2-dr. GTC Cpe-5P	16164	2863	Note 1
JCH	27	2-dr. Conv-4P	16884/17578	3010/3028	Note 1
JCP	27	2-dr. LX Conv-4P	20280	3184	Note 1
JCH	27	2-dr. GTC Conv-4P	18985	3010	Note 1
APP	41	4-dr. Sedan-6P	13998/14962	2882/2951	Note 2
APX	41	4-dr. LX Sed-6P	15287	2970	Note 2
ACP	41	4-dr. Landau Sed-6P	15710/16404	2984/3055	Note 2

Note: Where applicable, LeBaron prices and weights to left of slash for four-cylinder engine, to right for V-6.

Note 1: LeBaron two-door production totaled 45,940 (5,656 coupes and 40,284 convertibles) with no further breakout available.

Note 2: LeBaron four-door production totaled 33,862 with no further breakout available.

NEW YORKER (V-6)

CCS	41	4-dr. Salon Sed-6P	18849	3273	17,237
YCS	41	4-dr. Fifth Ave. Sed-6P	22074	3365	34,363

IMPERIAL (V-6)

YCP	41	4-dr. Sed-6P	28453	3519	7,069

ENGINE DATA: BASE FOUR (LeB, LeB Landau): Inline, overhead cam four-cylinder. Cast iron block; aluminum head. Displacement: 153 cu. in. (2.5 liters). Bore & stroke: 3.44 x 4.09 in. Compression ratio: 8.9:1. Brake horsepower: 100 at 4800 RPM. Torque: 135 lb.-ft. at 2800 RPM. Five main bearings. Hydraulic valve lifters. Throttle-body fuel injection. OPTIONAL TURBOCHARGED FOUR (LeB cpe/conv, LeB GTC): Same as 2.5-liter four above, except turbocharged. Compression ratio: 7.8:1. Brake horsepower: 152 at 4800 RPM. Torque: 211 lb.-ft. at 2800 RPM. BASE V-6 (LeB LX, LeB GTC); OPTIONAL (LeB, LeB Landau): Overhead cam V-6. Displacement: 181 cu. in. (3.0 liters). Bore & stroke: 3.59 x 2.99 in. Compression ratio: 8.9:1. Brake horsepower: 141 at 5000 RPM. Torque: 171 lb.-ft. at 2800 RPM. Hydraulic valve lifters. Sequential fuel injection. BASE V-6 (N.Y.): Overhead valve V-6. Displacement: 201 cu. in. (3.3 liters). Bore & stroke: 3.66 x 3.19 in. Compression ratio: 8.9:1. Brake horsepower: 147 at 4800 RPM. Torque: 183 lb.-ft. at 3600 RPM. Hydraulic valve lifters. Multi-Port fuel injection. BASE V-6 (Imperial); OPTIONAL (N.Y. Fifth Ave.): Overhead valve V-6. Displacement: 230 cu. in. (3.8 liters). Bore & stroke: 3.78 x 3.42 in. Compression ratio: 9.0:1. Brake horsepower: 150 at 4400 RPM. Torque: 203 lb.-ft. at 3200 RPM. Hydraulic valve lifters. Multi-Port fuel injection.

CHASSIS DATA: Wheelbase: (LeB cpe/conv) 100.5 in.; (LeB sed) 103.5 in.; (N.Y. Salon) 104.5 in.; (N.Y. Fifth Ave., Imperial) 109.5 in. Overall length: (LeB cpe/conv) 184.8 in.; (LeB sed) 182.7 in.; (N.Y. Salon) 193.6 in.; (N.Y. Fifth Ave.) 198.6 in.; (Imperial) 203.0 in. Height: (LeB cpe) 53.3 in.; (LeB conv) 52.4 in.; (LeB sed) 53.7 in.; (N.Y. Salon) 53.6 in.; (N.Y. Fifth Ave.) 55.1 in.; (Imperial) 55.3 in. Width: (LeB cpe/conv) 69.2 in.; (LeB sed) 68.1 in.; (N.Y., Imperial) 68.9 in. Front tread: (LeB conv/sed) 57.6 in.; (LeB cpe) 57.5 in.; (N.Y.) 57.6 in.; (Imperial) 57.6 in. Rear tread: (LeB conv/cpe) 57.6 in.; (LeB sed) 57.2 in.; (N.Y.) 57.6 in.; (Imperial) 57.6 in. Standard Tires: (LeB) P195/70R14; (LeB GTC) P205/55R16; (N.Y., Imperial) P195/75R14.

1992 Chrysler, LeBaron GTC coupe with optional Performance Handling Suspension package (OCW)

TECHNICAL: Transmission: Five-speed manual standard on LeB GTC. Three-speed automatic standard on LeB and LeB Landau. Four-speed automatic standard on LeB LX, N.Y., and Imperial. Steering: (all) Power rack and pinion. Front Suspension: (LeB) Iso-Strut w/coil springs, gas-

charged hydraulic shock absorbers and stabilizer bar; (N.Y., Imperial) Iso-Strut w/coil springs and stabilizer bar. Rear Suspension: (LeB, N.Y., Imperial) Trailing flex-arm w/track bar, coil springs, gas-charged hydraulic shock absorbers and stabilizer bar. Brakes: Front disc, rear drum (power-assisted) except (Imperial) anti-lock four-wheel disc. Body construction: Unibody. Fuel tank: (LeB cpe/conv) 14 gal.; (LeB sed, N.Y., Imperial) 16 gal.

DRIVETRAIN OPTIONS: Engines: Turbocharged four: LeB cpe/conv ($694); LeB GTC (NC). 3.0-liter V-6: LeB cpe/conv ($694). 3.8-liter V-6: N.Y. Fifth Ave. ($262). Transmission/Differential: H.D. five-speed manual trans.: LeB GTC (NC). Three-speed automatic trans.: LeB GTC ($392). Four-speed automatic trans.: LeB cpe/conv ($93). LeB GTC w/V-6 ($640). Brakes: Hi-Perf four-wheel disc: LeB GTC ($183). Anti-lock four-wheel disc: LeB sed ($899); N.Y. ($899). Suspension: Rear automatic load-leveling: N.Y. Salon ($225). Elect. Controlled Air Susp.: N.Y. Fifth Ave. ($650); Imperial ($650).

1992 Chrysler, LeBaron LX sedan (OCW)

LEBARON COUPE/CONVERTIBLE CONVENIENCE/APPEARANCE OPTIONS: LeBaron: Pkg. 22A: stnd equip. (NC). Pkg. 25A: 22A plus 3.0L V-6 and 5-spd man. trans. ($137). Pkg. 22B: 22A plus air cond. ($831). Pkg. 22C (cpe only): 22B plus floor mats, dlx. convenience grp., and remote decklid release ($500). Pkg. 22C (conv. only): 22B plus floor mats, dlx. convenience grp., remote decklid release and bodyside stripes ($1124). Pkg. 24B: Turbo I 2.5L four-cylinder engine ($1525). Pkg. 24C (cpe only): 22C plus Turbo I engine ($1194). Pkg. 24C (conv only): 22C plus Turbo I engine ($1818). Pkg. 25B (conv only): 25A plus air cond ($968). Pkg. 25C (cpe only): 22C plus 3.0L V-6 and 5-spd man. trans. ($637). Pkg. 25C (conv only): 22C plus 3.0L V-6 and 5-spd man. trans. ($1301). Pkg. 26B (conv only): 3.0L V-6 and 4-spd auto. trans. and air cond ($1658). Pkg. 26C (cpe only): 22C plus 3.0L V-6 and 4-spd auto. trans. ($1288). Pkg. 26C (conv only): 22C plus 3.0L V-6 and 4-spd auto. trans. ($1951). Pkg. 22D (cpe only): 22A plus air cond, floor mats, dlx convenience grp., remote decklid release, pwr convenience group, bodyside stripe, light grp., overhead console, six-way pwr driver's seat and leather-wrapped stng whl ($1714). Pkg. 24D (cpe only): 22D plus Turbo I four-cylinder engine ($2408). Pkg. 25D (cpe only): 22D plus 3.0L V-6 and 5-spd man. trans. ($1851). Pkg. 26D (cpe only): 22D plus 3.0L V-6 and 4-spd auto. trans. ($2541). LeBaron LX: Pkg. 26W: stnd equip. (NC). Pkg. 26D (cpe only): 26W plus floor mats, light grp., overhead console, 8-way pwr driver's seat and remote decklid release ($925). LeBaron GTC: Pkg. 25G: stnd equip. (NC). Pkg. 26G (cpe only): 25G plus 4-spd auto. trans. ($690). Pkg.23H: 25G plus GTC Perf Grp. Pkg. incl. Turbo I engine, H.D. 5-spd man. trans., enthusiast bucket seats w/12-way pwr driver's seat, 4-whl disc brakes w/anti-lock, turbo boost gauge, Perf Handling Susp., P205/55R16 tires, 16-in. cast alum. whls: cpe ($1877); conv ($2614). Pkg. 24H: 23H plus 3-spd auto. trans.: cpe ($2269); conv ($3006). Other: (AJW) Power Convenience Pkg.: Incl. Pwr. Dr Locks, Dual Pwr. Heated Remote Control Mirrors ($338). Pwr. 6-way Driver's Seat ($306). Pwr. 8-way Driver's Seat ($367). (ADS) Sport Grp. (N/A LX or GTC): incl. body color grille and lace wheel covers: cpe ($50); conv ($100). Security Alarm ($149). 4-whl disc brakes w/anti-lock ($899). (AJK) Deluxe Convenience Pkg.: Incl. Elect. Spd Control, Tilt Strg Col ($372). Overhead console, GTC cpe ($265). Digital Instrument Cluster, LX ($305). Calif. Emissions ($102). Extra cost paint, base & LX only ($97). Compact Disc Player ($449). AM/FM Stereo Radio w/Cass & Clock, base ($165). AM/FM Stereo Radio w/Cass & Seek/Scan ($299). AM/FM Stereo Radio w/Cass, Seek/Scan, Graphic Equalizer, Clock and Infinity Spkrs ($899). Leather seat trim ($1006). Leather seat trim w/pwr driver's seat ($639). Vinyl trim, conv ($103). Trip computer ($93). Vehicle Info Center, N/A base: cpe ($690); conv ($678). 14-in. cast alum. whls. ($328). (AY3) Handling Pkg.: Incl. 15-in. Cast Alum Wheels, Sport Handling Suspension, P205/60R15 Tires ($532). (AY4) Handling Pkg.: Incl. 16-in. Cast Alum Wheels, Sport Handling Suspension, P205/55R16 Tires ($188). P195/70R14 WSW ($74). P205/60R15 WSW ($78).

LEBARON SEDAN CONVENIENCE/APPEARANCE OPTIONS: LeBaron: Pkg. 22P: stnd equip. (NC). Pkg. 22U: 22P plus air cond, pwr mirrors/dr locks/windows, P195/70R14 tires ($700). Pkg. 26U: 22U plus 3.0L V-6 ($1394). Pkg. 28U: 22U plus 3.0L V-6 and 4-spd auto.

trans. ($1327). LX: Pkg. 28X: stnd equip. (NC). Pkg. 28U: 28X plus air cond, pwr mirrors/dr locks/windows, AM/FM stereo radio w/cass & clock ($792). Landau: Pkg. 22K: stnd equip. (NC). Pkg. 22K: 22K plus 3.0L V-6 and 4-spd auto. trans. ($827). Pkg. 22L: 22K plus Int. Convenience Grp., leather-wrapped stng whl, Illum. Grp., Pwr Equip. Grp. and wire wheel covers ($756). 28L: 22L plus 3.0L V-6 and 4-spd auto. trans. ($1583). Other: (AJP) Pwr Equip. Grp.: Incl. Pwr Dr Locks/Mirrors/Windows (NC). Pwr driver's seat ($306). 4-whl disc brakes w/antilock ($899). (ADM) Elect. Display Grp.: Incl. Elect. Instrument Panel Cluster and Trip Computer ($317). Calif. emissions ($103). (AFH) Int. Convenience Grp.: Incl. Overhead Console w/F&R Reading Lamps/Outside Temp Readout/Compass/Storage for Garage Opener and Illum. Grp. ($400). (AJN) Int. Illum. Grp.: incl. Illum. entry and Dual Illum. Visor Vanity Mirrors ($195). Extra Cost Paint ($97). AM/FM Stereo Radio w/Cass & Clock, base only ($165). AM/FM Stereo Radio w/Cass, Seek/Scan, Graphic Equal., Clock, N/A base ($500-$530). AM/FM Stereo Radio w/Cass, Seek/Scan, Clock & 4 Spkrs ($285-$440). Leather seat trim w/leather-wrapped stng whl, Landau only ($668). Cloth 50/50 frnt seat ($109). Wire whl covers, Landau only ($240). Alum. whls, base only ($255). Conventional spare tire ($95).

1992 Chrysler, New Yorker Fifth Avenue sedan with optional cast aluminum wheels (OCW)

NEW YORKER CONVENIENCE/APPEARANCE OPTIONS: Salon: Pkg. 26A: stnd equip. (NC). Pkg. 26C: 26A plus floor mounted console, Dlx Convenience Grp., floor mats, pwr dr locks, AM/FM stereo radio w/cass & clock, bodyside stripe, P195/75R14 tires, undercoating ($730). Pkg. 26D: 26C plus headlamps w/timed delay, auto day/night mirror, pwr 6-way driver and pass. seats, cell phone prewire, leather-wrapped stng whl, wire whl covers ($2037). Other: (AJW) Pwr Accessories Grp.: incl. decklid pulldown, pwr antenna ($169). Pwr dr locks ($331). Pwr. 6-way driver's seat ($306). Pwr. 8-way driver & pass. seat w/memory ($396). Pwr. sunroof ($792). 4-whl disc anti-lock brakes ($899). (AJK) Deluxe Convenience Grp.: incl. Elect. Spd Control, Tilt Strg Col. ($372). Calif. emissions ($102). Extra cost paint ($97). AM/FM Stereo Radio w/cass & clock ($165). AM/FM Stereo Radio w/Cass, Seek & Scan, Graphic Equal., clock ($283). AM/FM Stereo Radio w/Cass, Seek & Scan, Graphic Equal., w/10 Spkrs & Trunk-Mounted Amp ($668). Vinyl landau roof ($325). 50/50 leather trim ($590). Wire whl covers ($228). Cast alum. whls ($50). P195/75R14 tires ($73). Conventional spare tire ($85). Fifth Ave.: Pkg. 26A: stnd equip. (NC). Pkg. 28A: 26A plus 3.8L V-6 ($2190). Pkg. 26B: 26A plus floor mounted console, light grp., auto. day/night mirror, pwr 8-way driver & pass seats w/memory, floor mats, AM/FM stereo radio w/cass & clock, leather-wrapped stng whl, wire whl covers, cell phone prewire, undercoating ($1294). Pkg. 28B: 26B plus 3.8L V-6 ($1556). Pkg. 26C: 26B plus Mark Cross Edition leather ($1871). Pkg. 28C: 26B plus Mark Cross Edition leather and 3.8L V-6 ($2183). Other: (AJW) Pwr Accessories Grp.: incl. pwr antenna and pwr decklid pulldown ($169). Pwr sunroof ($792). Auto. temp control air cond ($152). 4-whl disc anti-lock brakes ($899). (ADM) Electric Grp.: incl. overhead console w/Elect. Vehicle Info Center, Elect. Instrument Cluster ($1159). Calif. Emissions ($102). Extra cost paint ($97). AM/FM Stereo Radio w/Cass & Graphic Equal. ($438). Infinity Syst. w/10 Spkrs & Trunk-Mounted Amp ($395). (GWA) Security Grp.: incl. Alarm w/Panel Warning Light, Remote Keyless Entry, Remote Dr Lock & decklid activation ($292). Wire whl covers ($240). Cast alum. whls ($50-$278). Conventional spare tire ($85).

1992 Chrysler, Imperial sedan (OCW)

IMPERIAL CONVENIENCE/APPEARANCE OPTIONS: Pkg. 28A: stnd equip. (NC). Pkg. 28D: 28A plus Mark Cross Edition leather and 8-way pwr driver & pass seat w/memory ($1025). Other: 8-way pwr driver &

pass seat w/memory ($376). (ADN) Electronic Grp.: incl. Overhead Console w/Elect. Vehicle Info Center, Elect. Instrument Cluster, Auto Day/Night Adjustment, Infinity Syst. w/10 Spkrs & Trunk-Mounted Amp, cell phone prewire, auto headlamp w/time delay ($1011). Calif. Emissions ($102). Extra cost paint ($97). Conventional spare tire ($85).

HISTORY: Model year production: 138,471. Calendar year sales: 148,010 (including 9,971 1993 Concorde sedans). Robert J. Eaton was hired by Chrysler in March 1992 to take over the chairman/CEO slot vacated by Lee Iacocca, who retired on December 31, 1992. Eaton was the president of General Motors (Europe) AG. Chrysler also announced in late-1992 that it would relocate its headquarters from Highland Park to Auburn Hills, Michigan.

1993 CHRYSLER

It was a year of sweeping change at Chrysler, with a new CEO, Robert Eaton, at the helm (replacing retired Lee "The Legend" Iacocca), and almost a completely new lineup on deck or being readied for launch in early-1993 as 1994 models (see 1994 listings). Ending production during 1993 were the "flagship" Imperial, C/Y-platform New Yorker and LeBaron coupe, while the Concorde sedan was launched as an example of both Chrysler's revolutionary new "team approach" to building and marketing automobiles and the "cab forward" design. The LeBaron sedan lineup was again revised. Base and LX trim level sedans were discontinued and an LE level joined the existing Landau sedan.

1993 Chrysler, LeBaron LE sedan (OCW)

LEBARON — SERIES J (coupe and convertible)/SERIES A (sedan) — FOUR/V-6 — LeBaron's days were numbered with the onslaught of cab-forward design Chrysler products coming on-line. The LeBaron lineup was tweaked, with the previously offered base and LX sedans discontinued. An LE sedan joined the existing Landau sedan that now used the 3.0-liter V-6 and four-speed automatic transmission as its standard powertrain. The LE was powered by the 2.5-liter four-cylinder engine paired with a three-speed automatic. This was also the final year of production for the LeBaron coupe body style. The grille and headlights of the LeBaron coupe and convertible were updated, otherwise LeBarons were carried over from the previous year mostly unchanged with the same standard powertrain combinations. The previously optional Turbo I 2.5-liter turbocharged four-cylinder engine was no longer available.

1993 Chrysler, New Yorker Salon sedan (OCW)

NEW YORKER — SERIES C — V-6 — Production of the Fifth Avenue ended in May 1993 while the Salon's production continued through to the end of the model year. Both were essentially carryover models, with one notable exception being the updating of the Salon's interior trim. Powertrain combinations were unchanged from the year previous. An all-new "cab forward" New Yorker LH was launched in April 1993 as a 1994 model to carry on the exalted New Yorker name.

IMPERIAL — SERIES Y — V-6 — Production of the Imperial also was discontinued in May 1993, so the luxury sedan was a carryover, with powertrain offered the previous year intact. One notable upgrade was a

sound system upgrade to include a Chrysler/Infinity Spatial Imaging system. Unlike the New Yorker, no cab forward Imperial replacement model was announced. Fewer than 6,300 Imperials were sold in the car's final, shortened model year, an ending somehow less-than-fitting for Chrysler's flagship.

CONCORDE — SERIES H — V-6 — The pioneering cab-forward-design Concorde sedan was built on the all-new LH platform, Chrysler's first totally new platform in 10 years. Concorde's sleek, aerodynamic styling was startlingly new. Power was supplied by the sequentially fuel-injected 3.3-liter V-6 paired with an electronically controlled four-speed automatic transmission with overdrive. Optional was the all-new 24-valve 3.5-liter V-6 rated at 214 horsepower. Concorde's standard equipment included dual airbags, four-wheel disc brakes with anti-lock, air conditioning, electric rear window defroster, intermittent wipers with high volume vehicle speed sensitive fluidic washers, solar control windshield glass and stainless steel exhaust. Options included low-speed traction control, fold-away integrated child's seat and automatic temperature control. Concorde also featured fully independent suspension with two tuning options: road and touring. Exterior colors offered were: Black Cherry, Radiant Red, Metallic Red, Light Driftwood, Char-Gold, Emerald Green, Teal, Sapphire Blue, Black and Bright White. Interior colors offered were: Dark Gray, Agate/Medium Quartz, Agate/Medium Driftwood and Agate/Slate Blue. The Concorde's wheelbase was 113 inches with an overall length of 202.8 inches.

I.D. DATA: As before, Chrysler's 17-symbol Vehicle Identification Number (VIN) was on the upper left corner of the instrument panel, visible through the windshield. Coding was similar to 1986-92. The model year code changed to 'P' for 1993.

1993 Chrysler, LeBaron Landau sedan (OCW)

LEBARON (FOUR/V-6)

Model No.	Body/ Style No.	Body Type & Seating	Factory Price	Shipping Weight	Prod. Total
JCH	21	2-dr. Cpe-5P	13999/14693	2863/2882	Note 1
JCP	21	2-dr. LX Cpe-5P	16676	3019	Note 1
JCH	21	2-dr. GTC Cpe-5P	16676	3019	Note 1
JCH	27	2-dr. Conv-4P	17399/17578	3010/3028	Note 1
JCP	27	2-dr. LX Conv-4P	21165	3184	Note 1
JCH	27	2-dr. GTC Conv-4P	20380	3010	Note 1
ACM	41	4-dr. LE Sed-6P	14497/15191	2854/2937	Note 2
ACP	41	4-dr. Landau Sed-6P	17119	3014	Note 2

Note: Where applicable, LeBaron prices and weights to left of slash for four-cylinder engine, to right for V-6.

Note 1: LeBaron two-door production totaled 32,783 (6,007 coupes and 26,776 convertibles) with no further breakout available.

Note 2: LeBaron four-door production totaled 26,474 with no further breakout available.

NEW YORKER (V-6)

CCS	41	4-dr. Salon Sed-6P	18705	3231	20,852
YCS	41	4-dr. Fifth Ave. Sed-6P	21948	3311	27,351

IMPERIAL (V-6)

YCP	41	4-dr. Sed-6P	29381	3469	6,233

CONCORDE (V-6)

HLP	41	4-dr. Sed-6P	18341	3327	48,326

ENGINE DATA: BASE FOUR (LeB, LeB LE): Inline, overhead cam four-cylinder. Cast iron block; aluminum head. Displacement: 153 cu. in. (2.5 liters). Bore & stroke: 3.44 x 4.09 in. Compression ratio: 8.9:1.

Brake horsepower: 100 at 4800 RPM. Torque: 135 lb.-ft. at 2800 RPM. Five main bearings. Hydraulic valve lifters. Throttle-body fuel injection. **BASE V-6 (LeB LX, LeB GTC, LeB Landau); OPTIONAL (LeB, LeB LE):** Overhead cam V-6. Displacement: 181 cu. in. (3.0 liters). Bore & stroke: 3.59 x 2.99 in. Compression ratio: 8.9:1. Brake horsepower: 141 at 5200 RPM. Torque: 171 lb.-ft. at 2800 RPM. Hydraulic valve lifters. Sequential fuel injection. **BASE V-6 (N.Y., Concorde):** Overhead valve V-6. Displacement: 201 cu. in. (3.3 liters). Bore & stroke: 3.66 x 3.19 in. Compression ratio: 8.9:1. Brake horsepower: (N.Y.) 147 at 4800 RPM; (Concorde) 153 at 5300 RPM. Torque: (N.Y.) 183 lb.-ft. at 3600 RPM; (Concorde) 177 lb.-ft. at 2800 RPM. Sequential fuel injection. **BASE V-6 (Imperial); OPTIONAL (N.Y. Fifth Ave.):** Overhead valve V-6. Displacement: 230 cu. in. (3.8 liters). Bore & stroke: 3.78 x 3.42 in. Compression ratio: 9.0:1. Brake horsepower: 150 at 4400 RPM. Torque: 203 lb.-ft. at 3200 RPM. Hydraulic valve lifters. Multi-Port fuel injection. **OPTIONAL V-6 (Concorde):** Overhead cam V-6. Displacement: 214 cu. in. (3.5 liters). Bore & stroke: 3.78 x 3.19 in. Compression ratio: 10.4:1. Brake horsepower: 214 at 5800 RPM. Torque: 221 lb.-ft. at 2800 RPM. Sequential fuel injection.

CHASSIS DATA: Wheelbase: (LeB cpe) 100.5 in.; (LeB conv) 100.6 in.; (LeB sed) 103.5 in.; (N.Y. Salon) 104.5 in.; (N.Y. Fifth Ave., Imperial) 109.5 in.; (Concorde) 113.0 in. Overall length: (LeB cpe/conv) 184.8 in.; (LeB sed) 182.7 in.; (N.Y. Salon) 193.6 in.; (N.Y. Fifth Ave.) 198.6 in.; (Imperial) 203.0 in.; (Concorde) 202.8 in. Height: (LeB cpe) 53.3 in.; (LeB conv) 52.4 in.; (LeB sed) 55.9 in.; (N.Y. Salon) 53.6 in.; (N.Y. Fifth Ave.) 55.1 in.; (Imperial) 55.3 in.; (Concorde) 56.3 in. Width: (LeB cpe/conv) 69.2 in.; (LeB sed) 68.1 in.; (N.Y., Imperial) 68.9 in.; (Concorde) 74.4 in. Front tread: (LeB conv/sed) 57.6 in.; (LeB cpe) 57.5 in.; (N.Y.) 57.6 in.; (Imperial) 57.6 in.; (Concorde) 62.0 in. Rear tread: (LeB conv/cpe) 57.6 in.; (LeB sed) 57.2 in.; (N.Y.) 57.6 in.; (Imperial) 57.6 in.; (Concorde) 62.0 in. Standard Tires: (LeB, LeB LE) P195/70R14; (LeB LX, LeB GTC, LeB Landau) P205/60R15; (N.Y., Imperial) P195/75R14; (Concorde) P205/70R15.

1993 Chrysler, New Yorker Fifth Avenue sedan (OCW)

TECHNICAL: Transmission: Five-speed manual standard on LeB GTC. Three-speed automatic standard on LeB and LeB LE. Four-speed automatic standard on LeB LX, LeB Landau, N.Y., Imperial and Concorde. Steering: (all) Power rack and pinion. Front Suspension: (LeB) Iso-Strut w/coil springs, gas-charged hydraulic shock absorbers and stabilizer bar; (N.Y., Imperial) Iso-Strut w/coil springs and stabilizer bar; (Concorde) MacPherson strut w/coil springs, gas-charged hydraulic shock absorbers and stabilizer bar. Rear Suspension: (LeB, N.Y., Imperial) Trailing flex-arm w/track bar, coil springs, gas-charged hydraulic shock absorbers and stabilizer bar; (Concorde) Independent rear, multi-link w/coil springs, gas-charged hydraulic shock absorbers and stabilizer bar. Brakes: Front disc, rear drum (power-assisted) except (Imperial, Concorde) anti-lock four-wheel disc. Body construction: Unibody. Fuel tank: (LeB cpe/conv) 14 gal.; (LeB sed, N.Y., Imperial) 16 gal.; (Concorde) 18 gal.

1993 Chrysler, LeBaron GTC convertible (OCW)

DRIVETRAIN OPTIONS: Engines: 3.0-liter V-6: LeB cpe/conv ($694). 3.8-liter V-6: N.Y. Fifth Ave. ($262). Transmission/Differential: Three-speed automatic trans.: LeB ($392). Four-speed automatic trans.: LeB cpe/conv ($93). LeB GTC w/V-6 ($640). Brakes: Anti-lock four-wheel disc: LeB ($899); N.Y. ($899). Suspension: Rear automatic load-leveling: N.Y. Salon ($225). Elect. Controlled Air Susp.: N.Y. Fifth Ave. ($650); Imperial ($650). Traction control: Concorde ($175).

1993 Chrysler, LeBaron GTC coupe (OCW)

LEBARON COUPE/CONVERTIBLE CONVENIENCE/APPEARANCE OPTIONS: LeBaron cpe: Pkg. 22A: stnd equip. (NC). Pkg. 22C: 22A plus air cond, floor mats, dlx. convenience grp., bodyside mldgs, AM/FM stereo radio w/cass & clock and remote decklid release ($747). Pkg. 25C: 22C plus 3.0L V-6 and 5-spd man. trans. ($884). Pkg. 26C: 22C plus 3.0L V-6 and 4-spd auto. trans. ($1574). Pkg. 26D: 22C plus 3.0L V-6 and 4-spd auto. trans., overhead console, pwr convenience grp., and 6-way pwr driver's seat ($2483). LeBaron conv: Pkg. 22A: stnd equip. (NC). Pkg. 26A: 22A plus 3.0L V-6 and 4-spd auto. trans. ($827). Pkg. 22C: 22A plus air cond, floor mats, dlx. convenience grp., bodyside mldgs, AM/FM stereo radio w/cass & clock and remote decklid release ($1322). Pkg. 25C: 22C plus 3.0L V-6 and 5-spd man. trans. ($1459). Pkg. 26C: 22C plus 3.0L V-6 and 4-spd auto. trans. ($2149). Pkg. 22D: 22C plus 2.5L four-cylinder engine and 3-spd auto. trans., pwr convenience grp., and 6-way pwr driver's seat ($1866). Pkg. 25D: 22D plus 3.0L V-6 and 5-spd man. trans. ($2003). Pkg. 26D: 22D plus 3.0L V-6 and 4-spd auto. trans. ($2693). LeBaron LX: Pkg. 26W: stnd equip. (NC). Pkg. 26D (cpe only): 26W plus floor mats, light grp., overhead console, 8-way pwr driver's seat, AM/FM stereo radio w/cass & clock, and remote decklid release ($1100). LeBaron GTC: Pkg. 25G: stnd equip. (NC). Pkg. 26G: 25G plus 4-spd auto. trans. ($690). Other: (AJK) Deluxe Convenience Grp.: Incl. Elect. Spd Control, Tilt Strg Col ($372). (AJW) Pwr Convenience Grp.: Incl. Pwr. Dr Locks, Dual Pwr. Heated Remote Control Mirrors ($338). Air cond., base conv only ($831). Pwr. 6-way Driver's Seat, base ($306). Pwr. 8-way Driver's Seat, LX and GTC ($377). Elect. Instrument Cluster, LX ($305). Elect. Vehicle Info Center, LX and GTC ($690). Calif. Emissions ($102). (AY3) Handling Pkg.: Incl. 15-in. Cast Alum Wheels, Sport Handling Suspension, P205/60R15 Tires, LX ($532). (AY4) Handling Pkg.: Incl. 16-in. Cast Alum Wheels, Sport Handling Suspension, P205/55R16 Tires ($188). (ADA) Light Grp., base and GTC ($196). Mini-trip computer ($93). Overhead console, GTC ($265). AM/FM Stereo Radio w/Cass & Clock, base and LX ($165). AM/FM Stereo Radio w/Cass, Seek/Scan, Pwr Amp, Graphic Equalizer, Clock and Infinity Spkrs ($529-$694). AM/FM Stereo Radio w/CD Player, Seek/Scan, Pwr Amp, Graphic Equalizer, Clock and Infinity Spkrs ($699-$894). Security Alarm ($149). (ADS) Sport Grp. (base): incl. body color grille and Triad wheel covers: cpe ($50); conv ($100). 14-in. cast alum. whls. ($328). 15-in. cast alum. whls. ($328). P195/70R14 WSW ($74). P205/60R15 WSW ($78).

LEBARON SEDAN CONVENIENCE/APPEARANCE OPTIONS: LeBaron LE: Pkg. 22P: stnd equip. (NC). Pkg. 22U: 22P plus air cond, pwr mirrors/dr locks/windows ($627). Pkg. 26U: 22U plus 3.0L V-6 and 3-spd auto. trans. ($1321). Pkg. 28U: 22U plus 3.0L V-6 and 4-spd auto. trans. ($1454). Pkg. 28X: 22U plus 3.0L V-6 and 4-spd auto. trans., AM/FM stereo radio w/cass & clock, 15-in. alum. whls & tires and handling suspension ($2013). Landau: Pkg. 28K: stnd equip. (NC). Pkg. 28L: 28K plus int. illum. grp., leather-wrapped stng whl, overhead console, pwr equip. grp., and wire whl covers ($756). Other: (AJP) Pwr Equip. Grp.: Incl. Pwr Dr Locks/Mirrors/Windows, Landau ($85). 6-way pwr driver's seat, Landau ($306). Pwr driver's seat, LE ($306). (ADM) Elect. Display Grp.: Incl. Elect. Instrument Panel Cluster and Mini-Trip Computer, Landau ($317). Calif. emissions ($103). (AJN) Int. Illum. Grp.: incl. Illum. entry and Dual Illum. Visor Vanity Mirrors ($195). AM/FM Stereo Radio w/Cass, Seek/Scan, Graphic Equal., Clock, and Infinity Spkrs: LE ($520); Landau ($355). AM/FM Stereo Radio w/CD player, Graphic Equal., Clock & 4 Spkrs: LE ($690); Landau ($525). Wire whl covers, Landau ($240). P195/70R14 ($73). Conventional spare tire ($95).

NEW YORKER CONVENIENCE/APPEARANCE OPTIONS: Salon: Pkg. 26A: stnd equip. (NC). Pkg. 26C: 26A plus floor mounted console, Dlx Convenience Grp., floor mats, pwr dr locks, AM/FM stereo radio w/cass & clock, bodyside stripe, P195/75R14 tires, undercoating ($730). Pkg.

26D: 26C plus headlamps w/timed delay, auto day/night mirror, pwr 8-way driver and pass. seats w/memory, leather-wrapped stng whl, wire whl covers ($2073). Other: (AJW) Pwr Accessories Grp.: incl. decklid pulldown ($169). Pwr dr locks ($331). (AJK) Deluxe Convenience Grp.: incl. Elect. Spd Control, Tilt Strg Col. ($372). (AJB) Security Grp.: incl. alarm w/panel warning light, remote keyless entry and remote activation of dr locks ($292). Calif. emissions ($102). AM/FM Stereo Radio w/cass & clock ($165). AM/FM Stereo Radio w/Cass, Graphic Equal., and clock ($273). (ARB) Infinity RS Grp.: incl. AM/FM Stereo Radio w/Cass & clock, Infinity Syst., w/10 Spkrs & Trunk-Mounted Amp ($668). Vinyl landau roof ($325). Wire whl covers ($240). Cast alum. whls ($39). P195/75R14 tires ($73). Conventional spare tire ($85). Fifth Ave.: Pkg. 26A: stnd equip. (NC). Pkg. 26B: 26A plus pwr antenna, pwr decklid pulldown, floor mats, illum. entry, illum. visor vanity mirrors, leather-wrapped stng whl, undercoating, wire whl covers, and AM/FM stereo radio w/cass & clock ($495). Pkg. 28B: 26B plus 3.8L V-6 ($757). Pkg. 26C: 26B plus graphic equalizer on stereo, floor mounted console, integrated info center, fender-mounted cornering lights, headlamps w/timed delay, day/night rearview mirror, and 8-way pwr driver & pass seats w/memory ($1475). Pkg. 28C: 26B plus 3.8L V-6 ($1737). Other: (AJW) Pwr Accessories Grp.: incl. pwr antenna and pwr decklid pulldown ($169). Pwr sunroof ($792). Auto. temp control air cond ($152). (ADM) Elect. Features Grp.: incl. overhead console w/Elect. Vehicle Info Center, Elect. Instrument Cluster ($1159). Calif. Emissions ($102). Flr mats, F&R ($46). AM/FM Stereo Radio w/Cass & clock. ($165). AM/FM Stereo Radio w/Cass, Graphic Equal., Clock & Spkrs ($273). AM/FM Stereo Radio w/CD player, graphic equal., and Infinity Spkrs ($569). (ARB) Infinity RS Grp.: incl. AM/FM Stereo w/Cass & Clock, Infinity Syst. w/10 Spkrs & Trunk-Mounted Amp ($395-$668). (AJB) Security Grp.: incl. Alarm w/Panel Warning Light, Remote Keyless Entry, Remote Dr Lock & Decklid Activation ($292). Wire whl covers ($240). Cast alum. whls ($39). Conventional spare tire ($85).

1993 Chrysler, Concorde sedan with optional Touring Group wheel package (OCW)

IMPERIAL CONVENIENCE/APPEARANCE OPTIONS: Pkg. 28A: stnd equip. (NC). Pkg. 28D: 28A plus leather trim and 8-way pwr driver & pass seat w/memory ($1025). Other: 8-way pwr driver & pass seat w/memory ($376). (ADN) Elect. Features Grp.: incl. Overhead and Flr Mounted Consoles - OH w/Elect. Vehicle Info Center, Elect. Instrument Cluster, Auto Day/Night Adjustable Mirror, Infinity Syst. w/10 Spkrs & Trunk-Mounted Amp, auto headlamp w/time delay ($947). (AJB) Security Grp.: incl. alarm w/panel warning light, remote keyless entry, remote activation of decklid and dr locks ($292). Calif. Emissions ($102). AM/FM Stereo Radio w/CD player, graphic equal., seek/scan, pwr amp, clock and Infinity Spkrs ($174-$569). Conventional spare tire ($85).

CONCORDE CONVENIENCE/APPEARANCE OPTIONS: Pkg. 22A: stnd equip. (NC). Pkg. 22B: 22A plus pwr dr locks, floor mats, spd control, pwr windows, AM/FM stereo radio w/cass ($887). Pkg. 22C: 22B plus auto. temp air cond., 8-way pwr driver's seat, remote illum. entry, dual illum. visor vanity mirrors ($1616). Pkg. 26C: 22C plus 3.5L V-6 ($2241). Pkg. 26D: 26C plus Chrysler/Infinity Spatial Imaging Cass Sound Syst. (delete AM/FM unit from 22C), traction control and overhead console ($3277). Other: (AJF) Remote Illum. Entry Grp.: incl. remote

keyless entry ($221). Integrated child's seat ($100). Calif. emissions ($102). Pwr dr locks ($250). 8-way pwr driver's seat ($377). Chrysler/Infinity Spatial Imaging Sound Syst. w/Cass. ($713); w/CD player ($882), exc. w/Pkg. 26D ($169). (AGC) 16-in. Whl & Touring Grp.: incl. 16-in. Spiralcast alum whls, handling suspension and touring tires ($524). Conventional spare tire ($95).

HISTORY: Model year production: 162,019. Calendar year sales: 156,598. Slated to end production in 1993, LeBaron sedan production was continued until mid-year 1994.

1994 CHRYSLER

Chrysler's lineup was vastly different from the previous year, with the "new" New Yorker LH sedan and LHS sedan joining the remaining LeBaron models and the Concorde sedan. The LeBaron ranks were thinned considerably. Gone were all coupe models and the base and LX convertibles. The LE and Landau sedans and GTC convertible were again offered, but it was the final year for sedan availability (production was halted mid-year 1994).

1994 Chrysler, LeBaron GTC convertible (OCW)

LEBARON — SERIES J (convertible)/SERIES A (sedan) — FOUR/V-6 — The LeBaron coupe was no longer available, and only one convertible, the GTC, and two sedans, LE and Landau, comprised the lineup. In 1994, the V-6 dominated in Chrysler cars, the lone exception being the LeBaron LE sedan that again used the 2.5-liter four-cylinder engine paired with a three-speed automatic transmission. The 3.0-liter V-6 that was newly standard in the GTC convertible and again in the Landau sedan was optional in the LE. Both GTC and Landau models used a refined 41TE four-speed automatic transmission with overdrive, the option unit in the LE when the 3.0-liter V-6 was ordered. The first convertible with an airbag (driver's side), GTCs in 1994 received a passenger-side airbag and knee bolster supplemental passive restraint system for added safety. Also new in the LeBaron ragtop was the use of non-CFC R-134A refrigerant in the air conditioning system, a column-mounted turn signal switch replaced the previously offered instrument panel-mounted switch, seat fabric was updated and a low-cost leather seat trim was used. The GTC also featured increased structural rigidity for improved ride quality. The LeBaron sedans, in their final year, were updated slightly receiving a motorized torso belt and knee bolster passive restraint system for the front passenger. Also, 50/50 front seating was made standard and one new exterior color was offered: Sky Blue.

CONCORDE — SERIES H — V-6 — In its sophomore year, the Concorde sedan received flexible fuel capability available with its 3.3-liter V-6. The "normal" gasoline-fueled 3.3-liter V-6 that was standard also was refined, with eight more horsepower (161 vs. the previous 153) and increased torque (181 pound-feet vs. the previous 177). The 42LE electronically controlled four-speed automatic transmission was also upgraded for smoother shifting. New standard features for 1994 included variable-assist speed-proportional power steering, touring suspension (formerly optional), aluminized exhaust system coating, solar control glass in rear window, bar-type manual seat adjuster, additional head restraint adjustment, and door beams and structural reinforcements for dynamic side impact protection. New optional features included a power moonroof, vehicle theft security alarm, 50/50 front seating, eight-way power passenger seat with cloth trim, and automatic day/night rearview mirror. The 3.5-liter V-6 was again the option engine.

NEW YORKER LH — SERIES H — V-6 — Introduced early in May 1993 as a 1994 model, the LH-platformed New Yorker sedan featured the cab-forward design incorporated into most other new Chrysler Corp. automobiles. Due to its early launch, New Yorkers were classified first as "spring introduction" models followed by "fall introduction" models.

Running changes occurred from one model to the next. Standard features of the New Yorker included dual airbags, anti-lock four-wheel disc brakes, air conditioning with non-CFC R-134A refrigerant, stainless steel dual exhaust, solar control glass windshield/side windows/back window, windshield wipers with vehicle speed sensitive intermittent operation and high-volume washers, courtesy lamps with fade-off and time-out features and electronic indicator for transmission gear selection. The "fall" New Yorker added variable-assist speed-proportional power steering, aluminized exhaust system coating, "Simplex" wheel covers, and touring tires and wheels were made standard. Optional equipment included low-speed traction control, automatic temperature control, vehicle theft security alarm system, eight-way power driver and passenger seats, automatic headlights with delay feature, automatic day/night rearview mirror and power moonroof. New Yorker's powertrain consisted of the 24-valve, overhead cam 3.5-liter V-6 paired with the electronically controlled four-speed automatic transmission with overdrive.

1994 Chrysler, New Yorker sedan (OCW)

LHS — SERIES H — V-6 — The new top-of-the-line Chrysler was similar to the New Yorker in that it, too, was an early-1993 launch as a 1994 model and was classed as both "spring" and "fall" models with running changes made from one to the next. The LHS sedan's powertrain was the same as New Yorker's as was most of its standard equipment. The difference was in what was optional on the New Yorker was standard on LHS, including low-speed traction control, automatic temperature control, vehicle theft security alarm system, eight-way power driver and passenger seats, automatic headlights with delay feature, automatic day/night rearview mirror and power moonroof. LHS shared New Yorker's 113-inch wheelbase and 207.4-inch overall length. Exterior colors available were Black Cherry, Radiant Red, Char-Gold, Emerald Green, Black, Bright White and Bright Metallic Silver. Interior colors were Agate, Medium Driftwood, Medium Quartz and Slate Blue.

1994 Chrysler, LHS sedan (OCW)

I.D. DATA: As before, Chrysler's 17-symbol Vehicle Identification Number (VIN) was on the upper left corner of the instrument panel, visible through the windshield. Coding was similar to 1986-93. The model year code changed to 'R' for 1994.

LEBARON (FOUR/V-6)

Model No.	Body/ Style No.	Body Type & Seating	Factory Price	Shipping Weight	Prod. Total
JCH	27	2-dr. GTC Conv-4P	17024	3122	37,052
ACM	41	4-dr. LE Sed-6P	15121/16551	2744/2971	Note 1
ACP	41	4-dr. Landau Sed-6P	17933	2938	Note 1

Note: Where applicable, LeBaron prices and weights to left of slash for four-cylinder engine, to right for V-6.

Note 1: LeBaron sedan production totaled 26,031 with no further breakout available.

1994 Chrysler, Concorde sedan (OCW)

CONCORDE (V-6)

HLP	41	4-dr. Sed-6P	19457	3379	70,181

NEW YORKER LH (V-6)

HCH	41	4-dr. Sed-6P	25386	3457	31,383

LHS (V-6)

HCP	41	4-dr. Sed-5P	30283	3483	44,739

ENGINE DATA: BASE FOUR (LeB LE): Inline, overhead cam four-cylinder. Cast iron block; aluminum head. Displacement: 153 cu. in. (2.5 liters). Bore & stroke: 3.44 x 4.09 in. Compression ratio: 8.9:1. Brake horsepower: 100 at 4800 RPM. Torque: 135 lb.-ft. at 2800 RPM. Five main bearings. Hydraulic valve lifters. Throttle-body fuel injection. BASE V-6 (LeB GTC, LeB Landau); OPTIONAL (LeB LE): Overhead cam V-6. Cast iron block, aluminum heads. Displacement: 181 cu. in. (3.0 liters). Bore & stroke: 3.59 x 2.99 in. Compression ratio: 8.9:1. Brake horsepower: 142 at 5200 RPM. Torque: 171 lb.-ft. at 2400 RPM. Hydraulic valve lifters. Sequential fuel injection. BASE V-6 (Concorde): Overhead valve V-6. Cast iron block, aluminum heads. Displacement: 201 cu. in. (3.3 liters). Bore & stroke: 3.66 x 3.19 in. Compression ratio: 8.9:1. Brake horsepower: 161 at 5300 RPM. Torque: 181 lb.-ft. at 3200 RPM. Sequential fuel injection. OPTIONAL V-6 (Concorde): same as 3.3-liter above except flexible fuel capability. Brake horsepower: 167 at 5400 RPM. Torque: 185 lb.-ft. at 3000 RPM. BASE V-6 (New Yorker, LHS); OPTIONAL (Concorde): 24-valve, overhead cam V-6. Cast iron block, aluminum heads. Displacement: 214 cu. in. (3.5 liters). Bore & stroke: 3.78 x 3.19 in. Compression ratio: 10.5:1. Brake horsepower: 214 at 5800 RPM. Torque: 221 lb.-ft. at 2800 RPM. Sequential fuel injection.

CHASSIS DATA: Wheelbase: (LeB conv) 100.6 in.; (LeB sed) 103.5 in.; (Concorde, N.Y., LHS) 113.0 in. Overall length: (LeB conv) 184.8 in.; (LeB sed) 182.7 in.; (Concorde) 202.8 in.; (N.Y., LHS) 207.4 in. Height: (LeB conv) 52.4 in.; (LeB sed) 53.7 in.; (Concorde) 56.3 in.; (N.Y., LHS) 55.7 in. Width: (LeB conv) 69.2 in.; (LeB sed) 68.1 in.; (Concorde, N.Y., LHS) 74.4 in. Front tread: (LeB conv/sed) 57.6 in.; (Concorde, N.Y., LHS) 62.0 in. Rear tread: (LeB conv) 57.6 in.; (LeB sed) 57.2 in.; (Concorde, N.Y., LHS) 62.0 in. Standard Tires: (LeB sed) P195/70R14; (LeB GTC) P205/60R15; (Concorde, N.Y.) P205/70R15; (LHS) P225/60R16.

TECHNICAL: Transmission: Three-speed automatic standard on LeB LE. Four-speed automatic standard on LeB GTC, LeB Landau, Concorde, N.Y., LHS. Steering: (all) Rack and pinion. Front Suspension: (LeB) Iso-Strut w/integral gas-charged shock absorbers, asymmetrical lower control arms, coil springs, and linkless stabilizer bar; (Concorde, N.Y., LHS) Iso-Strut w/integral gas-charged shock absorbers, coil springs, single transverse lower links, tension struts, and link-type stabilizer bar. Rear Suspension: (LeB) Beam axle, trailing flex-arm w/track bar, coil springs, gas-charged shock absorbers and frameless tubular stabilizer bar; (Concorde, N.Y., LHS) Chapman struts w/integral gas-charged shock absorbers and concentric coil springs, dual transverse lower links, lower trailing links, and link-type stabilizer bar. Brakes: (LeB) Front disc, rear drum (power-assisted); (Concorde, N.Y., LHS) anti-lock four-wheel disc. Body construction: Unibody. Fuel tank: (LeB conv) 14 gal.; (LeB sed) 16 gal.; (Concorde, N.Y., LHS) 18 gal.

DRIVETRAIN OPTIONS: Engines: 3.0-liter V-6: LeB LE (N/A). 3.3-liter V-6 w/flex fuel capability: Concorde (N/A). 3.5-liter V-6: Concorde (N/A).

Transmission/Differential: Four-speed automatic trans.: LeB LE (N/A). Brakes: Anti-lock four-wheel disc: LeB ($699). Traction control: Concorde ($175); N.Y. ($175).

LEBARON CONVERTIBLE CONVENIENCE/APPEARANCE OPTIONS: Pkg. 26A: stnd equip. (NC). Pkg. 26T: 26A plus Dlx. and Pwr Convenience Grps., remote decklid release, flr mats, 6-way pwr driver's seat ($1000). Pkg. 26W: 26T plus leather int. incl. seating & stng whl, Light Grp., 15-in. "Cathedral" cast alum whls ($2000). anti-lock four-wheel disc brakes ($699). (AJK) Deluxe Convenience Grp.: Incl. Elect. Spd Control, Tilt Strg Col ($372). (AJW) Pwr Convenience Grp.: Incl. Pwr. Dr Locks, Dual Pwr. Heated Remote Control Mirrors ($338). (ASW) Decor Grp.: Incl. bright grille, bright pentastar medallion & nameplates, bright mldgs, 15-in. "Conclave" whl covers ($50). (ADA) Light Grp.: Incl. illum. entry, illum. visor vanity mirrors ($196). (AY4) Performance Grp.: Incl. 16-in. cast alum "Spiralcast" whls, Perf. Handling Suspension, P205/55R16 tires ($516). Calif. emissions ($102). Mini-Trip Computer ($93). Security Alarm ($149). Vinyl bucket seats, rear bench ($102). Leather bucket seats w/6-way pwr driver's seat, rear bench ($668). Premium leather bucket seats w/12-way pwr driver's seat, rear bench ($424-$1092). AM/FM Stereo Radio w/Cass & Clock, Graphic Equal., and 6 Infinity Spkrs ($524). AM/FM Stereo Radio w/CD Player, Graphic Equal., Clock and 6 Infinity Spkrs ($694). 15-in. "Cathedral" cast alum. whls. ($328).

LEBARON SEDAN CONVENIENCE/APPEARANCE OPTIONS: LE: Pkg. 26U: stnd equip. (NC). Pkg. 28U: 26U plus 4-spd auto. trans. ($173). Pkg. 28X: 28U plus 3.0L V-6 and 4-spd auto. trans., AM/FM stereo radio w/cass & clock, 15-in. alum. whls., P205/60R15 tires and handling susp. ($812). Landau: Pkg. 28K: stnd equip. (NC). Pkg. 28L: 28K plus int. illum. grp., leather-wrapped stng whl, overhead console, and wire whl covers ($750). Other: (ADM) Elect. Display Grp.: Incl. Elect. Instrument Panel Cluster and Mini-Trip Computer, Landau ($317). (AJN) Int. Illum. Grp.: incl. Illum. entry and Dual Illum. Visor Vanity Mirrors ($195). 6-way pwr driver's seat, Landau ($306). Calif. emissions ($103). Leather front 50/50 bench seat w/6-way pwr driver's seat, leather-wrapped stng whl, and rear bench seat, Landau ($974). AM/FM Stereo Radio w/Cass & Clock, LE ($170). AM/FM Stereo Radio w/Cass, Graphic Equal., Clock & 4 Spkrs: LE ($520); Landau ($350). Wire whl covers, Landau ($240). P195/70R14 tires, LE ($73). Conventional spare tire, LE ($95).

CONCORDE CONVENIENCE/APPEARANCE OPTIONS: Pkg. 22A: stnd equip. (NC). Pkg. 22B: 22A plus pwr dr locks, pwr windows, dual illum. visor vanity mirrors ($596). Pkg. 22C: 22B plus auto. temp air cond., 8-way pwr driver's seat, remote illum. entry ($1226). Pkg. 26C: 22C plus 3.5L V-6 ($1951). Pkg. 22D: 22C plus overhead console, auto. day/night rearview mirror, Chrysler/Infinity Spatial Imaging Cass Sound Syst., security alarm, spd sensitive stng ($2350). Pkg. 26D: 22D plus 3.5L V-6 ($3075). (AJF) Remote Illum. Entry Grp.: incl. remote keyless entry ($221). Integrated child's seat ($100). Calif. emissions ($102). 8-way pwr driver's seat ($377). 8-way pwr driver & pass seats ($754). Leather bucket seats w/8-way pwr driver & pass seats, leather-wrapped stng whl & shift knob, rear bench seat ($1069). Security alarm ($149). Overhead console w/trip computer, compass and storage ($378). Pwr moonroof ($716-$1094). Eng. block htr ($20). Chrysler/Infinity Spatial Imaging Sound Syst. w/Cass. ($708); w/CD player ($877), exc. w/Pkg. 26D ($169). (AGC) 16-in. Whl & Handling Grp.: incl. 16-in. "Spiralcast" alum whls, variable-assist spd-proportional stng and touring tires ($524-$628). Conventional spare tire ($95).

1994 Chrysler, New Yorker LH sedan (OCW)

NEW YORKER LH CONVENIENCE/APPEARANCE OPTIONS: Pkg. 26A: stnd equip. (NC). Pkg. 26B: 26A plus auto. temp air cond, mini-overhead console w/trip computer/compass/reading lamps, dual illum. visor vanity mirrors, Remote Illum. Entry Grp., Chrysler/Infinity Spatial Imaging Sound Syst. w/Cass. ($1338). Pkg. 26C: 26B plus Leather Int. Grp., 8-way pwr driver & pass seats, conventional spare tire, traction control ($2633). Calif. emissions ($102). Eng. block htr ($20). Pwr moonroof ($792). Chrysler/Infinity Spatial Imaging Sound Syst. w/CD Player ($169). Pwr 8-way driver & pass seats ($377). Conventional spare tire ($95). 16-in. "Spiralcast" alum whls ($328). Leather 50/50 front seat w/8-way pwr driver & pass seats, rear bench seat ($1075).

LHS CONVENIENCE/APPEARANCE OPTIONS: Pkg. 26J: stnd equip. (NC). Calif. Emissions ($102). Eng. block htr ($20). Extra cost paint: Bright Platinum Metallic ($200); other colors ($97). Chrysler/Infinity Spatial Imaging Sound Syst. w/CD Player ($169). Premium cloth bucket seats, rear bench seats (replacement for stnd leather seats (NC).

HISTORY: Model year production: 209,386. Calendar year sales: 202,038. In February 1994, Chrysler Corp. and Harris Corp. announced joint development of a microcomputer for an electronic superhighway system for automobiles of the future.

1995 CHRYSLER

The void created when the LeBaron coupe and sedan were dropped was filled by two more-than-capable replacements in the form of Chrysler's new Sebring coupe and Cirrus sedan. The LeBaron series now consisted of one car, the GTC convertible, which was in its final year. The GTC's phase-out was done to make room for the Sebring JX convertible, a 1996 model.

1995 Chrysler, Sebring LXi coupe (OCW)

LEBARON — SERIES J — V-6 — The LE and Landau sedans offered the previous year were discontinued, leaving the LeBaron lineup comprised of only the GTC convertible. The ragtop was in its final year and changes were kept to a minimum with one notable exception being the availability of remote keyless entry. The 3.0-liter V-6 and 41TE four-speed automatic transmission with overdrive again powered the GTC.

SEBRING — SERIES J — FOUR/V-6 — Borrowing a name from Florida's legendary sports car racing circuit, the Sebring luxury sport coupe was a late arrival in the model year being launched in January 1995. The Sebring was offered in two trim levels: LX and the more upscale LXi. The LX was powered by a 16-valve, dual overhead cam 2.0-liter four-cylinder engine coupled with a five-speed manual transmission. LXi coupes used a 24-valve 2.5-liter V-6 paired with an electronically controlled four-speed automatic with overdrive, which was also the option powertrain for the LX. Sebring's standard features included dual airbags, anti-lock brakes, stainless steel exhaust, rear window defroster, tinted glass, foglights, intermittent wipers and tilt steering column. To this list, the LXi added four-wheel disc brakes, power door locks, power windows, dual exhaust, remote keyless entry/security alarm system, electronic speed control and 16-inch cast aluminum wheels. A power sunroof was optional on the LXi. Sebring's wheelbase measured 103.7 inches while its overall length was 187.4 inches. Its coefficient of drag was 0.35. Exterior colors offered were Bright White, Black, Wildberry, Char-Gold, Medium Gray, Silver Mist, Deep Green and Medium Gray-Blue. Interior color choices were Gray, Brownstone, and, in LXi only, Gray-Blue.

1995 Chrysler, Cirrus LX sedan (OCW)

CIRRUS — SERIES A — V-6 — Cirrus was Chrysler's new mid-size sports sedan offered in two trim levels: LX and the more upscale LXi. Both were powered by the 24-valve 2.5-liter V-6 paired with the electronically controlled four-speed automatic transmission with overdrive. Mid-model year (January 1995), a dual overhead cam 2.4-liter four-cylinder engine was offered in the LX, also mated with the four-speed automatic transmission. Standard features of the cab-forward design Cirrus included dual airbags, anti-lock brakes, climate control air conditioning, electric rear window defroster, power windows, power door locks, fog lights, solar control glass all-around, personal security group including remote keyless entry and illuminated entry, electronic speed control with steering wheel switches, tilt steering column and speed-sensitive variable delay wipers. The LXi added a theft alarm as part of the personal security group, 8-way power driver's seat and "Finale" cast aluminum wheels. The Cirrus featured short/long arm suspension front and rear, a four-point powertrain mounting system and dynamic side impact protection. Its coefficient of drag was 0.31. The overall length of the Cirrus measured 186.0 inches while its wheelbase was 108.0 inches. Exterior colors offered were Dark Rosewood, Light Rosewood, Metallic Red, Wild Orchid, Light Silverfern, Medium Fern Green, Light Iris, Medium Blue, Black and White.

CONCORDE — SERIES H — V-6 — Concorde entered its third year of availability with no change in powertrains offered, both as standard and optional equipment. The 3.3-liter V-6 was again standard, with a flex fuel version optional. The 3.5-liter V-6 was also again the more powerful option engine. All of these powerplants used the 42LE electronically controlled four-speed automatic transmission, which was upgraded for smoother shifting. Other updates to the Concorde sedan for 1995 (matching those of the New Yorker and LHS) were modifications to the emissions control and remote keyless entry systems as well as a cancel feature added to the speed control.

NEW YORKER LH — SERIES H — V-6 — Notable changes to the New Yorker paralleled those listed for the Concorde involving the emissions control and remote keyless entry systems and the cancel feature added to the speed control. Powertrain for the New Yorker sedan was again the 3.5-liter V-6 paired with the electronically controlled four-speed automatic transmission with overdrive (also upgraded for smoother shifting).

LHS — SERIES H — V-6 — Updates to the LHS sedan mirrored those listed for the New Yorker and Concorde. Powertrain was again the 3.5-liter V-6 paired with the 42LE four-speed automatic transmission.

I.D. DATA: As before, Chrysler's 17-symbol Vehicle Identification Number (VIN) was on the upper left corner of the instrument panel, visible through the windshield. Coding was similar to 1986-94. The model year code changed to 'S' for 1995.

LEBARON (FOUR/V-6)

Model No.	Body/ Style No.	Body Type & Seating	Factory Price	Shipping Weight	Prod. Total
JCH	27	2-dr. GTC Conv-4P	17469	3122	35,760

SEBRING (FOUR/V-6)

JCS	22	2-dr. LX Cpe-5P	15434/16108	2816/N/A	Note 1
JCP	22	2-dr. LXi Cpe-5P	19029	2980	Note 1

Note: Where applicable, prices and weights to left of slash for four-cylinder engine, to right for V-6.

Note 1: Sebring coupe production totaled 20,560 with no further breakout available.

CIRRUS (V-6)

ACP	41	4-dr. LX Sed-5P	17435	2911	Note 1
ACP	41	4-dr. LXi Sed-5P	19365	3118	Note 1

Note 1: Cirrus sedan production totaled 61,407 with no further break-out available.

CONCORDE (V-6)

HLP	41	4-dr. Sed-6P	20550	3369	51,306

NEW YORKER LH (V-6)

HCH	41	4-dr. Sed-6P	25596	3457	20,316

LHS (V-6)

HCP	41	4-dr. Sed-5P	29595	3483	29,418

ENGINE DATA: BASE FOUR (Sebring LX): Inline, dual overhead cam four-cylinder. Cast iron block; aluminum head. Displacement: 121 cu. in. (2.0 liters). Bore & stroke: 3.44 x 3.27 in. Compression ratio: 9.6:1. Brake horsepower: 140 at 6000 RPM. Torque: 130 lb.-ft. at 4800 RPM. Sequential fuel injection. OPTIONAL FOUR (Cirrus LX): Inline, dual overhead cam four-cylinder. Cast iron block; aluminum head. Displacement: 148 cu. in. (2.4 liters). Bore & stroke: 3.29 x 2.99 in. Compression ratio: 9.4:1. Brake horsepower: 138 at 5200 RPM. Torque: 156 lb.-ft. at 4000

RPM. Sequential fuel injection. BASE V-6 (Sebring LXi, Cirrus LX, Cirrus LXi): Overhead cam V-6. Cast iron block, aluminum heads. Displacement: 152 cu. in. (2.5 liters). Bore & stroke: 3.29 x 2.99 in. Compression ratio: 9.4:1. Brake horsepower: (Sebring) 155 at 5500 RPM; (Cirrus) 164 at 5900 RPM. Torque: (Sebring) 161 lb.-ft. at 4400 RPM; (Cirrus) 163 lb.-ft. at 4350 RPM. Sequential fuel injection. BASE V-6 (LeB GTC): Overhead cam V-6. Cast iron block, aluminum heads. Displacement: 181 cu. in. (3.0 liters). Bore & stroke: 3.59 x 2.99 in. Compression ratio: 8.9:1. Brake horsepower: 142 at 5200 RPM. Torque: 171 lb.-ft. at 2400 RPM. Sequential fuel injection. BASE V-6 (Concorde): Overhead valve V-6. Cast iron block, aluminum heads. Displacement: 201 cu. in. (3.3 liters). Bore & stroke: 3.66 x 3.19 in. Compression ratio: 8.9:1. Brake horsepower: 161 at 5300 RPM. Torque: 181 lb.-ft. at 3200 RPM. Sequential fuel injection. OPTIONAL V-6 (Concorde): same as 3.3-liter above except flexible fuel capability. Brake horsepower: 167 at 5400 RPM. Torque: 185 lb.-ft. at 3000 RPM. BASE V-6 (New Yorker, LHS): OPTIONAL (Concorde): 24-valve, overhead cam V-6. Cast iron block, aluminum heads. Displacement: 214 cu. in. (3.5 liters). Bore & stroke: 3.78 x 3.19 in. Compression ratio: 10.5:1. Brake horsepower: 214 at 5800 RPM. Torque: 221 lb.-ft. at 2800 RPM. Sequential fuel injection.

CHASSIS DATA: Wheelbase: (LeB) 100.6 in.; (Sebring) 103.7 in.; (Cirrus) 108.0 in.; (Concorde, N.Y.) 113.0 in. Overall length: (LeB) 184.8 in.; (Sebring) 187.4 in.; (Cirrus) 186.0 in.; (Concorde) 201.5 in.; (N.Y., LHS) 207.4 in. Height: (LeB) 52.4 in.; (Sebring) 53.0 in.; (Cirrus) 54.1 in.; (Concorde) 56.3 in.; (N.Y., LHS) 55.9 in. Width: (LeB) 69.2 in.; (Sebring) 69.7 in.; (Cirrus) 71.0 in.; (Concorde) 74.4 in.; (N.Y., LHS) 74.5 in. Front tread: (LeB) 57.6 in.; (Sebring) 59.5 in.; (Cirrus) 60.2 in.; (Concorde, N.Y., LHS) 62.0 in. Rear tread: (LeB) 57.6 in.; (Sebring) 59.3 in.; (Cirrus) 60.2 in.; (Concorde, N.Y., LHS) 62.0 in. Standard Tires: (LeB) P205/60R15; (Sebring LX) P195/70HR14; (Sebring LXi) P205/55HR16; (Cirrus) P195/65R15; (Concorde, N.Y.) P205/70R15; (LHS) P225/60R16.

TECHNICAL: Transmission: Five-speed manual standard on Sebring LX. Four-speed automatic standard on LeB GTC, Sebring LXi, Cirrus, Concorde, N.Y., LHS. Steering: (all) Rack and pinion. Front Suspension: (LeB) Iso-Strut w/integral gas-charged shock absorbers, asymmetrical lower control arms, coil springs, and linkless stabilizer bar; (Sebring) Double wishbone w/coil springs, direct acting shock absorbers and stabilizer bar; (Cirrus) Unequal length upper and lower control arms, coil springs, tubular shock absorbers and (LX) stabilizer bar; (LXi) higher rate springs; (Concorde, N.Y., LHS) Iso-Strut w/integral gas-charged shock absorbers, coil springs, single transverse lower links, tension struts, and link-type stabilizer bar. Rear Suspension: (LeB) Beam axle, trailing flex-arm w/track bar, coil springs, gas-charged shock absorbers and frameless tubular stabilizer bar; (Sebring) Double wishbone w/coil springs, direct acting shock absorbers and stabilizer bar; (Cirrus) Unequal length upper and lower control arms, trailing arms, coil springs, tubular shock absorbers and (LX) stabilizer bar; (LXi) stabilizer bar and higher rate springs; (Concorde, N.Y., LHS) Chapman struts w/integral gas-charged shock absorbers and concentric coil springs, dual transverse lower links, lower trailing links, and link-type stabilizer bar. Brakes: (LeB) Front disc, rear drum (power-assisted); (Sebring LX, Cirrus LX, Cirrus LXi) Front disc, rear drum w/anti-lock (power-assisted); (Sebring LXi, Concorde, N.Y., LHS) anti-lock four-wheel disc. Body construction: Unibody. Fuel tank: (LeB) 14 gal.; (Sebring, Cirrus) 16 gal.; (Concorde, N.Y., LHS) 18 gal.

DRIVETRAIN OPTIONS: Engines: 2.4-liter four-cylinder engine: Cirrus LX ($699 credit). 2.5-liter V-6: Sebring LX (N/A). 3.3-liter V-6 w/flex fuel capability: Concorde (N/A). 3.5-liter V-6: Concorde (N/A). Transmission/Differential: Four-speed automatic trans.: Sebring LX ($683). Brakes: Anti-lock four-wheel disc: LeB ($699). Traction control: Concorde ($175); N.Y. ($175).

LEBARON CONVENIENCE/APPEARANCE OPTIONS: Pkg. 26A: stnd equip. (NC). Pkg. 26T: 26A plus Dlx. and Pwr Convenience Grps., remote decklid release, flr mats, 6-way pwr driver's seat ($1113). Pkg. 26W: 26T plus leather int. incl. seating & stng whl, Light Grp., 15-in. "Cathedral" cast alum whls ($2433). (AJK) Deluxe Convenience Grp.: Incl. Elect. Spd Control, Tilt Strg Col ($372). (AJW) Pwr Convenience Grp.: Incl. Pwr. Dr Locks, Dual Pwr. Heated Remote Control Mirrors ($338). (ASW) Decor Grp.: Incl. bright grille, bright pentastar medallion & nameplates, bright mldgs, 15-in. "Conclave" whl covers ($60). (ADA) Light Grp.: Incl. illum. entry, remote keyless entry, illum. visor vanity mirrors ($324). (AY4) Performance Grp.: Incl. 16-in. cast alum "Spiralcast" whls, Perf. Handling Suspension, P205/55R16 tires (N/A). Calif. emissions ($102). Extra cost paint ($97). Mini-Trip Computer ($93). Security Alarm ($149). Vinyl bucket seats, rear bench ($102). Leather bucket seats w/6-way pwr driver's seat, rear bench ($668). AM/FM Stereo Radio w/Cass & Clock, Graphic Equal., and 6 Infinity Spkrs ($524). AM/FM Stereo Radio w/CD Player, Graphic Equal., Clock and 6 Infinity Spkrs ($694). 15-in. "Cathedral" cast alum. whls. ($328).

SEBRING CONVENIENCE/APPEARANCE OPTIONS: (LX): Pkg. 21G: stnd equip. (NC). Pkg. 22G: 21G plus 4-spd. auto. trans. ($683). Pkg. 21W: 21G plus pwr dr locks/windows/mirrors, floor mats, trunk cargo net, spd control, dual illum. visor mirrors and AM/FM stereo radio w/cass

& clock ($984). Pkg. 22H: 21H plus 4-spd. auto. trans. ($1667). Pkg. 24H: 22H plus 2.5L V-6, 16-in. tires & whl covers, rear disc brakes and suspension and battery upgrade ($2341). (LXi): Pkg. 24J: stnd equip. (NC). Pkg. 24K: 24J plus pwr sunroof, leather seats and 6-way pwr driver's seat ($1266). Other: 6-way pwr driver's seat ($203). Calif. emissions (NC). Security alarm incl. remote keyless entry, stnd LXi ($272). Elect. spd control, stnd LXi ($203). AM/FM stereo radio w/cass., clock & 4 spkrs ($174). Premium AM/FM stereo w/cass., equalizer & 8 spkrs ($550). Premium AM/FM stereo w/CD player, equalizer & 8 spkrs ($707).

1995 Chrysler, Cirrus LXi sedan (OCW)

CIRRUS CONVENIENCE/APPEARANCE OPTIONS: LX: Pkg. 24J: stnd equip. and 2.4-liter 4-cyl. engine in place of 2.5-liter V-6 ($699 credit). Pkg. 26J: stnd equip. only (NC). LXi: Pkg. 26K: stnd equip. plus LXi appliqués, leather int. incl. seating/shift knob/strg whl, AM/FM stereo radio w/cass & clock & 6 spkrs, pwr antenna, 8-way pwr driver's seat, security alarm, sport-tuned suspension, P195/65R15 tires and cast alum whls ($1930). Other: 8-way pwr driver's seat, stnd LXi ($377). Calif. emissions ($102). Eng. block htr ($30). Extra cost paint ($97). Integrated child's seat ($100). AM/FM stereo radio w/cass., clock & 6 spkrs, stnd LXi ($368). AM/FM stereo radio w/CD player, clock & 6 spkrs: LX ($491); LXi ($122). Cloth front bucket seats (NC). Leather front bucket seats, LXi only (NC). Security alarm, stnd LXi ($149). Conventional spare tire ($95).

CONCORDE CONVENIENCE/APPEARANCE OPTIONS: Pkg. 22B: stnd equip. (NC). Pkg. 22C: 22B plus auto. temp air cond., 8-way pwr driver's seat, remote illum. entry ($630). Pkg. 26C: 22C plus 3.5L V-6 ($1355). Pkg. 22D: 22C plus overhead console, auto. day/night rearview mirror, Chrysler/Infinity Spatial Imaging Cass Sound Syst., security alarm, spd sensitive stng ($1755). Pkg. 26D: 22D plus 3.5L V-6 ($2480). (AJF) Remote Illum. Entry Grp.: incl. remote keyless entry ($221). Integrated child's seat ($100). Calif. emissions ($102). 8-way pwr driver's seat ($377). 8-way pwr driver & pass seats ($377-$754). Leather bucket seats w/8-way pwr driver & pass seats, leather-wrapped stng whl & shift knob, rear bench seat ($1069). Security alarm ($149). Overhead console w/trip computer, compass and storage ($378). Pwr moonroof ($716-$1094). Eng. block htr ($20). Bright Platinum Metallic Paint ($200). Extra cost paint ($97). Chrysler/Infinity Spatial Imaging Sound Syst. w/Cass. ($708); w/CD player ($877), exc. w/Pkg. 26D ($169). (AGC) 16-in. Whl & Handling Grp.: incl. 16-in. "Spiralcast" alum whls, variable-assist spd-proportional stng and touring tires ($524-$628). Conventional spare tire ($95).

NEW YORKER LH CONVENIENCE/APPEARANCE OPTIONS: Pkg. 26A: stnd equip. (NC). Pkg. 26B: 26A plus auto. temp air cond, mini-overhead console w/trip computer/compass/reading lamps, dual illum. visor vanity mirrors, Remote Illum. Entry Grp., Chrysler/Infinity Spatial Imaging Sound Syst. w/Cass ($1338). Pkg. 26C: 26B plus Leather Int. Grp., 8-way pwr driver & pass seats, conventional spare tire, traction control, 16-in. "Spiralcast" alum whls ($2743). Calif. emissions ($102). Eng. block htr ($20). Pwr moonroof ($792). Bright Platinum Metallic Paint ($200). Extra cost paint ($97). Chrysler/Infinity Spatial Imaging Sound Syst. w/CD Player ($169). Pwr 8-way driver & pass seats ($377). Conventional spare tire ($95). 16-in. "Spiralcast" alum whls ($2743).

LHS CONVENIENCE/APPEARANCE OPTIONS: Pkg. 26J: stnd equip. (NC). Calif. Emissions ($102). Eng. block htr ($20). Bright Platinum Metallic Paint ($200). Extra cost paint ($97). Chrysler/Infinity Spatial Imaging Sound Syst. w/CD Player ($169).

HISTORY: Model year production: 218,767. Calendar year sales: 215,164. The Chrysler Atlantic concept vehicle debuted at the North American International Auto Show in Detroit on January 7, 1995. The coupe, finished in Silver Beige with a two-tone Rosewood leather interior, was designed in the spirit of luxury French custom coachbuilders of the late-1930s. The Atlantic was powered by an 4.0-liter, dual overhead cam inline eight-cylinder engine. The "straight eight" was rated at 325 horsepower. The concept coupe featured 21-inch front tires and 22-inch tires at the rear. The new Cirrus sedan was named Motor Trend magazine's 1995 "Car of the Year."

1996 CHRYSLER

1996 Chrysler, Sebring LX coupe (OCW)

Both the Sebring and Concorde lineups gained models for 1996, with the new Sebring convertible launched to replace the discontinued Le-Baron ragtop. The Sebring softtop was offered in two trim levels: JX and JXi. The previously one sedan Concorde series was doubled with the lineup now consisting of an LX sedan and more upscale LXi sedan. The New Yorker LH sedan was in its final year of production in 1996, which was also another poor sales year for the car that got "lost" between the Concorde and LHS.

SEBRING — SERIES J (coupe)/SERIES X (convertible) — FOUR/V-6 — Sharing the cab forward design of its Chrysler stablemates, a four-passenger convertible joined the Sebring series in 1996. The Sebring ragtop was offered in two trim levels: JX and JXi, similar to the existing Sebring LX and LXi coupes introduced the year previous. While the Sebring coupe was based on the FJ platform, the Sebring convertible was based on the JA platform also used for the Cirrus sedan (the convertible's platform was renamed JX by Chrysler engineers to avoid confusion with the Cirrus platform). The JX convertible was powered by the dual overhead cam 2.4-liter four-cylinder engine linked to an electronically controlled four-speed automatic transmission with overdrive. The more upscale JXi model used the 24-valve 2.5-liter V-6 and four-speed automatic as its powertrain. This pair was also optional in the JX. All powertrains were now equipped with the OBD II on-board diagnostics system. Standard features of the convertible included dual airbags, climate control air conditioning, power convertible top with glass rear window, stainless steel exhaust system, electric rear window defroster and tinted glass all-around. The JXi added anti-lock brakes, touring suspension, 16-inch cast aluminum wheels, power door locks, dual exhaust, fog lamps and illuminated entry system. The Sebring convertible's overall length measured 193 inches while its wheelbase was 106 inches. The LX coupe was again powered by the dual overhead cam 2.0-liter four-cylinder engine paired with a five-speed manual transmission. LXi models again used the 2.5-liter V-6 coupled with an electronically controlled four-speed automatic with overdrive, which was again optional in the LX. New features for the Sebring coupe were an enhanced evaporative emission control system, all powertrains were equipped with OBD II as well as the SBEC III Powertrain Control Module and three new exterior colors were offered: Polo Green, Spanish Olive and Light Autumnwood. New standard equipment for the LXi (and optional for the LX) featured a "panic" alarm added to the remote keyless entry system and the addition of a HomeLink three-channel universal transmitter for opening garage doors.

CIRRUS — SERIES A — FOUR/V-6 — The LX and LXi sedans again comprised the Cirrus lineup, both models now available with an optional power sunroof that was introduced in mid-year 1996. The dual overhead cam 2.4-liter four-cylinder engine introduced the previous year was now standard in the LX. The LXi was again powered by the 2.5-liter V-6 (optional on the LX), which featured a revised torque converter for more responsive performance. Both engines were equipped with an SBEC III Powertrain Control Module, and were again paired with the electronically controlled four-speed automatic transmission with overdrive. Other new features of the 1996 Cirrus were an enhanced evaporative emission control system, OBD II on-board diagnostics for all powertrains, front and rear "pillow" head rests, HomeLink three-channel universal transmitter for opening garage doors, Camel interior color and four exterior color choices: Candy Apple Red Metallic, Light Gold Pearl, Forest Green and Stone White. Late in the model year, the LXi could be ordered with optional chrome-plated aluminum wheels.

CONCORDE — SERIES H — V-6 — The Concorde lineup was expanded from its previous one sedan offering to now having two trim levels: LX and the more upscale LXi. The LX was powered by the 3.3-liter V-6 while the LXi used the 3.5-liter V-6. Only available in California, New York, Maine and Massachusetts was a 3.3-liter TLEV (transitional low emission vehicle) engine, optional on both LX and LXi sedans. All Concorde engines were linked to an electronically controlled four-speed automatic transmission with overdrive. In addition to several new audio offerings including a more powerful Infinity Spatial Imaging Cassette system, new features of the Concorde were improved headlight illumination, OBD II on-board diagnostics for all powertrains, seat fabric upgrade, refined NVH (noise, vibration, harshness) Control Package, SBEC III Powertrain Control Module, revised exterior appearance (exterior cladding was dropped in favor of a single color styling), and four new exterior color choices: Candy Apple Red Metallic, Opal, Island Teal and Stone White. The LX received 16-inch wheels as standard fare, as well as "Vanguard" bolt-on style wheel covers. The LXi featured "Sparkle Gold" cast aluminum wheels.

1996 Chrysler, Concorde LXi sedan (OCW)

NEW YORKER LH — SERIES H — V-6 — A sales disappointment since its launch in early-1993 as a redesigned cab-forward 1994 model, the long-running New Yorker name would be shelved after the 1996 model year. In its final year of production, the sedan's new standard features list included a HomeLink three-channel universal transmitter for opening garage doors, integral rear window radio antenna, OBD II on-board diagnostics capability, SBEC III Powertrain Control Module, refined NVH Control Package and four new exterior color selections: Candy Apple Metallic Red, Opal, Island Teal and Stone White. Also, previously optional equipment that was made standard included the automatic temperature control feature of the air conditioning system; mini overhead console with compass, thermometer and trip computer; illuminated entry system; remote keyless entry; Chrysler/Infinity Spatial Imaging Cassette Sound System with CD Changer; vehicle theft security alarm and power windows with driver override and one-touch down features. The New Yorker was again powered by the 3.5-liter V-6 linked to the electronically controlled four-speed automatic transmission with overdrive.

LHS — SERIES H — V-6 — New standard features of the LHS sedan mirrored those listed for New Yorker with exceptions being the addition of a more comfortable console armrest and a Drama Gold exterior color choice instead of the Opal and Island Teal selections. The LHS again was powered by the 3.5-liter V-6 linked to an electronically controlled four-speed automatic transmission with overdrive.

I.D. DATA: As before, Chrysler's 17-symbol Vehicle Identification Number (VIN) was on the upper left corner of the instrument panel, visible

through the windshield. Coding was similar to 1986-95. The model year code changed to 'T' for 1996.

SEBRING (FOUR/V-6)

Model No.	Body/ Style No.	Body Type & Seating	Factory Price	Shipping Weight	Prod. Total
XCH	27	2-dr. JX Conv.-4P	19460/20290	3244/3340	Note 1
XCP	27	2-dr. JXi Conv.-4P	24675	3432	Note 1
JCS	22	2-dr. LX Cpe-5P	16441/17271	2908/N/A	Note 2
JCP	22	2-dr. LXi Cpe-5P	20150	3157	Note 2

Note: Where applicable, prices and weights to left of slash for four-cylinder engine, to right for V-6.

Note 1: Sebring convertible production totaled 47,809 with no further breakout available.

Note 2: Sebring coupe production totaled 32,506 with no further breakout available.

CIRRUS (FOUR/V-6)

ACP	41	4-dr. LX Sed-5P	17560/18360	3148/N/A	Note 1
ACP	41	4-dr. LXi Sed-5P	20430	3153	Note 1

Note: Where applicable, prices and weights to left of slash for four-cylinder engine, to right for V-6.

Note 1: Cirrus sedan production totaled 43,367 with no further breakout available.

CONCORDE (V-6)

HLP	41	4-dr. LX Sed-6P	19445	3492	Note 1
HLP	41	4-dr. LXi Sed-6P	24100	N/A	Note 1

Note 1: Concorde sedan production totaled 49,994 with no further breakout available.

NEW YORKER LH (V-6)

HCH	41	4-dr. Sed-6P	27300	3587	3,295

LHS (V-6)

HCP	41	4-dr. Sed-5P	30225	3596	34,900

1996 Chrysler, LHS sedan with optional moonroof (OCW)

ENGINE DATA: BASE FOUR (Sebring LX): Inline, dual overhead cam four-cylinder. Cast iron block; aluminum head. Displacement: 121 cu. in. (2.0 liters). Bore & stroke: 3.44 x 3.27 in. Compression ratio: 9.6:1. Brake horsepower: 140 at 6000 RPM. Torque: 130 lb.-ft. at 4800 RPM. Sequential fuel injection. BASE FOUR (Sebring JX, Cirrus LX): Inline, dual overhead cam four-cylinder. Cast iron block; aluminum head. Displacement: 148 cu. in. (2.4 liters). Bore & stroke: 3.44 x 3.98 in. Compression ratio: 9.4:1. Brake horsepower: 150 at 5200 RPM. Torque: 167 lb.-ft. at 4000 RPM. Sequential fuel injection. BASE V-6 (Sebring JXi, Sebring LXi, Cirrus LXi); OPTIONAL (Sebring JX, Sebring LX, Cirrus LX): Overhead cam V-6. Cast iron block, aluminum heads. Displacement: 152 cu. in. (2.5 liters). Bore & stroke: 3.29 x 2.99 in. Compression ratio: 9.4:1. Brake horsepower: (Sebring LXi) 163 at 5500 RPM; (Sebring JXi, Cirrus LXi) 168 at 5800 RPM. Torque: (Sebring LXi) 170 lb.-ft. at 4400 RPM; (Sebring JXi, Cirrus LXi) 170 lb.-ft. at 4350 RPM. Sequential fuel injection. BASE V-6 (Concorde): Overhead valve V-6.

Cast iron block, aluminum heads. Displacement: 201 cu. in. (3.3 liters). Bore & stroke: 3.66 x 3.19 in. Compression ratio: 8.9:1. Brake horsepower: 161 at 5300 RPM. Torque: 181 lb.-ft. at 3200 RPM. Sequential fuel injection. OPTIONAL V-6 (Concorde): same as 3.3-liter above except transitional low emission vehicle engine offered in California, New York, Maine and Massachusetts. BASE V-6 (New Yorker, LHS): OPTIONAL (Concorde): 24-valve, overhead cam V-6. Cast iron block, aluminum heads. Displacement: 214 cu. in. (3.5 liters). Bore & stroke: 3.78 x 3.19 in. Compression ratio: 9.6:1. Brake horsepower: 214 at 5850 RPM. Torque: 221 lb.-ft. at 3100 RPM. Sequential fuel injection.

CHASSIS DATA: Wheelbase: (Sebring conv) 106.0 in.; (Sebring cpe) 103.7 in.; (Cirrus) 108.0 in.; (Concorde, N.Y., LHS) 113.0 in. Overall length: (Sebring conv) 193.0 in.; (Sebring cpe) 187.4 in.; (Cirrus) 186.0 in.; (Concorde) 202.8 in.; (N.Y., LHS) 207.4 in. Height: (Sebring conv) 54.8 in.; (Sebring cpe) 51.0 in.; (Cirrus) 52.5 in.; (Concorde) 56.3 in.; (N.Y., LHS) 55.7 in. Width: (Sebring conv) 69.2 in.; (Sebring cpe) 69.7 in.; (Cirrus) 71.7 in.; (Concorde, N.Y., LHS) 74.4 in. Front tread: (Sebring conv) 60.2 in.; (Sebring cpe) 59.5 in.; (Cirrus) 60.2 in.; (Concorde, N.Y., LHS) 62.0 in. Rear tread: (Sebring conv) 60.2 in.; (Sebring cpe) 59.3 in.; (Cirrus) 60.2 in.; (Concorde, N.Y., LHS) 62.0 in. Standard Tires: (Sebring JX) P205/65R15; (Sebring JXi) P215/55R16; (Sebring LX) P195/70R14; (Sebring LXi) P205/55HR16; (Cirrus) P195/65R15; (Concorde, N.Y., LHS) P225/60R16.

TECHNICAL: Transmission: Five-speed manual standard on Sebring LX. Four-speed automatic standard on Sebring JX, Sebring JXi, Sebring LXi, Cirrus, Concorde, N.Y., LHS. Steering: (all) Rack and pinion. Front Suspension: (Sebring conv) Unequal length upper and lower control arms, coil springs and (JX) tubular shock absorbers and stabilizer bar: (JXi) touring tuned springs and shock absorbers; (Sebring cpe) Modified double wishbone w/coil springs, direct acting shock absorbers and link-type stabilizer bar; (Cirrus) Unequal length upper and lower control arms, coil springs, tubular shock absorbers and (LX) stabilizer bar: (LXi) higher rate springs; (Concorde, N.Y., LHS) Iso-Strut w/integral gas-charged shock absorbers, coil springs, single transverse lower links, tension struts, and link-type stabilizer bar. Rear Suspension: (Sebring conv) Unequal length upper and lower control arms, trailing arms, coil springs and (JX) tubular shock absorbers and stabilizer bar; (JXi) touring tuned springs, shock absorbers and stabilizer bar; (Sebring cpe) Modified double wishbone w/coil springs and direct acting shock absorbers; (Cirrus) Unequal length upper and lower control arms, trailing arms, coil springs, tubular shock absorbers and (LX) stabilizer bar and higher rate springs; (Concorde, N.Y., LHS) Chapman struts w/integral gas-charged shock absorbers and concentric coil springs, dual transverse lower links, lower trailing links, and link-type stabilizer bar. Brakes: (Sebring JX, Concorde LX) Front disc, rear drum (power-assisted); (Sebring JXi, Sebring LX, Cirrus LX, Cirrus LXi) Front disc, rear drum w/anti-lock (power-assisted); (Sebring LXi, Concorde LXi, N.Y., LHS) anti-lock four-wheel disc. Body construction: Unibody. Fuel tank: (Sebring, Cirrus) 16 gal.; (Concorde, N.Y., LHS) 18 gal.

DRIVETRAIN OPTIONS: Engines: 2.5-liter V-6: Sebring JX (N/A); Sebring LX ($830); Cirrus LX ($800). 3.3-liter TLEV V-6: Concorde (N/A). 3.5-liter V-6: Concorde (N/A). Transmission/Differential: Four-speed automatic trans.: Sebring LX ($683). Anti-lock Brakes: Sebring JX ($565). Concorde LX ($600). Traction control: Concorde LX ($175); N.Y. ($175).

SEBRING CONVENIENCE/APPEARANCE OPTIONS: (JX): Pkg. 24A: stand equip. (NC). Pkg. 24B: 24A plus Pwr Convenience Grp., AM/FM stereo radio w/cass. & CD changer, auto. spd control, pwr decklid release, floor mats, remote keyless entry w/panic alarm, premium cloth seat trim, 6-way pwr driver's seat, illum. entry, dual illum. visor mirrors and headlamps w/time delay ($1635). Pkg. 26B: 24B plus 2.5L V-6, anti-lock brakes and dual exhaust ($3000). (JXi): Pkg. 26D: stnd equip. (NC). (LX): Pkg. 21G: stnd equip. (NC). Pkg. 22G: 21G plus 4-spd. auto. trans. ($683). Pkg. 21H: 21G plus trunk cargo net, pwr dr locks/windows/mirrors, spd control and dual illum. visor mirrors ($759). Pkg. 22H: 21H plus 4-spd. auto. trans. ($1442). Pkg. 24H: 22H plus 2.5L V-6 ($2272). (LXi): Pkg. 24J: stnd equip. (NC). Pkg. 24K: 24J plus pwr sunroof, leather seats and 6-way pwr driver's seat ($1266). Other: (AJW) Convenience Grp.: programmable pwr door locks and pwr heated outside mirrors, JX ($360). (AJB) Security Grp.: HomeLink garage dr opener and security alarm, JX ($240). HomeLink garage door opener, LX ($108). 6-way pwr driver's seat ($203). Security alarm incl. remote keyless entry, LX ($274). Pwr sunroof, N/A conv ($640). Auto. spd control, stnd JXi ($240). Extra cost paint: Candy Apple Red Metallic, conv ($150); other colors, conv ($100). Radio systems: RBN, LX ($550). RAZ: LX ($842); LXi ($292). RBS, JX ($275). RBR, JX ($170-$445). RDR, JX ($500). ARA, stnd JXi ($355). ARD: JX ($695); JXi ($340). Premium seat cloth trim: JX ($95); JX ($250 credit). (AY4) Touring Grp.: 16-in. cast alum whls, P215/55R16 tires, touring suspension and firm feel pwr stng, JX ($475).

CIRRUS CONVENIENCE/APPEARANCE OPTIONS: LX: Pkg. 24J: stnd equip. (NC). Pkg. 26J: 24J plus 2.5-liter V-6 ($800). LXi: Pkg. 26K: 26J plus LXi appliqués, leather int. incl. seating/shift knob/stng whl, AM/FM stereo radio w/cass & 8 spkrs, pwr antenna, 8-way pwr driver's seat, security alarm, and sport-tuned suspension ($2870). Other: 8-way

pwr driver's seat, stnd LXi ($380). Eng. block & battery htr ($30). Extra cost paint: Metallic ($150); other colors ($100). Integrated child's seat ($100). Pwr sunroof ($580). AM/FM stereo radio w/cass. & 8 spkrs, stnd LXi ($370). AM/FM stereo radio w/CD player & 8 spkrs: LX ($495); LXi ($125). Security alarm w/remote keyless entry, stnd LXi ($150). Conventional spare tire ($125).

CONCORDE CONVENIENCE/APPEARANCE OPTIONS: LX: Pkg. 22B: stnd equip. (NC). Pkg. 22C: 22B plus auto. temp air cond., 8-way pwr driver's seat, remote illum. entry, full overhead console, spd proportional stng, AM/FM stereo radio w/cass. & 8 spkrs and auto. day/night rearview mirror ($1620). LXi: Pkg. 26D: 22C exc. pwr driver's seat replaced w/8-way pwr driver and pass. seat and radio replaced by Chrysler/Infinity Spatial Imaging Cass Sound Syst., plus 3.5L V-6, Decor Grp., traction control, security alarm, 16-in. "Camelot" cast alum whls w/Sparkle Gold graphics ($4655). Other: (ALC) Luxury Appearance Pkg.: incl. 50/50 leather bench seats, 8-way pwr driver & pass seats, Sparkle Silver whls, overhead console and leather-wrapped stng whl ($1135). Integrated child's seat ($100). 8-way pwr driver & pass seats, LX ($380). Security alarm, LX ($150). Pwr Moonroof w/trip computer, compass and storage, auto. day/night rearview mirror, dual illum. visor mirrors ($720). Eng. block htr ($20). Chrysler/Infinity Spatial Imaging Sound Syst. w/Cass., LX ($300); w/CD player: LX ($600); LXi ($300). 16-in. Sparkle Silver "Camelot" alum whls, LX ($365). Conventional spare tire ($125). Extra cost paint: Metallic ($200); other colors ($100).

1996 Chrysler, Sebring JXi convertible (OCW)

NEW YORKER LH CONVENIENCE/APPEARANCE OPTIONS: Pkg. 26B: stnd equip. (NC). Pkg. 26C: 26B plus Leather Int. Grp. incl. seating and stng whl, 8-way pwr driver & pass seats, conventional spare tire and traction control ($1135). Eng. block htr ($20). Pwr moonroof ($795). Bright Platinum Metallic or Candy Apple Red Paint ($200). Char-Gold, Orchid or Spruce Paint ($100). Chrysler/Infinity Spatial Imaging Sound Syst. w/CD Player ($300). Pwr 8-way driver & pass seats ($380). Leather seat trim incl. leather-wrapped stng whl ($1080). Conventional spare tire ($95). 16-in. "Spiralcast" alum whls ($328).

LHS CONVENIENCE/APPEARANCE OPTIONS: Pkg. 26J: stnd equip. (NC). Pwr Moonroof ($795). Eng. block htr ($20). Bright Platinum Metallic Paint ($200). Other colors ($100). Chrysler/Infinity Spatial Imaging Sound Syst. w/CD Player ($300).

HISTORY: Model year production: 211,871. Calendar year sales: 212,021 (including 1,062 1995 LeBaron convertibles sold in 1996). In August 1996, Chrysler-Plymouth and Jeep-Eagle divisions of Chrysler Corp. were consolidated.

1997 CHRYSLER

Aside from the discontinuation of the New Yorker, Chrysler's 1997 lineup carried over unchanged from the previous year. The Sebring coupe was the first to wear Chrysler's new "winged" logo as part of its restyled front end. The Sebring convertible debuted Chrysler's AutoStick shiftable four-speed automatic transmission. Powertrain combinations for Sebring, Cirrus and Concorde changed for 1997, including the dropping of Concorde LX's 3.3-liter V-6. It was replaced by the LX's previously optional 3.5-liter V-6. The production of the LHS sedan was suspended after the 1997 model year, awaiting the arrival of an all-new 1999 LHS (launched in mid-1998) that was based on Chrysler's 1996 LHX concept car.

1997 Chrysler, Sebring LX coupe (OCW)

SEBRING — SERIES J (coupe)/SERIES X (convertible) — FOUR/V-6 — The Sebring returned in both coupe and convertible body styles, each again offered in two trim levels: JX and JXi for the ragtop and LX and LXi for the hardtop. The LX was again powered by the 2.0-liter four-cylinder engine mated to a five-speed manual transmission. A four-speed automatic transmission was again optional when the LX was ordered with the 2.0-liter four. The LXi again used the 2.5-liter V-6 and electronically controlled four-speed automatic transmission with overdrive for its powertrain, which was again optional on the LX. The 2.4-liter four-cylinder engine and four-speed automatic combination that was previously standard in the JX continued powering that convertible, but also became standard in the JXi. JXi's previously standard 2.5-liter V-6 was now the option engine for both the JX and JXi, which also both used the four-speed automatic with that V-6. The 2.4-liter powerplant featured a redesigned intake manifold for 1997 to quiet operation noise. The Sebring coupe received substantial restyling for 1997, including the first use of Chrysler's new "winged" logo up front. Revisions included a redesigned front fascia and grille, new bodyside cladding and headlamp mask turn lamps at the leading edge. In back, the fascia was reshaped and included new combination taillamps, dimensional fascia badging and Chrysler seal, and, on the LXi only a rear spoiler. Also new was dimensional bodyside badging, a woodgrain center stack bezel, black-and-tan interior scheme and two exterior color choices: Pewter Blue (replaced Medium Gray) and Paprika (replaced Spanish Olive). The LX offered new-style 14- and 16-inch wheel covers. The LXi received an automatic day/night rearview mirror, 17-inch cast aluminum wheels and P215/50HR17 tires and handling suspension with a rear anti-sway bar as new standard equipment. The Sebring convertible entered its second year of availability not resting on the laurels of a successful launch. Refinements were many, including Chrysler's new AutoStick Transmission Control System that was available when the optional 2.5-liter V-6 was ordered. AutoStick blended the performance of a manual shift with the smooth control of an electronic automatic transmission. Other new features of the ragtop were electroluminescent illumination for the automatic transmission console PRNDL indicators, an agate steering wheel cover, agate/light camel color scheme with camel interior and two exterior color choices: Flame Red and Deep Amethyst Pearl. Exclusive to the JXi was the addition of a trip computer with compass and thermometer. New optional equipment included an enhanced vehicle theft alarm system that deactivated the HomeLink transmitter and trunk release, damage-resistant power antenna, electrochromic rearview mirror and trunk unlock/panic alarm/rolling code features were added to the remote keyless entry system.

1997 Chrysler, Cirrus LX sedan (OCW)

CIRRUS — SERIES A — FOUR/V-6 — Both the LX and LXi sedans again comprising the Cirrus lineup featured the dual overhead cam 2.4-liter four-cylinder engine paired with the electronically controlled four-speed automatic transmission with overdrive as their standard powertrain in 1997. The 2.5-liter V-6 that was previously standard on the LXi and optional on the LX was now the option engine for both sedans. The 2.5-liter V-6, when ordered, was also linked to the four-speed automatic. The 2.4-liter four received both a revised intake manifold and oil pan for quieter operation. In addition to several upgrades in audio system availability,

the Cirrus sedan featured new map lamps that operated as courtesy lamps, a new floor console with armrest and storage, electroluminescent illumination for the automatic transmission console PRNDL indicators, and increased flow to the rear seat heat ducts. Inside, the Cirrus had updated interior decor featuring an agate instrument panel with camel interior, black instrument panel air outlets and rustic birdseye maple woodgrain accents. Exterior color selections were revised with Dark Chestnut Pearl replacing Orchid and Deep Amethyst Pearl replacing Light Gold. In the spring of the previous year, Cirrus buyers could order the optional Gold Package with select colors and this was continued for 1997. Cast aluminum wheels were now optional on the LX while chrome-plated aluminum wheels were standard on the LXi. Newly optional on both the LX and LXi was a mini-trip computer with compass and thermometer.

CONCORDE — SERIES H — V-6 — Both the LX and LXi sedans offered in the Concorde lineup were now powered by the 24-valve 3.5-liter V-6 that was formerly optional on the LX and standard on the LXi. The only transmission available to Concorde buyers was the adaptive electronically controlled four-speed automatic with overdrive, which underwent software refinements for 1997. The 3.3-liter V-6 previously standard in the LX was discontinued. Due to an all-new Concorde set for 1998 release, the 1997 version was basically a carryover from the previous year. Minor refinements that were carried out included the addition of hood-mounted windshield washer nozzles and a new exterior color choice: Deep Amethyst Pearl, which replaced Orchid.

LHS — SERIES H — V-6 — Production of the LHS sedan was stopped after the 1997 production run ended to make way for an all-new 1999 LHS sedan. In its pre-hiatus version, the LHS was again powered by the 3.5-liter V-6 linked to an adaptive electronically controlled four-speed automatic transmission with overdrive. Changes from the year previous model were minimal including software refinements to the transmission and Deep Amethyst Pearl added as an exterior color choice.

I.D. DATA: As before, Chrysler's 17-symbol Vehicle Identification Number (VIN) was on the upper left corner of the instrument panel, visible through the windshield. Coding was similar to 1986-96. The model year code changed to 'V' for 1997.

SEBRING (FOUR/V-6)

Model No.	Body/ Style No.	Body Type & Seating	Factory Price	Shipping Weight	Prod. Total
XCH	27	2-dr. JX Conv.-4P	20150/20950	3350/N/A	Note 1
XCP	27	2-dr. JXi Conv.-4P	24660/25460	3365/N/A	Note 1
JCS	22	2-dr. LX Cpe-5P	16540/17370	2888/3117	Note 2
JCP	22	2-dr. LXi Cpe-5P	21020	3197	Note 2

Note: Where applicable, prices and weights to left of slash for four-cylinder engine, to right for V-6.

Note 1: Sebring convertible production totaled 55,887 with no further breakout available.

Note 2: Sebring coupe production totaled 33,097 with no further breakout available.

CIRRUS (FOUR/V-6)

ACP	41	4-dr. LX Sed-5P	18030/18730	3099/N/A	Note 1
ACP	41	4-dr. LXi Sed-5P	20365/21065	N/A/N/A	Note 1

Note: Where applicable, prices and weights to left of slash for four-cylinder engine, to right for V-6.

Note 1: Cirrus sedan production totaled 27,913 with no further breakout available.

CONCORDE (V-6)

HLP	41	4-dr. LX Sed-6P	20435	3468	Note 1
HLP	41	4-dr. LXi Sed-6P	24665	N/A	Note 1

Note 1: Concorde sedan production totaled 50,913 with no further breakout available.

LHS (V-6)

HCP	41	4-dr. Sed-5P	30255	3625	36,525

ENGINE DATA: BASE FOUR (Sebring LX): Inline, dual overhead cam four-cylinder. Cast iron block; aluminum head. Displacement: 121 cu. in. (2.0 liters). Bore & stroke: 3.44 x 3.27 in. Compression ratio: 9.6:1. Brake horsepower: 140 at 6000 RPM. Torque: 130 lb.-ft. at 4800 RPM. Sequential fuel injection. **BASE FOUR (Sebring JX, Sebring JXi, Cirrus LX, Cirrus LXi):** Inline, dual overhead cam four-cylinder. Cast iron block; aluminum head. Displacement: 148 cu. in. (2.4 liters). Bore & stroke: 3.44 x 3.98 in. Compression ratio: 9.4:1. Brake horsepower: 150 at 5200 RPM. Torque: 167 lb.-ft. at 4000 RPM. Sequential fuel injection.

BASE V-6 (Sebring LXi); OPTIONAL (Sebring JX, Sebring JXi, Sebring LX, Cirrus LX, Cirrus LXi): Overhead cam V-6. Cast iron block, aluminum heads. Displacement: 152 cu. in. (2.5 liters). Bore & stroke: 3.29 x 2.99 in. Compression ratio: 9.4:1. Brake horsepower: (Sebring LXi) 163 at 5500 RPM; (Sebring JX, Sebring JXi, Cirrus LX, Cirrus LXi) 168 at 5800 RPM. Torque: (Sebring LXi) 170 lb.-ft. at 4400 RPM; (Sebring JX, Sebring JXi, Cirrus LX, Cirrus LXi) 170 lb.-ft. at 4350 RPM. Sequential fuel injection. **BASE V-6 (Concorde, LHS):** 24-valve, overhead cam V-6. Cast iron block, aluminum heads. Displacement: 214 cu. in. (3.5 liters). Bore & stroke: 3.78 x 3.19 in. Compression ratio: 9.6:1. Brake horsepower: 214 at 5850 RPM. Torque: 221 lb.-ft. at 3100 RPM. Sequential fuel injection.

CHASSIS DATA: Wheelbase: (Sebring conv) 106.0 in.; (Sebring cpe) 103.7 in.; (Cirrus) 108.0 in.; (Concorde, LHS) 113.0 in. Overall length: (Sebring conv) 193.0 in.; (Sebring cpe) 191.1 in.; (Cirrus) 186.0 in.; (Concorde) 202.8 in.; (LHS) 207.4 in. Height: (Sebring conv) 54.8 in.; (Sebring cpe) 53.0 in.; (Cirrus) 52.5 in.; (Concorde) 56.3 in.; (LHS) 55.7 in. Width: (Sebring conv) 69.2 in.; (Sebring cpe) 69.4 in.; (Cirrus) 71.7 in.; (Concorde, LHS) 74.4 in. Front tread: (Sebring conv) 60.2 in.; (Sebring cpe) 59.5 in.; (Cirrus) 60.2 in.; (Concorde, LHS) 62.0 in. Rear tread: (Sebring conv) 60.2 in.; (Sebring cpe) 59.3 in.; (Cirrus) 60.2 in.; (Concorde, LHS) 62.0 in. Standard Tires: (Sebring JX) P205/65R15; (Sebring JXi) P215/55R16; (Sebring LX) P195/70R14; (Sebring LXi) P215/50HR17; (Cirrus) P195/65R15; (Concorde, LHS) P225/60R16.

1997 Chrysler, Concorde LXi sedan (OCW)

TECHNICAL: Transmission: Five-speed manual standard on Sebring LX. Four-speed automatic standard on Sebring JX, Sebring JXi, Sebring LXi, Cirrus, Concorde, LHS. Steering: (all) Rack and pinion. Front Suspension: (Sebring conv) Unequal length upper and lower control arms, coil springs and (JX) tubular shock absorbers and stabilizer bar: (JXi) touring tuned springs and shock absorbers; (Sebring cpe) Modified double wishbone w/coil springs, direct acting shock absorbers and link-type stabilizer bar; (Cirrus) Unequal length upper and lower control arms, coil springs, tubular shock absorbers and (LX) stabilizer bar: (LXi) higher rate springs; (Concorde, LHS) Iso-Strut w/integral gas-charged shock absorbers, coil springs, single transverse lower links, tension struts, and tubular link-type stabilizer bar. Rear Suspension: (Sebring conv) Unequal length upper and lower control arms, trailing arms, coil springs and (JX) tubular shock absorbers and stabilizer bar; (JXi) touring tuned springs, shock absorbers and stabilizer bar; (Sebring cpe) Modified double wishbone w/coil springs and direct acting shock absorbers (LXi added link-type stabilizer bar); (Cirrus) Unequal length upper and lower control arms, trailing arms, coil springs, tubular shock absorbers and (LX) stabilizer bar: (LXi) stabilizer bar and higher rate springs; (Concorde, LHS) Chapman struts w/integral gas-charged shock absorbers and concentric coil springs, dual transverse lower links, lower trailing links, and link-type stabilizer bar. Brakes: (Sebring JX, Concorde LX) Front disc, rear drum (power-assisted); (Sebring JXi, Sebring LX, Cirrus LX, Cirrus LXi) Front disc, rear drum w/anti-lock (power-assisted); (Sebring LXi, Concorde LXi, LHS) anti-lock four-wheel disc. Body construction: Unibody. Fuel tank: (Sebring conv, Cirrus) 16 gal.; (Sebring cpe) 16.9 gal.; (Concorde, LHS) 18 gal.

DRIVETRAIN OPTIONS: Engines: 2.5-liter V-6: Sebring JX ($1365); Sebring JXi ($800); Sebring LX ($830); Cirrus LX ($800); Cirrus LXi ($800). Transmission/Differential: Four-speed automatic trans.: Sebring LX ($695). Anti-lock Brakes: Sebring JX ($565). Sebring LX, four-wheel disc w/ABS ($599). Concorde LX ($600). Traction control: Concorde LX ($175).

SEBRING CONVENIENCE/APPEARANCE OPTIONS: (JX): Pkg. 24A: stand equip. (NC). Pkg. 24B: 24A plus Pwr Convenience Grp., AM/FM

stereo radio w/cass. & CD changer, auto. spd control, pwr decklid release, floor mats, remote keyless illum. entry w/panic alarm, Ultrahide bucket seats, 6-way pwr driver's seat, Light Grp., dual heated foldaway outside mirrors and headlamps w/time delay ($1585). Pkg. 26B: 24B plus 2.5L V-6 ($2950). Pkg. 26C: 26B plus AutoStick transmission ($3145). (JXi): Pkg. 24D: stnd equip. (NC). Pkg. 26D: 24D plus 2.5L V-6 ($800). Pkg. 26E: 26D plus AutoStick transmission ($995). (LX): Pkg. 21G: stnd equip. (NC). Pkg. 22G: 21G plus 4-spd. auto. trans. ($695). Pkg. 21H: 21G plus trunk cargo net, pwr dr locks/windows/mirrors, spd control, dual pwr outside mirrors and dual illum. visor mirrors ($771). Pkg. 22H: 21H plus 4-spd. auto. trans. ($1466). Pkg. 24H: 22H plus 2.5L V-6, 16-in. tires & whl covers, rear disc brakes, suspension upgrade and dual exhaust ($2296). (LXi): Pkg. 24J: stnd equip. (NC). Pkg. 24K: 24J plus leather seats and 6-way pwr driver's seat ($626). Other: (AJW) Pwr Convenience Grp.: programmable pwr door locks and pwr heated outside mirrors, conv ($360). (AJB) Security Grp.: security alarm and central locking, JX ($150). (AWK) Luxury Grp.: HomeLink garage door opener and auto. day/night rearview mirror, conv ($175). Security alarm incl. remote keyless entry, LX ($287). Pwr sunroof, N/A conv ($640). Auto. spd control, JX ($240). Extra cost paint: Candy Apple Red Metallic, conv ($200). Radio systems: RBX, LX ($435). RAZ: LX ($760); LXi ($326). RBS, JX ($275). RBR, JX ($170-$445). ARA, stnd JX ($440). ARD: JX ($780); JXi ($340). CD changer, conv ($500). Auto. day/night rearview mirror, LX ($86). Premium seat cloth trim: JX ($95); JXi ($250 credit). (AY4) Touring Grp.: 16-in. cast alum whls, P215/55R16 tires, touring suspension and firm feel pwr stng, JX ($495). (AY9) Wheel Grp.: 16-in. cast alum whls, P205/55HR15 tires, LX ($333-$490).

1997 Chrysler, LHS sedan (OCW)

CIRRUS CONVENIENCE/APPEARANCE OPTIONS: LX: Pkg. 24J: stnd equip. (NC). Pkg. 26J: 24J plus 2.5-liter V-6 ($800). LXi: Pkg. 24K: 24J plus LXi appliqués, trunk cargo net, body color grille, leather int. incl. seating/shift knob/stng whl, folding rear headrests, AM/FM stereo radio w/cass & CD changer & 8 spkrs and 8-way pwr driver's seat ($2335). Pkg. 26K: 24K plus 2.5L V-6 ($3135). Other: (ALJ) Gold Pkg.: LX: incl. C-pillar LX badging, gold Chrysler door nameplates, gold fascia accent side mldgs; LXi: incl. painted grille w/gold emblem, camel int., and "Finale" cast alum whls w/gold pockets ($450). 8-way pwr driver's seat, stnd LXi ($380). Eng. block & battery htr ($30). Extra cost paint: Candy Apple Red Metallic ($200). Integrated child's seat, LX ($100). Pwr sunroof ($580). AM/FM stereo radio w/cass., CD changer & 8 spkrs, LX ($340). AM/FM stereo radio w/CD player & 4 spkrs: LX ($200). Premium AM/FM stereo radio w/cass., in-dash CD changer & 4 spkrs ($550). CD changer ($500). Security alarm, LX ($150). Conventional spare tire ($125). Mini trip computer w/compass and thermometer ($160). 15-in. "Finale" cast alum whls ($320).

1997 Chrysler, Sebring JXi convertible (OCW)

CONCORDE CONVENIENCE/APPEARANCE OPTIONS: LX: Pkg. 26B: stnd equip. (NC). Pkg. 26C: 26B plus auto. temp air cond., trunk cargo net, 8-way pwr driver's seat, remote keyless illum. entry, dual illum. visor mirrors, full overhead console, AM/FM stereo radio w/cass. & CD changer & 8 spkrs and auto. day/night rearview mirror ($1280). LXi: Pkg. 26D: 26C exc. radio replaced by Chrysler/Infinity Spatial Imaging Cass Sound Syst., plus anti-lock brakes, Decor Grp., 8-way pwr driver & pass seats, leather seating/stng whl/shift knob, spd sensitive stng, traction control, security alarm, 16-in. "Camelot" cast alum whls w/Spar-

kle Gold graphics ($4230). Other: (ALC) Luxury Appearance Pkg.: incl. 50/50 leather bench seats, 8-way pwr driver & pass seats, Sparkle Silver whls, and leather-wrapped stng whl, LX ($1135). 8-way pwr driver & pass seats, LX ($380). Security alarm, LX ($150). Pwr Moonroof w/trip computer, compass and storage, auto. day/night rearview mirror, dual illum. visor mirrors ($720). Eng. block htr ($20). Chrysler/Infinity Spatial Imaging Sound Syst. w/Cass., LX ($215); w/CD player: LX ($515); LXi ($300). 16-in. Sparkle Silver "Camelot" alum whls, LX ($365). Conventional spare tire ($125). Extra cost paint: Metallic ($200).

1997 Chrysler, Cirrus LXi sedan (OCW)

LHS CONVENIENCE/APPEARANCE OPTIONS: Pkg. 26J: stnd equip. (NC). Pwr Moonroof ($795). Eng. block htr ($20). Extra cost paint ($200). Chrysler/Infinity Spatial Imaging Sound Syst. w/CD Player ($300).

HISTORY: Model year production: 204,334. Calendar year sales: 188,929. Embracing and contemporizing the classic design cues from historic touring automobiles of the 1930s and 1940s, Chrysler debuted its Phaeton concept car at the 1997 North American International Auto Show in Detroit. The Phaeton was a dual cowl four-door convertible with detachable hardtop, which was inspired by the 1940 Newport parade car that also paced the 1941 Indianapolis 500. The Phaeton was powered by a 48-valve 5.4-liter aluminum V-12 rated at 425 horsepower. Its overall length spanned 215 inches with a 132-inch wheelbase. It was finished in two-tone champagne pearl and featured a two-tone leather interior with wood accents.

1998 CHRYSLER

1998 Chrysler, Sebring JXi convertible (OCW)

The 1998 Chrysler ranks were thinned due to the discontinuation of the Cirrus LX sedan and the hiatus of the LHS sedan (the 1999 LHS debuted mid-year 1998-see 1999 listing). The "second-generation" cab-forward design Concorde sedan was introduced, remaining available in LX and LXi trim levels. Two new engines powered the Concorde sedan, the LX using a 2.7-liter V-6 and the LXi featuring a 3.2-liter V-6. Both the Sebring JXi convertible and Cirrus LXi sedan returned to the 2.5-liter V-6 as their standard powerplant after the previous year's foray into using the 2.4-liter four as base engine. Sebring also offered an optional trim package called Limited that featured chrome wheels, leather and woodgrain interior trim and special exterior badging.

SEBRING — SERIES J (coupe)/SERIES X (convertible) — FOUR/V-6 — After extensive restyling the previous year, the Sebring LX and LXi coupes returned basically as carryover models for 1998. Powertrain combinations remained unchanged, the LX powered by the dual overhead cam 2.0-liter four-cylinder engine linked to a five-speed manual transmission and the LXi using the 2.5-liter V-6 mated to an electronically controlled four-speed automatic with overdrive (again the option combi-

nation for the LX). Notable changes to the Sebring coupe were a new black and gray interior color scheme and one new exterior color choice: "Caffe Latte." In addition to the JX and JXi convertibles that were offered previously, the Sebring lineup now included an optional trim level called Limited. For $1,550 over the cost of a JXi, a buyer could have a Limited that featured a 2.5-liter V-6 linked to an AutoStick four-speed automatic transmission, anti-lock four-wheel disc brakes, traction control, chrome-plated cast aluminum wheels, leather- and woodgrain-trimmed interior finished in an agate color scheme, instrument cluster with electroluminescent lighting and special "Limited" and Chrysler "winged" exterior badging. The JX convertible was again powered by the dual overhead cam 2.4-liter four-cylinder engine mated to a four-speed automatic. The JXi, after one year of relying on the 2.4-liter four as standard powerplant, again featured the 2.5-liter V-6 and four-speed automatic, with AutoStick optional. The 2.5-liter V-6 was again optional on the JX. Refinements to the JX and JXi included "next-generation" airbags, a new agate interior color and five new exterior color choices: Champagne Pearl, Alpine Green, Platinum Silver, Intense Blue and Deep Slate. The JXi featured new 16-inch cast aluminum performance wheels and gold tone badging and wheel accents for 1998. New optional equipment included a refined anti-lock four-wheel disc brake system that incorporated traction control and a "Smart Key" vehicle immobilizer feature added to the personal security and theft package. "Smart Key" required a computer match between the key and the ignition for the car to start.

1998 Chrysler, Cirrus LXi sedan (OCW)

CIRRUS — SERIES A — V-6 — The Cirrus LX sedan was dropped so the LXi was the lone offering in the series. As with the Sebring JXi convertible, the Cirrus LXi returned to using the 2.5-liter V-6 as its standard engine after a year away using the 2.4-liter four-cylinder engine. The LXi again used the adaptive electronically controlled four-speed automatic transmission with overdrive. New features of the Cirrus LXi included "next-generation" airbags and five new exterior color choices: Champagne Pearl, Alpine Green, Bright Platinum, Deep Cranberry and Deep Slate.

1998 Chrysler, Concorde LXi sedan (OCW)

CONCORDE — SERIES H — V-6 — While the trim levels offered in the Concorde sedan lineup sounded familiar, LX and LXi, the car itself was completely redesigned for the first time since its introduction as a 1993 model. All-new powerplants and a "second-generation" cab-forward design were part of the Concorde's makeover, the reshaped exterior so slippery its coefficient of drag measured 0.298. The LX's powertrain

consisted of the all-new, all-aluminum, 24-valve 2.7-liter V-6 paired with an adaptive electronically controlled four-speed automatic transmission. The LXi used an all-aluminum, 24-valve 3.2-liter V-6 linked to a four-speed automatic, the all-new engine up to 25 percent more powerful and 10 percent more fuel efficient than the discontinued 3.5-liter V-6 that was formerly standard in both the LX and LXi. The 2.7-liter V-6 churned out 200 horsepower while the 3.2-liter version was rated at 220 horses. The 1998 Concorde also represented Chrysler's first "paperless" car program whereby all design and engineering were done using the automaker's advanced CATIA computer system. New Concordes featured a lower hood profile with less front overhang, and all 1998 models wore Chrysler's "winged" emblem that originated in similar fashion on Walter P. Chrysler's first car in 1924. Inside, Concorde featured more interior and trunk room than its predecessor and its rear passenger compartment was lengthened by 2.5 inches. A long list of new features included a pass-through between rear seat and the trunk, "next-generation" airbags, redesigned instrument panel that featured an industry-first soft-touch TPU (thermal plastic urethane) outer layer with integrally molded urethane foam padding, repositioned multi-function switch stalk on the steering column, remote trunk release repositioned from the glovebox to left of the steering column, larger headlamps with new quad bulb and reflector design, high-strength steel replaced mild steel for front/rear rails and B-pillars for increased impact resistance, aluminum hood to reduce weight and corrosion, battery saver, revised anti-lock and anti-lock/traction control system for quieter operation, higher-capacity defroster system for quicker windshield clearing, bolt-on wheel covers to reduce theft, magnesium steering wheel structure to reduce weight, isolated aluminum rear suspension crossmember to reduce NVH (noise, vibration and harshness) and weight, structural headliner to reduce NVH, and Chrysler Corp.'s first use of On-board Refueling Vapor Recovery system (ORVR).

I.D. DATA: As before, Chrysler's 17-symbol Vehicle Identification Number (VIN) was on the upper left corner of the instrument panel, visible through the windshield. Coding was similar to 1986-97. The model year code changed to 'W' for 1998.

SEBRING (FOUR/V-6)

Model No.	Body/ Style No.	Body Type & Seating	Factory Price	Shipping Weight	Prod. Total
XCH	27	2-dr. JX Conv.-4P	20575/21940	3344/N/A	Note 1
XCP	27	2-dr. JXi Conv.-4P	25840	3406	Note 1
JCS	22	2-dr. LX Cpe-5P	16840/17670	2888/2959	Note 2
JCP	22	2-dr. LXi Cpe-5P	20775	3197	Note 2

Note: Where applicable, prices and weights to left of slash for four-cylinder engine, to right for V-6.

Note 1: Sebring convertible production totaled 50,814 with no further breakout available.

Note 2: Sebring coupe production totaled 35,010 with no further breakout available.

CIRRUS (V-6)

ACP	41	4-dr. LXi Sed-5P	19460	3181	37,290

CONCORDE (V-6)

HLP	41	4-dr. LX Sed-6P	21305	3451	Note 1
HLP	41	4-dr. LXi Sed-6P	24220	3531	Note 1

Note 1: Concorde sedan production totaled 46,535 with no further breakout available.

ENGINE DATA: BASE FOUR (Sebring LX): Inline, dual overhead cam four-cylinder. Cast iron block; aluminum head. Displacement: 121 cu. in. (2.0 liters). Bore & stroke: 3.44 x 3.27 in. Compression ratio: 9.6:1. Brake horsepower: 140 at 6000 RPM. Torque: 130 lb.-ft. at 4800 RPM. Sequential fuel injection. **BASE FOUR (Sebring JX):** Inline, dual overhead cam four-cylinder. Cast iron block; aluminum head. Displacement: 148 cu. in. (2.4 liters). Bore & stroke: 3.44 x 3.98 in. Compression ratio: 9.4:1. Brake horsepower: 150 at 5200 RPM. Torque: 167 lb.-ft. at 4000 RPM. Sequential fuel injection. **BASE V-6 (Sebring JXi, Sebring LXi, Cirrus LXi); OPTIONAL (Sebring JX, Sebring LX):** Overhead cam V-6. Cast iron block, aluminum heads. Displacement: 152 cu. in. (2.5 liters). Bore & stroke: 3.29 x 2.99 in. Compression ratio: 9.4:1. Brake horsepower: (Sebring JXi, Sebring LXi) 163 at 5500 RPM; (Cirrus LXi) 168 at 5800 RPM. Torque: 170 lb.-ft. at 4350 RPM. Sequential fuel injection. **BASE V-6 (Concorde LX):** 24-valve, dual overhead cam V-6. Aluminum block and heads. Displacement: 167 cu. in. (2.7 liters). Bore & stroke: 3.38 x 3.09 in. Compression ratio: 9.7:1. Brake horsepower: 200 at 6000 RPM. Torque: 188 lb.-ft. at 4900 RPM. Sequential fuel injection. **BASE V-6 (Concorde LXi):** 24-valve, overhead cam V-6. Aluminum block and heads. Displacement: 197 cu. in. (3.2 liters). Bore & stroke: 3.62 x 3.19 in. Compression ratio: 9.5:1. Brake horsepower:

220 at 6600 RPM. Torque: 222 lb.-ft. at 4000 RPM. Sequential fuel injection.

CHASSIS DATA: Wheelbase: (Sebring conv) 106.0 in.; (Sebring cpe) 103.7 in.; (Cirrus) 108.0 in.; (Concorde) 113.0 in. Overall length: (Sebring conv) 192.6 in.; (Sebring cpe) 191.1 in.; (Cirrus) 187.0 in.; (Concorde) 209.1 in. Height: (Sebring conv) 54.8 in.; (Sebring cpe) 53.0 in.; (Cirrus) 52.5 in.; (Concorde) 55.9 in. Width: (Sebring conv) 70.1 in.; (Sebring cpe) 69.4 in.; (Cirrus) 71.7 in.; (Concorde) 74.7 in. Front tread: (Sebring conv) 60.2 in.; (Sebring cpe) 59.5 in.; (Cirrus) 60.2 in.; (Concorde) 62.0 in. Rear tread: (Sebring conv) 60.2 in.; (Sebring cpe) 59.3 in.; (Cirrus) 60.2 in.; (Concorde) 62.0 in. Standard Tires: (Sebring JX) P205/65R15; (Sebring JXi) P215/55R16; (Sebring LX) P195/70R14; (Sebring LXi) P215/50HR17; (Cirrus) P195/65R15; (Concorde) P205/70R15.

TECHNICAL: Transmission: Five-speed manual standard on Sebring LX. Four-speed automatic standard on Sebring JX, Sebring JXi, Sebring LXi, Cirrus LXi, Concorde. Steering: (all) Rack and pinion. Front Suspension: (Sebring conv) Unequal length upper and lower control arms, coil springs and (JX) tubular shock absorbers and stabilizer bar; (JXi) touring tuned springs and shock absorbers; (Sebring cpe) Modified double wishbone w/coil springs, direct acting shock absorbers and link-type stabilizer bar; (Cirrus LXi) Unequal length upper and lower control arms, coil springs, tubular shock absorbers and higher rate springs; (Concorde) Iso-Strut w/integral gas-charged shock absorbers, coil springs, single transverse lower links, tension struts, and tubular link-type stabilizer bar. Rear Suspension: (Sebring conv) Unequal length upper and lower control arms, trailing arms, coil springs and (JX) tubular shock absorbers and stabilizer bar; (JXi) touring tuned springs, shock absorbers and stabilizer bar; (Sebring cpe) Modified double wishbone w/coil springs and direct acting shock absorbers (LXi added link-type stabilizer bar); (Cirrus) Unequal length upper and lower control arms, trailing arms, coil springs, tubular shock absorbers and stabilizer bar and higher rate springs; (Concorde) Chapman struts w/integral gas-charged shock absorbers and concentric coil springs, dual transverse lower links, lower trailing links, and link-type stabilizer bar. Brakes: (Sebring JX) Front disc, rear drum (power-assisted); (Sebring JXi, Sebring LX, Cirrus LXi) Front disc, rear drum w/anti-lock (power-assisted); (Concorde LX) four-wheel disc (power-assisted); (Sebring LXi, Concorde LXi) anti-lock four-wheel disc. Body construction: Unibody. Fuel tank: (Sebring conv, Cirrus) 16 gal.; (Sebring cpe) 16.9 gal.; (Concorde) N/A.

DRIVETRAIN OPTIONS: Engines: 2.5-liter V-6: Sebring JX ($1365); Sebring LX ($830). Transmission/Differential: Four-speed automatic trans.: Sebring JX ($695). Anti-lock Brakes: Sebring JX ($565). Sebring LX, four-wheel disc w/ABS ($600). Concorde LX ($600). Traction control: Sebring JX ($225-$790). Sebring JXi ($225). Concorde LX ($175).

SEBRING CONVENIENCE/APPEARANCE OPTIONS: (JX): Pkg. 2A: stand equip. (NC). Pkg. 2B: 2A plus Pwr Convenience Grp., AM/FM stereo radio w/cass. & CD changer, auto. spd control, pwr decklid release, floor mats, remote keyless illum. entry w/panic alarm, 6-way pwr driver's seat, Light Grp., dual heated foldaway outside mirrors and headlamps w/time delay ($1585). Pkg. 2C: 2B plus 2.5L V-6 and AutoStick 4-spd. auto. trans. ($2610). (JXi): Pkg. 2D: stnd equip. (NC). Pkg. 2E: 2D plus 2.5L V-6 and AutoStick 4-spd. auto. trans. ($1025). Pkg. 2G: Limited incl. 2.5L V-6 and AutoStick 4-spd. auto. trans., traction control w/4-whl disc brakes, Luxury Convenience Grp., and Limited Decor Grp. ($1550). (LX): Pkg. 2G: stnd equip. (NC). Pkg. 2H: 2G plus trunk cargo net, pwr dr locks/windows/mirrors, spd control, and dual illum. visor mirrors ($780). (LXi): Pkg. 2J: stnd equip. (NC). Pkg. 2K: 2J plus leather seats and 6-way pwr driver's seat (NC). Other: (AJW) Pwr Convenience Grp.: incl. programmable pwr door locks and pwr heated outside mirrors, conv ($360). (AJB) Security Grp.: incl. Smart Key eng. immobilizer, security alarm and central locking, JX ($175). (AWK) Luxury Grp.: incl. garage door opener and auto. day/night rearview mirror, JX ($175). Eng. block heater ($30). Security alarm incl. remote keyless entry, LX ($290). Pwr sunroof, N/A conv ($640). Auto. spd control, JX ($240). 6-way pwr driver's seat ($205). Cloth seat trim: JX ($95); JXi ($250 credit). Candy Apple Red Metallic Paint, conv ($200). Radio systems: RBX, LX ($435). RAZ: LX ($760); LXi ($326). RBS: JXi ($275); LXi ($275). RBR, JX ($170-$445). ARA, JX ($355). ARD: JX ($695); JXi ($340). CD changer, conv ($500). Premium seat cloth trim: JX ($95); JXi ($250 credit). (AY4) Touring Grp.: 16-in. cast alum whls, P215/55R16 tires, touring suspension and firm feel pwr stng, JX ($495). (AY9) Wheel Grp.: 16-in. cast alum whls, P205/55HR15 tires, LX ($335-$490).

CIRRUS CONVENIENCE/APPEARANCE OPTIONS: LXi: Pkg. 26K: stnd equip. (NC). Other: (ALJ) Gold Pkg.: incl. gold badging, gold fascia accents and 15-in. chrome-plated whls w/gold pockets ($500). 8-way pwr driver's seat, stnd LXi ($380). Eng. block & battery htr ($30). Candy Apple Red Metallic Paint ($200). Pwr sunroof ($580). AM/FM stereo radio w/cass., CD changer & 8 spkrs, LX ($340). AM/FM stereo radio w/cass., in-dash CD changer & 4 spkrs ($550). Security alarm ($150). Conventional spare tire ($125).

CONCORDE CONVENIENCE/APPEARANCE OPTIONS: LX: Pkg. 22C: stnd equip. (NC). Pkg. 22D: 22C plus 8-way pwr driver & pass seats, 16-in. whl & tire grp., garage door opener, trip computer, Premium cass. player w/amp & 8 spkrs and auto. day/night rearview mirror ($1265). LXi: Pkg. 24F: 22D exc. 16-in. whl & tire grp. replaced by 16x7 alum whls, plus auto. temp air cond., LXi gold badging, 4-whl anti-lock disc brakes, Premium CD player w/amp & 8 spkrs, leather bucket seats/stng whl/shift knob, security alarm, Sentry Key theft deterrent syst., full-size spare tire, and traction control ($3725). Other: Candy Apple Red Paint ($200). Eng. block & battery htr ($30). Pwr sunroof, LXi ($795). Leather 50/50 bench seat ($100). Premium cloth 50/50 split bench seat ($100). AM/FM stereo radio w/CD & cass., equal., amp and 9 spkrs ($370). Premium AM/FM stereo radio w/CD changer, amp and 8 spkrs, LX ($145-$435). (AGC) 16-in. Wheel & Tire Grp.: incl. P225/60R16 touring tires and 16-in. whl covers, LX ($200). Full-size spare tire, LX ($125).

HISTORY: Model year production: 169,649. Following the previous year's positive reaction to the Phaeton, Chrysler returned to the 1998 auto show circuit with a new concept car called the Chronos, inspired by the 1953 Chrysler D'Elegance concept vehicle. The four-door Chronos was powered by a 350-horsepower 6.0-liter V-10 linked to a 46RE electronically controlled four-speed automatic transmission. It was finished in Sterling Blue clear coat and featured a dark blue and yellow two-tone leather interior. The Chronos' overall length measured 205.4 inches with a 131.0-inch wheelbase. It rode on 20-inch front tires and 21-inch rears.

1999 CHRYSLER

Chrysler Corp. shocked the automotive industry in 1999 after it announced a merger with German automaker Daimler-Benz. This merger was renamed DaimlerChrysler, and it effectively shattered the "Big Three" environment that domestic manufacturers Chrysler, Ford and General Motors had operated in for decades. The DaimlerChrysler lineup was expanded in 1999 with the return of the LHS sedan as well as a return of sorts of the letter series performance sedans that left off in 1965 with the 300L, now in the fold as the 300M. Both additions were powered by an all-new, all-aluminum 3.5-liter V-6 rated at 253 horsepower.

1999 Chrysler, Cirrus LXi sedan (OCW)

SEBRING — SERIES J (coupe)/SERIES X (convertible) — FOUR/V-6 — The Sebring lineup remained intact from the previous year with LX and LXi coupes and JX and JXi convertibles as well as the optional Limited trim level. Powertrains also remained unchanged with the LX powered by the dual overhead cam 2.0-liter four-cylinder engine mated to a five-speed manual transmission and the LXi using the 2.5-liter V-6 paired with an electronically controlled four-speed automatic with overdrive (again the option combination for the LX). The JX convertible again used the dual overhead cam 2.4-liter four-cylinder engine and four-speed automatic while the JXi was again powered by the 2.5-liter V-6 and four-speed automatic, with AutoStick optional. The 2.5-liter V-6 was again optional on the JX. The Sebring coupe sported several new features for 1999 including body-colored exterior mirrors and body-colored wheel packages for Caffe Latte and White body colors. Two new exterior colors were Shark Blue and Plum.

CIRRUS — SERIES A — V-6 — The LXi sedan again comprised the Cirrus lineup and it was again powered by the 2.5-liter V-6 paired with the adaptive electronically controlled four-speed automatic transmission with overdrive. For 1999, the LXi adopted Chrysler's "winged" emblem on its front grille. Other new standard features included 15-inch chrome wheel covers, revised suspension tuning to improve ride control and reduce harshness, revised instrument cluster with improved graphics, and two exterior color choices: Inferno Red and Light Cypress Green.

New optional equipment included 15-inch aluminum wheels and the Sentry Key vehicle immobilizer.

1999 Chrysler, Concorde LXi sedan (OCW)

CONCORDE — SERIES H — V-6 — After a complete redesign the previous year, the Concorde LX and LXi sedans received minor updating for 1999. New standard features included premium carpeting, a revised headliner, a stitched boot design for the shift lever that provided a richer look to the interior, and one exterior color choice: Light Cypress Green. New leather seating was standard in the LXi while upgraded fabric seating was found in the LX. The Concorde also received more robust sway bar links and tubular rear trailing arms for improved road isolation. Outside, the LXi added 16-inch Medallion alloy wheels as standard equipment. Sentry Key vehicle immobilizer was a new option. The LX was again powered by the all-aluminum 2.7-liter V-6 paired with an adaptive electronically controlled four-speed automatic transmission. The LXi again used the all-aluminum 3.2-liter V-6 linked to a four-speed automatic.

1999 Chrysler, 300M sedan (OCW)

300M — SERIES H — V-6 — Picking up almost 35 years later where the 300L letter series performance sedan left off in 1965 was the 1999 300M. Original 300 letter series cars were produced between 1955 and 1965. According to Chrysler, the 300M-launched in May 1998-was a "modern interpretation" of those early alphabet cars, offering a balance of performance, fuel efficiency and precise handling. The car was identified by "300M" chrome badging on the fenders and trunklid. Chrysler's "winged" emblem graced the grille. The 300M was powered by an all-new, all-aluminum high-output 3.5-liter V-6 coupled to an AutoStick high-performance four-speed automatic transmission with overdrive. For cars sold outside the United States (30 international markets), the 300M relied on the 2.7-liter V-6 also found under the hood of the Concorde LX. The list of 300M's standard equipment included leather-trimmed and heated eight-way power front seats and a personalized memory system for the driver's seat, mirrors and radio pre-sets; leather-wrapped steering wheel and shift knob; 60/40 split rear folding seat; soft-touch instrument panel with natural wood inserts; "next-generation" dual airbags; solar control glass all around; Sentry Key theft deterrent system; automatic day/night rearview mirror; electronic speed control; tilt steering column; four-wheel anti-lock disc brakes with traction control; dual ex-

haust and 17-inch wheels with P225/55R17 touring tires. "Razorstar" 17-inch chrome wheels, a power moonroof and a Handling Group were optional equipment. The Handling Group featured firmer struts, taller rear jounce bumpers, firm-feel response steering, 16-inch "Medallion" cast aluminum wheels, high-performance four-wheel anti-lock disc brakes, P225/60VR 16 tires and unlimited top speed Powertrain Control Module. Interior color choices were Light Pearl Beige, Agate and Camel Tan and exterior color choices were Light Cypress Green, Bright Platinum, Candy Apple Red, Champagne Pearl, Cinnamon Glaze, Deep Amethyst, Deep Cranberry, Deep Slate, Forest Green and Stone White. The 300M's coefficient of drag measured 0.312.

LHS — SERIES H — V-6 — After a hiatus of one model year, the LHS sedan returned to Chrysler's 1999 lineup completely redesigned from its predecessor that was introduced in 1994. The five-passenger luxury sedan featured a sloping roofline and more aggressive stance than the previous-design LHS. It featured "second-generation" cab-forward styling that pushed wheels to the corners of the car and increased cabin and cargo space. The LHS used the same 3.5-liter V-6 and AutoStick transmission powertrain combination found in the 300M. Chassis improvements included a new road touring suspension that delivered "crisper" handling and greater steering feel than that of the first-generation LHS. A stiffer body, quieter engine and use of sound-deadening materials in the body also provided for overall quieter operation. Standard features of the LHS mirrored those found in the 300M.

1999 Chrysler, LHS sedan (OCW)

I.D. DATA: As before, Chrysler's 17-symbol Vehicle Identification Number (VIN) was on the upper left corner of the instrument panel, visible through the windshield. Coding was similar to 1986-98. The model year code changed to 'X' for 1999.

*Note: At the time this book went to press, 1999 production totals were not yet available.

SEBRING (FOUR/V-6)

Model No.	Body/ Style No.	Body Type & Seating	Factory Price	Shipping Weight	Prod. Total
XCH	27	2-dr. JX Conv.-4P	23870/N/A	3331/N/A	*
XCP	27	2-dr. JXi Conv.-4P	26185	3382	*
JCS	22	2-dr. LX Cpe-5P	17125/17820	2967/N/A	*
JCP	22	2-dr. LXi Cpe-5P	21225	3203	*

Note: Where applicable, prices and weights to left of slash for four-cylinder engine, to right for V-6.

CIRRUS (V-6)

ACP	41	4-dr. LXi Sed-5P	19460	3146	*

CONCORDE (V-6)

HLP	41	4-dr. LX Sed-6P	21510	3446	*
HLP	41	4-dr. LXi Sed-6P	25235	3556	*

300M (V-6)

HYS	41	4-dr. Sedan-5P	28700	3567	*

LHS (V-6)

HCP	41	4-dr. Sedan-5P	28700	3689	*

ENGINE DATA: BASE FOUR (Sebring LX): Inline, dual overhead cam four-cylinder. Cast iron block; aluminum head. Displacement: 121 cu. in. (2.0 liters). Bore & stroke: 3.44 x 3.27 in. Compression ratio: 9.6:1. Brake horsepower: 140 at 6000 RPM. Torque: 130 lb.-ft. at 4800 RPM. Sequential fuel injection. **BASE FOUR (Sebring JX):** Inline, dual overhead cam four-cylinder. Cast iron block; aluminum head. Displacement: 148 cu. in. (2.4 liters). Bore & stroke: 3.44 x 3.98 in. Compression ratio:

9.4:1. Brake horsepower: 150 at 5200 RPM. Torque: 167 lb.-ft. at 4000 RPM. Sequential fuel injection. BASE V-6 (Sebring JXi, Sebring LXi, Cirrus LXi); OPTIONAL (Sebring JX, Sebring LX): Overhead cam V-6. Cast iron block, aluminum heads. Displacement: 152 cu. in. (2.5 liters). Bore & stroke: 3.29 x 2.99 in. Compression ratio: 9.4:1. Brake horsepower: (Sebring JXi, Sebring LXi) 163 at 5500 RPM; (Cirrus LXi) 168 at 5800 RPM. Torque: 170 lb.-ft. at 4350 RPM. Sequential fuel injection. BASE V-6 (Concorde LX): 24-valve, dual overhead cam V-6. Aluminum block and heads. Displacement: 167 cu. in. (2.7 liters). Bore & stroke: 3.38 x 3.09 in. Compression ratio: 9.7:1. Brake horsepower: 200 at 6000 RPM. Torque: 188 lb.-ft. at 4900 RPM. Sequential fuel injection. BASE V-6 (Concorde LXi): 24-valve, overhead cam V-6. Aluminum block and heads. Displacement: 197 cu. in. (3.2 liters). Bore & stroke: 3.62 x 3.19 in. Compression ratio: 9.5:1. Brake horsepower: 220 at 6600 RPM. Torque: 222 lb.-ft. at 4000 RPM. Sequential fuel injection. BASE V-6 (300M, LHS): High-output, 24-valve, overhead cam V-6. Aluminum block and heads. Displacement: 215 cu. in. (3.5 liters). Bore & stroke: 3.78 x 3.19 in. Compression ratio: 10.1:1. Brake horsepower: 253 at 6400 RPM. Torque: 255 lb.-ft. at 3950 RPM. Sequential fuel injection.

1999 Chrysler, Sebring JX convertible (OCW)

CHASSIS DATA: Wheelbase: (Sebring conv) 106.0 in.; (Sebring cpe) 103.7 in.; (Cirrus) 108.0 in.; (Concorde, 300M, LHS) 113.0 in. Overall length: (Sebring conv) 192.6 in.; (Sebring cpe) 191.1 in.; (Cirrus) 187.0 in.; (Concorde) 209.1 in.; (300M) 197.8 in.; (LHS) 207.7 in. Height: (Sebring conv) 54.8 in.; (Sebring cpe) 53.0 in.; (Cirrus) 52.5 in.; (Concorde) 55.9 in.; (300M, LHS) 56.0 in. Width: (Sebring conv) 69.4 in.; (Sebring cpe) 71.7 in.; (Concorde) 74.5 in.; (300M) 74.4 in.; (LHS) 74.5 in. Front tread: (Sebring conv) 60.2 in.; (Sebring cpe) 59.5 in.; (Cirrus) 59.7 in.; (Concorde) 62.4 in.; (300M, LHS) 61.9 in. Rear tread: (Sebring conv) 60.2 in.; (Sebring cpe) 59.3 in.; (Cirrus) 59.7 in.; (Concorde) 62.0 in.; (300M, LHS) 61.6 in.. Standard Tires: (Sebring JX) P205/65R15; (Sebring JXi) P215/55R16; (Sebring LX) P195/70HR14; (Sebring LXi) P215/50HR17; (Cirrus) P195/65R15; (Concorde) P205/70R15; (300M, LHS) P225/55R17.

1999 Chrysler, Concorde LXi sedan (OCW)

TECHNICAL: Transmission: Five-speed manual standard on Sebring LX. Four-speed automatic standard on Sebring JX, Sebring JXi, Sebring LXi, Cirrus LXi, Concorde, 300M and LHS. Steering: (all) Rack and pinion. Front Suspension: (Sebring conv) Unequal length upper and lower control arms, coil springs and (JX) tubular shock absorbers and stabilizer bar: (JXi) touring tuned springs and shock absorbers; (Sebring cpe) Modified double wishbone w/coil springs, direct acting shock absorbers and link-type stabilizer bar; (Cirrus LXi) Unequal length upper and lower control arms, coil springs, tubular shock absorbers and higher rate springs; (Concorde) Iso-Strut w/integral gas-charged shock absorbers, coil springs, single transverse lower links, tension struts, and tubular link-type stabilizer bar; (300M, LHS) Iso-Strut w/integral gas-charged shock absorbers, coil springs, single transverse lower links, tension struts, link-type stabilizer bar and urethane jounce bumpers. Rear Suspension: (Sebring conv) Unequal length upper and lower control arms, trailing arms, coil springs and (JX) tubular shock absorbers and stabilizer bar: (JXi) touring tuned springs, shock absorbers and stabilizer bar; (Sebring cpe) Modified double wishbone w/coil springs and direct acting shock absorbers (LXi

added link-type stabilizer bar); (Cirrus) Unequal length upper and lower control arms, trailing arms, coil springs, tubular shock absorbers and stabilizer bar and higher rate springs; (Concorde) Chapman struts w/integral gas-charged shock absorbers and concentric coil springs, dual transverse lower links, lower trailing links, and link-type stabilizer bar; (300M, LHS) Chapman struts w/integral gas-charged shock absorbers and concentric coil springs, dual transverse lower links, lower trailing links, link-type stabilizer bar and urethane jounce bumpers. Brakes: (Sebring JX) Front disc, rear drum (power-assisted); (Sebring JXi, Sebring LX, Cirrus LXi) Front disc, rear drum w/anti-lock (power-assisted); (Concorde LX) four-wheel disc (power-assisted); (Sebring LXi, Concorde LXi, 300M, LHS) anti-lock four-wheel disc. Body construction: Unibody. Fuel tank: (Sebring conv, Cirrus) 16 gal.; (Sebring cpe) 16.9 gal.; (Concorde) N/A; (300M, LHS) 17 gal.

DRIVETRAIN OPTIONS: Engines: 2.5-liter V-6: Sebring JX ($1365); Sebring LX ($830). Transmission/Differential: Four-speed automatic trans.: Sebring LX ($695). Anti-lock Brakes: Sebring JX ($565). Sebring LX, four-wheel disc w/ABS ($600). Concorde LX ($600). Traction control: Sebring JXi ($225-$790). Sebring JXi ($225). Concorde LX ($175).

SEBRING CONVENIENCE/APPEARANCE OPTIONS: (JX): Pkg. 26B: stand equip. (JXi): Pkg. 26D: stnd equip. (NC). (Limited): Pkg. 26G: 26D plus AutoStick 4-spd. auto. trans., traction control w/4-whl anti-lock disc brakes, Luxury Convenience Grp., and Limited Decor Grp. ($1890). (LX): Pkg. 21G: stnd equip. (NC). Pkg. 22G: 21G plus 4-spd. auto. trans. ($695). Pkg. 24H: 21G plus 4-whl disc brakes, trunk cargo net, pwr dr locks/windows/mirrors, spd control, P205/55R16 tires, and dual illum. visor mirrors ($2305). (LXi): Pkg. 24J: stnd equip. (NC). Pkg. 24K: 2J plus leather bucket seats and 6-way pwr driver's seat (NC). Other: (ALL) All Season Grp.: incl. 4-whl anti-lock disc brakes, Luxury Convenience Grp., and AM/FM stereo radio w/CD & cass., JXi ($400). (AJB) Security Grp.: incl. Sentry Key eng. immobilizer, security alarm and central locking, JX ($175). (AWK) Luxury Convenience Grp.: incl. garage door opener and auto. day/night rearview mirror, JXi ($175). Eng. block & battery heater ($30). Pwr sunroof, N/A conv ($640). 6-way pwr driver's seat ($205). Inferno Red Paint, conv w/camel or black top ($200). Keyless entry w/panic alarm, LX ($305). Radio systems: RBX, LX ($435). RAZ: cpe ($760); conv ($340). AR5, JXi ($160). CD changer, JXi ($500). Premium seat cloth trim: JX ($95); JXi ($250 credit). (AY4) Touring Grp.: 16-in. cast alum whls, P215/55R16 tires, touring suspension and firm-feel pwr stng, JX ($495). 16-in. alum whls, cpe ($335).

CIRRUS CONVENIENCE/APPEARANCE OPTIONS: LXi: Pkg. 26K: stnd equip. (NC). Other: (ALJ) Gold Pkg.: incl. gold badging, gold fascia accents and 15-in. chrome-plated whls w/gold pockets ($615). Eng. block & battery htr ($30). Inferno Red Paint ($200). Pwr sunroof ($580). AM/FM stereo radio w/cass., CD changer & 8 spkrs, LX ($340). AM/FM stereo radio w/cass., in-dash CD changer & 4 spkrs ($550). Security alarm w/Sentry Key theft deterrent syst. ($175). Conventional spare tire ($125). 15-in. alum whls ($295).

CONCORDE CONVENIENCE/APPEARANCE OPTIONS: LX: Pkg. 22C: stnd equip. (NC). Pkg. 22D: 22C plus 8-way pwr driver & pass seats, 16-in. whl & tire grp., garage door opener, trip computer, Premium cass. player w/amp & 8 spkrs and auto. day/night rearview mirror ($1265). LXi: Pkg. 24F: 22D exc. 16-in. whl & tire grp. replaced by 16x7 alum whls, plus auto. temp air cond., LXi gold badging, 4-whl anti-lock disc brakes, Premium CD player w/amp & 8 spkrs, leather bucket seats/stng whl/shift knob, security alarm, Sentry Key theft deterrent syst., full-size spare tire, and traction control ($3725). Other: Candy Apple Red Paint ($200). Eng. block & battery htr ($30). Pwr sunroof, LXi ($795). Leather 50/50 bench seat ($100). Premium cloth 50/50 split bench seat ($100). AM/FM stereo radio w/CD & cass, equal., amp and 9 spkrs ($370). Premium AM/FM stereo radio w/CD changer, amp and 8 spkrs, LX ($145-$435). (AGC) 16-in. Wheel & Tire Grp.: incl. P225/60R16 touring tires and 16-in. whl covers, LX ($200). Conventional spare tire, LX ($125).

300M CONVENIENCE/APPEARANCE OPTIONS: Pkg. 26M: stnd equip. (NC). Other: (AWT) Performance Handling Grp.: Hi-perf. 4-whl anti-lock disc brakes, hi-spd engine controller, perf. stng, perf. susp., P225/60VR16 tires, 16-in. alum whls ($400). Eng. block & battery heater ($30). Pwr moonroof ($795). Candy Apple Red Metallic Paint ($200). AM/FM stereo radio w/CD & cass., equal., amp and 11 spkrs. ($215). Conventional spare tire ($215-$365). 17-in. chrome whls ($600).

LHS CONVENIENCE/APPEARANCE OPTIONS: Pkg. 26J: stnd equip. (NC). Other: Eng. block & battery heater ($30). Pwr moonroof ($795). AM/FM stereo radio w/CD & cass., equal., amp and 11 spkrs. ($215). Conventional spare tire ($215-$365). 17-in. chrome whls ($600).

HISTORY: DaimlerChrysler announced the creation of "Chrysler Showcase," which featured Chrysler brand vehicles as well as interactive kiosks and a staff of Chrysler product "ambassadors" (not salespeople) to answer questions as well as raise consumer awareness of DaimlerChrysler products. The Showcase was set up in locations nationwide, including shopping malls, festivals and golf tournaments.

In its first model year under the new, DaimlerChrysler banner, Chrysler's millennium-ending 2000 lineup remained unchanged from 1999, with the exception of the re-introduction of a four-cylinder Cirrus LX, absent since 1997. Much anticipated, however, was the introduction - scheduled for spring 2000 - of Chrysler's next "retro-style" offering, the PT Cruiser, a Neon-based wagon reminiscent in appearance of a late-'30s Ford sedan, but classified as a minivan by the EPA.

2000 Chrysler, Sebring LX coupe (OCW)

SEBRING — SERIES J (coupe)/SERIES X (convertible) — V-6 — The Sebring lineup remained intact for the fifth consecutive year with LX and LXi coupes and JX and JXi convertibles as well as the optional Limited trim level on the JXi. Gone, however, was the dual overhead cam, 2.0-liter four-cylinder engine that had been mated to a five-speed manual transaxle on the LX and to a four-speed automatic on the JX. Instead, the base drivetrain for all models was a 2.5-liter V-6 paired with an electronically controlled four-speed automatic with overdrive. While bearing the same model name, the Sebring "twins" were anything but identical. The convertible shared its platform, chassis, and drivetrain components with the Cirrus sedan, making it one of the few, true, four-passenger soft tops on the planet. The coupe, with its Mitsubishi-based components, was more closely related to the Dodge Avenger. While both coupe and convertible used 2.5-liter V-6s, the convertible's Chrysler-built engine had a slight power edge over the coupe's Mitsubishi unit. AutoStick four-speed automatic, with its manual shift capability, was again part of the JXi Limited option package. The Sebring coupe for 2000 featured a longer standard equipment list, updated LX trim fabric, and Ice Silver as a new exterior color. The convertible's rear suspension was retuned for a better ride and four new colors (Shale Green, Bright Silver, Black, and Taupe Frost) were added to its palette.

2000 Chrysler, Cirrus LXi sedan (OCW)

CIRRUS — SERIES A — FOUR/V-6 — An entry-level, four-cylinder LX, absent from the Cirrus lineup since 1997, returned for 2000. It rejoined the LXi sedan, which was again powered by a 2.5-liter V-6 paired with the adaptive electronically controlled four-speed automatic transmission with overdrive. With a major redesign anticipated for 2001, styling remained unchanged for 2000. Aluminum wheels and an eight-speaker

AM/FM cassette stereo moved from optional to standard on the LXi, the same four new colors as Sebring became available, and rear child seat anchorages were added to both models.

2000 Chrysler, Concorde LX sedan (OCW)

2000 Chrysler, Concorde LXi sedan (OCW)

CONCORDE — SERIES H — V-6 — After a complete redesign for 1998, the Concorde LX and LXi sedans received only minor updating for 1999 and again for 2000. New standard features included chrome nameplates and speed-sensitive steering on LXi, 16-inch wheels and tires on LX, and new instrument clusters and rear suspension modifications on both. New options included a moon roof for LX and chrome, 16-inch Medallion alloy wheels on LXi. Also new were six exterior colors in adddition to the four previously offered. The LX was again powered by the all-aluminum 2.7-liter V-6 paired with an adaptive electronically controlled four-speed automatic transmission. The LXi again used the more powerful all-aluminum 3.2-liter V-6 linked to a four-speed automatic.

2000 Chrysler, 300M sedan (OCW)

300M — SERIES H — V-6 — In its second model year as a "modern interpretation" of the original 300 letter series cars produced between 1955 and 1965, the 300M was again touted as offering a balance of performance, fuel efficiency, and precise handling. Sort of a sports version of the Chrysler Concorde, it continued to be powered by the potent, all-aluminum, high-output 3.5-liter V-6 shared with the LHS and, now, Plymouth Prowler. Standard on the 300M was Chrysler's AutoStick high-performance four-speed automatic transmission with overdrive. For units sold outside the United States, the 300M again relied on the 2.7-liter V-6 also found under the hood of the Concorde LX. The list of 300M's standard equipment included leather-trimmed and heated eight-way

power front seats and a personalized memory system for the driver's seat, mirrors and radio pre-sets; leather-wrapped steering wheel and shift knob; 60/40 split rear folding seat; analog gauges with electroluminescent lighting; "next-generation" dual airbags; solar control glass all around; Sentry Key theft deterrent system; automatic day/night rearview mirror; electronic speed control; tilt steering column; four-wheel anti-lock disc brakes with traction control; dual exhaust and 17-inch wheels with P225/55R17 touring tires. "Razorstar" 17-inch chrome wheels, a power moonroof and a Handling Group remained optional equipment. The Handling Group featured firmer struts, taller rear jounce bumpers, Firm-Feel Enhanced Response Steering, 16-inch "Medallion" cast aluminum wheels, high-performance four-wheel anti-lock disc brakes, P225/60VR16 tires and unlimited top speed engine controller. Interior color choices were Light Pearl Beige, Agate, and Camel Tan teamed with exterior color options that included: Light Cypress Green, Champagne Pearl, Cinnamon Glaze, Deep Slate, and Stone White carried over from 1999 and new additions: Dark Garnet Red, Inferno Red, Shale Green Metallic, Steel Blue, and Bright Silver Metallic. The 300M's coefficient of drag measured 0.313.

2000 Chrysler, LHS sedan (OCW)

LHS — SERIES H — V-6 — If the 300M was a refined sports version of the Concorde, The LHS could be thought of as its luxury iteration. After a complete redesign for 1999, the LHS joined Chrysler's 2000 lineup largely unchanged in appearance. Standard features on the five-passenger luxury sedan echoed those of the 300M and only three major options were offered: chrome wheels, power sunroof, and an upgraded sound system with four-disc, in-dash CD changer. The LHS used the same 253-hp, 3.5-liter V-6 as the 300M, but did not offer its performance-oriented AutoStick transaxle. Chassis improvements included rear suspension modifications to reduce noise, vibration, and harshness. With four exterior colors new for this year, the LHS could be had in all the same hues as the 300M, with the exception of Inferno Red.

I.D. DATA: As before, Chrysler's 17-symbol Vehicle Identification Number (VIN) was on the upper left corner of the instrument panel, visible through the windshield. Coding was similar to 1986-99. The model year code changed to 'Y' for 2000.

* At the time this book went to press, 2000 production totals were not yet available.

SEBRING (V-6)

Model No.	Body/ Style No.	Body Type & Seating	Factory Price	Shipping Weight	Prod. Total
XCH	27	2-dr. JX Conv.-4P	24245	3440	*
XCP	27	2-dr. JXi Conv.-4P	26560	3444	*
JCS	22	2-dr. LX Cpe-5P	19765	3155	*
JCP	22	2-dr. LXi Cpe-5P	22100	3203	*

CIRRUS (FOUR/V-6)

ACH	41	4-dr. LX Sed-5P	16230	2911	*
ACP	41	4-dr. LXi Sed-5P	20085	3168	*

CONCORDE (V-6)

HCH	41	4-dr. LX Sed-6P	22145	3452	*
HCH	41	4-dr. LXi Sed-6P	26385	3532	*

300M (V-6)

HYS	41	4-dr. Sed-5P	29085	3567	*

LHS (V-6)

HCP	41	4-dr. Sed-5P	28240	3564	*

ENGINE DATA: BASE FOUR: (Cirrus LX): Inline, single overhead cam four-cylinder. Cast iron block; aluminum head. Displacement: 121 cu. in. (2 liters). Bore & stroke: 3.44 x 3.27 in. Compression ratio 9.8:1. Brake horsepower: 132 at 6000 RPM. Torque: 129 lb.-ft. at 4950 RPM.

Sequential fuel injection. **BASE V-6** (Sebring JX, Sebring JXi, Cirrus LXi); Overhead cam V-6. Cast iron block, aluminum heads. Displacement: 152 cu. in. (2.5 liters). Bore & stroke: 3.29 x 2.99 in. Compression ratio: 9.4:1. Brake horsepower: 168 at 5800 RPM. Torque: 170 lb.-ft. at 4350 RPM. Sequential fuel injection. (Sebring LX, Sebring LXi): Overhead cam V-6. Cast iron block, aluminum heads. Displacement: 152 cu. in. (2.5 liters). Bore & stroke: 3.29 x 2.99 in. Compression ratio: 9.4:1. Brake horsepower: 163 at 5500 RPM. Torque: 170 lb.-ft. at 4350 RPM. Sequential fuel injection. **BASE V-6** (Concorde LX): 24-valve, dual overhead cam V-6. Aluminum block and heads. Displacement: 167 cu. in. (2.7 liters). Bore & stroke: 3.38 x 3.09 in. Compression ratio: 9.7:1. Brake horsepower: 200 at 5800 RPM. Torque: 190 lb.-ft. at 4800 RPM. Sequential fuel injection. **BASE V-6** (Concorde LXi): 24-valve, overhead cam V-6. Aluminum block and heads. Displacement: 197 cu. in. (3.2 liters). Bore & stroke: 3.62 x 3.19 in. Compression ratio: 9.5:1. Brake horsepower: 225 at 6300 RPM. Torque: 225 lb.-ft. at 3800 RPM. Sequential fuel injection. **BASE V-6** (300M, LHS): High-output, 24-valve, overhead cam V-6. Aluminum block and heads. Displacement: 215 cu. in. (3.5 liters). Bore & stroke: 3.78 x 3.19 in. Compression ratio: 9.9:1. Brake horsepower: 253 at 6400 RPM. Torque: 255 lb.-ft. at 3950 RPM. Sequential fuel injection.

CHASSIS DATA: Wheelbase: (Sebring conv) 106.0 in.; (Sebring cpe) 103.7 in.; (Cirrus) 108.0 in.; (Concorde, 300M, LHS) 113.0 in. Overall length: (Sebring conv) 192.6 in.; (Sebring cpe) 190.9 in.; (Cirrus) 187.0 in.; (Concorde) 209.1 in.; (300M) 197.8 in.; (LHS) 207.7 in. Height: (Sebring conv) 54.8 in.; (Sebring cpe LX) 53.0 in. (LXi) 53.3 in.; (Cirrus) 54.3 in.; (Concorde) 55.9 in.; (300M, LHS) 56.0 in. Width: (Sebring conv) 70.1 in.; (Sebring cpe) 69.4 in.; (Cirrus) 71.7 in.; (Concorde) 74.6 in.; (300M) 74.4 in.; (LHS) 74.4 in. Front tread: (Sebring conv) 59.7 in.; (Sebring cpe) 59.5 in.; (Cirrus) 59.7 in.; (Concorde) 62.4 in.; (300M, LHS) 61.9 in. Rear tread: (Sebring conv) 59.9 in.; (Sebring cpe) 59.3 in.; (Cirrus) 59.9 in.; (Concorde) 62.0 in.; (300M, LHS) 61.6 in.. Standard Tires: (Sebring JX) P205/65R15; (Sebring JXi) P215/55R16; (Sebring LX) P205/55HR16; (Sebring LXi) P215/50HR17; (Cirrus) P195/65R15; (Concorde) P225/60R16; (300M, LHS) P225/55R17.

2000 Chrysler, Sebring JX convertible (OCW)

TECHNICAL: Transmission: Five-speed OD manual standard on Cirrus LX. Four-speed automatic standard on Sebring JX, Sebring JXi, Sebring LX, Sebring LXi, Cirrus LXi, Concorde, 300M and LHS. Steering: (all) Power-assisted rack and pinion. Front Suspension: (Sebring conv) Unequal length upper and lower control arms, coil springs and tubular shock absorbers and stabilizer bar (JX): touring tuned springs and shock absorbers (JXi); (Sebring cpe) Modified double wishbone w/coil springs, direct-acting shock absorbers and link-type stabilizer bar; (Cirrus LXi) Unequal length upper and lower control arms, coil springs, tubular shock absorbers and stabilizer bar; (Concorde) Iso struts w/integral gas-charged shock absorbers, coil springs, single transverse lower links, tension struts, and tubular link-type stabilizer bar; (300M, LHS) Iso struts w/integral gas-charged shock absorbers, coil springs, single transverse lower links, tension struts, link-type stabilizer bar and urethane jounce bumpers. Rear Suspension: (Sebring conv) Unequal length upper and lower control arms, trailing arms, coil springs and tubular shock absorbers and stabilizer bar (JX): touring tuned springs, shock absorbers and stabilizer bar (JXi); (Sebring cpe) Double wishbone w/coil springs and direct acting shock absorbers (LXi added link-type stabilizer bar); (Cirrus) Unequal length upper and lower control arms, trailing arms, coil springs, tubular shock absorbers and stabilizer bar; (Concorde) Chapman struts w/integral gas-charged shock absorbers and concentric coil springs, dual transverse lower links, lower trailing links, and link-type stabilizer bar; (300M, LHS) Chapman struts w/integral gas-charged shock absorbers and concentric coil springs, dual transverse lower links, lower trailing links, link-type stabilizer bar and urethane jounce bumpers. Brakes: (Cirrus LX) Front disc, rear drum (power-assisted); (Sebring JX, Sebring JXi) Front disc, rear drum w/anti-lock (power-assisted); (Sebring LX, Sebring LXi, Concorde LX) four-wheel disc (power-assisted); (Cirrus LXi, Concorde LXi,

300M, LHS) anti-lock four-wheel disc. Body construction: Unibody. Fuel tank: (Sebring conv, Cirrus) 16 gal.; (Sebring cpe) 15.9 gal.; (Concorde, 300M, LHS) 17 gal.

DRIVETRAIN OPTIONS: (Cirrus LX) 2.4-liter, dual overhead cam four-cylinder engine (NC). (Sebring LX, Sebring LXi, Concorde LX) four-wheel disc brakes w/ABS ($600).

2000 Chrysler, Sebring Limited convertible (OCW)

SEBRING CONVENIENCE/APPEARANCE OPTIONS: (JX): Pkg. 26B: stand equip. (NC). (JXi): Pkg. 26D: stand equip. (NC). (Limited): Pkg. 26G: 26D plus AutoStick 4-spd. auto. trans., traction control w/4-whl anti-lock disc brakes, Luxury Convenience Grp., and Limited Decor Grp. ($1890). (LX): Pkg. 24H: stnd equip. (NC), (LXi): Pkg. 24K: stnd equip. (NC) Other: All Season Grp.: incl. 4-whl anti-lock disc brakes, Luxury Convenience Grp., and AM/FM stereo radio w/CD & cass., JXi ($400). Security Grp.: incl. security alarm and central locking, JX ($175). Luxury Convenience Grp.: incl. garage door opener and auto. day/night rearview mirror, JXi ($175). Eng. block & battery heater, JX, JXi ($30). 4-whl anti-lock disc brakes, LX, LXi ($600). Pwr sunroof, LX, LXi, N/A conv ($685). 6-way pwr driver's seat ($205). Inferno Red Paint w/camel or black vinyl top, JX, JXi w/black or sandalwood cloth top, JXi ($200). Keyless entry w/panic alarm, LX ($305). Radio systems: AM/FM Stereo w/cassette, CD & equalizer, LX ($435). AM/FM Stereo w/cassette, CD, equalizer & Infinity speaker system, LX ($760), LXi ($325). Premium AM/FM w/cassette, 6-disc CD changer in-dash and CD changer control, JXi ($160). 6-disc in-dash CD changer, JXi ($500). Premium seat cloth trim, JX ($95). Touring Grp.: 16-in. cast alum whls, P215/55R16 tires, touring suspension and firm-feel pwr strg, JX ($495). 16-in. alum whls, cpe ($335).

CIRRUS CONVENIENCE/APPEARANCE OPTIONS: LX: Pkg. 21A: stnd equip. (NC). Other: Pkg. 21A: includes front and rear floor mats, speed sensitive power locks, pwr mirrors, 8-way pwr driver's seat, and pwr windows (NC); requires (EDZ) 2.4-liter 4-cyl engine (NC) and (DGB) 4-spd auto transmission ($1,050). Anti-lock front disc/rear drum brakes ($565). Remote illuminated entry grp ($170). Premium radio w/cassette and CD ready ($340), Premium radio w/cassette and 6-disc CD changer ($550). Premium radio w/CD player ($200). Eng. block & battery htr ($30). Inferno Red Paint ($200). Pwr sunroof ($695). Conventional spare tire ($125). 15-in. alum whls ($365). LXi: Pkg. 26K: stnd equip. (NC). Other: Gold Pkg.: incl. silver accents, LXi badge, gold badging, and 15-in. chrome-plated whls w/gold accents ($500). Eng. block & battery htr ($30). Inferno Red Paint ($200). Pwr sunroof ($580). Premium cassette w/6-disc CD changer ($210). Front ash tray and cigar lighter ($20). AM/FM stereo radio w/cass., CD changer & 8 spkrs, LX ($340). AM/FM stereo radio w/cass., in-dash CD changer & 4 spkrs ($550). Security alarm w/Sentry Key theft deterrent syst. ($175). Conventional spare tire ($125). 15-in. alum whls ($295).

CONCORDE CONVENIENCE/APPEARANCE OPTIONS: LX: Pkg. 22C: stnd equip. (NC). Pkg. 22D: 22C plus 8-way pwr driver & pass seats, garage door opener, trip computer, Premium cass. player w/amp & 8 spkrs, and auto. day/night rearview mirror ($1125). LXi: Pkg. 24F: stnd equip. 22D exc. 16-in. whl & tire grp. replaced by 16x7 alum whls, plus auto. temp air cond., LXi gold badging, 4-whl anti-lock disc brakes, Premium CD player w/amp & 8 spkrs, leather bucket seats/strg whl/shift knob, security alarm, Sentry Key theft deterrent syst., full-size spare tire, and traction control (NC). Other: Inferno Red Paint ($200). Eng. block & battery htr ($30). Front & rear ash trays and cigar lighter ($20). Pwr sunroof ($895). Leather 50/50 bench seat ($100). Premium cloth 50/50 split bench seat, LX ($100). AM/FM stereo radio w/CD & cass., equal., amp and 8 spkrs, LX ($225-$575). Premium AM/FM stereo radio w/4-disc, in-dash CD changer, amp and 9 Infinity spkrs, LXi ($500). Leather & Wheel Grp.: incl. leather-trimmed bucket seats, leather-wrapped shift knob & strg whl, and 16-in. alum whls, LX ($760). 16-in. alum whls, LX ($365). 16-in. chrome-plated alum whls, LXi ($600).Traction control, LX ($175). 4-whl disc anti-lock brakes, LX ($600). Conventional spare tire, LX ($125) LXi ($90-$240).

300M CONVENIENCE/APPEARANCE OPTIONS: Pkg. 26M: stnd equip. (NC). Other: Performance Handling Grp.: Hi-perf. 4-whl anti-lock disc brakes, hi-spd engine controller, perf. strg, perf. susp., P225/60VR16 tires, 16-in. alum whls ($500). Eng. block & battery heater ($30). Front & rear ash trays and cigar lighter ($20). Pwr moonroof ($895). Inferno Red Paint ($200). AM/FM stereo radio w/4-disc, in-dash CD & cass., equal., amp and 11 Infinity spkrs. ($515). Conventional spare tire ($215-$365). 16-in. chrome-plated alum whls ($750). 17-in. chrome-plated alum whls ($750).

LHS CONVENIENCE/APPEARANCE OPTIONS: Pkg. 26J: stnd equip. (NC). Other: Eng. block & battery heater ($30). Front & rear ash trays and cigar lighter ($20). Pwr moonroof ($895). AM/FM stereo radio w/CD & cass., equal., amp and 11 Infinity spkrs. ($515). Conventional spare tire ($215-$365). 17-in. chrome-plated alum whls ($750).

2000 Chrysler, Sebring LXi coupe (OCW)

HISTORY: On January 26, 2000, Robert J. Eaton, Chairman of DaimlerChrysler AG, announced that he would retire as of March 31. Eaton, who had become Chairman and CEO of Chrysler Corporation seven years earlier, presided over the most successful period in the company's history and forged the alliance with Daimler-Benz that resulted in the formation of DaimlerChrysler AG. During Eaton's tenure, Chrysler posted all-time record earnings. It introduced a new lineup of products that were among the most successful in their categories. In 1996, Chrysler Corporation was named "Company of the Year" by Forbes Magazine. In making his announcement, Eaton said, "The merger is complete. The structure and future leadership is in place. The two companies are one, my goal has been accomplished. This is the right time for me to go."

DeSoto

DeSOTO

1928-1961

The DeSoto was a phenomenon. In its first 12 months in the industry, a total of 81,065 cars were delivered, a first-year sales record that eclipsed the previous high marks made by Graham-Paige (1928), Pontiac (1926), and Chrysler (1924), and a record that would endure far longer, for nearly three decades in fact. If any car seemed destined to be a winner, it was the DeSoto. "Most emphatically, it is not just another model, to be dragged along by the tractive effort of Chrysler advertising, prestige, and popularity," Automobile Topics enthused upon its introduction. "Nor is it to suffer the unkindly fate that so often befalls the proverbial stepchild." But that is precisely what happened, ultimately, though the unkindly fate of this companion car was more leisurely in coming than most. Actually, the DeSoto wasn't a necessary car when it arrived, for the market gap it was intended to fill between the Chrysler and the new Plymouth could nicely be plugged by Dodge, which company Walter Chrysler had just managed to buy. Indeed, there is reason to believe that the DeSoto had been planned by Chrysler to intimidate the bankers controlling Dodge into selling the company to him. By the time that happened and the papers were signed, the DeSoto was on the assembly line, however.

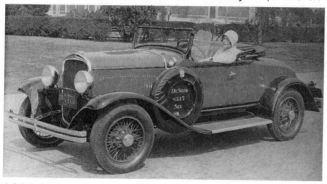
1929 DeSoto Six Series K roadster (OCW)

In the heady optimism of the 1920s, its sensational first year seemed to indicate that the car, though somewhat superfluous, could do nicely on its own. It was a nice automobile, though not extraordinary in any way, its 174.9-cid, L-head, six-cylinder engine delivering 55 hp for a pleasantly snappy and vigorous performance, and Lockheed hydraulic brakes, Lovejoy shock absorbers, Hotchkiss drive, and the same thin-profile (or "ribbon") radiator of the more expensive Chrysler making for an admirable $845 DeSoto package. The car was named, of course, for the Spanish explorer Hernando de Soto who, comparatively, probably encountered no more difficulties in discovering the Mississippi in 1541 than DeSoto would in surviving the 1930s. The car's fortunes plummeted during the Depression. In 1930, the DeSoto line of sixes was augmented by a straight-eight, its engine and chassis similar to the new Dodge eight also introduced that year. During 1930, 34,889 DeSotos and 68,159 Dodges were produced, the same vis-a-vis ratio of the two cars since 1928, which seemed to auger well. The eight was discontinued after 1932, replaced by a fine new 75-hp six, the first DeSoto featuring a body design completely its own, though it shared the new Plymouth PB chassis with free-wheeling and Floating Power engine mounts. In that depth-of-Depression year, DeSoto's sales of more than 25,000 cars prac-

tically equalled Dodge's. By 1933, however, two decisions were made for the car, one of which perhaps wasn't wise, the other an unmitigated disaster. First, the DeSoto's price range was modified; from a car priced somewhat less than the Dodge, it now became a car priced somewhat higher. Since this moved the DeSoto closer to the Chrysler than heretofore, it perhaps followed that the car would become more Chrysler-like. In 1934 that meant the Airflow. DeSoto sold just over 15,000 of them that year, which was better than Chrysler's 11,000 Airflows, but Chrysler also offered a conventionally-styled car (DeSoto didn't) that brought overall Chrysler sales up to a more respectable near 37,000. Meanwhile Dodge passed the 100,000 mark.

1934 DeSoto Airflow four-door sedan (OCW)

In 1935 and 1936, only 11,797 DeSoto Airflows were built, though the more conventional Airstream introduced in 1935 helped to boost respective production figures to 34,276 and 52,789 cars during those years. But Dodge was up past the 200,000 mark now. And so it would go. Still, DeSoto did enjoy some good fortune in the later 1930s. The beginnings of a lucrative taxicab business and an upswing in sales following introduction of the completely conventional Ray Dietrich-designed cars of 1937 were positives in the DeSoto history. The superlative arrived for 1942, the most expensive DeSotos ever, with scads of chrome and disappearing headlights. Just 24,771 of them were built before February 9, 1942, when all production stopped. When it resumed after the war, the DeSoto continued its teeter-totter life within Chrysler Corporation for a decade and a half. Ironically, the car's last year, 1960, was also the year the new Ford Falcon took away the sales record that DeSoto had enjoyed holding since 1929.

1935 DeSoto Airstream four-door sedan (OCW)

1942 DeSoto Custom four-door sedan (OCW)

During the war, DeSoto was responsible for assemblies of fuselage sections for the Martin B-26 Marauder, the manufacture of parts for Bofors anti-aircraft cannon, the building of Hell-Diver airplane wing sections, and construction of B-29 aircraft nose sections (using parts supplied from Chrysler and Plymouth factory assembly lines). With the end of the war, plans to convert back to a civilian economy were fraught with many difficulties, including materials shortages and labor problems. The actual work of converting plants also delayed 1946 model introductions. Finally, in March of that calendar year, the postwar DeSoto arrived.

1946 DeSoto Custom seven-passenger four-door sedan (OCW)

Based on the same body as the short-lived 1942 offering, the latest DeSoto deviated, stylingwise, in a number of areas. There were new front fenders with conventional, exposed headlights, a redesigned grille, redone doors, new bumpers, and updated ornamentation. The Suburban was a late addition to the line, arriving in November 1946. The initial postwar series was carried forth for 1947 and 1948, plus into the first part of the next calendar year, as an early 1949 line.

1948 DeSoto Custom convertible (OCW)

The updated S-13 models were delayed in production, due to labor unrest in the tooling plants during 1948. Finally, they appeared as second-series 1949 models. These practical, newly-styled automobiles were advertised as, "The Car With You In Mind." Essentially, this fresh, new postwar look would remain in production through the 1954 model year. There were, however, a number of styling refinements within this period, which paralleled those found in Chrysler counterparts.

Magazine ad for the 1949 DeSoto (OCW)

The DeSoto Firedome V-8, with its free-breathing, hemispherical-segment-shaped combustion chambers, was introduced in 1952. The following year marked the division's 25th Anniversary, which was suitably celebrated by creation of the Adventurer show car. This "dream car" was wrought by Italian coachbuilder Ghia, but was based on a near-standard DeSoto Firedome chassis. A number of new options appeared the same season, including refrigerated air conditioning and authentic chrome wire spoke wheels. It was the first time this style of wheel rim had been seen on DeSotos in over 20 years!

For model year 1954, DeSoto sales declined dramatically, despite introduction of the PowerFlite two-speed, fully-automatic transmission. This new gearbox, although a giant technical improvement, was priced $45 lower than the inconvenient, semi-automatic unit it replaced. The Adventurer II "idea car," with even sleeker design work by Ghia, was heralded as a "Car of the Future," when seen by the public at many new car shows.

1954 DeSoto Adventurer I experimental car, designed by Virgil Exner (OCW)

A major turning point in the fortunes of the division occurred in 1955, as Chrysler's highly-promoted "Forward Look" debuted and brought an 85-percent sales boost in DeSoto Land. The

all-modern styling erased the stodgy appearance of the past, replacing it with designs of a new, youthful flair. In some cases, three-tone paint treatments were added for extra buyer appeal. These "Styled-For-Tomorrow" models helped lead the corporation to a banner sales year and it was hard to imagine that DeSoto had but six years to live.

In 1956, the Adventurer nameplate was seen on a production car for the first time. This was DeSoto's shot at the enthusiast market, shared with such magical Mopar models as the Chrysler 300, Dodge D-500, and Plymouth Fury. Other offerings for the year were characterized by a slight styling face-lift, front and rear, with a new emphasis placed on the height of tail fins.

A new DeSoto Fireflite convertible acted as pace car for the 1956 Indianapolis 500 Mile Race (OCW)

The year 1957 saw the DeSoto redesigned again, with even more of an upward tail fin sweep. Such styling, coupled with a lower bodyside color sweep panel, served to enhance the cars' length and beauty. Sales climbed over the previous season, but not to the same degree as the other Chrysler products' sales improved.

Disastrous sales were the 1958 trend for DeSotos, as production plunged more than 60 percent, to a level not seen since the dark days of 1938. These cars would also be the last company products to leave the famous Wyoming Avenue factory, in Detroit.

Separate body/frame construction was in its final year when the 1959 DeSoto line was introduced. Continuing to be marketed as a specialty model was the low-production Adventurer, which came only fully-equipped and custom finished in specific colors. Sales continued to decline, dropping yet another notch, while Chrysler went forward with plans to integrate DeSoto assemblies with those of the corporation's other automotive divisions. Already, some observers were predicting the demise of the marque and a close to DeSoto history.

Still, the DeSoto was carried into 1960, with production quartered alongside that of Chryslers in the Jefferson Avenue plant. The unibody method of construction was the primary engineering advance of the year, but could not offset an additional 40 percent falloff from the low totals of 1959.

A 1961 model with restyled headlight, grille, and taillight treatments was unveiled in mid-October, but on Nov. 30, 1960, production of the once popular DeSoto automobile came to its end. Noted always for solid value and regarded as a marque "Built to Last," the proud DeSoto nameplate had been affixed to a total of 2,024,629 cars since its inception in the summer of 1928. More than half of these cars were built in the postwar era.

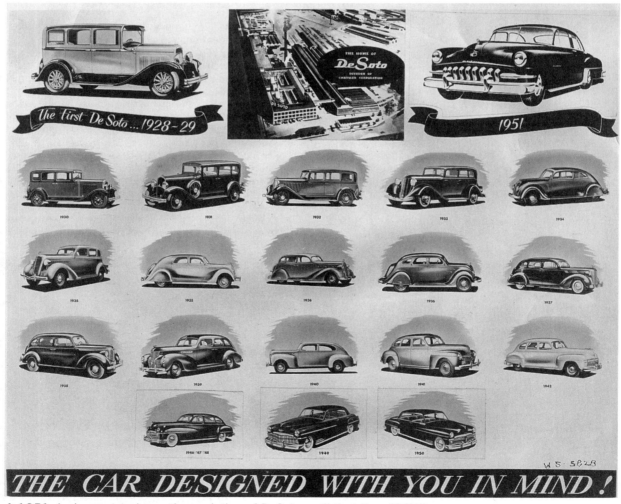

A 1951 dealer poster shows the evolution of DeSoto until that time (OCW)

1929 DeSOTO

DESOTO — SERIES K — SIX: The DeSoto was introduced in the middle of 1928 as a 1929 automobile. The new marque was named after the Spanish explorer and aimed at the low-priced six market. After its August 4 introduction, the DeSoto sold at a record setting pace and hit an all-time high for any American car in its first year at this point in time. Appearance features included an arched headlamp tie-bar, triple groups of vertical hood louvers, and cowl lamps integral with the surcingle molding. Deluxe equipment included fender wells, six wheel equipment, special paint, chrome headlamp tie-bar and richer upholstery. Standard equipment included Delco-Remy ignition, hydraulic brakes, Lovejoy shock absorbers and rubber mounted motor suspension.

1929 DeSoto Six, Series K, sedan (OCW)

1929 DeSoto Six, Series K, roadster (OCW)

I.D. DATA: Serial numbers followed the Fedco coding system. They were located on a plate built into the center of the instrument board. Starting: KW000P. Ending: KL300L. Engine numbers were located on the upper left side of cylinder block between No. 1 and No. 2 cylinders, just below cylinder head. Starting: K1001. Ending: K83099.

Model No.	Body Type & Seating	Price	Weight	Prod. Total
K	2-dr. Rds.-2/4P	845	2350	Note 1
K	4-dr. Phae.-5P	845	2445	Note 1
K	2-dr. Bus. Cpe.-2P	845	2465	Note 1
K	2-dr. Del. Cpe.-2/4P	885	2525	Note 1
K	2-dr. Coach-5P	845	2580	Note 1
K	4-dr. Sed.-5P	885	2645	Note 1
K	4-dr. Del. Sed.-5P	955	2655	Note 1

Note 1: Total production was over 80,000 cars.

ENGINE: Inline. L-head. Six. Cast iron block. B & S: 3 x 4-1/8 in. Disp.: 174.9 cu. in. C.R.: 5.2:1. Brake H.P.: 55 @ 3000 R.P.M. N.A.C.C. H.P.: 21.6. Four main bearings. Solid valve lifters. Carb.: Stromberg IV. Torque: 110 lb.-ft. @ 1200 R.P.M.

CHASSIS: [Series K] W.B.: 109.75 in. O.L.:169 in. Tires: 5.00 x 19.

TECHNICAL: Selective sliding gear transmission. Speeds: 3F/1R. Floor shift control. Conventional clutch. Shaft drive. Semi-floating rear axle. Overall ratio: 4.7:1. Lockheed hydraulic four-wheel brakes. Wood spoke wheels.

OPTIONS: Front bumper. Rear bumper. Single sidemount. Dual sidemount. Sidemount cover(s). Rear spare. Wire spoke wheels. Special paint. Special upholstery. Cigar lighter. High compression cylinder head. Trippe lights. Spotlight(s). Cowl lamps.

HISTORICAL: Introduced August 6, 1928. All new light six-cylinder from Chrysler Corp. Calendar year registrations: (1928) 14,538; (1929) 59,614. Calendar year production: (1929) 64,911; (1928) 33,345. Model year production: (1929) 62,191. Corporate president: Walter P. Chrysler. First announced in the *Detroit Free Press* on May 6, 1928. Over 500 dealers signed up immediately and by the end of 1928, over 34,000 cars were shipped to a dealer network of 1,500. J.E. Fields, a Chrysler vice-president of sales, was named president of DeSoto Division.

1930 DeSOTO

1930 DeSoto Six, Series K, roadster (OCW)

DESOTO — SERIES K — SIX: The Series K DeSoto six continued to be marketed when the 1930 model year began in July 1929. The cars were unchanged in terms of appearance features or equipment. The model year designation was simply changed to make the cars seem more up-to-date. Refer to the previous listing for models, prices, weights and technical specifications.

1930 DeSoto Eight, Series CF, coupe (JAC)

DESOTO — SERIES CF — EIGHT: In January 1930, DeSoto continued to market the Series K six as a 1930 model, but also introduced the new Series CF eight. This was a low-priced eight-cylinder car. It had undivided vertical hood louvers, instead of the three separate groupings used on sixes. The radiator had a deeper, chrome plated shell. A unit grouped instrument panel was featured. Standard equipment included NorthEast ignition, hydraulic brakes, mono-piece body construction, fuel pump,

rubber spring shackles, downdraft carburetor, Lovejoy shock absorbers, and a seven crossmember frame.

FINER DESOTO — SERIES CK — SIX: The CK DeSoto six was introduced in May 1930. Its appearance features included a deeper radiator shell and cowl lamps mounted on top of the front fenders. Otherwise it looked much like the original DeSoto six. Standard equipment additions included Delco-Remy ignition and a larger bore engine.

1930 DeSoto Eight, Series CF, phaeton (JAC)

I.D. DATA: [Series K] Serial numbers were in the same location. Starting: KL300E. Ending: KK142W. Engine numbers were in the same location. Starting: K83100. Ending: K113744. [Series CF] Serial numbers were in the same location. Both Fedco and conventional type numbers were used. Starting: L001WP. Ending: L172PH. (Conventional) 6000001 to 6000212. Engine numbers were in the same location. Starting: CF1001. Ending: CF19388. [Series CK] DeSoto switched completely to the use of conventional serial numbers. They were in the same location. Starting: 5000001. Ending: 5006932. Engine numbers were in the same location. Starting: CK-1001. Ending: CK-8443.

Model No.	Body Type & Seating	Price	Weight	Prod. Total
K	2-dr. Rds.-2/4P	845	2350	Note 1
K	4-dr. Phae.-5P	845	2445	Note 1
K	2-dr. Bus. Cpe.-2P	845	2465	Note 1
K	2-dr. Del. Cpe.-2/4P	885	2525	Note 1
K	2-dr. Sed.-5P	845	2580	Note 1
K	4-dr. Sed.-5P	885	2645	Note 1
K	4-dr. Del. Sed.-5P	955	2655	Note 1

Note 1: See 1929 Series K production totals.

CF	2-dr. Rds.-2/4P	985	2720	1457
CF	4-dr. Phae.-5P	1035	2800	179
CF	2-dr. Bus. Cpe.-2P	965	2835	1015
CF	2-dr. Del. Cpe.-2/4P	1025	2875	2735
CF	2-dr. Conv. Cpe.-2/4P	1075	2845	524
CF	4-dr. Sed.-5P	995	2965	9653
CF	4-dr. Del. Sed.-5P	1065	2975	4139
CF	Chassis	NA	NA	373

Note 2: Total series production was 20,075.

CK	2-dr. Rds.-2/4P	810	2385	1086
CK	4-dr. Phae.-5P	830	2475	209
CK	2-dr. Bus. Cpe.-2P	830	2515	858
CK	2-dr. R/S Cpe.-2/4P	860	2585	1521
CK	2-dr. Conv. Cpe.-2/4P	945	2540	184
CK	4-dr. Sed.-5P	875	2705	8248
CK	Chassis	NA	NA	94

Note 3: Total series production was 12,200.

1930 DeSoto Six, Series CK, roadster (JAC)

ENGINE: [Series K] Inline. L-head. Six. Cast iron block. B & S: 3 x 4-1/8 in. Disp.: 174.9 cu. in. C.R.: 5.2:1. Brake H.P.: 55 @ 3000 R.P.M. N.A.C.C. H.P.: 21.6. Four main bearings. Solid valve lifters. Carb.: Stromberg one-barrel. Torque: 110 lb.-ft. @ 1200 R.P.M. [Series CF] Inline. L-head. Eight. Cast iron block. B & S: 2-7/8 x 4 in. Disp 207.7 cu. in. C.R.: 5.2:1. Brake H.P.: 70 @ 3400 R.P.M. N.A.C.C. H.P.: 26.45. Five main bearings. Solid valve lifters. Carb.: Carter model 188 SR. Torque: 132 lb.-ft. @ 1200 R.P.M. [Series CK] Inline. L-head. Six. Cast iron block. B & S: 3-1/8 x 4-1/8 in. Disp.: 189.8 cu. in. C.R.: 5.2:1. Brake H.P.: 60 @ 3400 R.P.M. Four main bearings. Solid valve lifters. Carb.: Stromberg one-barrel model DX3. Torque: 120 lb.-ft. @ 1200 R.P.M.

CHASSIS: [Series K] W.B.: 109 in. O.L.: 169 in. Tires: 19 x 5.00. [Series CF] W.B.: 114 in. O.L.: 177 in. Tires: 19 x 5.25. [Series CK] W.B.: 109 in. O.L.: 169 in. Tires: 19 x 5.00.

TECHNICAL: Selective sliding gear transmission. Speeds: 3F/1R. Floor shift controls. Single-plate dry disc clutch. Shaft drive. Semi-floating rear axle. Overall ratios: (K) 4.7:1; (CF) 4.9:1; (CK) 4.7:1. Four wheel hydraulic brakes. Wood spoke wheels.

OPTIONS: Front bumper. Rear bumper. Single sidemount. Dual sidemount. Sidemount cover(s). Wire wheels. Bumper guards. Outside rear view mirror. Heater. Clock. Cigar lighter. Special paint. Special upholstery. Wind wings. Spotlight(s). Cowl lamps. Trumpet horn. Pedestal sidemount mirrors. Fender wells.

HISTORICAL: Date of Introduction: (K) July 1929; (CF) January 1930; (CK) May 1930. Innovations: First DeSoto Eight. Larger more powerful "CK" six. Delco-Remy ignition. Calendar year registrations: 35,267. Calendar year production: 34,889. Model year production: 32,091. DeSoto was America's 15th largest automaker in model year 1930. The 100,000th DeSoto was built this year.

1930-31 DeSOTO

DESOTO (FINER) SERIES CK — SIX: The Finer Six was carried over as an early 1931 series. There were no obvious styling or equipment changes. The rear axle ratio was numerically lowered and new serial number ranges were used. July 1, 1930, was the date after which CKs were considered first series 1931 DeSotos.

DESOTO — SERIES CF — EIGHT: The DeSoto Eight was carried over as an early 1931 model. There were no obvious styling or equipment changes. The rear axle ratio was numerically lowered and a new range of serial numbers was used. July 1, 1930, was the date after which CFs were considered first series 1931 models.

I.D. DATA: [Series CK] Serial numbers were in the same locations. Starting: 5006933. Ending: 5011672. Engine numbers were in the same location. Starting: CK8444. Ending: CK13217. [Series CF] Serial numbers were in the same location. Starting: L172PR. Ending: L185PC. Engine numbers were in the same location. Starting: CF19389. Ending: CF21448.

NOTE: Body styles, prices, weights and production totals for the 1930-31 DeSoto CK models are given in the 1930 section. Body styles, prices, weights and production totals for the 1930-31 CF models are also given in the 1930 section.

ENGINE: Specifications for the DeSoto six- and eight-cylinder engines were unchanged. See 1930 charts above.

CHASSIS: Chassis specifications were the same as 1930 model specifications.

TECHNICAL: Drivetrain specifications were the same as 1930 model specifications except cars now had a 4.6:1 rear axle ratio.

OPTIONS: Options available for the 1930-31 series were the same as offered for the 1930 models.

HISTORICAL: See 1930 DeSoto historical notes. Calculations based on serial and engine numbers suggest that approximately 4,800 sixes (CK) and 2,100 eights (CF) were sold as 1931 first series cars.

1931 DeSOTO

DESOTO — SERIES SA — SIX: The 1931 DeSoto Six SA was introduced in January 1931 at the New York Automobile Show. The restyled body appearance emphasized a longer hood. Other styling features included a narrow profile radiator, vertical radiator shutters and hood louvers, twin cowl ventilators, new type swinging windshield and an oval instrument board. Standard equipment included Delco-Remy ignition, hydraulic brakes, double drop frame and hydraulic shock absorbers.

DESOTO — SERIES CF* — EIGHT: The 1931 DeSoto CF* Eight used a new headlamp cross-bar with the DeSoto crest in the center of it to distinguish it from the six. The eight had two-bar bumpers, a stripe on the sun visor and matching body and fender finish. Other features included a new, narrow profile radiator shell, vertical radiator shutters and hood louvers, twin cowl ventilators, an oval instrument panel and new French type sun visor and top. Standard equipment included Delco-Remy ignition, hydraulic brakes, new counterbalanced crankshaft, a non-glare slanting windshield, adjustable front seats and hydraulic shock absorbers.

I.D. DATA: [Series SA] Serial numbers were in the same location. Starting: 5011801. Ending: 5030806. Engine numbers were in the same location. Starting: SA1001. Ending: SA20305. [Series CF*] Serial numbers were in the same locations. Both Fedco and conventional numbers were used on the eights. Starting: L-185PH. Ending: L-192LD. Conventional serial numbers 6000801 to 6001888 were also used. Engine numbers were in the same locations. Starting: CF*22001. Ending: CF*24308.

Model No.	Body Type & Seating	Price	Weight	Prod. Total
SA	2-dr. Rds.-2/4P	795	2520	1949
SA	4-dr. Phae.-5P	795	2645	100
SA	2-dr. Std. Cpe.-2P	740	2630	1309
SA	2-dr. Del. Cpe.-2/4P	775	2685	2663
SA	2-dr. Conv. Cpe.-2/4P	825	2630	638
SA	2-dr. Sed.-5P	695	2715	2349
SA	4-dr. Sed.-5P	775	2745	17,866
SA	4-dr. Del. Sed.-5P	825	2835	1450
SA	Chassis	—	—	32

Note 1: Total series production was 28,356.

CF*	2-dr. Rds.-2/4P	995	2825	73
CF*	2-dr. Bus. Cpe.-2P	965	2935	102
CF*	2-dr. Del. Cpe.-2/4P	995	2970	486
CF*	2-dr. Conv. Cpe.-2/4P	1110	2970	48
CF*	4-dr. Sed.-5P	995	3065	3490
CF*	4-dr. Del. Sed.-5P	1065	3115	Note 3
CF*	Chassis	NA	NA	3

Note 2: Total series production was 4,224.

Note 3: Production of the Deluxe sedan is included in the total for the regular four-door sedan.

1931 DeSoto Six, Series SA, roadster (OCW)

ENGINE: [Series SA] Inline. L-head. Six. Cast iron block. B & S: 3-1/4 x 4-1/8 in. Disp.: 205.3 cu. in. C.R.: 5.4:1. Brake H.P.: 72 @ 3400 R.P.M. N.A.C.C. H.P.: 25.35. Four main bearings. Solid valve lifters. Carb.: Carter one-barrel model 188SR. Torque: 139 lb.-ft. @ 1200 R.P.M. [Series CF*] Inline. L-head. Eight. Cast iron block. B & S: 2-7/8 x 4-1/4 in. Disp.: 220.7 cu. in. C.R.: 5.4:1. Brake H.P.: 77 @ 3400 R.P.M. N.A.C.C. H.P.: 26.45. Five main bearings. Solid valve lifters. Carb.: Stromberg one-barrel model DX3. Torque: 140 lb.-ft. @ 1200 R.P.M.

CHASSIS: [Series SA] W.B.: 109 in. Tires: 19 x 5.00. [Series CF*] W.B.: 114 in. Tires: 19 x 5.25.

TECHNICAL: Selective sliding gear transmission. Speeds: 3F/1R. Floor shift controls. Single plate dry disc clutch. Shaft drive. Semi-floating rear axle. Overall ratios: (SA) 4.33:1; (CF*) 4.60:1. Hydraulic four wheel brakes. Wood spoke wheels (except convertibles).

OPTIONS: Front bumper. Rear bumper. Single sidemount. Dual sidemounts. (standard on CF convertible). Metal sidemount cover(s). Leather sidemount covers. Outside rear view mirrors. Wire spoke wheels (standard on convertibles). Heater. Clock. Cigar lighter. Wind wings. Trunk rack. Touring trunk. Spotlight(s). Cowl lamps. Trumpet horn. Spare tire(s). Chrome headlights.

1931 DeSoto Six, Series SA, deluxe coupe (JAC)

HISTORICAL: Introduced January 1, 1931. Innovations: (Six) Double drop frame. Hydraulic shock absorbers. Visor-less styling on closed cars. (Eight) Unisteel enclosed bodies. Increased stroke. Heavier crankshaft. New rubber center clutch hub. Calendar year registrations: 28,430. Calendar year production: 32,091. DeSoto was America's 15th ranked producer in terms of model year production. Some depot hack bodies for the DeSoto chassis were custom built by J.T. Cantrell & Co. Peter De Paolo drove a DeSoto Eight across the country as a promotional stunt. Production figures above cover 1931 models (built January to June 1931) and 1931-32 models (built July to December 1931). About 75 percent of the sixes and 50 percent of the eights were sold as "true" 1931 models.

1931-32 DeSOTO

DESOTO — SERIES SA — SIX: The Series SA DeSoto Six was carried over as an early 1932 series. There were no obvious styling changes. New technical features included "Easy-Shift" transmission with silent second gear and the optional availability of freewheeling at $20 extra. July 1, 1931, was the date after which SAs were considered 1932 models.

DESOTO — CF* — EIGHT: The Series CF* DeSoto Eight was carried over as an early 1932 series. There were no obvious styling changes. New technical features included "Easy-Shift" transmission with silent second gear and the optional availability of freewheeling at $20 extra. July 1, 1931, was the date after which CF* models were considered 1932 automobiles.

I.D. DATA: [Series SA] Serial numbers were in the same location. Starting: 5030807. Ending: 5040056. Engine numbers were in the same location: Starting: SA20306. Ending: SA29328. [Series CF*] Serial numbers were in the same location. Both Fedco and conventional numbers were used on the eights. Starting: L192EW. Ending: L192DS. Conventional serial numbers 6001889 to 6004021 were also used. Engine numbers were in the same location. Starting: CF* 24309. Ending: CF* 26621.

Note 1: Body styles, prices, weights and production totals for the 1931-32 DeSoto SA models are given in the 1931 section. About 25 percent of the sixes were sold as 1932 models.

Model No.	Body Type & Seating	Price	Weight	Prod. Total
CF*	4-dr. Phae.-5P	1035	2750	22

Note 1: The four-door phaeton was an all-new model produced only in the early 1932 series. Body styles, prices, weights and production totals for other 1931-32 DeSoto CF* models are given in the 1931 section. About 50 percent of the eights were sold as 1932 models.

ENGINE: [Series SA] DeSoto Six engine specifications were unchanged from 1931 specifications. See data in charts above. [Series CF*] DeSoto Eight engine specifications were unchanged from 1931 specifications. See data in charts above.

CHASSIS: Chassis specifications were the same as 1931 model specifications.

TECHNICAL: Drivetrain specifications were the same as 1931 model specifications except the transmission now had a silent second gear and freewheeling was an available option.

OPTIONS: Options available for the 1931-32 series were the same as offered for the 1931 models.

HISTORICAL: See 1931 DeSoto historical notes. Calculations based on serial numbers suggest that approximately 9,022 sixes (CA) and 2,312 eights (CF*) were sold as 1932 first series cars.

1932 DeSOTO

DESOTO — SERIES SC — SIX: Introduced in January 1932, the SC series was characterized by a rounded grille that resembled that of a Miller racing car. It had horizontal bars divided by three vertical bars. New styling features included one-piece fenders, twin cowl ventilators, wider body belt moldings, interior (instead of exterior) sun visors and wire wheels. Standard equipment included Delco-Remy ignition, hydraulic brakes, "Floating Power," freewheeling, fuel pump, double drop X-type frame, safety all-steel body, silent gear selector, synchromesh transmission, and a rear spare wheel. Buyers could have their car with a painted grille shell or a chrome plated one (at extra cost). There was also a custom SC sub-series in which all models featured external trumpet horns, dual taillamps, dual windshield wipers, safety glass, cigar lighters, adjustable seats, and fenders painted to match the body color. Both standard and custom models could also be ordered with "deluxe" equipment including bumpers and six wire wheels. Chrome headlights were standard on all SCs. The Custom roadster and coupe were models with a rumbleseat and six wheel equipment was standard on the custom SC convertible sedan.

I.D. DATA: Serial numbers were in the same location, Starting: (std.) 5040201; (cus.) 6005001. Ending: (std.) 5055921; (cus.) 6012580. Engine numbers were in the same location. Starting: (std.) SC1001; (cus.) SC1001. Ending: (std.) SC23584; (cus.) SC24800.

Model No.	Body Type & Seating	Price	Weight	Prod. Total
(Standard SC)				
SSC	2-dr. Rds.-2P	675	2720	(894)
SSC	2-dr. Cpe.-2P	695	2843	1691
SSC	2-dr. R/S Cpe.-2/4P	735	2888	(2897)
SSC	2-dr. Brgm.-5P	695	2903	3730
SSC	4-dr. Sed.-5P	775	2993	8924
SSC	4-dr. Sed.-7P	925	3148	221
SSC	Chassis	NA	NA	83
(Custom SC)				
CSC	2-dr. Rds.-2/4P	775	2738	(894)
CSC	2-dr. Cpe.-2/4P	790	2913	(2897)
CSC	2-dr. Conv. Cpe.-2/4P	845	2858	960
CSC	4-dr. Sed.-5P	835	3028	4791
CSC	2-dr. Conv. Sed.-5P	975	3043	275
CSC	4-dr. Phae.-5P	775	NA	30

Note 1: Total series production was 24,496.

Note 2: Figures in brackets are combined totals for standard and custom models and are shown in both places.

1932 DeSoto Six, Series SC, convertible sedan (OCW)

ENGINE: Inline. L-head. Six. Cast iron block. B & S: 3-1/4 x 4-3/8 in. Disp.: 217.8 cu. in. C.R.: 5.4:1. Brake H.P.: 75 @ 3400 R.P.M. N.A.C.C. H.P.: 25.35. Four main bearings. Solid valve lifters. Carb.: Ball & Ball one-barrel model 6B2. Torque: 140 lb.-ft. @ 1400 R.P.M.

CHASSIS: [Series SC (std.)] W.B.: 112-3/8 in. Tires: 18 x 5.25. [Series SC (cus.)] W.B.: 112-3/8 in. Tires: 17 x 5.50. [Series SC (Sed.-7P)] W.B.: 121 in. Tires: 18 x 5.25.

TECHNICAL: Transmission: Selective sliding w/constant mesh and freewheeling. Speeds: 3F/1R. Floor shift controls. Single disc dry plate clutch. Shaft drive. Semi-floating rear axle. Overall ratio: 4.62:1. Four wheel hydraulic brakes. Wire wheels.

Note: A vacuum-operated automatic clutch was available at extra cost.

OPTIONS: Front bumper. Rear bumper. Single sidemount. Dual sidemount(s). Sidemount cover(s). Wood spoke wheels. Spare tire. Radio. Heater. Clock. Cigar lighter. Radio antenna. Special upholstery. Wind wings. Spotlight(s). Cowl lamps. Trumpet horns (std. models). Trunk rack. Touring trunk. Safety glass (std. models). Dual taillights (std. models). Chrome radiator shell. Dual sun visors (std. models). Chrome sidemount trim bands. Special paint.

1932 DeSoto Six, Series SC, sedan (JAC)

HISTORICAL: Introduced January 1932. Innovations: Fuel pump. Automatic clutch option. Constant mesh transmission. New double drop X-frame. Freewheeling standard. Longer wheelbase. "Floating Power" engine mounting system. Calendar year registrations: 25,311. Calendar year production: 27,441. Model year production: 24,496. For the calendar year, DeSoto was the ninth ranked U.S. automaker. The company placed 12th in model year production. At least two SC Custom town cars were constructed on the 121-inch wheelbase chassis. The 1932 DeSoto was advertised as "America's Smartest Low-Priced Car." Race driver Peter DePaolo made a 10-day cross-country promotional run in a new DeSoto SC. It culminated with a 300-mile race track trial at speeds up to 80 mph. Production and sales of the SC DeSoto continued into 1933 in Great Britain, where a badge-engineered version was marketed as the Chrysler Mortlake Six.

1933 DeSOTO

1933 DeSoto Six, Series SD, convertible coupe (OCW)

DESOTO — SERIES SD — SIX: The 1933 DeSotos had a horizontal radiator grille and front fenders that came to the center of the radiator. One way to tell standard models was that they did not have a vertical trim divider on the headlight lenses. Twin sun visors, taillights and trumpet horns were standard on only the Customs early in the year, but later became standard equipment on the low-priced cars as well. Other 1933 DeSoto features included Delco-Remy ignition, hydraulic brakes, "Floating Power," automatic vacuum clutch, coincidental starter, automatic choke, double drop X-type frames and safety plate glass. Six wire wheel equipment was standard on the Custom convertible sedan.

I.D. DATA: Serial numbers were in the same location. Starting: (std.) 5056001; (cus.) 6013001. Ending: (std.) 5068056; (cus.) 60234023. Engine numbers were in the same location. Starting: SD-1001. Ending: SD23800.

Model No.	Body Type & Seating	Price	Weight	Prod. Total
(Standard SD)				
SD	2-dr. Cpe.-2P	665	2905	800
SD	2-dr. R/S Cpe.-2/4P	705	2975	(2705)
SD	2-dr. Brgm.-5P	665	2995	2436
SD	2-dr. Spl. Brgm.-5P	725	3015	8133
SD	4-dr. Sed.-5P	735	3070	(7890)
(Custom SD)				
SD	2-dr. R/S Cpe.-2/4P	750	2995	(2705)
SD	2-dr. Conv. Cpe.-2/4P	775	2990	412
SD	4-dr. Sed.-5P	795	3150	(7890)
SD	2-dr. Conv. Sed.-5P	875	NA	132
SD	Chassis	NA	NA	124
SD	4-dr. Exp. Sed.-7P	NA	NA	104

Note 1: Total series production was 22,736.

Note 2: Figures in parenthesis indicate combined production totals for standard and custom models. No additional breakouts are available.

1933 DeSoto Six, Series SD, standard brougham (JAC)

ENGINE: Inline. L-head. Six. Cast iron block. B & S: 3-1/4 x 4-3/8 in. Disp.: 217.8 cu. in. C.R.: 6.2:1. Brake H.P.: 100 @ 3400 R.P.M.

N.A.C.C. H.P.: 25.35. Five main bearings. Solid valve lifters. Carb.: Ball & Ball one-barrel model E6A3. Torque: 160 lb.-ft. @ 1200 R.P.M.

CHASSIS: [Series SD] W.B.: 114-3/8 in. Tires: (std.) 17 x 5.50; (cus.) 15 x 7.00.

TECHNICAL: All-silent helical gear transmission. Speeds: 3F/1R. Floor shift controls. Single plate dry disc clutch. Shaft drive. Semi-floating rear axle. Overall ratio: 4.375:1. Four wheel hydraulic brakes. Wire wheels supplied on standard models. Goodyear "Airwheels" standard on Custom models.

OPTIONS: Front bumper. Rear bumper. Single sidemount. Dual sidemount(s). Sidemount cover(s). Trumpet horns. Bumper guards. Radio (all cars wired for radios). Heater. Clock. Cigar lighter. Radio antenna. Seat covers. Outside rear view mirror(s). Spotlight(s). Cowl lamps. Rear spare tire. Wind wings. Special paint. Special upholstery. Trunk rack. Touring trunk.

HISTORICAL: Introduced December 1932. Automatic choke. Automatic manifold heat control. All helical-gear transmission. Coincidental starter operated by accelerator pedal. Calendar year registrations: 21,260. Calendar year production: 20,186. Model year production: 22,736. Race driver Harry Hartz drove a specially modified DeSoto backwards across the U.S. this year. The stunt was designed to herald the 1934 DeSoto Airflows. The SD was sold in Great Britain as the Chrysler Wimbledon this year only.

1933 DeSoto Six, Series SD, custom coupe (JAC)

1934 DeSOTO

DESOTO — SERIES SE — SIX: All 1934 DeSotos featured Chrysler Corp.'s new, streamlined Airflow design. They had built-in headlamps. Wider front seats accommodated three passengers. The hood extended beyond the front axle. The rear fenders were shrouded with full fender skirts. Other design features included horizontal hood louvers, a rounded radiator grille and a modified, vee-shaped windshield. Standard equipment included Delco-Remy ignition, four-wheel hydraulic brakes, unit body construction, "Floating Power," and Goodyear "Airwheels."

I.D. DATA: Serial numbers were in the same location. Starting: 5068501 and up. Engine numbers were in the same location. Starting: SE1001 and up.

Model No.	Body Type & Seating	Price	Weight	Prod. Total
SE	2-dr. Cpe.-5P	995	3323	1584
SE	2-dr. Brgm.-6P	995	3323	522
SE	4-dr. Sed.-6P	995	3378	11,713
SE	4-dr. Twn. Sed.-6P	995	3343	119
SE	Chassis	NA	NA	2

Note: Total series production was 13,940.

ENGINE: Inline. L-head. Six. Cast iron block. B & S: 3-3/8 x 4-1/2 in. Disp.: 241.5 cu. in. C.R.: 6.2:1. Brake H.P.: 100 @ 3400 R.P.M. N.A.C.C. H.P.: 27.34. Four main bearings. Solid valve lifters. Carb.: Ball & Ball one-barrel model E6BI. Torque: 185 lb.-ft. @ 1200 R.P.M.

CHASSIS: W.B.: 115-1/2 in. Tires: 16 x 6.50.

TECHNICAL: Manual transmission with freewheeling. Speeds: 3F/1R. Floor shift controls. Conventional clutch. Shaft drive. Semi-floating rear axle. Overall ratio: 4.11:1. Four wheel hydraulic brakes. Goodyear "Airwheels."

OPTIONS: Front bumper. Rear bumper. Fender skirt ornament. Fender skirts (std. models). Bumper guards. Radio. Heater. Clock. Cigar lighter. Radio antenna. Seat covers. Steel artillery spoke wheels (no extra cost). Spotlight. Steel disc wheels (no extra cost). License plate frames. Automatic vacuum clutch.

1934 DeSoto Airflow, Series SE, four-door sedan (OCW)

HISTORICAL: Introduced January 1934. Innovations: Radically new Airflow design. Balanced weight distribution. Unit body construction. Extra long leaf springs. Low radiator core. Fresh air ventilation. Calendar year registrations: 11,447. Calendar year production: 15,825. Model year production: 13,940. DeSoto ranked 13th in terms of U.S. model year output. Byron C. Foy was president of DeSoto. He helped promote sales of the new model at Chrysler's exhibit at the "Century of Progress" exposition in Chicago. Airflows were capable of up to 22 mpg fuel economy. Race driver Harry Hartz set 32 stock car records driving a DeSoto Airflow at Muroc Dry Lake Bed in California. Hartz also made a New York to San Francisco cross-country trip with a total fuel bill of just $33.06. The SE was sold in Great Britain as the Chrysler Croydon.

1935 DeSOTO

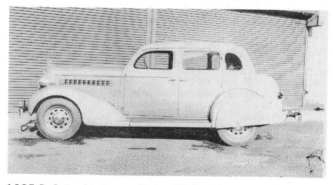

1935 DeSoto, Airstream, Series SF, four-door sedan (OCW)

AIRSTREAM — SERIES SF — SIX: Because of the Airflow's lack of acceptance, DeSoto added the conventional Airstream series as a companion car this year. Styling features included a sloping vee-type radiator grille, two rows of horizontal windstream hood louvers and bullet shaped headlights mounted on pedestals above the front fender catwalks. The bumper had a vee-shaped dip in its center and three vertical chrome "hash marks" decorated the lower front fender aprons. The Airstreams were about $220 cheaper than comparable Airflows in the DeSoto line. Standard equipment included Autolite ignition, hydraulic brakes, independent front suspension, balanced weight distribution, "Floating Power" and new centrifuse brake drums. A Deluxe equipment package including two-tone paint, small front fender lamps, dual taillights, dual trumpet horns, two windshield wipers, wheel trim rings, chrome fender and run-

ningboard moldings, a cigar lighter and front compartment carpeting was available for $35 extra after June 1935.

1935 DeSoto Airstream, Series SF, convertible coupe (JAC)

AIRFLOW — SERIES SG — SIX: In an attempt to make it look slightly less radical, the DeSoto Airflow was given a new front end with a slightly vee-shaped radiator. The 1935 grille was more sloping than rounded, increasing the length of the hood. There were now only three horizontal hood louvers instead of 11. Standard equipment included Autolite ignition, Lockheed four-wheel hydraulic brakes, balanced weight distribution, centrifuse brake drums, "Floating Power," and fender skirts. A hypoid rear axle was adopted this year and the anti-sway stabilizer bar was moved from the rear of the car to the front. Freewheeling was no longer used.

1935 DeSoto Airflow, Series SG, four-door sedan (OCW)

I.D. DATA: [Series SF] Serial numbers were in the same location. Starting: 6023501. Ending: 6043679. Engine numbers were in the same locations. Starting: SF-1001. Ending: SF-21874. [Series SG] Serial numbers were in the same location. Starting: 5082201. Ending: 5088967. Engine numbers were in the same location. Starting: SG-1001. Ending: SG-7843.

Model No.	Body Type & Seating	Price	Weight	Prod. Total
SF	2-dr. Bus. Cpe.-2P	695	2840	1760
SF	2-dr. R/S Cpe.-2/4P	760	2925	900
SF	2-dr. Conv. Cpe.-2/4P	835	3035	226
SF	2-dr. Sed.-5P	745	2915	1350
SF	2-dr. Tr. Sed.-5P	775	2960	2035
SF	4-dr. Sed.-5P	795	2990	5714
SF	4-dr. Tr. Sed.-5P	825	3035	8018

Note 1: Total series production was 20,784.

SG	2-dr. Bus. Cpe.-3P	1015	3390	70
SG	2-dr. Cpe.-5P	1015	3390	418
SG	4-dr. Sed.-6P	1015	3390	6269
SG	4-dr. Twn. Sed.-6P	1015	3400	40

Note 2: Total series production was 6,797.

Note 3: Above factory prices (for Airflows) in effect after February 7, 1935. Earlier price was $1,195 for all models.

ENGINE: [Series SF] Inline. L-head. Six. Cast iron block. B & S: 3-3/8 x 4-1/2 in. Disp.: 241.5 cu. in. C.R.: 6.0:1. Brake H.P.: 93 @ 3400 R.P.M. N.A.C.C. H.P.: 27.34. Four main bearings. Solid valve lifters. Carb.: Ball & Ball one-barrel model E6F2. Torque: 180 lb.-ft. @ 1200 R.P.M. [Series SG] Inline. L-head. Six. Cast iron block. B & S: 3-3/8 x 4-1/2 in. Disp.: 241.5 cu. in. C.R.: 6.5:1. Brake H.P.: 100 @ 3400 R.P.M. N.A.C.C. H.P.: 27.34. Four main bearings. Solid valve lifters. Carb.: Ball & Ball one-barrel E6F2. Torque: 185 lb.-ft. @ 1200 R.P.M.

CHASSIS: [Series SF] W.B.: 116 in. Tires: 16 x 6.25. [Series SG] W.B.: 115-1/2 in. Tires: 16 x 6.50.

TECHNICAL: Manual transmission (synchromesh). Speeds: 3F/1R. Floor shift controls. Conventional clutch. Shaft drive. Hypoid rear axle. Overall ratio: (SF) 3.89:1; (SG) 4.0:1. Lockheed four-wheel centrifuse hydraulic brakes. Steel spoke wheels with Goodyear "Airwheel" tires.

OPTIONS: Front bumper. Rear bumper. Whitewall tires. Dual sidemount (Airstream). Sidemount covers (Airstream). Fender skirts. Bumper guards. Radio. Heater. Clock. Cigar lighter. Radio antenna. Seat covers. Chrome wheel trim rings. Spotlight(s). Parking lamps. Trumpet horns. Fender skirt ornaments. Fender moldings. Runningboard moldings. Carpets. Twin wipers. Right-hand taillight. Right-hand interior sun visor. Spare tire metal cover. Overdrive transmission. Special paint colors.

HISTORICAL: Production began November 1934. Production ended: (SF) August 1935; (SG) September 1935. Introduced January 2, 1935. Innovations: Both models have engine over axles and redistribution of weight. Improved hydraulic brakes on centrifuse drums. Freewheeling eliminated. Independent front suspension on Airstreams. Hypoid rear axle. Ventilated clutch in Airflow. Calendar year registrations: 26,952. Calendar year production: 34,276. Model year production: 27,581. Company president was Byron C. Foy. DeSoto was America's 13th largest producer on a model year basis. For the second year in-a-row, the DeSoto Airflow won the Grand Prix Award for aerodynamic styling at the Monte Carlo Concours d' Elegance. Taxicab specials were produced in some quantities this year. DeSoto provided dealers with a kit that could be used to update 1934 Airflows to give them generally the same appearance as 1935 models. DeSoto experimented with a streamlined compact car this year. The SG was sold in Great Britain as the Chrysler Croydon; leftover 1934 models were slightly modified and sold into 1935.

1936 DeSOTO

AIRSTREAM — SERIES S-1 — SIX: The DeSoto Airstream came in Deluxe and Custom car-lines for 1936. Both carried conventional body work with a new horizontal bar radiator grille and "pennon" style hood louvers. DeLuxes had one-piece flat windshields. Customs (except the convertibles) had split vee-type windshields, chrome moldings on top of headlamps, fender skirt and runningboard moldings and rear wheel shrouds (fender skirts). Standard equipment included Autolite ignition, hydraulic brakes, "Floating Power," extra-long springs, independent front suspension, ride stabilizer and Goodyear's "Airwheel Magic Carpet" ride. The Custom Traveler and limousine were built on a long-wheelbase chassis. Special seven-passenger taxicabs had the long wheelbase Custom bodies, Deluxe-type windshields and sliding sun roofs (in 2,200 cars).

1936 DeSoto Airstream, Series S-1, coupe (OCW)

AIRFLOW III — SERIES S-2 — SIX: The DeSoto Airflow had a new, flanged steel roof panel insert. It was bolted to the perimeter of the roof, acoustically treated and electrically insulated to serve as a radio antenna. New styling features included a die-cast grille with vertical moldings and curved diagonal trim, twin "pennon" style hood louvers, new bumpers, redesigned bodyside moldings, new taillights and an updated instrument panel. Standard equipment included Autolite ignition, four-wheel hydraulic brakes, balanced weight distribution, "Floating Power," unitized body construction and Goodyear "Airwheels."

I.D. DATA: [Series S-1] Serial numbers were in the same location. Starting: (Del.) 6043701; (Cust.) 5500001. Ending: (Del.) 6061693; (Cust.) 5517216. Engine numbers were in the same location. Starting: S1-1001. Ending: S1-39756. [Series S-2] Serial numbers were in the same

location. Starting: 5089001. Ending: 5093971. Engine numbers were in the same location. Starting: S2-1001. Ending: S2-6038.

1936 DeSoto Airflow, Series S-2, four-door sedan (OCW)

Model No.	Body Type & Seating	Price	Weight	Prod. Total
(Deluxe)				
S-1	2-dr. Bus. Cpe.-2P	695	2941	2592
S-1	2-dr. Tr. Brgm,-5P	770	3051	2207
S-1	4-dr. Tr. Sed.-5P	810	3111	13,093
S-1	Chassis	NA	NA	99
(Custom)				
S-1	2-dr. Bus. Cpe.-2P	745	3000	940
S-1	2-dr. R/S Cpe.-2/4P	795	3085	641
S-1	2-dr. Conv. Cpe.-2/4P	895	3031	350
S-1	2-dr. Tr. Brgm.-5P	825	3031	1120
S-1	4-dr. Tr. Sed.-5P	865	3126	13,801
S-1	4-dr. Conv. Sed.-5P	1095	3246	215
(LWB Custom)				
S-1	4-dr. Trav. Sed.-5P	1075	3256	23
S-1	4-dr. Sed.-7P	1075	3340	208
S-1	4-dr. N.Y. Taxi-7P	NA	NA	2500
S-1	Chassis	NA	NA	460
S-1	4-dr. Calif. Taxi-7P	NA	NA	451

Note 1: Total Deluxe series production was 17,991; Total Custom series production was 20,719. Grand total Series S-1 production was 38,710.

S-2	2-dr. Cpe.-5P	1095	3540	250
S-2	4-dr. Sed.-6P	1095	3540	4750

Note 2: Total series production was 5,000.

ENGINE: [Series S-1] Inline. L-head. Six. Cast iron block. B & S: 3-3/8 x 4-1/2 in. Disp.: 241.5 cu. in. C.R.: 6.0:1. Brake H.P.: 93 @ 3400 R.P.M. N.A.C.C. H.P.: 27.34. Four main bearings. Solid valve lifters. Carb.: Ball & Ball one-barrel model E6GI. Torque: 180 lb.-ft. @ 1200 R.P.M. [Series S-2] Inline. L-head. Six. Cast iron block. B & S: 3-3/8 x 4-1/2 in. Disp.: 241.5 cu. in. C.R.: 6.5:1. Brake H.P.: 100 @ 3400 R.P.M. N.A.C.C. H.P.: 27.34. Four main bearings. Solid valve lifters. Carb.: Ball & Ball model E6GI. Torque: 185 lb.-ft. @ 1200 R.P.M.

1936 DeSoto Airstream, Series S-1, four-door sedan (JAC)

CHASSIS: [Series S-1] W.B.: 118 in. Tires: 16 x 6.25. [Series (LWB) S-1] W.B.: 130 in. Tires: 16 x 6.25. [Series S-2] W.B.: 115-1/2 in. Tires: 16 x 6.50.

TECHNICAL: Manual transmission (synchromesh). Speeds: 3F/1R. Floor shift controls. Conventional clutch. Shaft drive. Spiral bevel gear

axle (hypoid with overdrive). Overall ratio: (S-1) 3.89:1; (S-1) 4.1:1. Lockheed four-wheel centrifuse brakes. Steel spoke wheels with Goodyear "Airwheel" tires.

OPTIONS: Front bumper. Rear Bumper. Whitewalls. Dual sidemount(s). Fender skirts. Bumper guards. Radio. Heater. Clock. Cigar lighter. Radio antenna. Seat covers. Spotlight(s). Fog lamps. Trumpet horn (Airstreams). Overdrive (Deluxe Airstream). Wind wings (convertibles). Chrome wheel covers. Special paint. Outside rear view mirror. Right-hand taillight (Deluxe). Right-hand sun visor (Deluxe). Twin wipers (Deluxe).

HISTORICAL: Production began September 1935. Production ended August 1936. Introduced November 2, 1935. Steel top insert. One-inch lower Airstream chassis is claimed to be "twice as rigid." Airstream wheelbase increased two inches. DeSoto officially enters the taxi building business with New York City "Sunshine" cabs. Calendar year registrations: 45,088. Calendar year production: 52,789. Model year production: 43,710. Company president: Byron C. Foy. DeSoto was America's 13th ranked automaker for model year 1936. The convertible sedan was reintroduced in the Airstream Custom series. This was the last year for the DeSoto Airflow. DeSoto production facilities were expanded this season and also separated from Chrysler production facilities. The DeSoto S-1 was sold as the Chrysler Richmond in Great Britain.

1937 DeSOTO

1937 DeSoto, Series S-3, four-door sedan (OCW)

DESOTO — SERIES S-3 — SIX: There was just one DeSoto series in 1937. These cars had a new hood that was hinged at the cowl. The grille featured horizontal bars divided by a vertical center panel finished in body color. The six upper grille bars swept back along the sides of the hood. The DeSoto name was spelled out by vertically stacked chrome letters on the center panel. Bullet shaped headlamps were attached to the sides of the hood. A wide, ribbed bumper was used. Standard equipment included Autolite ignition, hydraulic brakes, all-steel body construction with 14 rubber float body mountings, hypoid rear axle and independent front suspension. A "safety-styled" interior was a 1937 innovation. The speedometer was mounted in front of the steering column, instrument panel knobs were recessed, gauges were flush-mounted and door handles curved inward to prevent snagging. The top of the front seat back was heavily padded and even the overhead windshield wiper knob was made of soft rubber. Several accessories including bumpers, bumper guards, spare tire and safety glass were standard equipment for the first time this year. Dual wipers, taillights, sun visors, horns and door armrests were standard in convertibles.

I.D. DATA: Serial numbers were in the same location. Starting: 5517301. Ending: 5597700. Engine numbers were in the same location. Starting: S3-1001. Ending: S3-77210.

Model No.	Body Type & Seating	Price	Weight	Prod. Total
S-3	2-dr. Bus. Cpe.-3P	770	3038	11,050
S-3	2-dr. R/S Cpe.-3/5P	820	3088	1,030
S-3	2-dr. Conv. Cpe.-3/5P	975	3225	992
S-3	2-dr. Fs Bk. Brgm.-6P	830	3123	1200
S-3	2-dr. Tr. Brgm.-6P	840	3148	11,660
S-3	4-dr. Fs Bk. Sed.-6P	870	3123	2265
S-3	4-dr. Tr. Sed.-6P	880	3148	51,889
S-3	4-dr. Conv. Sed.-5P	1300	3441	426

Model No.	Body Type & Seating	Price	Weight	Prod. Total
(Long Wheelbase [LWB])				
S-3	4-dr. Tr. Sed.-7P	1120	3451	695
S-3	4-dr. Limo. Sed.-7P	1220	3536	71
S-3	4-dr. Calif. Taxi-7P	NA	NA	225
S-3	Chassis	NA	NA	497

Note 1: Total series production was 82,000.

ENGINE: Inline. L-head. Six. Cast iron block. B & S: 3-3/8 x 4-1/4 in. Disp.: 228.1 cu. in. C.R.: 6.5:1. Brake H.P.: 93 @ 3600 R.P.M. N.A.C.C. H.P.: 27.34. Four main bearings. Solid valve lifters. Carb.: Ball & Ball one-barrel model E6K4. Torque: 168 lb.-ft. @ 1200 R.P.M.

CHASSIS: [Series S-3] W.B.: 116 in. Tires: 16 x 6.00. [Series (LWB) S-3] W. B.: 133 in. Tires: 16 x 6.50.

TECHNICAL: Synchromesh manual transmission, Speeds: 3F/1R. Floor shift controls. Conventional clutch. Shaft drive. Hypoid rear axle. Overall ratio: (SWB)4.11:1; (LWB) 4.33:1. Four-wheel hydraulic brakes. Steel disc wheels.

1937 DeSoto, Series S-3, coupe (JAC)

OPTIONS: Front bumper (standard). Rear bumper (standard). Whitewall tires. Dual sidemounts. Sidemount cover(s). Fender skirts. Bumper guards (standard). Transitone radio. Heater. Clock. Cigar lighter (std. in convertibles). Radio antenna. Seat covers. External sun shade. Spotlight(s). Fog lamps. "Gas-Saver" overdrive transmission ($35). Wheel trim rings. Sliding sun roof. License plate frames. Outside rear view mirror. Vent wings (convertibles).

1937 DeSoto, Series S-3, convertible sedan (JAC)

HISTORICAL: Production started September 1936. Production ended August 1937. Introduced September 1936. Innovations: Shorter stroke engine. Safety styled interior. Alligator hood with removable side panels. Steel roof construction. One-piece flat windshield on all DeSotos. First DeSoto station wagons built by J.C. Cantrell on DeSoto S-3 chassis. Rubber body mounting. Calendar year registrations: 74,424. Calendar year production: 86,541. Model year production: 82,000. DeSoto was America's 12th ranked automaker for model year 1937. World's first three-way radios installed in Eastchester, New York, Police Department's 1937 DeSoto squad cars. A specially finished Silver DeSoto convertible sedan was used as an "Official Car" at the 1937 Indy 500. DeSoto claimed its "Gas Saver" transmission was so economical that it gave one free mile for every four miles the car was driven. The 1937 DeSotos were designed by former custom coachbuilder Ray Dietrich, Chrysler Corp.'s new chief designer. The S-3 DeSoto continued to be sold in Great Britain as a Chrysler Richmond.

1938 DeSOTO

DESOTO SERIES S-5 SIX: The 1938 DeSotos had a new, die-cast grille. It was shorter than last year's grille and had a chrome chevron effect at the bottom on the fender apron. The DeSoto had a three-inch longer wheelbase. The bullet-shaped headlamps were recessed into the fenders. A cowl vent was used to draw fresh air into the car; eliminating the use of crank-open windshields. Wipers were moved from the windshield header, back to the cowl. Standard equipment included Autolite ignition, hydraulic brakes, independent front suspension, semi-elliptic rear leaf springs, 10 percent larger brake drums, a new and stronger chassis frame, dash mounted emergency brake and rubber mounted steering system. Two seven-passenger body styles were again available on the long wheelbase chassis. Optional this year was a high-compression engine with an aluminum cylinder head.

1938 DeSoto, Series S-5, four-door sedan (OCW)

I.D. DATA: Serial numbers were in the same location. Starting: 5598301. Ending: 5632912. Engine numbers were in the same location. Starting: S5-1001. Ending: S5-39664.

Model No.	Body Type & Seating	Price	Weight	Prod. Total
S-5	2-dr. Bus. Cpe.-3P	870	3039	5160
S-5	2-dr. R/S Cpe.-3/5P	920	3089	38
S-5	2-dr. Tr. Brgm.-6P	930	3119	5367
S-5	2-dr. FsBk Sed.-6P	920	3104	11
S-5	4-dr. Tr. Sed.-6P	970	3139	23,681
S-5	4-dr. FsBk Sed.-6P	958	3134	498
S-5	4-dr. Conv. Sed.-5P	1375	3394	431
(LWB)				
S-5	4-dr. Tr. Sed.-7P	1195	3439	513
S-5	4-dr. Sed. Limo.-7P	1285	3524	81
S-5	4-dr. Calif. Taxi.-7P	NA	NA	372
(Chassis)				
S-5	Chassis	NA	NA	413
S-5	4-dr. Cantrell Sta. Wag.	NA	NA	NA
S-5	4-dr. Derham Town Car	NA	NA	(1)

Note 1: Total series production was 39,203.

Note 2: The Cantrell station wagons and Derham town car were among models built on the chassis that DeSoto supplied to coachbuilders for special bodies or professional conversions.

1938 DeSoto, Series S-5, coupe (JAC)

ENGINE: Inline. L-head. Six. Cast iron block. B & S: 3-3/8 x 4-1/4 in. Disp.: 228.1 cu. in. C.R.: (std.) 6.5:1; (opt.) 7.0:1. Brake H.P.: (std.) 93 @ 3600 R.P.M.; (opt.) 100 @ 3600 R.P.M. N.A.C.C. H.P.: 27.34. Four main bearings. Solid valve lifters. Carb.: Carter one-barrel model E6M1 (Ball & Ball). Torque: (std.) 172 lb.-ft. @ 1200 R.P.M.; (opt.) 176 lb.-ft. @ 1200 R.P.M.

CHASSIS: [Series S-5] W.B.: 119 in. Tires: 16 x 6.00. [Series (LWB) S-5] W.B.: 136 in. Tires: 16 x 6.50.

TECHNICAL: Synchromesh manual transmission. Speeds: 3F/1R. Floor shift controls. Conventional clutch. Shaft drive. Hypoid rear axle. Overall ratio: 4.1:1. Four wheel hydraulic brakes. Steel disc wheels.

OPTIONS: Front bumper. Rear bumper. Whitewall tires. Outside rear view mirror. "Butterfly" ventipanes (convertible). Fender skirts. Bumper guards. Radio. Heater. Clock. Cigar lighter. Radio antenna. Seat covers. External sun shade. Spotlight(s). Fog lamps. Wheel trim rings. Right-hand sun visor (std. on convertible). Right-hand taillight (std. on convertible). Dual horns (std. on convertible). Right-hand windshield wiper (std. on convertible). High-compression aluminum cylinder head. Leather driver's seat (limousine). "Gas Saver" overdrive transmission.

HISTORICAL: Production started September 1937. Production ended July 1938. Introduced September 1, 1937. Innovations: New rubber mounted steering gear. Parking brake control positioned below instrument panel. Cowl mounted wipers. Non-opening one-piece windshields. High-compression engine with aluminum head (used on all long wheelbase models). Calendar year registrations: 35,259. Calendar year production: 32,688. Model year production: 39,203. DeSoto was America's 13th ranked automaker in model year 1938.

1939 DeSOTO

DESOTO — SERIES S-6 — SIX: The 1939 DeSoto had more streamlined styling with a newly designed hood. The nose of the car had horizontal chrome grille bars running rearward. There were also chrome horizontal bars running across the front splash aprons. The headlamps were entirely recessed in the fenders. The DeSoto name appeared on both sides of the nose and there were horizontal decorations with four square vents on the rear end of the hood side panels. Two-piece vee-type windshields made their return this year. DeSoto again marketed two bodies on an extended wheelbase chassis and all models, except the Custom club coupe, were available in deluxe or custom trim. Custom models had all features of deluxe cars plus dual sun visors, dual horns, dual taillights and richer interiors with darker colored fabrics. Innovations for 1939 included column mounted gearshift levers, constant speed electric windshield wipers and "Superfinish," an exclusive Chrysler Corp. method of giving engine parts a smooth, mirror-like surface. Standard equipment included Solar Spark ignition, hydraulic brakes and coil spring independent front suspension. The Custom club coupe came with "Airfoam" rubber cushion front seats. There was no convertible in the DeSoto line this year and an optional sliding sun roof was introduced as an alternative sports feature. All 1939 sedans, limousines and taxis were fastback models.

I.D. DATA: Serial numbers were in the same location. Starting: 5634001. Ending: 5687134. Engine numbers were in the same location. Starting: S6-1001. Ending: S6-55461.

Model No.	Body Type & Seating	Price	Weight	Prod. Total
(DeLuxe Line)				
S-6	2-dr. Bus. Cpe.-2P	870	3064	5176
S-6	2-dr. All Season Cpe.-2/4P	925	3089	2124
S-6	2-dr. Tr. Sed.-5P	930	3129	7472
S-6	4-dr. Tr. Sed.-5P	970	3174	31,513
(LWB DeLuxe Line)				
S-6	4-dr. Calif. Taxi-7P	NA	NA	1250
S-6	4-dr. Tr. Sed.-7P	1195	3454	425
S-6	4-dr. Sed. Limo.-7P	1285	3549	84
S-6	Chassis	NA	NA	154
(Custom Line)				
S-6	2-dr. Bus. Cpe.-2P	923	3069	498
S-6	2-dr. Cus. AS Cpe.-2/4P	978	3094	287
S-6	2-dr. Cus. Clb. Cpe.-4P	1145	3164	264
S-6	2-dr. Tr. Sed.-5P	983	3134	424
S-6	4-dr. Tr. Sed.-5P	1023	3179	5993
(LWB Custom Line)				
S-6	4-dr. Tr. Sed.-7P	1248	3459	30
S-6	4-dr. Limo. Sed.-7P	1338	3554	5

Note 1: Total series production was 55,699.

Note 2: The all-season coupe had auxiliary (jump) seats.

Note 3: The Custom club coupe was built by Hayes Body Co.

ENGINE: Inline. L-head. Six. Cast iron block. B & S: 3-3/8 x 4-1/4 in. Disp.: 228.1 cu. in. C.R.: (std.) 6.5:1; (opt.) 7.0:1. Brake H.P.: (std.) 93 @ 3600 R.P.M.; (opt.) 100 @ 3600 R.P.M. N.A.C.C. H.P.: 27.34. Four main bearings. Solid valve lifters. Carb.: Ball & Ball one-barrel model E6N1. Torque: (std.) 172 lb.-ft. @ 1200 R.P.M.; (opt.) 176 lb.-ft. @ 1200 R.P.M.

CHASSIS: [Series S-6] W.B.: 119 in. Tires: 16 x 6.00. [Series (LWB) S-6] W.B.: 136 in. Tires: 16 x 6.50.

TECHNICAL: Manual synchromesh transmission. Speeds: 3F/1R. Column mounted gearshift. Conventional multiple disc clutch. Shaft drive. Hypoid rear axle. Overall ratio: 4.1:1. Four wheel hydraulic brakes. Steel disc wheels.

1939 DeSoto, Series S-6, four-door sedan (JAC)

OPTIONS: Whitewall tires. Chrome beauty rings. Outside rear view mirror(s). Vent wings. Bumper wing guards. Fender skirts. Bumper guards. Radio. Heater. Clock. Cigar lighter. Radio antenna. Seat covers. External sun shade. Spotlight(s). Fog lamps. Dual tone horns (std. on Custom). Right-hand sun visor (deluxe). Right-hand taillight (deluxe). Sliding sun roof. "Perfected Controlled" overdrive transmission. "Airfoam" seat cushions (except Custom club coupe). License plate frames. Special paint colors.

1939 DeSoto, Series, S-6, four-door sedan (OCW)

HISTORICAL: Started production August 1938. Ended production July 1939. Introduced October 1938. Innovations: New streamlined bodies including limited production Custom club coupe made by Hayes Body Co. Remote control gearshift. Improved overdrive. "Superfinish" engine parts. Calendar year registration: 51,951. Calendar year production: 53,269. Model year production: 55,699. DeSoto was America's 13th ranked automaker for model year 1939. DeSoto claimed that its new step-down type overdrive gave the equivalent of five forward speeds. Spencer Tracy, Walt Disney and Myrna Loy were among personalities who participated in DeSoto's advertising and promotional campaign this year.

1940 DeSOTO

DESOTO — SERIES S-7 — SIX: The 1940 DeSotos were even more streamlined. They had more massive fenders and concealed door hinges. The frontal design featured horizontal chrome grille bars in a special configuration having two separate grilles on either side of a vee-shaped body color panel in the center. The vee pointed downward. DeSoto script nameplates were positioned on either side of the center panel on the nose of the car. Conventional runningboards were available on all models, but optional on customs, which had chrome trimmed rocker panels as standard equipment. All of the cars had wider front and back seats and larger windows. Both the Deluxe and Custom lines included long wheelbase models. New innovations included sealed beam headlights and an "All-Weather" air control system with dual heater and blower units. Also available, as an option, was "Simplimatic" Fluid-Drive — a type of semi-automatic transmission. A chrome script applied to the rear of the hood sides, below beltline level, identified each car as a "Custom" or "Deluxe" trimmed car. Custom models also had chrome moldings around the windshield and windows and chrome trim above and below the taillights. Deluxe models did not have such brightwork.

1940 DeSoto, Series S-7, Deluxe coupe (JAC)

I.D. DATA: Serial numbers were in the same locations. Starting: (Del.) 6064301; (Cus.) 5688001. Ending: (Del.) 6095928; (Cus.) 5720329. Engine numbers were in the same location. Starting: (All) S7-1001. Ending: (All) S7-67427.

Model No.	Body Type & Seating	Price	Weight	Prod. Total
(Deluxe)				
S-7	2-dr. Bus. Cpe.-2P	845	3001	3650
S-7	2-dr. All Season Cpe.-2/4P	905	3026	2098
S-7	2-dr. Tr. Sed.-5P	905	3066	7072
S-7	4-dr. Tr. Sed.-5P	945	3086	18,666
(LWB Deluxe)				
S-7	4-dr. Tr. Sed.-7P	1175	3490	142
S-7	4-dr. Calif. Taxi-7P	NA	NA	2323
(Custom)				
S-7	2-dr. Cus. Cpe.-2P	885	3024	1898
S-7	2-dr. All Season Cus. Cpe.-2/4P	945	3044	2234
S-7	2-dr. Conv. Cpe.-4P	1095	3329	1085
S-7	2-dr. Tr. Sed.-5P	945	3084	3109
S-7	4-dr. Tr. Sed.-5P	985	3104	25,221
(LWB Custom)				
S-7	4-dr. Tr. Sed.-7P	1215	3490	206
S-7	4-dr. Limo.-7P	1290	3635	34
S-7	Chassis	NA	NA	52

Note 1: Total series production was 67,790.

1940 DeSoto, Series S-7, four-door sedan (OCW)

ENGINE: Inline. L-head. Six. Cast iron block. B & S: 3-3/8 x 4-1/4 in. Disp.: 228.1 cu. in. C.R.: (std.) 6.5:1 (opt.) 6.8:1. Brake H.P.: (std.) 100 @ 3600 R.P.M. (opt.) 105 @ 3600 R.P.M. N.A.C.C. H.P.: 27.34.

Four main bearings. Solid valve lifters. Carb.: Ball & Ball two-barrel model E6N2. Torque: (std.) 176 lb.-ft. @ 1200 R.P.M.; (opt.) 178 lb.-ft. @ 1200 R.P.M.

CHASSIS: [Series S-7] W.B.: 122.5 in. Tires: 16 x 6.00. [Series (LWB) S-7] W.B.: 139.5 in. Tires: 16 x 6.50.

TECHNICAL: Manual synchromesh transmission. Speeds: 3F/1R. Column mounted gearshift. Conventional multiple disc clutch. Shaft drive. Hypoid rear axle. Overall ratio: 4.1:1. Four wheel hydraulic brakes. Steel disc wheels.

OPTIONS: Whitewall tires. Chrome beauty trim rings. Outside rear view mirror(s). Bumper wind guards. Master grille guard. Fender skirts. Bumper guards. Radio. Heater. Clock. Cigar lighter. Radio antenna. Seat covers. External sun shade. Spotlight(s). Fog lamps. Dual note horns. Conventional runningboards (on Customs). Two-tone "Sportsman" exterior finish (four-door sedan). Special paint colors. License plate frames.

HISTORICAL: Production started August 1939. Production ended July 1940. Introduced September 1939. Innovations: Sealed beam headlights. Fluid drive semi-automatic transmission. "All-Weather" fresh air circulation system. Autolite ignition. New "high-lift" camshaft. Stronger and lower chassis frame. Sportsman sedan introduced at mid-year. Calendar year registrations: 71,943. Calendar year production: 83,805. Model year production: 67,790. Walter P. Chrysler died on August 18, 1940. DeSoto, a Chrysler Corp. company, was America's 13th ranked automaker for model year 1940. The company had a much higher 10th place ranking in terms of calendar year sales. Production of early 1940 models was delayed by a strike. DeSoto was advertised as "America's Family Car."

1941 DeSOTO

1941 DeSoto, Series S-8, Custom brougham (OCW)

DESOTO — SERIES S-8 — SIX: DeSoto's 1941 styling changes started with longer, lower, wider "Rocket" bodies. They had flatter windshields and alligator hoods with the lock control inside the driver's compartment. The grille consisted of 14 curved, vertical bars on either side of a body color center panel. There were three, short, horizontal strips on either side of the nose. Headlamps were round with ornamental trim extensions top and bottom. Runningboards were fully concealed. Standard equipment included Autolite ignition, hydraulic brakes, Fluid Drive, Simplimatic transmission, flipper windows for rear seat ventilation, "Hold-open" front doors, Safety-Rim wheels, oil bath air cleaner, a new steering wheel with a single horizontal spoke and a speedometer with a needle that glowed red when driving over 50 mph. Custom models also had "Air Foam" seat cushions, chrome window moldings and dual electric wipers. Both lines — Custom and Deluxe — included long wheelbase models. Rear vision was greatly improved by enlarged rear windows.

I.D. DATA: Serial numbers were in the same location. Starting: (Del.) 6096001; (Cust.) 5720401. Ending: (Del.) 6141720; (Cust.) 5770881. Engine numbers were in the same location. Starting: (All) S8-1001. Ending: (All) S8-100247.

Model No.	Body Type & Seating	Price	Weight	Prod. Total
(Deluxe)				
S-8	2-dr. Bus. Cpe.-2P	945	3134	4449
S-8	2-dr. Cpe.-5P	1025	3219	5603
S-8	2-dr. Sed.-5P	1008	3224	9228
S-8	4-dr. Sed.-5P	1035	3254	26,417
(Deluxe LWB)				
S-8	4-dr. Sed.-7P	1270	3629	101
S-8	4-dr. Calif. Taxi-7P	NA	NA	2502
(Custom)				
S-8	2-dr. Cus. Cpe.-2P	982	3144	2033
S-8	2-dr. Clb. Cpe.-5P	1080	3239	6726
S-8	2-dr. Conv. Cpe.-5P	1240	3494	2937
S-8	2-dr. Brgm.-5P	1060	3264	4609
S-8	4-dr. Sed.-5P	1085	3269	30,876
S-8	4-dr. Twn. Sed.-5P	1133	3329	4362
(Custom LWB)				
S-8	4-dr. Sed.-7P	1310	3649	120
S-8	4-dr. Limo.-7P	1390	3754	35
S-8	Chassis	NA	NA	1

Note 1: Total series production was 99,999.

ENGINE: Inline. L-head. Six. Cast iron block. B & S: 3-3/8 x 4-1/4 in. Disp.: 228.1 cu. in. C.R.: (Del.) 6.5:1; (Cust.) 6.8:1. Brake H.P.: (Del.) 100 @ 3600 R.P.M.; (Cust.) 105 @ 3600 R.P.M. N.A.C.C. H.P.: 28.36. Four main bearings. Solid valve lifters. Carb.: Carter one-barrel model EE-1. Torque: (Del.) 176 lb.-ft. @ 1200 R.P.M.; (Cust.) 178 lb.-ft. @ 1200 R.P.M.

1941 DeSoto, Series S-8, Custom coupe (HAC)

CHASSIS: [Series S-8] W.B.: 121.5 in. O.L.: 208 in. Tires: 16 x 6.25. [Series S-8 (LWB)] W.B.: 139.5 in. Tires: 16 x 6.50.

TECHNICAL: Transmission: Synchromesh (manual). Speeds: 3F/1R. Column mounted gearshift. Multiple-disc clutch. Shaft drive. Hypoid rear axle. Overall ratio: 4.1:1. Four wheel hydraulic brakes. Safety-Rim wheels.

OPTIONS: Whitewall tires. Chrome beauty trim rings. Outside rear view mirror(s). Bright fender edge molding (standard at mid-year). Fender guardrails. Fender skirts. Bumper guards. Radio. Heater. Clock. Cigar lighter. Radio antenna. Seat covers. External sun shade. Spotlight(s). Fog lamps. Twin horns. Sportsman club coupe trim package. Two-tone paint. Special paint colors. Fluid drive. Simplimatic transmission. "Skyview" taxicab window. Front fender parking lamps. Conventional runningboards. Oversize tires.

HISTORICAL: Production started August 1940. Production ended July 1941. Introduction October 8, 1940. Innovations: Simplimatic semi-automatic transmission. Higher second gear ratio. Battery located under left fender shield. Oil bath air cleaner. Single spoke steering wheel. Alligator type hood. Safety-rim wheels. Calendar year registrations: 91,004. Calendar year production: 85,980. Model year production: 99,999. Chrysler was America's 10th ranked automaker in calendar year 1941. Model year output was also 10th highest for a domestic manufacturer. DeSoto prices increased $42.50 in the middle of the year.

1942 DeSOTO

DESOTO — SERIES S-10 — SIX: Styling characteristics for 1942 included headlights that were concealed behind retractable doors. The grille featured S-shaped vertical bars running fully across the front. More massive wraparound bumpers curved around the front and rear fenders. Rectangular parking lamps were mounted in the front fenders. The upper grille bar was trimmed with a center ornament, on the nose, and also wrapped around and down the front fenders. Standard equipment in-

cluded Autolite ignition, hydraulic brakes, concealed runningboards, a larger-bore "Powermaster" six-cylinder engine, and key lock front doors. Custom line models also had bolster type upholstery, "Air Foam" seat cushions, dual electric wipers, front and rear door armrests, and a folding rear seat armrest on sedans, limousines and broughams. Both trim levels came on standard and long wheelbase chassis.

1942 DeSoto, Series S-10, sedan (OCW)

I.D. DATA: Serial numbers were in the same location. Starting: (Del.) 6142001; (Cust.) 5771001. Ending: (Del.) 6153101; (Cust.) 5783503. Engine numbers were in the same locations. Starting: (Both) S10-1001. Ending: (Both) S10-25551.

Model No.	Body Type & Seating	Price	Weight	Prod. Total
(Deluxe)				
S-10	2-dr. Bus. Cpe.-2P	1010	3190	469
S-10	2-dr. Cpe.-5P	1092	3270	1968
S-10	2-dr. Sed.-5P	1075	3270	1781
S-10	4-dr. Sed.-5P	1103	3315	6463
S-10	4-dr. Twn. Sed.-5P	1147	3335	291
S-10	2-dr. Del. Conv. Cpe.-5P	1250	3495	79
(Deluxe LWB)				
S-10	4-dr. Sed.-7P	1455	3705	49
S-10	4-dr. Calif. Taxi-7P	NA	NA	756
(Custom)				
S-10	2-dr. Cus. Cpe.-2P	1046	3205	120
S-10	2-dr. Clb. Cpe.-5P	1142	3270	2236
S-10	2-dr. Conv. Cpe.-5P	1317	3510	489
S-10	2-dr. Brgm.-5P	1142	3305	913
S-10	4-dr. Sed.-5P	1152	3330	7974
S-10	4-dr. Twn. Sed.-5P	1196	3365	1084
(Custom LWB)				
S-10	4-dr. Sed.-7P	1504	3725	79
S-10	4-dr. Limo.-7P	1580	3820	20

Note 1: Total series production is 24,771.

1942 DeSoto, Series S-10, custom convertible coupe (HAC)

ENGINE: Inline. L-head. Six. Cast iron block. B & S: 3-7/16 x 4-1/4 in. Disp.: 236.7 cu. in. C.R.: 6.6:1. Brake H.P.: 115 @ 3800 R.P.M. N.A.C.C. H.P.: 28.36. Four main bearings. Solid valve lifters. Carb.: Carter one-barrel model EE-1. Torque: 190 lb.-ft. @ 1600 R.P.M.

CHASSIS: [Series S-10] W.B.: 121.5 in. Tires: 16 x 6.25. [Series S-10 (LWB)] W.B.: 139.5 in. Tires: 16 x 6.50.

TECHNICAL: Transmission: Synchromesh (manual). Speeds 3F/1R. Column mounted gearshift. Multiple disc clutch. Shaft drive. Hypoid rear axle. Overall ratio: 3.9:1. Four wheel hydraulic brakes. Safety-rim wheels.

OPTIONS: Whitewall tires. Whitewall plastic wheel discs. Outside rear view mirror(s). Chrome rear fender edge shields. Chrome wheel trim

rings. Fender skirts. Bumper guards. Radio. Heater. Clock. Cigar Lighter. Radio antenna. Seat covers. External sun shade. Spotlight(s). Fog lamps. Dual horns. Fluid Drive. Simplimatic transmission. Directional signals. License plate frame. "Skyview" taxicab window. Sportsman interior trim package. Two-tone paint. Special paint colors. Oversize tires.

HISTORICAL: Production started August 1941. Production ended January 1942. Introduction September 1, 1941. Hidden "Airfoil" headlights. Higher horsepower engine. Larger valves. Numerically lower rear axle ratio. Key locks on both front doors. Calendar year registrations: none. Calendar year production: 4,186. Model year production: 24,771. DeSoto fell from 10th place to 14th in calendar year sales. Its model year output was 13th highest in the auto industry. A specially trimmed DeSoto was driven around the country promoting sales of U.S. War Bonds. DeSoto's prewar production ended February 9, 1942.

1946 DeSOTO

DELUXE SERIES — (6-CYL) — The first postwar DeSoto models were based on the short-lived 1942 line. Major changes included new hoods, grilles, wraparound bumpers, front fenders that blended into the doors and redesigned rear fenders. There were additional changes in exterior trim and interior design. Burl and grain garnish moldings, large full vision steering wheels and chrome trim and fine appointments were seen. The hidden headlamps of 1942 were not carried over. An interesting feature was a speedometer that changed colors in increments: green to 39 mph, amber to 50 mph and red at higher speeds. The body structure was all-steel, a longtime Chrysler Corp. characteristic. Separate chassis/frame construction was used. Body insulation included the interior structure of the body, roof, side panels, floor, cowl and trunk. Postwar developments were Safe Guard hydraulic brakes and a permanent Oilite fuel tank filter. Rustproofing now protected even the interior structure of the body. Identification of series was provided by nameplates found on the sides of the hood. Standard equipment on Deluxes included dual sun visors, dual two-speed electric wipers, directional signals with parking brake light, cigar lighter, illuminated glove box with lock, dual outside door locks, map light, counter balanced luggage compartment lid, illuminated luggage compartment, right and left front door armrests, interior door locks and bumper guards front and rear.

I.D. DATA: Early 1946 cars had serial number codes on right front door hinge pillar post. After March 1, 1946, on left front door hinge pillar post. Letters shown in midsection of lines, before the serial numbers, identified the assembly plant as follows: D=Detroit, Mich.; LA=Los Angeles, Calif.; W=Windsor, Ontario, Canada. These letters were not part of the serial number. Serial numbers 6154001 to 6172862 appeared on Deluxes. Serial numbers 5784001 to 5825784 appeared on Customs. Serial numbers 5102501 to 5105413 appeared on taxis. Engine numbers were located on the left side of the block below cylinder head between first and second cylinders. Engine numbers ran from S111001 and up.

DELUXE SERIES

Model No.	Body/Style No.	Body Type & Seating	Factory Price	Shipping Weight	Prod. Total
S11S	Note 1	2-dr Cpe-3P	1315	3257	(1,950)
S11S	Note 1	2-dr Clb Cpe-6P	1435	3347	(8,580)
S11S	Note 1	2-dr Sed-6P	1410	3352	(12,751)
S11S	Note 1	4-dr Sed-6P	1445	3382	(32,213)

Note 1: Owners seeking parts were advised: "There is no way to positively identify the type of body. When in doubt specify vehicle serial number and vehicle body number in ordering parts."

Note 2: Production totals are in parenthesis because they are combined totals for 1946, 1947, 1948 and early (first series) 1949 models. DeSoto recorded these only as a combined total, with no model year breakouts.

ENGINE: L-head. Six-cylinder. Cast iron block. Displacement: 236.7 cid. Bore and stroke: 3.438 x 4.25 inches. Compression ratio: 6.6:1. Brake hp: 109 at 3600 rpm. Four main bearings. Solid valve lifters. Carburetors: (Taxi) B-B EL1L or EX3R; (Fluid Drive and Vacumatic) B-B EV1 or B-B EV2 or E7L4; (Standard transmission) B-B EX1, B-B EX2 or B-B EX3.

1946 DeSoto, Custom four-door nine-passenger Suburban, 6-cyl (AA)

CUSTOM SERIES — (6-CYL) — Custom models were clearly identified by the nameplates on the sides of the hood. The front compartment was equipped with tailored carpets and chrome-plated window sashes. Front seat cushions included a foam rubber pad. The Custom represented an upgraded, high-line version of the Deluxe. A suburban was added to the Custom line in November 1946. Delon plastic upholstery was featured. Standard equipment on Customs included white plastic trim rings (prior to introduction of white sidewall tires), plastic steering wheel, foam rubber seat cushions and tailored front carpets. Three colors of broadcloth upholstery were available: green, blue and tan. The convertible coupe had Bedford cord and leather in various colors.

1946 DeSoto, Custom two-door convertible, 6-cyl

CUSTOM SERIES

Model No.	Body Style Style No.	Body Type & Seating	Factory Price	Shipping Weight	Prod. Total
(Standard Wheelbase)					
S11C	Note 1	2-dr Clb Cpe-6P	1485	3337	(38,720)
S11C	Note 1	2-dr Conv Cpe-6P	1745	3375	(8,100)
S11C	Note 1	2-dr Sed-6P	1475	3377	(1,600)
S11C	Note 1	4-dr Sed-6P	1495	3390	(126,226)
(Long Wheelbase)					
S11C	Note 1	4-dr Sub-8P	2175	4000	(7,500)
S11C	Note 1	4-dr Sedan-8P	1875	3837	(3,530)
S11C	Note 1	4-dr Limo-8P	1995	3937	(120)

Note 1: See 1946 DeSoto Deluxe series specifications chart. Eight-passenger models were on the long wheelbase chassis.

Note 2: Production totals are in parenthesis because they are combined totals for 1946, 1947, 1948 and early (first series) 1949 models. DeSoto recorded these only as a combined total, with no model year breakouts.

ENGINE: L-head. Six-cylinder. Cast iron block. Displacement: 236.7 cid. Bore and stroke: 3.438 x 4.25 inches. Compression ratio: 6.6:1. Brake hp: 109 at 3600 rpm. Four main bearings. Solid valve lifters. Carburetors: (Fluid Drive and Vacumatic) B-B EV1 or B-B EV2 or E7L4; (Standard transmission) B-B EX1, B-B EX2 or B-B EX3.

CHASSIS FEATURES: Wheelbase: (long wheelbase models) 139-1/2 inches; (all others) 121-1/2 inches. Tires: long wheelbase cars used 6.50 x 16 tires until car number 5802797 and 7.00 x 15 tires thereafter. Short wheelbase cars used 6.50 x 16 tires. Whitewalls were not available in 1946. Three-speed manual transmission was standard in Deluxes.

Gyrol Fluid Drive with Tip-Toe Shift four-speed was standard in Customs and optional in Deluxes.

HISTORICAL FOOTNOTES: Calendar year production was 62,368 units, making DeSoto the 13th largest automaker in the U.S. The model year started on March 1, 1946, for DeSoto. The company produced only 2.8 percent of the nation's cars.

1947 DeSOTO

DELUXE SERIES — (6-CYL) — There were virtually no changes in the 1947 DeSoto models. Prices for Deluxe editions were slightly changed and published specifications charts indicate that a weight increase of just a few pounds was registered. Whitewall tires were reintroduced, as an option, after April 1, 1947. Standard equipment features remained as before.

1947 DeSoto, Deluxe three-passenger coupe, 6-cyl (AA)

I.D. DATA: Serial number codes located on left door hinge pillar post. Letters shown in midsection of lines, before the serial numbers, identified the assembly plant as follows: D=Detroit, Mich.; LA=Los Angeles, Calif.; W=Windsor, Ontario, Canada. These letters were not part of the serial number. Serial numbers 6172863 to 6190369 appeared on Deluxes. Serial numbers 5825785 to 5885815 appeared on Customs. Serial numbers 5102501 to 5105413 appeared on taxis. Engine numbers were located on the left side of the block below cylinder head between first and second cylinders. Engine numbers ran from S111001 and up.

DELUXE SERIES

Model No.	Body/ Style No.	Body Type & Seating	Factory Price	Shipping Weight	Prod. Total
S11S	Note 1	2-dr Cpe-3P	1331	3303	(1,950)
S11S	Note 1	2-dr Clb Cpe-6P	1451	8393	(8,580)
S11S	Note 1	2-dr Sed-6P	1426	3398	(12,751)
S11S	Note 1	4-dr Sed-6P	1461	3428	(32,213)

Note 1: Owners were again advised that there was no way to positively identify the type of body by code numbers.

Note 2: Production totals are in parenthesis because they are combined totals for 1946, 1947, 1948 and eary (first series) 1949 models. DeSoto recorded these only as a combined total, with no model year breakouts.

ENGINE: L-head. Six-cylinder. Cast iron block. Displacement: 236.6 cid. Bore and stroke: 3.438 x 4.25 inches. Compression ratio: 6.6:1. Brake hp: 109 at 3600 rpm. Four main bearings. Solid valve lifters. Carburetors: (Taxi) B-B EL1L or EX3R; (Fluid Drive and Vacumatic) B-B EV1 or B-B EV2 or E7L4; (Standard transmission) B-B EX1, B-B EX2 or B-B EX3.

CUSTOM SERIES — (6-CYL) — Custom models were indiscernible from their 1946 counterparts. Once again, prices and weights were slightly increased. Custom models were basically Deluxes with upgraded trim and appointments, except in the case of the long wheelbase models, which were totally distinctive offerings built off a stretched platform.

CUSTOM SERIES

Model No.	Body/ Style No.	Body Type & Seating	Factory Price	Shipping Weight	Prod. Total
(Standard Wheelbase)					
S11C	Note 1	2-dr Clb Cpe-6P	1501	3378	(38,720)
S11C	Note 1	2-dr Conv Cpe-5P	1761	3618	(8,100)
S11C	Note 1	2-dr Sed-6P	1491	3423	(1,600)
S11C	Note 1	4-dr Sed-6P	1511	3433	(126,226)

Model No.	Body/ Style No.	Body Type & Seating	Factory Price	Shipping Weight	Prod. Total
(Long Wheelbase)					
S11C	Note 1	4-dr Sedan-7P	1893	3837	(3,530)
S11C	Note 1	4-dr Limo-7P	2013	3995	(120)
S11C	Note 1	4-dr Sub-9P	2193	4012	(7,500)

Note 1: Owners were again advised that there was no way to positively identify the type of body through code numbers.

Note 2: Production totals are in parenthesis because they are combined totals for 1946, 1947, 1948 and early (first series) 1949 models. DeSoto recorded these only as a combined total, with no model year breakouts.

ENGINE: L-head. Six-cylinder. Cast iron block. Displacement: 236.6 cid. Bore and stroke: 3.438 x 4.25 inches. Compression ratio: 6.6:1. Brake hp: 109 at 3600 rpm. Four main bearings. Solid valve lifters. Carburetors: (Fluid Drive and Vacumatic) B-B EV1 or B-B EV2 or E7L4. (Standard transmission) B-B EX1, B-B EX2 or B-B EX3.

1947 DeSoto, Custom four-door sedan, 6-cyl (AA)

CHASSIS FEATURES: Wheelbase: (long wheelbase models) 139-1/2 inches; (all others) 121-1/2 inches. Tires: long wheelbase cars now used 7.00 x 15 inch tires. Short wheelbase cars again used 6.50 x 16 inch tires, switching to 7.60 x 15 late in the year. Whitewalls became available (optionally) in mid-1947. Three-speed manual transmission was standard. Fluid Drive was optional. Fluid Drive with Tip-Toe shift was $121 extra.

HISTORICAL FOOTNOTES: Calendar year production of 82,232 cars put DeSoto in 14th rank in the auto industry. The DeSoto model year started Jan. 1, 1947, and corresponded with the calendar year. In April 1947, white sidewall tires were returned to the optional equipment list.

1948 DeSOTO

1948 DeSoto, Custom two-door Club Coupe, 6-cyl

DELUXE SERIES — (6-CYL) — Minimal physical change marked the DeSoto S-11 models built in the final production run, although rather steep price increases and decreases in weights were recorded. They averaged $298 and 38 pounds, respectively. Low-pressure tires were adopted and stainless steel wheel beauty rings were seen, after the use of white plastic 'whitewalls' was dropped. Cars built after December 1, 1948, were officially considered as 1949 models, although the only difference from previous offerings was the serial numbers used.

I.D. DATA: Serial number codes located on the left door hinge pillar post. Letters shown in midsection of chart, before the serial numbers, identified the assembly plant as follows: D=Detroit, Mich.; LA=Los Angeles, Calif.; W=Windsor, Ontario, Canada. These letters were not part of the serial number. Serial numbers 6190370 to 6209494 appeared on Deluxes. Serial numbers 5885816 to 5962601 appeared on Customs made in Detroit; 62001001 to 62001894 on Customs made in Los Angeles. Effective Dec. 1, 1948, Detroit-built Deluxes with serial numbers 6205976 to 6209494 were considered 1949 models for purposes of registration only. Effective the same date, Customs with serial numbers 5948453 to 5962601 were considered 1949 models for purposes of registration only. Serial numbers 5102501 to 5105413 appeared on taxis. Engine numbers were located on the left side of the block below cylinder head between first and second cylinders. Engine numbers continued from 1946-1947.

DELUXE SERIES

Model No.	Body/ Style No.	Body Type & Seating	Factory Price	Shipping Weight	Prod. Total
S11S	Note 1	2-dr Cpe-3P	1699	3285	(1,950)
S11S	Note 1	2-dr Clb Cpe-6P	1815	3385	(8,580)
S11S	Note 1	2-dr Sed-6P	1788	3375	(12,751)
S11S	Note 1	4-dr Sed-6P	1825	3435	(32,213)
S11S	Note 1	4-dr Cal Taxi-6P	N/A		(11,600)

Note 1: Owners were again advised that there was no way to positively identify the type of body by code numbers.

Note 2: Production totals are in parenthesis because they are combined totals for 1946, 1947, 1948 and early (first series) 1949 models. DeSoto recorded these only as a combined total, with no model year breakouts.

ENGINE: L-head. Six-cylinder. Cast iron block. Displacement: 236.6 cid. Bore and stroke: 3.438 x 4.25 inches. Compression ratio: 6.6:1. Brake hp: 109 at 3600 rpm. Four main bearings. Solid valve lifters. Carburetors: (Taxi) B-B EL1L or EX3R; (Fluid Drive and Vacumatic) B-B EV1 or B-B EV2 or E7L4; (Standard transmission) B-B EX1, B-B EX2 or B-B EX3.

1948 DeSoto, four-door nine-passenger Suburban, 6-cyl

CUSTOM SERIES — (6-CYL) — There were virtually no differences, externally, between 1946-1947 DeSoto Custom models and their 1948 counterparts. Low-pressure tires were adopted for standard wheelbase models.

CUSTOM SERIES

Model No.	Body/ Style No.	Body Type & Seating	Factory Price	Shipping Weight	Prod. Total
(Standard Wheelbase)					
S11C	Note 1	4-dr Sed-6P	1892	3439	(126,226)
S11C	Note 1	2-dr Sed-6P	1860	3399	(1,600)
S11C	Note 1	2-dr Clb Cpe-6P	1874	3389	(38,720)
S11C	Note 1	2-dr Conv Cpe-6P	2296	3599	(8,100)
(Long Wheelbase)					
S11C	Note 1	4-dr Sed-7P	2315	3819	(3,530)
S11C	Note 1	4-dr Limo-7P	2442	3995	(120)
S11C	Note 1	4-dr Sub-9P	2631	3974	(7,500)
S11C	Note 1	Chassis Only	N/A	N/A	(105)

Note 1: Owners were again advised that there was no way to positively identify the type of body by code numbers.

Note 2: Production totals are in parenthesis because they are combined totals for 1946, 1947, 1948 and early (first series) 1949 models. DeSoto recorded these only as a combined total, with no model year breakouts. Chassis only were supplied to professional carmakers.

ENGINE: L-head. Six-cylinder. Cast iron block. Displacement: 236.6 cid. Bore and stroke: 3.438 x 4.25 inches. Compression ratio: 6.6:1. Brake hp: 109 at 3600 rpm. Four main bearings. Solid valve lifters. Carburetors: (Taxi) B-B EL1L or EX3R; (Fluid Drive and Vacumatic) B-B EV1 or B-B EV2 or E7L4; (Standard transmission) B-B EX1, B-B EX2 or B-B EX3.

CHASSIS FEATURES: Wheelbase: (long wheelbase models) 139-1/2 inches; (all others) 121-1/2 inches. Tires: long wheelbase cars used 7.00 x 15 size tires; short wheelbase cars used 7.60 x 15 size tires, which were adopted late in 1947. Three-speed manual transmission was standard. Fluid Drive with Tip-Toe shift transmission was available at $121 extra.

HISTORICAL FOOTNOTES: The model year started Jan. 1, 1948, corresponding directly with the calendar year. Calendar year production of 93,369 cars put DeSoto in 15th rank in the industry.

1949 DeSOTO

DELUXE SERIES — (6-CYL) — The 1946-1948 models were carried over during the first part of the model year. Those built from Dec. 1, 1948, to about March 1, 1949 (when the new, redesigned models appeared) are known as first-series 1949s. The second series 1949 DeSoto line featured an all-new postwar body shell and was marketed as "The Car Designed With You In Mind." Styling was characterized by sheet metal panels with shorter overhangs front and rear. When coupled with the new, taller roof structure, this gave the second series 1949 models a short, stubby look. A tooth-like grille theme was adopted and had a noticeable peak in line with the front of the hood. Conventional bustleback contours were seen where the roofline ended at the deck lid. The rear license plate was mounted in a slightly recessed housing on the deck lid. Taillamps were set into long, narrow housings attached atop the rear fenders. A totally new style was called the Carry-All sedan. It featured a modified, fold-down rear seat that, when folded, provided nearly eight feet of storage space from the rear of the body to the rear of the front seatback. The station wagon was a new addition to the DeSoto line; the first body of this type seen since the Cantrell-bodied chassis of the 1930s. It did not enter production until July. The wagon featured steel body construction with ash wood exterior framing. The convertible came with a full-width vinyl rear window.

1949 DeSoto, Deluxe station wagon, 6-cyl

I.D. DATA: Serial numbers were located on the left front door hinge pillar post. Letters shown in midsection of lines, before the serial numbers, identified the assembly plant as follows: D=Detroit, Mich.; LA=Los Angeles, Calif.; W=Windsor, Ontario, Canada. These letters were not part of the serial number. Deluxes built in Detroit used numbers 6212001 to 6232740; those built in Los Angeles used numbers 60002001 to 600004755. Taxis were numbered 5115001 to 5115680. Customs built in Detroit used numbers 500001001 to 50061189; those built in Los Angeles used numbers 620004001 to 62011187. Engine numbers were located on the left side of the block below cylinder head between first and second cylinders. Engine numbers began with S13-1001 and ran through S13-93581.

DELUXE SERIES

Model No.	Body/Style No.	Body Type & Seating	Factory Price	Shipping Weight	Prod. Total
S13-1	Note 1	2-dr Clb Cpe-6P	1871	3455	6,807
S13-1	Note 1	4-dr Sed-6P	1881	3520	13,148
S13-1	Note 1	4-dr Carry-All-6P	2075	3455	2,690
S13-1	Note 1	4-dr Sta Wag-9P	2805	3915	850

Note 1: Owners were again advised that there was no way to positively identify the type of body by code number. The production figures include 680 taxicabs in the Deluxe line.

ENGINE: L-head. Six-cylinder. Cast iron block. Displacement: 236.7 cid. Bore and stroke: 3.438 x 4.25 inches. Compression ratio: 7.0:1. Brake hp: 112 at 3600 rpm. Carburetors: (standard shift) Ball and Ball Model B-B EX1R or B-B EX2R; (Fluid Drive or M-6 transmission) Ball and Ball Model B-B E7L1-L2.

CUSTOM SERIES — (6-CYL) — The new Custom line was externally identified by extra chrome trim. It consisted of two short strips mounted low on front fenders, behind the wheel opening. The interior was enriched, with a rear armrest as an option. Fluid Drive and Tip-Toe shift transmission were standard features. The Suburban had a roof-mounted luggage rack as standard equipment. Production began late, due to a strike affecting tooling, in 1948.

CUSTOM SERIES

(Standard Wheelbase)

S13-2	Note 1	2-dr Clb Cpe-6P	2042	3585	18,431
S13-2	Note 1	2-dr Conv Cpe-6P	2443	3785	3,385
S13-2	Note 1	4-dr Sed-6P	2059	3645	48,589

(Long Wheelbase)

S13-2	Note 1	4-dr Sed-8P	2863	4200	342
S13-2	Note 1	4-dr Sub-9P	3179	4410	129

Note 1: Owners were again advised that there was no way to positively identify the type of body by code number.

ENGINE: L-head. Six-cylinder. Cast iron block. Displacement: 236.7 cid. Bore and stroke: 3.438 x 4.25 inches. Compression ratio: 7.0:1. Brake hp: 112 at 3600 rpm. Carburetors: (standard shift) Ball and Ball Model B-B EX1R or B-B EX2R; (Fluid Drive or M-6 transmission) Ball and Ball Model B-B E7L1-L2.

CHASSIS FEATURES: Wheelbase (long wheelbase models) 139.5 inches; (all others) 125.5 inches. Tires: 7.60 x 15 for all standard wheelbase models; 8.20 x 15 for others. Three-speed manual transmission was standard on Deluxes. Tip-Toe Hydraulic shift with Gyrol Fluid Drive was standard equipment on Customs and $121 extra on Deluxes.

HISTORICAL FOOTNOTES: Calendar year production of 107,174 cars registered as 1949 models put DeSoto in 13th spot in the U.S. auto production race.

1950 DeSOTO

1950 DeSoto, Custom two-door Club Coupe, 6-cyl

DELUXE SERIES — (6-CYL) — A minor face lift on the previous year's model was advertised as the "New DeSoto" and referred to as a "Car built for owner satisfaction." The rear fenders now had a peaked design, as the only change in the sheet metal. Grille textures and ornamentation features were slightly revised. An easy way to spot cars built to 1950 specifications is to look for the body color vertical grille divider, which was unlike any previous or later DeSoto design. Series identification was carried on a plate at the top front of the front doors.

I.D. DATA: Serial numbers were located on the left front door hinge pillar post. Letters shown in midsection of lines, before the serial numbers, identified the assembly plant as follows: D=Detroit, Mich.; LA=Los Angeles, Calif.; W=Windsor, Ontario, Canada. These letters were not part of the serial number. Deluxes built in Detroit had serial numbers 6233501 to 6262653; those built in Los Angeles had serial numbers

60005001 to 60009175. Taxis were numbered 5116001 to 5118350. Customs built in Detroit had serial numbers 50062001 to 50148412. Cars built in Los Angeles had serial numbers 62011501 to 62023225. Engine numbers were located on the left side of the block below cylinder head between first and second cylinders. Engine numbers began with S13-1001 and ran through S13-93581.

1950 DeSoto, Custom four-door eight-passenger sedan, 6-cyl (AA)

DELUXE SERIES

Model No.	Body/ Style No.	Body Type & Seating	Factory Price	Shipping Weight	Prod. Total
(Standard Wheelbase)					
S14-1	Note 1	2-dr Clb Cpe-6P	1976	3450	10,703
S14-1	Note 1	4-dr Sed-6P	1986	3525	18,489
S14-1	Note 1	4-dr Carry-All-6P	2191	3600	3,900
(Long Wheelbase)					
S14-1	Note 1	4-dr Sed-8P	2676	3995	235

Note 1: Code numbers identifying body style were not used.

Note 2: The production totals above include 2,350 taxicabs in the Deluxe series.

ENGINE: L-head. Six-cylinder. Cast iron block. Displacement: 236.7 inches. Bore and stroke: 3.438 x 4.25 inches. Compression ratio: 7.0:1. Brake hp: 112 at 3600 rpm. Carburetors: (Fluid Drive or M-6) B-B E7L3 or B-B E7L4; (standard transmission) EX2R or EX3R.

CUSTOM SERIES — (6-CYL) — The Custom series reflected the same minor styling changes seen on 1950 Deluxe models. Identification could be made by spotting the word Custom on front doors of all styles, except the Suburban, which featured suitable identification letters. The word Sportsman appeared on the hardtop model. Factory literature showed the lettering under the vent window, although there are photos of cars with the name on the door. The Sportsman was an all-new, two-door pillarless coupe. Another innovation seen on the Suburban was all-steel panel construction. Whitewalls and full wheel covers were standard on the Sportsman and the convertible coupe.

CUSTOM SERIES

Model No.	Body/ Style No.	Body Type & Seating	Factory Price	Shipping Weight	Prod. Total
(Standard Wheelbase)					
S14-2	Note 1	4-dr Sed-6P	2174	3640	72,664
S14-2	Note 1	2-dr Clb Cpe-6P	2156	3575	6,100
S14-2	Note 1	2-dr SptMn HT-6P	2489	3735	4,600
S14-2	Note 1	2-dr Conv Cpe-6P	2578	3815	2,900
S14-2	Note 1	4-dr Sta Wag-6P	3093	4035	600
S14-2	Note 1	4-dr Stl Sta Wag-6P	2717	3900	100
(Long Wheelbase)					
S14-2	Note 1	4-dr Sed-8P	2863	4115	734
S14-2	Note 1	4-dr Sub-8P	3179	4400	623

Note 1: Code numbers identifying body style were not used.

ENGINE: L-head. Six-cylinder. Cast iron block. Displacement: 236.7 inches. Bore and stroke: 3.438 x 4.25 inches. Compression ratio: 7.0:1. Brake hp: 112 at 3600 rpm. Carburetor: (Fluid Drive or M-6) B-B E7L3 or B-B E7L4; (Standard transmission) EX2R or EX3R.

CHASSIS FEATURES: Wheelbase (long wheelbase models) 139.5 inches; (all others) 125.5 inches. Tires: 7.60 x 15 for all standard wheelbase models; 8.20 x 15 for others. Three-speed manual transmission was standard on Deluxes. Tip-Toe Hydraulic shift with Gyrol Fluid Drive was standard equipment on Customs and $121 extra on Deluxes.

OPTIONS: Tip-Toe Hydraulic Shift with Gyrol Fluid Drive on Deluxe models ($121); standard on Custom models. Radio. Heater. Chrome full wheel covers. Directional signals (Deluxe). Backup lights (Deluxe). Whitewalls. Electric clock. Lighted hood ornament. Two-tone paint.

HISTORICAL FOOTNOTES: DeSoto came in 14th in the production race with 127,430 assemblies for the 1950 calendar year.

1951 DeSOTO

DELUXE SERIES — (6-CYL) — The 1951 DeSoto S15 lineup continued with the same models as the previous year. The most noticeable of several obvious, but not major, design changes was a re-shaped hood that sloped towards a flatter, broader looking grille. A more massive front bumper was adopted along with rounder front fender contours. Deluxe models lacked front door nomenclature and came standard with small hubcaps. Equipment highlights included Oriflow shock absorbers; high-compression engine; Floating Power engine mounts; 'Featherlight' steering; long wheelbase stance; chair-high seating; Hotchkiss drive; super rim wheels; Safety Cushion tires; Big 12-inch brakes; new parking brakes; heavy-duty generator; hypoid rear axle; removable bearings; full-length engine water jacket; Synchromesh silent gears; roller bearing universals; Oilite gas filter; oil bath air cleaner and automatic choke. A woodgrained dashboard was standard on closed cars.

1951 DeSoto, Custom four-door sedan, 6-cyl

I.D. DATA: Serial numbers were located on the left front door hinge pillar post. Letters shown in midsection of lines, before the serial numbers, identified the assembly plant as follows: D=Detroit, Mich.; LA=Los Angeles, Calif.; W=Windsor, Ontario, Canada. These letters were not part of the serial number. Only serial numbers were to be used for identification purposes. Deluxe models built in Detroit had serial numbers 6269001 to 6283459. Deluxe models built in Los Angeles had serial numbers 60011001 to 60012889. Custom models built in Detroit had serial numbers 50155001 to 50230003. Custom models built in Los Angeles had serial numbers 62024001 to 62032486. Engine numbers were located on the left side of the block below cylinder head between first and second cylinders. Engine numbers were S15-1001 and up for models and series and were continued into 1952 without interruption.

DELUXE SERIES

Model No.	Body/ Style No.	Body Type & Seating	Factory Price	Shipping Weight	Prod. Total
(Standard Wheelbase)					
S15-1	Note 1	4-dr Sed-6P	2227	3570	Note 2
S15-1	Note 1	2-dr Clb Cpe-6P	2215	3475	Note 2
S15-1	Note 1	4-dr Carry-All-6P	2457	3685	Note 2
(Long Wheelbase)					
S15-1	Note 1	4-dr Sed-8P	3001	4005	Note 2

Note 1: Body style code numbers were not provided.

Note 2: Production for 1951 and 1952 was lumped together, with no breakouts available for individual model year production. See Historical Footnotes for additional production data.

ENGINE: L-head. Six-cylinder. Cast iron block. Displacement: 250.6 cid. Bore and stroke: 3.438 x 4.50 inches. Compression ratio: 7.0:1. Brake hp: 116 at 3600 rpm. Five main bearings. Carburetors: Stromberg 380359; (with M-6 transmission) Stromberg 380349; (also with M-6 transmission) Carter E9AI.

CUSTOM SERIES — (6-CYL) — Various models in the Custom series were distinguished by the words Custom, Sportsman or Suburban on the front fenders. Body panel changes were the same as seen on the Deluxes, as were most regular equipment features. These 1951 models were carried into the 1952 model year due to manufacturing sanctions imposed by involvement in the Korean War.

CUSTOM SERIES

Model No.	Body/Style No.	Body Type & Seating	Factory Price	Shipping Weight	Prod. Total
(Standard Wheelbase)					
S15-2	Note 1	4-dr Sed-6P	2438	3685	Note 2
S15-2	Note 1	2-dr Clb Cpe-6P	2418	3585	Note 2
S15-2	Note 1	2-dr SptMn HT-6P	2761	3760	Note 2
S15-2	Note 1	2-dr Conv Cpe-6P	2862	3840	Note 2
S15-2	Note 1	4-dr Sta Wag-6P	3047	3960	Note 2
(Long Wheelbase)					
S15-2	Note 1	4-dr Sed-8P	3211	4155	Note 2
S15-2	Note 1	4-dr Sub-9P	3566	4395	Note 2

Note 1: Body style code numbers were not provided.

Note 2: Production for 1951 and 1952 was lumped together, with no breakouts available for individual year production. See Historical Footnotes for additional production data.

ENGINE: L-head. Six-cylinder. Cast iron block. Displacement: 250.6 cid. Bore and stroke: 3.438 x 4.50 inches. Compression ratio: 7.0:1. Brake hp: 116 at 3600 rpm. Five main bearings. Carburetors: Stromberg 380359; (with M-6 transmission) Stromberg 380349; (also with M-6 transmission) Carter E9AI.

CHASSIS FEATURES: Wheelbase: (long wheelbase models) 139.5 inches; (all others) 125.5 inches. Three-speed manual transmission was standard in Deluxe models. Tip-Toe Shift Fluid Drive (Prest-O-Matic) was optional on Deluxes and standard on Customs. As an option it was priced at $132. The number of cars built with automatic transmission (semi-automatic in DeSotos) was governed by rules established by the National Price Administration (NPA). The permissible NPA attachment rates varied in relation to a car's sales price bracket. In the DeSoto price class, the limit was established at 65 percent. Tire sizes: (short wheelbase models) 7.60 x 15; (long wheelbase models) 8.20 x 15.

OPTIONS: Radio. Heater. Whitewall tires. Full wheel covers. Lighted hood ornament. Directional signals. Back-up lights. Two-tone paint.

HISTORICAL FOOTNOTES: The 1951 DeSotos were introduced at showroom level on Jan. 27, 1951. Due to the Korean War, production for the 1951 and 1952 model years was counted as a single total. However, industry sources record that 121,794 DeSotos (2.28 percent of total industry output) were built in the 1951 model year. Of these, 3,910 were Custom convertibles; 6,775 were Custom hardtops and 1,637 were Custom station wagons. Calendar year production stood at 120,757 units, which put DeSoto 12th in the industry. On Dec. 16, 1950, the Economic Stabilization Agency (ESA) froze prices of automobiles at the Dec. 1 level. This freeze lasted until March 1, 1951.

1952 DeSOTO

DELUXE SERIES — (6-CYL) — The 1952 DeSotos were introduced to the public on Nov. 15, 1951. The DeSoto Firedome V-8 became an addition to the line on Valentine's Day 1952. The cars available early in the season were basically a carryover series from the previous model run. Minor exterior changes included rear taillamp frames, which tapered towards the top and had integral back-up lights. The name DeSoto was placed on the hood in block letters, a variation from the script style logo used in 1951. The hood medallion became taller and narrower than that used on earlier models. After the introduction of the Firedome V-8, Deluxe cars adopted a newly designed hood. It had an air scoop and a medallion similar to the 1951 style medallion. In all cases, the word Deluxe was seen on front fendersides. Features receiving promotional backing included Cyclebond brake linings; box-type frame construction; full waterproof ignition; narrow corner posts; electric windshield wipers; bolted-on fenders; air foam seat cushions; internal expanding positive action parking brake; Super Cushion tires; a new wider frame; tapered leaf rear springs; coil front springs; straddle mounted steering gear and fuel filter in gasoline tank. Other features promoted during 1951 appeared again, too.

I.D. DATA: Serial numbers were located on the left front door hinge pillar post. Letters shown in midsection of lines, before the serial numbers, identified the assembly plant as follows: D=Detroit, Mich.; LA=Los Angeles, Calif.; W=Windsor, Ontario, Canada. These letters were not part of the serial number. Only serial numbers were to be used for identification purposes. Deluxe models built in Detroit had serial numbers 6283601

to 6288250. Deluxe models built in Los Angeles had serial numbers 60013001 to 60013651. An important phase of DeSoto operations was the manufacture of taxicabs built on the long wheelbase platform with body shell furnished to taxicab manufacturer's specifications. Taxis had serial numbers 5121401 to 5122684. Custom models built in Detroit had serial numbers 50203101 to 50261940. Custom models built in Los Angeles had serial numbers 62032601 to 62036371. Firedome models built in Detroit had serial numbers 5500001 to 55040155. Firedome models built in Los Angeles had serial numbers 64001001 to 64005899. Six-cylinder engine numbers were located on the left side of the block below cylinder head between first and second cylinders. These numbers were S15-145987 and up for Deluxes and Customs and continued into 1952 without interruption. On the V-8, the engine number was positioned atop the engine block under the water outlet elbow. Engine numbers S17-1001 to S17-46488 were used at both assembly plants.

1952 DeSoto, Custom Sportsman two-door hardtop, 6-cyl

DELUXE SERIES

Model No.	Body/Style No.	Body Type & Seating	Factory Price	Shipping Weight	Prod. Total
(Standard Wheelbase)					
S15-1	Note 1	4-dr Sed-6P	2333	3540	13,506
S15-1	Note 1	2-dr Clb Cpe-6P	2319	3435	6,100
S15-1	Note 1	4-dr Carry-All-6P	2572	3650	1,700
(Long Wheelbase)					
S15-1	Note 1	4-dr Taxi-6P	N/A	N/A	3550
S15-1	Note 1	4-dr Sed-8P	3142	4035	343

Note 1: Code numbers identifying body style were not used.

Note 2: Production totals are a combination of 1951 and 1952 output, with no breakouts per model year available. See Historical Footnotes in 1951 section for additional production data. Totals for Deluxe models include 3,550 California taxicabs. For the 1952 calendar year, DeSoto produced 97,585 cars, including 5,325 hardtops, 1,319 station wagons and 1,150 convertibles. These body styles were available with Custom trim only.

ENGINES: L-head. Six-cylinder. Cast iron block. Displacement: 250.6 cid. Bore and stroke: 3.438 x 4.50 inches. Compression ratio: 7.0:1. Brake hp: 116 at 3600 rpm. Five main bearings. Carburetors: Stromberg 380359; (with M-6 transmission) Stromberg 380349; (also with M-6 transmission) Carter E9AI.

CUSTOM SERIES — (6-CYL) — The Custom six was also a carryover from 1951 with the same changes outlined in Deluxe models plus upgraded upholstery choices. The word Custom appeared on the front fenders. Late models used the Air-Vent-type hood similar to the Firedome V-8. This hood was also slightly lower than the previous type.

CUSTOM SERIES

Model No.	Body/Style No.	Body Type & Seating	Factory Price	Shipping Weight	Prod. Total
(Standard Wheelbase)					
S15-2	Note 1	4-dr Sed-6P	2552	3660	88,491
S15-2	Note 1	2-dr Clb Cpe-6P	2531	3565	19,000

Model No.	Body/ Style No.	Body Type & Seating	Factory Price	Shipping Weight	Prod. Total
S15-2	Note 1	2-dr SptMn HT-6P	2890	3720	8,750
S15-2	Note 1	2-dr Conv Cpe-6P	2996	3865	3,950
S15-2	Note 1	4-dr Sta Wag-6P	3189	4020	1,440
(Long Wheelbase)					
S15-2	Note 1	4-dr Sed-8P	3362	4155	769
S15-2	Note 1	4-dr Sub-9P	3734	4370	600

Note 1: Code numbers identifying the body style were not used.

Note 2: Production totals are a combination of 1951 and 1952 output, with no breakouts per model year available. See 1952 DeSoto Deluxe specifications chart notes for additional production data.

ENGINE: L-head. Six-cylinder. Cast iron block. Displacement: 250.6 cid. Bore and stroke: 3.438 x 4.50 inches. Compression ratio: 7.0:1. Brake hp: 116 at 3600 rpm. Five main bearings. Carburetor: Stromberg 380359; (with M-6 transmission) Stromberg 380349; (also with M-6 transmission) Carter E9AI.

1952 DeSoto, Firedome four-door sedan, V-8 (AA)

FIREDOME SERIES — (V-8) — The big news from DeSoto for 1952 was the introduction of the spherical segment combustion chamber engine in the DeSoto chassis. This is commonly referred to as the DeSoto Hemi V-8. It had been available in specific Chrysler models since 1951 and was the first eight-cylinder engine offered in a DeSoto since the inline eight of 1930-1931. Essentially, the Firedome models were Customs with suitable modifications to accommodate the new V-8. Nomenclature consisted of the name 'Firedome 8' placed on front fender sides and an '8' positioned on the deck lid. Shortly after introduction, the '8' emblems were replaced by a V-8 insignia for the deck.

FIREDOME SERIES

Model No.	Body/ Style No.	Body Type & Seating	Factory Price	Shipping Weight	Prod. Total
(Standard Wheelbase)					
S17	Note 1	4-dr Sed-6P	2740	3760	35,651
S17	Note 1	2-dr Clb Cpe-6P	2718	3675	5,699
S17	Note 1	2-dr SptMn HT-6P	3078	3850	3,000
S17	Note 1	2-dr Conv Cpe-6P	3183	3950	850
S17	Note 1	4-dr Sta Wag-6P	3377	4080	550
(Long Wheelbase)					
S17	Note 1	4-dr Sed-8P	3547	4325	80

Note 1: Code numbers identifying the body style were not used. This series was offered exclusively in 1952 and production totals for Firedome models are for this model year only.

ENGINE: V-8. Overhead valve. Hemispherical combustion chambers. Displacement: 276.1 cid. Bore and stroke: 3.626 x 3.344 inches. Compression ratio: 7.0:1. Brake hp: 160 at 4400 rpm. Five main bearings. Hydraulic valve lifters. Carburetors: Carter WCD two-barrel Models 884S, 884SA and 884SC. Also used were Models 901S with Fluid Drive or Torque Convertor and M-6 transmission; 905S with standard transmission; 906S with standard transmission in combination with overdrive. Later Firedome V-8s used Models 908S, 909S and 910S, which carried over into 1953 production.

CHASSIS FEATURES: Wheelbase: (long wheelbase models) 139-1/2 inches; (short wheelbase models) 125-1/2 inches. Overall length: (long wheelbase models) 224-3/8 inches; (short wheelbase models) 208-3/8 inches. Front tread: (all) 56-5/16 inches. Rear tread: (all) 59-9/16 inches. Tires: (eight-passenger) 8.20 x 15; (all others) 7.60 x 15.

OPTIONS: Power steering ($199). Overdrive ($102). Tip-Toe Shift with Fluid Torque Drive ($257). Tip-Toe Shift with Fluid Drive ($132). Solex tinted glass. Electric window lids. Radio. Heater. White sidewall tires. Power brakes. Two-tone paint.

HISTORICAL FOOTNOTES: Actual building of Firedome V-8s commenced Oct. 18, 1951. About 85 percent of DeSotos were built at the Wyoming Ave. assembly plant in Detroit. Engines were built at the Warren Ave. plant, a so-called 'push-button' facility. The transfermatic machinery

in this factory had a capacity of 60 V-8 powerplants per hour. Calendar year output of 97,585 cars put DeSoto 12th in the industry.

1953 DeSOTO

POWERMASTER SIX SERIES — (6-CYL) — A new series debuted with this 25th Anniversary model. Gone were the Deluxe and Custom names. The 1953s had an appearance similar to the previous series, yet the design was a major sheet metal revamp. The front fender line extended front to rear and the back fenders were now integral with the body structure. Only the station wagon continued with 1952 fender styling. The new Sportsman used the 1952-style roof structure and three-piece rear window treatment, while the eight-passenger sedan used the 1952 body with the new one-piece curved windshield, pioneered by Chrysler in 1934 on the Series CW Airflow. All other models featured curved, one-piece windshields and rear windows. The new 'grinning' grille added two more teeth, versus the nine on the 1952 DeSoto offerings. Side chrome was more evident, as Korean War demands abated. In addition, the roofline now faded into the rear deck in a more pleasing fashion. It was much improved over the abrupt styling of 1952. The Club Coupe was now more sedan-like than the previous year's counterpart. For identification purposes, the word Powermaster was on both front fenders, which had no additional chrome trim.

1953 DeSoto, Firedome Sportsman two-door hardtop (prototype), V-8 (AA)

DESOTO I.D. NUMBERS: Serial numbers were located on the left front door hinge pillar post. Letters shown in midsection of lines, before the serial numbers, identified the assembly plant as follows: D=Detroit, Mich.; LA=Los Angeles, Calif.; W=Windsor, Ontario, Canada. These letters were not part of the serial number. Only serial numbers were to be used for identification purposes. Powermasters built in Detroit had serial numbers 50266001 to 50304981. Powermasters built in Los Angeles had serial numbers 6209001 to 62042345. Taxis were numbered 5124001 to 5125701. Firedome models built in Detroit had serial numbers 55050001 to 55127622. Firedome models built in Los Angeles had serial numbers 64008001 to 64015691. Six-cylinder engine numbers were located on the left side of the block below cylinder head between first and second cylinders. These numbers were S18-1001 and up for Powermasters. On the V-8, the engine number was positioned atop the engine block under the water outlet elbow. Engine numbers S16-1001 and were used.

POWERMASTER SIX SERIES

Model No.	Body/ Style No.	Body Type & Seating	Factory Price	Shipping Weight	Prod. Total
S18	Note 1	2-dr Clb Cpe-6P	2434	3495	8,063
S18	Note 1	4-dr Sed-6P	2456	3555	33,644
S18	Note 1	4-dr Sed-8P	3266	4070	225
S18	Note 1	2-dr Sptmn HT-6P	2781	3596	1,470
S18	Note 1	4-dr Sta Wag-6P	3093	3855	500

Note 1: Code numbers identifying the body style were not used. Production totals include 1,700 California taxicabs. Eight-passenger models were on the long wheelbase chassis.

ENGINE: L-head. Six-cylinder. Cast iron block. Displacement: 250.6 cid. Bore and stroke: 3.438 x 4.50 inches. Compression ratio: 7.0:1. Brake hp: 116 at 3600 rpm. Five main bearings. Carburetor: Stromberg 380359; (with M-6 transmission) Stromberg 380349; (also with M-6 transmission) Carter E9AI.

FIREDOME SERIES — (V-8) — This was the second year for the V-8 models. They shared most features of the six-cylinder series and offered

the same six body styles as seen in 1952. Highlights included brakes with 12-inch drums; Cyclebond brake linings; Oriflow shock absorbers; coil front springs; waterproof ignition; full-length water jackets; full-pressure lubrication; air vent hoods and an improved frame designed to resist twisting. Changes from 1952 included new combination tail, stop and back-up lights and a gas cap positioned below the deck lid on the left side. The words 'Firedome V-8' appeared on both front fenders and the word 'Eight' was affixed on the right side, below the deck lid. A chrome trim slash was seen on the front fenders of all models except the eight-passenger sedan and the station wagon.

1953 DeSoto, Firedome station wagon, V-8

FIREDOME SERIES

Model No.	Body/ Style No.	Body Type & Seating	Factory Price	Shipping Weight	Prod. Total
S16	Note 1	2-dr Clb Cpe-6P	2718	3640	14,591
S16	Note 1	4-dr Sed-6P	2740	3705	64,211
S16	Note 1	4-dr Sed-8P	3544	4290	200
S16	Note 1	2-dr Conv Cpe-6P	3172	3965	1,700
S16	Note 1	2-dr Sptmn HT-6P	3069	3675	4,700
S16	Note 1	4-dr Sta Wag-6P	3366	3990	1,100

Note 1: Code numbers identifying body style were not used. Eight-passenger models were on the long wheelbase chassis.

ENGINE: V-8. Overhead valve. Hemispherical combustion chambers. Displacement: 276.1 cid. Bore and stroke: 3.626 x 3.344 inches. Compression ratio: 7.0:1. Brake hp: 160 at 4400 rpm. Five main bearings. Hydraulic valve lifters. Carburetors: Same as 1952 late-year models.

CHASSIS FEATURES: Wheelbase: (long wheelbase models) 139-1/2 inches; (short wheelbase models) 125-1/2 inches. Overall length: (long wheelbase models) 224 inches; (short wheelbase models) 213-3/8 inches; (station wagon) 212-3/4 inches. Front tread: (all) 56-5/16 inches. Rear tread: (all) 59-9/16 inches. Tires: (eight-passenger) 8.20 x 15; (all others) 7.60 x 15.

OPTIONS: Overdrive ($98). Tip-Toe Shift with Fluid Torque Drive ($237). Tip-Toe Shift with Fluid Drive ($130). Power steering ($177). Power brakes. Solex safety glass. Electric window lifts. White sidewall tires. Air conditioning. Continental tire kit. Wire spoke wheel covers. Full wheel covers. Radio. Heater.

HISTORICAL FOOTNOTES: Calendar year production of 129,959 units put DeSoto 12th in the industry this year. Chrysler purchased the Briggs Manufacturing Co. this year for $35,000,000. This was the 25th Anniversary for DeSoto, but no special models were offered. The DeSoto Adventurer experimental show car was seen during 1953. The model year started in November 1952. Air conditioning was introduced in January, which seems a bit odd.

1954 DeSOTO

POWERMASTER SERIES — (6-CYL) — The annual model changeover this year brought a DeSoto with the same basic styling as the 1953 model. Exterior changes were revisions to trim moldings, grille, bumpers and taillights. The grille reverted to a nine-tooth look with parking lamps floating inside the grille outline. The protector guards were redesigned and looked a bit more massive. New step down chrome moldings were seen on front fenders and doors. The rear fender side moldings now stretched completely to the rear of the cars, and the gravel shields were redesigned. Headlight and taillight clusters were updated with decorative bezels on top. The word Powermaster was incorporated on front fender moldings and a Powermaster crest adorned the hood. A horizontal chrome handle dressed up the deck lid. Completely new interior styling was adopted with upholstery, instrument panel and all appointments color-keyed to better harmonize with exterior finish. Highlighted in ad-

vertisements were a number of technical features including: No-Sway ride control; Oriflow shocks; Safe Guard hydraulic brakes; safety rim wheels; box-type frame side rails; independent parking brake; waterproof ignition; rubber-insulated body moldings; tapered leaf sply-mounted rear springs and rubber insulated rear spring shackles. Compression ratios were raised and horsepower ratings also jumped. A new, fully automatic transmission with the industry's highest starting ratio and torque convertor multiplication ratio was optional. It was said to provide instant response with no lagging or lurching between shifts.

1954 DeSoto, Powermaster station wagon, 6-cyl

I.D. DATA: Serial numbers were located on the left front door hinge pillar post. Letters shown in midsection of lines, before the serial numbers, identified the assembly plant as follows: D=Detroit, Mich.; LA=Los Angeles, Calif.; W=Windsor, Ontario, Canada. These letters were not part of the serial number. Only serial numbers were to be used for identification purposes. Powermasters built in Detroit were numbered 50306001 to 50322514; in Los Angeles 62043001 to 62043897; taxicabs 5126001 to 5128005. Firedomes built in Detroit were numbered 55130001 to 55182504; in Los Angeles 64017001 to 64020704. Six-cylinder engine numbers were located on the left side of the block below cylinder head between first and second cylinders. These numbers were S20-1001 through S20-21082. On the V-8, the engine number was positioned atop the engine block under the water outlet elbow. Engine numbers S19-1001 to S19-57604 were used.

POWERMASTER SIX SERIES

Model No.	Body/ Style No.	Body Type & Seating	Factory Price	Shipping Weight	Prod. Total
S20	Note 1	2-dr Clb Cpe-6P	2364	3525	3,499
S20	Note 1	4-dr Sed-6P	2386	3590	14,967
S20	Note 1	4-dr Sed-8P	3281	4120	263
S20	Note 1	2-dr Spl Clb Cpe-6P	2893	3815	250
S20	Note 1	4-dr Sta Wag-6P	3108	3855	225

Note 1: Code numbers identifying body style were not used. Powermaster production totals include 2,005 taxicabs.

Note 2: Records show no Powermaster hardtops were sold in the U.S. They were sold in Canada only and were called Powermaster 6 Special Club Coupes (not Sportsman) although they were true pillarless hardtops.

Note 3: Eight-passenger sedan was on the long wheelbase chassis.

ENGINE: L-head. Six-cylinder. Displacement: 250.6 cid. Bore and stroke: 3.438 x 4.50 inches. Compression ratio: 7.0:1. Brake hp: 116 at 3600 rpm. Carburetors: Carter BBD two-barrel: (with standard transmission) Model 2067S; (with overdrive) Model 2068S; (with PowerFlite) Model 2070S.

1954 DeSoto, Firedome Sportsman two-door hardtop, V-8 (AA)

FIREDOME SERIES — (V-8) — The word Firedome, incorporated between the step down front fender moldings, identified the V-8 models for 1954. There were also prominent V-8 emblems on the front of the hood and rear fender sides, plus a V-shaped insignia on the rear deck lid. Seven models appeared at introduction time and a luxury four-door Coronado sedan was added in the spring. Outside embellishments on

this car included special rear fender signature logos and small medallions on the rear roof C-pillar. A one-piece rear window was seen on the Sportsman V-8.

FIREDOME SERIES

Model No.	Body/ Style No.	Body Type & Seating	Factory Price	Shipping Weight	Prod. Total
S19	Note 1	2-dr Clb Cpe-6P	2652	3685	5,762
S19	Note 1	4-dr Sed-6P	2673	3750	45,095
S19	Note 1	4-dr Sed-8P	3559	4275	165
S19	Note 1	2-dr Conv Cpe-6P	3144	3995	1,025
S19	Note 1	2-dr Sptmn HT-6P	2923	3775	4,382
S19	Note 1	4-dr Sta Wag-6P	3361	4025	946

Note 1: Code numbers to provide positive identification of type of body were not provided.

Note 2: The eight-passenger sedan was on the long wheelbase platform.

Note 3: Six-passenger sedan total includes Coronado production.

ENGINE: V-8. Overhead valve. Cast iron block. Displacement: 276.1 cid. Bore and stroke: 3.625 x 3.344 inches. Compression ratio: 7.5:1. Brake hp: 170 at 4400 rpm. Five main bearings. Hydraulic valve lifters. Carburetor: Carter BBD two-barrel Model 2070S; (with standard transmission) Models 2067S or 2129S; (with overdrive) Models 2068S or 2130S. Carter Models 2250S and 2131S also saw applications on PowerFlite-equipped cars. Larger diameter valves were used in some Firedome V-8 models late in the year.

CHASSIS FEATURES: Three-speed manual column-mounted transmission was standard. Overdrive manual transmission was optional at $98 extra. PowerFlite automatic transmission was optional at $189 extra. Wheelbase: (standard) 125-1/2 inches; (eight-passenger) 139-1/2 inches. Overall length: (standard) 214-1/2 inches; (eight-passenger) 223-7/8 inches. Front tread: (all) 56-5/16 inches. Rear tread: (all) 59-5/8 inches. Tires: (eight-passenger) 8.20 x 15; (all others) 7.60 x 15.

OPTIONS: Power steering ($140). Power brakes ($37). Power windows ($101). Radio ($101). Heater ($78). Air Temp air conditioning ($643). Electric clock ($33). Solex tinted glass ($33). Fog lights ($33). White sidewall tires ($33 exchange). Wire spoke wheel rims. Wheel covers. Rear seat radio speaker. Windshield washers. Outside rearview mirror.

HISTORICAL FOOTNOTES: DeSoto ranked as the 12th largest volume manufacturer in the industry this year, based on calendar year production of 69,844 cars. Only 1.27 percent of American cars were DeSotos. The 1954 models were promoted as 'DeSoto Automatics' to spotlight the new, fully-automatic PowerFlite transmission. The Coronado was a midyear spring model. Chrysler Corp. held elaborate dedication ceremonies for its new proving grounds, at Chelsea, Michigan, during 1954. The Ghia-built Adventurer II show car appeared this year.

1955 DeSOTO

1955 DeSoto, Firedome Sportsman two-door hardtop, V-8 (AA)

FIREDOME — (V-8) — Styling changes were evident as an all-new "Forward Look" made its debut. A six was no longer provided in DeSotos and the Firedome V-8 became the low rung line. New exterior sheet metal was highlighted by lower, longer, wider body contours. A wraparound windshield appeared. The redesigned seven-tooth grille featured integrated bumper guards and floating parking lamps. Styling on the interior was of 'cockpit' inspiration with the radio and clock option centered in dash. The glovebox, a series nameplate and the radio speaker graced the right-hand side of the dashboard. All gauges and a dash-

mounted automatic shift lever were to the left. Hood ornaments and taillamp clusters had fresh treatments. Cars in this line were identifiable by the Firedome name, in script, on front fenders. Bodyside decorations took the form of constant width chrome moldings running front to rear, with a slight kickup above the rear wheel housing. There were nameplates and round medallions, mounted to the rear roof pillar, to help in picking out Sportsman models. Shortly after production began, Fireflite color sweep treatments became a Firedome option, as did sun cap visors. Standard equipment included five tubeless tires; waterproof ignition; adjustable speed electric windshield wipers; Oriflow shock absorbers and Safety Rim wheels.

FIREDOME I.D. DATA: Serial numbers and engine numbers were in the previous locations, only the former usable for identification. Cars built in Detroit were numbered 55185001 to 55256392; in Los Angeles 64022001 to 64026847; taxicab numbers began at 5130001. Engine numbers were S22-1001 to S22-76620.

FIREDOME SERIES

Model No.	Body/ Style No.	Body Type & Seating	Factory Price	Shipping Weight	Prod. Total
S22	Note 1	4-dr Sed-6P	2498	3870	46,388
S22	Note 1	2-dr Conv Cpe-6P	2824	4010	625
S22	Note 1	2-dr Sptmn HT-6P	2654	3805	28,944
S22	Note 1	2-dr Spl Cpe-6P	2541	3810	(See Notes)
S22	Note 1	4-dr Sta Wag-6P	3125	4175	1,803

Note 1: Code numbers to provide positive identification of body type were not provided.

Note 2: Production totals include taxicabs. The production of Fireflite Special two-door hardtop coupes was counted in the figures for Sportsman hardtops. All DeSotos were on a common wheelbase this season.

1955 DeSoto, Fireflite four-door sedan, V-8

FIREFLITE SERIES — (V-8) — DeSoto's top line also offered new aircraft-inspired Forward Look styling. Identification features included Fireflite front fender script; chrome fender top ornaments running back from headlamps; and rocker panel beauty trim. Four-door models had a single, flared, chrome side molding with slight kickup above the rear wheel housing. Special side color sweep beauty panels were standard on Fireflite convertibles and hardtops, optional on other DeSoto models. The Coronado was an added springtime model. It was a sedan featuring a leather interior and three-tone exterior finish treatment. The fuel filler was now located behind a door on the right rear quarter panel. There were V-8 emblems on the rear quarter panel, set lower and forward inside the color sweep. Cars without color sweep styling treatments had the V-8 emblem slightly offset, forward of the gas filler and even with the taillamp centerline. A sun cap visor treatment was seen. Genuine leather trimmed upholstery was provided in the Fireflite Sportsman. Others had silky nylon upholstery and nylon carpeting, too. A 200-hp four-barrel V-8 with hemispherical segment combustion chambers was another Fireflite standard.

FIREFLITE I.D. DATA: Code number locations were the same as previous. Detroit numbers were 50330001 to 50364093; Los Angeles numbers were 62045001 to 62047586. Engine numbers were S21-1001 to S21-35660.

FIREFLITE SERIES

Model No.	Body/ Style No.	Body Type & Seating	Factory Price	Shipping Weight	Prod. Total
S21	Note 1	4-dr Sed-6P	2727	3395	26,637
S21	Note 1	4-dr Coronado Sed-6P	N/A	N/A	(Note 2)
S21	Note 1	2-dr Conv Cpe-6P	3151	4090	775
S21	Note 1	2-dr Sptmn-6P	2939	3490	10,313

Note 1: Code numbers to provide positive identification of body type were not provided.

Note 2: Coronado sedan production included in total for Fireflite four-door sedan.

ENGINES:

(FIREDOME) V-8. Overhead valve. Cast iron block. Displacement: 291 cid. Bore and stroke: 3.72 x 3.344 inches. Compression ratio: 7.5:1. Brake hp: 185 at 4400 rpm. Five main bearings. Hydraulic valve lifters. Carburetors: (standard transmission) Carter BBD two-barrel Model 2067S; (overdrive transmission) Carter BBD Model 2177S-SA; (Power-Flite transmission) Carter BBD Model 2178S-SA.

(FIREFLITE) V-8. Overhead valve. Cast iron block. Displacement: 291 cid. Bore and stroke: 3.72 x 3.344 inches. Compression ratio: 7.5:1. Brake hp: 200 at 4400 rpm. Five main bearings. Hydraulic valve lifters. Carburetor: Carter WCFB four-barrel Model 2210S.

CHASSIS FEATURES: Three-speed manual column-mounted transmission was standard. Overdrive manual transmission was optional at $108 extra. PowerFlite automatic transmission with 'Flight Control' selector lever protruding from dashboard was $189 extra. Wheelbase: (all) 126 inches. Overall length: (station wagon) 218.6 inches; (all others) 217.9 inches. Front tread: (all) 60.2 inches. Rear tread: (all) 59.6 inches. Tires: tubeless blackwalls of 7.60 x 15 size.

OPTIONS: Power steering ($113). Power brakes ($40). Power front seat ($70). Four-barrel power package for Firedome series ($40). Radios ($110 and $128). Heater ($92). Power windows ($102). Air conditioning ($567). Directional signals. White sidewall tires. Other standard accessories.

HISTORICAL FOOTNOTES: Dual exhaust were available on all models, except station wagons, at extra cost. Three famous Ghia-built experimental show cars with DeSoto running gear appeared this year at auto shows. They were the Falcon roadster; Flight Sweep I convertible and Flight Sweep II coupe.

1956 DeSOTO

FIREDOME — (V-8) — A new perforated mesh grille with a large 'V' in the center dominated the 1956 DeSoto frontal revamping. Redesigned taillight clusters had three tiers of turret-shaped lenses and tailfin rear fenders appeared. Color sweep two-toning remained a feature, although the shape of the contrast panels was revised. New front bumper guards incorporated park lamps. A large, V-shaped emblem dominated the rear deck. Cars in the Firedome series had suitable nameplates on front fenders, chrome-plated headlamp hoods and plain top front fenders. Standard side trim was a plain, full-length molding of consistent width, while color sweep two-toning was optional on hardtop models. This option took a shape that was distinctive to the Firedome line, although another pattern was available for cars in the Fireflite series. Station wagons could be ordered with a third type of color sweep pattern and had chrome-plated bolt-on-type rear fins. Standard equipment included full-time power steering; independent parking brake; safety rim wheels; Oriflow shock absorbers; constant speed electric windshield wipers; new safety door latches; all-weather headlights; Super Highway taillamp clusters and center plane brakes. A 12-volt electrical system was adopted. Low-priced hardtops were designated as Sevilles and a four-door pillarless model was introduced.

1956 DeSoto, Firedome Seville two-door hardtop, V-8

FIREDOME I.D. DATA: Serial and engine numbers were in the usual locations. Use serial number only for identification purposes. Cars built in Detroit were numbered 55258001 to 55329506; in Los Angeles 64028001 to 64034406. Engine numbers S23-1001 to S23-79267 were used.

1956 DeSoto, Fireflite Sportsman two-door hardtop, V-8

FIREDOME SERIES

Model No.	Body/ Style No.	Body Type & Seating	Factory Price	Shipping Weight	Prod. Total
S23	Note 1	2-dr SeV HT-6P	2684	3865	19,136
S23	Note 1	4-dr SeV HT-6P	2833	3940	4,030
S23	Note 1	2-dr SptMn-6P	2783	3910	4,589
S23	Note 1	4-dr SptMn-6P	2954	3920	1,645
S23	Note 1	4-dr Sed-6P	2805	3855	44,909
S23	Note 1	2-dr Conv Cpe-6P	3032	4230	646
S23	Note 1	4-dr Sta Wag-6P	3321	4230	2,950

Note 1: Code numbers to provide positive identification of body type were not used.

1956 DeSoto, Fireflite four-door sedan, V-8 (AA)

FIREFLITE — (V-8) — Fireflite models had suitable front fender nameplates and painted headlight hoods with chrome strips on top extending back along the peak of the front fenders. The upper arm of color sweep panels on Fireflites extended in a solid line from in back of headlights to the extreme tip of the tailfin. A double molding was used and grew wider at the front edge of the front door spreading to an even wider flare at the rear fender. On four-door sedans, the side trim could be had in the color sweep format or an optional format that utilized the upper double molding only. Fireflite four-doors with the latter choice are considered rare today. All Fireflite cars had PowerFlite automatic transmission as standard equipment. This transmission now incorporated push-button gear selection controls. On Jan. 11, 1956, DeSoto announced that a Fireflite convertible with heavy-duty underpinnings, but standard engine, would pace the Indianapolis 500 and that a limited-edition 'Pacesetter' convertible would be available to the public These cars had the same special features and a heavy complement of power accessories, but were not lettered like the authentic pace car.

FIREFLITE I.D. DATA: Serial and engine numbers were in the usual locations with serial numbers meant for identification purposes. Cars built in Detroit were numbered 50366001 to 50392114; in Los Angeles 62048001 to 62051424. Engine numbers S24-1001 to S24-29811 were used.

FIREFLITE SERIES

Model No.	Body/ Style No.	Body Type & Seating	Factory Price	Shipping Weight	Prod. Total
S24	Note 1	2-dr SptMn-6P	3256	4030	7,479
S24	Note 1	4-dr Sed-6P	3029	4005	18,207
S24	Note 1	4-dr SptMn-6P	3341	4015	3,350
S24	Note 1	2-dr Conv Cpe-6P	3454	4125	1,485
S24	Note 1	2-dr Conv Pace Car-6P	3565	4070	(Note 2)

Note 1: Code numbers to provide positive identification of body type were not used.

Note 2: Production of Pacesetter convertibles is included in base convertible totals.

ADVENTURER — (V-8) — The Adventurer two-door hardtop coupe was introduced as a limited production specialty car on Feb. 18, 1956. It

was technically a Fireflite sub-series and was sometimes called the Golden Adventurer. It had a special high-performance engine, dual exhaust and custom appointments and finish. Standard equipment included power brakes, whitewall tires, dual tailpipe extensions, dual outside rearview mirrors, rear-mounted manual radio antennas, padded instrument panel, power front seat, electric windows, windshield washers, electric clock and heavy-duty suspension.

1956 DeSoto, Adventurer two-door hardtop, V-8

ADVENTURER I.D. NUMBERS: Coding on Adventurers was the same as on Detroit-built Fireflites in terms of serial numbers. Engine numbers S24A-1001 to S24A-29811 were used in Adventurers.

ADVENTURER SUB-SERIES

S24A	Note 1	2-dr HT Cpe-6P	3678	3870	996

Note 1: Code numbers to provide positive identification of body type were not used.

ENGINES:

(FIREDOME) V-8. Overhead valve. Cast iron block. Displacement: 330.4 cid. Bore and stroke: 3.72 x 3.80 inches. Compression ratio: 8.5:1. Brake hp: 230 at 4400 rpm. Five main bearings. Hydraulic valve lifters. Carburetors: Carter BBD two-barrel (with standard transmission) Model 2308S; (overdrive transmission) Model 2309S; (PowerFlite transmission) 2310S.

(FIREFLITE) V-8. Overhead valve. Cast iron block. Displacement: 330.4 cid. Bore and stroke: 3.72 x 3.80 inches. Compression ratio: 8.5:1. Brake hp: 255 at 4400 rpm. Five main bearings. Hydraulic valve lifters. Carburetors: Carter WCFB four-barrel Model 2311S (primary and secondary).

(ADVENTURER) V-8. Overhead valve with enlarged valve ports, high-lift camshaft, large diameter valves and stiffer valve springs. Cast iron block with modified slipper pistons, heavy-duty connecting rods and shot-peened crankshaft. Displacement: 341.4 cid. Bore and stroke: 3.78 x 3.80 inches. Compression ratio: 9.25:1. Brake hp: 320 at 5200 rpm. Five main bearings. Hydraulic valve lifters. Carburetors: Carter dual four-barrel WCFB type: (front) Model 2476S; (rear) Model 2445S.

CHASSIS FEATURES: Three-speed column-mounted transmission was standard on Firedome and not normally available on Fireflite. Overdrive transmission $108 on Firedome and not normally available on Fireflite. PowerFlite automatic transmission was optional on Firedome for $189 extra and standard on Fireflite. Push-button PowerFlite controls were adopted. Wheelbase: (all) 126 inches. Overall length: (four-door sedan and Sportsman) 217.9 inches; (all two-doors) 220.9 inches; (station wagon) 218.6 inches. Front tread: (all) 60.4 inches. Rear tread: (all) 59.6 inches. Tires: 7.60 x 15.

OPTIONS: Power steering ($97). Power brakes ($40). Power front seat ($70). Highway Hi-Fi record player. Air Temp air conditioning. Electric window lifts. Power radio antenna. Hot water heater. Instant heat. Conditionair (operates on gasoline burner). Solex safety glass. Whitewall tires. Steering wheel mounted clock. Seat belts. Other standard accessories.

HISTORICAL FOOTNOTES: An Adventurer hardtop paced the 1956 Pike's Peak Hill Climb. Another Adventurer competed in Daytona Speed-Weeks.

1957 DeSOTO

FIRESWEEP SERIES — (V-8) — All new styling and chassis engineering characterized 1957 DeSotos. Changes from 1956 included new bodies that were lower and longer; new side trim and color sweep treatments; a massive new bumper grille combination; new upswept rear fender

tailfins and a new Firesweep series, which was essentially a 1957 Dodge under its skin and built by Dodge Division. Identification features for this line were Firesweep rear fender nameplates; a wide continuous metal band on tops and side of the headlamp hoods; optional dual color sweep moldings or a standard trim treatment that had a molding starting at the rear of the car and extending forward across two-thirds of the front door. Standard features now included Torsionare torsion bar front suspension, Oriflow shocks, Safety-Lock door latches, Total Contact brakes and Power-Tip spark plugs.

FIRESWEEP I.D. DATA: Serial numbers and engine numbers were in their familiar locations. Cars built in Detroit were numbered 58001001 to 58038408; in Los Angeles 60014001 to 60017360. Engine numbers KDS-1001 to KDS-287531 were used. Firesweep models were actually manufactured by Chrysler Corporation's Dodge Division.

FIRESWEEP SERIES

Model No.	Body/ Style No.	Body Type & Seating	Factory Price	Shipping Weight	Prod. Total
S27	Note 1	2-dr SptMn-6P	2836	3645	13,333
S27	Note 1	4-dr Sed-6P	2777	3675	17,300
S27	Note 1	4-dr SptMn-6P	2912	3720	7,168
S27	Note 1	4-dr Sta Wag-6P	3169	3965	2,270
S27	Note 1	4-dr Sta Wag-9P	3310	3970	1,198

Note 1: Code numbers designating body style were not provided. The six-passenger station wagon was called the 'Shopper'; the nine-passenger station wagon was called the 'Explorer'.

1957 DeSoto, Firedome four-door sedan, V-8 (AA)

FIREDOME SERIES — (V-8) — The former low-priced DeSoto was the middle series for 1957. This was a true DeSoto in the sense that it shared no parts with a Dodge though, of course, it did share the major body structure of all Chrysler products. The triple round taillamp theme was a carryover from 1956. The grille was now part of the bumper structure and the color sweep was located low on the body panels. Exhaust tips were integrated with the rear bumper and were of a flat oval or elliptical shape, suggestive of the styling used for the grille. Sedans had six windows and the license plate housing was recessed into the deck lid. Twin rear antennas and dual headlamps were available in this series. There were rear fender nameplates, a Firesweep-like standard molding treatment and optional color sweep-style side moldings.

FIREDOME I.D. DATA: Serial numbers and engine numbers were in their familiar locations. Cars built in Detroit were numbered 55332001 to 55377868; in Los Angeles 64035001 and up. Engine numbers S25-1001 to S25-47060 were used.

FIREDOME SERIES

S25	Note 1	2-dr SptMn-6P	3085	3910	12,179
S25	Note 1	4-dr Sed-6P	2958	3955	23,339
S25	Note 1	4-dr SptMn-6P	3142	3960	9,050
S25	Note 1	2-dr Conv Cpe-6P	3361	4065	1,297

Note 1: Code numbers designating body style were not provided.

1957 DeSoto, Fireflite Sportsman four-door hardtop, V-8 (AA)

FIREFLITE SERIES — (V-8) — For identification, models in the top line series had Fireflite rear fender nameplates. In addition, medallions were seen at the front fender side moldings. Headlights were positioned separate of the grille (as on Firedomes) with cutback notches in the sides of the hood. Dual color sweep moldings were standard on all models. The six-passenger station wagon was again referred to as the 'Shopper,' while the nine-passenger model was called the 'Explorer.' The convertible coupe used a distinctive, dome-like windshield, which became standard on all Sportsman models for 1958. Front fendertop chrome ornaments

appeared in mixed applications on some Fireflite models. TorqueFlite automatic transmission; foam seat cushions; back-up lights and full wheel covers were standard.

1957 DeSoto, Fireflite four-door sedan, V-8

FIREFLITE I.D. DATA: Serial numbers and engine numbers were in their familiar locations. Cars built in Detroit were numbered 50396001 to 50426380; in Los Angeles 62053001 and up. Engine numbers S26-1001 to S26-29541 were used.

FIREFLITE SERIES

Model No.	Body/ Style No.	Body Type & Seating	Factory Price	Shipping Weight	Prod. Total
S26	Note 1	2-dr SptMn-6P	3614	4000	7,217
S26	Note 1	4-dr Sed-6P	3487	4025	11,565
S26	Note 1	4-dr SptMn-6P	3671	4125	6,726
S26	Note 1	2-dr Conv Cpe-6P	3890	4085	1,151
S26	Note 1	4-dr Sta Wag-6P	3982	4250	837
S26	Note 1	4-dr Sta Wag-9P	4124	4290	934

Note 1: Code numbers designating body style were not used.

ADVENTURER SERIES — (V-8) — This was a high-powered, performance car line. The Adventurer hardtop coupe was introduced two months after regular DeSoto introductions on Oct. 30, 1956. An Adventurer convertible was marketed even later. Both models had special gold-colored trim accents to carry forward the tradition begun in 1956. They also featured TorqueFlite automatic transmission; power brakes; dual exhaust; dual rear radio antenna; dual outside rearview mirrors; white sidewall tires; padded dashboards and special paint and trim as standard equipment. Distinctive nameplates appeared on the rear fender and bright metal strips graced the rear deck lid. Dual headlamps were seen and had now become accepted as legal equipment in all states. A special V-8 with dual four-barrel carburetors was installed. This engine provided one horsepower per cubic inch of displacement.

1957 DeSoto, Adventurer two-door hardtop, V-8 (AA)

ADVENTURER I.D. DATA: Serial numbers and engine numbers were in their familiar locations. All Adventurers were built at the Detroit factory, according to reference sources, with serial numbers 50396001 to 50426380 utilized. This range of numbers is the same as listed for Detroit-built Fireflites, which indicates the Adventurer was a sub-series of this line. Engine numbers also fell into the previously listed Fireflite sequence.

ADVENTURER SERIES

S26A	Note 1	2-dr HT Cpe-6P	3997	4040	1,650
S26A	Note 1	2-dr Conv Cpe-6P	4272	4235	300

Note 1: Code numbers designating body style were not used.

ENGINES:

(FIRESWEEP) V-8. Overhead valve. Cast iron block. Displacement: 325 cid. Bore and stroke: 3.69 x 3.80 inches. Compression ratio: 8.5:1. Brake hp: 245 at 4400 rpm. Five main bearings. Hydraulic valve lifters. Carburetor: Carter two-barrel Model 2532S.

(FIREDOME) V-8. Overhead valve. Cast iron block. Displacement: 341.4 cid. Bore and stroke: 3.78 x 3.80 inches. Compression ratio: 9.25:1.

Brake hp: 270 at 4600 rpm. Five main bearings. Hydraulic valve lifters. Carburetor: Carter two-barrel Model 2522S.

(FIREFLITE) V-8. Overhead valve. Cast iron block. Displacement: 341.4 cid. Bore and stroke: 3.78 x 3.80 inches. Compression ratio: 9.25:1. Brake hp: 295 at 4600 rpm. Five main bearings. Hydraulic valve lifters. Carburetor: Carter four-barrel Model 2588S.

(ADVENTURER) V-8. Overhead valve. Cast iron block. Displacement: 345 cid. Bore and stroke: 3.80 x 3.80 inches. Compression ratio: 9.25:1. Brake hp: 345 at 5200 rpm. Five main bearings. Hydraulic valve lifters. Carburetor: Carter dual-quad induction.

CHASSIS FEATURES: Automatic transmissions were now considered standard DeSoto equipment at slight additional cost for lower cost models; no extra cost for Fireflites and Adventurers. PowerFlite automatic transmission was offered only in Firesweep models at approximately $180 extra. TorqueFlite automatic transmission was offered in all lines at approximately $220 extra. Push-button gear shifting was featured with both transmissions. Three-speed manual transmission with column-mounted gear shifting was an infrequently ordered 'deduct option.' Wheelbase: (S27) 122 inches; (all others) 126 inches. Overall length: (S27 station wagon) 217.4 inches; (S27 passenger cars) 215.8 inches; (Adventurer) 221 inches; (all other station wagons) 219.5 inches; (all other passenger cars) 218 inches. Front tread: (S27) 60.9 inches; (all others) 61 inches. Rear tread: (all) 59.7 inches. Tires: (S26A) 9.00 x 14; (S26 and S25) 8.50 x 14 and (S27) 8.00 x 14.

OPTIONS: Power brakes ($39). Power steering ($106). Power window lifts ($106). Six-Way power seat ($101). Dual exhaust, except standard on Adventurer, ($34). Whitewalls, except standard on Adventurer ($42-$45). Radio with antenna ($120). Electro Tune radio with antenna ($120). Dual rear antenna ($16). Rear seat speaker ($15). Single rear power antenna ($24). Fresh Air heater ($89). Instant Air heater ($157). Standard two-tone finish ($19). Special finish, solid or two-tone ($71). Tinted glass ($32). Electric clock ($18). Self-winding steering wheel clock ($30). Windshield washer ($12). Variable speed windshield wiper, except standard on Firedome and Fireflite ($7). Air Foam seat cushions, except standard on Fireflite and Firedome ($11). Armrest on four-door and sport models ($27). Air Conditioning with Fresh Air heater ($493). Air conditioning group order ($404). Padded safety panel (dash) except standard on Adventurer ($21). Firesweep back-up lights ($12). Engine four-barrel power-pack, Firesweep only ($45). Undercoating ($14). Wheel covers ($16). Front and rear carpets in Firesweep ($14). Rear window defogger ($21). Non-Slip differential ($50). Outside mirror ($6).

HISTORICAL FOOTNOTES: The 1957 DeSoto Adventurer was the first base model U.S. car to provide one horsepower per cubic inch of displacement, as the 345-hp engine was not considered optional equipment. The 1956 Chrysler 300-B and 1957 Chevrolet were also available with one-horsepower-per-cubic-inch V-8s as optional equipment. DeSoto earned 1.63 percent of total U.S. auto sales for 1957. It was the third best year in the division's history. The Firesweep line made DeSoto the only maker in the medium-low price field to achieve a gain in new car sales over the previous season. The offering of an overdrive transmission was discontinued this year. When equipped with the optional Power-Pack four-barrel V-8, the 1957 DeSoto Firesweep models were rated 260 hp at 4400 rpm, a gain of 15 hp over the base two-barrel engine.

1958 DeSOTO

FIRESWEEP SERIES — (V-8) — This series continued to use the Dodge chassis. Styling was characterized by a minor face lift of the 1957 model. Changes included a honeycomb grille insert, a dip in the center of the middle grille bar and round parking lights at the outboard ends of the lower grille opening. Dual headlamps were seen on all models. Bodyside trim was redesigned so that the upper molding ran at an angle to the upper corner of the tailfin. There were Firesweep rear fender nameplates and a continuous band of metal again decorated the front lip of the hood and climbed over the headlamp hoods. Sportsman models had the dome-like windshield seen on 1957 convertibles, while sedans continued with a visored windshield header. An upgraded interior, similar to that fitted inside Firedome models, was an available option. Electric windshield wipers were employed and a new V-8 engine with wedge-shaped combustion chambers and full-flow oil filter was standard.

1958 DeSoto, Firesweep Explorer station wagon, V-8 (AA)

1958 DeSoto, Firesweep two-door convertible, V-8

FIRESWEEP I.D. NUMBERS: Serial numbers and engine numbers were in the familiar locations. Cars built in Detroit had serial numbers LS1-1001 to 18900; in Los Angeles LS1L-1001 and up. Engine numbers L350-1001 and up were used.

FIRESWEEP SERIES

Model No.	Body/ Style No.	Body Type & Seating	Factory Price	Shipping Weight	Prod. Total
LS1-L	Note 1	2-dr SptMn-6P	2890	3660	5,635
LS1-L	Note 1	4-dr Sed-6P	2819	3660	7,646
LS1-L	Note 1	4-dr SptMn-6P	2953	3720	3,003
LS1-L	Note 1	2-dr Conv Cpe-6P	3219	3850	700
LS1-L	Note 1	4-dr Sta Wag-6P	3266	3955	1,305
LS1-L	Note 1	4-dr Sta Wag-9P	3408	3980	1,125

Note 1: Code numbers designating body style were not used. The six-passenger station wagon was the Shopper. The nine-passenger station wagon was the Explorer.

FIREDOME SERIES — (V-8) — Firedome nameplates on the rear fenders identified DeSoto's one-step-up line. Firedome models had the same side trim as Firesweeps, but not the same frontal molding treatment. Windsplit ornaments for tops of front fenders were optional. A richer interior was featured. Upholstery materials were defined as Frontier Homespun fabric in combination with grained vinyl, colored to harmonize with exterior finish. These same interiors could be had in selected Firesweep models at slight extra cost.

FIREDOME I.D. NUMBERS: Serial numbers and engine numbers were in the familiar locations. Cars built in Detroit had serial numbers LS2-1001 to 17409. Some reference sources indicate no Los Angeles production. Others indicate that Los Angeles numbers ran from LS2L-1001 and up. Engine numbers L360-1001 and up were used.

FIREDOME SERIES

LS2-M	Note 1	4-dr Sed-6P	3085	3855	9,505
LS2-M	Note 1	2-dr SptMn-6P	3178	3825	4,325
LS2-M	Note 1	4-dr SptMn-6P	3235	3920	3,130
LS2-M	Note 1	2-dr Conv Cpe-6P	3489	4065	519

Note 1: Code numbers designating body style were not used.

FIREFLITE SERIES — (V-8) — Identifiers for the top rung series included specific rear fender nameplates and a distinctive upper bodyside molding that extended the full length of the car and incorporated special medallions on the sides of front fenders. Windsplit fendertop ornaments were standard equipment. Color sweep trim was standard on hardtops and convertibles. Eighty-six two-tone and 14 solid color schemes were offered for DeSotos. The Fireflites used the same new V-8 that featured a rigid, deep skirt block; inline overhead valves employing a single shaft in each cylinder head; a reduced weight of 640 pounds; and wedge-shaped combustion chambers. A springtime trim package was released as an option for all models except Adventurers. It featured two groups of four vertical bright metal deck lid slashes, with one group affixed to each side of the recessed license plate housing. New exterior colors were announced about the same time. Fireflite interiors were done in metallic Damask and vinyl and incorporated integrated armrests with aluminum finish recesses above them.

1958 DeSoto, Fireflite Sportsman two-door hardtop, V-8 (AA)

FIREFLITE I.D. DATA: Serial numbers and engine numbers were in their familiar locations. Reference sources give Detroit numbers only. They run from LS3-1001 to 13552. Engine numbers were L360-1001 and up.

FIREFLITE SERIES

Model No.	Body/ Style No.	Body Type & Seating	Factory Price	Shipping Weight	Prod. Total
LS3-H	Note 1	4-dr Sed-6P	3583	3990	4,192
LS3-H	Note 1	2-dr SptMn-6P	3675	3920	3,284
LS3-H	Note 1	4-dr SptMn-6P	3731	3980	3,243
LS3-H	Note 1	2-dr Conv Cpe-6P	3972	4105	474
LS3-H	Note 1	4-dr Sta Wag-6P	4030	4225	318
LS3-H	Note 1	4-dr Sta Wag-9P	4172	4295	609

Note 1: Code numbers designating body style were not used. The six-passenger station wagon was the Shopper; the nine-passenger station wagon was the Explorer.

ADVENTURER SERIES — (V-8) — The Adventurer models again represented a sub-series. Like the Fireflites that they were based on, these high-performance cars came standard with TorqueFlite transmission, back-up lamps and full wheel covers. But there were some other extras, too, such as power brakes, dual exhaust, dual rear radio antennas, dual outside rearview mirrors, white sidewall tires, dashboard safety panel and special paint and trim. The latter included gold highlights, twin groupings of four deck lid bars, triangular rear side sweep inserts and special upholstery. This specialty series was announced at the 1958 Chicago Auto Show on January 4 of the year. Other De-Soto models had been introduced Nov. 1, 1957. A new option was an electronic fuel injection system manufactured by Bendix. Cars so-equipped wore special nameplates above the front fender medallions and were later recalled to the factory for reconversion into 'standard,' dual-quad carburetor form.

1958 DeSoto, Adventurer two-door hardtop, V-8 (AA)

ADVENTURER I.D. DATA: As a Fireflite sub-series, the Adventurers used corresponding serial and engine numbers.

ADVENTURER SERIES

LS3-S	Note 1	2-dr HT Cpe-6P	4071	4000	350
LS3-S	Note 1	2-dr Conv Cpe-6P	4369	4180	82

Note 1: Code numbers designating body style were not used.

ENGINES:

(FIRESWEEP) V-8. Overhead valve. Cast iron block. Displacement: 350 cid. Bore and stroke: 4.06 x 3.38 inches. Compression ratio: 10.0:1. Brake hp: 280 at 4600 rpm. Five main bearings. Hydraulic valve lifters. Carburetor: Carter two-barrel (part number 1855633).

(FIREDOME) V-8. Overhead valve. Cast iron block. Displacement: 361 cid. Bore and stroke: 4.12 x 3.38 inches. Compression ratio: 10.0:1. Brake hp: 295 at 4600 rpm. Five main bearings. Hydraulic valve lifters. Carburetor: Carter two-barrel (part number 1855633).

(FIREFLITE) V-8. Overhead valve. Cast iron block. Displacement: 361 cid. Bore and stroke: 4.12 x 3.38 inches. Compression ratio:10.0:1. Brake hp: 305 at 4600 rpm. Five main bearings. Hydraulic valve lifters. Carburetor: Carter (part number 1822053).

(ADVENTURER) V-8. Overhead valve. Cast iron block. Displacement: 361 cid. Bore and stroke: 4.12 x 3.38 inches. Compression ratio: 10.25:1. Brake hp: 345 at 5000 rpm. Five main bearings. Hydraulic valve lifters. Carburetor: two four-barrel Carter carburetors (front carburetor part number 1826081; rear carburetor part number 1826082).

CHASSIS FEATURES: Automatic transmission was still considered "standard" DeSoto equipment, but again cost extra on Firesweep and Firedome models. There was no charge for automatic transmission in Fireflite and Adventurer models. PowerFlite two-speed automatic transmission was available only in Firesweeps at $180 extra. TorqueFlite three-speed automatic transmission was offered in all lines and cost $220 extra in Firesweeps and Firedomes. Push-button gear shifting was used again, too. Three-speed manual transmission with column-mounted controls was an infrequently ordered 'deduct option.' The Bendix-built EFI (fuel-injection) system was a $637.20 option in Adventurers only. It was installed in a limited number of 1958 Adventurers, Chrysler 300-Ds, Dodge D-500s and Plymouth Furys. These cars were originally built with dual-quad carburetors and were then converted to fuel injection at the DeSoto factory. Adventurers so-equipped were rated 355 hp at 5000 rpm. As previously noted, these cars were factory recalled for reconversion to 'standard' carburetion systems, although some may have escaped the call-back. Wheelbase: (LS1-L) 122 inches; (all others) 126 inches. Overall length: (LS1-L station wagon) 218.1 inches; (LS1-L passenger cars) 216.5 inches; (Adventurer) 221 inches; (all other station wagons) 220.2 inches; (all passenger cars) 218.6 inches. Front tread: (LS1-L) 60.9 inches; (all others) 61 inches. Rear tread: (all) 59.7 inches. Tires: (Adventurer) 9.00 x 14; (LS1-L and LS2-M) 8.50 x 14 and (LS3-H) 8.00 x 14. Several sources indicate that 9.00 x 14 tires were used on 1957 and 1958 Adventurers and that six-ply 8.50 x 14 tires were used on Explorer station wagons. Other references do not confirm this information, however.

OPTIONS: Power brakes ($39). Power steering ($106). Power window lifts ($106). Six-way power seat ($101). Dual exhaust, except standard on Adventurer ($34). Whitewalls, except standard on Adventurer ($42-$45). Radio with antenna ($120). Electro Tune radio with antenna ($120). Dual rear antenna ($16). Rear seat speaker ($15). Single rear power antenna ($24). Fresh Air heater ($89). Instant Air heater ($157). Standard two-tone finish ($19). Special finish, solid or two-tone ($71). Tinted glass ($32). Electric clock ($18). Self-winding steering wheel clock ($30). Windshield washer ($12). Variable speed windshield wiper, except standard Firedome and Fireflite ($7). Air Foam seat cushions, except standard on Fireflite and Firedome ($11). Armrest on four-door and sport models ($27). Air Conditioning with Fresh Air heater ($493). Air conditioning group order ($404). Padded safety panel (dash), except standard on Adventurer ($21). Firesweep back-up lights ($12). Engine four-barrel power-pack, Firesweep only ($45). Undercoating ($14). Wheel covers ($16). Front and rear carpets in Firesweep ($14). Rear window defogger ($21). Non-Slip differential ($50). Outside mirror ($6). EFI fuel injection ($637.20).

1959 DeSOTO

1959 DeSoto, Firesweep four-door sedan, V-8 (AA)

FIRESWEEP — (V-8) — Air scoops were 'in' for 1959. DeSotos had three and they were built right into the bi-level front bumper. At the bottom was a full-width scoop. Above it, on either side of the license plate indentation

(in the lower grille bar), were two more. A rectangular cross-hatched grille insert, where the parking lights were placed, stretched between the headlights. On the sides of the body, full-length sweep spears were narrower and redesigned. They took a dip behind the rear wheel openings and then curved upward towards the tips of tall tailfins. Tri-cluster, turret-shaped taillight lenses were again seen. Also characterizing the rear end styling was a large double bumper, with beauty panels between the top and bottom members. There were no series nameplates on Firesweeps and silver colored inserts along the sides were optional. The four-door sedan had painted side window trim. At the start of the season, four body styles appeared in this line, but two Seville hardtops were introduced as midrun additions. Standard equipment included front foam cushions, dual exhaust on the convertible, four black nylon Captive Air tires on three-seat station wagons and front and rear carpets (except on the six-passenger station wagon and four-door sedan).

1959 DeSoto, Firedome Sportsman two-door hardtop, V-8

FIRESWEEP I.D. NUMBERS: Serial numbers and engine numbers were in their familiar locations. Cars built in Detroit were numbered M412-100001 and up; in Los Angeles M414-100001 and up. Station wagons were numbered M471-100001 and up and were all assembled in Detroit.

FIRESWEEP SERIES MS1-L

Model No.	Body/ Style No.	Body Type & Seating	Factory Price	Shipping Weight	Prod. Total
413	41	4-dr Sed-6P	2904	3670	9,649
414	43	4-dr SptMn-6P	3038	3700	2,875
412	23	2-dr SptMn-6P	2967	3625	5,481
415	27	2-dr Conv Cpe-6P	3315	3840	596
476	45A	4-dr Sta Wag-6P	3366	3950	1,054
477	45B	4-dr Sta Wag-9P	3508	3980	1,179

Notes: Two-digit body model (style) numbers were now provided. Two- and four-door Seville hardtops were midyear models included in production figures for two- and four-door Sportsman. The six-passenger four-door station wagon was the Shopper; the nine-passenger four-door station wagon was the Explorer.

1959 DeSoto, Firedome Sportsman two-door hardtop (with simplified side trim molding), V-8 (AA)

FIREDOME — (V-8) — For identification a series nameplate was affixed to front fenders. Silver color sweeps were optional. Side window trim on four-door sedans was of bright metal. Standard equipment was the same as in Firesweeps plus back-up lights, padded dash panel, rear foam cushions, front and rear carpets, wheel covers, special steering wheel and vari-speed windshield wipers.

FIREDOME I.D. NUMBERS: Serial numbers and engine numbers were in their familiar locations. Cars built in Detroit were numbered M43-10001 and up. No California production is noted in standard reference sources.

FIREDOME SERIES MS2-M

Model No.	Body/ Style No.	Body Type & Seating	Factory Price	Shipping Weight	Prod. Total
433	41	4-dr Sed-6P	3234	3840	9,171
434	43	4-dr SptMn-6P	3398	3895	2,862
432	23	2-dr SptMn-6P	3341	3795	2,744
435	27	2-dr Conv Cpe-6P	3653	4015	299

Note 1: Seville two- and four-door hardtops added at midyear are included in Sportsman production figures.

1959 DeSoto, Fireflite Sportsman four-door hardtop, V-8

FIREFLITE SERIES — (V-8) — Fireflites looked similar to Firedomes, but could be distinguished by a different series nameplate on front fenders and by large medallions above the dip in the side trim on the rear fenders. Standard equipment matched all found on Firedomes plus TorqueFlite transmission; front and rear bumper guards; electric clock; handbrake warning light; color sweep molding; roof molding package; molding package number 2; windshield washer and 8.50 x 14 tires. Three-seat station wagons came with a power tailgate and four-ply black nylon Captive Air tires as regular features.

FIREFLITE I.D. DATA: Serial numbers and engine numbers were in their familiar locations. All cars were built in Detroit and were numbered M451-100001 and up.

FIREFLITE SERIES MS4-M

Model No.	Body/ Style No.	Body Type & Seating	Factory Price	Shipping Weight	Prod. Total
453	41	4-dr Sed-6P	3763	3920	4,480
454	43	4-dr SptMn-6P	3888	3950	2,364
452	23	2-dr SptMn-6P	3831	3910	1,393
455	27	2-dr Conv Cpe-6P	4152	4105	186
478	45A	4-dr Sta Wag-6P	4216	4170	271
479	45B	4-dr Sta Wag-9P	4358	4205	433

Notes: The six-passenger station wagon was the Shopper; the nine-passenger station wagon was the Explorer.

ADVENTURER SERIES — (V-8) — Cars in this line had Adventurer nameplates on their front fenders. Gold color sweep inserts were affixed and the grille was also finished in gold. A narrow vertical medallion was placed at the dip in the side trim on rear fenders. Wheel cutout moldings were used. The two-door hardtop had simulated Scotch-grain leather finish for the roof. Standard equipment was the same as for Fireflites plus power steering; power brakes; dual exhaust; dual rear radio antennas; dual outside rearview mirrors; white sidewall tires constructed of Rayon (size 8.50 x 14); brushed aluminum sweep insert; deck lid moldings; swivel front driver's seat; and high-performance Adventurer dual four-barrel carbureted V-8 with high-lift camshaft.

ADVENTURER I.D. DATA: Serial numbers and engine numbers were in their familiar locations. Adventurers were assembled in Detroit and had serial numbers M491-100001 and up.

ADVENTURER SERIES MS3-H

492	23	2-dr SptMn-6P	4427	3980	590
495	27	2-dr Conv Cpe-6P	4749	4120	97

ENGINES:

(FIRESWEEP) V-8. Overhead valve. Cast iron block. Displacement: 361 cid. Bore and stroke: 4.12 x 3.38 inches. Compression ratio: 10.0:1. Brake hp: 295 at 4600 rpm. Five main bearings. Hydraulic valve lifters. Carburetor: Carter BBD two-barrel Model 2870S.

(FIREDOME) V-8. Overhead valve. Cast iron block. Displacement: 383 cid. Bore and stroke: 4.25 x 3.38 inches. Compression ratio: 10.1:1. Brake hp: 305 at 4600 rpm. Five main bearings. Hydraulic valve lifters. Carburetor: Carter BBD two-barrel Model 2871S.

(FIREFLITE) V-8. Overhead valve. Cast iron block. Displacement: 383 cid. Bore and stroke: 4.25 x 3.38 inches. Compression ratio: 10.1:1. Brake hp: 325 at 4600 rpm. Five main bearings. Hydraulic valve lifters. Carburetor: Carter BBD four-barrel Model 2794.

(ADVENTURER) V-8. Overhead valve. Cast iron block. Displacement: 383 cid. Bore and stroke: 4.25 x 3.38 inches. Compression ratio: 10.1:1. Brake hp: 350 at 5000 rpm. Five main bearings. Hydraulic valve lifters. Carburetor: Two Carter AFB four-barrel Model 2794.

CHASSIS FEATURES: Three-speed manual transmission was the base price attachment on Firesweep and Firedome models, although automatic transmission was often referred to as standard equipment. Torque-Flite automatic transmission was included in the price of Fireflite and Adventurer models. Wheelbase: (Firesweep) 122 inches; (all others) 126 inches. Overall length: (MS1-L passenger cars) 217.1 inches; (MS1-L station wagons) 216.1 inches; (MS3-H station wagons) 220.1 inches;

(all other passenger cars) 221.1 inches. Tires: (Firesweep) 8.00 x 14; (all others) 8.50 x 14.

OPTIONS: TorqueFlite transmission as option ($227). PowerFlite transmission ($189). Power steering ($106). Power brakes ($43). Power window lifts ($106). Six-way seat ($101). Firedome/Fireflite power front swivel seat ($187). Adventurer power swivel passenger seat ($101). Manual swivel seat ($86). Note: Swivel seats not available on Firedome four-door sedan and Fireflite station wagon; available in Firesweep Sportsman. Dual exhaust as option ($34). Whitewall 8.00 x 14 four-ply Rayon tires on all, but Explorer ($42). Whitewall 8.50 x 14 four-ply Rayon tires on all, but Explorer ($46). Whitewall 9.80 x 14 four-ply Rayon tires ($147). Radio with antenna ($94). Electric Tuner radio with antenna ($94). Rear seat speaker ($17). Manual dual rear antenna ($16). Hot water heater ($98). Instantaneous heater ($135). Standard two-tone paint ($21). Special solid or two-tone paint ($71). Color sweep trim ($21). Solex tinted glass ($43). Electric clock ($18). Windshield washer ($12). Variable speed windshield wiper ($7). Air foam cushion as option ($11). Air conditioning with hot water heater ($501). Air conditioning with accessory groups ($404). Dual air conditioning with hot water heater for station wagons ($710). Padded dash as option ($21). Firesweep back-up lights ($12). Undercoating ($14). Full wheel covers ($18). Firesweep front and rear carpets ($14). Rear window defogger ($21). Sure-Grip differential ($50). Outside rearview mirror ($6). Remote control outside rearview mirror on Adventurer ($11); on others ($18). Photo electric tilt rearview mirror ($23). Power tailgate on six-passenger station wagon ($40). Rear air suspension ($140). Aluminum sweep insert ($21). Automatic headlamp beam changer ($50). Front bumper guards ($12). Front and rear bumper guards ($24). Adventurer dual four-barrel V-8 for Firesweep ($142); for Firedome ($122); for Fireflite ($108). Station wagon luggage locker ($31). Adventurer deck lid molding ($11). Sill and lower deck molding package ($27). Number 1 roof molding package for four-door sedans and station wagons ($14). Number 2 roof molding package for Firesweep and Firedome Sportsman ($38). Special plastic steering wheel ($10). Panoramic rear window ($24). Air suspension (rear only).

HISTORICAL FOOTNOTES: Special appointments, including plaid upholstery, padded dash and custom steering wheel were added to the Firedome standard equipment list in the spring. This was the last season for DeSoto convertibles and station wagons as well as the final year for separate frame and body construction.

1960 DeSOTO

FIREFLITE — (V-8) — Formerly a high-priced line, this series was relegated to low-rung status for 1960, while cheaper nameplates were dropped altogether. New styling was actually a pleasant departure from the past few seasons, with cleaner renditions of the same general dart-shaped theme. Chrysler Corp.'s new unitized body construction was used. The DeSotos, in fact, were Chrysler-like in appearance. Plain, full-length moldings adorned the bodysides and no sweep spear inserts were seen. The frontal treatment was dominated by a drop-center bumper, a flat, but distinctively shaped, grille and horizontal dual headlamps. Fins on the rear fenders were canted outward and ended with boomerang-shaped notches that housed the taillamp lenses. There were no convertibles or station wagons and the Sportsman designation for pillarless styles was dropped. Standard equipment was comprised of turn signals, front foam seat cushions and five 8.00 x 14 Rayon black tires.

1960 DeSoto, Fireflite four-door sedan, V-8

FIREFLITE I.D. DATA: Vehicle numbers were on the left front door hinge pillar post. Engine numbers were found on top of the engine, below the water outlet elbow. Fireflite vehicle numbers were 7103-100001 and up.

FIREFLITE SERIES PS1-L

Model No.	Body/Style No.	Body Type & Seating	Factory Price	Shipping Weight	Prod. Total
713	41	4-dr Sed-6P	3017	3865	9,032
712	23	2-dr HT Cpe-6P	3102	3885	3,494
714	43	4-dr HT Sed-6P	3167	3865	1,958

1960 DeSoto, Adventurer two-door hardtop, V-8 (AA)

ADVENTURER — (V-8) — While Fireflites had no signature script for identification, three models in a new Adventurer series did. Such nameplates were affixed to the tailfins. Two-tone paint treatments were limited to roofs finished in contrasting color. The only big news of the year — and the only throwback to previous high-performance Adventurer models — was the use of Ram-Tuned induction with dual four-barrel carburetors. Standard equipment included all features found on Fireflites, plus padded dash panel; variable speed windshield wipers; full wheel covers; special steering wheel; roof molding package; rear stone deflectors; bumper guards; back-up lamps; rear foam seat cushions and TorqueFlite automatic transmission with push-button controls.

ADVENTURER I.D. DATA: Vehicle numbers and engine numbers were positioned as on Fireflites. Adventurer numbers began at 7203-100001 and up. All production was at one assembly point.

ADVENTURER SERIES PS3-M

722	23	2-dr HT Cpe-6P	3663	3945	3,092
723	41	4-dr Sed-6P	3579	3895	5,746
724	43	4-dr HT Sed-6P	3727	3940	2,759

ENGINES:

(FIREFLITE) V-8. Overhead valve. Cast iron block. Displacement: 361 cid. Bore and stroke: 4.12 x 3.38 inches. Compression ratio: 10.0:1. Brake hp: 295 at 4600 rpm. Five main bearings. Hydraulic valve lifters. Carburetor: Carter BBD two-barrel Model 2923S.

(ADVENTURER) V-8. Overhead valve. Cast iron block. Displacement: 383 cid. Bore and stroke: 4.25 x 3.38 inches. Compression ratio: 10.0:1. Brake hp: 305 at 4600 rpm. Five main bearings. Hydraulic valve lifters. Carburetor: Carter BBD two-barrel Model 2923S.

CHASSIS FEATURES: Three-speed manual transmission was regular cost equipment on Fireflite models. TorqueFlite automatic transmission was standard in Adventurer. Wheelbase: (all) 122 inches. Overall length: (Fireflite) 215.4 inches; (Adventurer) 217 inches. Tires: 8.00 x 14.

OPTIONS: Four-barrel 383-cid V-8, with dual exhaust and TorqueFlite required, in Fireflites ($85); same engine for Adventurer ($54). Ram-induction 383-cid dual four-barrel V-8 with dual exhaust and 12-inch brakes in Adventurer only ($283). Rear foam seat cushion as option ($11). Heater ($98). License plate frame ($4). Safe-T-Matic door lock in two-door model ($36); in four-door model ($43). Back-up lights for Fireflite ($12). Parking brake light ($4). Left outside rearview mirror ($6). Left remote control outside mirror ($18). Right outside rearview mirror ($6). Three-way Prismatic mirror ($5). Vanity mirror ($2). Front fender ornament ($9). Two-tone paint ($21). Power brakes with automatic only ($43). Six-way power seat ($101). Power steering. Automatic transmission required ($106). Power windows ($106). Push-button radio ($89). Radio with rear seat speaker ($106). Rear speaker with accessory groups ($17). RCA Automatic Record Player, radio required ($52). Fireflite four-door roof molding ($14). Fireflite two-door roof molding package ($38). Padded instrument panel in Fireflites ($21). Solex glass ($43). Easy Grip steering wheel ($10). Rear stone deflectors on Fireflites ($8). Sure-Grip differential ($50). Automatic swivel seats ($106). Five 8.00 x 14 Rayon whitewall tires ($42). Five 8.00 x 14 nylon whitewall tires ($59). Five 8.50 x 14 nylon whitewall tires ($83). PowerFlite transmission with 383-cid V-8 in Fireflites only ($189). TorqueFlite transmission in Fireflites ($227). Undercoating with fiberglass pad ($15). Wheel covers on Fireflites ($19). Windshield washers ($12). Variable speed wipers in Fireflites ($7). Same with washers in Fireflites ($18).

HISTORICAL FOOTNOTES: This was the next-to-last year for DeSotos. The Ram-Tuned induction Adventurer V-8 produced 330 hp at 4800 rpm. The Fireflite V-8 was again called a TurboFlash engine. The four-barrel Adventurer V-8 was called the Mark I powerplant. The ram-inducted dual-quad V-8 was called the Ramcharger option. Manual transmission was considered a special order feature and automatic transmission was referred to as standard equipment, although it cost extra in Fireflites. Air suspension was dropped from the option list.

1961 DeSOTO

DESOTO — (V-8) — DeSoto's long and illustrious history came to an end on Nov. 30, 1960, just 47 days after models built to 1961 specifications were introduced. New styling had reflected a minor face lift of the 1960 Adventurer series, with Chrysler-like themes. Rear taillamp design was altered, as were features of the bodyside trim. The fins were modified just ever so slightly but not enough to draw extra sales. Canted headlamps had been adopted as part of the annual change and were integrated into an unusual double-tiered grille. Horizontal front bumpers were used. Series nomenclature disappeared for all practical purposes. The two available models were based on the former Fireflites, but referred to only as DeSotos. The end of production marked a sad close to 32 years of DeSotos and untold miles of practical use by millions of owners.

I.D. DATA: Serial numbers and engine numbers were found in the previous locations. Vehicle numbers 6113-100001 and up were used.

1961 DeSoto, Adventurer four-door hardtop, V-8 (AA)

DESOTO SERIES RS1-L

Model No.	Body/Style No.	Body Type & Seating	Factory Price	Shipping Weight	Prod. Total
612	23	2-dr HT Sed-6P	3102	3760	911
614	43	4-dr HT Sed-6P	3166	3820	2,123

ENGINE: V-8. Overhead valve. Cast iron block. Displacement: 361 cid. Bore and stroke: 4.12 x 3.38 inches. Compression ratio: 9.0:1. Brake hp: 265 at 4400 rpm. Five main bearings. Hydraulic valve lifters. Carburetor: Stromberg WWC two-barrel Model 3-188.

CHASSIS FEATURES: TorqueFlite automatic transmission was considered standard. Manual transmission was a deduct option. Wheelbase: 122 inches. Overall length: 215.6 inches. Tires: 8.00 x 14.

OPTIONS: Air conditioning including heater ($501). Air conditioning with Basic Group ($403). Permanent antifreeze ($5). Crankcase vent system ($5). Heater ($98). Back-up lights ($12). Left-hand remote control outside rearview mirror ($18). Three-way Prismatic rearview mirror ($5). Two-tone paint ($21). Power brakes ($43). Six-way power seat ($101). Power steering ($106). Power windows ($106). Push-button radio ($89). RCA Automatic Record Player, radio required ($52). Four-door roof molding package ($14). Two-door roof molding package ($38). Padded instrument panel ($21). Solex glass ($43). Easy Grip steering wheel ($10). Sure-Grip differential ($50). Five 8.00 x 14 Rayon white-wall tires ($50). Five 8.00 x 14 Rayon whitewall tires ($42). TorqueFlite transmission ($227). Undercoating with fiberglass pad ($14). Full wheel covers ($19). Windshield washers and variable speed windshield wipers ($19). Basic Group, including heater; radio; power steering; power brakes; windshield washer; variable speed windshield wipers; electric clock; and wheel covers ($390). Deluxe Group, including left-hand remote control outside rearview mirror; rear foam seat cushion; rear bumper guards; padded instrument panel, sill and wheelhouse moldings and stone deflectors ($93). Light package including glovebox, trunk, map, backup and parking brake lights ($23).

HISTORICAL FOOTNOTES: Good-bye DeSoto!

Dodge

DODGE
1914-2000

The U.S. Army employed at least one 1914 Dodge Brothers in its recruiting efforts (OCW)

In 1914, the announcement was likened in the trade press to "another Comstock lode or a second Klondike." The famous Dodge brothers were about to build a car. From the turn of the century when they established a small machine shop in Detroit, John and Horace Dodge had supplied engines and transmissions to Ransom Eli Olds, then engines, transmissions and axles to Henry Ford. As both manufacturers for and stockholders in the Ford venture, they made a fortune, but by 1913 had recognized the Ford company was moving toward self-sufficiency and, as John Dodge put it, "being carried around in Henry Ford's vest pocket" had become tiresome. And so, now, these respected engine builders would produce an automobile called, like their company itself, Dodge Brothers. Planning began in 1913, and the first Dodge Brothers vehicle left the factory on November 14, 1914. The brothers were never ones to rush things, nor were they particularly loath to change once they felt they had things right. Probably there was no more sturdy a car built in America in 1915 than the Dodge Brothers. Its 35-hp, L-head, four-cylinder engine was strength personified, as was its welded all-steel body by Budd, though the brothers would add rivets here and there for a few years just for safety's sake. The Dodge Brothers was America's first mass-produced automobile with an all-steel body. Distinctive, too, was the car's 12-volt electrical system and its three-speed selective transmission with enclosed heat-treated vanadium gears and "back-to-front" gear change. The wheelbase was 110 inches, and its dimension (raised to 114 for 1917 and 116 for 1924) would represent just about the only change made to the Dodge Brothers for the next decade. The car was immediately successful, with some 45,000 units built in 1915, the best first year for a new car thus far in American automobile history. In 1916 Dodge stood in fourth place in the industry. Certainly, the brothers' renown in the industry was partly responsible for this splendid beginning, but responsible, too, was the reputation their car quickly earned for its straightforward honesty and dependability. In 1916, General Pershing used a Dodge Brothers to chase Pancho Villa over much of Mexico, and probably more of the brothers' cars saw overseas service during World War I than those of any other single manufacturer. Following the Armistice, John and Horace Dodge added an all-steel sedan for 1919 that, at $1,900, was their most expensive car to date. For 1920 they slightly raked the windshield on all models, which for the conservative Dodge Brothers was a styling move that almost bordered on the risque. Nineteen-twenty was the year that Dodge moved into second place in the industry; it was also the year that both brothers died, John of pneumonia in January, Horace of cirrhosis in December. That the Dodge brothers were raucous and roistering big drinkers had been widely known; John had wrecked at least one saloon and though his drinking habits may have hastened his death, it was his death that hastened Horace's. The brothers had been incredibly close. Dodge Brothers company now fell to their widows, with Frederick Haynes, a longtime company man, installed in the presidency in January 1921. Unfortunately, also in 1921, the company fell to third place in the industry. This didn't make Haynes' position very tenable, though he endured in it into 1925, during which year Dodge Brothers dropped to fifth and the Dodge widows decided to sell out to the New York banking house of Dillon, Read & Company for $146 million, the largest cash transaction thus far in the history of industrial finance. (A facsimile of the check was widely published in the press.) A financial man with no automobile experience, one E.G. Wilmer, was installed as Dodge Brothers' president that year. The company's position continued downward. Continued too, were the traditional cars, though the wood-framed Fisher-bodied coach offered in 1925 would have been abhorred by the brothers. In 1927 a new Fast Four (40 hp, 108-inch wheelbase) and for 1928 an L-head, 60-hp six (designed by Dodge, but built by Continental) were added to the line. In 1928 Dillion, Read sold the company (for $170 million—a stock transaction, not cash) to Walter P. Chrysler, who had first tried to buy Dodge two years earlier.

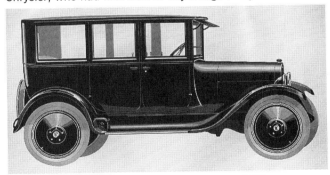

1923 Dodge Brothers four-door sedan (OCW)

Though a relative newcomer in the industry, Walter Chrysler's Chrysler was an immensely popular medium-priced car, but he needed the formidable Dodge facilities and distributorship network in order to crack the lower-priced field. That he wished to lose no time is indicated by Clarence Dillon's phone call to him the morning following the sale to say everything was in order at the Dodge Brothers factory and it could run itself sight unseen for three months. "Hell, Clarence, our boys moved in yesterday" was Walter Chrysler's response. And so they had; E.G. Wilmer and crew were immediately informed their services were no longer needed. From an unlucky 13th place in the industry in 1928, the Dodge Brothers moved into the lucky seven spot within a year under Chrysler Corporation aegis. Most cars were sixes by 1928, with the hydraulic front-wheel brakes and standard gearshift adopted the year before being retained; retained, too, for the next few years was the car's individual identity.

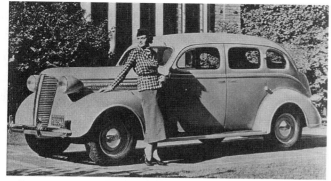

1937 Dodge four-door Touring Sedan (OCW)

The transition of its name from Dodge Brothers to simply Dodge took place around 1930. A radio as standard equipment was offered on the top-of-the-line six that year. Gradually, the Dodge moved into a specific niche within the multi-division corporate framework; Chrysler was the top-market car, Plymouth the mass-volume car, and the Dodge and DeSoto were in between, with Dodge initially the more expensive, later the less, of the two. A straight-eight was offered from 1930 to 1933; sixes only were produced from 1934 to the war. In 1933, the Dodge be-

came the industry's fourth best-seller (behind Plymouth), a position it would hold through 1937, the result, no doubt, of the car being spared the calamitous Airflow styling of the Chrysler and the DeSoto. Though Dodge did not weather the "depression within the depression" of the later '30s as well as other makers, the division did bounce back to an above 200,000-unit-per-year mark in 1940. When production ceased in early 1942, and Chrysler Corporation turned its efforts to war work, the position of Dodge on the American automotive scene was as solid as it had been during John and Horace's Dodge Brothers days.

1946 Dodge Custom convertible (OCW)

A 1951 dealer poster shows the evolution of Dodge until that time. (OCW)

1950 Dodge Wayfarer sport roadster (OCW)

After World War II, Dodge re-entered the auto market with face-lifted prewar models. Like other Chrysler cars, they changed little, until 1949, when new midyear models appeared as a "Second Series." Introduced was a boxy exterior look. Deluxe and Custom names gave way to those such as Coronet or Meadowbrook. Especially interesting were Wayfarer coupes and Sportabout roadsters. An all-steel Sierra station wagon was introduced for 1950 and Sportabouts and eight-passenger sedans were dropped in 1951.

Despite model cutting, 1951 was a good year. Dodge operated at its highest level. W.C. Newberg, president of the Hamtramck, Mich.-based firm, ruled over Chrysler's largest plant, known as Dodge Main. While most popular with Easterners, many Dodges were made in the huge San Leandro, Calif., plant or another in Los Angeles.

A Meadowbrook Special Series replaced the Wayfarer in 1952. The big news of 1953 was a "Red Ram" V-8 in some series. In 1954, Dodge brought out the Firearrow show car and PowerFlite fully-automatic transmission for production models. With 10 extra horsepower, the 1954 Dodge V-8 set 196 speed records at the Bonneville Salt Flats.

All-new 1955s came in three series with longer, lower, wider bodies, plus new hardtops, three-tone paint, and more upmarket trim variations. Some economy models disappeared, but luxurious Custom Royals were added. The styling program clicked, as Dodge sales jumped 160.3 percent. Even more cars could have been sold, except Dodge and Plymouth shared the same V-8 plant. This created a production jam-up, but Dodge still made 237,000 V-8s in a 273,000-unit year!

1956 Dodge Custom Royal Lancer four-door hardtop (OCW)

Restyling was seen at the tail of 1956s. Back fenders grew into fins. An innovative, push-button transmission was introduced. The D-500 was introduced for performance buffs. Unfortunately, there was no magic push button to help sales, which tumbled 22.4 percent. M.C. Patterson became president of Dodge in 1957, and new swept-wing styling appeared. Anticipating an improved market, renovations began at the home plant and led to 42-percent higher sales.

On Oct. 27, 1957, over 65,000 Dodge employee families attended Family Day, at Dodge Main, to preview 1958 models. They retained the swept-wing look and added a superpowerful B-block engine package. (A handful of electronic fuel-injected 1958s were built and later recalled.) Unfortunately, sales by the end of the year amounted to just over two cars for every "Dodge Boy" at the party. Dodge dropped to 3.1 percent of industry, after holding 4.5 percent the year before. Then, 1959 got off to a worse start. Labor problems, in 1958, resulted in a late production start. Potential buyers had to wait weeks for delivery, since showroom units were needed for display. What a way to begin the 45th year of Dodge history!

Aimed at competition with the Big Three was Dodge's expanded 1960 line of 118-inch wheelbase Darts, plus full-size Polaras and Monacos. Unitized bodies and a host of convenience options were new. Buyer reaction to the multi-size program was great and Dodge nearly caught Plymouth, after moving less than half as many cars in 1959!

Dodge entered the compact field in 1961. Under the direction of a new General Manager, B.J. Nichols, the Dodge Lancer appeared. It was a Plymouth Valiant with a slightly altered look. The Polara, on the "big" chassis, had new medium prices. The Matador was dropped. Americans went on a big car buying binge and Dodge felt a substantial 2.15 percent drop in market share.

Nineteen sixty-two Darts had a Lancer-inspired image. Wheelbase was down to 116 inches for a leaner size. Big Dodges were dropped, but returned at midyear as the Custom 880s. The 1962 Lancer, with a brighter grille and bucket seat GT, was a hit in an otherwise bad run. For 1963, the 111-inch wheelbase Dart replaced Lancer as a family-sized compact. Polaras got a 119-inch wheelbase, abandoning 1962's "lean-bred" theme. Flatter rooflines, squared-off decks, and bolder grilles contributed to a high-performance image and helped output soar.

Dodge had a successful year in 1964. Darts were changed little. Full-size Dodges had more glass area, larger doors, and "Golden Anniversary" styling updates. Aluminum grilles and downward tapering roof pillars were new appearance accents. The 880 and Custom 880 models gave buyers a big-car option from 1962 through 1964. Performance V-8s ranged from 265 to 425 hp. The 1965 Dodge was offered in 17 models, including a plush, new Monaco with front and rear bucket seats. Coronets were resized and poised for performance. The option list provided 426-cid Hemi V-8s, floor shifts, bucket seats, and consoles. Model year output of 550,795 units eclipsed 1964's record 475,672 cars.

The 1966 Dodge Charger was a fastback show car brought to life. It was based on the new Coronet and both models combined high-performance and luxury. New Dart options included improved power steering and front disc brakes. Polaras came in seven varieties, ranging from economy sedan to sporty hardtop. Tilt and telescope steering wheels and front disc brakes were optional. Advertised as Dodge's "Rebellion," the sales battle registered a gain, with a 6.6 percent market share. Model year output, however, tumbled to its first decline since 1962.

R.B. McCurry, Jr., became vice-president and general manager of Dodge in 1967, when Darts and Polaras were restyled. America's largest compact had a new unit body, curved side glass, and delta-shaped taillamps. Polara was 6.3 inches larger and innovated a new, blind quarter hardtop roofline. The face-lifted Charger/Coronet received a new R/T option package for the performance crowd. But, again, Dodge popularity declined.

Moderate styling changes were seen on the smallest and largest 1968 Dodges, while Coronet/Chargers adopted a slim, rounded, "Coke-bottle" theme. No longer slope-backed, the Charger had conventional hardtop styling on a Coronet body tipped by a unique wind-splitting nose. It came V-8-powered only, up to the hefty Hemi Charger. The popular 1968 lineup gave Dodge its fifth sales record in six years.

1968 Dodge Charger two-door hardtop (OCW)

Hailed as "Dodge Fever," the brand's popularity saw only a small decline for 1969, which was still the second best year in Dodge history. The division hit a strong 6.8 percent market share. Big styling changes were reserved for the Polara/Monaco full-sized models, which took on the Chrysler "fuselage" look with smooth, convex bodysides and curved, ventless side window glass.

1970 Dodge Challenger R/T convertible (OCW)

As the 1970s dawned, Dodge continued to emphasize sportiness and performance, but the market began to change rapidly with governmental regulation and oil embargoes. The sporty, all-new Challenger, introduced in 1970 as a companion to Plymouth's Barracuda, was too late to find large success in the waning days of the muscle-car era. It survived only through 1974, although the name was reintroduced later for a Japanese model imported by Dodge.

As gas mileage became more of a sales factor, the large cars gradually lost ground, and model offerings were pared down as a consequence. Restyled for 1971, the mid-range was split between the Charger two-door sport models and the Coronet sedans and station wagons, all of which were reasonably successful through the styling cycle, which ran through 1974.

There was more buyer interest in the Dart line, which, in response, expanded to include additional luxury sedans and sporty, performance coupes with names such as Demon and Swinger. Dodge imported its entries for the sub-compact market, the Colt line.

The full-size Polara and Monaco lines were restyled in 1974. When Coronets received a major face-lift in 1975, hardtop coupes were again included. The Charger nameplate went onto a personal luxury model based on the new Chrysler Cordoba's body shell. High-performance engines were gradually toned down, while options and luxury appointments were expanded.

Calendar year builds placed Dodge in seventh place for 1970, 1971, 1972, 1973, and 1975. In 1974, however, Dodge was able to pass Buick in annual production.

Recalls plagued Dodge's new Aspen, introduced for 1976 as compact replacement for the venerable Dart (which hung on one more year). Sales never took off like Dart's had, either. While performance wasn't forgotten in the Dodge camp, the high-potency Chargers and Challengers were mainly memories. Four hardtop coupe models (or option packages) carried on the Charger and Daytona nameplates, with a 240-hp, 400-cid V-8 possible underhood; but such temptations wouldn't last much

longer. Aspen's R/T package, on the other hand, could combine with a 360-cid V-8 on a lighter-weight coupe chassis. Dart's model selection reached out for fuel economy with a Dart Lite package, which sounded more like a new brand of beer. Pillarless hardtops were still available from Dodge, but top-line mid-sizes displayed opera windows. Full-size Monacos and Royal Monacos were the only models to offer the big 440-cid V-8. While model-year sales rose in 1976, they hardly matched the record set three years earlier. Compacts were finding plenty of customers, but the bigger Dodges were losing appeal.

Monaco became the name for mid-sizes in 1977, as the well-known Coronet badge disappeared. Full-sizes kept the "Royal" prefix. Aspen coupes could have not only the former R/T package, but a Super R/T, as well as a T-Bar roof or sunroof. Those Aspens are most likely to appeal to collectors. So might the sporty Daytona package, which went on 5,225 Charger SE models. Dodge's new Diplomat, mid-size at the time, would still be around a decade later as the last remaining "big" rear-drive model.

Subcompacts, not full-size models, were the big news in 1978, though. As the biggest Dodges faded away, the L-body Omni (and near-twin Plymouth Horizon) arrived—the first of the American-built front-drives. Few realized at the time that Omni signaled a major trend, paving the way for front-wheel drive to virtually take over the marketplace over the next decade. Sporty Aspens came in additional forms this time: R/T (again), R/T Sport Pak and Super Coupe, along with a Street Kit Car. Farther up the line, the Magnum XE, with its distinctive slat-style grille, took over from Daytona as the sporty mid-size. Magnum's GT package might be the one to look over now. Monaco had a couple of special packages, too—SS and Gran Coupe— but those hardly rivaled the appeal of a Magnum.

Important as Omni was, it didn't help Dodge sales enough as the 1970s ended. Totals fell slightly in both 1978 and '79, then far lower for the 1980 model year. Big Dodges were gone for 1979, replaced by a new and lighter St. Regis. A front-drive 024 coupe joined the original Omni sedan. Not many Aspens carried the R/T package this year, but quite a few were Sunrise Coupes. Among other moves, new Chrysler Chairman Lee Iacocca tried to promote a wider gulf between Dodge and the Chrysler-Plymouth Division.

Mirada, similar in appearance to the restyled Chrysler Cordoba, but with slat grille, claimed the personal-luxury coupe niche from Magnum XE for 1980. Mirada's CMX package— especially one with the high-output 360-cid V-8 and dual exhaust—is the one to seek out today. Aspen R/T and new 024 DeTomaso options may not seem as attractive to latter-day enthusiasts, but are comparatively rare. Fewer are likely to grow excited by the sight of a Touring Edition St. Regis or a Diplomat S coupe.

1981 Dodge Omni hatchback sedan (OCW)

Excitement isn't the word that comes to mind for Aries, either, which entered the Dodge lineup for 1981, along with the related Plymouth Reliant. Yet this front-drive compact sedan worked wonders for Dodge sales and reputation. Motor Trend gave it "Car of the Year" honors. Omni added a stripped-down

Miser and a step-up Euro-Sedan. More appealing nowadays, though, might be the subcompact coupe's option choices, the rather rare De Tomaso, and the new Charger 2.2 package, both with 2.2-liter engine. Aries' popularity helped Dodge sales rise by a healthy amount.

St. Regis didn't return for 1982, a victim of sagged sales. Diplomat came only in four-door sedan form. Charger was the name on the subcompact coupe's performance edition, hardly a rival to its predecessors with that badge, but appealing in its own way. Aries' chassis was stretched a bit to produce the new 400 series, which even included a convertible—something not seen in Dodge ranks since 1971.

Charger performance took a leap upward with the addition of a (Carroll) Shelby edition for 1983. A 107-hp four, after all, could propel a lightweight subcompact coupe quite nicely. Mirada was in its final year, but another numbered front-drive Dodge model arrived, the 600 sedan. "Talking dashboards" available on 400 and 600, were not universally loved. Sales looked good this year as Dodge's market share rose.

The next year, the 600 nameplate went on former 400 models and the 600 ES (Euro-Sport) came with gas-filled shocks. Dodge had a much different, smaller-scale offering for performance-minded prospects, though. It was the new Daytona, available with a 142-hp turbocharged engine in regular or Turbo Z trim. Performance also came in tiny packages: not only the Shelby Charger, but a new Omni GLH option. With Mirada gone, Diplomat was the only rear-drive Dodge remaining, popular mainly with police agencies. After a long life, the old Slant Six engine was retired.

Just as Daytona had been near twin to Chrysler's Laser, the new Lancer for 1985 was closely related to LeBaron GTS. Turbo power was now standard on the Shelby Charger, and available under Omni GLH hoods as well as in larger models. Model-year sales hit their highest peak since 1978, and rose again for 1986 (but only with the help of captive import sales).

Performance fans tend to overlook Omni's GLH, described as "ferocious" and "a savage." Whether truly collectible or not, they serve as interesting examples of potent power in lightweight packages. Shelby Chargers are perhaps more likely to attract collector interest, if only for their name. Other recent possibilities that may hold future appeal include the 600 ES Turbo convertible, Daytona Turbo Z, and Mirada CMX.

Dodge Division operated as a separate branch of Chrysler Motors Corp. in 1987, with its main office at Chrysler Corp. headquarters in Highland Park, Michigan. The division was headed by E. Thomas Pappert, Chrysler Group VP of Sales, with J.B. York, VP for Dodge Car and Truck, overseeing day-to-day Dodge operations.

Chrysler's game plan for this period was to better define the identities of its divisions and this included making the corporate G-body car exclusive to Dodge as the Daytona. (The G-bodied Chrysler Laser was dropped). Emphasizing the image of Dodge as a mass market excitement car was the all-new Shadow subcompact, which sold nearly 76,000 copies.

Overall, Dodge Division product sales (including the Mitsubishi-built Colt, Conquest, and Vista models) tumbled 15 percent from 1986. Only the Vista and Dodge 600 four-door outpaced previous year deliveries and both only by small margins. Part of the decline was due to a temporary suspension of Dodge Omni production, in the spring, when the Belvidere, Illinois facility was converted to building new C-bodied Chrysler New Yorkers. However, the Omni went back into production, at the former AMC plant in Kenosha, Wisconsin, a month after Chrysler bought American Motors in August 1987.

Production-wise, Dodge's 1987 model year total for U.S.-built cars climbed from 456,896 units to 501,926 for a 6.79 percent share of industry. The division's most popular 1987 model was the Aries sedan, with 71,216 builds.

Dodge was shooting for sales of 470,000 cars as the 1988 model year kicked off. This was exceeded by nearly 10,000

units, despite the disappearance of the Vista (a captive import) and the domestically-built Dodge 600 two-door. In fact, the only Dodge to see a sales decline was the H-body Lancer, built in Sterling Heights, Michigan.

Among the year's big wins were continued buyer acceptance of the P-body Shadow and the instant popularity of the all-new Dynasty, a full-sized C-body front-drive that earned nearly 60,000 customers. "America" versions of the Aries coupes, sedans, and wagons drove deliveries of these models 5,000 above the goal of 100,000. These cars had a sticker price that was $1,400 lower than in 1987, due to a reduction in the number of standard options from 25 to nine.

A new five-door Colt wagon was introduced for 1988, along with the Shelby-Lancer (a car aimed at enthusiasts). This hot-performing sporty car came with a 2.2-liter/174-hp, inter-cooled, Turbo II four-cylinder engine as standard equipment. Adding more excitement to the Dodge lineup were the Turbo I-engined Daytona Pacifica and the Turbo II-powered Shelby-Daytona Z. Daytona model sales more than doubled from 1987, climbing to 70,986 units. This figure included a limited number of Shelby versions with a C/S "lite" competition package.

J.B. Damoose took over as vice-president for Dodge car and truck, leading the division into a 1989 model year that witnessed a modest decline in sales to 474,989 units. Competition from Ford and imported makers, combined with the elimination of five Dodge car lines (Charger, 600, Lancer, Diplomat, and Aries), accounted for much of the drop. These cutbacks were a reflection of Chrysler Corp. financial woes, which brought about the closing of several plants. They included the Jefferson Avenue facility, where Omnis were built, and the St. Louis factory, which produced Daytonas.

Dodge's version of the new Chrysler A-body sedan was the Spirit, which sold close to 60,000 copies. It was the introduction of this mid-market family car that led to dropping of the Aries K-car in mid-season. Remaining popular was the Daytona, which earned a strong 68,032 sales. Of these, nearly one-fifth were equipped with optional turbocharged engines.

Management changes continued for model year 1990, with Lawrence W. Baker becoming general manager—a new position—for Dodge car and truck. The season's new car was one with an old name, the Monaco. It was a midsize, front-drive sedan with prices starting at just above $15,000. Based on Chrysler's Canadian-built Eagle Premier platform, the Monaco used a Regie Renault-made 3.0-liter aluminum V-6.

Several technical innovations highlighted Dodge's 1990 carryover cars. The Daytona, Spirit, and Shadow were made available with a new five-speed manual transmission built by Chrysler's Acustar parts subsidiary. Turbo-four-powered Shadows and Daytonas received a variable nozzle turbocharger. Other improvements included a 3.0-liter Mitsubishi V-6 option for the Daytona and a new, American-made, 3.3-liter V-6 top engine for the full-sized Dynasty.

Also available for model year 1990 were the Mitsubishi-built Colt/Colt Vista and (until February 2, 1990) the Omni. The latter was discontinued after suffering a 15 percent decline in sales during 1989.

Throughout the decade of the 1990s, auto racing would play a big part in Dodge Division products. In 1991, the Daytona Shelby was renamed the IROC Shelby to promote the fact that Dodge was the supplier of cars for the International Race of Champions. The IROC series pitted a dozen professional race drivers competing in identically prepared Dodge IROC Shelby-bodied (with NASCAR-type underpinnings) stock cars at four events for gobs of prize money. At Indianapolis, a prototype V-10-powered 1992 Dodge Viper paced the 1991 Indianapolis 500 with the legendary Carroll Shelby at the wheel. Also new to the lineup that year was the imported Stealth 2+2—a derivative of the Mitsubishi 3000GT. All domestically produced 1991 Dodges featured a driver's side airbag as standard equipment.

Production of the Monaco ceased in late 1991, with carry-over models sold as 1992 models. Shortly after, the production Viper roadster hit showrooms, and the American automotive industry would never be the same. The "throwback," brutish Viper defied all Detroit logic, but the public loved it and the image of owning one said, "Politically correct, be damned! I want a gas-guzzling road rocket, where every stretch of open asphalt will be my own personal racetrack." Mid-year in 1992, the cab forward revolution began at Dodge with the early release of the 1993 Intrepid, a midsize sedan built on the shared LH platform with Chrysler (Concorde) and Eagle (Vision).

Both 1993 and 1994 were transition years at Dodge, with the division geared up to be completely (well, almost) cab forward by 1995. Daytona and Dynasty were gone after the 1993 model year. Shadow and the imported Colt ended production the following year. Spirit was also slated to cease production in 1994, but was carried over into 1995 until the new Stratus sedan came online in mid-model year. Other new products joining the Stratus were the Neon and Avenger. The much-anticipated coupe version (not to be confused with the detachable hardtop that became optional equipment on the roadster in 1996) of the Viper, named GTS, was displayed as a concept car on the 1993 auto show circuit. The GTS coupe's design paid homage to the immortal GT racing cars of the 1960s, such as the Shelby Cobra Daytona coupe and Ferrari 250 GTO. While just about every muscle-car enthusiast lusted after a GTS, it would be a few more years before that could become reality.

1996 Dodge Viper GTS coupe (OCW)

The Viper GTS coupe paced the 1996 Indianapolis 500, and while "mass" production of the car—packing an all-alumi-num, 450-hp V-10—was set for 1996 (with an announced price of $66,700, not including gas and luxury taxes), it was not readily available until spring 1997. While Dodge gained a muscle car with the Viper GTS, it also lost one at the end of the 1996 model year as the imported Stealth was discontinued.

Not to be lost among all the Viper buzz, Dodge's Neon was also making racing history, mopping up on the showroom stock circuit. In its first several years of availability, the Neon lineup was juggled with models added and dropped or turned into option packages. The dust pretty much settled by 1998 when Neon was offered in a trio of packaged formats: Highline, Competition, and R/T. The second-generation cab forward Intrepid also debuted in 1998. Not resting on its laurels, on that year's auto show tour Dodge was already showcasing its 2001 Intrepid R/T, which factored large in the automaker's then-secret motorsports plans for the future.

In 1999, after 22 years away from victory lane, the newly-formed (see Chrysler listing for details) DaimlerChrysler announced that its Dodge Division would return to NASCAR competition in 2001 with the Intrepid. Just prior to that announcement, to the dismay of "spec" racers everywhere, Chrysler Corp. pulled the plug on its involvement in showroom stock racing with the Neon, citing rules that were unfairly advantageous to rival manufacturers' cars.

Dodge's millennium-ending 2000 lineup remained unchanged from 1999. Totally new, however—along with its Plymouth counterpart—was the Neon, which was redesigned front to rear, inside and out. The 2000 Neons were actually introduced midyear of 1999. Detail refinements characterized the other 2000 offerings, although the full-size Intrepid was heated up with a new R/T performance option featuring a 242-hp version of the corporate 3.5-liter V-6, while the base four-cylinder engine and manual transmission was dropped for Avenger and replaced by a standard 2.5-liter V-6 coupled with a four-speed automatic.

The list of modern Dodge automobiles likely to strike the fancy of future collectors is varied. Certainly the Viper, in all its configurations, will head that list. The Neon Sport and Competition models should appeal to enthusiasts who favor collector cars that also serve as fun, daily drivers. Imported Stealth models, especially the turbocharged R/T all-wheel-drive coupes, may also find favor. And finally, due to the minimal number of modern convertible models, Dodge soft-tops from 1982-'86 will likely be an affordable choice for collectors to pursue.

1914 DODGE

1914 Dodge Brothers, touring (OCW)

DODGE — MODEL 30-35 — FOUR: Horace and John Dodge took delivery of the first Dodge car on November 14, 1914. Cars built during 1914 carried serial numbers 1-370. Most historians consider all of these cars to be 1915 models, although many collectors prefer to call them 1914 models. Standard equipment included leather seats, a folding top, electric lighting, an electric self-starter, windshield, speedometer and demountable rims. The only model available was a touring car with "four" doors, one of which (driver's) was non-opening. Styling characteristics of early Dodge cars included headlights positioned high on the fenders and set back from the radiator, splash aprons that angled back and down and no splash aprons below the radiator.

I.D. DATA: Serial numbers were located on a plate on the toe board. Also prior to car number 761408 the serial number is stamped on the center crossmember of the frame on the right side under the rear floorboard. Starting: 1. Ending: 370. Engine numbers were located on the front flange of cylinder block just ahead of the starter generator. Engine numbers are not available.

Model No.	Body Type & Seating	Price	Weight	Prod. Total
30-35	4-dr. Tr.-5P	785	2200	Note 1

Note 1: Total series production has been established as 370 cars in calendar year 1914.

ENGINE: Inline, L-head. Four. Cast iron block. B. & S.: 3-7/8 x 4-1/2 in. Disp.: 212.3 cu. in. C.R.: 4.0:1. Brake H.P.: 35 @ 2000 R.P.M. N.A.C.C. H.P.: 24. Main bearings: four. Valve lifters: solid.

CHASSIS: W.B.: 110 in. Tires: 33 x 4.

TECHNICAL: Selective sliding transmission. Speeds: 3F/1R. Floor shift controls. Cone type clutch. Shaft drive. Two wheel mechanical brakes. Demountable wood spoke wheels.

OPTIONS: Spare tire. Side curtains. Tool kit. Runningboard. Luggage rack. Horn. Wind wings. Moto-meter. Windshield wiper. Spotlight. Wire wheels.

HISTORICAL: Introduced November 14, 1914. First Dodge car. Unique manual transmission gearshift pattern. Calendar year production: 370 (built in calendar 1914). Dodge Brothers was organized on July 17, 1914. John and Horace Dodge capitalized the company with $5 million in common stock. The Dodge factory was located in Hamtramck, Michigan. The first car to leave the factory was photographed extensively. It had hood louvers, but production models had plain side hoods.

1915 DODGE

DODGE — MODEL 30-35 — FOUR: There were no styling changes on 1915 Dodge touring cars. A new roadster was introduced. It had a slanting deck with an integral storage compartment and a spare tire carrier. Standard equipment for both models was leather seats, folding tops, electric lights, electric self-starters, windshields, speedometers and demountable wheel rims.

1915 Dodge Brothers, touring (HAC)

I.D. DATA: Serial numbers were in the same locations. Starting: 371. Ending: 45,000. Engine numbers were in the same location. Engine numbers are not available.

Model No.	Body Type & Seating	Price	Weight	Prod. Total
30-35	4-dr. Tr.-5P	785	2200	Note 1
30-35	2-dr. Rds.-2P	785	2155	Note 1

Note 1: Total 1914-1915 series production was 45,000.

ENGINE: Same as 1914 engine. See previous specifications.

CHASSIS: W.B.: 110 in. Tires: 33 x 4.

TECHNICAL: Selective sliding transmission. Speeds: 3F/1R. Floor shift controls. Leather-faced cone clutch. Shaft drive. Two wheel mechanical brakes. Demountable wood spoke wheels.

OPTIONS: Spare tire. Side curtains. Tool kit. Runningboard. Luggage rack. Horn. Wind wings. Moto-meter. Windshield wiper. Spotlight. Wire wheels.

HISTORICAL: Introduced January 1, 1915. Calendar year production: 45,000 (includes 1914 models). Due to start-up costs, John and Horace Dodge lost money on the production of their earliest Dodge cars. Dodge was ranked America's number three automaker in 1915.

1916 DODGE

1916 Dodge Brothers, touring (OCW)

DODGE — MODEL 30-35 — FOUR: History books are in dispute over the specific models and features offered in Dodge Brothers' 1916 line. *The Manual of Automobile Liability Insurance*, which was published January 1, 1916, by The Fidelity and Casualty Co. of New York, indicates that the 1916 line had no basic changes from the 1915 offerings. According to this book, these cars were still rated 30-35 horsepower and still came in only two body styles - roadster and touring. The book describes them as 1915-1916 models, indicating the 1916 (model year) Dodges were a direct carryover from 1915. This information also agrees with a similar insurance guide published in 1918. It can thus be assumed that other sources showing several minor changes in "1916" Dodges

have confused the true 1916 models with cars built in that calendar year, but marketed as 1917 models. We are going to consider the 1916 models a continuation of the 1915 series, using these contemporary sources for documentation. These cars had no styling changes. Standard equipment included leather seats, folding tops, electric lights, electric self-starter, windshield, speedometer and demountable wheel rims.

I.D. DATA: Serial numbers were in the same locations. Starting 45001. Ending: 110000. Engine numbers were in the same location. Engine numbers are not available.

1916 Dodge Brothers, California top touring (OCW)

Model No.	Body Type & Seating	Price	Weight	Prod. Total
30-35	2-dr. Rds.-2P	785	2155	Note 1
30-35	2-dr. Tour.-5P	785	2200	Note 1

Note 1: Total series production was 71,400.

ENGINE: Same as 1914-15 engine. See previous specifications.

CHASSIS: W.B.: 110 in. Tires: 33 x 4 in.

TECHNICAL: Selective sliding transmission. Speeds: 3F/1R. Floor shift controls. Leather-faced cone clutch. Shaft drive. Two wheel mechanical brakes. Demountable wood spoke wheels.

OPTIONS: Spare tire. Side curtains. Tool kit. Runningboard. Luggage rack. Horn. Wind wings. Moto-meter. Windshield wiper. Spotlight. Wire wheels.

HISTORICAL: Introduced July 1915. The true 1916 models seem to be a continuation of the 1915 models and had no more than minor running production changes. Calendar year production: 71,400.

Dodge coined the slogan "It speaks for itself" in 1916 and started stressing the dependability of its products. U.S. Army General John Pershing placed an order for 150 Dodge Brothers touring cars for delivery July 15, 1916. The cars were used in the campaign against Mexican bandit Pancho Villa. Lt. George Patton, Jr. led the first mechanized cavalry charge with three of these cars and 15 soldiers.

1917 DODGE

DODGE — MODEL 30 — FOUR: According to the contemporary sources used for our research, the 1917 Dodge was referred to as the Dodge Model 30. It was rated at 35 advertised horsepower. These cars had a longer 114 inch wheelbase. There were four new models, in addition to the roadster and touring. Two of these were simply "Rex" top models. This term referred to a type of removable hardtop fitted with snap-on glass windows and detachable side panels. Built by the Rex Manufacturing Co. of Connersville, Indiana, these tops allowed the owner to "convert" his roadster or touring car into a variety of configurations: open car, open-side hardtop or fully enclosed. The other models were a permanently enclosed center door sedan coupe with lowerable windows. Mechanically, a multiple disc clutch was used in place of the leather-faced cone type. Cars built after approximately October 1, 1916 (for model year 1917), also had higher radiators, headlights mounted ahead of the radiator, splash aprons on the inner sides of the fenders and a rear cross bar (inside the spare tire carrier) supporting the rear license plate bracket and an electric taillamp.

1917 Dodge Brothers, Rex touring (OCW)

I.D. DATA: Serial numbers were in the same location. Starting: 116339. Ending: 210000. Engine numbers were in the same location. Engine numbers are not available.

Model No.	Body Type & Seating	Price	Weight	Prod. Total
30	2-dr. Rds.-2P	835	2200	Note 1
30	4-dr. Tour.-5P	835	2200	Note 1
30	2-dr. Rex Rds.-2P	1000	2500	Note 1
30	4-dr. Rex Tour.-5P	1000	2700	Note 1
30	2-dr. C/D Sed.-5P	1265	2795	Note 1
30	2-dr. Cpe.-2P	1265	2520	Note 1

Note 1: Total series production was 90,000.

ENGINE: Same as 1914-16 engines. See previous specifications.

CHASSIS: W.B.: 114 in. Tires: 33 x 4.

TECHNICAL: Selective sliding transmission. Speeds: 3F/1R. Floor shift controls. Multiple dry disc clutch. Shaft drive. Two-wheel mechanical brakes. Wood spoke wheels.

OPTIONS: Spare tire. Side curtains. Tool kit. Runningboard. Luggage rack. Horn. Wind wings. Moto-meter. Windshield wiper. Spotlight. Wire wheels.

HISTORICAL: Introduced July 1916. Innovations: Longer wheelbase. Multiple dry disc clutch. Four new body styles. New hood styling. Repositioned headlights and taillights. New splash aprons. Calendar year production: 90,000. Dodge entered the commercial vehicle field in 1917, building both civilian and military trucks. Dodge dropped to fifth sales rank in the American auto industry.

1918 DODGE

DODGE — MODEL 30 — FOUR: There were no significant changes in the 1918 Dodges. Styling was of the later 1917 type with high radiators, headlights ahead of radiator, inner side fender aprons and rear accessories mounted on a cross bar inside the spare tire carrier. Standard equipment included leather seats, windshield, self-starter, electric lights, speedometer, demountable rims and side curtains. Prices were up and civilian production was down due to the outbreak of World War I in Europe. Wire wheels seem to have received heavy promotion in ads this year.

I.D. DATA: Serial numbers were in the same locations. Starting: 217926. Ending: 300000. Engine numbers were stamped above the carburetor on the left side of the cylinder block. Engine numbers were also stamped on the left side of the engine rear support. In 1918, the right side of a few engine rear supports were also stamped with engine numbers. The engine numbers are not available.

Model No.	Body Type & Seating	Price	Weight	Prod. Total
30	2-dr. Rds.-2P	985	2200	Note 1
30	4-dr. Tour.-5P	985	2200	Note 1
30	2-dr. Rex Rds.-2P	1150	2500	Note 1
30	4-dr. Rex Tr.-5P	1150	2700	Note 1

Model No.	Body Type & Seating	Price	Weight	Prod. Total
30	2-dr. C/D Sed.-5P	1425	2795	Note 1
30	2-dr. Cpe.-2P	1425	2520	Note 1

Note 1: Total series production was 62,000.

ENGINE: Same as 1914-17 engine. See previous specifications.

CHASSIS: W.B.: 114 in. Tires: 33 x 4.

TECHNICAL: Selective sliding transmission. Speeds: 3F/1R. Floor shift controls. Multiple dry disc clutch. Shaft drive. Two-wheel mechanical brakes. Wood spoke wheels.

OPTIONS: Spare tire(s). Side curtains. Tool kit. Runningboard. Luggage rack. Horn. Wind wings. Moto-meter. Windshield wiper. Spotlight. Wire wheels. Sidemounts (on commercial vehicles).

HISTORICAL: Introduced July 1, 1917. Calendar year production: 62,000. Dodge continued as the fifth largest automaker in the U.S. Commercial vehicles ranged from a panel delivery truck called the "Business Car" to a chemical fire truck ordered by the Clear Lake, Minnesota, Fire Department.

1919 DODGE

1919 Dodge Brothers, four-door sedan (JAC)

DODGE — MODEL 30 — FOUR: Originating as a carryover series, the 1919 Dodge Brothers' line underwent a number of running production changes during the model year. One was the adoption of narrower windshields for all open cars. A four-door sedan with standard wire wheels was introduced in February 1919. In April, the Rex "convertible" roadster/coupe was replaced with a conventional five window coupe. General styling characteristics and equipment features were the same as seen on 1918 models.

I.D. DATA: Serial numbers were in the same locations. Starting: 303107. Ending: 420000. Engine numbers were in the same locations. Engine numbers are not available.

Model No.	Body Type & Seating	Price	Weight	Prod. Total
30	2-dr. Rds.-2P	1085	NA	Note 1
30	4-dr. Tour.-5P	1085	NA	Note 1
30	2-dr. Rex Rds.-2P	1250	NA	Note 1
30	4-dr. Rex Tour.-5P	1250	NA	Note 1
30	2-dr. C/D Sed.-5P	1425	NA	Note 1
30	4-dr. Sed.-5P	1900	2815	Note 1
30	2-dr. 5W Cpe.-3P	1750	NA	Note 1
30	4-dr. Cus. Limo.-6P	NA	NA	Note 1
30	4-dr. Taxi-3/6P	1650	NA	Note 1

Note 1: Total series production was 106,000.

ENGINE: Same as 1914-18 engine. See previous specifications.

CHASSIS: W.B.: 114 in. Tires: 33 x 4.

TECHNICAL: Selective sliding transmission. Speeds: 3F/1R. Multiple dry disc clutch. Shaft drive. Two-wheel mechanical brakes. Wood spoke wheels.

OPTIONS: Spare tire(s). Side curtains. Tool kit. Runningboard. Luggage rack. Horn. Wind wings. Moto-meter. Windshield wiper. Spotlight. Wire wheels (standard four-door sedan). Side-mounts (commercial vehicles). Kerosene coach lamps (on limousine). Front bumper. Rear fender guards.

HISTORICAL: Announced July 1, 1918. New models including four-door sedan, five window coupe, town car taxicab and custom-built limousine. Thinner windshield on open cars as a running production change. Calendar year production: 106,000. Dodge capacity was up to 500 cars per day this year. The company put its 400,000th car together. The number of commercial vehicle offerings enjoyed a large increase.

1920 DODGE

1920 Dodge Brothers, touring (OCW)

DODGE — MODEL 30 — FOUR: Dodge continued to follow its policy of phasing in minor alterations as running production changes and avoiding annual styling updates. When introduced on July 1, 1919, the 1920 Dodges looked much like the company's original designs. During the model run, a slanted windshield was adopted on both open models and the touring car was fitted with new, longer rear fenders. There was also a new convertible top, with wraparound rear curtains. And longer, 45-inch rear springs provided a smoother ride. General styling and equipment features were the same as on previous models. The Rex top models were no longer offered.

I.D. DATA: Serial numbers were in the same locations. Starting: 424146. Ending: 569548. Engine numbers were in the same location. Engine numbers are not available.

Model No.	Body Type & Seating	Price	Weight	Prod. Total
30	2-dr. Rds.-2P	1085	2240	Note 1
30	4-dr. Tour.-5P	1085	2425	Note 1
30	2 dr. Cpe.-3P	1750	2520	Note 1
30	4-dr. Sed.-5P	1900	2795	Note 1
30	4-dr. Taxi-5P	1650	2710	Note 1

Note 1: Total series production was 141,000.

ENGINE: The 1920 engine was the same as the 1914-19 engine. See previous specifications.

CHASSIS: W.B.: 114 in. Tires 33 x 4.

TECHNICAL: Selective sliding transmission. Speeds: 3F/1R. Floor shift controls. Multiple disc clutch. Shaft drive. Two-wheel mechanical brakes. Wood spoke wheels (wire wheels on sedan).

OPTIONS: Front bumper. Rear bumper. Single sidemount (commercial). Wire wheels (except sedan). Spare tire cover. Runningboard. Luggage rack. Moto-meter. Outside rear view mirror. Wind wings (open cars). Spare tire. "Fat Man" steering wheel. Side curtains. Spotlight(s).

HISTORICAL: Introduced July 1, 1919. Longer rear springs. Slant windshields on open cars. New style top. Longer rear fenders on touring car. Calendar year production: 141,000.

Dodge was America's second best selling car in 1920. John Dodge died on January 14, 1920, after a bout with pneumonia. Horace Dodge died December 20, 1920, after contracting the flu. Soon thereafter, Frederick J. Hayes became president of Dodge Brothers, Inc. Commercial vehicles offered this year included a panel truck and screen side delivery van.

1921 DODGE

1921 Dodge Brothers, touring (OCW)

DODGE — MODEL 30 — FOUR: There were additional minor changes in Dodge Brothers' cars this season. On the touring car the "cathedral" style windows used since 1914 were replaced with a horizontal, rectangular glass window. Closed cars got a new, full-width front seat. The diameter of the wood spoke wheels was reduced by one inch to 24 inches, with a corresponding reduction in tire size. A brand new feature was a heater. Wire wheels were now standard on the coupe and sedan and were used on roadsters built late in the model year. Some 1921 Dodges still came with cathedral style tops and some had a new headlamp tie-bar.

I.D. DATA: Serial numbers were in the same locations. Starting: 569549. Ending: 663096. Engine numbers were in the same location. Engine numbers were not available.

Model No.	Body Type & Seating	Price	Weight	Prod. Total
30	2-dr. Rds.-2P	1235	2305	Note 1
30	4-dr. Tr.-5P	1285	2500	Note 1
30	2-dr. Cpe.-3P	1900	2590	Note 1
30	4-dr. Sed.-5P	2150	2890	Note 1

Note 1: Total calendar year production was 81,000.

ENGINE: The 1921 engine was the same as the 1914-20 engine. See previous specifications.

CHASSIS: W.B.: 114 in. Tires: 33 x 4.

TECHNICAL: Selective sliding transmission. Speeds: 3F/1R. Floor shift controls. Multiple dry disc clutch. Shaft drive. Two-wheel mechanical brakes. Wood spoke or wire wheels.

OPTIONS: Front bumper. Rear bumper. Single sidemount (commercial). Spare tire. Spare tire cover. Runningboard. Luggage rack. Wire wheels (open cars except late roadsters). Moto-meter. Heater. Outside rear view mirror. Wind wings (open cars). "Fat Man" steering wheel. Side curtains. Window shades (coupe/sedan). Spotlight(s).

HISTORICAL: Introduced July 1920. Smaller diameter wheels and tires. Rectangular rear window design adopted as a running change. Full width front seat for closed cars. Calendar year production: 81,000. Dodge placed third in the U.S. sales race for calendar 1921. Frederick J. Haynes was the new president of Dodge Brothers, Inc. A custom-bodied landau touring with disc wheels was built on a 1921 Dodge chassis by Stratton-Bliss. Graham Brothers, of Evansville, Indiana, made an agreement to market its trucks through the Dodge dealer network in mid-1921. Graham became an independent affiliate of Dodge Brothers, Inc.

1922 DODGE

DODGE — FIRST SERIES — FOUR: There were two series of 1922 Dodges. The first series models had "low" hoods of the 1921 style. There

were, however, changes in some body styles. On the sedan, the roof was four inches lower, the beltline was straighter and the rear side window opening was now square-cornered. Budd-Michelin steel discs replaced the former wire wheels. This model had the spare tire mounted at the rear. A small taillight and license plate holder were mounted on the left rear fender and a new semi-floating rear axle was used. Similar changes were used in the three-passenger coupe. Open models were nearly a direct carryover from 1921. Due to the economic effects of a postwar (World War I) recession, Dodge prices were lowered considerably.

1922 Dodge Brothers, touring (OCW)

DODGE SECOND SERIES — FOUR: Second series models had an altered radiator, hood, cowl line that was raised 3-1/2 inches. Other changes included outside door handles, fluted headlamp lenses, a slanted instrument panel, windshield visors and buttonless upholstery. Prices were again lowered, although major specifications were unchanged. A new body style was a two-passenger business coupe with fabric-covered blind rear roof quarters. The cowl on the second series models had a more curved appearance and the windshield on open cars was bowed slightly outward.

I.D. DATA: [First Series] Serial numbers were in the same locations. Starting: 663097. Ending: 761407. Engine numbers were in the same location. Engine numbers are not available. [Second Series] Serial numbers were located on a plate on the toe board and were now also stamped on the right side frame member just to the rear of the front spring rear hanger. Starting: 761408. Ending: 826401. Engine numbers were in the same location. Engine numbers are not available.

Model No.	Body Type & Seating	Price	Weight	Prod. Total
S/1	2-dr. Rds.-2P	935	2305	Note 1
S/1	4-dr. Tour.-5P	985	2450	Note 1
S/1	2-dr. Cpe.-3P	1585	2650	Note 1
S/1	4-dr. Sed.-5P	1785	2940	Note 1

Note 1: There is no separate breakout available for first series production. Serial numbers indicate that approximately 98,310 cars were built in this series.

Note 2: The S/1 designation indicates "Series One" and is not a factory designation.

S/2	2-dr. Rds.-2P	850	2300	Note 1
S/2	4-dr. Tour.-5P	880	2500	Note 1
S/2	2-dr. Bus. Cpe.-2P	980	2600	Note 1
S/2	4-dr. Bus. Sed.-5P	1195	2965	Note 1
S/2	4-dr. Sed.-5P	1440	2940	Note 1

Note 1: There is no separate breakout available for first series production. Serial numbers indicate that approximately 65,000 cars were built in this series.

Note 2: The S/2 designation indicates "Series Two" and is not a factory designation.

ENGINE: [First Series] Inline. L-head. Four. Cast iron block. B & S: 3-7/8 x 4-1/2 in. Disp.: 212.3 cu. in. C.R.: 4.0:1. Brake H.P.: 35 @ 2000 R.P.M. N.A.C.C. H.P.: 24.03. Main bearings: four. Valve lifters: solid. [Second Series] Selective sliding transmission. Speeds: 3F/1R. Floor shift controls. Multiple dry disc clutch. Shaft drive. Semi-floating rear axle. Two-wheel mechanical brakes. Wood spoke wheels.

CHASSIS: (All Series) W.B.: 114 in. Tires: 32 x 4.

OPTIONS: Front bumper. Rear bumper. Single sidemount (commercial). Spare tire. Spare tire cover. Wire spoke wheels. Budd-Michelin steel disc wheels. "Fat Man" steering wheel. Heater. Moto-meter. Wind wings (open cars). Outside rear view mirror. Spotlights. Side curtains. Runningboard. Luggage rack.

HISTORICAL: First series introduced July 1921. Square window sedan introduced August 1921. Square window coupe introduced September 1921. Second series introduced June 1922. Higher radiator and hood. Higher, rounder cowl styling. Disc wheels. Windshield visor. Buttonless upholstery. Semi-floating rear axle. Lower rooflines. Calendar year pro-

duction: 142,000. Model year production: 152,673. Dodge set record breaking sales figures this season and regained third rank in the U.S. industry. The company expanded its production facilities, achieving the 600 vehicle per day level. The Babcock Body Co. built a luxurious town car brougham on the Dodge chassis this year. The commercial vehicle lineup of Dodge and Graham Brothers models included over six models and numerous funeral vehicles were built on Dodge running gear by various specialty manufacturers.

1923 DODGE

1923 Dodge Brothers, four-door sedan (OCW)

DODGE — SERIES 116 — FOUR: A 1923 Dodge Brothers innovation was the introduction of the automotive industry's first all-steel bodies. A business coupe, introduced in June 1922 (as a 1923 model) was the first car to ever feature this type of construction. The Type B four-door sedan, also featuring an all-steel body, made its debut in September. Other 1923 models were carried over from the previous season with only minor changes in specifications. A number of special, custom-bodied Dodges were also built during the year. Around October 1, the design of the new coupe was updated to include a sun visor and a larger rear window. The Type B business sedan also had a sun visor. The front seat was hinged to fold forward and the rear seat was completely removable. With the seat removed, the rear compartment became a cargo carrying area. The Type A sedan had mohair velvet upholstery. The all-steel Type B business sedan had genuine Spanish leather upholstery.

I.D. DATA: Serial numbers were in the same locations. Starting: 826402. Ending: 1000000. Engine numbers were in the same locations. Engine numbers are not available.

Model No.	Body Type & Seating	Price	Weight	Prod. Total
(Standards)				
Std. A	2-dr. Rds.-2P	850	2375	Note 1
Std. A	4-dr. Tr.-5P	880	2545	Note 1
Std. A	4-dr. Sed.-5P	1440	2990	Note 1
Std. B	2 dr. Bus. Cpe.-2P	980	2590	Note 1
Std. B	4-dr. Bus. Sed.-5P	1195	2965	Note 1
(Customs)				
Cus.	4-dr. Sed.-7P	NA	NA	Note 1
Cus.	2-dr. Lang. Cpe.-4P	NA	NA	Note 1
Cus.	2-dr. C.C. Cpe.-4P	NA	NA	Note 1
Cus.	3-dr. Depot Wag.-7P	NA	NA	Note 1

Note 1: Total calendar year production was 151,000.

ENGINE: Inline. L head. Four. Cast iron block. B & S: 3-7/8 x 4-1/2 in. Disp.: 212.3 cu. in. C.R. 4.0:1. Brake H.P.: 35 @ 2000 R.P.M. N.A.C.C. H.P.: 24.03. Main bearings: three. Valve lifters: slid.

CHASSIS: W.B.: 114 in. Tires: 32 x 4.

TECHNICAL: Selective sliding transmission. Speeds: 3F/1R. Floor shift controls. Multiple dry disc clutch. Shaft drive. Semi-floating rear axle. Two wheel mechanical brakes. Wood spoke wheels.

OPTIONS: Front bumper. Rear bumper. Single sidemount (commercial). Steel disc wheels. Moto-meter. Spare tire. Custom bodies. "Fat Man" steering wheel. Heater. Outside rear view mirror. Runningboard. Luggage rack. Spotlight(s).

HISTORICAL: Introduced June 1922. Industry's first all-steel bodies. Baker enamel finish replaces varnish type paint on all-steel models. Last year for the 114-inch wheelbase. Calendar year registrations: 114,076. Calendar year production: 151,000. Model year production: 171,421.

Dodge was America's sixth best selling car in 1923. A total of 6,971 Dodge/Graham Brothers trucks were made this year. J.T. Cantrell & Co. built a limited number of depot hack bodies for the Dodge chassis. A wide range of Dodge funeral vehicles were also produced.

1924 DODGE

1924 Dodge Brothers, touring (OCW)

DODGE — SERIES 116 — FOUR: This was a year of big changes in Dodge Brothers products. Appearance updates included a taller radiator and a higher hood line. The side hood panels now had vertical louvers. Drum headlights were another new styling feature. The cars had a longer wheelbase and lower overall height. The former three-quarter elliptic springs were replaced with those of semi-elliptic configuration. Inside, the seats were lowered. Gear and brake levers were moved forward, providing more usable leg room. Budd-Michelin steel disc wheels were now available for the roadster, as well as the closed body styles. All closed cars had a flat, slanted sun visor supported by curved corner brackets. A rear brake light was now made standard equipment for all models. Introduced at the New York Automobile Show in January 1924 was a line of "special" models with deluxe equipment features such as nickel-plated radiators, bumpers, automobile windshield wipers, moto-meter type radiator caps and bright metal runningboard step plates. Custom bodies appearing on the 1924 Dodge chassis included an open-drive taxi, enclosed-drive taxi and landau sedan.

I.D. DATA: Serial numbers were in the same locations. Starting: A-1. Ending: A-132706. Engine numbers were in the same location. Engine numbers are not available.

Model No.	Body Type & Seating	Price	Weight	Prod. Total
Std.	2-dr. Rds.-2P	865	2513	Note 1
Std.	4-dr. Tour.-5P	880	2610	Note 1
Std.	2-dr. Bus. Cpe.-2P	1035	2755	Note 1
Std.	2-dr. Cpe.-4P	1375	2809	Note 1
Std.	4 dr. Bus. Sed.-5P	1250	3050	Note 1
Std.	4 dr. Std. Sed.-5P	1385	3098	Note 1
(Special)				
Spec.	2-dr. Rds.-2P	1025	2653	Note 1
Spec.	4-dr. Tour.-5P	1055	2755	Note 1
Spec.	2 dr. Bus. Cpe.-2P	1035	2865	Note 1
Spec.	2-dr. Cpe.-4P	1535	2929	Note 1
Spec.	4-dr. Bus. Sed.-5P	1545	3050	Note 1
Spec.	4-dr. Sed.-5P	1385	3195	Note 1
(Custom Bodies)				
Cus.	4-dr. O.D. Taxi-6P	NA	NA	Note 1
Cus.	4-dr. E.D. Taxi-6P	NA	NA	Note 1
Cus.	4-dr. Lan. Sed.-6P	NA	NA	Note 1

Note 1: Total calendar year production was 193,861.

Note 2: Taxi prices were usually determined by the quantity ordered. Taxi weights depended upon final equipment specifications.

ENGINE: Inline. L-head. Four. Cast iron block. B & S: 3-7/8 x 4-1/2 in. Disp.: 212.3 cu. in. C.R.: 4.0:1. Brake H.P.: 35 @ 2000 R.P.M. Net H.P. 24.03. Main bearings: three. Valve lifters: solid.

CHASSIS: [Standard Series] W.B.: 116 in. Tires: 32 x 4. [Special Series] W.B.: 116 in. Tires: 30 x 5.77.

TECHNICAL: Selective sliding transmission. Speeds: 3F/1R. Floor shift controls. Multiple dry disc clutch. Semi-floating rear axle. Two wheel mechanical brakes. Wood-spoke wheels.

OPTIONS: Front bumper (std. on Spec.). Rear bumper (std. on Spec.) Spare tire. Budd-Michelin steel disc wheels (std. on Spec.). Rear taillight (std. on all). Moto-meter (std. on all). Goodyear balloon tires (std. on Spec.). Runningboard step plates (std. on Spec.). Heater. Outside rear view mirror. Wind wings (open models). Nickel-plated radiator (std. on Spec.). Sidemount spare tire (commercial vehicles). "Fat Man" steering wheel. Spot light(s). Cowl lamps (std. on Spec.). Automatic windshield wiper (std. on Spec.). Custom-built bodies. Deluxe equipment packages.

HISTORICAL: Introduced July 1923. Calendar year registrations: 157,982. Calendar year production: 193,861. Model year production: 207,687. Innovations: New styling. Optional balloon tires. Semi-elliptic rear springs. Increased wheelbase. Increased front seat legroom. Lower center of gravity. Drum headlights. Increased cooling system with 2-1/2 quart capacity.

Dodge regained its former position as third ranked U.S. auto producer. Additional plant expansion was accomplished this year. New Canadian assembly plant starts operation in Walkerville, Ontario. Roy Chapman Andrew took three Dodges on a 10,000 mile fossil-hunting expedition into China and inner Mongolia.

1925 DODGE

DODGE — SERIES 116 — FOUR: The 1925 Dodges looked nearly identical to the previous year's models. New features included automatic windshield wipers, lift-open rear windows, cowl vents and a one-piece windshield. All cars had 20-inch wheels and balloon-type tires. Technical improvements included silichrome exhaust valves, rubber motor mountings and new oil-drain piston rings. Introduced at the New York Automobile Show in January 1925 was a coach (two-door sedan) with a Fisher body. A new "cadet" style sun visor was used on this model. All Dodge Brothers body styles were available with special equipment features at modestly higher prices. The Special equipment again included double bar bumpers and rear fender guards, nickel-plated radiator shell, Budd-Michelin steel disc wheels, a moto-meter type radiator cap, runningboard step plates, rear taillamp, Goodyear balloon tires and cowl lamps on closed body cars. Among custom creations turned out on the 1925 Dodge Brothers chassis were a depot hack type station wagon built by J.T. Cantrell, Inc. and a custom town car built for Thomas J. Doyle, a Dodge distributor in the Detroit area.

1925 Dodge Brothers, four-door sedan (OCW)

I.D. DATA: Serial numbers were located on toe board on either right or left side; also on crossmember under floorboard. Starting: A132707. Ending: A372474. Engine numbers located above carburetor on left side of cylinder block. Engine numbers not available.

Model No.	Body Type & Seating	Price	Weight	Prod. Total
(Standard Line)				
Std.	2-dr. Rds.-2P	855	2494	Note 1
Std.	4-dr. Tr.-5P	885	2591	Note 1
Std.	2-dr. Bus. Cpe.-2P	995	2725	Note 1
Std.	2-dr. Cpe.-4P	1375	2793	Note 1
Std.	4-dr. Bus. Sed.-5P	1095	3011	Note 1
Std.	4-dr. Sed.-5P	1245	3063	Note 1
Std.	2-dr. Coach-5P	1095	2783	Note 1

Model No.	Body Type & Seating	Price	Weight	Prod. Total
(Special Line)				
Spec.	2-dr. Rds.-2P	955	2650	Note 1
Spec.	4-dr. Tr.-5P	985	2750	Note 1
Spec.	2-dr. Bus. Cpe.-2P	1095	2865	Note 1
Spec.	2-dr. Cpe.-4P	1475	2932	Note 1
Spec.	4-dr. Bus. Sed.-5P	1195	3150	Note 1
Spec.	4-dr. Sed.-5P	1330	3195	Note 1
Spec.	2-dr. Coach-5P	1110	2823	Note 1
(Customs)				
Cus.	4-dr. Cant. Sta. Wag.-8P	NA	NA	Note 1
Cus.	4-dr. Twn. Car.-6P	NA	NA	Note 1

Note 1: Total calendar year production was 201,000.

ENGINE: Inline. L-head. Four. Cast iron block. B & S: 3-7/8 x 4-1/2 in. Disp.: 212.3 cu. in. C.R.: 4.0:1. Brake H.P.: 35 @ 2000 R.P.M. Net H.P.: 24.03. Main bearings: three. Valve lifters: solid.

CHASSIS: [Standard series] W.B.: 116 in. Tires: 30 x 5.77. [Special Series] W.B.: 116 in. Tires: 30 x 5.77.

TECHNICAL: Selective sliding gear transmission. Speeds: 3F/1R. Floor shift controls. Multiple dry disc clutch. Semi-floating rear axle. Two-wheel mechanical brakes. Wood-spoke wheels.

OPTIONS: Front bumper (std. on Spec.). Rear bumper (std. on Spec.). Spare tire. Budd-Michelin steel disc wheels (std. on Spec.). Rear taillight (std. on Spec.). Moto-meter (std. on Spec.). Goodyear balloon tires (std. on Spec.). Runningboard step plates (std. on Spec.). Heater. Outside rear view mirror. Wind wings (open models). Nickel-plated radiator (std. on Spec.). Sidemount spare tires (commercial vehicles). "Fat Man" steering wheel. Spotlight(s). Cowl lamps (std. on Spec. closed cars). Automatic windshield wiper (std. on Spec.). Deluxe equipment packages. Whitewall tires.

HISTORICAL: Introduced July 1925. Calendar year registrations: 167,686. Calendar year production: 201,000. Innovations: Automatic wipers. Lift open rear windows. Cowl vents. One-piece windshield. Silichrome exhaust valves. Oil drain piston rings. New 20-inch wheels and balloon tires on all models after November 1, 1924.

Dodge was the fifth best-selling American nameplate this year. A consortium of New York bankers purchased the Dodge Brothers properties for $146 million. E.J. Wilmer was appointed chief executive officer of the company by the new owners.

1926 DODGE

1926 Dodge Brothers, touring (OCW)

DODGE — SERIES 126 — FOUR: There were no major differences in the 1926 Dodges, although the company continued its policy of making running changes and introducing new models during the season. The gearshift pattern was changed to the conventional three-speed "H" system standardized by the Society of Automotive Engineers. This took place about January 1926. Another change was a two-inch reduction in the overall height of the "Type B" all-steel bodied business sedan. In March, the use of the hinged front seat in this model was discontinued. The business sedan and the standard roadster switched to one-piece windshields late in the year, while the standard touring retained a two-piece type. Triple door hinges were used on all 1926 Dodges and the "cadet" style sun visor was used on all closed cars. A new sports roadster was introduced at the New York Automobile Show in January 1926. It had

a dark green finish, natural finish wood spoke wheels, bumpers, kick-plates, nickel radiator shell, gray Spanish leather upholstery, bullet-shaped headlights, a one-piece windshield and a storage compartment built into the rear deck. The two-door sedan or coach was discontinued at mid-year.

I.D. DATA: Serial numbers were located on the toe board on either right or left side; also on crossmember under floorboard. Starting: A372475. Ending: A702242. Engine numbers were located above carburetor on left side of cylinder block. Engine numbers are not available.

Model No.	Body Type & Seating	Price	Weight	Prod. Total
(Standard Line)				
Std.	2 dr. Rds.-2P	855	2475	Note 1
Std.	4 dr. Tour.-5P	875	2565	Note 1
Std.	2-dr. Cpe.-2P	960	2658	Note 1
Std.-A	4-dr. Sed.-5P	1195	3020	Note 1
Std.-B	4 dr. Bus. Sed.-5P	1045	2995	Note 1
Std.	2-dr. Coach-5P	1035	2783	Note 1
(Special Line)				
Spec.	2-dr. Rds.-2P	955	2595	Note 1
Spec.	4-dr. Tour.-5P	975	2695	Note 1
Spec.	2-dr. Cpe.-2P	1060	2718	Note 1
Spec.-A	2-dr. Sed.-5P	1295	3107	Note 1
Spec.-B	4-dr. Bus. Sed.-5P	1145	3077	Note 1
Spec.	2-dr. Coach-5P	1135	2823	Note 1
(Deluxe/Sport Models)				
Del.	2-dr. Spt. Rds.-2P	880	2497	Note 1
Del.	4-dr. Sed.-5P	1075	2930	Note 1
Del.	4-dr. Spt. Tour.-5P	880	2617	Note 1
(Customs)				
Cus.	4-dr. Lan. Sed.-6P	NA	NA	Note 1
Cus.	4-dr. Est. Car.-8p	NA	NA	Note 1

Note 1: Total calendar year production was 265,000.

Note 2: The prices shown for Standard and Special Line models are early year prices. These were reduced by an average of $135 later in the year when the Deluxe and Sport models were introduced.

ENGINE: Inline. L-head. Four. Cast iron block. B & S: 3-7/8 x 4-1/2 in. Disp.: 212.3 cu. in. C.R.: 4.0:1. Brake H.P.: 35 @ 2000 R.P.M. Net H.P. 24.03. Main bearings: three. Valve lifters: solid.

(Special Line)				
Spec.	2-dr. Rds.-2P	955	2595	Note 1
Spec.	4-dr. Tour.-5P	975	2695	Note 1
Spec.	2-dr. Cpe.-2P	1060	2718	Note 1
Spec. A	4 dr. Sed.-5P	1295	3107	Note 1
Spec. B	4-dr. Bus. Sed.-5P	1145	3077	Note 1
Spec.	2-dr. Coach-5P	1135	2823	Note 1
(Deluxe/Sport Models)				
Del.	2-dr. Spt. Rds.-2P	880	2497	Note 1
Del.	4-dr. Sed.-5P	1075	2930	Note 1
Del.	4-dr. Spt. Tour.-5P	880	2617	Note 1
(Customs)				
Cus.	4-dr. Lan. Sed.-6P	NA	NA	Note 1
Cus.	4-dr. Est. Car.-8P	NA	NA	Note 1

Note 1: Total calendar year production was 265,000.

Note 2: The prices shown for Standard and Special Line models are early year prices. These were reduced by an average of $135 later in the year when the Deluxe and Sport models were introduced.

ENGINE: Inline. L-head. Four. Cast iron block. B & S: 3-7/8 x 4-1/2 in. Disp.: 212.3 cu. in. C.R.: 4.0:1. Brake H.P.: 35 @ 2000 R.P.M. Net H.P. 24.03. Main bearings: three. Valve lifters: solid. Carb.: Stromberg one-barrel.

CHASSIS: [Series 126] W.B.: 116 in. Tires: (early) 30 x 5.77; (late) 31 x 5.25.

TECHNICAL: Selective sliding transmission. Speeds: 3F/1R. Floor shift controls. Multiple dry disc clutch. Semi-floating rear axle. Two-wheel mechanical brakes. Wood-spoke wheels.

Note 3: In January 1926, all Dodges switched to 21-inch wheels and larger balloon tires.

OPTIONS: Front bumper. Rear fender guards. Spare tire: Steel disc wheels. Taillight. Moto-meter. Step plates. Outside rear view mirror. Heater. Wind wings (open cars). Nickel-plated radiator. Automatic windshield wiper. Whitewall tires. Special paint. Spotlight(s). Cowl lamps. Nickel-plated headlight rims.

Note 4: Special, Deluxe and Sport models had a front bumper, rear fender guards, disc wheels, taillight, moto-meter, step plates, nickel-plated radiator and automatic windshield wiper as standard equipment. Special models and early De-luxe sedans had nickel-plated headlight rims. Sport models and late Deluxe sedans had new bullet-shaped headlights with nickel-plated rims.

HISTORICAL: Introduced July 1925. Calendar year registrations: 219,446. Calendar year production: 265,000. Model year production: 249,869. Innovations: Two-unit six-volt electrical system introduced. SAE standard "H" gearshift pattern introduced. Bullet-shaped headlights on Sport and late Deluxe models. Triple door hinges on all Dodge Brothers cars.

Dodge came in fourth in the U.S. auto sales race this season. Custom models included a padded top, oval rear quarter-window landau sedan built by E.J. Thompson Co. of Pittsburgh, Pennsylvania, and a wood-bodied estate car, with cane accent panels, built by H.H. Babcock Co., of Watertown, New York. The Graham Brothers resigned from Dodge Brothers to begin a new firm known as Graham-Paige.

1927 DODGE

1927 Dodge Brothers, four-door sedan (OCW)

1927 Dodge Brothers, Special, coupe (HAC)

DODGE — SERIES 126/124 — FOUR: In the appearance department, 1927 Dodges were much the same as in the past. Standard models had painted radiators and no cowl lamps. Special models had nickel-plated radiators, cowl lamps, moto-meters, runningboard step plates, bumpers, and drum headlights with nickel-plated rims. Deluxe and Sport models had special equipment plus bullet-shaped headlamps. New body styles included a convertible cabriolet introduced in April and an all-purpose sedan. The latter model was built by Millspaugh & Irish Corp. of Indianapolis. It had a curb-side opening rear door similar to the type used on sedan deliveries and panel trucks. Standard equipment on 1927 Dodges included a speedometer, ammeter, electric horn, coincidental lock, bumpers (extra cost on std.), rear tire carrier, headlamp dimmer, inside rear view mirror, tool kit and jack. Special models also had an exhaust body heater. The Special coupe was now of the three-window type. The new convertible cabriolet was built for only 2-1/2 months. It had genuine Spanish leather upholstery, landau irons, door glass window regulators, a rumble seat and Armory green finish.

I.D. DATA: Serial numbers were located on toe board on either side and also on the crossmember under the floorboard. First series (126) serial

numbers were A702243 to A875379. Second series (124) serial numbers were A875380 to A934104. Engine numbers were located above carburetor on left side of cylinder block. Engine numbers are not available.

Model No.	Body Type & Seating	Price	Weight	Prod. Total
(Std.)				
Std.	2-dr. Rds.-2P	795	2448	Note 1
Std.	4-dr. Tour.-5P	795	2584	Note 1
Std.	2-dr. Cpe.-2P	845	2568	Note 1
Std.	4-dr. Sed.-5P	895	2816	Note 1
(Spec.)				
Spec.	2-dr. Rds.-2P	845	2541	Note 1
Spec.	4-dr. Tr.-5P	845	2669	Note 1
Spec.	2-dr. Cpe.-2P	895	2672	Note 1
Spec.	4-dr. Sed.-5P	975	2893	Note 1
Spec.	4-dr. AP Sed.-5P	1245	NA	Note 1
(Del./Spt.)				
Del.	4-dr. Sed.-5P	1075	2609	Note 1
Spt.	2-dr. Rds.-2/4P	975	2604	Note 1
Spt.	4-dr. Tr.-5P	895	2633	Note 1
Del.	2-dr. Cabr.-2/4P	995	2727	Note 1
(Custom)				
Cus.	2-dr. Clb. Cpe.-4P	[4951]	NA	Note 1

Note 1: Total calendar year production was 146,000.

Note 2: The Custom club coupe was built by Pioneer Body Co. of Sidney, Ohio, and the price shown in brackets is the price of the body only. There was also a $30 destination change.

ENGINE: Inline. L-head. Four. Cast iron block. B & S: 3-7/8 x 4-1/2 in. Disp.: 212.3 cu. in. C.R.: [Series 126] 4.0:1; [Series 124] 4.1:1. Brake H.P.: 35 @ 2000 R.P.M. Net H.P.: 24.03. Main bearings: five. Valve lifters: solid.

CHASSIS: W.B.: 116 in. Tires: 31 x 5.25.

TECHNICAL: Selective sliding transmission. Speeds: 3F/1R. Floor shift controls. Multiple dry disc clutch. Semi-floating rear axle. Two-wheel mechanical brakes. Wood-spoke wheels.

Note 3: Wire wheels were standard equipment on the convertible cabriolet.

OPTIONS: Front bumper. Rear bumper. Spare tire. Spare tire cover. Steel disc wheels. Wire wheels (std. on cabriolet). Taillight. Outside rear view mirror. Heater. Automatic windshield wipers. Moto-meter. Wind wings. Nickel-plated radiator. Nickel-plated headlight rims. Spotlight(s). Cowl lamps. Step plates. Special colors. Trunk rack. Touring trunk.

Note 4: Special equipment features were again standard on some Special, Deluxe and Sport models.

HISTORICAL: Introduced [Series 126] July 1926-January 1927 [Series 124] January 1927-July 1927. Calendar year registrations: 123,918. Calendar year production: 146,000. Model year production: 146,001. Innovations: [Series 126] Five main bearing crankshaft. New instrument panel with white faced gauges having black figures. [Series 124] Four-point engine mounting. Nickel-plated drum headlights. Higher compression ratio. New convertible cabriolet produced between April 25, 1927, and August 7, 1927, then discontinued.

Dodge slipped to seventh position on the U.S. auto sales charts this season. The Graham Brothers truck factory built all 1927 Dodge commercial vehicles. This was to be the last full season that the New York based banking firm Dillon, Read and Co. would retain ownership of the Dodge Brothers name and facilities.

1927-28 DODGE

DODGE SENIOR — SERIES 2249 — SIX: The Dodge Senior Six Series was the first of three new lines that the company introduced in late 1927 for the 1928 model year. Appearance features included a narrow, nickel-plated radiator shell, new horizontal hood louvers, double body bead moldings and swinging type windshields. The Senior Six was aimed at the high-priced market and had a 116-inch wheelbase. Standard equipment included a Stromberg carburetor, NorthEast ignition, four-wheel hydraulic brakes, worm and sector steering and an I-beam front axle. The Senior Six entered production in May 1927.

DODGE FAST FOUR — SERIES 128 — FOUR: The Dodge Fast Four (or Fastest Four) Model 128 was the second of three new lines that were introduced in late 1927 for the 1928 model year. Appearance features

on these cars included "cadet" type sun visors, new lower bodies, a shorter wheelbase, new type body molding and vertical hood louvers. These cars looked similar to earlier four-cylinder Dodges but had more rounded rear roof corners and window openings, "cadet" type visors, lower body sills and a slightly concave type of A-pillar that blended more smoothly into the cowl area. Standard, Special and Deluxe trim models were available. Standard equipment included a Stewart carburetor, NorthEast ignition, mechanical two-wheel brakes, speedometer, ammeter, horn, coincidental lock, rear tire carrier, headlamp dimmer, inside rear view mirror, tool kit and jack. This series entered production in July 1927.

DODGE FAST FOUR — SERIES 129 — FOUR: The Dodge Fast Four Model 129 was the last of three new lines that were introduced in late 1927 for the 1928 model year. These cars were the same as those in the Fast Four Model 128 series except they now had four wheel steeldraulic brakes. This increased the shipping weights of some models although prices did not change. This series entered production in August 1927.

I.D. DATA: [Series 2249] Serial numbers were located on a plate on the toe board near the steering column; also stamped on right front frame, below fender. Starting: 1S10001. Ending: 1S29156. Engine numbers were located on the left rear side of cylinder block, right side of cylinder block and right side (either front or rear) below exhaust manifold. Starting: S10001. Ending: S25109. [Series 128] Serial numbers were in the same locations. Starting: A934105. Ending: A961722. Engine numbers were in the same locations. Starting: A1005968. Ending: A1037113. [Series 129] Serial numbers were in the same locations. Starting: A961723. Ending: A1019544. Engine numbers were in the same locations. Starting: A1037114. Ending: A1104269.

Model No.	Body Type & Seating	Price	Weight	Prod. Total
2249	2-dr. Cpe.-2P	1495	3236	NA
2249	2-dr. Cpe.-4P	1570	3315	NA
2249	2-dr. Cabr.-2/4P	1595	3353	NA
2249	4-dr. Sed.-5P	1595	3421	NA
128	2-dr. Cpe.-2P	855	2428	NA
128	2-dr. Spl. Cpe.-2P	895	2725	NA
128	2-dr. Cabr.-2/4P	955	2463	NA
128	4-dr. Sed.-5P	875	2600	NA
128	4-dr. Spl. Sed.-5P	945	2924	NA
128	4-dr. Del. Sed.-5P	950	2609	NA
129	2-dr. Cpe.-2P	855	2486	NA
129	2-dr. Spl. Cpe.-2P	895	2725	NA
129	2-dr. Cabr.-2/4P	955	2521	NA
129	4-dr. Sed.-5P	875	2694	NA
129	4-dr. Spl. Sed.-5P	945	2924	NA
129	4-dr. Del. Sed.-5P	950	2695	NA

ENGINE: [Series 2249] Inline. L-head. Six. Cast iron block. B & S: 3- 1/4 x 4-1/2 in. Disp.: 224.3 cu. in. C.R.: 5.3:1. Brake H.P.: 60 @ 2800 R.P.M. Net H.P.: 25.34. Valve lifters: solid. Carb.: Stromberg one-barrel. [Series 128] Inline. L-head. Four. Cast iron block. B & S: 3-7/8 x 4-1/2 in. Disp.: 212.3 cu. in. C.R.: 4.1:1. Brake H.P.: 44 @ 2700 R.P.M. Net H.P.: 24.03. Main bearings: five. Valve lifters: solid. Carb.: Stewart one-barrel. [Series 129] See Series 128 engine specifications.

CHASSIS: [Series 2249] W.B.: 116 in. Tires: 31 x 6. [Series 128] W.B.: 108 in. Tires: 29 x 5. [Series 129] W.B.: 108 in. Tires: 29 x 5.

TECHNICAL: Selective sliding gear transmission. Speeds: 3F/1R. Floor shift controls. Single plate dry disc clutch. Hotchkiss drive. Overall ratio: [128/129] 3.76:1; [2249] 4.45:1. [128] Two-wheel mechanical brakes [129] Four-wheel steeldraulic brakes; [2249] Four-wheel hydraulic brakes. Wood-spoke or wire wheels.

OPTIONS: Front bumper. Rear bumper. Spare tire. Dual sidemounts (Senior Six sport models). Sidemount cover(s). Moto-meter. Wood spoke wheels. Wire wheels. Heater. Nickel-plated radiator. Nickel headlight rims. Nickel-plated headlight buckets. Taillight(s). Outside rear view mirror. Spotlight(s). Cowl lamps. Steel disc wheels. Trunk rack. Touring trunk. Automatic windshield wiper. Special paint colors. Wind wings (open models).

HISTORICAL: Introduced: [2249] May 1927; [128] July 1927, [129] August 1927.

Note: For calendar year production information see 1927 section. No separate breakout is available for the early 1928 (1927-1928) series. All of the cars in this series were built during the 1927 calendar year. Innovations: New Dodge Six. Steel body framework eliminated; new construction features welded inner reinforcement panels. Four wheel hydraulic brakes on Senior Six. Hotchkiss drive. Four-point motor suspension.

1928 DODGE

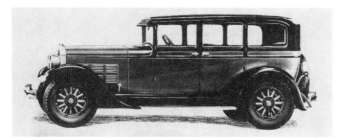

1928 Dodge Brothers, Senior Six, four-door sedan (OCW)

DODGE VICTORY — SERIES 130/131 — SIX: The Victory Six entered production in November 1927 and was introduced on January 7, 1928, at the New York Automobile Show. These all-new cars were recognized as the fastest and smartest vehicles in their price class available from an American automaker. They had a 1-1/2 inch wheelbase. Victory Six bodies were built by the Budd Manufacturing Co. and featured a prominent beltline molding that ran entirely around the back of the cars, small sun visors and round cornered windows. The hood had four separate groups of vertical louvers inside a raised rectangular panel. There were three louvers in each of the first three groups and two louvers in the rearmost group. Other features included nickel-plated drum type headlights, nickel-plated radiators and one-piece crown fenders. The difference between the 130 and 131 series was that the latter had larger wheels for added road clearance. Standard equipment on all Victory Sixes included NorthEast ignition, internal hydraulic brakes, a large frame, Zerk chassis lubrication and aluminum alloy pistons. Deluxe/Sport equipment included bumpers, sidemount spares and wire wheels.

DODGE SENIOR — SERIES 2251/2252 — SIX: In January 1928, the Senior Six received a few changes and became a "true" 1928 series designated with the number 2251. One change was the addition of sport models with welled fenders, sidemount spares, wire spoke wheels, larger headlamps with a nickel-plated tie-bar and vertical stanchions, cowl lamps, a nickel-plated cowl molding and folding trunk rack. The sport sedan was the first to appear. It debuted in January. Sport equipment became available for other body styles later in the year. There was also a change in the engine, which increased its horsepower to 68. When equipped with standard size tires, the Senior Six was designated Series 2251; with oversize tires, Series 2252.

1928 Dodge Brothers, Victory Six, sedan (JAC)

DODGE STANDARD — SERIES 140/141 — SIX: The Standard Six was the third new line from Dodge and was offered in two Series 140 and 141, the latter using larger wheels for improved road clearance. These cars had 22 multiple vertical hood louvers, cadet type sun visors and painted drum type headlights. Standard equipment included a NorthEast ignition system, steeldraulic brakes and a starting system with the starter control mounted on the instrument board. The rumbleseat cabriolet came with "sport" type equipment including nickel-plated drum headlights and wire spoke wheels. The sedan also came in "deluxe" type trim with contrasting body color and nickel-plated drum headlights. These cars entered production in March 1928 and were introduced on April 27, 1928, with additional body styles added later in the year.

I.D. DATA: [Series 130/131] Serial numbers were in the same location. Starting: M1. Ending: M51929. Engine numbers were in the same location. Starting: M10001. Ending: M69396. [Series 2251/2252] Serial numbers and engine numbers were continued from 1927-28. See number listed in the previous section. [Series 140/141] Serial numbers were in the same locations. Starting: J1. Ending: J42686. Engine numbers were in the same locations. Starting: J10001. Ending: J55556.

Model No.	Body Type & Seating	Price	Weight	Prod. Total
130-1	4-dr. Tour.-5P	1030	2785	NA
130-1	2-dr. Cpe.-2P	1045	2660	NA
130-1	2-dr. Cpe.-4P	1170	2860	NA
130-1	2-dr. Brgm.-5P	1170	2849	NA
130-1	4-dr. Sed.-5P	1095	2767	NA
130-1	4-dr. Del. Sed.-5P	1170	2867	NA
2251-2	2-dr. Cpe.-2P	1495	3236	NA
2251-2	2-dr. Spt. Cpe.-2/4P	1725	3410	NA
2251-2	2-dr. Clb. Cpe.-4P	1570	3315	NA
2251-2	2-dr. Spt. Clb. Cpe.-4P	1800	3495	NA
2251 2	2-dr. Cabr.-2/4P	1595	3353	NA
2251-2	2-dr. Spt. Cabr.-2/4P	1720	3533	NA
2251-2	4-dr. Sed.-5P	1595	3421	NA
2251-2	4-dr. Spt. Sed.-5P	1770	3643	NA
140-1	2-dr. Cpe.-2P	875	2502	NA
140 1	2-dr. Spt. Cabr.-2/4P	945	2585	NA
140-1	4-dr. Sed.-5P	895	2721	NA
140-1	4-dr. Del. Sed.-5P	970	2790	NA

ENGINE: [Series 130/131] Inline. L-head. Six. Cast iron block. B & S: 3-3/8 x 3-7/8 in. Disp.: 208 cu. in. C.R.: 5.2:1. Brake H.P.: 58 @ 3000 R.P.M. Net H.P.: 27.34. Valve lifters: solid. Carb.: Stromberg one-barrel. [Series 2251/2252] Inline. L-head. Six. Cast iron block. B & S: 3-1/4 x 4-1/2 in. Disp.: 224 cu. in. Brake H.P.: 68 @ 2800 R.P.M. Net H.P.: 25.34. Valve lifters: solid. Carb.: Stromberg one-barrel. [Series 140/141] Inline. L-head. Six. Cast iron block. B & S: 3-3/8 x 3-7/8 in. Disp.: 208 cu. in. Brake H.P.: 58 @ 3000 R.P.M. Net H.P.: 27.3. Valve lifters: solid. carb.: Stromberg one-barrel.

CHASSIS: [Victory Six] W.B.: 112 in. Tires: 29 x 5. [Senior Six] W.B.: 116 in. Tires: 31 x 6. [Standard Six] W.B.: 110 in. Tires: 29 x 5.00.

TECHNICAL: Selective sliding transmission. Speeds: 3F/1R. Column shift controls. Single plate dry disc clutch. Semi-floating rear axle. Overall ratio: [Victory] 4.45:1, [Senior] 4.45:1, [Standard] 4.45:1. [Standard] Steeldraulic brakes; (others) hydraulic brakes. Wood-spoke or wire-spoke wheels. Hotchkiss drive.

OPTIONS: Front bumper. Rear bumper. Spare tire. Dual sidemount. Sidemount cover(s). Nickel-plated headlights. Wire-spoke wheels. Steel disc wheels. Heater. Moto-meter. Outside rear view mirror. Special paint colors. Oversize tires and wheels. Taillight(s). Spotlight(s). Cowl lamps. Wind wings. Trunk rack. Touring trunk.

HISTORICAL: Introduced January 1928; (Standard Six) March 1928. Calendar year registrations: 149,004. Calendar year sales: 67,327.
Note: The above calendar year totals also include 1929 (model year) cars built during calendar year 1928. Innovations: Senior Six sport models introduced. All-new Victory Six series introduced. All-new Standard Six series introduced. Horsepower of Senior Series six-cylinder engine increased. New aluminum alloy pistons in Victory engine.

HISTORY: Walter P. Chrysler purchased Dodge from Dillon, Read & Co. (a New York banking firm) for a $170 million stock exchange merger on July 30, 1928. This led to a major reorganization of the company and caused Dodge to drop to 13th sales rank in the U.S. auto industry.

1928-29 DODGE

DODGE STANDARD — SERIES J — SIX: Beginning in July 1928, the Dodge Standard Six line was carried over as a "new" series for the first part of the 1929 model year. There were no major changes in specifications from the 1928 Standard Six, except that the shipping weights of two models increased slightly for an undetermined reason. A new molding, running from the radiator to the windshield pillar, was added on these cars and fender beading was slightly changed. Beginning in September, bullet headlights were used on cabriolets and sedans.

DODGE VICTORY — SERIES M — SIX: Beginning in July 1928, the Dodge Victory Six line was also carried over as a "new" series for the first part of the 1929 model year. There were no major changes in specifications from the 1928 Victory Six, except that prices were lowered and several new body styles were added. These cars had lower, longer bodies with three-inch wider doors and smaller rear quarter windows on sedans.

DODGE SENIOR — SERIES S — SIX: New styling was used on Senior Sixes marketed after July 1928 as "new" first series 1929 models. Appearance features included a new, higher radiator shell, vertical hood louvers, automatic radiator shutters, cadet type sun visors and a new type instrument panel with silver finish. Standard equipment included a larger, more powerful six-cylinder engine, NorthEast ignition, hydraulic brakes, Lovejoy shock absorbers and a new type emergency brake handle. These cars also had automatic windshield wipers, complete gauges, front and rear bumpers, a cigar lighter, two smoking cases and interior courtesy lamps. Rich interior appointments included plush velvet mohair upholstery, a mahogany finish steering wheel, rear door assist straps and the frosted silver dash treatment. The Senior Six wheelbase also increased four inches, bringing a corresponding increase in overall body proportions.

I.D. DATA: [Series J] Serial numbers were in the same locations. Starting: J42687. Ending: J75519. Engine numbers were in the same locations. Starting: J55557. Ending: J91561. [Series M] Serial numbers were in the same locations. Starting: M51930. Ending: M87759. Engine numbers were in the same locations. Starting: M69397. Ending: M128387. [Series S] Serial numbers were in the same locations. Starting: S50001. Ending: S60487. Engine numbers were in the same locations. Starting: S60001. Ending: S70595.

Model No.	Body Type & Seating	Price	Weight	Prod. Total
J	2-dr. Cpe.-2P	875	2515	NA
J	2-dr. Cabr.-2/4P	945	2585	NA
J	4-dr. Sed.-5P	895	2721	NA
J	4-dr. Del. Sed.-5P	970	2827	NA
M	2-dr. Rds.-2/4P	995	2673	NA
M	4-dr. Tr.-5P	995	2703	NA
M	2-dr. Cpe.-2P	1045	2629	NA
M	2-dr. Del. Cpe.-4P	1170	2860	NA
M	4-dr. Sed.-5P	1095	2870	NA
M	4-dr. Del. Sed.-5P	1170	2943	NA
M	4-dr. Spt. Sed.-5P	1295	3100	NA
S	2-dr. Rds.-2/4P	1615	3303	NA
S	2-dr. Cpe.-2P	1545	3389	NA
S	2-dr. Spt. Cpe.-2/4P	1627	3438	NA
S	2-dr. Brgm. Vic.-5P	1575	3468	NA
S	2-dr. Sed.-5P	1495	3403	NA
S	4-dr. Sed.-5P	1545	3507	NA
S	4-dr. Lan. Sed.-5P	1595	3470	NA
S	4-dr. Spt. Sed.-5P	1795	3719	NA

ENGINE: [Series J] See 1928 Standard Six engine specifications. [Series M] See 1928 Victory Six engine specifications. [Series S] Inline. L-head, Six. Cast iron block. B & S: 3-3/8 x 4-1/2 in. Disp.: 241.6 cu. in. C.R. 5.2:1. Brake H.P.: 78 @ 3000 R.P.M. Net H.P.: 27.34. Valve lifters: solid. Carb.: Stromberg one-barrel.

CHASSIS: [Standard Six] W.B.: 110 in. Tires: 29 x 5.00. [Victory Six] W.B.: 112 in. Tires: 29 x 5.00. [Senior Six] W.B.: 120 in. Tires: 31 x 6.00.

TECHNICAL: Lightweight selective sliding gear transmission. Speeds 3F/1R. Floor shift controls. Single plate dry disc clutch. Semi-floating rear axle. Overall ratio: (all) 4.45:1. (std.) Steeldraulic brakes, (others) hydraulic brakes. Wood-spoke or wire-spoke wheels. Hotchkiss drive.

OPTIONS: Front bumper. Rear bumper. Spare tire. Dual sidemounts. Gordon sidemount cover(s): Nickel-plated headlamps. Wire-spoke wheels. Steel disc wheels. Heater. Moto-meter. Cigar lighter. Ouside rear view mirror. Special paint colors. Oversize tires and wheels. Spotlight(s). Cowl lamps. Wind wings. Dual taillights. Trunk rack. Touring trunk. Clock. Dual chrome trumpet horns. Trippe lights. Trunk cover.

HISTORICAL: Introduced July 1928.
Note: The cars in these series were built during calendar year 1928. For production information, see the 1928 section.

INNOVATIONS: Corrosion resistant fenders introduced. Styling refinements on Standard Six. Larger, lower bodies on Victory Six. Senior Six has longer wheelbase, Lovejoy shock absorbers, automatic radiator shutters and larger bore engine with increased horsepower. The Standard Six and Victory Six were discontinued in December 1928, while the Senior Six was carried over, until June 1929, as a First Series 1929 line.

1929 DODGE

1929 Dodge Brothers, Standard Six, four-door sedan (OCW)

DODGE — SERIES DA — SIX: The DA Six was an offshoot of the Victory Six. New styling characteristics reflective of the Chrysler design influence were headlamps mounted on a bowed tie-bar and a narrow, bright metal molding attached to the rear edge of the hood. The hood was longer, the fenders were of one-piece full crown design and the bodies were of monopiece construction. Chromium plating was used on exterior hardware, in place of nickel-plating. Standard equipment included NorthEast ignition, a gasoline filter, Lovejoy shock absorbers and a new exhaust manifold that ran to the front of the motor instead of the rear. The DAs had new bowl-shaped headlights that were painted on standard models and chrome-plated on sporty or Deluxe cars.

1929 Dodge Brothers, Victory Six, brougham (HAC)

1929 Dodge Brothers, Senior Six, two-door sedan (HAC)

DODGE SENIOR — SERIES S — SIX: Beginning in January 1929, the Dodge Senior Six line was carried over as a "second series" 1929 offering. There were no basic alterations in styling or engineering features. Serial numbers, models, prices, weights and engine specifications were identical to those listed for 1928-29 models. Refer to the previous section for information.

I.D. DATA: Serial numbers were in the same locations. Starting: DA1. Ending: DA83714. Engine numbers were in the same locations. Starting Engine No.: H1001. Ending: H99485.

Model No.	Body Type & Seating	Price	Weight	Prod. Total
DA	2-dr. Rds.-2/4P	995	2695	NA
DA	4-dr. Phae.-5P	1025	2730	NA
DA	2-dr. Bus. Cpe.-2P	945	2770	NA
DA	2-dr. Del. Cpe.-2/4P	1025	2812	NA
DA	2-dr. Vic. Cpe.-4P	1025	2831	NA
DA	2-dr. Brgm.-5P	995	2830	NA
DA	4-dr. Sed.-5P	995	2900	NA
DA	4-dr. Del. Sed.-5P	1065	2920	NA

ENGINE: Inline. L-head. Six. Cast iron block. B & S: 3-3/8 x 3-7/8 in. Disp.: 208 cu. in. C.R.: 5.2:1. Brake H.P.: 63 @ 3000 R.P.M. Net H.P.: 27.34. Valve lifters: solid. Carb.: Stromberg one-barrel.

CHASSIS: [DA Six] W.B.: 112 in. Tires: 29 x 5.00. [Senior Six] W.B.: 120 in. Tires: 31 x 6.00.

TECHNICAL: Selective sliding gear transmission. Speeds: 3F/1R. Floor shift controls. Single plate dry disc clutch. Semi-floating rear axle. Overall ratio: [DA Six] 4.45:1 to 4.72:1. [Senior Six] 4.45:1. Hydraulic brakes. Wood-spoke or wire-spoke wheels. Hotchkiss drive.

OPTIONS: Front bumper. Rear bumper. Spare tire. Dual sidemounts. Gordon sidemount cover(s). Plated headlamps. Wire wheels. Motometer. Heater. Clock. Cigar lighter. Outside rear view mirror. Special paint colors. Wind wings. Spotlight(s). Cowl lamps. Dual taillights. Trunk rack. Touring trunk. Dual chrome trumpet horns. Trippe lights. Trunk cover. Whitewall tires. Chrome hood molding. Rear windscreen (phaeton).

HISTORICAL: Introduced January 1929. Calendar year registrations: 115,774. Calendar year production: 124,557.
Note: The above calendar year totals also include 1930 (model year) cars built during calendar year 1929.

MODEL YEAR PRODUCTION: 121,457.
Note: The preceding model year production figure includes cars built in calendar 1929 as 1930 models. Innovations: Chrysler influence reflected in design of new DA Six. Horsepower on small six increased. Shock absorbers on smaller Dodge DA series. New pastel colors available. Dodge first in U.S. industry to adopt downdraft carburetors. Dodge sales improved considerably. The company was America's seventh ranked automaker of 1929 on both calendar and model year basis. Production of the DA Six continued into March 1930, while the S Series Senior Six was replaced by a new DB Series Senior Six in June of 1929. The DB is considered a 1930 model.

1929-30 DODGE

DODGE — SERIES DA — SIX: Starting July 1, 1929, the DA Six was redesignated a "first series" 1930 Dodge. One new model was added to the line and the shipping weights for several other body styles changed slightly. Gemmer worm and sector type steering gear was now listed as a feature of these cars. General specifications were, however, the same as 1929 models.

DODGE SENIOR — SERIES DB — SIX: A new series in Dodge's "first series" 1930 model lineup was the DB Senior Six. It was introduced in July 1929. Specifications and appearance features were basically the same as those for the 1929 Senior Six. New technical features included a four-speed transmission and rubber mounted engine suspension system. In the styling department, chrome-plated vertical supports were added below the headlights. Standard equipment included NorthEast ignition, hydraulic brakes, Lovejoy shock absorbers and automatic radiator shutters.

I.D. DATA: [Series DA] Serial numbers were in the same locations. Starting: DA83715. Ending: DA123481. Engine numbers were in the same locations. Starting: H99486. Ending: H149821. [Series DB] Serial numbers were in the same locations. Starting: DB1. Ending: DB2999. Engine numbers were in the same locations. Starting: 0-1. Ending: 0-3019.

DA	2-dr. Rds.-2/4P	995	2687	NA
DA	4-dr. Phae.-5P	1025	2730	NA
DA	2-dr. Bus. Cpe.-2P	945	2750	NA
DA	2-dr. Del. Cpe.-2/4P	1025	2812	NA
DA	2-dr. Cpe. Vic.-4P	1025	2846	NA

Model No.	Body Type & Seating	Price	Weight	Prod. Total
DA	2-dr. Sed.-5P	925	2876	NA
DA	2-dr. Brgm.-5P	995	2834	NA
DA	4-dr. Sed.-5P	995	2867	NA
DA	4-dr. Del. Sed.-5P	1065	2898	NA
DB	2-dr. Rds.-2/4P	1615	3303	NA
DB	2-dr. Cpe.-2/4P	1595	3426	NA
DB	2-dr. Brgm. Vic.-5P	1545	3419	NA
DB	4-dr. Sed.-5P	1595	3513	NA

ENGINE: [Series DA] See 1929 DA Series engine specifications. [Series DB] See 1929 Senior Six Series engine specifications.

CHASSIS: [DA Series] W.B.: 112 in. Tires: 19 x 5.50. [DB Series] W.B.: 120 in. Tires: 19 x 6.00.

TECHNICAL: Selective sliding gear transmission. Speeds: [DA] 3F/1R, [DB] 4F/1R. Floor shift controls. Single-plate dry disc clutch. Semi-floating rear axle. Overall ratio: (both) 4.72:1. Hydraulic brakes. Wood spokes or wire spoke wheels.

OPTIONS: Front bumper. Rear bumper. Spare tire. Dual sidemounts. Sidemount cover(s). Wire spoke wheels. Trunk rack. Touring trunk. Heater. Clock. Cigar lighter. Spotlight(s). Cowl lamps. Trunk cover. Dual windshield wipers. Outside rear view mirror. Chrome-plated headlamps. Twin wipers. Twin taillights. Twin trumpet horns. Special paint colors. Wind wings.
Note: Some of these accessories were standard equipment on DeLuxe models.

HISTORICAL: Introduced July 1, 1929. See 1929 section for calendar year production figures. Model year production figures same as 1930. Innovations: Four-speed transmission on Series DB Senior Six. Also, four-point engine mounting system. Both the DA and DB Series were continued into calendar year 1930. The Dodge DA Six was produced until March 1930. The Dodge DB Six was produced until June 1930.

1930 DODGE

1930 Dodge Six, Series DD, convertible coupe (JAC)

DODGE — SERIES DD — SIX: Introduced in January 1930, the DD Six was an all-new, "second series" 1930 Dodge car line. Appearance characteristics included a smaller 109-inch wheelbase, monopiece body construction, wider radiator and a V.V. (vision and ventilating) type windshield. Early DD models had uniform size vertical hood louvers and no cowl lamps. Later DD models also had vertical hood louvers, but the louvers grew smaller in size towards the front and the rear. This gave them an arch-like pattern. The later cars also had cowl lamps. Headlamps were of the bowl type with the buckets finished in black enamel and trimmed with chrome-plated rims. They were mounted on a bow-shaped, chrome plated tie-bar. Standard equipment included NorthEast ignition, hydraulic brakes, AC fuel pump, new type instrument panel and a three-spoke steering wheel.

DODGE — SERIES DA — SIX: After January 1, the Dodge DA Six continued to be produced and sold as part of the "second series" 1930 line. There are no separate serial number breakouts for the cars built between January and the end of production in March. Appearance and equipment features, models, prices, weights and engine specifications are believed to be the same as listed in the 1929 section for this series.

DODGE — SERIES DC — EIGHT: The new Dodge DC Eight was said to be "more attractive, more powerful, longer and roomier." It was brought out in January 1930, despite the worsening depression in America. Appearance characteristics included all-steel monopiece body construction, a wide shell radiator, chrome-plated bowl-shaped headlights, a chrome-plated bow-shaped headlight tie-bar and cowl lamps. The hood had vertical louvers that were fatter than those used on sixes. They formed an arch pattern, top and bottom, as they grew progressively smaller towards the front and rear. The eights measured a sizable 163 inches overall and were mounted on a 114-inch wheelbase. Standard equipment included Delco-Remy ignition, hydraulic brakes, a new type slanting windshield, new instrument panel, AC fuel pump, hydraulic shock absorbers, three-spoke steering wheel, rubber shackled springs, wood-spoke wheels and a rumbleseat in the roadster and convertible. A badge at the upper center of the radiator read "DODGE 8." Six wheel equipment (with wire wheels) was standard with phaetons.

1930 Dodge Eight, Series DC, four-door sedan (JAC)

DODGE SENIOR — SERIES DB — SIX: After January 1, the Dodge DB Senior Six continued to be produced and sold as part of the 1930 "second series" line. There are no separate serial number breakouts for the cars built between January and the end of production in June. Appearance and equipment features, models, prices, weights and engine specifications are believed to be the same as listed in the 1929 section covering this series.

ENGINE: [Series DD] For the new 1930 models, Dodge adopted the Fedco serial numbering system. Fedco plates were mounted on the center of the instrument panel, above the instruments. Conventional numbers were also used. Conventional numbers were in the same locations on a plate on the toe board, also on a plate on the right front door hinge pillar post and also on the frame below the right front fender. For DD models the Fedco numbers were D001WP to D255P0 and the conventional numbers were 3500001 to 3504188. Engine numbers were on the right rear side of cylinder block below exhaust manifold. Starting: DD1001. Ending: DD32787. [Series DC] Serial numbers were in the same location as on the DD sixes. Starting: (Fedco) E001WC; (conventional) 4500001. Ending: (Fedco) E191HY; (conventional) 4501083. Engine numbers were in the same location as on the DD sixes. Starting: DC1001. Ending: DC22400.

Model No.	Body Type & Seating	Price	Weight	Prod. Total
DD	2-dr. Rds.-2/4P	855	2462	772
DD	2-dr. Bus. Cpe.-2P	835	2534	3877
DD	2-dr. Cpe.-2/4P	855	2603	3363
DD	2-dr. Conv. Cpe.-2/4P	935	2605	620
DD	4-dr. Sed.-5P	865	2668	33,432
DD	Chassis	NA	NA	899

Note 1: Total series production was 42,963. (This includes DD sixes sold as 1931 models).

DC	2-dr. Rds.-2/4P	1095	2802	598
DC	4-dr. Phae.-5P	1225	2960	234
DC	2-dr. Cpe.-2/4P	1125	2981	2999
DC	2-dr. Conv. Cpe.-2/4P	1195	2938	728
DC	4-dr. Sed.-5P	1145	3043	20,315
DC	Chassis	NA	NA	253

Note 1: Total series production was 25,127. (This includes DC eights sold as 1931 models.)

ENGINE: [Series DD] Inline. L-head. Six. Cast iron block. B & S: 3-1/8 x 4-1/8 in. Disp.: 189.8 cu. in. C.R.: 5.2:1. Brake H.P.: 60 @ 3400 R.P.M. Net H.P.: 23.44. Main bearings: four. Valve lifters: solid. Carb.: Carter one-barrel. Torque: 120 lb.-ft. @ 1200 R.P.M. [Series DC] Inline. L-head. Eight. Cast iron block. B & S: 2-7/8 x 4-1/2 in. Disp.: 220.7 cu. in. C.R.: 5.4:1. Brake H.P.: 75 @ 3400 R.P.M. Net H.P.: 26.45. Main bearings: five. Valve lifters: solid. Carb.: Stromberg. Torque: 145 lb.-ft. @ 1400 R.P.M.

CHASSIS: [Series DD Six] W.B.: 109 in. O.L.: 155-7/8 in. Tires: 19 x 5.00 [Series DA Six] W.B.: 112 in. Tires: 19 x 5.50. [Series DC Eight] W.B.: 114 in. O.L.: 163 in. Tires: 18 x 5.50. [Series DB Senior Six] W.B.: 120 in. Tires: 19 x 6.00.

TECHNICAL: Selective sliding transmission. Speeds: [DB] 4F/1R; [others] 3F/1R. Floor shift controls. Single plate dry disc clutch. Semi-floating rear axle. Overall ratio: [DA/DB] 4.72:1; [DC] 4.6:1 and [DD] 4.9:1. Hydraulic brakes. Wood-spoke wheels.

OPTIONS: Front bumper. Rear bumper. Single sidemount. Dual sidemounts. Sidemount cover(s). Spare tire. Wire-spoke wheels. Silvertone radio. Heater. Clock. Cigar lighter. Radio antenna. Trunk rack. Touring trunk. Spotlight(s). Cowl lamps. Trumpet horns. Twin taillights. Twin horns. Folding bed option. Wind wings (open cars). Trunk cover. Outside rear view mirror. Special paint. Dual windshield wipers.

Note: Some accessories standard equipment on higher-priced models.

HISTORICAL: Introduced January 1, 1930. Calendar year registrations: 64,105. Calendar year production: 68,158. Model year production: 90,755. Innovations: First Dodge eight introduced. Fuel pumps used on all-new 1930 models (vacuum tanks on carryover models). New instrument panels. Vision and ventilating windshields on all-new models. Hydraulic shock absorbers. For the model year, Dodge was fifth in U.S. sales. The company also ranked seventh in calendar year output. About 80 percent of DC Series production was sold as 1930 models. About 70 percent of DD Series production sold as 1930 models. These series were produced into the 1931 calendar year ending May 1931 and September 1931, respectively.

1930-31 DODGE

STANDARD DODGE — SERIES DD — SIX: After July 1930, the Dodge DD Six was slightly updated and carried over as part of the 1931 "first series." Changes included a new Delco-Remy ignition system, the relocation of the starter control to the instrument panel and the addition of a new five-passenger phaeton. Prices were lowered $100 and shipping weights did not change. A new radiator featured a slanting "DODGE 6" emblem.

STANDARD DODGE — SERIES DC — EIGHT: After July 1930, the Dodge DC Eight was slightly updated and carried over as part of the 1931 "first series." Changes included a lower overall body height, the addition of twin cowl vents, a sloping windshield, oblong type windows, and a new radiator emblem with a figure "8". Prices were cut $100-145.

I.D. DATA: [Series DD] Serial numbers were in the same locations. Starting: (Fedco) D255CW; (conventional) 3504189. Ending: (Fedco) D257PH; (conventional) 3516105. Engine numbers were in the same location. Starting: DD32788. Ending: DD44576. [Series DC] Serial numbers were in the same locations. Starting: (Fedco) E191HS (conventional) 4501084. Ending: (Fedco) E192EL, (conventional) 4504533. Engine numbers were in the same location. Starting: DC22401. Ending: DC26018.

Model No.	Body Type & Seating	Price	Weight	Prod. Total
DD	2-dr. Rds.-2/4P	755	2462	Note 1
DD	4-dr. Phae.-5P	775	2521	542
DD	2-dr. Bus. Cpe.-2P	735	2534	Note 1
DD	2-dr. Cpe.-2/4P	755	2603	Note 1
DD	2-dr. Conv. Cpe.-2/4P	835	2605	Note 1
DD	4-dr. Sed.-5P	765	2668	Note 1
DD	Chassis	NA	NA	Note 1

Note 1: For carryover models see 1930 production totals.

Note 2: Total production of this series for the 1931 model year was approximately 12,900. The DD Six remained in actual production until May 1931.

DC	2-dr. Rds.-2/4P	995	2802	Note 1
DC	4-dr. Phae.-5P	1080	2960	Note 1
DC	2-dr. Bus. Cpe.-2P	1025	2910	123
DC	2-dr. Cpe.-2/4P	1065	2981	Note 1
DC	2-dr. Conv. Cpe.-2/4P	1095	2938	Note 1
DC	4-dr. Sed.-5P	1045	3043	Note 1
DC	Chassis	NA	NA	Note 1

Note 1: For carryover models see 1930 production totals.

Note 2: Total production of this series for the 1931 model year was approximately 4,300. The DC Eight remained in actual production until September 1931.

ENGINE: [Series DD] See 1930 DD Series engine specifications. [Series DC] See 1930 DD Series.

CHASSIS: [Series DD] W.B.: 109 in. O.L.: 155-7/8 in. Tires: 19 x 5.00 [Series DC] W.B.: 114 in. O.L.: 163 in. Tires: 18 x 5.50.

TECHNICAL: Selective sliding transmission. Speeds: 3F/1R. Floor shift controls. Single plate dry disc clutch. Semi-floating rear axle. Overall ratio: [DD] 4.9:1; [DC] 4.6:1. Hydraulic brakes. Wood-spoke wheels.

OPTIONS: Front bumper. Rear bumper. Single sidemount. Dual sidemounts. Sidemount cover(s). Spare tire. Wire-spoke wheels. Radio. Heater. Clock. Cigar lighter. Radio antenna. Trunk rack. Touring trunk. Spotlight(s). Cowl lamps. Trumpet horn(s). Twin taillights. Twin horns. Folding bed option. Wind wings. Trunk cover. Outside rear view mirror. Special paint. Dual windshield wipers.

Note: Some accessories standard on some models.

HISTORICAL: Introduced July 1930. See 1929 section for calendar year production figures. Model year production figures same as 1931. Innovations: Lower DC Eight bodies. Starting control on dashboard. New DD Phaeton. Twin cowl vents on Eight.

The Model DC was nicknamed the "Marathon Eight" after one car was driven over 102,000 miles during the year. Many Dodge chassis were supplied to taxicab companies. They had special features such as steel disc wheels, leather front seats and special lighting. Some station wagons were also turned out by J. Cantrell & Co. of Huntington, New York.

1931 DODGE

DODGE — SERIES DD — SIX: Starting in January 1931, the Dodge DD Six was carried over as a part of the true 1931 series. There were no changes in the appearance features, standard equipment, availability of models, factory prices, shipping weights or engine specifications. Refer to the 1930-31 section for specifications and production information. The DD Six line remained in production through May 1931.

1931 Dodge Six, Series DH, four-door sedan (JAC)

DODGE — SERIES DH — SIX: The new DH models entered production in November 1930, as a "true" 1931 series. The line was made up of six medium-priced six-cylinder cars on a five-inch longer wheelbase. Appearance features included a wider and deeper radiator grille, lever type radiator, shutters, twin cowl ventilators, fuller crown front fenders, a longer hood, a new front bumper with a vee-shaped upper bar, a beaded sun visor and an ebony finished instrument panel. Standard equipment included a double drop frame, Delco-Remy ignition, hydraulic brakes, a new vibration dampener, adjustable seats and wire spoke wheels.

DODGE — SERIES DC — EIGHT: Starting in January 1931, the Dodge DC Eight was carried over as part of the true 1931 series. There were no changes in the appearance features, standard equipment, model availability, factory prices, shipping weights or engine specifications. Refer to the 1930-31 section for specifications and production information.

DODGE — SERIES DG — EIGHT: The new DG models entered production in January 1931, as a "true" 1931 series. The line was initially made up of four eight-cylinder cars. Appearance characteristics included a wider radiator, lever operated radiator shutters, twin cowl ventilators, new instrument panel and a swinging windshield. These cars were the first to

use the Rocky Mountain ram as a hood ornament. Equipment features included Delco-Remy ignition, hydraulic brakes, double drop frame, downdraft Stromberg carburetor, rubber mounted motor suspension, three-spoke steering wheel, adjustable seats and five wire spoke wheels. The wheelbase was over four inches longer than that of the DC Eight.

I.D. DATA: [Series DH] Serial numbers were located on a plate on the toe board, also on the front right door hinge pillar post and also on frame below right front fender. Starting: 3518001. Ending: 3548559. Engine numbers were in the same location. Starting: DH1001. Ending: DH33442. [Series DG] Serial numbers were in the same locations. Starting: 4508001. Ending: 4517521. Engine numbers were in the same location. Starting: DG1003. Ending: DG11086.

Model No.	Body Type & Seating	Price	Weight	Prod. Total
DH	4-dr. Phae.-5P	865	2655	164
DH	2-dr. Bus. Cpe.-2P	815	2661	3178
DH	2-dr. R/S Cpe.-2/4P	853	2745	4187
DH	4-dr. Sed.-5P	845	2820	33,090
DH	2-dr. Rds.-2/4P	825	2638	160
DH	2-dr. Conv. Cpe.-2/4P	895	NA	NA
DH	Chassis	NA	NA	47

Note 1: Total production in the 1931 series was approximately 20,558 based on the range of serial numbers.

Note 2: The individual totals given in the right-hand column above include DH Sixes carried over into the 1932 "first series."

Note 3: Dodge records do not show any production figures for the DH convertible coupe, although this model does appear in sales literature.

DG	2-dr. Rds.-2/4P	1095	NA	64
DG	2-dr. Cpe.-2/4P	1095	3094	2181
DG	2-dr. Conv. Cpe.-2/4P	1170	NA	NA
DG	4-dr. Sed.-5P	1135	3175	8937
DG	Chassis	NA	NA	20

Note 1: Total production in the 1931 series was approximately 9,500 based on the range of serial numbers.

Note 2: The individual totals given in the right-hand column above include DG Eights carried over into the 1932 "first series."

Note 3: Dodge records do not show any production figures for the DG convertible coupe, although this model does appear in sales literature.

ENGINE: [Series DH] Inline. L-head. Six. Cast iron block. B & S: 3-1/4 x 4-1/4 in. Disp.: 211.5 cu. in. C.R.: 5.2:1. Brake H.P.: 68 @ 3200 R.P.M. Net H.P.: 25.35. Main bearings: four. Valve lifters: solid. Carb.: Carter one-barrel model 197S. Torque: 140 lb.-ft. @ 1400 R.P.M. [Series DG] Inline. L-head. Eight. Cast iron block. B & S: 3 x 4-1/4 in. Disp.: 240.3 cu. in. C.R.: 5.2:1. Brake H.P.: 84 @ 3400 R.P.M. Net H.P.: 28.8. Main bearings: five. Valve lifters: solid. Carb.: Stromberg one-barrel model DXC-3. Torque: 158 lb.-ft. @ 1400 R.P.M.

CHASSIS: [Series DD] W.B.: 109 in. O.L.: 155-7/8 in. Tires: 19 x 5.00 [Series DH] W.B.: 114 in. Tires: 19 x 5.00. [Series DC] W.B.: 114 in. O.L.: 163 in. Tires: 18 x 5.50. [Series DG] W.B.: 118-1/4 in. Tires: 18 x 5.50.

TECHNICAL: Selective sliding transmission. Speeds: 3F/1R. Floor shift controls. Conventional clutch. Semi-floating rear axle. Overall ratio: [DD] 4.9:1; [DH] 4.66:1 to 4.3:1; [DC] 4.6:1; [DG] 4.6:1 to 4.3:1. Hydraulic brakes. Wood-spoke or wire-spoke wheels.

OPTIONS: Front bumper. Rear bumper. Spare tire. Dual sidemounts. Leather sidemount cover(s). Metal sidemount covers. Wire wheels. Disc wheels (taxi). Radio. Heater. Clock. Cigar lighter. Radio antenna. Trunk rack. Touring trunk. Spotlights. Cowl lamps. Trumpet horns. Wind wings. Trunk cover. Trippe lights. Outside rear view mirror. Special paint.

HISTORICAL: Introduced January 1931. Calendar year registrations: 53,090. Calendar year production: 56,003. Model year production: 52,364. Innovations: Fully rust proof bodies. Valve seat inserts. Fully automatic spark control. Dodge was America's ninth ranked automaker for the model year. This was the last time a Dodge roadster would be offered until 1949.

1931-32 DODGE

DODGE — SERIES DD — SIX: Chrysler Corp. records indicate that production of the Series DD Dodge Six ended in May of 1931. However,

Red Book *National Used Car Market Report* (1935 edition) contains a listing for this series as an "early" 1932 line. This would suggest that the Depression kept sales so low that Dodge continued to sell these cars even after production had ended. The cars marketed after July 1, 1931, were sold as part of the "first series" for 1932 and had serial numbers 3516106 and up; engine numbers DD44501 and up. Appearance features, standard equipment, model listings, factory prices, shipping weights and engine specifications did not change. Refer to the 1930-31 section for specifications and production information. Serial numbers indicate that only nine of these cars were sold as 1932 models.

1932 Dodge Four, Series DM, four-door sedan (JB)

DODGE — SERIES DH — SIX: Beginning in July 1931, the Series DH Dodge Six was carried over as part of the company's "first series" for 1932. Appearance features were slightly changed in that swinging type windshields and lever operated radiator shutters were adopted. Standard equipment included a new type gearshifter and freewheeling. Brake horsepower was slightly increased due to a higher compression ratio being used. Other features were the same as on 1931 Dodge DH Sixes.

DODGE — SERIES DC — EIGHT: Starting in July 1931, the Series DC Dodge Eight was carried over as part of the company's "first series" for 1932. These cars can be identified by a new instrument panel with three control buttons. Other appearance features, standard equipment, models, factory prices, shipping weights and engine specifications were unchanged. Cars sold as 1932 models had Fedco serial numbers E192EE to E193PS and conventional serial numbers 4504534 to 4505165. Engine numbers were DC26019 to DC26774. The DC Eight remained in production until September 1931 and was then discontinued.

DODGE — SERIES DG — EIGHT: Starting in July 1931, the Series DG Dodge Eight was carried over as part of the company's "first series" for 1932. These cars can be identified by a new type mahogany instrument panel, new type gearshift and new rubber bushed spring shackles. There were a number of changes in the body style offerings with the convertible coupe being deleted and a phaeton and two new coupes being added.

I.D. DATA: [Series DH] Serial numbers were in the same locations. Starting: 3548560. Ending: 3557371. Engine numbers were in the same location. Starting: DH33443. Ending: DH41772. [Series DG] Serial numbers were in the same locations. Starting: 4517522. Ending: 4519534. Engine numbers were in the same locations. Starting: DG11807. Ending: DG13028.

Model No.	Body Type & Seating	Price	Weight	Prod. Total
DH	4-dr. Phae.-5P	865	2655	Note 1
DH	2-dr. Bus. Cpe.-2P	815	2661	Note 1
DH	2-dr. R/S Cpe.-2/4P	835	2745	Note 1
DH	4-dr. Sed.-5P	845	2840	Note 1
DH	2-dr. Rds.-2/4P	850	2638	Note 1

Note 1: See 1931 Dodge DH Six section for production totals. About 8,800 cars were built in the 1931-32 Series.

DG	2-dr. Rds.-2/4P	1095	2976	Note 1
DG	4-dr. Phae.-5P	1155	2985	43
DG	2-dr. Bus. Cpe.-2P	1095	3003	119
DG	2-dr. R/S Cpe.-2/4P	1095	3094	Note 1
DG	2-dr. Clb. Cpe.-5P	1145	3240	500
DG	4-dr. Sed.-5P	1135	3175	Note 1
DG	Chassis	NA	NA	Note 1

Note 1: Production totals for the roadster, r/s coupe, sedan and chassis — only are listed in the 1931 Series DG Eight section.

Note 2: About 2,000 cars were built and sold as 1932 models, according to the range of serial numbers.

ENGINE: [Series DH] Inline, L-head. Six. Cast iron block. B & S: 3-1/4 x 4 1/4 in. Disp.: 211.5 cu. in. C.R.: 5.4:1. Brake H.P.: 74 @ 3400 R.P.M. Net H.P. 25.35. Main bearings: four. Valve lifters: solid. Carb.: Carter IV. Torque: 140 lb. ft. @ 1400 R.P.M. [Series DG] See 1931 Series DG Eight engine specifications.

CHASSIS: [Series DD] W.B.: 109 in. O.L.: 155-7/8 in. Tires: 19 x 5.00 [Series DH] W.B.: 114-1/4 in. Tires: 19 x 5.00. [Series DC] W.B.: 114 in. O.L.: 163 in. Tires: 18 x 5.50. [Series DG] W.B.: 118-1/4 in. Tires: 18 x 5.50.

TECHNICAL: Selective sliding transmission. Speeds: 3F/1R. Floor shift controls. Conventional clutch. Semi-floating rear axle. Overall ratio: [DD] 4.9:1. [DH] 4.66:1; [DC] 4.6:1; [DG] 4.6:1. Hydraulic brakes. Wood-spoke or wire-spoke wheels. Freewheeling.

OPTIONS: Front bumper. Rear bumper. Spare tire. Dual sidemounts. Leather sidemount cover(s). Metal sidemount covers. Wire wheels. Disc wheels (taxi). Radio. Heater. Clock. Cigar lighter. Radio antenna. Trunk rack. Touring trunk. Spotlights. Cowl lamps. Trumpet horns. Wind wings. Trunk cover. Trippe lights. Outside rear view mirror. Special paint.

HISTORICAL: Introduced July 1931. See 1931 section for calendar year production. See 1932 section for model year production. Innovations: DH Six has new type gearshifter and freewheeling feature; engine compression and horsepower rating increased. DG Eight has new dash, new gearshifter and rubber shackled springs. DC Eight has new instrumentation controls. The Depression had a negative effect on Dodge sales and led to all of the late 1931 models being carried over into the early part of the 1932 selling season.

1932 DODGE

1932 Dodge Six, Series DL, four-door sedan (OCW)

DODGE — SERIES DL — SIX: A new DL Series Dodge Six entered production in November 1931 and was introduced in January 1932. Appearance characteristics included a rakishly sloped windshield with no external sun visor, a new Dodge ram hood ornament, a curved-vee double bar bumper, a higher and more rounded cowl line, chrome-plated bowl type headlamps, longer, lower body feature lines and cowl lamps mounted further back on the surcingle molding. Standard equipment included Delco-Remy ignition, hydraulic brakes, double drop bridge type frame and a silent second gear transmission with an optional automatic vacuum-operated clutch and freewheeling device operated by a button on the instrument panel. A single control on the new satin-finished instrument panel locked both the automatic clutch and the freewheeling unit in or out. Monopiece all-steel body construction was featured again and there were two, hand-operated ventilators on the top of the cowl.

DODGE — SERIES DK — EIGHT: Known as the "New Eight," the DK Series Dodge lineup entered production in November 1931 for January 1932 auto show introduction. Cars in this series were mounted on a larger double drop bridge frame and had a 122-inch wheelbase. Appearance features included a sloping windshield, interior (only) sun visors, longer and lower body feature lines and wire-spoke wheels. On these cars, only the top bar of the bumper was curved and "veed" downward at its center. The bottom bar was straight. Standard equipment included Delco-Remy ignition, hydraulic brakes, "Floating Power" type engine suspension, silent second gear transmission, hydraulic shocks and an adjustable windshield. Freewheeling and an automatic clutch were standard on the New Eight. Cars built after mid-year had a high-compression cylinder head and 10 additional horsepower.

1932 Dodge Eight, Series DK, coupe (JAC)

DODGE — SERIES DM — FOUR: Beginning in 1932 and continuing until Pearl Harbor, Chrysler Corporation built a series of "junior" Dodges, based on the Plymouth body shell and drivetrain, for sale in the Canadian and export markets. This move came as a result of the corporate structural organization outside the U.S. Dodge dealers in these markets were not dualed with Plymouth, which eliminated the dealer from pursuing sales in the low-priced end of the market. The DM was an answer to these problems. Engine and chassis for the DM was supplied by the PB model Plymouth, with Dodge supplying the body and trim. In succeeding years Plymouth would supply even the body with Dodge lookalike grilles and trim applied. A total of 1,173 Dodge DMs were built in the United States for foreign export, with an additional 16 cars built in Windsor, Ontario.

I.D. DATA: [Series DL] Serial numbers were in the same locations. Starting: 3558101. Ending: 3578392. Engine numbers were in the same location. Starting: DL1001. Ending: DL21030. [Series DK] Serial numbers were in the same locations. Starting: 4520101. Ending: 4526087. [Series DM] Serial numbers on a tag on the right front door post. Starting: 9905001. Ending: 9906173. Engine numbers on flat spot on left side of block, beginning number DM-1001.

Note: Starting with serial number 4524540 the higher compression cylinder head was used. Engine numbers were in the same location. Starting: DK1001. Ending: DK7123.

Note: Engines above number DK5667 had the high compression cylinder head.

Model No.	Body Type & Seating	Price	Weight	Prod. Total
DL	2-dr. Bus. Cpe.-2P	795	2928	1963
DL	2-dr. R/S Cpe.-2/4P	835	2995	1815
DL	2-dr. Conv. Cpe.-2/4P	895	2988	224
DL	2-dr. Conv. Sed.-5P	915	3068	12
DL	2-dr. Vic. Cpe.-5P	865	3085	1
DL	4-dr. Sed.-5P	845	3094	16,901
DL	Chassis	NA	NA	126

Note 1: Total series production was 21,042.

DK	2-dr. R/S Cpe.-2/4P	1115	3417	821
DK	2-dr. Bus. Cpe.-2P	1095	3350	57
DK	2-dr. Conv. Cpe.-2/4P	1220	3438	88
DK	4-dr. Sed.-5P	1145	3527	4422
DK	4-dr. Conv. Sed.-5P	1395	3706	88
DK	2-dr. Vic. Cpe.-5P	1145	3504	651
DK	Chassis	NA	NA	22

Note 1: Total series production was 6,187.

DM	Phaeton	NA	NA	92
DM	Roadster	NA	NA	54
DM	4-dr. Sed.	NA	NA	760
DM	Conv.Sed.	NA	NA	48
DM	Sta. Wag.	NA	NA	1
DM	Chassis	NA	NA	235

ENGINE: [Series DL] Inline. L-head. Six. Cast iron block. B & S: 3-1/4 x 4-3/8 in. Disp.: 217.8 cu. in. C.R.: (std.) 5.35:1; (opt.) 6.35:1. Brake H.P.: 79 @ 3400 R.P.M. Net H.P.: 25.35. Main bearings: four. Valve lifters: solid. Carb.: Carter one-barrel. Torque: 150 lb.-ft. @ 1200 R.P.M. [Series DK] Inline. L-head. Eight. Cast iron block. B & S: 3-1/4 x 4-1/4 in. Disp.: 282.1 cu. in. C.R.: (std.) 5.2:1; (opt.) 6.2:1 with "Red Head" engine. Brake H.P.: (std.) 90 @ 3400 R.P.M; (opt.) 100 @ 3400 R.P.M. Net H.P.: 33.8. Main bearings: five. Valve lifters: solid. Carb.: Stromberg one-barrel model DXR-3. Torque: (std.) 185 lb.-ft. @ 1200 R.P.M.; (opt.) 195 lb.-ft. @ 1200 R.P.M. [Series DM] Inline. L-head. Four. Cast iron block. B & S: 3-5/8 x 4-3/4 in. Disp.: 196.1 cu. in. Brake H.P.: 65 @ 3400 R.P.M.

CHASSIS: [Series DL] W.B.: 114-1/2 in. Tires: 18 x 5.50. [Series DK] W.B.: 122 in. Tires: 18 x 6.00. [Series DM] W.B.: 112 in.

TECHNICAL: Selective sliding transmission. Speeds: 3F/1R. Floor shift controls. Single plate dry disc clutch. Semi-floating rear axle. Overall ratio: [DL] 4.6:1-4.3:1; [DK] 4.1:1. Hydraulic brakes. Wood-spoke or wire-spoke wheels. Drivetrain options: Freewheeling (std. on DK). Vacuum clutch (std. on DK).

OPTIONS: Front bumper. Rear bumper. Spare tire. Dual sidemounts. Metal sidemount covers. Chrome sidemount trim ring. Wire wheels (on DL Six). Radio. Heater. Clock. Cigar lighter. Radio antenna. Trunk rack. Touring trunk. Spotlight(s). Cowl lamps. Dual trumpet horns. Whitewall tires. Outside rear view mirror. Special paint. Dual windshield wipers. Right-hand taillight. Right-hand sun visor. Wheel trim rings.

HISTORICAL: Introduced January 1932. Calendar year registrations: 28,111. Calendar year production: 30,216. Model year production: 27,555. Innovations: Lower center of gravity. Freewheeling. Vacuum operated automatic clutch. Double drop bridge frame. Silent gear transmission. "Floating Power" engine suspension. "Red Head" high compression engine. Dodge was America's seventh largest automaker in model year 1932. The company held eighth rank in sales for the calendar year. Shipments of Dodge DMs began in April and ended in December of 1932.

1933 DODGE

1933 Dodge Six, Series DP, coupe (JAC)

DODGE — SERIES DP — SIX: The all-new Series DP Dodge Six was introduced on November 23, 1932, as a 1933 model. At this time, Series DK Dodge Eights were still being made and sold in Dodge showrooms, but they were considered 1932 models since the company had changed to an annual model year policy. The DP Six had front-opening doors that were popular at this time and were often called "suicide" doors. Other appearance characteristics included a vee-type radiator that was slanted and slightly curved at the bottom, double interior sun visors, single bar front bumper (and rear bumper), fuller crowned fenders, chrome-plated bowl-type headlights, no cowl lamps and a generally more streamlined look. Standard equipment included Delco-Remy ignition, hydraulic brakes, "Floating Power" engine suspension, double drop "X-type" frame construction, freewheeling, automatic vacuum clutch, tubular front axle, downdraft carburetor, air cleaner, safety glass windshield and Zerk chassis lubrication. Dodge DP Sixes built from November 1932 to April 1933 had a 111-1/4 in. wheelbase. Those made after April 1933 had a 115-inch wheelbase. The two types of DP Sixes are considered separate series, although factory records combine the body style production totals of both.

DODGE — SERIES DO — EIGHT: The DO Series Dodge Eight entered production in December 1932 for introduction January 1, 1933. It was the last eight-cylinder Dodge product marketed before the outbreak of World War II. These luxurious cars rode on a 122-inch wheelbase. Appearance characteristics included a sloping vee-type radiator that curved forward at the bottom, "beaver-tail" rear body styling, single bar bumpers, vertical hood louvers, chrome-plated bullet-shaped headlamps, a visorless slanting windshield, dual chrome-plated horns and front-hinged, rear opening door. Standard equipment included Delco-Remy ignition, hydraulic brakes, Tri-beam headlights, coincidental transmission lock, I-beam front axle, downdraft carburetor, "Floating Power" engine suspension, freewheeling and a safety glass windshield.

DODGE — SERIES DP — SIX: The long wheelbase version of the Series DP Dodge Six was introduced on April 5, 1933. Other specifications

were identical to the 1933 DP first series. The extra length of these cars was apparent in the design of the front sheet metal, particularly the forward edge of the hood where the space between the radiator and the louvers was increased. The runningboards and sill plates were also obviously longer. Otherwise the styling of the short and long wheelbase cars was identical. Prices were also unchanged. Factory records do not breakout the body style production figures separately for the two lines.

1933 Dodge Six, Series DP, four-door sedan (JAC)

DODGE — SERIES DQ — SIX: Once again, Plymouth provided the base for Dodge to build this model. Differing from the DM of 1932, Plymouth now also supplied the body as well as the engine and chassis for this conversion for the Canadian and overseas markets. Each car was fitted with a Dodge-appearing grille and other various trim pieces to differentiate it from its Plymouth heritage.

1933 Dodge Six, Series DP, convertible coupe (JAC)

I.D. DATA: [Series DP] Serial numbers were located on a plate on the right front door hinge pillar post. Starting: 3579001. Ending: 3594421. Engine numbers located on left side of engine block just below cylinder head. Starting: DP1001. Ending: DP17793. [Series DO] Serial numbers were in the same location. Starting: 4527001. Ending: 4528601. Engine numbers were in the same location. Starting: DO1001. Ending: DO2649. [Series DP] Serial numbers were in the same locations. Starting: 3594422. Ending: 3680000. Engine numbers were in the same location. Starting: DP17794. Ending: DP105429. Canadian built cars located serial number on right front door post. Starting: 9452951. Ending: 9455705. Engine numbers located on flat spot on left corner of block.

Model No.	Body Type & Seating	Price	Weight	Prod. Total
DP	2-dr. Bus. Cpe.-2P	595	2452	11,236
DP	2-dr. R/S Cpe.-2/4P	640	2506	8879
DP	2-dr. Conv. Cpe.-2/4P	695	2511	1563
DP	2-dr. Sed.-5P	630	2591	8523
DP	2-dr. Salon Brgm.-5P	660	2620	(4200)
DP	4-dr. Sed.-5P	675	2632	69,074
DP	2-dr. Del. Salon Brgm.-5P	775	2825	(4200)
DP	Chassis	NA	NA	980

Note 1: Production totals above are for both short and long wheelbase versions of the DP Six. Serial numbers indicate that approximately 15,420 short wheelbase cars were built.

Note 2: The production total in parentheses represents the combined total (4200) for the Standard and Deluxe two-door Salon Brougham. No further breakout is available.

Model No.	Body Type & Seating	Price	Weight	Prod. Total
DO	2-dr. R/S Cpe.-2/4P	1115	3451	212
DO	2-dr. Vic. Cpe.-5P	1145	3540	159
DO	2-dr. Conv. Cpe.-2/4P	1185	3465	56
DO	4-dr. Sed.-5P	1145	3580	1173
DO	4-dr. Conv. Sed.-5P	1395	3961	39
DO	Chassis	NA	NA	13

Note 1: Total series production was 1,652.

Model No.	Body Type & Seating	Price	Weight	Prod. Total
DP	2-dr. Bus. Cpe.-2P	595	2501	Note 1
DP	2-dr. R/S Cpe.-2/4P	640	2551	Note 1
DP	2-dr. Conv. Cpe.-2/4P	695	2556	Note 1
DP	2-dr. Sed.-5P	630	2591	Note 1
DP	4-dr. Sed.-5P	675	2661	Note 1
DP	2-dr. Salon Brgm.-5P	660	2651	Note 1
DP	Chassis	NA	NA	Note 1

Note 1: See production totals listed above for the 1933 DP first series.

Serial numbers indicate that approximately 87,635 long wheelbase cars were built.

ENGINE: [Series DP] Inline. L-head. Six. Cast iron block. B & S: 3-1/8 x 4-3/8 in. Disp.: 201.3 cu. in. C.R.: (std.) 5.5:1; (opt.) 6.2:1. Brake H.P.: (std.) 75 @ 3600 R.P.M.; (opt.) 81 @ 3600 R.P.M. Net H.P.: 23.44. Main bearings: four. Valve lifters: solid. Carb.: Stromberg one-barrel model EX-22. Torque: (std.) 136 lb.-ft. @ 1200 R.P.M.; (opt.) 144 lb.-ft. @ 1200 R.P.M. [Series DO] Inline. L-head. Eight. Cast iron block. B & S: 3-1/4 in. x 4-1/4 Disp.: 282.1 cu. in. C.R.: (std.) 6.5:1; (opt.) 5.2:1. Brake H.P.: (std.) 100 @ 3400 R.P.M.; (opt.) 94 @ 3400 R.P.M. Net H.P.: 33.8. Main bearings: five. Valve lifters: solid. Carb.: Ball & Ball two-barrel model ESA. Torque: (std.) 200 lb.-ft. @ 1200 R.P.M.; (opt.) 184 lb.-ft. @ 1200 R.P.M. [Series DP] Inline. L-head. Six. Cast iron block. B & S: 3-1/8 x 4-3/8 in. Disp.: 201.3 cu. in. C.R.: (std.) 5.5:1; (opt.) 6.2:1. Brake H.P.: (std.) 75 @ 3600 R.P.M, (opt.) 81 @ 3600 R.P.M. Net H.P.: 23.44. Main bearings: four. Valve lifters: solid. Carb.: Stromberg one barrel model EX-22. Torque: (std.) 136 lb.-ft. @ 1200 R.P.M.; (opt.) 144 lb.-ft. @ 1200 R.P.M. [Series DQ] Inline. L-head. Six. Cast iron block. B & S: 3-1/8 x 4-1/8 in. Disp.: 189.8 cu. in. Brake H.P. 70 @ 3600 R. P. M.

CHASSIS: [Series DP] W.B.:111-1/4 in. Tires: 16 x 6.00. [Series DO] W.B.: 122 in. Tires: 17 x 6.50. [Series DP] W.B.: 115 in. Tires: 16 x 6.00

TECHNICAL: Selective sliding transmission. Speeds: 3F/1R. Floor shift controls. Single plate dry disc clutch. Semi-floating rear axle. Overall ratio: 4.375:1. Hydraulic brakes. Artillery or wire-spoke wheels. Drivetrain options: Freewheeling. Vacuum clutch.

OPTIONS: Front bumper. Rear bumper. Dual sidemounts. Metal sidemount cover(s). Chrome sidemount trim bands. Rear spare metal cover. Radio. Heater. Clock. Cigar lighter. Radio antenna. Trunk rack. Touring trunk. Spotlights. Outside rear view mirror. Dual chrome trumpet horns (std. on "DO" Eight). Built-in trunk. Dual taillights. Dual windshield wipers. Wind wings. License plate frames. Goodyear "Airwheel" tires. White stripe tires.

HISTORICAL: Introduced: [DP/SWB] 11/23/32; [DO] 1/1/33, [DP/LWB] 4/5/33. Calendar year registrations: 86,062. Calendar year production: 91,403. Model year production: 106,103. Innovations: Silent helical gear transmissions. First 100 horsepower Dodge; most powerful model up to 1933. New long wheelbase Six. New pressed steel artillery spoke wheels. New six-cylinder engine. Dodge was America's fourth ranked automaker for model year 1933. A Dodge DP convertible competed in the 1933 Elgin Road Races. Numerous Dodge promotions including a "Hell Driver's" demonstration highlighted the Chrysler display at the 1933 "Century of Progress Exposition" in Chicago.

1934 DODGE

1934 Dodge Six, Series DR, four-door sedan (OCW)

DODGE DELUXE — SERIES DR — SIX: The 1934 Dodge was completely restyled to reflect a much more streamlined look. Appearance

characteristics included a new vee-type radiator, skirted front and rear fenders, multiple horizontal hood louvers of descending length, larger bullet-shaped chrome-plated headlamps and a single-bar bumper with a flat dip in its center. Standard equipment included Delco-Remy ignition, hydraulic brakes, new independent front suspension, "Floating Power," X-type frame, new type ventilating system, steel spoke wheels, dual horns and a new "leaping ram" hood ornament. Pin striping highlighted the body feature lines of the DR Series Dodge Six. An optional high-compression engine featured an aluminum "Silver Dome" cylinder head. Also standard was "Duplate" safety glass windshields and the automatic vacuum clutch. These models were retroactively designated "DeLuxe Sixes" after the Standard Six was introduced in June. At this point, the design of the hood side panels was changed replacing the multiple louvers with four plainer louvers, as used on the Standard Six.

1934 Dodge Six, Series DS, aero brougham (JAC)

DODGE SPECIAL — SERIES DS — SIX: The DS sub-series was basically a long wheelbase version of the DR containing only two distinctive body styles. They were an aerodynamically-styled four-door "slantback" sedan and a four-door convertible sedan, also with a "slantback" body. These cars were known as Specials and had a 121-inch stance. Appearance features included the vee-shaped radiator, skirted fenders, horizontal hood louvers, large chrome bullet-shaped headlights, dual trumpet horns and body pin striping. As standard equipment, these cars had Delco-Remy ignition, hydraulic brakes, independent front suspension, X-type frame, the new seven point "Finger Touch" ventilation system with control on dash, "Floating Power" engine suspension and "Floating Cushion" wheels with Goodyear "Airwheel" tires. An automatic vacuum clutch and "Duplate" safety glass were also featured. The four-door Special Aero-dynamic Brougham was also known as a close-coupled sedan.

1934 Dodge Six, Series DRXX, four-door sedan (JAC)

DODGE STANDARD — SERIES DRXX — SIX: The 1934 Dodge DRXX series was introduced on June 2, 1934, to sell alongside the DR and DS models. These cars were part of a mid-season economy line designed to offer buyers cars with the same general appearance as Deluxe Sixes, but slightly less features. They did not have safety-type "Duplate" glass, or an automatic vacuum clutch or the ventilating body. Other characteristics of the two lines were practically the same, except most standard models had body colored radiator shells and no pin striping (although both of these trim features were optional at slight extra cost). As mentioned earlier, the Standard Six introduced the plainer hood design with only four horizontal louvers.

DODGE — SERIES DT — SIX: Continuing the practice of providing Canadian and overseas Dodge dealers with a smaller, less expensive car to sell, Plymouth again supplied body, chassis and running gear for a junior series Dodge. Again, only minor trim differences were made to the basic Plymouth to make it look like a smaller Dodge.

I.D. DATA: [Series DR] Serial numbers were in the same location. Starting: 3680001. Ending: 3756367. Engine numbers were in the same location. Starting: DR-1001. Ending: DR-95158. [Series DS] Serial numbers were in the same location, Starting: 4528651. Ending: 4530400. Engine numbers were in the same location. Starting: DR1009 and up. [Series DRXX] Serial numbers were in the same location. Starting: 4000001. Ending: 4015004. Engine numbers were in the same location. Starting: DRXX-59585. Ending: DRXX-95861. Canadian-built cars located serial numbers on right front door post. Starting: 9455721. Ending: 9460020. Engine numbers were located on flat spot on left front corner of block.

Model No.	Body Type & Seating	Price	Weight	Prod. Total
DR	2-dr. Bus. Cpe.-2P	665	2695	8723
DR	2-dr. R/S Cpe.-2/4P	715	2745	5323
DR	2-dr. Conv. Cpe.-2/4P	765	2725	1239
DR	2-dr. Sed.-5P	715	2855	7308
DR	4-dr. Sed.-5P	765	2940	53,479
DR	4-dr. Sed.-7P	NA	NA	710
DR	Chassis	NA	NA	1475

Note 1: Total series production was 78,257

DS	4-dr. Spl. Aero. Brgm.-5P	845	2905	1397
DS	4-dr. Spl. Aero. Conv. Sed.-5P	875	2915	350
DS	Chassis	NA	NA	3

Note: Total series production was 1,750.

DRXX	2-dr. Bus. Cpe.-2P	645	2695	2284
DRXX	2-dr. R/S Cpe.-2/4P	690	2745	105
DRXX	2-dr. Conv. Cpe.-2/4P	745	2845	NA
DRXX	2-dr. Sed.-5P	695	2855	3133
DRXX	4-dr. Sed.-5P	745	2940	9481
DRXX	Chassis	NA	NA	1

Note 1: Total series production (excluding convertible coupe) was 15,004.

Note 2: Convertible coupe production is not included in available factory records; possibly none were built.

ENGINE: [Series DR] Inline. L-head. Six. Cast iron block. B & S: 3-1/4 x 4-3/8 in. Disp.: 217.8 cu. in. C.R.: (std.) 5.6:1; (opt.) 6.5:1. Brake H.P. (std.) 82 @ 3600 R.P.M.: (opt.) 87 @ 3600 R.P.M. Net H.P.: 25.35. Main bearings: four. Valve lifters: solid. Carb.: Stromberg one-barrel model EX-22. Torque: (std.) 150 lb.-ft. @ 1200 R.P.M.: (opt.) 160 lb.-ft. @ 1200 R.P.M. [Series DS] Inline. L-head. Six. Cast iron block. B & S: 3-1/4 x 4-3/8 in. Disp.: 217.8 cu. in. C.R.: 6.5:1. Brake H.P.: 87 @ 3600 R.P.M. Net H.P.: 25.35. Main bearings: four. Valve lifters: solid. Carb.: Stromberg one-barrel model EX-22. Torque: 160 lb.-ft. @ 1200 R.P.M. [Series DRXX] Inline. L-head. Six. Cast iron block. B & S: 3-1/4 x 4-3/8 in. Disp.: 217.8 cu. in. C.R. 5.6:1. Brake H.P.: 82 @ 3600 R.P.M. Net H.P.: 25.35. Main bearings: four. Valve lifters: solid. Carb.: Stromberg one-barrel model EX-22. Torque: 150 lb.-ft. @ 1200 R.P.M. [Series DT] Inline. L-head. Six. Cast iron block. B & S: 3-1/8 x 4-3/8 in. Disp.: 201 cu. in. Brake H.P.: 77 @ 3600 R.P.M.

CHASSIS: [Deluxe Six] W.B.: 117 in. Tires: 16 x 6.25. [Special Six] W.B.: 121 in. Tires: 16 x 6.25. [Standard Six] W.B.: 117 in. Tires: 16 x 6.25.

TECHNICAL: Selective sliding transmission. Speeds: 3F/1R. Floor shift controls. Single plate dry disc clutch. Semi-floating rear axle. Overall ratio: [DR] 3.8:1 or 5.1:1; [DS] 3.4:1 or 5.1:1; [DRXX] 3.8:1 or 5.1:1. Hydraulic brakes. "Floating Cushion" steel spoke wheels. Drivetrain options: Vacuum clutch (std. on Deluxe and Special). Overdrive.

OPTIONS: Front bumper. Rear bumper. Dual sidemount(s). Metal sidemount cover(s). Wire spoke wheels. Bumper guards. Radio. Heater. Clock. Cigar lighter. Radio antenna. Seat covers. Outside rear view mirror(s). Spotlight(s). Chrome-plated radiator shell (on Standard). Metal spare tire cover. Body pin striping (on Standard. Six). Wind wings (open models). License plate frame. Special paint.

HISTORICAL: Introduced: [DR/DS] January 2, 1934; [DRXX] June 2, 1934. Calendar year registrations: 90,139. Calendar year production: 108,687. Model year production: 95,011. Innovations: Synchronized front and rear springs. Larger, improved brake drums. "Draft Free" body ventilation. First automatic overdrive. Independent front suspension.

Dodge was America's fourth ranked automaker in model year 1934. This was the year that Dodge began promoting "showdowns." These comparison tests with contemporary cars were highlighted in many filmstrips produced by Chrysler's advertising agency Ross Roy. This technique is still used to sell Dodge products today. Production of the DR/DS Series started in January 1934 and ended the following November.

1935 DODGE

1935 Dodge Six, Series DU, convertible coupe (JAC)

DODGE NEW VALUE — SERIES DU — SIX: Dodge's "New Value" line for 1935 was totally restyled. Appearance characteristics included a narrower, more sloping radiator grille, horizontal "Wind Stream" hood louvers, all-steel bodies that extended down to the runningboards, lower rooflines, a 3-3/4 inch lower floor, a more fastback rear body treatment and parking lamps mounted on the front fender aprons. The new "humpback" touring sedans were advertised as "Century" sedans. Standard equipment included Autolite ignition, hydraulic brakes, ventilated clutch, "Floating Power," automatic choke, leaf spring front suspension, concealed radiator cap, "Finger Tip" steering, "Air-Glide" ride and a crank-open windshield. The engine was moved eight inches forward in the chassis this season and the seats were also moved forward for better weight distribution. Two models, the Caravan sedan and seven-passenger sedan, had a foot longer wheelbase and correspondingly longer bodies

1935 Dodge Six, Series DU, touring sedan (OCW)

DODGE — SERIES DV & DV-6 — SIX: This was once again a Plymouth-based small Dodge for the Canadian and overseas export markets. While full production figures are unknown, 1,170 right-hand-drive DVs were built in Detroit for export. In Canada the DV was sold in two trim levels, the DV or standard, and the DV-6 or Deluxe. Again, only minor trim differences were made to the Plymouth to make it look like a Dodge.

I.D. DATA: Serial numbers were in the same location. Starting: 3756501. Ending: 3913106. Engine numbers were in the same location. Starting: DU-1011. Ending: DU-159821. Canadian-built cars located serial numbers on right front door post. DV starting: 9460021. DV ending: 9464305. DV-6 starting: 9316226. DV-6 ending: 9316895. Engine numbers were located on left front corner of block.

Model No.	Body Type & Seating	Price	Weight	Prod. Total
DU	2-dr. Bus. Cpe.-2P	645	2731	17,800
DU	2-dr. R/S Cpe.-2/4P	710	2801	4499
DU	2-dr. Conv. Cpe.-2/4P	770	2883	950
DU	2-dr. Sed.-5P	690	2821	7891
DU	2-dr. Tr. Sed.-5P	715	2868	18,069

Model No.	Body Type & Seating	Price	Weight	Prod. Total
DU	4-dr. Sed.-5P	735	2861	33,118
DU	4-dr. Tr. Sed.-5P	760	2903	74,203
(Long Wheelbase)				
DU	4-dr. Caravan Sed.-5P	995	3118	193
DU	4-dr. Sed.-7P	995	3221	1018
DU	Chassis	NA	NA	1258

Note 1: Total series production was 158,999.

Model No.	Body Type & Seating	Price	Weight	Prod. Total
DV	Bus. Cpe.-2P	755	2745	—
DV	2-dr. Sed.-5P	810	2795	—
DV-6	Bus. Cpe.-2P	770	NA	—
DV-6	R/S Cpe.-4P	840	2840	—
DV-6	2-dr. Sed.-5P	835	NA	—
DV-6	2-dr. Tr. Sed.-5P	880	2865	—
DV-6	4-dr. Sed.-5P	880	2875	—
DV-6	4-dr. Tr. Sed.-5P	910	2910	—

Note: Prices shown in 1935 Canadian dollars.

ENGINE: Inline. L-head. Six. Cast iron block. B & S: 3-1/4 x 4-3/8 in. Disp.: 217.8 cu. in. C.R.: 6.5:1. Brake H.P.: 87 @ 3600 R.P.M. Net H.P.: 25.35. Main bearings: four. Valve lifters: solid. Carb.: Stromberg one-barrel model EX-22. Torque: 155 lb.-ft. @ 1200 R.P.M. [Series DV & DV-6] Inline. L-head. Six. Cast iron block. B & S: 3-1/8 x 4-3/8 in. Disp.: 201 cu. in. Brake H.P.: 82 @ 3600 R.P.M.

CHASSIS: [Standard DU] W.B.: 116 in. Tires: 16 x 6.00. [Long Wheelbase DU] W.B.: 128 in. Tires: 16 x 6.00. [Series DV & DV-6] W.B.: 113 in. Tires: 5.25 x 17 standard, 6.00 x 16 deluxe.

TECHNICAL: Selective sliding transmission. Speeds: 3F/1R. Floor shift controls. Single plate dry disc clutch. Semi-floating rear axle. Overall ratio: 4.7:1. Hydraulic brakes. Steel spoke wheels. Drivetrain options: Vacuum clutch. Overdrive.

OPTIONS: Front bumper. Rear bumper. Dual sidemounts. Metal side-mount cover(s). Wheel trim rings. Bumper guards. Radio. Heater. Clock. Cigar lighter. Radio antenna. Seat covers. Dual windshield wipers. Spotlight(s). Outside rear view mirror. Trunk rack. Touring trunk. Police equipment package. License plate frames. Special paint.

HISTORICAL: Introduced January 2, 1935. Calendar year registrations: 178,770. Calendar year production: 211,752. Model year production: 158,999. Innovations: Synchromatic gearshift control. Easier front steering. Leaf springs replace coil springs in front suspension. Sliding windows replace pivot type vent windows. High strength carbon molybdenum steel used for chassis parts. Dodge slipped one place to fifth position in U.S. model year production for 1935. The three millionth Dodge in history was built this year. Abram VanderZee was general sales manager of Dodge Division of Chrysler Corp. A number of wood-bodied Westchester Suburban station wagons were constructed on Dodge chassis by U.S. Body & Forging Co. of Tell City, Indiana. Production of 1935 Dodges started in November 1934 and ended in September 1935.

1936 DODGE

DODGE BEAUTY WINNER — SERIES D-2 — SIX: Dodge's new "Beauty Winner" Six line entered production in September 1935. Styling characteristics included a more rounded, but slightly convex radiator grille with four horizontal bars on each side, twin rows of transverse hood louvers with five chrome horizontal stripes, built-in horn housings below the torpedo-shaped headlamps and an all-steel top that blended smoothly into the roof surface and also was wired for a radio antenna. Only one long wheelbase car, the seven-passenger sedan, remained in the D-2 series. Standard equipment included Autolite ignition, hydraulic brakes, a built-in foot rest in the rear compartment, "Silent" front spring shackles and a new instrument panel design with a large, airplane type speedometer in the center and horizontal chrome moldings. Dodge headlight buckets were now finished in body color with chrome trim rings. Chair height seats were used inside the cars, which also featured more interior space. A four-door convertible sedan reappeared in the Dodge line this year and the U.S. Body & Forging Co. continued to build Westchester Suburban station wagons on Dodge chassis. These wood-bodied wagons had fabric roof inserts and snap-on canvas side curtains at the rear of the body. Also available from the factory was a new "Commercial" sedan that represented a cross between a passenger car and a sedan delivery truck.

1936 Dodge Six, Series D-2, touring sedan (JAC)

DODGE — SERIES D-3 & D-4 — SIX: Advertised as "The Money Saving Dodge," the D-3 standard and D-4 deluxe Dodges were once again based on the 1936 Plymouth P-1 and P-2 series cars. Built for export and the Canadian market, these "junior" Dodges put Dodge in the low-priced field in their respective selling markets. These cars varied only in grille and trim differences from the Plymouths upon which they were based, with Plymouth again supplying the engine, drivetrain and body for the conversion. These models were built in the United States for export and in the Windsor, Ontario, plant for Canadian consumption. Almost 3,100 D-3s were built in Detroit for export, with 36 cars being shipped with a small bore (2-7/8 inch) export engine and right-hand drive.

1936 Dodge Six, Series D-2, touring sedan (OCW)

I.D. DATA: Serial numbers were in the same locations. Starting: 4015051. Ending: 4276687. Engine numbers were in the same locations. Starting: D2-1001. Ending: D2-266089. Canadian-built cars: [D-3] Starting: 9316901. Ending: 9318219. [D-4] Starting: 9464311. Ending: 9469955.

Model No.	Body Type & Seating	Price	Weight	Prod. Total
D2	2-dr. Bus. Cpe.-2P	640	2773	32,952
D2	2-dr. R/S Cpe.-2/4P	695	2823	4317
D2	2-dr. Conv. Cpe.-2/4P	795	2887	1525
D2	2-dr. Sed.-5P	695	2903	2453
D2	2-dr. Tr. Sed.-5P	720	2893	37,468
D2	4-dr. Sed.-5P	735	2923	5996
D2	4-dr. Tr. Sed.-5P	760	2958	174,334
D2	4-dr. Conv. Sed.-5P	995	3018	750
D2	4-dr. Sed.-7P	975	3238	1942
D2	Chassis	NA	NA	1910
D2	4-dr. Comm. Sed.	665	1935	1358

Note 1: Total series production was 265,005.

D3	Bus. Cpe.-2P	730	2770	—
D3	2-dr. Sed.-5P	785	2840	—
D3	4-dr. Sed.-5P	825	2890	—
D3	2-dr. Tr. Sed.-5P	815	2850	—
D3	4-dr. Tr. Sed.-5P	855	2920	—
D3	Sed. Del.	800	2890	—
D4	Bus. Cpe.-2P	775	2805	—
D4	R/S Cpe.-4P	830	2890	—
D4	R/S Conv.-4P	965	2960	—
D4	2-dr. Tr. Sed.-5P	860	2920	—
D4	4-dr. Tr. Sed.-5P	900	2980	—

Note: Prices shown in 1936 Canadian dollars.

ENGINE: Inline. L-head. Six. Cast iron block. B & S: 3-1/4 x 4-3/8 in. Disp.: 217.8 cu. in. C.R.: 6.5:1. Brake H.P.: 87 @ 3600 R.P.M. Net H.P.: 25.35. Main bearings: four. Valve lifters: solid. Carb.: Stromberg one-barrel model EXV-2. Torque: 155 lb.-ft. @ 1200 R.P.M. [Series D-3 & D-4] Inline. L-head. Six. Cast iron block. B & S: 3-1/8 x 4-1/8 in. Disp.: 201 cu. in. Brake H.P.: 82 @ 3600 R.P.M.

CHASSIS: [Regular Chassis] W.B.: 116 in. Tires: 16 x 6.00. [Extended Chassis] W.B.: 128 in. Tires: 16 x 6.00. [Series D-3 & D-4] W.B.: 113 in. Tires: D-3 5.50 x 17, D-4 6.00 x 16.

TECHNICAL: Selective sliding transmission. Speeds: 3F/1R. Floor shift controls. Single plate dry disc clutch. Semi-floating rear axle. Overall ratio: 4.125:1 or 3.88:1. Hydraulic brakes. Steel artillery spoke wheels. Drivetrain options: Vacuum clutch. Overdrive.

OPTIONS: Front bumper. Rear bumper. Single sidemount (commercial sedan). Dual sidemounts. Metal sidemount cover(s). Fender skirts. Bumper guards. Radio. Heater. Clock. Cigar lighter. Radio antenna. Seat covers. Dual windshield wipers. Spotlights. Chrome wheel beauty trim rings. Outside rear view mirror. Chrome license plate frames. Whitewall tires. Metal spare tire cover. Special paint.

HISTORICAL: Introduced November 2, 1935. Calendar year registrations: 248,518. Calendar year production: 274,904. Model year production: 263,647. Innovations: All-steel top construction wired for radio antenna. New commercial sedan introduced. Silent front spring shackles.

Dodge battled its way back into fourth place in U.S. model year production for 1936. Although Dodge did not produce Airflow passenger cars, the company manufactured 112 distinctive Airflow trucks between January 1935 and December 1936. For more information on Dodge trucks consult Krause Publication's *Encyclopedia of American Work Trucks.* Production of 1936 models ended in August of that year.

1937 DODGE

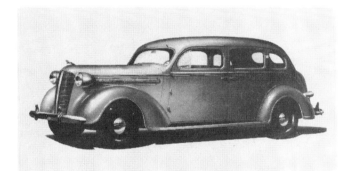

1937 Dodge Six, Series D-5, touring sedan (OCW)

DODGE — SERIES D5 — SIX: For 1937, the Dodge styling theme was patterned after that of other Chrysler products. A new split grille featured several vertical chrome moldings running down the center that were paralleled by wider body colored panels. The grilles on either side had multiple chrome-plated horizontal strips. Larger, more deeply crowned bullet-shaped headlamps were mounted on either side of the grille. There were no longer any horn parts in the fender aprons, the horns being moved into a new behind-the-grille location. A chrome drip molding now extended the full length of the all-steel body on all models and door handles were curved inward for safety. Hood louvers were again of a transverse design, but had slightly fewer vents and chrome moldings. Standard equipment included Autolite ignition, hydraulic brakes, all-steel disc wheels, "No-Draft" ventilation, reading lamps over rear windows (in lieu of dome lamps), ventipane type windows, new 16-gallon fuel tanks, dual taillamps, divided rear windows on all sedans and single windshield wipers. A new hypoid rear axle allowed a flat floor in the rear compartment as well as a lower driveshaft tunnel. Interior safety was emphasized this year with the introduction of non-snag door handles, recessed dash knobs and flush-mounted gauges. Built-in defroster vents were another new Dodge feature.

DODGE — SERIES D6 & D7 — SIX: The junior Dodge was once again Plymouth based, the D6 corresponding to the P3 business line with the D7 in deluxe trim like the P4 Plymouth. Plymouth once again supplied the engine, chassis and body, with Dodge supplying the grille and other corporate identity items. Detroit-built conversions were shipped overseas to the tune of better than 7,000 cars, including 39 fitted with a small-

bore (2-1/8 inch) export engine. These cars were shipped both completed and knocked down for overseas final assembly. Total Canadian production is uncertain.

I.D. DATA: Serial numbers were in the same location. (Detroit factory) Starting: 4530451. Ending: 4789907. (Evansville, Indiana, factory) Starting: 9118501. Ending: 9149361. Engine numbers were in the same location. Starting: D5-1001. Ending: D5-295935. (Canadian-built cars) D6 Starting: 9318226 and 9387361. D6 Ending: 9319000 and 9388420. D7 Starting: 9469961. D7 Ending: 9478110.

Model No.	Body Type & Seating	Price	Weight	Prod. Total
D5	2-dr. Bus. Cpe.-2P	715	2902	41,702
D5	2-dr. R/S Cpe.-2/4P	770	2967	3500
D5	2-dr. Conv. Cpe.-2/4P	910	3057	1345
D5	2-dr. FsBk. Sed.-5P	780	2992	5302
D5	2-dr. Tr. Sed.-5P	790	2997	44,750
D5	4-dr. FsBk. Sed.-5P	820	2982	7555
D5	4-dr. Tr. Sed.-5P	830	2997	185,483
D5	4-dr. Conv. Sed.-5P	1230	3262	473
(Long Wheelbase)				
D5	4-dr. Sed.-7P	1075	3367	2207
D5	4-dr. Limo.-5P	1175	NA	216
D5	Chassis	NA	NA	2514
D5	2-dr. Murray Conv. Vic.-5P	NA	NA	(Chassis)
D6	Bus. Cpe.-2P	720	2850	—
D6	2-dr. Sed.-5P	775	2880	—
D6	4-dr. Sed.-5P	820	2930	—
D6	2-dr. Tr. Sed.-5P	795	2895	—
D6	4-dr. Tr. Sed.-5P	840	2950	—
D7	Bus. Cpe.-2P	760	2895	—
D7	R/S Cpe.-4P	820	2995	—
D7	2-dr. Tr. Sed.-5P	850	2970	—
D7	4-dr. Tr. Sed.-5P	890	2975	—

Note: Prices shown in 1937 Canadian dollars.

Note 1: Total series production was 295,047.

Note 2: The custom-built Murray convertible victoria was constructed on the Dodge chassis by Murray Body Corp. This car was first used by engineering executive Fred Zeder and later used by Dean Clark, a Chrysler designer who worked in the Art & Colour Studio.

ENGINE: Inline. L-head. Six. Cast iron block. B & S: 3-1/4 x 4-3/8 in. Disp.: 217.8 cu. in. C.R.: 6.5:1. Brake H.P.: 87 @ 3600 R.P.M. Net H.P.: 25.35. Main bearings: four. Valve lifters: solid. Carb.: Stromberg one-barrel model EXV-2. Torque: 155 lb.-ft. @ 1200 R.P.M. [Series D6 & D7] Inline. L-head. Six. Cast iron block. B & S: 3-1/8 x 4-1/8 in. Disp.: 201 cu. in. Brake H.P.: 82 @ 3600 R.P.M.

CHASSIS: [Series D5; regular chassis] W.B.: 115 in. Tires: 6.00 x 16. [Series DS, extended chassis] W.B.: 132 in. Tires: 6.50 x 16. [Series D6 & D7] W.B. 112 in. Tires: D6 5.50 x 16; D7 6.00 x 16.

TECHNICAL: Selective sliding transmission. Speeds: 3F/1R. Floor shift controls. Single plate dry disc clutch. Hypoid rear axle. Overall ratio: 4.1:1; (coupes) 3.9:1. Hydraulic brakes. Steel disc wheels. Drivetrain options: Vacuum clutch. Overdrive.

OPTIONS: Front bumper. Rear bumper. Chrome wheel beauty trim rings. Dual sidemounts (Westchester Suburban). Metal sidemount covers. Fender skirts. Bumper guards. Radio. Heater. Clock. Cigar lighter. Radio antenna. Seat covers. Outside rear view mirror. Spotlights. Whitewall tires. Chrome license plate frames. Dual windshield wipers. Special paint.

HISTORICAL: Introduced October 1936. Calendar year registrations: 255,258. Calendar year production: 288,841. Model year production: 295,047. Innovations: First in auto industry to feature fully-insulated rubber body mountings. Safety padding on front seatbacks. Steel disc wheels made standard equipment. Safety recessed door handles and gauges. Hypoid rear axles. Longer wheelbase on extended chassis models.

Dodge remained America's fourth largest automaker in model year 1937. The wood-bodied Westchester Suburban was again available for the Dodge chassis this season. Actor Clark Gable owned a 1937 Dodge Westchester Suburban fitted with dual sidemounted spares and twin spotlights. Production of 1937 models started in September 1936 and ended in August 1937.

1938 DODGE

DODGE — SERIES D8 — SIX: The 1938 Dodge was mildly face lifted from 1937. The new radiator grille had narrower stripes down the center, with narrower horizontal bars on either side. These bars harmonized with the new, horizontal hood louvers. The headlamps were moved on top of the fenders. A Dodge Brothers type emblem was again used on the grille, but this would be the last time for such identification. A leaping ram hood ornament was on top of the nose of the cars. The factory offered 10 body styles, with the seven-passenger sedan and division window limousine on a lengthened wheelbase. New 1938 features were all-steel, "silent-safety" body construction with insulated roofs, rear quarters, body, cowl and door panels and adjustable seats with a lever at the driver's left hand. Standard equipment included Autolite ignition, hydraulic brakes, single windshield wipers, dual taillights, improved engine mountings, self-lubricating clutch and 16-gallon fuel tank. The limousine again had a leather front seat, velvet mohair rear seat and division window between the driver's and passenger's compartment. The seven-passenger sedan had a pair of folding jump seats in the passenger's compartment.

1938 Dodge Six, Series D8, two-door sedan (JAC)

1938 Dodge Six, Series D8, touring sedan (AA)

DODGE — SERIES D9 & D10 DELUXE — SIX: Dodge juniors this year were based on the Plymouth P5 and P6 models. Again, Plymouth supplied body, chassis and drivetrain while Dodge supplied the grille and other identity items. Conversions were built in both the U.S. (for export) and in Windsor (for the Canadian market). Only the D9 was built in the U.S., with nearly 7,500 units shipped, 81 with the small-bore (2-7/8 inch) engine; 4,285 of these had right-hand drive as well. Canadian production came to over 10,000 units.

I.D. DATA: Serial numbers were in the same location. (Detroit) Starting: 3001001. Ending: 30097065. (Evansville) Starting: 4001001. Ending: 4001625. Engine numbers were in the same location. Starting: D8-1001. Ending: D8-114530. (Canada) D9 Starting: 9388426. Ending: 9390904. D10 Starting: 9478116. Ending: 9486415.

Model No.	Body Type & Seating	Price	Weight	Prod. Total
D8	2-dr. Bus. Cpe.-2P	808	2877	15,552
D8	2-dr. R/S Cpe.-2/4P	858	2952	950
D8	2-dr. Conv. Cpe.-2/4P	960	3122	701
D8	2-dr. FsBk. Sed.-5P	858	2977	999
D8	2-dr. Tr. Sed.-5P	870	2957	17,282
D8	4-dr. FsBk. Sed.-5P	898	2977	714
D8	4-dr. Tr. Sed.-5P	910	2967	73,417
D8	4-dr. Conv. Sed.-5P	1275	3308	132
(Long Wheelbase)				
D8	4-dr. Tr. Sed.-7P	1095	3332	1953
D8	4-dr. Limo.-5P	1185	3380	153
D8	Chassis	NA	NA	2301
(Semi-Custom)				
D8	4-dr. W'chest. Sub.-7P	1028	3200	375

Note 1: Total series production was 114,529

Model No.	Body Type & Seating	Price	Weight	Prod. Total
D9	Bus. Cpe.-2P	850	2875	—
D9	2-dr. Sed.-5P	913	2915	—
D9	2-dr. Tr. Sed.-5P	928	2925	—
D9	4-dr. Sed.-5P	960	2950	—
D9	4-dr. Tr. Sed.-5P	975	2955	—
D10	Bus. Cpe.-2P	915	2925	—
D10	R/S Cpe.-4P	964	3005	—
D10	2-dr. Sed.-5P	966	3005	—
D10	2-dr. Tr. Sed.-5P	981	3020	—
D10	4-dr. Sed.-5P	1003	3000	—
D10	4-dr. Tr. Sed.-5P	1018	3035	—

Note: Prices given in 1938 Canadian dollars.

1938 Dodge Six, Series D9, four-door sedan (JB)

ENGINE: Inline. L-head. Six. Cast iron block. B & S: 3-1/4 x 4-3/8 in. Disp.: 217.8 cu. in. C.R.: 6.5:1. Brake H.P.: 87 @ 3600 R.P.M. Net H.P.: 25.35. Main bearings: four. Valve lifters: solid. Carb.: Stromberg one-barrel model EXV-2. Torque: 155 lb.-ft. @ 1200 R.P.M. [Series D9 & D10] Inline. L-head. Six. Cast iron block. B & S: 3-1/8 x 4-3/4 in. Disp.: 201 cu. in. Brake H.P.: 82 @ 3600 R.P.M.

CHASSIS: [D8; regular chassis] W.B.: 115 in. Tires: 6.00 x 16. [Series D8; extended chassis] W.B.: 132 in. Tires: 6.50 x 16. [Series D9 & D10] W.B.: 112 in.

TECHNICAL: Selective sliding transmission. Speeds: 3F/1R. Floor shift controls. Single plate dry disc clutch. Hypoid rear axle. Overall ratio: [sedan] 4.1:1 [coupe] 3.9:1; [opt.] 4.3:1. Hydraulic brakes. Steel disc wheels. Drivetrain options: Vacuum clutch. Overdrive.

OPTIONS: Front bumper. Rear bumper. Single sidemount (station wagon). Metal sidemount cover (station wagon). Fender skirts. Bumper guards. Radio. Heater. Clock. Cigar lighter. Radio antenna. Seat covers. Dual windshield wipers. Spotlight(s). Whitewall tires. Chrome wheel beauty trim rings. Master grille guard. Chrome license plate frames. Special paint. Outside rear view mirror.

HISTORICAL: Introduced October 1937. Calendar year registrations: 104,881. Calendar year production: 106,370. Model year production: 114,529. Innovations: Improved body insulation. Parking brake mounted on cowl to right of driver. Longer life engine mountings. Larger, self-lubricating clutch bearing. Rubber windshield mountings without metal frames. Dodge placed fifth in model year production during this recession year. The company continued to build Airflow type heavy trucks this season and introduced a new route van type truck. A new Dodge truck factory was opened in Detroit, Michigan. Production of 1938 models began in September 1937 and ended in July 1938.

1939 DODGE

DODGE LUXURY LINER — SERIES D11 — SIX: Heralding the 25th anniversary of the Dodge nameplate were 10 cars featuring all-new styling. There were three cars in the low-priced Special sub-series and seven in the Deluxe line. Two of the Deluxe models were on the extended length chassis, which now had a 134-inch wheelbase. The regular chassis also grew about two inches. Appearance characteristics of these "Luxury Liners" included a rounded hood with narrow, horizontal grille bars in the nose, near the top center. Below this were larger grilles (with horizontal bars) in the fender splash aprons, divided by a "vee" extending up to the sides of the hood. The all-new bodies were longer and wider, with the door bottoms flared outward. Headlamps were fully recessed into the front fenders. Each side of the hood had two groupings of short, horizontal louvers with one group at the front and the other at the rear. New features included a "Remote Control" gearshift mounted on the steering column and independent front suspension with coil springs. Two-piece split windshields were used and a new "Safety Light" speedometer had a lighted bead that glowed different colors depending on car speed. Standard equipment included Autolite ignition, hydraulic brakes, dual taillights, door safety buttons on garnish moldings, 18-gallon fuel tank, steel disc wheels and No-Draft ventilation. A special turret-top coupe with a rear "split window" look was built by the Hayes Body Corp. and known as the town coupe.

1939 Dodge, Deluxe Six, Series D11, four-door sedan (OCW)

DODGE — SERIES D12 & D13 DELUXE — SIX: Continuing the practice of offering a junior series Dodge in the Canadian and export markets, Plymouth again supplied body, chassis and running gear to Dodge. A Dodge grille and trim gave the cars separate identity. Export junior Dodges were again built in the U.S. while Windsor built conversions mainly for the Canadian marketplace. Nearly 6,800 D12 Sixes of U.S. origin were sold, 3,438 were right-hand drive, 38 fitted with the small-bore (2-7/8 inch) export engine; 2,924 were shipped as built-up units, the remaining 3,885 as CKD (completely knocked down) units for final overseas assembly. Windsor accounted for an additional 10,328 units for the Canadian trade.

I.D. DATA: Serial numbers were in the same location. Starting: (Spl.) 4276701; (Del.) 30100001. Ending: (Spl.) 4347700; (Del.) 30214458. Engine numbers were in the same location. Starting: (Spl.) D11-1001; (Del.) D11-1001. Ending: (Spl.) D11-186148. (Del.) D11-186527. (Canada) D12 Starting: 9390906. Ending: 9393277. D13 Starting: 9486416. Ending: 9494715.

Model No.	Body Type & Seating	Price	Weight	Prod. Total
Special				
D11	2-dr. Bus. Cpe.-2P	756	2905	12,300
D11	2-dr. Sed.-5P	815	2955	26,700
D11	4-dr. Sed.-5P	855	2995	32,000
Deluxe				
D11	2-dr. Bus. Cpe.-2P	803	2940	Note 2
D11	2-dr. A/S Cpe.-2/4P	860	2985	Note 2
D11	2-dr. Twn. Cpe.-5P	1055	3075	602
D11	2-dr. Sed.-5P	865	3010	Note 2
D11	4-dr. Sed.-5P	905	3045	Note 2
Deluxe Long Wheelbase				
D11	4-dr. Sed.-7P	1095	3440	Note 2
D11	4-dr. Limo.-7P	1185	3545	Note 2

Note 1: The range of serial numbers suggests that approximately 70,999 Special and 114,457 Deluxe Dodge "Luxury Liners" were built.

Note 2: Several books show production totals for the D13 Series built in Canada and apply these figures to the Deluxe D11 Series. We believe this to be an error and feel that production totals for U.S.-built Specials are not available at this time.

Note 3: Hayes Body Corp. supplied 1,000 town coupe bodies to Chrysler. Since 264 DeSoto town coupes and 134 Chrysler town coupes were made, it can be assumed that the remaining 602 cars were Dodge town coupes.

D12	Bus. Cpe.-2P	860	2850	—
D12	2-dr. Sed.-5P	927	2900	—
D12	2-dr. Tr. Sed.-5P	944	2895	—
D12	4-dr. Sed.-5P	979	2935	—
D12	4-dr. Tr. Sed.-5P	995	2935	—
D13	Bus. Cpe.-2P	948	2900	—
D13	2-dr. Sed.-5P	1004	2985	—
D13	2-dr. Tr. Sed.-5P	1020	2990	—
D13	4-dr. Tr. Sed.-5P	1061	2995	—
D13	4-dr. Sed.-5P	1044	3000	—

Note: Prices given in 1939 Canadian dollars.

1939 Dodge Six, Series D12, coupe (JB)

1939 Dodge, Deluxe Six, Series D11, Town Coupe, Hayes (OCW)

ENGINE: Inline. L-head. Six. Cast iron block. B & S: 3-1/4 x 4-3/8 in. Disp.: 217.8 cu. in. C.R.: 6.5:1. Brake H.P.: 87 @ 3600 R.P.M. Net H.P.: 25.35. Main bearings: four. Valve lifters: solid. Carb.: Stromberg one-barrel model BXV-3. Torque: 158 lb.-ft. @ 1200 R.P.M. [Series D12 & D13] Inline. L-head. Six. Cast iron block. B & S: 3-1/8 x 4-3/8 in. Disp.: 201 cu. in. Brake H.P.: 82 @ 3600 R.P.M.

CHASSIS: [Special Series] W.B.: 117 in. Tires: 16 x 6.00. [Deluxe SWB Series] W.B.: 117 in. Tires: 16 x 6.00. [Deluxe LWB Series] W.B.: 134 in. Tires: 16 x 6.50. [Series D12 & D13] W.B.: 114 in.

TECHNICAL: Selective sliding transmission. Speeds: 3F/1R. Column shift controls. Single plate dry disc clutch. Hypoid rear axle. Overall ratio: [Reg. W.B.] 4.1:1; [Extended W.B.] 4.3:1. Hydraulic brakes. Steel disc wheels.

OPTIONS: Front bumper. Rear bumper. Whitewall tires. Chrome beauty rings. Outside rear view mirror. Fender skirts. Bumper guards. Radio. Heater. Clock. Cigar lighter. Radio antenna. Seat covers. Dual taillight (on business coupe). Spotlights. Front bumper guard extension rails. Fender mounted parking lamps. Directional signals. Chrome license plate frames. Special paint.

HISTORICAL: Introduced October 1938. Calendar year registrations: 176,585. Calendar year production: 186,474. Model year production: 179,300. Innovations: Column gearshift controls. Cowl mounted windshield wipers. Independent front suspension with coil springs. "Safety Light" speedometer. Roomier interiors with wider seats. Improved carburetion. Increased torque. Dodge was America's fifth largest automaker in model year 1939, which was also the company's 25th anniversary year. Production of 1939 models started in August 1938 and ended in July 1939.

1940 DODGE

DODGE LUXURY LINER SPECIAL — SERIES D17 — SIX: A longer wheelbase and larger body highlighted the restyled 1940 Dodge "Luxury

Liner." The year's new frontal treatment sported a two-piece grille with horizontal chrome bars extending across the radiator and fender aprons. The upper and lower grilles were separated by a horizontal, body color panel. The upper grille tapered to a sharp point on the nose of the car, which had a ram hood ornament on top and the Dodge name on either side. A horizontal chrome molding trimmed the hoodside. It had short, slanting chrome hash marks at the front, center and rear. A wide chrome molding ran from the grille down the center of the hood. Sealed beam headlights were fully recessed into the front fenders, with parking lights incorporated into the chrome bezels. The front fenders were decorated with three, long "wind stream" bead moldings along their sides. Base trim features were found on the D17 Specials, which had no lower body-side moldings. The beltline was decorated with a paint stripe instead of chrome molding. Standard equipment included Autolite ignition, hydraulic brakes, single vacuum windshield wiper, standard steering wheel, regular seat cushions, instrument panel safety signals, wider front and rear seats, full-floating suspension system and concealed door hinges. Conventional runningboards were now optional equipment.

1940 Dodge, Series D17, two-door sedan (OCW)

1940 Dodge, Deluxe Six, Series D14, four-door sedan (OCW)

DODGE LUXURY LINER DELUXE — SERIES D14 — SIX: The Deluxe Series for 1940 was again separated into standard and extended chassis car-lines, both of which had D14 model designations. The smaller cars had a 2-1/2 inch longer wheelbase than 1939 Dodges, while the big, seven-passenger wheelbase grew 5-1/2 inches. Deluxe models had the same basic appearance as the Specials, but carried slightly more trim and equipment. Interior appointments were also plusher. Some of the distinctive Deluxe features included "Air Foam" seat cushions, dual electric windshield wipers, chrome beltline trim moldings, deluxe steering wheel with horn ring, chrome moldings on the lower bodysides (or runningboards) and richer upholstery. As in 1939, the fancier version of the Deluxe coupe carried folding auxiliary seats inside the body, rather than a rumbleseat. The larger, seven-passenger models had wider doors, door windows and front sheet metal. The long wheelbase sedan featured folding jump seats and the limousine also had a leather front seat and glass partition window. Optional two-tone finish was available for the Deluxe four-door sedan and included a harmonizing interior with special dress-up trim and a chrome exterior molding between the upper and lower sections of the grille.

DODGE — SERIES D14 KINGSWAY, D15 DELUXE & D15 DELUXE SPECIAL — SIX: This year's junior Dodge series expanded into three distinct groups, at least in the Canadian market, although the Deluxe Special differed from the Deluxe only in being equipped with dual sun visors and horns, horn rings, cigar lighter and front door armrests. Whether three models were offered in the foreign export cars is unknown. Again, these cars were based on the Plymouth body shell and chassis with a Canadian sourced engine; a Dodge grille and trim differentiated from the Plymouth. Only the D15 version was built in the U.S. for export, pro-

duction totaling 4,317 units, nearly two-thirds of which were right-hand drive vehicles; none had the small bore export engine fitted, however.

I.D. DATA: [D17] Serial numbers in same location. Starting: 4349001. Ending: 4415505. Engine numbers in same location. Starting: D14-1001. Ending: D14-19385.
Note: Since both series used the same engine, all engines are coded "D14." [D14] Serial numbers in same location. Starting: 30216001. Ending: 30342333. Engine numbers in same location. Starting: D14-1001. Ending: D14-193835.

(Canadian) D14 Starting: 9420231. Ending: 9422897. D15 Starting: 9669926. Ending: 9673662.

Model No.	Body Type & Seating	Price	Weight	Prod. Total
D17	2-dr. Bus. Cpe.-2P	755	2867	12,001
D17	2-dr. Sed.-5P	815	2942	27,700
D17	4-dr. Sed.-5P	855	2997	26,803

Note 1: Total series production was 66,504.
Note 2: Add 25 pounds for cars with conventional runningboards.

D14	2-dr. Bus. Cpe.-2P	803	2905	12,750
D14	2-dr. A/S Cpe.-2/4P	855	2973	8028
D14	2-dr. Conv. Cpe.-5P	1030	3190	2100
D14	2-dr. Sed.-5P	860	2990	19,838
D14	4-dr. Sed.-5P	905	3028	84,976
(Extended Chassis)				
D14	4-dr. Sed.-7P	1095	3460	932
D14	4-dr. Limo.-7P	1170	3550	79
D14	Chassis	NA	NA	298

Note 1: Total series production was 129,001.
Note 2: Add 25 pounds for cars with conventional runningboards.

D14	4-dr. Sed.-6P	995	2980	—
D14	2-dr. Sed.-6P	944	2965	—
D14	Bus. Cpe.-3P	860	2890	—
D15	Deluxe 4-dr. Sed.-6P	1061	3060	—
D15	Deluxe 2-dr. Sed.-6P	1020	3010	—
D15	Deluxe Bus. Cpe.-3P	948	2930	—
D15	Del. Spec. 4-dr. Sed.-6P	1088	3060	—
D15	Del. Spec. 2-dr. Sed.-6P	1048	3020	—
D15	Del. Spec. Bus. Cpe.-3P	975	2950	—
D15	Del. Spec. Clb. Cpe.-4P	1037	3000	—

Note: Prices shown in 1940 Canadian dollars.

1940 Dodge, sedan (Australian) (JB)

ENGINE: Inline. L-head. Six. Cast iron block. B & S: 3-1/4 x 4-3/8 in. Disp.: 217.8 cu. in. C.R.: 6.5:1. Brake H.P.: 87 @ 3600 R.P.M. Net H.P.: 25.35. Main bearings: four. Valve lifters: solid. Carb.: Stromberg one-barrel model BXV-3. Torque: 166 lb.-ft. @ 1200 R.P.M. [Canada/Export] Inline. L-head. Six. Cast iron block. B & S: 3-1/4 x 4-3/8 in. Disp.: 218 cu. in. Brake H.P.: 84 @ 3600 R.P.M.

CHASSIS: [Special Series] W.B.: 119-1/2 in. Tires: 16 x 6.00. [Deluxe SWB Series] W.B.: 119-1/2 in. Tires: 16 x 6.00. [Deluxe LWB Series] W.B.: 139-1/2 in. Tires: 16 x 6.50. [Canada/Export] W.B.: 117 in. Tires: D14 5.50 x 16, D15 6.00 x 16.

TECHNICAL: Selective sliding transmission. Speeds: 3F/1R. Column shift controls. Single plate dry disc clutch. Hypoid rear axle. Overall ratio: [Sed.] 4.1:1; [Cpe.] 3.9:1. Hydraulic brakes. Steel disc wheels.

OPTIONS: Front bumper. Rear bumper. Whitewall tires. Wheel trim rings. Oversize tires. Fender skirts. Bumper guards. Radio. Heater. Clock. Cigar lighter. Radio antenna. Seat covers. External sun shade. Spotlights. Master grille guard. Two-tone paint (Deluxe four-door sedan). Special paint. Chrome license plate frames. Deluxe trim package (Special models). Conventional runningboards. Rear fender rubber scuff pads. Outside rear view mirror.

HISTORICAL: Introduced September 1939. Calendar year registrations: 197,252. Calendar year production: 225,595. Model year production: 195,505. Innovations: Sealed beam headlights. Longer wheelbase. Increased torque rating. Two leading shoe front wheel brakes. Safety wheel rims introduced. Dodge fell to seventh position in the model year production charts. Dodge accounted for 26 percent of Chrysler Corp.'s sales volume this year. Production of 1940 models began in August 1939 and ended in July 1940.

1941 DODGE

1941 Dodge, Custom, Series D19, six-passenger town sedan (OCW)

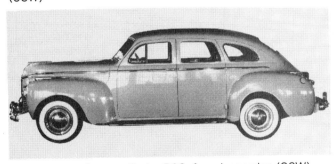

1941 Dodge, Custom, Series D19, four-door sedan (OCW)

DODGE — SERIES D19 — SIX: The 1941 Dodge models featured larger, vee-shaped windshields. The size of rear windows was also increased. Two large, horizontal-bar grilles were separated by a vee-shaped panel done in body color. The grilles stretched completely over the fender aprons to the headlamps. A chrome molding ran over the nose and down the center of the hood. Decorative elements included a winged crest bearing the Dodge family coat-of-arms mounted at the front of the nose and a streamlined ram ornament mounted on top. All models had a chrome beltline molding running from the front of the hood to the rear of the body. Although all 1941 Dodges had the same D19 series designation, there were still three types of cars. The base trim level now used "Deluxe" nomenclature, while the fancier models were called "Customs." The Custom Six featured certain extras such as "Air Foam" seat cushions, dual electric windshield wipers, a right-hand inside armrest, Deluxe steering wheel and chrome beading around the outside windows. The third type of Dodge was the extended chassis models that accommodated seven passengers with the addition of jump seats in the rear. Standard equipment included Autolite ignition, hydraulic brakes, hump-rim safety wheels, vertical uplift door handles, oil bath air cleaner and more powerful engine. Fluid drive was optional on all Dodge products.

DODGE — SERIES D20 KINGSWAY, D21 DELUXE & D21 DELUXE SPECIAL — SIX: Once again, at least for the Canadian market, the junior Dodges were broken down into three categories although differences among them were minimal — the Deluxe Special being noted only as having a cigar lighter and front door armrests to differentiate it from the Kingsway and Deluxe versions. Based on the P11 and P12 Plymouth

series, the junior Dodges were built in the U.S. for export and in Windsor for the Canadian markets. Leaving the Detroit assembly line were 1,180 D20s and 2,094 D20 Deluxes, while nearly 14,000 units came off the Windsor line. Again Plymouth supplied the body and chassis with a Dodge 218-cubic inch engine (which Plymouth would begin using in its 1942 U.S. production).

I.D. DATA: Serial numbers in same location. Starting: 30342401. Ending: 30576861. Engine numbers in same location. Starting: D19-1001. Ending: D19-235536. [Canadian] D20 Starting: 9673666. Ending: 9681156. D21 Starting: 9503606. Ending: 9510870.

Model No.	Body Type & Seating	Price	Weight	Prod. Total
Deluxe Series				
D19	2-dr. Bus. Cpe.-2P	862	3034	22,318
D19	2-dr. Sed.-5P	915	3109	34,566
D19	4-dr. Sed.-5P	954	3149	49,579
Custom Series, 119.5" wb				
D19	2-dr. Clb. Cpe.-6P	995	3154	18,024
D19	2-dr. Conv. Cpe.-5P	1162	3384	3554
D19	2-dr. Brgm.-6P	962	3169	20,146
D19	4-dr. Sed.-6P	999	3194	72,067
D19	4-dr. Twn. Sed.-6P	1062	3234	16,074
Custom Series, 137.5" wb				
D19	4-dr. Sed.-7P	1195	3579	601
D19	4-dr. Limo.-7P	1262	3669	50
D19	Chassis	NA	NA	20

Note 1: Total series production was 236,999.

Note 2: The Custom club coupe was a five-window coupe; the convertible coupe now had rear quarter windows; the Custom brougham was a two-door sedan with vent panes in the rear side window; the four-door sedan had separate rear quarter windows; the town sedan had large rear door windows with vent panes at the rear.

Kingsway Series				
D20	Cpe.-3P	1079	2945	—
D20	Clb. Cpe.-5P	1167	3010	—
D20	2-dr. Sed.-6P	1178	3015	—
D20	4-dr. Sed.-6P	1241	3030	—
Kingsway Special Series				
D20	Cpe.-3P	1105	2960	—
D20	Clb. Cpe.-5P	1192	3025	—
D20	2-dr. Sed.-6P	1203	3030	—
D20	4-dr. Sed.-6P	1266	3045	—
Deluxe Series				
D21	Cpe.-3P	1191	2990	—
D21	2-dr. Sed.-6P	1277	3060	—
D21	4-dr. Sed.-6P	1327	3100	—
Deluxe Special Series				
D21	Cpe.-3P	1222	3015	—
D21	Clb. Cpe.-5P	1297	3085	—
D21	2-dr. Sed.-6P	1309	3080	—
D21	4-dr. Sed.-6P	1359	3135	—
D21	4-dr. Sed.-7P	1676	3565	—

Note: Prices given in 1941 Canadian dollars.

ENGINE: Inline. L-head. Six. Cast iron block. B & S: 3-1/4 x 4-3/8 in. Disp.: 217.8 cu. in. C.R.: 6.5:1. Brake H.P.: 91 @ 3800 R.P.M. Net H.P.: 25.35. Main bearings: four. Valve lifters: solid. Carb.: Stromberg one-barrel model BXV-3. Torque: 170 lb.-ft. @ 1200 R.P.M. [Canada/Export] Inline. L-head. Six. B & S: 3-3/8 x 4-1/6 in. Disp.: 218 cu. in. Brake H.P.: 88 @ 3800 R.P.M.

CHASSIS: [Deluxe Series] W.B.: 119.5 in. Tires: 16 x 6.00. [Custom SWB Series] W.B.: 119.5 in. Tires: 16 x 6.00. [Custom LWB Series] W.B.: 137.5 in. Tires: 16 x 6.50. [Canada/Export] W.B.: 117-1/2 in.

TECHNICAL: Selective sliding transmission. Speeds: 3F/1R. Column shift controls. Single plate dry disc clutch. Hypoid rear axle. Overall ratio: 4.3:1. Hydraulic brakes. Safety steel disc wheels. Drivetrain options: Fluid drive.

OPTIONS: Front bumper. Rear bumper. Whitewall tires. Wheel trim beauty rings. Oversize tires. Fender skirts. Bumper guards. Radio. Heater. Clock. Cigar lighter. Radio antenna. Seat covers. External sun shade. Spotlights. Fender mounted turn signals. Outside rear view mirror. Conventional runningboards. Master grille guards. Full wheel discs. Chrome fender speed line moldings. Special paint. Chrome license plate frames. Custom trim package.

HISTORICAL: Introduced September 1940. Calendar year registrations: 215,563. Calendar year production: 215,575. Model year production: 236,999. Innovations: Fluid Drive. Safety rim wheels. Shorter wheelbase on seven-passenger models. Taillights mounted in chrome, fin-like housings on top of rear fenders. Higher horsepower six-cylinder engine. Torque rating increased again. Dodge came in as the seventh most active U.S.

automaker for the 1941 model year. Production of the D19 Series began in August 1940 and ended in September 1941.

1942 DODGE

1942 Dodge, Deluxe, Series D22, two-door sedan (OCW)

DODGE — SERIES D22 — SIX: The 1942 Dodge had a more massive front end appearance. The front grille design had a square effect with heavy horizontal bars extending to the head lamps. The hood was hinged at the rear and opened with a pull control button mounted below the instrument panel. The fenders were of a more sweeping, streamlined design. Dual "Air-Line" moldings were placed low on the front and rear fenders. Other features included concealed runningboards and an airplane type speedometer. At the rear, rectangular taillamps were moved back onto the body and mounted flush in small chrome housings. Deluxe models represented the base trim car-line. Custom models included "Air-Foam" seat cushions, dual electric windshield wipers and chrome beading around the outside windows as standard equipment. All models had Autolite ignition, hydraulic brakes, a new "Power Flow" six-cylinder engine and a heavier crankshaft. New "All-Fluid" drive was optional at extra cost. Dodge sales ceased on February 21, 1942, after the outbreak of World War II. Cars built between mid-December and January had "blackout" style trim with most bright metal parts painted.

1942 Dodge, Custom, Series D22, convertible coupe (OCW)

DODGE — SERIES D23S DELUXE & D23C SPECIAL DELUXE — SIX: The Plymouth-based junior series Dodge enjoyed brisk sales in Canada, while U.S. production for export dropped dramatically as a result of World War II: 1,113 units compared to Canada's 6,461. Again two distinct series were offered corresponding to the similar P14S and P14C models from Plymouth on which the cars were based. Canadian-built cars utilized the 25-inch "long-block" engine from the Canadian foundry while U.S. sourced vehicles continued to use the shorter 23-inch block.

I.D. DATA: Serial numbers in same location. Starting: 30577001. Ending: 30644378. Engine numbers in same location. Starting: D22-1001. Ending: D22-68416. [Canada] D23 Starting: 9681161. Ending: 9687621.

Model No.	Body Type & Seating	Price	Weight	Prod. Total
Deluxe Series				
D22	2-dr. Cpe.-3P	895	3056	5257
D22	2-dr. Clb. Cpe.-6P	995	3131	3314
D22	2-dr. Sed.-6P	958	3131	9767
D22	4-dr. Sed.-6P	998	3171	13,343

Model No.	Body Type & Seating	Price	Weight	Prod. Total
Custom Series, 119.5" wb				
D22	2-dr. Clb. Cpe.-6P	1045	3171	4659
D22	2-dr. Conv. Cpe.-5P	1245	3476	1185
D22	2-dr. Brgm.-6P	1008	3171	4685
D22	4-dr. Sed.-6P	1048	3206	22,055
D22	4-dr. Twn. Sed.-6P	1105	3256	4047
Custom Series, 137.5" wb				
D22	4-dr. Sed.-7P	1395	3693	201
D22	4-dr. Limo.-7P	1475	3768	9

Note 1: Total series production was 68,522.

ENGINE: Inline. L-head. Six. Cast iron block. B & S: 3-1/4 x 4-5/8 in. Disp.: 230.2 cu. in. C.R.: 6.7:1. Brake H.P.: 105 @ 3600 R.P.M. Net H.P.: 25.35. Main bearings: four. Valve lifters: solid. Carb.: Stromberg one-barrel model BXV-3. Torque: 185 lb.-ft. @ 1600 R.P.M.

CHASSIS: [Deluxe Series] W.B.: 119.5 in. Tires: 16 x 6.00. [Custom SWB Series] W.B.: 119.5 in. Tires: 16 x 6.00. [Custom LWB Series] W.B.: 137.5 in. Tires: 16 x 6.50.

TECHNICAL: Selective sliding transmission. Speeds: 3F/1R. Column shift controls. Single plate dry disc clutch. Hypoid rear axle. Overall ratio: (std.) 3.9:1; (opt.) 3.73:1 or 4.1:1. Hydraulic brakes. Safety rim steel disc wheels. Drivetrain options: All-Fluid Drive.

OPTIONS: Front bumper. Rear bumper. Whitewall tires. Wheel trim rings. Full wheel discs. Fender skirts. Bumper guards. Radio. Heater. Clock. Cigar lighter. Radio antenna. Seat covers. External sun shade. Spotlights. Outside rear view mirror. Turn signals. Parking brake "on" buzzer. Master grille guard. Chrome license plate frames. Oversize tires. Special paint. Custom trim package.

1942 Dodge, Custom, Series D22, town sedan (OCW)

HISTORICAL: Introduced September 1941. Calendar year production: 11,675. Model year production: 68,522. Innovations: Longer stroke "Power Flow" six has higher compression with more horsepower and torque. Improved Fluid Drive feature optional. Heavier crankshaft. Stoplight mounted in center of trunk lid. For the war-shortened 1942 model run, Dodge wound up as America's sixth largest automaker. Production of 1942 models began in August 1941 and ended in January 1942.

1946 DODGE

1946 Dodge, Deluxe two-door three-passenger coupe, 6-cyl (JL)

DELUXE SERIES — (6-CYL) — The Deluxe was the base trim level and the least expensive of the 1946 Dodges. Postwar Dodges used the bodies and mechanical parts from 1942 models, with slight restyling. A new

checkerboard pattern grille replaced the 1942 grille and the parking lights were mounted low on the fenders, directly below the headlights. Several new mechanical innovations were included in the 1946 models. Among them were the introduction of the famous Fluid-Drive, a push-button starter system. Micronic filtration of the oil, twin-cylinder front wheel brakes and Oilite fuel filters. All Dodges built between 1946 and 1948 were classified as Series D-24 models, regardless of the particular body style.

DELUXE I.D. DATA: All Dodges, if assembled in Detroit, began at 30645001 and went up to 30799737 and if assembled in Los Angeles began at 45000001 and went up to 45002145. The Deluxe models were identified by the suffix 'S' after the D24 model designation.

DELUXE SERIES

Model No.	Body/ Style No.	Body Type & Seating	Factory Price	Shipping Weight	Prod. Total
D24S	Note 1	4-dr Sed-6P	1339	3256	Note 2
D24S	Note 1	2-dr Sed-6P	1299	3236	Note 2
D24S	Note 1	2-dr Cpe-3P	1229	3146	Note 2

Note 1: Owners seeking parts were advised, "There is no way to positively identify type of body. When in doubt, specify vehicle serial number and vehicle body number when ordering parts."

Note 2: No model year breakdown of production figures was available from Chrysler. Figures shown for 1948 Dodge represent total production of 1946, 1947, 1948 and first series 1949 models.

CUSTOM SERIES — (6-CYL) — Dodge Custom series models looked identical to the base offerings at first glance. Standard extras included: Air Foam front seat cushions, dual electric windshield wipers and a chrome bead around the outside windows. Interiors were of a slightly richer trim. The Town Sedan had four doors, all of which opened from the rear.

1946 Dodge, Deluxe two-door sedan, 6-cyl

CUSTOM I.D. NUMBERS: All Dodges, if assembled in Detroit, began at 30645001 and went up to 30799737 and if assembled in California began at 45000001 and went up to 45002145. The Custom models were identified by the suffix 'C' after the D24 model designation.

CUSTOM SERIES

D24C	Note 1	4-dr Sed-6P	1389	3281	Note 2
D24C	Note 1	4-dr Twn Sed-6P	1444	3331	Note 2
D24C	Note 1	4-dr Sed-7P	1743	3757	Note 2
D24C	Note 1	2-dr Clb Cpe-6P	1384	3241	Note 2
D24C	Note 1	2-dr Conv-5P	1649	3461	Note 2

Note 1: Owners seeking parts were advised, "There is no way to positively identify type of body. When in doubt, specify vehicle serial number and vehicle body number when ordering parts."

Note 2: No model year breakdown of production figures was available from Chrysler. Figures shown for 1948 Dodge represent total production of 1946, 1947, 1948 and first series 1949 models.

PRODUCTION NOTE: Total series output was 170,986 Deluxe models and 479,013 Custom models. Included in the Custom production totals are two limousines and 302 chassis.

ENGINE: L-head. Inline. Six-cylinder. Cast iron block. Displacement: 230 cid. Bore and stroke: 3.25 x 4.38 inches. Compression ratio: 8.6:1. Brake hp: 102. Four main bearings. Solid valve lifters. Carburetor: Stromberg BXV-2 single-barrel.

CHASSIS FEATURES: Wheelbase: (seven-passenger sedan) 137.5 inches; (others) 119.5 inches. Overall length: (seven-passenger sedan) 222.5 inches; (others) 204.5 inches. Tires: 6.00 x 16 tube-type black sidewall (white sidewall tires were not available in 1946). Three-speed manual transmissions were standard, with the Fluid-Drive as an option.

Fluid-Drive "provides fluid transfer to the drive line with no metal-to-metal contact between the power source and drive."

CONVENIENCE OPTIONS: Electric clock. Turn signals. Radio. Heater. White wheel trim rings. Back up lights.

HISTORICAL FOOTNOTES: The five-millionth Dodge ever made was constructed this season, a year in which model year output peaked at 156,148 units. That left Dodge with a 7.4 percent share of the U.S. market. L.L. "Tex" Colbert was the president of Dodge.

1947 DODGE

1947 Dodge, Custom four-door sedan (with optional Helms grille guard), 6-cyl

DELUXE SERIES — (6-CYL) — 1947 Dodges were identical to the 1946 models. The only change in the entire car was that the Ram ornament on the hood became slightly more detailed than the previous year. Dodge made a running change to 15-inch wheels during the year.

DELUXE I.D. DATA: All Dodges, if assembled in Detroit, began at 30799738 and went up to 31011765 and if assembled in Los Angeles began at 45002146 and went up to 45022452. The Deluxe models were identified by the suffix 'S' after the D24 model designation.

DELUXE SERIES

Model No.	Body/ Style No.	Body Type & Seating	Factory Price	Shipping Weight	Prod. Total
D24S	Note 1	4-dr Sed-6P	1457	3256	Note 2
D24S	Note 1	2-dr Sed-6P	1417	3236	Note 2
D24S	Note 1	2-dr Cpe-3P	1347	3147	Note 2

Note 1: Owners seeking parts were advised, "There is no way to positively identify type of body. When in doubt, specify vehicle serial number and vehicle body number when ordering parts."

Note 2: Production figures given for 1948 represent total production for 1946, 1947, 1948 and first series 1949 models. No model year breakouts were available from Chrysler.

CUSTOM SERIES — (6-CYL) — The Custom line Dodges continued to be just a little richer than Deluxes on close inspection. Dual electric wipers, pencil-stripe seats and rear fender moldings were the primary differentiation points. Dodge made a running change to 15-inch wheels during the year.

CUSTOM I.D. DATA: All Dodges, if assembled in Detroit, began at 30799738 and went up to 31011765 and if assembled in Los Angeles began at 45002146 and went up to 45022452. The Custom models were identified by the suffix 'C' after the D24 model designation.

CUSTOM SERIES

D24C	Note 1	4-dr Sed-6P	1507	3281	Note 2
D24C	Note 1	4-dr Twn Sed-6P	1577	3331	Note 2
D24C	Note 1	4-dr Sed-7P	1861	3757	Note 2
D24C	Note 1	2-dr Clb Cpe-6P	1502	3241	Note 2
D24C	Note 1	2-dr Conv-5P	1871	3461	Note 2

Note 1: Owners seeking parts were advised, "There is no way to positively identify type of body. When in doubt, specify vehicle serial number and vehicle body number when ordering parts."

Note 2: Production figures given for 1948 represent total production for 1946, 1947, 1948 and first series 1949 models. No model year breakouts were available from Chrysler.

ENGINE: Inline. L-head. Six-cylinder. Cast iron block. Displacement: 230 cid. Bore and stroke: 3.25 x 4.38 inches. Compression ratio: 6.6:1. Brake hp: 102 at 3800 rpm. Four main bearings. Solid valve lifters. Carburetor: Stromberg one-barrel Model BXV-3.

CHASSIS FEATURES: Wheelbase: (seven-passenger sedan) 137.5 inches; (other models) 119.5 inches. Overall length: (seven-passenger sedan) 222.5 inches; (other models) 204.5 inches. Tires: 6.00 x 16 tube-type black sidewall (7.10 x 15 after serial number 30993973). Three-speed manual transmissions were standard, with Fluid Drive as an option (see 1946 chassis features).

CONVENIENCE OPTIONS: Electric clock. Turn signals. Radio. Heater. Goodyear Super Cushion low-pressure tires. White wheel trim rings. Back-up lights.

HISTORICAL FOOTNOTES: Dodge Division of Chrysler Corp. was America's fifth ranked automaker this year. Calendar year production was recorded as 232,472 units for a 6.52 percent share of the total domestic market. State registration agencies totaled 209,552 registrations for the Dodge nameplate this year.

1948 DODGE

1948 Dodge, Custom four-door town sedan, 6-cyl

1948 Dodge, Custom two-door club coupe, 6-cyl

DELUXE SERIES — (6-CYL) — 1948 Dodges were identical to the 1947 models, with a price increase being the only change.

DELUXE I.D. DATA: All Dodges, if assembled in Detroit, began at 31011766 and went up to 31242628 and if assembled in Los Angeles began at 41022453 and went up to 45045426. The Deluxe models were identified by the suffix 'S' after the D24 model designation.

DELUXE SERIES

Model No.	Body/ Style No.	Body Type & Seating	Factory Price	Shipping Weight	Prod. Total
D24S	Note 1	4-dr Sed-6P	1718	3256	61,987
D24S	Note 1	2-dr Sed-6P	1676	3236	81,399
D24S	Note 1	2-dr Cpe-3P	1587	3146	27,600

Note 1: Owners were once again advised that there was no way to positively identify the type of body by code numbers (see Note 1, 1947).

Note 2: Production figures are totals for 1946, 1947, 1948 and first series 1949 models.

CUSTOM SERIES — (6-CYL) — If you learned to differentiate 1946 from 1947 Deluxes and Customs, you knew how to spot the 1948 (and first-series 1949) editions. They were identical.

CUSTOM I.D. DATA: All Dodges, if assembled in Detroit, began at 31011766 and went up to 37058328 and if assembled in Los Angeles began at 41022453 and went up to 45045426. The Custom models were identified by the suffix 'C' after the D24 model designation.

CUSTOM SERIES

Model No.	Body/ Style No.	Body Type & Seating	Factory Price	Shipping Weight	Prod. Total
D24C	Note 1	4-dr Sed-6P	1788	3281	333,911
D24C	Note 1	4-dr Twn Sed-6P	1872	3331	27,800
D24C	Note 1	4-dr Sed-7P	2179	3757	3,698
D24C	Note 1	2-dr Clb Cpe-6P	1774	3241	103,800
D24C	Note 1	2-dr Conv-5P	2189	3461	9,500

Note 1: Owners were once again advised that there was no way to positively identify the type of body by code numbers (see Note 1, 1947).

Note 2: Production figures are totals for 1946, 1947, 1948 and first series 1949 models.

Production Note: Total series output was 170,986 Deluxe models and 479,013 Custom models. Included in the Custom production totals are two limousines and 302 chassis.

ENGINE: Inline. L-head. Six-cylinder. Cast iron block. Displacement: 230 cid. Bore and stroke: 3.25 x 4.38 inches. Compression ratio: 6.6:1. Brake hp: 102 at 3600 rpm. Four main bearings. Solid valve lifters. Carburetor: Stromberg one-barrel Model BXV-3.

CHASSIS FEATURES: Wheelbase: (seven-passenger sedan) 137.5 inches; (other models) 119.5 inches. Overall length: (seven-passenger sedan) 222.5 inches; (other models) 204.5 inches. Tires: 7.10 x 15 tube-type black sidewall. Three-speed manual transmissions were standard with Fluid-Drive as an option (see 1946 chassis features).

CONVENIENCE OPTIONS: Electric clock. Turn signals. Radio. Heater. White sidewall tires. Back-up lights.

HISTORICAL FOOTNOTES: Effective Dec. 1, 1948, all Dodges being assembled were considered 1949 series models for registration purposes. This included units with serial numbers 31201087 and up built at Dodge Main, in Hamtramck, Mich., plus units with serial numbers 45041546 to 45045426 built at the Los Angeles assembly plant. Dodge built 378,048 cars during calendar 1948, earning a 6.12 percent share of market in the process.

1949 DODGE

1949 Dodge, Wayfarer two-door coupe, 6-cyl (TVB)

WAYFARER SERIES — (6-CYL) — February 1949 saw the introduction of the first new body styles since the war. New model names were adopted for the all-new sheet metal, with the Wayfarer making up the base trim level. The new Wayfarers featured longer and lower bodies than the previous year. Front fenders flared into the body easily and rear fenders continued to be bolted on. The checkerboard grille had a more pronounced peak in the center. Round parking lights were located below the headlights on the front fenders. The base Wayfarer line also included

an all-new roadster. It was introduced with detachable windows, but Dodge later substituted vent wings and roll-up windows during the model run. Fluid-Drive became standard for 1949, with the new Gyro-Matic semi-automatic transmission being the optional transmission.

WAYFARER I.D. DATA: Wayfarer models, if assembled in Detroit, began at 37000101 and went up to 37058328; if assembled in San Leandro, Calif., began at 48000101 and went up to 48003813; if assembled in Los Angeles began at 48500101 and went up to 48501977.

1949 Dodge, Wayfarer two-door roadster, 6-cyl

WAYFARER SERIES

Model No.	Body/ Style No.	Body Type & Seating	Factory Price	Shipping Weight	Prod. Tool
D29	Note 1	2-dr Sed-6P	1738	3180	49,054
D29	Note 1	2-dr Cpe-3P	1611	3065	9,342
D29	Note 1	2-dr Rds-3P	1727	3145	5,420

Note 1: See Note 1,1947 Deluxe models.

MEADOWBROOK SERIES — (6-CYL) — The Meadowbrook series was the base trim level four-door sedan, and the series was offered only in the four-door sedan configuration.

MEADOWBROOK I.D. DATA: Meadowbrook series sedans, if assembled in Detroit, began at 312450001 and went up to 31417330; if assembled in San Leandro, Calif., began at 45050001 and went up to 45063676; if assembled in Los Angeles began at 45500101 and went up to 45504688.

MEADOWBROOK SERIES

D30	Note 1	4-dr Sed-6P	1848	3355	Note 2

Note 1: See Note 1,1947 Deluxe models.

Note 2: Total Meadowbrook and Coronet four-door sedan production was 144,390.

CORONET SERIES — (6-CYL) — The Coronet series was the top trim level 1949 Dodge. The Coronet and Meadowbrook models differed only in interior appointments and minor exterior trim differences. Both differed from Wayfarers in having taillights housed in chrome fin-like appendages atop the fenders. The brake light was incorporated into the license housing/trunk handle ensemble in the center of the deck lid. The Town Sedan had an upgraded interior.

1949 Dodge, Coronet six-passenger station wagon, 6-cyl (TVB)

CORONET I.D. DATA: Coronets if assembled in Detroit, began at 31245001 and went up to 31417330; if assembled in San Leandro, Calif., began at 45050001 and went up to 45063676; if assembled in Los Angeles began at 45500101 and went up to 45504688.

DL	23	2-dr HT Cpe-6P	3001	3870	Note 1
DL	27	2-dr Conv-6P	3288	3930	Note 1
DL	45	4-dr Sta Wag-6P	3212	4400	Note 1
DL	46	4-dr Sta Wag-9P	3676	4450	Note 1
DL	23	2-dr HT Cpe-6P	3001	3870	Note 1
DL	27	2-dr Conv-6P	3288	3930	Note 1
DL	45	4-dr Sta Wag-6P	3212	4400	Note 1
DL	46	4-dr Sta Wag-9P	3676	4450	Note 1

CORONET SERIES

Model No.	Body/ Style No.	Body Type & Seating	Factory Price	Shipping Weight	Prod. Total
D30	Note 1	4-dr Sed-6P	1927	3380	Note 2
D30	Note 1	4-dr Twn Sed-6P	2030	3390	Note 2
D30	Note 1	2-dr Clb Cpe-6P	1914	3325	45,435
D30	Note 1	2-dr Conv-5P	2329	3570	2,411
D30	Note 1	2-dr Sta Wag-6P	2865	3830	800
D30	Note 1	4-dr Sed-8P	2635	4070	N/A

Note 1: See Note 1, 1947 Deluxe models.

Note 2: There was no breakout of four-door sedan production between the Meadowbrook and Coronet series. There were 144,390 four-doors produced in both series.

ENGINE: Inline. L-head. Six-cylinder. Cast iron block. Displacement: 230 cid. Bore and stroke: 3.25 x 4.38 inches. Compression ratio: 7.1:1. Brake hp: 103 at 3600 rpm. Four main bearings. Solid valve lifters. Carburetor: Stromberg Type BXVD one-barrel Model 3-93A.

CHASSIS FEATURES: Wheelbase: (Wayfarer) 115 inches; (Meadowbrook and Coronet) 123.5 inches; (eight-passenger) 137.5 inches. Overall length: (Wayfarer roadster) 194.38 inches; (Wayfarer sedan) 196.3 inches: (Meadowbrook and Coronet) 202.9 inches. Tires: (Wayfarer) 6.70 x 15 tube-type black sidewall; (Meadowbrook and Coronet) 7.10 x 15 tube-type black sidewall. Three-speed standard transmissions with Fluid-Drive were standard in all 1949 models.

CONVENIENCE OPTIONS: Electric clock. Turn signals. Radio. Heater. Gyromatic semi-automatic transmission (Coronets). White sidewall tires.

HISTORICAL FOOTNOTES: The regular 1949 Dodges were introduced in April 1949, and the roadster and station wagon appeared in dealer showrooms somewhat later. Model year production peaked at 260,000 units. Calendar year sales of 298,399 cars were recorded. L.L. "Tex" Colbert was the president of the division this year. Dodge was the number two maker in the medium-price class. Dodge had an 18.9 percent share of medium-price auto sales and a 5.82 percent share of America's total new car market. The company was ranked sixth for the industry as a whole. Dodge registrations totaled 273,350.

1950 DODGE

1950 Dodge, Wayfarer two-door roadster, 6-cyl (AA)

WAYFARER SERIES — (6-CYL) — The 1950 Dodges utilized the same body introduced in 1949 with minor restyling of trim and a completely new grille. The grille consisted of three heavy horizontal bars, with the upper bar curving down at the ends. The second and third bars formed a long oval with round parking lights incorporated at the ends. A large chrome center plaque contained the Dodge crest. A single horizontal chrome strip was located on each front and rear fender. The model name was located along the chrome strip on the front fenders, behind the front wheelwell. As in 1949, the Wayfarer was the base trim level. The model name Wayfarer was located on the front fenders.

WAYFARER I.D. DATA: Wayfarer numbers were: (Detroit) 37060001 to 37129622; (San Leandro, Calif.) 48004001 to 48007069; (Los Angeles) 48502001 to 48504748.

WAYFARER SERIES

D33	Note 1	2-dr Sed-6P	1738	3200	65,000
D33	Note 1	2-dr Cpe-3P	1611	3095	7,500
D33	Note 1	2-dr Rds-3P	1727	3190	2,903

Note 1: See Note 1, 1947 Deluxe models.

MEADOWBROOK SERIES — (6-CYL) — The Meadowbrook was the base trim level four-door sedan and the series was offered only in this configuration.

1950 Dodge, Meadowbrook four-door sedan, 6-cyl

MEADOWBROOK I.D. DATA: Meadowbrook numbers were: (Detroit) 31420001 to 31660411; (San Leandro, Calif.) 45064001 to 45077531; (Los Angeles) 45505001 to 45515652. Engine numbers began at D34-1001 and went to D34-341043.

MEADOWBROOK SERIES

Model No.	Body/ Style No.	Body Type & Seating	Factory Price	Shipping Weight	Prod. Total
D34	Note 1	4-dr Sed-6P	1848	3395	Note 2

Note 1: See Note 1, 1947 Deluxe models.

Note 2: Total Meadowbrook and Coronet four-door sedan production was 221,791.

1950 Dodge, Coronet four-door sedan, 6-cyl

CORONET SERIES — (6-CYL) — The Coronet series continued as the top trim level for 1950 and included all the features of the Meadowbrook plus chrome trim rings on the wheels, rear fender gravel guards and the Coronet name on the front fenders. New for 1950 was the Diplomat two-door hardtop, added in June 1950. The Town Sedan with the upgraded interior was dropped in February 1950.

CORONET I.D. DATA: Coronet numbers were: (Detroit) 31420001 to 31660411; (San Leandro, Calif.) 45064001 to 45077531; (Los Angeles) 45505001 to 45515652. Engine numbers began at D34-1001 and went to D34-341043.

CORONET SERIES

D34	Note 1	4-dr Sed-6P	1927	3405	Note 2
D34	Note 1	4-dr Twn Sed-6P	2030	3410	Note 2
D34	Note 1	2-dr Clb Cpe-6P	2012	3410	38,502
D34	Note 1	2-dr HT Cpe-6P	2223	3515	3,600
D34	Note 1	2-dr Conv-6P	2329	3590	1,800
D34	Note 1	4-dr Sta Wag-6P	2865	3850	600
D34	Note 1	4-dr Mtl Sta Wag-6P	2865	3726	100
D34	Note 1	4-dr Sed-8P	2617	4045	1,300

Note 1: See Note 1, 1947 Deluxe series.

Note 2: There was no breakout of four-door sedan production between the Meadowbrook and the Coronet series. Total production in both series was 221,791.

Note 3: The four-door metal station wagon is called the Sierra.

ENGINE: Inline. L-head. Six-cylinder. Cast iron block. Displacement: 230 cid. Bore and stroke: 3.25 x 4.33 inches. Compression ratio: 7.1:1. Brake hp: 103 at 3600 rpm. Four main bearings. Solid valve lifters. Carburetor: Stromberg BXVD 3-93.

CHASSIS FEATURES: Wheelbase: (Wayfarer) 115 inches; (Meadowbrook and Coronet) 123.5 inches; (eight-passenger) 137.5 inches. Overall length: (Wayfarer roadster) 194.38 inches; (Wayfarer sedan) 196.3 inches; (Meadowbrook and Coronet) 202.9 inches. Tires: (Wayfarer) 6.70 x 15 tube-type black sidewall; (Meadowbrook and Coronet) 7.10

x 15 tube-type black sidewall. Three-speed manual with Fluid-Drive was once again the standard transmission in 1950.

1950 Dodge, Coronet Diplomat two-door hardtop, 6-cyl

CONVENIENCE OPTIONS: Electric clock. Turn signals. Radio. Heater. Gyromatic semi-automatic transmission. White sidewall tires.

HISTORICAL FOOTNOTES: The standard Dodge line was introduced Jan. 4, 1950, and the Diplomat appeared in dealer showrooms June 11, 1950. Model year production peaked at 350,000 units. Calendar year sales of 332,782 cars were recorded. L.L. 'Tex' Colbert was again president of the Dodge Division. W.C. Newberg became the divisional vice-president, a role he would fill through 1951. Dodge held a 4.99 percent total market share.

1951 DODGE

WAYFARER SERIES — (6-CYL) — Considered by many to be the nicest looking car produced by the Dodge Division up to that point, the 1951 models were derived from the 1949-1950 models with new hood, grille and bumper styling. The hood sloped smoothly to the grille, which was dominated by a bold horizontal bar extending around the parking lights at both ends. Bumpers had a rounded cross-section. The Dodge crest was located in the center of the redesigned hood, directly above the Dodge name, in block letters. A single chrome strip appeared on both the front and rear fenders and the Wayfarer name appeared on the front fenders below the chrome strip and behind the front wheelwell.

WAYFARER I.D. DATA: Wayfarer numbers were: (Detroit) 37135001 to 37174914; (San Leandro, Calif.) 48008001 to 48009814, (Los Angeles) 48506001 to 48507517. Engine numbers began at D42-1001 and went up.

WAYFARER SERIES

Model No.	Body/ Style No.	Body Type & Seating	Factory Price	Shipping Weight	Prod. Total
D41	Note 1	2-dr Sed-6P	1895	3210	70,700
D41	Note 1	2-dr Cpe-3P	1757	3125	6,702
D41	Note 1	2-dr Rds-3P	1884	3175	1,002

Note 1: See Note 1, 1947 Deluxe models.

Note 2: Production figures are totals for 1951 and 1952 model years.

MEADOWBROOK SERIES — (6-CYL) — As in the past, the Meadowbrook was the base trim level four-door sedan, and the series was offered only in this configuration.

MEADOWBROOK I.D. DATA: Meadowbrook numbers were: (Detroit) 31663001 to 31867688; (San Leandro, Calif.) 45079001 to 45090488; (Los Angeles) 45518001 to 45527385. Engine numbers began at D42-1001 and went up.

MEADOWBROOK SERIES

D42	Note 1	4-dr Sed-6P	2016	3415	Note 2

Note 1: See Note 1, 1947 Deluxe models.

Note 2: Total Meadowbrook and Coronet four-door sedan production was 329,202. This figure is the total for 1951 and 1952 model years.

CORONET SERIES — (6-CYL) — The Coronet series continued as the top trim level for 1951 and included all the features of the Meadowbrook, plus chrome trim rings on the wheels and the name Coronet on the front fenders.

CORONET I.D. DATA: Coronet numbers were: (Detroit) 31663001 to 31867688; (San Leandro, Calif.) 45079001 to 45090488; (Los Angeles) 45518001 to 45527385. Engine numbers began at D42-1001 and went up. See Meadowbrook series.

CORONET SERIES

Model No.	Body/ Style No.	Body Type & Seating	Factory Price	Shipping Weight	Prod. Total
D42	Note 1	4-dr Sed-6P	2103	3415	Note 2
D42	Note 1	2-dr Clb Cpe-6P	2088	3320	56,103
D42	Note 1	2-dr Diplomat HT-6P	2426	3515	21,600
D42	Note 1	2-dr Conv-6P	2514	3575	5,550
D42	Note 1	4-dr Mtl Sta Wag-6P	2710	3750	4,000
D42	Note 1	4-dr Sed-6P	2855	3935	1,150

Note 1: See Note 1, 1947 Deluxe series.

Note 2: There was no breakout of four-door sedan production between the Meadowbrook and Coronet series. Total production in both series was 329,202.

Note 3: Production figures are totals for 1951 and 1952 model years.

Note 4: The metal station wagon is the Sierra.

1951 Dodge, Coronet four-door sedan, 6-cyl

ENGINE: Inline. L-head. Six-cylinder. Cast iron block. Displacement: 230 cid. Bore and stroke: 3.25 x 4.38 inches. Compression ratio: 7.1:1. Brake hp: 103 at 3600 rpm. Four main bearings. Solid valve lifters. Carburetor: Stromberg Type BXVD one-barrel Model 3-93.

CHASSIS FEATURES: Wheelbase: (Wayfarer) 115 inches; (Meadowbrook and Coronet) 123.5 inches; (eight-passenger) 137.5 inches. Overall length: (Wayfarer roadster) 194.38 inches; (Wayfarer sedan) 196.3 inches; (Meadowbrook and Coronet) 202.9 inches; (eight-passenger) 222.9 inches. Front tread: (all models) 56 inches. Rear tread: (all models) 59 inches. Tires: (Wayfarer) 6.70 x 15; (Meadowbrook and Coronet) 7.10 x 15; (Sierra) 7.60 x 15; (eight-passenger) 8.20 x 15.

POWERTRAIN OPTIONS: Fluid-Drive was standard. Gyromatic transmission ($95). Heavy-duty air cleaner. Available rear axle gear ratios: 3.73:1; 3.90:1; 4.00:1.

CONVENIENCE OPTIONS: Electric clock. Turn signals. Mopar radio. Heater (called the "All Weather Comfort System"). Chrome wheel trim rings (standard on Coronet). Back-up lights. Gyromatic semi-automatic transmission (with Sprint-Away passing gear). Whitewall tires.

HISTORICAL FOOTNOTES: The 1951 Dodges were introduced Jan. 20, 1951. Model year production peaked at 292,000 units. Calendar year sales of 325,694 cars were recorded. W.C. Newberg became president of Dodge Division this year. Dodge earned a 6.10 percent share of total market. The Sierra all-steel station wagon and eight-passenger sedans were discontinued late in the calendar year, when production of models built to 1952 specifications commenced (November 1951). Nearly 90 percent of Dodge Division output was quartered at its Hamtramck, Michigan, plant, which was called 'Dodge Main'. This large factory offered 5,480,312 square feet of floor space. Preparations began, late in the season, for production of an all-new Dodge V-8.

1952 DODGE

WAYFARER SERIES — (6-CYL) — While 1951 and 1952 Dodges are nearly identical, there are some minor revisions in the later year models. Dodge was involved heavily in the massive war effort during the Korean conflict and was so busy with the construction of military vehicles, that the passenger car line was continued nearly the same. Some of the subtle

changes included a painted lower grille louver; red reflector dot below the taillight lenses; minor hubcap restyling; a new trunk handle; interior trim and the finish of the dashboard. Also, the rear fender moldings and taillight bezels were no longer connected. It was the last year for the low trim level, short wheelbase Wayfarer series, which was identified by the Wayfarer name on the front fenders. The Wayfarer roadster was dropped.

WAYFARER I.D. DATA: Wayfarer models, if assembled in Detroit, began at 37175001 and went to 37207644. If assembled in San Leandro, Calif., began at 48009901 and went to 48011259 and if assembled in Los Angeles, began at 48507601 and went to 48508754. Engine numbers continued where 1951 models left off and went up to D42-419735.

WAYFARER SERIES

Model No.	Body/ Style No.	Body Type & Seating	Factory Price	Shipping Weight	Prod. Total
D41	Note 1	2-dr Sed-6P	2034	3140	Note 2
D41	Note 1	2-dr Cpe-3P	1886	3050	Note 2
D41	Note 1	2-dr Rds-3P	1924	3100	Note 2

Note 1: See Note 1, 1947 Deluxe models.

Note 2: Production figures were not separated between 1951 and 1952 models. Therefore, production figures shown for 1951 models represented totals for both 1951 and 1952 model years.

MEADOWBROOK SERIES — (6-CYL) — As in the past, the Meadowbrook was the base trim level four-door sedan and the series was offered only in that particular configuration.

MEADOWBROOK I.D. DATA: Meadowbrook series sedans, if assembled in Detroit, began at 31887801 and went to 32038822. If assembled in San Leandro, Calif., began at 45090601 and went to 45100113. If assembled in Los Angeles, began at 45527501 and went to 45534770. Engine numbers continued where 1951 models left off and went up to D42-419735.

MEADOWBROOK SERIES

D41	Note 1	4-dr Sed-6P	2164	3355	Note 2

Note 1: See Note 1, 1947 Deluxe models.

Note 2: See Note 2, 1952 Wayfarer series.

1952 Dodge, Coronet two-door convertible, 6-cyl (AA)

CORONET SERIES — (6-CYL) — The Coronet series continued as the top trim level for 1952 and included all the features of the Meadowbrook plus chrome trim rings on the wheels and the Coronet name on the front fenders. The eight-passenger sedan was dropped late in 1951.

CORONET I.D. DATA: Coronets, if assembled in Detroit, began at 31867801 and went to 32038822. If assembled in San Leandro, Calif., began at 45090601 and went to 45100113. If assembled in Los Angeles, began at 45527501 and went to 45534770. Engine numbers continued where 1951 models left off and went up to D42-419735.

CORONET SERIES

D42	Note 1	4-dr Sed-6P	2256	3385	Note 2
D42	Note 1	2-dr Clb Cpe-6P	2240	3290	Note 2
D42	Note 1	2-dr Diplomat HT-6P	2602	3475	Note 2
D42	Note 1	2-dr Conv-6P	2698	3520	Note 2
D42	Note 1	4-dr Sierra Wag-6P	2908	3735	Note 2
D42	Note 1	4-dr Sed-8P	3064	3935	Note 2

Note 1: See Note 1, 1947 Deluxe series.

Note 2: See Note 2, 1952 Wayfarer series.

ENGINE: Inline. L-head. Six-cylinder. Cast iron block. Displacement: 230 cid. Bore and stroke: 3.25 x 4.265 inches. Compression ratio: 7.0:1. Brake hp: 103 at 3600 rpm. Four main bearings. Solid valve lifters. Carburetor: Stromberg Type BXVD one-barrel Model 3-93.

CHASSIS FEATURES: Wheelbase: (Wayfarer) 115 inches; (Meadowbrook and Coronet) 123.5 inches; (eight-passenger) 137.5 inches. Overall length: (Wayfarer roadster) 194.3 inches; (Wayfarer sedan) 196.3 inches; (Meadowbrook and Coronet) 202.9 inches; (eight-passenger) 222.5 inches. Tires: (Wayfarer) 6.70 x 15 tube-type black sidewall; (Meadowbrook and Coronet) 7.10 x 15 tube-type black sidewall; (Sierra station wagon) 7.60 x 15 tube-type black sidewall; (eight-passenger) 8.20 x 15 tube-type black sidewall. A three-speed manual with Fluid-Drive continued to be the standard transmission, with Gyromatic semi-automatic as an option on all models except the Wayfarer roadster.

CONVENIENCE OPTIONS: Electric clock. Turn signals. Mopar radio. Heater (called the 'All Weather Comfort System'). Chrome wheel trim rings (standard on Coronet). Back-up lights. Gyromatic semi-automatic transmission (with Sprint-Away passing gear). Dodge safety tint glass. White sidewall tires.

HISTORICAL FOOTNOTES: The 1952 Dodges were introduced Nov. 10, 1951. Model year production peaked at 206,000 units. Calendar year sales of 259,519 cars were recorded. W.C. Newberg was the president of Dodge Division this year. The Meadowbrook Special series was introduced late in the calendar year, as was a new 'Red Ram' Dodge V-8. Dodge was America's sixth largest automaker. The company reported that the number of Dodges licensed to operate on the roads this year was approximately 2.5 million cars. On a calendar year basis, Dodge made an estimated 15,613 hardtop coupes; 25,504 convertibles and 58,546 station wagons during 1952.

1953 DODGE

1953 Dodge, Meadowbrook Suburban two-door station wagon, 6-cyl

MEADOWBROOK SERIES — (6-CYL) — 1953 was a significant year for Dodge for several reasons. Among them was the totally restyled body, the introduction of a fully automatic transmission and the introduction of the famous 241-cid 'Hemi' V-8 engine. In the styling department, the 1953 Dodge grille evolved from that of the 1950-52 models, now featuring two horizontal bars with five vertical dividing bars. On V-8-powered models, the hood featured a 'Jet Flow' scoop around the V-8 emblem. Also new for 1953 was the large one-piece curved windshield. The new doors opened wider and the top featured a larger, wraparound rear window, one-piece on sedans and three-piece on the Diplomat hardtop. The new doors also featured pull-type handles. Oval taillights were used and the fuel filter was relocated to the lower left side of the escutcheon panel. The Meadowbrook Special was the base trim level for 1953 and was included primarily as a salesman's car. The Specials were devoid of any chrome side trim and had rubber windshield and rear window moldings. The interiors were as stark as possible. There was also a standard Meadowbrook series. Meadowbrooks featured a Dodge crest on the hood, chrome windshield and rear window moldings and chrome side steps (which began low on the body, behind the front wheelwell, and ran horizontally back and swept up over the rear wheel opening). The Meadowbrook name was located at the tip of the front fenders.

MEADOWBROOK I.D. DATA: Meadowbrook series, if assembled in Detroit, began at 32042001 and went to 32152851. If assembled in San Leandro, Calif., began at 45102001 and went to 45105772, and if assembled in Los Angeles, began at 45536001 and went to 45538622. Engine numbers began at D46-1001 and went to D46-134677.

MEADOWBROOK SERIES

Model No.	Body/ Style No.	Body Type & Seating	Factory Price	Shipping Weight	Prod. Total
D46	Note 1	4-dr Spl Sed-6P	2000	3195	84,158
D46	Note 1	2-dr Spl Sed-6P	1958	3100	36,766
D46	Note 1	4-dr Sed-6P	2000	3175	Note 2
D46	Note 1	2-dr Sed-6P	1958	3085	Note 2
D47	Note 1	2-dr Sub-6P	2176	3190	15,751

Note 1: See Note 1, 1947 Deluxe models.

Note 2: There is no breakout between Meadowbrook Special models and standard Meadowbrook models. Therefore, figures given represent total Meadowbrook production for each of the body styles.

1953 Dodge, Coronet four-door sedan, V-8 (AA)

CORONET SERIES — (6-CYL/V-8) — The Coronet was the top trim level for 1953 and included all the Meadowbrook Series features, plus an air scoop with the nomenclature "Dodge V-8" located beneath the Ram hood ornament, chrome gravel deflector and the Coronet name, in script, on the sides of the front fenders. The two-door hardtop was once again called the Coronet Diplomat. Six-cylinder sedans appeared in March.

CORONET I.D. DATA: Coronet models powered by six-cylinder engines used the same serial number sequence as the Meadowbrook series and V-8-powered Coronets. If assembled in Detroit, numbers began at 3450001 and went to 34635734. If assembled in San Leandro, Calif., began at 4250001 and went to 42507899, and if assembled in Los Angeles, began at 41500001 and went to 41504467. Engine numbers began at D44-1001 and went to D44-176412.

CORONET SERIES

D46/44	Note 1	4-dr Sed-6P	2111/2220	3220/3385	Note 2
D46/44	Note 1	2-dr Sed-6P	2084/2198	3155/3325	Note 2
D48	Note 1	2-dr Diplomat HT-6P	2361	3310	17,334
D48	Note 1	2-dr Conv-6P	2494	3480	4,100
D48	Note 1	2-dr Sierra Wag-6P	2503	3425	5,400

Note 1: See Note 1, 1947 Deluxe models.

Note 2: See Note 2, 1953 Meadowbrook series. The note also applies to Coronet two-door and four-door sedans equipped with six-cylinder engines.

Note 3: The V-8 was considered a separate series, not an option. Factory prices and weights, on charts, give data for six-cylinder cars above slash and V-8 data below slash.

ENGINES:

(Six) Inline. L-head. Cast iron block. Displacement: 230 cid. Bore and stroke: 3.25 x 4.625 inches. Compression ratio: 7.1:1. Brake hp: 103 at 3600 rpm. Four main bearings. Solid valve lifters. Carburetor: Carter one-barrel Model D6H2.

(V-8) Hemi head overhead valve Cast iron block. Displacement: 241 cid. Bore and stroke: 3.44 x 3.25 inches. Compression ratio: 7.0:1. Brake hp: 140 at 4400 rpm. Five main bearings. Hydraulic valve lifters. Carburetor: Stromberg two-barrel Model WW3-108.

CHASSIS FEATURES: Wheelbase: (Diplomat hardtop, convertible, Suburban station wagon) 114 inches; (sedan and club coupe) 119 inches. Overall length: (Suburban and Sierra station wagons) 189.6 inches; (convertible and Diplomat) 191.3 inches; (four-door sedans and club coupes) 201.4 inches. Tires: (Meadowbrook) 6.70 x 15 tube-type black sidewall; (Coronet) 7.10 x 15 tube-type black sidewall. Three-speed manual transmission was once again the standard transmission, with Overdrive, Fluid-Drive and Gyro-Torque automatic as the optional transmissions.

CONVENIENCE OPTIONS: Electric clock. Turn signals. Mopar radio. Heater. Windshield washers. Back-up lights. Solex tinted glass. Wheel covers. Overdrive. Gyromatic drive (Fluid-Drive). Gyro-Torque automatic drive. White sidewall tires. Bright wheel opening trim. Chrome wire wheels. Continental spare wheel kit.

HISTORICAL FOOTNOTES: The 1953 Dodges were introduced Oct. 23, 1952, and the Coronet Six appeared in dealer showrooms March 18, 1953. Model year production peaked at 304,000 units. Calendar year sales of 293,714 cars were recorded. W.C. Newberg was the president of Dodge Division this year. The Meadowbrook Special series was introduced late in the calendar year as was a new 'Red Ram' Dodge V-8. On Jan. 15, 1953, the 100,000th Dodge built to 1953 specifications left the factory. A general price cut took effect on March 25, 1953. Sales of a new option, air-conditioning, began April 6, 1953, during the same month the Meadowbrook Special was discontinued and the Coronet Six was announced for mid-March availability. Dodge topped all other American Eights in the Mobilgas Economy Run. In September 1953, a 1954 Dodge set 196 AAA stock car speed records at the Bonneville Salt Flats in Utah. On Nov. 12, 1953, the Dodge Firearrow, a futuristic sports roadster, was put on display at leading U.S. auto shows. NASCAR drivers liked the powerful Dodges and drove them to six wins in 1953, the first such victories for Dodge.

1954 DODGE

MEADOWBROOK SERIES — (6-CYL/V-8) — For 1954, Dodges utilized the same body introduced in 1953, with minor changes. The new grille featured a prominent horizontal bar with a distinctive vertical post in the middle. The taillight clusters were redesigned and chrome stone shields were used on the rear fenders of the top trim levels. Rubber stone shields were used on the base trim level Meadowbrook series. The Meadowbrooks also included rubber windshield and rear window moldings; the Dodge crest in the center of the hood; the Meadowbrook name, in script, on the rear fenders and a short chrome strip along the sides of the front fenders and part of the front door.

MEADOWBROOK I.D. DATA: Meadowbrook series, if assembled in Detroit, began at 32152901 and went to 32189926; if assembled in San Leandro, Calif., began at 45105801 and went to 45110883. Engine numbers began at D51-1001 and went to D51-1877 and D51A-1001 and went to D51A-1877.

MEADOWBROOK SERIES

Model No.	Body/ Style No.	Body Type & Seating	Factory Price	Shipping Weight	Prod. Total
D50/51	Note 1	4-dr Sed-6P	2000/2151	3195/3390	11,193
D50/51	Note 1	2-dr Clb Cpe-6P	1958/2121	3120/3335	4,251

Note 1: See Note 1, 1947 Deluxe models.

Note 2: The figures to the left of slash marks represent six-cylinder models and the figures to the right represent V-8-powered models.

1954 Dodge, Coronet Sierra station wagon, V-8

CORONET SERIES — (6-CYL/V-8) — The Coronet was now the intermediate trim level Dodge and included all the Meadowbrook features plus chrome windshield and rear window moldings; a full-length chrome

strip along the middle of the body (which dipped down behind the front door to near the top of the rear wheelwell) and chrome rear fender stone shields. The Coronet name, in script, appeared on the sides of the rear fenders.

CORONET I.D. DATA: Coronet models powered by six-cylinder engines and assembled in Detroit began at 32160001 and went up to 32189926; if assembled in San Leandro, Calif., began at 45110001 and went up to 45110883. Coronets powered by V-8 engines and assembled in Detroit, began at 34642001 and went up to 34739536, and if assembled in San Leandro, began at 42510001 and went up to 42516879. Six-cylinder engine numbers began at D1-1001 and went to D1-35830. V-8 engine numbers began at D502-1001 and went up to D502-110857.

CORONET SERIES

Model No.	Body/ Style No.	Body Type & Seating	Factory Price	Shipping Weight	Prod. Total
D50/51	Note 1	4-dr Sed-6P	2111/2220	3235/3405	50,963
D50/51	Note 1	2-dr Clb Cpe-6P	2084/2198	3165/3345	12,499
D52/53	Note 1	2-dr Sub-6P	2204/2492	3185/3400	9,489
D52/53	Note 1	4-dr Sierra-6P	2694/2935	3430/3605	1,300
D53-2	Note 1	2-dr HT Cpe-6P	2355	3310	100
D53-2	Note 1	2-dr Conv-6P	2489	3505	50

Note 1: See Note 1, 1947 Deluxe model.

Note 2: The figures to the left of the slash marks represent six-cylinder models and the figures to the right represent V-8-powered models. Those models with only one set of figures were available only with V-8 power.

ROYAL SERIES — (V-8) — The Royal series was the new top trim level for 1954 and was available only with the 241-cid 'Hemi' engine. The Royal models included all the Coronet features, plus chrome rocker panel moldings; V-8 emblem; 'Jet Flow' scoop on the front of the hood and chrome fins along the tops of the rear fenders.

1954 Dodge, Royal four-door sedan, V-8 (AA)

ROYAL I.D. DATA: Royal models assembled in Detroit began at 34642001 and went up to 34799536. Those assembled in San Leandro, Calif., began at 42510001 and went up to 42516879. Engine numbers began at D502-1001 and went up to D502-110857.

ROYAL SERIES

D50-3	Note 1	4-dr Sed-6P	2348	3425	50,050
D50-3	Note 1	2-dr Clb Cpe-6P	2324	3385	8,900
D53-3	Note 1	2-dr HT Cpe-6P	2478	3355	3,852
D53-3	Note 1	2-dr Conv-6P	2607	3575	2,000

Note 1: See Note 1, 1947 Deluxe models.

ENGINES:

(Six) Inline. L-head. Cast iron block. Displacement: 230 cid. Bore and stroke: 3.25 x 4.625 inches. Compression ratio: 7.25:1. Brake hp: 110 at 3600 rpm. Four main bearings. Solid valve lifters. Carburetor: Carter one-barrel Model D6U1.

(V-8) Hemi head overhead valve. Cast iron block. Displacement: 241 cid. Bore and stroke: 3.312 x 3.25 inches. Compression ratio: 7.5:1 (7.1:1 on Meadowbrook models). Brake hp: 150 at 4400 rpm (140 at 4400 rpm on Meadowbrook models). Five main bearings. Solid valve lifters. Carburetor: Stromberg two-barrel Model WW-3-108.

CHASSIS FEATURES: Wheelbase: (hardtop, convertible and two-door station wagon models) 114 inches; (other models) 119 inches. Overall length: (short-wheelbase models) 196 inches; (long-wheelbase models) 205.5 inches. Tires: (Meadowbrook and six-cylinder-equipped Suburbans) 6.70 x 15 tube-type black sidewall; (other models) 7.10 x 15 tube-type black sidewall. Three-speed manual transmission was once again the standard transmission, with Overdrive ($98); Fluid-Drive ($20) and PowerFlite automatic transmission ($189) being the optional transmissions. Gyromatic Drive was also available ($130).

CONVENIENCE OPTIONS: Electric clock. Turn signals. Mopar radio. Power steering ($134). Back-up lights. Solex tinted glass. Air temp air conditioning ($643). White sidewall tires ($30). Windshield washers. Power brakes ($37). Chrome wire wheels. Wire wheel covers. Continental spare tire kit.

1954 Dodge, Royal 500 two-door convertible (with Jerry Lewis and Dean Martin), V-8 (IMS)

HISTORICAL FOOTNOTES: The full-size Dodge and Royal models were introduced Oct. 8, 1953, and the four-door Dodge Sierra station wagon appeared in dealer showrooms Dec. 8, 1953. Model year production peaked at 150,930 units. Calendar year sales of 151,766 cars were recorded. W.C. Newberg was president of Dodge Division, which earned a 2.75 percent share of the total U.S. market this year. In January 1954, Dodge Division initiated a heavy radio and television advertising campaign. On Feb. 7, 1954, an advertising contest to celebrate Dodge's 40th anniversary as a carmaker was launched. On Feb. 20, the Firearrow dream car was exhibited at the Chicago Auto Show. A new range of special spring paint colors was announced on March 22, 1954. On April 8, a Dodge equipped with overdrive transmission won out over all other low-medium priced U.S. cars in the Mobilgas Economy Run. It averaged 25.3873 mpg for the complete 1,335-mile course. On May 31, 1954, a specially-trimmed Dodge convertible paced the Indianapolis 500-Mile Race, and 701 Royal 500 pace car replica convertibles were produced; the figure is included in Royal convertible production totals. Pace car engines were equipped with four-barrel carburetors and dual exhaust. On June 16, 1954, the Firearrow proved itself to be a functional dream car, as it was used to establish a woman's world speed record of 143.44 mph for 4.7 miles at the Chrysler Proving Grounds, in Chelsea, Mich. There was only a single Dodge win in NASCAR racing this year.

1955 DODGE

CORONET SERIES — (6-CYL/V-8) — All Dodge models were totally restyled once again for 1955. They were more than six inches longer than the 1954 models. They were also lower and wider and were powered by a larger and more powerful V-8 engine. The six-cylinder engine also received a boost, to 123 hp, as the great performance race of the mid-'50s began. Dodge's advertising people called the new styling 'Flair-Fashion.' This styling was set off by the use of tri-color paint schemes. The new grille was divided into two separate openings. Each opening housed a single horizontal bar that wrapped around the fender and incorporated the parking light. All models featured a simulated hood scoop. The windshield was a wraparound affair, which Dodge referred to as a 'new horizon' windshield. The new taillights were emphasized by a chrome trim piece and the higher trim levels featured dual lenses on each side (the lower of which was often replaced with back-up lights). Six-cylinder-equipped models featured the large Dodge crest in the center of the hood and trunk lid. Those models with V-8 power featured the Dodge crest over a large 'V'. The Coronet was the base trim level for 1955 and featured chrome windshield and rear window moldings; chrome trim around the simulated hood scoop; chrome headlight doors and a single horizontal chrome strip running from the front fender to the rear of the front door. The Coronet name appeared, in script, along the side of the front fenders on cars with Lancer trim and just ahead of the taillights on those with standard trim. Late in the year, Lancer trim was made available on sedans and station wagons.

1955 Dodge, Coronet four-door sedan, 6-cyl (AA)

CORONET I.D. DATA: Six-cylinder-powered Coronets assembled in Detroit began at 32192001 and went to 32225514 and those assembled in Los Angeles began at 48016001 and went to 48016299. V-8-powered models assembled in Detroit began with 34740001 and went to 34970679 and those assembled in Los Angeles began at 42518001 and went to 42526800. Six-cylinder engine numbers began at D56-1001 and went up to D56-34905. V-8 engine numbers began at D551-1001 and went up to D551-149857.

CORONET SERIES

Model No.	Body/ Style No.	Body Type & Seating	Factory Price	Shipping Weight	Prod. Total
D55/56	Note 1	4-dr Sed-6P	2068/2171	3295/3395	46,074
D55/56	Note 1	2-dr Sed-6P	1988/2091	3235/3360	24,104
D55-1	Note 1	2-dr Lancer HT-6P	2256	3375	26,727
D55/56	Note 1	2-dr Sub-6P	2324/2427	3410/3550	8,115
D55/56	Note 1	4-dr Sierra Wag-6P	2438/2541	3480/3590	5,952
D55/56	Note 1	4-dr Sierra Wag-8P	2540/2643	3595/3695	Note 2

Note 1: See Note 1, 1947 Deluxe models.

Note 2: There is no breakout per six- and eight-passenger Sierra station wagon models. Production figures given under the six-passenger model represent the cumulative total for both styles.

Note 3: The figures to the left of the slash marks represent six-cylinder models and the figures to the right represent V-8 models. Those without a slash mark came only as V-8s.

ROYAL SERIES — (V-8) — The Royal was the intermediate trim level for 1955 and included all the Coronet features plus hooded, chrome headlight doors and the Royal name, in script, on the front or rear fenders. Lancer trim, standard on Lancers (as hardtops and convertibles were named in all lines), became optional on most other models. Narrow chrome strips trailed back from the hood scoop, dipped at the C-pillar, then continued high on the rear fenders to the taillight housings.

1955 Dodge, Royal Sierra station wagon, V-8 (AA)

ROYAL I.D. DATA: Royal V-8-powered models assembled in Detroit began with 34740001 and went to 34970679. Those assembled in Los Angeles began at 42518001 and went to 42526800. V-8 engine numbers began at D551-1001 and went up to D551-149857.

ROYAL SERIES

D55-2	Note 1	4-dr Sed-6P	2285	3425	45,323
D55-2	Note 1	2-dr Lancer HT-6P	2370	3425	25,831
D55-2	Note 1	4-dr Sierra Wag-6P	2634	3655	5,506
D55-2	Note 1	4-dr Sierra Wag-8P	2736	3730	Note 2

Note 1: See Note 1, 1947 Deluxe models.

Note 2: See Note 2, 1955 Coronet models.

CUSTOM ROYAL SERIES — (V-8) — The Custom Royal was the top trim level for 1955 and included all the Royal features, plus the Royal name and medallion on the rear fenders of the sedans with standard side trim and on the front fenders of models with Lancer sweep spear trim. The Lancer hardtop and convertible models featured chrome fins on the tops of the rear fenders. In April, a Royal Lancer four-door sedan appeared as an answer to the new four-door hardtops from General Motors. It had Lancer side trim. There was a midyear LaFemme option for the Custom Royal Lancer.

1955 Dodge, Royal Lancer two-door hardtop, V-8 (AA)

CUSTOM ROYAL I.D. DATA: Custom Royal V-8-powered models assembled in Detroit began with 34740001 and went to 34970679. Those assembled in Los Angeles began at 42518001 and went to 42526800. V-8 engine numbers began at D551-1001 and went up to D551-149857.

CUSTOM ROYAL SERIES

Model No.	Body/ Style No.	Body Type & Seating	Factory Price	Shipping Weight	Prod. Total
D55-3	Note 1	4-dr Sed-6P	2448	3485	55,503
D55-3	Note 1	2-dr Lancer HT-6P	2518	3480	30,499
D55-3	Note 1	2-dr Lancer Conv-6P	2723	3610	3,302
D55-3	Note 1	4-dr Lancer Sed-6P	N/A	N/A	N/A

Note 1: See Note 1, 1947 Deluxe models.

ENGINES:

(Six) Inline. L-head. Cast iron block. Displacement: 230 cid. Bore and stroke: 3.25 x 4.625 inches. Compression ratio: 7.4:1. Brake hp: 123 at 3600 rpm. Four main bearings. Solid valve lifters. Carburetor: Stromberg two-barrel Model WW3-124.

(Red Ram V-8) Overhead valve. Polysphere combustion chambers. Cast iron block. Displacement: 270 cid. Bore and stroke: 3.63 x 3.26 inches. Compression ratio: 7.6:1. Brake hp: 175 at 4400 rpm. Five main bearings. Hydraulic valve lifters. Carburetor: Stromberg two-barrel Model WW3-131.

(Super Red Ram V-8) Overhead valve. Hemispherical combustion chambers. Cast iron block. Displacement: 270 cid. Bore and stroke: 3.63 x 3.26 inches. Compression ratio: 7.6:1. Brake hp (std.) 183 at 4400 rpm; (opt.) 193 at 4400 rpm. Five main bearings. Hydraulic valve lifters. Carburetor: (std.) Stromberg two-barrel; (opt.) Carter four-barrel.

CHASSIS FEATURES: Wheelbase: 120 inches. Overall length: 212.1 inches. Tires: (Coronet six) 6.70 x 15 tube-type black sidewall; (V-8-powered models) 7.10 x 15 black sidewall. Three-speed manual transmission was the standard transmission, with PowerFlite being the two-speed fully automatic optional transmission ($178). Overdrive was an option on standard transmission-equipped models ($108).

CONVENIENCE OPTIONS: Electric clock. Turn signals. Mopar radio ($110). Power steering ($113). Power brakes ($38). Power seats ($70). Power windows ($102). Heater. Air temp air conditioning ($567). Windshield washers. White sidewall tires. Engine power package ($48). Spinner wheel covers. Chrome wire wheels. Tinted glass. Continental spare tire kit. Lancer trim offered a natural break for 16 two-tone and 16 three-tone color combinations.

1955 Dodge, La Femme (based on Custom Royal Lancer) two-door hardtop, V-8

HISTORICAL FOOTNOTES: The full-size Dodges were introduced Nov. 17, 1954, and the Coronet Sierra station wagon and Royal Lancer appeared in dealer showrooms Dec. 17, 1954. The Custom Royal Lancer four-door sedan debuted in April. Another midyear trim option, called LaFemme, was the industry's first appeal to women with special Heather Rose and Sapphire White color combinations and matching cape, boots, umbrella, shoulder bag and floral upholstery fabrics. Model year production peaked at 273,286 units. Calendar year sales of 313,038 cars were recorded. W.C. Newberg was president of Dodge Division this year. The capacity of the Dodge V-8 assembly plant was greatly increased during the final months of calendar 1955, when the Plymouth V-8 plant opened. *Motor Trend* magazine found its Custom Royal V-8 (with PowerFlite) capable of going 0-to-60 mph in 16.2 seconds and calculated a top speed of 101.8 mph for this model.

1956 DODGE

CORONET SERIES — (6-CYL/V-8) — Following a year of outstanding sales, Dodge chose wisely not to drastically restyle its cars for 1956. While the front end was nearly identical to the previous year, the side trim and taillights were altered slightly. Also, the rear fenders grew fins, as was the current rage in Detroit. A four-door hardtop was offered for the first time in all three series. Electrical systems changed from six-volt to 12-volt. This was the year of the great horsepower race of the '50s and Dodge was right in the thick of things. The division had V-8 engines all the way up to 295 hp. The year ushered in one of Chrysler's most famous trademarks: the push-button selector for the automatic transmission. Carried over unchanged from 1955 were some of the customizer's most sought after items: the beautiful Dodge Lancer wheel covers. No chopped and channeled custom of the '50s would be complete without a set of the Lancer spinners. The Coronet was the base trim level for 1956 and included chrome windshield and rear window moldings; chrome trim around the simulated hood scoop; chrome headlight doors; 'Saddle Sweep' chrome side trim and the Coronet name, in script, along the rear fenders.

1956 Dodge, Royal Custom Sierra eight-passenger station wagon, V-8

CORONET I.D. DATA: Six-cylinder-powered Coronets assembled in Detroit began at 32227001 and went to 32254093. Those assembled in Los Angeles began at 48016501 and went to 48018723. V-8-powered models assembled in Detroit began at 34972001 and went to 35167854. Those assembled in Los Angeles began at 42608001 and went to 42618518. Engine numbers were D62-1001 and up for six-cylinder engines and D63-1-1001 and up for V-8 engines.

CORONET SERIES

Model No.	Body/ Style No.	Body Type & Seating	Factory Price	Shipping Weight	Prod. Total
D62/63	Note 1	4-dr Sed-6P	2232/2340	3295/3435	Note 2
D62/63	Note 1	2-dr Clb Sed-6P	2159/2267	3250/3380	Note 2
D63	Note 1	4-dr Lancer HT-6P	2517	3560	Note 2
D63	Note 1	2-dr Lancer HT-6P	2403	3430	Note 2
D63	Note 1	2-dr Conv-6P	2643	3600	Note 2
D62/63	Note 1	2-dr Sub-6P	2456/2564	3455/3605	Note 2
D63	Note 1	4-dr Sierra Wag-6P	2681	3600	Note 2
D63	Note 1	4-dr Sierra Wag-8P	2787	3715	Note 2

Note 1: See Note 1, 1947 Deluxe models.

Note 2: Production figures were not given for individual models and body styles. Dodge produced a total of 220,208 cars during calendar year 1956, including 142,613 Coronets. Model year production amounted to some 241,000 cars in all series.

Note 3: Prices and weights to left of slash marks are for sixes, to right for V-8s.

1956 Dodge, Coronet Lancer two-door hardtop, V-8

ROYAL SERIES — (V-8) — The Royal was once again the intermediate trim level and included all the Coronet features plus six chrome fins on the top of the center bar in the grille, chrome rain gutters and smooth taillight and back-up light housings. The Royal name appeared in script on the rear fenders, along with the V-8 emblem.

ROYAL I.D. DATA: V-8-powered models assembled in Detroit began at 34972001 and went to 35167854. Those assembled in Los Angeles began at 42608001 and went to 42618518. Engine numbers were D63-1-1001 and up on V-8 engines.

ROYAL SERIES

Model No.	Body/ Style No.	Body Type & Seating	Factory Price	Shipping Weight	Prod. Total
D63-2	Note 1	4-dr Sed-6P	2478	3475	Note 2
D63-2	Note 1	4-dr Lancer HT-6P	2662	3625	Note 2
D63-2	Note 1	2-dr Lancer HT-6P	2548	3505	Note 2
D63-2	Note 1	2-dr Cus Sub-6P	2694	3620	Note 2
D63-2	Note 1	4-dr Cus Sierra-6P	2834	3710	Note 2
D63-2	Note 1	4-dr Cus Sierra-8P	2939	3800	Note 2

Note 1: See Note 1, 1947 Deluxe models.

Note 2: See Note 2, 1956 Coronet models. A total of 48,780 Royal models were built.

1956 Dodge, Custom Royal Lancer two-door hardtop, V-8

CUSTOM ROYAL SERIES — (V-8) — The Custom Royal was once again the top trim level Dodge and included all the Royal features plus hooded and painted headlight doors; grooved back-up and taillight housings; a strip of the lower body color extending up the rear edge of the rear fenders and the Custom Royal name, in script, on the rear fenders, along with the V-8 emblem. Midyear saw LaFemme and Golden Lancer options for the Custom Royal Lancer two-door hardtop.

CUSTOM ROYAL I.D. DATA: V-8-powered models assembled in Detroit began at 34972001 and went to 35167854. Those assembled in Los Angeles began at 42608001 and went to 42618518. Engine numbers were D63-1-1001 and up on V-8 engines.

CUSTOM ROYAL SERIES

Model No.	Body/ Style No.	Body Type & Seating	Factory Price	Shipping Weight	Prod. Total
D63-3	Note 1	4-dr Sed-6P	2588	3520	Note 2
D63-3	Note 1	4-dr Lancer HT-6P	2772	3675	Note 2
D63-3	Note 1	2-dr Lancer HT-6P	2658	3505	Note 2
D63-3	Note 1	2-dr Conv-6P	2878	3630	Note 2

Note 1: See Note 1, 1947 Deluxe models.

Note 2: See Note 2, 1956 Coronet models. A total of 49,293 Custom Royal models were built.

ENGINES:

(Six) Inline. L-head. Cast iron block. Displacement: 230 cid. Bore and stroke: 3.25 x 4.625 inches. Compression ratio: 7.6:1. Brake hp: 131 at 3600 rpm. Four main bearings. Solid valve lifters. Carburetor: Stromberg two-barrel Model WW3-124.

(Red Ram V-8) Overhead valve. Polysphere combustion chambers. Cast iron block. Displacement: 270 cid. Bore and stroke: 3.63 x 3.26 inches. Compression ratio: 7.6:1. Brake hp: 189 at 4400 rpm. Five main bearings. Hydraulic valve lifters. Carburetor: Stromberg two-barrel Model WW3-135.

(Super Red Ram V-8) Overhead valve. Polysphere combustion chambers. Cast iron block. Displacement: 315 cid. Bore and stroke: 3.63 x 3.80 inches. Compression ratio: 8.0:1. Brake hp: 218 at 4400 rpm. Five main bearings. Hydraulic valve lifters. Carburetor: Stromberg two-barrel Model WW3-148.

(Super Red Ram V-8) Overhead valve. Polysphere combustion chambers. Cast iron block. Displacement: 315 cid. Bore and stroke: 3.63 x 3.80 inches. Compression ratio: 8.0:1. Brake hp: 230 at 4400 rpm. Five main bearings. Hydraulic valve lifters. Carburetor: Carter four-barrel Model WCFB.

(D-500 V-8) Overhead valve. Hemispherical combustion chambers. Cast iron block. Displacement: 315 cid. Bore and stroke: 3.63 x 3.80 inches. Compression ratio: 9.25:1. Brake hp: 260 at 4400 rpm. Five main bearings. Solid valve lifters. Carburetor: Carter four-barrel Type WCFB.

(D-500-1) engine: same as above, but with dual Carter WCFB four-barrel carburetors and manual transmission. Brake hp: 295 at 4400 rpm. (These were midyear options.)

CHASSIS FEATURES: Wheelbase: 120 inches. Overall length: 212 inches. Tires: (six-cylinder Coronet and Suburban) 6.70 x 15 tubeless black sidewall; (Royal, Coronet and V-8 station wagons) 7.10 x 15 tubeless black sidewall; (Custom Royal) 7.60 x 15. Three-speed manual continued to be the standard transmission, with Overdrive ($102) and PowerFlite fully automatic ($184) being the optional transmissions.

CONVENIENCE OPTIONS: Electric clock. Turn signals. Mopar radio. Power steering ($92). Power brakes ($38). Power seats. Power windows. Heater. Air Temp air conditioning. Highway Hi-Fi automatic record player. Windshield washers. White sidewall tires.

HISTORICAL FOOTNOTES: The 1956 Dodge line was introduced on Oct. 7, 1955. Model year production peaked at exactly 233,686 units, giving the company a 3.7 percent share of the total market. Of this total (again on a model year basis) 1,687 had optional air conditioning. On a calendar year basis (Jan. 1956 to Jan. 1957), Dodge built 40,100 two-door hardtops, 10,900 four-door hardtops; 4,100 convertibles and 16,100 station wagons. These rounded off totals include 1957 models built in the fall of 1956, but 1956 models built in the fall of 1955 are not included, so this gives only a rough idea of how many of each particular body style were made. Calendar year production for Dodge totaled 205,727 cars. This was a decline of 22.4 percent over 1955. During 1956, Dodge installed automatic transmissions in 90.3 percent of all its cars; 94.8 percent had heaters; 62.6 percent had back-up lights; 60.2 percent had whitewalls; 17.3 percent had power brakes and 24.3 percent had power steering. M.C. Patterson became president and chief executive officer of Dodge Division this season. The company's address was 7900 Joseph Campau Avenue in Detroit. Some mention must be made of two special options introduced midyear in the Custom Royal series. The "La Femme" featured a lavender and white paint job and matching interior with gold flecks. It came with a matching umbrella, cap and purse hook. The Golden Lancer featured a Sapphire white body and top with Gallant Saddle Gold exterior and interior trim. In September 1955, a 1956 Dodge Custom Royal four-door sedan, was driven 31,224 miles in 14 days at the Bonneville Salt Flats, Utah, and set 306 speed records. Dodges won 11 NASCAR races, a figure that wouldn't be topped until 1964.

1957 DODGE

CORONET SERIES — (6-CYL/V-8) — The new Dodges were totally restyled from the previous year and were very much a part of the 'Forward Look' being promoted by Chrysler. They rode on longer wheelbases than any previous year since 1933 (except long wheelbase models), and were longer, lower and wider than any previous Dodge. Helping provide a low silhouette was a switch to 14-inch wheels. Front torsion bar suspension was also new. The headlights were now deeply recessed below large headlight 'brows' and the grille featured a gull-wing-shaped horizontal bar, which dipped in the center and surrounded a large Dodge crest. All models used a single horizontal chrome strip along the bodyside and chrome trim along the base of the large rear fender fins. Chrome trim surrounded the headlights and grille opening. The Dodge name, in block letters, was spaced along the front and the grille, directly below the

chrome jet-styled hood ornament. Among the more interesting features on the 1957 Dodges (and all 1957 Chrysler products) was the instrument panel-mounted inside rearview mirror. With two passengers in the car, rear vision was partially obstructed. With four or more passengers, there was virtually no rear vision. Yet, this mirror location lasted for several years, before returning to the conventional windshield mounting point. While the new Dodges were beautiful to look at, quality control problems abounded and Dodge sales suffered for the next few years. The Coronet was the base trim Dodge for 1957 and included chrome windshield and rear window moldings; chrome side trim; chrome trim along the fins and grille opening; wheel covers and the Coronet name on the front fenders above the chrome strip.

1957 Dodge, Coronet D-501 two-door Club Sedan, V-8

CORONET I.D. DATA: Six-cylinder-powered Coronets assembled in Detroit began at 32255081 and went to 32292657. V-8-powered Coronets assembled in Detroit began at 35172001 and went to 35303713. Those assembled in Los Angeles began at 42620001 and went to 45547041. Six-cylinder engine numbers began at D72-1001 and went to D72-9600. After Jan. 10, 1957, engine numbers began at KDS-6-9601 and went up to KDS-6-18892. V-8 engine numbers began at KDS-1001 and went to KDS-287536.

CORONET SERIES

Model No.	Body/ Style No.	Body Type & Seating	Factory Price	Shipping Weight	Prod. Total
D66/72	Note 1	4-dr Sed-6P	2416/2524	3470/3620	Note 2
D66/72	Note 1	2-dr Clb Sed-6P	2335/2443	3400/3530	Note 2
D66	Note 1	4-dr Lancer HT-6P	2630	3665	Note 2
D66	Note 1	2-dr Lancer HT-6P	2545	3570	Note 2
D66	Note 1	2-dr Lancer Conv-6P	2807	3815	Note 2

Note 1: See Note 1, 1947 Deluxe models.

Note 2: Production figures were not given for individual models and body styles. Dodge produced a total of 257,488 cars during calendar year 1957, including 160,979 Coronets. Coronet model year output, in round figures, was 160,500 cars.

Note 3: Prices and weights to left of slash marks are for sixes, to right for V-8s.

ROYAL SERIES — (V-8) — The Royal was once again the intermediate trim level and included all the Coronet features plus chrome headlight doors and a 'V' medallion on the rear deck lid. The Royal name appeared on the front fender above the chrome trim strip.

1957 Dodge, Coronet four-door sedan, V-8

ROYAL I.D. DATA: Royal models assembled in Detroit began at 37240001 and went to 37321614. Those assembled in Los Angeles began at 45540001 and went to 45631610. V-8 engine numbers began at KDS-1001 and went to KDS-287538.

ROYAL SERIES

D67-1	Note 1	4-dr Sed-6P	2677	3620	Note 2
D67-1	Note 1	4-dr Lancer HT-6P	2783	3690	Note 2
D67-1	Note 1	2-dr Lancer HT-6P	2734	3585	Note 2
D67-1	Note 1	2-dr Lancer Conv-6P	2996	3830	Note 2

Note 1: See Note 1, 1947 Deluxe models.

Note 2: Production figures were not given for individual models and body styles. Dodge produced a total of 257,488 cars during calendar year 1957. A total of 40,999 Royal models were built on a calendar year basis. Royal series model year output, in rounded off figures, was 41,000 cars.

1957 Dodge, Custom Royal Lancer two-door hardtop, V-8 (AA)

CUSTOM ROYAL SERIES — (V-8) — The Custom Royal was once again the top trim level Dodge and included all the Royal features plus six vertical bumper bars between the bumper and the horizontal grille bar; the Dodge name, in gold, on the hood and the trunk lid and the Custom Royal name on the sides of the front fenders, above the chrome trim strip.

CUSTOM ROYAL I.D. DATA: Custom Royal models assembled in Detroit began at 37240001 and went to 37321614. Those assembled in Los Angeles began at 45540001 and went to 45631610. V-8 engine numbers began at KDS-1001 and went to KDS-287536.

CUSTOM ROYAL SERIES

Model No.	Body/ Style No.	Body Type & Seating	Factory Price	Shipping Weight	Prod. Total
D67-2	Note 1	4-dr Sed-6P	2846	3690	Note 2
D67-2	Note 1	4-dr Lancer HT-6P	2956	3750	Note 2
D67-2	Note 1	2-dr Lancer HT-6P	2885	3670	Note 2
D67-2	Note 1	2-dr Conv-6P	3111	3810	Note 2

Note 1: See Note 1, 1947 Deluxe models.

Note 2: See Note 2, 1957 Coronet models. A total of 55,149 Custom Royal models were built on a calendar year basis. Custom Royal series output, on a model year basis, in round figures, was 47,000 units.

STATION WAGON SERIES — (V-8) — For the first time, station wagons were included in their own series. The two-door Suburban and four-door Sierra models were the base trim level and compared to the Coronet series of conventional cars. The Custom Sierra was the top trim level and compared to the Royal series of conventional cars. An interesting feature of the 1957 Dodge station wagons was the location of the spare tire. It was mounted behind the right rear wheel and was accessible from a removable fender skirt located behind the rear wheelwell.

STATION WAGON I.D. DATA: Station wagon models were assembled only in Detroit and began at 38001001 and went to 38022513 for the Suburban and Sierra models, or began at 38535001 and went to 38542217 for the Custom Sierra. Engine numbers corresponded to the Royal series of conventional cars.

STATION WAGON SERIES

D70	Note 1	2-dr Sub-6P	2826	3830	Note 2
D70	Note 1	4-dr Sierra-6P	2911	3930	Note 2
D70	Note 1	4-dr Sierra-9P	3038	4015	Note 2
D71	Note 1	4-dr Cus Sierra-6P	3052	3960	Note 2
D71	Note 1	4-dr Cus Sierra-9P	3180	4030	Note 2

Note 1: See Note 1, 1947 Deluxe models.

Note 2: See Note 2, 1957 Coronet models. A total of 30,481 station wagons were built on a calendar year basis. Station wagon model year output, in round figures, was 32,000 units.

D-500 SERIES — (V-8) — The D-500 was actually a high-performance engine option for all series. However, in this edition, we are listing it in series format, because of its importance to collectors. The representative prices and weights shown are based on adding the option to a pair of Custom Royal models. Dodge D-500s included all features of the base series models, plus the high-performance 285-, 310- or 340-hp V-8 engines.

D-500 I.D. DATA: See Dodge V-8 model I.D. numbers above. Engine numbers began at KD-501-1001 and went to KD-501-1102.

D-500 SERIES

D501	Note 1	2-dr Clb Sed-6P	3279	3885	Note 2
D501	Note 1	2-dr Conv-6P	3635	3975	Note 2

Note 1: See Note 1, 1947 Deluxe models.

Note 2: Production of 500 Dodge D-500s was scheduled. Approximately 101 cars were fitted with D-501 engines.

ENGINES:

(Six) Inline. L-head. Cast iron block. Displacement: 230 cid. Bore and stroke: 3.25 x 4.625 inches. Compression ratio: 8.0:1. Brake hp: 138 at 4000 rpm. Four main bearings. Solid valve lifters. Carburetor: Stromberg one-barrel Model WW3-159.

(Red Ram V-8) Overhead valve. Cast iron block. Displacement: 325 cid. Bore and stroke: 3.69 x 3.80 inches. Compression ratio: 8.5:1. Brake hp: 245 at 4400 rpm in Coronet and Royal series, 260 at 4400 rpm in Custom Royal series. Five main bearings. Hydraulic valve lifters. Carburetor: (245 hp) Stromberg two-barrel Model WW3-149; (260 hp) Carter WCFB-2532S.

(D-500 V-8) Overhead valve. Cast iron block. Displacement: 325 cid. Bore and stroke: 3.69 x 3.80 inches. Compression ratio: 10.0:1. Hemispherical heads. Brake hp: 285 at 5200 rpm. Solid valve lifters. Carburetor: Carter four-barrel Type WCFB.

(Super D-500) engine: same as above but with dual Carter WCFB four-barrel carburetors. Brake hp: 310 at 5200 rpm.

(D-501 V-8) Overhead valve. Cast iron block. Displacement: 354 cid. Bore and stroke: 3.94 x 3.63 inches. Compression ratio: 10.0:1. Hemispherical heads. Brake horsepower: 340 at 5200 rpm. Hydraulic valve lifters. Carburetor: Two Carter WCFB four-barrel (midyear offering).

CHASSIS FEATURES: Wheelbase: 122 inches. Overall length: (station wagon) 214.4 inches; (other models) 212.2 inches. Tires: (Coronet) 7.50 x 14 tubeless black sidewall; (D-500) 7.60 x 15 tubeless black sidewall; (Royal, Custom Royal, station wagons and convertibles) 8.00 x 14 tubeless black sidewall.

CONVENIENCE OPTIONS: Electric clock. Turn signals. Mopar radio. PowerFlite or TorqueFlite automatic transmissions. Power steering. Power brakes. Power windows. Power seats. Heater. Air Temp air conditioning. Highway Hi-Fi automatic record player. Windshield washers. White sidewall tires.

HISTORICAL FOOTNOTES: This year saw the introduction of the famous torsion bar front suspension that Chrysler used from 1957 on. The 1957 Dodge lineup was introduced Oct. 30, 1958, the same day that all other Chrysler products debuted that season. The division's total model year production peaked at 281,359 cars, which gave Dodge a 4.5 percent market share. On a 1957 calendar year basis, Dodge manufactured 82,220 two-door hardtops; 6,960 two-door convertibles; 8,100 two-door station wagons and 34,210 four-door station wagons. This does not include 1957 models built in the fall of 1956 but it does include 1958 models built in calendar 1957. Therefore it can only be used as an indication of body style popularity in calendar 1957. On a model year basis, 96.5 percent of all 1957 Dodges had automatic transmissions; 25.9 percent had power brakes; 2.2 percent had power seats; 2.1 percent had power windows; 53.7 percent had radios; 15.1 percent had dual exhaust and 93.4 percent had V-8 engines. M.C. Patterson was president of the division again this year.

1958 DODGE

CORONET SERIES — (6-CYL/V-8) — The 1958 Dodges continued to use the 1957 body shell with only minor restyling. The major change was a completely revised grille and quad headlights. The grille had abbreviated horizontal center bars, which housed the parking lights at their inside edge. A major concentration at Dodge in 1958 was power. All engines were of the "wedge" single rocker head design. The ultimate, an electronically fuel-injected 361-cid version, put out 333 hp. The Coronet was the base trim level for 1958 and included chrome windshield and rear window moldings; chrome trim around the grille opening and headlights; a single chrome strip along the bodyside and base of the rear fender fins and the Coronet name, in script, along the back of the side chrome strip. The Dodge name, in block letters, was spaced along the front edge of the hood.

CORONET I.D. DATA: Six-cylinder-powered Coronets assembled in Detroit were numbered LD1-1001 and up. Those assembled in Newark were numbered LD1N-1001 and up. V-8 Coronets assembled in Detroit were numbered LD2-1001 and up. Those assembled in Los Angeles

were numbered LD2L-1001 and up. Those assembled at Newark were numbered LD2N-1001 and up. Engine numbers were L230-1001 and up for sixes and L325-1001 and up for V-8s.

1958 Dodge, Coronet two-door sedan, V-8

CORONET SERIES

Model No.	Body/ Style No.	Body Type & Seating	Factory Price	Shipping Weight	Prod. Total
LD1/2	Note 1	4-dr Sed-6P	2495/2602	3410/3555	Note 2
LD1/2	Note 1	2-dr Sed-6P	2414/2521	3360/3505	Note 2
LD2-L1	Note 1	4-dr Lancer HT-6P	2729	3605	Note 2
LD2-L1	Note 1	2-dr Lancer HT-6P	2644	3540	Note 2
LD2-L1	Note 1	2-dr Conv-6P	2907	3725	Note 2

Note 1: See Note 1, 1947 Deluxe models.

Note 2: Production figures were not given for individual models and body styles. Dodge produced a total of 135,505 cars during calendar year 1958, including 77,388 Coronets. Dodge model year output peaked at 133,953 units. In rounded figures, 77,000 of these cars were Coronets.

Note 3: Prices and weights to left of slash marks are for sixes, to right for V-8s.

ROYAL SERIES — (V-8) — The Royal was once again the intermediate trim level and included all the Coronet features. On this series, the chrome trim at the base of the rear fender fin flared out to a pointed dip, before angling up to the top of the fin. Twin chrome hood ornaments were another distinction.

ROYAL I.D. DATA: V-8 Royals assembled in Detroit were numbered LD2-1001 and up. Those assembled in Los Angeles were numbered LD2L-1001 and up. Those assembled at Newark were numbered LD2N-1001 and up. Engine numbers were L325-1001 and up.

ROYAL SERIES

LD2M	Note 1	4-dr Sed-6P	2757	3570	Note 2
LD2M	Note 1	4-dr Lancer HT-6P	2875	3640	Note 2
LD2M	Note 1	2-dr Lancer HT-6P	2814	3565	Note 2

Note 1: See Note 1, 1947 Deluxe models.

Note 2: Total Royal models built on a calendar year basis N/A. On a model year basis, using rounded off figures, Royal output was counted as 15,500 units.

1958 Dodge, Royal Lancer four-door hardtop, V-8

CUSTOM ROYAL SERIES — (V-8) — The Custom Royal was once again the top trim level Dodge and included all the Royal features plus 'knight's head' emblems on the front fenders, a gold Dodge name on the hood and trunk and chrome rain gutter moldings. The Regal Lancer was a midyear two-door hardtop introduced in early 1958. Also, a Spring Special trim package, introduced in the (what else?) spring, was offered on most Custom Royal models. It consisted of a grille medallion, blackout headlights, new side molding, rear fin trim and license box trim.

CUSTOM ROYAL I.D. DATA: Custom Royal models assembled in Detroit were numbered LD3-1001 and up. Those assembled in Los Angeles were numbered LD3L-1001 and up. Those assembled in Newark were numbered LD3N-1001 and up. Engine numbers were L350-1001 and up.

CUSTOM ROYAL SERIES

Model No.	Body/ Style No.	Body Type & Seating	Factory Price	Shipping Weight	Prod. Total
LD3H	Note 1	4-dr Sed-6P	2985	3640	Note 2
LD3H	Note 1	4-dr Lancer HT-6P	3097	3670	Note 2
LD3H	Note 1	2-dr Lancer HT-6P	3026	3610	Note 2
LD3H	Note 1	2-dr Conv-6P	3253	3785	Note 2
LD3H	Note 1	2-dr Reg Lan-6P	3200	3655	Note 2

Note 1: See Note 1, 1947 Deluxe models.

Note 2: A total of 23,949 Custom Royal models were built on a calendar year basis. On a model year basis, Custom Royal output was 21,000 units in rounded off figures.

STATION WAGON SERIES — (V-8) — For 1958, station wagons continued to be in their own series. As in 1957, the two-door Suburban was the base trim level and was comparable to the Coronet series of conventional cars. The Sierra was the intermediate trim level station wagon and was comparable to the Royal series of conventional cars. The Custom Sierra was the top trim level and was comparable to the Custom Royal series of conventional cars.

STATION WAGON I.D. DATA: Station wagon models used the same serial number sequence as the Custom Royal series.

1958 Dodge, Custom Sierra station wagon, V-8

STATION WAGON SERIES

LD3L	Note 1	2-dr Sub-6P	2930	3875	Note 2
LD3L	Note 1	4-dr Sierra-6P	2995	3930	Note 2
LD3L	Note 1	4-dr Sierra-9P	3137	3990	Note 2
LD3H	Note 1	4-dr Cus Sierra-6P	3172	3955	Note 2
LD3H	Note 1	4-dr Cus Sierra-9P	3314	4035	Note 2

Note 1: See Note 1, 1947 Deluxe models.

Note 2: A total of 30,481 station wagons were built in the calendar year. On a model year basis, 20,000 station wagons were built (rounded off figures).

ENGINES:

(Six) Inline. L-head. Cast iron block. Displacement: 230 cid. Bore and stroke: 3.25 x 4.825 inches. Compression ratio: 8.0:1. Brake hp: 138 at 4000 rpm. Four main bearings. Solid valve lifters. Carburetor: Stromberg one-barrel Model WW3-159.

(Red Ram V-8) Overhead valve. Cast iron block. Displacement: 325 cid. Bore and stroke: 3.69 x 3.80 inches. Compression ratio: 8.0:1. Brake hp: 245 at 4400 rpm (265 at 4600 rpm in Royal models). Five main bearings. Hydraulic valve lifters. Carburetor: (Coronet V-8) Stromberg Model WW3-163 two-barrel; (Royal V-8) Carter WCFB-2660S two-barrel.

(Ram Fire V-8) Overhead valve. Cast iron block. Displacement: 350 cid. Bore and stroke: 4.05 x 3.38 inches. Compression ratio: 10.0:1. Brake hp: 295 at 4600 rpm. Five main bearings. Hydraulic valve lifters. Carburetor: Carter four-barrel.

(D-500 V-8) Overhead valve. Cast iron block. Displacement: 361 cid. Bore and stroke: 4.12 x 3.38 inches. Compression ratio: 10.0:1. Brake hp: 305 at 4600 rpm. Five main bearings. Hydraulic valve lifters. Carburetor: Carter four-barrel Model WCFB.

(Super D-500 V-8) Overhead valve. Cast iron block. Displacement: 361 cid. Bore and stroke: 4.12 x 3.38 inches. Compression ratio: 10.0:1. Brake hp: 320 at 4600 rpm. Carburetor: Two Carter four-barrel Model WCFB.

(Electronic Fuel Injection V-8) Overhead valve. Cast iron block. Displacement: 361 cid. Bore and stroke: 4.12 x 3.38 inches. Compression ratio: 10.0:1. Brake hp: 333 at 4800 rpm. Five main bearings. Hydraulic valve lifters. Fuel system: Bendix electronic fuel injection.

CHASSIS FEATURES: Wheelbase: 122 inches. Overall length: (station wagons) 214.4 inches; (other models) 212.2 inches. Tires: (Coronet) 7.50 x 14; (Royal, Custom Royal and station wagons) 8.00 x 14 tubeless black sidewall.

CONVENIENCE OPTIONS: Electric clock. Turn signals. Mopar radio. PowerFlite ($180). TorqueFlite ($220). Power steering ($92). Power brakes ($38). Power windows. Power seats. Heater. Air Temp air conditioning ($381). Highway Hi-Fi automatic record player. Windshield washer. White sidewall tires. Seat belts.

HISTORICAL FOOTNOTES: The 1958 Dodges were introduced Nov. 1, 1957. Model year production peaked at 133,953 units. Calendar year sales of 114,206 cars were recorded. M.C. Patterson was president of the division this year. The demand for Dodge sixes increased during 1958, rising from 4.6 percent to 9.7 percent. On a model year basis, 96.4 percent of all Dodges had automatic transmission; 62.5 percent had power steering; 34 percent had power brakes; 2.5 percent had power windows; 44.7 percent had radios; 23.4 percent had tinted glass; 4.4 percent had air conditioning and 7.2 percent had dual exhaust. The 1958 Regal Lancer was a limited edition two-door hardtop with special paint, trim and interior. It came only in bronze finish, combined with either black or white. Approximately 12 Dodges were built with the new Bendix EFI (electronic fuel injection) system. This option was later deleted and these cars were recalled for conversion to normal carburetion.

1959 DODGE

CORONET SERIES — (6-CYL/V-8) — The new Dodges were easily recognizable as Dodges, even though the styling of the 1957-1958 models was simply exaggerated. The fins were more rakish, the brows over the headlights were much larger and the entire car was longer, lower and wider than in previous years. The grille was a modification of the split bumper grille bar theme backed by an aluminum mesh. The great horsepower race of the 1950s was over, but Dodge continued to build high-performance cars. This year's offering in the high horsepower category was the first of the famous 383-cid V-8 engines, which Chrysler used for more than a decade. The 383 boasted 345 hp in its Super D-500 format. Also new for 1959 was the Swivel-Seat option. A simple motion of the lever, at the side of the seat, and the unit swung out to meet the occupant. Dodge experimented with self-leveling rear air suspension, called LevelFlite, as an option. The Coronet continued to be the base trim level and included chrome windshield and rear window moldings, a single horizontal chrome strip along the bodyside and chrome trim at the lower edge of the fender fin. The Dodge name, in block letters, appeared on the trunk lid (directly below a combination Dodge crest and trunk handle). The Coronet name, in script, appeared on the front fender. At midyear, a "Silver Challenger" option was available on the two-door sedan.

1959 Dodge, Coronet two-door Club Sedan, V-8

CORONET I.D. DATA: Six-cylinder-powered Coronets assembled in Detroit were numbered M302100001 and up. Those assembled in Newark were numbered M305100001 and up. V-8-powered models assembled in Detroit were numbered M312100001 and up. Those assembled in Newark were numbered M315100001 and up. V-8 models assembled in California were numbered M314100001 and up.

CORONET SERIES

Model No.	Body/Style No.	Body Type & Seating	Factory Price	Shipping Weight	Prod. Total
MD1/2L	41	4-dr Sed-6P	2537/2657	3425/3615	8,103
MD1/2L	21	2-dr Clb Sed-6P	2466/2586	3375/3565	5,432
MD1/2L	23	2-dr Lancer HT-6P	2594/2714	3395/3590	2,151

Model No.	Body/Style No.	Body Type & Seating	Factory Price	Shipping Weight	Prod. Total
MD2L	43	4-dr Lancer HT-6P	2792	3620	8,946
MD2L	27	2-dr Conv-6P	3039	3775	1,840

Note 1: A total of 96,782 Coronet models were produced during calendar year 1959. Exactly 151,851 Dodges were built

for the 1959 model year. In slightly rounded off figures, the model year output of Coronets was counted at 96,900 units.

Note 2: Prices and weights to left of slash marks are for sixes, to right for V-8s.

1959 Dodge, Custom Royal Lancer four-door hardtop, V-8

ROYAL SERIES — (V-8) — The Royal continued to be the intermediate trim level and included all Coronet features, plus a long horizontal chrome strip (from the front wheelwell to the rear of the car), which is wider than the trim used on the Coronet. Royals also featured horizontal scoring on this strip. A stylized V-8 emblem appeared on the front fenders and the Royal name appeared on a wide molding at the front of the rear fender fins.

ROYAL I.D. DATA: Royal models assembled in Detroit were numbered M332100001 and up. Those assembled in Newark were numbered M335100001 and up and those assembled in California were numbered M334100001 and up.

ROYAL SERIES

MD3M	41	4-dr Sed-6P	2884	3640	8,389
MD3M	43	4-dr Lancer HT-6P	3019	3690	2,935
MD3M	23	2-dr Lancer HT-6P	2940	3625	3,483

Note 1: A total of 14,807 Royal models were produced during calendar year 1959. In slightly rounded off figures, the model year output of Royals was counted at 14,900 units.

CUSTOM ROYALS SERIES — (V-8) — The Custom Royal continued to be the top trim level and included all the Royal features, plus the Custom Royal name on the wide molding at the front of the rear fender fins.

CUSTOM ROYAL I.D. DATA: Custom Royal models assembled in Detroit were numbered M352100001 and up. Those assembled in Newark were numbered M355100001 and up and those assembled in California were numbered M354100001 and up.

CUSTOM ROYAL SERIES

MD3H	41	4-dr Sed-6P	3095	3660	8,925
MD3H	43	4-dr Lancer HT-6P	3229	3745	5,019
MD3H	23	2-dr Lancer HT-6P	3151	3675	6,278
MD3H	27	2-dr Conv-6P	3372	3820	984

Note 1: A total of 21,206 Custom Royal models were produced during calendar year 1959. In slightly rounded off figures, the model year output of Custom Royals was counted at 16,500 units.

1959 Dodge, Custom Sierra station wagon, V-8

STATION WAGON SERIES — (V-8) — Station wagons continued to have their own series for 1959. The two-door Suburban was dropped, and the four-door Sierra replaced the Suburban as the base trim level. The Custom Sierra continued in the top trim level, equaling the Royal series of conventional cars in trim.

STATION WAGON I.D. DATA: Station wagon models assembled in Detroit were numbered 372100001 and up. Those assembled in Newark were numbered 375100001 and up and those assembled in California were numbered 374100001 and up.

STATION WAGON SERIES

Model No.	Body/ Style No.	Body Type & Seating	Factory Price	Shipping Weight	Prod. Total
MD3-L	45A	4-dr Sierra-6P	3053	3940	11,069
MD3-L	45B	4-dr Sierra-9P	3174	4015	6,650
MD3-H	45A	4-dr Cus Sierra-6P	3268	3980	2,434
MD3-H	45B	4-dr Cus Sierra-9P	3389	4020	3,437

Note 1: A total of 23,590 station wagons were produced during calendar year 1959. In slightly rounded off figures, the model year output of Dodge station wagons was 23,500.

ENGINES:

(Six) L-head. Inline. Cast iron block. Displacement: 230 cid. Bore and stroke: 3.25 x 4.38 inches. Compression ratio: 8.0:1. Brake hp: 135 at 3600 rpm. Four main bearings. Solid valve lifters. Carburetor: Stromberg one-barrel.

(Red Ram V-8) Overhead valve. Cast iron block. Displacement: 326 cid. Bore and stroke: 3.95 x 3.31 inches. Compression ratio: 9.2:1. Brake hp: 255 at 4400 rpm. Five main bearings. Hydraulic valve lifters. Carburetor: Carter two-barrel.

(Ram Fire V-8) Overhead valve. Cast iron block. Displacement: 361 cid. Bore and stroke: 4.12 x 3.38 inches. Compression ratio: 10.1:1. Brake hp: 295 at 4600 rpm on Royal and Sierra models, 305 at 4600 rpm on Custom Royal and Custom Sierra models. Five main bearings. Hydraulic valve lifters. Carburetor: (295 hp) Carter two-barrel; (305 hp) Carter four-barrel.

(D-500 V-8) Overhead valve. Cast iron block. Displacement: 383 cid. Bore and stroke: 4.25 x 3.38 inches. Compression ratio: 10.1:1. Brake hp: 320 at 4600 rpm. Five main bearings. Hydraulic valve lifters. Carburetor: Carter four-barrel.

(Super D-500 V-8) Overhead valve. Cast iron block. Displacement: 383 cid. Bore and stroke: 4.25 x 3.38 inches. Compression ratio: 10.0:1. Brake hp: 345 at 5000 rpm. Five main bearings. Hydraulic valve lifters. Carburetor: Two Carter four-barrel.

CHASSIS FEATURES: Wheelbase: 122 inches. Overall length: 217.4 inches (216.4 inches on station wagons). Tires: (Coronet) 7.50 x 14; (all others) 8.00 x 14 tubeless black sidewalls.

CONVENIENCE OPTIONS: TorqueFlite transmission, all V-8 models ($226.90). PowerFlite transmission, Coronet and Royal ($189.10). Power steering, V-8 only ($92.15). Power brakes ($42.60). Power window lifts ($102.30). Power tailgate window, two-seat wagons ($34.10). Six-Way power seat ($95.70). Dual exhaust ($30.90). Push-button radio ($86.50). Rear speaker ($14.95). Radio with dual antenna ($14.05). Heater and defroster ($93.55). Tires: white sidewall 7.50 x 14, Coronet except convertible ($33.35); 8.00 x 14, other models ($41.75). Two-tone paint standard colors ($18.55); Deluxe colors ($34.10). Solex glass ($42.60); windshield only ($18.55). Back-up lights ($10.70). Wheel covers ($14.30); Deluxe ($30.50). Electric clock ($15.95). Windshield washer ($11.80). Variable speed windshield wipers ($6.60). Windshield washer and Vari-speed wipers ($18.25). Front and rear Air Foam seat ($10.70). Undercoating ($12.85). Air conditioning with heater, V-8s only ($468.55); wagons ($662.95). Carpets ($11.80). Rear window defroster ($20.60). Sure-Grip differential, all except convertible ($49.70). Padded instrument panel ($20.00). Padded sun visors ($8.00). Automatic headlight beam changer ($49.70). Heavy-duty 70-amp battery ($8.60). Custom trim package, Coronet except convertible ($56.00). D-500 383 cid/320 hp four-barrel carb engine with dual exhaust and TorqueFlite transmission, Coronet convertible ($368.00); Coronet V-8 except convertible ($398.90); Royal and Sierra station wagons ($328.10); Custom Royal convertible ($273.35); Custom Royal and Custom station wagons ($304.15). Super D-500 345 hp engine, Coronet V-8 except convertible ($540.45); Coronet convertible ($509.60); Royal and Sierra station wagons ($469.65); Custom Royal convertible ($414.95); Custom Royal and Custom station wagons ($445.75). LevelFlite, V-8s only ($127.55). Outside rearview mirror ($6.45). Remote control left outside rearview mirror ($17.75); right ($8.60). Co-Pilot speed warning device ($12.85). Storage compartment with lock, two-seat station wagons ($28.20). Swivel seat ($70.95).

HISTORICAL FOOTNOTES: The 1959 Dodges were introduced on Oct. 10, 1958. Model year production peaked at 151,851 units, of which approximately 15,600 were sixes and 136,200 were V-8 powered. Dodge assembled 13,515 two-door sedans; 65,752 four-door sedans; 29,610 two-door hardtops; 16,704 four-door hardtops; 2,733 convertibles; 13,515 four-door two-seat station wagons and 10,022 four-door three-seat station wagons in the 1959 model year. Dodge Division's calendar year output was 192,798 units this year, accounting for a 3.44

percent share of the total market. M.C. Patterson continued as president and general manager of Dodge Division this season. For the model run, about 94 percent of all Dodges had automatic transmissions; 68.9 percent had power steering; 27.4 percent had power brakes; 23.2 percent had windshield washers; 84.7 percent had back-up lights; 4.5 percent had air conditioning and only 0.7 percent had the rare air suspension, an option that did not last long.

1960 DODGE

DART SENECA — SERIES PD3/PD4 — (6-CYL/V-8) — The year 1960 was a significant one for Dodge. In addition to the full-size Dodges, a line of slightly smaller cars was introduced. This new Dart series rode on a smaller 118-inch wheelbase and was four inches shorter, overall, than the larger Dodge. Like all new Dodges, the Dart Seneca had unitized body/chassis construction for the first time. While standard Dodges used the 361-cid V-8 engine as base equipment, the new Dart was offered with the 225-cid 'Slant Six.' This engine was slanted toward the passenger side of the car to allow easier maintenance on the carburetor and spark plugs. This also allowed the use of longer intake manifold runners, which added considerably to power output. Styling of the new Darts left little doubt that they were products of Dodge Division, but the general appearance was more subdued than in 1959. The headlight 'eyebrows' were replaced by more conventional chrome bezels and the height of the fins was reduced substantially. The side styling was simple, with a single horizontal chrome strip beginning at the rear of the front wheelwell and going back to the rear bumper. The taillamps were enclosed in a chrome bezel, which bore an interesting resemblance to the air intake scoop of an F-88 Sabre Jet. The Dodge name, in script, appeared on the lower right side of the trunk lid. At the front, the grille featured a vertical bar theme with five dividers, which was complemented by a split front bumper. A new Dodge crest, more contemporary than in previous years, was located on the front of the hood. The Seneca series was the base trim level Dart and included chrome windshield and rear window moldings; a single chrome strip along the bodyside; chrome trim along the back edge of the fin; chrome license plate frame recessed into the trunk lid; front armrests; electric windshield wipers; sun visors; turn signals and the Seneca name, in script, along the side of the rear fender, just in front of the taillights.

SENECA I.D. DATA: Serial numbers are stamped/embossed on a plate on left front door pillar and use the form 410()100001 and up. The first symbol indicates car-line/engine: 4=Dart six-cyl.; 5=Dart V-8; 6=Dodge V-8. The second symbol indicates series: 1=Seneca/Matador; 2=Pioneer; 3=Phoenix/Polara; 5=Seneca/Matador station wagon; 6=Pioneer station wagon; 7=Polara station wagon; 8=Taxicab and 9=Police Special. The third symbol indicates model year: 0=1960. The fourth symbol indicates assembly plant: 1=Lynch Rd.; 2=Dodge Main; 3=Detroit (Jefferson); 5=Los Angeles, Calif.; 6=Newark; 7=St. Louis, Mo.; and 8=Clairpointe, Mo. The last six symbols are the sequential production number starting at 100001 for each series at each factory. Body number plates are located under the hood on fenders, cowl or radiator crossmember. They carry symbols that tell the production schedule dates, body production number, body series and trim, paint and accessory codes. A three-digit body number identifies each model and appears in the Model Number column of the charts below, replacing series codes that appeared in earlier editions of this catalog. Model codes with alpha prefixes are also employed as follows: L=low-priced; M=medium-priced; H=high-priced; P=premium-priced and S=specially-priced. These appear in charts below in the Body/Style Number column. Engine codes were stamped on the right side of most engines and the left side of 318-cid V-8s, as follows: P-22 on 225-cid Slant Six; P-318 on 318-cid V-8; P-36 on 361-cid V-8 and P-38 on 383-cid V-8.

SENECA SERIES

Model No.	Body/ Style No.	Body Type & Seating	Factory Price	Shipping Weight	Prod. Total
413/513	L41	4-dr Sed-6P	2330/2449	3420/3600	Notes 1 & 2
411/511	L21	2-dr Sed-6P	2278/2397	3385/3530	Notes 1 & 2
456/556	L45	4-dr Sta Wag-6P	2695/2815	3805/3975	Notes 1 & 2

Note 1: Exactly 306,603 Dodge Darts were built during the 1960 model year. In rounded off figures, this included 111,600 Dodge Dart Seneca passenger cars and an undetermined number of Seneca station wagons. (Station wagons were a separate series. A total of some 51,600 station wagons were built in all lines.)

Note 2: During model year 1960, Dodge built exactly 44,719 two-door sedans; 162,420 four-door sedans; 54,345 two-door hardtops; 20,216 four-door hardtops; 8,817 convertibles; 38,275 four-door station wagons with two seats and 13,379 station wagons with three seats. Unfortunately, no breakouts are available as to how many of each body style were built in specific series or car-lines.

Note 3: Prices and weights to left of slash marks are for sixes, to right for V-8s.

1960 Dodge, Dart Pioneer station wagon, 6-cyl

DART PIONEER — PD3/PD4 SERIES — (6-CYL/V-8) — The Pioneer was the intermediate trim level Dart. It included all Seneca features, plus rear armrests; front foam cushions and cigarette lighter. Nine-passenger station wagons also included a power tailgate window.

PIONEER I.D. DATA: See Seneca I.D. Data section above.

PIONEER SERIES

Model No.	Body/ Style No.	Body Type & Seating	Factory Price	Shipping Weight	Prod. Total
423/523	M41	4-dr Sed-6P	2459/2578	3430/3610	Note 1
421/521	M21	2-dr Sed-6P	2410/2530	3375/3540	Note 1
422/522	M23	2-dr HT Cpe-6P	2488/2607	3410/3610	Note 1
466/566	M45A	4-dr Sta Wag-6P	2787/2906	3820/4000	Note 1
467/567	M45B	4-dr Sta Wag-9P	2892/3011	3875/4065	Note 1

Note 1: Exactly 306,603 Dodge Darts were built during the 1960 model year. In rounded off figures, this included 80,000 Pioneer passenger cars and an undetermined number of Pioneer station wagons. (Station wagons were in a separate series. A total of some 51,600 station wagons were built in all lines.)

Note 2: Body style production of 1960 Dodges is available in terms of total output only and cannot be broken-out by series or car-line at the current time. See Seneca series Note 2 above.

Note 3: Prices and weights above slash mark are for sixes, below for V-8.

1960 Dodge, Dart Phoenix four-door hardtop, V-8

PHOENIX SERIES — (6-CYL/V-8) — The Phoenix was the top trim level Dart for 1960 and included all the Pioneer features plus exterior moldings, Custom upholstery, Custom interior trimmings and back-up lights.

PHOENIX I.D. DATA: See Seneca I.D. Data section above.

PHOENIX SERIES

433/533	H41	4-dr Sed-6P	2595/2715	3420/3610	Note 1
434/534	H43	4-dr HT Sed-6P	2677/2796	3460/3655	Note 1
432/532	H23	2-dr HT Cpe-6P	2618/2737	3410/3605	Note 1
435/535	H27	2-dr Conv-6P	2868/2988	3460/3690	Note 1

Note 1: Exactly 306,603 Dodge Darts were built during the 1960 model year. In rounded off figures, this included 70,700 Dodge Dart Phoenix passenger cars. (No station wagons were built in the Phoenix car line.)

Note 2: Body style production of 1960 Dodges is available in terms of total output only and cannot be broken out by series or car line. See Seneca series Note 2 above.

Note 3: Prices and weights above slash mark are for sixes, below for V-8.

DODGE MATADOR — SERIES PD1L — (V-8) — The Matador was the base trim Dodge for 1960. Like all full-size Dodges, it featured styling similar to the smaller Dart models, but with slightly exaggerated fins and more deeply tunneled taillights. The fin ended three-quarters of the way down the rear fender. It was capped with chrome rear trim and a reflector. A single horizontal chrome strip ran the entire length of the bodyside. The Matador name, in script, was located on the front fender, just behind the wheelwell. A highly stylized star was located on the side of the tailfin.

MATADOR I.D. DATA: See Seneca I.D. Data section above.

MATADOR SERIES

Model No.	Body/ Style No.	Body Type & Seating	Factory Price	Shipping Weight	Prod. Total
643	41	4-dr Sed-6P	2930	3725	Note 1
644	43	4-dr HT Sed-6P	3075	3820	Note 1
642	23	2-dr HT Cpe-6P	2996	3705	Note 1
678	45A	4-dr Sta Wag-6P	3239	4045	Note 1
679	45B	4-dr Sta Wag-9P	3354	4120	Note 1

Note 1: Exactly 42,517 Dodges (Matador/Polara) were built during the 1960 model year. In figures rounded off to the nearest 100, this included 23,600 Matador passenger cars and an undetermined number of Matador station wagons. (Station wagons were in a separate series. A total of some 51,600 station wagons were built in all car lines.)

Note 2: Body style production of 1960 Dodges is available in terms of total output only and cannot be broken out by series or car line. See Seneca series Note 2 above.

1960 Dodge, Polara two-door convertible, V-8

DODGE POLARA — SERIES PD2H — (V-8) — The Polara was the top trim level Dodge for 1960 and included all Matador features plus dual exhaust; Deluxe interior appointments; rear fender aluminum stone shields; front fender ornaments and the Polara name, in script, on the front fender, just behind the front wheelwell. The Polara station wagon featured pillarless hardtop styling. It was one of the nicest looking station wagons to come out of the Chrysler Corp. assembly plants.

POLARA I.D. DATA: See Seneca I.D. Data section above.

POLARA SERIES

543	41	4-dr Sed-6P	3141	3735	Note 1
544	43	4-dr HT Sed-6P	3275	3815	Note 1
542	23	2-dr HT Cpe-6P	3196	3740	Note 1
578	46A	4-dr Sta Wag-6P	3506	4085	Note 1
579	46B	4-dr Sta Wag-9P	3621	4220	Note 1
545	27	2-dr Conv-6P	3416	3765	Note 1

Note 1: Exactly 42,517 Dodges (Matador/Polara) were built during the 1960 model year. In figures rounded off to the nearest 100, this included 11,600 Polara passenger cars and an undetermined number of Polara station wagons. (Station wagons were in a separate series. A total of some 51,600 station wagons were built in all car lines.)

Note 2: Body style production of 1960 Dodges is available in terms of total output only and cannot be broken out by series or car line. See Seneca series Note 2 above.

ENGINES:

(Slant Six) Overhead valve. Cast iron block. Displacement: 225 cid. Bore and stroke: 3.41 x 4.13 inches. Compression ratio: 8.5:1. Brake hp: 145 at 4000 rpm. Four main bearings. Solid valve lifters. Carburetor: Carter one-barrel BBS-2985S.

(V-8) Overhead valve. Cast iron block. Displacement: 318 cid. Bore and stroke: 3.91 x 3.31 inches. Compression ratio: 9.0:1. Brake hp: 230 at 4400 rpm. Five main bearings. Hydraulic valve lifters. Carburetor: Carter two-barrel BBD-2921S. Another available version of this engine had a four-barrel carburetor and produced 255 hp.

(Super Red Ram V-8) Overhead valve. Cast iron block. Displacement: 361 cid. Bore and stroke: 4.12 x 3.38 inches. Compression ratio: 10.0:1. Brake hp: 295 at 4600 rpm. Five main bearings. Hydraulic valve lifters. Carburetor: Stromberg two-barrel WWC-3-188.

(Ram Fire V-8) Overhead valve. Cast iron block. Displacement: 383 cid. Bore and stroke: 4.25 x 3.38 inches. Compression ratio: 10.0:1. Brake hp: 325 at 4600 rpm. Five main bearings. Hydraulic valve lifters. Carburetor: Holley four-barrel R-1971-A.

(D-500 V-8) Ram Induction (Dart models). Overhead valve. Cast iron block. Displacement: 381 cid. Bore and stroke: 4.12 x 3.38 inches. Compression ratio: 10.0:1. Brake hp: 320 at 4800 rpm. Five main bearings. Hydraulic valve lifters. Carburetor: Two Carter four-barrel on 30-inch "cross ram induction" manifolds.

CHASSIS FEATURES:

(Dart) Wheelbase: 118 inches (122 inches on station wagons). Overall length: 208.6 inches (214.8 inches on station wagons). Tires: 7.50 x 14 tubeless black sidewall on sedans (8.00 x 14 on station wagons).

(Dodge) Wheelbase: 122 inches. Overall length: 212.6 inches (214.8 inches on station wagons). Tires: 8.00 x 14 tubeless black sidewall.

CONVENIENCE OPTIONS: Electric clock ($15). Music Master radio ($59). PowerFlite ($189). TorqueFlite ($211). Power steering ($77). Power brakes ($43). Power seats ($96). Power windows ($102). Air Temp air conditioning ($446). Deluxe dual station wagon air conditioning ($640). Windshield washer ($12). Remote-control side mirror ($18). Swivel seats ($87). D-500 engine in Polara ($359); in Matador ($379) and in Dart Phoenix ($418). White sidewall tires on Darts ($33); on Dodges ($58).

HISTORICAL FOOTNOTES: In 1960, a modified Dart Phoenix driven by Norm Thatcher set three world records at Bonneville in the B-Class for supercharged gas coupes. The supercharged 383-cid V-8-powered hardtop achieved a speed of 191.8 mph over the measured course.

1961 DODGE

DART SENECA — SERIES RD3/RD4 — (6-CYL/V-8) — The year 1961 saw the introduction of a major face lift for the Dart. The most unusual feature of the 1961 models was reverse-slanting fins They appeared to grow out of the fenders, at the base of the roof 'C' pillar and then tapered toward the rear of the car. They then wrapped around and formed a chrome-trimmed feature line, which moved forward, to the back of the rear door. The front end was shaped like a single large air intake. The large grille opening contained grillework with a concave grid pattern, with the quad headlights set at either end. The Dodge name, in block letters, was located across the front of the hood and across the trunk lid, directly above the recessed license plate. The Seneca was the base level Dart and included chrome windshield and rear window moldings; a single chrome strip along the top of the fin (that wrapped around the bodyside); front armrests; electric windshield wipers; sun visors; turn signals and the Seneca name, in script, directly below the fins.

1961 Dodge, Dart Phoenix four-door hardtop, V-8

DART SENECA I.D. DATA — (6-CYL/V-8) — Serial numbers are stamped/embossed on a plate on left front door pillar and use the form 411()100001 and up. The first symbol indicates car-line/engine: 4=Dart six-cyl.; 5=Dodge V-8; 7=Lancer six-cyl. The second symbol indicates series: 1=Seneca Lancer 170; 2=Pioneer; 3=Phoenix/Lancer 770; 4=Polara; 5=Seneca/Lancer 170 wagon; 6=Pioneer station wagon; 7=Polara station wagon; 8=Taxicab; 9=Police Special; 0=Fleet car.

The third symbol indicates model year: 1=1961. The fourth symbol indicates assembly plant: 2=Dodge Main; 3=Detroit (Jefferson); 5=Los Angeles, Calif.; 6=Newark, Del.; 7=St. Louis, Mo. The last six symbols are the sequential production number starting at 100001 for each series at each factory. Body number plates are located under the hood on fenders, cowl or radiator crossmember. They carry symbols that tell the production schedule dates, body production number, body series and trim, paint and accessory codes. A three-digit body number identifies each model and appears in the Model Number column of the charts below, replacing series codes that appeared in earlier editions of this catalog. Model codes with alpha prefixes are also employed, as follows: L=low-priced; M=medium-priced; H=high-priced; P=premium-priced and S=specially-priced. These appear in charts below in the Body/Style Number column. Engine codes were stamped on the right side of most engines and the left side of 318-cid V-8s, as follows: R-17 on 170-cid Slant Six; R-22 on 225-cid Slant Six; R-318 on 318-cid V-8; R-36 on 361-cid V-8; R-38 on 383-cid V-8 and R-41 on 413-cid V-8.

DART SENECA SERIES

Model No.	Body/Style No.	Body Type & Seating	Factory Price	Shipping Weight	Prod. Total
413/513	L41	4-dr Sed-6P	2330/2449	3335/3515	Note 1
411/511	L21	2-dr Sed-6P	2278/2397	3290/3470	Note 1
456/556	L45	4-dr Sta Wag-6P	2695/2815	3740/3920	Note 1

Note 1: A total of 66,100 Seneca passenger cars were built during the model year. During the 1961 model year, Dodge built 20,625 two-door sedans; 97,201 four-door sedans; 22,156 two-door hardtops; 9,665 four-door hardtops; 4,361 convertibles; 20,697 six-passenger station wagons and 7,005 nine-passenger station wagons. There are no available breakouts per series, only by body style.

Note 2: Data above slash marks is for sixes, below for V-8.

DART PIONEER — RD3/RD4 SERIES — (6-CYL/V-8) — The Pioneer was the intermediate trim level Dart and included all Seneca features plus rear armrests, front foam cushion and cigarette lighter. Nine-passenger station wagons also included a power tailgate window. The "Pioneer" name appeared in script at the rear of the rear fender fins.

DART PIONEER I.D. DATA: See 1961 Dart Seneca I.D. Data listing. All models began at 100001 and went up in the unit number sequence.

DART PIONEER SERIES

Model No.	Body/Style No.	Body Type & Seating	Factory Price	Shipping Weight	Prod. Total
423/523	M41	4-dr Sed-6P	2459/2478	3335/3510	Note 1
421/521	M21	2-dr Sed-6P	2410/2530	3290/3460	Note 1
422/522	M23	2-dr HT Cpe-6P	2488/2607	3335/3500	Note 1
466/566	M45A	4-dr Sta Wag-6P	2787/2906	3740/3940	Note 1
467/567	M54B	4-dr Sta Wag-9P	2892/3011	3825/4005	Note 1

Note 1: A total of 38,600 Pioneer passenger cars were built during model year 1961. No production breakout is provided for individual body styles in each series. See Seneca series for total production of each body style during 1961.

Note 2: Data above slash marks for sixes, below for V-8s.

DART PHOENIX — RD3/RD4 SERIES — (6-CYL/V-8) — The Phoenix was the top trim level Dart for 1961 and included all Pioneer features plus exterior moldings; Custom interior upholstery and trim and back-up lights.

DART PHOENIX I.D. DATA: See 1961 Seneca series I.D. Data listing. All models began at 100001 and went up in the unit number sequence.

DART PHOENIX SERIES

Model No.	Body/Style No.	Body Type & Seating	Factory Price	Shipping Weight	Prod. Total
433/533	H41	4-dr Sed-6P	2595/2715	3350/3535	Note 1
434/534	H43	4-dr HT Sed-6P	2677/2796	3385/3555	Note 1
432/532	H23	2-dr HT Cpe-6P	2618/2737	3325/3520	Note 1
435/535	H27	2-dr Conv-6P	2988	3580	Note 1

Note 1: A total of 37,300 Phoenixes were built during calendar year 1961. No production breakout is provided for individual body styles in each series. See Seneca series for total production of each body style during 1961.

Note 2: Data above slash marks is for sixes, below for V-8s. The Phoenix convertible came only with V-8 power.

POLARA — RD1 SERIES — (V-8) — The Polara was the only full-size Dodge offered in 1961. All Polaras utilized the 361-cid V-8 engine as standard equipment. The 383-cid V-8 was optional. Polara models featured chrome windshield and rear window moldings. A split chrome strip, with an aluminum insert, changed back into a single strip behind the

front door, then ran to the rear of the car, sweeping up, over the tailfin. Taillights recessed into bezels, like jet airplane exhaust, were contained in the wraparound sweep of the tailfins. Polaras used Dart grilles, with a crossbar ornament in the center. The Polara name, in script, was located on the front fender ahead of the wheelwell.

1961 Dodge, Polara four-door hardtop station wagon, V-8

POLARA I.D. DATA: See Dart Seneca I.D. Data listing. All models began at 100001 and went up in the unit number sequence.

POLARA SERIES

Model No.	Body/ Style No.	Body Type & Seating	Factory Price	Shipping Weight	Prod. Total
543	L41	4-dr Sed-6P	2966	3700	Note 1
544	L43	4-dr HT Sed-6P	3110	3740	Note 1
542	L23	2-dr HT Cpe-6P	3032	3690	Note 1
545	L27	2-dr Conv-6P	3252	3765	Note 1
578	L46A	4-dr Sta Wag-6P	3294	4115	Note 1
579	L46B	4-dr Sta Wag-9P	3409	4125	Note 1

Note 1: A total of 14,032 Polaras were built during model year 1961. No production breakout is provided for individual body styles in each series. See Seneca series for total production of each body style during 1961.

LANCER 170 — RW1 SERIES — (6-CYL) — The big news for 1961 was the introduction of the compact Lancer series. An offshoot of the Plymouth Valiant, the Lancer was nearly two feet shorter and 700 pounds lighter than a standard Dodge. The Lancer used the basic Valiant body shell, but with more attractive trim and much finer interior appointments. Powering the new Lancer was a smaller, 170-cid version of the Slant Six engine. The Lancer 170 was the base trim level and included chrome windshield and rear window moldings; a short chrome strip on the rear fender feature line (terminating at the taillights) and the Lancer name, in block letters, on the side of the front door (below the feature line). A Dodge crest was located on the front of the hood above the horizontal bar grille. The Dodge name, also in block letters, was located on the trunk lid. A grille of thin horizontal bars ran full width and incorporated quad headlights. Concave, round taillights were set into the rear fender fins.

1961 Dodge, Lancer 770 station wagon, 6-cyl

LANCER 170 I.D. DATA: See Dart Seneca I.D. Data listing. All models began at 100001 and went up in the unit number sequence.

LANCER 170 SERIES

711	L41	4-dr Sed-6P	2069	2595	Note 1
713	L21	2-dr Sed-6P	2007	2585	Note 1
756	L45	4-dr Sta Wag-6P	2382	2760	Note 1

Note 1: The exact model year output of Dodge Lancers was 74,773 units. In rounded figures, this included 20,800 Lancer 170 passenger cars; 44,300 Lancer 770 passenger cars and 9,700 Lancer station wagons (both series).

Note 2: The model year output of 74,733 units included 12,637 two-door sedans; 44,884 four-door sedans; 7,552 two-door hardtops and 9,720 two-seat four-door station wagons. There is no further breakout by series.

LANCER 770 — RW1 SERIES — (6-CYL) — The 770 series was the top trim level Lancer for 1961 and included all the 170 series trim plus more exterior bright trim and more plush interior appointments.

LANCER 770 I.D. DATA: See Dart Seneca I.D. Data listing. All models began at 100001 and went up in the unit number sequence.

LANCER 770 SERIES

Model No.	Body/ Style No.	Body Type & Seating	Factory Price	Shipping Weight	Prod. Total
733	H41	4-dr Sed-6P	2154	2605	Note 1
732	H23	2-dr HT Cpe-6P	2181	2595	Note 1
731	N/A	2-dr Spt Cpe-6P	2092	N/A	Note 1
776	H45	4-dr Sta Wag-6P	2466	2775	Note 1

Note 1: See Note 1 under 1961 Dodge Lancer '170' listing.

ENGINES:

(170 Slant Six) Overhead valve. Cast iron block. Displacement: 170 cid. Bore and stroke: 3.40 x 3.13 inches. Compression ratio: 8.2:1. Brake hp: 101 at 4400 rpm. Four main bearings. Solid valve lifters. Carburetor: Carter one-barrel BBS-3093S.

(225 Slant Six) Overhead valve. Cast iron block. (Some 225 engines were built with aluminum blocks.) Displacement: 225 cid. Bore and stroke: 3.41 x 4.13 inches. Compression ratio: 8.2:1. Brake hp: 145 at 4000 rpm. Four main bearings. Solid valve lifters. Carburetor: Carter one-barrel BBS-3098S.

(Hyper-Pak 225 Slant Six) Overhead valve. Cast iron block (See Historical Footnotes). Displacement: 225 cid. Bore and stroke: 3.41 x 4.13 inches. Compression ratio: 8.2:1. Brake hp: 195 at 5200 rpm. Four main bearings. Solid valve lifters. Carburetor: Carter AFB 3083S four-barrel. Tuned exhaust headers leading to tuned exhaust system.

(V-8) Overhead valve. Cast iron block. Displacement: 318 cid. Bore and stroke: 3.91 x 3.31 inches. Compression ratio: 9.0:1. Brake hp: 230 at 4400 rpm. Five main bearings. Hydraulic valve lifters. Carburetor: Stromberg two-barrel WW-1543.

(Polara V-8) Overhead valve. Cast iron block. Displacement: 361 cid. Bore and stroke: 4.12 x 3.38 inches. Compression ratio: 9.0:1. Brake hp: 265 at 4400 rpm. Five main bearings. Hydraulic valve lifters. Carburetor: Stromberg two-barrel WWC-3-188.

(Dart D-500 V-8) Overhead valve. Cast iron block. Displacement: 361 cid. Bore and stroke: 4.12 x 3.38 inches. Compression ratio: 9.0:1. Brake hp: 305 at 4800 rpm. Five main bearings. Hydraulic valve lifters. Carburetor: Carter AFB-3105S four-barrel.

(Polara D-500 V-8) Overhead valve. Cast iron block. Displacement: 383 cid. Bore and stroke: 4.25 x 3.38 inches. Compression ratio: 10.0:1. Brake hp: 325 at 4800 rpm. Five main bearings. Hydraulic valve lifters. Carburetor: Two Carter AFB-2903S four-barrel.

(Polara Ram-Induction D-500 V-8) Overhead valve. Cast iron block. Displacement: 383 cid. Bore and stroke: 4.25 x 3.38 inches. Compression ratio: 10.0:1. Brake hp: 330 at 5000 rpm. Five main bearings. Hydraulic valve lifters. Carburetor: Two Carter AFB-3084S four-barrel.

(Super D-500 V-8) Overhead valve. Cast iron block. Displacement: 413 cid. Bore and stroke: 4.19 x 3.75 inches. Compression ratio: 10.0:1. Brake hp: 350 at 4600 rpm. Five main bearings. Carburetor: Two Carter AFB-3108S four-barrel. (Option added at midyear.)

(Super Ram-Tuned D-500 V-8) Overhead valve. Cast iron block. Displacement: 413 cid. Bore and stroke: 4.19 x 3.75 inches. Compression ratio: 10.0:1. Brake hp: 375 at 5000 rpm. Five main bearings. Hydraulic valve lifters. Carburetor: Two Carter AFB-3084S four-barrel. (Option added at midyear; includes "short" ram-tuned induction system.)

CHASSIS FEATURES:

(Lancer) Wheelbase: 106.5 inches. Overall length: 188.8 inches. Tires: 6.50 x 13 tubeless black sidewall. Three-speed manual transmission was standard on all Lancers, with the three-speed TorqueFlite automatic transmission optional.

(Dart) Wheelbase: 118 inches (122 inches on station wagons). Overall length: 209.4 inches (214.8 inches on station wagons). Tires: 7.00 x 14 tubeless black sidewall on sedans; 8.00 x 14 on station wagons. Three-speed manual transmission was standard on all Darts, with the three-speed TorqueFlite automatic transmission optional.

(Polara) Wheelbase: 122 inches. Overall length: 212.5 inches (214.8 inches on station wagons). Tires: 8.00 x 14 tubeless black sidewall. Three-speed manual transmission was standard on all Polaras with three-speed TorqueFlite automatic transmission optional.

CONVENIENCE OPTIONS: Electric clock ($16). Music Master radio ($59). TorqueFlite automatic transmission ($211). Power steering ($77). Power brakes ($43). Power seats ($96). Power windows ($102). Air Temp air conditioning ($446); dual unit used in station wagons ($640). Windshield washer ($12). Remote-control outside mirror ($18). Tinted glass ($43). Ram-induction D-500 V-8 ($313). White sidewall tires on Darts ($33); on Polaras ($64).

HISTORICAL FOOTNOTES: Beginning in mid-1961, the 225-cid Slant Six engine was produced with an aluminum engine block. Exact production dates are unavailable. There is no record of the number of these blocks produced. A special Hyper-Pak was available for the Slant Six. A competition engine, the Hyper-Pak featured a much more radical cam; a Carter AFB four-barrel carburetor mounted on an intake manifold with long ram passages; steel tubing exhaust headers; higher compression pistons and a special tuned exhaust system. Advertised at 195 hp, Hyper-Pak engines actually put out in excess of 275 bhp. They were the rulers of the lower stock classes at the drag races. The Hyper-Pak was available as a dealer-installed option. The D-500 and Super D-500 V-8 engines featured an unusual intake system, with two Carter AFB four-barrel carburetors mounted on 30-inch long intake manifolds. The carburetor mounted over the right valve cover actually fed the left bank of the engine and vice-versa. These extremely long manifolds produced incredible low-end torque.

1962 DODGE

DART SERIES — (6-CYL/V-8) — Completely restyled for 1962, the Dart was new from the ground up. Riding on a two-inch shorter, 116-inch wheelbase, the new 202-inch overall length was 10 inches shorter than in 1961. The redesigned grille featured an unusual headlight arrangement. The inboard lights were mounted higher than the outer ones. An oval grille featured vertical bars, with five larger division bars spaced across the insert. Taillamps continued the angular theme of the front and, again, the inboard lenses were positioned higher than the outer ones. Heavy feature lines characterized the bodysides. They originated as a 'brow' over the headlights and flared around the side of the fender. From there, they continued along the side, to the trailing edge of the front door. Another heavy feature line began immediately in front of the rear wheelwell. It swept up, along the wheel opening, and angled back to a point even with the inboard rear taillamp elevation. A chrome strip highlighted each feature line and continued across the trunk lid, between the uppermost taillights. The Dodge name, in block letters, was spaced along the edge of the hood. A Dodge crest was located above the chrome strip, on the trunk lid. The Dart was the base trim model and featured chrome windshield and rear window moldings; chrome headlight doors; turn signals; electric windshield wipers; driver's side inside sun visor and front armrests. The Dart name, in script, appeared on the front door edge.

DART I.D. DATA: Serial numbers are stamped/embossed on a plate on left front door pillar and use the form 412()100001 and up. The first symbol indicates car-line/engine: 4=Dart six-cyl.; 5=Dart V-8/Polara; 6=Dodge Custom 880 V-8; 7=Lancer 170/770/GT. The second symbol indicates series: 1=Lancer 170/Dart/880; 2=Dart 330; 3=Lancer 770/Dart 440; 5=Lancer 170/Dart Custom station wagon; 6=Dart 330 station wagon; 7=Lancer 770/Dart 440 station wagon; 8=Taxicab; 9=Police Special; 10=Fleet car. The third symbol indicates model year: 2=1962. The fourth symbol indicates assembly plant: 2=Dodge Main; 3=Detroit (Jefferson); 5=Los Angeles, Calif.; 6=Newark, Del.; 7=St. Louis, Mo. The last six symbols are the sequential production number starting at 100001 for each series at each factory. Body number plates are located under the hood on fenders, cowl or radiator crossmember. They carry symbols that tell the production schedule dates, body production number, body series and trim, paint and accessory codes. A three-digit body number identifies each model and appears in the Body/Style Number column of the charts below. Engine codes were stamped on the right side of most engines and the left side of 318-cid V-8s, as follows: S-17 on 170-cid Slant Six; S-22 on 225-cid Slant Six; S-318 on 318-cid V-8; S-36 on 361-cid V-8; S-38 on 383-cid V-8; S-41 on 413-cid V-8.

DART SERIES

Model No.	Body/ Style No.	Body Type & Seating	Factory Price	Shipping Weight	Prod. Total
SD1/2	413/513	4-dr Sed-6P	2297/2404	3000/3170	Note 1
SD1/2	411/511	2-dr Sed-6P	2241/2348	2970/3435	Note 1
SD1/2	456/556	4-dr Sta Wag-6P	2644/2751	3270/3435	Note 1

Note 1: The exact model year output of full-size Dodges was 165,861 units. In rounded totals, this included 48,200 Darts; 25,500 Dart 330s; 37,800 Dart 440s; 12,500 Polara 500s; 24,400 Dart station wagons; 15,400 Custom 880s and 2,100 Custom 880 station wagons.

Note 2: The exact model year production total given above included 13,500 two-door sedans; 85,163 four-door sedans; 21,499 two-door hardtops; 13,130 four-door hardtops; 6,024 convertibles; 19,124 four-door two-seat station wagons and 7,421 four-door three-seat station wagons. Unfortunately, there is no way to break out these individual body style totals, per series.

Note 3: Data above slash marks for sixes, below for V-8s.

Note 4: In rounded off totals, the series production figures in Note 1 include 35,500 Dart sixes; 8,800 Dart 330 sixes; 3,200 Dart 440 sixes and 5,300 six-cylinder Dart station wagons. All other Darts (some 95,600) were V-8 powered. All Polara 500s and Custom 880s had standard V-8 power.

1962 Dodge, Dart 330 two-door hardtop, V-8

DART 330 SERIES — (6-CYL/V-8) — The Dart 330 was the intermediate trim level Dart and included all the features of the Dart series plus a cigarette lighter; front foam cushion; rear armrests; and a power tailgate window (on nine-passenger station wagons).

DART 330 I.D. DATA: See Dart I.D. Data listing. All models began at 100001 and went up in the unit number sequence.

DART 330 SERIES

Model No.	Body/ Style No.	Body Type & Seating	Factory Price	Shipping Weight	Prod. Total
SD1/2M	423/523	4-dr Sed-6P	2432/2540	3000/3170	Note 1
SD1/2M	421/521	2-dr Sed-6P	2375/2482	2965/3135	Note 1
SD1/2M	422/522	2-dr HT Cpe-6P	2463/2570	2985/3155	Note 1
SD1/2M	466/566	4-dr Sta Wag-6P	2739/2848	3275/3435	Note 1
SD2M	567	4-dr Sta Wag-9P	2949	3500	Note 1

Note 1: See all notes under 1962 Dodge Dart series listing.

DART 440 SERIES — (6-CYL/V-8) — The Dart 440 was the top trim level Dart for 1962 and included all the Dart 330 features plus back-up lights; Custom interior upholstery and trim; exterior moldings and a power tailgate window on nine-passenger station wagons. A Sportsweep trim package was available for the 440 series models, which consisted of a Polara-type color sweep molding on the hood, belt and trunk.

DART 440 I.D. DATA: See Dart I.D. Data listing. All models began at 100001 and went up in the unit number sequence.

1962 Dodge, Dart 440 four-door hardtop, V-8

DART 440 SERIES

Model No.	Body/ Style No.	Body Type & Seating	Factory Price	Shipping Weight	Prod. Total
SD1H/2H	433/533	4-dr Sed-6P	2584/2691	3045/3205	Note 1
SD1H/2H	432/532	2-dr HT Cpe-6P	2606/2731	3025/3185	Note 1
SD2H	534	4-dr HT Sed-6P	2763	3260	Note 1
SD2H	535	2-dr Conv-6P	2945	3285	Note 1
SD2H	576	4-dr Sta Wag-6P	2989	3460	Note 1
SD2H	477	4-dr Sta Wag-9P	3092	3530	Note 1

Note 1: See all notes under 1962 Dodge Dart series listing.

POLARA 500 SERIES — (V-8) — Polara 500 was the top trim level Dodge for 1962. It shared body and chassis components with the Dart series and included all the features of the Dart 440 plus bucket seats; carpeting; dual exhaust; 361-cid V-8 engine; padded instrument panel; Deluxe steering wheel; wheel covers; outside rearview mirror on the left door and the Polara name, in script, where the 'Dart' name appeared on Darts. Special exterior trim, in contrasting colors, was also a part of the Polara 500 package. The four-door hardtop was added on Nov. 5, 1961.

POLARA 500 I.D. DATA: See Dart I.D. Data listing. All models began at 100001 and went up in the unit number sequence.

POLARA 500 SERIES

Model No.	Body/ Style No.	Body Type & Seating	Factory Price	Shipping Weight	Prod. Total
SD2P	544	4-dr HT Sed-6P	2960	3360	Note 1
SD2P	542	2-dr HT Cpe-6P	3019	3315	Note 1
SD2P	545	2-dr Conv-6P	3263	3430	Note 1

Note 1: See all notes under 1962 Dodge Dart series listing. All Polara 500s were V-8 powered.

1962 Dodge Custom 880, four-door hardtop station wagon, V-8

CUSTOM 880 SERIES — (V-8) — The Custom 880 was the luxury Dodge offering for 1962. It was introduced on Jan. 21, 1962, to flesh out the line with a 'big' Dodge and to plug the gap left with the demise of the DeSoto. Dodge combined the 1962 Chrysler body with the front end of a 1961 Dodge, creating an attractive combination. Offering a full line of body styles, the Custom 880 also included a beautifully styled hardtop station wagon. The Custom 880 was, undoubtedly, the best looking of the 1962 Dodges. All Custom 880s were V-8 powered.

CUSTOM 880 I.D. DATA: See Dart I.D. Data listing. All models began at 100001 and went up in the unit number sequence.

CUSTOM 880 SERIES

SD3L	613	4-dr Sed-6P	2964	3655	11,141
SD3L	614	4-dr HT Sed-6P	3109	3680	1,855
SD3L	612	2-dr HT Cpe-6P	3030	3615	1,761
SD3L	615	2-dr Conv-6P	3251	3705	684
SD3L	658	4-dr Sta Wag-6P	3292	4025	1,174
SD3L	659	4-dr Sta Wag-9P	3407	4055	890

Note 1: See all notes under 1962 Dodge Dart series listings. All Custom 880s were V-8 powered.

1962 Dodge, Lancer GT two-door hardtop coupe, 6-cyl

LANCER 170 SERIES — (6-CYL) — The year 1962 was the last for the Lancer name on Dodge's compact line. Styling was virtually the same as in 1961, with some minor trim updating. The convex grille featured a combination of vertical and horizontal bars in place of the horizontal bars used in 1961. The taillights were slightly re-trimmed. The Lancer 170 continued to be the base trim level and included chrome windshield and rear window moldings; a short chrome strip on the rear fender feature line (terminating at the taillights) and the Lancer name, in block letters, on the side of the front door below the front feature line. A Dodge crest

was located on the front of the hood, above the grille. The Dodge name, also in block letters, was located on the trunk lid.

LANCER 170 I.D. DATA: See Dart I.D. Data listing. All models began at 100001 and went up in the unit number sequence.

LANCER 170 SERIES

Model No.	Body/ Style No.	Body Type & Seating	Factory Price	Shipping Weight	Prod. Total
SL1L	713	4-dr Sed-6P	2011	2525	Note 1
SL1L	711	2-dr Sed-6P	1951	2495	Note 1
SL1L	756	2-dr Sta Wag-6P	2306	2685	Note 1

Note 1: The exact model year output of Dodge Lancers was 64,271 units. In rounded off figures, this included 17,100 Lancer 170s; 26,100 Lancer 770s; 14,100 GT hardtops and 7,000 Lancer station wagons with two-seats.

Note 2: The exact model year production total given above included 14,333 two-door sedans; 28,793 four-door sedans; 14,140 hardtops and 7,005 four-door two-seat station wagons. Unfortunately, there is no further breakout of these individual body style totals, per series.

Additional Note: All 1962 Dodge Lancers were six-cylinder powered.

LANCER 770 SERIES — (6-CYL) — The 770 series was the top trim level Lancer for 1962 and included all the 170 series trim plus extra exterior trim and plusher interior appointments. A sport version of the 770 series, called the 'GT,' was offered in two-door hardtop configuration only. It featured the larger 225-cid Slant Six engine.

LANCER 770 I.D. DATA: See Dart I.D. Data listing. All models began at 100001 and went up in the sequence unit numbers.

LANCER 770 SERIES

SL1H	733	4-dr Sed-6P	2114	2540	Note 1
SL1H	731	2-dr Sed-6P	2052	2520	Note 1
SL1H	776	4-dr Sta Wag-8P	2408	2705	Note 1
SL1P	742	2-dr GT/HT Cpe-5P	2257	2560	(14,140)

Note 1: Except in one case (figure in parenthesis), it is not possible to break out individual body style production between the Lancer 170 and Lancer 770 series. See all notes under 1962 Dodge Lancer 170 series.

ENGINES:

(170 Slant Six) Overhead valve. Aluminum block. Displacement: 170 cid. Bore and stroke: 3.40 x 3.13 inches. Compression ratio: 8.2:1. Brake hp: 101 at 4400 rpm. Four main bearings. Solid valve lifters. Carburetor: Carter one-barrel BBS-3229S.

(225 Slant Six) Overhead valve. Aluminum block. Displacement: 225 cid. Bore and stroke: 3.41 x 4.13 inches. Compression ratio: 8.2:1. Brake hp: 145 at 4000 rpm. Four main bearings. Solid valve lifters. Carburetor: Carter one-barrel BBS-3231S.

(Hyper-Pak 225 Slant Six) Overhead valve. Cast iron block. Displacement: 225 cid. Bore and stroke: 3.41 x 4.13 inches. Compression ratio: 8.2:1. Brake hp: 195 at 5200 rpm. Four main bearings. Solid valve lifters. Carburetor: Carter AFB 3083S four-barrel. Tuned exhaust headers leading to tuned exhaust system. (Available as a dealer-installed option. Installations at dealer level may have included kits left over from 1961.)

(Dart V-8) Overhead valve. Cast iron block. Displacement: 318 cid. Bore and stroke: 3.91 x 3.31 inches. Compression ratio: 9.0:1. Brake hp: 230 at 4400 rpm. Five main bearings. Hydraulic valve lifters. Carburetor: Carter two-barrel BBD-3240S.

(Dart V-8) Overhead valve. Cast iron block. Displacement: 318 cid. Bore and stroke: 3.91 x 3.31 inches. Compression ratio: 9.0:1. Brake hp: 260 at 4400 rpm. Five main bearings. Hydraulic valve lifters. Carburetor: Carter AFB four-barrel.

(Polara V-8) Overhead valve. Cast iron block. Displacement: 361 cid. Bore and stroke: 4.12 x 3.38 inches. Compression ratio: 9.0:1. Brake hp: 305 at 4800 rpm. Five main bearings. Hydraulic valve lifters. Carburetor: Carter AFB 3252S four-barrel.

(Ram-Charger "Max Wedge" V-8) Overhead valve. Cast iron block. Displacement: 413 cid. Bore and stroke: 4.19 x 3.75 inches. Compression ratio: 11.0:1. Brake hp: 410 at 5400 rpm. Five main bearings. Solid valve lifters. Carburetor: Two Carter AFB 3084S four-barrel. (Midyear option.)

(Ram-Charger "Max Wedge" V-8) Overhead valve. Cast iron block. Displacement: 413 cid. Bore and stroke: 4.19 x 3.75 inches. Compression ratio: 13.5:1. Brake hp: 420 at 5400 rpm. Five main bearings. Solid

valve lifters. Carburetor: Two Carter AFB 3084S four-barrel. (Midyear option.)

CHASSIS FEATURES:

(Lancer) Wheelbase: 106.5 inches. Overall length: 188.8 inches. Tires: 6.50 x 13 tubeless black sidewall. Three-speed manual transmission was standard on all Lancers, with the three-speed TorqueFlite automatic transmission optional.

(Dart and Polara) Wheelbase: 116 inches. Overall length: 202 inches (210 inches on station wagons). Tires: 6.50 x 14 tubeless black sidewall (7.00 x 14 on Polaras and station wagons). Three-speed manual transmission was standard on all Darts and Polaras, with the three-speed TorqueFlite automatic transmission optional.

(Custom 880) Wheelbase: 122 inches. Overall length: 213.5 inches (215 inches on station wagons). Tires: 8.00 x 14 tubeless black sidewall. Three-speed manual transmission was standard on all Custom 880s, with the three-speed TorqueFlite automatic optional.

CONVENIENCE OPTIONS: Electric clock ($16). Music Master radio ($58). TorqueFlite automatic transmission on six-cylinders ($192); on V-8s ($211). Power steering ($77). Power brakes ($43). Power seats ($96). Power windows ($102). Air Temp air conditioning ($445). Windshield washer ($12). 413-cid Ramcharger V-8 engine ($400). Four-speed manual transmission ($146). White sidewall tires ($33-$48).

HISTORICAL FOOTNOTES: The 1962 Dodge/Dart/Polara line was introduced on Sept. 28, 1961. The Custom 880 arrived in January 1962. Model year production hit exactly 165,861 units. Calendar year output included 35,564 Lancers and 216,158 Dodges. Lancer production was discontinued in August 1962. The new 'senior-compact' size Dodge Dart would replace the Lancer in 1963. C.E. Briggs was the vice-president and general manager of Dodge Division. While the Ram-Tuned engines of 1961 were extremely powerful, with their huge intake manifolds, they were a mechanic's nightmare. Chrysler Corp. solved this problem with the midyear introduction of the famous Ram-Charger 413 engine, which utilized ram passages only 15 inches long. As the name implied, this engine represented the maximum performance state of tune for the 413-cid V-8. The intake and exhaust ports were 25 percent larger than in 1961 and there were dozens of other performance features, such as mechanical valve lifters and a cast-aluminum ram-induction manifold. Dodges proved themselves to be the car to beat on the dragstrip in 1962. Four National Hot Rod Association (NHRA) records were taken by Ram-Charger 413 Dodges. In SS/S class, Dick Landy did the quarter-mile in 12.71 seconds. In SS/SA class, Bill "Maverick" Golden hit 12.50 seconds. The Golden Lancer, owned by Dode Martin and Jim Nelson, featured the 413 in a compact Lancer. Running in A/FX class, it made a record 12.26 second run. In the even wilder AA/D class, Nelson registered 8.59 seconds with another car. Once again, Norm Thatcher drove a specially-prepared Dart, equipped with a modified Ram-Charger V-8, to a Class B Production record of 167.3 mph in the Flying Mile at the Bonneville Salt Flats in Utah.

1963 DODGE

DART 170 SERIES — (6-CYL) — The Dart series was the new compact in the Dodge lineup and was slightly larger than the Lancer it replaced. Overall, it was 4-1/2 inches longer than the previous models. For the first time, the Dart was offered with a convertible, both in the top line GT and the intermediate 270 series. Styling was smooth. A concave grille, featuring a vertical theme, was located between the single headlights. A Dodge crest was located on the hood and a single body feature line ran horizontally at the belt. A smaller feature line ran horizontally at the lower side of the body, swept up over the rear wheelwell and continued horizontally back to the rear bumper. The single round taillights were housed in a small chrome bezel and the Dodge name, in block letters, appeared on the vertical section of the trunk lid. The Dart 170 was the base trim level and included chrome windshield and rear window moldings; chrome headlight doors; a Dart emblem on the roof 'C' pillar; turn signals; electric windshield wipers; sun visors; dual horns; saddle moldings; cigar lighter; front armrests and the Dart name, in script, along the bodyside, at the back of the rear fender.

DART I.D. DATA: Serial numbers are stamped/embossed on a plate on left front door pillar and use the form 713( )100001 and up. The first symbol indicates car-line/engine: 4=Dart six-cyl.; 5=Dodge 880 V-8; 6=Dodge V-8; 7=Dart 170/270/GT. The second symbol indicates series: 1=170/330/Custom 880; 2=440; 3=270/Polara; 4=Dart

GT/Polara 500; 5=170/330/880/Custom station wagon; 6=440 station wagon; 7=Polara/270 station wagon; 8=Taxicab; 9=Police Special; 10=880/fleet. The third symbol indicates model year: 3=1963. The fourth symbol indicates assembly plant: 2=Dodge Main; 3=Detroit (Jefferson); 5=Los Angeles, Calif.; 6=Newark, Del.; 7=St. Louis, Mo. The last six symbols are the sequential production number starting at 100001 for each series at each factory. Body number plates are located under the hood on fenders, cowl or radiator crossmember. They carry symbols that tell the production schedule dates, body production number, body series and trim, paint and accessory codes. A three-digit body number identifies each model and appears in the Body/Style Number column of the charts below. Engine codes were stamped on the right side of most engines and the left side of 318-cid V-8s, as follows: T-170 on 170-cid Slant Six; T-22 on 225-cid Slant Six; T-318 on 318-cid V-8; T-36 on 361-cid V-8; T-38 on 383-cid V-8; T-41 on 413-cid V-8 and T-42 on 426 Max Wedge V-8.

DART 170 SERIES

Model No.	Body/ Style No.	Body Type & Seating	Factory Price	Shipping Weight	Prod. Total
TL1L	713	4-dr Sed-6P	2041	2634	Note 1
TL1L	711	2-dr Sed-6P	1983	2614	Note 1
TL1L	756	4-dr Sta Wag-6P	2309	2735	Note 1

Note 1: A total of 51,300 Dart 170s were built during model year 1963, all six-cylinder powered. In addition, a total of 13,000 station wagons were built in all of the Dart lines. All were sixes. There is no breakout of station wagon production by series, so this total includes both 170 and 270 station wagons. (All figures rounded off to the nearest 100 units.)

DART 270 SERIES — (6-CYL) — The Dart 270 was the intermediate trim level and included all the 170 features plus carpeting, special upholstery and trim.

DART 270 I.D. DATA: See Dart I.D. Data listing. All models began at 100001 and went up in the unit number sequence.

DART 270 SERIES

TL1H	733	4-dr Sed-6P	2135	2644	Note 1
TL1H	731	2-dr Sed-6P	2079	2624	Note 1
TL1H	735	2-dr Conv-6P	2385	2710	Note 1
TL1H	776	4-dr Sta Wag-6P	2433	2745	Note 1

Note 1: A total of 55,300 Dart 270 passenger cars were built during model year 1963, all six-cylinder powered. (Figures rounded off to nearest 100 units.)

Note 2: Dart 270 station wagon production totals are included with Dart 170 station wagon production totals. See Dart 170 series Note 1 above.

1963 Dodge, Dart GT two-door hardtop coupe, 6-cyl

DART GT SERIES — (6-CYL) — The GT was the top trim level Dart for 1963 and included all the 270 features plus padded instrument panel, wheel covers and bucket seats.

DART GT I.D. DATA: See Dart I.D. Data listing. All models began at 100001 and went up in the unit number sequence.

DART GT SERIES

TL1P	742	2-dr HT Cpe-5P	2290	2661	Note 1
TL1P	745	2-dr Conv-5P	2512	2740	Note 1

Note 1: A total of 34,300 Dart GTs were built during model year 1963, all six-cylinder powered. (Figures rounded off to the nearest 100 units.)

DODGE 330 SERIES — (6-CYL/V-8) — The full-size Dodge was once again totally restyled for 1963 and rode on a wheelbase stretched three inches to 119 inches. This season represented the end of the 'ugly' Dodge era. Styling at both ends of the automobile was attractive. In the case of the Dodge, a massive full-width grille, featuring a vertical theme and convex styling, contained the inboard headlights. These were located lower than the outboard units, exactly the opposite of the 1962 design. A nearly horizontal feature line angled back from the front fenders, to the rear of the car, and dropped down to just in front of the taillights. Large rectangular taillights were used and a three-pointed stylized star, located on the trunk lid, housed the trunk lock. The license plate was recessed in the escutcheon panel. The 1963 Dodges were the absolute terror of the country's dragstrips during 1963. When powered by the new 426-cid Ram-Charger Max Wedge V-8, almost no other car could

catch them. The Dodge 330 was the base trim level Dodge for 1963 and included chrome windshield and rear window moldings; turn signals; electric windshield wipers; sun visors; PCV system; power tailgate window on nine-passenger station wagons and the Dodge name, in block letters, on the right side of the trunk lid. The '330' model designation was carried on the roof 'C' pillars.

DODGE 330 I.D. DATA: See Dart I.D Number listing. All models began at 100001 and went up in the sequence unit numbers.

DODGE 330 SERIES

Model No.	Body/ Style No.	Body Type & Seating	Factory Price	Shipping Weight	Prod. Total
TD1L/2L	413/613	4-dr Sed-6P	2301/2408	3064/3253	Note 1
TD1L/2L	411/611	2-dr Sed-6P	2245/2352	3029/3218	Note 1
TD1L/2L	456/656	4-dr Sta Wag-6P	2648/2756	3293/3478	Note 1
TD1L/2L	457/657	4-dr Sta Wag-9P	2749/2857	3358/3543	Note 1

Note 1: A total of 64,100 Dodge 330 passenger cars were built during model year 1963. Of these, 40,100 were sixes and 24,000 were V-8s. In addition, a total of 26,100 station wagons were built in the Dodge 330 and 440 lines. This included 5,400 station wagons with sixes and 20,700 with V-8s. There is no breakout of station wagon production by series, except in the case of the Dodge 880 series. The total includes both Dodge 330 and 440 station wagons. (Figures rounded off to the nearest 100 units.)

DODGE 440 SERIES — (6-CYL/V-8) — The Dodge 440 was the intermediate trim level Dodge and included all the features of the 330 models plus front foam cushions, carpeting and power tailgate window on nine-passenger station wagons. The '440' model designation was carried on the roof 'C' pillars.

DODGE 440 I.D. DATA: See Dart I.D. Data listing. All models began at 100001 and went up in the unit number sequence.

DODGE 440 SERIES

TD1M/2M	423/623	4-dr Sed-6P	2438/2546	3068/3262	Note 1
TD1M/2M	421/621	2-dr Sed-6P	2381/2489	3038/3232	Note 1
TD1M/2M	422/622	2-dr HT Cpe-6P	2470/2477	3053/3242	Note 1
TD2M	666	4-dr Sta Wag-6P	2854	3487	Note 1
TD2M	667	4-dr Sta Wag-9P	2956	3552	Note 1

Note 1: A total of 44,300 Dodge 440 passenger cars were built during model year 1963. Of these, 10,000 were sixes and 34,300 were V-8s. (Figures rounded off to the nearest 100.)

Note 2: Dodge 440 station wagon production totals are included with Dodge 330 station wagon production totals. See Dodge 330 series Note 1 above.

1963 Dodge, Polara two-door convertible, V-8 (AA)

POLARA SERIES — (6-CYL/V-8) — The Polara was, once again, the top trim level Dodge. It included all the features on the 440, plus back-up lights; Custom interior and upholstery trim; exterior moldings and a power top on the convertible. The Polara designation was carried on the roof 'C' pillars. A special high-performance sport model, called the Polara 500, was also available. It included all the features of the Polara plus bucket seats; rear foam cushions; padded instrument panel; Deluxe steering wheel; special wheel covers and the 383 cid/265 hp V-8 engine. Polara 500 models also included special exterior trim on the rear quarter panels behind the rear wheelwell.

POLARA AND POLARA 500 I.D. DATA: See Dart I.D. Data listing. All models began at 100001 and went up in the unit number sequence.

POLARA SERIES

TD1H/2H	433/633	4-dr Sed-6P	2602/2709	3096/3262	Note 1
TD1H/2H	432/632	2-dr HT Cpe-6P	2624/2732	3071/3280	Note 1
TD2H	634	4-dr HT Sed-6P	2781	3370	Note 1
TD2H	635	2-dr Conv-6P	2963	3380	Note 1

POLARA 500

Model No.	Body/ Style No.	Body Type & Seating	Factory Price	Shipping Weight	Prod. Total
TD2P	642	2-dr HT Cpe-6P	2965	3426	Note 1
TD2P	645	2-dr Conv-6P	3196	3546	Note 1

Note 1: A total of 39,800 Polaras were built during model year 1963. Of these, 2.200 were sixes and 37,600 were V-8s. A total of 7,300 Polara 500s were built during model year 1963, all V-8s. (Figures rounded off to the nearest 100 units.)

880 AND CUSTOM 880 SERIES — (V-8) — The 880 was the top trim level in conventional Dodges for 1963. While continuing to utilize the Chrysler body from the windshield back, a completely new front end was styled for 1963. This gave the car an identity all its own. The full-width grille was made up of fine convex vertical bars. The Dodge name, in block letters, was located in the center of the hood. It also appeared, in script, on the front fenders behind the headlights. Rear end styling featured new circular taillights and chrome housings. The Custom 880 was identical to the 880, with the addition of a few minor trim pieces. The 361 cid/265 hp V-8 engine was standard in all 880s and Custom 880s.

1963 Dodge, Custom 880 four-door sedan, V-8

880 AND CUSTOM 880 I.D. DATA: See Dart I.D. Data listing. All models began at 100001 and went up in the unit number sequence.

880 AND CUSTOM 880 SERIES

880 LINE

TA3E	503	4-dr Sed-6P	2813	3790	7,197
TA3E	556	4-dr Sta Wag-6P	3142	4135	1,727
TA3E	557	4-dr Sta Wag-9P	3257	4185	907

CUSTOM 880 LINE

TA3L	513	4-dr Sed-6P	2964	3730	9,233
TA3L	514	4-dr HT Sed-6P	3109	3745	2,564
TA3L	512	2-dr HT Cpe-6P	3030	3705	2,804
TA3L	515	2-dr Conv-6P	3251	3770	822
TA3L	558	4-dr Sta Wag-6P	3292	4110	1,647
TA3L	559	4-dr Sta Wag-9P	3407	4165	1,365

Note 1: A total of 7,200 Dodge 880 and 15,400 Custom 880 passenger cars were built during model year 1963. In addition, some 5,600 station wagons (all V-8s) were built in both series, combined, during model year 1963. (Figures rounded off to the nearest 100 units.)

ENGINES:

(170 Slant Six) Overhead valve. Cast iron block. Displacement: 170 cid. Bore and stroke: 3.40 x 3.13 inches. Compression ratio: 8.2:1. Brake hp: 101 at 4400 rpm. Four main bearings. Solid valve lifters. Carburetor: Carter one-barrel BBS-3462S.

(225 Slant Six) Overhead valve. Cast iron block. Displacement: 225 cid. Bore and stroke: 3.41 x 4.13 inches. Compression ratio: 8.2:1. Brake hp: 145 at 4000 rpm. Four main bearings. Solid valve lifters. Carburetor: Holley one-barrel R2418A.

(V-8) Overhead valve. Cast iron block. Displacement: 318 cid. Bore and stroke: 3.91 x 3.31 inches. Compression ratio: 9.0:1. Brake hp: 230 at 4400 rpm. Five main bearings. Hydraulic valve lifters. Carburetor: Stromberg two-barrel 3-222A.

(V-8) Overhead valve. Cast iron block. Displacement: 361 cid. Bore and stroke: 4.13 x 3.38 inches. Compression ratio: 9.0:1. Brake hp: 265 at 4400 rpm. Five main bearings. Hydraulic valve lifters. Carburetor: Carter two-barrel BBD-34763.

(Polara V-8) Overhead valve. Cast iron block. Displacement: 383 cid. Bore and stroke: 4.25 x 3.38 inches. Compression ratio: 10.1:1. Brake hp: 330 at 4600 rpm. Five main bearings. Hydraulic valve lifters. Carburetor: Carter four-barrel BBD-3684-S.

(413 V-8) Overhead valve. Cast iron block. Displacement: 413.2 cid. Bore and stroke: 4.188 x 3.75 inches. Compression ratio: 10.0:1. Brake

hp: 340 at 4800 rpm. Five main bearings. Hydraulic valve lifters. Carburetor: Carter AFB four-barrel.

(413 V-8) Overhead valve. Cast iron block. Displacement: 413.2 cid. Bore and stroke: 4.188 x 3.75 inches. Compression ratio: 10.1:1. Brake hp: 360 at 4800 rpm. Hydraulic valve lifters. Carburetor: Carter AFB four-barrel.

(413 V-8) Overhead valve. Cast iron block. Displacement: 413.2 cid. Bore and stroke: 4.188 x 3.75 inches. Compression ratio: 10.1:1. Brake hp: 390 at 4800 rpm. Five main bearings. Hydraulic valve lifters. Carburetor: Two Carter AFB four-barrel.

(Note: The Ram-Charger 413 "Max Wedge" engine was not available in 1963.)

(426 "Max Wedge Stage II" Ramcharger V-8) Overhead valve. Cast iron block. Displacement: 426 cid. Bore and stroke: 4.25 x 3.75 inches. Compression ratio: 11.0:1. Brake hp: 415 at 5800 rpm. Five main bearings. Solid valve lifters. Carburetor: Two Carter four-barrel.

(426 "Max Wedge Stage II" Ramcharger V-8) Overhead valve. Cast iron block. Displacement: 426 cid. Bore and stroke: 4.25 x 3.75 inches. Compression ratio: 13.5:1. Brake hp: 425 at 5600 rpm. Five main bearings. Solid valve lifters. Carburetor: Two Carter four-barrel.

(Note: Dodge changed the spelling of "Ram-Charger" to "Ramcharger" for identification of Chrysler's new 426-cid Max Wedge Stage II engine. This was an all-out racing mill. The Plymouth version had a black seven-blade fan, while Dodge's had a chrome fan in sales literature.)

CHASSIS FEATURES:

(Dart) Wheelbase: 111 inches (106 inches on station wagons). Overall length: 195.9 inches (190.2 inches on station wagons). Tires: 6.50 x 13 tubeless black sidewall. Three-speed manual transmission was standard on all Darts, with the three-speed TorqueFlite automatic transmission optional.

(Dodge) Wheelbase: 119 inches (116 inches on station wagons). Overall length: 208.1 inches (210.7 inches on station wagons). Tires: 7.00 x 14 tubeless black sidewall. Three-speed manual transmission was standard on all Dodges, with the three-speed TorqueFlite automatic transmission optional.

(880 and Custom 880) Wheelbase: 122 inches. Overall length: 214.8 inches (216.3 inches on station wagons). Tires: 8.00 x 14 tubeless black sidewall. Three-speed manual transmission was standard on all 880s and Custom 880s, with the three-speed TorqueFlite automatic transmission optional.

DART CONVENIENCE OPTIONS: AM radio, on 170 and 270 series ($169); on GT series ($153). Carpets in 170 ($17). 225-cid aluminum Slant Six engine ($47). Tinted glass ($14). Heater and defroster ($74). Back-up lights ($11). Luggage rack on station wagons ($48). Outside rearview mirror on left front fender ($5). Padded instrument panel ($16). Two-tone paint ($16). Power steering ($73). Power tailgate window on station wagons ($33). Front seat belts ($19). TorqueFlite automatic transmission ($172). Wheel covers ($16). Windshield washers ($12). White sidewall tires ($29).

DODGE CONVENIENCE OPTIONS: Electric clock ($16). Music Master radio ($58). TorqueFlite automatic transmission with six-cylinders ($192); with V-8s ($211). Power steering ($77). Power brakes ($43). Power seats ($96). Power windows ($102). Air Temp air conditioning ($45). Windshield washer ($12). 426-cid Ramcharger V-8 engine ($445). Four-speed manual transmission ($146). White sidewall tires ($33-$48).

HISTORICAL FOOTNOTES: During calendar year 1963, Dodge built exactly 33,708 Dart two-door sedans; 67,265 Dart four-door sedans; 28,475 Dart two-door hardtops; 11,390 Dart convertibles and 13,083 Dart two-seat station wagons. These figures include Dart 170, Dart 270 and Dart GT models with no series breakouts available. The company also built 18,339 full-size Dodge two-door sedans; 118,135 Dodge four-door sedans; 24,406 Dodge two-door hardtops; 11,832 Dodge four-door hardtops; 5,358 Dodge convertibles; 20,794 Dodge six-passenger station wagons and 10,977 Dodge nine-passenger station wagons. These figures include Dodge 330, 440, Polara, 880 and Custom 880 models, with no series breakouts available. Dodge discontinued the aluminum block for the 225 Slant Six engine because buyer demand did not warrant the extra cost involved in producing the lighter alloy block. Dodge also continued to be the brand to catch on the dragstrips of America. Teams such as the Ramchargers, of Michigan, competed in several different classes with their 426-cid powered sedans and station wagons. The popular team painted their cars white with red stripes running along the top surfaces of the cars. The manual transmission-equipped cars were called 'Candysticks' and the automatic transmission-equipped cars were called 'Candymatics'. At least one of these cars has been restored to

original racing condition as an outgrowth of the current boom in nostalgic drag racing. The later 426 single four-barrel carb engine was primarily for stock car racing and street use, while the two Ramcharger dual four-barrel carb engines were used for drag racing. Dodge re-launched its NASCAR racing program in 1963, but no wins were registered this year.

1964 DODGE

DART 170 SERIES — (6-CYL/V-8) — The Dart received a new grille and other minor trim changes, but overall was the same car offered in 1963. The big news for 1964, in addition to it being Dodge's Golden Anniversary, was the addition of the new 273-cid V-8 engine to the powertrain options. Joining the 170- and 225-cid sixes, the 273 cid/180 hp V-8 proved to be a reliable and powerful engine in the light car. The Dart 170 once again was the base trim level and included chrome windshield and rear window moldings; chrome headlight doors; a Dart emblem on the roof 'C' pillar; turn signals; electric windshield wipers; sun visors; dual horns; chrome trim around the simulated scoop on the hood; a revised grille; the Dodge name in block letters, dividing the grille horizontally; cigar lighter; front armrests and the Dart name, in block letters, on a front fender tip emblem.

DART I.D. DATA: Serial numbers are stamped/embossed on a plate on left front door pillar and use the form 714( )100001 and up. The first symbol indicates car-line/engine: 4=Dart six-cyl.; 5=Dodge 880 V-8; 6=Dodge V-8; 7=Dart 170/270/GT. The second symbol indicates series: 1=170/330/880; 2=Custom 880/440; 3=270/Polara; 4=Dart GT/Polara; 5=170/330/880 station wagon; 6=440/Custom 880 station wagon; 7=270 station wagon; 8=Taxicab; 9=Police Special. The third symbol indicates model year: 4=1964. The fourth symbol indicates assembly plant: 2=Dodge Main; 3=Detroit (Jefferson); 5=Los Angeles, Calif.; 6=Newark, Del.; 7=St. Louis, Mo. The last six symbols are the sequential production number starting at 100001 for each series at each factory. Body number plates are located under the hood on fenders, cowl or radiator crossmember. They carry symbols that tell the production schedule dates, body production number, body series and trim, paint and accessory codes. A three-digit body number identifies each model and appears in the Body/Style Number column of the charts below. Engine codes were stamped on the right side of most engines and the left side of 318-cid V-8s, as follows: V-17 on 170-cid Slant Six; V-22 on 225-cid Slant Six; V-273 on 273-cid V-8; V-318 on 318-cid V-8; V-36 on 361-cid V-8; V-38 on 383-cid V-8 and V-426 on 426-cid V-8.

DART 170 SERIES

Model No.	Body/Style No.	Body Type & Seating	Factory Price	Shipping Weight	Prod. Total
VL1L/2L	713	4-dr Sed-6P	2053/2161	2620/2800	Note 1
VL1L/2L	711	2-dr Sed-6P	1988/2096	2585/2765	Note 1
VL1L/2L	756	4-dr Sta Wag-6P	2315/2423	2730/2910	Note 1

Note 1: A total of 70,200 Dart 170s were built during model year 1964. Of these, 68,000 were sixes and 2,200 were V-8s. In addition, a total of 14,000 station wagons were built in all of the Dart series. This included 12,900 station wagons with sixes and 1,100 with V-8s. There is no breakout of station wagon production by series, so this total includes both 170 and 270 station wagons. (Figures rounded off to the nearest 100 units.)

DART 270 SERIES — (6-CYL/V-8) — The Dart 270 was, once again, the intermediate trim level. It included all the 170 features plus carpeting, special upholstery and extra trim.

DART 270 I.D. DATA: See Dart I.D. Data listing. All models began at 100001 and went up in the unit number sequence.

DART 270 SERIES

Model No.	Body/Style No.	Body Type & Seating	Factory Price	Shipping Weight	Prod. Total
VL1H/2H	733	4-dr Sed-6P	2160/2268	2630/2810	Note 1
VL1H/2H	731	2-dr Sed-6P	2094/2202	2595/2775	Note 1
VL1H/2H	742	2-dr HT Cpe-6P	2182/2290	2640/2820	Note 1
VL1H/2H	776	2-dr Sta Wag-6P	2414/2522	2740/2920	Note 1
VL1H/2H	735	2-dr Conv-6P	2389/2497	2710/2890	Note 1

Note 1: A total of 60,400 Dart 270s were built during model year 1964. Of these, 53,700 were sixes and 6,700 were V-8s. (Figures rounded off to the nearest 100 units.)

ADDITIONAL NOTE: Dart 270 station wagon production totals are included with Dart 170 station wagon production totals. See Dart 170 series Note 1 above.

DART GT SERIES — (6-CYL/V-8) — The GT was the top trim level Dart for 1964 and included all the 270 features, plus padded instrument panel, wheel covers and bucket seats.

DART GT I.D. DATA: See Dart I.D. Data listing. All models began at 100001 and went up in the unit number sequence.

DART GT SERIES

Model No.	Body/ Style No.	Body Type & Seating	Factory Price	Shipping Weight	Prod. Total
VL1P/2P	742	2-dr HT-6P	2318/2426	2650/2830	Note 1
VL1P/2P	745	2-dr Conv-6P	2536/2644	2740/2920	Note 1

Note 1: A total of 50,700 Dart GTs were built during model year 1964. Of these, 38,200 were sixes and 12,500 were V-8s. (Figures rounded off to the nearest 100 units.)

DODGE 330 SERIES — (6-CYL/V-8) — For 1964, Dodges were totally restyled once again. Many Dodge enthusiasts consider the 1964 models to be one of the most attractive ever built. Smooth styling was the keynote and every line seemed to flow into the next line. The grille was the epitome of simplicity. It began as small chrome moldings around the outboard headlights, narrowed slightly at the inboard headlights and featured a vertical bar theme. The Dodge name, in block letters, was spaced equally across the front of the hood. From the windshield back, the 1964 Dodges shared bodies with the previous models, except at the 'C' pillar of two-door hardtops, which was wider at the top than at the bottom. The basic 1963 body shell, combined with the new front end, produced an attractive car, indeed. The 330 was the base trim level Dodge and included chrome windshield and rear window moldings; turn signals; electric windshield wipers; sun visors; PCV system; power tailgate window on nine-passenger station wagons and the Dodge name, in block letters, on the right side of the trunk lid. The '330' model designation was carried on the roof 'C' pillars.

DODGE 330 I.D. DATA: See Dart I.D. Data listing. All models began at 100001 and went up in the unit number sequence.

DODGE 330 SERIES

VD1L/2L	413/613	4-dr Sed-6P	2317/2424	3105/3300	Note 1
VD1L/2L	411/611	2-dr Sed-6P	2264/2372	3075/3270	Note 1
VD1L/2L	456/656	4-dr Sta Wag-6P	2654/2762	3375/3555	Note 1
VD1L/2L	457/657	4-dr Sta Wag-9P	2755/2863	3445/3560	Note 1

Note 1: A total of 76,400 Dodge 330s were built during model year 1964. Of these, 44,800 were sixes and 31,600 were V-8s. In addition, a total of 30,300 full-size Dodge station wagons were built in the 330 and 440 series. This included 5,700 station wagons with sixes and 24,600 with V-8s. There is no breakout of station wagon production by series, so this total includes both 330 and 440 station wagons. (Figures rounded off to nearest 100 units.)

1964 Dodge, Dart GT two-door hardtop, 6-cyl (PH)

DODGE 440 SERIES — (6-CYL/V-8) — The Dodge 440 was the intermediate trim level Dodge and included all the features of the Dodge 330 models plus front foam cushions, carpeting and the '440' model designation on the roof 'C' pillars.

DODGE 440 I.D. DATA: See Dart I.D. Data listing. All models began at 100001 and went up in the unit number sequence.

DODGE 440 SERIES

VD1M/2M	423/623	4-dr Sed-6P	2454/2562	3115/3310	Note 1
VD1M/2M	421/621	2-dr Sed-6P	2401/2508	3085/3280	Note 1
VD1M/2M	422/622	2-dr HT Cpe-6P	2483/2590	3090/3285	Note 1
VD2M	666	4-dr Sta Wag-6P	2861	3615	Note 1
VD2M	667	4-dr Sta Wag-9P	2962	3620	Note 1

Note 1: A total of 58,700 Dodge 440s were built during model year 1964. Of these, 10,200 were sixes and 48,500 were V-8s. (Figures rounded off to nearest 100.)

Additional Note: Dodge 440 station wagon production totals are included with Dodge 330 station wagon production totals. See Dodge 330 series Note 1.

1964 Dodge, Polara two-door hardtop, V-8 (PH)

POLARA SERIES — (6-CYL/V-8) — The Polara was, once again, the top trim level Dodge. It included all the features of the Dodge 440 plus back-up lights; Custom interior and upholstery trim; special exterior moldings and a power top on the convertible. The Polara model designation was carried on the roof 'C' pillar. The Polara convertible and two-door hardtop were also offered with the special Polara 500 trim package, which consisted of bucket seats; a console and console-mounted shifter; padded instrument panel and Deluxe wheel covers. Special Polara 500 identification badges and swirl-finish side trim moldings were also included.

POLARA SERIES

Model No.	Body/ Style No.	Body Type & Seating	Factory Price	Shipping Weight	Prod. Total
VD1H/2H	433/633	4-dr Sed-6P	2615/2722	3150/3310	Note 1
VD1H/2H	432/632	2-dr HT Cpe-6P	2637/2745	3115/3310	Note 1
VD2H	634	4-dr HT Sed-6P	2794	3390	Note 1
VD2H	635	2-dr Conv-6P	2976	3415	Note 1

Note 1: A total of 64,900 Polaras were built during model year 1964. Of these, 2,200 were sixes and 62,700 were V-8s. In addition, a total of 18,400 Polara 500s were built during model year 1964. All of these were V-8s. (Figures rounded off to the nearest 100 units.)

1964 Dodge, Custom 880 two-door convertible, V-8 (PH)

880 AND CUSTOM 880 SERIES — (V-8) — The 880 and Custom 880 lines on the 122-inch wheelbase chassis continued with the same body as 1963. Rear quarter panels and taillights and a revised grille gave them a more modern look. The grille was concave and featured a central horizontal divider in the same shell as used in 1963. A single horizontal trim strip, at belt level, highlighted the smooth sides. It dipped down to form a front molding for the large, wraparound taillights. A polished aluminum rocker panel molding was used on the Custom 880 models. They also featured slightly more posh interiors than the standard 880 models. The Dodge name appeared, in block letters, on the center of the hood and along the rear fender. It also appeared, in script, along the right side of the trunk lid. A grooved aluminum panel was located between the taillights and highlighted the rear of the 880 models.

880 AND CUSTOM 880 I.D. DATA: See Dart I.D. Data listing. All models began at 100001 and went up in the unit number sequence.

880 AND CUSTOM 880 SERIES

880 LINE

VA3E	503	4-dr Sed-6P	2826	3790	7,536
VA3E	556	4-dr Sta Wag-6P	3155	4135	1,908
VA3E	557	4-dr Sta Wag-9P	3270	4185	1,082

CUSTOM 880 LINE

VA3L	513	4-dr Sed-6P	2977	3800	9,309
VA3L	514	4-dr HT Sed-6P	3122	3820	3,634
VA3L	512	2-dr HT Cpe-6P	3043	3785	3,798

Model No.	Body/Style No.	Body Type & Seating	Factory Price	Shipping Weight	Prod. Total
VA3L	515	2-dr Conv-6P	3264	3845	1,058
VA3L	558	4-dr Sta Wag-6P	3305	4135	1,639
VA3L	559	4-dr Sta Wag-9P	3420	4230	1,796

Note 1: A total of 7,500 Dodge 880s and 17,800 Custom 880s were built during model year 1964. In addition, 6,500 Dodge 880 and Custom 880 station wagons were built during model year 1964, all V-8s.

ENGINES:

(170 Slant Six) Overhead valve. Cast iron block. Displacement: 170 cid. Bore and stroke: 3.40 x 3.13 inches. Compression ratio: 8.2:1. Brake hp: 101 at 4000 rpm. Four main bearings. Solid valve lifters. Carburetor: Carter one-barrel BBS-3675S.

(225 Slant Six) Overhead valve. Cast iron block. Displacement: 225 cid. Bore and stroke: 3.41 x 4.13 inches. Compression ratio: 8.4:1. Brake hp: 145 at 4000 rpm. Four main bearings. Solid valve lifters. Carburetor: Carter one-barrel BBS-3679S.

(V-8) Overhead valve. Cast iron block. Displacement: 273 cid. Bore and stroke: 3.63 x 3.31 inches. Compression ratio: 8.8:1. Brake hp: 180 at 4200 rpm. Five main bearings. Hydraulic valve lifters. Carburetor: Carter two-barrel BBD-3843S.

(318 V-8) Overhead valve. Cast iron block. Displacement: 318 cid. Bore and stroke: 3.91 x 3.31 inches. Compression ratio: 9.0:1. Brake hp: 230 at 4400 rpm. Five main bearings. Hydraulic valve lifters. Carburetor: Carter two-barrel BBD-3682S.

(361 V-8) Overhead valve. Cast iron block. Displacement: 361 cid. Bore and stroke: 4.13 x 3.38 inches. Compression ratio: 9.0:1. Brake hp: 265 at 4400 rpm. Five main bearings. Hydraulic valve lifters. Carburetor: Stromberg two-barrel WWC-3-244.

(383 V-8) Overhead valve. Cast iron block. Displacement: 383 cid. Bore and stroke: 4.25 x 3.38 inches. Compression ratio: 10.0:1. Brake hp: 305 at 4600 rpm. Five main bearings. Hydraulic valve lifters. Carburetor: Carter two-barrel BBD-3476S.

(383 V-8) Overhead valve. Cast iron block. Displacement: 383 cid. Bore and stroke: 4.25 x 3.38 inches. Compression ratio: 10.0:1. Brake hp: 330 at 6400 rpm. Five main bearings. Hydraulic valve lifters. Carburetor: Carter four-barrel BBD-3684S.

(Ramcharger V-8) Overhead valve. Cast iron block. Displacement: 426 cid. Bore and stroke: 4.25 x 3.75 inches. Compression ratio: 10.3:1. Brake hp: 415 at 5600 rpm. Five main bearings. Solid valve lifters. Carburetor: Carter AFB 3859S four-barrel.

(Ramcharger 'Eight-Barrel' V-8) Overhead valve. Cast iron block. Displacement: 426 cid. Bore and stroke: 4.25 x 3.75 inches. Compression ratio: 11.0:1 (12.5:1 also available). Brake hp: 425 at 5600 rpm. Five main bearings. Solid valve lifters. Carburetor: Two Carter AFB 3084S four-barrel.

(Hemi-Charger (NASCAR) V-8) Overhead valve with hemispherical segment combustion chambers. Cast iron block. Displacement: 426 cid. Bore and stroke: 4.25 x 3.75 inches. Compression ratio: 12.5:1. Brake hp: 400 at 5600 rpm. Five main bearings. Solid valve lifters. Carburetor: Holley four-barrel.

(Hemi-Charger V-8) Overhead valve with hemispherical segment combustion chambers. Cast iron block. Displacement: 426 cid. Bore and stroke: 4.25 x 3.75 inches. Compression ratio: 11.0:1. Brake hp: 415 at 5600 rpm. Five main bearings. Solid valve lifters. Carburetor: Two Carter AFB 3859S four-barrel.

(Hemi-Charger 'Eight Barrel' V-8) Overhead valve with hemispherical segment combustion chambers. Cast iron block. Displacement: 426 cid. Bore and stroke: 4.25 x 3.75 inches. Compression ratio: 12.5:1. Brake hp: 425 at 5600 rpm. Five main bearings. Solid valve lifters. Carburetor: Two Carter AFB 3084S four-barrel.

CHASSIS FEATURES:

(Dart) Wheelbase: 111 inches (106 inches on station wagons). Overall length: 195.9 inches (190.2 inches on station wagons). Tires: 6.50 x 13 tubeless black sidewall. Three-speed manual transmission was standard on all Darts, with the three-speed TorqueFlite automatic transmission optional.

(Dodge) Wheelbase: 119 inches (116 inches on station wagons). Overall length: 209.8 inches (212.3 inches on station wagons). Tires: 7.00 x 14 tubeless black sidewall (7.50 x 14 on station wagons). Three-speed manual transmission was standard on all Dodges, with the three-speed TorqueFlite automatic transmission optional.

(880 and Custom 880) Wheelbase: 122 inches. Overall length: 214.8 inches (216.3 inches on station wagons). Tires: 8.00 x 14 tubeless black sidewall. Three-speed manual transmission was standard on all Dodge 880s and Custom 880s, with the three-speed TorqueFlite automatic transmission optional.

DART CONVENIENCE OPTIONS: AM radio group on 170 and 270 series ($169); on GT series ($153). Carpets in 170s ($17). 225-cid six-cylinder engine ($47). 273-cid V-8 engine. Tinted glass ($14). Heater and defroster ($74). Back-up lights ($11). Luggage rack on station wagons ($48). Outside rearview mirror on left front fender ($5). Padded instrument panel ($16). Two-tone paint ($16). Power steering ($73). Power tailgate window on station wagon ($33). Front seat belts ($19). TorqueFlite automatic transmission ($172). Wheel covers ($16). Windshield washers ($12). White sidewall tires ($29).

DODGE CONVENIENCE OPTIONS: Electric clock ($16). Music Master radio ($56). TorqueFlite automatic transmission on six-cylinder ($192); on V-8s ($211). Power steering ($77). Power brakes ($43). Power seats ($96). Power windows ($102). Air Temp air conditioning ($445). Windshield washers ($12). 426-cid Ramcharger V-8 engine ($445). Four-speed manual transmission ($146). White sidewall tires ($33-$48).

HISTORICAL FOOTNOTES: The year 1964 was significant for Dodge for several reasons, one it being the Golden Anniversary for the marque, but also for the reputation Dodge was gaining in the performance market. The awesome Ramcharger was setting records on the nation's dragstrips. Roger Lindamood, driving the incredible 'Color Me Gone' Dodge 330 two-door sedan took the NHRA Top Eliminator title at the Winter Nationals event that year. Ramcharger-powered Dodges also garnered the top four positions at the Super Stock Invitationals in York, Pa., and a Ramcharger-equipped rail dragster set a new national NHRA record for AA/D (unlimited displacement rail dragster) of 190.26 mph at East Hudson, Conn., dragstrip. While the Ramcharger was tearing up the opposition on the dragstrips, it was not doing as well on the NASCAR ovals and Chrysler decided to reintroduce the hemispherical segment heads for the Ramcharger. This resulted in the 'Hemi-Charger' available for competition use only, in Dodges and Plymouths. The 'Hemi' immediately replaced the Ramcharger as the engine to beat. Conservatively rated at 410 hp with a four-barrel (or 425 hp with two-barrel), actual output was more in the neighborhood of 500 or 550 hp, respectively. A pair of Dodge 330 two-door sedans powered by supercharged Hemi engines were used for exhibition runs during the summer of 1964. The Dodge 'Chargers' turned standing start quarter-mile speeds in the 135 mph range and were the forerunners of today's Funny Cars.

1965 DODGE

DART 170 SERIES — (6-CYL/V-8) — Continuing to use the same body as in the previous two years, the 1965 Dart nonetheless looked much different than before. A new grille was a flat grid design. At the rear, new oval taillights were used in place of the former round type. Minor trim changes rounded out the new Dart styling for 1965. As in the past, the Dart 170 was the base trim level and included chrome windshield and rear window moldings; a Dodge crest on the hood; a single horizontal chrome strip along the center of the bodyside; the Dodge name, in block letters, at the back of the rear fender chrome strip; heater and defroster; front seat belts; electric windshield wipers and the 170-cid Slant Six engine.

DART I.D. DATA: Serial numbers are stamped/embossed on a plate on left front door pillar and use the form 715( )100001 and up. The first symbol indicates car-line/engine: 2=Dart six-cyl.; L=Dart V-8; 4=Coronet six-cyl.; W=Coronet V-8. The second symbol indicates series: 1=170/Deluxe Polara; 2=Coronet; 3=270/Coronet 440/Custom 880; 4=Dart GT/Coronet 440/Monaco; 5=170/Deluxe Polara/station wagons; 7=270/Coronet 440/Custom 880 station wagon; 9=Police Special. The third symbol indicates model year: 5=1965. The fourth symbol indicates assembly plant: 2=Dodge Main; 3=Detroit (Jefferson); 5=Los Angeles, Calif.; 6=Newark, Del.; 7=St. Louis, Mo. The last six symbols are the sequential production number starting at 100001 for each series at each factory. Body number plates are located under the hood on fenders, cowl or radiator crossmember. They carry symbols that tell the production schedule dates, body production number, body series and trim, paint and accessory codes. A three-digit body number identifies each model and appears in the Body/Style Number column of the charts below. Engine codes were stamped on the right side of most engines and the left side of 318-cid V-8s, as follows: A-170 on 170-cid Slant Six; A-22 on 225-cid Slant Six; A-273 on 273-cid V-8; A-31 on 318-

cid V-8; A-361 on 361-cid V-8; A-38 on 383-cid V-8 and T-42 on 426 Hemi V-8.

DART 170 SERIES

Model No.	Body/ Style No.	Body Type & Seating	Factory Price	Shipping Weight	Prod. Total
AL1L/2L	L13	4-dr Sed-6P	2112/2208	2660/2840	Note 1
AL1L/2L	L11	2-dr Sed-6P	2049/2145	2645/2825	Note 1
AL1L/2L	L56	4-dr Sta Wag-6P	2375/2471	2770/2950	Note 1

Note 1: A total of some 73,800 Dart 170 passenger cars were built during model year 1965. Of these, 70,900 were sixes and 2,900 were V-8s. In addition, a total of 29,400 station wagons were built in all of the Dart series. This included 23,400 station wagons with sixes and 6,000 with V-8s. There is no breakout of station wagon production by series, so this includes both Dart 170 and Dart 270 station wagons. (Figures rounded off to the nearest 100 units.)

DART 270 SERIES — (6-CYL/V-8) — The Dart 270 was, once again, the intermediate trim level. It included all the 170 features plus carpeting, Deluxe two-spoke steering wheel, full horn ring and vinyl trim on the convertible.

DART 270 I.D. DATA: See Dart I.D. Data listing. All models began at 100001 and went up in the unit number sequence.

DART 270 SERIES

AL1H/2H	L33	4-dr Sed-6P	2218/2314	2670/2850	Note 1
AL1H/2H	L31	2-dr Sed-6P	2153/2249	2650/2830	Note 1
AL1H/2H	L32	2-dr HT-6P	2245/2341	2675/2855	Note 1
AL1H/2H	L35	2-dr Conv-6P	2447/2543	2765/2945	Note 1
AL1H/2H	L76	4-dr Sta Wag-6P	2472/2568	2770/2950	Note 1

Note 1: A total of some 62,800 Dart 270 passenger cars were built during model year 1965. Of these, 52,900 were sixes and 9,900 were V-8s. (Figures rounded off to the nearest 100 units.)

Additional Note: Dart 270 station wagon production totals are included with Dart 170 station wagon production totals. See Dart 270 series Note 1 above.

1965 Dodge, Dart GT two-door hardtop, V-8 (PH)

DART GT SERIES — (6-CYL/V-8) — The GT was the top trim level Dart for 1965. It included all the 270 features, plus padded instrument panel, wheel covers and bucket seats. In addition, the GTs had a special emblem on the roof 'C' pillar, three chrome louvers behind the front wheel opening and stone shields on the rear fenders.

DART GT I.D. DATA: See Dart I.D. Data listing. All models began at 100001 and went up in the unit number sequence.

DART GT SERIES

AL1P/2P	L42	2-dr HT-5P	2372/2468	2715/2895	Note 1
AL1P/2P	L45	2-dr Conv-5P	2591/2687	2795/2975	Note 1

Note 1: A total of some 40,700 Dodge Dart GTs were built during model year 1965. All were passenger car models, as no station wagons were offered in this series. Of the total, 22,700 were sixes and 18,000 were V-8s. (Figures rounded off to the nearest 100 units.)

CORONET SERIES — (6-CYL/V-8) — The Coronet name, last used by Dodge in 1959, was revived for the intermediate-size Dodge models for 1965. While larger than Ford's Fairlane and Chevrolet's Chevelle, it was nevertheless smaller than full-size Polara models. It was built on a 117-inch wheelbase platform, two inches shorter than the 1964 Polara/440/330 models. Styling was simple. The grille and rear end treatments were quite flat. There was a slab-sided look with only a belt-level feature line. Vertical bars patterned the grille and the taillights were also vertically positioned. The plain Coronet (330 call-out was no longer used) was the base trim level. It included the 225-cid six-cylinder engine; 7.35 x 14 tubeless tires; heater and defroster; electric windshield wipers; front seat belts; the Dodge name, in block letters, across the front of the hood (and on the right side of the trunk lid) and the Coronet name, in script, on the front fender tip.

CORONET I.D. DATA: See Dart I.D. Data listing. All models began at 100001 and went up in the unit number sequence.

CORONET SERIES

Model No.	Body/ Style No.	Body Type & Seating	Factory Price	Shipping Weight	Prod. Total
AW1L/2L	W13	4-dr Sed-6P	2267/2361	3140/3210	Note 1
AW1L/2L	W11	2-dr Sed-6P	2228/2322	3090/3160	Note 1
AW1L/2L	W56	4-dr Sta Wag-6P	2556/2650	3390/3470	Note 1

Note 1: A total of some 63,100 Coronet passenger cars were built during model year 1965. Of these, 37,100 were sixes and 26,000 were V-8s. In addition, a total of some 25,600 intermediate-size Dodge station wagons were built in the Coronet and Coronet 440 series. This included 3,800 sixes and 21,800 V-8s. There is no breakout of station wagon production by series, so these figures include both Coronet and Coronet 440 station wagons. (Figures rounded off to the nearest 100 units.)

1965 Dodge, Coronet 440 four-door sedan, V-8

CORONET 440 SERIES — (6-CYL/V-8) — The Coronet 440 was the intermediate trim level of the new Coronet series. It included all the features of the base Coronet series plus back-up lights, air foam front seats, carpeting in all models, power top and vinyl interior on the convertible and, in the nine-passenger station wagon, the 273-cid V-8 engine and a power tailgate window as standard equipment.

CORONET 440 I.D. DATA: See Dart I.D. Data listing. All models began at 100001 and went up in the unit number sequence.

CORONET 440 SERIES

AW1/2H	W33	4-dr Sed-6P	2346/2440	3125/3230	Note 1
AW1/2H	W32	2-dr HT-6P	2371/2465	3100/3180	Note 1
AW1/2H	W35	2-dr Conv-6P	2586/2680	3230/3295	Note 1
AW1/2H	W76	4-dr Sta Wag-6P	2637/2731	3395/3490	Note 1
AW2H	W77	4-dr Sta Wag-9P	2827	3560	Note 1

Note 1: A total of some 87,500 Coronet 440 passenger cars were built during model year 1965. Of these, 11,900 were sixes and 75,600 were V-8s. (Figures rounded off to the nearest 100.)

Additional Note: Dodge Coronet 440 station wagon production totals are included with Dodge Coronet station wagon totals. See Dodge Coronet Note 1 above.

CORONET 500 SERIES — (V-8) — The Coronet 500 was the top trim level of the Coronet series and included all the 440 features plus padded instrument panel; console and bucket seats; wheel covers; 273-cid V-8 engine; a single horizontal chrome strip at the beltline and the Coronet 500 name, in script, at the rear of the wheelwell on the front fenders.

CORONET 500 I.D. DATA: See Dart I.D. Data listing. All models began at 100001 and went up in the unit number sequence.

CORONET 500 SERIES

AW2P	W42	2-dr HT-6P	2637	3255	Note 1
AW2P	W45	2-dr Conv-6P	2852	3340	Note 1

Note 1: A total of some 33,300 Coronet 500 passenger cars were built during model year 1965, all V-8s.

POLARA SERIES — (V-8) — The Polara for 1965 filled the position formerly held by the Dodge 880 in the completely restyled full-size car line. The 121-inch wheelbase of the Polara, Custom 880 and Monaco models was an inch shorter than the 1964 Custom 880. The Polara included chrome windshield and rear window moldings; the Dodge name, in block letters, across the center of the hood face (directly above the bustle-shaped grille and across the rear escutcheon panel). Also included were the 383 cid/270 hp V-8; engine heater and defroster; front seat belts; power convertible top and 8.25 x 14 tubeless tires. All station wagons included a vinyl interior and the nine-passenger station wagon also had a power tailgate window and rear bumper guards with step pads.

POLARA I.D. DATA: See Dart I.D. Data listing. All models began at 100001 and went up in the unit number sequence.

POLARA SERIES

Model No.	Body/ Style No.	Body Type & Seating	Factory Price	Shipping Weight	Prod. Total
AD2L	D13	4-dr Sed-6P	2770	3905	Note 1
AD2L	D14	4-dr HT-6P	2874	3965	Note 1
AD2L	D12	2-dr HT-6P	2800	3850	Note 1
AD2L	D15	2-dr Conv-6P	3088	3940	Note 1
AD2L	D56	4-dr Sta Wag-6P	3110	4220	Note 1
AD2L	D57	4-dr Sta Wag-9P	3214	4255	Note 1

Note 1: A total of some 75,100 Polara passenger cars were built during model year 1965, all V-8s. In addition, a total of 22,800 station wagons (all V-8s) were built in the Polara and Custom 880 series combined. There is no breakout of station wagon production by series so this figure included both Polara and Custom 880 station wagons. (All figures rounded off to the nearest 100 units.)

CUSTOM 880 SERIES — (V-8) — The Custom 880 was a higher trim level than the Polara series and included all the features of the Polara plus air foam front seats and stainless steel window frames on station wagons and four-door sedans. The hardtops had vinyl interior trim.

1965 Dodge, Custom 880 two-door convertible, V-8

CUSTOM 880 I.D. DATA: See Dart I.D. Data listing. All models began at 100001 and went up in the unit number sequence.

CUSTOM 880 SERIES

AD2H	D38	4-dr Sed-6P	2970	3915	9,380
AD2H	D34	4-dr HT-6P	3107	4155	7,966
AD2H	D32	2-dr HT-6P	3043	3945	4,850
AD2H	D35	2-dr Conv-6P	3288	3965	1,416
AD2H	D76	4-dr Sta Wag-6P	3373	4270	4,499
AD2H	D77	4-dr Sta Wag-9P	3476	4335	5,923

Note 1: A total of some 23,700 Custom 880 passenger cars were built during model year 1965, all V-8s. (Figures rounded off to the nearest 100 units.)

Additional Note: Dodge Custom 880 station wagon production totals are included with Dodge Polara station wagon production totals. See 1965 Dodge Polara series Note 1 above.

1965 Dodge, Monaco two-door hardtop, V-8

MONACO SERIES — (V-8) — The Monaco was the specialty coupe built by Dodge to compete directly with Pontiac's Grand Prix. Monacos were available only in the two-door hardtop configuration. Elegant simplicity describes the looks of the original edition for 1965. The Monaco featured all the standard equipment offered on the Custom 880 plus a 383 cid/315 hp V-8 engine; front and rear foam seats; electric clock; remote-control outside rearview mirror; console; inside glare-proof mirror; padded instrument panel; three-spoke steering wheel; special wheel covers with spinners and the Monaco name, in script, on the front fenders just behind the wheelwells.

MONACO I.D. DATA: See Dart I.D. Data listing. All models began at 100001 and went up in the unit number sequence.

MONACO SERIES

Model No.	Body/ Style No.	Body Type & Seating	Factory Price	Shipping Weight	Prod. Total
AD2P	D42	2-dr HT-6P	3308	4000	13,200

ENGINES:

(170 Slant Six) Overhead valve. Cast iron block. Displacement: 170 cid. Bore and stroke: 3.41 x 3.13 inches. Compression ratio: 8.4:1. Brake hp: 101 at 4400 rpm. Four main bearings. Solid valve lifters. Carburetor: Carter one-barrel BBS-3833S.

(225 Slant Six) Overhead valve. Cast iron block. Displacement: 225 cid. Bore and stroke: 3.41 x 4.13 inches. Compression ratio: 8.4:1. Brake hp: 145 at 4000 rpm. Four main bearings. Solid valve lifters. Carburetor: Carter one-barrel BBS-3839S.

(V-8) Overhead valve. Cast iron block. Displacement: 273 cid. Bore and stroke: 3.63 x 3.31 inches. Compression ratio: 8.8:1. Brake hp: 180 at 4200 rpm. Five main bearings. Hydraulic valve lifters. Carburetor: Carter two-barrel BBD-3943S.

(318 V-8) Overhead valve. Cast iron block. Displacement: 318 cid. Bore and stroke: 3.91 x 3.31 inches. Compression ratio: 9.0:1. Brake hp: 230 at 4400 rpm. Five main bearings. Hydraulic valve lifters. Carburetor: Carter two-barrel BBD-3947S.

(361 V-8) Overhead valve. Cast iron block. Displacement: 361 cid. Bore and stroke: 4.13 x 3.38 inches. Compression ratio: 9.0:1. Brake hp: 265 at 4400 rpm. Five main bearings. Hydraulic valve lifters. Carburetor: Carter two-barrel BBD-3849S.

(383 V-8) Overhead valve. Cast iron block. Displacement: 383 cid. Bore and stroke: 4.25 x 3.38 inches. Compression ratio: 10.0:1. Brake hp: 330 at 4400 rpm (330 hp with dual exhaust). Five main bearings. Hydraulic valve lifters. Carburetor: Carter AFB 3855S four barrel.

(413 V-8) Overhead valve. Cast iron block. Displacement: 413 cid. Bore and stroke: 4.19 x 3.75 inches. Compression ratio: 10.1:1. Brake hp: 340 at 4600 rpm. Five main bearings. Hydraulic valve lifters. Carburetor: Carter AFB 3858S four-barrel.

(426 V-8) Overhead valve. Cast iron block. Displacement: 426 cid. Bore and stroke: 4.25 x 3.75 inches. Compression ratio: 10.1:1. Brake hp: 365 at 4800 rpm. Five main bearings. Hydraulic valve lifters. Carburetor: Carter AFB 3959S four-barrel.

(426 'Hemi' V-8) Overhead valve with hemispherical combustion chambers. Cast iron block. Displacement: 426 cid. Bore and stroke: 4.25 x 3.75 inches. Compression ratio: 11.0:1. Brake hp: 415 at 5600 rpm. Five main bearings. Solid valve lifters. Carburetor: Carter AFB 3859S four-barrel.

(426 'Hemi Eight-Barrel' V-8) Overhead valve with hemispherical combustion chambers. Cast iron block. Displacement: 426 cid. Bore and stroke: 4.25 x 3.75 inches. Compression ratio: 12.0:1. Brake hp: 425 at 5600 rpm. Five main bearings. Solid valve lifters. Carburetor: Two Carter AFB 3084S four-barrel.

CHASSIS FEATURES:

(Dart) Wheelbase: 111 inches (106 inches on station wagons). Overall length: 195.9 inches (190.2 inches on station wagons). Tires: 6.50 x 13 tubeless black sidewall. Three-speed manual transmission was standard on all Darts, with the three-speed TorqueFlite automatic and four-speed transmissions optional.

(Coronet) Wheelbase: 117 inches. Overall length: 204.2 inches (209.3 inches on station wagons). Tires: 7.35 x 14 tubeless black sidewall (7.75 x 14 on station wagons). Three-speed manual transmission was standard on all Coronets, with the three-speed TorqueFlite automatic and four-speed manual transmissions optional.

(Polara/Custom 880/Monaco) Wheelbase: 121 inches. Overall length: 212.3 inches (217.1 inches on station wagons). Tires: 7.35 x 14 tubeless black sidewall on Polaras; 8.25 x 14 tubeless blackwall on Custom 880s and Monacos; 8.55 x 14 tubeless black sidewall on station wagons. Three-speed manual transmission was standard on all Polaras, Custom 880s and Monacos, with the three-speed TorqueFlite automatic and four-speed manual transmissions optional.

DART CONVENIENCE OPTIONS: AM radio group ($79); on GTs ($67). Carpets in 170 ($13). Slant Six, 225-cid engine ($39). 273-cid V-8 ($81). Four-speed manual transmission with Slant Six ($152); with V-8 ($146). TorqueFlite automatic transmission with Slant Six ($140); with V-8 ($148). Power convertible top ($42). Tinted glass ($22). Back-up lights ($8). Luggage rack on station wagons ($37). Left-hand outside rearview mirror ($4). Padded instrument panel, on GT (standard equipment); on others ($13). Two-tone paint ($12). Power steering ($67).

Power tailgate window in station wagon ($25). Wheel covers ($12). Windshield washers and variable speed wipers ($13). White sidewall tires ($23-$25).

DODGE CONVENIENCE OPTIONS: Music Master AM radio ($45). Astrophonic AM radio ($69). AM/FM radio ($103). Rear speaker with reverberation ($28-$41 depending on model). Polara 500 Sport package for Polara two-door hardtops and convertibles (bucket seats, console, identification badges and deluxe spinner wheel covers ($171). Air conditioning ($282-$315). Dual air conditioning in station wagon ($481). Auto Pilot ($66). Power steering ($67-$74). Power brakes ($33). Electric clock ($12). Rear window defogger ($16). Sure-Grip differential ($39). Power door locks ($43). Tinted glass ($31). Two-tone paint ($13). Power bench seats ($74). Power bucket seats, in Monaco ($61-$121). Tachometer ($39). TorqueFlite automatic transmission ($165-$181). Four-speed manual transmission ($146-$180). 230-hp V-8 engine ($25). 270-hp V-8 engine ($73). 316-hp V-8 engine ($86). 363-hp V-8 engine ($344-$444). 425-hp 'Hemi' V-8 engine (approximately $1,800).

HISTORICAL FOOTNOTES: The 1965 Dodge line was introduced Sept. 25, 1964. The company's exact model year production was 550,795 cars for a 6.2 percent share of the total U.S. market. This included 206,631 Dodge Darts; 209,393 Coronets and 134,771 Polara/Custom 880/Monaco models. (See charts above for breakouts per series in figures rounded off to the nearest 100 units.) The 426-cid 'Hemi-Charger' powered Dodges continued to dominate the action on the dragstrips across the country. A few Hemis were produced for street use and were sold 'as is', meaning Chrysler Corp. was not responsible for their use and all warranty provisions, normally associated with a new car, did not apply to the Hemi Dodges.

1966 DODGE

DART SERIES — (6-CYL/V-8) — Continuing to use the same body as in the past three years, the new Dart featured a restyled anodized aluminum grille and large, oval taillights as the styling changes for 1966. As in the past, the Dart was the base trim level, and included chrome windshield and rear window moldings, no side chrome and the Dodge name, in block letters, across the vertical section of the trunk lid and on the front of the hood. Also included was the heater and defroster, electric windshield wipers, 170-cid Slant Six engine and manual transmission. Newly enacted Federal Safety Standards dictated that the new Darts also be equipped with back-up lights and emergency flashers as standard equipment, as well as the outside rearview mirror becoming standard.

DART I.D. DATA: Chrysler Corp. changed the numbering system and code locations for 1966 and they can be broken down as follows: The first symbol was a letter designating the car line: "D" = Polara and Monaco, "W" = Coronet and Charger and "L" = Dart. The second symbol designated the price class: "E" = Economy, "M" = Middle, "H" = High, "S" = Special and "P" = Premium. The third and fourth symbols indicated Body/Style, as indicated in the chart below. The fifth symbol, a letter, designated the type and displacement of the engine: "A" = 170-cid Slant Six, "B" = 225-cid Slant Six, "C" = Special 225-cid Slant Six, "E" = Special Order, "G" = 318-cid V-8, "H" = 273-cid four-barrel carb V-8, "J" = 340-cid V-8, "K" = 360-cid V-8, "L" = 383-cid V-8, "M" = 400-cid V-8, "N" = 383-cid four-barrel carb V-8, "P" = 400-cid V-8, "R" = 426-cid V-8, "T" = 440-cid V-8, "U" = 440-cid V-8, "V" = 440-cid V-8, "Z" = Special Order. The sixth represented the year produced ("6" = 1966) and the remaining six digits were the sequential unit number. Assembly plants were identified as follows: "A" = Lynch Road, "B" = Hamtramck, "C" = Jefferson, "D" = Belvedere, "A" = Newark, "G" = St. Louis and "R" = Windsor.

DART 170 SERIES

Model No.	Body/ Style No.	Body Type & Seating	Factory Price	Shipping Weight	Prod. Total
BL1L/2L	41	4-dr Sed-6P	2158/2286	2695/2895	Note 1
BL1L/2L	21	2-dr Sed-6P	2094/2222	2670/2860	Note 1
BL1L/2L	45	4-dr Sta Wag-6P	2436/2564	2780/2990	Note 1

Note 1: A total of 29,800 Darts were built during calender year 1966. Of these, 28,400 were sixes and 1,400 were V-8s. A total of 29,300 station wagons were built that year. Of these, 20,900 were sixes and 8,400 were V-8s. No breakout is provided for individual models and the production figure represents total station wagon production.

DART 270 SERIES — (6-CYL/V-8) — The Dart 270 was, once again, the intermediate trim level and included all the Dart features plus carpeting, Deluxe two-spoke steering wheel, full horn ring and vinyl trim on the convertible.

DART 270 I.D. DATA: See Dart I.D. Data listing. All models began at 100001 and went up in the unit number sequence.

DART 270 SERIES

Model No.	Body/ Style No.	Body Type & Seating	Factory Price	Shipping Weight	Prod. Total
BL1/2H	41	4-dr Sed-6P	2280/2408	2680/2895	Note 1
BL1/2H	21	2-dr Sed-6P	2214/2342	2665/2860	Note 1
BL1/2H	23	2-dr HT-6P	2307/2435	2720/2890	Note 1
BL1/2H	27	2-dr Conv-6P	2570/2698	2805/2995	Note 1
BL1/2H	45	4-dr Sta Wag-6P	2533/2661	2795/3020	Note 1

Note 1: A total of 35,100 Dart 270s were built during calender year 1966. Of these, 28,500 were sixes and 6,600 were V-8s.

1966 Dodge, Dart GT two-door convertible, V-8 (PH)

DART GT SERIES — (6-CYL/V-8) — The GT was the top trim level Dart for 1966 and included all the 270 features plus padded instrument panel, wheel covers and bucket seats. In addition, the GTs had a special emblem on the roof 'C' pillar and chrome rocker panel trim.

DART GT I.D. DATA: See Dart I.D. Data listing. All models began at 100001 and went up in the unit number sequence.

DART GT SERIES

Model No.	Body/ Style No.	Body Type & Seating	Factory Price	Shipping Weight	Prod. Total
BL1P/2P	23	2-dr HT-6P	2417/2545	2735/2915	Note 1
BL1P/2P	27	2-dr Conv-6P	2700/2828	2830/2995	Note 1

Note 1: A total of 18,700 GTs were built during calendar year 1966. Of these, 8,700 were sixes and 10,000 were V-8s.

DART CONVENIENCE OPTIONS: Prices and availability were similar to 1965.

CORONET/CORONET DELUXE SERIES — (6-CYL/V-8) — The Coronet continued as the intermediate size model for 1966. Completely restyled for the new year, the Coronet was to become one of the most attractive of that model ever to be produced. The 1966 models were nearly an inch shorter than the previous year and wider. They featured a mesh grille with the parking lights at the extreme ends and larger rectangular taillights that blended in nicely with the overall styling of the rear of the Coronet models. The Coronet was the base trim level and included the 225-cid six-cylinder engine, 7.35 x 14 tubeless tires, heater and defroster, electric windshield wipers, chrome windshield and rear window moldings, a single horizontal chrome strip along the bodyside and the Dodge name, in block letters, across the center of the front of the hood and the vertical section of the trunk lid.

CORONET I.D. DATA: See Dart I.D. Data listing. All models began at 100001 and went up in the unit number sequence.

CORONET/CORONET DELUXE SERIES

Model No.	Body/ Style No.	Body Type & Seating	Factory Price	Shipping Weight	Prod. Total
BW1/2L	41	4-dr Sed-6P	2302/2396	3075/3240	Note 1
BW1/2L	21	2-dr Sed-6P	2264/2358	3050/3215	Note 1
BW1/2L	41	4-dr DeL Sed-6P	2341/2435	3075/3240	Note 1
BW1/2L	21	2-dr DeL Sed-6P	2303/2397	3050/3215	Note 1
BW1/2L	45	4-dr DeL Sta Wag-6P	2631/2725	3480/3595	Note 1

Note 1: A total of 10,700 Coronets were built during calendar year 1966. Of these, 7,700 were sixes and 3,000 were V-8s. A total of 46,200 Coronet Deluxe models were built during that year. Of these, 25,600 were sixes and 20,600 were V-8s. A total of 27,700 station wagons were built during that year. Of these, 3,100 were sixes and 24,600 were V-8s. No breakout is provided for individual models, and the production figure represents total station wagon production.

CORONET 440 SERIES — (6-CYL/V-8) — The Coronet 440 was the intermediate trim level of the Coronet series and included all the features of the base Coronet series plus air foam front seat, power top and vinyl

interior on the convertible and carpets. The nine-passenger station wagons had the 273-cid V-8 engine and power tailgate window as standard equipment.

CORONET 440 I.D. DATA: See Dart I.D. Data listing. All models began at 100001 and went up in the unit number sequence.

CORONET 440 SERIES

Model No.	Body/ Style No.	Body Type & Seating	Factory Price	Shipping Weight	Prod. Total
BW1/2H	41	4-dr Sed-6P	2432/2526	3095/3220	Note 1
BW1/2H	23	2-dr HT-6P	2457/2551	3075/3235	Note 1
BW1/2H	27	2-dr Conv-6P	2672/2766	3185/3310	Note 1
BW1/2H	45	4-dr Sta Wag-6P	2722/2816	3515/3585	Note 1
BW2H	46	4-dr Sta Wag-9P	2926	3680	Note 1

Note 1: A total of 110,600 440s were built during calendar year 1966. Of these, 14,000 were sixes and 96,600 were V-8s. See Coronet series Note 1 for station wagon production.

1966 Dodge, Coronet 500 two-door hardtop, V-8

CORONET 500 SERIES — (6-CYL/V-8) — The Coronet 500 was the top trim level Coronet for 1966 and included all the 440 features plus padded instrument panel, console and bucket seats; wheel covers; 225-cid Slant Six in the four-door sedan and 273-cid V-8 engine in all others; four vertical chrome louvers on the rear fenders just ahead of the rear wheelwell and the Coronet 500 name, in script, at the front of the front fenders.

CORONET 500 I.D. DATA: See Dart I.D. Data listing. All models began at 100001 and went up in the unit number sequence.

CORONET 500 SERIES

BW1P/2P	41	4-dr Sed-6P	2586/2680	3120/3280	Note 1
BW1P/2P	23	2-dr HT-6P	N/A/2705	N/A/3275	Note 1
BW1P/2P	27	2-dr Conv-6P	2829/2921	3180/3345	Note 1

Note 1: A total of 55,700 500s were built during calendar year 1966. Of these, 500 were sixes and 55,200 were V-8s.

1966 Dodge, Charger two-door fastback hardtop, V-8

ADDITIONAL CORONET/DELUXE/440/500 NOTE: The following are known production figures for models equipped with the 426-cid Hemi V-8, according to Mopar authority Galen V. Govier: Coronet - 34 two-door sedans, Coronet Deluxe - 49 two-door sedans, Coronet 440 - 288 two-door hardtops and 6 convertibles, Coronet 500 - 340 two-door hardtops and 21 convertibles. Additionally, two Coronet four-door sedans have been authenticated as being produced with 426 Hemi power, but more may exist.

CHARGER SERIES — (V-8) — The Charger was Dodge's entry into the current 'fastback' craze. The Charger used Coronet chassis and running gear components, but the body was completely different. The Charger's frontal area was filled with a convex grille with fine vertical bars and a round Charger crest in the center. The rear end used a single, full-width taillight with the Charger name in block letters spaced evenly across the entire length. Hidden headlights were becoming the rage and the Charger featured these items along with the full-width taillights. Two fine feature lines were used along the bodyside and the fastback terminated at the rear of the car. Inside, the Charger's rear bucket seats folded individually to provide a spacious luggage compartment. The instrument panel was unique to the Charger in that four large, round pods contained all the instruments and located them directly in front of the driver. The floor shift (standard or automatic) was located in a full-length console that divided both front and rear seats.

CHARGER I.D. DATA: See Dart I.D. Data listing. All models began at 100001 and went up in the unit number sequence.

CHARGER SERIES

Model No.	Body/ Style No.	Body Type & Seating	Factory Price	Shipping Weight	Prod. Total
BX2P	29	2-dr HT-4P	3122	3499	37,300

ADDITIONAL CHARGER NOTE: The following is a known production figure for models equipped with the 426-cid Hemi V-8, according to Mopar authority Galen V. Govier: Charger - 468 two-door hardtops.

POLARA SERIES — (V-8) — The Polara continued as the base trim level full-size Dodge. A slightly revised grille and large, delta-shaped taillights highlighted the minor restyling for 1966. The Polara had chrome windshield and rear window moldings. The Dodge name, in block letters, across the center of the hood, directly above the hourglass-shaped grille. Also included were the 383 cid/270 hp V-8 engine, heater and defroster, power top on convertibles and 8.25 x 14 tubeless tires. The station wagons also included a vinyl interior and the nine-passenger station wagons also included power tailgate window and rear bumper guards with step pads. A sporty version of the Polara, called the Polara 500 was also offered and was intended to compete directly with the Chevrolet Impala SS and the Ford Galaxie 500XL models. The Polara 500s featured all the standard Polara items plus bucket seats and console with floor shift. Small round '500' emblems on the front fenders identified the 500s from the standard Polaras.

POLARA I.D. DATA: See Dart I.D. Data listing. All models began at 100001 and went up in the unit number sequence.

POLARA SERIES

BD2L	41	4-dr Sed-6P	2838	3765	Note 1
BD2L	43	4-dr HT-6P	2948	3880	Note 1
BD2L	23	2-dr HT-6P	2874	3820	Note 1
BD2L	27	2-dr Conv-6P	3161	3885	Note 1
BD2L	45	4-dr Sta Wag-6P	3183	4265	Note 1
BD2L	46	4-dr Sta Wag-9P	3286	4295	Note 1

Note 1: A total of 75,400 Polaras were built during calendar year 1966, including 12,400 low priced "Polara 318" economy models. All Polaras were V-8 powered. A total of 29,300 station wagons were produced during that year, although no breakout is provided for six- and nine-passenger models.

MONACO SERIES — (V-8) — The Monaco line was expanded during 1966 to include four separate models. The position held by the 1965 Monaco was filled by a new more luxurious Monaco 500 version of the Monaco. For 1966, the Monaco shared the Polara body and was merely a more highly trimmed Polara and shared drivetrain features with the Polara. The Monaco 500 was powered by the 325-hp four-barrel version of the 383-cid V-8 engine. All Monacos featured air foam front seats and stainless steel window frames on station wagons and four-door sedans. The hardtops had vinyl interior trim. The Monaco 500 featured all the Monaco standard equipment plus special exterior trim, bucket seats and a center console, wheel covers with spinners and the Monaco name, in script, on the left side of the trunk lid.

MONACO I.D. DATA: See Dart I.D. Data listing. All models began at 100001 and went up in the unit number sequence.

1966 Dodge, Monaco 500 two-door hardtop, V-8

MONACO SERIES

Model No.	Body/ Style No.	Body Type & Seating	Factory Price	Shipping Weight	Prod. Total
BD2H	41	4-dr Sed-6P	3033	3890	Note 1
BD2H	43	4-dr HT-6P	3170	3835	Note 1
BD2H	23	2-dr HT-6P	3107	3855	Note 1
BD2H	45	4-dr Sta Wag-6P	3183	4265	Note 1
BD2H	46	4-dr Sta Wag-9P	3539	4315	Note 1
BD2P	23	2-dr 500 HT-6P	3604	4270	Note 1

Note 1: A total of 30,600 Monacos and 7,300 Monaco 500s were built during calendar year 1966, all V-8s. See Note 1, Polara series for station wagon production.

CORONET/POLARA/MONACO CONVENIENCE OPTIONS: Prices and availability were similar to 1965.

ENGINES:

(170 Slant Six) Overhead valve. Cast iron block. Displacement: 170 cid. Bore and stroke: 3.41 x 3.13 inches. Compression ratio: 8.5:1. Brake hp: 101 at 4400 rpm. Four main bearings. Solid valve lifters. Carburetor: Carter one-barrel BBS-4099S.

(225 Slant Six) Overhead valve. Cast iron block. Displacement: 225 cid. Bore and stroke: 3.41 x 4.13 inches. Compression ratio: 8.4:1. Brake hp: 145 at 4000 rpm. Four main bearings. Solid valve lifters. Carburetor: Holley one-barrel R-3271-A.

(273 V-8) Overhead valve. Cast iron block. Displacement: 273 cid. Bore and stroke: 3.63 x 3.31 inches. Compression ratio: 8.8:1. Brake hp: 180 at 4200 rpm. Five main bearings. Hydraulic valve lifters. Carburetor: Carter two-barrel BBD-4113S.

(High-Performance 273 V-8) Overhead valve. Cast iron block. Displacement: 273 cid. Bore and stroke: 3.63 x 3.31 inches. Compression ratio: 10.5:1. Brake hp: 235 at 5200 rpm. Five main bearings. Hydraulic valve lifters. Carburetor: Carter AFB 3855S four-barrel.

(318 V-8) Overhead valve. Cast iron block. Displacement: 318 cid. Bore and stroke: 3.91 x 3.31 inches. Compression ratio: 9.0:1. Brake hp: 230 at 4400 rpm. Five main bearings. Hydraulic valve lifters. Carburetor: Stromberg two-barrel WW3-258.

(361 V-8) Overhead valve. Cast iron block. Displacement: 361 cid. Bore and stroke: 4.13 x 3.38 inches. Compression ratio: 9.0:1. Brake hp: 265 at 4400 rpm. Five main bearings. Hydraulic valve lifters. Carburetor: Carter two-barrel BBD-3849S.

(383 V-8) Overhead valve. Cast iron block. Displacement: 383 cid. Bore and stroke: 4.25 x 3.38 inches. Compression ratio: 9.2:1. Brake hp: 270 at 4400 rpm. Five main bearings. Hydraulic valve lifters. Carburetor: Carter two-barrel BBD-4125S.

(383 V-8) Overhead valve. Cast iron block. Displacement: 383 cid. Bore and stroke: 4.24 x 3.38 inches. Compression ratio: 10.0:1. Brake hp: 325 at 4800 rpm. Five main bearings. Hydraulic valve lifters. Carburetor: Carter AFB 3855S four-barrel.

(426 'Hemi' V-8) Overhead valve with hemispherical combustion chambers. Cast iron block. Displacement: 426 cid. Bore and stroke: 4.25 x 3.75 inches. Compression ratio: 12.0:1. Brake hp: 425 at 5600 rpm. Five main bearings. Solid valve lifters. Carburetor: Two Carter AFB 3084S four-barrel.

(426 'Street Hemi' 'Eight-Barrel' V-8) Same as 'Race Hemi' except hydraulic valve lifters and 10.25:1 compression ratio.

(440 Wedge) Cast iron block. Displacement: 440 cid. Bore and stroke: 4.32 x 3.75. Compression ratio: 10.0:1. Brake hp: 365 at 4400 rpm. Five main bearings. Hydraulic valve lifters. Carburetor: Carter AFB 4130S.

CHASSIS FEATURES:

(Dart) Wheelbase: 111 inches (106 inches on station wagons). Overall length: 195.9 inches (190.2 inches on station wagons). Tires: 6.50 x 13 tubeless black sidewall (7.00 x 13 on V-8s). Three-speed manual transmission was standard on all Darts, with the three-speed TorqueFlite automatic and four-speed manual transmissions optional.

(Coronet) Wheelbase: 117 inches. Overall length: 203 inches (207.9 inches on station wagons). Tires: 7.35 x 14 tubeless black sidewall on sixes; 7.75 x 14 on V-8s and 8.25 x 14 on station wagons. Three-speed manual transmission was standard on all Coronets, with the three-speed TorqueFlite and four-speed manual transmissions optional.

(Polara/Monaco/Monaco 500) Wheelbase: 121 inches. Overall length: 213.3 inches (217.1 inches on six-passenger station wagons and 218.4 inches on nine-passenger station wagons). Tires: 8.25 x 14 tubeless black sidewall on Monaco 500s and 8.55 x 14 tubeless black sidewall on all others. Three-speed manual transmission was standard on all Polara, Monaco and Monaco 500 models, with three-speed TorqueFlite and four-speed manual transmissions optional.

HISTORICAL FOOTNOTES: Dodge production totaled 532,026 for the calendar year, maintaining Dodge as the seventh ranked U.S. automaker in the industry.

1967 DODGE

DART SERIES — (6-CYL/V-8) — The 1967 Darts all featured completely new styling from the ground up. Riding on the same chassis as in 1966, the new Darts looked larger than their predecessors, even though they were, in fact, half an inch shorter. The full-width grille housed single headlights and featured a vertical bar arrangement with a large vertical dividing bar in the center of the concave grille. The side profile was slightly more rounded than in previous years and carried basically the same lines as in the past. The rear end treatment featured large, nearly square taillights and a vertical section on the trunk lid, which was as wide as the taillights were high. The Dart was the base trim level and included chrome windshield and rear window moldings, no side chrome and the Dart name, in block letters, along the side of the rear fenders. The Dodge name, also in block letters, appeared on the front of the hood and across the vertical section of the trunk lid. Also included was a heater and defroster, electric windshield wipers, the 170-cid Slant Six engine and manual three-speed transmission.

DART I.D. DATA: See 1966 Dart I.D. Data listing. All models began at 100001 and went up in the unit number sequence.

DART SERIES

Model No.	Body/ Style No.	Body Type & Seating	Factory Price	Shipping Weight	Prod. Total
CL1L/2L	41	4-dr Sed-6P	2224/2352	2725/2910	Note 1
CL1L/2L	21	2-dr Sed-6P	2187/2315	2710/2895	Note 1

Note 1: In figures rounded off to the nearest 100 units, a total of 53,100 Dodge Darts were built during model year 1967. Of these, 50,900 were sixes and 2,200 were V-8s. No additional breakouts by body style are available.

Note 2: For all 1967 Dodge specifications listings in this catalog, model numbers, prices and weights above slash are for sixes/below slash for V-8s.

DART 270 SERIES — (6-CYL/V-8) — The Dart 270 continued as the intermediate trim level and included all the Dart features plus carpeting; Deluxe two-spoke steering wheel; full horn ring and vinyl interior trim.

DART 270 I.D. DATA: See 1966 Dart I.D. Data listing. All models began at 100001 and went up in the unit number sequence.

DART 270 SERIES

Model No.	Body/ Style No.	Body Type & Seating	Factory Price	Shipping Weight	Prod. Total
CL1H/2H	41	4-dr Sed-6P	2362/2490	2735/2915	Note 1
CL1H/2H	23	2-dr HT Cpe-6P	2388/2516	2725/2910	Note 1

Note 1: In figures rounded off to the nearest 100 units, a total of 63,200 Dodge Dart 270s were built during model year 1967. Of these 49,700 were sixes and 13,500 were V-8s. No additional breakouts by body style are available.

DART GT SERIES — (6-CYL/V-8) — The GT was the top trim level Dart for 1967 and included all of the Dart 270 features plus padded instru-

ment panel, wheel covers and bucket seats. In addition, the GTs had a special emblem on the roof 'C' pillar and chrome rocker panel trim.

1967 Dodge, Dart GT two-door hardtop, V-8

DART GT I.D. DATA: See 1966 Dart I.D. Data listing. All models began at 100001 and went up in the unit number sequence.

DART GT SERIES

Model No.	Body/ Style No.	Body Type & Seating	Factory Price	Shipping Weight	Prod. Total
CL1P/2P	23	2-dr HT Cpe-6P	2499/2627	2750/2930	Note 1
CL1P/2P	27	2-dr Conv-6P	2732/2860	2850/3030	Note 1

Note 1: In figures rounded off to the nearest 100 units, a total of 38,200 Dodge Dart GTs were built during the model year 1967. Of these 16,600 were sixes and 21,600 were V-8s. No additional breakouts by body style are available.

CORONET DELUXE SERIES — (6-CYL/V-8) — The Coronet Deluxe was the intermediate size model for 1967. Using the 1966 body shell, the new Coronets adopted the Charger grille and featured a slightly revised rear end treatment. The Coronet was the base trim level and featured chrome windshield and rear window moldings and the Coronet name in block letters, along the sides of the rear fenders. The Dodge name, also in block letters, was seen across the front of the grille and on the vertical section of the trunk lid. Standard equipment included front and rear seat belts; windshield washer; 7.75 x 14 tubeless black sidewall tires (8.25 x 14 on V-8s); heater and defroster; two-speed electric wipers; left and right outside rearview mirrors; dual parking system and warning light; padded instrument panel and sun visors; emergency warning flashers; prismatic inside mirror; 225-cid Slant Six engine; back-up lights and black rubber floor mats.

CORONET DELUXE I.D. DATA: See 1966 Dart I.D. Data listing. All models began at 100001 and went up in the unit number sequence.

CORONET DELUXE SERIES

CW1/2L	41	4-dr Sed-6P	2397/2491	3070/3235	Note 1
CW1/2L	21	2-dr Sed-6P	2359/2453	3045/3210	Note 1
CW1/2L	45	4-dr Sta Wag-6P	2693/2787	3495/3625	Note 2

Note 1: In figures rounded off to the nearest 100 units, a total of 27,800 Dodge Coronet Deluxe passenger cars were built during model year 1967. Of these, 14,100 were sixes and 13,700 were V-8s.

Note 2: Production of all Coronet-bodied station wagons, including those in both Deluxe and 440 trim lines, was grouped together. In figures rounded off to the nearest 100 units this production total was 24,200 units, including 3,300 sixes and 20,900 V-8s.

CORONET 440 SERIES — (6-CYL/V-8) — The Coronet 440 continued as the intermediate trim level of the Coronet series and included all features of the standard Coronet plus carpeting; foam front seats and vinyl interiors on convertibles, hardtops and station wagons. Station wagons also included a power tailgate window and, on nine-passenger styles, a 273-cid V-8; rear bumper guards; step pads and cargo light were standard.

CORONET 440 I.D. DATA: See 1966 Dart I.D. Data listing. All models began at 100001 and went up in the unit number sequence.

CORONET 440 SERIES

CW1/2H	41	4-dr Sed-6P	2475/2569	3060/3225	Note 1
CW1/2H	23	2-dr HT Cpe-6P	2500/2594	3065/3235	Note 1
CW1/2H	27	2-dr Conv-6P	2740/2634	3140/3305	Note 1
CW1/2H	45	4-dr Sta Wag-6P	2771/2865	3495/3605	Note 2
CW2H	46	4-dr Sta Wag-9P	2975	3705	Note 2

Note 1: In figures rounded off to the nearest 100 units, a total of 92,500 Dodge Coronet 440 passenger cars were built in model year 1967. Of these, 8,600 were sixes and 83,900

were V-8s. This does not include station wagons. No additional body style breakouts are available.

Note 2: See 1967 Dodge Coronet Deluxe series Note 2.

CORONET 500 SERIES — (6-CYL/V-8) — The Coronet 500 was the top trim level for 1967 and included all the 440 features plus wheel covers, console, bucket seats and vinyl interior. The Coronet 500 name, in block letters, appeared on the sides of the rear fenders.

CORONET 500 I.D. DATA: See 1966 Dart I.D. Data listing. All models began at 100001 and went up in the unit number sequence.

CORONET 500 SERIES

Model No.	Body/ Style No.	Body Type & Seating	Factory Price	Shipping Weight	Prod. Total
CW1/2P	41	4-dr Sed-6P	2654/2748	3075/3235	Note 1
CW1/2P	23	2-dr HT Cpe-6P	2679/2773	3115/3280	Note 1
CW1/2P	27	2-dr Conv-6P	2919/3013	3190/3355	Note 1

Note 1: In figures rounded off to the nearest 100 units, a total of 29,300 Dodge Coronet 500 passenger cars were built during model year 1967. This includes 400 sixes and 28,900 V-8s. No additional breakouts by body style are available.

CORONET R/T SERIES — (V-8) — The Coronet R/T was the high-performance model of the Coronet series and included all Coronet 500 features plus the 440-cid Magnum V-8 engine (with four-barrel carburetor and dual exhaust); TorqueFlite automatic transmission; a special paint stripe; 7.75 x 14 Red Streak nylon tires; heavy-duty shock absorbers and torsion bars; special hood (with scoops); 70 amp/hour battery and heavy-duty brakes. The convertible also included map and courtesy lights.

1967 Dodge, Coronet 500 two-door hardtop, V-8

CORONET R/T I.D. DATA: See 1966 Dart I.D. Data listing. All models began at 100001 and went up in the unit number sequence.

CORONET R/T SERIES

CW2P	23	2-dr HT Cpe-6P	3199	3565	Note 1
CW2P	27	2-dr Conv-6P	3438	3640	Note 1

Note 1: A total of 10,181 Dodge Coronet R/T passenger cars were built in model year 1967. All were V-8s. Of this total, 628 were R/T convertibles.

ADDITIONAL CORONET/DELUXE/440/500/R/T NOTE: The following are known production figures for models equipped with the 426-cid Hemi V-8, according to Mopar authority Galen V. Govier: Coronet 440 (S/S) - 55 two-door hardtops, Coronet R/T - 283 two-door hardtops and convertibles (combined, separate breakouts N/A). Additionally, one Coronet Deluxe two-door sedan has been authenticated as being produced with 426 Hemi power, but more may exist. Also, Coronet 500 two-door hardtop production with 426 Hemi power has been authenticated, but the total number equipped this way is N/A.

CHARGER SERIES — (V-8) — The 1967 Charger utilized the same body introduced in 1966, with front fender mounted turn signal indicators and a few new chrome pieces added. The Chargers, being mounted on the Coronet chassis, included all the features found in Coronet 500 models plus paint stripes; map and courtesy lights; front and rear bucket seats; rear center armrests; cigar lighter; 318-cid V-8 engine; tinted rear window; oil pressure gauge; tachometer and rear pillar interior lights.

1967 Dodge, Charger two-door fastback hardtop, V-8

CHARGER I.D. DATA: See 1966 Dart I.D. Data listing. All models began at 100001 and went up in the unit number sequence.

CHARGER SERIES

Model No.	Body/ Style No.	Body Type & Seating	Factory Price	Shipping Weight	Prod. Total
CW2P	29	2-dr HT-6P	3128	3480	15,788

Note: The production total above is an exact model year output figure. All Chargers were V-8 powered.

Additional Charger Note: The following is a known production figure for models equipped with the 426-cid Hemi V-8, according to Mopar authority Galen V. Govier: Charger - 118 two-door hardtops.

1967 Dodge, Polara two-door convertible, V-8

POLARA SERIES — (V-8) — Completely restyled for 1967 the new full-size Polara series featured longer, lower and wider bodies than its 1966 counterpart. Large, delta-shaped plastic taillights were featured and this shape was duplicated, to a much lesser extent, in the grille. Top styling of four-door models was the same as 1965 and 1966 models, while two-door hardtops had a new semi-fastback roof style with a reverse slant to the rear quarter window opening. Two feature lines were used on the bodysides, one at the belt level and the other on the lower bodyside, which flared out slightly just in front of the rear wheel opening. The Polara was the base trim level and included chrome windshield and rear window moldings; 383-cid V-8 engine (318 engine in Polara '318' models); 8.25 x 14 tubeless black sidewall tires (8.55 x 14 on station wagons); outside left rearview mirror; two-speed wipers; rear bumper guards with step pads on nine-passenger station wagons; carpeting; right outside rearview mirror on station wagon; dual braking system and warning light; padded instrument panel and sun visors; emergency flasher system; vinyl interior on convertibles and station wagons; front and rear seat belts and back-up lights. The Polara name, in block letters, was located along the sides of the rear fenders and the Dodge name, in block letters, appeared on the front of the hood and across the vertical section of the trunk lid. A Polara 500 trim option including bucket seats and center console was available in two-door hardtop and convertible styles.

POLARA I.D. DATA: See 1966 Dart I.D. Data listing. All models began at 100001 and went up in the unit number sequence.

POLARA SERIES

CD2L	41	4-dr '318' Sed-6P	2843	3765	Note 1
CD2L	41	4-dr Sed-6P	2918	3885	Note 1
CD2L	43	4-dr HT Sed-6P	3028	3920	Note 1
CD2L	23	2-dr HT Cpe-6P	2953	3870	Note 1
CD2L	27	2-dr Conv-6P	3241	3930	Note 1
CD2L	45	4-dr Sta Wag-6P	3265	4400	Note 2
CD2L	46	4-dr Sta Wag-9P	3368	4450	Note 2

Note 1: In figures rounded off to the nearest 100 units, a total of 24,000 Polaras; 5,600 Polara 318s and 3,200 Polara 500 passenger cars were built during model year 1967. No additional body style breakouts are available.

Note 2: In addition to the totals in Note 1, some 8,900 full-size Dodge (Polara and Monaco) station wagons were built during the 1967 model run, with no additional breakout as to trim level or passenger/seating configurations.

MONACO SERIES — (V-8) — The Monaco line adopted the Polara body and was considered the top trim level of that line. Monacos included all Polara features plus glovebox light; ashtray light; map and courtesy lights; parking brake light; foam front seat cushions and wheel covers. Hardtops and station wagons had vinyl trim and the nine-passenger station wagon had a power tailgate window. The top line Monaco 500 had all the Monaco features plus console; paint stripes; electric clock; three-spoke Deluxe steering wheel; four-barrel carburetor; TorqueFlite or four-speed manual transmission; front bucket seats and a brushed stainless steel rocker panel molding. The Monaco or Monaco 500 name appeared, in block letters, across the sides of the rear fenders.

1967 Dodge, Monaco four-door hardtop, V-8

MONACO I.D. DATA: See 1966 Dart I.D. Data listing. All models began at 100001 and went up in the unit number sequence.

MONACO AND MONACO 500 SERIES

Model No.	Body/ Style No.	Body Type & Seating	Factory Price	Shipping Weight	Prod. Total
MONACO					
CD2H	41	4-dr Sed-6P	3138	3895	Note 1
CD2H	43	4-dr HT Sed-6P	3275	3945	Note 1
CD2H	23	2-dr HT Cpe-6P	3213	3885	Note 1
CD2H	45	4-dr Sta Wag-6P	3542	4425	Note 2
CD2H	45	4-dr Sta Wag-9P	3646	4475	Note 2
MONACO 500					
CD2P	23	2-dr HT Cpe-6P	3712	3970	Note 1

Note 1: In figures rounded off to the nearest 100 units, a total of 11,400 Monacos and 2,500 Monaco 500 passenger cars were built during the 1967 model year. All were V-8s. No additional breakouts are available.

Note 2: See 1967 Polara series Note 2 for the combined total of 1967 Monaco and Polara station wagons. No additional breakout by trim level or passenger/seating configuration is available.

ENGINES:

(170 Slant Six) Overhead valve. Cast iron block. Displacement: 170 cid. Bore and stroke: 3.41 x 3.13 inches. Compression ratio: 8.5:1. Brake hp: 101 at 4400 rpm. Four main bearings. Solid valve lifters. Carburetor: Carter one-barrel BBS-4099S.

(225 Slant Six) Overhead valve. Cast iron block. Displacement: 225 cid. Bore and stroke: 3.41 x 4.13 inches. Compression ratio: 8.4:1. Brake hp: 145 at 4000 rpm. Four main bearings. Solid valve lifters. Carburetor: Holley one-barrel R-3271-A.

(273 V-8) Overhead valve. Cast iron block. Displacement: 273 cid. Bore and stroke: 3.63 x 3.31 inches. Compression ratio: 8.6:1. Brake hp: 180 at 4200 rpm. Five main bearings. Hydraulic valve lifters. Carburetor: Carter two-barrel BBD-4113S.

(High-Performance 273 V-8) Overhead valve. Cast iron block. Displacement: 273 cid. Bore and stroke: 3.63 x 3.31 inches. Compression ratio: 10.5:1. Brake hp: 235 at 5200 rpm. Five main bearings. Hydraulic valve lifters. Carburetor: Carter AFB 3855S four-barrel.

(318 V-8) Overhead valve. Cast iron block. Displacement: 318 cid. Bore and stroke: 3.91 x 3.31 inches. Compression ratio: 9.0:1. Brake hp: 230 at 4400 rpm. Five main bearings. Hydraulic valve lifters. Carburetor: Stromberg two-barrel WW3-258.

(383 V-8) Overhead valve. Cast iron block. Displacement: 383 cid. Bore and stroke: 4.25 x 3.38 inches. Compression ratio: 9.2:1. Brake hp: 270 at 4400 rpm. Five main bearings. Hydraulic valve lifters. Carburetor: Carter two-barrel BBD-4125S.

(383 V-8) Overhead valve. Cast iron block. Displacement: 383 cid. Bore and stroke: 4.24 x 3.38 inches. Compression ratio: 10.0:1. Brake hp: 325 at 4800 rpm. Five main bearings. Hydraulic valve lifters. Carburetor: Carter AFB 3855S four-barrel.

(426 'Street Hemi' V-8) Overhead valve with hemispherical combustion chambers. Cast iron block. Displacement: 426 cid. Bore and stroke: 4.25 x 3.75 inches. Compression ratio: 10.25:1. Brake hp: 425 at 5600 rpm. Five main bearings. Solid valve lifters. Carburetor: Two Carter AFB 3084S four-barrel.

(440 Wedge V-8) Cast iron block. Displacement: 440 cid. Bore and stroke: 4.32 x 3.75 inches. Compression ratio: 10.0:1. Brake hp: 375 at 4400 rpm. Five main bearings. Hydraulic valve lifters. Carburetor: Carter AFB 4130S.

(440 Magnum V-8) Cast iron block. Displacement: 440 cid. Bore and stroke: 4.32 x 3.75 inches. Compression ratio: 10.0:1. Brake hp: 375 at 4400 rpm. Five main bearings. Hydraulic valve lifters. Carburetor: Carter AFB 4130S.

CHASSIS FEATURES:

(Dart) Wheelbase: 111 inches. Overall length: 195.4 inches. Tires: 6.50 x 13 tubeless black sidewall on sixes and 7.00 x 13 tubeless black sidewall on V-8. Three-speed manual transmission was standard on all Darts, with the three-speed TorqueFlite automatic or four-speed manual transmissions optional.

(Coronet) Wheelbase: 117 inches. Overall length: 203 inches (207.9 inches on station wagons). Tires: 7.35 x 14 tubeless black sidewall on six-cylinder sedans; 7.75 x 14 on six-cylinder station wagons; 7.35 x 14 on V-8 sedans and 8.25 x 14 on V-8 station wagons. Three-speed manual transmission was standard on all Coronets except the R/T, with the three-speed TorqueFlite and four-speed manual transmissions optional (TorqueFlite standard on R/T).

(Polara/Monaco/Monaco 500) Wheelbase: 122 inches. Overall length: 219.6 inches (221.3 inches on nine-passenger station wagon). Tires: 8.25 x 14 black sidewall on 318 sedans; 8.45 x 14 on all others. Three-speed manual transmission was standard on all Polara and Monaco models, with the three-speed TorqueFlite and four-speed standard on Monaco 500 models and optional on all others.

DART CONVENIENCE OPTIONS: 225-cid Slant Six engine ($38). 273-cid V-8 engine ($79). TorqueFlite automatic transmission for sixes ($139); for V-8s ($147). Four-speed manual transmission ($145). Power steering ($65). Power brakes ($32). Power front disc brakes ($54). Console on GTs ($38). Tinted glass ($22). Headrests for bucket seats ($32). Buffed paint on 270s and GTs ($18). Two-tone paint ($15). Music Master AM radio ($44). Rallye suspension ($11). Tachometer on GTs with console ($38). Vinyl top ($58). Wheel covers on 13-inch wheels ($14); on 14-inch wheels ($16). Simulated 'mag' wheel covers on GTs ($13); on 270s ($57). White sidewall tires ($34).

CORONET/POLARA/MONACO CONVENIENCE OPTIONS: 318-cid V-8 engine ($24). 383-cid V-8 engine, in Charger ($56); in others ($81). 383-cid four-barrel V-8 engine in Polara ($28); in Charger ($97); in other models ($121). 440-cid V-8 engine, in Monaco 500 ($69); in Monaco ($97); in Polaras and Monaco station wagons ($133). 426-cid 'Hemi' V-8, in Coronet R/T ($457); in Dodge Charger ($712). TorqueFlite automatic transmission, on six-cylinders ($153); depending on engine with V-8s ($183-$176). Four-speed manual transmission ($145-$175). Air conditioning on Coronets and Chargers ($274); on Polaras and Monacos ($311). Auto Pilot cruise control ($64). Power steering ($73). Power brakes ($16). Power front disc brakes ($54). Electric clock ($11). Console ($20). Sure-Grip differential ($29-$37). Heavy-duty differential ($107). Power door locks ($42). Dual exhaust ($24). Buffed paint ($16). Music Master AM radio on Coronets and Chargers ($44); on Polaras and Monacos ($47). Tilt & Telescope steering wheel ($67). Woodgrained steering wheel on Coronets and R/T ($20); on Chargers ($16); on Polaras and Monacos ($12). Tachometer ($38). Vinyl top on four-door sedans ($58); on hardtops ($70). Bucket seats ($75). Wheel covers ($14-$22). Simulated 'mag' wheel covers ($41-$57). Road wheels ($59-$75). Three-speed windshield wipers ($4).

HISTORICAL FOOTNOTES: Dodge retained its seventh ranking in the industry with production totaling 497,380 vehicles for the calendar year.

1968 DODGE

DART SERIES — **(6-CYL/V-8)** — The 1968 Darts continued to use the same body as introduced in 1967 with only minor trim updating. The Dart continued as the base trim level and included chrome windshield and rear window moldings, no side chrome and the Dart name, in block letters, along the side of the rear fenders. The Dodge name, also in block letters, appeared on the front of the hood and across the vertical section of the trunk lid. Also included in the standard Dart package, was the federally mandated Cleaner Air System; heater and defroster; 170-cid Slant Six engine and three-speed manual transmission.

DART I.D. DATA: See 1966 Dart I.D. Data listing. All models began at 100001 and went up in the unit number sequence.

DART SERIES

Model No.	Body/ Style No.	Body Type & Seating	Factory Price	Shipping Weight	Prod. Total
CL1L/2L	41	4-dr Sed-6P	2334/2462	2725/2910	Note 1
CL1L/2L	21	2-dr Sed-6P	2297/2425	2710/2895	Note 1

Note 1: Some 60,300 Darts were built during model year 1968. Of those, 58,900 were sixes and 3,400 were V-8s.

Additional Notes: For all 1968 Dodge listings: Model numbers, prices and weights above slash are for sixes/below slash for V-8s. All 1968 Dodge model year production totals given in this catalog are expressed in figures rounded off to the nearest 100 units, unless otherwise noted.

DART 270 SERIES — **(6-CYL/V-8)** — The Dart 270 was once again the intermediate trim level and included all the Dart features plus carpeting; cigar lighter; half horn ring and dual horns. Hardtops also included a full-width all-vinyl bench seat.

DART 270 I.D. DATA: See 1966 Dart I.D. Data listing. All models began at 100001 and went up in the unit number sequence.

DART 270 SERIES

CL1H/2H	41	4-dr Sed-6P	2473/2601	2735/2915	Note 1
CL1H/2H	23	2-dr HT Cpe-6P	2499/2627	2725/2910	Note 1

Note 1: Some 76,500 Dart 270s were built during model year 1968. Of those, 55,200 were sixes and 21,300 were V-8s.

1968 Dodge, Dart 'GTS' two-door hardtop, V-8

DART GT SERIES — **(6-CYL/V-8)** — The GT was the top trim level Dart for 1968 and included all the 270 features plus 14- or 15-inch wheels and tires with Deluxe wheel covers. The hardtops had bucket seats and the convertibles had power tops and full-width all-vinyl bench seats. The GTS was a special high-performance version of the GT and was equipped with the new 340-cid V-8 engine; hubcaps; firm-ride shock absorbers; Rallye suspension and E70-14 Red Streak Wide Oval tires; TorqueFlite three-speed automatic (or four-speed manual transmission); Bumblebee stripes across the sides of the rear fenders and trunk lid and an engine dress-up kit (consisting of black crinkle-finished aluminum valve covers and a special black, crinkle-finished aluminum air cleaner). The GT and GTS models included the appropriate model designation on the sides of the front fenders, just behind the front wheel openings.

DART GT I.D. DATA: See 1966 Dart I.D. Data listing. All models began at 100001 and went up in the unit number sequence.

DART GT SERIES

DART GT

CL1P/2P	23	2-dr HT Cpe-5P	2611/2739	2750/2930	Note 1
CL1P/2P	27	2-dr Conv-6P	2831/2959	2850/3030	Note 1

DART GTS

CL2	23	2-dr HT Cpe-5P	3163	3038	Note 1
CL2	27	2-dr Conv-6P	3383	3310	Note 1

Note 1: Some 35,000 Dart GT and GTS models were built during model year 1968. Of those, 10,900 were sixes and 24,100 were V-8s. All GTS models were V-8 powered.

Additional Dart Note: The following is a known production figure for models equipped with the 426-cid Hemi V-8, according to Mopar authority Galen V. Govier: Dart (S/S) - 80 two-door hardtops.

CORONET DELUXE SERIES — **(6-CYL/V-8)** — Completely restyled for 1968, the new Coronet Deluxe models presented a smoother, more rounded profile than in the previous year. To many, they are one of the most attractive Coronets ever produced. A full-width grille housed the quad headlights and its insert design was a fine, eggcrate arrangement. The taillights were housed in a full-width concave escutcheon panel. The Coronet Deluxe was the base trim level and featured chrome windshield and rear window moldings; the Coronet name, in block letters, along the sides of the rear fenders and the Dodge name, also in block letters, on

the vertical section of the escutcheon panel. Also included in the base Coronet were all federally mandated safety equipment; ashtray light; cigarette lighter; heater and defroster; window sill moldings; color keyed rubber floor mats; rear armrests and ashtrays; the 225-cid Slant Six (or 273-cid V-8) engine and double-acting tailgate on station wagons.

CORONET DELUXE I.D. DATA: See 1966 Dart I.D. Data listing. All models began at 100001 and went up in the unit number sequence.

CORONET DELUXE SERIES

Model No.	Body/ Style No.	Body Type & Seating	Factory Price	Shipping Weight	Prod. Total
WL	41	4-dr Sed-6P	2499/2593	3070/3235	Note 1
WL	21	2-dr Cpe-6P	2461/2555	3045/3210	Note 1
WL	45	4-dr Sta Wag-6P	2816/2910	3455/3590	Note 1

Note 1: Some 45,000 Coronet Deluxe passenger cars were built during model year 1968. Of those, 19,300 were sixes and 25,700 were V-8s. Also included in Coronet passenger car production were 4,844 police and taxi six-cylinder units and 2,206 police and taxi V-8 units. A total of 33,100 intermediate size Dodge station wagons were built during the year. Of those, 2,600 were six-cylinders and 30,500 were V-8s. No breakout is provided for individual lines and the production figure represents total production of all Coronet station wagons.

Additional Note: Exact production of all Coronet models for model year 1968 was 196,242 units.

CORONET 440 SERIES — (6-CYL/V-8) — The Coronet 440 continued as the intermediate trim level of the Coronet series and included all the features of the Coronet plus carpeting; dual horns; steering wheel with horn ring and padded hub. The hardtops and station wagons had all-vinyl bench seats and the hardtops and sedans had window sill moldings. A midyear offering, the Super Bee, was based on the Coronet 440 "pillared" coupe. Standard equipment for the Super Bee included: 383 cid/335 hp V-8; four-speed transmission with Hurst "Competition Plus" floor shifter; dual exhaust; heavy-duty suspension; bench seat interior; bumblebee striping and a power bulge hood. Coronet 440 four-door sedans and station wagons included drip rail moldings and station wagons included wheel lip moldings. Nine-passenger station wagons included a power tailgate window.

CORONET 440 I.D. DATA: See 1966 Dart I.D. Data listing. All models began at 100001 and went up in the unit number sequence.

1968 Dodge, Coronet Super Bee two-door coupe, V-8

CORONET 440 SERIES

WH	41	4-dr Sed-6P	2577/2683	3060/3225	Note 1
WH	23	2-dr HT Cpe-6P	2601/2707	3065/3235	Note 1
WH	45	4-dr Sta Wag-6P	2898/3004	3495/3605	Note 1
WH	46	4-dr Sta Wag-9P	3114	3705	Note 1

Note 1: Some 103,500 Coronet 440 passenger cars were built during model year 1968. Of those, 8,200 were sixes and 95,300 were V-8s. Super Bee production number breakout is N/A. See Note 1, Coronet series for station wagon production data.

CORONET 500 SERIES — (6-CYL/V-8) — The Coronet 500 was the top trim level for 1968 and included all the Coronet 440 features plus front air foam seats; all-vinyl bench seats; power top on convertible; all-vinyl bench seats and simulated woodgrain on the bodyside and tailgate panels of station wagons. All-vinyl front bucket seats were featured in sedans and hardtops. Sedans had an alternate choice of front bucket seats with cloth inserts. Bench seat models had foam padded rear seat cushions. Four-door sedans and station wagons had drip rail moldings and rear door automatic lamp switch with upper door frame moldings and quarter window moldings on station wagons. Sedans also included a fold-down center front armrest. The standard engine in the Coronet 500 was the 318-cid V-8.

CORONET 500 I.D. DATA: See 1966 Dart I.D. Data listing. All models began at 100001 and went up in the unit number sequence.

CORONET 500 SERIES

Model No.	Body/ Style No.	Body Type & Seating	Factory Price	Shipping Weight	Prod. Total
WP	41	4-dr Sed-6P	2886	3235	Note 1
WP	23	2-dr HT Cpe-6P	2836	3280	Note 1
WP	27	2-dr Conv-6P	3036	3355	Note 1
WP	45	4-dr Sta Wag-6P	3186	3615	Note 1
WP	46	4-dr Sta Wag-9P	3296	3715	Note 1

Note 1: Some 30,100 Coronet 500 passenger cars were built during model year 1968. All were V-8 powered. See Note 1, Coronet series for station wagon production data.

CORONET R/T SERIES — (V-8) — The Coronet R/T continued as the high-performance model of the Coronet series. It included all Coronet 500 features plus the 440-cid Magnum V-8 engine with four-barrel carburetor and dual exhaust; ashtray light; front all-vinyl bucket seats; carpeting; cigarette lighter; drip rail, wheel lip and window sill moldings; 150 mph speedometer; steering wheel with padded hub and horn ring; bodyside or Bumblebee stripes; TorqueFlite three-speed automatic transmission; R/T emblems on the grille; fender and rear latch panel medallions; 70 amp/hour battery; heavy-duty drum brakes; dual horns; rear armrests and ashtrays; firm-ride shock absorbers; Rallye suspension and F70-14 wide-tread black sidewall tires. The convertible also included power top, map and courtesy lights.

CORONET R/T I.D. DATA: See 1966 Dart I.D. Data listing. All models began at 100001 and went up in the unit number sequence.

CORONET R/T SERIES

WS	23	2-dr HT Cpe-5P	3353	3565	Note 1
WS	27	2-dr Conv-5P	3613	3640	Note 1

Note 1: Some 10,900 Coronet R/Ts were built during model year 1968, all V-8 powered. No breakout is provided for individual body styles. Therefore, production figures represent total R/T production.

1968 Dodge, Charger two-door hardtop, V-8 (AA)

ADDITIONAL CORONET/SUPER BEE/440/R/T NOTE: The following are known production figures for models equipped with the 426-cid Hemi V-8, according to Mopar authority Galen V. Govier: Super Bee - 125 two-door coupes, R/T - 220 two-door hardtops and 9 convertibles. Additionally, two Coronet 440 two-door coupes have been authenticated as being produced with 426 Hemi power, but more may exist.

CHARGER SERIES — (6-CYL/V-8) — Completely restyled for 1968, the new Chargers went from a fastback body style to a semi-fastback style, which produced one of the best looking Dodge models ever built. A full-width grille was featured and a smooth, slightly rounded 'coke-bottle' shape was used. At the rear end two round taillights on each side were located in a flat-black-finished escutcheon panel. The Charger was the base trim level and included all federally mandated safety features plus all-vinyl front bucket seats; carpeting; three-spoke steering wheel

with padded hub and partial horn ring; heater and defroster; electric clock; cigarette lighter; ashtray light; heavy-duty suspension (including sway bar); heavy-duty rear springs and torsion bars; front and rear bumper guards; wheel opening moldings; concealed headlights; quick-fill gasoline cap; the 318-cid V-8 engine and 7.35 x 14 tubeless black sidewall tires. The Charger R/T was the high-performance version of the Charger and included all the standard Charger features plus the 440-cid Magnum V-8 engine; TorqueFlite three-speed automatic transmission; dual exhaust (with chrome tips); heavy-duty brakes; R/T handling package; racing stripes and F70-14 Red Streak or white sidewall tires.

CHARGER I.D. DATA: See 1966 Dart I.D. Data listing. All models began at 100001 and went up in the unit number sequence.

CHARGER AND CHARGER R/T SERIES

Model No.	Body/ Style No.	Body Type & Seating	Factory Price	Shipping Weight	Prod. Total
XP	29	2-dr HT Cpe-5P	3014	3500	Note 1
XS	29	2-dr R/T HT-5P	3480	3650	Note 1

Note 1: Some 96,100 Chargers and R/Ts were built during model year 1968, all were V-8 powered. No breakout is provided for individual model, therefore, production figures represent total Charger production.

Additional Charger Note: The following is a known production figure for models equipped with the 426-cid Hemi V-8, according to Mopar authority Galen V. Govier: Charger R/T - 467 two-door hardtops (one Charger 500 prototype was also equipped with the 426 Hemi engine).

1968 Dodge, Polara four-door hardtop, V-8

POLARA SERIES — (6-CYL/V-8) — Only slightly restyled for 1968, the new Polara relied on trim updating to complete the changes for the year. The Polara was the base trim level and included chrome windshield and rear window moldings; 318-cid V-8 engine; heater and defroster; carpeting; cigar lighter; rear seat cushion foam pad; all-vinyl interior on station wagons and convertibles, plus power top on convertibles. The nine-passenger station wagons also had seat belts on the third seat; power tailgate window and rear bumper guards. The Polara name, in block letters, appeared on the sides of the front fenders and the Dodge name, also in block letters, appeared on the right side of the trunk lid. The Polara 500 was the top trim level of the Polara series and included all the standard Polara features plus Deluxe wheel covers, window sill and wheel lip moldings and front air foam vinyl bucket seats (with center folding armrests). A console was optional at no extra charge.

MONACO SERIES — (6-CYL/V-8) — The Monaco was the base trim level of the Monaco series, which utilized the Polara body and chassis. Standard Monacos included all the Polara features plus the Polara Light Package; 383-cid two-barrel V-8 engine; wheel lip and window sill moldings; air foam front seats and Deluxe wheel covers. Four-door sedans also had upper door frame moldings and station wagons also included upper door and quarter window moldings; power tailgate window; rear bumper guards and rear compartment lock. The Monaco 500 was the top trim level of the Monaco series and included all the standard Monaco features plus front foam vinyl bucket seats (with center folding armrests), electric clock and TorqueFlite three-speed automatic transmission. A console was optional at no extra charge.

POLARA I.D. DATA: See 1966 Dart I.D. Data listing. All models began at 100001 and went up in the unit number sequence.

POLARA SERIES

POLARA

DL	41	4-dr Sed-6P	3001	3765	Note 1
DL	43	4-dr HT Sed-6P	3074	3920	Note 1

POLARA 500

DM	23	2-dr HT Cpe-5P	3200	3875	Note 1
DM	27	2-dr Conv-5P	3487	3935	Note 1

MONACO I.D. DATA: See 1966 Dart I.D. Data listing. All models began at 100001 and went up in the unit number sequence.

MONACO SERIES

Model No.	Body/ Style No.	Body Type & Seating	Factory Price	Shipping Weight	Prod. Total
DH	41	4-dr Sed-6P	3268	3895	Note 1
DH	43	4-dr HT Sed-6P	3406	3945	Note 1
DH	23	2-dr HT Cpe-6P	3343	3885	Note 1
DH	45	4-dr Sta Wag-6P	3676	4425	Note 1
DH	46	4-dr Sta Wag-9P	3809	4475	Note 1

MONACO 500

DP	23	2-dr HT Cpe-5P	3843	3970	Note 1

Note 1: Some 70,100 Polara passenger cars were built during model year 1968, all were V-8 powered. This figure includes 2,206 special Polara '318' units used in police and taxi operation. A total of 4,000 Polara 500s were built during the year, also all V-8s. A total of 21,100 Monacos and 3,400 Monaco 500 passenger cars were built during model year 1968, all V-8s. A total of 16,900 Polara and Monaco station wagons were also built during the year, although no breakout by series is provided for station wagons. Therefore, the total represents production of all station wagons in the full-size lineup.

Additional Note: Exact production of all full-size Dodges was 138,933 units.

CHASSIS FEATURES: Wheelbase: (Dart) 111 inches; (Coronet/Charger) 117 inches; (Polara/Monaco) 122 inches. Overall length: (Dart) 196 inches; (Coronet wagon) 210 inches; (Coronet) 207 inches; (Charger) 208 inches; (Polara/Monaco wagon) 220 inches; (Polara/Monaco) 219 inches. Width: (Dart) 70 inches; (Coronet/Charger) 77 inches. Tires: (base Dart) 6.50 x 13; (Dart V-8/convertible) 7.00 x 13; (Dart GTS) E70-14; (Coronet/Charger) 7.35 x 14; (Coronet wagon) 8.25 x 14; (Coronet/Charger R/T) F70-14; (Polara/Monaco) 8.25 x 14; (Polara/Monaco wagon) 8.55 x 14.

1968 Dodge, Monaco 500 two-door hardtop, V-8

ENGINES: Same as 1967, with the addition of:

(V-8) Overhead valve. Cast iron block. Displacement: 340 cid. Bore and stroke: 4.04 x 3.31 inches. Compression ratio: 10.5:1. Brake hp: 275 at 5000 rpm. Five main bearings. Hydraulic valve lifters. Carburetor: Carter Thermo-Quad four barrel.

(383 V-8) two-barrel was now rated at 290 hp with the same specifications. 383 V-8 four-barrel was now rated at 300 hp with the same specifications.

DART CONVENIENCE OPTIONS: Power brakes ($16). Power steering ($80). Air conditioning ($335). 273-cid V-8 ($128). TorqueFlite transmission, with six ($172); with V-8 ($181). Four-speed transmission ($179). Music Master AM radio ($44). Tachometer ($38). 'Mag' styled wheel covers ($55).

CORONET/CHARGER/POLARA/MONACO CONVENIENCE OPTIONS: 318-cid V-8 engine ($24). 383-cid V-8 engine ($58-$81). 383-cid four-barrel V-8 engine ($97-$121). 383-cid four-barrel V-8 in Polaras ($28). 440-cid Magnum V-8 engine ($88-$133). 426-cid 'Hemi' V-8 engine

($457-$712). TorqueFlite automatic transmission on six-cylinders ($153); on V-8s ($163-$176). Four-speed manual transmission ($145-$175). Air conditioning on Coronets and Chargers ($274); on Polaras and Monacos ($311). Auto Pilot cruise control ($64). Power steering ($73). Power brakes ($16). Power front disc brakes ($54). Electric clock ($11). Console ($20). Sure-Grip differential ($29-$37). Heavy-duty differential ($107). Power door locks ($42). Dual exhaust ($24). Buffed paint ($16). Music Master AM radio on Coronets and Chargers ($44); on Polaras and Monacos ($47). Tilt & Telescope steering wheel ($87). Woodgrained steering wheel on Coronets and R/Ts ($20); on Chargers ($16); on Polaras and Monacos ($12). Tachometer ($38). Vinyl top on four-door sedans ($58); hardtops ($70). Simulated 'mag' wheel covers ($41-$57). Road wheels ($59-$75). Three-speed windshield wipers ($4).

HISTORICAL FOOTNOTES: Dodges, for 1968, were advertised under the high-performance 'Scat Pack' theme. At Daytona, the 'Coke bottle' shaped Coronets were capable of lapping the NASCAR oval at speeds up to 185 mph. A low-priced performance model, the Super Bee, with basic appointments and a 383 cid/335 hp V-8 as the base engine, was introduced in the spring. Five checkered flags were captured by Dodges, on the Grand National stock car racing circuit. Available this season was the 'Hemi' Dart, a stripped edition with special, lightweight body parts, that qualified for Super Stock drag racing classes.

1969 DODGE

DART SERIES — (6-CYL/V-8) — The 1969 Darts featured new grilles; headlights; taillights and other exterior trim mounted on the same basic body shell as used in 1968. Dodge Dart was the base trim level for 1969 and included chrome windshield and rear window moldings and the Dodge name, in block letters, across the vertical section of the trunk lid and on the left front corner of the hood. Also included were all the mandatory safety equipment; heater and defroster; 6.50 x 13 black sidewall tubeless tires on six-cylinder-equipped cars and 7.00 x 13 tubeless black sidewall tires on V-8s.

DART I.D. DATA: See 1966 Dart I.D. Data listing. All models began at 100001 and went up in the unit number sequence.

DART SERIES

Model No.	Body/ Style No.	Body Type & Seating	Factory Price	Shipping Weight	Prod. Total
DART					
LL41	N/A	4-dr Sed-6P	2413/2524	2726/2894	Note 1
SWINGER					
LL23	N/A	2-dr Cpe-6P	2400/2511	2711/2879	Note 1

General Note: All 1969 Dodge model year production figures listed in this catalog are series production totals expressed to the nearest 100 units. No additional breakouts by trim level, model or body style are available. In all of the specifications charts the prices and weights above slash are for sixes and below slash for V-8s.

Note 1: Some 86,400 Dodge Dart passenger cars were built during calendar year 1969. Of these, 61,800 were sixes and 24,600 were V-8s.

1969 Dodge, Dart Swinger two-door hardtop, V-8

DART SWINGER SERIES — (V-8) — The Swinger was a new economy sports performance two-door hardtop in the Dart line. Standard Swingers could be equipped with any of the engines from the basic six to the 383 Magnum V-8. A special package called the Swinger 340 featured the 340-cid V-8 engine; Rallye Suspension; Firm Ride Shocks; 'Power Bulge' hood; Bumblebee stripes; chrome dual exhaust outlets; D70-14 wide-oval tires; four-speed manual transmission (or TorqueFlite automatic) and carpeting.

DART SWINGER SERIES

Model No.	Body/ Style No.	Body Type & Seating	Factory Price	Shipping Weight	Prod. Total
LM23	N/A	2-dr HT Cpe-6P	2836	3097	20,000

DART CUSTOM SERIES — (6-CYL/V-8) — The Custom was the intermediate trim level Dart for 1969 and included all the Dart series features plus cigarette lighter; carpeting and three-spoke steering wheel. The hardtop also had vinyl bench seats and the sedan had cloth and vinyl seats. A single horizontal chrome strip was used along the bodyside and ran the entire length of the car.

DART CUSTOM I.D. DATA: See 1966 Dart I.D. Data listing. All models began at 100001 and went up in the unit number sequence.

DART CUSTOM

LH41	N/A	4-dr Sed-6P	2550/2661	2726/2894	Note 1
LH23	N/A	2-dr HT Cpe-6P	2577/2688	2711/2879	Note 1

Note 1: Some 63,700 Dodge Dart Custom passenger cars were built during model year 1969. Of these. 41,600 were sixes and 22,100 were V-8s.

DART GT AND GTS SERIES — (6-CYL/V-8) — The GT continued as the top trim level Dodge Dart for 1969 and included all Dart series features plus a special blacked-out grille with center horizontal divider bar and the Dart GT name, in block letters, on the side of the rear fenders just in front of the rear wheelwells. The GTS version of the GT included all the GT features plus E70-14 Red Line tires; 340-cid V-8 engine; TorqueFlite automatic transmission; three-spoke steering wheel; dual exhaust; carpeting and engine dress-up kit. All GTS models also included the Bumblebee stripe across the trunk lid and down the sides of the body.

DART GT AND GTS I.D. Data: See 1966 Dart I.D Data listing. All models began at 100001 and went up in the unit number sequence.

DART GT AND GTS SERIES

DART GT

LP23	N/A	2-dr HT Cpe-6P	2672/2783	2716/2884	Note 1
LP27	N/A	2-dr Conv-6P	2865/2976	2821/2979	Note 1

DART GTS

LS23	N/A	2-dr HT Cpe-6P	3226	3105	Note 1
LS27	N/A	2-dr Conv-6P	3419	3210	Note 1

Note 1: Some 20,900 Dodge Dart GT passenger cars were built during model year 1969. Of these, 5,600 were sixes and 15,300 were V-8s. A total of some 6,700 GTS hardtops and convertibles were built during the model year, all V-8 powered.

CORONET DELUXE SERIES — (6-CYL/V-8) — New grilles and taillights adorned the Coronet Deluxe for 1969 and presented an attractive package to the buyer. The grille continued Dodge's trend to delta shapes while the taillights had long oval-shaped lenses. The high-performance model Super Bee, introduced in February of 1968 and originally based on a 440 "pillared" coupe, was added to the Coronet Deluxe line for 1969. It offered outstanding performance without a high price tag. The Coronet Deluxe was the base trim level and included a 225-cid Slant Six engine; heater and defroster; 7.35 x 14 tubeless black sidewall tires on sixes and 7.75 x 14 tires on V-8 models. Station wagons also included dual-action tailgates and automatic rear door interior lamp switches. The nine-passenger station wagon also included the 318-cid V-8 engine as standard equipment. The Super Bee had all the standard Coronet Deluxe passenger car features plus the 383-cid engine (modified with 440 heads and a stronger cam), heavy-duty 11-inch drum brakes, Rallye Suspension with sway bar, Firm Ride shock absorbers, 'Power Bulge' hood; Bumblebee stripes; F70-14 Red Line wide-oval tires and four-speed manual transmission.

CORONET DELUXE I.D. Data: See 1966 Dart I.D. Data listings. All models began at 100001 and went up in the unit number sequence.

SUPER BEE

WM21	N/A	2-dr Cpe-6P	3076	3440	Note 1
WM23	N/A	2-dr HT Cpe-6P	3138	3470	Note 1

Note 1: Some 30,400 standard Coronet Deluxe passenger cars and station wagons were built during model year 1969. Of these, 12,500 were sixes and 17,900 were V-8s. Some 27,800 Super Bees were built during the model year, all V-8 powered.

CORONET DELUXE SERIES

Model No.	Body/ Style No.	Body Type & Seating	Factory Price	Shipping Weight	Prod. Total
CORONET DELUXE					
WL41	N/A	4-dr Sed-6P	2589/2692	3018/3176	Note 1
WL21	N/A	2-dr Cpe-6P	2554/2657	2988/3146	Note 1
WL45	N/A	4-dr Sta Wag-6P	2992/3095	3498/3606	Note 1

CORONET 440 SERIES — (6-CYL/V-8) — The Coronet 440 was the intermediate trim level Coronet for 1969 and included all the Coronet features plus carpeting and polished aluminum wheel lip moldings. A brushed aluminum escutcheon panel was located on the trunk lid (between the taillights) and the Coronet 440 name, in block letters, was located behind the front wheel cutouts.

CORONET 440 I.D. DATA: See 1966 Dart I.D. Data listing. All models began at 100001 and went up in the unit number sequence.

1969 Dodge, Coronet Super Bee two-door hardtop, V-8 (AA)

CORONET 440 SERIES

Model No.	Body/ Style No.	Body Type & Seating	Factory Price	Shipping Weight	Prod. Total
WH41	N/A	4-dr Sed-6P	2670/2773	3023/3181	Note 1
WH21	N/A	2-dr Cpe-6P	2630/2733	2983/3151	Note 1
WH23	N/A	2-dr HT Cpe-6P	2692/2795	3018/3176	Note 1
WH45	N/A	4-dr Sta Wag-6P	3033/3136	3503/3606	Note 1
WH46	N/A	4-dr Sta Wag-9P	3246	3676	Note 1

Note 1: Some 105,900 Dodge Coronet 440 passenger cars and station wagons were built during model year 1969. Of these, some 4,700 were sixes and 101,200 V-8s.

CORONET 500 SERIES — (6-CYL/V-8) — The Coronet 500 was the top trim level and included all the 440 series features plus the 318-cid V-8 engine; simulated woodgrain applique on instrument panel; extra thick foam seat cushions; map, ashtray and glovebox lights; wheel lip moldings; pedal dress-up kit; power top on convertible; and bucket seats. Sedans and station wagons also have rear door automatic interior lamp switches. The station wagon also had simulated woodgrain body appliques.

CORONET 500 I.D. DATA: See 1966 Dart I.D. Data listing. All models began at 100001 and went up in the unit number sequence.

CORONET 500 SERIES

Model No.	Body/ Style No.	Body Type & Seating	Factory Price	Shipping Weight	Prod. Total
WP41	N/A	4-dr Sed-6P	2963	3206	Note 1
WP23	N/A	2-dr HT Cpe-6P	2929	3171	Note 1
WP27	N/A	2-dr Conv-6P	3069	3306	Note 1
WP45	N/A	4-dr Sta Wag-6P	3280	3611	Note 1
WP46	N/A	4-dr Sta Wag-9P	3392	3676	Note 1

Note 1: Some 32,100 Dodge Coronet 500 passenger cars and station wagons were built during model year 1969. All were V-8 powered.

CORONET R/T SERIES — (V-8) — The Coronet R/T continued as the high-performance model in the Coronet series and included all the features of the Coronet 500 plus the Magnum 440-cid V-8 engine; TorqueFlite automatic transmission; light group; sill moldings and 'R/T' nomenclature (in the Bumblebee stripe) across the trunk lid and down the fendersides. Two simulated scoops were also located on the rear fenders, just ahead of the rear wheelwell openings on each side.

CORONET R/T I.D. DATA: See 1966 Dart I.D. Data listing. All models began at 100001 and went up in the unit number sequence.

CORONET R/T SERIES

Model No.	Body/ Style No.	Body Type & Seating	Factory Price	Shipping Weight	Prod. Total
WS23	N/A	2-dr HT Cpe-6P	3442	3601	Note 1
WS27	N/A	2-dr Conv-6P	3660	3721	Note 1

Note 1: Some 7,200 Dodge Coronet R/T hardtops and convertibles were built during model year 1969, all V-8 powered.

Additional Coronet Super Bee/R/T Note: The following are known production figures for models equipped with the 426-cid Hemi V-8, according to Mopar authority Galen V. Govier: Super Bee - 166 two-door coupes and 92 two-door hard-

tops, R/T - 97 two-door hardtops and 10 convertibles. Additionally, the following are known production figures for models equipped with the 440-cid "Six-Pak" V-8, according to Galen V. Govier: Super Bee - 1,487 two-door coupes and 420 two-door hardtops.

1969 Dodge, Charger Daytona two-door hardtop, V-8

CHARGER SERIES — (6-CYL/V-8) — The 1969 Charger continued to use the beautifully styled body introduced with the 1968 models. The main changes in the two years was the new divided grille for the 1969 models and a new taillight treatment. Even though a mere 500 were built, the base engine for the Charger was the 225-cid Slant Six, with the 318-cid V-8 a much more popular 'base' powerplant for the performance-oriented Chargers. The R/T was the high-performance model in the Charger and Coronet lines. R/Ts featured all standard Charger trim, plus the Magnum '440' four-barrel carb V-8; dual exhaust with chrome tips; TorqueFlite automatic transmission; heavy-duty, manually-adjusted brakes; F70-14 Red Line tires, R/T handling package and Bumblebee stripes. The Charger SE was the sports/luxury model and included all the standard Charger features plus leather and vinyl front bucket seats; simulated woodgrain steering wheel; deep-dish wheel covers; hood-mounted turn signal indicators; simulated woodgrain instrument panel trim and the light group. A limited number of super high-performance Charger 500s were built to fulfill a requirement for NASCAR stock car racing. The 500s were based on standard Chargers with a flush-mounted grille (not recessed into the oval grille opening), fixed headlights and a flush-mounted rear window glass for lower wind resistance.

CHARGER I.D. DATA: See 1966 Dart I.D. Data listing. All models began at 100001 and went up in the unit number sequence.

1969 Dodge, Charger 500 two-door hardtop, V-8

CHARGER SERIES

Model No.	Body/ Style No.	Body Type & Seating	Factory Price	Shipping Weight	Prod. Total
BASE LINE					
XP29	N/A	2-dr HT Cpe-6P	3020/3126	3103/3256	Note 1
R/T LINE					
XS29	N/A	2-dr HT Cpe-6P	3592	3646	Note 1
SE/500 LINE					
XX29	N/A	2-dr SE HT Cpe-6P	3860	3671	Note 1
XX29	N/A	2-dr HT Cpe-6P	3860	3671	Note 1

Note 1: Some 69,100 Dodge Chargers and 20,100 Charger RTs were built during model year 1969. Of these, some 500 standard Chargers were sixes and 68,600 were V-8s. All R/Ts were V-8 powered.

Additional Charger R/T/Daytona/500 Note: The following are known production figures for models equipped with the 426-cid Hemi V-8, according to Mopar authority Galen V. Govier: Charger R/T - 232 two-door hardtops, Charger Daytona (see Historical Footnotes) - 70 two-door hardtops. Additionally,

52 Charger 500 two-door hardtops have been authenticated as being produced with 426 Hemi power, but more may exist.

POLARA/MONACO — (V-8) — Completely restyled once again for 1969, the new Polaras featured what Chrysler advertising people called 'fuselage styling'. Smoother and more rounded than in the past, the new models were a long 18-plus feet overall. The Polara was the base trim level and included all the federally mandated safety features plus the 318-cid V-8 engine; concealed windshield wipers; carpeting; heater and defroster; rear seat foam cushion; 8.25 x 15 tubeless black sidewall tires; cloth and vinyl trim in the hardtops and sedans and all-vinyl trim in convertibles and station wagons. The station wagons also included rear-mounted air deflector and dual action tailgate plus larger, 8.85 x 15 tubeless black sidewall tires. The Polara 500 was the intermediate trim level and included all features found in the Polara plus front bucket seats (with centerfolding armrest) and Deluxe wheel covers. The Monaco was the top trim level of the Polara series. It included all Polara features plus the light group and front and rear seat cushion pads. Sedans had cloth and vinyl interior trim. Two- and four-door hardtops had all-vinyl interior trim. Station wagons had cloth and vinyl interior trim, power tailgate window and, on the nine-passenger model, a lockable third seat well.

POLARA I.D. DATA: See 1966 Dart I.D. Data listing. All models began at 100001 and went up in the unit number sequence.

1969 Dodge, Polara station wagon, V-8

POLARA SERIES

Model No.	Body/ Style No.	Body Type & Seating	Factory Price	Shipping Weight	Prod. Total
BASE LINE					
DL41	N/A	4-dr Sed-6P	3095	3701	Note 1
DL43	N/A	4-dr HT Sed-6P	3188	3731	Note 1
DL23	N/A	2-dr HT Cpe-6P	3117	3646	Note 1
DL27	N/A	2-dr Conv-6P	3377	3791	Note 1
DL45	N/A	4-dr Sta Wag-6P	3522	4161	Note 1
DL46	N/A	4-dr Sta Wag-9P	3629	4211	Note 1
500 LINE					
DM23	N/A	2-dr HT Cpe-6P	3629	3681	Note 1
DM27	N/A	2-dr Conv-5P	3576	3801	Note 1
MONACO LINE					
DH41	N/A	4-dr Sed-6P	3452	3846	Note 1
DH43	N/A	4-dr HT Sed-6P	3591	3891	Note 1
DH23	N/A	2-dr HT Cpe-6P	3528	3811	Note 1
DH46	N/A	4-dr Sta Wag-6P	3917	4306	Note 1
DH46	N/A	4-dr Sta Wag-9P	4046	4361	Note 1

Note 1: Some 117,152 Polara and Monaco passenger cars and station wagons were built during model year 1969. All were V-8-powered. No additional breakouts by model, body style or trim level are available.

CHASSIS FEATURES:

(Dart) Wheelbase: 111 inches. Overall length: 195.4 inches. Tires: 6.50 x 13 tubeless black sidewall on sixes and sedans; 6.95 x 14 on V-8 sedans and 7.00 x 13 on six-cylinder convertibles. Three-speed manual transmission was standard on all Darts, with the three-speed TorqueFlite automatic or four-speed manual transmissions optional.

(Coronet and Charger) Wheelbase: 117 inches. Overall length: 206.6 inches on Coronet sedans, 207.9 inches on Chargers and 210 inches on Coronet station wagons. Tires: 7.75 x 14 tubeless black sidewall on Coronet sedans, 8.25 x 14 on station wagons; F70-14 on Coronet Super Bee, Charger, Charger R/T and Charger 500. The three-speed manual transmission was standard transmission on all models unless noted, with the TorqueFlite three-speed automatic and four-speed manual transmissions optional.

(Polara and Monaco) Wheelbase: 112 inches. Overall length: 220.4 inches on station wagons and 220.8 inches on sedans. Tires: 8.25 x 15 tubeless black sidewall on sedans, 8.85 x 15 on station wagons. Three-speed manual transmission was standard on all models unless

noted, with the three-speed TorqueFlite automatic and four-speed manual transmissions optional.

ENGINES: Same as 1967 with these changes:

(170 Slant Six) 115 hp.383 Magnum V-8. Overhead valve. Cast iron block. Displacement: 383 cid. Bore and stroke: 4.25 x 3.38 inches. Compression ratio: 10.0:1. Brake hp: 335 at 5200 rpm. Five main bearings. Hydraulic valve lifters. Carburetor: one four-barrel.

CONVENIENCE OPTIONS FOR DART: 225-cid Slant Six engine ($46). 273-cid V-8 engine ($79). TorqueFlite automatic transmission ($176 with Slant Six; $191 with small V-8s; $28 with 383-cid V-8). Four-speed manual transmission ($188). Power steering ($85). Power brakes ($43). Console ($53 - GT and GTS models only). Tinted glass ($33). Air conditioning ($361). Two-tone paint ($23). Music Master AM radio ($62). AM/FM radio ($135). AM/FM 8-Track stereo ($196). Custom steering wheel with full horn ring ($15). Simulated woodgrain Sport steering wheel ($32). White sidewall tires ($34).

CONVENIENCE OPTIONS FOR CORONET/CHARGER/POLARA/MONACO: '383' two-barrel V-8 ($70). '383' four-barrel V-8 ($68-$138). 440-cid 'Magnum' V-8 ($268). 426-cid 'Hemi' V-8 engine in Coronet Super Bee ($831); in Coronet R/T ($718); in Charger R/T ($648). TorqueFlite automatic transmission ($39-$206). Four-speed manual transmission ($197 - no charge on R/T models). Air conditioning on Coronets and Chargers ($358); on Polaras and Monacos ($395). Power steering on Coronets and Chargers ($100); on Polaras and Monacos ($106). Power brakes ($43). Power front disc brakes ($49). Power seats ($100). Power windows, on Coronets and Chargers ($105); on Polaras and Monacos ($109). Electric clock on Coronets ($18); on Polaras and Monacos ($16). Console ($54). Sure-Grip differential on Coronets and Chargers ($42); on Polaras and Monacos ($48). Super-Light in Polaras and Monacos ($50). Two-tone paint on Coronets ($23); on Polaras and Monacos ($28). Music Master AM radio on Coronets and Chargers ($62); on Polaras and Monacos ($68). AM/FM radio on Coronets ($135). AM/FM Multiplex stereo radio, on Polara and Monaco ($184). AM/8-track stereo, in Coronets and Chargers ($196); in Polaras and Monacos ($200). Automatic speed control on Coronets and Chargers with 383-cid V-8 engines ($58), on Polaras and Monacos ($61). Sun roof in Chargers with vinyl top ($461). Rallye suspension, on Coronets and Chargers ($23); on Polaras and Monacos ($14). Woodgrain steering wheels, on Coronets and Chargers ($27); on Polara ($32). Tilt steering wheel on Polaras ($47). Vinyl top, on Coronets ($89); on Chargers ($94) and on Polaras and Monacos ($104); Chrome stamped 14-inch wheels, on Coronets and Chargers ($86); on Charger SE and Charger 500 ($48). White sidewall tires ($34).

HISTORICAL FOOTNOTES: With the factories backing NASCAR entries, a no-holds war for speedway supremacy was taking place. Aerodynamics became even more important than in the past. Dodge Division found that even the smoothed-over Charger 500 models were not aerodynamic enough to make for a clear-cut advantage over the super-powerful Fords. As a solution, the Daytona Charger was introduced. With an elongated fiberglass nose piece covering the standard grille opening and a huge, roof-high spoiler mounted on the trunk, these wild looking creations could navigate the super speedways at nearly 200 mph, with their big 'Hemi' engines. Bobby Isaac won the Daytona 500 in February 1969 with one of the Hemi-powered Daytona Chargers. To meet NASCAR's rules for homologation, approximately 1,000 Daytona Chargers were built during 1969, for sale to the general public for street use. While not particularly important from a historically significant point of view, the most widely recognized Dodge in the world today is the 'General Lee', a 1969 Dodge Charger used in the television series 'Dukes of Hazzard'. The little Dart Swinger 340s proved to be popular to the economy-minded performance enthusiast. While devoid of conventional creature comforts such as carpeting, what 340s lacked in luxuries, they made up for with outstanding performance. The 340 remains, to this day, as one high point of the 1960's Supercar Era. 1969 also saw the introduction of the famous 'Six-Pak' option on the 340- and 440-cid V-8 engines. Three Holley two-barrel carburetors mounted on an Edelbrock aluminum intake manifold provided a 15-hp boost in power. The result was a strong, fairly economical (when driven on the center carburetor only) engine. 1969 also saw the introduction of the novel 'Super-Light' option for Polaras and Monacos. A single, quartz-halogen light (mounted in the driver's side of the grille) threw out a broad, flat beam of bluish light, which provided much more illumination for the driver, without blinding oncoming traffic. This option was continued for 1970, but was discontinued after only two years. The idea was several years ahead of its time and also met with limited-acceptance from law enforcement officials; in some states this option was illegal.

1970 DODGE

DART SERIES — (6-CYL/V-8) — While new Dodge Darts continued to use the same basic body, restyling of the front and rear ends made it look completely new. The styling was more rakish, with a grille that sloped forward at the top and was divided in the center. The rear had a lower sloped-back look and the taillights were inserted in the simple rear bumper. With introduction of the sporty Challenger the compact line was cut to five versions. The standard Dart was the base trim level of the line and included chrome windshield and rear window moldings; the Dodge name, in script, on the right side of the trunk lid and a similar signature in the center of the hood. The Dart name, in block letters, appeared at the rear of the front fenders, just behind the front wheelwell. Also included was all federally mandated safety equipment; heater and defroster and 6.50 x 13 tubeless black sidewall tires on six-cylinder-equipped cars (7.00 x 13 tubeless black sidewall tires on V-8s). The Dart Swinger 340 was the high-performance version of the Swinger two-door hardtop model and included all standard Dart features plus 340-cid V-8 engine; three-speed manual transmission; 3.23 rear axle ratio; front disc brakes; Firm Ride shock absorbers; Rallye Suspension; E78-14 blackwall fiberglass tires and Dart 340 nameplates on the front fenders, just behind the front wheelwells.

1970 Dodge, Dart Swinger two-door hardtop, V-8

DODGE I.D. DATA: The Vehicle Identification Number was located on a plate attached to left-hand side of dashboard, visible through windshield. The VIN has 13 symbols. (The first four symbols, together, are the Model Number in second column of charts below.) The first symbol identifies the car-line or marque: D=Polara/Monaco; J=Challenger; L=Dart; W=Coronet and X=Charger. The second symbol indicates trim/price level as follows: E=Economy; H=High; K=Police; L=Low; M=Medium; P=Premium; T=Taxi, S=Special. The next two symbols identify the body style as follows: 21=two-door sedan; 23=two-door hardtop; 27=convertible; 29=two-door Sports hardtop; 41=four-door sedan; 43=four-door hardtop; 45=six-passenger station wagon; 46=nine-passenger station wagon. The fifth symbol denotes the engine as follows: (six-cylinder) B=198 cid; C=225 cid; E=special order; (V-8) G=318 cid 2V; H=340 cid 4V (high-performance); J=340 cid 3x2V (high-performance); K=360 cid 2V; L=383 cid 2V; N=383 cid 4V (high-performance); R=426 cid "Street Hemi" 2x4V; T=440 cid 4V; U=440 cid 4V (high-performance); V=440 3x2V (high-performance); Z=special order. The sixth symbol denotes the model year as follows: 0=1970. The seventh symbol denotes the assembly plant, as follows: A=Lynch Rd. (Detroit); B=Hamtramck, Mich.; C=Jefferson Ave. (Detroit); D=Belvedere, Ill.; E=Los Angeles, Calif.; F=Newark, Del.; G=St. Louis Mo.; R=Windsor, Ont. (Canada). The last six symbols are the sequential production number starting at 100001 for each series at each plant. Body code plate located under hood, on left (fender shield, wheelhousing or radiator support) includes S.O. number and trim/paint codes, too numerous to list.

DART SERIES

Model No.	Body/Style No.	Body Type & Seating	Factory Price	Shipping Weight	Prod. Total
LL41	41	4-dr Sed-6P	2485/2595	2843/2963	35,449
LL23	23	2-dr Swinger HT-6P	2468/2579	2261/2461	119,883
LL23	23	2-dr 340 HT-6P	2808	3179	13,785

Note 1: Exactly 191,986 Dodge Dart/Dart Custom/Dart Swinger and Dart Swinger 340 passenger cars were built during

model year 1970. In rounded off totals this included only 3,900 units built in the United States. The additional cars, some 188,100, were manufactured in Canada for the U.S. market. Six-cylinder engines were installed in 69.7 percent of these cars and the rest were V-8s.

Note 2: Data above slash for six/below slash for V-8.

DART CUSTOM SERIES — (6-CYL/V-8) — The Custom was the top trim level Dart for 1970 and included all standard Dart features plus dual horns; wheel lip moldings on hardtop; bodyside moldings on sedan; steering wheel with partial horn ring; pile carpeting and, in sedans, cloth and vinyl bench seats. The Dart Custom name, in block letters, was located on the sides of the front fender, just behind the front wheelwell.

DART CUSTOM I.D. DATA: See 1970 Dodge I.D. Data listing. All models began at 100001 and went up in the unit number sequence.

DART CUSTOM SERIES

Model No.	Body/Style No.	Body Type & Seating	Factory Price	Shipping Weight	Prod. Total
LH42	42	4-dr Sed-6P	2650/2761	2833/2955	23,779
LH23	23	2-dr HT-6P	2677/2788	2843/2965	17,208

Note 1: Data above slash for six/below slash for V-8

1970 Dodge, Coronet R/T two-door convertible, V-8

CORONET DELUXE SERIES — (6-CYL/V-8) — The new Coronet Deluxe was face-lifted with the addition of a new grille. The front bumper consisted of a heavy molding around the grille, which had two, large, oval openings. The rear received an updating also, with the addition of large, delta-shaped taillights. The Coronet Deluxe was the base trim level and included all the federally mandated safety features; the 225-cid Slant Six engine or the 318-cid V-8 engine; all-vinyl front bench seat; color-keyed floor mats; heater and defroster; cigarette lighter; and F78-14 fiberglass belted black sidewall tires. The Dodge name, in block letters, appeared in the center of the rear escutcheon panel and beside the left high-beam headlight, in the grille. No model designation appeared on the outside of the cars. The Coronet Super Bee continued as the high-performance, intermediate-size counterpart to the Dart Swinger 340s. Super Bees included all the Coronet Deluxe features plus a special 383-cid Magnum V-8 engine; three-speed manual transmission with floor-mounted shifter; heavy-duty, automatic adjusting drum brakes; dual horns; heavy-duty front shock absorbers; Rallye Suspension with sway bar (or extra-heavy-duty suspension); three-speed windshield wipers; carpeting; F70-14 fiberglass belted white sidewall or black sidewall tires with raised white letters; and a three-spoke steering wheel with partial horn ring.

CORONET DELUXE I.D. DATA: See 1970 Dodge I.D. Data listing. All models began at 100001 and went up in the unit number sequence.

CORONET DELUXE SERIES

Model No.	Body/Style No.	Body Type & Seating	Factory Price	Shipping Weight	Prod. Total
WL41	41	4-dr Sed-6P	2704/2806	3113/3268	7,894
WL21	21	2-dr Cpe-6P	2669/2771	3068/3238	2,978
WL45	45	4-dr Sta Wag-6P	3048/3150	3628/3728	3,694
WM21	21	2-dr Sup Bee Cpe-6P	3012	3425	3,966
WM23	23	2-dr Sup Bee HT-6P	3074	3390	11,540

Note 1: Data above slash for six/below slash for V-8.

CORONET 440 SERIES — (6-CYL/V-8) — The Coronet 440 was the intermediate trim level Coronet for 1970 and included all the Coronet Deluxe features plus cloth and vinyl front bench seats on sedans; carpeting; three-spoke steering wheel with partial horn ring; and the Coronet 440 name, in block letters, on the leading corners of front fenders.

CORONET 440 I.D. DATA: See 1970 Dodge I.D. Data listing. All models began at 100001 and went up in the sequence unit numbers.

CORONET 440 SERIES

Model No.	Body/Style No.	Body Type & Seating	Factory Price	Shipping Weight	Prod. Total
WH41	41	4-dr Sed-6P	2783/2885	3108/3263	33,258
WH21	21	2-dr Cpe-6P	2743/2845	3088/3243	1,236

Model No.	Body/Style No.	Body Type & Seating	Factory Price	Shipping Weight	Prod. Total
WH23	23	2-dr HT-6P	2805/2907	3108/3263	24,341
WH45	45	4-dr Sta Wag-6P	3156/3258	3623/3778	3,964
WH46	46	4-dr Sta Wag-9P	3368	3803	3,772

Additional Note: In figures rounded off to the nearest 100 units, some 58,800 Dodge Coronet 440 passenger cars were built during the 1970 model year, including 2,000 sixes and 56,800 V-8s.

Note 1: Data above slash for six/below slash for V-8.

CORONET 500/R/T SERIES — (6-CYL/V-8) — The Coronet 500 was the top trim level Coronet and included all the 440 features plus belt moldings on hardtops and convertibles; pedal dress-up kit; deluxe 14-inch wheel covers; all-vinyl front bucket seats; G78-14 fiberglass belted tires and the Coronet 500 model designation in block letters, on the front fender. The R/T continued to be the high-performance version of the Coronet 500 series and included all the 500 features plus the 440-cid Magnum V-8 engine; TorqueFlite automatic transmission; heavy-duty 70 amp/hour battery; heavy-duty automatic adjusting drum brakes; heavy-duty front and rear shock absorbers; extra-heavy-duty suspension; three-speed windshield wipers; all-vinyl front bucket seats; carpeting; cigar lighter; F70-14 fiberglass belted white sidewall tires or black sidewall tires with raised white letters. Also included were two hood scoops near the outside edges of the hood. R/T model designations were carried on the simulated hood scoops (located on the rear quarter panels) and in the center of the rear escutcheon panel below the Dodge name. All R/T models included blacked-out escutcheon panels and bumblebee stripes across the trunk lid and down the rear fendersides.

CORONET 500 AND R/T I.D. DATA: See 1970 Dodge I.D. Data listing. All models began at 100001 and went up in the unit number sequence.

CORONET 500 AND R/T SERIES

Model No.	Body/Style No.	Body Type & Seating	Factory Price	Shipping Weight	Prod. Total
CORONET 500 SERIES					
WP41	41	4-dr Sed-5P	3082	3283	2,890
WP23	23	2-dr HT-5P	3048	3263	8,247
WP27	27	2-dr Conv-5P	3188	3373	924
WP45	45	4-dr Sta Wag-6P	3404	3743	1,857
WP46	46	4-dr Sta Wag-8P	3514	3813	1,779
R/T SERIES					
WS23	23	2-dr R/T HT-5P	3569	3573	2,319
WS27	27	2-dr R/T Conv-5P	3785	3638	296

Additional Coronet Super Bee/R/T Note: The following are known production figures for models equipped with the 426-cid Hemi V-8, according to Mopar authority Galen V. Govier: Super Bee - 32 two-door hardtops and 4 two-door coupes, Coronet R/T - 13 two-door hardtops and production of 426 Hemi-powered convertibles has been authenticated but the total production number is N/A. Additionally, the following are known production figures for models equipped with the 440-cid "Six Pak" V-8, according to Galen V. Govier: Super Bee - 1,072 two-door hardtops and 196 two-door coupes, Coronet R/T - 194 two-door hardtops and 16 convertibles.

1970 Dodge, Charger R/T two-door hardtop, V-8

CHARGER SERIES — (6-CYL/V-8) — The 1970 Charger continued to use the same body as in 1969, with minor trim changes. The high-performance version of the Charger for 1970 was again the Charger R/T, powered by the 440-cid Magnum V-8, and was a strong performer. A special interior and exterior trim package, called the Special Edition (SE), was offered for both Charger 500s and Charger R/Ts. It included deep-dish wheel covers; hood-mounted turn signal indicators; leather bucket seats and woodgrain steering wheel and instrument panel trim. The standard Charger was the base trim level and included all federally mandated safety features; the 225-cid Slant Six engine or 318-cid V-8 engine; vinyl front bench seat; carpeting; three-spoke steering wheel (with partial horn ring); heater and defroster; cigar lighter; heavy-duty suspension; heavy-duty front sway bar; rear bumper guards; concealed headlights; and F78-14 fiberglass belted black sidewall tires on sixes, G78-14 on V-8s. The

Charger 500 was the intermediate trim level Charger and included all the standard Charger trim plus vinyl front bucket seats, electric clock and wheel lip moldings. The Charger R/T was the high-performance entry in the Charger lineup and included (in addition to the 440-cid V-8 engine) heavy-duty 70 amp/hour battery; heavy-duty automatic adjusting drum brakes; front and rear heavy-duty shock absorbers; front and rear Rally Suspension with sway bar; TorqueFlite automatic transmission; three-speed windshield wipers; dual exhaust; R/T handling package; bumble-bee stripe or longitudinal tape stripe; F70-14 fiberglass belted white or black sidewall tires (with raised white letters) and special R/T identification on the left side of the grille and on the simulated bodyside scoops.

CHARGER I.D. DATA: See 1970 Dodge I.D. Data listing. All models began at 100001 and went up in the unit number sequence.

CHARGER SERIES

Model No.	Body/Style No.	Body Type & Seating	Factory Price	Shipping Weight	Prod. Total
CHARGER					
XH29	N/A	2-dr HT-6P	3001/3108	3228/3363	Note 1
CHARGER 500					
XP29	N/A	2-dr HT-5P	3139/3246	3228/3362	Note 1
CHARGER R/T					
XS29	N/A	2-dr HT-5P	3711	3638	10,337

Note 1: The combined production of Models XH29 and XP29 was recorded as 39,431 units. No further breakout between the two models is available.

Note 2: In figures rounded off to the nearest 100 units, some 49,800 Dodge Chargers were built during model year 1970, including 300 sixes and 49,500 V-8s. (Only 7.4 percent of these cars had four-speed manual transmission attachment and 38.1 percent had an optional V-8.) The base V-8 was installed in 61.4 percent of the remaining Chargers, while another 0.5 percent were the scarce, but not highly collectible, six-cylinder cars.

Note 3: Data above slash for six/below slash for V-8.

Additional ChargerR/T Note: The following is a known production figure for models equipped with the 426-cid Hemi V-8, according to Mopar authority Galen V. Govier: Charger R/T - 112 two-door hardtops. Additionally, the following is a known production figure for models equipped with the 440-cid "Six-Pak" V-8, according to Galen V. Govier: Charger R/T - 116 two-door hardtops.

1970 Dodge, Monaco four-door hardtop, V-8

POLARA SERIES — (6-CYL/V-8) — Slightly restyled for 1970, the new full-size Dodge series was completely reshuffled. A massive grille molding formed the front bumper on the Polara models and the large, oblong taillights were housed in a new rear bumper. The Polara Special was the base trim level for 1970 and included all federally mandated safety features plus chrome windshield and rear window moldings and the Dodge name, in block letters, spaced across the front of the hood. Dodge nameplates were also seen on the right side of the trunk. Midyear Polara Specials were introduced primarily for fleet, taxi and police duty. These were introduced on March 17 and represented an economy model with a 225 cid/145 hp six standard in the sedan while the 318-cid V-8 was standard in station wagons. The Polara was the intermediate trim level in the series and included all the Special features plus the 318-cid V-8 engine; cloth and vinyl interior trim in hardtop and sedan models; vinyl interiors in the convertible and station wagon models; color-keyed vinyl bodyside moldings; concealed wipers; pile carpeting; three-spoke steering wheel with padded hub; heater and defroster; cigarette lighter; glovebox lock; sway bar and thick padded front and rear seat foam cushions. The convertible also had a power top and station wagons had roof-mounted air deflectors and dual action tailgate. Two-door hardtops and four-door sedans had G78-15 fiberglass belted tires, four-door hardtops and convertibles had H78-15 fiberglass belted tires and station wagons had J78-15 fiberglass belted black sidewall tires. The Polara Custom was the top trim level and included all the Polara features plus Deluxe wheel covers; 290-hp V-8 engine; wide sill moldings on four-door models; belt molding

on hardtops; steering wheel with partial horn ring; H78-15 fiberglass belted black sidewall tires and the interior light group. The Monaco was the luxury version of the Polara series and included all the Polara Custom features (except side moldings) plus simulated walnut instrument panel trim and door inserts; pedal dress-up kit; two-door hardtop and station wagon all-vinyl interiors (with split front bench seat and center armrests); and four-door sedan and hardtop vinyl and cloth interiors (with front center armrests). Station wagons also had J78-15 fiberglass belted black sidewall tires, cargo compartment carpeting and the nine-passenger station wagons had a lockable third seat well.

POLARA I.D. DATA: See 1970 Dodge I.D. Data listing. All models began at 100001 and went up in the unit number sequence.

POLARA SERIES

Model No.	Body/Style No.	Body Type & Seating	Factory Price	Shipping Weight	Prod. Total
POLARA SPECIAL					
DE41	41	4-dr Sed-6P	2960/3065	3745/3805	Note 1
DE45	45	4-dr Sta Wag-6P	3513	4180	Note 1
DE46	46	4-dr Sta Wag-9P	3621	4325	Note 1
POLARA					
DL41	41	4-dr Sed-6P	3222	3828	18,740
DL43	43	4-dr HT-6P	3316	3873	19,223
DL23	23	2-dr HT-6P	3244	3973	15,243
DL27	27	2-dr Conv-6P	3527	3853	842
DL45	45	4-dr Sta Wag-6P	3670	4203	3,074
DL46	46	4-dr Sta Wag-9P	3778	4258	3,548
POLARA CUSTOM					
DM41	41	4-dr Sed-6P	3426	3998	Note 1
DM43	43	4-dr HT-6P	3528	4028	Note 1
DM23	23	2-dr HT-6P	3458	3948	Note 1
MONACO					
DH41	41	4-dr Sed-6P	3604	4033	4,721
DH43	43	4-dr HT-6P	3743	4068	10,974
DH23	23	2-dr HT-6P	3679	3973	3,522
DH45	45	4-dr Sta Wag-6P	4110	4443	2,211
DH46	46	4-dr Sta Wag-9P	4242	4498	3,284

Note 1: Production of similar body styles in all Polara series was recorded together, which is listed under the Polara series grouping in the chart above. The only additional breakouts available are by passenger car-line and engine. They were recorded (in figures rounded off to the nearest 100 units) as follows: Polara: A total of 50,400 passenger cars including 132 sixes and 50,268 V-8s. Polara Custom: A total of 9,300 passenger cars, all V-8s. Polara station wagon totals cannot be segregated in this manner, since they were combined with totals for Monaco station wagons.

Note 2: Data above slash for six/below slash for V-8.

1970 Dodge, Challenger R/T two-door convertible, V-8

CHALLENGER SERIES — (6-CYL/V-8) — The Challenger was Dodge's answer to the Mustang and Camaro and was offered in two body styles: a two-door hardtop and convertible. Challengers featured a low profile with a full-width, scoop-like grille opening. Bodysides had the familiar 'Coke-bottle' profile, with raised rear fenders tapering down at the taillights. Two large, rectangular taillights nearly filled the rear escutcheon panel, with a small, license plate-width aluminum panel left to hold the Dodge name, in block letters. The Challenger Special Edition was the luxury version of the line and included a padded vinyl roof with a small rear window, luxurious interior appointments and special exterior ornamentation. The R/T was the high-performance version of the Challenger and included all the standard Challenger features plus electric clock; 383-cid four-barrel V-8 engine; instrument panel Rallye cluster; front and rear Rallye Suspension with sway bar; heavy-duty drum brakes; F70-14 fiberglass belted black sidewall tires (with raised white letters); longitudinal tape or bumblebee stripes and special R/T exterior ornamentation. On Jan. 8, 1970, the Challenger T/A two-door hardtop was announced to legalize the model for Sports Car Club of America (SCCA)

Trans-Am racing. It had a 340-cid "Six-Pak" (three two-barrel carbs) V-8. It listed for $4,056 and a production run of 2,500 units (one for each dealer) was planned. On March 17, 1970, a lower-priced Challenger called "The Deputy" was announced. It came with a 198-cid six-cylinder engine with a single-barrel carburetor and listed for $2,724. A 318 cid/230 hp engine was also available in this model. Among its economy features was fixed rear quarter windows.

CHALLENGER I.D. DATA: See 1970 Dodge I.D. Data listing. All models began at 100001 and went up in the unit number sequence.

CHALLENGER SERIES

Model No.	Body/Style No.	Body Type & Seating	Factory Price	Shipping Weight	Prod. Total
JH23	23	2-dr HT-4P	2851/2953	3006/3118	53,337
JH29	29	2-dr SE Fml HT-4P	3083/3185	3028/3148	6,584
JH27	27	2-dr Conv-4P	3120/3198	3535/3470	3,173
LH23	23	2-dr HT-4P	2724/2803	N/A/N/A	N/A

R/T SERIES

JS23	23	2-dr HT-4P	3266	3402	14,889
JS29	29	2-dr SE Fml HT-4P	3498	3437	3,979
JS27	27	2-dr Conv-4P	3535	3467	1,070

T/A SERIES

SS23	23	2-dr HT-4P	4056	N/A	1,000+

Note 1: The combined model year output of Challenger and Challenger R/T models was 83,032 cars. Of this total, 13.4 percent were sixes; 60 percent had the standard V-8 and 26.6 percent had optional V-8 installations. In addition, 12.7 percent had four-speed manual transmission; 36.2 percent had styled steel wheels; 63.2 percent wore vinyl tops; 94.3 percent had front bucket seats and 36.5 percent had dual exhaust.

Note 2: Data above slash for six/below slash for V-8.

Additional Challenger R/T Note: The following are known production figures for models equipped with the 426-cid Hemi V-8, according to Mopar authority Galen V. Govier: Challenger R/T - 287 two-door hardtops and 9 convertibles, Challenger R/T SE - 60 two-door hardtops. Additionally, the following are known production figures for models equipped with the 440-cid "Six-Pak" V-8, according to Galen V. Govier: Challenger R/T - 1,640 two-door hardtops and 99 convertibles, Challenger R/T SE - 296 two-door hardtops.

ENGINES:

(198 Slant Six) Overhead valve. Cast iron block. Displacement: 198 cid. Bore and stroke: 3.40 x 3.64 inches. Compression ratio: 8.4:1. Brake hp: 125 at 4400 rpm. Four main bearings. Solid valve lifters. Carburetor: one-barrel.

(225 Slant Six) Overhead valve. Cast iron block. Displacement: 225 cid. Bore and stroke: 3.41 x 4.13 inches. Compression ratio: 8.4:1. Brake hp: 145 at 4000 rpm. Four main bearings. Solid valve lifters. Carburetor: one-barrel.

(318 V-8) Overhead valve. Cast iron block. Displacement: 318 cid. Bore and stroke: 3.91 x 3.31 inches. Compression ratio: 9.0:1. Brake hp: 230 at 4400 rpm. Five main bearings. Hydraulic valve lifters. Carburetor: two-barrel.

(340 V-8) Overhead valve. Cast iron block. Displacement: 340 cid. Bore and stroke: 4.04 x 3.31 inches. Compression ratio: 10.0:1. Brake hp: 275 at 5600 rpm. Five main bearings. Hydraulic valve lifters. Carburetor: Carter 'Thermo-Quad' four-barrel.

(340 'Six-Pak' V-8) Overhead valve. Cast iron block. Displacement: 340 cid. Bore and stroke: 4.04 x 3.31 inches. Compression ratio: 10.0:1. Brake hp: 290 at 4400 rpm. Five main bearings. Hydraulic valve lifters. Carburetor: three Holley two-barrel.

(383 two-barrel V-8) Overhead valve. Cast iron block. Displacement: 383 cid. Bore and stroke: 4.25 x 3.38 inches. Compression ratio: 9.2:1. Brake hp: 290 at 4400 rpm. Five main bearings. Hydraulic valve lifters. Carburetor: Carter BBD two-barrel.

(383 four-barrel V-8) Overhead valve. Cast iron block. Displacement: 383 cid. Bore and stroke: 4.25 x 3.38 inches. Compression ratio: 10.0:1. Brake hp: 330 at 5200 rpm. Five main bearings. Hydraulic valve lifters. Carburetor: four-barrel.

(383 four-barrel V-8) Overhead valve. Cast iron block. Displacement: 383 cid. Bore and stroke: 4.25 x 3.38 inches. Compression ratio: 10.0:1. Brake hp: 335 at 5000 rpm. Five main bearings. Hydraulic valve lifters. Carburetor: Carter BBD four-barrel.

(440 Magnum V-8) Overhead valve. Cast iron block. Displacement: 440 cid. Bore and stroke: 4.32 x 3.75 inches. Compression ratio: 10.0:1. Brake hp: 350 at 4000 rpm. Five main bearings. Hydraulic valve lifters. Carburetor: Carter AFS four-barrel.

(440 Magnum V-8) Overhead valve. Cast iron block. Displacement: 440 cid. Bore and stroke: 4.32 x 3.75 inches. Compression ratio: 10.0:1. Brake hp: 375 at 4000 rpm. Five main bearings. Hydraulic valve lifters. Carburetor: Carter AFS four-barrel.

(440 'Six-Pack' V-8) Overhead valve. Cast iron block. Displacement: 440 cid. Bore and stroke: 4.32 x 3.75 inches. Compression ratio: 10.1:1. Brake hp: 390 at 4700 rpm. Five main bearings. Hydraulic valve lifters. Carburetor: three Holley two-barrel.

(426 'Street Hemi' V-8) Overhead valve with hemispherical combustion chamber. Cast iron block. Displacement: 426 cid. Bore and stroke: 425 x 3.75 inches. Compression ratio: 10.25:1. Brake hp: 425 at 5000 rpm. Five main bearings. Hydraulic valve lifters. Carburetor: two Carter AFB four-barrel.

DODGE/DART/CHARGER/CHALLENGER POWERTRAIN OPTIONS: Dart '225' Slant Six ($46). Dart '318' V-8 ($79). TorqueFlite in Dart with Slant Six ($175); with V-8 ($191). Dart four-speed manual transmission ($188). Dodge/Charger/Challenger 383 cid/290 hp V-8 ($70). High-performance 383 cid/350 hp V-8, in R/T and Super Bee (standard); in other Challenger/Coronet models ($138). Magnum 440 cid/375 hp V-8, in Challenger R/T ($131). Magnum 440 cid/350 hp V-8 in Challenger R/T, base Coronet and Super Bee ($250); same in Coronet R/T, Polara Custom and Monaco ($119); same in base Polara ($189). Street Hemi 428 cid/425 hp V-8, in Challenger ($779); in Charger R/T ($648); in Coronet Super Bee ($848); in Coronet R/T ($718).

DODGE/DART/CHARGER/CHALLENGER CONVENIENCE OPTIONS: Power steering ($85). Power brakes ($43). Tinted glass ($33). Air conditioning ($361). Two-tone paint ($23). Music Master AM radio ($62). AM/FM radio ($135). AM radio with 8-track tape ($196). Simulated woodgrain Sport steering wheel ($32). White sidewall tires ($34).

CHASSIS FEATURES:

(Dart) Wheelbase: 111 inches. Overall length: 197 inches. Tires: D78-14 fiberglass belted black sidewalls (E70-14 on Swinger 340). Three-speed manual transmission was standard on all Darts, with the three-speed TorqueFlite automatic or four-speed manual transmissions optional.

(Coronet and Charger) Wheelbase: 117 inches. Overall length: 210 inches on Coronet sedans; 212 inches on Coronet station wagons and 208 inches on Chargers. Tires: F78-14 on Coronets and Charger V-8s, G78-14 on Coronet station wagons and F70-14 fiberglass belted black sidewall on Coronet and Charger R/T. Three-speed manual transmission was standard on all models unless noted, with TorqueFlite three-speed automatic and four-speed manual transmissions optional.

(Polara and Monaco) Wheelbase: 122 inches. Overall length: 220 inches on sedans and 224 inches on station wagons. Tires: H78-15 fiberglass belted black sidewall on all sedans, J78-15 on all station wagons. Three-speed manual transmission was standard on all models unless noted, with TorqueFlite three-speed automatic and four-speed manual transmissions optional.

HISTORICAL FOOTNOTES: 1970 was a significant year for Dodge for several reasons. It was the last time a convertible would be offered in either the Coronet line or the Polara line. The Super-Light optional driving light for Polara and Monaco models was also discontinued because of less-than-enthusiastic public and official acceptance. Dodge introduced 1970 models on Sept. 23, 1969, and a total of 503,392 Dodges were produced during that year, which was 7.07 percent of the market in 1970. The little Dart Swinger 340s continued to be popular, in spite of the introduction of the sexy looking Challengers. The 340 Swingers were quick cars and earned considerably lower insurance premiums than the 'pony cars' such as Challengers. With the popularity of Trans American sedan racing during 1970, Dodge jumped on the bandwagon with the introduction of the Challenger T/A. This special version of the Challenger included the 340-cid V-8 engine and four-speed manual transmission as standard equipment as well as special T/A exterior ornamentation. Unfortunately this was meant to be a limited-production model and little more than 1,000 of the T/As were built. Chrysler built 1,543 "Street Hemi" engines for Dodges and Plymouths this year. Of these 482 were used in Dodge models, as follows: (Coronet Super Bee hardtop) 21 four-speed and 11 TorqueFlite; (Coronet Super Bee coupe) 4 four-speeds and no TorqueFlite; (Coronet R/T hardtop) 4 four-speed and 9 TorqueFlite; (Coronet R/T convertible) one with four-speed; (Charger R/T) 112 with no transmission break-out; (Challenger R/T hardtop) 137 four-speed and 150 TorqueFlite; (Challenger R/T convertible) 5 four-speed and 4 Torque-Flite; (Challenger R/T SE hardtop) 23 four-speed and 37 TorqueFlite.

1971 DODGE

1971 Dodge, Demon '340' two-door coupe, V-8

DEMON SERIES — (6-CYL/V-8) — Given only slight grille and trim restyling for 1971, the Dart sedan and hardtop continued as popular Dodge products. A new coupe version of the Dart, utilizing Plymouth's Duster body, was also introduced. Dubbed the Demon, this model rode on a chassis with a three-inch shorter wheelbase and overall length was reduced about four inches. The Demon was the base 'value package' version of the Dart series and included all the federally mandated safety features; pivoting rear quarter windows; 198-cid Slant Six engine; black rubber floor mats; and 6.45 x 14 polyester black sidewall tires. On cars with V-8 power, 6.95 x 14 black sidewall tires were substituted. Demon nameplates were located on the right side of the rear escutcheon panel and on the front fenders, just behind the front wheelwells. A special, high-performance Demon 340 was powered by a 340-cid V-8 engine with three-speed manual transmission as standard equipment. Also included in the 340 package were E70-14 belted black sidewall tires; performance bodyside and rear deck panel tape stripes; front and rear Rallye Suspension (with sway bar); and floor-mounted transmission shifter. A Demon "Sizzler" was introduced Feb. 9, 1971, as a package for the base Demon. Its price of $141 ($131 V-8) included side hood stripes; rallye wheels; racing mirrors and a special steering wheel among 13 extras. Later, an optional hood was announced for the Demon 340 featuring dual air scoops and a pair of tie-down pins.

DODGE I.D. DATA: The Vehicle Identification Number was located on a plate attached to left-hand side of dashboard, visible through windshield. The VIN has 13 symbols. (The first four symbols, together, are the Model Number in second column of charts below.) The first symbol identifies the car-line or marque: D=Polara/Monaco; J=Challenger; L=Dart; W=Coronet and X=Charger. The second symbol indicates trim/price level as follows: E=Economy; H=High; K=Police; L=Low; M=Medium; P=Premium; T=Taxi; S=Special. The next two symbols identify the body style, as follows: 21=two-door sedan; 23=two-door hardtop; 27=convertible; 29=two-door Sports hardtop; 41=four-door sedan; 43=four-door hardtop; 45=six-passenger station wagon; 46=nine-passenger station wagon. The fifth symbol denotes the engine as follows: (six-cylinder) B=198 cid; C=225 cid; E=special order; (V-8) G=318 cid 2V; H=340 cid 4V (high-performance); J=340 cid 3x2V (high-performance); K=360 cid 2V; L=383 cid 2V; N=383 cid 4V (high-performance); R=426 cid "Street Hemi" 2x4V; T=440 cid 4V; U=440 cid 4V (high-performance); V=440 3x2V (high-performance); Z=special order. The sixth symbol denotes the model year as follows: 1=1971. The seventh symbol denotes the assembly plant, as follows: A=Lynch Rd. (Detroit); B=Hamtramck, Mich.; C=Jefferson Ave. (Detroit); D=Belvedere, Ill.; E=Los Angeles, Calif.; F=Newark, Del.; G=St. Louis, Mo.; R=Windsor, Ont. (Canada). The last six symbols are the sequential production number starting at 100001 for each series at each plant. Body code plate located under hood, on left (fender shield, wheel-housing or radiator support) includes S.O. number and trim/paint codes, too numerous to list.

DEMON SERIES

Model No.	Body/ Style No.	Body Type & Seating	Factory Price	Shipping Weight	Prod. Total
LL29	29	2-dr Cpe-6P	2343/2476	2845/2995	69,861
LM29	29	2-dr 340 Cpe-6P	2721	3165	10,098

Note 1: Data above slash for six/below slash for V-8.

DART SERIES — (6-CYL/V-8) — Dart was the base trim level in the Dart sedan and hardtop lineup and included all federally mandated safety and pollution systems, front and rear armrests, ashtrays, cigarette lighter, concealed spare tire, rubber floor mats, glovebox with rotary latch, heater and defroster, dome light, parking brake and brake system warning lights,

all-vinyl bench seats, three-spoke steering wheel with padded horn button, two-speed electric windshield wipers, 198-cid Slant Six (or 318-cid V-8) and vent wings. Dart Swinger and Custom models also included dual note horns, drip rail and wheel lip moldings, three-spoke steering wheel (with padded hub and horn tabs) and carpeting. Custom trim added bodyside moldings and ventless side windows. Each entry earned model identification on the front sides just behind the front wheel openings. A lower priced Swinger Special two-door hardtop was announced in October 1970.

DART I.D. DATA: See 1971 Dodge I.D. Data listing. All models began at 100001 and went up in the unit number sequence.

DART/SWINGER/CUSTOM SERIES

Model No.	Body/ Style No.	Body Type & Seating	Factory Price	Shipping Weight	Prod. Total
DART SERIES					
LL41	41	4-dr Sed-6P	2450/2600	2900/3050	32,711
LL23	23	2-dr Spec HT-6P	2402/2552	2900/3050	13,485
SWINGER SERIES					
LH23	23	2-dr HT-6P	2561/2601	2900/3050	102,480
CUSTOM SERIES					
LH41	41	4-dr Sed-6P	2609/2759	2900/3050	21,785

Note 1: Data above slash for six/below slash for V-8.

1971 Dodge, Coronet Crestwood station wagon, V-8

CORONET SERIES — (6-CYL/V-8) — In an effort to further segregate the Coronet from the Charger, 1971 saw the introduction of an all-new Coronet that was mounted on a chassis with a wheelbase of 118 inches. Styling was slightly more rounded than in the previous year. A full-width grille opening was accented by a large surround that served as the front bumper. Horizontal grille bars were highlighted by the triangular Dodge symbol, first introduced in 1964. A subtle 'Coke bottle' profile led to a simply styled rear end with two large rectangular taillights (plus the license holder) housed in the rear bumper. For 1971, Coronet intermediate-size Dodges were offered only in four-door sedan and station wagon models. The Coronet was the base trim level and included all federally mandated safety and pollution equipment; 225-cid Slant Six or 318-cid V-8 engine; color-keyed rubber floor mats; a single horn and no exterior moldings (except on windshield and rear window). Also included were a three-spoke steering wheel, rear ashtray and extra-thick foam seat cushions. Station wagons added heavy-duty brakes; drip rail moldings and three-way tailgate. The Coronet model designation was carried, in script, on the front fenders, just behind the wheelwell.

CORONET I.D. DATA: See 1971 Dodge I.D. Data listing. All models began at 100001 and went up in the unit number sequence.

CORONET SERIES

WL41	41	4-dr Sed-6P	2777/2872	3245/3360	11,794
WL45	45	4-dr Sta Wag-6P	3101/3196	3745/3810	5,470

Note 1: Data above slash for six/below slash for V-8.

CORONET CUSTOM SERIES — (6-CYL/V-8) — The Custom was the intermediate trim level in the Coronet series and included all the standard Coronet features plus color-keyed carpeting; dual note horns; wheel opening, bodyside and drip rail moldings; and three-spoke steering wheel (with padded horn bars).

CORONET CUSTOM I.D. DATA: See 1971 Dodge I.D. Data listing. All models began at 100001 and went up in the unit number sequence.

CORONET CUSTOM SERIES

Model No.	Body/ Style No.	Body Type & Seating	Factory Price	Shipping Weight	Prod. Total
WH41	41	4-dr Sed-6P	2951/3046	3250/3365	37,817
WH45	45	4-dr Sta Wag-6P	3278/3373	3750/3815	5,365
WH46	46	4-dr Sta Wag-9P	3454	3890	5,717

Note 1: Data above slash for six/below slash for V-8.

1971 Dodge, Coronet Brougham four-door sedan, V-8

BROUGHAM/CRESTWOOD SERIES — (6-CYL/V-8) — The Brougham was the top trim level sedan and the Crestwood was the top trim level station wagon in the Coronet series. These cars included all Custom features. The Brougham sedan added folding front seat center armrest; ashtray; glovebox light; ignition with time delay lamp; map and courtesy lights; pedal dress-up kit; upper door frame moldings; rear door automatic entrance light; and deluxe wheel covers. The Crestwood station wagon also included wheel opening moldings; bright upper door frame and quarter window moldings; woodgrain side panels (with bright moldings) and, in its nine-passenger form, a tailgate inside safety latch.

BROUGHAM/CRESTWOOD I.D. DATA: See 1971 Dodge I.D. Data listing. All models began at 100001 and went up in the unit number sequence.

BROUGHAM/CRESTWOOD SERIES

WP41	41	4-dr Sed-6P	3332	3375	4,700
WP45	45	4-dr Sta Wag-6P	3601	3845	2,884
WP46	46	4-dr Sta Wag-6P	3682	3900	3,981

CHARGER SERIES — (6-CYL/V-8) — The Charger was completely restyled for 1971 to further segregate it from the Coronet series. Chargers rode on a new 115-inch wheelbase chassis and were expanded to six coupes and hardtops in three series. All models were semi-fastback coupes featuring rear quarter window styling that swept up from the fender to meet the sloping upper window frame. The full-width bumper/grille shell was split by a large vertical divider on all Chargers and the rear end featured a small trunk lip spoiler and six square taillights located in the oval rear bumper. The standard Charger was the base trim level and included all federally mandated safety and pollution equipment; 225-cid Slant Six (or 318-cid V-8); cigarette lighter; dual horns; color-keyed carpeting; inside day/night minor; roof drip rail and wheelwell moldings and two-speed windshield wipers. The Charger 500 was the intermediate trim level Charger and included all the standard Charger features plus ashtray lights; glovebox, map and courtesy lights; pedal dress-up kit; sill moldings; bucket seats; deluxe wheel covers; and '500' exterior badges. The Charger Super Bee was patterned after the Coronet Super Bee to offer the buyer a low-cost, high-performance package. In addition to the standard Charger features, Super Bees also included a 59 amp/hour battery; heavy-duty brakes; heavy-duty shock absorbers; Rallye Suspension; Rallye instrument cluster; floor-mounted three-speed manual transmission; and 383-cid V-8 engine. The R/T was the more luxurious high-performance version of the Charger and included all the features of the Charger 500 plus 70 amp/hour battery; heavy-duty brakes and shock absorbers; pedal dress-up kit; extra heavy-duty Rallye suspension; TorqueFlite automatic transmission or four-speed manual transmission; 440-cid Magnum V-8 engine; and the R/T designation on the exterior of the body.

1971 Dodge, Charger Super Bee two-door hardtop, V-8

CHARGER I.D. DATA: See 1971 Dodge I.D. Data listing. All models began at 100001 and went up in the unit number sequence.

CHARGER SERIES

Model No.	Body/ Style No.	Body Type & Seating	Factory Price	Shipping Weight	Prod. Total
WL21	21	2-dr Cpe-6P	2707/2802	3215/3325	Note 1
WH23	23	2-dr HT-6P	2975/3070	3240/3350	Note 1

500 SERIES

WP23	23	2-dr HT-5P	3223	3350	11,948
WP23	23	2-dr Sup Bee HT-5P	3271	3640	5,054
WP29	29	2-dr SE HT-5P	3422	3375	15,811

R/T SERIES

WS23	23	2-dr HT-5P	3777	3685	3,118

Note 1: Production of styles WL21 and WH23 was recorded as a single total: 46,183 units. Since Dodge combined rounded off totals of Coronets and Chargers this season, it is impossible to determine how many Chargers were equipped with sixes or V-8s.

Note 2: Data above slash for six/below slash for V-8.

ADDITIONAL CHARGER SUPER BEE/R/T NOTE: The following are known production figures for models equipped with the 426-cid Hemi V-8, according to Mopar authority Galen V. Govier: Charger Super Bee - 22 two-door hardtops, Charger R/T - 63 two-door hardtops. Additionally, the following are known production figures for models equipped with the 440-cid "Six-Pak" V-8, according to Galen V. Govier: Charger Super Bee - 99 two-door hardtops, Charger R/T - 178 two-door hardtops.

1971 Dodge, Monaco two-door hardtop, V-8

POLARA/MONACO SERIES — (6-CYL/V-8) — Continuing to use the same body as introduced in 1969, the 1971 Polara featured slight trim updating to separate it from the previous year's models. A new grille, featuring horizontal bars with two wider center bars, ran the full width of the car. The rear end treatment consisted of tail and back-up lights housed behind a horizontal slotted bar arrangement that was raised slightly, at the center of the bottom bar, to house the license plate. Polara was the base trim level and included all federally mandated safety and pollution equipment; air control system; front and rear armrests; front and rear ashtrays; 46 amp/hour battery; cigarette lighter; color-keyed carpeting; dual horns; dome and parking brake system warning lights; inside day/night mirror; outside left manual mirror; three-spoke steering wheel (with padded hub); electric windshield washers and wipers; and the '225' six or '318' V-8. The Dodge name, in block letters, was spaced evenly across the front of the hood and trunk lid and the Polara model designation was located directly below the rear fender marker lights on each side. Polara Custom was the intermediate trim level in the Polara series and included all Polara features plus bodyside moldings with a vinyl insert; wheel opening moldings; foam rubber seat cushions; and the Custom model designation on the rear fenders. The base Polara four-door hardtop was a midyear model announced on Jan. 20, 1971. Brougham was the top trim level of the Polara series and included all features of the Custom plus folding front center armrest; 59 amp/hour battery; ashtray, glovebox and trunk lights; headlight-on warning signal; front bumper surround moldings; pedal dress-up kit; upper door sill moldings; rear door automatic entrance light switches; deluxe wheel covers and 383-cid two-barrel V-8 engine. Monaco was the luxury model of the Polara line and included all Brougham features plus nylon carpeting; cornering lights; dome/map lights; upper door frame moldings on four-door models and a steering wheel with padded hub and horn tabs. Monacos featured a grille of die-cast zinc, in a rectangular slot pattern, which was duplicated at the rear and featured side-to-side taillights. The Monaco name appeared, in script, directly above the bodyside feature line and on the right side of the trunk lid.

POLARA/MONACO I.D. DATA: See 1971 Dodge I.D. Data listing. All models began at 100001 and went up in the unit number sequence.

POLARA/MONACO SERIES

POLARA SERIES

DE41	41	4-dr Sed-6P	3298/3409	3755/3820	21,578
DE23	23	2-dr HT-6P	3319/3430	3715/3795	11,535
DE43	43	4-dr HT-6P	3497	3875	2,487
DL41	41	4-dr Cus Sed-6P	3593	3835	13,860
DL43	43	4-dr Cus HT-6P	3681	3875	17,458

Model No.	Body/ Style No.	Body Type & Seating	Factory Price	Shipping Weight	Prod. Total
DL23	23	2-dr Cus HT-6P	3614	3805	9,682
DL45	45	4-dr Cus Wag-6P	3992	3280	Note 1
DL46	46	4-dr Cus Wag-9P	4098	4335	Note 1
DM43	43	4-dr Brghm HT-6P	3884	4035	2,570
DM23	23	2-dr Brghm HT-6P	3818	3965	2,024

MONACO SERIES

DH41	41	4-dr Sed-6P	4223	4050	Note 2
DH43	43	4-dr HT-6P	4362	4080	Note 2
DH23	23	2-dr HT-6P	4298	4000	3,195
DH45	45	4-dr Sta Wag-6P	4689	4525	Note 3
DH46	46	4-dr Sta Wag-9P	4821	4580	Note 3

Note 1: Total production of Polara Custom station wagons was 9,682 units, which included both DL45 and DL46 models.

Note 2: In figures rounded off to the nearest 100 units, 16,900 Monaco four-door passenger cars were built during the 1971 model year. All were V-8 powered. No breakout between Monaco four-door sedans and four-door hardtops is available.

Note 3: A total of 5,449 units for combined production of both DH45 and DH46 models is given in Dodge records. However, rounded off totals provided in industry statistics show a slightly higher figure, which varies by 1,480 units. This may be due to inclusion of station wagons built in Canada or, perhaps, station wagons built for police, taxi, emergency and other professional-use purposes.

Note 4: Data above slash for six/below slash for V-8.

Note 5: The totals given in the chart above for Models DE23 and DL41 are estimates, based on calculations from known records and should be considered 'ballpark' figures only. The total given for Model DE41 includes 308 taxicabs and 6,826 police cars.

CHALLENGER SERIES — (6-CYL/V-8) — The Challenger continued to use the same body as originally introduced back in 1970 with minor trim changes, namely slightly revised grille and taillight treatments. The Challenger was the base trim level and included all the federally mandated safety and pollution equipment; 225-cid Slant Six (198-cid Slant Six on coupe) or 318-cid V-8 engine; front and rear side armrests and ashtrays; cigarette lighter (except coupe); color-keyed carpeting; ventless side windows; glovebox with rotary latch (locking on convertible); heater and defroster; dual horns (except coupe); dome and parking brake/brake system warning lights; outside left manual mirror; inside day/night mirror (except coupe); bucket seats; front foam seat cushion; three-spoke steering wheel with simulated woodgrain and padded hub; electric windshield washer and concealed two-speed wipers. The Challenger R/T continued as the high-performance model in the Challenger lineup and included all the base line Challenger equipment plus heavy-duty drum brakes; chrome exhaust tips; Rallye instrument cluster with simulated woodgrain trim; Rallye suspension; bodyside tape stripe; variable speed wipers and 383-cid four-barrel V-8 engine. The convertible also had front courtesy and pocket panel lights and a collapsible spare tire.

1971 Dodge, Challenger R/T two-door hardtop, V-8

CHALLENGER I.D. DATA: See 1971 Dodge I.D. Data listing. All models began at 100001 and went up in the unit number sequence.

CHALLENGER SERIES

CHALLENGER

JL23	23	2-dr Cpe-4P	2727/2853	3020/3080	Note 1
JH23	23	2-dr HT-4P	2848/2950	3065/3120	Note 1
JH27	27	2-dr Conv-4P	3105/3207	3150/3210	2,165

R/T SERIES

JS23	23	2-dr HT-4P	3273	3495	4,630

Note 1: A total of 23,088 units was recorded for Models JL23 and JH23, with no additional breakout between the two models available.

Note 2: In figures rounded off to the nearest 100 units, Challenger output included 2,000 sixes and 27,900 V-8s. Of the grand total of 29,883 Challengers built during 1971, only 5.3 percent had four-speed manual gearboxes; 6.7 percent were sixes; 76.5 percent featured standard V-8 power and 16.8 percent were equipped with optional V-8 engines.

Note 3: Data above slash for six/below slash for V-8.

Additional Challenger R/T Note: The following is a known production figure for models equipped with the 426-cid Hemi V-8, according to Mopar authority Galen V. Govier: Challenger R/T - 71 two-door hardtops. Additionally, the following is a known production figure for models equipped with the 440-cid "Six-Pak" V-8, according to Galen V. Govier: Challenger R/T - 250 two-door hardtops.

COLT SERIES — (I-4) — The Colt was Dodge's offering into the new sub-compact field shared by the Ford Pinto, Chevy Vega and AMC's Gremlin. Manufactured in Japan by Mitsubishi Motors Corp., and sold by Dodge dealers in this country, the Colt became the first of the 'Captive Imports', which along with the Plymouth Cricket, was produced by Chrysler U.K. (formerly Rootes). It was sold overseas as the Hillman Avenger. Pleasantly styled, these little cars bore a resemblance to the Toyota Corolla models and Datsun 510 models from that era. The 97.5-cid (1600 cubic centimeters) engine was the only engine available with the Colt. Since the Colt was not a true American-built automobile, it will not be covered further in the following sections of this catalog that are devoted to Dodge.

COLT I.D. DATA: See 1971 Dodge I.D. Data listing. All models began at 100001 and went up in the unit number sequence.

COLT SERIES

Model No.	Body/ Style No.	Body Type & Seating	Factory Price	Shipping Weight	Prod. Total
6H41	41	4-dr Sed-4P	1995	2020	Note 1
6L21	21	2-dr Sed-4P	1924	2045	Note 1
6H23	23	2-dr HT-4P	2074	2055	Note 1
6H45	45	2-dr Sta Wag-4P	2225	2120	Note 1

Note 1: Sales of the Colt for 1971 were 28,381 units.

ENGINES:

(Colt four-cylinder) Overhead valve. Cast iron block. Displacement: 97.5 cid (1600 cubic centimeters). Bore and stroke: 3.03 x 3.39 inches. Brake hp: 100. Five main bearings. Hydraulic valve lifters.

(198 Slant Six) Overhead valve. Cast iron block. Displacement: 198 cid. Bore and stroke: 3.40 x 3.64 inches. Compression ratio: 8.4:1. Brake hp: 125 at 4000 rpm. Four main bearings. Solid valve lifters. Carburetor: one-barrel.

(225 Slant Six) Overhead valve. Cast iron block. Displacement: 225 cid. Bore and stroke: 3.41 x 4.13 inches. Compression ratio: 8.4:1. Brake hp: 145 at 4000 rpm. Four main bearings. Solid valve lifters. Carburetor: one-barrel.

(318 V-8) Overhead valve. Cast iron block. Displacement: 318 cid. Bore and stroke: 3.91 x 3.31 inches. Compression ratio: 9.0:1. Brake hp: 230 at 4400 rpm. Five main bearings. Carburetor: two-barrel.

(340 V-8) Overhead valve. Cast iron block. Displacement: 340 cid. Bore and stroke: 4.04 x 3.31 inches. Compression ratio: 10.0:1. Brake hp: 275 at 5600 rpm. Five main bearings. Hydraulic valve lifters. Carburetor: Carter 'Thermo-Quad' four-barrel.

(360 V-8) Overhead valve. Cast iron block. Displacement: 360 cid. Bore and stroke: 4.00 x 3.58 inches. Compression ratio: 8.7:1. Brake hp: 255 at 4000 rpm. Five main bearings. Hydraulic valve lifters. Carburetor: two-barrel.

(383 V-8) Overhead valve. Cast iron block. Displacement: 383 cid. Bore and stroke: 4.25 x 3.38 inches. Compression ratio: 9.2:1. Brake hp: 275 at 4400 rpm. Five main bearings. Hydraulic valve lifters. Carburetor: two-barrel.

(383 V-8) Overhead valve. Cast iron block. Displacement: 383 cid. Bore and stroke: 4.25 x 3.38 inches. Compression ratio: 9.5:1. Brake hp: 300 at 4800 rpm. Five main bearings. Hydraulic valve lifters. Carburetor: four-barrel.

(440 Magnum V-8) Overhead valve. Cast iron block. Displacement: 440 cid. Bore and stroke: 4.32 x 3.75 inches. Compression ratio: 9.7:1. Brake hp: 370 at 4800 rpm. Five main bearings. Hydraulic valve lifters. Carburetor: four-barrel.

(440 'Six-Pack' V-8) Overhead valve. Cast iron block. Displacement: 440 cid. Bore and stroke: 4.32 x 3.75 inches. Compression ratio: 10.5:1. Brake hp: 385 at 5200 rpm. Five main bearings. Hydraulic valve lifters. Carburetor: three Holley two-barrel.

(428 'Street Hemi' V-8) Overhead valve with hemispherical combustion chamber. Cast iron block. Displacement: 426 cid. Bore and stroke: 4.25 x 3.75 inches. Compression ratio: 10.25:1. Brake hp: 425 at 5600 rpm. Five main bearings. Hydraulic valve lifters. Carburetor: two Carter AFB four-barrel.

CHASSIS FEATURES:

(Colt) Wheelbase: 95.3 inches. Overall length: 160.6 inches (165 inches on station wagon). Tires: 6.00 x 13 tubeless black sidewall. Four-speed manual transmission was standard on all Colts with the three-speed automatic optional.

(Demon) Wheelbase: 108 inches. Overall length: 192.5 inches. Tires: 8.45 x 14 tubeless black sidewall (E70-14 belted black sidewall with raised white letters on Demon 340 models). Three-speed manual transmission was standard on all Demons with the TorqueFlite automatic or four-speed manual transmissions optional.

(Dart) Wheelbase: 111 inches. Overall length: 197 inches. Tires: D78-14 belted black sidewall. Three-speed manual transmission was standard on all Darts, with the TorqueFlite automatic or four-speed manual transmissions optional.

(Challenger) Wheelbase: 110 inches. Overall length: 192 inches. Tires: 7.35 x 14 tubeless black sidewall (F70-14 belted black sidewall with raised white letters on R/T models). Three-speed manual transmission was standard on all Challengers unless otherwise noted, with the Torque-Flite automatic or four-speed manual transmissions optional.

(Charger) Wheelbase: 115 inches. Overall length: 206 inches. Tires: E78-14 belted black sidewall (F70-14 belted black sidewall with raised white letters on Super Bee and R/T models). Three-speed manual transmission was standard on all Chargers unless otherwise noted, with the TorqueFlite automatic or four-speed manual transmissions optional.

(Coronet) Wheelbase: 118 inches. Overall length: 207 inches on sedans and 214 inches on station wagons. Tires: E78-14 belted black sidewalls on sedans and H78-14 belted black sidewall on station wagons. Three-speed manual transmission was standard on all Coronets with the TorqueFlite automatic and four-speed manual transmissions optional.

(Polara/Monaco) Wheelbase: 122 inches. Overall length: 221 inches on sedans and 224 inches on station wagons. Tires: H78-15 on sedans and J78-15 on station wagons. All tires were belted black sidewalls. TorqueFlite automatic transmission was standard on all Polara and Monaco models.

CONVENIENCE OPTIONS: (average prices) — Power brakes ($45). Power disc brakes ($66). Challenger '340' four-barrel carb V-8 ($253). Dart/Demon/Challenger '225' Slant Six ($39). Challenger/Coronet/Super Bee '383' V-8 ($71). Challenger/Coronet/Super Bee '383' four-barrel carb V-8 ($145). Polara/Monaco '383' two-barrel carb V-8 ($73). Polara/Monaco '383' four-barrel carb V-8 ($145). Polara/Monaco '440' four-barrel carb V-8 ($198). Coronet 'Track-Pack' ($138). Coronet 'Super Track-Pack' ($202). Monaco Brougham option ($220). Air conditioning, in Monaco/Polara ($423), in other models ($380). Hemi '426' V-8 in Super Bee ($837), in Charger R/T ($707); in Challenger ($790). (Colt) Automatic transmission. Full wheel covers. Air conditioning. White sidewall tires.

HISTORICAL FOOTNOTES: Dodge offered many convenience options for the 1971 models. New items ranged from slightly wider rearview mirrors to cassette tape players. An optional 'lock door' and 'low fuel' warning lights were also featured. Flow-through ventilation for the upper level of the car was a popular option. The top-line station wagons featured a translucent woodgrain film that allowed the color of the main body to 'bleed' through, creating an unusual effect. When its winged 1969 Daytona was effectively outlawed by NASCAR, Dodge cut back heavily on factory backing of stock car racing. After 22 Grand National wins in 1969 and 17 in 1970, there were only eight in 1971. Unfortunately, 1971 was also the last time the famous and awesome 'Hemi' V-8 engine was offered to the public, either as the street version, or in the race form. Insurance premiums were astronomical on high-performance cars and, beginning in 1972, all cars had to be able to run on regular gasoline. Rather than compromise the incredible 'Hemi', Chrysler wisely decided to retire it as a winner. Dodge installed a mere 156 of the engines in three 1971 models, as follows: (Charger Super Bee) 9 four-speed and 13 TorqueFlite; (Charger R/T) 30 four-speed and 33 TorqueFlite; (Challenger R/T hardtop) 59 four-speed and 12 TorqueFlite. Chrysler announced in 1992 that it would start making 426-cid Hemi engines again

for sale to racers and restorers through its Chrysler Performance (formerly Direct Connection) high-performance parts division.

1972 DODGE

DEMON SERIES — (6-CYL/V-8) — Basically unchanged for 1972, the new Darts received only revised grilles and updated interiors to separate them from the previous year's models. The Demon continued to be the base 'value package' of the Dart lineup. Demons included all the federally mandated safety and pollution equipment, pivoting rear quarter windows, the 198-cid Slant Six engine, black rubber floor mats, 6.45 x 14 black sidewall tires on six-cylinder models and 6.95 x 14 black sidewall tires on V-8 models. The Demon model designation was once again carried on the right side of the rear escutcheon panel and on the front fenders. The Demon 340 continued as the high-performance version of the Demon and included all standard Demon features plus the 340-cid V-8 engine with three-speed manual transmission; E70-14 belted black sidewall tires; performance bodyside and rear deck panel tape stripes; front and rear Rallye Suspension with sway bar and floor-mounted shifter.

DODGE I.D. DATA: The Vehicle Identification Number was located on a plate attached to left-hand side of dashboard, visible through windshield. The VIN has 13 symbols. (The first four symbols, together, are the Model Number in second column of charts below.) The first symbol identifies the car-line or marque: D=Polara/Monaco; J=Challenger; L=Dart; W=Coronet and X=Charger. The second symbol indicates trim/price level as follows: G=Dodge Taxi; H=High; K=Police; L=Low; M=Medium; P=Premium; T=Taxi; S=Special. The next two symbols identify the body style, as follows: 21=two-door sedan; 23=two-door hardtop; 29=two-door Sports hardtop; 41=four-door sedan; 43=four-door hardtop; 45=six-passenger station wagon; 46=nine-passenger station wagon. The fifth symbol denotes the engine as follows: (six-cylinder) B=198 cid; C=225 cid; (V-8) E=318 cid 2V; G=318 cid 2V; H=340 cid 4V (high-performance); K=360 cid 2V; M=400 cid 2V; P=400 cid 4V (high-performance); T=440 cid 4V; U=440 cid 4V (high-performance); V=440 3x2V (high-performance); Z=special order. The sixth symbol denotes the model year as follows: 2=1972. The seventh symbol denotes the assembly plant as follows: A=Lynch Rd. (Detroit); B=Hamtramck, Mich.; C=Jefferson Ave. (Detroit); D=Belvedere, Ill.; F=Newark, Del.; G=St Louis, Mo.; R=Windsor, Ont. (Canada). The last six symbols are the sequential production number starting at 100001 for each series at each plant. Body code plate located under hood, on left (fender shield, wheelhousing or radiator support) includes S.O. number and trim/paint codes, too numerous to list.

DEMON SERIES

Model No.	Body/ Style No.	Body Type & Seating	Factory Price	Shipping Weight	Prod. Total
LL29	29	2-dr Cpe-6P	2316/2449	2800/2995	39,880
LM29	29	2-dr 340 Cpe-6P	2759	3125	8,700

Note 1: The production total for Model LM29 is based on rounded off model year records that include only U.S. built cars. The production total for Model LL29 appears to be an exact model year record covering all cars built in the U.S. and Canada, for the U.S. market.

Note 2: Data above slash for six/below slash for V-8.

1972 Dodge, Dart Swinger two-door hardtop, 6-cyl

DART SERIES — (6-CYL/V-8) — The Dart was the standard base trim level in the Dart model lineup and included all federally mandated safety and pollution systems; front and rear armrests; ashtrays; cigarette lighter; concealed spare tire; rubber floor mats; glovebox with rotary latch; heater and defroster; dome light; parking brake and brake system warning lights; all-vinyl bench seats; three-spoke steering wheel (with padded horn button); two-speed electric windshield wipers; '198' Slant Six (or '318' V-8

engine) and vent wings. Dart Swinger and Custom models also included dual note horns; drip rail and wheel lip moldings; three-spoke steering wheel (with padded hub and horn tabs) and carpeting. The Custom models also included bodyside moldings and ventless side windows. Each model carried identification on the front fender sides just behind the front wheel openings.

DART/SWINGER/CUSTOM I.D. DATA: See 1972 Dodge I.D. Data listing. All models began at 100001 and went up in the unit number sequence.

DART/SWINGER/CUSTOM SERIES

Model No.	Body/ Style No.	Body Type & Seating	Factory Price	Shipping Weight	Prod. Total
LL41	41	4-dr Sed-6P	2420/2570	2855/3005	26,019
LL23	23	2-dr Spec HT-6P	2373/2523	2845/2995	19,210
LH23	23	2-dr Swinger HT-6P	2528/2678	2835/2985	119,618
LH41	41	4-dr Cus Sed-6P	2574/2724	2855/3005	49,941

Note 1: Data above slash for six/below slash for V-8.

1972 Dodge, Coronet Custom four-door sedan, V-8

CORONET SERIES — (6-CYL/V-8) — Simplification was the key word in the Coronet lineup for 1972. Minor restyling, in the form of new grilles and taillights, highlighted the new Coronets. As in 1971, all Coronets were four-door models, either sedans or station wagons. The Coronet was the base trim level and included all federally mandated safety and pollution equipment; '225' Slant Six or '318' V-8 engine; color-keyed rubber floor mats; a single horn; and no exterior moldings, except windshield and rear window moldings. Also included was the three-spoke steering wheel, rear ashtray and extra-thick foam seat cushions. Station wagons added heavy-duty brakes; drip rail moldings; and three-way tailgate. The Coronet model designation was carried, in block letters, on the front fenders behind the wheelwell. The Coronet Custom was the top trim level in the Coronet series and included all standard Coronet features plus color-keyed carpeting; dual note horns; wheel opening, bodyside and drip rail moldings; and a three-spoke steering wheel (with padded horn bar). Also included were upper door frame moldings, rear door automatic entrance light and Deluxe wheel covers. The Crestwood station wagon added wheelwell moldings; bright upper door frame and quarter window moldings; woodgrain side panels and, on the nine-passenger Crestwood, an inside tailgate safety latch. Three Coronet and "Topper" trim packages were made available as a midyear option for the Custom four-door sedan.

CORONET I.D. DATA: See 1972 Dodge I.D. Data listing. All models began at 100001 and went up in the unit number sequence.

CORONET SERIES

Model No.	Body/ Style No.	Body Type & Seating	Factory Price	Shipping Weight	Prod. Total
WL41	N/A	4-dr Sed-6P	2721/2828	3350/3375	11,293
WL45	N/A	4-dr Sta Wag-6P	3209	3795	Note 1
WH41	N/A	4-dr Cus Sed-6P	2891/2998	3310/3370	43,132
WH45	N/A	4-dr Cus Wag-6P	3382	3800	Note 1
WH46	N/A	4-dr Cus Wag-9P	3460	3840	Note 1
WP45	N/A	4-dr Crstwd-6P	3604	3810	Note 2
WP46	N/A	4-dr Crstwd-9P	3683	3850	Note 2

Note 1: Data above slash for six/below slash for V-8.

Note 2: The production of Model WL45 was counted together with production of Models WH45 and WH46. The total for all three was 5,452 units.

Note 3: The production of Models WP45 and WP46 was counted together as 6,471 units.

CHARGER SERIES — (6-CYL/V-8) — As in 1971, all intermediate models were considered Chargers. The Charger lineup was simplified like the Coronet's, with three models replacing the six offered in 1971. The R/T Super Bee and 500 models were dropped and a new Rallye model was added. The standard Charger continued as the base trim level and included all federally mandated safety and pollution equipment; '225' Slant Six or '318' V-8 engine; cigarette lighter; dual horns; color-keyed carpeting; inside day/night mirror; roof drip rail and wheelwell moldings; and two-speed windshield wipers. The Charger Rallye included all standard Charger features plus front and rear sway bars; F70-14 white sidewall tires; special instrumentation; louvered taillights; and various types of exterior performance ornamentation. The Charger SE continued as the top trim level and included all the standard Charger features plus a landau vinyl top and hidden headlights. The 440-cid 'Six-Pak' engine continued to be offered, but only in the Rallye-optioned Charger. Three midyear Topper trim packages were released for Charger hardtops.

CHARGER SERIES

Model No.	Body/ Style No.	Body Type & Seating	Factory Price	Shipping Weight	Prod. Total
WL21	21	2-dr Cpe-6P	2652/2759	3245/3318	7,803
WL23	23	2-dr HT-6P	2913/3020	3260/3325	45,361
WH23	23	2-dr SE HT-6P	3249	3325	22,430

Note: Data above slash for six/below slash for V-8.

Additional Charger Rallye Note: According to Mopar authority Galen V. Govier, Charger Rallye models were produced with the 440-cid "Six-Pak" V-8. Two Charger Rallye two-door hardtops have been authenticated as being produced with this engine, but more may exist. The number of Charger Rallye two-door coupes equipped with the 440-cid "Six-Pak" is N/A.

POLARA/MONACO SERIES — (6-CYL/V-8) — Nineteen seventy-two was a year for a major face lift in the Polara lineup. A more formal appearance was evident, with the addition of new rooflines to the two- and four-door hardtops. Both grille and headlights were housed in a more massive, full-width bumper. The rear bumper was also redesigned and contained the large rectangular taillights. The Polara was the base trim level full-size Dodge and included all federally mandated safety and pollution equipment; air control system; front and rear armrests; front and rear ashtrays; 46 amp/hour battery; cigarette lighter; color-keyed carpeting; dual horns; dome and parking brake system warning lights; inside day/night mirror; outside left manual mirror; three-spoke steering wheel (with padded hub); electric windshield washers and two-speed wipers and the 318-cid V-8 engine. The 225-cid six was available in Polaras made for fleet use. The Dodge name, in block letters, was spaced evenly across the front of the hood and across the center of the rear bumper. The Polara model designation, in script, was located on the rear fenders, just above the side marker lights. The Polara Custom was the intermediate trim level and included all the Polara features plus bodyside moldings (with a vinyl insert); wheel opening moldings; and foam rubber seat cushions. The Custom model designation was located on the rear fenders. A greater attempt was made to segregate the Monaco from the Polara for 1972. Concealed headlights and special front and rear end treatments made the two models appear completely different. The Monaco included all Polara Custom features plus folding front center armrest; 59 amp/hour battery; ashtray; glovebox and trunk lights; headlight-on warning light; pedal dress-up trim; upper door and sill moldings; rear door automatic entrance light switches; Deluxe wheel covers; 360-cid V-8 engine; nylon carpeting; cornering lamps; dome/map lights; and the Monaco name, in script, on the rear fenders (just above the side marker lights).

1972 Dodge, Polara Custom four-door hardtop, V-8

POLARA/MONACO I.D. DATA: See 1972 Dodge I.D. Data listing. All models began at 100001 and went up in the unit number sequence.

POLARA/MONACO SERIES

POLARA SERIES

DL41	41	4-dr Sed-6P	3335	3965	16,766
DL43	43	4-dr HT-6P	N/A	3875	8,212
DL23	23	2-dr HT-6P	3356	3930	7,022
DM45	45	4-dr Sta Wag-6P	3712	4445	3,013

POLARA CUSTOM SERIES

Model No.	Body/ Style No.	Body Type & Seating	Factory Price	Shipping Weight	Prod. Total
DM41	41	4-dr Cus Sed-6P	3515	3975	19,739
DM43	43	4-dr Cus HT-6P	3898	3890	22,505
DM23	23	2-dr Cus HT-6P	3536	3945	15,039
DM45	45	4-dr Cus Sta Wag-6P	4262	4320	3,497
DM46	46	4-dr Cus Sta Wag-9P	4371	4370	7,660

MONACO SERIES

DP41	41	4-dr Sed-6P	4095	3980	6,474
DP43	43	4-dr HT-6P	4216	4030	15,039
DP23	23	2-dr HT-6P	4153	3960	7,786
DP45	45	4-dr Sta Wag-6P	4627	4445	2,569
DP46	46	4-dr Sta Wag-9P	4756	4490	5,145

Note 1: The production total listed for Model DL23 is an estimate of model year production, excluding shipments to Canada. This should be considered a 'ballpark' figure only. All other totals above are exact model year records, including Canadian shipments.

Note 2: Data above slash for six/below slash for V-8.

1972 Dodge, Challenger two-door hardtop, V-8

CHALLENGER SERIES — (6-CYL/V-8) — The Challenger redesign for 1972 had a few cosmetic changes. Only two body styles were offered in 1972, with the convertible deleted. This was significant in that the Challenger was the last Dodge convertible to be produced until 10 years later. The Challenger was the base trim level hardtop and included all federally mandated safety and pollution equipment; '225' Slant Six engine; front and rear side armrests; front ashtray; cigarette lighter; color-keyed carpeting; ventless side windows; glovebox with rotary latch; heater and defroster; dual horns; dome and parking brake/brake system warning lights; outside left manual mirror; inside day/night mirror; bucket seats; front foam seat cushion; three-spoke steering wheel (with simulated woodgrain padded hub); electric windshield washer and concealed two-speed wipers. The Challenger Rallye was the high-performance option for the series and included all the standard Challenger features plus the 318-cid V-8 engine; a side scoop behind the front wheels and strobe-type tape stripes that ran the full length of the car.

CHALLENGER I.D. DATA: See 1972 Dodge I.D. Data listing. All models began at 100001 and went up in the unit number sequence.

CHALLENGER SERIES

JH23	23	2-dr HT-4P	2790/2902	3070/3125	18,535
JS23	23	2-dr Rallye HT-4P	3082	3225	8,123

Note: Data above slash for six/below slash for V-8.

ENGINES:

(198 Slant Six) Overhead valve. Cast iron block. Displacement: 198 cid. Bore and stroke: 3.40 x 3.84 inches. Compression ratio: 8.4:1. Net hp: 100 at 4400 rpm. Four main bearings. Solid valve lifters. Carburetor: one-barrel.

(225 Slant Six) Overhead valve. Cast iron block. Displacement: 225 cid. Bore and stroke: 3.41 x 4.13 inches. Compression ratio: 8.4:1. Net hp: 110 at 4000 rpm. Four main bearings. Solid valve lifters. Carburetor: one-barrel.

(V-8) Overhead valve. Cast iron block. Displacement: 318 cid. Bore and stroke: 3.91 x 3.31 inches. Compression ratio: 8.6:1. (Net hp: 150 at 4000 rpm) Four main bearings. Hydraulic valve lifters. Carburetor: two-barrel.

(V-8) Overhead valve. Cast iron block. Displacement: 340 cid. Bore and stroke: 4.04 x 3.31 inches. Compression ratio: 8.5:1. Net hp: 240 at

4800 rpm. Five main bearings. Hydraulic valve lifters. Carburetor: Carter Thermo-Quad four-barrel.

(V-8) Overhead valve. Cast iron block. Displacement: 360 cid. Bore and stroke: 4.00 x 3.58 inches. Compression ratio: 8.8:1. Net hp: 175 at 4000 rpm. Five main bearings. Hydraulic valve lifters. Carburetor: two-barrel.

(V-8) Overhead valve. Cast iron block. Displacement: 400 cid. Bore and stroke: 4.34 x 3.38 inches. Compression ratio: 8.2:1. Net hp: 190 at 4400 rpm. Five main bearings. Hydraulic valve lifters. Carburetor: two-barrel.

(V-8) Overhead valve. Cast iron block. Displacement: 400 cid. Bore and stroke: 4.34 x 3.38 inches. Compression ratio: 8.2:1. Net hp: 255 at 4400 rpm. Five main bearings. Hydraulic valve lifters. Carburetor: four-barrel.

(Magnum V-8) Overhead valve. Cast iron block. Displacement: 440 cid. Bore and stroke: 4.32 x 3.75 inches. Compression ratio: 8.2:1. Net hp: 280 at 4800 rpm. Five main bearings. Hydraulic valve lifters. Carburetor: four-barrel.

('Six-Pak' V-8) Overhead valve. Cast iron block. Displacement: 440 cid. Bore and stroke: 4.32 x 3.75 inches. Compression ratio: 10.3:1. Net hp: 330 at 4800 rpm. Five main bearings. Hydraulic valve lifters. Carburetor: three Holley two-barrel.

CHASSIS FEATURES:

(Demon) Wheelbase: 108 inches. Overall length: 192.5 inches. Tires: 6.45 x 14 tubeless black sidewall (E70-14 belted black sidewall with raised white letters on Demon 340 models). Three-speed manual transmission was standard on all Demons, with the TorqueFlite automatic optional.

(Dart) Wheelbase: 111 inches. Overall length: 197 inches. Tires: D78-14 belted black sidewall. Three-speed manual transmission was standard on all Darts, with the TorqueFlite automatic or four-speed manual transmissions optional.

(Challenger) Wheelbase: 110 inches. Overall length: 192 inches. Tires: 7.35 x 14 tubeless black sidewall on standard Challenger, F70-14 belted black sidewall on Rallye models. Three-speed manual transmission was standard on all Challengers unless otherwise noted with the TorqueFlite automatic or four-speed manual transmissions optional.

(Coronet) Wheelbase: 118 inches. Overall length: 207 inches on sedans and 214 inches on station wagons. Tires: E78-14 belted black sidewall on sedans and H78-14 belted black sidewall on station wagons. Three-speed manual transmission was standard on all Coronets, with the TorqueFlite automatic and four-speed manual transmissions optional.

(Charger) Wheelbase: 115 inches. Overall length: 206 inches. Tires: E78-14 belted black sidewall (F70-14 belted black sidewall with raised white letters on Rallye models). Three-speed manual transmission was standard on all Chargers unless otherwise noted, with the TorqueFlite automatic or four-speed manual transmissions optional.

(Polara/Monaco) Wheelbase: 122 inches. Overall length: 220 inches on sedans and 223 inches on station wagons. Tires: F78-15 belted black sidewall on Polara sedans, G78-15 belted black sidewall on Monaco sedans, and J78-15 belted black sidewall on Polara six-passenger station wagons and L84-15 belted black sidewall on Polara nine-passenger station wagons. TorqueFlite automatic transmission was standard on all Polara and Monaco models.

CONVENIENCE OPTIONS FOR DEMON/DART/CHALLENGER: 225-cid Slant Six engine in Demons ($37.85). TorqueFlite automatic transmission ($177.75-$208.40). Four-speed manual transmission ($184.50). Power steering ($92.25). Power brakes, drum type ($40.45); disc type ($62.30). All tinted glass ($35.85); windshield only ($24.35). Air conditioning ($354). Two-tone paint ($30.40). Music Master AM radio ($59.40). AM/FM radio ($124.55). AM/8-track stereo ($196.25). Simulated woodgrain Sport steering wheel ($18.40-$28.00).

CONVENIENCE OPTIONS FOR CORONET/CHARGER/POLARA/MONACO: 340-cid V-8 engine in Chargers ($209.70). 440-cid Six-Pak V-8 engine in Charger Rallyes ($306.45). 440-cid V-8 in Polaras and Monacos ($193.35-$148.60). TorqueFlite automatic transmission ($203.45-$231.65). Power steering ($102.65-$113.70). Power brakes, disc only required on station wagons ($68.05). Power seats ($90.95-$102.65). Power windows ($125). Power front disc brakes ($68.05). Air conditioning, single type ($364.80-$412.95). AM radio ($64.90). AM/FM radio ($209). AM/FM stereo radio with 8-track tape player ($358). Four-speed manual transmission ($20.85). Heavy-duty suspension ($13-$14). Deep Dish wheel covers ($31.15-$57.85). Deluxe wheel covers ($26.75). Wire wheel covers ($41.95-$68.50). Rallye

road wheels ($28.35-$57.85). Limited-slip differential ($44.75-$47.65). Vinyl top ($94).

HISTORICAL FOOTNOTES: 1972 was a significant year for several reasons in the mechanical aspect of the Dodges offered. A new federal law required that all automobiles produced that year have the ability to run on low lead or no lead gasoline, requiring the compression ratio on the high-performance engines to be lowered. Also, all engines were rated at SAE net horsepower, rather than brake horsepower, as in previous years. This is the theoretical horsepower with all accessories in place. Richard Petty switched from racing a Plymouth to a Dodge Charger midway through the 1972 NASCAR Grand National season. He would run these cars into 1978. Dodge won five events that year.

1973 DODGE

1973 Dodge, Dart Sport two-door coupe, 6-cyl

DART SPORT SERIES — (6-CYL/V-8) — Continuing to use the same body as in the previous few years, the new Darts were separated from their predecessors by an entirely new front end arrangement. It featured a new hood, with a ridge in the middle. An all-new grille protruded forward at the center. This was the first year for the new, federally mandated safety bumpers on the front ends of cars. The Dart's new bumper carried the theme initiated by the grille. All new Chrysler products featured electronic ignition for 1973. The Demon nomenclature was dropped for the 'value package' Dart and the new name was Dart Sport. Dart Sports included all safety and pollution equipment; pivoting rear quarter windows; 198-cid Slant Six engine; black rubber floor mats; and 6.95 x 14 tubeless black sidewall tires. The Dart Sport designation was carried, in block letters, on the front fenders, behind the front wheelwells. The Dodge name, also in block letters, was carried on the right side of the rear escutcheon panel. The Dart Sport 340 continued as the high-performance version of the standard Dart Sport. It included all the standard Dart Sport features plus the 340-cid V-8 engine with three-speed manual transmission; E70-14 belted black sidewall tires; 'performance' bodyside tape stripes; front and rear Rallye Suspension (with sway bar); and floor-mounted shift lever. A Rallye package for the base Dart Sport was available, at midyear, as was a 'Topper' trim option.

DODGE I.D. DATA: The Vehicle Identification Number was located on a plate attached to left-hand side of dashboard, visible through windshield. The VIN has 13 symbols. (The first four symbols, together, are the Model Number in second column of charts below.) The first symbol identifies the car-line or marque: D=Polara/Monaco; J=Challenger; L=Dart; W=Coronet and X=Charger. The second symbol indicates trim/price level as follows: G=New York Taxi; H=High; L=Low; M=Medium; P=Premium; S=Special. The next two symbols identify the body style as follows: 21=two-door coupe; 23=two-door hardtop; 29=two-door Sports hardtop; 41=sedan; 43=hardtop sedan; 45=six-passenger station wagon; 46=nine-passenger station wagon. The fifth symbol denotes the engine, as follows: (six-cylinder) B=198 cid; C=225 cid; E=special order; (V-8) G=318 cid 2V; H=340 cid 4V; K=360 cid 2V; M=400 cid 2V; P=400 cid 4V (high-performance); T=440 cid 4V; U=440 cid 4V (high-performance). The sixth symbol denotes the model year as follows: 3=1973. The seventh symbol denotes the assembly plant as follows: A=Lynch Rd. (Detroit); B=Hamtramck, Mich.; C=Jefferson Ave. (Detroit); D=Belvedere, Ill.; F=Newark, Del.; G=St. Louis, Mo.; H=New Stanton, RI; R=Windsor, Ont. (Canada). The last six symbols are the sequential induction number

starting at 100001 for each series at each plant. Body code plate located under hood, on left (fender shield, wheelhousing or radiator support) includes S.O. number and trim/paint codes, too numerous to list.

DART SPORT SERIES

Model No.	Body/ Style No.	Body Type & Seating	Factory Price	Shipping Weight	Prod. Total
LL	29	2-dr Cpe-6P	2424/2557	2850/3045	68,113
LM	29	2-dr '340' Cpe-6P	2853	3205	11,315

Note 1: Data above slash for six/below slash for V-8s.

1973 Dodge, Dart Swinger two-door hardtop
(with optional sun roof), 6-cyl

DART SERIES — (6-CYL/V-8) — The Dart was the standard base trim level in the Dart model lineup and included all federally mandated safety and pollution equipment; front and rear armrests; ashtrays; cigarette lighter; concealed spare tire; rubber floor mats; glovebox with rotary latch; heater and defroster; dome light; parking brake and brake system warning lights; all-vinyl bench seats; three-spoke steering wheel (with padded horn button); two-speed electric windshield wipers; 198-cid Slant Six engine (or 318-cid V-8 engine); and vent wings. Dart Swinger and Custom models also included dual note horns; drip rail and wheel lip moldings; three-spoke steering wheel (with padded hub and horn tabs) and carpeting. The Custom models also included bodyside moldings and ventless side windows. Each model carried the model designation on the front fender sides, behind the front wheel opening.

DART/SWINGER/CUSTOM I.D. DATA: See 1973 Dodge I.D. Data listing. All models began at 100001 and went up in the unit number sequence.

DART/SWINGER/CUSTOM SERIES

DART
LL	41	4-dr Sed-6P	2504/2654	2910/3060	21,539
LL	23	2-dr HT Cpe-6P	2462/2612	2895/3045	17,480

SWINGER
LH	23	2-dr HT Cpe-6P	2617/2767	2890/3040	107,619

CUSTOM
LH	41	4-dr Sed-6P	2658/2808	2910/3060	62,626

Note 1: Data above slash for six/below slash for V-8s.

CORONET SERIES — (6-CYL/V-8) — Even though they continued to use the same body as in previous years, the new Coronets were much more pleasant cars due to the concentration on comfort and ride during 1973. More sound deadeners and insulation material were added and the suspension contained redesigned components that contributed to a smoother ride. Again offered only in four-door sedan and station wagon configuration, the new Coronets featured slightly restyled taillights and grilles. They used new colors and updated interiors, too. The Coronet was the base trim level and included all federally mandated safety and pollution equipment; the 225-cid Slant Six (or 318-cid V-8 engine); color-keyed rubber floor mats; a single horn; and no exterior moldings (except on windshield and rear windows). Also included was the three-spoke steering wheel; rear ashtray; and extra thick foam seat cushion. Station wagons also included heavy-duty brakes; drip rail moldings and three-way tailgate. The Coronet model designation was carried, in block letters, on the front fenders behind the front wheelwell. The Coronet Custom was the top trim level in the Coronet series and included all the standard Coronet features plus color-keyed carpeting; dual note horns;

wheel opening, bodyside and drip rail moldings; and three-spoke steering wheel with padded horn bars. Also included were upper door frame moldings, rear door automatic entrance light and Deluxe wheel covers. The Crestwood station wagons also included wheelwell moldings; bright upper door frame moldings and quarter window moldings; woodgrain side panels and, on the nine-passenger Crestwood, tailgate inside safety latch.

CORONET I.D. DATA: See 1973 Dodge I.D. Data listing. All models began at 100001 and went up in the unit number sequence.

CORONET SERIES

Model No.	Body/ Style No.	Body Type & Seating	Factory Price	Shipping Weight	Prod. Total
CORONET					
WL	41	4-dr Sed-6P	2867/2979	3440/3505	14,395
WL	45	4-dr Sta Wag-6P	3314	3955	4,874
CORONET CUSTOM					
WH	41	4-dr Sed-6P	3017/3129	3430/3495	46,491
WH	45	4-dr Sta Wag-6P	3442	3955	Note 1
WH	46	4-dr Sta Wag-9P	3560	4000	Note 1
CRESTWOOD					
WP	45	4-dr Sta Wag-6P	3671	3970	Note 2
WP	46	4-dr Sta Wag-9P	3791	4005	Note 2

Note 1: Exactly 13,018 Coronet Custom station wagons were built, including both six- and nine-passenger styles.

Note 2: Exactly 8,755 Coronet Crestwood station wagons were built, including both six- and nine-passenger styles.

Note 3: Data above slash for six/below slash for V-8s.

1973 Dodge, Coronet Custom four-door sedan, V-8

CHARGER SERIES — (6-CYL/V-8) — Continuing the policy of the past two years, all two-door intermediate models were considered Chargers. The grille was revised slightly from the previous models, but the most noticeable change was in the new roofline around the quarter windows. The new window line was more conservative than in the past, but was also more pleasing to many. New taillights, featuring 22 individual lenses, were used for 1973. The standard Charger continued as the base trim level and included all federally mandated safety and pollution equipment; 225-cid Slant Six (or 318-cid V-8) engine; cigarette lighter; dual horns; color-keyed carpeting; inside day/night mirror; roof drip rail and wheelwell moldings and two-speed windshield wipers. The Charger Rallye option included all the standard Charger features plus front and rear sway bars; F70-14 raised white letter black sidewall tires; power bulge hood; Rallye instrument cluster; body tape stripes; hood pins and special exterior ornamentation. The Charger SE continued as the top trim level and included all the standard Charger features plus a landau vinyl top with three-section opera windows, replacing the quarter windows. The 440-cid Magnum V-8 engine continued as the largest engine option, but was offered only on the Rallye.

1973 Dodge, Charger SE two-door coupe, V-8

CHARGER I.D. DATA: See 1973 Dodge I.D. Data listing. All models began at 100001 and went up in the unit number sequence.

CHARGER SERIES

Model No.	Body/Style No.	Body Type & Seating	Factory Price	Shipping Weight	Prod. Total
CHARGER COUPE					
WL	21	2-dr Cpe-6P	2810/2922	3395/3460	11,995
CHARGER HARDTOP					
WH	23	2-dr HT Cpe-6P	3060/3171	3450/3480	45,415
CHARGER SE					
WP	29	2-dr HT Cpe-6P	3375	3540	61,908

1973 Dodge, Monaco two-door hardtop, V-8

POLARA/MONACO SERIES — (6-CYL/V-8) — The new Polara was only slightly updated from the previous year. The new frontal treatment featured a rectangular grille with a rectangular grid pattern insert. Quad headlights and a new bumper were now separate from the grille. Taillights made up of multiple rectangular sections were set into the rear bumper. The Polara was the base trim level full-size Dodge and included all federally mandated safety and pollution equipment; air control system; front and rear armrests; front and rear ashtrays; 46 amp/hour battery; cigarette lighter; color-keyed carpeting; dual horns; dome and parking brake system warning lights; inside day/night mirror; outside left manual mirror; three-spoke steering wheel (with padded hub); electric windshield washers; two-speed wipers and the 318-cid V-8 engine. The Dodge name, in block letters, was spaced evenly across the top of the grille surround trim and on the right side of the trunk lid. The Polara Custom was the intermediate trim level and included all the Polara features plus bodyside moldings with a vinyl insert; wheel opening moldings; foam seat cushions and the Custom model designation located on the rear fenders. Continuing as the top trim level was the Monaco series. As in the previous year, the Monaco was somewhat segregated from the basic Polara series with a completely different front end. A revised grille insert and a new rear bumper and taillights distinguished the 1973 models from the 1972s. The six-cylinder base Polara for fleet use was still offered.

1973 Dodge, Polara Custom station wagon, V-8

POLARA/MONACO I.D. DATA: See 1973 Dodge I.D. Data listing. All models began at 100001 and went up in the unit number sequence.

POLARA/MONACO SERIES

Model No.	Body/Style No.	Body Type & Seating	Factory Price	Shipping Weight	Prod. Total
POLARA					
DL	41	4-dr Sed-6P	3729	3865	15,015
DL	23	2-dr HT Cpe-6P	3752	3835	6,432
DL	45	4-dr Sta Wag-6P	4186	4420	3,327
POLARA CUSTOM					
DM	41	4-dr Sed-6P	3911	3870	23,939
DM	43	4-dr HT Sed-6P	4001	3905	29,341

Model No.	Body/Style No.	Body Type & Seating	Factory Price	Shipping Weight	Prod. Total
DM	23	2-dr HT Cpe-6P	3928	3835	17,406
DM	45	4-dr Sta Wag-6P	4370	4440	3,702
DM	46	4-dr Sta Wag-9P	4494	4485	8,839
MONACO					
DP	41	4-dr Sed-6P	4218	4020	6,316
DP	43	4-dr HT Sed-6P	4339	4060	9,031
DP	23	2-dr HT Cpe-6P	4276	3985	6,133
DP	45	4-dr Sta Wag-6P	4730	4470	2,337
DP	46	4-dr Sta Wag-9P	4859	4515	5,579

Note 1: A Brougham option package for the Monaco four-door passenger cars included special nameplates; lower body moldings with front and rear extensions; 50/50-type split-back front center armrest (reclining passenger seatback); rear seat center armrests; carpeted trunk compartment; spare tire cover and cornering lamps. This package was installed on 4,200 sedans and 1,564 four-door hardtop sedans.

Note 2: Data above slash for six/below slash for V-8s.

CHALLENGER SERIES — (6-CYL/V-8) — The only change in the Challenger from the 1972 version was a revised grille insert and big rubber bumper guards to meet safety bumper regulations. The Challenger was the base trim level hardtop and included all the federally mandated safety and pollution equipment; 318-cid V-8 engine; front and rear side armrests; front ashtrays; cigarette lighter; color-keyed carpeting; ventless side windows; glovebox with rotary latch; heater and defroster; dual horns; dome and parking brake/brake system warning lights; outside left manual mirror; inside day/night mirror; bucket seats; front foam seat cushion; three-spoke steering wheel (with simulated woodgrain and padded hub); electric windshield washer; and concealed two-speed wipers. The Challenger Rallye option also included a side scoop (located behind the front wheels) and strobe-type tape stripes that ran the full length of the car.

1973 Dodge, Challenger Rallye two-door hardtop, V-8

CHALLENGER I.D. DATA: See 1973 Dodge I.D. Data listing. All models began at 100001 and went up in the unit number sequence.

CHALLENGER SERIES

Model No.	Body/Style No.	Body Type & Seating	Factory Price	Shipping Weight	Prod. Total
JH	23	2-dr HT Cpe-4P	3011	3155	32,596

ENGINES:

(198 Slant Six) Overhead valve. Cast iron block. Displacement: 198 cid. Bore and stroke: 3.40 x 3.64 inches. Compression ratio: 8.4:1. Net hp: 95 at 4400 rpm. Four main bearings. Solid valve lifters. Carburetor: one-barrel.

(225 Slant Six) Overhead valve. Cast iron block. Displacement: 225 cid. Bore and stroke: 3.41 x 4.13 inches. Compression ratio: 8.4:1. Net hp: 105 at 4000 rpm. Four main bearings. Solid valve lifters. Carburetor: one-barrel.

(V-8) Overhead valve. Cast iron block. Displacement: 318 cid. Bore and stroke: 3.91 x 3.31 inches. Compression ratio: 8.6:1. Net hp: 150 at 4000 rpm. Four main bearings. Hydraulic valve lifters. Carburetor: two-barrel.

(V-8) Overhead valve. Cast iron block. Displacement: 340 cid. Bore and stroke: 4.04 x 3.31 inches. Compression ratio: 8.5:1. Net hp: 240 at 4800 rpm. Five main bearings. Hydraulic valve lifters. Carburetor: Carter Thermo-Quad four-barrel.

(V-8) Overhead valve. Cast iron block. Displacement: 360 cid. Bore and stroke: 4.00 x 3.58 inches. Compression ratio: 8.4:1. Net hp: 170 at 4000 rpm. Five main bearings. Hydraulic valve lifters. Carburetor: two-barrel.

(V-8) Overhead valve. Cast iron block. Displacement: 400 cid. Bore and stroke: 4.34 x 3.38 inches. Compression ratio: 8.2:1. Net hp: 175 at 4400 rpm. Five main bearings. Hydraulic valve lifters. Carburetor: two-barrel.

(V-8) Overhead valve. Cast iron block. Displacement: 400 cid. Bore and stroke: 4.34 x 3.38 inches. Compression ratio: 8.2:1. Net hp: 260 at

4400 rpm. Five main bearings. Hydraulic valve lifters. Carburetor: four-barrel.

(Magnum V-8) Overhead valve. Cast iron block. Displacement: 440 cid. Bore and stroke: 4.32 x 3.75 inches. Compression ratio: 8.2:1. Net hp: 280 at 4800 rpm. Five main bearings. Hydraulic valve lifters. Carburetor: four-barrel.

CHASSIS FEATURES: Wheelbase: (Dart coupe) 108 inches; (Dart hardtop/sedan) 111 inches; (Challenger) 110 inches; (all Coronets) 118 inches; (Charger) 115 inches; (Polara/Monaco) 122 inches. Overall length: (Dart coupe) 200 inches; (Dart hardtop/sedan) 204 inches; (Challenger) 199 inches; (Coronet station wagon) 218 inches; (Coronet/Charger) 213 inches; (Polara station wagon) 228 inches; (Monaco station wagon) 231 inches; (Polara) 227 inches; (Monaco) 229 inches. Width: (Dart coupe) 72 inches; (Dart hardtop/sedan) 70 inches; (Challenger) 77 inches; (Charger) 77 inches; (Coronet station wagon) 79 inches; (Coronet) 78 inches; (Polara/Monaco) 80 inches. Tires: (Dart '340') E70-14 (all other Darts) 6.95 x 14; (Challenger) 7.35 x 14; (Coronet/Charger) E78-14; (Coronet station wagon) H78-14; (Polara/Monaco three-seat station wagon) L84-15; (Polara/Monaco two-seat station wagon) J78-15; (Polara passenger) G78-15; (Monaco passenger) H78-15.

POWERTRAIN OPTIONS: Four-barrel 340-cid V-8 engine, in Coronet, Charger and Crestwood station wagon ($209). Four-barrel 340-cid V-8 engine, in Challenger ($181). Four-barrel 400-cid engine, in Coronet, Charger and Crestwood station wagon ($176). Automatic transmission standard in Polara, Polara Custom and Monaco. Two-barrel 318-cid V-8 engine in Dodge Dart ($143).

POPULAR CONVENIENCE OPTIONS: Vinyl top, on Dart ($61). Air conditioning, in Dart ($358). Vinyl top on Coronet ($95). Coronet/Charger AM/FM stereo ($211). Coronet/Charger AM/FM stereo with tape deck ($362). Regular vinyl top on Charger, standard on SE models; on other models ($115). Sun roof and canopy top on Charger ($251). Sun roof with full vinyl top, on Charger ($286). Sun roof with formal style vinyl roof, on Charger ($171). Vinyl top, on Challenger ($81). AM/FM stereo, in Challenger ($194). Challenger Rallye Package ($162). Air conditioning, in Challenger ($369). Vinyl top, on Monaco/Polara ($108). Monaco Brougham Package ($319). AM/FM stereo in Monaco/Polara ($212). AM/FM stereo with tape in Monaco/Polara ($363). Power windows, in Monaco/Polara ($126).

HISTORICAL FOOTNOTES: The full-size Dodges were introduced in September 1972 and the Dodge Darts appeared in dealer showrooms the same time. Model year production peaked at 675,161 units. Richard Petty accounted for six of eight Dodge wins in NASCAR Grand National stock car races in 1973, driving a Charger.

1974 DODGE

DART SPORT SERIES — (6-CYL/V-8) — Once again sporting the same body as in the previous three years, the 1974 Darts were updated only with new taillight, rear bumper and rear valance treatments. The balance of the car remained unchanged. The Dart Sport continued as the base trim level and included all federally mandated safety and pollution equipment; pivoting rear quarter windows; the 198-cid Slant Six engine; black rubber floor mats, 6.95 x 14 black sidewall tubeless tires, and the Dart Sport designation in block letters on the front fenders (just behind the wheelwells). The Dodge name, also in block letters, was carried on the right side of the rear escutcheon panel. With a large displacement engine replacing the previous year's '340', the Dart Sport 360 was the high-performance version of the Sport lineup and included all Dart Sport features plus the 360-cid two-barrel V-8 engine; ventless side windows; E70-14 black sidewall tires; grille surround moldings; front and rear bumper guards; power front disc brakes; heavy-duty suspension and shock absorbers; wheel covers; tape stripes; three-speed manual transmission with floor-mounted shifter; electronic ignition; and cigar lighter. Special 360 exterior identification was also included in the 360 package. A "Hang Ten" option package was available, after midyear, for Dart Sport coupes. A special striped interior and exterior were part of the surfing-oriented package. A 'Topper' trim package was available, midyear, for the base Dart Sport coupe.

DODGE I.D. DATA: The Vehicle Identification Number was located on a plate attached to left-hand side of dashboard, visible through windshield. The VIN has 13 symbols. (The first four symbols, together, are the Model Number in second column of charts below.) The first symbol identifies the car-line or marque: D=Monaco; J=Challenger; L=Dart; W=Coronet/Charger. The second symbol indicates trim/price level as follows: G=Grand; H=High; L=Low; M=Medium; P=Premium; S=Special. The next two symbols identify the body style, as follows:

21=two-door coupe; 23=two-door hardtop; 29=two-door Special hardtop; 41=sedan; 43=hardtop sedan; 45=six-passenger station wagon; 46=nine-passenger station wagon. The fifth symbol denotes the engine as follows: (six-cylinder) B=198 cid; C=225 cid; E=special order; (V-8) G=318 cid 2V; H=340 cid 4V (high-performance); J=360 cid 4V; K=360 cid 2V; L=360 cid 4V (high-performance); M=400 cid 2V; N=400 cid 4V; P=400 cid 4V (high-performance); T=440 cid 4V; U=440 cid 4V (high-performance). The sixth symbol denotes the model year as follows: 4=1974. The seventh symbol denotes the assembly plant as follows: A=Lynch Rd. (Detroit); B=Hamtramck, Mich.; C=Jefferson Ave. (Detroit); D=Belvedere, Ill.; F=Newark, Del.; G=St. Louis, Mo. The last six symbols are the sequential production number starting at 100001 for each series at each plant. Body code plate located under hood, on left (fender shield, wheelhousing or radiator support) includes S.O. number and trim/paint codes, too numerous to list.

DART SPORT SERIES

Model No.	Body/ Style No.	Body Type & Seating	Factory Price	Shipping Weight	Prod. Total
DART SPORT					
LL	29	2-dr Cpe-6P	2878/3029	2990/3140	Note 1
DART SPORT '360'					
LM	29	2-dr Cpe-6P	3320	3330	Note 1

Note 1: Some 63,518 Dart Sports were built during model year 1974. Of those, 40,293 were sixes and 23,225 were V-8s. Some 3,951 Dart Sport 360s were built during the year, all V-8s.

Note 2: Exact model year production totals are not available for 1974 Dodges. Figures given in the footnotes are model year totals for cars built in the U.S. for domestic sales and are expressed in exact amounts. Cars built in Canada for the domestic market are not included.

Note 3: Data above slash for six/below slash for V-8s.

1974 Dodge, Dart Swinger two-door hardtop, V-8

DART SERIES — (6-CYL/V-8) — The Dart was the standard base trim level in the Dart model lineup and included all federally mandated safety and pollution equipment; front and rear armrests; ashtrays; cigarette lighter; concealed spare tire; rubber floor mats; glovebox with rotary latch; heater and defroster; dome light; parking brake and brake system warning lights; all-vinyl bench seats; three-spoke steering wheel (with padded horn button); two-speed windshield wipers; 198-cid Slant Six (or 318-cid V-8 engine) and vent wings. Dart Swingers included all the standard Dart features plus dual note horns; deluxe steering wheel; carpeting; and drip rail and door edge moldings. The Custom included all the Swinger features plus cloth and vinyl seats. The Special Edition was a new, luxury version Dart model and included all the Custom features plus padded vinyl top, brocade cloth seating surfaces and color-keyed Deluxe wheel covers. The Special Edition was released Jan. 13, 1974, as a midyear addition to the lineup.

DART/SWINGER/CUSTOM/SPECIAL EDITION I.D. DATA: See 1974 Dodge I.D. Data listing. All models began at 100001 and went up in the unit number sequence.

DART/SWINGER/CUSTOM/SPECIAL EDITION SERIES

BASE/SPECIAL

LL	41	4-dr Sed-6P	2961/3112	3055/3205	Note 1
LL	23	2-dr Spl HT Cpe-6P	2918/3069	3035/3185	Note 1

SWINGER/CUSTOM

LH	23	2-dr Swinger-6P	3077/3228	3030/3180	Note 1
LH	41	4-dr Cus Sed-6P	3119/3270	3055/3205	Note 1

SPECIAL EDITION

Model No.	Body/ Style No.	Body Type & Seating	Factory Price	Shipping Weight	Prod. Total
LP	41	4-dr Sed-6P	3837/3988	3641/3791	Note 1
LP	23	2-dr HT Cpe-6P	3794/3945	3599/3749	Note 1

Note 1: Some 16,155 Swinger Specials were built during model year 1974. Of those, 14,211 were sixes and 1,944 were V-8s. Some 89,242 Swingers were built during that year. Of those, 56,126 were sixes and 33,116 were V-8s. During model year 1974 some 78,216 Customs were built. Of those, 50,047 were sixes and 28,169 were V-8s. Some 12,385 Special Editions were built during that year. Of those, 3,111 were sixes and 9,274 were V-8s.

Note 2: Data above slash for six/below slash for V-8.

1974 Dodge, Coronet Custom four-door sedan, V-8

CORONET SERIES — (6-CYL/V-8) — Coronets received a front end restyling, changed rear bumper and new taillights for 1974. The full-width grille enclosed the quad headlights and the grille was an eggcrate design with rectangular openings. The Dodge name, in block letters, was spaced across the center of the hood and also appeared on the right side of the trunk lid. The Coronet was the base trim level and included all federally mandated safety and pollution equipment; the 225-cid Slant Six (or 318-cid V-8) engine; color-keyed rubber floor mats; vinyl bench seats; front and rear bumper guards; day/night inside mirror; foam cushion rear seat; three-spoke steering wheel; front and rear ashtrays and armrests; dome light; chrome hubcaps; cigarette lighter; glovebox lock; dual horns; sill moldings; and E78-14 black sidewall tubeless tires. The Coronet Custom was the top trim level in the Coronet series and included all the Coronet trim plus carpeting; roof drip rail moldings; wheel lip opening and bodyside moldings; dual note horns and deluxe steering wheel. The Crestwood was the top trim level station wagon and included all the standard station wagon features plus roof-mounted air deflectors; Deluxe wheel covers; map and glovebox lights; cargo area carpeting; woodgrain bodyside panels; bright upper door frame and quarter window moldings and H78-14 black sidewall tires.

CORONET I.D. DATA: See 1974 Dodge I.D. Data listing. All models began at 100001 and went up in the unit number sequence.

CORONET SERIES

CORONET

WL	41	4-dr Sed-6P	3271/3386	3610/3685	Note 1
WL	45	4-dr Sta Wag-6P	3699	4185	Note 1

CORONET CUSTOM

WH	41	4-dr Sed-6P	3374/3489	3500/3575	Note 1
WH	45	4-dr Sta Wag-6P	3882	4090	Note 1
WH	46	4-dr Sta Wag-9P	4196	4130	Note 1

CRESTWOOD

WP	45	4-dr Sta Wag-6P	4117	4100	Note 1
WP	46	4-dr Sta Wag-9P	4433	4135	Note 1

Note 1: Some 6,013 Coronets and Chargers were built during model year 1974. Of those, 3,315 were sixes and 2,698 were V-8s. Some 55,599 Coronet Customs were built during the year. Of those, 2,252 were sixes and 53,347 were V-8s.

CHARGER SERIES — (6-CYL/V-8) — Featuring only slight changes in the grille and taillights, the 1974 Chargers continued to be popular with the public. The standard Charger continued as the base trim level and included all federally mandated safety and pollution equipment; 225-cid Slant Six (or 318-cid V-8) engine; cigarette lighter; dual horns; color-keyed carpeting; inside day/night mirror; roof drip rail and wheelwell moldings; and two-speed windshield wipers. The Charger Rallye option included all the standard Charger features plus front and rear sway bars; F70-14 raised white letter black sidewall tires; power bulge hood; Rallye instrument cluster; body tape stripes; hood pins and special exterior ornamentation. The Charger SE continued as the top trim level and included all the standard Charger features plus landau vinyl top with filled quarter windows and six opera windows; electric clock; concealed headlights; inside hood release; belt and rear hood moldings; front stone shield molding; Deluxe wheel covers; front bench seat with folding center armrests, Light Group; Rallye instrument cluster; and F78-14 black sidewall tires.

CHARGER I.D. DATA: See 1974 Dodge I.D. Data listing. All models began at 100001 and went up in the unit number sequence.

1974 Dodge, Charger two-door hardtop, V-8

CHARGER SERIES

Model No.	Body/ Style No.	Body Type & Seating	Factory Price	Shipping Weight	Prod. Total
WL	21	2-dr Cpe-6P	3212/3327	3470/3550	Note 1
WL	23	2-dr HT Cpe-6P	3412/3526	3490/3565	Note 1
WP	29	2-dr SE HT-6P	3742	3625	Note 1

Note 1: Some 6,013 Coronets and Chargers were built during model year 1974. Of those, 3,315 were sixes and 2,698 were V-8s. Some 30,957 Charger SEs were built during model year 1974, all V-8s.

Note 2: Data above slash for six/below slash for V-8.

1974 Dodge, Monaco Brougham station wagon, V-8

MONACO SERIES — (6-CYL/V-8) — For the first time since 1960, the Polara name was not included in the full-size Dodge lineup. All full-size 1974 models were called Monacos. Completely restyled for the year, the new Monacos were, perhaps, the most pleasant looking of all 1974 Dodges. The rounded look of the previous few years was replaced by a leaner and less bulky body style. The grille was similar to the Buicks of that era and, when combined with the squarer sides, more angular rooflines and conservative use of chrome trim produced a nice looking car. The Monaco was the base trim level and included all federally mandated safety and pollution equipment; front ashtrays and armrests; cigar lighter; carpeting; dual headlights and horns; dome and parking brake/brake system warning lights; inside day/night mirror; concealed wipers; air control system; power steering; TorqueFlite automatic transmission; power front disc brakes; front and rear bumper guards; front seatback latches; truck compartment rubber mats; 360-cid V-8 engine; and G78-15 tubeless black sidewall tires. Monaco station wagons also had a power tailgate window; 400-cid V-8 engine and J78-15 tubeless black sidewall tires. The Custom was the intermediate trim level Monaco and included all the standard Monaco features plus a glovebox lock; adjustable front seat; rear armrests with ashtrays; ignition switch light; front and rear foam padded seats; wheel lip moldings; trunk mat; and dome light. The two-door hardtop also included a rear pillar interior courtesy light. Four-door models added upper door frame moldings and Custom station wagons also included a cargo area dome light and heavy-duty brakes. The Brougham was the top trim level Monaco and included all the Custom features plus nylon carpeting; cornering lights; electric clock; all-vinyl seats (with fold-down center armrest); headlights-on reminder; Deluxe wheel covers and HR78-15 radial black sidewall tires. Brougham station wagons added rear compartment lock; bright upper door frame and quarter rear door automatic entrance switches; Deluxe

wheel covers; woodgrain side panels with surround moldings and cargo compartment carpeting. The 400-cid V-8 engine was also standard on all Brougham models.

MONACO I.D. DATA: See 1974 Dodge I.D. Data listing. All models began at 100001 and went up in the unit number sequence.

MONACO SERIES

Model No.	Body/ Style No.	Body Type & Seating	Factory Price	Shipping Weight	Prod. Total
MONACO					
DM	41	4-dr Sed-6P	4259	4170	Note 1
DM	23	2-dr HT Cpe-6P	4283	4150	Note 1
DM	45	4-dr Sta Wag-6P	4706	4760	Note 1
MONACO CUSTOM					
DH	41	4-dr Sed-6P	4446	4175	Note 1
DH	43	4-dr HT Sed-6P	4539	4205	Note 1
DH	23	2-dr HT Cpe-6P	4464	4155	Note 1
DH	45	4-dr Sta Wag-6P	4839	4770	Note 1
DH	46	4-dr Sta Wag-9P	4956	4815	Note 1
MONACO BROUGHAM					
DP	41	4-dr Sed-6P	4891	4410	Note 1
DP	43	4-dr HT Sed-6P	4999	4445	Note 1
DP	23	2-dr HT Cpe-6P	4951	4370	Note 1
DP	45	4-dr Sta Wag-6P	5360	4860	Note 1
DP	46	4-dr Sta Wag-9P	5477	4905	Note 1

Note 1: Some 20,810 Monacos, 4,874 Monaco Specials (police and taxi), 34,414 Customs and 18,226 Broughams were built during model year 1974, all V-8s.

1974 Dodge, Challenger two-door hardtop, V-8

CHALLENGER SERIES — (6-CYL/V-8) — Appearing for the last time in this configuration (the name would be revived for a Japanese-built Dodge Sport compact), the 1974 Challenger was unchanged from the 1973 models. The Challenger continued to be the base trim level and included all federally mandated safety and pollution equipment; vinyl bucket seats; front foam seat cushions; concealed wipers; three-speed manual transmission with floor-mounted shifter; the 318-cid V-8 engine; 7.35 x 14 tubeless black sidewall tires; three-spoke steering wheel; front and rear bumper guards; heavy-duty suspension; ventless side windows; roof drip rail and wheel lip moldings; heavy-duty suspension; ventless windows; cigar lighter; carpeting; day/night inside mirror and electronic ignition. The Challenger Rallye option added a side scoop, behind the front wheels, with strobe-type tape stripes that ran the full length of the car, plus two hood scoops and special cast wheels with trim rings and F70-14 raised white letter tires.

CHALLENGER I.D. DATA: See 1974 Dodge I.D. Data listing. All models began at 100001 and went up in the unit number sequence.

CHALLENGER SERIES

JH	23	2-dr HT Cpe-4P	3143	3225	16,437

ENGINES:

(198 Slant Six) Overhead valve. Cast iron block. Displacement: 198 cid. Bore and stroke: 3.40 x 3.64 inches. Compression ratio: 8.4:1. Net hp: 95 at 4400 rpm. Four main bearings. Solid valve lifters. Carburetor: one-barrel.

(225 Slant Six) Overhead valve. Cast iron block. Displacement: 225 cid. Bore and stroke: 3.41 x 4.13 inches. Compression ratio: 8.4:1. Net hp: 105 at 4000 rpm. Four main bearings. Solid valve lifters. Carburetor: one-barrel.

(V-8) Overhead valve. Cast iron block. Displacement: 318 cid. Bore and stroke: 3.91 x 3.31 inches. Compression ratio: 8.6:1. Net hp: 150 at 4000 rpm. Hydraulic valve lifters. Carburetor: two-barrel.

(V-8) Overhead valve. Cast iron block. Displacement: 360 cid. Bore and stroke: 4.00 x 3.58 inches. Compression ratio: 8.4:1. Net hp: 200 at 4000 rpm. Five main bearings. Hydraulic valve lifters. Carburetor: two-barrel.

(V-8) Overhead valve. Cast iron block. Displacement: 360 cid. Bore and stroke: 4.00 x 3.58 inches. Compression ratio: 8.4:1. Net hp: 245 at 4000 rpm. Five main bearings. Hydraulic valve lifters. Carburetor: four-barrel.

(V-8) Overhead valve. Cast iron block. Displacement: 400 cid. Bore and stroke: 4.34 x 3.38 inches. Compression ratio: 8.2:1. Net hp: 205 at 4400 rpm. Five main bearings. Hydraulic valve lifters. Carburetor: four-barrel.

(V-8) Overhead valve. Cast iron block. Displacement: 400 cid. Bore and stroke: 4.34 x 3.38 inches. Compression ratio: 8.2:1. Net hp: 250 at 4400 rpm. Five main bearings. Hydraulic valve lifters. Carburetor: four-barrel.

(V-8) Overhead valve. Cast iron block. Displacement: 440 cid. Bore and stroke: 4.32 x 3.75 inches. Compression ratio: 8.2:1. Net hp: 230 at 4400. Five main bearings. Hydraulic valve lifters. Carburetor: four-barrel.

(Magnum V-8) Overhead valve. Cast iron block. Displacement: 440 cid. Bore and stroke: 4.32 x 3.75 inches. Compression ratio: 8.2:1. Net hp: 275 at 4800. Five main bearings. Hydraulic valve lifters. Carburetor: four-barrel.

CHASSIS FEATURES: Wheelbase: (Dart coupe) 108 inches; (Dart hardtop/sedan) 111 inches; (Challenger) 110 inches; (all Coronets) 118 inches; (Charger) 115 inches; (Monaco) 121.5 inches. Overall length: (Dart coupe) 200 inches; (Dart hardtop/sedan) 204 inches; (Challenger) 199 inches; (Coronet station wagon) 218 inches; (Coronet/Charger) 213 inches; (Monaco station wagon) 231 inches; (Monaco sedan) 224 inches; (Monaco Custom) 226 inches; (Monaco station wagon) 227 inches; (Brougham station wagon) 229 inches. Width: (Dart coupe) 72 inches; (Dart hardtop/sedan) 70 inches; (Challenger) 77 inches; (Charger) 77 inches; (Coronet station wagon) 79 inches; (Coronet) 78 inches; (Monaco) 80 inches. Tires: G78-15 tubeless black sidewall on sedans, J78-15 on Broughams and LR78-15B radial black sidewall on station wagons. TorqueFlite automatic transmission was standard on all Monaco models.

POWERTRAIN OPTIONS: Automatic transmission was standard on Monaco, Monaco Custom and Monaco Brougham. Charger '360' V-8 engine ($222). Challenger '360' V-8 engine ($259). Charger '400' V-8 engine ($188). Dart '318' V-8 engine ($151).

CONVENIENCE OPTIONS: Vinyl top, on Dart ($88). Air conditioning, on Dart ($384). Sun roof, on Dart ($154). Vinyl top on Coronet ($103). AM/FM stereo in Coronet/Charger ($230). Regular vinyl top, on Charger SE (standard equipment); on all other Chargers ($125). Sun roof with vinyl canopy top, on Charger ($261). Vinyl top on Monaco ($117). AM/FM stereo, in Monaco ($254). AM/FM stereo with tape, in Monaco ($397). Power windows, in Monaco ($137). Sun roof, in Monaco ($521). RV7 Package on Monaco ($400). Vinyl top on Challenger ($84). AM/FM stereo, in Challenger ($202). Rallye Package, on Challenger ($190). Sun roof with vinyl canopy top, on Challenger ($261).

HISTORICAL FOOTNOTES: The full-size Dodges were introduced on Sept. 25, 1973, and the Darts appeared in dealer showrooms at the same time. As in the past several years, the production of certain models was quartered at specific factories in the United States and Canada. The series production totals listed in this catalog are exact figures, but cover only cars built in the United States. Cars built in Canada for the U.S. market will not be reflected in these records. Therefore, such totals should be considered only a guide to how many cars of a certain type were manufactured. For some series, the number of units actually sold by U.S. franchised dealers could be much larger. Dodge marked its 60th year as an automaker during 1974. Dodge NASCAR drivers won 10 NASCAR Grand National races, of which six went to Richard Petty. It was the company's best racing year since 1970.

1975 DODGE

DART SPORT SERIES — (6-CYL/V-8) — Continuing to use the basic body introduced in 1970, the new Darts received a slightly revised grille. A 'trademark' of the mid-1970s automobile - the spring-loaded hood ornament - was a new sight on Darts. The base Dart Sport models featured redesigned roof tape stripe treatments and lower escutcheon panel appliques. Integrated taillight bezels were also adopted. The remainder of the car stayed generally the same as before. Dart Sports included all

federally mandated safety and pollution equipment; pivoting rear quarter windows; the 225-cid Slant Six (or 318-cid V-8) engine; black rubber floor mats and 6.95 x 14B tubeless black sidewall tires. The designation Dart Sport appeared, in block letters, on the front fender sides. The Dart Sport '360' continued as the high-performance entry in this series. It included all base features plus the 360-cid V-8; ventless side windows; E78-14 black sidewall tires, grille surround moldings; front and rear bumper guards; power front disc brakes; heavy-duty suspension and shock absorbers; wheel covers; tape stripes; three-speed manual transmission with floor-mounted shifter; electronic ignition; cigar lighter and special '360' exterior identification.

DODGE I.D. DATA: The Vehicle Identification Number was located on a plate attached to left-hand side of dashboard, visible through windshield. The VIN has 13 symbols. (The first four symbols, together, are the Model Number in second column of charts below.) The first symbol identifies the car-line or marque D=Monaco; L=Dart; W=Coronet; X=Charger. The second symbol indicates trim/price level, as follows: D=Dodge Taxi; T=Taxi; S=Special; G=Grand; H=High; L=Low; M=Medium; P=Premium; S=Special. The next two symbols identify the body style, as follows: 21/22=two-door coupe; 23=two-door hardtop; 29=two-door Special hardtop; 41=sedan; 43=hardtop sedan; 45=six-passenger station wagon; 46=nine-passenger station wagon. The fifth symbol denotes the engine as follows: (six-cylinder) C=225 cid; E=special order; (V-8) G=318 cid 2V; J=360 cid 4V; K=360 cid 2V; L=360 cid 4V (high-performance); M=400 cid 2V; N=400 cid 4V; P=400 cid 4V (high-performance); T=440 cid 4V; U=440 cid 4V (high-performance); Z=Special Order V-8. The sixth symbol denotes the model year as follows: 5=1975. The seventh symbol denotes the assembly plant, as follows: A=Lynch Rd. (Detroit); B=Hamtramck, Mich.; C=Jefferson Ave. (Detroit); D=Belvedere, Ill.; F=Newark, Del.; G=St. Louis, Mo.; R=Canada. The last six symbols are the sequential production number starting at 100001 for each series at each plant. Body code plate located under hood, on left (fender shield, wheelhousing or radiator support) includes S.O. number and trim/paint codes, too numerous to list.

1975 Dodge, Dart Custom four-door sedan, 6-cyl

ART SPORT SERIES

Model No.	Body/ Style No.	Body Type & Seating	Factory Price	Shipping Weight	Prod. Total
SPORT					
LL	29	2-dr Cpe-6P	3297/3447	2980/3130	Note 1
SPORT '360'					
LM	29	2-dr Cpe-6P	4014	3335	Note 1

Note 1: Some 37,192 Dart Sports were built during model year 1975. Of those, 28,391 were sixes and 8,801 were V-8s.

Note 2: The production totals given in the charts are exact figures for cars produced in the U.S. with breakouts by model year and series. No body style breakouts are available. Cars built in Canada for the U.S. market are not included. Therefore, these totals should serve only as 'ballpark' guidelines in determining the number of units produced for domestic sales.

Note 3: Data above slash for six/below slash for V-8.

DART SERIES — (6-CYL/V-8) — A grille with a more formal look and matching parking light arrangement highlighted exterior changes in the standard Dart models for 1975. Base trim level features included all federally mandated safety and pollution equipment; front and rear ashtrays; armrests; cigarette lighter; concealed spare tire; rubber floor mats; glovebox with rotary latch; heater and defroster; dome light; parking brake (and warning system); all-vinyl bench seats; three-spoke steering wheel (with padded horn button); two-speed windshield wipers and vent wings. Power was supplied by either the '225' Slant Six or '318' V-8. Dart Swingers added dual horns, deluxe steering wheel, carpeting and drip rail and door edge moldings. The Dart Custom models also included plush cloth and vinyl seats. The top trim level was the Dart Special Edition, which included all Dart Custom equipment plus a padded vinyl top, velour interior seating surfaces and color-keyed wheel covers. A Dart

Swinger decorator package called the Spring Special debuted at midyear, featuring a special interior.

1975 Dodge, Dart Special Edition two-door hardtop, V-8

DART SERIES

Model No.	Body/ Style No.	Body Type & Seating	Factory Price	Shipping Weight	Prod. Total
DART					
LL	41	4-dr Sed-6P	3269/3419	3060/3210	Note 1
LL	23	2-dr Spl HT Cpe-6P	3341/3491	3045/3195	Note 1
DART CUSTOM					
LH	23	2-dr Swinger HT-6P	3518/3666	3035/3185	Note 1
LH	41	4-dr Cus Sed-6P	3444/3594	3060/3210	Note 1
DART SPECIAL EDITION					
LP	41	4-dr Sed-6P	4159/4309	3260/3430	Note 1
LP	23	2-dr HT Cpe-6P	4232/4362	3260/3410	Note 1

Note 1: Some 19,349 Darts were built during model year 1975. Of those, 17,600 were sixes and 1,749 were V-8s. Some 7,028 Swinger Specials were built during model year 1975. Of those, 6,705 were sixes and 323 were V-8s. Some 93,557 Swingers and Dart Customs were built during model year 1975. Of those, 75,105 were sixes and 18,452 were V-8s. Some 13,971 Dart Special Editions were built during model year 1975. Of those, 7,393 were sixes and 6,598 were V-8s.

Note 2: Model year U.S. dealer sales of 1975 Dodge Darts (all series) totaled exactly 164,434 cars. Calendar year registrations of Darts hit exactly 163,639 cars. The variations between production and sales totals are due to the splitting of production between the U.S. and Canada.

Note 3: Data above slash for six/below slash for V-8.

1975 Dodge, Coronet Brougham two-door hardtop, V-8

CORONET SERIES — (6-CYL/V-8) — Once again (since 1970) offering a two-door model, the new Coronet line featured a restyled grille. It was characterized by a horizontal theme and divided in the center. The new single unit headlights were housed in rectangular doors. Sharply sculptured feature lines accented the revived hardtops, which were further highlighted by vertical taillights and a full-width bumper that housed the back-up lamps. Coronet was the base trim level and incorporated all federally mandated safety and pollution equipment; the '225' Slant Six (or '318' V-8) engine; color-keyed rubber floor mats; vinyl bench seats; front and rear bumper guards; inside day/night mirrors; foam rear seat cushion; three-spoke steering wheel; front and rear ashtrays and armrests; dome light; chrome hubcaps; cigarette lighter; glovebox lock; dual horns; sill moldings and E78-14 black sidewall tubeless tires. Coronet Customs added carpeting; roof drip rail, wheel lip and bodyside moldings; dual note horns and deluxe steering wheel. The Coronet Brougham was the top trim level, incorporating all Custom features plus special bodyside moldings (with vinyl inserts); stand-up hood ornament; special exterior

rearview mirrors; padded vinyl top and turbine-style wheel covers. The Crestwood was the high-level station wagon and included all standard station wagon features plus roof-mounted air deflector; deluxe wheel covers; map and glovebox lights; cargo area carpeting; woodgrain body-side paneling; bright upper door frame and quarter window moldings and H78-14 tubeless black sidewall tires.

CORONET I.D. DATA: See 1975 Dodge I.D. Data listing. All models began at 100001 and went up in the unit number sequence.

CORONET SERIES

Model No.	Body/ Style No.	Body Type & Seating	Factory Price	Shipping Weight	Prod. Total
CORONET					
WL	41	4-dr Sed-6P	3641/3769	3595/3710	Note 1
WL	21	2-dr HT Cpe-6P	3591/3719	3565/3675	Note 1
WL	45	4-dr Sta Wag-6P	4358	4165	Note 2
CORONET CUSTOM					
WH	41	4-dr Sed-6P	3754/3883	3635/3750	Note 1
WH	23	2-dr HT Cpe-6P	3777/3904	3645/3760	Note 1
WH	45	4-dr Sta Wag-6P	4560	4240	Note 2
WH	46	4-dr Sta Wag-9P	4674	4290	Note 2
BROUGHAM/CRESTWOOD STATION WAGON					
WP	23	2-dr HT Cpe-6P	4154	3600	Note 1
WP	45	4-dr Sta Wag-6P	4826	4230	Note 2
WP	46	4-dr Sta Wag-9P	4918	4290	Note 2

Note 1: Some 11,608 Coronet passenger cars were built during model year 1974, including 1,697 sixes and 9,911 V-8s. Some 41,893 Custom Coronet passenger cars were built during model year 1975, including 2,854 sixes and 39,039 V-8s. Some 9,975 Coronet Brougham passenger cars were built during model year 1975, all V-8s.

Note 2: Some 8,019 intermediate-size Dodge station wagons were built during model year 1975. This included all Coronet/Coronet Custom and Crestwood station wagons, with no further breakout by line. All station wagons were V-8 powered.

Note 3: Data above slash for six/below slash for V-8.

CHARGER SE SERIES — (6-CYL/V-8) — Introduced to compete in the popular specialty car market occupied by the Chevrolet Monte Carlo and Ford Elite, the new Charger SE utilized formal styling and was available only in a two-door hardtop coupe configuration. It used a popular long hood/short rear deck styling approach and the padded top featured opera windows with six horizontal louvers for accent. The front end treatment was highlighted by a large rectangular grille opening featuring three horizontal divider bars and single headlights housed in round, chrome bezels. Double horizontal taillights gave a traditional Dodge look to the highly sculptured rear. The license plate was recessed in the center of the rear end, directly below the trunk lid. The dipped beltline provided a low-appearing silhouette. The Charger SE featured more standard equipment than any intermediate-size Dodge previously offered. As well as the federally mandated safety and pollution equipment, all Charger SEs included the 360-cid two-barrel V-8 engine; TorqueFlite automatic transmission; power steering; power front disc brakes; electronic digital clock; radial white sidewall tires; dual horns; inside hood release and front and rear sway bars. On March 4, 1975, a Daytona option package was announced for the Charger SE. It came in three color combinations and featured two-tone exterior paint with Daytona lettering. The package, for $132, featured vinyl bucket seats. It was the first use of the Daytona name since the 1969 winged version. Ironically, for 1975, Dodge drivers in NASCAR avoided the 1975 SE and drove 1974 Chargers, which accounted for 14 Grand National wins.

1975 Dodge, Charger SE two-door hardtop, V-8

CHARGER SE I.D. DATA: See 1975 Dodge I.D. Data listing. All models began at 100001 and went up in the unit number sequence.

CHARGER SE SERIES

Model No.	Body/ Style No.	Body Type & Seating	Factory Price	Shipping Weight	Prod. Total
XS	22	2-dr HT Cpe-6P	4903	3950	Note 1

Note 1: Production of the Charger SE was included with that of the Dodge Coronet lines since cars in both series were built off the same platform.

Note 2: A total of exactly 30,812 Charger SE hardtops were sold by U.S. automobile dealers during the 1975 model year. Such sales figures do not conform exactly to production totals, but fall in the same general 'ballpark'.

Note 3: Data above slash for six/below slash for V-8.

MONACO SERIES — (6-CYL/V-8) — Utilizing the same body as in 1974, the new models seemed different, if for no other reason than a massive change in model nomenclature. The base trim level Monaco continued to use the same name as in 1974 and included all federally mandated safety and pollution equipment; front ashtrays and armrests; cigar lighter; carpeting; dual headlights and horns; dome and parking brake/brake system warning lights; inside day/night mirror; concealed wipers; air control system; power steering; TorqueFlite automatic transmission; power front disc brakes; front and rear bumper guards; front seatback latches; trunk compartment rubber mats; 360-cid V-8 engine and G78-15 tubeless black sidewall tires. Monaco station wagons also included power tailgate window, 400-cid V-8 engine and J78-15 tubeless black sidewall tires. The 1974 Monaco Custom became the Royal Monaco for 1975. It included all the standard Monaco features plus a glovebox lock; adjustable front seat; rear armrests; ashtrays; ignition switch light; front and rear foam padded seat; wheel lip moldings; trunk mat and dome light. The two-door hardtop also included a rear pillar courtesy light. Four-door models also included upper door frame moldings. Royal station wagons also included a cargo area dome light and heavy-duty brakes. The top trim level 1974 Monaco Brougham became the luxurious Royal Monaco Brougham for 1975 and included all the Royal Monaco features plus nylon carpeting; cornering lights; electric clock; all-vinyl bench seats (with fold-down center armrest); headlights-on reminder; Deluxe wheel covers and HR78-15 radial black sidewall tires. Royal Monaco Brougham station wagons also included rear compartment lock; bright upper door frames and quarter window moldings; rear door automatic entrance switches; Deluxe wheel covers; woodgrain side panels with surround moldings and cargo compartment carpeting. A special, ultra-luxurious trim package was available for Royal Monaco Brougham two-door hardtops. Called the Diplomat, the package consisted of a wide, brushed aluminum trim band that crossed the roof. It was similar to the Ford Crown Victoria. The Diplomat also featured side opera windows; padded landau roof, special velour interior trim and distinctive exterior ornamentation. Royal Monaco and Royal Monaco Brougham models utilized the 400-cid V-8 engine as standard equipment. A Diplomat formal roof option was announced Dec. 13, 1974, for the Royal Monaco Brougham two-door hardtop. It featured a stainless steel band over the top of the roof at the door post.

MONACO I.D. DATA: See 1975 Dodge I.D. Data listing. All models began at 100001 and went up in the unit number sequence.

MONACO SERIES

Model No.	Body/ Style No.	Body Type & Seating	Factory Price	Shipping Weight	Prod. Total
MONACO					
DM	41	4-dr Sed-6P	4605	4260	Note 1
DM	23	2-dr HT Cpe-6P	4631	4225	Note 1
DM	45	4-dr Sta Wag-6P	5109	4885	Note 2
ROYAL MONACO					
DH	41	4-dr Sed-6P	4848	4285	Note 1
DH	43	4-dr HT Sed-6P	4951	4310	Note 1
DH	23	2-dr HT Cpe-6P	4868	4240	Note 1
DH	45	4-dr Sta Wag-6P	5292	4905	Note 2
DH	46	4-dr Sta Wag-9P	5415	4945	Note 2
ROYAL MONACO BROUGHAM					
DP	41	4 dr Sed-6P	5262	4455	Note 1
DP	43	4-dr HT Sed-6P	5382	4485	Note 1
DP	29	2-dr FT Cpe-6P	5460	4370	Note 1
DP	45	4-dr Sta Wag-6P	5779	4980	Note 1
DP	46	4-dr Sta Wag-9P	5905	5025	Note 1

Note 1: Some 34,802 Monaco/Royal Monaco passenger cars (combined series) were built during the 1975 model year. Some 22,218 Monaco Brougham passenger cars were built during the 1975 model year. All Monacos were V-8 powered.

Note 2: Some 8,019 full-size Dodge station wagons were built during the 1975 model year. This included all Monaco/Royal Monaco and Monaco Brougham station wagons, with no further breakouts by line. All station wagons were V-8 powered.

Note 3: Data above slash for six/below slash for V-8s.

ENGINES:

(Inline Six) Overhead valve. Cast iron block. Displacement: 225 cid. Bore and stroke: 3.40 x 4.12 inches. Compression ratio: 8.4:1. SAE Net hp: 95 at 3600 rpm. Four main bearings. Solid valve lifters. Carburetor: one-barrel.

(V-8) Overhead valve. Cast iron block. Displacement: 318 cid. Bore and stroke: 3.91 x 3.31 inches. Compression ratio: 8.5:1. SAE Net hp: 145 at 4000 rpm. Five main bearings. Hydraulic valve lifters. Carburetor: two-barrel.

(V-8) Overhead valve. Cast iron block. Displacement: 360 cid. Bore and stroke: 4.00 x 3.58 inches. Compression ratio: 8.4:1. SAE Net hp: 180 at 4000 rpm. Five main bearings. Hydraulic valve lifters. Carburetor: two-barrel.

(V-8) Overhead valve. Cast iron block. Displacement: 360 cid. Bore and stroke: 4.00 x 3.58 inches. Compression ratio: 8.4:1. SAE Net hp: 200 at 4400 rpm. Five main bearings. Hydraulic valve lifters. Carburetor: four-barrel.

(V-8) Overhead valve. Cast iron block. Displacement: 400 cid. Bore and stroke: 4.34 x 3.38 inches. Compression ratio: 8.2:1. SAE Net hp: 175 at 4000 rpm. Five main bearings. Hydraulic valve lifters. Carburetor: two-barrel.

(V-8) Overhead valve. Cast iron block. Displacement: 400 cid. Bore and stroke: 4.34 x 3.38 inches. Compression ratio: 8.2:1. SAE Net hp: 190 at 4200 rpm. Five main bearings. Hydraulic valve lifters. Carburetor: four-barrel.

(V-8) Overhead valve. Cast iron block. Displacement: 440 cid. Bore and stroke: 4.32 x 3.75 inches. Compression ratio: 8.2:1. SAE Net hp: 215 at 4000 rpm. Five main bearings. Hydraulic valve lifters. Carburetor: four-barrel.

Note: When equipped with dual exhaust the two-barrel '400' V-8 was rated 185 hp and the four-barrel '400' V-8 was rated 235 hp.

CHASSIS FEATURES: Wheelbase: (Dart sedan and hardtop) 111 inches; (Dart coupe) 108 inches; (Coronet/Charger hardtop) 115 inches; (other Coronet models) 117.5 inches; (Monaco station wagon) 124 inches; (Monaco passenger cars) 121.5 inches. Overall length: (Dodge Dart sedan and hardtop) 204 inches; (Dart coupe) 201 inches; (Coronet hardtop) 214 inches; (Coronet station wagon) 226 inches; (other Coronets) 218 inches; (Charger hardtop) 218 inches; (all Monaco station wagons) 229 inches; (Monaco Royal/Brougham) 226 inches; (Monaco) 224 inches. Width: (Dart sedan and hardtop) 70 inches; (Dart coupe) 72 inches; (Coronet station wagons) 79 inches; (other Coronets) 78 inches; (Charger) 78 inches; (all Monacos) 80 inches. Tires: Refer to text above.

POWERTRAIN OPTIONS: Automatic transmission was standard in Dart '360' Sport/Dart Special Edition/Charger SE/Crestwood/Monaco. Automatic transmission was also standard with V-8s. Three-speed manual transmission standard with all six-cylinder attachments. Two-barrel '360' V-8 in Coronet ($89). Four-barrel '360' V-8 in Charger SE ($153). Four-barrel '360' V-8 in Coronet ($202). Four-barrel '400' in Coronet ($122). Four-barrel '400' V-8 in Charger SE ($73). Two-barrel '318' V-8 in Dart ($151).

CONVENIENCE OPTIONS: Bucket seats, in Dart ($133). Power disc brakes in Dart ($65). Fold-down seats, in Dart ($99). Vinyl top, on Dart SE (standard); on other Darts ($88). Air conditioning in Dart ($407). Sun roof, on Dart ($178). Dart Rallye Package ($594). Dart 'Sport Topper' roof treatment ($251). Dart 'Hang Ten' Package ($254). Coronet/Charger/Monaco AM/FM stereo ($254); same with tape deck ($397). Coronet station wagon luggage rack ($67). Coronet power windows ($139). Coronet power seats ($119). Easy Order Option Package, on Coronet/Charger SE ($812). Coronet Rallye Package ($225). Coronet/Charger SE sun roof ($296). Coronet/Charger Road Wheels ($109). Charger SE power seat ($117). Charger SE power windows ($97). Vinyl top, on Charger ($109). Vinyl top, on Monaco Brougham (standard); on Monaco ($117). Monaco sun roof ($634). Monaco station wagon luggage rack ($79). Easy Order Option Package, Monaco station wagons ($460); Royal Monaco ($435). Electric rear defroster, in Monacos ($73). Cornering lights, on Monacos ($41). Burglar alarm system, in Monaco ($112). Reclining passenger seat, includes special interior trim, for Monacos ($151).

Note: Power steering was standard on Special Edition/Charger SE/Monaco series. Power brakes were standard on Dart '360' Sport/Charger SE/Crestwood/Monaco series.

HISTORICAL FOOTNOTES: The full-size Dodges were introduced Oct. 1, 1974, and the compact Dart series appeared in showrooms on the same day. Model year production through Aug. 31, 1975, included 160,568 Darts; 70,351 Coronet/Charger models; 38,455 Charger SE models and 45,647 Monacos. (NOTE: In this footnote only, the Dart and Charger SE production figures include cars built in Canada for the U.S. market). Model year sales by U.S. franchised dealers peaked at the

following levels: Dart - 164,434 units; Coronet - 68,191 units; Charger SE - 30,812 units and Monaco - 42,511 units. R.K. Brown, Group Vice-President for U.S. Auto Sales, was chief executive officer of Dodge Division this year.

1976 DODGE

Dodge's model lineup was similar to that offered in 1975, but this would be the final year for the venerable Dodge Dart. Its place would be taken up by the new Aspen compact, which debuted this year. Dodge covered much of the market with its model lineup, which included the mid-size Coronet, a selection of four Charger specialty coupes, and the full size Monaco and Royal Monaco. Fuel mileage got a major push this year, with axle ratios geared in that direction. Chrysler's Electronic Lean Burn System went on all 400 and 440 cu. in. V-8s. Its miniature computer received data from sensors on throttle position, engine rpm, manifold vacuum, and coolant temperature; then adjusted spark timing to produce the leanest air/fuel mixture. Monaco was the only Dodge to have a 440 cu. in. V-8 option. Engines destined for California Dodges differed in horsepower and/or carburetor configuration from those offered in the other 49 states. Pillarless hardtops were still available, but top-line mid-sizes had opera windows.

1976 Dodge, Dart Lite coupe (OCW)

1976 Dodge, Dart sedan (OCW)

DART — SERIES L — SIX/V-8 — "The value car" came in four models for 1976, with no change in styling. Most of them could have either the base 225 cu. in. Slant Six, or a 318 or 360 cu. in. V-8 engine. Coupes rode a 108-in. wheelbase, while 111 in. was used for two-door hardtops and four-door sedans. Dart Sport was the cheapest; others were the Swinger, Swinger Special, and Dart Sedan. Several variants also were available. Single round headlamps set into the ends of Dart's full-width grille, made up of horizontal bars. Wide parking lamps were inset into the recessed portion of the grille on each side, just inboard of the head-lamps. The full-width grille header (which surrounded the entire head-lamp/grille unit) contained 'Dodge' block lettering. The grille's center came to a slight forward peak. At the rear were twin rectangular taillamps at each end of a full-width trim panel, wrapping slightly around the quarter panels. Dart Lite was the name for a Sport with fuel economy package, 150 pounds lighter than its mate. The economy Slant Six had an aluminum intake manifold and modified engine block. Aluminum was used for bumper reinforcements, as well as hood and decklid inner panels. An Overdrive4 transmission was used, with 2.94:1 axle ratio (2.76:1 with automatic). Lites also carried a shorter option list. Cloth/vinyl bench seats were standard on Swinger Special and Sport. A Decorator package containing low-back vinyl seats, Boca Raton cloth inserts, woodgrained dash and deluxe steering wheel was optional on Sport. A Custom package for the Dart sedan included deluxe cloth/vinyl seats, rear armrests, woodgrain dash, plus special moldings, nameplates and appliqués. Dart

Sport offered a Convertriple option: sunroof and fold-down rear seat (with security panel) that converted the rear seat and trunk into a carpeted cargo area. Also optional: the Overdrive4 transmission, manual sunroof, and Rallye wheels. A Special Edition package (RPO code A76) went on 7.3 percent of Darts.

1976 Dodge, Aspen sedan (OCW)

1976 Dodge, Aspen station wagon with optional roof rack and wind deflector (OCW)

1976 Dodge, Aspen Special Edition coupe (OCW)

1976 Dodge, Aspen Special Edition sedan (OCW)

ASPEN — SERIES N — SIX/V-8 — Dart's new replacement was dubbed "the family car of the future." Like the similar F-bodied Plymouth Volare, it arrived as a mid-year entry. Three bodies were offered: four-door sedan, semi-fastback coupe with large triangular quarter windows, and four-door wagon with one-piece liftgate. (That was the first compact wagon since 1966.) The two-door coupe rode a 108.5-in. wheelbase, while the four-door sedan and wagon measured 112.5 in. Three trim levels were offered:

standard, Custom and SE. Coupes carried five passengers; others six. Aspen used a new transverse (crosswise) torsion bar front suspension, rather than the conventional longitudinal torsion bars. Fully isolated from the body shell, it was supposed to give a "big car" ride. Leaf springs provided the rear suspension. Base engine was the 225 cu. in. Slant Six. Optional: 318 and 360 cu. in. V-8s. An Overdrive4 floor-shift transmission was available, to replace the standard three-speed. Four axle ratios were available, as was three-speed TorqueFlite automatic. Front disc brakes were power-assisted on wagons and V-8 models. Aspen's grille was made up of horizontal strips, with a wide center portion that protruded forward. A bright upper header molding held inset 'Dodge' block letters. Single round headlamps sat in square, bright housings. Parking lamps set into the bumper, below the headlamps, while the bumper center pushed forward to match the grille shape. Front fenders held 'Aspen' nameplates, ahead of the door. Small horizontal side marker lamps went on front fenders, roughly in line with wheel opening tops. The windshield had narrow roof pillars. Wide horizontal rectangular taillamps were directly above similarly-shaped but shorter backup lamps, in a single unit, set at ends of a wide trim panel with 'Dodge' lettering in the center. The license plate was mounted at the bumper. An 'Aspen' nameplate was on the decklid. Base Aspen coupes had low-back cloth-vinyl bench seats; the sedan and wagon used vinyl. Standard equipment included a heater/defroster, hubcaps, drip moldings, driver's mirror, armrests, two-speed wipers, three-spoke steering wheel, plus windshield and backlight moldings. Coupes and wagons had quarter-window moldings. Aspen's Custom coupe could have either standard Oxford vinyl bench seats or optional sporty buckets. Custom sedans had a standard cloth/vinyl bench seat or optional all-vinyl. Custom models also added rear armrests with ashtrays, a rear deck appliqué, wide bodyside moldings, belt moldings, cigarette lighter, and woodgrained dash. Special Edition models held a 60/40 split vinyl seat with dual recliners and center armrest. Coupes had special body striping and a formal landau vinyl roof with opera windows. Other coupes had much larger triangular rear windows. Special Edition wagons had lockable storage compartments in side panels. SE models also included dual horns, a woodgrained glove box door with lock, TorqueFlite transmission, color-keyed wide vinyl bodyside moldings, full wheel lip moldings, hood paint stripe, hood ornament and wind-split molding, day/night mirror, and electric clock. Sedans added a vinyl roof. Body colors were: Big Sky Blue, Spitfire Orange, Claret Red, Parchment, Saddle Tan, Harvest Gold, Eggshell White, and Black; plus metallic Silver Cloud, Jamaican Blue, Jade Green, Tropic Green, Deep Sherwood, Caramel Tan, Cinnamon, and Spanish Gold. Aspen's R/T coupe package had a blackout grille with bright moldings and 'R/T' medallion, special body and decklid striping, large 'R/T' decal just ahead of the rear wheel, and Rallye road wheels with wide E70 x 14 raised white-letter tires. The R/T rear end looked different, with much wider upper taillamps above the narrower backup lamps and no center trim panel. Twin wide stripes ran across the deck and through the full bodyside length. R/T Aspens came with either the 318 or 360 cu. in. V-8 engine. The R/T package was popular, installed on 79 percent of the 7,916 V-8 powered NL29 coupes.

1976 Dodge, Coronet sedan with optional vinyl roof (OCW)

CORONET — SERIES W — SIX/V-8 — Dodge's mid-size four-door, with 117.5-in. wheelbase, showed little body change for 1976. Coronet's split grille had a body-color center divider, like the base Charger coupe. Each side contained a crosshatch pattern dominated by three horizontal bars. Single round headlamps sat in square housings. Curved-side amber parking lamps were mounted in the bumper, below the headlamps. Wide horizontal taillamps were set into the back bumper, with backup lenses in the center of each unit and a recessed license plate housing in the middle. A 'Dodge' nameplate was on the decklid and grille; 'Coronet' script on front fenders. Decklids had a center crease. Coronets had a hood ornament in this, their final year. Only sedan and wagon bodies were offered. Wagons had a standard 360 cu. in. V-8, while the sedan was powered by a 225 cu. in. Slant Six or optional 318 V-8. The standard cloth/vinyl front bench seat came in five color choices. Brougham added a velour and vinyl front seat with center armrest and deluxe wheel covers, plus a distinctive hood ornament. Minor instrument changes included speedometer calibration in miles and kilometers. New to the option list: tilt steering. V-8s could have a no-cost optional 2.45:1 axle for extended cruising.

CHARGER — SERIES W — SIX/V-8 — Formerly part of the Coronet line, the Charger nameplate went on four separate hardtop coupe models or packages this year: base Charger and Charger Sport, plus the Charger Special Edition and Daytona (listed separately). The basic Charger had a split blackout grille. Each side had a bright surrounding molding and three horizontal dividers over a subdued fine-mesh pattern. Between

them was a body-color divider. A 'Dodge' nameplate sat on the driver's side of the grille. Single round headlamps rested in square housings. Horizontal amber parking lamps with curved edges were inset into the bumper. 'Charger' script was on front fenders, just ahead of the door. Vertical taillamps sat at fender tips, each with a vertical divider. Standard Charger equipment included a heater/defroster, single horn, day/night mirror, two-speed wipers, hubcaps, and woodgrain (simulated) dash trim; plus moldings for backlight, windshield, belt, bodyside, deck-lid, taillamp surround, drip, bodyside, and partial wheel lips. A low-back vinyl bench seat was standard, cloth/vinyl optional. Bucket seats were available in all-vinyl or cloth/vinyl. A canopy vinyl roof with louvered quartered windows was optional. Charger Sport had color-keyed vinyl insert bodyside moldings. Sport models also added dual horns and deluxe wheel covers, plus 'Sport' nameplates and medallions on rear roof pillars. Standard velour seats had a fold-down center armrest, but all-vinyl bucket seats were offered at no extra charge. In addition to the canopy vinyl roof with louvered windows, a halo vinyl roof that stood back from standard hardtop coupe windows was available. Charger/Sport body colors were: Powder Blue, Bright Red, Yellow Blaze, Golden Fawn, Black, or Eggshell White; plus metallic Silver Cloud, Jamaican Blue, Vintage Red, Bittersweet, Jade Green, Tropic Green, Deep Sherwood, Caramel Tan, Moondust, Cinnamon, Inca Gold, and Spanish Gold. New options included a 60/40 bench seat and tilt steering wheel.

CHARGER SE — SERIES X — V-8 —

Dodge's sporty SE, introduced in 1975, featured a Cordoba-like appearance, with round parking lamps between the grille and single round headlamps. Sheetmetal differed from the basic Charger. The SE grille consisted of just two horizontal and three vertical divider bars over a horizontal pattern. That pattern repeated in bumper slots below. Near front fender tips were small vertical side marker lenses, split into three sections. Louvers were optional for the narrow opera windows. The instrument panel had simulated rosewood trim. Standard bucket seats were upholstered in Oxford vinyl in black, blue, green, gold, red, tan or white. Base engine was the 318 cu. in. V-8. Charger SE was meant to rival Chevrolet's Monte Carlo and Ford's Elite. Daytona was actually an option package that was installed on 17.3 percent of SE models, featuring two-tone paint treatments with special body taping. Dual sport mirrors and bodyside moldings were color-keyed. Daytona decals stood on doors, fenders and decklid. The black-textured grille had bright accents in a 6 x 4 hole pattern, with horizontal bars dominant. A 'Dodge' nameplate was on the driver's side of the grille. Round parking lamps stood between the grille and single round headlamps, as on the SE, and the grille pattern was repeated in a wide bumper slot below. Underneath was a standard rear sway bar, plus whitewall steel-belted radials. Wraparound taillamps protruded along the quarter panel tips, but extended inward to the edge of the protruding decklid. Each taillamp held a horizontal divider strip. Backup lamps were inset into the bumper, roughly halfway in toward the center. Daytonas had plain, small opera windows. Distinctive two-tone paint treatments put the accent color on hood, deck and roof front, as well as the lower body. "Charger Daytona" lettering was low on the bodyside. Standard Daytona equipment included dual horns, power steering, TorqueFlite, hood ornament, and wheel lip moldings. Options included a 360 or 400 cu. in. V-8 and floor-shift TorqueFlite. A "Tuff" steering wheel was optional, along with urethane-styled road wheels. Standard interior was all-vinyl front bucket seats in red, black, blue and white. Daytona/SE colors were similar to base Chargers, but included Platinum metallic, Astral Blue metallic, Starlight Blue metallic, Saddle Tan, and Light Chestnut metallic. Powder Blue, Tropic Green, Moondust and Cinnamon were not available. The Daytona package cost only $345. A Brougham package that cost even less went on nearly 48 percent of Charger SE models.

1976 Dodge, Royal Monaco sedan (OCW)

MONACO — SERIES D — SIX/V-8 —

Full-size Dodges split into several levels: basic Monaco, Royal Monaco, and Royal Monaco Brougham (introduced in 1975). Monaco came in four-door sedan or two-seat wagon form. The more costly Royal Monacos came with two-door hardtop and four-door sedan bodies, and either a two- or three-seat wagon. Wagons rode a 124-in. wheelbase; others 122 in. All could be spotted by their hidden headlamps. Royal Monaco's grille was a curious upright design in tight crosshatch pattern, with flat horizontal elements that contained columns of rounded vertical pieces. The bottom row extended outward on each side, below the concealed headlamp doors. The grille pattern repeated in bumper slots below. On the driver's side headlamp door was

a 'Royal Monaco' script. At the fender tips were wraparound marker lenses. Royal Monaco taillamps were just above recessed openings in the bumper top. Each rectangular unit consisted of two tri-section red lenses on either side of a square center backup lamp. The license plate mounting was on the bumper, below a center hump. Between the taillamp was a trim panel with 'Royal Monaco' italic lettering. Standard equipment included TorqueFlite automatic transmission, power steering and brakes, and a V-8 engine. Monaco had a standard 318 cu. in. V-8; Royal Monaco a 360 cu. in.; and Royal Monaco Brougham (and all wagons) the 400 cu. in. V-8. A 440 cu. in. V-8 was optional on all models. Monaco sedans had standard cloth/vinyl upholstery. Royal Monaco offered true hardtop styling with roll-down quarter windows. Other coupes had opera windows. Royal Monaco Brougham added opera windows, vinyl roof, and individually adjustable 50/50 front seats. A "Diplomat" package for the Royal Monaco Brougham two-door hardtop included a landau vinyl roof, opera windows, and distinctive steel roof band.

I.D. DATA: Dodge's 13-symbol Vehicle Identification Number (VIN) was on the upper left corner of the instrument panel, visible through the windshield. Symbol one indicates car line: 'L' Dart; 'N' Aspen; 'W' Coronet; 'X' Charger SE; 'D' Monaco. Symbol two is series (price class): 'L' low; 'H' high; 'P' premium; 'M' medium; 'S' special. Symbols 3-4 show body type: '22' 2-dr. pillared hardtop; '23' 2-dr. hardtop; '29', 2-dr. special; '41' 4-dr. sedan; '45' two-seat station wagon; '46' three-seat wagon. Symbol five is the engine code: 'C' L6225; 'G' V8318; 'K' V8360 2Bbl.; 'J' V8360 4Bbl.; 'L' Hi-perf. V8360 4Bbl.; 'M' V8400 2Bbl.; 'N' V8400 4Bbl.; 'P' Hi-perf. V8400 4Bbl.; 'T' V8440 4Bbl. Symbol six is the model year code: '6' 1976. Symbol seven indicates assembly plant: 'A' Lynch Road; 'B' Hamtramck, MI; 'C' Jefferson; 'D' Belvidere, IL; 'F' Newark, DE; 'G' St. Louis; 'R' Windsor, Ontario. The final six digits make up the sequential serial number, starting with 100001. An abbreviated version of the VIN is also stamped on a pad on the engine block: below No. 6 spark plug on six-cylinder engines, and to rear of right engine mount on V-8s. Serial numbers for 318 and 360 cu. in. V-8s are coded as follows: first letter series (model year); second assembly plant; next three digits displacement (cu. in.); next one or two letters model; next four digits show build date; and final four digits are the engine sequence number. Coding of other engines is: first letter series (model year); next three digits displacement; next one or two letters model; next four digits build date; and the final digit reveals the shift on which the engine was built. Information on over/undersized parts is stamped on six-cylinder engines on the joint face at right corner, adjacent to No. 1 cylinder; on 318/360 V-8s, at left front of block just below the head; on 400 V-8, just ahead of No. 2 cylinder, next to distributor; and on 440 V-8, on left bank pad adjacent to front tappet rail. A Vehicle Safety Certification Label that displays (among other data) the date of manufacture is attached to the rear facing of the driver's door. A Body Code Plate is on the left front fender side shield, wheel housing, or left side of upper radiator support.

DART (SIX/V-8)

Model No.	Body/ Style No.	Body Type & Seating	Factory Price	Shipping Weight	Prod. Total
LL	41	4-dr. Sedan-6P	3268/3405	3070/----	27,849

DART SPORT FASTBACK (SIX/V-8)

Model No.	Body/ Style No.	Body Type & Seating	Factory Price	Shipping Weight	Prod. Total
LL	29	2-dr. Spt Cpe-6P	3233/3370	2990/----	13,642

DART SWINGER (SIX/V-8)

Model No.	Body/ Style No.	Body Type & Seating	Factory Price	Shipping Weight	Prod. Total
LH	23	2-dr. HT Cpe-6P	3485/3622	3035/----	8,937

DART SWINGER SPECIAL (SIX/V-8)

Model No.	Body/ Style No.	Body Type & Seating	Factory Price	Shipping Weight	Prod. Total
LL	23	2-dr. HT Cpe-6P	3312/3449	3050/----	3,036

ASPEN (SIX/V-8)

Model No.	Body/ Style No.	Body Type & Seating	Factory Price	Shipping Weight	Prod. Total
NL	29	2-dr. Spt Cpe-5P	3336/3501	3160/3285	22,249
NL	41	4-dr. Sedan-6P	3371/3536	3190/3315	13,981
NL	45	4-dr. Sta Wag-6P	3658/3771	3560/3650	33,265

ASPEN CUSTOM (SIX/V-8)

Model No.	Body/ Style No.	Body Type & Seating	Factory Price	Shipping Weight	Prod. Total
NH	29	2-dr. Spt Cpe-5P	3518/3683	3170/3295	21,064
NH	41	4-dr. Sedan-6P	3553/3718	3200/3325	28,632

ASPEN SPECIAL EDITION (SIX/V-8)

Model No.	Body/ Style No.	Body Type & Seating	Factory Price	Shipping Weight	Prod. Total
NP	29	2-dr. Spt Cpe-5P	4413/4526	3375/3490	18,604
NP	41	4-dr. Sedan-6P	4400/4513	3410/3530	21,323
NH	45	4-dr. Sta Wag-6P	3988/4222	3565/3695	30,782

CORONET (SIX/V-8)

Model No.	Body/ Style No.	Body Type & Seating	Factory Price	Shipping Weight	Prod. Total
WL	41	4-dr. Sedan-6P	3700/3938	3625/3860	10,853
WL	45	4-dr. Sta Wag-6P	----/4625	----/4285	1,840
WL	46	4-dr. 3S Wag-9P	----/4767	----/4350	3,039

CORONET BROUGHAM (SIX/V-8)

Model No.	Body/ Style No.	Body Type & Seating	Factory Price	Shipping Weight	Prod. Total
WH	41	4-dr. Sedan-6P	3989/4227	3645/3875	12,831

CORONET CRESTWOOD STATION WAGON (V-8)

Model No.	Body/ Style No.	Body Type & Seating	Factory Price	Shipping Weight	Prod. Total
WH	45	4-dr. 2S Wag-6P	----/5014	----/4285	1,092
WH	46	4-dr. 3S Wag-9P	----/5156	----/4360	2,154

CHARGER (SIX/V-8)

Model No.	Body/ Style No.	Body Type & Seating	Factory Price	Shipping Weight	Prod. Total
WL	23	2-dr. HT Cpe-6P	3666/3904	3595/3830	6,613
WH	23	2-dr. Spt HT-6P	3955/4193	3600/3835	10,811

CHARGER SPECIAL EDITION (V-8)

Model No.	Body/ Style No.	Body Type & Seating	Factory Price	Shipping Weight	Prod. Total
XS	22	2-dr. HT Cpe-5P	4763	3945	35,337

MONACO (V-8)

Model No.	Body/ Style No.	Body Type & Seating	Factory Price	Shipping Weight	Prod. Total
DM	41	4-dr. Sedan-6P	4388	4160	3,686
DM	45	4-dr. Sta Wag-6P	4948	4910	597

ROYAL MONACO (V-8)

Model No.	Body/ Style No.	Body Type & Seating	Factory Price	Shipping Weight	Prod. Total
DH	23	2-dr. HT Cpe-6P	4778	4280	1,591
DH	41	4-dr. Sedan-6P	4763	4325	9,049
DH	45	4-dr. Sta Wag-6P	5241	4915	547
DH	46	4-dr. 3S Wag-9P	5364	4950	1,006

ROYAL MONACO BROUGHAM (V-8)

Model No.	Body/ Style No.	Body Type & Seating	Factory Price	Shipping Weight	Prod. Total
DP	29	2-dr. Formal HT-6P	5382	4430	2,742
DP	41	4-dr. Sedan-6P	5211	4520	3,890
DP	46	4-dr. 3S Wag-9P	5869	4995	1,873

Factory Price and Weight Note: Prices and weights to left of slash are for six-cylinder, to right for V-8 engine.

Production Note: In addition to the figures shown, a total of 3,852 Coronet and 2,426 Monaco police four-door sedans were shipped.

ENGINE DATA: BASE SIX (Dart, Aspen, Coronet, Charger): Inline, overhead-valve six. Cast iron block and head. Displacement: 225 cu. in. (3.7 liters). Bore and stroke: 3.40 x 4.12 in. Compression ratio: 8.4:1. Brake horsepower: 100 at 3600 R.P.M. Torque: 170 lb.-ft. at 1600 R.P.M. Four main bearings. Solid valve lifters. Carburetor: 1Bbl. Holley 1945 (R7356A). VIN Code: C. BASE V-8 (Charger SE, Monaco); OPTIONAL (Dart, Aspen, Coronet, Charger): 90-degree, overhead valve V-8. Cast iron block and head. Displacement: 318 cu. in. (5.2 liters). Bore and stroke: 3.91 x 3.31 in. Compression ratio: 8.5:1. Brake horsepower: 150 at 4000 R.P.M. Torque: 255 lb.-ft. at 1600 R.P.M. Five main bearings. Hydraulic valve lifters. Carburetor: 2Bbl. Carter BBD 8068S or 8069S. VIN Code: G. BASE V-8 (Coronet wagon, Royal Monaco); OPTIONAL V-8 (Aspen, Coronet, Charger/SE, Monaco, Royal Monaco): 90-degree, overhead valve V-8. Cast iron block and head. Displacement: 360 cu. in. (5.9 liters). Bore and stroke: 4.00 x 3.58 in. Compression ratio: 8.4:1. Brake horsepower: 170 at 4000 R.P.M. Torque: 280 lb.-ft. at 2400 R.P.M. Five main bearings. Hydraulic valve lifters. Carburetor: 2Bbl. Holley 2245 (R7364A). VIN Code: K. CALIFORNIA V-8: Same as 360 cu. in. V-8 above, exc. with Carter TQ 4Bbl. carburetor. Brake H.P.: 175 at 4000 R.P.M. Torque: 270 lb.-ft. at 1600 R.P.M. VIN Code: J. OPTIONAL V-8 (Dart): Same as 360 V-8 above, with Carter TQ9002S 4Bbl. carburetor, exc. Brake H.P. 220 at 4400 R.P.M. Torque: 280 lb.-ft. at 3200 R.P.M. VIN Code: L. BASE V-8 (Royal Monaco Brougham, Monaco/Royal Monaco wagon): OPTIONAL V-8 (Coronet, Charger, SE, Monaco, Royal Monaco): 90-degree, overhead valve V-8. Cast iron block and head. Displacement: 400 cu. in. (6.6 liters). Bore and stroke: 4.34 x 3.38 in. Compression ratio: 8.2:1. Brake horsepower: 175 at 4000 R.P.M. Torque: 300 lb.-ft. at 2400 R.P.M. Five main bearings. Hydraulic valve lifters. Carburetor: 2Bbl. Holley 2245 (R7366A). VIN Code: M. CALIFORNIA V-8: Same as 400 cu. in. V-8 above, with Carter TQ9056S 4Bbl. carburetor. Brake H.P.: 185 at 3600 R.P.M. Torque: 285 lb.-ft. at 3200 R.P.M. VIN Code: N. OPTIONAL V-8 (Monaco, Royal Monaco): Same as 400 cu. in. 4Bbl. V-8 above, except Carter TQ9064S carburetor. Brake H.P.: 210 at 4400 R.P.M. Torque: 305 lb.-ft. at 3200 R.P.M. OPTIONAL V-8 (Coronet, Charger/SE, Royal Monaco Brougham): Same as 400 4Bbl. V-8 above, with Carter TQ9054S carburetor and dual exhaust. Brake H.P.: 240 at 4400 R.P.M. Torque: 325 lb.-ft. at 3200

R.P.M. VIN Code: P. OPTIONAL V-8 (Monaco, Royal Monaco): 90-degree, overhead valve V-8. Cast iron block and heads. Displacement: 440 cu. in. (7.2 liters). Bore and stroke: 4.32 x 3.75 in. Compression ratio: 8.2:1. Brake horsepower: 205 at 3600 R.P.M. Torque: 320 lb.-ft. at 2000 R.P.M. Five main bearings. Hydraulic valve lifters. Carburetor: 4Bbl. Carter TQ9058S. VIN Code: T.

CHASSIS DATA: Wheelbase: (Dart) 111.0 in.; (Dart Sport) 108.0 in.; (Aspen cpe) 108.5 in.; (Aspen sed/wag) 112.5 in.; (Coronet) 117.5 in.; (Coronet/Charger HT cpe) 115.0 in.; (Monaco) 121.5 in.; (Monaco wag) 124.0 in. Overall Length: (Dart) 203.4 in.; (Dart Sport) 200.9 in.; (Aspen cpe) 197.5 in.; (Aspen sed/wag) 201.5 in.; (Coronet sed) 218.4 in.; (Coronet wag) 225.6 in.; (Charger/Sport) 213.7 in.; (Charger SE) 215.3 in.; (Monaco) 225.7 in.; (Monaco wag) 229.5 in. Height: (Dart 2-dr.) 53.0 in.; (Dart 4-dr.) 54.0 in.; (Dart Sport) 53.4 in.; (Aspen cpe) 53.1 in.; (Aspen sed/wag) 54.8 in.; (Coronet sed) 54.0 in.; (Coronet wag) 55.8 in.; (Charger) 52.6 in.; (Monaco 2-dr.) 54.1 in.; (Monaco 4-dr.) 54.8 in.; (Monaco wag) 57.6 in. Width: (Dart) 69.8 in.; (Dart Sport) 71.7 in.; (Aspen) 72.8 in.; (Coronet sed) 77.7 in.; (Coronet wag) 78.8 in.; (Charger/Sport) 77.7 in.; (Charger SE) 77.1 in.; (Monaco) 79.8 in.; (Monaco wag) 79.4 in. Front Tread (Dart) 59.2 in.; (Aspen) 60.0 in.; (Coronet/Charger) 61.9 in.; (Monaco) 64.0 in. Rear Tread: (Dart) 55.6 in.; (Aspen) 58.5 in.; (Coronet/Charger) 62.0 in.; (Coronet wag) 63.4 in.; (Monaco) 63.4 in. Wheel size: (Dart) 14 x 4.5 in.; (Aspen cpe/sed) 14 x 5.5 in.; (Charger) 14 x 5.0 in.; (Charger SE) 15 x 5.5 in.; (Coronet) 14 x 5.0 in. exc. wag, 6.0 in. (Monaco) 15 x 5.5 in. exc. wag, 6.5 in. Standard Tires: (Dart six) 6.95 x 14; (Dart V-8) D78 x 14; (Aspen) D78 x 14 BSW exc. wag, F78 x 14 glass-belted; (Coronet) F78 x 14 exc. wag, H78 x 14; (Charger) F78 x 14 BSW; (Charger SE) G78 x 15 BSW glass-belted exc. Daytona, GR78 x 15 WSW; (Monaco) GR78 x 15 exc. wag, LR78 x 15; (Royal Monaco) HR78 x 15 exc. wag, LR78 x 15.

TECHNICAL: Transmission: Three-speed manual transmission (column shift) standard on Dart, Aspen, Coronet and Charger. Gear ratios: (lst) 3.08:1; (2nd) 1.70:1; (3rd) 1.00:1; (Rev) 2.90:1 exc. six-cylinder Dart: (lst) 2.99:1; (2nd) 1.75:1; (3rd) 1.00:1; (Rev) 3.17:1. Column or floor lever on Dart/Aspen. Four-speed overdrive manual gearbox available on Dart/Aspen: (lst) 3.09:1; (2nd) 1.67:1; (3rd) 1.00:1; (4th) 0.73:1; (Rev) 3.00:1. Three-speed automatic standard on Charger SE and Monaco, optional on others. Gear ratios: (lst) 2.45:1; (2nd) 1.45:1; (3rd) 1.00:1; (Rev) 2.22:1. Floor lever available for all exc. Monaco. Standard final drive ratio: (Dart six) 3.23:1 w/overdrive, various ratios w/auto.; (Dart V8318) 2.45:1 exc. 2.94:1 or 3.21:1 w/overdrive, various ratios w/auto.; (Dart V8360) 2.94:1 w/auto.; (Aspen six) 3.23:1 exc. 2.76:1 w/auto., 2.94:1 in wag.; (Aspen V8318) 2.45:1 exc. 2.94:1 w/4spd; (Aspen V8360) 2.76:1 exc. 2.71:1 in wagon; (Coronet/Charger six) 3.21:1 w/3spd, 2.94:1 w/auto.; (Coronet/Charger V-8) 2.94:1 w/3spd, 2.71:1 or 3.21:1 w/auto; (Charger SE) 2.71:1; (Monaco) 2.71:1. Steering: Recirculating ball. Suspension: (Dart) longitudinal front torsion bars w/lower trailing links, semi-elliptic rear leaf springs w/rigid axle; (Aspen) transverse front torsion bars and anti-sway bar, asymmetrical semi-elliptic rear leaf springs; (others) longitudinal front torsion bars and anti-sway bar, semi-elliptic rear leaf springs; rear anti-sway bar on Charger SE. Brakes: Front disc, rear drum exc. Dart six, front/rear drum. Ignition: Electronic. Body construction: (Dart) unibody; (Aspen/Monaco) unibody w/front auxiliary frame; (Coronet/Charger) unibody w/isolated front crossmembers. Fuel tank: (Dart) 16 gal.; (Aspen) 18 gal.; (Coronet) 25.5 gal. exc. wag, 20 gal.; (Charger six) 20.5 gal.; (Charger V-8) 25.5 gal.; (Monaco) 26.5 gal. exc. wag, 24 gal.

DRIVETRAIN OPTIONS: Engines: 360 cu. in., 2Bbl. V-8: Aspen ($50); Charger/SE, Coronet ($54); Monaco ($55); 360 cu. in., 4Bbl. V-8: Charger/SE, Coronet ($99) exc. wag ($45); Monaco ($100); Royal Monaco ($45). 360 cu. in., 4Bbl. V-8 w/dual exhaust: Dart Spt ($376). 400 cu. in., 2Bbl. V-8: Charger/SE, Coronet ($102) exc. wag ($48); Monaco ($104); Royal Monaco ($49). 400 cu. in., 4Bbl. V-8: Charger/SE, Coronet ($147) exc. wag ($93); Monaco ($149); Royal Monaco ($94); Monaco Brghm/wag ($45). 400 cu. in., 4 Bbl. V-8 w/dual exhaust: Charger/SE, Coronet ($198) exc. wag ($144). 440 cu. in., 4Bbl. V-8: Monaco ($273); Royal Monaco ($218); Monaco Brghm/wag ($169). Transmission/Differential: Three-speed manual trans. w/floor shift: Dart/Aspen ($28). Four-speed overdrive manual trans. w/floor lever: Dart/Aspen ($127). TorqueFlite auto. trans.: Dart/Aspen ($250); Charger/Coronet ($273). Sure Grip differential: Dart/Aspen ($49); Charger/SE/Coronet ($54); Monaco ($58). Optional axle ratio: Aspen ($13); Charger/SE/Coronet/Monaco ($15). Brakes and Steering: Manual front disc brakes: Dart six ($25). Power front disc brakes ($56-$81) but std. w/Aspen V-8; Charger/Coronet ($61). Power steering: Dart/Aspen ($131); Charger/Coronet six ($143). Suspension: Automatic height control: Monaco ($100). Front sway bar: Dart ($14). H.D. susp.: Dart/Aspen ($9-$23); Charger /SE/Coronet ($25); Monaco ($18-$25). H.D. shock absorbers: Charger/SE/Coronet/Monaco ($7). Other: Long-life battery: Monaco ($30). Engine temp and oil pressure gauge: Monaco ($20). Trailer towing pkg.: Dart/Aspen ($68). Light trailer towing pkg.: Charger/SE/Coronet ($298); Monaco ($75). Heavy trailer towing pkg.: Charger/SE/Coronet ($345); Monaco ($302).

DART/ASPEN CONVENIENCE/APPEARANCE OPTIONS: Option Packages: Dart decorator trim pkg. ($178). Dart Special Edition pkg. ($291-$438). Dart exterior decor pkg.: Spt ($84). Dart interior decor group:

Spt ($92). Dart radial tire roadability pkg. ($17). Dart custom pkg.: base ($176-$218). Dart Lite pkg: Spt ($68). Dart overdrive decor pkg.: Spt ($19). Aspen R/T pkg.: base cpe ($196). Aspen R/T decor group: base cpe/sed ($95). Aspen two-tone paint pkg.: Cust cpe ($158). Light pkg. ($33). Deluxe insulation pkg. ($23-$51). Easy order pkg. ($604-$772) exc. Aspen SE ($221). Protection group ($18-$27). Comfort/Convenience: Air cond. ($431). Rear defogger, blower type ($41). Rear defroster, electric ($74). Automatic speed control: Aspen ($70). Power seat: Aspen ($119). Power windows: Aspen ($95-$135). Power door locks: Aspen ($60-$95); all windows ($44). Tinted windshield ($35). Luxury steering wheel ($15-$26). Tilt steering wheel: Aspen ($54). Electric clock: Aspen ($18). Inside hood release ($11). Horns and Mirrors: Dual horns ($6). Remote left mirror ($14). Dual sport mirrors, left remote: Dart ($15-$29). Dual remote mirrors: Aspen ($27-$40). Dual remote sport mirrors: Aspen ($33-$47). Day/night mirror ($7). Entertainment: AM radio ($72). AM/FM radio ($65-$137). AM/FM stereo radio: Aspen ($160-$233). Rear speaker ($20). Exterior Trim: Manual sunroof: Dart Spt, Aspen cpe ($186). Full vinyl roof: Dart Spt, Aspen sed ($17-$92). Canopy vinyl roof: Dart Spt ($76). Halo vinyl roof: Aspen cpe ($92-$107). Landau vinyl roof: Aspen cpe ($45-$137). Vinyl bodyside moldings ($18-$37). Belt moldings: Aspen ($15). Door edge protectors ($7-$11). Upper door frame moldings: sed ($27). Wheel lip moldings ($18). Drip rail molding: Dart ($15). Sill moldings: Dart ($16). Tape stripe (up/over): Dart Spt ($44). Bumper guards ($35). Rear air deflectors: Aspen wag ($22). Luggage rack: Aspen wag ($65). Interior Trim/Upholstery: Console: Dart Spt, Aspen cpe ($68). Cloth/vinyl bench seat: Dart sed ($64). Vinyl bench seat: Dart cpe ($64); Aspen wag ($32). Splitback vinyl bench seat: Dart ($105). Cloth 60/40 split bench seat: Aspen SE ($51). Vinyl 60/40 split bench seat: Aspen SE wag ($114). Vinyl bucket seats: Dart Spt ($87-$150); Swinger ($128); Aspen ($87-$119). Carpets: Dart ($22). Cargo area carpets and bins: Aspen wag ($45). Wheels and Tires: Rallye wheels ($36-$66). Deluxe wheel covers ($29). Premier wheel covers: Aspen ($25-$54). Wire wheel covers: Aspen ($32-$86). 6.95 x 14 WSW: Dart (NC to $32). D78 x 14 BSW: Dart ($16). D78 x 14 WSW: Dart (NC to $75); Aspen (NC to $32). DR78 x 14 WSW: Dart ($85-$132). E78 x 14 BSW: Aspen ($16). E78 x 14 WSW: Dart ($16-$63); Aspen (NC to $75). E70 x 14 RWL: Dart ($61-$109); Aspen ($61-$93). ER78 x 14 WSW: Dart ($23-$148); Aspen ($85-$132). F78 x 14 BSW: Aspen ($44-$60). F78 x 14 WSW: Aspen (NC to $96). FR78 x 14 WSW: Aspen ($41-$153). GR78 x 14 WSW: Aspen ($75-$110).

CORONET/CHARGER/CHARGER SE CONVENIENCE/APPEARANCE OPTIONS: Option Packages: Charger SE Daytona pkg. ($345). Charger SE Brougham pkg. ($287-$303). Easy order pkg.: Charger SE ($1027); others ($347-$870). Luxury equipment pkg. ($1369-$1739) exc. SE. Exterior decor pkg. ($92-$175) exc. SE. Deluxe insulation pkg. ($55) exc. SE. Light pkg. ($24-$45). Comfort/Convenience: Air cond. ($490). Rear defroster, electric ($81). Automatic speed control ($77). Tinted windshield ($38); all windows ($52). Power seat ($130). Power windows ($104-$147). Power tailgate window: wag ($41). Power door locks ($65-$94). Power decklid release: SE ($19). Luxury steering wheel ($17). Tilt steering wheel ($59). Tachometer ($62). Electric clock ($20) exc. SE. Digital clock: SE ($45). Inside hood release ($12) exc. SE. Horns and Mirrors: Dual horns ($6) exc. SE. Left remote mirror ($15). Dual remote mirrors ($29-$44). Dual sport styled remote mirrors ($37-$52). Entertainment: AM radio ($79). AM/FM radio ($71-$149). AM radio w/8track tape player ($48-$220). AM/FM stereo radio ($83-$254). w/8track ($186-$357). Search tune AM/FM stereo radio: Charger SE ($214-$314). Rear speaker ($22). Exterior Trim: Manual sunroof: cpe ($311). Full vinyl roof ($15-$115). Landau vinyl roof: Charger SE ($100). Canopy vinyl roof: HT cpe ($83). Canopy vinyl roof w/louvered quarter window: HT cpe ($32-$115). Vinyl bodyside moldings ($20-$40). Sill moldings: sed/wag ($25). Door edge protectors ($7-$13). Performance hood treatment: HT cpe ($28) exc. SE. Hood/deck stripes: Charger SE ($40). Hood stripe ($20). Bodyside stripes: HT cpe ($40). Side/deck Rallye stripe: HT cpe ($20). Air deflector: base wag ($24). Auto-lock tailgate: wag ($35). Luggage rack: wag ($71). Bumper guards ($38); front only, sed/wag ($19). Undercoating ($30). Interior Trim/Upholstery: Console: HT cpe ($18). 60/40 split bench seats: HT cpe cloth/vinyl sedan velour/vinyl or wagon vinyl ($124). Vinyl bucket seats: base HT cpe ($206). Cloth/vinyl bucket seats w/sun gold trim: HT cpe ($31-$237). Cargo area carpet: base wag ($28). Charger SE Upholstery: Console ($90). Cloth/vinyl bench seat ($72). Velour/vinyl bench seat ($89). Velour/vinyl 60/40 bench seat w/recliners ($196). Wheels and Tires: Rallye wheels ($43-$75). Styled wheels ($113-$145). Deluxe wheel covers ($32) exc. SE. Wire wheel covers ($62-$94). F78 x 14 WSW (NC to $39). G78 x 14 BSW ($19). G78 x 14 WSW (NC to $58). H78 x 14 BSW ($32-$40). H78 x 14 WSW (NC to $83). G70 x 14 RWL ($53-$110). GR78 x 15 WSW ($111-$169). HR78 x 15 WSW ($111-$194). GR70 x 15 RWL ($164-$221). NOTE: optional tires do not apply to Charger SE.

MONACO CONVENIENCE/APPEARANCE OPTIONS: Option Packages: Luxury equipment pkg. ($1509-$1836). Wagon pkg. ($63). Deluxe sound insulation pkg. ($41). Comfort/Convenience: Air cond. ($504); auto-temp ($590) exc. ($85) w/luxury pkg. Rear defroster, electric ($82). Automatic speed control ($78). Power seat ($132). Power windows ($110-$167). Power door locks ($66-$95). Tinted glass ($66). Luxury

steering wheel ($17). Tilt/telescope steering wheel ($83-$100). Electric clock ($20). Digital clock ($25-$45). Lighting, Horns and Mirrors: Cornering lights: Royal ($43). Dual horns ($6). Remote left mirror ($15). Dual remote mirrors ($30-$45). Day/night mirror ($8). Entertainment: AM radio ($80). AM/FM radio ($76-$155). AM radio w/8track tape player ($62-$239). AM/FM stereo radio ($80-$257); w/8track stereo tape ($184-$362). Rear speaker ($22). Exterior Trim: Sunroof w/vinyl roof ($627-$758). Door edge protectors ($8-$13). Upper door frame moldings: base ($29). Bumper guards ($45). Rear air deflector: base wag ($25). Auto-lock tailgate: wag ($35). Luggage rack: wag ($86). Wheels and Tires: Styled chrome wheels ($77-$147). Deluxe wheel covers ($32). Premium wheel covers ($38-$70). G78 x 15 WSW ($39). GR78 x 15 BSW ($99). GR78 x 15 WSW (NC to $158). HR78 x 15 BSW ($22-$121). HR78 x 15 WSW (NC to $164). JR78 x 15 WSW ($31-$195). L78 x 15 WSW ($49). LR78 x 15 BSW ($99). LR78 x 15 WSW (NC to $148).

HISTORY: Introduced: October 16, 1975. Model year production: Chrysler reported a total of 359,163 passenger cars shipped. Total production for the U.S. market of 336,381 units included 163,307 six-cylinder and 173,074 V-8s. Calendar year production (U.S.): 547,916 (incl. 50,946 Sportsman vans). Calendar year sales by U.S. dealers: 478,960, for a 5.6 percent share of the market. Model year sales by U.S. dealers: 421,122 (not incl. 47,383 Colts and 42,303 Sportsman vans).

HISTORICAL FOOTNOTES: The new Aspen, built at half of Chrysler's six U.S. final assembly plants, sold well. Over a third of Aspens sold were station wagons. The combination of Dart and Aspen amounted to some 54 percent of total sales, as mid-size and full-size models were losing ground. Sales for the model year were up 26.7 percent, but well under the 1973 record. (Figures include the imported Colt and Sportsman van). That Colt had a new 2.0-liter four, in addition to the standard 1.6-liter powerplant. Charger SE was made only at Windsor, Ontario. Before too long, both Aspen and its sister Plymouth Volare would be subjected to a succession of recalls, to achieve one of the worst recall records of their era.

1977 DODGE

Several Dodge nameplates changed this year, but not much else. This would be the final year for the full-size Royal Monaco. The Coronet name was gone, as all mid-sizes were now called Monaco. Full-size Dodges now fell under the Royal Monaco banner. Charger SE had its own identity again, as the basic Charger name was dropped. Dart had disappeared during the 1976 model year. A new model joined the lineup at mid-year: the upper-level compact Diplomat, kin to Chrysler's new Le-Baron. Electronic Lean Burn was now on the 360 cu. in. V-8 as well as bigger versions. The familiar Slant Six appeared in an additional form with two-barrel carburetor, called "Super Six." Aspen again offered an R/T package. Aspen coupes could have an optional T-Bar roof as well as a sunroof.

1977 Dodge, Aspen Custom coupe with optional landau vinyl roof and wire wheel covers (OCW)

1977 Dodge, Aspen Special Edition station wagon with optional Rallye wheels, roof rack, wind deflector and woodgrain decor package (OCW)

1977 Dodge, Aspen R/T coupe (OCW)

ASPEN — SERIES N — SIX/V-8 — Introduced for the 1976 model year, the compact Aspen changed little in appearance this year. Again, it came in base, Custom, and Special Edition dress. Base engine was the one-barrel 225 cu. in. Slant Six, except for wagons which carried the new two-barrel Super Six. Optional were 318 and 360 cu. in. V-8s. Base coupes had cloth/vinyl bench seating; sedans and wagons had all vinyl. Custom coupes added all-vinyl seats, special bodyside moldings, woodgrained instrument panel, lighter, and rear armrests. Custom sedans had standard Revere cloth/vinyl bench seating in blue, green, red, parchment or tan. Special Edition Aspens carried 60/40 vinyl reclining seats with fold-down center armrest (same colors as Custom), door pull straps, glass-belted radial tires, power brakes and steering. Otherwise, standard equipment was similar to 1976. A T-Bar roof with removable panels was optional on all coupes. Aspen's R/T package was offered again, along with an R/T Super Pak. The basic package included a floor-shift three-speed manual transmission, E70 x 14 raised white letter tires on Rallye wheels, blackout grille, bold stripes, and 'R/T' decals between doors and rear wheel openings. Super Pak added front and rear spoilers, special tape stripes that included an 'R/T' insignia on the rear spoiler, wheel opening flares, and louvered rear quarter windows. Both could have a 360 two-barrel or the 360 four-barrel with Electronic Lean Burn. R/T was Dodge's only "performance" model. A total of 4,465 Aspen coupes had the R/T package, while 2,284 carried the Super R/T package.

1977 Dodge, Diplomat sedan with optional wire wheel covers (OCW)

DIPLOMAT — SERIES G — V-8 — Classed as a "premium specialty intermediate," the new Diplomat arrived as a mid-year addition, offered in base and Medallion form. Riding a 112.7-in. wheelbase, the M-bodied Diplomat was closely related to the similarly new Chrysler LeBaron. Described in the catalog as "fiendishly seductive," Diplomat was also promoted for its "manageable new size," suggesting the start of the downsizing that was soon to arrive. Two bodies were offered: a fixed-pillar coupe and four-door sedan. Underneath the unibody design were transverse front torsion bars, plus a leaf-spring rear (live axle). Diplomat's upright grille showed a tight crosshatch pattern, divided into four side-by-side sections by three wider vertical strips. 'Dodge' block lettering highlighted the driver's side of the grille header. Side-by-side rectangular headlamps stood directly above quad rectangular park/signal lamps, which continued into twin-lensed (clear/amber) wraparound side marker lamps. (LeBaron's layout was just the opposite, with headlamps below.) 'Diplomat' lettering went on the front fender, ahead of the door. Wide wraparound taillamps were divided into three side-by-side sections, the outer one wrapping onto the quarter panel. Each taillamp unit also contained a bright horizontal divider bar, making six sections in all. Back-up lamps were near the ends of the bumper, with license plate housing in the center. A 'Diplomat' nameplate sat on the right side of the decklid,

just above the taillamp. 'Dodge' lettering stood below the decklid, on a center panel between the taillamps on base Diplomats; or above the lock on Medallion's center decklid extension. Rather large opera windows were four-sided, in a curious shape with sharp corners. Four-door sedans had standard fully padded vinyl roofs, available in seven colors. A landau roof was optional on two-doors. Back windows were slightly peaked at the center. Inside, the modular instrument panel had woodtone appliqué and deeply-inset gauges. A curved left section of the dash put radio and heat controls near the driver. Fuel, alternator and temp gauges were displayed. Two-door models had reading lamps in the windshield header. Base Diplomats had cloth/vinyl bench seating. Medallion offered standard cloth/velour 60/40 seating, with leather/vinyl optional. Standard were door-pillar assist handles, plenty of courtesy lamps, and premium wheel covers. Base engine was the 318 cu. in. Lean Burn V-8 with TorqueFlite automatic transmission, power steering and brakes. Standard equipment also included FR78 x 15 GBR blackwall tires, space-saving spare tire, stand-up hood ornament, wide rocker moldings and extensions, and dual horns. Medallion added a remote-control driver's mirror and trunk dress-up package. Medallion added a remote-control driver's mirror and trunk dress-up package, wheel opening moldings, dual chrome quarter-window stripes (two-doors), bodyside tape accent stripes (two-doors), and lower deck accent stripes (four-door). Thirteen body colors were available: Dove Gray, Classic Cream, and Eggshell White; plus metallic Pewter Gray, Charcoal Gray Sunfire, Cadet Blue, Starlight Blue Sunfire, Tapestry Red Sunfire, Mint Green, Augusta Green Sunfire, Caramel Tan, Sable Tan Sunfire, and Black Sunfire. Vinyl roofs came in silver, blue, red, green, tan, white, or black. Options included air conditioning, vinyl roof, cruise control, electric rear defroster, tilt steering, power windows, power seats, power door locks, and sliding steel sunroof. The Slant Six engine could be ordered as a credit option.

1977 Dodge, Diplomat Medallion coupe with optional wire wheel covers (OCW)

MONACO — SERIES W — SIX/V-8 — After a long history at Dodge, the Coronet name disappeared, but its place in the mid-size lineup was taken over by Monaco. Wheelbase was the same as Coronet: 115 in. for two-doors, 117.5 for four-doors. Base and Brougham trim levels were offered, with two-door hardtop, four-door or Crestwood station wagon bodies. Most noticeable in appearance were the new vertically stacked quad headlamps, which replaced former round units. The split grille consisted of two side-by-side inserts, separated by a vertical divider. Each rectangular half was divided into a 3 x 2 pattern; and each of these sections showed an internal crosshatch pattern. Parking lights were in the bumper, below the headlamps. 'Monaco' script was on front fenders. Small side marker lenses at front and rear aligned with each wheel opening top (considerably higher than Royal Monaco). Each small wraparound taillamp was divided by two thin horizontal strips into three segments. The license plate was mounted in a recess that dipped down into the bumper and into a notch at the lower decklid. Backup lamps were in the bumper; their outer edges were angled. Coupes had opera windows and a wide rear roof pillar. Base engine was the new two-barrel Super Six. Optional: a 318 cu. in. V-8, or 360 or 400 V-8 with Lean Burn. Standard equipment included power brakes, and simulated woodgrain instrument panel accents.

CHARGER SE — SERIES X — V-8 — With the abandonment of the Coronet name, Charger switched from a sub-model (as in 1975-76) to a separate model. Appearance was basically the same as 1976, but

Charger's grille now showed a tight crosshatch pattern divided into three rows by two wide horizontal bars. As before, the pattern repeated in bumper slots. Charger still carried round parking lights and headlamps, revealing its relationship to Chrysler's Cordoba. Standard engine was the 318 cu. in. V-8, with TorqueFlite three-speed automatic. Both 360 and 400 cu. in. V-8s were optional. Charger had front torsion bars and rear leaf springs, with front and rear sway bars. Vinyl bucket seats were standard; corduroy/vinyl optional. Power brakes and steering also were standard. Charger SE wore GR78 x 15 glass-belted radial tires. Options included a T-Bar roof, with removable glass panel that could be stored in the trunk. A total of 2,937 Chargers had a Spring Special package (RPO code A58). More significant, 5,225 Charger SEs carried the sporty Daytona package. Daytona was basically similar to 1976, with 'Charger Daytona' decals on front fender and door. A new (and weird) "eye-catching" two-tone treatment put accent color at the front and rear of bodysides. That color extended into the door but left a center patch of basic color between, which also ran forward and back beneath the accented sections. Accent color was also on the forward roof. Four two-tone combinations were offered. Wraparound taillamps held two body-color horizontal divider strips. Daytona also had decklid, roof and cowl striping.

1977 Dodge, Monaco Brougham coupe with optional styled wheels and manual sunroof (OCW)

1977 Dodge, Monaco Brougham sedan with optional wire wheel covers (OCW)

ROYAL MONACO — SERIES D — V-8 — Last of the traditional full-size Dodges, this year's Royal Monaco came in seven models: base and Brougham hardtop coupe, four-door sedan, or station wagon (two- or three-seat). Appearance was the same as 1976, except for new rear bumper corner guards (required by Federal standards). The two-door was one of the last remaining "true" (pillarless) hardtops. The lower portion of Royal Monaco's grille extended outward below the concealed headlamps. Low side marker lights stood just ahead of wheel openings. Wide taillamps were made up of three squarish sections, with two vertical divider bars in each taillamp square and backup lenses in the center. Base engine was the 318 cu. in. V-8, but Broughams carried the 360 V-8 and wagons the 400. Optional: the big 440 cu. in. V-8. Standard equipment included TorqueFlite automatic transmission, power steering and brakes, and an inside hood release. Also standard: two front ashtrays, cigarette lighter, glove box coin holder, wheel lip and door frame moldings, two-speed wipers, cloth/vinyl bench seats, fiberglass-belted radial tires, and hubcaps. Brougham added glovebox and instrument panel lighting, courtesy lights, a split-back vinyl front bench seat with center armrest, hood stripes, and body accent stripes. Brougham sedans had upper door frame moldings.

I.D. DATA: Dodge's 13-symbol Vehicle Identification Number (VIN) was on the upper left corner of the instrument panel, visible through the windshield. Symbol one indicates car line: 'N' Aspen; 'G' Diplomat; 'W' Monaco; 'X' Charger SE; 'D' Royal Monaco. Symbol two is series (price

class): 'L' low; 'M' medium; 'H' high; 'P' premium; 'S' special. Symbols 3-4 show body type: '22' 2-dr. pillared hardtop; '23' 2-dr. hardtop; '29' 2-dr. coupe; '41' 4-dr. sedan; '45' two-seat station wagon; '46' three-seat wagon. Symbol five is the engine code: 'C' L6225 1Bbl.; 'D' L6225 2Bbl.; 'G' V8318; 'K' V8360 2Bbl.; 'L' Hi-perf. V8360 4Bbl.; 'N' V8400 4Bbl.; 'T' V8440 4Bbl. Symbol six is the model year code: '7' 1977. Symbol seven indicates assembly plant: 'A' Lynch Road; 'B' Hamtramck, MI; 'D' Belvidere, IL; 'F' Newark, DE; 'G' St. Louis; 'R' Windsor, Ontario. The final six digits make up the sequential serial number, starting with 100001. Engine number coding, Safety Certification Label and Body Code Plate are the same as 1976.

1977 Dodge, Royal Monaco Brougham sedan (OCW)

ASPEN (SIX/V-8)

Model No.	Body/ Style No.	Body Type & Seating	Factory Price	Shipping Weight	Prod. Total
NL	29	2-dr. Spt Cpe-5P	3582/3752	3180/3290	24,378
NL	41	4-dr. Sedan-6P	3631/3801	3235/3345	25,838
NL	45	4-dr. Sta Wag-6P	3953/4037	3445/3540	59,458

ASPEN CUSTOM (SIX/V-8)

NH	29	2-dr. Spt Cpe-5P	3764/3934	3185/3295	26,389
NH	41	4-dr. Sedan-6P	3813/3983	3240/3350	40,455

ASPEN SPECIAL EDITION (SIX/V-8)

NP	29	2-dr. Spt Cpe-5P	4317/4430	3375/3480	15,908
NP	41	4-dr. Sedan-6P	4366/4479	3440/3545	21,522
NH	45	4-dr. Sta Wag-6P	4283/4488	3450/3585	52,064

DIPLOMAT (V-8)

GH	22	2-dr. Cpe-6P	4943	3510	12,335
GH	41	4-dr. Sedan-6P	5101	3560	8,092

DIPLOMAT MEDALLION (V-8)

GP	22	2-dr. Cpe-6P	5313	3615	9,155
GP	41	4-dr. Sedan-6P	5471	3675	4,631

MONACO (SIX/V-8)

WL	23	2-dr. HT Cpe-6P	3911/4172	3630/3860	10,368
WL	41	4-dr. Sedan-6P	3988/4249	3655/3890	15,433
WL	45	4-dr. Sta Wag-6P	----/4724	----/4335	3,037
WL	46	4-dr. 3S Wag-9P	----/4867	----/4395	4,297

MONACO BROUGHAM (SIX/V-8)

WH	23	2-dr. HT Cpe-6P	4146/4408	3635/3870	11,405
WH	41	4-dr. Sedan-6P	4217/4478	3665/3900	14,908

MONACO CRESTWOOD STATION WAGON (V-8)

Model No.	Body/ Style No.	Body Type & Seating	Factory Price	Shipping Weight	Prod. Total
WH	45	4-dr. 2S Wag-6P	----/5224	----/4330	1,341
WH	46	4-dr. 3S Wag-9P	----/5367	----/4405	2,895

MONACO SPECIAL (SIX/V-8)

WS	23	2-dr. HT Cpe-6P	3995/4256	N/A/N/A	N/A

CHARGER SPECIAL EDITION (V-8)

XS	22	2-dr. HT Cpe-5P	5098	3895	36,204

ROYAL MONACO (V-8)

DM	23	2-dr. HT Cpe-6P	4731	4050	1,901
DM	41	4-dr. Sedan-6P	4716	4125	9,491
DM	45	4-dr. Sta Wag-6P	5353	4905	1,333

ROYAL MONACO BROUGHAM (V-8)

DH	23	2-dr. Formal HT-6P	5011	4205	6,348
DH	41	4-dr. Sedan-6P	4996	4270	18,361
DH	45	4-dr. Sta Wag-6P	5607	4900	906
DH	46	4-dr. 3S Wag-9P	5730	4935	3,493

Factory Price and Weight Note: Prices and weights to left of slash are for six-cylinder, to right for V-8 engine.

Production Note: In addition to the figures shown, a total of 4,963 Monaco and 2,206 Royal Monaco police four-door sedans were shipped.

1977 Dodge, Charger Daytona coupe (limited edition option package) (OCW)

ENGINE DATA: BASE SIX (Aspen): Inline, overhead-valve six. Cast iron block and head. Displacement: 225 cu. in. (3.7 liters). Bore and stroke: 3.40 x 4.12 in. Compression ratio: 8.4:1. Brake horsepower: 100 at 3600 R.P.M. Torque: 170 lb.-ft. at 1600 R.P.M. Four main bearings. Solid valve lifters. Carburetor: 1Bbl. Holley 1945 (R7764A). VIN Code: C. BASE SIX (Aspen wag, Monaco); OPTIONAL (Aspen): Same as 225 cu. in. six above, but with 2Bbl. Carter BBD 8086S carburetor. Brake horsepower: 110 at 3600 R.P.M. Torque: 180 lb.-ft. at 2000 R.P.M. VIN Code: D. BASE V-8 (Diplomat, Charger SE, Royal Monaco); OPTIONAL (Aspen, Monaco): 90-degree, overhead valve V-8. Cast iron block and head. Displacement: 318 cu. in. (5.2 liters). Bore and stroke: 3.91 x 3.31 in. Compression ratio: 8.5:1. Brake horsepower: 145 at 4000 R.P.M. Torque: 245 lb.-ft. at 1600 R.P.M. Five main bearings. Hydraulic valve lifters. Carburetor: 2Bbl. Carter BBD 8093S or 8094S. VIN Code: G. BASE V-8 (Monaco wag, Royal Monaco Brougham); OPTIONAL V-8 (Aspen, Monaco, Charger SE, Royal Monaco): 90-degree, overhead valve V-8. Cast iron block and head. Displacement: 360 cu. in. (5.9 liters). Bore and stroke: 4.00 x 3.58 in. Compression ratio: 8.4:1. Brake horsepower: 155 at 3600 R.P.M. Torque : 275 lb.-ft. at 2000 R.P.M. Five main bearings. Hydraulic valve lifters. Carburetor: 2Bbl. Holley 2245 (R7671A). VIN Code: K. OPTIONAL V-8 (Aspen): Same as 360 cu. in. V-8 above, but with Carter TQ 4Bbl. carburetor and Lean Burn system. Compression: 8.0:1. Horsepower: 175 at 4000 R.P.M. Torque: 275 lb.-ft. at 2000 R.P.M. VIN Code: L. BASE V-8 (Royal Monaco wag); OPTIONAL (Charger SE, Monaco, Royal Monaco): 90-degree, overhead valve V-8. Cast iron block and head. Displacement: 400 cu. in. (6.6 liters). Bore and stroke: 4.34 x 3.38 in. Compression ratio: 8.2:1. Brake horsepower: 190 at 3600 R.P.M. Torque: 305 lb.-ft. at 3200 R.P.M. Five main bearings. Hydraulic valve lifters. Carburetor: 4Bbl. Carter TQ9102S. VIN Code: N. OPTIONAL V-8 (Royal Monaco): 90-degree, overhead valve V-8. Cast iron block and head. Displacement: 440 cu. in. (7.2 liters). Bore and stroke: 4.32 x 3.75 in. Compression ratio: 8.2:1. Brake horsepower: 195 at 3600 R.P.M. Torque: 320 lb.-ft. at 2000 R.P.M. Five main bearings. Hydraulic valve lifters. Carburetor: 4Bbl. Carter TQ9078S. VIN Code: T.

CHASSIS DATA: Wheelbase: (Aspen cpe) 108.7 in.; (Aspen sed/wag) 112.7 in.; (Diplomat) 112.7 in.; (Charger/Monaco cpe) 115.0 in.; (Monaco sed) 117.4 in.; (Monaco wag) 117.5 in.; (Royal Monaco) 121.4

in.; (Royal wag) 124.0 in. Overall length: (Aspen cpe) 197.5 in.; (Aspen sed/wag) 201.5 in.; (Diplo cpe) 204.1 in.; (Diplo sed) 206.1 in.; (Monaco cpe) 213.7 in.; (Monaco sed) 218.4 in.; (Monaco wag) 225.6 in.; (Charger SE) 215.3 in.; (Royal Monaco) 225.7 in.; (Royal wag) 229.5 in. Height: (Aspen cpe) 53.3 in.; (Aspen sed) 55.0 in.; (Aspen wag) 55.2 in.; (Diplo cpe) 53.3 in.; (Diplo sed) 55.3 in.; (Monaco sed) 54.0 in.; (Monaco wag) 55.8 in.; (Monaco/Charger SE cpe) 52.6 in.; (Royal Monaco 2-dr.) 54.1 in.; (Royal 4-dr.) 54.8 in.; (Royal wag) 56.9 in. Width: (Aspen) 72.8 in.; (Diplo cpe) 73.5 in.; (Diplo sed) 72.8 in.; (Monaco) 77.7 in.; (Charger SE) 77.1 in.; (Royal Monaco) 79.8 in.; (Royal wag) 79.4 in. Front Tread: (Aspen/Diplo) 60.0 in.; (Monaco/Charger) 61.9 in.; (Royal Monaco) 64.0 in. Rear Tread: (Aspen/Diplo) 58.5 in.; (Monaco/Charger) 62.0 in.; (Monaco wag) 63.4 in.; (Royal Monaco) 63.4 in. Wheel size: (Aspen cpe/sed) 14 x 5.5 in.; (Diplo) 15 x 5.5 in.; (Charger SE) 15 x 5.5 in.; (Monaco/Royal) 15 x 5.5 in. exc. wag, 6.5 in. Standard Tires: (Aspen) D78 x 14 BSW exc. DR78 x 14 GBR BSW on SE cpe/sed, E78 x 14 or ER78 x 14 with V-8, and F78 x 14 on wag; (Diplo) FR78 x 15 GBR; (Monaco) F78 x 15 exc. wag, H78 x 15; (Monaco V8400) G78 x 15 exc. wag, H78 x 15; (Charger SE) GR78 x 15; (Royal Monaco) GR78 x 15 exc. wag, LR78 x 15.

1977 Dodge, Aspen R/T Super Pak coupe (OCW)

TECHNICAL: Transmission: Three-speed manual transmission (column shift) standard on Aspen and Monaco. Gear ratios: (1st) 3.08:1; (2nd) 1.70:1; (3rd) 1.00:1; (Rev) 2.90:1. Column or floor lever on Aspen; column on Monaco. Four-speed overdrive manual gearbox available on Aspen: (1st) 3.09:1; (2nd) 1.67:1; (3rd) 1.00:1; (4th) 0.73:1; (Rev) 3.00:1. TorqueFlite three-speed automatic standard on other models, optional on all. Gear ratios: (1st) 2.45:1; (2nd) 1.45:1; (3rd) 1.00:1; (Rev) 2.22:1. Floor lever available for all exc. Royal Monaco. Standard final drive ratio: (Aspen six) 3.23:1 exc. 2.76:1 w/auto., 2.94:1 in wag.; (Aspen V8318) 2.94:1 exc. 2.71:1 w/auto.; (Aspen V8360) 2.45:1 exc. 2.71:1 in wag, 3.23:1 w/Lean Burn 4Bbl.; (Diplomat) 2.7:1; (Monaco six) 3.21:1 w/3spd, 2.94:1 w/auto.; (Monaco V-8) 2.94:1 w/3spd but 2.71:1, 2.45:1 or 3.21:1 w/auto.; (Charger SE) 2.71:1 except 2.45:1 w/V8360; (Royal Monaco) 2.71:1. Steering: Recirculating ball. Suspension: (Aspen/Diplomat) isolated transverse front torsion bars and anti-sway bar, semi-elliptic rear leaf springs; (others) longitudinal front torsion bars w/lower trailing links and anti-sway bar, semi-elliptic rear leaf springs; rear anti-sway bar on Charger SE. Brakes: Front disc, rear drum. Ignition: Electronic. Body construction: (Diplomat) unibody; (Aspen/Royal Monaco) unibody w/front auxiliary frame; (Monaco/Charger) unibody w/isolated front crossmembers. Fuel tank: (Aspen) 18 gal. exc. V-8 or wagon, 20 gal.; (Diplomat) 19.5 gal.; (Monaco) 25.5 gal. exc. wag, 20 gal.; (Charger SE) 25.5 gal.; (Royal Monaco) 26.5 gal. exc. wag, 24 gal. and V8318, 20.5 gal.

DRIVETRAIN OPTIONS: Engines: 225 cu. in., 2Bbl. six: Aspen ($38). 360 cu. in., 2Bbl. V-8: Aspen ($53); Charger SE, Monaco ($57); Royal ($58). 360 cu. in., 4 Bbl. V-8: Aspen cpe ($219-$241); Charger SE, Monaco ($105) exc. wag ($47); Royal ($106); Royal Brghm ($48). 400 cu. in., 4Bbl. V-8: Charger SE, Monaco ($156) exc. wag ($98); Royal Monaco ($158); Royal Brghm ($99). 440 cu. in., 4Bbl. V-8: Royal Monaco ($289); Royal Brghm ($231); Royal wag ($132). Transmission/Differential: Three-speed manual trans. w/floor shift: Aspen ($30). Four-speed overdrive manual trans. w/floor lever: Aspen ($134). TorqueFlite auto. trans.: Aspen ($270); Monaco ($295). Sure Grip differential: Aspen ($52); Charger SE/Monaco ($57). Optional axle ratio: Aspen ($14); Charger SE/Monaco/Royal ($16). Brakes and Steering: Power front disc brakes: Aspen ($59). Power steering: Aspen ($140); Monaco six ($153). Suspension: Automatic height control: Royal Monaco ($109). H.D. susp.: Aspen ($23); Charger SE ($25); Monaco, Royal ($18-$25). H.D. shock absorbers: Charger SE/Monaco/Royal ($7). Other: Long-life battery ($29-$32). Fuel pacer system ($18-$36). En-

gine block heater: Royal ($18). Engine temp and oil pressure gauge: Royal Monaco ($21). Trailer towing pkg.: Aspen ($72). Light trailer towing pkg.: Charger SE/Monaco ($79); Royal ($80). Heavy trailer towing pkg.: Charger/Monaco ($316); Royal ($321). California emission system ($67-$75). High-altitude emission system ($21-$24).

ASPEN CONVENIENCE/APPEARANCE OPTIONS: Option Packages: R/T pkg.: base cpe ($184-$207). R/T decor group: base cpe ($82-$101). R/T "Super Pak": base cpe ($318). Two-tone paint pkg.: Cust/SE cpe ($120-$158). Light pkg. ($35). Deluxe insulation pkg. ($35-$65). Easy order pkg. ($594-$801). Fold-down rear seat pkg. ($110). Protection group ($19-$28). Comfort/Convenience: Air cond. ($454). Rear defogger, blower-type ($45); electric ($79). Automatic speed control ($77). Power seat ($131). Power windows ($104-$145). Power door locks ($65-$92). Tinted windshield ($37); all windows ($48). Luxury steering wheel ($28). Tuff steering wheel ($7-$35). Tilt steering wheel ($54). Electric clock ($19). Inside hood release ($11). Deluxe wipers ($9). Lighter: base ($6). Locking gas cap ($6). Locking glove box ($5). Horns and Mirrors: Dual horns ($6). Remote left mirror ($15). Dual remote mirrors ($28-$43). Dual remote sport mirrors ($35-$50). Day/night mirror ($8). Entertainment: AM radio ($69). AM/FM radio ($67-$137). AM/FM stereo radio ($145-$215); w/8track player ($235-$304). Exterior: T-Bar roof: cpe ($540-$554). Manual sunroof: cpe ($198). Full vinyl roof: sed ($92). Halo vinyl roof: cpe ($92-$107). Landau vinyl roof: cpe ($56-$148). Vinyl bodyside moldings ($19-$38). Belt moldings ($15). Door edge protectors ($8-$12). Upper door frame moldings: sed ($28). Wheel lip moldings ($19). Bumper guards ($37); rub strips ($30). Rear air deflector: wag ($25). Luggage rack: wag ($68). Undercoating ($30). Interior: Console: cpe ($72). Vinyl bench seat: base wag ($34). Cloth 60/40 split bench seat: SE ($54); SE wag ($198). Vinyl 60/40 split bench seat: wag ($121-$155). Vinyl bucket seats: cpe ($92-$126). Rear armrest w/ashtray: base ($11). Color-keyed mats ($16). Cargo area carpets: wag ($47). Wheels and Tires: Rallye wheels ($32-$68). Chrome wheels ($51-$119). Deluxe wheel covers ($32). Premium wheel covers ($25-$57). Wire wheel covers ($42-$99). Space-saving spare tire ($41).

DIPLOMAT CONVENIENCE/APPEARANCE OPTIONS: Option Packages: Easy-order pkg. Deluxe insulation pkg. Light pkg. Heavy-duty (trailering) pkg. Comfort/Convenience: Air conditioning. Rear defroster, electric. Automatic speed control. Power bench seat (base only). Power 60/40 split-bench seat, driver's side (Medallion). Power windows. Power door locks. Power decklid release. Tinted glass. Luxury three-spoke steering wheel. Tilt steering wheel. Digital clock. Deluxe wiper/washer. Locking gas cap. Lighting and Mirrors: Cornering lights. Remote driver's mirror (std. on Medallion). Remote passenger mirror (Medallion only). Dual remote-control mirrors (base only). Lighted vanity mirror. Entertainment: AM, AM/FM, and AM/FM stereo radios. AM/FM stereo with 8track tape player. Rear speaker. Exterior: Power sunroof (steel or glass). Front bumper guards. Door edge protectors. Undercoating. Interior: Color-keyed floor mats. Pedal dress-up (std. on Medallion). Wheels: Premium wheel covers (std. on Medallion). Wire wheel covers. Forged aluminum wheels.

1977 Dodge, Charger SE coupe with optional T-bar roof package (OCW)

CHARGER SE CONVENIENCE/APPEARANCE OPTIONS: Option Packages: Daytona pkg. ($166). Easy order pkg. ($987). Light pkg. ($26). Comfort/Convenience: Air cond. ($518). Rear defroster, electric ($86). Automatic speed control ($84). Tinted windshield ($40): all windows ($57). Power seat ($143). Power windows ($113). Power door locks ($71). Power decklid release ($21). Luxury steering wheel ($18). Padded leather steering wheel ($53). Tilt steering wheel ($59). Tachometer ($66). Digital clock ($47). Locking gas cap ($7). Deluxe wipers ($10). Mirrors: Left remote mirror ($16). Dual remote mirrors ($31-$47). Dual sport styled remote mirrors ($39-$55). Lighted vanity mirror ($45). Entertainment: AM radio ($76). AM/FM radio ($74-$149). AM/FM stereo

radio ($134-$234); w/8track ($232-$332). Search tune AM/FM stereo radio ($214-$314). Rear speaker ($24). Exterior: T-Bar roof ($605). Manual sunroof ($330). Full vinyl roof ($5-$116). Landau vinyl roof ($112). Quarter window louvers (NC) w/vinyl roof. Vinyl bodyside moldings ($42). Door edge protectors ($9). Hood/deck stripes ($42). Bodyside stripes ($42). Undercoating ($32). Upholstery: Console ($18-$94). Cloth/vinyl bench seat ($76). Velour/vinyl 60/40 bench seat ($208). Corduroy/vinyl bucket seats ($137). Center front cushion ($76). Color-keyed mats ($18). Trunk dress-up ($45). Wheels and Tires: Rallye wheels ($45). Styled wheels ($120). Wire wheel covers ($73). GR78 x 15 GBR WSW ($43). GR78 x 15 SBR WSW ($50-$93). HR78 x 15 SBR WSW ($77-$120). GR70 x 15 RWL ($40-$82). Conventional spare tire (NC).

MONACO CONVENIENCE/APPEARANCE OPTIONS: Option Packages: Luxury equipment pkg.: Brghm/Crestwood ($1461-$1792). Easy-order pkg.: ($350-$872). Roadability pkg.: V-8 HT/sed ($33). Deluxe insulation pkg.: six-cyl. ($62). Light pkg. ($41-$48). Comfort/Convenience: Air cond. ($518). Rear defroster, electric ($86). Auto. speed control: V-8 ($84). Power windows ($113-$158). Power tailgate window: wag ($44). Power door locks ($71-$101). Power seat ($143). Auto-lock tailgate: wag ($37). Tinted glass ($57); windshield only ($40). Luxury steering wheel ($18). Tilt steering wheel ($59). Electric clock ($21). Deluxe wipers ($10). Inside hood release ($13). Locking gas cap ($7). Horns and Mirrors: Dual horns: base ($6). Remote driver's mirror ($16). Dual chrome remote mirrors ($31-$47). Dual sport remote mirrors, chrome or painted: HT ($39-$55). Entertainment: AM radio ($76). AM/FM radio ($74-$149). AM/FM stereo ($61-$234); w/8track tape player ($159-$332). Rear speaker ($24). Exterior: Manual sunroof: HT ($330). Full vinyl roof ($116) exc. Brghm HT ($22). Canopy vinyl roof: HT ($95). Canopy roof w/opera windows ($22-$116). Vinyl bodyside molding: base ($42). Belt moldings: base HT ($16). Door edge protectors ($8-$14). Sill moldings: sed, base wag ($27). Upper door frame moldings: base sed/wag ($31). Deck tape stripes: HT ($21). Bodyside tape stripes: HT ($42). Bumper rub strips; front ($16); front/rear, HT ($32). Luggage rack: wag ($75). Undercoating ($32). Interior: Console: Brghm HT ($18). Vinyl bench seat: base ($45). Cloth/vinyl 60/40 bench seat: HT/Crestwood ($132). Velour/vinyl 60/40 seat: Brghm sed ($132). Vinyl 60/40 seat: Crestwood, Brghm sed ($132). Cloth/vinyl bucket seats: Brghm HT ($32). Color-keyed mats ($18). Pedal dress-up ($9). Trunk dress-up: sed ($45). Wheels and Tires: Deluxe wheel covers ($35). Wire wheel covers ($73-$108). Rallye wheels ($45-$80). Styled wheels ($119-$154).

ROYAL MONACO CONVENIENCE/APPEARANCE OPTIONS: Option Packages: Diplomat pkg.: Brghm HT ($646-$834). Luxury equipment pkg.: ($1876-$1969). Easy-order pkg. ($508-$581). Wagon pkg. ($67). Light pkg. ($69-$82). Deluxe sound insulation pkg. ($43). Comfort/Convenience: Air cond. ($546): auto-temp ($630) exc. ($83) w/luxury pkg. Rear defroster, electric ($87). Automatic speed control ($88). Power seat ($145). Power windows ($119-$179). Power door locks ($72-$102). Auto-lock tailgate: wag ($37). Decklid release ($21). Tinted glass ($72). Luxury steering wheel ($18). Tilt/telescope steering wheel ($88-$106). Electric clock ($21). Digital clock ($27-$48). Deluxe wiper/washer ($17). Locking gas cap ($8). Lighting, Horns and Mirrors: Cornering lights: Brghm ($46). Dual horns ($6). Remote left mirror ($16). Dual remote mirrors ($31-$48). Day/night mirror: base ($9). Entertainment: AM radio ($77). AM/FM radio ($79-$155). AM/FM stereo radio ($58-$237); w/8track stereo tape ($157-$337). Rear speaker ($25). Exterior: Power sunroof w/vinyl roof ($626-$768). Full vinyl roof ($60-$141). Canopy vinyl roof w/opera windows: HT ($141). Vinyl bodyside moldings ($22). Manual vent windows: sed ($43). Door edge protectors ($9-$14). Upper door frame moldings: base sed ($31). Rear air deflector: base wag ($28). Luggage rack: wag ($104). Assist handles: wag ($24). Rear bumper step pads: wag ($15). Undercoating ($33). Interior: Vinyl bench seat: base sed ($22). Cloth/vinyl bench seat: base wag ($59). Cloth/vinyl 50/50 bench seat: Brghm ($198). Vinyl 50/50 bench seat: Brghm wag ($198). Color-keyed mats ($18). Trunk dress-up ($45). Wheels and Tires: Chrome wheels ($81-$156). Deluxe wheel covers ($35). Premier wheel covers ($39-$74).

HISTORY: Introduced: October 1, 1976. Model year production: Chrysler reported a total of 449,559 passenger cars shipped. Total North American production for the U.S. market of 512,229 units (incl. 62,512 Sportsman vans) consisted of 181,083 six-cylinder and 331,146 V-8s. Calendar year production (U.S.): 450,871 (not incl. 46,362 Sportsman vans). Calendar year sales by U.S. dealers: 413,297 (plus 45,380 Sportsman vans). Model year sales by U.S. dealers: 418,644 (not incl. 69,963 Colts and 45,841 Sportsman vans).

HISTORICAL FOOTNOTES: Dodge sales rose 5 percent for model year 1977, while production leaped 23 percent (though production fell for the calendar year). Aspen sales went up by 44 percent, reaching 254,532. Diplomat, introduced during the '77 model year, found 23,912 buyers even in the short period. The related Chrysler LeBaron also sold well from the start. Dodge's Mitsubishi-built Colt, imported from Japan, was selling well too, rising 47 percent for the model year after introduction of a smaller, cheaper version. An economy Colt version was added (slightly smaller).

1978 DODGE

Biggest news for 1978 was the January debut of the new front-drive subcompact Omni (and twin Plymouth Horizon). This was also the final year for big Dodges. Aspen, Diplomat and Monaco lost weight this year in their windshields, inner body panels, interior trim, and bumpers. Electronic Lean Burn was not only on many V-8s now, but even installed on the new subcompact Omni four. A new lock-up torque converter on many TorqueFlite transmissions engaged when shifted into third gear, and disengaged below about 30 mph (or when the transmission downshifted). It was intended to minimize slippage. All Dodge models had unibody construction. Differences between California and 49-state engines peaked in the late 1970s. Variants such as a four-barrel carbureted version of the 318 cu. in. V-8 were offered strictly for California and/or high-altitude regions.

1978 Dodge, Omni hatchback sedan with optional graphics package (OCW)

OMNI — SERIES ZL — FOUR — Omni "does it all." That's what the factory sales catalog promised, at any rate, to prospective buyers of Dodge's new subcompact four-wheel drive hatchback. This was the first front-wheel drive subcompact manufactured in America. The 99-in. wheelbase, L-body design was shared by Plymouth's Horizon, which differed in little more than grille appearance. Omni's rectangular grille was made up of horizontal bars only, with a center medallion. Single rectangular headlamps were recessed, and flanked by amber wraparound park/signal lamps. Above the driver's side headlamp was 'Dodge' lettering. 'Omni' lettering went on the front fender, ahead of the door. At the rear, large rectangular three-row taillamps (upper rows red, bottom row amber on the outside with clear backup lens inside) wrapped around slightly onto the quarter panels. The license plate holder sat in the center of the back panel, below the lift-up hatch. Under the hood was a transverse-mounted overhead-cam four-cylinder engine with 104.7 cu. in. (1.7 liter) displacement. The engine actually came from Volkswagen, but was enlarged and modified to meet Chrysler's requirements. Both the cylinder head and intake manifold were aluminum. It drove a standard four-speed manual transaxle, but TorqueFlite automatic was available. Front suspension was an Iso-Strut design with coil springs and anti-sway bar. At the rear were trailing-arm independent coil springs with integral anti-sway provision. Rack-and-pinion steering was used. Tires were P155/80R13 glass-belted radial whitewalls. Standard equipment included bodyside moldings with black vinyl inserts, four-speed transmission, lighter, door armrests, color-keyed visors, two coat hooks, folding rear shelf security panel, built-in diagnostics connector, three-spoke steering wheel, manual disc/drum brakes, and cut-pile carpeting. Colors were: Spitfire Orange, Sunrise Orange, Light Mocha Tan, Yellow Blaze, Eggshell White, and Black; plus metallic Tapestry Red Sunfire, Caramel Tan, Citron, Augusta Green Sunfire, Regatta Blue, Starlight Blue Sunfire, and Pewter Gray. Five two-tone paint and tape options were available. Standard high-back vinyl bucket seats came in blue, tan, red or black. Optional cloth/vinyl upholstery was red or black. A Custom Interior Package could have all-vinyl high-back seats, either solid color or two-tone. A Premium Interior Package included dual reclining seatbacks, upholstered in embossed vinyl or suede-like cloth. On the dashboard was a mile/kilometer speedometer, ammeter, and temperature gauge. An AM radio and inside hood release were standard. A multi-function steering column lever controlled turn signals, dimmer, and wiper/washer with standard pulse-wipe. Options included a roof rack, AM/FM stereo radio, remote-control mirrors, air conditioning, rear defroster and wiper/washer, and power brakes. Basic Omni had a bright grille, bright bumpers with rub strips, plus bright windshield and liftgate window moldings. A Custom Package added bright trim to hood, fender, wheel lip, door sill, and roof drip rail. The Premium Exterior Package added bright accents on door frames, belt, and center pillars; plus full-length bodyside and liftgate moldings, and Rallye wheel hubs with bright acorn nuts. Inside were a three-spoke simulated woodgrain steering wheel, visor vanity mirror (passenger), and premium door trim

panels. One step further along was the Premium Wood-Grained Package, with simulated wood appliqué on bodysides and lower liftgate.

1978 Dodge, Aspen sedan with Special Edition decor package (OCW)

ASPEN — SERIES N — SIX/V-8 — Similar in overall appearance to the 1977 version, this year's compact Aspen sported a revised front end. The new, narrower one-piece grille was made up of horizontal bars, but without the former recessed side portions. Instead, those twin areas between grille and headlamps were occupied by square amber parking lamps, each with two horizontal trim strips. (Parking lamps had previously been in the bumper.) Round headlamps were again recessed in bright square housings. Rear end appearance changed too, with revised taillamps. Each rectangular unit, about one-third the car width (with backup lamps toward the center of the car) was split by two horizontal trim strips that continued across the center trim panel. That panel displayed 'Dodge' block letters in the center row. As before, the standard model had no bodyside molding. This year's Aspen weighed less, as a result of changes in the windshield, inner body panels, headlining materials, and brakes. Ten new body colors were offered: Bright Canyon Red, Tapestry Red Sunfire metallic, Citron and Cadet Blue metallic, Caramel Tan and Mint Green metallic, Augusta Green Sunfire metallic, Classic Cream, Black, and Pewter Gray metallic. Eggshell White, Spitfire Orange, Starlight Blue Sunfire metallic and Light Mocha Tan were carried over. Only one trim level was offered, rather than the three choices of 1977. Instead, option packages allowed buyers to modify their Aspens. As before, two-door coupe, four-door sedan, and two-seat wagon bodies were available. Base engine was the one-barrel Slant Six, though wagons carried the two-barrel Super Six version. Three-speed manual shift was standard; four-speed available. TorqueFlite automatic transmissions (optional) added a new lock-up torque converter. Aspen's sporty coupes were offered again, in three versions: Super Coupe, R/T, and R/T Sport Pak. The Super Coupe (arriving later in the season) included dark brown body paint with black-finish hood, front fender tops, headlamps, wiper arms, front/rear bumpers, and remote-control racing mirrors. Bodyside and roof tape striping was included, along with wheel flares, front/rear spoilers, quarter-window louvers, GR60 x 15 Aramid fiber-belted raised white letter radial tires on 8-in. GT wheels, heavy-duty suspension with rear anti-sway bar, and the 360 cu. in. four-barrel V-8. The basic R/T had FR78 x 14 GBR BSW tires on Rallye wheels; heavy-duty suspension; red grille treatment; multi-color bodyside, hood and rear tape stripes; R/T decals and grille medallion; rocker panel moldings with black paint below; and dual remote racing mirrors. The R/T Sport Pak added a front spoiler, wheel flares, quarter-window louvers, rear-deck spoiler, and full-length tricolor stripes on white or black body. The R/T package (RPO Code A57) went on 3.2 percent of Aspen coupes, while Super Coupes (code A67) amounted to 1.1 percent. R/T Sport Pak (code A66) was installed on 1.3 percent of Aspen coupes. A Sunrise package went on 7.5 percent, and rarest of the lot is the Street Kit Car, with an installation rate of only 0.3 percent.

DIPLOMAT — SERIES G — SIX/V-8 — Introduced during the 1977 model year, Diplomat added a four-door station wagon for its first full season. Offered only in base trim, the wagon had wraparound horizontally-divided taillamps, simulated teakwood-grain body panels, a shorter rear end, wide back pillars, and an all-vinyl split-back bench seat with fold-down center armrest. Appearance of the two-door coupe and four-door sedan did not change, but a low-priced 'S' series was added to the original base and Medallion selection. Diplomats had a large grille, quad rectangular headlamps, and wraparound taillamps, plus full wheelhouse plastic splash shields. TorqueFlite and a 318 V-8 had been standard in the first Diplomats, but this year's edition switched to the new 225 cu. in. two-barrel Super Six, coupled to four-speed manual overdrive gearbox. Automatic and V-8 power were now optional. A thin-back bench seat was standard. Options included a 40-channel CB transceiver/stereo radio, and a search-tune stereo radio.

CHARGER SE — SERIES XP — V-8 — Appearance of the Dodge's carryover coupe did not change for 1978. Charger's front end still revealed its Cordoba relationship. Standard engine was the 318 cu. in. 5.2-liter V-8 with Electronic Lean Burn, hooked to TorqueFlite three-speed automatic (now with a lock-up torque converter). Options reached all the way to the 400 cu. in. (6.6-liter) four-barrel V-8. Standard equipment

included power steering, cloth bench seat, dual horns, and rear anti-sway bar. Door outer panels were one-sided galvanized metal. Joining the option list was a power sliding metal sunroof, as well as a T-Bar roof with removable tinted-glass panels. A new optional wiper gave intermittent operation. Thin-back bucket seats were also available. Other options: forged aluminum wheels and a three-spoke leather-wrapped steering wheel.

1978 Dodge, Magnum XE coupe with optional T-bar roof (OCW)

MAGNUM XE — SERIES XS — V-8 — In another attempt to capture the performance-minded market, Dodge added a second sporty hardtop coupe to join Charger SE, replacing the abandoned Daytona. Ads called Magnum "the totally personal approach to driving excitement." Distinctive aero-inspired front-end styling featured quad rectangular headlamps behind horizontally-scored clear covers, which retracted when lights were switched on. The headlamp units extended outward to encompass wraparound parking/signal lenses. The grille merely consisted of four big, wide slots with thin bright trim on the body-colored horizontal divider bars. The thin outer grille molding extended outward on each side, a bit below the headlamps, to wrap around the fenders below the marker lenses. 'Magnum' block letters and a medallion stood on front fenders, ahead of the door. Narrow opera windows could be plain or display thin horizontal louvers (available at no charge with vinyl roof). Twin bulges in each door extended into front fenders and quarter panels. At the rear were wraparound taillamps with horizontal trim strips. Four roof styles were optional: full or landau vinyl, T-Bar, or a power-operated sunroof. Base engine was the Lean Burn 318 cu. in. V-8 with TorqueFlite three-speed automatic. Power steering and brakes were standard, as were thin-back low-profile vinyl bucket seats with adjustable head restraints. Cloth 60/40 seating and leather/vinyl buckets were available. Magnum's Gran Touring package, arriving later, included color-keyed polyurethane fender flares that blended into the body, plus heavy-duty shock absorbers. GT Magnums rode GR60 x 15 Aramid fiber-belted radial tires with raised white letters on 7-in. wheels with functional air slots, deep-dish trim rings, a bright centerpiece, and bright lug nuts. Inside, the Gran Touring had engine-turned instrument panel appliqués, a two-spoke leather-wrapped steering wheel, and firm-feel power steering. GT colors were: Classic Cream, Eggshell White, Bright Canyon Red, Black, and metallic Pewter Gray, Starlight Blue Sunfire, or Tapestry Red Sunfire. Other Magnums could also have Charcoal Gray Sunfire metallic, Dove Gray, Cadet Blue or Mint Green metallic, Augusta Green or Sable Tan Sunfire metallic, or Caramel Tan metallic. GT packages (RPO Code A75) were installed in 1.8 percent of Magnums, and the model as a whole sold far better than Charger.

MONACO — SERIES W — SIX/V-8 — When the traditional full-size Royal Monaco was dropped, Monaco became the biggest Dodge, even though the hardtop rode a mid-size 115-in. wheelbase and sedans/wagons measured just over 117 in. Monaco came in base or luxury Brougham trim, including two station wagon series (standard and Crestwood). An 'SS' package, installed on 20.5 percent of the base Monaco coupes, featured tri-color striping and vinyl bucket seats with center armrest. Base engine was the two-barrel Super Six with three-speed manual column shift. Power brakes were standard. Two- and three-seat wagons carried the 360 cu. in. V-8 with TorqueFlite, and added power steering. The automatic transmission now had a lock-up torque converter. Monacos had vertically stacked headlamps and a split horizontal-style grille, each section containing one dominant horizontal and two vertical bars. Hardtops had new wraparound taillamps. Regency cloth/vinyl bench seats were standard. Options included aluminum-fascia wheels, and AM or AM/FM stereo radios with built-in CB transceivers. Sedans could get a full vinyl roof; two-door hardtops a halo roof or canopy roof, the latter with or without opera windows. A Gran Coupe package was installed on 19.1 percent of the total production. Available only V-8 powered, it included a halo vinyl roof, bodyside accent stripes, cloth/vinyl bucket seats, luxury steering wheel, color-keyed seatbelts, hood ornament with windsplit molding, sill moldings, G78 x 15 whitewalls, and dual sport remote mirrors (chromed or painted).

I.D. DATA: Dodge's 13-symbol Vehicle Identification Number (VIN) was on the upper left corner of the instrument panel, visible through the windshield. Symbol one indicates car line: 'Z' Omni; 'N' Aspen; 'G' Diplomat; 'W' Monaco; 'X' Charger SE or Magnum XE. Symbol two is series (price class): 'L' low; 'M' medium; 'H' high; 'P' premium; 'S' special. Symbols 3-4 show body type: '22' 2-dr. pillared hardtop; '23' 2-dr. hardtop; '29' 2-dr. coupe; '41' 4-dr. sedan; '44' 4-dr. hatchback; '45' two-seat station wagon; '46' three-seat wagon. Symbol five is the engine code: 'A' L4105; 'C' L6225 1Bbl.; 'D' L6225 2Bbl.; 'G' V8318; 'K' V8360 2Bbl.; 'J' V8360 4Bbl.; 'L' Hi-perf. V8360 4Bbl.; 'N' V8400 4Bbl.; 'P' Hi-perf. V8400 4Bbl. Symbol six is the model year code: '8' 1978. Symbol seven indicates assembly plant: 'A' Lynch Road; 'B' Hamtramck, MI; 'D' Belvidere, IL; 'F' Newark, DE; 'G' St. Louis; 'R' Windsor, Ontario. The final six digits make up the sequential serial number, starting with 100001. Six/V-8 engine number coding was similar to 1976-77. The engine number for the new Omni four-cylinder was located on a pad, just above the fuel pump. As before, a Vehicle Safety Certification Label that displays (among other data) the date of manufacture was attached to the rear facing of the driver's door. A Body Code Plate was on the left front fender side shield, wheel housing, or left side of upper radiator support.

1978 Dodge, Omni hatchback sedan with optional roof rack and Premium Woodgrain package (OCW)

1978 Dodge, Omni hatchback sedan with optional Premium Exterior package (OCW)

OMNI (FOUR)

Model No.	Body/ Style No.	Body Type & Seating	Factory Price	Shipping Weight	Prod. Total
ZL	44	4-dr. Hatch-4P	3976	2145	70,971

ASPEN (SIX/V-8)

Model No.	Body/ Style No.	Body Type & Seating	Factory Price	Shipping Weight	Prod. Total
NL	29	2-dr. Spt Cpe-5P	3747/3917	3135/3255	48,311

Model No.	Body/ Style No.	Body Type & Seating	Factory Price	Shipping Weight	Prod. Total
NL	41	4-dr. Sedan-6P	3865/4035	3175/3295	64,320
NL	45	4-dr. Sta Wag-6P	4207/4336	3405/3490	53,788

DIPLOMAT (SIX/V-8)

GH	22	2-dr. Cpe-6P	4991/5167	3420/3550	11,294
GH	41	4-dr. Sedan-6P	5147/5323	3465/3505	12,951
GH	45	4-dr. Sta Wag-6P	5486/5660	3555/3640	10,906

DIPLOMAT 'S' (SIX/V-8)

GM	22	2-dr. Cpe-6P	4771/4957	3315/3400	1,655
GM	41	4-dr. Sedan-6P	4937/5123	3395/3480	1,667

DIPLOMAT MEDALLION (SIX/V-8)

GP	22	2-dr. Cpe-6P	5361/5537	3495/3580	11,986
GP	41	4-dr. Sedan-6P	5517/5693	3550/3635	10,841

CHARGER SE (V-8)

XP	22	2-dr. HT Cpe-6P	5307	3895	2,735

MAGNUM XE (V-8)

XS	22	2-dr. HT Cpe-6P	5448	3895	47,827

MONACO (SIX/V-8)

WL	23	2-dr. HT Cpe-6P	4230/4406	3610/3865	7,509
WL	41	4-dr. Sedan-6P	4310/4385	3635/3885	16,333
WL	45	4-dr. Sta Wag-6P	----/5043	----/4310	1,665
WL	46	4-dr. 3S Wag-8P	----/5186	----/4375	2,544

MONACO 'SS' (SIX/V-8)

WL	23	2-dr. HT Cpe-6P	4322/4498	N/A/N/A	Note 1

Note 1: Production included in base HT Coupe total above (approximately 1,540 'SS' packages were installed).

MONACO BROUGHAM (SIX/V-8)

WH	23	2-dr. HT Cpe-6P	4476/4652	3615/3870	4,727
WH	41	4-dr. Sedan-6P	4527/4703	3650/3900	6,937

MONACO CRESTWOOD STATION WAGON (V-8)

WH	45	4-dr. 2S Wag-6P	----/5486	----/4305	668
WH	46	4-dr. 3S Wag-8P	----/5629	----/4380	1,588

Factory Price and Weight Note: Prices and weights to left of slash are for six-cylinder, to right for V-8 engine.

ENGINE DATA: BASE FOUR (Omni): Inline, overhead-cam four-cylinder. Cast iron block; aluminum head. Displacement: 104.7 cu. in. (1.7 liters). Bore and stroke: 3.13 x 3.40 in. Compression ratio: 8.2:1. Brake horsepower: 75 at 5600 R.P.M. Torque: 90 lb.-ft. at 3200 R.P.M. Five main bearings. Solid valve lifters. Carburetor: 2Bbl. Holley 5220. VIN Code: A. BASE SIX (Aspen): Inline, overhead-valve six. Cast iron block and head. Displacement: 225 cu. in. (3.7 liters). Bore and stroke: 3.40 x 4.12 in. Compression ratio: 8.4:1. Brake horsepower: 100 at 3600 R.P.M. Torque: 170 lb.-ft. at 1600 R.P.M. Four main bearings. Solid valve lifters. Carburetor: 1Bbl. Holley 1945. VIN Code: C. BASE SIX (Aspen, Diplomat, Monaco). OPTIONAL (Aspen): Same as 225 cu. in. six above, but with 2Bbl. Carter BBD carburetor. Brake horsepower: 110 at 3600 R.P.M. Torque: 180 lb.-ft. at 2000 R.P.M. VIN Code: D. BASE V-8 (Charger SE, Magnum XE): OPTIONAL (Aspen, Diplomat, Monaco): 90-degree, overhead valve V-8. Cast iron block and head. Displacement: 318 cu. in. (5.2 liters). Bore and stroke: 3.91 x 3.31 in. Compression ratio: 8.5:1. Brake horsepower: 140 at 4000 R.P.M. Torque: 245 lb.-ft. at 1600 R.P.M. Five main bearings. Hydraulic valve lifters. Carburetor: 2Bbl. Carter BBD. VIN Code: G. BASE V-8 (Monaco wag); OPTIONAL V-8 (Aspen, Diplomat, Charger SE, Magnum XE, Monaco): 90-degree, overhead valve V-8. Cast iron block and head. Displacement: 360 cu. in. (5.9 liters). Bore and stroke: 4.00 x 3.58 in. Compression ratio: 8.4:1. Brake horsepower: 155 at 3600 R.P.M. Torque: 270 lb.-ft. at 2400 R.P.M. Five main bearings. Hydraulic valve lifters. Carburetor: 2Bbl. Holley 2245. VIN Code: K. OPTIONAL V-8 (Aspen): Same as 360 cu. in. V-8 above, but with Carter TQ 4Bbl.

carburetor. Compression ratio: 8.0:1. Brake horsepower: 175 at 4000 R.P.M. Torque: 260 lb.-ft. at 2400 R.P.M. VIN Code: J. OPTIONAL V-8 (Charger SE, Magnum XE, Monaco): 90-degree, overhead valve V-8. Cast iron block and head. Displacement: 400 cu. in. (6.6 liters). Bore and stroke: 4.34 x 3.38 in. Compression ratio: 8.2:1. Brake horsepower: 190 at 3600 R.P.M. Torque: 305 lb.-ft. at 3200 R.P.M. Five main bearings. Hydraulic valve lifters. Carburetor: 4Bbl. Carter TQ. VIN Code: N. HIGH-OUTPUT V-8 (Charger SE, Magnum XE, Monaco): Heavy-duty version of 400 cu. in. V-8 above. Specs N/A. VIN Code: P.

CHASSIS DATA: Wheelbase: (Omni) 99.2 in.; (Aspen cpe) 108.7 in.; (Aspen sed/wag) 112.7 in.; (Diplomat) 112.7 in.; (Charger/Magnum/Monaco cpe) 114.9 in.; (Monaco sed) 117.4 in.; (Monaco wag) 117.5 in. Overall length: (Omni) 163.2 in.; (Aspen cpe) 197.2 in.; (Aspen sed/wag) 201.2 in.; (Diplo cpe) 204.1 in.; (Diplo sed) 206.1 in.; (Diplo wag) 202.8 in.; (Charger) 215.3 in.; (Magnum) 215.8 in.; (Monaco cpe) 213.2 in.; (Monaco sed) 218.0 in.; (Monaco wag) 225.1 in. Height: (Omni) 53.4 in.; (Aspen cpe) 53.3 in.; (Aspen sed) 55.3 in.; (Aspen wag) 55.7 in.; (Diplo cpe) 53.3 in.; (Diplo sed) 55.3 in.; (Diplo wag) 55.7 in.; (Monaco/Charger cpe) 52.9 in.; (Magnum) 53.1 in.; (Monaco sed) 54.3 in.; (Monaco wag) 56.9 in. Width: (Omni) 66.2 in.; (Aspen) 73.3 in.; (Diplo cpe) 73.5 in.; (Diplo sed/wag) 73.3 in.; (Charger/Magnum) 77.1 in.; (Monaco) 77.7 in.; (Monaco wag) 78.8 in. Front Tread: (Omni) 55.5 in.; (Aspen/Diplo) 60.0 in.; (Charger/Magnum/Monaco) 61.9 in. Rear Tread: (Omni) 55.1 in.; (Aspen/Diplo) 58.5 in.; (Chgr/Mag/Monaco) 62.0 in.; (Monaco wag) 63.4 in. Wheel size: (Omni) 13 x 4.5 in.; (Aspen cpe/sed) 14 x 5.0 in. exc. wagon, 14 x 5.5 in.; (Diplo/Chgr/Magnum) 15 x 5.5 in.; (Monaco) 15 x 5.5 in. exc. wagon, 15 x 6.5 in. Standard Tires: (Omni) P155/80R13 GBR WSW; (Aspen) D78 x 14 BSW exc. wag, F78 x 14; (Diplo) FR78 x 15 GBR BSW; (Charger/Magnum) FR78 x 15 GBR BSW; (Monaco) F78 x 15 BSW exc. wag, H78 x 15.

TECHNICAL: Transmission: Three-speed manual transmission standard on Aspen, Monaco six. Gear ratios: (1st) 3.08:1; (2nd) 1.70:1; (3rd) 1.00:1; (Rev) 2.90:1. Floor lever on Aspen; column on Monaco. Four-speed manual (floor lever) standard on Omni: (1st) 3.45:1; (2nd) 1.94:1; (3rd) 1.29:1; (4th) 0.97:1; (Rev) 3.17:1. Four-speed overdrive manual gearbox available on Aspen, standard on Diplomat: (1st) 3.09:1; (2nd) 1.67:1; (3rd) 1.00:1; (4th) 0.73:1; (Rev) 3.00:1. TorqueFlite three-speed automatic standard on other models, optional on all. Gear ratios: (1st) 2.45:1; (2nd) 1.45:1; (3rd) 1.00:1; (Rev) 2.22:1. Floor lever available for all. Omni TorqueFlite gear ratios: (1st) 2.47:1; (2nd) 1.47:1; (3rd) 1.00:1; (Rev) 2.10:1. Standard final drive ratio: (Omni) 3.48:1; (Aspen six) 3.23:1; (Aspen V-8) 2.94:1; (Aspen V8360) 2.45:1 or 3.21:1; (Aspen wag) 3.21:1; (Diplomat six) 3.23:1; (Diplo V-8) 2.94:1 or 2.45:1; (Diplo V-8 wag) 2.71:1; (Charger/Magnum) 2.71:1 exc. 2.45:1 w/V8360/400, 3.2:1 w/hi-perf. V8400; (Monaco six) 3.21:1; (Monaco V-8) 2.71:1; (Monaco V8360) 2.45:1 or 2.71:1. Steering: (Omni) rack and pinion; (others) recirculating ball. Suspension: (Omni) Iso-Strut independent coil front w/anti-sway bar, trailing arm independent coil rear w/integral anti-sway; (Aspen/Diplomat) isolated transverse front torsion bars and anti-sway bar, semi-elliptic rear leaf springs; (others) longitudinal front torsion bars w/lower trailing links and anti-sway bar, semi-elliptic rear leaf springs; rear anti-sway bar on Charger SE/Magnum XE. Brakes: Front disc, rear drum. Ignition: Electronic. Body construction: (Omni) unibody; (Aspen/Diplomat) unibody w/front auxiliary frame; (Monaco/Charger/Magnum) unibody w/isolated front crossmembers. Fuel tank: (Omni) 13 gal.; (Aspen six) 18 gal.; (Aspen V-8/wag) 19.5 gal.; (Diplomat) 19.5 gal.; (Charger/Magnum) 25.5 gal.; (Monaco six) 20.5 gal.; (Monaco V-8) 25.5 gal. exc. wag, 20 gal.

DRIVETRAIN OPTIONS: Engines: 225 cu. in., 2Bbl. six: Aspen ($41). 318 cu. in., 2Bbl. V-8: Aspen cpe/sed ($170); Aspen wag ($129); Diplomat/Monaco ($176). 318 cu. in., 4Bbl. V-8 (Calif.): Aspen cpe/sed ($439-$463); Aspen wag ($399); Chgr/Mag ($45); Diplo/Monaco ($221). 360 cu. in., 2Bbl. V-8: Aspen cpe/sed ($275); Aspen wag ($234); Chgr/Mag ($109); Diplomat/Monaco ($285). H.D. 360 cu. in., 2Bbl. V-8: Aspen sed ($332); Aspen wag ($292); Diplo ($345). 360 cu. in., 4Bbl. V-8: Aspen cpe ($439-$463); Diplo ($330); Charger/Magnum ($154); Monaco ($330) exc. wag ($45) H.D. 360 cu. in., 4Bbl. V-8: Charger/Magnum ($305); Diplo/Monaco ($481). 400 cu. in., 4Bbl. V-8: Charger/Magnum ($203); Monaco ($379) exc. wag ($94). H.D. 400 cu. in., 4Bbl. V-8: Chgr/Mag ($330); Monaco ($507) exc. wag ($222). Transmission/Differential: Four-speed overdrive manual trans. w/floor lever: Aspen ($142). TorqueFlite auto. trans.: Omni ($303); Aspen ($293); Diplo ($165); Monaco ($320). SureGrip differential: Aspen ($56); Diplo/Chgr/Mag/Monaco ($62). Optional axle ratio: Aspen ($15). Brakes and Steering: Power front disc brakes: Omni ($68); Aspen cpe/sed ($66). Power steering: Omni ($148); Aspen ($145); Monaco HT/sed ($159). Suspension: H.D. susp.: Aspen ($24); Diplo/Charger/Magnum ($26); Monaco ($19-$26). Sport susp.: Omni ($24). H.D. shock absorbers: Chgr/Mag/Monaco ($7). Other: Long-life battery ($30-$33). H.D. trailer towing pkg.: Aspen sed/wag ($150); Diplo ($154); Chgr/Mag ($183); Monaco ($157). California emission system ($72-$79). High-altitude emission system ($31-$34).

OMNI CONVENIENCE/APPEARANCE OPTIONS: Option Packages: Classic two-tone paint pkg. ($73-$107). Custom exterior pkg. ($71). Premium exterior pkg. ($167). Custom interior pkg. ($62-$82). Premium interior pkg. ($214-$242). Premium woodgrain pkg. ($312). Popular equipment group ($250). Light pkg. ($44). Comfort/Convenience: Air cond. ($493). Tinted glass ($56). Luxury steering wheel ($15). Electric clock w/trip odometer ($26). Rear wiper/washer ($59). Locking gas cap ($7). Glove box lock ($5). Horns and Mirrors: Dual horns ($7). Remote left mirror ($16). Dual remote mirrors ($30-$46). Day/night mirror ($9). Entertainment: AM/FM radio ($74). AM/FM stereo radio ($143). Exterior: Full vinyl roof ($93). Moldings: belt ($16); drip ($18); sill ($19); upper door frame ($30); wheel lip ($27). Door edge protectors ($20). Bumper guards ($41). Multi-color tape stripe ($78). Luggage rack ($81). Undercoating ($31). Interior: Console: storage ($21); shift lever ($30). Cloth/vinyl bucket seats ($21). Cargo area carpet ($43). Color-keyed floor mats ($26). Wheels and Tires: Wheel trim rings ($36). Rallye wheels ($36-$73). Bright Rallye hubs ($37). 165/75 x 13 GBR WSW ($16). 165/75 x 13 SBR WSW ($48). Conventional spare tire ($12-$24).

ASPEN CONVENIENCE/APPEARANCE OPTIONS: Option Packages: Super Coupe pkg. ($1351-$1420). "Street Kit Car" pkg.: cpe ($1085), R/T pkg.: cpe ($289). R/T decor group: cpe ($51). R/T "Sport Pak": cpe ($340-$499). Special Edition wagon woodgrain group ($221). Special Edition interior pkg. ($180-$483). Special Edition exterior pkg. ($128-$157). Sunrise pkg.: cpe ($77). Sunrise decor pkg.: cpe ($170-$186). Custom exterior pkg. ($73-$86). Custom interior pkg. ($144-$224). Basic group ($653-$655). Value bonus pkg. A ($229); B ($656-$673). Two-tone paint pkg.: cpe ($188). Two-tone decor pkg. ($62). Light pkg. ($44). Deluxe insulation pkg. ($38-$47). Protection group ($28-$35). Comfort/Convenience: Air cond. ($484). Rear defogger, blower-type ($48); electric ($83). Automatic speed control ($86). Power seat ($142). Power windows ($113-$157). Power door locks ($71-$98). Power tailgate release: wag ($21). Tinted windshield ($39); all windows ($53). Luxury steering wheel ($29). Tuff steering wheel ($37). Tilt steering wheel ($65). Digital clock ($46). Inside hood release ($12). Intermittent wipers ($31). Lighter ($6). Locking gas cap ($7). Locking glove box ($5). Horns and Mirrors: Dual horns ($6). Remote left mirror ($16). Dual remote mirrors ($30-$46). Dual remote sport mirrors ($38-$53). Day/night mirror ($9). Entertainment: AM radio ($74); w/8track player ($143-$217); w/CB ($305-$379). AM/FM radio ($74-$148). AM/FM stereo radio ($143-$217); w/8track player ($234-$308); w/CB ($448-$522). Rear speaker ($23). Exterior: T-Bar roof: cpe ($572). Full vinyl roof: sed ($93). Halo vinyl roof: cpe ($93-$109). Landau vinyl roof: cpe ($164). Vinyl bodyside moldings ($40). Belt moldings ($16). Door edge protectors ($10-$18). Upper door frame moldings: sed/wag ($30). Wheel lip moldings ($20). Bumper guards ($39). rub strips ($31). Rear air deflector: wag ($27). Luggage rack: wag ($81). Undercoating ($21-$31). Interior: Console: cpe ($55). Vinyl bucket seats ($102). Cloth/vinyl bucket seats ($160). Rear armrest ($11). Color-keyed mats ($20). Color-keyed seatbelts ($15). Cargo area carpets and storage bin: wag ($50). Pedal dress-up ($9). Trunk dress-up ($43). Wheels and Tires: Rallye wheels ($33-$72). Styled wheels ($55-$127). Deluxe wheel covers ($36). Premium wheel covers ($36-$71). Wire wheel covers ($91-$127). D78 x 14 WSW. DR78 x 14 GBR BSW. DR78 x 14 GBR WSW. E78 x 14 GBR BSW. E78 x 14 GBR WSW. ER78 x 14 GBR SSW. ER78 x 14 GBR WSW. ER78 x 14 SBR WSW. FR70 x 14 RWL Aramid-belted. FR78 x 14 GBR BSW. FR78 x 14 GBR WSW. FR78 x 14 SBR WSW. GR78 x 14 SBR WSW. Space-saving spare tire: cpe/sed (NC). Conventional spare tire (NC).

DIPLOMAT CONVENIENCE/APPEARANCE OPTIONS: Option Packages: Basic group ($1055-$1219). Deluxe insulation pkg. ($9-$80). Light pkg. ($69-$80). Comfort/Convenience: Air cond. ($563). Rear defroster ($91). Auto. speed control ($94). Power seat ($155). Power windows ($129-$179). Power door locks ($83-$116). Power decklid/tailgate release ($22-$23). Tinted glass ($65). Luxury steering wheel ($19). Leather-covered steering wheel ($57). Tilt steering wheel ($71). Digital clock ($50). Deluxe wiper/washer ($41). Locking gas cap ($7). Lighting and Mirrors: Cornering lights ($48). Remote driver's mirror: base ($17). Remote passenger mirror: Medallion ($33). Dual remote-control mirrors: base ($33-$50). Lighted vanity mirror ($48). Entertainment: AM radio ($81); w/CB ($333-$414). AM/FM radio ($81-$161). AM/FM stereo ($157-$237). w/8-track tape player ($256-$336); w/CB ($490-$570). Search-tune AM/FM stereo ($284-$365). Rear speaker ($25). Power antenna ($46). Exterior: T-Bar roof: cpe ($643). Power sunroof: metal ($626); glass ($788). Landau vinyl roof: cpe ($137). Vinyl bodyside moldings ($44). Front bumper guards ($21). Hood tape stripe: Medallion ($23). Door edge protectors ($11-$20). Air deflector: wag ($29). Luggage rack: wag ($89). Woodgrain: wag (NC). Undercoating ($24). Interior: Vinyl bench seat: base cpe/sed ($48). Cloth 60/40 seat: wag ($140). Leather 60/40 seat: wag ($410). Medallion ($270). Color-keyed floor mats ($58). Color-keyed seatbelts: base ($16). Pedal dress-up: base ($10). Wheels/Tires: Premium wheel covers: base ($41). Wire wheel covers ($58-$99). Forged aluminum wheels ($208-$248). FR78 x 15 GBR WSW ($48). FR78 x 15 SBR WSW ($57-$106). Conventional spare (NC).

CHARGER SE/MAGNUM XE CONVENIENCE/APPEARANCE OPTIONS: Option Packages: Gran Touring 'GT' pkg.: Magnum ($497). Basic group: Charger ($1030); Magnum ($988). Light pkg. ($28). Comfort/Convenience: Air cond. ($563). Rear defroster, electric ($91). Automatic speed control ($94). Tinted windshield ($42); all windows ($65). Power seat ($155). Power windows ($129). Power door locks ($83). Power decklid release ($23). Luxury steering wheel ($19). Leather steering wheel ($57). Tilt steering wheel ($57). Tachometer ($70). Digital clock ($50). Locking gas cap ($7). Deluxe wipers ($34). Mirrors: Left remote ($17). Dual remote ($33-$50). Dual sport remote ($41-$58). Lighted vanity ($48). Entertainment: AM radio ($81); w/8track player ($157-$237); w/CB ($333-$414). AM/FM radio ($81-$161). AM/FM stereo radio ($157-$237); w/8track ($256-$336); w/CB ($490-$570). Search-tune AM/FM stereo ($284-$365). Rear speaker ($25-$26). Power antenna ($46). Exterior: T-Bar roof ($643). Power sunroof ($516). Full vinyl roof ($5-$121). Landau vinyl roof ($117). Quarter window louvers: Magnum (NC) w/vinyl roof. Fender-mount turn signals: Mag ($15). Vinyl bodyside moldings ($44). Wheel lip moldings: Mag ($98). Door edge protectors ($11). Bumper rub strips: Mag ($35). Hood/deck or bodyside stripes: Mag ($45). Wheel lip tape stripes: Mag ($23). Undercoating ($34). Interior: Console ($58-$90). Velour/vinyl 60/40 bench seat: Mag ($216). Vinyl bucket seats: Chgr ($187). Velour/vinyl bucket seats: Mag ($146). Leather bucket seats: Mag ($346). Center front cushion: Mag ($41). Color-keyed mats ($22). Color-keyed seatbelts ($16). Trunk dress-up ($47). Pedal dress-up ($10). Wheels and Tires: Aluminum-fascia wheels: Magnum ($87). Styled wheels ($248). Wire wheel covers ($99). GR78 x 15 GBR BSW ($21). GR78 x 15 GBR WSW ($48). GR78 x 15 SBR WSW ($57-$106). HR78 x 15 SBR WSW ($83-$131). GR60 x 15 RWL Aramid-belted ($219-$267). Conventional spare tire (NC).

MONACO CONVENIENCE/APPEARANCE OPTIONS: Option Packages: Gran Coupe pkg. ($686). Basic group ($254-$739). Value pkg. ($168-$214). Roadability pkg.: V-8 HT/sed ($35). Deluxe insulation pkg.: six-cyl. ($32-$68). Light pkg. ($43-$51). Comfort/Convenience: Air cond. ($563). Rear defroster, electric ($91). Auto. speed control: V-8 ($94). Power windows ($129-$179). Power tailgate window: wag ($46). Power door locks ($83-$116). Power seat ($155). Auto-lock tailgate: wag ($38). Tinted glass ($65); windshield only ($42). Luxury steering wheel ($19). Tilt steering wheel ($71). Electric clock ($22). Deluxe wipers ($34). Inside hood release ($13). Locking gas cap ($7). Horns and Mirrors: Dual horns: base ($7). Remote driver's mirror ($17). Dual chrome remote mirrors ($33-$50). Dual sport remote mirrors, chrome or painted: HT ($41-$58). Entertainment: AM radio ($81); w/8track player ($157-$237); w/CB ($333-$414). AM/FM radio ($81-$161). AM/FM stereo ($157-$237); w/8track tape player ($256-$336); w/CB ($490-$570). Rear speaker ($25). Exterior: Full vinyl roof: sed ($121). Halo vinyl roof: HT ($121). Canopy vinyl roof: HT ($100). Canopy roof w/opera windows ($121). Vinyl bodyside molding: base ($22-$44). Wide bodyside molding: Crestwood (NC). Belt moldings: base HT ($17). Door edge protectors ($11-$20). Sill moldings: sed, base wag ($25). Upper door frame moldings: base sed/wag ($33). Wheel lip moldings: sed ($22). Deck stripes: HT ($23). Tri-color bodyside stripes: HT ($45). Bumper rub strips: front ($17); front/rear, HT ($35). Air deflector: wag ($29). Luggage rack: wag ($89). Undercoating ($34). Interior: Console: Brghm ($58). Vinyl bench seat: base ($48); Brghm sed ($31). Cloth/vinyl 60/40 bench seat: Brghm ($140). Vinyl 60/40 seat: Crestwood ($140). Color-keyed mats ($22). Color-keyed seatbelts ($16). Wheels and Tires: Deluxe wheel covers ($39). Wire wheel covers ($99-$138). Aluminum-fascia wheels ($87-$126). F78 x 15 WSW ($48). G78 x 15 BSW ($21). G78 x 15 WSW ($21-$69). H78 x 15 BSW ($45). H78 x 15 WSW ($47-$95). GR78 x 15 SBR WSW ($130-$178). GR60 x 15 RWL Aramid-belted ($327-$376). 215 x 15 SBR WSW ($109-$204). Space-saving spare tire (NC).

HISTORY: Introduced: October 7, 1977. Model year production: Chrysler reported a total of 391,223 passenger cars shipped. Total North American production for the U.S. market of 424,934 units (incl. 30,599 Sportsman vans) included 71,000 four-cylinder, 129,659 six-cylinder and 224,275 V-8s. Calendar year production (U.S.): 412,821 (not incl. 33,220 Sportsman vans). Calendar year sales by U.S. dealers: 398,219 (plus 44,376 Sportsman vans). Model year sales by U.S. dealers: 398,151 (not incl. 47,931 Colts, 14,196 Challengers and 46,292 Sportsman vans).

HISTORICAL FOOTNOTES: This was not a great sales year for either Dodge or Plymouth. Dodge ranked No. 8, just behind Plymouth, with model year sales down 5 percent. Production fell even further, by 21 percent. A sporty new Challenger model, imported from Japan, was expected to help sales. Omni's engine block came from Volkswagenwerk AG in Germany, but was modified at Chrysler. That meant lengthening its stroke and adding a Lean Burn system. Manual gearboxes also came from Volkswagen, while automatics were Chrysler-made. Omni reached a composite (city/highway) EPA mileage figure of 30 mpg. Dodge ads in this era featured the Sherlock Holmes character.

1979 DODGE

Two nameplates left the lineup this year: Charger and Monaco. Magnum XE remained as Dodge's sporty performance coupe, while a new rear-drive St. Regis filled the big-car spot. That new R-bodied St. Regis, though, weighed some 700 pounds less than the full-size Dodges of a few years earlier. The average Dodge, in fact, weighed 160 pounds less this year, in an attempt to boost gas mileage. Omni added a new two-door 024 coupe to match the original four-door hatchback. Sixes and V-8s had aluminum intake manifolds. A new diagnostic connector on all models helped isolate electrical problems. A 430-amp maintenance-free battery was included with the 360 cu. in. V-8 on Aspen, Diplomat and St. Regis, and available on Omnis. A 500-amp battery was optional with all sixes and V-8s. Batteries had a new test indicator. Both Aspen and Diplomat continued to use the unique transverse torsion bar front suspension, while all rear-drives had multi-leaf rear springs. Omni and St. Regis had new sill-mounted jack pads for use with a scissors jack. A new compact spare tire arrived on Aspen, Diplomat and St. Regis coupes and sedans. TorqueFlite transmissions with all normal-duty V-8s (and some sixes) had the direct-drive lock-up torque converter clutch, introduced a year earlier.

1979 Dodge, Omni O24 hatchback coupe with optional sunroof (OCW)

OMNI/024 — SERIES ZL — FOUR

OMNI/024 — SERIES ZL — FOUR — Four-door Omnis looked the same as they had in their opening season of 1978. Body features included single rectangular headlamps, combined park/signal/marker lamps with bright accents in leading edges of front fenders, tri-color taillamp lenses with bright accents, and rear side marker lamps in quarter panels. Omnis had black vinyl bodyside moldings and bumper rub strips. Inside were standard high-back vinyl bucket front seats and a deep-dish three-spoke steering wheel, plus a rear bench seat with fold-down seatback. An electric rear defroster and AM radio were standard. So were the folding rear shelf security panel and a multi-function control lever on column. This year's solid colors were: Nightwatch Blue, Chianti Red, Flame Orange, Light Cashmere, Black, or Eggshell White; plus metallic Ensign Blue, Cadet Blue, Turquoise, Teal Green Sunfire, Teal Frost, Medium Cashmere, and Pewter Gray. Six two-tones also were offered. Standard engine was again the 1.7-liter four with four-speed transaxle. High-strength aluminum bumpers helped cut weight. Omni options included a custom equipment package, premium interior package (vinyl seats with head restraints and passenger seatback recliner), maintenance-free battery, sunroof, and locking glovebox. In addition to the four-door

econobox, however, Omni now offered a two-door hatchback coupe, dubbed 024, on a wheelbase 2.5 inches shorter (96.7 in.) than the sedan. The six-window design included a narrow quarter window just to the rear of the door window, plus a sharply angled far-rear window that followed the line of the hatch. 024 had an aero-shaped, soft-feel molded urethane front end (including grille, bumper facing and fender caps) and a soft urethane rear bumper fascia, plus a sports suspension. Its grille was a simple set of wide horizontal slots, three on each side, in the sloping body-color panel, with 'Dodge' lettering above on the driver's side. Single rectangular headlamps were deeply recessed, with parking lamps recessed down below the bumper strip area. Large curved slots flanked the front license plate. An 'Omni 024' nameplate adorned front fenders, ahead of the door. Amber side marker lamps were on front fenders. Bodysides displayed dual pin stripes, plus a black aero driver's mirror. 024 also had belt, drip rail, sill and wheel lip moldings, along with black wiper arms and blades. Nearly full-width, bright-accented tri-color taillamps were red on the outside (wrapping onto quarter panels), then amber, with clear backup lenses toward the center. Each taillamp was divided by a pair of horizontal ribs. Solid body colors were the same as for the four-door Omni, along with Bright Yellow. Three two-tones were offered, plus three with the Sport package. Like the basic Omni, 024 had front-wheel drive and an Iso-Strut front suspension. A transverse-mounted four-cylinder engine and four-speed manual gearbox provided the power. Whitewall tires and wheel trim rings were standard; bumper rub strips optional. Inside were high-back all-vinyl bucket seats with integral head restraints, and a rear bench seat with fold-down seatback. Cloth/vinyl upholstery was optional. Standard equipment included an AM/FM radio, remote power liftgate release, electric rear defroster, glovebox lock, multi-function column lever, deep-dish three-spoke steering wheel, and simulated woodgrain instrument panel. A Sport package included black accent striping with reflective red accents at the taillamp area, louvered quarter window appliqué, black bumper rub strips, black backlight and quarter window moldings, black belt moldings, and black windshield molding. Also included: dual black remote sport mirrors, four-spoke black sport steering wheel, Rallye instrument cluster (including tachometer), body-color wheels with bright trim rings, and large '024' decals on forward edges of quarter panels and rear spoiler. A total of 15,369 two-door Omnis had the Sport package, while 4,156 carried the Rallye package.

1979 Dodge, Aspen sedan with optional Custom decor package (OCW)

ASPEN — SERIES NL — SIX/V-8

ASPEN — SERIES NL — SIX/V-8 — As in 1978, Aspen came in only one trim level, but Custom and Special Edition packages were available. Coupe, sedan and station wagon bodies were offered, all looking about the same as the '78 versions. Aspen's grille had bright horizontal and vertical bars. Two-segment taillamps had red outboard lenses and clear (backup) lenses inboard. New body colors included: Teal Green Sunfire and Teal Frost metallic, Light Cashmere, Medium Cashmere metallic, Chianti Red, Regent Red Sunfire metallic, Ensign Blue metallic, and (coupe only) Light Yellow. On the dash was a new 85 mph speedometer. Standard three-speed manual transmission was available only with a floor lever and one-barrel 225 cu. in. six. TorqueFlite had a lock-up torque converter clutch, except on wagons with the two-barrel six and some 360 cu. in. V-8s. Six-cylinder models used a new, quieter air conditioner compressor. A high-pressure compact spare tire became standard on coupe and sedan. Also new: an aluminum intake manifold, and aluminum/plastic master cylinder and ignition lock housing. A diagnostic connector allowed hookup to an electronic engine performance analyzer. New options included a Sunrise Coupe package with tape striping, R/T package, Sport Wagon package with flared wheel openings and

bucket seats, and aluminum wheels. A total of 75 Aspens had the R/T package, while 8,159 had the Sunrise coupe package. A 40-channel CB was optional on all models, with AM or AM/FM stereo.

1979 Dodge, Diplomat Salon sedan with optional forged aluminum wheels (OCW)

1979 Dodge, Diplomat Salon station wagon with optional roof rack and wind deflector (OCW)

DIPLOMAT — SERIES G — SIX/V-8 — Once again, seven Diplomat models were offered. They included a new medium-price base two- and four-door; highline two- and four-door (now called Salon); premium models, again called Medallion; and Salon station wagon. Appearance was similar to before, but with modifications. Diplomat's new chromed grille had bold, rectangular openings framing fine vertical bars. It was divided into an 8 x 3 overall pattern, with crosshatching in each section and a heavy upper header. Quad rectangular parking lamps were mounted just above quad rectangular headlamps. Chromed framing for headlamps and parking lamps wrapped around bodysides, to frame the amber marker/cornering lenses with Diplomat crest. On the hood was a distinctive crest ornament. At the rear were restyled two-segment wraparound taillamps. Each consisted of four sections, arranged 2 x 2 and separated by a vertical trim bar. At closer glance, each of the four sections was split in two horizontally. Backup lamps again were mounted in the bumper. Salon two- and four-doors had new bodyside accent tape stripes. Medallions had bodyside, decklid and deck lower panel accent stripes. A padded full vinyl roof was standard on Salon and Medallion four-doors. A restyled Landau vinyl roof with rectangular opera window was optional on two-doors. Medallions had a map/courtesy reading lamp, as well as rear-pillar vanity mirrors with lamps on the four-door. Wagons displayed teakwood-grain woodtone appliqués with light woodtone stripes on bodysides and liftgate (which could be deleted). New cloth/vinyl bucket seats

were optional on Salon. Other new options: halogen headlamps and wire wheel covers. Eleven body colors were available for coupes and sedans, seven for wagons . Choices were: Dove Gray, Chianti Red, Black, Light Cashmere, Eggshell White, and metallic Cadet Blue, Ensign Blue, Regent Red Sunfire, Sable Tan Sunfire, Teal Frost, Teal Green Sunfire, and Medium Cashmere (wagons only). Overdrive-4 manual transmission was standard with the one-barrel Slant Six. TorqueFlite had a lock-up clutch in all normal-duty V-8s and the two-barrel six (two-doors) without air conditioning; but not in models with a heavy-duty trailer assist package. The electric choke heater was redesigned to improve cold-weather startup; the Slant Six carburetor revised; and the oil-change interval doubled. Power brakes and steering were standard on all Diplomats. A total of 594 Diplomats had the Sport Appearance package, while only 72 were reported to have the heavy-duty package.

1979 Dodge, Diplomat Medallion coupe with optional T-bar roof (OCW)

1979 Dodge, Magnum XE coupe with optional T-bar roof (OCW)

MAGNUM XE — SERIES XS — V-8 — Modest appearance changes, notably new taillamps, hit the Magnum in its second year. With Charger out of the lineup, it remained the only Dodge performance coupe model. New wraparound two-segment taillamps had bright horizontal ribs to match the front styling. Magnum's sloping, aero-look front end featured a grille with widely-spaced horizontal bars and transparent, sealed (retractable) covers over quad headlamps. Parking/signal/marker lamps wrapped around the corners of front fender extensions behind a curved transparent cover. Horizontal ribs on that cover (and headlamp covers) blended with horizontal grille bars. Front fenders and decklid held bold 'Magnum' block letters. XE medallions went on front fenders and headlamp lenses. The 'Dodge' name was on the driver's side headlamp cover and decklid. Raised, sculptured sections on front fenders and rear quarter panels extended into doors. Wheel covers showed XE center medallions. New body colors included Nightwatch Blue, Teal Green, and Light Cashmere. Fourteen solid colors and four two-tones were available. Inside were low-back vinyl bucket seats, front/rear ashtrays, cigarette lighter, woodtone instrument panel trim, and two-spoke padded steering wheel. Standard TorqueFlite had a lock-up torque converter (except with heavy-duty 360 V-8 or 3.2:1 axle). Base engine was the 318 cu. in. V-8. New options included a unique two-tone paint package and Roadability package. Magnum was considered roughly equivalent to Chrysler's 300, but cost about the same as a base Cordoba. Magnum's Gran Touring (GT) package was offered again, with bold fender flares, GR60 x 15 Aramid-belted tires with raised white letters on 15 x 7-in. wheels, leather-wrapped three-spoke steering wheel, and engine-turned instrument panel appliqué to replace the standard woodtone. GT medallions highlighted front fenders. The package also included firm-feel suspension and power steering. A total of 1,670 Magnums had the GT package (RPO Code A75).

1979 Dodge, St. Regis pillared hardtop with optional two-tone paint and forged aluminum wheels (OCW)

ST. REGIS — SERIES EH — SIX/V-8 — Dodge's new "full size" four-door model would actually have been considered a mid-size a couple of years earlier. In fact, it was now called a "regular size" or family-size, with a design that had its roots in the departed Monaco. Though it offered a big-car look, St. Regis rode a 118.5-in. wheelbase and weighed 700 pounds less than prior full-size models. Chromed aluminum bumpers were one of many weight-cutting features. The R-body design, referred to as a "four-door pillared hardtop," was related to Chrysler's Newport and New Yorker. Basic grille shape was similar to Magnum's, but with a much different pattern of wide segments and a thick, bright header. The unusual pattern of the swing-away chrome grille was made up of separate small wide rectangles, arranged in six columns and seven rows. A pair of wider rectangular elements extended outward at the base, below the headlamps, to wrap around front fenders. Transparent headlamp doors with embossed horizontal ribs (similar to Magnum) swung down when lights were switched on. Wide parking lamps were inset in the bumper. Marker lenses mated with the headlamp covers. Separate cornering lamps (if ordered) were farther down on the fender, ahead of the

wheel openings. Standard equipment included the two-barrel Slant Six engines, power steering and brakes, TorqueFlite three-speed automatic, tinted glass, a trip odometer, and aero flag-type mirrors. Standard 60/40 split bench seats with folding center armrest and passenger seatback recliner came in Saxony and Whittier cloth. Also standard: front/rear ashtrays, protective bumper rub strips, lighter, gauges, dual horns, two-spoke steering wheel with woodtone trim, P195/75R15 GBR tires, and deluxe wheel covers. St. Regis colors were: Dove Gray, Frost Blue metallic, Nightwatch Blue, Teal Frost metallic, Teal Green or Regent Red Sunfire metallic, Light Cashmere, Medium Cashmere metallic, Sable Tan Sunfire metallic, Eggshell White, and Black; plus four two-tones. Three new interior trim colors were offered: Midnight Blue, Teal Green and Cashmere; plus carryover Canyon Red and Dove Gray. A multi-switch lever on the steering column controlled turn signals, dimmer and wiper/washer. St. Regis had a two-spoke steering wheel with woodtone trim, new hi/lo heater/defroster, and compact spare tire. Bumper guards were optional. So was the 360 cu. in. V-8, which wouldn't be around much longer. Other options included power windows and driver's seat, search-tune AM/FM stereo radio with digital display, 40-channel CB with AM or AM/FM stereo radio, intermittent wipers, cornering lamps, power glass sunroof, leather-wrapped or tilt steering wheel, trailer towing package, and wire wheel covers or aluminum wheels. An Open Road Handling Package had firm-feel suspension and power steering, like that on police cars. A total of 640 St. Regis models came with the handling package.

I.D. DATA: Dodge's 13-symbol Vehicle Identification Number (VIN) was on the upper left corner of the instrument panel, visible through the windshield. Symbol one indicates car line: 'Z' Omni/024; 'N' Aspen; 'G' Diplomat; 'X' Magnum XE; 'E' St. Regis. Symbol two is series (price class): 'L' low; 'M' medium; 'H' high; 'P' premium; 'S' special. Symbols 3-4 show body type: '22' 2-dr. pillared hardtop; '24' 2-dr. hatchback; '29' 2-dr. coupe; '41' 4-dr. sedan; '42' 4-dr. pillared hardtop; '44' 4-dr. hatchback; '45' two-seat station wagon. Symbol five is the engine code: 'A' L4105; 'C' L6225 1Bbl.; 'D' L6225 2Bbl.; 'G'-V8318 2Bbl.; 'K' V8360 2Bbl.; 'L' V8360 4Bbl. Symbol six is the model year code: '9' 1979. Symbol seven indicates assembly plant: 'B' Hamtramck, MI; 'D' Belvidere, IL; 'F' Newark, DE; 'G' St. Louis; 'R' Windsor, Ontario. The final six digits make up the sequential serial number, starting with 100001. An abbreviated version of the VIN is also stamped on a pad on the engine block: below No. 6 spark plug on six-cylinder engines, and to rear of right engine mount on V-8s. Serial numbers for V-8s are coded as follows: first letter series (model year); second assembly plant; next three digits displacement (cu. in.); next one or two letters model; next four digits show build date; and final four digits are the engine sequence number. Omni's engine number is on a pad just above the fuel pump. Information on over/undersized parts is stamped on six-cylinder engines on the joint face at right corner, adjacent to No. 1 cylinder; on 318/360 V-8s, at left front of block just below the head. A Body Code Plate is on the left front fender side shield, wheel housing, or left side of upper radiator support.

1979 Dodge, Omni hatchback sedan with optional roof rack and Classic two-tone paint package (OCW)

OMNI (FOUR)

Model No.	Body/Style No.	Body Type & Seating	Factory Price	Shipping Weight	Prod. Total
ZL	44	4-dr. Hatch-4P	4122	2135	71,556

OMNI 024 (FOUR)

ZL	24	2-dr. Hatch-4P	4482	2195	46,781

ASPEN (SIX/V-8)

NL	29	2-dr. Cpe-5P	3968/4184	3050/3170	Note 1
NL	41	4-dr. Sedan-6P	4069/4285	3115/3235	Note 1
NL	45	4-dr. Sta Wag-6P	4445/4661	3325/3435	33,086

Note 1: Total Aspen coupe/sedan production, 88,268.

DIPLOMAT (SIX/V-8)

GM	22	2-dr. Cpe-6P	4901/5137	3270/3365	Note 2
GM	41	4-dr. Sedan-6P	4999/5235	3330/3425	Note 2

Note 2: Total base model production, 13,929.

DIPLOMAT SALON (SIX/V-8)

GH	22	2-dr. Cpe-6P	5138/5374	3285/3385	Note 3
GH	41	4-dr. Sedan-6P	5366/5602	3350/3450	Note 3
GH	45	4-dr. Sta Wag-6P	5769/6005	3545/3630	7,785

Note 3: Total Salon coupe/sedan production, 17,577.

DIPLOMAT MEDALLION (SIX/V-8)

GP	22	2-dr. Cpe-6P	5612/5848	3345/3440	Note 4
GP	41	4-dr. Sedan-6P	5840/6076	3425/3520	Note 4

Note 4: Total Medallion production, 12,394.

MAGNUM XE (V-8)

XS	22	2-dr. HT Cpe-6P	5709	3675	25,367

ST. REGIS (SIX/V-8)

EH	42	4-dr. Pill. HT-6P	6216/6455	3565/3640	34,434

Factory Price and Weight Note: Prices and weights to left of slash are for six-cylinder, to right for V-8 engine.

1979 Dodge, Aspen coupe with optional R/T package (OCW)

ENGINE DATA: BASE FOUR (Omni): Inline, overhead-cam four-cylinder. Cast iron block; aluminum head. Displacement: 104.7 cu. in. (1.7 liters). Bore and stroke: 3.13 x 3.40 in. Compression ratio: 8.2:1. Brake horsepower: 70 at 5200 R.P.M. Torque: 85 lb.-ft. at 2800 R.P.M. Five main bearings. Solid valve lifters. Carburetor: 2Bbl. Holley 5220. VIN Code: A. BASE SIX (Aspen, Diplomat): Inline, overhead-valve six. Cast iron block and head. Displacement: 225 cu. in. (3.7 liters). Bore and stroke: 3.40 x 4.12 in. Compression ratio: 8.4:1. Brake horsepower: 100 at 3600 R.P.M. Torque: 165 lb.-ft. at 1600 R.P.M. Four main bearings. Solid valve lifters. Carburetor: 1Bbl. Holley 1945. VIN Code: C. BASE SIX (St. Regis); OPTIONAL (Aspen, Diplomat): Same as 225 cu. in. six above, but with 2Bbl. Carter BBD carburetor. Horsepower: 110 at 3600 R.P.M. Torque: 180 lb.-ft. at 2000 R.P.M. VIN Code: D. BASE V-8 (Magnum XE); OPTIONAL (Aspen, Diplomat, St. Regis): 90-degree, overhead valve V-8. Cast iron block and head. Displacement: 318 cu. in. (5.2 liters). Bore and stroke: 3.91 x 3.31 in. Compression ratio: 8.5:1. Brake horsepower: 135 at 4000 R.P.M. Torque: 250 lb.-ft. at 1600 R.P.M. Five main bearings. Hydraulic valve lifters. Carburetor: 2Bbl. Holley 2280 (R8448A). VIN Code: G. OPTIONAL V-8 (Diplomat, Magnum XE, St. Regis): 90-degree, overhead valve V-8. Cast iron block and

head. Displacement: 360 cu. in. (5.9 liters). Bore and stroke: 4.00 x 3.58 in. Compression ratio: 8.4:1. Brake horsepower: 150 at 3600 R.P.M. Torque: 265 lb.-ft. at 2400 R.P.M. Five main bearings. Hydraulic valve lifters. Carburetor: 2Bbl. Holley 2245. VIN Code K. OPTIONAL V-8 (Aspen cpe, Diplomat, Magnum, St. Regis): Same as 360 cu. in. V-8 above, but with Carter TQ 4Bbl. carburetor. Compression ratio: 8.0:1. Brake horsepower: 195 at 4000 R.P.M. Torque: 280 lb.-ft. at 2400 R.P.M. VIN Code: L.

CHASSIS DATA: Wheelbase: (Omni) 99.2 in.; (024) 96.7 in.; (Aspen cpe) 108.7 in.; (Aspen sed/wag) 112.7 in.; (Diplomat) 112.7 in.; (Magnum) 114.9 in.; (St. Regis) 118.5 in. Overall length: (Omni) 164.8 in.; (024) 172.7 in.; (Aspen cpe) 197.2 in.; (Aspen sed/wag) 201.2 in.; (Diplo cpe) 204.1 in.; (Diplo sed) 206.1 in.; (Diplo wag) 202.8 in.; (Magnum) 215.8 in.; (St. R.) 220.2 in. Height: (Omni) 53.7 in.; (024) 51.4 in.; (Aspen cpe) 53.3 in.; (Aspen sed) 55.3 in.; (Aspen wag) 55.7 in.; (Diplo cpe) 53.0 in.; (Diplo sed) 55.3 in.; (Diplo wag) 55.7 in.; (Magnum) 53.1 in.; (St. R.) 54.5 in. Width: (Omni) 66.2 in.; (024) 66.0 in.; (Aspen) 72.8 in.; (Diplo cpe) 73.5 in.; (Diplo sed/wag) 72.8 in.; (Magnum) 77.1 in.; (St. R.) 77.1 in. Front Tread: (Omni/024) 56.0 in.; (Aspen/Diplo) 60.0 in.; (Magnum/St. Regis) 61.9 in. Rear Tread: (Omni/024) 55.6 in.; (Aspen/Diplo) 58.5 in.; (Mag/St. R.) 62.0 in. Standard Tires: (Omni) P155/80R13 GBR WSW; (024) P165/75R13 GBR WSW; (Aspen) D78 x 14 exc. wag, ER78 x 14; (Diplo/Magnum) FR78 x 15 GBR BSW; (St. R.) P195/75R15 GBR BSW.

1979 Dodge, Aspen station wagon with optional Special Edition decor package (OCW)

1979 Dodge, Aspen station wagon with optional Sport Wagon package (OCW)

TECHNICAL: Transmission: Three-speed manual trans. (floor lever) standard on Aspen six. Gear ratios: (lst) 3.08:1; (2nd) 1.70:1; (3rd) 1.00:1; (Rev) 2.90:1. Four-speed manual (floor lever) standard on Omni: (lst) 3.45:1; (2nd) 1.94:1; (3rd) 1.29:1; (4th) 0.97:1; (Rev) 3.17:1. Overdrive-4 manual gearbox standard on Diplomat, available on Aspen: (1st) 3.09:1; (2nd) 1.67:1; (3rd) 1.00:1; (4th) 0.71:1; (Rev) 3.00:1.

TorqueFlite three-speed automatic standard on other models, optional on all. Gear ratios: (1st) 2.45:1; (2nd) 1.45:1; (3rd) 1.00:1; (Rev) 2.22:1. Floor lever available for all. Omni TorqueFlite gear ratios: (1st) 2.47:1; (2nd) 1.47:1; (3rd) 1.00:1; (Rev) 2.10:1. Standard final drive ratio; (Omni) 3.37:1 w/4-spd, 3.48:1 w/auto.; (Aspen/Diplo six) 3.23:1; (Aspen V-8) 2.47:1 or 2.45:1; (Magnum) 2.71:1 except 2.45:1 w/V8360 or 3.21:1 w/4Bbl. V8360; (St. R. six) 2.94:1; (St. R. V-8) 2.45:1 exc. 3.21:1 w/4Bbl. V8360. Steering (Omni) rack and pinion; (others) recirculating ball. Suspension: (Omni) Iso-Strut independent coil front w/anti-sway bar, trailing arm independent coil rear w/integral anti-sway; (Aspen/Diplomat) isolated transverse front torsion bars and anti-sway bar, semi-elliptic rear leaf springs; (others) longitudinal front torsion bars w/anti-sway bar, semi-elliptic rear leaf springs. Brakes: Front disc, rear drum. Ignition: Electronic. Body construction: Unibody. Fuel tank: (Omni) 13 gal.; (Aspen six) 18 gal.; (Aspen V-8/wag) 19.5 gal.; (Diplomat) 19.5 gal.; (Magnum/St. R.) 21 gal.

1979 Dodge, Aspen coupe with optional Sunrise decor package (OCW)

DRIVETRAIN OPTIONS: Engines: 225 cu. in., 2Bbl. six: Aspen ($43); Diplo (NC). 318 cu. in., 2Bbl. V-8: Aspen ($216); Diplomat ($236); St. Regis ($239). 318 cu. in., 4Bbl. V-8 (Calif.): Aspen ($271); Diplo ($296); Mag ($61); St. R ($300). 360 cu. in., 2Bbl. V-8: Diplo ($426); Mag ($191); St. R. ($432). 360 cu. in., 4Bbl. V-8 (Calif.): Diplo ($487); Mag ($251); St. R. ($493). H.D. 360 cu. in., 4Bbl. V-8: Aspen ($575-$600); Diplo ($655); Magnum ($420); St. R. ($664). Transmission/Differential: Four-speed overdrive manual trans. w/floor lever: Aspen six ($149). TorqueFlite auto. trans.: Omni/Aspen ($319); Diplo ($193). SureGrip differential: Aspen ($61); Diplo/Mag/St R ($67). Optional axle ratio: Omni/Aspen ($18); others ($20). Brakes and Steering: Power front disc brakes: Omni/Aspen ($72). Power steering: Omni/Aspen ($156). Suspension: H.D. susp.: Omni 4-dr., Aspen ($25); Diplo/Mag/St. R. ($28). Sport susp.: 024 ($41). H.D. shock absorbers: Mag/St. R. ($8). Other: Long-life battery: Omni ($20); others ($32-$35). H.D. trailer assist pkg.: Aspen sed/wag ($157); Diplo ($170); Mag ($150); St. R. ($152). California emission system ($79-$88).

OMNI/024 CONVENIENCE/APPEARANCE OPTIONS: Option Packages: Sport pkg.: 024 ($278-$340). Rallye equipment pkg.: 024 ($177-$352). Sport/Classic two-tone paint pkg.: 4-dr. ($114-$164). Custom exterior pkg.: 4-dr. ($74). Premium exterior pkg. ($78-$199). Custom interior pkg.: 4-dr. ($79-$101). Premium interior pkg. ($146-$270). Premium woodgrain pkg.: 4-dr. ($290-$507). Popular equipment group ($267-$279). Light pkg. ($31-$46). Comfort/Convenience: Air cond. ($507). Tinted glass ($61). Tinted windshield ($43). Luxury steering wheel: 4-dr. ($18). Rallye instrument cluster: 024 ($76). Electric clock w/trip odometer ($28). Rear wiper/washer: 4-dr. ($62). Locking gas cap ($7). Locking glovebox ($5). Horns and Mirrors: Dual horns ($9). Remote left mirror: 024 ($17). Dual remote mirrors: 4-dr. ($32-$49). Dual sport remote mirrors: 024 ($61). Day/night mirror ($11). Entertainment: AM/FM radio: 4-dr. ($73). AM/FM stereo radio ($67-$141). Rear speaker: 024 ($24). Exterior Trim: Removable glass sunroof ($176). Rear spoiler: 024 ($53). Flip-out quarter windows: 024 ($54). Moldings, 4-dr.: belt ($16); drip ($18); sill ($20); upper door frame ($31); wheel lip ($28). Black vinyl bodyside molding: 024 ($41). Door edge protectors ($12-$20). Bumper guards: 4-dr. ($43). Bumper rub strips: 024 ($34). Multi-color tape stripe: 4-dr. ($82). Luggage rack ($86). Undercoating ($33). Interior: Console: storage ($22); shift lever ($32). Cloth/vinyl bucket seats: 024 ($22-$52). Tonneau cover: 024 ($44). Cargo area dress-up ($43). Color-keyed floor mats ($27). Color-keyed seatbelts ($31). Wheels and Tires: Wheel trim rings: 4-dr. ($41). Deluxe wheel covers (NC). Cast aluminum wheels ($165-$246). Rallye wheels ($39-$80). Bright Rallye hubs ($39). 165/75R13 WSW ($17). 165/75R13 SBR WSW ($34-$51). 175/75R13 WSW ($51-$68). 185/70R13 OWL ($136). Conventional spare tire ($13-$25).

ASPEN CONVENIENCE/APPEARANCE OPTIONS: Option Packages: R/T pkg.: cpe ($651). Sport pkg.: cpe ($630). Handling/performance

pkg.: cpe ($218). Special Edition wagon woodgrain group ($232). Special Edition interior pkg. ($275-$499). Special Edition exterior pkg. ($100-$165). Sunrise pkg.: cpe ($30-$60). Sunrise decor pkg.: cpe ($90). Custom exterior pkg. ($75-$89). Custom interior pkg. ($162-$196). Basic group ($626-$712). Two-tone paint pkg. ($142). Two-tone decor pkg. ($65-$96). Light pkg. ($46). Deluxe insulation pkg. ($39-$50). Protection group ($30-$38). Comfort/Convenience: Air cond. ($507). Rear defogger blower-type ($52); electric ($90). Automatic speed control ($98). Power seat ($153). Power windows ($120-$169). Power door locks ($76-$106). Power liftgate release: wag ($23). Tinted windshield ($43); all windows ($61). Luxury steering wheel ($31). Tuff steering wheel ($8-$39). Tilt steering wheel ($32-$71). Digital clock ($51). Inside hood release ($13). Intermittent wipers ($36). Lighter ($7). Locking gas cap ($7). Locking glovebox ($5). Horns and Mirrors: Dual horns ($9). Remote left mirror ($17). Dual remote mirrors ($32-$49). Dual remote sport mirrors ($44-$61). Day/night mirror ($11). Entertainment: AM radio ($79); w/8track player ($152-$231); w/CB ($262-$342). AM/FM radio ($73-$153). AM/FM stereo radio ($141-$220); w/8track player ($235-$314); w/CB ($403-$482). Rear speaker ($24). Exterior: T-Bar roof: cpe ($600). Full vinyl roof: sed ($95). Halo vinyl roof: cpe ($95-$111). Landau vinyl roof: cpe ($174). Vinyl bodyside moldings ($41). Belt moldings ($16). Door edge protectors ($12-$20). Upper door frame moldings: sed/wag ($34). Wheel lip moldings ($22). Hood strobe stripe: cpe ($42). Bumper guards ($43); rub strips ($34). Rear air deflector: wag ($28). Luggage rack: wag ($86). Undercoating ($23-$33). Interior: Console: cpe/wag ($55-$95). Vinyl bench seat: sed ($30). Vinyl bucket seats ($107). Center cushion w/armrest: cpe ($39). Rear armrest ($12). Color-keyed mats ($23). Color-keyed seatbelts ($18). Cargo area carpets and storage bin: wag ($53). Pedal dress-up ($9). Trunk dress-up ($43). Wheels and Tires: Cast aluminum wheels ($144-$280). Styled wheels ($94-$136). Deluxe wheel covers ($41). Premium wheel covers ($37-$79). Wire wheel covers ($94-$136). D78 x 14 WSW ($45). DR78 x 14 BSW ($56). DR78 x 14 WSW ($56-$101). ER78 x 14 BSW ($75). ER78 x 14 WSW ($45-$119). FR70 x 14 OWL ($129-$248). FR78 x 14 WSW ($72-$192). Conventional spare tire (NC).

DIPLOMAT CONVENIENCE/APPEARANCE OPTIONS: Option Packages: Sport appearance pkg. ($110-$219). Basic group ($1130-$1385). Deluxe insulation pkg. ($10-$93). Light pkg. ($72-$84). Comfort/Convenience: Air conditioning ($584). Rear defroster, electric ($98). Automatic speed control ($107). Power seat ($167). Power windows ($137-$194). Power door locks ($89-$124). Power decklid/tailgate release ($25). Tinted glass ($73). Luxury steering wheel ($20). Leather-covered steering wheel ($40-$60). Tilt steering wheel ($58-$77). Digital clock ($56). Deluxe wiper/washer ($47). Locking gas cap ($7). Lighting, Horns and Mirrors: Halogen headlamps ($26). Cornering lights ($51). Dual horns: base ($9). Remote driver's mirror: base/Salon ($19). Remote passenger mirror: Medallion ($35). Dual remote-control mirrors: base/Salon ($35-$54). Dual remote sport mirrors ($48-$67). Lighted vanity mirror ($50). Day/night mirror: base ($12). Entertainment: AM radio ($87); w/CB ($287-$373). AM/FM radio ($80-$167). AM/FM stereo ($154-$240); w/8track tape player ($256-$343); w/CB ($440-$527). Search-tune AM/FM stereo ($281-$368). Rear speaker ($26). Power antenna ($48). Exterior: T-Bar roof: cpe ($675). Power glass sunroof ($827). Full vinyl roof: base sed ($165). Landau vinyl roof: cpe ($148). Vinyl bodyside moldings ($45). Front bumper guards ($24). Bumper rub strips ($37). Hood tape stripe: Medallion ($24). Door edge protectors ($13-$22). Air deflector: wag ($30). Luggage rack: wag ($94). Undercoating ($25-$36). Interior: Vinyl bench seat: cpe/sed ($50-$67). Cloth 60/40 seat: wag ($175). Leather 60/40 seat: wag ($430); Medallion ($283). Cloth/vinyl bucket seats: Salon ($110). Color-keyed floor mats ($25). Color-keyed seatbelts ($20). Pedal dress-up ($10). Wheels/Tires: Deluxe wheel covers: base ($45). Premium wheel covers: base ($45-$90). Wire wheel covers ($111-$300). Forged aluminum wheels ($116-$305). FR78 x 15 GBR WSW ($50). FR78 x 15 SBR WSW ($60-$110). Conventional spare (NC).

MAGNUM XE CONVENIENCE/APPEARANCE OPTIONS: Option Packages: Gran Touring pkg. ($528-$601). Basic group ($1018-$1054). Two-tone paint pkg. ($203-$221). Roadability pkg. ($29). Light pkg. ($29). Comfort/Convenience: Air cond. ($584); auto-temp ($628) exc. ($44) w/option pkg. Rear defroster, electric ($98). Automatic speed control ($107). Tinted windshield ($47); all windows ($73). Power seat ($167). Power windows ($137). Power door locks ($89). Power decklid release ($26). Luxury steering wheel ($20). Leather-covered steering wheel ($60). Tilt steering wheel ($77). Tachometer ($73). Digital clock ($56). Locking gas cap ($7). Deluxe wipers ($40). Lighting and Mirrors: Halogen headlamps ($26). Left remote mirror ($19). Dual remote mirrors ($35-$54). Dual sport remote mirrors ($48-$67). Lighted vanity mirror ($50). Entertainment: AM radio ($87); w/8track player ($166-$252); w/CB ($287-$373). AM/FM radio ($80-$167). AM/FM stereo radio ($154-$240); w/8track ($256-$343); w/CB ($440-$527). Search-tune AM/FM stereo ($281-$368). Rear speaker ($26). Power antenna ($48). Exterior: T-Bar roof ($675). Power sunroof ($546). Landau vinyl roof ($132). Fender-mount turn signals ($16). Vinyl bodyside moldings

($45). Wheel lip flares ($102). Door edge protectors ($13). Bumper rub strips ($37). Hood/deck or bodyside stripes ($47). Wheel lip tape stripes ($24). Undercoating ($36). Interior: Console ($60-$103). Cloth/vinyl 60/40 bench seat ($226). Leather bucket seats ($363). Center front cushion ($43). Color-keyed mats ($25). Color-keyed seatbelts ($20). Trunk dress-up ($47). Pedal dress-up ($10). Wheels and Tires: Aluminum-fascia wheels ($93-$164). Aluminum wheels w/trim rings ($142-$213). Forged aluminum wheels ($189-$260). Premier wheel covers ($45). FR78 x 15 WSW ($50). GR78 x 15 BSW ($22). GR78 x 15 WSW ($22-$72). HR78 x 15 SBR WSW ($87-$160). GR60 x 15 RWL ($230-$302). Conventional spare tire (NC).

ST. REGIS CONVENIENCE/APPEARANCE OPTIONS: Option Packages: Basic group ($1176). Two-tone paint pkg. ($160). Open road handling pkg. ($216). Light pkg. ($96). Comfort/Convenience: Air cond. ($628); auto-temp ($673) exc. ($45) w/option pkg. Rear defroster, electric ($107). Auto. speed control ($112). Power windows ($212). Power door locks ($126). Power seat ($170). Power decklid release ($27-$35). Luxury steering wheel ($20). Leather-covered steering wheel ($60). Tilt steering wheel ($79). Digital clock ($57). Deluxe wipers ($41). Locking gas cap ($9). Lighting and Mirrors: Halogen headlamps ($27). Cornering lights ($51). Remote driver's mirror ($20). Dual chrome remote mirrors ($24-$44). Lighted vanity mirror ($50). Entertainment: AM radio ($106); w/CB ($290-$396). AM/FM radio ($76-$182). AM/FM stereo ($147-$253); w/8track tape player ($254-$360); w/CB ($437-$543). Search-tune AM/FM stereo ($266-$372). Rear speaker ($28). Power antenna ($50). Exterior: Power glass sunroof ($993). Full vinyl roof ($152). Vinyl bodyside molding ($51). Door edge protectors ($23). Bodyside/hood tape stripes ($72). Bumper guards ($60). Undercoating ($30). Interior: Vinyl 60/40 bench seat ($33). Color-keyed mats ($26). Color-keyed seatbelts ($21). Pedal dress-up ($10). Trunk dress-up ($67). Litter container ($8). Wheels and Tires: Premier wheel covers ($54). Wire wheel covers ($259). Aluminum wheels ($175). Aluminum wheels w/trim rings ($216). P195/75R15 WSW ($51). P205/75R15 BSW ($23). P205/75R15 WSW ($23-$134). P225/70R15 WSW ($24-$75). Conventional spare tire (NC).

HISTORY: Introduced: October 5, 1978. Model year production: Chrysler reported a total of 351,177 passenger cars shipped. Total North American production for the U.S. market of 336,979 units (not incl. 25,451 Sportsman vans) included 115,733 four-cylinder, 105,520 six-cylinder, and 115,726 V-8s. Calendar year production: 366,387 (not incl. 17,067 Sportsman vans). Calendar year sales by U.S. dealers: 342,925 (plus 24,917 Sportsman vans). Model year sales by U.S. dealers: 371,003 (not incl. 60,646 Colts, 16,920 Challengers and 32,070 Sportsman vans).

HISTORICAL FOOTNOTES: Model year sales slipped by more than five percent for 1979, with big cars faring the worst. Sales of the new downsized St. Regis fell well below expectations. Omni, on the other hand, found quite a few buyers: 120,218 this year. But a shortage of engines kept Dodge from meeting the rising demand for small cars. Production for model year 1979 dropped even more. For the first time, though, Dodge outsold Plymouth for the model year (including imports). Many rebates were offered during this period (except on Omni/Horizon). On the import front, a new Colt two-door hatchback was added. Colt/Challenger sales amounted to an impressive 16 percent of Dodge's total. After this year, captive imports (Colt/Challenger) could no longer be counted in the figures to meet CAFE standards. Dodge Division, like the parent Chrysler Corp., faced enormous financial problems that would eventually require federal loan guarantees. Lee Iacocca, the new corporate chairman, pushed for a sharper distinction between Dodge and the Chrysler-Plymouth Division, as had been the case years before.

1980 DODGE

One new nameplate joined the lineup for 1980: the two-door Mirada, a replacement for the specialty Magnum XE. Otherwise, this was a year mainly of waiting for the new front-drive Aries, which would replace the rear-drive Aspen for 1981.

OMNI/024 — SERIES ZL — FOUR — Both the four-door hatchback sedan and two-door 024 coupe changed little in appearance this year. The sedan's grille consisted of six wide holes, each divided by another horizontal strip, making a 5 x 13 pattern of thin, wide holes. In the grille's center was a rectangular crest badge. Wraparound park/signal lamps had amber lenses. 'Dodge' letters stood above the left headlamp; 'Omni' lettering ahead of doors and on the hatch. Taillamps wrapped around slightly. Their tri-section design had two red segments, with the bottom

split between clear and amber. Individually adjustable bucket seats were standard on the four-door, in cashmere or black. Powerplant was still the VW-built 1.6-liter four. Standard equipment included tinted glass, electric rear defroster, and trip odometer. New options: intermittent wipers and automatic speed control. Halogen headlamps also were available. Though they looked drastically different, the sport coupe was mechanically identical to the sedan. As before, the Omni sedan came in base form, or could be ordered with optional Custom or Premium interior and exterior packages, or a Premium Woodgrain Exterior package. 024 could have a Premium Exterior package with bright and black rub strips, bodyside and rear tape stripes, and whitewalls; or a Sport Appearance package with black molding accents and blackout lower body paint, '024' decals, black mirrors, rear spoiler, Rallye wheels and whitewalls. Body colors this year were: Graphic Blue, Baron Red, Natural Suede Tan, Light Cashmere, Nightwatch Blue, Formal Black, Bright Yellow, and Spinnaker White; plus metallic Mocha Brown, Frost Blue, Teal Tropic Green, Crimson Red, and Burnished Silver. Four two-tones were available on the sedan, three on the coupe, and four on the coupe with Sport package. A new De Tomaso sport coupe package came in graphic red or bright yellow body color with black accents, highlighted by a front airdam, wheel flares, vertically-louvered rear quarter windows, rear spoiler, cast aluminum wheels, and bright brushed transverse roof band. 'De Tomaso' badges were easy to spot on bodyside, spoiler, and windshield top. Inside De Tomaso were black bucket seats, a Rallye gauge cluster, leather-wrapped sport steering wheel and shift knob, plus 'De Tomaso' identification on front floor mats and a special dash plaque. Apart from a special sport suspension and wider (P185/70R13) Aramid-belted tires, though, De Tomaso's chassis was the same as the standard coupe. A total of 1,333 Omni coupes came with the De Tomaso package.

ASPEN — SERIES N — SIX/V-8 — This would be Aspen's final year, as a new front-drive Dodge compact was soon to arrive. Aspen's new full-width grille now had only three horizontal divider elements, which made it look like four separate sections (one above the other). Single rectangular headlamps were new. Basic lineup was the same as before: two-door coupe, four-door sedan, and four-door wagon. In addition, a new Special series (coupe and sedan only) was offered, sporting minimal chrome trim but with automatic transmission, power steering and wheel lip moldings. Otherwise, standard equipment was similar to 1979. Base engine was again the 225 cu. in. Slant Six, with 318 cu. in. V-8 optional. A Sport Wagon option package, introduced in 1979, included an airdam, wheel arch flares, bucket seats, tape stripes, and styled wheels. The R/T coupe package, installed on only 285 Aspens, had a blackout front end treatment, black drip moldings, new tape-stripe graphics, and painted wheels. Aspen's Sunrise package came with plaid bucket seats, deluxe wheel covers, and new body/decklid tape stripes. A total of 11,542 Aspens had the Premier package.

1980-1/2 Dodge, Diplomat Special Sport Coupe (OCW)

DIPLOMAT — SERIES G — SIX/V-8 — Though similar in overall appearance to the 1979 version, Diplomat enjoyed a restyle this year, with squared-off fenders and a formal-look roofline. Models included a two-door coupe, four-door sedan and four-door wagon, in base and Salon dress. Coupes and sedans also came in top-line Medallion form. Added a bit later was a new Special Sport Coupe. Available only with Slant Six engine, it had two-tone paint, wheel lip moldings, dual sport remote

mirrors, belt moldings, luxury steering wheel, and deluxe wheel covers. The lowest-priced wagon lacked woodgrain side paneling. Two-door models now rode a shorter (108.7 in.) wheelbase; sedans and wagons measured 112.7 inches again. Wheelbases, in fact, were identical to Aspen's. Diplomat's new grille showed a fine-mesh pattern, separated into eight side-by-side vertical sections with bright framing around each one. Similarly-patterned, smaller sections extended outward below the quad rectangular headlamps, to wrap around the front fenders. Those smaller sections held segmented parking lamps at the front and sectioned marker lenses at the side. As before, the hood was creased on each side. Fenderline creases were sharper. 'Diplomat' lettering sat on front fenders, ahead of the door. Full-width taillamps wrapped around the quarter panels and held backup lenses toward the center of the car. The license plate mounted in a recessed housing between the taillamps. The revised roofline was most noticeable in the coupe body, which had a more horizontal look and narrow opera windows to the rear of fairly wide 'B' pillars. Standard equipment included cloth/vinyl bench seating, 225 cu. in. six-cylinder engine, power brakes and steering, TorqueFlite, multi-function steering column switch, trip odometer, temp/fuel/alternator gauges, inside hood release, whitewall radial tires, and protective bumper rub strips. Also standard: a bright hood ornament; bright windshield, back window, quarter window and roof drip moldings; tinted quarter-window (coupe) glass; bright driver's mirror; front bumper guards and hubcaps. Diplomat Salon added bright belt, sill, center pillar and wheel opening moldings, plus dual horns. Medallion came with bodyside and deck accent stripes, remote driver's mirror, and padded landau or full vinyl roof, plus crushed velour 60/40 seating. Body colors were: Baron Red, Light Cashmere, Eggshell White, Nightwatch Blue, Black, Light Heather Gray, and Natural Suede Tan; plus metallic Burnished Silver, Mocha Brown, Light Heather Gray, Frost Blue, Teal Frost, Teal Tropic Green and Crimson Red. New two-tone paint combinations were available. A new 'S' package for the Salon coupe cost $549 to $569. It included dual remote sport mirrors, bold body stripes, high-back cloth bucket seats, luxury steering wheel, and brushed-aluminum finish instrument cluster cover, door moldings and glovebox door insert. Also included: halogen headlamps and P205/75R15 steel-belted radial whitewall tires on color-keyed wheels. A total of 2,188 Diplomats had the 'S' package. Salon coupes could also have a console for $109.

1980 Dodge, Mirada coupe with optional CMX package (OCW)

MIRADA — SERIES X — SIX/V-8 — New this year, Mirada served as replacement for the departed Magnum XE coupe. Its side view showed off what was described as a "striking roof motif" and aerodynamic profile (the latter a phrase that would soon come to describe just about any vehicle that wasn't squarely upright). Mirada was over 6 inches shorter than Magnum, and some 400 pounds lighter. And whereas Magnum had been V-8 powered, Mirada carried a base Slant Six; a 318 cu. in. V-8 was optional. As before, this was Dodge's version of the Chrysler Cordoba, which was also reworked this year. Mirada featured a soft front fascia with sloping, slat-style grille, single rectangular headlamps, and simulated front fender louvers. The grille consisted of four wide slots separated by five bright horizontal strips, each of which bent back at the ends to meet the angled front panel. A horizontal lip sat ahead of each headlamp's base. On front fenders were small horizontal side marker lenses, just ahead of the wheel opening and aligned with the bumper strip. A set of four angled louvers stood ahead of the door. 'Mirada' lettering was below the bodyside crease line. A 'CMX' nameplate (if applicable) sat below that lettering. Bodysides displayed sculptured-look creases near the top and bottom, as well as down the middle. Miradas had sharp-cornered opera windows at the far rear, plus a grooved bright band alongside the smaller forward quarter windows. Each rectangular taillamp had three horizontal trim strips, with backup lenses toward the center of the car. Though large, the taillamps didn't extend either to quarter panel tips or the license plate opening. The license plate housing was recessed, below the decklid (which held 'Mirada' lettering). Inside was a brushed-metal instrument panel that held a set of gauges. Standard equipment included the 225 cu. in. Slant Six, TorqueFlite, power steering and brakes, multi-function steering column lever, high-back vinyl bucket seats, AM radio, lighter, tinted glass, and dual horns. Also standard: chrome driver's side mirror, two-spoke padded steering wheel with brushed aluminum appliqué, compact spare tire, trip odometer, premier wheel covers, P195/75R15 GBR WSW tires, and two-speed wiper/washers. Body colors were: Light Heather Gray, Nightwatch Blue, Baron Red,

Natural Suede Tan, Eggshell White, Black, and Light Cashmere, plus metallic Light Heather Gray, Frost Blue, Crimson Red, Mocha Brown, and Burnished Silver. Two models were offered: standard and 'S' versions, as well as a CMX package. A high-performance 360 cu. in. V-8 with dual exhaust was optional with that CMX package, which also included an up-and-over roof accent molding, color-keyed bumper strips with bright insert, front fender nameplates, dual remote mirrors, unique bodyside tape stripes, forged aluminum ten-spoke wheels, and larger (P205) whitewall tires. CMX came only in Baron Red, Nightwatch Blue, Frost Blue, or Burnished Silver. Options also included a cabriolet simulated-convertible roof, AM/FM stereo with cassette player, automatic speed control, intermittent wipers, illuminated entry system, forged aluminum wheels, and turbine wheel covers. A total of 5,384 Miradas had the CMX package, while 936 had the convertible-style roof (and only seven of those were on the XS22 model).

1980 Dodge, St. Regis pillared hardtop with optional wire wheel covers (OCW)

ST. REGIS — SERIES EH — SIX/V-8 — Little change was evident in Dodge's "regular size" four-door, except for side trim and striping. Full-width taillamps stretched from the license plate to wraparound quarter panels, each lens divided into a crosshatch pattern. Sculptured lines included notable twin bodyside creases that stretched full length. Again, St. Regis had transparent headlamp covers and a distinctive grille made up of small rectangles. Standard interior held a split-back bench seat with folding center armrest of Verdi II cloth/vinyl (or optional Oxford all-vinyl). 60/40 seating was also available. Standard equipment included the 225 cu. in. Slant Six, power brakes and steering, three-speed Torque-Flite, tinted glass, two-speed wiper/washers, two-spoke steering wheel with woodgrain trim, flag-type mirrors, dual horns, lighter, bumper rub strips, and temp/alternator/fuel gauges. Options included both the 318 and 360 cu. in. V-8 engines, as well as an illuminated entry system. St. Regis had a new high-strength steel back bumper. A new Touring Edition was available, priced at $1,677 and up. The package included a padded full vinyl roof with special medallion inset into the rear post, a formal backlight, unique body pin striping, cornering lamps, dual remote chrome mirrors, and bright rear sill extensions. Wide whitewall SBR tires rode forged aluminum ten-spoke wheels, color-keyed in red or gold to match the interior. Inside was red or cashmere 60/40 leather seating, plus a leather-wrapped tilt steering wheel, power windows, and door courtesy lights. The instrument cluster cover held a Featherwood woodgrain-textured appliqué. A total of 438 St. Regis models had the Touring Edition package, while 222 had the Special Promotional Package (RPO Code A84).

I.D. DATA: Dodge's 13-symbol Vehicle Identification Number (VIN) was on the upper left corner of the instrument panel, visible through the windshield. Symbol one indicates car line: 'Z' Omni/024; 'N' Aspen; 'G' Diplomat; 'X' Mirada; 'E' St. Regis. Symbol two is series (price class): 'E' economy; 'L' low; 'M' medium; 'H' high; 'P' premium; 'S' special. Symbols 3-4 show body type: '22' 2-dr. special coupe or 'B' pillared hardtop; '24' 2-dr. hatchback; '29' 2-dr. coupe; '41' 4-dr. sedan; '42' 4-dr. 'B' pillared hardtop; '44' 4-dr. hatchback; '45' two-seat station wagon. Symbol five is the engine code: 'A' L4105; 'C' L6225 1Bbl.; 'G' V8318 2Bbl.; 'K' V8360 2Bbl.; 'L' V8360 4Bbl. Symbol six is the model year code: 'A' 1980. Symbol seven indicates assembly plant: 'A' Lynch Road; 'B' Hamtramck, MI; 'D' Belvidere, IL; 'F' Newark, DE; 'G' St. Louis; 'R' Windsor, Ontario. The final six digits make up the sequential serial number, starting with 100001. Engine number coding and locations are similar to 1978-79.

OMNI (FOUR)

Model No.	Body/ Style No.	Body Type & Seating	Factory Price	Shipping Weight	Prod. Total
ZL	44	4-dr. Hatch-4P	4925	2095	67,279

OMNI 024 (FOUR)

Model No.	Body/ Style No.	Body Type & Seating	Factory Price	Shipping Weight	Prod. Total
ZL	24	2-dr. Hatch-4P	5271	2135	51,731

ASPEN (SIX/V-8)

Model No.	Body/Style No.	Body Type & Seating	Factory Price	Shipping Weight	Prod. Total
NL	29	2-dr. Cpe-5P	4742/4953	3110/3260	9,454
NL	41	4-dr. Sedan-6P	4859/5070	3165/3320	20,938
NL	45	4-dr. Sta Wag-6P	5101/5312	3340/3480	12,388

ASPEN SPECIAL (SIX)

NE	29	2-dr. Cpe-5P	4977	3155	9,684
NE	41	4-dr. Sedan-6P	4994	3210	14,854

DIPLOMAT (SIX/V-8)

GM	22	2-dr. Cpe-6P	5681/5911	3220/3300	4,213
GM	41	4-dr. Sedan-6P	5832/6062	3300/3385	5,671
GM	45	4-dr. Sta Wag-6P	5971/6201	3455/3535	1,569

DIPLOMAT SPECIAL SPORT (SIX)

GL	22	2-dr. Cpe-6P	5995	3130	2,597

DIPLOMAT SALON (SIX/V-8)

GH	22	2-dr. Cpe-6P	5997/6227	3230/3310	5,778
GH	41	4-dr. Sedan-6P	6119/6349	3325/3405	4,251
GH	45	4-dr. Sta Wag-6P	6661/6891	3485/3565	2,104

DIPLOMAT MEDALLION (SIX/V-8)

GP	22	2-dr. Cpe-6P	6551/6781	3285/3360	2,103
GP	41	4-dr. Sedan-6P	6698/6928	3400/3485	2,086

MIRADA (SIX/V-8)

XH	22	2-dr. HT Cpe-6P	6364/6594	3280/3360	27,165

MIRADA 'S' (SIX/V-8)

XS	22	2-dr. HT Cpe-6P	6645/6740	3280/3375	1,468

ST. REGIS (SIX/V-8)

EH	42	4-dr. Pill. HT-6P	6724/6957	565/3650	14,010

Factory Price and Weight Note: Prices and weights to left of slash are for six-cylinder, to right for V-8 engine. Prices for 318 cu. in. V-8 engines dropped during the model year, to under $100.

ENGINE DATA: BASE FOUR (Omni): Inline, overhead-cam four-cylinder. Cast iron block; aluminum head. Displacement: 104.7 cu. in. (1.7 liters). Bore and stroke: 3.13 x 3.40 in. Compression ratio: 8.2:1. Brake horsepower: 65 at 5200 R.P.M. Torque: 85 lb.-ft. at 2400 R.P.M. Five main bearings. Solid valve lifters. Carburetor: 2Bbl. Holley 5220. VIN Code: A. BASE SIX (Aspen, Diplomat, Mirada, St. Regis): Inline, overhead-valve six. Cast iron block and head. Displacement: 225 cu. in. (3.7 liters). Bore and stroke: 3.40 x 4.12 in. Compression ratio: 8.4:1. Brake horsepower: 90 at 3600 R.P.M. Torque: 160 lb.-ft. at 1600 R.P.M. Four main bearings. Solid valve lifters. Carburetor: 1Bbl. Holley 1945. VIN Code: C. OPTIONAL V-8 (Aspen, Diplomat, Mirada, St. Regis): 90-degree, overhead valve V-8. Cast iron block and head. Displacement: 318 cu. in. (5.2 liters). Bore and stroke: 3.91 x 3.31 in. Compression ratio: 8.5:1. Brake horsepower: 120 at 3600 R.P.M. Torque: 245 lb.-ft. at 1600 R.P.M. Five main bearings. Hydraulic valve lifters. Carburetor: 2Bbl. Carter BBD. VIN Code: G. OPTIONAL V-8 (St. Regis): 90-degree, overhead V-8. Cast iron block and head. Displacement: 360 cu. in. (5.9 liters). Bore and stroke: 4.00 x 3.58 in. Compression ratio: 8.4:1. Brake horsepower: 150 at 3600 R.P.M. Torque: 265 lb.-ft. at 2400 R.P.M. Five main bearings. Hydraulic valve lifters. Carburetor: 2Bbl. Carter BBD. VIN Code: K. OPTIONAL V-8 (Mirada): Same as 360 cu. in. V-8 above, but with Carter TQ 4Bbl. carburetor. Compression ratio: 8.0:1. Brake horsepower: 185 at 4000 R.P.M. Torque: 275 lb.-ft. at 2000 R.P.M. VIN Code: L.

CHASSIS DATA: Wheelbase: (Omni) 99.2 in.; (024) 96.7 in.; (Aspen/Diplomat cpe) 108.7 in.; (Aspen/Diplo sed/wag) 112.7 in.; (Mirada) 112.7 in.; (St. Regis) 118.5 in. Overall length: (Omni) 164.8 in.; (024) 173.3 in.; (Aspen cpe) 200.3 in.; (Aspen sed/wag) 204.3 in.; (Diplo cpe) 201.2 in.; (Diplo sed/wag) 205.2 in.; (Mirada) 209.5 in.; (St. R.) 220.2 in. Height: (Omni) 53.5 in.; (024) 51.2 in.; (Aspen cpe) 53.6 in.; (Aspen sed) 55.3 in.; (Aspen wag) 55.5 in.; (Diplo cpe) 53.4.; (Diplo sed) 55.3 in.; (Diplo wag) 55.5 in.; (Mirada) 53.3 in.; (St. R.) 54.5 in. Width: (Omni) 65.8 in.; (024) 66:7 in.; (Aspen)

72.4 in.; (Diplo) 74.2 in.; (Mirada) 72.7 in.; (St. R.) 77.6 in. Front Tread: (Omni/024) 56.1 in.; (Aspen Diplo/Mirada) 60.0 in.; (Magnum/St. Regis) 61.9 in. Rear Tread: (Omni/024) 55.6 in.; (Aspen/Diplo/Mirada) 59.5 in.; (St. R.) 62.0 in. Standard Tires: (Omni) P155/80R13 GBR WSW; (024) P175/75R13 GBR WSW; (Aspen) P195/75R14; (Diplo) P195/75R15 GBR BSW; (Mirada/St. R.) P195/75R15 GBR WSW.

TECHNICAL: Transmission: Three-speed manual trans. (floor lever) standard on Aspen six. Gear ratios: (1st) 3.08:1; (2nd) 1.70:1; (3rd) 1.00:1; (Rev) 2.90:1. Four-speed manual (floor lever) standard on Omni: (1st) 3.45:1; (2nd) 1.94:1; (3rd) 1.29:1; (4th) 0.97:1; (Rev) 3.17:1. Overdrive-4 manual gearbox available on Aspen: (1st) 3.09:1; (2nd) 1.67:1; (3rd) 1.00:1; (4th) 0.71:1; (Rev) 3.00:1. TorqueFlite three-speed automatic standard on other models, optional on all. V-8 gear ratios: (1st) 2.45:1; (2nd) 1.45:1; (3rd) 1.00:1; (Rev) 2.22:1. Six-cylinder: (1st) 2.74:1; (2nd) 1.54:1; (3rd) 1.00:1; (Rev) 2.22:1. Omni TorqueFlite gear ratios: (1st) 2.47:1; (2nd) 1.47:1; (3rd) 1.00:1; (Rev) 2.10:1. Standard final drive ratio: (Omni) 3.37:1 w/4-spd, 3.48:1 w/auto.; (Aspen six) 3.23:1 w/manual, 2.76:1 or 2.71:1 w/auto.; (Aspen Special) 2.76:1; (Aspen V-8) 2.47:1 exc. wag, 2.45:1; (Diplo six) 2.76:1; (Diplo wag) 2.94:1; (Diplo V-8) 2.47:1 exc. wag, 2.45:1; (Mirada six) 2.76:1; (Mirada V-8) 2.47:l; (Mirada V8360) 2.94:1; (St. R. six) 2.94:1; (St. R. V-8) 2.45:1. Steering: (Omni) rack and pinion; (others) recirculating ball. Susp.: (Omni) MacPherson strut w/anti-sway bar, trailing arm independent coil rear w/integral anti-sway; (Aspen/Diplomat/Mirada) transverse front torsion bars and anti-sway bar, semi-elliptic rear leaf springs; (St. Regis) longitudinal front torsion bars w/anti-sway bar, semi-elliptic rear leaf springs. Brakes: Front disc, rear drum. Ignition: Electronic. Body construction: Unibody. Fuel tank: (Omni) 13 gal.; (Aspen) 18 gal.; (Aspen wag) 19.5 gal.; (Diplomat/Mirada) 18 gal.; (St. Regis) 21 gal.

DRIVETRAIN OPTIONS: Engines: 318 cu. in., 2Bbl. V-8: Aspen ($211); Diplomat/Mirada ($230); St. Regis ($233). 318 cu. in., 4Bbl. V-8 (Calif.): Aspen ($266); Diplo/Mirada ($291); St. R. ($295). 360 cu. in., 2Bbl. V-8: St. R. ($457). 360 cu. in., 4Bbl. V-8: Mirada CMX ($545). Transmission/Differential: Four-speed overdrive manual trans. w/floor lever: Aspen six ($153). TorqueFlite auto. trans.: Omni/Aspen ($340). SureGrip differential: Aspen ($63); Diplo ($71); Mirada ($72); St. R. ($77). Brakes and Steering: Power front disc brakes: Omni/Aspen ($77). Power steering: Omni ($161); Aspen ($166). Suspension: H.D. susp.: Omni 4-dr., Aspen ($26); Diplo/Mirada ($28); St. R. ($30). Sport susp.: 024 ($43). H.D. shock absorbers: Mirada/St. R. ($8). Other: Long-life battery: Omni ($21); others ($33-$36). H.D. trailer assist pkg.: St. R. ($258). Max. cooling: Aspen ($34-$58); Diplo/Mirada ($37-$63); St. R. ($77-$104). California emission system ($254).

OMMI/024 CONVENIENCE/APPEARANCE OPTIONS: Option Packages: De Tomaso pkg.: 024 ($1484-$1575). Sport pkg.: 024 ($340-$431). Sport/Classic two-tone paint pkg. ($131-$137). Custom exterior pkg.: 4-dr. ($101). Premium exterior pkg. ($126-$207). Custom interior pkg. ($89-$112). Premium interior pkg. ($239-$355). Premium woodgrain pkg.: 4-dr. ($300-$344). Popular equipment group ($267-$273). Comfort/Convenience: Air cond. ($541). Automatic speed control ($101). Power liftgate release: 024 ($24). Luxury steering wheel: 4-dr. ($18). Sport steering wheel ($18-$40). Rallye instrument cluster w/tachometer ($65). Intermittent wipers ($38). Rear wiper/washer: 4-dr. ($63). Lighter ($8). Locking gas cap ($7). Locking glovebox: 4-dr. ($5). Lighting, Horns and Mirrors: Halogen headlamps ($37). Dual horns ($9). Remote left mirror: 4-dr. ($19). Dual remote mirrors: 4-dr. ($38-$57). Dual sport remote mirrors: 024 ($69). Day/night mirror ($11). Entertainment: AM/FM radio: 4-dr. ($58). AM/FM stereo radio ($35-$93). Rear speaker: 024 ($19). Exterior: Removable glass sunroof ($182). Rear spoiler: 024 ($55). Moldings, 4-dr.: belt ($17); drip ($19); sill ($21); upper door frame ($32); wheel lip ($29). Vinyl bodyside molding: 024 ($44). Door edge protectors ($13-$21). Bumper guards: 4-dr. ($45). Bumper rub strips: 024 ($35). Multi-color tape stripe: 024 ($72). Hood/bodyside/deck stripe: 4-dr. ($45). Bodyside/deck stripe: 024 ($31). Luggage rack ($90). Undercoating ($34). Lower body protective coating ($31). Interior: Console: storage ($22); shift lever ($33). Cloth/vinyl bucket seats ($22). Vinyl bucket seats: 4-dr. Vinyl bucket seats w/recliner: 024. Tonneau cover: 024 ($46). Cargo area carpet ($31). Cargo area dress-up ($45). Floor mats: front ($24); front/rear ($42). Color-keyed seatbelts ($23). Wheels and Tires: Wheel trim rings: 4-dr. ($44). Deluxe wheel covers: 4-dr. ($44); 024 (NC). Cast aluminum wheels ($171-$254). Rallye wheels ($39-$83). P165/75R13 WSW ($17). P175/75R13 WSW ($43). P175/75R13 SBR WSW ($78-$86). P185/70R13 Aramid-belted BSW ($45-$131). P185/70R13 Aramid-belted OWL ($106-$192). Conventional spare tire ($13-$26).

ASPEN CONVENIENCE/APPEARANCE OPTIONS: Option Packages: R/T pkg.: cpe ($586). Sport appearance pkg.: cpe ($192-$254). Handling/performance pkg.: base cpe/wag ($385). Wagon Sport pkg. ($721). Special Edition pkg. ($513-$814). Sunrise Coupe pkg. ($155). Custom pkg. ($258-$386). Basic group: base ($246-$403). Two-tone paint pkg.: base cpe/sed ($148). Light pkg. ($46). Deluxe insulation

pkg. ($40-$51). Protection group ($56-$64). Comfort/Convenience: Air cond. ($543). Rear defogger, blower-type ($53); electric ($97). Automatic speed control ($106). Power seat ($163). Power windows ($130-$183). Power door locks ($83-$117). Power liftgate release: wag ($24). Tinted windshield ($44); all windows ($66). Luxury steering wheel ($32). Tuff steering wheel ($24-$56). Tilt steering wheel ($44-$76). Digital clock ($55). Inside hood release ($13). Intermittent wipers ($39). Tailgate wiper/washer: wag ($64). Lighter ($8). Locking gas cap ($7). Locking glovebox ($6). Lighting, Horns and Mirrors: Halogen headlamps ($37). Dual horns ($10). Remote left mirror ($18). Dual remote mirrors ($36-$54). Dual remote sport mirrors ($50-$68). Day/night mirror ($11). Entertainment: AM radio ($90); w/8track player ($143-$233). AM/FM radio ($58-$148). AM/FM stereo radio ($93-$183); w/8track player ($166-$256); w/cassette ($220-$310); w/CB ($351-$441). Rear speaker ($19). Delete AM radio ($51 credit). Exterior: T-Bar roof: cpe ($614). Full vinyl roof: sed ($97). Landau vinyl roof: cpe ($161-$178). Vinyl bodyside moldings ($44). Belt moldings ($17). Door edge protectors ($13-$21). Upper door frame moldings: sed/wag ($34). Wheel lip moldings: base ($24). Sill moldings: Special ($28). Bumper rub strips ($36). Rear air deflector: wag ($28). Luggage rack ($91). Undercoating ($23-$34). Interior: Console: cpe/wag ($34-$99). Vinyl bench seat: sed ($30). Vinyl bucket seats ($110). Cloth/vinyl bench seat. Cloth/vinyl bucket seats. Vinyl bucket seats w/cushion and center armrest. 60/40 seating (cloth or vinyl). Center cushion w/armrest: cpe/wag ($44). Rear armrest w/ashtray ($12). Color-keyed mats: front ($24); rear ($19). Color-keyed seatbelts ($23). Cargo area carpets: wag ($69); w/storage bin ($93). Cargo security cover: wag ($46). Pedal dress-up ($9). Trunk dress-up ($45). Wheels and Tires: Cast aluminum wheels ($133-$287). Styled spoke wheels ($110-$154). Deluxe wheel covers ($44). Premium wheel covers ($37-$81). Wire wheel covers ($106-$150). P195/75R14 GBR WSW ($49). P205/75R14 SBR WSW ($84-$133). FR70 x 14 Aramid-belted OWL ($150-$199). Conventional spare tire ($25).

DIPLOMAT CONVENIENCE/APPEARANCE OPTIONS: Option Packages: 'S' pkg.: Salon cpe ($549-$569). Sport appearance pkg. ($166-$290). Basic group ($961-$1267). Two-tone paint pkg. ($162). Handling pkg. ($151). Deluxe insulation pkg. ($10-$110). Light pkg. ($85-$98). Protection group ($61-$70). Comfort/Convenience: Air conditioning ($623); auto-temp ($673) but ($50) w/option pkg. Rear defroster, electric ($106). Auto. speed control ($116). Power seat ($179). Power windows ($148-$209). Power door locks ($96-$136). Power decklid/tailgate release ($27). Illuminated entry system ($58). Tinted glass ($78). Luxury steering wheel ($20). Tuff steering wheel ($36-$56). Leather-covered steering wheel ($41-$61). Tilt steering wheel ($63-$83). Digital clock ($60). Deluxe wiper/washer ($51). Liftgate wiper/washer: wag ($69). Locking gas cap ($8). Lighting, Horns and Mirrors: Halogen headlamps ($41). Cornering lights ($55). Dual horns: base ($10). Remote driver's mirror: base/Salon ($20). Remote passenger mirror: Medallion ($41). Dual remote-control mirrors: base/Salon ($41-$61). Dual remote sport mirrors ($56-$76). Lighted vanity mirror ($51). Day/night mirror: base ($12). Entertainment: AM radio ($99). AM/FM radio ($63-$162). AM/FM stereo ($101-$200); w/ 8track tape player ($181-$280); w/cassette ($240-$339); w/CB ($383-$482). Search-tune AM/FM stereo ($227-$326). Rear speaker ($21). Power antenna ($52). Exterior: T-Bar roof: cpe ($715). Power glass sunroof ($871). Full vinyl roof: base/Salon sed ($129). Landau vinyl roof: base/Salon cpe ($176). Vinyl bodyside moldings ($46). Belt moldings: base ($21). Upper door frame molding: base wag ($40). Wheel lip moldings: base ($26). Door edge protectors ($14-$23). Rear bumper guards ($25). Hood tape stripe ($24). Bodyside stripe ($50). Bodyside/decklid stripe: Salon ($73). Air deflector: wag ($32). Luggage rack: wag ($100). Undercoating ($25). Interior: Console: Salon cpe ($109). Vinyl bench seat: base/Salon ($51-$69). Cloth 60/40 seat: wag, Salon cpe ($160-$281). Vinyl 60/40 seat: base wag, Salon ($212-$281). Cloth/vinyl 60/40 seat: Salon sed ($230). Leather 60/40 seat ($371-$619). Cloth/vinyl bucket seats: Salon cpe ($103). Color-keyed floor mats: front ($26); rear ($21). Cargo area carpet: base wag ($75); w/storage bins ($101). Cargo security cover: wag ($61). Color-keyed seatbelts ($27). Pedal dress-up ($10). Trunk dress-up ($49). Wheels and Tires: Deluxe wheel covers: base ($48). Premier wheel covers ($45-$93). Premium wheel covers ($45-$138). Wire wheel covers ($114-$308). Forged aluminum wheels ($118-$380). Styled wheels ($101-$194). P205/75R15 SBR WSW ($89). P205/75R15 Aramid-belted white/gold ($86-$175). Conventional spare ($27).

MIRADA CONVENIENCE/APPEARANCE OPTIONS: Option Packages: CMX pkg. ($614-$1426). Cabriolet roof pkg. ($738-$950). Basic group ($958-$1034). Sport handling pkg. ($192). Roadability pkg. ($29). Light pkg. ($104). Protection pkg. ($61). Comfort/Convenience: Air cond. ($623); auto-temp ($675) exc. ($52) w/option pkg. Rear defroster, electric ($106). Automatic speed control ($116). Power seat ($179). Power windows ($148). Power door locks ($96). Power decklid release ($28-$44). Illuminated entry system ($58). Luxury steering wheel ($22). Tuff steering wheel ($56). Leather-covered steering wheel ($61). Tilt steering wheel ($83). Digital clock ($60). Locking gas cap ($8).

Intermittent wipers ($43). Lighting, Horns and Mirrors: Halogen headlamps ($41). Cornering lights ($21). Triad horns ($22). Left remote mirror ($20). Dual remote mirrors, chrome or painted ($57-$77). Lighted vanity mirror ($51). Entertainment: AM radio w/8track player ($156). AM/FM radio ($63). AM/FM stereo radio ($101); w/8track ($181); w/cassette ($240); w/CB ($383). Search-tune AM/FM stereo ($227). Rear speaker ($21). Power antenna ($52). Delete radio ($56 credit). Exterior: T-Bar roof ($715). Power sunroof ($787). Landau vinyl roof ($141). Vinyl bodyside moldings ($48). Wheel lip moldings ($26). Sill moldings ($30). Door edge protectors ($14). Bumper guards, rear ($25); rub strips ($20). Bodyside tape stripes ($51). Undercoating ($25). Interior: Console ($66-$109). Cloth/vinyl 60/40 bench seat ($232). Leather bucket seats ($550). Center front cushion ($43). Color-keyed mats: front ($26); rear ($21). Color-keyed seatbelts ($27). Trunk dress-up ($49). Pedal dress-up ($10). Wheels and Tires: Forged aluminum wheels ($334). Premium wheel covers ($92). P205/75R15 GBR WSW ($22). P205/75R15 SBR WSW ($89). P205/75R15 Aramid-belted white/gold ($86-$175). P215/70R15 SBR RWL ($25-$114). Conventional spare tire ($27).

ST. REGIS CONVENIENCE/APPEARANCE OPTIONS: Option Packages: Touring Edition pkg. ($1677-$1904). Two-tone paint pkg. ($168). Open Road handling pkg. ($269). Comfort/Convenience: Air cond. ($670); auto-temp ($720) exc. ($50) w/option pkg. Rear defroster, electric ($113). Auto. speed control ($122). Power windows ($228). Power door locks ($139). Power seat ($183). Power decklid release ($30-$46). Illuminated entry system ($62). Luxury steering wheel ($20). Leather-covered steering wheel ($62). Tilt steering wheel ($85). Digital clock ($61). Intermittent wipers ($44). Locking gas cap ($9). Lighting, Horns and Mirrors: Halogen headlamps ($42). Cornering lights ($55). Triad horns ($22). Remote driver's mirror ($21). Dual remote mirrors ($31-$52). Lighted vanity mirror ($53). Entertainment: AM radio ($106). AM/FM radio ($58-$164). AM/FM stereo ($103-$209); w/8track tape player ($181-$287); w/cassette ($241-$347); w/CB ($389-$495). Search-tune AM/FM stereo ($224-$330). Rear speaker ($22). Power antenna ($54). Exterior: Power glass sunroof ($1053). Full vinyl roof ($162). Vinyl bodyside molding ($55). Door edge protectors ($24). Bodyside tape stripes ($49). Bumper guards ($62). Undercoating ($31). Interior: Vinyl bench seat ($34). Vinyl 60/40 bench seat ($186). Cloth/vinyl 60/40 seat ($152). Leather 60/40 seat ($528). Color-keyed mats: front ($26); rear ($21). Color-keyed seatbelts ($27). Pedal dress-up ($10). Trunk dress-up ($70). Litter container ($9). Wheels and Tires: Premier wheel covers ($44). Premium wheel covers ($91). Wire wheel covers ($266). Forged aluminum wheels ($336). P205/75R15 SBR WSW ($92). P205/75R15 Aramid-belted white/gold ($179). P225/70R15 ($186). Conventional spare tire ($27).

HISTORY: Introduced: October 1, 1979. Model year production: Chrysler reported a total of 259,343 passenger cars shipped. Total North American production for the U.S. market of 258,792 units included 119,014 four-cylinder, 94,489 six-cylinder, and 45,289 V-8s. Calendar year production (U.S.): 269,446. Calendar year sales by U.S. dealers: 266,460. Model year sales by U.S. dealers: 325,036 (incl. 54,313 Colts and 13,059 Challengers). Note: Beginning this year, Sportsman vans were counted as trucks rather than passenger cars in production/sales figures.

HISTORICAL FOOTNOTES: Dodge sales slipped drastically for the model year, down over 32 percent, though the division at least beat Plymouth again. Aspen and full-size models made the worst showing, but every model posted a decline. Rebates and incentive programs during the year didn't help enough. A weak national economy was hurting car sales nationwide. In fact, 1980 was considered the worst year ever for the domestic auto industry. Production also fell sharply, down from 418,215 in 1979 to just 286,703 this year. Dodge (and Chrysler as a whole) was pinning much of its hopes on the new-for-1981 K-car. All through this dark period, Chrysler Corp. was instituting economy measures, including the purchase of more components from outside sources. Thus, Dodge workers endured not only layoffs but some plant closings.

1981 DODGE

At last, the long-awaited Chrysler front-drive compacts arrived, holding out a promise of improved sales. The company promoted fuel economy and six-passenger capacity for both Dodge Aries and its K-car twin, the Plymouth Reliant. The new 2.2-liter Trans-4 engine that powered Aries was the first Chrysler-built four-cylinder since the 1930s. Its overhead-cam design featured an aluminum head and cast iron block. The new four produced 84 horsepower at 4800 rpm, and 111 pound-feet of torque at 2800 rpm. It also became available as an Omni option. Also

offered as an Aries option was a 2.6-liter four, built by Mitsubishi. On the subcompact level, Omni added a stripped "Miser" edition to both the two- and four-door models. Also new: a Euro-Sedan package for the Omni sedan. Otherwise, the lineup remained much the same as in 1980. The old familiar Slant Six engine finally added hydraulic valve lifters. Omni managed to grow from its original four-passenger seating to a claimed five-passenger capacity, without gaining in size.

1981 Dodge, Omni 024 hatchback coupe with optional cast aluminum wheels (OCW)

OMNI/024 — SERIES Z — FOUR — Although basic sedan appearance changed little, Omni's revised grille had only four bright horizontal divider bars (formerly five) over a fine-mesh pattern. A new vertical divider bar at the center replaced the former emblem. Tri-section wraparound tail-lamps were similar to 1978-80, with clear bottom sections. Some formerly standard equipment (such as tinted glass and a rear defroster) was now made optional. Two new variants of interest appeared: a Euro-Sedan and Miser, aimed at two different portions of the market. The Euro-Sedan package included blacked-out accent trim, P175/75R13 SBR tires on cast aluminum wheels, a Sport interior with corded-cloth front bucket seats, Rallye instrument cluster with tachometer and clock, four-spoke sport steering wheel, and carpeted cargo area. A total of 557 sedans had the Euro-Sedan package (RPO code A69). Miser managed a 28 mpg (43 highway) EPA estimate because of its lower weight, special engine calibrations, and 2.6:1 overall drive ratio. Misers also had a limited equipment list. Newly optional was the Chrysler-built 135 cu. in. (2.2-liter) Trans-4 engine, made available during the model year instead of the standard 104.7 cu. in. (1.7-liter) four. Revised four-speed over-drive manual transaxle gearing came only with the larger engine; Torque-Flite automatic was available with both. Standard Omni interior had high-back vinyl bucket seats in blue, cashmere, red or black (Miser only cashmere and black). Body colors for 1980 were: Black, Sunlight Yellow, Graphic Yellow, Pearl White, Ginger, Baron Red, Graphic Red, Spice Tan Starmist, Nightwatch Blue, Vivid Blue Starmist, and metallic Burnished Silver, Daystar Blue, or Glencoe Green. Three two-tone combinations were offered. Options included a Tri-Lite sunroof, automatic speed control, intermittent wiper system, air conditioning, roof rack, and rear wiper/washer. AM/FM stereo radios were available with either 8-track or cassette, and Dolby noise reduction. Two-door 024 coupes were no longer listed in the same factory catalog as the Omni sedan, but remained part of the family. Coupe appearance changed little this year. 024's grille, consisting of three slots on each side of the sloping panel (each slot split by twin vertical dividers), looked a bit like a set of side-by-side stepladders. Turismo and De Tomaso packages were offered again, but revised a bit. The De Tomaso option, installed on 619 vehicles, included the new 2.2-liter engine and 14-in. wheels. A total of 7,306 coupes had a new Charger 2.2 package (RPO code A54), which cost $399 extra. That one included a hood scoop, quarter-window appliqués, fender exhausters, 3.13:1 gearing with four-speed (2.71:1 w/automatic), rear spoiler, high-back bucket seats, P195/60R14 SBR RWL tires, and 'Charger 2.2' tape graphics. Basic 024 models could have either cast aluminum or Rallye 14-in. wheels as an option.

1981 Dodge, Aries sedan with optional vinyl roof (OCW)

1981 Dodge, Aries Custom two-door sedan (OCW)

ARIES — SERIES D — FOUR — The eagerly-awaited compact K-car came in two-door, four-door or station wagon form, in Custom and SE trim as well as the base model. Carrying six passengers on a front-wheel drive chassis. Aries was a near twin to Plymouth Reliant. The two looked similar, but Plymouth used a more formal grille pattern. A simple slat-style grille (not unlike Mirada's) consisted of four wide, bright horizontal bars and a thin, subdued vertical divider set farther back. On the body-colored upper header panel was 'Dodge' block lettering. Vertical rectangular parking lamps sat between the grille and single rectangular head-lamps. A single frame on each side enclosed parking lamps, headlamps and large amber-lensed marker lamps at front fender tips. 'Aries' lettering sat just ahead of the door, and on the rear panel just above the right taillamp. The letter 'K' to identify the K-car stood alongside that lettering at the rear. On each side were tri-section taillamps consisting of two outer red lenses and an inner backup lens, adjoining the license plate mount. Bodyside moldings followed the same line from front to back, meeting the bumper rub strips. Aries' unibody design was much shorter and lighter than the Aspen it replaced, and its shape was more aerodynamic. At 99.6 inches, wheelbase was shorter than General Motors' new X-car, though overall design was similar. The suspension used Iso-struts with coil springs at the front, and coil springs at the rear with a beam axle and trailing arms. Aries had front and rear anti-roll control, and rack-and-pinion steering. The K-car managed a 25 mpg EPA estimate (41 highway). Base engine was a transverse-mounted 135 cu. in. (2.2-liter) trans-verse-mounted overhead-cam four, called the Trans-4. Built by Chrysler, it had hydraulic valve lifters and an electronic feedback carburetor. The 2.2 came with standard four-speed overdrive manual transaxle, or optional TorqueFlite. For added performance, a Mitsubishi hemi Silent Shaft 156 cu. in. (2.6-liter) engine was available, with three-valve MCA-JET cylinder head. Also used in the imported Challenger coupe, that one came only with automatic. Standard equipment included an electric engine fan, fiberglass-belted radial tires, compact spare tire, bumper rub strips, wide bodyside moldings, drip rail moldings, cloth/vinyl bench seat, multi-function steering column lever, AM radio, lighter, day/night mirror, front/rear ashtrays, dome light, and carpeting. Four-doors and wagons had back door vent windows. Two-doors (sometimes referred to as coupes, but usually as sedans) had quarter-window louvers. Aries Special Edition (SE) had woodtone door panel and dash appliqués plus dual horns, upper door frame moldings, remote-control driver's mirror, belt moldings, deluxe wheel covers, and cloth bench seat. Wagons in each series had power brakes. Body colors were: Nightwatch Blue, Baron Red, Graphic Red, Sunlight Yellow, Spice Tan Starmist, Pearl White, Formal Black and Natural Suede Tan; plus metallic Burnished Silver, Daystar Blue, Light Seaspray Green, or Glencoe Green. Designed with easy servicing in mind, K-cars had an ample option list. Extras included 14-in. tires and wheels, air conditioning, digital clock, automatic transmission, speed control, AM/FM stereo radio with cassette player and Dolby sound, remote-control right mirror, power steering, and six-way power seat. A total of 537 Aries sedans had the simulated convertible roof.

1981 Dodge, Diplomat Salon station wagon with optional roof rack and wind deflector (OCW)

DIPLOMAT — SERIES G — SIX/V-8 — Following its 1980 restyle, Diplomat received no significant appearance change this year. Diplomat's model lineup was slightly revised, though, adding a new Sport Coupe to replace the former base two-door. No base sedan was announced at first. Both two- and four-door models came in mid-level Salon and upper-notch Medallion trim. Wagons came in the base or Salon level. The Sport Coupe included bright windshield, center pillar, rear quarter window, backlight and wheel opening moldings, as well as rocker panel moldings. It featured a two-tone paint treatment with landau effect (accent color on the lower body and rear roof). Sport Coupes also had bodyside and deck accent stripes, sport wheel covers, front bumper guards, front/rear bumper rub strips, and dual remote chrome sport mirrors. Diplomat's Salon included a remote driver's mirror and deluxe wheel covers, plus bright moldings for windshield, center pillar, back window, roof drip, quarter window, belt, sill and wheel openings. Medallions added a padded vinyl roof as well as bodyside and deck accent stripes. Salon and Medallion also had dual horns and a day/night inside mirror. Diplomat body colors were: Pearl White, Light Cashmere, Baron Red, Nightwatch Blue, Light Heather Gray, Black, Spice Tan Starmist, Mahogany Starmist, and Graphic Red; plus metallic Burnished Silver, Daystar Blue, Glencoe Green, or Light Seaspray Green. Four two-tone combinations were offered. New hydraulic valve lifters went on the standard Slant Six engine. Standard equipment included wide-ratio TorqueFlite three-speed automatic, along with power steering and brakes. Radio and tape player options were improved this year. Thicker primer coats and increased use of galvanized steel (and plastics) was intended to improve corrosion resistance, as well as cut weight. Like the related Chrysler LeBaron, Diplomat was now promoted as a mid-size.

1981 Dodge, Mirada coupe (simulated convertible top) with optional CMX package (OCW)

MIRADA — SERIES X — SIX/V-8 — Dodge's distinctively-styled coupe appeared about the same this year, with its wide slat grille in an angled front end. As in 1980, large vertical rectangular parking lamps sat back from the grille in the same housing as the adjoining single rectangular headlamps. Non-functional angled fender louvers again were standard. For the first time, the base 225 cu. in. Slant Six had hydraulic valve lifters. Standard equipment included an AM radio, wide-ratio TorqueFlite three-speed automatic, trip odometer, brushed aluminum dash appliqué, gauges, cloth/vinyl bucket seats, and locking glovebox. Options included the 318 cu. in. V-8, Sport Handling or Roadability packages, leather-wrapped steering wheel, sunroof, wire wheel covers, and forged aluminum wheels. The 318 V-8 added a three-way catalyst emission control and electronic feedback carburetor this year, while Mirada's back bumper switched from aluminum to high-strength steel. Mirada's CMX package was offered again, including a simulated convertible top (tan, dark blue, dark red, black or white), P205/75R15 whitewall tires, black bumper rub strips with bright inserts, front fender CMX nameplates, and color-keyed rear bumper guards. CMX came in Baron Red, Nightwatch Blue, Pearl White, Graphic Red, Black, Light Cashmere, Silver, Spice Tan Starmist, or Daystar Blue metallic. Standard Miradas could also be painted Light Heather Gray or Mahogany Starmist. A total of 1,683 CMX packages were installed. The simulated convertible top was no longer offered separately.

1981 Dodge, St. Regis pillared hardtop (OCW)

ST. REGIS — SERIES E — SIX/V-8 — Essentially unchanged in appearance, St. Regis was promoted as having more standard equipment this year, but the list revealed nothing startling. The current list included bumper rub strips, a two-spoke steering wheel, trip odometer, lane-change turn signals, and twin outside mirrors. St. Regis came with a

full-length padded vinyl roof, bodyside accent stripes, cloth/vinyl seat trim with folding front center armrest, premier wheel covers and steel-belted whitewall tires, power brakes and steering, TorqueFlite automatic transmission, and tinted glass. This year's colors were: Pearl White, Mahogany Starmist, Light Cashmere, Black, Light Heather Gray, Nightwatch Blue, Baron Red, and metallic Heather Mist, Daystar Blue, or Coffee Brown. As before, only one model was offered: a formal-look four-door pillared hardtop sedan. Both the base Slant Six and optional 318 V-8 had improved catalytic emission control. Corrosion resistance was improved through use of a thicker primer coat and specially treated chrome. Like the related Plymouth Gran Fury, St. Regis remained popular with families, but its days were numbered anyway. The Touring Edition was dropped this year, so buyers had no option packages available other than a Basic Group priced at $1,010.

1981 Dodge, Aries Special Edition station wagon (OCW)

I.D. DATA: Dodge had a new 17-symbol Vehicle Identification Number (VIN) on the upper left corner of the instrument panel, again visible through the windshield. The first digit indicates Country: '1' U.S.A.; '2' Canada. The second symbol is Make: 'B' Dodge. Third is Vehicle Type: '3' passenger car. The next symbol ('B') indicates manual seatbelts. Symbol five is Car Line: 'L' Omni; 'K' Aries; 'M' Diplomat; 'J' Mirada; 'R' St. Regis. Symbol six is Series (price class): '1' Economy; '2' Low; '3' Medium; '4' High'; '5' Premium; '6' Special. Symbol seven is Body Style: '1' 2-dr. sedan; '2' 2-dr. specialty hardtop; '4' 2-dr. "22" hatchback; '6' 4-dr. sedan; '7' 4-dr. pillared hardtop; '8' 4-dr. hatchback; '9' 4-dr. wagon. Eighth is the Engine Code: 'A' L4105 2Bbl.; 'B' L4135 2Bbl.; 'D' L4156 2Bbl.; 'E' L6225 1Bbl.; 'K' V8318 2Bbl.; 'M' V8318 4Bbl. Next comes a check digit: 0 through 9 (or X). Symbol ten indicates Model Year: 'B' 1981. Symbol eleven is Assembly Plant: 'A' Lynch Road; 'C' Jefferson; 'D' Belvidere, IL; 'F' Newark, DE; 'G' or 'X' St. Louis; 'R' Windsor, Ontario. The last six digits make up the sequential serial number, starting with 100001. Four-cylinder engine identification numbers are on the rear face of the block, directly under cylinder head (left side in vehicle) except for 2.6-liter, which is on left side of block between core plug and rear face of block (radiator side). Engine serial numbers (for parts replacement) are located on the block as follows: 1.7-liter, above fuel pump; 2.2-liter, on rear face just below head (below identification number); 2.6-liter, on right front of block adjacent to exhaust manifold stud. Six-cylinder engine identification numbers are stamped on a pad at the right of the block, below No. 6 spark plug. On V-8s, that pad is on the right of the block to the rear of the engine mount. An engine serial number is on the right of the block below No. 1 spark plug on six-cylinder engines, and on the left front corner of the block below the cylinder head on V-8s. A Body Code Plate is on the left upper radiator support, left front fender side shield, or wheelhousing.

OMNI (FOUR)

Model No.	Body/ Style No.	Body Type & Seating	Factory Price	Shipping Weight	Prod. Total
ZL	24	2-dr. 024 Hatch-4P	6149	2205	35,983
ZL	44	4-dr. Hatch-5P	5690	2130	41,056

OMNI MISER (FOUR)

ZE	24	2-dr. Hatch-4P	5299	2137	Note 1
ZE	44	4-dr. Hatch-5P	5299	2060	Note 1

Note 1: Total Miser production, 37,819.

ARIES (FOUR)

Model No.	Body/ Style No.	Body Type & Seating	Factory Price	Shipping Weight	Prod. Total
DL	21	2-dr. Sedan-6P	5880	2305	Note 2
DL	41	4-dr. Sedan-6P	5980	2300	Note 2

Note 2: Total coupe/sedan production, 47,679.

ARIES CUSTOM (FOUR)

DH	21	2-dr. Sedan-6P	6315	2315	Note 3
DH	41	4-dr. Sedan-6P	6448	2310	Note 3
DH	45	4-dr. Sta Wag-6P	6721	2375	31,380

Note 3: Total Custom coupe/sedan production, 46,792.

ARIES SPECIAL EDITION (FOUR)

DP	21	2-dr. Sedan-6P	6789	2340	Note 4
DP	41	4-dr. Sedan-6P	6933	2340	Note 4
DP	45	4-dr. Sta Wag-6P	7254	2390	9,770

Note 4: Total Special Edition coupe/sedan production, 20,160.

DIPLOMAT (SIX/V-8)

GL	22	2-dr. Spt Cpe-6P	6495/6557	3210/3335	Note 5
GL	41	4-dr. Spt Sed-6P	6672/6734	3275/3400	Note 5
GM	45	4-dr. Sta Wag-6P	7089/7151	3470/3590	1,806

Note 5: Total Sport Coupe and Sedan production, 4,608.

DIPLOMAT SALON (SIX/V-8)

GH	22	2-dr. Cpe-6P	7134/7196	3200/3325	Note 6
GH	41	4-dr. Sedan-6P	7268/7330	3305/3430	Note 6
GH	45	4-dr. Sta Wag-6P	7670/7732	3505/3625	1,206

Note 6: Total Salon coupe/sedan production, 15,023.

DIPLOMAT MEDALLION (SIX/V-8)

GP	22	2-dr. Cpe-6P	7645/7707	3255/3380	Note 7
GP	41	4-dr. Sedan-6P	7777/7839	3365/3490	Note 7

Note 7: Total Medallion coupe/sedan production, 1,527.

MIRADA (SIX/V-8)

XS	22	2-dr. HT Cpe-6P	7700/7764	3290/3410	11,899

ST. REGIS (SIX/V-8)

EH	42	4-dr. Pill. HT-6P	7674/7738	3535/3640	5,388

Factory Price and Weight Note: Prices and weights to left of slash are for six-cylinder, to right for V-8 engine.

Model Number Note: Some sources identify models using the new VIN data to indicate Car Line, Price Class and Body Style. Example: Aries four-door (DL41) has the equivalent number K26, which translates to Aries line, Low price class, and four-door sedan body. See I.D. Data section for breakdown.

ENGINE DATA: BASE FOUR (Omni): Inline, overhead-cam four-cylinder. Cast iron block; aluminum head. Displacement: 104.7 cu. in. (1.7 liters). Bore and stroke: 3.13 x 3.40 in. Compression ratio: 8.2:1. Brake horsepower: 63 at 5200 R.P.M. Torque: 83 lb.-ft. at 2400 R.P.M. Five main bearings. Solid valve lifters. Carburetor: 2Bbl. Holley 6520 (R9052A). VIN Code: A. **BASE FOUR (Aries); OPTIONAL (Omni):** Inline, overhead-cam four-cylinder. Cast iron block; aluminum head. Displacement: 135 cu. in. (2.2 liters). Bore and stroke: 3.44 x 3.62 in. Compression ratio: 8.5:1. Brake horsepower: 84 at 4800 R.P.M. Torque: 111 lb.-ft. at 2800 R.P.M. Five main bearings. Hydraulic valve lifters. Carburetor: 2Bbl. Holley 6520 (R9060A). VIN Code: B. **OPTIONAL FOUR (Aries):** Inline, overhead-cam four-cylinder. Cast iron block; aluminum head. Displacement: 156 cu. in. (2.6 liters). Bore and stroke: 3.59 x 3.86 in. Compression ratio: 8.2:1. Brake horsepower: 92 at 4500 R.P.M. Torque: 131 lb.-ft. at 2500 R.P.M. Five main bearings. Carburetor: 2Bbl. Mikuni. VIN Code: D. **BASE SIX (Diplomat, Mirada, St. Regis):** Inline, overhead-valve six. Cast iron block and head. Displacement: 225 cu. in. (3.7 liters). Bore and stroke: 3.40 x 4.12 in. Compression ratio: 8.4:1. Brake horsepower: 85 at 3600 R.P.M. Torque: 165 lb.-ft. at 1600 R.P.M. Four main bearings. Hydraulic valve lifters. Carburetor: 1Bbl. Holley 1945 (R9253A). VIN Code: E. **OPTIONAL V-8 (Diplomat, Mirada, St. Regis):** 90-degree, overhead valve V-8. Cast iron block and head. Displacement: 318 cu. in. (5.2 liters). Bore and stroke: 3.91 x 3.31 in. Compression ratio: 8.5:1. Brake horsepower: 130 at 4000 R.P.M. Torque: 230 lb.-ft. at 2000 R.P.M. Five main bearings. Hydraulic valve lifters. Carburetor: 2Bbl. Carter BBD 8291S. VIN Code: K. **OPTIONAL V-8 (St. Regis):** Same as 318 cu. in. V-8 above, but with 4Bbl. Carter TQ 9293S carburetor. Brake horsepower: 165 at 4000 R.P.M. Torque: 240 lb.-ft. at 2000 R.P.M. VIN Code: M.

CHASSIS DATA: Wheelbase: (Omni) 99.1 in.; (024) 96.6 in.; (Aries) 99.6 in.; (Diplomat cpe) 108.7 in.; (Diplo sed/wag) 112.7 in.; (Mirada) 112.7 in.; (St. Regis) 118.5 in. Overall Length: (Omni) 164.8 in.; (024) 174.0 in.; (Aries sed) 176.0 in.; (Aries wag) 176.2 in.; (Diplo cpe) 201.7 in.; (Diplo sed) 205.7 in.; (Diplo wag) 206.0 in.; (Mirada) 209.5 in.; (St. R.) 220.2 in. Height: (Omni) 53.1 in.; (024) 51.2 in.; (Aries 2-dr.) 52.4 in.; (Aries 4-dr.) 52.7 in.; (Aries wag) 52.8 in.; (Diplo cpe) 53.3 in.; (Diplo sed) 55.3 in.; (Diplo wag) 55.5 in.; (Mirada) 53.2 in.; (St. R.) 54.5 in. Width: (Omni) 65.8 in.; (024) 66.7 in.; (Aries) 68.6 in.; (Diplo) 74.2 in.; (Mirada) 72.7 in.; (St. R.) 77.6 in. Front Tread: (Omni/024) 56.1 in.; (Aries) 57.6 in.; (Diplo/Mirada) 60.0 in.; (St. Regis) 61.9 in. Rear Tread: (Omni/024) 55.6 in.; (Aries) 57.0 in.; (Diplo/Mirada) 59.5 in.; (St. R.) 62.0 in. Standard Tires: (Omni) P155/80R13 GBR WSW; (024) P175/75R13 GBR; (Aries) P175/75R13 GBR BSW; (Diplo/Mirada/St. R.) P195/75R15 GBR WSW.

TECHNICAL: Transmission: Four-speed manual (floor lever) standard on Omni. Gear ratios: (1st) 3.45:1; (2nd) 1.94:1; (3rd) 1.29:1; (4th) 0.97:1; (Rev) 3.17:1. Four-speed manual (floor lever) standard on Aries and Omni w/2.2-liter engine: (1st) 3.29:1; (2nd) 1.89:1; (3rd) 1.21:1; (4th) 0.88:1; (Rev) 3.14:1. TorqueFlite three-speed automatic standard on other models, optional on all. Omni 1.7-liter and Aries gear ratios: (1st) 2.69:1; (2nd) 1.55:1; (3rd) 1.00:1; (Rev) 2.10:1. Diplomat/Mirada/St. Regis: (1st) 2.74:1; (2nd) 1.54:1; (3rd) 1.00:1; (Rev) 2.22:1. Omni 2.2-liter: (1st) 2.47:1; (2nd) 1.47:1; (3rd) 1.00:1; (Rev) 2.10:1. Standard final drive ratio: (Omni) 3.37:1 w/4-spd, 3.48:1 w/auto.; (Omni Miser) 2.69:1; (Omni w/2.2-liter four) 2.69:1 w/4-spd, 2.78:1 w/auto.; (Aries) 2.69:1 w/4-spd, 2.78:1 w/auto.; (Diplo six) 2.76:1; (Diplo V-8) 2.26:1; (Diplo V-8 wag) 2.45:1; (Mirada six) 2.76:1; (Mirada V-8) 2.26:1; (St. R. six) 2.94:1; (St. R. V-8 2Bbl.) 2.24:1; (St. R. V-8 4Bbl.) 2.45:1. Steering: (Omni/Aries) rack and pinion; (others) recirculating ball. Suspension: (Omni) Iso-strut independent coil front w/anti-sway bar, trailing arm semi-independent coil rear w/integral anti-sway; (Aries) Iso-strut front w/coil springs, flex-arm beam rear axle w/trailing links and coil springs; (Diplomat/Mirada) transverse front torsion bars and anti-sway bar, semi-elliptic rear leaf springs; (St. Regis) longitudinal front torsion bars w/anti-sway bar, semi-elliptic rear leaf springs. Brakes: Front disc, rear drum. Ignition: Electronic. Body construction: Unibody. Fuel tank: (Omni/Aries) 13 gal.; (Diplomat/Mirada) 18 gal.; (St. Regis) 21 gal.

DRIVETRAIN OPTIONS: Engines: 2.2-liter four: Omni ($104). 2.6-liter four: Aries ($159). 318 cu. in. V-8: Diplomat/Mirada/St. Regis ($62). Transmission/Differential: TorqueFlite auto. trans.: Omni ($359); Aries ($360). SureGrip differential: Diplo ($70-$109); Mirada ($110); St. R. ($114). Brakes and Steering: Power front disc brakes: Omni/Aries ($82). Power steering: Omni ($165); Aries ($174). Suspension: H.D. susp.: Omni 4-dr. ($28); Aries ($23); Diplo/Mirada ($27); St. R. ($29). Sport susp.: 024 ($46). H.D. shock absorbers: Mirada/St. R. ($8). Other: Long-life battery: Omni ($23); others ($36-$38). H.D. trailer assist pkg.: St. R. ($253). Max. engine cooling ($127). California emission system ($46).

OMNI/024 CONVENIENCE/APPEARANCE OPTIONS: Option Packages: De Tomaso pkg.: 024 ($1511-$1866). Euro-Sedan pkg.: 4-dr. ($613-$865). Charger 2.2 pkg.: 024 ($399). Charger 2.2 two-tone paint pkg. ($151). Sport appearance pkg.: 024 ($331-$435). Sport/Classic two-tone paint pkg. ($111-$164). Sport interior pkg. ($147-$200). Custom exterior pkg.: 4-dr. ($188). Premium exterior pkg.: 024 ($92-$166); 4-dr. ($250-$290). Premium interior pkg. ($212-$311). Popular equipment group ($423-$477). Light pkg. ($49). Comfort/Convenience: Air cond. ($554). Rear defroster, electric ($102). Automatic speed control ($136). Power liftgate release: 024 ($27). Tinted windshield: 4-dr. ($45). Tinted glass ($71). Luxury steering wheel: 024 ($20). Sport steering wheel: 4-dr. ($23-$43). Leather-wrapped steering wheel ($17-$60). Rallye instrument cluster w/tachometer ($70-$100). Electric clock w/trip odometer ($30). Intermittent wipers ($42). Rear wiper/washer: 4-dr. ($83). Locking gas cap ($8). Light/Horn/Mirror: Halogen lamps ($40). Two horns ($10). Remote left mirror: ($20). Remote right mirror, black: 4-dr. ($20). Dual remote chrome mirrors: 4-dr. ($41-$60). Dual sport remote mirrors: 024 ($74). Entertainment: AM radio: Miser ($92). AM/FM radio ($59-$151). AM/FM stereo radio ($94-$186); w/8track player ($168-$260); w/cassette ($223-$315). Rear speaker: 024 ($20). Exterior: Removable glass sunroof ($213). Rear spoiler: 024 ($59). Starmist paint ($49). Moldings, 4-dr.: belt ($19); drip ($21); upper door frame ($35); wheel lip ($32). Black vinyl bodyside molding ($46). Door edge protectors ($13-$23). Bumper guards: 4-dr. ($48). Multi-color tape stripe: 4-dr. ($99). Hood/bodyside/deck stripe: 024 ($34). Bodyside/deck stripe ($48). Luggage rack ($92). Undercoating ($37). Lower body protective coating ($34). Interior: Console: storage ($24); shift lever ($36). Cloth/vinyl bucket seats ($25). Tonneau cover: 024 ($49). Cargo area carpet ($34); w/sound insulation ($15-$49). Floor mats: front ($25); rear ($18). Color-keyed seatbelts ($25). Wheels and Tires: Wheel trim rings: 4-dr. ($48). Deluxe wheel covers: 4-dr. ($48). Cast aluminum 13-in. wheels: 4-dr. ($215-$263). Cast aluminum 14-in. wheels: 024

($175). 13-in. Rallye wheels: 4-dr. ($40-$88). 14-in. Rallye wheels: 024 (NC). P155/80R13 WSW: 4-dr. ($52). P165/75R13 WSW: 4-dr. ($33-$85). P175/75R13 GBR WSW: 024 ($58). P175/75R13 SBR BSW: 4-dr. ($17-$102). P175/75R13 SBR WSW: 4-dr. ($89-$174). P185/70R13 SBR BSW: 024 ($116-$174). P195/60R14 SBR BSW: 024 ($79-$137). P195/60R14 SBR RWL: 024 ($39-$205). Conventional spare tire ($39).

ARIES CONVENIENCE/APPEARANCE OPTIONS: Option Packages: Basic group ($701-$784). Light pkg. ($75-$83). Protection group ($95-$103). Comfort/Convenience: Air cond. ($605). Rear defroster ($107). Auto. speed control ($132). Power seat ($173). Power door locks ($93-$132). Power decklid/liftgate release ($27). Tinted windshield ($48); all windows ($75). Luxury steering wheel ($46). Sport steering wheel ($7-$53). Tilt steering wheel ($81). Digital clock ($59). Intermittent wipers ($41). Tailgate wiper/washer: wag ($82). Locking gas cap ($7). Lighting, Horns and Mirrors: Halogen headlamps ($36). Dual horns ($10). Remote left mirror ($19). Remote right mirror: SE ($49). Dual remote mirrors ($49-$68). Vanity mirror ($5). Entertainment: AM radio: base ($90). AM/FM radio ($64-$150). AM/FM stereo radio ($100); w/8track player ($174); w/cassette ($224); w/CB ($361). Rear speaker ($19). Dual front speakers ($25) w/mono radio. Premium speakers ($92). Delete AM radio ($85 credit). Exterior: Glass sunroof ($246). Full vinyl roof: 4-dr. ($131). Canopy vinyl roof: 2-dr. ($131). Spice Tan Starmist paint ($55). Door edge protectors ($13-$20). Upper door frame moldings ($58-$67). Sill moldings ($20). Bumper guards, front or rear ($24). Luggage rack ($90). Special sound insulation ($75). Undercoating ($37). Vinyl lower body protection ($34). Interior: Vinyl bench seat ($27). Vinyl bucket seats ($51-$78) but (NC) on SE. Cloth bucket seats: SE ($91). Color-keyed mats: front ($25); rear ($19). Tonneau cover: wag ($50). Pedal dress-up ($9). Trunk dress-up ($45). Wheels and Tires: Styled wheels ($36-$82). Deluxe wheel covers ($46). Luxury wheel covers ($36-$82). P175/75R13 GBR wide WSW ($51). P185/70R13 SBR wide WSW ($124-$175). P185/65R14 GBR wide WSW ($82-$133). P185/65R14 SBR wide WSW ($136-$187). Conventional spare tire ($39).

DIPLOMAT CONVENIENCE/APPEARANCE OPTIONS: Option Packages: Sport appearance pkg. ($154-$238). Appearance pkg.: spt cpe (NC). Basic group ($937-$1147). Two-tone paint pkg. ($158). Handling pkg. ($163). Deluxe insulation pkg. ($10-$109). Light pkg. ($85-$99). Protection group ($58-$67). Comfort/Convenience: Air conditioning ($606); auto-temp ($656) but ($50) w/option pkg. Rear defroster, electric ($107). Auto. speed control ($136). Power seat ($177). Power windows ($145-$202). Power door locks ($96-$136). Power decklid/tailgate release ($29). Illuminated entry system ($57). Tinted glass ($78). Luxury steering wheel ($39). Sport steering wheel ($16-$55). Leather-covered steering wheel ($21-$60). Tilt steering wheel ($83). Digital clock ($56). Deluxe wiper/washer ($51). Liftgate wiper/washer: wag ($82). Locking gas cap ($8). Lighting, Horns and Mirrors: Halogen headlamps ($40). Cornering lights ($54). Dual horns: base ($10). Remote passenger mirror ($41). Dual remote sport mirrors ($56). Lighted vanity mirror ($50). Day/night mirror: base ($13). Entertainment: AM radio ($92). AM/FM radio ($59-$151). AM/FM stereo ($94-$186); w/8track tape player ($169-$261); w/cassette ($223-$315); w/CB ($355-$447). Search-tune AM/FM stereo ($211-$303). Rear speaker ($20). Dual front speakers ($26). Premium speakers ($93). Power antenna ($49). Exterior: T-Bar roof: cpe ($695). Power glass sunroof ($865). Full vinyl roof: Salon ($131). Landau padded vinyl roof: base/Salon cpe ($173). Starmist paint ($55). Vinyl bodyside moldings ($43). Belt moldings: base wag ($21). Upper door frame moldings: base wag ($38). Door edge protectors ($13-$22). Rear bumper guards ($25). Hood tape stripe ($24). Bodyside stripe ($50). Bodyside/decklid stripe: Salon ($72). Air deflector: wag ($31). Luggage rack: wag ($98). Undercoating ($25). Interior: Console: Salon ($108). Vinyl bench seat: spt cpe, base wag ($69); Salon ($50). Cloth 60/40 seat: wag ($208-$276). Vinyl 60/40 seat: base wag, Salon ($208-$276). Cloth/vinyl 60/40 seat: Salon ($226). Leather 60/40 seat: wag, Medallion ($364-$608). Cloth/vinyl bucket seats: Salon cpe ($101). Center armrest cushion: Salon ($42). Color-keyed floor mats: front ($25); rear ($20). Cargo area carpet: base wag ($74); w/storage bins ($25-$99). Cargo security cover: wag ($50). Pedal dress-up ($10). Trunk dress-up ($47). Wheels and Tires: Premier wheel covers ($45). Premium wheel covers ($43-$88). Wire wheel covers ($106-$249). Forged aluminum wheels ($183-$326). Styled wheels ($98-$143). Conventional spare ($39).

MIRADA CONVENIENCE/APPEARANCE OPTIONS: Option Packages: CMX pkg. ($780). Basic group ($922). Sport handling pkg. ($139-$240). Roadability pkg. ($31). Light pkg. ($117). Protection group ($68). Comfort/Convenience: Air cond. ($606); auto-temp ($654) exc. ($48) w/option pkg. Rear defroster, electric ($107). Auto. speed control ($136). Power seat ($177). Power windows ($145). Power door locks ($96). Power decklid release ($28-$43). Illuminated entry system ($57). Luxury steering wheel (NC). Leather-covered two-spoke steering wheel (NC). Tilt steering wheel ($83). Digital clock ($59). Locking gas cap ($8). Intermittent wipers ($43). Lighting, Horns and Mirrors: Halo-

gen headlamps ($40). Cornering lights ($54). Reading lamp ($20). Triad horns ($22). Lighted vanity mirror ($50). Entertainment: AM/FM radio ($59). AM/FM stereo radio ($95); w/8track ($169): w/cassette ($211); w/CB ($355). Search-tune AM/FM stereo ($223). Rear speaker ($20). Dual front speakers ($26). Premium speakers ($93). Power antenna ($49). Delete radio ($85 credit). Exterior: T-Bar roof ($695). Power sunroof ($758). Landau vinyl roof ($131). Premium paint ($68). Vinyl bodyside moldings ($45). Wheel lip moldings ($26). Sill moldings ($30). Door edge protectors ($13). Bumper guards, rear ($25); rub strips ($20). Hood/deck tape stripes ($50). Undercoating ($25). Interior: Console ($66-$108). Vinyl bucket seats ($42). Leather bucket seats ($451-$493). Center cushion w/armrest ($42). Color-keyed mats: front ($25); rear ($20). Trunk dress-up ($47). Pedal dress-up ($11). Litter container ($10). Wheels and Tires: Forged aluminum wheels ($238-$329). Premium wheel covers ($91). Wire wheel covers ($161-$252). P205/75R15 GBR WSW ($27). P205/75R15 SBR WSW ($101). P215/70R15 SBR WSW ($56-$161). P215/70R15 SBR RWL ($60-$157). Conventional spare tire ($39).

ST. REGIS CONVENIENCE/APPEARANCE OPTIONS: Option Packages: Open Road handling pkg. ($281). Basic group ($993). Light pkg. ($103). Comfort/Convenience: Air cond. ($646); auto-temp ($692) exc. ($46) w/option pkg. Rear defroster, electric ($112). Auto. speed control ($139). Power windows ($218). Power door locks ($138). Power seat ($179). Power decklid release ($30-$45). Illuminated entry system ($60). Luxury steering wheel ($39). Leather-covered steering wheel ($60). Tilt steering wheel ($84). Digital clock ($62). Intermittent wipers ($44). Locking gas cap ($9). Lighting, Horns and Mirrors: Halogen headlamps ($41). Cornering lights ($54). Triad horns ($22). Remote driver's mirror ($21). Dual remote mirrors ($30-$51). Lighted vanity mirror ($51). Entertainment: AM radio ($97). AM/FM radio ($54-$151). AM/FM stereo ($95-$192); w/8track tape player ($166-$263); w/cassette ($221-$318); w/CB ($356-$453). Search-tune AM/FM stereo ($206-$303). Rear speaker ($21). Dual front speakers ($26). Premium speakers ($95). Power antenna ($50). Exterior: Power glass sunroof ($934). Special paint ($68). Vinyl bodyside molding ($51). Door edge protectors ($23). Bumper guards ($60). Undercoating ($31). Interior: Vinyl bench seat ($34). Cloth/vinyl 60/40 bench seat ($148). Color-keyed mats: front ($25); rear ($20). Pedal dress-up ($11). Trunk dress-up ($65). Litter container ($10). Wheels and Tires: Premium wheel covers ($86). Wire wheel covers ($251). Forged aluminum wheels ($321). P205/75R15 SBR WSW ($101). P225/70R15 SBR WSW ($192). Conventional spare tire ($39).

HISTORY: Introduced: October 13, 1980. Model year production: Chrysler reported a total of 312,096 passenger cars shipped. Total North American production for the U.S. market of 356,513 units included 255,120 four-cylinder, 79,314 six-cylinder and 22,079 V-8s. Calendar year production (U.S.): 328,631. Calendar year sales by U.S. dealers: 305,757. Model year sales by U.S. dealers: 371,528 (incl. 41,288 imported Colts and 12,371 Challengers).

HISTORICAL FOOTNOTES: At introduction time, the new Aries was priced several hundred dollars lower than competitive X-cars from General Motors. After slow early sales and amid plenty of publicity, Aries soon began to sell strongly. Aries' catalog headline, "America's not going to be pushed around anymore!" made clear Chrysler's attitude toward the new K-car as an import fighter. Also promoted was the fact that Chrysler had begun front-wheel drive production (of the Omni) two or three years earlier than GM and Ford. The new Omni "Miser" was intended to rival Ford's new Escort/Lynx. To help sell Omnis and some other models, many dealers even offered a 30-Day/1,000-Mile Money-Back Guarantee. Model year sales rose by over 14 percent, due mainly to success of front-drive Dodge models, led by Aries. Over 81 percent of Dodges sold had front-drive, and Aries accounted for over two-fifths of the total. Even so, the final figure stood well below the 1979 level. St. Regis faded away at the end of 1980, largely because of minimal sales (only 7,556 for the model year). Model year production rose by 26 percent, again led by Aries, which amounted to half the total. Dodge's share of the industry production total for calendar year 1981 was 5.3 percent (up from 4.2 percent in 1980).

1982 DODGE

Several models came and went this year. Diplomat lost its coupe and station wagon body styles, leaving only a four-door sedan. The renowned Charger name went on a performance version of the Omni-based subcompact coupe. Dodge added one all-new model: the 400, which was

a stretched version of the K-car (Aries) but more luxurious. And the full-size St. Regis was gone. Compacts were getting more standard equipment without equivalent price increases. Engineering changes were aimed at a better ride and gas mileage. Biggest engine was the two-barrel 318 cu. in. V-8 (four-barrel in California). At mid-year the new 400 series added a convertible, a mate to Chrysler's LeBaron.

1982 Dodge, Omni Custom hatchback sedan (OCW)

OMNI/024 — SERIES Z — FOUR — This year's Omni sedan looked similar to the 1981 version, but added a pentastar emblem atop the vertical divider of its horizontal-bar grille. 'Omni' lettering was no longer on the front fenders, though it remained on the hatch. A 'Dodge' nameplate was also on the hatch, as well as above the driver's side headlamp. The base Omni sedan was now called Custom. New standard equipment included a driver's remote outside mirror, dual horns, and bright wheel hub nuts. Euro-Sedan became a separate model, and the stripped-down Miser was offered again. Omni's chassis held a new linkless sway bar. At its rear were low-rate springs and retuned shocks, intended to give a softer ride and greater stability. A simplified catalytic converter was used; the dual-bed version dropped. The Custom held new standard cloth/vinyl Sport high-back bucket seats with integral headrests and dual recliners, plus a four-spoke color-keyed sport steering wheel and padded instrument panel with woodtone accents. Far fewer option packages were offered this year. New individual options included a lighted passenger vanity mirror and an engine block heater, as well as nerf strips. Reclining front seatbacks were available. Standard engine was again the 1.7-liter OHC four, with 2.2 optional. Automatic TorqueFlite was available to replace the standard four-speed manual gearbox. Omni Miser returned with its specially calibrated 1.7-liter engine, four-speed manual transaxle, and 2.69:1 overall drive ratio. Miser's vinyl interior came in red, blue, cashmere or black. Standard fittings included a locking glovebox, day/night mirror, remote driver's outside mirror, and inside hood release. Such extras as air conditioning and power steering weren't available on the Miser. Omni's sporty E-Type Euro-Sedan had blacked-out trim, dual black remote-control mirrors, bumper rub strips, special bodyside and mirror stripes, Rallye instrument cluster with tachometer and trip odometer, shift-lever console, and high-back cloth/vinyl bucket seats with recliners. This year's body colors were: Black, Pearl White, Graphic Yellow or Red, Morocco Red, and Manila Cream; plus metallic Charcoal Gray, Spice Tan, Medium Seaspray Green, Daystar Blue, Ensign Blue, Navy Blue, and Burnished Silver. Three two-tones were available. The 024 two-door hatchback coupe also came in Custom and Miser form again, marketed separately from the sedan. Custom coupes had thicker C-pillar appliqués. New this year was a performance variant called Charger 2.2 (listed next).

1982 Dodge, Omni Charger 2.2 hatchback coupe (OCW)

(OMNI) CHARGER 2.2 — SERIES Z — FOUR — Charger, a well-known name in Dodge performance-car history, returned on the Omni-based coupe with standard 135 cu. in. (2.2-liter) Trans-4 engine. In addition to snappy performance, Charger offered an EPA mileage estimate of 26 mpg (41 highway). Appearance was similar to the basic 024, but more dramatic. Charger's grille consisted of six wide slots, three on each side, in a sharply-slanted front panel. Single rectangular headlamps were deeply recessed, with parking lamps below. At the front of the hood was a round laydown ornament with pentastar emblem. Bodies displayed easy-to-spot tape graphics, including large 'Charger 2.2' lettering as part of the bodyside and rear spoiler striping and a huge 'Charger 2.2' decal on the simulated hood scoop. Tape graphics came in several color combinations (red, black or gold), depending on the body color. A black lower body accent paint package was also available. On the fender just ahead of the door was a simulated front fender exhaust outlet. The sporty fastback roofline was similar to earlier 024s, except that the center side window did not come to a point at the rear. Two horizontal divider bars split each wide taillamp into three segments. Charger 2.2 standard equipment included manual front disc brakes, heater/defroster, AM radio, lighter, bumper rub strips, passenger and cargo area carpet, performance exhaust system, and tinted glass all around. Also standard: dual horns, padded instrument panel with woodtone appliqué, glovebox lock, power liftgate release, dual remote color-keyed mirrors, day/night inside mirror, black windshield and rear window moldings, black belt moldings, and a Sport suspension with rear anti-sway bar. Body colors were Black, Graphic Red, Pearl White, Burnished Silver metallic, and Ensign Blue metallic. Rallye steel wheels held P195/60R14 raised white-letter tires. Inside were Sport high-back reclining bucket seats upholstered in corded cloth/vinyl, plus a four-spoke steering wheel and Rallye instrument cluster (including tachometer, clock and trip odometer).

1982 Dodge, Aries Special Edition station wagon (OCW)

1982 Dodge, Aries Special Edition two-door sedan with optional landau vinyl roof (OCW)

ARIES — SERIES D — FOUR — Except for a stand-up hood ornament and elimination of an 'Aries' nameplate from front fenders, the Dodge K-car didn't change much for its second season. Separate 'Dodge' letters stood above the slat-type grille. As before, vertical parking lamps were between the grille and single recessed headlamps, which connected with amber marker lenses. Lower bodyside moldings ran into the front and rear bumper strips for a unified look. Standard engine was again the 2.2-liter OHC Trans-4, with 2.6-liter Mitsubishi optional. The 2.2-liter four got a new cooling fan for improved fuel efficiency, plus a high-altitude compensator that adjusted spark advance electronically. Idle speed was modified, for smoother running. Silver/black was the underhood color scheme, and Aries had a new counterbalanced hood. Underneath was a new linkless front sway bar with new geometry in the Iso-strut suspension for better steering control on rough roads. As before, models included two- and four-door sedans and a four-door wagon; in base, Custom and SE trim. Base Aries models had all-vinyl bench seats. Aries Custom had standard pleated cloth/vinyl bench seating in red, green, blue or cashmere. Custom also added door frame moldings, color-keyed quarter-window louvers, and bright taillamp accents. The Special Edition had cloth seats with a folding center armrest, plus power brakes and steering,

a remote control driver's mirror, deluxe wheel covers, bright decklid molding, and Special Edition plaque on rear roof pillars. Aries colors for 1982 were: Black, Pearl White, Manila Cream, Nightwatch Blue, and Morocco Red; plus metallic Burnished Silver, Medium Seaspray Green, Spice Tan, Daystar Blue, Charcoal Gray, Goldenrod Tan, and Light Seaspray Green. A new cabriolet roof package was offered for Custom and SE, but Chrysler reports that only 86 of the simulated convertible tops were installed. Also added to the option list: power front windows, center console (with manual shift), leather-covered steering wheel, Rallye wheels, and 14-in. cast aluminum wheels. Spring Special packages (RPO code A07) were installed on 2,082 Aries models.

1982 Dodge, 400 convertible with optional wire wheel covers (OCW)

1982 Dodge, 400 LS coupe (OCW)

400 — SERIES V — FOUR — Riding a K-car chassis with 99.9 in. wheelbase, the sporty new mid-size front-drive "Super K" arrived first only in two-door form, with a four-door added later. Both were offered in base or premium LS trim. Added at mid-year was a convertible model, similar to Chrysler's new LeBaron ragtop, converted from a coupe by Cars and Concepts in Brighton, Michigan. Dimensions, drivetrains, suspensions and dashboards were similar to Aries, but 400 had a body-color horizontal-bar grille like Mirada. Fenders held twin vertical louvers (simulated) at the cowl. The convertible had a small back window and wide rear quarters. The 135 cu. in. (2.2-liter) Trans-4 served as base engine, with the Mitsubishi-built 156 cu. in. (2.6-liter) four optional (and standard on the convertible). Four-speed manual shift was standard, along with power brakes and rack-and-pinion steering. Three-speed TorqueFlite was optional. Tires were P185/70R14 steel-belted radial wide-whitewall tires. Better equipped than Aries, the 400 came with a standard AM radio, carpeting, door-ajar chimes, seatbelt and headlamps-on warnings, lighter, digital clock, dual horns, courtesy lights, locking glovebox, dual chrome mirrors, and day/night inside mirror. Moldings were provided for windshield, hood rear edge, lower deck, upper door frame, drip rail, partial wheel lip, and bodyside (color-keyed vinyl). Cloth/vinyl standard seats had a center armrest and door trim panels were carpeted. Also standard: a padded landau vinyl roof with color-keyed surround moldings and Frenched back window, luxury wheel covers, and luxury steering wheel. The instrument panel held a brushed-finish cluster with two-tone woodgrain treatment and padded top. LS added a velvet bench seat, halogen headlamps, light/gauge alert group, cornering lights, dual remote-controlled mirrors, and bodyside tape stripes.

1982 Dodge, Diplomat Medallion sedan (OCW)

DIPLOMAT — SERIES G — SIX/V-8 — Only the four-door sedan remained in the Diplomat lineup, in Salon and Medallion trim. Both the coupe and station wagon were dropped. No base model was offered. Diplomat looked similar to the 1981 edition, with the same rectangular-element grille that extended outward at the base to enclose parking and marker lamps. With St. Regis gone, Diplomat was Dodge's biggest car and one of only two rear-drives. Salon had standard cushioned foam cloth/vinyl bench seats, while Medallion carried 60/40 seating. Both included folding center armrests. Standard equipment included the 225 cu. in. (3.7-liter) Slant Six engine, TorqueFlite three-speed automatic, power brakes and steering, glass-belted radial whitewalls, tinted glass, front bumper guards, bumper rub strips, and bright rear door glass division bar; plus moldings for windshield, belt, sill, wheel openings, and roof drip. Medallion added bright upper door frame moldings, a full vinyl roof with bright vinyl termination molding, map/dome reading light and headlamp switch with time delay, remote left mirror, and trunk dress-up equipment. This year's colors were: Black, Manila Cream, Morocco Red, Nightwatch Blue, and Pearl White; plus metallic Charcoal Gray, Spice Tan, Burnished Silver, and Daystar Blue. Automatic transmissions with the optional 318 cu. in. V-8 had a lock-up torque converter. A four-way power seat was available for the front passenger, as well as six-way for the driver. New to the option list: an electronic-tuning AM/FM stereo radio with cassette player. A total of 11,787 Police packages (RPO code A38) were installed on Diplomats. That was nearly half the total production.

1982 Dodge, Mirada coupe (simulated convertible roof) with optional CMX package (OCW)

MIRADA — SERIES X — SIX/V-8 — No significant appearance changes hit the Cordoba-related mid-size coupe, with its sleek profile and wide-slat grille. As before, rectangular parking lamps sat right next to the single rectangular headlamps in their set-back housings. Twin hood creases came forward to meet the grille sides. Mirada carried only modest bright ornamentation, but fenders again held angled simulated louvers above the 'Mirada' nameplates. Taillamps again displayed horizontal trim strips. The front end was made of flexible plastic. Body colors were: Morocco Red, Manila Cream, Nightwatch Blue, Black, and Pearl White; plus metallic Charcoal Gray, Mahogany, Daystar Blue, Burnished Silver, and Spice Tan. Standard Miradas had grooved-look moldings at the rear of the center side windows, but many carried a simulated convertible top that offered a much different look. A T-Bar roof also was available. Base engine was again the 225 cu. in. Slant Six, with 318 V-8 optional. TorqueFlite three-speed automatic was standard. The instrument panel displayed round gauges. Standard high-back cloth Sport bucket seats could also have an optional center cushion and folding center armrest. Vinyl and leather/vinyl bucket seats were available, as was 60/40 seating. Also optional: a new electronic-tuning AM/FM stereo radio with cassette player, and a rear anti-sway bar. New standard equipment included halogen headlamps, rear bumper rub strips (formerly front only), and color-keyed two-spoke steering wheel. Mirada's CMX package included a sailcloth-textured simulated convertible vinyl top, bright touchdown moldings, front fender 'CMX' nameplates, color-keyed door handle inserts, premium wheel covers, and P205/75R15 SBR wide whitewall tires. A total of 1,474 CMX packages were installed.

I.D. DATA: Dodge's 17-symbol Vehicle Identification Number (VIN), as before, was on the upper left corner of the instrument panel, visible through the windshield. The first digit indicates Country: '1' U.S.A.; '2' Canada. The second symbol is Make: 'B' Dodge. Third is Vehicle Type: '3' passenger car. The next symbol ('B') indicates manual seatbelts. Symbol five is Car Line: 'Z' Omni; 'D' Aries; 'G' Diplomat; 'X' Mirada; 'V' 400. Symbol six is Series (price class): '1' Economy; '2' Low; '4' High; '5' Premium; '6' Special. Symbol seven is Body Style: '1' 2-dr. sedan; '2' 2-dr. specialty hardtop; '4' 2-dr. "22" hatchback; '5' 2-dr. convertible; '6' 4-dr. sedan; '8' 4-dr. hatchback; '9' 4-dr. wagon. Eighth is the Engine Code: 'A' L4105 2Bbl.; 'B' L4135 2Bbl.; 'D' L4156 2Bbl.; 'E' L6225 1Bbl.; 'K' V8318 2Bbl. Next comes a check digit. Symbol ten indicates Model Year: 'C' 1982. Symbol eleven is Assembly Plant: 'C' Jefferson; 'D' Belvidere, IL; 'F' Newark, DE; 'G' or 'X' St. Louis; 'R' Windsor, Ontario. The last six digits make up the sequential serial number, starting with 100001. Engine number coding is the same as 1981.

OMNI CUSTOM (FOUR)

Model No.	Body/ Style No.	Body Type & Seating	Factory Price	Shipping Weight	Prod. Total
ZH	24	2-dr. 024 Hatch-5P	6421	2205	11,287
ZH	44	4-dr. Hatch-5P	5927	2175	14,466

OMNI MISER (FOUR)

ZE	24	2-dr. 024 Hatch-5P	5799	2180	14,947
ZE	44	4-dr. Hatch-5P	5499	2110	16,105

OMNI EURO-SEDAN (FOUR)

ZP	44	4-dr. Hatch-5P	6636	2180	639

OMNI CHARGER 2.2 (FOUR)

ZP	24	2-dr. Hatch-5P	7115	2315	14,420

ARIES (FOUR)

DL	21	2-dr. Sedan-6P	5990	2315	10,286
DL	41	4-dr. Sedan-6P	6131	2310	28,561

ARIES CUSTOM (FOUR)

DH	21	2-dr. Sedan-6P	6998	2320	8,127
DH	41	4-dr. Sedan-6P	7053	2320	19,438
DH	45	4-dr. Sta Wag-6P	7334	2395	26,233

ARIES SPECIAL EDITION (FOUR)

DP	21	2-dr. Sedan-6P	7575	2365	1,374
DP	41	4-dr. Sedan-6P	7736	2385	4,269
DP	45	4-dr. Sta Wag-6P	8101	2470	6,375

400 (FOUR)

VH	22	2-dr. Cpe-6P	8043	2470	12,716
VH	41	4-dr. Sedan-6P	8137	N/A	3,595
VH	27	2-dr. Conv-4P	12300	N/A	5,541

400 LS (FOUR)

VP	22	2-dr. Cpe-6P	8308	2475	6,727
VP	41	4-dr. Sedan-6P	8402	N/A	2,870

DIPLOMAT SALON (SIX/V-8)

GL	41	4-dr. Sedan-6P	7750/7820	3275/3415	19,773

DIPLOMAT MEDALLION (SIX/V-8)

GH	41	4-dr. Sedan-6P	8799/8869	3305/3445	3,373

MIRADA (SIX/V-8)

XS	22	2-dr. HT Cpe-5P	8619/8689	3305/3455	6,818

Factory Price and Weight Note: Prices and weights to left of slash are for six-cylinder, to right for V-8 engine.

Model Number Note: Some sources identify models using the new VIN data to indicate Car Line, Price Class and Body Style. Example: Aries four-door (DL41) has the equivalent number D26, which translates to Aries line, Low price class, and four-door sedan body. See I.D. Data section for breakdown.

ENGINE DATA: BASE FOUR (Omni): Inline, overhead-cam four-cylinder. Cast iron block; aluminum head. Displacement: 104.7 cu. in. (1.7 liters). Bore and stroke: 3.13 x 3.40 in. Compression ratio: 8.2:1. Brake horsepower: 63 at 4800 R.P.M. Torque: 83 lb.-ft. at 2400 R.P.M. Five main bearings. Solid valve lifters. Carburetor: 2Bbl. Holley 6520. VIN Code: A. BASE FOUR (Aries, 400); OPTIONAL (Omni): Inline, overhead-cam four-cylinder. Cast iron block; aluminum head. Displacement: 135 cu. in. (2.2 liters). Bore and stroke: 3.44 x 3.62 in. Compression ratio: 8.5:1. Brake horsepower: 84 at 4800 R.P.M. Torque: 111 lb.-ft. at 2400 R.P.M. Five main bearings. Hydraulic valve lifters. Carburetor:

2Bbl. Holley 6520 or 5220. VIN Code: B. OPTIONAL FOUR (Aries, 400): Inline, overhead-cam four-cylinder. Cast iron block; aluminum head. Displacement: 156 cu. in. (2.6 liters). Bore and stroke: 3.59 x 3.86 in. Compression ratio: 8.2:1. Brake horsepower: 92 at 4500 R.P.M. Torque: 131 lb.-ft. at 2500 R.P.M. Five main bearings. Solid valve lifters. Carburetor: 2Bbl. Mikuni. VIN Code: D. BASE SIX (Diplomat, Mirada): Inline, overhead-valve six. Cast iron block and heads. Displacement: 225 cu. in. (3.7 liters). Bore and stroke: 3.40 x 4.12 in. Compression ratio: 8.4:1. Brake horsepower: 90 at 3600 R.P.M. Torque: 160 lb.-ft. at 1600 R.P.M. Four main bearings. Hydraulic valve lifters. Carburetor: 1Bbl. Holley 1945. VIN Code: E. OPTIONAL V-8 (Diplomat, Mirada): 90-degree, overhead valve V-8. Cast iron block and heads. Displacement: 318 cu. in. (5.2 liters). Bore and stroke: 3.91 x 3.31 in. Compression ratio: 8.5:1. Brake horsepower: 130 at 4000 R.P.M. Torque: 230 lb.-ft. at 2000 R.P.M. Five main bearings. Hydraulic valve lifters. Carburetor: 2Bbl. Carter BBD. VIN Code: K.

CHASSIS DATA: Wheelbase: (Omni) 99.1 in.; (024) 96.6 in.; (Aries/400) 99.9 in.; (Diplomat) 112.7 in.; (Mirada) 112.7 in. Overall Length: (Omni Miser) 162.6 in.; (Omni Cust) 164.8 in.; (Omni E Type) 163.2 in.; (024) 174.0 in.; (Aries sed) 176.0 in.; (Aries wag) 176.2 in.; (400) 181.2 in.; (Diplomat) 205.7 in.; (Mirada) 209.6 in. Height: (Omni) 53.1 in.; (024) 50.8 in.; (Aries 2-dr.) 52.3 in.; (Aries 4-dr.) 52.7 in.; (Aries wag) 52.4 in.; (40 2-dr.) 52.6 in.; (400 4-dr.) 53.0 in.; (400 conv.) 54.1 in.; (Diplomat) 55.3 in.; (Mirada) 53.2 in. Width: (Omni) 65.8 in.; (024) 66.7 in.; (Aries) 68.6 in.; (400) 68.5 in.; (Diplo) 74.2 in.; (Mirada) 72.7 in. Front Tread: (Omni/024) 56.1 in.; (Aries/400) 57.6 in.; (Diplo/Mirada) 60.0 in. Rear Tread: (Omni/024) 55.6 in.; (Aries/400) 57.0 in.; (Diplo/Mirada) 59.5 in. Wheel size: (Omni/Aries) 13 x 5.5 in.; (024/400) 14 x 5.5 in.; (Diplo/Mirada) 15 x 5.5 in. Standard Tires: (Omni/Aries) P175/75R13 GBR BSW; (024) P195/60R14 SSR BSW; (400) P185/70R14 SBR; (Diplo/Mirada) P195/75R15 GBR WSW.

TECHNICAL: Transmission: Four-speed manual (floor lever) standard on Omni. Gear ratios: (1st) 3.45:1; (2nd) 1.94:1; (3rd) 1.29:1; (4th) 0.97:1; (Rev) 3.17:1. Four-speed manual (floor lever) standard on Aries, 400, Omni Miser, and Omni w/2.2-liter engine: (1st) 3.29:1; (2nd) 1.89:1; (3rd) 1.21:1; (4th) 0.88:1; (Rev) 3.14:1. TorqueFlite three-speed automatic standard on other models, optional on all. Omni, Aries and 400 gear ratios: (1st) 2.69:1; (2nd) 1.55:1; (3rd) 1.00:1; (Rev) 2.10:1. Diplomat/Mirada: (1st) 2.74:1; (2nd) 1.54:1; (3rd) 1.00:1; (Rev) 2.22:1. Standard final drive ratio: (Omni 4-spd) 3.37:1; (Miser 4-spd) 2.69:1; (Omni 2.2-liter 4-spd) 3.13:1; (Omni auto.) 2.78:1; (Aries/400) 2.69:1 w/4-spd, 2.78:1 w/auto.; (Diplo/Mirada six) 2.94:1; (Diplo/Mirada V-8) 2.20:1. Steering: (Omni/Aries/400) rack and pinion; (others) recirculating ball. Suspension: (Omni) Iso-strut independent coil front w/anti-sway bar, trailing arm semi-independent coil rear w/integral anti-sway; (Aries/400) MacPherson strut front w/coil springs and anti-sway bar, flex-arm beam rear axle w/trailing arms, coil springs and anti-sway bar; (Diplomat/Mirada) transverse front torsion bars and anti-sway bar, semi-elliptic rear leaf springs. Brakes: Front disc, rear drum. Ignition: Electronic. Body construction: Unibody. Fuel tank: (Omni/Aries/400) 13 gal.; (Diplomat/Mirada) 18 gal.

DRIVETRAIN OPTIONS: Engines: 2.2-liter four: Omni ($112). 2.6-liter four: Aries/400 ($171). 318 cu. in., 2Bbl. V-8: Diplomat/Mirada ($70). Transmission: TorqueFlite auto. trans.: Omni/Aries/400 ($396). Brakes and Steering: Power front disc brakes: Omni/Aries ($93). Power steering: Omni ($190); Aries ($195). Suspension: H.D. susp.: Aries/Diplo ($26); 400 ($27); Mirada ($31). Sport susp.: 024 ($52). Rear sway bar: Mirada ($34). Other: Long-life battery: Omni ($26); others ($43). Engine block heater: Omni ($18). H.D. engine cooling ($141). California emission system ($65). High-altitude emission (NC).

OMNI/024 CONVENIENCE/APPEARANCE OPTIONS: Option Packages: Sport appearance pkg.: 024 ($138). Bright exterior accent group ($85-$121). Two-tone paint pkg. ($113-$186). Charger blackout graphics ($127). Light group ($74). Comfort/Convenience: Air cond. ($612). Rear defroster, electric ($120). Automatic speed control ($155). Tinted glass: 4-dr. ($82). Rallye instrument cluster ($127). Electric clock w/trip odometer ($48). Intermittent wipers ($47). Rear wiper/washer: 4-dr. ($117). Mirrors: Dual remote chrome: 4-dr. ($47). Dual sport remote: 024 ($55). Lighted vanity ($50). Entertainment: AM radio: Miser ($78). AM/FM stereo radio ($106-$184); w/8track player ($192-$270); w/cassette ($242-$320). Exterior: Removable glass sunroof: 024 ($275). Rear spoiler: base 024 ($68). Black vinyl bodyside molding: 4-dr. ($45). Bumper guards: 4-dr. ($56). Front nerf strips: 4-dr. ($25). Rear nerf strips ($25). Bodyside/deck stripe: 4-dr. ($39). Luggage rack: 4-dr. ($93). Undercoating ($39). Lower body protective coating ($39). Interior: Console, shift lever ($41). Cloth/vinyl bucket seats: Miser ($27). Vinyl bucket seats (NC) exc. Miser. Tonneau cover: 024 ($64). Cargo area carpet w/sound insulation ($56). Wheels and Tires: Deluxe wheel covers: 4-dr. (NC). Luxury wheel covers (NC). Cast aluminum 14 in. wheels: 024 ($231). 13 in. Rallye wheels: Euro ($45). 14 in. Rallye wheels: 024 (NC). P175/75R13 WSW ($58). P175/75R13 SBR WSW ($134). P195/60R14 SBR BSW: 024 ($173). P195/75R14 SBR RWL: 024 ($257). Conventional spare tire ($51).

ARIES CONVENIENCE/APPEARANCE OPTIONS: Option Packages: Cabriolet roof pkg,: Cust/SE ($696). Light pkg. ($89-$98). Comfort/Convenience: Air cond. ($676). Rear defroster ($125). Automatic speed control ($155). Power seat ($197). Power front windows ($165). Power door locks ($106-$152). Power decklid/liftgate release ($32). Tinted glass ($88). Steering wheel: Luxury ($40); Sport ($50-$90); Leatherwrapped ($50-90); Tilt ($95). Digital clock ($61). Intermittent wipers ($47). Liftgate wiper/washer: wag ($117). Lighting, Horns and Mirrors: Halogen headlamps ($41). Dual horns ($12). Remote left mirror ($22). Dual remote mirrors ($64-$86). Lighted vanity mirror, right ($50). Entertainment: AM radio: base ($78). AM/FM stereo radio ($106-$184); w/8track player ($192-$270); w/cassette ($242-$320); w/CB ($364-$442). Dual front speakers ($27). Premium speakers ($126). Delete AM radio ($56 credit). Exterior: Removable glass sunroof ($275). Full vinyl roof: 4-dr. ($157). Padded landau roof: 2-dr. ($157). Door edge protectors ($15-$25). Sill moldings ($23). Bumper guards, front or rear ($28). Bodyside tape stripe: 4-dr. ($48). Luggage rack ($106). Special sound insulation ($87). Undercoating ($39). Vinyl lower body protection ($39). Interior: Console: Cust/SE ($100). Vinyl bench seat: Cust (NC). Cloth/vinyl bench seat: base ($31). Vinyl reclining bucket seats: Cust ($132-$151); SE (NC). Cloth reclining bucket seats: Cust ($249-$270); SE ($98). Color-keyed mats: front ($25); rear ($20). Color-keyed seatbelts ($28). Tonneau cover: wag ($64). Trunk dress-up ($51). Wheels and Tires: Deluxe 13 in. wheel covers ($52). Luxury 14 in. wheel covers ($41-$93). 14 in. wire wheel covers ($257-$309). Rallye wheels, 13 or 14 in. ($41-$93). Cast aluminum 14 in. wheels ($357-$409). P175/75R13 GBR wide WSW ($58). P185/70R13 SBR wide WSW ($194). P185/70R14 GBR wide WSW ($207). Conventional spare tire ($51).

400 CONVENIENCE/APPEARANCE OPTIONS: Option Packages: Light/gauge alert group: base ($79). Sport appearance pkg. ($210-$309). Exterior appearance pkg. ($113-$212). Comfort/Convenience: Air cond. ($676). Auto. speed control ($155). Power windows ($165). Power door locks ($106). Power seat ($197). Power decklid release ($32). Tinted glass ($88). Sport steering wheel ($50). Leather-wrapped steering wheel ($51) but (NC) w/option pkg. Tilt steering wheel ($95). Deluxe wipers ($47). Lighting and Mirrors: Halogen headlamps: base ($15). Cornering lights: base ($57). Reading lamp: base ($24). Remote-control mirror: base ($55). Lighted vanity mirror ($50). Entertainment: AM/FM stereo ($106); w/8track tape player ($192); w/CB ($364). Electronic-tuning AM/FM stereo ($250); w/cassette ($455). Dual front speakers ($27). Premium speakers ($126). Radio delete ($56 credit). Exterior: Glass sunroof ($275). Crystal Coat paint ($99). Two-tone paint: base ($113-$212). Sill moldings ($23). Door edge protectors ($15). Bodyside tape stripe ($48). Bumper guards, front or rear ($23). Undercoating ($39). Vinyl lower body protection ($39). Interior: Console ($100). Vinyl bucket seats w/dual recliners: base 2-dr. ($92). Cloth/vinyl bucket seats: LS ($151). Leather bucket seats: LS ($263-$414). Center armrest ($59). Color-keyed mats: front ($25); rear ($20). Trunk dress-up: base ($51). Wheels/Tires: Wire wheel covers ($219). Cast aluminum wheels ($316). Conventional spare tire ($51).

DIPLOMAT CONVENIENCE/APPEARANCE OPTIONS: Option Packages: Basic group ($923-$1143). Light pkg. ($106-$139). Protection group ($119). Comfort/Convenience: Air cond. ($731). Rear defroster, electric ($125). Auto. speed control ($155). Power seat, each ($197). Power windows ($235). Power door locks ($152). Power decklid release ($32). Illuminated entry system ($72). Leather-wrapped steering wheel ($50). Tilt steering wheel ($95). Digital clock ($61). Intermittent wipers ($47). Mirrors: Remote driver's ($22). Dual remote chrome ($43-$65). Lighted vanity ($58). Entertainment: AM/FM stereo radio ($106); w/8track tape player ($192); w/CB ($364). Search-tune AM/FM stereo ($239). Electronic-tuning AM/FM stereo w/cassette ($455). Dual front speakers ($28). Premium speakers ($126). Power antenna ($55). Radio delete ($56 credit). Exterior: Power glass sunroof ($982). Full vinyl roof: Salon ($157). Vinyl bodyside moldings ($46). Upper door frame moldings: Salon ($41). Bodyside/deck/hood stripe ($109). Body sound insulation ($30). Undercoating ($39). Interior: Vinyl bench seat: Salon ($57). Leather 60/40 seat: Medallion ($416). Trunk dress-up ($50). Wheels and Tires: Premium wheel covers ($93). Wire wheel covers ($257). Forged aluminum wheels ($364). P205/75R15 SBR WSW ($116). Conventional spare tire ($51).

MIRADA CONVENIENCE/APPEARANCE OPTIONS: Option Packages: CMX pkg. ($935). Basic group ($1072-$1229). Light pkg. ($159). Protection pkg. ($137). Comfort/Convenience: Air cond. ($731). Rear defroster, electric ($125). Auto. speed control ($155). Power seat ($197); dual ($394). Power windows ($165). Power door locks ($106). Power decklid release ($32-49). Illuminated entry system ($72). Sport steering wheel ($50). Leather-covered steering wheel ($50). Tilt steering wheel ($95). Digital clock ($61). Intermittent wipers ($47). Lighting, Horns and Mirrors: Cornering lights ($57). Triad horns ($25). Lighted vanity mirror ($58). Entertainment: AM/FM stereo radio ($106); w/8track ($192); w/CB ($364). Search-tune AM/FM stereo ($239).

Electronic-tuning AM/FM stereo w/cassette ($455). Dual front speakers ($28). Premium speakers ($126). Power antenna ($55). Delete radio ($56 credit). Exterior: T-Bar roof ($790). Landau vinyl roof ($157). Wheel lip moldings ($30). Sill moldings ($34). Bodyside/hood/deck tape stripes ($96). Undercoating ($39). Interior: Console ($75-$124), Cloth/vinyl 60/40 seat ($202-$251). Vinyl bucket seats ($48). Leather bucket seats ($515-$564). Center armrest ($49). Trunk dress-up ($60). Wheels and Tires: Forged aluminum wheels ($270-$323). Premium wheel covers ($53). Wire wheel covers ($163-$216). P205/75R15 SBR WSW ($115). P215/70R15 SBR RWL ($66-$181). Conventional spare tire ($51).

HISTORY: Introduced: October 4, 1981 except 400, October 29; and 400 convertible, mid-April 1982. Model year production: Chrysler reported a total of 237,940 passenger cars shipped. Total North American production for the U.S. market of 272,407 units included 241,359 four-cylinder, 9,795 six-cylinder and 21,253 V-8s. Calendar year production (U.S.): 244,878. Calendar year sales by U.S. dealers: 261,105. Model year sales by U.S. dealers: 250,392 (not incl. 41,577 imported Colts and 14,340 Challengers).

HISTORICAL FOOTNOTES: Model year sales slipped considerably, from 371,548 in 1981 (including captive imports) to just 306,309 in 1982. Nevertheless, Dodge's market share held almost steady at 4.0 percent. Figuring domestic models only, Dodge's share was 4.5 percent of the market (down from 4.8 percent). Only the imported Colt and Challenger showed a sales increase. Omni/024 sales dropped by 27 percent for the model year; rear-drive models by 44 percent. In fact, only 10 percent of Dodge sales were rear-drives (Mirada/Diplomat). Calendar year production fell by over 25 percent. Motor Trend had named Aries its 1981 "Car of the Year." Aries was Dodge's top seller by far, but even its sales fell by 18 percent. The Charger 2.2 sales catalog directed customers to Direct Connection, Chrysler's Performance Parts Program, if they felt the need for additional dress-up items as well as mechanical components for off-road driving. In fall 1982, Batten, Barton, Durstine and Osborne Inc. was named Dodge's ad agency, taking over from Kenyon and Eckhardt Inc. (which had previously handled all Chrysler products). This was part of Chrysler Vice-President of Marketing Joseph A. Campana's strategy of giving Dodge Division a stronger independent identity. At midyear a Rampage car/pickup debuted, based on the 024 design.

1983 DODGE

In the factory sales catalogs, Dodges were billed as "America's Driving Machines." All Omni-based coupes adopted the Charger nameplate this year, dropping the 024 designation. Dodge hoped to attract customers who might recognize the familiar name from the much larger performance-oriented models of the 1970s. A new high-performance Charger model, modified by Carroll Shelby, was aimed at younger buyers. This would be the final season for the rear-drive Mirada. One new model emerged late in 1982: a stretched version of the K-car, called 600. Chrysler's 2.2-liter Trans-4 engine added 10 horsepower this year with a boost to 9.0:1 compression, reworked manifolds, and recalibrated fuel/spark control. Five-speed manual transmission was now standard on 400, optional on Omni/Charger/Aries. A 'Message Center' displayed warning lights indicating door is open or fuel is low, on a car diagram. Electronic Voice Alert, optional on 400 and 600, added audio. The system monitored 11 functions. Galvanized sheet metal panels, pre-coated steel in critical areas, and a seven-step dip-and-spray process improved rust resistance.

1983 Dodge, Omni hatchback sedan (OCW)

OMNI — SERIES Z — FOUR — Appearance of Dodge's subcompact sedan was similar to 1982, but with red (upper) portions of taillamps split into separate side-by-side sections, rather than divided horizontally. Base Omnis were better equipped this year. New standard features included halogen headlamps, reclining bucket seats, a quartz clock, power brakes, and a trip odometer. Standard engine was again the 104.7 cu. in. (1.7-liter four) with four-speed manual transaxle. But a new 1.6-liter four (from Peugeot) took its place at mid-year. Omnis now had standard power front disc/self-adjusting rear drum brakes. Chrysler's pentastar sat in the center of the grille, which had one vertical bar and four horizontal bars forming 10 sections, plus subdued horizontal bars within each section. Amber parking/turn lamps wrapped around onto fenders. A 'Dodge' nameplate was on the left front lip of the hood. At the rear were small amber side reflectors. Omnis had full-length blackout bodyside moldings and new, longer bumper end caps. Interiors held standard reclining cloth-and-vinyl low-back premium bucket seats. All-vinyl buckets were available at no extra cost. Upholstery colors were: red, silver, dark blue/medium blue, or dark brown/beige. Standard equipment included wheel trim rings, a black outside mirror, vanity mirror, luggage compartment light, intermittent wipers, color-keyed four-spoke sport steering wheel, and P175/75R13 GBR tires. Base and Custom sedans were offered; the low-budget Miser was gone. So was the E-Type (Euro-Sedan). Omni Custom had dual reclining high-back sport bucket seats with integral headrests in cloth-and-vinyl (same colors as base model); woodgrain appliqué on instrument panel; wide whitewall GBR tires; deluxe wheel covers; cargo area carpeting and sound insulation. Body colors were: Silver Crystal Coat, Crimson Red, Charcoal Gray metallic, Black, Beige Crystal Coat, Glacier Blue Crystal Coat, Pearl White, and Graphic Red; Custom could also have Sable Brown or Nightwatch Blue. Two-tones (Custom only) were: Silver Crystal Coat/Charcoal Gray metallic; Glacier Blue Crystal Coat/Nightwatch Blue; Beige Crystal Coat/Sable Brown. Options included a new manual five-speed transaxle with 2.20:1 or 2.57:1 performance gear ratio. TorqueFlite automatic was available with the optional 2.2-liter engine. An optional Rallye cluster held a tachometer, trip odometer, quartz clock, alternator gauge, fuel gauge, temp and oil pressure lights, and brake system warning light. An electronic-tuning radio was now available, with or without a cassette player.

1983 Dodge, Charger 2.2 hatchback coupe (OCW)

1983-1/2 Dodge, Shelby Charger hatchback coupe (OCW)

CHARGER/2.2 — SERIES Z — FOUR — A 'Charger' nameplate on wide pillars between the subcompact coupe's side windows demonstrated its name change this year. Coupes came in three levels: base model with standard 1.7-liter four and four-speed manual shift, Charger 2.2 with the Trans-4 engine, and (as a mid-year addition) a new Shelby Charger performance model. The Miser edition was dropped. As with the Omni sedan, a 1.6-liter became the base engine at mid-year. Charger's front end featured a sharply sloped grille that was actually six simple horizontal slots, accompanied by tunneled halogen headlamps. Standard cloth-and-vinyl high-back bucket seats had integral headrests and reclining seatbacks. The back seat folded down. Upholstery colors were red, brown/beige, silver, black, and dark blue/medium blue. All-vinyl was available at no extra cost. A standard Rallye instrument cluster held an alternator gauge, temp/oil pressure warning light, fuel gauge, speedometer, tachometer, trip odometer, and quartz clock. Chargers had a color-keyed four-spoke sport steering wheel and P175/75R13 GBR tires. Body colors were: Glacier Blue Crystal Coat, Charcoal Gray Metallic, Crimson Red, Nightwatch Blue, Beige Crystal Coat, Pearl White, Black, Silver Crystal Coat, Sable Brown, or Graphic Red. Three two-tones were offered:

Black/Burnished Silver metallic; Glacier Blue Crystal Coat/Nightwatch Blue; or Beige Crystal Coat/Sable Brown. Options included the new five-speed manual transaxle, TorqueFlite automatic (which required the 2.2-liter engine), air conditioning (not with 1.6 engine) and a manual sunroof. Charger 2.2 was noticeable by its simulated hood scoop, topped by a large 'Charger 2.2' decal, and simulated front fender exhausters. Additional 'Charger 2.2' graphics in red, black or beige went on bodysides (to rear of door) and rear spoiler, along with black accent trim. Otherwise, appearance was similar to the base Charger, with a six-slot body grille (each slot containing twin vertical elements) topped by 'Dodge' nameplate and deep-set headlamps. Standard engine was the 135 cu. in. (2.2-liter) four with five-speed manual transaxle, with 10 more horsepower this year. Raised white letter low-profile P195/60R14 SBR tires rode 14 in. steel Rallye road wheels. Standard equipment included a performance exhaust (rather loud), firm-feel sport suspension, power brakes, cockpit-like interior with console, dual remote sport mirrors, front storage, and maintenance-free battery. Upholstery came in red, brown/beige, or black. High-back cloth-and-vinyl seats were like the base Charger; all-vinyl optional at no extra cost. Electronic-tuning radios, with or without cassette player, were newly optional. Charger 2.2 body colors were: Graphic Red, Pearl White, Black, Silver Crystal Coat, or Sable Brown. An optional Black graphics package consisted of flat black lower body paint, lower accent stripes on bodysides, and front/rear bumper rub strips. It was available with silver, red or white body color. The heavily reworked Shelby Charger, developed at Santa Fe Springs, California, carried a high-performance 2.2-liter four rated at 107 horsepower. Compression was boosted to 9.6:1, the camshaft revised, and exhaust restriction lessened. Shelby had a blue or silver body with contrasting stripes, a front airdam, rear roof appliqués, rocker-panel (ground effects) extensions, rear lip spoiler, and special paint/tape treatment. Rather than the standard two-section quarter windows, Shelby had a one-piece design. Wide 15 in. aluminum wheels carried 50-series Eagle GT tires. Color-keyed bucket seats had a 'CS' logo. Gas/brake pedals were revised for heel/toe shifting. Five-speed manual shift was standard. So were heavy-duty shocks and higher-rate springs. All this effort paid off, as Shelby Chargers ran a claimed 0-60 mph time of 8.5 seconds.

1983 Dodge, Aries Special Edition two-door sedan with optional landau vinyl roof (OCW)

1983 Dodge, Aries Special Edition station wagon with optional roof rack (OCW)

ARIES — SERIES D — FOUR — Aries, according to the Dodge catalog, was "America's Family Driving Machine.... The car that put America back on the road again." Appearance was just about the same as 1982, including the stand-up pentastar hood ornament, but with new bright metal accents. The grille consisted of five horizontal bars (including top and bottom bars) with 'Dodge' block letters on the body-color header above. Vertical rectangular clear parking lights sat between grille and headlamps, with amber cornering lamps on the outside. Integrated front and rear bumpers were intended to be part of its design, not 'hung' on as an afterthought. Only the wagon remained in the Custom series; sedans came in base or SE trim. Power brakes were now standard. So were brighter, longer-lasting halogen headlamps, as well as self-adjusting rear brakes, a tethered gas cap, and a maintenance-free battery. New optional air conditioning had bi-level cooling to eliminate 'cold zones.' Instrument panels had a new soft cover. A new flasher allowed signaling with headlamps when passing in daylight. Under the hood, the base 2.2-liter OHC engine got a horsepower boost from 84 to 94, to improve acceleration.

That powerplant had chrome valve stems, cobalt alloy valve seats, moly-faced compression rings, and an electric thermo-controlled fan. Optional again was the 2.6-liter from Mitsubishi, on SE models as well as the Custom wagon. A new heater system improved air distribution, and there was a new maintenance-free battery. Four-speed manual transaxle was standard, five-speed overdrive optional. The five-speed used a cable shift linkage rather than the customary rod, which was supposed to shorten lever travel and improve its 'feel.' Three-speed TorqueFlite was standard with the 2.6-liter engine, optional with the 2.2-liter. Rack and pinion steering was power-assisted on the SE wagon. All-vinyl bench seats went in the standard interior, along with carpeted lower door trim panels. SE models had a plush new standard split-back all-cloth bench seat with fold-down center armrest, carpeted door trim panels with detailed wood-tone inserts, and matching woodtone lower instrument panel trim. Two- and four-door sedans had new rear quarter window louvers, bright decklid lower molding, and 'SE' pillar medallion. All SE models carried 10-ounce cut pile carpeting, a digital clock, dome light, cloth-covered headliner, day/night inside mirror, AM radio, and two-speed wiper/washers. SE wagons had woodgrain bodyside and liftgate appliqués. Optional reclining cloth buckets and a center console with free-standing center armrest were available on the SE and Custom wagon. Standard upholstery colors were: brown/beige, dark/medium blue, or red. SE sedans could also have silver. Wagons could have the same colors in saddle vinyl. Upholstery options for base Aries were Kingsley cloth in brown/beige, Madison cloth in dark/medium blue, or red cloth-and-vinyl. Nine body colors were offered: Black, Nightwatch Blue, Charcoal Gray metallic, Pearl White, Silver Crystal Coat, Beige Crystal Coat, Crimson Red, Sable Brown, or Glacier Blue Crystal Coat. Also two-tone Charcoal Gray/Burnished Silver metallic. Three easy-order packages were available, along with a new electronic-tuning stereo radio option.

1983 Dodge, 400 coupe (OCW)

1983 Dodge, 400 convertible (OCW)

400 — SERIES V — FOUR — Only one series was offered in the 400 line this year, as the original LS was dropped. A two-door coupe, four-door sedan and convertible were available again, the latter two having been added during the 1982 model year. A slat-style grille consisted of six wide, bright horizontal bars. Quad headlamps were mounted in separate, deeply recessed housings. Small parking lamps were below the bumper rub strip. Front fenders displayed twin vertical louvers. Bodyside moldings met with bumper strips at front and rear. Coupes had narrow opera windows, while the full vinyl roof on sedans extended to the rear portion of the back door, creating a narrow window shape. New standard equipment included a ram-air heat/vent system with an extra dash vent, tethered gas cap, wide rear bumper guards, self-adjusting rear brakes, and a maintenance-free battery. The ample list also included power brakes and steering, bumper rub strips, digital clock, 2.2-liter Trans-4 engine with electric fan, and halogen high/low beam headlamps. All models also had a pentastar hood ornament, dual horns, day/night mirror, dual outside chrome mirrors, color-keyed vinyl roof surround molding, AM radio, landau (coupe) or full (sedan) padded vinyl roof, and standard vinyl bucket seats with center armrest. Also standard: a two-spoke steering wheel, P185/70R14 SBR whitewall tires, two-speed wipers, deluxe wheel covers, and inside hood release. Bodies held bright moldings for belt, bodyside (with vinyl inserts), decklid, windshield, upper door frame, and drip rail. Convertibles included a console with center armrest, power top, visor vanity mirror, and dual color-keyed remote-control mirrors. The four-door and convertible had standard TorqueFlite transmission; two-doors came with a standard five-speed manual transaxle. The standard sedan interior held a Kimberley cloth bench seat with center armrest,

while the coupe and convertible had low-back vinyl bucket seats with adjustable head restraints and seatback recliners. Body colors were: Black, Crimson Red, Nightwatch Blue, Sable Brown, and Pearl White; plus metallic Charcoal Gray, Beige Crystal Coat, Silver Crystal Coat, and Glacier Blue Crystal Coat. Two-door models could also have a choice of four two-tone paint packages; four-doors, three selections. New options included an Electronic Voice Alert System to augment the standard message center. Also optional: an electronic travel computer cluster, tilt steering, power windows and door locks, air conditioning with new bi-level ventilation, automatic speed control, electronic-tuning AM/FM stereo radio with cassette player, and rear window defroster. Two easy-order packages were available, one for $640 and the other priced over $2,100. A Roadability package included the Sport handling suspension (larger diameter sway bars, firm-feel power steering and special drive ratio) and P185/70R14 Goodyear Eagle GT SBR tires. Dodge's 400 was closely related to Chrysler LeBaron.

1983 Dodge, 600 ES sedan with optional Sport Handling Suspension package (OCW)

600 — SERIES E — FOUR — Yet another front-drive joined the Dodge lineup this year (actually introduced late in 1982), the E-bodied 600 and more sporty 600 ES. According to Dodge, the 600 was a Euro-sport touring car that "begs to be driven." Wheelbase was 3 in. longer than the K-car; 10 in. longer overall. The six-window, four-door sedan was a mate to Chrysler's E-Class. A sculptured hood with pentastar stand-up hood ornament stood behind a grille with six bright horizontal bars, somewhat akin to Mirada and 400. Quad recessed rectangular halogen headlamps were used. Clear parking lights set into an integrated bumper. A wide slot in the front bumper was approximately grille width. Twin front fender louvers appeared just ahead of the front door. Unlike the Aries/400 back window, which was nearly vertical, the 600 version slanted somewhat. The rear end might remind some observers of Mercedes. Chassis and suspension were similar to Aries and 400: Iso-strut front with linkless anti-sway bar and coil springs, and a flex-arm beam rear axle with trailing links and coil springs. Improved power brakes had bigger rotor and caliper assemblies; rear drums were now self-adjusting. An electronic feedback carburetor went on the standard 2.2-liter engine. Standard equipment included power brakes and steering, electric fuel filler door and decklid releases, dual bright mirrors, AM radio, and digital clock. The base 600 came with standard wide-ratio three-speed Torque-Flite; 600 ES carried a standard manual five-speed transaxle. Mitsubishi's 2.6-liter four was optional. An "optical" horn let the driver blink lights when passing. Standard cloth and vinyl bench seats had a folding center armrest and adjustable head restraints. Interiors also held padded door trim panels with cloth and carpet inserts, woodtone bezels, full-length armrests, pull straps, and courtesy lamps. Interior colors were blue, silver, red, and beige. Silver, red or beige vinyl also was available. Also optional: cloth-and-vinyl 50/50 seating with dual armrests and recliners, center consolettes and seatback pockets in blue, silver, red, beige, or brown. Body colors were: Crimson Red, Glacier Blue Crystal Coat, Beige Crystal Coat, Charcoal metallic, and Bright Silver Crystal Coat. The base 600 could also get Pearl White, Sable Brown, Black, or Nightwatch Blue Crystal Coat. Two-tones included Sable Brown/Beige Crystal Coat, Nightwatch Blue/Glacier Blue Crystal Coat, and Black/Silver Crystal Coat. For a more dramatic look, the 600 ES displayed a blackout exterior including black moldings, outside mirrors, bodyside and decklid stripes, and outside door handle inserts. Inside were cloth and vinyl high-back bucket seats with integral head restraints and reclining backs, a center console with freestanding armrest (silver, red or beige), and sport steering

wheel. Standard Electronic Voice Alert monitored 10 conditions: door ajar, brake on, low fuel, belts unbuckled, etc. A Sport Handling Suspension Package consisted of larger front/rear sway bars, higher-control shocks, firm-feel power steering with quicker ratio, and Goodyear SBR Eagle GT tires on aluminum wheels. Two easy-order packages were available, one for around $600 and the other over three times that figure.

DIPLOMAT — SERIES G — SIX/V-8 — Once again, Diplomat arrived only in four-door sedan form, in Salon and Medallion trim levels. Apart from four new body colors available, appearance was similar to 1982, including the same grille and stand-up pentastar hood ornament. The formal-style eight-section grille had cross-hatched segments within each vertical section. Six small squarish sections tapered outward toward the fender edge on each side, to join twin rectangular amber reflectors. 'Dodge' letters stood on the wide upper bar. Quad rectangular headlamps were used. 'Diplomat' insignias were on front fenders, ahead of the door. Standard engine was again the 225 cu. in. (3.7-liter) Slant Six, with 318 cu. in. V-8 optional. Diplomat's Salon included tinted glass, Sherwood woodtone trim on the instrument panel, cloth-and-vinyl bench seat with folding center armrest, power steering/brakes, and three-speed TorqueFlite. Upholstery colors were dark blue, red, beige, or silver. Optional: a beige vinyl bench seat. Medallion offered a more luxurious interior and formal roof styling. 60/40 cloth-and-vinyl seating had a folding center armrest and passenger recliner (dark blue, red, beige or silver), plus dress-up trunk. As for outside trim, Salon had bright windshield, roof drip, belt, sill and wheel opening moldings; bright rear door glass division bar; bumper protective rub strips; and front bumper guards. Medallion added bright upper door frame moldings, a full vinyl roof, and bright vinyl roof termination molding. Body colors were: Nightwatch Blue, Sable Brown, Crimson Red, Pearl White, Charcoal Gray metallic, Formal Black, Glacier Blue Crystal Coat, Beige Crystal Coat, and Silver Crystal Coat. Diplomat, it was said, was aimed at motorists who "couldn't afford to operate one of yesterday's behemoths." Most of its customers, though, were fleet buyers. A total of 13,106 Diplomats (over half the total production) had the Police package.

1983 Dodge, Mirada coupe (simulated convertible roof) with optional CMX package (OCW)

MIRADA — SERIES X — SIX/V-8 — For its final stab at attracting buyers, "America's sporty driving machine" kept the same eye-catching appearance as in 1982, but offered some new body colors. The factory catalog claimed that owning a four-drive Mirada displayed "a clear statement of your personality." The familiar 225 cu. in. (3.7-liter) Slant Six was standard again, 318 cu. in. (5.2-liter) V-8 optional. All Miradas had three-speed TorqueFlite automatic and a "driver-oriented" dash filled with round gauges. Standard equipment included dual horns, inside hood release, color-keyed seat belts, power steering/brakes, and an AM radio. Mirada's chassis was the same as that used on the four-door Diplomat, but the resemblance stopped there. Mirada had a flexible plastic front end. A sculptured hood top merged into the sleek grille with five horizontal bars tipped by thin bright strips; half a dozen vertical bars set well behind. Some observers compared Mirada's grille to that of the 1936-37 Cord. Vertical rectangular amber park/turn lights sat between headlamps and grille. An integrated front bumper held twin wide slots in its center. 'Mirada' block letters were evident at the rear of front fenders; 'CMX' badge (if that package was included) immediately below. Both 'Dodge' and 'Mirada' letters could be seen on the decklid. Trim consisted of bright hood rear edge, fender edge, windshield, drip rail, belt, rear quarter side window, opera window, and rear window moldings; a bright/black wide-louvered up-and-over roof molding; and simulated (angled) front fender louvers. Also standard: bumper rub strips and tinted glass. Standard cloth-and-vinyl high-back bucket seats came in red, beige, dark blue, or silver, Optional cloth-and-vinyl 60/40 seats could be red, beige, dark blue or silver, with folding center armrest and passenger seat recliner. Also optional: leather and vinyl low-back bucket seats with center cushion and folding center armrest, in beige or silver. Body colors were: Glacier Blue Crystal Coat, Beige Crystal Coat, Silver Crystal Coat, Pearl White, Charcoal Gray metallic, Black, Nightwatch Blue, Sable Brown, or Crimson Red. The optional CMX package included a sailcloth-textured vinyl simulated convertible roof; bright touchdown moldings; color-keyed door handle inserts; cloth and vinyl bucket seats with center armrest; premium wheel covers and P205/75R15 SBR WSW tires. A total of 1,841 Miradas had the CMX package, while 638 came with the Sport Equipment package (RPO code A76). Also optional: aluminum road wheels.

1983 Dodge, Diplomat Salon sedan (OCW)

I.D. DATA: Dodge's 17-symbol Vehicle Identification Number (VIN), as before, was on the upper left corner of the instrument panel, visible through the windshield. The first digit indicates Country: '1' U.S.A.; '2' Canada. The second symbol is Make: 'B' Dodge. Third is Vehicle Type: '3' passenger car. The next symbol ('B') indicates manual seatbelts. Symbol five is Car Line: 'Z' Omni/Charger; 'D' Aries; 'E' 600; 'G' Diplomat; 'X' Mirada; 'V' 400. Symbol six is Series (price class): '1' Economy; '2' Low; '4' High'; '5' Premium; '6' Special. Symbol seven is Body Style: '1' 2-dr. sedan; '2' 2-dr. specialty hardtop; '4' 2-dr. hatchback; '5' 2-dr. convertible; '6' 4-dr. sedan; '8' 4-dr. hatchback; '9' 4-dr. wagon. Eighth is the Engine Code: 'A' L498 2Bbl.; 'B' L4105 2Bbl.; 'C' L4135 2Bbl.; 'F' or '8' Shelby L4135 2Bbl.; 'G' L4156 2Bbl.; 'H' L6225 1 Bbl.; 'P' V8318 2Bbl. Next comes a check digit (0-9 or X). Symbol ten indicates Model Year: 'D' 1983. Symbol eleven is Assembly Plant: 'C' Jefferson (Detroit); 'D' Belvidere, IL; 'F' Newark, DE; 'G' or 'X' St. Louis; 'R' Windsor, Ontario. The last six digits make up the sequential serial number, starting with 100001. Engine numbers and Body Code Plates are in the same locations as 1981-82.

OMNI (FOUR)

Model No.	Body/ Style No.	Body Type & Seating	Factory Price	Shipping Weight	Prod. Total
ZE	44	4-dr. Hatch-5P	5841	2165	33,264
ZE	44	4-dr. Hatch-5P	6071	2195	9,290

CHARGER (FOUR)

ZH	24	2-dr. Hatch-5P	6379	2210	22,535

CHARGER 2.2 (FOUR)

ZP	24	2-dr. Hatch-5P	7303	2330	10,448

SHELBY CHARGER (FOUR)

ZS	24	2-dr. Hatch-5P	8290	N/A	8,251

ARIES (FOUR)

DL	21	2-dr. Sedan-6P	6577	2300	14,218
DL	41	4-dr. Sedan-6P	6718	2300	51,783
DH	45	4-dr. Cust Wag-6P	7636	2410	29,228

ARIES SPECIAL EDITION (FOUR)

DH	21	2-dr. Sedan-6P	7260	2310	4,325
DH	41	4-dr. Sedan-6P	7417	2340	8,962
DP	45	4-dr. Sta Wag-6P	8186	2465	4,023

400 (FOUR)

VP	22	2-dr. Cpe-6P	8014	2430	11,504
VP	41	4-dr. Sedan-6P	8490	2480	9,560
VP	27	2-dr. Conv.-4P	12500	2475	4,888

400 Price Note: The convertible's price was cut sharply during the model year, down to $9,995.

600 (FOUR)

EH	41	4-dr. Sedan-6P	8841	2525	21,065
EH	41	4-dr. ES sedan-6P	9372	2540	12,423

DIPLOMAT SALON (SIX/V-8)

GL	41	4-dr. Sedan-6P	8248/8473	3320/3455	21,368

DIPLOMAT MEDALLION (SIX/V-8)

GH	41	4-dr. Sedan-6P	9369/9594	3390/3525	3,076

MIRADA (SIX/V-8)

XS	22	2-dr. HT Cpe-5P	9011/9236	3310/3450	5,597

Factory Price and Weight Note: Prices and weights to left of slash are for six-cylinder, to right for V-8 engine.

Model Number Note: Some sources identify models using the new VIN data to indicate Car Line, Price Class and Body Style. Example: Aries four-door (DL41) has the equivalent number D26, which translates to Aries line, Low price class, and four-door sedan body. See I.D. Data section for breakdown.

ENGINE DATA: BASE FOUR (Omni, Charger): Inline, overhead-cam four-cylinder. Cast iron block; aluminum head. Displacement: 104.7 cu. in. (1.7 liters). Bore and stroke: 3.13 x 3.40 in. Compression ratio: 8.2:1. Brake horsepower: 63 at 4800 R.P.M. Torque: 83 lb.-ft. at 2400 R.P.M. Five main bearings. Solid valve lifters. Carburetor: 2Bbl. Holley 6520. VIN Code: B. BASE FOUR (late Omni, Charger): Inline, overhead-cam four-cylinder. Cast iron block; aluminum head. Displacement: 97.3 cu. in. (1.6 liters). Bore and stroke: 3.17 x 3.07 in. Compression ratio: 8.8:1. Brake horsepower: 62 at 4800 R.P.M. Torque: 86 lb.-ft. at 3200 R.P.M. Five main bearings. Solid valve lifters. Carburetor: 2Bbl. VIN Code: A. BASE FOUR (Charger 2.2, Aries, 400, 600); OPTIONAL (Omni, Charger): Inline, overhead-cam four-cylinder. Cast iron block; aluminum head. Displacement: 135 cu. in. (2.2 liters). Bore and stroke: 3.44 x 3.62 in. Compression ratio: 9.0:1. Brake horsepower: 94 at 5200 R.P.M. (Charger 2.2, 100 at 5200 R.P.M.). Torque: 111 lb.-ft. at 2400 R.P.M. (Charger 2.2, 122 lb.-ft. at 3200 R.P.M.) Five main bearings. Hydraulic valve lifters. Carburetor: 2Bbl. Holley 6520. VIN Code: C. BASE FOUR (Shelby Charger): Same as 135 cu. in. four above, exc. Compression ratio: 9.6:1. Horsepower: 107 at 5600 R.P.M. Torque: 127 lb.-ft. at 3200 R.P.M. VIN Code: F. OPTIONAL FOUR (Aries, 400, 600): Inline, overhead-cam four-cylinder. Cast iron block; aluminum head. Displacement: 156 cu. in. (2.6 liters). Bore and stroke: 3.59 x 3.86 in. Compression ratio: 8.2:1. Brake horsepower: 93 at 4500 R.P.M. Torque: 132 lb.-ft. at 2500 R.P.M. Five main bearings. Solid valve lifters. Carburetor: 2Bbl. Mikuni. Mitsubishi-built. VIN Code: G. BASE SIX (Diplomat, Mirada): Inline, overhead-valve six. Cast iron block and head. Displacement: 225 cu. in. (3.7 liters). Bore and stroke: 3.40 x 4.12 in. Compression ratio: 8.4:1. Brake horsepower: 90 at 3600 R.P.M. Torque: 165 lb.-ft. at 1600 R.P.M. Four main bearings. Hydraulic valve lifters. Carburetor: 1Bbl. Holley 6145. VIN Code: H. OPTIONAL V-8 (Diplomat, Mirada): 90-degree, overhead valve V-8. Cast iron block and head. Displacement: 318 cu. in. (5.2 liters). Bore and stroke: 3.91 x 3.31 in. Compression ratio: 8.5:1. Brake horsepower: 130 at 4000 R.P.M. Torque: 230 lb.-ft. at 1600 R.P.M. Five main bearings. Hydraulic valve lifters. Carburetor: 2Bbl. Carter BBD. VIN Code: P.

CHASSIS DATA: Wheelbase: (Omni) 99.1 in.; (Charger) 96.6 in.; (Aries) 100.1 in.; (400) 100.3 in.; (600) 102.9 in.; (Diplomat/Mirada) 112.7 in. Overall length: (Omni) 164.8 in.; (Chgr) 173.7 in.; (Aries sed) 176.0 in.; (Aries wag) 176.2 in.; (400) 181.2 in.; (600) 187.2 in.; (Diplomat) 205.7 in.; (Mirada) 209.5 in. Height: (Omni) 53.1 in.; (Chgr) 50.8 in.; (Aries 2-dr.) 52.3 in.; (Aries 4-dr.) 52.7 in.; (Aries wag) 52.4 in.; (400 2-dr.) 52.5 in.; (400 4-dr.) 52.9 in.; (400 conv.) 54.1 in.; (600) 53.9 in.; (Diplomat) 55.3 in.; (Mirada) 53.2 in. Width: (Omni) 65.8 in.; (Chgr) 66.7 in.; (Aries) 68.6 in.; (400) 68.5 in.; (600) 68.0 in.; (Diplo) 74.2 in.; (Mirada) 72.7 in. Front Tread: (Omni/Chgr) 56.1 in.; (Aries/400/600) 57.6 in.; (Diplo/Mirada) 60.0 in. Rear Tread: (Omni/Chgr) 55.6 in.; (Aries/400/600) 57.0 in.; (Diplo/Mirada) 59.5 in. Standard Tires: (Omni/Charger/Aries) P175/75R13 GBR; (Charger 2.2) P195/60R14 SBR RWL; (400) P185/70R14; (600) P185/70R14 SBR WSW; (600ES) P185/70R14 SBR RBL; (Diplo/Mirada) P195/75R15 GBR WSW.

TECHNICAL: Transmission: Four-speed manual (floor lever) standard on Omni/Charger w/1.7-liter four. Gear ratios: (1st) 3.45:1; (2nd) 1.94:1; (3rd) 1.29:1; (4th) 0.97:1; (Rev) 3.17:1. Four-speed manual (floor lever) standard on other Omni/Charger and Aries. (1st) 3.29:1; (2nd) 1.89:1; (3rd) 1.21:1; (4th) 0.88:1; (Rev) 3.14:1. Five-speed manual standard on 400 and 600ES, optional on Omni/Charger/Aries: (1st) 3.29:1; (2nd) 1.89:1; (3rd) 1.21:1; (4th) 0.88:1; (5th) 0.72:1; (Rev) 3.14:1. TorqueFlite three-speed automatic standard on other models, optional on all. Front-wheel drive gear ratios: (1st) 2.69:1; (2nd) 1.55:1; (3rd) 1.00:1; (Rev) 2.10:1. Diplomat/Mirada: (1st) 2.74:1; (2nd) 1.54:1; (3rd) 1.00:1; (Rev) 2.22:1. Standard final drive ratio: (Omni/Charger) 2.69:1 w/4-spd, 2.59:1 or 2.20:1 w/5-spd, 2.78:1 w/auto.; (Aries) 2.69:1 w/4-spd, 2.20:1 w/5-spd, 2.78:1 w/auto.; (400) 2.57:1 w/manual, 2.78:1 w/auto.; (400 w/2.6-liter) 2.78:1 or 3.02:1 w/auto.; (600) 2.57:1 w/5-spd, 2.78:1 w/auto., 3.02:1 w/2.6-liter and auto.; (Diplo) 2.94:1 (Mirada six) 2.94:1; (Mirada V-8) 2.26:1. Steering: (Omni/Charger/Aries/400/600) rack and pinion; (others) recirculating ball. Suspension: (Omni/Charger) MacPherson Iso-strut independent coil front w/anti-sway bar, trailing arm semi-independent coil rear w/beam axle and integral anti-sway; (Aries/400/600) Iso-strut front w/coil springs and linkless anti-sway bar, and flex-arm beam rear axle w/trailing links, coil springs and anti-sway bar; (Diplomat/Mirada) transverse front torsion bars and anti-sway bar, semi-elliptic rear leaf springs. Brakes: Front disc, rear drum. Ignition: Electronic. Body construction: Unibody. Fuel tank: (Omni/Chgr/Aries/400/600) 13 gal.; (Diplomat/Mirada) 18 gal.

DRIVETRAIN OPTIONS: Engines: 2.2-liter four: Omni ($134). 2.6-liter four: Aries/400/600 ($259). 318 cu. in., 2Bbl. V-8: Diplomat/Mirada ($225). Transmission and Axle: Five-speed manual trans.: Omni/Chgr, Aries Cust/SE ($75). TorqueFlite auto. trans.: Omni/Aries/400/600 ($439). Performance axle: Omni/Chgr, Aries Cust/SE ($22). Steering and Suspension: Power steering: Omni/Aries ($214). H.D. susp.: Omni 4-dr. ($34); Aries/Diplo ($26); Mirada ($36). Sport susp.: 400 2-dr., 600 ($55). Rear sway bar: Mirada ($36). Other: H.D. battery ($43) exc. Omni/Chgr. H.D. engine cooling ($141). California emission system ($75). High-altitude emission (NC).

OMNI/CHARGER CONVENIENCE/APPEARANCE OPTIONS: Option Packages: Bright exterior accent group: Chgr ($64). Two-tone paint ($134-$155). Light group ($44-$62). Protection group ($125-$181). Cold weather group ($174). Comfort/Convenience: Air cond. ($632). Rear defroster, electric ($127). Automatic speed control ($174). Tinted glass: 4-dr. ($90). Rallye instrument cluster: 4-dr. ($79). Rear wiper/washer: 4-dr. ($117). Mirrors: Dual remote: 4-dr. ($48). Dual sport remote: Chgr ($56). Entertainment: AM radio ($83). AM/FM stereo radio ($109-$192). Electronic-tuning AM/FM stereo ($263-$346); w/cassette ($402-$485). Exterior: Removable glass sunroof: Chgr ($310). Rear spoiler: Chgr ($72). Black vinyl bodyside molding: 4-dr. ($45). Luggage rack: 4-dr. ($93). Interior: Console ($76-$84). Vinyl bucket seats (NC). Center armrest ($46). Tonneau cover: Chgr ($68). Cargo area carpet: Chgr ($41); w/sound insulation, base 4-dr. ($59). Wheels and Tires: Deluxe wheel covers: Chgr (NC). Cast aluminum 14 in. wheels: Chgr ($250-$298). 13-in. Rallye wheels: 4-dr. ($48). 14-in. Rallye wheels: Chgr ($48). P175/75R13 wide WSW: base ($59). P175/75R13 SBR BSW ($54). P175/75R13 SBR wide WSW ($81-$135). P195/60R14 SBR BSW: Chgr ($225). P195/60R14 SBR RWL: Chgr ($310). 2.2 ($85). Conventional spare tire ($63).

ARIES CONVENIENCE/APPEARANCE OPTIONS: Option Packages: Easy-order pkg. A91 ($132-$238); A92 ($761-$1203); A93 ($1607-$1943). Light pkg. ($93-$103). Security pkg. ($687-$810). Comfort/Convenience: Air cond. ($732). Rear defroster ($137). Auto. speed control ($174). Power driver's bucket seat ($210). Power windows ($180-$255). Power door locks ($120-$170). Power decklid/liftgate release ($40). Tinted glass ($105). Luxury steering wheel: base ($40). Tilt steering wheel ($105). Intermittent wipers ($52). Liftgate wiper/washer: wag ($117). Mirrors: Remote left ($22). Dual remote ($66-$88). Lighted vanity, right: Cust/SE ($50). Entertainment: AM radio: base ($78). AM/FM stereo radio ($109-$187). Electronic-tuning AM/FM stereo ($263-$341); w/cassette ($402-$480). Delete AM radio ($56 credit). Exterior: Full vinyl roof: 4-dr. ($172). Padded landau roof: 2-dr. ($177). Two-tone paint: 2-dr. ($176). Door edge protectors ($15-$25). Sill moldings ($23). Bumper guards, front or rear ($28). Bodyside tape stripe ($48). Luggage rack: wag ($106). Special sound insulation ($43). Undercoating ($41). Vinyl lower body protection ($39). Interior: Vinyl bench seat: Cust/SE (NC). Cloth/vinyl bench seat: base ($31). Cloth bucket seats: Cust/SE ($156). Center armrest: Cust/SE ($63). Color-keyed mats: front ($25); rear ($20). Color-keyed seatbelts ($28). Tonneau cover: wag ($68). Trunk dress-up: base ($51). Wheels and Tires: Deluxe 13-in. wheel covers ($52). Luxury 13-in. wheel covers ($47-$99). P175/75R13 GBR wide WSW ($58). P185/70R13 SBR WSW ($194). P185/70R14 SBR wide WSW ($207). Conventional spare tire ($63).

400/600 CONVENIENCE/APPEARANCE OPTIONS: Option Packages: Sport appearance pkg.: 400 ($176-$218). Easy-order pkg. A ($556-$676); B ($1832-$2288). Roadability pkg.: 400 ($123). Protection pkg.: 600 ($64-$120). Comfort/Convenience: Air cond. ($732). Rear defroster ($137-$138). Auto. speed control ($174). Power windows ($180-$255). Power door locks ($120-$170). Power seat ($210). Power decklid release: 400 ($40). Tinted glass ($105). Audible message center ($63). Travel Computer cluster ($206). Sport steering wheel: 400 ($50). Leather-wrapped steering wheel ($50). Tilt steering wheel ($105). Intermittent wipers ($52). Lighting and Mirrors: Cornering lights ($60). Reading lamp: 400 ($24). Dual remote-control mirrors ($57); power ($104-$107). Lighted vanity mirror ($50-$58). Entertainment: AM/FM stereo radio ($109). Electronic-tuning AM/FM stereo ($263); w/cassette ($402). Premium speakers ($126). Radio delete ($56 credit). Exterior: Two-tone paint ($170-$176). Sill moldings ($23). Door edge protectors ($15-$25). Bodyside tape stripe: 400 ($42). Bodyside/deck stripes: 600 ($63). Bumper guards, front or rear ($23-$28). Undercoating ($41). Vinyl lower body protection ($39). Interior: Console: 400 sed ($100). Cloth/vinyl bench seat: 400 cpe (NC). Vinyl bench seat: 600 (NC). Cloth 50/50 bench seat: 600 ($267). Vinyl bucket seats w/dual recliners: 400 sed (NC). Cloth/vinyl bucket seats: 400 cpe/sed ($160). Center armrest: 400 ($59). Color-keyed mats: front ($25); rear ($20). Trunk dress-up ($51). Wheels/Tires: Wire wheel covers ($219). Cast aluminum wheels ($316-$336). Conventional spare tire ($63).

DIPLOMAT CONVENIENCE/APPEARANCE OPTIONS: Option Packages: Basic group ($1101-$1308). Light pkg. ($112-$147). Protection group ($132). Comfort/Convenience: Air conditioning, semi-auto

($787). Rear defroster, electric ($138). Auto. speed control ($174). Power seat, left: Salon ($199). Power windows ($255). Power door locks ($159). Power decklid release ($40). Illuminated entry system ($75). Leather-wrapped steering wheel ($75). Tilt steering wheel ($99). Digital clock ($64). Intermittent wipers ($52). Mirrors: Remote driver's: Salon ($23). Dual remote, chrome ($44-$67). Lighted vanity, right ($61). Entertainment: AM/FM stereo radio ($109). Electronic-tuning AM/FM stereo ($154-$263); w/cassette ($293-$402). Dual front speakers ($28). Premium speakers ($126). Power antenna ($60). Radio delete ($56 credit). Exterior: Power glass sunroof ($1041). Full vinyl roof: Salon ($172). Vinyl bodyside moldings ($57). Upper door frame moldings: Salon ($44). Bodyside/deck/hood stripe ($109). Body sound insulation: Salon ($43). Undercoating ($41). Interior: Vinyl bench seat: Salon ($60). Trunk dress-up: Salon ($54). Wheels/Tires: Premium wheel covers ($94). Wire wheel covers ($257). P205/75R15 SBR WSW ($123). Conventional spare tire ($63).

MIRADA CONVENIENCE/APPEARANCE OPTIONS: Option Packages: CMX pkg. ($982). Basic group ($1048-$1146). Light pkg. ($168). Protection pkg. ($146). Comfort/Convenience: Air cond., semi-auto ($787). Rear defroster, electric ($138). Auto. speed control ($174). Power seat ($199). Power windows ($180). Power door locks ($120). Power decklid release ($40-$58). Illuminated entry system ($75). Leather-wrapped steering wheel ($53). Tilt steering wheel ($99). Digital clock ($64). Intermittent wipers ($52). Lighting, Horns and Mirrors: Cornering lights ($60). Triad horns ($27). Lighted vanity mirror ($61). Entertainment: Same as Diplomat. Exterior: Wheel lip moldings ($30). Sill moldings ($34). Bodyside/hood/deck tape stripes ($98). Undercoating ($41). Interior: Console ($75-$124). Cloth/vinyl 60/40 seat ($217-$266). Leather bucket seats ($549-$598). Center armrest ($49). Trunk dress-up ($48). Wheels and Tires: Forged aluminum wheels ($270-$327). Premium wheel covers ($56). Wire wheel covers ($187-$244). P205/75R15 SBR WSW ($116); Michelins available. P215/70R15 SBR RWL ($66-$193). Conventional spare tire ($63).

HISTORY: Introduced: October 1, 1982. Model year production: Chrysler reported a total of 285,808 passenger cars shipped. Total North American production for the U.S. market of 334,505 units included 304,464 four-cylinder, 9,443 six-cylinder, and 20,598 V-8s. Calendar year production (U.S.): 358,602. Calendar year sales by U.S. dealers: 313,977. Model year sales by U.S. dealers: 309,056 (not incl. 34,701 Colts, 14,735 Challengers and 71 other imports).

HISTORICAL FOOTNOTES: Like Chrysler Corp. as a whole, Dodge enjoyed an ample sales increase for model year 1983, gaining 17 percent. Dodge's newest model, the front-drive 400, showed the greatest gain, up one-third over the 1982 figure. Only the rear-drive Mirada slipped, and it dropped out of the lineup before the '84 model year. Dodge's market share rose to 4.8 percent, which gave it an eighth place ranking. A new assembly plant at Sterling Heights was purchased from Volkswagen of America this year and readied for production of an anticipated H-body compact. Dodges came with a 5-year/50,000-mile powertrain limited warranty (plus outer panel rust-through protection), applicable after the regular 12-month/12,000-mile warranty expired. It had a deductible, though. New Computer-Assisted Design and Manufacturing techniques were being used.

1984 DODGE

Two-door 400 models were renamed 600 this year, joining the four-door of that name (or number). The 400 designation was abandoned. Daytona was the all-new model this year, aimed at the youth market. A 142-horsepower turbocharged engine was a major attraction. The new turbo was also available in the 600 series. Electronic Voice Alert was improved, to deliver more significant comments. Better yet, a shutoff switch in the glovebox allowed drivers who found the comments irritating to eliminate them completely. Later in the year, a fuel-injected 2.2-liter four, standard in the new Daytona, replaced the carbureted version. Mirada was dropped, making Diplomat the only rear-drive Dodge remaining, now available only with the 318 cu. in. V-8 engine. Radios now incorporated electronic tuning.

OMNI — SERIES Z — FOUR — Touted as "the car that started the Dodge revolution," the Omni sedan came in base and step-up SE trim for 1984. Also available was a new GLH package, said to denote an Omni that "goes like h---," carrying a hefty $1,528 price tag. The base model's grille was similar in shape to 1983, but with more and thinner horizontal bars (all black except the two center ones). A pentastar emblem

again went in its center. Omni displayed "Euro-type" blacked-out trim. Inside was a four-spoke sport steering wheel, plus a revised dashboard with gauges that looked easier to read. Unlike the base model, Omni SE had distinct bright door frame, belt, sill and liftgate window moldings, plus bodyside and liftgate moldings, deluxe wheel covers, and a body-color center pillar. SE was described as looking "American" because of its bright moldings and whitewall tires. Body colors were: Black, White, Graphic Red, Nightwatch Blue, Spice metallic, Charcoal metallic, Garnet Red Pearl Coat, and three Crystal Coats: Radiant Silver, Beige, or Glacier Blue. Three two-tones were available. Standard interiors had cloth/vinyl low-back bucket seats with dual recliners and adjustable headrest, and a fold-down back seat. SE held cloth/vinyl high-back bucket seats with dual recliners and integral headrests. The base 1.6-liter four-cylinder engine was offered only with four-speed manual shift. The optional 2.2-liter came with five-speed or automatic. Standard equipment included power brakes, halogen headlamps, intermittent wipers, and a tethered fuel cap. Omni SE had an electronic-tuning AM radio with digital clock. The 110-horsepower high-performance engine, formerly offered only on the Shelby Charger, was now available on all models for $256 extra. A total of 3,285 GLH performance packages (RPO code AGB) were installed on Omnis.

1984 Dodge, Charger 2.2 hatchback coupe (OCW)

1984 Dodge, Shelby Charger hatchback coupe (OCW)

1984 Dodge, Daytona Turbo Z hatchback coupe (OCW)

CHARGER/2.2 — SERIES Z — FOUR — A restyled nose and simpler grille helped give Charger a different look this year. The sharply angled side window at the far rear was gone, leaving "only" two windows on each side for a more conventional appearance. A totally different grille consisted of just two wide slots between new quad rectangular halogen headlamps (formerly dual). Twin side-by-side slots were also evident below the bumper strip, along with parking lamps. A shallow depression in the hood held a laydown pentastar ornament. Grillework patterning to the rear of quarter windows ran back to the hatch, in line with window bases. Wraparound, horizontally-ribbed taillamp lenses held square backup lamps toward the license plate housing at the center. Taillamps also displayed black graphics. 'Dodge' and 'Charger' block lettering, plus a center pentastar, were on the rear panel. Charger 2.2 lost its simulated hood scoop. A 'Charger 2.2' decal (if applicable) was now on the upper quarter panel, where the rearward window used to be. Charger 2.2's quarter panels now looked similar to Shelby's. A new liftgate spoiler was standard on Charger 2.2, optional on the base coupe. Base engine remained the Peugeot 1.6-liter four, with four-speed manual transaxle. Options included the regular 2.2-liter four, as well as the high-performance edition (priced at $256). Power brakes and hatch release were standard, along with a color-keyed four-spoke sport steering wheel. Contoured cloth/vinyl low-back bucket seats had individually adjustable front seatback recliners. A redesigned, full-gauge Rallye instrument cluster included a tachometer and trip odometer. Body colors were: Black, White, Nightwatch Blue, Graphic Red, Charcoal or Spice metallic, Glacier Blue or Beige Crystal Coat, Radiant Silver Crystal Coat, or Garnet Red Pearl Coat. Four two-tones were offered. Shelby Charger's 2.2-liter engine gained a rephased camshaft and a compression boost to 9.6:1, as well as recalibrated electronics. It produced 110 horsepower at 5600 rpm. Overall top gear ratio switched from 2.57:1 to 2.78:1. Shelby added an aerodynamic front airdam, bodyside ground-effect spoilers, and unique "Porsche-like" rear spoiler, which helped produce a drag coefficient of only 0.37. Shelby also had a "free-breathing" exhaust, chrome valve cover, stiffer shocks/springs, 14:1 fast-ratio power steering, and low-profile 50-series Eagle GT speed-rated radial tires on 15-in. cast aluminum wheels. The gas pedal was redesigned for heel-and-toe shifting. Shelby had its own look with single headlamps and a grille made up of two wide slots: one above the bumper rub strip, the other below. The hood sloped downward onto the panel between the headlamps, with pentastar at the center. A 'Shelby' decal went on the bodyside, between door and rear wheel opening. As before, Shelby came only in Radiant Silver with Santa Fe Blue trim (or the reverse combination). High-back bucket seats with dual recliners and integral headrests were upholstered in blue and silver cloth with Shelby logo. This performance edition was named after Carroll Shelby, the famed racing car designer and driver. It cost about $2,000 more than a base Charger. As for performance, Shelby was claimed to go 0-50 mph in 5.5 seconds and do the quarter-mile in under 16 seconds (based on National Hot Road Association testing of an '83 model).

1984 Dodge, Daytona Turbo hatchback coupe (OCW)

DAYTONA — SERIES GV — FOUR — Close kin to Chrysler's new Laser, the sporty new Daytona four-passenger coupe was created to draw youthful, performance-minded buyers. Essentially a variant of the K-car, on a shorter wheelbase and developed as a G24 coupe, Daytona came with either a standard 2.2-liter four-cylinder engine (now fuel injected) or a new turbocharged edition. That was the first front-drive turbo. Rated at 142 horsepower with multi-point fuel injection, the Daytona Turbo still managed an EPA mileage estimate of 22 mpg (35 highway). The base four produced 99 horsepower, with throttle-body fuel injection. Daytona Turbo had a close-ratio five-speed manual transaxle, performance seats, performance handling package, Goodyear Eagle GT tires, and aluminum wheels. It cost nearly $2,000 more than a base Daytona. Stepping up further yet, buyers could choose a Turbo Z. A total of 9,422 of those packages (RPO code AGS) were installed vs. 4,194 for the "plain" Turbo package (code AGT). Turbo Z had two-tone paint and a deep airdam, ground-effects rocker extensions, tape stripes, bodyside moldings, and unique rear spoiler. Chrysler's Laser differed little, but Laser offered no Turbo Z equivalent. Developed by Garrett AIResearch, the turbocharger unit delivered 7.5 psi maximum boost and had a water-cooled turbine end-shaft bearing. Multi-point fuel injection used Bosch injectors at each cylinder. Dished-top pistons cut compression down to 8.0:1. Turbo engines had a detonation sensor and could use no-lead regular gasoline (though premium was recommended). They also had a racier camshaft,

bigger oil pump, 2.5 in. low-restriction exhaust, and tighter internal sealing. Equal-length half-shafts helped reduce torque-steer during acceleration, to improve handling. Turbo dashes held analog gauges. Suspensions used gas-filled shocks, as well as higher spring rates than the Aries line. Turbos included a Performance Handling Package with firmer spring/shock rates, larger stabilizer bars, and 60-series 15-in. tires. Turbo seats also had inflatable lumbar/thigh support bolsters. All Daytonas had a center console, plus bucket seats in front and rear (really tight in the back). Chrysler claimed a 0-60 mph acceleration time of 8.5 seconds or less with turbo and manual shift. Non-turbo Daytonas managed to hit 60 mph in about 10 seconds. Daytona's rivals included Porsche, Camaro/Firebird, and Datsun/Nissan 280ZX.

1984 Dodge, Aries Special Edition two-door sedan (OCW)

ARIES — SERIES D — FOUR — Revisions were modest on Dodge's front-drive compact K-car sedans and wagons, offered in base and SE form (along with a Custom wagon). The new black-accented grille showed a similar pattern of bright horizontal bars, but added a large pentastar in the center instead of the former pentastar stand-up hood ornament. 'Dodge' block letters no longer stood above the grille. Taillamps kept their full-width design with three square sections on each side of the license plate housing, but now had horizontal ribbing (two horizontal strips across each section). Also, backup lenses (alongside the license plate) were larger than before. 'Dodge' and 'Aries' lettering was on the decklid, along with a center pentastar. Wagon taillamps were tri-section vertical wraparound style, with a small backup lens in the bottom section. Standard deluxe wheel covers were new. So was the instrument panel with a full set of gauges, including fuel/temp/voltage indicators and trip odometer. The gas tank grew from 13 to 14 gallons. New standard tires were P175/80R13 all-season steel-belted radial blackwalls. A multi-function control was on the steering column. Body colors this year were: Crimson Red, Pearl White, Nightwatch Blue, and Black; plus Beige, Glacier Blue, Charcoal or Radiant Silver Crystal Coat; or Garnet Red or Mink Brown Pearl Coat. Also available, a pair of two-tones. An all-vinyl bench seat went in the base interior. Aries SE sported an all-cloth split-back front bench seat with fold-down center armrests and adjustable head restraints. Base engine again was the 2.2-liter Trans-4 with two-barrel carburetor. That engine had chrome valve stems, cobalt alloy valve seats, and moly-faced compression rings. A fuel-injected version was anticipated for later in the model year, but failed to materialize. Optional once more was the Mitsubishi-built 2.6-liter four, which gained 8 horsepower as a result of carburetor and ignition recalibration. A four-speed manual transaxle was standard again, with five-speed and TorqueFlite optional. New options included Rallye 13-in. and cast aluminum 14-in. wheels. Low-back cloth bucket seats were available. All radios had electronic-tuning and a built-in digital clock.

1984 Dodge, 600 convertible (OCW)

600 COUPE/CONVERTIBLE — SERIES KV — FOUR — Both the club coupe and convertible in this year's 600 series were actually the 400 models from 1983. Only the four-door sedan (listed next) carried over with the same designation as before. The coupe was promoted for its "classic elegance;" the convertible for "classic styling." The two-door front end looked the same as 1983, with a grille made up of horizontal strips and a wide empty slot below the bumper rub strip. Quad rectangular headlamps were recessed. Parking lamps stood below the bumper strip. Twin vertical fender louvers were standard again. New wide wraparound taillamps each were divided into six side-by-side sections, with backup

lenses at the inner ends, next to the license plate housing. Each was also split horizontally by a divider bar that went all the way across the full width. On the decklid were 'Dodge' and '600' lettering and a center pentastar. The club coupe had a padded formal landau roof and narrow opera windows. Inside were high-back cloth/vinyl bucket seats (same as the 600 ES sedan but without a standard console). Base club coupe and convertible engine was the carbureted 2.2-liter four, but this year a turbocharged version was available, as well as the Mitsubishi-built 2.6-liter four. The 2.6 was offered only with automatic transmission. A five-speed manual transaxle was standard with 2.2-liter coupe engines, but convertibles came only with TorqueFlite. All models had an electronic-tuning AM radio with digital clock, but that unit could be deleted. Halogen headlamps were standard; cornering lamps optional. Inside was a new standard luxury steering wheel; underneath, a larger 14-gallon gas tank. Added to the option list: an illuminated entry system. Body colors were: Black, Crimson Red, Nightwatch Blue, and Pearl White; Garnet Red, Mink Brown or Gunmetal Blue Pearl Coat; Radiant Silver, Beige or Charcoal Crystal Coat. Two two-tones were offered. Not all colors were available on every model. Dodge claimed to have "brought back the American convertible to the American road," offering the lowest-priced ragtop on the domestic market. Convertibles had a wider back seat and tinted glass back window this year, along with new power side (quarter) windows. The soft top had narrower quarters, too. Vinyl low-back bucket seats had dual recliners and console. A visual message center on the dash was standard, as were dual remote color-keyed mirrors. A total of 1,786 ES Turbo convertibles (RPO code AGT) were produced in the 600 series. Not a bad figure, considering that the package cost a whopping $3,378.

1984 Dodge, Omni hatchback sedan (OCW)

600 SEDAN — SERIES E — FOUR — Sedans had a longer wheelbase than the coupe and convertible (103.3 in. vs. 100.3 in.), thus qualifying as mid-sizes rather than compacts. Styling was similar, with the same slatted grille. On the decklid was 'Dodge' and '600' (or '600 ES') lettering, along with the center pentastar. The base sedan was promoted for its "sophistication," the 600ES for performance. Both models had a standard fuel-injected version of the 2.2-liter Trans-4 engine, with both the 2.6-liter and turbo 2.2 optional. The base sedan came with TorqueFlite, whereas the 600ES could have either a five-speed manual or automatic gearbox. Kimberley cloth/vinyl bench seating was standard on the base sedan, with fold-down center armrest and adjustable head restraints. Billed as a "Euro-Sport" touring model, the 600ES came with a standard Sport Handling Suspension Package that included gas-filled shocks and quicker power steering. A standard electronic instrument cluster included self-diagnostics and a distinctive digital tachometer. Blackout styling consisted of black moldings, black dual power remote-control mirrors, and black bodyside stripes. P185/70R14 SBR Goodyear Eagle GT tires with raised black letters rode cast aluminum wheels. Cloth/vinyl high-back bucket seats had integral head restraints and reclining seatbacks. The standard center console included a freestanding center armrest. Dark woodtone accented the instrument panel. Taillamps displayed two horizontal divider bars rather than one. Both 600 sedans had a power decklid release.

1984 Dodge, Diplomat SE sedan with optional wire wheel covers (OCW)

DIPLOMAT — SERIES G — V-8 — Once again, Diplomat proved most popular for fleet applications, since 10,330 Police packages were installed. This year, the familiar Slant Six finally disappeared. Only the 318 cu. in. V-8 was offered, with TorqueFlite three-speed automatic. Two models were available: basic Salon and, added later, a new SE (to replace the former Medallion). Salon appearance was similar to 1983. The grille again consisted of seven vertical bars and a heavy upper header, with a pattern of squares extending outward below the quad rectangular headlamps. Those squares held parking/signal lamps and wrapped around the fenders. A markedly different front end look for the new SE was highlighted by quad park/signal lamps over the quad rectangular headlamps, and a simple bright crossbar grille fronting a black pattern. Each of Diplomat's wide wraparound taillamps were subtly divided into four side-by-side sections, with backup lenses in inner sections alongside the license plate housing. Diplomat featured "classic" squared-off fenders and a formal-look roofline. All-season P205/75R15 wide-whitewall steel-belted radial tires were standard. Body colors were: Crimson Red, Formal Black, Sable Brown, White, and Nightwatch Blue; plus Charcoal Gray, Glacier Blue, Radiant Silver or Beige Crystal Coat. Salon's interior contained a cloth/vinyl bench seat with folding center armrest. SE turned to a cloth/vinyl 60/40 individually-adjustable seat with folding center armrest and passenger recliner. Also inside was a new luxury steering wheel, along with new black velvet-finish instrument panel bezels. An electronic-tuning AM radio with digital clock was now standard. SE Diplomats could have cast aluminum wheels.

I.D. DATA: Dodge's 17-symbol Vehicle Identification Number (VIN), as before, was on the upper left corner of the instrument panel, visible through the windshield. The first digit indicates Country: '1' U.S.A. The second symbol is Make: 'B' Dodge. Third is Vehicle Type: '3' passenger car. The next symbol ('B') indicates manual seatbelts. Symbol five is Car Line: 'Z' Omni/Charger; 'A' Daytona; 'D' Aries; 'E' 600 sedan; 'V' 600 coupe/convertible; 'G' Diplomat. Symbol six is Series (price class): '1' Economy; '2' Low; '4' High; '5' Premium; '6' Special. Symbol seven is Body Style: '1' 2-dr. sedan; '4' 2-dr. hatchback; '5' 2-dr. convertible; '6' 4-dr. sedan; '8' 4-dr. hatchback; '9' 4-dr. wagon. Eighth is the Engine Code: 'A' L498 2Bbl.; 'C' L4135 2Bbl.; 'D' L4135 FI; 'E' Turbo L4135 FI; 'F' or '8' Hi-perf. (Shelby) L4135 2Bbl.; 'G' L4156 2Bbl.; 'P' V8318 2Bbl. Next comes a check digit (0-9 or X). Symbol ten indicates Model Year: 'E' 1984. Symbol eleven is Assembly Plant: 'C' Jefferson (Detroit); 'D' Belvidere, IL; 'F' Newark, DE; 'G' or 'X' St. Louis. The last six digits make up the sequential serial number, starting with 100001. Engine numbers and Body Code Plates are in the same locations as 1981-83.

OMNI (FOUR)

Model No.	Body/ Style No.	Body Type & Seating	Factory Price	Shipping Weight	Prod. Total
ZE	44	4-dr. Hatch-5P	5830	2095	54,584
ZH	44	4-dr. SE Hatch-5P	6148	2120	13,486

CHARGER (FOUR)

ZH	24	2-dr. Hatch-5P	6494	2160	34,763

CHARGER 2.2 (FOUR)

ZP	24	2-dr. Hatch-5P	7288	2305	11,949

SHELBY CHARGER (FOUR)

ZS	24	2-dr. Hatch-5P	8541	2350	7,552

DAYTONA (FOUR)

GVH	24	2-dr. Hatch-4P	8308	2520	21,916

DAYTONA TURBO (FOUR)

GVS	24	2-dr. Hatch-4P	10227	2630	27,431

ARIES (FOUR)

DL	21	2-dr. Sedan-6P	6837	2335	11,921
DL	41	4-dr. Sedan-6P	6949	2340	55,331
DH	45	4-dr. Cust Wag-6P	7736	2430	31,421

ARIES SPECIAL EDITION (FOUR)

DH	21	2-dr. Sedan-6P	7463	2345	4,231
DH	41	4-dr. Sedan-6P	7589	2375	12,314
DP	45	4-dr. Sta Wag-6P	8195	2480	4,814

600 COUPE/CONVERTIBLE (FOUR)

VP	22	2-dr. Cpe-5P	8376	2445	13,296
VP	27	2-dr. Conv.-4P	10595	2530	10,960

600 ES SEDAN (FOUR)

EH	41	4-dr. Sedan-6P	8903	2530	28,646
ES	41	4-dr. ES Sed-5P	9525	2530	8,735

DIPLOMAT SALON (V-8)

GL	41	4-dr. Sedan-6P	9180	3465	16,261

DIPLOMAT SE (V-8)

GP	41	4-dr. Sedan-6P	N/A	N/A	5,902

Model Number Note: Some sources identify models using the VIN data to indicate Car Line, Price Class and Body Style. Example: Aries four-door (DL41) has the equivalent number D26, which translates to Aries line, Low price class, and four-door sedan body. See I.D. Data section for breakdown.

ENGINE DATA: BASE FOUR (Omni, Charger): Inline, overhead-cam four-cylinder. Cast iron block; aluminum head. Displacement: 97.3 cu. in. (1.6 liters). Bore and stroke: 3.17 x 3.07 in. Compression ratio: 8.8:1. Brake horsepower: 64 at 4800 R.P.M. Torque: 87 lb.-ft. at 2800 R.P.M. Five main bearings. Solid valve lifters. Carburetor: 2Bbl. Holley 6520. VIN Code: A. BASE FOUR (Charger 2.2, Aries, 600); OPTIONAL (Omni, Charger): Inline, overhead-cam four-cylinder. Cast iron block; aluminum head. Displacement: 135 cu. in. (2.2 liters). Bore and stroke: 3.44 x 3.62 in. Compression ratio: 9.0:1. Brake horsepower: 96 at 5200 R.P.M. (Charger 2.2, 101 at 5200 R.P.M.) Torque: 119 lb.-ft. at 3200 R.P.M. (Charger 2.2, 124 lb.-ft. at 3200 R.P.M.) Five main bearings. Hydraulic valve lifters. Carburetor: 2Bbl. Holley 6520. VIN Code: C. BASE FOUR (Shelby Charger); OPTIONAL (Omni, Charger): Same as 135 cu. in. four above, exc. Compression ratio: 9.6:1. Brake horsepower: 110 at 5600 R.P.M. Torque: 129 lb.-ft. at 3600 R.P.M. VIN Code: F. BASE FOUR (Daytona, 600 sedan): Same as 135 cu. in. four above, but with electronic fuel injection. Brake horsepower: 99 at 5600 R.P.M. Torque: 121 lb.-ft. at 3200 R.P.M. VIN Code: D. TURBOCHARGED FOUR; BASE (Daytona Turbo); OPTIONAL (Daytona, 600): Same as 135 cu. in. four above, with electronic fuel injection and turbocharger. Compression ratio: 8.0:1. Brake horsepower: 142 at 5600 R.P.M. Torque: 160 lb.-ft. at 3200 R.P.M. VIN Code: E. OPTIONAL FOUR (Aries, 600): Inline, overhead-cam four-cylinder. Cast iron block; aluminum head. Displacement: 156 cu. in. (2.6-liters). Bore and stroke: 3.59 x 3.86 in. Compression ratio: 8.7:1. Brake horsepower: 101 at 4800 R.P.M. Torque: 140 lb.-ft. at 2800 R.P.M. Five main bearings. Solid valve lifters. Carburetor: 2Bbl. Mikuni, Mitsubishi-built. VIN Code: G. BASE V-8 (Diplomat): 90-degree, overhead valve V-8. Cast iron block and head. Displacement: 318 cu. in. (5.2 liters). Bore and stroke: 3.91 x 3.31 in. Compression ratio: 8.5:1. Brake horsepower: 130 at 4000 R.P.M. Torque: 235 lb.-ft. at 1600 R.P.M. Five main bearings. Hydraulic valve lifters. Carburetor: 2Bbl. Carter BBD. VIN Code: P. POLICE V-8 (Diplomat): Same as 318 cu. in. V-8 above, with 4Bbl. Carter TQ 9295 carburetor. Brake horsepower: 165 at 4000 R.P.M. Torque: 240 lb.-ft. at 2000 R.P.M.

CHASSIS DATA: Wheelbase: (Omni) 99.1 in.; (Charger) 96.6 in.; (Daytona) 97.0 in.; (Aries/600) 100.3 in.; (600 sedan) 103.3 in.; (Diplomat) 112.7 in. Overall Length: (Omni) 164.8 in.; (Chgr) 174.8 in.; (Daytona) 175.0 in.; (Aries) 176.0 in.; (600) 179.5 in.; (600 sedan) 187.4 in.; (Diplomat) 205.7 in. Height: (Omni) 53.0 in.; (Chgr) 50.8 in.; (Daytona) 50.3 in.; (Aries 2-dr.) 52.3 in.; (Aries 4-dr.) 52.7 in.; (Aries wag) 52.4 in.; (600 cpe) 52.6 in.; (600 conv.) 54.1 in.; (600 sedan) 52.9 in.; (Diplomat) 55.3 in. Width: (Omni) 66.2 in.; (Chgr) 66.7 in.; (Aries) 68.6 in.; (Daytona) 69.3 in.; (600) 68.5 in.; (600 sed) 68.3 in.; (Diplo) 74.2 in. Front Tread: (Omni/Chgr) 56.1 in.; (Aries/Daytona/600) 57.6 in.; (Diplo) 60.0 in. Rear Tread: (Omni) 55.6 in.; (Chgr) 55.9 in.; (Aries/600) 57.0 in.; (Daytona) 57.2 in.; (Diplo) 59.5 in. Standard Tires: (Omni/Charger) P165/80R13 SBR; (Charger 2.2) P195/60R14 SBR RBL; (Shelby) P195/50R15 SBR RBL; (Daytona) P185/70R14; (Aries) P175/80R13 SBR; (600) P185/70R14 SBR; (600ES) P185/70R14 SBR RBL; (Diplomat) P205/75R15 SBR WSW.

TECHNICAL: Transmission: Four-speed manual (floor lever) standard on Omni/Charger and Aries: (1st) 3.29:1; (2nd) 1.89:1; (3rd) 1.21:1; (4th) 0.88:1; (Rev) 3.14:1. Five-speed manual standard on 600 two-door and Daytona, optional on Omni/Charger/Aries: (1st) 3.29:1; (2nd) 2.08:1; (3rd) 1.45:1; (4th) 1.04:1; (5th) 0.72:1; (Rev) 3.14:1. Torque-Flite three-speed automatic standard on Diplomat, optional on all other models. Diplomat gear ratios: (1st) 2.74:1; (2nd) 1.54:1; (3rd) 1.00:1; (Rev) 2.22:1. Other models: (1st) 2.69:1; (2nd) 1.55:1; (3rd) 1.00:1; (Rev) 2.10:1. Standard final drive ratio: (Omni/(Charger) 2.69:1 w/4-spd, 2.20:1 w/5-spd, 3.02:1 w/auto.; (Omni/Chgr w/H.O. 2.2-liter) 2.78:1 w/5-spd; (Daytona) 2.57:1 w/5-spd, 3.22:1 w/auto.; (Aries) 2.69:1 w/4-spd, 2.20:1 w/5-spd, 2.78:1 or 3.02:1 w/auto.; (600) 2.57:1 w/5-spd, 3.02:1 w/auto.; (Diplo) 2.26:1. Steering: (Diplomat) recirculating ball; (others) rack and pinion. Suspension: (Omni/Chgr) MacPherson Iso-strut independent coil front w/anti-sway bar, trailing arm semi-independent coil rear w/beam axle and integral anti-sway; (Daytona) Iso-strut front w/anti-sway bar, rigid rear axle w/radius arms and track bar; (Aries/600) MacPherson Iso-strut front w/coil springs and linkless anti-sway bar, flex-arm beam rear axle w/trailing links and transverse track bar; (Diplomat) transverse front torsion bars and anti-sway bar, semi-elliptic rear leaf springs. Brakes: Front disc, rear drum. Ignition: Electronic. Body construction: Unibody. Fuel tank: (Omni/Chgr) 13 gal.; (Daytona/Aries/600) 14 gal.; (Diplomat) 18 gal.

DRIVETRAIN OPTIONS: Engines: 2.2-liter four: Omni/Chgr ($134). Hi-perf. 2.2-liter four: Omni/Chgr ($256); Chgr 2.2 ($122). Turbocharged 2.2-liter four: base Daytona ($934); 600 ($610). 2.6-liter four: Aries/600 ($271). Transmission and Axle: Five-speed manual trans.: Omni/Chgr, Aries Cust/SE ($75). TorqueFlite auto. trans.: Omni/Chgr/Daytona/Aries, 600 Cpe/ES ($439). High-altitude axle: Omni/Chgr/Aries ($22). Steering and Suspension: Power steering: Omni/Chgr/Daytona, 600 conv. ($219). H.D. susp.: Omni 4-dr. ($36); Aries wag, Diplo ($26). Sport handling susp.: 600 ($57) exc. conv. ($276). Other: H.D. battery: Aries/600/Diplo ($44). H.D. engine cooling: Omni/Chgr/Aries/600 ($141). California emission system ($99).

OMNI/CHARGER CONVENIENCE/APPEARANCE OPTIONS: Option Packages: GLH pkg.: base Omni ($1528). Light group ($38-$57). Protection group ($88-$144). Cold weather group ($180). Comfort/Convenience: Air cond. ($643). Rear defroster, electric ($132). Automatic speed control ($179). Tinted glass: Omni ($95). Rallye instrument cluster: Omni ($121). Rear wiper/washer: Omni ($120). Mirrors: Dual remote: Omni ($49). Dual black remote: Chgr ($57). Electronic-tuning radios: AM: base ($113). AM/FM stereo ($125-$238). Seek/scan AM/FM stereo w/cassette ($264-$502). Exterior: Removable glass sunroof: Chgr ($315). Rear spoiler: base Chgr ($72). Pearl Coat paint ($40). Two-tone paint ($151) exc. base Omni. Black vinyl bodyside molding: Omni ($45). Luggage rack: Omni ($100). Interior: Console ($79-$88). Low-back vinyl bucket seats: SE/Chgr (NC). High-back vinyl bucket seats: base Omni (NC). High-back cloth bucket seats: Chgr ($65). Center armrest ($48). Tonneau cover: Chgr ($69). Cargo area carpet ($43-$62). Wheels/Tires: Cast aluminum 14-in. wheels: Chgr ($305); 2.2 ($255). 13-in. Rallye wheels ($50) exc. 2.2/Shelby. P165/80R13 SBR WSW: base ($59). P195/60R14 SBR RWL: base Chgr ($286); 2.2 ($22). P195/60R14 SBR RWL w/sport susp.: base Chgr ($308). Conventional spare tire ($63-$93).

DAYTONA CONVENIENCE/APPEARANCE OPTIONS: Option Packages: Turbo pkg.: base ($934). Turbo Z pkg.: Turbo model ($1277). Basic group ($1294-$1319). Cargo trim/quiet sound group: base ($154). Light group: base ($97). Comfort/Convenience: Air cond. ($737). Rear defroster ($143-$168). Auto. speed control ($179). Electronic navigator ($272). Electronic voice alert ($66). Power driver's seat ($215). Power windows ($185). Power door locks ($125). Illuminated entry system ($75). Tinted glass ($110). Tilt steering wheel ($110). Liftgate wiper/washer ($120). Dual power remote mirrors: base ($48). Electronic-tuning radios: AM/FM stereo: base ($125). Seek/scan AM/FM stereo ($160-$285); w/cassette ($299-$424). Premium speakers ($126). Delete radio ($56 credit). Exterior: Removable glass sunroof ($322). Thin black bodyside molding: base ($55). Interior: Low-back vinyl bucket seats: base (NC). Low-back cloth/vinyl bucket seats w/adjustable driver's lumbar/thigh support: base ($362). Low-back leather bucket seats w/adjustable driver's lumbar/thigh support: base ($929); Turbo ($567). Front/rear mats ($45). Wheels/Tires: Aluminum wheels: base ($316). P185/70R14 RBL: base ($62); Turbo (NC). P185/70R14 RWL: base ($22-$84).

ARIES CONVENIENCE/APPEARANCE OPTIONS: Option Packages: Easy-order pkg. AAA ($130-$243); AAB ($795-$1235); AAC ($1594-$1947). Light pkg. ($70-$108). Comfort/Convenience: Air cond. ($737). Rear defroster ($143). Auto. speed control ($179). Power driver's bucket seat: Cust/SE ($215). Power windows ($185-$260). Power door locks ($125-$175). Power decklid/liftgate release ($40). Tinted glass ($110). Tilt steering wheel ($110). Intermittent wipers ($53). Liftgate wiper/washer: wag ($120). Mirrors: Remote left ($24). Dual remote ($88). Electronic-tuning radios: AM: base ($113). AM/FM stereo ($125-$238). Seek/scan AM/FM stereo: Cust/SE ($250); w/cassette ($389). Delete AM radio ($56 credit). Exterior: Full vinyl roof: SE 4-dr. ($179). Padded landau roof: 2-dr. ($184). Two-tone paint ($186). Pearl Coat paint ($40). Sill moldings ($26). Bumper guards, front/rear ($56). Bodyside tape stripe ($48). Luggage rack: wag ($106). Special sound insulation ($43). Undercoating ($43). Interior: Vinyl bench seat (NC). Cloth/vinyl bench seat: base ($31). Cloth bucket seats: Cust/SE ($161). Color-keyed mats ($45). Trunk dress-up: SE ($51). Wheels/Tires: Wire wheel covers, 14 in.: Cust/SE ($263). Luxury wheel covers, 13 in. ($48). Rallye wheels, 13 in. ($60). Cast aluminum wheels, 14 in.: Cust/SE ($370). P175/80R13 WSW ($58). P185/70R14 SBR wide WSW ($143). Conventional spare tire ($73-$83).

600 CONVENIENCE/APPEARANCE OPTIONS: Extra-cost option packages: 600 ES Turbo convertible ($3378). Easy-order pkg. A ($530-$710); B ($1570-$2013). Comfort/Convenience: Air cond. ($737). Rear defroster ($143). Auto. speed control ($179). Power windows ($185-$260). Power door locks ($125-$175). Power seat ($215). Power decklid release: 2-dr. ($40). Illuminated entry system ($75). Tinted glass ($110). Electronic voice alert ($66). Leather-wrapped steering wheel ($50). Tilt steering wheel ($110). Intermittent wipers ($53). Lighting and Mirrors: Cornering lamps ($60). Dual remote-control mirrors ($59); power ($82-$107). Lighted vanity mirror ($58). Electronic-tuning radios: AM/FM stereo ($125). Seek/Scan AM/FM stereo ($285); w/cas-

sette ($139-$424). Premium speakers ($126). Radio delete ($56 credit). Exterior: Two-tone paint ($232). Pearl Coat paint ($40). Vinyl bodyside moldings ($55). Door edge protectors: sed ($25). Bodyside tape stripe ($45). Bumper guards ($56). Undercoating ($43). Interior: Cloth/vinyl bench seat: cpe (NC). Vinyl bench seat: sed (NC). Cloth 50/50 bench seat: sed ($278). Center armrest: cpe ($61). Color-keyed mats: front, conv. ($25); front/rear, others ($45). Trunk dress-up ($51). Wheels/Tires: Wire wheel covers, locking ($266). Cast aluminum wheels ($370). P185/70R14 SBR WSW: conv. ($58). Conventional spare tire ($83).

DIPLOMAT CONVENIENCE/APPEARANCE OPTIONS: Option Packages: Basic group ($1129-$1351). Light pkg. ($118-$153). Protection group ($133). Comfort/Convenience: Air conditioning, semi-auto ($792). Rear defroster, electric ($143). Auto. speed control ($179). Power seat, left: SE ($215). Power windows ($260). Power door locks ($175). Power decklid release ($40). Illuminated entry system ($75). Leather-wrapped steering wheel ($60). Tilt steering wheel ($110). Intermittent wipers ($53). Mirrors: Remote driver's: Salon ($24). Dual remote, chrome ($67). Lighted vanity, right ($58). Electronic-tuning radios: AM/FM stereo ($125). Seek/scan AM/FM stereo ($125-$250); w/cassette ($264-$389). Premium speakers ($126). Power antenna ($60). Radio delete ($39 credit). Exterior: Power glass sunroof ($1041). Full vinyl roof: Salon ($185). Vinyl bodyside moldings ($57). Upper door frame moldings: Salon ($46). Bodyside/deck/hood stripe: Salon ($109). Body sound insulation: Salon ($66). Undercoating ($43). Interior: Vinyl split-back bench seat: Salon ($60). Trunk dress-up ($57). Wheels/Tires: Premium wheel covers ($96). Wire wheel covers ($215-$263). Cast aluminum wheels: SE ($262). Conventional spare tire ($93).

HISTORY: Introduced: October 2, 1983. Model year production: Chrysler reported a total of 375,513 passenger cars shipped. Calendar year production: 465,885. Calendar year sales by U.S. dealers: 369,255. Model year sales by U.S. dealers: 353,954 (not incl. 35,113 Colts, 1,424 Challengers, 3,341 Conquests and 7,672 Colt Vistas).

HISTORICAL FOOTNOTES: Prices rose less than 2 percent (average) as the 1984 model year began, though Aries jumped by 10 percent. On the other hand, the 600 convertible enjoyed a 12 percent price cut. Though full-size models were gaining renewed popularity, Dodge no longer had any such models to compete with. Diplomat, Dodge's largest model, sold mainly to police and taxi fleets. Model year sales edged over 400,000 this time, marking a 12 percent gain over 1983 (including import sales of four Mitsubishi models, which fell slightly). The new Daytona was a strong seller, arriving as an early 1984 model and finding over 42,000 buyers. Aries sales dropped 12 percent, though. On the import scene, a new Conquest replaced the Challenger, and there was a new Colt Vista wagon. Also new this year was the Caravan minivan. Nearly 70 percent of '84 Daytonas carried one of the turbo packages, helping to make Chrysler the leader in turbo sales among domestic producers. The 600 convertible sold fairly well too, though not as strongly as Chrysler's LeBaron version (or Ford's Mustang ragtop). Dodge/Chrysler's CAFE rating was right in line with government standards. The financial picture looked good too, with impressive earnings to offset those huge losses of a few years earlier. In October 1984, NHTSA launched an investigation into alleged stalling problems with various engines used in the Omni, Aries and 400: a total of 2.7 million Chrysler-built cars built between 1978 and 1984. Up to that point, Chrysler's recall record had been better than either General Motors or Ford.

1985 DODGE

"The revolution continues." So proclaimed Dodge's sales catalog, at any rate, as an all-new H-bodied Lancer joined the lineup. Similar to Chrysler's new LeBaron GTS, Lancer was built at the Sterling Heights, Michigan, plant. The turbocharged four-cylinder engine, with four more horsepower than before, was now standard on Shelby Charger and optional on several models. A new electronic wastegate control varied maximum turbo boost from 7.2 to 9.0 psi. The close-ratio five-speed manual gearbox got a revised dual-rail selector mechanism. Omni/Charger, Aries, and 600 all had dual-path Iso-strut front suspensions with a linkless anti-sway bar. Daytona also had the dual-path Iso-struts, while the new Lancer used gas-charged struts and shocks. A number of items left the option lists, either becoming standard or dropping out completely. Ultimate Sound stereo systems with cassette player became optional, with provision for AM stereo as well as FM stereo reception. Model numbering now included a prefix letter to indicate body type.

1985 Dodge, Omni hatchback sedan with optional GLH package (OCW)

OMNI — SERIES LZ — FOUR — Not much changed on the Omni four-door hatchback. As before, base Omnis featured Euro-inspired blackout trim, while the SE sported bright metal trim. Standard engine was again the Peugeot-built 1.6 four with four-speed manual transaxle. "No more Mr. nice guy" was how Dodge described the performance-oriented Omni GLH. "This ferocious contender," it was said, "qualifies as one of the fastest production cars in America." Rather than being priced as an option, as in 1984, Omni GLH was given an actual list price of $7,620 (over $1,600 higher than base Omni). A total of 6,513 Omnis had the GLH package (RPO code AGB). Equipped somewhat like the Shelby Charger, GLH came with a high-output 110-horsepower 2.2-liter engine and five-speed manual gearbox, black grille and trim, airdam, sill spoilers, foglamps, and aluminum wheels. GLH could also have the turbocharged 2.2 engine.

1985 Dodge, Shelby Charger hatchback coupe (OCW)

CHARGER/2.2 — SERIES LZ — FOUR — Three versions made up the Charger series again: base Charger with standard 1.6-liter four, Charger 2.2 with the high-performance 2.2-liter engine (formerly in Shelby), and Shelby Charger, now carrying the turbocharged 2.2-liter. Styling of the standard Charger was the same as in 1984. Three body colors were new, as was one interior trim color. A four-speed transaxle remained standard in the base model. Low-back Embassy cloth bucket seats had individually adjustable front seatback recliners. Charger had a four-spoke sport steering wheel and Rallye full-gauge instrument cluster. Deluxe 13-in. wheel covers were new. So was a shift indicator on manual-gearbox models (except with turbo engine). In addition to the 110-horsepower engine and standard five-speed transmission, Charger 2.2 revealed a bold new look with fresh graphics. Charger 2.2 lost its wide bodyside moldings, but now had a performance-look airdam and fender extensions, plus side sill ground-effect spoilers. Rallye wheels were standard, with cast aluminum 14-in. wheels a new option. 'Charger 2.2' lettering no longer appeared to the rear of the quarter window, but as a portion of bodyside striping, just to rear of the door. A 'Charger 2.2' decal was also on the hatch, as part of its striping. Otherwise, appearance was similar to 1984. A Sun-Sound-Shade discount package included a removable sunroof with vinyl storage bag, black rear window louvers, and electronic-tuning AM/FM stereo radio with digital clock. "Awe-inspiring" was Dodge's description of the Shelby Charger, now powered by a 2.2-liter four with Garrett AIResearch T3 turbocharger that delivered boost up to 8.0 psi. Appearance was about the same as 1984, but with 'Turbo' lettering on the side of the hood's bulge as well as hood louvers. The 146-horsepower engine had Chrysler/Bosch multi-point fuel injection. Shelby had a performance-geared close-ratio five-speed (overdrive) transaxle, 2.57:1 overall top gear ratio, gas-charged front struts and rear shocks, bigger rear drum brakes, and new standard P205/50VR15 speed-rated steel-belted radial tires. Premium high-back bucket seats displayed an embroidered Shelby logo. A Rallye instrument cluster held a 7000 rpm tachometer and trip odometer. Shelby's wider gas pedal was positioned for heel/toe shifting. Shelby now carried a standard AM/FM stereo radio (formerly AM). Body colors this year were: Black, Ice Blue, Cream, Gold Dust, Radiant Silver, Spice or White Crystal Coat; Charcoal or Garnet Red Pearl Coat. Three two-tones were available. Shelby Charger expanded to four two-tone combinations: Santa

Fe Blue and Radiant Silver Crystal Coat (or vice versa), Black and Radiant Silver Crystal Coat, or Garnet Red pearl and Radiant Silver Crystal Coat. Charger's interior contained cloth/vinyl low-back bucket seats with reclining seatbacks, in charcoal/silver, blue, red or tan. Shelby had high-back full-contour premium bucket seats with integral head restraints, reclining seatbacks, and increased lateral support. Shelby upholstery came in blue/silver or charcoal/silver.

DAYTONA — SERIES GV — FOUR — Dodge's sporty hatchback coupe, with a distinctive wraparound rear spoiler, bodyside rocker panel extensions, molded front airdam and aircraft-style doors, was touted as "the ultimate moving experience." As in 1984, Daytona came in three versions: base, Turbo, and Turbo Z. Rather than being priced merely as an option package, Turbo Z was given its own list price this year, over $1,300 higher than the standard Daytona Turbo. Changes this year included a switch to wider (P205/60HR15) raised black-letter tires for the Turbo, a slightly more powerful turbo 2 2-liter engine, modified dual-rail shift linkage, and two new body colors. A new body-color three-piece wraparound rear spoiler, similar to that used on the '84 Turbo Z, now appeared on all Daytonas. Fuel filler door and hatch releases moved from the console glovebox to the sill alongside the driver's seat. Newly optional: an Ultimate Sound stereo system with graphic equalizer. As for performance, a Turbo four could match many six and V-8 coupes. A standard Graphic Message Center showed an incandescent display. Base Daytonas carried an AM radio; Turbos an AM/FM stereo and leather-wrapped steering wheel. Turbos also had black hood louvers and a handling suspension, plus cast aluminum 15-in. wheels, while base Daytonas rode P185/70R14 tires on 14-in. wheels. Turbo Z added a distinctive wraparound rear spoiler, lower body ground effects and specially-molded front airdam. The Turbo Z package featured a unique front fascia and rear fascia that wrapped to wheel openings; integrated wide black bodyside moldings; black headlamp surround moldings; black bumper rub strips; front fascia extension; subtle accent tape striping; Turbo Z decal; dual electric aero-style remote mirrors; and rear sunvisors. Daytonas came in Black Crystal Coat or a choice of 10 Pearl Coat and Crystal Coat two-tone combinations. Turbo Z came only in Black or two two-tone possibilities. Standard Daytona interior had cloth low-back bucket seats with reclining seatbacks and adjustable head restraints in black, red, silver/charcoal, or light/medium tan. Turbo model enthusiast driver's seats, with adjustable (pneumatic) lumbar and thigh support, were available in Corinthian leather as well as cloth. Turbos got much of the attention, but the base Daytona came with a standard fuel-injected 2.2-liter four. A new system retarded spark knock in one or more cylinders, instead of all four at once. A total of 8,023 Daytonas were reported to have the Turbo Z package (code AGS), while 3,539 had the Electronic Features Package I (code ADM) and 391 had the T-Bar roof package.

ARIES — SERIES KD — FOUR — A wider grille tapered inward at its base, helped give Aries a much different front-end look in its first major facelift. Simple bright crossbars covered a subdued black pattern, with center pentastar emblem. Billed as having new "sweeping curves and softened lines," Aries' basic shape remained close to 1984, though truly more rounded with a slightly longer nose and higher deck. Plastic halogen headlamps had integral turn signals. Wraparound amber lenses served as parking lamps, without the separate park lamps next to the grille as in 1984. Prior tri-section full-width taillamps changed to five sections this year, with backup lenses at the inner ends, and new wraparound sections at the outside. As before, though, two horizontal ribs ran across each lens panel. Rear side marker lenses were now part of the bodyside molding, no longer separate as in 1984. New black bodyside moldings were integrated (continuous) with bumper rub strips. Bright moldings now surrounded the entire side-window segment, while each window held black moldings. Also new were soft bumper coverings, black headlamp bezels, hood and decklid. Inside, a new soft padded cover topped the instrument panel. A new flat-face climate control panel eliminated protruding buttons, and door panels held new map pockets. The Custom wagon was dropped, but a whole new top-rung LE (Luxury Edition) series was added: sedans and the wagon. Aries gained standard equipment and more black trim this year. SE added an AM radio and intermittent wipers. LE added black sill moldings, wide black bodyside moldings with argent stripe, and a trunk light. Wire wheel covers left the option list, as did vinyl roofs. Added to that list were electronic-tuning radios with AM stereo, reclining bucket seats with full-length console, and a heavy-duty suspension with gas-filled shocks. Base engine was the 2.2-liter four, with 2.6-liter optional. An electronic feedback carburetor was used. A four-speed manual transaxle was standard; five-speed and TorqueFlite available. Manual-shift models had a new upshift indicator light. Aries colors were: Black, Ice Blue, Nightwatch Blue, Cream, Gold Dust, Crimson Red, Radiant Silver, or White Crystal Coat; Gunmetal Blue, Mink Brown, or Garnet Red Pearl Coat. Base interiors held an all-vinyl bench seat with adjustable head restraints (split-back on two-door sedan). Aries LE and SE had cloth split-back bench seating with folding center armrest.

1985 Dodge, Lancer hatchback sedan (OCW)

1985 Dodge, Lancer ES hatchback sedan with optional Sport Handling Suspension package (OCW)

LANCER — SERIES HD — FOUR — Dodge's new hatchback six-window, four-door aero-styled touring sedan rode a 103.1-in. wheelbase, just a trifle shorter than the 600 sedan. Described as a "world-class automotive achievement," Lancer featured a front airdam, flush windshield and liftback glass, sloping hood with available (functional) turbo louvers, plus black bumper strips and bodyside moldings. Doors were aircraft-style (extending slightly into the roof), and the aerowrap windshield displayed a sharp 58-degree slant. Lancer had a black crossbar grille, as opposed to the bright vertical-bar grille used on the similar H-bodied Chrysler LeBaron GTS. Two trim levels were offered: base and ES. Standard engine was the fuel-injected 2.2-liter four, with turbocharged edition optional. With that option came a 'Turbo' nameplate on front fenders. A close-ratio five-speed gearbox was standard. TorqueFlite three-speed automatic was available with either engine. Remote cable releases operated the liftback and fuel door. Base Lancer dashboards held a Graphic Message Center and mechanical (analog) instrument cluster. La Corde II cloth upholstered, contoured low-back bucket seats had back wings and reclining seatbacks. Standard equipment also included power brakes, soft-fascia bumpers, warning chimes, side window demisters, tethered gas cap, halogen quad headlamps, bi-level Ram Air heater, front-door map pockets, driver's remote aero-style mirror, and a day/night inside mirror. Lancer had bright-edge belt moldings, narrow black bodyside moldings with bright edge, black windshield molding, multi-function steering column lever, AM/FM stereo radio with digital clock, power rack and pinion steering, and two-speed wipers. The padded instrument panel had an integral console. A heel-and-toe gas pedal went into manual-shift models. The road touring suspension used nitrogen-charged front dual-path Iso-struts and rear shocks, with front/rear anti-sway bars and rear track support bar. P185/70R14 steel-belted radial tires were standard. Lancer's sportier ES added a black front airdam with black trim and bodyside moldings, along with both bodyside and liftback accent stripes. Sport bucket seats had reclining seatbacks; standard cloth, or available Corinthian leather. Seats offered adjustable lumbar and thigh support. A 60/40 split-back rear seat contained integral headrests. An electronic instrument cluster included fluorescent displays for digital speedometer/odometer/trip odometer, plus graphic flashing tachometer and graphic gauges. ES also had a Euro-sport steering wheel, P195/70R14 raised black-letter tires on styled steel wheels, sport handling suspension, black upper door frame and pillar appliqué tape, black sill moldings, time-delay headlamp switch, and courtesy lights. All paints were Crystal Coat or Pearl Coat. Lancer colors were: Black, Ice Blue,

Nightwatch Blue, Cream, Gold Dust and Radiant Silver Crystal Coat; Gunmetal Blue, Desert Bronze, Mink Brown and Garnet Red Pearl Coat. Three two-tone combinations were offered. Two "Sport Handling" suspension packages were available. The standard one, installed on 992 cars, included P185/70R14 all-season Goodyear Vector or Michelin XA4 tires. A Premium version added full electronic instrument cluster, rear headrests, and 60/40 fold-down rear seatback. That one is reported to have gone on 4,639 Lancers. A total of 4,581 Lancers carried the Turbo Sport I package (code AGT).

1985 Dodge, 600 SE sedan with optional wire wheel covers (OCW)

600 SEDAN — SERIES EE — FOUR — Moving to the longer-wheelbase sedan, which measured the same as Chrysler's New Yorker, changes also were minimal. The 600ES Euro-style sedan was dropped, partly because of the new Lancer. But a 600SE edition replaced it, offering more luxury touches. Standard equipment was similar to the 600 coupe, but with front center armrest, assist handles, power decklid release, remote fuel filler door release, cloth/vinyl split-back bench seats, and bright/black rear quarter window moldings. No vinyl roof was included.

1985 Dodge, 600 ES convertible with optional cast aluminum wheels (OCW)

600 COUPE/CONVERTIBLE — SERIES KV — FOUR — Little change was evident in either the shorter-wheelbase two-door 600 or the longer sedan. New this year were upper bodyside accent stripes, improved seatbelt refractors, and a maintenance-free 400-amp battery. Both the carbureted 2.2-liter engine and five-speed transaxle were dropped. The club coupe had a formal roofline and Laredo-grain landau roof with opera windows. A total of 5,621 ES Turbo convertible packages (code AGT) were installed. The ES convertible carried P195/60VR15 SBR Eagle GT RBL tires, while other 600s had P185/70R14. Base engine was the fuel-injected 2.2-liter four with automatic transaxle. Mitsubishi's MCA-Jet 2.6-liter was optional again, along with a turbo 2.2. In addition to the turbocharged engine, the 600 ES Turbo featured leather upholstery.

1985 Dodge, Diplomat SE sedan with optional wire wheel covers (OCW)

DIPLOMAT — SERIES MG — V-8 — Changes to the biggest Dodge focused mainly on the standard 318 cu. in. (5.2-liter) V-8 engine. Compression jumped from 8.4:1 to 9.0:1, roller cam followers were installed, and horsepower rose by 10 (to 140). Two trim levels were offered: Salon and Luxury SE (the latter added late in the 1984 model year), both four-door sedans only. SE had a distinctive quad crossbar grille, Laredo grain full vinyl roof, Gibson velour upholstery, door courtesy lights, dual remote-

control mirrors, and improved sound insulation. Vinyl bodyside moldings were new this year. So was a new standard 400-amp maintenance-free battery. Lower bodyside panels were treated with a urethane protective coating to resist chips/corrosion. An electronic-tuning stereo radio with cassette player was a new option. Diplomat, a near twin to Plymouth's Gran Fury, continued to sell mainly to fleet operators (and large families). A total of 14,834 Diplomats had the Police package (code AHB).

I.D. DATA: Coding of Dodge's 17-symbol Vehicle Identification Number (VIN), on the upper left corner of the instrument panel visible through the windshield, is similar to 1984. Under Car Line, code 'X' (Lancer) was added. Model Year code changed to 'F' 1985. Code 'N' was added for the new assembly plant at Sterling Heights, MI. Engine numbers and Body Code Plates are in the same locations as 1981-84.

OMNI (FOUR)

Model No.	Body/Style No.	Body Type & Seating	Factory Price	Shipping Weight	Prod. Total
LZE	44	4-dr. Hatch-5P	5977	2095	54,229
LZH	44	4-dr. SE Hatch-5P	6298	2120	13,385

OMNI GLH (FOUR)

LZE	44/AGB	4-dr. Hatch-5P	7620	2320	6,513

CHARGER (FOUR)

LZH	24	2-dr. Hatch-5P	6584	2160	38,203

CHARGER 2.2 (FOUR)

LZP	24	2-dr. Hatch-5P	7515	2305	10,645

SHELBY CHARGER (FOUR)

LZS	24	2-dr. Hatch-5P	9553	2350	7,709

DAYTONA (FOUR)

GVH	24	2-dr. Hatch-4P	8505	2520	29,987

DAYTONA TURBO (FOUR)

GVS	24	2-dr. Hatch-4P	10286	2630	9,509

DAYTONA TURBO Z (FOUR)

GVS	24/AGS	2-dr. Hatch-4P	11620	N/A	8,023

ARIES (FOUR)

KDL	21	2-dr. Sedan-6P	6924	2335	9,428
KDL	41	4-dr. Sedan-6P	7039	2340	39,580

ARIES SE (FOUR)

KDM	21	2-dr. Sedan-6P	7321	2345	7,937
KDM	41	4-dr. Sedan-6P	7439	2375	23,920
KDH	45	4-dr. Sta Wag-6P	7909	2480	22,953

ARIES LE (FOUR)

KDH	21	2-dr. Sedan-6P	7659	2345	3,706
KDH	41	4-dr. Sedan-6P	7792	2375	5,932
KDP	45	4-dr. Sta Wag-6P	8348	2480	4,519

LANCER (FOUR)

HDH	44	4-dr. Spt Hatch-5P	8713	N/A	30,567
HDS	44	4-dr. ES Hatch-5P	9690	N/A	15,286

600 COUPE/CONVERTIBLE (FOUR)

KVP	22	2-dr. Cpe-5P	9060	2445	12,670
KVP	27	2-dr. Conv.-4P	10889	2530	8,188
KVP	27/AGT	2-dr. ES Conv-4P	13995	2530	5,621

600 SE SEDAN (FOUR)

EEH	41	4-dr. Sedan-6P	8953	2530	32,368

DIPLOMAT SALON (V-8)

MGL	41	4-dr. Sedan-6P	9399	3465	25,398

DIPLOMAT SE (V-8)

MGP	41	4-dr. Sedan-6P	10418	N/A	13,767

Model Number Note: Some sources identify models using the VIN data to indicate Car Line, Price Class and Body Style. Example: Aries four-door (KDL41) has the equivalent number D26, which translates to Aries line, Low price class, and four-door sedan body. See I.D. Data section for breakdown.

ENGINE DATA: BASE FOUR (Omni, Charger): Inline, overhead-cam four-cylinder. Cast iron block; aluminum head. Displacement: 97.3 cu. in. (1.6 liters). Bore and stroke: 3.17 x 3.07 in. Compression ratio: 8.8:1. Brake horsepower: 64 at 4800 R.P.M. Torque: 87 lb.-ft. at 2800 R.P.M. Five main bearings. Solid valve lifters. Carburetor: 2Bbl. Holley 6520. Peugeot-built. VIN Code: A. BASE FOUR (Aries); OPTIONAL (Omni,

Charger): Inline, overhead-cam four-cylinder. Cast iron block; aluminum head. Displacement: 135 cu. in. (2.2 liters). Bore and stroke: 3.44 x 3.62 in. Compression ratio: 9.0:1. Brake horsepower: 96 at 5200 R.P.M. Torque: 119 lb.-ft. at 3200 R.P.M. Five main bearings. Hydraulic valve lifters. Carburetor: 2Bbl. Holley 6520. VIN Code: C. BASE FOUR (Daytona, Lancer, 600); OPTIONAL (Aries): Same as 135 cu. in. four above, but with electronic fuel injection. Brake horsepower: 99 at 5600 R.P.M. Torque: 121 lb.-ft. at 3200 R.P.M. VIN Code: D. BASE FOUR (Omni GLH, Charger 2.2): High-performance carbureted version of 135 cu. in. four above. Compression ratio: 9.6:1. Brake horsepower: 110 at 5600 R.P.M. Torque: 129 lb.-ft. at 3600 R.P.M. VIN Code: F. TUR-BOCHARGED FOUR, BASE (Shelby Charger); OPTIONAL (Omni GLH, Daytona, Lancer, 600): Same as 135 cu. in. four above, with electronic fuel injection and turbocharger. Compression ratio: 8.1:1. Horsepower: 146 at 5200 R.P.M. Torque: 168 lb.-ft. at 3600 R.P.M. VIN Code: E. OPTIONAL FOUR (Aries, 600): Inline, overhead-cam four-cylinder. Cast iron block; aluminum head. Displacement: 156 cu. in. (2.6 liters). Bore and stroke: 3.59 x 3.86 in. Compression ratio: 8.7:1. Brake horsepower: 101 at 4800 R.P.M. Torque: 140 lb.-ft. at 2800 R.P.M. Five main bearings. Solid valve lifters. Carburetor: 2Bbl. Mikuni. Mitsubishi-built. VIN Code: G. BASE V-8 (Diplomat): 90-degree, overhead valve V-8. Cast iron block and head. Displacement: 318 cu. in. (5.2 liters). Bore and stroke: 3.91 x 3.31 in. Compression ratio: 8.7:1. Brake horsepower: 140 at 3600 R.P.M. Torque: 265 lb.-ft. at 1600 R.P.M. Five main bearings. Hydraulic valve lifters. Carburetor: 2Bbl. Holley 6280. VIN Code: P.

Note: Dodge's police V-8 was the same as the above 318 cu. in. engine, exc.: Compression ratio: 8.0:1. Brake horsepower: 175 at 4000 R.P.M. Torque: 250 lb.-ft. at 3200 R.P.M.

CHASSIS DATA: Wheelbase: (Omni) 99.1 in.; (Charger) 96.5 in.; (Daytona) 97.0 in.; (Aries/600 coupe) 100.3 in.; (600 Sedan) 103.3 in.; (Lancer) 103.1 in.; (Diplomat) 112.7 in. Overall length: (Omni) 164.8 in.; (Charger) 174.8 in.; (Daytona) 175.0 in.; (Aries) 178.6 in.; (Aries wagon) 179.0 in.; (Lancer) 180.4 in.; (600 coupe) 180.7 in.; (600 sedan) 186.6 in.; (Diplomat) 205.7 in. Height: (Omni) 53.0 in.; (Charger) 50.7 in.; (Shelby) 50.2 in.; (Daytona) 50.3 in.; (Aries 2-dr.) 52.7 in.; (Aries 4-dr.) 52.9 in.; (Aries wag) 53.2 in.; (Lancer) 53.0 in.; (600 cpe) 52.7 in.; (600 conv.) 53.7 in.; (600 sedan) 53.1 in.; (Diplomat) 55.3 in. Width: (Omni) 66.8 in.; (Chgr) 66.7 in.; (Aries/600) 68.0 in.; (Daytona) 69.3 in.; (Lancer) 68.3 in.; (Diplo) 74.2 in. Front Tread: (Omni/Chgr) 56.1 in.; (Aries/Daytona/Lancer/600) 57.6 in.; (Diplo) 60.0 in. Rear Tread: (Omni/Chgr) 55.7 in.; (Aries/Daytona/Lancer/600) 7.2 in.; (Diplo) 59.5 in. Standard Tires: (Omni/Charger) P165/80R13 SBR; (Charger 2.2) P195/60R14 SBR RBL; (Shelby) P205/50VR15 SBR RBL unidirectional; (Daytona) P185/70R14 SBR BSW; (Daytona Turbo) P205/60HR15 SBR RBL; (Aries) P175/80R13 SBR BSW; (Lancer) P185/70R14 SBR BSW; (Lancer ES) P195/70R14 SBR RBL; (600) P185/70R14 SBR BSW; (600 ES conv) P195/60VR15 SBR Eagle GT RBL; (Diplomat) P205/75R15 SBR WSW.

TECHNICAL: Transmission: Four-speed manual (floor lever) standard on Omni/Charger and Aries 2.2-liter: (1st) 3.29:1; (2nd) 1.89:1; (3rd) 1.21:1; (4th) 0.88:1; (Rev) 3.14:1. Five-speed manual standard on Omni/Charger 2.2-liter, Lancer and Daytona; optional on Aries: (1st) 3.29:1; (2nd) 2.08:1; (3rd) 1.45:1; (4th) 1.04:1; (5th) 0.72:1; (Rev) 3.14:1. TorqueFlite three-speed automatic standard on Diplomat, Aries 2.6-liter and 600; optional on all other models. Diplomat gear ratios: (1st) 2.74:1; (2nd) 1.54:1; (3rd) 1.00:1; (Rev) 2.22:1. Other models: (1st) 2.69:1; (2nd) 1.55:1; (3rd) 1.00:1; (Rev) 2.10:1. Standard final drive ratio: (Omni/Charger) 2.69:1 w/4-spd, 2.20:1 or 2.78:1 w/5-spd, 3.02:1 w/auto.; (Shelby) 2.57:1; (Daytona/Lancer) 2.57:1 w/5-spd, 3.02:1 w/auto.; (Aries) 2.69:1 w/4-spd, 2.20:1 w/5-spd, 3.02:1 w/auto.; (600) 3.02:1; (Diplo) 2.26:1. Steering: (Diplomat) recirculating ball; (others) rack and pinion. Suspension: (Omni/Chgr) Dual path Iso-strut independent coil front w/anti-sway bar, trailing arm semi-independent coil rear w/anti-sway bar on Charger 2.2 and Shelby; (Daytona) Dual path Iso-strut front, trailing arm rear w/gas-charged shock absorbers, front/rear anti-sway bars; (Lancer) Dual path gas-charged front Iso-struts, gas-charged rear shocks, front/rear anti-sway bars and rear track support bars; (Aries/600) Dual path Iso-strut front w/coil springs and linkless anti-sway bar, beam rear axle w/trailing arms and coil springs; (Diplomat) transverse front torsion bars and anti-sway bar, semi-elliptic rear leaf springs. Brakes: Front disc, rear drum. Ignition: Electronic. Body construction: Unibody. Fuel tank: (Omni/Chgr) 13 gal.; (Daytona/Aries/Lancer/600) 14 gal.; (Diplomat) 18 gal.

DRIVETRAIN OPTIONS: Engines: 2.2-liter four: Omni/Chgr ($134). Turbocharged 2.2-liter four: Omni GLH ($872); base Daytona ($964); Lancer/600 ($610). 2.6-liter four: Aries/600 ($271). Transmission/Axle: Five-speed manual trans.: Omni/Chgr, Aries Cust/SE ($75). TorqueFlite auto. trans.: Omni/Chgr/Daytona/Aries ($439); Lancer ($464). High-altitude axle: Omni/Chgr/Aries ($22). Steering/Suspension: Power steering: Omni/Chgr/Aries, base 600 conv. ($219). H.D. susp.: Aries ($58); Diplo ($26). Sport handling susp.: 600 ($57) exc. base conv. ($276).

Other: H.D. battery: Aries/600/Lancer/Diplo ($44). H.D. engine cooling: Omni/Chgr/Aries ($141). California emission system ($99).

OMNI/CHARGER CONVENIENCE/APPEARANCE OPTIONS: Option Packages: Sun/Sound/Shade pkg.: Shelby/2.2 ($512-$623). Auto. trans. discount pkg. ($765-$886). 2.2-liter engine and five-speed discount pkg. ($295-$408). Light group ($55-$88). Protection group ($88-$189). Comfort/Convenience: Air cond. ($643), Rear defroster ($132). Automatic speed control ($179). Rear wiper/washer: Omni ($120). Dual remote mirrors: Omni/SE ($49); Chgr ($57). Electronic-tuning radios: AM: base ($113), AM/FM stereo ($125-$238). Seek/scan AM/FM stereo w/cassette ($264-$502). Ultimate sound stereo w/cassette: Chgr ($210-$712). Exterior: Removable glass sunroof: Chgr ($315). Rear spoiler: base Chgr ($72). Pearl Coat paint ($40). Two-tone paint: SE/Chgr ($150). Interior: Low-back vinyl bucket seats ($31) exc. SE (NC). High-back cloth bucket seats ($107). Center armrest ($48). Tonneau cover: Chgr ($69). Cargo area carpet ($43-$62). Wheels/Tires: Cast aluminum 14-in. wheels: Chgr ($255-$305). P165/80R13 SBR WSW: base ($59). P195/60R14 SBR RWL: Chgr 2.2 ($22). P195/60R14 SBR RWL w/sport susp.: base Chgr ($350). Conventional spare tire ($63-$187).

DAYTONA CONVENIENCE/APPEARANCE OPTIONS: Option Packages: Equipment discount pkg.: Popular ($417-$763); Luxury ($1156-$1269). Electronic features pkg.: voice alert and navigator ($338-$362). Cargo trim/quiet sound group: base ($154-$173). Light group ($138). Protection pkg. ($88-$142). Comfort/Convenience: Air cond. ($737). Rear defroster ($143-$168). Auto. speed control ($179). Power driver's seat ($215). Power windows ($185). Power door locks ($125). Illuminated entry system ($75). Tinted glass ($110). Tilt steering wheel ($110). Liftgate wiper/washer ($120). Dual power remote mirrors ($48). Electronic-tuning radios w/digital clock: AM/FM stereo: base ($160). Premium AM/FM stereo w/cassette ($264-$424). Ultimate sound seek/scan AM/FM stereo w/cassette ($474-$634). Delete radio ($56 credit). Exterior: Removable glass sunroof ($322). Interior: Low-back vinyl bucket seats: base ($31). Low-back cloth/vinyl bucket seats w/adjustable driver's lumbar/thigh support: base ($362). Low-back leather bucket seats w/adjustable driver's lumbar/thigh support: base ($929); Turbo ($567). Wheels/Tires: Aluminum wheels: base ($322). P195/70R14 RBL: base ($92). Conventional spare tire ($83-$93).

ARIES CONVENIENCE/APPEARANCE OPTIONS: Option Packages: Equipment pkg.: Basic, base ($247); Popular, LE/SE ($516-$603); Premium, LE ($742-$887). Light pkg. ($56-$119). Comfort/Convenience: Air cond. ($737). Rear defroster ($143). Auto. speed control ($179). Power windows ($185-$260). Power door locks ($125-$175). Tinted glass ($110). Tilt steering wheel ($110). Intermittent wipers ($53). Liftgate wiper/washer: wag ($120). Mirrors: Remote left ($24). Dual black remote ($64-$88). Electronic-tuning radios: AM: base ($113). AM/FM stereo ($125-$238). Seek/scan AM/FM stereo w/cassette ($264-$389). Exterior: Pearl Coat paint ($40). Sill moldings, black ($26). Bumper guards, front/rear ($56). Bodyside tape stripe ($48). Luggage rack: wag ($116). Special sound insulation: base ($43). Undercoating ($43). Interior: Vinyl bench seat: SE, wag ($31). Cloth/vinyl bench seat: base ($31). Cloth/vinyl bucket seats: SE ($284); LE, wag ($210). Color-keyed mats ($45). Trunk dress-up: SE ($51). Wheels/Tires: Deluxe wheel covers: base ($52). Luxury wheel covers: base ($48-$100). Styled 13-in. wheels ($12-$112). Cast aluminum wheels, 14-in.: SE/LE ($322-$370). P175/80R13 WSW ($58). P185/70R14 SBR BSW ($36-$94). P185/70R14 SBR WSW ($94-$152). Conventional spare tire ($73-$83).

LANCER CONVENIENCE/APPEARANCE OPTIONS: Option Packages: Turbo sport pkg. ($1098-$1397). Equipment discount pkg.: Popular ($509-$664); Luxury ($1102-$1257). Electronic features pkg. I: ES ($515); II ($382). Sport handling pkg.: base ($118). Sport handling pkg. II ($180-$668). Light pkg.: base ($76). Comfort/Convenience: Air cond. ($757). Rear defroster ($148). Auto. speed control ($179). Power windows ($270). Power door locks ($180). Power seat ($225). Illuminated entry system ($75). Tinted glass ($115). Mechanical instrument cluster: ES (NC). Tilt steering wheel ($110). Intermittent wipers ($53). Liftgate wiper/washer ($125). Mirrors: Dual black remote-control ($64); power ($48-$112). Lighted vanity, right ($58). Electronic-tuning radios w/digital clock: Seek/scan AM stereo/FM stereo w/cassette ($305). Ultimate sound AM stereo/FM stereo w/cassette ($515). Radio delete ($152 credit). Exterior: Removable glass sunroof ($332). Two-tone paint ($210). Pearl Coat paint ($40). Premium sound insulation: base ($43). Undercoating ($43). Interior: Leather bucket seats: ES ($566). Folding armrest: base ($43). Vinyl console/armrest: base ($79). Color-keyed mats ($45). Wheels/Tires: Styled 14-in. wheels: base ($60). Cast aluminum wheels, 14 in. or 15 in. ($310-$370) but (NC) w/base Turbo sport pkg. P185/70R14 SBR WSW ($58). P195/70R14 SBR RBL: base ($92). P205/60R15 SBR RBL ($180-$272). Conventional spare tire: base ($83).

600 CONVENIENCE/APPEARANCE OPTIONS: Option Packages: Equipment discount pkg.: Popular ($593-$1055); Luxury, cpe/sed

($1272-$1397). Protection pkg.: sed ($81). Comfort/Convenience: Air cond. ($757). Rear defroster ($143). Auto. speed control ($179). Power windows ($195-$270). Power door locks ($130-$180). Power seat ($225). Power decklid release: 2-dr. ($40). Illuminated entry system ($75). Tinted glass ($115). Electronic voice alert: sed ($66). Euro/sport three-spoke steering wheel: cpe/conv. ($10). Leather-wrapped steering wheel ($50). Tilt steering wheel ($110). Lighting/Mirrors: Cornering lamps ($60). Dual power remote-control mirrors ($86). Lighted vanity mirror ($58). Electronic-tuning radios w/digital clock: AM/FM stereo ($125). Seek/scan AM/FM stereo w/cassette ($299-$424). Ultimate sound stereo w/cassette ($210-$634). Premium speakers ($126). Radio delete ($56 credit). Exterior: Two-tone paint: cpe/sed ($187). Pearl Coat paint ($40). Vinyl bodyside moldings ($55). Door edge protectors: sed ($25). Bumper guards ($56). Undercoating ($43). Interior: Cloth/vinyl bench seat: cpe (NC). Vinyl bench seat: sed ($31). Cloth 50/50 bench seat: sed ($287). Center armrest: cpe ($61). Color-keyed mats: front, conv. ($25); front/rear, others ($45). Trunk dress-up ($51). Wheels/Tires: Wire wheel covers, locking ($224). Cast aluminum wheels ($107-$322). P185/70R14 SBR WSW: conv. ($58). Conventional spare tire ($83).

DIPLOMAT CONVENIENCE/APPEARANCE OPTIONS: Option Packages: Equipment pkg.: Popular ($414-$537); Luxury, SE ($1868). Light pkg. ($120-$158). Comfort/Convenience: Air conditioning, semi-auto ($812). Rear defroster ($148). Auto. speed control ($179). Power seat, left: SE ($225). Power windows ($270). Power door locks ($180). Power decklid release ($40). Illuminated entry system ($75). Leather-wrapped steering wheel: SE ($60). Tilt steering wheel ($115). Intermittent wipers ($53). Mirrors: Remote driver's: Salon ($24). Dual remote, chrome ($67). Lighted vanity, right ($58). Electronic-tuning radios w/digital clock: AM/FM stereo ($125). Seek/scan AM/FM stereo w/cassette ($264-$389). Ultimate sound AM stereo/FM stereo w/cassette ($474-$599). Power antenna: SE ($65). Radio delete ($56 credit). Exterior: Power glass sunroof ($1076). Full vinyl roof: Salon ($185). Pearl Coat paint ($40). Vinyl bodyside moldings ($57). Upper door frame moldings: Salon ($46). Body sound insulation: Salon ($66). Undercoating ($43). Interior: Vinyl split-back bench seat: Salon ($60). Trunk dress-up ($56). Wheels/Tires: Premium wheel covers: Salon ($96). Wire wheel covers: SE ($224). Cast aluminum wheels: SE ($262). Conventional spare tire ($93).

HISTORY: Introduced: October 2, 1984, except Lancer, January 2, 1985. Model year production: Chrysler reported a total of 440,043 passenger cars shipped. Of the 400,878 four-cylinder engines, 65,854 were turbos. Calendar year production: 482,388. Calendar year sales by U.S. dealers: 434,325. Model year sales by U.S. dealers: 438,494.

HISTORICAL FOOTNOTES: Chrysler Corp. prices rose only an average 1.2 percent ($125) for 1985; half that amount on smaller Dodge models. The previous year's increases had been modest, too; far different from the hefty jumps of a few years earlier. Model year sales (including Japanese imports) reached the highest total since 1978, and 21 percent over the 1984 figure. Every domestic model except the 600 showed a sales increase for the model year, including Diplomat, which jumped from 21,932 in 1984 to 37,350 for a 70 percent increase. Plenty of buyers, it appeared, still craved a V-8 engine. The P-body Dodge Shadow (and Plymouth Sundance), scheduled for arrival in mid-1986, were originally intended to become the Omni/Horizon replacement. But renewed vigor in sales of those old L-bodies caused Chrysler Corp. to retarget the upcoming models into a higher price level of the market, between Omni and Aries.

1986 DODGE

No new models were introduced for 1986, but Dodge added a new engine to replace the Mitsubishi 2.6-liter four. Optional in Aries, Daytona, Lancer and 600, the 153 cu. in. (2.5 liter) fuel-injected four used two counter-rotating balance shafts to counteract the vibrations ordinarily inherent in four-cylinder powerplants. They were mounted in a cast aluminum housing beneath the crankshaft, in the oil pan. The engine produced 100 horsepower at 4800 rpm. An electronic control unit monitored engine operation and adjusted fuel/air mixture, timing, and emission control components. It even maintained a "diary" of operations that assisted in diagnosis if a fault were detected. The new engine was essentially a stroked variant of the 2.2-liter. The cylinder head of the 2.2-liter four was modified to hasten burning of the air/fuel mixture by creating turbulence, allowing gases to ignite closer to TDC. This allowed a compression jump to 9.5:1, without the need for higher-octane fuel. The same

"fast-burn" head was used on the new 2.5-liter. New Chrysler/Bosch low-pressure single-point fuel injection operated at 14.7 psi (less than half the previous pressure); it was used in all Chrysler fours. All fours also had a new labyrinth distributor with fewer parts. Fuel-injected engines, and the carbureted 2.2, had on-board diagnostics that monitored 23 functions. All Dodges had the required center high-mounted stop lamp, either mounted inside the car and sealed against the backlight, built into a rear spoiler or, on convertibles, mounted in a separate pod attached to the decklid. On the less dramatic side, all Dodges except Omni/Charger got a new ignition key design. Intermittent rear window wipers became optional on Daytona and Lancer. All domestic front-drives now had the "precision-feel" power steering introduced in 1985.

1986 Dodge, Omni hatchback sedan with optional GLH Turbo package (OCW)

OMNI — SERIES LZ — FOUR — Buyers could choose either a "lean or mean" Omni. Even though the base Omni hatchback and step-up SE were sensible small cars, Omni GLH was described as "a well-behaved savage." Appearance of each model changed little this year, except for the newly-required center stop lamp, which was attached to the lower hatchback lip. As before, base Omni's Euro-styling included black grille, headlamp bezels and trim, while SE turned to bright body trim. Base engine was again the 1.6-liter Peugeot four, with four-speed manual transaxle; optional, the 2.2-liter with close-ratio five-speed manual or three-speed TorqueFlite. Manual transaxles included a shift indicator light. A Rallye instrument cluster held large analog gauges. This year's body colors were: Black, Ice Blue, Cream, Charcoal Pearl Coat, Gold Dust, Garnet Red Pearl Coat, Graphic Red, Radiant Silver, Spice, White, and Santa Fe Blue. Three two-tones were available only on Omni SE. Both models had standard cloth/vinyl low-back bucket seats, while SE's were the high-back design. SE also had standard P165/80R13 whitewall tires. National Hot Rod Association tests in 1984 had demonstrated that Omni GLH could hit 50 mph in 5.75 seconds, and this year's version was expected to beat that figure. GLH came with the 110-horsepower, high-output 2.2-liter four, which had a chrome valve cover and performance exhaust; or optional 146-horsepower turbo edition. Close-ratio five-speed was standard, along with a higher final drive ratio. The GLH package included black bumpers, dual black remote mirrors, black front airdam with side extensions, black grille and headlamp bezels, a black painted panel between taillamps, black side sill spoilers, dual Bosch foglamps integrated into front airdam, and GLH identification. Red striping went on the airdam and sill spoilers. Inside was an AM stereo/FM stereo radio with digital clock, and a heel-and-toe gas pedal. Speed-rated Eagle GT P195/50HR15 SBR tires rode 15-in. cast aluminum wheels. Trenton cloth high-back sport bucket seats were standard, and the special sport suspension used gas-charged front struts and rear shocks. Turbo GLH models also had a functional louvered hood and stainless steel exhaust, as well as a GLH Turbo decal on each sill spoiler and on passenger side of hatch. A total of 3,629 Omnis had the GLH performance package.

1986 Dodge, Shelby Charger hatchback coupe (OCW)

CHARGER/2.2 — SERIES LZ — FOUR — Like the closely-related Omni sedan, the shorter-wheelbase Charger showed no significant change for 1986 beyond the new center stop lamp. Once again, a base model, Charger 2.2 and Shelby Charger were offered. Base engine was the 1.6-liter with four-speed, while Charger 2.2 had a five-speed with its high-output (110 horsepower) 2.2-liter four, and Shelby carried a 146-horse-power turbo. A 2.2-liter engine rated 96 horsepower was also available for the base model. A shift indicator light, called Fuel Pacer, went on manual-transaxle models. Cloth/vinyl low-back bucket seats with recliners and adjustable head restraints made up the standard interior. Charger colors were: Black, Ice Blue, Charcoal Pearl Coat, Cream, Gold Dust, Garnet Red Pearl Coat, Graphic Red, Radiant Silver, Spice and White. Shelby came only in one of four two-tone combinations (silver/blue, blue/silver, silver/red, or silver/black); base Chargers had two two-tone options. In addition to turbo power, Shelby had gas-charged front Iso-struts and rear shocks, quick 14:1 steering, ventilated front disc brakes, large anti-sway bars, and 15-in. cast aluminum Shelby wheels holding P205/50VR15 blackwall Eagle GT SBR tires with unidirectional tread. Body features included a "turbo bulge" hood with louvers and special badges, aero front airdam, side sill spoilers, and functional rear spoiler. Cloth/vinyl high-back bucket seats were embroidered with the Carroll Shelby logo. A 1985 Shelby had managed 0-50 mph in 5.34 seconds, in NHRA testing.

1986 Dodge, Daytona Turbo Z hatchback coupe with optional CS (Carroll Shelby) Handling Package (OCW)

DAYTONA — SERIES GV — FOUR — For its third season, Daytona changed only modestly in appearance. This year's lineup consisted of a base model and the Turbo Z. The former "ordinary" Turbo model was dropped. Front and rear fascias were modified. New nerf extensions and integrated bodyside moldings now offered full 360-degree protection. Tinted glass became standard, as did new 14-in. cast aluminum wheels. Both models had a standard AM stereo/FM stereo radio with six speakers. New low-travel switches controlled optional power door locks, windows, rear defogger, and a new intermittent rear wiper/washer. There was also a new four-way adjustable head restraint. Base Daytonas had 14-in. cast aluminum wheels, a standard 2.2-liter four with fuel injection, and five-speed manual transaxle. The new 2.5-liter four with balancing shafts was optional, as was three-speed TorqueFlite. Daytona colors were: Black, Ice Blue, Radiant Silver, Golden Bronze or Garnet Red Pearl Coat, and White. Turbo Z came in Black, Flash Red, Radiant Silver, White, or Gunmetal Blue Pearl Coat. Daytona's Turbo Z showed a specially molded single-piece front airdam and functional three-piece rear spoiler. P205/60HR15 raised black-letter Eagle GT tires rode distinctive 15 x 6-in. Shelby cast aluminum wheels. Turbo Z had standard wraparound front and rear fascias that extended to wheel openings; integrated wide bodyside moldings; accent tape striping; and 'Turbo Z' lettering below taillamp lenses. An enthusiast driver's seat offered orthopedic support, especially in lumbar/thigh areas, using pneumatic adjustment. Turbo Z also added black functional hood louvers, a leather-wrapped Euro-sport steering wheel, lower bodyside sill spoilers, and a handling suspension with gas-charged struts and shocks. New this year was an optional C/S Handling Package (named for Carroll Shelby) for the Turbo Z. Priced at $189, it included solid 32mm front and 28mm rear anti-sway bars (standard bars were tubular), performance-tuned struts/shocks, and P225/50VR15 unidirectional speed-rated tires on unique C/S 15 x 6.5-in. cast aluminum wheels. A new optional T-Bar roof package had twin removable tinted glass panels and anti-theft locks. That package also included power windows and larger aero-look power mirrors. A total of 7,704 Daytonas had the C/S Handling Package, while 5,984 had the T-Bar roof package. The turbocharged engine was also optional on the base model. While the closely-related Chrysler Laser promoted luxury, Dodge focused more on performance with its Daytona.

ARIES K — SERIES KD — FOUR — A square 'K' emblem joined the 'Aries' lettering on the decklid, emphasizing the basic body type. Otherwise, Aries looked the same as in 1985. Base, SE and LE versions were offered. Base engine was the 2.2-liter four, now fuel-injected, with fully synchronized five-speed close-ratio transaxle. Optional: the new 2.5-liter, and TorqueFlite three-speed automatic. The four-speed gearbox

was abandoned. Bodies included the two- and four-door sedan, and four-door station wagon. Base models had a standard all-vinyl bench seat (split-back on two-door sedan). LE had Kincaid and Classic cloth/vinyl split-back bench seating with folding center armrest and adjustable head restraints, and cloth door trim panels. SE also used cloth/vinyl, but with vinyl door trim panels. Bucket seats were available in SE/LE. An AM radio with digital clock and a remote driver's mirror were standard in SE, while Aries LE carried a standard AM stereo/FM stereo sound system. Base models had two-speed wipers and black narrow bodyside moldings. Both SE and LE switched to intermittent wipers and wide black bodyside moldings with argent stripe. Standard tires were P175/80R13 steel-belted radial blackwalls except LE, which carried P185/70R14. Aries K colors were: Black, Ice Blue, Gunmetal Blue Pearl Coat, Golden Bronze Pearl Coat, Dark Cordovan Pearl Coat, Light Cream, Gold Dust, Garnet Red Pearl Coat, Radiant Silver, and White. Revised discount option packages were available for SE/LE.

1986 Dodge, Aries LE two-door sedan with optional cast aluminum wheels (OCW)

1986 Dodge, Lancer ES hatchback sedan with optional turbocharged engine and cast aluminum wheels (OCW)

LANCER — SERIES HD — FOUR — Not much change was evident in the four-door hatchback Lancer, but its option list lost quite a few items. As in its opening season, base and ES versions were available. New this year were a refined electro-mechanical instrument cluster (including 125 mph speedometer); tinted glass; passenger-assist straps; and child-proof safety rear door locks. Base Lancers had reclining low-back bucket seats in cloth/vinyl, with two-way headrests. ES carried new standard cloth/vinyl low-back reclining performance bucket seats with four-way adjustable head restraints and increased lateral support, plus intermittent wipers and new 14-in. styled road wheels. Standard 60/40 split-back rear seat-backs folded down. Engine choices included the base fuel-injected 2.2-liter four, new optional 2.5-liter, or turbocharged 2.2 rated at 146 horse-power. Five-speed manual shift was standard; TorqueFlite optional (required with the 2.5-liter engine). Lancer body colors were: Garnet Red, Dark Cordovan, Light Rosewood Mist, Golden Bronze or Gunmetal Blue Pearl Coat; Gold Dust; Light Cream; Ice Blue; Black; and Radiant Silver. Three two-tone combinations were offered. An electronic instrument cluster with fluorescent displays was available only on ES. Base Lancers showed electro-mechanical analog gauges. An Electronic Navigator was optional only on ES. A road touring suspension was standard, but buyers had two step-up alternatives. Sport Handling Pkg. I included P195/70R14 SBR RBL tires and sport handling suspension. Package II added P205/60HR15 SBR RBL tires on cast aluminum wheels. A total of 2,508 ES Lancers had the Turbo Sport package (code AGT) installed. That one included black belt, door window frame, and quarter window moldings; P205/60HR15 SBR RBL tires on cast aluminum wheels; dual remote mirrors; lower bodyside and door window frame surround tape stripes; two-tone paint; and the turbo engine.

600 COUPE/CONVERTIBLE — SERIES KV — FOUR — Shaped similar to the prior version, 600 nevertheless had a significantly altered appearance with completely different grille and restyled back end. Front fender louvers were gone. The new crossbar grille contained a pentastar emblem attached to wide vertical and horizontal bars, over a black crosshatch pattern. The grille had a thick, bright upper header molding, with sides slightly tapered inward at the base. This year's front-end treatment used

quad rectangular headlamps with side marker lamps and reflectors integral to the bezel. Amber park/signal lamps went into the front bumper, which was modified to hold air intake slots. A new soft bumper fascia had integral nerf rub strips with bright insert. A new square gas filler door replaced the former round one. Taillamps looked similar to 1985, but more tapered in their wraparound portion, with integral side markers and turn signals shining through new lenses. Also new: bright trunk lid and rear quarter extension moldings and bodyside accent stripes. A 'Turbo' badge (if applicable) went on front fenders, just below the bodyside molding line. On the dash, a new convenience light bar indicated door ajar, low fuel, low washer fluid, and trunk lid ajar. As before, the Club Coupe and convertible rode on a shorter wheelbase than the 600 ES sedan (listed next). Also available was a 600 ES Turbo convertible. The option list lost a number of individual items, but added some new accessory packages. Base engine was the 2.2-liter four (fuel injected), with the new 2.5-liter four or 2.2-liter turbo optional. The Club Coupe had a classic formal landau roof and opera windows, plus standard cloth front bench seat with folding center armrest. Convertibles carried Saddle Grain vinyl low-back reclining bucket seats. 600 body colors were: Garnet Red or Gunmetal Blue Pearl Coat, Radiant Silver, Black, Ice Blue, White, Nightwatch Blue, Dark Cordovan or Light Rosewood Mist Pearl Coat, Light Cream, or Golden Bronze Pearl Coat. One two-tone was offered on all models, another on Club Coupe only. Besides the turbocharged Trans-4 2.2-liter engine, the 600 ES Turbo convertible added a special sports/handling suspension. The package also included Corinthian leather/vinyl low-back bucket seats, aero dual remote mirrors, Euro/sport leather-wrapped steering wheel, electronic instrument cluster with tachometer, AM stereo/FM stereo radio with cassette player, accent tape striping, color-keyed protective rub strips, and black door handles. P195/60R15 Goodyear Eagle GT SBR RBL tires went on Shelby cast aluminum wheels. Bodies displayed blackout exterior trim, plus a '600 ES' insignia on the decklid. A total of 4,759 ES Turbo convertibles were produced. Options this year included a padded vinyl landau roof with opera windows (coupe); narrow bodyside moldings color-keyed to bumper nerfs; and color-coordinated front/rear bumper guards. Several new discount packages were offered, including interior lighting, cold-weather protection, and power conveniences.

1986 Dodge, 600 coupe with optional turbocharged engine and wire wheel covers (OCW)

1986 Dodge, 600 ES convertible with optional wire wheel covers (OCW)

600 SEDAN — SERIES EE — FOUR — As before, the 600 sedan, though similar in appearance to coupe and convertible, qualified as a mid-size rather than compact by virtue of its longer wheelbase. Chassis was the same as Chrysler's New Yorker and Plymouth Caravelle. A base model was added to the former SE. New standard equipment on four-doors included an easier-to-read instrument cluster, plus 50/50 front seats (on SE only).

DIPLOMAT — SERIES MG — V-8 — Offered again in Salon and SE dress, Diplomat carried on with minimal change apart from the newly required center stop lamp. Diplomat's interior used Sherwood woodtone trim and a padded instrument panel. Standard equipment included tinted

glass and dual remote mirrors. Salons had a cloth/vinyl split-back front bench seat with folding center armrest. SE had all-cloth velour 60/40 front seating with folding center armrest and passenger recliner, plus a full vinyl roof and door courtesy lights. Colors this year were: Crimson Red, Ice Blue, Gold Dust, Nightwatch Blue, White, Radiant Silver, Black, and Mink Brown or Gunmetal Blue Pearl Coat. Sole engine remained the 318 cu. in. (5.2-liter) V-8 with two-barrel carburetor, but a four-barrel version was installed in Police Diplomats. A total of 10,372 Diplomats had the Police package. Three-speed TorqueFlite was standard. A standard lower body protective coating included stone-resistant urethane primer. Joining the option list was an AM stereo/FM stereo radio. A Luxury Equipment discount package for the SE cost $2,010 extra. Virtually identical to Plymouth's Gran Fury, Diplomat was offered only as a four-door sedan.

1986 Dodge, Diplomat SE sedan with optional sunroof and wire wheel covers (OCW)

I.D. DATA: Dodge's 17-symbol Vehicle Identification Number (VIN), as before, was on the upper left corner of the instrument panel, visible through the windshield. The first digit indicates Country: '1' U.S.A. The second symbol is Make: 'B' Dodge. Third is Vehicle Type: '3' passenger car. The next symbol ('B') indicates manual seatbelts. Symbol five is Car Line: 'Z' Omni/Charger; 'A' Daytona; 'D' Aries; 'E' 600 sedan; 'V' 600 coupe/convertible; 'X' Lancer; 'G' Diplomat. Symbol six is Series (price class): '1' Economy; '2' Low; '3' Medium; '4' High; '5' Premium; '6' Special. Symbol seven is Body Style: '1' 2-dr. sedan; '4' 2-dr. hatchback; '5' 2-dr. convertible; '6' 4-dr. sedan; '8' 4-dr. hatchback; '9' 4-dr. wagon. Eighth is the Engine Code: 'A' L498 2Bbl.; 'C' L4135 2Bbl.; 'D' L4135 FI; 'E' Turbo L4135 FI; '8' Hi-perf. L4135 2Bbl.; 'K' L4153 FI; 'P' V8318 2Bbl. Next comes a check digit. Symbol ten indicates Model Year: 'G' 1986. Symbol eleven is Assembly Plant: 'C' Jefferson (Detroit); 'D' Belvidere, IL; 'F' Newark, DE: 'N' Sterling Heights, MI; 'G' or 'X' St. Louis. The last six digits make up the sequential serial number, starting with 100001. Engine numbers and Body Code Plates are in the same locations as 1981-85.

1986 Dodge, Aries SE station wagon with optional roof rack (OCW)

OMNI (FOUR)

Model No.	Body/ Style No.	Body Type & Seating	Factory Price	Shipping Weight	Prod. Total
LZE	44	4-dr. Hatch-5P	6209	2100	61,812
LZH	44	4-dr. SE Hatch-5P	6558	2120	8,139

OMNI GLH (FOUR)

LZE	44/AGB	4-dr. Hatch-5P	7918	2295	3,629

CHARGER (FOUR)

LZH	24	2-dr. Hatch-5P	6787	2170	38,172

CHARGER 2.2 (FOUR)

LZP	24	2-dr. Hatch-5P	7732	2325	4,814

SHELBY CHARGER (FOUR)

LZS	24	2-dr. Hatch-5P	9361	2390	7,669

DAYTONA (FOUR)

Model No.	Body/ Style No.	Body Type & Seating	Factory Price	Shipping Weight	Prod. Total
GVH	24	2-dr. Hatch-4P	9013	N/A	26,771

DAYTONA TURBO (FOUR)

Model No.	Body/ Style No.	Body Type & Seating	Factory Price	Shipping Weight	Prod. Total
GVS	24	2-dr. Hatch-4P	11301	N/A	17,595

ARIES (FOUR)

Model No.	Body/ Style No.	Body Type & Seating	Factory Price	Shipping Weight	Prod. Total
KDL	21	2-dr. Sedan-6P	7184	2380	2,437
KDL	41	4-dr. Sedan-6P	7301	2390	14,445

ARIES SE (FOUR)

Model No.	Body/ Style No.	Body Type & Seating	Factory Price	Shipping Weight	Prod. Total
KDM	21	2-dr. Sedan-6P	7639	2400	9,084
KDM	41	4-dr. Sedan-6P	7759	2415	40,254
KDM	45	4-dr. Sta Wag-6P	8186	2470	17,757

ARIES LE (FOUR)

Model No.	Body/ Style No.	Body Type & Seating	Factory Price	Shipping Weight	Prod. Total
KDH	21	2-dr. Sedan-6P	8087	2440	2,475
KDH	41	4-dr. Sedan-6P	8207	2455	5,638
KDH	45	4-dr. Sta Wag-6P	8936	2560	5,278

LANCER (FOUR)

Model No.	Body/ Style No.	Body Type & Seating	Factory Price	Shipping Weight	Prod. Total
HDH	44	4-dr. Spt Hatch-5P	9426	2610	34,009
HDS	44	4-dr. ES Hatch-5P	10332	2665	17,888

600 COUPE/CONVERTIBLE (FOUR)

Model No.	Body/ Style No.	Body Type & Seating	Factory Price	Shipping Weight	Prod. Total
KVP	22	2-dr. Club Cpe-6P	9577	2470	11,714
KVP	27	2-dr. Conv-4P	11695	2535	11,678
KVP	27/AGT	2-dr. ES Conv-4P	14856	2580	4,759

600/SE SEDAN (FOUR)

Model No.	Body/ Style No.	Body Type & Seating	Factory Price	Shipping Weight	Prod. Total
EEM	41	4-dr. Sedan-6P	9370	2535	16,235
EEH	41	4-dr. SE Sed-6P	10028	2545	15,291

DIPLOMAT SALON (V-8)

Model No.	Body/ Style No.	Body Type & Seating	Factory Price	Shipping Weight	Prod. Total
MGL	41	4-dr. Sedan-6P	10086	3475	15,469

DIPLOMAT SE (V-8)

Model No.	Body/ Style No.	Body Type & Seating	Factory Price	Shipping Weight	Prod. Total
MGP	41	4-dr. Sedan-6P	11166	3530	11,484

Model Number Note: Some sources identify models using the VIN data to indicate Car Line, Price Class and Body Style. Example: Aries four-door (KDL41) has the equivalent number D26, which translates to Aries line, Low price class, and four-door sedan body. See I.D. Data section for breakdown.

ENGINE DATA: BASE FOUR (Omni, Charger): Inline, overhead-cam four-cylinder. Cast iron block; aluminum head. Displacement: 97.3 cu. in. (1.6 liters). Bore and stroke: 3.17 x 3.07 in. Compression ratio: 8.8:1. Brake horsepower: 64 at 4800 R.P.M. Torque: 87 lb.-ft. at 2800 R.P.M. Five main bearings. Solid valve lifters. Carburetor: 2Bbl. Holley 6520. Peugeot-built. VIN Code: A. OPTIONAL FOUR (Omni, Charger): Inline, overhead-cam four-cylinder. Cast iron block; aluminum head. Displacement: 135 cu. in. (2.2 liters). Bore and stroke: 3.44 x 3.62 in. Compression ratio: 9.0:1. Brake horsepower: 96 at 5200 R.P.M. Torque: 119 lb.-ft. at 3200 R.P.M. Five main bearings. Hydraulic valve lifters. Carburetor: 2Bbl. Holley 6520. VIN Code: C. BASE FOUR (Aries, Daytona, Lancer, 600): Same as 135 cu. in. four above, but with electronic fuel injection. Compression ratio: 9.5:1. Brake horsepower: 97 at 5200 R.P.M. Torque: 122 lb.-ft. at 3200 R.P.M. VIN Code: D. BASE FOUR (Omni GLH, Charger 2.2): High-performance carbureted version of 135 cu. in. four above: Compression ratio: 9.6:1. Brake horsepower: 110 at 5600 R.P.M. Torque: 129 lb.-ft. at 3600 R.P.M. VIN Code: 8. TURBOCHARGED FOUR, BASE (Shelby Charger, Daytona Turbo); OPTIONAL (Omni GLH, Daytona, Lancer, 600): Same as 135 cu. in. four above, with electronic fuel injection and turbocharger. Compression ratio: 8.1:1. Horsepower: 146 at 5200 R.P.M. Torque: 170 lb.-ft. at 3600 R.P.M. VIN Code: E. OPTIONAL FOUR (Aries, Daytona, Lancer, 600): Inline, overhead-cam four-cylinder. Cast iron block; aluminum head. Displacement: 153 cu. in. (2.5 liters). Bore and stroke: 3.44 x 4.09 in. Compression ratio: 9.0:1. Brake horsepower: 100 at 4800 R.P.M. Torque: 136 lb.-ft. at 2800 R.P.M. Five main bearings. Hydraulic valve lifters. Electronic fuel injection. VIN Code: K. BASE V-8 (Diplomat): 90-degree, overhead valve V-8. Cast iron block and heads. Displacement: 318 cu. in. (5.2 liters). Bore and stroke: 3.91 x 3.31 in. Compression ratio: 9.0:1. Brake horsepower: 140 at 3600 R.P.M. Torque: 265 lb.-ft. at 1600 R.P.M. Five main bearings. Hydraulic valve lifters. Carburetor: 2Bbl. Holley 6280. VIN Code: P.

Note: Police V-8 was same as 318 cu. in. V-8 above, but with 4Bbl. Rochester carburetor. Compression ratio: 8.0:1. Brake horsepower: 175 at 4000 R.P.M. Torque: 250 lb.-ft. at 3200 R.P.M.

CHASSIS DATA: Wheelbase: (Omni) 99.1 in.; (Charger) 96.5 in.; (Daytona) 97.0 in.; (Aries/600) 100.3 in.; (Aries wag, 600 conv.) 100.4

in.; (600 sedan) 103.3 in.; (Lancer) 103.1 in.; (Diplomat) 112.6 in. Overall Length: (Omni) 163.2 in.; (Chgr) 174.8 in.; (Shelby) 174.7 in.; (Daytona) 175.0 in.; (Daytona Turbo Z) 176.9 in.; (Aries) 178.6 in.; (Aries wag) 179.0 in.; (Lancer) 180.4 in.; (600) 179.2 in.; (600 sedan) 185.2 in.; (Diplomat) 204.6 in. Height: (Omni) 53.0 in.; (Chgr) 50.7 in.; (Shelby) 50.2 in.; (Daytona) 50.4 in.; (Aries 2-dr.) 52.5 in.; (Aries 4-dr.) 52.9 in.; (Aries wag) 53.2 in.; (Lancer) 53.0 in.; (600 cpe) 52.5 in.; (600 conv.) 52.9 in.; (600 sedan) 53.1 in.; (Diplomat) 55.1 in. Width: (Omni) 66.8 in.; (Chgr) 66.1 in.; (Aries/600) 68.0 in.; (Daytona) 69.3 in.; (Lancer) 68.3 in.; (Diplo) 72.4 in. Front Tread: (Omni/Chgr) 56.1 in.; (Aries/Daytona/Lancer/600) 57.6 in.; (Diplo) 60.0 in. Rear Tread: (Omni/Chgr) 55.7 in.; (Aries/Daytona/Lancer/600) 57.2 in.; (Diplo) 59.5 in. Standard Tires: (Omni/Charger) P165/80R13 SBR BSW; (Charger 2.2) P195/60R14 SBR RBL; (Shelby) P205/50VR15 SBR RBL unidirectional; (Daytona) P185/70R14 SBR BSW; (Daytona Turbo) P205/60HR15 SBR RBL; (Aries) P175/80R13 SBR BSW; (Aries LE, Lancer) P185/70R14 SBR BSW; (Lancer ES) P195/70R14 SBR RBL; (600) P185/70R14 SBR; (Diplomat) P205/75R15 SBR WSW.

TECHNICAL: Transmission: Four-speed manual (floor lever) standard on Omni/Charger. Five-speed manual standard on Omni/Charger 2.2-liter, Aries, Lancer and Daytona. TorqueFlite three-speed automatic standard on Diplomat, Aries/Lancer 2.5-liter and 600; optional on all other models. Diplomat gear ratios: (1st) 2.74:1; (2nd) 1.54:1; (3rd) 1.00:1; (Rev) 2.22:1. Other models: (1st) 2.69:1; (2nd) 1.55:1; (3rd) 1.00:1; (Rev) 2.10:1. Standard final drive ratio: (Omni/Charger) 2.69:1 w/4-spd, 2.20:1 or 2.78:1 w/5-spd, 2.78:1 or 3.02:1 w/auto.; (Omni GLH/Shelby turbo) 2.57:1; (Daytona/Lancer) 2.57:1 w/5-spd, 3.02:1 w/auto. exc. (Daytona 2.5-liter) 3.02:1 w/5-spd; (Aries) 2.20:1 w/5-spd, 2.78:1 or 3.02:1 w/auto.; (600) 3.02:1; (Diplo) 2.26:1. Steering: (Diplomat) recirculating ball; (others) rack and pinion. Suspension: (Omni/Chgr) Dual path Iso-strut independent coil front w/anti-sway bar, trailing arm semi-independent coil rear w/anti-sway bar on Charger 2.2; (Shelby) same as Omni/Charger but gas-charged rear shocks and front/rear anti-sway bars; (Daytona) Dual path Iso-strut front, trailing arm rear w/gas-charged shock absorbers, front/rear anti-sway bars; (Daytona Turbo) same as Daytona but gas-charged front Iso-struts; (Lancer) Dual path gas-charged front Iso-struts, gas-charged rear shocks, front/rear anti-sway bars; (Aries/600) Dual path Iso-strut front w/coil springs and linkless anti-sway bar, beam rear axle w/trailing arms and coil springs; (Diplomat) transverse front torsion bars and anti-sway bar, semi-elliptic rear leaf springs. Brakes: Front disc, rear drum. Ignition: Electronic. Body construction: Unibody. Fuel tank: (Omni/Chgr) 13 gal.; (Daytona/Aries/Lancer/600) 14 gal.; (Diplomat) 18 gal.

1986 Dodge, Daytona Turbo Z hatchback coupe (OCW)

DRIVETRAIN OPTIONS: Engines: 2.2-liter four: Omni/Chgr ($138). Turbocharged 2.2-liter four: Omni GLH ($898); base Daytona ($993); Lancer/600 ($628). 2.5-liter four: Aries/Lancer/600, base Daytona ($279). Transmission/Axle: Five-speed manual trans.: Omni/Chgr ($77). TorqueFlite auto. trans.: Omni/Chgr/Daytona/Aries/Lancer ($478). High-altitude axle: Omni/Chgr/Aries ($23). Steering/Suspension: Power steering: Omni/Chgr/Aries/ base 600 conv. ($226). H.D. susp.: Aries ($60); Diplo ($27). Sport handling susp.: 600 ($58) exc. base conv. ($284). Sport handling susp. w/14-in. tires: base Lancer ($122). Other: H.D. battery: Aries/600/Diplo ($45). H.D. engine cooling: Omni/Chgr ($145). California emission system ($102).

OMNI/CHARGER CONVENIENCE/APPEARANCE OPTIONS: Option Packages: Sun/Sound/Shade pkg.: Shelby/2.2 ($562-$634). Auto. trans. discount pkg. ($808-$933). 2.2-liter engine and five-speed discount pkg. ($304-$420). Light group ($52-$86). Protection group ($90-$194). Comfort/Convenience: Air cond. ($683). Rear defroster ($141). Automatic speed control ($184). Rear wiper/washer: Omni ($129). Dual remote mirrors: Omni/SE ($50); Chgr ($59). Electronic-tuning radios: AM: base ($116). AM/FM stereo ($149-$265). Seek/scan AM/FM stereo w/cassette ($251-$516). Ultimate sound stereo w/cassette: Chgr ($216-$732). Exterior: Removable glass sunroof: Chgr ($335). Pearl Coat paint ($155). Two-tone paint: SE/Chgr ($155). Interior: Low-back vinyl bucket seats ($32). High-back cloth bucket seats ($110). Center armrest ($49). Tonneau cover: Chgr ($71). Cargo area carpet ($44-$64). Wheels/Tires: Cast aluminum 14-in. wheels: Chgr

($263-$314). P165/80R13 SBR WSW: base ($61). P195/60R14 SBR RWL: base Chgr ($358); Chgr 2.2 ($23). Conventional spare tire ($65-$193).

DAYTONA CONVENIENCE/APPEARANCE OPTIONS: Option Packages: Sun/Sound/Shade discount pkg. ($639). Popular equipment discount pkg. ($260-$354); w/air ($840-$934). Electronic features pkg. w/navigator: base ($280); w/navigator and electronic instruments: Turbo ($600). Cargo trim/quiet sound group: Turbo ($239-$258). C/S handling pkg.: Turbo ($189). Protection pkg. ($90). Comfort/Convenience: Air cond. ($780). Rear defroster ($152-$188). Auto. speed control ($184). Power driver's seat ($232). Power windows ($201). Power door locks ($134). Tilt steering wheel ($118). Liftgate wiper/washer ($129). Dual power remote mirrors ($58). Electronic-tuning radios w/digital clock: Premium AM/FM stereo w/cassette ($251). Ultimate sound AM/FM stereo w/cassette ($216-$467). Exterior: Removable glass sunroof ($342). Pearl Coat paint ($41). interior: Low-back cloth/vinyl bucket seats w/adj. driver's lumbar/thigh support: base ($404). Low-back leather bucket seats w/adj. driver's lumbar/thigh support: base ($988); Turbo ($584). Tires: P195/70R14 RBL: base ($95). Conventional spare tire ($85).

ARIES CONVENIENCE/APPEARANCE OPTIONS: Option Packages: Equipment pkg.: Basic, base ($256); Popular, LE/SE ($219-$702); Premium, LE ($758-$1076). Protection pkg. ($148). Comfort/Convenience: Air cond. ($780). Rear defroster ($152). Auto. speed control ($184). Power door locks ($134-$185). Tinted glass ($118). Tilt steering wheel ($118). Liftgate wiper/washer: wag ($129). Electronic-tuning radios: AM stereo/FM stereo: base ($149-$265). AM stereo/FM stereo w/cassette: SE/LE ($251-$400). Exterior: Pearl Coat paint ($41). Luggage rack: wag ($119). Interior: Vinyl bench seat: SE ($32); LE (NC). Cloth/vinyl bench seat: base ($32). Cloth/vinyl bucket seats: SE ($275); LE ($216). Wheels/Tires: Deluxe wheel covers: SE ($49). Cast aluminum wheels, 14-in.: LE ($332-$381). P175/80R13 WSW: base/SE ($60). P185/70R14 BSW: SE ($97). P185/70R14 WSW: SE ($157); LE ($60). Conventional spare tire ($75-$85).

LANCER CONVENIENCE/APPEARANCE OPTIONS: Option Packages: Turbo Sport pkg.: ES ($413-$1415). Equipment discount pkg.: Popular ($667-$1839); Luxury ($688-$1078). Electronic features pkg.: ES ($637-$681). Deluxe convenience pkg. ($118-$302). Power convenience pkg. ($463). Highline upgrade pkg.: base ($125). Sport handling pkg. I with P195/70R14 tires ($118). Sport handling pkg. II with P205/60HR15 SBR RBL tires on 15-in. cast aluminum wheels ($180-$668). Cold weather pkg. ($197). Protection pkg. ($90). Comfort/Convenience: Air cond. ($760). Power seat ($232). Liftgate wiper/washer ($129). Mirrors: Dual black remote-control ($66); power ($49-$115). Lighted vanity, right ($60). Electronic-tuning radios w/digital clock: Premium AM stereo/FM stereo w/cassette ($293). Ultimate sound AM stereo/FM stereo w/cassette ($509). Exterior: Removable glass sunroof ($342). Two-tone paint ($216). Pearl Coat paint ($41). Interior: Leather bucket seats: ES ($583). Folding cloth armrest: base ($44). Console/armrest: base ($81). Wheels/Tires: Styled 14-in. wheels: base ($62). Cast aluminum wheels, 14 in. or 15 in. ($319-$381). P185/70R14 SBR WSW ($60). P195/70R14 SBR: base ($95). Conventional spare tire: base ($85).

600 CONVENIENCE/APPEARANCE OPTIONS: Option Packages: Equipment discount pkg.: Popular ($382-$531); Luxury ($915-$1238). Deluxe convenience pkg. ($302). Power convenience pkg. ($335-$463). Interior illumination pkg.: cpe ($137). Center console pkg.: cpe ($208). Cold weather pkg.: cpe ($197). Protection pkg.: 2-dr. ($115). Light pkg.: base sed ($139). Comfort/Convenience: Air cond. ($780). Rear defroster ($152). Power seat ($232). Power decklid release: 2-dr. ($41). Illuminated entry system: conv. ($77). Leather-wrapped steering wheel ($52). Intermittent wipers ($55). Mirrors: Left remote: base sed ($25). Dual power remote-control: cpe ($88); sed ($88-$113). Lighted vanity, pair: sed ($120). Electronic-tuning radios w/digital clock: AM stereo/FM stereo: base sed ($149). Seek/scan AM stereo/FM stereo w/cassette ($287-$436). Ultimate sound stereo w/cassette ($216-$652). Exterior: Two-tone paint: cpe ($193). Pearl Coat paint ($41). Vinyl bodyside moldings: sed ($57). Bumper guards: sed ($58). Undercoating ($44). Interior: Cloth bucket seats: cpe ($171). Color-keyed mats: front, conv. ($26); front/rear, others ($46). Trunk dress-up ($53). Wheels/Tires: Wire wheel covers, locking: 2-dr. ($280). Cast aluminum wheels: 2-dr. ($381). P185/70R14 SBR WSW: conv. ($60). Conventional spare tire ($85).

DIPLOMAT CONVENIENCE/APPEARANCE OPTIONS: Option Packages: Equipment pkg.: Popular ($461-$588); Luxury, SE ($2010). Light pkg. ($93-$132). Protection group ($137). Comfort/Convenience: Air conditioning, semi-auto ($836). Rear defroster ($152). Auto. speed control ($184). Power seat, left: SE ($232). Power windows ($278). Power door locks ($185). Power decklid release ($41). Illuminated entry system: SE ($77). Leather-wrapped steering wheel: SE ($62). Tilt steering wheel ($118). Intermittent wipers ($55). Mirrors: Remote driver's: Salon ($25). Dual remote, chrome: Salon ($69). Lighted vanity, right: SE ($60). Electronic-tuning radios w/digital clock: AM stereo/FM stereo

($149). Seek/scan AM stereo/FM stereo w/cassette ($251-$400). Ultimate sound AM stereo/FM stereo w/cassette ($467-$616). Power antenna: Salon ($67). Radio delete ($56 credit). Exterior: Power glass sunroof: Salon ($1108). Full vinyl roof: Salon ($191). Pearl Coat paint ($41). Vinyl bodyside moldings ($59). Upper door frame moldings: Salon ($47). Body sound insulation: Salon ($68). Undercoating ($44). Interior: Vinyl split-back bench seat: Salon ($62). Trunk dress-up: Salon ($58). Wheels/Tires: Premium wheel covers: Salon ($99). Wire wheel covers: SE ($231). Cast aluminum wheels: SE ($39-$270). Conventional spare tire ($96).

HISTORY: Introduced: October 1, 1985. Model year production: Chrysler reported a total of 404,496 passenger cars shipped. Of the four-cylinder engines, 66,272 were turbos. Calendar year production: 506,404. Calendar year sales by U.S. dealers: 456,777. Model year sales by U.S. dealers: 432,205 (not incl. imports or early '87 Dodge Shadows).

HISTORICAL FOOTNOTES: Chrysler Corp. predicted a decline in domestic car sales for the model year. Yet Dodge Division beat the 1985 figure, posting the highest total since 1978. That rise was due largely to the three Mitsubishi-built imports, however (Colt, Colt Vista, and Conquest). Domestic sales declined a bit (down about 6,300) for the model year. Daytona expected to remain for 1987, even though sales were down, whereas Chrysler's Laser was to be dropped. Omni/Charger sales had been rather good during 1985 as a result of option discount packages and low-rate financing. Omni sales improved after the new "America" campaign, which included price cuts. Aries declined somewhat in model year sales, while Lancer rose by 20 percent. Diplomats were hit with a gas guzzler tax, yet sold fairly well, down only moderately for the model year. Dodge's market share for 1986 was 5.3 percent (not including the imports). High-performance versions of GLH, Charger and Daytona were tested on a track of the Chrysler Shelby Performance Center at Santa Fe Springs, California. Dodge, according to General Marketing Manager John Damoose served as "the performance division of the Corporation."

1987 DODGE

Only one model was all-new this year: the Shadow, a close relation to Plymouth's Sundance. Chrysler dropped its Laser version of the front-drive sport coupe, but the similar Dodge Daytona carried on. The 600 coupe and convertible were gone, but the sedans remained. Three high-performance Shelby editions were offered, in the Charger, Daytona and Lancer lines. Dodge also continued to produce the Caravan minivan and to import the Colt and Colt Vista, both built by Mitsubishi.

1987 Dodge, Omni America hatchback sedan (OCW)

OMNI AMERICA — SERIES L — FOUR — Reduction of the hatchback subcompact sedan to a single series brought a substantial price cut. Only three separate options were offered, and three option packages. The only engine choice was the 2.2-liter four, rated at 96 horsepower, with standard five-speed manual shift or optional three-speed automatic. Standard equipment included power brakes, a rear defogger, rear wiper/washer, tinted glass, black bodyside moldings, and right visor mirror.

CHARGER — SERIES L — FOUR — Like the Omni sedan, Dodge's hatchback coupe came with a standard carbureted 2.2-liter four. But performance-minded buyers had the option of a turbocharged Shelby Charger, with a 146-horsepower engine and close-ratio five-speed gearbox. The Shelby came with power steering, sport suspension, AM/FM stereo with cassette player, lighted right visor mirror, sport front seats, removable glass sunroof, two-tone paint, front and rear spoilers, side sill extensions, and P205/50VR15 tires on aluminum wheels.

1987 Dodge, Daytona Pacifica hatchback coupe (OCW)

1987 Dodge, Daytona Shelby Z hatchback coupe with optional T-bar roof (OCW)

1987 Dodge, Shelby Charger hatchback coupe (OCW)

DAYTONA — SERIES G — FOUR — Restyling hit Dodge's front-drive sport coupe, highlighted up front by new concealed headlamps to replace the former exposed quad units. Rear-end styling was new too, including wide taillamps that contained the required high-mount stoplamp. Three models were offered: base, Pacifica and Shelby Z. The latter two each displayed a new three-piece spoiler, but had different front airdams and bodyside moldings. Base Daytona engine was the 2.5-liter four, rated at 100 horsepower, with 146-horsepower turbo optional. That turbo was standard in the Pacifica, while the Shelby held a 174-horsepower Turbo II edition with an intercooler and higher boost pressure. The Shelby also used a stronger five-speed manual gearbox, and wasn't available with automatic (except with the lower-powered turbo). Analog instrumentation on all models included a 125 mph speedometer. Standard equipment included a five-speed manual transmission, power brakes and steering, dual remote mirrors, remote hatch and fuel-filler releases, AM/FM stereo, rear defogger, and soft feel steering wheel. Pacifica added air conditioning, an overhead console, trumpet air horns, heated power mirrors, Electronic Navigator computer, leather-wrapped steering wheel, and Enthusiast front seats (six-way power on driver's side). The Shelby Z included disc brakes, aerodynamic body treatment (including rear spoiler and front airdam), performance seats and suspension, and tilt steering.

1987 Dodge, Shadow sedan (OCW)

SHADOW — SERIES P — FOUR — Chrysler's P-body arrived before the start of the model year in four-door hatchback form, joined later by a two-door hatchback. Shadows had a sizable amount of standard equipment and a fairly firm suspension, Two powerplants were available: the base 2.2-liter four, and a turbocharged version rated at 146 horsepower. Turbo models came with high-performance tires, but in the same size as the others. An ES package included P205/50VR15 unidirectional radial tires on cast aluminum wheels. Standard equipment included a five-speed manual gearbox, power brakes and steering, cloth upholstery,

tachometer, reclining front bucket seats, AM radio, remote manual mirrors, side-window demisters, remote hatch release, and wide bodyside moldings.

1987 Dodge, Aries LE two-door sedan (OCW)

1987 Dodge, Aries LE station wagon with optional roof rack (OCW)

ARIES K — SERIES K — FOUR — Only two series were left in the compact front-drive family sedan lineup, as the SE dropped out. Base and LE models remained, in two- and four-door body styles along with the station wagon. Front bucket seats were now standard, but LE buyers could get a bench seat (with folding center armrest) at no extra charge. Otherwise, little was new this year.

1987 Dodge, Lancer ES sedan with optional turbocharged engine (OCW)

LANCER — SERIES H — FOUR — Two mechanical changes appeared in Lancer for 1987: a new stainless steel exhaust system and a lockup torque converter for the available automatic transmission, the latter offered only with the optional 2.5-liter engine. The new converter was supposed to boost fuel mileage. A near twin to Chrysler's LeBaron GTS, the Lancer four-door sedan came with a standard 2.2-liter four. Both the 2.5-liter and a turbocharged 2.2 (rated at 146 horsepower) were optional. A new optional electronic cruise control replaced the former vacuum-actuated unit. Also added to the option list were an overhead console (with compass and thermometer) and, later, a six-speaker Infinity sound system. A high-performance Lancer Shelby became available in limited number (see 1988 listing for details).

1987 Dodge, 600 SE sedan with optional turbocharged engine and wire wheel covers (OCW)

600 SEDAN — SERIES E — FOUR — Chrysler's new LeBaron coupe and convertible served as replacements for the Dodge K-body versions, which dropped out this year. The remaining 600 sedan, riding a lengthened K-body platform, had only minor changes. They included a new stainless steel exhaust system, plus a lockup torque converter in the

automatic transmission supplied with the optional 2.5-liter engine. Base engine was a 2.2-liter four. A new electronic cruise control was optional, replacing the former vacuum-type unit.

1987 Dodge, Diplomat SE sedan with optional sunroof and wire wheel covers (OCW)

DIPLOMAT — SERIES M — V-8 — Nothing was new in Dodge's full-size, traditional rear-drive model. Base engine remained the 318 cu. in. (5.2-liter) V-8, delivering 140 horsepower to a TorqueFlite three-speed automatic transmission.

I.D. DATA: Dodge's 17-symbol Vehicle Identification Number (VIN), as before, was on the upper left corner of the instrument panel, visible through the windshield. Coding is similar to 1986. Symbol ten (model year) changed to 'H' for 1987. Engine numbers and Body Code Plates are in the same locations as 1981-86.

OMNI AMERICA (FOUR)

Model No.	Body/Style No.	Body Type & Seating	Factory Price	Shipping Weight	Prod. Total
LZE	44	4-dr. Hatch-5P	5499	2237	66,907

CHARGER (FOUR)

LZH	24	2-dr. Hatch-5P	6999	2290	24,275

SHELBY CHARGER (FOUR)

LZS	24	2-dr. Hatch-5P	9840	2483	2,011

DAYTONA (FOUR)

GVH	24	2-dr. Hatch-4P	9799	2676	18,485

DAYTONA PACIFICA (FOUR)

GVP	24	2-dr. Hatch-4P	13912	2862	7,467

DAYTONA SHELBY Z (FOUR)

GVS	24	2-dr. Hatch-4P	12749	2812	7,152

SHADOW (FOUR)

PDH	24	2-dr. Sedan-5P	7499	2459	38,497
PDH	44	4-dr. Sedan-5P	7699	2494	37,559

ARIES (FOUR)

KDL	21	2-dr. Sedan-6P	7655	2409	204
KDL	41	4-dr. Sedan-6P	7655	2415	4,710

ARIES LE (FOUR)

KDM	21	2-dr. Sedan-6P	8134	2468	7,517
KDM	41	4-dr. Sedan-6P	8134	2484	66,506
KDM	45	4-dr. Sta Wag-6P	8579	2588	20,362

LANCER (FOUR)

HDH	44	4-dr. Spt Hatch-5P	9474	2645	17,040
HDS	44	4-dr. ES Hatch-5P	10428	2692	9,529

LANCER SHELBY (FOUR)

HDS	44	4-dr. Sedan-5P	N/A	N/A	N/A

600 SEDAN (FOUR)

EEM	41	4-dr. Sedan-6P	9891	2594	20,074
EEH	41	4-dr. SE Sed-6P	10553	2601	20,317

DIPLOMAT SALON (V-8)

MGL	41	4-dr. Sedan-6P	10598	3566	11,256

DIPLOMAT SE (V-8)

MGP	41	4-dr. Sedan-6P	11678	3627	9,371

ENGINE DATA: BASE FOUR (Omni, Charger): Inline, overhead-cam four-cylinder. Cast iron block; aluminum head. Displacement: 135 cu. in. (2.2-liters). Bore and stroke: 3.44 x 3.62 in. Compression ratio: 9.0:1. Brake horsepower: 96 at 5200 R.P.M. Torque: 119 lb.-ft. at 3200 R.P.M. Five main bearings. Hydraulic valve lifters. Carburetor 2Bbl. BASE FOUR (Aries, Shadow, Lancer, 600): Same as 135 cu. in. four above exc. with throttle-body fuel injection. Compression ratio: 9.5:1.

Horsepower: 97 at 5200 R.P.M. Torque: 122 lb.-ft. at 3200 R.P.M. BASE TURBOCHARGED FOUR (Shelby Charger, Daytona Pacifica): OPTIONAL (Daytona, Shadow, Lancer, 600): Same as 135 cu. in. four above, with electronic fuel injection and turbocharger. Compression ratio: 8.1:1. Horsepower: 146 at 5200 R.P.M. Torque: 170 lb.-ft. at 3600 R.P.M. BASE TURBOCHARGED FOUR (Shelby Z Daytona): Same as turbocharged 135 cu. in. four above exc.: Brake horsepower: 174 at 4800 R.P.M. Torque: 200 lb.-ft. at 3200 R.P.M. BASE FOUR (Daytona); OPTIONAL (Aries, Lancer, 600): Inline, overhead-cam four-cylinder. Cast iron block; aluminum head. Displacement: 153 cu. in. (2.5-liters). Bore and stroke: 3.44 x 4.09 in. Compression ratio: 9.0:1. Brake horsepower: 100 at 4800 R.P.M. Torque: 136 lb.-ft. at 2800 R.P.M. Five main bearings. Hydraulic valve lifters. Throttle-body fuel injection. BASE V-8 (Diplomat): 90-degree, overhead valve V-8. Cast iron block and heads. Displacement: 318 cu. in. (5.2-liters). Bore and stroke: 3.91 x 3.31 in. Compression ratio: 9.0:1. Brake horsepower: 140 at 3600 R.P.M. Torque: 265 lb.-ft. at 1600 R.P.M. Five main bearings. Hydraulic valve lifters. Carburetor 2Bbl.

CHASSIS DATA: Wheelbase: (Omni) 99.1 in.; (Charger) 96.5 in.; (Daytona) 97.0 in.; (Shadow) 97.0 in.; (Aries) 100.3 in.; (Aries wag) 100.4 in.; (600) 103.3 in.; (Lancer) 103.1 in.; (Diplomat) 112.7 in. Overall Length: (Omni) 163.2 in.; (Charger) 174.8 in.; (Shelby) 174.7.; (Daytona) 175.0 in.; (Shadow) 171.7 in.; (Daytona Shelby Z) 176.9 in.; (Aries) 178.9 in.; (Aries wag) 179.0 in.; (Lancer) 180.4 in.; (600) 179.2 in.; (Diplomat) 204.6 in. Height: (Omni) 53.0 in.; (Charger) 50.7 in.; (Shelby) 50.2 in.; (Daytona) 50.4 in.; (Shadow) 52.7 in.; (Aries 2-dr.) 52.5 in.; (Aries 4-dr.) 52.9 in.; (Aries wag) 53.3 in.; (Lancer) 53.0 in.; (600) 53.1 in.; (Diplomat) 55.3 in. Width: (Omni) 66.8 in.; (Charger) 66.1 in.; (Aries) 67.9 in.; (Daytona) 69.3 in.; (Shadow) 67.3 in.; (Lancer) 68.3 in.; (600) 68.0 in.; (Diplomat) 74.2 in. Front Tread: (Omni/Charger) 56.1 in.; (Aries/Daytona/Shadow/Lancer/600) 57.6 in.; (Diplomat) 60.0 in. Rear Tread: (Omni/Charger) 55.7 in.; (Aries/Shadow/Lancer/600) 57.2 in.; (Daytona) 59.5 in. Standard Tires: (Omni/Charger) P165/80R13; (Shelby Charger) P205/50VR15; (Daytona) P185/70R14 SBR BSW; (Daytona Shelby) P205/60R15; (Shadow) P185/70R14; (Aries) P175/80R13; (Lancer) P185/70R14; (Lancer ES) P195/70R14; (600) P185/70R14; (Diplomat) P205/75R15.

TECHNICAL: Transmission: Five-speed manual standard on Omni/Charger, Shadow, Aries, Lancer and Daytona. TorqueFlite three-speed automatic standard on Diplomat and 600; optional on all other models. Steering: (Diplomat) recirculating ball; (others) rack and pinion. Suspension: (Omni/Charger) MacPherson front struts with coil springs and anti-sway bar, beam rear axle with coil springs (anti-sway bar on Charger); (Aries/Daytona/Shadow/Lancer 600) MacPherson front struts with coil springs and anti-sway bar, beam rear axle with coil springs and anti-sway bar; (Diplomat) transverse front torsion bars and anti-sway bar, semi-elliptic rear leaf springs. Brakes: Front disc, rear drum. Body construction: Unibody. Fuel tank: (Omni/Charger) 13 gal.; (Daytona/Shadow/Aries/Lancer/600) 14 gal.; (Diplomat) 18 gal.

DRIVETRAIN OPTIONS: Engines: Turbo 2.2-liter: Shadow ($815); Daytona ($990); Lancer/600 ($685). 2.5-liter four: Daytona ($279); Aries LE/Lancer/600 ($287). Transmission: TorqueFlite auto. trans.: Daytona ($504); Shadow/Aries/Lancer ($534).

OMNI/CHARGER CONVENIENCE/APPEARANCE OPTIONS: Basic Pkg. (auto. trans. and pwr stng) ($776). Manual Trans. Pkg. Pwr stng, AM/FM stereo ET, highback front bucket seats, upgraded cargo area trim, center console with coin holder, cubby box, cupholder, ash receiver light (N/A Shelby) ($575). Auto. Trans. Pkg. Manual Transmission discount Pkg. plus 3-spd auto. trans. (NA Shelby) ($1009). Air cond. (discount pkg. reg'd) ($701). California emission pkg. ($99). AM/FM stereo cassette (discount pkg. reg'd) ($246).

DAYTONA CONVENIENCE/APPEARANCE OPTIONS: Air cond. ($757). Popular Equipment Pkg. w/A/C. Air cond., pwr remote mirrors, tilt stng column, rear defogger, cruise control, light group. Base ($757). Base w/T-Bar roof ($841). Turbo Z ($897). Popular Equipment w/o A/C. Base ($249). Base w/T-Bar roof ($284). Turbo Z ($340). Cargo Trim/Quiet Sound Group. Added cargo area carpeting and sound insulation, tonneau cover. Turbo Z ($252). Turbo Z w/Popular Equipment ($233). Sun/Sound/Shade Pkg. rear window louvers. AM/FM stereo ET cassette ($626). W/T-bar roof ($294). C/S Handling Pkg., Turbo Z ($183). Pwr door locks ($130). Pwr windows ($195). Pwr driver's seat ($225). Cruise control ($179). Rear window wiper/washer ($125). Pwr remote mirrors ($56). Tilt stng column ($115). AM/FM stereo cassette ($244). AM/FM stereo cassette w/graphic EQ (Ultimate Sound) w/Sun/Sound/Shade ($454). w/o Sun/Sound/Shade ($210). Flip up/removable glass sunroof ($332). Sport seats w/inflatable driver's side supports, Leather, base ($959). Leather, Turbo Z ($674). Cloth and vinyl, base ($392). Conventional spare tire ($83). With P195/70R14 tires, base ($92). Electronic Features (voice alert and trip computer). Base ($583). Turbo Z ($272). T-Bar roof (incl. pwr windows and mirrors, reading lamps) w/o Popular Equipment ($1372). Base w/Popular Equipment ($1351). Turbo Z w/Popular Equipment ($1295).

1987 Dodge, Shadow two-door sedan with optional ES performance package and sunroof (OCW)

SHADOW CONVENIENCE/APPEARANCE OPTIONS: ES pkg. 2.2-liter turbocharged engine, full console w/center armrest, 60/40 folding rear seatback, dual pwr mirrors, AM/FM stereo, leather-wrapped stng whl, premium bucket seats, map light, P205/50VR15 unidirectional tires on alum whls ($1755). W/Popular Equipment ($1598). W/Light Pkg. ($1731). Popular Equipment Pkg., rear defogger, light pkg. AM/FM stereo ($284). Deluxe Convenience Pkg., cruise control and tilt stng column ($310). Light Pkg., 2-dr ($91). 4-dr ($103). Protection Pkg. ($90). Air cond. (tinted glass req'd) ($701). Full console w/armrest ($150). Rear window defogger ($149). California emission pkg. ($102). Tinted glass ($106). Dual pwr mirrors (console req'd) ($49). Pwr windows (console req'd), 2-dr ($212). 4-dr ($288). Pwr door locks, 2-dr ($146). 4-dr ($197). Sound systems: AM/FM stereo ($157). AM/FM stereo cassette ($403). W/ES or Popular Equipment ($246). Removable glass sunroof ($369). Conventional spare tire (N/A w/ES) ($85). 14-in. alum whls (N/A w/ES) ($315). Pearl Coat paint ($41).

ARIES CONVENIENCE/APPEARANCE OPTIONS: Air cond. (tinted glass req'd) ($790). Pearl Coat paint ($41). Cloth and vinyl bench seat, base (NC). Vinyl bench seat w/center armrest, LE (NC) w/cloth and vinyl LE (NC). Basic Equipment Pkg., AM mono, left remote mirror, intermittent wipers, deluxe wheel covers, base ($260). Popular Equipment Pkg. Auto. trans., pwr stng, tinted glass, AM/FM stereo ET, dual remote mirrors, uprated sound insulation, trunk dress-up, tonneau cover (wag), deluxe wheel covers, P185/70R14 blackwall tires. LE sedans ($740). Wag ($760). Premium Equipment Pkg., Popular Equipment plus rear defogger, pwr door locks, cruise control, tilt stng column, rear wiper/washer and luggage rack (wag), LE 2-dr ($1261). LE 4-dr ($1312). Wag ($1589). Light Pkg. ($59). Tinted glass ($121). Full console ($157). Rear window defogger ($152). Calif. emissions pkg. ($102). Front and rear floor mats ($46). Luggage rack, wag ($127). Pwr door locks, LE 2-dr ($146). LE 4-dr, wag ($197). Pwr stng ($242). Sound systems AM/FM stereo base ($271). Base w/Basic Equipment, LE ($157). AM/FM stereo cassette, LE (Popular or Premium Equipment req'd) ($257). Conventional spare tire (13-in.) ($75). Conventional spare tire (14-in.) ($85). Cruise control ($184). Tilt stng col. (cruise req'd) ($126). Heavy-duty suspension ($61). Undercoating ($44). Cast aluminum 14-in. road wheels, LE w/Popular or Premium Equipment ($332). W/o Popular or Premium Equipment ($381). Rear wiper/washer, wag ($130). Woodtone exterior appliqué, wag w/o Popular or Premium Equipment ($282). W/Popular or Premium Equipment ($233). P185/70R14 tires, LE w/o Popular or Premium Equipment ($164). W/Popular or Premium Equipment ($67).

LANCER CONVENIENCE/APPEARANCE OPTIONS: Air cond. ($790). Pearl Coat paint ($41). Leather seats, ES ($644). Popular Equipment Pkg., Base: air cond., light pkg., front and rear floor mats, cruise control, tilt stng column, undercoating. ES: base content plus 2.2-liter turbo engine, P205/60 15-in. tires on cast alum whls ($901). Base incl. auto. trans. ($1245). ES ($1468). ES incl. auto. trans. ($1852). Console/Lights Convenience Pkg. Overhead console w/compass, outside temperature thermometer, garage door opener holder, map lights, lighted visor mirrors, console w/armrest, light pkg. Base w/o Popular Equip. ($236). Base w/Popular Equip. ($166). ES ($279). Deluxe Convenience Pkg.; cruise control, tilt stng column, front and rear floor mats, undercoating ($401). Electronic Features Pkg.: Electronic instrument cluster, electronic navigator, voice alert, 500-amp battery, headlamp extinguish feature. ES ($701). ES w/rear window defogger ($656). Rear window defogger ($198). Calif. emission pkg. ($102). Pwr Convenience Pkg. Pwr windows and door locks ($481). Pwr driver's seat ($242). Sound systems AM/FM stereo cassette ($298). W/graphic EQ (Ultimate Sound) ($510). Removable glass sunroof w/Pwr Convenience Pkg. ($376). Sport handling suspension ($27). Cast aluminum 14-in. whls ($319). 15-in. whls and tires, base (NC on ES) ($285). W/alum whls, base ($604). W/alum whls, ES ($192). Rear wiper/washer ($130). P195/70R14 SBR handling tires, base ($102).

600 CONVENIENCE/APPEARANCE OPTIONS: Popular Equipment Pkg., Rear window defogger, 500-amp battery, air cond., cruise control, tilt stng column, AM/FM stereo ET, intermittent wipers, left remote and right manual mirrors, base ($928). SE ($997). Rear window defroster

pkg. ($197). Protection pkg. ($209). Deluxe Convenience Pkg., cruise control, tilt stng column ($310). Light pkg. ($138). Air cond. ($790). Calif. emissions pkg. ($102). Dual pwr mirrors, base ($113). Base w/Popular Equip., SE ($88). Dual illum. visor mirrors ($119). Pwr Convenience Pkg., Pwr windows and door locks ($436). Pwr seat (left or bench), SE ($242) AM/FM stereo cassette ($438). Base w/Popular Equip., SE ($292). Pearl Coat paint ($41). Vinyl bodyside mldg ($61). Conventional spare tire ($85). Sport handling suspension ($59) Trunk dress-up ($53). Locking wire whl covers ($280). Cast alum whls ($381).

DIPLOMAT CONVENIENCE/APPEARANCE OPTIONS: Heavy-duty suspension ($26). Auto temp air cond. ($837). Pearl Coat paint ($40). Full vinyl roof ($200). Vinyl bodyside mldg ($62). Light Pkg., Salon ($128). SE ($90). Popular Equipment Pkg., rear window defogger, dual remote mirrors, Protection Grp., AM/FM stereo ET, tilt stng column, intermittent wipers, Salon ($597). SE ($474). Luxury Equipment Pkg., Popular Equipment content plus auto. air cond., pwr windows and door locks, cruise control, illum. right side visor mirror, wire whl covers, SE ($2027). Protection Grp. ($138). 500-amp battery ($44). Rear window defogger ($148). Calif. emissions pkg. ($99). Illum. entry system (tilt stng req'd) ($75). Special body sound insulation ($66). Remote left mirror, Salon ($24). Dual remote mirrors, SE ($67). Illum. right visor mirror, SE ($58). Upper door frame mldg ($46). Pwr decklid release ($50). Pwr door locks ($195). Pwr driver's seat ($240). Sound systems AM/FM stereo ($155). AM/FM stereo cassette w/o Popular or Luxury Equip. ($399). W/Popular or Luxury Equip. ($254). W/graphic EQ (Ultimate Sound) w/Popular or Luxury Equip. ($464). Pwr antenna ($70). Delete stnd radio ($56 credit). Conventional spare tire ($93). Cruise control ($179). Leather-wrapped stng whl, SE ($60). Tilt stng column ($125). Pwr glass sunroof ($1076). Trunk dress-up ($56). Undercoating ($43). Premium whl covers, Salon ($96). Wire whl covers, SE ($224). Cast alum whls, SE w/o Luxury Equip. ($262). SE w/Luxury Equip. ($38). Intermittent wipers ($58).

HISTORY: Model year production: 501,926. Calendar year production: 414,684. Calendar year sales by U.S. dealers: 348,294.

1988 DODGE

Charger was gone, retiring an old familiar Dodge nameplate; but Dynasty was new this year. That family sedan was related to the Chrysler New Yorker, but lacked the New Yorker's concealed headlamps. Aries slipped down to a single series this time around.

1988 Dodge, Omni America hatchback sedan (OCW)

OMNI AMERICA — SERIES L — FOUR — Fuel injection replaced the old carburetor on the subcompact hatchback's 2.2-liter four-cylinder engine. In addition, the optional three-speed automatic transmission gained a lockup torque converter for improved gas mileage. A five-speed manual gearbox was standard. Both Omni and its near twin, the Plymouth Horizon, were now manufactured at the former AMC plant in Kenosha, Wisconsin, following takeover of that company by Chrysler. As in 1987, few options were available and Omni came in only one trim level.

DAYTONA — SERIES G — FOUR — Once again, the sporty coupe came in three forms: base model with a 96-horsepower, 2.5-liter four; Pacifica, powered by a 146-horsepower Turbo I engine; or the all-out Shelby Z, with a 174-horsepower Turbo II beneath its hood. Running with a new lightweight turbocharger, the Turbo I also was part of a new C/S performance package for the base Daytona. That package included four-wheel disc brakes, special P205/60R15 tires on aluminum wheels, and a performance handling suspension. New Infinity sound systems and a compact-disc player joined the option list.

1988 Dodge, Shadow sedan with optional ES performance package (OCW)

1988 Dodge, Daytona Shelby Z hatchback coupe with optional rear window louver (OCW)

SHADOW — SERIES P — FOUR — Little was new in the basic sub-compact Shadow, but its ES turbo option package changed this year. In addition to the turbocharged four-cylinder engine, the package now included a revised front fascia with integral airdam and built-in foglamps. The ES also contained a new rear spoiler, front fender flares, tape striping, and ES graphics. Inside the ES were reclining front bucket seats with four-way head restraints and driver's lumbar support, plus power door locks and a rear window defogger. The ES came only in a two-door hatchback form, while the base Shadow came as a two- or four-door hatchback. Base powertrain was a 2.2-liter four with five-speed manual gearbox, with 2.5-liter four and automatic optional. The automatic had a new lockup torque converter.

1988 Dodge, Aries America LE sedan (OCW)

ARIES AMERICA — SERIES K — FOUR — Like the Omni a year earlier, Aries was reduced to a single trim level as a cost-cutting (and price-cutting) measure. Its option list also shrank, with most extras grouped in packages instead of priced separately. Two- and four-door sedans were available, along with the four-door station wagon. Base engine was a fuel-injected 2.2-liter four, with a 2.5-liter four optional. The bigger engine was available only with automatic shift, but a five-speed manual gearbox was standard.

1988 Dodge, Lancer Shelby hatchback sedan (OCW)

LANCER — SERIES H — FOUR — Base Lancers, with a standard 2.2-liter four-cylinder engine and five-speed gearbox, changed little this year. A rear-window defogger was now standard. A 125 mph electronic speedometer went into the base model's analog instrument cluster. Lancer ES came with a 2.5-liter four rated at 96 horsepower, and included air conditioning, dual power mirrors, lighted visor vanity mirrors, and power door locks. Both the base and ES could have the optional 146-horsepower turbocharged engine. Introduced in small quantities for 1987, the Lancer Shelby became a full-fledged model this year. The Shelby had a body-color grille, side sill extensions, and front and rear spoiler. Driving lights sat in the front spoiler. Shelby's engine was the Turbo II, with 174-horsepower output, hooked to a five-speed manual gearbox. No options were offered for the Shelby except for a power glass sunroof.

1988 Dodge, 600 SE sedan (OCW)

600 — SERIES E — FOUR — This year's engine for the step-up 600 SE was the 2.5-liter four, while the 2.2-liter four remained standard in the base model. Both could be ordered with a 146-horsepower turbo instead. The three-speed automatic transmission had a lockup torque converter to boost gas mileage. Dodge's mid-size four-door sedans were related to the Plymouth Caravelle and the short-lived Chrysler New Yorker Turbo.

1988 Dodge, Dynasty LE sedan with optional cast aluminum wheels (OCW)

DYNASTY — SERIES C — FOUR/V-6 — Dodge's new model was a C-bodied front drive sedan, related to the Chrysler New Yorker and second only to the rear-drive Diplomat in size. Unlike the New Yorker, Dynasty kept its aero headlamps exposed. Full width wraparound taillamps stood at the rear. Base and LE trim levels were offered. Base engine was a 2.5-liter four with three-speed automatic transmission. A Mitsubishi-built 3.0-liter V-6 was optional. Standard equipment included power brakes and steering, AM/FM stereo, analog instruments, clearcoat paint, a stainless steel exhaust system, cornering lamps, rear window defogger, and a bench seat with armrest. The premium model added a 50/50 bench seat and leather-wrapped steering wheel. Anti-lock braking was optional on the LE. So was a rear load-leveling system and a power glass sunroof.

1988 Dodge, Diplomat SE sedan with optional wire wheel covers (OCW)

DIPLOMAT — SERIES M — V-8 — Changes in the full-size, rear-drive Dodge centered on its standard equipment list. Added this year to the step-up SE were cruise control, AM/FM stereo, tilt steering, rear window defogger, driver's seat recliner, and intermittent wipers. A driver's side airbag became standard late in the model year. Two options joined the list: twin lighted visor mirrors and twin power remote-control door mirrors. Sole powertrain was the 5.2-liter V-8 with three-speed automatic.

I.D. DATA: Dodge's 17-symbol Vehicle Identification Number (VIN), as before, was on the upper left corner of the instrument panel, visible through the windshield. Coding is similar to 1986-87. Symbol ten (model year) changed to 'J' for 1988.

OMNI AMERICA (FOUR)

Model No.	Body/ Style No.	Body Type & Seating	Factory Price	Shipping Weight	Prod. Total
LZE	44	4-dr. Hatch-5P	5999	2225	59,887

DAYTONA (FOUR)

GVH	24	2-dr. Hatch-4P	10025	2676	54,075

DAYTONA PACIFICA (FOUR)

GVP	24	2-dr. Hatch-4P	14513	2862	4,752

DAYTONA SHELBY Z (FOUR)

GVS	24	2-dr. Hatch-4P	13394	2812	7,850

SHADOW (FOUR)

PDH	24	2-dr. Sedan-5P	7875	2513	36,452
PDH	44	4-dr. Sedan-5P	8075	2544	55,857

ARIES AMERICA (FOUR)

KDH	21	2-dr. Sedan-6P	6995	2485	6,578
KDH	41	4-dr. Sedan-6P	6995	2459	85,613
KDH	45	4-dr. Sta Wag-6P	7695	2537	19,172

LANCER (FOUR)

HDH	44	4-dr. Spt Hatch-5P	10482	2646	6,580
HDS	44	4-dr. ES Hatch-5P	12715	2702	2,484

LANCER SHELBY (FOUR)

HDS	44/AFP	4-dr. Spt Hatch-5P	N/A	N/A	279

600 (FOUR)

EEM	41	4-dr. Sedan-6P	10659	2595	26,653
EEH	41	4-dr. SE Sed-6P	11628	2633	28,897

DYNASTY (FOUR/V-6)

CDH	41	4-dr. Sedan-6P	11666	2956	26,653
CDP	41	4-dr. Prem Sed-6P	12226	2966	28,897

DIPLOMAT (V-8)

MGE	41	4-dr. Sedan-6P	12127	3584	444
MGP	41	4-dr. Sedan-6P	14221	3634	5,737

DIPLOMAT SALON (V-8)

MGL	41	4-dr. Sedan-6P	11407	3567	12,992

ENGINE DATA: BASE FOUR (Omni, Shadow, Aries, Lancer, 600): Inline, overhead-cam four-cylinder. Cast iron block; aluminum head. Displacement: 135 cu. in. (2.2 liters). Bore and stroke: 3.44 x 3.62 in. Compression ratio: 9.5:1. Brake horsepower: 93 at 4800 R.P.M. Torque: 122 lb.-ft. at 3200 R.P.M. Five main bearings. Throttle-body fuel injection. BASE TURBOCHARGED FOUR (Daytona Pacifica); OPTIONAL (Daytona, Shadow, Lancer, 600): Same as 135 cu. in. four above, with electronic fuel injection and turbocharger. Compression ratio: 8.0:1. Brake horsepower: 146 at 5200 R.P.M. Torque: 170 lb.-ft. at 2400 R.P.M. BASE TURBOCHARGED FOUR (Shelby Z Daytona, Lancer Shelby): Same as turbocharged 135 cu. in. four above exc.: Brake horsepower: 174 at 5200 R.P.M. Torque: 200 lb.-ft. at 2400 R.P.M. BASE FOUR (Daytona, Lancer ES, 600 SE, Dynasty); OPTIONAL (Shadow, Aries, Lancer, 600): Inline, overhead-cam four-cylinder. Cast iron block; aluminum head. Displacement: 153 cu. in. (2.5 liters). Bore and stroke: 3.44 x 4.09 in. Compression ratio: 8.9:1. Brake horsepower: 96 at 4400 R.P.M. Torque: 133 lb.-ft. at 2800 R.P.M. Five main bearings. Throttle-body fuel injection. OPTIONAL V-6 (Dynasty): Overhead cam V-6. Displacement: 181 cu. in. (3.0 liters). Bore and stroke: 3.59 x 2.99 in. Compression ratio: 8.9:1. Brake horsepower: 136 at 4800 R.P.M. Torque: 168 lb.-ft. at 2800 R.P.M. Port fuel injection. BASE V-8 (Diplomat): 90-degree, overhead valve V-8. Cast iron block and heads. Displacement: 318 cu. in. (5.2 liters). Bore and stroke: 3.91 x 3.31 in. Compression ratio: 9.1:1. Brake horsepower: 140 at 3600 R.P.M. Torque: 265 lb.-ft. at 1600 R.P.M. Five main bearings. Hydraulic valve lifters. Carburetor: 2Bbl.

CHASSIS DATA: Wheelbase: (Omni) 99.1 in.; (Daytona) 97.0 in.; (Shadow) 97.0 in.; (Aries) 100.3 in.; (600) 103.3 in.; (Lancer) 103.1 in.; (Dynasty) 104.3 in.; (Diplomat) 112.7 in. Overall Length: (Omni) 163.2 in.; (Daytona) 175.0 in.; (Shadow) 171.7 in.; (Aries) 178.9 in.; (Aries wag) 179.0 in.; (Lancer) 180.4 in.; (600) 179.2 in.; (Dynasty) 192.0 in.; (Diplomat) 204.6 in. Height: (Omni) 53.0 in.; (Daytona) 50.4 in.; (Shadow) 52.7 in.; (Aries 2-dr.) 52.5 in.; (Aries 4-dr.) 52.9 in.; (Aries wag) 53.3 in.; (Lancer) 53.0 in.; (600) 53.1 in.; (Dynasty) 53.5

in.; (Diplomat) 55.3 in. Width: (Omni) 66.8 in.; (Aries) 67.9 in.; (Daytona) 69.3 in.; (Shadow) 67. in.; (Lancer) 68.3 in.; (600) 68.0 in.; (Dynasty) 68.5 in.; (Diplomat) 74.2 in. Front Tread: (Omni) 56.1 in.; (Aries/Daytona/Shadow/Lancer/Dynasty/600) 57.6 in.; (Diplomat) 60.0 in. Rear Tread: (Omni) 55.7 in.; (Aries/Shadow/Lancer/600) 57.2 in.; (Daytona/Dynasty) 57.6 in.; (Diplomat) 59.5 in. Standard Tires: (Omni) P165/80R13; (Daytona) P185/70R14 SBR; (Daytona Pacifica) P205/60HR15; (Daytona Shelby) P225/50VR15; (Shadow) P185/70R14; (Aries) P185/70R13; (Aries wag) P185/70R14; (Lancer) P185/70R14; (Lancer ES) P195/70R14; (600) P185/75R14; (Dynasty) P195/75R14; (Diplomat) P205/75R15.

TECHNICAL: Transmission: Five-speed manual standard on Omni, Shadow, Aries, Lancer, and Daytona. TorqueFlite three-speed automatic standard on Dynasty, Diplomat, and 600; optional on all other models. Steering: (Diplomat) recirculating ball; (others) rack and pinion. Brakes: Front disc, rear drum. Body construction: Unibody. Fuel tank: (Omni) 13 gal.; (Daytona/Shadow/Aries/Lancer/600) 14 gal.; (Dynasty) 16 gal.; (Diplomat) 18 gal.

DRIVETRAIN OPTIONS: Engines: Turbo 2.2-liter: Shadow ($809) Daytona ($864); Lancer ($700); 600 ($412-$700). 2.5-liter four: Shadow/Aries/Lancer/600 ($288). Transmission: TorqueFlite auto. trans.: Daytona/Shadow/Lancer ($546).

OMNI CONVENIENCE/APPEARANCE OPTIONS: Basic Pkg. ($769). Manual Trans. Discount Pkg. incl. dual recliners, high back bucket seats ($705). Auto. Trans. Discount Pkg. ($1179). Air cond. ($694). Frt. license plate bracket (NC). Calif. emissions system ($99). AM/FM premium stereo w/cass. ($254). Conventional spare tire ($73).

DAYTONA CONVENIENCE/APPEARANCE OPTIONS: Pearl coat paint, GVH24 ($40); GVS24 and GVP24 ($40). Low back, cloth and vinyl pwr seat w/elect. adjust. lumbar and thigh supports ($392). Low back, leather pwr seat w/elect. adjust. lumbar and thigh supports ($488); GVS24 ($939). Low back, cloth bucket seats w/4-way headrests ($305). Popular Equipment Pkg. GVH24 ($907); GVS24 ($900). Popular Equipment w/o air ($322). Luxury Equipment Discount Pkg. ($506). Cargo Trim/Quiet Sound ($203). Lights and locks discount ($287). Turbo I Eng. Pkg. ($837). Auto. Trans. Pkg. (NC). T-Bar roof, GVH24 ($1468); GVH24 w/(ADD) ($1352); GVS24 ($1258); GVS24 w/(ADF) ($1246). Sun/Sound/Shade discount, GVH24 ($801); GVH24 w/(AET) ($417); GVP24 ($442); GVH24 or GVP24 w/(AET) ($245); GVS24 ($629); GVS24 w/(ADF) ($617). C/S Performance Pkg. ($1394). Electronic inst. cluster ($311). Calif. emissions ($99). Pwr windows ($210). Prem. AM stereo/FM stereo w/cass.; incl. Infinity spkrs on GVP24 and GVS24 and w/(AJS) on GVH24 ($254). Infinity II sound system w/cass. and graphic equalizer ($210). CD player ($400). Auto. spd control ($175). Leather-wrapped stng whl ($59). Rear window sun louver ($210). Conventional spare tire ($171). Security tonneau cover ($69). 14-in. cast alum whls ($310). Liftgate wiper/washer ($125).

SHADOW CONVENIENCE/APPEARANCE OPTIONS: Pearl coat paint ($40). Popular Equip. Discount Pkg., 2-dr. ($438); 4-dr. ($450). Deluxe Convenience Pkg. ($310/385). Pwr Assist Pkg. w/(AGN) ($232); 2-dr. w/o(AGN) ($363); 4-dr. w/(AGN) ($300); 4-dr. w/o(AGN) ($475). Turbo Eng. Pkg. ($780). Shadow 'ES' Pkg., 2-dr. ($2053); 4-dr. ($2115). Air cond. ($694). Frt. lic. plate bracket (NC). Elect. rear window defroster ($145). Calif. emissions ($99). Tinted glass ($105). Pwr door locks, 2-dr. ($145); 4-dr. ($195). AM stereo/FM stereo and 4 spkrs ($155). AM stereo/FM stereo w/cass. and 4 spkrs ($254). Removable glass sunroof ($365). Cast alum whls ($306); w/(AJK) ($363).

1988 Dodge, Aries America LE two-door sedan (OCW)

ARIES CONVENIENCE/APPEARANCE OPTIONS: Basic Equipment Pkg., KDH21 and KDH41 ($769); KDH45 ($529). Popular Equip. Discount Pkg. NA w/man. trans., KDH21 and KDH41 ($1294); w/H3 Seat ($1194); KDH45 ($988); w/H3 seat ($888). Premium Equip. Discount Pkg. NA w/man. trans., KDH21 ($1732); w/H3 seat ($1632); KDH41 ($1782); w/H3 seat ($1682); w/H3 seat ($1476); w/H3 seat ($1376). Wagon Convenience Pkg. KDH45 ($252). Road touring suspension KPD45 ($59). Air cond., tinted glass req'd ($775). Tinted glass ($120). Frt. lic. plate bracket ($120). Rear window defroster ($145). Calif. emissions ($99). AM/FM stereo radio w/cass. player w/seek and scan ($254).

Pwr stng ($240). Road touring suspension KPG45 ($59). P185/70R14 SBS WSW tires ($68). Conventional spare tire, w/13-in. whls ($73); w/14-in. whls ($83). Pearl coat paint ($40). Bench seat (NC).

LANCER CONVENIENCE/APPEARANCE OPTIONS: Turbo Sport Discount Pkg. ($1465). Lancer Shelby Pkg. ($3830); w/Turbo I eng. and auto. trans. ($3651). Deluxe Convenience Pkg., HDH44 ($300). Electronic Features Pkg. ($571). Basic Equip. Discount Pkg. ($964). Popular Equip. Discount Pkg. w/man. trans.($1361); w/auto. trans. ($1797). Luxury Equip. Discount Pkg., HDH44 w/man. trans.($1888); w/auto trans. ($2324); HDS44 w/manual trans.($903); w/auto. trans. ($1339). Air cond. ($775). Frt. license plate bracket (NC). Calif. emissions ($99). Pwr door locks ($195). Pwr Convenience Discount Pkg. ($514). Pwr driver's seat, HDH44 ($240). Pwr windows ($285). Prem. AM/FM stereo w/cass. (incl. 6 spkrs), HDH44 ($463). Ultimate sound AM/FM stereo w/cass., Infinity spkrs and graphic equalizer ($673). Pwr sunroof ($774); w/(AFF) ($599). Sport handling suspension ($85). P185/70R14 steel radial WSW ($68). P195/70R14 steel radial ($112). 15-in. whl covers/tires ($278). 15-in. road whl/tire ($178). Liftgate wiper/washer ($128). Pearl coat paint ($40). Two-tone paint ($226). Leather low back prem. power bucket seats ($566).

600 CONVENIENCE/APPEARANCE OPTIONS: Popular Equip. Discount Pkg., EEM41 ($1193); EEH41 ($1081). Luxury Equipment Discount Pkg., EEM41 ($1847); EEH41 ($1461). Protection Pkg., EEM41 ($159). Air cond. ($775). Frt. lic. plate bracket (NC). Rear window defroster ($145). Calif. emissions ($99). Pwr driver's seat ($240). AM/FM stereo w/cass. Player and 4 spkrs ($254). Road touring suspension ($57). Conventional spare tire ($83). Wire whl covers ($272). 14-in. cast alum whls ($370). Pearl coat paint ($40).

DYNASTY CONVENIENCE/APPEARANCE OPTIONS: Pearl coat paint ($40). Popular Equipment Discount Pkg., CDH41 ($1223); CDP41 ($1549). Luxury Equipment Discount Pkg. CDP41 ($2375). Protection Pkg. ($88). Deluxe Convenience Pkg. ($300). Interior Illum. ($192). Pwr Convenience Pkg. ($338). Air cond. ($775). Frt. license plate bracket (NC). Pwr door locks ($285). Calif. emissions ($99). AM/FM Stereo Cass. Sound Pkg. ($557). AM/FM stereo cass. radio w/5-band graphic equalizer ($767). AM/FM stereo w/cass. player ($254). Pwr 6-way driver's seat ($240). Pwr sunroof ($776). Road handling suspension ($57). Auto. rear load leveling suspension ($180). Conventional spare tire ($83). Wire whl covers ($224). Cast alum whls ($273); w/(AFF) ($49).

DIPLOMAT CONVENIENCE/APPEARANCE OPTIONS: Tilt stng column ($125). H.D. suspension ($26). Clear/pearl coat paint ($40). Full vinyl roof ($200). Popular Equipment Discount Pkg. ($1230). Luxury Equipment Discount Pkg. ($1163). Protection Grp. ($180). Light Pkg., MGL41 ($130); MGP41 ($119). Auto-temp air cond. ($830). Frt. license plate (NC). Rear window defroster ($145). Calif. emissions ($99). Illum. entry system ($76). Dual pwr remote mirrors ($159). Pwr door locks ($195). Pwr windows ($285). AM/FM stereo prem. radio w/cass. and 4 spkrs ($254). Pwr antenna ($70). Pwr sunroof ($1076). Trunk dress-up ($56). Conventional spare tire ($93). Wire whl covers ($224).

HISTORY: Model year production: 489,645. Calendar year production: 511,133. Calendar year sales: 455,787.

1989 DODGE

A new Spirit joined the Dodge lineup this year, replacing the departed 600. Though closely related to the Plymouth Acclaim, Dodge's version was considered the sportier of the pair. Daytonas added disc brakes all around, Shadow switched to a body-color grille, and a new 150-horsepower turbocharged version of the 2.5-liter four-cylinder engine was available in several models.

OMNI AMERICA — SERIES L — FOUR — Little was new on Dodge's hatchback subcompact sedan, which again carried the "America" nameplate and had a shrunken option list. Sole engine was the fuel-injected 2.2-liter four, with five-speed manual gearbox; three-speed automatic optional. Standard equipment included a tachometer, tinted glass, folddown rear seat, rear wiper/washer, rear defogger, and black bodyside moldings.

DAYTONA — SERIES G — FOUR — Every Daytona this year gained all-wheel disc brakes. Each one also got a new front-end look and wraparound taillamps. As ES model replaced the former Pacifica. The ES Turbo had a new Turbo I engine, delivering 150 horsepower. A more potent Turbo II (174 horsepower) again went into the Shelby, which lost its 'Z' designation but gained 16-inch unidirectional tires. Body paint on the Shelby now took a charcoal tone on the bottom, gradually turning to

the regular color on upper panels. A driver's airbag had been added late in the 1988 model year, and continued this year. The optional T-Bar roof now included a removable sunshade. Base models again could be ordered with a C/S Competition Package that included the Turbo II engine and 15-inch tires.

1989 Dodge, Daytona ES Turbo hatchback coupe (OCW)

1989 Dodge, Shadow two-door sedan with optional ES performance package (OCW)

SHADOW — SERIES P — FOUR — Appearance changes in the front-drive hatchback duo included a new body-color grille with crossbar pattern to replace the former crosshatching, plus aero-type headlamps. Base engine remained the 2.2-liter four, with 2.5-liter optional. Replacing the former turbo option, however, was a 150-horsepower 2.5-liter Turbo I engine. The Turbo was available only with an ES option package, which included foglamps and wider tires (P195/60HR15) on new "pumper" alloy wheels. The ES also gained some suspension refinements to boost its performance potential. A new competition package for the two-door hatchback included ES-level tires, a rear spoiler, sport suspension, and the Turbo I engine. A six-way power driver's seat was added to the option selection.

1989 Dodge, Aries America LE sedan (OCW)

ARIES AMERICA — SERIES K — FOUR — Sedans continued with few changes, but the Aries station wagon was dropped. Base engine remained the fuel-injected 2.2-liter four, with a 2.5-liter four optional. Five-speed manual shift remained standard; three-speed automatic available as part of a basic equipment package. Except for identifying paint markings under the hood, and a four-speaker stereo system, nothing was new. Only a few individual options were available, including air conditioning and power steering.

LANCER — SERIES H — FOUR — Three Lancer four-door hatchback models were available this year: base, ES and Shelby. Base engine was the 2.2-liter four, rated at 93 horsepower, with the 2.5-liter four optional. A new 2.5-liter Turbo I option was available, delivering 150 horsepower. That replaced the former 146-horsepower 2.2-liter turbo. Blackout body trim made the ES easily identifiable, and it came with either the standard turbo or optional non-turbo engine. Shelby was more potent yet, with a 174-horsepower, 2.2-liter intercooled Turbo II engine. The Shelby came in a choice of three body colors (white, red or black) and carried foglamps and a selection of aero body components as well as a sport/handling suspension. Shelby interiors held leather bucket seats, with six-way power for the driver.

SPIRIT — SERIES A — FOUR/V-6 — Like its near A-body twin, the Plymouth Acclaim, the new mid-size Spirit was a front-drive four-door notchback sedan that served as a replacement for the 600. Aero-style headlamps stood alongside the crossbar-patterned grille. Standard engine for the base and LE models was the 2.5-liter four, rated at 100 horsepower. A turbocharged version went under the hood of the sporty ES edition; or it could get an optional Mitsubishi-built 3.0-liter V-6 instead. The V-6 came with Chrysler's new four-speed overdrive automatic transmission, while four-cylinder Spirits had either the standard five-speed manual or a three-speed automatic. Standard equipment included cloth reclining front bucket seats, remote fuel-door and trunk releases, power brakes and steering, AM/FM stereo, and visor mirrors. LE added tinted glass, dual remote mirrors, a rear window defogger, cruise control, tilt steering, and lumbar support adjustment for the driver's seat. ES included a cassette player, lighted visor mirrors, sill extensions, a front airdam with foglights, and larger (P205/60R14) Goodyear Eagle GT tires on alloy wheels.

1989 Dodge, Dynasty sedan (OCW)

1989 Dodge, Dynasty LE sedan (OCW)

DYNASTY — SERIES C — FOUR/V-6 — Four horsepower was added to Dynasty's base four-cylinder engine for its second year in the lineup. The step-up LE model came with a Mitsubishi-built 3.0-liter V-6, delivering 141 horsepower (five more than before). That one had Chrysler's new four-speed overdrive transmission, while the four-cylinder Dynasty ran with a three-speed automatic. Anti-lock braking remained optional. Joining the option list were a six-way power driver's seat (with position memory) and an anti-theft system. The four-door, front-drive Dynasty was related to Chrysler's New Yorker.

DIPLOMAT — SERIES M — V-8 — Dodge's six-passenger, full-size, rear-drive sedan entered its final season in the lineup with no significant changes. Two trim levels were available: Salon and SE. Standard equipment included a driver's airbag, tilt steering, tinted glass, AM/FM stereo, intermittent wipers, bench seat with center armrest, and the 5.2-liter V-8 with three-speed automatic. SE added a vinyl roof, automatic air conditioning, 60/40 front seat, rear defogger, remote-control mirrors, cruise control, and lighted passenger visor mirror.

I.D. DATA: Dodge's 17-symbol Vehicle Identification Number (VIN), as before, was on the upper left corner of the instrument panel, visible through the windshield. Coding is similar to 1986-88. Symbol ten (model year) changed to 'K' for 1989.

OMNI AMERICA (FOUR)

Model No.	Body/ Style No.	Body Type & Seating	Factory Price	Shipping Weight	Prod. Total
LZE	44	4-dr. Hatch-5P	6595	2237	37,720

DAYTONA (FOUR)

GVL	24	2-dr. Hatch-4P	9295	2751	Note 1
GVH	24	2-dr. ES Hatch-4P	10395	2822	Note 1

DAYTONA ES TURBO (FOUR)

GVS	24	2-dr. Hatch-4P	11995	2936	Note 1

DAYTONA SHELBY (FOUR)

GVX	24	2-dr. Hatch-4P	13295	2951	Note 1

Note 1: Daytona production totaled 69,998 with no further breakout available.

Model No.	Body/ Style No.	Body Type & Seating	Factory Price	Shipping Weight	Prod. Total
SHADOW (FOUR)					
PDH	24	2-dr. Sedan-5P	8395	2520	31,508
PDH	44	4-dr. Sedan-5P	8595	2558	46,183
ARIES AMERICA (FOUR)					
KDH	21	2-dr. Sedan-6P	7595	2317	3,359
KDH	41	4-dr. Sedan-6P	7595	2323	49,837
LANCER (FOUR)					
HDH	44	4-dr. Spt Hatch-5P	11195	2646	Note 1
HDS	44	4-dr. ES Hatch-5P	13695	2702	Note 1
LANCER SHELBY (FOUR)					
HDX	44	4-dr. Spt Hatch-5P	17395	2838	Note 1

Note 1: Lancer production totaled 2,793 with no further breakout available.

SPIRIT (FOUR/V-6)					
ADH	41	4-dr. Sedan-6P	9995	2765	Note 1
ADP	41	4-dr. ES Sed-6P	12495	2842	Note 1
ADX	41	4-dr. LE Sed-6P	11195	2901	Note 1

Note 1: Spirit production totaled 60,546 with no further breakout available.

DYNASTY (FOUR/V-6)					
CDH	41	4-dr. Sedan-6P	12295	2992	Note 1
CDP	41	4-dr. LE Sedan-6P	13595	3066	Note 1

Note 1: Dynasty production totaled 115,623 with no further breakout available.

DIPLOMAT (V-8)					
MGL	41	4-dr. Salon Sed-6P	11995	3582	Note 1
MGP	41	4-dr. SE Sedan-6P	14795	3732	Note 1

Note 1: Dynasty production totaled 5,709 with no further breakout available.

ENGINE DATA: BASE FOUR (Omni, Shadow, Aries, Lancer): Inline, overhead-cam four-cylinder. Cast iron block; aluminum head. Displacement: 135 cu. in. (2.2 liters). Bore and stroke: 3.44 x 3.62 in. Compression ratio: 9.5:1. Brake horsepower: 93 at 4800 R.P.M. Torque: 122 lb.-ft. at 3200 R.P.M. Five main bearings. Throttle-body fuel injection. BASE TURBOCHARGED FOUR (Shelby Daytona, Lancer Shelby): Same as 2.2-liter four above exc.: Compression ratio: 8.1:1. Brake horsepower: 174 at 5200 R.P.M. Torque: 200 lb.-ft. at 2400 R.P.M. BASE FOUR (Daytona, Spirit, Dynasty); OPTIONAL (Shadow, Aries, Lancer): Inline, overhead cam four-cylinder. Cast iron block; aluminum head. Displacement: 153 cu. in. (2.5 liters). Bore and stroke: 3.44 x 4.09 in. Compression ratio: 9.0:1. Brake horsepower: 100 at 4400 R.P.M. Torque: 135 lb.-ft. at 2800 R.P.M. Five main bearings. Throttle-body fuel injection. BASE TURBOCHARGED FOUR (Spirit ES); OPTIONAL (Shadow, Daytona, Spirit, Lancer): Same as 2.5-liter four above exc.: Compression ratio: 7.8:1. Brake horsepower: 150 at 4800 R.P.M. Torque: 180 lb.-ft. at 2000 R.P.M. BASE V-6 (Dynasty LE); OPTIONAL (Spirit ES, base Dynasty): Overhead cam V-6. Displacement: 181 cu. in. (3.0 liters). Bore and stroke: 3.59 x 2.99 in. Compression ratio: 8.9:1. Brake horsepower: 141 at 5000 R.P.M. Torque: 171 lb.-ft. at 2800 R.P.M. Port fuel injection. BASE V-8 (Diplomat): 90-degree, overhead valve V-8. Cast iron block and heads. Displacement: 318 cu. in. (5.2 liters). Bore and stroke: 3.91 x 3.31 in. Compression ratio: 9.1:1. Brake horsepower: 140 at 3600 R.P.M. Torque: 265 lb.-ft. at 1600 R.P.M. Five main bearings. Hydraulic valve lifters. Carburetor: 2Bbl.

CHASSIS DATA: Wheelbase: (Omni) 99.1 in.; (Daytona) 97.0 in.; (Shadow) 97.0 in.; (Aries) 100.3 in.; (Spirit) 103.3 in.; (Lancer); 103.1 in.; (Dynasty) 104.3 in.; (Diplomat) 112.7 in. Overall Length: (Omni) 163.2 in.; (Daytona) 175.0 in.; (Shadow) 171.7 in.; (Aries) 178.9 in.; (Lancer) 180.4 in.; (Spirit) 181.2 in.; (Dynasty) 192.0 in.; (Diplomat) 204.6 in. Height: (Omni) 53.0 in.; (Daytona) 50.4 in.; (Shadow) 52.7 in.; (Aries) 52.5 in.; (Lancer) 53.0 in.; (Spirit) 55.5 in.; (Dynasty) 53.5 in.; (Diplomat) 55.3 in. Width: (Omni) 66.8 in.; (Daytona) 69.3 in.; (Shadow) 67.3 in.; (Aries) 67.9 in.; (Lancer) 68.3 in.; (Spirit) 68.1 in.; (Dynasty) 68.5 in.; (Diplomat) 74.2 in. Front Tread: (Omni) 56.1 in.; (Spirit) 57.5 in.; (Aries/Daytona/Shadow/Lancer/Dynasty) 57.6 in.; (Diplomat) 60.0 in. Rear Tread: (Omni) 55.7 in.; (Aries/Shadow/Lancer/Spirit) 57.2 in.; (Daytona/Dynasty) 57.6 in.; (Diplomat) 59.5 in. Standard Tires: (Omni) P165/80R13; (Daytona) P185/70R14; (Daytona Shelby) P205/55VR16; (Shadow) P185/70R14; (Aries) P185/70R13; (Lancer) P195/70R14; (Lancer Shelby) P205/60R15; (Spirit) P195/70R14; (Spirit ES) P205/60R14; (Dynasty) P195/75R14; (Diplomat) P205/75R15.

TECHNICAL: Transmission: Five-speed manual standard on Omni, Shadow, Aries, Lancer, Spirit and Daytona. TorqueFlite three-speed au-

tomatic standard on Dynasty and Diplomat; optional on other models. Four-speed overdrive automatic standard on Spirit V-6 and Dynasty LE. Steering: (Diplomat) recirculating ball; (others) rack and pinion. Brakes: Front disc, rear drum exc. (Daytona) four-wheel disc. Body construction: Unibody. Fuel tank: (Omni) 13 gal.; (Daytona/Shadow/Aries/Lancer) 14 gal.; (Spirit/Dynasty) 16 gal.; (Diplomat) 18 gal.

DRIVETRAIN OPTIONS: Engines: 2.5-liter four; Aries ($279); Shadow/Lancer ($287). Turbo 2.5-liter four: Lancer ($839); Spirit ($678). Turbo engine pkg.: Shadow ($950): 3.0-liter V-6: Dynasty ($774). Spirit ES (NC). Transmission: Three-speed auto. trans.; Shadow/Daytona/Lancer ($552). Spirit ($536). Four-speed automatic: Spirit ES V-6 ($615). Brakes: Anti-lock braking: Dynasty LE ($954).

1989 Dodge, Omni America hatchback sedan (OCW)

OMNI CONVENIENCE/APPEARANCE OPTIONS: Basic Option Pkgs. incl. auto. trans.; pwr stng ($776). Manual Trans. Discount Pkg. incl. console; pwr stng, AM/FM stereo w/digital clock; cloth spt seats w/dual recliners; trunk dress-up ($710). Auto Trans. Discount Pkg. incl. auto. trans. console; pwr stng, AM/FM stereo w/digital clock, cloth spt seats w/dual recliners; trunk dress-up ($1201). Clear Coat paint (NC). Tinted glass ($105). Manual air cond. ($694). Frt. lic. plate bracket (NC); Calif. emissions ($100). AM/FM stereo radio w/cass. ($152). Conventional spare tire ($73).

1989 Dodge, Daytona Shelby hatchback coupe (OCW)

1989 Dodge, Daytona hatchback coupe (OCW)

DAYTONA CONVENIENCE/APPEARANCE OPTIONS: Popular Equipment Discount Pkg. incl. air cond., frt. fitted floor mats, light grp., dual pwr heated mirrors; tilt stng col. ($952). Light and locks discount, incl. headlights "on" delay; illum. entry lighting system; pwr door locks; dual lighted vanity visor mirrors ($292). C/S Performance Discount Pkg. incl. Turbo I eng., perf. cloth bucket seats; T125/90R15 spare tire, perf. handling suspension; turbo accessories perf. handling; cast alum 15 x 6.0-in. whls ($1443). Popular Equipment incl. frt. fitted floor mats; light grp.; dual pwr heated mirrors; tilt stng column ($327). C/S Competition, incl. Turbo II; perf. cloth seats; T125/90R15 spare tire; rear spoiler; tilt stng col.; max perf. Shelby suspension; P225/50VR15 SBR unidirectional tires; high output 5-spd; turbo accessories; cast alum 15 x 6.5-in. whls ($2879). T-Bar roof, incl. dual illum. vanity visor mirrors; T-

Bar roof w/Sunshades; pwr windows; cargo straps ($1513). W/(ADD) ($1397). Popular Equip. Discount incl. air cond., frt. fitted floor mats; light grp.; dual pwr heated mirrors; tilt stng col., ES (AGVH24) ($952). Lights and Locks Discount Pkg. incl. headlights "on" extinguish delay; illum. entry lighting system; pwr door locks, dual illum. vanity visor mirrors, ES ($292). T-Bar roof, incl. dual illum. visor mirrors, pwr windows; T-Bar roof w/sunshades; cargo straps, ES ($1513). W/(ADD) ($1397). Popular Equip. Discount incl. air cond., frt. fitted floor mats; light grp., dual pwr heated mirrors, pwr door locks; pwr windows; tilt stng col., ES Turbo ($1010). T-Bar roof, incl. pwr windows; T-bar roof and sunshades; dual illum. visor mirrors, cargo strap ($1298). Electronic Equip. Discount Pkg. incl. overhead console w/compass and temp. readout; electronic navigator, headlights "on" extinguish delay; illum. entry lighting system; dual illum. vanity visor mirrors, ES Turbo ($579). w/Sunroof ($404). W/T-bar roof ($333). Popular Equip Discount Pkg.; incl. air cond., frt. fitted floor mats, light grp., dual pwr heated mirrors, pwr door locks, pwr windows, tilt stng col., Shelby ($1010). Electronic Equip. Discount Pkg. incl. console w/compass and temp. readout; electronic navigator; headlights "on" extinguish delay; illum. entry lighting system; dual illum. vanity visor mirrors, Shelby ($579). W/sunroof, ($404). W/T-bar roof ($333). T-bar roof and sunshades; dual illum. vanity visor mirrors, Shelby ($1298). Pearl/clear paint ($40). Cloth, Perf. low back bucket seats ($305). Cloth, Enthusiast low back bucket seats ($391). Leather, Enthusiast seats ($879). ES Turbo ($938). Elect. instrument cluster ($311). Calif. emissions ($100). Pwr windows ($215). AM/FM stereo w/cass. ($152). AM/FM stereo w/cass., ES Turbo and Shelby (NC). AM/FM stereo w/cass., w/5-band graphic equalizer ($632). ES Turbo and Shelby ($210). CD player, ES Turbo and Shelby ($400). Elect. spd control ($180). Rear window sun louver ($210). Removable sunroof ($384). Security tonneau cover ($69). Liftgate wiper/washer ($126). Cast alum 14-in. whl ($322).

1989 Dodge, Shadow two-door sedan (OCW)

SHADOW CONVENIENCE/APPEARANCE OPTIONS: Popular Equip. Pkg. incl. console, light grp., elect. rear window defroster; 4 spkrs, 3-dr. ($253). 5-dr. ($265). Deluxe Convenience Pkg. incl. conventional spare tire; floor mats, elect. spd control, tilt stng col. ($213). 15-in. alum whls/tires vs. conventional spare ($300). Power Assist Pkg. incl. pwr door locks, dual black pwr mirrors, 3-dr. ($178). 5-dr. ($223). W/(AGN) ($48). Power Assist Pkg. incl. pwr driver's seat; pwr windows, 3-dr. ($409). 5-dr. ($477). ES Pkg. incl. AM/FM stereo cass. with seek & scan; Perf. buckets; console, conventional spare tire, elect. rear window defroster; eng. dress-up; flr. mats, foglights, heel/toe type pedals w/man. trans., light grp., ES liftgate nameplate, stainless steel exhaust, pwr door locks, prem. int. w/rear fldg bench seat, P195/60HR15 SBR ASP tires; sill mldg w/frt. flares; sill mldg tape stripe ES, tape graphic, 4 spkrs, rear spoiler, firm feel sport suspension, leather-wrapped stng whl, turbo boost gauge; warning lights message center, cast alum 15-in. whls, 125 mph speedometer, 2.5-liter MPI turbo eng., 3-dr. ($1977). 5-dr. ($2039). (AGT) Turbo Eng. Pkg. incl. eng. dress-up, heel/toe type pedals w/man. trans., stainless steel exhaust syst., pwr bulge hood w/Turbo decal; P185/70R14 SBR tires; turbo boost gauge; warning lights message center; 125 mph speedometer; turbo eng., 3-dr. and 5-dr. ($923). Competition Pkg. eng. dress-up, heel/toe type pedals w/man. trans., stainless steel exhaust, pwr bulge hood w/Turbo decal P195/60HR15 SBR tires, 4 spkrs, decklid spoiler, firm feel sport suspension, turbo boost gauge; warning lights message center, cast alum 15 whls, 125 mph speedometer, 2.5-liter turbo eng. (DH24 only) ($1515). Pearl/clear coat paint ($40). Air cond. ($775). Tinted glass ($105). 500-amp battery ($44). Frt. lic. plate bracket (NC). Elect. rear window defroster ($145). Calif. emissions ($100). Pwr door locks: 2-dr ($150). 4-dr ($200). AM/FM stereo w/cass. ($201). W/(AAM) or (ANA) Pkg. ($152). AM/FM stereo w/cass. ($254). Removable sunroof ($372). 14-in. alum whls ($306). W/(AJK) ($383).

ARIES CONVENIENCE/APPEARANCE OPTIONS: Basic Equipment Pkg. incl. auto. trans., pwr stng ($776). Basic radio discount, incl. auto. trans.; pwr stng, AM/FM stereo w/4 spkrs ($929). Popular Equipment Discount Pkg. incl. auto. trans., pwr stng, AM/FM stereo w/4 spkrs, tinted glass, dual remote mirrors, bodyside tape stripes, sound insulation,

console, P185/70R14 steel radials; trunk dress-up, whl covers ($1392). W/bench seat ($1292). Prem. Discount Pkg. incl. elect. spd control, tilt stng col., pwr door locks; luxury stng whl, light grp. 2-dr. ($1845). w/bench seat ($1745). Premium discount, 4-dr. ($1895). W/bench seat ($1795). Pearl paint ($40). Air cond. ($775). Tinted glass ($120). 50-amp battery ($44). Frt. lic. plate bracket (NC). Rear window defroster ($145). Calif. emissions ($100). AM/FM stereo/cass. radio ($152). Pwr stng ($240). Conventional spare tire, 14-in. ($83). P185/70R14 WSW tires ($68).

1989 Dodge, Lancer ES hatchback sedan (OCW)

LANCER CONVENIENCE/APPEARANCE OPTIONS: Basic Equipment Discount Pkg., air cond., console extension w/armrest; light grp. (AHDH44) ($873). Popular Equip. Discount w/manual trans., incl. air cond., console extension w/armrest; elect. spd control, flr. mats, light grp. illum. entry, AM/FM stereo w/cass., tilt stng, undercoating ($1443). W/auto or turbo ($1879). W/auto and turbo ($2315). Luxury Equip. Discount Pkg. incl. air cond., console extension w/armrest, pwr door locks, elect. spd control, flr. mats, light grp., illum. entry, dual pwr heated mirror; AM/FM stereo w/cass., tilt stng col., leather-wrapped stng whl, undercoating, dual illum. vanity mirrors, pwr windows ($2064). Sport Appearance Discount Pkg. incl. Turbo I eng., Ground Effects, Precision Feel power steering, P205/60R15 BSW tires, cast alum 15-in. Euro whls ($1200). Power Convenience Discount Pkg. incl. pwr door locks, dual pwr heated black mirrors, pwr windows ($514). Spt Handling Pkg. incl. leather-wrapped stng whl, sport handling suspension, P195/70R14 BSW tires ($153). W/(AFF) Pkg. ($94). Deluxe Convenience Pkg.: elect. spd. control, tilt stng col. ($300). Luxury Equip. Discount Pkg. incl. console w/compass and outside temp. gauge, elect. spd control, fog lamps, illum. entry, AM/FM stereo/cass./Infinity, pwr driver's seat, tilt stng col., undercoating, pwr windows, ES ($194). Sport Appearance Discount Pkg. incl. fog lamps, ground effects, illum. entry, precision-feel pwr stng; pwr sunroof, sport handling suspension, P205/60R15 BSW tires, cast alum 15-in. Euro whls ($1693). Sport Handling Pkg. incl. P195/70R14 BSW tires, sport handling suspension ($94). Deluxe Convenience Pkg. incl. elect. spd control, tilt stng col. ($300). Pearl/clear paint ($40). Two-tone paint, incl. whl lip mldg ($226). Leather prem. bucket seats w/vinyl ($566). Air cond. ($775). Frt. lic. plate bracket (NC). Pwr door locks ($195). Elect. instrument cluster ($299). Calif. emissions ($100). Elect. navigator ($272). Pwr driver's seat ($240). Pwr windows ($285). AM/FM stereo w/cass. ($152). AM/FM stereo/cass. with seek/scan ($458). W/(AFF) or (AAM) ($306). AM/FM stereo cass. with seek/scan and graphic equalizer ($210). Glass pwr sunroof ($776). W/(AFF) on S44 ($601). P205/60R15 RBL SBR tires/cast alum 15-in. whls ($262). W/(AGA) ($194). Cast alum 14-in. whls ($322). Liftgate wiper/washer ($126).

SPIRIT CONVENIENCE/APPEARANCE OPTIONS: Super Discount Pkg., air cond.; console extension w/armrest; rear window defroster; flr. mats; tinted glass; ignition time delay lights; elect. spd control; 4-spkr system; tilt stng; ADH41 ($934). Super Discount Pkg. above plus pwr remote heated dual mirrors; pwr windows; pwr door locks ($1202). Super Discount Pkg., air cond.; pwr remote heated dual mirrors; pwr windows; pwr door locks; ADP41 and ADX41, ADH41 ($593). Popular Equipment Discount Pkg., air cond.; console extension w/armrest; elect. rear defroster; tinted glass; 4-spkr system ($893). Premium Equipment Discount Pkg., prem. body sound insulation; courtesy lights; ignition time delay; 6 function message center; split rear seat ($239). W/bench seat ($339). Basic Group Discount Pkg., console extension, P205/60R15 SBR BSW ($164). Cast alum 15-in. whls ($322). Conventional spare tire ($93). Power Equipment Discount Pkg., pwr remote heated dual black mirrors; pwr windows; pwr door locks; ADP41/ADX41 ($533). Pearl/clear paint ($40). Cloth 50/50 frt. bench seat APH41 ($100). W/(AAM) or (ADG) ($60). Cloth 50/50 frt. bench w/split fold down rear ($100). W/(AAM) or (ADG) pkgs. ($60). Cloth 50/50 frt. premium bench seat w/55/45 split fold down rear, DP41 ($60). Air cond. ($775). Frt. lic. plate bracket (NC). Elect. rear window defroster DH41 ($145). Calif. emissions ($100). Pwr door locks ($200). Pwr driver's seat ($240). AM/FM stereo w/cass. ($201). W/(AAK) or (ADG) pkgs. DH41 ($152). AM/FM stereo/cass./seek/scan, incl. 4 Infinity spkrs ($422). DX41 ($270). Stereo cass. with graphic equalizer, incl. 4 Infinity spkrs ADP41 ($632). ADX41 ($480). Pop-up sunroof ($397).

DYNASTY CONVENIENCE/APPEARANCE OPTIONS: Pwr Convenience Pkg., heated pwr dual remote control mirrors; pwr windows ($343). Popular Equipment Pkg., air cond.; elect. spd control; flr. mats; pwr door locks; tilt stng col.; undercoating ($1138). Interior Illumination Pkg., illum. entry; illum. vanity mirrors ($192). Popular Equipment Pkg., air cond.; elect. spd control; flr. mats; pwr door locks, heated pwr dual remote control mirrors; pwr windows; tilt stng col.; undercoating CDP41 ($1469). Luxury Equipment Pkg. incl. air cond.; elect. spd control; flr. mats; illum. entry; illum. vanity mirrors; pwr door locks; heated dual remote control mirrors; pwr 6-way seats; pwr windows; security alarm; tilt stng. col.; undercoating; wire whl covers; leather-wrapped stng whl ($2500). Interior Illumination Pkg., illum. entry; illum. vanity mirrors ($192). Deluxe Convenience Pkg., elect. spd control; security alarm ($310). Pearl/coat paint ($40). Air cond. ($775). Frt. lic. plate bracket (NC). Pwr door locks, spd activated ($290). Calif. emissions ($100). Road handling suspension ($57). Rear auto. load leveling suspension ($180). AM/FM stereo/cass. radio ($152). AM/FM stereo/cass. w/seek/scan ($254). AM/FM Stereo/Cass. Sound Pkg. incl. 6 Infinity spkrs, pwr antenna, digital clock ($552). AM/FM Stereo/Cass. w/5-Band Graphic Equalizer Sound Pkg. incl. graphic equalizer, 6 Infinity spkrs, pwr antenna, digital clock ($762). Pwr 6-way driver's seat ($240). Pwr 8-way driver's and pass. seat w/memory and pwr recliner ($341). Security alarm ($146). Conventional spare tire ($83). Pwr sunroof, incl. sunshade and wind deflector ($776). Wire whl covers ($224). Cast alum whls w/(AFF) ($49). W/o (AFF) ($273).

DIPLOMAT CONVENIENCE/APPEARANCE OPTIONS: Popular Equipment Discount Pkg., auto. temp air cond.; rear window defroster; dual pwr remote mirrors; spd control, premium whl covers ($1147). Protection Pkg., bodyside mldg.; rear bumper guards; flr. mats; undercoating ($185). Light Pkg. ($133). Luxury Equipment Discount Pkg., light grp.; pwr decklid; pwr door locks, pwr left seat; pwr windows; leather-wrapped stng whl; illum. vanity mirrors; wire whl covers ($1202). Light Pkg. MGP41 ($122). H.D. suspension ($27). Pearl/clear paint ($41). Auto temp air cond. ($855). Frt. lic. plate bracket (NC). Rear window defroster ($149). Calif. emissions ($102). Illum. entry system ($78). Dual pwr remote control mirrors ($164). Pwr door locks ($201). Pwr windows ($294). AM/FM stereo w/cass. ($262). Pwr antenna ($72). Pwr sunroof ($1108). Trunk dress-up ($58). Conventional spare tire ($96). Full vinyl roof ($206). Wire whl covers ($231). Deluxe Convenience Discount Pkg., flr. mats; ignition time delay; elect. spd control; tilt stng col. ($316). W/(AAC) pkg. ($305). Power Equipment Discount Pkg., pwr remote heated dual black mirrors; pwr windows; pwr door locks ($533).

HISTORY: Model year production: 423,276. Model year sales: 435,419 (representing a 5.9 share of the U.S. market compared with 427,937 and 5.8 the year previous).

1990 DODGE

Dodge seemed to shrink to a shadow of its former self, as three well-known models disappeared: Aries, Lancer and Diplomat. Nothing new replaced them as the model year began, either, though Spirit and Dynasty were comparatively recent additions. Later in the model year came a new mid-size Monaco, reviving an old Dodge nameplate. It was related to the Eagle Premier and powered by a Renault-built 3.0-liter V-6, but early sales were sluggish. With the demise of the Diplomat, all remaining Dodges were front-wheel drive.

1990 Dodge, Omni hatchback sedan (OCW)

OMNI — SERIES L — FOUR — Dodge's Wisconsin-built subcompact added a driver's side airbag and lost its former "America" designation. The option list remained short, however. Inside was a new instrument panel and steering wheel, along with back-seat shoulder belts. Externally, little was different except for a revised mirror design. As before, the 2.2-liter four-cylinder engine came with a standard five-speed manual gearbox or extra-cost automatic, the latter available only in an option package.

1990 Dodge, Daytona ES Turbo hatchback coupe (OCW)

1990 Dodge, Daytona Shelby hatchback coupe with optional rear window louver (OCW)

DAYTONA — SERIES G — FOUR/V-6 — Six-cylinder power was available under the hood of Dodge's base or ES performance coupe this year, in the form of a 141-horsepower, 3.0-liter V-6, built by Mitsubishi (Chrysler's Japanese partner). Base gearbox was Chrysler's new five-speed manual unit, with two automatics available: a three-speed or overdrive four-speed. A new turbo version of the old 2.2-liter four also became available: standard on the Shelby, optional with the C/S competition package. Available only with five-speed manual shift, that turbo IV engine developed 174 horsepower with its variable-nozzle turbocharger (VNT), while cutting down on turbo lag during acceleration. Base engine remained the 2.5-liter four (non-turbo), while a turbocharged version went into the ES Turbo model. Minor body changes were evident on the Shelby, which could be ordered with a new three-way electronic variable suspension; console switches selected a firm, normal or soft ride. Inside each Daytona was a new steering wheel (with airbag) and dashboard.

SHADOW — SERIES P — FOUR — Performance-minded Shadow buyers had a tempting choice this year: 174-horsepower, 2.2-liter VNT Turbo IV, formerly available only in the modified Shelby Shadow CSX model. Offered only with five-speed manual shift, the Turbo IV was designed for quicker throttle response with minimal turbo lag. Only Shadows with the ES or Competition package could get that top-rung turbo, but any model might have the 150-horsepower, 2.5-liter Turbo I. ES versions got revised front and rear fascias this year, with built-in foglights. Bodyside tape graphics were new; so were the ground-effects lower body

panels. ES also had four-wheel disc brakes and P195/60HR15 tires on alloy wheels, rather than the usual P185/70R14 size. All Shadows had a driver's side airbag this year.

SPIRIT — SERIES A — FOUR/V-6 — Four-wheel disc brakes became standard in the ES edition of the A-body four-door notchback sedan, which had been introduced several months after the start of the 1989 model year. Self-restoring bumpers were designed to snap back to their original position after a low-speed (five mph) collision. A driver's side airbag also was new, mounted in a tilt steering column. Any of the three models could have the Mitsubishi-built V-6 engine, offered only with four-speed overdrive automatic transmission. Base engine was the 2.5-liter four, while the ES had a standard 2.5-liter turbo. Both of these came with a standard five-speed manual gearbox, or extra-cost automatic. The mid-level LE included cruise control, a rear window defroster, tilt steering, and adjustable lumbar support for the driver. ES stepped up to aero body panels and foglamps, with sport bucket seats inside.

1990 Dodge, Spirit ES sedan (OCW)

DYNASTY — SERIES C — FOUR/V-6 — By this time, Dodge's biggest car had also become its biggest seller. In addition to the base 2.5-liter four and available 3.0-liter V-6, a new 3.3-liter (201 cubic-inch) V-6 became optional with the step-up LE model. That engine was built by Chrysler, whereas the 3.0 came from Mitsubishi. A four-speed overdrive automatic transmission was required with the big V-6 and available with the 3.0-liter, which normally came with a three-speed automatic. A restyled two-spoke steering wheel held a driver's side airbag. Cruise control was now handled right at the steering wheel, instead of from the turn-signal stalk. Side marker lights now flashed along with the regular turn signal lights. Anti-lock brakes were again available.

1990 Dodge, Monaco ES sedan (OCW)

MONACO — SERIES B — V-6 — At mid-year came a new mid-size Dodge four-door model, a little bigger than the Dynasty. Two versions were offered, an entry-level LE and performance-oriented ES, both with a 3.0-liter V-6 under the hood and a floor-shifted four-speed automatic transmission. Up front was a crossbar-style grille with 'DODGE' block letters in its lower corner, flanked by aero-type headlamps. Standard LE equipment included reclining bucket seats, a center console, rear window defroster, AM/FM stereo radio, and stainless steel exhaust. ES added air conditioning, four-wheel disc brakes, leather-wrapped steering wheel, two-tone paint, cassette player, P205/70R14 tires on polycast wheels, and a touring suspension with gas-charged front struts and rear shocks and a rear anti-sway bar. Built at Bramalea, Ontario, Canada, the Monaco was a close relative of the Eagle Premier.

I.D. DATA: Dodge's 17-symbol Vehicle Identification Number (VIN), as before, was on the upper left corner of the instrument panel, visible through the windshield. Coding is similar to 1986-89. Symbol ten (model year) changed to 'L' for 1990.

OMNI AMERICA (FOUR)

Model No.	Body/Style No.	Body Type & Seating	Factory Price	Shipping Weight	Prod. Total
LZE	44	4-dr. Hatch-5P	6995	2100	16,531

DAYTONA (FOUR)

GVL	24	2-dr. Hatch-4P	9795	2550	Note 1
GVH	24	2-dr. ES Hatch-4P	10995	N/A	Note 1

DAYTONA ES TURBO (FOUR)

GVS	24	2-dr. Hatch-4P	12895	N/A	Note 1

DAYTONA SHELBY (FOUR)

GVX	24	2-dr. Hatch-4P	14295	2665	Note 1

Note 1: Daytona production totaled 38,488 with no further breakout available.

SHADOW (FOUR)

PDH	24	2-dr. Sedan-5P	8735	2513	27,232
PDH	44	4-dr. Sedan-5P	8935	2544	44,390

SPIRIT (FOUR/V-6)

ADH	41	4-dr. Sedan-6P	10485	2765	Note 1
ADP	41	4-dr. LE Sed-6P	11845	2842	Note 1
ADX	41	4-dr. ES Sed-6P	13145	N/A	Note 1

Note 1: Spirit production totaled 79,498 with no further breakout available.

DYNASTY (FOUR/V-6)

CDH	41	4-dr. Sedan-6P	12995	2907	Note 1
CDP	41	4-dr. LE Sedan-6P	14395	N/A	Note 1

Note 1: Dynasty production totaled 94,683 with no further breakout available.

MONACO (V-6)

BDP	41	4-dr. LE Sedan-6P	14995	3083	Note 1
BDS	41	4-dr. ES Sedan-6P	17595	3121	Note 1

Note 1: Monaco production totaled 7,153 with no further breakout available.

ENGINE DATA: BASE FOUR (Omni, Shadow): Inline, overhead-cam four-cylinder. Cast iron block; aluminum head. Displacement: 135 cu. in. (2.2 liters). Bore and stroke: 3.44 x 3.62 in. Compression ratio: 9.5:1. Brake horsepower: 93 at 4800 R.P.M. Torque: 122 lb.-ft. at 3200 R.P.M. Five main bearings. Throttle-body fuel injection. **BASE TURBOCHARGED FOUR** (Daytona Shelby): OPTIONAL (Shadow): Same as 2.2-liter four above exc.: Compression ratio: 8.1:1. Brake horsepower: 174 at 5200 R.P.M. Torque: 200 lb.-ft. at 2400 R.P.M. **BASE FOUR** (Daytona, Spirit, Dynasty); OPTIONAL (Shadow): Inline, overhead-cam four-cylinder. Cast iron block; aluminum head. Displacement: 153 cu. in. (2.5 liters). Bore and stroke: 3.44 x 4.09 in. Compression ratio: 8.9:1. Brake horsepower: 100 at 4800 R.P.M. Torque: 135 lb.-ft. at 2800 R.P.M. Five main bearings. Throttle-body fuel injection. **BASE TURBOCHARGED FOUR** (Spirit ES); OPTIONAL (Shadow, Daytona, Spirit): Same as 2.5-liter four above exc.: Compression ratio: 7.8:1. Brake horsepower: 150 at 4800 R.P.M. Torque: 180 lb.-ft. at 2000 R.P.M. **BASE V-6** (Dynasty LE); OPTIONAL (Daytona, Spirit, base Dynasty): Overhead cam V-6. Displacement: 181 cu. in. (3.0 liters). Bore and stroke: 3.59 x 2.99 in. Compression ratio: 8.9:1. Brake horsepower: 141 at 5000 R.P.M. Torque: 171 lb.-ft. at 2800 R.P.M. Port fuel injection. **BASE V-6** (Monaco): Overhead cam V-6. Displacement: 180 cu. in. (3.0 liters). Bore and stroke: 3.66 x 2.87 in. Compression ratio: 9.3:1. Brake horsepower: 150 at 5000 R.P.M. Torque: 171 lb.-ft. at 3600 R.P.M. Port fuel injection. **OPTIONAL V-6** (Dynasty): Overhead valve V-6. Displacement: 201 cu. in. (3.3 liters). Bore and stroke: 3.66 x 3.19 in. Compression ratio: 8.9:1. Brake horsepower: 147 at 4800 R.P.M. Torque: 183 lb.-ft. at 3800 R.P.M. Port fuel injection.

CHASSIS DATA: Wheelbase: (Omni) 99.1 in.; (Daytona) 97.0 in.; (Shadow) 97.0 in.; (Spirit) 103.3 in.; (Dynasty) 104.3 in.; (Monaco) 106.0 in. Overall Length: (Omni) 163.2 in.; (Daytona) 179.2 in.; (Shadow) 171.7 in.; (Spirit) 181.2 in.; (Dynasty) 192.0 in.; (Monaco) 192.8 in. Height: (Omni) 53.0 in.; (Daytona) 50.1 in.; (Shadow) 52.6 in.; (Spirit) 53.5 in.; (Dynasty) 54.8 in.; (Monaco) 56.5 in. Width: (Omni) 66.8 in.; (Daytona) 69.3 in.; (Shadow) 67.3 in.; (Spirit) 68.1 in.; (Dynasty) 68.5 in.; (Monaco) 70.0 in. Front Tread: (Omni) 56.1 in.; (Daytona/Shadow/Dynasty) 57.6 in.; (Monaco) 58.1 in. Rear Tread: (Omni) 55.7 in.; (Shadow/Spirit) 57.2 in.; (Daytona/Dynasty) 57.6 in.; (Monaco) 57.1 in. Standard Tires: (Omni) P165/80R13; (Day-tona) P185/70R14; (Daytona ES) P205/60HR15; (Daytona Shelby) P205/55VR16; (Shadow) P185/70R14; (Spirit) P195/70R14; (Spirit ES) P205/60R15; (Dynasty) P195/75R14; (Monaco ES) P205/70R14.

TECHNICAL: Transmission: Five-speed manual standard on Omni, Shadow, Spirit and Daytona. Three-speed automatic standard on Dynasty. Four-speed overdrive automatic standard on Spirit V-6 and Monaco and required on Dynasty with 3.3-liter V-6. Steering: Rack and pinion. Brakes: Front disc, rear drum exc. (Spirit ES, Monaco ES) four-wheel disc. Body construction: Unibody. Fuel tank: (Omni) 13 gal.; (Daytona/Shadow) 14 gal.; (Spirit/Dynasty) 16 gal.; (Monaco) 17 gal.

DRIVETRAIN OPTIONS: Engines: 2.5-liter four: Shadow ($288). Turbo 2.5-liter four: Spirit ($700). Competition pkg. (Turbo IV): Shadow ($2619). 3.0-liter V-6: Daytona/Dynasty/Spirit ($700). 3.3-liter V-6: Dynasty LE ($103). Transmission: Three-speed automatic: Daytona/Shadow/Spirit ($552). Four-speed automatic: Daytona V-6 ($646); Spirit ($646); base Dynasty ($94). Brakes: Anti-lock braking: Daytona ES ($184): Dynasty V-6 ($954).

OMNI CONVENIENCE/APPEARANCE OPTIONS: Basic Equipment Pkg. incl. auto. trans.; pwr stng ($799). Manual Trans Discount Pkg., pwr stng; AM/FM stereo radio w/digital clock; cloth hi-back spt. seat; w/dual recliners; trunk dress-up; floor mats; dual remote outside mirrors; Rallye-type 13-in. whls ($786). Auto. Trans. Discount Pkg., auto. trans.; pwr stng; AM/FM stereo w/digital clock, cloth hi-back spt. seat; w/dual re-cliners; trunk dress-up; floor mats; dual remote outside mirrors; Rallye-type 13-in. whls ($1290). Air cond. ($798). Frt. lic. plate bracket (NC). Rear window defroster ($155). Calif. emissions ($103). Tinted glass ($108). AM/FM stereo radio with cass. ($157). Conventional spare tire ($75). P165/80R13 WSW tire ($65).

DAYTONA CONVENIENCE/APPEARANCE OPTIONS: Popular Equipment Discount Pkg. incl. air cond., frt. floor mats; glovebox, cargo, underhood dual map/reading lights; dual pwr heated remote mirrors; tilt stng col. VL24 and VH24 ($1007). VS24 and VX24 Pkg. incl. air cond., frt. floor mats; glove box, cargo, underhood, dual map/reading lights; dual pwr heated remote control mirrors; pwr door locks, pwr windows; spd control; tilt stng col. ($1317). Value Pkg., pwr door locks; elect. spd control, AM/FM stereo radio w/cass. VL24 ($554). VL24 w/(AJP) ($348). C/S Performance Discount Pkg. incl. pwr 4-whl disc brakes; turbo engine; rear spoiler; performance handling suspension; P205/60R15 SBR perf. tires w/15-in. compact spare; turbo accessories, incl. boost gauge, perf. tuned stainless steel exhaust, pwr bulge hood; Eurocast alum 15 x 6.0-in. whls; VL24 ($1550). V-6 Performance Discount Pkg., pwr 4-whl brakes w/15-in. compact spare tire, additional cargo area carpet over wheelhouse; 3.0 V-6 w/perf. tuned exhaust, enthusiast cloth bucket seats; map pockets; leather-wrapped stng whl; performance handling suspension; AM/FM stereo radio w/cass. and seek/scan, 6 Infinity spkrs, VH24 w/(AJP) ($1782). VH24 Pkg., same as VH24 w/(AJP) plus pwr door locks and windows ($2215). Popular Equipment Pkg. incl. frt. fitted mats; glovebox, cargo, underhood, dual map/reading mirrors; dual pwr heated remote control mirrors; tilt stng col., VL24 ($338). Premium Light Pkg. incl. illum. entry, lighting system; dual illum. vanity visor mirrors VL24 and VH24 ($197). VL24 w/(AET) and VH24 w/)AET) Pkg. incl. illum. entry, light system ($78). T-bar roof; incl. pwr windows; w/cargo tie down straps and storage covers; dual illum. vanity visor mirrors VL24 and VH24 ($1563). VS24, VX24, VL24 w/(AJP), and VH24 w/(AJP) Pkg. incl. all above exc. pwr windows ($1336). Overhead Convenience Pkg. w/T-bar roof or sunroof; overhead console w/compass and temp. readout; dual illum. vanity visor mirrors; VS24 and VX24 ($387). C/S Competition Pkg. incl. 120-amp alternator; pwr 4-whl disc brakes; Turbo IV eng.; rear spoiler; tilt stng col.; max perf. Shelby suspension; P225/50VR15 SBR unidirectional tires w/15-in. compact spare; H.D. 5-spd man. trans.; turbo accessories incl. boost gauge, perf. tuned stainless steel exhaust, pwr bulge hood, 15 x 6.5-in. cast alum whl ($2778). Security Pkg., illum. entry, lighting system; security system, anti theft; VS24 and VX24 ($228). Power Convenience Pkg. incl. pwr door locks; pwr windows; VL24 and VH24 ($433). V-6 Discount Pkg., pwr 4-whl disc brakes; 3.0L V-6 ($794). Auto. Trans. Pkg. incl. 90-amp alternator; Turbo I eng.; spd control, 3-spd auto. trans.; turbo accessories, VX24 (NC). VX24 w/(AAM) Pkg. incl. all of VX24 exc. spd control ($191). Frt. lic. plate bracket (NC). Overhead console; incl. garage door opener storage, compass and temp. readout; dome and map lights; VH24 ($268). Calif. emissions ($103). Pearl coat/clear coat paint VL24 ($75). AM/FM stereo cass. VL24 and VH24 ($157). AM/FM stereo cass., seek and scan; w/6 Infinity spkrs ($497). AM/FM stereo cass., seek and scan; w/6 infinity spkrs and 5-band graphic equalizer, VL24 and VH24 ($713). VS24 and VX24 ($216). Pwr. 6-way seat, VL24 and VH24 ($258). Enthusiast pwr 8-way seat ($324). Enthusiast pwr 8-way leather seat ($983). Elect. spd control ($191). Rear window sun louver ($216). Removable sunroof ($409). Conventional spare tire, 14-in. VL24 ($85). Conventional spare tire 15-in. w/Eurocast whl, VH24 and VS24 ($244). Security tonneau cover VL24 ($75). Liftgate wiper/washer ($130). Aero whls 14-in. ($103). Cast alum 14-in. whls ($332).

1990 Dodge, Shadow two-door sedan with optional ES performance package (OCW)

SHADOW CONVENIENCE/APPEARANCE OPTIONS: Competition Pkg. incl. 4-whl pwr disc brakes; Turbo IV eng.; remote liftgate release; message center, warning lights; dual remote black mirrors; perf. front bucket seats; and 60/40 split folding rear; 4-spkrs; rear spoiler; sport suspension; P195/60R15 SBR tires; turbo accessories incl. boost gauge, perf. tuned stainless steel exhaust, eng. dress-up, pwr bulge hood; heel/toe-type pedals; 15 x 6-in. cast alum whls; DH24 ($2619). Air cond. ($798). Frt. lic. plate bracket (NC). Rear window defroster ($155). Calif. emissions ($103). Floor mats, F&R ($46). Pearl coat/clear coat paint ($75). Pwr door locks: 2-dr ($160). 4-dr ($211). Pwr windows: 2-dr. ($227). 4-dr. ($304). Pwr dual outside mirrors ($58). AM/FM stereo w/cass., 4 spkrs w/o seek and scan ($207). AM/FM stereo w/cass., seek and scan, Infinity spkrs ($435). Elect. spd control ($191). Tilt stng col. ($134). Removable sunroof, incl. tie down straps and storage pouch ($383). Tinted glass ($108). Conventional spare tire 14-in. ($85). w/2.5L Turbo, Shadow ES turbo ($215); engine ($104). Conventional spare tire 15-in. w/(ANA) pkg. or Shadow ES (non turbo) ($185). Cast alum whls ($332).

1990 Dodge, Spirit LE sedan (OCW)

SPIRIT CONVENIENCE/APPEARANCE OPTIONS: Super Discount Pkg. incl. air cond.; elect. rear defroster; F&R floor mats; tinted glass; ignition light w/time delay; 4 spkr system; spd control; tilt stng col. DH41 ($1110). Super Discount B Pkg. incl. all above plus dual pwr remote heated black mirrors; pwr windows; pwr door locks; DH41 ($1411). Super Discount C Pkg. incl. pwr equip.; air cond.; dual pwr remote heated mirrors; pwr windows; pwr door locks, DP41 and DX41 ($775). Popular Equip. Discount Pkg. air cond. incl. elect. rear defroster; tinted glass; 4 spkrs; DH41 ($941). Premium Equip. Discount Pkg. incl. bucket front seats; split folding 55/45 rear; center armrest; premium body sound; courtesy, map, underhood lights; cigarette lighter; ignition lights, w/time delay; message center; DH41 ($301). DH41 w/(AWN), (AWP), or (AJK) Pkg., same as PH41 exc. ignition lights w/time delay ($293). Deluxe Convenience Discount Pkg. incl. floor mats, ignition lights w/time delay; elect. spd control, tilt stng col. DH41 ($329). Power Equipment Discount Pkg. incl. dual pwr remote heated black mirrors; pwr windows; pwr door locks, DH41, DP41 and DX41 ($568). Air cond. ($819). Frt. license plate bracket (NC). Elect. rear window defroster ($155). Pwr door locks ($221). Calif. emissions ($103). Pearl coat/clear coat paint ($75). AM/FM stereo w/cass., digital clock, 4 spkrs, DH41 ($207). w/Pkg. (AWN), (AWP), or (AAM) on DH41 ($157). AM/FM stereo w/cass., digital clock, seek and scan, 4 Infinity spkrs, DP41 ($435). DX41 ($278). AM/FM stereo w/cass., digital clock, seek and scan, 4 Infinity spkrs, graphic equalizer, DP41 ($651). DX41 ($494). Power driver's seat ($258). Frt. bench seat; rear full fixed bench, DH41 ($103). Frt. bench seat, rear 55/45 split fold down bench; DH41 ($62). Premium frt. bench

seat; rear 55/45 split fold down bench, DP41 ($62). Pop-up sunroof incl. deflector, removable shade, storage bag, tie down straps ($409). P195/70R14 SBR WSW tires DH41 ($74). P205/60R15 SBR BSW tires ($169). Conventional spare tire 14-in., DH41 and DP41 ($95). 15-in. Eurocast alum whls ($332).

1990 Dodge, Dynasty LE sedan (OCW)

DYNASTY CONVENIENCE/APPEARANCE OPTIONS: Popular Equip. Discount Pkg. incl. Deluxe Convenience Pkg. on DH41 and DP41, and Pwr Convenience Pkg. on DP41; incl. air cond.; pwr door locks; floor mats; spd control; tilt stng col.; undercoating, CDH41 ($1212). CDP41, also incl. 3.3L V-6; dual pwr heated remote control mirrors; pwr windows ($1589). Luxury Equip. Discount Pkg. incl. popular equip. incl. illum. pwr convenience and dlx convenience plus auto. day/night rearview mirror; pwr 6-way driver's and pass. seats; security alarm; leather-wrapped stng whl; wire whl covers; CDP41 ($2785). Deluxe Convenience Pkg.; elect. spd control; tilt stng col., CDP41 ($325). Pwr Convenience Discount Pkg. incl. dual pwr remote control heated mirrors; pwr windows, CDH41 ($360). Interior Illumination Pkg., illum. entry, illum. visor vanity mirrors; CDH41 and CDP41 ($197). Power Accessories Pkg. incl. pwr decklid pulldown; pwr antenna, CDP41 ($154). Air cond. ($819). Frt. license plate bracket (NC). Pwr door locks ($304). Calif. emissions ($103). Pearl coat/clear coat paint ($75). AM/FM stereo/cass. ($157). Infinity I prem. AM/FM stereo cass. ($497). Premium AM/FM stereo cass. radio w/graphic equalizer w/seek and scan plus 6 Infinity spkrs ($713). Pwr 8-way driver's & pass. seats w/memory and pwr recliner ($372). Pwr 6-way driver's seat ($258). Security alarm ($150). Conventional spare tire ($85). Pwr sunroof ($799). Road handling suspension ($59). Rear auto. load leveling suspension ($185). Wire whl covers ($231). Cast alum whls ($281) w/(AFF) ($50).

HISTORY: Model year production: 307,935. Calendar year sales: 334,839.

1991 DODGE

Since 1978, the Dodge lineup included the Omni name but it was no more in 1991. The Shadow lineup was greatly expanded, its ranks increased to eight models in three different trim levels as opposed to the previous year's two model offering. The Shadow was also now offered in a convertible body style. The Shelby hatchback of the Daytona series was renamed the IROC Shelby, the sporty model inspired by the International Race of Champions series. The Spirit series gained a turbocharged four-cylinder R/T sedan for 1991 and an all-new Stealth 2+2 sports coupe also joined Dodge's ranks. Because the Stealth was built by Mitsubishi Motors of Japan it is considered an import and not included in this catalog. The compact Dodge Colt, also produced by Mitsubishi Motors, also falls into this category. All domestically produced 1991 Dodges (as well as the Stealth) featured a driver's side airbag as standard equipment.

DAYTONA — SERIES G — FOUR/V-6 — Daytona was again available in base, ES and Shelby trim levels although by midyear, the Shelby was renamed the IROC Shelby in honor of the International Race of Champions series in which Dodge participated in the early-1990s. Also in midyear, a Daytona Sport Package became available. This option included a color-keyed spoiler and front fascia and 15-inch wheels and tires as well as four exterior color choices. The 2.5-liter "High Torque" multiport fuel-injected Turbo I four-cylinder engine with five-speed manual transmission was the new standard powertrain for the Shelby. Peak torque of the 2.5-liter four was increased 16 percent - to 210 pound-feet - compared to the Shelby's previously used 2.2-liter turbocharged four. This torque upgrade was accomplished by recalibrating the turbocharger for more low-speed boost. A new exhaust system with lower back pressure was included with the Turbo I engine. Base and ES models were again powered by the non-turbo 2.5-liter electronically fuel-injected four paired with a five-speed manual transmission. A three-speed auto-

matic was optional on both models. The Turbo I four was also optional on base Daytonas. Again optional on base or ES hatchbacks was the 3.0-liter multi-port fuel-injected V-6 mated to either a five-speed manual or four-speed automatic transmission. New-for-1991 features included a modified clutch release system with starter interlock that prevented starting in gear when the 2.5-liter four was equipped with the five-speed manual transmission. Top gear ratio in the manual transmission was raised from 2.52 to 2.76 for better acceleration. The steering ratio was increased for reduced steering effort, and upgraded lower control arms, struts, steering knuckle and sway bar were incorporated into a revised suspension system. Front disc brakes used a new caliper for a firmer brake feel. Also new was four-wheel disc anti-lock as an option on ES and Shelby models. Four-wheel disc brakes were standard on Shelby and optional on base and ES models. Interior refinements included redesigned air conditioning controls, low center console, turn signal switch with rotary motion for better driver operation, and a manual front seat mechanism for improved fore/aft adjustment. Daytona's optional equipment list included air conditioning, overhead console, electric rear window defroster, power door locks, power seats, driver enthusiast power seat, speed control, tilt steering, sunroof, rear window sun louver, power windows, liftgate wiper/washer and steel or aluminum road wheels.

1991 Dodge, Shadow America hatchback coupe (OCW)

1991 Dodge, Shadow ES convertible (OCW)

SHADOW — SERIES P — FOUR — The compact Shadow enhanced its 1991 lineup with the addition of an entry-level America trim level as well as offering a convertible in two trim levels. Shadow was now available in the aforementioned America, base or ES trim, with the base and ES lines offering four-passenger convertibles. Five-passenger hatchbacks in either three- or five-door configurations comprised the remainder of the lineup. All Shadows were built on a 97-inch wheelbase and measured 171.7 inches overall. America models, in addition to Shadow and ES hatchbacks, were powered by Chrysler's 2.2-liter electronically fuel-injected four-cylinder engine mated to a five-speed manual transmission. A three-speed automatic was optional. Standard features of the America hatchback included a driver's side airbag, power steering and power brakes. Optional were air conditioning, tinted glass, rear window defroster, dual remote outside mirrors, bodyside moldings and convenience lights. Convertibles were powered by the 2.5-liter electronically fuel-injected four-cylinder engine paired with a five-speed manual transmission. Optional powertrain choice was the 2.5-liter "High Torque" Turbo I four with three-speed automatic transmission. Ordering the five-speed manual transmission with the Turbo I four increased the unit's torque rating to 181 pound-feet. A gas, prop-assisted manual folding soft top with attached rear and quarter windows permitted easy folding and storage of the Shadow convertible's top. Standard features of the convertible included power brakes, power steering, power windows, center console with armrest, body-color grille, premium sound insulation, floor-mounted shifter and driver's side airbag. Optional were air conditioning, power door locks, performance bucket seats, driver power seat, and speed control. Base hatchbacks could be ordered with the optional 2.5-liter multi-port fuel-injected four coupled to either a five-speed manual or four-speed automatic transmission. Shadow's suspension was upgraded for 1991 including front and rear sway bars. New front disc brake calipers provided a firmer brake feel and revised disc brake pads incorporated aramid synthetic fiber, which eliminated the use of asbestos. Redesigned front and rear seats provided improved comfort and roominess. Rear seats featured outboard bolsters and a folding center section. Midyear, a Shadow Sport Package became available, and included color-keyed front fascia and spoiler and 14-inch cast aluminum wheels.

SPIRIT — SERIES A — FOUR/V-6 — The Spirit sedan attempted to shake its sedate, family-transport image in 1991 with the addition of R/T model. This sports sedan joined a lineup that already consisted of base, LE and ES sedans. The R/T retained Spirit's contemporary four-door sedan appearance, but gained its performance stance from Chrysler's new dual overhead cam 2.2-liter turbocharged four-cylinder engine with intercooler and twin balance shafts. This engine, with a broad, flat torque curve for superior mid-range acceleration, had the highest specific power output - more than 100 horsepower per liter - of any production engine ever developed by Chrysler Corp. to that time. It delivered 224 horsepower at 6000 rpm and 217 pound-feet of torque at 2800 rpm. Engine redline was 6500 rpm. Combined with the standard five-speed manual transmission, the R/T was capable of 0-60 mph speed in 6.8 seconds. In addition to the suspension redesign of all Dodge front-drive cars in 1991 (see Daytona and Shadow listings), the R/T also featured specific performance-tuned suspension. These modifications included increased spring rates in both front and rear, increased control conventional valving in front, increased control performance-oriented rear shock absorbers, 70-millimeter progressive-rate front jounce bumpers and a 28.6-millimeter solid-rod rear sway bar. In addition, the R/T featured P205/60HR15 Michelin tires and 15x6-inch wheels. R/T sedans were offered in bright white or Indy red and featured a rear spoiler, unique bodyside molding with accent stripes and "DOHC INTER-COOLED/MULTI-VALVE" graphics. Inside, the R/T had front sport bucket seats with improved lateral support and a leather-wrapped gearshift knob. Medium Quartz was the only interior trim color offered. Base and LE Spirits were again powered by the 2.5-liter electronically fuel-injected four paired with a five-speed manual transmission (base) or three-speed automatic (LE). Optional on these models were the Turbo I 2.5-liter four or the 3.0-liter V-6. The Spirit ES again used the Turbo I 2.5-liter four mated to a five-speed manual transmission as its standard powertrain. Both the 3.0-liter V-6 and an electronically controlled four-speed automatic transmission were optional. The ES was aerodynamically designed with styled wrap-to-wheel openings and bumper fascias. The front fascia had fog lights and add-on ground effects and the sedan rode on P205/60R15 performance tires mounted on Eurocast aluminum wheels. Four-wheel disc brakes were standard equipment on the ES and all Spirits offered four-wheel anti-lock brakes as an option in 1991.

1991 Dodge, Dynasty sedan (OCW)

DYNASTY — SERIES C — FOUR/V-6 — Dynasty sedans were again available in base and LE trims levels. The 2.5-liter electronically fuel-injected four-cylinder engine coupled to a three-speed automatic transmission again powered the base model while the LE again used the 3.0-liter multi-port fuel-injected V-6 paired with the Ultradrive four-speed automatic transmission. This latter combination was optional on the base sedan. Both the base and LE offered the 3.3-liter multi-port fuel-injected V-6 with Ultradrive as an option engine. Both the base and LE sedans were built on a 104.3-inch wheelbase, measured 192 inches overall and provided 16.5 cubic feet of luggage space. For 1991, the Ultradrive transmission was refined for improved internal cooling, smoother down-shifting, "crisper" upshifting and more accurate diagnostic analysis. As with other front-drive Dodges, Dynasty's steering, suspension and brakes were upgraded. Key standard features of the Dynasty included power steering, power brakes, electric rear window defroster, tinted glass, dual remote outside rearview mirrors, dual vanity mirrors, remote trunk release, message center and driver's side airbag. Optional equipment included air conditioning, power windows, power antenna, four-wheel anti-lock brakes, power seats with memory, speed control, tilt steering, power sunroof, automatic load-leveling suspension and power door locks. A new option was the Visorphone "hands-free" sun visor-mounted cell phone. Two other portable floor-mounted cell phones were also optional.

MONACO — SERIES B — V-6 — The midsize Monaco sedan returned in both LE and ES trim levels, both powered by the 3.0-liter multi-port fuel-injected V-6 linked to a four-speed automatic transmission with overdrive. Refinements for 1991 included revised transmission cooling, driveline shafts, fuel pump, engine cooling, engine control computer and the addition of a direct (distributorless) ignition system. Also upgraded were the front and rear suspension systems to reduce ride harshness. Increased use of silencing materials also reduced noise, vibration and harshness coming from the road, engine and wind. Outside, Monaco was freshened by the appearance of a raised black section to

front and rear fascias. Five new exterior color choices were available. Monaco was built on a 106-inch wheelbase, measured 192.8 inches overall and provided 17 cubic feet of luggage space. Monaco's standard features included center console with transmission shifter, electric rear window defroster, tinted glass, full instrument panel gauges, dual remote outside rearview mirrors, power steering, halogen headlights, inside hood release, intermittent wipers and body-color grille on the ES sedan (bright on the LE). Options included air conditioning, speed control, tilt wheel, power door locks, message center, power antenna, compact disc player, power seats, trip computer, leather-wrapped steering wheel and four-wheel disc brakes (standard on the ES). Four-wheel anti-lock brakes were a new option for Monacos in 1991.

I.D. DATA: Dodge's 17-symbol Vehicle Identification Number (VIN), as before, was on the upper left corner of the instrument panel, visible through the windshield. Coding is similar to 1986-90. Symbol ten (model year) changed to 'M' for 1991.

DAYTONA (FOUR/V-6)

Model No.	Body/ Style No.	Body Type & Seating	Factory Price	Shipping Weight	Prod. Total
GVL	24	2-dr. Hatch-4P	10150/10844	2798/2880	Note 1
GVH	24	2-dr. ES Hatch-4P	11395/12089	2873/2955	Note 1
GVX	24	2-dr. IROC Hatch-4P	-----/12940	----/3030	Note 1

Note: Prices and weights to left of slash for four-cylinder, to right for V-6.

Note 1: Daytona hatchback production totaled 17,523 with no further breakout available.

SHADOW AMERICA (FOUR)

PDL	24	2-dr. Hatch-5P	7599	2615	Note 1
PDL	44	4-dr. Hatch-5P	7799	2652	Note 2

SHADOW (FOUR)

PDH	24	2-dr. Hatch-5P	9070	2632	Note 1
PDH	44	4-dr. Hatch-5P	9270	2669	Note 2
PDH	27	2-dr. Conv-4P	12995	2882	Note 3

SHADOW ES (FOUR)

PDS	24	2-dr. Hatch-5P	10545	2708	Note 1
PDS	44	4-dr. Hatch-5P	10745	2746	Note 2
PDS	27	2-dr. Conv-4P	14068	2910	Note 3

Note 1: Shadow two-door hatchback production totaled 28,756 with no further breakout available.

Note 2: Shadow four-door hatchback production totaled 33,839 with no further breakout available.

Note 3: Shadow convertible production totaled 20,043 with no further breakout available.

SPIRIT (FOUR/V-6)

ADH	41	4-dr. Sedan-6P	10905/11599	2801/2884	Note 1
ADP	41	4-dr. LE Sed-6P	12905/13599	2905/2976	Note 1
ADX	41	4-dr. ES Sed-6P	13689/14383	3009/3058	Note 1
ADS	41	4-dr. R/T Sed-6P	17800/-----	3060/----	Note 1

Note: Prices and weights to left of slash for four-cylinder, to right for V-6.

Note 1: Spirit sedan production totaled 95,311 with no further breakout available.

DYNASTY (FOUR/V-6)

CDH	41	4-dr. Sedan-6P	13625/14319	3006/3066	Note 1
CDP	41	4-dr. LE Sedan-6P	-----/15065	----/3078	Note 1

Note: Prices and weights to left of slash for four-cylinder, to right for V-6.

Note 1: Dynasty sedan production totaled 112,438 with no further breakout available.

MONACO (V-6)

BDP	41	4-dr. LE Sedan-6P	13895	3017	Note 1
BDS	41	4-dr. ES Sedan-6P	16595	3103	Note 1

Note 1: Monaco sedan production totaled 12,436 with no further breakout available.

ENGINE DATA: BASE FOUR (Shadow America, Shadow, Shadow ES): Inline, overhead cam four-cylinder. Cast iron block; aluminum head.

Displacement: 135 cu. in. (2.2 liters). Bore & stroke: 3.44 x 3.62 in. Compression ratio: 9.5:1. Brake horsepower: 93 at 4800 RPM. Torque: 122 lb.-ft. at 3200 RPM. Throttle-body fuel injection. **BASE TURBO-CHARGED FOUR** (Spirit R/T): Inline, dual overhead cam four-cylinder. Cast iron block; aluminum head. Displacement: 135 cu. in. (2.2 liters). Bore & stroke: 3.44 x 3.62 in. Compression ratio: 8.5:1. Brake horsepower: 224 at 2800 RPM. Torque: 217 lb.-ft. at 6000 RPM. Multi-port fuel injection. **BASE FOUR** (Shadow conv, Daytona, Daytona ES, Spirit, Spirit LE, Dynasty); **OPTIONAL** (Shadow America, Shadow, Shadow ES): Inline, overhead cam four-cylinder. Cast iron block; aluminum head. Displacement: 153 cu. in. (2.5 liters). Bore & stroke: 3.44 x 4.09 in. Compression ratio: 8.9:1. Brake horsepower: 100 at 4800 RPM. Torque: 135 lb.-ft. at 2800 RPM. Throttle-body fuel injection. **BASE TURBO-CHARGED FOUR** (Daytona IROC Shelby, Spirit ES); **OPTIONAL** (Daytona, Shadow conv, Spirit, Spirit LE): Inline, overhead cam four-cylinder. Cast iron block; aluminum head. Displacement: 153 cu. in. (2.5 liters). Bore & stroke: 3.44 x 4.09 in. Compression ratio: 7.8:1. Brake horsepower: 152 at 4800 RPM. Torque: 210 lb.-ft. at 2000 RPM. Multi-port fuel injection. **BASE V-6** (Dynasty LE); **OPTIONAL** (Daytona, Daytona ES, Spirit, Spirit LE, Spirit ES, Dynasty): Overhead cam V-6. Displacement: 181 cu. in. (3.0 liters). Bore & stroke: 3.59 x 2.99 in. Compression ratio: 8.9:1. Brake horsepower: 141 at 5000 RPM. Torque: 171 lb.-ft. at 2800 RPM. Multi-port fuel injection. **BASE V-6** (Monaco LE, Monaco ES): Overhead cam V-6. Displacement: 180 cu. in. (3.0 liters). Bore & stroke: 3.66 x 2.87 in. Compression ratio: 9.3:1. Brake horsepower: 150 at 5000 RPM. Torque: 171 lb.-ft. at 3600 RPM. Multi-port fuel injection. **OPTIONAL V-6** (Dynasty, Dynasty LE): Overhead valve V-6. Displacement: 201 cu. in. (3.3 liters). Bore & stroke: 3.66 x 3.19 in. Compression ratio: 8.9:1. Brake horsepower: 147 at 4800 RPM. Torque: 183 lb.-ft. at 3600 RPM. Multi-port fuel injection.

1991 Dodge, Spirit R/T sedan (OCW)

CHASSIS DATA: Wheelbase: (Daytona) 97.0 in.; (Shadow) 97.0 in.; (Spirit) 103.3 in.; (Dynasty) 104.3 in.; (Monaco) 106.0 in. Overall length: (Daytona) 179.2 in.; (Shadow) 171.7 in.; (Spirit) 181.2 in.; (Dynasty) 192.0 in.; (Monaco) 192.8 in. Height: (Daytona) 50.1 in.; (Shadow) 52.6 in.; (Spirit) 53.5 in.; (Dynasty) 54.8 in.; (Monaco) 56.5 in. Width: (Daytona) 69.3 in.; (Shadow) 67.3 in.; (Spirit) 68.1 in.; (Dynasty) 68.5 in.; (Monaco) 69.3 in. Front Tread: (Daytona) 57.5 in.; (Shadow) 57.6 in.; (Spirit) 57.6 in.; (Dynasty) 57.6 in.; (Monaco) 58.1 in. Rear Tread: (Daytona) 57.6 in.; (Shadow) 57.2 in.; (Spirit) 57.2 in.; (Dynasty) 57.6 in.; (Monaco) 57.1 in. Standard Tires: (Daytona) P185/70R14; (Daytona ES) P205/60HR15; (Daytona Shelby) P205/55R16; (Shadow) P185/70R14; (Spirit) P195/70R14; (Spirit ES, Spirit R/T) P205/60R15; (Dynasty) P195/75R14; (Monaco LE) P195/70R14; (Monaco ES) P205/60R15.

TECHNICAL: Transmission: Five-speed manual standard on Daytona (all), Shadow (all), Spirit, Spirit ES and Spirit R/T. Three-speed automatic standard on Spirit LE and Dynasty. Four-speed automatic standard on Dynasty LE and Monaco (all). Steering: (all) Rack and pinion. Front suspension: (Daytona, Spirit, Dynasty) Iso-strut w/coil springs, gas-charged hydraulic shock absorbers and stabilizer bar; (Shadow) Iso-strut w/coil springs, direct hydraulic shock absorbers and stabilizer bar; (Monaco) MacPherson strut w/steering arm on strut, cast iron lower "A" arm w/plastic ball joint, coil springs, MacPherson strut twin-tube shock absorbers and stabilizer bar. Rear suspension: (Daytona, Spirit, Dynasty) Trailing flex arm w/track bar, coil springs, gas-charged hydraulic shock absorbers and stabilizer bar; (Shadow) Trailing flex arm w/track bar, coil springs, direct hydraulic shock absorbers and stabilizer bar; (Monaco) Trailing arms w/integral twist beam torsion bars, twin-tube high-pressure gas shock cartridge shock absorbers and dual function torsion bars. Brakes: Front disc, rear drum (power-assisted) except (Daytona Shelby, Spirit ES, Spirit R/T and Monaco ES) four-wheel disc. Body construction: Unibody. Fuel tank: (Daytona) 14 gals.; (Shadow) 14 gals.; (Spirit) 16 gals.; (Dynasty) 16 gals.; (Monaco) 16 gals.

DRIVETRAIN OPTIONS: Engines: 2.5-liter four: Shadow ($286). Turbo 2.5-liter four: Shadow ($729); Spirit ($694). 3.0-liter V-6: Daytona/Dynasty/Spirit ($694). 3.3-liter V-6: Dynasty ($694). Transmission: Three-speed auto. trans.: Daytona/Shadow/Spirit ($557). Four-speed auto.

trans.: Daytona/Spirit ($640); Dynasty ($93). Brakes: Four-wheel disc w/anti-lock: Spirit ($899); Dynasty ($899); Monaco ($799). Auto load-leveling susp.: Dynasty ($225).

1991 Dodge, Daytona Shelby hatchback coupe (OCW)

DAYTONA CONVENIENCE/APPEARANCE OPTIONS: Daytona: Pkg. 21A: incl. 2.5L four and 5-spd manual trans., Sport Pkg. w/body-color spoiler, striping, P205/60R15 tires, Sport whl covers ($10845). Pkg. 22A: 21A plus 3-spd trans. ($11402). Pkg. 21B: incl. 2.5L four and 5-spd manual trans., tinted glass, floor mats, Light Pkg., pwr dual remote outside mirrors, tilt stng, pwr door locks, elect. spd control, AM/FM stereo radio w/cass. ($11777). Pkg. 22B: 21B exc. 3-spd auto. trans. replaces 5-spd manual ($12334). Pkg. 25B: 21B exc. 3.0L V-6 replaces 2.5L four ($12471). Pkg. 26B: 25B exc. 4-spd auto. trans. replaces 5-spd manual ($13121). Pkg. 21C: 21B plus Sport Pkg. ($12122). Pkg. 22C: 21C exc. 3-spd auto. trans. replaces 5-spd manual ($12679). Pkg. 25C: 21C plus 3.0L V-6 and 5-spd manual trans. ($12816). Pkg. 26C: 25C exc. 4-spd. auto. trans. replaces 5-spd manual ($13466). Other: (AWN) Super Discount Pkg.: incl. air cond., front floor mats, dual pwr remote outside mirrors, tilt stng, pwr door locks, elect. spd control, RAS audio syst. ($1068). (AAM) Popular Equipment Pkg.: AWN exc. delete pwr door locks, elect. spd control, RAS audio syst., Shelby ($994). (AAN) Popular Equipment Pkg.: incl. front floor mats, dual pwr remote outside mirrors, tilt stng, N/A Shelby ($313). (AAW) Value Discount Pkg.: incl. pwr door locks, elect. spd control, RAS audio syst. ($404). (AGY) V-6 Performance Pkg.: incl. pwr 4-whl disc brakes, 3.0L V-6 w/perf. tuned exhaust, leather-wrapped stng whl & shift knob, Performance Handling Susp., ES ($1013). (ADK) Premium Light Pkg.: incl. illum. entry, dual illum. visor mirrors, ES or Shelby ($196). (ADS) Sport Pkg.: incl. body-color stripe, rear spoiler, P205/60R15 tires, Sport whl covers, base ($345). (AGX) Shelby Performance Pkg.: incl. Turbo I 2.5L four and high-output 5-spd manual trans., pwr bulge hood, "Shelby" & "Turbo" graphics, Shelby ($165). (AY5) Steel Wheel Discount Pkg.: incl. P205/60R14 touring tires, 14-inch styled steel whls, base ($110). (AY6) Aluminum Wheel Discount Pkg.: incl. P205/60R14 touring tires, 14-inch cast alum whls, base ($336). Overhead console w/storage, compass & thermometer, ES or Shelby ($265). Elect. rear window defroster ($209). Calif. emission ($102). Extra cost paint ($77). (RAN) AM/FM stereo radio w/cass., seek/scan & 6 spkrs, ES or Shelby ($338-$493). (RAY) AM/FM stereo radio w/cass., graphic equal., seek/scan & 6 spkrs, ES or Shelby ($551-$706). CD player, ES or Shelby ($449). Pwr 6-way driver's seat, base or ES ($296). Pwr 8-way driver's seat ($751). Leather seat trim ($1402). Security alarm, ES or Shelby ($149). Sun louver ($214). Sunroof ($405). Tonneau cover, base ($74). Pwr windows ($265). Liftgate wiper/washer ($129).

SHADOW CONVENIENCE/APPEARANCE OPTIONS: America: Pkg. 21X: incl. 2.2L four and 5-spd manual trans., rear window defroster, Light Pkg., dual remote outside rearview mirrors, floor mats, AM/FM stereo radio: 2-dr. ($8370); 4-dr. ($8682). Pkg. 22X: incl. 21X exc. 3-spd auto. trans. replaces 5-spd manual: 2-dr. ($8927); 4-dr. ($9239). Pkg. 21Y: 21X plus air cond., tinted glass: 2-dr. ($9278); 4-dr. ($9590). Pkg. 22Y: 22X plus air cond., tinted glass: 2-dr. ($9835); 4-dr. ($10147). Shadow: Pkg. 21B: incl. 2.2L four and 5-spd manual trans., air cond., tinted glass, tilt stng, rear window defroster: 2-dr. ($9952); 4-dr. ($10252). Pkg. 22B: 21B exc. 3-spd auto. trans. replaces 5-spd manual trans.: 2-dr. ($10509); 4-dr. ($10809). Pkg. 23B: 21B exc. 2.5L four replaces 2.2L four: 2-dr. ($10238); 4-dr. ($10538). Pkg. 24B: 23B exc. 3-spd auto. trans. replaces 5-spd manual: 2-dr. ($10795); 4-dr. ($11095). Pkg. 23C: incl. 2.5L four and 5-spd manual trans., rear window defroster, tilt stng, Light Pkg., floor console, Liftgate release, dual note horn, wide mldgs, bodyside stripes, intermittent wipers, tach w/125 mph speedometer, dual outside remote mirrors: 2-dr. ($9912); 4-dr. ($10224). Pkg. 24C: 23C exc. 3-spd auto. trans. replaces 5-spd manual: 2-dr. ($10469); 4-dr. ($10781). Pkg. 23D: 23C plus air cond., tinted glass: 2-dr. ($10520); 4-dr. ($10832). Pkg. 24D: 24C plus air cond., tinted glass: 2-dr. ($11077); 4-dr. ($11389). Pkg. 23E: 23D exc. delete dual outside remote mirrors and replace w/dual pwr outside mirrors plus elect. spd control, pwr door locks, floor mats, AM/FM stereo radio w/cass.: 2-dr. ($11201); 4-dr. ($11554). Pkg. 24E: 23E plus 3-spd auto. trans.: 2-dr. ($11758); 4-dr. ($12111). ES: Pkg. 23H: 2.5L four and 5-spd manual trans., air cond., tinted glass, Light Pkg., rear window defroster, tilt stng, elect. spd control, pwr door

locks, dual pwr outside remote mirrors, liftgate release, floor mats, dual note horn, AM/FM stereo radio w/cass.: 2-dr. ($12054); 4-dr. ($12407). Pkg. 24H: 23H exc. 3-spd auto. trans. replaces 5-spd manual: 2-dr. ($12611); 4-dr. ($12694). Pkg. 25H: 23H exc. Turbo I 2.5L four replaces 2.5L four: 2-dr. ($12783); 4-dr. ($13136). Pkg. 26H: 25H exc. 3-spd auto. trans. replaces 5-spd manual: 2-dr. ($13340); 4-dr. ($13693). Shadow Conv: Pkg. 23B: incl. 2.5L four and 5-spd manual trans., tilt stng, air cond., tinted glass ($13851). Pkg. 24B: 23B exc. 3-spd auto. trans. replaces 5-spd manual ($14408). Pkg. 23C: incl. 2.5L four and 5-spd manual trans., tilt stng, Light Pkg., intermittent wipers, dual note horn, bodyside mldg, bodyside stripes, tach cluster ($13408). Pkg. 24C: 23C exc. 3-spd auto. trans. replaces 5-spd manual ($13965). Pkg. 23D: 23C plus air cond., tinted glass ($13966). Pkg. 24D: 24C plus air cond., tinted glass ($14523). Pkg. 23E: 23D plus dual pwr outside remote mirrors, elect. spd control, pwr door locks, floor mats, AM/FM stereo radio w/cass. ($14647). Pkg. 24E: 23E exc. 3-spd auto. trans. replaces 5-spd manual ($15204). Pkg. 25E: 23E exc. Turbo I 2.5L four replaces 2.5L four ($15407). Pkg. 26E: 25E exc. 3-spd auto. trans. replaces 5-spd manual ($15964). ES Conv: Pkg. 23H: incl. 2.5L four and 5-spd manual trans., tilt stng, air cond., tinted glass, Light Pkg., dual note horn, dual pwr outside remote mirrors, elect. spd control, pwr door locks, floor mats, Infinity I audio syst. ($15491). Pkg. 24H: 23H exc. 3-spd auto. trans. replaces 5-spd manual ($16048). Pkg. 25H: 23H exc. Turbo I 2.5L four replaces 2.5L four ($16220). Pkg. 26H: 25H exc. 3-spd auto. trans. replaces 5-spd manual ($16777). Other: Air conditioning ($801). Tinted glass ($107). Overhead console incl. storage, compass & thermometer ($265). Elect. rear window defroster ($173). Pwr door locks: 2-dr. ($199); 4-dr. ($240). Calif. emissions ($102). Front & rear floor mats ($46). Intermittent wipers ($66). Dual outside remote mirrors, stnd conv ($69). Dual pwr outside remote mirrors, Shadow or ES ($57). Extra cost paint ($77). Pwr driver's seat ($296). Pwr windows: 2-dr. ($255); 4-dr. ($321). (RAL) AM/FM stereo radio w/digital clock ($284). (RAS) Dlx AM/FM stereo radio w/cass. & 4 spkrs, America ($205-$489); others ($155). (RAN) Infinity I audio syst.: Shadow ($275); ES ($430). Elect. spd control ($224). Sunroof ($379). Tilt stng ($148). Conventional spare tire, N/A conv ($85); w/alum whl ($213). Cast alum whls ($328).

1991 Dodge, Spirit ES sedan (OCW)

SPIRIT CONVENIENCE/APPEARANCE OPTIONS: Spirit: Pkg. 22D: incl. 2.5L four and 3-spd auto. trans., air cond., rear window defroster, floor mats, tinted glass, tilt stng, elect. spd control ($12488). Pkg. 28D: 22D exc. 3.0L V-6 and 4-spd auto. trans. replaces 2.5L four and 3-spd auto. ($13275). Pkg. 22E: 22D plus pwr mirrors, pwr door locks, pwr windows ($13074). Pkg. 28E: 28D plus pwr mirrors, pwr door locks, pwr windows ($13861). LE: Pkg. 22U: incl. 2.5L four and 3-spd auto. trans., air cond., pwr mirrors, pwr door locks, pwr windows ($13978). Pkg. 28U: 22U exc. 3.0L V-6 and 4-spd auto. trans. replaces 2.5L four and 3-spd auto. ($14755). ES: Pkg. 24U: 22U exc. Turbo I 2.5L four replaces 2.5L four ($15309). Pkg. 28U: 3.0L V-6 and 4-spd auto. trans., air cond., pwr mirrors, pwr door locks, pwr windows ($15392). Other: (AWN) Super Discount A Pkg.: incl. air cond., elect. rear window defroster, front & rear floor mats, tinted glass, elect. spd control, tilt stng, Spirit ($965). (AWP) Super Discount B Pkg.: AWN plus dual pwr remote outside mirrors, pwr windows, pwr door locks, Spirit ($1541). (AWR) Super Discount C Pkg.: incl. air cond., dual pwr remote outside mirrors, pwr windows, pwr door locks, LE or ES ($992). (AAC) Premium Equipment Discount Pkg.: incl. 55/45 split folding rear seats, premium sound insulation, message center, lighter, Spirit ($241). (AJK) Deluxe Convenience Discount Pkg.: incl. front & rear floor mats, elect. spd control, tilt stng, Spirit ($379). (AJP) Power Equipment Discount Pkg.: incl. dual pwr remote outside mirrors, pwr windows, pwr door locks, Spirit R/T ($543). (AFH) Overhead Convenience Discount Pkg.: incl. overhead console w/storage, compass, thermometer, reading lamps, dual illum visor mirrors, LE or ES ($333). Air cond., Spirit ($831). Console-mounted armrest ($81-$155). Elect. rear window defroster ($173). Pwr door locks ($250). Calif. emissions ($102). Extra cost paint ($77). (RAS) AM/FM radio w/cass. & clock, Spirit ($155-$205). (RAN) AM/FM stereo radio w/cass. & clock, seek/scan & 4 spkrs: Spirit ($430); ES or R/T ($275). (RAY) AM/FM stereo radio w/cass. & clock, graphic equal., seek/scan & 4 spkrs: LE ($645); ES or R/T ($490). Pwr driver's seat,

Spirit ($296). Bench seats, Spirit ($102). Rear 55/45 bench seat ($61). P195/70R14 tires, Spirit ($73). P205/60R15 tires, Spirit or LE ($146). Conventional 14-inch spare tire, Spirit or LE ($95). 15-in. Eurocast alum whls, Spirit or LE ($328).

DYNASTY CONVENIENCE/APPEARANCE OPTIONS: Dynasty: Pkg. 22B: 2.5L and 3-spd auto. trans., air cond., P195/75R14 tires ($14611). Pkg. 24B: 22B exc. 3.0L V-6 and 4-spd auto. trans. replaces 2.5L and 3-spd auto. ($15388). Pkg. 26B: 22B exc. 3.3L V-6 and 4-spd auto. trans. replaces 2.5L and 3-spd auto. ($15388). Pkg. 24C: 24B plus floor mats, undercoating, elect. spd control, tilt stng, pwr door locks, message center, bodyside stripes ($15915). Pkg. 26C: 24C exc. 3.3L V-6 replaces 3.0L V-6 ($15915). LE: Pkg. 24E: incl. 3.0L V-6 and 4-spd auto. trans., air cond., P195/75R14 tires ($16041). Pkg. 26E: 24E exc. 3.3L V-6 replaces 3.0L V-6 ($16041). Pkg. 26F: 26E plus floor mats, undercoating, elect. spd control, tilt stng, pwr door locks, pwr windows, pwr mirrors ($16808). Pkg. 26G: 26F plus auto. adjustable rearview mirror, illum. entry & visor mirrors, leather-wrapped stng whl, pwr 6-way driver's & pass. seats, wire whl covers, cell phone pre-wire ($18032). Other: (AAB) Dynasty Popular Equipment Discount Pkg.: incl. Deluxe Convenience Pkg., air cond., pwr door locks, front & rear floor mats, message center, elect. spd control, bodyside stripe, tilt stng, undercoating ($1353). (AAB) LE Popular Equipment Discount Pkg.: incl. 3.3L V-6, pwr windows, dual pwr remote outside mirrors, Deluxe Convenience Pkg., air cond., pwr door locks, front & rear floor mats, elect. spd control, tilt stng, undercoating, Pwr Convenience Pkg. ($1393). (AFF) LE Luxury Equipment Discount Pkg.: incl. Popular Equipment Pkg., Pwr Convenience Pkg., illum. entry, auto. day/night rearview mirror, dual illum. visor mirrors, pwr 6-way driver's & pass. seats, leather-wrapped stng whl, wire whl covers, cell phone pre-wire ($2817). (AJK) LE Deluxe Convenience Pkg.: incl. elect. spd control, tilt stng ($372). (AJP) Dynasty Pwr Convenience Pkg.: incl. pwr dual remote outside mirrors, pwr windows ($384). (AJB) Security Pkg.: incl. security alarm w/panel warning light, keyless remote entry, remote activation of door locks & decklid, illum. entry, illum. visor mirrors: Dynasty ($473); LE ($277). (AJW) LE Pwr Accessories Pkg.: incl. pwr decklid pulldown, pwr antenna ($159). Air cond. ($831). Pwr door locks ($331). Calif. emissions ($102). Extra cost paint ($77). (RAS) AM/FM radio w/cass. ($155). (RAY) AM/FM stereo radio w/cass., graphic equal., seek/scan & 4 spkrs ($428). (ARB) Infinity RS audio syst. ($812). 8-way pwr driver's & pass. seats w/memory & pwr recliner ($396). Pwr 6-way driver's seat ($296). 50/50 front bench seat ($372). Leather 50/50 front bench seat ($590). Conventional spare tire ($85). Pwr sunroof ($792). P195/75R14 tires ($73). Wire whl covers ($228). Cast alum whls ($50-$279).

1991 Dodge, Monaco ES sedan (OCW)

MONACO CONVENIENCE/APPEARANCE OPTIONS: (ADC) Deluxe Convenience Pkg.: incl. elect. spd control w/stng whl controls, tilt stng ($372). (ADN) Electronic Features Pkg.: incl. trip computer w/multiple elect. functions ($237). (AWC) LE Enthusiast Pkg.: incl. pwr 4-whl disc brakes, touring susp., P205/60R15 touring tires, alum lace whls ($660). (AAY) Family Value Discount Pkg.: incl. auto. temp control air cond., pwr windows, pwr door locks, elect. spd control w/stng whl controls, tilt stng, LE ($1580). (AFF) Luxury Equipment Discount Pkg.: incl. Popular Equip. Pkg., Elect. Features Pkg., illum. entry syst., keyless entry syst., dual illum. visor mirrors, Premium AM/FM stereo radio w/cass. & graphic equal. & 6 spkrs, pwr antenna, leather-wrapped stng whl: LE ($3232); ES ($1777). (AAM) LE Popular Equipment Discount Pkg.: incl. auto. air cond., front & rear floor mats, pwr decklid release, pwr door locks, pwr mirrors, 6-way pwr driver's seat, pwr windows, AM/FM stereo radio w/cass., remote fuel filler door release, cruise control, tilt stng, Polycast Eurosport whls ($2326). (AAM) ES Popular Equipment Discount Pkg.: incl. front & rear floor mats, illum. entry syst., keyless entry syst., pwr door locks, 6-way pwr driver's seat, pwr windows, pwr decklid release, remote fuel filler door release, cruise control, tilt stng, P205/60HR15 performance tires, Alum lace whls ($1170). Air cond., LE ($887). Pwr door locks ($240). Calif. emissions ($102). Illum. entry syst., ES ($78). Keyless entry syst., ES ($128). Decklid luggage rack ($117). Color-keyed f&r floor mats ($46). (RAF) AM/FM stereo radio w/cass., LE ($239). (ARA) Premium AM/FM stereo radio w/cass. & graphic equal. & 6 spkrs ($381). (RBB) Premium AM/FM stereo radio w/cass. & CD player, pwr antenna & 6 spkrs ($279-$660). Pwr 6-way driver's seat ($296). Dual pwr 6-way leather seats: LE ($993); ES ($891). 14-in. Polycast Eurosport whls, LE ($104). Alum lace whls w/P205/60R15 tires, LE ($419-

$523); w/P205/60HR15 tires, ES ($386). Pwr windows ($331). Conventional spare tire ($95).

HISTORY: Model year production: 320,346. Calendar year sales: 287,396 (including 561 1990 Omni hatchbacks sold in 1991 and not including imported Stealth or Colt sales). A prototype 1992 Dodge Viper with V-10 power paced the 1991 Indianapolis 500 with Carroll Shelby as the driver. Production of the Monaco was stopped in December 1991. Cars produced as 1992 Monacos in those few months of the early 1992 model year were carryover '91s.

1992 DODGE

Dodge took the automotive industry by storm with the introduction in January 1992 of its "brutish" Dodge Viper RT/10 roadster. A V-10-powered muscle car, the Viper was initially assembled at a rate of three cars per day. It featured a curvaceous retro look and plenty of "snort" (0-60 mph in 4.5 seconds and a top speed of 165 mph). Another new Dodge also debuted in mid-model year 1992, the Daytona IROC R/T. It was powered by a dual overhead cam Turbo III 2.2-liter four-cylinder engine. The 1992 Monaco was in production only until December 1991, and then dropped from the lineup. It was basically a carryover model from the previous year.

1992 Dodge, Daytona hatchback coupe (OCW)

1992 Dodge, Daytona ES hatchback coupe (OCW)

1992 Dodge, Daytona IROC hatchback coupe (OCW)

DAYTONA — SERIES G — FOUR/V-6 — The Daytona ranks were bolstered in mid-model year 1992 with the addition of the IROC R/T, a brother trim level to the Spirit R/T and imported Stealth R/T (built by Mitsubishi of Japan). The IROC R/T's powertrain was comprised of a dual overhead cam 2.2-liter Turbo III four-cylinder engine paired with the heavy-duty version five-speed manual transmission. The existing IROC hatchback offered a revised engine lineup with the multi-port fuel-injected 3.0-liter V-6 now standard, replacing the formerly used Turbo I four that was now optional. The five-speed manual transmission was the IROC's standard unit while the heavy-duty version of the five-speed as well as three- and four-speed automatics were optional. Base and ES models were again powered by the non-turbo 2.5-liter electronically fuel-

injected four mated to a five-speed manual transmission. A four-speed automatic was optional on both models. Again optional on base or ES hatchbacks was the 3.0-liter V-6. New features for 1992 included a clutch/ignition interlock system for manual transmission-equipped Daytonas and a park/ignition interlock system for automatic-equipped Daytonas. Also new were three exterior color choices: Aqua, Raspberry and Light Blue, and two interior color choices: Crimson and Agate. Daytonas received an appearance "freshening" at both ends including new aero headlamps and new bodyside moldings or ground effects appliqués, exterior mirrors, wheels and wheelcovers, and side daylight opening moldings. Anti-lock brakes were standard equipment on IROC R/T models and optional on ES and IROC hatchbacks.

1992 Dodge, Shadow convertible (OCW)

1992 Dodge, Shadow ES hatchback coupe (OCW)

SHADOW — SERIES P — FOUR — Shadow returned in 1992 with its three levels of trim: America, Shadow and ES. America was again offered in three- and five-door hatchback body styles while both the Shadow and ES models were again available as three- and five-door hatchbacks and convertibles. America and Shadow hatchbacks were again powered by the 2.2-liter electronically fuel-injected four-cylinder engine linked to a five-speed manual transmission. A three-speed automatic was again optional on all models in the series. The Shadow convertible and all ES models used the 2.5-liter multi-port fuel-injected four-cylinder engine paired with a five-speed manual transmission. Optional powertrain choice was the 2.5-liter "High Torque" Turbo I four with three-speed automatic transmission. America and Shadow hatchbacks offered the 2.5-liter four as their option engine. New-for-1992 was the ES models offering the sequentially fuel-injected 3.0-liter V-6 as an option powerplant. This engine was paired with a four-speed automatic transmission. Other new features included body-color front and rear bumpers, one interior color choice: Crimson, and two exterior color choices: Aqua and Bright Silver Quartz.

1992 Dodge, Spirit R/T sedan (OCW)

SPIRIT — SERIES A — FOUR/V-6 — Spirit's lineup remained unchanged from what was offered the year previous, the all-sedan series again available in base, LE, ES and R/T trim levels. Base and LE Spirits were again powered by the 2.5-liter electronically fuel-injected four-cylinder engine mated to a five-speed manual transmission (base) or three-speed automatic (LE, optional on base). Optional on these models were the Turbo I 2.5-liter four or the 3.0-liter V-6 that was now sequentially fuel-injected. Also optional was an electronically controlled four-speed automatic transmission. The Spirit ES again used the Turbo I 2.5-liter four mated to a five-speed manual transmission as its standard power-

train. Both the 3.0-liter V-6 and a four-speed automatic were optional. Spirit R/T again used the dual overhead cam 2.2-liter Turbo III four-cylinder engine coupled to a five-speed manual transmission. New features included revised gear ratios for the five-speed manual transmission, both a redesigned 14-inch wheel cover and 15-inch cast aluminum wheel, and one new exterior color choice: Bright Silver Quartz.

1992 Dodge, Dynasty sedan (OCW)

DYNASTY — SERIES C — FOUR/V-6 — Both the Dynasty's lineup and powertrain availability carried over from the year previous. The base and LE trim levels returned, with the Dynasty again powered by the 2.5-liter electronically fuel-injected four-cylinder engine paired with a three-speed automatic transmission and the LE again used the 3.0-liter sequentially fuel-injected V-6 paired with a four-speed automatic. This latter combination was optional on the base sedan, while the 3.3-liter multi-port fuel-injected V-6 was optional on both the base and LE sedans. Four new exterior color choices were offered on Dynastys: Claret Red, Beryl Green, Dark Quartz Grey Metallic and Bright Silver Quartz. Two new interior color choices were also available: Agate and Crimson. Other new features included an overhead light module with storage bin, child-proof door locks, and, in package availability only, a lower floor console.

MONACO — SERIES B — V-6 — Production of Monacos was stopped in December 1991 shortly after the beginning of the 1992 model year. Aside from two new exterior color choices, the LE and ES sedans offered were carryovers from the year previous.

1992 Dodge, Viper RT/10 roadster (OCW)

VIPER RT/10- SERIES R — V-10 — After years of inappropriate use, the term muscle car could rightly be applied to Dodge's Viper RT/10. Powered by an all-aluminum 8.0-liter V-10 engine paired with a fully synchronized Borg-Warner T56 six-speed manual transmission, the two-seat Viper was Dodge's performance-oriented flagship model. The V-10 engine held 11 quarts of motor oil and featured a bottom-fed fuel injection system, the first such unit used in a Chrysler Corp. vehicle. Its list of standard features included a continuous fiber reinforced composite body attached to a steel tubing space frame, four-wheel disc brakes, foglamps, aero halogen headlamps, distributorless ignition system, leather-wrapped steering wheel, 16-pound removable folding soft top with side curtains, snap-in tonneau cover, tachometer, and 17-inch cast aluminum wheels. Structural urethane foam trim was used throughout its interior, the first U.S.-produced car to feature this material. Viper was the product of a platform team approach to vehicle development, going from concept to public introduction in less than 36 months. The Viper's final drive ratio was 3.07:1. It rode on a 96.2-inch wheelbase and measured 175.1 inches overall, and featured twin, side-of-car exhaust systems that incorporated space-age technology. To grip the road, Viper used P275/40ZR17 tires up front and P335/35ZR17 tires in back.

I.D. DATA: Dodge's 17-symbol Vehicle Identification Number (VIN), as before, was on the upper left corner of the instrument panel, visible through the windshield. Coding is similar to 1986-91. Symbol ten (model year) changed to 'N' for 1992.

DAYTONA (FOUR/V-6)

Model No.	Body/ Style No.	Body Type & Seating	Factory Price	Shipping Weight	Prod. Total
GVL	24	2-dr. Hatch-4P	10997/11691	2779/2819	Note 1
GVH	24	2-dr. ES Hatch-4P	11871/12565	2864/2905	Note 1
GVX	24	2-dr. IROC Hatch-4P	-----/13333	----/2950	Note 1
GVS	24	2-dr. IROC R/T Hatch-4P	18532/-----	2942/----	Note 1

Note: Prices and weights to left of slash for four-cylinder, to right for V-6.

Note 1: Daytona hatchback production totaled 10,937 with no further breakout available.

SHADOW AMERICA (FOUR)

PDL	24	2-dr. Hatch-5P	7984	2613	Note 1
PDL	44	4-dr. Hatch-5P	8384	2649	Note 2

SHADOW (FOUR)

PDH	24	2-dr. Hatch-5P	9246	2636	Note 1
PDH	44	4-dr. Hatch-5P	9646	2672	Note 2
PDH	27	2-dr. Conv-4P	13457	2884	Note 3

SHADOW ES (FOUR)

PDS	24	2-dr. Hatch-5P	10912	2672	Note 1
PDS	44	4-dr. Hatch-5P	11234	2757	Note 2
PDS	27	2-dr. Conv-4P	14685	2924	Note 3

Note 1: Shadow two-door hatchback production totaled 38,822 with no further breakout available.

Note 2: Shadow four-door hatchback production totaled 37,402 with no further breakout available.

Note 3: Shadow convertible production totaled 3,185 with no further breakout available.

SPIRIT (FOUR/V-6)

ADH	41	4-dr. Sedan-6P	11470/12195	2788/2871	Note 1
ADP	41	4-dr. LE Sed-6P	13530/14255	2879/2949	Note 1
ADX	41	4-dr. ES Sed-6P	14441/14441	2939/2995	Note 1
ADS	41	4-dr. R/T Sed-6P	18674/-----	3089/----	Note 1

Note: Prices and weights to left of slash for four-cylinder, to right for V-6.

Note 1: Spirit sedan production totaled 66,904 with no further breakout available.

DYNASTY (FOUR/V-6)

CDH	41	4-dr. Sedan-6P	14447/15171	2971/3041	Note 1
CDP	41	4-dr. LE Sedan-6P	-----/15967	----/3065	Note 1

Note: Prices and weights to left of slash for four-cylinder, to right for V-6.

Note 1: Dynasty sedan production totaled 85,238 with no further breakout available.

MONACO (V-6)

BDP	41	4-dr. LE Sedan-6P	14354	2991	Note 1
BDS	41	4-dr. ES Sedan-6P	17203	3068	Note 1

Note 1: Monaco sedan production totaled 1,960 with no further breakout available.

VIPER RT/10 (V-10)

RDS	27	2-dr. Rdstr-2P	50000	3399	Note 1

Note 1: Viper production is listed at 155, but this figure includes both 1992 and 1993 models introduced early in 1992.

ENGINE DATA: BASE FOUR (Shadow America, Shadow): Inline, overhead cam four-cylinder. Cast iron block; aluminum head. Displacement: 135 cu. in. (2.2 liters). Bore & stroke: 3.44 x 3.62 in. Compression ratio: 9.5:1. Brake horsepower: 93 at 4800 RPM. Torque: 122 lb.-ft. at 3200 RPM. Throttle-body fuel injection. BASE TURBOCHARGED FOUR (Spirit R/T, Daytona IROC R/T): Inline, dual overhead cam four-cylinder. Cast iron block; aluminum head. Displacement: 135 cu. in. (2.2 liters). Bore & stroke: 3.44 x 3.62 in. Compression ratio: 8.5:1. Brake horsepower: 224 at 2800 RPM. Torque: 217 lb.-ft. at 6000 RPM. Multi-port fuel injection. BASE FOUR (Shadow conv, Shadow ES, Daytona, Daytona ES, Spirit, Spirit LE, Dynasty); OPTIONAL (Shadow America, Shadow): Inline, overhead cam four-cylinder. Cast iron block; aluminum head. Displacement: 153 cu. in. (2.5 liters). Bore & stroke: 3.44 x 4.09 in. Compression ratio: 8.9:1. Brake horsepower: 100 at 4800 RPM. Torque: 135 lb.-ft. at 2800 RPM. Throttle-body fuel injection. BASE TURBOCHARGED FOUR (Spirit ES); OPTIONAL (Shadow conv, Shadow ES, Daytona IROC, Spirit, Spirit LE): Inline, overhead cam four-cylinder. Cast iron block; aluminum head. Displacement: 153 cu. in. (2.5 liters). Bore & stroke: 3.44 x 4.09 in. Compression ratio: 7.8:1. Brake horsepower: 152 at 4800 RPM. Torque: 210 lb.-ft. at 2400 RPM. Multi-port fuel injection. BASE V-6 (Daytona IROC, Dynasty LE); OPTIONAL (Daytona, Daytona ES, Spirit, Spirit LE, Spirit ES, Dynasty): Overhead cam V-6. Displacement: 181 cu. in. (3.0 liters). Bore & stroke: 3.59 x 2.99 in. Compression ratio: 8.9:1. Brake horsepower: 141 at 5000 RPM. Torque: 171 lb.-ft. at 2800 RPM. Sequential fuel injection. BASE V-6 (Monaco LE, Monaco ES): Overhead cam V-6. Displacement: 180 cu. in. (3.0 liters). Bore & stroke: 3.66 x 2.87 in. Compression ratio: 9.3:1. Brake horsepower: 150 at 5000 RPM. Torque: 171 lb.-ft. at 3600 RPM. Multi-port fuel injection. OPTIONAL V-6 (Dynasty, Dynasty LE): Overhead valve V-6. Displacement: 201 cu. in. (3.3 liters). Bore & stroke: 3.66 x 3.19 in. Compression ratio: 8.9:1. Brake horsepower: 147 at 4800 RPM. Torque: 183 lb.-ft. at 3600 RPM. Multi-port fuel injection. BASE V-10 (Viper): Overhead valve V-10. Aluminum block and heads. Displacement: 488 cu. in. (8.0 liters). Bore & stroke: 4.00 x 3.88 in. Compression ratio: 9.1:1. Brake horsepower: 400 at 4600 RPM. Torque: 450 lb.-ft. at 3600 RPM. Sequential fuel injection.

CHASSIS DATA: Wheelbase: (Daytona) 97.2 in.; (Shadow) 97.0 in.; (Spirit) 103.5 in.; (Dynasty) 104.5 in.; (Monaco) 106.0 in.; (Viper) 96.2 in. Overall length: (Daytona) 179.8 in.; (Shadow) 171.7 in.; (Spirit) 181.2 in.; (Dynasty) 192.0 in.; (Monaco) 192.8 in.; (Viper) 175.1 in. Height: (Daytona) 51.8 in.; (Shadow hatch) 52.7 in.; (Shadow conv) 52.6 in.; (Spirit) 53.5 in.; (Dynasty) 53.6 in.; (Monaco) 54.7 in.; (Viper) 43.9 in. Width: (Daytona) 69.3 in.; (Shadow) 67.3 in.; (Spirit) 68.1 in.; (Dynasty) 68.9 in.; (Monaco) 70.0 in.; (Viper) 75.7 in. Front Tread: (Daytona) 57.5 in.; (Shadow) 57.6 in.; (Spirit) 57.6 in.; (Dynasty) 57.6 in.; (Monaco) 58.1 in.; (Viper) 59.6 in. Rear Tread: (Daytona) 57.6 in.; (Shadow) 57.2 in.; (Spirit) 57.2 in.; (Dynasty) 57.6 in.; (Monaco) 57.1 in.; (Viper) 60.6 in. Standard Tires: (Daytona) P185/70R14; (Daytona ES) P205/60HR15; (Daytona IROC) P205/55R16; (Shadow) P185/70R14; (Spirit) P185/70R14; (Spirit ES, Spirit R/T) P205/60R15; (Dynasty) P195/75R14; (Monaco LE) P195/70R14; (Monaco ES) P205/60R15; (Viper) P275/40ZR17 front/P335/35ZR17 rear.

TECHNICAL: Transmission: Five-speed manual standard on Daytona (all), Shadow (all), Spirit, Spirit ES and Spirit R/T. Three-speed automatic standard on Spirit LE and Dynasty. Four-speed automatic standard on Dynasty LE and Monaco (all). Six-speed manual standard on Viper. Steering: (all) Rack and pinion. Front suspension: (Daytona, Spirit, Dynasty) Iso-strut w/coil springs, gas-charged hydraulic shock absorbers and stabilizer bar; (Shadow) Iso-strut w/coil springs, direct hydraulic shock absorbers and stabilizer bar; (Monaco) MacPherson strut w/steering arm on strut, cast iron lower "A" arm w/plastic ball joint, coil springs, MacPherson strut twin-tube shock absorbers and stabilizer bar; (Viper) Independent w/unequal length upper and lower control arms, coil over shock units, micro-grain alloy coil springs, dynamic acting hydraulic/low-pressure gas charged shock absorbers w/adjustable rebound and tubular anti-roll bar. Rear suspension: (Daytona, Spirit, Dynasty) Trailing flex arm w/track bar, coil springs, gas-charged hydraulic shock absorbers and stabilizer bar; (Shadow) Trailing flex arm w/track bar, coil springs, direct hydraulic shock absorbers and stabilizer bar; (Monaco) Trailing arms w/integral twist beam torsion bars, twin-tube high-pressure gas shock cartridge shock absorbers and dual function torsion bars; (Viper) Independent w/unequal length upper and lower control arms w/separate toe link, micro-grain alloy coil springs, dynamic acting hydraulic/low-pressure gas charged shock absorbers w/adjustable rebound and tubular anti-roll bar. Brakes: Front disc, rear drum (power-assisted) except (Daytona IROC, Spirit ES, Spirit R/T, Monaco ES and Viper) four-wheel disc. Body construction: Unibody except (Viper) tubular space frame. Fuel tank: (Daytona) 14 gals.; (Shadow) 14 gals.; (Spirit) 16 gals.; (Dynasty) 16 gals.; (Monaco) 16 gals.; (Viper) 22 gals.

DRIVETRAIN OPTIONS: Engines: 2.5-liter four: Shadow ($286). Turbo 2.5-liter four: Shadow conv/Shadow ES (N/A); Daytona IROC (N/A); Spirit/Spirit LE ($725). 3.0-liter V-6: Shadow conv ($905). Shadow ES ($694); Daytona/Daytona ES ($694); Spirit/Spirit LE/Spirit ES ($725); Dynasty ($827). 3.3-liter V-6: Dynasty/Dynasty LE ($827). Transmission: Three-speed auto. trans.: Daytona IROC (N/A); Shadow/Spirit ($557). Four-speed auto. trans.: Daytona/Daytona ES/Daytona IROC ($690); Spirit/Spirit LE/Spirit ES (N/A); Dynasty ($827). Brakes: Four-wheel disc w/anti-lock: Spirit ($899); Dynasty ($899); Monaco ($799). Auto load-leveling susp.: Dynasty ($225).

DAYTONA CONVENIENCE/APPEARANCE OPTIONS: Daytona: Pkg. 21A: stnd equip. (NC). Pkg. 22A: 21A plus 3-spd auto. trans. ($557). Pkg. 21B: incl. 2.5L four and 5-spd manual trans., air cond., rear window defroster, floor mats, Light Pkg., pwr dual remote outside mirrors, tilt stng, pwr door locks, elect. spd control, AM/FM stereo radio w/cass. ($1207). Pkg. 22B: 21B exc. 3-spd auto. trans. replaces 5-spd manual ($1764). Pkg. 25B: 21B exc. 3.0L V-6 replaces 2.5L four ($1901). Pkg. 26B: 21B exc. 3.0L V-6 replaces 2.5L four and 4-spd auto. trans. replaces 5-spd manual ($2591). ES: Pkg. 21A: stnd equip. (NC). Pkg. 22A: 21A plus 3-spd auto. trans. ($557). Pkg. 25A: incl. 3.0L V-6 and 5-spd manual trans. ($694). Pkg. 21B: incl. 2.5L four and 5-spd manual trans., air cond., rear window defroster, floor mats, Light pkg., pwr dual remote outside mirrors, tilt stng, liftgate release, pwr door locks, elect. spd control, AM/FM stereo radio w/cass. ($1207). Pkg. 22B: 21B exc. 3-spd auto. trans. replaces 5-spd manual ($1764). Pkg. 25B: 21B exc. 3.0L V-6 replaces 2.5L four ($1901). Pkg. 26B: 21B exc. 3.0L V-6 replaces 2.5L four and 4-spd auto. trans. replaces 5-spd manual ($2591). IROC: Pkg. 25A: stnd equip. (NC). Pkg. 25B: 25A plus air cond., rear window defroster, floor mats, Light Pkg., pwr dual remote outside mirrors, tilt stng, pwr door locks, liftgate release, elect. spd control, AM/FM stereo radio w/cass. & 4 spkrs ($1207). Pkg. 26B: 25B exc. 4-spd auto. trans. replaces 5-spd manual ($1897). IROC R/T: Pkg. 27A: stnd equip. (NC). Pkg. 27B: 27A plus rear window defroster, floor mats, Light Pkg., pwr dual remote outside mirrors, tilt stng, pwr door locks, liftgate release, elect. spd control, AM/FM stereo radio w/cass. & 4 spkrs ($787). Other: (AAW) Value Grp.: incl. tilt stng, pwr door locks, elect. spd control, AM/FM stereo radio w/cass., base or LE ($640). (AGY) V-6 Performance Pkg.: incl. pwr 4-whl disc brakes, 3.0L V-6, leather-wrapped stng whl, Performance Handling Susp., ES ($1007). (ADK) Premium Light Pkg.: incl. illum. entry, dual illum. visor mirrors, ES, IROC, IROC R/T ($196). (ADS) Sport Pkg.: incl. body-color stripe, rear spoiler, P205/60R15 touring tires, Sport whl covers, base ($395). Overhead console, ES, IROC, IROC R/T ($265). Elect. rear window defroster ($209). Calif. emission ($102). Extra cost paint, N/A IROC or IROC R/T ($97). (RAN) AM/FM stereo radio w/cass., seek/scan & 6 spkrs, N/A base ($348). (RAY) AM/FM stereo radio w/cass., graphic equal., seek/scan & 6 spkrs, N/A base ($561). CD player, N/A base ($449). Pwr 6-way driver's seat, base or ES ($306). Pwr 12-way driver's seat, N/A base: cloth ($761); leather ($1412). Leather seat trim ($1402). Security alarm, N/A base ($149). Sun louver ($214). Sunroof ($405). Tonneau cover, base ($74). Pwr windows ($275). Liftgate wiper/washer ($129). 15-in. cast alum whls, base ($328).

SHADOW CONVENIENCE/APPEARANCE OPTIONS: America: Pkg. 21W: stnd equip. (NC). Pkg. 22W: incl. 2.2L four and 3-spd auto. trans. ($557). Pkg. 21Y: 22W plus air cond., tinted glass, rear window defroster, Light Grp., floor mats, dual visor mirrors, dual remote outside mirrors, dlx wipers, whl trim rings, AM/FM stereo radio w/clock & 2 spkrs: 2-dr. ($1450); 4-dr. ($1462). Pkg. 22Y: 21Y exc. 3-spd auto. trans. replaces 5-spd manual: 2-dr. ($2007); 4-dr. ($2019). Pkg. 23Y: 21Y exc. 2.5L four replaces 2.2L four: 2-dr. ($1736); 4-dr. ($1748). Pkg. 24Y: 23Y exc. 3-spd auto. trans. replaces 5-spd manual: 2-dr. ($2293); 4-dr. ($2305). Shadow: Pkg. 21A: stnd equip. (NC). Pkg. 22A: incl. 2.2L four and 3-spd auto. trans. ($557). Pkg. 23A: incl. 2.5L four and 5-spd manual trans. ($286). Pkg. 24A: incl. 2.5L four and 3-spd auto. trans. ($843). Pkg. 23D: 23A plus air cond., tinted glass, tilt stng, rear window defroster, dual horns, floor mats, bodyside mldg, dlx wipers, tach, Light Grp., floor-mounted console, liftgate release, bodyside striping, dual remote outside mirrors: 2-dr. ($1276); 4-dr. ($1288). Pkg. 24D: 23D exc. 3-spd auto. trans. replaces 5-spd manual: 2-dr. ($1833); 4-dr. ($1845). Shadow conv: Pkg. 23A: stnd equip. (NC). Pkg. 24A: incl. 2.5L four and 3-spd auto. trans. ($557). Pkg. 27A: incl. 3.0L V-6 and 5-spd manual trans. ($905). Pkg. 28A: 3.0L V-6 and 4-spd auto. trans. ($1595). Pkg. 23D: incl. 2.5L four and 5-spd manual trans., air cond., tinted glass, tilt stng, rear window defroster, dual horns, floor mats, bodyside mldg, dlx wipers, tach, headlights-on/seatbelts/key-in-ignition warning chimes, Light Grp., bodyside striping, dual visor mirrors, AM/FM stereo radio w/cass. & 4 spkrs ($627). Pkg. 24D: 23D exc. 3-spd auto. trans. replaces 5-spd manual: ($1184). Pkg. 27D: 23D exc. 3.0L V-6 replaces 2.5L four ($1532). Pkg. 28D: 27D exc. 4-spd auto. trans. replaces 5-spd manual ($2222). ES: Pkg. 23G: stnd equip. (NC). Pkg. 24G: incl. 2.5L four and 3-spd auto. trans. ($557). Pkg. 27G: incl. 3.0L V-6 and 5-spd manual trans. ($694). Pkg. 28G: incl. 3.0L V-6 and 4-spd auto. trans. ($1384). Pkg. 23H: incl. 2.5L four and 5-spd manual trans., air cond., tinted glass, rear window defroster, floor mats, foglamps, Light Pkg., floor-mounted console, liftgate release, dual note horn, premium sound insulation, dlx wipers, tach, dual visor mirrors, headlights-on/seatbelts/key-in-ignition warning chimes, AM/FM stereo radio w/cass. & 4 spkrs ($1016). Pkg. 24H: 23H exc. 3-spd auto. trans. replaces 5-spd manual ($1573). Pkg. 27H: 23H exc. 3.0L V-6 replaces 2.5L four and H.D. 5-spd manual trans. replaces 5-spd manual ($1710). Pkg. 28H: 27H exc. 4-spd auto. trans. replaces H.D. 5-spd manual ($2400). ES conv: Pkg. 23G: stnd equip. (NC). Pkg. 24G: incl. 2.5L four and 3-spd auto. trans. ($557). Pkg. 27G: incl. 3.0L V-6 and 5-spd manual trans. ($905). Pkg. 28G: incl. 3.0L V-6 and 4-spd auto. trans. ($1595). Pkg. 23H: incl. 2.5L four and 5-spd manual trans., air cond.,

tinted glass, floor mats, Light Pkg., dual note horn, dlx wipers, tach, dual visor mirrors, headlights-on/seatbelts/key-in-ignition warning chimes, AM/FM stereo radio w/cass. & 4 spkrs ($531). Pkg. 24H: 23H exc. 3-spd auto. trans. replaces 5-spd manual trans. ($1088). Pkg. 27H: 23H exc. 3.0L V-6 replaces 2.5L four and H.D. 5-spd manual trans. replaces 5-spd manual ($1436). Pkg. 28H: 27H exc. 4-spd auto. trans. replaces H.D. 5-spd manual ($2126). Other: (ADA) Light Grp: 2-dr. and conv ($65); 4-dr. and ES hatch ($77). (ALE) Deluxe Decor Pkg.: incl. body-color fascias, wide bodyside mldgs, bodyside stripes, 14-in. whl covers ($142). Air cond. ($900). Overhead console incl. storage, compass & thermometer ($265). Elect. rear window defroster ($173). Pwr door locks: 2-dr. ($199); 4-dr. ($240). Calif. emissions ($102). Front & rear floor mats ($46). Intermittent wipers ($66). Dual outside remote mirrors, stnd conv ($69). Dual pwr outside remote mirrors, Shadow or ES ($57). Extra cost paint ($97). Pwr driver's seat, N/A America ($306). Pwr windows, Shadow and ES: 2-dr. ($265); 4-dr. ($331). (RAL) AM/FM stereo radio w/digital clock & 2 spkrs, America ($284). (RAS) AM/FM stereo radio w/cass. & 4 spkrs, America ($215-$499); others ($165-$215). (RAN) Infinity I audio syst.: Shadow ($275-$440); ES ($275-$490). (RBC) AM/FM stereo radio w/CD player, seek/scan, equalizer, clock & 4 spkrs, ES ($645-$860). Elect. spd control ($224). Sunroof ($379). Tilt stng ($148). Conventional spare tire, N/A conv ($85); w/alum whl ($213). Cast alum whls ($328).

1992 Dodge, Spirit ES sedan (OCW)

SPIRIT CONVENIENCE/APPEARANCE OPTIONS: Spirit: Pkg. 21A: stnd equip. (NC). Pkg. 22A: incl. 2.5L four and 3-spd auto. trans. ($557). Pkg. 21C: incl. 2.5L four and 5-spd manual trans., air cond., rear window defroster, floor mats, tinted glass, tilt stng, elect. spd control ($505). Pkg. 22D: 21C exc. 3-spd auto. trans. replaces 5-spd manual ($1062). Pkg. 26D: 21C exc. 3.0L V-6 replaces 2.5L four and 3-spd auto. trans. replaces 5-spd manual plus P195/70R14 tires ($1787). Pkg. 22E: 22D plus air cond., rear window defroster, floor mats, tinted glass, tilt stng, elect. spd control, pwr mirrors, pwr door locks, pwr windows, pwr trunk release ($1734). Pkg. 26E: 22E exc. 3.0L V-6 replaces 2.5L four plus P195/70R14 tires ($2459). Pkg. 28E: 22E exc. 3.0L V-6 replaces 2.5L four and 4-spd auto. trans. replaces 3-spd auto. trans. plus P195/70R14 tires ($2592). LE: Pkg. 22P: stnd equip. (NC). Pkg. 22U: incl. 2.5L four and 3-spd auto. trans., air cond., pwr mirrors, pwr door locks, pwr windows ($627). Pkg. 24U: 22U exc. 2.5L Turbo I four replaces 2.5L four plus P195/70R14 tires ($1352). Pkg. 26U: 22U exc. 3.0L V-6 replaces 2.5L four plus P195/70R14 ($1352). Pkg. 28U: 22U exc. 3.0L V-6 replaces 2.5L four and 4-spd auto. trans. replaces 3-spd auto. trans. plus P195/70R14 tires ($1485). ES: Pkg. 23X: stnd equip. (NC). Pkg. 23U: incl. 2.5L Turbo I four and 5-spd manual trans., air cond., pwr mirrors, pwr door locks, pwr windows ($627). Pkg. 24U: 23U exc. 3-spd auto. trans. replaces 5-spd manual trans. ($1184). Pkg. 28U: 23U exc. 3.0L V-6 replaces 2.5L Turbo I four and 4-spd auto. trans. replaces 5-spd manual ($1317). R/T: Pkg. 29S: stnd equip. (NC). Other: (AJN) Illum. Grp.: incl. illum. entry, dual illum. visor mirrors: base ($293); LE or ES ($195). (AJP) Power Equipment Grp.: incl. pwr windows, pwr door locks, R/T ($553). (AFH) Convenience Grp.: incl. storage, compass, temp. display, reading lamps, AJN Illum. Grp., LE, ES, R/T ($400). Air cond., Spirit ($831). Console-mounted armrest ($81-$155). Elect. rear window defroster ($173). Pwr door locks ($250). Calif. emissions ($102). Extra cost paint ($97). (RAS) AM/FM radio w/cass. & clock & 4 spkrs, base or LE ($165). (RAN) AM/FM stereo radio w/cass. & clock, seek/scan & 4 spkrs: LE ($440); ES ($285-$440). (RAY) AM/FM stereo radio w/cass. & clock, graphic equal., seek/scan & 4 spkrs: ES or R/T ($500). Pwr driver's seat, N/A base ($306). Bench seats, base ($150). Front 50/50 bench seat, base ($298). Front bucket seats, base ($148). Front 50/50 bench seat, LE ($109). P195/70R14 tires, base ($73-$104). P205/60R15 tires, LE ($146-$177). Conventional spare tire, base or LE ($95). 15-in. cast alum whls, LE ($328).

DYNASTY CONVENIENCE/APPEARANCE OPTIONS: Dynasty: Pkg. 22A: stnd equip. (NC). Pkg. 24A: incl. 3.0L V-6 and 4-spd auto. trans. ($827). Pkg. 26A: incl. 3.3L V-6 and 4-spd auto. trans. ($827). Pkg. 22C: 22A plus air cond., P195/75R14 tires, floor-mounted console, elect. speed control, tilt stng, floor mats, message center warning lights for door ajar and decklid ajar, pwr door locks, bodyside stripe, under-

coating, AM/FM stereo radio w/cass. & 4 spkrs ($1146). Pkg. 24C: 22C exc. 3.0L V-6 replaces 2.5L four and 4-spd auto. trans. replaces 3-spd auto. ($1973). Pkg. 26C: 24C exc. 3.3L V-6 replaces 3.0L V-6 ($1973). LE: Pkg. 24A: stnd equip. (NC). Pkg. 26A: incl. 3.3L V-6 and 4-spd auto. trans. (NC). Pkg. 26C: 26A plus air cond., floor mounted console, tilt stng, elect. spd control, floor mats, pwr door locks, pwr heated mirrors, pwr windows, AM/FM stereo radio w/cass. & 4 spkrs, P195/75R14 tires, undercoating ($1396). Pkg. 26D: 26C plus illum. entry, illum. visor mirrors, auto. day/night rearview mirror, 6-way pwr driver's & pass. seats, leather-wrapped stng whl, cell phone pre-wire, wire whl covers ($2602). Other: (AJK) Convenience Grp.: incl. elect. spd control, tilt stng, LE ($372). (AJP) Pwr Convenience Grp.: incl. pwr dual remote outside mirrors, pwr windows, base ($394). (AJB) Security Grp.: incl. security alarm w/panel warning light, keyless remote entry w/activation of door locks ($292). (AJW) Power Accessories Grp.: incl. pwr decklid pulldown, pwr antenna, LE ($169). Air cond. ($831). Pwr door locks ($331). Calif. emissions ($102). Extra cost paint ($97). (RAS) AM/FM radio w/cass. ($165). (RAY) AM/FM stereo radio w/cass., graphic equal., seek/scan & 4 spkrs ($283). (ARB) Infinity RS audio syst., LE ($668). 8-way pwr driver's & pass. seats w/memory, LE ($396). Pwr 6-way driver's seat, LE ($306). 50/50 front bench seat, base ($372). Leather 50/50 front bench seat, LE ($590). Conventional spare tire ($85). Pwr sunroof, LE ($792). P195/75R14 tires ($73). Wire whl covers ($240). Cast alum whls ($50-$279).

MONACO CONVENIENCE/APPEARANCE OPTIONS: LE: Pkg. 24J: stnd equip. (NC). Pkg. 24K: incl. auto. temp air cond., elect. spd control, tilt stng, pwr door locks, pwr windows ($1590). Pkg. 24L: 24K plus floor mats, dual pwr heated mirrors, 6-way pwr driver's seat, AM./FM stereo radio w/cass., remote fuel door release, remote decklid release, 14-in. Polycast whls ($2366). ES: Pkg. 24N: stnd equip. (NC). Pkg. 24P: incl. elect. spd control, tilt stng, floor mats, illum. entry, keyless entry syst., pwr door locks, 6-way pwr driver's seat, pwr windows, remote fuel door release, remote decklid release, P205/60R15 tires, 15-in. cast alum whls ($1768). Pkg. 24R: 24P plus premium audio syst. and trip computer ($1768). Other: Calif. emissions ($102). Decklid luggage rack ($117). (RAF) AM/FM stereo radio w/cass., LE ($249). (ARA) Premium AM/FM stereo radio w/cass. & graphic equal. & 6 spkrs ($381). Pwr 6-way driver's seat ($306). Leather trim, ES ($891). Polycast whls, LE ($104). Cast alum whls w/P205/60R15 tires, LE ($419-$523). Conventional spare tire ($95).

VIPER CONVENIENCE/APPEARANCE OPTIONS: (N/A).

HISTORY: Model year production: 244,603. Calendar year sales: 246,559 (not including 13,367 1993 Intrepid sedans sold in 1992 nor imports). Intrepid, Dodge's 1993 midsize sedan built on the cab-forward LH platform, debuted in August 1992.

1993 DODGE

It was a transition year for Dodge in 1993, with two series making their final appearance and one all-new sedan coming on-line. New-for-1993 was the cab-forward-design Intrepid sedan built on the all-new LH platform. Intrepid was offered in two trim levels: base and ES, and offered the all-new sequentially fuel-injected 3.5-liter V-6 as an option engine while relying on the 3.3-liter V-6 as its standard powerplant. Making their last stand were the Daytona and Dynasty series. Shadow offerings were scaled back with the discontinuation of the America trim level hatchbacks. Also, Spirit halved its available models via the dropping of both the LE and R/T sedans.

1993 Dodge, Daytona IROC hatchback coupe (OCW)

1993 Dodge, Daytona IROC R/T hatchback coupe (OCW)

DAYTONA — SERIES G — FOUR/V-6 — In its shortened final model year (production ended March 1993), Daytona returned basically as a carryover from the year previous with its existing all-hatchback lineup intact: base, ES, IROC and IROC R/T. With one exception, powertrain availability was unchanged from the year previous. The single change was that the IROC hatchback no longer offered the Turbo I 2.5-liter four-cylinder engine as an option due to its discontinuation. One other change of note was that the base Daytona offered 15-inch anti-lock brakes as optional equipment.

1993 Dodge, Shadow ES hatchback sedan (OCW)

SHADOW — SERIES P — FOUR — With the America trim level dropped, Shadow was now the entry level car of the same-named series while Shadow ES remained the upscale model. Both Shadow and ES each continued to be offered in two- and four-door hatchback and convertible body styles. Standard powertrain continued intact from the year previous, but the optional engine offering changed due to the dropping of the Turbo I four-cylinder powerplant that was formerly available in the Shadow convertible and ES models. Those Shadows now exclusively used the 3.0-liter V-6 as their option engine. The notable change for 1993 was that Shadows now offered anti-lock brakes as an option.

1993 Dodge, Spirit sedan (OCW)

SPIRIT — SERIES A — FOUR/V-6 — Spirit model availability was cut in half for 1993 with the formerly four trim level series pared back to two. Both the LE and R/T Spirit sedans were dropped, with the base and ES models now comprising the series. Spirit sedans received a redesigned grille to "freshen" their appearance, which helped boost sales by almost 10,000 units in 1993 with only half the lineup compared to the year previous. As with Daytona and Shadow, the discontinued Turbo I four-cylinder engine that was formerly optional on the base Spirit left the 3.0-liter V-6 as the lone option powerplant in the series. The Spirit ES now featured a three-speed automatic transmission as standard equipment, replacing the formerly used five-speed manual unit. Aside from those changes, powertrain availability mirrored what was offered the year previous.

DYNASTY — SERIES C — FOUR/V-6 — Making its final appearance in 1993, the Dynasty sedan was essentially carried over from the year previous, again offered in base and LE trim levels. One new feature was

that an optional body-color landau vinyl roof was offered for both trim levels. Powertrain availability remained the same as what was offered in the prior model year.

INTREPID — SERIES H — V-6 — Intrepid was Dodge's first cab-forward-design automobile-built on the all-new LH platform along with the 1993 Chrysler Concorde and Eagle Vision-and it was offered in two trim levels: base and ES. Built in Bramalea, Ontario, Canada, the Intrepid sedan rode on a 113-inch wheelbase and measured 201.7 inches in overall length. Standard powertrain for the Intrepid was the sequentially fuel-injected 3.3-liter V-6 hooked to an electronically controlled four-speed automatic transmission with overdrive. Optional was the all-new 24-valve 3.5-liter V-6. Intrepid's list of standard features included dual airbags, child protection rear door locks, stainless steel exhaust system, instrument cluster including tach and warning lights for multiple functions, electric rear window defroster, tilt steering column, solar control glass windshield and speed-sensitive intermittent wipers. The ES sedan added four-wheel disc brakes, foglamps, message center, luggage compartment cargo net, ground effects wrap-around molding, power decklid release, leather-wrapped steering wheel and 16-inch "Polystar" cast wheels with touring tires and touring suspension. Optional equipment included air conditioning, overhead storage console, power door locks, illuminated entry, dual heated exterior power mirrors, power windows, Chrysler/Infinity Spatial Imaging Sound System (cassette or CD), remote keyless entry, speed control and conventional spare tire. Options exclusive to Intrepid ES included traction control with anti-lock braking, a leather interior package, 16-inch "Extender" aluminum wheels and a performance suspension package with firm-feel steering. Exterior color choices were Black Cherry, Metallic Red, Indy Red, Light Driftwood, Char-Gold, Emerald Green, Teal, Nighthawk Blue Metallic, Black and Bright White. Interior color choices were Dark/Medium Quartz, Dark Slate/Slate Blue, Dark Crimson/Crimson Red and Dark/Medium Driftwood.

1993 Dodge, Intrepid sedan (OCW)

VIPER RT/10 — SERIES R — V-10 — In its second year of availability, Dodge's "red rocket" Viper continued to be powered by the 400-horsepower V-10 linked to the T56 six-speed manual transmission. New exterior colors were slated for 1993 Vipers, but were delayed until the 1994 model arrived later in the year. As was the case in its debut year, buyers of the Viper were again forced to pay an additional $2,600 "gas guzzler" tax to Uncle Sam.

I.D. DATA: Dodge's 17-symbol Vehicle Identification Number (VIN), as before, was on the upper left corner of the instrument panel, visible through the windshield. Coding is similar to 1986-92. Symbol ten (model year) changed to 'P' for 1993.

DAYTONA (FOUR/V-6)

Model No.	Body/ Style No.	Body Type & Seating	Factory Price	Shipping Weight	Prod. Total
GVL	24	2-dr. Hatch-4P	10874/11568	2746/2793	Note 1
GVH	24	2-dr. ES Hatch-4P	12018/12712	2822/2869	Note 1
GVX	24	2-dr. IROC Hatch-4P	-----/13309	----/2926	Note 1
GVS	24	2-dr. IROC R/T Hatch-4P	19185/-----	N/A/----	Note 1

Note: Prices and weights to left of slash for four-cylinder, to right for V-6.

Note 1: Daytona hatchback production totaled 9,062 with no further breakout available.

Standard Catalog of Chrysler

Model No.	Body/ Style No.	Body Type & Seating	Factory Price	Shipping Weight	Prod. Total
SHADOW (FOUR)					
PDL	24	2-dr. Hatch-5P	8397	2575	Note 1
PDL	44	4-dr. Hatch-5P	8797	2610	Note 2
PDH	27	2-dr. Conv-4P	14028	2861	Note 3
SHADOW ES (FOUR)					
PDS	24	2-dr. Hatch-5P	9804	2690	Note 1
PDS	44	4-dr. Hatch-5P	10204	2713	Note 2
PDS	27	2-dr. Conv-4P	14167	2879	Note 3

Note 1: Shadow two-door hatchback production totaled 50,218 with no further breakout available.

Note 2: Shadow four-door hatchback production totaled 45,883 with no further breakout available.

Note 3: Shadow convertible production totaled 6,313 with no further breakout available.

SPIRIT (FOUR/V-6)

Model No.	Body/ Style No.	Body Type & Seating	Factory Price	Shipping Weight	Prod. Total
ADH	41	4-dr. Sedan-6P	11941/12666	2757/2852	Note 1
ADP	41	4-dr. ES Sed-6P	14715/15440	2848/2930	Note 1

Note: Prices and weights to left of slash for four-cylinder, to right for V-6.

Note 1: Spirit sedan production totaled 76,499 with no further breakout available.

DYNASTY (FOUR/V-6)

Model No.	Body/ Style No.	Body Type & Seating	Factory Price	Shipping Weight	Prod. Total
CDH	41	4-dr. Sedan-6P	14736/15430	2925/2996	Note 1
CDP	41	4-dr. LE Sedan-6P	-----/16267	----/3020	Note 1

Note: Prices and weights to left of slash for four-cylinder, to right for V-6.

Note 1: Dynasty sedan production totaled 58,402 with no further breakout available.

1993 Dodge, Intrepid ES sedan (OCW)

INTREPID (V-6)

Model No.	Body/ Style No.	Body Type & Seating	Factory Price	Shipping Weight	Prod. Total
HDH	41	4-dr. Sedan-6P	15930	3217	Note 1
HDP	41	4-dr. ES Sedan-6P	17189	3315	Note 1

Note 1: Intrepid sedan production totaled 70,046 with no further breakout available.

VIPER RT/10 (V-10)

Model No.	Body/ Style No.	Body Type & Seating	Factory Price	Shipping Weight	Prod. Total
RDS	27	2-dr. Rdstr-2P	50700	3476	895

ENGINE DATA: BASE FOUR (Shadow): Inline, overhead cam four-cylinder. Cast iron block; aluminum head. Displacement: 135 cu. in. (2.2 liters). Bore & stroke: 3.44 x 3.62 in. Compression ratio: 9.5:1. Brake horsepower: 93 at 5200 RPM. Torque: 122 lb.-ft. at 3200 RPM. Throttle-body fuel injection. **BASE TURBOCHARGED FOUR** (Daytona IROC R/T): Inline, dual overhead cam four-cylinder. Cast iron block; aluminum head. Displacement: 135 cu. in. (2.2 liters). Bore & stroke: 3.44 x 3.62 in. Compression ratio: 8.5:1. Brake horsepower: 224 at 2800 RPM. Torque: 217 lb.-ft. at 6000 RPM. Multi-port fuel injection. **BASE FOUR** (Shadow conv, Shadow ES, Daytona, Daytona ES, Spirit, Spirit ES, Dynasty); **OPTIONAL (Shadow):** Inline, overhead cam four-cylinder. Cast iron block; aluminum head. Displacement: 153 cu. in. (2.5 liters). Bore & stroke: 3.44 x 4.09 in. Compression ratio: 9.5:1. Brake horsepower: 100 at 4800 RPM. Torque: 135 lb.-ft. at 2800 RPM. Throttle-body fuel injection. **BASE V-6** (Daytona IROC, Dynasty LE); **OPTIONAL** (Daytona, Daytona ES, Shadow ES, Spirit, Spirit ES, Dynasty): Overhead cam V-6. Displacement: 181 cu. in. (3.0 liters). Bore & stroke: 3.59 x 2.99 in. Compression ratio: 8.9:1. Brake horsepower: 141 at 5200 RPM. Torque: 171 lb.-ft. at 2800 RPM. Sequential fuel injection. **BASE V-6** (Intrepid, Intrepid ES); **OPTIONAL V-6** (Dynasty, Dynasty LE): Overhead valve V-6. Cast iron block; aluminum heads. Displacement: 201 cu. in. (3.3 liters). Bore & stroke: 3.66 x 3.19 in. Compression ratio: 8.9:1. Brake horse-

power: 153 at 5300 RPM. Torque: 171 lb.-ft. at 2800 RPM. Sequential fuel injection. OPTIONAL V-6 (Intrepid, Intrepid ES): Overhead cam V-6. Cast iron block; aluminum heads. Displacement: 214 cu. in. (3.5 liters). Bore & stroke: 3.78 x 3.19 in. Compression ratio: 10.5:1. Brake horsepower: 214 at 5800 RPM. Torque: 221 lb.-ft. at 2800 RPM. Sequential fuel injection. BASE V-10 (Viper): Overhead valve V-10. Aluminum block and heads. Displacement: 488 cu. in. (8.0 liters). Bore & stroke: 4.00 x 3.88 in. Compression ratio: 9.1:1. Brake horsepower: 400 at 4600 RPM. Torque: 450 lb.-ft. at 3600 RPM. Sequential fuel injection.

CHASSIS DATA: Wheelbase: (Daytona) 97.2 in.; (Shadow) 97.2 in.; (Spirit) 103.5 in.; (Dynasty) 104.5 in.; (Intrepid) 113.0 in.; (Viper) 96.2 in. Overall length: (Daytona) 179.8 in.; (Shadow) 171.9 in.; (Spirit) 181.2 in.; (Dynasty) 192.0 in.; (Intrepid) 201.7 in.; (Viper) 175.1 in. Height: (Daytona) 51.8 in.; (Shadow) 52.7 in.; (Spirit) 55.5 in.; (Dynasty) 53.6 in.; (Intrepid) 56.3 in.; (Viper) 43.9 in. Width: (Daytona) 69.3 in.; (Shadow) 67.3 in.; (Spirit) 68.1 in.; (Dynasty) 68.9 in.; (Intrepid) 74.4 in.; (Viper) 75.1 in. Front Tread: (Daytona) 57.5 in.; (Shadow) 57.6 in.; (Spirit) 57.6 in.; (Dynasty) 57.6 in.; (Intrepid) 62.0 in.; (Viper) 59.6 in. Rear Tread: (Daytona) 57.6 in.; (Shadow) 57.2 in.; (Spirit) 57.2 in.; (Dynasty) 57.6 in.; (Intrepid) 62.0 in.; (Viper) 60.6 in. Standard Tires: (Daytona) P185/70R14; (Daytona ES) P205/60R15; (Daytona IROC) P205/55VR16; (Daytona IROC R/T) P205/55ZR16; (Shadow, Shadow conv, Shadow ES conv) P185/70R14; (Shadow ES hatch) P195/60HR15; (Spirit) P185/70R14; (Spirit ES) P205/60R15; (Dynasty) P195/75R14; (Intrepid) P205/70R15; (Intrepid ES) P225/60R16; (Viper) P275/40ZR17 front/P335/35ZR17 rear.

TECHNICAL: Transmission: Five-speed manual standard on Daytona (all), Shadow (all) and Spirit. Three-speed automatic standard on Spirit ES and Dynasty. Four-speed automatic standard on Dynasty LE and Intrepid (all). Six-speed manual standard on Viper. Steering: (all) Rack and pinion. Front suspension: (Daytona, Spirit, Dynasty) Iso-strut w/coil springs, gas-charged hydraulic shock absorbers and stabilizer bar; (Shadow) Iso-strut w/coil springs, direct hydraulic shock absorbers and stabilizer bar; (Intrepid) MacPherson strut w/coil springs, gas-charged hydraulic shock absorbers and stabilizer bar; (Viper) Independent w/unequal length upper and lower control arms, coil over shock units, micrograin alloy coil springs, dynamic acting hydraulic/low-pressure gas charged shock absorbers w/adjustable rebound and tubular anti-roll bar. Rear suspension: (Daytona, Spirit, Dynasty) Trailing flex arm w/track bar, coil springs, gas-charged hydraulic shock absorbers and stabilizer bar; (Shadow) Trailing flex arm w/track bar, coil springs, direct hydraulic shock absorbers and stabilizer bar; (Intrepid) Independent rear, multilink w/coil springs, gas-charged hydraulic shock absorbers and stabilizer bar; (Viper) Independent w/unequal length upper and lower control arms w/separate toe link, micro-grain alloy coil springs, dynamic acting hydraulic/low-pressure gas charged shock absorbers w/adjustable rebound and tubular anti-roll bar. Brakes: Front disc, rear drum (power-assisted) except (Daytona IROC, Spirit ES, Intrepid ES and Viper) four-wheel disc. Body construction: Unibody except (Viper) tubular space frame. Fuel tank: (Daytona) 14 gals.; (Shadow) 14 gals.; (Spirit) 16 gals.; (Dynasty) 16 gals.; (Intrepid) 18 gals.; (Viper) 22 gals.

DRIVETRAIN OPTIONS: Engines: 2.5-liter four: Shadow ($286). 3.0-liter V-6: Shadow conv/Shadow ES conv ($905). Shadow ES ($694); Daytona/Daytona ES ($694); Spirit/Spirit ES ($694); Dynasty ($827). 3.3-liter V-6: Dynasty/Dynasty LE ($827). 3.5-liter V-6: Intrepid/Intrepid ES ($525). Transmission: Three-speed auto. trans.: Daytona/Daytona ES/Daytona IROC ($557); Shadow/Spirit ($557). Four-speed auto. trans.: Daytona/Daytona ES/Daytona IROC ($690); Shadow ($690); Spirit/Spirit ES ($858); Dynasty ($827). Brakes: Anti-lock: Daytona ($899); Shadow ($899). Four-wheel disc w/anti-lock: Spirit ($899); Dynasty ($899); Intrepid ($599-$624). Auto load-leveling susp.: Dynasty ($225). Handling susp.: Spirit ($26). Traction control: w/ABS on Intrepid ES ($774).

DAYTONA CONVENIENCE/APPEARANCE OPTIONS: Daytona: Pkg. 21A: stnd equip. (NC). Pkg. 22A: 21A plus 3-spd auto. trans. ($557). Pkg. 21B: incl. 2.5L four and 5-spd manual trans., air cond., rear window defroster, floor mats, Light Pkg., tilt stng, remote liftgate release, AM/FM stereo radio w/cass. & 4 spkrs ($826). Pkg. 22B: 21B exc. 3-spd auto. trans. replaces 5-spd manual ($1383). Pkg. 25B: 21B exc. 3.0L V-6 replaces 2.5L four ($1520). Pkg. 26B: 21B exc. 3.0L V-6 replaces 2.5L four and 4-spd auto. trans. replaces 5-spd manual ($2210). ES: Pkg. 21A: stnd equip. (NC). Pkg. 21B: incl. 2.5L four and 5-spd manual trans., air cond., rear window defroster, floor mats, Light pkg., pwr heated outside mirrors, tilt stng, remote liftgate release, pwr door locks, elect. spd control, AM/FM stereo radio w/cass. & 4 spkrs ($1207). Pkg. 22B: 21B exc. 3-spd auto. trans. replaces 5-spd manual ($1764). Pkg. 25B: 21B exc. 3.0L V-6 replaces 2.5L four ($1901). Pkg. 26B: 21B exc. 3.0L V-6 replaces 2.5L four and 4-spd auto. trans. replaces 5-spd manual ($2591). IROC: Pkg. 25A: stnd equip. (NC). Pkg. 25B: 25A plus air cond., rear window defroster, floor mats, Light Pkg., pwr heated outside mirrors, pwr windows, tilt stng, pwr door locks, remote liftgate release, elect. spd control, AM/FM stereo radio w/cass. & 4 spkrs

($1482). Pkg. 26B: 25B exc. 4-spd auto. trans. replaces 5-spd manual ($2172). IROC R/T: Pkg. 27A: stnd equip. (NC). Pkg. 27B: 25B exc. air cond. stnd ($1062). Other: (AAW) Value Grp.: incl. tilt stng, pwr door locks, elect. spd control, AM/FM stereo radio w/cass., base or ES ($640). (AGY) V-6 Performance Pkg.: incl. pwr 4-whl disc brakes, leather-wrapped stng whl & manual shifter knob, Performance Handling Susp., ES ($319). (ADK) Light Grp.: incl. illum. entry, dual illum. visor mirrors, ES, IROC, IROC R/T ($196). (ADS) Sport Grp.: incl. rear spoiler, P205/60R15 touring tires, "Triad" whl covers ($299). Overhead console, ES, IROC, IROC R/T ($265). Elect. rear window defroster ($173). Pwr heated mirrors, base or ES ($93). Calif. emission ($102). (RBC) AM/FM stereo radio w/CD player, graphic equalizer & 6 spkrs, N/A base ($506). (RAY) AM/FM stereo radio w/cass., graphic equal., seek/scan & 6 spkrs, N/A base ($336). Speed control, base ($224). Pwr 6-way driver's seat, base ($306). Security alarm, N/A base ($149). Sun louver, N/A base ($214). Sunroof ($405). Tonneau cover, base ($74). Pwr windows ($275). Pwr door locks, base ($245). Liftgate wiper/washer ($129). 15-in. cast alum whls, base ($328).

SHADOW CONVENIENCE/APPEARANCE OPTIONS: Shadow: Pkg. 21W: stnd equip. (NC). Pkg. 22W: incl. 2.2L four and 3-spd auto. trans. ($557). Pkg. 23W: incl. 2.5L four and 5-spd manual trans. ($286). Pkg. 24W: incl. 2.5L four and 3-spd auto. trans. ($843). Pkg. 21Y: 2.2L four and 5-spd manual trans. plus air cond., tinted glass, body-color fascias, rear window defroster, floor mats, color-keyed bodyside mldg & instrument panel bezels, dlx wipers, Light Grp., bodyside striping, dual remote outside mirrors, dual visor mirrors, 14-in. whl covers ($1545). Pkg. 22Y: 21Y exc. 3-spd auto. trans. replaces 5-spd manual ($2102). Pkg. 23Y: 21Y exc. 2.5L four replaces 2.2L four ($1831). Pkg. 24Y: 21Y exc. 2.5L four replaces 2.2L four and 3-spd auto. trans. replaces 5-spd manual ($2388). Shadow conv: Pkg. 23A: stnd equip. (NC). Pkg. 24A: incl. 2.5L four and 3-spd auto. trans. ($557). Pkg. 27A: incl. 3.0L V-6 and 5-spd manual trans. ($905). Pkg. 28A: 3.0L V-6 and 4-spd auto. trans. ($1595). Pkg. 23D: incl. 2.5L four and 5-spd manual trans., air cond., tinted glass, tilt stng, rear window defroster, dual horns, floor mats, dlx wipers, tach, headlights-on/seatbelts/key-in-ignition warning chimes, Light Grp., dual visor mirrors, AM/FM stereo radio w/cass. & 4 spkrs ($531). Pkg. 24D: 23D exc. 3-spd auto. trans. replaces 5-spd manual: ($1088). Pkg. 27D: 23D exc. 3.0L V-6 replaces 2.5L four ($1436). Pkg. 28D: 23D exc. 3.0L V-6 replaces 2.5L four and 4-spd auto. trans. replaces 5-spd manual ($2126). ES: Pkg. 23G: stnd equip. (NC). Pkg. 24G: incl. 2.5L four and 3-spd auto. trans. ($557). Pkg. 27G: incl. 3.0L V-6 and 5-spd manual trans. ($694). Pkg. 28G: incl. 3.0L V-6 and 4-spd auto. trans. ($1384). Pkg. 23H: incl. 2.5L four and 5-spd manual trans., air cond., tinted glass, rear window defroster, floor mats, foglamps, Light Pkg., floor-mounted console, remote liftgate release, dual note horn, dlx wipers, tach, dual visor mirrors, headlights-on/seatbelts/key-in-ignition warning chimes, AM/FM stereo radio w/cass. & 4 spkrs ($973). Pkg. 24H: 23H exc. 3-spd auto. trans. replaces 5-spd manual ($1530). Pkg. 27H: 23H exc. 3.0L V-6 replaces 2.5L four and H.D. trans. replaces 5-spd manual ($1667). Pkg. 28H: 23H exc. 4-spd auto. trans. replaces H.D. 5-spd manual ($2357). ES conv: Pkg. 23G: stnd equip. (NC). Pkg. 24G: incl. 2.5L four and 3-spd auto. trans. ($557). Pkg. 27G: incl. 3.0L V-6 and 5-spd manual trans. ($905). Pkg. 28G: incl. 3.0L V-6 and 4-spd auto. trans. ($1595). Pkg. 23H: incl. 2.5L four and 5-spd manual trans., air cond., tinted glass, floor mats, Light Pkg., dual note horn, dlx wipers, tach, dual visor mirrors, headlights-on/seatbelts/key-in-ignition warning chimes, AM/FM stereo radio w/cass. & 4 spkrs ($531). Pkg. 24H: 23H exc. 3-spd auto. trans. replaces 5-spd manual trans. ($1088). Pkg. 27H: 23H exc. 3.0L V-6 replaces 2.5L four and H.D. 5-spd manual trans. replaces 5-spd manual ($1436). Pkg. 28H: 23H exc. 4-spd auto. trans. replaces H.D. 5-spd manual ($2126). Other: (ADA) Light Grp.: conv ($65); hatch ($77). Air cond. ($900). Overhead console incl. storage, compass & thermometer ($265). Elect. rear window defroster, N/A conv ($173). Pwr door locks: 2-dr. ($199); 4-dr. ($240). Calif. emissions ($102). Front & rear floor mats ($46). Intermittent wipers ($66). Dual outside remote mirrors, stnd conv ($69). Dual pwr outside remote mirrors, conv or ES ($57). Pwr driver's seat ($306). Pwr windows: 2-dr. ($265); 4-dr. ($331). (RAL) AM/FM stereo radio w/digital clock & 2 spkrs, base ($284). (RAS) AM/FM stereo radio w/cass. & 4 spkrs: base ($165-$499); others ($215). (RAY) AM/FM stereo radio w/cass., graphic equal. & 4 spkrs ($305-$520). (RBC) AM/FM stereo radio w/CD player, seek/scan, graphic equal. & 4 spkrs, conv or ES ($475-$690). Remote liftgate release ($24). Elect. spd control ($224). Sunroof ($379). Tilt stng ($148). Conventional spare tire, N/A conv ($85). Cast alum whls ($328). 15-in. "Turbostar" alum whls, ES conv ($646).

SPIRIT CONVENIENCE/APPEARANCE OPTIONS: Spirit: Pkg. 21A: stnd equip. (NC). Pkg. 22A: incl. 2.5L four and 3-spd auto. trans. ($557). Pkg. 21C: incl. 2.5L four and 5-spd manual trans., air cond., rear window defroster, floor mats, tilt stng, elect. spd control ($472). Pkg. 22D: 21C exc. 3-spd auto. trans. replaces 5-spd manual ($1029). Pkg. 26D: 21C exc. 3.0L V-6 replaces 2.5L four and 3-spd auto. trans. replaces 5-spd manual plus P195/70R14 tires ($1754). Pkg. 22E: 21C plus pwr mirrors, pwr door locks, pwr windows, pwr trunk release ($1701). Pkg.

26E: 22E exc. 3.0L V-6 replaces 2.5L four plus P195/70R14 tires ($2426). Pkg. 28E: 22E exc. 3.0L V-6 replaces 2.5L four and 4-spd auto. trans. replaces 3-spd auto. trans. plus P195/70R14 tires ($2559). ES: Pkg. 22P: stnd equip. (NC). Pkg. 22U: incl. 2.5L four and 3-spd auto. trans., air cond., pwr mirrors, pwr door locks, pwr windows, AM/FM stereo radio w/cass. ($627). Pkg. 26U: 22U exc. 3.0L V-6 replaces 2.5L four ($1321). Pkg. 28U: 22U exc. 4-spd auto. trans. replaces 3-spd auto. ($1454). Other: (AJN) Interior Illum. Grp.: incl. illum. entry, message center, dual illum. visor mirrors: base ($293); ES ($195). (AFH) Interior Convenience Grp.: incl. overhead console storage, compass, temp. display, reading lamps, AJN Illum. Grp., ES ($400). Console-mounted armrest ($155). Elect. rear window defroster, base ($173). Pwr door locks, base ($250). Calif. emissions ($102). Pwr driver's seat ($306). (RAS) AM/FM radio w/cass. & clock & 4 spkrs, base ($165). (RAY) AM/FM stereo radio w/cass. & clock, graphic equal. & 4 spkrs, ES ($355). (RBC) AM/FM stereo radio w/CD player, graphic equal., clock & 4 spkrs: base ($690); ES ($525). P195/70R14 tires, base ($73-$104). Conventional spare tire, base ($95).

DYNASTY CONVENIENCE/APPEARANCE OPTIONS: Dynasty: Pkg. 22A: stnd equip. (NC). Pkg. 24A: incl. 3.0L V-6 and 4-spd auto. trans. ($827). Pkg. 26A: incl. 3.3L V-6 and 4-spd auto. trans. ($827). Pkg. 22C: 22A plus air cond., P195/75R14 tires, floor-mounted console, Deluxe Convenience Grp., floor mats, message center warning lights for door ajar and decklid ajar, pwr door locks, bodyside stripe, undercoating, AM/FM stereo radio w/cass. & 4 spkrs ($1146). Pkg. 24C: 22C exc. 3.0L V-6 replaces 2.5L four and 4-spd auto. trans. replaces 3-spd auto. ($1973). Pkg. 26C: 22C exc. 3.3L V-6 replaces 3.0L V-6 and 4-spd auto. trans. replaces 3-spd auto.($1973). LE: Pkg. 24A: stnd equip. (NC). Pkg. 26A: incl. 3.3L V-6 and 4-spd auto. trans. (NC). Pkg. 24C: 3.0L V-6 and 4-spd auto. trans. plus air cond., floor mounted console, floor mats, pwr door locks, pwr heated mirrors, pwr windows, AM/FM stereo radio w/cass. & 4 spkrs, P195/75R14 tires, undercoating ($1396). Pkg. 26C: 24C exc. 3.3L V-6 replaces 3.0L V-6 ($1396). Pkg. 24D: 24C plus illum. entry, illum. visor mirrors, auto. day/night rearview mirror, 6-way pwr driver's & pass. seats, leather-wrapped stng whl, wire whl covers ($2503). Pkg. 26D: 24D incl. 3.3L V-6 and 4-spd auto. trans. ($2538). Other: (AJK) Convenience Grp.: incl. elect. spd control, tilt stng ($372). (AJP) Pwr Convenience Grp.: incl. pwr dual remote outside mirrors, pwr windows, base ($394). (AJB) Security Grp.: incl. security alarm w/panel warning light, keyless remote entry w/activation of door locks, LE ($292). (AJW) Power Accessories Grp.: incl. pwr decklid pulldown, pwr antenna, LE ($169). Air cond., base ($831). Pwr door locks, LE ($331). Calif. emissions ($102). (RAS) AM/FM radio w/cass. & 4 spkrs ($165). (RAY) AM/FM stereo radio w/cass., graphic equal. & 4 spkrs, LE ($273). (ARB) Infinity RS audio syst., LE ($668). 8-way pwr driver's & pass. seats w/memory, LE ($396). Pwr 6-way driver's seat, LE ($306). Vinyl landau roof ($325). Conventional spare tire ($85). P195/75R14 tires ($73). Wire whl covers ($240). Cast alum whls ($39-$279).

INTREPID CONVENIENCE/APPEARANCE OPTIONS: Intrepid: Pkg. 22A: stnd equip. (NC). Pkg. 22B: incl. 22A plus air cond., floor mats, elect. spd control ($925). Pkg. 22C: 22B plus pwr door locks, pwr windows, AM/FM stereo radio w/cass. ($1585). Pkg. 22D: 22C plus 4-whl disc brakes, pwr remote decklid release, 8-way pwr driver's seat, message center, dual pwr heated outside mirrors ($2207). Pkg. 26D: 22D incl. 3.5L V-6 ($2832). Pkg. 26E: 26D plus overhead console, remote illum. entry grp., leather-wrapped stng whl, 16-in. whl & touring grp. ($4334). ES: Pkg. 22J: stnd equip. (NC). Pkg. 22K: 22J plus elect. spd control, air cond., AM/FM stereo radio w/cass. ($1250). Pkg. 26K: 22K plus 3.5L V-6 replaces 3.3L V-6 ($1875). Pkg. 22L: 22K plus pwr door locks, 8-way pwr driver's seat, pwr remote heated mirrors, leather-wrapped stng whl, pwr windows, 16-in. "Extender" alum whls ($2180). Pkg. 26L: 22L incl. 3.5L V-6 ($2805). Pkg. 26M: 22L exc. Chrysler/Infinity Spatial Imaging Cass. Sound Syst. replaces AM/FM stereo radio w/cass. plus auto. temp. air cond., Perf. Handling Grp., Anti-lock brakes w/traction control, overhead console, remote illum. entry, conventional spare tire ($5018). Other: (AJF) Remote Illum. Entry Grp.: incl. remote keyless entry, illum. entry, dual illum. visor mirrors ($339); w/overhead console ($221). (AGC) Perf. Handling Grp.: incl. perf. susp., 16-in. perf. tires, firm-feel stng ($217). (AGC) 16-in. Whl & Touring Grp.: incl. 16-in. "Polystar" whls, 16-in. touring tires, touring susp. ($300). Air cond. ($831); w/auto. temp., ES ($152). Full overhead console ($463). Mini overhead console, base ($387). Calif. emissions ($102). Pwr decklid release, base ($61). Integrated child seat ($100). Pwr door locks ($250). Pwr windows, ES ($341). (RAS) AM/FM stereo radio w/cass. & 6 spkrs ($195). (RAY) Chrysler/Infinity Spatial Imaging Cass. Sound Syst. ($713). (RBC) Chrysler/Infinity Spatial Imaging CD Sound Syst.: base ($882); ES ($169). "Extender" alum whls, ES ($224). Conventional spare tire ($95).

VIPER CONVENIENCE/APPEARANCE OPTIONS: (N/A).

HISTORY: Model year production: 317,318. Calendar year sales: 337,757 (not including imports). The Dodge Viper GTS concept car was displayed on the 1993 auto show circuit. A coupe, the GTS was designed

to capture the spirit of the immortal GT racing cars of the 1960s, such as Shelby Cobra Daytona Coupe and the Ferrari 250 GTO. Elements of the GTS that exemplified its race car image included a hood-mounted NACA intake for cold ram air induction to the engine, hood-mounted exhaust louvers for scavenging pressure and heat from the engine compartment and front wheel housings, roof "blisters" for greater head/helmet clearance, dual rear-routed exhaust pipes, fuel filler located under a cast aluminum quick release racing fuel cap feeding a bladder-type fuel cell, and competition five-point aircraft-type belt harness with a wrist-turn quick release.

1994 DODGE

Dodge was a much leaner division in 1994 with two fewer series than the year previous and thinner ranks among half the remaining series. Gone were the Daytona and Dynasty. Shadow convertibles were discontinued, as was the Spirit ES sedan trim level. The remaining Shadow models were making their final appearance. Dodge's transition to cab-forward models was still in its infancy, with the Intrepid and the early launch of the 1995 Neon (February 1994 in four-door body style only) the lone representatives for the division to that point. That would change dramatically with the arrival of the 1995 model year.

1994 Dodge, Shadow ES hatchback coupe (OCW)

SHADOW — SERIES P — FOUR — The ragtop Shadow was history, leaving the Viper as the only open-top Dodge in the 1994 lineup. In its final year of production, the Shadow series was now comprised of two- and four-door hatchbacks in both base and ES trim levels. Shadow was again powered by the 2.2-liter four-cylinder engine while the ES model again used the 2.5-liter four, which was optional on the base models. Both offered the five-speed manual transmission as standard equipment and the electronically controlled three-speed automatic as optional. The Shadow ES could also be ordered with the optional 3.0-liter V-6 and 41TE electronically controlled four-speed automatic with overdrive, which was refined for 1994. New features included non-CFC R-134A refrigerant used in the optional air conditioning system. Right front passengers in Shadows were now protected by a motorized torso belt and knee bolster passive restraint system. Bright turquoise was a new exterior color choice while interior color selections were reduced to two: Quartz and Champagne. The Shadow achieved a 0.42 coefficient of drag in two-door body style and 0.43 as a four-door model. The Shadow's list of standard features included a stainless steel exhaust system, aero halogen headlamps and counter-balanced hood with inside release. Optional equipment included the aforementioned air conditioning (with tinted glass all-around as part of the package), electric rear window defroster, electronic speed control with steering wheel-mounted switches, tilt steering column, sunroof, conventional spare tire and intermittent wipers.

1994 Dodge, Spirit sedan (OCW)

SPIRIT — SERIES A — FOUR/V-6 — And then there was one.... With the discontinuation of the ES sedan, the Spirit series was now comprised of the base (also called Highline) sedan. This model could be ordered

as a flexible fuel vehicle (FFV) using the standard electronically fuel-injected 2.5-liter four-cylinder engine, which in FFV mode was sequentially fuel injected. With either engine setup, the electronically controlled three-speed automatic transmission was standard replacing the five-speed manual previously used in base sedans. Optional on Spirit was the sequentially fuel injected 3.0-liter V-6 and 41TE electronically controlled four-speed automatic, which was updated for 1994. With the FFV setup, the Spirit's trip computer featured a fuel concentration function. New Spirit features included 50/50 front seats were made standard, right front passengers were now protected by a motorized torso belt and knee bolster passive restraint system, and Sky Blue was added as an exterior color choice. Spirit achieved a 0.40 coefficient of drag. For 1994, Spirit was available with an optional Argent Special Equipment Group that included a luggage rack, P195/70R14 tires and "Teardrop" cast aluminum wheels. It could also be ordered with the optional Gold Special Equipment Group that featured gold badging and molding inserts, luggage rack, P195/70R14 tires and "Teardrop" cast aluminum wheels with gold accents. The Spirit's standard features list included air conditioning, electric rear window defroster, stainless steel exhaust system, tinted glass all-around, body-color grille, aero halogen headlamps, counter-balanced hood with inside release, dual note horn, "Austin" cloth seat trim, electronic speed control, tilt steering column, "Centrifuge" wheel covers and intermittent wipers. Optional equipment included power door locks, dual power heated outside mirrors, six-way power driver's seat, conventional spare tire, remote trunk release, trip computer and power windows.

1994 Dodge, Intrepid ES sedan (OCW)

INTREPID — SERIES H — V-6 — Intrepid returned for its second year again offering base and ES trim level sedans. Powertrain availability was unchanged from the year previous with the exception that Intrepid-like the Spirit-could be ordered as a flexible fuel vehicle (FFV) also using the standard sequentially fuel-injected 3.3-liter V-6 in this capacity. The 3.3-liter V-6 was refined for 1994 and offered increased horsepower and torque. Intrepids also offered the sequentially fuel-injected 3.5-liter V-6 as an option, and whatever engine was ordered was paired with the 42LE electronically controlled four-speed automatic transmission with overdrive, which was refined for 1994. The coefficient of drag for Intrepid was 0.31. New standard features included variable-assist speed-proportional power steering, touring suspension, aluminized exhaust system coating, door beams and structural reinforcements for dynamic side intrusion protection, solar control glass added to the rear window, additional head restraint adjustment and upgraded NVH (noise, vibration, harshness) control. New optional equipment included a power moonroof, and, exclusive to the ES, a vehicle theft security alarm system, automatic day/night rearview mirror and eight-way power passenger seat available with cloth trim.

VIPER RT/10 — SERIES R — V-10 — The Viper achieved a new look for 1994 due to two additional exterior color choices available: Emerald Green and Dandelion Yellow. Exclusive to the Emerald Green finish was a new interior color combination: black and tan. Factory-installed air conditioning was a new option for 1994, and the system used the non-CFC R-134A refrigerant. Other new features were the Viper's Borg-Warner T56 six-speed manual transmission received a reverse lock-out function and a windshield-mounted radio antenna with amplifier was installed to improve audio sound quality. The Viper continued to be built in limited numbers at the New Mack facility in Detroit, Michigan. Its powerplant was again the all-aluminum 8.0-liter V-10 that used unleaded fuel with an octane rating of 89 or greater. With top off, the Viper's coefficient of drag was 0.55.

I.D. DATA: Dodge's 17-symbol Vehicle Identification Number (VIN), as before, was on the upper left corner of the instrument panel, visible through the windshield. Coding is similar to 1986-93. Symbol ten (model year) changed to 'R' for 1994.

SHADOW (FOUR)

Model No.	Body/Style No.	Body Type & Seating	Factory Price	Shipping Weight	Prod. Total
PDL	24	2-dr. Hatch-5P	8806	2608	Note 1
PDL	44	4-dr. Hatch-5P	9206	2643	Note 2

SHADOW ES (FOUR)

Model No.	Body/Style No.	Body Type & Seating	Factory Price	Shipping Weight	Prod. Total
PDS	24	2-dr. Hatch-5P	10252	2672	Note 1
PDS	44	4-dr. Hatch-5P	10652	2757	Note 2

Note 1: Shadow two-door hatchback production totaled 41,000 with no further breakout available.

Note 2: Shadow four-door hatchback production totaled 47,929 with no further breakout available.

SPIRIT (FOUR/V-6)

Model No.	Body/Style No.	Body Type & Seating	Factory Price	Shipping Weight	Prod. Total
ADH	41	4-dr. Sedan-6P	12470/13195	2744/2824	68,333

Note: Prices and weights to left of slash for four-cylinder, to right for V-6.

INTREPID (V-6)

Model No.	Body/Style No.	Body Type & Seating	Factory Price	Shipping Weight	Prod. Total
HDH	41	4-dr. Sedan-6P	17251	3271	Note 1
HDP	41	4-dr. ES Sedan-6P	19191	3370	Note 1

Note 1: Intrepid sedan production totaled 128,190 with no further breakout available.

VIPELR RT/10 (V-10)

Model No.	Body/Style No.	Body Type & Seating	Factory Price	Shipping Weight	Prod. Total
RDS	27	2-dr. Rdstr-2P	54500	3476	2890

ENGINE DATA: BASE FOUR (Shadow): Inline, overhead cam four-cylinder. Cast iron block; aluminum head. Displacement: 135 cu. in. (2.2 liters). Bore & stroke: 3.44 x 3.62 in. Compression ratio: 9.5:1. Brake horsepower: 93 at 5200 RPM. Torque: 122 lb.-ft. at 3200 RPM. Throttle-body fuel injection. BASE FOUR (Shadow ES, Spirit); OPTIONAL (Shadow): Inline, overhead cam four-cylinder. Cast iron block; aluminum head. Displacement: 153 cu. in. (2.5 liters). Bore & stroke: 3.44 x 4.09 in. Compression ratio: 8.9:1. Brake horsepower: 100 at 4800 RPM. Torque: 135 lb.-ft. at 2800 RPM. Throttle-body fuel injection. BASE FOUR (Flex Fuel-equipped Shadow): same as 2.5-liter four above exc.: Brake horsepower: 106 at 4400 RPM. Torque: 145 lb.-ft. at 2400 RPM. Sequential fuel injection. OPTIONAL V-6: (Shadow ES, Spirit): Overhead cam V-6. Cast iron block; aluminum head. Displacement: 181 cu. in. (3.0 liters). Bore & stroke: 3.59 x 2.99 in. Compression ratio: 8.9:1. Brake horsepower: 142 at 5000 RPM. Torque: 171 lb.-ft. at 2400 RPM. Sequential fuel injection. BASE V-6 (Intrepid, Intrepid ES): Overhead valve V-6. Cast iron block; aluminum heads. Displacement: 201 cu. in. (3.3 liters). Bore & stroke: 3.66 x 3.19 in. Compression ratio: 8.9:1. Brake horsepower: 153 at 5300 RPM. Torque: 171 lb.-ft. at 2800 RPM. Sequential fuel injection. BASE V-6 (Flex Fuel-equipped Intrepid or Intrepid ES): same as 3.3-liter V-6 above exc.: Brake horsepower: 167 at 5400 RPM. Torque: 185 lb.-ft. at 3000 RPM. OPTIONAL V-6 (Intrepid, Intrepid ES): Overhead cam V-6. Cast iron block; aluminum heads. Displacement: 214 cu. in. (3.5 liters). Bore & stroke: 3.78 x 3.19 in. Compression ratio: 10.5:1. Brake horsepower: 214 at 5800 RPM. Torque: 221 lb.-ft. at 2800 RPM. Sequential fuel injection. BASE V-10 (Viper): Overhead valve V-10. Aluminum block and heads. Displacement: 488 cu. in. (8.0 liters). Bore & stroke: 4.00 x 3.88 in. Compression ratio: 9.1:1. Brake horsepower: 400 at 4600 RPM. Torque: 450 lb.-ft. at 3600 RPM. Sequential fuel injection.

CHASSIS DATA: Wheelbase: (Shadow) 97.2 in.; (Spirit) 103.5 in.; (Intrepid) 113.0 in.; (Viper) 96.2 in. Overall length: (Shadow) 171.9 in.; (Spirit) 181.2 in.; (Intrepid) 201.7 in.; (Viper) 175.1 in. Height: (Shadow) 52.7 in.; (Spirit) 55.5 in.; (Intrepid) 56.3 in.; (Viper) 43.9 in. Width: (Shadow) 67.3 in.; (Spirit) 68.1 in.; (Intrepid) 74.4 in.; (Viper) 75.1 in. Front Tread: (Shadow) 57.6 in.; (Spirit) 57.6 in.; (Intrepid) 62.0 in.; (Viper) 59.6 in. Rear Tread: (Shadow) 57.2 in.; (Spirit) 57.2 in.; (Intrepid) 62.0 in.; (Viper) 60.6 in. Standard Tires: (Shadow) P185/70R14; (Shadow ES) P195/60HR15; (Spirit) P185/70R14; (Intrepid) P205/70R15; (Intrepid ES) P225/60R16; (Viper) P275/40ZR17 front/P335/35ZR17 rear.

TECHNICAL: Transmission: Five-speed manual standard on Shadow and Shadow ES. Three-speed automatic standard on Intrepid and Intrepid ES. Four-speed automatic standard on Intrepid and Intrepid ES. Six-speed manual standard on Viper. Steering: (all) Rack and pinion. Front suspension: (Shadow, Spirit) Iso-strut w/integral gas-charged hydraulic shock absorbers, asymmetrical lower control arms, coil springs and linkless stabilizer bar; (Intrepid) Iso-strut w/integral gas-charged shock absorbers, coil springs, single transverse lower links, tension struts and link-type stabilizer bar; (Viper) Unequal length upper and lower control arms, coil springs, low-pressure gas-charged shock absorbers w/adjustable rebound and stabilizer bar. Rear suspension: (Shadow, Spirit) Beam axle, trailing flex arms w/track bar, coil springs, gas-charged shock absorbers and frameless tubular stabilizer bar; (Intrepid) Chapman struts w/integral gas-charged shock absorbers, concentric coil springs, dual transverse lower links, lower trailing links and link-type stabilizer bar; (Viper) Unequal length upper and lower control arms w/toe-control links, coil springs, low-pressure gas-charged shock absorbers w/adjustable rebound and stabilizer bar. Brakes: Front disc, rear drum (power-assisted) except (Intrepid ES and Viper) four-wheel disc. Body construction: Unibody except (Viper)

tubular space frame. Fuel tank: (Shadow) 14 gals.; (Spirit) 16 gals.; (Intrepid) 18 gals.; (Viper) 22 gals.

DRIVETRAIN OPTIONS: Engines: 2.5-liter four: Shadow ($286). 3.0-liter V-6: Shadow ES ($694); Spirit ($694). 3.5-liter V-6: Intrepid/Intrepid ES ($725). Transmission: Three-speed auto. trans.: Shadow ($557). Four-speed auto. trans.: Shadow ES ($730); Spirit ($971). Brakes: Anti-lock: Shadow ($699). Four-wheel disc w/anti-lock: Spirit ($699); Intrepid ($599-$624). Traction control: w/ABS on Intrepid ES ($175).

SHADOW CONVENIENCE/APPEARANCE OPTIONS: Shadow: Pkg. 21W: stnd equip. (NC). Pkg. 22W: incl. 2.2L four and 3-spd auto. trans. ($557). Pkg. 23W: incl. 2.5L four and 5-spd manual trans. ($286). Pkg. 24W: incl. 2.5L four and 3-spd auto. trans. ($843). Pkg. 21Y: 2.2L four and 5-spd manual trans. plus air cond., tinted glass, body-color fascias, rear window defroster, floor mats, color-keyed bodyside mldg & instrument panel bezels, dlx wipers, Light Grp., bodyside striping, dual remote outside mirrors, dual visor mirrors, 14-in. whl covers ($1545). Pkg. 22Y: 21Y exc. 3-spd auto. trans. replaces 5-spd manual ($2102). Pkg. 23Y: 21Y exc. 2.5L four replaces 2.2L four ($1831). Pkg. 24Y: 21Y exc. 2.5L four replaces 2.2L four and 3-spd auto. trans. replaces 5-spd manual ($2388). ES: Pkg. 23G: stnd equip. (NC). Pkg. 24G: incl. 2.5L four and 3-spd auto. trans. ($557). Pkg. 27G: incl. 3.0L V-6 and 5-spd manual trans. ($694). Pkg. 28G: incl. 3.0L V-6 and 4-spd auto. trans. ($1424). Pkg. 23H: incl. 2.5L four and 5-spd manual trans., air cond., tinted glass, rear window defroster, floor mats, foglamps, Light Pkg., floor-mounted console, remote liftgate release, dual note horn, dlx wipers, tach, dual visor mirrors, headlights-on/seat-belts/key-in-ignition warning chimes, AM/FM stereo radio w/cass. & 4 spkrs ($978). Pkg. 24H: 23H exc. 3-spd auto. trans. replaces 5-spd manual ($1535). Pkg. 27H: 23H exc. 3.0L V-6 replaces 2.5L four and H.D. 5-spd manual trans. replaces 5-spd manual ($1672). Pkg. 28H: 23H exc. 4-spd auto. trans. replaces H.D. 5-spd manual ($2402). Other: (ADA) Light Grp. ($77). Air cond. ($900). Overhead console incl. storage, compass & thermometer ($265). Elect. rear window defroster ($173). Pwr door locks: 2-dr. ($199); 4-dr. ($240). Calif. emissions ($102). Front & rear floor mats ($46). Intermittent wipers ($66). Dual outside remote mirrors, base ($69). Dual pwr outside remote mirrors, ES ($57). Pwr driver's seat ($306). Pwr windows: 2-dr. ($265); 4-dr. ($331). (RAL) AM/FM stereo radio w/digital clock & 2 spkrs, base ($284). (RAS) AM/FM stereo radio w/cass. & 4 spkrs: base ($170-$504); others ($220). (RAY) AM/FM stereo radio w/cass., graphic equal. & 4 spkrs ($300-$520). (RBC) AM/FM stereo radio w/CD player, seek/scan, graphic equal. & 4 spkrs, ES ($470-$690). Remote liftgate release ($24). Elect. spd control ($224). Sunroof ($379). Tilt stng ($148). Conventional spare tire ($85). Cast alum whls ($328). 14-in. "Teardrop" alum whls, base ($376).

SPIRIT CONVENIENCE/APPEARANCE OPTIONS: Spirit: Pkg. 21A: stnd equip. (NC). Pkg. 24D: 21A exc. 2.5L Flex Fuel four replaces 2.5L gas four (NC). Pkg. 26D: 21A exc. 3.0L V-6 replaces 2.5L four plus P195/70R14 tires ($798). Pkg. 28D: incl. 3.0L V-6 and 4-spd auto. trans. plus P195/70R14 tires ($971). Pkg. 24E: 24D plus dual pwr mirrors, pwr door locks, pwr windows, pwr trunk release, rear split folding bench seat ($883). Pkg. 28E: 24E exc. 3.0L V-6 replaces 2.5L Flex Fuel four and 4-spd auto. trans. replaces 3-spd auto. trans. plus P195/70R14 tires ($1854). Other: (ADS) Argent Special Equipment Grp.: incl. luggage rack, P195/70R14 tires, 14-in. "Teardrop" cast alum whls ($200). (ASH) Gold Special Equipment Grp.: incl. gold badging & mldg, luggage rack, P195/70R14 tires, 14-in. "Teardrop" cast alum whls w/gold accents ($200). Elect. rear window defroster ($173). Pwr door locks ($250). Calif. emissions ($102). Pwr driver's seat ($306). (RAS) AM/FM radio w/cass. & clock & 4 spkrs ($170). Mini Trip Computer ($93). P195/70R14 tires ($73-$104). Conventional spare tire ($95).

1994 Dodge, Intrepid sedan (OCW)

INTREPID CONVENIENCE/APPEARANCE OPTIONS: Intrepid: Pkg. 22B: stnd equip. (NC). Pkg. 22C: incl. 22B plus floor mats, elect. spd control, pwr door locks, pwr windows, AM/FM stereo radio w/cass. & 6 spkrs ($891). Pkg. 22D: 22C plus 4-whl disc brakes, pwr remote decklid release, 8-way pwr driver's seat, message center, dual pwr heated outside mirrors ($1653). Pkg. 26D: 22D exc. 3.5L V-6 replaces 3.3L V-6 ($2378). ES: Pkg. 22K: stnd equip. (NC). Pkg. 22L: 22K plus pwr door locks, 8-way pwr driver's seat, pwr remote heated mirrors, leather-wrapped stng whl, pwr windows ($1268). Pkg. 26L: 22L exc. 3.5L V-6

replaces 3.3L V-6 ($1993). Pkg. 26M: 26L plus Chrysler/Infinity Spatial Imaging Cass. Sound Syst., auto. temp. air cond., auto. day/night rear-view mirror, anti-lock brakes w/traction control, overhead console, security alarm, conventional spare tire ($3741). Other: (AJF) Remote Illum. Entry Grp.: incl. remote keyless entry, illum. entry ($221). (AWT) Perf. Handling Grp.: incl. 16-in. perf. tires, perf. susp., ES ($217). (AGC) 16-in. Wheel & Handling Grp.: incl. 16-in. "Polystar" whls, 16-in. touring tires, variable-assist spd-proportional steering ($404). (AJP) Convenience Grp.: incl. pwr door locks, pwr windows, dual pwr mirrors, ES ($684). Auto. temp air cond., ES ($152). Full overhead console: base ($296); ES ($378). Calif. emissions ($102). Pwr decklid release, base ($61). Integrated child seat ($100). Pwr door locks ($250). Floor mats ($46). Pwr moonroof: base ($1012); ES ($716-$1094). Speed control ($224). 8-way pwr driver's & pass. seats, ES ($377). Leather front bucket seats w/8-way pwr driver's & pass. seats & leather shift knob, ES ($1009). Security alarm, ES ($149). Extra cost paint ($97). (RAS) AM/FM stereo radio w/cass. & 6 spkrs ($200). (ARA) Chrysler/Infinity Spatial Imaging Cass. Sound Syst. ($708). (ARB) Chrysler/Infinity Spatial Imaging CD Sound Syst.: base ($877); ES w/26M pkg. ($169). "Extender" alum whls, ES ($224). Conventional spare tire ($95).

1994 Dodge, Viper RT/10 roadster (OCW)

VIPER CONVENIENCE/APPEARANCE OPTIONS: Air cond. ($1200).

HISTORY: Model year production: 288,342. Calendar year sales: 244,189 (not including imports nor 93,300 1995 Neon models sold in 1994). The 1994 auto show circuit was introduced to Dodge's latest concept car, the Venom. Cast in the heritage of high-performance machines such as the Dodge Charger, Dodge Viper and Plymouth Barracuda, the Venom was, in the words of Neil Walling, Chrysler's Director of Advanced Design, "a redefinition of the American muscle car." The Venom was a combination of the Dodge Coronet's handlebar grille, the Viper's side scoop, and the Dodge Challenger's and Barracuda's rear end. Cab forward in design and using a modified Neon floor pan, the Venom coupe was powered by a High Output overhead cam 3.5-liter V-6 rated at 245 horsepower. Its rear-driven wheels were fed power through a T56 six-speed manual transmission. The Venom's wheelbase measured 106.0 inches within an overall length of 185.2 inches. It featured four-wheel disc brakes and was finished in Venom Yellow Green Pearl with an Agate interior featuring Agate perforated leather seats with Nitro Green accents.

1995 DODGE

The cab-forward revolution was completed in 1995 as three all-new Dodges came online, the Neon, Avenger and, late in the model year, the Stratus. In the case of the Stratus, it was a replacement for the Spirit, which was carried over from the year previous and sold for part of 1995 before being discontinued. Also gone from the lineup was the Shadow as well as the imported Colt (not covered in this catalog).

1995 Dodge, Neon sedan (OCW)

NEON — SERIES L — FOUR — In a unique approach to marketing an automobile-although certainly not the first in the industry to do so-the compact, five-passenger Neon was a Chrysler Corp. product that served two masters. Badged as either a Dodge or a Plymouth, the Neon for both brands was identical. Introduced in early-1994 (in four-door configuration, the two-door model did not debut until the fall of 1994) as a 1995 model, the Neon's duality was explained by Chrysler's Vice-President of Marketing and Communications, A.C. "Bud" Liebler thusly: "This marketing approach breaks from industry tradition, but is clearly in line with the Neon's 'dare to be different' product philosophy." The Neon was available in three trim levels: base, Highline and Sport. All were assembled in Belvidere, Illinois. The base model was offered in sedan only configuration while the Highline and Sport each came in both coupe and sedan body styles. All Neons with the exception of the Sport coupe were powered by a sequentially fuel injected 2.0-liter four-cylinder engine paired with a five-speed manual transmission. Sport coupes used a dual overhead cam version of the 2.0-liter four. Optional was an electronically controlled three-speed automatic. Neon was also the first passenger car to feature "returnless" fuel injection as well as the industry-first direct ignition system with sensor technology for quick starts. Neon's standard features included dual airbags and knee bolster passive restraint system, stainless steel exhaust system, side impact door beam protection, aero-style halogen headlights, analog instrument cluster with 120 mph speedometer, rear door child safety locks (sedans), warning chime feature for key-in-ignition/headlights on/seatbelt reminder, and climate control. Sport models added four-wheel anti-lock brakes, electric rear window defogger, power door locks, foglights, tinted glass, dual aero power black exterior mirrors, power steering, tilt steering column, touring suspension, remote trunk release, and intermittent wipers. Much of this equipment was available as optional or in packaged form only on base or Highline models. Air conditioning was an across-the-board package-only feature. The base sedan featured an interior consisting of "Naples" cloth and "Classic" vinyl. Highline and Sport models also used the same vinyl, but the former featured "Prism" cloth while the latter used "Pesto" cloth. "Pyramid" cloth and "Phoenix" vinyl was optional at the Sport trim level. The Neon's coefficient of drag measured 0.328. Its wheelbase was 104.0 inches and overall length 171.8 inches. Exterior color choices were Flame Red, Bright White, and Black across-the-board; Aqua and Light Iris on base and Highline models; and Strawberry, Emerald Green, and Brilliant Blue on Highline and Sport models. Medium/Dark Quartz was an interior color choice for all Neons, while Medium/Dark Driftwood was offered in Highline and Sport coupes and sedans and Sport models only—late in the model year—also had available a "Flash" decor in Medium/Dark Quartz. Several versions of an extra cost Competition Package were available as the Neon was used extensively in "showroom stock" sports car racing events.

1995 Dodge, Avenger ES coupe (OCW)

AVENGER — SERIES J — FOUR/V-6 — The Avenger sport coupe was made famous in its first year of availability by being selected as the car-

in highly modified form-used in the International Race of Champions (IROC) series pitting a dozen professional racing drivers in identically prepared stock cars in a "winner-takes-all" format on four different high-banked speedways. The public version of the Avenger-based on the Mitsubishi Galant-was offered in two trim levels: base and ES. It featured a "Viper-inspired" nose and 2+2 seating within 104 cubic feet of interior room as well as 13.1 cubic feet of trunk space made possible due to its cab-forward design. The base coupe was powered by a dual overhead cam 2.0-liter four-cylinder engine, rated at 140 horsepower, mated to a five-speed manual transmission. The ES coupe used a 24-valve 2.5-liter V-6, rated at 155 horsepower, paired with an electronically controlled four-speed automatic with selectable overdrive. This combination was optional in the base model. Avengers rode on fully independent front and rear suspension. All four wheels featured a double-wishbone suspension with a high-mounted upper control arm, lower arm and trailing arm that formed a kingpin axis resulting in enhanced "bite" in the turns and superior traction. The ES added Sport-Tuned Suspension featuring 16-inch speed-rated performance tires and five-spoke cast aluminum wheels. Standard equipment included dual airbags, steel beam side impact protection, speed-sensitive power steering, rear window defroster, stainless steel exhaust (dual on ES), halogen headlamps with polycarbonate lenses, intermittent wipers, and tilt steering column. The ES added four-wheel anti-lock disc brakes, six-way power driver's seat, air conditioning, decklid spoiler, electronic speed control, foglamps, and leather-wrapped steering wheel. Avenger's optional features included security alarm with remote keyless entry, cell phone, power windows, a variety of audio systems, sunroof and, on ES, leather upholstery. Avengers rode on a 103.7-inch wheelbase and measured 187.2 inches overall. Coefficient of drag measured 0.36.

1995 Dodge, Spirit sedan with optional Gold Appearance Package (OCW)

SPIRIT — SERIES A — FOUR/V-6 — Until the Stratus came online in mid-model year, the previous year's Spirit was carried over as a 1995 model for a short time and then dropped. Even in that abbreviated timeframe, it still was able to rack up production of almost 25,000 units. Powertrain availability was unchanged from the previous year with the exception that the formerly optional four-speed automatic transmission was no longer available. The optional Gold Appearance Package was again a Spirit extra.

1995 Dodge, Stratus sedan (OCW)

STRATUS — SERIES A — FOUR/V-6 — Launched in mid-model year, the all-new, cab-forward Stratus replaced the Spirit in the compact family sedan category. Offered in two trim levels, base and ES, the five-passenger Stratus was Dodge's counterpart to the also-new-for-1995

Chrysler Cirrus. A product of computer-aided design, the unibody Stratus featured a "ladder" underbody that increased the car's torsional stiffness by 24 percent over the Spirit. Standard powertrain was the 16-valve 2.0-liter sequentially fuel-injected four-cylinder engine mated to a five-speed manual transmission. Optional for both trim levels was the dual overhead cam 2.4-liter sequentially fuel-injected four-cylinder linked to the 41TE electronically controlled four-speed automatic with overdrive. Additionally, the ES sedan could be ordered with the Mitsubishi-developed four-valve 2.5-liter sequentially fuel-injected V-6 paired with the 41TE unit. Standard features included dual airbags, dynamic side impact protection, child guard rear door locks, climate control air conditioning with non-CFC R-134A refrigerant, electric rear window defroster, stainless steel exhaust, driver's left footrest, solar-control glass all-around, aero-style halogen headlamps with adjustable reflectors, electrical accessory power outlet, electronic speed control with steering wheel switches, tilt steering, remote decklid release, intermittent wipers, and warning chime for key-in-ignition/headlights on/seatbelt reminder. The ES sedan added four-wheel anti-lock brakes, power door locks, dual power heated black exterior mirrors, speed-sensitive variable-assist power steering, and "Extensor" cast aluminum wheels. Optional equipment for both trim levels included power windows, conventional spare tire, power sunroof (introduced late), rear child's safety seat, and personal security group with remote keyless entry, "panic" alarm and illuminated entry. The Stratus measured 186.0 inches long with a 108.0-inch wheelbase. Its coefficient of drag measured 0.314. Exterior color choices were Dark Rosewood, Light Rosewood, Metallic Red, Orchid Pearl, Light Silverfern, Medium Fern Green, Light Iris, Medium Blue, Black, and Bright White. Interior color choices were Mist Gray, Silverfern, and Rosewood.

1995 Dodge, Intrepid sedan (OCW)

INTREPID — SERIES H — V-6 — Base and ES sedans again comprised the Intrepid lineup. Powertrain availability remained the same as the year previous, but the 42LE electronically controlled four-speed automatic transmission with overdrive was modified for smoother operation. Also upgraded was the emissions control system for the optional 3.5-liter V-6 as well as the optional-for-ES sedan's remote keyless entry system. A cancel feature was added to Intrepid's standard automatic speed control and outside the headlights were refined to offer better visibility when in use. A new optional exterior color choice was Bright Platinum Metallic.

1995 Dodge, Viper RT/10 roadster (OCW)

VIPER RT/10 — SERIES R — V-10 — The Viper carried over to 1995 with no major changes. In testing, the roadster achieved 1.0 g in lateral acceleration on a skid pad with a 300-foot circle.

I.D. DATA: Dodge's 17-symbol Vehicle Identification Number (VIN), as before, was on the upper left corner of the instrument panel, visible through the windshield. Coding is similar to 1986-94. Symbol ten (model year) changed to 'S' for 1995.

NEON (FOUR)

Model No.	Body/ Style No.	Body Type & Seating	Factory Price	Shipping Weight	Prod. Total
LDL	42	4-dr. Sedan-5P	9500	2320	Note 2

NEON HIGHLINE (FOUR)

LDH	22	2-dr. Coupe-5P	11240	2377	Note 1
LDH	42	4-dr. Sedan-5P	11240	2388	Note 2

NEON SPORT (FOUR)

LDS	22	2-dr. Coupe-5P	13567	2439	Note 1
LDS	42	4-dr. Sedan-5P	13267	2449	Note 2

Note: Plymouth Neon production totals are separate and can be found in the Plymouth listings.

Note 1: Dodge Neon two-door production totaled 30,342 with no further breakout available.

Note 2: Dodge Neon four-door production totaled 112,511 with no further breakout available.

AVENGER (FOUR)

JDH	22	2-dr. Coupe-4P	13341	2822	Note 1

AVENGER ES (V-6)

JDS	22	2-dr. ES Coupe-4P	17191	3084	Note 1

Note 1: Avenger production totaled 32,870 with no further breakout available.

SPIRIT (FOUR/V-6)

ADH	41	4-dr. Sedan-6P	14323/15121	2771/2795	24,553

Note: Prices and weights to left of slash for four-cylinder, to right for V-6.

STRATUS (FOUR/V-6)

ADH	41	4-dr. Sedan-5P	13965/-----	2911/----	Note 1
ADP	41	4-dr. ES Sedan-5P	15565/17265	N/A/3145	Note 1

Note: Prices and weights to left of slash for four-cylinder, to right for V-6.

Note 1: Stratus production totaled 47,500 with no further breakout available.

INTREPID (V-6)

HDH	41	4-dr. Sedan-6P	17974	3308	Note 1
HDP	41	4-dr. ES Sedan-6P	20844	3370	Note 1

Note 1: Intrepid sedan production totaled 150,474 with no further breakout available.

VIPER RT/10 (V-10)

RDS	27	2-dr. Rdstr-2P	56000	3476	1418

ENGINE DATA: BASE FOUR (Neon, Neon Highline, Neon Sport sed, Stratus, Stratus ES): Inline, overhead cam four-cylinder. Cast iron block; aluminum head. Displacement: 121 cu. in. (2.0 liters). Bore & stroke: 3.44 x 3.27 in. Compression ratio: 9.8:1. Brake horsepower: 132 at 6000 RPM. Torque: 129 lb.-ft. at 5000 RPM. Sequential fuel injection. **BASE FOUR** (Neon Sport cpe, Avenger): Inline, dual overhead cam four-cylinder. Cast iron block; aluminum head. Displacement: 121 cu. in. (2.0 liters). Bore & stroke: 3.44 x 3.27 in. Compression ratio: (Neon Sport cpe) 9.8:1; (Avenger) 9.6:1. Brake horsepower: (Neon Sport cpe) 150 at 6500 RPM; (Avenger) 140 at 6000 RPM. Torque: (Neon Sport cpe) 133 lb.-ft. at 5500 RPM; (Avenger) 130 lb.-ft. at 4800 RPM. Sequential fuel injection. **OPTIONAL FOUR** (Stratus, Stratus ES): Inline, dual overhead cam four-cylinder. Cast iron block; aluminum head. Displacement: 148 cu. in. (2.4 liters). Bore & stroke: 3.44 x 3.98 in. Compression ratio: 9.4:1. Brake horsepower: 140 at 5200 RPM. Torque: 160 lb.-ft. at 4000 RPM. Sequential fuel injection. **BASE FOUR** (Spirit): Inline, overhead cam four-cylinder. Cast iron block; aluminum head. Displacement: 153 cu. in. (2.5 liters). Bore & stroke: 3.44 x 4.09 in. Compression ratio: 8.9:1. Brake horsepower: 100 at 4800 RPM. Torque: 135 lb.-ft. at 2800 RPM. Throttle-body fuel injection. **BASE V-6** (Avenger ES); **OPTIONAL V-6** (Stratus ES): Overhead cam V-6. Cast iron block; aluminum head. Displacement: 152 cu. in. (2.5 liters). Bore & stroke: 3.29 x 2.99 in. Compression ratio: 9.4:1. Brake horsepower: (Avenger ES) 155 at 5500 RPM; (Stratus ES) 164 at 5900 RPM. Torque: (Avenger ES) 161 lb.-ft. at 4400 RPM; (Stratus ES) 163 lb.-ft. at 4350 RPM. Sequential fuel injection. **OPTIONAL V-6:** (Spirit): Overhead cam V-6. Cast iron block; aluminum head. Displacement: 181 cu. in. (3.0 liters). Bore & stroke: 3.59 x 2.99 in. Compression ratio: 9.4:1. Brake horsepower: 142 at 5000 RPM. Torque: 171 lb.-ft. at 2400 RPM. Sequential fuel injection. **BASE V-6** (Intrepid, Intrepid ES): Overhead valve V-6. Cast iron block; aluminum heads. Displacement: 201 cu. in. (3.3 liters). Bore & stroke: 3.66 x 3.19 in. Compression ratio: 8.9:1. Brake horsepower: 161 at 5300 RPM. Torque: 181 lb.-ft. at 3200 RPM. Sequential fuel

injection. BASE V-6 (Flex Fuel-equipped Intrepid or Intrepid ES): same as 3.3-liter V-6 above exc.: Brake horsepower: 167 at 5400 RPM. Torque: 185 lb.-ft. at 3000 RPM. OPTIONAL V-6 (Intrepid, Intrepid ES): Overhead cam V-6. Cast iron block; aluminum heads. Displacement: 214 cu. in. (3.5 liters). Bore & stroke: 3.78 x 3.19 in. Compression ratio: 10.5:1. Brake horsepower: 214 at 5800 RPM. Torque: 221 lb.-ft. at 3100 RPM. Sequential fuel injection. BASE V-10 (Viper): Overhead valve V-10. Aluminum block and heads. Displacement: 488 cu. in. (8.0 liters). Bore & stroke: 4.00 x 3.88 in. Compression ratio: 9.1:1. Brake horsepower: 400 at 4600 RPM. Torque: 480 lb.-ft. at 3600 RPM. Sequential fuel injection.

CHASSIS DATA: Wheelbase: (Neon) 104.0 in.; (Avenger) 103.7 in.; (Stratus) 108.0 in.; (Spirit) 103.5 in.; (Intrepid) 113.0 in.; (Viper) 96.2 in. Overall length: (Neon) 171.8 in.; (Avenger) 187.2 in.; (Stratus) 186.0 in.; (Spirit) 181.2 in.; (Intrepid) 201.7 in.; (Viper) 175.1 in. Height: (Neon cpe) 52.8 in.; (Neon sed) 54.8 in.; (Avenger) 53.0 in.; (Stratus) 54.1 in.; (Spirit) 55.5 in.; (Intrepid) 56.3 in.; (Viper) 43.9 in. Width: (Neon) 67.2 in.; (Avenger) 68.5 in.; (Stratus) 71.0 in.; (Spirit) 68.1 in.; (Intrepid) 74.4 in.; (Viper) 75.1 in. Front Tread: (Neon) 57.4 in.; (Avenger) 59.5 in.; (Stratus) 60.2 in.; (Spirit) 57.6 in.; (Intrepid) 62.0 in.; (Viper) 59.6 in. Rear Tread: (Neon) 57.4 in.; (Avenger) 59.5 in.; (Stratus) 60.2 in.; (Spirit) 57.2 in.; (Intrepid) 62.0 in.; (Viper) 60.6 in. Standard Tires: (Neon) P165/80R13: (Neon Highline) P185/70R13; (Neon Sport) P185/65R14; (Avenger) P195/70HR14; (Avenger ES) P205/55HR16; (Stratus) P195/70SR14; (Stratus ES) P195/65HR15; (Spirit) P185/70R14; (Intrepid) P205/70R15; (Intrepid ES) P225/60R16; (Viper) P275/40ZR17 front/P335/35ZR17 rear.

TECHNICAL: Transmission: Five-speed manual standard on Neon (all), Avenger, Stratus (all). Three-speed automatic standard on Spirit. Four-speed automatic standard on Avenger ES, Intrepid (all). Six-speed manual standard on Viper. Steering: (all) Rack and pinion. Front suspension: (Neon) MacPherson struts, asymmetrical lower control arms, coil springs and (opt. on base; stnd on Highline, Sport) link-type stabilizer bar; (Avenger) Modified double-wishbone w/coil springs, direct acting shock absorbers and link-type stabilizer bar; (Stratus) Unequal length upper and lower control arms, coil springs, tubular shock absorbers and stabilizer bar (higher rate springs on ES); (Spirit) Iso-strut w/integral gas-charged hydraulic shock absorbers, asymmetrical lower control arms, coil springs and linkless stabilizer bar; (Intrepid) Iso-strut w/integral gas-charged shock absorbers, coil springs, single transverse lower links, tension struts and link-type stabilizer bar; (Viper) Cast aluminum unequal length upper and lower control arms, coil springs, low-pressure gas-charged shock absorbers w/adjustable rebound and stabilizer bar. Rear suspension: (Neon) Chapman struts, coil springs, dual lower transverse links, lower trailing links; (Avenger) Double wishbones, coil springs, direct acting shock absorbers and (ES only) link-type stabilizer bar; (Stratus) Unequal length upper and lower control arms, trailing arms, coil springs, tubular shock absorbers and stabilizer bar (larger stabilizer bar and higher rate springs on ES); (Spirit) Beam axle, trailing flex arms w/track bar, coil springs, gas-charged shock absorbers and frameless tubular stabilizer bar; (Intrepid) Chapman struts w/integral gas-charged shock absorbers, concentric coil springs, dual transverse lower links, lower trailing links and link-type stabilizer bar; (Viper) Cast aluminum unequal length upper and lower control arms w/toe-control links, coil springs, low-pressure gas-charged shock absorbers w/adjustable rebound and stabilizer bar. Brakes: Front disc, rear drum (power-assisted) exc. (Neon Sport, Stratus ES) Front disc, rear drum w/anti-lock (power-assisted); (Avenger ES, Intrepid ES) four-wheel disc w/anti-lock; (Viper) four-wheel disc. Body construction: Unibody exc. (Viper) tubular space frame. Fuel tank: (Neon) 11.2 gals.; (Avenger) 15.8 gals.; (Stratus) 16 gals.; (Spirit) 16 gals.; (Intrepid) 18 gals.; (Viper) 22 gals.

DRIVETRAIN OPTIONS: Engines: SOHC 2.0-liter four: Neon Sport cpe ($100 credit). 2.4-liter four: Stratus/Stratus ES ($699). 2.5-liter V-6: Stratus ES (N/A). 3.0-liter V-6: Spirit ($798). 3.3-liter flex fuel V-6: Intrepid/Intrepid ES ($150). 3.5-liter V-6: Intrepid/Intrepid ES ($725). Transmission: Three-speed auto. trans.: Neon ($557). Four-speed auto. trans.: Avenger ($683); Stratus/Stratus ES ($467). Brakes: Anti-lock: Neon base/Highline ($565); Avenger ($599); Stratus ($565). Four-wheel disc w/anti-lock: Spirit ($699); Intrepid ($599-$624). Traction control: w/ABS on Intrepid ES ($175).

NEON CONVENIENCE/APPEARANCE OPTIONS: Base: Pkg. 21A: stnd equip. (NC). Pkg. 22A: 21A exc. 3-spd auto. trans. replaces 5-spd manual ($557). Competition Pkg. 25A: 21A plus ACR Competition Pkg. and extra cost paint ($1575). Pkg. 21B: 21A plus air cond., rear window defroster, dual remote outside mirrors, bodyside mldg, AM/FM stereo radio w/clock & 4 spkrs, pwr stng, tinted glass, touring susp., intermittent wipers ($1861). Pkg. 22B: 21B exc. 3-spd auto. trans. replaces 5-spd manual ($2418). Competition Pkg. 25B: 25A plus air cond., rear window defroster, dual remote outside mirrors, AM/FM stereo radio w/clock & 4 spkrs, intermittent wipers ($3315). Highline: Pkg. 21C: stnd equip. (NC). Competition Pkg. 23C: incl. DOHC 2.0L four and 5-spd manual trans. plus ACR Competition Pkg. and extra cost paint ($1140). Pkg. 21D: 21C plus air cond., floor-mounted console, remote decklid release,

rear window defroster ($703). Pkg. 22D: 21D exc. 3-spd auto. trans. replaces 5-spd manual ($1260). Competition Pkg. 23D: 23C plus air cond., floor-mounted console, remote decklid release, rear window defroster, extra cost paint, cpe only ($2177). Pkg. 21F: 21D plus pwr door locks, floor mats, Light Grp., dual illum. visor mirrors, tilt stng, tach, low fuel light, P185/65R14 tires, 14-in. whl covers: cpe ($1330); sed ($1351). Pkg. 22F: 21F exc. 3-spd auto. trans. replaces 5-spd manual: cpe ($1887); sed ($1928). Sport cpe: Pkg. 21J: incl. SOHC 2.0L four and 5-spd manual trans. ($100 credit). Pkg. 22J: 21J exc. 3-spd auto. trans. replaces 5-spd manual ($457). Pkg. 23J: stnd equip. (NC). Pkg. 24J: 23J exc. 3-spd auto. trans. replaces 5-spd manual ($557). Pkg. 21K: 21J plus air cond., floor mats, Light Grp., AM/FM stereo radio w/prem. cass. & CD changer & 6 spkrs ($627). Pkg. 22K: 21K exc. 3-spd auto. trans. replaces 5-spd manual ($1184). Pkg. 23K: 23J plus air cond., floor mats, Light Grp., AM/FM stereo radio w/prem. cass. & CD changer & 6 spkrs ($727). Pkg. 24K: 23K exc. 3-spd auto. trans. replaces 5-spd manual ($1284). Sport sed: Pkg. 21J: stnd equip. (NC). Pkg. 22J: 21J exc. 3-spd auto. trans. replaces 5-spd manual ($557). Pkg. 21K: 21J plus air cond., floor mats, Light Grp., AM/FM stereo radio w/prem. cass. & CD changer & 6 spkrs ($727). Pkg. 22K: 21K exc. 3-spd auto. trans. replaces 5-spd manual ($1284). Other: (AJP) Convenience Grp.: incl. dual pwr remote mirrors, pwr door locks, stnd Sport: cpe ($256); sed ($297). (ACR) Competition Pkg.: incl. 14-in. 4-whl disc brakes, unlimited spd eng. controller, body-color fascias, body-color grille bar, tinted glass, dual manual remote mirrors, bodyside mldg, H.D. radiator, radio delete, pwr stng w/16:1 ratio, competition susp., tach, low fuel light, 14-in. cast alum whls, P175/65HR14 perf. tires on base/P185/60HR14 touring tires on Highline (NC). Integrated child seat ($100). Rear window defroster ($173). Calif. emissions ($102). Floor mats, base or Highline ($46). Roof rack ($100). Dual remote manual mirrors, base ($70). Body-side mldg, base ($30). (RAL) AM/FM stereo radio w/clock & 4 spkrs, base ($334). (RAS) AM/FM stereo radio w/cass., clock & 6 prem. spkrs ($250). (RBS) AM/FM stereo radio w/prem. cass., CD changer, clock & 6 prem. spkrs ($356). (RBG) Elect. AM/FM stereo radio w/CD player, clock & 6 prem. spkrs ($132-$488). Speed control, N/A base ($224). Tilt stng, Highline ($148). Tach & Low Fuel Warning Light, Highline ($93). (AYC) Wheel Cover Pkg., Sport ($500 credit). (AY7) Wheel Dress-Up Pkg., Highline ($80). Intermittent wipers, base ($66). Pwr windows, Sport sed ($210). "Flash" Decor cloth bucket seats, Sport ($120). Leather bucket seats, Sport ($649). Extra cost paint, N/A Sport ($97).

1995 Dodge, Neon Sport sedan (OCW)

1995 Dodge, Avenger coupe (OCW)

AVENGER CONVENIENCE/APPEARANCE OPTIONS: Base: Pkg. 21A: stnd equip. (NC). Pkg. 22A: 21A exc. 4-spd auto. trans. replaces 5-spd manual ($683). Pkg. 21B: 21A plus air cond., floor mats, spd control, AM/FM stereo radio w/cass., clock & 4 spkrs ($1216). Pkg. 22B: 21B exc. 4-spd auto. trans. replaces 5-spd manual ($1899). Pkg. 21C: 21B plus pwr door locks, cargo net, pwr windows, dual pwr remote mirrors ($1750). Pkg. 22C: 21C exc. 4-spd auto. trans. replaces 5-spd manual ($2433). ES: Pkg. 24D: stnd equip. (NC). Pkg. 24E: 24D plus pwr door locks, dual pwr remote mirrors, pwr windows, dual illum. visor mirrors ($534). Pkg. 24F: 23F plus pwr driver's seat, security alarm, pwr sunroof, AM/FM stereo radio w/cass., equal., clock & Infinity spkrs ($2199). Other: pwr driver's seat ($203). Calif. emissions ($102). Security alarm w/remote keyless entry ($272). (RAS) Elect. AM/FM stereo radio w/cass., clock & 4 spkrs, stnd ES ($174). (RAY) Elect. AM/FM stereo radio w/cass., equal., clock & Infinity spkrs ($550). (RBC) Elect. AM/FM stereo radio w/CD player, equal., clock & Infinity spkrs ($157-$707). Leather seats, ES ($423).

STRATUS CONVENIENCE/APPEARANCE OPTIONS: Base: Pkg. 21A: stnd equip. (NC). Pkg. 24A: incl. 2.4L four and 4-spd auto. trans. ($1166). Pkg. 21B: 21A plus pwr door locks, dual pwr remote heated mirrors, pwr windows, driver's seat height adj. ($684). Pkg. 24B: 24A plus pwr door locks, dual pwr remote heated mirrors, pwr windows, driver's seat height adj. ($1850). ES: Pkg. 26J: stnd equip. (NC). Pkg. 26K: incl. 2.4L four and 4-spd auto. trans. plus Personal Security Grp., convenience net, security alarm, leather-trimmed seats/stng whl/shift knob, 8-way pwr driver's seat, pwr antenna, prem. AM/FM stereo radio w/cass., clock & 6 spkrs ($1731). Other: (AJF) Personal Security Grp.: incl. illum. entry, remote keyless entry, panic alarm ($168). Integrated child seat ($100). Security alarm, ES ($149). Calif. emissions ($102). Eng. block & battery heater ($30). Extra cost paint ($97). (RBS) Elect. prem. AM/FM stereo radio w/cass., clock & 6 spkrs ($368). (RBG) Elect. AM/FM stereo radio w/CD player, seek, clock & 6 spkrs ($122-$491). Conventional spare tire ($95).

SPIRIT CONVENIENCE/APPEARANCE OPTIONS: Pkg. 22D: stnd equip. (NC). Pkg. 26D: 22D exc. 3.0L V-6 replaces 2.5L four plus P195/70R14 tires ($798). Pkg. 26E: 26D plus dual pwr mirrors, pwr door locks, pwr windows, pwr trunk release ($1533). Other: (ASH) Gold Decor Grp.: incl. gold badging & mldg, luggage rack, P195/70R14 tires, 14-in. "Teardrop" cast alum whls w/gold accents ($200). Pwr door locks ($250). Calif. emissions ($102). Pwr driver's seat ($306). Eng. block heater ($20). Extra cost paint ($97). Conventional spare tire ($95).

INTREPID CONVENIENCE/APPEARANCE OPTIONS: Intrepid: Pkg. 22B: stnd equip. (NC). Pkg. 24B: 22B exc. flex fuel 3.3L V-6 replaces 3.3L V-6 ($150). Pkg. 22C: incl. 22B plus floor mats, elect. spd control, pwr door locks, pwr windows ($723). Pkg. 24C: 22C exc. flex fuel 3.3L V-6 replaces 3.3L V-6 ($873). Pkg. 22D: 22C plus 4-whl disc brakes, pwr remote decklid release, 8-way pwr driver's seat, message center, dual pwr heated outside mirrors ($1407). Pkg. 26D: 22D exc. 3.5L V-6 replaces 3.3L V-6 ($2132). ES: Pkg. 22K: stnd equip. (NC). Pkg. 22K plus 8-way pwr driver's seat, dual illum. visor mirrors, leather-wrapped stng whl ($693). Pkg. 26L: 22L exc. 3.5L V-6 replaces 3.3L V-6 ($1418). Pkg. 22M: 22L incl. upgraded air cond. & audio syst. plus full overhead console, security alarm, conventional spare tire, traction control ($2085). Pkg. 26M: 22M exc. 3.5L V-6 replaces 3.3L V-6 ($2810). Other: (AJF) Remote Illum. Entry Grp.: incl. remote keyless entry, illum. entry, remote decklid release ($221). (AWT) Perf. Handling Grp.: incl. P225/60R16 perf. tires, perf. susp., ES ($217). (AGC) 16-in. Wheel & Handling Grp.: incl. 16-in. "Polystar" whls, P225/50R16 touring tires, variable-assist spd-proportional steering, base ($404). Auto. temp air cond., ES ($152). Full overhead console: base ($296); ES ($378). Calif. emissions ($102). Pwr decklid release, base ($61). Integrated child seat ($100). Pwr door locks ($250). Floor mats ($46). Pwr moonroof: base ($1012); ES ($716-$1094). Speed control ($224). 8-way pwr driver's & pass. seats, ES ($377). Leather front bucket seats w/8-way pwr driver's & pass. seats & leather shift knob, ES ($1009). Security alarm, ES ($149). Extra cost paint ($97). Bright Platinum Metallic paint, ES ($200). (ARA) Chrysler/Infinity Spatial Imaging Cass. Sound Syst. ($708). (ARB) Chrysler/Infinity Spatial Imaging CD Sound Syst., ES ($169-$877). Conventional spare tire ($95).

VIPER CONVENIENCE/APPEARANCE OPTIONS: Air cond. ($1200).

HISTORY: Model year production: 399,668. Calendar year sales: 397,070 (not including imports). At the North American International Auto Show in Detroit, Dodge unveiled the Avenger R/T show car. The R/T was powered by a 24-valve 3.0-liter V-6 that generated in excess of 200 horsepower. It featured drilled front and rear disc brakes utilizing a four-caliper per disc system also found on the imported Stealth R/T Turbo and Viper RT/10. The R/T's bodywork differed from the public Avenger in that its hood was modified and it sported unique front and rear fascias and an aggressive rear spoiler. The R/T also rode on 18-inch chrome-plated aluminum alloy wheels and low-profile, speed-rated tires. One unique feature of the R/T was its cockpit-controlled shock absorbers. The R/T could travel 0-60 mph in an estimated seven seconds.

1996 DODGE

The Spirit was discontinued early in the previous model year and a base coupe was added to the Neon series, otherwise Dodge's lineup carried over intact from 1995. The Avenger ES coupe could now be ordered with a 2.0-liter four-cylinder engine after previously offering only a V-6. Available only as a dealer-installed option, the 1996 Viper roadster featured a removable hardtop with sliding side curtains.

1996 Dodge, Neon sedan (OCW)

NEON — SERIES L — FOUR — With the addition of a base coupe, all three trim levels of Neon-base, Highline and Sport-each now offered a coupe and sedan. Also added to the Highline models was an optional Expresso package that included "Expresso" graphics, a power bulge hood, "Flash Decor" interior trim, decklid spoiler and tach. The Expresso could also be ordered with a three-speed automatic transmission in place of the Highline's standard five-speed manual unit. The Neon's standard powertrain lineup was revised slightly from the year previous with all models now using the sequentially fuel injected 2.0-liter four-cylinder engine linked to a five-speed manual transmission. The dual overhead cam version of the 2.0-liter four that previously was standard in the Sport coupe was now optional in Sport coupes and sedans as well as base Neon coupes equipped with the optional Competition Package. An electronically controlled three-speed automatic transmission was optional across-the-board. Also optional in all California (or states requiring California Emission Controls) Neons was a TLEV (transitional low emission vehicle) version of the 2.0-liter four. An upgraded noise, vibration and harshness (NVH) reduction package was standard on all 1996 Neons. Base models received more standard equipment including touring suspension, intermittent wipers, remote trunk release and tinted glass, all of which was previously optional. Other new features included a 12.5 gallon molded plastic gas tank (which replaced the former 11.2 gallon unit), SBEC III Powertrain Control Module, four-spoke steering wheel with center horn pad, mist gray interior color choice and two new exterior color choices: Magenta and Bright Jade. New optional features of the Neon included four-wheel anti-lock disc brakes available on all models; power windows on coupes; and a power sunroof, remote keyless entry with "panic" alarm and dome and map lamp time out feature offered on Highline and Sport models.

1996 Dodge, Avenger coupe (OCW)

AVENGER — SERIES J — FOUR/V-6 — Again available in base and ES trim levels, the Avenger coupe received several upgrades for 1996. The base coupe was again powered by a dual overhead cam 2.0-liter four-cylinder engine paired with a five-speed manual transmission. New for 1996, this combination was optional on the ES coupe. The ES coupe again used the 2.5-liter V-6 mated to an electronically controlled four-speed automatic with selectable overdrive. The four-speed automatic was optional in the base Avenger. Both engines received upgrades to their Evaporative Emission Control Systems and all Avenger powertrains now featured OBD II on-board diagnostics as well as the SBEC III Powertrain Control Module. Three new exterior color choices were available:

Polo Green, Spanish Olive and Prism Blue. The ES featured new "Fresno" and "Hudson" cloth seat fabrics. New optional equipment included a "panic" alarm added to the remote keyless entry system, HomeLink universal transmitter for emergency situations, and Infinity cassette and CD audio system upgrades.

1996 Dodge, Stratus sedan (OCW)

1996 Dodge, Stratus ES sedan (OCW)

STRATUS — SERIES A — FOUR/V-6 — Stratus was again offered in base and ES trim level sedans. Powertrain availability remained unchanged from the year previous with the 2.0-liter sequentially fuel-injected four-cylinder engine linked to a five-speed manual transmission the standard combination. Again optional for both base and ES sedans was the dual overhead cam 2.4-liter sequentially fuel-injected four-cylinder engine paired with an 41TE electronically controlled four-speed automatic with overdrive. The ES sedan could again be ordered with the 2.5-liter sequentially fuel-injected V-6 paired with the 41TE unit. In line with other Dodges, upgrades for the 1996 Stratus included improved engine Evaporative Emission Control Systems and the addition of OBD II on-board diagnostics (to all Stratus powertrains offered) as well as the SBEC III Powertrain Control Module. The ES sedan's 2.5-liter V-6 received a revised torque converter for more responsive performance. Camel was a new interior color choice while there were four new exterior color choices: Candy Apple Red Metallic, Light Gold, Forest Green and Stone White. A power sunroof (introduced late the year previous) was added to the option list for both trim levels.

1996 Dodge, Intrepid sedan (OCW)

INTREPID — SERIES H — V-6 — The Intrepid's lineup of base and ES sedans carried over from the previous year. Powertrain availability was revised with the addition of an optional TLEV (transitional low emission vehicle) version of the base sedan's 3.3-liter V-6 for use in California, New York, Maine and Massachusetts as well as the previously optional 3.5-liter V-6 now standard in the ES. The 42LE electronically controlled four-speed automatic transmission with overdrive was used with both engines. Both the base and ES sedans received enhanced NVH (noise, vibration and harshness) reduction for 1996. As with other Dodges, the Intrepid also featured improved engine Evaporative Emission Control Systems and the addition of OBD II on-board diagnostics as well as the SBEC III Powertrain Control Module. The base Intrepid offered several new standard features including 16-inch wheels and "Fortress" bolt-on wheel covers. Inside, a premium cloth seat fabric was new. Outside, four new exterior color choices were available: Candy Apple Red Metallic, Opal, Island Teal and Stone White. Several audio system upgrades were also offered, including a more powerful Infinity Spatial Imaging cassette system wit CD changer controls.

1996 Dodge, Viper GTS coupe (OCW)

VIPER RT/10 — SERIES R — V-10 — For the first time since its 1992 introduction, the Viper was "overhauled," receiving several major modifications. Foremost among the upgrades, the V-10 engine powering the Viper offered higher output, now rated at 415 horsepower (up from the previous 400) and 488 pound-feet of torque (up from 465). It remained paired with the T56 six-speed manual transmission with overdrive. Other new features included a low restriction rear outlet exhaust system (which replaced the original side-mounted exhaust), an increased torque-capacity drive line, five-spoke forged aluminum wheels, JTEC Powertrain Control Module, OBD II on-board diagnostics, improved convertible top seals, all-aluminum front and rear suspension components and a lighter, stiffer frame. The 1996 Viper was the industry-first domestic car to use Michelin Pilot MXX3 Maximum Speed-Rated tires. The Viper's fuel tank capacity was reduced from the previous 22 gallons to 19 gallons. New exterior color choices consisted of three combinations: red with yellow wheels, black with silver stripe and silver wheels, and white with blue stripe and white wheels. For $2,500, the Viper buyer could order an optional, dealer-installed removable hardtop with sliding side curtains. After its debut as the Indianapolis 500 pace car, the Viper GTS coupe began extremely limited production in Viper Blue with white striping finish (see 1997 Viper listing for specifications).

I.D. DATA: Dodge's 17-symbol Vehicle Identification Number (VIN), as before, was on the upper left corner of the instrument panel, visible through the windshield. Coding is similar to 1986-95. Symbol ten (model year) changed to 'T' for 1996.

1996 Dodge, Neon Sport coupe (OCW)

NEON (FOUR)

Model No.	Body/Style No.	Body Type & Seating	Factory Price	Shipping Weight	Prod. Total
LDL	22	2-dr. Coupe-5P	9495	N/A	Note 1
LDL	42	4-dr. Sedan-5P	9995	2343	Note 2

NEON HIGHLINE (FOUR)

LDH	22	2-dr. Coupe-5P	11300	2385	Note 1
LDH	42	4-dr. Sedan-5P	11500	2416	Note 2

NEON SPORT (FOUR)

LDS	22	2-dr. Coupe-5P	12500	2469	Note 1
LDS	42	4-dr. Sedan-5P	12700	2456	Note 2

Note: Plymouth Neon production totals are separate and can be found in the Plymouth listings.

Note 1: Dodge Neon two-door production totaled 34,641 with no further breakout available.

Note 2: Dodge Neon four-door production totaled 96,702 with no further breakout available.

AVENGER (FOUR/V-6)

JDH	22	2-dr. Coupe-4P	14040/-----	2879/----	Note 1
JDS	22	2-dr. ES Coupe-4P	16829/18121	N/A/3124	Note 1

Note: Prices and weights to left of slash for four-cylinder, to right for V-6.

Note 1: Avenger production totaled 38,812 with no further breakout available.

STRATUS (FOUR/V-6)

ADH	41	4-dr. Sedan-5P	14460/-----	2899/----	Note 1
ADP	41	4-dr. ES Sedan-5P	16110/17360	N/A/3117	Note 1

Note: Prices and weights to left of slash for four-cylinder, to right for V-6.

Note 1: Stratus production totaled 98,929 with no further breakout available.

INTREPID (V-6)

HDH	41	4-dr. Sedan-6P	18445	3318	Note 1
HDP	41	4-dr. ES Sedan-6P	22260	3415	Note 1

Note 1: Intrepid sedan production totaled 145,167 with no further breakout available.

VIPER RT/10 (V-10)

RDS	27	2-dr. Rdstr-2P	58600	3445	1234
RDS	29	2-dr. GTS Cpe-2P	66000	3383	N/A

ENGINE DATA: BASE FOUR (Neon, Neon Highline, Neon Sport, Stratus, Stratus ES): Inline, overhead cam four-cylinder. Cast iron block; aluminum head. Displacement: 121 cu. in. (2.0 liters). Bore & stroke: 3.44 x 3.27 in. Compression ratio: 9.8:1. Brake horsepower: 132 at 6000 RPM. Torque: 129 lb.-ft. at 5000 RPM. Sequential fuel injection. OPTIONAL FOUR (Neon, Neon Highline, Neon Sport): Inline, dual overhead cam four-cylinder. Cast iron block; aluminum head. Displacement: 121 cu. in. (2.0 liters). Bore & stroke: 3.44 x 3.27 in. Compression ratio: 9.8:1. Brake horsepower: 150 at 6800 RPM. Torque: 131 lb.-ft. at 5600 RPM. Sequential fuel injection. BASE FOUR (Avenger); OPTIONAL FOUR (Avenger ES): Inline, dual overhead cam four-cylinder. Cast iron block; aluminum head. Displacement: 121 cu. in. (2.0 liters). Bore & stroke: 3.44 x 3.27 in. Compression ratio: 9.6:1. Brake horsepower: 140 at 6000 RPM. Torque: 130 lb.-ft. at 4800 RPM. Sequential fuel injection. OPTIONAL FOUR (Stratus, Stratus ES): Inline, dual overhead cam four-cylinder. Cast iron block; aluminum head. Displacement: 148 cu. in. (2.4 liters). Bore & stroke: 3.44 x 3.98 in. Compression ratio: 9.4:1. Brake horsepower: 150 at 5200 RPM. Torque: 167 lb.-ft. at 4000 RPM. Sequential fuel injection. BASE V-6 (Avenger ES); OPTIONAL V-6 (Stratus ES): Overhead cam V-6. Cast iron block; aluminum heads. Displacement: 152 cu. in. (2.5 liters). Bore & stroke: 3.29 x 2.99 in. Compression ratio: 9.4:1. Brake horsepower: (Avenger ES) 163 at 5800 RPM; (Stratus ES) 168 at 5800 RPM. Torque: (Avenger ES) 170 lb.-ft. at 4400 RPM; (Stratus ES) 170 lb.-ft. at 4350 RPM. Sequential fuel injection. BASE V-6 (Intrepid): Overhead valve V-6. Cast iron block; aluminum heads. Displacement: 201 cu. in. (3.3 liters). Bore & stroke: 3.66 x 3.19 in. Compression ratio: 8.9:1. Brake horsepower: 161 at 5300 RPM. Torque: 181 lb.-ft. at 3200 RPM. Sequential fuel injection. BASE V-6 (Intrepid ES): Overhead cam V-6. Cast iron block; aluminum heads. Displacement: 214 cu. in. (3.5 liters). Bore & stroke: 3.78 x 3.19 in. Compression ratio: 9.6:1. Brake horsepower: 214 at 5850 RPM. Torque: 221 lb.-ft. at 3100 RPM. Sequential fuel injection. BASE V-10 (Viper): Overhead valve V-10. Aluminum block and heads. Displacement: 488 cu. in. (8.0 liters). Bore & stroke: 4.00 x 3.88 in. Compression ratio: 9.1:1. Brake horsepower: 415 at 5200 RPM. Torque: 488 lb.-ft. at 3600 RPM. Sequential fuel injection.

CHASSIS DATA: Wheelbase: (Neon) 104.0 in.; (Avenger) 103.7 in.; (Stratus) 108.0 in.; (Intrepid) 113.0 in.; (Viper) 96.2 in. Overall length: (Neon) 171.8 in.; (Avenger) 187.2 in.; (Stratus) 186.0 in.; (Intrepid) 201.8 in.; (Viper) 175.1 in. Height: (Neon cpe) 53.0 in.; (Neon sed) 52.8 in.; (Avenger) 53.0 in.; (Stratus) 54.2 in.; (Intrepid) 56.3 in.; (Viper) 43.5 in. Width: (Neon) 67.5 in.; (Avenger) 68.5 in.; (Stratus) 71.7 in.; (Intrepid) 74.4 in.; (Viper) 75.7 in. Front Tread: (Neon) 57.4 in.; (Avenger) 59.5 in.; (Stratus) 60.2 in.; (Intrepid) 62.0 in.; (Viper) 59.6 in. Rear Tread: (Neon) 57.4 in.; (Avenger) 59.3 in.; (Stratus) 60.2 in.; (Intrepid) 62.0 in.; (Viper) 60.6 in. Standard Tires: (Neon - all) P185/65R14; (Avenger) P195/70HR14; (Avenger ES) P205/55HR16; (Stratus) P195/70R14; (Stratus ES) P195/65HR15; (Intrepid - all) P225/60R16; (Viper) P275/40ZR17 front/P335/35ZR17 rear.

TECHNICAL: Transmission: Five-speed manual standard on Neon (all), Avenger, Stratus (all). Four-speed automatic standard on Avenger ES, Intrepid (all). Six-speed manual standard on Viper. Steering: (all) Rack and pinion. Front suspension: (Neon) MacPherson struts, asymmetrical lower control arms, coil springs and link-type stabilizer bar; (Avenger) Modified double-wishbone w/coil springs, direct acting shock absorbers and link-type stabilizer bar; (Stratus) Unequal length upper and lower control arms, coil springs, tubular shock absorbers and stabilizer bar (higher rate springs on ES); (Intrepid) Iso-strut w/integral gas-charged shock absorbers, coil springs, single transverse lower links, tension struts and link-type stabilizer bar; (Viper) Cast aluminum unequal length upper and lower control arms, coil springs, low-pressure gas-charged shock absorbers w/adjustable rebound and stabilizer bar. Rear suspension: (Neon) Chapman struts, coil springs, dual lower transverse links, lower trailing links; (Avenger) Double wishbones, coil springs, direct acting shock absorbers and (ES only) link-type stabilizer bar; (Stratus) Unequal length upper and lower control arms, trailing arms, coil springs, tubular shock absorbers and stabilizer bar (larger stabilizer bar and higher rate springs on ES); (Intrepid) Chapman struts w/integral gas-charged shock absorbers, concentric coil springs, dual transverse lower links, lower trailing links and link-type stabilizer bar; (Viper) Cast aluminum unequal length upper and lower control arms w/toe-control links, coil springs, low-pressure gas-charged shock absorbers w/adjustable rebound and stabilizer bar. Brakes: Front disc, rear drum (power-assisted) exc. (Stratus ES) Front disc, rear drum w/anti-lock (power-assisted); (Avenger ES, Intrepid ES) four-wheel disc w/anti-lock; (Viper) four-wheel disc. Body construction: Unibody exc. (Viper) backbone tubular space frame w/separate cowl structure. Fuel tank: (Neon) 12.5 gals.; (Avenger) 15.9 gals.; (Stratus) 16 gals.; (Intrepid) 18 gals.; (Viper) 19 gals.

DRIVETRAIN OPTIONS: Engines: DOHC 2.0-liter four: Neon cpe (N/A); Neon sed (N/A); Neon Sport ($150); Avenger ES ($1292 credit). 2.4-liter four: Stratus/Stratus ES ($700). 2.5-liter four: Stratus ES ($800). Transmission: Performance five-speed manual trans.: Neon Sport ($150). Three-speed auto. trans.: Neon ($600). Four-speed auto. trans.: Avenger ($683); Stratus/Stratus ES ($475). AutoStick four-speed auto. trans.: Stratus ES ($970). Brakes: Anti-lock: Neon, all ($565); Avenger, base ($599); Stratus, base ($565). Four-wheel disc w/anti-lock: Intrepid, base ($600-$625). Traction control: w/ABS on Intrepid ES ($175).

NEON CONVENIENCE/APPEARANCE OPTIONS: Base: Pkg. 21A: stnd equip. (NC). Pkg. 22A: 21A exc. 3-spd auto. trans. replaces 5-spd manual ($600). ACR Competition Pkg.: incl. pwr asst. 14-in. disc brakes, unlimited spd engine controller, body-color fascias, dual exterior manual remote mirrors, H.D. radiator, 16:1 pwr asst. steering, competition susp., tach, compact spare tire, P175/65HR14 perf. tires, 14-in. cast alum whls: cpe ($1800); sed ($1630). Highline: Pkg. 21C: stnd equip. (NC). Pkg. 22C: 21C exc. 3-spd auto. trans. replaces 5-spd manual ($600). Pkg. 21D: 21C plus air cond., floor-mounted console, rear window defroster ($785). Pkg. 22D: 21D exc. 3-spd auto. trans. replaces 5-spd manual ($1385). Expresso Pkg. 21G: 21D plus "Expresso" graphics, pwr bulge hood, "Flash Decor" interior trim, decklid spoiler, tach ($965). Expresso Pkg. 22G: 21G exc. 3-spd auto. trans. replaces 5-spd manual ($1565). Sport: Pkg. 21J: stnd equip. (NC). Pkg. 22J: 21J exc. 3-spd auto. trans. replaces 5-spd manual ($600). Pkg. 23J: 21J exc. Perf. 5-spd manual trans. replaces 5-spd manual ($150). Pkg. 24J: 23J exc. 3-spd auto. trans. replaces Perf. 5-spd manual trans. ($750). Pkg. 21K: 21J plus air cond., floor mats, AM/FM stereo radio w/prem. cass. & CD changer & 6 spkrs ($1050). Pkg. 22K: 21K exc. 3-spd auto. trans. replaces 5-spd manual ($1650). Pkg. 23K: 21K exc. DOHC 2.0L four replaces SOHC 2.0L four and Perf. 5-spd manual trans. replaces 5-spd manual ($1200). Pkg. 24K: 23K exc. 3-spd auto. trans. replaces Perf. 5-spd manual ($1800). Other: (AJP) Pwr Convenience Grp.: incl. dual pwr remote mirrors, pwr door locks, stnd Sport: cpe ($260); sed ($300). (AJK) Dlx Convenience Grp.: incl. auto. spd control, tilt stng, Highline ($350). Integrated child seat ($100). Air cond. ($1000). Rear window defroster, base and Highline ($205). Calif. emissions ($105). Floor mats ($50). Light Grp., Highline and Sport ($130). Dual remote manual mirrors, base ($70). Bodyside mldg., base ($60). Pwr moonroof, Highline and Sport ($595). (RAL) AM/FM stereo radio w/clock & 4 spkrs, base ($334). (RAS) AM/FM stereo radio w/cass., clock & 6 prem. spkrs: base ($585); Highline ($250). (RBS) AM/FM stereo radio w/prem. cass., CD changer, clock & 6 prem. spkrs, Highline ($300). (RBG) AM/FM

stereo radio w/CD player, clock & 6 prem. spkrs, Highline and Sport ($180-$480). Remote keyless entry w/panic alarm, Highline and Sport ($155). Speed control, Sport ($224). Tilt stng, base and Highline ($150). Tach & Low Fuel Warning Light, Highline ($95). Extra cost paint, N/A Sport ($100). Pwr windows, Highline and Sport ($265). "Flash" Decor cloth bucket seats, Sport ($120). 14-in. cast alum whls, Sport ($355).

1996 Dodge, Avenger ES coupe (OCW)

AVENGER CONVENIENCE/APPEARANCE OPTIONS: Base: Pkg. 21A: stnd equip. (NC). Pkg. 22A: 21A exc. 4-spd auto. trans. replaces 5-spd manual ($683). Pkg. 21B: 21A plus air cond., floor mats, spd control, AM/FM stereo radio w/cass., clock & 4 spkrs ($1216). Pkg. 22B: 21B exc. 4-spd auto. trans. replaces 5-spd manual ($1899). Pkg. 21C: 21B plus pwr door locks, cargo net, pwr windows, dual pwr remote mirrors ($1750). Pkg. 22C: 21C exc. 4-spd auto. trans. replaces 5-spd manual ($2433). ES: Pkg. 21D: 2.0L four replaces 2.5L V-6 and 5-spd manual trans. replaces 4-spd auto. ($1292 credit). Pkg. 24D: stnd equip. incl. 2.5L V-6 and 4-spd auto. trans. (NC). Pkg. 21E: 21D plus pwr door locks, dual pwr remote mirrors, pwr windows, dual illum. visor mirrors ($1068 credit). Pkg. 24E: 21E plus 2.5L V-6 and 4-spd auto. trans. ($534). Pkg. 21F: 21E plus garage door opener, HomeLink Universal Transmitter, AM/FM stereo radio w/cass./equal./8 spkrs, 6-way pwr driver's seat, sunroof, security alarm ($1017). 24F 21F plus 2.5L V-6 and 4-spd auto. trans. ($2309). Other: Air cond., base ($788). HomeLink garage door opener ($108). 6-way pwr driver's seat ($203). Pwr sunroof ($640). Security alarm w/remote keyless entry and panic alarm ($274). (RAS) Elect. AM/FM stereo radio w/cass., clock & 4 spkrs, stnd ES ($174). (RBN) AM/FM stereo radio w/cass., equal., & 8 Infinity spkrs ($550). (RAZ) AM/FM stereo radio w/cass., CD player, equal., & 8 Infinity spkrs ($292-$842). Leather seats, ES ($423). 16-in. whl grp. incl. P205/55HR16 tires, base ($464).

STRATUS CONVENIENCE/APPEARANCE OPTIONS: Base: Pkg. 21A: stnd equip. (NC). Pkg. 24A: 21A exc. 2.4L four replaces 2.0L four and 4-spd auto. trans. replaces 5-spd manual, incl. cruise control ($1500). Pkg. 21B: 21A plus pwr door locks, dual pwr remote heated mirrors, pwr windows, driver's seat height adj. ($655). Pkg. 24B: 24A plus pwr door locks, dual pwr remote heated mirrors, pwr windows, driver's seat height adj. ($2155). ES: Pkg. 21J: stnd equip. (NC). Pkg. 24J: 21J exc. 2.4L four replaces 2.0L four and 4-spd auto. trans. replaces 5-spd manual ($1275). Pkg. 26R: 21J plus 2.5L V-6 and AutoStick 4-spd auto. trans. ($2225). Pkg. 21K: 21J plus Personal Security Grp., convenience net, security alarm, leather-trimmed seats/stng whl/shift knob, 8-way pwr driver's seat, pwr antenna, prem. AM/FM stereo radio w/cass., clock & 6 spkrs ($1920). Pkg. 24K: 21K plus 2.4L four and 4-spd auto. trans. ($3195). Pkg. 26S: 21K plus 2.5L V-6 and AutoStick 4-spd auto. trans. ($4145). Other: (AJF) Personal Security Grp.: incl. illum. entry, remote keyless entry, panic alarm ($170). Pwr sunroof: base ($695); ES ($580). Integrated child seat ($100). Security alarm, ES ($150). Calif. emissions ($105). Eng. block & battery heater ($30). Extra cost paint: metallic ($150); other ($100). (AR3) Prem. AM/FM stereo radio w/cass., & 8 spkrs ($370). (AR4) Prem. AM/FM stereo radio w/CD player & 8 spkrs ($125-$495). Conventional spare tire ($125).

INTREPID CONVENIENCE/APPEARANCE OPTIONS: Intrepid: Pkg. 22C: stnd equip. (NC). Pkg. 22D: 22C plus 4-whl disc brakes, 8-way pwr driver's seat, message center, dual illum. visor mirrors, AM/FM stereo radio w/cass. & 8 spkrs, remote/illum. entry grp., dual pwr heated outside mirrors ($1235). ES: Pkg. 26L: stnd equip. (NC). Pkg. 26R: 26L exc. AutoStick 4-spd auto. trans. replaces 4-spd auto. trans. plus auto. temp air cond., Chrysler Infinity Spatial Imaging Cass. Sound Syst., full overhead console, security alarm, conventional spare tire, traction control ($1275). Other: (AWT) Perf. Handling Grp.: incl. P225/60R16 perf. tires, perf. susp., ES ($220). Auto. temp air cond., ES ($155). Full overhead console, ES ($385). Calif. emissions ($105). Integrated child seat ($100). Pwr moonroof: base ($1100); ES ($720-$1100). Eng. block heater ($30). 8-way pwr driver's & pass. seats, ES ($380). Leather front bucket seats w/8-way pwr driver's & pass. seats & leather shift knob, ES ($1015). Security alarm, ES ($150). Extra cost paint: metallic ($200); other ($100). (ARH) AM/FM stereo radio w/cass. & 8 spkrs, base ($350). (ARA) Chrysler/Infinity Spatial Imaging Cass. Sound Syst., ES ($300). (ARD) Chrysler/Infinity Spatial Imaging CD Sound Syst., ES ($300-$600). 16-in. Polycast whl, base ($105). Conventional spare tire ($125).

VIPER CONVENIENCE/APPEARANCE OPTIONS: Air cond. ($1200). Body-color detachable hardtop w/sliding side curtains ($2500).

HISTORY: Model year production: 415,485. Calendar year sales: 420,669 (not including imports). A prototype Viper GTS coupe was selected as the pace car for the 1996 Indianapolis 500. The GTS would enter into limited production mid-model year in 1996 as a "companion" model to the RT/10 roadster. The Dodge Intrepid ESX hybrid car made its debut at the North American International Auto Show in Detroit in January 1996. The ESX featured a diesel/electric powerplant coupled with advanced lead/acid batteries to drive twin electric motors, one in each rear-wheel hub. The ESX's unibody was constructed of 100 percent aluminum and the car, overall, weighed 2,880 pounds. The ESX was finished in Chili Pepper Red with two-tone Chili Pepper Red and Driftwood interior colors.

1997 DODGE

The "buzz" created by the Dodge Viper GTS 1996 Indianapolis 500 pace car carried over to the production 1997 GTS coupe, which was not available until mid-model year. Hailed as one of the world's great grand touring cars, the GTS coupe was worthy of the title "instant collectible." The Neon lineup was thinned with the discontinuation of the Sport trim level, but an optional Sport package was offered for Neon Highline coupes and sedans. A Sport package was also available on the base Intrepid sedan. The Avenger ES now used the dual overhead cam 2.0-liter four-cylinder engine as its standard powerplant while the previously standard 2.5-liter V-6 was now optional on both the ES and base Avenger. The imported Dodge Stealth (not covered in this catalog) was also no longer offered.

1997 Dodge, Neon coupe (OCW)

1997 Dodge, Neon Highline sedan (OCW)

1997 Dodge, Neon coupe with optional Sport package (OCW)

NEON — SERIES L — FOUR — The Sport trim level previously offered in the Neon lineup was dropped, but an optional Sport package was offered on the Highline coupe and sedan. Also returning to the lineup was the base coupe and sedan. When the Sport package was ordered,

the resulting Highline coupe or sedan featured the standard 2.0-liter four-cylinder engine paired with a five-speed manual transmission, but the dual overhead cam version of the 2.0-liter four was a no-charge option. Also optional were a three-speed automatic or the performance five-speed manual transmission. The Sport package also consisted of a power bulge hood (when the DOHC engine was ordered) with specific graphics, rear spoiler, fog lights, 14-inch bolt-on wheel covers, silver "Sport" bodyside decals, low-back front bucket seats, Tango cloth interior, 60/40 split-folding rear seatback, 8000-rpm tach and front-passenger grab handle. Eleven exterior colors were offered with the Sport package: Black, Bright White, Light Iris, Brilliant Blue, Bright Jade, Flame Red, Emerald Green, Magenta, Strawberry, Lapis Blue and (new for 1997 on Highline or Sport models) Deep Amethyst. The Transitional Low Emission Vehicle (TLEV) version of the Neon was again offered for California and markets requiring California emission controls. For 1997, Neons received a structural oil pan for quieter operation, reduced evaporative emissions, dynamic side impact protection (sedans only), redesigned bolt-on wheel covers and two new interior color choices: Agate and Camel. New optional equipment included "Tango" cloth interior fabric and CD player (Highline only).

1997 Dodge, Avenger coupe (OCW)

1997 Dodge, Avenger ES coupe (OCW)

AVENGER — SERIES J — FOUR/V-6 — The Avenger lineup continued to feature base and ES trim levels, but the series' powertrain availability was juggled from what was previously offered. The standard powertrain for both base and ES coupes was now the dual overhead cam 2.0-liter four-cylinder engine mated to a five-speed manual transmission. Formerly standard on the ES, the Mitsubishi-built 2.5-liter V-6 was now optional on both Avenger trim levels. An electronically controlled four-speed automatic transmission with overdrive was optional on base models with either engine, but available only on the ES when the V-6 was ordered. The Avenger's exterior was revised for 1997. Up front changes included a new fascia featuring headlamp masks and turn lamps and different badge location. Base Avengers also received new 14-inch wheel covers while ES coupes added fog lamps. At the rear, the new fascia contained combination lamps and dimensional badging. ES models added a decklid spoiler. New exterior color choices were Pewter Blue (replaced Medium Gray), Bright Jade (replaced Prism Blue), and Paprika. Inside, a new black and tan color scheme was offered. When the ES coupe was ordered with the V-6, equipment included a handling suspension featuring 17-inch cast aluminum wheels fitted with P215/50HR17 tires.

STRATUS — SERIES A — FOUR/V-6 — Base and ES sedans again comprised the Stratus sedan lineup. Powertrain availability carried over from the year previous with the exception of the ES sedan's optional 2.5-liter V-6 that was now paired with the AutoStick four-speed automatic transmission (which debuted late in the model year the previous year). Also, the 2.4-liter four-cylinder engine that was optional across-the-board received both a redesigned intake manifold and oil pan for quieter operation. Among the new features found in the Stratus were improved audio systems (both cassette and CD), monochrome fascias, a floor console with armrest and covered storage, electroluminescent PRNDL display in console, automatic transmission shifter boot, increased-flow rear seat heat ducts, map lamps that operated as courtesy lamps (ES only) and two new exterior color choices: Dark Chestnut (replaced Orchid) and Deep Amethyst (replaced Light Gold).

1997 Dodge, Intrepid sedan (OCW)

INTREPID — SERIES H — V-6 — This was the final year for the original cab-forward-design Intrepid, launched in 1993, as an all-new model was scheduled to debut in 1998. The base and ES trim levels returned with an optional Sport package available on base sedans. The powertrain lineup consisted of the 3.3-liter V-6 linked to an electronically controlled four-speed automatic transmission with overdrive again standard in the base Intrepid, the 3.5-liter V-6 paired with a four-speed automatic again used in the ES sedan, and the 3.5-liter V-6 mated to an AutoStick four-speed automatic installed when the Sport sedan was ordered. AutoStick was also optional on the ES sedan. Other features of the Sport package included an eight-way power driver's seat, leather-wrapped steering wheel and shift knob, instrument panel message center, "Sport" badging, and "Fortress" wheel covers (white or silver). New features for the 1997 Intrepid included software refinements for the automatic transmission for smoother shifting, upgraded cassette audio system and one exterior color choice: Deep Amethyst.

1997 Dodge, Viper GTS coupe (OCW)

VIPER — SERIES R — V-10 — The Viper lineup now included a GTS coupe as a companion to the RT/10 roadster, both launched mid-model year 1997. The detachable hardtop with sliding side curtains was again offered as a delete-option with the roadster, which the buyer could cancel to save money on the overall price of the car. The mid-model year debut of the (very) limited edition GTS the year previous also introduced the second-generation V-10, which also found its way under the hood of the RT/10. The new V-10 mimicked the all-aluminum composition and 488 cubic inch displacement of its predecessor, but weighed less (80 pounds) and offered higher output with 450 horsepower (compared to the previous 415) and 490 pound-feet of torque (vs. the former 488). The next-generation 8.0-liter V-10 featured aluminum, ram-tuned intake manifolds with dual plenums and sequential multipoint fuel injection with bottom-fed, high-impedance injectors. In both the GTS and RT/10 this engine was again paired with a performance six-speed manual transmission. While the GTS coupe appeared similar in design to the RT/10 roadster, 90 percent of the car was new including its body and interior. Inside, the GTS featured dual airbags, a new instrument panel with revised gauge location and a pioneering adjustable pedal system whereby the driver could move the clutch, brake and accelerator pedals up to four inches closer by simply turning a knob mounted under the steering column. This system was also incorporated into the RT/10 along with tilt steering and an adjustable seat that allowed 5.2 inches of fore-and-aft travel. The Viper braking system consisted of power-assisted four-piston caliper front disc brakes and a single-piston rear disc design. The instrument panel featured full analog instrumentation with a 7000-rpm tach, 200-mph speedometer, engine coolant gauge, oil pressure gauge, fuel gauge and voltmeter. Both Viper hardtops and ragtops rode on Michelin Pilot SX MXX3 performance tires on 17-inch cast aluminum wheels. Exterior color schemes were Viper Blue with white stripes (GTS and RT/10) and Viper Red (both) with gold wheels (RT/10) or yellow wheels (GTS).

I.D. DATA: Dodge's 17-symbol Vehicle Identification Number (VIN), as before, was on the upper left corner of the instrument panel, visible through the windshield. Coding is similar to 1986-96. Symbol ten (model year) changed to 'V' for 1997.

NEON (FOUR)

Model No.	Body/ Style No.	Body Type & Seating	Factory Price	Shipping Weight	Prod. Total
LDL	22	2-dr. Coupe-5P	10395	2389	Note 1
LDL	42	4-dr. Sedan-5P	10595	2399	Note 2

NEON HIGHLINE (FOUR)

Model No.	Body/Style No.	Body Type & Seating	Factory Price	Shipping Weight	Prod. Total
LDH	22	2-dr. Coupe-5P	12470	2416	Note 1
LDH	42	4-dr. Sedan-5P	12670	2459	Note 2

Note: Plymouth Neon production totals are separate and can be found in the Plymouth listings.

Note 1: Dodge Neon two-door production totaled 29,551 with no further breakout available.

Note 2: Dodge Neon four-door production totaled 85,559 with no further breakout available.

AVENGER (FOUR/V-6)

JDH	22	2-dr. Coupe-4P	14620/15450	2822/N/A	Note 1
JDS	22	2-dr. ES Coupe-4P	17490/18205	3084/N/A	Note 1

Note: Prices and weights to left of slash for four-cylinder, to right for V-6.

Note 1: Avenger production totaled 32,601 with no further breakout available.

STRATUS (FOUR/V-6)

ADH	41	4-dr. Sedan-5P	14960/-----	2911/----	Note 1
ADP	41	4-dr. ES Sedan-5P	16665/17815	2968/N/A	Note 1

Note: Prices and weights to left of slash for four-cylinder, to right for V-6.

Note 1: Stratus production totaled 96,757 with no further breakout available.

INTREPID (V-6)

HDH	41	4-dr. Sedan-6P	19405	3349	Note 1
HDP	41	4-dr. ES Sedan-6P	22910	3440	Note 1

Note 1: Intrepid sedan production totaled 151,404 with no further breakout available.

VIPER (V-10)

RDS	27	2-dr. RT/10 Rdstr-2P	58600	3319	N/A
RDS	29	2-dr. GTS Cpe-2P	66000	3383	954

ENGINE DATA: BASE FOUR (Neon, Neon Highline, Stratus, Stratus ES): Inline, overhead cam four-cylinder. Cast iron block; aluminum head. Displacement: 121 cu. in. (2.0 liters). Bore & stroke: 3.44 x 3.27 in. Compression ratio: 9.8:1. Brake horsepower: 132 at 6000 RPM. Torque: 129 lb.-ft. at 5000 RPM. Sequential fuel injection. OPTIONAL FOUR (Neon, Neon Highline): Inline, dual overhead cam four-cylinder. Cast iron block; aluminum head. Displacement: 121 cu. in. (2.0 liters). Bore & stroke: 3.44 x 3.27 in. Compression ratio: 9.6:1. Brake horsepower: 150 at 6500 RPM. Torque: 133 lb.-ft. at 5500 RPM. Sequential fuel injection. BASE FOUR (Avenger, Avenger ES): Inline, dual overhead cam four-cylinder. Cast iron block; aluminum head. Displacement: 121 cu. in. (2.0 liters). Bore & stroke: 3.44 x 3.27 in. Compression ratio: 9.6:1. Brake horsepower: 140 at 6000 RPM. Torque: 130 lb.-ft. at 4800 RPM. Sequential fuel injection. OPTIONAL FOUR (Stratus, Stratus ES): Inline, dual overhead cam four-cylinder. Cast iron block; aluminum head. Displacement: 148 cu. in. (2.4 liters). Bore & stroke: 3.44 x 3.98 in. Compression ratio: 9.4:1. Brake horsepower: 150 at 5200 RPM. Torque: 165 lb.-ft. at 4000 RPM. Sequential fuel injection. OPTIONAL V-6 (Avenger, Avenger ES, Stratus ES): Overhead cam V-6. Cast iron block; aluminum heads. Displacement: 152 cu. in. (2.5 liters). Bore & stroke: 3.29 x 2.99 in. Compression ratio: 9.4:1. Brake horsepower: (Avenger, Avenger ES) 163 at 5500 RPM; (Stratus ES) 168 at 5800 RPM. Torque: (all) 170 lb.-ft. at 4350 RPM. Sequential fuel injection. BASE V-6 (Intrepid): Overhead valve V-6. Cast iron block; aluminum heads. Displacement: 201 cu. in. (3.3 liters). Bore & stroke: 3.66 x 3.19 in. Compression ratio: 8.9:1. Brake horsepower: 161 at 5300 RPM. Torque: 181 lb.-ft. at 3200 RPM. Sequential fuel injection. BASE V-6 (Intrepid ES): Overhead cam V-6. Cast iron block; aluminum heads. Displacement: 214 cu. in. (3.5 liters). Bore & stroke: 3.78 x 3.19 in. Compression ratio: 9.6:1. Brake horsepower: 214 at 5850 RPM. Torque: 221 lb.-ft. at 3100 RPM. Sequential fuel injection. BASE V-10 (Viper): Overhead valve V-10. Aluminum block and heads. Displacement: 488 cu. in. (8.0 liters). Bore & stroke: 4.00 x 3.88 in. Compression ratio: 9.6:1. Brake horsepower: 450 at 5200 RPM. Torque: 490 lb.-ft. at 3700 RPM. Sequential fuel injection.

CHASSIS DATA: Wheelbase: (Neon) 104.0 in.; (Avenger) 103.7 in.; (Stratus) 108.0 in.; (Intrepid) 113.0 in.; (Viper) 96.2 in. Overall length: (Neon) 171.8 in.; (Avenger) 190.4 in.; (Stratus) 186.0 in.; (Intrepid) 201.8 in.; (Viper RT/10) 175.1 in.; (Viper GTS) 176.7 in. Height: (Neon cpe) 53.0 in.; (Neon sed) 52.8 in.; (Avenger) 53.0 in.; (Stratus) 54.1 in.; (Intrepid) 56.3 in.; (Viper RT/10) 44.0 in.; (Viper GTS) 47.0 in.

Width: (Neon) 67.5 in.; (Avenger) 69.1 in.; (Stratus) 71.7 in.; (Intrepid) 74.4 in.; (Viper) 75.7 in. Front Tread: (Neon) 57.4 in.; (Avenger) 59.5 in.; (Stratus) 60.2 in.; (Intrepid) 62.0 in.; (Viper) 59.6 in. Rear Tread: (Neon) 57.4 in.; (Avenger) 59.3 in.; (Stratus) 60.2 in.; (Intrepid) 62.0 in.; (Viper) 60.6 in. Standard Tires: (Neon) P175/70R14; (Neon Highline) P185/65R14; (Avenger) P195/70HR14; (Avenger ES) P205/55HR16; (Stratus) P195/70R14; (Stratus ES) P195/65HR15; (Intrepid - all) P225/60R16; (Viper) P275/40ZR17 front/P335/35ZR17 rear.

TECHNICAL: Transmission: Five-speed manual standard on Neon (all), Avenger (all), Stratus (all). Four-speed automatic standard on Intrepid (all). Six-speed manual standard on Viper (all). Steering: (all) Rack and pinion. Front suspension: (Neon) MacPherson struts, asymmetrical lower control arms, coil springs and link-type stabilizer bar; (Avenger) Modified double-wishbone w/coil springs, direct acting shock absorbers and link-type stabilizer bar; (Stratus) Unequal length upper and lower control arms, coil springs, tubular shock absorbers and stabilizer bar (higher rate springs on ES); (Intrepid) Iso-strut w/integral gas-charged shock absorbers, coil springs, single transverse lower links, tension struts and link-type stabilizer bar (stiffer springs and firmer shock absorbers optional on ES); (Viper) Cast aluminum unequal length upper and lower control arms, coil springs, low-pressure gas-charged shock absorbers w/adjustable rebound and stabilizer bar. Rear suspension: (Neon) Chapman struts, coil springs, dual lower transverse links, lower trailing links; (Avenger) Double wishbones, coil springs, direct acting shock absorbers and (ES only) link-type stabilizer bar; (Stratus) Unequal length upper and lower control arms, trailing arms, coil springs, tubular shock absorbers and stabilizer bar (larger stabilizer bar with optional 2.5-liter V-6 and higher rate springs on ES); (Intrepid) Chapman struts w/integral gas-charged shock absorbers, concentric coil springs, dual transverse lower links, lower trailing links and link-type stabilizer bar (stiffer springs and firmer shock absorbers optional on ES); (Viper) Cast aluminum unequal length upper and lower control arms w/toe-control links, coil springs, low-pressure gas-charged shock absorbers w/adjustable rebound and stabilizer bar. Brakes: Front disc, rear drum (power-assisted) exc. (Stratus ES) Front disc, rear drum w/anti-lock (power-assisted) (Avenger ES, Intrepid ES) four-wheel disc w/anti-lock; (Viper) four-wheel disc. Body construction: Unibody exc. (Viper) backbone tubular space frame w/separate cowl structure. Fuel tank: (Neon) 12.5 gals.; (Avenger) 16 gals.; (Stratus) 16 gals.; (Intrepid) 18 gals.; (Viper) 19 gals.

DRIVETRAIN OPTIONS: Engines: DOHC 2.0-liter four: Neon cpe (N/A); Neon Highline ($300). 2.4-liter four: Stratus/Stratus ES ($700). 2.5-liter four: Avenger/Avenger ES ($673); Stratus ES ($800). Transmission: Three-speed auto. trans.: Neon ($600). Four-speed auto. trans.: Avenger ($695); Stratus/Stratus ES ($475). AutoStick four-speed auto. trans.: Stratus ES ($970); Intrepid ES (N/A). Brakes: Anti-lock: Neon, all ($565); Avenger, base ($599); Stratus, base ($565). Four-wheel disc w/anti-lock: Intrepid, base ($600-$625). Traction control: w/ABS on Intrepid ES ($175).

NEON CONVENIENCE/APPEARANCE OPTIONS: Base: Pkg. 21A: stnd equip. (NC). Pkg. 22A: 21A exc. 3-spd auto. trans. replaces 5-spd manual ($600). Highline: Pkg. 21D: stnd equip. (NC). Pkg. 22D: 21D exc. 3-spd auto. trans. replaces 5-spd manual ($600). Sport Pkg. 21G: 21D plus "Sport" graphics, pwr bulge hood, "Tango" interior trim, decklid spoiler, tach, 14-in. Sport whl covers, painted fascias, foglamps, low-back bucket seats, 60/40 rear fldng bench seat ($300). Pkg. 22G: 21G exc. 3-spd auto. trans. replaces 5-spd manual ($900). Pkg. 23G: 21G exc. DOHC 2.0L four replaces SOHC 2.0L four ($300). Pkg. 24G: 21G exc. DOHC 2.0L four replaces SOHC 2.0L four and 3-spd auto. trans. replaces 5-spd manual ($900). Competition: Pkg. 23A: ACR Competition Pkg.: incl. pwr asst. 14-in. disc brakes, DOHC 2.0L four (N/A base sed), pwr bulge hood, unlimited spd engine controller, body-color fascias, dual exterior manual remote mirrors, H.D. radiator, 16:1 pwr asst. steering, competition susp., tach, compact spare tire, P175/65HR14 perf. tires (sed)/P185/60HR14 perf. tires (cpe), 14-in. cast alum whls: cpe ($1750); sed w/SOHC 2.0L four ($1560). Other: (ANC) National Champion Int. Pkg.: incl. "Tango" cloth int. trim, low-back bucket seats, 60/40 rear fldng bench seat, leather-wrapped stng whl & shift knob, base ($500). (AJP) Pwr Convenience Grp.: incl. dual pwr remote mirrors, pwr door locks, Highline: (cpe $260); sed ($300). (AJK) Dlx Convenience Grp.: incl. auto. spd control, tilt stng, Highline ($350). Integrated child seat ($100). Air cond. ($1000). Rear window defroster ($205). Calif. emissions ($170). Floor mats ($50). Light Grp., Highline ($130). Body-color mldg ($60). Pwr moonroof ($595). (RAL) AM/FM stereo radio & 4 spkrs, base ($335). (RAS) AM/FM stereo radio w/cass. & 8 spkrs: base ($595); Highline ($260). (RBS) AM/FM stereo radio w/prem. cass., CD changer & 8 spkrs, Highline ($285). (RBR) AM/FM stereo radio w/CD player & 8 spkrs ($395). Remote keyless entry w/panic alarm, Highline ($155). Tilt stng, base ($150). Tach & Low Fuel Warning Light, Highline ($100). Pwr windows, Highline ($265). 14-in. cast alum whls, Highline ($355).

AVENGER CONVENIENCE/APPEARANCE OPTIONS: Base: Pkg. 21A: stnd equip. (NC). Pkg. 22A: 21A exc. 4-spd auto. trans. replaces 5-spd manual ($695). Pkg. 21B: 21A plus air cond., floor mats, spd control, AM/FM stereo radio w/cass. & 6 spkrs ($1308). Pkg. 22B: 21B exc. 4-spd auto. trans. replaces 5-spd manual ($2003). Pkg. 21C: 21B plus pwr door locks, cargo net, pwr windows, dual pwr remote mirrors ($1844). Pkg. 22C: 21C exc. 4-spd auto. trans. replaces 5-spd manual ($2539). Pkg. 24V: 21C exc. 2.5L V-6 replaces 2.0L four and 4-spd auto. trans. replaces 5-spd manual plus 16-in. whl grp. ($3702). ES: Pkg. 21D: stnd equip. (NC). Pkg. 24D: 21D exc. 2.5L V-6 replaces 2.0L four and 4-spd auto. trans. replaces 5-spd manual ($1410). Pkg. 21E: 21D plus pwr door locks, dual pwr remote mirrors, pwr windows, dual illum. visor mirrors ($536). Pkg. 24E: 21E plus 2.5L V-6 and 4-spd auto. trans. replaces ($1946). Pkg. 21F: 21E plus garage door opener, HomeLink Universal Transmitter, AM/FM stereo radio w/cass./CD player/6 spkrs, 6-way pwr driver's seat, security alarm ($1569). Pkg. 24F: 21F plus 2.5L V-6 and 4-spd auto. trans. ($2979). Other: Air cond., base ($788). 6-way pwr driver's seat ($203). Pwr sunroof ($640). Security alarm w/remote keyless entry and panic alarm ($287). Calif. emissions ($170). (RBX) AM/FM stereo radio w/CD & cass. & 6 spkrs ($435). (RAZ) AM/FM stereo radio w/CD & cass., equal. & 8 Infinity spkrs, ES ($326-$760). Leather seats, ES ($423). 16-in. whl grp. incl. P205/55HR16 tires, base ($490).

1997 Dodge, Stratus sedan (OCW)

STRATUS CONVENIENCE/APPEARANCE OPTIONS: Base: Pkg. 21A: stnd equip. (NC). Pkg. 24A: 21A exc. 2.4L four replaces 2.0L four and 4-spd auto. trans. replaces 5-spd manual, incl. elect. spd control ($1500). Pkg. 21B: 21A plus pwr door locks, dual pwr remote heated mirrors, pwr windows, driver's seat height adj. ($685). Pkg. 24B: 21B incl. 2.4L four replaces 2.0L four and 4-spd auto. trans. replaces 5-spd manual, incl. elect. spd control ($2185). ES: Pkg. 21J: stnd equip. (NC). Pkg. 24J: 21J exc. 2.4L four replaces 2.0L four and 4-spd auto. trans. replaces 5-spd manual ($1275). Pkg. 26R: 24J exc. 2.5L V-6 replaces 2.4L four and AutoStick 4-spd auto. trans. replaces 4-spd auto. trans. ($2225). Pkg. 21K: 21J plus Personal Security Grp., convenience net, security alarm, leather-trimmed seats/stng whl/shift knob, 8-way pwr driver's seat, prem. AM/FM stereo radio w/cass., CD changer & 8 spkrs ($1805). Pkg. 24K: 21K incl. 2.4L four and 4-spd auto. trans. ($3080). Pkg. 26S: 24K exc. 2.5L V-6 replaces 2.4L four and AutoStick 4-spd auto. trans. replaces 4-spd auto. trans. ($4030). Other: (AJF) Personal Security Grp.: incl. illum. entry, remote keyless entry, panic alarm, head-lamp time delay ($170). Integrated child seat ($100). Security alarm, ES ($150). Calif. emissions ($170). Eng. block & battery heater ($30). (AR3) Prem. AM/FM stereo radio w/cass., CD changer & 8 spkrs ($340). (AR4) Prem. AM/FM stereo radio w/CD player & 4 spkrs ($200). (AR5) Prem. AM/FM stereo radio w/cass., CD changer & 4 spkrs ($550). In-dash CD changer, ES ($500). Conventional spare tire ($125).

INTREPID CONVENIENCE/APPEARANCE OPTIONS: Intrepid: Pkg. 22C: stnd equip. (NC). Sport Pkg. 22E: 22C exc. 3.5L V-6 replaces 3.3L V-6 and AutoStick 4-spd auto. trans. replaces 4-spd auto. trans. plus "Sport" badging, message center, 8-way pwr driver's seat, leather-wrapped stng whl & shift knob ($800). ES: Pkg. 26L: stnd equip. (NC). Pkg. 26R: 26L exc. AutoStick 4-spd auto. trans. replaces 4-spd auto. trans. plus auto. temp air cond., Chrysler Infinity Spatial Imaging Cass. Sound Syst., full overhead console, security alarm, conventional spare tire, traction control ($1400). Other: (AJK) Convenience Grp.: incl. message center, illum. visor mirrors, remote/illum. keyless entry, remote decklid release, base ($395-$420). (AWT) Perf. Handling Grp.: incl. P225/60VR16 perf. tires, perf. susp., ES ($220). Auto. temp air cond.,

ES ($155). Full overhead console, ES ($385). Calif. emissions ($170). Pwr moonroof: base ($1100-$1275); ES ($720-$1100). Eng. block heater ($20). 8-way pwr driver's & pass. seats, ES ($380). Leather front bucket seats w/8-way pwr driver's & pass. seats & leather shift knob, ES ($1015). Security alarm, ES ($150). Extra cost paint: metallic ($200). (ARH) AM/FM stereo radio w/cass., seek/scan, CD changer & 8 spkrs, base ($350). (ARA) Chrysler/Infinity Spatial Imaging Cass. Sound Syst., ES ($215). (ARD) Chrysler/Infinity Spatial Imaging CD Sound Syst., ES ($300-$515). 16-in. Polycast whl, base ($105). Conventional spare tire ($125).

VIPER CONVENIENCE/APPEARANCE OPTIONS: RT/10: Air cond. ($1200). Body-color detachable hardtop w/sliding side curtains ($2500). Yellow Gold cast alum whls (NC). GTS: Viper Blue pearlcoat paint w/dual white stripes ($1200). Polished cast alum whls ($300). Sparkle Gold cast alum whls (NC).

HISTORY: Model year production: 396,826. Calendar year sales: 372,832. It had been over 65 years since a Chrysler-badged vehicle entered the 24 Hours of Le Mans in France. Chrysler Corp. returned in 1996, fielding a GTS-R (production-based racing version of the GTS coupe). In 1997, Viper GTS-Rs garnered two FIA GT2 class world motorsports championships, the first time a U.S. automaker had won a world championship with a production-based vehicle.

1998 DODGE

An all-new Intrepid debuted in 1998 and featured second-generation cab-forward design. The Neon lineup was revamped with the former base coupe and sedan discontinued. Neons were now available in three package formats: Highline, Sport and R/T. An optional Sport package was available to "gussy up" the Avenger coupe. The Stratus ES sedan's previously optional 2.4-liter four-cylinder engine and four-speed automatic transmission powertrain combination was now standard.

1998 Dodge, Stratus ES sedan (OCW)

NEON — SERIES L — FOUR — Flush with success in Sports Car Club of America Showroom Stock competition, the Neon series was revamped in 1998 to reflect the car's racing prowess. Gone were the previously offered base coupe and sedan, that entry level position filled by the former second tier Highline coupe and sedan. In addition to the Highline trim level (or package), two other Neon packages available were the Sport and R/T coupes and sedans. An optional ARC Competition Group package was also offered and included four-wheel disc brakes, firm-feel power steering, competition suspension, and leather-wrapped steering wheel and shift knob. The Neon R/T paid homage to Dodge's famed R/T performance models of earlier eras. Underneath its "Viper stripes" with a Flame Red, Intense Blue or Bright White exterior colors was the dual overhead cam 2.0-liter four-cylinder engine, rated at 150 horsepower, linked to five-speed manual transmission. Inside, the R/T carried on the performance theme with unique bucket seats and leather-wrapped steering wheel and shift knob. The R/T also featured a sport suspension with sway bars front and rear, along with unique springs and rear spring isolators. A 16:1 steering gear ratio, four-wheel disc brakes and 14-inch polished aluminum wheels rounded out the package. All 1998 Neons benefited from NVH (noise, vibration and harshness) reduction including a new transmission housing structural collar. As did other Chrysler products, the Neon received next-generation airbags for driver and passenger. Highline models were powered by the 2.0-liter four-cylinder engine paired with a five-speed manual transmission. Standard features of this newly-entry level Neon included an upgraded interior, low-back bucket seats, remote trunk release and fold-down rear seat. Sport coupes featured the same powertrain as the R/T while Sport sedans used the Highline engine/transmission combination with the DOHC 2.0-liter four a no-cost option.

AVENGER — SERIES J — FOUR/V-6 — In addition to the returning base and ES trim levels, the Avenger lineup now included an optional Sport package that dressed up the base coupe. The Sport model featured new 16-inch aluminum wheels, decklid spoiler, leather-wrapped steering wheel and was powered by the 2.5-liter V-6 linked to an electronically controlled four-speed automatic transmission with overdrive. This combination was again optional for base and ES coupes. All Avengers again used the dual overhead cam 2.0-liter four-cylinder engine paired with a five-speed manual transmission as standard power source. The four-speed automatic was also optional with the 2.0-liter four on the base coupe only. New features included dynamic side impact protection, dual airbags with an accident response system that electronically unlocked all doors and lit the interior after a deployment, revised cloth interior fabrics, a gray/black interior color scheme, and one new exterior color choice: Caffe Latte. The ES coupe added a six-way power driver's seat and leather-trimmed seating to complement either the black and tan or black and gray interior color schemes. The 2.0-liter ES model also received a rear sway bar, which was formerly only available when the V-6 was ordered.

1998 Dodge, Intrepid ES sedan (OCW)

STRATUS — SERIES A — FOUR/V-6 — Stratus was again available in base and ES trim levels, with the base sedan again powered by the 2.0-liter four-cylinder engine paired with a five-speed manual transmission. New for 1998, the ES sedan's standard powertrain was the previously optional dual overhead cam 2.4-liter four mated to an electronically controlled four-speed automatic with overdrive, which remained optional on the base Stratus. Optional powertrain for the ES model was again the 2.5-liter V-6 linked to the AutoStick four-speed automatic. Both TLEV (transitional low emissions vehicle) and LEV versions of Stratus power-plants were available markets requiring those standards. The ES sedan also received a leather-wrapped steering wheel and shift knob as standard fare. New safety features included next-generation dual airbags, dynamic side impact protection, front seat height adjustable shoulder belts and an optional personal security package. Five new exterior color choices were Deep Cranberry, Alpine Green, Bright Platinum, Champagne Pearl and Deep Slate.

INTREPID — SERIES H — V-6 — The second-generation cab-forward design 1998 Intrepid retained only the base and ES trim level designations of its predecessor, otherwise it was an all-new automobile. Gone were the 3.3-liter and 3.5-liter V-6s that previously powered the base and ES sedans, respectively. The new engine lineup was comprised of two all-aluminum V-6s that were 25 percent more powerful and 10 percent more fuel efficient than the units they replaced. Both engines featured direct coil-on-plug ignition systems and platinum-tipped spark plugs that provided 100,000-mile intervals between tune-ups. The base Intrepid's power source was a 24-valve 2.7-liter V-6, rated at 200 horse-power, linked to an electronically controlled four-speed automatic transmission with overdrive. The ES sedan used a 220-horsepower 3.2-liter V-6 paired with the AutoStick four-speed automatic that allowed drivers to shift gears without using a clutch. The exterior appearance of the new Intrepid borrowed heavily from the 1998 ESX concept car's streamlined, muscular shape. Specific design cues for the 1998 Intrepid sedan included a prominent "cross hair" grille while its roofline and shortened rear deck resulted in a coupe-like profile and resulted in the car achieving a low 0.30 coefficient of drag. New, larger quad-system headlamps

wrapped into the front fenders allowing for a "sportier" stance. The headlamp's low beam output was 50 percent brighter and high beam output was 100 percent brighter compared to the previous units. The new Intrepid could accommodate up to six passengers due to the car's floor console being integrated into the center of the instrument panel for the five-passenger version while a separate center console lower section was created for the optional 50/50 front seat for six passenger use. Other new features included next-generation dual airbags, four-wheel disc brakes on the base sedan (already standard with anti-lock braking system on ES), a softer steering wheel rim with centered horn function, remote trunk release repositioned from inside the glovebox to the left side of the steering column, flush-mounted stereo and ventilation system controls and, on the ES, a 60/40 split-folding rear seat for increased cargo space.

1998 Dodge, Viper GTS coupe (OCW)

VIPER — SERIES R — V-10 — The RT/10 roadster and GTS coupe again comprised the Viper lineup, both receiving subtle upgrades for 1998. After being lightened the previous year, the Viper's 8.0-liter V-10's weight was further reduced through the use of tubular stainless steel exhaust manifolds. A low-overlap camshaft helped to reduce emissions and improve fuel economy while an electronic radiator fan control reduced noise. Vipers continued to use a six-speed manual transmission. New safety features included next-generation dual airbags including a passenger airbag cut-off switch, leak-resistant battery case and battery saver. Security was also improved with revised key locks and a keyless entry system. The Viper's 1998 colors included Bright Metallic Silver and Red, both matched with a black monochromatic interior.

I.D. DATA: Dodge's 17-symbol Vehicle Identification Number (VIN), as before, was on the upper left corner of the instrument panel, visible through the windshield. Coding is similar to 1986-97. Symbol ten (model year) changed to 'W' for 1998.

NEON HIGHLINE (FOUR)

Model No.	Body/ Style No.	Body Type & Seating	Factory Price	Shipping Weight	Prod. Total
LDH	22	2-dr. Coupe-5P	11155	2470	Note 1
LDH	42	4-dr. Sedan-5P	11355	2507	Note 2

NEON SPORT (FOUR)

LDL	22	2-dr. Coupe-5P	12980	N/A	Note 1
LDL	42	4-dr. Sedan-5P	13160	N/A	Note 2

NEON R/T (FOUR)

N/A	22	2-dr. Coupe-5P	13895	N/A	Note 1
N/A	42	4-dr. Sedan-5P	14095	N/A	Note 2

Note: Plymouth Neon production totals are separate and can be found in the Plymouth listings.

Note 1: Dodge Neon two-door production totaled 29,886 with no further breakout available.

Note 2: Dodge Neon four-door production totaled 99,989 with no further breakout available.

AVENGER (FOUR/V-6)

JDH	22	2-dr. Coupe-4P	14930/15605	2888/N/A	Note 1
JDS	22	2-dr. ES Coupe-4P	17310/17920	2989/N/A	Note 1

Note: Prices and weights to left of slash for four-cylinder, to right for V-6.

Note 1: Avenger production totaled 26,603 with no further breakout available.

STRATUS (FOUR/V-6)

ADH	41	4-dr. Sedan-5P	14840/-----	2919/----	Note 1
ADP	41	4-dr. ES Sedan-5P	17665/18465	2958/N/A	Note 1

Note: Prices and weights to left of slash for four-cylinder, to right for V-6.

Note 1: Stratus production totaled 107,136 with no further breakout available.

INTREPID (V-6)

HDH	41	4-dr. Sedan-6P	19685	3422	Note 1
HDP	41	4-dr. ES Sedan-6P	22465	3517	Note 1

Note 1: Intrepid sedan production totaled 70,266 with no further breakout available.

VIPER (V-10)

RDS	27	2-dr. RT/10 Rdstr-2P	64000	3319	74
RDS	29	2-dr. GTS Cpe-2P	66500	3383	848

ENGINE DATA: BASE FOUR (Neon Highline, Neon Sport sed, Stratus): Inline, overhead cam four-cylinder. Cast iron block; aluminum head. Displacement: 121 cu. in. (2.0 liters). Bore & stroke: 3.44 x 3.27 in. Compression ratio: 9.8:1. Brake horsepower: 132 at 6000 RPM. Torque: 129 lb.-ft. at 5000 RPM. Sequential fuel injection. BASE FOUR (Neon Sport cpe, Neon R/T); OPTIONAL FOUR (Neon Highline): Inline, dual overhead cam four-cylinder. Cast iron block; aluminum head. Displacement: 121 cu. in. (2.0 liters). Compression ratio: 9.6:1. Brake horsepower: 150 at 6500 RPM. Torque: 133 lb.-ft. at 5500 RPM. Sequential fuel injection. BASE FOUR (Avenger, Avenger ES): Inline, dual overhead cam four-cylinder. Cast iron block; aluminum head. Displacement: 121 cu. in. (2.0 liters). Bore & stroke: 3.44 x 3.27 in. Compression ratio: 9.6:1. Brake horsepower: 140 at 6000 RPM. Torque: 130 lb.-ft. at 4800 RPM. Sequential fuel injection. BASE FOUR (Stratus ES); OPTIONAL FOUR (Stratus): Inline, dual overhead cam four-cylinder. Cast iron block; aluminum head. Displacement: 146 cu. in. (2.4 liters). Bore & stroke: 3.44 x 3.98 in. Compression ratio: 9.4:1. Brake horsepower: 150 at 5200 RPM. Torque: 167 lb.-ft. at 4000 RPM. Sequential fuel injection. OPTIONAL V-6 (Avenger, Avenger ES, Stratus ES): Overhead cam V-6. Cast iron block; aluminum heads. Displacement: 152 cu. in. (2.5 liters). Bore & stroke: 3.29 x 2.99 in. Compression ratio: (Avenger, Avenger ES) 9.2:1; (Stratus ES) 9.4:1. Brake horsepower: (Avenger, Avenger ES) 163 at 5500 RPM; (Stratus ES) 168 at 5800 RPM. Torque: (all) 170 lb.-ft. at 4350 RPM. Sequential fuel injection. BASE V-6 (Intrepid): Overhead valve V-6. Aluminum block and heads. Displacement: 167 cu. in. (2.7 liters). Bore & stroke: 3.38 x 3.09 in. Compression ratio: 9.7:1. Brake horsepower: 200 at 5800 RPM. Torque: 190 lb.-ft. at 4850 RPM. Sequential fuel injection. BASE V-6 (Intrepid ES): Overhead cam V-6. Aluminum block and heads. Displacement: 197 cu. in. (3.2 liters). Bore & stroke: 3.62 x 3.19 in. Compression ratio: 9.5:1. Brake horsepower: 220 at 6300 RPM. Torque: 225 lb.-ft. at 4000 RPM. Sequential fuel injection. BASE V-10 (Viper): Overhead valve V-10. Aluminum block and heads. Displacement: 488 cu. in. (8.0 liters). Bore & stroke: 4.00 x 3.88 in. Compression ratio: 9.6:1. Brake horsepower: 450 at 5200 RPM. Torque: 490 lb.-ft. at 3700 RPM. Sequential fuel injection.

CHASSIS DATA: Wheelbase: (Neon) 104.0 in.; (Avenger) 103.7 in.; (Stratus) 108.0 in.; (Intrepid) 113.0 in.; (Viper) 96.2 in. Overall length: (Neon) 171.8 in.; (Avenger) 190.4 in.; (Stratus) 186.0 in.; (Intrepid) 203.7 in.; (Viper RT/10) 175.1 in.; (Viper GTS) 176.7 in. Height: (Neon Highline, Neon Sport) 54.9 in.; (Neon R/T cpe) 53.0 in.; (Neon R/T sed) 52.8 in.; (Avenger) 53.0 in.; (Stratus) 54.1 in.; (Intrepid) 55.9 in.; (Viper RT/10) 44.0 in.; (Viper GTS) 47.0 in. Width: (Neon cpe) 67.4 in.; (Neon sed) 67.2 in.; (Avenger) 69.1 in.; (Stratus) 71.7 in.; (Intrepid) 74.7 in.; (Viper) 75.7 in. Front Tread: (Neon) 57.4 in.; (Avenger) 59.5 in.; (Stratus) 60.2 in.; (Intrepid) 62.4 in.; (Viper) 59.6 in. Rear Tread: (Neon) 57.4 in.; (Avenger) 59.3 in.; (Stratus) 60.2 in.; (Intrepid) 62.0 in.; (Viper) 60.6 in. Standard Tires: (Neon Highline, Neon Sport) P185/65R14; (Neon R/T) P185/65HR14; (Avenger) P195/70HR14; (Avenger ES) P215/50HR17; (Stratus) P195/70R14; (Stratus ES) P195/65R15; (Intrepid) P205/70R15; (Intrepid ES) P225/60R16; (Viper) P275/40ZR17 front/P335/35ZR17 rear.

TECHNICAL: Transmission: Five-speed manual standard on Neon (all), Avenger (all), Stratus. Four-speed automatic standard on Stratus ES, Intrepid (all). Six-speed manual standard on Viper (all). Steering: (all) Rack and pinion. Front suspension: (Neon) MacPherson struts, asymmetrical lower control arms, coil springs and link-type stabilizer bar (R/T has performance-tuned struts and higher rate springs); (Avenger) Modified double-wishbone w/coil springs, direct acting shock absorbers and link-type stabilizer bar; (Stratus) Unequal length upper and lower control arms, coil springs, tubular shock absorbers and stabilizer bar (higher rate springs on ES); (Intrepid) Iso-strut w/integral gas-charged shock absorbers, coil springs, single transverse lower links, tension struts and link-type stabilizer bar (stiffer springs and firmer shock absorbers optional on ES); (Viper) Cast aluminum unequal length upper and lower control arms, coil springs, low-pressure gas-charged shock absorbers w/adjustable rebound and stabilizer bar. Rear suspension: (Neon) Chapman struts, coil springs, dual lower transverse links, lower trailing links (R/T has performance-tuned struts, higher rate springs and link-type stabilizer bar); (Avenger) Double wishbones, coil springs, direct acting shock absorbers and (ES only) link-type stabilizer bar; (Stratus) Unequal length

upper and lower control arms, trailing arms, coil springs, tubular shock absorbers and stabilizer bar (larger stabilizer bar with optional 2.5-liter V-6 and higher rate springs on ES); (Intrepid) Chapman struts w/integral gas-charged shock absorbers, concentric coil springs, dual transverse lower links, lower trailing links and link-type stabilizer bar (stiffer springs and firmer shock absorbers optional on ES); (Viper) Cast aluminum unequal length upper and lower control arms w/toe-control links, coil springs, low-pressure gas-charged shock absorbers w/adjustable rebound and stabilizer bar. Brakes: Front disc, rear drum (power-assisted) exc. (Stratus ES) Front disc, rear drum w/anti-lock (power-assisted); (Avenger ES, Intrepid ES) four-wheel disc w/anti-lock; (Intrepid, Viper) four-wheel disc. Body construction: Unibody exc. (Intrepid) Unibody w/isolated engine/suspension cradle and rear cross member; (Viper) Backbone tubular space frame w/separate cowl structure. Fuel tank: (Neon) 12.5 gals.; (Avenger) 16 gals.; (Stratus) 16 gals.; (Intrepid) 17 gals.; (Viper) 19 gals.

DRIVETRAIN OPTIONS: Engines: DOHC 2.0-liter four: Neon Highline ($150). 2.4-liter four: Stratus ($450). 2.5-liter four: Avenger ($675); Avenger ES ($610); Stratus ES ($800). Transmission: Three-speed auto. trans.: Neon Highline ($600). Four-speed auto. trans.: Avenger ($695); Stratus, incl. spd control ($1050). Brakes: Anti-lock: Neon Highline ($515-$565); Avenger, base ($600); Stratus, base ($565). Four-wheel anti-lock: Intrepid, base ($600).

NEON CONVENIENCE/APPEARANCE OPTIONS: Highline: Pkg. 21D: stnd equip. (NC). Pkg. 22D: 21D exc. 3-spd auto. trans. replaces 5-spd manual ($600). Sport: Pkg. 23G: incl. DOHC 2.0L four and perf. 5-spd manual trans., air cond., "Sport" graphics, pwr bulge hood, decklid spoiler, tach, 14-in. Sport whl covers, foglamps, cloth bucket seats ($1300). Pkg. 24G: 23G exc. 3-spd auto. trans. replaces perf. 5-spd manual ($1900). R/T: Pkg. 23H: 23G plus R/T badging, 4-whl disc brakes, unlimited spd engine controller, body-color door handles, AM/FM stereo radio w/cass. & CD changer, cloth low-back bucket seats, firm-feel pwr stng, leather-wrapped stng whl & shift knob, sport susp., P185/65HR14 perf. tires, 14-in. alum whls ($2140). Other: (ACR) Competition Grp.: incl. 4-whl disc brakes, unlimited spd engine controller, radio delete, cloth low-back bucket seats, firm-feel pwr stng, leather-wrapped stng whl & shift knob, competition susp., tach, P175/65HR14 perf. tires (sed)/P185/65HR14 perf. tires (cpe), 14-in. cast alum whls: cpe ($2080); sed ($2060). (AJP) Pwr Convenience Grp.: incl. dual pwr remote mirrors, pwr door locks, Highline: cpe ($260); sed ($300). (AJK) Dlx Convenience Grp.: incl. auto. spd control, tilt stng, Highline ($350). (ALT) Value Grp.: incl. Pwr Convenience Grp., pwr windows, AM/FM stereo radio w/cass. & CD changer, Highline ($540). (ALF) Value/Fun Grp.: incl. Pwr. Convenience Grp., pwr windows, pwr sunroof, AM/FM stereo radio w/prem. cass. & CD changer, Highline ($775-$935). Integrated child seat ($100). Air cond. ($1000). Rear window defroster, Competition ($205). Calif. emissions ($170). Floor mats ($50). Light Grp., Highline ($130). Pwr sunroof ($595). (RAS) AM/FM stereo radio w/cass. & 8 spkrs: Highline ($265); Competition ($565). (RBS) AM/FM stereo radio w/prem. cass., CD changer & 8 spkrs, Highline ($285). (RBR) AM/FM stereo radio w/prem. CD player & 8 spkrs ($110-$395). Remote keyless entry w/panic alarm, Highline ($155). Tilt stng, Highline ($150). Tach, Highline ($100). Pwr windows, Highline ($265). 14-in. cast alum whls, Highline ($355).

AVENGER CONVENIENCE/APPEARANCE OPTIONS: Base: Pkg. 21A: stnd equip. (NC). Pkg. 22A: 21A exc. 4-spd auto. trans. replaces 5-spd manual ($695). Pkg. 21C: 21A plus air cond., floor mats, cargo net, pwr door locks/mirrors/windows, spd control ($1595). Pkg. 22C: 21C exc. 4-spd auto. trans. replaces 5-spd manual ($2290). Sport Pkg. 24S: 21C exc. 2.5L V-6 replaces 2.0L four and 4-spd auto. trans. replaces 5-spd manual plus decklid spoiler, leather-wrapped stng whl, 16-in. whl grp. ($3660). ES: Pkg. 21D: stnd equip. (NC). Pkg. 21F: 21D plus Universal garage door opener, keyless entry w/panic alarm, pwr door locks, illum. visor mirrors, pwr mirrors, AM/FM stereo radio w/cass. & CD player ($1375). Pkg. 24F: 21F exc. 2.5L V-6 replaces 2.4L four and 4-spd auto. trans. replaces 5-spd manual ($2680). Other: Air cond., base ($790). 6-way pwr driver's seat ($205). Pwr sunroof ($640). Security alarm w/remote keyless entry and panic alarm ($290). Calif. emissions ($170). (RBX) AM/FM stereo radio w/CD & cass. & 6 spkrs ($435). (RAZ) AM/FM stereo radio w/CD & cass., equal. & 8 Infinity spkrs, ES ($325). Leather bucket seats, ES (NC). 16-in. whl grp. incl. P205/55HR16 tires, base ($490).

STRATUS CONVENIENCE/APPEARANCE OPTIONS: Base: Pkg. 21A: stnd equip. (NC). Pkg. 24A: 21A exc. 2.4L four replaces 2.0L four and 4-spd auto. trans. replaces 5-spd manual, incl. elect. spd control ($1500). Pkg. 21B: 21A plus spd sensitive pwr door locks, dual pwr remote heated mirrors, pwr windows, driver's seat height adj. ($685). Pkg. 24B: 21B incl. 2.4L four replaces 2.0L four and 4-spd auto. trans. replaces 5-spd manual, incl. elect. spd control ($2545). ES: Pkg. 24J: stnd equip. (NC). Pkg. 26R: 24J exc. 2.5L V-6 replaces 2.4L four and AutoStick 4-spd auto. trans. replaces 4-spd auto. trans. ($1145). Pkg. 26S: 26R plus cargo net, remote/illum. entry grp., 8-way pwr driver's seat, low-back bucket seats ($870). Other: (AJF) Remote/Illum. Grp.:

incl. illum. entry, remote keyless entry ($170). Integrated child seat, base ($100). Security alarm, ES ($150). Calif. emissions ($170). Eng. block & battery heater ($30). Extra cost Candy Apple Red paint ($200). (AR3) Prem. AM/FM stereo radio w/cass., CD changer & 8 spkrs ($340). (AR4) Prem. AM/FM stereo radio w/CD player & 4 spkrs, base ($200). (AR5) Prem. AM/FM stereo radio w/cass., CD changer & 4 spkrs ($550). Pwr sunroof: base ($695); ES ($580). Conventional spare tire ($125).

INTREPID CONVENIENCE/APPEARANCE OPTIONS: Intrepid: Pkg. 22C: stnd equip. (NC). Pkg. 22D: 22C plus rear reading/courtesy lamps, illum. visor mirrors, prem. cass. w/amp & 8 spkrs, Remote/Illum. Entry Grp., 8-way pwr driver's seat, leather-wrapped stng whl & shift knob ($1140). ES: Pkg. 24L: stnd equip. (NC). Pkg. 24M: 24L plus auto. temp. air cond., overhead trip computer/garage door opener, cass. w/amp & 9 Infinity spkrs, security alarm, full-size spare tire, traction control ($1130). Other: (AJK) Comfort/Security Grp.: incl. auto. temp. air cond., security alarm, ES ($305). (AJF) Remote Keyless/Illum. Entry Grp.: incl. keyless entry w/2 transmitters, illum entry, base ($225). Calif. emissions ($170). Overhead trip computer/garage door opener, ES ($310). Head-liner module, base ($170). Auto. day/night mirror, ES ($85). Pwr sunroof ES ($795). Eng. block & battery heater ($30). Cloth 50/50 front bench seat, base (NC). 8-way pwr driver's seat, base ($380). 8-way pwr pass. seat, ES ($380). Leather front bucket seats and rear bench seat, ES ($1000). Extra cost Candy Apple Red paint ($200). (AR1) AM/FM stereo radio w/cass., amp & 8 spkrs ($350). (AR2) AM/FM stereo radio w/CD changer, amp & 8 spkrs: base ($145-$435); ES ($145). (ARB) AM/FM stereo radio w/CD changer, amp & 9 Infinity spkrs, ES ($145). (AR6) AM/FM stereo radio w/cass. & CD changer, amp & 9 Infinity spkrs, ES ($300-$515) Wheel & Tire Grp.: incl. P225/60R16 touring tires and 16-in. bolt-on whl covers, base ($200). Conventional spare tire ($125).

VIPER CONVENIENCE/APPEARANCE OPTIONS: RT/10: Pkg. 21A: stnd equip. (NC). Tonneau cover ($250). Air cond. delete ($1000 credit). Body-color (red or silver) detachable hardtop w/sliding side curtains ($2500). GTS: Pkg. 21A: stnd equip. (NC). Extra cost paint ($1500). Polished cast alum whls ($500).

HISTORY: Model year production: 334,802. In 1998, Dodge unveiled its second-generation hybrid concept car called the Intrepid ESX2. The sleek ESX2, an improved version of the 1996 ESX diesel/electric-powered concept, featured an extreme cab-forward design and room for six passengers as well as having 19.9 cubic feet of cargo space. The car's unique rear suspension and lowered floor allowed for the batteries and electronics to be packaged behind the rear seat. The main structure of the ESX2 consisted of six thermoplastic polyester panels that weighed 50 percent less than the 80 steel pieces they replaced on a traditional car.

1999 DODGE

For the second year in-a-row, the Stratus ES received a new standard powertrain. After upgrading from the 2.0-liter four-cylinder engine and five-speed manual transmission to the 2.4-liter four and four-speed automatic the year previous, the (formerly optional) 2.5-liter V-6 paired with AutoStick four-speed automatic was now standard equipment as was four-wheel anti-lock disc brakes.

1999 Dodge, Neon R/T coupe (OCW)

NEON — SERIES L — FOUR — Following on the heels of record sales for the compact, Dodge carried over the Neon lineup intact for the 1999 model year, again consisting of the three package offerings: Highline, Sport, and R/T, as well as the optional ARC Competition Group package for the "race on Sunday, drive on Monday" crowd. Powertrain availability was unchanged from the previous year. New features for 1999 included Neon complying with California's LEV (low emission vehicle) standards. Standard safety equipment now also included dynamic side impact/intrusion protection.

1999 Dodge, Avenger coupe (OCW)

AVENGER — SERIES J — FOUR/V-6 — The Avenger lineup was again comprised of base and ES trim level coupes as well as the return of the optional Sport package for "revving up" the base model. Powertrain availability carried over intact from the previous year. Next-generation dual airbags were installed in all Avengers and two new exterior color choices were offered for 1999: Plum and Shark Blue.

1999 Dodge, Stratus ES sedan (OCW)

STRATUS — SERIES A — FOUR/V-6 — The base and ES trim level sedans continued as the Stratus lineup offerings for 1999. The base sedan was again powered by the 2.0-liter four-cylinder engine linked to a five-speed manual transmission. New-for-1999, the Stratus ES revised its standard powertrain for the second time in two model years. Use of the dual overhead cam 2.4-liter four-cylinder engine paired with an electronically controlled four-speed automatic transmission with overdrive was discontinued (it remained the optional powertrain for the base sedan) in favor of the 2.5-liter V-6 mated to an AutoStick four-speed automatic, which was formerly optional in the ES. Also for 1999, the Stratus series sedans received improved damping and retuning of their suspension. This resulted in an improved "on center" steering feel and increased ride control. A new package of standard equipment included power windows, door locks and mirrors as well as a driver's seat height adjuster and rear floor mats. Also newly standard on the ES sedan were four-wheel anti-lock disc brakes, five-spoke aluminum wheels and an improved instrument cluster with revised graphics. Two new exterior color choices were Inferno Red and Light Cypress Green. A new option was Sentry Key vehicle immobilizer.

1999 Dodge, Intrepid ES sedan (OCW)

INTREPID — SERIES H — V-6 — After a complete redesign the year previous, the Intrepid received minor upgrades for 1999. The series was again comprised of base and ES trim level sedans. The base Intrepid was again powered by the 2.7-liter V-6 paired with an electronically controlled four-speed automatic transmission with overdrive. The ES sedan again used the 3.2-liter V-6 mated to the AutoStick four-speed automatic. Inside, new features included upgraded carpeting and headliner, enhanced interior fabrics and leather seating surfaces, and a stitched boot for the gearshift lever. Both the base and ES sedans received more "robust" sway bar links and tubular trailing arms that better isolated road harshness. Newly optional was Sentry Key vehicle immobilizer.

1999 Dodge, Viper GTS coupe with optional ACR package (OCW)

1999 Dodge, Viper RT/10 roadster (OCW)

VIPER — SERIES R — V-10 —

Vipers received "more bite" in 1999 as both the RT/10 roadster and the GTS coupe were now fitted with 18-inch polished aluminum wheels shod with Michelin Pilot MXX3 speed-rated tires, which replaced the 17-inch wheels and tires previously standard. New tire sizes were P275/35ZR18 in front and P335/30ZR18 in back. Other changes for 1999 included reintroducing black to the existing color choices of red and silver. On the GTS coupe, wide dual silver stripes were offered with the red or black exterior, while the RT/10 was available in red or black sans stripes. Silver came with wide dual blue stripes on the GTS coupe, with monotone silver offered on the RT/10. Interior upgrades to both Viper models included power sideview mirrors, cloth-covered sun visors, and a satin aluminum finish on components including the gauge trim rings, parking brake handle and release button, shift lever shaft, gearshift knob and inside door release handles. A new interior option offered on both the RT/10 and GTS was a Cognac-colored leather accent package. It included Cognac trim panels and carpeting with Cognac leather seats, steering wheel, shift knob and parking brake boot and grip. The package was only offered with Vipers finished in either black or silver monotone exterior colors or black with silver stripes. A ViperACR package was also optional and included a higher output V-10 (460 horsepower and 500 pound-feet of torque vs. 450 and 490 on production versions), one-piece BBS 18-in. wheels, Koni racing shock absorbers, Meritor springs, K&N air filter, five-point restraint system and specific ACR badging and graphics.

I.D. DATA: Dodge's 17-symbol Vehicle Identification Number (VIN), as before, was on the upper left corner of the instrument panel, visible through the windshield. Coding is similar to 1986-98. Symbol ten (model year) changed to 'X' for 1999.

*Note: Production figures for 1999 Dodges were not available at the time this book went to press.

NEON HIGHLINE (FOUR)

Model No.	Body/ Style No.	Body Type & Seating	Factory Price	Shipping Weight	Prod. Total
LDH	22	2-dr. Coupe-5P	10550	2470	*
LDH	42	4-dr. Sedan-5P	10750	2507	*

NEON SPORT (FOUR)

LDL	22	2-dr. Coupe-5P	11225	N/A	*
LDL	42	4-dr. Sedan-5P	11425	N/A	*

NEON R/T (FOUR)

N/A	22	2-dr. Coupe-5P	13365	N/A	*
N/A	42	4-dr. Sedan-5P	13565	N/A	*

AVENGER (FOUR/V-6)

JDH	22	2-dr. Coupe-4P	15370/15980	2897/N/A	*
JDS	22	2-dr. ES Coupe-4P	17645/18255	2996/N/A	*

Note: Prices and weights to left of slash for four-cylinder, to right for V-6.

STRATUS (FOUR)

ADH	41	4-dr. Sedan-5P	15140	3007	*

STRATUS ES (V-6)

ADP	41	4-dr. Sedan-5P	18960	3169	*

INTREPID (V-6)

HDH	41	4-dr. Sedan-6P	19890	3423	*
HDP	41	4-dr. ES Sedan-6P	22640	3518	*

VIPER (V-10)

RDS	27	2-dr. RT/10 Rdstr-2P	65725	3319	*
RDS	29	2-dr. GTS Cpe-2P	68225	3383	*

ENGINE DATA: BASE FOUR (Neon Highline, Neon Sport sed, Stratus): Inline, overhead cam four-cylinder. Cast iron block; aluminum head. Displacement: 121 cu. in. (2.0 liters). Bore & stroke: 3.44 x 3.27 in. Compression ratio: 9.8:1. Brake horsepower: 132 at 6000 RPM. Torque: 129 lb.-ft. at 5000 RPM. Sequential fuel injection. BASE FOUR (Neon Sport cpe, Neon R/T); OPTIONAL FOUR (Neon Highline): Inline, dual overhead cam four-cylinder. Cast iron block; aluminum head. Displacement: 121 cu. in. (2.0 liters). Bore & stroke: 3.44 x 3.27 in. Compression ratio: 9.6:1. Brake horsepower: 150 at 6500 RPM. Torque: 133 lb.-ft. at 5500 RPM. Sequential fuel injection. BASE FOUR (Avenger, Avenger ES): Inline, dual overhead cam four-cylinder. Cast iron block; aluminum head. Displacement: 121 cu. in. (2.0 liters). Bore & stroke: 3.44 x 3.27 in. Compression ratio: 9.6:1. Brake horsepower: 140 at 6000 RPM. Torque: 130 lb.-ft. at 4800 RPM. Sequential fuel injection. OPTIONAL FOUR (Stratus): Inline, dual overhead cam four-cylinder. Cast iron block; aluminum head. Displacement: 148 cu. in. (2.4 liters). Bore & stroke: 3.44 x 3.98 in. Compression ratio: 9.4:1. Brake horsepower: 150 at 5200 RPM. Torque: 167 lb.-ft. at 4000 RPM. Sequential fuel injection. BASE V-6 (Stratus ES); OPTIONAL V-6 (Avenger, Avenger ES): Overhead cam V-6. Cast iron block; aluminum heads. Displacement: 152 cu. in. (2.5 liters). Bore & stroke: 3.29 x 2.99 in. Compression ratio: 9.4:1. Brake horsepower: (Avenger, Avenger ES) 163 at 5500 RPM; (Stratus ES) 168 at 5800 RPM. Torque: (all) 170 lb.-ft. at 4350 RPM. Sequential fuel injection. BASE V-6 (Intrepid): Overhead valve V-6. Aluminum block and heads. Displacement: 167 cu. in. (2.7 liters). Bore & stroke: 3.38 x 3.09 in. Compression ratio: 9.7:1. Brake horsepower: 200 at 5800 RPM. Torque: 190 lb.-ft. at 4850 RPM. Sequential fuel injection. BASE V-6 (Intrepid ES): Overhead cam V-6. Aluminum block and heads. Displacement: 197 cu. in. (3.2 liters). Bore & stroke: 3.62 x 3.19 in. Compression ratio: 9.5:1. Brake horsepower: 225 at 6300 RPM. Torque: 225 lb.-ft. at 3800 RPM. Sequential fuel injection. BASE V-10 (Viper): Overhead valve V-10. Aluminum block and heads. Displacement: 488 cu. in. (8.0 liters). Bore & stroke: 4.00 x 3.88 in. Compression ratio: 9.6:1. Brake horsepower: 450 at 5200 RPM. Torque: 490 lb.-ft. at 3700 RPM. Sequential fuel injection.

CHASSIS DATA: Wheelbase: (Neon) 104.0 in.; (Avenger) 103.7 in.; (Stratus) 108.0 in.; (Intrepid) 113.0 in.; (Viper) 96.2 in. Overall length: (Neon) 171.8 in.; (Avenger) 190.2 in.; (Stratus) 186.0 in.; (Intrepid) 203.7 in.; (Viper RT/10) 175.1 in.; (Viper GTS) 176.7 in. Height: (Neon Highline, Neon Sport) 54.9 in.; (Neon R/T cpe) 54.9 in.; (Neon R/T sed) 52.8 in.; (Avenger) 53.0 in.; (Stratus) 54.2 in.; (Intrepid) 55.9 in.; (Viper RT/10) 44.0 in.; (Viper GTS) 47.0 in. Width: (Neon cpe) 67.4 in.; (Neon sed) 67.2 in.; (Avenger) 69.1 in.; (Stratus) 71.7 in.; (Intrepid) 74.7 in.; (Viper) 75.7 in. Front Tread: (Neon) 57.4 in.; (Avenger) 59.5 in.; (Stratus) 60.2 in.; (Intrepid) 62.4 in.; (Viper) 59.6 in. Rear Tread: (Neon) 57.4 in.; (Avenger) 59.3 in.; (Stratus) 60.2 in.;

(Intrepid) 62.0 in.; (Viper) 60.6 in. Standard Tires: (Neon Highline) P185/65R14; (Neon Sport) P175/70R14; (Neon R/T) P185/65HR14; (Avenger) P195/70HR14; (Avenger ES) P215/50HR17; (Stratus) P195/70R14; (Stratus ES) P195/65R15; (Intrepid) P205/70R15; (Intrepid ES) P225/60R16; (Viper) P275/35ZR18 front/P335/30ZR18 rear.

TECHNICAL: Transmission: Five-speed manual standard on Neon (all), Avenger (all), Stratus. Four-speed automatic standard on Stratus ES, Intrepid (all). Six-speed manual standard on Viper (all). Steering: (all) Rack and pinion. Front suspension: (Neon) MacPherson struts, asymmetrical lower control arms, coil springs and link-type stabilizer bar (R/T has performance-tuned struts and higher rate springs); (Avenger) Modified double-wishbone w/coil springs, direct acting shock absorbers and link-type stabilizer bar; (Stratus) Unequal length upper and lower control arms, coil springs, tubular shock absorbers and stabilizer bar (higher rate springs on ES); (Intrepid) Iso-strut w/integral gas-charged shock absorbers, coil springs, single transverse lower links, tension struts and link-type stabilizer bar (stiffer springs and firmer shock absorbers optional on ES); (Viper) Cast aluminum unequal length upper and lower control arms, coil springs, low-pressure gas-charged shock absorbers w/adjustable rebound and stabilizer bar. Rear suspension: (Neon) Chapman struts, coil springs, dual lower transverse links, lower trailing links (R/T has performance-tuned struts, higher rate springs and link-type stabilizer bar); (Avenger) Double wishbones, coil springs, direct acting shock absorbers and (ES only) link-type stabilizer bar; (Stratus) Unequal length upper and lower control arms, trailing arms, coil springs, tubular shock absorbers and stabilizer bar (larger stabilizer bar with optional 2.5-liter V-6 and higher rate springs on ES); (Intrepid) Chapman struts w/integral gas-charged shock absorbers, concentric coil springs, dual transverse lower links, lower trailing links and link-type stabilizer bar (stiffer springs and firmer shock absorbers optional on ES); (Viper) Cast aluminum unequal length upper and lower control arms w/toe-control links, coil springs, low-pressure gas-charged shock absorbers w/adjustable rebound and stabilizer bar. Brakes: Front disc, rear drum (power-assisted) exc. (Avenger ES, Stratus ES, Intrepid ES) four-wheel disc w/anti-lock; (Intrepid, Viper) four-wheel disc. Body construction: Unibody exc. (Intrepid) Unibody w/isolated engine/suspension cradle and rear cross member; (Viper) Backbone tubular space frame w/separate cowl structure. Fuel tank: (Neon) 12.5 gals.; (Avenger) 16 gals.; (Stratus) 16 gals.; (Intrepid) 17 gals.; (Viper) 19 gals.

DRIVETRAIN OPTIONS: Engines: DOHC 2.0-liter four: Neon Highline ($150). 2.4-liter four: Stratus ($450). 2.5-liter four: Avenger ($675); Avenger ES ($610). Transmission: Three-speed auto. trans.: Neon Highline ($600). Four-speed auto. trans.: Avenger ($695); Stratus, incl. spd control ($1050). Brakes: Anti-lock: Neon Highline ($515-$565); Avenger, base ($600); Stratus, base ($565). Four-wheel disc w/anti-lock: Avenger Sport ($600); Intrepid, base ($600).

NEON CONVENIENCE/APPEARANCE OPTIONS: Highline: Pkg. 21D: stnd equip. (NC). Pkg. 22D: 21D exc. 3-spd auto. trans. replaces 5-spd manual ($600). Sport: Pkg. 23G: incl. DOHC 2.0L four and perf. 5-spd manual trans., air cond., "Sport" graphics, pwr bulge hood, decklid spoiler, tach, 14-in. Sport whl covers, foglamps, cloth low-back bucket seats ($1300). Pkg. 24G: 23G exc. 3-spd auto. trans. replaces perf. 5-spd manual ($1900). R/T: Pkg. 23H: 23G plus R/T badging, 4-whl disc brakes, unlimited spd engine controller, body-color door handles, AM/FM stereo radio w/cass. & CD changer, cloth low-back bucket seats, firm-feel pwr stng, leather-wrapped stng whl & shift knob, sport susp., P185/65HR14 perf. tires, 14-in. alum whls ($2140). Other: (ACR) Competition Grp.: incl. 4-whl disc brakes, unlimited spd engine controller, radio delete, cloth low-back bucket seats, firm-feel pwr stng, leather-wrapped stng whl & shift knob, competition susp., tach, P175/65HR14 perf. tires (sed)/P185/65HR14 perf. tires (cpe), 14-in. cast alum whls: cpe ($2080); sed ($2060). (AJP) Pwr Convenience Grp.: incl. dual pwr remote mirrors, pwr door locks, Highline: cpe ($260); sed ($300). (AJK) Dlx Convenience Grp.: incl. auto. spd control, tilt stng, tach, Highline ($350-$400). (ALT) Value Grp.: incl. Pwr Convenience Grp., pwr windows, AM/FM stereo radio w/cass. & CD changer, Highline ($540). (ALF) Value/Fun Grp.: incl. Pwr. Convenience Grp., pwr windows, pwr sunroof, AM/FM stereo radio w/prem. cass. & CD changer, Highline ($775-$935). Air cond. ($1000). Rear window defroster, stnd Highline ($205). Calif. emissions ($200). Light Grp., Highline ($130). (RBS) AM/FM stereo radio w/prem. cass., CD changer & 8 spkrs, Highline ($285). (RBR) AM/FM stereo radio w/prem. CD player & 8 spkrs, Highline ($110-$395). Pwr windows, Highline ($265). Remote keyless entry w/panic alarm, Highline ($165). 14-in. cast alum whls, Highline ($355).

AVENGER CONVENIENCE/APPEARANCE OPTIONS: Base: Pkg. 21A: stnd equip. (NC). Pkg. 22A: 21A exc. 4-spd auto. trans. replaces 5-spd manual ($695). Pkg. 21C: 21A plus air cond., floor mats, cargo net, pwr door locks/mirrors/windows, spd control, P205/55R16 tires, 16-in. whl covers ($1750). Pkg. 22C: 21C exc. 4-spd auto. trans. replaces 5-spd manual ($2445). Sport: Pkg. 24S: 21C exc. 2.5L V-6 replaces 2.0L

four and 4-spd auto. trans. replaces 5-spd manual plus 4-whl disc brakes, decklid spoiler, leather-wrapped stng whl, 16-in. alum. whls ($3660). ES: Pkg. 21D: stnd equip. (NC). Pkg. 21F: 21D plus Universal garage door opener, keyless entry w/panic alarm, pwr door locks and windows, illum. visor mirrors, pwr mirrors, AM/FM stereo radio w/cass. & CD player, 6-way leather low-back bucket seats ($1390). Pkg. 24F: 21F exc. 2.5L V-6 replaces 2.4L four and 4-spd auto. trans. replaces 5-spd manual ($2695). Other: Air cond., base ($790). 6-way pwr driver's seat, base ($205). Pwr sunroof ($640). Security alarm w/remote keyless entry and panic alarm, base ($305). Calif. emissions ($200). (RBX) AM/FM stereo radio w/CD & cass. & 6 spkrs ($435). (RAZ) AM/FM stereo radio w/CD & cass., equal. & 8 Infinity spkrs, ES ($325).

STRATUS CONVENIENCE/APPEARANCE OPTIONS: Base: Pkg. 21A: stnd equip. (NC). Pkg. 24A: 21A exc. 2.4L four replaces 2.0L four and 4-spd auto. trans., incl. elect. spd control ($1500). Pkg. 21B: 21A plus floor mats, spd sensitive pwr door locks, dual pwr remote heated mirrors, pwr windows, driver's seat height adj. (NC). Pkg. 24B: 21B incl. 2.4L four replaces 2.0L four and 4-spd auto. trans. replaces 5-spd manual, incl. elect. spd control ($1500). ES: Pkg. 26R: stnd equip. (NC). Pkg. 26S: 26R plus cargo net, remote/illum. entry grp., 8-way pwr driver's seat, leather bucket seats ($500). Other: (AJF) Remote/Illum. Grp.: incl. illum. entry, remote keyless entry ($170). Security alarm ($175). Calif. emissions ($200). Eng. block & battery heater ($30). Extra cost Inferno Red paint ($200). (ARR) Prem. AM/FM stereo radio w/CD & 6 spkrs, base ($200). (AR3) Prem. AM/FM stereo radio w/cass., CD changer & 8 spkrs ($340). (AR5) Prem. AM/FM stereo radio w/cass., CD changer & 6 spkrs ($550). Pwr sunroof: base ($695); ES ($580). Conventional spare tire ($125).

INTREPID CONVENIENCE/APPEARANCE OPTIONS: Intrepid: Pkg. 22C: stnd equip. (NC). Pkg. 22D: 22C plus rear reading/courtesy lamps, illum. visor mirrors, prem. cass. w/amp & 8 spkrs, Remote/Illum. Entry Grp., 8-way pwr driver's seat, leather-wrapped stng whl & shift knob ($1140). ES: Pkg. 24L: stnd equip. (NC). Pkg. 24M: 24L plus auto. temp. air cond., overhead trip computer/garage door opener, prem. CD radio w/amp & 8 spkrs, security alarm, full-size spare tire, traction control ($1170). Other: (AJK) Comfort/Security Grp.: incl. auto. temp. air cond., security alarm, ES ($330). (AJF) Remote Keyless/Illum. Entry Grp.: incl. keyless entry w/2 transmitters, illum entry, base ($225). Calif. emissions ($200). Headliner module w/overhead trip computer/garage door opener, ES ($395). Pwr sunroof, ES ($795). Eng. block & battery heater ($30). Cloth 50/50 front bench seat, base ($100). 8-way pwr driver's seat, base ($380). 8-way pwr driver's & pass. seat, ES ($380). Leather bucket seats, ES ($1000). Extra cost Candy Apple Red paint ($200). (AR2) AM/FM stereo radio w/CD changer, amp & 8 spkrs: base ($145-$435); ES ($145). (AR6) AM/FM stereo radio w/cass. & CD changer, amp & 9 Infinity spkrs, ES ($370-$515) Wheel & Tire Grp.: incl. P225/60R16 touring tires and 16-in. bolt-on whl covers, base ($200). Conventional spare tire ($125).

VIPER CONVENIENCE/APPEARANCE OPTIONS: RT/10: Pkg. 21A: stnd equip. (NC). Tonneau cover ($250). Body-color (red, black or silver) detachable hardtop w/sliding side curtains ($2500). GTS: Pkg. 21A: stnd equip. (NC). Extra cost paint ($2000). Other: Cognac Leather Interior Grp. ($500). ACR package incl. high output V-10, radio and air cond. delete, ACR badging, racing shock absorbers, 18-in. racing whls, higher rate springs, five-point harness ($10000). Comfort Grp. ACR req'd (restores radio and air cond. to ACR package) ($910).

HISTORY: At the 1999 North American International Auto Show in Detroit, Dodge debuted its 2001 Intrepid R/T, powered by a 242-horsepower 3.5-liter V-6 paired with an AutoStick four-speed automatic transmission. The Viper Red Intrepid R/T featured performance-tuned suspension, four-wheel disc brakes, specific aluminum wheels and performance tires, body-color rear spoiler, dual chrome exhaust tips, foglamps, unique taillights with black surrounds and white back-up lamps with amber bulbs. Dodge also announced it was resurrecting the Charger R/T name from the 1960s. The former muscle car moniker was slated for use on a concept sedan powered by a supercharged 4.7-liter V-8 fueled by compressed natural gas, capable of generating 325 horsepower yet meeting the ULEV (ultra low emission vehicle) standards. The concept Charger R/T measured 187 inches in overall length (compared to 203 for the 1968 Charger R/T) and weighed 3,000 pounds (vs. 3,650 for the 1968 version). The concept sedan featured rear-wheel drive and also used a five-speed manual transmission. Under new DaimlerChrysler management, it was announced in August 1999 that the automaker was severing all ties with the SCCA's (Sports Car Club of America) Showroom Stock racing series in which the Neon had been ultra-successful for many years. Company officials cited unfair rules that favored competing makes over the Neon for pulling its monetary and factory support from the series.

2000 DODGE

In its first model year under the new, DaimlerChrysler banner, Dodge's millennium-ending 2000 lineup brought significant changes from 1999. The compact 2000 Dodge Neon sedan (along with its Plymouth twin) was completely redesigned with attention paid to increased acceleration and reduced engine noise.

Also, a sunroof option became available and a R/T performance package was announced for midyear availability. The slower-selling coupe was dropped. The four-cylinder engine and manual transmission disappeared from the Avenger coupe equipment list with V-6 power and four-speed automatic becoming standard. A five-speed manual driven by four-cylinders remained standard on the Stratus sedan, however. An R/T package was also announced for the full-size Intrepid and the Viper saw the addition of one new color and changes made to its ACR (American Club Racer) package.

2000 Dodge, Neon Highline sedan (OCW)

NEON — SERIES L — FOUR — The totally redesigned Neon for 2000 was improved in many ways. It offered more interior room, a larger trunk, quieter operation and refinement in other areas. Standard equipment included: driver- and passenger-side airbags, power steering, tilt steering wheel, cloth bucket seats, storage armrest, cupholders, 60/40 split folding rear seatbacks, AM/FM/cassette radio with CD changer controls and six speakers, variable intermittent wipers, rear defroster, passenger-side visor mirror, auxilary power outlet, remote trunk lid release, floor mats, dual outside mirrors, and wheel covers. Initially, the Neon was offered only as the base Highline four-door sedan (the coupe having been dropped) with an ES luxury upgrade option package available. Later in the year a performance-oriented R/T version would be offered with a 150-hp SOHC four-cylinder engine, quick-shifting five-speed transaxle, sport suspension, 16-inch aluminum wheels, performance tires, and other sporting touches.

2000 Dodge, Avenger coupe (OCW)

AVENGER — SERIES J — V-6 — The Avenger lineup was again comprised of base and ES trim level coupes, but the 2.0-liter, four-cylinder engine and five-speed manual transmission of the former base version was dropped in favor of the ES's 2.5-liter V-6 and four-speed overdrive automatic. Standard equipment for the base Avenger now also included: driver- and passenger-side airbags, four-wheel disc brakes, air conditioning, variable-assist power steering, tilt steering wheel, cruise control, cloth upholstery, front bucket seats, height-adjustable driver seat, center console, cupholders, split folding rear seat, power mirrors, power windows, power door locks, rear defogger, AM/FM/cassette radio with six speakers, digital clock, tachometer, variable intermittent wipers, map lights, visor mirrors, remote fuel door and deck lid release, floor mats, rear deck spoiler, 205/55HR16 tires, and wheel covers. Over and above these features, the ES came with leather upholstery, six-way power driver seat, leather-wrapped steering wheel, remote keyless entry, AM/FM/cassette radio with CD player, garage door opener, theft-deterrent system, performance suspension, fog lights, and 215/50HR17 tires on alloy wheels.

2000 Dodge, Stratus ES sedan (OCW)

STRATUS — SERIES A — FOUR/V-6 — The base model became SE and, along with the ES trim level, the two four-door sedans comprised the Stratus lineup for 2000. Standard drivetrain for the SE was the 2.0-liter four-cylinder engine linked to a five-speed manual transmission, but this could be upgraded to the 2.4-liter four at no extra cost when the optional (at extra cost) four-speed automatic was selected. The Stratus ES continued use of the 2.5-liter V-6 mated to an AutoStick four-speed automatic for its standard powertrain.

SE standard equipment also included: driver- and passenger-side air bags, air conditioning, power steering, tilt steering wheel, cloth upholstery, front bucket seats, console, cupholders, folding rear bench seat, AM/FM/cassette radio w/six speakers, digital clock, tachometer, rear defogger, variable intermittent wipers, remote deck lid release, auxiliary power outlet, visor mirrors, front floor mats, dual remote mirrors, 195/70R14 tires, and wheel covers. In addition to these, the ES featured anti-lock four-wheel disc brakes, cruise control, variable-assist power steering, leather-wrapped steering wheel and shift knob, power mirrors, map lights, illuminated visor mirrors, rear floor mats, fog lamps, and 195/65R15 tires on alloy wheels.

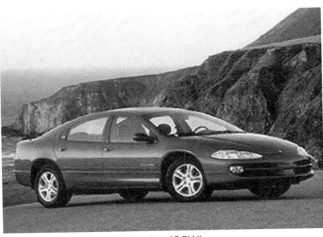

2000 Dodge, Intrepid ES sedan (OCW)

INTREPID — SERIES H — V-6 — After a complete redesign for 1998, the Intrepid received only minor upgrades for 1999, and again for 2000. These included five new colors, new seat fabric in the base models, in-dash CD changer availability on ES, child seat anchors behind the rear seats, and LEV standards met on cars sold in California. The big news was the introduction of a performance-oriented R/T model in addition to the base and ES trim level sedans. The base Intrepid was again powered by the 2.7-liter V-6 paired with an electronically controlled four-speed automatic transmission with overdrive. The ES sedan used a version of the 2.7-liter V-6 that produced slightly more power and torque and was mated to the AutoStick four-speed automatic, but it could be optioned even higher to the 3.2-liter V-6. At the top of the performance heap, R/T came equipped with the same 3.5-liter V-6 and AutoStick used in the Chrysler 300M and LHS, although rated at 11 fewer horsepower. Base level standard equipment also included: driver- and passenger-side air bags, four-wheel disc brakes, air conditioning, power steering, tilt steering wheel, cruise control, cloth upholstery, front bucket seats, center console, power mirrors, power windows, power door locks, rear defogger, variable intermittent wipers, AM/FM/cassette radio w/four speakers, digital clock, tachometer, visor mirrors, map lights, power remote deck lid release, automatic-off headlights, floor mats, 225/60R16 tires on steel wheels, and wheel covers. Selecting the ES added stainless steel exhaust with a chrome tip, additional exterior lighting (including front fog/driving lights), remote keyless entry, panic alarm, driver's side power seat, lumbar support, 60/40 folding rear bench seat w/fixed head rests, center arm rest, premium cloth seats, leather-wrapped gear shift knob, two door curb lights, illuminated entry, leather-wrapped tilt steering wheel, and 16-inch aluminum wheels. For an even sweeter package, the R/T added a 3.66 axle ratio, sport tuned suspension, four-wheel anti-lock disc brakes, a premium AM/FM/cassette stereo radio w/CD and eight speakers, four-way driver's seat direction control, and P225/55VR17 performance tires on silver alloy wheels.

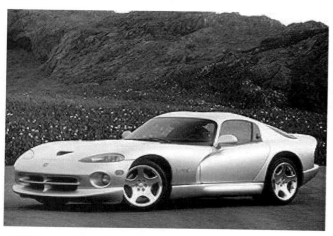

2000 Dodge, Viper GTS coupe (OCW)

VIPER — SERIES R — V-10 — Entering its ninth year of production, Viper was largely unchanged from 1999 except for additional tweaks to the ACR (American Club Racer) option on the GTS coupe, and steel gray replacing silver on the Viper color palette. For both the RT/10 roadster and GTS coupe, options were few with both powered by the 450-hp, 8-liter V-10 - still America's largest and most powerful automobile engine - driving through a six-speed manual gearbox. Neither anti-lock brakes nor traction control was available, but standard equipment was extensive and on the RT/10 included: limited-slip differential, driver- and passenger-side air bags, four-wheel disc brakes, air conditioning, power steering with tilt wheel, leather-wrapped steering wheel and shifter knob, adjustable pedals, leather reclining front bucket seats with lumbar adjustment, center console, power windows, power door locks, remote keyless entry, tachometer, AM/FM/cassette radio with CD player and five speakers, map lights, fog lights, theft-deterrent system, removable folding soft top, and alloy wheels. Selecting the GTS coupe added rear defogger, six speakers, overhead mesh storage compartment, trunk light, and - of course - deleted the folding soft top and map lights. Color choices were red, black, and the new steel gray on the RT/10, and the same colors with or without silver stripes on the GTS.

I.D. DATA: Dodge's 17-symbol Vehicle Identification Number (VIN), as before, was on the upper left corner of the instrument panel, visible through the windshield. Coding is similar to 1986-99. Symbol ten (model year) changed to 'Y' for 2000

* Note: Production figures for 2000 Dodges were not available at the time this book went to press.

NEON HIGHLINE (FOUR)

Model No.	Body/ Style No.	Body Type & Seating	Factory Price	Shipping Weight	Prod. Total
LDH	41	4-dr. Sed-5P	12460	2559	*

AVENGER (V-6)

JDH	22	2-dr. Cpe-4P	18970	3137	*
JDS	22	2-dr. ES Cpe-4P	121215	3172	*

STRATUS SE (FOUR)

ADH	41	4-dr. Sed-5P	16080	2940	*

STRATUS ES (V-6)

ADP	41	4-dr. Sed-5P	19980	3058	*

INTREPID (V-6)

HDH	41	4-dr. Sed-6P	20545	3471	*
HDP	41	4-dr. ES Sed-6P	22235	3489	*
HDX	41	4-dr. R/T Sed-6P	24435	3511	*

VIPER (V-10)

RDS	27	2-dr. RT/10 Rdstr-2P	67225	3440	*
RDS	29	2-dr. GTS Cpe-2P	69725	3460	*

ENGINE DATA: BASE FOUR (Neon Highline, Stratus SE): Inline, overhead cam four-cylinder. Cast iron block; aluminum head. Displacement: 121 cu. in. (2.0 liters). Bore & stroke: 3.44 x 3.27 in. Compression ratio: 9.8:1. Brake horsepower: 132 at 5600 RPM. Torque: 130 lb.-ft. at 4600 RPM. Sequential fuel injection. **OPTIONAL FOUR** (Stratus SE): Inline, dual overhead cam four-cylinder. Cast iron block; aluminum head. Displacement: 148 cu. in. (2.4 liters). Bore & stroke: 3.44 x 3.98 in. Compression ratio: 9.4:1. Brake horsepower: 150 at 5200 RPM. Torque: 167 lb.-ft. at 4000 RPM. Sequential fuel injection. **BASE V-6** (Stratus ES); **BASE V-6** (Avenger, Avenger ES): Overhead cam V-6. Cast iron block; aluminum heads. Displacement: 152 cu. in. (2.5 liters). Bore & stroke: 3.29 x 2.99 in. Compression ratio: 9.4:1. Brake horsepower: (Avenger, Avenger ES) 163 at 5500 RPM; (Stratus ES) 168 at 5800 RPM. Torque: (all) 170 lb.-ft. at 4350 RPM. Sequential fuel injection. **BASE V-6** (Intrepid): Overhead valve V-6. Aluminum block and heads. Displacement: 167 cu. in. (2.7 liters). Bore & stroke: 3.38 x 3.09 in. Compression ratio: 9.7:1. Brake horsepower: 200 at 5800 RPM. Torque: 190 lb.-ft. at 4850 RPM. Sequential fuel injection. **BASE V-6** (Intrepid ES): Overhead valve V-6. Aluminum block and heads. Displacement: 167 cu. in. (2.7 liters). Bore & stroke: 3.38 x 3.09 in. Compression ratio: 9.7:1. Brake horsepower: 202 at 5800 RPM. Torque: 195 lb.-ft. at 4200 RPM. Sequential fuel injection. **OPTIONAL V-6** (Intrepid ES): Overhead cam V-6. Aluminum block and heads. Displacement: 197 cu. in. (3.2 liters). Bore & stroke: 3.62 x 3.19 in. Compression ratio: 9.5:1. Brake horsepower: 225 at 6300 RPM. Torque: 225 lb.-ft. at 3800 RPM. Sequential fuel injection. **BASE V-6** (Intrepid R/T) Overhead cam V-6. Aluminum block and heads. Displacement: 215 cu. in. (3.5 liters). Bore & stroke: 3.78 x 3.19 in. Compression ratio: 9.9:1. Brake horsepower: 242 at 6400 RPM. Torque: 248 lb.-ft. at 3950 RPM. Sequential fuel injection. **BASE V-10** (Viper): Overhead valve V-10. Aluminum block and heads. Displacement: 488 cu. in. (8.0 liters). Bore & stroke: 4.00 x 3.88 in. Compression ratio: 9.6:1. Brake horsepower: 450 at 5200 RPM. Torque: 490 lb.-ft. at 3700 RPM. Sequential fuel injection.

CHASSIS DATA: Wheelbase: (Neon) 105.0 in.; (Avenger) 103.7 in.; (Stratus) 108.0 in.; (Intrepid) 113.0 in.; (Viper) 96.2 in. Overall length: (Neon) 174.4 in.; (Avenger) 190.2 in.; (Stratus) 186.0 in.; (Intrepid) 203.7 in.; (Viper RT/10) 176.2 in.; (Viper GTS) 176.7 in. Height: (Neon) 56.0 in.; (Avenger) 53.0 in.; (Stratus) 54.2 in.; (Intrepid) 55.9 in.; (Viper RT/10) 44.0 in.; (Viper GTS) 47.0 in. Width: (Neon) 67.4 in.; (Avenger) 69.1 in.; (Stratus) 71.7 in.; (Intrepid) 74.7 in.; (Viper) 75.7 in. Front Tread: (Neon) 58.0 in.; (Avenger) 59.5 in.; (Stratus) 60.2 in.; (Intrepid) 62.4 in.; (Viper) 59.6 in. Rear Tread: (Neon) 58.0 in.; (Avenger) 59.3 in.; (Stratus) 60.2 in.; (Intrepid) 62.0 in.; (Viper) 60.6 in. Standard Tires: (Neon Highline) P185/65R14; (Avenger) P205/55HR16; (Avenger ES) P215/50HR17; (Stratus SE) P195/70R14; (Stratus ES) P195/65R15; (Intrepid, Intrepid ES) P225/60R16 (Intrepid R/T) P225/55R17; (Viper) P275/35ZR18 front/P335/30ZR18 rear.

TECHNICAL: Transmission: Five-speed manual standard on Neon, Stratus SE. Four-speed automatic standard on Avenger, Stratus ES, Intrepid (all). Six-speed manual standard on Viper (all). Steering: (all) Rack and pinion. Front suspension: (Neon) MacPherson struts, asymmetrical lower control arms, coil springs and link-type stabilizer bar; (Avenger) Modified double-wishbone w/coil springs, direct acting shock absorbers and link-type stabilizer bar; (Stratus) Unequal length upper and lower control arms, coil springs, tubular shock absorbers and stabilizer bar; (Intrepid) Iso-strut w/integral gas-charged shock absorbers, coil springs, single transverse lower links, tension struts and link-type stabilizer bar; (Viper) Cast aluminum unequal length upper and lower control arms, coil springs,

low-pressure gas-charged shock absorbers w/adjustable rebound and stabilizer bar. Rear suspension: (Neon) Chapman struts, coil springs, dual lower transverse links, lower trailing links, link-type stabilizer bar; (Avenger) Double wishbones, coil springs, direct acting shock absorbers and (ES only) link-type stabilizer bar; (Stratus) Unequal length upper and lower control arms, trailing arms, coil springs, tubular shock absorbers and stabilizer bar (larger stabilizer bar with 2.5-liter V-6 in ES); (Intrepid) Chapman struts w/integral gas-charged shock absorbers, concentric coil springs, dual transverse lower links, lower trailing links and link-type stabilizer bar ("sport ride "suspension on R/T); (Viper) Cast aluminum unequal length upper and lower control arms w/toe-control links, coil springs, low-pressure gas-charged shock absorbers w/adjustable rebound and stabilizer bar. Brakes: Front disc, rear drum (power-assisted) exc. (Avenger (all), Stratus ES, Intrepid ES) four-wheel disc w/anti-lock; (Intrepid, Viper) four-wheel disc. Body construction: Unibody exc. (Intrepid) Unibody w/isolated engine/suspension cradle and rear cross member; (Viper) Backbone tubular space frame w/separate cowl structure w/resin transfer & SMC body panels and alum sills. Fuel tank: (Neon) 12.5 gals.; (Avenger) 16 gals.; (Stratus) 16 gals.; (Intrepid) 17 gals.; (Viper) 18 gals., (RT/10) 18.5 gals. (GTS).

DRIVETRAIN OPTIONS: Engines: 2.4-liter four, Stratus (NC, required with 4-spd auto. trans.); 3.2-liter V-6, Intrepid ES ($500); Transmission: Three-speed auto. trans.: Neon Highline ($600). Four-speed auto. trans.: Stratus SE, incl. spd control ($1050). Brakes: Anti-lock: Neon Highline ($515-$565); Stratus SE ($565). Four-wheel disc w/anti-lock: Avenger ES ($600); Intrepid, base ($600).

NEON CONVENIENCE/APPEARANCE OPTIONS: Highline: Pkg. 21D: stnd equip. (NC). ES: Pkg. 21G: incl. ES badging, air conditoning, color-keyed instrument panel bezel, keyless entry, pwr door locks with central locking, pwr heated exterior mirrors, security alarm. Sentry key theft deterrent system, leather-wrapped strg whl and shift knob, pwr trunk lid release, pwr windows, premium cloth low-back bucket seats, passenger assist handles, fog lamps, tachometer, P185/60R15 BSW touring tires, and 15-in. whl covers ($1760). R/T: Details regarding the specifications and cost of the R/T package were not available at the time of publication. Other: (Highline) Air conditioning ($1000). Dlx Convenience Grp.: incl. automatic spd cntrl w/strg whl switches & tilt strg column—must have A/C ($350). Pwr Convenience Grp.: Pwr heated fold-away mirrors & pwr frnt windows—must have Sentry key security grp. and A/C ($380). Sentry Key Security Grp.: Security alarm, Sentry key theft deterrent system, four-function keyless entry, tachometer, pwr automatic door locks w/lighted switches, central locking, lock-out protection & enhanced accident response system, pwr trunk lid release—must have A/C ($315). (Highline, ES) 3-spd auto. trans. replaces 5-spd manual ($600). Speed control ($225). 4-disc instrument panel-mounted CD changer ($125). Engine blk htr ($20). 15-in. alum whls w/P185/60R15 Goodyear Eagle LS all-season touring tires - must have A/C ($355). Anti-lock Brake Grp.: incl. anti-lock 4-whl-disc brakes, tachometer, & traction cntrl ($595). Light Grp.: incl. illuminated visor vanity mirrors, inside rear view mirror w/reading lamps, glove compartment lamp, underhood lamp, & console flood lamp—must have A/C ($130). Front ash tray & cigar lighter ($20).

AVENGER CONVENIENCE/APPEARANCE OPTIONS: Base: Pkg. 24E: stnd equip. (NC). AM/FM stereo radio w/CD & cass. & 6 spkrs ($435). Security alarm w/remote keyless entry and panic alarm ($305). ES: Pkg. 24F: stnd equip. (NC). 4-whl anti-lock disc barakes ($600). AM/FM stereo radio w/CD & cass., equal. & 8 Infinity spkrs ($325). Other: Pwr sunroof ($685).

STRATUS CONVENIENCE/APPEARANCE OPTIONS: SE: Pkg. 21A: stnd equip. (NC). Pkg. 24B: Includes floor mats, spd sensitive pwr door locks, dual pwr remote heated mirrors, pwr windows, 8-way pwr driver's seat. (NC). Prem. AM/FM/cassette stereo radio w/CD & 6 spkrs ($200). ES: Pkg. 26S: incl cargo net, remote/illum. entry grp., 8-way pwr driver's seat, leather bucket seats, premium AM/FM/cassette radio w/8 spkrs, & security alarm ($280). 8-way pwr leather driver's seat ($380). Security

alarm ($175). Other: Remote/Illum. Grp.: incl. illum. entry, remote keyless entry ($170). Eng. block & battery heater ($30). Cigar lighter and front ash tray ($20). Inferno Red paint ($200). Prem. AM/FM stereo radio w/cass., CD changer & 8 spkrs ($340). Prem. AM/FM stereo radio w/cass., CD changer & 6 spkrs, SE ($550) ES ($210). Pwr sunroof: SE ($695); ES ($580). Conventional spare tire ($125).

INTREPID CONVENIENCE/APPEARANCE OPTIONS: Intrepid: Pkg. 22C: stnd equip. (NC). Remote Keyless/Illum. Entry Grp.: incl. keyless entry w/2 transmitters, illum entry ($225). Cloth 50/50 bench seat ($100). 8-way pwr driver's seat ($380). ES: Pkg. 23L & 24L: stnd equip. ($115 credit). Pkg. 24M(a): 24L plus auto. temp. air cond., overhead trip computer/garage door opener, auto day/night mirror, security alarm, full-size spare tire, traction control ($1170). Pkg. 24M(b): 24L plus auto. temp. air cond., overhead trip computer/garage door opener, auto day/night mirror, illum visor vanity mirrors, AM/FM stereo w/cassette and CD changer control, 4-disc in-dash changer & 9 Infinity speakers, leather-trimmed bucket seats, 8-way pwr driver's & passenger's seats, security alarm, Sentry theft deterrent system, & full-size spare tire ($2560). Comfort/Security Grp.: incl. auto. temp. air cond., security alarm, ($330). 8-way pwr driver's & pass. seat ($1000). R/T: Driver Conv Grp.: Incl. illum. entry, keyless entry system & 8-way pwr driver's seat ($605). Other: Front & rear ash tray & cigar lighter ($20).) Pwr sunroof ($895). Eng. block & battery heater ($30). Inferno Red paint ($200). Full-size spare tire & whl ($90-$125) base & ES ($215) R/T. AM/FM/cassette stereo radio w/CD changer, amp & 8 spkrs, base & ES ($575). Anti-lock brakes, base & ES ($600). Anti-lock brakes w/traction control, ES ($775).

VIPER CONVENIENCE/APPEARANCE OPTIONS: RT/10: Pkg. 21A: stnd equip. (NC). Tonneau cover ($250). Body-color (red, black or steel gray) detachable hardtop ($2500). GTS: Pkg. 21A: stnd equip. (NC). Dual silver painted stripes ($2500). ACR Competition Grp.: incl. low restriction air cleaner, radio, air cond. & fog lamp delete, ACR badging, competition suspension, 18-in. racing whls, five-point harness ($10000.). Comfort Grp.: ACR req'd) restores radio and air cond. to ACR package ($910).

OTHER: Cognac-colored Connolly Leather Interior Grp.: incl. Connolly leather seats w/carpeted backs, Connolly leather-wrapped steering wheel, shift knob, parking brake handle & brake handle boot, color-keyed carpet, knee blocker, console, door trim panel inserts, speaker grilles & door panel assist handles ($750, available w/select colors, not available w/ACR Grp.)

HISTORY: At the 2000 North American International Auto Show, in Detroit, Dodge unveiled its 2001 Intrepid R/T Winston Cup show car, less than 100 days after the October 1999 announcement of the division's intention to return to NASCAR Winston Cup racing beginning with the 2001 Daytona 500. Long positioned as the performance-oriented division of Chrysler Corporation, and fueled by successes in the NASCAR Craftsman Truck racing series, Dodge Division was determined to return to the Winston Cup racing venue where it had seen so much success in the past. In February 2000 Dodge officially announced the complement of teams and drivers slated to help carry the Dodge banner in its Winston Cup return. Bill Davis Racing and Petty Enterprises were named to partner with Evernham Motorsports, which had been at work developing the company's Dodge Intrepid R/T Winston Cup program since its October announcement. "We have created a strategic alliance that blends some of the very best racing minds and driving talent in Winston Cup racing today," said Jim Julow, Vice President - Dodge Division. It was a pair of legendary Pettys—Lee and Richard—who had much to do with Dodge's first successful run in the NASCAR Winston Cup ranks from the '50s through the '70s. Along with notable drivers such as David Pearson and Buddy Baker, the Pettys helped Dodge amass 160 Winston Cup victories and two manufacturers titles.

Safe Passage — Sight Unseen

THROUGH blinding fog and sleet in the North Atlantic, across the vast, dazzling expanse of the South Pacific, into strange harbors and along mountainous coasts move the Allied convoys and their escorting ships of war.

On hundreds of them is that magic instrument—the Sperry Gyro-Compass—made by Dodge for the surer guidance and safer passage of those valiant ships and crews.

Making the great Gyro Compass called for tooling of the highest order. Making it in quantity production was one of the most exacting of manufacturing jobs; with some ten thousand individual parts for every compass —with tolerances, balance, and perfection of final performance such as gallant ships and lives might depend upon.

Nothing in the history of Dodge surpasses this production accomplishment—unless it is the same kind of precision work on the great Bofors guns for the same ships, or the thousands of Dodge fighting trucks that have gone to battle areas as part of the cargo.

The two million Dodge cars and trucks at home are doing a good wartime job. Their tire mileage is remarkably high and their gas consumption extremely low. The engineering features that became famous in peace time are of vital importance now.

DODGE
Division of Chrysler Corporation

A War Record to Read and Remember!

43

The Chrysler Imperial Series CG roadster for 1931 sported a semi-custom body by LeBaron. Weighing in at 4,530 pounds and priced at $3,220, this beauty is one of just 100 built.

A 1934 Plymouth Deluxe four-door sedan like this one was the one-millionth Plymouth built; it was driven off the assembly line by Walter P. Chrysler on August 8th of that year. The family shown here was sold on their Plymouth's safety features, which included Hydraulic Brakes, Safety-Steel Body, Floating Power engine mounts, and Individual Front Wheel Springing.

"WE FOUND WHAT WE WANTED
A Carefree Car!"

"It's a Plymouth with _All_ _Four_ Features we need"

MGM film star Spencer Tracy appeared in print ads for the 1939 DeSoto. He is shown here with a Custom Four-Door Touring Sedan. Other contemporary Hollywood personalities to associate their names with DeSoto included Myrna Loy and Walt Disney.

During its 10-year production run (1941-1950), Chrysler's wood-trimmed Town & Country series was offered in station wagon, convertible, four-door sedan, and two-door hardtop form. Shown here is a '47 Town & Country sedan.

Newly restyled and down-sized for 1953, 35,185 copies of the Plymouth Cranbrook Belvedere two-door hardtop were built. Genuine wire wheels were optional that year and could be had chrome-plated (shown) or painted.

250 HP Chrysler New Yorker Deluxe St. Regis in Navajo Orange and Desert Sand

ANNOUNCING America's most smartly different car

CHRYSLER FOR 1955
WITH THE NEW 100-MILLION-DOLLAR LOOK

Chrysler Corporation's "New 100-Million-Dollar Look" for 1955 featured totally new styling in all lines and bright, new color combinations imaginatively applied.

Nineteen fifty-six was the second year for Imperial's unique "sparrow-strainer," free-standing taillight design, a styling cue that was to be echoed in one form or another through the 1962 model year.

Available as a two-door hardtop or a convertible, the '57 Chrysler 300C was powered by a standard 375-hp, 392-cid version of Chrysler's legendary Hemi V-8, with 390 hp available optionally. Just 484 convertibles hit the streets that year.

During the '50s, popular TV personality Lawrence Welk and his Champagne Musicmakers were sponsored by Dodge. Here Welk poses in his personalized '57 Dodge Custom Royal Lancer convertible equipped with a dealer-installed B&W Continental Wheel Kit.

This 1958 DeSoto Fireflite Sportsman two-door hardtop displays the spring dress-up group available that year and consisting of anodized aluminum inserts defined by the sidesweep moldings, plus eight trunk lid accent strips and a lower body molding of stainless steel.

For 1959, its last year of station wagon production, the heaviest DeSoto was the Fireflite Explorer nine-passenger wagon. It weighed in at a road-hugging 4,205 pounds and, with its $4,358 price tag, attracted 433 buyers.

Best of show ...and GO!

Among the many "hyphen-ated" standard features of this 1960 Plymouth Fury four-door hardtop were Torsion-Aire Suspension, Custom-Positioned Front Seats, Safety-Rim Wheels, and Total-Contact Brakes.

Dodge's entire compact Dart line was restyled for 1965. The top-end GT models – available only as two-door hardtops and convertibles – all had padded dashboards, full wheel covers, bucket seats, and distinctive body markings.

With 8,426 examples built, the Imperial LeBaron four-door hardtop for 1970 outsold the less costly Crown Series version by more than six to one.

This close-up of a '71 Plymouth Hemi 'Cuda engine compartment clearly shows the "shaker" air cleaner – so-called because it "shakes" with every vibration of the engine – and the hood opening through which it protrudes.

As the last rear-drive holdout in the Plymouth line, Chrysler's marketing mavens called the '83 Gran Fury four-door sedan "The American Way to Get Your Money's Worth." Popular as a police vehicle, it soldiered on, continuing to offer V-8 power, through 1989.

The second in Chrysler's series of "retro-style" dream cars come true (after the Dodge Viper RT/10, introduced in 1992) the '97 Plymouth Prowler took the automotive world by storm. Dubbed a "factory hot rod," the Prowler Purple roadster evoked uniquely American visions of cruisin', drive-ins, and drag strips, but became available only to a fortunate few.

For 2000, Chrysler's rakish Sebring convertible, which replaced the LeBaron GTC in 1996, carried Chrysler's cab-forward design onward for yet another year. The drop-top Sebring proved far more popular than its predecessor with sales averaging some 50,000 per year.

Eagle

EAGLE
1988-1998

After Chrysler Corp. formally acquired American Motors Corp. on August 5, 1987, for a reported $1.5 billion, it established a new Jeep-Eagle Division to market the products previously adorned with the AMC badge. With this move, 1,453 former AMC dealers became Jeep-Eagle dealers. While the Jeep end of the division continued the success that the rugged machine had known for years (it was, after all, the main reason why Chrysler Corp. acquired AMC), the Eagle portion of the division was launched carrying some "baggage" acquired from AMC. Looming large was the inherited joint venture projects with automaker Renault of France, which were forged in the AMC era.

The Renault-shared automobiles acquired were simply folded into the newly launched Eagle division of Chrysler Corp. This attempted meshing of products was, from the start, too much of an identity crisis to overcome. Because of it, the Eagle brand would never gain the autonomy that Chrysler had wanted—and spent many dollars to attain—for its fledgling division. Eagle models imported from Renault of France (Medallion), models imported from Japan that were eventually produced in the United States (Summit), and even the former AMC model built in Canada (Premier) never found enough buyers to justify their continuation and were eventually discontinued. If Eagle ever did hit any kind of stride, it was after borrowing an idea from the very company it sought distance from, AMC.

1990 Eagle Talon coupe (OCW)

Just as the cult-favorite AMC Eagle line featured all-wheel-drive (AWD), Eagle's introduction of the Talon sports coupe in 1990, available in both front- and all-wheel drive, allowed the division a moment of glory. That, too, though, was short-lived. Sales of fewer than 35,000 Talons (in both drive configurations) in each of the first two years of its existence and dropping to approximately 28,000 and 27,000 in its third and fourth years, respectively, was not cause for celebration among Chrysler brass.

By 1993, the Eagle division was purged of AMC/Renault-borne products, now offering the Talon and the Vision sedan—Chrysler Corp.'s "cab-forward" contribution to the Eagle lineup—as well as the Mitsubishi-inspired Summit. The stigma of buyer reluctance to Eagle products, though, when first year sales figures for Vision and its two shared-platform counterparts are compared: Dodge Intrepid - 89,127, Chrysler Concorde - 56,029, and Eagle Vision - 24,429.

Eagle's Talon/Vision domestic lineup would carry on through 1997, annually combining to sell around 50,000 cars until the bottom fell out in 1996 when only 15,100 Talons and 12,806 Visions found buyers. Already rumors were thick that Chrysler was ready to pull the plug on its Eagle division, rumors that were vehemently denied at Chrysler's top level. In a move to bolster Eagle products, Chrysler-Plymouth and Jeep-Eagle divisions were consolidated in August 1996. It didn't change the downward spiral of Eagle sales as only 9,788 Talons and 5,874 Visions were sold in 1997, and that abysmal showing ended the Vision (both the car and Chrysler's outlook for making the Eagle division a player of the same stature as its other divisions).

1991 Eagle Premier four-door sedan (OCW)

The Talon returned for one more year, selling a paltry 4,308 units (both front- and all-wheel-drive versions) in 1998. Chrysler then announced the demise of Eagle, which left the Jeep as the lone survivor of the American Motors buyout in 1987. But, then, isn't that what Chrysler wanted from the start?

In the collector-car marketplace, the last few years of all-wheel-drive Talons should spark high interest. These cars were the beneficiary of several years of "improving the breed" as well as being smartly styled automobiles with the ruggedness of AWD built in.

1988 EAGLE

The new Eagle automobile division of Chrysler Corp. was launched with two series - one already terminated before the model year really got underway - and two others on the way. The 1988 Eagle Premier sedan, built in Brampton, Ontario, Canada, was launched on December 26, 1987. The 1988 Eagle station wagon - a carry-over four-wheel-drive AMC model that was also assembled in Brampton - was discontinued in December 1987. On May 6, 1988, the Medallion sedan and station wagon were introduced as 1989 Eagle models. Medallion models were produced by Renault in France and imported into the United States, and for that reason are not covered in this catalog beyond the aforementioned introductory mention. Also debuted in 1988 as a 1989 model was the Eagle Summit, launched in August 1988. The Summit, a joint-venture product of Chrysler Corp. and Mitsubishi Motors of Japan, began production in May 1989 at the new Diamond-Star Motors Corp. (DSM) in Normal, Illinois. DSM was a Chrysler/Mitsubishi 50:50 joint-ownership facility that also produced the Mitsubishi Eclipse, Plymouth Laser and soon-to-come-online 1989 Eagle Talon.

1988 Eagle, Premier ES sedan (OCW)

EAGLE — SERIES N/A — SIX — It was now officially the Eagle Eagle! In its ninth and final year on the market, the way-ahead-of-its-time Eagle station wagon was powered by the 258-cid six-cylinder engine with five-speed overdrive transmission, but an automatic transmission (floor shift with select drive) was offered as a no-cost option. The car was basically carried over from its days as an AMC product (see 1985-1986 AMC Eagle listings). Production of the four-wheel-drive station wagon (which has since established a cult following among collector car enthusiasts) was terminated in December 1987—a mere four months after Chrysler Corp. acquired AMC. Most of the previously optional equipment for Eagle, such as air conditioning, automatic transmission and tilt steering wheel, was made standard in a move to both use up existing stocks of parts quicker and to make assembly easier by limiting variations in equipment levels.

PREMIER — SERIES B — FOUR/V-6 — The Premier name was also a carry-over from the American Motors buy-out (a joint AMC/Renault model built in Canada). The midsize, front-wheel-drive Eagle Premier sedan was available in two trim levels: LX and the more upscale ES. The car was designed by Giorgetto Giugiaro, the head of Ital Design in Turin, Italy. The LX sedan was powered by a throttle-body fuel-injected 2.5-liter four-cylinder engine paired with an AR4 electronically controlled four-speed automatic transmission with overdrive that was jointly developed by Renault and Volkswagen. The AR4 had a reverse gear lock-out feature that would not allow the car to be shifted into reverse while it was moving forward. The 2.5-liter four produced 111 horsepower and 142 pound-feet of torque. It allowed the Premier to travel 0-60 mph in 11.6 seconds, and featured a computer-controlled engine management system. The ES sedan used the all-aluminum, multi-point fuel-injected 3.0-liter V-6 linked to a ZF 4HP18 four-speed automatic with overdrive, also equipped with reverse gear lock-out. This powertrain combination was optional on LX models. The 3.0-liter V-6 was a joint venture project involving Renault, Peugeot and Volvo and also featured a microprocessor-controlled engine management system. It generated 150 horsepower and 171 pound-feet of torque and propelled the Premier from 0-60 mph in less than 10 seconds. Attesting to its aerodynamic body design, the Premier achieved a low 0.33 coefficient of drag - among the best for a mass-production passenger car. Exterior features of the Premier included limousine-type doors for easy entry and exit, quad halogen headlamps, full-width taillights, urethane encapsulated rocker panels for enhanced corrosion protection, and, on ES models, wide lower bodyside cladding. Inside, standard features of the LX included dual front seat recliners, rear seat center armrest, digital clock, leather-wrapped steering wheel, rear door child safety locks, and analog instrumentation. Standard inside the ES were luxury front bucket seats, full-length console with armrest, and rallye instrumentation including a vehicle maintenance monitor and trip com-

puter. The ES also featured turbine polycast sport wheels, dual exhaust, and bodyside accent stripes as exterior standard fare. Exterior color choices were Dover Gray, Sterling, Light Baltic, Dark Baltic, Vivid Red, Driftwood, Dark Driftwood and Dark Cherry (all metallic clearcoat) as well as Pearl White and Classic Black. Interior color choices (in pin stripe velour and cloth) were Charcoal, Navy, Brownstone and Cordovan. Premier offered 16.3 cubic feet of trunk space and 121.3 cubic feet of interior room. Optional equipment included remote keyless entry, rear window defroster and power sunroof.

1988 Eagle, Premier LX sedan (OCW)

I.D. DATA: Eagle's 17-symbol Vehicle Identification Number (VIN) was embossed on a metal plate riveted to the top left surface of the instrument panel, visible through the windshield. Model year (symbol ten) was 'J' for 1988.

EAGLE (SIX)

Model No.	Body/ Style No.	Body Type & Seating	Factory Price	Shipping Weight	Prod. Total
N/A	N/A	4-dr Sta Wag-5P	12995	3502	2,305

PREMIER LX (FOUR)

BXP	41	4-dr Sed-6P	13104	2858	Note 1

PREMIER ES (V-6)

BXS	41	4-dr Sed-5P	14079	2960	Note 1

Note 1: Premier sedan production totaled 45,546 with no further breakout available.

ENGINE DATA: BASE FOUR (Premier LX): Inline, overhead valve four-cylinder. Cast iron block; aluminum head. Displacement: 150 cu. in. (2.5 liters). Bore & stroke: 3.86 x 3.19 in. Compression ratio: 9.2:1. Brake horsepower: 111 at 4750 RPM. Torque: 142 lb.-ft. at 2500 RPM. Bendix throttle-body fuel injection. BASE V-6 (Premier ES); OPTIONAL V-6 (Premier LX): 90 degree, overhead cam V-6. Aluminum block and heads. Displacement: 182 cu. in. (3.0 liters). Bore & stroke: 3.66 x 2.87 in. Compression ratio: 9.3:1. Brake horsepower: 150 at 5000 RPM. Torque: 171 lb.-ft. at 3750 RPM. Multi-point fuel injection. BASE SIX (Eagle): Inline, overhead valve six-cylinder. Cast iron block and head. Displacement: 258 cu. in. (4.2 liters). Bore & stroke: 3.75 x 3.90 in. Compression ratio: 9.2:1. Brake horsepower: 110 at 3200 RPM. Torque: 210 lb.-ft. at 1800 RPM. Carburetor: 2Bbl.

CHASSIS DATA: Wheelbase: (Eagle) 109.3 in.; (Premier) 105.5 in. Overall length: (Eagle) 180.9 in.; (Premier) 192.6 in. Height: (Eagle) 54.4 in.; (Premier) 55.8 in. Width: (Eagle) 72.3 in.; (Premier) 69.8 in. Front Tread: (Eagle) 59.6 in.; (Premier) 58.1 in. Rear Tread: (Eagle) 57.6 in.; (Premier) 57.0 in. Standard Tires: (Eagle) P195/75R15; (Premier LX) P195/70R14; (Premier ES) P205/70HR14.

TECHNICAL: Transmission: (Eagle) Five-speed manual with overdrive (select drive automatic offered as a no-cost option). (Premier) Four-speed automatic with overdrive. Steering: (Eagle) Recirculating ball; (Premier) Rack and pinion. Front suspension: (Eagle) Independent front w/coil springs; (Premier) MacPherson-type w/inclined coil springs and stabilizer bar. Rear suspension: (Eagle) Semi-elliptic leaf springs; (Premier) Independent w/trailing arms, twin tube shock absorbers and four transverse torsion bars. Brakes: (Eagle) Front disc, rear drum; (Premier) Front disc, rear drum (power assisted). Body construction: (Eagle) Body on frame; (Premier) Unibody. Fuel tank: (Eagle) 22 gals.; (Premier) 17 gals.

DRIVETRAIN OPTIONS: Eagle: Three-speed floor-shift automatic transmission (NC). Optional 2.73:1 axle ratio ($35). H.D. engine cooling ($82). Automatic load leveling air shocks ($192). Extra-duty suspension pkg. ($91). Front suspension skid plate ($91). Trailer towing package A (to 2,000 pounds) ($123). Trailer towing package B (to 3,500 pounds) ($262). H.D. battery ($34). Cold climate group ($68). Premier: 3.0L V-6, LX ($680). ZF 4-spd auto. trans., LX w/3.0L V-6 only (NC).

EAGLE CONVENIENCE/APPEARANCE OPTIONS: Protection Grp.: incl. front/rear bumper guards, front/rear mats, stainless steel door edge guards ($90). Convenience Grp.: incl. headlight-on buzzer, intermittent wipers, lighted vanity mirror ($87). Gauge pkg. ($107). Light Grp. ($72). Right remote control ($37). Cruise control ($200). Halogen headlamps ($18). Halogen foglamps ($97). AM/FM radio ($197). Electronic-tuning AM/FM/Stereo radio ($258). Electronic-tuning AM/FM/cassette stereo radio ($474). Power door locks ($205). Power windows and door locks

($503). Power six-way driver's seat ($224). Power six-way driver/pass. seats ($357). Floor shift console ($76). Parcel shelf ($32). Rear wiper/washer ($146). Rear window defroster ($160). Leather-wrapped sport steering wheel ($29). Woodgrain paneling ($170). Black scuff moldings ($65). Roof rack ($136). Bumper guards ($62). Sport 15-in. alum. whls ($239). Wire wheel covers ($171). Tires: P195/75R15 ($25). P195/75R15B w/whitewall ($87).

PREMIER CONVENIENCE/APPEARANCE OPTIONS: LX: (AFF) LX Luxury Option Grp.: incl. Popular Option Grp., dual elect. remote control mirrors, dual illum. visor mirrors, pwr windows, prem. audio syst. ($2201). (ADN) Electronic Information Pkg.: incl. vehicle maintenance monitor and trip computer ($300). (AWC) Enthusiast Grp.: incl. fabric bucket seats, touring susp., P205/70HR14 tires, 14-in. alum whls ($640). ES: (AFF) ES Luxury Option Grp.: incl. Popular Option Grp., dual elect. remote control mirrors, pwr windows, prem. audio syst. ($1962). Other: (AAM) Popular Option Grp.: incl. air cond., Convenience Grp., Pwr Lock Grp. ($1305). (AWF) Power Lock Grp.: incl. pwr door locks, pwr decklid release, remote fuel door release, remote door lock feature w/illum. entry ($405). (ADC) Convenience Grp.: incl. cruise control, tilt stng whl ($310). 45/45 fabric bucket seats, LX ($100). 45/45 leather bucket seats, ES ($566). Air cond. ($830). Calif. emissions ($100). Luggage rack ($115). Pwr windows ($290). 6-way pwr driver's/pass. seats ($480). (RAF) AM/FM stereo radio w/cass. ($234). (ARA) AM/FM stereo radio w/cass., graphic equal., pwr antenna & 8 Jensen spkrs: LX ($602); ES ($295). 14-in. cast alum whls: LX ($370); ES ($295). Conventional spare tire ($83).

HISTORY: Model year production: 47,851 (not including imported Medallion). Model year sales by U.S. dealers: 32,789 (not including imported Medallion). Sales of 29,878 Premiers was a disappointment for Chrysler as 40,000 were projected to leave showrooms for the first-year Eagle product.

1989 EAGLE

With Chrysler Corp. trying to mold the Eagle division into "one of its own," work was underway in both the Jeep and Eagle arenas to distance those products from their American Motors heritage. Gone was the four-wheel-drive Eagle station wagon that was produced briefly the previous model year until its remaining parts supplies were used up. (In actuality, it was gone when the purchase of AMC was completed in August 1987.) Chrysler would not abandon the four-wheel-drive format, though, with the all-wheel drive Eagle Talon coming onboard in 1990. Also, the Renault-based Medallion import that Chrysler Corp. "acquired" in the AMC deal would be sold through the 1989 model year and then dropped. This after a meager 15,658 Medallion sales were recorded in 1988. New for 1989 was the Eagle Summit sedan, which was available in two trim levels: DL and LX. Also, a Premier ES Limited sedan joined the existing LX and ES sedans.

1989 Eagle, Summit LX sedan (OCW)

SUMMIT — SERIES 2 — FOUR — While in its first year it was technically an import, the 1989 Summit is being included in this catalog because Chrysler Corp.'s intent was to produce the car at its 50 percent-owned Diamond-Star Motors Corp. facility in Normal, Illinois. Due to delays, this did not happen until the 1991 model year, but we include the first two years of Summit production (imported from Mitsubishi Motors Corp. of Japan—the other 50 percent owner of Diamond-Star Motors Corp.) for consistency. In its launch year, the subcompact Summit sedan was available in DL and more upscale LX trim levels. Standard powertrain for the DL and LX models was the multi-port fuel-injected 1.5-liter four-cylinder engine paired with a five-speed manual transmission with overdrive. A three-speed automatic was optional for both models. A special performance package was also available for the LX sedan that featured a dual

overhead cam 1.6-liter four linked to a five-speed manual transmission. A four-speed automatic with overdrive was optional with this "power" package. The more potent Summit LX also featured a sport suspension that included heavy-duty front anti-sway bar and coil springs and gas-charged shock absorbers. Four-wheel disc brakes were part of the package as well as special exterior colors, interior trim and sport bucket seats. DL models featured cloth seats, floor console and manual rack-and-pinion steering. The front suspension utilized independent MacPherson-type struts and coils while the rear was comprised of a three-link trailing arm and coil system. The luxury-oriented LX sedan had full-face velour on seating surfaces, bucket seats with adjustable height control on the driver's seat, power rack-and-pinion steering, and a tilt/telescoping steering column. Optional equipment on both Summit trim levels included power windows and door locks, electronically-tuned radio, air conditioning, dual remote electrically adjusted mirrors, cruise control and 13- or 14-inch aluminum wheels.

1989-1/2 Eagle, Premier ES Limited sedan (PH)

PREMIER — SERIES B — FOUR/V-6 — An ES Limited sedan was added to the Premier lineup in the spring of 1989, joining the existing LX and ES intermediate sedans. The ES Limited model, built in the tradition of European performance touring sedans, featured an all-white monochromatic exterior including grille, fascias, side cladding and wheels, offset by black window molding. Other special features included four-wheel disc brakes, leather seating, and 15-inch aluminum wheels. Power source was the 3.0-liter V-6 mated to a four-speed automatic transmission with overdrive, which was modified for smoother downshifting. This powertrain was also again standard on the ES and optional on the LX (which again used the 2.5-liter four paired with the AR4 electronically controlled four-speed automatic with overdrive). Standard equipment on the ES Limited included air conditioning, power windows/locks/mirrors/seats, and a Premium Audio sound system. For 1989, the Premier LX and ES received increased levels of standard equipment, including items that were optional the previous year such as electric rear window defogger and floor mats. On the LX, full analog instrumentation (including tach) was also made standard. In response to feedback from consumers, the Premier's steering effort was reduced for 1989. Over one-half of Premier's functions were controlled by ten on-board computers including its "smart" heater that delayed blower operation until warm air could be provided.

I.D. DATA: Eagle's 17-symbol Vehicle Identification Number (VIN) was embossed on a metal plate riveted to the top left surface of the instrument panel, visible through the windshield. Model year (symbol ten) was 'K' for 1989.

SUMMIT (FOUR)

Model No.	Body/ Style No.	Body Type & Seating	Factory Price	Shipping Weight	Prod. Total
2XM	41	4-dr DL Sed-5P	9347	2271	Note 1
2XM	41	4-dr LX Sed-5P	10364/11169	2337/2513	Note 1

Note: Summit LX price and weight to left of slash for SOHC four, to right for DOHC four.

Note 1: Summit sedan production for 1989 N/A. U.S. sales totaled 27,213 with no further breakout available.

PREMIER LX (FOUR)

BXP	41	4-dr Sed-6P	13956	2938	Note 1

PREMIER ES (V-6)

BXS	41	4-dr Sed-5P	15259	2899	Note 1
BXS	41	4-dr Ltd. Sed-5P	19181	N/A	Note 1

Note 1: Premier sedan production totaled 41,349 with no further breakout available.

ENGINE DATA: BASE FOUR (Summit DL, Summit LX): Inline, overhead cam four-cylinder. Cast iron block; aluminum head. Displacement: 90 cu. in. (1.5 liters). Bore & stroke: 2.97 x 3.23 in. Compression ratio: 9.4:1. Brake horsepower: 81 at 6500 RPM. Torque: 91 lb.-ft. at 3000 RPM. Multi-point fuel injection. OPTIONAL FOUR (Summit LX): Inline, dual overhead cam four-cylinder. Cast iron block; aluminum head. Displacement: 97 cu. in. (1.6 liters). Bore & stroke: 3.24 x 2.95 in. Com-

pression ratio: 9.2:1. Brake horsepower: 113 at 6500 RPM. Torque: 99 lb.-ft. at 5000 RPM. Multi-point fuel injection. BASE FOUR (Premier LX): Inline, overhead valve four-cylinder. Cast iron block; aluminum head. Displacement: 150 cu. in. (2.5 liters). Bore & stroke: 3.86 x 3.19 in. Compression ratio: 9.2:1. Brake horsepower: 111 at 4750 RPM. Torque: 142 lb.-ft. at 2500 RPM. Bendix throttle-body fuel injection. BASE V-6 (Premier ES, Premier ES Limited); OPTIONAL V-6 (Premier LX): 90 degree, overhead cam V-6. Aluminum block and heads. Displacement: 182 cu. in. (3.0 liters). Bore & stroke: 3.66 x 2.87 in. Compression ratio: 9.3:1. Brake horsepower: 150 at 5000 RPM. Torque: 171 lb.-ft. at 3750 RPM. Multi-point fuel injection.

CHASSIS DATA: Wheelbase: (Summit) 96.7 in.; (Premier) 106.0 in. Overall length: (Summit) 170.1 in.; (Premier) 192.8 in. Height: (Summit) 52.8 in.; (Premier) 53.3 in. Width: (Summit) 65.7 in.; (Premier) 70.0 in. Front Tread: (Summit) 56.3 in.; (Premier) 58.2 in. Rear Tread: (Summit) 56.3 in.; (Premier) 57.1 in. Standard Tires: (Summit DL) P155/80R13; (Summit LX) P175/70R13; (Premier LX) P195/70R14; (Premier ES) P205/70HR14; (Premier ES Limited) P205/60HR15.

TECHNICAL: Transmission: (Summit) Five-speed manual with overdrive. (Premier) Four-speed automatic with overdrive. Steering: (Summit, Premier) Rack and pinion. Front suspension: (Summit) Independent strut w/coil springs, strut-type shock absorbers and stabilizer bar; (Premier) MacPherson strut w/steering arm on strut cast, iron lower A-arm w/plastic ball joint-type. Rear suspension: (Summit) Three-link torsion axle w/coil springs, and telescopic-type shock absorbers; (Premier) Trailing arms w/integral twist beam torsion bars, suspension/stabilizer bar and monotube high-pressure gas shock cartridges. Brakes: (Summit, Premier) Front disc, rear drum (power assisted) exc. Summit LX w/DOHC 1.6-liter four (four-wheel disc). Body construction: (Summit) Monocock body; (Premier) Unibody. Fuel tank: (Summit) 13.2 gals.; (Premier) 17.0 gals.

DRIVETRAIN OPTIONS: Transmission: Three-speed floor-shift auto., Summit DL and LX ($505). Four-speed floor-shift auto., Summit LX w/DOHC pkg. ($682); w/column-shift, Premier (NC). Engine: DOHC 1.6-liter four, Summit LX (N/A). 3.0-liter V-6, Premier LX ($680).

SUMMIT CONVENIENCE/APPEARANCE OPTIONS: DL: IFA Pkg.: stnd equip. (NC). IFB Pkg.: incl. IFA plus digital clock, pwr stng, tinted glass, elect. AM/FM stereo radio ($680). IFC Pkg.: incl. IFB plus elect. stereo radio w/cass., dual elect. mirrors ($215). IFD Pkg.: incl. IFC plus 13-in. alum. whls ($300). LX: IFA Pkg.: stnd equip. (NC). IFB Pkg.: incl. IFA plus dual elect. mirrors and elect. AM/FM stereo radio ($350). IFC Pkg.: incl. IFB plus elect. stereo radio w/cass., pwr windows, pwr door locks ($610). IFF Pkg.: IFC plus 13-in. Eurocast alum. whls ($272). LX w/DOHC four: IFD Pkg.: incl. 1.6L four and 5-spd manual trans., DOHC Pkg., dual elect. mirrors, elect. AM/FM stereo radio w/cass. ($1331). IFE Pkg.: incl. IFD plus prem. audio syst., pwr windows, pwr door locks, cruise control, 14-in. Sport alum. whls ($1225). Other: (AYB) DOHC Pkg.: incl. 1.6L four, sport susp., 4-whl disc brakes, unique interior/exterior treatments, LX ($805). (AJP) Pwr windows and door locks ($440). Two-tone paint ($159). Air cond. ($748). Decklid luggage rack ($94). Floor mats ($28). Cruise control incl. intermittent wipers, LX ($211). Dual elect. mirrors: DL ($49); LX ($55). Digital clock, DL ($55). Pwr stng, DL ($262). Tinted glass, DL ($63). (RAT) Elect. AM/FM stereo radio w/6 spkrs ($301). (RAW) Elect. AM/FM stereo radio w/cass. & 6 spkrs ($471). (RAX) Elect. AM/FM stereo radio w/cass., graphic equal. & 6 spkrs ($743). 13-in. Eurocast alum. whls ($272). 14-in. Sport alum. whls, LX w/DOHC Pkg. ($302).

PREMIER CONVENIENCE/APPEARANCE OPTIONS: LX: (AFF) LX Luxury Option Grp.: incl. Popular Option Grp., dual elect. remote control mirrors, dual illum. visor mirrors, pwr windows, prem. audio syst. ($2201). (ADN) Electronic Information Pkg.: incl. vehicle maintenance monitor and trip computer ($300). (AWC) Enthusiast Grp.: incl. fabric bucket seats, touring susp., P205/70HR14 tires, 14-in. alum whls ($640). ES: (AFF) ES Luxury Option Grp.: incl. Popular Option Grp., dual elect. remote control mirrors, pwr windows, prem. audio syst. ($1962). ES Limited: (AGG) ES Limited Pkg.: incl. Bright White Monochromatic exterior, leather bucket seats, body-color fascias/grille/body-side cladding, air cond., Convenience Grp. incl. cruise control & tilt stng whl, dual elect. remote control mirrors, Pwr Lock Grp., pwr windows, pwr 4-whl disc brakes, 6-way pwr driver's & pass. seats, Prem. audio syst., pwr antenna, leather-wrapped stng whl, P205/60HR15 tires, 15-in. Sport alum. whls., accent stripes ($3322). Other: (AAM) Popular Option Grp.: incl. air cond., Convenience Grp., Pwr Lock Grp. ($1305). (AWF) Power Lock Grp.: incl. pwr door locks, pwr decklid release, remote fuel door release, remote door lock feature w/illum. entry ($405). (ADC) Convenience Grp.: incl. cruise control, tilt stng whl ($310). 45/45 fabric bucket seats, LX ($100). 45/45 leather bucket seats: ES ($566); ES Limited (NC). Air cond. ($830). Calif. emissions ($100). Luggage rack ($115). Pwr windows ($290). 6-way pwr driver's/pass. seats ($480). (RAF) AM/FM stereo radio w/cass. ($234). (ARA) AM/FM stereo radio w/cass., graphic equal., pwr antenna & 8 Jensen spkrs: LX ($602); ES ($434). 14-in. cast alum whls: LX ($370); ES ($295). Conventional spare tire: LX, ES ($83); ES Limited ($93).

HISTORY: Model year production: 41,349 (not including imported Summit or Medallion). The 1990 all-wheel drive Eagle Talon was displayed at the 1989 Chicago Auto Show to promote both the car and its assembly site down the road in Normal, Illinois.

1990 EAGLE

The imported Medallion (not covered in this catalog) was discontinued. Beginning in May of 1989, Chrysler Corp.'s 50-percent-owned Diamond-Star Motors Corp. facility in Normal, Illinois, began producing 1990 Eagle Talon coupes in both front- and all-wheel-drive versions. Even though it sold poorly in its initial model year, available models in the Summit series doubled from the previous year with base and ES trim levels joining the existing DL and LX levels. All Premier sedans were now powered by the 3.0-liter V-6. The 2.5-liter four-cylinder engine that was previously standard in the Premier LX was dropped.

1990 Eagle, Talon TSi sports coupe with all-wheel-drive (AWD) (OCW)

1990 Eagle, Premier ES sedan (OCW)

TALON — SERIES D — FOUR — A counterpart to the Mitsubishi Eclipse and Plymouth Laser, the all-new Talon sports coupe was offered in two trim levels: base and TSi. Base models were available in front-wheel drive configuration only while the turbocharged TSi coupe was offered in both front- and all-wheel-drive (AWD) formats. Talon featured an aerodynamic exterior design, cockpit-style interior, and, on the TSi, all-wheel-drive for added grip on slippery surfaces. The base coupe was powered by a 16-valve, dual overhead cam 2.0-liter four-cylinder engine linked to a five-speed manual transmission with overdrive. On this model only a four-speed automatic with overdrive was optional. Both the front- and all-wheel-drive versions of the TSi coupe also used the 2.0-liter four and five-speed manual transmission, but the engine was enhanced by an inter-cooled turbocharger that boosted horsepower to 190 compared with 135 for the non-turbo unit. Talon rode on a 97.2-inch wheelbase contained within a 172.4-inch overall length. The TSi's AWD system operated through a center-mounted viscous limited-slip differential that helped prevent slip between the front and rear axles. Standard equipment on all Talon models included four-wheel power disc brakes, independent front and rear suspension, power rack-and-pinion steering, dual power remote control mirrors, rear spoiler, full analog sport instrumentation and 16-inch wheels. TSi coupes added adjustable driver's seat, exterior aero-effect lower body treatment and leather-wrapped steering wheel and gear-shift knob. Optional equipment included air conditioning, five-spoke alloy wheels and a sunroof.

SUMMIT — SERIES 2 — FOUR — The previous two-sedan Summit lineup doubled in 1990 with the addition of entry-level base and high-end ES trim levels sandwiching the existing DL and LX models. Summit, DL and LX models used the multi-port fuel-injected 1.5-liter four-cylinder engine linked to a five-speed manual transmission with overdrive as standard powertrain. A three-speed automatic was optional for those three models. The ES was powered by the dual overhead cam 1.6-liter four matched to a five-speed manual transmission, which was again the option powertrain on the LX. A four-speed automatic with overdrive was optional on both the LX and ES with the 1.6-liter four. The upscale ES sedan's standard features included sport suspension, cloth sport bucket seats with see-through headrests, monochromatic exterior treatment

(grille insert, door handles and bodyside moldings), split-folding rear seats with center armrest, power rack-and-pinion steering, tilt-and-telescope sport-style urethane steering wheel and turbine-style 14-inch sport wheel covers. Optional equipment for the ES included 14-inch spoke-style aluminum wheels and charcoal lower bodyside paint treatment. A new safety feature for 1990 was the addition of shift-lock to the Summit's optional automatic transmissions.

1990 Eagle, Premier LX sedan with optional luggage rack and lace wheels (OCW)

PREMIER — SERIES B — V-6 — The previous year's Premier lineup consisting of LX, ES and ES Limited sedans carried over to 1990 with the big change occurring under the hood of the LX. Its formerly standard 2.5-liter four-cylinder engine was dropped, making the 3.0-liter V-6 the exclusive engine of the Premier series. All Premiers also used a four-speed automatic transmission with overdrive, which for 1990 featured a floor shift configuration due to the previously used column shifter being discontinued. Also new across-the-board were nameplate graphics, four-wheel power disc brakes, expanded use of exterior blackout trim and stainless steel exhaust system as standard equipment. New options included a CD player, 15-inch lace aluminum wheels. Unique to the ES sedan's list of new standard features were 15-inch Polycast wheels and P205/60R15 performance tires. Also, the touring suspension that was standard on both the ES and ES Limited was upgraded for a more responsive ride.

I.D. DATA: Eagle's 17-symbol Vehicle Identification Number (VIN) was embossed on a metal plate riveted to the top left surface of the instrument panel, visible through the windshield. Model year (symbol ten) was 'L' for 1990.

TALON (FOUR)

Model No.	Body/ Style No.	Body Type & Seating	Factory Price	Shipping Weight	Prod. Total
DXH	24	2-dr Cpe-4P	12995	2711	Note 1
DXP	24	2-dr TSi Cpe-4P	14753	2777	Note 1
DFP	24	2-dr AWD TSi Cpe-4P	16437	3101	Note 1

Note 1: Talon coupe production totaled 32,708 with no further breakout available.

SUMMIT (FOUR)

2XM	41	4-dr Sed-5P	8895	2271	Note 1
2XM	41	4-dr DL Sed-5P	9456	2271	Note 1
2XH	41	4-dr LX Sed-5P	10408	2337	Note 1
2XS	41	4-dr ES Sed-5P	11257	2513	Note 1

Note: Summit ES exclusively used 1.6-liter DOHC four as its standard engine.

Note 1: Summit sedan production for 1990 N/A. U.S. sales totaled 13,772 with no further breakout available.

PREMIER (V-6)

BXP	41	4-dr LX Sed-6P	15350	2941	Note 1
BXS	41	4-dr ES Sed-5P	17845	3121	Note 1
BXS	41	4-dr ES Ltd. Sed-5P	20284	3121	Note 1

Note 1: Premier sedan production totaled 14,243 with no further breakout available.

ENGINE DATA: BASE FOUR (Talon): Inline, dual overhead cam four-cylinder. Cast iron block; aluminum head. Displacement: 121 cu. in. (2.0 liters). Bore & stroke: 3.34 x 3.46 in. Compression ratio: 9.0:1. Brake horsepower: 135 at 6000 RPM. Torque: 125 lb.-ft. at 5000 RPM. Multi-point fuel injection. **BASE FOUR (Talon TSi):** Inline turbocharged, dual overhead cam four-cylinder. Cast iron block; aluminum head. Displacement: 121 cu. in. (2.0 liters). Bore & stroke: 3.34 x 3.46 in. Compression ratio: 7.8:1. Brake horsepower: (fwd) 190 at 6000 RPM; (awd) 195 at 6000 RPM. Torque: 203 lb.-ft. at 5000 RPM. Multi-point fuel injection. **BASE FOUR (Summit, Summit DL, Summit LX):** Inline, overhead cam four-cylinder. Cast iron block; aluminum head. Displacement: 90 cu. in.

(1.5 liters). Bore & stroke: 2.97 x 3.23 in. Compression ratio: 9.4:1. Brake horsepower: 81 at 5500 RPM. Torque: 91 lb.-ft. at 3000 RPM. Multi-point fuel injection. **BASE FOUR (Summit ES); OPTIONAL FOUR (Summit LX):** Inline, dual overhead cam four-cylinder. Cast iron block; aluminum head. Displacement: 97 cu. in. (1.6 liters). Bore & stroke: 3.24 x 2.95 in. Compression ratio: 9.2:1. Brake horsepower: 113 at 6500 RPM. Torque: 99 lb.-ft. at 5000 RPM. Multi-point fuel injection. **BASE V-6 (Premier LX, Premier ES, Premier ES Limited):** 90 degree, overhead cam V-6. Aluminum block and heads. Displacement: 180 cu. in. (3.0 liters). Bore & stroke: 3.66 x 2.87 in. Compression ratio: 9.3:1. Brake horsepower: 150 at 5000 RPM. Torque: 171 lb.-ft. at 3600 RPM. Multi-point fuel injection.

CHASSIS DATA: Wheelbase: (Talon) 97.2 in.; (Summit) 96.7 in.; (Premier) 106.0 in. Overall length: (Talon) 172.4 in.; (Summit) 170.1 in.; (Premier) 192.8 in. Height: (Talon) 52.0 in.; (Summit) 52.8 in.; (Premier) 54.7 in. Width: (Talon) 66.9 in.; (Summit) 65.7 in.; (Premier) 70.0 in. Front Tread: (Talon) 57.7 in.; (Summit) 56.3 in.; (Premier) 58.1 in. Rear Tread: (Talon) 57.1 in.; (Summit) 56.3 in.; (Premier) 57.1 in. Standard Tires: (Talon) P205/60HR16; (Talon TSi) P205/55VR16; (Summit, Summit DL) P155/80R13; (Summit LX) P175/70R13; (Summit ES) P195/60R14; (Premier LX) P195/70R14; (Premier ES) P205/60R15; (Premier ES Limited) P205/60HR15.

TECHNICAL: Transmission: (Talon, Summit) Five-speed manual with overdrive. (Premier) Four-speed automatic with overdrive. Steering: (Talon, Summit, Premier) Rack and pinion. Front suspension: (Talon) Independent strut-type w/fixed upper pivots, lower control arms, upper strut surrounded by coil springs, hydraulic shock absorbers and stabilizer bar; (Summit) Independent strut w/coil springs, strut-type shock absorbers and stabilizer bar; (Premier) MacPherson strut w/steering arm on strut cast, iron lower A-arm w/plastic ball joint, coil springs and MacPherson strut twin-tube shock absorbers. Rear suspension: (Talon) Three-link, trailing arm, torsion bar, integral stabilizer bar w/inverted U-section beam axle, coil springs, hydraulic shock absorbers and stabilizer bar (TSi AWD: double wishbone, fully independent, upper and lower lateral arms, single trailing arm that included toe link and cross member); (Summit) Three-link torsion axle w/coil springs, and telescopic-type shock absorbers; (Premier) Trailing arms w/integral twist beam torsion bars, suspension/stabilizer bar and monotube high-pressure gas shock cartridges. Brakes: (Talon, Summit ES, Premier) Four-wheel disc (power assisted); (Summit, Summit DL, Summit LX) Front disc, rear drum (power assisted). Body construction: (Summit) Monocock body; (Talon, Premier) Unibody. Fuel tank: (Talon) 15.9 gals.; (Summit) 13.2 gals.; (Premier) 17.0 gals.

DRIVETRAIN OPTIONS: Transmission: Three-speed floor-shift auto., Summit, Summit DL and LX ($505). Four-speed floor-shift auto.: Summit LX and Summit ES w/DOHC pkg. ($682); Talon ($682). Engine: DOHC 1.6-liter four, Summit LX (N/A).

TALON CONVENIENCE/APPEARANCE OPTIONS: Talon: AAA Pkg.: stnd equip. (NC). (AAM) Popular Equip. Pkg.: incl. air cond., cruise control, pwr windows, pwr door locks, liftgate wiper/washer ($1495). (AAF) Luxury Equip. Pkg.: incl. AAM plus prem. audio syst., alloy whls ($2021). TSi w/fwd: AAA Pkg.: stnd equip. (NC). (AAM) Popular Equip. Pkg.: incl. air cond., cruise control, pwr windows, pwr door locks, liftgate wiper/washer ($1495). (AAF) Luxury Equip. Pkg.: incl. AAM plus prem. audio syst., alloy whls ($2021). TSi w/awd: AAA Pkg.: stnd equip. (NC). (AAM) Popular Equip. Pkg.: incl. air cond., cruise control, pwr windows, pwr door locks, liftgate wiper/washer ($1495). (AAF) Luxury Equip. Pkg.: incl. AAM plus prem. audio syst., alloy whls, security alarm syst. ($2186). Other: Air cond. ($802). Sunroof ($378). Calif. emissions ($103). Leather seating, TSi ($430). Malibu fabric seats, TSi ($430). (RAY) Prem. audio syst. incl. cass., digital clock, graphic equal. & 6 spkrs: Talon, TSi w/fwd ($242); TSi w/awd ($407). (RDP) Elect. AM/FM stereo radio w/CD player, clock & equal.: Talon, TSi w/fwd ($656); TSi w/awd ($414-$821). 5-spoke alloy whls ($284).

SUMMIT CONVENIENCE/APPEARANCE OPTIONS: Base: IFE Pkg.: stnd equip. (NC). IFF Pkg.: incl. IFE plus rear window defroster, tinted glass ($130). IFG Pkg.: incl. IFF plus AM/FM stereo radio ($434). IFH Pkg.: incl. IFG plus pwr stng ($696). DL: IFA Pkg.: stnd equip. (NC). IFB Pkg.: incl. IFA plus digital clock, pwr stng, elect. AM/FM stereo radio ($621). IFC Pkg.: incl. IFB plus elect. stereo radio w/cass., dual elect. mirrors ($839). IFD Pkg.: incl. IFC plus 13-in. alum. whls ($1135). LX: IFA Pkg.: stnd equip. plus dual elect. mirrors, elect. AM/FM stereo radio ($353). IFB Pkg.: incl. IFA plus elect. AM/FM stereo radio w/cass., pwr windows, pwr door locks ($962). IFC Pkg.: incl. IFB plus 13-in. Eurocast alum. whls ($1234). LX w/DOHC four: IFD Pkg.: incl. 1.6L four and 5-spd manual trans., DOHC Pkg., dual elect. mirrors, elect. AM/FM stereo radio w/cass. ($1319). IFE Pkg.: incl. IFD plus pwr windows, pwr door locks, cruise control w/intermittent wipers ($1970). IFF Pkg.: incl. IFE plus 14-in. Sport alum whls ($2242). ES: IFA Pkg.: stnd equip. plus dual elect. mirrors, elect. AM/FM stereo radio ($365). IFB Pkg.: incl. IFA plus elect. AM/FM stereo radio w/cass., cruise control w/intermittent wipers, 14-in. Sport alum whls ($1017). IFC Pkg.: incl. IFB plus 13-in. Prem. audio syst., pwr windows, pwr door locks ($1729). Other: (AYB) DOHC Pkg.: incl. 1.6L four, extra-duty brake syst., 14-in. turbine whl covers, dual chrome exhaust tips, P195/60R14 tires, LX (N/A). (AJP) Pwr windows

and door locks, LX and ES (N/A). Air cond. ($748). Decklid luggage rack ($94). Floor mats ($50). Cruise control incl. intermittent wipers, LX and ES (N/A). Dual elect. mirrors: DL and LX (N/A); ES (N/A). Pwr stng, base and DL (N/A). Tinted glass, base (N/A). Rear window defroster, base (N/A). Charcoal lower body paint treatment, ES ($159). (RAT) Elect. AM/FM stereo radio w/6 spkrs (N/A). (RAW) Elect. AM/FM stereo radio w/cass. & 6 spkrs, N/A base (N/A). (RAX) Elect. AM/FM stereo radio w/cass., graphic equal. & 6 spkrs, ES (N/A). Bright whl trim rings, base ($56). 13-in. Eurocast alum. whls, DL and LX (N/A). 14-in. Sport alum. whls, LX and ES w/1.6L engine (N/A).

1990 Eagle, Summit ES sedan with optional spoke wheels (OCW)

PREMIER CONVENIENCE/APPEARANCE OPTIONS: LX: AAA Pkg.: stnd equip. (NC). (AAM) Popular Equip. Grp.: incl. air cond., Convenience Grp. incl. cruise control & tilt stng, Pwr Lock Grp. incl. pwr door locks, remote decklid release, remote fuel door release & remote control door lock feature w/illum. entry ($1387). (AFF) Luxury Equip. Grp.: incl. AAM plus dual elect. remote control mirrors, dual illum. visor mirrors, pwr windows, pwr antenna, prem. audio syst. ($2316). **ES:** AAA Pkg.: stnd equip. (NC). (AAM) Popular Equip. Grp.: incl. Convenience Grp. incl. cruise control & tilt stng, Pwr Lock Grp. incl. pwr door locks, remote decklid release, remote fuel door release & remote control door lock feature w/illum. entry ($652). (AFF) Luxury Equip. Grp.: incl. AAM plus pwr windows, pwr antenna, prem. audio syst. ($1087). **ES Limited:** (AGG) ES Limited Pkg.: incl. Convenience Grp. incl. cruise control & tilt stng, pwr antenna, Pwr Lock Grp. incl. pwr door locks, remote decklid release, remote fuel door release & remote control door lock feature w/illum. entry, 6-way pwr driver's & pass. seats, prem. audio syst., 15-in. Sport alum. whls, full-size spare tire (NC). Other: (ADN) Electronic Information Pkg.: incl. vehicle maintenance monitor and trip computer, LX ($300). (AWF) Power Lock Grp.: incl. pwr door locks, pwr decklid release, remote fuel door release, remote door lock feature w/illum. entry, stnd ES Limited ($437). (ADC) Convenience Grp.: incl. cruise control, tilt stng whl, stnd ES Limited ($330). Leather/vinyl bucket seats, ES ($566). Air cond., LX ($860). Sunroof ($776). Calif. emissions ($100). Luggage rack ($115). Pwr windows, stnd ES Limited ($305). 6-way pwr driver's/pass. seats, stnd ES Limited ($540). (RAF) Elect. AM/FM stereo radio w/cass., LX ($234). (ARA) Elect. AM/FM stereo radio w/cass., graphic equal., pwr amp & 8 Jensen spkrs: LX ($532); ES ($130). (RBB) Elect. AM/FM stereo radio w/CD player, pwr amp & 8 Jensen spkrs: LX ($806); ES Limited ($274). 15-in. lace cast alum whls: LX w/P205/60R15 tires ($466); ES ($295). Conventional spare tire: LX, ES ($83).

HISTORY: Model year production: 46,951 (not including imported Summit). Calendar year sales: 60,646 (including 475 imported Medallions). Showcasing Chrysler's next-generation "cab-forward" design on the auto show circuit was the 1990 Eagle Optima concept car. Powered by an experimental, all-aluminum, 32-valve V-8 designed by Chrysler, the Optima rode on a 112-inch wheelbase with an overall length of 193.7 inches. Outside, the Optima was finished in three coats of pearlescent white with a quartz gray with blue accents interior color.

1991 EAGLE

For 1991, Summit sedans were no longer imported from Mitsubishi Motors Corp. of Japan, but instead entered production at Chrysler Corp.'s 50-percent owned Diamond-Star Motors facility in Normal, Illinois. It was a revised Summit lineup, though, that was now produced stateside. The previously offered DL and LX trim levels were discontinued. The existing base and ES levels now offered both sedan and all-new hatchback body styles, although the hatchbacks were produced by Mitsubishi in Japan and imported to the United States. Talon received anti-lock brakes (ABS) as an option as well as a four-speed automatic transmission being available on TSi models after previously being optional only on base coupes. Premier ES Limited sedans also received ABS as standard equipment, while it was optional on LX and ES sedans.

1991 Eagle, Talon TSi sports coupe with all-wheel-drive (AWD) (OCW)

TALON — SERIES D — FOUR — Base and TSi coupes again comprised the Talon lineup, with the base again offered in front-wheel drive (fwd) configuration while the TSi was again available in either front- or all-wheel-drive (awd) formats. Previously optional on only the base coupe, a four-speed automatic transmission with overdrive was now optional for all Talons as was anti-lock braking. The dual overhead cam 2.0-liter four-cylinder engine was again the powerplant for all Talons with the difference being the TSi again using the intercooled turbocharged unit and the base coupe the non-turbo version. The five-speed manual transmission with overdrive was again standard across-the-board. Talon, with a coefficient of drag of 0.29, added two exterior color choices for 1991: Dark Spectrum Blue Metallic and Medium Quartz Metallic. Power windows and door locks, liftgate wiper/washer and CD player were optional on all Talons while leather seating and a security alarm system were available on TSi coupes. New-for-1991, base and TSi fwd coupes received a split folding rear seat as standard equipment.

1991 Eagle, Summit ES hatchback (import model) (OCW)

SUMMIT — SERIES 2 — FOUR — Summit sedans were now produced at the Diamond-Star Motors Corp. assembly plant in Normal, Illinois, instead of being imported from Japan's Mitsubishi Motors Corp. What was imported from Japan with the Summit name was an all-new hatchback, which joined the existing sedan body style. (Technically an import, the hatchback will be included in this catalog to avoid confusion due to the "split" nature of Summit production, with half occurring in Japan and half in Illinois. DL and LX trim levels offered previously were dropped, leaving Summits available in either base or the monochromatic ES dress. Newly standard for 1991 was a 12-valve, multi-point fuel-injected 1.5-liter four-cylinder engine that produced 92 horsepower. This powerplant replaced the eight-valve 1.5-liter four, rated at 81 horsepower, that was formerly standard in all but the ES sedan. The dual overhead cam 1.6-liter four that was previously standard in the ES sedan was dropped. Both the base sedan and ES sedan and hatchback used a five-speed manual transmission with overdrive as their standard unit, while the base hatchback employed a four-speed manual transmission. Optional were a three-speed automatic on Summit hatchback models and four-speed automatic with overdrive on sedans. Summit sedans featured new exterior styling that included a color-keyed grille and tri-color taillamps, new seat and door trim fabrics and several new exterior color choices: Black Cherry, Dark Spectrum Blue, Medium Quartz and Pewter Mist for the base model only and Black, Light Spectrum Blue, Rallye Red and Bright White for both the base and ES sedans. Standard equipment for the base sedan included power-assisted front disc brakes, center console, dual mirrors, reclining front bucket seats, rack-and-pinion steering and 13-inch steel wheels. The ES sedan added rear window defroster, remote fuel door release, dual remote power mirrors, power-assisted rack-and-pinion steering, split folding rear seat with center armrest, tilt/telescoping steering wheel, intermittent wipers and wheel covers. The Summit sedan's option list included air conditioning, speed control, AM/FM cassette stereo radio, power windows and door locks, aluminum wheels and (standard on ES) rear window defroster, power steering and dual electric mirrors. The hatchback's standard features included reclining front bucket seats, power-assisted front disc brakes, console, stainless steel exhaust system, rack-and-pinion steering and 13-inch steel wheels. Optional were tinted glass, air conditioning, rear window defroster and AM/FM radio. The ES hatchback's option list added power steering, intermittent wipers, rear wiper/washer, digital clock, aluminum wheels, rear spoiler and tach.

1991 Eagle, Premier ES Limited sedan (OCW)

PREMIER — SERIES B — V-6 — The Premier's lineup and powertrain combination carried over intact from the previous year. All three Premier trim levels, LX, ES and ES Limited, now offered automatic temperature control air conditioning, dual remote control mirrors, speed control and tilt steering wheel as standard equipment. Anti-lock brakes were newly standard in the ES Limited sedan and optional in LX and ES sedans. The 3.0-liter V-6 that exclusively powered Premier sedans now featured a distributorless ignition system. Other newly standard equipment included power door locks and revised seat fabrics for the ES. The ES Limited featured a revised grille and taillamp treatment for 1991. The Limited's short option list was comprised of a luggage rack and audio system with CD player.

I.D. DATA: Eagle's 17-symbol Vehicle Identification Number (VIN) was embossed on a metal plate riveted to the top left surface of the instrument panel, visible through the windshield. Model year (symbol ten) was 'M' for 1991.

TALON (FOUR)

Model No.	Body/ Style No.	Body Type & Seating	Factory Price	Shipping Weight	Prod. Total
DXH	24	2-dr Cpe-4P	12990	2651	Note 1
DXP	24	2-dr TSi Cpe-4P	14609	2777	Note 1
DFP	24	2-dr AWD TSi Cpe-4P	16513	2800	Note 1

Note 1: Talon coupe production totaled 33,537 with no further breakout available.

SUMMIT (FOUR)

2XE	24	2-dr Hatch-5P	6949	2205	Note 1
2XM	41	4-dr Sed-5P	8618	2271	Note 2
2XL	24	2-dr ES Hatch-5P	7845	2249	Note 1
2XP	41	4-dr ES Sed-5P	9623	2337	Note 2

Note 1: Summit hatchback production for 1991 N/A. U.S. sales totaled 8,363 with no further breakout available.

Note 2: Summit sedan production totaled 9,257 with no further breakout available.

PREMIER (V-6)

BXP	41	4-dr LX Sed-6P	15250	2983	Note 1
BXS	41	4-dr ES Sed-5P	17455	3060	Note 1
BXS	41	4-dr ES Ltd. Sed-5P	19695	3060	Note 1

Note 1: Premier sedan production totaled 11,634 with no further breakout available.

ENGINE DATA: BASE FOUR (Talon): Inline, dual overhead cam four-cylinder. Cast iron block; aluminum head. Displacement: 121 cu. in. (2.0 liters). Bore & stroke: 3.34 x 3.46 in. Compression ratio: 9.0:1. Brake horsepower: 135 at 6000 RPM. Torque: 125 lb.-ft. at 5000 RPM. Multi-point fuel injection. BASE FOUR (Talon TSi): Inline turbocharged, dual overhead cam four-cylinder. Cast iron block; aluminum head. Displacement: 121 cu. in. (2.0 liters). Bore & stroke: 3.34 x 3.46 in. Compression ratio: 7.8:1. Brake horsepower: (fwd) 190 at 6000 RPM; (awd) 195 at 6000 RPM. Torque: 203 lb.-ft. at 5000 RPM. Multi-point fuel injection. BASE FOUR (Summit, Summit ES): Inline, overhead cam four-cylinder. Cast iron block; aluminum head. Displacement: 90 cu. in. (1.5 liters). Bore & stroke: 2.97 x 3.23 in. Compression ratio: 9.2:1. Brake horsepower: 92 at 6000 RPM. Torque: 93 lb.-ft. at 3000 RPM. Multi-point fuel injection. BASE V-6 (Premier LX, Premier ES, Premier ES Limited): 90 degree, overhead cam V-6. Aluminum block and heads. Displacement: 180 cu. in. (3.0 liters). Bore & stroke: 3.66 x 2.87 in. Compression ratio: 9.3:1. Brake horsepower: 150 at 5000 RPM. Torque: 171 lb.-ft. at 3600 RPM. Multi-point fuel injection.

CHASSIS DATA: Wheelbase: (Talon) 97.2 in.; (Summit hatch) 93.9 in.; (Summit sed) 96.7 in.; (Premier) 106.0 in. Overall length: (Talon) 172.4 in.; (Summit hatch) 158.7 in.; (Summit sed) 170.1 in.; (Premier) 192.8 in. Height: (Talon) 52.0 in.; (Summit hatch) 51.9 in.; (Summit sed) 52.8

in.; (Premier) 54.7 in. Width: (Talon) 66.9 in.; (Summit hatch) 65.7 in.; (Summit sed) 65.7 in.; (Premier) 70.0 in. Front Tread: (Talon) 57.7 in.; (Summit) 56.3 in.; (Premier) 58.1 in. Rear Tread: (Talon) 57.1 in.; (Summit) 56.3 in.; (Premier) 57.1 in. Standard Tires: (Talon) P205/60HR16; (Talon TSi) P205/55VR16; (Summit) P155/80R13; (Summit ES) P175/70R13; (Premier LX) P195/70R14; (Premier ES) P205/60R15; (Premier ES Limited) P205/60HR15.

TECHNICAL: Transmission: (Talon, Summit sed, Summit ES hatch and sed) Five-speed manual with overdrive. (Summit hatch) Four-speed manual. (Premier) Four-speed automatic with overdrive. Steering: (Talon, Summit, Premier) Rack and pinion. Front suspension: (Talon) Independent strut-type w/fixed upper pivots, lower control arms, upper strut surrounded by coil springs, hydraulic shock absorbers and stabilizer bar; (Summit) Independent strut w/coil springs, strut-type shock absorbers and stabilizer bar; (Premier) MacPherson strut w/steering arm on strut cast, iron lower A-arm w/plastic ball joint, coil springs and MacPherson strut twin-tube shock absorbers. Rear suspension: (Talon) Three-link, trailing arm, torsion bar, integral stabilizer bar w/inverted U-section beam axle, coil springs, hydraulic shock absorbers and stabilizer bar (TSi AWD: double wishbone, fully independent, upper and lower lateral arms, single trailing arm that included toe link and cross member); (Summit) Three-link torsion axle w/coil springs, and telescopic-type shock absorbers; (Premier) Trailing arms w/integral twist beam torsion bars, suspension/stabilizer bar and monotube high-pressure gas shock cartridges. Brakes: (Talon, Premier LX, Premier ES) Four-wheel disc (power assisted); (Summit, Summit ES) Front disc, rear drum (power assisted); (Premier ES Limited) Four-wheel disc w/anti-lock. Body construction: (Talon, Summit, Premier) Unibody. Fuel tank: (Talon) 15.9 gals.; (Summit) 13.2 gals.; (Premier) 17.0 gals.

DRIVETRAIN OPTIONS: Transmission: Three-speed auto.: Summit hatch ($601); Summit ES hatch ($499). Four-speed auto.: Summit sed, Summit ES sed ($673); Talon, Talon TSi ($771). Anti-lock brakes: Talon, Talon TSi fwd ($925). Premier LX, Premier ES ($799).

TALON CONVENIENCE/APPEARANCE OPTIONS: Talon: Pkg. 23B: incl. air cond. ($811). Pkg. 23C: incl. 23B plus cruise control, pwr windows, pwr door locks, liftgate wiper/washer ($1595). Pkg. 23D: incl. 23C plus elect. AM/FM stereo radio w/cass., digital clock, graphic equal. & 6 spkrs, alloy whls ($2081). Pkg. 24B: incl. 4-spd auto. trans. ($1499). Pkg. 24C: incl. 24B plus air cond., cruise control, rear window wiper/washer, pwr windows, pwr door locks ($2282). Pkg. 24D: incl. 24C plus elect. AM/FM stereo radio w/cass., graphic equal., digital clock & 6 spkrs, alloy whls ($2589). TSi w/fwd: Pkg. 25F: incl. air cond., cruise control, pwr windows, pwr door locks, liftgate wiper/washer ($1595). Pkg. 25G: incl. 25F plus elect. AM/FM stereo radio w/cass., digital clock, graphic equal. & 6 spkrs, alloy whls ($2081). Pkg. 26E: incl. 4-spd auto. trans. ($823). Pkg. 26F: incl. 26E plus air cond., cruise control, rear window wiper/washer, pwr windows, pwr door locks ($2417). Pkg. 26G: incl. 26F plus elect. AM/FM stereo radio w/cass., digital clock, graphic equal. & 6 spkrs, alloy whls ($2904). TSi w/awd: Pkg. 25J: incl. air cond., cruise control, pwr windows, pwr door locks, liftgate wiper/washer ($1595). Pkg. 26H: incl. 4-spd auto. trans. ($823). Pkg. 26J: incl. 26H plus air cond., cruise control, pwr windows, pwr door locks, liftgate wiper/washer ($2417). Other: Alarm syst., TSi ($163). Sunroof ($366). Leather seating, TSi ($427). (RAY) Prem. audio syst. incl. cass., digital clock, graphic equal. & 6 spkrs: TSi w/awd ($209). (RDP) Elect. AM/FM stereo radio w/cass. & CD player, clock & equal. & 6 spkrs: TSi w/fwd ($495); TSi w/awd ($704). Alloy whls, base ($278).

1991 Eagle, Summit ES sedan (OCW)

SUMMIT CONVENIENCE/APPEARANCE OPTIONS: Base sed: Pkg. 22A: incl. 4-spd auto. trans. ($673). Pkg. 21B: incl. remote fuel filler door release, remote decklid release, trunk trim, dual visor mirrors, intermittent wipers, rear window defroster ($142). Pkg. 21C: incl. 21B plus digital clock, pwr stng, elect. AM/FM stereo radio w/6 spkrs, dual pwr mirrors ($755). Pkg. 22C: incl. 21C plus 4-spd auto. trans. ($1428). Pkg. 21D: incl. 21B plus digital clock, pwr stng, elect. AM/FM stereo radio w/6 spkrs ($970). Pkg. 22D: incl. 21D plus 4-spd auto. trans. ($1643). ES sed: Pkg. 22E: incl. 4-spd auto. trans. ($673). Pkg. 21F:

incl. elect. AM/FM stereo radio w/6 spkrs, cruise control, intermittent wipers ($508). Pkg. 22F: incl. 21F plus 4-spd auto. trans. ($1181). Pkg. 21G: elect. AM/FM stereo radio w/cass. & 6 spkrs, cruise control, intermittent wipers ($675). Pkg. 22G: incl. 21G plus 4-spd. auto. trans. ($1348). Pkg. 21H: incl. 21G plus pwr windows, pwr door locks ($1110). Pkg. 22H: incl. 21H plus 4-spd auto. trans. ($1783). Pkg. 21J: incl. 21H plus alum whls ($1385). Pkg. 22J: incl. 21J plus 4-spd auto. trans. ($2058). Base hatch: IFB Pkg.: incl. rear window defroster ($66). IFC Pkg.: incl. tinted glass ($63). IFD Pkg. incl. rear window defroster, tinted glass ($129). ES hatch: IFC Pkg.: incl. rear window defroster, tinted glass ($129). IFD Pkg.: incl. IFC plus pwr stng, intermittent wipers ($416). IFE Pkg.: incl. IFD plus rear window wiper/washer, digital clock ($603). IFF Pkg.: incl. IFE plus alum whls ($872). IFG Pkg. incl. IFF plus rear spoiler, tach ($1058). Other: Cruise control incl. intermittent wipers, base sed ($236). Air cond. ($753). Rear window defroster, base sed ($66). Floor mats, hatch ($28). Pwr steering, base sed ($259). Bright whl trim rings, base hatch ($55). (RAG) AM/FM stereo radio w/2 spkrs, hatch ($217). (RAT) Elect. AM/FM stereo radio w/6 spkrs, base sed ($300).

PREMIER CONVENIENCE/APPEARANCE OPTIONS: LX: AAD Pkg.: incl. spd control, tilt stng, elect. AM/FM stereo radio w/cass. ($511). AAE Pkg.: incl. AAD plus dual illum. visor mirrors, pwr door locks, pwr windows ($800). AAF Pkg.: incl. AAE exc. radio plus pwr driver's seat, Prem. audio syst., trip computer/vehicle monitor and Pwr Grp. incl. keyless entry, pwr rear decklid release, remote fuel door release, illum. entry ($1798). ES: AAE Pkg.: incl. pwr windows and Pwr Grp. incl. keyless entry, pwr rear decklid release, remote fuel door release, illum. entry ($540). AAE Pkg. w/pwr driver's seat ($186). AAF Pkg.: incl. AAE plus Prem. audio syst., pwr antenna ($821). AAF Pkg. w/pwr driver's seat ($467). AAF Pkg. w/leather seats ($1340). ES Limited: AGG Pkg.: incl. anti-lock brakes, spd control, tilt stng, pwr windows, pwr leather driver's & pass. seats, Prem. audio syst., P205/60HR15 tires, 15-in. Sport alum whls, monochromatic exterior appearance, unique grille & taillamps and Pwr Grp. incl. keyless entry, pwr rear decklid release, remote fuel door release, illum. entry (NC). Other: (ADN) Vehicle monitor/trip computer, LX ($237). (AWF) Power Grp.: incl. keyless entry, pwr decklid release, remote fuel door release, illum. entry, LX ($309). 45/45 leather bucket seats incl. pwr driver's & pass. seats, ES Limited ($1169). Calif. emissions ($102). Spd control, LX ($224). Tilt stng, LX ($148). Luggage rack ($117). Pwr windows, stnd ES Limited ($331). Pwr door locks, LX ($240). 6-way pwr driver's seat, stnd ES Limited ($296). (ARA) Elect. AM/FM stereo radio w/cass., graphic equal., pwr amp, pwr antenna & 6 Jensen spkrs, stnd ES Limited ($381). (RBB) Elect. AM/FM stereo radio w/cass. & CD player, pwr amp, pwr antenna & 6 Jensen spkrs: LX ($279-$660); ES ($279-$660); ES Limited ($279). 15-in. lace cast alum whls: LX w/P205/60R15 tires ($523); ES ($301). Conventional spare tire, stnd ES Limited ($95).

HISTORY: Model year production: 54,428 (not including imported Summit hatchback). Calendar year sales: 57,779 (including 8,363 imported Summit hatchbacks).

1992 EAGLE

The Premier had a short model year run for 1992 and was then dropped. Production ended in December 1991, on what was basically a carry-over series from the year previous. The other change in the Eagle lineup occurred within the Summit lineup with the addition of a station wagon model imported from Japan. Even though it was called a station wagon, its characteristics were that of a minivan, therefore that model will not be covered in this catalog.

1992 Eagle, Talon TSi sports coupe with front-wheel-drive (FWD) (OCW)

TALON — SERIES D — FOUR — It was an all-new-look Talon that hit the streets in 1992. Again offered in base and TSi trim levels, the Talon

coupe received an aerodynamic "makeover" that included redesigned front and rear fascias, front fenders, hood, taillamps, spoiler, bodyside cladding (now also standard on base coupes), aero-styled headlamps, and aluminum wheels. An additional appearance change involved the TSi models as these coupes were now monochromatic in finish. TSi coupes were again available in both front- and all-wheel-drive configurations. Base coupes again were powered by the non-turbocharged dual overhead cam 2.0-liter four-cylinder engine while the TSi models again used the more potent intercooled turbo version of that same engine. The five-speed manual transmission with overdrive was again the standard unit across-the-board, with a four-speed automatic with overdrive again optional on all Talons. Talon received new seat fabrics for 1992 and the TSi's optional leather seating was now only offered in buckskin color.

1992 Eagle, Summit sedan (OCW)

SUMMIT — SERIES 2 — FOUR — The big change to the Summit lineup was the addition of an imported (assembled at Mitsubishi Motors Corp. in Japan along with the Summit hatchback) station wagon to the series. Due to this "station wagon" having more in common with a minivan than an automobile, it will not be covered in this catalog. Otherwise, the Summit series was carried over unchanged from the year previous. Powertrain combinations also remained the same. A new option available for base Summits was cloth-faced seats.

PREMIER — SERIES B — V-6 — Aside from minor grille and taillamp revisions on the LX and ES sedans and two new exterior colors: Teal and Radiant Red, the Premier series carried over unchanged from the previous year. Premier was produced as a 1992 model until December of 1991 (most likely to use up existing parts supplies) and then dropped from the Eagle lineup. The Bramalea, Ontario, Canada plant where the Premier was produced was then retooled for assembly of the cab-forward Eagle Vision that debuted in fall 1992 as a 1993 model.

I.D. DATA: Eagle's 17-symbol Vehicle Identification Number (VIN) was embossed on a metal plate riveted to the top left surface of the instrument panel, visible through the windshield. Model year (symbol ten) was 'N' for 1992.

TALON (FOUR)

Model No.	Body/Style No.	Body Type & Seating	Factory Price	Shipping Weight	Prod. Total
DXH	24	2-dr Cpe-4P	13631	2711	Note 1
DXP	24	2-dr TSi Cpe-4P	14963	2791	Note 1
DFP	24	2-dr AWD TSi Cpe-4P	16905	3108	Note 1

Note 1: Talon coupe production totaled 27,945 with no further breakout available.

SUMMIT (FOUR)

2XE	24	2-dr Hatch-5P	7302	2205	Note 1
2XM	41	4-dr Sed-5P	8981	2271	Note 2
2XL	24	2-dr ES Hatch-5P	8122	2249	Note 1
2XP	41	4-dr ES Sed-5P	9998	2337	Note 2

Note 1: Summit hatchback production for 1992 N/A. U.S. sales totaled 6,881 with no further breakout available.

Note 2: Summit sedan production totaled 3,348 with no further breakout available.

PREMIER (V-6)

BXP	41	4-dr LX Sed-6P	15716	3039	Note 1
BXS	41	4-dr ES Sed-5P	18057	3095	Note 1
BXS	41	4-dr ES Ltd. Sed-5P	20212	3095	Note 1

Note 1: Premier sedan production totaled 4,730 with no further breakout available.

ENGINE DATA: BASE FOUR (Talon): Inline, dual overhead cam four-cylinder. Cast iron block; aluminum head. Displacement: 121 cu. in. (2.0 liters). Bore & stroke: 3.34 x 3.46 in. Compression ratio: 9.0:1. Brake horsepower: 135 at 6000 RPM. Torque: 125 lb.-ft. at 5000 RPM. Multi-point fuel injection. BASE FOUR (Talon TSi): Inline turbocharged, dual overhead cam four-cylinder. Cast iron block; aluminum head. Displacement: 121 cu. in. (2.0 liters). Bore & stroke: 3.34 x 3.46 in. Compression ratio: 7.8:1. Brake horsepower: 195 at 6000 RPM. Torque: 203 lb.-ft. at 5000 RPM. Multi-point fuel injection. BASE FOUR (Summit, Summit ES): Inline, overhead cam four-cylinder. Cast iron block; aluminum head.

Displacement: 90 cu. in. (1.5 liters). Bore & stroke: 2.97 x 3.23 in. Compression ratio: 9.2:1. Brake horsepower: 92 at 6000 RPM. Torque: 93 lb.-ft. at 3000 RPM. Multi-point fuel injection. BASE V-6 (Premier LX, Premier ES, Premier ES Limited): 90 degree, overhead cam V-6. Aluminum block and heads. Displacement: 180 cu. in. (3.0 liters). Bore & stroke: 3.66 x 2.87 in. Compression ratio: 9.3:1. Brake horsepower: 150 at 5000 RPM. Torque: 171 lb.-ft. at 3600 RPM. Multi-point fuel injection.

CHASSIS DATA: Wheelbase: (Talon) 97.2 in.; (Summit hatch) 93.9 in.; (Summit sed) 96.7 in.; (Premier) 106.0 in. Overall length: (Talon) 172.4 in.; (Summit hatch) 158.7 in.; (Summit sed) 170.1 in.; (Premier) 192.8 in. Height: (Talon) 52.0 in.; (Summit hatch) 51.9 in.; (Summit sed) 52.8 in.; (Premier) 54.7 in. Width: (Talon) 66.9 in.; (Summit hatch) 65.7 in.; (Summit sed) 65.7 in.; (Premier) 70.0 in. Front Tread: (Talon) 57.7 in.; (Summit) 56.3 in.; (Premier) 58.1 in. Rear Tread: (Talon) 57.1 in.; (Summit) 56.3 in.; (Premier) 57.1 in. Standard Tires: (Talon, Talon TSi) P205/55R16; (Summit) P155/80R13; (Summit ES) P175/70R13; (Premier LX) P195/70R14; (Premier ES) P205/60R15; (Premier ES Limited) P205/60HR15.

TECHNICAL: Transmission: (Talon, Summit sed, Summit ES hatch and sed) Five-speed manual with overdrive. (Summit hatch) Four-speed manual. (Premier) Four-speed automatic with overdrive. Steering: (Talon, Summit, Premier) Rack and pinion. Front suspension: (Talon) Independent strut-type w/fixed upper pivots, lower control arms, upper strut surrounded by coil springs, hydraulic shock absorbers and stabilizer bar; (Summit) Independent strut w/coil springs, strut-type shock absorbers and stabilizer bar; (Premier) MacPherson strut w/steering arm on strut cast, iron lower A-arm w/plastic ball joint, coil springs and MacPherson strut twin-tube shock absorbers. Rear suspension: (Talon) Three-link, trailing arm, torsion bar, integral stabilizer bar w/inverted U-section beam axle, coil springs, hydraulic shock absorbers and stabilizer bar (TSi AWD: double wishbone, fully independent, upper and lower lateral arms, single trailing arm that includes toe link and cross member); (Summit) Three-link torsion axle w/coil springs, and telescopic-type shock absorbers; (Premier) Trailing arms w/integral twist beam torsion bars, suspension/stabilizer bar and monotube high-pressure gas shock cartridges. Brakes: (Talon, Premier LX, Premier ES) Four-wheel disc (power assisted); (Summit, Summit ES) Front disc, rear drum (power assisted); (Premier ES Limited) Four-wheel disc w/anti-lock. Body construction: (Talon, Summit, Premier) Unibody. Fuel tank: (Talon) 15.9 gals.; (Summit) 13.2 gals.; (Premier) 17.0 gals.

1992 Eagle, Talon TSi sports coupe with all-wheel-drive (AWD) (OCW)

DRIVETRAIN OPTIONS: Transmission: Three-speed auto.: Summit hatch ($613); Summit ES hatch ($508). Four-speed auto.: Summit sed, Summit ES sed ($687); Talon, Talon TSi ($701). Anti-lock brakes: Talon, Talon TSi fwd ($943). Premier LX, Premier ES ($799).

TALON CONVENIENCE/APPEARANCE OPTIONS: Talon: Pkg. 23B: incl. stnd equip. plus air cond. ($827). Pkg. 24B: 23B exc. 4-spd auto. trans. replaces 5-spd manual ($1528). Pkg. 23C: incl. 23B plus spd control, pwr windows, pwr door locks, liftgate wiper/washer ($1624). Pkg. 24C: 23C exc. 4-spd auto. trans. replaces 5-spd manual ($2325). Pkg. 23D: incl. 23C plus elect. AM/FM stereo radio w/cass., digital clock, graphic equal. & 6 spkrs, 16-in. alloy whls ($2120). Pkg. 24D: incl. 23D exc. 4-spd auto. trans. replaces 5-spd manual ($2821). TSi w/fwd: Pkg. 25F: incl. stnd equip. plus air cond., spd control, pwr windows, pwr door locks, liftgate wiper/washer ($1624). Pkg. 26F: incl. 25F exc. 4-spd auto. trans. replaces 5-spd manual ($2464). Pkg. 25G: incl. 25F plus elect. AM/FM stereo radio w/cass., digital clock, graphic equal. & 6 spkrs, 16-in. alloy whls ($2120). Pkg. 26G: incl. 25G exc. 4-spd auto. trans. replaces 5-spd manual ($2960). TSi w/awd: Pkg. 25J: incl. stnd. equip. plus air cond., spd control, pwr windows, pwr door locks, liftgate wiper/washer ($1624). Pkg. 26J: 25J exc. 4-spd auto. trans. replaces 5-spd manual ($2464). Other: Sunroof ($373). Leather seating, TSi ($435). (RAY) Prem. audio syst. incl. cass., digital clock, graphic equal. & 6 spkrs: TSi w/awd ($212). (RDP) Elect. AM/FM stereo radio w/cass. & CD player, clock & equal. & 6 spkrs: TSi w/fwd ($506); TSi w/awd ($718). 16-in. alloy whls, base ($284).

SUMMIT CONVENIENCE/APPEARANCE OPTIONS: Base sed: Pkg. 21A: incl. stnd equip. (NC). Pkg. 22A: incl. 21A exc. 4-spd auto. trans.

replaces 5-spd manual ($687). Pkg. 21B: incl. stnd equip. plus remote fuel filler door release, trunk trim, dual visor mirrors, intermittent wipers, rear window defroster, digital clock, pwr stng, elect. AM/FM stereo radio ($755). Pkg. 22B: 21B exc. 4-spd auto. trans. replaces 5-spd manual ($1442). Pkg. 21C: incl. 21B plus air cond. ($1508). Pkg. 22C: 21C exc. 4-spd auto. trans. replaces 5-spd manual ($2195). Pkg. 21D: incl. stnd equip. plus AM/FM radio w/cass., dual elect. mirrors ($1723). Pkg. 22D: 21D exc. 4-spd auto. trans. replaces 5-spd manual ($2410). ES sed: Pkg. 21E: incl. stnd equip. (NC). Pkg. 22E: 21E exc. 4-spd auto. trans. replaces 5-spd manual ($687). Pkg. 21F: incl. stnd equip. plus air cond., elect. AM/FM stereo radio w/cass., spd control, intermittent wipers ($1428). Pkg. 22F: 21F exc. 4-spd auto. trans. replaces 5-spd manual ($2115). Base hatch: Pkg. 21A: incl. stnd equip. (NC). Pkg. 24A: 21A exc. 3-spd auto. trans. replaces 4-spd manual ($613). Pkg. 21B: incl. 21A plus rear window defroster ($66). Pkg. 24B: 21B exc. 3-spd auto. trans. replaces 4-spd manual ($679). Pkg. 21C: incl. stnd equip. plus rear window defroster, tinted glass, AM/FM radio w/2 spkrs ($346). Pkg. 24C: 21C exc. 3-spd auto. trans. replaces 4-spd manual ($959). Pkg. 21D: incl. 21C plus rear shelf, fabric seats ($470). Pkg. 24D: 21D exc. 3-spd auto. trans. replaces 4-spd manual ($1083). ES hatch: Pkg. 23G: incl. stnd equip. plus tinted glass, rear window defroster, AM/FM radio w/2 spkrs ($346). Pkg. 24G: 23G exc. 3-spd auto. trans. replaces 4-spd manual ($854). Pkg. 23H: incl. stnd equip. plus air cond., tinted glass, rear window defroster, pwr stng, intermittent wipers, AM/FM radio w/cass. ($814). Pkg. 24H: 23H exc. 3-spd auto. trans. replaces 4-spd manual ($1322). Pkg. 23K: incl. stnd equip. plus rear wiper/washer, digital clock ($1001). Pkg. 24K: 23K exc. 3-spd auto. trans. replaces 4-spd manual ($1509). Other: Spd control incl. intermittent wipers, base sed ($208). Air cond. ($753). Rear window defroster, base sed ($66). Pwr steering, base sed ($259). Pwr door locks/windows, ES sed ($435). (RAG) AM/FM stereo radio w/2 spkrs, base hatch ($217). (RAT) Elect. AM/FM stereo radio w/6 spkrs, base sed ($300). (RAW) Elect. AM/FM stereo radio w/cass., base sed ($167). Alum whls, ES sed ($275).

1992 Eagle, Premier LX sedan (OCW)

PREMIER CONVENIENCE/APPEARANCE OPTIONS: LX: Pkg. 24A: stnd equip. (NC). Pkg. 24B: incl. 24A plus spd control, tilt stng, elect. AM/FM stereo radio w/cass. ($511). Pkg. 24C: incl. 24B plus dual illum. visor mirrors, pwr door locks, pwr windows ($800). Pkg. 24D: incl. 24C exc. Prem. audio syst. replaces AM/FM stereo radio w/cass. plus 6-way pwr driver's seat, trip computer, keyless entry syst., pwr rear decklid release, remote fuel door release, illum. entry ($1798). ES: Pkg. 24E: stnd equip. (NC). Pkg. 24F: incl. 24E plus pwr windows, keyless entry syst., pwr rear decklid release, remote fuel door release, illum. entry syst., 6-way pwr driver's seat ($726). Pkg. 24G: incl. 24F plus Prem. audio syst. ($467). ES Limited: Pkg. 24H: stnd equip. (NC). Other: (AWF) Power Lock Grp.: incl. illum. keyless entry, pwr decklid release, remote fuel door release, illum. entry, LX ($309). 45/45 leather bucket seats incl. pwr driver's & pass. seats, ES ($873). Calif. emissions ($102). Spd control, LX ($224). Tilt stng, LX ($148). Pwr door locks, LX ($240). 6-way pwr driver's seat, stnd ES Limited ($296). (ARA) Elect. AM/FM stereo radio w/cass., graphic equal., pwr amp, pwr antenna & 6 spkrs, stnd ES Limited ($381). (RBB) Elect. AM/FM stereo radio w/cass. & CD player, pwr amp, pwr antenna & 6 spkrs, ES Limited ($279). 15-in. lace cast alum whls: LX w/P205/60R15 tires ($523); ES ($301). Conventional spare tire, stnd ES Limited ($95).

HISTORY: Model year production: 38,555 (not including imported Summit hatchbacks). Calendar year sales: 51,909 (including 6,881 imported Summit hatchbacks, but not including 7,307 imported Summit station wagons—a vehicle constructed more like a minivan and not covered in this catalog).

1993 EAGLE

The Eagle division underwent sweeping change in 1993 as Chrysler Corp.'s "cab-forward revolution" began shaping the products Eagle was marketing. Gone was the three-sedan Premier series, replaced by one of

Chrysler's next-generation LH platform sports sedans called Vision. The Eagle Vision was offered in two trim levels: ESi and the more upscale TSi. The Talon lineup was also juggled as its offerings increased. Replacing the base Talon was a DL trim level coupe in addition to an ES coupe joining the existing pair of TSi models in front- and all-wheel-drive versions. Summit, no longer produced in Normal, Illinois, became a total import series consisting of DL and ES coupes and DL and ES sedans produced along with the Summit station wagon by Mitsubishi Motors Corp. in Japan. Due to this complete import nature of the Summit, it will no longer be included in this catalog.

1993 Eagle, Talon DL sports coupe (OCW)

TALON — SERIES D — FOUR — The 1993 Talon series offered four trim levels of coupe, with an entry-level DL model replacing the base coupe that was previously offered. In addition to the DL model, there was an ES coupe as well as the existing TSi models in front- and all-wheel-drive configurations. The DL coupe was fitted with an all-new sequentially fuel-injected 1.8-liter four-cylinder engine paired with a five-speed manual transmission with overdrive. The ES model used the sequentially fuel-injected, dual overhead cam 2.0-liter four, linked to a five-speed manual transmission, that formerly powered the TSi front-wheel-drive coupe. Both the front- and all-wheel-drive TSi models were now powered by the intercooled turbocharged version of the 2.0-liter four, also mated to a five-speed manual transmission with overdrive. The four-speed automatic with overdrive was optional across-the-board. The DL coupe's standard equipment included four-wheel disc brakes, stainless steel exhaust system, tinted glass, high-back front bucket seats with recliner, split folding rear seat, tilt steering, sport suspension and intermittent wipers. The ES model added a rear spoiler, rear window defroster, foglamps, color-keyed floor mats, removable tonneau cover, performance suspension and Polycast wheels. Optional equipment on DL and ES coupes included air conditioning, electronic speed control and sunroof. The ES added anti-lock brakes, five-spoke cast aluminum wheels and power windows and door locks.

1993 Eagle, Vision ESi sedan (OCW)

VISION — SERIES H — V-6 — One of three (the others being the Chrysler Concorde and Dodge Intrepid) initial cab-forward sedans built on the next-generation LH platform, the Eagle Vision replaced the poor-selling Premier series that was acquired when Chrysler bought out American Motors Corp. in 1987. The Vision was offered in two trim levels: ESi and the more upscale TSi. The ESi sedan was powered by a sequentially fuel-injected 3.3-liter V-6 rated at 153 horsepower while the TSi used a 24-valve 3.5-liter V-6 rated at 214 horsepower. Both engines were paired with an electronically controlled four-speed automatic transmission with overdrive. Vision featured a wide-stance design with a low cowl and steeply raked windshield that both maximized interior space (104.1 cubic feet) and optimized coefficient of drag (0.31). Wheelbase was 113 inches contained within a 201.6-inch overall length. Standard features of the Vision included dual airbags, four-wheel disc brakes, air conditioning, child-protection rear door locks, instrument cluster with tach/warning lights/message center, stainless steel exhaust system, foglamps, rear window defroster, tilt steering, intermittent wipers and tinted glass. Additionally, standard on TSi and optional on ESi were anti-lock brakes, power door locks, automatic temperature control and speed control. The Vision's option list included illuminated entry, power windows, Chrysler/Infinity Spatial Imaging Sound System (either cassette or CD), remote keyless entry, eight-way power driver's seat, integrated child's seat and conventional spare tire. The ESi model rode on a touring suspension, and was equipped with 15-inch touring tires. The TSi sedan, also featuring a touring

suspension, used 16-inch "Caisson" aluminum wheels fitted with touring tires. Specific wheel and handling packages were optional on both models.

I.D. DATA: Eagle's 17-symbol Vehicle Identification Number (VIN) was embossed on a metal plate riveted to the top left surface of the instrument panel, visible through the windshield. Model year (symbol ten) was 'P' for 1993.

TALON (FOUR)

Model No.	Body/ Style No.	Body Type & Seating	Factory Price	Shipping Weight	Prod. Total
DXM	24	2-dr DL Cpe-4P	11752	2550	Note 1
DXH	24	2-dr ES Cpe-4P	14197	2712	Note 1
DXP	24	2-dr TSi Cpe-4P	15703	2791	Note 1
DFP	24	2-dr AWD TSi Cpe-4P	17772	3108	Note 1

Note 1: Talon coupe production totaled 26,740 with no further break-out available.

VISION (V-6)

HXP	41	4-dr ESi Sed-5P	17387	3290	Note 1
HXS	41	4-dr TSi Sed-5P	21104	3422	Note 1

Note 1: Vision sedan production totaled 28,678 with no further breakout available.

ENGINE DATA: BASE FOUR (Talon DL): Inline, overhead cam four-cylinder. Cast iron block; aluminum head. Displacement: 107 cu. in. (1.8 liters). Bore & stroke: 3.17 x 3.39 in. Compression ratio: 9.0:1. Brake horsepower: 92 at 5000 RPM. Torque: 105 lb.-ft. at 3500 RPM. Sequential fuel injection. BASE FOUR (Talon ES): Inline, dual overhead cam four-cylinder. Cast iron block; aluminum head. Displacement: 121 cu. in. (2.0 liters). Bore & stroke: 3.34 x 3.46 in. Compression ratio: 9.0:1. Brake horsepower: 135 at 6000 RPM. Torque: 125 lb.-ft. at 5000 RPM. Sequential fuel injection. BASE FOUR (Talon TSi): Inline turbocharged, dual overhead cam four-cylinder. Cast iron block; aluminum head. Displacement: 121 cu. in. (2.0 liters). Bore & stroke: 3.34 x 3.46 in. Compression ratio: 7.8:1. Brake horsepower: 195 at 6000 RPM. Torque: 203 lb.-ft. at 3000 RPM. Sequential fuel injection. BASE V-6 (Vision ESi): 60 degree, overhead valve V-6. Cast iron block; aluminum heads. Displacement: 201 cu. in. (3.3 liters). Bore & stroke: 3.66 x 3.19 in. Compression ratio: 8.9:1. Brake horsepower: 153 at 5300 RPM. Torque: 177 lb.-ft. at 2800 RPM. Sequential fuel injection. BASE V-6 (Vision TSi): 60 degree, overhead cam V-6. Cast iron block; aluminum heads. Displacement: 214 cu. in. (3.5 liters). Bore & stroke: 3.78 x 3.19 in. Compression ratio: 10.4:1. Brake horsepower: 214 at 5800 RPM. Torque: 221 lb.-ft. at 2800 RPM. Sequential fuel injection.

CHASSIS DATA: Wheelbase: (Talon) 97.2 in.; (Vision) 113.0 in. Overall length: (Talon) 172.4 in.; (Vision) 201.6 in. Height: (Talon) 51.4 in.; (Vision) 55.8 in. Width: (Talon) 66.9 in.; (Vision) 74.4 in. Front Tread: (Talon) 57.7 in.; (Vision) 62.0 in. Rear Tread: (Talon) 57.1 in.; (Vision) 62.0 in. Standard Tires: (Talon DL) P185/70R14; (Talon ES, Talon TSi) P205/55R16; (Vision ESi) P205/70R15; (Vision TSi) P225/60R16.

TECHNICAL: Transmission: (Talon) Five-speed manual with overdrive. (Vision) Four-speed automatic with overdrive. Steering: (Talon, Vision) Rack and pinion. Front suspension: (Talon) Iso-strut w/integral shock absorbers (gas-charged on TSI AWD), coil springs, asymmetrical lower arms and link-type stabilizer; (Vision) Iso-strut w/integral gas-charged shock absorbers, coil springs, single transverse lower links, tension struts and link-type stabilizer bar. Rear suspension: (Talon - all fwd) Trailing arms, beam axle w/integral stabilizer bar, track bar, shock absorbers w/concentric coil springs; (Talon TSi AWD) Semi-trailing arms w/toe-control links, unequal length lateral links, stabilizer bar, gas-charged shock absorbers w/concentric coil springs; (Vision) Chapman struts w/integral gas-charged shock absorbers, concentric coil springs, dual transverse lower links, lower trailing links and link-type stabilizer bar. Brakes: (Talon, Vision ESi) Four-wheel disc (power assisted); (Vision TSi) Four-wheel disc w/anti-lock. Body construction: (Talon, Vision) Unibody. Fuel tank: (Talon) 15.8 gals.; (Vision) 18.0 gals.

DRIVETRAIN OPTIONS: Transmission: Four-speed auto.: Talon DL ($716); Talon ES ($716); Talon TSi ($857). Anti-lock brakes: Talon ES ($943); Talon TSi ($943); Vision ESi ($599). Traction control: Vision TSi ($175).

1993 Eagle, Vision TSi sedan (OCW)

TALON CONVENIENCE/APPEARANCE OPTIONS: Talon DL: Pkg. 21K: stnd equip. (NC). Pkg. 21L: incl. 21K plus rear window defroster, front floor mats, pwr stng, tonneau cover, console cupholder ($515). Pkg. 22L: incl. 21L exc. 4-spd auto. trans. replaces 5-spd manual ($1231). Pkg. 21M: incl. 21L plus air cond., spd control, elect. AM/FM stereo radio w/cass. ($1758). Pkg. 22M: incl. 21M exc. 4-spd auto. trans. replaces 5-spd manual ($2474). Talon ES: Pkg. 23B: incl. stnd equip. plus air cond., spd control ($1045). Pkg. 24B: 23B exc. 4-spd auto. trans. replaces 5-spd manual ($1761). Pkg. 23C: incl. 23B plus pwr windows, pwr door locks, liftgate wiper/washer ($1646). Pkg. 24C: 23C exc. 4-spd auto. trans. replaces 5-spd manual ($2362). Pkg. 23D: incl. 23C plus elect. AM/FM stereo radio w/cass. & graphic equal., 16-in. alloy whls ($2164). Pkg. 24D: incl. 23D exc. 4-spd auto. trans. replaces 5-spd manual ($2880). TSi w/fwd: Pkg. 25F: incl. stnd equip. plus air cond., spd control, pwr windows, pwr door locks, liftgate wiper/washer ($1646). Pkg. 25G: incl. 25F plus elect. AM/FM stereo radio w/cass. & graphic equal., 16-in. alloy whls ($2164). Pkg. 26G: 25G exc. 4-spd auto. trans. replaces 5-spd manual ($3021). TSi w/awd: Pkg. 25H: stnd equip. (NC). Pkg. 25J: incl. 25G exc. 16-in. alloy whls are stnd ($1862). Pkg. 26J: incl. 25J exc. 4-spd auto. trans. replaces 5-spd manual ($2719). Other: Sunroof ($373). Leather seating, TSi ($444). Rear window defroster, DL ($130). (RAN) Elect. AM/FM stereo radio w/digital clock & 6 spkrs, DL ($198). (RDP) Elect. AM/FM stereo radio w/cass. & CD player, digital clock, graphic equal. & 6 spkrs, TSi ($517). 16-in. alloy whls: ES ($302); TSi fwd ($302).

VISION CONVENIENCE/APPEARANCE OPTIONS: ESi: Pkg. 22A: stnd equip. (NC). Pkg. 22B: incl. 22A plus pwr door locks, pwr windows, elect. AM/FM stereo radio w/cass., spd control ($848). Pkg. 22C: incl. 22B plus dual illum. visor mirrors, 8-way pwr driver's seat, remote/illum. entry syst. ($1450). Pkg. 22D: incl. 22C plus auto. temp air cond., overhead console w/compass, AM/FM stereo radio w/cass. & graphic equal. ($2466). TSi: Pkg. 22J: stnd equip. (NC). Pkg. 26K: incl. 22J plus pwr windows, 8-way pwr driver's seat, remote/illum. entry syst. ($789). Pkg. 26L: incl. 26K exc. pwr driver's seat replaced with 8-way pwr driver's & pass. seats plus elect. AM/FM stereo radio w/cass. & graphic equal., traction control ($1851). Pkg. 26M: incl. 26L plus Handling Grp., leather seats, conventional spare tire ($2598). Other: (AJF) Illum. Entry Grp.: incl. remote keyless entry, illum. entry ($221). (AGC) Whl & Handling Grp.: incl. 16-in. Polycast whls, P225/60R16 touring tires, ESi ($270). Pwr windows, TSi ($341). Calif. emissions ($102). Spd control, ESi ($224). Integrated child's seat ($100). Pwr door locks, ESi ($250). 8-way pwr driver's seat, ESi ($377). 8-way pwr driver's & pass. seats, TSi ($377). Eng block heater ($20). Leather seats, TSi ($577). Dual illum. visor mirrors, ESi ($118). (RAY) Elect. AM/FM stereo radio w/cass. & graphic equal. ($713). (RBC) Elect. AM/FM stereo radio w/CD player & graphic equal.: ESi ($169-$882); TSi ($169). Conventional spare tire ($95).

HISTORY: Model year production: 55,418 (not including imported Summits). Calendar year sales: 71,225 (including 19,436 imported Summits).

1994 EAGLE

It was a "quiet" year for change within the Eagle division after the previous year's massive revamp of that brand's product lineup. The biggest change was that the Vision ESi was now offered with an optional FFV (flexible fuel vehicle) 3.3-liter V-6 for use in markets with tighter emissions standards. The first-generation Talon, introduced in 1990, was in its final year as the next-generation model was set to debut in 1995.

TALON — SERIES D — FOUR — With the next-generation, 1995 Talon already on the assembly line in mid-model year 1994, Talon received only minor upgrades for 1994. The lineup and powertrain combinations carried over unchanged from the previous year. Revised restraint system retractors for child seat retention, new gas-pressure shock absorbers for the TSi all-wheel-drive model, and one new exterior color, Silver Mint Metallic, headed the new features for Talons.

1994 Eagle, Vision ESi sedan (OCW)

VISION — SERIES H — V-6 — In its second year of availability, the Vision sedan was refined in several areas. The ESi model now offered an optional FFV (flexible fuel vehicle) 3.3-liter V-6 for buyers living in areas with more stringent emissions standards. Standard power source remained the sequentially fuel-injected 3.3-liter V-6 for the ESi sedan and 24-valve 3.5-liter V-6 for the TSi model. The ESi's 3.3-liter V-6 received both a power and torque boost for 1994, now rated at 161 horsepower (compared with 153 the year previous) and 181 pound-feet of torque (formerly 177). The 42LE electronically controlled four-speed automatic transmission with overdrive used in all Visions was also refined for smoother operation. Vision's NVH (noise, vibration and harshness) levels were reduced, and door beams and structural reinforcements were added for dynamic side impact protection. Outside, the bodyside cladding and two-tone fascias previously standard only on TSi sedans were added to ESi models. Inside, TSi cloth seats and trim were now also standard in the ESi. New standard features for 1994 Visions included variable-assist speed-proportional power steering, solar control glass rear window, bar-type manual seat adjuster, additional head restraint adjustment and upgraded AM/FM stereo radio with cassette player. New optional equipment included a vehicle theft security alarm system, power moonroof and automatic day/night rearview mirror.

I.D. DATA: Eagle's 17-symbol Vehicle Identification Number (VIN) was embossed on a metal plate riveted to the top left surface of the instrument panel, visible through the windshield. Model year (symbol ten) was 'R' for 1994.

TALON (FOUR)

Model No.	Body/ Style No.	Body Type & Seating	Factory Price	Shipping Weight	Prod. Total
DXM	24	2-dr DL Cpe-4P	11892	2549	Note 1
DXH	24	2-dr ES Cpe-4P	14362	2712	Note 1
DXP	24	2-dr TSi Cpe-4P	15885	2789	Note 1
DFP	24	2-dr AWD TSi Cpe-4P	17978	3109	Note 1

Note 1: Talon coupe production totaled 24,040 with no further breakout available.

VISION (V-6)

HXP	41	4-dr ESi Sed-5P	19308	3344	Note 1
HXS	41	4-dr TSi Sed-5P	22773	3486	Note 1

Note 1: Vision sedan production totaled 22,064 with no further breakout available.

ENGINE DATA: BASE FOUR (Talon DL): Inline, overhead cam four-cylinder. Cast iron block; aluminum head. Displacement: 107 cu. in. (1.8 liters). Bore & stroke: 3.17 x 3.39 in. Compression ratio: 9.0:1. Brake horsepower: 92 at 5000 RPM. Torque: 105 lb.-ft. at 3500 RPM. Sequential fuel injection. BASE FOUR (Talon ES): Inline, dual overhead cam four-cylinder. Cast iron block; aluminum head. Displacement: 121 cu. in. (2.0 liters). Bore & stroke: 3.34 x 3.46 in. Compression ratio: 9.0:1. Brake horsepower: 135 at 6000 RPM. Torque: 125 lb.-ft. at 5000 RPM. Sequential fuel injection. BASE FOUR (Talon TSi): Inline turbocharged, dual overhead cam four-cylinder. Cast iron block; aluminum head. Displacement: 121 cu. in. (2.0 liters). Bore & stroke: 3.34 x 3.46 in. Compression ratio: 7.8:1. Brake horsepower: 195 at 6000 RPM. Torque: 203 lb.-ft. at 3000 RPM. Sequential fuel injection. BASE V-6 (Vision ESi): 60 degree, overhead valve V-6. Cast iron block; aluminum heads. Displacement: 201 cu. in. (3.3 liters). Bore & stroke: 3.66 x 3.19 in. Compression ratio: 8.9:1. Brake horsepower: 161 at 5300 RPM. Torque: 181 lb.-ft. at 3200 RPM. Sequential fuel injection. BASE V-6 (Vision TSi): 60 degree, overhead cam V-6. Cast iron block; aluminum heads. Displacement: 214 cu. in. (3.5 liters). Bore & stroke: 3.78 x 3.19 in. Compression ratio: 10.5:1. Brake horsepower: 214 at 5800 RPM. Torque: 221 lb.-ft. at 2800 RPM. Sequential fuel injection.

1994 Eagle, Vision TSi sedan (OCW)

CHASSIS DATA: Wheelbase: (Talon) 97.2 in.; (Vision) 113.0 in. Overall length: (Talon) 172.4 in.; (Vision) 201.6 in. Height: (Talon) 51.4 in.; (Vision) 55.8 in. Width: (Talon) 66.9 in.; (Vision) 74.4 in. Front Tread:

(Talon) 57.7 in.; (Vision) 62.0 in. Rear Tread: (Talon) 57.1 in.; (Vision) 62.0 in. Standard Tires: (Talon DL) P185/70R14; (Talon ES, Talon TSi) P205/55R16; (Vision ESi) P205/70R15; (Vision TSi) P225/60R16.

TECHNICAL: Transmission: (Talon) Five-speed manual with overdrive. (Vision) Four-speed automatic with overdrive. Steering: (Talon, Vision) Rack and pinion. Front suspension: (Talon) Iso-strut w/integral shock absorbers (gas-charged on TSI AWD), coil springs, asymmetrical lower arms and link-type stabilizer; (Vision) Iso-strut w/integral gas-charged shock absorbers, coil springs, single transverse lower links, tension struts and link-type stabilizer bar. Rear suspension: (Talon - all fwd) Trailing arms, beam axle w/integral stabilizer bar, track bar, shock absorbers w/concentric coil springs; (Talon TSi AWD) Semi-trailing arms w/toe-control links, unequal length lateral links, stabilizer bar, gas-charged shock absorbers w/concentric coil springs; (Vision) Chapman struts w/integral gas-charged shock absorbers, concentric coil springs, dual transverse lower links, lower trailing links and link-type stabilizer bar. Brakes: (Talon, Vision ESi) Four-wheel disc (power assisted); (Vision TSi) Four-wheel disc w/anti-lock. Body construction: (Talon, Vision) Unibody. Fuel tank: (Talon) 15.8 gals.; (Vision) 18.0 gals.

DRIVETRAIN OPTIONS: Transmission: Four-speed auto.: Talon DL ($716); Talon ES ($716); Talon TSi ($555). Anti-lock brakes: Talon ES ($699); Talon TSi ($699); Vision ESi ($599). Traction control: Vision TSi ($175).

TALON CONVENIENCE/APPEARANCE OPTIONS: Talon DL: Pkg. 21K: stnd equip. (NC). Pkg. 21T: incl. 21K plus air cond., pwr stng ($1099). Pkg. 22T: incl. 21T exc. 4-spd auto. trans. replaces 5-spd manual ($1815). Pkg. 21L: incl. 21K plus pwr stng, cargo area cover, console, rear window defroster, front floor mats ($515). Pkg. 22L: incl. 21L exc. 4-spd auto. trans. replaces 5-spd manual ($1231). Pkg. 21M: incl. 21L plus air cond., spd control, elect. AM/FM stereo radio w/cass. & 6 spkrs ($1758). Pkg. 22M: incl. 21M exc. 4-spd auto. trans. replaces 5-spd manual ($2474). Talon ES: Pkg. 23A: stnd equip. (NC). Pkg. 23B: incl. 23A plus air cond., spd control ($1045). Pkg. 24B: 23B exc. 4-spd auto. trans. replaces 5-spd manual ($1761). Pkg. 23C: incl. 23B plus pwr windows, pwr door locks, liftgate wiper/washer ($1646). Pkg. 24C: 23C exc. 4-spd auto. trans. replaces 5-spd manual ($2362). Pkg. 23D: incl. 23C plus elect. AM/FM stereo radio w/cass. & graphic equal. & 6 spkrs, 16-in. alloy whls ($2164). Pkg. 24D: incl. 23D exc. 4-spd auto. trans. replaces 5-spd manual ($2880). TSi w/fwd: Pkg. 25F: stnd equip. (NC). Pkg. 25G: incl. 25F plus air cond., spd control, liftgate wiper/washer, pwr door locks, pwr windows, elect. AM/FM stereo radio w/cass., graphic equal. & 6 spkrs, 16-in. alloy whls ($2164). Pkg. 26G: incl. 25G exc. 4-spd auto. trans. replaces 5-spd manual ($3021). TSi w/awd: Pkg. 26J: incl. 25G exc. 4-spd auto. trans. replaces 5-spd manual ($2719). Other: Sunroof ($373). Rear window defroster, DL ($130). (RAN) Elect. AM/FM stereo radio w/cass. & 6 spkrs, DL ($198). (RDP) Elect. AM/FM stereo radio w/cass. & CD player & 6 spkrs: ES ($517); TSi ($517). 16-in. alloy whls, ES ($302).

VISION CONVENIENCE/APPEARANCE OPTIONS: ESi: Pkg. 22B: stnd equip. (NC). Pkg. 22C: incl. 22B plus dual illum. visor mirrors, 8-way pwr driver's seat, remote/illum. entry syst. ($601). Pkg. 22D: incl. 22C plus auto. temp air cond., overhead console w/compass, auto. day/night mirror, Chrysler/Infinity Spatial Imaging Sound Syst. w/cass., security alarm ($1767). TSi: Pkg. 26K: stnd equip. (NC). Pkg. 26L: incl. 26K plus 8-way pwr driver's & pass. seats, auto. day/night mirror, Chrysler/Infinity Spatial Imaging Sound Syst. w/cass. ($980). Pkg. 26M: incl. 26L plus security alarm, leather seats, conventional spare tire ($1706). Pkg. 26N: incl. 26M plus moonroof ($2307). Other: (AWT) Perf. Handling Grp.: incl. P225/60R16 perf. tires, perf. susp., conventional spare tire, traction control, TSi ($217). Calif. emissions ($102). Integrated child's seat ($100). 8-way pwr driver's seat ($377). Security alarm ($149). Eng block heater ($20). Leather seats, TSi ($620). Satin Glow paint ($97). Pearl Coat paint (NC). (ARA) Elect. AM/FM stereo radio w/cass., graphic equal., pwr antenna & 11 Infinity spkrs ($708). (ARB) Elect. AM/FM stereo radio w/CD player, graphic equal., pwr antenna & 11 Infinity spkrs, ($169). Conventional spare tire ($95). 16-in. Polycast whls, ESi ($374).

HISTORY: Model year production: 46,104 (not including imported Summits). Calendar year sales: 62,495 (including 11,021 imported Summits). In August 1994, Chrysler Corp. announced a $100 million advertising campaign aimed at increasing Eagle sales by 50 percent.

1995 EAGLE

The all-new, 1995 Talon coupe debuted early in summer 1994, in trim levels comparable to Vision's: ESi and TSi (again, the latter offered in front- and all-wheel-drive versions). Dropped from the series was the 1.8-

liter four-cylinder engine that previously powered the entry-level DL coupe, which was discontinued along with the ES model.

1995 Eagle, Talon ESi sports coupe (OCW)

TALON — SERIES J — FOUR — The next-generation Talon, produced at Chrysler Corp.'s half-owned Diamond-Star Motors facility in Normal, Illinois, featured a slimmed-down lineup with two trim levels offered instead of the previous year's three. Consistent with the Eagle Vision, Talon was now available in either ESi or TSi trim levels. ESi - a counterpart to the Mitsubishi Eclipse - was front-wheel-drive only, while the TSi again was available in both front- and all-wheel-drive configurations. Chrysler's new, naturally-aspirated dual overhead cam 2.0-liter four-cylinder engine powered the ESi coupe. It produced 140 horsepower and 130 pound-feet of torque. The TSi again used the Mitsubishi-built, intercooled turbocharged version of the 2.0-liter four. It received a power and torque boost, now rated at 210 horsepower (compared to the previous 195) and 214 pound-feet of torque (formerly 205). Both engines were paired with a specific synchronized five-speed manual transmission with overdrive as the standard unit with a specific electronically controlled four-speed automatic with overdrive as the option transmission. The new Talon's body was 50 percent stiffer than its predecessor, with torsional rigidity improved by 60 percent. All Talons were equipped with a new double wishbone, fully independent front and rear suspensions. TSi models included a specially-tuned enthusiast suspension package. Dual airbags were standard equipment in Talons, included in a totally redesigned interior anchored by a new instrument panel that extended uninterrupted into the doors. All models featured the Talon "signature" black roof and black rear spoiler, as well as four-wheel disc brakes, floor console, remote fuel door and liftgate release, tilt steering, warning chime for key-in-ignition/headlights-on/fasten seat belts, intermittent wipers, rear window wiper/washer and tinted glass. TSi's standard features list added foglamps, bodyside cladding, body-color heated exterior mirrors, painted 16-inch aluminum wheels and dual exhaust outside, while inside were leather-wrapped steering wheel and manual shift knob, driver's seat power/memory height and recline adjuster, plus a passenger seat power/memory system for fore and aft adjustments. Talons had four new exterior color choices: Medium Gray Metallic, Wildberry, Tropical Lime and Blue, as well as two new interior selections: two-tone Gray and two-tone Brownstone. Optional equipment included air conditioning, anti-lock brakes, color-keyed front floor mats, remote keyless entry/security alarm system and power sunroof.

VISION — SERIES H — V-6 — The 1994 Eagle Vision was not much different from the ESi and TSi sedans offered the year previous. Powertrain combinations remained the same. Changes included modifications to the emissions control system and remote keyless entry system (standard on TSi, optional on ESi). Also, a cancel feature was added to the automatic speed control that was standard on all Visions.

I.D. DATA: Eagle's 17-symbol Vehicle Identification Number (VIN) was embossed on a metal plate riveted to the top left surface of the instrument panel, visible through the windshield. Model year (symbol ten) was 'S' for 1995.

TALON (FOUR)

Model No.	Body/ Style No.	Body Type & Seating	Factory Price	Shipping Weight	Prod. Total
JXH	24	2-dr ESi Cpe-4P	14460	2756	Note 1
JXP	24	2-dr TSi Cpe-4P	17266	2866	Note 1
JFS	24	2-dr AWD TSi Cpe-4P	19448	3119	Note 1

Note 1: Talon coupe production totaled 25,066 with no further breakout available.

VISION (V-6)

HXP	41	4-dr ESi Sed-5P	19697	3374	Note 1
HXS	41	4-dr TSi Sed-5P	22871	3493	Note 1

ENGINE DATA: BASE FOUR (Talon ESi): Inline, dual overhead cam four-cylinder. Cast iron block; aluminum head. Displacement: 121 cu. in. (2.0 liters). Bore & stroke: 3.44 x 3.27 in. Compression ratio: 9.6:1. Brake horsepower: 140 at 6000 RPM. Torque: 131 lb.-ft. at 4800 RPM. Sequential fuel injection. BASE FOUR (Talon TSi): Inline turbocharged, dual overhead cam four-cylinder. Cast iron block; aluminum head. Displacement: 121 cu. in. (2.0 liters). Bore & stroke: 3.34 x 3.46 in. Compression

ratio: 8.5:1. Brake horsepower: 210 at 6000 RPM. Torque: 214 lb.-ft. at 3000 RPM. Sequential fuel injection. BASE V-6 (Vision ESi): 60 degree, overhead valve V-6. Cast iron block; aluminum heads. Displacement: 201 cu. in. (3.3 liters). Bore & stroke: 3.66 x 3.19 in. Compression ratio: 8.9:1. Brake horsepower: 161 at 5300 RPM. Torque: 181 lb.-ft. at 3200 RPM. Sequential fuel injection. BASE V-6 (Vision TSi): 60 degree, overhead cam V-6. Cast iron block; aluminum heads. Displacement: 214 cu. in. (3.5 liters). Bore & stroke: 3.78 x 3.19 in. Compression ratio: 10.5:1. Brake horsepower: 214 at 5800 RPM. Torque: 221 lb.-ft. at 2800 RPM. Sequential fuel injection.

CHASSIS DATA: Wheelbase: (Talon) 98.8 in.; (Vision) 113.0 in. Overall length: (Talon) 172.2 in.; (Vision) 201.6 in. Height: (Talon) 51.6 in.; (Vision) 56.3 in. Width: (Talon) 68.7 in.; (Vision) 74.4 in. Front Tread: (Talon) 59.7 in.; (Vision) 62.0 in. Rear Tread: (Talon) 59.4 in.; (Vision) 62.0 in. Standard Tires: (Talon) P195/70HR14; (Talon TSi FWD) P215/55HR16; (Talon TSi AWD) P215/55VR16; (Vision ESi) P205/70R15; (Vision TSi) P225/60R16.

TECHNICAL: Transmission: (Talon) Five-speed manual with overdrive. (Vision) Four-speed automatic with overdrive. Steering: (Talon, Vision) Rack and pinion. Front suspension: (Talon) Modified double wishbone, coil springs, direct acting shock absorbers and link-type stabilizer bar; (Vision) Iso-strut w/integral gas-charged shock absorbers, coil springs, single transverse lower links, tension struts and link-type stabilizer bar. Rear suspension: (Talon) Multiple links, coil springs, direct acting shock absorbers and (TSi AWD only) link-type stabilizer bar; (Vision) Chapman struts w/integral gas-charged shock absorbers, concentric coil springs, dual transverse lower links, lower trailing links and link-type stabilizer bar. Brakes: (Talon, Vision ESi) Four-wheel disc (power assisted); (Vision TSi) Four-wheel disc w/anti-lock. Body construction: (Talon, Vision) Unibody. Fuel tank: (Talon) 15.8 gals.; (Vision) 18.0 gals.

DRIVETRAIN OPTIONS: Transmission: Four-speed auto.: Talon ESi ($738); Talon TSi FWD ($883); Talon TSi AWD ($852). Anti-lock brakes: Talon ESi ($649); Talon TSi ($649); Vision ESi ($599). Limited Slip Differential: Talon TSi AWD ($266).

1995 Eagle, Talon TSi sports coupe with front-wheel-drive (FWD) (OCW)

TALON CONVENIENCE/APPEARANCE OPTIONS: Talon ESi: Pkg. 21A: stnd equip. (NC). Pkg. 21B: incl. 21A plus air cond., rear center shelf, rear window defroster, front floor mats, dual pwr mirrors, AM/FM stereo radio w/cass., clock & 6 spkrs, spd control ($1601). Pkg. 22B: 21B exc. 4-spd auto. trans. replaces 5-spd manual ($2339). Pkg. 21C: incl. 21B plus pwr windows, pwr door locks, cargo net, soft door trim ($2135). Pkg. 22C: 21C exc. 4-spd auto. trans. replaces 5-spd manual ($2873). TSi w/fwd: Pkg. 23D: stnd equip. (NC). Pkg. 24D: incl. 23D exc. 4-spd auto. trans. replaces 5-spd manual ($883). Pkg. 23P: incl. 23D plus air cond., spd control, pwr door locks, pwr windows, front floor mats ($1574). Pkg. 24P: incl. 23P exc. 4-spd auto. trans. replaces 5-spd manual ($2457). TSi w/awd: Pkg. 25F: stnd equip. (NC). Pkg. 26F: incl. 25F exc. 4-spd auto. trans. replaces 5-spd manual ($852). Pkg. 25S: incl. 25F plus air cond., front floor mats ($880). Pkg. 26S: incl. 25S exc. 4-spd auto. trans. replaces 5-spd manual ($1732). Pkg. 25H: incl. 25S plus AM/FM stereo radio w/cass., clock, equal. & 8 spkrs, pwr driver's seat, pwr sunroof, security alarm ($2983). Pkg. 26H: incl. 25H exc. 4-spd auto. trans. replaces 5-spd manual ($3835). Other: Pwr driver's seat, TSi AWD ($332). Security alarm w/remote keyless entry ($332). Pwr sunroof ($730). Rear window defroster, ESi ($162). Leather front bucket seats w/folding rear split folding bench seat ($457). (RAZ) Elect. AM/FM stereo radio w/CD player & cass., clock & 6 spkrs ($634). (RAY) Elect. AM/FM stereo radio w/cass., clock, equal. & 8 spkrs, TSi ($709).

VISION CONVENIENCE/APPEARANCE OPTIONS: ESi: Pkg. 22B: stnd equip. (NC). Pkg. 22C: incl. 22B plus dual illum. visor mirrors, 8-way pwr driver's seat, remote/illum. entry syst. ($601). Pkg. 22D: incl. 22C plus auto. temp air cond., overhead console w/compass, auto. day/night mirror, Chrysler/Infinity Spatial Imaging Sound Syst. w/cass., security alarm ($1767). TSi: Pkg. 26K: stnd equip. (NC). Pkg. 26L: incl. 26K plus 8-way pwr driver's & pass. seats, auto. day/night mirror, Chrysler/Infinity Spatial Imaging Sound Syst. w/cass., traction control ($1127). Pkg. 26M: incl. 26L plus security alarm, leather seats, conventional spare tire ($1853). Other: (AJF) Remote/Illum. Entry Grp.: incl. remote keyless entry, remote decklid release, illum. entry, ESi (NC). (AWT) Perf. Handling Grp.: incl. P225/60VR16 perf. tires, perf. susp., conventional spare tire, traction control, TSi ($217). Calif. emissions ($102). Integrated child's seat ($100). 8-way pwr driver's seat, ESi ($377). 8-way pwr driver's &

pass. seats, TSi ($377). Pwr moonroof: ESi ($1012); TSi ($716). Security alarm ($149). Eng block heater ($20). Leather seats, TSi ($620). Extra cost paint ($97). Bright Platinum Metallic paint ($200). (ARA) Elect. AM/FM stereo radio w/cass., graphic equal., & 11 Infinity spkrs ($708). (ARB) Elect. AM/FM stereo radio w/CD player, graphic equal., pwr antenna & 11 Infinity spkrs ($169). Conventional spare tire ($95). 16-in. Polycast "Pacifica" whls w/P225/60R16 touring tires, ESi ($374).

HISTORY: Model year production: 50,194 (not including imported Summits). Calendar year sales: 53,612 (including 9,443 imported Summits). The Eagle Jazz concept car debuted at the North American International Auto Show in Detroit on January 7, 1995. The Jazz pushed the cab-forward approach to car design further, extending the windshield bottom over the front wheels. Wheel wells were deep-seated to provide for 18-inch wheels and tires. The rear roofline sloped down to the bumpers, unlike the deckline of a typical sedan. Power was supplied by a 24-valve 2.5-liter V-6, rated at 175 horsepower, linked to an AutoStick four-speed automatic transmission. The front-wheel drive sedan featured four-wheel anti-lock disc brakes, a Blackberry exterior finish and Camel and Blackberry leather interior. Wheelbase measured 113.5 inches. Another concept car created by Eagle engineers to explore innovative automotive technology was the Vision Aerie. Looking similar to a production Vision, the "test-bed" Aerie featured electro-rheological fluid suspension, a compact navigational unit inside the car, and a 275-horsepower 3.5-liter V-6 with ram induction. Other state-of-the-art equipment included automatic traction control, automatic 911 communication with airbag deployment, Gentex Night Vision Safety interior/exterior mirrors and automatic dimming glass and interior air filtration system.

1996 EAGLE

Possibly a countermeasure to halt sagging sales, Eagle returned to offering an "entry-level" Talon coupe (a model that the division abandoned after the 1994 model year) in addition to its existing ESi and TSi trim levels. The Vision TSi sedan received the dual-mode AutoStick four-speed automatic transmission while the ESi sedan could be ordered with an optional transitional low-emission vehicle (TLEV) 3.3-liter V-6.

1996 Eagle, Talon ESi sports coupe (OCW)

TALON — SERIES J — FOUR — One model year removed from a similar strategy that was discontinued, Talon returned to a three-trim-level lineup including a base or "entry level" coupe priced more affordably than the existing ESi or TSi models. This base coupe shared the powertrain combination used in ESi models, that being the 140-horsepower dual overhead cam 2.0-liter four-cylinder engine and five-speed manual transmission with overdrive. TSi coupes, again offered in both front- and all-wheel-drive versions, again used the intercooled turbocharged 2.0-liter four, rated at 210 horsepower, paired with a five-speed manual transmission with overdrive. Four-speed automatic transmissions with overdrive that were specific to both the base and ESi coupes and TSi coupes in both drive versions were optional. New safety features for Talons included dynamic side impact protection and a "panic" alarm added to the optional remote keyless entry system. The base coupe's standard equipment list included dual airbags, front disc/rear drum brakes, center-mount console, full sport analog instrumentation including tach, remote fuel door release, four-spoke sport steering wheel, tilt steering, stainless steel exhaust, tinted glass and intermittent wipers. Base model exterior color choices were Medium Gray Metallic, Blue Metallic and Prism Blue. Interior color was Forest Cloth Brownstone. New standard equipment across-the-board included enhanced evaporative emission controls and OBDII on-board diagnostics for all powertrains, SBECIII Powertrain Control Module added to the base/ESi's 2.0-liter four, and two new exterior color choices: Polo Green (not available on base coupe) and Prism Blue. New options included a HomeLink three-channel universal remote transmitter for opening garage doors and, on ESi sedans, a 16-inch cast aluminum wheel and P205/55HR16 tire package.

VISION — SERIES H — V-6 — As it was since its inception in 1993, Vision continued with its two-trim-level lineup of ESi and TSi sedans. For 1996, Vision took on a monochromatic exterior appearance. The ESi model again was powered by the 3.3-liter V-6 linked to an electronically controlled four-speed automatic transmission with overdrive. New-for-1996 was an optional TLEV (transitional low-emission vehicle) version of the 3.3-liter V-6 for buyers in areas with stricter emissions standards. TSi sedans again used the 3.5-liter V-6, which was now paired with the dual-mode AutoStick four-speed automatic transmission that provided the control of manual shifting with the ease of an automatic. As with the Talon, new features of the Vision included OBDII on-board diagnostics for all powertrains and the addition of a SBECIII Powertrain Control Module. Upgrades included reduced NVH (noise, vibration and harshness) levels, improved headlight illumination, new seat fabrics and four new exterior color choices: Candy Apple Red Metallic, Opal, Island Teal and Stone White. The ESi received 16-inch Polycast wheels as standard fare while the TSi rode on 16-inch "Caisson" aluminum wheels that were now chrome-finished. Optional audio system upgrades included more powerful Chrysler/Infinity Spatial Imaging Sound Systems with either cassette or CD functions.

I.D. DATA: Eagle's 17-symbol Vehicle Identification Number (VIN) was embossed on a metal plate riveted to the top left surface of the instrument panel, visible through the windshield. Model year (symbol ten) was 'T' for 1996.

TALON (FOUR)

Model No.	Body/ Style No.	Body Type & Seating	Factory Price	Shipping Weight	Prod. Total
JXL	24	2-dr Cpe-4P	14059	2789	Note 1
JXH	24	2-dr ESi Cpe-4P	14830	2789	Note 1
JXP	24	2-dr TSi Cpe-4P	18015	2866	Note 1
JFS	24	2-dr AWD TSi Cpe-4P	20271	3120	Note 1

Note 1: Talon coupe production totaled 15,100 with no further break-out available.

VISION (V-6)

HXP	41	4-dr ESi Sed-5P	19245	3371	Note 1
HXS	41	4-dr TSi Sed-5P	23835	3494	Note 1

Note 1: Vision sedan production totaled 12,806 with no further breakout available.

ENGINE DATA: BASE FOUR (Talon, Talon ESi): Inline, dual overhead cam four-cylinder. Cast iron block; aluminum head. Displacement: 121 cu. in. (2.0 liters). Bore & stroke: 3.44 x 3.27 in. Compression ratio: 9.6:1. Brake horsepower: 140 at 6000 RPM. Torque: 131 lb.-ft. at 4800 RPM. Sequential fuel injection. BASE FOUR (Talon TSi): Inline turbocharged, dual overhead cam four-cylinder. Cast iron block; aluminum head. Displacement: 121 cu. in. (2.0 liters). Bore & stroke: 3.34 x 3.46 in. Compression ratio: 8.5:1. Brake horsepower: 210 at 6000 RPM. Torque: 214 lb.-ft. at 3000 RPM. Sequential fuel injection. BASE V-6 (Vision ESi): 60 degree, overhead valve V-6. Cast iron block; aluminum heads. Displacement: 201 cu. in. (3.3 liters). Bore & stroke: 3.66 x 3.19 in. Compression ratio: 8.9:1. Brake horsepower: 161 at 5300 RPM. Torque: 181 lb.-ft. at 3200 RPM. Sequential fuel injection. BASE V-6 (Vision TSi): 60 degree, overhead cam V-6. Cast iron block; aluminum heads. Displacement: 214 cu. in. (3.5 liters). Bore & stroke: 3.78 x 3.19 in. Compression ratio: 9.6:1. Brake horsepower: 214 at 5850 RPM. Torque: 221 lb.-ft. at 3100 RPM. Sequential fuel injection.

CHASSIS DATA: Wheelbase: (Talon) 98.8 in.; (Vision) 113.0 in. Overall length: (Talon) 172.2 in.; (Vision) 201.6 in. Height: (Talon) 51.6 in.; (Vision) 56.3 in. Width: (Talon) 68.7 in. (Vision) 74.4 in. Front Tread: (Talon) 59.7 in.; (Vision) 62.0 in. Rear Tread: (Talon) 59.4 in.; (Vision) 62.0 in. Standard Tires: (Talon, Talon ESi) P195/70HR14; (Talon TSi FWD) P205/55HR16; (Talon TSi AWD) P215/55VR16; (Vision ESi, Vision TSi) P225/60R16.

TECHNICAL: Transmission: (Talon) Five-speed manual with overdrive. (Vision ESi) Four-speed automatic with overdrive. (Vision TSi) AutoStick four-speed automatic. Steering: (Talon, Vision) Rack and pinion. Front suspension: (Talon) Modified double wishbone, coil springs, direct acting shock absorbers and link-type stabilizer bar; (Vision) Iso-strut w/integral gas-charged shock absorbers, coil springs, single transverse lower links, tension struts and link-type stabilizer bar. Rear suspension: (Talon) Multiple links, coil springs, direct acting shock absorbers and (TSi AWD only) link-type stabilizer bar; (Vision) Chapman struts w/integral gas-charged shock absorbers, concentric coil springs, dual transverse lower links, lower trailing links and link-type stabilizer bar. Brakes: (Talon) Front disc/rear drum (power assisted); (Talon ESi, Talon TSi, Vision ESi) Four-wheel disc (power assisted); (Vision TSi) Four-wheel disc w/anti-lock. Body construction: (Talon, Vision) Unibody. Fuel tank: (Talon) 15.8 gals.; (Vision) 18.0 gals.

DRIVETRAIN OPTIONS: Transmission: Four-speed auto.: Talon ($745). Talon ESi ($745); Talon TSi FWD ($891); Talon TSi AWD ($861). Anti-lock brakes: Talon ($649); Talon ESi ($649); Talon TSi ($649); Vision ESi ($600). Limited Slip Differential: Talon TSi AWD ($266).

TALON CONVENIENCE/APPEARANCE OPTIONS: Talon: Pkg. 21X: stnd equip. (NC). Pkg. 22X: 21X exc. 4-spd auto. trans. replaces 5-spd manual ($745). Talon ESi: Pkg. 21A: stnd equip. (NC). Pkg. 22A: 21A exc. 4-spd auto. trans. replaces 5-spd manual ($745). Pkg. 21B: incl. 21A plus air cond., rear center shelf, rear window defroster, front floor mats, dual pwr mirrors, AM/FM stereo radio w/cass., clock & 6 spkrs, spd control ($1664). Pkg. 22B: 21B exc. 4-spd auto. trans. replaces 5-spd manual ($2409). Pkg. 21C: incl. 21B plus pwr windows, pwr door locks, cargo net, soft door trim ($2198). Pkg. 22C: 21C exc. 4-spd auto. trans. replaces 5-spd manual ($2943). TSi w/fwd: Pkg. 23D: stnd equip. (NC). Pkg. 24D: 23D exc. 4-spd auto. trans. replaces 5-spd manual ($891). Pkg. 23P: incl. 23D plus air cond., spd control, pwr door locks, pwr windows, front floor mats ($1590). Pkg. 24P: 23P exc. 4-spd auto. trans. replaces 5-spd manual ($2481). TSi w/awd: Pkg. 25F: stnd equip. (NC). Pkg. 26F: 25F exc. 4-spd auto. trans. replaces 5-spd manual ($861). Pkg. 25S: incl. 25F plus air cond., front floor mats ($889). Pkg. 26S: 25S exc. 4-spd auto. trans. replaces 5-spd manual ($1750). Pkg. 25L: incl. 25S plus AM/FM stereo radio w/cass. & CD player, graphic equal. & 8 Infinity spkrs, 6-way pwr driver's seat, leather bucket seats, pwr sunroof, security alarm ($3535). Pkg. 26L: incl. 25L exc. 4-spd auto. trans. replaces 5-spd manual ($4396). Other: Air cond., base, ESi ($860). 6-way pwr driver's seat, TSi ($332). HomeLink Universal Transmitter for opening garage doors, N/A base ($113). Security alarm w/remote keyless entry, N/A base ($334). Pwr sunroof, N/A base ($730). Rear window defroster, base, ESi ($162). Leather front bucket seats w/folding rear split folding bench seat, TSi ($457). (RAL) Elect. AM/FM stereo radio w/4 spkrs, base ($232). (RBW) Elect. AM/FM stereo radio w/cass. & 6 spkrs, base ($500). (RBX) Elect. AM/FM stereo radio w/CD player & cass. & 6 spkrs, ESi, TSi ($390). (RAZ) Elect. AM/FM stereo radio w/CD player & cass., graphic equal. & 8 Infinity spkrs ($793). (AY9) Whl Grp.: incl. 16-in. cast alum whls w/P205/55HR16 tires, ESi ($489).

VISION CONVENIENCE/APPEARANCE OPTIONS: ESi: Pkg. 22B: stnd equip. (NC). Pkg. 22C: incl. 22B plus dual illum. visor mirrors, 8-way pwr driver's seat, remote/illum. entry syst., spd proportional stng ($705). TSi: Pkg. 26L: stnd equip. (NC). Pkg. 26M: incl. 26L plus cargo net, leather bucket seats, Chrysler/Infinity Spatial Imaging Sound Syst. w/cass., security alarm, conventional spare tire ($1050). Other: (AJF) Remote/Illum. Entry Grp.: incl. remote keyless entry, remote decklid release, illum. entry, ESi (NC). (AWT) Perf. Handling Grp.: incl. P225/60VR16 perf. tires, perf. susp., TSi ($220). Calif. emissions ($105). Integrated child's seat ($100). Pwr moonroof: ESi ($1015); TSi ($720). Security alarm, TSi ($150). Eng block heater ($20). Leather seats, TSi ($620). Extra cost paint ($100). Metallic paint ($200). (ARH) AM/FM stereo radio w/cass. & 8 spkrs ($350). (ARA) Elect. AM/FM stereo radio w/cass., graphic equal., pwr antenna & 11 Infinity spkrs: ESi ($650); TSi ($300). (ARD) Elect. AM/FM stereo radio w/CD player, graphic equal., pwr antenna & 11 Infinity spkrs, TSi ($300-$600). Conventional spare tire ($125). 16-in. Polycast "Pacifica" whls w/P225/60R16 touring tires, ESi ($374).

HISTORY: Model year production: 27,906 (not including imported Summits). Calendar year sales: 28,695 (including 3,416 imported Summits). Sales of Eagle automobiles dropped dramatically in 1996 to approximately just over half the number sold the previous year. Whether it was a move to bolster the Eagle division or the handwriting was on the wall as far as the division's demise, in August 1996, Chrysler Corp. consolidated its Chrysler-Plymouth and Jeep-Eagle divisions. By November, Chrysler officials were reassuring the media that the Eagle division would not be dropped. By the end of the 1996 model year, the imported Summit was discontinued, with only the Talon and Vision remaining in the Eagle lineup.

1997 EAGLE

It was the beginning of the end when the 1997 model year began at Eagle. The imported Summit was discontinued after the 1996 model year. Production of 1997 Eagles was but a blip on the Chrysler Corp. radar screen with fewer than 16,000 Talons and Visions built. Talon received a re-do of its exterior with a more "aggressive" frontal appearance in an attempt to breathe life into the series. Also done in an attempt to spur sales, Vision ESi could now be ordered with an optional 3.5-liter V-6 that was the standard power source of the more upscale Vision TSi. It was too little, too late, though, as 1997 was the Vision's final year of production.

TALON — SERIES J — FOUR — Base, ESi and TSi trim levels again comprised the Talon sports coupe lineup. TSi remained available in both front- and all-wheel-drive versions. Powertrain combinations carried over unchanged from the previous year. Talon's exterior appearance was revised, giving the car an even more "aggressive" look. Redesigned were the front fascia, grille and emblem, and, on the TSi, the addition of new

foglamps. There was also new bodyside appliqué (not available on base model) as well as a reworked rear fascia, dimensional rear fascia badging, and, for ESi and TSi, a revamped rear spoiler. Also new were a quarter window garnish panel and high-gloss black drip rails. Exterior color choice revisions were Bright Jade replaced Blue Metallic, Paprika replaced Prism Blue, and Pewter Blue replaced Medium Gray. Inside, the Talon featured a new black and tan interior scheme. The ESi coupe received redesigned 14-inch Sparkle Silver wheel covers while the TSi now had P215/50VR17 tires and 17-inch Sparkle Silver cast aluminum wheels as standard fare. As with the base Talon, the ESi coupe now featured front disc/rear drum brakes after using four-wheel disc brakes the previous year.

1997 Eagle, Vision TSi sedan (OCW)

VISION — SERIES H — V-6 — In its final appearance, the Vision sedan remained available in ESi and TSi trim levels. Due to the Vision's demise at the end of the model year, changes were minimal. The ESi sedan now offered as an option the 3.5-liter V-6 that was standard in the TSi. Again standard in the ESi was the 3.3-liter V-6, which was again optional in TLEV (transitional low-emission vehicle) configuration. Both engines were paired with an electronically controlled four-speed automatic transmission with overdrive, which received software refinements to provide smoother operation. The ESi model now also had front disc/rear drum brakes after using four-wheel disc brakes the previous year. One other change of note was that Deep Amethyst Pearl replaced Wildberry as an exterior color choice.

I.D. DATA: Eagle's 17-symbol Vehicle Identification Number (VIN) was embossed on a metal plate riveted to the top left surface of the instrument panel, visible through the windshield. Model year (symbol ten) was 'V' for 1997.

TALON (FOUR)

Model No.	Body/ Style No.	Body Type & Seating	Factory Price	Shipping Weight	Prod. Total
JXL	24	2-dr Cpe-4P	14594	2729	Note 1
JXH	24	2-dr ESi Cpe-4P	15365	2745	Note 1
JXP	24	2-dr TSi Cpe-4P	18550	2899	Note 1
JFS	24	2-dr AWD TSi Cpe-4P	20806	3142	Note 1

Note 1: Talon coupe production totaled 9,788 with no further breakout available.

VISION (V-6)

HXP	41	4-dr ESi Sed-5P	20305	3439	Note 1
HXS	41	4-dr TSi Sed-5P	24485	3535	Note 1

Note 1: Vision sedan production totaled 5,874 with no further breakout available.

ENGINE DATA: BASE FOUR (Talon, Talon ESi): Inline, dual overhead cam four-cylinder. Cast iron block; aluminum head. Displacement: 121 cu. in. (2.0 liters). Bore & stroke: 3.44 x 3.27 in. Compression ratio: 9.6:1. Brake horsepower: 140 at 6000 RPM. Torque: 131 lb.-ft. at 4800 RPM. Sequential fuel injection. BASE FOUR (Talon TSi): Inline turbocharged, dual overhead cam four-cylinder. Cast iron block; aluminum head. Displacement: 121 cu. in. (2.0 liters). Bore & stroke: 3.34 x 3.46 in. Compression ratio: 8.5:1. Brake horsepower: 210 at 6000 RPM. Torque: 214 lb.-ft. at 3000 RPM. Sequential fuel injection. BASE V-6 (Vision ESi): 60 degree, overhead valve V-6. Cast iron block; aluminum heads. Displacement: 201 cu. in. (3.3 liters). Bore & stroke: 3.66 x 3.19 in. Compression ratio: 8.9:1. Brake horsepower: 161 at 5300 RPM. Torque: 181 lb.-ft. at 3200 RPM. Sequential fuel injection. BASE V-6 (Vision TSi); OPTIONAL V-6 (Vision ESi): 60 degree, overhead cam V-6. Cast iron block; aluminum heads. Displacement: 214 cu. in. (3.5 liters). Bore & stroke: 3.78 x 3.19 in. Compression ratio: 9.6:1. Brake horsepower: 214 at 5850 RPM. Torque: 221 lb.-ft. at 3100 RPM. Sequential fuel injection.

CHASSIS DATA: Wheelbase: (Talon) 98.8 in.; (Vision) 113.0 in. Overall length: (Talon) 174.8 in.; (Vision) 201.6 in. Height: (Talon) 51.6 in.; (Vision) 56.3 in. Width: (Talon) 69.9 in.; (Vision) 74.4 in. Front Tread: (Talon) 59.7 in.; (Vision) 62.0 in. Rear Tread: (Talon) 59.4 in.; (Vision) 62.0 in. Standard Tires: (Talon, Talon ESi) P195/70HR14; (Talon TSi FWD) P205/55HR16; (Talon TSi AWD) P215/50VR17; (Vision ESi, Vision TSi) P225/60R16.

TECHNICAL: Transmission: (Talon) Five-speed manual with overdrive. (Vision ESi) Four-speed automatic with overdrive. (Vision TSi) AutoStick four-speed automatic. Steering: (Talon, Vision) Rack and pinion. Front

suspension: (Talon) Modified double wishbone, coil springs, direct acting shock absorbers and link-type stabilizer bar; (Vision) Iso-strut w/integral gas-charged shock absorbers, coil springs, single transverse lower links, tension struts and link-type stabilizer bar. Rear suspension: (Talon) Multiple links, coil springs, direct acting shock absorbers and (TSi AWD only) link-type stabilizer bar; (Vision) Chapman struts w/integral gas-charged shock absorbers, concentric coil springs, dual transverse lower links, lower trailing links and link-type stabilizer bar. Brakes: (Talon, Talon ESi, Vision ESi) Front disc/rear drum (power assisted); (Talon TSi) Four-wheel disc (power assisted); (Vision TSi) Four-wheel disc w/anti-lock. Body construction: (Talon, Vision) Unibody. Fuel tank: (Talon) 16.9 gals.; (Vision) 18.0 gals.

DRIVETRAIN OPTIONS: Transmission: Four-speed auto.: Talon ($745). Talon ESi ($745); Talon TSi FWD ($891); Talon TSi AWD ($891). Anti-lock brakes: Talon ($649); Talon ESi ($649); Talon TSi ($649); Vision ESi ($600). Limited Slip Differential: Talon TSi AWD ($266).

1997 Eagle, Talon ESi sports coupe (OCW)

1997 Eagle, Talon TSi sports coupe with all-wheel-drive (AWD) (OCW)

TALON CONVENIENCE/APPEARANCE OPTIONS: Talon: Pkg. 21X: stnd equip. (NC). Pkg. 22X: 21X exc. 4-spd auto. trans. replaces 5-spd manual ($745). Talon ESi: Pkg. 21A: stnd equip. (NC). Pkg. 22A: 21A exc. 4-spd auto. trans. replaces 5-spd manual ($745). Pkg. 21B: incl. 21A plus air cond., rear center shelf, rear window defroster, front floor mats, dual pwr mirrors, AM/FM stereo radio w/cass., clock & 6 spkrs, spd control ($1688). Pkg. 22B: 21B exc. 4-spd auto. trans. replaces 5-spd manual ($2433). Pkg. 21C: incl. 21B plus pwr windows, pwr door locks, cargo net, soft door trim ($2222). Pkg. 22C: 21C exc. 4-spd auto. trans. replaces 5-spd manual ($2967). TSi w/fwd: Pkg. 23D: stnd equip. (NC). Pkg. 24D: 23D exc. 4-spd auto. trans. replaces 5-spd manual ($891). Pkg. 23P: incl. 23D plus air cond., spd control, pwr door locks, pwr windows, front floor mats ($1614). Pkg. 24P: 23P exc. 4-spd auto. trans. replaces 5-spd manual ($2505). TSi w/awd: Pkg. 25F: stnd equip. (NC). Pkg. 26F: 25F exc. 4-spd auto. trans. replaces 5-spd manual ($891). Pkg. 25S: incl. 25F plus air cond., front floor mats, security alarm w/remote keyless entry ($1223). Pkg. 26S: 25S exc. 4-spd auto. trans. replaces 5-spd manual ($2114). Pkg. 25L: incl. 25S plus anti-lock brakes, AM/FM stereo radio w/cass. & CD player, graphic equal. & 8 Infinity spkrs, 6-way pwr driver's seat, leather bucket seats, pwr sunroof ($4184). Pkg. 26L: 25L exc. 4-spd auto. trans. replaces 5-spd manual ($5075). Other: Air cond. ($860). 6-way pwr driver's seat, TSi ($332). HomeLink Universal Transmitter for opening garage doors, TSi AWD ($113). Security alarm w/remote keyless entry, N/A base ($334). Calif. emissions ($170). Pwr sunroof, N/A base ($730). Rear window defroster, base, ESi ($162). Leather front bucket seats w/folding rear split folding bench seat, TSi ($457). (RAL) Elect. AM/FM stereo radio w/4 spkrs, base ($234). (RBW) Elect. AM/FM stereo radio w/cass. & 6 spkrs, N/A base ($502). (RBX) Elect. AM/FM stereo radio w/CD player & cass., ESi, TSi ($390). (RAZ) Elect. AM/FM stereo radio w/CD player & cass., graphic equal. & 8 Infinity spkrs, TSi ($793). (AY9) Whl Grp.: incl. 16-in. cast alum Sparkle Silver whls w/P205/55HR16 tires, ESi ($507).

VISION CONVENIENCE/APPEARANCE OPTIONS: ESi: Pkg. 26B: stnd equip. (NC). Pkg. 26C: incl. 26B plus dual illum. visor mirrors, 8-way pwr driver's seat, remote/illum. entry syst. ($600). TSi: Pkg. 26L: stnd equip. (NC). Pkg. 26M: incl. 26L plus cargo net, leather bucket seats, Chrysler/Infinity Spatial Imaging Sound Syst. w/cass., security alarm, conventional spare tire ($1155). Other: (AWT) Perf. Handling Grp.: incl. P225/60VR16 perf. tires, perf. susp., TSi ($220). Calif. emissions ($170). Pwr moonroof w/mini overhead console ($1100). Security alarm, TSi ($150). Eng block heater ($20). Leather seats, TSi ($620). Extra cost paint ($200). (ARH) Elect. AM/FM stereo radio w/cass. & 8 spkrs, ESi ($350). (ARA) Elect. AM/FM stereo radio w/cass., graphic equal., pwr antenna & 11 Infinity spkrs: ESi ($565); TSi ($215). (ARB) Elect. AM/FM stereo radio w/CD player & cass., graphic equal., pwr antenna & 11 Infinity spkrs, TSi ($300-$515). Conventional spare tire ($125). 16-in. Polycast "Pacifica" whls w/P225/60R16 touring tires, ESi ($374).

HISTORY: Model year production: 15,662. Calendar year sales: 15,352. The Vision was dropped after the 1997 model year, with only the Talon wearing the Eagle name for 1998. That was also Talon's final campaign. In October 1997, Chrysler officials announced that the Eagle division was history after the 1998 model year run of Talons.

1998 EAGLE

This was the Eagle division's last flight, the Talon going it solo after the Vision was discontinued at the end of the previous model year.

TALON — SERIES J — FOUR — Talon returned for its final model year (presumably to use up existing parts supplies), again offered in base, ESi and TSi trim levels with no change to powertrain combinations that were offered previously. The few minor changes that were implemented occurred inside the sports coupe. New seat fabrics and a new black and gray interior color scheme were standard. Also, the ESi model now offered an optional audio system with integrated cassette and CD player.

I.D. DATA: Eagle's 17-symbol Vehicle Identification Number (VIN) was embossed on a metal plate riveted to the top left surface of the instrument panel, visible through the windshield. Model year (symbol ten) was 'W' for 1998.

TALON (FOUR)

Model No.	Body/ Style No.	Body Type & Seating	Factory Price	Shipping Weight	Prod. Total
JXL	24	2-dr Cpe-4P	14505	2729	Note 1
JXH	24	2-dr ESi Cpe-4P	15275	2745	Note 1
JXP	24	2-dr TSi Cpe-4P	18460	2899	Note 1
JFS	24	2-dr AWD TSi Cpe-4P	20715	3142	Note 1

Note 1: Talon coupe production totaled 4,308 with no further breakout available.

ENGINE DATA: BASE FOUR (Talon, Talon ESi): Inline, dual overhead cam four-cylinder. Cast iron block; aluminum head. Displacement: 121 cu. in. (2.0 liters). Bore & stroke: 3.44 x 3.27 in. Compression ratio: 9.6:1. Brake horsepower: 140 at 6000 RPM. Torque: 131 lb.-ft. at 4800 RPM. Sequential fuel injection. **BASE FOUR** (Talon TSi): Inline turbo-charged, dual overhead cam four-cylinder. Cast iron block; aluminum head. Displacement: 121 cu. in. (2.0 liters). Bore & stroke: 3.34 x 3.46 in. Compression ratio: 8.5:1. Brake horsepower: 210 at 6000 RPM. Torque: 214 lb.-ft. at 3000 RPM. Sequential fuel injection.

CHASSIS DATA: Wheelbase: (Talon) 98.8 in. Overall length: (Talon) 174.8 in. Height: (Talon) 51.0 in. Width: (Talon) 69.9 in. Front Tread: (Talon) 59.7 in. Rear Tread: (Talon) 59.4 in. Standard Tires: (Talon, Talon ESi) P195/70HR14; (Talon TSi FWD) P205/55HR16; (Talon TSi AWD) P215/50VR17.

TECHNICAL: Transmission: (Talon) Five-speed manual with overdrive. Steering: (Talon) Rack and pinion. Front suspension: (Talon) Modified double wishbone, coil springs, direct acting shock absorbers and link-type stabilizer bar. Rear suspension: (Talon) Multiple links, coil springs, direct acting shock absorbers and (TSi AWD only) link-type stabilizer bar. Brakes: (Talon, Talon ESi) Front disc/rear drum (power assisted); (Talon TSi) Four-wheel disc (power assisted). Body construction: (Talon) Unibody. Fuel tank: (Talon) 16.9 gals.

DRIVETRAIN OPTIONS: Transmission: Four-speed auto.: Talon ($745). Talon ESi ($745); Talon TSi FWD ($891); Talon TSi AWD ($891). Anti-lock brakes: Talon ($650); Talon ESi ($650); Talon TSi ($650). Limited Slip Differential: Talon TSi AWD ($266).

TALON CONVENIENCE/APPEARANCE OPTIONS: Talon: Pkg. 21X: stnd equip. (NC). Pkg. 22X: 21X exc. 4-spd auto. trans. replaces 5-spd manual ($745). Talon ESi: Pkg. 21A: stnd equip. (NC). Pkg. 22A: 21A exc. 4-spd auto. trans. replaces 5-spd manual ($745). Pkg. 21B: incl. 21A plus air cond., rear center shelf, rear window defroster, front floor mats, dual pwr mirrors, AM/FM stereo radio w/cass., clock & 6 spkrs, spd control ($1695). Pkg. 22B: 21B exc. 4-spd auto. trans. replaces 5-spd manual ($2440). Pkg. 21C: incl. 21B plus pwr windows, pwr door locks, cargo net, soft door trim, 16-inch Whl Grp. ($2740). Pkg. 22C: 21C exc. 4-spd auto. trans. replaces 5-spd manual ($3485). TSi w/fwd: Pkg. 23D: stnd equip. (NC). Pkg. 24D: 23D exc. 4-spd auto. trans. replaces 5-spd manual ($891). Pkg. 23P: incl. 23D plus air cond., spd control, pwr door locks, pwr windows, front floor mats, AM/FM stereo radio w/CD player & cass. ($2005). Pkg. 24P: 23P exc. 4-spd auto. trans. replaces 5-spd manual ($2895). TSi w/awd: Pkg. 25F: stnd equip. (NC). Pkg. 26F: 25F exc. 4-spd auto. trans. replaces 5-spd manual ($891). Pkg. 25S: incl. 25F plus air cond., front floor mats, security alarm w/remote keyless entry ($1225). Pkg. 26S: 25S exc. 4-spd auto. trans. replaces 5-spd manual ($2115). Pkg. 25L: incl. 25S plus anti-lock brakes, AM/FM stereo radio w/cass. & CD player, graphic equal. & 8 Infinity spkrs, 6-way pwr driver's seat, leather bucket seats, pwr sunroof ($4195). Pkg. 26L: incl. 25L exc. 4-spd auto. trans. replaces 5-spd manual ($5085). Other: Air cond. ($860). 6-way pwr driver's seat, TSi ($335). Security alarm w/remote keyless entry, N/A base ($334). Calif. emissions ($170). Pwr sunroof, N/A base ($730). Rear window defroster, base, ESi ($165). Leather front bucket seats w/folding rear split folding bench seat, TSi ($460). (RAL) Elect. AM/FM stereo radio w/4 spkrs, base ($234). (RBW) Elect. AM/FM stereo radio w/cass. & 6 spkrs, base ($500). (RBX) Elect. AM/FM stereo radio w/CD player & cass. & 6 spkrs, ESi, TSi ($390). (RAZ) Elect. AM/FM stereo radio w/CD player & cass., graphic equal. & 8 Infinity spkrs, TSi ($795). (AY9) Whl Grp.: incl. 16-in. cast alum Sparkle Silver whls w/P205/55HR16 tires, ESi ($510).

HISTORY: Model year production: 4,308. At the end of the 1998 model year, Chrysler Corp. placed the Eagle name into the automotive history books, leaving the Jeep as the lone survivor of the American Motors Corp. buyout of 1987.

Imperial

The postwar Imperial began as an extra-fancy Chrysler. Although larger and more luxurious, its styling was not particularly distinctive from the corporation's less expensive series.

There wasn't all that much reason to be different. From 1946 to mid-1953, automakers enjoyed a seller's market. As the Salesman's Data Book for 1946 Chryslers told dealers, "you have a car that puts you in a perfect position to pick your owners . . . to select the type of person who appreciates a fine motor car . . . one whose prestige and pride of ownership will reflect credit on the car and on your organization."

Chrysler styling seemed to reflect this attitude. At a time when customers demanded flash and glamour, the Imperial was sedate. It had a rather clean, practical design that didn't change dramatically until 1955. Engineering and passenger comfort had priority over appearance.

1956 Imperial four-door sedan (OCW)

Imperial became a separate brand of Chrysler Corp. in 1954. But, it wasn't until a year later that it started to develop its own personality. The swank 1955 and 1956 models, with their free-standing taillights, were a tremendous boost to Imperial's image. They also showed that a car could have style without looking like "a jukebox on wheels," as noted industrial designer Raymond Loewy put it.

"The flying saucers have landed at last!" That's what a bit character in an Elvis Presley movie exclaimed when he saw a 1957 Imperial convertible. It was easy to see why. Imperial styling this year was to the left of "Wow!" The public loved it. This would be the best sales year ever for the make.

Four years later, Imperial made an attempt to capture the beauty of the classic era by using free-standing headlights. Whether or not it succeeded is a matter of personal opinion. Yet, at least no one could accuse the company of not being innovative.

In 1964, Imperial styling reflected the influence of the handsome 1961-1963 Lincoln Continental. While not as original as the previous models, they were handsome. They seemed more in tune with the pre-1955 conservative designs (but a bit flashier).

Although luxurious and attractive, by 1967 the make was drifting back to its former fancy Chrysler image. At a time when Ford was trying to make Mercurys resemble Lincolns and Chevrolets received Cadillac-inspired styling, Imperial began to look more like the lower-cost Chryslers. However, other than the free-standing headlights and taillights, there wasn't really an "Imperial look" that the corporation could bestow on its less expensive cars. And the fact that just about everyone referred to the make as Chrysler-Imperial didn't help matters.

The fuselage-styled Imperials, introduced in 1969, were the sleekest cars in their price class. They were also quite popular, at least initially. Sales dropped the next year to their lowest level since 1958.

1973 Imperial LeBaron four-door hardtop (OCW)

From 1971 until 1975, Imperial was just a top-of-the-line Chrysler. It was no surprise that the 1976 New Yorker looked virtually the same as the previous year's Imperial. Still, to a lot of people, there will always be something special about owning an Imperial.

1946 IMPERIAL

1946 Chrysler Crown Imperial, four-door limousine, 8-cyl (AA)

CROWN IMPERIAL SERIES — SERIES C40 — The 1946 Crown Imperial had a new criss-cross pattern grille with wraparound top, center and lower horizontal pieces. Yet, the basic 1942 styling remained. Because of the shortage of whitewall tires, white metal beauty rings were used.

IMPERIAL I.D. DATA: For 1946 models, the serial number on Chrysler-Imperials was located on the right-hand front door hinge post. Serial numbers ranged from 7810001 to 7810166. Engine numbers were located on the left side of the engine block below the cylinder head and between cylinders number 1 and number 2. Engine numbers for 1946 Crown Imperials were C40-1001 and up. Body/Style Numbers were not used.

CROWN IMPERIAL SERIES

Model No.	Body/ Style No.	Body Type & Seating	Factory Price	Shipping Weight	Prod. Total
C40	N/A	4-dr Limo-8P	3875	4814	Note 1

Note 1: A total of 750 Crown Imperial limousines were made from 1946 to 1948.

ENGINE: Inline. L-head 8. Cast iron block. Displacement: 323.5 cid. Bore and stroke: 3.25 x 4.87 inches. Compression ratio: 6.8:1. Brake hp: 135 at 3400 rpm. Five main bearings. Solid valve lifters. Carburetor: Stromberg two-barrel Model AAV-2.

CHASSIS FEATURES: Wheelbase: 145.5 inches. Overall length: 235 inches. Front tread: 58 inches. Rear tread: 62 inches. Tires: 7.50 x 15.

OPTIONS: Mopar heater and defroster. Mopar radio. Electric clock. Spotlights. Fog lights. Directional signals. Fluid Drive, four-speed hydraulic semi-automatic transmission. Heavy-duty air cleaner. Available rear axle gear ratio: 3.58:1.

HISTORICAL FOOTNOTES: The Chrysler Crown Imperial was introduced in March 1946. Calendar year sales of 76,753 cars were recorded. Fluid Drive was standard equipment on Crown Imperials. A limited number of Derham Customs were built off the 1946 Chrysler Custom Imperial platform. A one-off 'Pullman' limousine was made for Post Brand cereal heiress Margery Merryweather. Also constructed on this chassis, for commercial emergency use, were a number of sedan ambulances made by McClintock Co. of Lansing, Mich.

1947 IMPERIAL

CROWN IMPERIAL SERIES — SERIES C40 — Styling was virtually unchanged for 1947. The high-beam indicator was moved from the top of the speedometer into the speedometer dial, replacing the left turn signal arrow. Red taillamp buttons replaced the white ones used previously. The details of the door locks and lock covers were modified slightly. White sidewall tires were made optional after April 1, 1947. Most of these were running changes that took effect during the 1947 calendar year. However, all of the 1946-1948 models were in the same C40 series. Cars with serial numbers higher than 7810167 and assembled after Jan. 1, 1947, were registered as 1947 automobiles.

IMPERIAL I.D. DATA: The serial number was located on a plate on the left front door hinge pillar post. Engine number was on top front center of engine block. Serial numbers ranged from 7810167 to 7810907. Engine numbers were in the same series as in 1946 and continued through consecutively, with no record of the first number for the year.

1947 Chrysler Crown Imperial, four-door limousine, 8-cyl (AA)

CROWN IMPERIAL SERIES

Model No.	Body/ Style No.	Body Type & Seating	Factory Price	Shipping Weight	Prod. Total
C40	N/A	4-dr Sed-8P	4205	4865	Note 1
C40	N/A	4-dr Limo-8P	4305	4875	Note 2

Note 1: A total of 650 Crown Imperial sedans were made from 1947 to 1948.

Note 2: See 1946 Production Total.

ENGINE: Inline. L-head 8. Cast iron block. Displacement: 323.5 cid. Bore and stroke: 3.25 x 4.87 inches. Compression ratio: 6.8:1. Brake hp: 135 at 3400 rpm. Five main bearings. Solid valve lifters. Carburetor: Stromberg two-barrel Model AAV-2.

CHASSIS FEATURES: Wheelbase: 145.5 inches. Overall length: 235 inches. Front tread: 58 inches. Rear tread: 62 inches. Tires: 7.50 x 15.

OPTIONS: Mopar heater and defroster. Mopar radio. Electric clock. Spotlights. Fog lights. Directional signals. Fluid Drive, four-speed hydraulic semi-automatic transmission. Heavy-duty air cleaner. Available rear axle gear ratio: 3.58:1.

HISTORICAL FOOTNOTES: The 1947 Crown Imperials were introduced in January 1947. This was the first season for the non-limousine eight-passenger sedan. This model was the same size as the 'limo' and also had the same type of jump seats, but did not feature a division window between the driver's compartment and rear passenger area. Cameramen at Paramount Studios crossed a Dodge pickup truck with an Imperial chassis and came up with a unique mobile camera rig.

1948 IMPERIAL

1948 Chrysler Crown Imperial, four-door limousine, 8-cyl

CROWN IMPERIAL SERIES — SERIES C40 — The new 1948 Crown Imperial looked the same as last year's model. It was still in the same C40 series, too. The major change was that larger, low-pressure tires were used. Two models were again offered this year. The limousine had a separate driver's compartment, with the front and rear sections split by a division window. The chauffeur's compartment was usually trimmed in leather, while the rear compartment was done in luxury cloth and had folding jump seats. Jump seats were also a feature of eight-passenger sedans, but division windows were not. The C40 series was actually carried into the next calendar year, with units assembled late in the run intended to be registered as 1949 cars. This fact sometimes causes confusion today.

IMPERIAL I.D. DATA: The serial number was located on a plate on the left front door hinge pillar post. Engine number was on top front center of the engine block. Serial numbers 7810908 to 7811347 were used

on 1948 Chrysler Crown Imperials. Effective Dec. 1, 1948, Crown Imperials bearing serial numbers 7811348 and higher were to be considered part of the 1949 series for purposes of registration only. For evaluation purposes, then and now, these cars were comparable to 1948 models. Engine numbers were continued from 1947, with no record of the year's starting or ending numbers.

CROWN IMPERIAL SERIES

Model No.	Body/ Style No.	Body Type & Seating	Factory Price	Shipping Weight	Prod. Total
C40	N/A	4-dr Sed-8P	4712	4865	Note 1
C40	N/A	4-dr Limo-8P	4817	4875	Note 2

Note 1: See 1947 Production Total.

Note 2: See 1946 Production Total.

ENGINE: Inline. L-head 8. Cast iron block. Displacement: 323.5 cid. Bore and stroke: 3.25 x 4.87 inches. Compression ratio: 6.8:1. Brake hp: 135 at 3400 rpm. Five main bearings. Solid valve lifters. Carburetor: Stromberg two-barrel Model AAV-2.

CHASSIS FEATURES: Wheelbase: 145.5 inches. Overall length: 235 inches. Front tread: 58 inches. Rear tread: 82 inches. Tires: 8.90 x 15.

OPTIONS: Mopar heater and defroster. Mopar radio. Spotlights. Front and rear center bumper guard. Wheel trim rings. Left outside rearview mirror. Right outside rearview mirror. White sidewall tires. Fluid Drive, four-speed hydraulic semi-automatic transmission. Heavy-duty air cleaner. Available rear axle gear ratio: 3.58:1.

HISTORICAL FOOTNOTES: The 1948 Chryslers were introduced Jan. 1, 1948, and were continued into the next calendar year as First Series 1949 models. Model year production is combined with 1946-1947 unit totals. Calendar year sales were part of the full Chrysler total. Derham Customs continued to be built on the 1948 Imperial chassis. Derham also converted one such unit into a four-door phaeton, under a commission from King Ibn Saud, of Saudi Arabia. It was used for gazelle hunting. Some of these custom-built cars may be eligible for recognition as full Classics, upon owner application to the Classic Car Club of America.

1949 IMPERIAL

1949 Chrysler Crown Imperial, four-door limousine, 8-cyl

IMPERIAL SERIES — SERIES C46-2 — The new custom-built Imperial sedan was based on the New Yorker. It shared the same trim, but had a canvas-covered roof and leather and broadcloth Imperial upholstery. These features were installed, by Derham, on the all-new postwar Chrysler sheet metal.

IMPERIAL I.D. DATA: The serial number was located on a plate on the left front door hinge pillar post. Engine number was on top front center of the engine block. Imperial sedan and Deluxe sedan serial numbers were 7107801 to 7107850. Engine numbers C46-1001 to 28838 were used in mixed production with other Chrysler Eights. The first symbol 'C' designated Chrysler division. The second and third symbols designated consecutive series code. Body/Style Numbers were not used. Note: Production halted when the C-47 was introduced.

IMPERIAL SERIES [Early 1948-1/2]

C46-2	N/A	4-dr Sed-6P	4665	4300	50

ENGINE: Inline. L-head 8. Cast iron block. Displacement: 323.5 cid. Bore and stroke: 3.25 x 4.87 inches. Compression ratio: 7.25:1. Brake hp: 135 at 3400 rpm. Five main bearings. Solid valve lifters. Carburetor: Carter Type Ball & Ball two-barrel Model BB-E7J1-2.

CROWN IMPERIAL SERIES — SERIES C47 — Early 1949s were actually just leftover 1948s. The really new models didn't arrive until March of 1949. Their styling was sleeker than previous Imperials, yet conservative. Fewer, but heavier, bars were used in the criss-cross pattern grille.

The upper and center horizontal pieces wrapped around the front fenders. Rocker panel moldings, rear fender stoneguards, full-length lower window trim and horizontal chrome strips on the rear fenders (and from the headlights to about half-way across the front doors) were used to decorate the side body.

IMPERIAL I.D. DATA: The serial number was located on a plate on the left front door hinge pillar post. Engine number was on top of engine block at front water outlet elbow. Chrysler Crown Imperials had serial numbers 7813001 to 7813088. Engine number C47-1001 to 1095 were used. These were distinct numbers for Custom Imperials. The first symbol 'C' designated Chrysler Division. The second and third symbol designated consecutive series code. Body/Style Numbers were not used.

CROWN IMPERIAL SERIES

Model No.	Body/ Style No.	Body Type & Seating	Factory Price	Shipping Weight	Prod. Total
C47	N/A	4-dr Sed-8P	5229	5250	40
C47	N/A	4-dr Limo-8P	5334	5295	45

ENGINE: Inline. L-head 8. Cast iron block. Displacement: 323.5 cid. Bore and stroke: 3.25 x 4.87 inches. Compression ratio: 7.25:1. Brake hp: 135 at 3400 rpm. Five main bearings. Solid valve lifters. Carburetor: Carter Type Ball & Ball two-barrel Model BB-E7J1-2.

CHASSIS FEATURES: Wheelbase: (Imperial) 131.5 inches. (Crown Imperial) 145.5 inches. Overall length: (Imperial) 210 inches; (Crown Imperial) 234.75. Front tread: (Imperial) 57 inches; (Crown Imperial) 57 inches. Rear tread: (Imperial) 58 inches; (Crown Imperial) 64 inches. Tires: (Imperial) 8.20 x 15; (Crown Imperial) 8.90 x 15.

OPTIONS: Mopar heater and defroster. Mopar radio. Electric clock. Spotlights. Fog lights. Whitewall tires. Wing vent deflectors. Middle bumper guards. Exhaust deflector. Grille guard. Weatherproof ignition. Auto compass. Underhood light. Windshield washer. Spare tire valve extension. Prestomatic transmission and Fluid Drive were standard. Heavy-duty air cleaner. Available rear axle gear ratios: 3.90:1; 4.00:1.

HISTORICAL FOOTNOTES: The 1949 Imperials entered production in January 1949 and the cars appeared in dealer showrooms by March. Model year production peaked at 135 units. Calendar year sales of 15,000 Chrysler Eights was recorded. D.A. Wallace was president of Chrysler Division this year. Cycle bonded brake linings were used. Another Imperial-based mobile camera car was built by MGM studios this year. The Imperial Eight sedan carried Chrysler New Yorker nameplates and wheel covers.

1950 IMPERIAL

1950 Chrysler Crown Imperial, four-door limousine, 8-cyl (AA)

IMPERIAL SERIES — SERIES C49-N — The new Imperial was essentially a New Yorker with custom interior. It had a Cadillac-style grille treatment that included circular signal lights enclosed in a wraparound, ribbed chrome piece. Side trim was similar to last year's model, but the front fender strip ended at the front doors and the rear fender molding was at tire-top level and integrated into the stone guard.

IMPERIAL I.D. DATA: The serial number was located on a plate on the left front door hinge pillar post. Engine number was on top front center of engine block. Serial numbers 7146001 to 7156654 were used only on Series C49 Imperials. Serial numbers 7813501 to 7813916 were used on Series C50 Crown Imperials. Engine numbers on regular Imperials were shared with the other 1950 Chrysler Eights. They fell within the range C49-1001 to 43041. The engine numbers used on Crown Imperials were distinct and ranged from C50-1001 to 1433.

IMPERIAL SERIES

C49-N	N/A	4-dr Sed-6P	3055	4245	9,500
C49-N	N/A	4-dr DeL Sed-6P	3176	4250	1,150

CROWN IMPERIAL SERIES — SERIES C50 — Unlike the standard Imperial, the Crown had a side trim treatment in which the rear fender

molding and stone guard were separate. Body sill moldings were used on all Imperials, but were of a less massive type on the more massive Crown models. A special version of the limousine was available. It featured a unique leather interior and a leather-covered top that blacked out the rear quarter windows. Power windows were standard.

CROWN IMPERIAL SERIES

Model No.	Body/ Style No.	Body Type & Seating	Factory Price	Shipping Weight	Prod. Total
C50	N/A	4-dr Sed-8P	5229	5235	209
C50	N/A	4-dr Limo-8P	5334	5305	205

ENGINE: Inline. L-head 8. Cast iron block. Displacement: 323.5 cid. Bore and stroke: 3.25 x 4.87 inches. Compression ratio: 7.25:1. Brake hp: 135 at 3200 rpm. Five main bearings. Solid valve lifters. Carburetor: Carter one-barrel Model BB-E7J4.

CHASSIS FEATURES: Wheelbase: (Imperial) 131.5 inches; (Crown Imperial) 145.5 inches. Overall length: (Imperial) 214 inches; (Crown Imperial) 230.25 inches. Front tread: (Imperial) 57 inches; (Crown Imperial) 57 inches. Rear tread: (Imperial) 58 inches; (Crown Imperial) 64 inches. Tires: (Imperial) 8.20 x 15; (Crown Imperial) 8.90 x 15. The industry's first disc brakes, Ausco-Lambert "self-energizing" disc brakes, were standard in Crown Imperial series.

OPTIONS: White sidewall tires. Wing vent deflectors. Exhaust deflector. Mopar radio. Mopar heater. Locking gas cap. Weatherproof ignition. Mopar auto compass. Windshield washer. Spare tire valve extension. A brand new option (also available on Chrysler Eights) was electrically operated power windows. Prestomatic transmission with Fluid Drive was standard. Heavy-duty oil bath air cleaner. Vacuum booster fuel pump.

HISTORICAL FOOTNOTES: The 1950 Chrysler Imperial models were introduced in January 1950. Model year production began in December 1949. D.A. Wallace was president of the Chrysler Division of Chrysler Corp., with offices at 12200 East Jefferson Avenue in Detroit. The Derham custom body company, of Rosemont, Pa., continued to create some beautiful vehicles on the Imperial chassis.

1951 IMPERIAL

1951 Chrysler Imperial, four-door sedan, V-8

1951 Chrysler Imperial, two-door convertible, V-8

IMPERIAL SERIES — SERIES C54 — In an unusual move for the 1950s, the Imperial had less chrome than the lower-priced New Yorker that it was based on. It had three horizontal grille bars (one across center); parking lights between the bars and a chrome vertical center piece. Aside from its front fender nameplate, side body trim was limited to moldings below the windows; rocker panel moldings; bright metal stone shields and a heavy, horizontal molding strip running across the fender skirts.

IMPERIAL I.D. DATA: The serial number was located on a plate on the left front door hinge pillar post. Engine number was on top front center of engine block. Series C54 Imperial Eights had serial numbers 7736501 to 7753512. Engine numbers used on these cars were in the same range of numbers (C51-8-1001 to 67967) used on other 1951 Chrysler Eights, with the engines in mixed production sequence. Series C53 Crown Imperials had serial numbers 7814501-7815000. Engine numbers on these cars were also in the same range as for other Chrysler Eights.

IMPERIAL SERIES

Model No.	Body/ Style No.	Body Type & Seating	Factory Price	Shipping Weight	Prod. Total
C54	N/A	4-dr Sed-8P	3699	4350	21,711
C54	N/A	2-dr Clb Cpe-6P	3687	4230	1,189
C54	N/A	2-dr HT-6P	4067	4380	3,450
C54	N/A	2-dr Conv-6P	4427	4570	650

Note 1: Production Totals include 1952 models.

CROWN IMPERIAL SERIES — SERIES C53 — In addition to its size and increased passenger capacity, center-opening rear doors and a concealed gas filler cap were a couple of distinguishing features for the Crown Imperial. The hood ornament had a 'crown' medallion in the center of the 'V' on the car's nose. Imperial models did not have lower front fender belt moldings. Power steering and Fluid Torque Drive were standard in Crown Imperials.

CROWN IMPERIAL SERIES

C53	N/A	4-dr Sed-8P	6623	5360	360
C53	N/A	4-dr Limo-8P	6740	5450	338

Note 1: Production Total includes 1952 models.

ENGINE: V-8. Overhead valve. Cast iron block. Displacement: 331.1 cid. Bore and stroke: 3.81 x 3.62 inches. Compression ratio: 7.5:1. Brake hp: 180 at 4000 rpm. Five main bearings. Hydraulic valve lifters. Carburetor: Carter two-barrel Model WCD-830S.

CHASSIS FEATURES: Wheelbase: (Imperial) 131.5 inches; (Crown Imperial) 145.5 inches. Front tread: (Imperial) 56 inches; (Crown Imperial) 60 inches. Rear tread: (Imperial) 58 inches; (Crown Imperial) 66 inches. Tires: (Imperial) 8.20 x 15; (Crown Imperial) 8.90 x 15.

OPTIONS: Hydraguide power steering, in Imperial Eight ($226); standard in Crown Imperial Eight. Power brakes. Power disc brakes standard on Crown Imperial. Power steering. Air conditioning. All Weather Comfort System. Electric lift windows. Mopar Radio. White sidewall tires. External sun visor. Fog lights. Spotlights. Exhaust deflector. Outside rearview mirror.

HISTORICAL FOOTNOTES: The 1951 Chrysler line (including Imperials) was introduced to the public on Feb. 9, 1951. On May 28, 1951, the Economic Stabilization Agency permitted the company to change its prices, to cover increased costs of the new V-8s. The increases were $251.19 for New Yorkers and Imperial Eights and $261.38 for the Crown Imperials. New features of this year included the Firepower V-8 engine (with hemispherical-segment cylinder heads); Hydraguide power steering and Oriflow shock absorbers. Assemblies of 1951 models began in December 1950 and the model year ran until November 1951. In this time span an estimated 156,000 units were built to 1951 specifications (Chrysler and Imperials together). A total of three special 'parade phaetons' were built on the Crown Imperial chassis and used by the cities of Los Angeles, New York and Detroit. These cars were later updated with mid-'50s styling. The 'Imperial Rose' was a special C54 series show car custom-made by the factory this year.

1952 IMPERIAL

1952 Chrysler Imperial, four-door sedan, V-8

IMPERIAL SERIES — SERIES C54 — If you liked the 1951 Imperial, you'd feel the same way about the 1952 models, since they were practically identical. The best way to separate cars of both years is through reference to serial numbers. The convertible body style was dropped. Unlike the case with Chryslers, the Imperial's taillights were not changed. Power steering was standard.

IMPERIAL I.D. DATA: The serial number was located on a plate on the left front door hinge pillar post. Engine number was on top front center of engine block. Serial numbers for C54 Imperials built as 1952 models were recorded as C-7753601 to 7763596. Engine numbers C52-

8-1001 to 59631 were used in this series, as well as in other Chrysler Eights, with engines built in mixed production sequence. Crown Imperials had serial numbers 7815101 to 7815306. Engine numbers, however, were shared with Chrysler V-8s.

IMPERIAL SERIES

Model No.	Body/ Style No.	Body Type & Seating	Factory Price	Shipping Weight	Prod. Total
C54	N/A	4-dr Sed-6P	3884	4350	Note 1
C54	N/A	2-dr Clb Cpe-6P	3851	4230	Note 1
C54	N/A	2-dr HT-6P	4249	4380	Note 1

Note 1: See 1951 Production Total.

CROWN IMPERIAL SERIES — SERIES C53 — The 'new' Crown Imperial was unchanged for 1952. Only 338 of these cars were made in the 1951-1952 model run and serial numbers indicate that 205 were registered as 1952 automobiles. A minor change was a one-inch reduction in front tread measurement.

CROWN IMPERIAL SERIES

C53	N/A	4-dr Sed-8P	6922	5360	Note 1
C53	N/A	4-dr Limo-8P	7044	5450	Note 1

Note 1: See 1951 Production Total.

ENGINE: V-8. Overhead valve. Cast iron block. Displacement: 331.1 cid. Bore and stroke: 3.81 x 3.62 inches. Compression ratio: 7.5:1. Brake hp: 180 at 4000 rpm. Five main bearings. Hydraulic valve lifters. Carburetor: Carter two-barrel Model WCD-884S.

CHASSIS FEATURES: Wheelbase: (Imperial) 131.5 inches; (Crown Imperial) 145.5 inches. Overall length: (Imperial) 213-1/8 inches; (Crown Imperial) 145-1/2 inches. Front tread: (Imperial) 57 inches; (Crown Imperial) 57 inches. Rear tread: (Imperial) 58 inches; (Crown Imperial) 66 inches. Tires: (Imperial) 8.20 x 15; (Crown Imperial) 8.90 x 15. Ausco-Lambert "self-energizing" disc brakes standard in Crown Imperial series.

OPTIONS: Power brakes. (Power disc brakes standard on Crown Imperial.) Power steering, on C54 ($199); on C53 (standard equipment). Air conditioning. Solex glass (new option). White sidewall tires. Electric window lids. Sun visor. Radio. Heater and defroster. Exhaust deflector. Spare tire valve extension. Locking gas cap. Windshield washer. Fog lamps. Spotlights. Outside rearview mirror. Vanity mirror. Fluid-Torque drive was $167 extra on C54 Imperials and standard equipment on C53 Crown Imperials. Heavy-duty oil bath air cleaner. Vacuum booster fuel pump. Oil filter.

HISTORICAL FOOTNOTES: The 1952 Chrysler models, including Imperials, were introduced Dec. 14, 1951. The Office of Price Stabilization (OPS), which set pricing policies during the Korean War, allowed Chrysler to make an across-the-board increase in retails on Feb. 11, 1952. On August 23, the OPS abandoned the policy of placing ceilings on new car prices and Chrysler again boosted its tags from $18-$30. D.A. Wallace remained as president of the division. Model year production for all Chryslers was estimated at 91,253 units. The Imperial convertible, introduced only one year earlier, was dropped and not replaced until 1957.

1953 IMPERIAL

1953 Chrysler Custom Imperial, Newport two-door hardtop, V-8

CUSTOM IMPERIAL SERIES — SERIES C58 — Although the Custom Imperial resembled the New Yorker, it had a different wheelbase, taillights and side trim. Clean front fenders and a higher rear fender stone shield set it apart from the 'ordinary' Chryslers. This was the first year for the stylized eagle hood ornament. Power brakes, power windows, center folding armrests (front and rear) and a padded dash were standard. Parking lights on all Imperials were positioned between the top and center grille moldings, a variation from the design used on other Chrysler cars. The Custom Imperial six-passenger limousine had, as standard equipment, electric windows; electric division window; floor level courtesy lamps;

near compartment heater; fold-up footrests; seatback mounted clock and special, luxury cloth or leather interiors. On March 10, 1953, the Custom Imperial Newport hardtop was added to the Imperial line at $325 over the price of the eight-passenger sedan. However, Chrysler instituted a general price cut on March 25, and the new model was then reduced $45. A week later, the delivery and handling charges for Imperials were raised $10, so the customer came out $35 ahead in the long run.

IMPERIAL I.D. DATA: The serial number was located on a plate on the left front door hinge pillar post. Engine number was on top of engine block at front water outlet elbow. Serial numbers C58-7765001 to 7773869 were used on 1953 Custom Imperials. Engine numbers fell in the range C53-8-1001 to 86292, which were shared with other Chrysler V-8 series. Crown Imperials had serial numbers C59-7816001 to 7816162. Engine numbers were in the same range used for Custom Imperials, as well as other Chrysler V-8s.

CUSTOM IMPERIAL SERIES

Model No.	Body/ Style No.	Body Type & Seating	Factory Price	Shipping Weight	Prod. Total
C58	N/A	4-dr Sed-8P	4260	4305	7,793
C58	N/A	4-dr Limo-6P	4797	4525	243
C58	N/A	2-dr HT-6P	4560	4290	823

CROWN IMPERIAL SERIES — SERIES C59 — The eagle hood ornament was about the only thing new on the 1953 Crown Imperial. The nameplate was changed slightly and the limousine featured moldings on top of rear fenders. It had a 12-volt electrical system (the Custom had a six-volt system). Power steering was standard and PowerFlite fully-automatic transmission was installed in a small number of late-in-the-year cars for testing and evaluation.

CROWN IMPERIAL SERIES

C59	N/A	4-dr Sed-8P	6922	5235	48
C59	N/A	4-dr Limo-8P	7044	5275	111

ENGINE: V-8. Overhead valve. Cast iron block. Displacement: 331.1 cid. Bore and stroke: 3.81 x 3.62 inches. Compression ratio: 7.5:1. Brake hp: 180 at 4000 rpm. Five main bearings. Hydraulic valve lifters. Carburetor: Carter WCD-935S.

CHASSIS FEATURES: Wheelbase: (Custom Imperial hardtop) 131.5 inches; (sedan and limousine) 133.5 inches; (Crown Imperial) 145.5 inches. Overall length: (Custom Imperial) 219 inches; (Crown Imperial) 229 inches. Front tread: (Custom Imperial) 57 inches; (Crown Imperial) 57 inches. Rear tread: (Custom Imperial) 57 inches; (Crown Imperial) 66 inches. Tires: (Custom Imperial) 8.20 x 15; (Crown Imperial) 8.90 x 15. Ausco-Lambert "self-energizing" disc brakes standard in Crown Imperial series.

OPTIONS: Power disc brakes were standard on C59 Crown Imperials. Power steering was optional on Custom Imperials ($177) and standard in Crown Imperials. Air conditioning. Power windows. At the start of the model year, Fluid-Torque transmission was standard equipment on all Imperials. In June 1953, PowerFlite fully-automatic transmission was selectively introduced and was subsequently made standard equipment in all 1954 Imperials.

HISTORICAL FOOTNOTES: The 1953 Chrysler line, including Imperials, was introduced Oct. 30, 1952. The Custom Imperial Newport hardtop was introduced on March 18, 1953. E.C. Quinn became president of Chrysler Division this year. Chrysler Corp. unveiled its PowerFlite transmission early in the summer. At that time, it had been under "road test" by a number of specially-selected customers whose use of the fully-automatic transmission was monitored. By the time the production go-ahead was given, assembly of 1953 Imperials had ended. Thus, it is possible to find 1953 Imperials with PowerFlite, although the first general-sales installations were made in 1954 models. It was made standard in Imperials and optional in other Chrysler cars.

1954 IMPERIAL

CUSTOM IMPERIAL SERIES — SERIES C64 — The new Custom Imperial had a grille consisting of a heavy, wraparound horizontal center bar (with five ridges on top) and integrated circular signal lights. Its front fender nameplate was above a chrome strip, which ran the length of the front door to the front wheel opening. The rear fender stone guard was larger than in 1953, but the rocker panel molding and rear fender chrome strip style were still the same. The back-up lights were now located directly below the taillights, rather than dividing the lights as in the previous year's model.

IMPERIAL I.D. DATA: The serial number was located on a plate on the left front door hinge pillar post. Engine number was on top of engine block

at front water outlet elbow. Serial numbers C64-7775001 to 7780767 were found on Custom Imperials. Serial numbers C64-7817001 to 7817100 were used on 1954 Crown Imperials. The engine numbers C542-8-1001 to 40478 were used on all 1954 Chrysler Eights.

1954 Chrysler Custom Imperial, four-door sedan, V-8

CUSTOM IMPERIAL SERIES

Model No.	Body/ Style No.	Body Type & Seating	Factory Price	Shipping Weight	Prod. Total
C64	N/A	4-dr Sed-6P	4260	4355	4,324
C64	N/A	2-dr HT-6P	4560	4345	1,249
C64	N/A	4-dr Limo-6P	4797	4465	85

1954 Chrysler Crown Imperial, four-door limousine, V-8

CROWN IMPERIAL SERIES — SERIES C66 — The Crown Imperial shared basic styling with the Custom. However, it had center-opening rear doors and Cadillac-like rear fender taillights. Air conditioning was standard.

CROWN IMPERIAL SERIES

C66	N/A	4-dr Sed-8P	6922	5220	23
C66	N/A	4-dr Limo-8P	7044	5295	77

ENGINE: V-8. Overhead valve. Cast iron block. Displacement: 331.1 cid. Bore and stroke: 3.81 x 3.62 inches. Compression ratio: 7.5:1. Brake hp: 235 at 4400 rpm. Five main bearings. Hydraulic valve lifters. Carburetor: Carter four-barrel Model WCFB-2041S.

CHASSIS FEATURES: Wheelbase: (Custom Imperial hardtop) 131.5 inches; (Custom Imperial sedan and hardtop) 133.5 inches; (Crown Imperial) 145.5 inches. Overall length: (C64 Newport) 221.75 inches; (C64) 223.75 inches; (C66) 236-3/8 inches. Tires: (Custom Imperial) 8.20 x 15; (Crown Imperial) 8.90 x 15. Ausco-Lambert "self-energizing" disc brakes standard in Crown Imperial series.

OPTIONS: Power disc brakes were standard on Crown Imperial. Power drum brakes optional on Custom Imperial. Power steering standard on Crown Imperial. Power steering optional on Custom Imperial. Air conditioning. Electric lift windows.

HISTORICAL FOOTNOTES: Derham Custom Body Co. built a special Custom Imperial Landau Victoria this year, with a Victoria-style half-roof and open driver's compartment. This Contessa show car was seen at the 1954 automobile shows. It was based on the Custom Imperial Newport hardtop with modifications including a vinyl-and-plexiglas roof; continental tire extension kit; chromed Kelsey-Hayes wire wheels and custom pink and white interior and exterior finish.

1955 IMPERIAL

IMPERIAL SERIES — SERIES C69 — Imperial, like all Chrysler Corp. cars, was completely restyled for 1955. It had bumper-integrated signal lights. Each section of the two-piece split grille consisted of two large

vertical bars, crossed by like-size horizontal ones. The Imperial eagle crest was placed between the sections. Side trim consisted of fender-to-fender mid-body molding and full-length lower body trim. Unique to the make were free-standing rear fender-mounted taillights.

1955 Imperial, Newport two-door hardtop, V-8

IMPERIAL I.D. DATA: The serial number was located on a plate on the left front door hinge pillar post. Engine number was on top of engine block at front water outlet elbow. Imperials and Crown Imperials were numbered C55-1001 to 12464. Engine numbers CE55-1001 to 12490 were used in mixed series production.

IMPERIAL SERIES

Model No.	Body/ Style No.	Body Type & Seating	Factory Price	Shipping Weight	Prod. Total
C69	N/A	4-dr Sed-6P	4483	4565	7,840
C69	N/A	2-dr HT-6P	4720	4490	3,418

CROWN IMPERIAL SERIES — SERIES C70 — The center-opening rear doors of previous Crown sedans and limousines were replaced by conventional ones in 1955. It shared the same basic styling as the standard Imperial but had a different roof with a smaller, rectangular rear window. New features included power disc brakes and a 12-volt electrical system.

CROWN IMPERIAL SERIES

C70	N/A	4-dr Sed-8P	7603	5145	45
C70	N/A	4-dr Limo-8P	7737	5205	127

ENGINE: V-8. Overhead valve. Cast iron block. Displacement: 331.1 cid. Bore and stroke: 3.81 x 3.82 inches. Compression ratio: 8.50:1. Brake hp: 250 at 4600 rpm. Carburetor: Carter four-barrel Model WCFB-2126S.

CHASSIS FEATURES: Wheelbase: (Imperial) 130 inches; (Crown Imperial) 149.5 inches; Tires: (Imperial) 8.20 x 15; (Crown Imperial) 8.90 x 15.

OPTIONS: Power brakes and power steering were standard with all Imperials. A Four-Way power seat was standard in eight-passenger styles. Extra-cost options: Air conditioning. Power windows. Signal-seeking radio.

HISTORICAL FOOTNOTES: The Custom Imperial Town Limousine was dropped for 1955. Model year introductions were scheduled on Nov. 17, 1954. E.C. Quinn was president of Chrysler Division this year. Beginning this season, Chrysler considered the Imperial to be a separate 'marque' or 'make' and duly registered it as such with the U.S. Government. Therefore, Imperial production figures were broken out from the totals for the rest of the Chrysler line. Chrysler Division's New Yorker and Imperial series climbed to second rank in the high-priced field, with 84,330 new car registrations in calendar 1955. This total included some 1954 "Chrysler-Imperials" and could be a misleading figure to some degree. The Imperial/New Yorker Division competed with Cadillac, Lincoln and Packard and Packard was the only one of those companies the Imperial "outsold" by itself (New Yorkers were targeted against senior Buicks). Genuine leather interior trims were offered in the front seat of Crown Imperial Limousines and eight-passenger sedans and in combinations for the Imperial Southampton four-door. In 1955, Imperial production was moved to the Jefferson Ave. plant in Detroit.

1956 IMPERIAL

IMPERIAL SERIES — SERIES C73 — Front end styling resembled last year's model, but the rear fenders were taller and the full-length mid-body side molding wrapped around them. The rear bumpers were attractively redesigned and seemed integrated into the rear fenders. Taillights were once again mounted on the fenders.

IMPERIAL I.D. DATA: The serial number was located on a plate on the left front door hinge pillar post. Engine number was on top of engine block at front water outlet elbow. Serial numbers for C73 series models were C56-1001 to 11715. Serial numbers for C70 models were C56-1001 to 9826. Engine numbers CE56-1001 to 11750 were used in cars of both series.

1956 Imperial, four-door sedan, V-8

IMPERIAL SERIES

Model No.	Body/ Style No.	Body Type & Seating	Factory Price	Shipping Weight	Prod. Total
C73	N/A	4-dr Sed-6P	4832	4575	6,821
C73	N/A	4-dr HT-6P	5225	4680	1,543
C73	N/A	2-dr HT-6P	5094	4555	2,094

CROWN IMPERIAL SERIES — SERIES C70 — Styling changes were minimal. About the only difference between the 1956 and last year's Crown was the side trim. The new version had mid-body moldings that extended only from the tip of the front fender to slightly beyond the beginning of the rear fender. There were five slanted slashes and a chrome outline of the tailfin on the rear fenders.

CROWN IMPERIAL SERIES

C70	N/A	4-dr Sed-8P	7603	5145	51
C70	N/A	4-dr Limo-8P	7737	5205	119

ENGINE: V-8. Overhead valve. Cast iron block. Displacement: 353.1 cid. Bore and stroke: 3.94 x 3.63 inches. Compression ratio: 9.0:1. Brake hp: 280 at 4600 rpm. Carburetor: Carter four-barrel Model WCFB-2314S.

CHASSIS FEATURES: Wheelbase: (Imperial) 133 inches; (Crown Imperial) 149.5 inches. Tires: (Imperial) 8.20 x 15; (Crown Imperial) 8.90 x 15.

OPTIONS: Power steering, power brakes and Four-Way power seats were standard equipment. Options included power windows and air conditioning. PowerFlite automatic transmission, now with push-button control, was standard in all Imperials when the model year started. A new three-speed TorqueFlite automatic transmission became available on all Imperials in the spring.

HISTORICAL FOOTNOTES: The 1956 Imperials were introduced Oct. 21, 1955. Model year production peaked at 10,685 cars. Calendar year production was counted as 12,130 units. This was the first calendar year that Imperial production records were recorded separate from Chrysler figures for the entire 12 months. E.C. Quinn was president of the Chrysler Division this year. Imperial was emerging as a strong selling luxury car in this period. Separate production lines for Imperials were setup at Chrysler's Kercheval and Jefferson plants in Detroit. The 1956 Imperial could go from 0-to-60 mph in 12.8 seconds. It had a top speed of over 104 mph.

1957 IMPERIAL

1957 Imperial, Southampton four-door hardtop, V-8 (FK)

IMPERIAL SERIES — SERIES IM-1 — Imperial styling moved further away from that of other Chrysler Corp. cars in 1957. Hardtop models featured a distinctive "overlapping" rear-section roof. The taillights were now integrated into the tips of the tailfins. Wraparound "eyebrow" trim above the headlights extended half the length of the front fenders. Mid-body chrome trim ran from the rear deck panel to the front tire well. The grille looked like a mesh of chrome pieces. Signal lights were sandwiched between the two horizontal bumpers. A simulated spare-tire cover trunk lid was optional on all 1957 Imperials.

IMPERIAL I.D. DATA: The serial number was located on a plate on the left front door hinge pillar post. Engine number was on top of engine block at front water outlet elbow. Imperial, Imperial Crown, LeBaron and Crown Imperial serial numbers were C57-1001 to 36890. Engine numbers were CE57-1001 to 36950.

IMPERIAL SERIES

Model No.	Body/ Style No.	Body Type & Seating	Factory Price	Shipping Weight	Prod. Total
IM1-1	N/A	4-dr Sed-6P	4838	4640	5,654
IM1-1	N/A	4-dr HT-6P	4838	4780	7,527
IM1-1	N/A	2-dr HT-6P	4736	4640	4,885

IMPERIAL CROWN SERIES — SERIES IM1-2 — Like all Imperial series, the Imperial Crown (not to be confused with the plusher Crown Imperial, of course) had recessed door handles. Exterior styling was basically the same as that used on the standard Imperial. However, Imperial Crowns had a tiny crown emblem above the second 'I' in the Imperial nameplate. A convertible was offered for the first time since 1951.

IMPERIAL CROWN SERIES

IM1-2	N/A	4-dr Sed-6P	5406	4740	3,642
IM1-2	N/A	4-dr HT-6P	5406	4920	7,843
IM1-2	N/A	2-dr HT-6P	5269	4755	4,199
IM1-2	N/A	2-dr Conv-6P	5598	4830	1,167

IMPERIAL LEBARON SERIES — SERIES IM1-4 — A distinctive front-fender emblem in place of the Imperial signature was the easiest way to tell the plush LeBaron from other Imperials.

IMPERIAL LEBARON SERIES

IM1-4	N/A	4-dr Sed-6P	5743	4765	1,729
IM1-4	N/A	4-dr HT-6P	5743	4900	911

CROWN IMPERIAL SERIES — The 1957 Crown Imperials were custom-built by Ghia in Turin, Italy. Several coats of blue, maroon, black or green lacquer were applied to them for an unsurpassed finish. The Crown Imperials had 1958-style grilles and their doors extended into the roof. Carpeting, air conditioning and power windows were just a few of the standard features.

CROWN IMPERIAL SERIES

Model No.	Body/ Style No.	Body Type & Seating	Factory Price	Shipping Weight	Prod. Total
N/A	N/A	4-dr Limo-8P	12,000	5960	36

ENGINE: V-8. Overhead valve. Cast iron block. Displacement: 392.7 cid. Bore and stroke: 4.0 x 3.9 inches. Compression ratio: 9.25:1. Brake hp: 325 at 4600 rpm. Carburetor: Carter Type four-barrel Model WCFB-2590S.

CHASSIS FEATURES: Wheelbase: (Imperial, Crown and LeBaron) 129 inches; (Crown Imperial) 149.5 inches. Tires: 9.50 x 14.

OPTIONS: Power brakes (standard). Power steering (standard). Four-Way power seat. Air conditioning ($590). Radio ($176). Solex glass ($50). Power windows ($125). TorqueFlite automatic transmission with push-button shift control was standard equipment.

HISTORICAL FOOTNOTES: The new Imperials were introduced, with other Chryslers, on Oct. 30, 1956. Quad headlights were offered on all Imperials sold in states where this setup was legal. The Ghia-built Crown Imperial limousine was announced on Jan. 2, 1957. Originally programmed for production of 75 units, the car sold less than half that amount. Model year output for Imperial peaked at 35,734 cars including, in rounded figures, 17,500 Imperials; 16,000 Crown Imperials and 2,500 LeBarons. Calendar year production was recorded as 37,946 units. E.C. Quinn was again president of Chrysler Division this year.

1958 IMPERIAL

IMPERIAL SERIES — SERIES LY1-L — "America's most distinctive fine car" is how advertisements described the new Imperial. Styling changes

were confined primarily to the grille. The mesh pattern of 1957 was replaced by four "stacks" of horizontal bars. The front bumper was now one solid piece with circular signal light pods extending from its lower section. Standard equipment included power brakes, power steering, back-up lights, windshield washer, and quad headlights. A simulated spare-tire-cover trunk lid was optional on all 1958 Imperials.

1958 Imperial Crown, two-door convertible, V-8

1958 Imperial Crown, four-door hardtop, V-8

IMPERIAL I.D. DATA: The serial number was located on a plate on the left front door hinge pillar post. Engine number was on top of engine block at front water outlet elbow. Serial numbers were LY1-1001 to 17325 for Imperial, Imperial Crown and Imperial LeBaron models. Engine numbers 58C-1001 and up were used in these series. Crown Imperial limousines were numbered C57-1001 and up and had engine numbers CE57-1001 and up.

IMPERIAL SERIES

Model No.	Body/ Style No.	Body Type & Seating	Factory Price	Shipping Weight	Prod. Total
LY1-L	N/A	4-dr Sed-6P	4945	4950	1,926
LY1-L	N/A	4-dr HT-6P	4839	4795	3,336
LY1-L	N/A	2-dr HT-6P	4945	4640	1,901

IMPERIAL CROWN SERIES — SERIES LY1-M — A tiny crown emblem above the second 'I' in the Imperial nameplate remained the easiest way to tell the Imperial Crown from the standard Imperial. It came with a Six-Way power seat, power windows and an outside rearview mirror.

IMPERIAL CROWN SERIES

Model No.	Body/ Style No.	Body Type & Seating	Factory Price	Shipping Weight	Prod. Total
LY1-M	N/A	4-dr Sed-6P	5632	4755	1,240
LY1-M	N/A	4-dr HT-6P	5632	4915	4,146
LY1-M	N/A	2-dr HT-6P	5388	4730	1,939
LY1-M	N/A	2-dr Conv-6P	5759	4820	675

IMPERIAL LEBARON SERIES — SERIES LY1-H — LeBarons had a distinctive emblem on the front fenders, instead of the Imperial name in script.

IMPERIAL LEBARON SERIES

LY1-H	N/A	4-dr Sed-6P	5969	4780	501
LY1-H	N/A	4-dr HT-6P	5969	4940	538

1958 Crown Imperial, four-door limousine, V-8

CROWN IMPERIAL SERIES — Because of its late introduction in 1957, the 'new' custom-built Crown Imperial was the same as last year's model. Great care was taken in the construction of this car. In fact, reportedly as much as 17 hours were spent on every auto just to make sure the doors fit perfectly. Carpeting, air conditioning, power steering, power windows and power brakes were only some of the many standard features.

CROWN IMPERIAL SERIES

N/A	N/A	4-dr Limo-8P	15,075	5960	31

ENGINE: V-8. Overhead valve. Cast iron block. Displacement: 392.7 cid. Bore and stroke: 4.0 x 3.9 inches. Compression ratio: 10.0:1. Brake hp: 345 at 4600 rpm. Carburetor: Carter four-barrel Model AFB-2651S.

CHASSIS FEATURES: Wheelbase: (Imperial, Crown and LeBaron) 129 inches: (Crown Imperial) 149.5 inches. Tires: 9.50 x 14.

OPTIONS: Power brakes. Power steering. Air conditioning ($590.20). Rear window defogger ($21.45). Custom heater ($140.60). Instant heater ($177.50). Six-Way power seat ($118.30). Power windows ($125.00). Electric touch radio with rear speaker and power antenna ($76.00). Solex glass ($50.40). White sidewall rayon tires, 9.50 x 14 ($55.10). Standard two-tone paint ($20.45). Auto pilot ($88.70). Electric door locks (two-door hardtop) with power windows ($40.70). Electric door locks (four-door models) with power windows ($65.80).

HISTORICAL FOOTNOTE: The 1958 Imperial line was introduced to the public Nov. 1, 1957. Most 1958 Imperials, 93.6 percent, had power seats; 92.9 percent had power windows; 86 percent had whitewall tires and 33.3 percent had air conditioning.

1959 IMPERIAL

1959 Imperial Crown, two-door hardtop, V-8 (AA)

IMPERIAL CUSTOM SERIES — SERIES MY1-L — The front-end treatment was jazzed up for 1959. Chrome-encased headlight pods were linked together by a large, center grille bar with five curved vertical pieces. Side trim, roof designs and the protruding tailfin taillight resembled the previous year's model. A lower rear-quarter panel stone shield and the Imperial name printed on the front fenders were two other changes. Buyers had their choice of three optional hardtop roof treatments. The Landau had a simulated rear canopy. The Silvercrest featured a stainless steel section covering the front half of the roof. The Silvercrest Landau was a combination of the first two. All 1959 Imperials came with power brakes, power steering, dual exhaust, electric clock, windshield washer and undercoating.

1959 Imperial Crown, two-door convertible, V-8

IMPERIAL I.D. DATA: The serial number was located on a plate on the left front door hinge pillar post. Engine number was stamped behind water pump on engine. Serial numbers took the form: M617100001 and up. The first symbol designated year ('M' = 1959). The second symbol designated make ('6' = Imperial). The third symbol designated series ('1' = Custom, '3' = Crown, '5' = LeBaron). The fourth symbol designated manufacturing plant ('7' = Detroit). The fifth to tenth symbols designated production numbers. Body number plates located below the hood, in various locations, indicate schedule date, body production number, and body series (see column 2 in charts below), plus trim, paint and accessories data.

IMPERIAL CUSTOM SERIES

Model No.	Body/ Style No.	Body Type & Seating	Factory Price	Shipping Weight	Prod. Total
MY1-L	613	4-dr Sed-6P	5016	4735	2,071
MY1-L	614	4-dr HT-6P	5016	4745	3,984
MY1-L	612	2-dr HT-6P	4910	4675	1,743

IMPERIAL CROWN SERIES — SERIES MY1-M —

Crown emblems on the front fenders were about the only way to distinguish the exterior of a Crown from a Custom. Standard features included Six-Way power seat, power windows, outside rearview mirror, vanity mirror and license plate frame.

IMPERIAL CROWN SERIES

Model No.	Body/ Style No.	Body Type & Seating	Factory Price	Shipping Weight	Prod. Total
MY1-M	633	4-dr Sed-6P	5647	4830	1,335
MY1-M	634	4-dr HT-6P	5647	4840	4,714
MY1-M	632	2-dr HT-6P	5403	4810	1,728
MY1-M	635	2-dr Conv-6P	5774	4850	555

IMPERIAL LEBARON SERIES — SERIES MY1-H — Its nameplate on the front fenders and special emblem on the chrome rear quarter panels were exterior features of the LeBaron. In addition to the standard equipment found on the other series, LeBarons had two-tone paint and whitewall tires.

IMPERIAL LEBARON SERIES

MY1-H	653	4-dr Sed-6P	6103	4865	510
MY1-H	654	4-dr HT-6P	6103	4875	622

CROWN IMPERIAL SERIES — Custom-built by Ghia of Italy, the Crown Imperial remained one of the finest custom-built luxury cars in the world. Basic styling was like that used on the standard Imperials. It came with air conditioning, power windows, carpeting, and many other features.

CROWN IMPERIAL SERIES

N/A	N/A	4-dr Limo-8P	16,000	5,960	7

ENGINE: V-8. Overhead valve. Cast iron block. Displacement: 413.2 cid. Bore and stroke: 4.18 x 3.75 inches. Compression ratio: 10.0:1. Brake hp: 350 at 4600 rpm. Carburetor: Carter four-barrel Model AFB-2797S.

CHASSIS FEATURES: Wheelbase: (Custom, Crown and LeBaron) 129 inches; (Crown Imperial) 149.5 inches. Tires: (all models) 9.50 x 14.

OPTIONS: Power brakes, standard. Power steering. Air conditioning ($590.20). Air suspension ($156). Rear window defogger ($21.45). Custom conditioned heater ($136.30). Instant heater ($164.95). Six-Way power seat ($124.80). Power windows ($125). Electric Touch radio, plus speaker and power antenna ($168.80). Electric Touch radio, plus speaker and power antenna for convertibles ($153.40). Solex glass ($53.75). Whitewall Rayon tires ($55.10). Whitewall nylon tires ($76.55). Whitewall nylon tires on LeBaron ($27.50). Two-tone paint ($20.45). Landau two-tone paint ($31.20). Auto pilot ($96.80). Electric door locks on two doors with power windows ($47.40). Electric door locks on four-doors with power windows ($72.50). Automatic beam changer ($54.90). Flitesweep deck lid ($55.45). Extra heavy-duty 40-amp generator ($42.60). Mirror-matic on Imperial Custom ($22.20); on Crown and LeBaron ($18.20). Outside remote control mirror on custom ($18.75); on Crown and LeBaron ($11. 90). Outside manual mirror ($6.85). Power swivel seat on Custom ($226.15); on Crown and LeBaron ($101.35). Stainless steel roof, hardtops ($139.80). Sure-grip differential ($57.45). True-level ride ($159.90). Leather trim Crown hardtops and convertible ($52.70).

HISTORICAL FOOTNOTES: The vast majority of 1959 Imperials, 97.1 percent had radios; 37.5 percent had air conditioning and 81.1 percent came with tinted glass.

1960 IMPERIAL

1960 Imperial Crown, two-door convertible, V-8 (AA)

IMPERIAL CUSTOM SERIES — SERIES PY1-L — Imperials had new bodies for 1960. The headlights were somewhat recessed under the overhanging front fenders. The grille had a clean, fine vertical and horizontal pieces treatment. Circular signal light pods were mounted on the lower half of the stylized 'wing' bumpers. The Imperial name was written on the grille and front fenders. Side trim started above the headlights and ran at a slightly downward angle almost to the end of the rear fender. Chrome trimmed taillights once again protruded from the tailfins. The roof had chrome trim pieces running from the rear quarter panel to the top of the windshield. This trim curved inward above the doors, giving the roof an overlapping effect. All 1960 Imperials had power steering, power brakes, dual exhaust, undercoating, electric clock and windshield washers.

IMPERIAL I.D. DATA: The serial number was located on a plate on the left front door hinge pillar post. First symbol: 9=Imperial. Second symbol: 1=Imperial Custom; 2=Imperial Crown; 3=Imperial LeBaron; 9=Crown Imperial limousine. Third symbol: 0=1960. Fourth symbol: 4=Imperial assembly plant in Detroit. Last six symbols are sequential production number. Engine number stamped on boss behind water pump: P-41 indicates 413 cid/350 hp V-8. Body number plate on fender, cowl or radiator support under hood indicates (50) schedule date; (NUMBER) body production number; (BDY) body series code [see second column in charts below]; (TRM) trim code; and (PNT) paint code.

IMPERIAL CUSTOM SERIES

Model No.	Body/ Style No.	Body Type & Seating	Factory Price	Shipping Weight	Prod. Total
PY1-L	913	4-dr Sed-6P	5029	4700	2,335
PY1-L	914	4-dr HT-6P	5029	4670	3,953
PY1-L	912	2-dr HT-6P	4923	4655	1,498

IMPERIAL CROWN SERIES — SERIES PY1-M — The word Crown printed beneath the Imperial nameplate was the easiest way to distinguish the Imperial Crown from the lower-produced Custom. Like all 1960 Imperials, a simulated spare-tire-cover trunk lid was optional. A Six-Way power seat, license frame, vanity mirror and outside rearview mirror were standard.

IMPERIAL CROWN SERIES

PY1-M	923	4-dr Sed-6P	5647	4770	1,594
PY1-M	924	4-dr HT-6P	5647	4765	4,510
PY1-M	922	2-dr HT-6P	5403	4720	1,504
PY1-M	925	2-dr Conv-6P	5774	4820	618

IMPERIAL LEBARON SERIES — SERIES PY1-H — LeBarons had a distinctive rectangular (rather than wraparound) rear window. It added a limousine quality to the series styling. The model name was also written, in chrome, on the trunk lid and front fenders. Power windows and two-tone paint were among the standard features.

IMPERIAL LEBARON SERIES

PY1-H	933	4-dr Sed-6P	6318	4860	692
PY1-H	934	4-dr HT-6P	6318	4835	999

CROWN IMPERIAL SERIES — The 1960 Imperial styling looked good on the custom-built Crown Imperial. It came with equipment such as: automatic headlight dimmer, auto pilot, dual radios, power windows, speaker phone and three heaters. The standard exterior color was black, but other combinations were available. The interior could be had in beige or gray.

CROWN IMPERIAL SERIES

N/A	N/A	4-dr Limo-8P	16,000	5960	16

ENGINE: V-8. Overhead valve. Cast iron block. Displacement: 413.2 cid. Bore and stroke: 4.18 x 3.75 inches. Compression ratio: 10.0:1. Brake hp: 350 at 4800 rpm. Carburetor: Carter four-barrel Model AFB-2927S.

CHASSIS FEATURES: Wheelbase: (Custom Imperial, Imperial Crown and LeBaron) 129 inches; (Crown Imperial) 149.5 inches. Tires: (Custom Imperial, Imperial Crown and LeBaron) 8.20 x 15; (Crown Imperial) 8.90 x 15.

OPTIONS: Air conditioning ($590.20). Auto pilot ($96.80). Automatic beam changer ($46.00). Rear window defogger ($21.45). Door guards: for two-doors ($4.40); for four-doors ($6.50). Electric door locks: for two-door hardtop and convertible with power windows ($47.40); for four-door models with power windows ($72.10). Flitesweep deck lid ($55.45). Extra heavy-duty 40-amp generator ($42.60). Heater ($136.30). Custom rear license plate frame ($6.05). Mirrormatic, except on convertibles ($18.20). Outside, left remote control mirror ($11.90). Outside, right-hand manual mirror ($6.85). Sill molding ($27.60). Standard two-tone paint ($20.45). Six-Way power front seat, in Custom ($124.80). Automatic power swivel seat ($121.00). Power vent windows ($76.60). Power windows in Custom ($125.00). Electric Touch-Tuner radio with power antenna and rear speaker ($168.80). Electric Touch-Tuner radio with power antenna, in convertible ($153.30). Solex glass ($53.75). Stainless steel roof, for Custom and Crown four-door models only ($62.40). Sure-Grip differential ($57.45). Whitewall Rayon tires ($55.10). Whitewall nylon tires ($76.55). Whitewall nylon tires on LeBaron ($27.50). Leather trim, in Crown four-door sedan and hardtop ($104.30).

HISTORICAL FOOTNOTES: Chrysler sales were up this year, but Imperial deliveries dropped around 19.7 percent. A total of 17,707 units were made during the model year. In rounded figures, that total included 7,800 Custom Imperials; 8,200 Crown Imperials and 1,700 LeBarons. On a calendar year basis, production was counted at 16,829 units or just .25 percent of the total American market. This year, as in 1959, the cars were built by the Chrysler-Imperial Division of Chrysler Corp., headed by C.E. Briggs, as vice-president and general manager. Plans were made to begin transfer of Imperial production from the Warren Road factory, Dearborn, to the Jefferson-Detroit facility, which had formerly housed Imperial assembly lines until August 1958. Most 1960 Imperials, 84.6 percent, had tinted glass, 44.7 percent had air conditioning and 92.9 percent had power windows.

1961 IMPERIAL

1961 Imperial Crown, Southampton four-door hardtop, V-8

IMPERIAL CUSTOM SERIES — SERIES RY1-L — A new horizontal bar grille and slightly recessed free-standing headlights dramatically changed the front end appearance of the 1961 Imperial. The make's name was now printed on the top section of the grille. The tailfins were more prominent and came to a point. The taillight pods stuck out from the lower section of the fins. A highly stylized flying eagle was placed on the rear fender part of the slightly slanted mid-body molding. Wheelwell openings and rocker panels were also trimmed with chrome. The unusual overlapping styled roof treatment, used in 1960, was continued. Power steering and power brakes were standard.

IMPERIAL I.D. DATA: The serial number was located on a plate on the left front door hinge pillar post. First symbol: 9=Imperial. Second symbol: 1=Imperial Custom; 2=Imperial Crown; 3=Imperial LeBaron; 10=Crown Imperial limousine. Third symbol: 1=1961. Fourth symbol: 4=Imperial assembly plant in Detroit. Last six symbols are sequential production number. Engine number stamped on boss behind water pump: R-41 indicates 413 cid/350 hp V-8. Body number plate on fender cowl or radiator support under hood indicates (SO) schedule date; (NUMBER) body production number; (BDY) body series code [see second column in charts below]; (TRM) trim code; and (PNT) paint code.

IMPERIAL CUSTOM SERIES

Model No.	Body/ Style No.	Body Type & Seating	Factory Price	Shipping Weight	Prod. Total
RY1-L	914	4-dr HT-6P	5111	4740	4,129
RY1-L	912	2-dr HT-6P	4925	4715	889

IMPERIAL CROWN SERIES — SERIES RY1-M — The Imperial Crown looked virtually the same as the Custom. It came with power seat; rear license plate frame; vanity mirror; carpeting; power windows; and outside rearview mirror.

IMPERIAL CROWN SERIES

RY1-M	924	4-dr HT-6P	5649	4855	4,769
RY1-M	922	2-dr HT-6P	5405	4790	1,007
RY1-M	925	2-dr Conv-6P	5776	4865	429

IMPERIAL LEBARON SERIES — SERIES RY1-H — Its unique formal roof treatment set the LeBaron apart from the other series. Power vent windows, stone shield moldings and whitewall tires were among standard features.

IMPERIAL LEBARON SERIES

RY1-H	934	4-dr HT-6P	6428	4875	1,026

CROWN IMPERIAL SERIES — The few Crown Imperials built in 1961 came with 1960 styling. Air conditioning; auto pilot; automatic headlight dimmer; three heaters; and power windows were just some of the many standard luxury features on this custom-built car.

CROWN IMPERIAL SERIES

Model No.	Body/ Style No.	Body Type & Seating	Factory Price	Shipping Weight	Prod. Total
N/A	N/A	4-dr Limo-8P	16,000	5960	9

ENGINE: V-8. Overhead valve. Cast iron block. Displacement: 413.2 cid. Bore and stroke: 4.18 x 3.75 inches. Compression ratio: 10.0:1. Brake hp: 350 at 4600 rpm. Carburetor: Carter Type four-barrel Model AFB-3108S.

CHASSIS FEATURES: Wheelbase: (Imperial Custom, Imperial Crown and Imperial LeBaron) 129 inches; (Crown Imperial) 149.5 inches. Tires: (Imperial Custom, Imperial Crown and Imperial LeBaron) 8.20 x 15; (Crown Imperial) 8.90 x 15.

OPTIONS: Power brakes. Power steering. Air conditioning ($590.20). Auto pilot ($96.80). Automatic beam changer ($46). Crankcase ventilation system ($5.20). Rear window defogger ($21.45). Door guards, two-doors ($4.40); four-doors ($6.50). Electric door locks, two-doors with power windows ($47.40); four-doors with power windows ($72.10). Flitesweep deck lid ($55.45). Heater ($136.30). Rear license plate frame in Custom ($6.05). Outside, left remote control mirror ($11.90); right remote-control mirror ($6.85). Wheelhouse, stone shields and sill molding ($39.60). Six-Way power front seat in Custom ($124.80). Power vent windows ($76.60). Power windows in Custom ($125). Electric Touch-Tuner radio with rear speaker and power antenna ($168.80). Electric Touch-Tuner radio with power antenna in convertibles ($153.30). Solex glass ($53.75). Stainless steel roof in Custom ($62.40). Sure-Grip differential ($57.45). Swivel seat, manual power seat required ($101.35). Whitewall rayon tires ($55.10). Leather trim in Crown ($104.30); in LeBaron ($69.70). Basic group, two-doors ($396.60); four doors ($398.70). Basic group includes: heater; radio with rear speaker and power antenna; door edge protectors; remote-control outside rear mirror on left; solex glass; rear window defogger. Convenience group: power seat; power windows; license plate frame in Custom ($255.85). Decor group: Flitesweep deck lid; stone shields; sill moldings; manual right outside rearview mirror, except LeBaron ($101.90).

HISTORICAL FOOTNOTES: The last gasp of the finned Imperials was heard this year. Some people christened them "Batmobiles." Chrysler's luxury line returned to body-on-frame construction. Just over half of all 1961 Imperials came equipped with air conditioning.

1962 IMPERIAL

1962 Imperial Custom, Southampton four-door hardtop, V-8

IMPERIAL CUSTOM SERIES — SERIES SY1-L — The Imperial Custom featured a new hood ornament and a split, thin, horizontal bar grille. The recessed free-standing headlights, introduced in 1961, were used again. Trim, starting at the headlight eyebrows, extended at a slight angle to the rear quarter panel. Wheelwell openings and rocker panel moldings also helped to decorate the sides. The taillights were mounted atop the rear fenders. Power brakes and power steering were standard.

IMPERIAL I.D. DATA: The serial number was located on a plate on the left front door hinge pillar post. First symbol: 9=Imperial. Second symbol: 1=Imperial Custom; 2=Imperial Crown; 3=Imperial LeBaron. Third symbol: 2=1962. Fourth symbol: 3=Imperial assembly plant in Detroit. Last six symbols are sequential production number. Engine number stamped on boss behind water pump: S-41 indicates 413 cid/340 hp V-8. Body number plate on fender, cowl or radiator support under hood indicates (SO) schedule date; (NUMBER) body production number; (BDY) body series code [see second column in charts below]; (TRM) trim code; and (PNT) paint code.

IMPERIAL CUSTOM SERIES

Model No.	Body/ Style No.	Body Type & Seating	Factory Price	Shipping Weight	Prod. Total
SY1-L	914	4-dr HT-6P	5106	4620	3,587
SY1-L	912	2-dr HT-6P	4920	4540	826

CROWN IMPERIAL SERIES — SERIES SY1-M — With deletion of the custom-built Crown Imperial limousines, the cars formerly known as Imperial Crowns became Crown Imperials. The Crown name and emblem on the rear fenders, below the taillights, was one way to tell the high-dollar Imperial from the lower-priced series. It came with the same standard equipment as the Custom, plus handbrake warning signal; electric clock; power windows; center armrest and Six-Way power front seat.

CROWN IMPERIAL SERIES

SY1-M	924	4-dr HT-6P	5644	4680	6,911
SY1-M	922	2-dr HT-6P	5400	4650	1,010
SY1-M	925	2-dr Conv-6P	5770	4765	554

IMPERIAL LEBARON SERIES — SERIES SY1-H — A distinctive rectangular rear window and formal roof were styling features of the top-of-the-line LeBaron.

IMPERIAL LEBARON SERIES

SY1-H	934	4-dr HT-6P	6422	4725	1,449

ENGINE: V-8. Overhead valve. Cast iron block. Displacement: 413.2 cid. Bore and stroke: 4.18 x 3.75 inches. Compression ratio: 10.0:1. Brake hp: 340 at 4600 rpm. Carburetor: Carter four-barrel Model AFB-3215S.

CHASSIS FEATURES: Wheelbase: (all) 129 inches. Tires: (all) 8.20 x 15.

OPTIONS: Power brakes. Power steering. Air conditioning ($590.20). Auto pilot ($98.80). Automatic beam changer ($46). Crankcase ventilation system ($5.20). Rear window defogger ($21.45). Door guards, two-doors ($4.40); four-doors ($6.50). Electric door locks, two-doors with power windows ($47.40); four-doors with power windows ($72.10). Heater ($136.30). Rear license plate frame, Custom, ($6.05). Rear license plate frame and door edge protectors. Custom and two-door hardtops ($10.45). Rear license plate frame and door edge protectors. Custom four-door hardtops ($12.55). Outside, left remote-control mirror ($11.90). Outside right manual mirror ($6.85). Wheelhouse, stone shields and sill molding ($40.90). Six-Way power front seat, Custom ($124.80). Power vent windows ($76.60). Electric Touch-Tuner radio with rear speaker and power antenna ($168.80). Electric Touch-Tuner radio with power antenna, convertible ($153.30). Tinted glass ($53.75). Sure-Grip differential ($57.45). Two front seat belts ($20.20). Whitewall Rayon tires ($55.10). Leather trim, Crown ($104.30); LeBaron ($69.70). Accessory Group, includes: heater; radio with rear speaker and power antenna; door edge protectors; remote-control outside rearview mirror on left; tinted glass; power seat and power windows. Accessory Group on Custom two-door hardtop ($624.95); on Custom four-door hardtop ($627.05); on Crown two-door hardtop ($375.15); on Crown and LeBaron four-door hardtop ($377.25).

HISTORICAL FOOTNOTES: The 1962 Imperials were introduced Sept. 26, 1961, one year and two days after the 1961 models first appeared. Total model year production hit 14,337 units, including 613 cars built for export markets. In rounded figures, this total included 4,400 Custom Imperials; 8,500 Crown Imperials and 1,400 LeBarons. For the calendar year, 14,787 units bearing Imperial nameplates were produced. The car's maker was now called the Chrysler-Plymouth Division of Chrysler Corp., which had been formed in 1961. C.E. Briggs remained as vice-president and general manager. Imperial sales were up 17 percent over the previous year and were the highest since late 1957. Most 1962 Imperials, 60.3 percent, came with air conditioning, 64.4 percent had power seats and 95.1 percent had power windows. No Ghia-built Crown Imperial limousines were sold in 1962.

1963 IMPERIAL

IMPERIAL CUSTOM SERIES — SERIES TY1-L — The 1963 Imperial Custom had a new stacked horizontal bar grille divided in the center by a rectangular section containing a stylized eagle emblem. Free-standing headlights were once again tucked under front fender 'eyebrows.' These were trimmed with a chrome piece that ran, at an angle, the entire length of the car and connected to the rear deck panel trim. The vertical taillights were now placed in the tailfins. Circular back-up lights were integrated into the rear bumpers. The roof design was less slanted than that of the previous year's models. Power steering, power brakes and power windows were standard.

1963 Imperial Custom, Southampton four-door hardtop, V-8

IMPERIAL I.D. DATA: The serial number was located on a plate on the left front door hinge pillar post. First symbol: 9=Imperial. Second symbol: 1=Imperial Custom; 2=Imperial Crown; 3=Imperial LeBaron. Third symbol: 3=1963. Fourth symbol: 3=Jefferson Ave. assembly plant in Detroit. Last six symbols are sequential production number. Engine number stamped on boss behind water pump: T-41 indicates 413 cid/340 hp V-8. Body number plate on fender, cowl or radiator support under hood indicates (SO) schedule date; (NUMBER) body production number; (BDY) body series code [see second column in charts below]; (TRM) trim code; and (PNT) paint code.

IMPERIAL CUSTOM SERIES

Model No.	Body/ Style No.	Body Type & Seating	Factory Price	Shipping Weight	Prod. Total
TY1-L	914	4-dr HT-6P	5243	4690	3,264
TY1-L	912	2-dr HT-6P	5058	4640	749

IMPERIAL CROWN SERIES — SERIES TY1-M — The Crown Imperial line returned, so the one-step-up (from Custom series) cars became Imperial Crowns again. The Crown name and emblem was in a small rectangular trim piece on the upper rear fenders, next to the taillights. It was the easiest way to distinguish the Crown from other Imperials.

IMPERIAL CROWN SERIES

TY1-M	924	4-dr HT-6P	656	4740	6,960
TY1-M	922	2-dr HT-6P	412	4720	1,067
TY1-M	925	2-dr Conv-6P	782	4795	531

IMPERIAL LEBARON SERIES — SERIES TY1-H — The fancy LeBaron crest on the roof quarter panels was subject to a federal jewelry excise tax. It, and the unique rectangular rear window were exclusive features of the top-of-the-line LeBaron.

IMPERIAL LEBARON SERIES

TY1-H	934	4-dr HT-6P	6434	4830	1,537

CROWN IMPERIAL SERIES — The exclusive, custom-built Crown Imperial returned this year forcing the previous year's Crown Imperial to retake its former name of Imperial Crown. Standard features of the custom-built car included carpeting; air conditioning; three heaters; Auto pilot; automatic headlight dimmer; power steering; power brakes and power windows.

CROWN IMPERIAL SERIES

N/A	N/A	4-dr Sed-8P	18,500	6000	1
N/A	N/A	4-dr Limo-8P	18,500	6100	12

ENGINE: V-8. Overhead valve. Cast iron block. Displacement: 413.2 cid. Bore and stroke: 4.18 x 3.75 inches. Compression ratio: 10.0:1. Brake hp: 340 at 4800 rpm. Carburetor: Carter Type four-barrel Model AFB-3256S.

CHASSIS FEATURES: Wheelbase: (Custom Imperial, Imperial Crown and LeBaron) 129 inches; (Crown Imperial) 149.5 inches. Tires: 8.20 x 15.

OPTIONS: Power brakes. Power steering. Air conditioning ($590.20). Auto pilot ($98.80). Automatic beam changer ($48). Flitesweep deck lid ($55.45). Rear window defogger ($21.45). Door guards, two-doors ($4.40); four-doors ($6.50). Electric door locks, two-doors ($47.40); four-doors ($72.10). Heater ($136.30). Rear license plate frame in Custom ($605). Rear license plate frame and door edge protectors in Custom two-door hardtop ($10.45); four-doors ($12.55). Outside right manual mirror ($6.85). Wheelhouse, stone shields and sill molding ($39.80). Six-Way power front seat in Custom ($124.80). Power vent windows ($76.60). Remote control power trunk lock ($53.15). Electric Touch-Tuner radio with rear speaker and power antenna ($168.80). Electric Touch-Tuner radio with power antenna in convertible ($153.30). Tinted glass ($53.75). Sure-Grip differential ($57.45). Two front seat belts ($18.75). Whitewall Rayon tires ($55.10). Leather trim in Crown ($104.30); in LeBaron ($69.70). Accessory group includes: heater; radio, rear speaker and power antenna; door edge protectors; tinted glass and power seat. Accessory group in Custom two-door hardtop ($488.05); four-door ($490.15). Accessory group in Imperial Crown two-door hardtop ($363.25); in Imperial Crown and LeBaron four-door hardtop ($365.35).

The 1963 Imperials were introduced Sept. 26, 1962. Calendar year production was up to 33,717 units or .44 percent of industry sales. P.N. Buckminster became vice-president and general manager of Chrysler-Plymouth Division. The majority of 1963 Imperials, 64.3 percent, had air conditioning, and 91.9 percent had tinted glass.

1964 IMPERIAL

1964 Imperial Crown, four-door hardtop, V-8

IMPERIAL CROWN SERIES — SERIES VY1-M — Imperial was attractively restyled for 1964. The model lineup was reduced to four cars in two series. Imperial Crown was now the base trim level. The free-standing headlights became chrome-ringed ones embedded in the slit, horizontal bar grille. Bodysides featured full-length, bumper-to-bumper upper body moldings and chrome-trimmed wheelwell openings and rocker panels. The taillights were integrated into the rear bumper and the trunk lid was designed with a simulated continental kit. The entire car seemed influenced by the crisp Lincoln-Continental styling. This was no doubt influenced by the fact that Chrysler had hired stylist Elwood Engle away from Ford two years earlier. Power steering, power windows and power brakes were standard.

IMPERIAL I.D. DATA: The serial number was located on a plate on the left front door hinge pillar post. First symbol: 9=Imperial. Second symbol: 2=Imperial Crown; 3=Imperial LeBaron. Third symbol: 4=1964. Fourth symbol: 3=Jefferson Ave. assembly plant in Detroit. Last six symbols are sequential production number. Engine number stamped on boss behind water pump: V-41 indicates 413 cid/340 hp V-8. Body number plate on fender, cowl or radiator support under hood indicates (SO) schedule date; (NUMBER) body production number; (BDY) body series code [see second column in charts below]; (TRM) trim code; and (PNT) paint code.

IMPERIAL CROWN SERIES

Model No.	Body/ Style No.	Body Type & Seating	Factory Price	Shipping Weight	Prod. Total
VY1-M	Y24	4-dr HT-6P	5581	4970	14,181
VY1-M	Y22	2-dr HT-6P	5739	4950	5,233
VY1-M	Y25	2-dr Conv-6P	6003	5185	922

IMPERIAL LEBARON SERIES — SERIES VY1-H — The LeBaron name on the front fenders and roof quarter panels was the main exterior difference between this top-of-the-line series and the Imperial Crown.

IMPERIAL LEBARON SERIES

VY1-H	934	4-dr HT-6P	6455	5005	2,949

CROWN IMPERIAL SERIES — Imperial's new styling was very becoming on the custom-built Crown Imperial. It was available with either six windows or with blind rear quarter roof panels.

CROWN IMPERIAL SERIES

N/A	N/A	4-dr Limo-8P	18,500	6100	10

ENGINE: V-8. Overhead valve. Cast iron block. Displacement: 413.2 cid. Bore and stroke: 4.18 x 3.75 inches. Compression ratio: 10.0:1. Brake hp: 340 at 4800 rpm. Carburetor: Carter four-barrel Model AFB-3644S.

CHASSIS FEATURES: Wheelbase: (Imperial Crown and LeBaron) 129 inches; (Crown Imperial) 149.5 inches. Tires: 8.20 x 15.

OPTIONS: Power brakes and power steering standard. Air conditioning ($461.95). Dual air conditioning ($649.85). Auto pilot ($96.80). Automatic beam changer ($46.00). Rear window defogger ($21.45). Door guard, two-door ($4.40); four-door ($6.50). Electric door locks, two-door ($47.40); four-door ($72.10). Left and right headrests ($45.60). Outside right mirror ($6.85). Two-tone paint ($20.85). Six-Way power front seat, in Imperial Crown four-door hardtop ($124.60). Positive crankcase vent

system ($5.10). Power trunk lock, remote control ($28.80). AM Touch Tuner radio with rear speaker and power antenna ($168.80). AM/FM radio with rear speaker and power antenna ($195.70). Rear reverberator speaker ($37.65). Two front retractable seat belts ($22.80). Adjustable steering wheel ($51.30). Sure-Grip differential ($57.45). Tinted glass ($53.75). Whitewall Rayon tires ($55.10). Leather trim ($104.30). Individual front seat trim, in Crown four-door hardtop ($506.10). Individual front seat trim in LeBaron ($381.40). Vinyl roof, in Crown coupe ($91.20). Vinyl roof, in LeBaron and Crown four-door hardtop ($110.80).

HISTORICAL FOOTNOTES: Imperials built to 1964 specifications were introduced Sept. 25, 1963. Chrysler-Plymouth Division, with P.N. Buckminster at the helm, produced exactly 23,285 Imperials during the model year. Most 1964 Imperials, 95 percent, had tinted glass, 77.5 percent had air conditioning, 28.8 percent had a tilting steering wheel and 98.8 percent had a radio. The Imperial Custom series disappeared and the Imperial Crown car-line became the base series. Use of the Southampton name to describe hardtops was also discontinued. Sales increased 65 percent over 1963 levels.

1965 IMPERIAL

1965 Imperial Crown, two-door hardtop, V-8

IMPERIAL CROWN SERIES — SERIES AY1-M — The basic styling originated in 1964 was kept. However, a new mesh-pattern grille, divided by chrome into four sections, was used. The headlights were recessed behind glass panels. The simulated spare-tire 'bulge' rear deck treatment was continued. Power brakes, power windows, power steering, carpeting, electric clock, padded dash and remote-control outside rearview mirror were standard.

IMPERIAL I.D. DATA: The serial number was located on a plate on the left front door hinge pillar post. First symbol: Y=Imperial. Second symbol: 2=Imperial Crown; 3=Imperial LeBaron. Third symbol: 5=1965. Fourth symbol: 3=Jefferson Ave. assembly plant in Detroit. Last six symbols are sequential production number. Engine number stamped on boss behind water pump: A-413 indicates 413 cid/340 hp V-8. Body number plate on fender, cowl or radiator support under hood indicates (SO) schedule date; (NUMBER) body production number; (BDY) body series code [see second column in charts below]; (TRM) trim code; and (PNT) paint code.

IMPERIAL CROWN SERIES

Model No.	Body/ Style No.	Body Type & Seating	Factory Price	Shipping Weight	Prod. Total
AY1-M	Y24	4-dr HT-6P	5772	5015	11,628
AY1-M	Y22	2-dr HT-6P	5930	5075	3,974
AY1-M	Y25	2-dr Conv-6P	6194	5345	633

IMPERIAL LEBARON SERIES — SERIES AY1-H — Aside from a fancier interior and its name written on the roof quarter panels, the LeBaron was the same basic car as the Imperial Crown. A Six-Way bench seat and whitewall tires were standard.

IMPERIAL LEBARON SERIES

AY1-H	934	4-dr HT-6P	6596	5080	2,164

CROWN IMPERIAL SERIES — This was the last year for the custom-built Ghia Crown Imperials. As before, they were available with either six windows or a blind rear roof quarter panel.

CROWN IMPERIAL SERIES

N/A	N/A	4-dr Limo-8P	16,000	Note 1	10

1965 Crown Imperial, four-door hardtop, V-8

ENGINE: V-8. Overhead valve. Cast iron block. Displacement: 413.2 cid. Bore and stroke: 4.18 x 3.75 inches. Compression ratio: 10.0:1. Brake hp: 340 at 4600 rpm. Carburetor: Carter four-barrel Model AFB-3871S.

CHASSIS FEATURES: Wheelbase: (Imperial Crown and LeBaron) 129 inches; (Crown Imperial) 149.5 inches. Tires: 8.20 x 15.

OPTIONS: Air conditioning ($461.95). Dual air conditioning ($649.85). Auto pilot ($96.80). Automatic beam changer ($46). Rear window defogger ($21.45). Door guards, two-door ($4.40); four-door ($6.50). Electric door locks, two-door ($47.40); four-door ($72.10). Left and right headrests ($45.60). Outside right mirror ($6.85). Two-tone paint ($20.85). Six-Way power front seat in Crown four-door hardtop ($124.80). Positive crankcase vent system ($5.10). Power trunk lock, remote-control ($28.80). AM Touch-Tuner radio with rear speaker and power antenna ($168.80). AM/FM radio with rear speaker and power antenna ($195.70). Rear reverberator speaker ($37.65). Two front retractable seat belts ($22.80). Adjustable steering wheel ($51.30). Sure-Grip differential ($57.45). Tinted glass ($53.75). Whitewall Rayon tires ($55.10). Leather trim ($104.30). Individual front seat trim, in Crown four-door hardtop ($506.10). Individual front seat trim in LeBaron ($381.40). Vinyl roof on Crown coupe ($91.20). Vinyl roof on LeBaron and Crown four-door hardtops ($110.80).

HISTORICAL FOOTNOTES: Introduced on Sept. 30, 1964, the new Imperial line earned Robert Anderson's Chrysler-Plymouth Division 18,399 assemblies for the model year. Calendar year production peaked at 16,422 units. Close to one in three 1965 Imperials came with a tilting steering wheel and 86.9 percent had air conditioning.

1966 IMPERIAL

1966 Imperial Crown, four-door hardtop, V-8

IMPERIAL CROWN SERIES — SERIES BY3-M — The 1966 Imperial Crown received a relatively minor face lift. It featured a new ice cube tray-style grille with the four headlights recessed into chrome panels. The same rear deck treatment used the last two years was continued. All 1966 Imperials came with power brakes, power steering, power windows, electric clock, carpeting, undercoating and vanity with mirror.

IMPERIAL I.D. DATA: The serial number was located on a plate on the left front door hinge pillar post. First symbol: Y=Imperial. Second symbol: M=Imperial Crown; H=Imperial LeBaron. Third and fourth symbols indicate body style: 23=two-door hardtop; 27=convertible; 43=four-door hardtop. Fifth symbol: J=440-cid V-8. Sixth symbol: 6=1966. Seventh symbol identifies assembly plant: 3=Jefferson Plant in Detroit. Last six symbols are sequential production number. Body number plate under hood gives (SO) schedule date; (NUMBER) body production sequence

number; (BDY) body code (column two of charts below); (TRM) trim code; and (PNT) paint code. Engine number on left of block, front, near water pump. Engine code B-440 for 440-cid V-8.

IMPERIAL CROWN SERIES

Model No.	Body/ Style No.	Body Type & Seating	Factory Price	Shipping Weight	Prod. Total
BY3-M	YM43	4-dr HT-6P	5733	4965	8,977
BY3-M	YM23	2-dr HT-6P	5887	5020	2,373
BY3-M	YM27	2-dr Conv-6P	6146	5295	514

IMPERIAL LEBARON SERIES — BY3-H — The LeBaron remained a slightly fancier version of the Crown. Except for its nameplate, exterior styling was the same. However, the LeBaron had a plusher interior, with standard Six-Way power seats.

IMPERIAL LEBARON SERIES

BY3-H	YH43	4-dr HT-6P	6540	5065	1,878

ENGINE: V-8. Overhead valve. Cast iron block. Displacement: 440 cid. Bore and stroke: 4.32 x 3.75 inches. Compression ratio: 10.1:1. Brake hp: 350 at 4400 rpm. Carburetor: Carter four-barrel Model AFB-4131S.

CHASSIS FEATURES: Wheelbase: 129 inches. Tires: 9.15 x 15.

OPTIONS: Automatic transmission was standard. Air conditioning ($452.25). Dual unit air conditioner ($636.15). Auto pilot ($94.90). Automatic beam changer ($45.10). Cleaner air package ($25.00). Rear window defogger ($26.20). Door edge guards in Crown two-door ($4.35); in four-door ($6.40). Left and right headrests ($52.45). Rear seat heater with defroster ($43.30). Front license plate frame ($5.95). Outside right mirror ($6.75). Mobile Director, in Crown coupe ($597.40). Power door locks in Crown two-doors ($46.50); in four-doors ($70.70). Six-Way left power seat, in Crown four-door hardtop ($105.50). Six-Way power seat, for driver and passenger, in Crown four-door hardtop ($210.85). Six-Way power bench seat, in Crown four-door sedan ($122.35). Power trunk release ($28.25). Power vent windows ($71.75). AM Touch-Tuner radio with rear speaker and power antenna ($165.45). AM/FM Touch-Tuner radio with rear speaker and power antenna ($227.75). Reverberator rear speaker ($36.90). Safeguard sentinel lighting ($36.10). Front center passenger seat belt ($9.20). Rear center passenger seat belt ($9.20). Front left and right shoulder belts ($26.80). Tilt-a-scope steering wheel ($92.45). Sure-Grip differential ($56.35). Tinted glass ($52.70). White three-ring tires ($54.05). Split bench seats, with leather trim, in four-door hardtops ($102.25). Vinyl roof ($129.70).

HISTORICAL FOOTNOTES: Sept. 30, 1965, was the big day when the 1966 Imperials appeared in dealer showrooms. By the model year's end, 13,742 of them had left the factory. Calendar year production was recorded as 17,653 cars. This year, Chrysler dropped the line of custombuilt Crown Imperial limousines for the second time. Lynn Townsend was pulling the strings at Chrysler Corp., although Robert Anderson was vice-president and general manager of the Chrysler-Plymouth Division. Model year sales were 25.3 percent off previous levels, although total market share was just about the same. Air conditioning was in 92.5 percent of 1966 Imperials. Only 30.4 percent had a tilting steering wheel. This was the last year for body-on-frame construction, as Imperials went to unit-body construction in 1967. The 440-cid V-8 replaced the 413-cid V-8 in Imperials, providing the cars with 10 additional horsepower.

1967 IMPERIAL

IMPERIAL SERIES — SERIES CY1-M — A new, two-model base series, Imperial also had a new look this year. Its name was printed in a rectangular box in the center of the fine horizontal bar grille. Wraparound signal lights were another new feature. Full-length upper tire-level moldings decorated the sides. The rear fenders were integrated into the bumpers. Power disc brakes; power steering; carpeting; electric clock and power windows were among the standard equipment.

IMPERIAL I.D. DATA: The serial number was located on a plate on the left front door hinge pillar post. First symbol: Y=Imperial. Second symbol: M=Imperial/Imperial Crown; H=Imperial LeBaron. Third and fourth symbols indicate body style: 23=two-door hardtop; 27=convertible; 41=four-door sedan; 43=four-door hardtop. Fifth symbol: L=440-cid V-8. Sixth symbol: 7=1967. Seventh symbol identifies assembly plant: 3=Jefferson Plant in Detroit. Last six symbols are sequential production number. Body number plate under hood gives (SO) schedule date; (NUMBER) body production sequence number; (BDY) body code (column two of charts below); (TRM) trim code; and (PNT) paint code. Engine number on left of block, front, near water pump. Engine code C-440 for 440-cid V-8.

1967 Imperial, two-door convertible, V-8

IMPERIAL SERIES

Model No.	Body/ Style No.	Body Type & Seating	Factory Price	Shipping Weight	Prod. Total
CY1-M	YM41	4-dr Sed-6P	5374	4830	2,193
CY1-M	YM27	2-dr Conv-6P	6244	4815	577

IMPERIAL CROWN SERIES — SERIES CY1-M — The Crown had an additional full-length side body trim, just below the door handles, to set it apart from the standard Imperial.

IMPERIAL CROWN SERIES

CY1-M	YM43	4-dr HT-6P	5836	4860	9,415
CY1-M	YM23	2-dr HT-6P	6011	4780	3,235

1967 Imperial LeBaron, four-door hardtop, V-8

IMPERIAL LEBARON SERIES — SERIES CY1-H — An easy way to identify the new LeBaron was to look at its sides. It featured distinctive upper tire-level molding. It also came with sliding assist straps; reading lights; power vents; Six-Way power seats and whitewall tires.

IMPERIAL LEBARON SERIES

CY1-H	YH43	4-dr HT-6P	6661	4970	2,194

ENGINE: V-8. Overhead valve. Cast iron block. Displacement: 440 cid. Bore and stroke: 4.32 x 3.75 inches. Brake hp: 350 at 4400 rpm. Carburetor: Holley four-barrel Model R-3667A.

CHASSIS FEATURES: Wheelbase: 127 inches. Tires: 9.15 x 15.

OPTIONS: TorqueFlite transmission was standard. Air conditioning ($452.25). Dual unit air conditioner ($636.15). Auto pilot ($94.90). Automatic beam changer ($45.10). Clean-Air package ($25). Rear window defogger ($26.20). Door edge guards, on two-doors ($4.35); on four-doors ($6.40). Left and right headrests ($52.45). Rear seat heater with defroster ($63.30). Front license plate frame ($5.95). Outside right mirror ($6.75). Mobile Director, in Crown coupe ($597.40). Power door locks, in Crown two-door ($46.50). Power door locks ($70.70). Six-Way left power seat, in Crown four-door hardtop ($105.50). Six-Way power seat, for driver and passenger, in Crown four-door hardtop ($210.85). Six-Way power bench seat in Crown four-door sedan ($122.35). Power trunk release ($28.25). Power vent windows ($71.75). AM Touch-Tuner radio with rear speaker and power antenna ($165.45). AM/FM Touch-Tuner radio with rear speaker and power antenna ($227.75). Reverberator rear speaker ($36.90). Safeguard sentinel lighting ($36.10). Front center passenger seat belt ($9.20). Rear center passenger seat belt ($9.20). Front left and right shoulder belts ($26.80). Tilt-A-Scope steering wheel ($92.45). Sure-Grip differential ($56.35). Tinted glass ($52.70). White three-ring tires ($54 05). Split bench seats leather trim, in four-door hardtops ($102.25). Vinyl roof ($129.70).

HISTORICAL FOOTNOTES: Robert Anderson, Chrysler-Plymouth general manager picked Sept. 29, 1966, to introduce the 1967 Imperial models to the public. It was the start of a 17,614 car model run. That total included some 15,400 Crown models and 2,200 LeBarons. As you can see, the 1967 Chrysler luxury car was somewhat of a success. On a calendar year basis, the line on the sales graph peaked at the 15,506 unit level, a decline over 12 months before. AM/FM stereo multiplex radio was a first-time option this year. Most 1967 Imperials, 98 percent, had tinted glass, 95.1 percent had air conditioning, 44.2 percent had vinyl roofs, 40.6 percent used speed control and 21.6 percent came with bucket seats.

1968 Imperial Crown, four-door hardtop, V-8

IMPERIAL CROWN SERIES — SERIES DY1-M — With the discontinuation of the previous year's Imperial lineup, the two models (sedan and convertible) from that series were absorbed into the Imperial Crown series for 1968. Although the rear end looked much the same as the previous year, the Imperial Crown received a new horizontal bar grille that wrapped around the front fenders. It was divided in the center by a vertical bar with a circular emblem. The headlights were recessed into the grille. The rectangular signal lights were located in the front bumpers. Full-length upper fender level trim and fender-to-fender tire level moldings were used on the sides. The Crown two-door hardtop came with vinyl covered quarter panels and rear roof. All 1968 Imperial Crowns came with power steering; power disc brakes; power windows; carpeting; energy-absorbing steering column; padded dash; undercoating; heater; electric clock and remote-control outside mirror.

IMPERIAL I.D. DATA: The serial number was located on a plate on the left front door hinge pillar post. First symbol: Y=Imperial. Second symbol: M=Imperial Crown; H=Imperial LeBaron. Third and fourth symbols indicate body style: 23=two-door hardtop; 27=convertible; 41=four-door sedan; 43=four-door hardtop. Fifth symbol: K=440-cid V-8; L=high-performance 440-cid V-8. Sixth symbol: 8=1968. Seventh symbol identifies assembly plant: 3=Jefferson Plant in Detroit. Last six symbols are sequential production number. Body number plate under hood gives (SO) schedule date; (NUMBER) body production sequence number; (BDY) body code (column two of charts below); (TRM) trim code; and (PNT) paint code. Engine number on left of block, front, near water pump. Engine code D-440 for 440-cid V-8.

IMPERIAL CROWN SERIES

Model No.	Body/ Style No.	Body Type & Seating	Factory Price	Shipping Weight	Prod. Total
DY1-M	YM41	4-dr Sed-6P	5653	4770	1,887
DY1-M	YM43	4-dr HT-6P	6114	4775	8,492
DY1-M	YM23	2-dr HT-6P	5721	4740	2,656
DY1-M	YM27	2-dr Conv-6P	6522	4845	474

IMPERIAL LEBARON SERIES — SERIES DY1-H — The LeBaron had a distinctive roof with a smaller back window than found on the Crown. It had all the standard features of the lower priced series, plus sliding assist straps, Six-Way power seats, reading lamps and whitewall tires.

IMPERIAL LEBARON SERIES

DY1-H	YH43	4-dr HT-6P	6939	4840	1,852

ENGINE: V-8. Overhead valve. Cast iron block. Displacement: 440 cid. Bore and stroke: 4.32 x 3.75 inches. Compression ratio: 10.1:1. Brake hp: 350 at 4400 rpm. Carburetor: Holley four-barrel Model R-3918A.

CHASSIS FEATURES: Wheelbase: 127 inches. Tires: 9.15 x 15.

OPTIONS: TorqueFlite transmission was standard. Power brakes. Power steering. Air conditioning ($493.45). Dual unit air conditioning ($771.40). Auto pilot ($94.90). Automatic beam changer ($50.15). Leather bucket seats, two-doors ($351.40). Rear window defogger ($26.20). Door edge guards, two-doors ($5.00); four-doors ($8.50). Dual 440, dual exhaust and air cleaner ($43.05). Right and left front head restraints ($52.45). Rear seat heater with defroster ($69.60). Front license plate frame ($5.95). Outside right manual mirror ($7.15). Mobile Director, Crown coupe ($317.60). Power door locks, two-doors ($46.50); four-doors ($70.70). Six-Way left power seat, Crown four-door hardtop ($105.50). Six-Way driver and passenger power seat ($210.85). Six-Way bench power seat ($122.35). Power trunk lid release ($29.60). Power vent windows ($71.75). AM Touch-Tuner radio with rear speaker and power antenna ($165 45). AM/FM Touch-Tuner radio with rear speaker and power antenna ($227.75). Multiplex AM/FM stereo with stereo speaker and power antenna ($294.85). Stereo tape player

($134.60). Safeguard Sentinel lighting ($36.10). Front, left and right shoulder belts ($26.80). Rear, left and right shoulder belts ($26.80). Front center passenger seat belt ($6.55). Rear center passenger seat belt ($6.55). Spare tire cover ($11.40). Tilt-A-Scope steering wheel ($92.45). Sure-Grip differential ($56.35). Tinted glass, all windows ($52.70). Trailer towing package, models without air conditioning ($63.85). Split bench seats with leather trim, four-door hardtops ($124.55). Vinyl roof, Crown coupe ($103.30). Vinyl roof, other models ($136.15). Trailer towing package, models with air conditioning ($53.55).

HISTORICAL FOOTNOTES: Over 80 percent of 1968 Imperials had a vinyl roof, 14.4 percent had bucket seats, 72.4 percent had tilting steering wheel, 64.8 percent had Cruise Control and 97.2 percent had air conditioning. This was the last year for the convertible.

1969 IMPERIAL

1969 Imperial Crown, four-door hardtop, V-8

IMPERIAL CROWN SERIES — SERIES EY-M — The sharp, crisp lines of the previous few years were replaced with 'fuselage' styling. Headlights were behind a grille consisting of fine vertical and horizontal pieces, with two larger bars in the center running from end-to-end. The grille and wraparound signal lights were framed in chrome. Upper signal light level full-length trim and three rectangular safety lights (between the front bumper and front wheelwell openings) graced the sides. The rear bumper was integrated into the rear deck and contained the rectangular taillights and back-up lights. Standard equipment included power front disc brakes; power steering; power windows; electric clock; carpeting and remote-control outside mirror.

IMPERIAL I.D. DATA: The serial number was located on a plate on the dash, visible through the windshield. First symbol: Y=Imperial. Second symbol: M=Imperial Crown; H=Imperial LeBaron. Third and fourth symbols indicate body style: 23=two-door hardtop; 41=four-door sedan; 43=four-door hardtop. Fifth symbol: K=440-cid V-8; L=high-performance 440-cid V-8. Sixth symbol: 9=1969. Seventh symbol identifies assembly plant: C=Jefferson Plant in Detroit. Last six symbols are sequential production number. Body number plate under hood gives (SO) schedule date; (NUMBER) body production sequence number; (BDY) body code (column two of charts below); (TRM) trim code; and (PNT) paint code. Engine number on left of block, front, near water pump. Engine code 440 for 440-cid V-8.

IMPERIAL CROWN SERIES

Model No.	Body/ Style No.	Body Type & Seating	Factory Price	Shipping Weight	Prod. Total
EY-M	YM41	4-dr Sed-6P	6411	4741	1,617
EY-M	YL43	4-dr HT-6P	6411	N/A	823
EY-M	YL23	2-dr HT-6P	6233	N/A	244

IMPERIAL LEBARON SERIES — SERIES EY-H — The LeBaron came with a vinyl covered roof, formal rear window, cloth and leather bench seats and storage compartments in all doors.

IMPERIAL LEBARON SERIES

EY-H	YM43	4-dr HT-6P	6772	4801	14,821
EY-H	YM23	2-dr HT-6P	6539	4795	4,572

ENGINE: V-8. Overhead valve. Cast iron block. Displacement: 440 cid. Bore and stroke: 4.32 x 3.75 inches. Compression ratio:10.1:1. Brake hp: 350 at 4400 rpm. Carburetor: Holley Type four-barrel Model R-4166A.

CHASSIS FEATURES: Wheelbase: 127 inches. Tires: 9.15 x 15.

OPTIONS: Power brakes. Power steering. Air conditioning ($732.05). Automatic beam changer ($51.65). Automatic speed control ($91.75). Rear window defogger ($27). Door edge guards, two-doors ($5.20); four-doors ($8.80). Right and left front head restraints ($26.40). Rear seat

heater with defroster ($71.65). Front and rear license plate frame ($11.80). Carpet protection mats ($13.75). Outside right manual mirror ($7.35). Power door locks, two-doors ($47.90); four-doors ($70.70). Six-Way left power seat ($108.55). Six-Way driver and passenger power seat ($217.10). Six-Way bench power seat ($122.35). Power trunk lid release ($30.50). Power vent windows ($73.85). AM Touch-Tuner radio with rear speaker and power antenna ($165.45). AM/FM Touch-Tuner radio with rear speaker and power antenna ($234.35). Multiplex AM/FM stereo tape with five speakers and power antenna ($350.70). Safeguard sentinel lighting ($36.10). Leather bucket seats ($361.60). Left and right rear shoulder belts ($26.80). Spare tire cover ($11.70). Tilt and telescope steering wheel ($96.70). Sure-Grip differential ($58). Tinted glass, all windows ($54.25). Whitewall two-ring fiberglass belted tires (9.15 x 15). Trailer towing package, models with air conditioning ($55.10); models without air conditioning ($65.70). Split bench seats with leather trim ($137.65). Vinyl roof ($152.05). TorqueFlite transmission was standard.

HISTORICAL FOOTNOTES: Only 12.3 percent of 1969 Imperials came with bucket seats, 99.7 percent had a radio, 96 percent had a vinyl roof and 61.3 percent had a tilting steering wheel.

1970 IMPERIAL

1970 Imperial Crown, two-door hardtop, V-8

IMPERIAL CROWN SERIES — SERIES FY-L — Styling changes for 1970 were mild. The four headlights were hidden behind a new, full-width grille of a grid pattern. A double pin stripe ran from upper signal light level to the rear bumper. There was a full-length lower body molding and a rectangular side marker light (located between the front bumper and front wheelwell opening). The rear side marker lights were incorporated into the bumpers and the taillights were decorated with thin chrome pieces. Standard equipment included power windows; trip odometer; electric clock; undercoating and pile carpeting.

IMPERIAL I.D. DATA: The serial number was located on a plate on the dash, visible through the windshield. First symbol: Y=Imperial. Second symbol: M=Imperial Crown; H=Imperial LeBaron. Third and fourth symbols indicate body style: 23=two-door hardtop; 43=four-door hardtop. Fifth symbol: T=440-cid V-8; U=high-performance 440-cid V-8. Sixth symbol: 0=1970. Seventh symbol identifies assembly plant: Jefferson Plant in Detroit. Last six symbols are sequential production number. Body number plate under hood gives (SO) schedule date; (NUMBER) body production sequence number; (BDY) body code (column two of charts below); (TRM) trim code; and (PNT) paint code. Engine number on left of block, front, near water pump. Engine code 440 for 440-cid V-8.

IMPERIAL CROWN SERIES

Model No.	Body/ Style No.	Body Type & Seating	Factory Price	Shipping Weight	Prod. Total
FY-L	YL43	4-dr HT-6P	5956	4775	1,333
FY-L	YL23	2-dr HT-6P	5779	4640	254

IMPERIAL LeBARON SERIES — SERIES FY-M — Outside of a standard vinyl roof, formal rear window and more luxurious cloth and leather interior, there was little difference between the Imperial LeBaron and Imperial Crown.

IMPERIAL LEBARON SERIES

FY-M	YM43	4-dr HT-6P	6328	4785	8,426
FY-M	YM23	2-dr HT-6P	6095	4665	1,803

ENGINE: V-8. Overhead valve. Cast iron block. Displacement: 440 cid. Bore and stroke: 4.32 x 3.75 inches. Compression ratio: 9.70:1. Brake hp: 350 at 4400 rpm. Carburetor: four-barrel.

CHASSIS FEATURES: Wheelbase: 127 inches. Overall length: 229.7 inches. Tires: L78-15.

OPTIONS: Power brakes. Power steering. Air conditioning ($474.95). Dual air conditioning ($713.53). Air conditioning with automatic temperature control ($493.45). Dual air conditioning with automatic temperature control ($732.05). Automatic beam changer ($51.65). Automatic speed control ($91.75). Rear-window defogger ($31.75). Door edge guards, two-doors ($5.20); four-doors ($8.80). Evaporative emissions control ($38.35). Rear seat heater with defroster ($75.90). Front and rear license plate frame ($11.80). Accessory floor mats ($13.75). Outside right manual mirror ($7.35). Power door locks, in two-doors ($47.90); in four-doors ($70.70). Six-Way left power seat ($108.55). Six-Way driver and passenger power seat ($217.10). Six-Way bench power seat ($122.35). Power trunk lid release ($33.45). Power vent windows ($73.85). AM Touch-Tuner radio with floor tuning switch, rear speaker and concealed antenna ($165.45). AM/FM Touch-Tuner with floor tuning switch, rear speaker and concealed antenna ($234.35). Multiplex AM/FM stereo type, with five speakers and concealed antenna ($403.75). Safeguard sentinel lighting ($36.10). Leather bucket seats ($361.60). Left and right rear shoulder belts ($26.80). Spare tire cover ($11.70). Tilt and telescope steering wheel ($96.70). Sure-Grip differential ($58.00). Tinted glass, all windows ($55.60). Whitewall L78-15 fiberglass-belted tires ($46.45). Trailer towing package ($56.35). Split bench seat with leather trim in LeBaron four-door hardtop ($137.65). Vinyl roof ($54.70). Vinyl bodyside protection moldings ($15.00). TorqueFlite transmission was standard.

HISTORICAL FOOTNOTES: The 1970 Imperials were introduced Sept. 23, 1969. Calendar year sales hit 10,555 units against a 12-month production total of 10,111 cars (15 percent penetration rate). On a model year basis, 11,816 Imperials left the assembly line, a whopping increase from 1969. Of these, some 1,600 were Crowns and 10,200 LeBarons. Lynn A. Townsend remained at the helm of Chrysler Corp., while R.D. McLaughlin, who held the title of general sales manager., was the top-ranked executive at Chrysler-Plymouth Division. On a model year basis, 90 percent of Imperial Crowns and 97.5 percent of LeBarons had power seats in 1970.

1971 IMPERIAL

1971 Imperial LeBaron, four-door hardtop, V-8

IMPERIAL LEBARON SERIES — SERIES GY-M — Imperial was down to one series this year. Styling changes were minimal. There were rectangular headlight doors on the grille. The Imperial name was printed on the face of the hood. The front side marker lights were divided into a square amber section and a rectangular white section. Imperial was printed on the rear quarter panels, above full-length upper tire-level moldings. The LeBaron name was written on the roof quarter panels. Among the standard features were cloth and leather individual adjustable seats (with passenger side recliner); switch-operated rear reading lights; door assist handles; burled walnut instrument panel; power windows; power steering; power disc brakes; fender skirts; vinyl roof and rim-blow steering wheel.

IMPERIAL I.D. DATA: The serial number was located on a plate on the left top of dash, visible through the windshield. First symbol: Y=Imperial. Second symbol: M=Imperial LeBaron. Third and fourth symbols indicate body style: 23=two-door hardtop; 43=four-door hardtop. Fifth symbol: T=440-cid V-8; U=high-performance 440-cid V-8. Sixth symbol: 1=1971. Seventh symbol identifies assembly plant: C=Jefferson Plant in Detroit. Last six symbols are sequential production number. Body number plate under hood gives schedule date, body production sequence number, body code (column two of chart below), trim and paint data. Engine number on left of block, front, near water pump. Engine code 440 for 440-cid V-8.

IMPERIAL LEBARON SERIES

Model No.	Body/ Style No.	Body Type & Seating	Factory Price	Shipping Weight	Prod. Total
GY-M	YM43	4-dr HT-6P	6276	4855	10,116
GY-M	YM23	2-dr HT-6P	6044	4705	1,442

ENGINE: V-8. Overhead valve. Cast iron block. Displacement: 440 cid. Bore and stroke: 4.32 x 3.75 inches. Compression ratio: 8.8:1. Brake hp: 335 at 4400 rpm. Carburetor: four-barrel.

CHASSIS FEATURES: Wheelbase: 127 inches. Overall length: 229.5 inches. Front tread: 62.4 inches. Rear tread: 62 inches. Tires: J78-15.

OPTIONS: Air conditioning ($489.95). Dual air conditioning ($728.60). Air conditioning with automatic temperature controls ($508.45). Dual air conditioning with automatic temperature control ($747.10). Automatic beam changer ($51.70). Automatic speed control ($95.10). Rear window defogger ($31.80). Door edge protectors, on two-doors ($6.55); on four-doors ($11.80). Power door locks, on two-doors ($50.35); on four-doors ($74.30). Engine block heater ($15.75). Exhaust emission control ($13.10). Accessory floor mats ($15.95). Four wheel Sure-Brake ($351.50). Tinted glass, all windows ($58.45). Rear seat heater and defroster ($79.75). Front and rear license plate frames ($11.30). Safeguard sentinel lighting ($38.00). Right manual mirror ($7.75). Microphone ($11.80). AM/FM search tuner radio ($250.20). AM/FM stereo radio ($308.20). AM/FM stereo with stereo tape cassette ($445.95). AM/FM stereo with 8-track ($419.70). Six-Way power bench seat, in two-doors ($122.45). Six-Way left-hand power 50/50 seat, in four-doors ($114.05). Six-Way power bucket seat or 50/50 left or right unit ($228.10). Rear shoulder belts ($26.85). Spare-tire cover ($12.35). Tilt and telescope steering wheel ($96.75). Power operated sun roof (two-doors) ($597.55). Sure-Grip differential ($58.05). Whitewall bias-belted tires L84-15 ($46.35). Trailer towing package ($59.20). Interior trim, two-door with leather bucket seats ($380.35). Interior trim, four-door with leather trim split bench seat ($157.40). Power trunk lid release ($33.45). Vent windows, in four-doors ($87.20). Headlamp washer and wipers ($29.65).

HISTORICAL FOOTNOTES: The Imperial returned this year to being a series of the overall Chrysler line rather than being a separate brand, which it had been since 1954.

1972 IMPERIAL

1972 Imperial LeBaron, two-door hardtop, V-8

IMPERIAL LEBARON SERIES — SERIES HY-M — The LeBaron received a new grille for 1972. The Imperial name was taken off the face of the hood and replaced by a small eagle emblem. The front side marker lights were raised a bit. They were now located above the full-length, upper tire-level side molding. The rear end styling featured narrow slanted vertical rear fender integrated taillights. Among the standard equipment was a vinyl roof, carpeting, power steering, power brakes, air conditioning and power windows. Although engine compression was lowered and engines were detuned to meet new federal emissions standards, the 1972 Imperial did offer "anti-skid" brakes as a $250 option. The brake system available on Imperials, designed by Bendix, was one of the first (Lincoln offered Sure-Trak in 1970) among U.S. makes going into the "ABS" era.

IMPERIAL I.D. DATA: The serial number was located on a plate on the left top of dash, visible through the windshield. First symbol: Y=Imperial. Second symbol: M=Imperial LeBaron. Third and fourth symbols indicate body style: 23=two-door hardtop; 43=four-door hardtop. Fifth symbol: T=440-cid V-8; U=high-performance 440-cid V-8. Sixth symbol: 2=1972. Seventh symbol identifies assembly plant: C=Jefferson Plant

in Detroit. Last six symbols are sequential production number. Body number plate under hood gives schedule date, body production sequence number, body code (column two of chart below), trim and paint data. Engine number on left of block, front, near water pump. Engine code 440 for 440-cid V-8.

IMPERIAL LEBARON SERIES

Model No.	Body/ Style No.	Body Type & Seating	Factory Price	Shipping Weight	Prod. Total
HY-M	YM43	4-dr HT-6P	6762	4955	13,472
HY-M	YM23	2-dr HT-6P	6534	4790	2,322

ENGINE: V-8. Overhead valve. Cast iron block. Displacement: 440 cid. Bore and stroke: 4.32 x 3.75 inches. Compression ratio: 8.2:1. Brake hp: 225 nhp at 4400 rpm (net horsepower rating system introduced). Carburetor: four-barrel.

CHASSIS FEATURES: Wheelbase: 127 inches. Overall length: 229.5 inches. Tires: L84-15.

OPTIONS: Power brakes, power steering, air conditioning and power windows were standard. Dual control air conditioner ($250.85). Automatic beam changer ($50.80). Automatic speed control ($93.10). Rear window defogger ($35.15). Power door locks, two-doors ($49.30); four-doors ($72.70). Engine block heater ($15.40). Exhaust emission control system ($28.30). Rear seat heater and defroster ($78.10). Safeguard sentinel lighting ($37.20). AM radio with stereo tape cassette ($271.50). AM/FM radio with five speakers ($301.60). AM/FM stereo with stereo tape cassette ($436.40). AM/FM stereo with 8-track stereo tape ($410.75). AM/FM radio with rear speaker ($244.80). Six-way power bench seat, two-doors ($119.80); four-doors ($111.60). Six-way power bucket or 50/50 bench seat ($223.20). Tilt and telescope steering wheel ($94.70). Power-operated sun roof ($584.75). Sure-Grip differential ($18). Four-wheel Sure-brake system ($344). Heavy-duty suspension ($18). Two-stripe whitewall tires L84-15, bias belted ($45.35). Whitewall tires L84-15, steel belted ($79.70). Bench seats with leather trim, four-doors ($154); two-doors ($372.20). Bucket seats with leather trim, two-doors ($372.20). Power vent windows, four-doors ($35.35). Accessory group includes floor mats, carpeted spare tire, right manual outside mirror, door protection guards. Accessory group, two-doors without H54 ($41.70); two-doors with H54 ($28.60); four-doors without H54 ($46.90); four-doors with H54 ($34.80). Trailer towing package ($71.70). Automatic transmission standard.

HISTORICAL FOOTNOTES: Most 1972 Imperials, 99.5 percent, were sold with a radio, 78.2 percent had an adjustable steering column, 83.8 percent had speed control and 11 percent came with bucket seats.

1973 IMPERIAL

LEBARON SERIES — SERIES 3Y-M — The biggest styling changes for the 1973 LeBaron were a new mesh-pattern grille and front bumper guards. Among the standard equipment were power steering; power brakes; air conditioning; power windows; carpeting and a vinyl roof.

IMPERIAL I.D. DATA: The serial number was located on a plate on the left top of dash, visible through the windshield. First symbol: Y=Imperial. Second symbol: M=Imperial LeBaron. Third and fourth symbols indicate body style: 23=two-door hardtop; 43=four-door hardtop. Fifth symbol: T=440-cid V-8; U=high-performance 440-cid V-8. Sixth symbol: 3=1973. Seventh symbol identifies assembly plant: C=Jefferson Plant in Detroit. Last six symbols are sequential production number. Body number plate under hood gives schedule date, body production, sequence number, body code (column two of chart below), trim and paint data. Engine number on left of block, front, near water pump. Engine code 440 for 440-cid V-8.

IMPERIAL LEBARON SERIES

Model No.	Body/ Style No.	Body Type & Seating	Factory Price	Shipping Weight	Prod. Total
3Y-M	YM43	4-dr HT-6P	7541	4940	14,166
3Y-M	YM23	2-dr HT-6P	7313	4775	2,563

ENGINE: V-8. Overhead valve. Cast iron block. Displacement: 440 cid. Bore and stroke: 4.32 x 3.75 inches. Compression ratio: 8.2:1. Brake hp: 215 nhp at 3600 rpm. Carburetor: four-barrel.

CHASSIS FEATURES: Wheelbase: 127 inches. Overall length: 229.6 inches. Tires: L84-15.

OPTIONS: Automatic transmission, power brakes, power steering, air conditioning were standard. Dual control air conditioner ($250.85). Automatic beam changer ($50.60). Automatic speed control ($93.10). Rear

window defogger ($35.15). Power door locks, two-doors ($49.30); four-doors ($72.70). Engine block heater ($15.40). Exhaust emission control system ($28.30). Rear seat heater and defroster ($78.10). Safeguard sentinel lighting ($37.20). AM radio with stereo tape cassette ($271.50). AM/FM radio with five speakers ($301.60). AM/FM stereo with stereo tape cassette ($436.40). AM/FM stereo with 8-track stereo tape ($410.75). AM/FM radio with rear speaker ($244.80). Six-Way power bucket or 50/50 bench seat ($223.20). Tilt and telescope steering wheel ($94.70). Power-operated sun roof ($584.75). Sure-Grip differential ($18). Four-wheel Sure-brake system ($344). Heavy-duty suspension ($18). Two-stripe whitewall tires L84-15, bias belted ($45.35). Whitewall tires L84-15, steel belted ($79.70). Bench seats with leather trim, four-doors ($154); two-doors ($372.20). Power vent windows, four-doors ($85.53). Accessory Group includes: floor mats, carpeted spare tire, right manual outside mirror, door protection guards. Accessory Group, two-doors without H54 ($41.70); Accessory Group, two-doors with H54 ($28.60); Accessory Group, four-doors without H54 ($46.90); Accessory Group, four-doors with H54 ($34.80). Trailer towing package ($71.70). Anti-Lock Brakes ($250).

1973 Imperial LeBaron, four-door hardtop, V-8

HISTORICAL FOOTNOTES: Most 1973 Imperials, 97.5 percent, had power seats, 99.9 percent had tinted glass and 83.7 percent had a tilting steering wheel.

1974 IMPERIAL

1974 Imperial LeBaron, four-door hardtop, V-8

IMPERIAL LEBARON SERIES — SERIES 4Y-M — The 1974 LeBaron received a major restyling (at least in the front). Its narrow, slightly protruding 'waterfall' grille gave it a definite Lincoln-Continental look. The wraparound front signal lights also were similar to Lincoln styling. The vertical slanting taillights resembled, but were larger than, the previous year's. The circular Imperial emblem was raised from the rear deck panel

to the trunk. Standard equipment included power steering; ribbed velour upholstery; windshield washer; four-wheel power disc brakes and power windows. The Crown Coupe, an option for the two-door hardtop, included opera windows and vinyl covering the front portion of the roof. It became available late in the year.

IMPERIAL I.D. DATA: The serial number was located on a plate on the left top of dash, visible through the windshield. First symbol: Y=Imperial. Second symbol: M=Imperial LeBaron. Third and fourth symbols indicate body style: 23=two-door hardtop; 43=four-door hardtop. Fifth symbol: T=440-cid V-8. Sixth symbol: 4=1974. Seventh symbol identifies assembly plant: C=Jefferson Plant in Detroit. Last six symbols are sequential production number. Body number plate under hood gives schedule date, body production sequence number, body code (column two of chart below), trim and paint data. Engine number on left of block, front, near water pump. Engine code 440 for 440-cid V-8.

IMPERIAL LEBARON SERIES

Model No.	Body/ Style No.	Body Type & Seating	Factory Price	Shipping Weight	Prod. Total
4Y-M	YM43	4-dr HT-6P	7230	4862	10,576
4Y-M	YM23	2-dr HT-6P	7793	4770	3,850
4Y-M	YM23	2-dr Crn Cpe-6P	7856	N/A	57

ENGINE: V-8. Overhead valve. Cast iron block. Displacement: 440 cid. Bore and stroke: 4.32 x 3.75 inches. Compression ratio: 8.2:1. Brake hp: 230 nhp at 4000 rpm. Carburetor: four-barrel.

CHASSIS FEATURES: Wheelbase: 124 inches. Overall length: 231.1 inches. Tires: LR78-15.

OPTIONS: Automatic transmission, power steering, power disc brakes, air conditioning and power windows were standard. Anti-lock brakes ($250). Automatic beam changer ($53.20). Automatic speed control ($97.95). Rear window defogger ($32.75). Sure-Grip differential ($59.80). Power door locks, two-doors ($51.85); four-doors ($76.45). Emission control testing system ($29.70). Engine block heater ($16.15). Locking gas cap ($4.95). Safeguard sentinel lighting ($39.10). AM/FM radio ($194.15). AM/FM search tuner with dual front and rear speakers ($332.80). AM/FM stereo with 8-track stereo tape, four speakers ($432.50). Power bench seat, left 50/50 four-doors ($117.45). 50/50 Power bench or power bucket seat, left and right ($234.90). Tilt and telescope steering wheel ($99.60). Power sun roof ($615.65). Security alarm system ($105.20). Heavy-duty shock absorbers ($5.40). Heavy-duty suspension ($18.90). Whitewall steel-belted radial tires LR84-15 ($30.80). Leather trim bench seats, in four-doors ($162.10). Power release trunk deck ($34.35). Manual vent windows, in four-doors ($35.10). Imperial accessory group: includes floor mats; carpeted spare cover; mirror; right outside rearview mirror and door edge guards, in two-doors ($50.00); in four-doors ($55.55). Trailer towing package ($276.20).

HISTORICAL FOOTNOTES: Most 1974 Imperials, 97.4 percent, came with power seats and 84.1 percent had a tilting steering wheel.

1975 IMPERIAL

IMPERIAL LEBARON SERIES — SERIES 5Y-M — This was the 'last' Imperial ... until 1981. Styling was basically the same as in 1974. Power steering; power disc brakes; power windows; air conditioning and tinted glass were among the many standard features. The 'final' Imperial built was a four-door hardtop, Serial Number YM43-T5C-182947.

IMPERIAL I.D. DATA: The serial number was located on a plate on the left top of dash, visible through the windshield. First symbol: Y=Imperial. Second symbol: M=Imperial LeBaron. Third and fourth symbols indicate body style: 23=two-door hardtop; 43=four-door hardtop. Fifth symbol: T=440-cid V-8. Sixth symbol: 5=1975. Seventh symbol identifies assembly plant: C=Jefferson Plant in Detroit. Last six symbols are sequential production number. Body number plate under hood gives schedule date, body production sequence number, body code (column two of chart below), trim and paint data. Engine number on left of block, front, near water pump. Engine code E-86 for 440-cid V-8.

IMPERIAL LEBARON SERIES

Model No.	Body/ Style No.	Body Type & Seating	Factory Price	Shipping Weight	Prod. Total
5Y-M	YM43	4-dr HT-6P	9046	5065	6,102
5Y-M	YM23	2-dr HT-6P	8900	4965	1,087
5Y-M	YM23	2-dr Crn Cpe-6P	9277	5165	1,641

ENGINE: V-8. Overhead valve. Cast iron block. Displacement: 440 cid. Bore and stroke: 4.32 x 3.75 inches. Compression ratio: 8.2:1. Brake hp: 215 at 4000 rpm. Carburetor: four-barrel.

CHASSIS FEATURES: Wheelbase: 124 inches. Overall length: 231.1 inches. Tires: LR78-15.

OPTIONS: Automatic transmission standard. Automatic beam changer ($53.20). Automatic speed control ($97.95). Rear window defogger ($32.75). Sure-Grip differential ($59.80). Power door locks, in two-door ($51.85); in four-door ($76.45). Emission control testing system ($29.70). Engine block heater ($16.15). Locking gas cap ($4.45). Safeguard sentinel lighting ($39.10). AM/FM radio ($194.15). AM/FM search tuner with dual front and rear speakers ($332.80). AM/FM stereo with 8-track stereo tape and four speakers ($432.50). Power bench seat, left 50/50 seat in four-doors ($117.45). 50/50 Power bench or power bucket seat, left and right ($234.90). Tilt and telescope steering wheel ($99.60). Power sun roof ($615.65). Security alarm system ($105.20). Heavy-duty shock absorbers ($5.40). Heavy-duty suspension ($18.90). White-wall steel-belted radial tires LR84-15 ($80.60). Leather trim bench seats, in four-doors ($162.10). Power release trunk deck ($34.35). Manual vent windows in four-door ($35.10). Imperial accessory group: includes floor mats; carpeted spare tire cover; mirror; right outside rearview mirror; door edge guards on two-door ($50.00); on four-doors ($55.55).

1975 Imperial LeBaron, two-door hardtop, V-8

HISTORICAL FOOTNOTES: This 'last' Imperial was introduced Oct. 1, 1974. For the 1975 model year, a total of exactly 8,830 Imperials were assembled. Calendar year production was a mere 1,930 units. R.B. McCurry, Jr. was group vice-president for U.S. automotive sales for Chrysler-Plymouth Division this year. Imperial new car dealer sales for 1975 models were recorded as 6,957 units. Lack of sales was the official reason for Imperial's phase-out. Production halted June 12, 1975. The final unit was an Imperial LeBaron four-door hardtop with the serial number given above in the 1975 introduction.

Plymouth

Because it typified "the endurance and strength, the rugged honesty, the enterprise, that determination of achievement and the freedom from old limitations of that Pilgrim band who were the first American colonists," the new car from Chrysler Corporation was to be called the Plymouth. Like the Chrysler, a perfect car for the 1920s, the stalwart little Plymouth was tailormade for the '30s. Though Walter P. Chrysler did not foresee the stock market upheaval when he introduced the Plymouth, there can be little doubt that, without it, Chrysler Corporation would have found survival in the Great Depression difficult at the very least.

A 1929 Plymouth roadster coming off the assembly line. (OCW)

In 1928, the Plymouth was intended, however, simply as a staid, inexpensive family car to take on America's best-sellers, Chevrolet and Ford. It debuted in July 1928, about six months after the hoopla accompanying the introduction of the Model A Ford had died down, and amid a good deal of hoopla itself, with dealers across the country dressed up like Pilgrims and Amelia Earhart sharing a platform with the Plymouth at New York's Madison Square Garden. The car, about which all the fuss had been made, was indeed new, though not revolutionary. It was evolutionary, redesigned from the four-cylinder Chrysler 52, which itself had metamorphosed from the venerable Maxwell four. Features such as four-wheel hydraulic brakes, full-pressure engine lubrication, aluminum alloy pistons, and an independent handbrake, however, made for a complete package that would not be offered by Chevrolet or Ford for a decade. The new Plymouth, which was introduced as a 1929 model, did not overwhelm its opposition, of course. Maiden year deliveries of something over 50,000 cars paled in comparison to the more than a half-million Fords and nearly a million Chevrolets. But the inroads in the marketplace made by the car as the Depression deepened were impressive. In 1931, Plymouth production passed the 100,000 mark for the first time, and displaced Buick in the number three spot in the industry. In 1933, the comparative figures were: 218,419 Plymouths, 271,994 Fords, and 438,888 Chevrolets. That Plymouth could accomplish this was due to factors in addition to the car itself. Walter Chrysler's purchase of Dodge was most significant in the estimable dealer organization it made available to sell the car. And Chrysler's gung-ho enthusiasm in seeing to a proper home for its assembly helped, too. Shortly after the Plymouth's introduction, a new factory was completed in Detroit in only three months' time, two crews of workmen building in from each of the ends, two more crews building out from the middle. The "New Finer" Plymouth for 1932 was on a 112-inch wheelbase (longer by three inches than the Chevrolet, by five-and-a-half than the Ford), and it had "Free Wheeling" and "Floating

Power." When Plymouth went to a six in 1933, the initial offering on a 107-inch wheelbase met with disappointing sales results, a matter quickly set right with the addition of a 112-inch wheelbase Deluxe model that offered a cavalcade of color and gadget options—one windshield wiper or two, two spare wheels or one, a flurry of paint and upholstery choices, rather like the "have it your way" campaign Burger King launched in its asserted attack on McDonald's supremacy. By the end of 1933, one out of four cars in America was a Plymouth; and two out of three Plymouths built that year were the "have it your way" Deluxe model. Independent front suspension was given a one-year run in the Plymouth for 1934, 85 hp arrived in 1935, and in 1936 Plymouth built more than 500,000 cars. On its 10th anniversary, in 1938, Plymouth could look back on a first decade of sales surpassing that of any other new automobile in American history. By the time World War II brought an end to automobile production in 1942, more than four million Plymouths had been built.

1942 Plymouth Special Deluxe Club Coupe (OCW)

With the momentum of its successful first 14 years of production, Plymouth entered the post-World War II market with restyled and mechanically refined versions of its 1942 models.

1946 Plymouth Special Deluxe four-door sedan (OCW)

Retaining its 117-inch wheelbase, Plymouth sported a new front grille and rear fenders, as well as a restyled interior and several chassis improvements. Escalating labor and material costs were reflected in higher model prices. No design changes were introduced until the spring of 1949.

The all-new 1949 Plymouths were based on the "box styling" philosophy of Chrysler Chairman K.T. Keller, who had succeeded Walter Chrysler in 1940. Emphasizing practicality over beauty, Keller is credited with the efficiency and roominess of the 1949 models. These new models, in DeLuxe and Special DeLuxe versions, sat on a longer wheelbase and were powered by Plymouth's L-head six-cylinder engine. This same year, Plymouth

also offered a shorter 111-inch wheelbase line with a coupe, sedan, and a new all-steel Suburban station wagon.

Although introducing the automatic electric choke and the combination ignition/starter switch to the low-priced field in 1950, Plymouth entered the '50s with no real styling changes. Sales dropped from third to fifth place in the industry by 1954. Plymouth added flow-through fenderlines and a one-piece windshield to its 1953 models, but all were powered by the same L-head six, which was quickly becoming dated and dull. The two-speed PowerFlite automatic transmission offered by Plymouth in 1954, however, proved popular.

Virgil Exner's all-new styling arrived with 1955 Plymouths and a brand new polyspherical-head V-8 engine brought even more excitement to the new lineup. In addition to new standard features, such as dashboard-controlled PowerFlite automatic transmission, suspended foot pedals, and tubeless tires, buyers could now opt for air conditioning, power windows, and power front seats. A total departure from Plymouth's past was the 1955 Belvedere. Called "A great new car for the young at heart," it included a sporty hardtop and convertible, the latter available only with a V-8 engine.

Along with the tail fins of Virgil Exner's "Forward Look," in 1956 Plymouth introduced an optional Highway Hi-Fi record player and expanded its Suburban, Belvedere, and Savoy series. Contributing to Plymouth's performance image in 1956 was the new limited-edition Fury hardtop, which was finished in white and gold and featured a 303-cid V-8 engine with four-barrel carburetor and dual exhausts.

1957 Plymouth Fury two-door hardtop (OCW)

From 1957 through the end of the decade, Plymouths were hailed as being ahead of their time. Daring styling and advanced performance helped push Plymouth back into third place in the industry in 1957. When Plymouth dropped its Plaza model in 1959, the Fury was elevated to a separate series and the Sport Fury moved in as the new high-performance entry. Also introduced, as an option in 1959, was the new 361-cid "Golden Commando" wedge-head V-8, which delivered 305 hp.

With the exception of the 1954 Belmont show car built in Plymouth's Briggs facility, Chrysler's Virgil Exner and Ghia coachworks of Italy collaborated on most of Plymouth's show cars during the 1950s. They included the XX-500 sedan, the 1954 Explorer grand tourer, the 1956 Plainsman station wagon, and the 1958 Cabana station wagon.

1960 Plymouth Valiant V-100 Suburban station wagon (OCW)

During the 1960s, Plymouth's sales plummeted with only sporadic recoveries. The tail-finned Savoy, Belvedere, Fury, and Suburban models for 1960 were coolly received by the buying public and, in 1962, the public shunned Plymouth's new, downsized models for larger Fords and Chevrolets. Only Plymouth's compact Valiant, with its strong Slant Six engine, was well received. In mid-1964, Plymouth also launched its successful sporty compact, the Barracuda. Along with more pleasing styling, Plymouth's success in racing competition spurred a remarkable sales recovery by 1965.

In the 1960s, the 426-cid/425-hp Hemi engine was offered as an option on Plymouth's Belvedere II and Satellite models, first in racing tune and then in a street performance edition to qualify it as a production option. The "Street Hemi" package included heavy-duty suspension and oversized brakes. In factory trim it qualified for A/Stock and AA/Stock drag racing and NASCAR's shorter circuits in 1966. Richard Petty won both the 1964 Daytona 500 and the 1967 NASCAR championship for Plymouth.

1967 Plymouth Barracuda two-door hardtop fastback (OCW)

For 1968, Plymouth restyled its intermediates with more rounded lines and introduced its hot Road Runner model available in hardtop and coupe. Identified by special wheels, a hood scoop, Road Runner emblems, and cartoon birds on sides and rear, the Road Runner could be had with either the 383-cid V-8 or the 426-cid Hemi. In addition to the Road Runner, Plymouth's GTX model, introduced in 1967, was continued for 1968.

In 1968 and 1969, Plymouth offered big-block models of its popular Barracuda, called the 'Cuda 340 and 'Cuda 383. In 1970, the Barracuda was completely restyled. It shared an all-new body shell with another Chrysler performance compact, the Dodge Challenger. A midyear variation of the Barracuda was the AAR (All-American Racers) 'Cuda 340, identifiable by its bold tape stripes. Fewer than 2,900 AAR models were built.

1970 Plymouth Road Runner Superbird two-door hardtop (OCW)

In 1970, Plymouth's Valiant was revived in the form of the Duster coupe and the optional Gold Duster. A high-performance variation, the Duster 340, used options similar to the AAR 'Cuda's to convert an otherwise mild Valiant into a skyrocket. Plymouth's most awesome newcomer in 1970 was the high-performance Superbird, which was part of the Road Runner series. With its droop-snout front end, sleek body, and deck lid carrying a stabilizer wing high above its tail, the Superbird was capable of over 220 mph in racing trim. In street form, the four-barrel 440-cid engine with TorqueFlite automatic transmission was standard. A six-barrel 440 engine, a racing 426 Hemi, and

four-speed manual transmission were optional. The Superbird accounted for 21 of 38 Chrysler victories on the Grand National circuit. When NASCAR changed its rules in 1971, however, the Superbird's dominance of high-speed ovals was over.

By 1972, the Barracuda series was severely cut and the optional 383, 440, and 426 Hemi engines were eliminated. A competition Hemi could still be had by professional racers, however, on special order. High insurance rates and government pressure for emission controls were contributors to a decline of the performance-car market. No longer around was the GTX. Due to sagging sales, it was dropped in 1971. That same year the Sport Fury was cast off in favor of the Gran Fury and all of the senior Plymouths were face-lifted.

In 1973, Plymouth made an exhaust gas recirculation system and an orifice spark advance and electrically-assisted choke standard on all models, to reduce air pollution. A new, five-mph-impact-absorbing front bumper was also introduced. By 1974, Plymouth's sales shrunk, hurt by the prior year's Arab oil embargo. Most models were carried over from 1973 with minor changes, due to the emphasis on unleaded fuel and other factors restricting power output. Plymouth stopped publishing passenger car horsepower ratings by 1975. This same year, Plymouth equipped most models with catalytic converters and an emission control device in the exhaust system requiring engines to use lead-free fuel.

Through most of its early life. Plymouth was thought of as a kind of kid brother to Dodge: same shape, same engines, and similar models appealing to ordinary families. Starting with the 1950s Fury, however, Plymouth also turned to performance, eventually turning out such eye-openers as the 1970 Road Runner Superbird with six-barrel carburetion, and a selection of potent Barracudas. Those were gone by 1976, and Plymouth seemed (with one or two exceptions) to have reverted to its family motor car origins—and would soon lose most of its familiar names.

The selection of Valiant and Duster models was still around, but scheduled for replacement by the new Volare (twin to Dodge's Aspen). Volare's Road Runner coupe package came with a 318-cid V-8, floor shift, and heavy-duty suspension, but hardly rivaled earlier models with that name. Basically, it was one more family car. So was the midsize Fury, restyled a year before, which offered one of the last pillarless two-door hardtop designs. Fury could have a 240-hp, 400-cid V-8, while the full-size Gran Fury's optional 440 rated just 205 hp.

Fury got another restyle for 1977, while the biggest Plymouths carried on for just one more year. Volare was the big seller in Plymouth's lineup. A selection of option packages helped, including the Road Runner and Sun Runner, plus a Super Pak with spoilers and louvered quarter windows. Super Coupe and a Street Kit Car were added to the Volare list for 1978, and a Gran Coupe to Fury's options. But the biggest event was the introduction of the subcompact Horizon. Like Dodge's nearly-identical Omni, Horizon had front-wheel drive and a transverse-mounted four-cylinder engine. The 440 V-8 was dropped as a Fury selection, and the name itself faded away before the 1979 model year. In fact, only two Plymouths were left by then: Horizon and Volare. A new TC3 hatchback coupe joined the Horizon sedan, though, with Sport and Rallye packages available. Volare coupes could still get a four-barrel 360-cid V-8, and the Road Runner extras.

Gran Fury returned for 1980, but in a new and shorter form. Volares were not selling well, and this would be their final try. A Turismo package was now available for the Horizon TC3 coupe, including blackout moldings and a rear spoiler. Plymouth sales were augmented by three captive imports: Arrow, Champ, and Sapporo.

Reliant was Plymouth's version of the new front-drive K-car, introduced for 1981. Economy-minded Miser models were added to the Horizon and TC3 list. TC3 had its Turismo option again, and Horizon a Euro-Sedan package. Gran Fury dropped

down to a single model, and was downsized to a 112.7-inch wheelbase for 1982. That version would remain in the lineup through the 1980s, appealing mainly to fleets and larger families. Gran Fury sedans sold to police departments carried a four-barrel, high-performance version of the V-8 engine. The Turismo 2.2 variant of TC3 came with a 2.2-liter engine. Model year sales slumped considerably, but they had risen substantially the year before, so all was just about even. Not until 1985 would a notable increase occur.

Horizon and Turismo engines for 1983 were smaller than before: 97-cid (1.6-liter) Peugeot-built versions, as opposed to the former 105 fours. Their optional powerplant was the 2.2-liter Trans-4, which began life as Reliant's base selection. The TC3 nameplate was dropped, as were the Miser and Euro-Sedan variants of the Plymouth subcompacts. Reliants could now have a five-speed manual transaxle.

It was almost like losing an old friend when the Slant Six engine dropped out, before the 1984 model year. But it just did not fit in with the trend toward front-drive. Gran Fury carried on with only the 318-cid V-8, adding roller lifters in 1985. Horizon showed the strongest sales increase for '84, but Gran Fury took the honors the next year. Also in 1985 came a new Plymouth, the front-drive Caravelle (which was actually a Chrysler E Class). The Turismo 2.2 got some performance-oriented styling features. In 1986, a brand new, fuel-injected, 2.5-liter engine replaced the Mitsubishi-built four as an option for Reliant and Caravelle.

This was not the greatest period for collectible Plymouths. Road Runner Volares? Passable, but not the most thrilling choice. Other Volare variants? Worth a look, but probably not worth traveling cross-country to find one. Even the moderately performance-oriented Turismo subcompact coupes were just adaptations of the Dodge design, not unique to Plymouth. No, Plymouth fanciers might do best to look to an earlier era—or switch to Dodge, which had a few more models of interest to choose from.

1987 Plymouth Horizon four-door hatchback (OCW)

Plymouth's identity in 1987 was linked with that of its parent make. The Chrysler-Plymouth Division was a branch of Chrysler Motors Corp., which was considered a subsidiary of Chrysler Corp. E. Thomas Pappert was Group VP of Sales for Chrysler-Plymouth (as well as Dodge), with Joseph A. Campana functioning as Marketing VP for Chrysler-Plymouth.

The year's lineup of Plymouths included three captive imports: Colt, Vista, and Conquest—which were also sold with Dodge nameplates—plus six domestically-built car lines. The latter were Turismo, Horizon, Reliant, Sundance, Gran Fury, and Caravelle.

Most of Plymouth's 1987 models declined in sales from 1986, although the Vista and Conquest earned modest gains. Another bright spot was the Sundance, an upscale compact introduced in mid-1986 as a 1987 model. It generated 75,080 model year sales, after a slow takeoff.

Operating cutbacks at Chrysler could be blamed, in part, for production losses. Horizon/Turismo sales were temporarily affected when an assembly site change (from Belvidere, Illinois, to Kenosha, Wisconsin) was made. Likewise, the transfer of Gran Fury production, from St. Louis to Kenosha, held down availability of this popular rear-drive M-body car.

Chrysler Corp. sales rose 21 percent in 1988, but this could not offset a decrease in earnings. Plymouth had a bad year. The nameplate's product line was unchanged and the only cars to gain in popularity were the Sundance, Reliant, and Gran Fury. All three had a noticeable increase in model year U.S. dealer sales.

The Sundance found nearly 7,000 more buyers, partly due to the release of a sporty new RS edition and the marketing of a convertible conversion sourced from American Sunroof Corp. The Sundance RS featured a 2.5-liter four linked to a five-speed manual transaxle. A 2.2-liter turbocharged four-cylinder engine was optional for all Sundances.

Chrysler's "America" marketing plan, which reduced costs through the cutting back of mandatory options, helped perk up Reliant sales by 13,000 units. Also benefiting from the program was the Horizon, which remained a volume seller despite a slight drop in deliveries.

Gran Furys received a midyear airbag option and enjoyed a nearly 3,000 unit sales increase. Caravelle buyers were also offered the 2.2-liter turbo option, but the model's popularity tapered off by nearly 50 percent!

For 1989, the new Acclaim midsize sedan was counted upon to revive Plymouth sales. This upscale, front-drive family car offered a 2.5-liter four and five-speed manual transaxle as standard equipment. There were Turbo four and 3.0-liter V-6 engine options and the V-6 could be coupled with a new, electronically controlled four-speed automatic transaxle. Sourced from Chrysler's Newark, New Jersey factory, the Acclaim was introduced in January 1989. By the end of the year, 69,243 were sold.

Another new Plymouth was the Laser, which was related to the previous G-body version of the nameplate in name only. The new Laser was a front-drive, two-plus-two sports specialty model built by Diamond-Star Motors (the Chrysler-Mitsubishi joint venture in Normal, Illinois). A derivative of the Mitsubishi Eclipse and Eagle Talon, the Laser was purchased by 14,576 customers in 1989. Other Plymouth developments for the year included an upgraded Turbo four available in the Sundance, a standard driver-side airbag system for Gran Fury, and the discontinuance of the Reliant station wagon.

Like its sister division Dodge, Chrysler-Plymouth got a new top management position for 1990. Michael V. Howe was appointed to the new role as divisional general manager. He had previously been Plymouth's general marketing manager.

Financial woes within Chrysler Corp. brought more belt-tightening. Disappearing from the Plymouth stable were the Conquest, Turismo, Reliant, Caravelle, and Gran Fury. The Horizon was dropped on February 2, 1990.

1990 Plymouth Acclaim four-door sedan

The 1990 Acclaim received a new 2.5-liter Turbo option, along with a three-speed automatic transmission. New for the Sundance was a steering wheel with speed control and an up-graded 2.5-liter base engine. The captive-import Colt/Colt Vista wagon got a new grille and new bodyside moldings.

Sundance, Laser, Acclaim, and the imported Colt anchored Plymouth's lineup through most of the first half of the 1990s. In 1992, Laser added a third model to its RS trim level, that being the Turbo AWD (all-wheel-drive) coupe. That same year, Plymouth dusted off the Duster name (not used since 1977) and applied it to the previously named Sundance RS hatchback. The Duster debuted V-6 power in the Sundance series, using the 3.0-liter engine that was also optional in the Acclaim.

Throughout the final half of the decade, rumors swirled that the Plymouth Division of Chrysler Corp. was being considered for termination—a fate that befell the Eagle Division at the end of the 1998 model year. One single act, though, that quieted those rumors (at least for the time being) was the unveiling of the Plymouth Prowler "factory hot rod." First seen on the 1993 auto show circuit as a concept car, the Prowler—a retro-looking roadster powered by a 240-hp, 3.5-liter V-6—defied the norm of Detroit thinking at that time; all cars must have a low coefficient of drag, every piece of safety equipment known to man, and affordable creature comforts to sell well. As with Dodge's Viper, working in the "opposite direction" worked wonders, both for Plymouth's image and bottom line. Again, as with the Viper, the Prowler was considered an "instant collectable." In 1993, Chrysler Corp. was also showcasing sketches of its new compact Plymouth, code-named PL. This car would enter showrooms in early 1994 as a 1995 model called the Neon.

Sundance, Laser, and the imported Colt were all discontinued at the end of the 1994 model year. Only the Neon and Acclaim were offered for 1995, with the Acclaim lasting only to January when its Sterling Heights, Michigan, assembly plant was shuttered for a $300 million re-do to tool up for the all-new, J-platform 1996 Breeze, which would enter showrooms one year later. In an image-enhancement move, Plymouth also revised its logo—a post-modern version of the original Mayflower sailing ship that debuted in 1928. The new logo was unveiled mid-model year on 1995 Neons and Voyager minivans.

Neon and Breeze anchored Plymouth's lineup for 1996, the same year that Chrysler Corp. consolidated its Chrysler-Plymouth and Jeep-Eagle Divisions. A year later, in March, the Prowler entered showrooms with a list price of $35,000, although what was actually being paid to dealers selling these "retro-rods" was much greater.

In 1998, a move was underway to individualize Plymouth Neon models from their Dodge counterparts. Different packaged models were offered to buyers of both brands, with those exclusive to Plymouth being the Expresso and Style packages. An optional Expresso package was also offered to dress-up the Breeze. There was no 1998 Prowler, the 1999 version launched early in spring 1998 with three new Prowler colors to go along with the traditional purple: red, yellow, and black. Prowler was now powered by the all-new, all-aluminum, High-Output 3.5-liter V-6 that was also under the hood of the 1999 Chrysler 300M and LHS sedans. Also, the all-new 2000 Neon sedan (the coupe body style was discontinued) was launched early in spring 1999.

In the fall of 1999, DaimlerChrysler announced that the Plymouth Division would be disbanded after model year 2001.

In the wake of that announcement, Plymouth's millennium-ending 2000 lineup remained the same as 1999: Neon, Breeze, and Prowler. Of these, most changed was the Neon, a complete redesign that actually had gone on sale, as a 2000 model, in spring of 1999.

1928 PLYMOUTH

CHRYSLER PLYMOUTH — MODEL Q — FOUR: Walter Chrysler's entry into the low-priced field was introduced at Madison Square Garden on July 7, 1928. The first car entering the arena was driven by famed aviatrix Amelia Earhart. Ironically, or shrewdly perhaps, the new car was not known solely as a Plymouth, but as the Chrysler Plymouth. The little four-cylinder car was the only four-cylindered car in the Chrysler lineup (it replaced the former Chrysler Model "52"), joining the six-cylinder Chrysler "65" and "75" models. The new "Chrysler" Plymouth shared many mechanical and body parts with the newly-introduced six-cylinder DeSoto and for the first years the Plymouth and DeSoto would share the same production facilities. Priced as low as $670, the new car was sold exclusively by Chrysler dealers and found a ready market, with nearly 60,000 units sold during its first model year. The new Model Q Plymouth, although sold throughout the remainder of the year 1928, was actually considered by the Corporation to be a 1929 model, but, with no definite Corporate guidelines, the Q and ensuing models through 1931 suffered from a lack of model year identity.

The Chrysler Plymouth styling closely matched that of its larger brethren and featured among other things, the Chrysler pioneered "thin-line" radiator shell in which most of the radiator chrome trim was concealed. Identifying features of the Model Q included the wording "Chrysler Plymouth" on the radiator medallion, two-piece front and rear bumpers that featured painted grooves on the flat surfaces, Depress Beam headlamps and hex headed hubcaps bearing a stylized letter "P". All cars used the Fedco numbering system, which consisted of a series of letters and numbers stamped onto a multi-piece medallion on the instrument panel for identification rather than a normal serial number plate. This Fedco code could be converted to a numerical sequence by converting the letters to their proper number using the following system:

WPCHRYSLER

0123456789, but this repeated the letter "R" so the solution was the substitution of "O" for the last "R".

Thus, HL-950-P would convert to the Numeric Serial Number 379501. Despite being a new make, Plymouth ended the sales year in 15th place.

I.D. DATA: Serial numbers on closed cars: medallion on center of upper dash rail. Open cars: medallion on instrument panel. (Fedco numbering system) Detroit, Michigan, starting: HL-950-P. Ending: HD-999-D. Detroit, Michigan, starting: RW-000-P. Ending RH-977-H. Windsor, Ontario, starting: GP-000-P. Ending: GP-582-E. Engine numbers on left front corner of cylinder block. (All model Q Plymouths had an engine serial number prefixed by the letter Q). Starting: Q175,000. Ending: Q242482.

Body No.	Body Type & Seating	Price	Weight	Prod. Total
NA	2-dr. Rds.-2P	670	2210	Note 1
R	2-dr. R/S Rds.-2/4P	675	2210	—
328	2-dr. DeL. Cpe.-2/4P	720	2345	—
T	4-dr. Tr.-5P	695	2305	—
321	2-dr. Sed.-5P	690	2485	—
320	4-dr. Sed.-5P	725	2510	Note 2
322	2-dr. Std. Cpe.-2P	670	NA	—

Note 1: Body style production figures are not available.

Note 2: Body code number 320 indicates Briggs body; body code number 88 indicates Hayes body on four-door sedans only.

ENGINE: Inline. Valve in block. Four. Cast iron block. B & S: 3-5/8 x 4-1/8 in. Disp.: 170.3 cu. in. C.R.: 4.6:1 Brake H.P.: 45 @ 2800 R.P.M. Taxable/A.L.A.M./N.A.C.C. H.P.: 21.03. Main bearings: three. Valve lifters: solid. Carb.: Carter RJHO8-112S (U.S.), DRJHO8-114S (L.H.D. export), DRJHO8-113S (R.H.D. export).

TECHNICAL: Sliding gear (spur gears) transmission. Speeds: 3F/1R. Floor shift controls. Single plate, dry clutch. Driveshaft, fabric universal discs. Semi-floating rear axle. Overall ratio: 4.3:1. Four wheel hydraulic brakes. Wood spoke standard wheels, wire wheel optional. Rim size: 4.75 x 20.

CHASSIS: [Series Q] W.B.: 109-3/4 in. O.L.: 169 in. Frt/Rear Tread: 56/56 in. Tires: 4.75 x 20.

OPTIONS: Front and rear bumpers, as a set ($15.00). Heater floor type, hot air heat (30.00). Clock eight-day, header board mount, dial wind (12.50). Cigar lighter in combination w/utility light (12.00). Disc wheels, set of five (25.00). Wire wheels (set of five) (35.00). Tire cover (1.50). Tire lock (Oakes stud type) (3.50). "Red Head" cylinder head (std. on roadster) (10.00). Spring covers (8.00). Trunk rack (only when sidemount equipped) (12.00). Trunk (20.00). Top boot (10.00). Top bow rest (2.00). Windshield wings for open cars (std. on roadster) (10.00). Monograms, painted type, black letters only (10.00). Monograms, sterling sil-

ver, applied type, three letters maximum (10.00). Special colors, body only (35.00). Special colors on fenders, splash guards, frame horns, rear deck, and tire carrier (35.00). Leather upholstery (closed models) (25.00). Mohair upholstery (coupe) (10.00). Broadcloth (two- and four-door sedan) (35.00). Broadcloth (coupe) (20.00). Sidemount fenders: When only one sidemount ordered, mounted in left fender. One fender with tire and tube (25.00). Two fenders with tire and tube (50.00). One fender, tire and tube when equipped with five disc wheels (50.00). Two fenders, tires and tubes when equipped with six disc wheels (75.00). One fender with tire and tube when equipped with five wire wheels (60.00). Two fenders with tires, tubes when equipped with six wire wheels (90.00). Cowl lamps with chrome cowl moldings, dealer installed (20.00).

HISTORICAL: Production began June 14, 1928, completed February 4, 1929. Model year production: 66,097. Plymouth shared the Chrysler/DeSoto production facilities at the Highland Park (Michigan) assembly plant until a new factory could be constructed. Each Plymouth engine was stamped with a serial number and a series of code letters to let garage owners and mechanics know that the engine installed in the car was fitted with certain undersize or oversize components. In addition, each engine had a code letter that corresponded to the model code of the ca - that is, that a PE engine was fitted into a PE chassis. There are some exceptions to that rule that have been noted under the individual engine specification charts for each model.

The engine number in all cases is located on the left front corner of the cylinder block on a flat boss, usually directly above the generator. A typical example is shown below:

A P12 123456 A

The first symbol (A) is the production number. The second symbol (P12) is the model code number.
The next group of symbols (123456) is the sequential serial 4.
The last symbol (A) is the letter size number (no letter-standard).

Letter Size Number Codes

A = .020 oversize cylinder bore
B = .010 undersize main and connecting rod bearings
C = .005 oversize rod bearings
AB = .020 oversize cylinders, .010 undersize main and connecting rod bearings
E = smaller carburetor (economy engine)

Export engines have the letter X following the model code number, indicating small bore engine (Example P12X)

Canadian engines have the letter C following the model code number, indicating the larger block engine (Example P12C)

1929 PLYMOUTH

1929 Plymouth, Model U, two-door sedan, AA

PLYMOUTH — MODEL U — FOUR: An updated version of the Model Q, the 1929 Plymouth Model U went into production in early January. It was the first "Plymouth" model, the "Chrysler" prefix being dropped and was fitted with a derivative engine that had been used in the early four-cylinder Chryslers and the Model Q. Notable changes in this new engine included relocation of the distributor to a vertical position and the moving of the exhaust pipe to the forward side of the engine. Internally the engine was only slightly larger and despite an increase of five cubic inches horsepower remained at 45.

Stylewise the Model U took a sharp eye to discern from its Model Q ancestry. Notable changes included only the word Plymouth on the radi-

ator medallion, two piece rounded bumpers, Twolite headlamps and mushroom shaped hubcaps.

The Model U continued in production into 1930 and was considered at various times by the factory as either a 1929 or 1930 model.

Body parts and most mechanical pieces, with the exception of the engine, were interchangeable between the Model Q and Model U.

Plymouth ended the year in 10th place in the national sales picture.

I.D. DATA: Serial numbers on closed cars: medallion on center of upper dash rail. Open cars: medallion on instrument panel. (Fedco numbering system) Detroit, Michigan, starting: RR-120-P. Ending RD-999-D. Detroit, Michigan, starting: Y-000-WP. Ending: Y-403-EP. Windsor, Ontario, starting: GP-583-W. Ending: GC-499-L. Engine numbers on left front corner of cylinder block. Starting: U-999. Ending: U-110000.

Body No.	Body Type & Seating	Price	Weight	Prod. Total
322	2-dr. Bus. Cpe.-2P	655	N/A	Note 1
328	2-dr. Del. R/S Cpe.-2/4P	695	N/A	—
321	2-dr. Sed.-5P	675	2485	—
320	4-dr. Sed.-5P	695	2510	Note 2
320	4-dr. Del. Sed.-5P	745	2590	Note 2
R	2-dr. R/S Rds.-2/4P	675	N/A	—
T	4-dr. Tr.-5P	695	N/A	—

Note 1: Body style production totals unavailable.

Note 2: Body code number 320 indicates Briggs body; body code number 88 indicates Hayes body on four-door sedans only. 3,999 Us were built with right-hand drive.

1929 Plymouth, Model U, deluxe rumbleseat coupe, HAC

ENGINE: Inline. Valve in block. Four. Cast iron block. B & S: 3-5/8 x 4-1/4 in. Disp.: 175.4 cu. in. C.R.: 4.6:1. Brake H.P.: 45 @ 2800 R.P.M. Taxable/A.L.A.M./N.A.C.C. H.P.: 21.03. Main bearings: three. Valve lifters: solid. Carb.: Carter 103-S (U.S.), 131-S and 121-SA (U.S. built for export); 132-SA all R.H.D.

TECHNICAL: Sliding gear (spur gears) transmission. Speeds: 3F/1R. Floor shift controls. Single plate, dry disc clutch. Driveshaft, with fabric universal discs. Semi-floating rear axle. Overall ratio: 4.3:1. Hydraulic brakes on four wheels. Wood spoke wheels, wire spoke optional. Rim size: 4.75 x 20 up to car #YO76LE, then 4.75 x 19.

CHASSIS: [Series U] W.B.: 109-3/4 in. O.L.: 169 in. Frt/Rear Tread: 56/56 in. Tires: 4.75 x 20/19.

OPTIONS: Front and rear bumper, as a set ($15.00). Heater hot air, under floor type (30.00). Clock eight-day, header board mount, dial wind (12.50). Cigar lighter in combo with utility light (12.00). Upholstery: leather (all closed models) (25.00). Velour (coupe only) (10.00). Broadcloth (two- or four-door sedan) (35.00). Broadcloth (coupe) (20.00). Disc wheels set of five (25.00) (rear mounted spare). Wire wheels, set of five, rear mount only (35.00). Tire covers (1.50). Oakes stud type tire lock (3.50). Spring covers, set of eight (8.00). Trunk rack, folding type available only with sidemounts (12.00). Trunk (20.00). Top boot (10.00). Top bow rests, set of four (2.00). Windshield wind wings (open cars only) (10.00). Monograms, painted, black letters only (10.00). Monograms, sterling silver, applied type, maximum of three (10.00). Special colors: body only (35.00). Special paint on fenders, splash pans, frame horns, rear deck and metal tire carriers (35.00). Special paint, chassis and running gear (20.00). Fender with well (including tires, tire lock and keys). When only one unit is supplied, left side is furnished. One fender well, one tire and tube (25.00). Two fenders w/well, two tires and tubes (50.00). Five disc wheels, spare tire and tube (50.00). Six disc wheels, two spare tires and tubes (75.00). Five wire wheels, tires and tubes (60.00). Six wire wheels, tires and tubes (90.00).

HISTORICAL: Production began January 7, 1929, ended April 5, 1930. Model year production: 108,345. W.P. Chrysler was corporate and division head. A Model U broke the world's endurance record by being driven nonstop for 632 hours and 36 minutes before being voluntarily stopped. During the time the car had covered 11,419 miles and was serviced while "on the go." To meet demand for Plymouths a crash program to build a new factory on Lynch Road in Detroit, was undertaken. Workmen toiled through the dead of winter to complete the structure, while a steam locomotive parked on a spur track provided steam heat to the assembly line workers inside. They were busily building new cars while the building went up around them!

1930 PLYMOUTH

PLYMOUTH — MODEL 30U — FOUR: An updated version of the Model U, the Model 30U went into production in April of 1930 and continued until early in 1931. Most notable of the changes in the 30U was a full width, chrome-plated radiator shell that replaced the "thin-line" shell of the preceding Q and U models. In other external appearances the 30U looked like its brethren but in fact the fenders were of a heavier design and did not interchange with previous models. Also new was an external mounted horn, centered on the headlamp bar. Headlamps were now painted, rather than stainless as had been the previous models.

Mechanically the 30U had a larger engine with an increase of horsepower. Throughout the year many other drivetrain improvements were made in the 30U, including a change to helical cut gears in the transmission, replacement of the fabric universal discs with universal joints, addition of a water pump and a fuel pump to replace the vacuum tank system.

It was during the 30U production year that Walter Chrysler announced that the Plymouth would now be sold by all corporate dealers, not just through Chrysler franchised dealers. It was this move that more than anything else can be credited with Plymouth's spectacular rises in the sales arena, the number of Plymouth dealers jumping from slightly over 3,000 to more than 10,000 dealers. Plymouth ended the year in eighth place but the stage was set for Plymouth's takeover of the number three sales position.

Many 30U sedans were fitted with an oval rear window as production continued, while most of the early models had been fitted with rectangular rear windows. New for the year was the introduction of a convertible coupe in addition to the roadster models, the convertible featuring a fixed windshield post, roll up side glass windows and a rumbleseat. A commercial (sedan) delivery was offered but sales were poor and the model was dropped. The Fedco identification system was dropped and all cars were now assigned a numerical serial number. Beginning with car number 1530245 the 30U was considered a 1931 model.

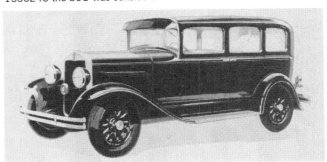

1930 Plymouth, Model 30U, four-door sedan, OCW

I.D. DATA: Serial numbers on right front door post. Detroit, Michigan, starting: 1500001. Ending: 1570188. Windsor, Ontario, starting: 9300001. Ending: 9305327. Engine numbers on left front corner of cylinder block. Starting: U200000. Ending: U277000.

Body No.	Body Type & Seating	Price	Weight	Prod. Total
R	2-dr. Spt. Rds.-2/4P	610	2280	2884
BR	2-dr. Bus. Rds.-2P	535	2245	169
383	2-dr. Bus. Cpe.-2P	590	2420	9189
382	2-dr. R/S Coupe-2/4P	625	2510	5850
T	4-dr. Spt. Phae.-5P	625	2340	632
384	2-dr. Conv.-2/4P	695	2450	1272
380	4-dr. Sedan-5P	625	2595	47,152
381	2-dr. Sedan-5P	565	2497	7980
NA	2-dr. Comm. Sedan-2P	750	N/A	80
NA	Chassis	—	—	302

Note: 1,627 Model 30Us were built with right-hand drive.

ENGINE: Inline. Valve in block. Four. Cast iron block. B & S: 3-5/8 x 4-3/4 in. Disp.: 196.1 cu. in. C.R.: 4.6:1. Brake H.P.: 48 @ 2800 R.P.M. Taxable/A.L.A.M./N.A.C.C. H.P.: 21.03. Main bearings: three. Valve lifters: solid. Carb.: Early production 30U: Carter 130S and 130SA; later production Carter 156-S; 158-S all export, 157-S all R.H.D. Torque (compression) 120 lb.-ft. @ 1200 R.P.M.

TECHNICAL: Sliding gear (early production had spur gears, mid-year change to helical type gears). Speeds: 3F/1R. Floor shift controls. Single disc, dry clutch. Driveshaft with fabric universal discs with a mid-year change to regular u-joints. Semi-floating rear axle. Overall ratio: 4.3:1. Hydraulic brakes on four wheels. Wood spoke wheels, wire spoke optional. Rim size: 4.75 x 19.

CHASSIS: [Series 30U] W.B.: 109-3/4 in. O.L.: 169 in. Frt/Rear Tread: 56-1/4/56-1/8 in. Tires: 4.75 x 19.

1930 Plymouth, Model 30U, convertible coupe, JAC

OPTIONS: Front bumper. Rear bumper. Single sidemount. Dual sidemounts. Clock (clock/mirror) also eight-day pull wind, 24-hour or electric. Cigar lighter. Six-bolt lug pattern wire wheels; five-bolt lug pattern wire wheels; trunk; windwings; gearshift knobs in onyx, french beige or ivory; radiator cap safety chain; Kool Kushion; umbrella and case; windshield defroster; spring covers.

HISTORICAL: Production began April 8, 1930; ended June 8, 1931. Model year production: 76,950. W.P. Chrysler was corporate head; F.L. Rockelman, division head.

1931 PLYMOUTH

1931 Plymouth, Model PA, four-door sedan, AA

PLYMOUTH — MODEL PA — FOUR: The Model PA signaled Plymouth's permanent takeover of the third place in the national new car sales picture, and the coining of the term "The Big Three." The redesigned PA was the result of a 2-1/2 million dollar investment by Chrysler Corporation. If nothing else can be said of Walter Chrysler, it must be said that he showed no fear to the face of the Great Depression. Offering more car for less money, the PA took the showrooms by storm as people lined up to buy this new model. Drawing much attention was the new "Floating Power" engine mountings - a unique system of mounting the engine in rubber and suspending the engine along its own center of gravity. Although still of four cylinders, the engine rocked in the chassis but the rubber mountings absorbed any shock resulting in a smoother ride to the passengers. Battling Chevy's six-cylinder engine and Ford's planned V-8, the car was touted as having the "Smoothness of a Six and the Economy of a Four!" With the first really all new design since its inception, the new Plymouth was quite handsome in appearance with its gently rounded radiator shell, bowl-shaped headlamps and oval rear windows. Offered with a full line of optional equipment the car found many ready buyers and with its heritage based on the DeSoto and Chrysler Sixes, many buyers who could not afford those models readily snapped up the new Plymouth.

The PA was the first Plymouth to have a built in radiator grille and each radiator cap was adorned with an attractive "short bodied" Flying Lady, and all 1931 enclosed models were factory wired with a radio antennae. The PA was also the last model to have been designated during two separate model years as both a 1931 and 1932 model, with future models all taking on certain year designations regardless of when they were built.

I.D. DATA: Serial numbers on right front door post. Detroit, Michigan, starting: 1570301. Ending: 1667963. Windsor, Ontario, starting: 9305401. Ending: 9307933. Detroit, Michigan, starting: 1668000. Ending: 1668001 (one car built PA Special Deluxe). Detroit, Michigan, starting: 1669001. Ending: 1669644 (PA Thrift). Detroit, Michigan, starting: 1670001. Ending: 1674250 (PA Thrift). Engine number location: left front corner of cylinder block. Starting: PA-1001. Ending: PA-107093.

Body No.	Body Type & Seating	Price	Weight	Prod. Total
480	4-dr. Thrift Sed.-5P	575	2655	Note 1
481	2-dr. Thrift Sed.-5P	495	2690	Note 1
T	4-dr. Phae.-5P	595	2545	528
BR	2-dr. Bus. Rds.-2P	535	2440	200
R	2-dr. Spt. Rds.-2/4P	595	2470	2680
483	2-dr. Std. Cpe.-2P	565	2600	12,079
482	2-dr. R/S Cpe.-2/4P	610	2645	9696
484	2-dr. Conv.-2/4P	645	2615	2783
480	4-dr. Sedan.-5P	635	2730	49,465
481	2 dr. Sed.-5P	575	2650	23,038
485	4-dr. Del. Sed.-5P	690	2795	4384
NA	4-dr. Taxi-5P	N/A	N/A	112
	Chassis	—	—	131

Note 1: PA Thrift models. Sources list 4,892 of both body types built but serial numbers assigned would indicate 4,894 built. 1,479 PAs and six PA Thrifts were built with right-hand drive.

1931 Plymouth, Model PA, two-door sedan, JAC

ENGINE: Inline. Valve in block. Four. Cast iron block. 3-5/8 x 4-3/4 in. Disp.: 196.1 cu. in. C.R.: 4.9:1. Brake H.P.: 56 @ 2800 R.P.M. Taxable/A.L.A.M./N.A.C.C. H.P.: 21.03. Main bearings: three. Valve lifters: solid. Carb.: Carter D-290S. Torque: 130 lb.-ft. @ 1600 R.P.M. Small bore export engines had a bore of 3-1/8 in. Only 85 PA and four PA Thrift cars were shipped with this engine.

TECHNICAL: Sliding gear transmission. Speeds: 3F/1R. Floor shift controls. Single disc, dry 8-7/8 in. clutch. Driveshaft. Semi-floating, spiral bevel rear axle. Overall ratio: 4.3:1. Hydraulic brakes on four wheels. Wire or wood spoke wheels. (PA Thrift first series had wood spoke, second series wire). Rim size: 4.75 x 19.

CHASSIS: [Series PA] W.B.: 109 in. O.L.: 169-3/4 in. Frt/Rear Tread: 56-1/4/56-1/8 in. Tires: 4.75 x 19.

OPTIONS: Front and rear bumper, as set ($15.00). Single sidemount w/five wire wheels or four wood, spare rim and tire lock (10.00), w/six wire wheels, two tire locks (30.00). Dual sidemount w/two spare rims for wood wheels, two locks (22.00). Radio Philco Transitone (99.80). Clock eight-day, header board mount (5.00). Cigar lighter in combination w/utility lamp (3.50). Cowl lamps including cowl molding, all chrome $7.50 factory installed option only. Special body colors (30.00). Special color, fenders and sheet metal (10.00). Leather upholstery, sedan (18.50), coupe (5.00). Trunk rack (sidemount cars) (10.00). Trunk (30.00). Top boot, roadster and phaeton (6.00). Convertible coupe (8.00). Tire covers (fabric) (1.50). Metal tire cover (10.50). Tire locks (3.50). Chrome headlamps and taillamp (5.00). Chrome radiator grille (5.00). Chrome radiator louvers (5.00). Spring covers (8.00). Windwings, open cars, non-shatterable glass (12.00). Plain glass (9.00). Flying lady radiator cap, safety glass, windshield only (5.00). All windows, sedan (30.00). All windows, coupe (20.00). On special order the running gear would be painted the fender color except for the engine. PA Thrift models: Only had three dash gauges, painted radiator shell and headlamps. Early models were only equipped with wood wheels, later ones with wire wheels.

HISTORICAL: Production began May 1, 1931; ended July 13, 1932 (see note 2). Model year production: 106,896. W.P. Chrysler, corporate head; F.L. Rockelman, division head. Overseas assembly plants were opened in England, Denmark and Sweden for final assembly of SKD or CKD (semi or completely knocked down) vehicles.

Note 2: PA Thrift production began January 1, 1932, and ended September 23, 1932. A 1931 PA four-door sedan, which had been picked at random from the Detroit assembly line, was shipped to San Francisco where it was fitted with an extra gas tank in the rear seat and a third spare tire in addition to twin fender-mounted spares. Driven by 57-year-old Louis B. Miller and co-driver Louis Pribek the car was driven from San Francisco to New York City and return in a time of 5 days, 12 hours, and 9 minutes, breaking the previous round trip speed record by 9-1/2 hours. Covering 6,287 miles they averaged 47.52 miles an hour for the trip. They were to have been greeted in New York City by Walter Chrysler himself but they were so far ahead of schedule that after an hour and a quarter's time spent servicing the car, they headed westward, without meeting Mr. Chrysler, to establish their record. They also bettered the time of "Cannonball" Baker, driving a Franklin, over the shorter Los Angeles to New York course.

1932 PLYMOUTH

1932 Plymouth, Model PB, coupe, AA

PLYMOUTH NEW FINER — MODEL PB — FOUR: Although the model PB saw one of Plymouth's shortest production years, it was without doubt Plymouth's zenith of four-cylinder car production and is the most "collectable" of all the four-cylinder models today. The model PB also has the distinction of being the first Plymouth model to have been assigned a model year classification by the Corporation; the PB was a 1932 model.

Armed with a vast array of body styles including five open models (business roadster, sport roadster, convertible coupe, convertible sedan and phaeton) and beautifully proportioned styling, the PB looked much ritzier than any four-cylinder automobile - and improvements in the engine, as well as an optional high compression cylinder head, gave the car sparkling performance.

1932 Plymouth, Model PB, four-door sedan, JAC

Style wise, the PB featured Plymouth's first one-piece front fenders, free standing, chrome-plated headlamps and on many models, chrome external trumpet horns mounted beneath the lamps. The hood stretched from the radiator shell (which itself was chrome-plated) over the cowl to the

windshield giving the illusion of a much longer car. Breaking the expanse of the hood were twin cowl ventilators mounted on either side of the hood centerline. Wire wheels and standard (on some models) twin fender mounted spare tires added to the attractive look of the new cars. An extended wheelbase also added much to the "big car" illusion of the PB and was, in fact, a move made to facilitate the installation of a six-cylinder engine in the chassis - a move that came late in 1932 with the succeeding model PC.

The PB was the first and only year for the two-door convertible sedan body style and it was also the last year that Plymouth offered a roadster body style. Sensing the public's rejection of drafty open cars, the PB was also the last year for a phaeton (touring car) body style as well. Those few that were built were all five-passenger models although extant photos show at least one prototype seven-passenger touring. The PB was Plymouth's last four-cylinder automobile until 1971.

In addition to the PB line, leftover PA models were sold as the PA Thrift model. These cars, available only as two- or four-door sedans, were made from a hodgepodge of leftover parts and were discontinued as supplies were used up.

I.D. DATA: Serial numbers on right front door post. Detroit, Michigan, starting: 1680001. Ending: 1758001. Windsor, Ontario, starting: 9307951. Ending: 9310965. Engine numbers on left front corner of cylinder block. Starting: PB-1001. Ending: PB-82450.

Body No.	Body Type & Seating	Price	Weight	Prod. Total
BR	2-dr. Bus. Rds.-2P	495	2545	325
RS	2-dr. Spt. Rds.-2/4P	595	2595	2163
T	4-dr. Phae.-5P	595	2655	259
532	2-dr. R/S Cpe.-2/4P	610	2750	8159
533	2-dr. Bus. Cpe.-2P	565	2695	11,126
531	2-dr. Sed.-5P	575	2825	13,031
530	4-dr. Sed.-5P	635	2870	38,066
534	2-dr. Conv.-2/4P	645	2730	4853
536	2-dr. Conv. Sed.-5P	785	2920	690
537	4-dr. Sed.-7P	725	3075	2179
NA	Chassis	—	—	159

Note: 928 PBs were built with right-hand drive.

ENGINE: Inline. Valve in block. Four. Cast iron block. B & S: 3-5/8 x 4-3/4 in. Disp.: 196.1 cu. in. C.R.: 4.9:1. Brake H.P.: 65 @ 3400 R.P.M. Taxable/A.L.A.M./N.A.C.C. H.P.: 21.03. Main bearings: three. Valve lifters: solid. Carb.: Carter 4A2 or 4A3. Torque: 136 lb.-ft. @ 1600 R.P.M. With optional high-compression cylinder head the compression ratio was 5.6:1. Small bore export engines had a bore of 3-7/64 in. but only 58 cars were shipped with this engine.

TECHNICAL: Sliding gear transmission. Speeds: 3F/1R. Floor shift. Single plate, dry disc clutch, Driveshaft. Semi-floating, spiral bevel rear axle. Overall ratio: 4.3:1. Hydraulic brakes on four wheels. Wire spoke wheels. Rim size: 4.75 x 19. Freewheeling standard.

CHASSIS: [Series PB] W.B.: 112 in. (seven-passenger 121 in.) O.L.: 175-1/32 in. (seven-passenger 184-1/32 in.) Frt/Rear Tread: 57-5/16/ 56-15/16 in. Tires: 5.25 x 18 in.

1932 Plymouth, Model PB, sport roadster, JAC

OPTIONS: Front and rear bumper as package ($15.00). Single sidemount. Dual sidemounts. Philco radio (69.50). Heater, several types offered, hot water and exhaust type. Clock. Cigar lighter (3.50). Automatic clutch (8.00). Leather upholstery (coupes) (8.00); (sedans) (18.50). Trunk rack (only for cars with sidemounts) (11.00). Front opening trunks (sedans only) (40.00). Suitcase set (45.00). Top boot for roadster or phaeton (6.00). Top boot for convertible coupe or convertible sedan (8.00). Fabric tire cover (1.50). Metal tire cover (9.00). Tire lock for rear mount (1.50). Twin chrome taillamps (6.00). External trumpet horns (10.00). "Red Head" cylinder head and decarbonizer (5.00). Right-hand windshield wiper (4.50). Chrome plated radiator louvers (5.00). Fabric spring covers (8.00). Windshield side wings for open cars, with safety glass (12.00 pair); same, with plate glass (9.00). Duplate safety glass for roadster (3.00). Phaeton (4.00). Closed cars (windshield only) (3.50). Closed cars (all windows) (17.50). Convertible sedan (14.50). Coupe (all windows) (9.50). 5.50 x 17 in. wire wheels (set of five) (10.00). Clocks:

eight-day, header board mount (8.00). Clock/mirror (10.00). Instrument panel mount (8.00). Instrument panel mount, electric (15.00).

HISTORICAL: Production began February 4, 1932; ended September 27, 1932. Public announcements date was April 3, 1932. Model year production: 83,910. W.P. Chrysler was corporate head. F.L. Rockelman, division head who was replaced by B.E. Hutchinson during the year. For $40 extra, Plymouth offered the Collegiate Special Roadster. The only distinguishing feature of the car was that for the extra money, the buyer got a car painted in his school colors, regardless of what that combination may have been. It was not noted how many cars were sold as such.

1933 PLYMOUTH

PLYMOUTH — MODEL PC — SIX: After spending $9 million in research and development, Chrysler Corporation unveiled its first six-cylinder Plymouth before the end of 1932. Considered a 1933 model the new model PC was completely redesigned but despite its low price (as low as $495, the same as the previous four-cylinder PB model) and the addition of two extra cylinders, the car met with heavy dealer and customer sales resistance. With its short wheelbase, slanted, chrome-plated radiator shell, and design of hood and louver slope that did not "synch" with the cut of the forward opening doors, the car took on a decidedly awkward appearance. To many people, the new six-cylinder car looked more like a four-cylinder car than had the four cylinder PB of the previous year!

Realizing their predicament Plymouth engineers put a crash program into gear to market a restyled car before the spring selling season. The result was the Deluxe model PD Plymouth; the PC was dropped altogether from production. In its place was the model PCXX, a car restyled to look much like the new PD.

The PC was distinguished by its short wheelbase, (which was increased by one inch early in production to accommodate fender mounted spare tires), chromed radiator shell with bolted-in-place Flying Lady ornament and painted headlamp shells in the shape of a bowl. On the interior the instruments were placed in an engine turned panel in the center of the dash, but the car lacked a temperature gauge.

The new six-cylinder engine, at 189 cubic inches was actually smaller internally than the four-cylinder that it replaced but developed five more horsepower and an optional high compression cylinder head added another six horsepower. The basic six-cylinder engine would remain in Plymouth production until the end of the 1959 model year - and into the 1960s in Dodge trucks!

1933 Plymouth, Model PD, convertible, OCW

PLYMOUTH STANDARD — MODEL PCXX — SIX: Replacing the PC model in mid-year, the PCXX was styled to closely match its PD big brother. The radiator shell now sat more upright, with a painted shell, removable external radiator cap (usually in the form of a Flying Lady) and large, painted, bowl-shaped headlamps. Various other differences between the PC and the PCXX were made, a fact that today can drive a 1933 Plymouth restorer up the wall in attempting to obtain correct parts for his car.

The PCXX was offered in a full range of body styles with the exception of a convertible coupe that was relegated to the Deluxe line only. Prices of the PCXX were lowered (to $445 for the business coupe) and sales were about equal to that of the PC that it replaced.

PLYMOUTH DELUXE — MODEL PD — SIX: When it became apparent to Chrysler personnel that the new six-cylinder PC was not being well received a crash program was put into effect to bring out a significantly restyled car before the spring selling season. To accomplish the task, Plymouth engineers took a Dodge Model DP frame, modified the wheel-

base slightly and, maintaining the basic body structure, proceeded to design a new front end for the car. By juggling hood panels, front fenders, runningboards and splash aprons the engineers could build a "new" car without excessive expense in redesigning a new body.

Built on a 112-inch wheelbase and with an additional four inches in overall length, the PD corrected all the "wrongs" of the original PC design. The painted radiator shell housed either a chrome-plated or painted grille, while the hood stretched back over the cowling to the windshield. The trailing edge of the hood, along with the hood louvers, now slanted on the same angle as did the leading edge of the forward opening doors. Chrome-plated, bullet-shaped headlamps added much to the looks of the car. Wood or wire wheels and long, flowing fenders also helped to alleviate the "stubby" look of the PC. A free flowing, long body "Flying Lady" radiator cap accented the front end of the car and many were fitted with the optional chrome-plated externally mounted trumpet horns beneath the headlamps.

The redesigned car remained mechanically the same as the previous PC and PCXX. With prices starting as low as $495, sales of the new car skyrocketed setting a new production record for Plymouth and placing the car solidly in third place in national car sales.

1933 Plymouth, Model PD, convertible coupe, JAC

I.D. DATA: [Model PC] Serial numbers on right front door post. Detroit, Michigan, starting: 1759001. Ending: 1817044. Los Angeles, California, starting: 3000001. Ending: 3000604. Windsor, Ontario, starting: 9311001. Ending: 9313273. Engine number location: Left front corner of cylinder block. Starting: PC-1001. Ending: PC-60979. [Model PCXX] Serial numbers on right front door post. Detroit, Michigan, starting: 1817101. Ending: 1858419. Los Angeles, California, starting: 3000610. Ending: 3001395. Windsor, Ontario, starting: 9315001. Ending: 9315375. Engine numbers in left front corner of cylinder block. Starting: PC75001. Ending: P118731. Plymouth also used the single letter "X" in its engine code numbers to designate a small bore, export engine. This practice was continued throughout the years of production. [Model PD] Serial numbers on right front door post. Detroit, Michigan, starting: 2000001. Ending: 2186951. Los Angeles, California, starting: 3002501. Ending: 3007678. Windsor, Ontario, starting: 9320001. Ending: 9321902. Windsor, Ontario, starting: 9395001. Ending: 9396071. Engine numbers on left front corner of cylinder block. Starting: PD-1001. Ending: PD-195997.

Body Code	Body Type & Seating	Price	Weight	Prod. Total
Plymouth PC				
BC	2-dr. Bus. Cpe.-2P	495	2418	10,853
TPC	2-dr. RS Cpe.-2/4P	545	2473	8894
585	2-dr. Sed.-5P	505	2498	4008
588	4-dr. Sed.-5P	575	2553	33,815
CC	2-dr. Conv. Cpe.-2/4P	595	2483	2034
NA	Chassis	—	—	396
Plymouth PCXX				
BC	2-dr. Bus. Cpe.-2P	445	2353	9200
TPC	2-dr. RS Cpe.-2/4P	485	2497	2497
588	4-dr. Sed.-5P	510	2523	13,661
585	2-dr. Sed.-5P	465	2443	17,736
NA	Chassis	—	—	309
Plymouth PD				
TPC	2-dr. RS Cpe.-2/4P	545	2545	20,821
BC	2-dr. Bus. Cpe.-2P	495	2485	30,728
588	4-dr. Sed.-5P	575	2645	88,404
585	2-dr. Sed.-5P	525	2560	49,826
CC	2-dr. Conv. Cpe.-2/4P	595	2530	4596
NA	Chassis	—	—	779

Note: 1,283 PCs, 625 PCXXs and 1,517 PDs were built with right-hand drive.

ENGINE: Inline. Valve in block. Six. Cast iron block. B & S: 3-1/8 x 4-1/8 in. Disp.: 189.8 cu. in. C.R.: 5.5:1. Brake H.P.: 70 @ 3600 R.P.M. Taxable/A.L.A.M./N.A.C.C. H.P.: 23.44. Main bearings: four. Valve lift-

ers: solid. Carb.: Carter C6A, C6A2, C6A3 or C6A4. Torque (compression): 130 lb.-ft. @ 1200 R.P.M. Optional "Redhead" high compression cylinder head; later replaced by high compression aluminum cylinder head. Small bore export engines had a bore of 2-7/8 in.; 437 PCs, 21 PCXXs and 193 PDs were shipped with this engine.

1933 Plymouth, Model PC, two-door, JAC

TECHNICAL: [Plymouth PC] Sliding gear transmission. Speeds: 3F/1R. Floor shift controls. Single plate, dry clutch. Driveshaft. Semi-floating rear axle. Overall ratio: 4.375:1. Hydraulic brakes on four wheels. Wire or wood spoke wheels. Rim size: 5.25 x 17. [Plymouth PCXX] Sliding gear transmission. Speeds: 3F/1R. Floor shift controls. Single disc, dry clutch. Driveshaft. Semi-floating rear axle. Overall ratio: 4.1:1. Hydraulic brakes on four wheels. Wire or wood spoke wheels. Rim size: 5.25 x 17. [Plymouth PD] Sliding gear transmission. Speeds: 3F/1R. Floor shift controls. Single disc, dry clutch. Driveshaft. Semi-floating rear axle. Overall ratio: 4.375:1. Hydraulic brakes on four wheels. Wire wheels, wood spoke optional. Rim size: 6.00 x 16/5.25 x 17. Vacuum clutch optional. Freewheeling standard.

CHASSIS: [Series PC] (Includes PCXX) W.B.: 107/108 in. (change early in production). O.L.: 174 in. Frt/Rear Tread: 56-1/4/56-1/4 in. Tires: 5.25 x 17. [Series PD] W.B.: 112 in. O.L.: 178-1/2 in. Frt/Rear Tread: 56/56-1/4 in. Tires: 5.25 x 17/6.00 x 16.

OPTIONS: Bumper optional as set ($15.00). Philco Transitone No. 5 radio (factory installed) (39.95). Radio antenna. Special paint, body (30.00). Special paint, fenders and sheetmetal (10.00). Automatic clutch (PD only) (8.00). Flying lady radiator ornament (2.50). Rubber mat for rear compartment of business coupe (1.50). Spare wheel lock (1.20). Thermostat (PC models) (1.50). Black enamel rear tire cover (1.00). Metal spare tire cover with emblem (5.00). Trunk rack (only for cars with sidemounts) (7.50). 16 in. wire "Airwheels", set of five with four tires and tubes (20.00) (PD Only) 16 in. wood ("Airwheels") with five wheels and four tires and tubes, PC or PD (20.06). Duplate safety glass. Dual rear mounted spare tires (12.00). Metal "form fit" trunk for sedans. 20 in. high clearance wheels. Accessory Group A for PD ($15.00); Same for PC ($17.00) included: dual horns, auxiliary windshield wiper, cigar lighter, dual taillamps on PD. Also included chrome headlamps and taillamp on PC. Antenna prices: all PC models without radio (5.00). with radio (1.00). For PD convertible coupe w/o radio (10.00). Antenna for convertible with radio, no charge. Single Sidemount (right fender only) available only on business coupe, either PC or PD: PC or PD with five 17 in. wire wheels (7.00). PC with five 17 in. painted wood wheels not available. PD with five 17 in. painted wood wheels (7.00). PD with five 16 in. wire "Airwheels" (27.00). PD with 5 16" wood "Airwheels" (27.00). PC with five 16 in. wood "Airwheels" (27.00). Two Sidemount Fenders PC or PD with six 17 in. wire wheels (15.00). PD with six 17 in. painted demountable wood wheels (15.00). PD with six 16 in. wire "Airwheels" (35.00). PC or PD with six 16 in. wood "Airwheels" (35.00). Note on sidemount fenders: early production PC models with the 107 in. wheelbase could not be fitted with sidemount fenders. Early in production the wheelbase on these cars was stretched to 108 in. to accommodate fender mount spare tires.

HISTORICAL: Plymouth PC production began November 11, 1932; ended April 7, 1933. Model year production: 60,000. Plymouth PCXX production began April 14, 1933, ended December 5, 1933. Model year production: 43,403. Plymouth PD production began March 17, 1933; ended January 27, 1934. Model year production: 195,154. W.P. Chrysler, corporate head; B.E. Hutchinson, division head.

Miss Irma Brandt became the first woman to compete in the Monte Carlo Rally driving a 1933 PC Plymouth coach in the 1934 Rally. She won her division, driving the car from Norway to Monte Carlo. The car remained in Miss Brandt's possession at her farm near Oslo, Norway. During the German occupation of Norway in World War II it was common practice for people to strip the wheels, tires or vital engine parts from their vehicles to keep the Nazi soldiers from confiscating the vehicle. Miss Brandt did likewise and the car has remained in her possession. The car was completely restored in 1984. Miss Brandt later drove a 1934 PE Plymouth to a second place finish in the 1935 running of the Monte Carlo Rally.

1934 PLYMOUTH

1934 Plymouth, Model PE, four-door sedan, AA

PLYMOUTH DELUXE — MODEL PE — SIX: The Deluxe Plymouth for 1934 perhaps reached an all-time high for Plymouth in the looks and equipment department. With a larger engine than the previous year (now at 201 cubic inches and 77 hp) the Deluxe Plymouth featured independent coil spring front suspension, an industry first in the low-price field. With a longer wheelbase, skirted fenders, a radiator cap located under the hood, and a special hood that featured not only rows of louvers but twin opening ventilating doors on either side, the PE Plymouth found itself in ready demand - so much so that before the year was over, the 1934 had surpassed the production record set in 1933 and had also seen the one millionth Plymouth built in August, a car that was driven off the line by Walter Chrysler himself. It had taken Plymouth only six years to build its first million cars - it had taken Henry Ford 12 years to reach that mark and Chevrolet nine years!

First offered in this year was the first factory available wooden bodied station wagon (the bodies were built by U.S. Body & Forging at a plant in Tell City, Indiana) and a close-coupled town sedan that featured a built-on metal trunk at the rear of the body. Although the official announcement date of the 1934 models was January 13, the cars were shown one week early to take advantage of the New York Automobile Show, which opened on January 6th. By the end of January production had reached 1,500 cars per day. Early PEs were equipped with a host of special equipment including freewheeling transmission and automatic vacuum controlled clutch, but this piece of equipment was made optional later in the model year.

Unique to the PE was a ventilating wind wing built into the front door window system. In normal operation the wind wing could be swung out via a crank handle and the side window rolled down in normal fashion. By closing both the wind wing and the side window, then locking them in place by throwing a lever, the entire system could be rolled down as one unit into the door for a completely unobstructed opening. The plant these cars were built in, located on Detroit's Lynch Road, was the largest automobile factory under one roof in the world.

PLYMOUTH SIX — MODEL PF — SIX: Introduced at the same time as the Deluxe PE, the PF was a lower priced, shorter wheelbased (by four inches) automobile. Closely resembling its bigger brother, the PF lacked the ventilating doors on the hood but retained the newly introduced independent front suspension system. Also missing was the combination vent window system and there was no provision for a glove compartment or ash receiver on the dash. In addition, the instrument gauges had white numerals on a black background rather than the gold type panel used on the Deluxe model.

The PF consisted of the entire range of body styles except for the convertible coupe, station wagon or the town sedan that was introduced in mid-year.

PLYMOUTH SPECIAL SIX — MODEL PFXX — SIX: Introduced in May for the spring selling season, the PF Special Six (better known as a PFXX) was a slightly higher priced car than its predecessor PF. Fitted with appointments such as a glove compartment, ash receiver (which could be replaced by the remote control head for a radio) and Accessory Group C that included such items as a Valchrome grille, dual externally mounted trumpet horns and twin taillamps, the PFXX was priced within $5 of the Ford Deluxe V-8. Whereas the original PF has been mostly equipped with wire wheels, the PFXX was fitted with the steel artillery wheels like the PE (wires were still optional if the purchaser desired them) with earlier cars carrying 17 in. wheels that were later changed to 16 in. like the Deluxe PE.

Although not considered by the factory as a separate sales line, production of the series nearly equalled that of the PF line. With the mid-year introduction of the town sedan, a model was offered on the PFXX chassis but only 574 were built.

Throughout the 1934 year, Plymouth juggled prices between its lines and at one point was forced by the government to reduce its prices after an announced price hike. PF prices did escalate after the introduction of the PG series, which took over the PF original price slots.

PLYMOUTH STANDARD SIX — MODEL PG — SIX: Introduced in March, three months after the PE and PF showings, the PG became the Plymouth business line. Offered in only two body styles, a coupe and a tudor (a handful of four-door sedans were built but were not cataloged) the PG had the same 108-inch wheelbase as its PF sister, but had a drop-forged I-beam front axle rather than independent front suspension like the PE and PF models. As the price leader, the PG's austerity was evident in its lack of trim that included no glove compartment, ash receiver or mechanical equipment such as that found on the other 1934 models. It was not possible to even order such equipment as freewheeling or automatic vacuum clutch even though they would have easily fit the car. As a cheap car for business people, the car was ideal and such options as a split front seat on the coupe allowed salesman to reach their samples in the trunk simply by folding the passenger seat forward. For those requiring extra road clearance oversize wheels and tires were offered. Despite its low cost, the PG line saw the least production of any models.

1934 Plymouth, Model PE, coupe, JAC

I.D. DATA: Plymouth PE Serial numbers on right front door post. Detroit, Michigan, starting: 2188001. Ending: 2397536. Los Angeles, California, starting: 3007701. Ending: 3019347. Windsor, Ontario, starting: 9321911. Ending: 9326544. Engine numbers on left front corner of cylinder block. Starting: PE-1001, all PE series engines began with prefix PE. Ending: PE-230836. Plymouth PF serial numbers on right front door post. Detroit, Michigan, starting: 1859001. Ending: 1894740. Los Angeles, California, starting: 3100001. Ending: 3101358. Windsor, Ontario, starting: 9315376. Ending: 9316221. Engine numbers on left front corner of cylinder block. Starting: PF-1001, all PF series engines began with prefix PF. Ending: PF-7232. Plymouth PFXX Serial number on right front door post. Detroit, Michigan, starting: 1909001. Ending: 1941945. Los Angeles, California, starting: 3092001. Ending: 3094353. Engine numbers on left front corner of cylinder block. All began with prefix PF. Starting: PF-41059. Ending: PF-96379. Plymouth PG Serial numbers on right front door post. Detroit, Michigan, starting: 10200001. Ending: 1039039. Los Angeles, California, starting: 3150001. Ending: 3151472. Engine numbers on left front corner of cylinder block. Starting: PF-7232. All PG series cars used PF series engines. Ending: PF-41049.

Body Code	Body Type & Seating	Price	Weight	Prod. Total
Plymouth PE				
BC	2-dr. Bus. Cpe.-2P	595	2668	28,433
TPC	2-dr. RS Cpe.-2/4P	630	2733	15,658
CC	2-dr. Conv. Cpe.-2/4P	685	2698	4,482
600	4-dr. Sed.-5P	660	2848	108,407
641	2-dr. Sed.-5P	610	2773	58,535
601	4-dr. Twn. Sed.-5P	695	2898	7,049
602	4-dr. Sed.-7P	1075	NA	891
NA	4-dr. Westchester Sub.-7/8P	820	NA	35
NA	Chassis	NA	NA	2,362

Note: Seven-passenger sedan price for 602 shown in 1934 Canadian dollars as most, if not all, of these were built in Canada.

Body Code	Body Type & Seating	Price	Weight	Prod. Total
Plymouth PF				
BC	2-dr. Bus. Cpe.-2P	540	2513	6,980
TPC	2-dr. RS Cpe.-2/4P	570	2573	2,061
NA	2-dr. Sed.-5P	560	2603	12,562
609	4-dr. Sed.-5P	600	2693	16,789
NA	Chassis	NA	NA	1,152

Body Code	Body Type & Seating	Price	Weight	Prod. Total
Plymouth PFXX				
BC	2-dr. Bus. Cpe.-2P	560	2563	3,721
TPC	2-dr. RS Cpe.-2/4P	590	2600	1,746
NA	2-dr. Sed.-5P	580	2658	12,497
604	4-dr. Sed.-5P	620	2708	16,760

Body Code	Body Type & Seating	Price	Weight	Prod. Total
NA	4-dr. Town Sed.-5P	655	2783	574
NA	Chassis	—	—	
Plymouth PG				
BC	2-dr. Bus. Cpe.-2P	485	2438	7,844
644	2-dr. Sed.-5P	510	2538	12,603
NA	4-dr. Sed.-5P	NA	NA	62
NA	Chassis	NA	NA	3

Engine specifications same for all PF and PE series. 6,682 PEs and 3,422 PFs were built with right-hand drive, no PGs were so built.

ENGINE: Inline. Valve in block. Six. Cast iron block. B & S: 3-1/8 x 4-3/8 in. Disp.: 201.3 cu. in. C.R.: 5.8:1. Brake H.P.: 77 @ 3600 R.P.M. Taxable/A.L.A.M./N.A.C.C. H.P.: 23.44. Main bearings: four. Valve lifters: solid. Carb.: Carter B & B C6B. Torque (compression) 140 lb.-ft. @ 1200 R.P.M. Optional aluminum high compression cylinder head. C.R.: 6.5:1. Brake H.P.: 82 @ 3600 R.P.M.

Note: Cars built for export were equipped with 170.4 cu. in. engine, 2-7/8 in. bore x 4-3/8 in. stroke. Engines were identified by engine number code PEX or PFX. 1,196 PEs and 333 PFs were equipped with this small-bore engine.

CHASSIS: [Series PE] 1934 W.B.: 114 in. (124 in. seven-passenger) O.L.: 181-5/16 in. coupe and convertible; 187-3/8 in. sedans. Frt/Rear Tread: 56-1/2/56-1/4 in. Tires: 6.00 x 16. [Series PF & PFXX] 1934 W.B.: 108 in. O.L.: 181-7/16 in. sedan; 176 in. coupes. Frt/Rear Tread: 56-1/8/56-3/8 in. Tires: 5.25 x 17/6.00 x 16. [Series PG] 1934 W.B.: 108 in. O.L.: 181-7/16 in. sedan; 176 in. coupe. Frt/Rear Tread: 56-1/8/56-3/8 in. Tires: 5/25 x 17.

1934 Plymouth, Model PG, coupe, AA

TECHNICAL: Sliding gear transmission. Speeds: 3F/1R. Floor shift controls. Single disc, dry nine inch clutch. Driveshaft. Semi-floating rear axle. Overall ratio: 4.375:1 sedans, 4.11:1 coupes. Hydraulic brakes on four wheels. Wire spoke or steel artillery wheels. Rim size: 6.00 x 16 in. (four in. rim) on PE and PFXX, 5.25 x 17 in. (three in. rim) on PF and PG. Freewheeling is standard on PE only.

Note: Although the vacuum clutch was an $8 option it was installed on all PE models produced through February production; from that point on the dealer had to specify its installation. It was not available on PF or PG models.

OPTIONS: Bumpers were still optional on all models in 1934. The complete bumper package, which includes front and rear bumper plates, spare tires and tube cost $22 on the PE series; $21 on PF and PG series. Single sidemount, all models 15.00 except town sedan (10.00); dual sidemounts PF-PG 40.00, PE 42.50, PE town sedan 37.50, PFXX town sedan 35.00. Sidemount covers). Fender skirts (9.00 pair). Bumper guards (3.00 for set of four). Radio in dash mount Philco Transitione (PE & PFXX) (55.00 Deluxe) (42.50 Standard). Heater: Several choices offered, all hot water type. Clock: Elgin eight-day dash clock (7.50). Waltham eight-day headerboard (12.50). Clock mirror (12.50). Cigar lighter (1.25). Radio antenna PE & PFXX factory wired, utilizing "chicken wire" fabric roof support (1.00 optional on PF & PG models). Seat covers: Several types offered including driver only "Keel Kushion." External sun shade. Spotlight (20.00). Form fit metal trunk for two-and four-door sedans (35.00). Fitted luggage (18.00). Hat box (6.50). Metal spare tire cover (std. on PE) (6.50). Right-hand taillamp (3.50). Klaxon K-26-M external mount dual horns (9.00). Right-hand windshield wiper (4.95). Wheel trim rings (6.75 for set of five). License plate frames (2.50 pair). Right-hand interior sunvisor (2.00). Locking gas cap (1.50). Automatic choke (5.25). Casco defroster (3.00). High compression aluminum cylinder head (5.00). Vacuum clutch (PE only) (8.00). Split front seat on coupe (for access to rear compartment without leaving vehicle) (5.00). "Mayflower" sailing ship ornament (3.50). Vent wings for PF or PG (7.50). Rear spring covers (3.50). Mohair upholstery (5.00). (Mohair was made optional at no extra cost later in the production year). 20 in. high clearance wheels. PE Accessory Group sold for $15 and included dual external horns, Right-hand taillamp, right-hand windshield wiper and cigar lighter. PF Accessory Group sold for $20 and included dual external horns, right-hand taillamp, right-hand windshield wiper, cigar lighter, chrome head-

lamps and a chrome grille. Note on PE grilles: At the start of production grilles on PE series were chrome-plated; around February the grilles were painted fender color; later in the year they received a treatment called Valchrome that gave a satiny "chrome" finish. During the painted grille period chrome grilles could be had for $17.50 extra, but this option was dropped when Valchrome use began.

1934 Plymouth, Model PF, four-door sedan, JAC

HISTORICAL: Plymouth PE production began December 19, 1933; ended September 28, 1934. Public announcement date for PE and PF models was January 13, 1934. Model year production: 225,817.

The one millionth Plymouth was built in August and was driven off the Detroit assembly line by Walter P. Chrysler himself. The car was then sold to Mrs. Ethel Miller of Turlock, California. Mrs. Miller had been the purchaser of the first Plymouth ever sold in 1928 and traded that car in on the one millionth Plymouth. The 1928 was subsequently put on display at the Chicago World's Fair.

A PE Plymouth placed second in the large car division of the 1935 Monte Carlo Rallye, driven by two women. Miss Irma-Darre Brandt and Miss Lena Christinsen. Another 1934 Plymouth won the 400 mile Durban to Johannesburg (South Africa) speed-endurance test, setting a new record over the course.

1935 PLYMOUTH

1935 Plymouth, Model PJ, station wagon, AA

PLYMOUTH DELUXE — MODEL PJ — SIX: The PJ was a completely new, from the frame up, automobile and marked Plymouth's styling change from "square" to "round". Starting with a heavier, X-braced frame, the new body was bolted to the frame both vertically and horizontally at 46 different points! This was called Unit Frame & Body Construction, making the frame an integral part of the body structure and the body an equal integral part of the frame.

The entire body, from the front fenders, to the radiator shell, to the rear of the body, now featured a gentle, more rounded styling, taking on a semblance of aerodynamics, and influenced, no doubt, by the Corporation's Airflow DeSoto and Chryslers.

Mechanically, the engine received a great deal of attention, including the addition of extra water jacketing in addition to a directional water cooling tube inside the water jacket that "directed" cool water to hot spots inside the engine. Additional changes were made to ventilate the clutch plate along with changes in the transmission. Oddly enough, Plymouth abandoned independent front suspension and returned to semi-elliptic springs and a tube front axle with the PJ models. Changes in spring lengths were credited with achieving "Balanced Weight" and improved ride qualities.

A line of sedans called "touring" models were now offered, which featured a built in "hump style" trunk on the rear of the body. These proved extremely popular despite a slightly higher price over the regular sedans. A line of long wheelbase five- and seven-passenger sedans was also offered.

Deluxe models are easily identified by their bullet-shaped, chrome-plated headlamps and hood trim that consisted of five chrome circles beneath three horizontal chrome bars.

PLYMOUTH BUSINESS SIX — MODEL PJ — SIX: Mechanically the same as other PJ models with the exception of a choke type thermostat rather than a by-pass type, the Business Six was Plymouth's price leader, starting at a low of $510. Plymouth's wooden bodied station wagon, the Westchester Suburban, was built on this chassis and in a return to a body style first offered in 1930, a return was made to the commercial sedan. This vehicle was based on a two-door sedan body style, with the addition of a single door at the rear of the body. Advertised as the perfect commercial vehicle for the small businessman, the commercial sedan was easily converted into a regular passenger sedan by the addition of an optional rear seat. The rear quarter windows, when used in a commercial capacity, were filled with window blanks that could be easily removed. The commercial sedan met with limited success but was carried on into future years' production. The Business Six was easily identified by its hood trim that consisted only of three horizontal chrome bars and painted headlamps.

PLYMOUTH — MODEL PJ — SIX: This was a limited series consisting of only two body styles. The series was mid-priced between the Business and Deluxe lines. It is identified by its Deluxe style hood chrome trim and painted headlamps. Most of these cars were built and sold in Canada.

I.D. DATA: [Plymouth PJ] Serial numbers on right front door post. Detroit, Michigan, starting: 1675001. Ending: 1675032. Windsor, Ontario, starting: 9386551. Ending: 9387355. [Plymouth PJ Business Six] Serial numbers on right front door post. Detroit, Michigan, starting: 1039101. Ending: 1111645. Los Angeles, California, starting: 3151501. Ending: 3157116. Windsor, Ontario, starting: 9396076. Ending: 9397345. [Plymouth PJ Deluxe] Serial numbers on right front door post. Detroit, Michigan, starting: 2397601. Ending: 2641320. Los Angeles, California, starting: 3019401. Ending: 3040567. Windsor, Ontario, starting: 9326551. Ending: 9332281. Engine numbers on left front corner of cylinder block. Starting: PJ-1001. Ending: PJ-359025.

1935 Plymouth, Model PJ, two-door sedan, JAC

Body Code	Body Type & Seating	Price	Weight	Prod. Total
Plymouth PJ Standard Six				
BC	2-dr. Bus. Cpe.-2P	565	2665	6664
651	2-dr. Sed.-5P	615	2670	7284
NA	Chassis	—	—	2680

Note 1: Chassis production is for all three PJ lines.

Body Code	Body Type & Seating	Price	Weight	Prod. Total
Plymouth PJ Business Six				
BC	2-dr. Bus. Cpe.-2P	510	2635	16,691
651	2-dr. Sed.-5P	535	2680	29,942
650	4-dr. Sed.-5P	570	2720	15,761
651-B	2-dr. Comm. Sed.-1p	635	2735	1142
NA	4-dr. Westchester-7/8P	765	N/A	119

Body Code	Body Type & Seating	Price	Weight	Prod. Total
Plymouth PJ Deluxe				
BC	2-dr. Bus. Cpe.-2P	575	2685	29,190
TPC	2-dr. RS Cpe.-2/4P	630	2730	12,118
654	2-dr. Conv. Cpe.-2/4P	695	2810	2308
651	2-dr. Sed.-5P	625	2730	12,424
656	2-dr. Tr. Sed.-5P	650	2790	45,203
650	4-dr. Sed.-5P	660	2790	66,083
655	4-dr. Tr. Sed.-5P	685	2834	82,068
NA	4-dr. Sed.-7P	895	3130	350***
NA	4-dr. Travelers Sed.-5P	N/A	—	77***

Note 1: Touring sedan refers to those cars with built in "humpback" style trunks.

Note 2: *** 128-inch wheelbase.

General Note: 10,375 PJ Deluxe and 240 PJ Standards were built with right-hand drive.

ENGINE: Inline. Valve in block. Six. Cast iron block. B & S: 3-1/8 x 4-3/8 in. Disp.: 201.3 cu. in. C.R.: 6.7:1. Brake H.P.: 82 @ 3600 R.P.M. Taxable/A.L.A.M./N.A.C.C. H.P.: 23.44. Main bearings: four. Valve lifters: solid. Carb. Carter BB439S. Torque: 145 lb.-ft. @ 1200 R.P.M. Small bore export engines had a bore of 2-7/8 in.; 748 PJ DeLuxe and six PJ Standards were shipped with this engine.

TECHNICAL: Sliding gear transmission. Speeds: 3F/1R. Floor shift controls. Single disc, dry 9-1/2 in. clutch. Driveshaft. Semi-floating rear axle. Overall ratio: 4.125:1. Hydraulic brakes on four wheels. Steel spoke "artillery" wheels.

CHASSIS: Series PJ (all) W.B.: 113 in. (128 in. five-passenger Traveler and seven-passenger sedan). O.L.: 187-7/8 in. sedan, 189-5/8 in. coupe and convertible. Frt/Rear Tread: 56-1/4/58 in. Tires: 5.25 x 17/6.00 x 16 in.

OPTIONS: Front and rear bumper, spare tire and tube plus tire cover covered in one package on all except touring models; $26.50 on touring as spare was carried inside trunk. ($33.00). Single sidemount (5.75). Dual sidemounts (39.50). Sidemount cover. Fender skirts (9.00 pair). Bumper guards. Philco Transitone dash mount radio (39.95 standard, 44.95 deluxe). Electric clock in glovebox door (11.75). Cigar lighter (1.00). Radio antenna chicken wire supporting roof fabric served as radio antennae. Seat covers several sets offered. Spotlight (15.95). Automatic choke (3.00). Clock mirror (3.95). Footrest (3.50). Locking gas cap (2.25). Dual Air Tone horns (externally mounted) (12.00). Keel Kushion (2.95). License plate frames (2.45). Radiator grille cover (1.25). Right-hand sun visor (1.75). Metal spring covers (6.00). Right-hand taillamp (3.30). Metal spare tire cover (6.50). Fabric spare tire cover (2.00). Visor vanity mirror (1.00). Wheel trim rings (1.35 each). Right-hand windshield wiper (4.95). Oil bath air cleaner (2.50). Duplate safety glass (7.50) coupes/(($10.00) sedans. Trunk rack (16.50). "Mayflower" sailing ship radiator ornament (3.50). Economy engine package. Heater packages included Duo-Airstream (19.95). Deluxe hot water (15.95) and Standard hot water (12.95). 20 in. high clearance wheels. Accessory Package AD for the Deluxe PJ series consisted of dual chrome external horns, right-hand taillamp, right-hand windshield wiper and right-hand interior sun visor, cigar lighter for $18.50. The same accessory package was also offered on the PJ Business series but included chrome headlamps. Package sold for $23.00.

HISTORICAL: Plymouth PJ Six production began November 17, 1934, ended August 15, 1935. Public announcement dates for the PJ models was January 5, 1935. Model year production: 13,948. Plymouth PJ Business Six production began November 10, 1934, ended August 15, 1935. Model year production: 63,536. PJ Deluxe production began November 6, 1934; ended August 15, 1935. Model year production: 249,940. K.T. Keller, corporate head; Dan S. Eddins, division head. Endurance racer Bob MacKenzie set a new coast to coast record in a PJ business coupe, driving from Los Angeles to New York City and return in a time of 121 hours and 52 minutes, covering 6,492 miles and averaging 53.7 miles per hour. Jimmy Lynch and his "Devil Dodgers" used PJ Plymouths exclusively in their thrill shows. Ole Fahlin and Swen Swanson built an experimental airplane powered by a 1935 Plymouth engine converted for aviation use to enter a government sponsored contest to come up with a practical design for a cheap "everyman's" airplane. The plane was certified and Fahlin was paid by Chrysler to bring the plane to Detroit for further examination. When the Fahlin-Swanson design (called the Plymocoupe or SF-2) failed to win the government contest and following the death of Swanson from pneumonia, the plane was sold to a party who attempted to set an endurance record from Anchorage, Alaska, to Mexico. Taking off in "marginal weather conditions" the pilot soon noticed a fluctuating oil gauge and crashed while attempting to land at the Juneau airport. Ultimately the Plymocoupe burned in a hangar fire. In an effort to capitalize on its Plymouth heritage the plane also used the 1935 hood trim on the cowling, a "sailing ship" radiator ornament on the radiator shrouding and passenger car instruments converted to aeronautical uses on the plane's instrument board. Walter P. Chrysler retired from active corporate duties, turning the company reins over to his longtime associate K.T. Keller. Overseas final assembly plants were opened in Ireland and New Zealand.

1935 Plymouth, Model PJ, four-door sedan, JAC

1936 PLYMOUTH

PLYMOUTH BUSINESS MODEL P1 — SIX: The P1 Business line was Plymouth's price leader and differed in trim levels to achieve its low price. Most noticeable difference externally was the lack of the three chrome chevrons on the headlamp stanchions and a painted rather than chrome-plated windshield frame. The station wagon was a part of this series as was a completely redesigned sedan delivery that was no longer built on a version of the two-door sedan as had been done the year before. Two unique options for 1936 included a removable pickup box, complete with tailgate, for the business coupe models and an ambulance/hearse conversion of the four-door sedans.

PLYMOUTH DELUXE — MODEL P2 — SIX: To many people the 1936 Plymouth was simply a rehashed version of the 1935, which had been an all new car. It was an error on the part of many, as the 1936 was also an all new car. Improving on the basic design of the 1935 frame, the 1936 frame featured not only boxed side rail members, but a large X unit riveted to an oval center section. Again the body was bolted both vertically and horizontally to the frame, giving the car extra rigidity. Other improvements included a kick shackle on the left front semi-elliptic spring and improvements in the transmission.

Style-wise, the car appeared much thinner than the 1935 with a high, narrow radiator shell with a three-piece grille insert, the center insert that was painted to match the body color. Also gone were the familiar chrome-plated bullet-shaped headlamps, replaced by free standing painted lamps in the fender catwalks. The fenders received beading over the wheel cutouts, which flowed into the line of the runningboards. The hood height, lower window opening height and top of the deck lid were all on one plane to give a balanced look.

A complete line of models, including both trunkless and humpback style two- and four-door sedans were offered with the trunk style sedans outselling the trunkless models by a wide margin. 1936 was the last year for fender mounted spare tire carriers in the passenger line and few cars were so equipped making a car with those options today quite rare. Deluxe models are most easily identified by the three chevron like chrome strips located on the headlamp stands at the front of the car. Coupe models had the spare tire mounted behind the passenger's seat for the first time and the gas tank filler was now relocated to the left rear fender from its former perch on the body itself. Taillamps on all models except the touring sedans were located on the rear fenders. On the interior, all the instruments were relocated to one huge dial in the center of the instrument panel. A glove compartment on the right side (on LHD cars) was matched by a dummy panel on the left in a perfectly symmetrical dash layout. A special trim and option package was offered with a deluxe, chrome-trimmed interior that included overstuffed seats and throw pillows. Plymouth production surpassed the half million unit per year mark with the 1936 models - a production record that would only stand until the next year.

I.D. DATA: Plymouth P1 Serial numbers on right front door post. Detroit starting: 1111701. Ending: 1183569. Los Angeles starting: 3157151. Ending: 3162365. Evansville, Indiana, starting: 9000101. Ending: 9012724. Windsor starting: 9397351. Ending: 9400000. All P1 and P2 series of 1936 used engine numbers beginning with the prefix P2. Plymouth P2 Serial numbers on right front door post. Detroit starting: 2641401. Ending: 2987635. Los Angeles starting: 3040601. Ending: 3077397. Evansville, Indiana, starting: 9025101. Ending: 9062168. Windsor starting: 9332286. Ending: 9339684. Engine numbers on left front corner of cylinder block. Starting: P2-1001. Ending: P2-532087.

Body Code	Body Type & Seating	Price	Weight	Prod. Total
Plymouth P1				
BC	2-dr. Bus. Cpe.-2P	510	2770	26,856
811	2-dr. Sed.-5P	545	2825	39,516
810	4-dr. Sed.-5P	590	2890	19,104
NA	2-dr. Comm. Sed.-1P	605	2880	3527
NA	Chassis	—	—	1211
806	2-dr. Tr. Sed.-5P	—	—	768
805	4-dr. Tr. Sed.-5P	—	—	1544
Plymouth P2				
BC	2-dr. Bus. Cpe.-2P	580	2800	54,601
TPC	2-dr. RS Cpe.-2/4P	620	2870	9663
804	2-dr. Conv. Cpe.-2/4P	725	2945	3297
811	2-dr. Sed.-5P	625	2785	6149
810	4-dr. Sed.-5P	660	2820	10,001
805	4-dr. Tr. Sed.-5P	680	2955	240,136
806	2-dr. Tr. Sed.-5P	645	2910	99,373
NA	4-dr. Sed.-7P	895	3265	1504

Body Code	Body Type & Seating	Price	Weight	Prod. Total
NA	4-dr. Westchester-7/8P	765	NA	309
NA	Chassis	—	—	2775

Note 1: Touring sedans have humpback styling.

Note 2: The seven-passenger sedan has a 125-in. wheelbase.

Note 3: The Westchester is the wood-bodied station wagon.

Engine specifications same for all 1936 models P1 and P2. 2,808 P1s and 11,102 P2s were built with right-hand drive.

ENGINE: Inline. Valve in block. Six. Cast iron block. 3-1/8 x 4-3/8 in. Disp.: 201.3 cu. in. C.R.: 6.7:1. Brake H.P.: 82 @ 3600 R.P.M. Taxable/A.L.A.M./N.A.C.C. H.P.: 23.44. Main bearings: four. Valve lifters: solid. Carb.: Carter BB439S or Carter B6FI or Carter C6EI-2. Torque (compression) 145 lb.-ft. @ 1200 R.P.M. Economy engine option has one inch carburetor, 65 bhp and 3.7:1 rear axle ratio.

Note: Cars built for export were equipped with 170.4 cu. in. engine, 2-7/8 in. bore x 4-3/8 in. stroke. Engines were identified by engine code number P2X. 88 P1 and 573 P2 models were shipped with this export engine.

1936 Plymouth, Model P1, coupe, AA

TECHNICAL: Sliding gear transmission. Speeds: 3F/1R. Floor shift controls. Single disc, dry 9-1/4 in. clutch. Driveshaft. Spiral bevel semifloating, Hotchkiss drive rear axle. Overall ratio: 4.125:1 (3.88:1 P1 business coupe). Hydraulic brakes on four wheels. Artillery (steel) spoke wheels. Rim size 5.25 x 17 on P1; 6.00 x 16 on P2.

CHASSIS: [Series P1 1936] W.B. 113 in. O.L.: 191-3/8 in. four-door touring sedan. 184-13/32 in. all except two-door sedan. 190-5/32 in. two-door sedan. Frt/Rear Tread: 55-7/8/58 in. Tires: 5.25 x 17. [Series P-2 1936] W.B.: 113 in. (128 in. seven-passenger) O.L.: same as listed for P1 models (seven-passenger 203-3/8 in.). Frt/Rear Tread: 56-1/16/58-3/16 in. Tires: 6.00 x 16.

OPTIONS: Bumpers were still extra cost in 1936 and came in three packages depending on the body style or model of the car. Bumper Group A sold for $35 for trunkless Deluxe four-door sedans, trunkless Deluxe two-door sedans and the convertible. It included front and rear bumpers, bumper guards, spare tire and tube, metal rear spring covers, spare tire lock and metal spare tire cover. Bumper Group B sold for $25.50 for all Business (P1) models. It included front and rear bumpers, spare tire and tube. Bumper Group C sold for $28.50 for all other Deluxe models not covered in Group A and included front and rear bumpers, bumper guards, spare tire and tube and metal rear spring covers. Single sidemount right-front fender (5.75). Dual sidemounts (38.00 on P2 Deluxe; 30.00 on P1 Business). Fender skirts (9.00 pair). Sidemount cover(s). Fender skirts. Radio in dash mount (49.50). Heater, several types optional, all hot water heat. Clock, 30-hour clock mirror (3.95) eight-day clock mirror (11.00). Cigar lighter (1.60). Radio antenna standard on all closed body styles, using the fabric roof "chicken wire" support. Seat covers several types offered. Spotlight (15.95). Heavy-duty air cleaner (2.50). Special body colors (30.00). Fender and sheet metal color (5.00). Safety glass (coupe) (7.50). (sedan) (10.00). Leather upholstery (coupe) (10.00). (sedan) (16.00). Radiator ornament (3.50). Metal rear springs covers (business series) (4.50). 16 in. wheels (business series) (15.00). Deluxe steering wheel (5.00). 20 in. high clearance wheels (15.00). Metal spare tire cover (6.50). Fabric rear tire cover (2.00). Trunk rack (15.00). Rear seat foot rests (3.50). Glovebox lock (1.00). Locking gas cap (1.50). Dual external "Airtone" horns (12.00). right-hand taillamp (2.85). right-hand wiper (4.50). right-hand inside sun visor (1.50). Radiator grille cover (1.25). Handbrake extension lever (1.50). Exhaust extension (1.00). Chrome wheel discs (2.30 each). Pair license plate frame (2.45). Defroster (1.50). Electric defrost fan (6.50). Ambulance conversion (40.00). Hearse conversion (65.00). (Ambulance and hearse conversion available only on four-door sedan models.) Removable pickup box for coupe body style, approximately (16.00). Accessory Group A: $17.50 included dual external "Airtone" horns, right-hand taillamp, right-hand windshield wiper, right-hand interior sun visor and cigar lighter. Accessory Group B: $5 included right-hand taillamp and right-hand windshield wiper.

Special Note On Paint: Although a complete line of colors was offered for the body of the car, unless the customer paid extra, the fenders and sheet metal were painted black - regardless of the body color. Today we tend to think of this "two-tone" as an option but on the 1936 models, if the customer wanted his car a solid color, he had to pay extra to get it!

1936 Plymouth, Model P2, four-door sedan, JAC

HISTORICAL: Plymouth P1 production began September 19, 1935; ended August 21, 1936. Model year production: 92,526. A Swedish woman, Greta Molander, drove a 1936 Plymouth in both the 1936 and 1937 Monte Carlo Rallye, winning the ladies division of the rallye. Plymouth P2 production began September 6, 1935, ended August 21, 1936. Model year production: 427,499. K.T. Keller, corporate head; Dan S. Eddins, division head.

1937 PLYMOUTH

PLYMOUTH BUSINESS — MODEL P3 — SIX: With Plymouth's introduction in 1937 of a truck chassis commercial car line that included a pickup, cab and chassis, station wagon and a sedan delivery, the business line consisted only of passenger type vehicles although the removable pickup box was offered for the business coupe. Distinguishing features of the business line included the lack of vent windows on front doors, less chrome trim and painted, rather than wood grain dashboards. All business models now rode on 16-inch wheels, with smaller tires fitted than those used on the DeLuxe lines. Fenders and sheet metal were painted black on all business models regardless of the body color unless the customer paid extra to have the car one solid color.

PLYMOUTH DELUXE — MODEL P4 — SIX: Despite a one-inch shorter wheelbase, the 1937 models grew in overall length and in general terms of styling, was "fattened" considerably over the "narrow" styling of the 1936 models. Despite a crippling labor strike, the 1937 set an overall production record, with the second year in-a-row of over half a million units produced - a record that would stand until 1951.

New was an all steel roof stamping that replaced the cloth insert found on previous models. Mechanically the car remained much the same as the previous year with the major mechanical change being in the fitting of a hypoid, rather than spiral bevel gear differential. All cars were now also fitted with airplane type shock absorbers for better handling. Wind wings in the front doors were also fitted to all DeLuxe models after an absence since the 1934 DeLuxe PE's complicated system.

On the interior new "Safety Styling" was emphasized, which included the removal of all protruding knobs from the instrument panel and placing them under the panel where they would be out of reach of passengers' knees in the event of an accident. Front seat backs were heavily padded to prevent injury to back seat passengers. The instrument gauges were now relocated in two dials directly in front of the driver. 1937 was to be the last year for opening windshields for ventilation.

PLYMOUTH COMMERCIAL CAR — MODEL PT50 — SIX: Plymouth entered the commercial car field in 1937 as the result of dealers' demands to have a commercial vehicle to sell when the dealer was not dualed with a Dodge dealership. Plymouth's entry into the field allowed Chrysler-Plymouth and DeSoto-Plymouth dealers extra opportunity for vehicle sales. Based on passenger car styling, in reality, no pieces interchanged between the passenger car line and the commercial line. Entering the

market with a full range of vehicles, including the wooden bodied Westchester station wagon and a sedan delivery, these models were short lived on the truck chassis and reverted back to the passenger car chassis in ensuing years.

1937 was the best year as far as sales were concerned for the Plymouth commercial line but the line's similarity to the Dodge commercial eventually spelled its doom. The Plymouth commercial was only a minor face lift of the basic Dodge commercial vehicle. In Canada, a similiar companion line called the Fargo was also introduced as no Plymouth commercials were ever built or sold in the Dominion. After the demise of Plymouth, the Fargo name was carried on as a companion make in Canada and the name was still used in various parts of the world until the late 1970s.

1937 Plymouth, Model P4, coupe, AA

I.D. DATA: [Plymouth P3] Serial numbers on right front door post. Detroit, Michigan, starting: 1184001. Ending: 1237460. Los Angeles, California, starting: 3101401. Ending: 3105159. Evansville, Indiana, starting: 9085551. Ending: 9097493. Windsor, Ontario, starting: 9376676. Ending: 9381157. All 1937 models P3 and P4 used engines with serial number prefix P4. [Plymouth P4] Serial numbers on right front door post. Detroit, Michigan, starting: 10101001. Ending: 10468044. Los Angeles, California, starting: 3162501. Ending: 3205879. Evansville, Indiana, starting: 9950001. Ending: 9999021. Windsor, Ontario, starting: 9339691. Ending: 9349561. Engine numbers on left front corner of cylinder block. Starting: P4-1001. Ending: P4-571569. [Plymouth PT50] The vehicle serial number appears on the plate showing model code, which is mounted on the engine side of the cowl over the steering column, or on the right front door front pillar post. Detroit, Michigan, starting: 8850101. Ending: 8861664. Los Angeles, California, starting: 9206601. Ending: 9208113. Evansville, Indiana, starting: 9182701. Ending: 9185187. Engine numbers on left front corner of cylinder block. Starting: T50-1001.

Body Code	Body Type & Seating	Price	Weight	Prod. Total
Plymouth P3				
911	2-dr. Sed.-5P	550	2770	28,685
BC	2-dr. Bus. Cpe.-2P	510	2700	18,202
910	4-dr. Sed.-5P	595	2770	16,000
915	4-dr. Tr. Sed.-5P	—	—	7,842
	2-dr. Tr. Sed.-5P	—	—	1,350
TPC	RS Cpe.-2/4P	—	—	540
—	Chassis	—	—	1,025

Note: The RS Coupe and most four-door touring sedans were built for export.

Plymouth P4

905	4-dr. Tr. Sed.-5P	680	2840	269,062
906	2-dr. Tr. Sed.-5P	650	2840	111,099
BC	2-dr. Bus. Cpe.-2P	575	2765	67,144
900	4-dr. Sed.-5P	670	2840	9,000
901	2-dr. Sed.-5P	640	2825	7,926
TPC	RS Cpe.-2/4P	625	2810	6,877
904	2-dr. Conv. Cpe.-2/4P	745	2920	3,110
—	4-dr. Sed.-7P	915	3255	1,840
—	4-dr. Taxi-7P	—	—	500
—	4-dr. Limo. Sed.-7P	—	—	63
—	Chassis	—	—	1,729

Plymouth PT50

K-8-2-LR	Pickup	525	—	10,709
NA	Cab & Chassis	495	—	158
NA	Sed. Del.	655	—	3256
NA	Sta. Wag.	740	—	602

7,114 P3s and 9,586 P4s were built with right-hand drive.

ENGINE: Specifications same for all 1937 models P3 and P4. Inline. Valve in block. Six. Cast iron block. B & S: 3-1/8 x 4-3/8 in. Disp.: 201.3 cu. in. C.R.: 6.7:1. Brake H.P.: 82 @ 3600 R.P.M. Tax-

able/A.L.A.M./N.A.C.C. H.P.: 23.44. Main bearings: four. Valve lifters: solid. Carb.: Carter BB439S or Carter C6HI or Carter B6GI or C6FI-5. Torque (compression): 145 lb.-ft. @ 1200 R.P.M. Plymouth also offered an "economy" engine package that developed 65 H.P. at 3500 R.P.M. Equipment included a one-inch carburetor and 3.73:1 rear axle ratio. [Plymouth PT50] Inline. Six. Cast iron block. B & S: 3-1/8 x 4-3/8 in. Disp.: 201 cu. in. C.R.: 6.7:1. Brake H.P.: 70 @ 3000 R.P.M. Taxable/A.L.A.M./N.A.C.C. H.P.: 23.44. Main bearings: four. Valve lifters: solid. Carb.: Chandler Groves A2. Torque (compression): 145 lb. ft. @ 1200 R.P.M.

Note: Cars built for export were equipped with 170.4 cu. in. engine, 2-7/8 in. bore x 4-3/8 in. stroke. Engines were identified by engine numbers coded P4X. 132 P3s and 525 P4s were shipped with this export engine.

CHASSIS: [Series P3] W.B.: 112 in. O.L.: 193-5/16 in. Frt/Rear Tread: 56/60 in. Tires: 5.50 x 16. [Series P4] W.B.: 112 in. (132 in. seven-passenger). O.L.: 193-5/16 in. (214-3/16 in. seven-passenger). Frt/Rear Tread: 56/60 in. Tires: 6.00 x 16. [Series PT50] W.B.: 116 in. Tires: 6.00 x 16.

1937 Plymouth, Model P4, four-door sedan, OCW

TECHNICAL: [Plymouth P3 and P4] Sliding gear transmission. Speeds: 3F/1R. Floor shift controls. Single disc, dry 9-1/4 in. clutch. Driveshaft. Hypoid, semi-floating, Hotchkiss drive. Overall ratio: 4.1:1 (DeLuxe sedans), 4.3:1 (seven-passenger); 3.9:1 [DeLuxe coupes and all business P3 models]. Hydraulic brakes on four wheels. Steel disc wheels. Rim size: 5.50 x 16 on P3, 6.00 x 16 on P4. [Plymouth PT50] Three-speed standard transmission. Floor shift controls. Single disc, dry 10 in. diameter clutch. Driveshaft. Hypoid, semi-floating rear axle. Hydraulic brakes on four wheels. Steel disc wheels. Rim size: 6.00 x 16.

1937 Plymouth, Model P4, convertible coupe, JAC

OPTIONS: Philco Transitone radio, with antenna ($53.95). Electric clock, in glovebox door (10.00). Heavy-duty air cleaner (2.50). Special body colors (30.00). Fender and sheet metal color other than black (5.00). Leather upholstery, coupes (10.00); sedans (16.00). Life guard tubes (35.00). Glove compartment lock (1.00). Radiator ornament (3.50). Metal spring cover (Business P3) (4.50). Deluxe steering wheel (5.00). 6.00 x 16 in. wheels and tires (Business P3) (15.00); 20 in. wheels (15.00). Junior model heater (8.95). Defroster attachment (1.25). Standard heater (12.95). Tri-Airstream Heater (15.95). Super Tri-Airstream Heater (19.95). Defroster attachment for Airstream heaters (3.45). Electric defrost fan (5.95). Rear seat speaker (5.95). Roadway radio (under runningboard) antenna (4.45). Accessory Group A including dual airtone trumpet horns, right-hand taillamp, right-hand windshield, right-hand sun visor and cigar lighter (17.50). Accessory Group B including right-hand taillamp and right-hand windshield wiper (5.00). Bumper groups: For Deluxe P4 consisting of bumpers, bumper guards, spare tire, tube and metal spring covers (28.50). For Business P3 consisting of bumpers, bumper guards, spare tire and tube (25.50). For seven-passenger models

consisting of bumpers, bumper guards, spare tires, tube and metal spring covers (32.50).

HISTORICAL: Plymouth P3 production began September 15, 1936, ended August 30, 1937. Public announcement date for the 1937 models was November 7, 1936. Model year production: 73,644. Plymouth P4 production began September 10, 1936, ended August 30, 1937. Model year production: 478,350.

The two millionth Plymouth was built during 1937. This car was sold to Mrs. Ethel Miller of Turlock, California. She had been the purchaser of the first Plymouth ever sold, as well as the purchaser of the one millionth Plymouth built in 1934.

Plymouth PT50 production began December, 1936, ended August 23, 1937. Model year production: 14,725. K.T. Keller, corporate president, Dan Eddins, division head. All corporate debt incurred when Chrysler purchased Dodge Brothers in 1928 was retired by the end of 1936.

An overseas assembly plant was opened in Norway for assembly of unfinished cars from the United States.

1938 PLYMOUTH

1938 Plymouth, Model P5, four-door sedan, AA

PLYMOUTH BUSINESS/ROADKING — MODEL P5 — SIX: Again the price leader, the "Business" series was renamed the "Roadking" midway through production to appease those people who objected to buying the business model just because they bought the cheaper series. Distinguishing features of the Business/Roadking was the lack of vent windows on all models, painted rather than wood grain instrument panels and 17-inch wheels while the Deluxe rode on 16-inch. For the first time, the windshield was permanently fixed on all models. Not only did the recession of 1938 hinder sales, but the fact that dealers' lots were full of used cars from the record sales set the year previous hurt as well.

1938 Plymouth, Model P6, convertible coupe, JAC

PLYMOUTH DELUXE — MODEL P6 — SIX: 1938 was not a good year for Plymouth. The recession of 1938 saw Plymouth's sales fall by nearly 50 percent (as did the rest of the industry). A restyled version of the 1937 models, the 1938 was not well received by either the dealer network or the buying public. With a "fatter" look resulting from a short, stubby waterfall grille and headlamps mounted high on the side of the radiator shell the car took on an "ugly duckling" appearance. Dealer unrest was so bad that the factory relocated the headlamps midway through production, lowering them two inches and moving them rearward another four inches, a move that did much to improve the looks of the car.

1938 was Plymouth's 10th anniversary year but the factory did little to exploit the occasion and no special models were offered. Some advertising did make mention of the "Jubilee Plymouth" however. 1938 would mark the first year that the Plymouth did not enjoy a gain in sales over the previous year since its introduction in 1928. "Safety Styling" continued on the interior with all protruding knobs again hidden to prevent injury in accidents and safety glass was standard on all models.

PLYMOUTH COMMERCIAL CAR — MODEL PT57 — SIX: With only a minor face lifting to match that of its passenger car counterpart, Plymouth's commercial entry for 1938 saw a drastic drop in sales for the model year, to less than one half of its introductory year, caused not only by an increase in prices but by the recession of 1938. This would be the last year that the pickup would bear passenger car styling but as in the year previous, no sheet metal or trim parts interchanged between the commercial and the passenger line. This would be the last year as well for the truck chassis sedan delivery as well as the final year for the spare tires to be fitted into the front fenders on the commercial car line.

I.D. DATA: [P5] Serial numbers on right front door post. Detroit, Michigan, starting: 1240001. Ending: 1296615. Los Angeles, California, starting: 3105301. Ending: 3109407. Evansville, Indiana, starting: 9097601. Ending: 9107725. Windsor, Ontario, starting: 9381161. Ending: 9385097. All P5 and P6 series used engines with P6 prefix. [P6] Serial numbers on right front door post. Detroit, Michigan, starting: 10470001. Ending: 10625650. Los Angeles, California, starting: 3206001. Ending: 3220997. Evansville, Indiana, starting: 20001001. Ending: 20025900. Windsor, Ontario, starting: 9349566. Ending 9358622. Engine numbers on left front corner of cylinder block. Starting: P6-1001. Ending: P6-286619. PT57 serial number appears on the plate showing the model code, which is mounted on the engine side of the cowl over the steering column, or on the right front door front pillar post. Detroit, Michigan, starting: 8618701. Ending: 8624135. Los Angeles, California, starting: 9208201. Ending: 9208797. Evansville, Indiana, starting: 9185301. Ending: 9186416. Engine numbers on left front corner of cylinder block. Starting: T57-1001.

Body Code	Body Type & Seating	Price	Weight	Prod. Total
P5 Business "Road King" Line				
BC	2-dr. Bus. Cpe.-2P	645	2694	15,932
406	2-dr. Tr. Sed.-5P	701	2779	16,413
416	2-dr. Sed.-5P	685	2744	15,393
405	4-dr. Tr. Sed.-5P	746	2824	18,664
415	4-dr. Sed.-5P	730	2774	6459
TPC	2-dr. RS Cpe.-2/4P	—	—	338

Note 1: The P5 rumbleseat coupe was built for export only.

Body Code	Body Type & Seating	Price	Weight	Prod. Total
P6 Deluxe Line				
BC	2-dr. Bus. Cpe.-2P	730	2754	27,181
TPC	2-dr. RS Cpe.-2/4P	770	2799	2000
406	2-dr. Tr. Sed.-5P	785	2819	46,669
416	2-dr. Sed.-5P	773	2814	1222
405	4-dr. Tr. Sed.-5P	815	2844	119,669
415	4-dr. Sed.-5P	803	2834	1446
404	2-dr. Conv. Cpe.-2/4P	850	2964	1900
NA	4-dr. Limo.-7P	1095	3289	75
408	4-dr. Sed.-7P	1005	3239	1824
NA	4-dr. Westchester-7/8P	880	3039	555
NA	4-dr. Taxi-7P	—	—	35
NA	Chassis	—	—	2004
NA	Chassis-7P	—	—	23

Body Code	Body Type & Seating	Price	Weight	Prod. Total
PT57 Commercial Line				
K-8-2-LR	2-dr. Pickup-2P	585	—	4620
NA	2-dr. Cab & Chassis-2P	560	—	95
K-1-3	2-dr. Sed. Del.-2P	695	—	1601

Engine specifications are the same for all 1938 Models P5 and P6. 7,046 P5s and 7,345 P6s were built with right-hand drive.

ENGINE: [Std.] Inline. Valve in block. Six. Cast iron block. B & S: 3-1/8 x 4-3/8 in. Disp.: 201.3 cu. in. C.R.: 6.7:1. Brake H.P.: 82 @ 3600 R.P.M. Taxable/A.L.A.M./N.A.C.C. H.P.: 23.44. Main bearings: four. Valve lifters: solid. Carb.: Carter BB439S, B6HI, B6JI, C6JI or C6KI. Torque (compression) 145 lb.-ft. @ 1200 R.P.M. [Opt. Engine] Inline. Valve in block. Six. Cast iron block. B & S: 3-1/8 x 4-3/8 in. Disp.: 201.3 cu. in. C.R.: 7.0:1. Brake H.P.: 86 @ 3600 R.P.M. Main bearings: four. Valve lifters: solid. Carb.: see above specs. Torque (compression) 156 lb.-ft. @ 1200 R.P.M. [Commercial Engine] Inline. Six. Cast iron block. B & S: 3-1/8 x 4-3/8 in. Disp.: 201 cu. in. C.R.: 6.7:1. Brake H.P.: 70 @ 3000 R.P.M. Taxable/A.L.A.M./N.A.C.C. H.P.: 23.44. Main bearings: four. Valve lifters: solid. Torque (compression) 145 lb.-ft. @ 1200 R.P.M.

Engine Note 1: Optional economy engine package with one-inch carb. developed 65 hp. All other specs the same.

Engine Note 2: Cars built for export were equipped with 170.4 cu. in. engine, 2-7/8 in. bore x 4-3/8 in. stroke. Engines were identified by engine number coded P6X. 109 P5s and 224 P6s were shipped with this export engine.

Engine Note 3: Some 1938 Canadian cars may have been fitted with a different "long block" Canadian engine.

413

TECHNICAL: [P5 and P6] Sliding gear transmission. Speeds: 3F/1R. Floor shift controls. Single disc, dry 9-1/4 in. clutch. Driveshaft. Hypoid, semi-floating Hotchkiss drive rear axle. Overall ratio: 4.1:1. Hydraulic brakes on four wheels. Steel disc wheels. Rim size: 5.50 x 16 on P5 , 6.00 x 16 on P6. [PT57] Three-speed standard with optional four speed w/power takeoff opening. Floor shift controls. Single disc, dry plate 10 in. diameter clutch. Hypoid gear, semi-floating rear axle. Overall ratio: 4.1:1. Hydraulic brakes on four wheels. Steel disc wheels. Rim size: 6.00 x 16 in.

CHASSIS: [P5] W.B.: 112 in. O.L.: 194-3/16 in. Frt/Rear Tread: 56/60 in. Tires: 5.50 x 16. [P6] W.B.: 112 in. (132 in. seven-passenger) O.L.: 194-3/16 in. (214-3/16 in. seven-passenger). Frt/ Rear Tread: 56/60 in. Tires: 6.00 x 16. [PT57] W.B.: 116 in. Frt/Rear Tread 56/57-7/8 in. Tires: 6.00 x 16.

1938 Plymouth, Model P6, business coupe, JAC

OPTIONS: Fender skirts ($12.00). Radio in dash, push-button (56.70). Electric clock in glovebox door (10.00). Cigar lighter. Spotlight. Heavy-duty air cleaner (2.50). Ambulance conversion (57.50). Glovebox lock (1.00). Oil filter (Roadking) (2.75). Rear seat speaker (5.95). Deluxe steering wheel (5.00). Metal rearspring covers (Roadking) (5.50). Chrome wheel rings (8.00 for set of five). Wiper vacuum booster pump (3.50). Rear compartment heater attachment (8.50). Roadway (runningboard mount) antennae (5.95). Skyway (cowl mount) antenna (5.95). Heaters offered included Duo-Airstream (18.95). Tri-Airstream (21.95). Super-Airstream (24.95). Defroster (4.50). Rubber bladed electric fan, trunk lamp; glareshield sun visor (inside); foglamps; front and rear center su-perguard bumper guard; radiator grille cover; adjustable radiator shutters; radiator insect screen; exhaust extention license plate frames, wheel trim rings; wheel discs; locking gas cap; 30-hour clock-mirror; 200-hour clock-mirror; glovebox lock. 20 inch high clearance wheels. Accessory Group A: right-hand taillamp, right-hand windshield wiper, right-hand interior sun visor, cigar lighter, dual trumpet horns (underhood) (19.00) ***. Accessory Group B: right-hand taillamp, right-hand windshield wiper (6.00). *** Accessory Group A cost $13 on convertible as twin taillamps were standard on it. Accessory Group C: Included all items in Group A in addition to special "pillow-type" upholstery, special door upholstery, carpet strips on door panel bottoms, chrome trim on door panels, special front seat-back trim, light wood grain, contrasting color on instrument panel, colored escutcheons on all handles, color steering wheel, front armrests on left and right doors, chrome horn ring, special gearshift knob, front bumper grille guard, two chrome license plate frames, chrome wind-shield wipers, wheel trim rings, glovebox lock and chrome trim on run-ningboards. Package price $35.00. Economy Group 1: one-inch diameter carburetor and intake manifold. 3.73:1 rear axle ratio on Deluxe P6 models, 3.54:1 rear axle on Business/Roadking P5 models. 65 hp at 3000 R.P.M. Economy Group 2: included items in Group 1 in addition to man-ifold heat shields and throttle stop at 45 mph.

1938 Plymouth PT57 Rear bumper chrome plated (8.50). Single side-mount standard, right side only. Dual sidemount included extra well, tire and tube, tire lock (10.00). Bumper guards (1.50 pair). Chassis Accessory Group included chrome radiator shell, chrome headlamps and double acting front and rear shocks (17.00). Dual horns (7.50). Coach lamps for commercial sedan (8.50). Long arm rear view mirror (1.50). Adjust-able long arm rear view mirror (2.50). Sun visors (2.00 each). Metal spare tire cover (6.50). Chrome windshield frame (3.00). Auxiliary tail-lamp (4.00). Economy Engine Package (Group 1) (2.50). Engine Econ-omy Package (Group 2) (3.00). Four-speed transmission (25.00). Painted sheet metal (fenders, splash aprons, runningboards) (5.00) (Note: Unless extra fees were paid these items remained black regardless of body color). Five 6.00 x 16 in. six ply tires (14.25). Five 20 in. wheels with 5.25 x 20 in. four ply tires and 4.78:1 rear axle (25.00). Six 20 in. wheels with 5 x 25 x 20 in. four ply tires and 4.78:1 rear axle (35.00). Oil bath air cleaner (3.75). Vortex air cleaner w/std. cap (17.50) with Vortex cap (19.50). Governor (5.00). Chrome headlamps (2.75). Oil filter (3.25). Chrome radiator shell (6.00). Auxiliary seat (commercial sedan) (10.00). Double acting shocks (4.75 front), (4.75 rear). Auxiliary wind-shield wiper (4.00).

HISTORICAL: P5 production began September 22, 1937; ended July 19, 1938. Public announcement date for the 1938 models was October 30, 1937. Model year production: 74,785. P6 production began Sep-tember 3, 1937; ended July 19, 1938. Model year production: 204,603. [PT57] Production began September 16, 1937; ended August 17, 1938. Model year production: 6,316. K.T. Keller, corporate head; Dan S. Eddins, division head.

1939 PLYMOUTH

1939 Plymouth, Model P8, business coupe, AA

PLYMOUTH ROADKING — MODEL P7 — SIX: Once again Plymouth's price leader, the Roadking series enjoyed brisk sales as the effects of the 1938 recession wore off. Easily identified by the belt line chrome trim that ends midway down the length of the hood, the Roadking truly became Plymouth's "business" line with the introduction of a "utility sedan" model and the return of the sedan delivery to the passenger car chassis from its two-year stint on the truck chassis. The utility sedan was simply a two-door with no rear seat or passenger's seat (although one was option-al). The utility could be fitted with a screen partition between driver and rear compartment and there was no partition between the passenger area and trunk. With a special body, the sedan delivery had two doors at the rear of the body. Causing much confusion was the fact that the spare tires on these models rode in fender mounts, which were not offered on the regular line of passenger cars. Because of their interchangeability these fenders have shown up in later years on other body styles although they are not aesthetically correct. Also offered in the Roadking line was the ambulance conversion (and on the Deluxe line as well) in addition to the optional removable pickup box with tailgate that could be fitted into the business coupe.

PLYMOUTH DELUXE — MODEL P8 — SIX: While the rest of the corpora-tion enjoyed new bodies, Plymouth was forced to make do with the old bodies in use since 1937. By clever face lifting most people then, as well as today, do not realize the relationship between the 1937-38 and 1939 models. A new cowling with a split, veed two-piece windshield added considerable length to the old body, effectively hiding the car's origins while a new roof stamping on sedans added more length to the rear of the bodies. A completely new, prow-shaped front end with headlamps mounted in the fenders completed the transformation. At the rear, teardrop shaped taillamps were fitted in to the fenders. Still retaining the old bulb/reflector type headlamps, 1939 would be the last year for cars with rumbleseats and saw the introduction of the first power operated con-vertible top in the entire automobile industry. Actuated by two vacuum cylinders located behind the front seat, the top moved up or down at the touch of a dashboard mounted control switch.

New for the year was an extended wheelbase four-door convertible sedan the first and last such offering from Plymouth. In reality the body was the same as that which had been used on the 1937 and 1938 DeSoto and Chrysler convertible sedans. Oddly enough, Plymouth offered the only open cars in the entire Chrysler Corporation in 1939 (not even GM's Chevrolet offered a convertible!). With its rectangular headlamps and multi-piece chrome grille the 1939 model has proven to be highly collectible.

Deluxe models all featured remote control gear shifting while Roadking models retained floor shifting and instrument panels featured the "Safety Signal" speedometer that changed colors as the speed of the vehicle increased. In addition the 1939 models returned to independent front suspension, which Plymouth had introduced with the 1934 models but had abandoned in 1935.

PLYMOUTH COMMERCIAL CAR — MODEL PT81 — SIX: Plymouth's commercial chassis entry this year was an entirely new body with a de-cidedly "truck" look to it. Without much doubt the Plymouth pickup now looked almost identical to its Dodge counterpart. A new "three-man cab" was touted to be the largest in the industry and a unique door latch located at the top of the door was designed to prevent the doors from popping

open when the vehicle was used on rough terrain. The body now sat farther ahead on the chassis while the box was enlarged in size. The spare tire now rode in a carrier underneath the pickup box. As in years past, the tailgate on some models was plain, while others spelled out the word "Plymouth" - no reason has ever been given for these two tailgate types! Cab and chassis models came factory equipped with full length running-boards and rear fenders. Prices were decreased slightly and sales increased by nearly 40 percent.

1939 Plymouth, Model P8, convertible sedan, JAC

I.D. DATA: [Plymouth P7] Serial numbers on right front door post. Detroit, Michigan, starting: 1298001. Ending: 1377475. Los Angeles, California, starting: 3110001. Ending: 3114680. Evansville, Indiana, starting: 9150401. Ending: 9164593. Windsor, Ontario, starting: 9603586. Ending: 9607605. All 1938 P7 and P8 engines began with prefix P8. [Plymouth P8] Serial numbers on right front door post. Detroit, Michigan, starting: 10630001. Ending: 10879874. Los Angeles, California, starting: 3222001. Ending: 3242203. Evansville, Indiana, starting: 20027001. Ending: 20062199. Windsor, Ontario, starting: 9358626. Ending: 9368510. Engine numbers on left front corner of cylinder block. Starting: P8-1001. Ending: P8-411923. [Plymouth PT81] Serial number appears on the plate showing the model code, which is mounted on the engine side of the cowl over the steering column, or on the front door front pillar post. Detroit, Michigan, starting: 8624201. Ending: 8630418. Los Angeles, California, starting: 9208851. Ending: 9209340. Engine numbers on left front corner of cylinder block. Starting: T81-1001.

Body Code	Body Type & Seating	Price	Weight	Prod. Total
P7 Road King Line				
103	2-dr. Bus. Cpe.-3P	645	2274	22,537
116	2-dr. Sed.-5P	685	2824	7,499
106	2-dr. Tr. Sed.-5P	699	2824	42,186
115	4-dr. Sed.-5P	726	2839	2,553
105	4-dr. Tr. Sed.-5P	740	2829	23,047
NA	2-dr. Utility Sed.-1P	685	NA	341
723	2-dr. Panel D'ly.-1P	715	NA	2,270
NA	2-dr. RS Cpe.-2/4P	NA	NA	222
NA	4-dr. Sta. Wag.-7/8P	NA	NA	97
NA	Chassis	NA	NA	1,616

Note 1: The P7 Rumbleseat Coupe and Station Wagon were built for export only.

P8 Deluxe Line				
103	2-dr. Bus. Cpe.-3P	725	2789	41,924
NA	2-dr. RS Cpe.-2/4P	755	2874	1,332
116	2-dr. Sed.-5P	761	2889	2,666
106	2-dr. Tr. Sed.-5P	775	2894	80,981
115	4-dr. Sed.-5P	791	2909	2,279
105	4-dr. Tr. Sed.-5P	805	2919	175,054
CS	4-dr. Conv. Sed.-5P	1150	NA	387
NA	4-dr. Sed.-7P	1005	3374	1,837
NA	4-dr. Limo.-7P	1095	3374	98
NA	4-dr. Sta. Wag.-7/8P	970**	3189	1,680
NA	2-dr. Utility Sed.-1P	NA	NA	13
NA	4-dr. Taxi-7P	NA	NA	12
NA	Chassis	NA	NA	900
NA	Chassis-7P Chassis	NA	NA	35

Note 2: Convertible sedan has body by Murray.

Note 3: **This wagon has glass in all windows; wagon with glass in windshield and front doors only was priced $930.

Plymouth PT81 Commericial				
M-1-2	Pickup	575	2800	6,181
NA	Cab & Chassis	545	2600	140

Specifications same for all 1939 models P7 and P8. 5,627 P7s and 4,938 P8s were built with right-hand drive.

STD. ENGINE: Inline. Valve in block. Six. Cast iron block. B & S: 3-1/8 x 4-3/8 in. Disp.: 201.3 cu. in. C.R.: 6.7:1. Brake H.P.: 82 @ 3600 R.P.M. Taxable/A.L.A.M./N.A.C.C. H.P.: 23.44. Main bearings: four.

Valve lifters: solid. Carb.: Carter B6KI, B6MI, DGAI-2 or D6CI-1. Torque (compression) 145 lb.-ft. @ 1200 R.P.M.

OPT. ENGINE: Aluminum cylinder head. Inline. Valve in block. Six. Cast iron block. B & S: 3-1/8 x 4-3/8 in. Disp.: 201.3 cu. in. C.R.: 7.0:1. Brake H.P.: 86 @ 3600 R.P.M. Main bearings: four. Valve lifters: solid. Carb.: Carter B6KI, B6MI, DGAI-2 or D6CI-2. Torque (compression) 156 lb.-ft. @ 1200 R.P.M.

Engine Note 1: Cars built for export were equipped with 170.4 cu. in. engine, 2-7/8 in. bore x 4-3/8 in. stroke. Engines were identified by engine code numbers P8X. 71 P7s and 202 P8s were shipped with this small-bore engine.

Engine Note 2: In 1938, an engine foundry was built in Windsor, Ontario, to produce engines solely for the Canadian built vehicles. Because of lower production demands it was deemed unneccesary to build two different engine blocks as was being done in the United States. In the U.S. the Plymouth and Dodge both shared the same 23 in. engine block, while Chrysler and DeSoto shared the larger 25 in. engine block. With fewer vehicles produced in the Canadian market it was decided that only the larger 25 in. block would be used in all Canadian built vehicles. With a bore of 3-3/8 in. and a stroke of 3-3/4 in. the engine displaced 201.3 cubic inches. (Note, despite the different bore and stroke size, the ultimate displacement remained the same as the smaller 23 in. U.S. built engine block.) This practice of using a larger block would continue through Plymouth production of the flathead six-cylinder engine in Canada.

These engines are also identified by the code letter C in the engine code serial numbe - example P8C.

COMMERCIAL ENGINE: Inline. Six. Cast iron block. B & S: 3-1/8 x 4-3/8 in. Disp.: 201 cu. in. C.R.: 6.7:1. Brake H.P.: 70 @ 3000 R.P.M. Main bearings: four. Valve lifters: solid. Torque (compression) 145 lb.-ft. @ 1200 R.P.M.

1939 Plymouth, Model P8, four-door sedan, OCW

CHASSIS: [Series P7 1939] W.B.: 114 in. O.L.: 182-3/16 in. Frt/Rear Tread: 56-1/4/60 in. Tires: 5.50 x 16. [Series P8 1939] W.B.: 114 in. (134 in. seven-passenger) Frt/Rear Tread: 56-1/4/60 in. Tires: 6.00 x 16. [Series P8 1939 Convertible Sedan] W.B.: 117 in. Frt/RearTread: 56-1/4/60 in. Tires: 6.00 x 16. [Series PT81] W.B.: 116 in. Frt/Rear Tread: 56/60 in. Tires: 6.00 x 16.

TECHNICAL: Sliding gear transmission. Speeds: 3F/1R. Floor shift on P7; column shift on P8 Deluxe. Single disc, dry 9-1/4 in. clutch. Driveshaft. Hyphoid, semi-floating axles; Hotchkiss drive rear axle. Overall ratio: 3.9:1. Hydraulic brakes on four wheels. Steel disc wheels. Rim size: 5.50 x 16 on P7; 6.00 x 16 on P8.

OPTIONS: Single sidemount available only on sedan delivery and station wagon although fenders will fit passenger cars and some were so fitted in the "aftermarket." Fender skirts ($8.25). Bumper guards (4.50 per pair). Electric clock (glovebox door) (10.00). Cigar lighter (2.00). Seat covers: several versions offered. Spotlight (14.50). Ambulance conversion (55.00). Chrome wheel discs (8.00). Economy Group 1 (2.50). Economy Group 2 (3.00). Stone deflector (1.00). Whitewall tires (15.75 for 6.00 x 16). Whitewalls (13.75 for 5.50 x 16). Heavy-duty air cleaner (2.00). Leather upholstery (coupes) (13.50). Leather upholstery sedans (22.00). 20 in. high clearance wheels (18.00). Glovebox lock (75 cents). Oil filter (Roadking) (2.75). Rear seat speaker (5.95). Deluxe steering wheel (5.00). Rear spring covers (Roadking) (3.00). Power gearshift (9.50). Clock mirror (3.95). Dual trumpet horns (underhood mount) (8.25). Rear body gravel deflector (2.50). Right-hand inside sun visor (1.75). License plate frames (pair) (1.75). Illuminated vanity mirror (1.95). Fog lamps (12.00). Outside rear view mirror (1.95). Spare tire outside valve extension (1.00). Runningboard side moldings (1.50). Glare shield (1.00). Exhaust extension (1.00). Locking gas cap (1.50). Removeable pickup box with tailgate and extended taillamp for installation in trunk area of

coupe (23.95). Heaters: Super-Airstream (24.45). Tri-Airstream (21.45). Deluxe (18.45). Duo-Airstream (15.45). Defroster (4.50). Fresh air attachment (7.00). Radio P8 (Deluxe) Push-button with Skyway antenna (51.00). Push-button with Roadway antenna (53.45). P7 (Roadking) Manual with Skyway antenna (41.50). Manual with Roadway antenna (43.95). Skyway antenna (cowl mounted external) (2.95). Roadway antenna (under runningboard mount) (6.25) (for dual antennas). Some accessories were also sold in package groups: Accessory Group A included right-hand taillamp, right-hand wiper, right-hand sun visor, cigar lighter and dual trumpet horns for $19. Accessory Group B included auxiliary taillamp and wiper for $6.

Plymouth 1939 PT81 Oil bath air cleaner (3.25). Auxiliary taillamp (4.00). Chrome headlamps (2.75). Dual horns (7.50). Colored sheet metal (5.00). Chrome radiator shell (6.00). Long arm stationary mirror (1.50).

Long arm adjustable mirror (2.50). Sun visor (2.00). Four-speed transmission (17.50). Chrome windshield frame (3.00). Right-hand windshield wiper (4.00). Express type rear bumper (6.00). Spare wheel lock (1.50).

HISTORICAL: Plymouth P7 production began August 18, 1938; ended August 18, 1939. Public announcement date for the 1939 models was September 24, 1938. Model year production: 102,368. Plymouth P8 production began August 18, 1938; ended August 18, 1939. Model year production: 315,161.

The three millionth Plymouth was built in 1939.

For its "Safety Signal" speedometer and other safety related items, the 1939 Plymouths were awarded the Eastern Safety Conference Award.

Plymouth PT81 production began November 1, 1938; ended August 31, 1939. Model year production: 6,321.

1940 PLYMOUTH

1940 Plymouth, Model P10, two-door sedan, OCW

PLYMOUTH DELUXE — MODEL P10 — SIX: Advertised as the "Low Priced Beauty with the Luxury Ride" the 1940 Plymouth finally received the new body the rest of the Corporation had received a year earlier. With a three-inch longer wheelbase, the engine moved forward four-inches and the rear axle aft 7-1/2 inches the car took on over 10 cubic feet of additional interior space over the 1939 models. Adding much to appearance of the car was a full length hood, and increased glass area (up 23 percent over 1939) and a one-piece rear window. Although the 1940 design followed the general styling theme set down by the 1939 models, the only interchangeable piece of sheet metal or trim was the radiator ornament!

With the discontinuance of the rumbleseat an auxiliary seat coupe was offered in its place - a model that would more commonly become known as the club coupe. In addition, a rear seat was added to the convertible coupe for additional passengers. Adding to the sleek appearance of these cars were the concealed front door hinges and concealed trunk lid hinges (on all models except the convertible and coupe). A stone deflector was now fitted between the rear of the body and the bumper face plate and runningboards were made a delete option. When not equipped with runningboards a chrome strip took their place on the body and a gravel pad was fitted to the leading edge of the rear fender. Sealed beam headlamps were fitted to all 1940 models replacing the old bulb/reflector lamps of previous years.

On the interior, the Safety Signal speedometer was continued and all models had column mounted gear shifting. An "All Weather Air Control System" provided a dual heater and defroster system for interior climate control. Full width rear doors and a new transmission that offered the passengers a completely flat floor along with suspension changes resulted in one of the best handling cars Plymouth had ever built. Early sales projections showed the new Plymouth would take over second place in sales from Ford, but a last minute blitz by Ford successfully thwarted this goal and Plymouth remained in third place.

PLYMOUTH COMMERCIAL CAR — MODEL PT105 — SIX: Only minor improvements were made for 1940, taking a sharp eye to discern the differences between this year and the previous year. Most obvious was the addition of sealed beam headlamps, replacing the old bulb/reflector units of the year past. With the addition of sealed beams, the parking lamps were now mounted in small pods on top of the headlamp shell. Also changed was the addition of three chromed grille bars to the otherwise steel stamped face of the grille. Despite a $10 price increase sales increased slightly over the PT81.

I.D. DATA: [P9] Serial numbers on right front door post. Detroit, Michigan, starting: 1378001. Ending: 1454303. Los Angeles, California, starting: 3114801. Ending: 3121385. Evansville, Indiana, starting: 9062201. Ending: 9081375. Windsor, Ontario, starting: 9368516. Ending: 9373193. Engine numbers on left front corner of cylinder block. Starting: P9-1001. Ending: P9-415461. [P10] Serial numbers on right front door post. Detroit, Michigan, starting: 10883001. Ending: 11122538. Los Angeles, California, starting: 3242501. Ending: 3269066. Evansville, Indiana, starting: 20063001. Ending: 20104165. Windsor, Ontario, starting: 9607611. Ending: 9616760. Engine numbers on left front corner of cylinder block. Starting: P10-1001. Ending: P10-15462. [PT105] Serial number appears on the plate showing the model code, which is mounted on the engine side of the cowl over the steering column, or on the right front door front pillar post. Detroit, Michigan, starting: 8631001. Ending: 8637730. Los Angeles, California, starting: 9209351. Ending: 9210053. Engine numbers on left front corner of cylinder block. Starting: PT105-1001. Ending: PT105-34654.

1940 Plymouth, Model P10, convertible coupe, JAC

Body Code	Body Type & Seating	Price	Weight	Prod. Total
P9 Road King				
TPC	2-dr. Bus. Cpe.-3P	645	2801	26,745
211	2-dr. Tr. Sed.-5P	699	2866	55,092
210	4-dr. Tr. Sed.-5P	740	2901	20,076
NA	2-dr. Utility Sed.-1P	699	2769	589
755	2-dr. Panel-1P	720	NA	2889
NA	2-dr. Clb. Cpe.-2P	—	—	360
NA	4-dr. Sta. Wag.-7/8P	—	—	80
NA	Chassis	—	—	907

Note 1: The P9 club coupe and station wagon were built for export only.

P10 Deluxe				
ASC	2-dr. Clb. Cpe.-5P	770	2881	32,244
TPC	2-dr. Bus. Cpe.-3P	725	2836	22,174
201	2-dr. Sed.-5P	775	2921	76,781
200	4-dr. Sed.-5P	805	2956	173,351
204	2-dr. Conv. Cpe.-5P	950	3081	6986
NA	4-dr. Sta. Wag.-7/8P	970	3144	3126
NA	4-dr. Sed.-7P	1005	3391	1179
NA	4-dr. Limo.-7P	1080	NA	68
NA	Chassis	—	—	18
NA	Chassis-7P	—	—	18

PT105 Commercial				
4012	Pickup	585	2800	6879
NA	Cab & Chassis	555	2600	174

Specifications same for all 1940 Models P9 and P10. 3,532 P9s and 3,377 P10s were built with right-hand drive.

STD. ENGINE: Inline. Valve in block. Six. Cast iron block. B & S: 3-1/8 x 4-1/8 in. Disp.: 201.3 cu. in. C.R.: 6.7:1. Brake H.P.: 84 @ 3600

R.P.M. Taxable/A.L.A.M./N.A.C.C. H.P.: 23.44. Main bearings: four. Valve lifters: solid. Carb.: Carter D6Al-2, D6Cl-2, D6Pl. Torque (compression): 154 lb.-ft. @ 1200 R.P.M. Cars built for export were equipped with 170.4 cu. in. engine, 2-7/8 in. bore x 4-3/8 in. stroke. Rated at 70 hp. Engines were identified by engine code number P9X or P10X - 6.07:1 compression ratio. Only one P9 and no P10 models are recorded as being shipped with this export engine, caused no doubt by the fact that most small bore engines were shipped to England for final assembly in the Kew plant; England was by this time at war with Germany and all car production had come to a halt.

OPT. ENGINE: Inline. Valve in block. Six. Cast iron block. B & S: 3-1/8 x 4-3/8 in. Disp.: 201.3 cu. in. C.R.: 7.0:1. Brake H.P.: 87 @ 3600 R.P.M. Main bearings: four. Valve lifters: solid. Torque (compression) 158 lb.-ft. @ 1200 R.P.M.

Engine Note: Canadian-built vehicles utilized the larger 25-inch block with 3-3/8 in. bore x 4-1/16 in. stroke, for a displacement of 218.6 cubic inches.

COMMERCIAL ENGINE: Inline. Six. Cast iron block. B & S: 3-1/8 x 4-3/8 in. Disp.: 210 cu. in. C.R.: 6.7:1. Brake H.P.: 79 @ 3000 R.P.M. Main bearings: four. Valve lifters: solid. Torque (compression) 154 lb.-ft. @ 1200 R.P.M.

TECHNICAL: [P9 and P10] Sliding gear transmission. Speeds: 3F/1R. Column shift controls (all models). Single disc, dry 9-1/4 in. clutch. Driveshaft. Hypoid, semi-floating ,Hotchkiss drive rear axle. Overall ratio: 4.1:1 on P10. 3.9:1 on Roadking P9. Hydraulic brakes on four wheels. Steel disc wheels. Rim size: 5.50 x 16 on P9 Roadking; 6.00 x 16 on P10 Deluxe. Four in. width. [PT105] Three-speed standard with option four-speed w/power takeoff opening. Floor shift controls. Single disc, dry plate 10 in. diameter clutch. Driveshaft. Hypoid, semi-floating rear axle. Overall ratio: 4.1:1 standard. Hydraulic brakes on four wheels. Steel disc wheels. Rim size: 6.00 x 16 standard (see list for other options). Optional rear axle ratios: 3.73:1, 4.3:1 or 4.78:1. Optional tire and wheel sizes included 5.25 x 20, four ply; 5.25 x 20, six ply; 6.00 x 16, six ply; 6.00 x 18, six ply; 6.25 x 16, six ply; 6.50 x 16, four ply or 6.50 x 16, six ply.

CHASSIS: [P9] W.B.: 117 in. O.L.: 194-1/2 in. Frt/Rear Tread: 57/59-15/16 in. Tires: 5.50 x 16. [P10] W.B.: 117 in. (137 in. seven-passenger) O.L.: 194-1/2 in. (214-1/2 in. seven-passenger). Frt/Rear Tread: 57/59-15/16 in. Tires: 6.00 x 16. [PT105] W.B.: 116 in. Frt/Rear Tread: 56/60 in. Tires: 6.00 x 16.

1940 Plymouth, Model P10, station wagon, OCW

OPTIONS: Radio push-button dash mount ($47.50). Heater all weather heat system (45.50). Electric clock electric mounted in glovebox door (12.00). Radio antenna "Skyway" external cowl mount. Seat covers, several varieties offered. Back up lamp (2.95). Exhaust extension (1.00). Fender grille guard (11.20). Fender protectors (6.25). Fog lamps (12.00). Locking gas cap (1.50). Grille guard (6.95). Rear seat heater (11.95). Dual trumpet horns (underhood mount) (8.50). License frames (1.50). Outside rear view mirror (1.95). Deluxe steering wheel (8.50). Bumper (center) "Superguard" (1.75). Rear bumper center "Superguard" (2.50). Wheel discs (1.50 each). Wheel trim rings (1.50 each). 20 inch high clearance wheel. PT105 oil bath air cleaner (2.50). Vortex air cleaner (17.50 w/standard cap or 19.50 with Vortex cap). Airfoam seat cushion and back (10.00). Auxiliary taillamp (2.50). Domelamp (3.50). Glovebox lock (1.50). 32 amp generator for slow speed operation (14.00). Governor (5.00). Chrome headlamps (3.50). Grille guard (7.50). Dual horns (7.50). Heater and defroster (25.00). Deluxe Purolator oil filter (5.00). Colored sheet metal (5.00). Long arm stationary mirror (1.50). Same for right side (2.50). Long arm adjustable mirror LH (2.50). Same right-hand (3.00). Sun visor (2.00). Inside rear view mirror (1.00). Four-speed transmission (17.50). Chrome windshield frame (3.00). Right-hand windshield wiper (vacuum) (4.00). Electric windshield wiper left-hand (6.00). Dual electric windshield wipers (13.00). Express type rear bumper (6.00). Spare wheel lock (1.50). Economy Group 1 (2.50). Economy Group 2 (3.00). Wheel and tire equipment (in sets of five) 5.25 x 20, four ply (18.00). 5.25 x 20, six ply (35.00). 6.00 x 16, six ply (14.50). 6.00 x 18, six ply (not listed). 6.25 x 16, six ply (23.50). 6.50 x 16, four ply (13.50). 6.50 x 16, six ply (28.25).

Standard Catalog of Chrysler

HISTORICAL: P9 production began August 15, 1939; ended July 12, 1940. Public announcement date for the 1940 models was Thursday, September 21, 1939. Model year production: 106,738. K.T. Keller, corporate head; Dan S. Eddins, division head. P10 production began August 15, 1939; ended July 12, 1940. Model year production: 316,417. For the second year in-a-row Plymouth was awarded the Eastern Safety Conference Award. PT105 production began September 26, 1939; ended August 20, 1940. Model year production: 7,053. Walter P. Chrysler died in August at the age of 65, after suffering a cerebral hemorrhage. He had been ill the last few years of his life.

1941 PLYMOUTH

PLYMOUTH — MODEL P11 — SIX: The "no frills" line this year was the "Plymouth" line. Identified by its lack of vent windows on the front doors, little chrome, one windshield wiper and one inside sun visor on the driver's side, the model was the division's price leader. Also identified by its "Plymouth" name plate on the hood side panels, many options were not available for this line and when they were, they were not as "deluxe" as other models - the optional vent wing package came with painted, rather than chrome trim for example. Despite this the line sold slightly better than the upgraded P11D Deluxe series.

1941 Plymouth, Model P12, convertible coupe, OCW

PLYMOUTH DELUXE — MODEL P11D — SIX: Considered by some to be merely a 1940 Plymouth with a "chrome plated bib for a grille," the 1941 Plymouth saw many refinements over the previous year. Most notable among the changes this year was the one-piece, "alligator" opening hood, the battery mounted under the hood rather than under the driver's seat and spring loaded hinges on the trunk lid, replacing the cam-locking device of years past. At the rear, the stop lamp was fitted in the center of the deck lid, incorporated with the license plate holder. This lamp, situated slightly higher than the taillamps, eliminated the "tailgating" driver not seeing the brake lights. Delete runningboards continued as an option but the high clearance wheel option was reduced from 20-inch wheels to 18-inch.

Although not considered by the factory as a separate line, the P11D featured better appointments than the P11 Deluxe but less than the Special Deluxe P12 series. Most noticeable among the P11D's features was chrome trim around the windshield and side windows and the word "Deluxe" on the hood side panels.

1941 Plymouth, Model P12, station wagon, JAC

PLYMOUTH SPECIAL DELUXE — MODEL P12 — SIX: Two-tone paints and upholstery were the most noted features of the 1941 Special Deluxe series. Carrying the two-toning even further, the wooden-bodied Westchester station wagon could be had in two trim levels, with the woodwork finished in one solid shade, or with the flat panels stained a darker shade

for contrast! Most Special Deluxes were fitted with the optional bumper end "wingtips" and a center "Superguard" - the rear guard of the folding type to prevent the guard from interfering with the opening of the deck lid. Sales were spectacular as more people became employed in industry catering to the war goods production for England and perhaps many saw the handwriting on the wall as this country edged closer to involvement in the conflict.

PLYMOUTH COMMERCIAL CAR — MODEL PT125 — SIX: 1941 would prove to be the final year for Plymouth's commercial car venture until the 1974 Trail Duster (which itself was based on a similar Dodge model). With minimal sales and Dodge needing the factory capacity to meet growing truck demands prior to our entry in World War II, the Plymouth commercial car production was discontinued at the end of the model run.

Still using the basic body introduced in 1939, the 1941 model saw the most changes. The sealed beam headlamps were moved outward and mounted on the crowning vee of the fender, giving the vehicle a bug-eyed look. The front grille piece now featured an overlay of chromed grille trim and the front bumper had a decided vee shape to it as well. In another change, the "Plymouth" name badge was moved from the radiator shell to a point midway on the side of the hood upper panels and the parking lamps were moved to the cowl just below the windshield. Prices were increased substantially, with production just below the level it had been the year before. With the introduction of the new body style in 1939 truck production had taken place only in the Detroit and Los Angeles assembly plants.

I.D. DATA: [Plymouth P11 and P11D] Serial numbers on right front door post. Detroit starting: 15000101. Ending: 15135030. Los Angeles starting: 3121501. Ending: 3133962. Evansville starting: 22001001. Ending: 22036667. Windsor starting: 9821241. Ending: 9829853. Engine numbers on left front corner of cylinder block. starting: P11-1001. Ending: P11-535085. [Plymouth P12] Serial numbers on right front door post. Detroit starting: 11123001. Ending: 11399250. Los Angeles starting: 3269301. Ending: 3296572. Evansville starting: 20105101. Ending: 20147921. Windsor starting: 9616761. Ending: 9624457. Engine numbers on left front corner of cylinder block. Starting: P12-1001. Ending: P12-535085. [Plymouth PT125] Serial number appears on the plate showing the model code, which is mounted on the engine side of the cowl over the steering column, or on the right front door pillar post. Detroit starting: 81000101. Ending: 81006107. Los Angeles starting: 9210101. Ending: 9210700. Engine numbers on left front corner of cylinder block. Starting: PT125-1001.

Body Code	Body Type & Seating	Price	Weight	Prod. Total
Plymouth P11 Deluxe				
303	2-dr. Bus. Cpe.-3P	685	2849	23,754
302	2-dr. Clb. Cpe.-4P	NA	NA	994
311	2-dr. Sed.-5P	739	2899	46,646
310	4-dr. Sed.-5P	780	2929	21,175
NA	2-dr. Utility Sed.-1P	739	2794	468
820	2-dr. Panel Del'y-1P	745	NA	3,200
NA	4-dr. Sta. Wag.-7/8P	NA	NA	217
NA	Chassis	NA	NA	676
P11D Deluxe				
311	2-dr. Sed.-5P	779	2939	46,138
310	4-dr. Sed.-5P	820	2964	32,336
303	2-dr. Bus. Cpe.-3P	729	2879	15,862
302	2-dr. Clb. Cpe.-4P	NA	NA	204
NA	2-dr. Utility Sed.-1P	NA	NA	1
820	2-dr. Panel Del'y-1P	NA	NA	1
P12 Special Deluxe				
303	2-dr. Bus. Cpe.-3P	760	2899	23,851
302	2-dr. Clb. Cpe.-4P	805	2974	37,352
301	2-dr. Sed.-5P	810	2974	84,810
300	4-dr. Sed.-5P	840	2999	190,513
304	2-dr. Conv. Cpe.-4P	970	3206	10,545
NA	4-dr. Sed.-7P	1045	3379	1,127
NA	4-dr. Limo.-7P	1120	3379	24
NA	4-dr. Sta. Wag.-7/8P	995	3194	5,594
NA	2-dr. Utility Sed.-1P	NA	NA	2
NA	Chassis	NA	NA	323
PT125				
4112	2-dr. Pickup-3P	625	2800	6,073
NA	Cab & Chassis-3P	590	2600	196

Body production code numbers also indicate by a series of letters the type of coupe body fitted: ASC indicates auxiliary seat (club) coupe; letters TPC indicate two-passenger (business) coupe.

Specifications same for all 1941 models P11 and P12 (Including P11D). 1,387 P11s, 1,046 P11Ds and 3,024 P12s were built with right-hand drive.

STD. ENGINE: Inline. Valve in block. Six. Cast iron block. B & S: 3-1/8 x 4-3/8 in. Disp.: 201.3 cu. in. C.R.: 6.7:1. Brake H.P.: 87 @ 3800 R.P.M. Taxable/A.L.A.M./N.A.C.C. H.P.: 23.44. Main bearings: four. Valve lifters: solid. Carb.: Carter D6AI-2, D6CI-2, B6PI. Torque (compression) 160 lb.-ft. @ 1200 R.P.M.

OPT. ENGINE: Aluminum cylinder head. Inline. Valve in block. Six. Cast iron block. B & S: 3-1/8 x 4-3/8 in. Disp.: 201.3 cu. in. C.R.: 7.25:1. Brake H.P.: 92 @ 3800 R.P.M. Main bearings: four. Valve lifters: solid. Carb.: Carter D6AI-2, D6CI-2, B6PI. Torque (compression) 164 lb.-ft. @ 1200 R.P.M. [Plymouth PT125] Inline. Six. Cast iron block. B & S: 3-1/8 x 4-3/8 in. Disp.: 201 cu. in. Brake H.P.: 82. Main bearings: four. Valve lifters: solid.

Engine Note: Canadian built vehicles utilized the larger 25-inch block with 3-3/8 in. bore x 4-1/16 in. stroke for 218.6 cubic inches.

CHASSIS: [P11] W.B.: 117 in. O.L.: 194-3/4 in. Frt/Rear Tread: 57/59-15/16 in. Tires: 6.00 x 16 [P11D and P12] W.B.: 117 in. O.L.: 198-1/4 in. Frt/Rear Tread: 57/59-15/16 in. Tires: 6.00 x 16, four-in. rim. [P12] W.B.: 137-1/2 in. O.L.: 220-13/16 in. Frt/Rear Tread: 57/60-9/32 in. Tires: 6.50 x 16 w/4-1/2 in. rim. [PT125] W.B.: 116 in. Frt/Rear Tread: 55-15/16/60 in. Tires: 6.00 x 16.

TECHNICAL: [P11, P11D and P12] Sliding gear transmission. Speeds: 3F/1R. Column shift controls. Single disc, dry 9-1/4 in. clutch. Driveshaft. Hypoid, semi-floating, Hotchkiss drive rear axle. Overall ratio: 4.1:1 [P11 and P11D, 4.3:1 P12] Four wheel-hydraulic brakes. Steel disc wheels 6.00 x 16 (seven-passenger 6.50 x 16). "Powermatic" vacuum shift opt. [PT125] Sliding gear transmission. Speeds: 3F/1R. four-speed with power takeoff opening opt. Single disc, dry 10 in. clutch. Driveshaft, hypoid, semi-floating Hotchkiss drive rear axle. Overall ratio: 4.1:1 std., optional 3.73:1, 4.3:1 or 4.78:1. Four wheel hydraulic brakes. Steel disc wheels. Rim size: 6.00 x 16.

OPTIONS: Accessory Group A (P11D and P12) including glovebox lock with steel glovebox, rear wheel shields, cigar lighter, stainless steel wheel trim rings, chrome wheel discs and chrome license plate frames (25.00). Accessory Group A for station wagon (does not include wheel shields) ($16.00). Accessory Group B (P11D and P12) including cigar lighter, glovebox lock with steel glovebox, stainless steel wheel trim rings (10.00). Accessory Group C (P11 only) right-hand windshield wiper and right-hand sun visor (5.00). Bumper fender guards (P11 only) (8.00). Bumper center guards (P11 only) (3.00). Chrome wheel discs (set of four) (6.00). Chrome wheel trim rings (set of five) (7.50). Electric clock (P12 only) (10.00). Front door armrest (1.75 each). Front door vent wings (P11 only) (12.00). Glovebox lock with steel glovebox (1.00). Dual horns (P11D and P12) (2.00). Dual horns (P11) (5.00). Powermatic shifting (6.50). Eight tube push-button radio (46.75). Six tube radio (35.15). Windshield antennae (excluding convertible) (6.20). Cowl mounted antennae (5.55). Rear wheel shields (9.00). Stainless steel window reveals (excluding seven-passenger) (7.50). Two-tone paint (P12 only) (10.00). Lifeguard inner tubes set of five, 6.00 x 16 (44.00) set of five, 6.50 x 16 (49.00). Economy Group 1, small bore carb, small bore intake manifold and 3.73:1 axle ratio (2.50). Economy Group 2, same as group one except includes throttle stop and heat shields (3.50). Taxi Cab Package 1 including heavy-duty springs, shock absorbers and special crankcase ventilation, 11 in. clutch plate (8.75). Taxi Cab Package 2, same equipment but 10 in. clutch plate (3.75). Back up signal, body side shields, emergency brake alarm, cigarette lighter, Kool Kushion, exhaust extension, foglights, locking gas cap, heater (six different models), cowl mounted outside rear view mirrors, grille guard, insect screen, rear window venetian blind, seat covers, spotlights (LH or RH) spare tire air valve extension, vanity case. [PT125] Vortex air cleaner with standard cap (17.50), with Vortex cap (19.50). Airfoam seat cushion and back (10.00). Extra taillamp (2.50). Dome light in cab (2.50). Economy Group 1 (3.00). Economy Group 2 (5.00). Economy Group 3 (7.50). Glovebox door lock (1.50). "Handy" Governor (5.00). 32 amp generator (slow speed operation) (8.00). Chrome windshield frame (3.00). Chrome headlamps and parking lamps (3.50). Radiator grille guard (7.50). Dual Air-tone horns (5.00). Heater and defroster (25.00). Purolator heavy-duty oil filter (6.00). Oil filter (3.25). Long arm rear view mirror, left-hand stationary (1.50), right-hand stationary (2.50), left-hand adjustable (2.50), right-hand adjustable (3.00). Extra inside rear view mirror (1.00). Sun visor (2.00). Four-speed transmission w/power takeoff opening (17.50). Right-hand vacuum windshield wiper (4.00). Dual electric wipers (13.00). Express type rear bumper (6.00). Spare wheel lock (1.00). Wheel and tire equipment 5.25 x 20, four ply (18.00), 5.25 x 20, six ply (35.00), 6.00 x 16, six ply (14.50), 6.00 x 18, 6 ply (not listed), 6.25 x 16, six ply (23.50), 6.50 x 16, six ply (28.25). P11 panel delivery and utility sedan options: Accessory Group C including right-hand windshield wiper, right-hand sun visor (5.00). Dual taillamps (3.00). Auxiliary seat for Panel Delivery (12.00). Screen partition for utility sedan (25.00). Rear seat conversion package including rear seat cushion and seat back, seat riser and side armrests (not listed).

HISTORICAL: Plymouth P11 and P11D production began August 8, 1940; Ended July 16, 1941. Model year production: 97,130 P11 models; 94,542 P11 D models. K.T. Keller, corporate head; Dan S. Eddins, division head.

On November 18, 1940, a specially prepared 1941 P11 four-door sedan left Detroit, Michigan, in an attempt to be the first to drive from Detroit to the tip of South America via the proposed route of the Pan American Highway. The Richardson Pan American Highway Expedition consisted

of three men, Sullivan C. Richardson, Arnold Whitaker and Kenneth C. Van Hee. Mapping out the proposed route of the Pan American Highway, it took the three men and their 1941 Plymouth eight months to reach Magallanes, Chile, via a route that included countless miles of swamp, mountain and desert terrain through Mexico, Central and South America. Their eight-month expedition covered 15,745 miles one way.

Plymouth P12 production began August 8, 1940; ended July 16, 1941. Model year production: 354,139.

The four millionth Plymouth was built in 1941, with young actor Mickey Rooney painting the symbolic numbers on a convertible at the Los Angeles assembly plant. Rooney was playing in the popular "Hardy Boys" series at the time.

Plymouth PT125 production began September 18, 1940. End of production not known. Model year production: 6,269.

An overseas assembly plant was opened in South Africa. It would close in 1942 for the duration of the war, then reopen in 1946.

1942 PLYMOUTH

PLYMOUTH DELUXE — MODEL P14S — SIX: Easily identified by the lack of chrome trim around the windshield, the Deluxe line continued to be the division's price leader. Available only in a limited amount of body styles the entire commercial lineup was eliminated from the sales picture. Gone were the sedan delivery and the ambulance conversion, but a small handful (less than 100) utility sedans were built. Also missing was the truck chassis commercial line as well for 1942. All models could be had with the normal list of options except for two-tone paint on the coupes. As production wore on and more materials were being taken for the war effort, many cars were either fitted with shortened pieces of chrome (especially the front fender trim) or the chrome trim was painted over in what would become known as "black out" models. Some cars were even reported to have been delivered to the military bearing wooden bumpers!

1942 Plymouth, Model P14C, Special Deluxe, town sedan, OCW

PLYMOUTH SPECIAL DELUXE — MODEL P14C — SIX: Despite the war shortened production year, Plymouth enjoyed brisk sales. Production began late in July and ended on January 31, 1942. Many of the new cars not already in consumers hands were impounded by the government with the result that many of these vehicles saw military service. The 1942 Plymouth was nearly an all new car. Gone was the old familiar X-braced frame, replaced by a box perimeter frame. The new body sat lower on the chassis and for the first time the runningboards, or what remained of them, were concealed by the doors that flared out at their lower extremities to cover them. At the front a new, massive grille with the headlamps placed at the outer ends was featured, along with a sheet metal air scoop (inspired by race cars so the advertising claimed) to help cool air entering the engine compartment. Highly touted as an accessory was the vacuum controlled shifting mechanism that had been offered the previous year. The system was not sold in any great quantities and disappeared forever after production ceased. This accessory may have been offered to appease those customers for the low priced Plymouth line not having any form of automatic transmission as higher priced Chrysler Corporation cars had.

Gone from the sales lineup was the seven-passenger sedan and the ambulance conversion. A one year offering was the town sedan which featured normal opening rear doors (rather than suicide style doors found on regular sedans). The town sedan, also placed the rear quarter window into the door frame itself. Convertibles were standard equipped with fender shields and leather upholstery. The station wagon was still offered with two choices

of wood trim and for this year only the wooden body was trimmed by full length belt moldings of chrome trim, at least those models built in early production, prior to cut-backs caused by war related material shortages.

1942 Plymouth, P14C, Special Deluxe, club coupe, AA

I.D. DATA: [Plymouth P14S] Serial numbers on right front door post. Detroit starting: 15135501. Ending: 15153935. Los Angeles starting: 3134501. Ending: 3136266. Evansville starting: 22037001. Ending: 22041356. Windsor starting: 9829856. Ending: 9836986. [P14C] Serial numbers on right front door post. Detroit starting: 11399501. Ending: 11494048. Los Angeles starting: 3297001. Ending: 3306756. Evansville starting: 20148001. Ending: 20164436. Windsor starting: 9829856. Ending: 9836986. Engine numbers on left front corner of cylinder block. Starting: P14-1001. Ending: P14-149161.

Body Code	Body Type & Seating	Price	Weight	Prod. Total
P14S Deluxe				
TPC	2-dr. Bus. Cpe.-2/3P	812	2930	3783
412	2-dr. Clb. Cpe.-4P	885	2990	2458
400	4-dr. Sed.-5P	889	3025	11,973
411	2-dr. Sed.-5P	850	2985	9350
NA	2-dr. Utility Sed.-1P	842	2985	80
NA	Chassis	—	—	1
P14C Special Deluxe				
TPC	2-dr. Bus. Cpe.-2/3P	855	2955	7258
402	2-dr. Clb. Cpe.-4P	928	3035	14,685
401	2-dr. Sed.-5P	895	3020	24,142
400	4-dr. Sed.-5P	935	3060	68,924
405	4-dr. Twn. Sed.-5P	980	3085	5821
404	2-dr. Conv. Cpe.-4P	1078	3255	2806
NA	4-dr. Sta. Wag.-7/8P	1145	NA	1136
NA	Chassis	—	—	10

Specifications same for all 1942 models P14S and P14C. 942 P14s and 1,457 P14Cs were built with right-hand drive.

ENGINE: Inline. Valve in block. Six. Cast iron block. B & S: 3-1/4 x 4-3/8 in. Disp.: 217.8 cu. in. C.R.: 6.8:1. Brake H.P.: 95 @ 3400 R.P.M. Taxable/A.L.A.M./N.A.C.C. H.P.: 25.35. Main bearings: four. Valve lifters: solid. Carb.: Carter 86PI, B6GI. Torque (compression) 172 lb.-ft. @ 1600 R.P.M.
Note: Canadian-built vehicles utilized the larger 25-inch block with 3-3/8 in. bore x 4-1/16 in. stroke for 218.6 cubic inches.

CHASSIS: [Series P14S] W.B.: 117 in. O.L.: 195-9/16 in. Frt/Rear Tread: 57/59-15/16 in. Tires: 6.00 x 16. [Series P14C] W.B.: 117 in. O.L.: 195-9/16 in. Frt/Rear Tread: 57/59-15/16 in. Tires: 6.00 x 16.

TECHNICAL: Sliding gear transmission. Speeds: 3F/1R. Column shift controls. Single disc, dry 9-1/4 in. clutch. Driveshaft. Hypoid, semi-floating, Hotchkiss drive rear axle. Overall ratio: 3.9:1. Hydraulic brakes on four wheels. Steel disc wheels. Rim size: 6.00 x 16. Other rear axle ratios: 3.73:1 with economy group package. 4.1:1 on Suburban (station wagon). 4.56:1 on Suburban with 18-inch wheel option. 4.78:1 on all export models.

OPTIONS: Fender skirts (std. on convertible) ($12.50). Radio eight tube push-button (type "801") (54.85). Heater all weather heating system (49.20). Electric clock electric (std. on convertible) (9.75). Cigar lighter (2.00). Radio antenna windshield header (5.50). Seat covers several types offered. Spotlight right or left side (15.80 each). Fog lamps (12.40). License plate frames (2.20). Windshield washer (3.95). Handbrake alarm (2.50). Locking gas cap (1.80). Rear window wiper (9.50). Outside rear view mirror (2.35). Powermatic shift (7.85). Direction signals (10.00). Rear fender wingtip guards; Rear bumper center "Superguard"; spare tire air valve extension (to fill spare tire from outside car without opening trunk!); rear window sunshade; exhaust extension; wheel trim discs, wheel trim

rings; buzzer type handbrake alarm; flashing light type handbrake alarm; other radios offered were type "601" six tube push-button radio and a universal mount radio. Other radio antennae offered included external "Skyway" cowl mounted; internal cowl mounted; crank operated "Cowl Concealed" and a power operated "Cowl Concealed" antennae. Delete option on the Deluxe series included no vent panes in front door glass, no right-hand windshield wiper and no front bumper guards to keep price down. A major option offered in 1942 was two-tone paint on all models except the business coupe. Standard upholstery in the convertible was red leather, but buyer could choose optional blue or tan leather if desired.

HISTORICAL: P14S production began July 25, 1941; ended January 31, 1942. Model year production: 27,645. Dan S. Eddins, division head. P14C production began July 25, 1941; ended January 31, 1942. Model year production: 124,782.

1946 PLYMOUTH

1946 Plymouth, Deluxe two-door business coupe, 6-cyl (TVB)

DELUXE SIX — (6-CYL) — SERIES P-15 — The Deluxe Six was the low-priced Plymouth in 1946. Styling was a carryover of the last prewar designs with a simpler grille bar pattern and a front bumper that wrapped around the corners of the body. The rear fenders were also new and had a lower, smaller wheel opening. Standard equipment was comprised of airplane-type shock absorbers; All-Weather ventilation; front-end sway bar; sealed beam headlights; burn resistant exhaust valve seat inserts; scuff-proof four-ring aluminum pistons; air-cooled soft action clutch; calibrated knock-free ignition; floating oil intake; full-pressure lubrication front coil springs; Hotchkiss drive; metal leaf spring covers; Oilite gas filter; rubber-mounted steering gear; instrument panel starter button; Rubber Poise body mountings and hypoid rear axle. Chrome trim consisted of small wheel center covers; heavy rocker sill strips; chrome headlamp rims; 'Mayflower' hood-nose emblem; horizontal bar grille front fender moldings; hood ornament; and an upper beltline molding running from the forward portion of the hood to the upper rear quarter area. A nameplate reading 'Plymouth Deluxe' was placed on the sides of the hood below the beltline trim. A black rubber windshield frame and rear window surround were used. The deck carried a massive, bright metal latching mechanism and 'Mayflower' emblem with light-up plastic lens.

PLYMOUTH I.D. NUMBERS: Serial number on a plate on left front door post (right front door post of early 1946 models) is the only code used for identification/registration purposes. It consists of a Plymouth prefix 'P' and two-symbol series number (P-15). The four or more symbols following this are the production sequence number starting with 1001 at each factory. Engine number near front upper left side of block between first and second cylinders takes same format as serial number, but may not match. Engine number should not be used for identification. Engine numbers sometimes had suffixes: A = .020 inch cylinder overbore; B = .010 inch undersize journals and diamond-shaped symbol = .008 inch oversize tappet bore. Plymouth factory codes are: M=Detroit, Mich.; LA=Los Angeles, Calif.; E=Evansville, Ind.; and SL=San Leandro, Calif. These codes do not appear in serial number. Chrysler did not use body/style numbers at this time. Serial numbers for 1946 were as follows: Deluxe Series: (M) 15154001-15206835; (LA) 26000001-36003588 and (E) 22042001-22053039. Special Deluxe Series: (M) 11496001-11643103; (LA) 25000001-25009752 and (E) 20165001-20185186.

DELUXE SIX SERIES

Series No.	Body/ Style No.	Body Type & Seating	Factory Price	Shipping Weight	Prod. Total
P-15	N/A	2-dr Cpe-3P	1089	2977	Note 1
P-15	N/A	2-dr Clb Cpe-6P	1159	3037	Note 1

Series No.	Body/ Style No.	Body Type & Seating	Factory Price	Shipping Weight	Prod. Total
P-15	N/A	2-dr Sed-6P	1124	3047	Note 1
P-15	N/A	4-dr Sed-6P	1164	3082	Note 1

Note 1: See 1948 section for 1946-1948 P-15 series production. No annual body style breakout available.

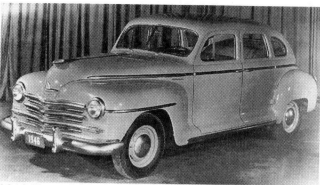

1946 Plymouth, Special Deluxe four-door sedan, 6-cyl

SPECIAL DELUXE SIX — (6-CYL) — SERIES P-15 — The Special Deluxe line was the second and higher-priced 1946 Plymouth model range. There were only small visual distinctions between cars in each series. Lettering at the rear corner of the hood, just ahead of the cowl area, carried the words 'Special Deluxe'. Bright metal moldings surrounded the windshield. Standard equipment included extra features such as dual windshield wipers and sun visors, glovebox lock, rear bumper fender guards, and rear window vents on sedans. The Special Deluxe could be ordered with either pencil stripe broad cloth upholstery or soft pile fabrics. Special Deluxe models were not quite as distinctive as in prewar times and weighed only slightly more than Deluxes. The convertible and wood-bodied station wagon came in the Special Deluxe series only. Both had their own unique interior appointments. The convertible featured genuine leather seats and the station wagon owner sat on leather-like upholstery. The station wagon came only in three-seats-for-eight-passengers format but the second and third seats were removable to create a large cargo deck. It had white ash wood framing and dark maple paneling. The top on the convertible coupe was of the blind rear quarter style, carried over from before the war.

SPECIAL DELUXE SIX SERIES

Series No.	Body/ Style No.	Body Type & Seating	Factory Price	Shipping Weight	Prod. Total
P-15	N/A	2-dr Cpe-3P	1159	2982	Note 1
P-15	N/A	2-dr Clb Cpe-6P	1234	3057	Note 1
P-15	N/A	2-dr Conv-5P	1439	3282	Note 1
P-15	N/A	2-dr Sed-6P	1199	3062	Note 1
P-15	N/A	4-dr Sed-6P	1239	3107	Note 1
P-15	N/A	4-dr Sta Wag-8P	1539	3402	Note 1

Note 1: See 1948 section for 1946-1948 P-15 series production. No annual body style breakout available.

ENGINE: PLYMOUTH SIX: Inline. L-head. Cast iron block. Displacement: 217.8 cid. Bore and stroke: 3-1/4 x 4-3/8 inches. Compression ratio: 6.6:1. Brake hp: 95 at 3600 rpm. Four main bearings. Solid valve lifters. Carburetor: Carter Type BB one-barrel Model DGG1.

CHASSIS FEATURES: Wheelbase: 117 inches. Overall length: (station wagon) 195-5/8 inches; (other styles) 196-3/4 inches. Front tread: 57 inches. Rear tread: 60-1/8 inches. Tires: 6.00 x 16.

OPTIONS: Heater and defroster. Radio and antenna. Large hubcaps (nine-inch hubcaps were standard on Deluxe, 10-inch were standard on Special Deluxe and optional on Deluxe). Directional signals. Seat covers. White sidewall discs. Wheel trim rings. Fog lamps. Spotlamp. Light-up hood ornament. Dual sun visors on Deluxe Six. Clock in Deluxe Six. Deluxe steering wheel. Deluxe Six rear fender molding (early in year only). Glovebox lock, in Deluxe Six. Dual windshield wipers, on Deluxe Six. External sun shade visor. Traffic light viewer. Bumper guards. Grille guard. Wing guards. License plate frames. Outside rearview mirrors. Three-speed manual transmission was standard. Heavy-duty air cleaner is available at extra cost. Available rear axle gear ratios (various).

HISTORICAL FOOTNOTES: The first postwar Plymouths were introduced in February 1946 and the P-15 series continued in production through early 1949. Calendar year production peaked at 242,534 units. Calendar year registrations of 211,800 cars were recorded. Plymouth was America's third largest producer of cars and accounted for 11.3 percent of U.S. auto production. Plymouth's 1946 sales slogan was "Now it's Plymouth: 50 new features and improvements." U.S. Body & Forging Co., of Franfurt, Ind., built wood-crafted bodies for Plymouth station wagons. The P-15 series, which entered production in February 1946, would continue being made for 39 consecutive months with only minor changes. You didn't need a crystal ball to predict what the next year's Plymouth was going to look like in the first few years after World War II.

1947 PLYMOUTH

1947 Plymouth, Deluxe two-door Club Coupe, 6-cyl

DELUXE SIX — (6-CYL) — SERIES P-15 — The Deluxe Six for 1947 was identical to the comparable 1946 model. Nomenclature was also the same. Plymouth simply continued with the same series for another year. Cars built after Jan. 1, 1947, were sold as 1947 models. The only way to pinpoint the model year is by reference to serial number codes. Even prices and weights stayed the same during the first part of 1947. The 154th edition of *Red Book*, dated April 1, 1947, reflects this consistency. Later, however, the price changes included in the charts below went into effect. Some models increased at retail, while others declined.

PLYMOUTH I.D. NUMBERS: Serial number on a plate on left front door post is the only code used for identification/registration purposes. It consists of a Plymouth prefix 'P' and two symbol series number (P-15). The four or more symbols following this are the production sequence number starting with 1001 at each factory. Engine number near front upper left side of block between first and second cylinders takes same format as serial number but may not match. Engine number should not be used for identification. Engine numbers sometimes had suffixes: A = .020 inch cylinder overbore; B = .010 inch undersize journals and diamond-shaped symbol = .008 inch oversize tappet bore. Plymouth factory codes are: M=Detroit, Mich.; LA=Los Angeles, Calif.; E=Evansville, Ind.; and SL=San Leandro, Calif. These codes do not appear in serial number. Chrysler did not use body/style numbers at this time. Serial numbers for 1947 were: Deluxe: (M) 15206936-15252278; (LA) 26003589-26010839; (E) 22043040-22063369. Special Deluxe: (M) 11643104-11854385; (LA) 25009753-25035585 and (E) 20185186-20233167.

DELUXE SIX SERIES

Series No.	Body/Style No.	Body Type & Seating	Factory Price	Shipping Weight	Prod. Total
P-15	N/A	2-dr Cpe-3P	1139	2977	Note 1
P-15	N/A	2-dr Clb Cpe-6P	1189	3037	Note 1
P-15	N/A	2-dr Sed-6P	1164	3047	Note 1
P-15	N/A	4-dr Sed-6P	1214	3082	Note 1

Note 1: See 1948 section for 1946-1948 P-15 series production. No annual body style breakout available.

1947 Plymouth, Special Deluxe four-door sedan, 6-cyl (TVB)

SPECIAL DELUXE SIX — (6-CYL) — SERIES P-15 — The Special Deluxe Six for 1947 was identical to the comparable 1946 model in appearance, construction and nomenclature. Cars built in the P-15 series, built after Jan. 1, 1947, were simply sold as 1947 models. Even prices remained unchanged at first but later increased due to the postwar seller's market

and inflationary spiral. Hoodside lettering, bright windshield frames and richer upholstery trims were telltale signs of a Special Deluxe. Serial numbers can be referred to for positive identification of year, but do not include body/style coding.

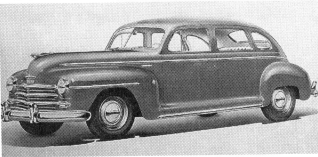

1947 Plymouth, Deluxe four-door sedan, 6-cyl

SPECIAL DELUXE SIX SERIES

Series No.	Body/Style No.	Body Type & Seating	Factory Price	Shipping Weight	Prod. Total
P-15	N/A	2-dr Cpe-3P	1209	2982	Note 1
P-15	N/A	2-dr Clb Cpe-6P	1264	3057	Note 1
P-15	N/A	2-dr Conv-5P	1565	3282	Note 1
P-15	N/A	2-dr Sed-6P	1239	3062	Note 1
P-15	N/A	4-dr Sed-6P	1289	3107	Note 1
P-15	N/A	4-dr Sta Wag-8P	1765	3402	Note 1

Note 1: See 1948 section for 1946-1948 P-15 series production. No annual body style breakout available.

ENGINE: PLYMOUTH SIX: Inline. L-head. Cast iron block. Displacement: 217.8 cid. Bore and stroke: 3-1/4 x 4-3/8 inches. Compression ratio: 6.6:1. Brake hp: 95 at 3600 rpm. Four main bearings. Solid valve lifters. Carburetor: Carter Type BB one-barrel Model DGG1.

1947 Plymouth, Special Deluxe two-door business coupe, 6-cyl (JL)

CHASSIS FEATURES: Wheelbase: (all models) 117 inches. Overall length: (station wagon) 195-5/8 inches; (all others) 196-3/4 inches. Front tread: (all models) 57 inches. Rear tread: (all models) 60-1/8 inches. Tires: (all models, early) 6.00 x 16; (all models, late) 6.70 x 15. The switch to 15-inch wheels was made in November and December 1947, and corresponded with the following serial numbers: Deluxe: (M) 15251917; (LA) 26010991; (E) 22063548; Special Deluxe: (M) 11851594; (LA) 25036148. (E) 20234249.

OPTIONS: Heater and defroster. Radio and antenna. Large hubcaps (nine-inch hubcaps were standard on Deluxe, 10-inch were standard on Special Deluxe and optional on Deluxe). Directional signals. Seat covers. White sidewall discs. Wheel trim rings. Fog lamps. Spotlamp. Light-up hood ornament. Dual sun visors on Deluxe Six. Clock in Deluxe Six. Deluxe steering wheel. Deluxe Six rear fender molding (early in year only). Glovebox lock, in Deluxe Six. Dual windshield wipers, on Deluxe Six. External sun shade visor. Traffic light viewer. Bumper guards. Grille guard. Wing guards. License plate frames. Outside rearview mirrors. Three-speed manual transmission was standard. Heavy-duty air cleaner was available at extra cost. Available rear axle gear ratios (various).

HISTORICAL FOOTNOTES: Plymouths of the P-15 series built after Dec. 1, 1946, were considered 1947 models and appeared in dealer showrooms after Jan. 1, 1947. Calendar year production peaked at 350,327 units. Calendar year registrations of 313,118 cars were recorded. Plymouth sales jumped 44.6 percent in 1947. The P-15 series ran from its 11th to 22nd consecutive months of production during calendar year 1947. Until late 1947, all models had 16-inch wheels and 6.00 x 16 tires. A full-size mock-up of a small-car proposal called the Plymouth "Cadet" was completed in 1947. This super-economy model resembled the soon-to-appear 1949 design. Project A-92 was another 1947 Plymouth styling concept for a larger postwar design car.

1948 PLYMOUTH

1948 Plymouth, Deluxe two-door sedan, 6-cyl (TVB)

DELUXE SIX — (6-CYL) — SERIES P-15 — The Plymouth P-15 series continued into 1948 without change as far as appearance, construction or nomenclature. Cars sold after Jan. 1, 1948, were designated 1948 models. Due to variations in state registration laws, it's possible to find 1947 models titled as 1948s. Some states issued license plates based on the date of sale. Check serial numbers for positive identification of Plymouths built as 1948 models. Prices increased substantially this season. A specifications change was in tire sizes. Fifteen-inch diameter-types replaced the 16-inch size of 1946-1947. (Some sources date the tire size change to late 1947, shortly before the Dec. 1 date designated as the start of 1948 production.) The smaller diameter tires gave the cars a lower look.

PLYMOUTH I.D. NUMBERS: Serial number on a plate on left front door post is the only code used for identification/registration purposes. It consists of a Plymouth prefix 'P' and two symbol series number (P-15). The four or more symbols following this are the production sequence number starting with 1001 at each factory. Engine number near front upper left side of block between first and second cylinders takes same format as serial number but may not match. Engine number should not be used for identification. Engine numbers sometimes had suffixes: A = .020 inch cylinder overbore; B = .010 inch undersize journals and diamond-shaped symbol = .008 inch oversize tappet bore. Plymouth factory codes are: M=Detroit, Mich.; LA=Los Angeles, Calif.; E=Evansville, Ind.; and SL=San Leandro, Calif. These codes do not appear in serial number. Chrysler did not use body/style numbers at this time. Serial numbers for 1948 were as follows: Deluxe: (M) 15252279-15284534; (LA) 26010840-26017025 and (E) 22063370-22071866. Special Deluxe: (M) 11854386-12066019; (LA) 25035586-25062782 and (E) 20233168-20287571.

1948 Plymouth, Special Deluxe four-door sedan, 6-cyl

DELUXE SIX SERIES

Series No.	Body/Style No.	Body Type & Seating	Factory Price	Shipping Weight	Prod. Total
P-15	N/A	4-dr Sed-6P	1441	3030	120,757
P-15	N/A	2-dr Sed-6P	1383	2995	49,918
P-15	N/A	2-dr Clb Cpe-6P	1409	3005	10,400
P-15	N/A	2-dr Cpe-3P	1346	2955	16,117

Note 1: 1946-1948 P-15 series production totals listed above. No annual body style breakout available.

Note 2: A total of 10 chassis only were also built.

1948 Plymouth, Special Deluxe two-door convertible, 6-cyl

SPECIAL DELUXE SIX — (6-CYL) — SERIES P-15 — Following corporate policy, the Special Deluxe Six was carried over into 1948 with no change in appearance, construction or nomenclature. Tire size changed to 15 inches. Prices went up, too. All 1946-1949 (First Series) Plymouths shared a few minor running changes, but none of these were of great significance. As previously mentioned, serial numbers should be referred to for dating and identifying P-15 series Plymouths, as to model year.

1948 Plymouth, Special Deluxe station wagon, 6-cyl

SPECIAL DELUXE SIX SERIES

Series No.	Body/Style No.	Body Type & Seating	Factory Price	Shipping Weight	Prod. Total
P-15	N/A	4-dr Sed-6P	1529	3045	514,986
P-15	N/A	2-dr Sed-6P	1471	3030	125,704
P-15	N/A	2-dr Clb Cpe-6P	1503	3020	156,629
P-15	N/A	2-dr Cpe-3P	1440	2950	31,399
P-15	N/A	2-dr Conv-5P	1857	3225	15,295
P-15	N/A	4-dr Sta Wag-8P	2068	3320	12,913

Note 1: 1946-1948 P-15 series production totals listed above. No annual body style breakout available.

Note 2: A total of 5,361 chassis only were also built.

ENGINE: PLYMOUTH SIX: Inline. L-head. Cast iron block. Displacement: 217.8 cid. Bore and stroke: 3-1/4 x 4-3/8 inches. Compression ratio: 6.6:1. Brake hp: 95 at 3600 rpm. Four main bearings. Solid valve lifters. Carburetor: Carter Type BB one-barrel Model DGG1.

CHASSIS FEATURES: Wheelbase: (all models) 117 inches. Overall length: (station wagon) 195-5/8 inches; (all others) 196-3/4 inches. Front tread: (all models) 57 inches. Rear tread: (all models) 60-1/8 inches. Tires: (all models) 6.70 x 15.

OPTIONS: Heater and defroster. Radio and antenna. Large hubcaps (nine-inch hubcaps were standard on Deluxe; 10-inch were standard on Special Deluxe and optional on Deluxe). Directional signals. Seat covers. White sidewall discs. Wheel trim rings. Fog lamps. Spotlamp. Light-up hood ornament. Dual sun visors on Deluxe Six. Clock in Deluxe Six. Deluxe steering wheel. Deluxe Six rear fender molding (early in year only). Glovebox lock in Deluxe Six. Dual windshield wipers, on Deluxe Six. External sun shade visor. Traffic light viewer. Bumper guards. Grille guard. Wing guards. License plate frames. Outside rearview mirrors. Three-speed manual transmission was standard. Heavy-duty air cleaner was available at extra cost. Available rear axle gear ratios (various). White sidewall tires. Two economy packages were offered. One had a smaller capacity carburetor and intake manifold, which reduced hp to 65 at 3000 rpm and a 3.73:1 rear axle ratio. Along with these changes, the second option also included a throttle stop limiting top speed to 45 mph.

HISTORICAL FOOTNOTES: Plymouths of the P-15 series built after Dec. 1, 1947, were considered 1948 models and appeared in dealer showrooms after Jan. 1, 1948. Calendar year production peaked at 378,048 units. Calendar year registrations of 347,174 cars were recorded. Plymouth sales rose 9.9 percent in 1948. The P-15 series ran from its 22nd consecutive month, at the beginning of 1948, to its 34th month in December.

1949 PLYMOUTH

(FIRST SERIES)

DELUXE AND SPECIAL DELUXE — (6-CYL) — From January to March of 1949, Plymouth continued to market P-15 series models built to 1948 model year specifications. These cars were officially built and sold as 1949 automobiles. They were, however, identical to 1948 models and carry approximately the same value to modern day car collectors. All of these cars were manufactured after Dec. 1, 1948, and had the following serial numbers at indicated factories: Deluxe Six: (Detroit) 15284535-15292209; (Evansville) 22071867-22073646 and (Los Angeles) 26017026-26018852. Special Deluxe Six: (Detroit) 12066020-12116123; (Evansville) 20287572-20299138 and (Los Angeles) 25062783-25071430. Owners of remaining examples should refer to the 1948 Plymouth section for information about fastback cars.

1949 Plymouth, Deluxe two-door Suburban, 6-cyl (PH)

(SECOND SERIES)

DELUXE (SHORT WHEELBASE) SIX — (6-CYL) — SERIES P-17 — Plymouth's first true postwar cars appeared in March 1949. The short wheelbase P-17 Deluxe models were the low-priced offering. Three two-door models - business coupe, Suburban and fastback sedan - were introduced successively. All had boxy lines reflecting the thinking of Chrysler's President K.T. Keller. They could be identified by their smaller, shorter sheet metal and Deluxe script on front fendersides. Frontal decorations consisted of a stylized 'Mayflower' hood ornament; Plymouth block lettering at the nose; chrome headlight rings and a massive horizontal plate above the grille bearing a 'Mayflower' emblem. The grille cavity was covered by a thick, horizontal bar between the headlights; two similar lower bars extending below the headlights (and housing rectangular parking lights at each outboard end); two thin horizontal moldings placed between the thicker ones (and equalling the top bar in length) plus three wide-spaced vertical moldings. Bumpers were of a triple-fluted design, with two vertical guards, and wrapped around the body corners. Other trim included a front fenderside molding; Deluxe front fender script; triple-fluted rocker panel steps; upper beltline molding; black rubber windshield surround; small hub center caps; trunk ornament emblem; trunk latch handle and rear bumper with guards. A rear fenderside spear was optional on early production units, but later became a regular feature. Upholstery was of the Deluxe level.

1949 Plymouth, Special Deluxe two-door Club Coupe, 6-cyl

PLYMOUTH I.D. NUMBERS: Serial number on plate on left front door post is the only code used for identification/registration purposes. It consists of a Plymouth prefix 'P' and two symbol series number (P-17, P-18). The four or more symbols following this are the production sequence number starting with 1001 at each factory. Engine number near front upper left side of block between first and second cylinders takes the same format as serial number, but may not match. Engine number should not be used for identification. Engine numbers sometimes had suffixes: A = .020 inch cylinder overbore; B = .010 inch undersize journals and diamond-shaped symbol = .008 inch oversize tappet bore. Plymouth factory codes are: M=Detroit, Mich.; LA=Los Angeles, Calif.; E=Evansville, Ind.; and SL=San Leandro, Calif. These codes do not appear in serial number. Chrysler did not use body/style numbers at this time. Serial numbers for 1949 at each factory were: P-17 Deluxe: (M) 18000101-18040467; (E) 24000001-24011890; (LA) 28000101-28003814 and (SL) 28500101-28503162. P-18 Deluxe: (M) 153000001-15358928; (E) 22080001-222096252; (LA) 26025001-26030100 and (SL) 26500101-26503423. P-18 Special Deluxe: (M) 1212000-112383178; (E) 20304001-20366486; (LA) 25075001-25097094 and (SL) 25500101-25510640. Engine Numbers for the three series were P-18-1001 through P-18-509050. P-17 = short wheelbase; Deluxe P-18 = long wheelbase, Deluxe or Special Deluxe. Production of Plymouths at San Leandro, California (code SL) began this year.

DELUXE (SHORT WHEELBASE) SIX SERIES

Series No.	Body/Style No.	Body Type & Seating	Factory Price	Shipping Weight	Prod. Total
P-17	N/A	2-dr Sed-6P	1492	2951	28,516
P-17	N/A	2-dr Cpe-3P	1371	2825	13,715
P-17	N/A	2-dr Sub-5P	1840	3105	19,220
P-17	N/A	Chassis only	—	—	4

1949 Plymouth, Special Deluxe two-door convertible, 6-cyl

DELUXE SIX — (6-CYL) — SERIES P-18 — Standard wheelbase Plymouths comprised the P-18 line. Two styles - sedan and club coupe - were offered with the basic Deluxe level of trim, equipment and appointments. External identification points for all P-17 and P-18 Deluxes included black rubber windshield surrounds, the lack of rear fender stone guards and Deluxe front fender side script. The Deluxe level interior had painted finish on the dashboard and window garnish panels and plainer upholstery fabrics. Important features found on all Plymouths this year were woven asbestos clutch facing; wider Safety-Rim wheels; Safe-Guard hydraulic brakes; shock-proof steering; rigid box-type frame; removable fenders; splash-proof distributors; resistor spark plugs; Floating-Power engine mountings; new Sea-Leg shock absorbers; engine splash shields; counterbalanced trunk lid; rotary door latches; rust-proof sheet metal; full-automatic spark control; theft-proof ignition cable; Oilite gasoline filter; and oil bath air cleaner. An electrically-operated automatic choke was one additional technical innovation and a redesigned intake manifold was another.

DELUXE SIX SERIES

P-18	N/A	4-dr Sed-6P	1551	3059	61,021
P-18	N/A	2-dr Clb Cpe-6P	1519	3034	25,687

SPECIAL DELUXE SIX — (6-CYL) — SERIES P-18 — The Special Deluxe Six represented the top level of trim for Plymouth again this year. Standard extras found with cars in this line included bright metal windshield and rear window trim moldings; mahogany grained dashboard and garnish moldings; richer upholstery fabrics; and special Deluxe front fenderside script. Only the standard wheelbase (P-18) models came with such trim and two exclusive body types were provided. The convertible had as standard equipment a power-operated folding top, convertible top boot and genuine leather upholstery. The Special Deluxe station wagon had three seats with leather-like coverings. The rear two were completely removable. The wood-trimmed bodies (by U.S. Steel & Forging Co.) were constructed with an all-steel roof and steel tailgate with integral spare tire enclosure. The roof pillars and rear upper hatch were of real wood. Station wagon bumpers, taillamps and trim were unique to this particular model. All Plymouths had new "bull's eye" headlight lenses with magnifier spots in the center. Taillights were housed in small fins mounted on top of the rear fenders on all standard wheelbase models except the station wagon.

SPECIAL DELUXE SIX SERIES

P-18	N/A	4-dr Sed-6P	1629	3079	252,878
P-18	N/A	2-dr Clb Cpe-6P	1603	3046	99,680
P-18	N/A	2-dr Conv-6P	1982	3323	15,240
P-18	N/A	4-dr Sta Wag-8P	2372	3341	3,443
P-18	N/A	Chassis only	—	—	981

ENGINE: PLYMOUTH SIX: Inline. L-head. Cast iron block. Displacement: 217.8 cid. Bore and stroke: 3.25 x 4.375 inches. Compression ratio: 7.0:1. Brake hp: 97 at 3600 rpm. Four main bearings. Solid valve lifters. Carburetor: Carter Type BB one-barrel Model D6H1.

CHASSIS FEATURES: Wheelbase: (P-17 series) 111 inches; (P-18 series) 118.5 inches. Overall length: (P-17 series) 185-5/16 inches; (P-18 series) 191-1/2 inches. Front tread: (all models) 55 inches. Rear tread: (all models) 56 inches. Tires: (P-17 series) 6.40 x 15; (P-18 series) 6.70 x 15.

OPTIONS: Heater and defroster. Radio and antenna. Full disc wheel covers. Wheel trim rings. White sidewall tires. License plate frames. Bumper guards. Grille guards. Dual windshield wipers, Deluxe. Dual horns, Deluxe. Dual sun visors, Deluxe. Chrome exhaust extension. Spotlight. Fog lamps. Back-up light. Outside rearview mirrors. Turn signals. Outside sun shade. Traffic light viewer. Seat covers. Stainless steel stone guards. Vent-I-Shades. Lockable glovebox. Deluxe lockable gas cap. Electric gas cap flipper. Three-speed manual transmission was standard. Heavy-duty air cleaner was optional, at extra cost. Available rear axle gear ratios (various).

HISTORICAL FOOTNOTES: The Second Series 1949 Plymouth P-18 models were introduced in March 1949 and the P-17 models appeared in dealer showrooms April 1949. Model year production peaked at 508,000 units. Calendar year sales of 574,734 cars were recorded. D.S. Eddins was the chief executive officer of the company this year. Plymouth retained its position as America's number three maker and held a 21.1 percent market share. The company was located at 6334 Lynch Road, Detroit, Mich. "The Great New Plymouth" was one of the slogans used to promote sales of the new 1949 postwar design. Production leaped 47.5 percent from 1948 and actually taxed Plymouth's ability to build enough cars. Toward the end of 1949, some cars were built with aluminum brake shoes due to a steel shortage. Some early versions of the all-new car had overly high riding heights. Shorter front coils and flatter rear leaf springs were adopted to lower them one-and-one-half inches. The Deluxe Suburban was a midyear model released in June 1949 and promoted as "the car with 101 uses." U.S. Body & Forging Co. continued to make the bodies for the "woodie" wagon, which began to decline in popularity.

1950 PLYMOUTH

1950 Plymouth, Deluxe two-door business coupe, 6-cyl (TVB)

DELUXE (SHORT WHEELBASE) SIX — (6-CYL) — SERIES P-19 — Styling changes for 1950 were of the bolt-on type. In addition to trim variations, they included new peaked rear fenders on most cars. This was a sheet metal revision, but one easily accomplished on Plymouths. The company heavily promoted the fact that rear fenders on all of its products were attached with bolts and readily replaceable in case of collision damage. Grille appearances were changed by reducing the number of horizontal blades. The two lower, thick bars remained, but the thin moldings were gone and a bowed upper bar was used. It had a trim molding right above it, with short extensions onto the fender edges. Plymouth lettering, a small nose emblem and the 'Mayflower' mascot were also seen on the hood. Triple-fluted bumpers were replaced with smoother, plainer ones, but ribbed rocker panel moldings were retained. Horizontal spears decorated both the front and rear fender sides and chrome headlamp rings and vertical bumper guards were seen once more. The side of the front fender earned a Deluxe script. At the rear, smaller trunk emblems, handles and taillights were featured. Deluxe models did not have rear gravel guards and used rubber windshield and rear window surrounds. Rear windows were made slightly larger. In September 1950, a fancy Special Suburban was offered. It had bright metal gravel guards and window frames, fancier upholstery and Special Suburban front fender script. Both Suburbans continued to use 1949-style rear fenders.

PLYMOUTH I.D. NUMBERS: Serial number on plate on left front door post is the only code used for identification/registration purposes. It consists of a Plymouth prefix 'P' and two symbol series number (P-19, P-20). The four or more symbols following this are the production sequence number starting with 1001 at each factory. Engine number near front upper left side of block between first and second cylinders takes same format as serial number, but may not match. Engine number should not be used for identification. Engine numbers sometimes had suffixes: A = .020 inch cylinder overbore; B = .010 inch undersize journals and diamond-shaped symbol = .008 inch oversize tappet bore. Plymouth factory codes are: M=Detroit, Mich.; LA=Los Angeles, Calif.; E=Evansville, Ind.; and SL=San Leandro, Calif. These codes do not appear in serial number. Chrysler did not use body/style numbers at this time. Serial numbers for 1950 at each factory were as follows: P-19 Deluxe: (M) 18041001-18119094; (E) 24012001-24035538; (LA) 28004001-28009848 and (SL) 28503501-28511177. P-20 Deluxe: (M) 15359501-15456084; (E) 22097001-22125803; (LA) 26030501-26035870 and (SL) 26504001-26510569. P-20 Special Deluxe: (M) 12384501-12627867; (E) 20367001-22125803; (LA) 26030501-26035870 and (SL) 26504001-26510569. Engine numbers for the three series were: P20-1001-P204.

DELUXE SIX SERIES

Series No.	Body/Style No.	Body Type & Seating	Factory Price	Shipping Weight	Prod. Total
P-19	N/A	2-dr Sed-6P	1492	2946	67,584
P-19	N/A	2-dr Cpe-3P	1371	2872	16,861
P-19	N/A	2-dr Sub-5P	1840	3116	34,457

SPECIAL DELUXE

P-19	N/A	2-dr Sub-5P	1946	3155	Note 1

Note 1: Special Deluxe Suburban Production Total included in the 34,457 Suburbans built.

Note 2: One chassis only was also built.

DELUXE SIX — (6-CYL) — SERIES P-20 — Styling changes for 1950 Plymouth P-20 models paralleled those of the lower-priced cars, although some of the parts (such as grille members) were actually larger in size. They looked the same, but were not interchangeable between both series. Two models continued to be offered in the low-level Deluxe trim line. Standard features included Deluxe front fender script; black rubber windshield and rear window moldings; painted dashboard and garnish moldings; and plainer upholstery fabrics. In base form, no rear fender gravel shields were provided. Unlike many other makers, Plymouth did not use black rubber stone guards on its cheaper models. However, chrome shields could be ordered as an option on all Plymouths. To increase rear vision, the rear window glass area was enlarged and now extended down to the rear deck region. Small hubcaps were standard equipment on Plymouth Deluxe automobiles.

DELUXE SIX SERIES

P-20	N/A	4-dr Sed-6P	1551	3068	87,871
P-20	N/A	2-dr Clb Cpe-6P	1519	3040	53,890

SPECIAL DELUXE — (6-CYL) — SERIES P-20 — The Special Deluxe P-20 series was Plymouth's high-dollar range. These cars had, as standard equipment, bright metal windshield and rear window frames; richer interior fabric choices; woodgrain finish on metal interior panels; and Special Deluxe front fender script. The convertible (officially described as a convertible club coupe) used leather upholstery and a power top riser mechanism and came with a simulated leather snap-on boot. The station wagon had the same features outlined for comparable 1949 models. In fact, its rear fenders and taillights were of the 1949 style. Factory photographs indicate Special Deluxes came with larger hubcaps, but not full wheel covers. Trim rings are seen on most of these cars. Also, as in 1949, the large cars had slightly bigger tires. Other features found as regular equipment in the Special Deluxe models were armrests on both front doors; cigar lighter and clock.

SPECIAL DELUXE SIX SERIES

P-20	N/A	4-dr Sed-6P	1629	3072	234,084
P-20	N/A	2-dr Clb Cpe-6P	1603	3041	99,361
P-20	N/A	2-dr Conv-6P	1982	3295	12,697
P-20	N/A	4-dr Sta Wag-8P	2372	3353	2,057
P-20	N/A	Chassis only	N/A	N/A	2,091

ENGINE: (PLYMOUTH SIX) Inline. L-head. Cast iron block. Displacement: 217.8 cid. Bore and stroke: 3.25 x 4.375 inches. Compression ratio: 7.0:1. Brake hp: 97 at 3600 rpm. Four main bearings. Solid valve lifters. Carburetor: Carter Type BB one-barrel Model D6H1.

CHASSIS FEATURES: Wheelbase: (P-19 series) 111 inches; (P-20 series) 118-1/2 inches. Overall length: (P-19 series) 186-1/2 inches; (P-20 series) 192-5/8 inches. Front tread: (all models) 55-7/16 inches. Rear tread: (all models) 58-7/16 inches. Tires: (P-19 series) 6.40 x 15; (P-20 series) 6.70 x 15.

OPTIONS: Heater and defroster. Radio and antenna. Full disc wheel covers. Wheel trim rings. White sidewall tires. License plate frames.

Bumper guards. Grille guards. Dual windshield wipers, Deluxe. Dual horns, Deluxe. Dual sun visors, Deluxe. Chrome exhaust extension. Spotlight. Fog lamps. Back-up light. Outside rearview mirrors. Turn signals. Outside sun shade. Traffic light viewer. Seat covers. Stainless steel stone guards. Vent-I-Shades. Lockable glovebox, Deluxe. Lockable gas cap. Electric gas cap flipper. Three-speed manual transmission was standard. Heavy-duty air cleaner was available, at extra cost. Available rear axle gear ratios (various).

1950 Plymouth, Special Deluxe station wagon, 6-cyl

HISTORICAL FOOTNOTES: The 1950 Plymouths were introduced Jan. 12, 1950. Model year production peaked at 590,000 units. Calendar year sales of 573,166 cars was recorded. D.S. Eddins was the chief executive officer of the company this year. Plymouth was still America's third largest automaker and held a 15.9 percent market share. Plymouth sales grew less than half a percent as the postwar boom in demand for autos subsided. A 100-day shutdown due to a labor strike didn't help either. The 1950 models were promoted as "The Beautifully New Plymouth." L.L "Tex" Colbert succeeded K.T. Keller as president of Chrysler Corp. in 1950. Keller became chairman of the board. This would be the last year for Plymouth "woodie" wagons with bodies by U.S. Body & Forging Co.

1951 PLYMOUTH

1951 Plymouth, Concord two-door sedan, 6-cyl

CONCORD — (6-CYL) — SERIES P-22 — The new Concord P-22 series played the same role, in the Plymouth lineup, as the short wheelbase Deluxe had in the past. Styling changes looked more extensive than they actually were. The sheet metal was nicely re-worked to create a more modern look without major re-tooling. The hood contour was lower, smoother and broader. Front fenders sloped downward at the front. The grille had a full-width, bow-shaped upper bar and a horizontal center blade, which was also slightly bowed. A trio of vertical elements looked more like misplaced bumper guards. Horizontal parking lights were set into vertical extensions of the upper bar. The full wraparound bumper was of more massive design and had two vertical guards. A plate, with the word Plymouth stamped into it, stretched above the grille. 'Mayflower' nose emblems and hood mascots appeared. Additional trim included front and rear fender moldings; rocker sill strips; black rubber windshield frame; new hubcaps; upper beltline trim; and Concord fender script. The Concord Suburban was now a two-seat economy station wagon, with spare tire carried inside. The Concord Savoy replaced the Special Deluxe Suburban and came with large hubcaps; chrome gravel guards; bright metal window frames; extra trim moldings; and special two-tone luxury upholstery. Standard equipment for the Concord Savoy included front and rear armrests; rear passenger assist straps; rear seat side storage compartments; and sliding central windows. Savoy nameplates were seen on the front fenders. This was now the company's fanciest station wagon-type vehicle, since the "woodie" was dropped from the P-23 series.

1951 Plymouth, Savoy two-door Suburban, 6-cyl (JL)

PLYMOUTH I.D. NUMBERS: Serial number on plate on left front door post is the only code used for identification/registration purposes. It consists of a Plymouth prefix 'P' and two symbol series number (P-22, P-23). The four or more symbols following this are the production sequence number starting with 1001 at each factory. Engine number near front upper left side of block between first and second cylinders takes same format as serial number, but may not match. Engine number should not be used for identification. Engine numbers sometimes had suffixes: A = .020 inch cylinder overbore; B = .010 inch undersize journals and diamond-shaped symbol = .008 inch oversize tappet bore. Plymouth factory codes are: M=Detroit, Mich.; LA=Los Angeles, Calif.; E=Evansville, Ind.; and SL=San Leandro, Calif. These codes do not appear in serial number. Chrysler did not use body/style numbers at this time. Serial numbers for 1951 at each factory were as follows: P-22 Deluxe Concord: (M) 18126001-18192309; (E) 24042001-24056628; (LA) 28011001-28015486 and (SL) 28513001-28518903. P-23 Deluxe Cambridge: (M) 15460001-15577561; (E) 22132001-22159468; (LA) 26040001-26045476 and (SL) 26512001-26517909. P-23 Special Deluxe Cranbrook: (M) 12635001-12906467; (E) 20435001-20482924; (LA) 25112001-25124987; (SL) 25531001-25545618. Engine numbers for all three series were P23-1001 and up.

1951 Plymouth, Concord two-door business coupe, 6-cyl

CONCORD SERIES

Series No.	Body/ Style No.	Body Type & Seating	Factory Price	Shipping Weight	Prod. Total
DELUXE TRIM					
P-22	N/A	2-dr Sed-6P	1673	2969	49,139
P-22	N/A	2-dr Cpe-3P	1537	2919	14,255
P-22	N/A	2-dr Sub-5P	2064	3124	76,520
SPECIAL SAVOY TRIM					
P-22	N/A	2-dr Sub-5P	2182	3184	Note 1

Note 1: Production Total of Savoy Special Suburban included in Suburban 76,520 total.

Note 2: Production Total covers both 1951 and 1952 Series P-22 Plymouths.

CAMBRIDGE — (6-CYL) — SERIES P-23 — The new Cambridge models played the same role in the Plymouth lineup as the former standard wheelbase Deluxes. Comparable styles were available, too. The word Cambridge appeared on fendersides, above the horizontal trim spear. All 1951 Plymouths came with interior colors selected to match the exterior finish. A completely new dash panel harmonized with other appointments and housed conveniently positioned controls. Outstanding new features included electric windshield wipers; chair high seats; downdraft carburetors; Synchro-Silent gears; a higher compression six-cylinder engine and Safety-Flow Ride. This latter enhancement claimed to utilize hydraulics to create "cushions of oil", which gave a smooth ride on the roughest roads

1951 Plymouth, Cambridge two-door Club Coupe, 6-cyl (TVB)

CAMBRIDGE SERIES

Series No.	Body/Style No.	Body Type & Seating	Factory Price	Shipping Weight	Prod. Total
P-23	N/A	4-dr Sed-6P	1739	3104	179,417
P-23	N/A	2-dr Clb Cpe-6P	1703	3059	101,784

Note 1: Production Total covers both 1951 and 1952 Plymouth P-23 series.

CRANBROOK — (6-CYL) — SERIES P-23 — The 1951 Cranbrook models played the starring role in the annual Plymouth revue. They replaced the former Special Deluxe line and embodied similar attributes. Block letters spelled out the model designation at the upper, trailing front fender area. A new body style was added in this range. The Belvedere two-door convertible hardtop had the fashionable pillarless 'hardtop convertible' look. It featured a smoothly wrapped-around three-piece backlight; wedge-shaped rear side windows; cloth and simulated leather upholstery and special Belvedere nameplates on the front fendersides. A convertible was another exclusive offering in Cranbrook level trim, but the station wagon was gone. Plymouth's classiest utility model this season was the Savoy in the short wheelbase P-22 series.

1951 Plymouth, Belvedere two-door hardtop, 6-cyl (TVB)

CRANBROOK SERIES

P-23	N/A	4-dr Sed-6P	1826	3109	388,735
P-23	N/A	2-dr Clb Cpe-6P	1796	3074	126,725
P-23	N/A	2-dr HT Cpe-6P	2114	3182	51,266
P-23	N/A	2-dr Conv-6P	2222	3294	15,650
P-23	N/A	Chassis Only	N/A	N/A	4,171

Note 1: Totals cover both 1951 and 1952 Plymouth P-23 models.

ENGINE: (PLYMOUTH SIX) Inline. L-head. Cast iron block. Displacement: 217.8 cid. Bore and stroke: 3.25 x 4.375 inches. Compression ratio: 7.0:1. Brake hp: 97 at 3600 rpm. Four main bearings. Solid valve lifters. Carburetor: Carter Type BB one-barrel Model D6H1.

CHASSIS FEATURES: Wheelbase (Concord) 111 inches; (Cambridge, Cranbrook) 118-1/2 inches. Overall length (Concord) 188-1/8 inches; (Cambridge, Cranbrook) 193-7/8 inches. Front tread (all models) 55-7/8 inches. Rear tread (all models) 58-7/16 inches. Tires: (Concord) 6.40 x 15; (Cambridge, Cranbrook) 6.70 x 15.

OPTIONS: Heater and defroster. Radio and antenna. Wheel trim rings. Full disc wheel covers. Solex tinted safety glass. Bumper guards. Grille guards. Spotlight. Fog light. Outside rearview mirror. White sidewall tires. External sun shade. Traffic light viewer. Rear fender chrome gravel shields. License plate frames. Seat covers. Rear seat speaker. Glove compartment lock. Electric clock. Special body colors. Mud guard flaps. Three-speed manual transmission was standard. Heavy-duty air cleaner was optional at extra cost. Available rear axle gear ratios: (P-22) 3.73:1 or 3.90:1; (P-23) 3.90:1 or 4.11:1.

HISTORICAL FOOTNOTES: The 1951 Plymouths were introduced Jan. 12, 1951, and the Belvedere hardtops appeared in dealer showrooms March 31, 1951. Model year production peaked at 576,000 units. Calendar year sales of 620,870 cars were recorded. D.S. Eddins was the chief executive officer of the company this year. On a calendar year basis Plymouth built 11,180 convertibles, 31,360 hardtops and 45,300 station wagons between Jan. 1, 1951, and the same date a year later. These would be close to model year figures since the model year at this time ran from Jan. 12, 1951, to November 1951, after which date production of cars built to 1952 specifications ensued. Overdrive transmission was not available in 1951. Plymouth set an all-time production record in 1951 and was the only auto manufacturer to do so that season. The company had an 11.63 percent market share and was responsible for 10.7 percent of all new car registrations. Plymouth's business climbed 8.2 percent in 1951, despite an overall decline in auto sales throughout the industry. Korean War material restrictions limited the supply of some parts. The Ghia-built Plymouth XX-500 dream car was made in Italy this year. It had futuristic features including slab sides, a one-piece curved windshield and fastback roof. It went on the auto show circuit in the mid-'50s. Plymouth also received a government contract to build seaplane hulls for the Grumman Albatross at its Evansville, Ind., plant.

1952 PLYMOUTH

1952 Plymouth, Concord two-door business coupe, 6-cyl

CONCORD — (6 CYL) — SERIES P-22 — Due to the outbreak of war in Korea, Plymouth continued its 1951 models into 1952, with only surface changes. The emblem on the nose of the cars was slightly redesigned. Signature style chrome script plates were used to adorn the front fenders as model identification trim. At the rear, the manufacturer's nameplate was repositioned from above the trunk emblem to a relief cut into the top of the emblem. Prices were increased, with permission from government agencies, but the series nomenclature was unchanged. Consequently, output figures for 1951 and 1952 Plymouths are recorded as a single total. Overdrive transmission was a Plymouth technical innovation this season. America's number three maker had not offered this feature on previous postwar models. By the end of the run, nearly 51,670 cars had this option installed. Neither automatic nor semi-automatic transmissions were yet available in Plymouth automobiles. The short wheelbase Concord was dropped from production in October 1952.

1952 Plymouth, Savoy two-door Suburban, 6-cyl

PLYMOUTH I.D. NUMBERS: Serial number on plate on left front door post is the only code used for identification/registration purposes. It consists of a Plymouth prefix 'P' and two symbol series number (P-22, P-23). The four or more symbols following this are the production sequence number starting with 1001 at each factory. Engine number near front upper left side of block between first and second cylinders takes same format as serial number, but may not match. Engine number should not be used for identification. Engine numbers sometimes had suffixes: A = .020 inch cylinder overbore; B = .010 inch undersize journals and diamond-shaped symbol = .008 inch oversize tappet bore. Plymouth factory codes are: M=Detroit, Mich.; LA=Los Angeles, Calif.; E=Evansville, Ind.; and SL=San Leandro, Calif. These codes do not appear in serial number. Chrysler did not use body style numbers at this time. Serial numbers for 1952 at each factory changed as follows: Concord: (M) 18192501-18223600; (E) 24056701-24063833; (LA) 28015701-2801555 and (SL) 28519101-28522352. Cambridge: (MA) 15577801-1566660; (E) 22159601-22181520; (LA) 26045701-26049991 and (SL)

26518201-26523546. Cranbrook: (M) 12906701-13066238; (E) 20485001-20516075; (LA) 25125301-25134190 and (SL) 25546101-25555957. Engine numbers for all series were P23-1001 and up.

CONCORD SERIES

Series No.	Body/ Style No.	Body Type & Seating	Factory Price	Shipping Weight	Prod. Total
DELUXE TRIM					
P-22	N/A	2-dr Sed-6P	1753	2959	Note 1
P-22	N/A	2-dr Cpe-3P	1610	2893	Note 1
P-22	N/A	2-dr Sub-5P	2163	3145	Note 1
SPECIAL SAVOY TRIM					
P-22	N/A	2-dr Sub-5P	2287	3165	Note 1

Note 1: See 1951 Plymouth production totals. Figures for both years are lumped together with no annual breakout available.

CAMBRIDGE — (6-CYL) — SERIES P-23 — The 1952 Cambridge was a mildly face-lifted version of the previous comparable model. The only variations between both years were number codes, prices and redesigned nameplates plus new hood and trunk emblems. It was also hard to buy a Plymouth equipped with optional whitewall tires this year. Raw material supplies were greatly diminished, due to restrictions imposed during the Korean conflict. Despite National Production Administration (NPA) ceilings on auto manufacturing during the Korean War, Plymouth continued as the output leader among Chrysler Corp. divisions. The company produced approximately 50 percent of all Chrysler automobiles built this year.

CAMBRIDGE SERIES

P-23	N/A	4-dr Sed-6P	1822	3068	Note 1
P-23	N/A	2-dr Clb Cpe-6P	1784	3030	Note 1

Note 1: See 1951 Plymouth production totals. Figures for both years are lumped together with no annual breakout available.

1952 Plymouth, Cranbrook two-door convertible, 6-cyl

CRANBROOK — (6-CYL) — SERIES P-23 — As is the case with other 1952 Plymouths, the Cranbrook models were merely a continuation of the basic 1951 product for another year. The only annual changes were new model identification script, redesigned hood mascots and slightly revised trim at the front and rear. Even the P-23 series designation was carried through again. The Belvedere, however, received some extra attention in that its identification badge was repositioned to the rear roof pillar and a different type of two-tone finish was employed. The top color with this paint scheme extended onto the rear quarter sheet metal. While the front and sides of the body were done in one tone, the roof, rear deck lid and deck lid surrounding area were painted a second shade that contrasted with the main color. Solex tinted glass was a new option available on all 1952 Plymouths.

CRANBROOK SERIES

P-23	N/A	4-dr Sed-6P	1914	3088	Note 1
P-23	N/A	2-dr Clb Cpe-6P	1883	3046	Note 1
P-23	N/A	2-dr HT Cpe-6P	2216	3105	Note 1
P-23	N/A	2-dr Conv-6P	2329	3256	Note 1

Note 1: See 1951 Plymouth production totals. Figures for both years are lumped together with no annual breakout available.

ENGINE: (PLYMOUTH SIX) Inline. L head. Cast iron block. Displacement: 217.8 cid. Bore and stroke: 3.25 x 4.375 inches. Compression ratio: 7.0:1. Brake hp: 97 at 3600 rpm. Four main bearings. Solid valve lifters. Carburetor: Carter Type BB one-barrel Model D6H2

CHASSIS FEATURES: Wheelbase: (Concord) 111 inches; (Cambridge, Cranbrook) 118-1/2 inches. Overall length: 188-1/2 inches; (Cambridge, Cranbrook) 193-7/8 inches. Front tread: (all models) 55-7/8 inches. Rear tread: (all models) 58-7/16 inches. Tires: (Concord sedan and coupe) 6.40 x 15; (Cranbrook) 6.70 x 15.

OPTIONS: Heater and defroster. Radio and antenna. Wheel trim rings. Full disc wheel covers. Solex tinted safety glass. Bumper guards. Grille guards. Spotlight. Fog light. Outside rearview mirror. White sidewall tires.

External sun shade. Traffic light viewer. Rear fender chrome gravel shields. License plate frames. Seat covers. Rear seat speaker. Glove compartment lock. Electric clock. Special body colors. Mudguard flaps. Three-speed manual transmission was standard. Overdrive transmission ($102). Heavy-duty air cleaner was available at extra cost. Available rear axle gear ratios: (P-22) 3.73:1 or 3.90:1; (P-23) 3.90:1 or 4.10:1.

HISTORICAL FOOTNOTES: The 1952 Plymouths were introduced Jan. 4, 1952. Sales went down 23.74 percent, largely due to the outbreak of fighting in Korea. Model year production peaked at 368,000 units. Calendar year sales of 474,836 cars were recorded. D.S. Eddins was the chief executive officer of the company this year. On a calendar year basis, Plymouth manufactured 21,290 Belvederes, 4,269 convertibles and 35,885 Suburbans between Jan. 1, 1952, and the same date a year later. Some of these were 1953 models, which entered production in the fall of 1952, earlier than usual. Overdrive transmission was a new option this year and was installed in 61,710 Plymouths built to 1952 specifications. The 111-inch wheelbase Concord line was dropped in October 1952. Plymouth bodies were built by Briggs Manufacturing Co. Plymouths were assembled at Detroit, Mich.; Evansville, Ind.; Los Angeles and San Leandro, Calif. The Detroit plant had 1,393,497 square feet under one roof and was one-half mile long. The National Production Administration (NPA) established production quotas this year, based on Korean war materials allotments. Aircraft hulls were constructed, under government contract, in the Evansville factory with the first one delivered late in 1952.

1953 PLYMOUTH

1953 Plymouth, Cambridge two-door business coupe, 6-cyl

CAMBRIDGE — (6-CYL) — SERIES P24-1 — The short wheelbase Concord line was not marketed after 1952. The Cambridge line was the base offering and used a 4-1/2-inch shorter stance, shared with all 1953 Plymouths. The company celebrated its 25th Anniversary this season by introducing all-new styling. Changes included a more modern body with one-piece windshield. Detachable rear fenders were finally abandoned, with stamped flairs decorating the front and rear quarter panels. The main grille bar and parking lights formed a horizontal V-shape. The 'Mayflower' hood ornament was fully redesigned. A new hood emblem incorporated the name Plymouth and the glove compartment was placed in the center of the instrument panel. The fuel filler pipe was located below the deck lid on the left side. Cambridge identification features included black rubber windshield frames, Cambridge front fender script on passenger cars and Suburban front fender script on station wagons. These cars had no side spears, no gravel shields, no tail ornaments and stationary rear vent windows. Small hubcaps were standard equipment. A new feature was a "one-third/two-third" type front seat, which was used in all two-door models. New equipment features included splay-mounted rear leaf springs, Oriflow shock absorbers, cyclebond brake linings and floating engine oil intake.

PLYMOUTH I.D. NUMBERS: Serial number located on plate on left door post. Serial number starts with prefix (P=Plymouth) and three digit series code: 24-1; 24-2, followed by sequential production number starting at 1001 at each factory. Factory codes: M=Detroit, Mich.; LA=Los Angeles, Calif.; E=Evansville, Ind.; and SL=San Leandro, Calif. These codes do not appear in serial number. Engine numbers near front upper left of block between cylinders one and two. Engine number resembles serial number, but may not match. Engine numbers should not be used for identification. Prefix symbols changed to P24-1=Cambridge and P24-2=Cranbrook. Serial numbers at each factory were: Cambridge: (M) 13070001-13505308; (E) 2052001-20657000; (LA) 25136001-25161846; and (SL) 25560001-25588345. Cranbrook: same number range as Cambridge. Engine numbers for both series were P24-1001 through P24-628721.

CAMBRIDGE SERIES

Series No.	Body/ Style No.	Body Type & Seating	Factory Price	Shipping Weight	Prod. Total
P24-1	N/A	4-dr Sed-6P	1745	2983	93,585
P24-1	N/A	2-dr Clb Cpe-6P	1707	2943	1,050
P24-1	N/A	2-dr Bus Cpe-3P	1598	2888	6,975
P24-1	N/A	2-dr Sub-6P	2044	3129	43,545
P24-1	N/A	2-dr Sed-6P	—	—	56,800

1953 Plymouth, Cranbrook four-door sedan, 6-cyl

CRANBROOK — (6-CYL) — SERIES P24-2 — Cranbrooks shared all 1953 styling changes such as the new sheet metal and grille design, but had a higher level of trim and appointments. Identification points included chrome windshield moldings; chrome sweep spears on front and rear fenders; chrome gravel shields; chrome 'fishtail' ornaments; operable vent wings in all doors and special front fender nameplates. The signature script on passenger cars read Cranbrook or Belvedere, while those on the Suburban station wagon read Savoy. The Belvedere was marketed as a luxury level, two-door pillarless hardtop. Its special features included a band of chrome and medallions on the rear roof pillar plus higher grade interior trim. The Savoy also had special upholstery and interior appointments to set it apart from the basic Suburban. The convertible, as usual, had leather grained trim; power top riser; special door panels and a new, zip-out pliable plastic rear window. Plymouth introduced Hy-Drive, a three-speed manual transmission with torque converter, which eliminated the need to use the clutch except when changing between reverse and forward gears. It was introduced in March 1953. By June, 3,000 cars per week were being built with this feature. On March 23, 1953, prices on all models were slashed an average of $100. This helped spur an all-time sales record for the model year.

CRANBROOK SERIES

P-24-2	N/A	4-dr Sed-6P	1853	3023	298,976
P-24-2	N/A	2-dr Clb Cpe-6P	1823	2971	92,102
P-24-2	N/A	2-dr Belv HT-6P	2044	3027	35,185
P-24-2	N/A	2-dr Savoy Sub-6P	2187	3170	12,089
P-24-2	N/A	2-dr Conv Cpe-6P	2200	3193	6,301
P2402		Chassis only	—	—	843

Note 1: 2,250 Belvedere sedans were built in addition to the above total.

Note 2: 760 Belvedere sport coupes were built in addition to the above total.

1953 Plymouth, Cranbrook Belvedere two-door hardtop, 6-cyl (JL)

ENGINE: (PLYMOUTH SIX) Inline. L-head. Cast iron block. Displacement: 217.8 cid. Bore and stroke: 3.24 x 4.375 inches. Compression ratio: 7.1:1. Brake hp: 100 at 3600 rpm. Four main bearings. Solid valve lifters. Carburetor: Carter Type BB one-barrel Model D6H2.

CHASSIS FEATURES: Wheelbase (all models) 114 inches. Overall length: (all models) 189-1/8 inches. Front tread: (all models) 55-7/8 inches. Rear tread: (all models) 58-7/16 inches. Tires: (all models) 6.70 x 15.

OPTIONS: Heater and defroster ($45). Radio ($100). Tinted glass ($31). Directional signals ($17). Windshield washer ($11). Back-up lights.

Chrome wheel discs. Chrome wire wheels ($293). Painted wire wheels. Wire spoke wheel covers, set ($99). White sidewall tires. Grille guard. Bumper wing guards. Front fender molding, Cambridge. Rear fender molding, Cambridge. Chrome grille molding, Cambridge. Chrome gravel shields. Chrome exhaust extension. Taxicab package. Wheel trim rings. Outside sun shade. Traffic light viewer. Spotlight. Fog lamps. Seat covers. License plate frames. Three-speed manual transmission was standard. Overdrive transmission ($98). Semi-automatic transmission ($146). Available rear axle gear ratios: (standard) 3.73:1; (overdrive) 4.10:1.

HISTORICAL FOOTNOTES: The 1953 Plymouths were introduced Nov. 20, 1952, and the XX-500 prototype appeared in dealer auto shows March 14-22, 1953. Sales increased 39.5 percent during Plymouth's 25th Anniversary year and the eight-millionth Plymouth was made in September. Model year production peaked at 636,000 units. Calendar year sales of 662,515 cars were recorded. J.P. Mansfield was the chief executive officer of the company this year. Hy-Drive transmission and Synchro Silent Drive were introduced. A total of 600,447 Plymouths were registered in calendar 1953. On March 23, 1953, Plymouth reduced prices on its models by an average of $100. The 1953 production totals marked a new, all-time high for Plymouth Division. Chrysler purchased the Briggs Manufacturing Co. on Dec. 29, 1953. Hy-Drive was first introduced in March 1953. By July, 25 percent of all Plymouths being produced were ordered with Hy-Drive. The Detroit factory accounted for 70 percent of Plymouth's total production. During the calendar year, 9,900 Plymouths were built with power steering (most likely all being 1954 models). For the model year, 109,300 Plymouths had overdrive attachments. Plymouth built its last Grumman Albatross.

1954 PLYMOUTH

1954 Plymouth, Belvedere two-door hardtop, 6-cyl

PLAZA — (6-CYL) — SERIES P25-1 — The Plaza line was the base Plymouth series for 1954. Annual styling revisions amounted to a minor face lift over the previous season, although model offerings were substantially rearranged. The word 'Plymouth' now appeared at the center of the main horizontal grille bar, with wraparound chrome moldings on each side. The headlights were given a recessed look by widening the chrome-plated surrounds. Circular front parking lamps were used and mounted at the outboard ends of the lower horizontal grille bar. Plaza models used black rubber gravel shields and had Plaza front fender script. Power steering was introduced as a new option, but was used in only about 20,000 cars built in this calendar year. Some of these were 1955 models, manufactured in the fall of 1954. On Feb. 26, 1954, fully-automatic Power-Flite transmission was added to the optional equipment list. Plymouth buyers could then order cars with three-speed manual overdrive, semi-automatic or automatic transmission. A total of about 75,000 of all 1954 Plymouths came with the latter unit attached. The Plaza four-door sedan had stationary rear ventipanes. Two-door styles featured the 'one-third/two-third' type front seat.

PLYMOUTH I.D. NUMBERS: Serial number located on plate on left door post. Serial number starts with prefix (P=Plymouth) and two symbol series code (P25-1=Plaza; P25-2=Savoy and P25-3=Belvedere) followed by sequential production number starting at 1001 at each factory. Factory codes: M=Detroit, Mich.; LA=Los Angeles, Calif.; E=Evansville, Ind.; and SL=San Leandro, Calif. These codes do not appear in serial number. Engine numbers near front upper left of block between cylinders one and two. Engine number resembles serial number, but may not match. Engine numbers should not be used for identification. Serial numbers at each factory were: (M) 13506001-13829336; (E) 20658001-20739829; (LA) 25163001-25175377; (SL) 25590001-25606284. Engine numbers P25-1001 through P25-243000 were used until Feb. 25, 1954. Engine numbers past this date were P25-243001 to P25-454271. The three series were manufactured in mixed production fashion and used the same range of serial and engine numbers.

PLAZA SERIES

Series No.	Body/ Style No.	Body Type & Seating	Factory Price	Shipping Weight	Prod. Total
P25-1	N/A	4-dr Sed-6P	1745	3004	43,077
P25-1	N/A	2-dr Clb Cpe-6P	1707	2943	27,976
P25-1	N/A	2-dr Bus Cpe-3P	1598	2889	5,000
P25-1	N/A	2-dr Sub-6P	2044	3122	35,937
P25-1	N/A	Chassis only	—	—	1
P25-1	N/A	2-dr Clb Cpe-6P	—	—	1,275

SAVOY — (6-CYL) — SERIES P25-2 — The Savoy nameplate changed from a model to a series designation this year. It was used to identify Plymouth's middle-priced line and also signified a higher level of trim and appointments. Identification features of the Savoy included full-length side body moldings; newly designed chrome gravel shields; and Savoy signatures placed on the cowl side area of front fenders. Bright metal windshield frames replaced the black rubber-type used with Plazas. The Savoy interior was a bit fancier, too, but most of its extras qualified as exterior trim. The highest grade fabrics and furnishings were reserved for Belvederes. A surprise was the fact that Suburbans were not normally provided with Savoy level trim, even though the name had been taken from the fancy all-steel station wagon model. However, the Chrysler Historical Archives indicate that a small number of Savoy Suburbans were manufactured.

SAVOY SERIES

P25-2	N/A	4-dr Sed-6P	1853	3036	139,383
P25-2	N/A	2-dr Clb Sed-6P	1815	2986	25,396
P25-2	N/A	2-dr Clb Cpe-6P	1823	2982	30,700
P25-2	N/A	2-dr Sub	—	—	450
P25-2	N/A	Chassis only	—	—	3,588

1954 Plymouth, Belvedere two-door Suburban, 6-cyl (JL)

BELVEDERE — (6-CYL) — SERIES P25-3 — The Belvedere nameplate no longer identified only the two-door pillarless hardtop. This designation was now used to label a four model lineup including this style, a sedan, a convertible and a fancy all-steel Suburban station wagon. Identification points included all extras found on Savoys plus full wheel discs; chrome 'fishtail' rear fender top fins; full-length rocker sill moldings and Belvedere front fender script. The hardtop and sedan also featured roof pillar medallions. The convertible had similar medallions behind the gravel shields and the station wagon (Suburban) had fin-less rear fenders, making each model slightly distinctive. Dressier interior furnishings were used on all of these cars. They included richer combinations of fabrics; extra armrests; special dashboard trim; Deluxe steering wheel; clock and fancier garnish moldings. In the spring, a special trim option was released for Belvedere hardtops and convertibles. It added a narrow, fin-shaped chrome molding below the side window openings, with the area above finished in contrasting color. When the production of 1954 Plymouths ended, on Aug. 20, 1954, the Hy-Drive semi-automatic transmission was dropped.

BELVEDERE SERIES

P25-3	N/A	4-dr Sed-6P	1933	3050	106,601
P25-3	N/A	2-dr HT Cpe-6P	2125	3038	25,592
P25-3	N/A	2-dr Conv Cpe-6P	2281	3273	6,900
P25-3	N/A	2-dr Sub-6P	2268	3186	9,241
P25-3	N/A	Chassis only	—	—	2,031

ENGINES:

(Plymouth Six) Inline. L-head. Cast iron block. Displacement: 217.8 cid. Bore and stroke: 3.24 x 4.375 inches. Compression ratio: 7.1:1. Brake hp: 100 at 3600 rpm. Four main bearings. Solid valve lifters. Carburetor: Carter Type BB one-barrel Model D6H2.

(Optional Plymouth Six) Inline. L-head. Cast iron block. Displacement: 230.2 cid. Bore and stroke: 3.25 x 4.625 inches. Compression ratio: 7.25:1. Brake hp: 110 at 3600 rpm. Four main bearings. Solid valve lifters. Carburetor: Carter Type BB one-barrel Model BB-D6H2. (This 'high head' engine was optional on cars late in 1954.)

CHASSIS FEATURES: Wheelbase: (all models) 114 inches. Overall length: (Suburban) 190-1/4 inches; (passenger cars) 193-1/2 inches. Front tread: (all models) 55-7/8 inches. Rear tread: (all models) 58-7/16 inches. Tires: (all models) 6.70 x 15.

OPTIONS: Power steering ($139.75). Radio ($82.50). Heater ($56.25). Directional signals ($13.30). Whitewall tires, exchange ($26.65). "Egg Cup" electric clock. Wire wheel covers ($59.15). Full wheel discs ($14). Wire wheels, chrome ($279.50). Wire wheels, painted ($102.15). Two-tone paint. Back-up lights. Bumper wing guards. Grille guard. Wheel trim rings. Seat covers. Vent-A-Shades. Solex tinted glass ($21). Wood weave door trim ($108). Custom trim, four-door ($188). Power brakes ($37). Three-speed manual transmission was standard. Overdrive transmission ($99.55). Semi-automatic transmission ($145.80); PowerFlite fully automatic transmission ($189). Six-cylinder 230.2 cid/110 hp 'high head' engine. Available rear axle gear ratios: (standard) 3.73:1; (overdrive) 4.10:1 and (Hy-Drive) 3.73:1.

HISTORICAL FOOTNOTES: The 1954 Plymouths were introduced Oct. 15, 1953, and the Belvedere appeared in dealer showrooms the same date. Model year production peaked at 433,000 units. Calendar year sales of 399,900 cars were recorded. J.P. Mansfield was the chief executive officer of the company this year. Robert Anderson, who later became Chrysler Division head officer, was Plymouth's chief engineer. Chrysler's Chelsea, Mich., proving grounds opened this year. When it was dedicated in June, one of the special cars seen was a Plymouth Belvedere hardtop with a gas turbine engine. On March 15, 1954, power brakes were introduced as a Plymouth option at $36.55. A total of 61,000 1954 models had PowerFlite fully automatic transmission and 75,000 had Hy-Drive semi-automatic attachments. Hy-Drive was dropped at the end of the 1954 model run. Production of 1954 models stopped on Aug. 13, 1954. Factory dream cars seen this year included the Plymouth-Ghia Explorer.

1955 PLYMOUTH

1955 Plymouth, Plaza four-door sedan, 6-cyl (AA)

1955 Plymouth, Plaza Suburban station wagon, 6-cyl

PLAZA — (6-CYL/V-8) — SERIES P26/P27 — The 1955 Plymouths were completely restyled with new longer, lower bodies. All sheet metal was new and more modern. The upper edge of the body line ran, in a straight line, from front to rear. A sweeping roofline was supported by wraparound glass at both ends. The side panels were slab shaped. Hood and deck were flatter. At the front, the fenders hooded the single headlamps. The grille cavity was highlighted by two wing-shaped, horizontal blades that were joined, at the center, by a ribbed horizontal tie-bar. The Plaza represented the low-priced line, but could be had with either six-cylinder or V-8 powerplants. No extraneous trim appeared on this series. Chrome ornamentation was limited to a large signature script, placed ahead of the front wheel opening. A fin-shaped hood ornament was used. Windshield framing was in black rubber. Cars with V-8 power had V-shaped emblems attached to the hood and trunk. A Plymouth badge was seen on the hood. At the rear, vertical taillights were set into the backwards pointing fender tips. Buyers were able to order side spear moldings as optional equipment after midyear. These moldings ran from below the taillight to the middle of the front door and then slanted forward, hitting the rocker sill at the door's front lower corner. Sales features included many new items such as tubeless tires; follow-through starter; push-button door handles and a dashboard-mounted automatic gear shift selector. Plainer-looking cloth upholstery was standard in the Plaza, but

vinyl combinations were available at slight extra cost. A business coupe was still provided in this model range. It used the two-door sedan body shell with only a front seat and storage space in the rear compartment. Suspended-type control pedals were another 1955 innovation.

PLYMOUTH I.D. NUMBERS: Serial number located on plate on left door post. Serial number starts with prefix (P=Plymouth) and series code (P26=six-cylinder; P27=V-8) followed by sequential production number starting at 1001 at each factory. Factory codes: M=Detroit, Mich.; LA=Los Angeles, Calif.; E=Evansville, Ind.; and SL=San Leandro, Calif. These codes do not appear in serial number. Six-cylinder engine numbers near front upper left of block between cylinders one and two. V-8 engine numbers on flat surface at front of block between two cylinder heads. Engine number resembles serial number, but may not match. Engine numbers should not be used for identification. Serial numbers at each factory were kept according to the type of engine and changed as follows: P26 six-cylinder: (M) 13835001-14119261; (E) 20745001-20819358 and (LA) 25180001-25200109. P27 V-8: (M) 15630001-15871476; (E) 22118201-22244749 and (LA) 26524001-26549993 and 26500000-26500290. Engine numbers were as follows: P26-1001 to P26-378770, P27-1001 to P27-60200 and P27-60201 to P27-298919.

PLAZA SERIES

Series No.	Body/ Style No.	Body Type & Seating	Factory Price	Shipping Weight	Prod. Total
P26/27	N/A	4-dr Sed	1756/1859	3129/3246	84,156
P26/27	N/A	2-dr Clb Sed-6P	1713/1816	3089/3202	53,610
P26	N/A	2-dr Bus Cpe-3P	1614/----	3025/----	4,882
P26/27	N/A	2-dr Sub-6P	2052/2155	3261/3389	31,788
P26/27	N/A	4-dr Sub-6P	2133/2237	3282/3408	15,442

Note 1: Data above slash for six-cylinder/below slash for V-8.

Note 2: The three-passenger business coupe came only with six-cylinder power.

SAVOY — (6-CYL/V-8) — SERIES P26/P27 — The Savoy was Plymouth's mid-priced model range in 1955. Standard equipment included slightly dressier interiors; chrome windshield frames; bright metal roof gutter rail; chrome trim on the rear deck overhang; horizontal sweep spear molding high on front fenders and doors; and Savoy front fender signature script. A Sport Tone trim option was available on the Savoy (after midyear) at slight extra cost. General styling features are the same as those outlined for 1955 Plazas. Cars with V-8 power had V-shaped hood and deck insignia. Sixes of all trim levels were designated as part of the P26 series; V-8s were P27 models.

SAVOY SERIES

Series No.	Body/ Style No.	Body Type & Seating	Factory Price	Shipping Weight	Prod. Total
P26/27	N/A	4-dr Sed-6P	1855/1958	3154/3265	162,741
P26/27	N/A	2-dr Clb Sed-6P	1812/1915	3109/3224	74,880

Note 1: Data above slash for six-cylinder/below slash for V-8.

1955 Plymouth, Belvedere two-door hardtop, V-8

BELVEDERE — (6-CYL/V-8) — SERIES P26/P27 — The Belvedere was the high-priced Plymouth line. It had the same general styling features described for other models, with richer interior and exterior finish. All body styles had Belvedere front fender script; chrome windshield and rear window moldings; chrome trim on the rear deck lid overhang; chrome trim inside the headlight hoods; moldings decorating the taillamps; and bright metal highlights on the rear roof pillar. Sedans and station wagons had full-length chrome sweep spears on their sides. The sport coupe and convertible had special contrasting 'color sweep' panels as standard equipment. The panel was formed by the side molding arrangement and two-tone paint treatment. A horizontal spear ran from the headlamp hood to the mid-door area. A second horizontal spear ran from above the taillamp to the middle of the door. Forward slanting moldings intersected the front spear below the front vent window and below the windshield post. The shorter one (below vent window) also intersected the lower horizontal piece. The longer one dropped to the rocker sill, at the mid-door point. Panels underneath the lower horizontal molding and between the slanting pieces were finished in a contrasting color, usually matching the roof color. A small crest-type emblem was placed between the slanting moldings on the door. Belvedere upholstery came in especially rich combinations, such as Jacquard 'Black Magic' Boucle. Deluxe steering wheels; dual ashtrays; armrests; clock; and special courtesy lights were included as regular attributes.

BELVEDERE SERIES

Series No.	Body/ Style No.	Body Type & Seating	Factory Price	Shipping Weight	Prod. Total
P26/27	N/A	4-dr Sed-6P	1954/2057	3159/3267	160,984
P26/27	N/A	2-dr Clb Sed-6P	1911/2014	3129/3228	41,645
P26/27	N/A	2-dr HT Cpe-6P	2088/2192	3149/3261	47,375
P27	N/A	2-dr Conv-6P	----/2326	----/3409	8,473
P26/27	N/A	4-dr Sub-6P	2297/2400	3330/3475	18,488

Note 1: Data above slash for six/below slash for V-8.

Note 2: Belvedere convertible came only as a V-8.

Note 3: 786 Belvedere four-door sedans; 100 club coupes; 93 hardtops and 21 Suburbans were built for Canada.

Note 4: Plymouth made 10 Savoy chassis-only and one Belvedere chassis-only.

ENGINES:

(Six) Inline. L-head. Cast iron block. Displacement: 230.2 cid. Bore and stroke: 3.25 x 4.625 inches. Compression ratio: 7.4:1. Brake hp: 117 at 3600 rpm. Four main bearings. Solid valve lifters. Carburetor: Carter Type BB one-barrel Model 2063SA.

(Hy-fire V-8) Overhead valve. Cast iron block. Displacement: 241 cid. Bore and stroke: 3.44 x 3.25 inches. Compression ratio: 7.6:1. Brake hp: 157 at 4400 rpm. Five main bearings. Hydraulic (non-adjustable) valve lifters. Carburetor: Carter Type BBD two-barrel Model 2262S.

(Optional V-8) Overhead valve. Cast iron block. Displacement: 259.2 cid. Bore and stroke: 3.563 x 3.25 inches. Compression ratio: 7.6:1. Brake hp: 167 (optional 177) at 4400 rpm. Five main bearings. Hydraulic (non-adjustable) valve lifters. Carburetor: Carter Type BBD two-barrel Model 2155S (optional Carter four-barrel Model WCFB-2253S).

CHASSIS FEATURES: Wheelbase: (all models) 115 inches. Overall length: (all models) 203.8 inches. Front tread: (all models) 58-13/32 inches. Rear tread: (all models) 58-1/2 inches. Tires: (all models) 6.70 x 15.

OPTIONS: Power brakes ($35). Power steering ($90). Air conditioning ($525). Power seat ($42). Power windows ($95). Radio ($83). Standard heater ($45). Deluxe heater ($70). Whitewalls, exchange ($25). Full wheel discs. Wire wheel discs. Grille guard. Seat covers. Dual exhaust. Oil filter. Rear seat speaker. Two-tone paint. Tinted Solex glass. Bumper guards. Variable speed electric wipers. Windshield washer. Three-speed manual transmission was standard. Overdrive transmission ($100). Automatic transmission ($165). V-8 240 cid/157 hp two-barrel engine. V-8 260 cid/167 hp two-barrel engine. V-8 260 cid/177 hp four-barrel engine. Available rear axle gear ratios: (standard) 3.73:1; (automatic) 3.54:1; (overdrive) 4.00:1.

HISTORICAL FOOTNOTES: The 1955 Plymouths were introduced Nov. 17, 1954, and the Suburbans appeared in dealer showrooms Dec. 22, 1954. Model year production peaked at 672,100 units. Calendar year sales of 742,991 cars were recorded. J.P. Mansfield was the chief executive officer this year. Plymouth created a new fleet sales department during 1955. The club coupe was dropped. Four-door Suburbans and Belvedere two-door sedans were new Plymouth styles. Detroit area dealers were shown the new models on Nov. 4, 1955, as the cars had entered actual production during September. Production lines at the Detroit factory were made 67 feet longer because the 1955 models were larger than past Plymouth products. On a calendar year basis, 35,664 Plymouths had power brakes; 33,000 had power steering; 348,771 (46 percent) had automatic transmission; 30,791 had overdrive and 60.8 percent had V-8 engines. The 157-hp V-8 was dropped (except for Canadian and export models) by the end of 1954 so Plymouth could advertise the highest standard horsepower V-8 ($167) in the low-priced field. Chevy and Ford both offered 162-hp V-8s.

1956 PLYMOUTH

PLAZA/DELUXE SUBURBAN — (6-CYL/V-8) — SERIES P28/P29-1 — For 1956, Plymouth face lifted the body introduced the previous season. Styling changes included fin-type rear fenders and a new grille with a grid pattern center piece (decorated with a gold V-shaped emblem on V-8s). Full-length taillights extended from the tip of the rear fins to the back-up lamp housing. Plymouth block lettering stretched across the edge of the hood. A wide jet airplane-type hood mascot was used. The Plaza range included the economy offerings. Identification features included: rubber windshield and rear window gaskets; painted taillight trim; Plaza rear fender side script; painted back-up light housings; small hubcaps; single horizontal front fender spears; and painted roof gutter rails. This year the Plymouth Suburbans (station wagons) were actually grouped in their own,

separate four model series. However the Deluxe Suburban was trimmed in Plaza fashion and will be included as such in this catalog. New technical features for 1956 included a 12-volt electrical system; independent safety handbrake and push-button automatic transmission controls.

PLYMOUTH I.D. NUMBERS: Serial number located on plate on left door post. Serial number starts with prefix (P=Plymouth) and series code (P28=six-cylinder; P29=V-8) followed by sequential production number starting at 1001 at each factory. Factory codes: M=Detroit, Mich.; LA=Los Angeles, Calif.; E=Evansville, Ind.; and SL=San Leandro, Calif. These codes do not appear in serial number. Six-cylinder engine numbers near front upper left of block between cylinders one and two. V-8 engine number on flat surface near front of block between two cylinder heads. Engine number resembles serial number, but may not match. Engine numbers should not be used for identification. Prefix symbols changed as follows: P28-1 = Plaza six; P28-2 = Savoy six and P28-3 = Belvedere six; P29-1 = Plaza V-8; P29-2 = Savoy V-8 and P29-3 = Belvedere V-8 and Fury. Serial numbers at each factory were changed as follows: Six-cylinder: (M) 14120001-14272723; (E) 20820001-20857927 and (LA) 25202001-25212960. V-8: (M) 15873001-16080450; (E) 22247001-22325907 and (LA) 26552001-26590897. Fury V-8: (M) 15873001-16080450; (E) 22247001-22325907 and (LA) 26552001-26590897. Engine numbers were: P28-1001 to P28-204591 (six); P29-40001 to P29-80000 (187 hp V-8); P29-250001 to P29-274000 (187 hp V-8): P29-1001 to P29-40000 (180 hp V-8); P29-80001 to P29-250000 (180 hp V-8) and P29-1001 to P29-329132 (Fury V-8).

PLAZA SERIES/DELUXE SUBURBAN

Series No.	Body/ Style No.	Body Type & Seating	Factory Price	Shipping Weight	Prod. Total
P28/29-1	N/A	4-dr Sed-6P	1868/1971	3145/3275	60,197
P28/29-1	N/A	2-dr Clb Sed-6P	1825/1928	3100/3250	43,022
P28/29-1	N/A	2-dr Bus Cpe-6P	1726/1829	3030/3170	3,728
P28/29	N/A	2-dr DeL Sub-6P	2138/2241	3285/3460	23,866

1956 Plymouth, Savoy two-door hardtop, V-8

SAVOY/CUSTOM SUBURBAN — (6-CYL/V-8) — P28/P29-2 — The Savoy line was the mid-range 1956 Plymouth offering and shared annual styling changes with other models. Standard equipment included: front fender horizontal sweep spear molding; chrome taillight molding; chrome headlight trim; painted back-up lamp housing; bright metal windshield and rear window frames; small hubcaps; and Savoy rear fender script. Although actually part of a separate series, two custom Suburbans came with Savoy-type features and trim, except for the rear fender script, which read Custom Suburban. One of these six-passenger station wagons was a two-door model and the other had four-doors. As usual, the interiors on the mid-priced Plymouths earned a few extra rich appointments. Buyers could also dress-up the exterior of Savoys (and Plazas) with the optional 'Sport Tone' molding treatment.

SAVOY SERIES/CUSTOM SUBURBAN

P28/29-2	N/A	4-dr Sed-6P	1967/2070	3160/3295	51,762
P28/29-2	N/A	2-dr Clb Sed-6P	1924/2027	3125/3255	57,927
P28/29-2	N/A	2-dr Spt Cpe-6P	2071/2174	3155/3275	16,473
P28/29	N/A	4-dr Cus Sub-6P	2255/2358	3375/3565	33,333
P28/29	N/A	2-dr Cus Sub-6P	2209/2312	3355/3500	9,489

Note 1: Data above slash for six/below slash for V-8.

1956 Plymouth, Belvedere four-door Sport Sedan, V-8

BELVEDERE/SPORT SUBURBAN/FURY — (6-CYL/V-8) — SERIES P28/P29-3 — The Belvedere was again Plymouth's high trim level car. The four-door Sport Wagon, in the Suburban series, also had Belvedere features. A new body style was the four-door hardtop Sport Sedan. Identifiers for these models included: front door model nameplates; chrome

back-up lamp housings; 'Forward Look' medallions; armrests; clock; Deluxe steering wheel; dressier interior trappings and bright metal moldings on the windshield, rear window, headlights and taillights; rear deck lid overhang and front edge of the hood. Belvederes (and Sport Suburbans) came standard with 'Sport Tone' side trim of a distinct, angled-back pattern. The Sport Suburban also had 'Forward Look' medallions on the rear fenders and tweed pattern seat cushions and backs plus a rooftop luggage carrier. Introduced as a midyear model, the Plymouth Fury high-performance sport coupe was actually part of the Belvedere V-8 series. Its custom features included: off-white exterior finish; tapering gold anodized aluminum side trim; gold-finished aluminum grille; directional signals; back-up lights; variable-speed wipers; dual exhaust system with chrome deflectors; windshield washers; dual outside rearview mirrors; prismatic inside rearview mirror; special tires; gold anodized spoke-style wheel covers and 240-hp V-8. There was also Fury rear fender script.

BELVEDERE/FURY SERIES/SPORT SUBURBAN

Series No.	Body/ Style No.	Body Type & Seating	Factory Price	Shipping Weight	Prod. Total
P28/29-3	N/A	4-dr Sed-6P	2051/2154	3170/3325	84,218
P28/29-3	N/A	4-dr Spt Sed-6P	2223/2326	3270/3415	17,515
P28/29-3	N/A	2-dr Clb Sed-6P	2008/2111	3125/3285	19,057
P28/29-3	N/A	2-dr Spt Cpe-6P	2155/2258	3165/3320	24,723
P29-3	N/A	2-dr Conv-6P	----/2478	----/3435	6,735
P28/29	N/A	4-dr Spt Sub-6P	2425/2528	3420/3605	15,104

1956 Plymouth, Fury two-door hardtop, V-8

FURY SUB-SERIES

P29-3	N/A	2-dr Spt Cpe-6P	2807	3650	4,485

Note 1: Data above slash for six/below slash for V-8.

Note 2: Belvedere convertible came only as a V-8.

ENGINES:

(Six) Inline. L-head. Cast iron block. Displacement: 230.2 cid. Bore and stroke: 3.25 x 4.625 inches. Compression ratio: 7.6:1. Brake hp: 125 (optional 131) at 3600 rpm. Four main bearings. Solid valve lifters. Carter Type BB one-barrel Model 2063SA (optional Carter Type BBS two-barrel Model 2293S).

(V-8) Overhead valve. Cast iron block. Displacement: 268.8 cid. Bore and stroke: 3.63 x 3.256 inches. Compression ratio: 8.0:1. Brake hp: 180 at 4400 rpm. Five main bearings. Hydraulic valve lifters. Carburetor: Carter Type BBD two-barrel Model 2259SB. Base V-8 for all except Fury.

(Fury V-8) Overhead valve. Cast iron block. Displacement: 303 cid. Bore and stroke: 3.81 x 3.31 inches. Compression ratio: 9.25:1. Brake hp: 240 at 4800 rpm. Five main bearings. Solid valve lifters. Carburetor: Carter Type WCFB four-barrel Model 2442S.

(Optional V-8) Overhead valve. Cast iron block. Displacement: 276.1 cid. Bore and stroke: 3.75 x 3.125 inches. Compression ratio: 8.0:1. Brake hp: 187 at 4400 rpm. Five main bearings. Hydraulic or solid valve lifters. Carburetor: Carter Type BBD two-barrel Model 2407S. NOTE: This is called the '277' engine and came with solid valve lifters when the optional four-barrel 'Power Pack' was installed.

CHASSIS FEATURES: Wheelbase: (all models) 115 inches. Overall length: (all models) 204.8 inches. Front tread: (all models) 58-13/32 inches. Rear tread: (Fury) 58-29/32 inches; (all other models) 58-1/2 inches. Tires: (Fury) 7.10 x 15; (all other models) 6.70 x 15.

OPTIONS: Power brakes ($40). Power steering ($81). Air conditioning, V-8 club sedan/sport coupe/four-door sedan/sport sedan only ($427). Power windows ($102). Power seat ($45). Standard radio ($90). Deluxe radio ($107). Heater ($75). Full wheel discs. Wheel trim rings. Wire wheel covers. White sidewall tires. Front safety belts. Rear safety belts. Hi-Way Hi-Fi. Undercoating. Padded dashboard. Outside rearview mirror. 'Sport Tone' moldings. Two-tone paint. Bumper guards. Station wagon rooftop luggage rack. Back-up lights. Directional signals. Windshield washer. Solex tinted glass. Three-speed manual transmission was standard. Overdrive transmission ($108). Automatic transmission ($184). V-8 276.1 cid/180 hp two-barrel engine. V-8 276.1 cid/187 hp two-barrel engine. V-8 276.1 cid/200 hp four-barrel engine. V-8 303 cid/240 hp Fury four-barrel engine. Four-barrel carburetor was standard with the Fury V-8 and available as 'Power Pack' equipment on the 276.1-cid V-8 (Carter WCFB-2442). Positive traction rear axle. Available rear axle gear ratios: (standard) 3.73:1; (automatic) 3.73:1; (overdrive) 4.11:1.

1957 PLYMOUTH

PLAZA/DELUXE SUBURBAN — (6-CYL/V-8) — SERIES KP30/KP31-1 — The 1957 Plymouths were completely redone. New touches included: a wraparound aluminum grid-style grille with vertical air slot bumper; tower-type tailfin rear fenders; dart-shaped body profile and parking lamps set alongside headlights for a quad-lamp effect. Plaza was the low-priced line. The Deluxe Suburban was part of a separate station wagon series, but had Plaza trim. Identification features included: model nameplates on rear fenders; untrimmed body sides; small hubcaps; painted roof gutter rails and V-shaped front fender top emblems on V-8 models. Tapered 'Sport Tone' side moldings were available at extra cost. Standard equipment included single speed windshield wipers; left-hand sun visor; dual horns; five tubeless tires; bumper jack and tire changing tools. Newly introduced features of the 1957 Plymouths included safety power frame construction and Torsion Air Ride (with torsion bar front suspension).

PLYMOUTH I.D. NUMBERS: Serial number located on plate on left door post. Serial number starts with P30-1 = Plaza six; P30-2 = Savoy six and P30-3 = Belvedere six; P31-1 = Plaza V-8; P31-2 = Savoy V-8 and P31-3 = Belvedere V-8 and Fury, followed by sequential production number starting at 1001 at each factory. Factory codes: M=Detroit, Mich.; LA=Los Angeles, Calif.; E=Evansville, Ind.; SL=San Leandro, Calif.; and (new) NJ=Newark, N.J. These codes do not appear in serial number. Six-cylinder engine numbers near front upper left of block between cylinders one and two; V-8 on top of block, near front, between cylinder heads. Engine number resembles serial number, but may not match. Engine numbers should not be used for identification. Serial numbers at each factory changed as follows: Six: (M) 14280001-14410539; (E) 20860001-20891720; (LA) 25215001-25222883 and (NJ) 28100001-28103737. V-8: (M) 1683001-16392956; (E) 22330001-22450693; (LA) 26595001-26643618 and (NJ) 28525001-28534683. Fury V-8: (M) 16083001-16392956. Engine numbers were: (Six) P30-1001 to P30-177184; (V-8) P31-1001 to P31-492995 and (Fury V-8) FP31-1001 to FP31-492995. Furys were assembled only at the Detroit factory.

PLAZA SERIES/DELUXE SUBURBAN

Series No.	Body/ Style No.	Body Type & Seating	Factory Price	Shipping Weight	Prod. Total
KP30/KP31-1	N/A	4-dr Sed-6P	2030/2130	3260/3405	70,248
KP30/KP31-1	N/A	2-dr Clb Sed-6P	1984/2084	3160/3330	49,137
KP30/KP31-1	N/A	2-dr Bus Cpe-3P	1874/1974	3155/3315	2,874
KP30/KP31-1	N/A	2-dr DeL Sub-6P	2305/2405	3555/3685	20,111
KP30/KP31-1	N/A	4-dr Taxi Spec-6P	2174/2274	3410/3515	N/A

Note 1: Data above slash for six/below slash for V-8.

SAVOY/CUSTOM SUBURBAN — (6-CYL/V-8) — SERIES KP30/KP31-2 — Savoys and Custom Suburbans shared the same general level of trim and appointments. They were Plymouth's mid-priced lines and had the same basic design changes as Plazas. The amount of standard equipment and decorative items was one step up the scale. The Savoy had all features of the lower priced car plus air foam seat cushions; armrests; horn-blowing ring; dual sun visors and a single horizontal side molding running from behind the headlights to just above the back-up lights. Dual, tapering 'Sport Tone' molding treatments were an option available at extra cost. Savoy block lettering was placed on the side of fins on passenger cars, while the comparable Suburban had double nameplates attached at mid-fin height. They read 'Custom' in script and 'Suburban' in block letters. The Suburbans had slightly different rear fenders than other models and also came with contrasting 'Sport Tone' finish, as an option.

1957 Plymouth, Savoy two-door sedan, 6-cyl

SAVOY SERIES/CUSTOM SUBURBAN

Series No.	Body/ Style No.	Body Type & Seating	Factory Price	Shipping Weight	Prod. Total
KP30/KP31-2	N/A	4-dr Sed-6P	2169/2269	3265/3415	53,093
KP30/KP31-2	N/A	4-dr Spt Sed-6P	2292/2392	3375/3480	7,601
KP30/KP31-2	N/A	2-dr Clb Sed-6P	2122/2222	3190/3335	55,590
KP30/KP31-2	N/A	2-dr HT Cpe-6P	2204/2304	3260/3410	31,373
KP30/KP31-2	N/A	4-dr Cus Sub-6P	2469/2569	3665/3840	40,227
KP30/KP31-2	N/A	4-dr Cus Sub-9P	2624/2724	N/A/N/A	9,357
KP30/KP31-2	N/A	2-dr Cus Sub	2415/2515	3580/3755	11,196

Note 1: Data above slash for six/below slash for V-8.

1957 Plymouth, Belvedere four-door sedan, V-8 (AA)

BELVEDERE/SPORT SUBURBAN/FURY — (6-CYL/V-8) — SERIES KP30/KP31-3 — The Belvedere group represented the top Plymouth line. The Sport Suburban was the comparably equipped station wagon and the Fury was a special high-performance model that had many standard extras. Belvederes had single side moldings as standard equipment and tapering dual side moldings, with 'Sport Tone' contrast panels as a slight extra cost option. Belvedere block letters were positioned at the middle sides of the rear tailfins, just above the moldings. Standard equipment included all items found on Savoys plus full wheel covers; rear quarter stone shields; electric clock; lockable glovebox; cigarette lighter and oil filter. The Sport Suburban had a special thick pillar roof treatment (also used on four-door Custom Suburbans); upright spare tire and rear-facing third seat. Model nameplates appeared at mid-fin level, above the rear tip of the horizontal side moldings or optional dual 'Sport Tone' moldings. The Fury came only as a two-door hardtop with Fury rear fender nameplates; Sand Dune White finish with gold anodized aluminum 'Sport Tone' trim inserts; upswept front bumper end extensions; safety padded dash; padded sun visors; foam seat, front and rear; special clock; back-up lights; directional signals; dual outside rearview mirrors; and a 290-hp V-8. The new three-speed TorqueFlite automatic transmission was offered only in the Belvedere and Fury lines.

BELVEDERE SERIES/SPORT SUBURBAN/FURY

Series No.	Body/ Style No.	Body Type & Seating	Factory Price	Shipping Weight	Prod. Total
KP30/KP31-3	N/A	4-dr Sed-6P	2285/2385	3270/3475	10,414
KP30/KP31-3	N/A	4-dr Spt Sed-6P	2394/2494	3350/3505	37,446
KP30/KP31-3	N/A	2-dr Clb Sed-6P	2239/2339	3235/3340	55,590
KP30/KP31-3	N/A	2-dr HT Cpe-6P	2324/2424	3280/3415	67,268
KP31-3	N/A	2-dr Conv-6P	----/2613	----/3585	9,866
KP30/KP31-3	N/A	4-dr Spt Sub-6P	2597/2697	3655/3840	15,444
KP30/KP31-3	N/A	4-dr Spt Sub-9P	2752/2852	N/A/N/A	7,988

FURY SUB-SERIES

Series No.	Body/ Style No.	Body Type & Seating	Factory Price	Shipping Weight	Prod. Total
KP31-3	N/A	2-dr HT Cpe-6P	2900	3595	7,438

Note 1: Data above slash for six/below slash for V-8.

Note 2: Belvedere convertible came only with V-8 power.

ENGINES:

(Six) Inline. L-head. Cast iron block. Displacement: 230.2 cid. Bore and stroke: 3.25 x 4.625 inches. Compression ratio: 8.0:1. Brake hp: 132 at 3600 rpm. Four main bearings. Solid valve lifters. Carburetor: Carter Type BBS one-barrel Model 2567S.

(V-8) Overhead valve. Cast iron block. Displacement: 276.1 cid. Bore and stroke: 3.75 x 3.125 inches. Compression ratio: 8.0:1. Brake hp: 197 at 4400 rpm. Five main bearings. Hydraulic valve lifters. Carburetor: Carter Type BBD two-barrel Model 2407S. NOTE: The Deluxe Suburban used the 299.6 cid '301' V-8 as standard equipment.

(Fury V-8) Overhead valve. Cast iron block. Displacement: 299.6 cid. Bore and stroke: 3.906 x 3.125 inches. Compression ratio: 8.5:1. Brake hp: 235 at 4400 rpm. Five main bearings. Solid valve lifters. Carburetor: Carter Type WCFB four-barrel Model 2631S.

(Optional V-8) Overhead valve. Cast iron block. Displacement: 299.6 cid. Bore and stroke: 3.906 x 3.125 inches. Compression ratio: 8.5:1. Brake hp: 215 at 9700 rpm. Five main bearings. Solid valve lifters. Carburetor: Carter Type BBD two-barrel Model 2512S. NOTE: This engine is normally referred to as the '301' V-8, although its actual displacement was 299.6 cid. It was standard in all 1957 Suburbans.

(Optional FURY V-8) Overhead valve. Cast iron block. Displacement: 317.6 cid. Bore and stroke: 3.906 x 3.312 inches. Compression ratio: 9.25:1. Brake hp: 290 at 5400 rpm. Five main bearings. Solid valve lifters. Carburetor: Two Carter Type WCFB four-barrel Model 2631S.

CHASSIS FEATURES: Wheelbase: (all passenger cars) 118 inches; (all Suburbans) 122 inches. Overall length: (Fury) 206.1 inches; (all passenger cars) 204.6 inches; (all station wagons) 208.6 inches. Front tread: (all models) 60-29/32 inches. Rear tread: (all models) 59-39/64 inches. Tires: (Fury and nine-passenger Suburbans) 8.00 x 14; (all other models) 7.50 x 14.

OPTIONS: Power brakes ($38). Power steering ($84). Air conditioning ($446). Power windows ($102). Two-Way power seat ($48). Push-button transistor radio with antenna ($73). Search Tune transistor radio with antenna ($106). Search Tune transistor radio with antenna and Hi-Fi ($187). Rear seat speaker ($12). Heater and defroster ($69). White sidewall tires, exchange ($33). Disc wheel covers on Plaza or Savoy ($18). 'Sport Tone' two-tone paint ($20). 'Sport Tone' on Suburbans ($24). Tinted Solex glass ($32). Back-up lights ($8). Suburban back-up lights ($10). Front and rear bumper guards ($34). Variable speed windshield wipers ($6). Windshield washer ($12). Electric clock on Plaza and Savoy ($14). Padded dashboard and sun visors ($24). Undercoating and hood panel ($13).

POWERTRAIN OPTIONS: Oil filter ($6). Three-speed manual transmission was standard. Overdrive transmission ($108). PowerFlite two-speed automatic transmission ($180). TorqueFlite three-speed automatic transmission was optional with V-8 engines only ($220). Dual exhaust was optional with V-8 engines only ($19.80). V-8 229.6 cid/215 hp two-barrel engine. V-8 299.6 cid/235 hp four-barrel engine. V-8 317.6 cid/290 hp dual four-barrel engine ($320). Four-barrel carburetor ($39). Positive traction rear axle ($50). Available rear axle gear ratios: (standard) 3.53:1; (overdrive) 3.90:1; (automatic) 3.54:1 or 3.35:1.

HISTORICAL FOOTNOTES: The 1957 Plymouths were introduced Oct. 25, 1956, and the Fury appeared in dealer showrooms on Dec. 18, 1956. Model year production peaked at 762,231 units. Calendar year sales of 655,526 cars were recorded. J.P. Mansfield was the chief executive officer this year. Plymouth retained the third rank in American auto sales. A unique station wagon prototype called the Cabana was built this year. It was based on the experimental Plainsman show car, but failed to reach the production stage. The Savoy Sport Sedan (four-door hardtop) was a midyear addition to the 1957 line introduced in March of the calendar year. The famous "Suddenly It's 1960" theme was used to promote the 1957 Plymouths. The Fury was re-introduced in January as a midyear high-performance model. With the 318 cid/290 hp engine it could do 0-to-60 mph in 8.6 seconds and cover the quarter-mile in 16.5 seconds.

1958 PLYMOUTH

PLAZA/DELUXE SUBURBAN — (6-CYL/V-8) — SERIES LP1/LP2-L — The Plaza group again represented the base Plymouth model range. The Deluxe Suburban was the counterpart station wagon. General styling revisions for the year included: a new, horizontal bar grille below the front bumper; fin-type front fender top ornaments on Belvederes and Savoys; new taillights; redesigned side trim treatments and four-beam headlamps on all models. Anodized aluminum 'Sport Tone' moldings and inserts were now optional on Belvederes and Sport Suburbans. Plazas (and Deluxe

Suburbans) could be identified by their respective rear fender nameplates. Normal side trim consisted of a straight sweep spear molding extending from the rear bumper to nearly across the front door. A molding arrangement forming a bullet-shaped side body cove with contrasting finish was optional at slight extra cost. Deluxe Suburbans had the same features as Plaza models, except for the rear fenderside nameplates. Basic equipment on the low-priced Plymouths included directional signals; dual headlights; single-speed electric windshield wipers; left-hand sun visor; dual horns; five tubeless tires; bumper jack and wheel lug wrench. Gold V-shaped emblems at the center of the grille were used to identify models with V-8 power.

1958 Plymouth, Fury two-door hardtop, V-8 (AA)

PLYMOUTH I.D. NUMBERS: Serial number located on plate on left door post. Six-cylinder engine numbers on front upper left side of block between cylinders one and two; V-8 engine numbers on flat surface, front top of block, between cylinder heads. Engine number resembles serial number, but may not match. Engine numbers should not be used for identification. Vehicle Identification Number: first symbol: L=1958; second symbol: P=Plymouth. The third symbol designated type of engine, as follows: 1=six-cylinder; 2=V-8. The fourth symbol designated the assembly plant as follows: Detroit, Mich. (no code used); Los Angeles=L; Evansville, Ind.=E and Delaware=N. The following group of symbols was the sequential unit production number, with series in mixed production, according to factory and engine type. Body/Style Numbers were not used, but a new method of coding trim levels shows up in the charts below. This code used the first three symbols of the serial number, followed by a letter that indicated the level of price and/or trim. These letters were 'L' for low; 'M' for medium; 'H' for high end and 'P' for premium. Serial numbers for 1958 models were as follows: (Six) LP1L-1001 to LP1L-6444; LP1N-1001 to LP1N-18176; LP1E-1001 to LP1E-23101 and LP1-1001 to LP1-66871. (V-8) LP2L-1001 to LP2L-39675; LP2N-1001 to LP2N-36506; LP2E-1001 to LP2E-84801 and LP2-1001 to LP2-140484. Engine numbers for 1958 sixes were LP6-1001 and up or LP230-100001 and up (after March 26,1958). Engine numbers for V-8s were LP8-1001 and up.

PLAZA SERIES/DELUXE SUBURBAN

Series No.	Body/Style No.	Body Type & Seating	Factory Price	Shipping Weight	Prod. Total
LP1/2-L	N/A	4-dr Sed-6P	2134/2242	3255/3415	54,194
LP1/2-L	N/A	2-dr Clb Sed-6P	2083/2190	3190/3315	39,062
LP1/2-L	N/A	2-dr Bus Cpe-3P	1993/2101	3170/3320	1,472
LP1/2-L	N/A	4-dr DeL Sub-6P	2451/2558	3580/3740	15,625
LP1/2-L	N/A	2-dr DeL Sub-6P	2397/2504	3475/3645	15,535

Note 1: Data above slash for six/below slash for V-8.

SAVOY/CUSTOM SUBURBAN — (6-CYL/V-8) — SERIES LP1/LP2-M — The Savoys played their traditional role as mid-priced Plymouth models and the Custom Suburbans were the comparable offerings in the Suburban series. Equipment for these cars included all Plaza features plus Air Foam (foam rubber) seat cushions; armrests; horn-blowing steering wheel ring; dual sun visors and slightly enriched upholstery combinations. Identification aids included model nameplates on rear fenders and front fender top ornaments. Standard bodyside trim was a full-length, single horizontal molding running from headlights to taillights. Finger-shaped 'Sport Tone' treatments were a $20 option on passenger car models and $24 extra on station wagons. With this type of trim the molding ran from the rear bumper to nearly the front edge of the front door, then looped back, along the doors and quarters, dropping down to the rocker sill just ahead of the rear wheel opening. The area within the moldings was painted a contrasting color, which usually matched that of the roof. In the spring, a special Silver Savoy Special was marketed. It was a club sedan with special 'Sport Toning'; front door and fender spears; metallic silver roof and wheels; turn signals; electric wipers and washers and a price tag that matched the model year. It sold for $1,958.

SAVOY SERIES/CUSTOM SUBURBAN

LP1/2-M	N/A	4-dr Sed-6P	2270/2378	3220/3400	67,933
LP1/2-M	N/A	4-dr HT Sed-6P	2365/2472	3310/3475	5,060
LP1/2-M	N/A	2-dr Clb Sed-6P	2219/2327	3220/3360	17,624
LP1/2-M	N/A	2-dr HT Cpe-6P	2294/2401	3240/3400	19,500
LP1/2-M	N/A	4-dr Cus Sub-6P	2572/2680	3575/3755	38,707
LP1/2-M	N/A	4-dr Cus Sub-9P	2712/2820	3685/3840	17,158
LP1/2-M	N/A	2-dr Cus Sub-6P	2518/2626	3570/3690	5,925

Note 1: Data above slash for six/below slash for V-8.

1958 Plymouth, Belvedere two-door hardtop, V-8

BELVEDERE/SPORT SUBURBAN/FURY — (6-CYL/V-8) — SERIES LP1/LP2-H

Belvedere represented the top full-line Plymouth series. The Sport Suburban was the comparable station wagon. The Fury was a Belvedere sub-series containing only the special high-performance sport coupe. Nameplates on the rear fender identified each particular car. The standard type of Belvedere side trim was a single, full-length horizontal molding of slightly distinctive design. Running with a slight downward slant, it moved from headlamp level towards the back fender. About a foot ahead of the taillights, the molding angled up towards the top of the fin. When optional 'Sport Tone' finish was added, a lower molding was added. It ran from above the back bumper and tapered towards the upper molding at the front fender tip. The area inside the moldings was then finished with contrasting colors, usually matching the roof. Belvederes and Sport Suburbans had all Savoy features plus full wheel covers; rear fender stone shields; electric clock; lockable glovebox; cigar lighter; oil filter and front fender top ornaments. The Fury was a limited-edition Buckskin beige two-door hardtop with Fury rear fender nameplates; 'Sport Tone' moldings (with gold anodized aluminum inserts); bumper wing guards; padded interior; front and rear foam seats; back-up lights; dual outside rearview mirrors and special Dual Fury or Golden Commando V-8.

BELVEDERE SERIES/SPORT SUBURBAN/FURY

Series No.	Body/ Style No.	Body Type & Seating	Factory Price	Shipping Weight	Prod. Total
LP1/2-H	N/A	4-dr Sed-6P	2404/2512	3255/3430	49,124
LP1/2-H	N/A	4-dr HT Sed-6P	2493/2600	3330/3520	18,194
LP1/2-H	N/A	2-dr Clb Sed-6P	2354/2461	3240/3370	4,229
LP1/2-H	N/A	2-dr HT Cpe-6P	2422/2529	3250/3410	36,043
LP2-H	N/A	2-dr Conv-6P	----/2727	----/3545	9,941
LP1/2-H	N/A	4-dr Spt Sub-6P	2725/2833	3615/3745	10,785
LP1/2-H	N/A	4-dr Spt Sub-9P	2865/2973	3685/3830	12,385

FURY SUB-SERIES

LP2-H	N/A	2-dr HT Cpe-6P	3032	3510	5,303

Note 1: Data above slash for six/below slash for V-8.
Note 2: The Belvedere convertible came only with V-8 power.

ENGINES:

(Six) Inline. L-head. Cast iron block. Displacement: 230.2 cid. Bore and stroke: 3.25 x 4.625 inches. Compression ratio: 8.0:1. Brake hp: 132 at 3600 rpm. Four main bearings. Solid valve lifters. Carburetor: Carter Type BBS one-barrel Model 2567S.

(V-8) Overhead valve. Cast iron block. Displacement: 317.6 cid. Bore and stroke: 3.906 x 3.312 inches. Compression ratio: 9.0:1. Brake hp: 225 at 4400 rpm. Five main bearings. Solid valve lifters. Carburetor: Carter Type BBS two-barrel Model 2644S.

(Fury V-8) Overhead valve. Cast iron block. Displacement: 317.6 cid. Bore and stroke: 3.906 x 3.312 inches. Compression ratio: 9.25:1. Brake hp: 290 at 5200 rpm. Five main bearings. Solid valve lifters. Carburetor: Two Carter Type WCFB four-barrel Model 2631S.

(Optional Golden Commando V-8) Overhead valve. Cast iron block. Displacement: 350 cid. Bore and stroke: 4.062 x 3.375 inches. Compression ratio: 10.0:1. Brake hp: 305 at 5000 rpm. Five main bearings. Hydraulic valve lifters. Carburetor: two Carter four-barrel Model 2631S. (An electronic fuel injection option rated at 315 hp was short-lived.)

CHASSIS FEATURES: (all passenger cars) 118 inches; (all Suburbans) 122 inches. Overall length: (Fury) 206 inches; (all other passenger cars) 204.6 inches; (all Suburbans) 213.1 inches. Front tread: (all models) 60-29/32 inches. Rear tread: (all models) 59-39/64 inches. Tires: (Fury and nine-passenger Suburban) 8.00 x 14; (all other models) 7.50 x 14.

OPTIONS: Power brakes ($38). Power steering ($77). Air conditioning ($446). Power windows ($102). Two-Way power seat ($48). Push-button transistor radio ($73). Search Tuner transistor radio ($106). Search Tuner transistor radio with HI-FI ($187). Rear seat speaker ($12). Heater and defroster ($69). Four-ply white sidewall tires, exchange ($33). Disc wheel covers, Plaza and Savoy ($18). 'Sport-Tone' finish, passenger cars ($20). 'Sport-Tone' finish, Suburbans ($24). Solex tinted glass ($32). Back-up lamps, passenger car ($8). Back-up lamps, Suburban ($10). Front and rear outer bumper guards ($34). Air Foam seat ($9). Variable-speed electric windshield wipers ($6). Windshield washers ($12). Electric

clock on Plaza and Savoy ($14). Padded panel and sun visors ($24). Undercoating and fiberglass hood pad ($13). Sure-Grip. Three-speed manual transmission was standard. Overdrive transmission ($108). PowerFlite automatic transmission with all but Golden Commando V-8 ($180). TorqueFlite automatic transmission with V-8 only ($220). 318 cid/225 hp two-barrel Fury V-8 'Fury' engine ($107). 318 cid/250 hp four-barrel Fury Super-Pak ($146). V-8 318 cid/290 hp dual four-barrel 'Dual Fury' engine ($324). V-8 350 cid/305 hp 'Golden Commando' engine ($324). V-8 350 cid/315 hp EFI engine ($500). Four-barrel carburetor ($39). Fuel injection ($500). Dual exhaust with V-8 engine only ($19.80). Oil filter ($6). Available rear axle gear ratios: 3.54:1; 3.73:1; 2.93:1; 3.15:1; 3.31:1; 3.90:1; 4.10:1.

HISTORICAL FOOTNOTES: The 1958 Plymouths were introduced Oct. 16, 1957, and the Fury appeared in dealer showrooms at the same time. Model year production peaked at 443,799 units. Calendar year sales of 367,296 cars were recorded. The term 'Power Pack' applied to cars having a four-barrel carburetor installed as optional equipment. The 'Dual Fury' V-8 came with two Carter WCFB-type four-barrel carburetors, 9.25:1 compression and 290 hp at 5200 rpm. The electronic fuel-injected (EFI) engine utilized a Bendix electronic fuel-injection system. All EFI equipped cars were Furys, which were first built with the 'Dual Fury' induction setup and then converted to EFI on a special assembly line in the DeSoto factory in Detroit. Cars with this option were later recalled so that most, if not all, could be re-converted to the 'Dual Fury' configuration. Plymouth retained its number three sales rank for the industry as a whole, with a 30.6 percent market share. Furys equipped with the wedge head 350 cid/305 hp big-block V-8 were capable of 0-to-60 mph in 7.7 seconds and could run the quarter-mile in 16.1 seconds.

1959 PLYMOUTH

SAVOY/DELUXE SUBURBAN — (6-CYL/V-8) — SERIES MP1-L/MP2-L

To upgrade its image for 1959, Plymouth discarded the Plaza name and shuffled its series designations one notch. The Plaza became the Savoy; the Savoy the Belvedere and the Belvedere the Fury. The special high-performance range, formerly known as the Fury, was now the Sport Fury series and had one new model, a two-door convertible. General styling features included: a twin section anodized aluminum eggcrate grille; new 'double-barrel' front fenders; longer, outward canted rear tailfins; oval-shaped horizontal taillights and flatter, more sweeping rear deck contours. The Savoy line was now the base series offering, as standard equipment: directional signals; dual headlights; single-speed electric windshield wipers; left-hand sun visor; dual horns; five tubeless tires; bumper jack and wheel lug wrench. Identification features included Savoy rear fender nameplates; single side spears, running from the front wheel opening to the back of the car; and small hubcaps. The Deluxe Suburbans (now available in two- or four-door styles) were the station wagon counterparts of Savoys. The two-door station wagons had thin, straight roof pillars, while the four-door models had a thicker 'C' pillar and 'flattop' rear roof look. Dual side trim moldings, with aluminum fin-shaped inserts below the 'green house' area, were optional on low-priced Plymouths.

PLYMOUTH I.D. NUMBERS: The Vehicle Identification Number was located on the left front hinge pillar of Savoys and Belvederes and on the left side of the cowl, below the hood on Furys. Engine numbers were found at the front of the engine block on the left side of sixes and on the top center of the V-8 block. Vehicle numbers began with a four symbol prefix. The first symbol: M=1959. The second symbol designated the engine as follows: 1=six-cylinder and 2=V-8. The third symbol designated the series as follows: 3=Savoy; 5=Belvedere; 6=Fury; 7=Suburban and 9=Sport Fury. The fourth symbol designated the manufacturing/assembly plant as follows: 1=Detroit; 2=Detroit (Dodge); 5=California; 6=Newark, Del.; 7=St. Louis, Mo. Then came the sequential unit production number with series mixed in production, according to engine and factory. Numbers began with 100001 and up at each factory. Ending serial numbers are not provided in standard reference sources. Body/Style Numbers were used this year and are shown in the second column of the specifications charts below.

SAVOY SERIES/DELUXE SUBURBAN

Series No.	Body/ Style No.	Body Type & Seating	Factory Price	Shipping Weight	Prod. Total
MP1/2-L	41	4-dr Sed-6P	2283/2402	3275/3425	84,274
MP1/2-L	21	2-dr Clb Sed-6P	2232/2352	3240/3390	46,979
MP1-L	22	2-dr Bus Cpe-3P	2143/----	3130/----	1,051
MP1/2-L	45A	4-dr Del Sub-6P	2641/2761	3625/3725	35,086
MP1/2-L	25	2-dr Del Sub-6P	2574/2694	3560/3690	15,074

Note 1: Data above slash for six/below slash for V-8.
Note 2: The Business Coupe came only as a six.

BELVEDERE/CUSTOM SUBURBAN — (6-CYL/V-8) — SERIES MP1-M/MP2-M

— Belvederes and Custom Suburbans represented middle-of-the-line Plymouths for 1959. The side trim moldings on these cars began behind the front wheel opening, flaring into a fin-shaped, tapering dual molding. This arrangement ran from just ahead of the front door, to the extreme rear of the body. Belvedere or Custom Suburban model nameplates appeared near the tops of the fins. Equipment included at regular prices began with all items found on Savoys and added foam seat cushions; armrests; horn ring; and dual sun visors. A special silver anodized insert could be ordered for $18.60 to fill the area between the bodyside moldings. As in the past, the Belvedere convertible was offered only with V-8 power. Many new options appeared for Plymouths this year and several became standard equipment on Sport Furys. Included were swivel-type front seats and deck lid tire cover impressions. Due to growth of the station wagon market in the late-1950s, Plymouth again offered three types of Custom Suburbans this season. Six-passenger editions came in two- and four-door styles, while the latter model could also be had with a rear-facing third seat. The nine-passenger Custom Suburban and two-door Custom Suburban also came with V-8 power only.

BELVEDERE SERIES/CUSTOM SUBURBAN

Series No.	Body/ Style No.	Body Type & Seating	Factory Price	Shipping Weight	Prod. Total
MP1/2-M	41	4-dr Sed-6P	2440/2559	3275/3430	67,980
MP1/2-M	43	4-dr HT Sed-6P	2525/2644	3275/3475	5,713
MP1/2-M	21	2-dr Clb Sed-6P	2389/2509	3225/3395	13,816
MP1/2-M	23	2-dr HT Spt Cpe-6P	2461/2581	3230/3405	23,469
MP2-M	27	2-dr Conv-6P	----/2814	----/3580	5,063
MP1/2-M	45A	4-dr Cus Sub-6P	2762/2881	3625/3730	35,024
MP2-M	45B	4-dr Cus Sub-9P	----/2991	----/3775	16,993
MP2-M	25	2-dr Cus Sub-6P	----/2814	----/3690	1,852

Note 1: Data above slash for six below slash for V-8.

1959 Plymouth, Sport Suburban station wagon, V-8 (AA)

FURY/SPORT SUBURBAN — (V-8) — SERIES MP2-H

— Furys and Sport Suburbans were marketed as higher-level offerings and came only with V-8 attachments. Standard features included all items mentioned for the Belvedere series plus disc wheel covers; rear quarter stone shields; Deluxe steering wheel with horn ring; electric clock; lockable glove compartment; cigar lighter; and oil filter. Fury signature script was positioned high on the tailfins. Side chrome was of a dual molding type, which began as a single spear behind the headlamps, flared into a double level arrangement behind the front wheel opening and tapered to a point in front of the taillamp wraparound edges. A single molding then continued around the rear body corner and fully across the rear deck lid overhang. A Plymouth signature in chrome, was placed at the left-hand corner of the deck lid. The rear bumper ran straight across the car and wrapped around the body corners, with a center depression below the license plate holder. All 1959 Plymouths with V-8 power including all Furys and Sport Suburbans had small V-shaped emblems near the Plymouth signature on the rear deck lid.

FURY SERIES/SPORT SUBURBAN

MP2-H	41	4-dr Sed-6P	2691	3455	30,149
MP2-H	43	4-dr HT Sed-6P	2771	3505	13,614
MP2-H	23	2-dr HT Cpe-6P	2714	3435	21,494
MP2-H	45A	4-dr Spt Sub-6P	3021	3760	7,224
MP2-H	45B	4-dr Spt Sub-9P	3131	3805	9,549

1959 Plymouth, Sport Fury two-door hardtop, V-8 (AA)

SPORT FURY — (V-8) — SERIES MP2-P

— The alphabetical suffixes appearing in Plymouth series codes were: L for low-priced; M for mid-priced; H for high-priced and P for premium-priced. In past years, the limited-edition Fury had been designated an 'H' model and was actually a Belvedere. This season the Belvedere moved down a notch and the new top dog was the Sport Fury. Two body styles, sport coupe and convertible, were marketed only with V-8 power. They had several special identification features. For example, the upper branch of the dual side spears curved upward on the rear fenders, to repeat the general contour of the fins. The lower branch wrapped around the rear body corners and ran fully across the deck lid overhang. A silver anodized aluminum insert panel was standard and Fury signature script was placed inside the dual moldings at the rear. Positioned directly behind the moldings were large, colorful 'Forward Look' medallions. Standard equipment for these cars included all Fury features plus swivel front seats; Sport deck lid tire cover stamping and custom, padded steering wheel. The 'Golden Commando' wedge head V-8 with four-barrel carburetor and 305 hp was optional.

SPORT FURY SERIES

Series No.	Body/ Style No.	Body Type & Seating	Factory Price	Shipping Weight	Prod. Total
MP2-P	23	2-dr HT Cpe-6P	2927	3475	17,867
MP2-P	27	2-dr Conv-6P	3125	3670	5,990

ENGINES:

(Savoy/Belvedere Six) Inline. L-head. Cast iron block. Displacement: 230.2 cid. Bore and stroke: 3.25 x 4.625 inches. Compression ratio: 8.0:1. Brake hp: 132 at 3600 rpm. Four main bearings. Solid valve lifters. Carburetor: Carter Type BBS one-barrel Model 2567S.

(Savoy/Belvedere/Fury/Station Wagon V-8) Overhead valve. Cast iron block. Displacement: 317.6 cid. Bore and stroke: 3.906 x 3.312 inches. Compression ratio: 9.0:1. Brake hp: 230 at 4400 rpm. Five main bearings. Solid valve lifters. Carburetor: Carter Type BBD two-barrel Model 2824S.

(Sport Fury V-8) Overhead valve. Cast iron block. Displacement: 317.6 cid. Bore and stroke: 3.906 x 3.312 inches. Compression ratio: 9.0:1. Brake hp: 260 at 4400 rpm. Five main bearings. Solid valve lifters. Carburetor: Carter Type AFB four-barrel Model 2813S.

(Golden Commando 395 V-8) Overhead valve. Cast iron block. Displacement: 360.8 cid. Bore and stroke: 4.12 x 3.38 inches. Compression ratio: 10.0:1. Brake hp: 305 at 4600 rpm. Five main bearings. Hydraulic valve lifters. Carburetor: Carter Type AFB four-barrel Model 2813S. (The '395' designation is based on this engine's output of 395 pound-feet of torque at 3000 rpm.)

CHASSIS FEATURES: Wheelbase: (all passenger cars) 118 inches; (all Suburbans) 122 inches. Overall length: (all passenger cars) 210 inches; (all Suburbans) 214.5 inches. Tires: (nine-passenger Suburban) 8.00 x 14; (all other models) 7.50 x 14.

1959 Plymouth, Sport Fury two-door convertible, V-8 (JL)

OPTIONS: Power brakes ($36). Power steering ($63). Air conditioning ($372); for station wagons ($531). Push-button radio ($59). Rear seat speaker ($11). Dual rear antenna ($10). Fresh air heater and defroster ($58). Instant Air gas heater ($86). Tinted glass ($36). Windshield washer ($10). Rear window defogger ($19). Variable speed windshield wipers ($6). Headlight dimmer ($40). Contour floor mats, pair ($8). Regular floor mats, pair ($4). Two-Way power seat ($40). Power windows ($84). Swivel seat ($57). Constant-Level air suspension ($88). Power tailgate window, standard on nine-passenger Sport Suburban ($28). Padded dashboard ($12). Padded sun visor ($6). Padded steering wheel, standard Sport Fury ($12). Clear plastic seat covers ($30). Anti-freeze ($6). Safety belts, each ($13). White sidewall tires ($28). Oversize tires, exchange ($13). Tutone paint ($15). Silver side moldings, standard Fury ($19). Station wagon storage compartment ($24). Bumper guards ($12). Front bumper guards ($10). Front bumper end guards ($16). Cigar lighter, standard Fury ($4). Wheel covers, standard Fury ($17). Rear foam seat cushion ($10). Tilt-type rearview mirror ($4). Automatic tilt mirror ($14). Left-hand remote control outside rearview mirror ($16). Dual mirrors, left-hand remote control ($23). Undercoating with hood pad ($13). Side view mirror ($6). Group 311: wheel covers, stone shields, electric clock and glovebox lock, standard Fury ($32). Group 312: back-up lights, windshield washer and variable speed wipers ($24). Group 313: right sun

visor; front armrests and front foam cushion, standard Belvedere and Fury ($20). Three-speed manual transmission was standard. PowerFlite automatic transmission was optional with all but Golden Commando V-8 ($189). Overdrive transmission ($84). TorqueFlite automatic transmission ($227). V-8 318 cid/260 hp 'Super Pack' engine ($32). V-8 360.8 cid/305 hp 'Golden Commando' engine ($74). Four-barrel carburetor ($32). Oil filter ($10). Dual exhaust, V-8 only ($23). Available rear axle gear ratios (various).

HISTORICAL FOOTNOTES: The 1959 Plymouths were introduced in October 1958. Plymouth sales leaped 11.6 percent. Model year production peaked at 458,261 units. Calendar year sales of 413,204 cars were recorded. Plymouth again held third rank on industry sales charts, but Rambler was closing the gap. Plymouth's market share was a declining 13.19 percent. Fuel-injection was deleted from the power options list, but new extras included air suspension, swiveling seats for driver and passenger, the "Flite Sweep" rear deck lid with spare tire embossment; an electric headlight dimmer and a self-dimming illuminated rearview mirror. This was Plymouth's 30th anniversary and General Manager Harry E. Cheesbrough marked the production of the company's 11-millionth vehicle in 1959. The Golden Commando 395 engine, named for the fact that it developed 395 pound-feet of torque, was optional in all Plymouths except the Savoy business coupe. A Fury four-door hardtop was converted into the latest in a series of Chrysler turbine-engined cars and made a 576-mile "cross-country" reliability run. Well, it certainly didn't cross the country, but Chrysler's promotional copywriters described the endurance trial that way.

1960 PLYMOUTH

1960 Plymouth, Valiant V-200 four-door sedan, 6-cyl

VALIANT V-100 — (6-CYL) — SERIES QX1-L — Chrysler Corp. introduced its compact Valiant as a 1960 model. This all-new car was not yet identified as a Plymouth and was officially considered a distinct brand of car, but a year later, it became a Plymouth. The Valiant was assembled by Dodge Division, but sold mainly by Plymouth dealers. It was an immediate success and enjoyed a high rate of sales. Features included unitized body construction; torsion bar front suspension; seven-dip rust proofing; Lustre-Bond exterior finish; light weight and small, but roomy size; 12-volt electrical system; and large trunk or station wagon cargo capacity (24.9 and 72 cubic feet, respectively). Valiant styling features included a long hood/short rear deck look; high degree of body sculpturing; large wheel cutouts; large trapezoid-shaped radiator grille with delicate criss-cross pattern insert; dual headlamps; 'cat's eyes' taillights and rear deck lid tire cover stamping. The low-priced V-100 models had a short, bright metal molding extending forward from the taillights. A new overhead valve 'Slant Six' engine and three-speed manual floor shift transmission were standard equipment. Gray cloth interiors were used for V-100 models.

PLYMOUTH I.D. NUMBERS: The Vehicle Identification Number is located on a plate attached to left front door pillar. First symbol identifies car-line: 1=Valiant; 2=Plymouth six-cylinder; 3=Plymouth V-8. Second symbol identifies series: 1=V-100/Savoy; 2=Belvedere; 3=V-200/Fury; 5=V-100 station wagon/Savoy station wagon; 6=Belvedere station wagon; 7=V-200 station wagon/Fury station wagon; 9=taxicab; 0=fleet car. Third symbol: 0=1960. Fourth symbol indicates factory: 3=Detroit; 6=Los Angeles; 7=St. Louis; 8=Clairpointe; 0=Canada. Body plate below hood on cowl, inner fenders or radiator support indicates schedule date (SO); sequential body production number; body/style number (second symbol in VIN plus numbers and letters in second column of charts below); trim code; and paint code. Six-cylinder engine numbers stamped on front or rear of left-hand side of block below cylinder head. V-8 engine numbers stamped on flat on top right-hand side of block behind water pump. Engine codes: P-17=170 cid/101 hp six and 170 cid/148 hp "hyper-pack" six; P-22=225 cid/145 hp six; P-318=318 cid/230 hp two-barrel V-8 or 318 cid/260 hp four-barrel V-8; P-36=361 cid/305 hp Golden Commando V-8 with four-barrel carb or 361 cid/310 hp Golden Commando V-8 with dual four-barrel carbs; P-38=383 cid/325 hp V-8 with four-barrel carb and 383 cid/330 hp V-8 with both dual four-barrel carbs and dual fours with Ram-Tuned induction.

VALIANT V-100 SERIES

Series No.	Body/Style No.	Body Type & Seating	Factory Price	Shipping Weight	Prod. Total
V-100	41	4-dr Sed-6P	2033	2635	52,788
V-100	45A	4-dr Sub Sta Wag-6P	2365	2815	12,018
V-100	45B	4-dr Sub Sta Wag-9P	2488	2845	1,928

VALIANT V-200 — (6-CYL) — SERIES QX1-H — The high-priced Valiant line was the V-200 series with bright metal side trim moldings extending from the front wheel opening into the taillight. They curved upward, below the rear ventipanes, to follow the rear fender contour. Interiors for the high-line cars were available in three choices of color and featured vinyl seat bolsters and nylon cloth inserts.

VALIANT V-200 SERIES

V-200	41	4-dr Sed-6P	2110	2655	106,515
V-200	45A	4-dr Sub Sta Wag-6P	2423	2855	16,368
V-200	45B	4-dr Sub Sta Wag-9P	2546	2860	4,675

1960 Plymouth, Deluxe Suburban two-door station wagon, 6-cyl

FLEET SPECIAL/SAVOY/DELUXE SUBURBAN — (6-CYL/V-8) — SERIES PP1-L/PP2-L — All 1960 Plymouths had a few common major styling changes. Most obvious was a new grille of close-spaced horizontal blades accented with thin, vertical division bars. The front fenders had a wing-like look, with feature lines wrapping around the body corners to the front wheel openings, creating a sort of a cove just ahead of the wheel cutout. Thin moldings were used to accent the sweep of this unique front fender treatment. Side trim moldings were rearranged and 'shark fin' rear fender panels appeared. The Savoy was the low-priced line in the regular market, but economy level 'Fleet Special' editions were provided for commercial customers. Standard equipment for the Savoy (and also Deluxe Suburbans) included: oil filter; turn signals; dual sun visors; and five tubeless blackwall tires. Single sun visors and other deletions characterized the Fleet Specials. Savoys had no model nameplates; straight side trim moldings from the front door back to the taillights and single 'Jet Age' missile medallions on the rear fins. Uni-body construction; Safety-Guard door latches; asymmetrical rear leaf springs and the new overhead valve Slant Six were technical innovations for 1960.

SAVOY SERIES/DELUXE SUBURBAN

FLEET SPECIAL LEVEL TRIM PASSENGER CAR

PP1/2-L	41	4-dr Sed-5P	2242/2394	N/A/N/A	N/A
PP1/2-L	21	2-dr Sed-5P	2192/2344	N/A/N/A	N/A

DELUXE LEVEL TRIM PASSENGER CAR

PP1/2-L	41	4-dr Sed-6P	2275/2395	3365/3500	51,384
PP1/2-L	21	2-dr Sed-6P	2225/2344	3330/3490	26,820

SUBURBANS

PP1/2-L	45	4-dr Sta Wag-6P	2623/2753	3740/3890	18,482
PP1/2-L	25	2-dr Sta Wag-6P	2567/2686	3680/3870	5,503

Note 1: Data above slash for six/below slash for V-8.

BELVEDERE/CUSTOM SUBURBAN — (6-CYL/V-8) — SERIES PP1-M/PP2-M — The Belvedere was Plymouth's medium range offering. The Custom station wagon was its utilitarian counterpart. Passenger cars had Belvedere script on the front fender 'coves' and three shield medallions on the tailfins. Standard equipment included all Savoy features plus front armrest and cigarette lighter. The station wagons did not carry front fender signatures. The nine-passenger Custom station wagon did, however, come standard with oversize tires and a power tailgate window.

BELVEDERE SERIES/CUSTOM SUBURBAN

PASSENGER CARS

PP1/2-M	41	4-dr Sed-6P	2404/2524	3375/3520	42,130
PP1/2-M	21	2-dr Sed-6P	2354/2473	3340/3505	6,529
PP1/2-M	23	2-dr HT Sed-6P	2426/2545	3370/3505	14,085

SUBURBANS

PP1/2-M	45A	4-dr Sta Wag-6P	2726/2845	3750/3890	17,308
PP2-M	45B	4-dr Sta Wag-9P	----/2955	----/4000	8,116

Note 1: Data above slash for six/below slash for V-8.

Note 2: Nine-passenger Custom Suburban came only as a V-8.

1960 Plymouth, Fury two-door convertible, V-8

FURY/SPORT SUBURBAN — (6-CYL/V-8) — PP1-H/PP2-H — The Fury was Plymouth's high-level offering. The Sport station wagon was its utilitarian counterpart. These models carried as standard equipment all items found on Belvederes plus electric clock; chrome stone shields; back-up lights; lockable glovebox; Fury front fender script (passenger cars only); large tailfin medallions of circular shape; wide, horizontally ribbed rocker panel underscores with rear extensions; and upper beltline moldings. The Sport Fury premium line was dropped. As in the lower lines, the Sport station wagon lacked front fender script and was equipped, at regular price, with oversize tires and power tailgate window when sold with rear-facing third seat. Plymouth started calling these "station wagons." They were part of a separate Suburban series, but each station wagon compared to the car-line they are grouped with here. The Sport Suburban was comparable to a Fury.

FURY SERIES/SPORT SUBURBAN

Series No.	Body/ Style No.	Body Type & Seating	Factory Price	Shipping Weight	Prod. Total
PASSENGER CARS					
PP1/2-H	41	4-dr Sed-6P	2540/2659	3400/3550	21,292
PP1/2-H	43	4-dr HT Sed-6P	2621/2740	3445/3610	9,036
PP1/2-H	23	2-dr HT Sed-6P	2564/2683	3395/3535	18,079
PP2-H	27	2-dr Conv-6P	----/2932	----/3630	7,080
SUBURBANS					
PP2-H	45A	4-dr Sta Wag-6P	2989	3895	3,333
PP2-H	45B	4-dr Sta Wag-9P	3099	4020	4,253

Note 1: Data above slash for six/below slash for V-8.

Note 2: Fury convertible and Sport Suburbans came only as V-8s.

ENGINES:

(Valiant V-100 Six) Inline. Overhead valve. Cast iron block. Displacement: 170.9 cid. Bore and stroke: 3.406 x 3.125 inches. Compression ratio: 8.5:1. Brake hp: 101 at 4400 rpm. Four main bearings. Solid lifters. Carburetor: Carter Ball and Ball Type BBS one-barrel model 2900S. In mid-model year an aluminum cylinder block was adopted.

(Savoy/Belvedere/Fury Six) Inline. Overhead valve. Cast iron or aluminum block. Displacement: 225.5 cid. Bore and stroke: 3.406 x 4.125 inches. Compression ratio: 8.5:1. Brake hp: 145 at 4000 rpm. Four main bearings. Solid valve lifters. Carburetor: Carter Type BBS one-barrel Model 2985S.

(Savoy/Belvedere/Fury/Station Wagon V-8) Overhead valve. Cast iron block. Displacement: 317.6 cid. Bore and stroke: 3.906 x 3.312 inches. Compression ratio: 9.0:1. Brake hp: 230 at 4400 rpm. Five main bearings. Solid valve lifters. Carburetor: Carter Type BBD two-barrel Model 2921S.

CHASSIS FEATURES: Wheelbase: (Valiant) 106.5 inches; (Suburban) 122 inches; (Plymouth passenger car) 118 inches. Overall length: (Valiant V-100 passenger car) 183.7 inches; (Valiant V-100 nine-passenger station wagon) 184.8 inches; (Valiant V-200 nine-passenger station wagon) 185.1 inches; (Valiant V-200 passenger car) 184 inches; (Plymouth passenger car) 209.4 inches; (Suburban) 214.9 inches. Tires: (all Valiants) 6.50 x 13; (Plymouth nine-passenger station wagon) 8.00 x 14; (all others) 7.50 x 14.

VALIANT OPTIONS: Power brakes ($41). Power steering ($73). Basic group ($102). Basic radio group ($160). Appearance group ($63). Convenience group, V-100 only ($16). Antifreeze ($4). Front and rear bumper guards ($12). Solex safety glass ($37). Deluxe V-200 floor covering ($17). Hot water heater with defroster ($74). Back-up lights ($11). Left-hand outside rearview mirror ($5). Power tailgate window ($33). Push-button radio ($59). Padded dashboard ($14). Station wagon third seat ($61). White sidewall tires ($29). Undercoating with underhood pad ($14). Deluxe wheel covers ($16). Variable speed windshield wipers ($17). Three-speed manual floor shift transmission was standard. Automatic transmission ($172). Six-cylinder 170 cid/148 hp 'Hyper Pack' engine. Four-barrel carburetor was optional as part of the 'Hyper Pack' option. When so-equipped, the Slant Six had 10.5:1 compression ratio and was rated 148 hp at 5200 rpm.

PLYMOUTH OPTIONS: Power brakes ($43). Power steering ($77). Air conditioning ($446); dual including heater ($640). Front fender Sport shield ($14). Heater and defroster ($75). Back-up lights ($11). Prismatic inside mirror ($4). Two-tone paint, except convertible ($17). Sport Tone paint ($21). Sport Tone paint, station wagon ($32). Six-Way power seat ($96). Power windows ($102). Hi-Fi radio ($84). Push-button radio ($59). RCA automatic record player, radio mandatory ($52). Padded dashboard ($14). Sport deck tire cover ($28). Deluxe steering wheel ($11). Rear stone shields, Savoy, Belvedere, Deluxe and Custom ($4). Station wagon stowage compartment and Captive Air tires, six-passenger ($62); nine-passenger ($91). Automatic swivel seats, Fury ($87). Four wheel covers ($19). Windshield washer ($12). Variable speed windshield wipers ($6). Left-hand remote control outside rearview mirror ($18). Safe-T-Matic power door locks, two-doors ($23); four-doors ($30). Clear Ski-Hi rear window in Belvedere sport coupe ($23). Solex tinted Ski-Hi rear window in Belvedere sport coupe ($66). Electric clock, Savoy, Belvedere, Deluxe and Custom ($16). Three-speed manual transmission was standard. PowerFlite automatic transmission was optional, except with Commando V-8 ($189). TorqueFlite automatic transmission with V-8 engine ($211). TorqueFlite automatic transmission with six only ($192). V-8 318 cid/260 hp 'Super Pack' four-barrel engine ($39). V-8 361 cid/305 hp 'Golden Commando' engine ($206). V-8 361 cid/310 hp 'Sonoramic Commando' engine ($389). V-8 383 cid/325 hp four-barrel engine. V-8 383 cid/330 hp 'Sonoramic Commando' engine ($405). Sure-Grip positive traction rear axle ($50). Dual exhaust, when not ordered in 'Super Pack' or standard with Commando V-8 ($27). Available rear axle gear ratios (various ratios). 'Sonoramic' engines used 30-inch tuned tubular intake manifolds with two four-barrel carburetors. See 1960 Dodge section for detailed engine specifications.

1960 Plymouth, Belvedere two-door hardtop, 6-cyl

HISTORICAL FOOTNOTES: Rambler moved into third rank with higher sales, dropping Plymouth into fourth position, but only by a margin of less than 1,800 units. Plymouth's new fleet sales department helped sell many taxicabs and police cars this year. A 1960 Fury experimental prototype with a gas-turbine engine evidenced Chrysler Corp.'s continued interest in this field. The Plymouth XNR sports-experimental dream car appeared this season. A fleet of 'Hyper-Pack' Valiants took the top seven positions in the 10-lap Compact Car Race at Daytona Speedway, Jan. 31, 1960. Three Valiants driven by Marvin Panch, Roy Schecter and Larry Frank then placed 1-2-3 in the 20-lap main event in front of coast-to-coast television cameras.

1961 PLYMOUTH

VALIANT V-100 — (6-CYL) — SERIES 1100 — Valiants were classified as Plymouths this year. There were few styling changes. A new look was achieved by blacking out the delicately patterned grille inserts, while leaving the wider horizontal and vertical blades in chrome finish. This gave an 'eggcrate' grille appearance. Script reading Valiant was again seen behind the front wheel opening, but Plymouth signatures now decorated the trunk lid. Once again, a simulated spare tire impression was seen on the deck lid. The Valiant had generous headroom and a spacious front compartment, but rear leg room was cramped for six-footers. The glove compartment was of a bin-type design, but its push-button latching mechanism was difficult to operate. The V-100 models composed the base offerings. Standard equipment included electric windshield wipers, turn signals, oil filter and five tubeless blackwall tires. In the middle of the 1961 model year, a version of the 225-cid Slant Six was released as a Valiant option. This engine had the same horsepower rating as the 1960 four-barrel 170-cid engine with 'Hyper-Pack' option.

PLYMOUTH I.D. NUMBERS: The Vehicle Identification Number is located on a plate attached to left front door pillar. First symbol identifies car-line: 1=Valiant; 2=Plymouth six-cylinder; 3=Plymouth V-8. Second

symbol identifies series: 1=V-100/Savoy; 2=Belvedere; 3=V-200/Fury; 5=V-100 station wagon/Savoy station wagon; 6=Belvedere station wagon; 7=V-200 station wagon/Fury station wagon; 8=taxicab; 9=law enforcement special; 0=fleet car. Third symbol: 1=1961. Fourth symbol indicates factory: 1=Detroit; 5=Los Angeles; 6=Newark, Del.; 7=St. Louis. Body plate below hood on cowl, inner fenders or radiator support indicates schedule date (SO); sequential body production number; body/style number (second symbol in VIN plus numbers and letters in second column of charts below); trim code and paint code. Six-cylinder engine numbers stamped on front or rear of left-hand side of block below cylinder head. V-8 engine numbers stamped on flat on top right-hand side of block behind water pump. Engine codes: R-17=170 cid/101 hp six and 170 cid/148 hp "Hyper-Pack" six; R-22=225 cid/145 hp six; R-318=318 cid/230 hp two-barrel V-8 or 318 cid/260 hp four-barrel V-8; R-36=361 cid/305 hp "Golden Commando" V-8 with four-barrel carb; R-38=383 cid/325 hp V-8 with four-barrel carb or 383 cid/330 hp V-8 with dual four-barrel carbs or 383 cid/330 hp V-8 with dual fours with "long-ram" induction or 318 cid/340 hp V-8 with dual fours and "short ram" induction. R-41=413 cid/350 hp four-barrel V-8 or 413 cid/375 hp V-8 with dual fours and "short ram" induction.

VALIANT V-100 SERIES

Series No.	Body/ Style No.	Body Type & Seating	Factory Price	Shipping Weight	Prod. Total
V1100	41	4-dr Sed-6P	2014	2590	25,695
V1100	21	2-dr Sed-6P	1953	2565	22,230
V1100	45	4-dr Sta Wag-6P	2327	2745	6,717

VALIANT V-200 — (6-CYL) — SERIES 1110 — The higher-priced Valiants were again grouped in the V-200 series and were immediately perceptible by their bright metal side window trim moldings and extra bodyside brightwork. An upper molding traveled along the front fender feature line and onto the flare on the front door, piercing a large circular medallion positioned below the vent window. The lower body crease had a second strip of stainless steel running from behind the front wheel openings, across the doors and partially up the rear fenders, with a touch of ribbing at the back. As with the base series, a two-door model was added. It was called a two-door sedan though it had no center post. (The new V-100 two-door was of the post style). Standard equipment for V-200s included all baseline items plus the convenience group features: front door armrests; cigar lighter; right side sun visor; and dual horns. The V-200 also used a lower compression base powerplant and, after midyear, could be had with an optional 225-hp engine.

VALIANT V-200 SERIES

V1110	41	4-dr Sed-6P	2110	2600	59,056
V1110	23	2-dr HT Sed-6P	2137	2605	18,586
V1110	45	4-dr Sta Wag-6P	2423	2770	10,794

FLEET SPECIAL/SAVOY/DELUXE SUBURBAN — (6-CYL/V-8) — SERIES RP1-L/RP2-L — Plymouth's sheet metal was drastically and uniquely altered by Virgil Exner's design team. Styling was based on straight lines, supplemented by sculptured curves. This sounds like a contradiction and looked like it, too. A straight beltline ran from the front body corners to the rear, across the deck overhang and continued entirely around to the opposite front corner. This created a flat, shelf-like upper beltline plane into which the hood and deck gently sloped. However, the front fender feature lines had an entirely different look, being rounded and canted at the same time. They came around the body corner running straight, but then angled into the stamped aluminum "eggcrate" grille, made an abrupt curve and ran into the dual individual headlights, which sat side-by-side at a slight angle. Below the 'shelf', the bodysides were a maze of concave and convex shapes, with flat doors thrown in for good measure. The front bumper ran straight across, with a rippled center section. The rear deck had a small thin dorsal fin and a concave latch panel. Large, missile-shaped taillights were hung on the lower rear bodysides. Sleek flowing rooflines were used on all models - even Suburbans. Standard equipment on base models included: oil filter; turn signals; sun visors; electric wipers; front foam cushions; front armrests; glovebox lock; and five tubeless blackwall tires. Savoys and Deluxe Suburbans had no trim to speak of. The 'Fleet Specials' had a few standard features deleted.

SAVOY SERIES/DELUXE SUBURBAN

FLEET LEVEL/PASSENGER CARS

RP1/2-L	41	4-dr Sed-6P	2242/2361	3305/3460	N/A
RP1/2-L	21	2-dr Sed-6P	2192/2311	3295/3435	N/A

DELUXE LEVEL/PASSENGER CARS

RP1/2-L	41	4-dr Sed-6P	2310/2430	3310/3465	44,913
RP1/2-L	21	2-dr Sed-6P	2260/2379	3300/3440	18,729

DELUXE SUBURBAN

RP1/2-L	45	4-dr Sta Wag-6P	2668/2788	3715/3885	12,980
RP1/2-L	25	2-dr Sta Wag-6P	2602/2721	3675/3845	2,464

Note 1: Data above slash for six/below slash for V-8.

BELVEDERE/CUSTOM SUBURBAN — (6-CYL/V-8) — SERIES RP1-M/RP2-M — Belvedere level trim included a tapering contrast panel along

the beltline from behind the rear most door edge to the rear body corner, with chrome louvers at its forward end. There was also slightly brighter window trim and Belvedere script plates on the left edge of the concave rear deck lid latch panel. Belvederes (and Custom Suburbans) had all Savoy/Deluxe-type equipment plus rear armrests; cigar lighter and, on nine-passenger station wagons, a power tailgate window and oversize tires. Plymouth paid quite a bit of attention to interior appointments for 1961. The transmission push buttons (automatic) were larger and rectangular for easier operation. A new, magnetic drive 'thermometer' type speedometer functioned with less noise. The previous system of gears was replaced with a cable-driven, 12-pole, annular-ceramic magnet with temperature compensator. This early analog gauge was more accurate. Body insulation was also improved. Square steering wheels - said to give a good instrument field of view - were a Belvedere option. Technical innovations included standardization of Ram-Tuned induction manifolding with the 383-cid engine option; the use of a cast iron intake manifold on the Slant Six; lower compression ratios for regular fuel adaptability; alternator electrical systems; and closed crankcase ventilation on all cars built for California sale.

1961 Plymouth, Belvedere two-door sedan, 6-cyl

BELVEDERE SERIES/CUSTOM SUBURBAN

Series No.	Body/ Style No.	Body Type & Seating	Factory Price	Shipping Weight	Prod. Total
PASSENGER CARS					
RP1/2-M	41	4-dr Sed-6P	2439/2559	3315/3470	40,090
RP1/2-M	23	2-dr HT Sed-6P	2461/2580	3320/3460	9,591
RP1/2-M	21	2-dr Sed-6P	2389/2508	3300/3450	4,740
CUSTOM SUBURBAN					
RP1/2-M	45A	4-dr Sta Wag-6P	2761/2880	3730/3885	13,553
RP2-M	45B	4-dr Sta Wag-9P	----/2990	----/3985	N/A

Note 1: Data above slash for six/below slash for V-8.

Note 2: Nine-passenger Custom Suburban came only as a V-8.

1961 Plymouth, Fury two-door hardtop, V-8

FURY/SPORT SUBURBAN — (6-CYL/V-8) — SERIES RP1-H/RP2-H — Furys and Sport Suburbans were Plymouth's richest models and the only real flashy cars of the year. They began at the Belvedere/Custom trim level and added upgraded upholstery; bright, full-length beltline trim; Fury or Sport signatures behind the front wheel openings; heavy slanted chrome louvers on the upper bodyside contrast panels (which also had aluminum inserts); a chrome base for the deck lid dorsal fin; full wheel discs; and, on two-door hardtop sedans, a larger 'Sky-Hi' rear window. Standard equipment extras were back-up lights and an electric clock. In addition, the missile-shaped taillight housings were fully chrome-plated. One outstanding performance attribute of all 1961 Plymouths was handling. The cars were extremely stable at all speeds and known, among enthusiasts, for excellent maneuverability. They could really go, too, when equipped with the Golden Commando (305 hp) V-8; Sonoramic Com-

mando Ram-Tuned (330 and 340 hp) 383-cid V-8 or 350 and 375 performance options on a new 413-cid block. The latter choices were midyear additions aimed at increased competition from Pontiac, Ford and Chevrolet in racing.

FURY SERIES/SPORT SUBURBAN

Series No.	Body/ Style No.	Body Type & Seating	Factory Price	Shipping Weight	Prod. Total
PASSENGER CARS					
RP1/2-H	41	4-dr Sed-6P	2575/2694	3350/3515	22,619
RP1/2-H	43	4-dr HT Sed-6P	2656/2775	3390/3555	8,507
RP1/2-H	23	2-dr HT Sed-6P	2599/2718	3300/3520	16,141
RP2-H	27	2-dr Conv-6P	----/2967	----/3535	6,948
SPORT SUBURBAN					
RP2-H	45A	4-dr Sta Wag-6P	3024	3890	2,844
RP2-H	45B	4-dr Sta Wag-9P	3134	3995	3,088

Note 1: Data above slash for six if offered/below slash for V-8.

Note 2: Fury convertible and Sport Suburban came only as V-8s.

ENGINES:

(Valiant V-100/V-200 Six) Inline. Overhead valve. Cast iron block. Displacement: 170.9 cid. Bore and stroke: 3.406 x 3.125 inches. Compression ratio: 8.2:1. Brake hp: 101 at 4400 rpm. Four main bearings. Solid lifters. Carburetor: Carter Ball and Ball Type BBS one-barrel Model 3093S.

(Savoy/Belvedere/Fury/Station Wagon SIX) Inline. Overhead valve. Aluminum block. Displacement: 225.5 cid. Bore and stroke: 3.406 x 4.125 inches. Compression ratio: 8.4:1. Brake hp: 145 at 4000 rpm. Four main bearings. Solid valve lifters. Carburetor: Carter Type BBS one-barrel Model 3679S.

(Savoy/Belvedere/Fury/Station Wagon V-8) Overhead valve. Cast iron block. Displacement: 317.6 cid. Bore and stroke: 3.906 x 3.312 inches. Compression ratio: 9.0:1. Brake hp: 230 at 4400 rpm. Five main bearings. Solid valve lifters. Carburetor: Carter Type BBD two-barrel Model 3682S.

CHASSIS FEATURES: Wheelbase (Valiant) 106.5 inches; (Plymouth Suburban) 122 inches; (Plymouth passenger car) 118 inches. Overall length: (Valiant) 183.7 inches; (Plymouth Suburban) 217.7 inches; (Plymouth passenger car) 209.5 inches. Front tread: (Valiant) 56 inches; (Plymouth) 60.9 inches. Rear tread: (Valiant) 55.5 inches; (Plymouth) 59.6 inches. Tires: (nine-passenger Suburban) 8.00 x 14; (other Plymouth V-8s) 7.50 x 14; (other Plymouth sixes) 7.00 x 14; (Valiant) 6.50 x 13.

1961 Plymouth, Valiant V-200 two-door hardtop, 6-cyl

VALIANT OPTIONS: Power brakes ($41). Power steering ($73). Basic group ($102). Basic radio group ($160). Appearance group ($63). Convenience group, V-100 only ($16). Antifreeze ($4). Front and rear bumper guards ($12). Solex safety glass ($37). Deluxe V-200 floor covering ($17). Hot water heater with defroster ($74). Back-up lights ($11). Left-hand outside rearview mirror ($5). Power tailgate window ($33). Push-button radio ($59). Padded dashboard ($13). Station wagon third seat ($61). White sidewall tires ($29). Undercoating with underhood pad ($14). Deluxe wheel covers ($16). Variable speed windshield wipers ($17). Three-speed manual floor shift transmission was standard. Automatic transmission ($172). Six-cylinder 225.5 cid/148 hp Slant Six engine. Positive crankcase ventilation system, mandatory on California-built cars ($5).

PLYMOUTH OPTIONS: Power brakes ($43). Power steering ($77). Air conditioning including heater ($446). Dual air conditioning with heater ($640). Front bumper grille bar ($14). All Solex glass ($43). Headlight trim plate ($18). Heater and defroster ($74). Saf-T-Matic power door locks, two-doors ($23); four-doors ($30). Locking spare tire compartment, six-passenger station wagon ($4). Two-tone paint, except convertible ($17). Six-Way power seat ($96). Power tailgate window, six-passenger station wagon ($33). Push-button radio ($59). Hi-fi radio ($84). RCA automatic record player, radio required ($52). Square-shaped Deluxe steering wheel ($11). Four wheel covers ($19). Left-hand outside rearview mirror ($5); same, remote control ($14); matching right-hand manual ($5). Inside Prismatic mirror ($4). Safety pad instrument panel ($14). Windshield wipers, variable ($6); washers ($12); both together ($17). Savoy/Deluxe options, clock ($16); cigar lighter ($4). Custom/Sport Wagon tailgate assist handle ($16). Undercoating and underhood pad ($14). Savoy/Deluxe, Belvedere/Custom back-up lights ($11).

Basic group ($92). Basic radio accessory group ($150). Appearance group ($47). Easy driving group ($98). Three-speed manual transmission was standard. TorqueFlite automatic transmission with standard V-8 ($189). TorqueFlite automatic transmission with V-8 engine options ($211). TorqueFlite automatic transmission with Slant Six ($192). Crankcase vent system mandatory on California-built cars ($5). Dual exhaust as optional equipment ($27). V-8 317.6 cid/260 hp four-barrel 'Super Fury' engine ($158). V-8 360.8 cid/305 hp four-barrel Golden Commando engine ($206). V-8 383 cid/325 hp four-barrel engine; V-8 383 cid/330 hp dual four-barrel Sonoramic Commando engine ($405). V-8 383 cid/340 hp dual four-barrel engine. V-8 413.2 cid/350 hp four-barrel engine. V-8 413.2 cid/375 hp dual four-barrel engine. Four-barrel carburetor ($119). All dual four-barrel engines used 'Sonoramic' tuned ram induction intake manifolds. Sure-Grip positive traction rear axle ($50). See 1961 Dodge section for detailed engine specifications.

HISTORICAL FOOTNOTES: The full-size Plymouths were introduced Sept. 29, 1960, and the Valiant appeared in dealer showrooms the same day. Model year production peaked at 198,444 units for Plymouths and 133,487 Valiants. This compared to 242,725 and 187,808, respectively, in 1960. General manager of the company this year was C.E. Briggs, who also held the title of Plymouth vice-president and chief executive officer. Chrysler-Plymouth Division was formed this year, joining together the marketing of the related nameplates. Plymouth sales alone dropped to seventh rank in the American industry. The radical new styling was one factor in this decline. Option installation rates showed the following percentage applications for Plymouths (and Valiants in parentheses): automatic transmission, 78 (62.1); V-8 engine, 63.7 (N/A); radio, 46.1 (34.6); heater, 97.6 (94.6); power steering, 51.7 (10.7); power seat, 0.8 (N/A); power brakes, 15.6 (0.8); air conditioning, 4.3 (N/A); dual exhaust, 4.8 (N/A); tinted glass, 18.3 (4.4) and windshield washers, 33.4 (24.4).

1962 PLYMOUTH

VALIANT V-100 — (6-CYL) — SERIES SV1-L — There were no major changes in 1962 Valiant styling, but minor refinements in appearance were visible from any angle. The inverted, trapezoid-shaped grille had a heavier chrome frame, which gave a richer look. The area ahead of the hood lip was flattened and had the Valiant name, in block letters, stamped into it. The grille insert consisted of six vertical 'stacks' of short horizontal blades, running top to bottom. They were segmented by means of five vertical division moldings. The center grille emblem was gone, replaced by a small rectangle of chrome at the top of the center divider. Side trim, on base models, was the same as in 1961. It consisted of just a Valiant chrome signature behind the front wheel opening. At the rear, the stamped 'continental tire' impression was gone. The 'cat's eye' taillamps of earlier years were replaced by round units at each lower body corner. A large, round chrome ring was placed on the rear deck and pierced by a strip of chrome running up the center. The V-100 series was the base line. Standard equipment included electric windshield wipers; turn signals; oil filter; front door armrests; cigar lighter; sun visors; dual horns; and five tubeless blackwall tires. Small hubcaps; unaccented window frames; and plain, but durable upholstery trims were seen.

PLYMOUTH I.D. NUMBERS: The Vehicle Identification Number is located on a plate attached to driver's side front door hinge pillar. First symbol identifies car-line: 1=Valiant; 2=Plymouth six; 3=Plymouth V-8. Second symbol identifies series: 1=Valiant 100/Savoy; 2=Belvedere; 3=Valiant 200/Fury; 4=Valiant Signet/Sport Fury; 5=Valiant 100 station wagon/Savoy station wagon; 6=Belvedere station wagon; 7=Valiant 200/Fury station wagon; 8=taxicab; 9=law enforcement special; 0=fleet car. Third symbol indicates model year: 2=1962. Fourth symbol identifies assembly plant: 1=Detroit, Mich.; 5=Los Angeles, Calif.; 6=Newark, Del.; 7=St. Louis, Mo. Last six symbols are sequential production number for series at factory. Body Number Plate on inner fenders, cowl or radiator support indicates SO number, body production sequence number, body style code (second column of charts below), trim code and paint code. Engine numbers stamped on right side of block: on six below cylinder head opposite number one cylinder; on V-8 below distributor. Engine number indicates year (S=1962), displacement (17=170 cid, etc.), month (1=Jan., etc.) and day (01=Jan. 1). Engine codes: S-17=170 cid/101 hp six; S-22=225 cid/145 hp six; S-318=318 cid/230 hp 2V V-8 or 318 cid/260 hp 4V V-8; S-361=361 cid/305 hp 4V V-8 or 361 cid/310 hp 2x4V V-8; S-38=383 cid/330 hp 4V V-8 or 383 cid/335 hp 2x4V V-8; S-41=413 cid/365 hp 4V V-8 or 413 cid/385 hp 2x4V V-8 or 413 cid/410 hp 2x4V "Ram-Tuned" V-8.

VALIANT V-100 SERIES

Series No.	Body/Style No.	Body Type & Seating	Factory Price	Shipping Weight	Prod. Total
SV1-L	113	4-dr Sed-6P	1991	2500	33,769
SV1-L	111	2-dr Sed-6P	1930	2480	19,679
SV1-L	156	4-dr Sta Wag-6P	2285	2660	5,932

VALIANT V-200 — (6-CYL) — SERIES SV1-H — The Valiant V-200 lineup continued with three styles that were somewhat better dressed than the lowest-priced cars. They had bright metal side window accents; a bright metal roof gutter rail; chrome taillamp rings; full wheel covers; and sweep spear side moldings. This trim began behind the front wheel opening and traced the lower body feature line to the rear quarters where three flat black 'dashes' were stamped into the molding. The trim then continued up over the rear wheel housing, across the upper fender line and around the rear upper body corners (short strips were used on all models to conceal a body weld at this point). The ring-type rear deck emblem was slightly fancier, too. The V-200 came with all the basic features plus special upholstery and trim and Deluxe carpeting. Technical advances for all Valiants included 32,000 mile interval chassis lubrication, a higher torque starting engine and electrical printed circuitry. Unibody construction was continued and was highly publicized. The V-200 two-door hardtop sedan of 1961 was replaced by a conventional (full-pillared) two-door sedan.

VALIANT V-200 SERIES

SV1-H	133	4-dr Sed-6P	2087	2510	55,789
SV1-H	131	2-dr Sed-6P	2026	2500	8,484
SV1-H	176	4-dr Sta Wag-6P	2381	2690	8,055

1962 Plymouth, Valiant Signet two-door hardtop, 6-cyl

SIGNET 200 — (6-CYL) — SV1-P — The Valiant two-door hardtop sedan of 1961 was turned into a separate series comprising one car. It was called the Signet 200 hardtop (the former and incorrect term "sedan" being dropped). This model had an exclusive appearance and unique appointments. The grille and headlight inserts were painted black and a large chrome ring was placed in the center of the grille. Special wheel covers were seen. A Signet 200 medallion was added behind the front wheel opening at each side. In addition, painted accent stripes highlighted the upper front fender contour. Standard equipment included all V-200 items plus bucket-type front seats and a padded instrument panel. Like the V-200, the Signet was available with the optional 145-hp engine, but it used the same base engine as other lines. The series code SV1-P indicated its premium-level status, the 'P' designating a 'premium' type Valiant.

SIGNET 200 SERIES

SV1-P	142	2-dr HT Cpe-5P	2230	2515	25,586

FLEET SPECIAL/SAVOY — (6-CYL/V-8) — SERIES SP1-L/SP2-L — The Valiant had proved a relatively successful addition to the Plymouth family so this year the full-size cars were given a Valiant look and scaled down by two inches in wheelbase and 7-1/2 inches in overall length. However, the rear side feature line stopped short of the Valiant's around-the-wheelhouse sweep. In fact, the back of the cars looked like the outcome of mating a Valiant with a regular 1962 Plymouth. The low, thin center dorsal fin remained atop the rear deck. The grille was not a Valiant inspiration either. It was concave, with a series of concave, vertically segmented fins. Dual horizontal headlamps were seen. The inner lenses were set into the grille and looked smaller than the outer lenses, which were positioned in large, tunneled, circular housings at each corner of the body. Rooflines were a radical departure from the past, most having wraparound backlights and a more formal look. A long hood/short deck theme was apparent throughout the line. Savoys were the basic models, with their script nameplates high on the front doors and no extraneous trim. Standard equipment included: oil filter; turn signals; sun visors; electric wipers; front armrests; glovebox lock; five tubeless blackwall tires; and small hubcaps. Fleet Specials were basically Savoys with less standard features.

FLEET SPECIAL/SAVOY SERIES

FLEET SPECIAL

N/A	203/303	4-dr Sed-6P	2913/2351	2955/3115	N/A
N/A	201/301	2-dr Sed-6P	2137/2295	2930/3080	N/A

SAVOY

Series No.	Body/Style No.	Body Type & Seating	Factory Price	Shipping Weight	Prod. Total
SP1/2-L	213/313	4-dr Sed-6P	2262/2369	2960/3115	49,777
SP1/2-L	211/311	2-dr Sed-6P	2206/2313	2930/3080	18,825
SP1/2-L	256/356	4-dr Sta Wag-6P	2609/2717	3225/3390	12,710

Note 1: Data above slash for six/below slash for V-8.

BELVEDERE — (6-CYL/V-8) — SERIES SP1-M/SP2-M — The Belvedere represented Plymouth's mid-priced full-size nameplate. These cars had a strip of stainless steel running along the fender feature line, from above the headlamps to mid-door, and ending there with a spear tip. Placed above the molding, on the door, were bright Belvedere signatures. Standard equipment was comprised of the Savoy assortment plus armrests; front foam seat cushions; cigar lighter; and power tailgate window on nine-passenger station wagons. Like the Valiant, the 1962 Plymouths promoted 32,000 mile intervals between chassis lubes. They also had printed electrical circuits; higher torque starters; unibody construction, and a new aluminum transmission case to brag about. This automatic transmission was a three-speed TorqueFlite unit, with push-button controls, available only on V-8 attachments. It allowed a lower transmission tunnel hump and shaved a few pounds as well. The year's early V-8 options included the 318 cid/260 hp 'Super Fury' V-8 with four-barrel carburetor, dual exhaust, 10.2:1 compression ratio and hydraulic lifters, plus the 361 cid/305 hp 'Golden Commando' engine with four-barrel induction, dual exhaust, 9.0:1 compression ratio and hydraulic lifters. Other choices were released as running additions to the high-performance equipment list.

BELVEDERE SERIES

SP1/2-M	223/323	4-dr Sed-6P	2399/2507	2960/3095	31,263
SP1/2-M	221/321	2-dr Sed-6P	2342/2450	2930/3070	3,128
SP1/2-M	222/322	2-dr HT Sed-6P	2341/2538	2945/3075	5,086
SP1/2-M	266/366	4-dr Sta Wag-6P	2708/2815	3245/3390	9,781
SP2-M	367	4-dr Sta Wag-9P	----/2917	----/3440	4,168

Note 1: Data above slash for six/below slash for V-8.

Note 2: Nine-passenger Belvedere station wagon came only as a V-8.

1962 Plymouth, Fury four-door hardtop, V-8

FURY — (6-CYL/V-8) — SP1-H/SP2-H — The Fury's SP1-H or SP2-H designation said a lot: S=1962; P=Plymouth; 1=six-cylinder/2=V-8. But it was the suffix 'H' that told the Fury story. It stood for high priced. High-level appointments and a high level of equipment were standard on Furys. Included were all Belvedere items plus aluminum exterior trim inserts (on rear door/body top edge); back-up lights; electric clock; and power tailgate window operation on nine-passenger station wagons. Also available were options such as all-vinyl trim in hardtops, rear foam seat cushion and Six-Way power seat. Wheel covers, however, were optional - not standard. A Fury signature script, quite large in size, was used for identification, being placed behind the front wheel opening. The front fender feature line was highlighted with a heavy chrome strip, which was fluted at the forward tip. Thin moldings outlined the front and rear wheel openings, too. Only two styles, sedan and two-door hardtop sedan, were marketed with a six.

FURY SERIES

SP1/2-H	233/333	4-dr Sed-6P	2563/2670	2990/3125	17,231
SP1/2-H	232/332	2-dr HT Sed-6P	2585/2693	2960/3105	9,589
SP2-H	334	4-dr HT Sed-6P	2742	3190	5,995
SP2-H	335	2-dr Conv-6P	2924	3210	4,349
SP2-H	377	4-dr Sta Wag-9P	3071	3455	2,411
SP2-H	376	4-dr Sta Wag-6P	2968	3395	2,352

Note 1: Data above slash for six/below slash; no slash is for V-8.

SPORT FURY — (V-8) — SERIES SP2-P — Announced about four months after the rest of the line, the revived Sport Fury became Plymouth's premium (P suffix) offering. It had extras such as bucket seats; center front console; full wheel covers; all-vinyl trim; rear foam seat cushions; and Deluxe steering wheel as standard equipment. Even the fanciest 1962 Plymouths looked quite plain. In response to dealer wishes, several tack-on items were added to all Furys and Sport Furys at midyear. They included a third taillamp on each side (total six); beltline trim extensions (full-length); and license plate recess trim. Sport Furys, however, were distinguished by their signature script placement (ahead of front wheel opening); deck lid license plates; and red, white and blue finished trim insert dimples. Also, the grille was given a more strongly segmented ap-

pearance by blacking out the wider division panels. The Sport Fury came as a two-door hardtop or convertible. Special engines were optional. Only V-8s were used in these cars, however. The 1962 Sport Fury convertible is quite a rare machine.

1962 Plymouth, Sport Fury two-door convertible, V-8

SPORT FURY SERIES

Series No.	Body/ Style No.	Body Type & Seating	Factory Price	Shipping Weight	Prod. Total
SP2-P	342	2-dr HT-5P	2851	3195	4,039
SP2-P	345	2-dr Conv-5P	3082	3295	1,516

ENGINES:

(Valiant V-100/V-200/Signet Six) Inline. Overhead valve. Cast iron block. Displacement: 170.9 cid. Bore and stroke: 3.406 x 3.125 inches. Compression ratio: 8.2:1. Brake hp: 101 at 4400 rpm. Four main bearings. Solid valve lifters. Carburetor: Carter Type BBS one-barrel Model 3462S.

(Fleet/Savoy/Belvedere/Fury Six) Inline. Overhead valve. Aluminum block. Displacement: 225 cid. Bore and stroke: 3-13/22 x 4-1/8 inches. Compression ratio: 8.2:1. Brake hp: 145 at 4000 rpm. Four main bearings. Solid valve lifters. Carburetor: Carter Type BBS one-barrel Model 3466S.

(Fleet/Savoy/Belvedere/Fury V-8) Overhead valve. Cast iron block. Displacement: 317.6 cid. Bore and stroke: 3-29/32 x 3-15/16 inches. Compression ratio: 9.0:1. Brake hp: 230 at 4400 rpm. Five main bearings. Solid valve lifters. Carburetor: Carter Type BBD two-barrel Model 3472S.

(Sport Fury V-8) Overhead valve. Cast iron block. Displacement: 360.8 cid. Bore and stroke: 4.125 x 3.375 inches. Compression ratio: 9.0:1. Brake hp: 305 at 4800 rpm. Five main bearings. Hydraulic valve lifters. Carburetor: Carter AFB-3252S four-barrel.

(See 1962 Dodge section for complete Mopar engine specifications.)

CHASSIS FEATURES: Wheelbase: (Valiant) 106.5 inches; (Plymouth) 116 inches. Overall length: (Valiant) 184.2 inches; (Plymouth station wagon) 210 inches; (other Plymouths) 202 inches. Front tread: (Valiant) 55.9 inches; (Plymouth) 59.4 inches. Rear tread: (Valiant) 55.6 inches; (Plymouth) 57.5 inches. Tires: (Valiant) 6.50 x 13; (all Plymouth station wagons/V-8s) 7.00 x 14; (other Plymouths) 6.50 x 14.

VALIANT OPTIONS: Power brakes ($41). Power steering ($73). Air conditioning, dealer installation. Anti-freeze ($4). Front and rear bumper guards ($11). Tinted windshield ($14); all tinted windows, Solex ($28). Heater and defroster ($74). Back-up lights ($11). Left-hand outside rearview mirror ($5). Day/Nite inside rearview mirror ($4). Two-tone exterior finish ($16). Radio ($63). Station wagon luggage carrier ($48). Front seat belts ($19). Front foam seat cushions, except Signet ($11). Padded instrument panel ($13). White sidewall tires size 6.50 x 13 ($29). Vinyl trim, V-200 four-door sedan ($20). Deluxe wheel covers ($16). Windshield washer ($12). Variable speed windshield wipers ($5). Basic Group, includes: heater, variable speed wipers, left-hand outside rearview mirror, windshield washer and back-up lights ($107). Basic Radio Group, includes: radio, plus Basic Group ($166). Appearance Group, includes: wheel covers, safety padded instrument panel and white sidewall tires, for V-200 only ($58). Three-speed manual transmission was standard. Six-cylinder 225 cid/145 hp aluminum engine. Crankcase vent system ($5).

PLYMOUTH OPTIONS: Power brakes ($43). Power steering ($77). Air conditioning including heater ($446). Air conditioning group ($375). Antifreeze ($5). Front bumper bar ($14). Savoy options: cigar lighter ($4); front foam seat ($11); clock ($16). Tinted glass, all windows ($43); windshield only ($22). Heater and defroster, standard with air conditioning ($75). Back-up lights ($11). Roof luggage rack, station wagon ($43). Six-passenger Suburban left-hand outside rearview mirror ($6). Day/Nite inside rearview mirror ($4). Two-tone paint ($17). Six-Way power seat, Fury only ($96). Six-passenger station wagon power tailgate window ($33). Power windows ($102). Standard push-button radio ($59). Deluxe radio ($84). Seat belts ($19). Padded dashboard ($14). Deluxe steering wheel ($11). All-vinyl trim, Fury hardtop ($30). Four wheel covers, except Sport Fury ($19). Windshield washer ($12). Variable speed windshield wipers ($6). Basic Group, Fury ($104); other models ($114). Basic Radio Group, Fury ($162); other models ($173). Safety Group ($107). Assist Lights Group, nine-passenger station wagon ($7); other

models ($12). Three-speed manual transmission was standard. Torque-Flite automatic transmission with six-cylinder ($192). Aluminum Torque-Flite automatic transmission with V-8 ($211). 'Super Fury' V-8 318 cid/260 hp four-barrel engine ($39). 'Golden Commando' V-8 361 cid/305 hp four-barrel engine ($103). Short ram V-8 413 cid/410 hp dual four-barrel engine ($545); short ram V-8 413 cid/420 hp dual four-barrel engine ($612). Sure-Grip positive traction rear axle ($50).

HISTORICAL FOOTNOTES: The full-size Plymouths were introduced Sept. 28, 1961, and the Valiants appeared in dealer showrooms the same day. Model year production peaked at 172,134 full-size units. Calendar year sales of 331,079 total cars were recorded. C.E. Briggs was the chief executive officer of the Chrysler-Plymouth Division this year. Plymouth's model year output included 6,143 exported cars. The compact Valiant's model year output was recorded at 145,353 units of which 28,200 cars were built for export. Total Plymouth-Valiant model year totals were 317,487 assemblies. A total of 4,992 Plymouths and 28,198 Valiants had bucket seats for the model run. This indicates that some Sport Furys were made with bench seats and that some non-Signet Valiants had bucket seats. A total of 98,800 Plymouths used V-8 engines. Two versions of the '413' V-8 with "short ram" intake manifolds became available in May 1962 and were used mostly for drag racing. Rare Plymouth options (with percentage installation rates in parentheses) include: power seat (0.6); power windows (0.8); back-up lights (5.2); tinted glass (10.8); and air conditioning (5.2). For Valiants: power steering (9.1); power brakes (0.7); seat belts (4.2); and tinted glass (3.0). Plymouth customers were not really options buyers. In August 1962, a specially-equipped Plymouth attained the fastest speed ever recorded for a stock-bodied automobile at this time. Running at the annual Bonneville National Speed Trials, the car reached 190.073 mph over a one-way run.

1963 PLYMOUTH

1963 Plymouth, Valiant Signet two-door hardtop, 6-cyl (PH)

VALIANT V-100 — (6-CYL) — SERIES TV1-L — A complete and major styling change was the first revamp for Valiants. The compact Plymouth was now two inches longer. It had a wide, flat hood and flat square rear deck. The roofline was flatter, sharpened in profile and more conventional than in the past. Advances in body structure, many accessories and a new spring-staged choke were promotional highlights. The grille was a variation of the inverted trapezoid shape that characterized contemporary Chryslers, with a fine mesh insert. The upper belt feature line ran from the rear body, in a gentle sweep, to the front fender tip. Here it was 'veed' back and down to the trailing edge of the front fender. A nameplate adorned the hood of all styles and the sides of station wagons (or new convertible in upper level lines). New, horizontal taillamps wrapped around the rear fender corners. Standard V-100 equipment included electric wipers; turn signals; front door armrests; cigar lighter; dual visors and horns and five blackwall tires. The 170-cid Slant Six continued as base powerplant. Early in the season the 225-cid, aluminum version of the Slant Six was an all-model option. However, it was later discontinued and replaced by a cast iron '225'.

PLYMOUTH I.D. NUMBERS: The Vehicle Identification Number is located on a plate attached to driver's side front door hinge pillar. First symbol identifies car-line: 1=Valiant; 2=Plymouth six; 3=Plymouth V-8. Second symbol identifies series: 1=Valiant 100/Savoy; 2=Belvedere; 3=Valiant 200/Fury; 4=Valiant Signet/Sport Fury; 5=Valiant 100 station wagon/Savoy station wagon; 6=Belvedere station wagon; 7=Valiant 200/Fury station wagon; 8=taxicab; 9=law enforcement special; 0=fleet car. Third symbol indicates model year: 3=1963. Fourth symbol identifies assembly plant: 1=Detroit, Mich.; 2=Hamtramck, Mich.; 5=Los Angeles, Calif.; 6=Newark, Del.; 7=St. Louis, Mo. Last six symbols are sequential production number for series at factory. Body Number Plate on inner fenders, cowl or radiator support indicates SO number, body production sequence number, body style code (second column of charts below), trim code and paint code. Engine numbers stamped on right side of block: on six below cylinder head opposite number one cylinder; on V-8 below distributor. Engine number indicates year (T=1963), displacement (17=170 cid, etc.), month (1=Jan., etc.) and day (01=Jan. 1).

441

Engine codes: T-17=170 cid/101 hp six; T-22=225 cid/145 hp six; T-318=318 cid/230 hp 2V V-8; T-361=361 cid/265 hp 2V V-8; T-38=383 cid/330 hp 4V V-8; T-42=Super Stock 426 cid/415 hp "Max Wedge Stage II" or Super Stock 426 cid/425 hp "Max Wedge Stage II" V-8.

VALIANT V-100 SERIES

Series No.	Body/ Style No.	Body Type & Seating	Factory Price	Shipping Weight	Prod. Total
TV1-L	113	4-dr Sed-6P	1973	2535	54,617
TV1-L	111	2-dr Sed-6P	1910	2515	32,761
TV1-L	156	4-dr Sta Wag-6P	2268	2700	11,864

VALIANT V-200 — (6-CYL) — SERIES TV1-H — Again there was no code 'M' (middle level) Valiant series. The high-priced line was the V-200, with the new styling. These models came with all basic features plus special upholstery, special trims and Deluxe carpeting. The convertible was a new body style. An extra trim feature was a thin, full-length upper beltline molding. Station wagons had roof pillar nameplates.

VALIANT V-200 SERIES

TV1-H	133	4-dr Sed-6P	2097	2555	57,029
TV1-H	131	2-dr Sed-6P	2035	2515	10,605
TV1-H	135	2-dr Conv-5P	2340	2640	7,122
TV1-H	176	4-dr Sta Wag-6P	2392	2715	11,147

VALIANT SIGNET — (6-CYL) — SERIES TV1-P — The Signet was classed as Valiant's 'premium' car range, above high-priced. Price, however, was in the compact car class and not really steep at all. Extra standard equipment on both body styles included bucket-type front seats, back-up lights with appliques and full wheel covers. The convertible came with a manually-operated top. A power top was not on the introductory accessories list, but may have been added during the year to stay competitive. Special Signet nameplates were attached at the front fendertips. On Dec. 1, 1962, an optional vinyl roof became available; the first offered on any Plymouth.

VALIANT SIGNET SERIES

TV1-P	142	2-dr HT Cpe-5P	2230	2570	30,857
TV1-P	145	2-dr Conv-5P	2454	2675	9,154

FLEET SPECIAL/SAVOY — (6-CYL/V-8) — SERIES TP1-L/TP2-L — A return to conventionality and more normal size characterized Plymouth's 1963 styling theme. The cars were three inches longer, an inch wider and had a flat roofline that angled into a flatter rear deck. The front had a square look. Oval parking lamps ran vertically at each body corner. Uniform-size appearing headlamps were housed, horizontally, within bright metal surrounds on the grille. The grille had a fine textured pattern, with prominent horizontal segments. Plymouth was spelled out in block letters across the edge of the hood. A stand-up hood ornament was used. The bodyside feature line ran from the upper front fender slanting just slightly downward as it moved to the rear. There it overlapped a square-shaped contour. Savoy features were comprised of oil filter; turn signals; electric wipers; glovebox lock; dual sun visors and front armrests. The nine-passenger station wagon had, in addition, a power rear window and cargo light. Passenger cars came with two-ply tires, station wagons with four-ply tires of similar size.

FLEET SERIES/SAVOY

FLEET SPECIAL

N/A	203/303	4-dr Sed-6P	N/A/N/A	3015/3215	N/A
N/A	201/301	2-dr Sed-6P	N/A/N/A	2970/N/A	N/A

SAVOY

TP1/2-L	213/313	4-dr Sed-6P	2262/2369	3020/3220	56,313
TP1/2-L	211/311	2-dr Sed-6P	2206/2313	2980/3200	20,281
TP1/2-L	257/357	4-dr Sta Wag-9P	2710/2818	3375/3560	4,342
TP1/2-L	256/356	4-dr Sta Wag-6P	2609/2717	3325/3475	12,874

Note 1: Data above slash for six/below slash for V-8s.

BELVEDERE — (6-CYL/V-8) — SERIES TP1-M/TP2-M — Belvedere was a full-size Plymouth's middle-priced nameplate. This model had a wide, colored molding along the bodyside feature line. Belvedere signatures replaced Savoy script, at mid-fender behind the front wheel cutout. A short molding was placed on the rear roof pillar. Belvederes could still be ordered with the Slant Six or base V-8 engines. Other equipment included rear armrests, front foam seats, and cigar lighter.

BELVEDERE SERIES

TP1/2-M	223/323	4-dr Sed-6P	2399/2507	3020/3235	54,929
TP1/2-M	221/321	2-dr Sed-6P	2342/2450	3000/3215	6,218
TP1/2-M	222/322	2-dr HT Cpe-6P	2431/2538	3025/3190	9,204
TP2-M	367	4-dr Sta Wag-9P	----/2917	----/3585	4,012
TP2-M	366	4-dr Sta Wag-6P	----/2815	----/3490	10,297

Note 1: Data above slash for six/below slash for V-8s.

Note 2: Belvedere station wagons came only as V-8s.

FURY — (6-CYL/V-8) — SERIES TP1-H/TP2-H — The Fury was Plymouth's high-level offering. In standard form it came with everything found in Belvederes plus a padded dashboard, back-up lamps and electric

clock. Trim features included a distinctive side molding (with color insert) that narrowed ahead of the front door. More window frame moldings were also added, and a rear deck panel beauty strip was applied. Identification was further increased with signatures behind the front wheel cutout; Fury block letters on the trunk and a rectangular emblem set into the right-hand end of the rear beauty panel. Two Furys still came with a Slant Six (cast iron block for most of the year), while V-8s included the '318' Commando, '383' Golden Commando and midyear '426' Commando; better known to enthusiasts as the 'Super Stock' or 'Max Wedge Stage II' powerplant. The four-speed transmission came only with V-8s, but another choice was a floor shifted three-speed manual unit with non-synchromesh first gear.

FURY SERIES

Series No.	Body/ Style No.	Body Type & Seating	Factory Price	Shipping Weight	Prod. Total
TP1/2-H	233/333	4-dr Sed-6P	2563/2670	3075/3265	31,891
TP1/2-H	232/332	2-dr HT Cpe-6P	2585/2693	3030/3215	13,832
TP2-H	334	4-dr HT Sed-6P	2742	3295	11,877
TP2-H	335	2-dr Conv-6P	2924	3340	5,221
TP2-H	377	4-dr Sta Wag-9P	3071	3590	3,368
TP2-H	376	4-dr Sta Wag-6P	2968	3545	3,304

Note 1: Data above slash for six/below slash or no slash for V-8.

1963 Plymouth, Sport Fury two-door hardtop, V-8 (PH)

SPORT FURY — (V-8) — SERIES TP2-P — The Sport Fury represented a premium-priced Plymouth, easily identified by bright rocker panel strips. The hardtop also had three hash marks on the rear roof pillar. Standard was everything regular Furys came with plus bucket seats; center console; all-vinyl upholstery; Deluxe steering wheel and rear foam seat cushions.

SPORT FURY SERIES

TP2-P	342	2-dr HT Cpe-5P	2851	3235	11,483
TP2-P	345	2-dr Conv-5P	3082	3385	3,836

ENGINES:

(Valiant V-100/V-200/Signet Six) Inline. Overhead valve. Cast iron block. Displacement: 170.9 cid. Bore and stroke: 3.406 x 3.125 inches. Compression ratio: 8.2:1. Brake hp: 101 at 4400 rpm. Four main bearings. Solid valve lifters. Carburetor: Carter Type BBS one-barrel Model 3675S.

(Savoy/Fleet Six) Inline. Overhead valve. Aluminum/cast iron block. Displacement: 225.5 cid. Bore and stroke: 3.406 x 4.125 inches. Compression ratio: 8.2:1. Brake hp: 145 at 4000 rpm. Four main bearings. Solid valve lifters. Carburetor: Carter Type BBS one-barrel Model 3466S. NOTE: Due to demand that was too low to justify extra production costs, Plymouth discontinued the cast aluminum six early in the 1963 model run.

(Savoy/Belvedere/Fury/Fleet/Sport Fury V-8) Overhead valve. Cast iron block. Displacement: 317.6 cid. Bore and stroke: 3.906 x 3.312 inches. Compression ratio: 9.0:1. Brake hp: 230 at 4400 rpm. Five main bearings. Solid valve lifters. Carburetor: Carter Type BBD two-barrel Model 3472S.

(See 1963 Dodge section for complete Mopar engine specifications.)

CHASSIS FEATURES: Wheelbase: (Valiant) 106 inches; (Plymouth) 116 inches. Overall length: (Valiant station wagon) 186.8 inches; (other Valiants) 186.2 inches; (Plymouth station wagon) 210.1 inches; (other Plymouths) 205 inches. Front tread: (Valiant) 55.9 inches; (Plymouth) 59.4 inches. Rear tread: (Valiant) 55.6 inches; (Plymouth) 57.5 inches. Tires: (Valiant) 6.50 x 13; (Plymouth) 7.00 x 14.

VALIANT OPTIONS: Power steering ($73). Air conditioning, dealer installation. Front and rear bumper guards ($12). Tinted glass, all windows ($28); windshield only ($14). Heater with defroster ($74). Back-up lights, V-100 ($11). Back-up lights, with applique, V-200 ($14). Left-hand outside rearview mirror ($5). Day/Nite inside rearview mirror ($4). Two-tone paint ($16). Power tailgate window ($33). Radio ($59). Roof luggage rack ($48). Front seat belts ($18). Front foam seats, except Signet ($11). Padded dash ($16). White sidewall tires ($29). Under-coating with hood pad ($13). Vinyl trim, V-200 four-door styles only ($20). Deluxe wheel covers ($16). Windshield washer ($12). Variable speed wipers ($5). Basic Group, V-100 ($102); V-200 ($105). Basic Radio Group, V-100 ($165); V-200 ($167). Custom Appearance Group,

V-100 ($50); V-200 ($34). Special Signet Group, Signet 200 only ($188). Three-speed manual transmission was standard. Automatic transmission ($172). Six-cylinder 225 cid/145 hp aluminum engine ($47). Six-cylinder 225 cid/145 hp cast iron engine. Heavy-duty 48-amp battery ($8).

PLYMOUTH OPTIONS: Power brakes ($43). Power steering ($77). Air conditioning ($446); as part of accessory group ($375). Front bumper bar ($14). Rear bumper guards ($14). Savoy options: cigar lighter ($4); foam seats ($11). Savoy and Belvedere options: electric clock ($16); padded dash ($14). Rear foam seats, Fury ($11). Tinted glass, all windows ($40); windshield only ($22). Heater and defroster, without air conditioning ($74). Back-up lights, standard Fury ($11). Left-hand outside rearview mirror ($6). Six-Way power seat, Fury only ($95). Power windows, Fury only ($102). Standard push-button radio ($59). Deluxe radio ($84). Deluxe steering wheel, standard Sport Fury ($11). All-vinyl Fury hardtop trim, standard Sport Fury ($25). Undercoating with hood pad ($14). Tailgate assist handles with rear wind deflector ($21). Four wheel covers, standard Sport Fury ($19). Windshield washer ($12). Variable speed wipers ($6). Basic Group, Fury ($104); others ($114). Basic Radio Group, Fury ($162); others ($173). Safety Group, Fury ($94); others ($107). Light Group, nine-passenger station wagon ($7); others ($12). 7.50 x 14 tires. Three-speed manual transmission was standard. Automatic transmission with six ($192). Four-speed manual floor shift transmission was available in midseason. 'Commando' V-8 361 cid/265 hp two-barrel 'Wedge' engine ($60). 'Golden Commando' V-8 383 cid/330 hp four-barrel 'Wedge' engine ($122). 'Super Stock' V-8 426 cid/415 hp four-barrel 'Max Wedge Stage II' engine (N/A). 'Super Stock' V-8 426 cid/425 hp dual four-barrel 'Max Wedge Stage II' engine (N/A). Sure-Grip positive traction rear axle ($50).

HISTORICAL FOOTNOTES: The full-size Plymouths were introduced Oct. 3, 1962, and the Valiant appeared in dealer showrooms the same day. Model year production peaked at 442,794 units. Calendar year sales of 496,412 cars were recorded. P.N. Buckminster was the chief executive officer of the company this year. The model year production total included 244,395 Plymouths (158,612 with V-8s) and 198,399 Valiants (all sixes). The Belvedere became a 'hot' car this year. In June 1963, Plymouth announced development of its 426-cid "Super-Stock" or "Max Wedge Stage II" V-8 engine for supervised drag racing and stock car racing. Cars with this engine finished first and second in USAC (United States Auto Club) competition. Four-speed manual transmissions were made available at about the same time. The power team worked best in the lighter weight cars. The Belvedere was such a machine and even looked good with its new colored body trim. Two versions of the Super Stock wedge engine with either 415 or 425 hp were available by special order. A total of just 2,130 Chrysler products (all brands) were made with 426-cid wedge engines. Some were Dodges, the rest Plymouths. Rare Plymouth options (percentage rates in parentheses) included: four-speed transmission (1.2); power seat (0.5); power windows (1.0); dual exhaust (4.1); and limited-slip differential (5.1). For Valiants, power steering (10.1); tinted glass (3.2); and air conditioning (1.6). The Satellite convertible, a show car, was seen this year.

1964 PLYMOUTH

VALIANT V-100 — (6-CYL) — SERIES VV1-L — For 1964, Plymouth re-trimmed the new Valiant body released in 1963. The most obvious styling change was a new grille with a horizontal bar theme. A medallion was placed at the center of the grille where the bars had a flat bulge. At the rear, the taillights were redone. They were now positioned vertically in the ends of the fenders. The ring-style rear deck decoration was replaced with a Valiant script located at the right-hand corner. The V-100 was in the base series. Heater and defroster; vinyl trim; turn signals; courtesy lights; front door armrests; and five tubeless black sidewall tires were listed as standard equipment. A new 273-cid V-8 was optional in all Valiants. However, there was no separate V-8 series. Passenger cars had V-100 identification on the rear roof 'C' pillar, but station wagons had Valiant signatures behind the front wheel housing and small V-100 nameplates on their narrow 'C' pillars.

PLYMOUTH I.D. NUMBERS: The Vehicle Identification Number is located on a plate attached to driver's side front door hinge pillar. First symbol identifies car-line: V=Valiant V-8; 1=Valiant six; 2=Plymouth six; 3=Plymouth V-8. Second symbol identifies series: 1=Valiant 100/Savoy; 2=Belvedere; 3=Valiant 200/Fury; 4=Valiant Signet/Sport Fury/Barracuda; 5=Valiant 100 station wagon/Savoy station wagon; 6=Belvedere station wagon; 7=Valiant 200/Fury station wagon; 8=taxicab; 9=law enforcement special; 0=fleet car. Third symbol indicates model year: 4=1964. Fourth symbol identifies assembly plant: 1=Detroit, Mich. (Lynch Rd.); 2=Hamtramck, Mich.; 3=Detroit, Mich. (Jefferson); 5=Los

Angeles, Calif.; 6=Newark, Del.; 7=St. Louis, Mo. Last six symbols are sequential production number for series at factory. Body Number Plate on inner fenders, cowl or radiator support indicates SO number, body production sequence number, body style code (second column of charts below), trim code and paint code. Engine numbers stamped on right side of block: on six below cylinder head opposite number one cylinder; on V-8 below distributor. Engine number indicates year (V=1964), displacement (17=170 cid, etc.), month (1=Jan., etc.) and day (01=Jan. 1). Engine codes: V-17=170 cid/101 hp six; V-22=225 cid/145 hp six; V-273=273 cid/180 hp V-8; V-318=318 cid/230 hp 2V V-8; V-36=361 cid/265 hp 2V V-8; V-38=383 cid/350 hp 4V V-8; V-42=426 cid/365 hp "Street Wedge" 4V V-8; V-426=426 cid/415 hp "Max Wedge Stage III" Super Stock V-8 (2x4V) and V-426+=426 cid/425 hp "Max Wedge Stage III" Super Stock V-8 (2x4V); VH-426=426 cid/415 hp "Race Hemi" V-8 (2x4V); VH-426HC=high-compression 426 cid/425 hp "Race Hemi" V-8 (2x4V).

VALIANT V-100 SERIES

Series No.	Body/ Style No.	Body Type & Seating	Factory Price	Shipping Weight	Prod. Total
VV1-L	113	4-dr Sed-6P	1992	2575	44,208
VV1-L	111	2-dr Sed-6P	1921	2540	35,403
VV1-L	156	4-dr Sta Wag-6P	2273	2725	10,759

VALIANT V-200 — (6-CYL) — VV1-H — The V-200 again represented the one-step-up Valiant. Trim distinctions were helpful in spotting these cars. A triangular badge on the deck lid centerline; a latch panel beauty molding; thin beltline moldings; bright metal roof gutter rails and lower bodyside moldings were a few identifiers. V-200s had all of the basic equipment plus full wheel covers; special upholstery; Deluxe carpeting; front and rear armrests; instrument panel; beauty moldings and cigarette lighter. A small plate bearing the series designation was placed under the Valiant signature at the right-hand corner of the deck lid. All 1964 Valiants had a bevelled feature line along the edge of the roof.

VALIANT V-200 SERIES

VV1-H	133	4-dr Sed-6P	2112	2570	63,828
VV1-H	131	2-dr Sed-6P	2044	2545	11,013
VV1-H	135	2-dr Conv-5P	2349	2670	5,856
VV1-H	176	4-dr Sta Wag-6P	2388	2730	11,146

VALIANT SIGNET — (6-CYL) — SERIES VV1-P — The Signet for 1964 came with foam rubber front seat cushions and attractively styled wheel covers. A lower bodyside molding stretched horizontally between the wheelhousings and was complemented by another molding on the lower rear quarter 'projectile' flare. The front fender ahead of the wheelhousing earned a chrome Signet signature and a 200 number plate. Bucket seats were standard. Cars with the optional 273-cid engine came with V-shaped emblems at the sides of the cowl. This engine became available until Jan. 1, 1964.

VALIANT SIGNET 200 SERIES

VV1-P	142	2-dr HT Cpe-5P	2256	2600	37,736
VV1-P	145	2-dr Conv-5P	2473	2690	7,636

1964-1/2 Plymouth, Valiant Barracuda two-door fastback coupe, V-8

BARRACUDA — (6-CYL) — SERIES VV1-P — April 1, 1964, was the Barracuda's launch date. The sporty new 'glassback' coupe went head-to-head against Ford's new Mustang, but lost in the sales race. It was an adaptation of Valiant sheet metal to a uniquely styled roof, deck and rear window. The roof received a wrapover look mated to an oversize, curved rear backlight with a fastback shape. The deck lid bulged up to meet the glass. Trim features, front to rear, were distinct for this model. They included a split, negative space grille with center insert and horizontal outer division bars, wide rocker sill panels and a chrome band across the rear window base housing a center medallion. Plymouth block letters decorated the trunk and Barracuda signatures were positioned on the sides of the cowl. Front fenders with a slimmer V-shaped feature line were seen. Standard equipment included: bucket front seats; bucket-shaped rear bench seat with folding backrest; special finned wheel covers with three-bar spinners or slotted wheel covers with simulated exposed hub and lugnuts; round chrome back-up light housings; and the base Valiant power team. For this year only, Barracudas earned Plymouth, Valiant and Barracuda identification plates.

BARRACUDA SERIES

Series No.	Body/Style No.	Body Type & Seating	Factory Price	Shipping Weight	Prod. Total
VV1-P	149	2-dr Spt HT-5P	2365	2740	23,443

SAVOY — (6-CYL/V-8) — SERIES VP1-L/VP2-L — Plymouth styling was face lifted for 1964. A bevelled edge feature line was used for the roofs of sedans, while hardtops had a new, cantilevered-type roof pillar. With this design, an extra large, wraparound backlight was employed and the pillars were much wider at the top than the bottom. A full-width grille was seen. It was 'veed' to the horizontal plane and featured an insert with six stacks of short horizontal blades, segmented by vertical division bars. There were wider horizontal blade sections at the outboard ends into which the dual headlamps were placed side-by-side. A more massive front bumper, housing the parking lamps, was used. At the rear, the 1963 look was further refined. Savoys had large, rectangular single taillamps. There was just a hint of a dorsal fin remaining. Plymouth block letters decorated the edge of the trunk. Savoy features were comprised of oil filter; turn signals; electric wipers; glovebox lock; dual sun visors and front armrests. The nine-passenger station wagon had, in addition, a power rear window and cargo light. Passenger cars came with two-ply tires, station wagons with four-ply tires of similar size. A Savoy identification script was positioned on the sides of front fenders, behind the wheel opening.

SAVOY SERIES

VP1/2-L	213/313	4-dr Sed-6P	2280/2388	3040/3210	51,024
VP1/2-L	211/311	2-dr Sed-6P	2224/2332	2990/3205	21,326
VP1/2-L	257/357	4-dr Sta Wag-9P	2721/2829	3400/3600	3,242
VP1/2-L	256/356	4-dr Sta Wag-6P	2620/2728	3345/3495	12,401

Note 1: Data above slash for six/below slash for V-8.

BELVEDERE — (6-CYL/V-8) — SERIES VP1-M/VP2-M — Plymouth's middle line was called the Belvedere again. This range could be identified by its full-length body side molding that was hook-shaped at the front end. Sedans also earned a horizontal 'C' pillar strip. Equipment feature extras were the same as seen the year before. A Belvedere signature script appeared behind the front wheel openings and on the right-hand side of the deck lid latch panel. However, there were no Plymouth letters on the rear edge of the trunk. The company was striving to give the Belvedere its own strong identity. An increased emphasis on performance was evident, too. However, Belvederes could still be ordered with the Slant Six or base V-8. Other standard equipment included rear armrests, front foam seats, and cigar lighter.

BELVEDERE SERIES

VP1/2-M	223/323	4-dr Sed-6P	2417/2524	3065/3225	57,307
VP1/2-M	221/321	2-dr Sed-6P	2359/2466	3000/3210	5,364
VP1/2-M	222/322	2-dr HT Cpe-6P	2444/2551	3010/3190	16,334
VP2-M	367	4-dr Sta Wag-9P	----/2928	----/3605	4,207
VP2-M	366	4-dr Sta Wag-6P	----/2826	----/3510	10,317

Note 1: Data above slash for six/below slash for V-8.

Note 2: Belvedere station wagons came only as V-8s.

1964 Plymouth, Fury station wagon, V-8 (PH)

FURY — (6-CYL/V-8) — SERIES VP1-H/VP2-H — Plymouth's high-priced line was the Fury series. It included four V-8 only models and two cars available with Slant Sixes. In standard form it came with everything found in Belvederes plus a padded dashboard, back-up lamps and electric clock. Furys included wide bodyside moldings with color inserts that tapered to a single spear on the front fenders. Also seen was Fury block lettering on the rear fender sides; Fury script on the right-hand edge of the trunk; rear deck panel 'grille'; dual taillamps; roof pillar medallions on sedans; and upgraded interior trim. Any Plymouth from Savoy up, could be ordered with the optional 'Commando 426-S' engine.

FURY SERIES

VP1/2-H	233/333	4-dr Sed-6P	2573/2680	3040/3230	34,901
VP1/2-H	232/332	2-dr HT Cpe-6P	2598/2706	3045/3215	26,303
VP2-H	334	4-dr HT Sed-6P	2752	3300	13,713
VP2-H	335	2-dr Conv-6P	2937	3345	5,173
VP2-H	377	4-dr Sta Wag-9P	3084	3630	4,482
VP2-H	376	4-dr Sta Wag-6P	2981	3530	3,646

Note 1: Data above slash for six/below slash, no slash for V-8.

1964 Plymouth, Sport Fury two-door hardtop, V-8 (PH)

SPORT FURY — (V-8) — SERIES VP2-P — The Sport Fury was the year's premium offering. Exterior trim was characterized by a wide bodyside feature line molding with color insert and a red, white and blue cowlside decorative panel. Sport Fury lettering and script were seen in the normal places. Special wheel covers with simulated knock-off hubs were used. Bucket seats were standard equipment, as was V-8 power. Cars ordered with the special 426 Super Sport "Max-Wedge Stage III" V-8 had unique external telltale signs. Numbers revealing the displacement were set against a black panel bridging the opening of the stand-up hood ornament. This subtle touch was an understated way to let the world know what kind of beast was lurking beneath the hood.

SPORT FURY SERIES

Series No.	Body/Style No.	Body Type & Seating	Factory Price	Shipping Weight	Prod. Total
VP2-P	342	2-dr HT Cpe-5P	2864	3270	23,695
VP2-P	345	2-dr Conv-5P	3095	3405	3,858

ENGINES:

(Valiant Six) Inline. Overhead valve. Cast iron block. Displacement: 170 cid. Bore and stroke: 3.40 x 3.125 inches. Compression ratio: 8.2:1. Brake hp: 101 at 4400 rpm. Four-main bearings. Solid valve lifters. Carburetor: Carter Type BBS one-barrel Model 3462S.

(Barracuda/Plymouth Six) Inline. Overhead valve. Cast iron block. Displacement: 225 cid. Bore and stroke: 3.40 x 4.125 inches. Compression ratio: 8.2:1. Brake hp: 145 at 4000 rpm. Four main bearings. Solid valve lifters. Carburetor: Carter Type BBS one-barrel Model 3839S.

(Valiant/Barracuda V-8) Overhead valve. Cast iron block. Displacement: 273 cid. Bore and stroke: 3.62 x 3.312 inches. Compression ratio: 8.8:1. Brake hp: 180 at 4200 rpm. Five main bearings. Solid valve lifters. Carburetor: Carter Type BBD two-barrel Model 3767S.

(Plymouth V-8) Overhead valve. Cast iron block. Displacement: 318 cid. Bore and stroke: 3.906 x 3.312 inches. Compression ratio: 9.0:1. Brake hp: 230 at 4400 rpm. Five main bearings. Solid valve lifters. Carburetor: Carter Type BBD two-barrel Model 3682S.

(See 1964 Dodge section for complete Mopar engine specifications.)

CHASSIS FEATURES: Wheelbase: (Valiant/Barracuda) 106 inches; (Plymouth) 116 inches. Overall length: (Valiant station wagon) 188.8 inches; (Valiant/Barracuda) 188.2 inches; (Plymouth station wagon) 211.5 inches; (Plymouth) 206.5 inches. Front tread: (Valiant/Barracuda) 55.9 inches; (Plymouth) 59.5 inches. Rear tread: (Valiant/Barracuda) 55.6 inches. (Plymouth) 59.6 inches. Tires: (Valiant six) 6.50 x 13; (Valiant V-8) 7.00 x 13; (Plymouth station wagon) 7.50 x 14; (other Plymouths) 7.00 x 14.

VALIANT OPTIONS: Power brakes ($43). Power steering ($82). Tinted glass, all windows ($29); windshield only ($14). Remote-control outside rearview mirror ($12). Barracuda racing stripes ($31). Special bubbled paint, Barracuda/Signet ($17). Two-tone finish, except Barracuda/Signet and convertible ($16). Power convertible roof ($54). Transaudio radio ($59). Station wagon rooftop luggage rack ($48). Retractable front seat belts ($7). Safety padded instrument panel ($16). Three-spoke steering wheel, except V-100 ($17). Heavy-duty shock absorbers and suspension package ($17). Vinyl trim in V-200 four-door styles ($20). Vinyl roof, Signet hardtop only ($77). Custom spinner wheel covers, Barracuda ($13); V-200 ($28). Bolt-on design sports wheel covers, Signet/Barracuda ($34); V-200 ($50). Deluxe wheel covers, V-100 and V-200 ($16). Variable speed wipers and washers ($17). Basic Group, includes: left-hand outside rearview mirror; windshield washer; variable speed wipers and radio ($84). Station Wagon Group, includes: power tailgate window; wind deflectors and luggage rack ($96). Sport Group, includes: simulated woodgrain three-spoke steering wheel; bolt-on design wheel covers; whitewalls ($80-$100). Performance Group, includes: suspension package, 273-cid four-barrel V-8 and power brakes, except station wagon ($156). Air conditioning ($364). Three-speed manual transmission was standard. Four-speed manual floor shift transmission ($180). Six-cylinder 225 cid/145 hp two-barrel engine ($47). V-8 273 cid/180 hp two-barrel engine ($131). Heavy-duty 48-amp battery ($8). Sure-Grip positive traction rear axle ($39).

PLYMOUTH OPTIONS: Power brakes ($43). Power steering, Belvedere ($86); Fury ($97). Dual air-conditioning, Fury station wagon ($550). Auto-Pilot speed control, Fury V-8 with automatic/power brakes ($85).

Electric clock, standard Sport Fury ($16). Rear window defogger, Fury ($21). Tinted glass, all windows ($40); windshield only ($22). Padded instrument panel ($19). Back-up lights, standard Sport Fury ($11). Four-Way power left-hand bucket seat, Sport Fury only ($78). Four-Way power left and right bucket seats, Sport Fury only ($156). Four power windows ($102). Transaudio radio ($59). Transaudio AM/FM radio ($129). Front foam seat cushions ($11). Deluxe steering wheel, Belvedere ($11). Adjustable steering wheel, automatic and power steering required ($46). Deluxe steering wheel, Fury ($15). Tachometer, Sport Fury only ($50). Tailgate assist handles, Belvedere station wagon ($21). Vinyl trim, sedans and hardtops ($25). Wheel covers, standard Sport Fury ($19). Bumper guards, front and rear except nine-passenger station wagon, Belvedere ($31); Fury ($34). Retractable seat belts, front and rear compartments ($30). Rear seat speaker with reverberator, except station wagon ($36). Basic Radio Group ($86). Six-passenger station wagon, Basic Radio Group ($91). Air conditioning ($417). Three-speed manual transmission was standard. Automatic transmission ($191-$210). Four-speed manual Hurst floor shift transmission ($188). 'Commando' V-8 361 cid/265 hp two-barrel engine ($59). 'Commando' V-8 383 cid/305 hp two-barrel engine ($71). 'Commando' V-8 383 cid/330 hp four-barrel engine ($122). 'Commando' (Street Wedge) V-8 426 cid/365 hp four-barrel engine ($483). 'Super Stock' (Max Wedge Stage III) V-8 426 cid/415 hp engine ($515). 'Super Stock' (Max Wedge Stage III) V-8 426 cid/425 hp engine ($545). 'Super Commando' V-8 426 cid/415 hp 'Hemi' engine ($1,800). 'Super Commando' V-8 426 cid/425 hp 'Hemi' engine ($2,000). Four-barrel carburetor on Commando '383' ($51). Sure-Grip positive traction rear axle ($50). Available rear axle gear ratios: 3.23:1; 3.31:1; 2.93:1 and 2.76:1.

HISTORICAL FOOTNOTES: The 1964 Plymouths and Valiants were introduced Sept. 20, 1963, and the Barracuda appeared in dealer showrooms in May 1964. Model year production of Plymouths peaked at 274,689 units. Calendar year sales of 330,440 cars were recorded. The Valiant saw model year production of 225,245 units this year and calendar year sales of 190,789 cars. Total calendar year production for Plymouth and Valiant combined was 571,339. P.N. Buckminster was the chief executive officer of the company this year. The 'Super Stock' Max Wedge Stage III 426-cid (426-R) V-8 was continued as a racing-only option in the $500 price range. Depending on compression ratio, it gave 415 or 425 hp. New was a street-tuned 426-S version of 365 advertised horsepower (about 410 actual horsepower). The 'Super Commando' 426-cid Hemi V-8 was released around Feb. 9, 1964, for competition use. The Hemi's in-the-crate price was approximately $1,800. Published power figures of 415 hp for the 11.0:1 compression version and 425 hp for the 12.5:1 high-compression version were considered conservative by most enthusiasts. A total of only 6,359 Chrysler products (Dodge and Plymouth) were built with 426-cid engines for model year 1964. Of these, only 271 were "Race Hemis". Rare Plymouth options and their percentage installation rates (in parentheses) included: four-speed transmission (4.1); power seat (0.6); power windows (1.1); and dual exhaust (8.3). For Valiants: four-speed transmission (6.7); power brakes (0.7); and air conditioning (2.3).

1965 PLYMOUTH

VALIANT V-100/V-200 — (6-CYL) — SERIES VV1-L — The Valiant was only slightly face lifted. The most obvious styling change was a new grille with more horizontal bars. The V-100 was in the base series. Heater and defroster; vinyl trim; turn signals; courtesy lights; front door armrests and five tubeless black sidewall tires were listed as standard equipment. A new 273-cid V-8 was optional in all Valiants. However, there was no separate V-8 series. Passenger cars had V-100 identification on the rear roof 'C' pillar, but station wagons had Valiant signatures behind the front wheel housing and small V-100 nameplates on their narrow 'C' pillars.

PLYMOUTH I.D. NUMBERS: The Vehicle Identification Number is located on a plate attached to driver's side front door hinge pillar. First symbol identifies car-line: B=Barracuda V-8; 1=Barracuda six; 3=Belvedere six; 5=Fury six; P=Fury V-8; R=Belvedere V-8. Second symbol identifies series: 1=Valiant 100/Belvedere I/Fury I; 2=Fury II; 3=Valiant 200/Belvedere II/Fury III; 4=Valiant Signet/Satellite/Sport Fury; 5=Valiant 100 station wagon/Belvedere I station wagon/Fury I station wagon; 6=Fury II station wagon; 7=Valiant 200/Belvedere II station wagon; 8=Barracuda; 9=law enforcement special; 0=fleet car. Third symbol indicates model year: 5=1965. Fourth symbol identifies assembly plant: 1=Detroit, Mich. (Lynch Rd.); 2=Hamtramck, Mich.; 5=Los Angeles, Calif.; 6=Newark, Del.; 7=St Louis, Mo. Last six symbols are sequential production number for series at factory. Body Number Plate on inner fenders, cowl or radiator support indicates SO number, body production sequence number, body style code (second column of charts below), trim

code and paint code. Engine numbers stamped on right side of block: on six below cylinder head opposite number one cylinder; on V-8 below distributor. Engine number indicates year (A=1965), displacement (170=170 cid, etc.), month (A=Jan., etc.) and day (A01=Jan. 1). Engine codes: A-170=170 cid/101 hp six; A-225=225 cid/145 hp six; A-273=273 cid/180 hp V-8 and 273 cid/235 hp 4V V-8; A-318=318 cid/230 hp 2V V-8; A-361=361 cid/265 hp 2V V-8; A-383=383 cid/270 hp 2V V-8 and 383 cid/330 hp 4V V-8; A-426=426 cid/365 hp "Street Wedge" 4V V-8; A-426R=426 cid/415 hp "Max Wedge Stage III" Super Stock V-8 (2x4V) and A-426S=426 cid/425 hp "Max Wedge Stage III" Super Stock V-8 (2x4V); AH-426=426 cid/415 hp "Race Hemi" V-8 (2x4V); AH-426HC=high compression 426 cid/425 hp "Race Hemi" V-8 (2x4V).

VALIANT V-100/V-200 SERIES

Series No.	Body/ Style No.	Body Type & Seating	Factory Price	Shipping Weight	Prod. Total
V-100					
AV1/2-L	V13	4-dr Sed-6P	2050/2178	2590/2770	42,857
AV1/2-L	V11	2-dr Sed-6P	1980/2108	2560/2740	40,434
AV1/2-L	V56	4-dr Sta Wag-6P	2330/2458	2750/2930	10,822
V-200					
AV1/2-H	V33	4-dr Sed-6P	2167/2295	2605/2795	41,642
AV1/2-H	V31	2-dr Sed-6P	2101/2229	2570/2750	8,919
AV1/2-H	V35	2-dr Conv-5P	2404/2532	2695/2875	2,769
AV1/2-H	V76	4-dr Sta Wag-6P	2442/2570	2755/2935	6,133

Note 1: Data above slash for six/below slash for V-8.

1965 Plymouth, Barracuda two-door fastback coupe, V-8 (PH)

VALIANT SIGNET/BARRACUDA — (6-CYL/V-8) — SERIES AV — The bucket seat Signet was the premium-level Valiant. Appearance extras included roof pillar trim; wheelhouse moldings; rocker panel moldings; front fendertop ornaments and circular medallions on the trunk and grille. Standard equipment was comprised of all V-200 features plus front foam seat cushions and full wheel covers. The Barracuda was a second type of premium compact from Plymouth and, technically, a sub-model in the Signet line. However, a Valiant nameplate no longer appeared on the deck lid's right-hand corner. This was about the only external change from the original. New was an optional 'Formula S' competition package that included a 235-hp edition of the 273-cid V-8 (four-barrel); heavy-duty front torsion bars; heavy-duty rear springs; firm ride shock absorbers; sway bar; rally stripes; extra wide wheel rims; Goodyear Blue Streak wide oval tires; and 'Formula S' medallions ahead of the front wheel openings. Barracuda sales took a big jump this season.

VALIANT SIGNET/BARRACUDA SERIES

VALIANT SIGNET

AV1/2-P	V42	2-dr HT Cpe-5P	2309/2437	2620/2820	10,999
AV1/2-P	V45	2-dr Conv-5P	2526/2654	2725/2905	2,578

BARRACUDA

AV1/2-P	V89	2-dr Spt HT-5P	2453/2535	2725/2930	64,596

Note 1: Data above slash for six/below slash for V-8.

BELVEDERE — (6-CYL/V-8) — SERIES AR — The Belvedere nameplate was no longer used to designate the level of trim and equipment. It was now used to classify intermediate size ranges. Actually, this was the same platform used for all Plymouths just one year earlier. There were three kinds of Belvederes. The low-level (L) offerings were in the Belvedere I series and had, as standard equipment, heater and defroster; front seat belts; oil filter; and five blackwall tires. Trim consisted of a straight, three-quarter length side body molding from the front door edge back and with Belvedere I script ahead of it. The high-level (H) Belvedere II models had, in addition, carpeting; special trim and upholstery; foam cushions; and back-up lights. Appearance distinctions were wide, full-length slanting horizontal moldings with color insert; Belvedere II signatures behind front wheel openings; and rocker panel steps. The premium-level (P) Belvedere

Satellite was endowed with a rich and sporty character. It had all equipment of the downscale models plus front bucket seats; center console; full wheel covers; and all-vinyl trim on the two-door hardtop. Side trim moldings were deleted, but louvers were seen on the Satellite's rear fenders and rocker panel moldings were used. Wheel opening moldings; Satellite signatures; and a rear horizontal beauty strip were nice accents. The 1965 Belvedere came with '318', '361', '383' and '426-S' (wedge head) V-8s. Professional auto racers could also get the 426-cid Hemi with 425 hp. Styling for these cars was a revamp of the 1964 body with single headlamps and a crossbar grille superimposed over a rectangular mesh background.

1965 Plymouth, Belvedere Satellite two-door hardtop, V-8

BELVEDERE SERIES

Series No.	Body/ Style No.	Body Type & Seating	Factory Price	Shipping Weight	Prod. Total
BELVEDERE I					
AR1/2-L	R13	4-dr Sed-6P	2236/2330	3105/3200	35,968
AR1/2-L	R11	2-dr Sed-6P	2198/2292	3045/3130	12,536
AP1/2-L	R56	4-dr Sta Wag-6P	2527/2621	3380/3465	8,338
BELVEDERE II					
AR1/2-M	R33	4-dr Sed-6P	2321/2415	3100/3155	41,445
AR1/2-M	R32	2-dr HT Cpe-6P	2347/2441	3075/3170	24,924
AR1/2-M	R35	2-dr Conv-6P	2561/2655	3195/3265	1,921
AR1/2-M	R77	4-dr Sta Wag-9P	2708/2802	3450/3525	3,294
AR1/2-M	R76	4-dr Sta Wag-6P	2612/2706	3385/3465	5,908
BELVEDERE SATELLITE					
AR2-P	R42	2-dr HT Cpe-5P	2612	3220	23,341
AR2-P	R45	2-dr Conv-5P	2827	3325	1,860

Note 1: Data above slash for six/below slash for V-8.

FURY — (6-CYL/V-8) — SERIES AP — There were four lines of Furys for 1965. The low-level (L) Fury I had heater and defroster; front seat belts; oil filter; and five blackwall tires. The Fury II (M) added front foam seats and carpets. The Fury III (H) also had a courtesy light package; electric clock; and back-up lamps. The Sport Fury (P) added bucket seats; console; special wheel covers; Deluxe Fury steering wheel; and rear fender skirts. All four full-size Plymouths were on a 119-inch wheelbase (121-inch for station wagons) and had unique sheet metal. Features included a long, narrow and high look; hooded, vertically stacked dual headlamps; V-shaped rear fender profile; full-length, rectangular bodyside depression; formal sedan roof treatment or semi-fastback cantilevered roofline on hardtops; and flat rear deck lid with peaked centerline and a cove-like latch panel treatment. Fury I trim consisted of a three-quarter-length horizontal molding from front door edge back. They had single taillamps. The Fury II had a full-length bodyside molding and single taillamps. The Fury III added a color insert to the side molding and had three, short horizontal bars of chrome on the cowl sides at mid-fender level. In addition, a twin taillamp treatment was used. The Sport Fury used two bars on the side of the cowl, with color treatment, and had Sport Fury signatures on front fenders and deck.

FURY SERIES

FURY

AP1/2-L	P13	4-dr Sed-6P	2401/2505	3490/3655	48,575
AP1/2-L	P11	2-dr Sed-6P	2348/2452	3430/3605	17,294
AP1/2-L	P56	4-dr Sta Wag-6P	2740/2844	3940/4120	13,360

FURY II

AP1/2-M	P23	4-dr Sed-6P	2500/2604	3485/3660	43,350
AP1/2-M	P21	2-dr Sed-6P	2448/2552	3445/3605	4,109
AP2-M	P67	4-dr Sta Wag-9P	3009	4160	6,445
AP2-M	P66	4-dr Sta Wag-6P	2908	4135	12,853

FURY III

AP1/2-H	P33	4-dr Sed-6P	2649/2754	3505/3685	50,725
AP1/2-H	P32	2-dr HT Cpe-6P	2656/2760	3485/3640	43,251
AP2-H	P34	4-dr HT Sed-6P	2825	3690	21,367
AP2-H	P35	2-dr Conv-6P	3006	3710	5,524
AP2-H	P77	4-dr Sta Wag-9P	3148	4200	9,546
AP2-H	P76	4-dr Sta Wag-6P	3047	4140	8,931

SPORT FURY

Series No.	Body/ Style No.	Body Type & Seating	Factory Price	Shipping Weight	Prod. Total
AP2-P	P42	2-dr HT Cpe-5P	2920	3715	38,348
AP2-P	P45	2-dr Conv-5P	3164	3755	6,272

Note 1: Data above slash for six/below slash, no slash for V-8.

1965 Plymouth, Sport Fury two-door convertible, V-8 (IMS)

ENGINES:

(Valiant/Signet Six) Inline. Overhead valve. Cast iron block. Displacement: 170 cid. Bore and stroke: 3.40 x 3.125 inches. Compression ratio: 8.5:1. Brake hp: 101 at 4400 rpm. Four main bearings. Solid valve lifters. Carburetor: Carter Type BBS one-barrel Model 3833S.

(Barracuda/Plymouth Six) Inline. Overhead valve. Cast iron block. Displacement: 225 cid. Bore and stroke: 3.40 x 4.125 inches. Compression ratio: 8.4:1. Brake hp: 145 at 4000 rpm. Four main bearings. Solid valve lifters. Carburetor: Carter Type BBS one-barrel Model 3839S.

(Valiant/Signet/Barracuda V-8) Overhead valve. Cast iron block. Displacement: 273 cid. Bore and stroke: 3.63 x 3.31 inches. Compression ratio: 8.8:1. Brake hp: 180 at 4200 rpm. Five main bearings. Solid valve lifters. Carburetor: Carter Type BBD two-barrel Model 3767S.

(Barracuda 'Formula' V-8) Commando 273. Overhead valve. Cast iron block. Displacement: 273 cid. Bore and stroke: 3.63 x 3.31 inches. Compression ratio: 10.5:1. Brake hp: 235 at 5200 rpm. Five main bearings. Solid valve lifters. Carburetor: Carter AFB four-barrel.

(Plymouth V-8) Overhead valve. Cast iron block. Displacement: 318 cid. Bore and stroke: 3.91 x 3.31 inches. Compression ratio: 9.0:1. Brake hp: 230 at 4400 rpm. Five main bearings. Solid valve lifters. Carburetor: Carter Type BBD two-barrel Model 3847S.

(See 1965 Dodge section for complete Mopar engine specifications.)

CHASSIS FEATURES: Wheelbase: (Valiant/Barracuda) 106 inches; (Belvedere/Satellite) 116 inches; (Fury station wagon) 121 inches; (Fury/Sport Fury) 119 inches. Overall length: (Valiant/Barracuda) 188.2 inches; (Valiant station wagon) 188.8 inches; (Belvedere/Satellite) 203.4 inches; (Belvedere station wagon) 208.5 inches; (Fury/Sport Fury) 209.4 inches; (Fury station wagon) 216.1 inches. Tires: (Valiant/Barracuda six) 6.50 x 13; (Valiant/Barracuda V-8) 7.00 x 13; (Plymouth passenger cars) 7.35 x 14; (Plymouth station wagon) 7.75 x 14 or 8.25 x 14.

VALIANT OPTIONS: Power brakes ($43). Power steering ($82). Tinted glass, all windows ($29); windshield only ($14). Remote-control outside rearview mirror ($12). Barracuda racing stripes ($31). Special buffed paint, Barracuda/Signet ($17). Two-tone finish, except Barracuda/Signet and convertibles ($16). Power convertible roof ($54). Transaudio radio ($59). Station wagon rooftop luggage rack ($48). Retractable front seat belts ($7). Safety padded instrument panel ($16). Three-spoke steering wheel, except V-100 ($17). Heavy-duty shock absorbers and suspension package ($17). Vinyl trim in V-200 four-door styles ($20). Vinyl roof, Signet hardtop only ($77). Custom spinner wheel covers, Barracuda ($13); V-200 ($28). Bolt-on design sports wheel covers, Signet/Barracuda ($34), V-200 ($50). Deluxe wheel covers, V-100 and V-200 ($16). Variable speed wipers and washers ($17). Basic Group, includes: left-hand outside rearview mirror; windshield washer; variable speed wipers and radio ($84). Wagon Group, includes: power tailgate window; wind deflectors and luggage rack ($96). Sport Group, includes: simulated woodgrain three-spoke steering wheel; bolt-on design wheel covers; whitewalls ($80-$100). Performance Group, includes: suspension package; 273-cid four-barrel V-8 and power brakes, except station wagon ($156). Air conditioning ($364). Three-speed manual transmission was standard. Four-speed manual floor shift transmission ($180). Six-cylinder 225 cid/145 hp two-barrel engine ($47). V-8 273 cid/180 hp two-barrel engine ($131). Heavy-duty 48-amp battery ($8). Sure-Grip positive traction rear axle ($39). Three-speed manual transmission was standard. TorqueFlite automatic transmission, with six ($172); with V-8 ($181). Four-speed manual floor shift transmission with '170' six ($179); with V-8 ($179). Four-speed manual transmission with floor shift and '225' six ($186). Valiant/Signet six-cylinder 225 cid/145 hp one-barrel engine ($46). Barracuda V-8 273 cid/235 hp four-barrel engine ($230). Crank-

case vent system, mandatory for California-built cars ($5). Sure-Grip positive traction rear axle ($39). Available rear axle gear ratios: (six) 3.23:1; (V-8) 2.93:1.

BARRACUDA OPTION PACKAGES: The Barracuda Formula S package included Commando 273 V-8 engine; rally suspension; heavy-duty shocks; 5.50 x 14 wheels; Goodyear Blue Streak tires; tachometer; 'open wheel' covers.

1965 Plymouth, Belvedere II four-door sedan (with optional bumper guards), V-8

PLYMOUTH OPTIONS: Power brakes ($43). Power steering, Belvedere ($86); Fury ($97). Air conditioning ($346). Dual air conditioning, Fury station wagon ($550). Auto Pilot speed control, Fury V-8 with automatic/power brakes ($85). Electric clock, standard Sport Fury and Fury III ($16). Rear window defogger, Fury ($21). Tinted glass, all windows ($40); windshield only ($22). Padded instrument panel ($19). Back-up lights, standard Sport Fury/Fury III/Satellite ($11). Six-Way power seat, Fury III only ($96). Four-Way power left-hand bucket seat, Sport Fury only ($78). Four-Way power left and right bucket seats, Sport Fury only ($156). Four power windows, except Belvedere I and Fury I/II ($102). Transaudio radio ($59). Transaudio AM/FM radio ($129). Front foam seat cushions, Fury I/Belvedere I ($11). Fender skirts, except station wagons and standard Sport Fury ($19). Deluxe steering wheel, Belvedere ($11). Adjustable steering wheel, automatic transmission and power steering required ($46). Deluxe steering wheel, Fury ($15). Tachometer, Sport Fury/Satellite only ($50). Tailgate assist handles, Belvedere station wagon ($21). Vinyl trim, Belvedere II/Fury III sedans and hardtops ($25). Wheel covers, standard Satellite/Sport Fury ($19). Bumper guards, front and rear except nine-passenger station wagon, Belvedere ($31); Fury ($34). Retractable seat belts, front and rear compartments ($30). Rear seat speaker with reverberator, except station wagon ($36). Basic Radio Group ($86). Six-passenger station wagon, Basic Wagon Group ($91). Three-speed manual transmission was standard. TorqueFlite automatic transmission, with six-cylinder ($192); with '273' V-8 ($203); with other V-8s ($211). Four-speed manual floor shift transmission with '361' and '383' V-8 ($188). 'Commando' V-8 318 cid/230 hp two-barrel engine ($31). 'Commando' V-8 361 cid/265 hp two-barrel engine ($88). 'Commando' V-8 383 cid/330 hp four-barrel engine ($153). Hemi V-8 426 cid/425 hp dual four-barrel engine ($1,800). '426-S' V-8 426 cid/365 hp four-barrel engine ($545). '426-R' Hemi V-8 426 cid/415 hp dual four-barrel engine ($1,150). Crankcase vent system, mandatory on California-built cars ($5). Sure-Grip positive traction rear axle ($39). Available rear axle gear ratios: (six) 3.31:1; (V-8) 3.23:1 or 2.93:1. (Race Hemi not available in Fury.)

HISTORICAL FOOTNOTES: The full-size Plymouths were introduced Sept. 25, 1964, and the Valiants appeared in dealer showrooms the same day. Model year production peaked at 683,456 units. Calendar year sales of 728,228 cars were recorded. P.N. Buckminster was the chief executive officer of the company this year. A Sport Fury convertible was the pace car at the 1965 Indianapolis 500. Plymouth released a special Pace Car drivetrain package, available in any Fury at extra cost. The XP-VIP experimental show car was built this year. The 1965 Fury body introduced the use of curved side window glass on Plymouth products. A total of 6,929 Chrysler Corp. products, including Plymouths, had 426-cid V-8s installed this year. Of these, only 360 were "Race Hemis" installed in Plymouths and Dodges. Four-speed transmissions were found in 2.6 percent of all Furys, 4.0 percent of all Belvederes, 19.4 percent of all Barracudas and 1.3 percent of all Valiants. Bucket seats were used in all Barracudas, 16 percent of Furys, 15.9 percent of Belvederes and 10.8 percent of Valiants. Some '65 Plymouths (and Dodges) had an altered wheelbase "drag package" for National Hot Rod Association (NHRA) Factory Experimental class drag racing.

VALIANT V-100/V-200 — (6-CYL/V-8) — SERIES BV — The Valiant V-100 was the base series. Standard features included: front fendertip series identification badges; chrome band at base of roof pillar; heater and defroster; vinyl interior; turn signals; courtesy lights; front seat belts; front door armrests; and five blackwall tires. The 170 cid/101 hp Slant Six was the base engine in the BV1-L line. The 273 cid/180 hp V-8 was base engine in the BV2-L line. The Valiant V-200 was the one-step-up line. It had all of the above features plus V-200 identification badges at front fendertips; straight, horizontal beltline molding; special upholstery and trim; Deluxe carpeting; front and rear armrests and cigar lighter. The V-200 two-door sedan and convertible were discontinued. Styling changes for the year included a split grille with fine-patterned insert; new front fenders; new rear fenders on sedans; new bevelled-edge rear deck lid; heavier rear bumper; and new, more formal roofline with large backlight. Station wagons had the new front end treatment, but carryover roof and rear styling. A lower body feature line ran at rear bumper height from the front to the rear quarter. It looped over both wheelhousings. On sedans, this line continued to the rear bumper. On station wagons, it stopped behind the rear wheel opening.

PLYMOUTH I.D. NUMBERS: The Vehicle Identification Number is located on a plate attached to driver's side front door hinge pillar. First symbol identifies car-line: B=Barracuda; R=Belvedere/Satellite; P=Fury; V=Valiant. Second symbol identifies series: L=Valiant 100/Belvedere I/Fury I; H=Signet/Valiant 200/Belvedere II/Fury III; M=Fury II; P=Barracuda/Satellite/Sport Fury; K=police; T=taxicab; S=VIP. Third and fourth symbols indicate body style and appear as the last two digits in Body/Style Number in charts below. Fifth symbol identifies engine: A=170-cid six; B=225-cid six; C=special order option six; D=273-cid V-8; E=318-cid V-8; F=361-cid V-8; G=383-cid V-8; H=426-cid "Street Hemi"; J=440-cid V-8; K=special order option V-8. Sixth symbol indicates model year: 6=1966. Seventh symbol identifies assembly plant: 1=Detroit, Mich. (Lynch Rd.); 2=Hamtramck, Mich.; 4=Belvedere, Ill.; 5=Los Angeles, Calif.; 6=Newark, Del.; 7=St. Louis, Mo.; 9=Windsor, Ontario, Canada. Last six symbols are sequential production number for series at factory. Body Number Plate on inner fenders, cowl or radiator support indicates SO number, body production sequence number, body style code (second column of charts below), trim code and paint code. Engine numbers stamped on right side of block: on six below cylinder head opposite number one cylinder; on V-8 below distributor. Engine number indicates year (B=1966), displacement (170=170 cid, etc.), month (A=Jan., etc.) and day (A01=Jan. 1). Engine codes: B-170=170 cid/101 hp six; B-225=225 cid/145 hp six; B-273=273 cid/180 hp V-8 and 273 cid/235 hp 4V V-8; B-318=318 cid/230 hp 2V V-8; B-361=361 cid/265 hp 2V V-8; B-383=383 cid/270 hp 2V V-8 and 383 cid/325 hp 4V V-8; BH-426=426 cid/425 hp "Street Hemi" V-8 (2x4V); B-440=440 cid/365 hp 4V V-8.

VALIANT V-100/V-200 SERIES

V-100

Series No.	Body/ Style No.	Body Type & Seating	Factory Price	Shipping Weight	Prod. Total
BV1/2-L	VL41	4-dr Sed-6P	2095/2223	2630/2820	36,031
BV1/2-L	VL21	2-dr Sed-6P	2025/2153	2600/2800	35,787
BV1/2-L	VL45	4-dr Sta Wag-6P	2387/2515	2780/2970	6,838

V-200

Series No.	Body/ Style No.	Body Type & Seating	Factory Price	Shipping Weight	Prod. Total
BV1/2-H	VH41	4-dr Sed-6P	2226/2354	2635/2820	39,392
BV1/2-H	VH45	4-dr Sta Wag-6P	2502/2630	2780/2985	4,537

Note 1: Data above slash for six/below slash for V-8.

1966 Plymouth, Valiant Signet two-door hardtop, V-8

447

1966 Plymouth, Barracuda 'Formula S' two-door fastback coupe, V-8

VALIANT SIGNET/BARRACUDA — (6-CYL/V-8) — SERIES BV — Standard features of Signets included front fender tip identification plates and script; front fender top turn indicators; wheel opening moldings; lower feature line moldings; (with full-length, satin-finish paint treatment below); bucket seats with front foam cushions; and special full wheel covers. Signet styling changes followed the Valiant pattern set by other lines, as did power teams. The two-door hardtop and convertible continued to be offered. The 1966 Barracuda was redesigned towards the front and largely unchanged at the rear and above the belt. It had the new split Valiant grille opening, but used an insert with a grid-style pattern and had a circular medallion on the horizontally ribbed body-colored center panel. Barracuda script appeared in front of the forward wheel openings. On cars having the Barracuda 'S' option package, small circular medallions were placed below the script. The 225 cid/145 hp Slant Six (optional on other Valiants) was standard in the BV1-P series Barracuda. The 273-cid two-barrel V-8 was standard in the BV2-P series Barracuda. Pin striping now appeared along the Barracuda's beltline and a vinyl top was a new option. Bucket seats; front fender turn indicators; rocker panel moldings; special full wheel covers; and carpets were among standard items.

VALIANT SIGNET/BARRACUDA SERIES

Series No.	Body/ Style No.	Body Type & Seating	Factory Price	Shipping Weight	Prod. Total
VALIANT SIGNET					
BV1/2-H	VH23	2-dr HT Cpe-5P	2261/2389	2635/2835	13,045
BV1/2-H	VH27	2-dr Conv-5P	2527/2655	2735/2925	2,507
VALIANT BARRACUDA					
BV1/2-P	VP29	2-dr Spt HT-5P	2556/2637	2800/2930	38,029

Note 1: Data above slash for six/below slash for V-8.

1966 Plymouth, Belvedere Satellite two-door hardtop, V-8

BELVEDERE — (6-CYL/V-8) — SERIES BR — The Belvedere received a major restyling in 1966. It had a square body. The fenders had a slab-like look, but were also gently sculptured forming a full-length rectangular depression panel above bumper top level. The large front wheel opening curved up into the rectangle, but the feature line passed over the rear wheel cutout. In profile, the edge of the front fender thrusted forward into a wide V-shaped form. Sedans had a square-angular roof with thick rear pillars. Hardtops retained the cantilevered roof treatment with a thicker base. This treatment was now seen at the rear of station wagons as well. Standard equipment on the Belvedere I included a Belvedere I nameplate behind the front wheelhousing; thin, straight moldings along the lower feature line (from behind front wheel housing to rear bumper); heater and defroster; front seat belts; oil filter; and five blackwall tires. Base power teams were three-speed manual transmission with the 225-cid Slant Six or 273-cid V-8. The Belvedere II series had its identification nameplate set a bit higher. It was adorned by a wide, full-length chrome spear placed above the bodyside centerline. The lower trunk lid panel was satin-finished. Carpeting; upgraded upholstery; front foam cushions; and back-up lights were featured. The Satellite had less side trim than other models, but came with the fancy trunk treatment; rocker panel moldings; bucket seats and console; wheel covers; and vinyl trims. A new powertrain option was a 'street' version of the 426 cid/425 hp Hemi V-8.

BELVEDERE SERIES

Series No.	Body/ Style No.	Body Type & Seating	Factory Price	Shipping Weight	Prod. Total
BELVEDERE I					
BR1/2-L	RL41	4-dr Sed-6P	2315/2409	3040/3210	31,063
BR1/2-L	RL21	2-dr Sed-6P	2277/2371	3015/3175	9,381
BR1/2-L	RL45	4-dr Sta Wag-6P	2605/2699	3470/3575	8,200
BELVEDERE II					
BR1/2-H	RH41	4-dr Sed-6P	2405/2499	3035/3195	49,911
BR1/2-H	RH23	2-dr HT Cpe-6P	2430/2524	3040/3205	36,644
BR1/2-H	RH27	2-dr Conv-6P	2644/2738	3115/3285	2,502
BR1/2-H	RH46	4-dr Sta Wag-9P	2804/2989	3565/3670	8,667
BR1/2-H	RH45	4-dr Sta Wag-6P	2695/2789	3465/3585	4,726
BELVEDERE SATELLITE					
BR2-P	RP23	2-dr HT Cpe-5P	2695	3255	35,399
BR2-P	RP27	2-dr Conv-5P	2910	3320	2,759

Note 1: Data above slash for six/below slash, no slash for V-8.

FURY — (6-CYL/V-8) — SERIES BP — Plymouth's full-size models for 1966 were face lifted. A new split grille with horizontal blades stretched between stacked headlights. The rear quarter panels and bumper were changed on passenger cars. The top face of the bumper had Plymouth block lettering. The deck lid had a flat center depression that carried over the rear panel, splitting it horizontally. The Fury I was the base model range. Equipment included model nameplates; full-length mid-bodyside moldings; heater and defroster; front seat belts; oil filter; and five blackwall tires. The Fury II had all the above features plus front foam seats; carpets; Fury II nameplates; and moldings along the upper feature line. A Spring Special Edition had metallic silver finish; blue vinyl seats; whitewalls; Deluxe wheel covers; and bright side window accents. It revived an old Plymouth tradition. The Fury III had all features of 'L' and 'M' suffix models plus the light package; electric clock; back-up lights; oversize tires on convertible; hooked 'candy cane' molding treatment; Fury III nameplates; and louver-style cowlside ornaments. The premium offering in this car line was the Sport Fury, which had all the above plus bucket seats; console; Deluxe Fury steering wheel; special finned wheel covers; fender skirts; and three decorative bars on front doors. A new offering, based on the full-size sheet metal, was the VIP line. It originally included only a four-door hardtop with VIP identification; special side moldings with woodgrain inserts; fender skirts; center armrest seats; and interior roof pillar reading lamps. After Jan. 1, 1966, a VIP two-door hardtop coupe was available.

FURY SERIES

Series No.	Body/ Style No.	Body Type & Seating	Factory Price	Shipping Weight	Prod. Total
FURY I					
BP1/2-L	PL41	4-dr Sed-6P	2479/2584	3485/3655	39,698
BP1/2-L	PL21	2-dr Sed-6P	2426/2531	3425/3610	12,538
BP1/2-L	PL45	4-dr Sta Wag-6P	2836/2941	3965/4130	9,690
FURY II					
BP1/2-M	PM41	4-dr Sed-6P	2579/2684	3480/3665	55,016
BP1/2-M	PM21	2-dr Sed-6P	2526/2631	3430/3630	2,503
BP2-M	PM46	4-dr Sta Wag-9P	3087	4175	5,580
BP2-M	PM45	4-dr Sta Wag-6P	2986	4145	10,718
FURY III					
BP1/2-H	PH41	4-dr Sed-6P	2718/2823	3505/3715	46,505
BP1/2-H	PH23	2-dr HT Cpe-6P	2724/2829	3480/3675	41,869
BP2-H	PH23	4-dr HT Sed-6P	2893	3730	33,922
BP2-H	PH27	2-dr Conv-6P	3074	3720	4,326
BP2-H	PH46	4-dr Sta Wag-9P	3216	4165	10,686
BP2-H	PH45	4-dr Sta Wag-6P	3115	4155	9,239
SPORT FURY					
BP2-P	PP33	2-dr HT Cpe-5P	3006	3730	32,523
BP2-P	PP27	2-dr Conv-5P	3251	3755	3,418
VIP					
BP2-H	PS43	4-dr HT Sed-6P	3133	3780	12,058
BP2-H	PS23	2-dr HT Cpe-6P	3069	3700	5,158

Note 1: According to Chrysler records, VIP two-door and four-door hardtop totals are also included in totals for what is believed to be Fury III two-door and four-door hardtops, respectively, although the Fury III is not specified by name.

Note 2: Data above slash for six/below slash, no slash for V-8.

ENGINES:

(Valiant/Signet Six) Inline. Overhead valve. Cast iron block. Displacement: 170 cid. Bore and stroke: 3.40 x 3.125 inches. Compression ratio: 8.5:1. Brake hp: 101 at 4400 rpm. Four main bearings. Solid valve lifters. Carburetor: Carter Type BBS one-barrel Model 3833S.

(Barracuda/Plymouth Six) Inline. Overhead valve. Cast iron block. Displacement: 225 cid. Bore and stroke: 3.40 x 4.125 inches. Compression

ratio: 8.4:1. Brake hp: 145 at 4000 rpm. Four main bearings. Solid valve lifters. Carburetor: Carter Type BBS one-barrel Model 3839S.

(Valiant/Signet/Barracuda/Belvedere V-8) Overhead valve. Cast iron block. Displacement: 273 cid. Bore and stroke: 3.63 x 3.31 inches. Compression ratio: 8.8:1. Brake hp: 180 at 4200 rpm. Five main bearings. Solid valve lifters. Carburetor: Carter Type BBD two-barrel Model 3767S.

('Formula' Barracuda V-8) Commando 273. Overhead valve. Cast iron block. Displacement: 273 cid. Bore and stroke: 3.63 x 3.31 inches. Compression ratio: 10.5:1. Brake hp: 235 at 5200 rpm. Five main bearings. Solid valve lifters. Carburetor: Carter AFB four-barrel.

(Fury/VIP V-8) Overhead valve. Cast iron block. Displacement: 318 cid. Bore and stroke: 3.91 x 3.31 inches. Compression ratio: 9.0:1. Brake hp: 230 at 4400 rpm. Five main bearings. Solid valve lifters. Carburetor: Carter Type BBD two-barrel Model 3847S.

(See 1966 Dodge section for complete Mopar engine specifications.)

1966 Plymouth, Sport Fury two-door hardtop, with Commando V-8

CHASSIS FEATURES: Wheelbase: (Valiant) 106 inches; (Belvedere station wagon) 117 inches; (other Belvederes/Satellite) 116 inches; (Fury station wagon) 121 inches; (other Furys/VIP) 119 inches. Overall length: (Valiant station wagon) 189 inches; (other Valiants/Barracuda) 188.3 inches; (Belvedere station wagon) 270.1 inches; (Belvedere Style 46 station wagon) 208.1 inches; (other Belvederes/Satellite) 200.5 inches; (Fury Style 45 station wagon) 216.1 inches; (Fury Style 46 station wagon) 217.4 inches; (other Furys/VIP) 209.8 inches. Tires: (Barracuda/Valiant six) 6.50 x 13; (Barracuda/Valiant V-8) 7.00 x 13; (Belvedere sedan/station wagon) 6.95 x 14 with six or 7.35 x 14 with V-8; (Belvedere convertible/Fury six) 7.35 x 14 or 7.75 x 14 on Style 45/8.25 x 14 on Style 46; (Fury V-8/VIP) 7.75 x 14 or 8.55 x 14 on all station wagons.

OPTIONS: [VALIANT/BARRACUDA] Power brakes ($42). Power steering ($80). Power disc brakes ($82). Air conditioning ($319). Three-speed manual transmission was standard. TorqueFlite automatic transmission, with six ($172); with V-8 ($181). Four-speed manual floor shift transmission with '170' six ($179); with V-8 ($179). Four-speed manual transmission with floor shift and '225' six ($186). Valiant Signet six-cylinder 225 cid/145 hp one-barrel engine ($46). Barracuda V-8 273 cid/235 hp four-barrel engine ($97). Crankcase vent system, mandatory on California-built cars ($5). Sure-Grip positive traction rear axle ($39). Available rear axle gear ratios: (six) 3.23:1; (V-8) 2.93:1. [FURY] Power brakes ($42). Disc brakes ($110). Power steering, Belvedere/Satellite ($84). Power steering, Fury/VIP ($95). Air conditioning, all ($338). Three-speed manual transmission was standard. Automatic transmission with six ($192); with V-8 ($211). Four-speed manual floor shift transmission with '383' or '440' V-8s. 'Commando' V-8 383 cid/270 hp two-barrel engine ($71). 'Commando' V-8 383 cid/325 hp four-barrel engine ($120). 'Commando' V-8 440 cid/365 hp four-barrel engine ($234). Crankcase vent system, mandatory on California-built cars ($5). Sure-Grip positive traction rear axle ($50). Available rear axle gear ratios: 3.23:1; 3.55:1; 2.93:1 and 2.94:1. [BELVEDERE] 'Commando' V-8 383 cid/325 hp four-barrel engine ($150). 'Street Hemi' V-8 426 cid/425 hp dual four-barrel engine ($1,105). 'Race Hemi' V-8 426 cid/425 hp dual four-barrel engine ($1,800). Crankcase vent system, mandatory for California-built cars ($5). Sure-Grip positive traction rear axle ($39). Available rear axle gear ratios: 3.23:1; 3.55:1; 2.93:1 and 2.94:1.

HISTORICAL FOOTNOTES: The Fury, Belvedere and Valiant were introduced Sept. 29, 1965, and the Barracuda appeared in dealer showrooms Nov. 25, 1965. A 1966 Sport Fury two-door hardtop with optional vinyl roof, built in late-1965, was the 14-millionth Plymouth assembled. Model year production peaked at 656,200 units. Calendar year sales of 687,514 cars were recorded. Robert Anderson was the chief executive officer of the company this year. The legendary Plymouth 'Street Hemi' engine was introduced this year. It had a bore and stroke of 4.25 x 3.75 inches; domed pistons with 10.25:1 compression; and dual four-barrel carburetors. It was conservatively rated for 425 hp at 5000 rpm. A total of 2,729 Street Hemi engines were installed in Dodges and Plymouths. Plymouth installations of the engine included 136 engines in Belvedere I two-door sedans (79 with four-speeds); 531 engines in Belvedere II hardtops (280 with four-speeds); 10 engines in Belvedere II convertibles (four with four-speeds); 817 engines in Belvedere Satellite hardtops (503 with four-speeds) and 27 engines in Belvedere Satellite convertibles (with no trans-

mission breakout available). Richard Petty won the Daytona 500 stock car race with an average speed of 160.627 mph driving a Belvedere hardtop with a de-stroked 404-cid 'Race Hemi'. Petty's engine produced over 550 hp. Industry trade journals indicate a total of 3,629 Chrysler products were built with 426-cid V-8s of Wedge and Hemi design this season. Only some of these were Plymouths. Four-speed manual transmission was used in 1.6 percent of all Furys; 4.8 percent of Belvederes, 14.9 percent of Barracudas and 0.5 percent of Valiants.

1967 PLYMOUTH

1967 Plymouth, Valiant Signet four-door sedan, V-8

VALIANT/SIGNET — (6-CYL/V-8) — SERIES CV — All-new bodies were used on 1967 Valiants. The general styling was straight and square, although the sides were mildly sculptured. They had a tapering lower feature line that widened toward the rear. The new fenders had a vertical 'slab' look. Features included a two-inch longer wheelbase; curved side glass; single headlamps in square bezels; a split grille that was subdivided horizontally; and vertical taillamps. The V-100 series was the low-level line. Standard equipment included all safety features now required by government mandate; front armrests on two-doors (front and rear on four-doors); heater and defroster; five blackwall tires; and small model name bars at mid-rear fender height. The trunk and center left-hand horizontal grille divider carried the Plymouth name. The V-200 was dropped, but a '200' decor group option was priced $71.95. It included body-side moldings; cloth and vinyl trim; Deluxe door panels; ashtray and rear armrest (in two-doors); colored rubber mats; partial horn ring; and '200' nameplates. Valiants came with either the 170-cid Slant Six or 273-cid V-8 series depending upon six or V-8 series. Horsepower rating for the six was raised to 115 by use of a Carter BBS Model 4286S one-barrel carb. The Signet was classed as the high-level series and included all the above features plus bright window accents; roof gutter rail moldings; rocker panel strips; fender-mounted turn indicator lamps; Signet rear fender script; cologne-grain vinyl seats; carpeting; map, courtesy, trunk and glovebox lamps; cigar lighter; custom padded dash with aluminum trim; padded sun visor; horn ring; and either the 225-cid Slant Six or 273-cid V-8.

PLYMOUTH I.D. NUMBERS: The Vehicle Identification Number is located on a plate attached to driver's side front door hinge pillar. First symbol identifies car-line: B=Barracuda; R=Belvedere; P=Fury; V=Valiant. Second symbol identifies series: E=Belvedere/Fury I; L=Valiant/Belvedere/Fury II; H=Signet/Belvedere II/Sport Fury; M=Fury III/Road Runner; P=Barracuda/Satellite/VIP; K=law enforcement special; T=taxicab; S=GTX/Sport Fury two-door; O=Super Stock. Third and fourth symbols indicate body style and appear as the last two digits in Body/Style Number in charts below. Fifth symbol identifies engine: A=170-cid six; B=225-cid six; C=special order option six; D=273-cid V-8; E=273-cid high-performance V-8; F=318-cid V-8; G=383-cid V-8; H=383-cid 4V high-performance V-8; J=426-cid "Street Hemi"; K=440-cid V-8; L=440-cid 4V high-performance V-8; M=special order option V-8. Sixth symbol indicates model year: 7=1967. Seventh symbol identifies assembly plant: 1=Detroit, Mich. (Lynch Rd.); 2=Hamtramck, Mich.; 4=Belvedere, Ill.; 5=Los Angeles, Calif.; 6=Newark, Del.; 7=St. Louis, Mo.; 8=Export; 9=Windsor, Ontario, Canada. Last six symbols are sequential production number for series at factory. Body Number Plate on inner fenders, cowl or radiator support indicates SO number, body production sequence number, body style code (second column of charts below), trim code and paint code. Engine numbers stamped on right side of block: on six below cylinder head opposite number one cylinder; on V-8 below distributor. Engine number indicates year (C=1967), displacement (170=170 cid, etc.), month (A=Jan., etc.) and day (A01=Jan. 1). Engine codes: C-170=170 cid/115 hp six; C-225=225 cid/145 hp six; C-273=273 cid/180 hp V-8 or 273 cid/235 hp V-8; C-318=318 cid/230 hp 2V V-8; C-383=383 cid/270 hp V-8 or [Barracuda] 383 cid/280 hp V-8 or 383 cid/325 hp 4V V-8; [Road Runner only] C-383=383 cid/375

hp V-8; C-426=426 cid/425 hp "Street Hemi" V-8 (2x4V); C-440=440 cid/350 hp 4V V-8 and 440 cid/375 hp 4V high-performance V-8.

VALIANT/SIGNET SERIES

Series No.	Body/ Style No.	Body Type & Seating	Factory Price	Shipping Weight	Prod. Total
VALIANT 100					
CV1/2-L	VL41	4-dr Sed-6P	2163/2291	2675/2850	46,638
CV1/2-L	VL21	2-dr Sed-6P	2117/2245	2655/2830	29,093
VALIANT SIGNET					
CV1/2-H	VH41	4-dr Sed-6P	2308/2436	2680/2855	26,395
CV1/2-H	VH21	2-dr Sed-6P	2262/2390	2660/2835	6,843

Note 1: Data above slash for six/below slash for V-8.

1967 Plymouth, 'Sports' Barracuda 'Formula S' two-door fastback coupe, V-8

BARRACUDA — (6-CYL/V-8) — SERIES CB — For 1967, the Barracuda shed its link to the Valiant family. It became a separate line with notchback, fastback and convertible available, all with totally new styling. They had curvy flowing features with a bare minimum of extraneous trim. Many magazines of the time compared the new Barracuda look to that of the Buick Riviera, but the two cars were actually world's apart. Characteristics for the redesigned Plymouth product included single headlights; concave roof pillars (on notchback coupe); curved side glass; a concave rear deck panel; wide wheel openings and a sleek fastback. The fastback had a flowing, streamlined rear roof treatment and less glass area for the rear window. The fastback was called the Sports Barracuda. Standard equipment on these cars included: three-speed manual transmission; carpeting; full instrumentation; grille-mounted Rally lights; heater and defroster; left-hand outside rearview mirror; padded dash rear fold-down seat (fastback); front bucket seats (convertible); all standard safety equipment, power top and glass rear window (convertible); and either the 225-cid Slant Six or 273-cid V-8. The new Barracudas were introduced Nov. 25, 1966, a bit later than other Plymouths.

BARRACUDA SERIES

CB1/2-H	BH23	2-dr HT Cpe-5P	2449/2530	2730/2855	28,196
CB1/2-H	BH29	2-dr FsBk Cpe-5P	2639/2720	2815/2940	30,110
CB1/2-H	BH27	2-dr Conv-5P	2779/2860	2840/2965	4,228

Note 1: Data above slash for six/below slash for V-8.

1967 Plymouth, Belvedere GTX two-door hardtop, V-8

BELVEDERE/SATELLITE/GTX — (6-CYL/V-8) — SERIES CR — The medium-size Belvedere and its derivative models were slightly face lifted. The horizontal grille blades were thinner and housed dual side-by-side headlights with small grille extensions between them. The parking lamps were moved into the bumper. The taillamps were redone. A new economy model was a plain station wagon simply called a Belvedere. It was intended to replace the Valiant station wagon in price. Features included: seat belts; dual outside rearview mirrors; dual brake system; flashers; energy absorbing steering column; Belvedere nameplates on front fender tips; and no bodyside moldings. Cars in the Belvedere I line included all the above features plus cigar lighter; padded dash; two-speed wipers with washers; back-up lights; front and rear armrests; tailgate filler panel on station wagons; rocker panel moldings; and Belvedere I nameplates. The Belvedere II line had all of the above plus front foam seats; parking brake warning lamp; wraparound taillights; carpeting; wheel opening moldings; full-length side moldings (along upper feature line); and Belvedere II nameplates. Three-seat station wagons in this series had all-vinyl seats; power tailgate window; two dome lamps; rear bumper step; and wall-to-wall carpeting. Convertibles had glass rear windows. The Satellite models had

additional extras including: front bucket seats with console (or center armrest seat); Deluxe wheel covers; glovebox light; fendertop turn signals; upper body accent stripe; courtesy lights; and aluma-plate full-length lower body trim panels. The high-performance GTX had all this and more including: a "Pit-Stop" gas cap; Red Streak tires; dual hood scoops; dual sport stripes; heavy-duty three-speed TorqueFlite transmission, brakes, suspension and battery; and a standard 440-cid four-barrel V-8 engine.

BELVEDERE/SATELLITE/GTX SERIES

Series No.	Body/ Style No.	Body Type & Seating	Factory Price	Shipping Weight	Prod. Total
BELVEDERE					
CR1/2-E	RE45	4-dr Sta Wag-6P	2579/2673	3455/3575	5,477
BELVEDERE I					
CR1/2-L	RL21	2-dr Sed-6P	2318/2412	3025/3185	4,718
CR1/2-L	RL41	4-dr Sed-6P	2356/2450	3065/3220	13,988
CR1/2-L	RL45	4-dr Sta Wag-6P	2652/2746	3470/3585	3,172
BELVEDERE II					
CR1/2-H	RH23	2-dr HT Cpe-6P	2457/2551	3050/3205	34,550
CR1/2-H	RH41	4-dr Sed-6P	2434/2528	3055/3210	42,694
CR1/2-H	RH27	2-dr Conv-6P	2695/2789	3120/3290	1,552
CR1/2-H	RH45	4-dr Sta Wag-6P	2729/2833	3485/3590	5,583
CR1/2-H	RH46	4-dr Sta Wag-9P	2836/2930	3555/3660	3,968
SATELLITE					
CR2-P	RP23	2-dr HT Cpe-5P	2747	3245	30,328
CR2-P	RP27	2-dr Conv-5P	2986	3335	2,050
GTX					
CR2-P	RS23	2-dr HT Cpe-5P	3178	3535	Note 1
CR2-P	RS27	2-dr Conv-5P	3418	3615	Note 1

Note 1: GTX production included in 1967 Satellite production totals.

Note 2: Data above slash for six/below slash for V-8, no slash for V-8.

FURY/VIP — (6-CYL/V-8) — SERIES CP — Completely new styling characterized full-size Plymouths. Features included larger, slab-sided bodies; 'coke-bottle' profiles; horizontally segmented grilles with fine pattern inserts and thin center division bar; stacked dual headlamps; and front fenders with a 'fanned-out' look. The cantilevered hardtop roofline was gone, replaced by a semi-fastback on some styles and a 'Fast Top' formal look on others. Standard on Fury I was carpeting; armrests; vinyl headliner; heater/defroster; glovebox lock; dual brake system; brake warning light; left-hand outside rearview mirror; back-up lights; inside mirror; energy absorbing steering column; two-speed wipers and washers; flasher; toggle/roller-type panel; panel dash and visors; seat belts and all-vinyl seats on station wagons. Fury IIs also had vinyl and cloth sedan interiors; foam seats; bright window accents; bodyside moldings; and special nine-passenger station wagon equipment. To all of this, the Fury IIIs added Deluxe cloth and vinyl interiors; electric clock; brake warning lamp; trunk light; glovebox light; torsion bar front suspension; Flow-Through ventilation (four-door hardtop); light group; glass rear window; and all-vinyl interior in convertible. Extras on the Sport Furys were bucket seats; Deluxe 15-inch wheels; armrest seat cushion center unit (or console); Deluxe steering wheel body accent stripes; Sport wheel covers; fender-mounted turn signals; and, on 'Fast Top' models, light group and Flow-Through ventilation. The VIP had all Fury III items plus simulated walnut paneling; Deluxe gold-fleck upholstery with vinyl trim; Deluxe wheel covers; lounge/sofa-type seats; center armrests; Deluxe 15-inch wheels; light group; and Flow-Through ventilation.

FURY/VIP SERIES

Series No.	Body/ Style No.	Body Type & Seating	Factory Price	Shipping Weight	Prod. Total
FURY I					
CP1/2-E	PE21	2-dr Sed-6P	2473/2578	3435/3535	6,647
CP1/2-E	PE41	4-dr Sed-6P	2517/2622	3490/3590	29,354
CP1/2-E	PE45	4-dr Sta Wag-6P	2884/2989	3945/4055	6,067
FURY II					
CP1/2-L	PL21	2-dr Sed-6P	2571/2676	3435/3540	2,783
CP1/2-L	PL41	4-dr Sed-6P	2614/2719	3470/3595	45,673
CP2-L	PL45	4-dr Sta Wag-6P	3021	4060	10,736
CP2-L	PL46	4-dr Sta Wag-9P	3122	4100	5,649
FURY III					
CP1/2-M	PM23	2-dr HT Cpe-6P	2767/2872	3475/3605	37,448
CP1/2-M	PM41	4-dr Sed-6P	2746/2851	3515/3615	52,690
CP2-M	PM43	4-dr HT Sed-6P	2922	3668	43,614
CP2-M	PM27	2-dr Conv-6P	3118	3670	4,523
CP2-M	PM45	4-dr Sta Wag-6P	3144	4080	9,270
CP2-M	PM46	4-dr Sta Wag-9P	3245	4125	12,533
SPORT FURY					
CP2-H	PH23	2-dr HT Cpe-5P	3033	3625	28,448
CP2-H	PH23	2-dr FsTp Cpe-5P	3062	3620	Note 1
CP2-H	PH27	2-dr Conv-5P	3279	3705	3,133

Series No.	Body/ Style No.	Body Type & Seating	Factory Price	Shipping Weight	Prod. Total
VIP					
CP2-P	PP23	2-dr HT Cpe-6P	3117	3630	7,912
CP2-P	PP43	4-dr HT Sed-6P	3182	3705	10,830

Note 1: Sport Fury two-door hardtop coupe/two-door Fast Top totals combined.

Note 2: Data above slash for six/below slash, no slash for V-8.

1967 Plymouth, Sport Fury two-door hardtop, V-8

ENGINES:

(Valiant 100 Six) Inline. Overhead valve. Cast iron block. Displacement: 170 cid. Bore and stroke: 3.40 x 3.125 inches. Compression ratio: 8.5:1. Brake hp: 115 at 4400 rpm. Four main bearings. Solid valve lifters. Carburetor: Carter Type BBS one-barrel Model 4286S.

(Signet/Barracuda/Plymouth Six) Inline. Overhead valve. Cast iron block. Displacement: 225 cid. Bore and stroke: 3.40 x 4.125 inches. Compression ratio: 8.4:1. Brake hp: 145 at 4000 rpm. Four main bearings. Solid valve lifters. Carburetor Carter Type BBS one-barrel Model 3839S.

(Valiant/Signet/Barracuda/Belvedere V-8) Overhead valve. Cast iron block. Displacement: 273 cid. Bore and stroke: 3.63 x 3.31 inches. Compression ratio: 8.8:1. Brake hp: 180 at 4200 rpm. Five main bearings. Solid valve lifters. Carburetor: Carter Type BBD two-barrel Model 3767S.

('Formula' Barracuda/Belvedere V-8) Commando 273. Overhead valve. Cast iron block. Displacement: 273 cid. Bore and stroke: 3.63 x 3.31 inches. Compression ratio: 10.5:1. Brake hp: 235 at 5200 rpm. Five main bearings. Solid valve lifters. Carburetor: Carter AFB four-barrel.

(Fury/VIP V-8) Overhead valve. Cast iron block. Displacement: 318 cid. Bore and stroke: 3.91 x 3.31 inches. Compression ratio: 9.0:1. Brake hp: 230 at 4400 rpm. Five main bearings. Solid valve lifters. Carburetor: Carter Type BBD two-barrel Model 3847S.

(GTX V-8) Overhead valve. Cast iron block. Displacement: 440 cid. Bore and stroke: 4.32 x 3.75 inches. Compression ratio: 10.1:1. Brake hp: 375 at 4600 rpm. Five main bearings. Hydraulic valve lifters. Carburetor: Carter Type AFB four-barrel Model 4326S.

(See 1967 Dodge section for complete Mopar engine specifications.)

1967 Plymouth, VIP four-door hardtop, with Commando V-8

CHASSIS FEATURES: Wheelbase: (Valiant/Barracuda) 108 inches; (Belvedere station wagon) 117 inches; (Belvedere passenger car) 116 inches; (Fury station wagon) 122 inches; (Fury passenger car) 119 inches. Overall length: (Valiant) 188.4 inches; (Belvedere six-passenger wagon) 207.1 inches; (Belvedere nine-passenger station wagon) 208.1 inches; (Belvedere/Satellite/GTX) 200.5 inches; (Fury six-passenger station wagon) 216 inches; (Fury nine-passenger station wagon) 217.3 inches; (Fury/Sport Fury/VIP) 213.1 inches. Front tread: (Valiant) 57.4 inches; (Belvedere) 59.5 inches; (Fury) 62.0 inches. Rear tread: (Valiant) 55.6 inches; (Belvedere) 58.5 inches; (Fury) 60.7 inches. Tires: (Valiant/Barracuda six) 6.50 x 13; (Valiant/Barracuda V-8) 7.00 x 13 (Belvedere/Satellite/GTX) 7.35 x 14; 7.75 x 14; 8.25 x 14 (Fury/Sport Fury/VIP) 7.75 x 14.

BARRACUDA/VALIANT OPTIONS: Power brakes ($42). Power steering ($80). Air conditioning ($319). Front and rear bumper guards ($22). Tinted glass, all windows ($28); windshield only ($14). Remote control outside rearview mirror ($7). Special buffed paint ($17). Two-tone paint ($19). Transaudio AM radio ($57). Signet, vinyl bucket seat interior ($75). Twin front shoulder belts ($26). Fast manual steering ($26). Deluxe steering wheel with full ring on V-100 ($11); on other models ($5). Signet, Deluxe woodgrain wheel ($26). Vinyl roof on Signet ($75). Vinyl trim in Signet ($23). Bolt-on design 14-inch wheels, Signet ($51). Deluxe 13-inch wheels ($18). Deluxe 14-inch wheels ($21). Heavy-duty suspension package ($14). Valiant 200 decor group package ($72). Basic group includes: AM radio, wheel covers, power steering and variable speed windshield wipers, with 13-inch wheels ($161); with 14-inch wheels ($164). Disc brakes. Three-speed manual transmission was standard. Automatic transmission, with six ($172); with V-8 ($181). Four-speed manual floor shift transmission, with V-8 only ($179). Valiant six-cylinder 225 cid/145 hp one-barrel engine ($46). Valiant V-8 273 cid/180 hp two-barrel engine ($97). Barracuda V-8 273 cid/235 hp four-barrel engine. Barracuda V-8 383 cid/280 hp four-barrel engine. Heavy-duty battery 70-amp/hour ($8). Sure-Grip positive traction rear axle ($39). Available rear axle gear ratios: 3.23:1; 2.93:1 and various options.

BELVEDERE/SATELLITE OPTIONS: Power brakes ($42). Power steering ($90). Front and rear bumper guards ($31). Cigar lighter, Belvedere station wagon ($4). Cleaner Air package with six ($18); with V-8 ($25). Electric clock ($15). GTX console in Satellite ($53). Disc brakes with V-8 ($70). Tinted glass, all windows ($40); windshield only ($21). Headrests with bucket or individual bench seats, pair ($26). Station wagon rooftop luggage rack ($47). Two-tone paint, except convertible ($22). Special buffed paint ($21). Power windows, two-doors ($100). Transaudio AM radio ($57). Transaudio AM/FM radio ($127). GTX front seat with folding center armrest, standard Satellite ($53). Heavy-duty shock absorbers, standard in GTX ($4). Twin front shoulder belts ($26). GTX sport stripes ($31). Full horn ring. Deluxe steering wheel, except station wagon ($5). Woodgrain Deluxe steering wheel, except station wagon ($26). Heavy-duty suspension package, except station wagon ($22). Satellite and GTX tachometer ($49). Vinyl roof, except station wagon and convertible ($75). Belvedere II vinyl trim ($24). Satellite Road Wheels ($77). Satellite 14-inch sport wheel covers ($18). Variable speed wipers ($5). Three-speed manual transmission was standard. TorqueFlite automatic transmission with six ($188); with '273' V-8 ($202); with other V-8s ($206). Four-speed manual floor shift transmission, all except GTX ($188). Note: Four-speed manual transmission not available with six or '273' and '318' V-8s. Commando V-8 318 cid/230 hp two-barrel engine ($30). Commando V-8 383 cid/270 hp two-barrel engine ($100). Commando V-8 383 cid/325 hp four-barrel engine ($150). 'Street Hemi' V-8 426 cid/425 hp dual four-barrel engine ($564). Super Commando V-8 440 cid/375 hp four-barrel engine (standard in GTX). Heavy-duty alternator ($11). Heavy-duty battery ($21). Heavy-duty Sure-Grip axle, GTX ($139). Sure-Grip positive traction rear axle ($38). Available rear axle gear ratios: 3.23:1; 3.55:1; 2.93:1, and other options. Note: The only optional V-8 in the GTX was the 426-cid 'Street Hemi'.

1967 Plymouth, Valiant (with 200 decor group option) four-door sedan, 6-cyl

1967 Plymouth, Satellite two-door hardtop, V-8

FURY/VIP OPTIONS: Power brakes ($42). Power steering ($95). Air conditioning ($338); dual system in Fury station wagon ($538). Auto Pilot ($83). Sport Fury center console (no charge). Rear window defogger ($20). Front disc brakes ($70). Sport Fury/VIP headrests, left ($21).

Power door locks, four-doors ($54); two-doors ($36). Six-Way power bench seat ($94). Left-hand Six-Way power bucket seat ($90). Power windows, VIP/Fury III/Sport Fury ($100). VIP two-door reclining passenger cloth/vinyl seat ($97). VIP four-door reclining passenger cloth/vinyl seat ($104). Bench seat leather trim, VIP only ($104). Tilt-A-Scope steering wheel ($87). Deluxe steering wheel, standard Sport Fury ($89). Tailgate assist handles, Fury station wagon ($16). Vinyl roof on hardtops ($75). Vinyl trim in Fury III hardtops and sedans ($24). Deluxe 15-inch wheels, standard VIP and Sport Fury ($21). Sport-type 14-inch wheels, standard Sport Fury ($40). Deep dish 14-inch wheels, Sport Fury only ($18). VIP Road Wheels ($76). Road Wheels on Fury I, Fury II, Fury III ($97). Road Wheels on Sport Fury ($58). Three-speed windshield wipers ($5). Three-speed manual transmission was standard. TorqueFlite automatic transmission, with six ($188); with '318' V-8 ($206); others ($216). Four-speed manual floor shift transmission; with '383' or '440' V-8 ($188). Commando V-8 383 cid/270 hp two-barrel engine ($70). Commando V-8 383 cid/325 hp four-barrel engine ($120). Station wagon V-8 440 cid/350 hp four-barrel engine ($234). Passenger car V-8 440 cid/375 hp four-barrel engine ($268). Heavy-duty alternator ($11). Heavy-duty battery ($21). Heavy-duty Sure-Grip axle ($139). Sure-Grip positive traction rear axle ($49). Available rear axle gear ratios: 3.23:1; 3.55:1; 2.93:1 and other options.

HISTORICAL FOOTNOTES: The Plymouths and Valiants were introduced Sept. 29, 1966, and the Barracuda appeared in dealer showrooms Nov. 25, 1966. Calendar year sales of 638,075 cars were recorded. Robert Anderson was the chief executive officer of the company this year. Plymouth factory installations of the "Street Hemi" in 1967 included two in Satellite hardtops (both four-speeds); one in a Satellite convertible (four-speed equipped); 55 engines in Belvedere II hardtops (no transmission attachment data for this model) and 720 in Belvedere GTX hardtops and convertibles (312 with four-speeds).

1968 PLYMOUTH

1968 Plymouth, Valiant Signet four-door sedan, 6-cyl

VALIANT/SIGNET — (6-CYL/V-8) — SERIES DV — Minor styling changes were seen on 1968 Valiants. The horizontal division bar was removed from the grille. A fine pattern cross-hatched insert was used and was framed by a segmented chrome surround. A Plymouth nameplate was placed on the left-hand grille insert. Vertical taillights were seen. They, too, were segmented and had a 'fanned-out' look. Model nameplates were moved from the rear fender to the front fender, ahead of the wheel opening. Standard equipment on the base V-100 models included: five 7.00 x 13 blackwall tires; seat belts; dual brake system with warning lamp emergency flashers; back-up lights; turn signals; heater and defroster; padded dash and visors; left-hand outside rearview mirror; inside day/nite mirror; energy-absorbing steering column; armrests: side marker lamps; windshield wipers and washers; and Safety-Rim wheels. Cars in the Signet series had all of these items plus body and wheel opening moldings; rocker moldings with front and rear extensions; cloth and vinyl interiors; cigar lighter; dual horns; carpeting; rear deck lid; horizontal beauty panel; and Signet front fender signature script. A 318 cid/230 hp V-8 was a Valiant option for the first time.

PLYMOUTH I.D. NUMBERS: The Vehicle Identification Number is located on a plate attached to driver's side front door hinge pillar. First symbol identifies car-line: B=Barracuda; R=Belvedere; P=Fury; V=Valiant. Second symbol identifies series: E=Belvedere/Fury II; L=Valiant/Belvedere/Fury II; H=Signet/Satellite/ Sport Fury; M=Fury III/Road Runner; P=Barracuda/Sport Satellite/VIP; T=taxicab; S=GTX/Sport Fury Fast Top; O=Super Stock; X=Fury III two-door Fast Top. Third and fourth symbols indicate body style and appear as the last two digits in Body/Style Number in charts below. Fifth symbol identifies engine: A=170-cid six; B=225-cid six; C=special order option six; D=273-cid V-8; F=318-cid V-8; G=383-cid V-8; H=383-cid 4V high-performance V-8; J=426-cid "Street Hemi"; K=440-cid V-8; L=440-

cid 4V high-performance V-8; M=special order option V-8; P=340-cid V-8. Sixth symbol indicates model year: 8=1968. Seventh symbol identifies assembly plant: A=Detroit, Mich. (Lynch Rd.); B=Hamtramck, Mich.; D=Belvedere, Ill.; E=Los Angeles, Calif.; F=Newark, Del.; G=St. Louis, Mo.; G=Windsor, Ontario, Canada. Last six symbols are sequential production number for series at factory. Body Number Plate on inner fenders, cowl or radiator support indicates SO number, body production sequence number, body style code (second column of charts below), trim code and paint code. Engine numbers stamped on right side of block: on six below cylinder head opposite number one cylinder; on V-8 below distributor. Engine number indicates year (PT=1968), displacement (170=170 cid, etc.), month (A=Jan., etc.) and day (A01=Jan. 1). Engine codes: PT-170=170 cid/115 hp six; PT-225=225 cid/145 hp six; PT-273=273 cid/190 hp V-8; PT-318=318 cid/230 hp 2V V-8; PT-383=383 cid/290 hp 2V V-8; 383 cid/300 hp 4V V-8; 383 cid/330 hp 4V V-8; [Road Runner only] 383 cid/335 hp 4V high-performance V-8; PT-426=426 cid/425 hp "Street Hemi" V-8 (2x4V); PT-440=440 cid/350 hp 4V V-8 and 440 cid/375 hp 4V high-performance V-8.

VALIANT SIGNET SERIES

Series No.	Body/ Style No.	Body Type & Seating	Factory Price	Shipping Weight	Prod. Total
VALIANT 100					
DV1/2-L	VL41	4-dr Sed-6P	2275/2456	2695/2895	49,446
DV1/2-L	VL21	2-dr Sed-6P	2228/2409	2675/2875	31,178
VALIANT SIGNET					
DV1/2-H	VH41	4-dr Sed-6P	2421/2602	2695/2895	23,906
DV1/2-H	VH21	2-dr Sed-6P	2374/2555	2675/2875	6,265

Note 1: Data above slash for six/below slash for V-8.

1968 Plymouth, Barracuda 'Formula S' two-door hardtop coupe, V-8

BARRACUDA — (6-CYL/V-8) — SERIES DB — The big news for Barracuda this year was the release of four new engine options. Buyers could now have '318', '340' or '383' cubic inches of V-8 below the hood and a special '383-S' engine was a Barracuda exclusive. Nameplates and script (plus engine identification badges) were moved to the cowlside front fender region. A vertical blade grille replaced the former cross-hatch mesh type. The word Plymouth appeared in block letters on the left-hand hood lip. Taillights were slightly changed and the rear deck panel received a black-out treatment. Standard equipment included either the 225-cid six or 318-cid V-8; three-speed manual transmission; carpeting; chromed hood louvers; full instrumentation; Rally lights; power top and glass window on convertible; heater and defroster; left-hand outside rearview mirror; energy absorbing steering column; dual brake system with warning lamp; emergency flasher; inside day/nite mirror; front and rear seat belts; padded sun visors; two-speed wipers with washers; padded dash; cleaner air package; fold-down rear seat (in fastback); front bucket seats (in convertible); and Deluxe wheel covers. The 'Formula S' package came in two forms, with both including: high-performance V-8; four-speed manual transmission with heavy-duty clutch or special automatic; wide wheels; heavy-duty suspension; white or red stripe wide oval tires; dual exhaust; sill moldings; and special instrumentation.

BARRACUDA SERIES

DB1/2-H	BH23	2-dr HT Cpe-5P	2579/2685	2715/2910	19,997
DB1/2-H	BH29	2-dr FsBk Cpe-5P	2736/2842	2810/3005	22,575
DB1/2-H	BH27	2-dr Conv-5P	2907/3013	2870/3070	2,840

Note 1: Data above slash for six/below slash for V-8.

PLYMOUTH INTERMEDIATES — (6-CYL/V-8) — SERIES DR — The Plymouth/Belvedere intermediate lines were restyled this season. The model lineup was rearranged and expanded, too. The economy station wagon was deleted. A new medium-priced high-performance entry was the Road Runner. It came between Belvedere and Satellite, in terms of price and features, except that its base engine was a 383-cid four-barrel V-8. The Belvedere I designation was no longer used for low-priced cars, since the Belvedere II and Belvedere III nameplates had disappeared entirely. The Satellite was the high-priced line and a Sport Satellite series was one rung higher. Then came the Satellite Sport Suburban series. Top offerings bore GTX identification and were considered "special" level cars. General styling changes centered around a sleek new body for all intermediate

models. The square look was gone. These cars had smooth-flowing lines that emphasized lowness and width. A 'coke bottle' image was evident. The grille was basically a low, horizontal opening with canted rectangles at each end housing dual headlights. Grille insert patterning differed with each line. The taillamps were housed in sculptured fender extensions with a sideways 'U-shaped' appearance. The rear deck lid was somewhat high and slightly 'veed' along its horizontal plane. Exterior trim was kept to a minimum on all models. The Belvedere grille was used on Belvederes, Satellites and Satellite station wagons. It had two horizontal rows of oval-rectangular openings framed in chrome. A narrow rocker panel molding appeared. Standard equipment included side marker lights; folding seatback latches (two-doors); padded dash; recessed controls; energy absorbing seatbacks and steering column; safety armrests; left-hand outside rearview mirror; Safety-Rim wheels; dual brake system with warning lamp; flashers; day/nite inside mirror; seat belts; padded visor; two-speed washer and wipers; turn signals; horn ring and carpeting. The Satellites had all of the above plus wider rocker moldings on station wagon; upper belt moldings; chrome window frames and gutter rails; Satellite fender script; vinyl door panels; armrests with ashtrays; and dual horns. The Sport Satellite had a blacked-out horizontal blade grille; foam seat cushions; base '318' V-8; and body accent stripes, plus wide rocker moldings like Satellite station wagons. The Road Runner had all Belvedere features plus base '383' four-barrel V-8; heavy-duty suspension and shocks; four-speed manual transmission; F70-14 white streak tires; chrome roof drip rails; armrests with ashtrays; special 'Beep-Beep' dual horns; simulated air scoop hood; wider rim wheels; Road Runner identification and cartoon emblems; and the Sport Satellite-type grille. The GTX was equipped like a Sport Satellite (with the same grille), but had many standard extras. They included the 440 'Super Commando' V-8; heavy-duty brakes, suspension, battery and shocks; dual scoop hood; and GTX identification. Station wagons had Belvedere features plus ashtray armrests and, on Satellite Sport Wagons, Satellite Sport trim and woodgrain exterior paneling.

PLYMOUTH INTERMEDIATE-SIZE SERIES

Series No.	Body/ Style No.	Body Type & Seating	Factory Price	Shipping Weight	Prod. Total
BELVEDERE					
DR1/2-L	RL41	4-dr Sed-6P	2457/2551	3010/3190	17,214
DR1/2-L	RL21	2-dr Cpe-6P	2418/2512	2975/3160	15,702
DR1/2-L	RL45	4-dr Sta Wag-6P	2747/2841	3450/3580	8,982
SATELLITE					
DR1/2-H	RH41	4-dr Sed-6P	2546/2640	3010/3195	42,309
DR1/2-H	RH23	2-dr HT Cpe-6P	2568/2662	2995/3180	46,539
DR1/2-H	RH27	2-dr Conv-6P	2824/2918	3075/3260	1,771
DR1/2-H	RH46	4-dr Sta Wag-9P	2972/3006	3525/3660	10,883
DR1/2-H	RH45	4-dr Sta Wag-6P	2865/2959	3445/3580	12,097

1968 Plymouth, Road Runner two-door coupe, V-8

Series No.	Body/ Style No.	Body Type & Seating	Factory Price	Shipping Weight	Prod. Total
ROAD RUNNER					
DR2-M	RM21	2-dr Cpe-6P	2870	3405	29,240
DR2-M	RM23	2-dr HT Cpe-6P	3034	3400	15,359
SPORT SATELLITE					
DR2-P	RP23	2-dr HT Cpe-5P	2796	3225	21,014
DR2-P	RP27	2-dr Conv-5P	3036	3290	1,523
SATELLITE SPORT WAGON					
DR2-P	RP46	4-dr Sta Wag-9P	3213	3660	Note 2
DR2-P	RP45	4-dr Sta Wag-6P	3105	3580	Note 2
GTX					
DR2-S	RS23	2-dr HT Cpe-5P	3329	3520	17,914
DR2-S	RS27	2-dr Conv-5P	3590	3620	1,026

Note 1: Chrysler records show 39,488 Belvedere two-door sedans were built in 1968.

Note 2: Style Numbers RH46/RH45 Production Totals include Satellite Sport station wagons.

Note 3: Data above slash for six/below slash; no slash for V-8.

PLYMOUTH FULL-SIZE — (6-CYL/V-8) — SERIES DP — Except in the case of station wagons, full-size Plymouths for 1968 received new rear end sheet metal including deck lids, quarter panels and rear doors of four-door styles. The deck now ran straight across with horizontal taillamps. It had a crisper and slimmer look. At the front, the basic elements of the 1967 design were retained, but grille surround moldings were reposi-

tioned in line with the new Plymouth theme of slim, horizontal shapes. Gone were the stand-up hood ornaments of the past. Standard equipment on Fury I models included untrimmed bodysides; front fender side nameplates; small rectangular taillights; Plymouth block lettering across concave rear panel; cloth/vinyl seats; foam padded cushions; front armrests; rear armrests with ashtrays; carpets; bright windshield frames; bright rear window moldings; back-up lights; cigar lighter; glovebox lock; dome and side marker lamps; padded dash; energy absorbing front seatbacks; left outside rearview mirror; dual brake system with warning light; emergency flasher; inside day/nite mirror; seat belts; padded visor; two-speed wipers with washers and Safety-Rim wheels. The Fury II had all the above items plus full-length mid-bodyside molding; Fury II nameplates; roof gutter moldings and rear deck moldings with satin aluminum insert area and Plymouth block letters across the edge of the deck lid. The Fury III models had all of the above plus wheel opening moldings; dual taillamps; bright upper door moldings (on four-door sedan); electric clock; lights in the glovebox and trunk; and a Fury III badge in the center of the satin aluminum rear insert. The Sport Furys had all Fury III items plus front grille with Sport Fury designation; bucket seats; all-vinyl interior; choice of console or center armrest bench seat; sport wheel covers; rocker panel moldings; fender-mounted turn signals; bright pedal moldings; combination map and courtesy lights; ignition switch lamp with time delay shutoff and Sport Fury front fenderside nameplates. The VIP came with most Sport Fury equipment (except bucket seats) and added the following extras: front grille with VIP designation; Deluxe cloth and vinyl interiors with front seat center armrest; nylon carpeting and rear pillar courtesy lamps. The basic Suburban was equipped in the manner of the Fury I. The Custom Suburban added the '318' V-8; electric tailgate window and assist strap; full-length bodyside molding; wheel opening moldings; bright upper door moldings; rear center dome light; and Custom Suburban fenderside nameplates. The Sport Suburban had all this equipment plus all-vinyl seats with individual seatbacks; nylon carpeting; woodgrain bodyside paneling; electric clock; glovebox lamp; and, on three-seat models, rear bumper guards and step pads.

PLYMOUTH FULL-SIZE SERIES

Series No.	Body/ Style No.	Body Type & Seating	Factory Price	Shipping Weight	Prod. Total
FURY I					
DP1/2-E	PE41	4-dr Sed-6P	2634/2739	3465/3605	23,208
DP1/2-E	PE21	2-dr Sed-6P	2591/2696	3410/3545	5,788
FURY II					
DP1/2-L	PL41	4-dr Sed-6P	2731/2836	3470/3605	49,423
DP1/2-L	PL21	2-dr Sed-6P	2689/2794	3425/3565	3,112
DP1/2-E	PE45	4-dr Sta Wag-6P	3022/3127	3950/4080	6,749
FURY III					
DP1/2-M	PM41	4-dr Sed-6P	2864/2969	3490/3625	57,899
DP1/2-M	PM23	2-dr HT Cpe-6P	2886/2991	3480/3680	60,472
DP1/2-M	PX23	2-dr FsTp Cpe-6P	2906/3011	3480/3620	Note 2
DP2-M	PM43	4-dr HT Sed-6P	3041	3670	45,147
DP2-M	PM27	2-dr Conv-6P	3236	3685	4,483
DP2-L	PL46	4-dr Sta Wag-9P	3327	4125	9,954
DP2-L	PL45	4-dr Sta Wag-6P	3226	4085	17,078
SPORT FURY					
DP2-H	PH23	2-dr HT Cpe-6P	3180	3645	6,642
DP2-H	PS23	2-dr FT Cpe-5P	3199	3645	17,073
DP2-H	PH27	2-dr Conv-5P	3425	3700	2,489
VIP					
DP2-P	PP43	4-dr HT Sed-6P	3300	3720	10,745
DP2-P	PP23	2-dr FsTp Cpe-6P	3234	3630	6,768
DP2-M	PM46	4-dr Sta Wag-9P	3517	4150	13,224
DP2-M	PM45	4-dr Sta Wag-6P	3416	4105	9,203

Note 1: Data above slash for six/below slash, no slash for V-8.

Note 2: Production Total for Fury III 'Fast Top' combined with the two-door hardtop total.

CHASSIS FEATURES: Wheelbase: (Valiant/Barracuda) 108 inches; (Belvedere/Satellite station wagon) 117 inches; (Belvedere/Satellite/GTX/Road Runner) 116 inches; (Fury/VIP station wagon) 122 inches; (Fury/VIP) 119 inches. Overall length: (Valiant) 188.4 inches; (Barracuda) 192.8 inches; (Belvedere/Satellite station wagon) 208 inches; (Belvedere/Satellite/GTX/Road Runner) 202.7 inches; (Fury/VIP nine-passenger station wagon) 217 inches; (Fury/VIP six-passenger station wagon) 216 inches; (Fury/VIP) 213 inches. Front tread: (Valiant) 58.4 inches; (Belvedere) 59.5 inches; (Satellite) 59.5 inches; (Fury) 62.0 inches. Rear tread: (Valiant) 55.6 inches; (Belvedere) 59.5 inches; (Satellite) 59.2 inches; (Fury) 60.7 inches. Tires: (Valiant six) 6.50 x 13; (Barracuda/Valiant V-8) 6.95 x 14; (Barracuda six) 7.00 x 14; (Belvedere station wagon, all engines) 8.25 x 14; (Fury, all engines) 8.25 x 14; (Fury station wagon, all engines) 8.55 x 14; (Belvedere/Satellite/GTX/Road Runner V-8) F70-14; (Belvedere 'RL' V-8) 7.35 x 14.

VALIANT OPTIONS: Power brakes ($44). Power steering ($84). Air conditioning ($335). Front and rear seat belts ($11). Pair of shoulder belts

($28). Signet vinyl bucket seats with paint stripe ($78). Front disc brake, 14-inch tires mandatory ($73). Front and rear bumper guards ($23). Rear window defogger ($21). Tinted glass, all windows ($30); windshield only ($15). Pair of head restraints ($44). Deluxe 13-inch wheel covers ($19). Deluxe 14-inch wheel covers ($22). Bolt-on design 14-inch wheel covers ($45). Wire wheel covers, 14-inch only ($67). Basic Group: includes AM radio, Deluxe wheel covers; remote-control left outside rearview mirror; foam front seat cushion, with 13-inch wheels and bench seats ($97); with 13-inch wheels and bucket seats ($89); with 14-inch wheels and bucket seats ($92); with 14-inch wheels and bench seat ($101). Valiant 200 Decor Group: includes three-spoke steering wheel with partial horn ring; color-keyed floor mats; cigar lighter; dual horns; body side molding; Valiant 200 nameplate; with cloth and vinyl ($76); with all-vinyl trim ($100). AM radio ($60). Vinyl roof hardtop ($79). Fast manual steering ($14). Sport simulated woodgrain steering wheel, with 200 group ($33). Three-speed manual transmission was standard. Automatic transmission with six ($180); with '273' V-8 ($190); with '318' V-8 ($194). Four-speed manual floor shift transmission, with V-8 only ($188). Six-cylinder 225 cid/145 hp one-barrel engine ($49). V-8 318 cid/230 hp two-barrel engine ($32). Heavy-duty battery ($8). Heavy-duty alternator, with air ($11); without air ($15). Positive traction rear axle ($45).

BARRACUDA OPTIONS: Power brakes ($44). Power steering ($84). Air conditioning ($335). Front disc brakes ($73). Bumper guards ($23). Console, with bucket seats, except three-speed ($51). Custom sill moldings ($21). Paint accent stripes ($15). Sport paint stripes ($20). Special buffed paint ($18). Wheelhouse liners, except convertible ($47). Deluxe wiper and washer package ($10). Undercoating with hood pad ($16). Vinyl roof, hardtop ($79). Fast manual steering ($14). Full horn ring steering wheel ($9). Woodgrain sport steering wheel ($27). Tachometer, V-8 only ($51). Performance gauge cluster, without clock or tachometer ($16). Deluxe wheel covers ($22). Bolt-on design wheel covers ($45). Wire wheel covers ($67). AM radio ($60). Basic Group: includes AM radio; power steering remote-control outside rearview mirror; variable-speed wipers and electric washers with '383' V-8 ($80); without '383' V-8 ($164). Rally Cluster: includes trip odometer; 150 mph speedometer and woodgrain dash trim ($6). 'Formula S' Group, as described in text, with '340' engine ($212); with '383' engine ($251). Three-speed manual transmission was standard. Automatic transmission, with six ($199); with '318' V-8 ($212); with other V-8s ($227). Four-speed manual floor shift transmission, with V-8s only ($188). 'Formula S' V-8 383 cid/300 hp four-barrel engine ($251). Heavy-duty battery ($6). Heavy-duty alternator ($11 or $15). Positive traction rear axle ($45). Transmissions available with 383-cid engine were four-speed manual or high-performance TorqueFlite with high-speed governor.

PLYMOUTH INTERMEDIATE OPTIONS: Power brakes ($44). Power steering ($94). Air conditioning ($355). Automatic speed control ($53). Armrest with ashtray ($8). Bumper guards front and rear, except station wagons ($14). Electric clock ($16). Rear window defogger ($21). Tinted glass, all windows ($42); windshield only ($22). Left and right head restraints ($44). Station wagon luggage rack ($49). Remote control left outside rearview mirror ($9). Right manual outside rearview mirror ($7). Road Runner, Satellite, Sport Wagon custom sill molding ($21). Upper belt moldings, two-door coupe and hardtop ($18). Two-tone paint, except convertible ($15). Road Runner body accent stripes ($15). Special buffed paint ($22). Road Runner and GTX performance black-out hood finish ($18). Solid state AM radio ($60). Firm Ride shocks, standard Road Runner and GTX ($4). Tachometer, V-8 only ($51). Vinyl roof, except station wagon ($79). Power windows, hardtop/convertible only ($26). Vinyl trim, Belvedere sedan and station wagon ($26). Vinyl trim, Satellite sedan and hardtop ($26). Road Wheels, except with 'Street Hemi' ($102). Deluxe wheel covers, 14-inch ($22); 15-inch ($26). Sport-style wheel covers, except 'Street Hemi' ($38). Three-speed manual transmission was standard. Automatic transmission in Road Runner only ($39). Automatic transmission, with six ($299); with '273' V-8 ($217); with other V-8s ($227). Four-speed manual floor shift transmission, with '383' or '426' only ($198). Four-speed manual transmission with floor shift, standard in Road Runner (no charge in GTX). Optional V-8 318 cid/230 hp two-barrel engine ($32). Optional V-8 383 cid/290 hp two-barrel engine ($105). Sport Satellite V-8 383 cid/290 hp two-barrel engine ($73). Optional V-8 383 cid/330 hp four-barrel engine ($176). Sport Satellite V-8 383 cid/330 hp four-barrel engine ($144). Road Runner V-8 426 cid/425 hp 'Street Hemi' dual four-barrel engine ($714). GTX V-8 426 cid/425 hp 'Street Hemi' four-barrel engine ($605). Heavy-duty Sure-Grip axle, Road Runner and GTX only ($146). Sure-Grip positive traction rear axle ($45). Note: Some V-8s listed above were standard in certain models; not available in others. Prices varied from one attachment to another. Some engines required specific transmission attachments.

PLYMOUTH FULL-SIZE OPTIONS: Power brakes ($44). Power steering ($94). Air conditioning ($355). Dual Suburban air conditioning ($565). Single Auto Temp air conditioning, V-8 only ($434). Dual Auto Temp air conditioning, station wagon only ($644). Front and rear bumper guards ($35). Electric clock, standard Fury II/Fury III/Sport Fury/VIP ($16). Console, Sport Fury only substitution (no charge). Rear window defogger ($21). Fender skirts, Fury III/Sport Fury/VIP only ($28). Tinted glass, all windows ($42); windshield only ($22). Station wagon luggage rack ($66). Solid state AM radio ($60). Solid state AM with stereo tape ($195). Solid state AM/FM radio ($140). Rear seat speaker ($15). Vinyl roof, Fury III/Sport Fury/VIP only ($79). Cloth and vinyl split bench seat, VIP four-door only ($109). Cloth and vinyl bucket seat, VIP two-door only ($102). Six-Way power bucket or split bench, Sport Fury/VIP only ($95). Six-Way power bench seat, Fury III/VIP/Sport Wagon only ($98). Leather-trimmed bench seat, VIP only ($109). Power windows, Fury III/Sport Fury/VIP/Sport Wagon only ($105). Road Wheels, VIP ($80); Sport Fury ($61); other models ($102). Deluxe 14-inch wheel covers ($22). Deluxe 15-inch wheel covers, standard Sport Fury/VIP ($26). Sport-style 14-inch wheel covers, VIP ($16); others ($38). Deep-dish 14-inch wheel covers, VIP ($30). Sport Fury ($11); others ($52). Three-speed windshield wipers ($5). Three-speed manual transmission was standard. Automatic transmission, with six ($199); with '383' ($217); with other V-8s ($227). Four-speed manual floor shift transmission, except station wagons or cars with six or '318' V-8 ($198). Commando V-8 383 cid/290 hp two-barrel engine ($73). Commando V-8 383 cid/330 hp four-barrel engine ($144). Suburban V-8 440 cid/350 hp four-barrel engine ($245). Super Commando V-8 440 cid/375 hp four-barrel engine ($281). Heavy-duty alternator ($11). Heavy-duty battery ($8). Heavy-duty Sure-Grip axle ($146). Positive traction rear axle ($51).

1968 Plymouth, Fury III four-door hardtop, V-8

HISTORICAL FOOTNOTES: The full-size Plymouths were introduced Sept. 14, 1967, and the compacts appeared in dealer showrooms the same date. Model year production peaked at 682,193 units. Calendar year sales of 683,678 cars were recorded. G.E. White was the chief executive officer of the company this year. Chrysler-Plymouth Division retail sales hit an all-time high this year. Plymouth was America's fourth largest automaker. The company held an 8.1 percent market share. Only 2,502 Chrysler products were sold with 426-cid 'Street Hemis' this season. Plymouth installations included 1,019 engines in Road Runner hardtops and coupes (576 with four-speeds) and 446 in Belvedere GTX hardtops and convertibles (234 four-speeds). A handful of Barracudas were also fitted with the 426 cid/425 hp Hemi V-8 for professional drag racing. With fiberglass hoods and front fenders and light steel doors these cars were capable of quarter-mile times of under 11 seconds at top speeds of over 130 mph. The rarest options for each line were four-speed transmission in Furys (only 0.2 percent installation rate); speed control in Belvederes (only 0.4 percent); disc brakes in Barracudas (6.1 percent) and four-speed manual transmission in Valiant (0.2 percent).

1969 PLYMOUTH

1969 Plymouth, Valiant Signet four-door sedan (with optional vinyl roof), V-8

VALIANT/SIGNET — (6-CYL/V-8) — SERIES EV — A new grille, new taillights and trim and a straight element rear window were featured in the 1969 Valiant 100 and Signet series. Standard engines were unchanged, although refinements in the Chrysler "Cleaner Air System" were said to produce better operating economy from the Slant Sixes. Improved brake adjusters, a more efficient power steering pump and improvements to the optional Sure-Grip differential were highlighted by the maker. The Valiant 100 was the base car-line and came with all safety features; vinyl

interior; three-spoke steering wheel; a new horizontal bar grille (with satin-finished surround); cowlside fender nameplates; small hubcaps and new lower prices. The Signet also had rear window, deck lid and ribbed rocker panel moldings; cigar lighter; front armrests; rear armrest with ashtray (in four-door sedan); carpets; dual horns; inverted 'V' shaped grille center badge; and Signet front fender script.

PLYMOUTH I.D. NUMBERS: The Vehicle Identification Number is located on a plate attached to driver's side front door hinge pillar. First symbol identifies car-line: B=Barracuda; R=Belvedere; P=Fury; V=Valiant. Second symbol identifies series: E=Fury I; L=Valiant/Belvedere/Fury II; H=Signet/Satellite/Sport Fury; M=Fury III/Road Runner; P=Barracuda/Sport Satellite/VIP; K=law enforcement special; T=taxicab; S=GTX; O=Super Stock. Third and fourth symbols indicate body style and appear as the last two digits in Body/Style Number in charts below. Fifth symbol identifies engine: A=170-cid six; B=225-cid six; C=special order option six; D=273-cid V-8; F=318-cid V-8; G=383-cid V-8; H=383-cid 4V high-performance V-8; J=426-cid "Street Hemi"; K=440-cid V-8; L=440-cid 4V high-performance V-8; M=440-cid "Six-Pack"; P=340-cid V-8. Sixth symbol indicates model year: 9=1969. Seventh symbol identifies assembly plant: A=Detroit, Mich. (Lynch Rd.); B=Hamtramck, Mich.; C=Detroit (Jefferson); D=Belvedere, Ill.; E=Los Angeles, Calif.; F=Newark, Del.; G=St. Louis, Mo. Last six symbols are sequential production number for series at factory. Body Number Plate on inner fenders, cowl or radiator support indicates SO number, body production sequence number, body style code (second column of charts below), trim code and paint code. Engine numbers stamped on right side of block: on six below cylinder head opposite number one cylinder; on V-8 below distributor. Engine number indicates year (PT=1969), displacement (170 for 170 cid, etc.), month (A=Jan., etc.) and day (A01=Jan. 1). Engine codes: PT-170=170 cid/115 hp six; PT-225=225 cid/145 hp six; PT-273=273 cid/190 hp V-8; PT-318=318 cid/230 hp V-8; [Barracuda only] PT-340=340 cid/275 hp 4V V-8; PT-383=383 cid/290 hp 2V V-8; [Barracuda only] 383 cid/300 hp 4V V-8; 383 cid/330 hp 4V V-8; [Road Runner only] 383 cid/335 hp 4V high-performance V-8; [Barracuda Super Stock/Road Runner/GTX] PT-426=426 cid/425 hp "Street Hemi" V-8 (2x4V); PT-440=440 cid/350 hp 4V V-8 and 440 cid/375 hp 4V high-performance V-8 and [Road Runner/GTX only] 440 cid/390 hp "Six-Pack" high-performance V-8.

VALIANT/SIGNET SERIES

Series No.	Body/ Style No.	Body Type & Seating	Factory Price	Shipping Weight	Prod. Total
VALIANT 100					
EV1/2-L	VL41	4-dr Sed-6P	2354/2465	2676/2844	49,409
EV1/2-L	VL21	2-dr Sed-6P	2307/2418	2656/2824	29,672
VALIANT SIGNET					
EV1/2-H	VH41	4-dr Sed-6P	2500/2611	2676/2844	21,492
EV1/2-H	VH21	2-dr Sed-6P	2453/2564	2656/2824	6,645

Note 1: Data above slash for six/below slash for V-8.

BARRACUDA — (6-CYL/V-8) — SERIES EB — The 'Cuda 340' was the new, high-performance 'option model' in the Barracuda line, with either fastback or hardtop styling. These styles, plus the convertible, also came as regular Barracudas. The 'Cuda' line of option-created models included four-speed manual transmission; sport tires; and heavy-duty suspension and brakes. The hardtop was available with an optional yellow flowered vinyl roof. The base Barracuda V-8 engine was the '318', with '383' and '340' engines available. The Barracuda six came with the tried-and-true 225-cid Slant Six. Installed on the basic models was all standard (government required) safety equipment; all-vinyl interior; bucket seats; Pit-Stop gas cap; rally lights; front shoulder belts (except convertible); beltline molding on fastback; red or white stripe tires (with V-8 engines); and aluminized horizontal rear deck panel with Barracuda block lettering. An easy way to tell a 1969 model from a 1968 edition is by the new side marker lamps, which were rectangular. Few other obvious differences are seen, however, the hoods and grilles were slightly face lifted.

BARRACUDA SERIES

Series	Body/Style	Body Type	Factory Price	Shipping Weight	Prod. Total
EB1/2-H	BH23	2-dr HT-5P	2674/2780	2731/2899	12,757
EB1/2-H	BH29	2-dr FsBk-5P	2707/2813	2816/2987	17,788
EB1/2-H	BH27	2-dr Conv-5P	2976/3082	2846/3034	1,442

Note 1: Data above slash for six/below slash for V-8.

PLYMOUTH INTERMEDIATES — (6-CYL/V-8) — SERIES ER — Two new models, the Sport Satellite four-door sedan and the Road Runner convertible were added to the intermediate Belvedere line for 1969. The GTX could be optionally equipped with an all-new cold-air induction package fed through functional hood scoops. All 18 models sported new grilles and new rear styling. The optional flowered vinyl roof and matching 'mod' interior were available for the Satellite two-door hardtop. Belvederes had the safety group; heater/defroster; lockable glovebox; nylon and vinyl trim (all-vinyl in coupe) and front shoulder belts. They had a twin level horizontal bar grille. Satellites added rear ashtray armrests; dual horns; roof drip and lower body (rocker) moldings; all-vinyl convertible trim; and vertical center grille divider. Sport Satellites also had 'B' pillar and wheel

opening moldings; accent striping; front foam seats; (convertible) bucket seats; and chrome door frames on sedans. The Road Runner had all this plus heavy-duty suspension, brakes and shocks; dash nameplate; deck lid nameplate; door nameplates; top opening hood scoops; chrome engine parts; unsilenced air cleaner; four-speed with Hurst shifter; fake walnut shift knob; reverse lamp and (except coupe) Deluxe steering wheel. The GTX featured all these items plus heavy-duty battery; exhaust trumpets; red or white reflective stripes; twin hood scoops; foam bucket seats; performance cam; big valve and ports; all-vinyl trim; heavy-duty TorqueFlite; and heavy-duty underpinnings. Station wagons followed the car trim levels, with exterior wood paneling on Sport Satellite models.

1969 Plymouth, Barracuda (with optional 383-S package) two-door fastback coupe, V-8

PLYMOUTH INTERMEDIATE SERIES

Series No.	Body/ Style No.	Body Type & Seating	Factory Price	Shipping Weight	Prod. Total
BELVEDERE (225/318)					
ER1/2-L	RL41	4-dr Sed-6P	2548/2638	3008/3156	12,914
ER1/2-L	RL21	2-dr Cpe-6P	2509/2599	2978/3126	7,063
ER1/2-L	RL45	4-dr Sta Wag-6P	2879/2969	3488/3591	7,038
ROAD RUNNER (383)					
ER2-M	RM21	2-dr Cpe-6P	2945	3435	33,743
ER2-M	RM23	2-dr HT Cpe-6P	3083	3450	48,549
ER2-M	RM27	2-dr Conv-5P	3313	3790	2,128
SATELLITE (225/318)					
ER1/2-H	RH41	4-dr Sed-6P	2635/2725	3013/3161	35,296
ER1/2-H	RH23	2-dr HT Cpe-6P	2659/2749	3008/3151	38,323
ER1/2-H	RH27	2-dr Conv-6P	2875/2965	3123/3276	1,137
ER1/2-H	RH46	4-dr Sta Wag-9P	3106/3196	3568/3656	4,730
ER1/2-H	RH45	4-dr Sta Wag-6P	2997/3087	3493/3586	5,837
SPORT SATELLITE (318)					
ER2-P	RP41	4-dr Sed-6P	2911	3196	5,836
ER2-P	RP23	2-dr HT Cpe-6P	2883	3156	15,807
ER2-P	RP27	2-dr Conv-5P	3081	3276	818
ER2-P	RP46	4-dr Sta Wag-9P	3350	3666	3,152
ER2-P	RP45	4-dr Sta Wag-6P	3241	3596	3,221

1969 Plymouth, GTX two-door hardtop, V-8

GTX (440)

Series	Body/Style	Body Type	Factory Price	Shipping Weight	Prod. Total
ER2-S	RS23	2-dr HT Cpe-5P	3416	3465	14,902
ER2-S	RS27	2-dr Conv-5P	3635	3590	700

Note 1: Data above slash for six/below slash, no slash for V-8.

PLYMOUTH FULL-SIZE — (6-CYL/V-8) — SERIES EP — With all-new sheet metal for 1969, the Fury came in 17 models and five series. They were named Fury I, Fury II, Fury III, Sport Fury and VIP. The cars were 1-1/2 inches longer and almost two inches wider than previous models. Engine choices included the '225' Slant Six or '318' V-8, with the '383' and '440' V-8s optional. Horizontal twin headlamps, a one-tier horizontal grille and rectangular side markers were car spotter aids. The Fury I came with all standard safety features; glovebox lock; heater/defroster; front fender side nameplates; and no side trim. The Fury II also had full-length bodyside moldings; bright roof side moldings and, on the coupe, frameless front door glass. The Fury III had all the above items plus vinyl/nylon foam padded bench seat carpeting; concealed wipers; clock and Deluxe steering wheel. The Sport Fury had all safety features; concealed wipers; sport wheel covers; dual paint stripes; red, white and blue body side markers; all-vinyl front bucket seats with console (or bench seat with fold-down

armrest); custom sill moldings; and upper door frame moldings. The VIP had all safety equipment plus Deluxe wheel covers; fender skirts; concealed wipers; die-cast grille; bench seats with fold-down center armrest; Safe-Flight dash; clock; front foam cushions; and Deluxe steering wheel. Station wagons had two-way tailgates; all-vinyl and trim equipment and trim matching next step-up passenger cars and integral rear roof deflector.

PLYMOUTH FULL-SIZE SERIES

Series No.	Body/ Style No.	Body Type & Seating	Factory Price	Shipping Weight	Prod. Total
FURY I					
PE1/2-E	PE41	4-dr Sed-6P	2744/2849	3488/3578	18,771
PE1/2-E	PE21	2-dr Sed-6P	2701/2806	3458/3548	4,971
PE1/2-E	PE45	4-dr Sta Wag-6P	3231/3336	4008/4103	6,424
FURY II					
PE1/2-L	PL41	4-dr Sed-6P	2841/2946	3488/3583	41,047
PE1/2-L	PL21	2-dr Cpe-6P	2813/2918	3458/3553	3,268
PE2-L	PL46	4-dr Sta Wag-9P	3527	4148	10,216
PE2-L	PL45	4-dr Sta Wag-6P	3436	4103	15,976
FURY III					
PE1/2-M	PM41	4-dr Sed-6P	2979/3084	3493/3588	72,747
PE1/2-M	PM23	2-dr HT Cpe-6P	3000/3105	3468/3563	44,168
PE1/2-M	PM29	2-dr FsTp Cpe-6P	3020/3125	3548/3653	22,738
PE2-M	PM43	4-dr HT Sed-6P	3155	3643	68,818
PE2-M	PM27	2-dr Conv-6P	3324	3704	4,129
PE2-M	PM46	4-dr Sta Wag-9P	3718	4173	13,502
PE2-M	PM45	4-dr Sta Wag-6P	3651	4123	8,201
SPORT FURY					
EP2-H	PH23	2-dr HT Cpe-5P	3283	3603	14,120
EP2-H	PH29	2-dr FsTp Cpe-5P	3303	3678	2,169
EP2-H	PH27	2-dr Conv-5P	3502	3729	1,579

1969 Plymouth, VIP two-door Formal Hardtop (with optional vinyl roof), V-8

VIP

EP2-P	PP43	4-dr HT Sed-6P	3433	3663	7,982
EP2-P	PP23	2-dr HT Cpe-6P	3382	3583	4,740
EP2-P	PP29	2-dr FsTp Cpe-6P	3382	3668	1,059

Note 1: Data above slash is for six/below slash, no slash for V-8.

ENGINES:

(Valiant V-100 Six) Inline. Overhead valve. Cast iron block. Displacement: 170 cid. Bore and stroke: 3.406 x 3.125 inches. Compression ratio: 8.5:1. Brake hp: 115 at 4400 rpm. Four main bearings. Solid valve lifters. Carburetor: Ball & Ball Type BBS Model 4601S.

(Signet/Barracuda/Plymouth Six) Inline. Overhead valve. Cast iron block. Displacement: 225 cid. Bore and stroke: 3.406 x 4.125 inches. Compression ratio: 8.4:1. Brake hp: 145 at 4000 rpm. Four main bearings. Solid valve lifters. Carburetor: Holley Type R one-barrel Model 4163A.

(Valiant/Barracuda/Belvedere V-8) Overhead valve. Cast iron block. Displacement: 273 cid. Bore and stroke: 3.63 x 3.31 inches. Compression ratio: 9.0:1. Brake hp: 190 at 4400 rpm. Four main bearings. Solid valve lifters. Carburetor: Carter BBD 4607S.

(Satellite/Fury/Sport Fury V-8) Overhead valve. Cast iron block. Displacement: 318 cid. Bore and stroke: 3.906 x 3.312 inches. Compression ratio: 9.2:1. Brake hp: 230 at 4400 rpm. Five main bearings. Hydraulic valve lifters. Carburetor: Carter Type BBD two-barrel Model 4607S.

(Road Runner V-8) Overhead valve. Cast iron block. Displacement: 383 cid. Bore and stroke: 4.250 x 3.375 inches. Compression ratio: 10.0:1. Brake hp: 335 at 5200 rpm. Five main bearings. Hydraulic valve lifters. Carburetor: Carter Type AVS four-barrel Model 4615S.

(GTX V-8) Overhead valve. Cast iron block. Displacement: 440 cid. Bore and stroke: 4.325 x 3.750 inches. Compression ratio: 10.1:1. Brake hp: 375 at 4600 rpm. Five main bearings. Hydraulic valve lifters. Carburetor: Carter Type AVS four-barrel Model 4617S.

CHASSIS FEATURES: Wheelbase: (Valiant/Barracuda) 108 inches; (Belvedere station wagon) 117 inches; (Belvedere passenger car) 116 inches; (Fury station wagon) 122 inches; (Fury passenger car) 120 inches.

Overall length: (Valiant) 188.4 inches; (Barracuda) 192.8 inches; (Belvedere station wagon) 208 inches; (other Belvederes) 202.7 inches; (Fury station wagon) 219.1 inches; (other Furys) 214.5 inches. Tires: (Valiant six) 6.50 x 13; (Barracuda six/V-8) 6.95 x 14; (Valiant V-8) 7.00 x 13; (Belvedere six/V-8) 7.35 x 14; (Fury six/V-8) 7.75 x 14; (Fury station wagon) 8.55 x 15; (Road Runner) 8.25 x 15; (GTX) 8.85 x 15.

1969 Plymouth, Fury III four-door hardtop (with optional fender skirts), V-8

OPTIONS: Air conditioning, Belvedere ($358); Fury ($365); Valiant ($361). Air Grabber scoop, with Road Runner and GTX ($55). Auto speed control, Belvedere ($58); Fury ($61). Disc front brakes, Belvedere, Fury and Valiant/Barracuda ($49). Bumper guards, front and rear, Belvedere ($32); Fury ($34); Valiant ($24). Color-keyed carpet mats, Belvedere and Fury ($14); Valiant ($11). Console with bucket seats, Road Runner/Sport Satellite ($54); Barracuda ($53). Fold-down rear seat, Barracuda fastback ($65). All-tinted glass, Belvedere ($41); Fury ($42); Valiant ($33). Tinted windshield, Belvedere ($26); Fury ($26); Valiant ($21). Dual head rests, all models ($27). Note: Head rests standard after Jan. 1, 1969. Headlights-on signal, Belvedere and Fury ($7). Cornering lamps, Fury series ($36). Station wagon roofrack, Belvedere-type ($52); Fury-type ($63). Power steering, Belvedere and Fury ($100); Valiant ($85). Performance hood paint, Road Runner/GTX ($18). Code '96' Air Grabber hood scoop, Road Runner/GTX ($55). Sport stripes paint treatment, Road Runner ($27); Barracuda ($26). Performance gauges, Barracuda without clock or tachometer ($17). Power brakes, all models ($43). Solid state AM radio ($62). Solid state AM/FM in Belvedere/Barracuda only ($135). Solid state AM with tape, Belvedere/Fury only ($196). Tilt adjustment steering wheel, Fury only ($47). Tachometer, Belvedere V-8/Fury I/Fury II/Barracuda V-8 ($50). Leather bench seats, VIP ($104). Floral roof treatment, Barracuda hardtop ($96). Floral interior, Barracuda hardtop with buckets and 'Cuda' ($113). Chrome-styled wheels, 14 inch, Belvedere except Hemi ($100). Formula 'S' option package, Barracuda '383' ($222). Formula 'S' option package, Barracuda '383' convertible ($198). Valiant '200' decor trim package with vinyl bench seats ($102). Turnpike package, Belvedere except Road Runner/GTX ($243). Turnpike package, Fury series, with Basic Group ($246). Super performance axle package, GTX, with Hemi ($242). Track Pack option Road Runner/GTX, required with four-speed ($143). Super Track Pack, Road Runner/GTX with '440' or '426' and four-speed ($256). Rally gauge cluster, Barracuda ($6). Barracuda Sport Group, except cars with 'Cuda' package ($51). Interior Decor Group, including fold-down rear seat (on fastback); woodgrain door and quarter panel trim; door map pouches; bright pedal trim; rear compartment carpet (required fastback); luxury vinyl bucket seats; rear armrests; ashtrays; and wheelhouse carpets (fastback), on fastback ($181). 'Cuda' 340 package, includes: four-speed manual transmission; hood scoops; hood tape stripe; lower black body stripes; dual exhaust with chrome tips; heavy-duty suspension; firm-ride shocks; E70-14 red stripe "Wide-Boot" tires; 14 x 5-1/2-inch wheel rims; black grille; vinyl bench seat and 340-cid V-8 ($309.35). 'Cuda' 383 package, includes: four-speed manual transmission; hood scoops; hood tape stripe; lower black body stripes; dual exhaust with chrome tips; heavy-duty suspension; firm-ride shocks; E70-14 red stripe "Wide-Boot" tires; 14 x 5-1/2-inch wheel rims; black grille; vinyl bench seat and 383-cid V-8 ($344.75). Powertrain options were about the same as in 1968, at the same or slightly higher prices, except that the '318' V-8 replaced the '273' as base powerplant in the Barracuda V-8 series. After midyear, the 440 cid/375 hp V-8 became available in limited quantities in the Barracuda. On cars with the 'Cuda' option, the '340' V-8 was standard. This powerplant, first used in 1968, had a 4.04 x 3.312 bore and stroke, 10.5:1 compression and offered 275 hp at 5000 rpm. The 'Street Hemi' was again provided as an $813.45 power option for the Road Runner and a $700.90 power option in the GTX.

HISTORICAL FOOTNOTES: The full-size Plymouths were introduced Sept. 19, 1968, and the Valiants appeared in dealer showrooms the same day. Model year production peaked at 645,130 units. Calendar year sales of 651,124 cars were recorded. G.E. White was the chief executive officer of the company this year. Domestic production of full-size models in the Fury line was declining, as this car was now being built in greater quantities in Canada. This was a result of the U.S. Canada Auto Trade Agreement of 1965. Over 100,000 Furys were made in Canada in 1968 and exported to the United States. A total of 1,702 "Street Hemi" engines were installed in Mopars this year. Plymouth installations of the engine included 422 Road Runner hardtops (234 with four-speed); 356 Road Runner coupes (194 with four-speed); 10 Road Runner con-

vertibles (four with four-speed); 198 Belvedere GTX hardtops (99 with four-speed) and 11 Belvedere GTX convertibles (five four-speeds).

1970 PLYMOUTH

1970 Plymouth, 'Cuda two-door hardtop, V-8

1970 Plymouth, Duster '340' two-door hardtop, V-8

VALIANT/VALIANT DUSTER — (6-CYL/V-8) — SERIES FV/FS — The Plymouth Valiant was carried over with minor detail changes. These revisions included a different grille for 1970. Grille elements were about the same, but had a refined look. The central portion bulged out and the horizontal bars were wider and finished in black-out style. New was the Valiant Duster, built on the same platform with the same front end sheet metal, but different from the cowl back. The Duster came only as a two-door coupe and bridged the gap between compact economy car and performance machine. Standard engine was a new 198-cid six, but selections ranged to the '340' V-8. Standard equipment on the Valiant included: turn signals; taillights; front armrests; the new six; and 6.95 x 14 blackwall tires. The Duster came comparably equipped in basic form. Regular equipment on the youth-market Duster 340 included: the 340-cid V-8; three-speed manual transmission with floor shift; special instrument panel; Road Wheels; performance stripes; high-rate torsion bars; heavy-duty springs and shocks; front anti-sway bar and disc brakes; and E70-14 fiberglass-belted black sidewall tires with raised white letters. Duster sales were extremely impressive and helped by the fact that some other makers stressed big cars this year. The special 'Gold Duster' appeared as a midyear 'package model'. It included the 225-cid six or 318-cid V-8; dual horns; whitewall tires; specific wheel covers; bright scalp rails; Argent Silver grille finish; golden tape stripes on sides and rear; front bucket seats; and cigarette lighter. No separate 'Gold Duster' production total is available.

PLYMOUTH I.D. NUMBERS: The Vehicle Identification Number is located on top left of dash. First symbol identifies model: B=Barracuda; V=Valiant; R=Belvedere/Satellite; P=Fury. Second symbol indicates carline price class: E=economy; L=low; M=medium; H=high; P=premium; S=special; K=police; T=taxicab. Third and fourth symbols indicate body style (first four symbols appear in second column of charts below). Fifth symbol indicates engine: A=198 cid/125 hp six; C=225 cid/145 hp six; E=special order six; G=318 cid/230 hp V-8; H=340 cid/275 hp high-performance V-8; ['R' Cuda only] J=340 cid/290 hp "Six-Pack" V-8; L=383 cid/290 hp V-8; N=383 cid/330 hp high-performance V-8; R=426 cid/425 hp "Street Hemi" V-8; T=440 cid/350 hp V-8; U=440 cid/375 hp high-performance V-8; V=440 cid/390 hp "Six-Pack" V-8; Z=Special Order V-8. The sixth symbol designated model year: O=1970. The seventh symbol indicated assembly plant: A=Lynch Rd., Detroit; B=Hamtramck, Mich.; C=Jefferson Ave., Detroit; D=Belvedere, Ill.; F=Newark, Del.; G=St. Louis, Mo.; P=Wyoming Ave., Detroit and R=Windsor, Canada. The last six symbols were the sequential unit production number. Number PH29GOC100050 would, therefore, indicate a Plymouth Sport Fury two-door Formal Top hardtop with base 318 cid/230 hp V-8 built in 1970 at the Jefferson factory, in Detroit, Mich. as the 50th car off the line at that plant.

VALIANT/VALIANT DUSTER

Series No.	Body/ Style No.	Body Type & Seating	Factory Price	Shipping Weight	Prod. Total
VALIANT VL					
FV1/2	VL41	4-dr Sed-6P	2250/2361	2795/2875	50,810
VALIANT DUSTER VL					
FV1/2	VL29	2-dr Cpe-6P	2172/2283	2790/2865	192,375
DUSTER 340 VS					
FV2	VS29	2-dr Cpe-5P	2547	3110	24,817

Note 1: Data above slash for six/below slash, no slash for V-8.

BARRACUDA/CUDA/GRAN COUPE — (6-CYL/V-8) — SERIES FB — Totally redesigned, the Barracuda line for 1970 offered buyers a wider choice of models and engines. Three styles were available with a total of nine models. Emphasis was placed on extending the racy image of long hoods, short decks and rakish windshields. The specialty/performance class 'Cuda' offered an innovative 'shaker' hood option. A classy Gran Coupe was the top-of-the-line. Even the 426-cid 'Street Hemi' was now offered in special Barracudas, built in limited numbers. Standard equipment in Barracudas included high-back bucket seats with all-vinyl trim; integral head rests; molded door and quarter trim panels; flood-lit instrument panel; three-spoke woodgrain steering wheel; floor shift; carpeting; 225-cid six and E78-15 fiberglass-belted tires. The Gran Coupe had all Barracuda items plus body sill, wheel lip, and beltline moldings; Gran Coupe emblems; leather bucket seats and consolette in Knit Jersey (hardtop only); molded headliner; and in convertible, leather bucket seats; DeLuxe vinyl or cloth and vinyl trims were available at lowered cost. The 'Cuda' carried all Gran Coupe equipment plus the four-barrel '383' V-8; heavy-duty suspension and drum brakes; 'Cuda' ornamentation; and F70-14 raised white letter tires. The 'Street Hemi' came as an $871.45 extra in TorqueFlite-equipped 'Cudas'. Few were ordered. The AAR 'Cuda' was offered in the spring of 1970 with special performance features for the Trans Am racing circuit, including an exclusive 290 hp version of the '340' V-8 with triple two-barrel carburetors, G60-15 rear tires and E60-15 front tires on 15 x 7-inch wheels. Production of 2,800 units was programmed, but the exact number of AAR 'Cudas' built is unknown.

BARRACUDA/GRAN COUPE/'CUDA

BARRACUDA SERIES

FB1/2	BH23	2-dr HT Cpe-5P	2764/2865	2790/3025	25,651
FB1/2	BH27	2-dr Conv-5P	3034/3135	3045/3100	1,554

GRAN COUPE SERIES

FB1/2	BP23	2-dr HT Cpe-5P	2934/3035	2990/3040	8,183
FB1/2	BP27	2-dr Conv-5P	3160/3260	3065/3115	596

'CUDA SERIES

FB2	BS23	2-dr HT Cpe-5P	3164	3395	18,880
FB2	BS27	2-dr Conv-5P	3433	3480	635

Note 1: Data above slash for six/below slash, no slash for V-8.

1970 Plymouth, Road Runner Superbird two-door hardtop, V-8

PLYMOUTH INTERMEDIATES — (6-CYL/V-8) — SERIES FR — Redesigned grilles, hoods, and fenders characterized Plymouth's 16-model intermediate-size lineup. Also new was a full-width rear panel housing arrow-shaped taillamps. The grille had a sort of 'telephone receiver' shape with integral dual headlamps at each end. Round park and back-up lamps graced the central bumper region front and rear. Belvederes had color-keyed floor mats; front armrests; rear ashtray/armrests/cigar lighter; glovebox lock; sill moldings; all-vinyl two-door coupe interior (cloth and vinyl in sedan); heavy-duty brakes (on station wagon); and 225-cid six or 318-cid V-8. The Road Runner featured three-on-the-floor heavy-duty goodies including suspension and brakes; carpets; dual exhaust; all-vinyl trim; front and rear armrests; cigar lighter; glovebox light; 'Beep-Beep' horn; performance hood; front bumper guards; 150 mph speedometer; cartoon emblems; F70-14 wide tires; safety wheel rims; three-speed wipers; roof drip rails and upper door frame moldings plus special shocks. The Superbird was a sub-series of the Road Runner featuring an aerodynamic extended nose, concealed headlights and a tall stabilizer wing on the rear. It was designed for NASCAR super speedway racing. To qualify for NASCAR, Plymouth built Superbirds on the basis of one for every two dealerships. The standard engine was the 440-cid V-8 with single four-barrel carburetor. Satellites had all Belvedere items plus Deluxe cloth and vinyl trim (all-vinyl in convertible); carpets; roof drip and wheelhouse

moldings; swing-away day/nite inside mirror; dual horns; and, on station wagons, heavy-duty brakes and rocker panel sill moldings. The Sport Satellite added Deluxe wheel covers; Deluxe all-vinyl interior (or cloth and vinyl sedan bench seat); bodyside pin stripes; wheel opening, 'B' pillar, upper door and quarter window moldings; custom rocker sill trim; scalp moldings and 318-cid V-8. Sport Satellite hardtops also had foam-cushioned front bucket seats, while station wagons had bigger brakes and comparable exterior trim (except for lack of custom sill moldings). Finally, the GTX took up where the Road Runner left off, adding extras to the basic performance package. They included heavy-duty TorqueFlite transmission; Deluxe vinyl interior with foam-cushioned bucket seats; reflective bodyside tape accent treatment; side markers; dual horns; 70-ampere battery; bright exhaust trumpets and big-block 440-cid 'Super-Commando' V-8 engine. In all, eight engines could be selected for the full line of Plymouth intermediates including a 390 hp version with 'Six-Pack' carburetion ($250 in Road Runner/$119 in GTX), and dual four-barrel 425 hp 'Street Hemi' ($841 in Road Runner/$711 in GTX). The performance V-8s were not available with three-speed manual transmission, air conditioning, automatic speed control, or trailer towing attachments.

PLYMOUTH INTERMEDIATES

BELVEDERE

Series No.	Body/ Style No.	Body Type & Seating	Factory Price	Shipping Weight	Prod. Total
FR1/2	RL41	4-dr Sed-6P	2641/2731	3085/3180	13,945
FR1/2	RL21	2-dr Cpe-6P	2603/2693	3050/3140	4,717
FR1/2	RL45	4-dr Sta Wag-6P	2985/3075	3610/3655	5,584

ROAD RUNNER

FR2	RM21	2-dr Cpe-6P	2896	3450	15,716
FR2	RM23	2-dr HT Cpe-6P	3034	3475	24,944
FR2	RM23	2-dr Superbird-6P	4298	3785	1,920
FR2	RM27	2-dr Conv-6P	3289	3550	824

SATELLITE

FR1/2	RH41	4-dr Sed-6P	2741/2831	3075/3175	30,377
FR1/2	RH23	2-dr HT Cpe-6P	2765/2855	3055/3155	28,200
FR1/2	RH27	2-dr Conv-6P	3006/3096	3175/3260	701
FR1/2	RH46	4-dr Sta Wag-9P	3211/3301	3685/3730	3,277
FR1/2	RH45	4-dr Sta Wag-6P	3101/3191	3615/3660	4,204

SPORT SATELLITE

FR2	RP41	4-dr Sed-6P	3017	3205	3,010
FR2	RP23	2-dr HT Cpe-6P	2988	3170	8,749
FR2	RP46	4-dr Sta Wag-9P	3455	3750	2,161
FR2	RP45	4-dr Sta Wag-6P	3345	3675	1,975

SATELLITE GTX

FR2	RS23	2-dr HT Cpe-6P	3535	3515	7,748

Note 1: Data above slash for six/below slash, no slash for V-8.

1970 Plymouth, Fury GT two-door hardtop, V-8

PLYMOUTH FULL-SIZE/FURY — (6-CYL/V-8) — SERIES FP — Integrated loop bumpers; non-wraparound horizontal taillamps; increased length; widened rear tread; new four-door styles; and generally more massive appearances were the elements of change in the big Plymouths this year. Several sporty option-created 'models' debuted during the year. Fury's had a loop front bumper; dual headlights; hubcaps; outside rearview mirror; gauges (but, oil pressure lamp); panel light dimmer; electric wiper/washers; padded dash, steering wheel and visors; crank-out ventipanes; and blackwall tires. Fury II had these plus integral back-up lamps and taillights in rear bumper; 120 mph speedometer; heater control and carpets. Fury III had all of this (except no ventipanes on hardtop coupe) plus vinyl body-side moldings; side markers; Deluxe steering wheel; ashtray and trunk lights; door frame trim; larger tires; and, on convertible, upper belt molding and pocket panel light. Sport Fury added concealed headlights; red, white and blue grille ornament deck medallion; glovebox light and wheelhouse moldings, but no vent windows or trunk light. The basic Suburban had a two-way tailgate; torsion bar suspension; integral rear wind deflector; power tailgate window; larger tires and '318' V-8. Custom

station wagons had upper door frame trim; bigger brakes; and carpets on nine-passenger model. The Sport Wagon had woodgrain exterior paneling; hidden headlights; Deluxe steering wheel and special grille. All models included regulation safety features. The Fury S-23 came with hood stripes; front anti-sway bar; Rally Road Wheels and 'Strobe Stripe' reflective tape treatment. The Fury GT came with 'Strobe Stripe' tape treatment; Rally Road Wheels; H70-15 fiberglass belted tires; a Super Commando 440-cid four-barrel V-8; chrome exhaust trumpets; heavy-duty suspension; heavy-duty brakes; 3.23:1 rear axle and hood striping.

1970 Plymouth, GTX two-door hardtop, V-8

PLYMOUTH FULL-SIZE/FURY

Series No.	Body/ Style No.	Body Type & Seating	Factory Price	Shipping Weight	Prod. Total
FURY I SERIES					
FP1/2	PE41	4-dr Sed-6P	2825/2930	3625/3655	14,813
FP1/2	PE21	2-dr Sed-6P	2790/2895	3575/3630	2,353
FURY II SERIES					
FP1/2	PL41	4-dr Sed-6P	2922/3027	3615/3650	27,694
FP1/2	PL21	2-dr Sed-6P	2903/3008	3565/3620	21,316
FP2	PL46	4-dr Sta Wag-9P	3518	4205	2,250
FP1/2	PL45	4-dr Sta Wag-6P	3303/3408	4090/4160	5,300
FURY GRAN COUPE (*)					
FP2	PL21 W/AC	2-dr Sed-6P	4216	3978	Note 2
FP2	PL21	2-dr Sed-6P	3833	3864	Note 2
FURY III SERIES					
FP1/2	PM41	4-dr Sed-6P	3069/3174	3625/3655	50,876
FP1/2	PM22	2-dr HT Cpe-6P	3091/3196	3600/3620	21,373
FP2	PM43	4-dr HT Sed-6P	3246	3690	47,879
FP2	PM29	2-dr FsTp Cpe-6P	3217	3615	12,367
FP2	PM27	2-dr Conv-6P	3415	3770	1,952
FP2	PM46	4-dr Sta Wag-9P	3603	4215	6,792
FP2	PM45	4-dr Sta Wag-6P	3527	4155	8,898
SPORT FURY SERIES					
FP2	PH41	4-dr Sed-6P	3291	3680	5,135
FP2	PH43	4-dr HT Sed-6P	3363	3705	6,854
FP2	PH23	2-dr HT Cpe-6P	3313	3630	8,018
FP2	PH29	2-dr FsTp Cpe-6P	3333	3645	5,688
FP2	PH46	4-dr Sta Wag-9P	3804	4260	9,170
FP2	PH45	4-dr Sta Wag-6P	3725	4200	4,403
S-23 (*)					
FP2	PS23	2-dr HT Cpe-5P	3379	3660	Note 3
FURY GT (*)					
FP2	PP23	2-dr HT Cpe-5P	3898	3925	Note 4

Note 1: (*) Option-created models with Fury body codes but specific options.

Note 2: Total for Fury Gran Coupe included with Fury II two-door sedan.

Note 3: Total for Fury S-23 hardtop included with Sport Fury two-door hardtop.

Note 4: Total for Fury GT coupe included with Sport Fury two-door hardtop.

Note 5: Data above slash for six/below slash, no slash for V-8.

ENGINES:

(Valiant/Duster Six) Inline. Overhead valve. Cast iron block. Displacement: 198 cid. Bore and stroke: 3.40 x 3.64 inches. Compression ratio: 8 4:1. Brake hp: 125 at 4400 rpm. Four main bearings. Solid valve lifters. Carburetor: Ball and Ball Type BBS one-barrel Model 4715S.

(Valiant/Duster/Barracuda/Fury/Satellite V-8) Overhead valve. Cast iron block. Displacement: 318 cid. Bore and stroke: 3.91 x 3.31 inches. Compression ratio: 8.8:1. Brake hp: 230 at 4400 rpm. Five main bearings. Hydraulic valve lifters. Carburetor: Carter Type BBD two-barrel Model 4721S.

(Duster 340 V-8) Overhead valve. Cast iron block. Displacement: 340 cid. Bore and stroke: 4.04 x 3.31 inches. Compression ratio: 10.5:1. Brake hp: 275 at 5000 rpm. Five main bearings. Hydraulic valve lifters. Carburetor: Carter Type AVS four-barrel Model 4933S.

(Barracuda/Fury/Satellite Six) Inline. Overhead valve. Cast iron block. Displacement: 225 cid. Bore and stroke: 3.40 x 4.12 inches. Compression ratio: 8.4:1. Brake hp: 145 at 4000 rpm. Four main bearings. Solid valve lifters. Carburetor: Holley one-barrel Model 1920-R4352A.

(Standard 'Cuda High-Performance/Road Runner V-8) Overhead valve. Cast iron block. Displacement: 383 cid. Bore and stroke: 4.25 x 3.38 inches. Compression ratio: 9.5:1. Brake hp: 335 at 5200 rpm. Five main bearings. Hydraulic valve lifters. Carburetor: Carter Type BBD four-barrel Model 4725S.

(Superbird/GTX/Fury GT V-8) Overhead valve. Cast iron block. Displacement: 440 cid. Bore and stroke: 4.32 x 3.75 inches. Compression ratio: 9.7:1. Brake hp: 375 at 4400 rpm. Five main bearings. Hydraulic valve lifters. Carburetor: Carter Type AVS four-barrel Model 4737S. NOTE: The GTX engine produced 375 hp at 4600 rpm.

1970 Plymouth, Fury III four-door hardtop, V-8

CHASSIS FEATURES: Wheelbase: (Valiant/Duster/Barracuda) 108 inches; (Belvedere station wagon) 117 inches; (Belvedere passenger car) 116 inches; (Fury station wagon) 122 inches; (Fury passenger car) 120 inches. Overall length: (Valiant/Duster) 188.4 inches; (Barracuda) 186.7 inches; (Belvedere station wagon) 209.1 inches; (Belvedere passenger car) 204 inches; (Fury station wagon) 220.6 inches; (Fury passenger car) 215.3 inches. Tires: (Valiant/Duster six) C78-14; (Barracuda six/V-8) E78-14; ('Cuda/Fury GT/Superbird/GTX) F70-14; (Duster '340') E60-15; (Belvedere/Fury) F78-14; (Belvedere/Fury station wagon) G78-14; (Sport Fury) H70-15.

OPTIONS: Power brakes ($43). Power steering, Valiant group ($85); Barracuda group ($90); Fury/Belvedere ($105). Air conditioning, Belvedere/Barracuda ($357); Fury ($365); Valiant ($347). Dual air conditioning, Fury station wagon ($581); or as part of option package ($217). Auto-Temp air conditioning, Fury passenger car ($440). Dual type in Fury station wagon ($663). Air Grabber hood scoop, Road Runner and GTX, standard with Hemi ($66). Barracuda black air scoop, quarter panel and lower body paint ($36). Automatic speed control, Fury V-8 ($61). Belvedere/Barracuda V-8 ($58). Heavy-duty brakes, Belvedere ($23); Fury ($22); Barracuda ($23). Front disc brakes, Valiant/Belvedere ($28); Fury, standard model with '440' ($28). Rear window defogger, all except convertible and station wagon ($27). Road Runner bright exhaust trumpets, standard with Hemi and GTX ($21). Headlight time delay warning signal, all except Fury III/Fury station wagon ($18). Hood hold-down pins, Road Runner and GTX only ($15). Racing mirrors, left-hand remote control on Barracuda ($11). Left outside rearview mirror remote control, Valiant/Belvedere/Fury ($10). Color-keyed racing mirrors, left-hand remote control on Barracuda ($26). Performance hood, Road Runner/GTX ($18). Sport striping, 'Cuda without side molding vinyl insert ($26). "Dust Trail" tape stripes, on Road Runner ($16). Power convertible top, on Barracuda ($53). Power windows, Belvedere convertible and hardtop/Fury/Barracuda ($105). Power bench seat, in Fury ($100). Power left-hand bucket seat, or left split bench, Fury III/Sport Fury/Sport Wagon ($93). Power door locks, Fury two-doors ($45); Fury four-doors ($69). Solid state AM radio, all models ($62). Solid state AM/FM radio, Belvedere ($135). Solid state AM radio with stereo tape, all except Valiant ($196). Multiplex AM/FM stereo system, Fury and Barracuda ($214). Bench seat, cloth and vinyl with center armrest, GTX/Sport Satellite (no charge). Vinyl bench seat with armrest and folding cushion, Barracuda ($17). Four-place style vinyl bench seats, Duster/Standard Duster '340' ($13). Bucket seat with vinyl trim, Road Runner ($100); Sport Satellite four-door sedan (no charge); Sport Satellite station wagon with center armrest and folding cushion ($103); Fury III two-door hardtop ($125); Sport Fury and Fury III convertible ($100), also standard in Sport Satellite and GTX. Leather bucket seat with consolette, Barracuda, also standard in Gran Coupe ($119). Leather bucket seat, in Barracuda convertible ($65). Center cushion and folding armrest, Road Runner/Sport Satellite/GTX ($54). Shaker hood fresh air package, 'Cuda only, standard with 'Hemi' ($97). Tilt adjustment steering wheel, Fury group only ($53). Tachometer, Duster '340'/Belvedere V-8 except Road Runner and GTX ($50). Tachometer including clock in Road Runner and GTX ($88). Floral vinyl roof, Barracuda group, except Gran Coupe ($96). Vinyl roof, passenger cars, Fury group ($106); Belvedere ($96); Valiant ($84). Duster vinyl and cloth

trim, includes carpets, Deluxe and '340' models ($39). Valiant/Duster vinyl and cloth trim, standard models ($52). Deluxe wheel covers as option on Belvedere/Fury/Valiant/Barracuda ($16). Sport wheel covers, as option, Fury without Basic Group ($28); with Basic Group ($12). Wire wheel covers, Belvedere except Sport Satellite/Barracuda/Valiant [except Duster 340] ($50). Rally Road Wheels, Belvedere/Barracuda/Valiant ($33); Belvedere ($17); Fury ($41). Chrome Road Wheels, Belvedere ($67); Fury ($75); Sport Fury ($34); Barracuda ($50). Fury Brougham package, includes luxury-style bucket seats and other luxury equipment ($118). Super Track Pak racing equipment package, Road Runner/GTX/'Cuda ($236). Three-speed manual transmission was standard; with floor shift in some models ($14). TorqueFlite automatic transmission, with six ($175-$190); with V-8 ($191-$227). Four-speed manual floor shift transmission, prices vary with model and engine ($188-$197). Six-cylinder 225 cid/145 hp Valiant engine ($25). Commando V-8 383 cid/290 hp in Belvedere/Fury/Barracuda ($70). Commando V-8 383 cid 330/335 hp in Belvedere/Fury/Barracuda ($138). Street Hemi V-8 426 cid/425 hp in Road Runner ($841). Street Hemi V-8 426 cid/425 hp engine in 'Cuda ($871). Street Hemi V-8 426 cid/425 hp in GTX ($711). Commando V-8 440 cid/350 hp in Fury ($234). Commando V-8 440 cid/350 hp Fury [w/air] engine ($164). "Six-Pack" V-8 440 cid/390 hp in Road Runner ($250). "Six-Pack" V-8 440 cid/390 hp engine in GTX ($119). "Six-Pack" V-8 440 cid/390 hp 'Cuda engine ($250). Commando V-8 440 cid/350 hp 'Cuda engine ($131). Heavy-duty, 70-ampere Valiant battery ($13). Heavy-duty, 59-ampere Valiant battery ($13). Heavy-duty 50-ampere Valiant alternator ($11-$15). Sure-Grip positive traction rear axle, in specific Belvederes/Valiants ($42); Furys ($49). Evaporative emissions control system ($38). Available rear axle gear ratios: 2.76:1 or 3.55:1 optional ($10).

HISTORICAL FOOTNOTES: The 1970 Plymouths were introduced Sept. 23, 1969, and the Valiant line appeared in dealer showrooms the same day. Model year production peaked at 725,600 units. Calendar year sales of 699,031 cars were recorded. This was the last year for convertibles in the Satellite and Fury lines. L.A. Townsend was the chief executive officer of the company this year. Of all Chrysler products built this model year, only 1,543 had 426-cid 'Street Hemi' engines and only a portion of these went into Plymouths. The cars that received these engines included 75 Road Runner hardtops (59 with four-speeds); 74 Road Runner coupes (44 with four-speeds); three Road Runner convertibles (one with the four-speed); 135 Superbirds (58 with four-speed); 72 GTX hardtops (43 with four-speeds); 652 'Cuda hardtops (284 with four-speeds); and 14 'Cuda convertibles (five with four-speeds). Besides Hemi 'Cudas, Plymouth put the following performance engine/transmission combinations in specific versions of its sports compact: ['Cuda 340 convertible] 19 three-speeds; 88 four-speeds and 155 automatics. ['Cuda 340 coupe] 1,872 three-speeds; 3,492 four-speeds and 3,392 automatics. ['Cuda 383 convertible] nine three-speeds; 63 four-speeds and 137 automatics. ['Cuda 383 coupe] 150 three-speeds; 1,905 four-speeds and 2,540 automatics. ['Cuda 440 four-barrel convertible] six four-speeds and 28 automatics. ['Cuda 440 four-barrel coupe] 334 four-speeds and 618 automatics. ['Cuda 440 Six-Pack convertible] 17 four-speeds and 12 automatics. ['Cuda 440 Six-Pack coupe] 903 four-speeds and 852 automatics. [AAR 'Cuda coupe] 1,120 four-speeds and 1,604 automatics. Rare options for Fury group models and their percentage of installation rates (in parentheses) were: six-cylinder engine (1.3); stereo tape (1.9); power door locks (1.5); Styled Road Wheels (1.2); and movable steering column (1.4). Rare Belvedere options and their percentage of installation rates (in parentheses) were: power side windows (0.5) and speed control (0.4). Eighty-three percent of all Barracudas had bucket seats and 18.5 percent had four-speed manual transmission. The rarest Valiant option was power drum brakes, used in just 1.6 percent of all Valiants built.

1971 PLYMOUTH

PLYMOUTH CRICKET — (4-CYL) — MODEL 4B21 — The sub-compact Plymouth Cricket was a new entry in the company's model lineup this year. This $1,915 four-door sedan was essentially a badge engineered vehicle made by Chrysler United Kingdom, Ltd., the English subsidiary that used to be Rootes Motors. The car was sold in Great Britain as the Hillman Avenger and the American market version was changed mainly in the design of nameplates used on the body. Since the *Standard Catalog of American Cars 1946-1975* is primarily concerned with vehicles produced in the United States, the Cricket will not be covered in detail.

VALIANT GROUP — (6-CYL/V-8) — SERIES GV — The Valiant group now included three different types of cars with totally different sheet metal: Valiant, Duster and Scamp. The basic Valiant was virtually unchanged. Small revisions included removal of the center grille emblem and a new kind of finish treatment on the grille surround. It now had a blacked-out

look instead of Satin Silver treatment. Regulation safety features were used on all Plymouth products. Valiants also had color-keyed door armrests (rear on four-door sedan only); clean air system; concealed spare tire; directionals with lane change; anti-theft lock and ignition buzzer; and two-speed electric wipers. New grilles and rear end appearances and 18 exterior colors gave the strong selling Duster a new look for 1971. It no longer carried Valiant nameplates and had the same cowl-back distinctions seen the previous year. Standard equipment began with all Valiant features plus swing-out rear quarter windows; ventless side glass; twin stacked horizontal slat taillights; and Duster emblems. The Duster '340' also had floor shift manual transmission; unique vertically segmented grille; tape accent stripes; cigar lighter; roof drip rail moldings; special instrument panel; heavy-duty suspension and the 340-cid V-8 with dual exhaust and twin snorkel air cleaner. A number of optional packages including Deluxe trim, Sports trim and the mid-season 'Twister' group allowed tailoring to individual taste. The Scamp was built off the Dodge Swinger platform with Dodge Dart sheet metal and a Valiant grille. It was larger and longer, but otherwise came with Valiant equipment features and identification. Both Dusters and Scamps used Valiant front end sheet metal, but were different types of vehicles from the cowl back.

1971 Plymouth, Valiant Scamp two-door hardtop, V-8

PLYMOUTH I.D. NUMBERS: The Vehicle Identification Number is located on top left of dash. First symbol identifies model: B=Barracuda; V=Valiant; R=Belvedere/Satellite; P=Fury. Second symbol indicates carline price class: E=Economy; L=Low; M=Medium; H=High; P=Premium; S=Special; K=Police; T=Taxicab. Third and fourth symbols indicate body style (first four symbols appear in second column of charts below). Fifth symbol indicates engine: B=198 cid/125 hp six; C=225 cid/145 hp six; E=special order six; G=318 cid/230 hp V-8; H=340 cid/275 hp V-8; [AAR 'Cuda only] J=340 cid/290 hp "Six Pack" V-8; K=360 cid/255 hp V-8; L=383 cid/275 hp V-8; N=383 cid/300 hp high-performance V-8; R=426 cid/425 hp "Street Hemi" V-8; T=440 cid/335 hp V-8; U=440 cid/370 hp high-performance V-8; V=440 cid/385 hp "Six-Pack" V-8; Z=Special Order V-8. The sixth symbol designated model year: 1=1971. The seventh symbol indicated assembly plant: A=Lynch Rd., Detroit; B=Hamtramck, Mich.; C=Jefferson Ave., Detroit; D=Belvedere, Ill.; F=Newark, Del.; G=St. Louis, Mo.; and R=Windsor, Canada. The last six symbols were the sequential unit production number.

VALIANT GROUP

Series No.	Body/ Style No.	Body Type & Seating	Factory Price	Shipping Weight	Prod. Total
VALIANT					
GV1/2	VL41	4-dr Sed-6P	2392/2516	2835/2925	42,660
DUSTER					
GV1/2	VL29	2-dr Cpe-6P	2313/2437	2825/2920	173,592
DUSTER '340'					
GV2	VS29	2-dr Cpe-6P	2703	3140	12,886
SCAMP					
GV1/2	VH23	2-dr HT Cpe-6P	2561/2685	2900/2985	48,253

Note 1: Data above slash for six/below slash, no slash for V-8.

BARRACUDA GROUP — (6-CYL/V-8) — SERIES GB — The Barracuda was again related to the Valiant, but listed as an entirely different series catering to the sports compact market. New grilles and rear lamps highlighted styling detail changes. Elastometric bumpers in a choice-of-colors were optionally available. Equipment for base models consisted of dual headlamps and horns; hubcaps; day/nite inside mirror; brake warning light; left outside rearview mirror; fuel, temperature and ammeter gauges; bucket seats; cigar lighter; heater and defroster and two-speed wipers. The base coupe came with the Valiant six-cylinder engine, while other Barracuda sixes used the Plymouth 225-cid version. A new grille with recessed vertically divided segments was used on all lines. Taillamps and back-up lights were now individual units. The second-step-up Barracuda was the Gran Coupe, which came with all the above features plus overhead consolette; pedal trim; leather bucket seats; formed headliner; wheel lip moldings; belt moldings; Gran Coupe ornamentation and a V-8. The high-performance 'Cuda was the flagship of the fleet and had all the above items plus chrome rocker sill moldings; special 'performance' hood (with

integral scoops); color-keyed grille; black-finished rear deck panel; heavy-duty suspension and brakes; 'Cuda ornamentation; whitewall tires; and the 383-cid four-barrel V-8. The 'Street Hemi' engine was a $884 option requiring the four-speed transmission and other mandatory extra-cost equipment.

1971 Plymouth, 'Cuda '340' two-door hardtop, V-8

BARRACUDA GROUP

Series No.	Body/ Style No.	Body Type & Seating	Factory Price	Shipping Weight	Prod. Total
BARRACUDA					
GB1/2	BH21	2-dr Cpe-5P	2654/2780	3010/3070	Note 2
GB1/2	BH23	2-dr HT Cpe-5P	2766/2867	3035/3090	9,459
GB1/2	BH27	2-dr Conv-5P	3023/3124	3115/3165	1,014
BARRACUDA GRAN COUPE					
GB2	BP23	2-dr HT Cpe-5P	3029	3105	1,615
'CUDA					
GB2	BS23	2-dr HT Cpe-5P	3156	3475	6,228
GB2	BS27	2-dr Conv-5P	3412	3550	374

Note 1: Data above slash for six/below slash, no slash for V-8.

Note 2: Production Total for Style BH21 is included in the total for Style BH23.

1971 Plymouth, Road Runner two-door hardtop, V-8

SATELLITE GROUP — (6-CYL/V-8) — SERIES GR — The so-called 'fuselage' body design was the hit of 1971 at Plymouth and different variations were seen on two-door and four-door models. Not a single panel of sheet metal interchanged on the two different basic types of cars. They looked different, too. The coupes and hardtop coupes seemed futuristic with their integral bumper/grilles, down-swooping curved panels and blending sail panel treatments. Styling feature lines gave the impression of the mid-body wrapping over the lower panel. On sedans and station wagons the look was completely different. It almost seemed as if someone had squashed down one of the old slab-sided cars until the body bulged out at the sides. The four-doors were much more conventional looking, with their regular-type grilles and slimmer horizontal taillamps. Many model names were changed and the model listings were confused by the practice of breaking out cars by body type, instead of the traditional series designations: L = Low; M = Medium; H = High; P = Premium and S = Special. The base for the line was simply called Satellite and had all-vinyl trim; color-keyed rubber floor coverings; dome light; transistorized voltage regulator; hubcaps; clean air system; heater/defroster and (except in coupes) cigar lighter and day/nite inside rearview mirror. Coded as an 'RM' model ('R' for Belvedere; 'M' for medium-priced) was the Road Runner, which had all the above equipment plus floor shift; heavy-duty

suspension; 'Beep-Beep' horn; Rally gauge cluster; deep pile carpets; performance hood; low-restriction dual exhaust; front foam seat cushions; drip rail moldings; heavy-duty shocks; and 383-cid high-performance V-8. The Satellite Sebring was the high-priced Belvedere two-door entry and came with the basic Satellite equipment assortment plus dual conventional horns; drip rail accents; sill moldings; wheelhouse trim and front foam cushions. Satellite Customs represented high-priced Satellites in four-door form and matched the regular Sebring in standard features. For premium-priced marketing, extra equipment (but not the same items) were added to each of the above cars. Then each body style in each level was given an identifiable name. Thus, there was the Sebring-Plus hardtop, the Satellite Brougham sedan, the Satellite Regent station wagon (with two or three seats) and the 'RS' coded ('R' for Belvedere; 'S' for Specialty) high-performance GTX. The Sebring-Plus came with vinyl bucket seats (or center armrest seat with cloth and vinyl trim); front foam cushions; Deluxe wheel covers and, if desired, wheel trim rings at no extra cost. Sebring Brougham sedans had the same thing (with center armrest seat mandatory); bright armrest bases; similar rear seat armrests; and bright upper door frame moldings. The Regent station wagon had all of this plus heavy-duty brakes and carpets, but used a vinyl bench seat instead of the bucket or armrest types. Unlike the Sebring-Plus and Satellite Brougham (and Road Runner, as well) the Regents did not come with whitewall tires. Last, but not least, was the GTX — a Road Runner with extra features. They included the 440-cid 'Super Commando' V-8; Torque-Flite transmission; bucket seats; low-restriction dual exhaust with chrome trumpets; dual horns; vinyl trim (cloth and vinyl, no charge); 70-ampere battery; custom sill moldings; wheel opening accents; drip rail trim; extra-heavy-duty suspension; and raised white letter tires. GTX buyers could have a cloth and vinyl center armrest seat, white sidewall tires or floor-mounted manual three-speed transmission as equipment substitutions with no change in price. Of course, in addition to all these different body styles, trim levels and nameplates, there was a host of individual options or pre-packaged accessory groups, including 'Air Grabber' hood scoops; louvered backlight (except in Pennsylvania); performance hood paint treatment; 'Strobe Stripes'; and aerodynamic spoiler.

SATELLITE GROUP

Series No.	Body/ Style No.	Body Type & Seating	Factory Price	Shipping Weight	Prod. Total
SATELLITE					
GR1/2	RL41	4-dr Sed-6P	2734/2829	3240/3340	11,059
GR1/2	RL21	2-dr Cpe-6P	2663/2758	3185/3295	Note 2
GR1/2	RL45	4-dr Sta Wag-6P	3058/3153	3725/3790	7,138
SATELLITE SEBRING					
GR1/2	RH23	2-dr HT Cpe-6P	2931/3026	3210/3320	46,807
SATELLITE CUSTOM					
GR1/2	RH41	4-dr Sed-6P	2908/3003	3240/3340	30,773
GR1/2	RH46	4-dr Sta Wag-9P	3315/3410	3800/3865	3,865
GR1/2	RH45	4-dr Sta Wag-6P	3235/3330	3730/3795	5,045
ROAD RUNNER					
GR2	RM23	2-dr HT Cpe-5P	3147	3640	14,218
SATELLITE SEBRING-PLUS					
GR2	RP23	2-dr HT Cpe-5P	3179	3330	16,253
SATELLITE BROUGHAM					
GR2	RP41	4-dr Sed-6P	3189	3300	3,020
SATELLITE REGENT WAGON					
GR2	RP46	4-dr Sta Wag-9P	3638	3885	2,985
GR2	RP45	4-dr Sta Wag-6P	3558	3815	2,161
GTX					
GR2	RS23	2-dr HT Cpe-5P	3733	3675	2,942

Note 1: Data above slash for six/below slash, no slash for V-8.
Note 2: Production Total for Style RL21 is included in total for Style RH23.

FURY GROUP — (6-CYL/V-8) — SERIES GP — At the beginning of the model year, standard-size Plymouths came in 19 models grouped into five series: Fury I, Fury II, Fury III, Sport Fury and Sport Fury GT. Around May 1971, TorqueFlite automatic transmission became standard in all full-size Plymouths. Prices were increased to cover this change and a well-equipped (but 'economy' coded) Fury Custom series was announced. Highlights for the season included: a new Fury II two-door hardtop; new front and rear appearances; ventless side window glass; more luxurious interiors and new cassette tape and sun roof options. Major technical improvements included: Torsion-Quiet Ride formerly available only on more expensive Chryslers and Imperials. A new isolation system was designed to cut vibration and noise and there was an optional regular-fuel 360-cid V-8. Sport Furys were available with color-keyed polyurethane rear inserts, while station wagons came with translucent woodgrain

trim that permitted the body color to show through. Standard Fury I equipment included: loop-type front bumpers; dual headlights; hubcaps; brake warning light; left outside rearview mirror; fuel-temperature gauges; ammeter-oil pressure warning lights; interior lights with panel dimmer; inside day/nite mirror; front and rear armrests; non-glare flood-lit instrumentation; two-speed electric wiper/washers; cigar lighter; glovebox lock; three-spoke steering wheel with integral horn button; dome lamp; courtesy lamp door switches; front and rear ashtrays; bright drip rail moldings; concealed wipers; side cowl ventilation and fresh air heater/defroster. The Fury II also had deep-pile carpets and full-length bodyside moldings. The Fury III had all of this plus color-keyed vinyl molding inserts; ashtray and trunk lights; wheel lip moldings; woodgrain door panel inserts and dash pad; woodgrain dash panel trim; glovebox light; wood-look steering wheel; bright metal armrest bases; and upper door frame accent moldings. The Sport Fury added door pull straps; lower door carpet panels; pull-down center armrest with integral headrest; sill molding; concealed headlamps; Sport Fury nameplates, ornaments and medallions; belt moldings (on all except the four-door sedan) and dome lamp rear courtesy switches on four-door sedan only. The Sport Fury GT had all features found on the lower level cars plus hood stripes; heavy-duty suspension; 70-ampere battery; 3.23:1 rear axle gear ratio; dual exhaust; power front disc brakes; Rally Road Wheels; white letter tires and the 'Super Commando' V-8. A side and rear 'Strobe Stripe' tape treatment replaced upper beltline moldings on the 'GT' and TorqueFlite transmission was standard in this model all year long. Interestingly, its price still increased in May but not as much as the window stickers on other models. Fury Suburbans had the basic Fury I equipment plus three-way tailgate; torsion bar suspension; rear integral wind deflector; power tailgate window and heavy-duty brakes. Custom Suburbans added lower foam seat cushions; carpets; and bright upper door frame, rocker sill and wheelhouse moldings. Sport Suburbans also had vinyl trim over a center armrest bench seat and woodgrain side body panels. The Fury Custom, which was mentioned earlier, came standard with Deluxe wheel covers; two-tone paint; vinyl side moldings; woodgrain dash appliques; Custom bodyside nameplates; paisley-pattern vinyl bench seats; extra-long front armrests with bright bases, and special Fury deck lid cover. This model was priced between Fury I and Fury II.

1971 Plymouth, Sport Fury two-door hardtop, V-8

FURY GROUP

Series No.	Body/ Style No.	Body Type & Seating	Factory Price	Shipping Weight	Prod. Total
FURY I					
GP1/2	PE41	4-dr Sed-6P	3146/3256	3705/3780	16,395
GP1/2	PE21	2-dr Sed-6P	3113/3223	3670/3750	5,152
FURY CUSTOM					
GP1/2	PE41	4-dr Sed-6P	3241/3351	3705/3780	Note 2
GP1/2	PE21	2-dr Sed-6P	3208/3318	3670/3750	Note 2
FURY II					
GP1/2	PL41	4-dr Sed-6P	3262/3372	3710/3785	20,098
GP1/2	PL23	2-dr HT Cpe-6P	3283/3393	3675/3750	7,859
GP2	PL46	4-dr Sta Wag-9P	3869	4290	2,662
GP2	PL45	4-dr Sta Wag-6P	3758	4245	4,877
FURY III					
GP1/2	PM41	4-dr Sed-6P	3437/3547	3715/3790	44,244
GP1/2	PM23	2-dr HT Cpe-6P	3458/3568	3680/3755	21,319
GP2	PM43	4-dr HT Sed-6P	3612	3820	55,356
GP2	PM29	2-dr FsTp Cpe-6P	3600	3750	24,465
GP2	PM46	4-dr Cus Sub-9P	3930	4300	11,702
GP2	PM45	4-dr Cus Sub-6P	3854	4240	10,874
SPORT FURY					
GP2	PH41	4-dr Sed-6P	3656	3845	2,823
GP2	PH43	4-dr HT Sed-6P	3724	3865	55,356
GP2	PH29	2-dr FsTp Cpe-6P	3710	3810	3,957
GP2	PH23	2-dr HT Cpe-6P	3677	3805	3,912
GP2	PH46	4-dr Spt Sub-9P	4146	4370	13,021
GP2	PH45	4-dr Spt Sub-6P	4071	4090	5,103
SPORT FURY 'GT'					
GP2	PP23	2-dr HT Cpe-6P	4111	4090	375

Note 1: Data above slash for six/below slash, no slash for V-8.

Note 2: Production Total of Fury Customs included with same Fury I body styles.

Note 3: 700 Fury IIs and 200 Fury IIIs built with six-cylinder engines.

ENGINES:

(Valiant/Duster Six) Inline. Overhead valve. Cast iron block. Displacement: 198 cid. Bore and stroke: 3.40 x 3.64 inches. Compression ratio: 8.4:1. Brake hp: 125 at 4000 rpm. Four main bearings. Solid valve lifters. Carburetor: one-barrel.

(Barracuda/Belvedere/FURY/Satellite Six) Inline. Overhead valve. Cast iron block. Displacement: 225 cid. Bore and stroke: 3.40 x 4.125 inches. Compression ratio: 8.4:1. Brake hp: 145 at 4000 rpm. Four main bearings. Solid valve lifters. Carburetor: Carter Type BBS two-barrel.

(Valiant/Duster/Barracuda/Belvedere/Fury V-8) Overhead valve. Cast iron block. Displacement: 318 cid. Bore and stroke: 3.91 x 3.31 inches. Compression ratio: 8.8:1. Brake hp: 230 at 4400 rpm. Five main bearings. Hydraulic valve lifters. Carburetor: two-barrel.

(Duster '340' V-8) Overhead valve. Cast iron block. Displacement: 340 cid. Bore and stroke: 4.04 x 3.31 inches. Brake hp: 275 at 5600 rpm. Compression ratio: 10.3:1. Five main bearings. Hydraulic valve lifters. Carburetor: four-barrel.

('Cuda/Road Runner V-8) Overhead valve. Cast iron block. Displacement: 383 cid. Bore and stroke: 4.25 x 3.375 inches. Compression ratio: 9.5:1. Brake hp: 335 at 4800 rpm. Carburetor: Carter four-barrel.

(GTX/Fury GT V-8) Overhead valve. Cast iron block. Displacement: 440 cid. Bore and stroke: 4.32 x 3.75 inches. Compression ratio: 9.7:1. Brake hp: 375 at 4300 rpm. Five main bearings. Hydraulic valve lifters. Carburetor: four-barrel.

CHASSIS FEATURES: Wheelbase: (Valiant/Duster/Barracuda) 108 inches; (Scamp) 111 inches; (Satellite two-door) 115 inches; (Satellite four-door) 117 inches; (Fury Suburban) 122 inches; (Fury Group) 120 inches. Overall length: (Valiant/Duster) 188.4 inches; (Scamp) 193 inches; (Barracuda Group) 186.6 inches; (Satellite two-door) 203.2 inches; (Satellite station wagon) 210.9 inches; (Satellite four-door) 204.6 inches; (Fury Suburban) 220.2 inches; (Fury Group) 215.1 inches. Tires: (Satellite) E78-14 (Satellite station wagon) H78-14; (Brougham) F78-14; (Fury) F78-15; (Fury Suburbans) J78-15; (Fury GT) H70-15; (Valiant) 6.95 x 14; (Duster) 6.45 x 14; (Barracuda) 7.35 x 14; ('Cuda/GTX) F70-14.

OPTIONS: Air conditioning, Valiant ($384); Barracuda, except '198' six and '426' or '440' V-8s ($370); Satellite ($383); Fury ($391). Dual air conditioning, all Suburbans and station wagons with automatic transmission ($608). 'Air Grabber' hood scoop for Road Runner or GTX ($67). Assist handles, in station wagons ($19). Automatic locking tailgate ($27). Heavy-duty front and rear brakes standard on station wagons on Valiant ($21); on Satellite ($23); on Barracuda ($23). Front disc brakes, Valiant ($32); on Satellite with power brakes ($24); on Barracuda with power brakes ($23). Front and rear bumper guards, Valiant ($25); Satellite, except station wagon ($34). Carpeted station wagon cargo compartment ($22). Electric clock, Barracuda ($13); Road Runner/Sebring-Plus center console ($58). Decorative exhaust tips on Road Runner, standard on GTX, but not available in California ($22). Hood pins, Barracuda, standard on 'Cuda ($15); Valiant, except sedan ($15); Road Runner/GTX ($17). Backlight louvers, Satellite Group except Brougham and station wagon and cars for Pennsylvania sale ($68). Dual outside racing mirrors, left remote-control and both color-keyed, on Valiants ($26); Barracuda ($26); Satellite ($28). Performance hood paint treatment, Duster coupe ($18); Duster '340' with engine 'callout' designation ($21). Paint treatment, rear fender 'Strobe' and C-pillar stripes ($34). Paint treatment, 'Strobe Stripes' on Fury III/Sport Fury two-door/Sport Fury Formal hardtop ($28). Rear tape stripe for Duster coupe, standard with Duster '340' ($13). Bodyside tape stripe on Barracuda sedan ($29); on Gran Coupe, replaces paint stripe ($14); on Duster coupe, standard with Duster '340' ($26); on GTX, not available with 'Air Grabber' hood scoop or Hemi V-8 ($23). Paint treatment, rear quarter panel 'Sport Stripe', on 'Cuda without vinyl side moldings ($38). Performance hood, Barracuda Group, except standard with 'Cuda ($20). Front disc brakes, power type on Fury Group ($70). Power deck lid release on Fury, except station wagon ($16). Power door locks, two-doors ($47); four-doors ($73). Power steering, Valiant ($100); Barracuda ($97); others ($111). Barracuda power lift convertible top ($49). Powerside windows, Satellite ($110); Fury ($120); Barracuda ($101). Inside hood release, Satellite ($11). Microphone tape recorder, Valiant ($21); Barracuda ($11); Satellite and Fury ($12). AM/FM radio with stereo and tape, Barracuda ($337); Satellite and Fury ($366). Vinyl roof, Barracuda ($82); Satellite, except station wagon ($96); Fury, except station wagon ($106). Canopy-style vinyl roof, Road Runner and Sebring-Plus ($67). Three-speed manual transmission was standard, except as indicated in text. Automatic transmission was standard in many models after midyear. Automatic transmission, in Valiant ($183); Barracuda coupe ($209); V-8 Valiant ($191). Automatic transmission, in Satellite/Fury six ($216); Satellite/Fury V-8 ($216-238). Three-speed manual floor shift transmission, in Satellite ($14); Valiant ($13). Four-speed manual floor shift transmission, in Barracuda ($198). Four-speed manual transmission with floor shift, in Satellite ($206). Four-speed manual trans-

mission with floor shift, in Road Runner ($206). Valiant six-cylinder 225 cid/145 hp one-barrel engine ($39). Barracuda coupe, six-cylinder 225 cid/145 hp one-barrel engine ($39). 'Cuda V-8 340 cid/275 hp four-barrel engine ($44). Road Runner and Fury V-8 440 cid/370 hp four-barrel engine ($46). Fury V-8 360 cid/255 hp two-barrel engine ($46). Satellite/Sport Fury V-8 383 cid/275 hp two-barrel engine ($73). Satellite/Fury V-8 383 cid/300 hp four-barrel engine ($145). 'Cuda/Road Runner V-8 426 cid/425 hp 'Street Hemi' engine ($884). GTX V-8 426 cid/425 hp 'Street Hemi' engine ($747). Fury V-8 440 cid/330 hp 'Six-Pack' engine ($253). Road Runner V-8 440 cid/335 hp 'Six-Pack' engine ($262). GTX V-8 440 cid/385 hp 'Six-Pack' engine ($125). Fury Suburban V-8 440 cid/370 hp four-barrel engine ($198). Barracuda V-8 383 cid/275 hp two-barrel engine ($71). Barracuda V-8 383 cid/300 hp four-barrel engine ($140). Sure-Grip axle ($42-49). Available rear axle gear ratios: 2.76:1; 3.23:1, 3.55:1.

HISTORICAL FOOTNOTES: The full-size Plymouths were introduced Oct. 6, 1970, and the Valiant line appeared in dealer showrooms Sept. 15, 1970. Model year production peaked at 625,812 units. Calendar year production of 636,592 units was recorded. L.A. Townsend was the chief executive officer of Chrysler Corp. this year. A total of 20,260 Crickets were marketed in the United States. This was the last year for the Barracuda convertible. Richard Petty continued to campaign a Hemi-powered Road Runner in NASCAR stock car racing this year. His brilliant blue #43 Plymouth helped him achieve his third Grand National championship. This was the last season for the offering of the "Street Hemi" and it was installed in just 356 Mopars. They included 55 Road Runners (28 with four-speeds); 30 GTXs (11 with four-speeds); 107 'Cuda hardtops (59 with four-speeds); and seven 'Cuda convertibles (two with four-speeds). The rest of the Hemi engines went into Dodges. In the 'Cuda series, the following additional engine/transmission attachments were made: ['Cuda 340 convertible] eight with three-speeds; 30 with four-speeds and 102 with automatics. ['Cuda 340 coupe] 51 with three-speeds; 1,141 with four-speeds and 2,008 with automatics. ['Cuda 383 convertible] eight with three-speeds; 33 with four-speeds and 87 with automatics. ['Cuda 383 coupe] 75 with three-speeds; 501 with four-speeds and 1,163 with automatics. ['Cuda 440 "Six-Pack" convertible] five with four-speeds and 12 with automatics. ['Cuda 440 "Six-Pack" coupe] 108 with four-speeds and 129 with automatics.

1972 PLYMOUTH

1972 Plymouth, Duster two-door coupe, 6-cyl

VALIANT GROUP — (6-CYL/V-8) — SERIES HV — The 1971 Valiant set sales records with 256,930 calendar year deliveries, so there was little motivation to change it. Only details of the taillights and grille were altered. The front side marker was slimmer and longer. This was the first year of the same basic four-door sedan body. The Dodge Dart-based Scamp was also little changed. New was a Scamp signature at the right-hand corner of the deck lid, just below the Plymouth block lettering. The base Duster models followed the pattern of minor revision, but the rear side marker lamps were moved an inch or two higher above the lower rear feature line. In addition, a nameplate was added to the sides of front fenders above the lower feature line and behind the wheel opening. This identification was not used on units with optional body striping packages, which had Duster decals at the front fender tip. The Twister included a stripe with a cartoon tornado at the rear tip and cartoon style "Twister" lettering, plus special hood paint treatment. Other ingredients included: dual racing mirrors (left remote control); drip rail moldings; wheel lip moldings; bodyside tape stripe; and lower deck tape. The Twister package was $98.20. 'Gold Duster' packages included a gold reptile-grain canopy-style vinyl top and special front fenderside decals. The Gold Duster package also included: harmonizing exterior; gold bodyside stripes; gold rear deck tape; whitewalls; wider wheels; special wheel covers; bright drip moldings; and special interior trim. It was a mid-year option (price not available). The high-performance Duster 340 had a beltline tape stripe

treatment and '340' rear fender lettering. Base Duster equipment included ventless side windows, concealed spare tire and two-speed wipers. The base Valiant added front and rear door armrests that were color-keyed to match the interior. The Scamp hardtop had the base Duster items plus color-keyed front door armrests; interior Decor Group trim and cigar lighter. The Duster 340 added lower deck tape stripe; bodyside tape stripe; three-speed manual floor shift; optional axle ratio; locking glovebox; heavy-duty suspension; a unique grille; dual snorkel air cleaner; roof drip rail moldings; cigar lighter; wide tires; and the 340-cid V-8 with dual exhaust. The 225-cid six was optional in all models, except the Duster '340'. The 340-cid V-8 was also extra in the other models.

PLYMOUTH I.D. NUMBERS: The Vehicle Identification Number is located on top left of dash. First symbol identifies model: B=Barracuda; V=Valiant; R=Satellite; P=Fury. Second symbol indicates car-line price class: L=Low; M=Medium; H=High; P=Premium; S=Special; K=Police; T=Taxicab. Third and fourth symbols indicate body style (first four symbols appear in second column of charts below). Fifth symbol indicates engine: B=198 cid/100 nhp six; C=225 cid/110 nhp six; E=special order six; G=318 cid/150 nhp V-8; H=340 cid/240 nhp V-8; K=360 cid/175 nhp V-8; M=400 cid/190 nhp 2V V-8; P=400 cid/255 nhp high-performance V-8; T=440 cid/225 nhp 4V V-8; U=440 cid/280 nhp high-performance V-8; V=440 cid/330 hp "Six-Pack" V-8; Z=Special Order V-8. The sixth symbol designated model year: 2=1972. The seventh symbol indicated assembly plant: A=Lynch Rd., Detroit; B=Hamtramck, Mich.; C=Jefferson Ave., Detroit; D=Belvedere, Ill.; F=Newark, Del.; G=St. Louis, Mo.; and R=Windsor, Ontario, Canada. The last six symbols were the sequential unit production number.

VALIANT GROUP

Series No.	Body/ Style No.	Body Type & Seating	Factory Price	Shipping Weight	Prod. Total
VALIANT					
HV1/2	VL41	4-dr Sed-6P	2355/2483	2800/2900	52,911
DUSTER					
HV1/2	VL29	2-dr Spt Cpe-6P	2287/2407	2780/2875	212,311
SCAMP					
HV1/2	VH23	2-dr HT Cpe-6P	2528/2648	2825/2915	49,470
DUSTER '340'					
HV2	VS29	2-dr Spt Cpe-6P	2728	3100	15,681

Note 1: Data above slash for six/below slash, no slash for V-8.

1972 Plymouth, 'Cuda '340' two-door hardtop, V-8

BARRACUDA GROUP — (6-CYL/V-8) — SERIES HB — Popularity of the Barracuda was on the decline as government and insurance company pressures combined to assault the pony car market with restrictive regulations or unbearable insurance rates. Deliveries had dropped 20,000 units in 1971. This season the Barracuda convertible disappeared and styling changes were limited to face lifting and repositioning of trim and equipment details. A split grille with louvered center divider and single headlamps was seen. Rectangular front parking lamps were moved towards the center on either side of the below-the-bumper license plate holder. Dual round taillamps appeared at each corner of the rear deck latch panel. The high-powered 'Cuda received a new twin scoop performance hood treatment and had a blacked-out rear panel (with 'Cuda lettering on the left side) and dual rectangular exhaust exits in the lower gravel pan, under the bumper. The model count was cut from nine to three. Standard equipment on the base coupe included: all regulation safety devices; dual headlamps and horns; hubcaps; inside day/nite mirror; brake warning lamp; left outside rearview mirror; bucket seats; cigar lighter; fuel, temperature and ammeter gauges; black sidewall tires; and either the 225-cid six or 318-cid V-8. The 'Cuda had all of these items plus chrome wheel lip and body sill moldings; performance hood; color-keyed grille; black-out rear deck panel; heavy-duty suspension and brakes; electronic ignition; wide profile tires with white sidewalls; and the 318-cid two-barrel V-8. New options included an electrically-operated sun

roof and Sport Decor Group trim package. The only Barracuda engine option was the '340' V-8 with four-barrel carburetion. Anything else was practically uninsurable and that included the famed 'Street Hemi'. The Hemi 'Cuda was a thing of the past.

BARRACUDA GROUP

Series No.	Body/ Style No.	Body Type & Seating	Factory Price	Shipping Weight	Prod. Total
BARRACUDA					
HB1/2	BH23	2-dr HT Cpe-4P	2710/2808	3040/3090	10,622
'CUDA					
HB2	BS23	2-dr HT Cpe-4P	2953	3330	7,828

1972 Plymouth, Satellite Sebring-Plus two-door hardtop, V-8

SATELLITE GROUP — (6-CYL/V-8) — SERIES HR — Plymouth's intermediate-size lineup for 1972 included one two-door coupe and three two-door hardtops on the 115-inch wheelbase platform, plus two sedans and six station wagons on a two-inch longer stance. Body restylings were minor. Engineering improvements were comprised of such things as a new 400-cid V-8; electronic ignition system; better alternator; improved transmissions; a solid stainless steel antenna; three-point safety belt system; better body sealing; stronger seats; reusable litter bag; and safer disc brakes. Station wagons featured a three-way tailgate that opened in a door-like manner without having to lower the window. A flatter-style grille insert was used on the lower-priced models and their side body nameplates were moved from in back of the front wheel opening to ahead of the rear opening. Standard features were a glovebox lock; dome light; hubcaps; soft coat hooks; inside day/nite mirror (except coupe); color-keyed rubber floor covering; all-vinyl interior; cigar lighter (except coupe); and 225-cid six or 318-cid V-8. The Sebring had the same equipment, but without the vinyl upholstery, plus dual horns; front foam seat cushions; and moldings for the drip rails, body sills and wheel cutouts with carpeting used on the floor. The Satellite Custom began with all Sebring items and added front armrests and rear armrests with ashtrays both with bright metal bases. The Sebring-Plus hardtop also had vinyl bucket seats up front; vinyl-covered rear bench seat; Deluxe wheel covers; bodyside moldings along the lower feature line (with Argent Silver finish below the molding) and standard V-8 power. In addition, the Sebring-Plus buyer could add wheel trim rings, at no extra cost, and substitute a cloth vinyl front seat with center armrest, in place of front buckets. Then came the Road Runner hardtop. It had all standard Satellite features plus the following additions or substitutions: three-speed floor shift; heavy-duty suspension and brakes; front and rear sway bars; deep-pile carpets; performance hood; low-restriction dual exhaust; 'Beep-Beep' horn; Rally instrument cluster; 150 mph speedometer; special deep recess split grille with Argent Silver inset; Road Runner front end medallion (with special lettering); specific inside and outside trim; rear deck cartoon decal; F70-14 white sidewall tires; and a 400-cid four-barrel V-8. On Satellite, Custom and Road Runner models the sidebody nameplates were repositioned. They were still just ahead of the rear wheel opening, but were on the lower body feature line (instead of at mid-body height as on Sebring and Sebring-Plus). The base Satellite station wagon had bright upper door frame moldings; vinyl-trimmed bench seats; front foam seat cushions; inside day/nite mirror; cigar lighter; hubcaps; color-keyed rubber floor coverings; and the new three-way tailgate. Drip rail, wheel opening and custom sill moldings were added to the Custom station wagon, which also had a thin full-length mid-body molding and an Argent Silver finished horizontal band across the tailgate. The top-of-the-line Regent station wagon had full wheel covers (except in some early factory photos) and woodgrain side paneling below a full-length molding that arched over each wheelhousing.

SATELLITE GROUP

SATELLITE

Series No.	Body/ Style No.	Body Type & Seating	Factory Price	Shipping Weight	Prod. Total
HR1/2	RL41	4-dr Sed-6P	2678/2770	3350/3345	12,794
HR1/2	RL21	2-dr Cpe-6P	2609/2701	3240/3300	10,507
HR2	RL45	4-dr Sta Wag-6P	3152	3785	7,377

SATELLITE SEBRING

HR1/2	RH23	2-dr HT Cpe-6P	2871/2963	3250/3315	34,353

SATELLITE CUSTOM

Series No.	Body/ Style No.	Body Type & Seating	Factory Price	Shipping Weight	Prod. Total
HR1/2	RH41	4-dr Sed-6P	2848/2940	3285/3350	34,973
HR2	RH45	4-dr Sta Wag-6P	3325	3780	5,485
HR2	RH46	4-dr Sta Wag-9P	3403	3825	5,637

REGENT WAGON

Series No.	Body/ Style No.	Body Type & Seating	Factory Price	Shipping Weight	Prod. Total
HR2	RP45	4-dr Sta Wag-6P	3547	3790	1,893
HR2	RP46	4-dr Sta Wag-9P	3625	3830	2,907

SEBRING-PLUS

Series No.	Body/ Style No.	Body Type & Seating	Factory Price	Shipping Weight	Prod. Total
HR2	RP23	2-dr HT Cpe-5P	3112	3320	21,399

ROAD RUNNER

Series No.	Body/ Style No.	Body Type & Seating	Factory Price	Shipping Weight	Prod. Total
HR2	RM23	2-dr HT Cpe-6P	3080	3495	7,628

Note 1: Data above slash for six/below slash, no slash for V-8.

1972 Plymouth, Fury Gran Coupe two-door hardtop, V-8

FURY GROUP — (6-CYL/V-8) — SERIES HP — Sixteen models made up the Fury line of full-size cars for 1972. The high-priced offerings were the Gran Coupe and Gran Sedan. All-new styling was evident in the sheet metal; bumpers; grilles; lamps and ornamentation. On base models, a more massive grille with larger body corner wraparounds was seen. It was divided into two individual openings, right and left, each of which housed dual headlamps with a horizontal bar between the headlights and wide center divider. The rear featured horizontal, rectangular taillights set into the bumper with the bumper having Plymouth lettering across its upper face bar. More expensive models had the two grille openings completely filled with fine vertical-blade inserts. There were hidden headlamps on these cars and larger taillamps with vertical segmentation. Rectangular nameplate badges were carried ahead of the front side markers and at the right-hand corner of the deck lid. Standard equipment on Fury I models included: automatic transmission; all-vinyl bench seats with adjustable head restraints; power steering; ventless side glass; left outside rearview mirror; inside day/nite mirror; front and rear armrests; two-speed electric wipers; electric washers; glovebox lock; front and rear side marker lamps; front and rear ashtrays; concealed wipers; front door courtesy light switches; brake warning light; keyless door locking; cigar lighter; bias-belted blackwall tires and inside hood release. A 318-cid two-barrel V-8 was the base engine. Fury II models had all the above plus deep-pile carpeting and bright, full-length sidebody moldings. The Fury III models added color-keyed vinyl insert-type side moldings; trunk light; upper door frame moldings on four-doors; wheel opening moldings; woodgrain dash and door panels; glovebox light; dual-sized taillamps with bright ornamentation; bright metal armrest bases; and carpeting. The Gran Coupe/Sedan was a Fury III with certain extras including: door-pull straps; carpeted lower door panels; folding center armrest seat; body sill and beltline moldings; color-keyed vinyl rear bumper pads; rear door courtesy light switches on sedans; and concealed headlamps. The base station wagon was comparable to the Fury I and also had a three-way tailgate; integral roof top air deflector; power tailgate window; and heavy-duty brakes. The next-step-up Custom Suburban added front foam seat cushions; carpets; bright upper door frames and wheel opening moldings. The Sport Suburban also had a vinyl trim bench seat with center armrest and woodgrain bodyside paneling. The Fury GT, like most other members of the Plymouth 'Rapid Transit System', had bit the dust. It was obvious that the high-performance era was dying and the day of the fully-equipped (and expensive) base model car had arrived. Buyers who wanted a cheap, economical Plymouth, with hardly any extras, would have to settle for a Cricket. This car was still around, but does not fit into the scope of this catalog covering American-built postwar cars.

FURY GROUP

FURY I

Series No.	Body/ Style No.	Body Type & Seating	Factory Price	Shipping Weight	Prod. Total
HP2	PL41	4-dr Sed-6P	3448	3840	14,006

FURY II

Series No.	Body/ Style No.	Body Type & Seating	Factory Price	Shipping Weight	Prod. Total
HP2	PM41	4-dr Sed-6P	3567	3830	20,051
HP2	PM23	2-dr HT Cpe-6P	3589	3790	7,515

FURY III

Series No.	Body/ Style No.	Body Type & Seating	Factory Price	Shipping Weight	Prod. Total
HP2	PH41	4-dr Sed-6P	3747	3830	46,713
HP2	PH43	4-dr HT Sed-6P	3813	3865	48,618
HP2	PH23	2-dr HT Cpe-6P	2769	3790	21,204
HP2	PH29	2-dr FsTp Cpe-6P	3802	3790	9,036

FURY GRAN COUPE/SEDAN

Series No.	Body/ Style No.	Body Type & Seating	Factory Price	Shipping Weight	Prod. Total
HP2	PP43	4-dr HT Sed-6P	3971	3865	17,551
HP2	PP23	2-dr HT Cpe-6P	3925	3735	15,840
HP2	PP29	2-dr FsTp Cpe-6P	3958	3805	8,509

SUBURBANS

Series No.	Body/ Style No.	Body Type & Seating	Factory Price	Shipping Weight	Prod. Total
HP2	PM45	4-dr Sta Wag-6P	3964	4315	5,368
HP2	PM46	4-dr Sta Wag-9P	4079	4360	2,773
HP2	PH45	4-dr Cus Wag-6P	4063	4315	11,067
HP2	PH46	4-dr Cus Wag-9P	4141	4365	14,041
HP2	PP45	4-dr Spt Wag-6P	4329	4335	4,971
HP2	PP46	4-dr Spt Wag-9P	4406	4395	15,928

Note 1: Data above slash for six/below slash, no slash for V-8.

ENGINES:

(Valiant/Duster Six) Inline. Overhead valve. Cast iron block. Displacement: 198 cid. Bore and stroke: 3.40 x 3.64 inches. Compression ratio: 8.4:1. SAE Net hp: 100. Four main bearings. Solid valve lifters. Carburetor: one-barrel.

(Barracuda/Satellite Six) Inline. Overhead valve. Cast iron block. Displacement: 225 cid. Bore and stroke: 3.40 x 4.12 inches. Compression ratio: 8.4:1. SAE Net hp: 100. Four main bearings. Solid valve lifters. Carburetor: one-barrel.

(Valiant/Duster/Barracuda/Satellite/Fury V-8) Overhead valve. Cast iron block. Displacement: 318 cid. Bore and stroke: 3.91 x 3.31 inches. Compression ratio: 8.6:1. SAE Net hp: 150. Five main bearings. Hydraulic valve lifters. Carburetor: two-barrel.

(Duster '340' V-8) Overhead valve. Cast iron block. Displacement: 340 cid. Bore and stroke: 4.04 x 3.31 inches. Compression ratio: 8.5:1. SAE Net hp: 240. Five main bearings. Hydraulic valve lifters. Carburetor: four-barrel.

(Road Runner V-8) Overhead valve. Cast iron block. Displacement: 400 cid. Bore and stroke: 4.34 x 3.38 inches. Compression ratio: 8.2:1. SAE Net hp: 255. Five main bearings. Hydraulic valve lifters. Carburetor: four-barrel.

CHASSIS FEATURES: Wheelbase: (Valiant/Duster) 108 inches; (Scamp) 111 inches; (Barracuda/'Cuda) 108 inches; (Satellite two-door) 115 inches; (Satellite four-door) 111 inches; (Fury Suburban) 122 inches; (Fury) 120 inches. Overall length: (Valiant/Duster) 188.4 inches; (Scamp) 192.1 inches; (Barracuda/'Cuda) 186.6 inches; (Satellite two-door) 203.2 inches; (Satellite station wagon) 210.9 inches; (Satellite four-door) 204.6 inches; (Fury Suburban) 222 inches; (Fury) 217.2 inches. Tires: See tire data in text.

OPTIONS: Power brakes, in Valiant only ($40). Power steering, in Valiant ($92); Satellite ($114); Barracuda ($104). Air conditioning, in Valiant ($353); in Barracuda ($365); in Satellite ($378); in Fury ($386). Automatic lock tailgate, in all station wagons ($27). Deluxe Dual air conditioning, in Fury station wagon ($598). Front end and rear bumper guards, Valiant ($24); Barracuda ($27); Satellite ($33); Fury ($38). Carpets, in base models as optional equipment ($19). Carpeted cargo compartment, all station wagons ($21). Electric clock, in Satellites without tachometer ($18); in Fury ($17). Center console, in Barracuda ($52); in Fury Gran Coupe/Sedan (no charge); in Satellite ($56). Rear window defogger, Valiant ($26); Barracuda ($28); others ($31). Engine block heater, Fury ($15). Decorative exhaust tips, on Satellites, except station wagon ($21). Luggage roof rack, Satellite station wagon ($56); Fury station wagon ($67). Accessory floor mats, Fury and Satellite ($14). Left-hand remote-control racing-type outside rearview mirror, Satellite two-doors ($16). Rear fender skirts, Furys without deep-dish wheel covers ($32). Road Runner C-pillar 'Strobe Stripe' ($33). Valiant performance hood paint treatment ($17). Valiant/Duster bodyside tape stripe ($25). Road Runner hood/fender tape stripe ($22). Hood or deck tape treatment on Satellite two-doors, each ($22). Power disc brakes, on Valiant ($62); on Fury/Satellite ($68); on Barracuda ($68). Power deck lid release, Fury ($15). Power door locks, Fury four-door sedan and station wagon ($71). Power bench seat, Fury ($103). Power seat, bucket-type or left-hand unit of 50/50 bench-type ($91). Power windows, on Satellite, except coupe ($119); on Fury ($125). AM radio, Fury/Satellite ($65); Barracuda ($59). AM/FM radio, Fury ($71); Valiant ($125 or $136). AM radio with stereo tape cassette, Fury/Satellite ($214); Barracuda ($196). Rooftop air deflector, Satellite station wagon ($20). Vinyl roof, Valiant ($75); Barracuda ($80); Satellite ($94); Fury ($108). Vinyl roof, Fury station wagon only ($139). Vinyl canopy roof, Satellite Group ($66). Vinyl bucket seats, Valiant including carpets ($120); Fury Gran Sport ($103). Center cushion armrest seat, Road Runner/Sebring ($56). 'Cuda performance hood paint treatment ($17). Rim-blow steering wheel, Fury ($26). Tilt steering with rim-blow, Satellite/Fury ($55). 'Tuff' steering

wheel, in Scamp ($28); in other Valiants ($18). 'Tuff' Rally steering wheel, Satellite/Road Runner ($20-$30). Sun roof, on Valiant with 6.95 x 14 or larger tires mandatory ($223). Vinyl roof with sun roof, Satellite with full vinyl top ($475); with canopy ($446). Barracuda Rally gauge package ($75-$85). Tachometer ($52). Deep-dish wheel covers, Fury ($31-$58). Wire wheel covers, Satellite ($42.69). Chrome styled Road Wheels, Satellite/Fury ($62-$101). Rally Road Wheels, Valiant/Sebring/Regent ($29-$58). Barracuda bodyside tape stripe ($28). Barracuda chrome styled Road Wheels ($81). Barracuda Rally-type Road Wheels ($28-$53). Barracuda vinyl roof ($80). Barracuda power sun roof with vinyl top covering ($434). Barracuda performance hood standard with 'Cuda ($20). Three-speed manual transmission was standard. Automatic transmission was standard in Fury. Automatic transmission, in Barracuda ($203-$223); in Valiant ($178-$208); in Satellite ($211-$231). Three-speed manual floor shift transmission, Valiant ($24). Four-speed manual floor shift transmission ($184-$201). Base Valiant six-cylinder 225 cid/100 hp one-barrel engine ($38). Road Runner V-8 340 cid/240 hp four-barrel engine ($64). Fury Group V-8 360 cid/175 hp two-barrel engine ($45). Fury/Satellite V-8 400 cid/190 hp two-barrel engine ($84). Satellite V-8 400 cid/225 hp four-barrel engine ($186). Fury V-8 400 cid/225 hp four-barrel engine ($193). Road Runner V-8 440 cid/280 hp four-barrel engine ($153). Road Runner V-8 440 cid/330 hp 'Six-Pack' V-8 (N/A). 'Cuda V-8 340 cid/240 hp four-barrel engine ($84). Barracuda V-8 340 cid/240 hp four-barrel engine ($210). Barracuda V-8 340 cid/240 hp four-barrel engine ($277). 'Air Grabber' air induction package, Road Runner only ($67). Positive traction rear axle ($41-$48). Available rear axle gear ratios: 2.76:1; 3.23:1; 3.55:1.

HISTORICAL FOOTNOTES: The full-size Plymouths were introduced Sept. 28, 1971, and the Valiant appeared in dealer showrooms the same day. Model year production peaked at 708,587 units. Calendar year sales of 733,124 cars were recorded. F.G. Hazelroth was general sales manager this year. Many options and accessories were offered. The Satellite Brougham package included cloth and vinyl bench seat with headrests and folding center armrest and woodstone lower door panels at $120. The Fury Brougham package included the same features plus a 50/50 bench seat with the left unit of the adjustable recliner-type. It was priced at $159 on Fury Gran Coupe/Sedan and Sport Suburban models and $184 on Custom Suburbans. Plymouth marketed a large variety of safety, convenience and performance features as individual groups (at special package prices). In addition, it was also possible to select an 'Easy Order Package' for Satellite and Fury models, which provided an assortment of popular groups as an all-inclusive package at prices in the $500-$550 range.

1973 PLYMOUTH

1973 Plymouth, Valiant four-door sedan, 6-cyl

VALIANT GROUP — (6-CYL/V-8) — SERIES JV — For 1973, Valiants continued to be marketed in three forms including Duster two-door coupes, Scamp two-door hardtops and Valiant sedans. New front and rear end treatments on all models gave the cars a fresh appearance. Interiors were considerably upgraded. Major improvements included an optional fold-down rear seat on the Duster; optional electrically heated window defogger; the inclusion of front and rear bumper guards as standard equipment; ventless side glass on Valiant Group hardtops; standard disc brakes on V-8 models; and an improved, quieter ride on all. New lowback-style seats were standard in Scamp and an option for Dusters and Valiants. With the above changes, the standard equipment distinctions were the same as in 1972. A new grille made the styling of the 1973 Valiant different than the previous year. It had single headlamps housed in square-shaped bezels at each end. Next to the headlamps were three oblong openings with vertical segmentation housing the rectangular parking lamps. Below the nose of the car were three larger oblong openings that 'veed' from the centerline and also had vertical segmentations. Above them was placed a chrome header bearing the word Plymouth in stamped

block letters. A Valiant script remained on the sides of the cowl. The Duster also had the same new grille and front safety bumper with rubber-faced guards flanking the license plate recess. Large single-lens taillamps replaced the former slat-type. 'Gold Duster' and 'Twister' packages were available again. The Gold Duster option package was priced at $161. The Duster 340 had a wide tape stripe running the full length of the car along the beltline and bold '340' lettering on the rear fender edge. The Scamp was changed at the front by the addition of the new Valiant-style grille. The only rear end alteration was a pair of more massive, rubber-faced bumper guards. The Scamp's ventless glass emphasized its hardtop look. The Duster '340' came standard with the 340-cid V-8. The '198' six or '318' V-8 were the base engines for the other Valiant Group entries. The only option this season was the '225' six, available only in base sixes, of course.

PLYMOUTH I.D. NUMBERS: The Vehicle Identification Number is located on a plate attached to upper left-hand top of dash, viewable through windshield. First symbol indicates model: B=Barracuda; P=Fury; R=Satellite/Sebring; V=Valiant/Duster. Second symbol indicates price class: L=low; M=medium; H=high; G=grand; P=premium; S=Special; T=taxicab; K=police. Third and fourth symbols indicate body style (first four symbols appear in Body/Style Number column of charts below). Fifth symbol indicates engine: B=198 cid/150 nhp six; C=225 cid/105 nhp six; E=special order six; G=318 cid/150 nhp 2V V-8; H=340 cid/240 nhp 4V high-performance V-8; K=360 cid/170 nhp 2V V-8; M=400 cid/175 nhp 2V V-8; P=400 cid/260 nhp high-performance 4V V-8; T=440 cid/220 nhp 4V V-8; U=440 cid/280 hp 4V TNT V-8; Z=special order V-8. Sixth symbol indicates model year: 3=1973. The seventh symbol indicated assembly plant: A=Lynch Rd., Detroit; B=Hamtramck, Mich.; C=Jefferson Ave., Detroit; D=Belvedere, Ill.; F=Newark, Del.; G=St. Louis, Mo.; and R=Windsor, Canada. The last six symbols were the sequential unit production number.

VALIANT GROUP

Series No.	Body/ Style No.	Body Type & Seating	Factory Price	Shipping Weight	Prod. Total
VALIANT					
JV1/2	VL41	4-dr Sed-6P	2447/2564	2865/2980	61,826
DUSTER					
JV1/2	VL29	2-dr Spt Cpe-6P	2346/2493	2830/2950	249,243
SCAMP					
JV1/2	VH23	2-dr HT Cpe-6P	2617/2734	2885/3000	53,792
DUSTER '340'					
JV2	VS29	2-dr Spt Cpe-6P	2822	3175	15,731

Note 1: Data above slash for six/below slash, no slash for V-8.

1973 Plymouth, Barracuda two-door hardtop, V-8

BARRACUDA GROUP — (V-8) — SERIES JB — The Barracuda and 'Cuda were now referred to as "specialty compacts" to downplay the high-performance image. Still, they continued to exhibit their previous sporty flavor. The six-cylinder engine was no longer available in either line. The 318-cid V-8, now including electronic ignition, was standard. The '340' V-8 was optional. Another new standard feature was manual disc brakes. Full-volume urethane foam cushioned bucket seats were used. A host of performance packages and decor packages were offered including sway bars, sport hoods and bodyside tape stripes. Revisions in appearance were seen mainly in bumper design. Rubber-faced guards were standard. The front side marker lamps were also moved to the sidebody feature line, instead of slightly below it. Cowlside signature script on base models was positioned slightly lower than before. 'Cudas were identified by bold model letters on the left-hand side of the rear panel and by the same twin-scoop performance hood of the previous year. With the exceptions noted above, standard equipment was a carryover from 1972, too.

BARRACUDA GROUP

BARRACUDA

JB2	BH23	2-dr HT Cpe-5P	2935	3140	11,587

'CUDA

JB2	BS23	2-dr HT Cpe-5P	3120	3235	10,626

1973 Plymouth, Satellite Custom four-door sedan, V-8

SATELLITE GROUP — (6-CYL/V-8) — SERIES JR — Styling of the two-door Satellite models was more conservative and de-emphasized the high-performance image in favor of a rich, luxury look. Standard equipment began with all items listed for 1972 models plus electronic ignition and manual disc brakes (with power discs standard in station wagon). Basic sheet metal was a carryover from the 1971-1972 design again with different wheelbases for two- and four-door cars. Details of the grille designs varied, helping car spotters in telling the different lines apart. On all models, the loop-type grille was gone. Satellites and Sebrings substituted a double-deck grid patterned insert. It stretched between quad headlights set into bright metal, rectangular housings. Satellite Custom and Regent station wagons had their quad headlamps set into Argent Silver finished housings. A recessed rectangle in the center housed a gridwork of chrome bars with square, honeycomb-like inserts. On these models the portion of the bumper face bar between the bumper guards had an upward curve. Road Runners combined the Satellite/Sebring-type grille with a hood having a wide center power bulge; taillights on all models were still rectangular. They were fatter, but not as long as the previous season. Engine availability included the 225-cid six and five V-8s up to the emasculated '440'. On all models (even the Road Runner) a 318-cid V-8 was standard equipment. 'Six-Pack' induction was no longer available. All 1973 Plymouth engines featured a new EGR (exhaust gas recirculation) system, electric choke and offset spark advance. The new bumpers on all models were intended to meet federal impact standards and steel beam door construction was adopted at midyear. Plymouths could not go as fast as before, but they were safer and cleaner and more sophisticated with more sophisticated pricing, as well.

SATELLITE GROUP

Series No.	Body/ Style No.	Body Type & Seating	Factory Price	Shipping Weight	Prod. Total
SATELLITE					
JR1/2	RL41	4-dr Sed-6P	2824/2936	3450/3515	14,716
JR1/2	RL21	2-dr Cpe-6P	2755/2867	3375/3440	13,570
SATELLITE CUSTOM					
JR1/2	RH41	4-dr Sed-6P	2974/3086	3445/3510	46,748
SATELLITE SEBRING					
JR1/2	RH23	2-dr HT Cpe-6P	2997/3109	3390/3460	51,575
SATELLITE-PLUS					
JR2	RP23	2-dr HT Cpe-5P	3258	3455	43,628
ROAD RUNNER					
JR2	RM23	2-dr HT Cpe-6P	3115	3525	19,056
SATELLITE WAGONS					
JR2	RL45	4-dr Sta Wag-6P	3272	3950	6,906
JR2	RH46	4-dr Cus Wag-9P	3518	3990	7,705
JR2	RH45	4-dr Cus Wag-6P	3400	3945	6,733
JR2	RP46	4-dr Spt Wag-9P	3740	4010	4,786
JR2	RP45	4-dr Spt Wag-6P	3621	3950	2,781

Note 1: Data above slash for six/below slash, no slash for V-8.

FURY GROUP — (V-8) — SERIES JP — Retaining the basic design configuration of 1972, the Fury Group had an altered frontal appearance with a new grille, new hood, bolt-on fender extensions and energy-absorbing bumper. Quad headlamps were now set into individual square-shaped bezels in the fender extension panels. A massive rectangular grille featured thin, horizontal blades and a Plymouth nameplate at the left-hand side. The bumper bar ran across the face of the grille and the blade-patterned insert showed underneath. This lower grille was split into two rectangles, one on either side of the license plate holder. Rear styling featured a massive bumper that was formed to dip under the taillamps at each end. High in the center, a rectangular depression with Plymouth lettering was seen. Integral, rubber-faced rear bumper guards were spaced wide apart, flanking the license plate recess on both sides. The vertical taillamps had the shape of a tall, thin triangle with rounded corners. They were deeply recessed into the fender extension caps and trimmed with chrome moldings on the outside and ribbed bands of bright metal around the inner lip. As the car-line's level of trim and appointments increased,

full-length horizontal side moldings were added and Fury Gran Sports also had front fender turn indicators, stand-up hood ornaments, body sill moldings and a small crest at the right side of the deck lid. The Fury Brougham package was priced at $160. Suburbans had wraparound horizontal taillamps with tailgate beauty bands and woodgrain side paneling on Sport models. Automatic transmission, V-8 engines, power disc brakes and electronic ignition were standard, with the remaining equipment distinctions for each line following the 1972 pattern. A four-door hardtop was added to the Fury III series and new options for the year included steel-belted radial tires and vent windows on four-door models. The '318' V-8 was standard in passenger cars; the '360' in Suburbans. A special option-created model appearing this season was the Fury Special. Its standard extras included: Chestnut metallic brown paint; a parchment textured vinyl top; color coordinated vinyl side molding inserts; rocker panel moldings; stand-up hood ornament; all-vinyl interior; tapestry cloth seat insert panels and special carpeting.

1973 Plymouth, Fury Gran Coupe two-door hardtop, V-8

FURY GROUP

Series No.	Body/ Style No.	Body Type & Seating	Factory Price	Shipping Weight	Prod. Total
FURY I					
JP2	PL41	4-dr Sed-6P	3575	3865	17,365
FURY II					
JP2	PM41	4-dr Sed-6P	3694	3845	21,646
FURY III					
JP2	PH41	4-dr Sed-6P	3866	3860	51,742
JP2	PH43	4-dr HT Sed-6P	3932	3880	51,215
JP2	PH23	2-dr HT Cpe-6P	3883	3815	34,963
GRAN FURY					
JP2	PP43	4-dr HT Sed-6P	4110	3890	14,852
JP2	PP23	2-dr HT Cpe-6P	4064	3845	18,127
SUBURBANS					
JP2	PM45	4-dr Sta Wag-6P	4150	4410	5,206
JP2	PH46	4-dr Cus Wag-9P	4354	4465	15,671
JP2	PH45	4-dr Cus Wag-6P	4246	4420	9,888
JP2	PP46	4-dr Spt Wag-9P	4599	4495	15,680
JP2	PP45	4-dr Spt Wag-6P	4497	4435	4,832

Note 1: 3,176 Fury II two-door hardtops were made, probably for Canadian sale.

ENGINES:

(Valiant/Duster Six) Inline. Overhead valve. Cast iron block. Displacement: 198 cid. Bore and stroke: 3.40 x 3.64 inches. Compression ratio: 8.4:1. SAE Net hp: 110. Four main bearings. Solid valve lifters. Carburetor: one-barrel.

(Satellite Six) Inline. Overhead valve. Cast iron block. Displacement: 225 cid. Bore and stroke: 3.40 x 4.12 inches. Compression ratio: 8.4:1. SAE Net hp: 110. Four main bearings. Solid valve lifters. Carburetor: one-barrel.

(Valiant/Duster/Barracuda/Satellite/Road Runner/Fury V-8) Overhead valve. Cast iron block. Displacement: 318 cid. Bore and stroke: 3.91 x 3.31 inches. Compression ratio: 8.6:1. SAE Net hp: 150. Five main bearings. Hydraulic valve lifters. Carburetor: two-barrel.

(Duster '340' V-8) Overhead valve. Cast iron block. Displacement: 340 cid. Bore and stroke: 4.04 x 3.31 inches. Compression ratio: 8.5:1. SAE Net hp: 235. Five main bearings. Hydraulic valve lifters. Carburetor: two-barrel.

CHASSIS FEATURES: Wheelbase: (Valiant/Duster) 108 inches; (Scamp) 111 inches; (Satellite two-door) 115 inches; (Satellite four-door) 117 inches; (Fury Suburban) 122 inches; (Fury) 120 inches; (Barracuda) 108 inches. Overall length: (Valiant/Duster) 195.8 inches; (Scamp) 199.6 inches; (Satellite station wagon) 216.1 inches; (Satellite two-door) 210.8 inches; (Satellite four-door) 213.3 inches; (Fury station wagon) 227.5 inches; (Fury) 223.4 inches; (Barracuda) 193 inches; (Road Runner) 210.8 inches. Tires: (Valiant/Duster/Scamp) 6.95 x 14; (Duster V-8) E78-14; (Barracuda) 7.35 x 14; ('Cuda) F70-14; (Satellite/Road Runner) E78-14; (Fury) F78-15.

OPTIONS: Barracuda, vinyl top ($81). Barracuda, air conditioning ($369). Barracuda, Rally Wheels ($53). Barracuda, AM/FM radio

($194). Barracuda, electric sun roof ($434). Barracuda, power disc brakes, standard in 'Cuda ($65). Valiant, disc brakes ($65). Duster, electric sun roof ($223). Valiant, air conditioning ($358). Valiant, vinyl roof ($76). Satellite Group, sun roof ($171). Satellite Group, vinyl top ($101). Satellite Group, AM/FM stereo ($212). Satellite Group, AM/FM stereo with tape ($363). Fury Group, vinyl top ($108). Fury Group, electric sun roof ($480). Fury Group, Deluxe Dual Suburban air conditioning ($598). Fury Group, AM/FM stereo ($212); Fury Group, AM/FM stereo with tape ($363). Three-speed manual transmission was standard. Automatic transmission was standard on Fury Group models. Automatic transmission, Valiant, six 225-cid one-barrel engine (N/A). Barracuda, V-8 340 cid/235 hp two-barrel engine ($90). 'Cuda, V-8 340 cid/235 hp two-barrel engine ($85). Satellite Group, V-8 400 cid/175 hp two-barrel engine. Satellite Group, 400 cid/260 hp four-barrel engine. Road Runner, V-8 400 cid/260 hp four-barrel engine. Road Runner, V-8 440 cid/280 hp four-barrel engine. Fury Group, V-8 360 cid/170 hp two-barrel engine. Fury Group, V-8 400 cid/185 hp two-barrel engine. Fury Group, V-8 440 cid/220 hp four-barrel engine. Positive traction rear axle.

HISTORICAL FOOTNOTES: The full-size 1973 Plymouths were introduced Sept. 26, 1972, and the Valiant Group appeared in dealer showrooms the same day. Model year production peaked at 746,821 units. Calendar year production of 742,957 cars was recorded. F.G. Hazelroth was the general sales manager this year. Plymouth Division held a 7.69 percent share of the total U.S. auto market and was America's sixth largest producer of automobiles.

1974 PLYMOUTH

1974 Plymouth, Duster '360' two-door coupe, V-8

VALIANT GROUP — (6-CYL/V-8) — SERIES 4V — For the Valiant Group the year's only styling changes were directly related to engineering revisions. These included a larger Valiant sedan and a new rear end treatment for Scamps. Otherwise, the only appearance variations were new decals, tape stripes and options packages. In most cases, not even grilles or taillights were redesigned. The four-door Valiant's sheet metal was adopted to the 111-inch Scamp wheelbase, with the extra inches showing behind the doors. The larger size resulted in thicker roof pillars and new rear fender contours. The front treatment was unchanged in any way, except for slimmer bumper guards, although even these became optional again. The basic Duster was also untouched, save for the new, optional bumper guards. Slightly different arrangements of decals and stripes were used with each of the cosmetic packages such as 'Twister', 'Gold Duster' or 'Space Duster' groupings. The regular Duster 'Twister' package cost $124.05 and included: lower deck and bodyside tape stripes; Rally wheels; front sway bar; dual racing mirrors; drip rail and wheel lip moldings; and 'Twister' decal. The 'Gold Duster' package cost $187.25 and included: canopy; vinyl top; Deluxe insulation; rear deck and bodyside tape stripes; Deluxe wheel covers; 'Gold Duster' decal and 6.95 x 14 white sidewall tires. The 'Gold Duster/Twister' combination cost $234.60 and included all 'Gold Duster' extras plus wheel lip moldings; Rally road wheels; dual racing mirrors; front sway bar; and wheel trim rings. The 'Space Duster' package cost $88.80 and included folding rear seatback; carpeted cargo area and security panel. The Duster 340 was replaced by the Duster 360 with a 360 cid/245 nhp four-barrel V-8. This car had the same stripes as the '340', but lacked the rear fender engine call-out decals. The Scamp had a shelf-like, energy absorbing rear bumper and new taillights to go with it. They wrapped around the back corners of the body and flanked a center beauty panel bearing Plymouth lettering. The midyear Valiant Brougham option included luxury appointments. It came either on the new four-door body or what was really a Scamp hardtop body with Valiant nameplates. Standard equipment for the base Valiant included all regulation safety features; two-speed wipers; ventless side windows; concealed spare; rubber floor mats; three-speed manual transmission; '198' six or '318' two-barrel V-8 and 6.95 x 14 blackwall tires. The Scamp had all of the above plus carpets; dual horns; cigar lighter;

Deluxe steering wheel; interior decor group; wheel opening and drip moldings and front door color-keyed armrests. The base Duster was equipped like a Valiant, while the Duster 360 had all the basics plus floor shift controls; lower deck and bodyside tape stripes; heavy-duty suspension; power front disc brakes; electronic ignition; drip moldings; cigar lighter; locking glovebox; optional axle ratios; E70-14 black sidewall tires and the 360-cid V-8.

PLYMOUTH I.D. NUMBERS: The Vehicle Identification Number is located on a plate attached to upper left-hand top of dash, viewable through windshield. First symbol indicates model: B=Barracuda; P=Fury; R=Satellite/Sebring; V=Valiant/Duster. Second symbol indicates price class: L=low; M=medium; H=high; P=premium; S=special; T=taxi-cab; K=police. Third and fourth symbols indicate body style (first four symbols appear in Body/Style Number column of charts below). Fifth symbol indicates engine: B=198 cid/95 nhp six; C=225 cid/105 nhp six; E=special order six; G=318 cid/150 nhp 2V V-8; H=360 cid/245 nhp high-performance 4V V-8; J=360 cid/200 nhp 4V V-8; K=360 cid/180 nhp 2V V-8; L=360 cid/245 hp high-performance 4V V-8; M=400 cid/175 nhp 2V V-8; N=400 cid/205 nhp 4V V-8; P=400 cid/250 hp 4V high-performance V-8; T=440 cid/230 nhp 4V V-8; U=440 cid/275 hp 4V TNT V-8; Z=special order V-8. The sixth symbol indicates model year: 4=1974. The seventh symbol indicates assembly plant: A=Lynch Rd., Detroit; B=Hamtramck, Mich.; C=Jefferson Ave., Detroit; D=Belvedere, Ill.; F=Newark, Del.; G=St. Louis, Mo.; and R=Windsor, Canada. The last six symbols are the production sequence number starting at 100001 at each factory.

VALIANT GROUP

Series No.	Body/ Style No.	Body Type & Seating	Factory Price	Shipping Weight	Prod. Total
VALIANT					
4V1/2	VL41	4-dr Sed-6P	2942/3093	3035/3135	127,430
DUSTER					
4V1/2	VL29	2-dr Spt Cpe-6P	2829/2980	2975/3010	277,409
SCAMP					
4V1/2	VH23	2-dr HT Cpe-6P	3077/3228	3010/3110	51,699
VALIANT BROUGHAM					
4V1/2	VP23	2-dr HT Cpe-6P	3794/3880	3180/3270	13,766
4V1/2	VP41	4-dr Sed-6P	3819/3905	3195/3285	2,545
DUSTER '360'					
4V2	VS20	2-dr Spt Cpe-6P	3288	3315	3,969

Note 1: Data above slash for six/below slash, no slash for V-8.

1974 Plymouth, 'Cuda '360' two-door hardtop, V-8

BARRACUDA GROUP — (V-8) — SERIES 4B — This was to be the final season of Barracuda production, as sales slid to the lowest level in the history of this nameplate. There were no styling changes from 1973. Even the tape stripe treatments stayed basically the same, although there may have been a few new color combinations. Standard equipment for the Barracuda included all regulation safety features; dual horns; hubcaps; inside day/nite mirror; brake warning light; left outside rearview mirror; vinyl bucket seats; cigar lighter; fuel, temperature and ammeter gauges; carpets; concealed windshield wipers; three-speed manual transmission with floor shift; 7.35 x 14 blackwall tires; and the 318-cid two-barrel V-8. The specialty 'Cuda also had power front disc brakes; performance hood; heavy-duty suspension; electronic ignition; wheel lip moldings; color-keyed grille; black-out finished rear deck panel; and F70-15 white sidewall tires. The sole engine option was the four-barrel '360' claiming a 245 hp SAE net output rating. There weren't even many options packages left for the sporty compact. The Basic Group option package included AM radio; chrome-plated remote-control left outside rearview mirror; day/nite inside mirror; three-speed wipers with electric washers; and Deluxe wheel covers (same as Valiant Basic Group package), plus power steering (Barracuda only) at $196. Buyers could also add the Code A51 Sport Decor Group with body sill and wheel lip moldings; bodyside tape stripe; and sport hood for $49.85 with the 360-cid V-8 or $70.55 with

the 318-cid V-8. This was the same feature the 'Cuda included in its regular equipment. A little more exciting was the Rally Instrument Panel Group, Code J97, which included tachometer; oil pressure gauge; trip odometer; 150 mph speedometer; three-speed wipers; and electric clock. It went for $39.45 in cars without basic options and $78.65 in those that also had the Basic Group. For the few remaining speed freaks who could afford the insurance rates, there was the Code A36 Performance Axle Package with Sure-Grip differential; high-performance radiator; and heavy-duty 3.55:1 rear axle ratio for $62.85 on Barracudas with the '360' V-8.

BARRACUDA

Series No.	Body/ Style No.	Body Type & Seating	Factory Price	Shipping Weight	Prod. Total
4B2	BH23	2-dr HT Cpe-5P	3067	3210	6,745

'CUDA

Series No.	Body/ Style No.	Body Type & Seating	Factory Price	Shipping Weight	Prod. Total
4B2	BS23	2-dr HT Cpe-5P	3252	3300	4,989

1974 Plymouth, Road Runner two-door hardtop, V-8

SATELLITE GROUP — (6-CYL/V-8) — SERIES 4R — Despite its 'Space Age' name, the Satellite was a 'Race Age' machine and the performance age had ended. This would be the final season for it. The intermediate line was carried over into 1974 with only minor changes. The grille had a more subdued look than the previous design. There were dual headlamps in large, rectangular bright metal housings at each corner of the front. Between them was grillework that emphasized negative space in the twin rectangular openings. Elements were stacked upon each other, with a horizontal center bar and an upright badge at the center. The more luxurious models substituted double-deck grid-patterned inserts in each of the main openings. Rear styling seemed unchanged, although the bumper was now of the energy absorbing-type with shock absorber mountings. Lower level models carried nameplates on the trailing edge of the front fender, just above the feature line. On other models they were moved onto or below the rear roof pillar. The Road Runner had cartoon bird emblems at the center of this pillar. Standard features for the Satellite were all regulation safety items; locking glovebox; dome lamp; hubcaps; vinyl interior trim; cigar lighter (except coupe); color-keyed rubber floor coverings; E78-14 belted blackwall tires and the '225' six or '318' two-barrel V-8. Station wagons also had power front disc brakes; two-way tailgate concealed storage compartment and H78-14 belted tires. Sebrings had all the above plus dual horns; drip rail and wheel lip moldings; cigar lighter; front foam cushions; carpets; and E78-14 bias-belted tires. The Sebring-Plus added a vinyl interior with bucket seats. Cloth and vinyl armrest-type seats were optional. Deluxe wheel covers (no charge for trim rings) and sidebody moldings also came on the Sebring-Plus. Satellite Customs had the same features as regular Sebrings plus Custom interior appointments and body sill moldings. The Regent was essentially a Satellite station wagon with Deluxe wheel covers; three-way tailgate; woodgrain exterior paneling and vinyl bench seat. The Road Runner offered buyers certain extras above base Satellite equipment. These included dual horns; three-speed floor shift manual transmission; heavy-duty suspension and brakes; front and rear sway bars; carpets; three-speed wipers; performance hood; Rally instrument cluster; dual exhaust and F70-14 white letter tires.

SATELLITE GROUP

SATELLITE

Series	Style No.	Body Type	Factory Price	Shipping Weight	Prod. Total
4R1/2	RL21	2-dr Cpe-6P	3155/3271	3435/3510	10,634
4R1/2	RL41	4-dr Sed-6P	3226/3342	3520/3590	12,726

SATELLITE CUSTOM

4R1/2	RH41	4-dr Sed-6P	3329/3445	3515/3585	45,863

SATELLITE SEBRING

4R1/2	RH23	2-dr HT Cpe-6P	3353/3468	3455/3530	31,980

SEBRING-PLUS

4R2	RP23	2-dr HT Cpe-5P	3621	3555	18,480

ROAD RUNNER

4R2	RM21	2-dr Cpe-5P	3545	3616	11,555

STATION WAGONS

4R2	RL45	4-dr Sta Wag-6P	3655	4065	4,622
4R2	RH45	4-dr Custom-6P	3839	4065	4,354

Series No.	Body/ Style No.	Body Type & Seating	Factory Price	Shipping Weight	Prod. Total
4R2	RH46	4-dr Custom-9P	4152	4110	5,591
4R2	RP45	4-dr Regent-6P	4066	4065	2,026
4R2	RP46	4-dr Regent-9P	4381	4130	3,132

Note 1: Data above slash for six/below slash, no slash for V-8.

1974 Plymouth, Fury Gran Sedan four-door hardtop, V-8

FURY GROUP — (V-8) — SERIES 4P — The full-size Plymouths were totally restyled and re-engineered for 1974. Two-door and four-door styles were now built off different wheelbase platforms. The new front bumper was a shelf-type, energy-absorbing design. Above it, dual headlamps were still housed in square bright metal bezels. However, they seemed more an integral part of the overall grille design, since the segmented styling motif was dropped. The new, multi-blade grille had a slimmer appearance, because horizontal lines were emphasized overall. However, it really wasn't much different in total area than the 1973 design and it still showed through the slots in the lower part of the bumper. The front bumper guards were moved closer together and nearer the center of the car. The front fenders had a more sweeping, downward slope while the back fenders had an angular kick-up at the upper rear quarter and also had a crisper, straight-line look at their trailing edge. The rear featured massive, horizontal taillamps with Plymouth lettering on the body-color panel between them. The bumper was also more massive and ran almost straight across, without the previous taillight dip. In mid-season, an opera window roof treatment became available for the Fury Gran Coupe. Fury I equipment included all-vinyl bench seats; automatic transmission; power steering; power front disc brakes; G78-14 blackwall tires; left outside rearview mirror; inside day/nite mirror; front and rear armrests; two-speed wipers; lockable glovebox; front and rear side marker lights; concealed wipers; cigar lighter; inside hood release; brake warning light and '360' two-barrel V-8. The Fury II had the same plus carpets and cloth and vinyl bench seats. The Fury III also had a three-spoke steering wheel with woodgrain inserts; glovebox, ashtray and trunk lights; bright armrest bases; body sill moldings; upper door frame moldings (on sedan); and front foam seat. The Gran Coupe/Sedan had all Fury III features plus Deluxe wheel covers; electric clock; vinyl center armrest seat; door-pull straps; carpeted lower door panels; rear door dome light switches (sedan); beltline moldings; stand-up hood ornament and concealed headlights. The base Suburban had Fury I equipment plus three-way tailgate; rear air deflector; power tailgate window; and heavy-duty brakes with J78-15 tires on two-seat models and L78-15s on three-seaters. Custom station wagons had carpets; foam seat cushions and wheel opening moldings. Sport Suburbans also had sill moldings; vinyl center armrest bench seats; woodgrain bodyside and surround panels; electric clock; Deluxe wheel covers and concealed headlamps. All nine-passenger station wagons also had bright upper door frame moldings. A Brougham package was available for the Fury Gran Coupe/Sedan, Custom Suburban and Sport Suburban at prices between $154.55 and $193.15. It included a cloth and vinyl-trimmed 50/50 Comfort Seat with adjustable left unit and folding center armrest; 'D' pillar Brougham nameplate on station wagons; deck lid nameplates on passenger cars; reclining front passenger seat backrest; and, in Gran Coupes only, cloth and vinyl bucket seats with armrest-type center cushion. It was also possible to purchase an all-inclusive Luxury Equipment Package (Code A08) for just about any Fury. It included all options that could possibly be installed on one car; everything from air conditioning and power windows, to speed control and a digital clock. The cost ran from $1,257.95 on the three-seat station wagon to $1,498.45 on the Fury III sedan with '400' or '440' V-8.

FURY GROUP

FURY I

4P2	PL41	4-dr Sed-6P	4101	4185	8,162

FURY II

4P2	PM41	4-dr Sed-6P	4223	4165	11,649

FURY III

4P2	PH41	4-dr Sed-6P	4400	4180	27,965
4P2	PH23	2-dr HT Cpe-6P	4418	4125	14,167
4P2	PH43	4-dr HT Sed-6P	4468	4205	18,778

GRAN FURY

Series No.	Body/Style No.	Body Type & Seating	Factory Price	Shipping Weight	Prod. Total
4P2	PP23	2-dr HT Cpe-6P	4627	4300	9,617
4P2	PP43	4-dr HT Sed-6P	4675	4370	8,191

SUBURBANS (V-8)

Series No.	Body/Style No.	Body Type & Seating	Factory Price	Shipping Weight	Prod. Total
4P2	PM45	4-dr Sta Wag-6P	4669	4745	2,490
4P2	PH45	4-dr Custom-6P	4767	4755	3,887
4P2	PH46	4-dr Custom-9P	4878	4800	5,628
4P2	PP45	4-dr Sport-6P	5025	4795	1,712
4P2	PP46	4-dr Sport-9P	5130	3850	6,047

ENGINES:

(Valiant/Duster Six) Inline. Overhead valve. Cast iron block. Displacement: 198 cid. Bore and stroke: 3.40 x 3.64 inches. Compression ratio: 8.4:1. SAE net hp: 95 at 4400 rpm. Four main bearings. Carburetor: one-barrel.

(Satellite Six) Inline. Overhead valve. Cast iron block. Displacement: 225 cid. Bore and stroke: 3.41 x 4.13 inches. Compression ratio: 8.4:1. SAE net hp: 105 at 4000 rpm. Four main bearings. Solid valve lifters. Carburetion: one-barrel.

(Barracuda/Duster/Valiant/Satellite/Road Runner V-8) Overhead valve. Cast iron block. Displacement: 318 cid. Bore and stroke: 3.91 x 3.31 inches. Compression ratio: 8.6:1. SAE net hp: 150 at 4000 rpm. Hydraulic valve lifters. Carburetion: two-barrel.

(Fury V-8) Overhead valve. Cast iron block. Displacement: 360 cid. Bore and stroke: 4.00 x 3.58 inches. Compression ratio: 8.4:1. SAE Net hp: 170. Five main bearings. Hydraulic valve lifters. Carburetor: two-barrel.

CHASSIS FEATURES: Wheelbase: (Valiant/Scamp) 111 inches; (Duster/Barracuda) 108 inches; (Satellite two-door) 115 inches; (Satellite four-door) 117 inches; (Fury I/Fury II) 120 inches; (Fury III/Gran Fury) 122 inches; (Fury Suburban) 124 inches. Overall length: (Valiant/Scamp) 197.6 inches; (Duster) 194.1 inches; (Barracuda) 195.6 inches; (Satellite two-door) 212.4 inches; (Satellite four-door) 208.9 inches; (Satellite station wagon) 217.1 inches; (Road Runner) 212.4 inches; (Sebring) 210.8 inches; (Fury I/Fury II) 223.4 inches; (Fury III/Gran Fury) 219.9 inches; (Suburban) 223.3 inches. Tires: See tire data in text.

OPTIONS: Air conditioning, Barracuda ($384); Fury ($406); Satellite ($398); Valiant ($384). Air conditioning, with automatic temperature control, Fury only ($484). Bumper guards, front and rear, Fury ($40); Satellite two-door ($17); Valiant ($31). Carpets, Valiant except Scamp ($18); Satellite/Road Runner/Fury I ($20). Electric clock, Barracuda ($17); Satellite ($19); Fury Group ($18). Digital electronic clock, Fury I/II/III ($40); Gran Fury/Suburban ($22). Console, bucket seats required, Road Runner/Sebring-Plus ($59). Console, bucket-seats required, Duster/Barracuda ($54). Front manual disc brakes, Valiant, except Duster 360 ($23). Engine block heater, Fury Group ($16). Gauges, temperature and oil pressure, Fury Group ($18). Tinted glass, all windows, Fury ($52); Satellite ($45); others ($37). Hood tie-down pins, Road Runner only ($17); Barracuda sport hood, standard with 'Cuda hardtop ($21). Left outside rearview mirror, remote control, Barracuda ($15); Satellite ($17). Remote-control dual outside rearview mirrors, Fury ($40). Performance hood paint treatment, Duster and '360' ($18). Hood and fender stripes, Road Runner only ($23). Duster lower deck stripes, standard Duster '360' ($13). Bodyside tape stripes, Barracuda ($29). Standard Duster ($26). Power front disc brakes, Valiant six ($66); Valiant V-8 ($43); Satellite ($46). Power door locks, two-door Fury ($49); four-door Fury ($75). Power steering, Valiant/Barracuda ($107); Satellite ($120). Power Six-Way bench seat, Fury Group ($108). Power left-hand bucket seat, Gran Coupe/Gran Sedan/Sport Wagon ($96). Power left-hand bucket seat, Fury III except Style PH23 ($96). Automatic locking tailgate, all station wagons ($28). Power windows, Satellite Group ($125); Fury Group ($31). Power tailgate window, Satellite station wagon ($36). AM/FM stereo radio, average price for all models ($202). AM/FM stereo radio with tape, average price for all Furys ($397). Vinyl top, compact-intermediate ($84-$99). Vinyl top, Fury Group, except station wagon ($112). Vinyl canopy top, Satellite two-door ($69); Duster ($63). Duster, vinyl trim bucket seats and carpets ($127). Vinyl trim split-bench seat with center armrest, Valiant Group ($78). Vinyl trim 50/50 split bench seat, Fury III four-door ($138). Cloth and vinyl bucket seat with center armrest, Sebring-Plus ($96). Security alarm system, Fury Group ($104). Automatic speed control, Fury and Satellite with TorqueFlite ($67). Tilt-A-Scope steering wheel, standard trim Fury ($92). 'Tuff' steering wheel, Valiant/Satellite/Road Runner Groups ($11-$31). Tachometer, Sebring-Plus/Road Runner ($54). Deluxe wheel covers ($26-$28). Premier-style wheel covers, Satellite ($51); Fury ($33-$61). Chrome styled Road Wheels, average price ($80). Rally Road Wheels, Valiant/Barracuda/Satellite, average price ($56). Manual vent windows, Fury Group four-doors ($35). Three-speed electric wipers and washers, Fury Group ($6-$11). Deluxe windshield wipers, Fury Group ($12). Code A06 Sebring 'Easy Order' package included AM radio; Light Group; power disc brakes; TorqueFlite; power steering; vinyl roof; left remote-control outside rearview mirror; whitewalls; three-speed wipers; station wagon luggage rack; Deluxe wheel covers; bright bumper guards; inside hood release and undercoating with hood pad at prices from $396 to $745. Salon package was available for

Fury III four-door models and the Custom Suburban after the middle of the year. It was priced at an average of $230. Three-speed manual transmission was standard in Valiant/Barracuda/Satellite Groups. Automatic transmission was standard in Fury Group; optional on others at various prices. Three-speed manual floor shift transmission optional in Valiant ($27). Four-speed manual floor shift transmission, optional ($195-$235). Valiant six-cylinder 225 cid/105 hp one-barrel engine ($39). Satellite V-8 360 cid/245 hp four-barrel engine ($86). Fury I/II/III V-8 360 cid/245 hp four-barrel engine ($39). Barracuda V-8 360 cid/245 hp four-barrel engine ($259). 'Cuda V-8 360 cid/245 hp four-barrel engine ($189). Road Runner V-8 360 cid/245 hp four-barrel engine ($161). Fury I/Satellite V-8 400 cid/205 hp four-barrel engine ($117). Fury I/II V-8 400 cid/205 hp four-barrel engine ($80). Gran Fury/Suburban V-8 400 cid/205 hp four-barrel ($39). Satellite coupe V-8 400 cid/250 hp four-barrel dual exhaust engine ($183). Road Runner V-8 400 cid/250 hp four-barrel dual exhaust engine ($127). Fury I/II/III V-8 440 cid/230 hp four-barrel engine ($156). Gran Fury/Suburban V-8 440 cid/230 hp four barrel engine ($115). Road Runner V-8 440 cid/275 hp four-barrel dual exhaust engine ($255). Satellite V-8 360 cid/180 hp two-barrel engine ($47). Positive traction rear axle, Fury Group ($50); Satellite ($47); Valiant/Barracuda ($43). Available rear axle gear ratios: 3.21:1, 3.23:1 ($13-$14 extra per Group).

HISTORICAL FOOTNOTES: The full-size Plymouths were introduced Sept. 25, 1973, and the Valiant line appeared in dealer showrooms the same day. Model year U.S. dealer sales peaked at 651,586 units. Calendar year production of 609,385 cars was recorded. R.K. Brown was the Group vice-president of U.S. sales this year. After a lapse of many years, Plymouth re-entered the commercial vehicle market with a line of van-type trucks bearing a new Voyager nameplate.

1975 PLYMOUTH

1975 Plymouth, Valiant Brougham four-door sedan, V-8

VALIANT GROUP — (6-CYL/V-8) — SERIES 5V — The Valiant lineup was expanded this year, and for good reason. One out of every four compact cars sold in 1974 was a member of Plymouth's Valiant Group. Improvements in styling and engineering details could be detected throughout the line. The Valiant Brougham returned and was the plushest edition yet. The popular Dusters and Scamps were carried over with minor revisions. On the technical side, several new items became available to buyers with increasing interest in fuel economy. Radial tires, a unique Fuel Pacer system, lower gear ratios and a lighter torque converter were designed specifically for gas savings. There were new 50,000-mile spark plugs and batteries and a 'Clincher' warranty that covered everything on the car except trim for 12 months with no mileage restrictions. Added to the former line of six sedans and coupes was a high-level Duster Custom sport coupe and Valiant Custom seda'n. The coupes were on the 108-inch wheelbase, with sedans and hardtops having a three-inch longer stance. The Duster 360 had an engine that matched the call-out part of its name, while other models offered, as base equipment, the '225' six or '318' V-8. Styling distinctions were limited to a new cross-hatched grille insert with stand-up Valiant identification badge in its center, a de-chromed wraparound taillight treatment on the Scamp-based bodies and, on the new Customs, full-length mid-body-side moldings, a wide selection of upholstery and seat designs, rocker sill moldings and loop-pile floor carpeting. Standard equipment for the carryover models followed the specifications outlined in the 1974 section, except for the Duster 360. This car again had heavy-duty suspension; special shock absorbers; front and rear sway bar and dual exhaust. But now it also featured a new rear panel and beltline tape stripe treatment and automatic transmission as standard equipment. The same tape stripes were optional on other Dusters and consisted of a thin, full-length stripe and a separate, wide upper rear fender tape panel.

PLYMOUTH I.D. NUMBERS: The Vehicle Identification Number is located on a plate attached to upper left-hand top of dash, viewable through windshield. First symbol indicates model: P=Gran Fury; R=Fury; V=Valiant. Second symbol indicates price class: L=low; M=medium; H=high; P=premium; S=special; K=police. Third and fourth symbols indicate

body style (first four symbols appear in Body/Style Number column of charts below). Fifth symbol indicates engine: C=225 cid/105 nhp six; E=special order six; G=318 cid 2V V-8; J=360 cid 4V V-8; K=360 cid 2V V-8; L=360 cid high-performance 4V V-8; M=400 cid 2V V-8; N=400 cid 4V V-8; P=400 cid/260 hp high-performance 4V V-8; T=440 cid/220 nhp 4V V-8; U=440 cid/280 4V TNT V-8; Z=special order V-8. The sixth symbol indicates model year: 5=1975. The seventh symbol indicates assembly plant: A=Lynch Rd., Detroit; B=Hamtramck, Mich.; C=Jefferson Ave., Detroit; D=Belvedere, Ill.; F=Newark, Del.; G=St. Louis, Mo.; and R=Windsor, Canada. The last six symbols are the production sequence number starting at 100001 at each factory.

VALIANT GROUP

VALIANT

Series No.	Body/Style No.	Body Type & Seating	Factory Price	Shipping Weight	Prod. Total
5V1/2	VL41	4-dr Sed-6P	3247/3369	3040/3185	44,471
5V1/2	VH41	4-dr Cus Sed-6P	3422/3544	3040/3185	56,258
5V1/2	VP41	4-dr Brgm Sed-6P	4139/4236	3250/3340	17,803

DUSTER

5V1/2	VL29	2-dr Cpe-6P	3243/3364	2970/3115	79,884
5V1/2	VH29	2-dr Cus Cpe-6P	3418/3539	2970/3115	38,826
5V2	VS29	2-dr '360' Cpe-6P	3979	3315	1,421

SCAMP

| 5V1/2 | VH23 | 2-dr HT Cpe-6P | 3518/3640 | 3020/3165 | 23,581 |
| 5V1/2 | VP23 | 2-dr Brgm HT-6P | 4232/4328 | 3240/3325 | 5,781 |

Note 1: Data above slash for six/below slash, no slash for V-8.

1975 Plymouth, Fury Sport two-door hardtop, V-8

FURY GROUP — (6-CYL/V-8) — SERIES 5R — For 1975, the intermediate-size Plymouths took the Fury name and the Satellite designation was dropped. (The standard-size models were then called Gran Furys.) The mid-size cars were completely redesigned, although the overall styling was still related to that seen previously on Satellites. The cars came on two different wheelbases. There were 115 inches between the hub centers of two-door hardtops and a 118-inch stance for sedans and station wagons. The only nameplate carried over from the past was Road Runner. This model was distinguished by a blacked-out grille treatment and a beltline tape stripe running from the front fender tip to the leading edge of the rear roof pillar and, from that point, up over the roof. The Road Runner came with heavy-duty suspension, dual exhaust and a choice of five V-8s ranging from the base 318-cid two-barrel version, to a 400-cid four-barrel high-output type. A unique new Road Runner option was a rear deck graphics decor package spelling the model name out boldly on back of the car. The appearance of the mid-size Furys was characterized by the use of large expanses of glass and a more tailored styling theme, which had some of the flair of Chrysler's new Cordoba. The two- and four-door models had the same look at the front, but used entirely different rear treatments. Two-door cars featured canted, vertical taillights and an angular center deck lid bulge with a trapezoid-shaped rear face that was mirrored in the bumper contours. Four-door cars had a Duster-like rear image, with a totally different bumper housing three-segment horizontal taillamps. The front end featured single headlights mounted in individual square bezels. The grille opening was of a round-cornered rectangular shape divided into 12 segments by vertical, bright metal bars. The outer segments housed vertical parking lamps and all of the segments were filled with a grid-patterned insert that, on Road Runners, was finished in black (bright-finished on other models). The bumper was a straight-across affair with integral bumper guards and no air slots or lower openings. A sleek, wrapover roof pillar treatment was seen on two-door models.

FURY GROUP

FURY CUSTOM/SPORT LINE

5R1/2	RL21	2-dr HT Cpe-6P	3542/3672	3555/3670	8,398
5R1/2	RH23	2-dr Cus HT-6P	3711/3840	3635/3750	27,486
5R2	RP23	2-dr Spt HT-6P	4105	3790	17,782
5R1/2	RL41	4-dr Sed-6P	3591/3720	3585/3685	11,432
5R1/2	RH41	4-dr Cus Sed-6P	3704/3834	3635/3750	31,080

Series No.	Body/Style No.	Body Type & Seating	Factory Price	Shipping Weight	Prod. Total

ROAD RUNNER LINE

| 5R2 | RM21 | 2-dr HT Cpe-6P | 3973 | 3760 | 7,183 |

SUBURBAN LINE

5R2	RL45	4-dr Sta Wag-6P	4309	4180	4,468
5R2	RH45	4-dr Cus Wag-6P	4512	4230	3,890
5R2	RH46	4-dr Cus Wag-9P	4632	4285	4,285
5R2	RP45	4-dr Spt Wag-6P	4770	4230	1,851
5R2	RP46	4-dr Spt Wag-9P	4867	4295	3,107

Note 1: Data above slash for six/below slash, no slash for V-8.

1975 Plymouth, Gran Fury Custom four-door hardtop, V-8

GRAN FURY GROUP — (V-8) — SERIES 5P — The Gran Fury designation that had formerly been used to identify two high-level offerings was now applied to all full-size Plymouths. The Gran Fury series supplied 111-inch wheelbase sedans and hardtops plus 124-inch wheelbase Suburban station wagons. At the top of the line were the Gran Fury Broughams and comparable Sport Suburbans. All of these cars used the same basic body with new grille and rear end treatments, which were different for each line. The Custom-style grilles and taillamps had only minor changes from the previous year. At the front, a horizontal center divider ran across the middle of the grille insert and carried an upright identification badge at its center. At the rear, the bumper guards were shorter and fatter. The standard Gran Fury had a bright metal mid-bodyside molding that was broken by the wheel opening contours. Custom models had a similar molding with color-keyed vinyl inserts, bright wheel lip opening trim and rocker sill moldings. Broughams had no side trim, except for cowlside signature script and rocker sill moldings, but featured a distinctive grille design. On the Brougham, single headlamps and vertical parking lamps were housed in a segmented rectangular surround with bright metal finish. The central grille insert was set in a separate round-cornered rectangular opening and had a square-grid pattern look. There was a stand-up hood ornament and Plymouth lettering across the lip of the hood. The front bumper was similar to the 1974 style, with slots on either side of the bumper guards allowing the grillework to show through. However, black vinyl protective strips were added. They moved, horizontally from below the headlamps to around the corners of the bumper. A formal roof treatment, complete with opera-style rear quarter windows, was standard on two-door Broughams. The standard engine for all Gran Furys was the '318' V-8, with options including the '360', '400' and '440' V-8s. Radial tires and wiper-mounted windshield washers were standard for Broughams. Other equipment variations between the various lines followed the pattern outlined for 1974 Plymouths, with standard models comparable to Fury II; Customs to Fury III and Broughams to the former Gran Coupe/Sedan.

GRAN FURY GROUP

GRAN FURY

5P2	PM41	4-dr Sed-6P	4565	4260	8,185
5P2	PH41	4-dr Cus Sed-6P	4761	4260	19,043
5P2	PH43	4-dr Cus HT Sed-6P	4837	4290	11,292
5P2	PH23	2-dr Cus HT Cpe-6P	4781	4205	6,041
5P2	PP29	2-dr Brgm HT Cpe-6P	5146	4310	6,521
5P2	PP43	4-dr Brgm HT Sed-6P	5067	4400	5,521

SUBURBANS

5P2	PM45	4-dr Sta Wag-6P	5067	4855	2,295
5P2	PH45	4-dr Cus Wag-6P	5176	4870	3,155
5P2	PH46	4-dr Cus Wag-9P	5294	4915	4,500
5P2	PP45	4-dr Spt Wag-6P	5455	4885	1,508
5P2	PP46	4-dr Spt Wag-9P	5573	4930	4,740

ENGINES:

(Valiant/Duster/Fury Six) Inline. Overhead valve. Cast iron block. Displacement: 225 cid. Bore and stroke: 3.40 x 4.12 inches. SAE Net hp: 95. Four main bearings. Solid valve lifters. Carburetor: one-barrel.

(Valiant/Duster/Fury/Road Runner V-8) Overhead valve. Cast iron block. Displacement: 318 cid. Bore and stroke: 3.91 x 3.31 inches. SAE Net hp: 145. Five main bearings. Hydraulic valve lifters. Carburetor: two-barrel.

(Duster '360' V-8) Overhead valve. Cast iron block. Displacement: 360 cid. Bore and stroke: 4.00 x 3.58 inches. SAE Net hp: 230. Five main bearings. Hydraulic valve lifters. Carburetor: four-barrel.

(Gran Fury/Custom V-8) Overhead valve. Cast iron block. Displacement: 360 cid. Bore and stroke: 4.00 x 3.58 inches. SAE Net hp: 180. Five main bearings. Hydraulic valve lifters. Carburetor: two-barrel.

(Suburban/Brougham V-8) Overhead valve. Cast iron block. Displacement: 400 cid. Bore and stroke: 4.34 x 3.38 inches. SAE Net hp: 175. Five main bearings. Hydraulic valve lifters. Carburetor: two-barrel.

CHASSIS FEATURES: Wheelbase: (Valiant Group sedan/hardtop) 111 inches; (Duster coupe) 108 inches; (Fury two-door) 115 inches; (Fury four-door/station wagon) 117.5 inches; (Road Runner) 115 inches; (Gran Fury Suburban) 124 inches; (Gran Fury passenger car) 121.5 inches. Overall length: (Valiant/Scamp) 200 inches; (Duster) 197 inches; (Fury two-door) 213.8 inches; (Fury four-door) 217.9 inches; (Road Runner) 213.8 inches; (Gran Fury Suburban) 219.9 inches; (Gran Fury passenger car) 223.3 inches. Tires: (Valiant Group coupe) 6.95 x 14; (other Valiants) D78-14; (Road Runner) G70-14; (Fury station wagon) H78-14; (other Furys) F78-14; (Gran Fury station wagon) LR78-15; (Brougham) HR78-15; (other Gran Furys) GR78-15.

OPTIONS: [VALIANT] Bucket seats ($83). Gold Duster package ($181). Electric rear window defroster ($67). Tinted glass, all windows ($44). Power disc brakes, average price ($65). Duster 'Decorator Special' package ($272). Power steering, standard in Valiant Brougham. Power brakes, standard on Duster 360. Factory air conditioning ($407). [FURY] Exterior Decor package ($116). Electric rear window defroster ($73). Power disc brakes, standard on station wagon, other models ($58). Station wagon luggage rack ($67). Sun roof ($296). AM/FM stereo with tape ($397). Power windows ($138). Power bench seats ($117). AM/FM stereo ($254). Salon package ($230). Exterior Decor package ($116). Electric rear window defroster ($73). Power disc brakes, standard on station wagon, other models ($58). Station wagon luggage rack ($67). Sun roof ($296). AM/FM stereo with tape ($397). Power windows ($138). Power bench seats ($117). AM/FM stereo ($254). [GRAN FURY] Reclining seat with special interior trim ($174). Sure-Grip axle ($52). Electric rear window defroster ($73). Security Alarm system ($112). Station wagon luggage rack ($79). Sun roof ($634). Automatic height control ($99). Vinyl top ($117). AM/FM stereo with tape ($397). Power seats ($117). AM/FM stereo ($254). Power brakes (standard). TorqueFlite automatic transmission was standard on all Gran Furys, mid-size Fury station wagons, Valiant Broughams and the Duster 360. Three-speed manual transmission was standard with all other models in base trim. The 360 cid/230 hp V-8 with four-barrel carburetor was optional in the Valiant Group. A 360 cid/180 hp V-8 was optional in mid-size Furys. A 360 cid/200 hp V-8 was also optional in mid-size Furys. A 318 cid/135 hp economy V-8 was also optional in mid-size Furys (the 318 cid/145 hp V-8 was standard). Four versions of the 400-cid V-8 with 175, 185, 190, or 235 net hp were also available in specific mid-size Furys. The standard Gran Fury/Custom V-8 was optional in Broughams and Suburbans, while the standard Brougham Suburban V-8 was optional in Gran Fury/Custom models. Also available in specific applications were a 360 cid/190 hp V-8 and 400 cid/200 hp V-8. Other options for full-size cars included a 400 cid/175 hp V-8 and a 440 cid/215 hp V-8. In some cases, a certain engine may have superseded another during the model year. In different cases, certain engines were available only in federally certified cars; others only in cars certified for sale in the state of California or designated high-altitude counties. The 360-cid four-barrel V-8 was a $202 option in Road Runners and Furys. The 400-cid two-barrel V-8 was a $93 option in Furys. The 400-cid two-barrel V-8 was a $44 option in Gran Furys. The 400-cid four-barrel V-8 was a $122 option in Furys. The 400-cid four-barrel V-8 was an $84 option in Gran Furys. These are the only prices available for 1975 Plymouths.

HISTORICAL FOOTNOTES: The full-size Plymouths were introduced Oct. 1, 1974, and the compact line appeared in dealer showrooms the same day. Model year dealer sales peaked at 403,169 units. Calendar year production of 447,403 cars was recorded. R.B. McCurry, Jr. was the Group vice-president for U.S. Automotive Sales at Chrysler-Plymouth Division this year. In mid-model year the Plymouth Arrow, a car built in Japan by Mitsubishi Industries, was added to the product line as an imported subcompact model.

1976 PLYMOUTH

Plymouth's lineup for 1976 included compact Valiants and Volares, the mid-size Fury, and full-size Gran Fury. This would be the final year for the Valiant group (which included Duster and Scamp), as the new Volare prepared to take over their spot. The familiar 225 cubic inch Slant Six

engine was standard on all except Gran Fury, with a selection of optional V-8s available. The big 400 and 440 cubic inch V-8s had Chrysler's Electronic Lean Burn System. Its mini-computer gathered data from sensors on throttle position, engine rpm, manifold vacuum and coolant temperature, and adjusted ignition timing for the leanest (most economical) air/fuel mixture.

1976 Plymouth, Feather Duster coupe (factory lightweight with aluminum components) (OCW)

1976 Plymouth, Duster custom coupe (OCW)

VALIANT/DUSTER/SCAMP — SERIES V — SIX/V-8 — Like the closely related Dodge Dart series, Valiant reached back to 1960 origin. For its final year, Plymouth's compact lineup included the Duster hardtop (semi-fastback) coupe on a 108 inch wheelbase, plus a Scamp hardtop and Valiant sedan on 111 inch wheelbases. The wide-look front end had a grille made up of many wide crosshatch elements, which stretched the full width between single round headlamps in squarish housings. Slightly rounded rectangular park/signal lamps sat in the grille insert. The center portion of that grille insert protruded forward slightly, and had a vertical rectangular emblem in the middle. On the thicker center portion of the upper header bar was 'Plymouth' block lettering. Duster's clean-look rear end held horizontal rectangular taillamps that reached to the quarter panel tips, surrounded by bright moldings and with a thin horizontal divider across each housing. Backup lenses were at the inner ends of each taillamp housing. Duster's bodyside sloped upward to the rear of the door, giving the quarter windows a tapered look. Scamp had a different back end appearance, with horizontal taillamps that wrapped slightly around the quarter panels and contained a horizontal divider bar. A sizable bright trim strip containing 'Plymouth' block letters on a darker panel ran between the taillamps. Scamp's side view was also different, with triangular, older-style quarter windows. The Valiant series offered torsion-bar front suspension, electric choke assist, hubcaps, fuel and temperature gauges, an ammeter, dome lamp switch, and unibody construction. V-8 models had front disc brakes; sixes kept drum brakes all around. V-8s also had front bumper guards. Duster had swing-out rear quarter windows; Scamp's were the roll-down type. Valiant sedans included vent windows. Duster held five passengers on standard cloth/vinyl bench seats. Valiant's base model could add a Custom or Brougham trim package. Brougham added such touches as simulated woodgrain inserts on the instrument panel, day/night mirror, and velour upholstery. Brougham packages were installed on 5.8 percent of hardtop and sedan models. Base engine was the old familiar 225 cubic inch Slant Six. A 318 cubic inch V-8 was optional. So was a 360 cubic inch V-8 (except in California), available only with TorqueFlite automatic transmission. Plymouth engines now had electronic ignition. Three-speed manual shift was standard, with four-speed overdrive optional. Body colors were: Powder Blue, Rallye Red, Sahara Beige, Yellow Blaze, Golden Fawn, Spinnaker White, and Formal Black; plus metallic Silver Cloud, Jamaican Blue, Vintage Red, Jade Green, Deep Sherwood, Caramel Tan, Cinnamon, Inca Gold, or Spanish Gold. A SpaceMaker option allowed the rear seat to fold down. Also among the options was a Fuel Pacer System, designed to conserve fuel. An optional Silver Duster decor package included unique bodyside stripes that twisted upward at the rear to meet the taillamps, and another stripe between the taillamp housings. It also included wheel moldings and a red interior. The Feather Duster fuel economy package turned to lightweight aluminum components, including the intake manifold, hood and deck inner panels, as well as economy (long) axle ratios. The overdrive

manual gearbox was mounted in an aluminum case. More than 22 percent of Duster coupes had the Feather Duster package, which had a limited option list. Scamp's Special was also aimed at economy buyers. Base Scamps had all-vinyl bench seating. Scamp Brougham went the other direction with velour cloth/vinyl upholstery, woodgrain instrument panel inserts, a hood ornament, wide sill moldings, and hood/deck accent stripes.

1976 Plymouth, Volare station wagon with optional roof rack and air deflector (OCW)

1976 Plymouth, Volare Premier coupe with optional wire wheel covers (OCW)

VOLARE — SERIES H — SIX/V-8 — Introduced this year as a replacement for the doomed Valiant, Volare was billed as "the new small car with the accent on comfort." Like the similar F-bodied Dodge Aspen, it debuted at mid-year. Base, Custom and top-rung Premier models were offered. Two-door coupes rode a 108.5 inch wheelbase, while four-door sedans and four-door station wagons measured 112.5 inches. Volare had a new Isolated Transverse Suspension System, with transverse-mounted front torsion bars and anti-sway bar, separated from the chassis by two sets of rubber mounts. This system of crosswise torsion bars (rather than the usual longitudinal mounting) was claimed to give a "big-car ride." Base engine was the 225 cubic inch Slant Six; 318 or 360 cubic inch V-8 optional, with TorqueFlite transmission. Overdrive four-speed manual shift also was available, instead of the standard three-speed. All Volares had standard front disc brakes; wagons and V-8s had power brakes. Volare's grille consisted of tiny squares arranged in three rows, divided by a vertical center bar. Single round headlamps sat in recessed square housings. Unusually large, clear park/signal lamps were recessed between the grille and headlamps. Volare's hood was higher in the center to match the grille width, sloping downward at the sides to meet the signal lamps. 'Volare' script was on front fenders, ahead of the door. Small horizontal amber side marker lenses stood on front fenders, near the headlamps. A horizontal strip divided each rectangular taillamp into upper and lower segments. A trim panel of the same height as the taillamps stretched between them. Backup lenses were at the inner end of each taillamp housing. Standard two-door Volares had large triangular quarter windows. A Landau vinyl roof, standard on Volare Premier, included square-look opera windows. Wagons had a large one-piece liftgate. Standard equipment included drip moldings, quarter-window reveal moldings, heater/defroster, and dome light. Volare Custom added a cigarette lighter, woodgrain instrument cluster trim, pleated vinyl or cloth/vinyl bench seats, rear deck lower appliqué, belt molding, B-pillar molding (on coupes), bodyside and partial wheel lip moldings, and rear armrests. Volare Premier added TorqueFlite, power steering, day/night mirror, electric clock, dual horns, locking glove box, color-keyed vinyl insert bodyside moldings, bodyside accent tape stripes, hood ornament and accent stripe, premium wheel covers, and a carpeted trunk. Inside was a 60/40 split bench seat with dual reclining seatbacks, carpeted lower door panels, door pull-handles, and luxury three-spoke steering wheel. Premier coupes had a landau vinyl roof; sedans had a full vinyl roof, Premier wagons had standard woodgrain bodyside appliqués. Body colors for Volare were: Big Sky Blue, Spitfire Orange, Claret Red, Sahara Beige, Saddle Tan, Harvest Gold, Spinnaker

White, and Formal Black. Metallic colors were: Silver Cloud, Jamaican Blue, Jade or Tropic Green, Deep Sherwood, Caramel Tan, Cinnamon, and Spanish Gold. Two-tone combinations arranged the colors in a way that looked almost like a three-tone. Performance-minded buyers could select a Volare Road Runner coupe package (like Dodge's Aspen R/T), which included a 318 cubic inch V-8, heavy-duty suspension, three-speed floor shift, and sporty interior trim. A hefty 83.8 percent of the 8,769 HL29 Volares with V-8 engine had the Road Runner package (code A57), while 21.7 percent carried the A66 Super Pak.

1976 Plymouth, Fury Sport hardtop with optional canopy vinyl roof and styled road wheels (OCW)

1976 Plymouth, Gran Fury Brougham hardtop with optional canopy vinyl roof and opera windows (OCW)

FURY — SERIES R — SIX/V-8 — Restyled for 1975, Plymouth's mid-size (descended from the old Satellite) entered this year with little change. The model lineup included a base two-door hardtop (true pillarless design) and four-door sedan; Salon four-door; Sport two-door hardtop; plus Suburban and Sport Suburban station wagons. Fury was closely related to Dodge's Coronet and Charger. The Road Runner performance package was announced again as a Fury option, but that name went on a Volare variant instead. Fury coupes rode a 115 inch wheelbase, while sedans and wagons measured 117.5 inches between hubs. Fury's grille consisted of many thin vertical bars, separated into a dozen sections by 11 dominant vertical dividers. Outer sections actually contained the parking lamps. Single round headlamps in squarish housings sat farther back than the grille. 'Plymouth' lettering was above the grille on the driver's side. Front fenders held 'Fury' script, just ahead of the door. Just inside the quarter panel tips of base and Sport Fury two-door models were vertical taillamps, surrounded by bright moldings, angled slightly inward. The triple-crease decklid had a sculptured look and 'Plymouth' block lettering. A recessed license plate housing extended into the bumper and lower decklid. Fury sedans had a different rear end, with large tri-section horizontal taillamps inset into the bumper. The license plate was deeply recessed in a housing built entirely into the bumper. Salon's decklid also had only a single crease running down its center, plus 'Plymouth' block lettering. On the decklid's side was a small 'Salon' script. A velour/vinyl seat with folding center armrest was standard on Salon, as was a hood ornament. The Fury Sport two-door hardtop was not a 'true' hardtop, but displayed opera windows. It had standard tape stripes and styled wheels, plus a standard 318 cubic inch V-8 engine. All-vinyl bucket seats with folding center armrest were a no-cost option to replace the standard velour split-back seating. The soft-touch steering wheel was new this year. Fury Sport could have optional louvered quarter windows with a canopy vinyl roof. Actually, that simply meant it had two skinny side-by-side opera window openings instead of one, in a design obviously meant for appearance rather than visibility. Base engine was the 225 cubic inch Slant Six. Optional: 318, 360 and 400 cubic inch V-8s. Wagons came with a standard 360 V-8 and automatic transmission, plus power steering and brakes. Standard equipment on the base Fury included hubcaps, F78x14 blackwall tires (H78x14 on wagons), front and rear armrests, sill moldings, decklid lower molding, dome light, lighter, heater/defroster, Torsion-Bar suspension with anti-sway bar, three-speed fully synchronized transmission (column shift), tuned exhaust system, and locking glovebox. Sedans and wagons had rear bumper guards. Fury Sport added deluxe wheel covers, dual horns, bodyside stripes, a bench seat with center armrest, premium door trim panels with pull handles, hood rear edge molding, hood ornament, and 'Sport' name on the C-pillar. Fury Salon added the hood ornament, Salon nameplate and crest, deluxe wheel covers, velour split-seat with center armrest, dual horns, and luxury door trim panels with pull handles. Newly introduced this year was 60/40 split-bench seating with dual reclining seatbacks.

GRAN FURY — SERIES P — V-8 — Full-size Plymouths changed little this year, except for a revised grille and parking lamp treatment. Dodge's Monaco was its near twin. The grille insert's crosshatch pattern was divided into four rows by three dominant horizontal dividers, each with 14 "holes" across and peaked forward at the center. Separate, large 'Plymouth' block letters stood above the grille, on the panel ahead of the hood. Vertical rectangular parking/signal lamps were between the grille and single round headlamps, mounted in square housings. A single bright molding surrounded both headlamps and parking lamps. Twin slots were in the front bumper, outboard of the bumper guards. Gran Fury came in base, Custom, or Brougham trim. Suburban wagons rode a 124 inch wheelbase, while the coupe and sedan measured 121.5 inches. A 318 cubic inch V-8 was standard on the base sedan (available at no cost on others); Customs had a 360 cubic inch V-8; and Broughams a 400 V-8. Both 400 and 440 cubic inch V-8 engines were offered as options. Standard equipment also included TorqueFlite automatic transmission, power brakes and steering, and heater/defroster. Broughams and Sport Suburbans had an electric clock and deluxe wheel covers. Wagons had a two-way tailgate and (optional) rear-facing third seat. Standard tires were G78x15 blackwalls; GR78x15 steel-belted radials on Brougham; LR78x15 steel-belted radials on Sport Suburban. The unibodied Gran Fury was lighter in weight than full-size Fords and Chevrolets, both of which used separate body/frame construction.

1976 Plymouth, Volare Premier sedan (OCW)

I.D. DATA: Plymouth's 13-symbol Vehicle Identification Number (VIN) was on the upper left corner of the instrument panel, visible through the windshield. Symbol one indicates car line: 'V' Valiant; 'H' Volare; 'R' Fury; 'P' Gran Fury. Symbol two is series (price class): 'L' low; 'M' medium; 'H' high; 'P' premium. Symbols 3-4 show body type: '23' 2-dr. hardtop coupe; '29' 2-dr. special coupe; '41' 4-dr. sedan; '45' two-seat station wagon; '46' three-seat wagon. Symbol five is the engine code: 'C' L6225; 'G' V8318; 'K' V8360 2Bbl.; 'J' V8360 4Bbl.; 'L' Hi-perf. V8360 4Bbl.; 'M' V8400 2Bbl.; 'N' V8400 4Bbl.; 'P' Hi-perf. V8400 4Bbl.; 'T' V8440 4Bbl. Symbol six is the model year code: '6' 1976. Symbol seven indicates assembly plant: 'A' Lynch Road; 'B' Hamtramck, MI; 'C' Jefferson; 'D' Belvidere, IL; 'F' Newark, DE; 'G' St. Louis. The final six digits make up the sequential serial number, starting with 100001. An abbreviated version of the VIN is also stamped on a pad on the engine block: below No. 6 spark plug on six-cylinder engines, and to rear of right engine mount on V-8s. Serial numbers for 318 and 360 cubic inch V-8s are coded as follows: first letter, series (model year); second, assembly plant; next three digits, displacement (cubic inch); next one or two letters model; next four digits show build date; and final four digits are the engine sequence number. Coding of other engines is: first letter, series (model year); next three digits, displacement; next one or two letters, model; next four digits, build date; and the final digit reveals the shift on which the engine was built. Information on over/undersized parts is stamped on six-cylinder engines on the joint face at right corner, adjacent to No. 1 cylinder; on 318/360 V-8s, at left front of block just below the head; on 400 V-8, just ahead of No. 2 cylinder, next to distributor; and on 440 V-8, on left bank pad adjacent to front tappet rail. A Vehicle Safety Certification Label that displays (among other data) the date of manufacture is attached to the rear facing of the driver's door. A Body Code Plate is on the left front fender side shield, wheel housing, or left side of upper radiator support.

Model No.	Body/ Style No.	Body Type & Seating	Factory Price	Shipping Weight	Prod. Total
VALIANT (SIX/V-8)					
VL	41	4-dr. Sedan-6P	3251/3388	3050/----	32,901
(VALIANT) SCAMP (SIX/V-8)					
VH	23	2-dr. HT Cpe-6P	3485/3622	3020/----	5,147
VL	23	2-dr. Spec HT-6P	3312/3449	3020/----	3,308
(VALIANT) DUSTER (SIX/V-8)					
VL	29	2-dr. Spt Cpe-5P	3216/3353	2975/----	26,688
VOLARE (SIX/V-8)					
HL	29	2-dr. Spt Cpe-5P	3324/3489	3160/3285	30,191
HL	41	4-dr. Sedan-6P	3359/3524	3190/3315	19,186
HL	45	4-dr. Sta Wag-6P	3646/3759	3560/3650	40,497

Model No.	Body/ Style No.	Body Type & Seating	Factory Price	Shipping Weight	Prod. Total
VOLARE CUSTOM (SIX/V-8)					
HH	29	2-dr. Spt Cpe-5P	3506/3671	3170/3295	27,656
HH	41	4-dr. Sedan-6P	3541/3706	3200/3325	32,765
VOLARE PREMIER (SIX/V-8)					
HP	29	2-dr. Spt Cpe-5P	4402/4515	3375/3490	27,442
HP	41	4-dr. Sedan-6P	4389/4502	3410/3530	33,080
HH	45	4-dr. Sta Wag-6P	3976/4210	3565/3695	44,191
FURY (SIX/V-8)					
RL	23	2-dr. HT Cpe-6P	3629/3867	3590/3830	11,341
RL	41	4-dr. Sedan-6P	3663/3901	3625/3860	18,006
RL	45	4-dr. 2S Wag-6P	----/4588	----/4285	3,765
RL	46	4-dr. 3S Wag-9P	----/4730	----/4350	3,810
FURY SPORT/SUBURBAN (SIX/V-8)					
RH	23	2-dr. HT Cpe-6P	3918/4156	3595/3835	23,312
RH	41	4-dr. Salon Sed-6P	3952/4109	3645/3875	16,768
RH	45	4-dr. 2S Wag-6P	----/4977	----/4285	1,567
RH	46	4-dr. 3S Wag-9P	----/5119	----/4360	3,143
GRAN FURY (V-8)					
PM	41	4-dr. Sedan-6P	4349	4140	5,560
PM	45	4-dr. 2S Wag-6P	4909	4880	1,046
GRAN FURY CUSTOM/SUBURBAN (V-8)					
PH	23	2-dr. HT Cpe-6P	4730	4265	1,513
PH	41	4-dr. Sedan-6P	4715	4305	12,088
PH	45	4-dr. 2S Wag-6P	5193	4895	1,018
PH	46	4-dr. 3S Wag-9P	5316	4940	1,700
GRAN FURY BROUGHAM (V-8)					
PP	29	2-dr. HT Cpe-6P	5334	4400	1,823
PP	41	4-dr. Sedan-6P	5162	4435	1,869
GRAN FURY SPORT SUBURBAN (V-8)					
PP	46	4-dr. 3S Wag-9P	5761	4975	1,794

Factory Price And Weight Note: Prices and weights to left of slash are for six-cylinder, to right for V-8 engine.

Production Note: In addition to totals shown, 4,427 Fury and 7,953 Gran Fury police four-door sedans were shipped this year.

ENGINE DATA: BASE SIX (Valiant/Scamp/Duster, Volare, Fury): Inline, overhead valve six-cylinder. Cast iron block and head. Displacement: 225 cu. in. (3.7-liters). Bore & stroke: 3.40 x 4.12 in. Compression ratio: 8.4:1. Brake horsepower: 100 at 3600 R.P.M. Torque: 170 lb.-ft. at 1600 R.P.M. Four main bearings. Solid valve lifters. Carburetor: 1 Bbl. Holley 1945 (R7356A). VIN Code: C. BASE V-8 (Gran Fury): OPTIONAL (all others): 90-degree, overhead valve V-8. Cast iron block and head. Displacement: 318 cu. in. (5.2-liters). Bore & stroke: 3.91 x 3.31 in. Compression ratio: 8.5:1. Brake horsepower: 150 at 4000 R.P.M. Torque: 255 lb.-ft. at 1600 R.P.M. Five main bearings. Hydraulic valve lifters. Carburetor: 2Bbl. Carter BBD 8068S or 8069S. VIN Code: G. BASE V-8 (Fury wagon, Gran Fury Custom); OPTIONAL (Volare, Fury, base Gran Fury): 90-degree, overhead valve V-8. Cast iron block and head. Displacement: 360 cu. in. (5.9-liters). Bore & stroke: 4.00 x 3.58 in. Compression ratio: 8.4:1. Brake horsepower: 170 at 4000 R.P.M. Torque: 280 lb.-ft. at 2400 R.P.M. Five main bearings. Hydraulic valve lifters. Carburetor: 2Bbl. Holley 2245 (R7364A). VIN Code: K. OPTIONAL V-8 (Valiant/Duster/Scamp): Same as 360 cu. in. V-8 above, but with Carter TQ9002S 4Bbl. carburetor. Horsepower: 220 at 4400 R.P.M. Torque: 280 lb.-ft. at 3200 R.P.M. VIN Code: L. BASE V-8 (Fury/Gran Fury wagon, Gran Fury Brougham); OPTIONAL (Fury, Gran Fury): 90-degree, overhead valve V-8. Cast iron block and head. Displacement: 400 cu. in. (6.6-liters). Bore & stroke: 4.34 x 3.38 in. Compression ratio: 8.2:1. Brake horsepower: 175 at 4000 R.P.M. Torque: 300 lb.-ft. at 2400 R.P.M. Five main bearings. Hydraulic valve lifters. Carburetor: 2Bbl. Holley 2245 (R7366A). VIN Code: M. OPTIONAL V-8 (Gran Fury): Same as 400 cu. in. V-8 above, but with Carter TQ9064S 4Bbl. carburetor. Horsepower: 210 at 4400 R.P.M. Torque: 305 lb.-ft. at 3200 R.P.M. VIN Code: N. OPTIONAL V-8 (Fury): Same as 400 cu. in. V-8 above, but with Carter TQ9054S 4Bbl. carburetor. Horsepower: 240 at 4400 R.P.M. Torque: 325 lb.-ft. at 3200 R.P.M. VIN Code: P. OPTIONAL V-8 (Gran Fury): 90-degree, overhead valve V-8. Cast iron block and head. Displacement: 440 cu. in. (7.2-liters). Bore & stroke: 4.32 x 3.75 in. Compression ratio: 8.2:1. Brake horsepower: 205 at 3600 R.P.M. Torque: 320 lb.-ft. at 2000 R.P.M. Five main bearings. Hydraulic valve lifters. Carburetor: 4Bbl. Carter TQ9058S. VIN Code: T.

CHASSIS DATA: Wheelbase: (Duster) 108.0 in.; (Volare cpe) 108.5 in.; (Valiant/Scamp) 111.0 in.; (Volare sed/wag) 112.5 in.; (Fury cpe) 115.0 in.; (Fury sed/wag) 117.5 in.; (Gran Fury) 121.5 in.; (Gran Fury wag) 124.0 in. Overall length: (Duster) 197.0 in.; (Volare cpe) 197.5 in.; (Valiant/Scamp) 199.6 in.; (Volare sed/wag) 201.5 in.; (Fury cpe) 213.7 in.; (Fury sed) 218.4 in.; (Fury wag) 224.2 in.; (Gran Fury) 222.4 in.; (Gran Fury wag) 226.4 in. Height: (Duster) 53.4 in.; (Valiant) 54.0 in.; (Scamp) 53.0 in.; (Volare cpe) 53.1 in.; (Volare sed/wag) 54.8 in.; (Fury

cpe) 52.6 in.; (Fury sed) 53.9 in.; (Fury wag) 56.5 in.; (Gran Fury cpe) 54.1 in.; (Gran Fury sed) 54.8 in.; (Fury wag) 57.6 in. Width: (Duster) 71.7 in.; (Valiant/Scamp) 71.0 in.; (Volare) 72.8 in.; (Fury) 77.7 in.; (Fury wag) 78.8 in.; (Gran Fury) 79.8 in.; (Gran Fury wag) 79.4 in. Front Tread: (Valiant) 59.2 in.; (Volare) 60.0 in.; (Fury) 61.9 in.; (Gran Fury) 64.0 in. Rear Tread: (Valiant) 55.6 in.; (Volare) 58.5 in.; (Fury) 62.0 in. exc. wag, 63.4 in. (Gran Fury) 63.4 in. Standard Tires: (Valiant six) 6.95x14 BSW; (Valiant V8318) D78x14 BSW; (Valiant V8360) E70x14 BSW; (Volare) D78x14, E78x14 or F78x14 BSW; (Fury) F78x14 or G78x14 BSW; (Fury wag) H78x14 BSW; (Gran Fury) GR78x15 exc. Brghm, HR78x15 and wagon, LR78x15.

TECHNICAL: Transmission: Three-speed manual transmission (column or floor shift) standard on all except Gran Fury. Gear ratios: (1st) 3.08:1; (2nd) 1.70:1; (3rd) 1.00:1; (Rev) 2.90:1, except Valiant six: (1st) 2.99:1; (2nd) 1.75:1; (3rd) 1.00:1; (Rev) 3.17:1. Four-speed overdrive available on Valiant/Volare: (1st) 3.09:1; (2nd) 1.67:1; (3rd) 1.00:1; (4th) 0.73:1; (Rev) 3.00:1. Three-speed automatic standard on Gran Fury (column shift), optional on others (column or floor lever). Gear ratios: (1st) 2.45:1; (2nd) 1.45:1; (3rd) 1.00:1; (Rev) 2.22:1. Standard final drive ratio: (Valiant/Duster six) 3.21:1 exc. 2.76:1 w/auto.; (Valiant/Duster V-8) 2.45:1 w/3spd, 2.94:1 w/4spd, 2.45:1 or 2.76:1 w/auto., 2.94:1 w/V8360; (Volare six) 3.23:1 w/3spd, 3.21:1 w/4spd, 2.71:1 w/auto.; (Volare V-8) 2.45:1 w/3spd, 2.94:1 w/4spd, 2.45:1 w/auto.; (Volare V8360) 2.76:1; (Fury) 2.94:1 exc. 3.21:1 w/six and 3spd, 2.71:1 w/V-8 and auto.; (Gran Fury) 2.71:1. Steering: Recirculating ball. Suspension: (Volare) isolated transverse front torsion bars, semi-elliptic rear leaf springs; (others) longitudinal front torsion bars, semi-elliptic rear leaf springs; front anti-sway bar on all except Valiant. Brakes: Front disc, rear drum except Valiant six, front/rear drum. Ignition: Electronic. Body construction: (Valiant/Duster/Volare/Fury) unibody; (Gran Fury) unibody w/auxiliary front frame. Fuel tank: (Valiant) 16 gal.; (Volare) 18 gal.; (Fury) 25.5 gal. exc. 20.5 gal. on wagons and six-cyl. models; (Gran Fury) 26.5 gal. exc. wagon, 24 gal.

DRIVETRAIN OPTIONS: Engines: 318 cu. in., 2Bbl. V-8: Gran Fury (NC). 360 cu. in., 2Bbl. V-8: Volare ($50); Fury ($54); base Gran Fury sedan ($55). 360 cu. in., 4Bbl. V-8: Fury ($99); Fury wag ($45); base Gran Fury ($100); Gran Fury Cust ($45). 360 cu. in., 4Bbl. V-8 w/dual exhaust: Duster ($392). 400 cu. in., 2Bbl. V-8: Fury ($102); Fury wag ($48); base Gran Fury ($104); Gran Fury Cust ($49). 400 cu. in., 4Bbl. V-8: Fury ($147); Fury wag ($93); base Gran Fury ($149); Gran Fury Cust ($94); Gran Fury Brghm, wag ($45). 400 cu. in., 4Bbl. V-8 w/dual exhaust: Fury ($198); Fury wag ($144). 440 cu. in., 4Bbl. V-8: base Gran Fury ($273); Gran Fury Cust ($218); Gran Fury Brghm, wag ($169). Transmission/Differential: TorqueFlite: Valiant/Scamp/Duster/Volare ($250); Fury ($273). Four-speed manual trans. w/floor lever: Valiant/Scamp/Duster/Volare ($127). Three-speed floor shifter: Valiant/Scamp/Duster/Volare ($28). Sure grip differential: Valiant/Scamp/Duster/Volare ($49); Fury ($54); Gran Fury ($58). Optional axle ratio: Valiant/Scamp/Duster/Volare ($13); Fury ($15). Gran Fury 3.21:1 axle ratio ($15); 2.45:1 (NC). Power Accessories: Power steering: Valiant/Scamp/Duster/Volare ($131); Fury ($143). Power brakes: Valiant/Scamp/Duster/Volare/Fury ($56-$81). Front disc brakes (manual): Valiant/Scamp/Duster six ($25). Suspension: H.D. susp.: Valiant/Scamp/Duster/Volare ($9-$25); Fury ($25); Gran Fury ($18-$25). Automatic height control: Gran Fury ($100). H.D. shock absorbers: Fury/Gran Fury ($7). Front sway bar: Valiant/Scamp/Duster ($14). Other: Trailer towing pkg.: Valiant/Scamp/Duster/Volare ($68). Fury trailer towing pkg.: light ($74); heavy ($298). Gran Fury trailer towing pkg.: light ($75); heavy ($302). Fuel pacer system: Valiant/Scamp/Duster/Volare ($19-$34). Long-life battery: Valiant/Scamp/Duster/Volare ($27); Fury ($29); Gran Fury ($30). California emission system: Valiant/Scamp/Duster/Volare ($53); Fury ($58).

VALIANT/SCAMP/DUSTER CONVENIENCE/APPEARANCE OPTIONS: Option Packages: Silver Duster trim pkg.: Duster ($178). Feather Duster pkg.: Duster ($51). Brougham pkg.: Scamp ($291); Valiant ($438). Easy-order pkg. ($698-$772). SpaceMaker pkg.: Duster ($104). Custom pkg.: Valiant ($176-$218). Radial tire roadability pkg. ($17). Exterior decor group: Duster ($84). Interior decor group: Duster ($92). Light pkg. ($33). Deluxe insulation pkg. ($23-$65). Protection group: Valiant ($22-$27). Comfort/Convenience: Air cond. ($431). Rear defroger, blower-type ($41); electric ($74). Tinted glass ($44). Tinted windshield ($35). Luxury steering wheel ($15-$26). Tuff steering wheel ($7-$33). Inside hood release ($11). Three-speed wipers ($8). Lighter ($6). Glovebox lock ($4). Locking gas cap ($6). Horns and Mirrors: Dual horns ($6). Remote driver's mirror ($14). Dual chrome sport mirrors, left remote: Duster ($15-$29). Day/night mirror ($7). Entertainment: AM radio ($72). AM/FM radio ($65-$137). Rear speaker ($20). Exterior Trim: Manual sunroof: Duster ($186). Full Vinyl roof ($17-$92). Canopy vinyl roof: Duster ($76). Vinyl bodyside molding ($18-$37). Bodyside tape stripe: Duster ($32). Bumper guards, front/rear: six-cyl. ($35). Bumper guards, rear: V-8 ($17). Door edge protectors ($7-$11). Drip rail moldings ($15). Sill moldings ($16). Upper door frame moldings: Valiant ($27). Wheel lip moldings ($18). Undercoating ($28). Interior Trim/Upholstery: Console: Duster ($68). Vinyl split-back bench seat: Valiant ($105). Cloth/vinyl bench seat: Valiant ($64). Vinyl bench seat: Duster ($64). Vinyl bucket seats:

Duster ($87-$150); Scamp ($128). Carpeting ($22). Color-keyed mats ($15). Wheels and Tires: Deluxe wheel covers ($29). Rallye wheels ($36-$66). 6.95x14 WSW ($32). D78x14 BSW ($16). D78x14 WSW ($16-$75). DR78x14 WSW ($85-$132). E78x14 WSW ($16-$63). E70x14 RWL ($61-$109). ER78x14 WSW ($23-$148).

VOLARE CONVENIENCE/APPEARANCE OPTIONS: Option Packages: Road Runner pkg.: base cpe ($205). Road Runner decor group: base cpe ($95). Two-tone paint pkg.: base cpe ($205). Easy-order pkg. ($221-$757). SpaceMaker Pkg.: cpe ($104). Light pkg. ($33). Protection group ($18-$27). Deluxe insulation pkg. ($23-$51). Comfort/Convenience: Air cond. ($431). Rear defogger, blower-type ($41); electric ($74). Automatic speed control ($70). Power seat ($119). Power windows ($95-$135) exc. wag. Power door locks ($60-$86) exc. wag. Tinted glass ($44). Tinted windshield ($35). Luxury steering wheel ($26). Tuff steering wheel ($7). Tilt steering wheel ($54). Three-speed wipers ($8). Electric clock ($18). Inside hood release ($11). Glovebox lock ($4). Lighter: base ($6). Locking gas cap ($6). Horns and Mirrors: Dual horns ($6). Remote left-hand mirror ($14). Dual remote mirrors ($27-$40). Dual remote sport mirrors ($33-$47). Day/night mirror ($7). Entertainment: AM radio ($72). AM/FM radio ($65-$137). AM/FM stereo radio ($160-$233). Rear speaker ($20). Exterior Trim: Manual sunroof: cpe ($186). Full vinyl roof: sed ($92). Canopy vinyl roof: cpe ($76-$90). Landau vinyl roof: cpe ($62-$137). Vinyl bodyside moldings: base ($15). Door edge protectors ($7-$11). Upper door frame moldings: base sed. ($27). Wheel lip moldings: base ($18). Bumper guards, front/rear ($35). Protective bumper rub strips ($28). Air deflector: wag ($22). Luggage rack; wag ($65). Undercoating ($28). Interior Trim/Upholstery: Console ($68). Rear armrest w/ashtray: base ($10). Vinyl bench seat: base wag ($32). Cloth 60/40 seat: Premier ($51). Vinyl 60/40 seat w/recliners: Premier wag ($114). Vinyl bucket seats: cpe ($87-$119). Color-keyed mats ($15). Cargo area carpets/storage bin: base wag ($45). Wheels and Tires: Deluxe wheel covers ($29). Premium wheel covers ($25-$54). Wire wheel covers ($32-$86). Rallye wheels ($36-$66). Styled wheels ($47-$113). D78x14 WSW ($32). E78x14 BSW ($16). E78x14 WSW ($16-$75). ER78x14 WSW ($85-$132). E70x14 RWL ($61-$93). F78x14 BSW ($44-$60). F78x14 WSW ($36-$96). FR78x14 WSW ($41-$153). GR78x14 WSW ($75-$110).

FURY CONVENIENCE/APPEARANCE OPTIONS: Option Packages: Easy order pkg. ($347-$870). Luxury equipment pkg.: Sport/Salon ($1393-$1779). Exterior decor pkg.: HT ($72-$155). Light pkg. ($38-$45). Deluxe insulation pkg.: six-cyl. ($55). Comfort/Convenience: Air cond. ($490). Rear defroster, electric ($81). Automatic speed control ($77). Power seat ($130). Power windows ($147). Power tailgate window: wag ($41). Auto-lock tailgate: wag ($35). Power door locks ($65-$94). Tinted glass ($52). Tinted windshield ($38). Strato ventilation ($20). Three-speed wipers ($9). Luxury steering wheel ($17). Tuff steering wheel ($24). Tilt steering wheel ($59). Inside hood release ($12). Tachometer ($42-$62). Electric clock ($20). Locking gas cap ($6). Horns and Mirrors: Dual horns ($8). Remote left mirror ($15). Dual chrome mirrors ($29-$44). Dual sport remote mirrors, painted or chrome ($37-$52). Entertainment: AM radio ($79); w/8track stereo tape player ($48-$220). AM/FM radio ($71-$149). AM/FM stereo radio ($83-$254); w/8track ($186-$357). Rear speaker ($22). Exterior Trim: Manual sunroof: HT ($311). Full vinyl roof ($115); w/easy-order ($32). Canopy vinyl roof: HT ($83). Canopy vinyl roof w/louvered quarter windows: HT ($115); w/easy-order ($32). Vinyl bodyside moldings ($40). Hood/deck tape stripes: HT ($40). Door edge protectors ($7-$13). Bumper guards, front: sed/wag ($19). Bumper guards, front/rear: HT ($38). Bumper strips, front: sed/wag ($15). Bumper strips, front/rear: HT ($31). Air deflector: wag ($24). Luggage rack: wag ($71). Undercoating ($30). Interior Trim/Upholstery: Console: Sport HT ($18). Vinyl bench seat: base ($42). Cloth/vinyl bucket seats: Sport HT ($31). Cloth/vinyl 60/40 bench seat: Sport HT ($124). Velour/vinyl 60/40 bench seat: Salon sed ($124). Vinyl 60/40 bench seat: Salon sed, Sport wag ($124). Pedal dress-up ($8). Trunk dress-up: sed ($42). Color-keyed mats ($17). Cargo area carpet: wag ($28). Wheels and Tires: Deluxe wheel covers ($32). Wire wheel covers ($62-$94). Rallye wheels ($43-$75). Styled wheels ($113-$145). F78x14 WSW ($39). G78x14 BSW ($19). G78x14 WSW ($39-$58). H78x14 BSW ($22-$40). H78x14 WSW ($25-$83). G70x14 RWL ($53-$110). GR78x15 WSW ($130-$169). HR78x15 WSW ($111-$181). GR70x15 RWL ($164-$203).

GRAN FURY CONVENIENCE/APPEARANCE OPTIONS: Option Packages: Easy order pkg. ($347-$522). Luxury equipment pkg. ($1488-$1811); N/A base. Light pkg. ($55-$74). Wagon pkg.: Sub ($63). Deluxe sound insulation pkg.: base/Cust HT/sed ($41). Comfort/Convenience: Air cond. ($504). Auto-temp air cond. ($15-$85). Rear defroster, electric ($82). Automatic speed control ($78). Power seat ($132). Power windows ($110-$167). Auto-lock tailgate: wag ($35). Power door locks ($66-$95). Tinted glass ($66). Deluxe wiper/washer pkg. ($16). Luxury steering wheel ($17). Tilt/telescope steering wheel ($83-$100). Gauges, temp & oil pressure ($20). Electric clock ($20). Digital clock ($25-$45). Horns and Mirrors: Remote left mirror ($15). Dual remote mirrors ($30-$45). Day/night mirror ($8). Entertainment: AM radio ($80); w/8track stereo tape player ($62-$239). AM/FM radio ($76-$155). AM/FM stereo radio ($80-$257); w/8track ($184-$362). Rear speaker ($22). Exterior

Trim: Sunroof w/vinyl roof ($627-$758). Vinyl roof ($131). Vinyl body-side moldings ($22-$31). Door edge protectors ($8-$13). Upper door frame moldings: 4dr. ($29). Bumper guards, rear ($23). Air deflector: base wag ($25). Assist handles: wag ($23). Luggage rack: wag ($86). Rear bumper step pads: wag ($14). Interior Trim/Upholstery: Vinyl bench seat: HT/sed ($28) exc. Brghm. Vinyl bench seat w/center armrest: Cust ($43). Wheels and Tires: Deluxe wheel covers ($32). Premier wheel covers ($38-$70). G78x15 WSW ($39). GR78x15 BSW ($99). GR78x15 WSW ($39-$138). HR78x15 BSW ($22-$121). HR78x15 WSW ($25-$164). JR78x15 WSW ($56-$195). L78x15 ($49). LR78x15 BSW ($99). LR78x15 WSW ($148).

HISTORY: Introduced: October 16, 1975. Model year production: Chrysler reported a total of 445,555 passenger cars shipped. Total North American passenger-car production for the U.S. market of 459,512 units included 221,765 six-cylinder and 237,747 V-8s. Calendar year production (U.S.): 658,019. Calendar year sales by U.S. dealers: 532,197 (not incl. 12,974 Voyagers). Model year sales by U.S. dealers: 515,347 (not incl. 20,769 imported Arrows and 13,009 Voyager vans).

Historical Footnotes: The new Volares (and Dodge Aspens) turned out to be the most recalled models of their day. Among other failings, their unibodies were notably prone to rusting. The Aspen/Volare duo was meant to rival Ford's Granada and Mercury Monarch. In mid-year 1975, a new Arrow subcompact, manufactured by Mitsubishi in Japan, had been added to the Plymouth line.

1977 PLYMOUTH

The Valiant bunch left the lineup this year, leaving the year-old Volare as Plymouth's compact offering. A two-barrel version of the Slant Six engine, dubbed Super Six, was now available. It was standard on Volare wagons and Fury, optional on other Volares. The big 440 cubic inch V-8 engine was back once more as a Gran Fury option, and Electronic Lean Burn went on the 360 V-8 as well as the bigger ones. Volare again offered a Road Runner option package, though its performance hardly ranked with earlier versions of that name. Volare's coupe could have an optional T-Bar roof as well as a sunroof.

1977 Plymouth, Volare coupe with optional Road Runner Super Pak package (OCW)

1977 Plymouth, Volare Custom coupe (OCW)

VOLARE — SERIES H — SIX/V-8 — For its second year in the Plymouth lineup, Volare looked identical to the 1976 version, again with large, clear-lensed parking/signal lamps between the single headlamps and grille. Eight new body colors were offered. The list included: French Racing Blue, Spitfire Orange, Spinnaker White, Yellow Blaze, Light Mocha Tan, and Mojave Beige; plus metallic Silver Cloud, Regatta Blue, Starlight Blue Sunfire, Vintage Red Sunfire, Jade Green, Forest Green Sunfire, Formal Black Sunfire, Spanish Gold, Caramel Tan, or Russet Sunfire. Nine two-tone combinations also were available (formerly just three). Standard equipment included a heater/defroster, drip moldings, bright grille surround moldings, dome light, and quarter-window reveal moldings. Base

Volares had low-back cloth/vinyl bench seating; Customs used pleated all-vinyl (or cloth/vinyl) with rear armrests and woodgrain instrument cluster inserts. Customs also added a rear deck lower appliqué, belt moldings, B-pillar molding (coupe) and cigarette lighter, as well as partial wheel lip moldings. Premiers had power brakes and steering, day/night mirror, clock, dual horns, bodyside and hood accent tape stripes, premium wheel covers, vinyl 60/40 split-bench seats, a chrome grille insert, hood medallion, and color-keyed vinyl bodyside moldings. The optional canopy vinyl roof had up-and-over stripes. Base engine was the one-barrel 225 cubic inch Slant Six, with three-speed manual shift. Options included a two-barrel Super Six (for $38 extra), rated 10 horsepower higher; a 318 cubic inch V-8; Overdrive-4 manual transmission; or a two-barrel 360 cubic inch V-8 with automatic. Wagons came with either the Super Six, 318 cubic inch V-8, or 360 V-8. Volare coupes could get a four-barrel 360 V-8, rated 175 horsepower. Power brakes were standard with V-8 models. Volare's Road Runner featured an identifying decal on doors, along the lower bodyside stripe, plus E70x14 raised-letter tires, heavy-duty suspension, Rallye wheels, blackout grille, and special "Beep-Beep" horn. A total of 4,585 Volares had the Road Runner package, while 2,390 were Super Road Runners. New Fun Runner option packages were offered for the coupe, including a "Sun Runner" and a "Front Runner" Super Pak that came with front and rear spoilers, louvered quarter windows, and flared wheel openings. The Front Runner came only in Spitfire Orange, with orange/yellow/black tape stripe. "Super Pak" cost $318 on the base coupe. A SpaceMaker Pak allowed the rear seat to fold down. There was also a new T-Bar roof option with removable glass panels.

1977 Plymouth, Fury Sport hardtop with optional canopy vinyl roof (OCW)

FURY — SERIES R — SIX/V-8 — A major restyle hit Plymouth's mid-size, along with cousin Dodge Monaco. Fury's revised front-end look was highlighted by new vertically-stacked quad rectangular headlamps that replaced the former single round units. The overall grille shape was similar to 1976, but had a heavier bright surrounding molding with 'Plymouth' block letters inset in the upper header. The grille pattern was altered too, now consisting of two rows of small vertical-style segments. Park/signal lamps were built into the bright front bumper, in half-curved openings below the headlamps. Small side marker lenses sat roughly midway between wheel openings and front fender tips. 'Fury' fender script was just ahead of the door. The Fury Sport two-door rode a 115 inch wheelbase; Salon sedan was 117.4 inches. As in 1976, Fury Sport (and the base two-door) had a different rear-end appearance than sedans, with vertical taillamps at quarter panel tips and a recessed license plate opening that extended down into the bumper, plus sculptured-look decklid with 'Plymouth' block lettering. 'Sport' script stood on the wide C-pillar, behind the swooping molding that accompanied the canopy roof's opera windows. Those optional opera windows were now single units instead of the extremely narrow side-by-side versions offered for 1976. Fury sedan's back end looked similar to 1976, with tri-section taillamps set into large rear bumper slots: but each tri-color (red/clear/amber) unit had a larger center backup lens, no longer inset into a red panel, The base Fury came in two-door hardtop or four-door (thin-pillar) sedan form, with standard Regency cloth/vinyl bench seat. Fury Sport's standard interior had crushed velour and vinyl split-back bench seats with folding center armrest. Engine choices included the new standard Super Six (two-barrel), 318 cubic inch V-8, 360 V-8, or Electronic Lean Burn 400 V-8 rated 190 horsepower, All models had power brakes. Three-speed manual shift was standard on the base Fury with 318 cubic inch V-8; TorqueFlite on the six-cylinder model (except in California and at high altitudes). Standard equipment included bumper guards, hubcaps, F78x15 blackwall tires, wheel opening moldings, lighter, dome light, lockable glovebox, and heater/defroster. Sedans had front and rear armrests; hardtops a decklid lower molding. Fury Sport added dual horns, hood rear edge and belt moldings, sill moldings, and hood ornament. Fury Salon included a hood ornament, Salon nameplate and crest, plush velour split-back bench seat, upper door frame moldings, deck molding, and dual horns. Fury colors were: Wedgewood Blue, Rallye Red, Spinnaker White, Golden Fawn, and Jasmine Yellow; plus metallic Silver Cloud, Cadet Blue, Starlight Blue Sunfire, Vintage Red Sunfire, Jade Green, Forest Green Sunfire, Formal Black Sunfire, Spanish or Inca Gold, Moondust, Coffee Sunfire, Russet Sunrise, or Burnished Copper. A total of 2,079 Fury models had the Police package, while 1,150 had a Taxi package.

GRAN FURY — SERIES P — V-8 — Gran Fury dropped the Custom line, but added a base two-door hardtop. This would be the last year for

the long (121.5 and 124 inch) wheelbase models. Base engine was the 318 cubic inch V-8, but Broughams had the 360 cubic inch two-barrel V-8, and wagons carried a 400 cubic inch four-barrel V-8. Also optional was a 440 V-8 rated 195 horsepower. Gran Fury could have a full vinyl roof, or a canopy vinyl roof with opera windows, for the same price. A sunroof was available again. Also on the option list were manual vent windows and chrome wheels. Appearance was virtually identical to 1976. Standard equipment included TorqueFlite automatic transmission, power brakes and steering, heater/defroster, carpeting, and electronic ignition. Base hardtops and sedans had G78x15 glass-belted radial tires; Broughams wore HR78x15; Suburban wagons had L78x15; and top-line Sport Suburban wagons carried LR78x15 tires. Steel-belted radials were optional. Sport Suburban wagons had either two or three seats; base Suburban, just two. Gran Fury now weighed some 450 pounds more than a freshly downsized Chevrolet Caprice. Nothing startling was new this year: just a lighter (yet heftier) battery; improved ignition switch and wiring harness; and new TorqueFlite torque converter.

1977 Plymouth, Fury Salon sedan with optional Luxury Equipment package (OCW)

I.D. DATA: Plymouth's 13-symbol Vehicle Identification Number (VIN) was on the upper left corner of the instrument panel, visible through the windshield. Symbol one indicates car line: 'H' Volare; 'R' Fury; 'P' Gran Fury. Symbol two is series (price class): 'L' low; 'M' medium; 'H' high; 'P' premium. Symbols 3-4 show body type: '23' 2-dr. hardtop coupe; '29' 2-dr. special coupe; '41' 4-dr. sedan; '45' two-seat station wagon; '46' three-seat station wagon. Symbol five is the engine code: 'C' L6225 1Bbl.; 'D' L6225 2Bbl.; 'G' V8318; 'K' V8360 2Bbl.; 'L' V8360 4Bbl.; 'N' V8400 4Bbl.; 'T' V8440 4Bbl. Symbol six is the model year code: '7' 1977. Symbol seven indicates assembly plant: 'A' Lynch Road; 'B' Hamtramck, MI; 'D' Belvidere, IL; 'F' Newark, DE; 'G' St. Louis. The final six digits make up the sequential serial number, starting with 100001. Engine number coding and Body Code Plate locations are the same as 1976. As before, a Vehicle Safety Certification Label that displays (among other data) the date of manufacture is attached to the rear facing of the driver's door.

VOLARE (SIX/V-8)

Model No.	Body/Style No.	Body Type & Seating	Factory Price	Shipping Weight	Prod. Total
HL	29	2-dr. Spt Cpe-5P	3570/3740	3180/3480	32,264
HL	41	4-dr. Sedan-6P	3619/3789	3235/3545	36,688
HL	45	4-dr. Sta Wag-6P	3941/4025	3445/3585	70,913

VOLARE CUSTOM (SIX/V-8)

Model No.	Body/Style No.	Body Type & Seating	Factory Price	Shipping Weight	Prod. Total
HH	29	2-dr. Spt Cpe-5P	3752/3922	3185/3295	30,230
HH	41	4-dr. Sedan-6P	3801/3971	3240/3350	45,130

VOLARE PREMIER (SIX/V-8)

Model No.	Body/Style No.	Body Type & Seating	Factory Price	Shipping Weight	Prod. Total
HP	29	2-dr. Spt Cpe-5P	4305/4418	3375/3480	17,852
HP	41	4-dr. Sedan-6P	4354/4467	3440/3545	26,050
HH	45	4-dr. Sta Wag-6P	4271/4476	3450/3585	68,612

FURY/SUBURBAN (SIX/V-8)

Model No.	Body/Style No.	Body Type & Seating	Factory Price	Shipping Weight	Prod. Total
RL	23	2-dr. HT Cpe-6P	3893/4154	3625/3855	11,909
RL	41	4-dr. Sedan-6P	3944/4205	3655/3890	20,103
RL	45	4-dr. 2S Wag-6P	----/4687	----/4335	5,626
RL	46	4-dr. 3S Wag-9P	----/4830	----/4390	5,141

FURY SPORT/SALON (SIX/V-8)

Model No.	Body/Style No.	Body Type & Seating	Factory Price	Shipping Weight	Prod. Total
RH	23	2-dr. Sport HT-6P	4132/4394	3630/3865	24,385
RH	41	4-dr. Salon Sed-6P	4185/4446	3665/3900	22,188
RH	45	4-dr. 2S Wag-6P	----/5192	----/4330	1,827
RH	46	4-dr. 3S Wag-9P	----/5335	----/4400	3,634

GRAN FURY (V-8)

Model No.	Body/Style No.	Body Type & Seating	Factory Price	Shipping Weight	Prod. Total
PM	23	2-dr. HT Cpe-6P	4692	4070	1,504
PM	41	4-dr. Sedan-6P	4697	4145	10,162
PM	45	4-dr. 2S Wag-6P	5315	4885	1,442

GRAN FURY BROUGHAM (V-8)

Model No.	Body/Style No.	Body Type & Seating	Factory Price	Shipping Weight	Prod. Total
PH	23	2-dr. HT Cpe-6P	4963	4190	3,242
PH	41	4-dr. Sedan-6P	4948	4250	15,021

GRAN FURY SPORT SUBURBAN (V-8)

Model No.	Body/Style No.	Body Type & Seating	Factory Price	Shipping Weight	Prod. Total
PH	45	4-dr. 2S Wag-6P	5558	4880	1,194
PH	46	4-dr. 3S Wag-9P	5681	4925	3,600

Factory Price And Weight Note: Prices and weights to left of slash are for six-cylinder, to right for V-8 engines.

Production Note: In addition to totals shown, 793 Volare (Model HK41), 7,204 Fury and 6,236 Gran Fury (Model PK41) police four-door sedans were shipped this year.

ENGINE DATA: BASE SIX (Volare): Inline, overhead-valve six-cylinder. Cast iron block and head. Displacement: 225 cu. in. (3.7-liters). Bore & stroke: 3.40 x 4.12 in. Compression ratio: 8.4:1. Brake horsepower: 100 at 3600 R.P.M. Torque: 170 lb.-ft. at 1600 R.P.M. Four main bearings. Solid valve lifters. Carburetor: 1Bbl. Holley 1945 (R7764A). VIN Code: C. BASE SIX (Volare wagon, Fury); OPTIONAL (Volare): Same as 225 cu. in. six above, but with 2Bbl. Carter BBD 8086S carburetor. Horse-power: 110 at 3600 R.P.M. Torque: 180 lb.-ft. at 2000 R.P.M. VIN Code: D. BASE V-8 (Gran Fury); OPTIONAL (Volare, Fury): 90-degree, overhead valve V-8. Cast iron block and head. Displacement: 318 cu. in. (5.2-liters). Bore & stroke: 3.91 x 3.31 in. Compression ratio: 8.5:1. Brake horsepower: 145 at 4000 R.P.M. Torque: 245 lb.-ft. at 1600 R.P.M. Five main bearings. Hydraulic valve lifters. Carburetor: 2Bbl. Carter BBD 8093S or 8094S. VIN Code: G. BASE V-8 (Fury wagon, Gran Fury Brougham); OPTIONAL (Volare, Fury, Gran Fury): 90-degree, overhead valve V-8. Cast iron block and head. Displacement: 360 cu. in. (5.9-liters). Bore & stroke: 4.00 x 3.58 in. Compression ratio: 8.4:1. Brake horsepower: 155 at 3600 R.P.M. Torque: 275 lb.-ft. at 2000 R.P.M. Five main bearings. Hydraulic valve lifters. Carburetor: 2Bbl. Holley 2245 (R7671A). VIN Code: K. OPTIONAL V-8 (Volare): Same as 360 cu. in. V-8 above, but with Carter TQ 4Bbl. carburetor. Horsepower: 175 at 4000 R.P.M. Torque: 275 lb.-ft. at 2000 R.P.M. VIN Code: L. BASE V-8 (Gran Fury wagon); OPTIONAL (Fury, Gran Fury/Brougham): 90-degree, overhead valve V-8. Cast iron block and head. Displacement: 400 cu. in. (6.6-liters). Bore & stroke: 4.34 x 3.38 in. Compression ratio: 8.2:1. Brake horsepower: 190 at 3600 R.P.M. Torque: 305 lb.-ft. at 3200 R.P.M. Five main bearings. Hydraulic valve lifters. Carburetor: 4Bbl. Carter TQ 9102S. VIN Code: N. OPTIONAL V-8 (Gran Fury): 90-degree, overhead valve V-8. Cast iron block and head. Displacement: 440 cu. in. (7.2-liters). Bore & stroke: 4.32 x 3.75 in. Compression ratio: 8.2:1. Brake horsepower: 195 at 3600 R.P.M. Torque: 320 lb.-ft. at 2000 R.P.M. Five main bearings. Hydraulic valve lifters. Carburetor: 4Bbl. Carter TQ 9101S. VIN Code: T.

CHASSIS DATA: Wheelbase: (Volare cpe) 108.7 in.; (Volare sed/wag) 112.7 in.; (Fury cpe) 115.0 in.; (Fury sed/wag) 117.4 in.; (Gran Fury) 121.4 in.; (Gran Fury wag) 124.0 in. Overall length: (Volare cpe) 197.5 in.; (Volare sed/wag) 201.5 in.; (Fury cpe) 213.7 in.; (Fury sed) 218.4 in.; (Fury wag) 225.6 in.; (Gran Fury) 222.4 in.; (Gran Fury wag) 226.4 in. Height: (Volare cpe) 53.3 in.; (Volare sed) 55.0 in.; (Volare wag) 55.2 in.; (Fury cpe) 52.6 in.; (Fury sed) 54.0 in.; (Fury wag) 55.8 in.; (Gran Fury cpe) 54.1 in.; (Gran Fury sed) 54.8 in.; (Gran Fury wag) 56.9 in. Width: (Volare) 72.8 in.; (Fury) 77.7 in.; (Fury wag) 78.8 in.; (Gran Fury) 79.8 in.; (Gran Fury wag) 79.4 in. Front Tread: (Volare) 60.0 in.; (Fury) 61.9 in.; (Gran Fury) 64.0 in. Rear Tread: (Volare) 58.5 in.; (Fury) 62.0 in. exc. wag, 63.4 in.; (Gran Fury) 63.4 in. Standard Tires: (Volare six/V8318) D78x14; (Volare V8360) E78x14; (Volare Premier six) DR78x14 GBR BSW; (Volare Premier V-8) ER78x14 GBR BSW; (Volare wag) F78x14 BSW; (Fury) F78x15; (Fury V8440) G78x15; (Fury wag) H78x15; (Gran Fury) GR78x15 exc. (V8440) HR78x15 and wagon, LR78x15.

TECHNICAL: Transmission: Three-speed manual transmission standard on all Volare and Fury V-8 (column shift on Fury, column or floor on Volare). Gear ratios: (1st) 3.08:1; (2nd) 1.70:1; (3rd) 1.00:1; (Rev) 2.90:1. Four-speed overdrive available on Volare: (1st) 3.09:1; (2nd) 1.67:1; (3rd) 1.00:1; (4th) 0.73:1; (Rev) 3.00:1. Three-speed automatic standard on Fury six and Gran Fury (column shift), optional on others (column or floor lever). Gear ratios: (1st) 2.45:1; (2nd) 1.45:1; (3rd) 1.00:1; (Rev) 2.22:1. Standard final drive ratio: (Volare six) 3.23:1 w/3spd, 3.2:1 w/4spd, 2.7:1 w/auto.; (Volare V8318) 2.94:1 w/manual, 2.71:1 w/auto.; (Volare V8360) 2.45:1; (Volare wag) 3.21:1, 2.94:1 or 2.71:1; (Fury six) 2.94:1; (Fury V8318) 2.94:1 w/3spd, 2.71:1 w/auto.; (Fury V8360/400) 2.45:1; (Gran Fury) 2.71:1. Steering: Recirculating ball. Suspension: (Volare) isolated transverse front torsion bars, semi-elliptic rear leaf springs; (others) longitudinal front torsion bars, semi-elliptic rear leaf springs; front anti-sway bar on all. Brakes: Front disc, rear drum. Ignition: Electronic. Body construction: (Volare/Fury) unibody; (Gran Fury) unibody w/auxiliary front frame. Fuel tank: (Volare) 18 gal. exc. V-8/wagon, 20 gal.; (Fury) 25.5 gal. exc. 20 gal. on wagons; (Gran Fury) 26.5 gal. exc. wagon, 24 gal. and V8318, 20.5 gal.

DRIVETRAIN OPTIONS: Engines: 225 cu. in., 2Bbl. six: Volare cpe/sed ($38). 360 cu. in., 2Bbl. V-8: Volare ($53); Fury ($57); base Gran Fury HT/sed ($58). 360 cu. in., 4Bbl. V-8: Volare cpe ($219-$241); Fury ($105); Fury wag ($47); base Gran Fury ($106); Gran Fury Brghm ($48). 400 cu. in., 4Bbl. V-8: Fury wag ($98); base Gran Fury ($158); Gran

Fury Brghm ($99). 440 cu. in., 4Bbl. V-8: base Gran Fury ($289); Gran Fury Brghm ($231); Gran Fury wag ($132). Transmission/Differential: TorqueFlite: Volare ($270); Fury ($295). Four-speed manual trans. w/floor lever: Volare ($134). Three-speed floor shifter: Volare ($30). Sure grip differential: Volare ($52); Fury ($57); Gran Fury ($61). Optional axle ratio: Volare ($14); Fury/Gran Fury ($16). Power Accessories: Power steering: Volare ($140); Fury six ($153). Power brakes: base Volare cpe/sed ($59). Suspension: H.D. susp.: Volare ($23); Fury/Gran Fury ($18-$25). Automatic height control: Gran Fury ($109). H.D. shock absorbers: Fury/Gran Fury ($7). Other: Trailer towing pkg.: Volare ($72). Fury trailer towing pkg.: light ($79); heavy ($316). Gran Fury trailer towing pkg.: light ($80); heavy ($321). Fuel pacer system: Volare ($20-$33); Fury ($22-$36); Gran Fury ($22). Engine block heater: Gran Fury ($18). Long-life battery: Volare ($29); Fury ($31); Gran Fury ($32). California emission system ($67-$75). High-altitude emission system ($21-$24).

1977 Plymouth, Volare Premier sedan (OCW)

VOLARE CONVENIENCE/APPEARANCE OPTIONS: Option Packages: Road Runner pkg.: base cpe ($193-$216). Road Runner decor group: base cpe ($82-$101). Road Runner "Super Pak": base cpe ($318). Two-tone paint pkg.: cpe ($120-$177). Easy-order pkg. ($594-$801). Space-Maker Pak: cpe ($110). Light pkg. ($35). Protection group ($19-$28). Deluxe insulation pkg. ($35-$65). Comfort/Convenience: Air cond. ($454). Rear defogger, blower-type ($45); electric ($79). Automatic speed control ($77). Power seat ($131). Power windows ($104-$145). Power door locks ($65-$92). Tinted glass ($48). Tinted windshield ($37). Luxury steering wheel ($28). Tuff steering wheel ($7-$35). Tilt steering wheel ($54). Deluxe wipers ($9). Electric clock ($19). Inside hood release ($11). Glove box lock ($5). Lighter: base ($6). Locking gas cap ($6). Horns and Mirrors: Dual horns ($6). Remote left-hand mirror ($15). Dual remote mirrors ($28-$43). Dual remote sport mirrors ($35-$50). Day/night mirror ($8). Entertainment: AM radio ($69). AM/FM radio ($67-$137). AM/FM stereo radio ($145-$215); w/8track tape player ($235-$304). Rear speaker ($22). Exterior: T-Bar roof ($540-$554). Manual sunroof: cpe ($198). Full vinyl roof: sed ($92). Canopy vinyl roof: cpe ($87-$101). Landau vinyl roof: cpe ($62-$148). Vinyl body-side moldings ($19-$38). Belt moldings: base ($15). Door edge protectors ($8-$12). Upper door frame moldings: sed ($28). Wheel lip moldings: base ($19). Bumper guards, front/rear ($37). Protective bumper rub strips ($30). Air deflector: wag ($25). Luggage rack ($68). Undercoating ($30). Interior: Console ($72). Vinyl armrest w/ashtray: base ($11). Vinyl bench seat: base wag ($34). Cloth 60/40 seat: Premier ($54); Cust wag ($198). Vinyl 60/40 seat w/recliners: wag ($121-$155). Vinyl bucket seats: cpe ($92-$126). Color-keyed mats ($16). Cargo area carpets/storage bin: base wag ($47). Wheels and Tires: Deluxe wheel covers ($32). Premium wheel covers ($25-$57). Wire wheel covers ($42-$99). Rallye Wheels ($32-$68). Chrome wheels ($51-$119). D78x14 WSW ($37). DR78x14 BSW ($51-$88). E78x14 BSW ($17). E78x14 WSW ($17-$54). ER78x14 BSW ($67). ER78x14 WSW ($67-$135). E70x14 RWL ($63-$101). FR78x14 BSW ($85). FR78x14 WSW ($87-$155). Space-saving spare tire ($41).

FURY CONVENIENCE/APPEARANCE OPTIONS: Option Packages: Easy order pkg. ($350-$872). Luxury equipment pkg.: Sport/Salon ($1461-$1837). Roadability pkg.: V-8 ($33). Light pkg. ($41-$48). Deluxe insulation pkg.: six-cyl. ($62). Comfort/Convenience: Air cond. ($518). Rear defroster, electric ($86). Automatic speed control ($84). Power seat ($143). Power windows ($113-$158). Power tailgate window: wag ($44). Auto-lock tailgate: wag ($37). Power door locks ($71-$101). Tinted glass ($57). Tinted windshield ($40). Deluxe wipers ($10). Luxury steering wheel ($18). Tilt steering wheel ($59). Inside hood release ($13). Electric clock ($21). Locking gas cap ($7). Horns and Mirrors: Dual horns ($6). Remote left mirror ($16). Dual chrome remote mirrors ($31-$47). Dual sport remote mirrors, painted or chrome ($39-$55). Entertainment: AM radio ($76). AM/FM radio ($74-$149). AM/FM stereo radio ($61-$234); w/8track ($159-$332). Rear speaker ($24). Exterior: Manual sunroof: HT ($330). Full vinyl roof ($116) exc. Sport w/option pkg. ($22). Canopy vinyl roof: HT ($95). Canopy vinyl roof w/louvered quarter win-

dows: HT ($116) exc. w/option pkg. ($22). Narrow bodyside moldings: base ($42). Wide bodyside moldings: Spt/Salon ($45). Hood tape stripe: sed ($21). Hood/deck tape stripes: HT ($42). Bodyside tape stripes: Spt ($42). Belt molding: base HT ($16). Sill moldings: base ($27). Upper door frame moldings: base sed/wag ($31). Door edge protectors ($8-$14). Bumper strips, front: sed/wag ($16). Bumper strips, front/rear: HT ($32). Air deflector: wag ($27). Luggage rack: wag ($75). Undercoating ($32). Interior: Console: Sport HT ($18). Vinyl bench seat: base ($45). Cloth/vinyl bucket seats: Sport ($32). 60/40 seat ($132). Pedal dress-up ($9). Trunk dress-up: sed ($45). Color-keyed mats ($18). Wheels and Tires: Deluxe wheel covers ($35). Wire wheel covers ($73-$108). Rallye wheels ($45-$85). Styled wheels ($119-$154). F78x15 WSW ($43). G78x15 BSW ($20). G78x15 WSW ($20-$63). H78x15 BSW ($43-$70). H78x15 WSW ($27-$90). G70x15 RWL ($56-$119). GR78x15 WSW ($103-$165). GR70x15 RWL ($159-$222). 215x15 WSW ($103-$192).

1977 Plymouth, Gran Fury Brougham hardtop with optional canopy vinyl roof and opera windows (OCW)

GRAN FURY CONVENIENCE/APPEARANCE OPTIONS: Option Packages: Easy order pkg. ($457-$530). Luxury equipment pkg.: Brghm ($1826-$1922). Light pkg. ($66-$79). Deluxe sound insulation pkg.: HT/sed ($43). Comfort/Convenience: Air cond. ($546). Auto-temp air cond. ($630) exc. w/option pkg. on Brhgm ($83). Rear defroster, electric ($87), Automatic speed control ($88). Power seat ($145). Power windows ($119-$179). Auto-lock tailgate: wag ($37). Power decklid release ($21). Tinted glass ($72). Deluxe wiper/washer pkg. ($17). Luxury steering wheel ($18). Tilt/telescope steering wheel ($88-$106). Gauges, temp & oil pressure ($21). Electric clock ($21). Digital clock ($27-$48). Locking gas cap: cpe/sed ($8). Horns and Mirrors: Dual horns ($6). Remote left mirror ($16). Dual remote mirrors ($31-$48). Day/night mirror ($9). Entertainment: AM radio ($77). AM/FM radio ($79-$155). AM/FM stereo radio ($58-$237); w/8track ($157-$337). Rear speaker ($25). Exterior: Sunroof w/vinyl top ($627-$768). Full vinyl roof ($141). Canopy vinyl roof w/opera windows ($141). Manual vent windows ($43). Vinyl bodyside moldings ($23). Door edge protectors ($9-$14). Upper door frame moldings: sed/wag ($31). Bumper guards, rear: wag ($24). Air deflector: base wag ($28). Assist handles: wag ($24). Luggage rack: wag ($104). Rear bumper step pads: wag ($15). Undercoating ($33). Interior: Cloth/vinyl bench seat: Spt wag ($59). Vinyl bench seat: base ($29). Vinyl bench seat w/center armrest: Brghm ($45). Cloth/vinyl 50/50 seat: Brghm ($198). Vinyl 50/50 seat: Spt wag ($198). Carpeting: wag ($26). Color-keyed mats ($18). Trunk dress-up ($45). Wheels and Tires: Deluxe wheel covers ($35). Premier wheel covers ($39-$74). Chrome wheels ($81-$156).

HISTORY: Introduced: October 1, 1976. Model year production: Chrysler reported a total of 472,910 passenger cars shipped. Total North American passenger-car production for the U.S. market of 473,748 units included 219,335 six-cylinder and 254,413 V-8s. Calendar year production (U.S.): 492,063. Calendar year sales by U.S. dealers: 444,063 (not incl. 13,767 Voyagers). Model year sales by U.S. dealers: 459,995 (not incl. 51,849 imported Arrows and 13,842 Voyager vans).

Historical Footnotes: This was the final year for the full-size Gran Fury, which slipped considerably in sales after once ranking No. 1 in the Plymouth lineup. Dodge/Plymouth mid-sizes not only looked alike at this time; they were assembled together. Volare sold strongly in 1977, reaching a total of 318,555 versus 239,528 in its opening year.

1978 PLYMOUTH

Biggest news this year was the new Plymouth Horizon, a twin to Dodge Omni, the first front-drive subcompacts built in America. No less significant was the abandonment of the Gran Fury badge, though it would return

later in another (smaller) form. A rather long list of 318, 360 and 400 cubic inch V-8s was optional, standard and heavy-duty, some available only in California and/or high-altitude regions. The big 440 V-8 was gone. Automatic transmissions added a lockup torque converter that cut in at about 27-31 mph.

1978 Plymouth, Horizon hatchback (OCW)

1978 Plymouth, Horizon hatchback with optional roof rack and Premium Woodgrain package (OCW)

HORIZON — SERIES M — FOUR — Plymouth's new L-body front-wheel drive subcompact, near twin to the Dodge Omni, had four doors and carried four passengers, with a liftgate (hatch) at the back. The two models differed mainly in grille appearance. Horizon's grille showed a tight cross-hatch pattern with horizontal divider bar and center shield-style emblem. Framing for the single rectangular headlamps, slightly recessed, extended outward to encircle wraparound amber park/signal lamps. Small 'Plymouth' block letters sat above the left headlamp. 'Horizon' script was on front fenders, and on passenger side of the liftgate. Taillamps consisted of fairly large wraparound red units at the outside, with smaller amber lens inside, above the matching clear backup lens. Small horizontal marker reflectors went on quarter panels, just ahead of the taillamps. Bodyside moldings continued around the back of the car. Sole engine was a transverse-mounted Lean Burn 104.7 cubic inch (1.7-liter) overhead-cam four, with standard four-speed manual shift. Engines came from Volkswagen, enlarged to the 1.7-liter displacement. In fact, the car itself had a VW Rabbit-like appearance. Horizon had rack-and-pinion steering, an Iso-Strut front suspension with anti-sway bar, plus "anti-sway characteristics" built into the trailing-arm, coil-spring beam axle rear suspension. Standard equipment included black vinyl bodyside moldings, bucket seats, AM radio, lighter, door dome light switch, folding rear shelf panel, fold-down rear seat, ammeter, temperature gauge, bin-type glove box, heater/defroster, three-spoke steering wheel, roll-down rear-door windows, multifunction steering column lever, and two-speed wiper/washers. Also standard: argent styled sport wheels with P155/80R13 glass-belted radial whitewall tires, anodized aluminum bumpers with protective strips, and stainless steel exhaust pipe. Options included a stereo radio, power steering, TorqueFlite transmission, roof rack, remote-control mirrors, air conditioning, and tinted glass. A selection of exterior and interior packages also was offered, essentially groupings of conventional add-ons. Body colors were: Sunrise Orange, Spitfire Orange, Formal Black, Spinnaker White, Yellow Blaze, and Light Mocha Tan; plus metallic Pewter Gray, Regatta Blue, Starlight Blue Sunfire, Tapestry Red Sunfire, Caramel Tan, Augusta Green Sunfire, and Mint Green. Five "classic" two-tone combinations were available.

VOLARE — SERIES H — SIX/V-8 — While Volare dropped down to a single series, an ample selection of option packages allowed buyers to vary their Volares considerably. They included Super Coupe and Street Kit Car packages that added over $1,000 to the coupe price, plus the cheaper Road Runner and Fun Runner. A two-door coupe, four-door sedan and two-seat station wagon made up the selection. Volare had a new "waffle-look" grille pattern, along with revised taillamps and trim. Otherwise, little change was evident. Bumpers were now built of high-strength steel to cut weight. Other weight reductions occurred in tires, glass and brakes, as well as the engine and air conditioner. "Super Pak" coupes

added such extras as spoilers and wheel arch flares, along with black paint, special striping, heavy-duty suspension, and the 360 cubic inch four-barrel V-8. Standard engine was again the 225 cubic inch Slant Six, with 318 or 360 V-8 optional. Wagons had the two-barrel Super Six, as well as power brakes. Three-speed manual shift was standard; four-speed and TorqueFlite (with new lockup clutch) optional. Coupes and sedans had D78x14 blackwall tires; wagons, F78x14 glass-belted tires. New optional thin-back front bucket seats had headrests and a center armrest. Also joining the option list: AM and AM/FM stereo radios with built-in CB transceivers. Galvanized metal and plastic front splash shields were now used to try and cut rusting.

1978 Plymouth, Fury Sport hardtop with optional vinyl roof (OCW)

FURY — SERIES R — SIX/V-8 — Plymouth's full-size Gran Fury disappeared, but the mid-size lineup amounted to eight models: base two-door hardtop and sedan, Sport hardtop, Salon sedan, plus Suburban and Sport Suburban wagons with either two or three seats. Styling was the same as 1977, though new thin-back front seats offered more knee room in back. Base engine was the 225 cubic inch two-barrel Super Six; optional, a 318 cubic inch (5.2-liter) Lean Burn V-8. Wagons had a standard 360 cubic inch (5.9-liter) Lean Burn or optional 400 Lean Burn V-8, also available on other models. Three-speed manual transmission was standard on six-cylinder models, but V-8s had TorqueFlite. Automatic transmissions added a lock-up torque converter. Standard equipment also included power brakes, power steering (on V-8 models), cigarette lighter, front/rear bumper guards, day/night mirror, locking glovebox, and F78x15 blackwall tires. Wagons had H78x15 tires. The Salon four-door added shag carpet, door trim panels, and a hood ornament with center molding. On the option list, a Fury Gran Coupe package was available for $686. So was a halo vinyl roof, as well as the canopy and full vinyl tops. Both AM and AM/FM stereo radios could have a built-in CB transceiver or tape player. Aluminum-fascia wheels and wire wheel covers were offered as options.

I.D. DATA: Plymouth's 13-symbol Vehicle Identification Number (VIN) again was on the upper left corner of the instrument panel, visible through the windshield. Symbol one indicates car line: 'M' Horizon; 'H' Volare; 'R' Fury. Symbol two is series (price class): 'L' low; 'H' high. Symbols 3-4 show body type: '23' 2-dr. hardtop coupe; '29' 2-dr. special coupe; '41' 4-dr. sedan; '44' 4-dr. hatchback; '45' two-seat station wagon; '46' three-seat wagon. Symbol five is the engine code: 'A' L4105 2Bbl.; 'C' L6225 1Bbl.; 'D' L6225 2Bbl.; 'G' V8318 2Bbl.; 'K' V8360 2Bbl.; 'J' V8360 4Bbl.; 'N' V8400 4Bbl. Symbol six is the model year code: '8' 1978. Symbol seven indicates assembly plant: 'A' Lynch Road; 'B' Hamtramck, MI; 'D' Belvidere, IL; 'F' Newark, DE. The final six digits make up the sequential serial number, starting with 100001. Six-cylinder/V-8 engine number coding is similar to 1976-77. Engine numbers for the new Horizon four-cylinder are on a pad just above the fuel pump. As before, a Vehicle Safety Certification Label that displays (among other data) the date of manufacture is attached to the rear facing of the driver's door. A Body Code Plate is on the left front fender side shield, wheel housing, or left side of upper radiator support.

HORIZON (FOUR)

Model No.	Body/ Style No.	Body Type & Seating	Factory Price	Shipping Weight	Prod. Total
ML	44	4-dr. Hatch-4P	3976	2145	95,817

VOLARE (SIX/V-8)

Model No.	Body/ Style No.	Body Type & Seating	Factory Price	Shipping Weight	Prod. Total
HL	29	2-dr. Spt Cpe-5P	3735/3905	3140/3255	61,702
HL	41	4-dr. Sedan-6P	3853/4020	3175/3295	85,365
HL	45	4-dr. Sta Wag-6P	4195/4324	3405/3490	70,728

FURY/SUBURBAN (SIX/V-8)

Model No.	Body/ Style No.	Body Type & Seating	Factory Price	Shipping Weight	Prod. Total
RL	23	2-dr. HT Cpe-6P	4212/4388	3600/3855	9,473
RL	41	4-dr. Sedan-6P	4292/4468	3635/3885	28,245
RL	45	4-dr. 2S Wag-6P	----/5024	----/4310	3,328
RL	46	4-dr. 3S Wag-9P	----/5167	----/4370	3,342

FURY SPORT/SALON (SIX/V-8)

Model No.	Body/ Style No.	Body Type & Seating	Factory Price	Shipping Weight	Prod. Total
RH	23	2-dr. Sport HT-6P	4452/4628	3610/3860	9,736
RH	41	4-dr. Salon Sed-6P	4527/4703	3645/3900	12,976

FURY SPORT SUBURBAN (V-8)

Model No.	Body/ Style No.	Body Type & Seating	Factory Price	Shipping Weight	Prod. Total
RH	45	4-dr. 2S Wag-6P	----/5482	----/4300	1,106
RH	46	4-dr. 3S Wag-9P	----/5625	----/4375	2,117

Factory Price And Weight Note: Prices and weights to left of slash are for six-cylinder, to right for V-8 engine.

ENGINE DATA: BASE FOUR (Horizon): Inline, overhead-cam four-cylinder. Cast iron block; aluminum head. Displacement: 104.7 cu. in. (1.7-liters). Bore & stroke: 3.13 x 3.40 in. Compression ratio: 8.2:1. Brake horsepower: 75 at 5600 R.P.M. Torque: 90 lb.-ft. at 3200 R.P.M. Five main bearings. Solid valve lifters. Carburetor: 2Bbl. Holley 5220. VIN Code: A. **BASE SIX (Volare):** Inline, overhead valve six-cylinder. Cast iron block and head. Displacement: 225 cu. in. (3.7-liters). Bore & stroke: 3.40 x 4.12 in. Compression ratio: 8.4:1. Brake horsepower: 100 at 3600 R.P.M. Torque: 170 lb.-ft. at 1600 R.P.M. Four main bearings. Solid valve lifters. Carburetor: 1Bbl. Holley 1945. VIN Code: C. **BASE SIX (Volare wagon, Fury); OPTIONAL (Volare):** Same as 225 cu. in. six above, but with 2Bbl. Carter BBD 8086S carburetor. Horsepower: 110 at 3600 R.P.M. Torque: 180 lb.-ft. at 2000 R.P.M. VIN Code: D. **OPTIONAL V-8 (Volare, Fury):** 90-degree, overhead valve V-8. Cast iron block and head. Displacement: 318 cu. in. (5.2-liters). Bore & stroke: 3.91 x 3.31 in. Compression ratio: 8.5:1. Brake horsepower: 140 at 4000 R.P.M. Torque: 245 lb.-ft. at 1600 R.P.M. Five main bearings. Hydraulic valve lifters. Carburetor: 2Bbl. Carter BBD, VIN Code: G. **BASE V-8 (Fury wagon); OPTIONAL (Volare, Fury):** 90-degree, overhead valve V-8. Cast iron block and head. Displacement: 360 cu. in. (5.9-liters). Bore & stroke: 4.00 x 3.58 in. Compression ratio: 8.4:1. Brake horsepower: 155 at 3600 R.P.M. Torque: 270 lb.-ft. at 2400 R.P.M. Five main bearings. Hydraulic valve lifters. Carburetor: 2Bbl. Holley 2245. VIN Code: K. **OPTIONAL V-8 (Volare):** Same as 360 cu. in. V-8 above, but with Carter TQ 4Bbl. carburetor. Horsepower: 175 at 4000 R.P.M. Torque: 260 lb.-ft. at 2400 R.P.M. VIN Code: J. **OPTIONAL V-8 (Fury):** 90-degree, overhead valve V-8, Cast iron block and head. Displacement: 400 cu. in. (6.6-liters). Bore & stroke: 4.34 x 3.38 in. Compression ratio: 8.2:1. Brake horsepower: 190 at 3600 R.P.M. Torque: 305 lb.-ft. at 3200 R.P.M. Five main bearings. Hydraulic valve lifters. Carburetor: 4Bbl. Carter TQ. VIN Code: N.

CHASSIS DATA: Wheelbase: (Horizon) 99.2 in.; (Volare cpe) 108.7 in.; (Volare sed/wag) 112.7 in.; (Fury cpe) 114.9 in.; (Fury sed) 117.4 in.; (Fury wag) 117.5 in. Overall Length: (Horizon) 163.2 in.; (Volare cpe) 197.2 in.; (Volare sed/wag) 201.2 in.; (Fury cpe) 213.2 in.; (Fury sed) 218.0 in.; (Fury wag) 225.1 in. Height: (Horizon) 53.4 in.; (Volare cpe) 53.3 in.; (Volare sed) 55.3 in.; (Volare wag) 55.7 in.; (Fury cpe) 52.9 in.; (Fury sed) 54.3 in.; (Fury wag) 56.9 in. Width: (Horizon) 66.2 in.; (Volare) 73.3 in.; (Fury) 77.7 in.; (Fury wag) 78.8 in. Front Tread: (Horizon) 55.5 in.; (Volare) 60.0 in.; (Fury) 61.9 in. Rear Tread: (Horizon) 55.1 in.; (Volare) 58.5 in.; (Fury) 62.0 in. exc. wag, 63.4 in. Standard Tires: (Horizon) P155/80R13 GBR WSW; (Volare) D78x14 BSW; (Volare wag) F78x14 BSW; (Fury) F78x15; (Fury wag) H78x15.

TECHNICAL: Transmission: Three-speed manual transmission standard on Volare and Fury six (column shift on Fury, floor on Volare). Gear ratios: (1st) 3.08:1; (2nd) 1.70:1; (3rd) 1.00:1; (Rev) 2.90:1. Four-speed overdrive available on Volare: (1st) 3.09:1; (2nd) 1.67:1; (3rd) 1.00:1; (4th) 0.71:1; (Rev) 3.00:1. Four-speed manual (floor shift) standard on Horizon: (1st) 3.45:1; (2nd) 1.94:1; (3rd) 1.29:1; (4th) 0.97:1; (Rev) 3.17:1. TorqueFlite three-speed automatic standard on Fury V-8, optional on others. Volare/Fury gear ratios: (1st) 2.45:1; (2nd) 1.45:1; (3rd) 1.00:1; (Rev) 2.22:1. Horizon gear ratios: (1st) 2.47:1; (2nd) 1.47:1; (3rd) 1.00:1; (Rev) 2.10:1. Standard final drive ratio: (Horizon) 3.48:1; (Volare six) 3.23:1 w/3spd, (Volare V8318) 2.94:1 w/manual, 2.47:1 or 2.45:1 w/auto.; (Volare V8360) 2.45:1 or 3.21:1; (Volare V8360 wag) 2.71:1; (Fury six) 3.21:1 w/manual, 2.71:1 w/auto.; (Fury V-8) 2.71:1 w/auto.; (Fury V8360) 2.45:1; (Fury V8360 wag) 2.71:1. Steering: (Horizon) rack and pinion; (others) recirculating ball. Suspension: (Horizon) Iso-Strut independent coil front w/anti-sway bar, independent trailing arm coil rear w/integral anti-sway; (Volare) isolated transverse front torsion bars w/anti-sway bar, semi-elliptic rear leaf springs; (Fury) longitudinal front torsion bars w/anti-sway bar, semi-elliptic rear leaf springs. Brakes: Front disc, rear drum. Ignition: Electronic. Body construction: Unibody. Fuel tank: (Horizon) 13 gal.; (Volare) 18 gal. exc. V-8/wagon, 19.5 gal.; (Fury) 25.5 gal. exc. wagon, 20 gal.

DRIVETRAIN OPTIONS: Engines: 225 cu. in., 2Bbl. six: Volare cpe/sed ($41). 318 cu. in., 2Bbl. V-8: Volare cpe/sed ($170); Volare wag ($129); Fury ($176). 318 cu. in., 4Bbl. V-8: Calif. Volare ($172-$213); Calif. Fury ($221). 360 cu. in., 2Bbl. V-8: Volare cpe/sed ($275); Volare wag ($234); Fury ($285). H.D. 360 cu. in., 2Bbl. V-8: Volare sed ($332); Volare wag ($292). 360 cu. in., 4Bbl. V-8: Volare cpe ($439-$463); high-altitude/Calif. Fury ($330-$481); high-alt./Calif. Fury wag ($45). 400 cu. in., 4Bbl. V-8: Fury HT/sed ($379); Fury wag ($94). H.D. 400 cu. in., 4Bbl. V-8: Fury HT/sed ($507); Fury wag ($222). Transmission/Differential: TorqueFlite: Horizon ($303); Volare ($293); Fury ($320). Four-speed manual trans. w/floor lever: Volare ($142). Sure grip differential: Volare ($56); Fury ($62). Optional axle ratio: Volare ($15). Power Accessories: Power steering: Horizon ($148); Volare ($145); Fury ($159). Power brakes: Horizon ($68); Volare ($66). Suspension: H.D. susp.: Volare ($24); Fury ($26). Sport susp.: Horizon ($24). H.D. shock absorbers: Fury ($7). Other: Trailer towing pkg.: Volare ($150); Fury ($157). Long-life battery: Volare ($30); Fury ($33). California emission system ($72-$79). High-altitude emission system ($31-$34).

HORIZON CONVENIENCE/APPEARANCE OPTIONS: Option Packages: Classic two-tone paint pkg. ($73-$107). Custom exterior pkg. ($71).

Premium exterior pkg. ($167). Custom interior pkg. ($62-$82). Premium interior pkg. ($214-$242). Premium woodgrain pkg. ($312). Popular equipment group ($250). Light pkg. ($44). Comfort/Convenience: Air cond. ($493). Rear defrostor ($80). Tinted glass ($56). Tinted windshield ($41). Luxury steering wheel ($15). Electric clock w/trip odometer ($26). Rear wiper/washer ($59). Locking gas cap ($7). Glovebox lock ($5). Horns and Mirrors: Dual horns ($7). Remote left mirror ($16). Dual remote mirrors ($30-$46). Day/night mirror ($9). Entertainment: AM/FM radio ($74). AM/FM stereo radio ($143). Exterior: Full vinyl roof ($93). Moldings: belt ($16); drip ($18); sill ($19); upper door frame ($30); wheel lip ($27). Door edge protectors ($20). Bumper guards ($41). Multi-color tape stripe ($66). Luggage rack ($81). Undercoating ($31). Interior: Console: storage ($21); Shift lever ($30). Cloth/vinyl bucket seats ($21). Cargo area carpet ($43). Color-keyed floor mats ($26). Wheels and Tires: Wheel trim rings ($36). Rallye wheels ($36-$73). Bright Rallye hubs ($37). 165/75x13 GBR WSW ($16). 165/75x13 SBR WSW ($48). Conventional spare tire ($12-$24).

1978 Plymouth, Volare Premier station wagon with optional Premier Woodgrain package, roof rack and air deflector (OCW)

VOLARE CONVENIENCE/APPEARANCE OPTIONS: Option Packages: Super Coupe pkg. ($1348-$1417). Street Kit Car pkg.: cpe ($1085). Road Runner pkg.: cpe ($289). Road Runner decor group: cpe ($51). Road Runner Sport Pak: cpe ($411-$499). Fun Runner Coupe pkg. ($77). Fun Runner decor pkg. ($180). Custom exterior pkg. ($73-$86). Custom interior pkg. ($144-$224). Premium exterior pkg. ($108-$138). Premium interior pkg. ($180-$483). Premier wagon woodgrain group ($221). Two-tone paint pkg.: cpe ($188). Two-tone decor pkg.: cpe ($62). Basic group ($653-$655). Light pkg. ($44). Protection group ($28-$35). Deluxe insulation pkg. ($35-$38). Comfort/Convenience: Air cond. ($484). Rear defogger, blower-type ($48); electric ($83). Automatic speed control ($86). Power seat ($142). Power windows ($113-$157). Power door locks ($71-$98). Tinted glass ($53). Tinted windshield ($39). Tilt steering wheel ($65). Intermittent wipers ($31). Digital clock ($46). Inside hood release ($12). Locking glovebox ($5). Lighter ($6). Locking gas cap ($7). Horns and Mirrors: Dual horns ($7). Remote left-hand mirror ($16). Dual remote mirrors ($30-$46). Dual remote sport mirrors: cpe ($37-$53). Day/night mirror ($9). Entertainment: AM radio ($74); w/8track player ($143-$217); w/CB ($305-$379). AM/FM radio ($74-$148). AM/FM stereo radio ($143-$217); w/8track player ($234-$308); w/CB ($448-$522). Rear speaker ($23). Exterior: T-Bar roof: cpe ($572). Full vinyl roof: sed ($93). Halo vinyl roof: cpe ($93-$109). Landau vinyl roof: cpe ($164). Vinyl bodyside moldings ($40). Belt moldings ($16). Door edge protectors ($10-$18). Upper door frame moldings: sed/wag ($30). Wheel lip moldings ($20). Bumper guards, front/rear ($39). Protective bumper rub strips ($32). Undercoating ($21-$31). Interior: Console: cpe ($55). Cloth/vinyl bucket seats: cpe ($160). Vinyl bucket seats: cpe ($102). Rear armrest ($11). Color-keyed mats ($20). Pedal dress-up ($9). Trunk dress-up ($43). Color-keyed seatbelts ($15). Wheels and Tires: Deluxe wheel covers ($36). Premium wheel covers ($36-$71). Wire wheel covers ($91-$127). Rallye wheels ($33-$72). Styled wheels ($55-$127). D78x14 WSW ($42). DR78x14 BSW ($54-$88). DR78x14 WSW ($42-$96). E78x14 BSW ($18). E78x14 WSW ($18-$60). ER78x14 GBR BSW ($18-$71). ER78x14 GBR WSW ($18-$113). ER78x14 SBR WSW ($86-$145). F78x14 WSW ($44). FR78x14 GBR BSW ($25-$73). FR78x14 GBR WSW ($25-$117). FR78x14 SBR WSW ($57-$149). FR70x14 Aramid-belt RWL ($127-$237). GR78x14 SBR WSW ($76-$120). Space-saving or conventional spare tire (NC).

FURY CONVENIENCE/APPEARANCE OPTIONS: Option Packages: Gran Coupe pkg.: HT ($686). Basic group ($254-$739). Light pkg. ($42-$51). Deluxe insulation pkg.: six-cyl. ($66). Roadability pkg. ($35). Comfort/Convenience: Air cond. ($563). Rear defroster, electric ($91). Automatic speed control ($94). Power seat ($155). Power windows ($129-$179). Power tailgate window: wag ($46). Auto-lock tailgate: wag ($38). Power door locks ($83-$116). Tinted glass ($53). Tinted windshield ($42). Deluxe wipers ($34). Luxury steering wheel ($19). Tilt steering wheel ($71). Inside hood release ($13). Electric clock ($22). Locking gas cap ($7). Horns and Mirrors: Dual horns ($7). Remote left mirror ($17). Dual chrome remote mirrors ($33-$45). Dual sport remote mirrors, painted or chrome ($41-$58). Entertainment: AM radio ($81); w/8track player ($157-$237); w/CB ($333-$414). AM/FM radio ($81-$161). AM/FM stereo radio ($157-$237); w/8track ($256-$336); w/CB

($490-$570). Rear speaker ($25). Exterior Trim: Halo vinyl roof: HT ($121). Full vinyl roof ($121). Canopy vinyl roof: HT ($100). Canopy vinyl roof w/louvered quarter windows: HT ($121). Narrow bodyside moldings ($44). Wide bodyside moldings: Salon ($48). Hood tape stripe: sed ($23). Hood/deck tape stripes: HT ($45). Bodyside tape stripes: Spt HT ($45). Belt molding: base HT ($17). Sill moldings: base sed/wag ($28). Wheel lip moldings: base sed ($22). Upper door frame moldings: base sed/wag ($33). Door edge protectors ($11-$20). Bumper strips, front: sed/wag ($17). Bumper strips, front/rear: HT ($35). Air deflector: wag ($29). Luggage rack: wag ($89). Undercoating ($34). Interior: Console: Sport HT ($58). Vinyl bench seat: base ($48); Salon ($31). Vinyl bucket seats: Sport HT (NC). Cloth/vinyl 60/40 seat: Spt/Salon ($140). Vinyl 60/40 seat: Spt wag ($140). Color-keyed mats ($22). Color-keyed seatbelts ($16). Wheels and Tires: Deluxe wheel covers ($39). Wire wheel covers ($99-$138). Aluminum-fascia wheels ($87-$246). F78x15 WSW ($48). G78x15 BSW ($21). G78x15 WSW ($21-$69). H78x15 BSW ($45). H78x15 WSW ($47-$95). GR78x15 SBR WSW ($130-$178). GR60x15 Aramid-belted RWL ($327-$376). 215x15 SBR WSW ($109-$204).

HISTORY: Introduced: October 7, 1977. Model year production: Chrysler reported a total of 383,935 passenger cars shipped. Total North American passenger-car production for the U.S. market of 385,068 units included 95,854 four-cylinder, 170,105 six-cylinder, and 119,109 V-8s. Calendar year production (U.S.): 443,619. Calendar year sales by U.S. dealers: 404,371 (not incl. 13,895 Voyagers). Model year sales by U.S. dealers: 393,368 (not incl. 36,693 imports and 14,138 Voyager vans).

Historical Footnotes: A poor year for sales, 1978 was also the final year for big cars from Chrysler Corp. Plymouth ranked No. 7 in production, just ahead of Dodge. Production of the new Horizon at the Belvidere, Illinois, plant began in November 1977. Chrysler thus became the first domestic automaker to build a front-drive subcompact. Volare sales dropped by 29 percent for the model year, due partly to success of the new Chrysler LeBaron. Fury faded away during the '78 model year, as had the Gran Fury before it. A new sporty Plymouth Sapporo to match the Dodge Challenger was now being imported from Mitsubishi in Japan.

1979 PLYMOUTH

After more than two decades in the lineup, the Fury name faded away, shrinking the Plymouth selection to just two models and a single (low) price class. A new Horizon-based hatchback coupe, on a shorter wheelbase but eight inches longer overall, was called Horizon TC3. Volare added a sports equipment package, but not much else.

HORIZON/TC3 — SERIES M — FOUR — "Horizons Unlimited," promised the 1979 factory sales catalog. Not quite, but Plymouth's front-drive subcompact now came in two forms: four-door hatchback and new two-door TC3 coupe. They were equivalent to Dodge's Omni and 024, respectively. Similar in design and basic equipment, the coupe and sedan differed significantly in appearance and size. TC3 rode a shorter wheelbase (96.7 inch versus 99.2 inch for the four-door), but the same basic chassis structure. Both models had Iso-Strut front suspension and rack-and-pinion steering. TC3 was promoted as "sporty," making use of a term that would, a few years later, become trendy throughout the industry. Four-door appearance was unchanged. TC3 had a grille consisting of five wide horizontal slots in a sloped body-color panel that extended forward from the hood. Above the grille on the driver's side was 'Plymouth' block lettering, just like the four-door. Single rectangular headlamps sat in recessed, trim-free housings. The inner fender lines extended back from the inner edge of the headlamp housings, so the hood was a bit lower than the fenders. Partly-curved parking/signal lamps were recess-mounted in the bumper area. Front side marker lenses were just ahead of the front wheels. 'Horizon' script sat on front fenders. TC3 had a six-window design, with a conventional quarter window just to the rear of the door, plus a triangular window at the very back that followed the sharp slope of the liftgate. Standard TC3 equipment included dual bodyside pin stripes, bright moldings, wheel trim rings, AM/FM radio, electric rear-window defroster, woodgrain instrument panel appliqué, luxury steering wheel, electric remote hatchback release, vinyl bucket front seats, and fold down rear seat. Tires were P165/75R13 glass-belted radial whitewalls. Larger steel-belted radials were available, as were Aramid-belted tires with outline white letters. Sport and Rallye TC3 packages were available, along with a "woody" look option for the four-door. The TC3 Sport Appearance package included a rear spoiler, blackout exterior treatment, 'TC3' decals, louvered quarter window appliqués, painted Rallye wheels, and four-spoke steering wheel. A Rallye instrument cluster contained a tachometer and trip odometer. A total of 14,709 coupes had the Sport package, while 4,154 carried the Rallye package. Cast aluminum wheels were also available. So were flip-out quarter windows. Four-door standard equipment included an AM

radio, electric rear-window defroster, lighter. whitewalls, and vinyl bodyside moldings. Both models carried the 104.7 cubic inch (1.7-liter) four with standard four-speed manual shift. Power steering, power brakes and TorqueFlite automatic were optional. Body colors this year were: Formal Black, Nightwatch Blue, Flame Orange, Light Cashmere, Chianti Red, and Spinnaker White, plus metallic Pewter Gray, Cadet Blue, Ensign Blue, Teal Frost, Teal Green Sunfire, Turquoise, or Medium Cashmere. TC3 could also have Bright Yellow, and both models had a choice of two-tones.

1979 Plymouth, Horizon hatchback with optional sunroof (OCW)

1979 Plymouth, Volare coupe with optional Duster decor package (OCW)

VOLARE — SERIES H — SIX/V-8 — Not much changed in Plymouth's compact, offered again with a base 225 cubic inch Slant Six engine and single-barrel carburetor. Volare's coupe could have a four-barrel 360 cubic inch V-8, rated 195 horsepower, for a price of $575 to $600. Otherwise, the standard engine upgrades for Volare were the two-barrel Slant Six ($41) and two-barrel 318 V-8 ($216). Volare six had a standard three-speed manual transmission with floor lever, with option of the four-speed overdrive unit ($149 extra). Volare V-8 came with TorqueFlite, and could get an optional maintenance-free battery. Only one trim level was offered, with sport coupe, four-door sedan or four-door station wagon body style. An electric choke heater was supposed to improve cold-weather startup. Galvanized metal body panels were installed to help protect against rust. The Duster name returned on a coupe package that cost only $30 (or $60 with quarter-window louvers). The Duster package included five-spoke painted wheels, two-tone paint, accent tape, performance options, louvered quarter windows, headlamp doors, and a rear deck spoiler. A Duster decor package added another $90. The wagon Sport package, priced considerably higher ($630), included a front air dam, tape stripes, blacked-out grille, and bucket seats. A total of 1,122 Volares had the Road Runner package (RPO code A57), which was also more costly. Cast aluminum wheels were optional this year.

I.D. DATA: Plymouth's 13-symbol Vehicle Identification Number (VIN) again was on the upper left corner of the instrument panel, visible through the windshield. Symbol one indicates car line: 'M' Horizon; 'H' Volare. Symbol two is series (price class): 'L' low. Symbols 3-4 show body type: '29' 2-dr. sport coupe; '41' 4-dr. sedan; '44' 4-dr. hatchback; '45' two-seat station wagon. Symbol five is the engine code: 'A' L4105 2Bbl.; 'C' L6225 1Bbl.; 'D' L6225 2Bbl.; 'G' V8318 2Bbl.; 'J' V8360 4Bbl. Symbol six is the model year code: '9' 1979. Symbol seven indicates assembly plant: 'B' Hamtramck, MI; 'D' Belvidere, IL; 'F' Newark, DE. The final six digits make up the sequential serial number, starting with 100001. Engine number coding is similar to 1976-78. As before, a Vehicle Safety Certification Label that displays (among other data) the date of manufacture is attached to the rear facing of the driver's door. A Body Code Plate is on the left front fender side shield, wheel housing, or left side of upper radiator support.

HORIZON (FOUR)

Model No.	Body/ Style No.	Body Type & Seating	Factory Price	Shipping Weight	Prod. Total
ML	44	4-dr. Hatch-4P	4122	2135	86,214

HORIZON TC3 (FOUR)

Model No.	Body/ Style No.	Body Type & Seating	Factory Price	Shipping Weight	Prod. Total
ML	24	2-dr. Hatch-4P	4482	2195	54,249

VOLARE (SIX/V-8)

Model No.	Body/ Style No.	Body Type & Seating	Factory Price	Shipping Weight	Prod. Total
HL	29	2-dr. Spt Cpe-5P	3956/4172	3050/3170	Note 1
HL	41	4-dr. Sedan-6P	4057/4273	3115/3235	Note 1
HL	45	4-dr. Sta Wag-6P	4433/4649	3325/3435	44,085

Note 1: Total coupe/sedan production, 134,734.

Factory Price And Weight Note: Prices and weights to left of slash are for six-cylinder, to right for V-8 engine.

ENGINE DATA: BASE FOUR (Horizon): Inline, overhead-cam four-cylinder. Cast iron block; aluminum head. Displacement: 104.7 cu. in. (1.7-liters). Bore & stroke: 3.13 x 3.40 in. Compression ratio: 8.2:1. Brake horsepower: 70 at 5200 R.P.M. Torque: 85 lb.-ft. at 2800 R.P.M. Five main bearings. Solid valve lifters. Carburetor: 2Bbl. Holley 5220. VIN Code: A. **BASE SIX (Volare):** Inline, overhead-valve six-cylinder. Cast iron block and head. Displacement: 225 cu. in. (3.7-liters). Bore & stroke: 3.40 x 4.12 in. Compression ratio: 8.4:1. Brake horsepower: 100 at 3600 R.P.M. Torque: 165 lb.-ft. at 1600 R.P.M. Four main bearings. Solid valve lifters. Carburetor: 1Bbl. Holley 1945. VIN Code: C. **OPTIONAL SIX (Volare):** Same as 225 cu. in. six above, but with 2Bbl. Carter BBD carburetor. Brake horsepower: 110 at 3600 R.P.M. Torque: 180 lb.-ft. at 2000 R.P.M. VIN Code: D. **OPTIONAL V-8 (Volare):** 90-degree, overhead valve V-8. Cast iron block and head. Displacement: 318 cu. in. (5.2-liters). Bore & stroke: 3.91 x 3.31 in. Compression ratio: 8.5:1. Brake horsepower: 135 at 4000 R.P.M. Torque: 250 lb.-ft. at 1600 R.P.M. Five main bearings. Hydraulic valve lifters. Carburetor: 2Bbl. Holley 2280. VIN Code: G. **OPTIONAL V-8 (Volare):** 90-degree, overhead valve V-8. Cast iron block and head. Displacement: 360 cu. in. (5.9-liters). Bore & stroke: 4.00 x 3.58 in. Compression ratio: 8.0:1. Brake horsepower: 195 at 4000 R.P.M. Torque: 280 lb.-ft. at 2400 R.P.M. Five main bearings. Hydraulic valve lifters. Carburetor: 4Bbl. Carter TQ VIN Code: J.

CHASSIS DATA: Wheelbase: (Horizon) 99.2 in.; (TC3) 96.7 in.; (Volare cpe) 108.7 in.; (Volare sed/wag) 112.7 in. Overall Length: (Horizon) 164.8 in. incl. optional bumper guards; (TC3) 172.7 in.; (Volare cpe) 197.2 in.; (Volare sed/wag) 201.2 in. Height: (Horizon) 53.7 in.; (TC3) 51.4 in.; (Volare cpe) 53.3 in.; (Volare sed) 55.3 in.; (Volare wag) 55.7 in. Width: (Horizon) 66.2 in.; (TC3) 66.0 in.; (Volare) 72.8 in. Front Tread: (Horizon/TC3) 56.0 in.; (Volare) 60.0 in. Rear Tread: (Horizon/TC3) 55.6 in.; (Volare) 58.5 in. Standard Tires: (Horizon) P155/80R13 GBR WSW; (TC3) P165/75R13 GBR WSW; (Volare) D78x14; (Volare wag) F78x14.

1979 Plymouth, Volare Premier sedan with optional wire wheel covers (OCW)

TECHNICAL: Transmission: Three-speed manual trans. (floor lever) standard on Volare six. Gear ratios: (1st) 3.08:1; (2nd) 1.70:1; (3rd) 1.00:1; (Rev) 2.90:1. Four-speed overdrive available on Volare six: (1st) 3.09:1; (2nd) 1.67:1; (3rd) 1.00:1; (4th) 0.71:1; (Rev) 3.00:1. Four-speed manual (floor shift) standard on Horizon: (1st) 3.45:1; (2nd) 1.94:1; (3rd) 1.29:1; (4th) 0.97:1; (Rev) 3.17:1. TorqueFlite three-speed automatic standard on Volare V-8, optional on others. Volare gear ratios: (1st) 2.45:1; (2nd) 1.45:1; (3rd) 1.00:1; (Rev) 2.22:1. Horizon gear ratios: (1st) 2.47:1; (2nd) 1.47:1; (3rd) 1.00:1; (Rev) 2.10:1. Standard final drive ratio: (Horizon/TC3) 3.37:1 w/4spd, 3.46:1 w/auto.; (Volare six) 3.23:1 w/3spd, 3.23:1 or 3.21:1 w/4spd, 2.7:1 or 2.76:1 w/auto.; (Volare V8318) 2.47:1 or 2.45:1; (Volare V8360) 2.71:1; (Volare wag) 2.94:1, 3.21:1 or 2.45:1. Steering: (Horizon) rack and pinion; (others) recirculating ball. Suspension: (Horizon/TC3) Iso-Strut independent coil front w/anti-sway bar, independent trailing arm coil rear w/integral anti-sway; (Volare) isolated transverse front torsion bars w/anti-sway bar, semi-elliptic rear leaf springs. Brakes: Front disc, rear drum. Ignition: Electronic. Body construction: Unibody. Fuel tank: (Horizon/TC3) 13 gal.; (Volare) 18 gal. exc. V-8/wagon, 19.5 gal.

DRIVETRAIN OPTIONS: Engines: 225 cu. in., 2Bbl. six: Volare ($43). 318 cu. in., 2Bbl. V-8: Volare ($216). 318 cu. in., 4Bbl. V-8: Calif. Volare ($271). 360 cu. in., 4Bbl. V-8: Volare ($575-$600). Transmission/Differential: TorqueFlite: Horizon/Volare ($319). Four-speed manual trans. w/floor lever: Volare ($149). Sure grip differential: Volare ($61). Optional axle ratio ($18) Power Accessories: Power steering ($155-$156). Power brakes ($72). Suspension: H.D. susp.: Horizon 4dr. ($25); Volare ($25). Sport susp.: TC3 ($41). Other: Trailer assist pkg.: Volare ($157). Maintenance-free battery: Horizon ($20). Long-life battery: Volare ($32). California emission system ($79).

HORIZON/TC3 CONVENIENCE/APPEARANCE OPTIONS: Option Packages: Rallye equipment pkg.: TC3 ($177-$352). Sport pkg.: TC3 ($278-$340). Sport/Classic two-tone paint pkg. ($114-$164). Custom exterior pkg.: 4dr. ($74). Premium exterior pkg.: TC3 ($78); 4dr. ($122-$199). Custom interior pkg.: 4dr. ($79-$101). Premium interior pkg. ($146-$270). Premium woodgrain pkg.: 4dr. ($290-$331). Popular equipment group ($267-$279). Comfort/Convenience: Air cond. ($507). Tinted glass ($61). Tinted windshield ($43). Luxury steering wheel: 4dr. ($18). Rallye instrument cluster: TC3 ($76). Electric clock w/trip odometer ($28). Rear wiper/washer ($62). Locking gas cap ($7). Locking glove box: 4dr. ($5). Horns and Mirrors: Dual horns ($9). Remote left mirror: 4dr. ($17). Dual remote mirrors ($32-$49). Dual remote sport mirrors: TC3 ($61). Day/night mirror ($11). Entertainment: AM/FM radio: 4dr. ($73). AM/FM stereo radio: 4dr. ($141); TC3 ($67). Rear speaker: TC3 ($24). Exterior: Removable glass sunroof ($176). Rear spoiler: TC3 ($53). Flip-out quarter windows: TC3 ($54). Black vinyl body-side moldings: TC3 ($41). Moldings (4dr.): belt ($16); drip rail ($18); upper door frame ($31); wheel lip ($28); sill ($20). Door edge protectors ($12-$20). Bumper guards: 4dr. ($43). Bumper rub strips: TC3 ($34). Multi-color tape stripe: 4dr. ($70). Luggage rack ($86). Undercoating ($33). Interior: Console: storage ($22); shift lever ($32). Cloth/vinyl bucket seats: TC3 ($22-$52). Vinyl or cloth/vinyl bucket seats: 4dr. (N/A). Tonneau cover: TC3 ($44). Cargo area dress-up ($43). Color-keyed floor mats ($27). Color-keyed seatbelts ($31). Wheels and Tires: Wheel trim rings: 4dr. ($41). Deluxe wheel covers: 4dr. ($41). Cast aluminum wheels ($165-$246). Rallye wheels ($39-$80). Bright Rallye hubs ($39). 165/75R13 GBR WSW ($17). 165/75R13 SBR WSW ($34-$51). 175/75R13 WSW ($51-$68). 185/70R13 OWL: TC3 ($136). Conventional spare tire ($13-$25).

VOLARE CONVENIENCE/APPEARANCE OPTIONS: Option Packages: Road Runner pkg.: cpe ($651). Sport pkg.: wag ($630). Handling/performance pkg.: cpe ($218). Duster Coupe pkg. ($30); w/quarter window louvers ($60). Duster decor pkg.: cpe ($90). Custom exterior pkg. ($75-$89). Custom interior pkg. ($151-$196). Premium exterior pkg. ($79-$144). Premium interior pkg. ($275-$499). Premier wagon woodgrain group ($232). Two-tone paint pkg. ($142). Two-tone decor pkg. ($78-$96). Basic group ($626-$712). Light pkg. ($46). Protection group ($30-$38). Deluxe insulation pkg. ($39-$50). Comfort/Convenience: Air cond. ($507). Rear defogger, blower-type ($52); electric ($90). Automatic speed control ($98). Power seat ($153). Power windows ($120-$169). Power door locks ($79-$106). Power liftgate release: wag ($23). Tinted glass ($61). Tinted windshield ($43). Luxury steering wheel ($31). Tuff steering wheel ($8-$39). Tilt steering wheel ($32-$71). Intermittent wipers ($36). Digital clock ($51). Inside hood release ($13). Locking glovebox ($5). Lighter ($7). Horns and Mirrors: Dual horns ($9). Remote left-hand mirror ($17). Dual remote mirrors ($32-$49). Dual remote sport mirrors: cpe ($44-$61). Day/night mirror ($11). Entertainment: AM radio ($79); w/8track player ($152-$231); w/CB ($262-$342). AM/FM radio ($73-$153). AM/FM stereo radio ($141-$220); w/8track tape player ($235-$314); w/CB ($403-$482). Rear speaker ($24). Exterior: T-Bar roof: cpe ($600). Full vinyl roof: sed ($95). Halo vinyl roof: cpe ($95-$111). Black vinyl bodyside moldings ($41). Belt moldings ($18). Door edge protectors ($12-$20). Upper door frame moldings: sed/wag ($31). Wheel lip moldings ($22). Hood strobe stripe: cpe ($42). Air deflector: wag ($28). Luggage rack: wag ($86). Bumper guards, front/rear ($43). Protective bumper rub strips ($34). Undercoating ($23-$33). Interior: Console: cpe/wag ($55-$95). Vinyl bench seat: sed ($30). Vinyl bucket seats: cpe/wag ($107). Center cushion w/armrest: cpe ($39). Rear armrest ($12). Cargo area carpet w/storage bins: wag ($53). Color-keyed mats ($23). Pedal dress-up ($9). Trunk dress-up ($43). Color-keyed seatbelts ($18). Wheels and Tires: Deluxe wheel covers ($41). Premium wheel covers ($37-$79). Wire wheel covers ($94-$136). Cast aluminum wheels ($144-$280). Styled wheels ($94-$136). D78x14 WSW ($45). DR78x14 BSW ($56). DR78x14 WSW ($56-$101). ER78x14 BSW ($75). ER78x14 WSW ($45-$119). FR78x14 wide WSW ($72-$192). FR70x14 OWL ($129-$248). Conventional spare tire (NC).

HISTORY: Introduced: October 5, 1978. Model year production: Chrysler reported a total of 319,282 passenger cars shipped. Total North American passenger-car production for the U.S. market of 311,008 units included 137,635 four-cylinder, 139,797 six-cylinder, and 33,576 V-8s. Calendar year production (U.S.): 358,863 (not incl. 4,874 Voyagers). Calendar year sales by U.S. dealers: 317,258 (not incl. 8,265 Voyagers). Model year sales by U.S. dealers: 337,895 (not incl. 59,576 imports and 10,653 Voyagers).

Historical Footnotes: Weight-cutting had become a major theme. The heaviest Chrysler product weighed less than 3,900 pounds at the curb. All models had aluminum and plastic master cylinders. All sixes and V-8s had lightweight radiators. To boost gas mileage, the big 400 and 440 cubic inch V-8s were abandoned. Plymouth added another import: the Champ hatchback coupe. The subcompact imports (Arrow/Sapporo/Champ) helped Chrysler meet this year's CAFE standards, but couldn't be counted for 1980 requirements. Horizon sales rose by almost 58 percent for the 1979 model year, but total volume was the lowest ever.

1980 PLYMOUTH

Two years after leaving the lineup, the Gran Fury nameplate returned, but on a shorter wheelbase than before. This would be Volare's final year, as the new K-car was being readied for 1981 introduction.

1980 Plymouth, Horizon TC3 hatchback with optional Sport Appearance package (OCW)

HORIZON/TC3 — SERIES M — FOUR — Neither the subcompact four-door hatchback sedan nor TC3 two-door sport coupe changed in appearance. New options included automatic speed control, halogen headlamps, and intermittent windshield wipers. Also available: a Tri-Lite sunroof with flip-up or removable glass panel. Both four-passenger models again had the standard 104.7 cubic inch (1.7-liter) four-cylinder engine and four-speed manual transaxle. Four-doors had a standard AM radio, tinted glass, three-spoke steering wheel, rear defroster, electric clock, and trip odometer. They could also have a selection of Premium and Custom exterior and interior packages to dress up the basic design. Standard vinyl bucket seats came in cashmere or black. The option list included a Premium Woodgrain package that added woodgrain appliqués along body-sides and the lower liftgate panel. A total of 1,701 Horizon coupes had a new Turismo package that cost around $1,200. That package included cast aluminum wheels, rear spoiler, blackout moldings, low-back vinyl premium bucket seats, and bright solid-color paint. A TC3 Sport Appearance Package included a 'TC3' decal between door and rear wheel opening. Coupe options also included quick-ratio power steering, power brakes, rear spoiler, and premium interior. Body colors were: Graphic Blue, Graphic Red, Baron Red, Natural Suede Tan, Light Cashmere, Nightwatch Blue, Formal Black. Bright Yellow, Spinnaker White, and a selection of metallics: Mocha Brown, Burnished Silver, Crimson Red, Teal Tropic Green, or Frost Blue. Four-doors could also have four two-tone combinations; TC3 had three; the TC3 Sport Package, four two-tones.

VOLARE — SERIES H — SIX/V-8 — For its final year in the Dodge lineup, Volare sported a new symmetrical crosshatch grille in five-row pattern, with large 'Plymouth' block letters inset into the upper header bar. Parking lamps again stood between grille and headlamps, but were narrower than earlier versions. Front side marker lenses were now vertical, at corner of fender, aligned with new single rectangular headlamps (formerly horizontal and set farther back). Halogen headlamps became optional. Two-doors had triangular sail-shaped quarter windows. Horizontal-style taillamps each were split into four sections: two narrow vertical lenses flanking wider red and white recessed lenses. Between the taillamps was a panel containing 'Plymouth' block lettering. 'Volare' script was on the decklid as well as front fenders. Bodyside ornamentation was new, and a landau vinyl top joined the option list. Base engine was again the 225 cubic inch Slant Six, with 318 cubic inch (5.2-liter) V-8 optional. Three-speed manual transmission was standard, as were cloth/vinyl bench seats. Volare body colors were: Natural Suede Tan, Baron Red, Graphic Red (coupe only), Nightwatch Blue, Light Cashmere, Formal Black, and Spinnaker White; plus metallic Burnished Silver, Crimson Red, Teal Tropic Green, Frost Blue, Teal Frost, and Mocha Brown. Three two-tones were offered. A new optional AM/FM stereo came with a cassette player and Dolby noise reduction. Quite a selection of option packages was available. The modestly-priced Duster Coupe package included colorful new bodyside and decklid tape stripes, 'Duster' front fender nameplates, and plaid cloth/vinyl high-back bucket seats. The Premier package's vinyl top covered up the standard triangular windows, showing wide, squarish opera-type windows instead. Premier coupes and sedans also had wheel opening and sill moldings, hood accent stripes, bodyside stripes, a stand-up hood medallion, rear lower deck appliqué, driver's remote mirror, day/night mirror, dual horns, and woodtone instrument panel. Wagons with a Premier package had woodtone trim on bodysides and tailgate, along with woodtone instrument panel cluster and glovebox door. A new Custom package included (among other extras) dual horns, an inside hood release, wheel lip and sill moldings, and belt moldings. Volare's Road Runner package included a black grille, headlamp doors

and parking lamp surround; black anodized moldings; dual remote sport mirrors; bright sill moldings with black surround; body accent stripes; rear spoiler; and unique gas cap. 'Road Runner' decals went on front fenders and spoiler; 'Plymouth' on the spoiler. Eight-spoke wheels with stainless steel ornamentation held P195/75R14 blackwall tires. Underneath was a heavy-duty suspension; inside, vinyl bucket seats and a "Tuff" steering wheel. The Sport Wagon package included wheel-opening flares, front air dam, tape stripe, and black-highlight grille; plus dual body-colored sport mirrors, "Tuff" three-spoke steering wheel, and eight-spoke road wheels. A total of 5,586 Duster coupe packages (RPO code A42) were installed, while 496 Volares had the Road Runner package and 12,644 the Premier package. In addition to the base two and four-door models, and a station wagon, Volare offered a new Special series. For a slightly higher price, the buyer got an automatic transmission, power steering, cloth/vinyl bench seat, whitewalls, deluxe wheel covers, body-side tape stripes, and wheel opening moldings. Specials came only with the Slant Six engine.

1980 Plymouth, Volare sedan with optional vinyl roof and custom exterior package (OCW)

GRAN FURY — SERIES J — SIX/V-8 — Out of the lineup for two years, Gran Fury was back again in downsized form, fully restyled on a 118.5 inch wheelbase. The four-door pillared hardtop had a long hood and a bold, blacked-out grille in 8x4 checkerboard pattern with chrome header. Recessed, side-by-side quad rectangular headlamps stood over wide parking lamps. Wide horizontal taillamps wrapped around the quarter panels. Unlike the old Gran Fury, this R-bodied version carried a base Slant Six engine with TorqueFlite automatic transmission. The 318 cubic inch two-barrel V-8 was optional. So was a 360 cubic inch V-8. required with the heavy-duty package. California models had a four-barrel 318 V-8. Turn signals and other controls went on the steering column. The suspension used front torsion bars with an anti-sway bar. Gran Fury was similar to Chrysler's Newport and Dodge St. Regis, and sold mainly to fleet buyers. Base and Salon versions were offered. Among the options was a heavy-duty trailer towing assist package. Only 31 Gran Fury models are reported to have had the optional handling package. Standard equipment included power steering and brakes. P195/75R15 glass-belted radial whitewall tires, tinted glass, dual flag mirrors, dual horns, cigarette lighter, day/night inside mirror, and inside hood release. Belt, drip and wheel opening moldings were included. Gran Fury Salon added protective bumper rub strips, sill moldings. and deluxe wheel covers.

I.D. DATA: Plymouth's 13-symbol Vehicle Identification Number (VIN) again was on the upper left corner of the instrument panel, visible through the windshield. Symbol one indicates car line: 'M' Horizon; 'H' Volare; 'J' Gran Fury. Symbol two is series (price class): 'E' economy; 'L' low; 'H' high. Symbols 3-4 show body type: '29' 2-dr. sport coupe; '41' 4-dr. sedan; '42' 4-dr. pillared hardtop; '44' 4-dr. hatchback; '45' two-seat station wagon. Symbol five is the engine code 'A' L4105 2Bbl.; 'C' L6225 1Bbl.; 'G' V8318 2Bbl.; 'K' V8360 2Bbl. Symbol six is the model year code: 'A' 1980. Symbol seven indicates assembly plant: 'A' Lynch Road; 'B' Hamtramck, MI; 'D' Belvidere, IL; 'F' Newark, DE. The final six digits make up the sequential serial number, starting with 100001. Engine number coding is similar to 1976-79. As before, a Vehicle Safety Certification Label that displays (among other data) the date of manufacture is attached to the rear facing of the driver's door. A Body Code Plate is on the left front fender side shield, wheel housing, or left side of upper radiator support.

HORIZON (FOUR)

Model No.	Body/ Style No.	Body Type & Seating	Factory Price	Shipping Weight	Prod. Total
ML	44	4-dr. Hatch-4P	4925	2135	85,751

HORIZON TC3 (FOUR)

Model No.	Body/ Style No.	Body Type & Seating	Factory Price	Shipping Weight	Prod. Total
ML	24	2-dr. Hatch-4P	5271	2095	59,527

VOLARE (SIX/V-8)

Model No.	Body/ Style No.	Body Type & Seating	Factory Price	Shipping Weight	Prod. Total
HL	29	2-dr. Spt Cpe-5P	4730/4941	3110/3260	14,453
HL	41	4-dr. Sedan-6P	4847/5058	3165/3320	25,768
HL	45	4-dr. Sta Wag-6P	5089/5300	3340/3480	16,895

VOLARE SPECIAL (SIX)

Model No.	Body/ Style No.	Body Type & Seating	Factory Price	Shipping Weight	Prod. Total
HE	29	2-dr. Cpe-5P	4977/----	3155/----	12,334
HE	41	4-dr. Sedan-6P	4994/----	3210/----	20,613

GRAN FURY (SIX/V-8)

Model No.	Body/ Style No.	Body Type & Seating	Factory Price	Shipping Weight	Prod. Total
JL	42	4-dr. Pill. HT-6P	6280/6513	3520/3605	12,576

GRAN FURY SALON (SIX/V-8)

Model No.	Body/ Style No.	Body Type & Seating	Factory Price	Shipping Weight	Prod. Total
JH	42	4-dr. Pill. HT-6P	6711/6944	3545/3630	2,024

Factory Price And Weight Note: Prices and weights to left of slash are for six-cylinder, to right for V-8 engine.

ENGINE DATA: BASE FOUR (Horizon/TC3): Inline, overhead-cam four-cylinder. Cast iron block; aluminum head. Displacement: 104.7 cu. in. (1.7-liters). Bore & stroke: 3.13 x 3.40 in. Compression ratio: 8.2:1. Brake horsepower: 65 at 5200 R.P.M. Torque: 85 lb.-ft. at 2400 R.P.M. Five main bearings. Solid valve lifters. Carburetor: 2Bbl. Holley 5220. VIN Code: A. **BASE SIX** (Volare, Gran Fury): Inline, overhead-valve six-cylinder. Cast iron block and head. Displacement: 225 cu. in. (3.7-liters). Bore & stroke: 3.40 x 4.12 in. Compression ratio: 8.4:1. Brake horse-power: 90 at 3600 R.P.M. Torque: 160 lb.-ft. at 1600 R.P.M. Four main bearings. Solid valve lifters. Carburetor: 1Bbl. Holley 1945, VIN Code: C. **OPTIONAL V-8** (Volare, Gran Fury): 90-degree, overhead valve V-8. Cast iron block and head. Displacement: 318 cu. in. (5.2-liters). Bore & stroke: 3.91 x 3.31 in. Compression ratio: 8.5:1. Brake horsepower: 120 at 3600 R.P.M. Torque: 245 lb.-ft. at 1600 R.P.M. Five main bearings. Hydraulic valve lifters. Carburetor: 2Bbl. Carter BBD. VIN Code: G. Note: High-altitude models could have a 4Bbl. V-8 318 rated 155 brake horse-power at 4000 R.P.M. **OPTIONAL V-8** (Gran Fury): 90-degree, overhead valve V-8. Cast iron block and head. Displacement: 360 cu. in. (5.9-liters). Bore & stroke: 4.00 x 3.58 in. Compression ratio: 8.4:1. Brake horsepower 130 at 3200 R.P.M. Torque: 255 lb.-ft. at 2000 R.P.M. Five main bearings. Hydraulic valve lifters. Carburetor: 2Bbl. Carter BBD. VIN Code: K.

CHASSIS DATA: Wheelbase: (Horizon) 99.2 in.; (TC3) 96.7 in.; (Volare cpe) 108.7 in.; (Volare sed/wag) 112.7 in.; (Gran Fury) 118.5 in. Overall Length: (Horizon) 164.8 in. incl. optional bumper guards; (TC3) 172.8 in.; (Volare cpe) 200.3 in.; (Volare sed/wag) 204.3 in.; (Gran Fury) 220.2 in. Height: (Horizon) 53.4 in.; (TC3) 51.1 in.; (Volare cpe) 53.6 in.; (Volare sed) 55.3 in.; (Volare wag) 55.5 in.; (Gran Fury) 54.5 in. Width: (Horizon) 65.8 in.; (TC3) 66.7 in.; (Volare) 72.4 in.; (Gran Fury) 77.6 in. Front Tread: (Horizon/TC3) 56.1 in.; (Volare) 60.0 in.; (Gran Fury) 61.9 in. Rear Tread: (Horizon/TC3) 55.6 in.; (Volare) 59.5 in.; (Gran Fury) 62.0 in. Standard Tires: (Horizon) P155/80R13 GBR WSW; (TC3) P175/75R13 GBR BSW; (Volare) P195/75R14 GBR BSW; (Gran Fury) P195/75R15 GBR WSW.

TECHNICAL: Transmission: Three-speed manual trans. (floor lever) standard on Volare six. Gear ratios: (1st) 3.08:1; (2nd) 1.70:1; (3rd) 1.00:1; (Rev) 2.90:1. Four-speed overdrive available on Volare six: (1st) 3.09:1; (2nd) 1.67:1; (3rd) 1.00:1; (4th) 0.71:1; (Rev) 3.00:1. Four-speed manual (floor shift) standard on Horizon/TC3: (1st) 3.45:1; (2nd) 1.94:1; (3rd) 1.29:1; (4th) 0.97:1; (Rev) 3.17:1. TorqueFlite three-speed automatic standard on Gran Fury, optional on others. Six-cylinder gear ratios: (1st) 2.74:1; (2nd) 1.54:1; (3rd) 1.00:1; (Rev) 2.22:1. V-8 ratios (1st) 2.45:1 (2nd) 1.45:1; (3rd) 1.00:1; (Rev) 2.22:1. Horizon ratios (1st) 2.47:1; (2nd) 1.47:1; (3rd) 1.00:1; (Rev) 2.10:1. Standard final drive ratio: (Horizon/TC3) 3.37:1 w/4spd, 3.48:1 w/auto.; (Volare six) 3.23:1 w/3spd, 3.23:1 or 3.21:1 w/4spd, 2.76:1 or 2.71:1 w/auto.; (Volare Special) 2.76:1; (Volare V-8) 2.47:1 or 2.24:1 w/auto. (Volare wag) 3.21:1 or 2.45:1; (Gran Fury six) 2.94:1; (G. Fury V-8) 2.45:1. Steering: (Horizon) rack and pinion; (others) recirculating ball. Suspension: (Horizon/TC3) Iso-Strut independent coil front w/anti-sway bar, independent trailing arm coil rear w/integral anti-sway; (Volare) isolated transverse front torsion bars w/anti-sway bar, semi-elliptic rear leaf springs; (Gran Fury) longitudinal front torsion bars, semi-elliptic rear leaf springs. Brakes: Front disc, rear drum. Ignition: Electronic. Body construction: Unibody. Fuel tank: (Horizon/TC3) 13 gal.; (Volare) 18 gal.; (Gran Fury) 21 gal.

DRIVETRAIN OPTIONS: Engines: 318 cu. in., 2Bbl. V-8: Volare ($211); Gran Fury ($233). 318 cu. in., 4Bbl. V-8: Calif. Volare ($266): G. Fury ($295). 360 cu. in., 2Bbl. V-8: G. Fury ($457). Transmission/Differential: TorqueFlite: Horizon ($322-$340); Volare ($340). Four-speed manual trans. w/floor lever: Volare ($153). Sure grip differential: Volare ($63); G. Fury ($77). Power Accessories: Power steering: Horizon ($161); Volare ($166). Power brakes: Horizon/Volare ($77). Suspension: H.D. susp.: Horizon 4-dr., Volare ($26); G. Fury ($30). Sport susp.: TC3 ($43). H.D. shock absorbers: G. Fury ($8). Other: Trailer assist pkg.: G. Fury ($258). Maintenance-free battery: Horizon ($21). Long-life battery: Volare ($33); G. Fury ($36). Max. cooling: Volare ($34-$58); G. Fury ($77-$104). California emission system ($254).

HORIZON/TC3 CONVENIENCE/APPEARANCE OPTIONS: Option Pack-ages: Turismo pkg.: TC3 ($1199-$1227). Sport pkg.: TC3 ($340-$431). Sport/Classic two-tone paint pkg. ($131-$137). Custom exterior pkg.: 4dr. ($101). Premium exterior pkg. ($126-$207). Custom interior pkg.: 4dr. ($89-$112). Premium interior pkg. ($239-$355). Premium woodgrain pkg.: 4dr. ($300-$344). Popular equipment group ($267-$273). Comfort/Convenience: Air cond. ($541). Auto. speed control ($101). Luxury steering wheel: 4dr. ($18). Sport steering wheel ($18-

$40). Rallye instrument cluster w/tach: TC3 ($65). Intermittent wiper ($38). Rear wiper/washer: 4dr. ($63). Lighter ($8). Locking gas cap ($7). Locking glovebox: 4dr. ($5). Lighting, Horns and Mirrors: Halogen headlamps ($37). Dual horns ($9). Remote left mirror: 4dr. ($19). Dual remote mirrors: 4dr. ($38-$57). Dual remote sport mirrors: TC3 ($69). Day/night mirror ($11). Entertainment: AM/FM radio: 4dr. ($58). AM/FM stereo radio: 4dr. ($93); TC3 ($35). Rear speaker: TC3 ($19). Exterior: Removable glass sunroof ($182). Rear spoiler: TC3 ($55). Black vinyl bodyside moldings: TC3 ($44). Moldings (4dr.): belt ($17); drip rail ($19); sill ($21); upper door frame ($32); wheel lip ($29). Door edge protectors ($13-$21). Bumper guards: 4dr. ($45). Bumper rub strips: TC3 ($35). Hood/bodyside/deck tape stripe: 4dr. ($45). Bodyside/deck stripe: TC3 ($31). Luggage rack ($90). Undercoating ($34). Lower body coating ($31). Interior: Console: storage ($22); shift lever ($33). Cloth/vi-nyl bucket seats: TC3 ($22-$53). Vinyl or cloth/vinyl bucket seats: 4dr. (NC). Bucket seats w/passenger recliner: TC3 (NC). Tonneau cover: TC3 ($46). Cargo area carpet: ($31); dress-up ($45). Color-keyed floor mats: front ($24); front/rear ($42). Color-keyed seatbelts ($23). Wheels and Tires: Wheel trim rings: 4dr. ($44). Deluxe wheel covers: 4dr. ($44). Cast aluminum wheels ($171-$254). Rallye wheels ($39-$83). P165/75R13 WSW: 4dr. ($17). P165/75R13 WSW: TC3 ($43). P175/75R13 SBR WSW ($78-$86). P185/70R13 Aramid BSW: TC3 ($45-$131). P185/70R13 Aramid OWL: TC3 ($106-$192). Conven-tional spare tire ($13-$26).

1980 Plymouth, Volare station wagon with optional Premier Woodgrain package and roof rack (OCW)

VOLARE CONVENIENCE/APPEARANCE OPTIONS: Option Packages: Road Runner pkg.: cpe ($586). Wagon Sport pkg. ($721). Sport appear-ance pkg. ($192-$254). Handling/performance pkg.: cpe/wag ($385). Duster Coupe pkg. ($155). Custom pkg. ($258-$386). Premier pkg. ($513-$814). Two-tone paint pkg. ($148). Basic group ($246-$403). Light pkg. ($46). Protection group ($56-$64). Deluxe insulation pkg. ($40-$51). Comfort/Convenience: Air Cond. ($543). Rear defogger, blower-type ($53); electric ($97). Automatic speed control ($106). Power seat ($163). Power windows ($130-$183). Power door locks ($83-$117). Power liftgate release: wag ($24). Tinted glass ($66). Tinted windshield ($44). Luxury steering wheel: wag ($32). Tuff steering wheel ($24-$56). Tilt steering wheel ($20-$76). Intermittent wipers ($39). Tailgate wiper/washer: wag ($64). Digital clock ($55). Inside hood release ($10). Locking glovebox ($6). Lighter ($8). Locking gas cap ($7). Light-ing, Horns and Mirrors: Halogen headlamps ($37). Dual horns ($10). Remote left-hand mirror ($18). Dual remote mirrors ($36-$54). Dual remote sport mirrors ($50-$68). Day/night mirror ($11). Entertainment: AM radio ($90); w/8track player ($143-$233). AM/FM radio ($58-$148). AM/FM stereo radio ($93-$183); w/8track tape player ($166-$256); w/cassette ($220-$310); w/CB ($351-$441). Rear speaker ($19). Radio delete ($51 credit). Exterior: T-Bar roof: cpe ($614). Full vinyl roof: sed ($97). Landau vinyl roof: cpe ($161-$178) Black vinyl bodyside moldings ($44). Belt moldings ($17). Door edge protectors ($13-$21). Upper door frame moldings: sed/wag ($34). Wheel lip mold-ings ($24). Air deflector: wag ($28). Luggage rack: wag ($91). Protective bumper rub strips ($36). Undercoating ($23-$34). Interior: Console: cpe/wag ($34-$99). Vinyl bench seat: sed ($30). Vinyl bucket seats: cpe/wag ($110). Center cushion w/armrest: cpe/wag ($44). Rear armrest ($12). Cargo area carpet: wag ($69); w/storage bins ($93). Cargo security cover: wag ($46). Color-keyed mats: front ($24); rear ($19). Pedal dress-up ($9). Trunk dress-up ($45). Color-keyed seatbelts ($23). Wheels and Tires: Deluxe wheel covers ($44). Premium wheel covers ($37-$81). Wire wheel covers ($106-$150). Cast aluminum wheels ($133-$287). Styled spoke wheels ($110-$154). P195/75R14 GBR WSW ($49). P205/75R14 SBR WSW ($84-$133). FR70x14 Aramid OWL ($150-$199). Conventional spare tire ($25).

GRAN FURY CONVENIENCE/APPEARANCE OPTIONS: Option Packag-es: Basic group ($1203). Two-tone paint pkg. ($168). Open Road han-dling pkg. ($269). Light pkg. ($87). Comfort/Convenience: Air conditioning ($670); auto-temp ($720) but ($50) w/option/pkg. Rear defroster, electric ($113). Auto. speed control ($122). Power seat ($183). Power windows ($228). Power door locks ($139). Power decklid release ($30-$46). Illuminated entry system ($62). Luxury steering wheel ($20). Leather-covered steering wheel ($62). Tilt steering wheel ($85). Digital clock ($61). Intermittent wipers ($44). Locking gas cap ($9). Lighting, Horns and Mirrors: Halogen headlamps ($42). Cornering lights ($55). Triad horns ($22). Remote driver's mirror ($21). Dual remote-

control mirrors ($31-$52). Lighted vanity mirror ($53). Entertainment: AM radio ($106). AM/FM radio ($58-$164). AM/FM stereo ($103-$209); w/8track tape player ($181-$287); w/cassette ($241-$347); w/CB ($389-$495). Search-tune AM/FM stereo ($224-$330). Rear speaker ($22). Power antenna ($54). Exterior: Power glass sunroof ($1053). Full vinyl roof ($162). Vinyl bodyside moldings ($55). Sill moldings: base ($31). Bumper guards ($62). Bumper rub strips: base ($41). Bodyside tape stripe ($49). Undercoating ($31). Interior: Vinyl bench seat ($34). Color-keyed floor mats: front ($26); rear ($21). Color-keyed seatbelts ($27). Pedal dress-up ($10). Trunk dress-up ($70). Litter container ($9). Wheels and Tires: Deluxe wheel covers: base ($49). Premier wheel covers ($44-$93). Premium wheel covers ($91-$140). Wire wheel covers ($266-$315). Forged aluminum wheels ($336-$385). P205/75R15 SBR WSW ($92). P205/75R15 Aramid-belted white/gold ($179). P225/70R15 SBR WSW ($186). Conventional spare ($27).

1980 Plymouth, Gran Fury pillared hardtop (OCW)

HISTORY: Introduced: October 1, 1979. Model year production: Chrysler reported a total of 249,941 passenger cars shipped. Total North American production for the U.S. market of 249,629 units included 145,284 four-cylinder, 82,165 six-cylinder, and 22,180 V-8s. Calendar year production: 287,065. Calendar year sales by U.S. dealers: 251,312. Model year sales by U.S. dealers: 239,627 (not incl. 57,598 imported Arrow/Champs and 10,311 Sapporos).

Historical Footnotes: Horizon TC3 was the only Chrysler-Plymouth domestic model to register a sales gain for the 1980 model year. Volare, which had sold well when introduced a few years earlier, slipped considerably (down over 50 percent this year). That loss resulted from its unimpressive fuel mileage, the popularity of GM's new X-cars, and the expectation of a "better" front-drive Dodge/Plymouth model for 1981. Even an aggressive advertising campaign and offers of rebates didn't help Volare much.

1981 PLYMOUTH

Both Plymouth and Dodge gained a new front-drive compact: the Reliant (and Aries) K-car. powered by a base 2.2-liter Trans4 engine. That aluminum-head, overhead-cam engine was the first four produced by Chrysler since the 1930s. It produced 84 horsepower and had 8.5:1 compression. Optional on Reliant was a 2.6-liter four, built by Mitsubishi in Japan. Elsewhere in the lineup, the subcompact coupe was now called just TC3, rather than Horizon TC3. Both the Horizon sedan and TC3 coupe added Miser models. All Plymouths had thick primer, precoated steel and plastic to improve corrosion resistance. A new 17-symbol Vehicle Identification Number was initiated this year. The electronic feedback carburetor, used in California models for 1980, was now in all fours and V-8s.

HORIZON — SERIES M — FOUR — The subcompact four-door's previous crosshatch-pattern grille was replaced by a simple pattern of thin vertical bars, running full width between the headlamps, unadorned by any emblem. As before, small 'Plymouth' block lettering was above the left headlamp. Single headlamps and wraparound parking/marker lamps were similar to 1980, though Plymouth promoted the parking lamps as new this year. As before, front fenders held 'Horizon' script. New two-color taillamps (red/clear) put turn signal, stop and taillamp functions in a single bulb. New interiors came in saddle grain vinyl, plus optional LaCorde and Monteverdi II cloth. Seven body colors were new. Tinted glass and a rear-window defroster, formerly standard, now became optional. Also added to the option list: a leather-wrapped steering wheel, and AM/FM stereo with cassette or 8track player. Various option packages were available too. Horizon wasn't any bigger than before, but passenger capacity as noted in the factory catalog grew from four to five. This year marked the first appearance of Miser, lighter in weight, with a specially calibrated 104.7 cubic inch (1.7-liter) engine and 2.6:1 overall top gear ratio. Reliant's new 135 cubic inch (2.2-liter) Trans4 engine became

optional on Horizon, but the 1.7 was standard. Body colors were: Ginger, Nightwatch Blue, Sunlight White, Graphic Yellow, Pearl White, Graphic Red, Formal Black, and Baron Red; plus metallic Glencoe Green, Daystar Blue, and Burnished Silver. Vivid Blue Starmist and Spice Tan Starmist were offered at extra cost. Three two-tones were available (except on Miser). With a price tag of $591 to $839, Horizon's Euro-Sedan package included blackout trim, moldings and bumpers; P175/75R13 SBR black-wall tires on cast aluminum wheels; and new bodyside stripes. Inside was a Rallye instrument cluster with tachometer, clock and trip odometer; four-spoke sport steering wheel; and LaCorde cloth/vinyl bucket seats. Mechanically, however, the Euro-Sedan offered nothing special beyond a stiffer suspension. A total of 2,483 cars had either the Euro or Turismo (coupe) package, which carried RPO code A69.

1981 Plymouth, TC3 Turismo hatchback (OCW)

TC3 — SERIES M — FOUR — For the first time, the subcompact two-door coupe veered away from its Horizon connection, billed simply as 'TC3.' Appearance was virtually unchanged from 1980, though official passenger capacity was enlarged to five (while size remained the same). TC3's grille again consisted of five wide slots in a sloped body-color panel, each row divided into six wide "holes." 'Plymouth' block lettering was on front fenders, just above the crease line. New TC3 Misers had the small 1.7-liter four under the hood, but standard models switched to the new Trans4 2.2-liter. Misers had standard vinyl high-back front bucket seats and tinted glass all around. Standard tires were P175/75R13 glass-belted radials, but TC3 could have optional P195/60R14 steel-belted tires, either blackwall or with raised white letters. Priced at $135 to $518, the Turismo package came with P195/60R14 SBR tires on steel Rallye wheels, Sport bucket front seats, Rallye instruments (tachometer, trip odometer and clock), and a four-spoke steering wheel. Also included: bodyside and rear spoiler identification, front fascia and wheel opening stripes, black moldings and bumper strips, and dual remote sport mirrors. Turismo had no 'TC3' nameplates, sill moldings, or wheel opening moldings. Solid TC3 body colors were the same as Horizon. Four two-tones were available, plus four with the Sport Appearance package. That option also included black moldings, a rear spoiler, P195/60R14 tires on Rallye wheels, 'TC3' quarter panel and spoiler identification, and Rallye instruments among its list of extras.

1981 Plymouth, Reliant Custom sedan with optional vinyl roof (OCW)

RELIANT K — SERIES P — FOUR — Plymouth's new K-body front-drive six-passenger compact, referred to as the K-car, was a near twin to the new Dodge Aries. Promoting fuel economy, Plymouth described Reliant as "The American way to beat the pump." The EPA gave Reliant a city rating of 25 mpg with manual shift. Mounted on a 99.6-inch wheelbase. Reliant was almost half a ton lighter and two feet shorter than Volare, with a squarish basic shape. Reliant's bright grille displayed a tiny crosshatch pattern, divided into eight larger sections by three horizontal bars and one vertical bar. A thin upper header molding had 'Plymouth' lettering on the driver's side. Clear vertical parking lamp lenses stood between bright-bezeled, single recessed rectangular headlamps and the grille. Amber side marker lenses extended rearward from the edge of the headlamp housings. 'Reliant' nameplates went on front fenders. Thin vertical marker lenses were at the rear edges of quarter panels. Reliant's soft color-keyed bumper wasn't a separate unit, but blended into the bodyside, with moldings that reached all around the car and served as protective bumper strips. Reliant's new Trans4 135 cubic inch (2.2-liter) engine weighed 298 pounds. It had same-side intake/exhaust valve porting and self-adjusting hydraulic lifters. An Electronic Fuel Control System used seven sensors and a tiny computer to adjust spark timing and air/fuel mixture. Optional was a Silent Shaft 156 cubic inch (2.6-liter) engine from Mitsubishi, which had a three-valve MCA JET cylinder head with

hemispherical combustion chambers. That engine was used in the imported Sapporo coupe. Both engines had five main bearings and an aluminum head, plus two-barrel carburetor and single overhead camshaft. The 2.2-liter rated 84 horsepower; the 2.6 produced 92. Both were transverse mounted. The fully synchronized manual gearbox included an overdrive fourth gear; three-speed TorqueFlite was available (standard with the 2.6-liter engine). An open back end in the four-speed's one-piece die-cast aluminum case would allow easy conversion to five-speed gearing in the future. Chrysler had designed Reliant's Iso-Strut front suspension, with one inch diameter front anti-sway bar. A three-point system of trailing links positioned the flex arm beam rear suspension, which included a transverse track bar. Rack-and-pinion steering was used. A steering column-mounted lever held controls for turn signals, dimmer, wiper/washer (and optional speed control). Two-door and four-door sedan and four-door station wagon bodies were offered; in base, Custom or Special Edition trim. There was no base wagon. Inside the base two-door was a cloth/vinyl split-back bench seat in cashmere color only. Reliant Custom had a standard cloth/vinyl bench seat in light blue, light green, red or cashmere; Custom wagons had an all-vinyl bench seat. SE held cloth bench seating in the same colors. Options included contoured vinyl bucket seats. Standard Custom equipment included blackwall fiberglass-belted radial tires, color-keyed protective bumper rub strips and wide vinyl bodyside moldings, AM radio, lighter, glove box lock, deluxe steering wheel, and day/night mirror. Also standard: an electric engine cooling fan, front disc brakes, high-pressure compact spare tire, woodtone instrument panel accents, dome light, rear door vent windows, and trunk mat. Wagons had power brakes. The base two-door had bright windshield moldings, bright headlamp bezels and grille surround, and came only in tan, white or black. It lacked the otherwise standard AM radio and other extras. Reliant Custom two-doors added quarter-window louvers. SE added bright decklid and window moldings, deluxe wheel covers, a Special Edition plaque on roof pillars, and body accent stripes. SE models also included dual horns, upper door frame moldings, belt moldings, and remote-control driver's mirror. SE wagons had woodtone bodyside and liftgate appliqués, while SE sedans displayed bodyside accent stripes. Reliant body colors were: Nightwatch Blue, Sunlight Yellow, Baron Red, Graphic Red, Natural Suede Tan, Formal Black, and Pearl White; plus metallic Burnished Silver, Daystar Blue, Light Seaspray Green, and Glencoe Green. Spice Tan Starmist cost extra. Vinyl roofs came in seven colors. Reliants were built for easy servicing, with such features as self-adjusting clutch linkage and cables, self-adjusting hydraulic tappets (2.2-liter), and easy-access drive belts and instrument panel. In addition to TorqueFlite, options included power brakes and steering, power decklid release, power seats, power door locks, tilt steering, automatic speed control, air conditioning, and color-keyed bodyside moldings. Also available: halogen headlamps, roof rack, flip-up sunroof, cargo tonneau cover, digital clock, bucket seats, and electric rear defroster. A total of 15,803 Reliants (9,097 sedans and 6,706 wagons) had a Spring Prom package installed.

1981 Plymouth, Gran Fury pillared hardtop (OCW)

GRAN FURY — SERIES J — SIX/V-8 — Only one Gran Fury model remained this year, as the Salon disappeared. Since fleet buyers continued to buy, the last remaining rear-drive Plymouth hung on longer. Not much changed in the four-door pillared hardtop body, apart from improved corrosion protection and a better optional (rear) radio speaker. Gran Fury's blacked-out grille consisted of rectangles within rectangles, with a huge chrome upper header. Horizontal taillamps wrapped around the rear quarter panels to serve also as side markers. Base engine once again was the 225 cubic inch Slant Six, with 318 cubic inch V-8 optional. Only 468 Gran Fury models had a six-cylinder engine installed.

I.D. DATA: Like other domestic makes, Plymouth had a new 17-symbol Vehicle Identification Number (VIN) on the upper left corner of the instrument panel, again visible through the windshield. The first digit indicates Country: '1' U.S.A. The second symbol is Make: 'P' Plymouth. Third is Vehicle Type: '3' passenger car. The next symbol ('B') indicates manual seatbelts. Symbol five is Car Line: 'L' Horizon; 'K' Reliant; 'R' Gran Fury. Symbol six is Series (price class); '1' Economy; '2' Low; '4' High ; '5' Premium. Symbol seven is Body Style: '1' 2-dr. sedan; '4' 2-dr. hatchback; '6' 4-dr. sedan; '7' 4-dr. pillared hardtop; '8' 4-dr. hatchback; '9' 4-dr. wagon. Eighth is the Engine Code: 'A' L4105 2Bbl.; 'B' L4135 2Bbl.; 'D' L4156 2Bbl.; 'E' L6-225 1Bbl.; 'K' V8318 2Bbl.; 'M' V8318 4Bbl. Next comes a check digit: 0 through 9 (or X). Symbol ten indicates Model

Year: 'B' 1981. Symbol eleven is Assembly Plant: 'A' Lynch Road; 'C' Jefferson; 'D' Belvidere, IL; 'F' Newark, DE. The last six digits make up the sequential serial number, starting with 100001. Four-cylinder engine identification numbers are on the rear face of the block, directly under cylinder head (left side in vehicle) except for 2.6-liter, which is on left side of block between core plug and rear face of block (radiator side). Engine serial numbers (for parts replacement) are located on the block as follows: 1.7-liter, above fuel pump; 2.2-liter, on rear face just below head (below identification number); 2.6-liter, on right front of block adjacent to exhaust manifold stud. Six cylinder engine identification numbers are stamped on a pad at the right of the block, below No. 6 spark plug. On V-8s, that pad is on the right of the block to the rear of the engine mount. An engine serial number is on the right of the block below No. 1 spark plug on six-cylinder engines, and on the left front corner of the block below the cylinder head on V-8s. A Body Code Plate is on the left upper radiator support, left front fender side shield, or wheelhousing.

HORIZON (FOUR)

Model No.	Body/ Style No.	Body Type & Seating	Factory Price	Shipping Weight	Prod. Total
ML	44	4-dr. Hatch-5P	5690	2130	58,547

HORIZON MISER (FOUR)

ME	44	4-dr. Hatch-5P	5299	2060	Note 1

TC3 (FOUR)

ML	24	2-dr. Hatch-5P	6149	2205	36,312

TC3 MISER (FOUR)

ME	24	2-dr. Hatch-5P	5299	2137	Note 1

Note 1: Total Miser production, 44,922.

RELIANT (FOUR)

PL	21	2-dr. Sedan-6P	5880	2305	Note 2
PL	41	4-dr. Sedan-6P	5980	2300	Note 2

Note 2: Total base Reliant production, 58,093

RELIANT CUSTOM (FOUR)

PH	21	2-dr. Sedan-6P	6315	2315	Note 3
PH	41	4-dr. Sedan-6P	6448	2310	Note 3
PH	45	4-dr. Sta Wag-6P	6721	2375	40,830

Note 3: Total Custom production, 13,587 coupes/sedans.

RELIANT SPECIAL EDITION (FOUR)

PP	21	2-dr. Sedan-6P	6789	2340	Note 4
PP	41	4-dr. Sedan-6P	6933	2340	Note 4
PP	45	4-dr. Sta Wag-6P	7254	2390	10,670

Note 4: Total Reliant SE production, 28,457 coupes/sedans.

GRAN FURY (SIX/V-8)

JL	42	4-dr. Pill. HT-6P	7387/7451	3485/3610	7,719

Factory Price And Weight Note: Gran Fury price and weight to left of slash is for six-cylinder, to right for V-8 engine.

Model Number Note: Some sources identify models using the new VIN data to indicate Car Line, Price Class and Body Style. Example: base Reliant four-door (PL41) has the equivalent number K26, which translates to Reliant line, Low price class, and four-door sedan body. See I.D. Data section for breakdown.

ENGINE DATA: BASE FOUR (Horizon, TC3): Inline, overhead-cam four-cylinder. Cast iron block; aluminum head. Displacement: 104.7 cu. in. (1.7-liters). Bore & stroke: 3.13 x 3.40 in. Compression ratio: 8.2:1. Brake horsepower: 63 at 5200 R.P.M. Torque: 83 lb.-ft. at 2400 R.P.M. Five main bearings. Solid valve lifters. Carburetor: 2Bbl. Holley 6520. VIN Code: A. **BASE FOUR (Reliant, late TC3); OPTIONAL (Horizon, TC3 Miser):** Inline, overhead-cam four-cylinder. Cast iron block: aluminum head. Displacement: 135 cu. in. (2.2-liters), Bore & stroke: 3.44 x 3.62 in. Compression ratio: 8.5:1. Brake horsepower: 84 at 4800 R.P.M. Torque: 111 lb.-ft. at 2800 R.P.M. Five main bearings. Hydraulic valve lifters. Carburetor: 2Bbl. Holley 6520. VIN Code: B. **OPTIONAL FOUR (Reliant):** Inline, overhead-cam four-cylinder. Cast iron block: aluminum head. Displacement: 156 cu. in. (2.6-liters). Bore & stroke: 3.59 x 3.86 in. Compression ratio: 8.2:1. Brake horsepower: 92 at 4500 R.P.M. Torque: 131 lb.-ft. at 2500 R.P.M. Five main bearings. Solid valve lifters. Carburetor: 2Bbl. Mikuni. VIN Code: D. **BASE SIX (Gran Fury):** Inline, overhead-valve six. Cast iron block and head. Displacement: 225 cu. in. (3.7-liters). Bore & stroke: 3.40 x 4.12 in. Compression ratio: 8.4:1. Brake horsepower: 85 at 3600 R.P.M. Torque: 165 lb.-ft. at 1600 R.P.M. Four main bearings. Hydraulic valve lifters. Carburetor: 1Bbl. Holley 1945. VIN Code: E. **OPTIONAL V-8 (Gran Fury):** 90-degree, overhead valve V-8. Cast iron block and head. Displacement: 318 cu. in. (5.2-liters). Bore & stroke: 3.91 x 3.31 in. Compression ratio: 8.5:1. Brake horsepower: 130 at 4000 R.P.M. Torque: 230 lb.-ft. at 2000 R.P.M. Five main bearings. Hydraulic valve lifters. Carburetor: 2Bbl. Carter BBD 8291S. VIN Code: K. **OPTIONAL V-8 (Gran Fury):** Same as 318 cu. in. V-8 above, but with Carter TQ 9283S 4Bbl. carburetor. Horsepower: 165 at 4000 R.P.M. Torque: 240 lb.-ft. at 2000 R.P.M. VIN Code: M.

CHASSIS DATA: Wheelbase: (Horizon) 99.1 in.; (TC3) 96.6 in.; (Reliant) 99.6 in.; (Gran Fury) 118.5 in. Overall Length: (Horizon) 164.8 in. incl. optional bumper guards; (TC3) 173.5 in.; (Reliant) 176.0 in.; (Reliant wag) 176.2 in.; (Gran Fury) 220.2 in. Height: (Horizon) 53.1 in.; (Reliant 2-dr.) 52.4 in.; (Reliant 4-dr.) 52.7 in.; (Reliant wag) 52.8 in.; (Gran Fury) 54.5 in. Width: (Horizon) 65.8 in.; (TC3) 66.7 in.; (Reliant) 68.6 in.; (Gran Fury) 77.6 in. Front Tread: (Horizon /TC3) 56.1 in.; (Reliant) 57.6 in.; (Gran Fury) 61.9 in. Rear Tread: (Horizon/TC3) 55.6 in.; (Reliant) 57.0 in.; (Gran Fury) 62.0 in. Standard Tires: (Horizon) P155/80R13 GBR BSW; (TC3/Reliant) P175/75R13 GBR BSW; (Gran Fury) P195/75R15 GBR WSW.

TECHNICAL: Transmission: Four-speed manual (floor shift) standard on Horizon/TC3: (1st) 3.45:1; (2nd) 1.94:1; (3rd) 1.29:1; (4th) 0.97:1; (Rev) 3.17:1. Four-speed manual (floor shift) standard on Reliant and Horizon/TC3 w/2.2-liter engine: (1st) 3.29:1; (2nd) 1.89:1; (3rd) 1.21:1; (4th) 0.88:1; (Rev) 3.14:1. TorqueFlite three-speed automatic standard on Gran Fury, optional on others. Gran Fury gear ratios: (1st) 2.74:1; (2nd) 1.54:1; (3rd) 1.00:1; (Rev) 2.22:1. Horizon/TC3/Reliant ratios: (1st) 2.69:1; (2nd) 1.55:1; (3rd) 1.00:1; (Rev) 2.10:1. Horizon/TC3 w/2.2-liter engine: (1st) 2.47:1; (2nd) 1.47:1; (3rd) 1.00:1; (Rev) 2.10:1. Standard final drive ratio: (Horizon/TC3) 3.37:1 w/4spd, 3.48:1 w/auto.; (Horizon/TC3 Miser) 2.69:1 w/4spd; (Horizon/TC3 w/2.2-liter four) 2.69:1 w/4spd, 2.7:1 w/auto.; (Reliant) 2.69:1 w/4spd, 2.78:1 w/auto. (Gran Fury six) 2.94:1; (G. Fury V-8 2Bbl.) 2.24:1; (G. Fury V-8 4Bbl.) 2.45:1. Steering: (Horizon/TC3/Reliant) rack and pinion; (Gran Fury) recirculating ball. Suspension: (Horizon/TC3) Iso-Strut independent coil front w/anti-sway bar, independent training arm coil rear w/integral anti-sway; (Reliant) Iso-Strut front, flex-beam rear axle w/trailing links and coil springs; (Gran Fury) front torsion bars, rear leaf springs. Brakes: Front disc, rear drum. Ignition: Electronic. Body construction: Unibody. Fuel Tank: 13 gal. exc. (Gran Fury) 21 gal.

DRIVETRAIN OPTIONS: Engines: 2.2-liter four: Horizon/TC3 ($104) exc. in California (NC). 2.6-liter four: Reliant ($159). 318 cu. in. V-8, 2Bbl. or 4Bbl.: Gran Fury ($64). Transmission/Differential: TorqueFlite: Horizon/TC3 ($359); Reliant ($360). Sure grip differential: G. Fury ($114). Power Accessories: Power steering: Horizon/TC3 ($165); Reliant ($174). Power brakes: Horizon/TC3/Reliant ($82). Suspension: H.D. susp.: Horizon 4-dr. ($28); Reliant ($23); G. Fury ($29). Sport susp.: TC3 ($46). H.D. shock absorbers: G. Fury ($8). Other: Trailer assist pkg.: G. Fury ($246). 430-amp battery: Horizon/TC3 ($23). 500-amp battery: Reliant/G. Fury ($38). Max. cooling ($127). California emission system ($46).

HORIZON/TC3 CONVENIENCE/APPEARANCE OPTIONS: Option Packages: Euro-Sedan pkg.: 4-dr. ($613-$865). Turismo pkg.: TC3 ($275-$655). Sport appearance pkg.: TC3 ($331-$435). Sport/Classic two-tone paint pkg. ($111-$164). Custom exterior pkg.: 4-dr. ($188). Premium exterior pkg.: 4-dr. ($250-$290); TC3 ($92-$166). Premium interior pkg. ($212-$311). Sport interior pkg. ($146-$196). Popular equipment group ($423-$477). Light pkg. ($49). Comfort/Convenience: Air cond. ($554). Rear defroster, electric ($102). Auto. speed control ($136). Tinted glass: 4-dr. ($71). Tinted windshield: 4-dr. ($45). Power liftgate release: TC3 ($27). Luxury steering wheel: 4-dr. ($20). Sport steering wheel ($23-$43). Leather-wrapped steering wheel ($17-$60). Rallye instrument cluster w/tach ($70-$100). Electric clock w/trip odometer ($30). Intermittent wiper ($42). Rear wiper/washer: 4-dr. ($83). Locking gas cap ($8). Lighting, Horns and Mirrors: Halogen headlamps ($40). Dual horns ($10). Remote left mirror, chrome: 4-dr. ($20). Remote right mirror, black: 4-dr. ($41). Dual remote mirrors, chrome: 4-dr. ($41-$60). Dual remote sport mirrors: TC3 ($74). Day/night mirror: Miser ($13). Entertainment: AM radio: Miser ($59-$151). AM/FM stereo radio ($94-$186); w/8track player ($168-$260); w/cassette ($223-$315). Radio upgrade ($14-$25). Rear speaker: TC3 ($20). Exterior: Glass sunroof ($213). Rear spoiler: TC3 ($59). Starmist paint ($49). Black vinyl bodyside moldings ($46). Moldings (4-dr.): belt ($19); drip rail ($21); upper door frame ($35); wheel lip ($32). Door edge protectors ($13-$23). Bumper guards: 4-dr. ($48). Hood/bodyside/deck tape stripe: 4-dr. ($48). Bodyside/deck stripe: TC3 ($34). Multi-color bodyside stripe: 4-dr. ($99). Luggage rack ($92). Undercoating ($37). Lower body coating ($34). Interior: Console: storage ($24); Shift lever ($36). Cloth/vinyl bucket seats ($25). Tonneau cover: TC3 ($49). Cargo area carpet ($34); w/sound insulation ($15-$49). Color-keyed floor mats: front ($25); rear ($18). Color-keyed seatbelts ($25). Wheels and Tires: Wheel trim rings: 4-dr. ($48). Deluxe wheel covers: 4dr. ($48); TC3 (NC). Cast aluminum wheels, 13-in. ($215-$263); 14-in., TC3 ($175). Rally wheels, 13-in.: 4-dr. ($40-$88); 14-in., TC3 (NC). P155/80R13 WSW: 4-dr. ($52). P165/75P13 WSW: 4-dr. ($33-$85). P175/75R13 SBR BSW: 4-dr. ($17-$102). P175/75R13 SBR WSW: 4-dr. ($89-$174). P175/75R13 GBR WSW: TC3 ($58). P185/70R13 SBR WSW: TC3 ($116-$174). P195/60R14 SBR BSW: TC3 ($79-$137). P195/60R14 SBR RWL: TC3 ($68-$205). Conventional spare tire ($39).

RELIANT CONVENIENCE/APPEARANCE OPTIONS: Option Packages: Basic group ($709-$784). Light pkg. ($75-$83). Protection group ($95-$103). Comfort/Convenience: Air cond. ($605). Rear defroster ($107). Automatic speed control ($132). Power seat ($173). Power door locks

($93-$132). Power decklid/liftgate release ($27). Tinted windshield ($48); all windows ($75). Luxury steering wheel: Cust ($46). Sport steering wheel: Cust ($53); SE ($7). Tilt steering wheel ($81). Digital clock ($59). Intermittent wipers ($41). Tailgate wiper/washer: wag ($82). Locking gas cap ($7). Lighting, Horns and Mirrors: Halogen headlamps ($36). Dual horns ($10). Remote left mirror ($19). Remote right mirror: SE ($49). Dual remote mirrors ($49-$68). Vanity mirror ($5), Entertainment: AM radio: base ($90): AM/FM radio ($64-$154). AM/FM stereo radio ($100); w/8track player ($174); w/cassette ($224); w/CB ($361). Rear speaker ($19). Dual front speakers ($25) w/mono radio. Premium speakers ($92). Delete AM radio ($85 credit). Exterior: Glass sunroof ($246). Full vinyl roof: 4-dr. ($131). Landau vinyl roof: 2-dr. ($131). Spice Tan Starmist paint ($55). Door edge protectors ($13-$21). Upper door frame moldings ($58-$67). Sill moldings ($20). Bumper guards, front or rear ($24). Luggage rack ($90). Special sound insulation ($75). Undercoating ($37). Vinyl lower body protection ($34). Interior: Console ($86). Vinyl bench seat: Cust ($27). Vinyl bucket seats ($51-$78) but (NC) on SE. Cloth bucket seats: SE ($91). Color-keyed mats: front ($25); rear ($19). Tonneau cover: wag ($50). Pedal dress-up ($9) Trunk dress-up ($45). Wheels and Tires: Rallye wheels ($36-$82). Deluxe wheel covers ($46). Luxury wheel covers ($36-$82). P175/75R13 GBR wide WSW ($51). P185/70R13 SBR wide WSW ($124-$175). P185/65R14 GBR wide WSW ($82-$133). P185/65R14 SBR wide WSW ($136-$187). Conventional spare tire: wag ($39).

1981 Plymouth, Reliant Custom SE two-door sedan with optional cabriolet roof (OCW)

GRAN FURY CONVENIENCE/APPEARANCE OPTIONS: Option Packages: Basic group ($993). Open Road handling pkg. ($281). Light pkg., ($103). Comfort/Convenience: Air conditioning ($646); auto-temp ($692) but ($46) w/option pkg. Rear defroster, electric ($112). Auto. speed control ($139). Power seat ($179). Power windows ($218). Power door locks ($138). Power decklid release ($30-$45). Illuminated entry system ($60). Luxury steering wheel ($39). Leather-covered steering wheel ($60). Tilt steering wheel ($84). Digital clock ($62). Intermittent wipers ($44). Locking gas cap ($9). Lighting, Horns and Mirrors: Halogen headlamps ($41). Cornering lights ($54). Triad horns ($22). Remote driver's mirror ($21). Dual remote-control mirrors ($30-$51). Lighted vanity mirror ($51). Entertainment: AM radio ($97). AM/FM radio ($54-$151). AM/FM stereo ($95-$192); w/8track tape player ($166-$263); w/cassette ($221-$318): w/CB ($356-$453). Search-tune AM/FM stereo ($206-$303). Dual front speakers ($26). Rear speaker ($21). Premium speakers ($95). Power antenna ($50). Exterior: Power glass sunroof ($934). Vinyl bodyside moldings ($51). Sill moldings ($31). Door edge protectors ($23). Bumper guards ($60). Bumper rub strips ($41). Bodyside tape stripe ($47). Undercoating ($31) Interior: Vinyl split-back bench seat ($69). Cloth/vinyl 60/40 bench seat ($182). Color-keyed floor mats: front ($25); rear ($20). Pedal dress-up ($11). Trunk dress-up ($65). Litter container ($10). Wheels and Tires: Deluxe wheel covers ($48). Premier wheel covers ($90). Premium wheel covers ($134). Wire wheel covers ($299). Forged aluminum wheels ($369). P205/75R15 SBR WSW ($101). P225/70R15 SBR WSW ($192). Conventional spare ($39).

HISTORY: Introduced: October 2, 1980 except Horizon/Gran Fury, October 16. Model year production: Chrysler reported a total of 348,985 passenger cars shipped. Total North American production for the U.S. market of 389,306 units included 310,101 four-cylinder, 71,209 six-cylinder, and 7,996 V-8s. Calendar year production: 363,702. Model year sales by U.S. dealers: 341,082 (not incl. 41,300 imported Champ/Arrows and 12,709 Sapporos).

Historical Footnotes: Reliants were produced in Detroit (at the Jefferson Ave. plant) and at Newark, Delaware. Not surprisingly, Reliant was the top seller for the model year, amounting to nearly two-fifths of total Chrysler-Plymouth Division sales. Almost three-fourths of the cars sold by CP were front-wheel drive (including the Japanese imports). The revived Gran Fury (and similar R-bodied Chrysler Newport) left the lineup soon after the model year began, only to return for 1982 with a totally different body on a shorter wheelbase.

1982 PLYMOUTH

Gran Fury took on a whole new, downsized form this year, but the rest of the Plymouth lineup enjoyed only engine/chassis refinements. Engine fans offered greater energy-efficiency, and a linkless sway bar was added to front-drive suspensions. Counterbalanced hoods replaced the old prop rods. New electronic-tuning radios had seek/scan and new seat fabrics appeared. New roll-down back window mechanisms were offered, along with new inertia-recliner bucket seats. Compacts added more standard equipment, without corresponding price rises.

1982 Plymouth, Horizon Custom hatchback with optional Deluxe wheel covers (OCW)

1982 Plymouth, Horizon TC3 Turismo hatchback (OCW)

HORIZON — SERIES M — FOUR — Except for modest revisions, Horizon appearance was the same as 1981. The grille had the same pattern of thin vertical bars, but added the Chrysler pentastar in the center. 'Horizon' script no longer appeared on front fenders, but remained on the hatch. Underneath was a new linkless front anti-sway bar. As usual, Horizon was nearly identical to Dodge's Omni, right down to the option list. Both were rated for five-passenger seating, but in a tight squeeze. Both served as Chrysler's "import fighters." Base, Custom, and E-Type Horizons were available this year. Horizon's EPA highway rating gained 2 mpg, as a result of changes in the catalytic converter and emissions control system. A base Miser reached an estimated 35 mpg city and 52 highway, with base 1.7-liter engine and four-speed manual transaxle. Customs had new corded cloth/vinyl Sport high-back bucket seats with dual recliners. Standard equipment included a color-keyed four-spoke sport steering wheel, deluxe wheel covers, bright body moldings, and woodgrain-trim instrument panel. Horizon Miser, offered again this year, carried a specially calibrated 1.7-liter four with four-speed manual transaxle and 2.69:1 overall top gear ratio. Miser had simpler trim and a smaller option selection. New vinyl high-back bucket seats and color-keyed seatbelts came in four colors. New standard Miser equipment also included a glovebox lock, day/night mirror, bright wheel hubs/nuts, and remote-control driver's mirror. Dual horns were standard. An optional light group included halogen headlamps, map/courtesy light, ignition switch light with time-delay, plus glovebox, ashtray and cargo area lights. A new blackout-trimmed E-Type (Euro-style) Horizon included Rallye instrumentation with tachometer, trip odometer, quartz clock, gauges, and a brake warning light. Standard high-back Sport bucket seats in corded cloth/vinyl had dual seatback recliners; optional, all-vinyl low-back buckets. A shift-lever console was included. Black moldings went on E-Type's windshield, liftgate window, drip rail and belt. Also standard: black upper door frames and center pillars; dual black remote-control mirrors with tape stripes; black door-handle inserts; and black bumpers with protective rub strips. Tape stripes ran from front to rear wheel openings. A four-speed manual transaxle with special 3.13:1 performance overall top gear ratio hooked up to either the standard 1.7-liter or optional 2.2-liter Trans4 engine (2.2 standard in California). E-Types were supposed to lure younger drivers. Thirteen body colors were available. They included: Formal Black, Graphic Red, Morocco Red, Pearl White, Manila Cream, and Graphic Yellow (except E-Type);

plus metallic Daystar Blue, Ensign Blue, Burnished Silver, Navy Blue, Spice Tan, Charcoal Gray, and Medium Seaspray Green. Three two-tones were offered on Custom only.

TC3 — SERIES M — FOUR — Side appearance of the subcompact two-door coupe was similar to 1981, except that 'Plymouth' block lettering on front fenders was dropped. Also, the center side window was made smaller, now triangular-shaped rather than squarish as before. The 'C' pillar also lost its ribbed trim, giving a wider appearance this year. Up front was a new front-end design with soft-fascia nose. TC3's body-color grille now consisted of 16 large square holes in the sloped panel, arranged in two rows of eight each. Below the bumper rub strip were three large slots. As before, 'Plymouth' block lettering stood above the driver's side of the grille, but a new round emblem also appeared at the hood front. Like Horizon, the TC3 carried a new linkless anti-sway bar and new single catalytic converter. Black wiper arms were installed, and a variety of items that had been optional became standard. They included a power hatch-back release, deluxe sound insulation, and tape stripes. Three price levels were offered: Miser, Custom and Turismo. Rated optimistically at five-passenger capacity, TC3 had a rear seat that folded down to create nearly 34 cubic feet of cargo space. The Custom model had a new quarter-window appliqué and standard Rallye road wheels, plus standard cloth/vinyl high-back Sport bucket seats with integral headrests and dual seatback recliners. TC3 Miser's design, though similar to the Custom, had much narrower C-pillars, allowing for a wider quarter window. Misers carried standard vinyl high-back bucket seats and a specially calibrated 1.7-liter four to deliver up to 51 mpg on the highway in EPA estimates. TC3 solid colors were the same as Horizon's. Four two-tones were offered on TC3 Custom; three more with the Sport Appearance package. A TC3 Turismo was offered this year, with equipment similar to the Horizon E-Type. Turismo had a claimed 0-50 mph time of 7 seconds with standard 2.2-liter engine and 3.13:1 overall top gear ratio. A performance exhaust system was optional. Many black accents highlighted Turismo's appearance, along with a rear spoiler, special tape striping and graphics, and low-profile blackwall steel-belted radial tires on 14-inch steel Rallye wheels (with bright hubs and trim rings). Inside was a Rallye instrument cluster and cloth/vinyl Sport bucket seats, or optional low-back Premium bucket seats. Buyers were also directed to Direct Connection, Chrysler's Performance Parts Program, as a source for such extras as air dams, wheels and engine chrome, along with off-road camshafts and pistons and an off-road suspension kit. Graphic Yellow body color wasn't available on Turismo. A separate factory sales catalog was distributed later for the Turismo 2.2. Though similar in appearance to the standard Turismo, the ultimate coupe showed special graphics including a 'Turismo' decal be-tween door and rear wheel opening, large '2.2' decal on the 'C' pillar, and two-color bodyside striping. Turismo 2.2 also added a simulated hood scoop and rear spoiler, dual remote-control sport mirrors, and P195/60R14 SBR blackwall tires on 14-inch Rallye wheels. A special sport suspension included heavy-duty shock absorbers and rear anti-sway bar. Naturally, the 2.2-liter engine was standard, with a "throaty" perfor-mance exhaust system. Turismo 2.2 came in five body colors: Morocco Red, Charcoal Gray metallic, Burnished Silver metallic, Black, or Pearl White. All graphics matched the narrow upper body stripe colors. A total of 3,208 cars had the Turismo 2.2 package.

1982 Plymouth, Reliant Custom sedan with optional vinyl roof and Luxury wheel covers (OCW)

RELIANT — SERIES P — FOUR — Changes in Plymouth's front-drive compact focused on engineering refinements rather than style for its sec-ond year in the lineup. Four-doors had new roll-down rear windows. Like other front-drives, Reliant added a linkless anti-sway bar in the front suspension. A counterbalanced hood replaced the former prop style. The 2.2-liter engine got new silver/black paint on the outside, a reworked intake manifold and repositioned camshaft on the inside. The engine fan was quieter, and the fuel-control computer was reworked to modify idle speed. Disc brake rotors were new. Base engine again was the 135 cubic inch (2.2-liter) four; optional, the Mitsubishi 156 cubic inch (2.6-liter), available only with automatic transmission. New options included power front windows, a Euro-style center console (with manual shift), lighted vanity mirror, bodyside tape stripes, wire wheel covers, and 14-inch cast aluminum wheels. Seven models included a base four-door sedan; Custom

and SE two and four-door sedans; and four-door (two-seat) wagon. Recliner bucket seats were optional in Custom and SE models. SE had new cloth/vinyl bench seating with center armrest; rosewood instrument panel and door trim appliqués; and power brakes/steering.

GRAN FURY — SERIES B — SIX/V-8 — Once again, the Gran Fury name went on a smaller model. This M-bodied four-door sedan, riding a 112.7 inch wheelbase, stood 14.5 inches shorter than its predecessor and some 230 pounds lighter. Actually, it was the '81 rear-drive LeBaron, which had been replaced by a new front-drive version. Gran Fury's grille lacked the usual eggcrate look. Instead, it showed what was described as "bold vertical lines (full depth) ... against a silvered background" to give a massive look. The standard seat, with center armrest, was upholstered in Madison cloth. Vinyl was available too. Upholstery colors were silver, blue, red, and cashmere. Body colors included Spice Tan, Daystar Blue, Nightwatch Blue, Manila Cream, Charcoal Gray, Morocco Red, Silver, White, and Black. Options included two new electronic-tuning AM/FM stereo radios made by Chrysler, with seek/scan to replace the prior search provision. One included a stereo cassette player with Dolby noise reduction. Engines were the same as before: either a 225 cubic inch Slant Six or 318 cubic inch V-8, both with TorqueFlite three-speed automatic transmission.

I.D. DATA: Plymouth again had a 17-symbol Vehicle Identification Number (VIN) on the upper left corner of the instrument panel, visible through the windshield. The first digit indicates Country: '1' U.S.A. The second symbol is Make: 'P' Plymouth. Third is Vehicle Type: '3' passenger car. The next symbol ('B') indicates manual seatbelts. Symbol five is Car Line: 'M' Horizon; 'P' Reliant; 'B' Gran Fury. Symbol six is Series (price class): '1' Economy; '2' Low; '4' High; '5' Premium. Symbol seven is Body Style: '1' 2-dr. sedan; '4' 2-dr. hatchback; '6' 4-dr. sedan; '8' 4-dr. hatchback; '9' 4-dr. wagon. Eighth is the Engine Code: 'A' L4105 2Bbl.; 'B' L4135 2Bbl.; 'D' L4156 2Bbl.; 'E' L6225 1Bbl.; 'K' V8318 2Bbl.; 'M' V8318 4Bbl. Next comes a check digit: 0 through 9 (or X). Symbol ten indicates Model Year: 'C' 1982. Symbol eleven is Assembly Plant: 'C' Jefferson; 'D' Belvidere, IL; 'F' Newark, DE; 'R' Windsor, Ontario. The last six digits make up the sequential serial number, starting with 100001. Engine number and Body Code Plate locations are the same as 1981.

HORIZON CUSTOM (FOUR)

Model No.	Body/Style No.	Body Type & Seating	Factory Price	Shipping Weight	Prod. Total
MH	44	4-dr. Hatch-5P	5927	2175	17,315

HORIZON MISER (FOUR)

Model No.	Body/Style No.	Body Type & Seating	Factory Price	Shipping Weight	Prod. Total
ME	44	4-dr. Hatch-5P	5499	2110	19,102

HORIZON EURO-SEDAN (FOUR)

Model No.	Body/Style No.	Body Type & Seating	Factory Price	Shipping Weight	Prod. Total
MP	44	4-dr. Hatch-5P	6636	2180	779

TC3 CUSTOM (FOUR)

Model No.	Body/Style No.	Body Type & Seating	Factory Price	Shipping Weight	Prod. Total
MH	24	2-dr. Hatch-5P	6421	2205	12,889

TC3 MISER (FOUR)

Model No.	Body/Style No.	Body Type & Seating	Factory Price	Shipping Weight	Prod. Total
ME	24	2-dr. Hatch-5P	5799	2180	18,359

TC3 TURISMO (FOUR)

Model No.	Body/Style No.	Body Type & Seating	Factory Price	Shipping Weight	Prod. Total
MP	24	2-dr. Hatch-5P	7115	2315	6,608

RELIANT (FOUR)

Model No.	Body/Style No.	Body Type & Seating	Factory Price	Shipping Weight	Prod. Total
PL	21	2-dr. Sedan-6P	5990	2315	12,026
PL	41	4-dr. Sedan-6P	6131	2310	37,488

RELIANT CUSTOM (FOUR)

Model No.	Body/Style No.	Body Type & Seating	Factory Price	Shipping Weight	Prod. Total
PH	21	2-dr. Sedan-6P	6898	2320	12,403
PH	41	4-dr. Sedan-6P	7053	2320	29,980
PH	45	4-dr. Sta Wag-6P	7334	2395	32,501

RELIANT SPECIAL EDITION (FOUR)

Model No.	Body/Style No.	Body Type & Seating	Factory Price	Shipping Weight	Prod. Total
PP	21	2-dr. Sedan-6P	7575	2365	2,536
PP	41	4-dr. Sedan-6P	7736	2385	4,578
PP	45	4-dr. Sta Wag-6P	8101	2470	7,711

GRAN FURY (SIX/V-8)

Model No.	Body/Style No.	Body Type & Seating	Factory Price	Shipping Weight	Prod. Total
BL	41	4-dr. Sedan-6P	7750/7820	3275/----	18,111

Factory Price And Weight Note: Gran Fury price and weight to left of slash is for six-cylinder, to right for V-8.

Model Number Note: Some sources identify models using the new VIN data to indicate Car Line, Price Class and Body Style. Example: base Reliant four-door (PL41) has the equivalent number P26, which translates to Reliant line, Low price class, and four-door sedan body. See I.D. Data section for breakdown.

ENGINE DATA: BASE FOUR (Horizon, TC3): Inline, overhead-cam four-cylinder. Cast iron block; aluminum head. Displacement: 104.7 cu. in. (1.7-liters). Bore & stroke: 3.13 x 3.40 in. Compression ratio: 8.2:1. Brake horsepower: 63 at 5200 R.P.M. Torque: 83 lb.-ft. at 2400 R.P.M. Five main bearings. Solid valve lifters. Carburetor: 2Bbl. Holley 6520. VIN Code: A. **BASE FOUR (Reliant, TC3 Turismo); OPTIONAL (Horizon, TC3):** Inline, overhead-cam four-cylinder. Cast iron block; aluminum

head. Displacement: 135 cu. in. (2.2-liters). Bore & stroke: 3.44 x 3.62 in. Compression ratio: 8.5:1. Brake horsepower: 84 at 4800 R.P.M. Torque: 111 lb.-ft. at 2400 R.P.M. Five main bearings. Hydraulic valve lifters. Carburetor: 2Bbl. Holley 6520 or 5220. VIN Code: B. **OPTIONAL FOUR (Reliant):** Inline, overhead-cam four-cylinder. Cast iron block: aluminum head. Displacement: 156 cu. in. (2.6-liters). Bore & stroke: 3.59 x 3.86 in. Compression ratio: 8.2:1. Brake horsepower: 92 at 4500 R.P.M. Torque: 131 lb.-ft. at 2500 R.P.M. Five main bearings. Solid valve lifters. Carburetor: 2Bbl. Mikuni. VIN Code: D. **BASE SIX (Gran Fury):** Inline. overhead-valve six. Cast iron block and head. Displacement: 225 cu. in. (3.7-liters). Bore & stroke: 3.40 x 4.12 in. Compression ratio: 8.4:1. Brake horsepower: 90 at 3600 R.P.M. Torque: 160 lb.-ft. at 1600 R.P.M. Four main bearings. Hydraulic valve lifters. Carburetor: 1Bbl. Holley 1945. VIN Code: E. **OPTIONAL V-8 (Gran Fury):** 90-degree, overhead valve V-8. Cast iron block and head. Displacement: 318 cu. in. (5.2-liters). Bore & stroke: 3.91 x 3.31 in. Compression ratio: 8.5:1. Brake horsepower: 130 at 4000 R.P.M. Torque: 230 lb.-ft. at 2000 R.P.M. Five main bearings. Hydraulic valve lifters. Carburetor: 2Bbl. Carter BBD. VIN Code: K. **CALIFORNIA V-8 (Gran Fury):** Same as 318 cu. in. V-8 above, but with Carter TQ 4Bbl. carburetor. Horsepower: 165 at 4000 R.P.M. Torque: 240 lb.-ft. at 2000 R.P.M. VIN Code: M.

CHASSIS DATA: Wheelbase: (Horizon) 99.1 in.; (TC3) 96.6 in.; (Reliant) 99.9 in.; (Gran Fury) 112.7 in. Overall Length: (Horizon) 162.6 in.; (Horizon E-Type) 163.2 in.; (TC3) 173.7 in.; (TC3 Turismo) 174.1 in.; (Turismo 2.2) 174.2 in.; (Reliant) 176.0 in.; (Reliant wag) 176.2 in.; (Gran Fury) 205.7 in. Height: (Horizon) 53.1 in.; (TC3) 50.8 in.; (Reliant 2-dr.) 52.3 in.; (Reliant 4-dr.) 52.7 in.; (Reliant wag) 52.4 in.; (Gran Fury) 55.3 in. Width: (Horizon) 65.8 in.; (TC3) 66.7 in.; (Reliant) 68.6 in.; (Gran Fury) 74.2 in. Front Tread: (Horizon/TC3) 56.1 in.; (Reliant) 57.6 in.; (Gran Fury) 60.0 in. Rear Tread: (Horizon/TC3) 55.6 in.; (Reliant) 57.0 in.; (Gran Fury) 59.5 in. Standard Tires: (Horizon/TC3) P175/75R13 GBR BSW; (Turismo) P195/60R14 SBR RBL; (Reliant) P175/75R13 GBR; (Gran Fury) P195/75R15 GBR.

TECHNICAL: Transmission: Four speed manual (floor shift) standard on Horizon/TC3: (1st) 3.45:1; (2nd) 1.94:1; (3rd) 1.29:1; (4th) 0.97:1; (Rev) 3.17:1. Four-speed manual (floor shift) standard on Reliant, Horizon/TC3 Miser, and Horizon/TC3 w/2.2-liter engine: (1st) 3.29:1; (2nd) 1.89:1; (3rd) 1.21:1; (4th) 0.88:1; (Rev) 3.14:1. TorqueFlite three-speed automatic standard on Gran Fury, optional on others. Gran Fury gear ratios: (1st) 2.74:1; (2nd) 1.54:1; (3rd) 1.00:1; (Rev) 2.22:1. Horizon/TC3/Reliant ratios: (1st) 2.69:1; (2nd) 1.55:1; (3rd) 1.00:1; (Rev) 2.10:1. Standard final drive ratio: (Horizon/TC3) 3.37:1 w/4spd; (Horizon/TC3 Miser) 2.69:1 w/4spd; (Horizon/TC3 w/2.2-liter four) 3.13:1 w/4spd, 2.78:1 w/auto.; (Reliant) 2.69:1 w/4spd, 2.78:1 w/auto.; (Gran Fury six) 2.94:1. Steering: (Horizon/TC3/Reliant) rack and pinion; (Gran Fury) recirculating ball. Suspension: (Horizon/TC3) Iso-Strut independent coil front w/anti-sway bar, semi-independent trailing arm coil rear w/integral anti-sway; (TC3 Turismo) sport susp., same as TC3 with rear anti-sway bar; (Reliant) Iso-Strut front, flex-beam rear axle w/trailing links and coil springs; (Gran Fury) front torsion bars and anti-sway bar, rear leaf springs. Brakes: Front disc, rear drum. Ignition: Electronic. Body construction: Unibody. Fuel tank: 13 gal exc. (Gran Fury) 18 gal.

DRIVETRAIN OPTIONS: Engines: 2.2-liter four: Horizon/TC3 ($112). 2.6-liter four: Reliant ($171). 318 cu. in., 2Bbl. V-8: Gran Fury ($70). 318 cu. in., 4Bbl. V-8: G. Fury ($70). Transmission: TorqueFlite: Horizon/TC3/Reliant ($396). Power Accessories: Power steering: Horizon/TC3 ($190); Reliant ($195). Power brakes: Horizon/TC3/Reliant ($93). Suspension: H.D. susp.: Reliant/G. Fury ($26). Sport susp.: TC3 ($52). Other: Performance exhaust system: TC3 Turismo ($31). 430-amp battery: Horizon/TC3 ($26). 500-amp battery: Reliant/G. Fury ($43). Engine block heater: Horizon/TC3 ($18). Max. cooling ($141). California emission system ($65). High-altitude emission system (NC).

HORIZON/TC3 CONVENIENCE/APPEARANCE OPTIONS: Option Packages: Sport appearance pkg.: TC3 Cust ($138). Bright exterior accent group: Cust ($85-$121). Two-tone paint pkg.: Cust ($113-$186). Light group ($74). Comfort/Convenience: Air cond. ($612). Rear defroster, electric ($120). Automatic speed control ($155). Tinted glass: 4-dr. ($82). Rallye instrument cluster: Cust ($127). Electric clock w/trip odometer ($48). Intermittent wipers ($47). Rear wiper/washer: 4-dr. ($117). Mirrors: Dual remote chrome: 4-dr. ($47). Dual sport remote: TC3 ($55). Lighted vanity ($50). Entertainment: AM radio: Miser ($78). AM/FM stereo radio ($106-$184); w/8track player ($192-$270); w/cassette ($242-$320). Radio upgrade ($15-$27). Exterior: Removable glass sunroof: TC3 ($275). Rear spoiler: TC3 Cust ($68). Black vinyl bodyside molding: Cust ($45). Bumper guards: Cust 4-dr. ($56). Front nerf strips: Cust 4-dr. ($25). Rear nerf strips: Cust ($25). Bodyside/deck trim stripe: Cust 4-dr. ($39). Luggage rack: 4-dr. ($93). Undercoating ($39). Lower body protective coating ($39). Interior: Console, shift lever: Cust ($41). Cloth/vinyl bucket seats: Miser ($27). Vinyl bucket seats (NC) exc. Miser. Tonneau cover: TC3 ($64). Cargo area carpet w/sound insulation: TC3 Cust ($56). Wheels and Tires: Luxury wheel covers (NC). Cast aluminum 14-in. wheels: TC3 ($231). 13-in. Rallye wheels: Cust/Euro 4-dr. ($45). 14-in. Rallye wheels: TC3 (NC). P175/75R13 WSW ($58). P175/75R13 SBR WSW ($134). P195/60R14 SBR BSW: TC3 Cust

($173). P195/60R14 SBR RWL: TC3 Cust ($257); Turismo ($84). Conventional spare tire ($51).

1982 Plymouth, Reliant SE station wagon with optional roof rack (OCW)

RELIANT CONVENIENCE/APPEARANCE OPTIONS: Option Packages: Cabriolet roof pkg.: Cust/SE 2-dr. ($696). Light pkg. ($89-$98). Comfort/Convenience: Air cond. ($676). Rear defroster ($125). Automatic speed control ($155). Power seat ($197). Power front windows ($165). Power door locks ($106-$152). Power decklid/liftgate release ($32). Tinted glass ($88). Steering wheel: Luxury ($50); Sport ($50-$90); Leather-wrapped ($50-$90); Tilt ($95). Digital clock ($61). Intermittent wipers ($47). Liftgate wiper/washer: wag ($117). Horns and Mirrors: Dual horns ($12). Remote left mirror ($22). Dual remote mirrors ($64-$86). Lighted vanity mirror, right ($50). Entertainment: AM radio: base ($78). AM/FM stereo radio ($106-$184); w/8track player ($192-$270); w/cassette ($242-$320); w/CB ($364-$442). Dual front speakers ($27). Premium speakers ($126). Delete AM radio ($56 credit). Exterior: Removable glass sunroof ($275). Full vinyl roof: 4-dr. ($157). Padded landau roof: 2-dr. ($157). Door edge protectors ($15-$25). Sill moldings ($23). Bumper guards, front or rear ($28). Bodyside tape stripe ($48) exc. SE wag (NC). Luggage rack ($106). Special sound insulation ($87). Undercoating ($39). Vinyl lower body protection ($39). Interior: Console: Cust/SE ($100). Vinyl bench seat: base (NC). Cloth/vinyl bench seat: base ($31). Vinyl reclining bucket seats: Cust ($132-$151); SE (NC). Cloth reclining bucket seats: Cust ($249-$270); SE ($98). Color-keyed mats: front ($25); rear ($20). Color-keyed seatbelts ($28). Tonneau cover: wag ($64). Trunk dress-up ($51). Wheels and Tires: Deluxe 13-in. wheel covers ($52). Luxury 14-in. wheel covers ($41-$93). 14-in. wire wheel covers ($257-$309). Rallye wheels, 13- or 14-in. ($41-$93). Cast aluminum 14-in. wheels ($357-$409). P175/75R13 GBR wide WSW ($58). P185/70R13 SBR wide WSW ($194). P185/70R14 GBR wide WSW ($207). Conventional spare tire ($50).

GRAN FURY CONVENIENCE/APPEARANCE OPTIONS: Option Packages: Basic group ($1143). Light pkg. ($139). Protection group ($119). Comfort/Convenience: Air cond. ($731). Rear defroster, electric ($125). Auto. speed control ($155). Power windows ($235), Power door locks ($152). Power decklid release ($32). Illuminated entry system ($72). Leather-wrapped steering wheel ($50). Tilt steering wheel ($95). Digital clock ($61). Intermittent wipers ($47). Mirrors: Remote driver's ($22). Dual remote chrome ($65). Lighted vanity ($58). Entertainment: AM/FM stereo radio ($106); w/8track tape player ($192); w/CB ($364). Search-tune AM/FM stereo ($239). Electronic-tuning AM/FM stereo w/cassette ($455). Dual front speakers ($28). Premium speakers ($126). Power antenna ($55). Radio delete ($56 credit). Exterior: Power glass sunroof ($982). Full vinyl roof ($158). Vinyl bodyside moldings ($46). Upper door frame moldings ($41). Bodyside/deck/hood stripe ($109). Body sound insulation ($30). Undercoating ($39). Interior: Vinyl bench seat ($58). Trunk dress-up ($51). Wheels and Tires: Premium wheel covers ($93). Wire wheel covers ($257). Forged aluminum wheels ($364). P205/75R15 SBR WSW ($116). Conventional spare tire ($51).

1982 Plymouth, Gran Fury sedan (OCW)

HISTORY: Introduced: October 14, 1981. Model year production: Chrysler reported a total of 232,386 passenger cars shipped. Calendar year production: 241,181. Calendar year sales by U.S. dealers: 251,628. Model year sales by U.S. dealers: 255,892 (not incl. 40,431 imported Colts and 12,607 Sapporos).

Historical Footnotes: Chrysler/Plymouth sales for the model year fell nine percent; but since other automakers fared even worse, the division gained a larger market share. Plymouth scored considerably worse, however, with each line except the rebodied rear-drive Gran Fury posting a sharp sales decline. Gran Fury sales almost doubled. Reliant remained the Division's best seller by far, taking one-third of CP sales even with a lagging total this year. TC3 coupes were now marketed separately from the Horizon sedan. At mid-year, a Rampage car/pickup based on the TC3/024 design went on the market.

1983 PLYMOUTH

Chrysler's Trans4 2.2-liter four-cylinder engine added 10 horsepower this year, with compression jacked up to 9.0:1. Standard on Reliant and optional on Horizon/Turismo, the 2.2 engine had reworked manifolds and cylinder head, and recalibrated fuel/spark control. A new (97 cubic inch) 1.6-liter four, built by Peugeot, replaced the former 105 cubic inch (1.7-liter) four as base Horizon/Turismo powerplant after the start of the model year. A five-speed manual transaxle became optional on Horizon, Turismo and Reliant. Little appearance change was evident on Plymouth models.

HORIZON — SERIES M — FOUR — Base and Custom Horizons were the two choices for 1983, as the low-budget Miser faded away. The Euro-Sedan disappeared as well. Taillamps, though similar in shape to 1983, showed horizontal lens ribbing and larger backup lenses. Otherwise, appearance changed little. After the model year began, a new 1.6-liter four, built by Peugeot, gradually began to replace the former Volkswagen-based 1.7-liter powerplant. A four-speed manual transaxle was standard again, but this year a new five-speed (overdrive) unit became available. Actually, it was the same old four-speed with an extra gear hooked up. The five-speed was offered with either the base 1.7-or optional 2.2-liter four. Horizons had standard power brakes and low-back reclining padded bucket seats. A restyled woodtone-finished instrument panel held a quartz clock and trip odometer. Standard equipment on the base model included bumper rub strips, lighter, quartz clock, locking glove box, dual horns, black body moldings, black remote-control driver's mirror, day/night mirror, trip odometer, and intermittent wipers. Custom added the woodtone instrument panel, chrome driver's mirror, deluxe wheel covers, and bright moldings for backlight, partial belt, liftgate, bodyside, sill and upper door frame.

1983 Plymouth, Turismo hatchback (OCW)

TURISMO — SERIES M — FOUR — The Horizon-based coupe changed its name from TC3 to Turismo this year, and the Miser disappeared. Otherwise, nothing drastic happened. Two models were offered: the base Turismo with 1.7-liter (later 1.6-liter) four, and the Turismo 2.2 with a high-performance, 100-horsepower version of the 2.2-liter engine. Actually, that powerplant didn't produce so much more power than the standard optional 2.2. which rose from 84 to 94 horsepower this year with a compression boost. Optional this year was a five-speed manual transaxle, to replace the basic four-speed. Standard power brakes were improved. Standard equipment included halogen headlamps, tachometer, trip odometer, maintenance-free battery, and cloth/vinyl sport high-back bucket seats with dual recliners. Also standard: tinted glass, front bumper rub strip, cigarette lighter, clock, dual horns, padded instrument panel with woodtone appliqué, power liftgate release, left remote (black) mirror, bodyside and hatchback stripes, intermittent wipers, and a four-spoke steering wheel. In addition to the high-output engine, Turismo 2.2 added an AM radio, sport suspension, 14-inch Rallye wheels, simulated hood scoop, and dual remote-control sport mirrors, Turismo 2.2 also included a performance exhaust system and unique tape graphics that included a wide bodyside stripe that dipped down at the front, along with a rear liftgate spoiler, front storage and shift lever console, and low-profile SBR tires. Chrysler claimed that a Turismo "leaves more expensive sport cars in the dust," while the most economical version warranted an EPA mileage estimate of 32 mpg (50 highway) with the base engine and four-speed.

RELIANT — SERIES P — FOUR — Model selection dwindled slightly, leaving only the station wagon in Reliant's Custom series, but retaining the base and SE editions as before. Choices included base and Special Edition two- or four-doors, and Custom or Special Edition wagons. The base overhead-cam, 2.2-liter four-cylinder engine gained 10 horsepower,

now producing 94 at 5200 rpm, partly as a result of a rise in compression ratio to 9.0:1. That engine used an electronic feedback two-barrel carburetor. As before, one engine option was offered: the Mitsubishi-built 2.6-liter MCA-Jet Silent Shaft four. This year, a five-speed manual transaxle was available, to replace the standard four-speed. Wide-ratio TorqueFlite automatic also remained on the option list, with high-ratio first and second gears. Chrysler called Reliant the "highest mileage, six-passenger front-wheel drive car in America," with an EPA estimate of 29 mpg in the city and 41 on the highway. Power brakes now were standard, as was a maintenance-free battery. A "Pass-Flasher" signal was added to the multi-function steering column lever. The fuel filler cap had a new plastic tether strap. Redesigned door latches were quieter. New ram-air features went into the heat/vent system, which added a dash vent. Optional air conditioning now offered bi-level operation through upper and lower outlets. Bodies featured a pentastar on the deck lid, along with 'Plymouth' and 'Reliant' letters on opposite sides. Vertical red reflectors stood at the rear of quarter panels. Full-width taillamps included square backup lamps flanking the license plate. Reliants had standard halogen headlamps and a stand-up pentastar hood ornament. The grille contained five bright horizontal bars and a center vertical bar. Inside was a color-keyed instrument panel with rosewood woodtone touches and deluxe two-spoke steering wheel. Standard upholstery consisted of an all-vinyl bench seat in blue, red, or beige. Optional: Madison (blue or red) or Kingsley (beige) cloth bench seat with vinyl door trim panels. Special Edition models (and Custom wagon) had an all-cloth bench seat with center armrest in silver (except wagon), blue, red, or beige. Optional at no cost was a saddle vinyl bench seat in the same colors. Optional at extra cost: all-cloth low-back bucket seats with dual recliners, also in the same colors. Body colors were: Formal Black, Nightwatch Blue, Pearl White, Silver crystal coat, Beige crystal coat, Crimson Red, Sable Brown, Charcoal Gray metallic, or Glacier Blue crystal coat. Also one two-tone combination: Charcoal Gray metallic/Silver crystal coat. All models carried bodyside moldings with vinyl inserts; bright drip rail moldings; bright windshield, quarter window and backlight moldings. Special Editions added rear door glass louvers, bright belt and decklid moldings, upper door frame moldings, bright taillamp accents, black paint graphics for the bright grille, bright front/rear rub strips with vinyl inserts, and Special Edition plaque on rear roof pillar. Optional at no cost was an all-cloth split back seat with center armrest. Custom and SE had a standard AM radio. SE wagons had woodgrain bodyside and liftgate appliqués with woodgrain surround moldings. Standard tires were P175/75R13 glass-belted radials.

GRAN FURY — SERIES B — SIX/V-8 — Apart from four new body colors, not much was different on the last rear-drive Plymouth. As before, only one four-door sedan model was offered. Base engine once again was the 225 cubic inch (3.7-liter) Slant Six with three-speed TorqueFlite automatic; optional, the 318 cubic inch (5.2-liter) V-8. Standard equipment included tinted glass, halogen headlamps, power steering and brakes, AM radio, cloth/vinyl bench seats with folding center armrest, and color-keyed seatbelts. Also standard: front bumper guards, front/rear bumper rub strips, dual horns, courtesy lights, day/night mirror, driver's outside mirror, wheel opening and belt moldings, drip rail and sill moldings, two-spoke steering wheel, two-speed wipers, and a trip odometer. Tires were P195/75R15 glass-belted radials, with deluxe wheel covers and a compact spare. A total of 8,400 police packages were installed on Gran Fury, which remained popular with fleet buyers and families.

I.D. DATA: Plymouth again had a 17-symbol Vehicle Identification Number (VIN) on the upper left corner of the instrument panel, visible through the windshield. Coding is similar to 1982. This year's engine codes (symbol eight) are: 'A' L497 2Bbl.; 'B' L4105 2Bbl.; 'C' L4135 2Bbl.; 'G' L4156 2Bbl.; 'H' L6225 1Bbl.; 'P' V8318 2Bbl. Model year code (symbol ten) changed to 'D' 1983. Symbol eleven is Assembly Plant: 'A' Detroit; 'D' Belvidere, IL; 'F' Newark, DE; 'G' or 'X' St. Louis; 'R' Windsor, Ontario. Engine number locations are the same as 1981-82.

HORIZON (FOUR)

Model No.	Body/ Style No.	Body Type & Seating	Factory Price	Shipping Weight	Prod. Total
ME	44	4-dr. Hatch-5P	5841	2165	35,796
MH	44	4-dr. Cust Hatch-5P	6071	2195	10,675

TURISMO (FOUR)

MH	24	2-dr. Hatch-5P	6379	2170	22,527

TURISMO 2.2 (FOUR)

MP	24	2-dr. Hatch-5P	7303	2330	9,538

RELIANT (FOUR)

PL	21	2-dr. Sedan-6P	6577	2300	16,109
PL	41	4-dr. Sedan-6P	6718	2300	69,112

RELIANT CUSTOM (FOUR)

PH	45	4-dr. Sta Wag-6P	7636	2410	38,264

RELIANT SPECIAL EDITION (FOUR)

PH	21	2-dr. Sedan-6P	7260	2310	5,852
PH	41	4-dr. Sedan-6P	7417	2340	13,434
PP	45	4-dr. Sta Wag-6P	8186	2465	3,791

GRAN FURY (SIX/V-8)

Model No.	Body/ Style No.	Body Type & Seating	Factory Price	Shipping Weight	Prod. Total
SL	41	4-dr. Sedan-6P	8248/8473	3320/3455	15,739

Factory Price And Weight Note: Gran Fury price and weight to left of slash is for six-cylinder, to right for V-8.

Model Number Note: Some sources identify models using the new VIN data to indicate Car Line, Price Class and Body Style. Example: base Reliant four-door (PL41) has the equivalent number P26, which translates to Reliant line, Low price class, and four-door sedan body. See I.D. Data section for breakdown.

ENGINE DATA: BASE FOUR (late Horizon, Turismo): Inline, overhead-cam four-cylinder. Cast iron block; aluminum head. Displacement: 97.3 cu. in. (1.6-liters). Bore & stroke: 3.17 x 3.07 in. Compression ratio: 8.8:1. Brake horsepower: 62 at 4800 R.P.M. Torque: 86 lb.-ft. at 3200 R.P.M. Five main bearings. Solid valve lifters. Carburetor: 2Bbl. VIN Code: A. BASE FOUR (early Horizon, Turismo): Inline, overhead-cam four-cylinder. Cast iron block; aluminum head. Displacement: 104.7 cu. in. (1.7-liters). Bore & stroke: 3.13 x 3.40 in. Compression ratio: 8.2:1. Brake horsepower: 63 at 4800 R.P.M. Torque: 83 lb.-ft. at 2400 R.P.M. Five main bearings. Solid valve lifters. Carburetor: 2Bbl. Holley 6520. VIN Code: B. BASE FOUR (Reliant, Turismo 2.2); OPTIONAL (Horizon, Turismo): Inline, overhead-cam four-cylinder. Cast iron block; aluminum head. Displacement: 135 cu. in. (2.2-liters). Bore & stroke: 3.44 x 3.62 in. Compression ratio: 9.0:1. Brake horsepower: 94 at 5200 R.P.M. (Turismo 2.2, 100 at 5200 R.P.M.). Torque: 117 lb.-ft. at 3200 R.P.M. (Turismo 2.2, 122 at 3200 R.P.M.). Five main bearings. Hydraulic valve lifters. Carburetor: 2Bbl. Holley 6520. VIN Code: C. OPTIONAL FOUR (Reliant): Inline, overhead-cam four-cylinder. Cast iron block; aluminum head. Displacement: 156 cu. in. (2.6-liters). Bore & stroke: 3.59 x 3.86 in. Compression ratio: 8.2:1. Brake horsepower: 93 at 4500 R.P.M. Torque: 132 lb.-ft. at 2500 R.P.M. Five main bearings. Solid valve lifters. Carburetor: 2Bbl. Mikuni. VIN Code: G. BASE SIX (Gran Fury): Inline, overhead-valve six. Cast iron block and head. Displacement: 225 cu. in. (3.7-liters). Bore & stroke: 3.40 x 4.12 in. Compression ratio: 8.4:1. Brake horsepower: 90 at 3600 R.P.M. Torque: 165 lb.-ft. at 1600 R.P.M. Four main bearings. Hydraulic valve lifters. Carburetor: 1Bbl. Holley 6145. VIN Code: H. OPTIONAL V-8 (Gran Fury): 90-degree, overhead valve V-8. Cast iron block and head. Displacement: 318 cu. in. (5.2-liters). Bore & stroke: 3.91 x 3.31 in. Compression ratio: 8.5:1. Brake horsepower: 130 at 4000 R.P.M. Torque: 230 lb.-ft. at 1600 R.P.M. Five main bearings. Hydraulic valve lifters. Carburetor: 2Bbl. Carter BBD. VIN Code: P.

CHASSIS DATA: Wheelbase: (Horizon) 99.1 in.; (Turismo) 96.6 in.; (Reliant) 100.1 in.; (Gran Fury) 112.7 in. Overall Length: (Horizon) 164.8 in.; (Turismo) 173.3 in.; (Reliant) 176.0 in.; (Reliant wag) 176.2 in.; (Gran Fury) 205.7 in. Height: (Horizon) 53.1 in.; (Turismo) 50.8 in.; (Reliant 2-dr.) 52.3 in.; (Reliant 4-dr.) 52.7 in.; (Reliant wag) 52.4 in.; (Gran Fury) 55.3 in. Width: (Horizon) 65.8 in.; (Turismo) 66.7 in.; (Reliant) 68.6 in.; (G. Fury) 74.2 in. Front Tread: (Horiz/Tur) 56.1 in.; (Reliant) 57.6 in.; (G. Fury) 60.0 in. Rear Tread: (Horiz/Tur) 55.6 in.; (Reliant) 57.0 in.; (G. Fury) 59.5 in. Standard Tires: (Horiz/Tur/Reliant) P175/75R13 GBR; (Turismo 2.2) P195/60R14 SBR RWL; (Gran Fury) P195/75R15.

TECHNICAL: Transmission: Four-speed manual (floor shift) standard on Horizon/Turismo w/1.7-liter engine: (1st) 3.45:1; (2nd) 1.94:1; (3rd) 1.29:1; (4th) 0.97:1; (Rev) 3.17:1. Four-speed manual (floor shift) standard on Reliant and Horizon/Turismo w/1.6- or 2.2-liter engine: (1st) 3.29:1; (2nd) 1.89:1; (3rd) 1.21:1; (4th) 0.88:1; (Rev) 3.14:1. Five-speed manual optional on Horizon/Turismo: (1st) 3.29:1; (2nd) 1.89:1; (3rd) 1.21:1; (4th) 0.88:1; (5th) 0.72:1; (Rev) 3.14:1. TorqueFlite three-speed automatic standard on Gran Fury and Reliant w/2.6-liter engine, optional on others. Gran Fury gear ratios: (1st) 2.74:1; (2nd) 1.54:1; (3rd) 1.00:1; (Rev) 2.22:1. Horizon/Turismo/Reliant ratios: (1st) 2.69:1; (2nd) 1.55:1; (3rd) 1.00:1; (Rev) 2.10:1. Standard final drive ratio: (Horizon/Turismo) 2.69:1 w/4spd, 2.59:1 w/auto.; (Horizon/Turismo w/2.2-liter four) 2.20:1 w/5spd, 2.78:1 w/auto.; (Reliant) 2.69:1 w/4spd, 2.20:1 w/5spd, 2.78:1 w/auto.; (Gran Fury) 2.94:1. Steering: (Horizon/Turismo/Reliant) rack and pinion; (Gran Fury) recirculating ball. Suspension: (Horizon/Turismo) Iso-Strut independent coil front w/anti-sway bar, semi-independent trailing arm coil rear w/available anti-sway bar; (Reliant) Iso-Strut front with integral linkless anti-sway bar, flex-arm beam rear axle w/trailing links and coil springs; (Gran Fury) front transverse torsion bars and anti-sway bar, semi-elliptic rear leaf springs. Brakes: Front disc, rear drum. Ignition: Electronic. Body construction: Unibody. Fuel tank: 13 gal. exc. (Gran Fury) 18 gal.

DRIVETRAIN OPTIONS: Engines: 2.2-liter four: Horizon/Turismo ($134). 2.6-liter four: Reliant ($259). 318 cu. in., 2Bbl. V-8: Gran Fury ($225). Transmission/Differential: Five-speed trans.: Horizon/Turismo/Reliant ($75). TorqueFlite: Horiz/Tur/Reliant ($439). Performance axle ratio: Horiz/Tur/Reliant ($22). Power Accessories: Power steering: Horiz/Tur/Reliant ($214). Suspension: H.D. susp.: Horizon 4-dr. ($34); Reliant/G. Fury ($26). Other: 500-amp battery: Reliant/G. Fury ($43). Max. cooling: Horizon/Turismo/Reliant ($141). California emission system ($75). High-altitude emission system (NC).

HORIZON/TURISMO CONVENIENCE/APPEARANCE OPTIONS: Option Packages: Same selection and prices as equivalent Dodge Omni and Charger models; see Dodge listing.

RELIANT CONVENIENCE/APPEARANCE OPTIONS: Same selection and prices as Dodge Aries; see Dodge listing.

GRAN FURY CONVENIENCE/APPEARANCE OPTIONS: Option Packages: Basic group ($1308). Light pkg. ($147). Protection group ($132). Comfort/Convenience: Air conditioning, semi-auto ($787). Rear defroster, electric ($138). Automatic speed control ($174). Power windows ($255). Power door locks ($159). Power decklid release ($40). Illuminated entry system ($75). Leather-wrapped steering wheel ($53). Tilt steering wheel ($99). Digital clock ($64). Intermittent wipers ($52). Mirrors: Remote driver's ($23). Dual remote, chrome ($67). Lighted vanity, right ($61). Entertainment: AM/FM stereo radio ($109). Electronic-tuning AM/FM stereo ($154-$263); w/cassette ($293-$402). Dual front speakers ($28). Premium speakers ($126). Power antenna ($60). Radio delete ($56 credit). Exterior Trim: Power glass sunroof ($1041). Full vinyl roof ($172). Vinyl bodyside moldings ($57). Upper door frame moldings ($44). Bodyside/deck/hood stripe ($109). Body sound insulation ($43). Undercoating ($41). Interior: Vinyl bench seat ($60). Trunk dress-up ($54). Wheels and Tires: Premium wheel covers ($94). Wire wheel covers ($257). P205/75R15 SBR WSW ($116). Conventional spare ($63).

HISTORY: Introduced: October 1, 1982. Model year production: Chrysler reported a total of 240,837 passenger cars shipped. Calendar year production: 310,748. Calendar year sales by U.S. dealers: 265,608. Model year sales by U.S. dealers: 265,564 (not incl. 44,534 captive imports).

Historical Footnotes: Horizon and Reliant sales enjoyed a modest rise in the 1983 model year, while the rear-drive Gran Fury slipped a bit. On the import scene, Champ switched to the Colt name at the start of the 1983 model year, but sales continued slow. In fact, no imports did Chrysler-Plymouth much good in sales.

1984 PLYMOUTH

After a long history under Chrysler product hoods, the old familiar Slant Six, engine was gone. Gran Fury now came only with the 318 cubic inch V-8. Reliant's optional 2.6-liter four, built by Mitsubishi, gained eight horsepower. "Match it. If you can" was this year's catalog slogan. The Turismo coupe got a significant restyle, while Horizon and Reliant added a new grille design.

1984 Plymouth, Horizon hatchback (OCW)

HORIZON — SERIES M — FOUR — Described as "an American Value Classic," Plymouth's subcompact sedan gained an altered front-end look this year. Horizon's new grille consisted of a bright surrounding frame that contained six narrow bright vertical bars, with center pentastar emblem, all over a horizontal-pattern black background. New single rectangular recessed halogen headlamps and amber wrap-around park/signal lamps were similar to 1983, with 'Plymouth' block lettering again above the left headlamp. Bodies were treated to chip-resistant lower bodyside urethane primer. The base model's Euro treatment included blackout bodyside and liftgate moldings, black windshield and back window moldings, black belt moldings and upper door frames, and black driver's remote mirror. Among its standard equipment, Horizon had a 335-amp maintenance-free battery. A new instrument panel held three round gauges, and a trip odometer. All-weather steel-belted radial tires rode 13-inch argent steel wheels with bright black hub covers, wheel nuts and trim rings. Bright bumpers held black rub strips and long end caps. Inside were new cloth/vinyl contoured low-back bucket seats with adjustable head restraints and recliners, a four-spoke sport steering wheel with center pad, passenger vanity mirror, and folding rear shelf security panel. The standard 1.6-liter engine and four-speed transaxle was rated 34 mpg (49 highway) in EPA mileage estimates. As before, a 2.2-liter four was available, and

either a five-speed manual or three-speed automatic transaxle. The high-output 2.2-liter, introduced in 1983 on Dodge's Shelby Charger, became optional on Horizon/Turismo this year. Horizon SE (which replaced the former Custom line) carried a new digital AM radio with electronic/manual tuning and digital clock, sport cloth/vinyl high-back bucket seats with integral headrests and recliners, carpeted cargo area trim panels, remote driver's chrome mirror, and SBR narrow whitewalls with new deluxe wheel covers. SE also included bright liftgate window, upper door frame, sill, and belt moldings; and bright/black bodyside and liftgate moldings. Body colors were: Spice Brown or Charcoal Gray metallic; Beige, Glacier Blue or Radiant Silver crystal coat; Nightwatch Blue; Graphic Red; White and Black. Garnet Red pearl coat cost extra, and SE could have a choice of three two-tones. Options included electronic-tuning stereo systems, cruise control, and a rear wiper/washer.

1984 Plymouth, Turismo 2.2 hatchback (OCW)

TURISMO — SERIES M — FOUR — Up front, Turismo's most noticeable appearance change was a switch from single headlamps to quad rectangular units, in a new soft front-end design. The grille was similar to 1983, though: just two wide slots (separated by a single horizontal bar) in the sloping body-color panel. Below the new integral bumper rub strip was a single, much larger slot, flanked by recessed parking/signal lamps. Along the bodysides ran new wide soft-touch protective moldings. Not only was a different quarter-window appliqué used, but the large far-rear triangular window of previous coupe models was gone. This year's design held only two side windows, with a horizontally-ribbed trim panel stretching from the quarter window back to the liftgate. Wide wrap-around taillamps with horizontally-ribbed lenses had square back-up lenses toward the center, near the license plate opening. New deluxe wheel covers highlighted the 13-inch steel-belted radial tires. This was the first significant restyle since the coupe's introduction in 1979. Standard equipment included the Peugeot-built 1.6-liter four-cylinder engine, four-speed manual transaxle, power brakes, tinted glass, a maintenance-free battery, power liftgate release, and driver's black remote mirror. Cloth/vinyl low-back bucket seats came in a choice of red, blue, beige or charcoal/silver or brown/saddle two-tone. Solid body colors were the same as Horizon, and Turismo could have a choice of four two-tones. Turismo 2.2 featured the high-output 2.2-liter engine and new close-ratio five-speed transaxle, along with a performance exhaust system, new rear spoiler, sport suspension, dual remote sport (black) mirrors, and new 14-inch Rallye wheels with low-profile SBR raised-black-letter tires. Large 'Turismo 2.2' tape graphics went near the base of each door, while the hood no longer held a simulated scoop. Turismo 2.2 came only in two-tone paint treatments, different from the standard model; but the secondary color was applied only along the lower edge of the body, making the two-tone less obvious. A new Rallye instrument cluster held a tachometer, trip odometer, voltmeter, temp, fuel and oil pressure gauges. An electronic-tuning AM radio with digital clock was standard. Cloth/vinyl low-back reclining bucket seats were standard, with high-back buckets available. Among the options was Ultimate Sound stereo with a cassette player, four speakers, and Dolby noise reduction. Turismos used an Iso-Strut front suspension with integral linkless anti-sway bar. At the rear was a beam axle and trailing arm system with coil springs, track bar, and torsion-tube anti-roll control. Turismo 2.2 added a rear anti-sway bar. Chrysler reported that 8,060 Duster packages were installed, though that option wasn't announced at introduction time.

1984 Plymouth, Reliant Custom station wagon (OCW)

RELIANT — SERIES P — FOUR — Plymouth's six-model compact lineup was the same as 1983: base two-door or four-door sedan, Custom wagon,

and SE two- or four-door sedan and wagon. Base engine remained the 2.2-liter Trans4. Optional again was the Mitsubishi-built 2.6-liter, which added horsepower and torque this year with a compression boost and recalibrated spark/carburetion. Brakes had a dual proportioning valve. Both a five-speed manual transaxle and three-speed TorqueFlite were available. This year's restyled grille consisted of two horizontal and one vertical thin bright bars, surrounded by a heavier upper and side molding, with pentastar emblem in the middle. Clear vertical rectangular parking lamps stood between the grille and recessed single rectangular head-lamps, with wraparound amber marker lenses at the outside. Color-keyed front/rear bumper strips were new. So were wide taillamps with horizontally-ribbed lenses, which didn't quite reach the quarter panel tips. Backup lenses sat toward the center, alongside the license plate opening. Wagons had new wraparound taillamps. Reliant's Iso-Strut front suspension with integral linkless anti-sway bar was reworked. Rear suspension was a beam axle and trailing arm design with track bar and torsion tube anti-roll control. The gas tank grew to 14 gallons this year. All radios had electronic tuning and a built-in digital clock. A new instrument cluster held analog gauges and a trip odometer. Standard equipment included a maintenance-free battery, halogen headlamps, new locking glovebox, vinyl bench seats, deluxe wheel covers, power brakes, two-speed wipers, P175/80R13 SBR tires, and bumper rub strips. SE carried a Special Edition plaque on the rear roof pillar. Standard SE fittings included twin vertical quarter-window (or back door window) louvers, plus bright moldings for decklid, backlight, windshield; upper door frames, belt, and tail-lamps. SE cloth-trim vinyl bench seats had a center armrest. Also inside was a new woodtone (upper/lower) instrument panel, as opposed to the base Reliant's upper woodtone treatment only. An AM radio was standard on SE, and on the Custom wagon. Body colors were: Crimson Red, Garnet Red or Mink Brown pearl coat, Beige or Glacier Blue crystal coat, Nightwatch Blue, Black, Charcoal or Radiant Silver crystal coat, or White. Two two-tones were available on four-door models.

1984 Plymouth, Gran Fury sedan (OCW)

GRAN FURY — SERIES B — V-8 — Apart from the loss of the six-cylinder powerplant, the M-bodied Gran Fury changed little. The 318 cubic inch (5.2-liter) V-8, optional for several years, now became standard. Gran Fury now rode larger (P205/75R15) steel-belted radial whitewall tires. The standard AM radio had digital readouts and a built-in clock. Other standard equipment included power brakes and steering, front bumper guards, carpeting, cigarette lighter, tinted glass, halogen headlamps, dual horns, courtesy lights, day/night mirror, and a cloth/vinyl bench seat with center armrest. Gran Fury displayed moldings for the drip rail, windshield, belt, wheel openings, and sill. Options included a full vinyl roof, power glass sunroof, power windows and door locks, and wire wheel covers. Available this year was a 60/40 cloth-upholstered front seat with center rear armrest. A total of 6,661 police packages were installed on Gran Fury models, 6,516 of which were reported as being for police use.

I.D. DATA: Plymouth again had a 17-symbol Vehicle Identification Number (VIN) on the upper left corner of the instrument panel, visible through the windshield. Coding was similar to 1983. Model year code changed to 'E' for 1984. Two engine codes were dropped ('B' for L4105 and 'H' for L6225) and one was added: 'F' H.O. L4135 2Bbl.; Code 'R' for Windsor assembly plant was dropped. Engine number locations are the same as 1981-83.

HORIZON (FOUR)

Model No.	Body/Style No.	Body Type & Seating	Factory Price	Shipping Weight	Prod. Total
ME	44	4-dr. Hatch-5P	6138	2095	62,903
MH	44	4-dr. SE Hatch-5P	6456	2160	15,661

TURISMO (FOUR)

Model No.	Body/Style No.	Body Type & Seating	Factory Price	Shipping Weight	Prod. Total
MH	24	2-dr. Hatch-5P	6868	2120	38,835

TURISMO 2.2 (FOUR)

Model No.	Body/Style No.	Body Type & Seating	Factory Price	Shipping Weight	Prod. Total
MP	24	2-dr. Hatch-5P	7662	2300	10,881

RELIANT (FOUR)

Model No.	Body/Style No.	Body Type & Seating	Factory Price	Shipping Weight	Prod. Total
PL	21	2-dr. Sedan-6P	7235	2335	14,533
PL	41	4-dr. Sedan-6P	7347	2340	72,595

RELIANT CUSTOM (FOUR)

Model No.	Body/Style No.	Body Type & Seating	Factory Price	Shipping Weight	Prod. Total
PH	45	4-dr. Sta Wag-6P	8134	2430	39,207

RELIANT SE (FOUR)

Model No.	Body/Style No.	Body Type & Seating	Factory Price	Shipping Weight	Prod. Total
PH	21	2-dr. Sedan-6P	7861	2345	5,287
PH	41	4-dr. Sedan-6P	7987	2375	16,223
PP	45	4-dr. Sta Wag-6P	8593	2480	4,338

GRAN FURY (V-8)

Model No.	Body/Style No.	Body Type & Seating	Factory Price	Shipping Weight	Prod. Total
BL	41	4-dr. Sedan-6P	9655	3470	14,516

Gran Fury Production Note: Of total production, 6,516 were for police use.

Model Number Note: Some sources identity models using the VIN data to indicate Car Line, Price Class and Body Style. Example: base Reliant four-door (PL41) has the equivalent number P26, which translates to Reliant line, Low price class, and four-door sedan body. See I.D. Data section for breakdown.

ENGINE DATA: BASE FOUR (Horizon, Turismo): Inline, overhead-cam four-cylinder. Cast iron block; aluminum head. Displacement: 97.3 cu. in. (1.6-liters). Bore & stroke: 3.17 x 3.07 in. Compression ratio: 8.8:1. Brake horsepower: 64 at 4800 R.P.M. Torque: 87 lb.-ft. at 2800 R.P.M. Five main bearings. Solid valve lifters. Carburetor: 2Bbl. Holley 6520. VIN Code: A. **BASE FOUR (Reliant, Turismo 2.2); OPTIONAL (Horizon, Turismo):** Inline, overhead-cam four-cylinder. Cast iron block; aluminum head. Displacement: 135 cu. in. (2.2-liters). Bore & stroke: 3.44 x 3.62 in. Compression ratio: 9.0:1. Brake horsepower: 96 at 5200 R.P.M. (Turismo 2.2, 101 at 5200 R.P.M.). Torque: 119 lb.-ft. at 3200 R.P.M. (Turismo 2.2, 124 at 3200 R.P.M.). Five main bearings. Hydraulic valve lifters. Carburetor: 2Bbl. Holley 6520. VIN Code: C. **OPTIONAL FOUR (Horizon, Turismo):** High-performance version of 135 cu. in. four above, with fuel injection. Horsepower: 110 at 5200 R.P.M. Torque: 129 lb.-ft. at 3600 R.P.M. VIN Code: F. **OPTIONAL FOUR (Reliant):** Inline, overhead-cam four-cylinder. Cast iron block; aluminum head. Displacement: 156 cu. in. (2.6-liters). Bore & stroke: 3.59 x 3.86 in. Compression ratio: 8.7:1. Brake horsepower: 101 at 4800 R.P.M. Torque: 140 lb.-ft. at 2800 R.P.M. Five main bearings. Solid valve lifters. Carburetor: 2Bbl. Mikuni. VIN Code: G. **BASE V-8 (Gran Fury):** 90-degree, overhead valve V-8. Cast iron block and head. Displacement: 318 cu. in. (5.2-liters). Bore & stroke: 3.91 x 3.31 in. Compression ratio: 8.7:1. Brake horsepower: 130 at 4000 R.P.M. Torque: 235 lb.-ft. at 1600 R.P.M. Five main bearings. Hydraulic valve lifters. Carburetor: 2Bbl. Carter BBD. VIN Code: P. **POLICE V-8 (Gran Fury):** Same as 318 cu. in. V-8 above, with 4Bbl. carburetor. Compression ratio: 8.4:1. Horsepower: 165 at 4400 R.P.M. Torque: 240 lb.-ft. at 1600 R.P.M.

CHASSIS DATA: Wheelbase: (Horizon) 99.1 in.; (Turismo) 96.6 in.; (Reliant) 100.3 in.; (Gran Fury) 112.7 in. Overall Length: (Horizon) 164.8 in.; (Turismo) 174.8 in.; (Reliant) 176.1 in.; (Reliant wag.) 176.2 in.; (Gran Fury) 205.7 in. Height: (Horizon) 53.1 in.; (Turismo) 50.8 in.; (Reliant 2-dr.) 52.3 in.; (Reliant 4-dr.) 52.7 in.; (Reliant wag.) 52.4 in.; (Gran Fury) 55.3 in. Width: (Horizon) 65.8 in.; (Turismo) 66.0 in.; (Reliant) 68.6 in.; (Gran Fury) 74.2 in. Front Tread: (Horizon/Turismo) 56.1 in.; (Reliant) 57.6 in.; (Gran Fury) 60.0 in. Rear Tread: (Horizon/Turismo) 55.6 in.; (Reliant) 57.0 in.; (Gran Fury) 59.5 in. Standard Tires: (Horizon/Turismo) P165/80R13 SBR; (Turismo 2.2) P195/60R14 SBR RBL; (Reliant) P175/80R13 SBR BSW; (Gran Fury) P205/75R15.

TECHNICAL: Transmission: Four-speed manual (floor shift) standard on Reliant and Horizon/Turismo w/1.6- or 2.2-liter engine: (1st) 3.29:1; (2nd) 1.89:1; (3rd) 1.21:1; (4th) 0.88:1; (Rev) 3.14:1. Five-speed manual optional on Horizon/Turismo/Reliant: (1st) 3.29:1; (2nd) 2.08:1; (3rd) 1.45:1; (4th) 1.04:1; (5th) 0.72:1; (Rev) 3.14:1. TorqueFlite three-speed automatic standard on Gran Fury and required on Reliant w/2.6-liter engine, optional on others. Gran Fury gear ratios: (1st) 2.74:1; (2nd) 1.54:1; (3rd) 1.00:1; (Rev) 2.22:1. Horizon/Turismo/Reliant ratios: (1st) 2.69:1; (2nd) 1.55:1; (3rd) 1.00:1; (Rev) 2.10:1. Standard final drive ratio: (Horizon/Turismo) 2.69:1 w/4spd; (Horizon/Turismo w/2.2-liter four) 2.20:1 w/5spd, 2.78:1 w/auto.; (Horizon/Turismo w/H.O. 2.2-liter) 2.57:1 w/5spd, 3.02:1 w/auto.; (Reliant) 2.69:1 w/4spd, 2.20:1 w/5spd, 2.78:1 w/auto., 3.02:1 w/2.6-liter; (Gran Fury) 2.26:1. Steering/Suspension/Brakes/Body: same as 1983. Fuel Tank: (Horizon/Turismo) 13 gal.; (Reliant) 14 gal.; (Gran Fury) 18 gal.

DRIVETRAIN OPTIONS: Engines: 2.2-liter four: Horizon/Turismo ($134). High-performance 2.2-liter: Horizon/Turismo ($256) exc. Turismo 2.2 ($122). 2.6-liter four: Reliant ($271). Transmission/Differential: Five-speed trans.: Horizon/Turismo/Reliant ($75). TorqueFlite: Horiz/Tur/Reliant ($439). Performance axle ratio: Horiz/Tur/Reliant ($22). Power Accessories: Power steering: Horiz/Tur/Reliant ($219). Suspension: H.D. susp.: Horizon 4-dr. ($36); Reliant wag, G. Fury ($26). Other: 500-amp battery: Reliant/G. Fury ($44). Max. cooling: Horiz/Tur/Reliant ($141). California emission system ($99).

HORIZON/TURISMO CONVENIENCE/APPEARANCE OPTIONS: Option Packages: Same selection and prices as equivalent Dodge Omni and Charger models (but without GLH package); see Dodge listing.

RELIANT CONVENIENCE/APPEARANCE OPTIONS: Same selection and prices as equivalent Dodge Aries models; see Dodge listing.

1984 Plymouth, Reliant SE sedan (OCW)

GRAN FURY CONVENIENCE/APPEARANCE OPTIONS: Option Packages: Basic group ($1351). Light pkg. ($153). Protection group ($133). Comfort/Convenience: Air conditioning, semi-auto ($792). Rear defroster, electric ($143). Automatic speed control ($179). Power windows ($260). Power door locks ($175). Power decklid release ($40). Illuminated entry system ($75). Leather-wrapped steering wheel ($60). Tilt steering wheel ($110). Intermittent wipers ($53). Mirrors: Remote driver's ($24). Dual remote, chrome ($67). Lighted vanity, right ($58). Electronic-Tuning Radios: AM/FM stereo ($125). Seek/scan AM/FM stereo ($125-$250); w/cassette ($264-$389). Premium speakers ($126). Power antenna ($60). Radio delete ($39 credit). Exterior: Power glass sunroof ($1041). Full vinyl roof ($185). Vinyl bodyside moldings ($57). Upper door frame moldings ($46). Bodyside/deck/hood stripe ($109). Body sound insulation ($66). Undercoating ($43). Interior: Vinyl split-back bench seat ($60). Trunk dress-up ($57). Wheels/Tires: Premium wheel covers ($96). Wire wheel covers ($263). Conventional spare ($93).

HISTORY: Introduced: October 2, 1983. Model year production: Chrysler reported a total of 294,979 passenger cars shipped. Calendar year production: 378,242. Calendar year sales by U.S. dealers: 289,244. Model year sales by U.S. dealers: 277,171 (not incl. 46,477 captive imports).

Historical Footnotes: Horizon sales rose 49.1 percent for the model year; Turismo, 24.5 percent. Reliant fared less well, as sales dropped nearly nine percent. Like other Chrysler products, Plymouths came with a 5/50 (five-year, 50,000-mile) powertrain and outer panel rust-through warranty that went into effect after the basic 12-month/12,000-mile warranty expired. As for Plymouth's captive imports, an optional turbo engine was added to Colt, a new Colt Vista appeared, and Sapporo was replaced by Conquest (based on Mitsubishi's Starion).

1985 PLYMOUTH

New to Plymouth was Chrysler's turbocharged 2.2-liter four, now offered as an option on the new Caravelle (which was actually the previous year's Chrysler E Class under another name). Instead of a new slogan for the full-line factory sales catalog, Plymouth just added a set of parentheses to the 1984 version, advising customers to "Match them. (If You Can!)" Also promoted was the 5/50 Protection Plan. Plymouth used more galvanized metal, to help prevent rusting. In addition to urethane lower body coating, all bodies got a final clear crystal coat over the acrylic paint. A selection of discount option packages could reduce the total price paid for extra equipment. All Plymouths had new high-output alternators. Manual-shift models had a new shift indicator light. This year's body colors (not available on every model) were: Black, Nightwatch Blue, Graphic Red, Cream, Gold Dust, Radiant Silver, Crimson Red, Spice, Ice Blue, and White crystal coat; plus Gunmetal Blue, Mink Brown, Garnet Red or Charcoal pearl coat. Five two-tone combinations also were offered: four on Horizon and/or Turismo, and two on Caravelle.

1985 Plymouth, Horizon hatchback (OCW)

HORIZON — SERIES M — FOUR — Three body colors were new, but Horizon looked just about the same this year, with its bright vertical grille bars over a black background and center pentastar. "An American value with European flair" was Chrysler's way of describing the subcompact base sedan, promoted for its Euro-styling. For the most part, all that meant was a set of black moldings rather than the bright-and-black ones mounted on the step-up SE model. A new shift indicator light came with manual-transaxle models. Tinted glass became standard, but the former dual-note horn changed back to single. Standard equipment included power brakes, 1.6-liter four-cylinder engine, four-speed manual transaxle, bumper rub strips, lighter, tethered gas cap, tinted glass, locking glove box, black remote-control driver's mirror, day/night mirror, and intermittent wipers. As before, the 2.2-liter Trans4 engine was available, along with a five-speed gearbox or three-speed TorqueFlite. Cloth/vinyl low-back bucket seats were standard on the base model; high-back buckets on the SE. Other SE extras included an electronic-tuning AM radio with built-in digital clock, remote-control chrome driver's mirror, and whitewall tires. New options included an AM stereo (and FM stereo) radio, and high-back bucket seats with dual recliners. Neither the luggage rack nor the heavy-duty suspension, formerly optional, were offered this year. One interior trim color was new.

1985 Plymouth, Turismo hatchback with optional Duster package (OCW)

TURISMO — SERIES M — FOUR — Plymouth's subcompact coupe carried on with the same overall appearance as in 1984, when it lost the old triangular back quarter windows and switched to quad headlamps. Turismo's grille consisted of two wide slots, one above the other in the body-color panel, with amber parking lamps below the bumper rub strip. Wide ribbed wraparound taillamps held backup lenses near their inner ends. Base engine, as before, was the Peugeot-built 1.6-liter four with four-speed manual transaxle. Cloth/vinyl low-back front bucket seats with dual recliners were standard. All Turismos had gauges in a Rallye cluster, while manual-shift models (except the Turismo 2.2) added a new shift indicator light. Standard equipment included a power liftgate release, tinted glass, halogen headlamps, driver's remote mirror, power brakes, and intermittent wipers. A new Ultimate Sound radio was available. Turismo 2.2, billed as "a serious driving machine," came with the High-Output 110-horsepower 2.2-liter engine and five-speed close-ratio manual gearbox. This year's version added an air dam, front fender extensions and sill spoilers. Also standard: a sport suspension including rear anti-sway bar, performance exhaust, and 14-inch Rallye wheels that held P195/60R14 raised-letter tires. An electronic-tuning AM radio with digital clock and dual black aero remote mirrors were standard, too. Available for the base Turismo was a Duster package, with a few sporty-look features but no powertrain changes. The package included a rear spoiler, bodyside and liftgate tape stripes, high-back cloth/vinyl bucket seats, 'Duster' and 'Plymouth' decals on front fenders and liftgate, and 13-inch Rallye wheels. A total of 27,444 Duster packages were installed. Chrysler's 2.2-liter four was available for the base Turismo, along with five-speed manual gearing or three-speed TorqueFlite.

1985 Plymouth, Reliant LE station wagon (OCW)

RELIANT — SERIES P — FOUR — Eight restyled models in three price classes made up this year's lineup, two more than in 1984. Modified body styling included more rounded corners. The rear deck was slightly higher, while the nose looked a bit longer. Reliant wore an all-new grille: a simple symmetrical crosshatch pattern within a bright frame that tapered inward at the base. In the grille's center was a pentastar emblem. Housings for the single rectangular headlamps tapered to match the grille edges. Outboard were amber wraparound parking/signal lamp lenses with two thin horizontal divider strips. Their housings curved a bit at the lower

outside corners. Though similar to the 1984 version, with backup lenses adjacent to the license plate opening, this year's taillamps grew larger and wrapped around the quarter panels, angled a bit at the front. Marker lenses moved down into the bodyside moldings. Reliants had a standard 2.2-liter Trans4 engine and four-speed manual transaxle, power brakes, dual-path Iso-Strut front suspension, rack-and-pinion steering, two-spoke steering wheel, vinyl bench seats and door trim panels, and inside hood release. A new padded-top instrument panel held a set of gauges, including a trip odometer and new fuel-economy shift indicator light (with manual transaxle only). Instrument panels showed more black trim than before. A new flat-face climate control panel eliminated protruding buttons. Door panels held new map pockets. Stepping up, Reliant SE added intermittent wipers, a cloth bench seat with fold-down center armrest, electronic-tuning AM radio with built-in digital clock, woodtone lower instrument panel bezel, passenger vanity mirror, and black upper door frames. LE added a passenger vanity mirror with map/reading light, cloth/vinyl bench seat with adjustable head restraints and fold-down center armrest, wood-tone upper/lower instrument panel bezels, dual horns, trunk light, and black remote left mirror. The LE station wagon had a standard tonneau cover. SE and LE also carried black/bright belt, C-pillar, and drip rail moldings. Two-doors had quarter-window louvers. Optional were the Mitsubishi-built 2.6-liter four, five-speed manual transaxle, and TorqueFlite. New options included an electronic-tuning radio with AM stereo, heavy-duty suspension with gas-filled shocks and struts, and full-length console (with bucket seats). Reliant's body colors were: Black, Ice Blue, Nightwatch Blue, Cream, Gold Dust, Radiant Silver, Crimson Red or White crystal coat; Garnet Red, Gunmetal Blue or Mink Brown pearl coat.

1985 Plymouth, Caravelle SE sedan with optional wire wheel covers (OCW)

CARAVELLE — SERIES J — FOUR — New to Plymouth, but not to the Chrysler product line, was a new six-passenger, front-drive four-door sedan, related to the K-car Reliant. Riding a longer 103.3 inch wheelbase, Caravelle measured 185.7 inches, overall. Base engine was the fuel-injected 2.2-liter overhead cam Trans4, with two options available: the Mitsubishi-built 2.6-liter, or Chrysler's own 146-horsepower turbocharged 2.2-liter four. Chrysler's was the only domestic turbo engine that used a water-cooled bearing housing. A simple crosshatch-patterned, slanted grille peaked forward at the center and aligned with the quad rectangular headlamps. Each pair of headlamps was separated by a narrow strip of the body-color panel. Small rectangular parking lamps went down below the narrow protective bumper strip, which ran back to the front wheel opening to contain marker lenses. The bumper strip also peaked forward at its center, to match the grille shape. Below it was a single wide slot, roughly grille width. Caravelle's bodysides featured a sculptured look, with twin creases: one just above the door handles, the other in line with bumper rub strips. The hood also held two creases, which ran forward to meet the grille. A stand-up pentastar hood ornament was standard. Described as "tastefully subtle," the wide taillamp lenses each were divided into six side-by-side sections, the inner one containing a backup lens and the outer red one wrapping around the quarter panel. Each unit also held two bright horizontal divider strips. On the decklid were 'Plymouth' and 'Caravelle' block letters, along with a center pentastar badge. The recessed license plate housing aligned with the taillamps. Bumper strips extended forward to the wheel opening and contained rear marker lenses to match the front lenses. Ample standard equipment included a Graphic Message Center with warning lights, power rack-and-pinion steering, power brakes, three-speed TorqueFlite, intermittent wipers, halogen headlamps, twin mirrors (left one remote-controlled), and an AM radio with built-in clock. Also standard: wheel covers, P185/70R14 steel-belted radial whitewall tires, remote decklid and fuel filler door releases, and warning chimes. Among the options: an 11-message Electronic Voice Alert system, Ultimate Sound stereo, cast aluminum wheels, and wire wheel covers. The six-window design held six passengers on standard cloth/vinyl bench seats with a fold-down center armrest up front. An optional 50/50 front seat had dual center armrests and recliners, as well as center consolettes and seatback pockets. A two-spoke steering wheel (both spokes aimed downward) was standard, as was a woodtone instrument panel. Only one price level was offered at first: the premium SE.

GRAN FURY — SERIES B — V-8 — With new roller lifters and a compression boost, Gran Fury's standard two-barrel carbureted 318 cubic inch V-8 gained 10 horsepower this year. Otherwise, not much was new

on Plymouth's full-size rear-drive four-door sedan, which continued to appeal mainly to fleet buyers. 'Plymouth' block letters were inset across the grille header. The grille itself had a 'busy' look, with crosshatching within each of eight side-by-side vertical segments. The crosshatch pattern continued in a series of squarish segments that extended outward beneath the quad rectangular headlamps. Those segments contained the parking lenses and met similarly-patterned amber side marker lenses at the fender tips. Backup lenses were inset into the inner ends of Gran Fury's wide wraparound taillamps. 'Gran Fury' script stood on front fenders, at the cowl. Bright moldings around wheel openings were standard, as was a cloth/vinyl front bench seat with folding center armrest. Other standards: tinted glass, power brakes and steering, front bumper guards, open-frame pentastar hood ornament, halogen headlamps, P205/75R15 steel-belted radial whitewalls, and electronic-tuning AM radio with digital clock. Sole engine was the 318 cubic inch (5.2-liter) V-8 with three-speed Torque-Flite. New this year was a standard 400-amp maintenance-free, low-profile battery. Newly optional: an Ultimate Sound AM stereo/FM stereo radio with cassette player and graphic equalizer. Color-keyed vinyl body-side moldings also were available. So was a 60/40 velour bench seat. As usual, a high-performance Police V-8 and heavy-duty suspension could be ordered. A total of 7,152 Gran Fury sedans had the AHB police package.

I.D. DATA: Plymouth again had a 17-symbol Vehicle Identification Number (VIN) on the upper left corner of the instrument panel, visible through the windshield. Coding was similar to 1984. The first digit indicates Country: '1' U.S.A. The second symbol is Make: 'P' Plymouth. Third is Vehicle Type: '3' passenger car. The next symbol ('B') indicates manual seatbelts. Symbol five is Car Line: 'M' Horizon; 'P' Reliant; 'J' Caravelle; 'B' Gran Fury. Symbol six is Series (price class): '1' Economy; '2' Low; '3' Medium; '4' High; '5' Premium. Symbol seven is Body Style: '1' 2-dr. sedan; '4' 2-dr. hatchback; '6' 4-dr. sedan; '8' 4-dr. hatchback; '9' 4-dr. wagon. Eighth is the Engine Code: 'A' L497 2Bbl.; 'C' L4135 2Bbl.; 'D' L4135 Fl; 'E' Turbo L4135 Fl; 'F' H.O. L4135 2Bbl.; 'G' L4156 2Bbl.; 'P' V8318 2Bbl. Next comes a check digit. Symbol ten indicates Model Year: 'F' 1985. Symbol eleven is Assembly Plant: 'A' Detroit; 'D' Belvidere, IL; 'F' Newark, DE; 'G' or 'X' St. Louis. The last six digits make up the sequential serial number, starting with 100001. Engine numbers and Body Code Plates are in the same locations as 1981-84.

HORIZON (FOUR)

Model No.	Body/Style No.	Body Type & Seating	Factory Price	Shipping Weight	Prod. Total
LME	44	4-dr. Hatch-5P	5999	2095	71,846
LMH	44	4-dr. SE Hatch-5P	6342	2120	16,165

TURISMO (FOUR)

Model No.	Body/Style No.	Body Type & Seating	Factory Price	Shipping Weight	Prod. Total
LMH	24	2-dr. Hatch-5P	6584	2160	44,377

TURISMO 2.2 (FOUR)

Model No.	Body/Style No.	Body Type & Seating	Factory Price	Shipping Weight	Prod. Total
LMP	24	2-dr. Hatch-5P	7515	2300	7,785

RELIANT (FOUR)

Model No.	Body/Style No.	Body Type & Seating	Factory Price	Shipping Weight	Prod. Total
KPL	21	2-dr. Sedan-6P	6924	2335	11,317
KPL	41	4-dr. Sedan-6P	7039	2340	46,972

RELIANT SE (FOUR)

Model No.	Body/Style No.	Body Type & Seating	Factory Price	Shipping Weight	Prod. Total
KPM	21	2-dr. Sedan-6P	7321	2345	9,530
KPM	41	4-dr. Sedan-6P	7439	2375	27,231
KPH	45	4-dr. Sta Wag-6P	7909	2480	27,489

RELIANT LE (FOUR)

Model No.	Body/Style No.	Body Type & Seating	Factory Price	Shipping Weight	Prod. Total
KPH	21	2-dr. Sedan-6P	7659	2345	4,110
KPH	41	4-dr. Sedan-6P	7792	2375	7,072
KPP	45	4-dr. Sta Wag-6P	8378	2480	4,017

CARAVELLE SE (FOUR)

Model No.	Body/Style No.	Body Type & Seating	Factory Price	Shipping Weight	Prod. Total
EJH	41	4-dr. Sedan-6P	9007	N/A	39,971

GRAN FURY (V-8)

Model No.	Body/Style No.	Body Type & Seating	Factory Price	Shipping Weight	Prod. Total
MBL	41	4-dr. Sedan-6P	9658	3470	19,102

Model Number Note: Some sources identify models using the VIN data to indicate Car Line, Price Class and Body Style. Example: base Reliant four-door (KPL41) has the equivalent number P26, which translates to Reliant line, Low price class, and four-door sedan body. See I.D. Data section for breakdown.

ENGINE DATA: BASE FOUR (Horizon, Turismo): Inline, overhead-cam four-cylinder. Cast iron block; aluminum head. Displacement: 97.3 cu. in. (1.6-liters). Bore & stroke: 3.17 x 3.07 in. Compression ratio: 8.8:1. Brake horsepower: 64 at 4800 R.P.M. Torque: 87 lb.-ft. at 2800 R.P.M. Five main bearings. Solid valve lifters. Carburetor: 2Bbl. Holley 6520. VIN Code: A. BASE FOUR (Reliant); OPTIONAL (Horizon, Turismo): Inline, overhead-cam four-cylinder. Cast iron block; aluminum head. Displacement: 135 cu. in. (2.2-liters). Bore & stroke: 3.44 x 3.62 in. Compression ratio: 9.0:1. Brake horsepower: 96 at 5200 R.P.M. Torque: 119 lb.-ft. at 3200 R.P.M. Five main bearings. Hydraulic valve lifters. Carburetor: 2Bbl. Holley 6520. VIN Code: C. BASE FOUR (Caravelle): Same as 135 cu. in. four above, but with electronic fuel injection. Horsepower: 99 at

5600 R.P.M. Torque: 121 lb.-ft. at 3200 R.P.M. VIN Code: D. BASE FOUR (Turismo 2.2): High-output version of 135 cu. in. four, with fuel injection. Compression: 9.6:1. Horsepower: 110 at 5600 R.P.M. Torque: 129 lb.-ft. at 3600 R.P.M. VIN Code: F. TURBO FOUR; OPTIONAL (Caravelle): Same as 135 cu. in. four above, with EFI and turbocharger. Compression: 8.1:1. Horsepower: 146 at 5200 R.P.M. Torque: 168 lb.-ft. at 3200 R.P.M. VIN Code: E. OPTIONAL FOUR (Reliant, Caravelle): Inline, overhead-cam four-cylinder. Cast iron block; aluminum head. Displacement: 156 cu. in. (2.6-liters). Bore & stroke: 3.59 x 3.86 in. Compression ratio: 8.7:1. Brake horsepower: 101 at 4800 R.P.M. Torque: 140 lb.-ft. at 2800 R.P.M. Five main bearings. Solid valve lifters. Carburetor: 2Bbl. Mikuni. VIN Code: G. BASE V-8 (Gran Fury): 90-degree, overhead valve V-8. Cast iron block and head. Displacement: 318 cu. in. (5.2-liters). Bore & stroke: 3.91 x 3.31 in. Compression ratio: 9.0:1. Brake horsepower: 140 at 3600 R.P.M. Torque: 265 lb.-ft. at 1600 R.P.M. Five main bearings. Hydraulic valve lifters. Carburetor: 2Bbl. Holley 6280. VIN Code: P. POLICE V-8 (Gran Fury): Same as 318 cu. in. V-8 above, with 4Bbl. carburetor. Compression ratio: 8.0:1. Horsepower: 175 at 4000 R.P.M. Torque: 250 lb.-ft. at 3200 R.P.M.

CHASSIS DATA: Wheelbase: (Horizon) 99.1 in.; (Turismo) 96.5 in.; (Reliant) 100.3 in.; (Caravelle) 103.3 in.; (Gran Fury) 112.7 in. Overall Length: (Horizon) 162.1 in.; (Turismo) 174.8 in.; (Reliant) 178.6 in.; (Reliant wag) 179.0 in.; (Caravelle) 185.7 in.; (Gran Fury) 205.7 in. Height: (Horizon) 53.0 in.; (Turismo) 50.7 in.; (Reliant 2-dr.) 52.7 in.; (Reliant 4-dr.) 52.9 in.; (Reliant wag) 53.2 in.; (Caravelle) 53.1 in.; (Gran Fury) 55.3 in. Width: (Horizon) 66.2 in.; (Turismo) 65.9 in.; (Reliant) 68.0 in.; (Caravelle) 68.4 in.; (Gran Fury) 74.2 in. Front Tread: (Horizon/Turismo) 56.1 in.; (Reliant/Caravelle) 57.6 in.; (Gran Fury) 60.0 in. Rear Tread: (Horizon/Turismo) 55.7 in.; (Reliant/Caravelle) 57.2 in.; (Gran Fury) 59.5 in. Standard Tires: (Horizon/Turismo) P165/80R13 SBR BSW exc. SE, WSW; (Turismo 2.2) P195/60R14 SBR RBL; (Reliant) P175/B0R13 SBR BSW; (Caravelle) P185/70R14 SBR WSW; (Gran Fury) P205/75R15 SBR WSW.

TECHNICAL: Transmission: Four-speed manual (floor shift) standard on Reliant and Horizon/Turismo w/1.6- or 2.2-liter engine: (1st) 3.29:1; (2nd) 1.89:1; (3rd) 1.21:1; (4th) 0.88:1; (Rev) 3.14:1. Five-speed manual optional on Horizon/Turismo, standard on 2.2-liter: (1st) 3.29:1; (2nd) 2.08:1; (3rd) 1.45:1; (4th) 1.04:1; (5th) 0.72:1; (Rev) 3.14:1. TorqueFlite three-speed automatic standard on Gran Fury and Caravelle, required on Reliant w/2.6-liter engine, optional on others. Gran Fury gear ratios: (1st) 2.74:1; (2nd) 1.54:1; (3rd) 1.00:1; (Rev) 2.22:1. Front-drive ratios: (1st) 2.69:1; (2nd) 1.55:1; (3rd) 1.00:1; (Rev) 2.10:1. Standard final drive ratio: (Horizon/Turismo) 2.69:1 w/4spd; (Horizon w/2.2-liter four) 2.20:1 w/5spd; (Horizon w/2.2-liter) 2.78:1 w/auto.; (Turismo w/2.2-liter) 2.20:1 w/5spd, 3.02:1 w/auto.; (Turismo w/H.O. 2.2-liter) 2.78:1 w/5spd; (Reliant) 2.69:1 w/4spd, 2.20:1 w/5spd, 2.78:1 w/auto.; (Reliant w/2.6-liter or wagon) 3.02:1 w/auto.; (Caravelle) 3.02:1; (Gran Fury) 2.26:1. Steering: (Horizon/Turismo/Reliant/Caravelle) rack and pinion; (Gran Fury) recirculating ball. Suspension: (Horizon/Turismo) Iso-Strut independent coil front w/anti-sway bar, semi-independent trailing arm coil rear; (Reliant) Dual path Iso-Strut front w/linkless anti-sway bar, rear axle w/trailing flex arm and track bar; (Caravelle) Iso-Strut front w/linkless anti-sway bar, beam rear axle w/trailing arms and coil springs; (Gran Fury) front transverse torsion bars and anti-sway bar, semi-elliptic rear leaf springs. Brakes: Front disc, rear drum. Ignition: Electronic. Body construction: Unibody. Fuel tank: (Horizon/Turismo) 13 gal.; (Reliant/Caravelle) 14 gal.; (Gran Fury) 18 gal.

DRIVETRAIN OPTIONS: Engines: 2.2-liter four: Horizon/Turismo ($134); Turismo 2.2 (NC). Turbo 2.2-liter four: Caravelle ($610). 2.6-liter four: Reliant/Caravelle ($271). Transmission/Differential: Five-speed trans.: Horizon/Turismo/Reliant ($75). TorqueFlite: Horiz/Tur/Reliant ($439). Performance axle ratio: Horiz/Tur/Reliant ($22). Power Accessories: Power steering: Horizon/Turismo/Reliant ($219). Suspension: H.D. susp.: Reliant ($58); G. Fury ($26). Euro handling susp.: Caravelle ($57). Other: 500-amp battery: Reliant/Caravelle/G. Fury ($44). Max. cooling: Horizon/Turismo/Reliant ($141). California emission system ($99). High-altitude emissions (NC).

HORIZON/TURISMO CONVENIENCE/APPEARANCE OPTIONS: Option Packages: Duster pkg.: Turismo ($96-$115). Sun/Sound/Shade pkg.: Turismo/2.2 ($512). Auto. trans. discount pkg. ($765-$886). 2.2-liter engine and five-speed discount pkg. ($295-$408). Light group ($55-$84). Protection group ($88-$189). Note: Other Horizon/Turismo options similar to equivalent Dodge Omni/Charger models; see Dodge listing.

RELIANT CONVENIENCE/APPEARANCE OPTIONS: Same selection and prices as equivalent Dodge Aries models; see Dodge listing.

CARAVELLE CONVENIENCE/APPEARANCE OPTIONS: Option Packages: Popular equipment discount pkg. ($609). Protection pkg. ($81). Comfort/Convenience: Air cond. ($757). Rear defroster ($148). Auto. speed control ($179). Power windows ($270). Power door locks ($180). Power seat ($225). Illuminated entry system ($75). Tinted glass ($115). Electronic voice alert ($66). Leather-wrapped steering wheel ($50). Tilt steering wheel ($115). Lighting and Mirrors: Cornering lamps ($60). Dual power remote-control mirrors ($86). Lighted vanity mirror ($58). Electronic-tuning radios w/digital clock: AM/FM stereo ($125). Seek/scan

AM/FM stereo w/cassette ($299-$424). Ultimate sound stereo w/cassette ($509-$634). Premium speakers ($126). Radio delete ($56 credit). Exterior: Two-tone paint: cpe/sed ($187). Pearl coat paint ($40). Vinyl bodyside moldings ($55). Door edge protectors ($25). Bumper guards ($56). Undercoating ($43). Interior: Vinyl bench seat ($31). Cloth 50/50 bench seat ($304). Color-keyed mats ($45). Trunk dress-up ($51). Wheels and Tires: Wire wheel covers, locking ($272). Cast aluminum wheels ($370). Conventional spare tire ($83).

1985 Plymouth, Gran Fury sedan (OCW)

GRAN FURY CONVENIENCE/APPEARANCE OPTIONS: Option Packages: Equipment pkg.: Popular ($537). Salon luxury pkg. ($536). Light pkg. ($158). Protection group ($133). Comfort/Convenience: Air conditioning, semi-auto ($812). Rear defroster, electric ($148). Automatic speed control ($179). Power windows ($270). Power door locks ($180). Power decklid release ($40). Illuminated entry system ($75). Tilt steering wheel ($115). Intermittent wipers ($53). Mirrors: Remote driver's ($24). Dual remote chrome ($67). Electronic-tuning radios w/digital clock: AM/FM stereo ($125). Seek/scan AM/FM stereo w/cassette ($264-$389). Ultimate sound AM stereo/FM stereo w/cassette ($474-$599). Radio delete ($56 credit). Exterior: Full vinyl roof ($185). Pearl coat paint ($40). Vinyl bodyside moldings ($57). Upper door frame moldings ($46). Body sound insulation ($66). Undercoating ($43). Interior: Vinyl split-back bench seat ($60). Cloth/vinyl 60/40 seat ($312). Trunk dress-up ($56). Wheels/Tires: Premium turbine wheel covers ($96). Conventional spare tire ($93).

HISTORY: Introduced: October 2, 1984. Model year production: Chrysler reported a total of 336,984 passenger cars shipped. Calendar year production (U.S.): 369,486. Calendar year sales by U.S. dealers: 329,731. Model year sales by U.S. dealers: 333,100 (not incl. 46,015 imports).

Historical Footnotes: Prices on most models were cut as the model year opened, though they rose again later on, passing the 1984 levels. Horizon's price reduction was intended to make the car more competitive with Escort and Chevette. The Caravelle name, found on a domestic Plymouth model for the first time, had been used on a bigger rear-drive made in Canada. Gran Fury sales rose 32 percent for the model year, reaching 18,734. Horizon/Turismo sold well also, up by some 17 percent. Reliant (and its twin Dodge Aries) remained Chrysler's best sellers.

1986 PLYMOUTH

A new 153 cubic inch (2.5-liter) engine replaced the Mitsubishi 2.6-liter as optional equipment in the front-drive Reliant and Caravelle. The fuel-injected, overhead cam design, with 9.0:1 compression, was rated 100 horsepower at 4800 rpm. Derived from the 2.2-liter, it had a longer stroke. Twin nodular iron balance shafts counter-rotated at twice crankshaft speed to improve the engine's smoothness. Only the Horizon/Turismo fours (1.6- and 2.2-liter) clung to carburetion. New single-point injection with a low-pressure fuel regulator and speed-compensating feature went into all the others. Its Electronic Control Unit not only adjusted the air/fuel mixture and spark timing, but kept a record of engine operations to spot malfunctions. A new air cleaner housing on 2.2- and 2.5-liter fours was easier to remove, and their cylinder heads were modified to speed up combustion and improve idling. A new four-cylinder labyrinth distributor was smaller and had fewer parts. All models had a new (required) center high-mounted stop lamp. Four-way adjustable head restraints became available on Caravelle. All front-drive models could have "precision-feel" power steering, which had been introduced in 1985.

HORIZON — SERIES M — FOUR — Little changed in Plymouth's five-passenger subcompact sedan, which again came in two models: blackout-trimmed base Horizon and bright-trimmed SE. The base model included 13-inch wheels with bright trim rings and P165/80R13 steel-belted radial tires, tinted glass, locking glove box, convenience lights, power brakes, halogen headlamps, fold-down rear seat, and security shelf panel. Horizon SE added high-back cloth/vinyl bucket seats, an AM radio with digital

clock, and whitewall tires. Standard engine, as before, was the 1.6-liter Peugeot four with four-speed manual transaxle. Optional: Chrysler's carbureted 2.2-liter with five-speed or TorqueFlite automatic.

TURISMO — SERIES M — FOUR — This was mainly a carryover year for Plymouth's two-door hatchback coupe. Base engine was again the Peugeot-built 1.6-liter four hooked to a four-speed manual transaxle. Optional: Chrysler's carbureted 2.2-liter four, five-speed manual transaxle, and three-speed TorqueFlite. Standard equipment included power brakes, bucket seats up front, inside hood and power hatch releases, locking glovebox, day/night mirror, remote-control driver's mirror, soft wide bodyside moldings, two-speed intermittent wipers, maintenance-free battery, tinted glass, and halogen headlamps. Base Turismos carried P165/80R13 steel-belted radial tires. Performance-minded buyers again could choose the Turismo 2.2, with high-output 2.2-liter engine and close-ratio five-speed, as well as a 2.78:1 final drive ratio and sport suspension. Its body sported sill extensions, a front air dam and fender extensions, along with paint and tape graphics and name decals. Standard 195/60R14 SBR raised-black-letter tires rode Rallye wheels. Equipment included dual remote mirrors, an AM radio with digital clock, heavy-duty radiator, and performance exhaust. For dress-up only, the Duster package contained SE Rallye instrumentation, 13-inch Rallye wheels with bright trim rings, body-side and liftgate striping, 'Duster' and 'Plymouth' decals, and high-back reclining cloth/vinyl bucket seats with increased lateral support. A total of 16,987 Duster packages were installed.

1986 Plymouth, Reliant SE two-door sedan with optional Sport wheel covers (OCW)

1986 Plymouth, Reliant LE sedan (OCW)

RELIANT K — SERIES P — FOUR — Appearance of the popular Reliant, near twin to Dodge's Aries, didn't change much this year. The crosshatch-patterned grille sat in a tapered-side frame, with center pentastar emblem. Housings for the single recessed rectangular headlamps were angled to follow the grille shape. Outboard were large wraparound amber parking lights. At the rear, large wraparound taillamps had lenses with wide horizontal ribs, with backup lenses alongside the recessed license plate opening. The decklid displayed 'Plymouth' block letters on the driver's side, 'Reliant K' on the right, and a pentastar in the middle. Two-door, four-door and station wagon bodies were offered again, in SE and top-level LE trim; as well as a base two-door and four-door. Standard equipment grew this year. Base Reliants had P175/80R13 SBR tires on 13-inch wheels with hubcaps; SE added wheel covers with 16 squarish holes around the rim. Standard equipment on the base Reliant included a maintenance-free battery, power brakes, lighter, halogen headlamps with bright bezels, vinyl bench seat, trip odometer, and two-speed wipers. SE added a trunk light, glovebox and map/reading light, intermittent wipers, cloth/vinyl bench seat with center armrest, remote black driver's mirror, and AM radio with digital clock. Also included: a passenger vanity mirror with map light, black upper door frames and quarter-window trim, and wide black bodyside moldings with argent stripe and bright insert. An optional SE Popular Equipment Discount package included tinted glass, power steering, TorqueFlite, and dual remote mirrors. Top-rung LE Reliants included an AM stereo/FM stereo radio with built-in digital clock, map/reading light, special sound insulation, 14-inch sport wheel covers with a pattern of four-rib segments radiating outward in six directions, and cloth/vinyl front bench seat with center armrest. The LE wagon had power steering and dual remote-control black mirrors; its bodyside/liftgate woodtone appliqué could be deleted for credit. Base engine was the fuel-injected 2.2-liter four, now coupled to a five-speed close-ratio manual overdrive transaxle (formerly four-speed). SE and LE models could have the new 2.5-liter four with twin balance shafts, as well as TorqueFlite automatic. Underneath was a dual-path Iso-Strut front suspension. Re-

liant K body colors were: Black, Light Cream, Radiant Silver, White, Gold Dust, Gunmetal Blue or Golden Bronze pearl coat, Ice Blue, and Garnet Red or Dark Cordovan pearl coat.

CARAVELLE — SERIES J — FOUR — For its second year in the Plymouth lineup, the spacious six-passenger sedan got a number of exterior and interior revisions. A new, less-equipped base model joined the original SE. The new vertically-oriented grille with center pentastar emblem had a crosshatch pattern, divided into six sections by five slightly wider vertical bars. Horizontal parking lamps set into the bumper. Wraparound side marker lenses stood outboard of recessed quad rectangular headlamps with new bezels. Also new this year: a soft bumper fascia, decklid panels and body moldings, and accent tape stripes. This year's taillamps had subtle horizontal ribbing, with a more curved look at the ends that wrapped around the quarter panels. Base engine was the fuel-injected 2.2-liter four; optional, either the new 2.5-liter or the turbocharged 2.2-liter. Standard equipment included power steering and brakes, digital clock, tethered gas cap, remote fuel filler door release, tinted glass, halogen headlamps, dual-note horn, twin outside mirrors, and P185/70R14 steel-belted radial whitewall tires. SE added a remote decklid release, remote-controlled dual outside mirrors, upper body tape stripes, and intermittent wipers. Base Caravelles had bench seats, while new individually-adjustable cloth/vinyl 50/50 front seats went into SE. Seats had armrests, recliners and seatback pockets. An AM stereo/FM stereo radio with digital clock became standard on SE; AM radio only on the base Caravelle.

1986 Plymouth, Gran Fury sedan (OCW)

GRAN FURY — SERIES B — V-8 — Traditional in style and powered again by the old familiar 318 cubic inch V-8 with two-barrel carburetor, Gran Fury managed to stick around in the lineup because of its popularity with fleet buyers and large families. The six passenger sedan had Torque-Flite automatic transmission as well as power brakes and steering. Also standard: front bumper guards, tethered gas cap, tinted glass, halogen headlamps, a hood ornament, wheel opening moldings, AM radio with built-in digital clock, and P205/75R15 steel-belted radial whitewalls. An optional Salon Luxury package included wire wheel covers, illuminated entry system, leather-wrapped steering wheel, and lighted passenger vanity mirror. The Popular Equipment Discount Package included an electric rear window defroster, tilt steering, dual remote chrome mirrors, and AM stereo/FM stereo radio with digital clock. As before, a high-performance engine with four-barrel carburetor and heavy-duty equipment was available only to law enforcement agencies. A total of 5,133 police packages were installed on Gran Fury sedans. Gran Fury was a near twin to Dodge's Diplomat.

I.D. DATA: Plymouth again had a 17-symbol Vehicle Identification Number (VIN) on the upper left corner of the instrument panel, visible through the windshield. Coding was similar to 1984. The first digit indicates Country: '1' U.S.A. The second symbol is Make: 'P' Plymouth. Third is Vehicle Type: '3' passenger car. The next symbol ('B') indicates manual seatbelts. Symbol five is Car Line: 'M' Horizon; 'P' Reliant; 'J' Caravelle; 'B' Gran Fury. Symbol six is Series (price class): '1' Economy; '2' Low; '3' Medium; '4' High; '5' Premium. Symbol seven is Body Style: '1' 2-dr. sedan; '4' 2-dr. hatchback; '6' 4-dr. sedan; '8' 4-dr. hatchback; '9' 4-dr. wagon. Eighth is the Engine Code: 'A' L497 2Bbl.; 'C' L4135 2Bbl.; 'D' L4135 FI; 'E' Turbo L4135 FI; '8' H.O. L4135 2Bbl.; 'K' L4153 FI; 'P' V8318 2Bbl. Next comes a check digit. Symbol ten indicates Model Year: 'G' 1986. Symbol eleven is Assembly Plant: 'A' Detroit; 'D' Belvidere, IL; 'F' Newark, DE; 'G' or 'X' St. Louis. The last six digits make up the sequential serial number, starting with 100001. Engine numbers and Body Code Plates are in the same locations as 1981-85.

HORIZON (FOUR)

Model No.	Body/ Style No.	Body Type & Seating	Factory Price	Shipping Weight	Prod. Total
LME	44	4-dr. Hatch-5P	6209	2105	76,458
LMH	44	4-dr. SE Hatch-5P	6558	2125	8,050

TURISMO (FOUR)

Model No.	Body/ Style No.	Body Type & Seating	Factory Price	Shipping Weight	Prod. Total
LMH	24	2-dr. Hatch-5P	6787	2170	41,899

TURISMO 2.2 (FOUR)

Model No.	Body/ Style No.	Body Type & Seating	Factory Price	Shipping Weight	Prod. Total
LMP	24	2-dr. Hatch-5P	7732	2300	4,488

RELIANT (FOUR)

Model No.	Body/ Style No.	Body Type & Seating	Factory Price	Shipping Weight	Prod. Total
KPL	21	2-dr. Sedan-6P	7184	2380	2,573
KPL	41	4-dr. Sedan-6P	7301	2390	26,220

RELIANT SE (FOUR)

Model No.	Body/Style No.	Body Type & Seating	Factory Price	Shipping Weight	Prod. Total
KPM	21	2-dr. Sedan-6P	7639	2400	10,707
KPM	41	4-dr. Sedan-6P	7759	2415	47,827
KPM	45	4-dr. Sta Wag-6P	8186	2470	22,154

RELIANT LE (FOUR)

Model No.	Body/Style No.	Body Type & Seating	Factory Price	Shipping Weight	Prod. Total
KPH	21	2-dr. Sedan-6P	8087	2440	2,482
KPH	41	4-dr. Sedan-6P	8207	2460	5,941
KPH	45	4-dr. Sta Wag-6P	8936	2560	5,101

CARAVELLE (FOUR)

Model No.	Body/Style No.	Body Type & Seating	Factory Price	Shipping Weight	Prod. Total
EJM	41	4-dr. Sedan-6P	9241	2535	18,968
EJH	41	4-dr. SE Sedan-6P	9810	2540	15,654

GRAN FURY (V-8)

Model No.	Body/Style No.	Body Type & Seating	Factory Price	Shipping Weight	Prod. Total
MBL	41	4-dr. Sedan-6P	10086	3470	14,761

Model Number Note: Some sources identify models using the VIN data to indicate Car Line, Price Class, and Body Style. Example: base Reliant four-door (KPL41) has the equivalent number P26, which translates to Reliant line, Low price class, and four-door sedan body. See I.D. Data section for breakdown.

ENGINE DATA: BASE FOUR (Horizon, Turismo): Inline, overhead-cam four-cylinder. Cast iron block; aluminum head. Displacement: 97.3 cu. in. (1.6-liters). Bore & stroke: 3.17 x 3.07 in. Compression ratio: 8.8:1. Brake horsepower: 64 at 4800 R.P.M. Torque: 87 lb.-ft. at 2800 R.P.M. Five main bearings. Solid valve lifters. Carburetor: 2Bbl. Holley 6520. VIN Code: A. **OPTIONAL FOUR (Horizon, Turismo):** Inline, overhead-cam four-cylinder. Cast iron block; aluminum head. Displacement: 135 cu. in. (2.2-liters). Bore & stroke: 3.44 x 3.62 in. Compression ratio: 9.5:1. Brake horsepower: 96 at 5200 R.P.M. Torque: 119 lb.-ft. at 3200 R.P.M. Five main bearings. Hydraulic valve lifters. Carburetor: 2Bbl. Holley 6520. VIN Code: C. **BASE FOUR (Reliant, Caravelle):** Same as 135 cu. in. four above, but with electronic fuel injection. Compression: 9.5:1. Horsepower: 97 at 5200 R.P.M. Torque: 122 lb.-ft. at 3200 R.P.M. VIN Code: D. **BASE FOUR (Turismo 2.2):** High-output carbureted version of 135 cu. in. four. Compression: 9.6:1. Horsepower: 110 at 5600 R.P.M. Torque: 129 lb.-ft. at 3600 R.P.M. VIN Code: 8. **TURBO FOUR; OPTIONAL (Caravelle):** Same as 135 cu. in. four above. with EFI and turbocharger. Compression: 8.1:1. Horsepower: 146 at 5200 R.P.M. Torque: 170 lb.-ft. at 3600 R.P.M. VIN Code: E. **OPTIONAL FOUR (Reliant, Caravelle):** Inline, overhead-cam four-cylinder. Cast iron block; aluminum head. Displacement: 153 cu. in. (2.5-liters). Bore & stroke: 3.44 x 4.09 in. Compression ratio: 9.0:1. Brake horsepower: 100 at 4800 R.P.M. Torque: 136 lb.-ft. at 2800 R.P.M. Five main bearings. Hydraulic valve lifters. Electronic fuel injection. VIN Code: K. **BASE V-8 (Gran Fury):** 90-degree, overhead valve V-8. Cast iron block and head. Displacement: 318 cu. in. (5.2-liters). Bore & stroke: 3.91 x 3.31 in, Compression ratio: 9.0:1. Brake horsepower: 140 at 3600 R.P.M. Torque: 265 lb.-ft. at 1600 R.P.M. Five main bearings. Hydraulic valve lifters. Carburetor: 2Bbl. Holley 6280. VIN Code: P. **POLICE V-8 (Gran Fury):** Same as 318 cu. in. V-8 above, with Rochester 4Bbl. carburetor. Compression ratio: 8.0:1. Horsepower: 175 at 4000 R.P.M. Torque: 250 lb.-ft. at 3200 R.P.M.

CHASSIS DATA: Wheelbase: (Horizon) 99.1 in.; (Turismo) 96.5 in.; (Reliant) 100.3 in.; (Reliant wag) 100.4 in.; (Caravelle) 103.3 in.; (Gran Fury) 112.6 in. Overall Length: (Horizon) 163.2 in.; (Turismo) 174.8 in.; (Reliant) 178.6 in.; (Reliant wag) 178.5 in.; (Caravelle) 185.2 in.; (Gran Fury) 204.6 in. Height: (Horizon) 53.0 in.; (Turismo) 50.7 in.; (Reliant 2-dr.) 52.5 in.; (Reliant 4-dr.) 52.9 in.; (Reliant wag) 53.2 in.; (Caravelle) 53.1 in.; (Gran Fury) 55.1 in. Width: (Horizon) 63.8 in.; (Turismo) 65.9 in.; (Reliant/Caravelle) 68.0 in.; (Gran Fury) 72.4 in. Front Tread: (Horizon/Turismo) 56.1 in.; (Reliant/Caravelle) 57.6 in.; (Gran Fury) 60.5 in. Rear Tread: (Horizon/Turismo) 55.7 in.; (Reliant/Caravelle) 57.2 in.; (Gran Fury) 60.0 in. Standard Tires: (Horizon/Turismo) P165/80R13 SBR BSW exc. SE, WSW; (Turismo 2.2) P195/60R14 SBR RBL; (Reliant) P175/80R13 SBR BSW; (Reliant LE, Caravelle) P185/70R14 SBR; (Gran Fury) P205/75R15 SBR WSW.

TECHNICAL: Transmission: Four-speed manual (floor shift) standard on Horizon/Turismo w/1.6-liter engine. Five-speed manual standard on Reliant and Turismo 2.2. TorqueFlite three-speed automatic standard on Caravelle and Gran Fury, optional on others. Gran Fury gear ratios: (1st) 2.74:1; (2nd) 1.54:1; (3rd) 1.00:1; (Rev) 2.22:1. Front-drive ratios: (1st) 2.69:1; (2nd) 1.55:1; (3rd) 1.00:1; (Rev) 2.10:1. Standard final drive ratio: (Horizon/Turismo) 2.69:1 w/4spd; (Horizon/Turismo w/2.2-liter four) 2.20:1 w/5spd, 2.78:1 w/auto.; (Turismo 2.2) 2.78:1 w/5spd; (Reliant) 2.20:1 w/5spd, 2.78:1 w/auto., (Reliant w/2.5-liter) 3.02:1 w/auto.; (Caravelle) 3.02:1; (Gran Fury) 2.26:1. Steering/Brakes/Body: same as 1985. Suspension: (Horizon/Turismo) Iso-Strut independent coil front w/anti-sway bar, semi-independent trailing arm coil rear; (Reliant) Dual-path Iso-Strut front w/linkless anti-sway bar, beam rear axle w/trailing arms and coil springs; (Caravelle) Iso-Strut front w/linkless anti-sway bar, beam rear axle w/trailing arms and anti-sway bar; (Gran Fury) front transverse torsion bars and anti-sway bar, semi-elliptic rear leaf springs. Fuel tank: (Horizon/Turismo) 13 gal.; (Reliant/Caravelle) 14 gal.; (Gran Fury) 18 gal.

DRIVETRAIN OPTIONS: Engines: 2.2-liter four: Horizon/Turismo ($138); Turismo 2.2 (NC). Turbo 2.2-liter four: Caravelle ($628). 2.5-liter four: Reliant/Caravelle ($279). Transmission/Differential: Five-speed trans.: Horizon/Turismo ($77). TorqueFlite: Horizon/Turismo/Reliant ($478). Performance (3.02:1) axle ratio: Horiz/Tur/Reliant ($23). Power Accessories: Power steering: Horizon/Turismo/Reliant ($226). Suspension: H.O. susp.: Reliant ($60); G. Fury ($27). Euro handling susp.: Caravelle ($58). Other: 500-amp battery: Caravelle/G. Fury ($45). Max. cooling: Horizon/Turismo ($145). California emission system ($102).

1986 Plymouth, Horizon hatchback (OCW)

HORIZON/TURISMO CONVENIENCE/APPEARANCE OPTIONS: Option Packages: Duster pkg.: Turismo ($99-$125). Sun/Sound/Shade pkg.: Turismo 2.2 ($562). Auto. trans. discount pkg. ($808-$933). 2.2-liter engine and five-speed discount pkg. ($304-$420). Light group ($57-$86). Protection group ($90-$194). Note: Individual Horizon/Turismo options are the same as those offered on equivalent Dodge Omni/Charger models; see Dodge listing.

RELIANT CONVENIENCE/APPEARANCE OPTIONS: Same selection and prices as equivalent Dodge Aries models; see Dodge listing. Reliant SE could get sport wheel covers rather than the deluxe wheel covers offered on Aries, for the same price ($49).

1986 Plymouth, Caravelle SE sedan with optional Turbo engine and wire wheel covers (OCW)

CARAVELLE CONVENIENCE/APPEARANCE OPTIONS: Option Packages: Popular equipment discount pkg. ($515-$689). Luxury equipment pkg.: SE ($960). Deluxe convenience pkg. ($302). Power convenience pkg. ($463). Light pkg. ($139). Comfort/Convenience: Air cond. ($780). Rear defroster ($152). Power seat: SE ($232). Intermittent wipers: base ($55). Mirrors: Left remote (right manual): base ($25). Dual power remote-control ($88-$113). Lighted vanity, pair ($120). Electronic-tuning radios w/digital clock: AM stereo/FM stereo: base ($149). Seek/scan AM stereo/FM stereo w/cassette ($287-$436). Ultimate sound AM stereo/FM stereo w/cassette ($503-$652). Exterior: Pearl coat paint ($41), Bodyside moldings ($57). Bumper guards ($58). Undercoating ($44). Interior: Color-keyed mats ($46). Trunk dress-up ($53). Wheels/Tires: Wire wheel covers, locking ($231-$280). Conventional spare tire ($85).

GRAN FURY CONVENIENCE/APPEARANCE OPTIONS: Option Packages: Popular equipment pkg. ($588). Salon luxury pkg. ($561). Light pkg. ($132). Protection group ($137). Comfort/Convenience: Air conditioning, semi-auto ($836). Rear defroster, electric ($152). Automatic speed control ($184). Power windows ($278). Power door locks ($185). Power decklid release ($41). Tilt steering wheel ($118). Intermittent wipers ($55). Mirrors: Remote driver's ($25). Dual remote chrome ($69). Electronic-tuning radios w/digital clock: AM stereo/FM stereo ($149). Seek/scan AM stereo/FM stereo w/cassette ($251-$400). Ultimate sound AM stereo/FM stereo w/cassette ($467-$616). Radio delete ($56 credit). Exterior: Full vinyl roof ($191). Pearl coat paint ($41). Vinyl bodyside moldings ($59). Upper door frame moldings ($47). Body sound insulation ($68). Undercoating ($44). Interior: Vinyl split-back bench seat ($62). Cloth/vinyl 60/40 split bench seat ($321). Trunk dress-up ($58). Wheels/Tires: Premium wheel covers ($99). Conventional spare ($96).

HISTORY: Introduced: October 1, 1985. Model year production: Chrysler reported a total of 303,283 passenger cars shipped. Calendar year production: 422,619 (incl. 36,856 early '87 Sundance models). Calendar year sales by U.S. dealers: 362,798. Model year sales by U.S. dealers: 335,079 (not incl. 69,402 imports).

Horizon sales grew as a result of the "America" advertising campaign, introduced in spring 1986. The subcompact became Chrysler-Plymouth's No. 3 best seller. Gran Fury sold well too, though it was subject to a gas guzzler penalty from the government, The carbureted V-8 just couldn't manage the 26 mpg requirement, it seemed, especially since no overdrive automatic transmission was offered. The new Plymouth Sundance was expected to begin production in spring 1986 as a 1987 model.

1987 PLYMOUTH

Sundance was a sporty new addition to the lineup this year, a well-equipped cousin to the new Dodge Shadow. The Horizon subcompact was reduced to a single, lower-cost model with few options. Other Plymouth models continued with little change.

1987 Plymouth, Horizon America hatchback (OCW)

HORIZON AMERICA — SERIES L — FOUR — A carbureted 2.2-liter four was the sole engine for Plymouth's subcompact hatchback sedan, which emerged ahead of the '87 model year under the new "America" name. Its option list was short, and only one model was offered. A five-speed manual gearbox was standard, with three-speed automatic available only as part of a package. The shrunken model lineup for Horizon and the nearly identical Dodge Omni enabled Chrysler to cut prices and simplify manufacture.

TURISMO — SERIES L — FOUR — Like the related Horizon sedan, the Turismo coupe was powered by the carbureted 2.2-liter four, with standard five-speed manual shift. Standard equipment included a rear defogger and wiper/washer, tinted glass, black bodyside moldings, power brakes, and remote liftgate release.

1987 Plymouth, Sundance hatchback coupe (OCW)

SUNDANCE — SERIES P — FOUR — During summer 1987, Plymouth introduced its sporty new four-door hatchback sedan, joined later by a two-door version. Compact in size, like the closely related Dodge Shadow, it was powered by a 2.2-liter four-cylinder engine with standard five-speed manual shift. A turbocharged four, rated 146 horsepower, was optional. So was a three-speed automatic transmission. Standard equipment included a tachometer, reclining front bucket seats, 60/40 fold-down rear seatbacks, quick-ratio power steering, power brakes, cloth upholstery, full carpeting (including lower door panels), and manual remote mirrors.

RELIANT — SERIES K — FOUR — Like its close kin, the Dodge Aries, Plymouth's compact K-car got a new stainless steel exhaust system and standard front bucket seats. The mid-range SE trim level dropped out, leaving only the base and LE series. Base powertrain remained the 2.2-liter four and five-speed manual transmission, with a 2.5-liter four and three-speed automatic optional.

CARAVELLE — SERIES E — FOUR — Except for a new stainless steel exhaust system, and a lockup torque converter for its three-speed automatic, the mid-size four-door sedan changed little this year. The lockup

unit came only with the optional 2.5-liter four-cylinder engine, not the base 2.2-liter or the 2.2 turbo. A new form of optional cruise control used electronic rather than vacuum actuation.

GRAN FURY — SERIES M — V-8 — Plymouth's full-size, rear-drive sedan, virtually identical to the Dodge Diplomat, continued as before. Sole powertrain remained the well-known 318 cubic inch (5.2-liter) V-8 with TorqueFlite three-speed automatic.

I.D. DATA: Plymouth again had a 17-symbol Vehicle Identification Number (VIN) on the upper left corner of the instrument panel, visible through the windshield. Coding was similar to 1986. Symbol ten (Model Year) changed to 'H' - 1987. Engine numbers and Body Code Plates are in the same locations as 1981-86.

HORIZON (FOUR)

Model No.	Body/ Style No.	Body Type & Seating	Factory Price	Shipping Weight	Prod. Total
LME	44	4-dr. Hatch-5P	5799	2237	79,449

TURISMO (FOUR)

LMH	24	2-dr. Hatch-5P	7199	2290	24,104

SUNDANCE (FOUR)

PPH	24	2-dr. Hatch-5P	7599	2527	35,719
PPH	44	4-dr. Hatch-5P	7799	2565	39,960

RELIANT (FOUR)

KPL	21	2-dr. Sedan-6P	7655	2209	204
KPL	41	4-dr. Sedan-6P	7655	2415	5,142

RELIANT LE (FOUR)

KPM	21	2-dr. Sedan-6P	8134	2468	9,127
KPM	41	4-dr. Sedan-6P	8134	2484	66,575
KPM	45	4-dr. Sta Wag-6P	8579	2588	22,905

CARAVELLE (FOUR)

EJM	41	4-dr. Sedan-6P	9762	2589	23,132
EJH	41	4-dr. SE Sedan-6P	10355	2596	19,333

GRAN FURY (V-8)

MBL	41	4-dr. Sedan-6P	10598	3599	10,377

ENGINE DATA: BASE FOUR (Horizon, Turismo): Inline, overhead-cam four-cylinder. Cast iron block; aluminum head. Displacement: 135 cu. in. (2.2-liters). Bore & stroke: 3.44 x 3.62 in. Compression ratio: 9.0:1. Brake horsepower: 96 at 5200 R.P.M. Torque: 119 lb.-ft. at 3200 R.P.M. Five main bearings. Hydraulic valve lifters. Carburetor: 2Bbl. BASE FOUR (Sundance, Reliant, Caravelle): Same as 135 cu. in. four above, but with throttle-body fuel injection. Compression: 9.5:1. Horsepower: 97 at 5200 R.P.M. Torque: 122 lb.-ft. at 3200 R.P.M. TURBO FOUR; OPTIONAL (Sundance, Caravelle): Same as 135 cu. in. four above, with EFI and turbocharger. Compression: 8.1:1. Horsepower: 146 at 5200 R.P.M. Torque: 170 lb.-ft. at 3600 R.P.M. Port fuel injection. OPTIONAL FOUR (Reliant, Caravelle): Inline, overhead-cam four-cylinder. Cast iron block; aluminum head. Displacement: 153 cu. in. (2.5-liters). Bore & stroke: 3.44 x 4.09 in. Compression ratio: 9.0:1. Brake horsepower: 100 at 4800 R.P.M. Torque: 133 lb.-ft. at 2800 R.P.M. Five main bearings. Hydraulic valve lifters. Throttle-body fuel injection. BASE V-8 (Gran Fury): 90-degree, overhead valve V-8. Cast iron block and head. Displacement: 318 cu. in. (5.2-liters). Bore & stroke: 3.91 x 3.31 in. Compression ratio: 9.0:1. Brake horsepower: 140 at 3600 R.P.M. Torque: 265 lb.-ft. at 1600 R.P.M. Five main bearings. Hydraulic valve lifters. Carburetor: 2Bbl.

1987 Plymouth, Reliant LE sedan with optional aluminum wheels (OCW)

CHASSIS DATA: Wheelbase: (Horizon) 99.1 in.; (Turismo) 96.5 in.; (Sundance) 97.0 in.; (Reliant) 100.3 in.; (Caravelle) 103.3 in.; (Gran Fury) 112.7 in. Overall Length: (Horizon) 163.2 in.; (Turismo) 174.8 in.; (Sundance) 171.7 in.; (Reliant) 178.9 in.; (Reliant wag) 179.0 in.; (Caravelle) 185.2 in.; (Gran Fury) 204.6 in. Height: (Horizon) 53.0 in.; (Turismo) 50.7 in.; (Sundance) 52.7 in.; (Reliant 2-dr.) 52.5 in.; (Reliant 4-dr.) 52.9 in.; (Turismo) 53.3 in.; (Caravelle) 53.1 in.; (Gran Fury) 55.3 in. Width: (Horizon) 66.8 in.; (Turismo) 66.1 in.; (Sundance) 67.3 in.; (Reliant) 67.9 in.; (Caravelle) 68.0 in.; (Gran Fury) 74.2 in. Front Tread: (Horizon/Turismo) 56.1 in.; (Sundance/Reliant/Caravelle) 57.6

in.; (Gran Fury) 60.0 in. Rear Tread: (Horizon/Turismo) 55.7 in.; (Sundance/Reliant/Caravelle) 57.2 in.; (Gran Fury) 59.5 in. Standard Tires: (Horizon/Turismo) P165/80R13; (Reliant) P175/80R13 BSW: (Sundance/Caravelle) P185/70R14; (Gran Fury) P205/75R15.

TECHNICAL: Transmission: Five-speed manual (floor shift) standard on Horizon/Turismo, Sundance, and Reliant. TorqueFlite three-speed automatic standard on Caravelle and Gran Fury, optional on others. Steering: Rack and pinion except (Gran Fury) recirculating ball. Suspension: (Horizon/Turismo) MacPherson front struts w/anti-sway bar, semi-independent trailing-arm coil-spring rear; (Sundance/Reliant/Caravelle) MacPherson front struts w/anti-sway bar; beam rear axle w/trailing arms, coil springs, and anti-sway bar; (Gran Fury) front transverse torsion bars and anti-sway bar, semi-elliptic rear leaf springs. Brakes: Front disc, rear drum. Fuel tank: (Horizon/Turismo) 13 gal.; (Sundance/Reliant/Caravelle) 14 gal.; (Gran Fury) 18 gal.

DRIVETRAIN OPTIONS: Engines: Turbo 2.2-liter four: Caravelle ($685). Turbo engine pkg.: Sundance ($815). 2.5-liter four: Reliant/Caravelle ($287). Transmission/Differential: TorqueFlite: Sundance/ Reliant ($534).

1987 Plymouth, Turismo hatchback with optional Duster package (OCW)

HORIZON/TURISMO CONVENIENCE/APPEARANCE OPTIONS: Basic Pkg. (auto trans. and power steering) ($776). Manual Transmission Discount Pkg. (Power steering, AM/FM stereo, highback front bucket seats, upgraded cargo area trim, center console with coin holder, cubby box, cupholder, ash receiver light.) ($575). Automatic Transmission Discount Pkg. (Manual Transmission Discount Pkg. plus 3-speed automatic transmission) ($1009). Air conditioning ($701). California emissions pkg. ($99). AM/FM stereo cassette ($246).

1987 Plymouth, Reliant LE station wagon with optional roof rack (OCW)

RELIANT CONVENIENCE/APPEARANCE OPTIONS: Heavy-duty suspension ($61). Power steering ($242). Air conditioning ($790). Pearl coat paint ($41). Cloth & vinyl bench seat, base (NC). Vinyl bench seat w/center armrest, LE (NC); w/cloth & vinyl, LE (NC). Basic Equipment Pkg. (AM mono radio, left remote mirror, intermittent wipers, deluxe wheel covers), base ($260). Popular Equipment Discount Pkg. (Automatic transmission, power steering, tinted glass, AM/FM stereo, dual remote mirrors, uprated sound insulation, trunk dress-up, tonneau cover (wagon), deluxe wheel covers, P185/70R14 blackwall tires. LE Sedan ($740); Wagon ($760). Premium Equipment Discount Pkg. (Popular Equipment plus rear defogger, power door locks, cruise control, tilt steering column, rear wiper/washer and luggage rack (wagon), LE 2-dr ($1261); LE 4-dr ($1312); Wagon ($1589). Light Pkg. ($59). Tinted glass ($121). Full console ($157). Rear defogger ($152). California emissions pkg. ($102). Front & rear floormats ($46). Luggage rack, wagon ($127). Power door locks, LE 2-dr ($146); LE 4-dr, wagon ($197). AM/FM Stereo, base ($271); Base w/Basic Equipment, LE ($157). AM/FM Stereo cassette, LE ($257). Conventional spare tire, 13-in. ($75); 14-in. ($85). Cruise control ($184). Tilt steering col. ($126). Undercoating ($44). Cast aluminum 14-in. wheels, LE: w/Popular or Premium Equipment ($332); w/o Popular or Premium Equipment ($381). Rear wiper/washer, wagon ($130). Woodtone exterior appliqué, wagon ($282); w/Popular or Premium Equipment ($233). P185/70R14 tires, LE ($164); w/Popular or Premium Equipment ($67).

1987 Plymouth, Caravelle SE sedan with optional wire wheel covers (OCW)

CARAVELLE CONVENIENCE/APPEARANCE OPTIONS: Popular Equipment Discount Pkg. (Rear defogger, 500-amp battery, air conditioning, cruise control, tilt steering column, AM/FM stereo, intermittent wipers, left remote and right manual mirrors), base ($928); SE ($997). Rear defogger pkg. ($197). Protection pkg. ($209). Deluxe Convenience Pkg. (Cruise control, tilt steering column) ($310). Light pkg. ($138). Air conditioning ($790). California emissions pkg. ($102). Dual power mirrors, base ($113); Base w/Popular Equip., SE ($88). Dual illuminated visor mirrors ($119). Power Convenience Pkg. (Power windows and door locks) ($436). Power driver's seat ($242). AM/FM stereo cassette, Base ($438); Base w/Popular Equipment, SE ($292). Conventional spare tire ($85). European handling suspension ($59). Trunk dress-up ($53). Pearl coat paint ($41). Bodyside protective molding ($61). Locking wire wheel covers, base ($280); SE ($231).

GRAN FURY CONVENIENCE/APPEARANCE OPTIONS: 60/40 split bench seat w/passenger recliner ($312). Popular Equipment Discount Pkg. (Dual remote mirrors, rear defogger, protection pkg., trunk dress-up, AM/FM stereo, tilt steering col., intermittent wipers ($597). Light pkg. ($128). Protection group ($138). Salon Luxury Pkg. (Illuminated entry system, lighted right visor mirror, leather-wrapped steering wheel, bodyside deck stripes, wire wheel covers) ($545). Auto temp control air conditioning ($837). 500-amp battery ($44). Rear defogger ($148). California emissions pkg. ($99). Special body sound insulation ($66). Driver's remote mirror ($24). Dual remote mirrors ($67). Upper door frame moldings ($46). Power decklid release ($50). Power door locks ($195). Power windows ($285). AM/FM stereo ($155). AM/FM stereo cassette ($399); w/Popular Equip. ($254). AM/FM stereo cassette w/graphic EQ Ultimate Sound ($609); w/Popular Equip. ($464). Delete standard radio ($56 credit). Conventional spare tire ($93). Cruise control ($179). Tilt steering col. ($125). Heavy-duty suspension ($26). Trunk dress-up ($56). Undercoating ($43). Premium wheel covers ($96). Intermittent wipers ($58). Pearl coat paint ($40). Full vinyl roof ($200). Vinyl bodyside molding ($62).

HISTORY: Model year production: 443,806. Calendar year production: 321,585. Calendar year sales: 289,112.

1988 PLYMOUTH

While the subcompact Horizon remained in the Plymouth lineup, its two-door companion, the Turismo, was gone. Reliant shrank to one lower-priced "America" series, as the Horizon had done earlier.

HORIZON AMERICA — SERIES M — FOUR — No more carburetors sent fuel to Horizon engines. The 2.2-liter four now had throttle-body fuel injection, with a loss of three horsepower but a comparable gain in torque. The optional three-speed automatic transmission gained an electronic lockup torque converter. Five-speed manual shift remained standard, with automatic available only as part of a package. Both Horizon and the nearly identical Dodge Omni were now produced at the former American Motors plant in Kenosha, Wisconsin, following Chrysler's takeover of AMC. Only three packages and three single items made up the Horizon option list.

SUNDANCE — SERIES P — FOUR — Little changed for Plymouth's latest subcompact in its second season, except for the addition of a sporty new Rallye Sport (RS) option package. That package included the larger (2.5-liter) engine, integral foglamps in a distinct front fascia, new front bucket seats (with driver's lumbar support), rear defogger, power door locks, and leather-wrapped steering wheel. Base engine was the 2.2-liter four with throttle-body fuel injection, rated 93 horsepower. Both the 2.5-liter and a turbocharged 2.2 were optional. Five-speed manual shift remained standard, and the optional three-speed automatic added a lockup torque converter.

1988 Plymouth, Reliant America two-door sedan (OCW)

RELIANT AMERICA — SERIES P — FOUR — Only one series remained in Plymouth's compact sedan, and its option list shrank. This allowed a substantial price cut for the year. Otherwise, little changed except that the lockup torque converter for the three-speed automatic was available with either engine, the base 2.2-liter four or the optional 2.5-liter. Automatic shift was required with the 2.5 engine.

1988 Plymouth, Caravelle SE sedan with optional Turbo engine and wire wheel covers (OCW)

CARAVELLE — SERIES J — FOUR — Other than the use of an electronic lockup torque converter on all Caravelle transmissions, nothing changed in the mid-size sedan. Base engine was the 2.2-liter four with throttle-body fuel injection; optional, either the 2.5-liter four or 146-horsepower turbo. Three-speed automatic was standard. The SE now had a standard rear-window defogger and came with the 2.5-liter engine.

GRAN FURY — SERIES B — V-8 — Plymouth's full-size sedan returned for yet another season with little change, apart from the addition of a driver's side airbag later in the model year. Sole powertrain remained the old familiar 318 cubic inch (5.2-liter) V-8 with three-speed TorqueFlite automatic.

I.D. DATA: Plymouth again had a 17-symbol Vehicle Identification Number (VIN) on the upper left corner of the instrument panel, visible through the windshield. Coding was similar to 1986-87. Symbol ten (Model Year) changed to 'J' - 1988.

HORIZON AMERICA (FOUR)

Model No.	Body/ Style No.	Body Type & Seating	Factory Price	Shipping Weight	Prod. Total
LME	44	4-dr. Hatch-5P	5999	2225	61,715

SUNDANCE (FOUR)

PPH	24	2-dr. Hatch-5P	7975	2513	34,827
PPH	44	4-dr. Hatch-5P	8175	2544	53,521

RELIANT AMERICA (FOUR)

KPH	21	2-dr. Sedan-6P	6995	2459	8,543
KPH	41	4-dr. Sedan-6P	6995	2485	95,551
KPH	45	4-dr. Sta Wag-6P	7695	2537	22,213

CARAVELLE (FOUR)

EJM	41	4-dr. Sedan-6P	10659	2594	9,718
EJH	41	4-dr. SE Sedan-6P	11628	2632	7,171

GRAN FURY (V-8)

MBL	41	4-dr. Salon Sed-6P	11407	3588	11,183
MBE	41	4-dr. Sedan-6P	12127	3576	238

ENGINE DATA: BASE FOUR (Horizon, Sundance, Reliant, Caravelle): Inline, overhead-cam four-cylinder. Cast iron block; aluminum head. Displacement: 135 cu. in. (2.2-liters). Bore & stroke: 3.44 x 3.62 in. Compression ratio: 9.5:1. Brake horsepower: 93 at 4800 R.P.M. (Sundance, 100 at 5200). Torque: 122 lb.-ft. at 3200 R.P.M. (Sundance, 133 at 3200). Five main bearings. Hydraulic valve lifters. Throttle-body fuel injection. **TURBO FOUR; OPTIONAL (Sundance, Caravelle):** Same as 2.2-liter four above, with EFI and turbocharger. Compression: 8.0:1. Horsepower: 146 at 5200 R.P.M. Torque: 170 lb.-ft. at 2400-3600 R.P.M. Port fuel injection. **BASE FOUR (Caravelle SE); OPTIONAL FOUR (Sundance, Reliant, Caravelle):** Inline, overhead-cam four-cylinder. Cast iron block; aluminum head. Displacement: 153 cu. in. (2.5-liters). Bore &

stroke: 3.44 x 4.09 in. Compression ratio: 8.9:1. Brake horsepower: 96 at 4400 R.P.M. Torque: 133 lb.-ft. at 2800 R.P.M. Five main bearings. Hydraulic valve lifters. Throttle-body fuel injection. **BASE V-8 (Gran Fury):** 90-degree, overhead valve V-8. Cast iron block and head. Displacement: 318 cu. in. (5.2-liters). Bore & stroke: 3.91 x 3.31 in. Compression ratio: 9.1:1. Brake horsepower: 140 at 3600 R.P.M. Torque: 265 lb.-ft. at 1600 R.P.M. Five main bearings. Hydraulic valve lifters. Carburetor: 2Bbl.

CHASSIS DATA: Wheelbase: (Horizon) 99.1 in.; (Sundance) 97.0 in.; (Reliant) 100.3 in.; (Caravelle) 103.3 in.; (Gran Fury) 112.7 in. Overall Length: (Horizon) 163.2 in.; (Sundance) 171.7 in.; (Reliant) 178.9 in.; (Reliant wag) 179.0 in.; (Caravelle) 179.2 in.; (Gran Fury) 204.6 in. Height: (Horizon) 53.0 in.; (Sundance) 52.7 in.; (Reliant 2-dr.) 52.5 in.; (Reliant 4-dr.) 52.9 in.; (Reliant wag) 53.3 in.; (Caravelle) 53.1 in.; (Gran Fury) 55.3 in. Width: (Horizon) 66.8 in.; (Sundance) 67.3 in.; (Reliant) 67.9 in.; (Caravelle) 68.0 in.; (Gran Fury) 74.2 in. Front Tread: (Horizon) 56.1 in.; (Sundance/Reliant/Caravelle) 57.6 in.; (Gran Fury) 60.0 in. Rear Tread: (Horizon) 55.7 in.; (Sundance/Reliant/Caravelle) 57.2 in.; (Gran Fury) 59.5 in. Standard Tires: (Horizon) P165/80R13; (Reliant) P175/80R13 BSW; (Reliant wag) P185/70R14; (Sundance) P185/70R14; (Caravelle) P185/75R14; (Gran Fury) P205/75R15.

TECHNICAL: Transmission: Five-speed manual (floor shift) standard on Horizon, Sundance, and Reliant. TorqueFlite three-speed automatic standard on Caravelle and Gran Fury, optional on others. Steering: Rack and pinion except (Gran Fury) recirculating ball. Suspension: Same as 1987. Brakes: Front disc, rear drum. Fuel tank: (Horizon) 13 gal.; (Sundance/Reliant/Caravelle) 14 gal.; (Gran Fury) 18 gal.

DRIVETRAIN OPTIONS: Engines: Turbo 2.2-liter four: Sundance ($774-$809); Caravelle ($412-$700). 2.5-liter four: Sundance ($546 plus popular equipment pkg.); Reliant ($288 plus equipment pkg.); Caravelle ($288). Transmission: TorqueFlite automatic: Sundance ($546).

HORIZON CONVENIENCE/APPEARANCE OPTIONS: Basic Pkg. ($769). Manual Trans. Discount Pkg. ($705). Auto Trans. Discount Pkg. ($1179). Air cond. ($694). Frt. lic. plate bracket (NC). Calif. Emissions Control System & Testing ($99). AM/FM Premium stereo radio w/cass. ($254). Conventional spare tire ($73).

1988 Plymouth, Sundance hatchback sedan with optional RS package and Turbo engine (OCW)

SUNDANCE CONVENIENCE/APPEARANCE OPTIONS: Pearl Coat Paint ($40); Popular Equipment Discount Pkg., 2-Dr ($538); 4-Dr ($550). Deluxe Convenience Pkg. ($385). Power Assist Pkg., 2-Dr w/AGH ($232); 2-Dr w/o AGH ($363); 4-Dr w/AGH ($300); 4-Dr w/o AGH ($475). Turbo Eng. Pkg., w/AGH ($467); w/o AGH ($780). 'RS' Pkg., 2-Dr ($1328); 4-Dr ($1390). Air Conditioning ($694). Frt. License Plate Bracket (NC). Electric Rear Defroster ($145). Calif. Emissions ($99). Tinted Glass ($105). Pwr. Door Locks, 2-Dr ($145); 4-Dr ($195). AM Stereo/FM Stereo & 4 Spkrs. ($155). AM/FM Stereo w/Cass. & 4 Spkrs. ($254). Removable Glass Sun Roof ($365). Cast Alum. 14-in. Wheels ($318); w/AJK ($397).

1988 Plymouth, Reliant America station wagon with optional roof rack (OCW)

RELIANT CONVENIENCE/APPEARANCE OPTIONS: Basic Equip. Pkg., KPH21 & KPH41 ($769); KPH45 ($529). Popular Equip. Discount Pkg., NA w/Man. Trans., KPH21 & KPH41 ($1294); w/H3 Seat ($1194); KPH45 ($968); w/H3 Seat ($888). Premium Equipment Discount Pkg.

NA w/Man. Trans., KPH21 ($1732); w/H3 Seat ($1632); KPH41 ($1782); w/H3 Seat ($1682); KPH45 ($1476); w/H3 Seat ($1376). Wagon Convenience Pkg. (KPH45 only) ($252). Pwr. Steering ($240). Road Touring Suspension (KPH45 only) ($59). Air conditioning ($775). Tinted Glass, All Windows ($120). Frt. Lic. Plate Bracket (NC). Rear Window Elect. Defroster, Heated ($145). Calif. Emissions ($99). AM/FM Stereo w/Cass Player w/Seek & Scan ($254). P185/70R14 SBR WSW Tires w/AAM or AAC ($68). Conventional Spare Tire w/13-in. Wheels ($73); w/14-in. Tires ($83).

CARAVELLE CONVENIENCE/APPEARANCE OPTIONS: Conventional Spare Tire ($83). Road Touring Suspension ($57). Wire Wheel Covers ($224). Popular Equipment Discount Pkg., EJM41 ($1193); EJH41 ($1117). Luxury Equip. Discount Pkg., EJM41 ($1847); EJH41 ($1497). Protection Pkg., EJM41 ($159). Air Cond. ($775). Frt. License Plate Bracket (NC). Rear Window Defroster ($145). Calif. Emission ($99). Pwr. Driver's Seat ($240). AM Stereo/FM Stereo w/Cass. Player & 4 Spkrs. ($254). Pearl Coat Paint ($40).

GRAN FURY CONVENIENCE/APPEARANCE OPTIONS: H.D. Suspension ($26). Clear/Pearl Coat Paint ($40). Full Vinyl Roof ($200). 60/40 Split Bench Seat With Pass. Recliner, Cloth/Vinyl ($343). Popular Equipment Discount Pkg. ($1230). Luxury Equipment Discount Pkg. ($2866). Protection Group ($180). Light Pkg. ($130). Auto-temp Air Cond. ($830). Frt. Lic. Plate Bracket (NC). Rear Window Defroster ($145). Calif. Emission ($99). Dual Remote Power Mirrors ($159). Power Door Locks ($195). Power Windows ($285). AM Stereo/FM Stereo w/Cass. Player & 4 Spkrs. ($254). Tilt Steering Column ($125). Trunk Dress Up ($56). Conventional Spare Tire ($93).

HISTORY: Model year production: 336,070. Calendar year production: 313,700. Calendar year sales: 291,059.

1989 PLYMOUTH

One new model arrived this year: the Acclaim, close kin to the Dodge Spirit. Caravelle left the lineup, and Reliant was in its final season.

1989 Plymouth, Horizon America hatchback (OCW)

HORIZON AMERICA — SERIES L — FOUR — First introduced for 1978, the Plymouth subcompact hatchback was back again with few changes. As it had been for the past two years, only a budget-priced "America" version was offered, with few options. Sole engine again was the 2.2-liter four with throttle-body fuel injection, rated 93 horsepower. Standard equipment included a tachometer, tinted glass, five-speed manual gearbox, and rear wiper/washer.

1989 Plymouth, Sundance hatchback coupe (OCW)

SUNDANCE — SERIES P — FOUR — For performance, Sundance buyers this year could get a 2.5-liter turbo instead of the former 2.2-liter, though it rated only slightly higher in horsepower. Sundance wore a new grille and taillamps, as well as new aero headlamps for a different front-end look. Base engine was again the 2.2-liter four with throttle-body fuel

injection; optional, a slightly more powerful 2.5-liter. The larger engine was included as part of the Rallye Sport (RS) package, along with fog lamps up front and two-tone body paint. Five-speed manual shift was standard; three-speed automatic optional.

1989 Plymouth, Reliant America two-door sedan (OCW)

RELIANT AMERICA — SERIES K — FOUR — No more station wagons were included in the Reliant line. Base engine remained the 93-horsepower, 2.2-liter four, but the optional 2.5-liter engine added four horsepower this year. Five-speed manual shift was standard, but three-speed automatic was required with the 2.5-liter engine. Up to six people fit into a Reliant with the optional bench seating; five with the standard front bucket seats. A four-speaker stereo system joined the option list.

ACCLAIM — SERIES A — FOUR/V-6 — Reliant's A-body replacement arrived a little late in the 1989 model year, with a similar upright appearance and front-drive platform, though three inches longer in wheelbase. The four-door sedan came in base, LE, or sporty LX trim. Base engine was the 2.5-liter four, rated 100 horsepower and hooked to a standard five-speed manual or optional three-speed automatic. LX came with a 3.0-liter V-6 and four-speed overdrive automatic transmission, and had larger (15-inch) tires and a firmer suspension than its mates. Up to six passengers could fit inside with an optional front bench seat; five people with the standard reclining front buckets. Standard equipment included power steering, tachometer, remote trunk and fuel-door releases, trip odometer, AM/FM stereo radio, and intermittent wipers. LE added cruise control, tilt steering, adjustable lumbar support for the driver's seat, a rear defogger, lighted visor mirrors, and message center. LX added the 3.0-liter V-6, sport suspension, decklid luggage rack, trip computer, cassette player, and leather-wrapped steering wheel.

GRAN FURY — SERIES M — V-8 — For what would be its final year in the Plymouth lineup, the rear-drive sedan (dating back to 1982) showed no changes. Sole engine was again the 5.2-liter V-8, hooked to three-speed automatic. Both the standard model and the special police versions (long popular with police departments) would disappear after 1989.

I.D. DATA: Plymouth again had a 17-symbol Vehicle Identification Number (VIN) on the upper left corner of the instrument panel, visible through the windshield. Coding was similar to 1988. Symbol ten (Model Year) changed to 'K' - 1989.

HORIZON AMERICA (FOUR)

Model No.	Body/ Style No.	Body Type & Seating	Factory Price	Shipping Weight	Prod. Total
LME	44	4-dr. Hatch-5P	6595	2237	37,794

SUNDANCE (FOUR)

Model No.	Body/ Style No.	Body Type & Seating	Factory Price	Shipping Weight	Prod. Total
PPH	24	2-dr. Hatch-5P	8395	2520	34,211
PPH	44	4-dr. Hatch-5P	8595	2558	51,350

RELIANT AMERICA (FOUR)

Model No.	Body/ Style No.	Body Type & Seating	Factory Price	Shipping Weight	Prod. Total
KPH	21	2-dr. Sedan-6P	6995	2459	4,032
KPH	41	4-dr. Sedan-6P	6995	2485	48,203

ACCLAIM (V-6)

Model No.	Body/ Style No.	Body Type & Seating	Factory Price	Shipping Weight	Prod. Total
APH	41	4-dr. Sedan-6P	9920	2753	Note 1
APP	41	4-dr. LE Sedan-6P	11295	2827	Note 1
APX	41	4-dr. LX Sedan-6P	13195	2968	Note 1

Note 1: Acclaim sedan production totaled 70,127 with no further breakout available.

GRAN FURY (V-8)

Model No.	Body/ Style No.	Body Type & Seating	Factory Price	Shipping Weight	Prod. Total
MBL	41	4-dr. Sedan-6P	11995	3556	4,484

ENGINE DATA: BASE FOUR (Horizon, Sundance, Reliant): Inline, overhead-cam four-cylinder. Cast iron block; aluminum head. Displacement: 135 cu. in. (2.2-liters). Bore & stroke: 3.44 x 3.62 in. Compression ratio: 9.5:1. Brake horsepower: 93 at 4800 R.P.M. Torque: 122 lb.-ft. at 3200 R.P.M. Five main bearings. Hydraulic valve lifters. Throttle-body fuel injection. **BASE FOUR** (Acclaim); **OPTIONAL** (Sundance, Reliant): Inline, overhead-cam four-cylinder. Cast iron block; aluminum head. Displacement: 153 cu. in. (2.5-liters). Bore & stroke: 3.44 x 4.09 in. Compression ratio: 9.0:1. Brake horsepower: 100 at 4400 R.P.M. Torque: 135 lb.-ft. at 2800 R.P.M. Five main bearings. Hydraulic valve lifters. Throttle-body fuel injection. **TURBO FOUR; OPTIONAL** (Sundance, Acclaim): Same as 2.5-liter four above, exc.: Compression: 8.1:1. Horsepower: 150 at 4800 R.P.M. Torque: 180 lb.-ft. at 2000 R.P.M. Port fuel injec-

tion. BASE V-6 (Acclaim LX); OPTIONAL (Acclaim): Overhead-cam V-6. Displacement: 181 cu. in. (3.0-liters). Bore & stroke: 3.59 x 2.99 in. Compression ratio: 8.9:1. Brake horsepower: 141 at 5000 R.P.M. Torque: 171 lb.-ft. at 2800 R.P.M. Hydraulic valve lifters. Port fuel injection. BASE V-8 (Gran Fury): 90-degree, overhead valve V-8. Cast iron block and head. Displacement: 318 cu. in. (5.2-liters). Bore & stroke: 3.91 x 3.31 in. Compression ratio: 9.0:1. Brake horsepower: 140 at 3600 R.P.M. Torque: 265 lb.-ft. at 1600 R.P.M. Five main bearings. Hydraulic valve lifters. Carburetor: 2Bbl.

CHASSIS DATA: Wheelbase: (Horizon) 99.1 in.; (Sundance) 97.0 in.; (Reliant) 100.3 in.; (Acclaim) 103.3 in.; (Gran Fury) 112.7 in. Overall Length: (Horizon) 163.2 in.; (Sundance) 171.7 in.; (Reliant) 178.9 in.; (Reliant wag) 179.0 in.; (Acclaim) 181.2 in.; (Gran Fury) 204.6 in. Height: (Horizon) 53.0 in.; (Sundance) 52.7 in.; (Reliant) 52.5 in.; (Acclaim) 55.5 in.; (Gran Fury) 55.3 in. Width: (Horizon) 66.8 in.; (Sundance) 67.3 in.; (Reliant) 67.9 in.; (Acclaim) 68.1 in.; (Gran Fury) 74.2 in. Front Tread: (Horizon) 56.1 in.; (Sundance/Reliant/Acclaim) 57.5-57.6 in.; (Gran Fury) 60.0 in. Rear Tread: (Horizon) 55.7 in.; (Sundance/Reliant/Acclaim) 57.2 in.; (Gran Fury) 59.5 in. Standard Tires: (Horizon) P165/80R13; (Reliant) P185/70R13; (Sundance) P185/70R14; (Acclaim) P185/75R14; (Acclaim LE) P195/70R14; (Acclaim LX) P205/60R15; (Gran Fury) P205/75R15.

TECHNICAL: Transmission: Five-speed manual (floor shift) standard Horizon, Sundance, Acclaim, and Reliant. TorqueFlite three-speed automatic standard on Gran Fury, optional on others. Four-speed overdrive automatic standard on Acclaim LX. Steering: Rack and pinion except (Gran Fury) recirculating ball. Suspension: Same as 1987-88. Brakes: Front disc, rear drum. Fuel Tank: (Horizon) 13 gal.; (Sundance/Reliant) 14 gal.; (Acclaim) 14 gal.; (Gran Fury) 18 gal.

DRIVETRAIN OPTIONS: Engines: Turbo 2.2-liter four package: Sundance ($628-$950). 2.5-liter four: Sundance ($287 plus RS or popular equipment pkg.); Reliant ($279 plus equipment pkg.). Transmission/Differential: Three-speed automatic: Sundance ($552).

HORIZON CONVENIENCE/APPEARANCE OPTIONS: Basic Pkg., Incl. Auto. Trans., Pwr. Stng ($776). Manual Trans. Discount Pkg., Incl. Console, Pwr. Stng, AM/FM Stereo w/Digital Clock; Cloth Sport Seats w/Dual Recliners, Trunk Dress-Up ($710). Auto. Trans, Discount Pkg., Incl. Auto. Trans., Console, Pwr Stng, AM/FM Stereo w/Digital Clock, Cloth Spt. Seats w/Dual Recliners, Trunk Dress-Up ($1201). Clear Coat Paint (NC). Tinted Glass ($105). Air Cond. ($775). Frt. Lic. Plate Bracket (NC). Calif. Emissions Control System & Testing ($100). AM/FM Stereo w/Cass ($152). Conventional Spare Tire ($73).

SUNDANCE CONVENIENCE/APPEARANCE OPTIONS: Popular Equipment Pkg., incl. Full Console, Electric Rear Window Defroster, Light Grp, 4 Spkrs: 3-Dr. ($353); 5-Dr. ($365). Dlx. Convenience Discount Pkg., incl. Conventional Spare Tire, Flr Mats, Electronic Speed Cntrl, Tilt Stng: 3-Dr. ($213); 5-Dr. ($213). Pwr. Assist I Discount Pkg. incl. Dual Pwr. Mirrors, Pwr. Dr. Locks: 3-Dr. ($178); 5-Dr. ($223); w/AGH ($48). Pwr. Assist II Discount Pkg., incl. Pwr. Driver's Seat, Pwr. Windows: 3-Dr. ($409); 5-Dr. ($477). Rallye Spt Discount, incl. Part. Cloth Buckets, Console, Electric Rear Window Defroster, Fog Lights w/Covers, Heel/Toe Type Pedals w/Man Trans, Light Grp, Liftgate Luggage Rack, Pwr. Dr. Locks, AM/FM Stereo Cass w/Seek & Scan, Leather-Wrapped Stng Wheel, Two-Tone Paint, Warning Lt. Message Center, 2.5L Eng, 125 mph Speedometer: 3-Dr. ($1198); 5-Dr. ($1260). Turbo Eng Pkg. incl. Air Dress-Up, Heel/Toe Type Pedals w/Man Trans, Pwr. Bulge Hood w/Turbo Decal, Stainless Steel Perf Exhaust Syst, Turbo Boost Gauge, Warning Lt. Message Center, P185/70R14 SBR Blk Letter Tires, 2.5L Turbo Eng, 125 mph Speedometer ($923); w/AGH ($610). Pearl/Clear Coat Paint ($93). Air Cond. ($775). Tinted Glass ($105). 500-Amp Battery ($44). Frt. Lic. Plate Bracket (NC). Electric Rear Window Defroster ($145). Calif. Emissions ($100). Pwr. Dr. Locks: 2-Dr. ($150); 4-Dr. ($200). AM/FM Stereo w/Cass ($201); w/AAM Pkg. ($152). AM/FM Stereo w/Cass, Seek & Scan ($254). Removable Sunroof ($372). 14-in. Alum. Wheels ($318); w/AJK ($397).

RELIANT CONVENIENCE/APPEARANCE OPTIONS: Basic Equipment Pkg., incl. Auto Trans., Pwr. Stng ($776), Basic Radio Discount Pkg., incl. Auto Trans, Pwr Stng, AM/FM Stereo w/4 Spkrs ($929). Popular Equip. Discount Pkg., incl. Auto Trans, Pwr. Stng, AM/FM Stereo w/4 Spkrs, Tinted Glass, Dual Remote Mirrors, Bodyside Tape Stripes, Sound Insulation, Console, P185/70R14 Tires, Trunk Dress-up, Sport Wheel Covers ($1392); w/Bench Seat ($1292). Premium Discount 2-Dr. Pkg., Incl. Elect. Spd Cntrl, Tilt Stng Col, Pwr. Dr. Locks, Lux Stng Wheel, Light Grp ($1845); w/Bench Seat ($1745). Premium Discount 4-Dr. Pkg., incl. Elect. Spd Cntrl, Tilt Stng Column, Pwr. Dr., Locks, Lux Stng Wheel, Light Grp ($1895); w/Bench Seat ($1795). Pearl Paint ($40). Air Cond. ($775). Tinted Glass ($120). 500-Amp Battery ($44). Frt. Lic Plates Bracket (NC). Electric Rear Window Defroster ($145). Calif. Emissions ($100). AM/FM Stereo Radio w/Cass ($152). Pwr. Stng ($240). Conventional Spare Tire ($73). 14-in. ($83). P185/70R14 Whitewall Tires ($68).

ACCLAIM CONVENIENCE/APPEARANCE OPTIONS: Super Discount Pkg., Incl. Manual Air Cond.; Console Extension w/Armrest, Electric Rear Window Defroster, Floor Mats, Tinted Glass, Ignition Time Delay Lights, 4 spkrs, Electronic Spd Control, Tilt Stng Col. APH41 ($934). Super

Discount Pkg., incl. above plus Pwr. Remote Heated Dual Mirrors, Pwr. Windows, Pwr. Dr. Locks APH41 ($1202). Super Discount Pkg., incl. Air Cond., Pwr. Remote Heated Dual Mirrors, Pwr. Windows, Pwr. Door Locks APP41 & APX41 ($593). Popular Equipment Discount Pkg., incl. Air Cond., Console w/Armrest, Electric Rear Window Defroster, Tinted Glass, 4 Spkrs System APH41 ($893). Premium Equipment Discount Pkg., incl. Premium Body Sound Insulation, Interior Lights, Cig. Lighter, Ignition Time Delay Lights, Message Center, Split Rear Seat APH41 ($239); w/Bench Seat ($339). Basic Group Discount Pkg., incl. Console Extension w/Armrest, 4 spkrs ($109). Dlx. Convenience Discount Pkg. incl. Flr. Mats, Ignition Time Delay Lights, Electronic Spd Control, Tilt Stng Column APH41 ($316); w/AAC Pkg., Incl. Flr. Mats, Electronic Spd Control, Tilt Stng Col. ($305). Pwr. Equipment Discount Pkg., incl. Pwr. Remote Heated Dual Mirrors, Pwr. Windows, Pwr. Door Locks ($533). Pwr. Equipment Discount Pkg., incl. Pwr. Remote Heated Dual Mirrors, Pwr. Windows, Pwr. Door Locks ($533). Pearl/Clear Paint, PH41 & PP41 ($40). Cloth 50/50 Frt. Bench Seat w/Full Fixed Rear, PH41 only ($100); w/AAM or ADG . Pkg., PH41 only ($60). Cloth 50/50 Frt. Bench w/Split Fold-Down Rear, PH41 only ($100); w/AAM or ADG. Pkgs., PH41 ($60). Cloth 50/50 Frt. Premium Bench Seat w/55/45 Split Fold-Down Rear, PP41 & PX41 ($60). Air Cond. ($775). Frt. License Plate Bracket (NC). Electric Rear Window Defroster ($145). Calif. Emissions Control & Testing ($100). Pwr. Door Locks ($200). Pwr. Driver's Seat ($240). Pwr. Windows (NC). AM/FM Stereo w/Cass ($201); w/AAM or ADG Pkgs. (H41 only) ($152). Stereo/Cass/Seek & Scan, incl. 4 Infinity Spkrs, PH41 & PP41 ($422); APX41 ($270). AM/FM Stereo/Cass/Seek & Scan w/Graphic Equalizer, incl. 4 Infinity Spkrs, PP41 ($632); PX41 ($480). Pop-up Sunroof ($397). P195/70R14 SBR BSW Tires ($30). P205/60R15 SBR BSW. PX41 only (NC). Conventional Spare Tire (w/185/70R14 Tires), PH41 ($83); (w/195/70R14 Tires) PH41 & PP41 ($93).

1989 Plymouth, Gran Fury sedan (OCW)

GRAN FURY CONVENIENCE/APPEARANCE OPTIONS: Popular Equipment Discount Pkg., incl. Auto Temp Cntrl Air Cond., Elect. Rear Window Defroster, Dual Pwr Remote Mirrors, Auto Spd Cntrl, Prem. Wheel Covers ($1147). Luxury Equipment Discount Pkg., incl. Auto Temp Air Cond., Elect. Rear Window Defroster, Light Grp, Dual Pwr. Remote Mirrors, Upper Door Frame Mldg, Pwr Decklid, Pwr Dr. Locks, Power Windows, 60/40 Cloth Seats w/Recliners, Auto Spd Cntrl, Leather-Wrapped Stng Wheel, Bodyside & Deck Stripe, Trunk Dress-up, Illum. Vanity Mirrors, Full Vinyl Roof, Wire Wheel Covers ($2835). Protection Pkg., Incl. Bodyside Mldg, Bumper Guards, Flr. Mats, Undercoating ($185). Light Pkg., incl. Light Grp ($133). H.D. Suspension ($27). Pearl/Clear Paint ($41). 60/40 Cloth Bench seat w/Dual Recliners ($353). Auto Temp Cntrl Air Cond. ($855). Frt. Lic. Plate Bracket (NC). Elect. Rear Window Defroster ($149). Calif. Emissions ($100). Dual Pwr Remote Mirrors ($164). Pwr. Dr. Locks ($201). Pwr. Windows ($294). AM/FM Stereo w/Cass, Elect. Tuning w/Digital Clock, 4 Spkrs. ($262). Trunk Dress-up ($58). Conventional Spare Tire ($96). Full Vinyl Roof ($206).

HISTORY: Model year production: 250,201 (not including 16,436 early-launch 1990 Lasers sold in the 1989 model year).

1990 PLYMOUTH

Plymouth scored a major coup for 1990 with the sporty new Laser, clearly the most important new model in years. Produced by Diamond-Star Motors in Normal, Illinois, as part of a joint venture between Chrysler and Mitsubishi, Laser was similar to the Mitsubishi Eclipse and the Talon (marketed under Chrysler's Eagle badge), but Dodge had no comparable offering. Reliant and Gran Fury were gone from the lineup. All Plymouths had a driver's side airbag this year.

HORIZON — SERIES L — FOUR — Little changed in Plymouth's long-lived compact, except that it dropped the "America" designation that it gained in 1987. As before, though, the option list was short and price kept low. A new steering wheel held the standard driver's airbag, and the instrument panel was revised. Only one engine was available: the 93-

horsepower, 2.2-liter four with standard five-speed manual or optional three-speed automatic.

1990 Plymouth, Sundance hatchback coupe with optional Turbo engine and aluminum wheels (OCW)

SUNDANCE — SERIES P — FOUR — A driver's airbag (in a new steering wheel) and revised instrument cluster were the only significant changes for 1990. Base engine remained the 2.2-liter four, with 2.5-liter optional (and standard with the RS package). A turbo package included a 150-horsepower engine. A reworked five-speed manual gearbox was standard, and three-speed automatic optional. Standard equipment included reclining cloth front bucket seats, tachometer, intermittent wipers, bodyside moldings, removable shelf panel, and remote liftgate release.

1990 Plymouth, Laser RS coupe with optional Twin Cam engine and alloy wheels (OCW)

LASER — SERIES D — FOUR — Even though the new Laser coupe went on sale in January 1989, it was considered a 1990 model. Except for the lack of a four-drive version, Laser was similar to Mitsubishi's Eclipse and to the Eagle Talon. Base engine was a Mitsubishi 1.8-liter four, rated at 92 horsepower. For a boost in power, the option list for the RS model included a 2.0-liter twin-cam four churning out 135 horsepower. And for all-out performance, the RS Turbo's version of that engine delivered 190 horsepower. A five-speed manual gearbox was standard on all models, with four-speed automatic available for the base and RS (but not the Turbo). Four-wheel disc brakes were standard. Standard equipment also included cloth/vinyl reclining bucket seats, tachometer, variable intermittent wipers, remote mirrors, remote fuel-door and hatch releases, AM/FM radio, and tilt steering. The RS added power steering, power mirrors, lumbar support adjustment for the driver's seat, a cargo cover, and cassette player. A performance suspension and bigger (P205/55VR16) tires came with the Turbo.

1990 Plymouth, Acclaim LX sedan with optional aluminum wheels (OCW)

ACCLAIM — SERIES A — FOUR/V-6 — Both the base and LE four-door Acclaims, which came with a standard 2.5-liter four, could get a 3.0-liter V-6 this year. That engine was standard in the LX. All Acclaims had a driver's airbag. Base models no longer had a standard tachometer and oil-pressure gauge. A new Rallye Sport package added those items, as well as a console armrest (with bucket seats). On the whole, Plymouth's version of this front-drive sedan were considered less sporty than Dodge's similar Spirit. A turbocharged 2.5-liter engine also was optional, rated 150 horsepower. Five-speed manual shift was standard with four-cylinder power, and three-speed automatic optional; but the LX came with a four-speed overdrive automatic.

I.D. DATA: Plymouth again had a 17-symbol Vehicle Identification Number (VIN) on the upper left corner of the instrument panel, visible through the windshield. Coding was similar to 1989. Symbol ten (Model Year) changed to 'L' - 1990.

HORIZON AMERICA (FOUR)

Model No.	Body/ Style No.	Body Type & Seating	Factory Price	Shipping Weight	Prod. Total
LME	44	4-dr. Hatch-5P	6995	2005	16,034

SUNDANCE (FOUR)

PPH	24	2-dr. Hatch-5P	8795	2513	Note 1
PPH	44	4-dr. Hatch-5P	8995	2544	Note 2
N/A	24	2-dr. RS Hatch-5P	10574	2515	Note 1
N/A	44	4-dr. RS Hatch-5P	10784	N/A	Note 2

Note 1: Sundance two-door production totaled 21,702 with no further breakout available.

Note 2: Sundance four-door production totaled 39,328 with no further breakout available.

LASER (FOUR)

DPM	24	2-dr. Coupe-4P	10855	2435	Note 1
DPH	24	2-dr. RS Coupe-4P	11900	2483	Note 1

LASER TURBO (FOUR)

DPH	24	2-dr. RS Coupe-4P	13905	N/A	Note 1

Note : Laser production total that follows does not include early-launch 1990 models built in 1989.

Note 1: Laser coupe production totaled 42,105 with no further breakout available.

ACCLAIM (FOUR/V-6)

APH	41	4-dr. Sedan-6P	10385	2765	Note 1
APP	41	4-dr. LE Sedan-6P	11815	2842	Note 1
APX	41	4-dr. LX Sedan-6P	13805	N/A	Note 1

Note 1: Acclaim sedan production totaled 95,710 with no further breakout available.

ENGINE DATA: BASE FOUR (Laser): Inline, overhead-cam four-cylinder. Displacement: 107 cu. in. (1.8-liters). Bore & stroke: 3.17 x 3.39 in. Compression ratio: 9.0:1. Brake horsepower: 92 at 5000 R.P.M. Torque: 107 lb.-ft. at 3500 R.P.M. Hydraulic valve lifters. Port fuel injection. **OPTIONAL FOUR (Laser):** Inline, dual-overhead-cam four-cylinder. Displacement: 122 cu. in. (2.0-liters). Bore & stroke: 3.35 x 3.45 in. Compression ratio: 9.0:1. Brake horsepower: 135 at 6000 R.P.M. Torque: 125 lb.-ft. at 5000 R.P.M. Hydraulic valve lifters. Port fuel injection. **BASE FOUR (Laser RS Turbo):** Same as 2.0-liter four above, exc.: Compression ratio: 7.8:1. Brake horsepower: 190 at 6000 R.P.M. Torque: 203 lb.-ft. at 5000 R.P.M. **BASE FOUR (Horizon, Sundance):** Inline, overhead-cam four-cylinder. Cast iron block; aluminum head. Displacement: 135 cu. in. (2.2-liters). Bore & stroke: 3.44 x 3.62 in. Compression ratio: 9.5:1. Brake horsepower: 93 at 4800 R.P.M. Torque: 122 lb.-ft. at 3200 R.P.M. Five main bearings. Hydraulic valve lifters. Throttle-body fuel injection. **BASE FOUR (Acclaim); OPTIONAL (Sundance):** Inline, overhead-cam four-cylinder. Cast iron block; aluminum head. Displacement: 153 cu. in. (2.5-liters). Bore & stroke: 3.44 x 4.09 in. Compression ratio: 8.9:1. Brake horsepower: 100 at 4400 R.P.M. Torque: 135 lb.-ft. at 2800 R.P.M. Five main bearings. Hydraulic valve lifters. Throttle-body fuel injection. **TURBO FOUR; OPTIONAL (Sundance, Acclaim):** Same as 2.5-liter four above, with turbocharger. Compression ratio: 7.8:1. Horsepower: 150 at 4800 R.P.M. Torque: 180 lb.-ft. at 2000 R.P.M. Port fuel injection. **BASE V-6 (Acclaim LX); OPTIONAL (Acclaim):** Overhead-cam V-6. Displacement: 181 cu. in. (3.0-liters). Bore & stroke: 3.59 x 2.99 in. Compression ratio: 8.9:1. Brake horsepower: 141 at 5000 R.P.M. Torque: 171 lb.-ft. at 2800 R.P.M. Hydraulic valve lifters. Port fuel injection.

CHASSIS DATA: Wheelbase: (Horizon) 99.1 in.; (Sundance) 97.0 in.; (Laser) 97.2 in.; (Acclaim) 103.3 in. Overall Length: (Horizon) 163.2 in.; (Sundance) 171.7 in.; (Laser) 170.5 in.; (Acclaim) 181.2 in. Height: (Horizon) 53.0 in.; (Sundance) 52.6 in.; (Laser) 51.4 in.; (Acclaim) 53.5 in. Width: (Horizon) 66.8 in.; (Sundance) 67.3 in.; (Laser) 66.5 in.; (Acclaim) 68.1 in. Standard Tires: (Horizon) P165/80R13; (Laser) P185/70R14; (Laser RS Turbo) P205/55R16; (Sundance) P185/70R14; (Acclaim) P185/75R14; (Acclaim LE) P195/70R14; (Acclaim LX) P205/60R15.

TECHNICAL: Transmission: Five-speed manual (floor shift) standard on all models except (Acclaim LX) four-speed overdrive automatic. Steering: Rack and pinion. Brakes: Front disc, rear drum except (Laser) four-wheel disc. Fuel tank: (Horizon) 13 gal.; (Sundance) 14 gal.; (Laser) 15.9 gal.; (Acclaim) 16 gal.

DRIVETRAIN OPTIONS: Engines: 2.0-liter DOHC four: Laser RS ($873). 2.5-liter four: Sundance ($288). Turbo 2.5-liter four: Acclaim ($700). 3.0-liter V-6: Acclaim ($700). Transmission/Differential: Three-speed automatic: Sundance/Acclaim ($552). Four-speed automatic: Laser ($682); Acclaim ($646).

HORIZON CONVENIENCE/APPEARANCE OPTIONS: Basic Equip Auto Trans, incl. Auto Trans, Pwr. Stng ($799). Manual Trans Discount Pkg., incl. Pwr. Stng. AM Stereo & FM Stereo Radio, w/Digital Clock, Cloth Hi-Back Seat w/Dual Recliners, Trunk Dress-Up, Flr Mats, O/S Dual Remote Mirrors, Rallye Type 13-in. Wheels ($786). Auto Trans Discount Pkg.,

Incl. Auto Trans, Pwr. Stng, AM/FM Stereo Radio, w/Digital Clock, Cloth Hi-Back Sport Seat w/Dual Recliners, Trunk Dress-Up, O/S Dual Remote Mirrors, Rallye Type 13-in. Wheels ($1290). Air Cond., incl. Tinted Glass & Conv. Spare ($798). Frt. License Plate Bracket (NC). Electric Rear Window Defroster ($155). Calif. Emissions ($103). Tinted Glass ($108). AM/FM Stereo Radio w/Cass. ($157). Conventional Spare Tire ($75). P165/80R13 WSW Tires ($65).

1990 Plymouth, Horizon hatchback (OCW)

SUNDANCE CONVENIENCE/APPEARANCE OPTIONS: Turbo Eng. Pkg., incl. 2.5L MPI Turbocharged Eng., Turbo Boost/Vacuum Gauge, Eng. Dress-up, Stainless Steel Perf Exhaust Syst, Heel/Toe Pedals w/Manual Trans only, P185/70R14 SBR Tires, Message Center (Prices vary). Light Pkg., incl. Lights for Ash Receiver, Cargo Compartment, Glovebox, Ignition Switch/Time Delay, Underhood & Rear Dome Light Switch, Dual Illum. Visor Vanity Mirrors (Prices vary). Sundance RS, incl. Light Pkg. Perf Bucket Seats, 60/40 Split Fldg Rear, Two-Tone Paint, Full Console w/Center Armrest, Electric Rear Window Defroster, Fascia Integral Fog Lamps, Remote Liftgate Release, Color-keyed Mldg, Luggage Rack, Dual O/S Remote Mirrors, Heel/Toe Pedals w/Manual Trans only, Radio, Cass. w/4 Spkrs, Tilt Stng Col, Lux Leather Stng Wheel, P185/70R14 SBR Tires, 14-in. Cast Alum, Message Center, Warning Lights (Prices vary). Air Cond., incl. Tinted Glass ($798). Frt. License Plate Bracket (NC). Elect. Rear Window Defroster ($155). Calif. Emissions ($103). Floor Mats ($46). Pearl Coat/Clear Coat Paint ($75). Pwr. Door Locks: 2-Dr ($160); 4-Dr ($211). Pwr. Windows: 2-Dr ($227); 4-Dr ($304). Pwr. Dual Outside Mirrors ($58). AM/FM Stereo Radio w/Cass. ($207). AM/FM Stereo Radio w/Cass., Seek, Scan, Infinity Spkrs ($228). Electronic Spd Control ($191). Tilt Steering Col ($134). Sunroof ($383). Tinted Glass ($108). Conventional Spare Tire ($85); w/2.5L Turbo Engine ($104); Sundance RS ($185). Cast Alum. 14-in. Wheels ($332).

ACCLAIM CONVENIENCE/APPEARANCE OPTIONS: Super Discount A Pkg., Incl. Popular Equip, Dlx Convenience, Air Cond., Electric Rear Window Defroster, Tinted Glass, Ignition Light w/Time Delay, 4 Spkrs Syst, Spd Control, Tilt Stng Col. ($1110). Super Discount B Pkg., A plus Dual Pwr. Remote Heated Mirrors, Pwr. Windows, Pwr. Door Locks ($1411). Super Discount C Pkg., incl. Air cond., Dual Pwr. Remote Heated Mirrors, Pwr. Windows, Pwr. Dr. Locks PP41 & PX41 ($775). Popular Equipment Discount Pkg. incl. Air Cond., Electric Rear Window Defroster, Tinted Glass, 4 Spkrs System ($941). Premium Equipment Discount Pkg., incl. Bucket Seats, Split Fldg 55/45 Rear Center Armrest, Premium Body Sound Insulation, Courtesy Lights (under instrument panel), Map Light, Underhood Light, Cigarette Lighter, Ignition Lights w/Time Delay, Message Center, PH41 ($301); PH41 w/AWN, AWP, or AJK ($293). Deluxe Convenience Discount Pkg., incl. Flr Mats, Ignition Light w/Time Delay, Electronic Spd Cntrl, Tilt Stng, PH41 ($329). Power Equipment Discount Pkg., incl. Dual Pwr. Remote Heated Mirrors, Power Windows, Pwr. Door Locks, PH41, PP41 & PX41 ($568). Rallye Sport Pkg., Cluster, Tachometer, Oil Pressure Gauge, & Check Gauges Warning Light PH1 ($163); PH41 w/AAC, BF, or NF, does not incl. Cluster, Tech, Oil Pressure Gauge Check Gauges Warning Light ($93). Air Cond. ($819). Frt. License Plate Gauge & Bracket (NC). Electric Rear Window Defroster ($155). Pwr. Dr. Locks ($221). Calif. Emissions ($103). Pearl Coat/Clear Coat Paint ($75). AM/FM Stereo w/Cass., Digital Clock, 4 Spkrs ($207); w/Pkg. on PH41 ($157). AM/FM Stereo w/Cass., Digital Clock, Seek & Scan, 4 Infinity Spkrs ($435). AM/FM Stereo w/Cass., Digital Clock, Seek & Scan, 4 Infinity Spkrs, Graphic Equalizer ($651); PX41 ($494). Pwr. Driver Seat ($258). Frt. Bench, Rear Full Fixed Bench Seats, N/A w/Manual Trans ($103). Frt. Bench, Rear 55/45 Split Fold Down seats ($62); Premium Frt. Bench, Rear 55/45 Split Fold Down Seats ($62). Pop-up Sunroof; incl. Deflector, Removable Shade, Storage Bag, Tie Down Straps ($409). P195/70R14 SBR BSW All Season Tires ($31). P195/70R14 SBR BSW All Season Tires ($105); PP41 ($74). Conventional Spare ($85); PH41 ($95). Cast Alum Wheels ($332).

LASER CONVENIENCE/APPEARANCE OPTIONS: Standard Vehicle Pkg., Air Cond., Electric Rear Window Defroster (NA). Basic Equipment Pkg., incl. Console Cup holder, Flr Mats, Spd Control, Pwr. Windows & Dr. Locks, Rear Liftgate Wiper/Washer, PH24 ($732). PM24 Popular Equipment Pkg., incl. Console Cup holder, Electric Rear Window Defroster, Flr. Mats, Power Stng, Tonneau Cover, Full Wheel Covers ($609). PH24 & PH24 w/BGDF Pkg. as above plus Air Cond., AM/FM Stereo Radio w/Cass., Digital Clock & 4 Spkrs, Spd Control, Rear Liftgate Wiper/Washer ($1398). PM24 Deluxe Equipment Pkg. incl. Air Cond., Con-

sole Cupholder, Electric Rear Window Defroster, Flr. Mats, AM/FM Stereo Radio w/Cass., Digital Clock & 4 Spkrs, Spd. Control, Pwr. Stng, Tonneau Cover, Full Wheel Covers ($1767). PH24 & PH24 w/BGDF as above plus AM/FM Stereo Radio w/Cass., Graphic Equalizer & 6 Spkrs, Pwr. Windows & Dr. Locks, Rear Liftgate Wiper/Washer ($1776). PH24 & PH w/BGDF Dlx Equipment w/Compact Disc Player, incl. Air Cond, Console Cup Holder, CD Player w/Premium Audio System, Flr Mats, Spd Control, 16-in. Alloy Wheels, Pwr. Windows & Dr. Locks, Rear Liftgate Wiper/Washer ($2190). Air Cond. ($802). Frt. License Plate Bracket (NC). Electric Rear Window Defroster ($150). Calif. Emissions ($103). AM/FM Stereo w/Cass., Digital Clock & 4 Spkrs ($170). AM/FM Stereo w/Cass., Graphic Equalizer & 6 Spkrs ($242). Removable Sunroof w/Parcel Strap ($378). 16-in. Alloy Wheels ($321).

HISTORY: Model year production: 214,879.

1991 PLYMOUTH

The Horizon, introduced in 1978, was dropped from the Plymouth lineup at the end of the 1990 model year. The remaining three series (not including the imported Colt, which is not covered in this catalog) of Plymouth automobiles consisted of Sundance, Laser and Acclaim. The models offered in the Sundance lineup increased from the previous year, now with three trim levels available: America, base and RS. Anti-lock brakes were now optional equipment on both the Laser and Acclaim.

1991 Plymouth, Sundance hatchback coupe with optional Turbo engine and aluminum wheels (OCW)

SUNDANCE — SERIES P — FOUR — A new "price leader" Sundance America hatchback joined the existing base and RS package trim levels in 1991, with the America being marketed as the "lowest priced car on the market available with a standard driver's side airbag." All three Sundance trim levels offered both two- and four-door hatchbacks. The America and base model were both powered by an electronically fuel-injected 2.2-liter four-cylinder engine paired with a five-speed manual transaxle. A three-speed automatic was optional on both. America's standard features included power-assisted front disc and rear drum brakes, power-assisted rack-and-pinion steering, front and rear fascias with a bright insert, corrosion protection through use of galvanized steel, side window demisters, two-speed windshield wipers, low-back performance bucket seats, quiet-tuned exhaust system and aero-styled headlights. Optional equipment on the America included air conditioning, tinted glass, rear window defroster, an interior lighting package, conventional spare tire, bodyside moldings, dual outside remote control mirrors and AM/FM stereo radio with cassette player and two or four speakers. Sundance's suspension was refined in 1991 to offer more directional stability, reduced body roll and improved steering response. Base Sundance models also featured cloth covered door trim panels with armrests and integral door handles, 14-inch sport wheel covers and black bodyside moldings. Options included an electronically fuel-injected 2.5-liter four-cylinder engine, center console, instrument cluster, bright accent bodyside moldings, inside remote liftgate release, tach, touring tires and intermittent wipers. The RS package was offered with either the 2.5-liter four or turbocharged version of that engine. The five-speed manual transaxle was standard with the three-speed automatic available. Other RS features included two-tone paint, leather-wrapped steering wheel, foglights, color-keyed fascia with rub strip and bright accent, cloth low-back contoured performance seats with lumbar support, touring tires, intermittent wipers, liftgate-mounted luggage rack, AM/FM stereo radio with cassette and four speakers and 50/50 split fold-down rear seat. Optional equipment included a message center, air conditioning, tinted glass, tilt steering, Infinity I audio system, power door locks, power driver's seat, power windows, speed control, rear window defroster and dual outside power remote control mirrors.

LASER — SERIES D — FOUR — The Laser sports coupe was again offered in base, RS and RS Turbo trim levels. Powertrain combinations were unchanged from the previous year with the base model again powered by the 1.8-liter four-cylinder engine, the RS again used the dual

overhead cam 2.0-liter four, and the RS Turbo the intercooled turbo-charged version of the 2.0-liter four. All Laser engines were paired with a five-speed manual transaxle as standard equipment while a four-speed automatic was now optional across-the-board. New-for-1991, RS models could be ordered with optional four-wheel anti-lock disc brakes and, for Turbo coupes only, a security alarm system. All Lasers featured tinted glass, stainless steel exhaust system and high-back bucket seats with rear fold-down seatbacks. RS models added a black roof panel, soft door trim with insert and lower carpet, unique seat fabric, adjustable driver's seat with lumbar support, full console with armrest, power steering, dual power exterior mirrors, rear window defroster and cassette player. Optional on RS models were air conditioning, sunroof, 16-inch alloy wheels and power door locks.

1991 Plymouth, Acclaim LX sedan with optional aluminum wheels (OCW)

ACCLAIM — SERIES A — FOUR/V-6 — Base, LE and LX sedans again comprised the Acclaim series. The Rallye Sport package that was offered the previous year was discontinued in 1991. Powertrain availability consisted of the base sedan using the electronically fuel-injected 2.5-liter four-cylinder engine matched with a close-ratio five-speed manual transaxle with overdrive, the LE powered by the same 2.5-liter four paired with a three-speed automatic and the LX using the 3.0-liter V-6 mated to an Ultradrive electronically controlled four-speed automatic. The 3.0-liter V-6 was optional on base and LE sedans, while the three-speed automatic was optional only on the base model. The four-speed automatic was optional on both the base and LE sedans. Standard features for the Acclaim included power rack-and-pinion steering, power front disc and rear drum brakes, remote trunk release, halogen headlights, dual remote control outside mirrors, bodyside moldings, accent stripes and cloth bucket seats with reclining seatbacks. The LE added tinted glass, rear window defroster, bright wheel lip moldings, lower bodyside protective cladding, tach, graphic message center, electronic speed control and tilt steering. The LX further added foglights, luggage rack, bumper fascias, cast aluminum wheels, leather-wrapped steering wheel, trip computer and AM/FM stereo radio with cassette player and four speakers. The option list for all Acclaim sedans included air conditioning, power door locks, power windows, power driver's seat, sunroof, portable cell phone and Chrysler/Infinity II AM/FM audio system. New-for-1991 features included optional four-wheel disc anti-lock brakes and an overhead console. The Acclaim's suspension and steering systems were also refined. When an automatic transaxle was ordered, either a column-mount or floor shift was available.

I.D. DATA: Plymouth again had a 17-symbol Vehicle Identification Number (VIN) on the upper left corner of the instrument panel, visible through the windshield. Coding was similar to 1987-1990. Symbol ten (Model Year) changed to 'M' - 1991.

SUNDANCE (FOUR)

Model No.	Body/ Style No.	Body Type & Seating	Factory Price	Shipping Weight	Prod. Total
PPL	24	2-dr. America Hatch-5P	7599	2617	Note 1
PPL	44	4-dr. America Hatch-5P	7799	2654	Note 2
PPH	24	2-dr. Hatch-5P	9070	2634	Note 1
PPH	44	4-dr. Hatch-5P	9270	2671	Note 2
PPS	24	2-dr. RS Hatch-5P	10270	2691	Note 1
PPS	44	4-dr. RS Hatch-5P	10495	2728	Note 2

Note 1: Sundance two-door production totaled 25,161 with no further breakout available.

Note 2: Sundance four-door production totaled 32,136 with no further breakout available.

LASER (FOUR)

DPM	24	2-dr. Cpe-4P	10864	2524	Note 1
DPH	24	2-dr. RS Cpe-4P	12770	2678	Note 1
DPH	24	2-dr. RS Turbo Cpe-4P	13954	2745	Note 1

Note 1: Laser coupe production totaled 30,198 with no further breakout available.

ACCLAIM (FOUR/V-6)

APH	41	4-dr. Sed-6P	10805/11499	2789/2872	Note 1
APP	41	4-dr. LE Sed-6P	12860/13554	2895/2966	Note 1
APX	41	4-dr. LX Sed-6P	-----/14360	----/2984	Note 1

Note: Price and weight figures to left of slash for four-cylinder engine, to right for V-6.

Note 1: Acclaim sedan production totaled 114,900 with no further breakout available.

ENGINE DATA: BASE FOUR (Laser): Inline, overhead cam four-cylinder. Displacement: 107 cu. in. (1.8 liters). Bore & stroke: 3.17 x 3.38 in. Compression ratio: 9.0:1. Brake horsepower: 92 at 5000 R.P.M. Torque: 105 lb.-ft. at 3500 R.P.M. Multi-port fuel injection. BASE FOUR (Laser RS): Inline, dual overhead cam four-cylinder. Displacement: 122 cu. in. (2.0 liters). Bore & stroke: 3.35 x 3.46 in. Compression ratio: 9.0:1. Brake horsepower: 135 at 6000 R.P.M. Torque: 125 lb.-ft. at 5000 R.P.M. Multi-port fuel injection. BASE TURBO FOUR (Laser RS Turbo): Intercooled turbocharged inline, dual overhead cam four-cylinder. Displacement: 122 cu. in. (2.0 liters). Bore & stroke: 3.35 x 3.46 in. Compression ratio: 7.8:1. Brake horsepower: 190 at 6000 R.P.M. Torque: 203 lb.-ft. at 3000 R.P.M. BASE FOUR (Sundance America, Sundance): Inline, overhead cam four-cylinder. Cast iron block; aluminum head. Displacement: 135 cu. in. (2.2 liters). Bore & stroke: 3.44 x 3.62 in. Compression ratio: 9.5:1. Brake horsepower: 93 at 4800 R.P.M. Torque: 122 lb.-ft. at 3200 R.P.M. Electronic fuel injection. BASE FOUR (Acclaim, Acclaim LE); OPTIONAL (Sundance): Inline, overhead cam four-cylinder. Cast iron block; aluminum head. Displacement: 153 cu. in. (2.5 liters). Bore & stroke: 3.44 x 4.09 in. Compression ratio: 8.9:1. Brake horsepower: 100 at 4800 R.P.M. Torque: 135 lb.-ft. at 2800 R.P.M. Electronic fuel injection. BASE TURBO FOUR (Sundance RS): Inline, overhead cam four-cylinder. Cast iron block; aluminum head. Displacement: 153 cu. in. (2.5 liters). Bore & stroke: 3.44 x 4.09 in. Compression ratio: 8.0:1. Horsepower: 152 at 4800 R.P.M. Torque: 210 lb.-ft. at 2400 R.P.M. Multi-port fuel injection. BASE V-6 (Acclaim LX); OPTIONAL (Acclaim, Acclaim LE): Overhead cam V-6. Displacement: 181 cu. in. (3.0-liters). Bore & stroke: 3.66 x 3.19 in. Compression ratio: 8.9:1. Brake horsepower: 141 at 5000 R.P.M. Torque: 171 lb.-ft. at 2800 R.P.M. Multi-port fuel injection.

CHASSIS DATA: Wheelbase: (Sundance) 97.0 in.; (Laser) 97.2 in.; (Acclaim) 103.3 in. Overall Length: (Sundance) 171.7 in.; (Laser) 170.5 in.; (Acclaim) 181.2 in. Height: (Sundance) 52.6 in.; (Laser) 51.4 in.; (Acclaim) 53.5 in. Width: (Sundance) 67.3 in.; (Laser) 66.5 in.; (Acclaim) 67.3 in. Standard Tires: (Sundance) P185/70R14; (Laser RS) P205/55HR16; (Laser RS Turbo) P205/55VR16; (Acclaim) P185/70R14; (Acclaim LE) P195/70R14; (Acclaim LX) P205/60R15.

TECHNICAL: Transmission: Five-speed manual standard on all exc. Acclaim LE, Acclaim LX. (Acclaim LE) Three-speed automatic. (Acclaim LX) Four-speed automatic. Steering: Rack and pinion. Front suspension: (Sundance) Iso-strut w/coil springs, direct-hydraulic shock absorbers and stabilizer bar; (Laser) Independent strut-type w/fixed upper pivots, lower control arms, upper strut surrounded by coil springs, strut-type shock absorbers and stabilizer bar; (Acclaim) Iso-strut w/coil springs, gas charged-hydraulic shock absorbers and stabilizer bar. Rear suspension: (Sundance) Trailing flex-arm w/track bar, coil springs, direct-hydraulic shock absorbers and stabilizer bar; (Laser) Three-link w/trailing arm, torsion bar, integral stabilized bar within inverted U-section beam axle, coil springs, telescopic-type shock absorbers and stabilizer bar; (Acclaim) Trailing flex-arm w/track bar, coil springs, gas charged-hydraulic shock absorbers and stabilizer bar. Brakes: Front disc/rear drum (power-assisted) exc. (Laser) four-wheel disc. Body construction: (Sundance, Acclaim) Unibody; (Laser) Unitized frame. Fuel tank: (Sundance) 14.0 gal.; (Laser) 15.9 gal.; (Acclaim) 16 gal.

DRIVETRAIN OPTIONS: Engines: 2.5-liter four: Sundance ($233). Turbo 2.5-liter four: Sundance RS ($676). 3.0-liter V-6: Acclaim/Acclaim LE ($694). Transmission/Differential: Three-speed automatic: Sundance ($504); Acclaim ($557). Four-speed automatic: Laser ($688); Acclaim/Acclaim LE ($640). Anti-lock Brakes: Laser ($925); Acclaim, w/four-wheel disc ($899).

1991 Plymouth, Sundance RS hatchback sedan with optional aluminum wheels (OCW)

SUNDANCE CONVENIENCE/APPEARANCE OPTIONS: America: Pkg. 22W: incl. 3-spd auto. trans. ($557). Pkg. 21X: incl. elect. rear window

defroster, Light Pkg., floor mats, dual manual remote mirrors, AM/FM stereo stereo radio ($671). Pkg. 22X: incl. 21X plus 3-spd auto. trans. ($1228). Pkg. 21Y: incl. 21X plus air cond., tinted glass ($1579). Pkg. 22Y: incl. 21Y plus 3-spd auto. trans. ($2136). Sundance: Pkg. 22A: incl. 3-spd auto. trans. ($504). Pkg. 23A: incl. 2.5L engine ($233). Pkg. 24A: incl. 2.5L engine and 3-spd auto. trans. ($790). Pkg. 21B: incl. air cond., tinted glass, elect. rear window defroster, tilt stng ($951). Pkg. 22B: incl. 21B plus 3-spd auto. trans. ($1508). Pkg. 23B: incl. 21B plus 2.5L engine ($1237). Pkg. 24B: incl. 23B plus 3-spd auto. trans. ($1794). Pkg. 23C: incl. 2.5L engine, elect. rear window defroster, tilt stng, Light Pkg., floor console, 4 radio spkrs, remote liftgate release, dual note horn, wide bodyside mldgs, bodyside accent stripes, intermittent wipers, tach, 125 mph speedometer, dual manual remote mirrors ($911). Pkg. 24C: incl. 23C plus 3-spd auto. trans. ($1468). Pkg. 23D: incl. 23C plus air cond., tinted glass ($1518). Pkg. 24D: incl. 23D plus 3-spd auto. trans. ($2076). Pkg. 23E: incl. 23D exc. dual pwr mirrors replace manual units plus pwr door locks, AM/FM stereo radio w/cass., cruise control, floor mats ($2200). Pkg. 24E: incl. 23E plus 3-spd auto. trans. ($2757). RS: Pkg. 24G: incl. 3-spd auto. trans. ($504). Pkg. 25G: incl. 2.5L Turbo engine ($676). Pkg. 26G: incl. 25G plus 3-spd auto. trans. ($1233). Pkg. 23H: incl. air cond., tinted glass, elect. rear window defroster, tilt stng, cruise control, pwr door locks, dual pwr mirrors, AM/FM stereo radio w/cass., floor mats ($1277). Pkg. 24H: incl. 23H plus 3-spd auto. trans. ($1834). Pkg. 25H: incl. 23H plus 2.5L Turbo engine ($2006). Pkg. 26H: incl. 25H plus 3-spd auto. trans. ($2573). Other: Air cond., tinted glass req'd, Sundance ($801). Overhead console w/thermometer & compass, base ($265). Cruise control, N/A America ($224). Rear window defroster ($173). Pwr door locks, N/A America: 2-dr ($199); 4-dr ($240). Calif. emissions ($102). Tinted glass ($107). F&R floor mats, N/A America ($46). Dual pwr mirrors, N/A America ($57). Dual manual remote mirrors, base ($69). Extra cost paint ($77). (RAL) AM/FM stereo radio w/2 spkrs, America ($284). (RAS) Elect. AM/FM stereo radio w/cass. & 4 spkrs: America ($489); base ($205); RS ($155). (RAN) Chrysler/Infinity audio syst., N/A America ($275). Sunroof, N/A America ($379). Pwr driver's seat, N/A America ($296). Tilt stng, N/A America ($138). Cast alum whls, N/A America ($328). Pwr windows, N/A America: 2-dr ($255); 4-dr ($321). Intermittent wipers, base ($66). Conventional spare tire: America/base ($85); RS ($103).

1991 Plymouth, Laser RS Turbo coupe with optional alloy wheels (OCW)

LASER CONVENIENCE/APPEARANCE OPTIONS: Laser: Pkg. 21B: incl. pwr stng, rear window defroster, whl covers, tonneau cover, floor mats, console ($596). Pkg. 21C: incl. 21B plus air cond. ($1407). Pkg. 21D: incl. 21C plus elect. AM/FM stereo radio w/cass., cruise control ($1787). Pkg. 22B: incl. 21B plus 4-spd auto. trans. ($1284). Pkg. 22C: incl. 21C plus 4-spd auto. trans. ($2095). Pkg. 22D: incl. 21D plus 4-spd auto. trans. ($2475). RS: Pkg. 23F: incl. air cond. ($811). Pkg. 23G: incl. 23F plus elect. AM/FM stereo radio w/cass., floor mats, console, cruise control, rear window wiper/washer ($1398). Pkg. 23H: incl. 23G plus pwr windows, pwr door locks ($1842). Pkg. 23J: incl. 23H plus CD player ($2337). Pkg. 24F: incl. air cond., 4-spd auto. trans. ($1499). Pkg. 24G: incl. 23G plus 4-spd auto. trans. ($2086). Pkg. 24H: incl. 24G plus pwr windows, pwr door locks ($2530). Pkg. 24J: incl. 24H plus CD player ($3025). RS Turbo: Pkg. 25F: incl. air cond. ($811). Pkg. 25G: incl. 25F plus elect. AM/FM stereo radio w/cass., floor mats, console, cruise control, rear window wiper/washer ($1398). Pkg. 25K: incl. 25G plus pwr windows, pwr door locks ($1842). Pkg. 25L: incl. 25K plus CD player ($2337). Pkg. 26F: incl. air cond., 4-spd auto. trans. ($1634). Pkg. 26G: incl. 25G plus 4-spd auto. trans. ($2221). Pkg. 26K: incl. 26G plus pwr windows, pwr door locks ($2665). Pkg. 26L: incl. 26K plus CD player ($3160). Other: Alarm syst., RS Turbo ($163). Rear window defroster, base ($123). Calif. emissions (NC). (RAN) Elect. AM/FM stereo radio w/cass. & 4 spkrs, base ($170). Sunroof ($366). Alloy whls, N/A base ($315).

ACCLAIM CONVENIENCE/APPEARANCE OPTIONS: (AWN) Super Discount A Pkg.: incl. Popular Equip., Dlx Convenience, Air Cond., Elect. Rear Window Defroster, Tinted Glass, 4 Spkrs System, Floor Mats ($955). (AWP) Super Discount B Pkg.: A plus Dual Pwr Remote Heated Mirrors, Pwr Windows, Pwr Door Locks ($1541). (AWR) Super Discount C Pkg.: incl. Air Cond., Dual Pwr Remote Heated Mirrors, Pwr Windows, Pwr Door Locks, N/A base ($992). (AAM) Popular Equip. Discount Pkg.: incl. Air Cond., Elect. Rear Window Defroster, Tinted Glass, 4 Spkrs

($941). (AAC) Premium Equip. Discount Pkg.: incl. Split Fldg 55/45 Rear Seat, Premium Body Sound Insulation, Courtesy Lights, 6-Function Message Center ($241). (AJK) Deluxe Convenience Discount Pkg.: incl. F&R Floor Mats, Elect. Spd Cntrl, Tilt Stng, base ($379). (AFH) Overhead Convenience Discount Pkg.: incl. Console w/Reading Lamps & Compass, Dual Illum Visor Mirrors, N/A base ($333). Other: Air Cond., base ($831). Elect. Rear Window Defroster ($173). Pwr Door Locks ($250). Calif. Emissions ($103). Extra Cost Paint ($77). (RAS) AM mono/FM stereo radio w/cass., digital clock & 4 spkrs, base ($155-$205). (RAN) AM/FM Stereo w/Cass, Digital Clock, Seek/Scan & 4 Infinity Spkrs: LE ($430); LX ($275). (RAY) AM/FM Stereo w/Cass., Digital Clock, Seek/Scan, Graphic Equal. & 4 Infinity Spkrs: LE ($645); LX ($490). Pwr Driver Seat ($296). Front Bench, Rear Full Fixed Bench Seats, N/A w/Manual Trans, base ($103). Front Bench, Rear 55/45 Split Fold Down Seats, base ($62). Premium Front Bench, Rear 55/45 Split Fold Down Seats, LE or LX ($62). Tach, base ($107). P195/70R14 Tires, base ($105). P195/70R14 Tires: base ($105); LE ($74). Conventional Spare Tire: base ($85); LE or LX ($95). 14-in. Cast Alum Whls, base or LE ($328).

HISTORY: Model year production: 202,395 (not including imported Colt or Vista models). Calendar year sales: 174,371 (not including 505 1990 Horizons sold in calendar year 1991 nor 17,317 imported Colt or Vista models).

1992 PLYMOUTH

Plymouth revamped its lineup in 1992 with the biggest change occurring in the Acclaim camp. The LE and LX trim level sedans previously offered were eliminated, leaving the base sedan the only Acclaim model offered. Laser added a third model to its RS trim level, this a Turbo all-wheel-drive (AWD) coupe. Sundance also revised its offerings, dropping the formerly used RS moniker in favor of bringing back a name from Plymouth's past, Duster. The Sundance Duster debuted V-6 power in that series, using the 3.0-liter powerplant that was also optional in the Acclaim.

SUNDANCE — SERIES P — FOUR/V-6 — A name missing from the Plymouth lineup since 1977 returned in 1992 with the debut of the V-6-powered Sundance Duster, available in both two- and four-door hatchback configurations. The Duster replaced the discontinued RS trim level offered previously. The remainder of the Sundance lineup again consisted of the America and base trim levels, both again using four-cylinder power and five-speed manual transaxle found in the cars the previous model year. The Duster, assembled in Toluca, Mexico, was powered by the 141-horsepower 3.0-liter V-6 paired with a five-speed manual transaxle that was the option powertrain in the Acclaim. A four-speed automatic was optional. As with other Plymouths, Duster featured a standard driver's side airbag. Optional equipment included a sunroof and 15-inch "Lace" aluminum wheels. New-for-1992, the America received a steel wheel while the base Sundance received body-color front and rear fascias. Two new exterior color choices were Aqua and Bright Silver while Crimson was new inside.

1992 Plymouth, Laser coupe (OCW)

LASER — SERIES D — FOUR — The RS Turbo sports coupe with front-wheel-drive gained an all-wheel-drive (AWD) companion for 1992. The rest of the Laser lineup and powertrain availability carried over unchanged from the previous year. The RS Turbo AWD coupe used only the dual overhead cam, turbocharged 2.0-liter four-cylinder engine coupled with a five-speed manual transaxle. Laser underwent an extensive restyling and featured new front and rear fascias (which added over two inches to the car's overall length), aerodynamic headlamps and taillamps and re-configured hood and fenders. Also new were seat fabrics as well as two

exterior color choices: Medium Red and Radiant Red. Base models received a new 14-inch wheelcover. RS coupes featured lower body appliqué with integral front wheel stone guard and new body-color power exterior mirrors. RS Turbo sports coupes, in mid-model year, received a new spoiler. Foglamps were added to the option list of RS models.

1992 Plymouth, Acclaim sedan (OCW)

ACCLAIM — SERIES A — FOUR/V-6 —
The Acclaim LE and LX sedans offered previously were discontinued, leaving only the base sedan to represent the series. Powertrain again was the electronically fuel-injected 2.5-liter four-cylinder engine paired with a close-ratio five-speed manual transaxle with overdrive. Again optional was the 3.0-liter V-6 matched with either a three-speed or Ultradrive electronically controlled four-speed automatic transaxle. As with the Sundance, Acclaim offered two new exterior and one interior color choice: Aqua and Bright Silver as well as Crimson, respectively. Fuel economy was improved through the use of new rolling resistant tires.

I.D. DATA: Plymouth again had a 17-symbol Vehicle Identification Number (VIN) on the upper left corner of the instrument panel, visible through the windshield. Coding was similar to 1987-1991. Symbol ten (Model Year) changed to 'N' - 1992.

SUNDANCE (FOUR)

Model No.	Body/Style No.	Body Type & Seating	Factory Price	Shipping Weight	Prod. Total
PPL	24	2-dr. America Hatch-5P	7984	2613	Note 1
PPL	44	4-dr. America Hatch-5P	8384	2649	Note 2
PPH	24	2-dr. Hatch-5P	9246	2637	Note 1
PPH	44	4-dr. Hatch-5P	9646	2673	Note 2

SUNDANCE (V-6)

PPS	24	2-dr. Duster Hatch-5P	9849	2718	Note 1
PPS	44	4-dr. Duster Hatch-5P	10249	2753	Note 2

Note 1: Sundance two-door production totaled 27,936 with no further breakout available.

Note 2: Sundance four-door production totaled 37,618 with no further breakout available.

LASER (FOUR)

DPM	24	2-dr. Cpe-4P	11184	2531	Note 1
DPH	24	2-dr. RS Cpe-4P	13332	2690	Note 1
DPH	24	2-dr. RS Turbo Cpe-4P	14811	2756	Note 1
DMH	24	2-dr. RS Turbo AWD Cpe-4P	16853	3073	Note 1

Note 1: Laser coupe production totaled 24,090 with no further breakout available.

ACCLAIM (FOUR/V-6)

APH	41	4-dr. Sed-6P	11470/12195	2784/2866	Note 1

Note: Price and weight figures to left of slash for four-cylinder engine, to right for V-6.

Note 1: Acclaim sedan production totaled 74,098 with no further breakout available.

ENGINE DATA: BASE FOUR (Laser): Inline, overhead cam four-cylinder. Displacement: 107 cu. in. (1.8 liters). Bore & stroke: 3.17 x 3.38 in. Compression ratio: 9.0:1. Brake horsepower: 92 at 5000 R.P.M. Torque: 105 lb.-ft. at 3500 R.P.M. Multi-port fuel injection. BASE FOUR (Laser RS): Inline, dual overhead cam four-cylinder. Displacement: 122 cu. in. (2.0 liters). Bore & stroke: 3.35 x 3.46 in. Compression ratio: 9.0:1. Brake horsepower: 135 at 6000 R.P.M. Torque: 125 lb.-ft. at 5000 R.P.M. Multi-port fuel injection. BASE TURBO FOUR (Laser RS Turbo): Intercooled turbocharged inline, dual overhead cam four-cylinder. Displacement: 122 cu. in. (2.0 liters). Bore & stroke: 3.35 x 3.46 in. Compression ratio: 7.8:1. Brake horsepower: 195 at 6000 R.P.M. Torque: 203 lb.-ft. at 3000 R.P.M. Multi-port fuel injection. BASE FOUR (Sundance America, Sundance): Inline, overhead cam four-cylinder. Cast iron block; aluminum head. Displacement: 135 cu. in. (2.2 liters). Bore & stroke: 3.44 x 3.62 in. Compression ratio: 9.5:1. Brake horsepower: 93 at 4800 R.P.M. Torque: 122 lb.-ft. at 3200 R.P.M. Electronic fuel in-

jection. BASE FOUR (Acclaim); OPTIONAL (Sundance): Inline, overhead cam four-cylinder. Cast iron block; aluminum head. Displacement: 153 cu. in. (2.5 liters). Bore & stroke: 3.44 x 4.09 in. Compression ratio: 8.9:1. Brake horsepower: 100 at 4800 R.P.M. Torque: 135 lb.-ft. at 2800 R.P.M. Electronic fuel injection. BASE V-6 (Sundance Duster); OPTIONAL V-6 (Acclaim): Overhead cam V-6. Displacement: 181 cu. in. (3.0-liters). Bore & stroke: 3.59 x 2.99 in. Compression ratio: 8.9:1. Brake horsepower: 141 at 5000 R.P.M. Torque: 171 lb.-ft. at 2800 R.P.M. Multi-port fuel injection.

CHASSIS DATA: Wheelbase: (Sundance) 97.0 in.; (Laser) 97.2 in.; (Acclaim) 103.5 in. Overall Length: (Sundance) 171.7 in.; (Laser) 172.8 in.; (Acclaim) 181.2 in. Height: (Sundance) 52.7 in.; (Laser) 51.4 in.; (Acclaim) 53.5 in. Width: (Sundance) 67.3 in.; (Laser) 66.7 in.; (Acclaim) 67.3 in. Standard Tires: (Sundance) P185/70R14; (Laser) P185/70R14; (Laser RS) P205/55HR16; (Laser RS Turbo) P205/55VR16; (Acclaim) P185/70R14.

TECHNICAL: Transmission: Five-speed manual standard on all. Steering: Rack and pinion. Front suspension: (Sundance) Iso-strut w/coil springs, direct-hydraulic shock absorbers and stabilizer bar; (Laser) Independent strut-type w/fixed upper pivots, lower control arms, upper strut surrounded by coil springs, strut-type shock absorbers and stabilizer bar; (Acclaim) Iso-strut w/coil springs, gas charged-hydraulic shock absorbers and stabilizer bar. Rear suspension: (Sundance) Trailing flex-arm w/track bar, coil springs, direct-hydraulic shock absorbers and stabilizer bar; (Laser) Three-link w/trailing arm, torsion bar, integral stabilized bar within inverted U-section beam axle, coil springs, telescopic-type shock absorbers and stabilizer bar; (Acclaim) Trailing flex-arm w/track bar, coil springs, gas charged-hydraulic shock absorbers and stabilizer bar. Brakes: Front disc/rear drum (power-assisted) exc. (Laser) four-wheel disc. Body construction: (Sundance, Acclaim) Unibody; (Laser) Unitized frame. Fuel tank: (Sundance) 14.0 gal.; (Laser) 15.9 gal.; (Acclaim) 16 gal.

DRIVETRAIN OPTIONS: Engines: 2.5-liter four: Sundance ($286). 3.0-liter V-6: Acclaim ($652). Transmission/Differential: Three-speed automatic: Sundance ($557); Acclaim ($557). Four-speed automatic: Sundance Duster ($640); Laser ($701); Acclaim ($735). Anti-lock Brakes: Laser ($943); Acclaim, w/four-wheel disc ($899).

1992 Plymouth, Sundance hatchback coupe (OCW)

1992 Plymouth, Sundance Duster hatchback coupe (OCW)

SUNDANCE CONVENIENCE/APPEARANCE OPTIONS: America: Pkg. 21W: stnd equip. (NC). Pkg. 22W: incl. 3-spd auto. trans. replaces 5-spd manual ($557). Pkg. 21Y: incl. 21W plus air cond., tinted glass, elect. rear window defroster, Light Pkg., dual visor mirrors, F&R floor mats, whl trim rings, dlx windshield wipers, dual manual remote mirrors, AM/FM stereo radio w/4 spkrs: 2-dr ($1450); 4-dr ($1462). Pkg. 22Y: incl. 21Y plus 3-spd auto. trans. replaces 5-spd manual: 2-dr ($2007); 4-dr ($2019). Pkg. 23Y: incl. 21Y plus 2.5L engine replaces 2.2L: 2-dr ($1736); 4-dr ($1748). Pkg. 24Y: incl. 23Y plus 3-spd auto. trans. replaces 5-spd manual: 2-dr ($2293); 4-dr ($2305). Sundance: Pkg. 21A: stnd equip. (NC). Pkg. 22A: incl. 21A plus 3-spd auto. trans. replaces 5-spd manual ($557). Pkg. 23A: incl. 21A plus 2.5L engine replaces 2.2L ($286). Pkg. 24A: incl. 21A plus 2.5L engine and 3-spd auto. trans. replaces 2.2L and 5-spd manual ($843). Pkg. 23D: incl. 21A plus 2.5L engine replaces 2.2L, air cond., tinted glass, tilt stng, elect. rear window defroster, dual horns, F&R floor mats, wide bodyside mldg, dlx windshield wipers, tach, Light Grp., floor-mounted console, bodyside/decklid striping, liftgate release, dual manual remote mirrors: 2-dr ($1276); 4-dr ($1288). Pkg. 24D: incl. 23D plus 3-spd auto. trans. replaces 5-spd manual: 2-dr ($1833); 4-dr ($1845). Duster: Pkg. 27G: stnd equip. (NC). Pkg. 28G: incl. 27G plus 4-spd auto. trans. replaces

5-spd manual ($640). Pkg. 27H: incl. 27G plus air cond., tinted glass, elect. rear window defroster, dual horns, dual visor mirrors, AM/FM stereo radio w/cass. & 4 spkrs, floor-mounted console, liftgate release, Light Grp., Prem. sound insulation, tach, dlx windshield wipers, F&R floor mats, warning chimes for headlights-on/key-in-ignition/seatbelts ($922). Pkg. 28H: incl. 27H plus 5-spd manual ($1562). Other: (ALE) Deluxe Decor Grp.: incl. body-color fascias, wide bodyside mldg., bodyside/decklid striping, 14-in. whl covers, America ($142). (ADA) Light Grp.: 2-dr ($65); 4-dr ($77). Air cond., tinted glass req'd ($900). Overhead console w/thermometer & compass ($265). Rear window defroster ($173). Pwr door locks, N/A America: 2-dr ($199); 4-dr ($240). Calif. emissions ($100). Tinted glass ($107). F&R floor mats ($46). Dual manual remote mirrors, stnd Duster ($69). Extra cost paint ($77). (RAL) AM/FM stereo radio w/cass., America ($284). (RAS) Elect. AM/FM stereo radio w/cass. & 4 spkrs: America ($205-$489); base or Duster ($155-$205). (RAN) Elect. AM/FM stereo radio w/cass., seek/scan & 4 Infinity spkrs: base ($430); Duster ($275-$480). (RBC) Elect. AM/FM stereo radio w/CD player, seek/scan & 4 spkrs, Duster ($645-$850). Sunroof, N/A America ($379). Spd control, N/A America ($224). Tilt stng, N/A America ($148). Cast alum whls, America or base ($328). 15-in. Lace alum whls, Duster ($328). Intermittent wipers ($66). Conventional spare tire: w/steel whl ($85); Duster ($213).

1992 Plymouth, Laser RS Turbo coupe (front-wheel-drive version) with optional foglamps and alloy wheels (OCW)

LASER CONVENIENCE/APPEARANCE OPTIONS: Laser: Pkg. 21A: stnd equip. (NC). Pkg. 21B: incl. 21A plus pwr stng, rear window defroster, whl covers, tonneau cover, floor mats, console ($608). Pkg. 22B: incl. 21B plus 4-spd auto. trans. replaces 5-spd manual ($1309). Pkg. 21C: incl. 21B plus air cond. ($1435). Pkg. 22C: incl. 21B plus air cond. and 4-spd auto. trans. replaces 5-spd manual ($2136). Pkg. 21D: incl. 21B plus air cond., spd control, elect. AM/FM stereo radio w/cass., clock, seek/scan & 6 spkrs ($1846). Pkg. 22D: incl. 21B plus air cond., spd control, elect. AM/FM stereo radio w/cass., clock, seek/scan & 6 spkrs and 4-spd auto. trans. replaces 5-spd manual ($2547). RS: Pkg. 23E: stnd equip. (NC). Pkg. 23F: incl. 23E plus air cond. ($827). Pkg. 24F: incl. 23F plus 4-spd auto. trans. replaces 5-spd manual ($1528). Pkg. 23R: incl. 23E plus air cond., spd control, elect. AM/FM stereo radio w/cass., clock, seek/scan & 6 spkrs, console, F&R floor mats, liftgate washer/wiper ($1423). Pkg. 24R: incl. 23R plus 4-spd auto. trans. replaces 5-spd manual ($2124). Pkg. 23H: incl. 23R plus foglamps, pwr windows, pwr door locks, spd control ($1931). Pkg. 24H: incl. 23H plus 4-spd auto. trans. replaces 5-spd manual ($2632). RS Turbo: Pkg. 25F: stnd equip. (NC). Pkg. 25G: incl. 25F plus air cond., elect. AM/FM stereo radio w/cass., seek/scan & 6 spkrs, floor mats, console, liftgate wiper/washer ($1210). Pkg. 26G: incl. 25G plus 4-spd auto. trans. replaces 5-spd manual ($2050). Pkg. 25H: incl. 25G plus foglamps, pwr windows, pwr door locks, spd control ($1931). Pkg. 26H: incl. 25H plus 4-spd auto. trans. replaces 5-spd manual ($2771). RS Turbo AWD: Pkg. 25M: stnd equip. (NC). Pkg. 25N: incl. 25M plus air cond. ($827). Pkg. 25P: incl. 25M plus air cond., console, F&R floor mats, elect. AM/FM stereo radio w/cass., seek/scan & 6 spkrs, liftgate washer/wiper ($1210). Pkg. 25Q: incl. 25P plus foglamps, pwr windows, pwr door locks, spd control ($1931). Other: Rear window defroster, base ($127). Calif. emissions (NC). (RAN) Elect. AM/FM stereo radio w/cass. & 6 spkrs, base ($198). CD player, N/A base ($506). Sunroof ($373). Alloy whls, N/A base or RS Turbo AWD ($321).

ACCLAIM CONVENIENCE/APPEARANCE OPTIONS: Pkg. 21A: stnd equip. (NC). Pkg. 22A: incl. 21A plus 3-spd auto. trans. replaces 5-spd manual ($557). Pkg. 21C: incl. 21A plus air cond., elect. rear window defroster, tinted glass, F&R floor mats, spd control, tilt stng ($505). Pkg. 22D: incl. 21C plus 3-spd auto. trans. replaces 5-spd manual ($1062). Pkg. 26D: incl. 21C plus 3.0L engine replaces 2.5L and 3-spd auto. trans. replaces 5-spd manual and P195/70R14 tires ($1787). Pkg. 22E: incl. 21A plus air cond., elect. rear window defroster, tinted glass, F&R floor mats, spd control, tilt stng, pwr windows, pwr door locks, pwr mirrors, pwr trunk release and 3-spd auto. trans. replaces 5-spd manual ($1734). Pkg. 26E: incl. 22E plus 3.0L engine replaces 2.5L and P195/70R14 tires ($2459). Pkg. 28E: incl. 22E plus 3.0L engine replaces 2.5L and 4-spd auto. trans. replaces 3-spd auto. trans. and P195/70R14 tires ($2542). Other: (AFD) Console & Armrest Grp. ($81-$155). (AJN) Illum. Grp. ($97-$293). Elect. Rear Window Defroster ($173). Calif. Emissions

($103). Extra Cost Paint ($97). (RAS) Elect. AM/FM stereo radio w/cass. ($165). (RAN) Elect. AM/FM Stereo w/Cass, Digital Clock, Seek/Scan & 4 Infinity Spkrs ($440). Pwr Driver Seat ($306). Front 50/50 Split Seat, Rear Fixed Bench ($150). Front 50/50 Split Seat, Rear Split-Fold Seat ($298). Front Bucket Seats, Rear Split-Fold Seat ($148). P195/70R14 Tires ($73-$104). Conventional Spare Tire ($95).

HISTORY: Model year production: 163,742 (not including imported Colt or Vista models). Calendar year sales: 164,448 (not including 17,728 imported Colt or Vista models).

1993 PLYMOUTH

The America name was dropped from the Sundance series, otherwise it was basically business as before for Plymouth in 1993. Anti-lock brakes were now optional on all Sundance models while the Laser RS Turbo AWD sports coupe offered a newly optional four-speed automatic trans-axle.

1993 Plymouth, Sundance Duster hatchback coupe with optional aluminum wheels (OCW)

SUNDANCE — SERIES P — FOUR/V-6 — Even though Plymouth discontinued use of the America name, the former "base" Sundance moved into the "price leader" slot previously the domain of the America. Returning for a second year as a member of the Sundance series was the Duster. The only revision in powertrain availability (a late running change the previous model year) was that the Duster could be ordered with a 2.5-liter four-cylinder engine (a $694 credit) instead of the standard 3.0-liter V-6. If a three-speed automatic transaxle was ordered with the four instead of the standard five-speed manual the credit was reduced to $137. Newly optional across-the-board for 1993 was anti-lock brakes. This was scheduled to be the final year of production for the Sundance, but it continued to early 1994 and was then dropped in favor of the Neon (launched early as a 1995 model).

LASER — SERIES D — FOUR — The four model lineup consisting of base, RS, RS Turbo and RS Turbo AWD sports coupes again represented the Laser series. Powertrain availability carried over intact from 1992 with the exception that the RS Turbo AWD model could now be ordered with an optional four-speed automatic transaxle. The all-wheel-drive coupe featured a limited-slip differential, alloy wheels and enthusiast suspension among its unique components. New optional features included a Gold Decor package that consisted of gold pin striping and badging.

ACCLAIM — SERIES A — FOUR/V-6 — Acclaim was carried over from the 1992 model year with no change in lineup, styling or powertrain availability.

I.D. DATA: Plymouth again had a 17-symbol Vehicle Identification Number (VIN) on the upper left corner of the instrument panel, visible through the windshield. Coding was similar to 1987-1992. Symbol ten (Model Year) changed to 'P' - 1993.

SUNDANCE (FOUR)

Model No.	Body/ Style No.	Body Type & Seating	Factory Price	Shipping Weight	Prod. Total
PPL	24	2-dr. Hatch-5P	8397	2575	Note 1
PPL	44	4-dr. Hatch-5P	8797	2610	Note 2

SUNDANCE (V-6)

Model No.	Body/ Style No.	Body Type & Seating	Factory Price	Shipping Weight	Prod. Total
PPS	24	2-dr. Duster Hatch-5P	10498	2727	Note 1
PPS	44	4-dr. Duster Hatch-5P	10898	2762	Note 2

Note 1: Sundance two-door production totaled 37,312 with no further breakout available.

Note 2: Sundance four-door production totaled 36,993 with no further breakout available.

LASER (FOUR)

Model No.	Body/ Style No.	Body Type & Seating	Factory Price	Shipping Weight	Prod. Total
DPM	24	2-dr. Cpe-4P	11406	2531	Note 1
DPH	24	2-dr. RS Cpe-4P	13749	2690	Note 1
DPH	24	2-dr. RS Turbo Cpe-4P	15267	2756	Note 1
DMH	24	2-dr. RS Turbo AWD Cpe-4P	17371	3073	Note 1

Note 1: Laser coupe production totaled 14,300 with no further breakout available.

ACCLAIM (FOUR/V-6)

APH	41	4-dr. Sed-6P	11941/12666	2756/2852	Note 1

Note: Price and weight figures to left of slash for four-cylinder engine, to right for V-6.

Note 1: Acclaim sedan production totaled 70,910 with no further breakout available.

ENGINE DATA: BASE FOUR (Laser): Inline, overhead cam four-cylinder. Displacement: 107 cu. in. (1.8 liters). Bore & stroke: 3.17 x 3.38 in. Compression ratio: 9.0:1. Brake horsepower: 92 at 5000 R.P.M. Torque: 105 lb.-ft. at 3500 R.P.M. Multi-port fuel injection. **BASE FOUR** (Laser RS): Inline, dual overhead cam four-cylinder. Displacement: 122 cu. in. (2.0 liters). Bore & stroke: 3.35 x 3.46 in. Compression ratio: 9.0:1. Brake horsepower: 135 at 6000 R.P.M. Torque: 125 lb.-ft. at 5000 R.P.M. Multi-port fuel injection. **BASE TURBO FOUR** (Laser RS Turbo): Intercooled turbocharged inline, dual overhead cam four-cylinder. Displacement: 122 cu. in. (2.0 liters). Bore & stroke: 3.35 x 3.46 in. Compression ratio: 7.8:1. Brake horsepower: 195 at 6000 R.P.M. Torque: 203 lb.-ft. at 3000 R.P.M. Multi-port fuel injection. **BASE FOUR** (Sundance): Inline, overhead cam four-cylinder. Cast iron block; aluminum head. Displacement: 135 cu. in. (2.2 liters). Bore & stroke: 3.44 x 3.62 in. Compression ratio: 9.5:1. Brake horsepower: 93 at 5200 R.P.M. Torque: 122 lb.-ft. at 3200 R.P.M. Electronic fuel injection. **BASE FOUR** (Acclaim); **OPTIONAL FOUR** (Sundance, Sundance Duster): Inline, overhead cam four-cylinder. Cast iron block; aluminum head. Displacement: 153 cu. in. (2.5 liters). Bore & stroke: 3.44 x 4.09 in. Compression ratio: 8.9:1. Brake horsepower: 100 at 4800 R.P.M. Torque: 135 lb.-ft. at 2800 R.P.M. Electronic fuel injection. **BASE V-6** (Sundance Duster); **OPTIONAL V-6** (Acclaim): Overhead cam V-6. Displacement: 181 cu. in. (3.0-liters). Bore & stroke: 3.59 x 2.99 in. Compression ratio: 8.9:1. Brake horsepower: 141 at 5200 R.P.M. Torque: 171 lb.-ft. at 2800 R.P.M. Multi-port fuel injection.

CHASSIS DATA: Wheelbase: (Sundance) 97.2 in.; (Laser) 97.2 in.; (Acclaim) 103.5 in. Overall Length: (Sundance) 171.9 in.; (Laser) 172.6 in.; (Acclaim) 181.2 in. Height: (Sundance) 52.7 in.; (Laser) 51.4 in.; (Acclaim) 53.5 in. Width: (Sundance) 67.3 in.; (Laser) 66.7 in.; (Acclaim) 68.1 in. Standard Tires: (Sundance) P185/70R14; (Sundance Duster) P195/60R15; (Laser) P185/70R14; (Laser RS) P205/55HR16; (Laser RS Turbo) P205/55VR16; (Acclaim) P185/70R14.

TECHNICAL: Transmission: Five-speed manual standard on all. Steering: Rack and pinion. Front suspension: (Sundance) Iso-strut w/integral gas-charged shock absorbers, asymmetrical lower control arms, coil springs and linkless stabilizer bar; (Laser) Iso-strut w/integral shock absorbers, coil springs, asymmetrical lower arms and link-type stabilizer bar; (Acclaim) Iso-strut w/integral gas-charged shock absorbers, asymmetrical lower control arms, coil springs and linkless stabilizer bar. Rear suspension: (Sundance) Beam axle, trailing flex-arm w/track bar, coil springs, gas-charged shock absorbers and frameless tubular stabilizer bar; (Laser w/front-drive) Trailing arms, beam axle w/integral stabilizer bar, track bar, shock absorbers and concentric coil springs; (Laser w/AWD) Semi-trailing arms w/toe-control links, unequal length lateral links, stabilizer bar, shock absorbers and concentric coil springs; (Acclaim) Beam axle, trailing flex-arms w/track bar, coil springs, gas-charged shock absorbers and frameless tubular stabilizer bar. Brakes: Front disc/rear drum (power-assisted) exc. (Laser) four-wheel disc. Body construction: (Sundance, Acclaim) Unibody; (Laser) Unibody w/isolated engine crossmember. Fuel tank: (Sundance) 14.0 gal.; (Laser) 15.8 gal.; (Acclaim) 16 gal.

DRIVETRAIN OPTIONS: Engines: 2.5-liter four: Sundance ($286); Sundance Duster ($694 credit). 3.0-liter V-6: Acclaim ($652). Transmission/Differential: Three-speed automatic: Sundance ($557); Sundance Duster ($137 credit w/2.5L four only); Acclaim ($557). Four-speed automatic: Sundance Duster ($690); Laser ($716); Laser RS ($516); Laser RS Turbo, FWD or AWD ($800). Acclaim ($735). Anti-lock Brakes: Sundance ($899); Laser ($943); Acclaim, w/four-wheel disc ($899). Handling suspension: Acclaim ($26).

SUNDANCE CONVENIENCE/APPEARANCE OPTIONS: Sundance: Pkg. 21W: stnd equip. (NC). Pkg. 22W: incl. 21W plus 3-spd auto. trans. replaces 5-spd manual ($557). Pkg. 23W: incl. 21W plus 2.5L engine replaces 2.2L ($286). Pkg. 24W: incl. 21W plus 2.5L engine and 3-spd auto. trans. replace 2.2L and 5-spd manual ($843). Pkg. 21Y: incl. air cond., tinted glass, elect. rear window defroster, F&R floor mats, narrow bodyside mldg., body-color fascias, color-keyed instrument panel bezels, dlx windshield wipers, Light Grp., bodyside/decklid striping, dual visor

mirrors, dual manual remote mirrors, 14-in. whl covers, AM/FM stereo radio w/4 spkrs ($1545). Pkg. 22Y: incl. 21Y plus 3-spd auto. trans. replaces 5-spd manual ($2102). Pkg. 23Y: incl. 21Y plus 2.5L engine replaces 2.2L ($1831). Pkg. 24Y: incl. 21Y plus 2.5L engine and 3-spd auto. trans. replace 2.2L and 5-spd manual ($2388). Duster: Pkg. 23G: incl. 2.5L engine replaces 3.0L ($694 credit). Pkg. 24G: incl. 2.5L engine and 3-spd auto. trans. replace 3.0L and 5-spd manual ($137 credit). Pkg. 27G: stnd equip. (NC). Pkg. 28G: incl. 27G plus 4-spd auto. trans. replaces 5-spd manual ($690). Pkg. 23H: incl. 27G exc. 2.5L engine replaces 3.0L plus air cond., tinted glass, elect. rear window defroster, dual horns, dual visor mirrors, AM/FM stereo radio w/cass. & 4 spkrs, floor-mounted console, liftgate release, Light Grp., foglamps, dlx windshield wipers, F&R floor mats, warning chimes for headlights-on/key-in-ignition/seatbelts ($279). Pkg. 24H: incl. 23H plus 3-spd auto. trans. replaces 5-spd manual ($836). Pkg. 27H: incl. 23H plus 3.0L engine replaces 2.5L ($973). Pkg. 28H: incl. 23H plus 3.0L engine and 4-spd auto. trans. replace 2.5L and 5-spd manual ($1663). Other: (ADA) Light Grp. ($77). Air cond., tinted glass req'd ($900). Overhead console w/thermometer & compass, Duster ($265). Rear window defroster ($173). Pwr door locks: 2-dr ($199); 4-dr ($240). Pwr windows, Duster: 2-dr ($265); 4-dr ($331). Calif. emissions ($102). Tinted glass ($107). F&R floor mats ($46). Dual manual remote mirrors, Duster ($69). Dual pwr mirrors, Duster ($57). Pwr driver's seat, Duster ($306). (RAL) AM/FM stereo radio w/2 spkrs, base ($284). (RAS) Elect. AM/FM stereo radio w/cass. & 4 spkrs: base ($165-$499); Duster ($215). (RAY) Elect. AM/FM stereo radio w/cass., graphic equal. & 4 Infinity spkrs: Duster ($305-$520). (RBC) Elect. AM/FM stereo radio w/CD player, graphic equal. & 4 spkrs, Duster ($475-$690). Remote liftgate release, base ($24). Sunroof ($379). Spd control ($224). Tilt stng ($148). 14-in. Bullet alum whls, base ($328). 15-in. Cathedral alum whls, Duster ($328). Intermittent wipers ($66). Conventional spare tire: w/steel whl ($85); Duster ($213).

LASER CONVENIENCE/APPEARANCE OPTIONS: Laser: Pkg. 21A: stnd equip. (NC). Pkg. 21B: incl. 21A plus pwr stng, rear spoiler, bodyside striping, rear window defroster, whl covers, tonneau cover, floor mats, console ($827). Pkg. 22B: incl. 21B plus 4-spd auto. trans. replaces 5-spd manual ($1543). Pkg. 21C: incl. 21B plus air cond. ($1654). Pkg. 22C: incl. 21C plus 4-spd auto. trans. replaces 5-spd manual ($2370). Pkg. 21D: incl. 21C plus spd control, elect. AM/FM stereo radio w/cass., clock & 6 spkrs ($2070). Pkg. 22D: incl. 21D plus 4-spd auto. trans. replaces 5-spd manual ($2786). RS: Pkg. 23E: stnd equip. (NC). Pkg. 23F: incl. 23E plus air cond., console, floor mats, bodyside striping ($921). Pkg. 24F: incl. 23F plus 4-spd auto. trans. replaces 5-spd manual ($1637). Pkg. 23G: incl. 23F plus spd control, elect. AM/FM stereo radio w/cass., clock, graphic equal. & 6 spkrs, liftgate washer/wiper ($1489). Pkg. 24G: incl. 23G plus 4-spd auto. trans. replaces 5-spd manual ($2205). Pkg. 23H: incl. 23G plus foglamps, pwr windows, pwr door locks, two-tone sill mldg ($2124). Pkg. 24H: incl. 23H plus 4-spd auto. trans. replaces 5-spd manual ($2840). RS Turbo: Pkg. 25F: stnd equip. (NC). Pkg. 25G: incl. 25F plus air cond., floor mats, console, liftgate wiper/washer, bodyside striping, spd control ($1273). Pkg. 25H: incl. 25G plus foglamps, pwr windows, pwr door locks, elect. AM/FM stereo radio w/cass., graphic equal. & 6 spkrs ($2013). Pkg. 26H: incl. 25H plus 4-spd auto. trans. replaces 5-spd manual ($2870). RS Turbo AWD: Pkg. 25M: incl. console, floor mats, bodyside striping ($94). Pkg. 25Q: incl. 25M plus air cond., foglamps, pwr windows, pwr door locks, spd control, liftgate washer/wiper, elect. AM/FM stereo radio w/cass., graphic equal. & 6 spkrs ($2013). Pkg. 26Q: incl. 25Q exc. foglamps deleted and 4-spd auto. trans. replaces 5-spd manual ($2813). Other: (ASH) Gold Decor Pkg.: incl. gold pin striping and badging, N/A base (NC). Rear window defroster, base ($130). Calif. emissions (NC). (RAN) Elect. AM/FM stereo radio w/cass. & 6 spkrs, base ($198). CD player, N/A base ($517). Sunroof ($373). Alloy whls: N/A base, stnd RS Turbo AWD.

ACCLAIM CONVENIENCE/APPEARANCE OPTIONS: Pkg. 21A: stnd equip. (NC). Pkg. 22A: incl. 21A plus 3-spd auto. trans. replaces 5-spd manual ($557). Pkg. 21C: incl. 21A plus air cond., elect. rear window defroster, floor mats, spd control, tilt stng ($472). Pkg. 22D: incl. 21C plus 3-spd auto. trans. replaces 5-spd manual ($1029). Pkg. 26D: incl. 21C plus 3.0L engine replaces 2.5L and 3-spd auto. trans. replaces 5-spd manual and P195/70R14 tires ($1754). Pkg. 22E: incl. 21C plus pwr windows, pwr door locks, dual pwr mirrors, remote trunk release and 3-spd auto. trans. replaces 5-spd manual ($1701). Pkg. 26E: incl. 22E plus 3.0L engine replaces 2.5L and P195/70R14 tires ($2426). Pkg. 28E: incl. 22E plus 3.0L engine replaces 2.5L and 4-spd auto. trans. replaces 3-spd auto. trans. and P195/70R14 tires ($2559). Other: (AFD) Console & Armrest Grp. ($155). (AJN) Interior Illum. Grp. ($293). Elect. Rear Window Defroster ($173). Calif. Emissions ($103). (RAS) Elect. AM/FM stereo radio w/cass. ($165). (RBC) Elect. AM/FM Stereo w/CD player, Graphic Equal. & 4 Infinity Spkrs ($690). Pwr Door Locks ($250). Pwr Driver Seat ($306). P195/70R14 Tires ($73-$104). Conventional Spare Tire ($95).

HISTORY: Model year production: 159,515 (not including imported Colt or Vista models). Calendar year sales: 181,014 (not including 19,122 imported Colt or Vista models). The Plymouth Prowler concept car made

its debut on the auto show circuit in 1993, promoted as Chrysler Corp.'s factory "hot rod." The Prowler concept roadster was powered by a 240-horsepower 3.5-liter V-6 linked to a rear-mounted four-speed transaxle. It featured an all-aluminum chassis and lightweight aluminum body panels. The Prowler also had a stowaway coupe top. At the 1993 Chicago Auto Show, Chrysler announced its new small car, code named PL, would go into production in late-1993 and be offered for sale in spring of 1994 as a 1995 model. The PL would later be known as the Plymouth (and Dodge) Neon.

1994 PLYMOUTH

This was the final production year (and an abbreviated one at that) for both the Sundance and Laser. It was also the last run for the imported Colt and Vista models (not covered in this catalog). The all-new Neon (a 1995 model) joined the Plymouth (and Dodge) lineup in January 1994.

1994 Plymouth, Sundance Duster hatchback coupe (OCW)

SUNDANCE — SERIES P — FOUR/V-6 — In its final appearance, the Sundance series was again comprised of the base and Duster trim levels, both again offered as two- and four-door hatchbacks. Production ended in March 1994 after the early-launch 1995 Plymouth Neon — the Sundance replacement — began filling dealership showrooms. The base model was again powered by the 2.2-liter four-cylinder engine mated to a five-speed manual transaxle with overdrive. Dusters used the 3.0-liter V-6 also paired with the five-speed manual transaxle. The 2.5-liter four and electronically controlled three-speed automatic were both optional across-the-board, but when the four was ordered in the Duster in place of its standard V-6 a $694 credit was offered. Also optional in the Duster was the 41TE electronically controlled four-speed automatic with overdrive, which was refined for 1994 to offer smoother operation. New features included the use of non-CFC R-134A refrigerant in the optional air conditioning system, easier-to-use restraint system buckles, the addition of a motorized torso belt and knee bolster passive restraint system for right front passenger and, for the base model, optional "Commodore" wheel covers. Bright Turquoise was a new exterior color choice while interior color choices were reduced to two: Quartz and Champagne. Standard equipment on all Sundance models included child protection door locks (four-door models only), stainless steel exhaust system (performance tuned on Dusters), halogen aero-style headlamps, tinted rear window, inside hood release, and console with front and rear storage. The Duster added color-keyed lower bodyside appliqués, body-color spoiler, dual manual exterior black mirrors, sport suspension and color-keyed "Triad" wheel covers. Optional equipment included air conditioning with tinted glass all-around, electric rear window defroster, power door locks, electronic speed control, tilt steering, sunroof, conventional spare tire and intermittent wipers.

LASER — SERIES D — FOUR — Laser, too, was making its last showing and again the series consisted of base, RS, RS Turbo and RS Turbo AWD sports coupes. Production of subcompact Laser sports coupes at the Diamond-Star Motors assembly plant in Normal, Illinois, ended June 1994. Powerplant availability again had the base model using the 1.8-liter four-cylinder engine, the RS the 2.0-liter four, and the RS Turbo models - again offered in both front- and all-wheel-drive (AWD) configurations - powered by the intercooled turbocharged version of the 2.0-liter four. All Lasers were fitted with a five-speed manual transaxle with overdrive as the standard unit. An electronically controlled four-speed automatic with overdrive was optional across-the-board. New features included an automatic locking rear outboard restraint system retractors for child seat protection, optional bodyside tape graphics and one new exterior color choice: Silver Mint Metallic. The RS Turbo AWD coupe received new gas-pressure shock absorbers in 1994. Laser featured a 0.36 coefficient of drag. Standard equipment included body-color bodyside moldings, power four-wheel disc brakes, stainless steel exhaust system (sport tuned with dual chrome tips on all except base coupe), tinted glass, driver's side footrest, remote fuel fill and liftgate release, tilt steering, headlights-on warning chime and intermittent wipers. RS models added a body-color rear spoiler,

electric rear window defroster, removable tonneau cover, dual power exterior body-color mirrors, driver's seat with adjustable lumbar support and "Turbine" wheel covers. Laser's option list included air conditioning, electronic speed control, sunroof, color-keyed floor mats and, available only on RS models, anti-lock brakes and foglights. The Gold Decor Package was again also offered as an option on RS models and featured gold pin striping and badging.

ACCLAIM — SERIES A — FOUR/V-6 — Acclaim was again a one-sedan-model, same-name series. The previously standard five-speed manual transaxle was discontinued, with the electronically controlled three-speed automatic its replacement. Standard powerplant was again the 2.5-liter four-cylinder engine, which was also again offered as a flex-fuel vehicle (FFV) option that was aimed primarily at fleet retail customers. The FFV model was designed to run on 100 percent gasoline as well as a blend of 85 percent methanol and 15 percent gas (M-85) or any fuel combination in between. For 1994, the FFV Acclaim featured a fuel concentration function on its mini-trip computer. Also optional on Acclaim was the 3.0-liter V-6 and newly refined 41TE electronically controlled four-speed automatic transaxle with overdrive. Other new features of the 1994 Acclaim included the addition of a motorized torso belt and knee bolster passive restraint system for right front passenger, "Commodore" wheel covers and one new exterior color choice: Sky Blue Satin-Glow. Previously optional equipment that was made standard included 50/50 front seats, speed control, tilt steering, air conditioning and electric rear window defroster. Two option packages available to Acclaim buyers were the Gold Special Edition and Argent Special Equipment Group. The Gold package included gold decals, unique body-color fascias with gold accents, luggage rack, bodyside molding with gold stripe, P195/70R14 tires and "Bullet" cast aluminum wheels with gold accents while the Argent package featured a luggage rack, P195/70R14 tires and "Bullet" cast aluminum wheels with argent accents.

I.D. DATA: Plymouth again had a 17-symbol Vehicle Identification Number (VIN) on the upper left corner of the instrument panel, visible through the windshield. Coding was similar to 1987-1993. Symbol ten (Model Year) changed to 'R' - 1994.

SUNDANCE (FOUR)

Model No.	Body/ Style No.	Body Type & Seating	Factory Price	Shipping Weight	Prod. Total
PPL	24	2-dr. Hatch-5P	8806	2608	Note 1
PPL	44	4-dr. Hatch-5P	9206	2643	Note 2

SUNDANCE (V-6)

PPS	24	2-dr. Duster Hatch-5P	10946	2672	Note 1
PPS	44	4-dr. Duster Hatch-5P	11346	2757	Note 2

Note 1: Sundance two-door production totaled 30,755 with no further breakout available.

Note 2: Sundance four-door production totaled 34,622 with no further breakout available.

LASER (FOUR)

DPM	24	2-dr. Cpe-4P	11542	2531	Note 1
DPH	24	2-dr. RS Cpe-4P	13910	2690	Note 1
DPH	24	2-dr. RS Turbo Cpe-4P	15444	2756	Note 1
DMH	24	2-dr. RS Turbo AWD Cpe-4P	17572	3073	Note 1

Note 1: Laser coupe production totaled 5,284 with no further breakout available.

ACCLAIM (FOUR/V-6)

APH	41	4-dr. Sed-6P	12470/13195	2831/2930	Note 1

Note: Price and weight figures to left of slash for four-cylinder engine, to right for V-6.

Note 1: Acclaim sedan production totaled 71,574 with no further breakout available.

ENGINE DATA: BASE FOUR (Laser): Inline, overhead cam four-cylinder. Cast iron block; aluminum head. Displacement: 107 cu. in. (1.8 liters). Bore & stroke: 3.17 x 3.38 in. Compression ratio: 9.0:1. Brake horsepower: 92 at 5000 R.P.M. Torque: 105 lb.-ft. at 3500 R.P.M. Multi-port fuel injection. **BASE FOUR (Laser RS):** Inline, dual overhead cam four-cylinder. Cast iron block; aluminum head. Displacement: 122 cu. in. (2.0 liters). Bore & stroke: 3.35 x 3.46 in. Compression ratio: 9.0:1. Brake horsepower: 135 at 6000 R.P.M. Torque: 125 lb.-ft. at 5000 R.P.M. Multi-port fuel injection. **BASE TURBO FOUR (Laser RS Turbo):** Intercooled turbocharged inline, dual overhead cam four-cylinder. Cast iron block; aluminum head. Displacement: 122 cu. in. (2.0 liters). Bore & stroke: 3.35 x 3.46 in. Compression ratio: 7.8:1. Brake horsepower: 195 at 6000 R.P.M. Torque: 203 lb.-ft. at 3000 R.P.M. Multi-port fuel injection. **BASE FOUR (Sundance):** Inline, overhead cam four-cylinder. Cast iron block; aluminum head. Displacement: 135 cu. in. (2.2 liters). Bore & stroke: 3.44 x 3.62 in. Compression ratio: 9.5:1. Brake horsepower: 93 at 4800 R.P.M. Torque: 122 lb.-ft. at 3200 R.P.M. Electronic fuel injection. **BASE FOUR (Acclaim); OPTIONAL FOUR (Sundance, Sun-**

dance Duster): Inline, overhead cam four-cylinder. Cast iron block; aluminum head. Displacement: 153 cu. in. (2.5 liters). Bore & stroke: 3.44 x 4.09 in. Compression ratio: 8.9:1. Brake horsepower: 100 at 4800 R.P.M. Torque: 135 lb.-ft. at 2800 R.P.M. Electronic fuel injection. FFV BASE FOUR (Acclaim w/M-85 fuel) Inline, overhead cam four-cylinder. Cast iron block; aluminum head. Displacement: 153 cu. in. (2.5 liters). Bore & stroke: 3.44 x 4.09 in. Compression ratio: 8.9:1. Brake horsepower: 106 at 4400 R.P.M. Torque: 145 lb.-ft. at 2400 R.P.M. Multiport fuel injection. BASE V-6 (Sundance Duster); OPTIONAL V-6 (Acclaim): Overhead cam V-6. Cast iron block; aluminum heads. Displacement: 181 cu. in. (3.0-liters). Bore & stroke: 3.59 x 2.99 in. Compression ratio: 8.9:1. Brake horsepower: 141 at 5000 R.P.M. Torque: 171 lb.-ft. at 2400 R.P.M. Multi-port fuel injection.

CHASSIS DATA: Wheelbase: (Sundance) 97.2 in.; (Laser) 97.2 in.; (Acclaim) 103.5 in. Overall Length: (Sundance) 171.9 in.; (Laser) 172.8 in.; (Acclaim) 181.2 in. Height: (Sundance) 52.7 in.; (Laser) 51.4 in.; (Acclaim) 53.5 in. Width: (Sundance) 67.3 in.; (Laser) 66.7 in.; (Acclaim) 68.1 in. Standard Tires: (Sundance) P185/70R14; (Sundance Duster) P195/60HR15; (Laser) P185/70R14; (Laser RS) P205/55HR16; (Laser RS Turbo) P205/55VR16; (Acclaim) P185/70R14.

TECHNICAL: Transmission: Five-speed manual standard on all exc. (Acclaim) three-speed automatic. Steering: Rack and pinion. Front suspension: (Sundance) Iso-strut w/integral gas-charged shock absorbers, asymmetrical lower control arms, coil springs and linkless stabilizer bar; (Laser) Iso-strut w/integral (gas-charged on AWD model) shock absorbers, coil springs, asymmetrical lower arms and link-type stabilizer bar; (Acclaim) Iso-strut w/integral gas-charged shock absorbers, asymmetrical lower control arms, coil springs and linkless stabilizer bar. Rear suspension: (Sundance) Beam axle, trailing flex-arm w/track bar, coil springs, gas-charged shock absorbers and frameless tubular stabilizer bar; (Laser w/front-drive) Trailing arms, beam axle w/integral stabilizer bar, track bar, shock absorbers and concentric coil springs; (Laser w/AWD) Semi-trailing arms w/toe-control links, unequal length lateral links, stabilizer bar, gas-charged shock absorbers and concentric coil springs; (Acclaim) Beam axle, trailing flex-arms w/track bar, coil springs, gas-charged shock absorbers and frameless tubular stabilizer bar. Brakes: Front disc/rear drum (power-assisted) exc. (Laser) four-wheel disc. Body construction: (Sundance, Acclaim) Unibody; (Laser) Unibody w/isolated engine crossmember. Fuel tank: (Sundance) 14.0 gal.; (Laser) 15.8 gal.; (Acclaim) 16 gal.; (Acclaim FFV) 18 gal.

DRIVETRAIN OPTIONS: Engines: 2.5-liter four: Sundance ($286); Sundance Duster ($694 credit). FFV 2.5-liter four: Acclaim (NC). 3.0-liter V-6: Acclaim ($652). Transmission/Differential: Three-speed automatic: Sundance ($557); Sundance Duster ($137 credit w/2.5L four only). Four-speed automatic: Sundance Duster ($730); Laser ($716); Laser RS ($716); Laser RS Turbo: FWD ($757); AWD ($800). Acclaim ($735). Anti-lock Brakes: Sundance ($699); Laser ($699); Acclaim, w/four-wheel disc ($699).

SUNDANCE CONVENIENCE/APPEARANCE OPTIONS: Sundance: Pkg. 21W: stnd equip. (NC). Pkg. 22W: incl. 21W plus 3-spd auto. trans. replaces 5-spd manual ($557). Pkg. 23W: incl. 21W plus 2.5L engine replaces 2.2L ($286). Pkg. 24W: incl. 23W plus 3-spd auto. trans. replaces 5-spd manual ($843). Pkg. 21Y: incl. air cond., tinted glass, elect. rear window defroster, floor mats, narrow bodyside mldg, body-color fascias, color-keyed instrument panel bezels, dlx windshield wipers, Light Grp., bodyside/decklid striping, dual visor mirrors, dual manual remote mirrors, 14-in. "Commodore" whl covers, AM/FM stereo radio w/4 spkrs ($1545). Pkg. 22Y: incl. 21Y plus 3-spd auto. trans. replaces 5-spd manual ($2102). Pkg. 23Y: incl. 21Y plus 2.5L engine replaces 2.2L ($1831). Pkg. 24Y: incl. 23Y plus 3-spd auto. trans. replaces 5-spd manual ($2388). Duster: Pkg. 23G: incl. 2.5L engine replaces 3.0L ($694 credit). Pkg. 24G: incl. 23G plus 3-spd auto. trans. replaces 5-spd manual ($137 credit). Pkg. 27G: stnd equip. (NC). Pkg. 28G: incl. 27G plus 4-spd auto. trans. replaces 5-spd manual ($730). Pkg. 23H: incl. 27G exc. 2.5L engine replaces 3.0L plus air cond., tinted glass, elect. rear window defroster, dual horns, dual visor mirrors, AM/FM stereo radio w/cass. & 4 spkrs, floor-mounted console, liftgate release, Light Grp., foglamps, dlx windshield wipers, floor mats, warning chimes for headlights-on/key-in-ignition/seatbelts ($284). Pkg. 24H: incl. 23H plus 3-spd auto. trans. replaces 5-spd manual ($841). Pkg. 27H: incl. 23H plus 3.0L engine replaces 2.5L ($978). Pkg. 28H: incl. 27H plus 4-spd auto. trans. replaces 5-spd manual ($1708). Other: (ADA) Light Grp. ($77). Air cond., tinted glass req'd ($900). Overhead console w/thermometer & compass, Duster ($265). Rear window defroster ($173). Pwr door locks: 2-dr ($199); 4-dr ($240). Pwr windows, Duster: 2-dr ($265); 4-dr ($331). Calif. emissions ($102). F&R floor mats ($46). Dual manual remote mirrors, stnd Duster ($69). Dual pwr mirrors, Duster ($57). Pwr driver's seat, Duster ($306). (RAL) AM/FM stereo radio w/2 spkrs, base ($284). (RAS) Elect. AM/FM stereo radio w/cass. & 4 spkrs: base ($170-$504); Duster ($220). (RAY) Elect. AM/FM stereo radio w/cass., graphic equal. & 4 Infinity spkrs: Duster ($300-$520). (RBC) Elect. AM/FM stereo radio w/CD player, graphic equal. & 4 spkrs, Duster ($470-$690). Remote liftgate release, base ($24). Sunroof ($379). Spd control ($224). Tilt stng ($148). 14-in. Bullet alum whls, base ($328-$376). 15-in.

Cathedral alum whls, Duster ($328). Intermittent wipers ($66). Conventional spare tire: w/steel whl ($85); Duster ($213).

1994 Plymouth, Laser RS coupe with optional foglamps and alloy wheels (OCW)

LASER CONVENIENCE/APPEARANCE OPTIONS: Laser: Pkg. 21A: stnd equip. (NC). Pkg. 21T: incl. 21A plus air cond., pwr stng ($1099). Pkg. 22T: incl. 21T plus 4-spd auto. trans. replaces 5-spd manual ($1815). Pkg. 21B: incl. 21A plus pwr stng, rear spoiler, bodyside striping, rear window defroster, whl covers, tonneau cover, floor mats, console ($827). Pkg. 22B: incl. 21B plus 4-spd auto. trans. replaces 5-spd manual ($1543). Pkg. 21C: incl. 21B plus air cond. ($1654). Pkg. 22C: incl. 21C plus 4-spd auto. trans. replaces 5-spd manual ($2370). Pkg. 21D: incl. 21C plus spd control, elect. AM/FM stereo radio w/cass., clock & 6 spkrs ($2070). Pkg. 22D: incl. 21D plus 4-spd auto. trans. replaces 5-spd manual ($2786). RS: Pkg. 23E: stnd equip. (NC). Pkg. 23F: incl. 23E plus air cond., console, floor mats, bodyside striping ($921). Pkg. 24F: incl. 23F plus 4-spd auto. trans. replaces 5-spd manual ($1637). Pkg. 23G: incl. 23F plus spd control, elect. AM/FM stereo radio w/cass., clock, graphic equal. & 6 spkrs, liftgate washer/wiper ($1489). Pkg. 24G: incl. 23G plus 4-spd auto. trans. replaces 5-spd manual ($2205). Pkg. 23H: incl. 23G plus foglamps, pwr windows, pwr door locks ($2013). Pkg. 24H: incl. 23H plus 4-spd auto. trans. replaces 5-spd manual ($2729). RS Turbo: Pkg. 25G: stnd equip. (NC). Pkg. 25H: incl. 25G plus air cond., floor mats, console, liftgate wiper/washer, bodyside striping, spd control, foglamps, pwr windows, pwr door locks, elect. AM/FM stereo radio w/cass., graphic equal. & 6 spkrs ($2013). Pkg. 26H: incl. 25H plus 4-spd auto. trans. replaces 5-spd manual ($2870). RS Turbo AWD: Pkg. 25M: stnd equip. (NC). Pkg. 25Q: incl. 25M plus air cond., foglamps, pwr windows, pwr door locks, bodyside striping, spd control, liftgate washer/wiper, elect. AM/FM stereo radio w/cass., graphic equal. & 6 spkrs ($2013). Pkg. 26Q: incl. 25Q exc. foglamps deleted and 4-spd auto. trans. replaces 5-spd manual ($2813). Other: (ASH) Gold Decor Pkg.: incl. gold pin striping and badging, N/A base (NC). Rear window defroster, base ($130). Calif. emissions (NC). (RAN) Elect. AM/FM stereo radio w/cass. & 6 spkrs, base ($198). CD player, N/A base ($517). Sunroof ($373). Alloy whls, N/A base, stnd RS Turbo AWD ($339).

ACCLAIM CONVENIENCE/APPEARANCE OPTIONS: Pkg. 21A: stnd equip. (NC). Pkg. 22D: incl. 21A plus 3-spd auto. trans. replaces 5-spd manual (NC). Pkg. 24D: incl. 22D plus FFV 2.5L engine replaces 2.5 (NC). Pkg. 26D: incl. 3.0L engine replaces FFV 2.5L and P195/70R14 tires ($725). Pkg. 24E: incl. 24D plus pwr windows, pwr door locks, dual pwr mirrors, remote trunk release, heated seats, rear split-folding bench seat ($883). Pkg. 28E: incl. 24E plus 3.0L engine and 4-spd auto. trans. replace 2.5L and 3-spd auto. trans. ($1781). Other: (ADS) Argent Special Equip. Grp.: incl. luggage rack, P195/70R14 tires and "Bullet" cast aluminum wheels with argent accents ($200). (ASH) Gold Special Equip. Grp.: incl. gold decals, unique body-color fascias with gold accents, luggage rack, bodyside molding with gold stripe, P195/70R14 tires and "Bullet" cast aluminum wheels with gold accents ($200). Mini-Trip Computer/Message Center ($93). Elect. Rear Window Defroster ($173). Calif. Emissions ($103). (RAS) Elect. AM/FM stereo radio w/cass., clock & 4 spkrs ($170). Pwr Door Locks ($250). Pwr Driver's Seat ($306). P195/70R14 Tires ($73-$104). Conventional Spare Tire ($95).

HISTORY: Model year production: 142,235 (not including 58,760 1995 Plymouth Neons produced in the 1994 model year nor imported Colt or Vista models). Calendar year sales: 106,043 (not including 85,660 1995 Plymouth Neons sold in calendar year 1994 nor 6,110 imported Colt or Vista models). The 1995 Plymouth/Dodge Neon sedan went on sale in January 1994. Shortly thereafter, production of the car was halted at its Belvidere, Illinois, assembly plant and a recall was enacted of all 15,000 Neons shipped to that point due to problems with the car's engine controller. Chrysler Corp.'s Sterling Heights, Michigan, plant received a $300 million redo to ready it for production of the J-platform cars including the Plymouth Breeze, a 1996 model.

1995 PLYMOUTH

With the discontinuation of both the Sundance and Laser, Plymouth offered just two series in 1995, the returning-for-its-final-year Acclaim and all-new Neon. The equally all-new Breeze was slated to replace the Acclaim in 1996. Because of its "lame duck" status, the Acclaim had an abbreviated model year, with production of the sedan halted at its Newark, Delaware, and Toluca, Mexico, assembly sites in January 1995. Neon, assembled in Belvidere, Illinois, was offered in three trim levels: base, Highline and Sport.

1995 Plymouth, Neon sedan (OCW)

NEON — SERIES L — FOUR — In a unique approach to marketing an automobile - although certainly not the first in the industry to do so - the compact, five-passenger Neon was a Chrysler Corp. product that served two masters. Badged as either a Plymouth or a Dodge, the Neon for both brands was identical. Introduced in early-1994 (in four-door configuration), the two-door model did not debut until the fall of 1994 as a 1995 model, the Neon's duality was explained by Chrysler's Vice-President of Marketing and Communications, A.C. "Bud" Liebler thusly: "This marketing approach breaks from industry tradition, but is clearly in line with the Neon's 'dare to be different' product philosophy." The Neon was available in three trim levels: base, Highline and Sport. All were assembled in Belvidere, Illinois. The base model was offered in sedan only configuration while the Highline and Sport each came in both coupe and sedan body styles. All Neons with the exception of the Sport coupe were powered by a sequentially fuel injected 2.0-liter four-cylinder engine paired with a five-speed manual transmission. Sport coupes used a dual overhead cam version of the 2.0-liter four. Optional was an electronically controlled three-speed automatic. Neon was also the first passenger car to feature "returnless" fuel injection as well as the industry-first direct ignition system with sensor technology for quick starts. Neon's standard features included dual airbags and knee bolster passive restraint system, stainless steel exhaust system, side impact door beam protection, aero-style halogen headlights, analog instrument cluster with 120 mph speedometer, rear door child safety locks (sedans), warning chime feature for key-in-ignition/headlights on/seatbelt reminder, and climate control. Sport models added four-wheel anti-lock brakes, electric rear window defogger, power door locks, foglights, tinted glass, dual aero power black exterior mirrors, power steering, tilt steering column, touring suspension, remote trunk release, and intermittent wipers. Much of this equipment was available as optional or in packaged form only on base or Highline models. Air conditioning was an across-the-board package-only feature. The base sedan featured an interior consisting of "Naples" cloth and "Classic" vinyl. Highline and Sport models also used the same vinyl, but the former featured "Prism" cloth while the latter used "Pesto" cloth. "Pyramid" cloth and "Phoenix" vinyl was optional at the Sport trim level. The Neon's coefficient of drag measured 0.328. Its wheelbase was 104.0 inches and overall length 171.8 inches. Exterior color choices were Flame Red, Bright White, and Black across-the-board; Aqua and Light Iris on base and Highline models; and Strawberry, Emerald Green, and Brilliant Blue on Highline and Sport models. Medium/Dark Quartz was an interior color choice for all Neons, while Medium/Dark Driftwood was offered in Highline and Sport coupes and sedans and Sport models only - late in the model year - also had available a "Flash" decor in Medium/Dark Quartz. Several versions of an extra cost Competition Package were available as the Neon was used extensively in "showroom stock" sports car racing events.

ACCLAIM — SERIES A — FOUR/V-6 — The Acclaim sedan returned for a short production run in 1995 and was then dropped to make way for its all-new J-platform replacement, the Breeze (a 1996 model that debuted in the fall of 1995). The Acclaim was basically carried over intact from the previous year, with the exception being the previously optional Argent Special Equipment Group was no longer offered. Also, the formerly optional four-wheel disc brake with anti-lock system was not promoted in Plymouth Acclaim press material as remaining available, but it may have been mistakenly overlooked.

I.D. DATA: Plymouth again had a 17-symbol Vehicle Identification Number (VIN) on the upper left corner of the instrument panel, visible through the windshield. Coding was similar to 1987-1994. Symbol ten (Model Year) changed to 'S' - 1995.

NEON (FOUR)

Model No.	Body/ Style No.	Body Type & Seating	Factory Price	Shipping Weight	Prod. Total
LPL	42	4-dr. Sedan-5P	9500	2320	Note 2

NEON HIGHLINE (FOUR)

Model No.	Body/ Style No.	Body Type & Seating	Factory Price	Shipping Weight	Prod. Total
LPH	22	2-dr. Coupe-5P	11240	2377	Note 1
LPH	42	4-dr. Sedan-5P	11240	2388	Note 2

NEON SPORT (FOUR)

Model No.	Body/ Style No.	Body Type & Seating	Factory Price	Shipping Weight	Prod. Total
LPS	22	2-dr. Coupe-5P	13567	2439	Note 1
LPS	42	4-dr. Sedan-5P	13267	2449	Note 2

Note: Dodge Neon production totals are separate and can be found in the Dodge listings.

Note 1: Plymouth Neon two-door production totaled 24,704 with no further breakout available.

Note 2: Plymouth Neon four-door production totaled 89,607 with no further breakout available.

ACCLAIM (FOUR/V-6)

Model No.	Body/ Style No.	Body Type & Seating	Factory Price	Shipping Weight	Prod. Total
APH	41	4-dr. Sedan-6P	14323/15121	2771/2795	Note 1

Note: Price and weight figures to left of slash for four-cylinder engine, to right for V-6.

Note 1: Acclaim sedan production totaled 23,763 with no further breakout available.

ENGINE DATA: BASE FOUR (Neon, Neon Highline, Neon Sport sed): Inline, overhead cam four-cylinder. Cast iron block; aluminum head. Displacement: 121 cu. in. (2.0 liters). Bore & stroke: 3.44 x 3.27 in. Compression ratio: 9.8:1. Brake horsepower: 132 at 6000 RPM. Torque: 129 lb.-ft. at 5000 RPM. Sequential fuel injection. **BASE FOUR** (Neon Sport cpe): Inline, dual overhead cam four-cylinder. Cast iron block; aluminum head. Displacement: 121 cu. in. (2.0 liters). Bore & stroke: 3.44 x 3.27 in. Compression ratio: 9.8:1. Brake horsepower: 150 at 6500 RPM. Torque: 133 lb.-ft. at 5500 RPM. Sequential fuel injection. **BASE FOUR** (Acclaim): Inline, overhead cam four-cylinder. Cast iron block; aluminum head. Displacement: 153 cu. in. (2.5 liters). Bore & stroke: 3.44 x 4.09 in. Compression ratio: 8.9:1. Brake horsepower: 100 at 4800 R.P.M. Torque: 135 lb.-ft. at 2800 R.P.M. Electronic fuel injection. **FFV BASE FOUR** (Acclaim w/M-85 fuel) Inline, overhead cam four-cylinder. Cast iron block; aluminum head. Displacement: 153 cu. in. (2.5 liters). Bore & stroke: 3.44 x 4.09 in. Compression ratio: 8.9:1. Brake horsepower: 106 at 4400 R.P.M. Torque: 145 lb.-ft. at 2400 R.P.M. Multi-port fuel injection. **OPTIONAL V-6** (Acclaim): Overhead cam V-6. Cast iron block; aluminum heads. Displacement: 181 cu. in. (3.0-liters). Bore & stroke: 3.59 x 2.99 in. Compression ratio: 8.9:1. Brake horsepower: 141 at 5000 R.P.M. Torque: 171 lb.-ft. at 2400 R.P.M. Multi-port fuel injection.

CHASSIS DATA: Wheelbase: (Neon) 104.0 in.; (Acclaim) 103.5 in. Overall Length: (Neon) 171.8 in.; (Acclaim) 181.2 in. Height: (Neon cpe) 52.8 in.; (Neon sed) 54.8 in.; (Acclaim) 53.5 in. Width: (Neon) 67.2 in.; (Acclaim) 68.1 in. Front Tread: (Neon) 57.4 in.; (Acclaim) 57.6 in. Rear Tread: (Neon) 57.4 in.; (Acclaim) 57.2 in. Standard Tires: (Neon) P165/80R13; (Neon Highline) P185/70R13; (Neon Sport) P185/65R14; (Acclaim) P185/70R14.

TECHNICAL: Transmission: (Neon) five-speed manual; (Acclaim) three-speed automatic. Steering: Rack and pinion. Front suspension: (Neon) MacPherson struts, asymmetrical lower control arms, coil springs and (opt. on base; stnd on Highline, Sport) link-type stabilizer bar; (Acclaim) Iso-strut w/integral gas-charged shock absorbers, asymmetrical lower control arms, coil springs and linkless stabilizer bar. Rear suspension: (Neon) Chapman struts, coil springs, dual lower transverse links, lower trailing links; (Acclaim) Beam axle, trailing flex-arms w/track bar, coil springs, gas-charged shock absorbers and frameless tubular stabilizer bar. Brakes: Front disc/rear drum (power-assisted) exc. (Neon Sport) Front disc/rear drum w/anti-lock (power-assisted). Body construction: (All) Unibody. Fuel tank: (Neon) 11.2 gals.; (Acclaim) 16.0 gals.; (Acclaim FFV) 18.0 gals.

DRIVETRAIN OPTIONS: Engines: 2.0-liter four: Neon Sport cpe ($100 credit). FFV 2.5-liter four: Acclaim (NC). 3.0-liter V-6: Acclaim ($694). Transmission/Differential: Three-speed automatic: Neon ($557). Four-speed automatic: Acclaim ($735). Anti-lock Brakes: Neon base/Highline ($565).

NEON CONVENIENCE/APPEARANCE OPTIONS: Base: Pkg. 21A: stnd equip. (NC). Pkg. 22A: 21A exc. 3-spd auto. trans. replaces 5-spd manual ($557). Competition Pkg. 25A: 21A plus ACR Competition Pkg. and extra cost paint ($1575). Pkg. 21B: 21A plus air cond., rear window

defroster, dual remote outside mirrors, bodyside mldg, AM/FM stereo radio w/clock & 4 spkrs, pwr strng, tinted glass, touring susp., intermittent wipers ($1861). Pkg. 22B: 21B exc. 3-spd auto. trans. replaces 5-spd manual ($2418). Competition Pkg. 25B: 25A plus air cond., rear window defroster, dual remote outside mirrors, AM/FM stereo radio w/clock & 4 spkrs, intermittent wipers ($3315). Highline: Pkg. 21C: stnd equip. (NC). Competition Pkg. 23C: incl. DOHC 2.0L four and 5-spd manual trans. plus ACR Competition Pkg. and extra cost paint ($1140). Pkg. 21D: 21C plus air cond., floor-mounted console, remote decklid release, rear window defroster ($703). Pkg. 22D: 21D exc. 3-spd auto. trans. replaces 5-spd manual ($1260). Competition Pkg. 23D: 23C plus air cond., floor-mounted console, remote decklid release, rear window defroster, extra cost paint, cpe only ($2177). Pkg. 21F: 21D plus pwr door locks, floor mats, Light Grp., dual illum. visor mirrors, tilt stng, tach, low fuel light, P185/65R14 tires, 14-in. whl covers: cpe ($1330); sed ($1351). Pkg. 22F: 21F exc. 3-spd auto. trans. replaces 5-spd manual: cpe ($1887); sed ($1928). Sport cpe: Pkg. 21J: incl. SOHC 2.0L four and 5-spd manual trans. ($100 credit). Pkg. 22J: 21J exc. 3-spd auto. trans. replaces 5-spd manual ($457). Pkg. 23J: stnd equip. (NC). Pkg. 24J: 23J exc. 3-spd auto. trans. replaces 5-spd manual ($557). Pkg. 21K: 21J plus air cond., floor mats, Light Grp., AM/FM stereo radio w/prem. cass. & CD changer & 6 spkrs ($627). Pkg. 22K: 21K exc. 3-spd auto. trans. replaces 5-spd manual ($1184). Pkg. 23K: 23J plus air cond., floor mats, Light Grp., AM/FM stereo radio w/prem. cass. & CD changer & 6 spkrs ($727). Pkg. 24K: 23K exc. 3-spd auto. trans. replaces 5-spd manual ($1284). Sport sed: Pkg. 21J: stnd equip. (NC). Pkg. 22J: 21J exc. 3-spd auto. trans. replaces 5-spd manual ($557). Pkg. 21K: 21J plus air cond., floor mats, Light Grp., AM/FM stereo radio w/prem. cass. & CD changer & 6 spkrs ($727). Pkg. 22K: 21K exc. 3-spd auto. trans. replaces 5-spd manual ($1284). Other: (AJP) Convenience Grp.: incl. dual pwr remote mirrors, pwr door locks, stnd Sport: cpe ($256); sed ($297). (ACR) Competition Pkg.: incl. 14-in. 4-whl disc brakes, unlimited spd eng. controller, body-color fascias, body-color grille bar, tinted glass, dual manual remote mirrors, bodyside mldg, H.D. radiator, radio delete, pwr stng w/16:1 ratio, competition susp., tach, low fuel light, 14-in. cast alum whls, P175/65HR14 perf. tires on base/P185/60HR14 touring tires on Highline (NC). Integrated child seat ($100). Rear window defroster ($173). Calif. emissions ($102). Floor mats, base or Highline ($46). Roof rack ($100). Dual remote manual mirrors, base ($70). Bodyside mldg, base ($30). (RAL) AM/FM stereo radio w/clock & 4 spkrs, base ($334). (RAS) AM/FM stereo radio w/cass., clock & 6 prem. spkrs ($250). (RBS) AM/FM stereo radio w/prem. cass., CD changer & 6 prem. spkrs ($356). (RBG) Elect. AM/FM stereo radio w/CD player, clock & 6 prem. spkrs ($132-$488). Speed control, N/A base ($224). Tilt stng, Highline ($148). Tach & Low Fuel Warning Light, Highline ($93). (AYC) Wheel Cover Pkg., Sport ($500 credit). (AY7) Wheel Dress-Up Pkg., Highline ($80). Intermittent wipers, base ($66). Pwr windows, Sport sed ($210). "Flash" Decor cloth bucket seats, Sport ($120). Leather bucket seats, Sport ($649). Extra cost paint, N/A Sport ($97).

1995 Plymouth, Neon Sport sedan (OCW)

ACCLAIM CONVENIENCE/APPEARANCE OPTIONS: Pkg. 22D: stnd equip. (NC). Pkg. 26D: incl. 22D plus 3.0L engine replaces 2.5L and P195/70R14 tires ($798). Pkg. 26E: incl. 26D plus pwr windows, pwr door locks, dual pwr remote heated mirrors, remote trunk release ($1533). Other: (ASH) Gold Special Equip. Grp.: incl. gold decals, unique body-color fascias with gold accents, luggage rack, bodyside molding with gold stripe, P195/70R14 tires and "Bullet" cast aluminum wheels with gold accents ($200). Calif. Emissions ($103). Pwr Door Locks ($250). Pwr Driver's Seat ($306). Extra Cost Paint ($97). P195/70R14 Tires ($73-$104). Conventional Spare Tire ($95).

HISTORY: Model year production: 138,074. Calendar year sales: 112,662 (not including 221 1996 Breeze sedans nor 682 imported 1994 Colts sold in the 1995 calendar year. The Mayflower sailing ship badge first appeared on Plymouth vehicles in 1928, and it was said to represent the "endurance and strength, rugged honesty...and freedom from limitations." A post-modern version of that badge returned in January 1995 to signify the brand's rejuvenated image of freedom and expressiveness. The new badge, unveiled at Detroit's North American International Auto Show, appeared later in the year on the Plymouth Neon and new Voyager minivan. The Mayflower badge, in its original form, appeared

on millions of Plymouth vehicles from 1928 through the 1950s. The "Plymouth Vitality Tour" traveled to the major auto shows in 1995 showcasing three concept vehicles from the automaker. The Breeze, Neon Wave (created in both coupe and sedan configurations) and Back Pack represented "motorized billboards for the new Plymouth," according to Chrysler-Plymouth Manager Steve Torok. The Breeze and Wave each featured a retractable "Vista Top" roof and youth-oriented features such as "hot" interior trim accents and exterior paint colors as well as trunk-and roof-mounted bike racks. The Back Pack was part utility, part pickup, part sporty coupe that "broke out of the car and truck paradigm." It was powered by a 16-valve 2.0-liter four-cylinder engine, rated at 135 horsepower, linked to a three-speed automatic transaxle. The front-wheel-drive Back Pack rode on a 91.7-inch wheelbase contained within an overall length of 142.0 inches. It was finished in Magic Green and featured a two-tone Black Olive and Silver Fern interior.

1996 PLYMOUTH

Plymouth's lineup was completely different than what was available just two model years previous with the Sundance, Laser and Acclaim. As it was in 1995, just two series comprised the 1996 Plymouth offerings: Neon and the all-new Breeze. A base coupe was added to the Neon series, now comprised of three trim levels each offering a coupe and sedan. The Breeze was represented by one sedan, which was the replacement for the discontinued Acclaim.

1996 Plymouth, Neon Highline coupe (OCW)

1996 Plymouth, Neon Highline sedan (OCW)

NEON — SERIES L — FOUR — With the addition of a base coupe, all three trim levels of Neon — base, Highline and Sport — each now offered a coupe and sedan. Also added to the Highline models was an optional Expresso package that included "Expresso" graphics, a power bulge hood, "Flash Decor" interior trim, decklid spoiler and tach. The Expresso could also be ordered with a three-speed automatic transmission in place of the Highline's standard five-speed manual unit. The Neon's standard powertrain lineup was revised slightly from the year previous with all models now using the sequentially fuel injected 2.0-liter four-cylinder engine linked to a five-speed manual transmission. The dual overhead cam version of the 2.0-liter four that previously was standard in the Sport coupe was now optional in Sport coupes and sedans as well as base Neon coupes equipped with the optional Competition Package. An electronically controlled three-speed automatic transmission was optional across-the-board. Also optional in all California (or states requiring California Emission Controls) Neons was a TLEV (transitional low emission vehicle) version of the 2.0-liter four. An upgraded noise, vibration and harshness (NVH) reduction package was standard on all 1996 Neons. Base models received more standard equipment including touring suspension, intermittent wipers, remote trunk release and tinted glass, all of which was previously

optional. Other new features included a 12.5 gallon molded plastic gas tank (which replaced the former 11.2 gallon unit), SBEC III Powertrain Control Module, four-spoke steering wheel with center horn pad, mist gray interior color choice and two new exterior color choices: Magenta and Bright Jade. New optional features of the Neon included four-wheel anti-lock disc brakes available on all models; power windows on coupes; and a power sunroof, remote keyless entry with "panic" alarm and dome and map lamp time out feature offered on Highline and Sport models.

1996 Plymouth, Breeze sedan (OCW)

BREEZE — SERIES A — FOUR —
The cab-forward design, midsize Breeze sedan debuted in showrooms in January 1996 already meeting 1997 federal dynamic side impact standards. It was built on the J-platform shared with both the Chrysler Cirrus and Dodge Stratus. Built at Chrysler Corp.'s Sterling Heights, Michigan, assembly plant, the Breeze was powered by a 16-valve 2.0-liter four-cylinder engine linked to a five-speed manual transaxle. The powerplant utilized a SBEC III Powertrain Control Module. The 41TE electronically controlled four-speed automatic with overdrive was optional and featured an EATX III (interactive automatic speed control) Transmission Control Module. Standard features of the Breeze included dual airbags, air conditioning with climate control, electric rear window defroster, AM/FM stereo radio with four speakers, child safety rear door locks, stainless steel exhaust system, solar control windshield and tinted glass side & rear, aero-style halogen headlights, power steering, tilt steering, remote trunklid release and intermittent wipers. Optional items included anti-lock brakes, power door locks, electronic speed control (automatic transaxle only), power sunroof (mid-model year introduction), full-size spare tire, power windows and a Personal Security Package that featured remote keyless entry with panic alarm, illuminated entry and headlight time delay. Breeze front and rear soft, rounded fascias were reaction-injection molded urethane and painted body color. Ornamentation included a Mayflower sailing ship badge mounted in the grille center, Plymouth script-letter nameplates on front doors and trunklid, script-letter Breeze decal nameplate on the trunklid, body-color bodyside molding and wheel covers with the Mayflower ship design molded into their outer surfaces. Breeze was offered with 10 exterior color choices: Dark Rosewood, Orchid, Light Silverfern, Light Gold, Medium Fern, Light Iris, Forest Green, Black, Stone White and Candy Apple Red Metallic. The interior featured Raven seat and door trim panel bolster fabric and color choices were Mist Gray, Silverfern and Camel. Breeze featured 15.7 cubic feet of cargo space and a 0.314 coefficient of drag.

I.D. DATA: Plymouth's 17-symbol Vehicle Identification Number (VIN), as before, was on the upper left corner of the instrument panel, visible through the windshield. Coding is similar to 1986-95. Symbol ten (model year) changed to 'T' for 1996.

NEON (FOUR)

Model No.	Body/Style No.	Body Type & Seating	Factory Price	Shipping Weight	Prod. Total
LPL	22	2-dr. Coupe-5P	9495	N/A	Note 1
LPL	42	4-dr. Sedan-5P	9995	2343	Note 2

NEON HIGHLINE (FOUR)

LPH	22	2-dr. Coupe-5P	11300	2385	Note 1
LPH	42	4-dr. Sedan-5P	11500	2416	Note 2

NEON SPORT (FOUR)

LPS	22	2-dr. Coupe-5P	12500	2469	Note 1
LPS	42	4-dr. Sedan-5P	12700	2456	Note 2

Note: Dodge Neon production totals are separate and can be found in the Dodge listings.

Note 1: Plymouth Neon two-door production totaled 28,129 with no further breakout available.

Note 2: Plymouth Neon four-door production totaled 75,684 with no further breakout available.

BREEZE (FOUR)

APH	41	4-dr. Sedan-5P	15110	2931	46,355

ENGINE DATA: BASE FOUR (Neon, Neon Highline, Neon Sport, Breeze): Inline, overhead cam four-cylinder. Cast iron block; aluminum head. Displacement: 121 cu. in. (2.0 liters). Bore & stroke: 3.44 x 3.27 in. Compression ratio: 9.8:1. Brake horsepower: 132 at 6000 RPM. Torque: 129 lb.-ft. at 5000 RPM. Sequential fuel injection. OPTIONAL FOUR

(Neon, Neon Highline, Neon Sport): Inline, dual overhead cam four-cylinder. Cast iron block; aluminum head. Displacement: 121 cu. in. (2.0 liters). Bore & stroke: 3.44 x 3.27 in. Compression ratio: 9.8:1. Brake horsepower: 150 at 6800 RPM. Torque: 131 lb.-ft. at 5600 RPM. Sequential fuel injection.

CHASSIS DATA: Wheelbase: (Neon) 104.0 in.; (Breeze) 108.0 in. Overall length: (Neon) 171.8 in.; (Breeze) 186.3 in. Height: (Neon cpe) 53.0 in.; (Neon sed) 52.8 in.; (Breeze) 51.9 in. Width: (Neon) 67.5 in.; (Breeze) 71.7 in. Front Tread: (Neon) 57.4 in.; (Breeze) 60.2 in. Rear Tread: (Neon) 57.4 in.; (Breeze) 60.2 in. Standard Tires: (Neon - all) P185/65R14; (Breeze) P195/70R14.

TECHNICAL: Transmission: (All) Five-speed manual. Steering: (All) Rack and pinion. Front suspension: (Neon) MacPherson struts, asymmetrical lower control arms, coil springs and link-type stabilizer bar; (Breeze) Unequal length upper/lower control arms, coil springs, tubular shock absorbers and stabilizer bar. Rear suspension: (Neon) Chapman struts, coil springs, dual lower transverse links, lower trailing links; (Breeze) Unequal length upper/lower control arms, trailing arms, coil springs, tubular shock absorbers and stabilizer bar. Brakes: (All) Front disc, rear drum (power-assisted). Body construction: (All) Unibody. Fuel tank: (Neon) 12.5 gals.; (Breeze) 16.0 gals.

DRIVETRAIN OPTIONS: Engines: DOHC 2.0-liter four: Neon cpe (N/A); Neon sed (N/A); Neon Sport ($150); Transmission: Performance five-speed manual trans.: Neon Sport ($150). Three-speed auto. trans.: Neon ($600). Four-speed auto. trans.: Breeze ($1050). Brakes: Anti-lock: Neon, all ($565); Breeze ($565).

NEON CONVENIENCE/APPEARANCE OPTIONS: Base: Pkg. 21A: stnd equip. (NC). Pkg. 22A: 21A exc. 3-spd auto. trans. replaces 5-spd manual ($600). ACR Competition Pkg.: incl. pwr asst. 14-in. disc brakes, unlimited spd engine controller, body-color fascias, dual exterior manual remote mirrors, H.D. radiator, 16:1 pwr asst. steering, competition susp., tach, compact spare tire, P175/65HR14 perf. tires, 14-in. cast alum whls: cpe ($1800); sed ($1630). Highline: Pkg. 21C: stnd equip. (NC). Pkg. 22C: 21C exc. 3-spd auto. trans. replaces 5-spd manual ($600). Pkg. 21D: 21C plus air cond., floor-mounted console, rear window defroster ($785). Pkg. 22D: 21D exc. 3-spd auto. trans. replaces 5-spd manual ($1385). Expresso Pkg. 21G: 21D plus "Expresso" graphics, pwr bulge hood, "Flash Decor" interior trim, decklid spoiler, tach ($965). Expresso Pkg. 22G: 21G exc. 3-spd auto. trans. replaces 5-spd manual ($1565). Sport: Pkg. 21J: stnd equip. (NC). Pkg. 22J: 21J exc. 3-spd auto. trans. replaces 5-spd manual ($600). Pkg. 23J: 21J exc. Perf. 5-spd manual trans. replaces 5-spd manual ($150). Pkg. 24J: 23J exc. 3-spd auto. trans. replaces Perf. 5-spd manual ($750). Pkg. 21K: 21J plus air cond., floor mats, AM/FM stereo radio w/prem. cass. & CD changer & 6 spkrs ($1050). Pkg. 22K: 21K exc. 3-spd auto. trans. replaces 5-spd manual ($1650). Pkg. 23K: 21K exc. DOHC 2.0L four replaces SOHC 2.0L four and Perf. 5-spd manual trans. replaces 5-spd manual ($1200). Pkg. 24K: 23K exc. 3-spd auto. trans. replaces Perf. 5-spd manual ($1800). Other: (AJP) Pwr Convenience Grp.: incl. dual pwr remote mirrors, pwr door locks, stnd Sport: cpe ($260); sed ($300). (AJK) Dlx Convenience Grp.: incl. auto. spd control, tilt stng, Highline ($350). Integrated child seat ($100). Air cond., base ($1000). Rear window defroster, base and Highline ($205). Calif. emissions ($105). Floor mats ($50). Light Grp., Highline and Sport ($130). Dual remote manual mirrors, base ($70). Bodyside mldg, base ($60). Pwr moonroof, Highline and Sport ($595). (RAL) AM/FM stereo radio w/clock & 4 spkrs, base ($334). (RAS) AM/FM stereo radio w/cass., clock & 6 prem. spkrs: base ($585); Highline ($250). (RBS) AM/FM stereo radio w/prem. cass., CD changer, clock & 6 prem. spkrs, Highline ($300). (RBG) AM/FM stereo radio w/CD player, clock & 6 prem. spkrs, Highline and Sport ($180-$480). Remote keyless entry w/panic alarm, Highline and Sport ($155). Speed control, Sport ($224). Tilt stng, base and Highline ($150). Tach & Low Fuel Warning Light, Highline ($95). Extra cost paint, N/A Sport ($100). Pwr windows, Highline and Sport ($265). "Flash" Decor cloth bucket seats, Sport ($120). 14-in. cast alum whls, Sport ($355).

BREEZE CONVENIENCE/APPEARANCE OPTIONS: Pkg. 21A: stnd equip. (NC). Pkg. 22A: incl. 21A plus 4-spd auto. trans. replaces 5-spd manual ($1050). Pkg. 21B: incl. 21A plus pwr windows, pwr door locks, dual pwr heated black mirrors, 4-way manual adjustable driver's seat ($665). Pkg. 22B: incl. 21B plus 4-spd auto. trans. replaces 5-spd manual ($1715). Other: (AJF) Personal Security Grp.: incl. remote keyless entry w/panic alarm, illum. entry ($170). Integrated child's seat ($100). Calif. emissions ($105). Eng block & battery heater ($30). Extra cost paint ($100). Candy Apple Red Metallic paint ($150). (RBS) AM/FM stereo radio w/Premium cass., CD changer & 4 spkrs ($275). (RBG) AM/FM stereo radio w/CD player & 4 spkrs ($400). Smokers Grp. w/ashtray & lighter ($15). Sunroof ($695). Conventional spare tire ($125).

HISTORY: Model year production: 150,168. Calendar year sales: 169,972. The 1997 Plymouth Prowler roadster — a factory "retro" rod —debuted at Detroit's North American International Auto Show in January 1996. By April, consumer interest in the Prowler included 14,000 letters, 8,000 Internet inquiries and 200 cash deposits from potential buyers. In August 1996, the Chrysler-Plymouth and Jeep-Eagle divisions of Chrysler Corp. were consolidated. Beginning in late-1995, Plymouth addressed how its vehicles were shopped and sold while attempting to make the

experience more enjoyable. The automaker introduced an innovative vehicle shopping process called Plymouth Place whereby consumers in over 60 U.S. markets could use interactive computer kiosks to "build" their own Plymouth on paper. On-site advisers assisted shoppers with lists of area dealerships and information on all aspects of Plymouth vehicles. Ray Fisher, general manager of Chrysler-Plymouth Division, said Plymouth Place offered a "...win-win situation all around. Customers like it because they are better informed before they enter a showroom. Dealers like it because customers are more often ready to buy by the time they enter a showroom."

1997 PLYMOUTH

The auto industry "buzz" in 1997 centered around Plymouth's launch (in March) of the production Prowler roadster — a modern tribute to the days of hot rods and cars that made statements of individualism. The "retro-style" two-passenger roadster used V-6 power and was finished in Prowler Purple, the only color available. The Sport trim level that was formerly part of the Neon lineup was dropped, but an optional Sport Package was offered for Neon Highline coupes and sedans.

1997 Plymouth, Neon Highline sedan with optional body-color aluminum wheels (OCW)

NEON — SERIES L — FOUR — The Sport trim level previously offered in the Neon lineup was dropped, but an optional Sport package was offered on the Highline coupe and sedan. Also returning to the lineup was the base coupe and sedan. When the Sport package was ordered, the resulting Highline coupe or sedan featured the standard 2.0-liter four-cylinder engine paired with a five-speed manual transmission, but the dual overhead cam version of the 2.0-liter four was a no-charge option. Also optional were a three-speed automatic or the performance five-speed manual transmission. The Sport package also consisted of a power bulge hood (when the DOHC engine was ordered) with specific graphics, rear spoiler, fog lights, 14-inch bolt-on wheel covers, low-back front bucket seats, silver "Sport" bodyside decals, low-back front bucket seats, Tango cloth interior, 60/40 split-folding rear seatback, 8000-rpm tach and front-passenger grab handle. Eleven exterior colors were offered with the Sport package: Black, Bright White, Light Iris, Brilliant Blue, Bright Jade, Flame Red, Emerald Green, Magenta, Strawberry, Lapis Blue and (new for 1997 on Highline or Sport models) Deep Amethyst. The Transitional Low Emission Vehicle (TLEV) version of the Neon was again offered for California and markets requiring California emission controls. For 1997, Neons received a structural oil pan for quieter operation, reduced evaporative emissions, dynamic side impact protection (sedans only), redesigned bolt-on wheel covers and two new interior color choices: Agate and Camel. New optional equipment included "Tango" cloth interior fabric and CD player (Highline only).

1997 Plymouth, Breeze sedan (OCW)

BREEZE — SERIES A — FOUR — The Breeze sedan returned for its second year with several improvements that were mainly "cosmetic" in nature. Powertrain availability carried over unchanged from the previous year. New features included a floor console with armrest and covered storage, revised rear seat heat ducts that allowed increased flow, an LED-lighted PRNDL display in console, and improved audio systems including

cassette and CD players. Buyers of the Stone White Breeze now received body-color wheel covers. Changes to exterior color choices were Dark Chestnut and Deep Amethyst replaced Light Gold and Orchid. Revised exterior ornamentation featured new dimensional decal nameplates.

1997 Plymouth, Prowler roadster (OCW)

PROWLER — SERIES R — V-6 — Production of the rear-wheel-drive Prowler roadster began in March 1997 at Chrysler Corp.'s Conner Avenue plant in Detroit. This plant also housed Dodge Viper production. The "factory hot rod's" powertrain consisted of a 24-valve 3.5-liter V-6 with stainless steel exhaust manifolds and a rear-mounted 4EATX electronically controlled four-speed with AutoStick transmission control system. Curb weight of the Prowler was approximately 2,800 pounds of which 900 was derived from aluminum components including body panels, frame and suspension pieces. Prowler's standard equipment included dual air-bags, dynamic side impact protection, air conditioning system charged with non-CFC R-134A refrigerant, four-wheel vented disc brakes, manual black cloth convertible top, remote hood and decklid releases, electric (convertible top) rear window defroster, power windows, power door locks with automatic time delay, dual power body-color exterior mirrors, remote keyless entry with theft alarm, color-keyed three-point Unibelt seat belts, leather low-back bucket seats with halo headrests, AM/FM stereo radio with cassette/CD player and seven speakers, composite aerodynamic quad projector beam headlights, electronic speed control, leather-wrapped steering wheel and shift knob, tilt steering column with tach, cast aluminum wheels and wet arm intermittent wipers. Optional was a lightweight body-color towed storage trailer (obviously, the Prowler lacked luggage space!). Prowler rode on "run flat" P225/45R17 tires up front and P295/40R20 tires in back. Wheelbase measured 113.0 inches while overall length was 165.0 inches. With its ragtop up, Prowler's height was 51.0 inches. Among the many unique features of the Prowler was the "motorcycle-type" front fenders that were attached to the rear of the spindle assembly and turned in conjunction with the direction the car was being steered.

I.D. DATA: Plymouth's 17-symbol Vehicle Identification Number (VIN), as before, was on the upper left corner of the instrument panel, visible through the windshield. Coding is similar to 1986-96. Symbol ten (model year) changed to 'V' for 1997.

NEON (FOUR)

Model No.	Body/ Style No.	Body Type & Seating	Factory Price	Shipping Weight	Prod. Total
LPL	22	2-dr. Coupe-5P	10395	2389	Note 1
LPL	42	4-dr. Sedan-5P	10595	2399	Note 2

NEON HIGHLINE (FOUR)

LPH	22	2-dr. Coupe-5P	12470	2416	Note 1
LPH	42	4-dr. Sedan-5P	12670	2459	Note 2

Note: Dodge Neon production totals are separate and can be found in the Dodge listings.

Note 1: Plymouth Neon two-door production totaled 22,108 with no further breakout available.

Note 2: Plymouth Neon four-door production totaled 60,713 with no further breakout available.

BREEZE (FOUR)

APH	41	4-dr. Sedan-5P	14795	2931	70,579

PROWLER (V-6)

RPS	27	2-dr. Rdstr-2P	35000	2800	Note 1

Note 1: Chrysler Corp. announced a first-year production goal of 3,000 Prowlers, but 1997 calendar year sales list only 120 Prowlers sold. No other information was available.

ENGINE DATA: BASE FOUR (Neon, Neon Highline, Breeze): Inline, overhead cam four-cylinder. Cast iron block; aluminum head. Displacement: 121 cu. in. (2.0 liters). Bore & stroke: 3.44 x 3.27 in. Compression ratio: 9.8:1. Brake horsepower: 132 at 6000 RPM. Torque: 129 lb.-ft. at 5000 RPM. Sequential fuel injection. OPTIONAL FOUR (Neon, Neon Highline): Inline, dual overhead cam four-cylinder. Cast iron block; aluminum head. Displacement: 121 cu. in. (2.0 liters). Bore & stroke: 3.44 x 3.27 in. Compression ratio: 9.6:1. Brake horsepower: 150 at 6500 RPM. Torque: 133 lb.-ft. at 5500 RPM. Sequential fuel injection. BASE V-6 (Prowler) High-output, 24-valve overhead cam V-6. Aluminum block and heads. Displacement: 215 cu. in. (3.5 liters). Bore & stroke: 3.78 x 3.19 in. Compression ratio: 10.1:1. Brake horsepower: 214 at 5800 RPM. Torque: 221 lb.-ft. at 3100 RPM. Sequential fuel injection.

CHASSIS DATA: Wheelbase: (Neon) 104.0 in.; (Breeze) 108.0 in.; (Prowler) 113.0 in. Overall length: (Neon) 171.8 in.; (Breeze) 186.3 in.; (Prowler) 165.0 in. Height: (Neon cpe) 53.0 in.; (Neon sed) 52.8 in.; (Breeze) 51.9 in.; (Prowler) 51.0 in. Width: (Neon) 67.5 in.; (Breeze) 71.7 in.; (Prowler) 76.0 in. Front Tread: (Neon) 57.4 in.; (Breeze) 60.2 in.; (Prowler) 62.0 in. Rear Tread: (Neon) 57.4 in.; (Breeze) 60.2 in.; (Prowler) 63.0 in. Standard Tires: (Neon) P175/70R14; (Neon Highline) P185/65R14; (Breeze) P195/70R14; (Prowler) P225/45R17 front and P295/40R20 rear.

TECHNICAL: Transmission: (Neon, Breeze) Five-speed manual; (Prowler) Four-speed automatic with AutoStick. Steering: (All) Rack and pinion. Front suspension: (Neon) MacPherson struts, asymmetrical lower control arms, coil springs and link-type stabilizer bar; (Breeze) Unequal length upper/lower control arms, coil springs, tubular shock absorbers and stabilizer bar; (Prowler) Semi-solid forged aluminum unequal length upper and lower control arms, pushrod-rocker arm-operated coil springs over low-pressure gas-charged rebound-adjustable shock absorbers and stabilizer bar. Rear suspension: (Neon) Chapman struts, coil springs, dual lower transverse links, lower trailing links; (Breeze) Unequal length upper/lower control arms, trailing arms, coil springs, tubular shock absorbers and stabilizer bar; (Prowler) Multi-link short/long arm independent, coil springs over low-pressure gas-charged rebound-adjustable shock absorbers and stabilizer bar. Brakes: (Neon, Breeze) Front disc, rear drum (power-assisted); (Prowler) Front/rear vented disc (power-assisted). Body construction: (Neon, Breeze) Unibody; (Prowler) Body on frame (bonded/riveted aluminum alloy frame). Fuel tank: (Neon) 12.5 gals.; (Breeze) 16.0 gals.; (Prowler) 12.0 gals.

DRIVETRAIN OPTIONS: Engines: DOHC 2.0-liter four: Neon cpe (N/A); Neon sed (N/A); Neon Highline ($300); Transmission: Three-speed auto. trans.: Neon ($600). Four-speed auto. trans.: Breeze ($1050). Brakes: Anti-lock: Neon, all ($565); Breeze ($565).

NEON CONVENIENCE/APPEARANCE OPTIONS: Base: Pkg. 21A: stnd equip. (NC). Pkg. 22A: 21A exc. 3-spd auto. trans. replaces 5-spd manual ($600). Highline: Pkg. 21D: stnd equip. (NC). Pkg. 22D: 21D exc. 3-spd auto. trans. replaces 5-spd manual ($600). Sport Pkg. 21G: 21D plus "Sport" graphics, pwr bulge hood, "Tango" interior trim, decklid spoiler, tach, 14-in. Sport whl covers, painted fascias, foglamps, low-back bucket seats, 60/40 rear fldng bench seat ($300). Pkg. 22G: 21G exc. 3-spd auto. trans. replaces 5-spd manual ($900). Pkg. 23G: 21G exc. DOHC 2.0L four replaces SOHC 2.0L four ($300). Pkg. 24G: 21G exc. DOHC 2.0L four replaces SOHC 2.0L four and 3-spd auto. trans. replaces 5-spd manual ($900). Competition: Pkg. 23A: ACR Competition Pkg.: incl. pwr asst. 14-in. disc brakes, DOHC 2.0L four (N/A base sed), pwr bulge hood, unlimited spd engine controller, body-color fascias, dual exterior manual remote mirrors, H.D. radiator, 16:1 pwr asst. steering, competition susp., tach, compact spare tire, P175/65HR14 perf. tires (sed)/P185/60HR14 perf. tires (cpe), 14-in. cast alum whls: cpe ($1750); sed w/SOHC 2.0L four ($1560). Other: (ANC) National Champion Int. Pkg.: incl. "Tango" cloth int. trim, low-back bucket seats, 60/40 rear fldng bench seat, leather-wrapped stng whl & shift knob, base ($500). (AJP) Pwr Convenience Grp.: incl. dual pwr remote mirrors, pwr door locks, Highline: cpe ($260); sed ($300). (AJK) Dlx Convenience Grp.: incl. auto. spd control, tilt stng, Highline ($350). Integrated child seat ($100). Air cond. ($1000). Rear window defroster ($205). Calif. emissions ($170). Floor mats ($50). Light Grp., Highline ($130). Body-color mirrors ($70). Body-color mldg ($60). Pwr moonroof ($595). (RAL) AM/FM stereo radio & 4 spkrs, base ($335). (RAS) AM/FM stereo radio w/cass. & 8 spkrs: base ($595); Highline ($260). (RBS) AM/FM stereo radio w/prem. cass., CD changer & 8 spkrs, Highline ($285). (RBR) AM/FM stereo radio w/CD player & 8 spkrs, Highline ($395). Remote keyless entry w/panic alarm, Highline ($155). Tilt stng, base ($150). Tach & Low Fuel Warning Light, Highline ($100). Pwr windows, Highline ($265). 14-in. cast alum whls, Highline ($355).

BREEZE CONVENIENCE/APPEARANCE OPTIONS: Pkg. 21A: stnd equip. (NC). Pkg. 22A: incl. 21A plus 4-spd auto. trans. replaces 5-spd manual ($1050). Pkg. 21B: incl. 21A plus pwr windows, pwr door locks, floor mats, dual pwr heated black mirrors, 4-way manual adjustable driver's seat ($685). Pkg. 22B: incl. 21B plus 4-spd auto. trans. replaces 5-spd manual and elect. cruise control ($1735). Other: (AJF) Personal Security Grp.: incl. remote keyless entry w/panic alarm, illum. entry, headlamp time delay ($170). Integrated child's seat ($100). Calif. emissions ($170). Eng block & battery heater ($30). Candy Apple Red Metallic

paint ($200). (RAS) AM/FM stereo radio w/cass. & 4 spkrs ($180). (ARR) Prem. AM/FM stereo radio w/CD player & 4 spkrs ($380). (AR5) Prem. AM/FM stereo radio w/cass., 6-Disc CD changer in dash & 4 spkrs ($730). Smokers Grp. w/ashtray & lighter ($20). Sunroof ($695). Conventional spare tire ($125).

PROWLER CONVENIENCE/APPEARANCE OPTIONS: Towed, body-color storage trailer (N/A).

HISTORY: Model year production: 153,400 (not including Prowler for which production figures were not available). Calendar year sales: 159,417. The Plymouth Pronto concept car was unveiled at Detroit's North America International Auto Show in January 1997. The Pronto was a five-door, four-passenger sedan that featured a roll-back fabric roof and Prowler-like stand-alone bumpers and frontal appearance. While the actual concept car was constructed of traditional automotive materials, the intent was to explore the use of all-composite plastic with molded-in color to form its body. The Pronto's wheelbase measured 101.0 inches contained within a 148.0-inch overall length. It was powered by a 2.0-liter four-cylinder engine linked to a three-speed automatic transaxle. Pronto's exterior finish was Cool Vanilla and featured a Vanilla with Sage Accents interior color scheme.

1998 PLYMOUTH

The Neon lineup was revamped for 1998 with the formerly available base coupe and sedan discontinued. Neons were now available in three package formats: Highline, Expresso and Style (sedan only). With the early (spring 1998) launch of the 1999 Prowler, there was no 1998 model. (Carry-over 1997 Prowlers were available up to the 1999 Prowler's release.) Breeze now also offered an optional Expresso package as well as an optional 2.4-liter four-cylinder engine, which was a running change in mid-model year 1997.

1998 Plymouth, Neon Highline sedan with optional Style package (OCW)

NEON — SERIES L — FOUR — The previously offered base coupe and sedan were discontinued, and that entry level position was filled by the former second-tier Highline coupe and sedan. Standard features of this newly-entry level Neon included an upgraded interior, low-back bucket seats, remote trunk release and fold-down rear seat. In addition to the Highline trim level (or package), two other Neon packages available were the Expresso coupe and sedan and Style (sedan only). An optional ARC Competition Group package was also offered and included four-wheel disc brakes, firm-feel power steering, competition suspension, and leather-wrapped steering wheel and shift knob. The Neon Style sedan's standard features included power sunroof, AM/FM stereo radio with cassette and CD changer controls, power windows and door locks, power mirrors, leather-wrapped steering wheel and shift knob, unique 14-inch wheel covers and specific bright badging. Exclusive to the Style were five exterior color choices: Candy Apple Red, Champagne, Deep Slate, Deep Cranberry and Bright Platinum. Interior color choices were Agate and Camel, both offered with special "Tango" cloth seat trim. All 1998 Neons benefited from NVH (noise, vibration and harshness) reduction including a new transmission housing structural collar, as well as a new ignition lock for improved security. As did other Chrysler products, the Neon received next-generation airbags for driver and passenger. All Plymouth Neon models were powered by the 2.0-liter four-cylinder engine - refined in 1998 to reduce noise - paired with a five-speed manual transmission. Optional on the Highline and Expresso models was the 150-horsepower dual overhead cam version of the 2.0-liter four. The three-speed automatic transaxle was optional on all Neons.

BREEZE — SERIES A — FOUR — The offerings in the Breeze series increased in 1998 through an Expresso option package available to "dress-up" the sedan. The Breeze Expresso featured specific badging, unique interior fabric, accent color on front and rear fascias, AM/FM stereo radio with cassette and unique 14-inch wheel covers. It was created as

a companion to the Neon Expresso and Voyager Expresso (minivan) models that Plymouth marketed. The Breeze was again powered by the 16-valve 2.0-liter four-cylinder engine - refined in 1998 to reduce noise - paired with a five-speed manual transaxle with overdrive. Optional was an electronically controlled four-speed automatic with speed control that could be linked to the 2.0-liter four or, beginning mid-model year 1997 as a running change, to the optional 150-horsepower, dual overhead cam 2.4-liter four. Also newly optional were a low emission vehicle (LEV) version of the 2.0-liter four or transitional low emission vehicle (TLEV) version of the 2.4-liter four. Breeze also received next-generation airbags for driver and passenger as well as a new ignition lock for improved security. New exterior color choices were: Flame Red, Deep Cranberry, Alpine Green, Bright Platinum, Champagne Pearl and Deep Slate.

PROWLER — SERIES R — V-6 — There was no "true" 1998 Prowler model, with the 1997 version being carried over for sale until the spring of 1998 when production of the 1999 Prowler began.

I.D. DATA: Plymouth's 17-symbol Vehicle Identification Number (VIN), as before, was on the upper left corner of the instrument panel, visible through the windshield. Coding is similar to 1986-97. Symbol ten (model year) changed to 'W' for 1998.

NEON HIGHLINE (FOUR)

Model No.	Body/Style No.	Body Type & Seating	Factory Price	Shipping Weight	Prod. Total
LPH	22	2-dr. Coupe-5P	11155	2470	Note 1
LPH	42	4-dr. Sedan-5P	11355	2507	Note 2

NEON EXPRESSO (FOUR)

LPL	22	2-dr. Coupe-5P	12980	N/A	Note 1
LPL	42	4-dr. Sedan-5P	13160	N/A	Note 2

NEON STYLE (FOUR)

N/A	42	4-dr. Sedan-5P	14095	N/A	Note 2

Note: Dodge Neon production totals are separate and can be found in the Dodge listings.

Note 1: Plymouth Neon two-door production totaled 18,545 with no further breakout available.

Note 2: Plymouth Neon four-door production totaled 68,521 with no further breakout available.

BREEZE (FOUR)

APH	41	4-dr. Sedan-5P	14675	2929	66,620

PROWLER (V-6)

RPS	27	2-dr. Rdstr-2P	35000	2800	Note 1

Note 1: In 1997, Chrysler Corp. announced a second-year (1998) production goal of between 4,500-5,000 Prowlers. With the "second-generation" 1999 Prowler launched early in spring 1998, production figures for the "1998" (carry-over 1997) Prowler were not available.

ENGINE DATA: BASE FOUR (Neon Highline, Neon Expresso, Neon Style, Breeze): Inline, overhead cam four-cylinder. Cast iron block; aluminum head. Displacement: 121 cu. in. (2.0 liters). Bore & stroke: 3.44 x 3.27 in. Compression ratio: 9.8:1. Brake horsepower: 132 at 6000 RPM. Torque: 129 lb.-ft. at 5000 RPM. Sequential fuel injection. OPTIONAL FOUR (Neon Highline, Neon Expresso): Inline, dual overhead cam four-cylinder. Cast iron block; aluminum head. Displacement: 121 cu. in. (2.0 liters). Bore & stroke: 3.44 x 3.27 in. Compression ratio: 9.6:1. Brake horsepower: 150 at 6500 RPM. Torque: 133 lb.-ft. at 5500 RPM. Sequential fuel injection. OPTIONAL FOUR (Breeze): Inline, dual overhead cam four-cylinder. Cast iron block; aluminum head. Displacement: 148 cu. in. (2.4 liters). Bore & stroke: 3.44 x 3.98 in. Compression ratio: 9.4:1. Brake horsepower: 150 at 5200 RPM. Torque: 167 lb.-ft. at 4000 RPM. Sequential fuel injection. BASE V-6 (Prowler) High-output, 24-valve overhead cam V-6. Aluminum block and heads. Displacement: 215 cu. in. (3.5 liters). Bore & stroke: 3.78 x 3.19 in. Compression ratio: 10.1:1. Brake horsepower: 214 at 5800 RPM. Torque: 221 lb.-ft. at 3100 RPM. Sequential fuel injection.

CHASSIS DATA: Wheelbase: (Neon) 104.0 in.; (Breeze) 108.0 in.; (Prowler) 113.0 in. Overall length: (Neon) 171.8 in.; (Breeze) 186.7 in.; (Prowler) 165.0 in. Height: (Neon) 54.9 in.; (Breeze) 54.9 in.; (Prowler) 51.0 in. Width: (Neon cpe) 67.4 in.; (Neon sed) 67.2 in.; (Breeze) 71.7 in.; (Prowler) 76.0 in. Front Tread: (Neon) 57.4 in.; (Breeze) 60.2 in.; (Prowler) 62.0 in. Rear Tread: (Neon) 57.4 in.; (Breeze) 60.2 in.; (Prowler) 63.0 in. Standard Tires: (Neon Highline, Neon Expresso, Neon Style) P185/65R14; (Breeze) P195/70R14; (Prowler) P225/45R17 front and P295/40R20 rear.

TECHNICAL: Transmission: (Neon, Breeze) Five-speed manual; (Prowler) Four-speed automatic with AutoStick. Steering: (All) Rack and pinion. Front suspension: (Neon) MacPherson struts, asymmetrical lower control arms, coil springs and link-type stabilizer bar; (Breeze) Unequal length upper/lower control arms, coil springs, tubular shock absorbers and stabilizer bar; (Prowler) Semi-solid forged aluminum unequal length upper and lower control arms, pushrod-rocker arm-operated coil springs over low-pressure gas-charged rebound-adjustable shock absorbers and sta-

bilizer bar. Rear suspension: (Neon) Chapman struts, coil springs, dual lower transverse links, lower trailing links; (Breeze) Unequal length upper/lower control arms, trailing arms, coil springs, tubular shock absorbers and stabilizer bar; (Prowler) Multi-link short/long arm independent, coil springs over low-pressure gas-charged rebound-adjustable shock absorbers and stabilizer bar. Brakes: (Neon, Breeze) Front disc, rear drum (power-assisted); (Prowler) Front/rear vented disc (power-assisted). Body construction: (Neon, Breeze) Unibody; (Prowler) Body on frame (bonded/riveted aluminum alloy frame). Fuel tank: (Neon) 12.5 gals.; (Breeze) 16.0 gals.; (Prowler) 12.0 gals.

DRIVETRAIN OPTIONS: Engines: DOHC 2.0-liter four: Neon Highline, Neon Expresso ($150). DOHC 2.4-liter four: Breeze ($450). Transmission: Three-speed auto. trans.: Neon Highline, Neon Expresso, Neon Style ($600). Four-speed auto. trans.: Breeze ($1050). Brakes: Anti-lock: Neon Highline ($515-$565); Breeze ($565).

1998 Plymouth, Breeze sedan with optional Expresso package (OCW)

NEON CONVENIENCE/APPEARANCE OPTIONS: Highline: Pkg. 21D: stnd equip. (NC). Pkg. 22D: 21D exc. 3-spd auto. trans. replaces 5-spd manual ($600). Style sed: Pkg. 21H: incl. air cond., body-color door handles, "Tango" cloth low-back bucket seats, leather-wrapped stng whl & shift knob, tach, Value Fun Grp., 14-in. whl covers ($2140). Pkg. 22H: 21H exc. 3-spd auto. trans. replaces 5-spd manual ($2740). Expresso: Pkg. 23G: incl. DOHC 2.0L four and perf. 5-spd manual trans., air cond., "Expresso" graphics, pwr bulge hood, decklid spoiler, tach, 14-in. Sport whl covers, foglamps, cloth bucket seats ($1300). Pkg. 24G: 23G exc. 3-spd auto. trans. replaces perf. 5-spd manual ($1900). Other: (ACR) Competition Grp.: incl. 4-whl disc brakes, unlimited jack engine controller, radio delete, cloth low-back bucket seats, firm-feel pwr stng, leather-wrapped stng whl & shift knob, competition susp., tach, P175/65HR14 perf. tires (sed)/P185/65HR14 perf. tires (cpe), 14-in. cast alum whls: cpe ($2080); sed ($2060). (AJP) Pwr Convenience Grp.: incl. dual pwr remote mirrors, pwr door locks, Highline: cpe ($260); sed ($300). (AJK) Dlx Convenience Grp.: incl. auto. spd control, tilt stng, Highline ($350). (ALT) Value Grp.: incl. Pwr Convenience Grp., pwr windows, AM/FM stereo radio w/cass. & CD changer, Highline ($540). (ALF) Value/Fun Grp.: incl. Pwr. Convenience Grp., pwr windows, pwr sunroof, AM/FM stereo radio w/prem. cass. & CD changer, Highline ($775-$935). Integrated child seat ($100). Air cond. ($1000). Rear window defroster, Competition ($205). Calif. emissions ($170). Floor mats ($50). Light Grp., Highline ($130). Pwr sunroof ($595). (RAS) AM/FM stereo radio w/cass. & 8 spkrs: Highline ($260); Competition ($565). (RBS) AM/FM stereo radio w/prem. cass., CD changer & 8 spkrs, Highline ($285). (RBR) AM/FM stereo radio w/prem. CD player & 8 spkrs ($110-$395). Remote keyless entry w/panic alarm, Highline ($155). Tilt stng, Highline ($150). Tach, Highline ($100). Pwr windows, Highline ($265). 14-in. cast alum whls, Highline ($355).

BREEZE CONVENIENCE/APPEARANCE OPTIONS: Pkg. 21A: stnd equip. (NC). Pkg. 22A: incl. 21A plus 4-spd auto. trans. replaces 5-spd manual ($1050). Pkg. 21B: incl. 21A plus pwr windows, pwr door locks, floor mats, dual pwr heated black mirrors, 4-way manual adjustable driver's seat ($685). Pkg. 22B: incl. 21B plus 4-spd auto. trans. replaces 5-spd manual and elect. cruise control ($1735). Pkg. 24B: incl. 22B plus 2.4L engine in place of 2.0L ($2185). Other: (ASG) Expresso Pkg.: incl. Expresso badging, body-color fascias w/accent striping, AM/FM stereo radio w/cass., unique seat trim & whl covers ($275). (AJF) Personal Security Grp.: incl. remote keyless entry w/panic alarm, illum. entry ($170). Integrated child's seat ($100). Calif. emissions ($170). Eng block heater ($30). Candy Apple Red Metallic paint ($200). (RAS) AM/FM stereo radio w/cass. & 4 spkrs ($180). (ARR) Prem. AM/FM stereo radio w/CD player & 4 spkrs: w/Expresso Pkg. ($200); w/o ($380). (AR5) Prem. AM/FM stereo radio w/cass., 6-Disc CD changer in dash & 4 spkrs: w/Expresso Pkg. ($550); w/o ($730). Smokers Grp. w/ashtray & lighter ($20). Sunroof ($695). Conventional spare tire ($125).

PROWLER CONVENIENCE/APPEARANCE OPTIONS: Towed, body-color storage trailer (N/A).

HISTORY: Model year production: 153,686 (not including Prowler for which production figures were not available). On the heels of the 1997

concept sedan, another Pronto concept car made its debut at Detroit's 1998 North American International Auto Show. This Pronto was a Spyder mid-engined sports racer and was, like its sedan predecessor, a simulated test vehicle for the use of thermoplastic body technology instead of steel. The Pronto Spyder, a roadster, featured a transverse, mid-mounted supercharged, dual overhead cam 2.4-liter four mated to a five-speed manual transaxle borrowed from the Neon ACR racing package. It featured leather racing shell seats, tortoise shell steering wheel rim with "banjo" spoke design, taillamps with neon tubes, wrap-around windshield and 18-inch cast aluminum wheels. The Pronto Spyder featured a Platinum Silver exterior finish and two-tone Sienna and Beige leather interior.

1999 PLYMOUTH

Big news from the Plymouth camp in 1999 was the return of the Prowler after a one-year absence. The 1999 version of the "retro" roadster was even bolder than before, now offered in Prowler Yellow to go along with the Prowler Purple color introduced in 1997. Mid-model year, Prowler Red and Prowler Black were added as color choices. Prowler's were now powered by the all-new, all-aluminum High-Output 3.5-liter V-6 that could also be found under the hood of the 1999 Chrysler 300M and LHS sedans. This was also slated to be the final year for the coupe body style in the Neon series. The all-new 2000 Neon sedan, in base and LX trim levels, was launched in spring 1999.

1999 Plymouth, Neon Highline sedan with optional sunroof and aluminum wheels (OCW)

NEON — SERIES L — FOUR — Neon's two-coupe and three-sedan lineup consisting of Highline, Expresso and Style (sedan only) trim levels was again offered by Plymouth. Powertrain availability carried over intact from the previous year and changes for 1999 were minimal, due to an all-new 2000 Neon sedan that debuted in showrooms in spring 1999. The Neon coupe body style was no longer produced after the 1999 model year.

1999 Plymouth, Breeze sedan (OCW)

BREEZE — SERIES A — FOUR — The Breeze sedan again comprised the series of the same name, with an Expresso package again optional. Powertrain availability mirrored the previous year with the exception that the optional 2.4-liter four-cylinder engine could now be ordered in LEV (low emission vehicle) configuration. For 1999, Breeze received the previously optional power windows/door locks/mirrors, floor mats and driver's seat height adjuster as standard equipment. Chrysler Corp.'s exclusive SentryKey vehicle immobilizer system was added to the option list. Also new was an upgraded NVH (noise, vibration and harshness) package for the interior, revised wheel covers, air induction resonator added to the 2.0-liter four-cylinder engine, improved suspension tuning to increase ride comfort and two exterior color choices: Inferno Red and Light Cypress Green.

PROWLER — SERIES R — V-6 — After a one-year hiatus, the Prowler returned in 1999 with major changes to its power source and appearance. Production of the "second-generation" Prowler began in the spring of

1998. It was now powered by the all-new, all-aluminum High-Output 3.5-liter V-6 also used in the 1999 Chrysler 300M and LHS sedans. Prowler's V-6 was recalibrated from the Chrysler sedan application to meet more aggressive performance demands. Modifications included the development of a quicker throttle cam and retuned intake and exhaust systems. The electronic controls for the engine and AutoStick four-speed automatic transmission were also revised, including changes to run on premium-grade fuel for optimum performance. The new engine, with its lower noise, vibration and harshness characteristics, reduced NVH levels throughout the car. Improved engine block stiffness and precision balancing of all rotating parts combined to isolate and reduce unwanted engine noise. Output of the new V-6 was 253 horsepower (an increase of 39 over the previously used V-6) while torque increased 34 pound-feet (255 compared to the former 221). The 1999 Prowler, even with more power, also had reduced hydrocarbon emissions in comparison to the 1997 version due to state-of-the-art computer engine management. Also new-for-1999, Prowler featured next-generation dual airbags including a key-operated passenger-side airbag disable switch. Interior changes included illuminated window switches with "express-down" on the driver's side as well as revised trim appearance for Prowler's 320-watt audio system speakers. Outside, three new color choices were available, Prowler Yellow, and added mid-model year, Prowler Red and Prowler Black.

I.D. DATA: Plymouth's 17-symbol Vehicle Identification Number (VIN), as before, was on the upper left corner of the instrument panel, visible through the windshield. Coding is similar to 1986-98. Symbol ten (model year) changed to 'X' for 1999.

*Note: Production totals for 1999 Plymouth automobiles were not available at the time this book went to press.

NEON HIGHLINE (FOUR)

Model No.	Body/ Style No.	Body Type & Seating	Factory Price	Shipping Weight	Prod. Total
LPH	22	2-dr. Coupe-5P	11735	2470	*
LPH	42	4-dr. Sedan-5P	11820	2507	*

NEON EXPRESSO (FOUR)

LPL	22	2-dr. Coupe-5P	12740	N/A	*
LPL	42	4-dr. Sedan-5P	12825	N/A	*

NEON STYLE (FOUR)

N/A	42	4-dr. Sedan-5P	13960	N/A	*

BREEZE (FOUR)

APH	41	4-dr. Sedan-5P	15290	2929	*

PROWLER (V-6)

RPS	27	2-dr. Rdstr-2P	39300	2838	*

ENGINE DATA: BASE FOUR (Neon Highline, Neon Expresso, Neon Style, Breeze): Inline, overhead cam four-cylinder. Cast iron block; aluminum head. Displacement: 121 cu. in. (2.0 liters). Bore & stroke: 3.44 x 3.27 in. Compression ratio: 9.8:1. Brake horsepower: 132 at 6000 RPM. Torque: 129 lb.-ft. at 5000 RPM. Sequential fuel injection. OPTIONAL FOUR (Neon Highline, Neon Expresso): Inline, dual overhead cam four-cylinder. Cast iron block; aluminum head. Displacement: 121 cu. in. (2.0 liters). Bore & stroke: 3.44 x 3.27 in. Compression ratio: 9.6:1. Brake horsepower: 150 at 6500 RPM. Torque: 133 lb.-ft. at 5500 RPM. Sequential fuel injection. OPTIONAL FOUR (Breeze): Inline, dual overhead cam four-cylinder. Cast iron block; aluminum head. Displacement: 148 cu. in. (2.4 liters). Bore & stroke: 3.44 x 3.98 in. Compression ratio: 9.4:1. Brake horsepower: 150 at 5200 RPM. Torque: 167 lb.-ft. at 4000 RPM. Sequential fuel injection. BASE V-6 (Prowler) High-output, 24-valve overhead cam V-6. Aluminum block and heads. Displacement: 215 cu. in. (3.5 liters). Bore & stroke: 3.78 x 3.19 in. Compression ratio: 10.1:1. Brake horsepower: 253 at 6400 RPM. Torque: 255 lb.-ft. at 3950 RPM. Sequential fuel injection.

CHASSIS DATA: Wheelbase: (Neon) 104.0 in.; (Breeze) 108.0 in.; (Prowler) 113.3 in. Overall length: (Neon) 171.8 in.; (Breeze) 186.7 in.; (Prowler) 165.3 in. Height: (Neon) 54.9 in.; (Breeze) 54.9 in.; (Prowler) 50.9 in. Width: (Neon cpe) 67.4 in.; (Neon sed) 67.2 in.; (Breeze) 71.7 in.; (Prowler) 76.5 in. Front Tread: (Neon) 57.4 in.; (Breeze) 60.2 in.; (Prowler) 62.2 in. Rear Tread: (Neon) 57.4 in.; (Breeze) 60.2 in.; (Prowler) 63.5 in. Standard Tires: (Neon Highline, Neon Expresso, Neon Style) P185/65R14; (Breeze) P195/70R14; (Prowler) P225/45HR17 front and P295/40HR20 rear.

TECHNICAL: Transmission: (Neon, Breeze) Five-speed manual; (Prowler) Four-speed automatic with AutoStick. Steering: (All) Rack and pinion. Front suspension: (Neon) MacPherson struts, asymmetrical lower control arms, coil springs and link-type stabilizer bar; (Breeze) Unequal length upper/lower control arms, coil springs, tubular shock absorbers and stabilizer bar; (Prowler) Semi-solid forged aluminum unequal length upper and lower control arms, pushrod-rocker arm-operated coil springs over low-pressure gas-charged rebound-adjustable shock absorbers and stabilizer bar. Rear suspension: (Neon) Chapman struts, coil springs, dual lower transverse links, lower trailing links; (Breeze) Unequal length upper/lower control arms, trailing arms, coil springs, tubular shock absorbers and stabilizer bar; (Prowler) Multi-link short/long arm independent, coil

springs over low-pressure gas-charged rebound-adjustable shock absorbers and stabilizer bar. Brakes: (Neon, Breeze) Front disc, rear drum (power-assisted); (Prowler) Front/rear vented disc (power-assisted). Body construction: (Neon, Breeze) Unibody; (Prowler) Body on frame (bonded/riveted aluminum alloy frame). Fuel tank: (Neon) 12.5 gals.; (Breeze) 16.0 gals.; (Prowler) 12.0 gals.

DRIVETRAIN OPTIONS: Engines: DOHC 2.0-liter four: Neon Highline, Neon Expresso ($150). DOHC 2.4-liter four: Breeze ($450). Transmission: Three-speed auto. trans.: Neon Highline, Neon Expresso, Neon Style ($600). Four-speed auto. trans.: Breeze ($1050). Brakes: Anti-lock: Neon Highline ($515-$565); Breeze ($565).

NEON CONVENIENCE/APPEARANCE OPTIONS: Highline: Pkg. 21D: stnd equip. (NC). Pkg. 22D: 21D exc. 3-spd auto. trans. replaces 5-spd manual ($600). Style sed: Pkg. 21H: incl. air cond., body-color door handles, "Tango" cloth low-back bucket seats, leather-wrapped stng whl & shift knob, tach, power windows, AM/FM stereo radio w/cass. & CD changer controls, 14-in. whl covers ($2140). Pkg. 22H: 21H exc. 3-spd auto. trans. replaces 5-spd manual ($2740). Expresso: Pkg. 23G: incl. DOHC 2.0L four and perf. 5-spd manual trans., air cond., "Expresso" graphics, pwr bulge hood, decklid spoiler, tach, 14-in. Premium whl covers, foglamps, cloth low-back bucket seats ($1300). Pkg. 24G: 23G exc. 3-spd auto. trans. replaces perf. 5-spd manual ($1900). Other: (ACR) Competition Grp.: incl. 4-whl disc brakes, unlimited spd engine controller, radio delete, cloth low-back bucket seats, firm-feel pwr stng, leather-wrapped stng whl & shift knob, competition susp., tach, P175/65HR14 perf. tires (sed)/P185/65HR14 perf. tires (cpe), 14-in. cast alum whls: cpe ($2080); sed ($2060). (AJP) Pwr Convenience Grp.: incl. dual pwr remote mirrors, pwr door locks, Highline: cpe ($260); sed ($300). (AJK) Dlx Convenience Grp.: incl. auto. spd control, tilt stng, Highline ($350-$400). (ALT) Value Grp.: incl. Pwr Convenience Grp., pwr windows, AM/FM stereo radio w/cass. & CD changer, Highline ($540). (ALF) Value/Fun Grp.: incl. Pwr. Convenience Grp., pwr windows, pwr sunroof, AM/FM stereo radio w/prem. cass. & CD changer, Highline ($775-$935). Air cond. ($1000). Rear window defroster, stnd Highline ($205). Calif. emissions (NC). Light Grp., Highline ($130). Pwr sunroof ($595). (RBS) AM/FM stereo radio w/prem. cass., CD changer & 8 spkrs: Highline ($285); w/ACR pkg. ($620). (RBR) AM/FM stereo radio w/prem. CD player & 8 spkrs, Highline ($110-$395). Remote keyless entry w/panic alarm, Highline ($165). Pwr windows, Highline ($265). 14-in. cast alum whls, Highline ($355).

1999 Plymouth, Prowler roadster (OCW)

BREEZE CONVENIENCE/APPEARANCE OPTIONS: Pkg. 21A: stnd equip. (NC). Pkg. 22A: incl. 21A plus 4-spd auto. trans. replaces 5-spd manual ($1050). Pkg. 24A: incl. 22A plus 2.4L engine replaces 2.0L ($1500). Pkg. 21B: incl. 21A plus pwr windows, pwr door locks, floor mats, dual pwr heated black mirrors, 4-way manual adjustable driver's seat (NC). Pkg. 22B: incl. 21B plus 4-spd auto. trans. replaces 5-spd manual ($1050). Pkg. 24B: incl. 22B plus 2.4L engine in place of 2.0L ($1500). Other: (ASG) Expresso Pkg.: incl. Expresso badging, body-color fascias w/accent striping, AM/FM stereo radio w/cass., unique seat trim & whl covers ($275). (AJF) Remote/Illum. Entry Grp.: incl. remote keyless entry w/panic alarm, illum. entry ($170). Calif. emissions ($200). Eng block & battery heater ($30). Extra cost paint ($200). (RAS) AM/FM stereo radio w/cass. & 4 spkrs ($180). (ARR) Prem. AM/FM stereo radio w/CD player & 4 spkrs: w/Expresso Pkg. ($200); w/o ($380). (AR5) Prem. AM/FM stereo radio w/cass., 6-Disc CD changer in dash & 4 spkrs: w/Expresso Pkg. ($550); w/o ($730). Smokers Grp. w/ashtray & lighter ($20). Sunroof ($695). Conventional spare tire ($125).

PROWLER CONVENIENCE/APPEARANCE OPTIONS: Towed, body-color storage trailer (N/A).

HISTORY: Plymouth Division's parent company, DaimlerChrysler, announced in late-1999 that after model year 2001, production of Plymouth cars and minivans would cease.

In its first model year under the new, DaimlerChrysler banner, Plymouth's millennium-ending 2000 lineup saw the most changes in the compact Neon sedan, which, along with its Dodge twin, was completely redesigned for 2000 with attention paid to increased acceleration and reduced engine noise. The all-new 2000 Neon sedan, in base and LX trim levels, was launched in spring 1999, but the slower-selling coupe was dropped. The mid-size Breeze returned again with four-cylinder-only power plants (choice of two), but with an enhanced list of no-cost options including a power driver's seat. Breeze was the lowest-cost version of the higher-line Dodge Stratus and Chrysler Cirrus, both of which were available with V-6 power. For 2000, the audacious retro-styled Prowler lost its purple plumage (as well as yellow) to be replaced by silver. The Prowler palette now consisted of red, black, and silver. There were also refinements to Prowler's suspension system aimed toward better ride and handling.

2000 Plymouth, Neon Highline sedan (OCW)

NEON — SERIES L — FOUR — Neon's lineup now consisted only of sedans, the coupe having been dropped due to sluggish sales, which were available in Highline (base) and LX trim levels. The standard 2.0-liter four carried over from 1999, but no longer was the optional and more powerful dual-overhead-cam version available. Standard equipment included: driver- and passenger-side air bags, power steering w/tilt steering wheel, cloth bucket seats, storage armrest, cupholders, split folding rear seat, AM/FM/cassette stereo radio w/CD changer controls, variable intermittent wipers, rear defogger, passenger-side visor mirror, auxiliary power outlet, remote trunk release, floor mats, dual outside mirrors, and 185/65R14 tires on steel wheels with wheel covers. The optional LX package added comfort and luxury features plus larger wheels and tires.

2000 Plymouth, Breeze sedan (OCW)

519

BREEZE — SERIES A — FOUR — The Breeze sedan continued as the lowest priced member of the Chrysler Cirrus, Dodge Stratus, and Plymouth Breeze triad and came in just one trim level. Engines were again restricted to four cylinders with the 2-liter version as base and the 2.4-liter a no-cost option. A five-speed manual transaxle came standard with the base engine, but an optional four-speed automatic could be had with the larger four. Standard equipment included: driver- and passenger-side air bags, air conditioning, power steering and tilt wheel, cloth upholstery, front bucket seats, folding rear seat, center storage console, cupholders, tachometer, 6-speaker AM/FM/cassette stereo, digital clock, rear defogger, variable intermittent wipers, auxiliary power outlet, remote trunk lid release, visor mirrors, front floor mats, dual remote mirrors, and 195/70R14 tires on steel wheels with wheel covers. Four new exterior colors became available; they were: Shale Green Metallic, Bright Silver Metallic, Black, and Taupe Frost Metallic.

2000 Plymouth, Prowler Roadster (OCW)

PROWLER — SERIES R — V-6 — For the second consecutive year, Prowler returned in 2000 powered by the all-aluminum high-output 3.5-liter V-6 also used in the Chrysler 300M and LHS sedans. Prowler's V-6, however, was warmed up somewhat from the sedan application to meet more aggressive performance demands. The rear-wheel-drive two-seater also continued to use the manually-shiftable AutoStick four-speed automatic transaxle from the 300M. Braking was accomplished by a four-wheel-disc system, but anti-lock brakes and traction control remained unavailable. New for 2000 were tweaks to improve ride and handling through the use of softer springs and recalibrated shock absorbers. Other, minor changes included a chrome bezel and leather boot for the shifter, illuminated gear selector indicator, and an automatic-dimming rear view mirror with integral compass, outside temperature display, and mini trip computer. On the safety front, a new automatic transmission brake-shift interlock prevented the driver from shifting out of Park unless the brake was applied, and a child seat tether anchorage was added. Only two factory options were catalogued for the 2000 Prowler, chrome-plated cast aluminum wheels and the "Woodward Edition" red and black, two-tone paint scheme with red pinstripe. The standard equipment list, however, was quite extensive. It included: 3.5-liter, 253-hp V-6 engine, four-speed AutoStick automatic transmission w/manual-shift capability, driver- and passenger-side air bags, four-wheel disc brakes, air conditioning, power steering w/tilt steering wheel, leather-wrapped steering wheel and shifter, cruise control, leather bucket seats, 6-way manual driver seat w/height adjuster, 2-way manual passenger seat, center console w/armrest, storage, and cupholder, power mirrors, power windows, power door locks, remote keyless entry, tachometer, AM/FM/cassette stereo w/6-disc CD changer, steering-wheel radio controls, auxiliary power outlet, intermittent wipers, rear defogger, power remote trunk lid release, floor mats, theft-deterrent system, manually-operated cloth convertible top, plus 225/45HR17 extended-mobility front tires w/low-pressure sensors and 295/40HR20 extended-mobility rear tires w/low-pressure sensors all mounted on cast aluminum wheels. Outside, one new color choice appeared, but two former colors were dropped. Prowler Yellow and Prowler Purple went bye-bye while Prowler Silver joined Prowler Red and Prowler Black to trim down monotone color selections to three.

I.D. DATA: Plymouth's 17-symbol Vehicle Identification Number (VIN), as before, was on the upper left corner of the instrument panel, visible through the windshield. Coding is similar to 1986-99. Symbol ten (model year) changed to 'Y' for 2000.

*****Note:** Production totals for 2000 Plymouth automobiles were not available at the time this book went to press.

NEON HIGHLINE (FOUR)

Model No.	Body/ Style No.	Body Type & Seating	Factory Price	Shipping Weight	Prod. Total
LPH	41	4-dr. Sed-5P	12490	2559	*

BREEZE (FOUR)

Model No.	Body/ Style No.	Body Type & Seating	Factory Price	Shipping Weight	Prod. Total
APH	41	4-dr. Sed-5P	16080	2945	*

PROWLER (V-6)

Model No.	Body/ Style No.	Body Type & Seating	Factory Price	Shipping Weight	Prod. Total
RPS	27	2-dr. Rdstr-2P	42800	2838	*

ENGINE DATA: BASE FOUR (Neon, Breeze): Inline, overhead cam four-cylinder. Cast iron block; aluminum head. Displacement: 121 cu. in. (2.0 liters). Bore & stroke: 3.44 x 3.27 in. Compression ratio: 9.8:1. Brake horsepower: 132 at 5600 RPM (Neon) 6000 RPM (Breeze). Torque: 130 lb.-ft. at 4600 RPM (Neon) 129 lb.-ft. at 4950 RPM (Breeze). Sequential fuel injection. **OPTIONAL FOUR (Breeze):** Inline, dual overhead cam four-cylinder. Cast iron block; aluminum head. Displacement: 148 cu. in. (2.4 liters). Bore & stroke: 3.44 x 3.98 in. Compression ratio: 9.4:1. Brake horsepower: 150 at 5200 RPM. Torque: 167 lb.-ft. at 4000 RPM. Sequential fuel injection. **BASE V-6 (Prowler)** High-output, 24-valve overhead cam V-6. Aluminum block and heads. Displacement: 215 cu. in. (3.5 liters). Bore & stroke: 3.78 x 3.19 in. Compression ratio: 9.9:1. Brake horsepower: 253 at 6400 RPM. Torque: 255 lb.-ft. at 3950 RPM. Sequential fuel injection.

CHASSIS DATA: Wheelbase: (Neon) 105.0 in.; (Breeze) 108.0 in.; (Prowler) 113.3 in. Overall length: (Neon) 174.4 in.; (Breeze) 186.7 in.; (Prowler) 165.3 in. Height: (Neon) 56.0 in.; (Breeze) 54.9 in.; (Prowler) 50.9 in. Width: (Neon) 67.4 in.; (Breeze) 71.7 in.; (Prowler) 76.5 in. Front Tread: (Neon) 58.0 in.; (Breeze) 60.2 in.; (Prowler) 62.2 in. Rear Tread: (Neon) 58.0 in.; (Breeze) 60.2 in.; (Prowler) 63.5 in. Standard Tires: (Neon) P185/65R14; (Breeze) P195/70R14; (Prowler) P225/45HR17 front and P295/40HR20 rear.

TECHNICAL: Transmission: (Neon, Breeze) Five-speed manual; (Prowler) Four-speed automatic with AutoStick. Steering: (All) Rack and pinion. Front suspension: (Neon) MacPherson struts, asymmetrical lower control arms, coil springs and link-type stabilizer bar; (Breeze) Unequal length upper/lower control arms, coil springs, tubular shock absorbers and stabilizer bar; (Prowler) Anodized cast aluminum unequal length upper and lower control arms, pushrod-rocker arm-operated coil springs over low-pressure gas-charged rebound-adjustable shock absorbers and stabilizer bar. Rear suspension: (Neon) Chapman struts, coil springs, dual lower transverse links, lower trailing links and link-type stabilizer bar; (Breeze) Unequal length upper/lower control arms, trailing arms, coil springs, tubular shock absorbers and stabilizer bar; (Prowler) Multiple lateral upper links, lower A arm, coil springs over low-pressure gas-charged rebound-adjustable shock absorbers and stabilizer bar. Brakes: (Neon, Breeze) Front disc, rear drum (power-assisted); (Prowler) Disc front (vented) and rear (power-assisted). Body construction: (Neon, Breeze) Unibody; (Prowler) Body on frame (bonded/riveted aluminum alloy frame). Fuel tank: (Neon) 12.5 gals.; (Breeze) 16.0 gals.; (Prowler) 12.2 gals.

DRIVETRAIN OPTIONS: DOHC 2.4-liter four: Breeze (NC). Transmission: Three-speed auto. trans.: Neon ($600). Four-speed auto. trans., includes electronic speed control: Breeze ($1050). Brakes: Anti-lock: Neon Highline ($515-$565); Breeze ($565).

NEON CONVENIENCE/APPEARANCE OPTIONS: Highline: Pkg. 21D/22D: stnd equip. (NC). LX: Pkg. 21G/22G: incl. LX badging, air conditioning, color-keyed instrument cluster bezel, keyless entry, pwr door locks w/central locking, pwr heated exterior mirrors, security alarm, Sentry key theft-deterrent system, leather-wrapped strg whl & shift knob, pwr trunk lid release, pwr windows, premium cloth low-back bucket seats, passenger assist handles, fog lamps, tachometer, and P185/60R15 touring tires on 15-inch whls w/wheel covers ($1820). Other: (Highline) Air conditioning ($1000). Dlx Convenience Grp.: incl. automatic spd cntrl w/strg whl switches & tilt strg column—must have A/C ($350). Pwr Convenience Grp.: Pwr heated fold-away mirrors & pwr frnt windows—must have Sentry key security grp. and A/C ($380). Sentry Key Security Grp.: Security alarm, Sentry key theft-deterrent system, four-function keyless entry, tachometer, pwr automatic door locks w/lighted switches, central locking, lock-out protection & enhanced accident response system, pwr trunk lid release—must have A/C ($315). (Highline, LX) 3-spd auto. trans. replaces 5-spd manual ($600). Speed control ($225). 4-disc instrument panel-mounted CD changer ($125). Engine blk htr ($20). 15-in. alum whls w/P185/60R15 Goodyear Eagle LS all-season touring tires—must have A/C ($355-$410). Anti-lock Brake Grp.: incl. anti-lock 4-whl-disc brakes, tachometer, & traction cntrl ($595). Light Grp.: incl. illuminated visor vanity mirrors, inside rear view mirror w/reading lamps, glove compartment lamp, underhood lamp, & console flood lamp ($130). Front ash tray & cigar lighter ($20).

BREEZE CONVENIENCE/APPEARANCE OPTIONS: Pkg. 21A: stnd equip. (NC). Pkg. 24B: Incl. front & rear floor mats, speed sensitive pwr door locks, pwr mirrors, 8-way pwr driver's seat & pwr windows (NC). 4-spd auto. trans. & 2.4-liter four replace 5-spd manual & 2.0-liter four ($1050). Other: Premium AM/FM/cassette stereo radio w/6-disc in-dash CD changer w/control & 6 spkrs ($550). Premium AM/FM/cassette stereo radio w/CD changer control & 8 spkrs ($340). Premium AM/FM w/CD & 6 spkrs ($200). Remote/Illum. Entry Grp.: incl. remote keyless entry w/panic alarm, illum. entry ($170). Eng block & battery heater ($30). Inferno Red paint ($200). Smokers Grp. w/front ash tray & lighter ($20). Pwr sunroof ($695). Conventional spare tire ($125).

PROWLER CONVENIENCE/APPEARANCE OPTIONS: Woodward Edition Grp.: Dramatic '50s rod & custom-style, red & black, two-tone paint combination w/red, handpainted pinstripe, and initialed by customizer/artist Dr. Ru.

HISTORY: After years of rumors of its impending demise, it was finally official. The venerable and proud Plymouth nameplate would become history after the 2001 model year, the first marque casualty of Chrysler Corporaton's merger with Daimler-Benz to form DaimlerChrysler AG. It seems that there was no room in DC's worldwide expansion plans for the redundancies that existed between Plymouth products and those of the Dodge Division. Said DaimlerChrysler President James P. Holden, "As we move forward in our global growth strategy, Plymouth . . . did not contribute to that growth." So, after nearly three-quarters of a century, Plymouth production was to cease.

A WORD ABOUT OLD CHRYSLERS . . .

The market for cars more than 15 years old may be stronger now than ever. Some buyers of pre-1985 cars are collectors who purchase vehicles that they particularly enjoy, or feel are likely to increase in value the older they get. Other buyers prefer the looks, size, performance, and reliability of what they perceive as yesterday's better-built automobiles.

With a typical year 2000 model selling for around $20,000, many Americans find themselves priced out of the new-car market. Late-model used cars can be pricey too, although often short on distinctive looks and roominess. The older cars may use more fuel, but their purchase prices are typically a whole lot lower.

New cars and late-model used cars tend to depreciate rapidly in value. Many can't tow large trailers or mobile homes and their high-tech engineering is often expensive to maintain or repair. In contrast, well-kept older cars are mechanically simpler, but often very powerful. In addition, they generally appreciate in value as they grow scarce and collectable. Even insuring them is generally cheaper.

Selecting a car and paying the right price for it are two considerations old-Chrysler-product buyers face. When did Plymouth first offer a V-8 engine? When was DeSoto introduced to the market and why? Were all Chrysler Town & Countries of the '40s convertibles? What is the horsepower and displacement of a Dodge Viper engine? What specific models were marketed under the Eagle banner?

Standard Catalog of Chrysler 1914-2000 answers these questions and many more. The Price Guide section shows models built between 1914 and 1993 and points out what they sell for today in six different, graded conditions. Cars built since 1993 are generally considered "used cars" of which few, as yet, have excited the interest of collectors.

The price estimates contained in this book are current as of the publication date, February 2000. After that date, more current prices may be obtained by referring to *Old Cars Price Guide*, which is available at many book stores, newsstands, and supermarket magazine departments or directly from Krause Publications, 700 E. State St., Iola, WI 54990-0001, telephone 1-800-258-0929, Code AUBR.

HOW TO USE THE CHRYSLER PRICE GUIDE

On the following pages is a **CHRYSLER PRICE GUIDE**, which lists price estimates for Chrysler-built automobiles (including pre-Chrysler Corp. Dodge Brothers) from 1914 through 2000. These prices are derived from national and regional data compiled by the editors of *Old Cars Weekly News & Marketplace* and *Old Cars Price Guide*. These data include prices actually paid at collector-car auctions and sales, verified reports of private sales, and input from experts. The figures in this book are amounts that fall within a reasonable range of each car's value to both buyers and sellers. The figures are not to be interpreted as "wholesale" or "retail." Rather, each price reflects what an informed buyer might pay a knowledgeable seller for his car in an arm's length transaction without duress to either party. Special cases, where nostalgia or other factors enter into the picture, must be judged on an individual basis.

Price estimates are listed for cars in six different states of condition. These conditions (1-to-6) are illustrated and explained in the **VEHICLE CONDITION SCALE** on the following three pages. Values are for complete vehicles—not

parts cars—except as noted. Values for modified cars are not included, but can be estimated by figuring the cost of restoring the subject vehicle to original condition and adjusting the figures shown here accordingly.

Appearing below is a section of chart taken from the **CHRYSLER PRICE GUIDE** to illustrate the following elements:

A. MAKE The make of car, or marque name, appears in large, boldface type at the beginning of each value section.

B. DESCRIPTION The extreme left-hand column indicates vehicle year, model name, body type, engine configuration, and—in some cases—wheelbase.

C. CONDITION CODE The six columns to the right are headed by the numbers one through six (1-6), which correspond to the conditions described in the **VEHICLE CONDITION SCALE** on the following pages.

D. PRICE The price estimates, in dollars, appear below their respective condition code headings and across from the vehicle descriptions.

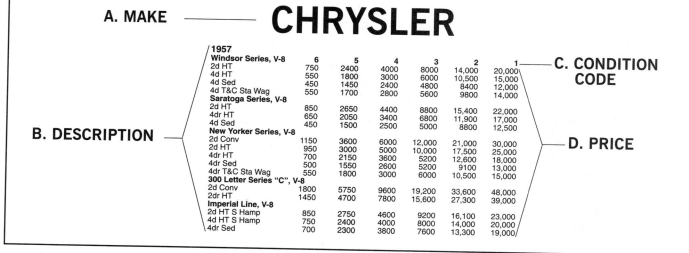

A. MAKE ——— **CHRYSLER**

B. DESCRIPTION / **C. CONDITION CODE** / **D. PRICE**

1957	6	5	4	3	2	1
Windsor Series, V-8						
2d HT	750	2400	4000	8000	14,000	20,000
4d HT	550	1800	3000	6000	10,500	15,000
4d Sed	450	1450	2400	4800	8400	12,000
4d T&C Sta Wag	550	1700	2800	5600	9800	14,000
Saratoga Series, V-8						
2d HT	850	2650	4400	8800	15,400	22,000
4dr HT	650	2050	3400	6800	11,900	17,000
4d Sed	450	1500	2500	5000	8800	12,500
New Yorker Series, V-8						
2d Conv	1150	3600	6000	12,000	21,000	30,000
2d HT	950	3000	5000	10,000	17,500	25,000
4dr HT	700	2150	3600	5200	12,600	18,000
4dr Sed	500	1550	2600	5200	9100	13,000
4dr T&C Sta Wag	550	1800	3000	6000	10,500	15,000
300 Letter Series "C", V-8						
2d Conv	1800	5750	9600	19,200	33,600	48,000
2dr HT	1450	4700	7800	15,600	27,300	39,000
Imperial Line, V-8						
2d HT S Hamp	850	2750	4600	9200	16,100	23,000
4d HT S Hamp	750	2400	4000	8000	14,000	20,000
4dr Sed	700	2300	3800	7600	13,300	19,000

VEHICLE CONDITION SCALE

Excellent

1) EXCELLENT: Restored to current maximum professional standards of quality in every area, or perfect original with components operating and appearing as new. A 95-plus point show vehicle that is not driven.

Fine

2) FINE: Well-restored, or a combination of superior restoration and excellent original. Also, an *extremely* well-maintained original showing very minimal wear.

Very Good

3) VERY GOOD: Completely operable original or "older restoration" showing wear. Also, a good amateur restoration, all presentable and serviceable inside and out. Plus, combinations of well-done restoration and good operable components or a partially restored vehicle with all parts necessary to complete and/or valuable NOS parts.

Good

4) GOOD: A drivable vehicle needing no or only minor work to be functional. Also, a deteriorated restoration or a very poor amateur restoration. All components may need restoration to be "excellent," but the vehicle is mostly usable "as is."

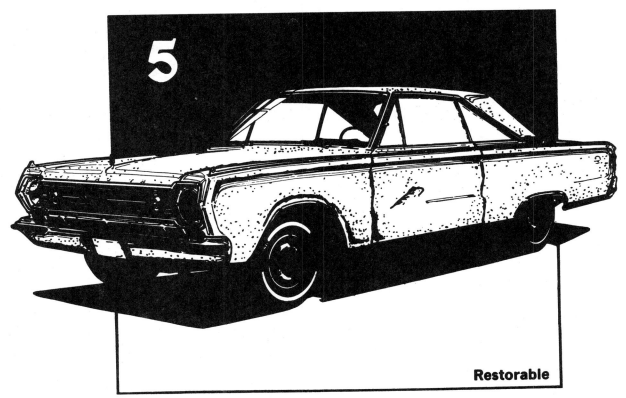

Restorable

5) RESTORABLE: Needs *complete* restoration of body, chassis and interior. May or may not be running, but isn't weathered, wrecked or stripped to the point of being useful only for parts.

Parts Car

6) PARTS VEHICLE: May or may not be running, but is weathered, wrecked and/or stripped to the point of being useful primarily for parts.

CHRYSLER

1924

Model B, 6-cyl., 112.75" wb	6	5	4	3	2	1
2d Rds	700	2300	3800	7600	13,300	19,000
4d Phae	750	2400	4000	8000	14,000	20,000
4d Tr	700	2150	3600	7200	12,600	18,000
2d RS Cpe	450	1450	2400	4800	8400	12,000
4d Sed	400	1200	2000	4000	7000	10,000
2d Brgm	400	1250	2100	4200	7400	10,500
4d Imp Sed	400	1300	2200	4400	7700	11,000
4d Crw Imp	450	1450	2400	4800	8400	12,000
4d T&C	550	1700	2800	5600	9800	14,000

1925

Model B-70, 6-cyl., 112.75" wb	6	5	4	3	2	1
2d Rds	700	2300	3800	7600	13,300	19,000
4d Phae	750	2400	4000	8000	14,000	20,000
4d Tr	700	2150	3600	7200	12,600	18,000
2d Roy Cpe	450	1450	2400	4800	8400	12,000
4d Sed	400	1200	2000	4000	7000	10,000
2d Brgm	400	1250	2100	4200	7400	10,500
4d Imp Sed	400	1300	2200	4400	7700	11,000
4d Crw Imp	450	1450	2400	4800	8400	12,000
4d T&C	550	1700	2800	5600	9800	14,000

1926

Series 58, 4-cyl., 109" wb	6	5	4	3	2	1
2d Rds	700	2150	3600	7200	12,600	18,000
4d Tr	700	2300	3800	7600	13,300	19,000
2d Clb Cpe	400	1300	2200	4400	7700	11,000
2d Sed	350	1000	1650	3300	5750	8200
4d Sed	350	950	1500	3050	5300	7600
Series 60, 6-cyl., 109" wb						
Introduced: May, 1926.						
2d Rds	700	2150	3600	7200	12,600	18,000
4d Tr	700	2300	3800	7600	13,300	19,000
2d Cpe	400	1300	2200	4400	7700	11,000
2d Sed	450	1050	1750	3550	6150	8800
4d Lthr Tr Sed	450	1080	1800	3600	6300	9000
4 dr Sed	350	1040	1700	3450	6000	8600
4d Lan Sed	450	1050	1750	3550	6150	8800
Series G-70, 6-cyl., 112.75" wb						
2d Rds	700	2300	3800	7600	13,300	19,000
4d Phae	750	2400	4000	8000	14,000	20,000
2d Roy Cpe	450	1400	2300	4600	8100	11,500
2d Sed	450	1080	1800	3600	6300	9000
4d Lthr Trm Sed	450	1140	1900	3800	6650	9500
2d Brgm	400	1250	2100	4200	7400	10,500
4d Sed	450	1140	1900	3800	6650	9500
4d Roy Sed	400	1300	2150	4300	7500	10,700
4d Crw Sed	400	1300	2200	4400	7700	11,000
Series E-80 Imperial, 6-cyl., 120" wb						
2d RS Rds	850	2650	4400	8800	15,400	22,000
4d Phae	850	2750	4600	9200	16,100	23,000
2d Cpe	500	1550	2600	5200	9100	13,000
4d 5P Sed	450	1450	2400	4800	8400	12,000
4d 7P Sed	500	1550	2600	5200	9100	13,000
4d Berl	500	1600	2700	5400	9500	13,500

1927

Series I-50, 4-cyl., 106" wb	6	5	4	3	2	1
2d 2P Rds	700	2150	3600	7200	12,600	18,000
2d RS Rds	700	2300	3800	7600	13,300	19,000
4d Tr	700	2150	3600	7200	12,600	18,000
2d Cpe	450	1140	1900	3800	6650	9500
2d Sed	350	1020	1700	3400	5950	8500
4d Lthr Trm Sed	450	1080	1800	3600	6300	9000
4d Sed	350	1000	1650	3350	5800	8300
4d Lan Sed	350	1020	1700	3400	5950	8500
Series H-60, 6-cyl., 109" wb						
2d 2P Rds	800	2500	4200	8400	14,700	21,000
2d RS Rds	850	2650	4400	8800	15,400	22,000
4d Tr	800	2500	4200	8400	14,700	21,000
2d 2P Cpe	400	1200	2000	4000	7000	10,000
2d RS Cpe	400	1250	2100	4200	7400	10,500
2d Sed	450	1090	1800	3650	6400	9100
4d Lthr Trm Sed	450	1140	1900	3800	6650	9500
4d Sed	350	975	1600	3250	5700	8100
Series 'Finer' 70, 6-cyl., 112.75" wb						
2d RS Rds	800	2500	4200	8400	14,700	21,000
4d Phae	850	2650	4400	8800	15,400	22,000
4d Spt Phae	850	2750	4600	9200	16,100	23,000
4d Cus Spt Phae	900	2900	4800	9600	16,800	24,000
2d RS Cabr	750	2400	4000	8000	14,000	20,000
2d 2P Cpe	400	1200	2000	4000	7000	10,000
2d RS Cpe	400	1250	2100	4200	7400	10,500
2d 4P Cpe	450	1190	2000	3950	6900	9900
2d Brgm	450	1150	1900	3850	6700	9600
4d Lan Brgm	450	1160	1950	3900	6800	9700
4d Roy Sed	450	1170	1975	3900	6850	9800
4d Crw Sed	450	1190	2000	3950	6900	9900

1927-Early 1928

Series E-80 Imperial, 6-cyl., 120" & 127" wb	6	5	4	3	2	1
2d RS Rds	1000	3100	5200	10,400	18,200	26,000
2d Spt Rds	1000	3250	5400	10,800	18,900	27,000
4d 5P Phae	1000	3250	5400	10,800	18,900	27,000
4d Spt Phae	1050	3350	5600	11,200	19,600	28,000
4d 7P Phae	1000	3100	5200	10,400	18,200	26,000
2d RS Cabr	950	3000	5000	10,000	17,500	25,000
2d Bus Cpe	500	1550	2600	5200	9100	13,000
2d 4P Cpe	500	1600	2700	5400	9500	13,500

2d 5P Cpe	450	1450	2400	4800	8400	12,000
4d Std Sed	400	1200	2000	4000	7100	10,100
4d Sed	400	1200	2000	4000	7000	10,000
4d Lan Sed	400	1300	2200	4400	7700	11,000
4d 7P Sed	400	1350	2250	4500	7800	11,200
4d Limo	500	1550	2600	5200	9100	13,000
4d T&C	550	1700	2800	5600	9800	14,000

1928

Series 52, 4-cyl., 106" wb	6	5	4	3	2	1
2d RS Rds	850	2750	4600	9200	16,100	23,000
4d Tr	400	1250	2100	4200	7400	10,500
2d Clb Cpe	450	1140	1900	3800	6650	9500
2d DeL Cpe	400	1300	2200	4400	7700	11,000
2d Sed	400	1200	2000	4000	7000	10,000
4d Sed	400	1200	2000	4000	7000	10,000
4d DeL Sed	450	1170	1975	3900	6850	9800
Series 62, 6-cyl., 109" wb						
2d RS Rds	900	2900	4800	9600	16,800	24,000
4d Tr	850	2750	4600	9200	16,100	23,000
2d Bus Cpe	350	1020	1700	3400	5950	8500
2d RS Cpe	450	1400	2300	4600	8100	11,500
2d Sed	400	1200	2000	4000	7000	10,000
4d Sed	450	1170	1975	3900	6850	9800
4d Lan Sed	400	1200	2000	4000	7100	10,100
Series 72, 6-cyl., 120.5" wb						
2d RS Rds	850	2750	4600	9200	16,100	23,000
2d Spt Rds	950	3000	5000	10,000	17,500	25,000
2d Conv	800	2500	4200	8400	14,700	21,000
2d RS Cpe	450	1450	2400	4800	8400	12,000
2d 4P Cpe	400	1300	2200	4400	7700	11,000
4d CC Sed	400	1300	2200	4400	7700	11,000
4d Roy Sed	400	1200	2000	4000	7000	10,000
4d Crw Sed	400	1300	2200	4400	7700	11,000
4d Twn Sed	450	1400	2300	4600	8100	11,500
4d LeB Imp Twn Cabr	550	1700	2800	5600	9800	14,000
Series 80 L Imperial, 6-cyl., 136" wb						
2d RS Rds	950	3000	5000	10,000	17,500	25,000
4d Sed	400	1300	2200	4400	7700	11,000
4d Twn Sed	450	1400	2300	4600	8100	11,500
4d 7P Sed	450	1450	2400	4800	8400	12,000
4d Limo	500	1550	2600	5200	9100	13,000
Series 80 L Imperial, 6-cyl., 136" wb, Custom Bodies						
4d LeB DC Phae	2200	6950	11,600	23,200	40,600	58,000
4d LeB CC Conv Sed	1900	6100	10,200	20,400	35,700	51,000
2d LeB RS Conv	1800	5750	9600	19,200	33,600	48,000
2d LeB Clb Cpe	850	2750	4600	9200	16,100	23,000
2d LeB Twn Cpe	850	2650	4400	8800	15,400	22,000
4d LeB Lan Limo	1700	5400	9000	18,000	31,500	45,000
4d Der Conv Sed	1900	6000	10,000	20,000	35,000	50,000
4d Dtrch Conv Sed	2050	6600	11,000	22,000	38,500	55,000
4d 4P Dtrch Phae	2200	6950	11,600	23,200	40,600	58,000
4d 7P Dtrch Phae	2200	6950	11,600	23,200	40,600	58,000
4d Dtrch Sed	1150	3700	6200	12,400	21,700	31,000
4d Lke Phae	1700	5400	9000	18,000	31,500	45,000

1929

Series 65, 6-cyl.), 112.75" wb	6	5	4	3	2	1
2d RS Rds	1000	3100	5200	10,400	18,200	26,000
4d Tr	1000	3250	5400	10,800	18,900	27,000
2d Bus Cpe	600	1900	3200	6400	11,200	16,000
2d RS Cpe	650	2050	3400	6800	11,900	17,000
2d Sed	500	1550	2600	5200	9100	13,000
4d Sed	500	1600	2700	5400	9500	13,500
Series 75, 6-cyl.						
2d RS Rds	1150	3600	6000	12,000	21,000	30,000
4d 5P Phae	1150	3700	6200	12,400	21,700	31,000
4d DC Phae	1200	3850	6400	12,800	22,400	32,000
4d 7P Phae	1150	3600	6000	12,000	21,000	30,000
2d RS Conv	1100	3500	5800	11,600	20,300	29,000
4d Conv Sed	1050	3350	5600	11,200	19,600	28,000
2d RS Cpe	650	2050	3400	6800	11,900	17,000
2d Cpe	600	1900	3200	6400	11,200	16,000
4d Roy Sed	550	1700	2800	5600	9800	14,000
4d Crw Sed	550	1800	3000	6000	10,500	15,000
4d Twn Sed	600	1850	3100	6200	10,900	15,500

1929-30

Series 80 L Imperial, 6-cyl., 136" wb	6	5	4	3	2	1
2d RS Phae	2200	7100	11,800	23,600	41,300	59,000
4d Lke DC Spt Phae	2650	8400	14,000	28,000	49,000	70,000
4d Lke 7P Phae	2500	7900	13,200	26,400	46,200	66,000
4d Lke Conv Sed	2400	7700	12,800	25,600	44,800	64,000
2d Lke RS Conv	1950	6250	10,400	20,800	36,400	52,000
2d 2P Cpe	750	2400	4000	8000	14,000	20,000
2d RS Cpe	850	2750	4600	9200	16,100	23,000
4 dr Sed	650	2050	3400	6800	11,900	17,000
4d Twn Sed	700	2150	3600	7200	12,600	18,000
4d 7P Sed	650	2050	3400	6800	11,900	17,000
4d Limo	800	2500	4200	8400	14,700	21,000

1930-1931 (through December)

Series Six, 6-cyl, 109" wb	6	5	4	3	2	1
(Continued through Dec. 1930).						
2d RS Rds	950	3000	5000	10,000	17,500	25,000
4d Tr	900	2900	4800	9600	16,800	24,000
2d RS Conv	850	2750	4600	9200	16,100	23,000
2d Bus Cpe	550	1700	2800	5600	9800	14,000
2d Roy Cpe	550	1800	3000	6000	10,500	15,000
4d Roy Sed	500	1550	2600	5200	9100	13,000

1930-1931

	6	5	4	3	2	1
Series 66, 6-cyl, 112 3/4" wb						
(Continued through May 1931).						
2d RS Rds	1000	3100	5200	10,400	18,200	26,000
4d Phae	1000	3250	5400	10,800	18,900	27,000
2d Bus Cpe	550	1800	3000	6000	10,500	15,000
2d Roy Cpe	600	1850	3100	6200	10,900	15,500
2d Brgm	500	1550	2600	5200	9100	13,000
4d Roy Sed	550	1700	2800	5600	9800	14,000
Series 70, 6 cyl, 116 1/2" wb						
(Continued through Feb. 1931).						
2d RS Rds	1150	3600	6000	12,000	21,000	30,000
2d RS Conv	1000	3250	5400	10,800	18,900	27,000
4d Phae	1150	3700	6200	12,400	21,700	31,000
2d Bus Cpe	550	1800	3000	6000	10,500	15,000
2d Roy Cpe	600	1850	3100	6200	10,900	15,500
2d Brgm	550	1700	2800	5600	9800	14,000
4d Roy Sed	550	1800	3000	6000	10,500	15,000
Series 77, 6-cyl., 124.5" wb						
2d RS Rds	1600	5050	8400	16,800	29,400	42,000
4d DC Phae	1400	4450	7400	14,800	25,900	37,000
2d RS Conv	1200	3850	6400	12,800	22,400	32,000
2d Bus Cpe	600	1900	3200	6400	11,200	16,000
2d Roy RS Cpe	600	2000	3300	6600	11,600	16,500
2d Crw Cpe	600	1900	3200	6400	11,200	16,000
4d Roy Sed	550	1800	3000	6000	10,500	15,000
4d Crw Sed	600	1900	3200	6400	11,200	16,000

1931-1932

	6	5	4	3	2	1
New Series Six, CM, 6-cyl., 116 wb						
(Produced Jan. -Dec. 1931).						
2d RS Rds	1150	3700	6200	12,400	21,700	31,000
4d Tr	1150	3600	6000	12,000	21,000	30,000
2d RS Conv	1100	3500	5800	11,600	20,300	29,000
2d Bus Cpe	600	1900	3200	6400	11,200	16,000
2d Roy Cpe	600	2000	3300	6600	11,600	16,500
4d Roy Sed	550	1800	3000	6000	10,500	15,000
Series 70, 6-cyl, 116 1/2" wb						
2d Bus Cpe	600	2000	3300	6600	11,600	16,500
2d Roy Cpe	650	2050	3400	6800	11,900	17,000
2d Brgm	600	1900	3200	6400	11,200	16,000
4d Roy Sed	600	1900	3200	6400	11,200	16,000
First Series, CD, 8--cyl., 80 hp, 124" wb						
(Built 7/17/30 -1/31).						
2d RS Rds	1250	3950	6600	13,200	23,100	33,000
2d Spt Rds	1350	4300	7200	14,400	25,200	36,000
2d Conv	1200	3850	6400	12,800	22,400	32,000
2d Cpe	750	2400	4000	8000	14,000	20,000
2d Spl Cpe	700	2300	3800	7600	13,300	19,000
4d Roy Sed	600	1900	3200	6400	11,200	16,000
4d Spl Roy Sed	650	2050	3400	6800	11,900	17,000
Second Series, CD, 8-cyl., 88 hp, 124" wb						
(Built 2/2/31 -5/18/31).						
2d RS Spt Rds	1900	6100	10,200	20,400	35,700	51,000
4d Lke DC Phae	1800	5750	9600	19,200	33,600	48,000
2d RS Conv	1550	4900	8200	16,400	28,700	41,000
2d Roy Cpe	850	2650	4400	8800	15,400	22,000
2d Spl Roy Cpe	850	2750	4600	9200	16,100	23,000
4d Roy Sed	600	1900	3200	6400	11,200	16,000
2nd Series CD						
4d Spl Roy Sed	650	2050	3400	6800	11,900	17,000
DeLuxe Series, CD, 8-cyl., 100 hp, 124" wb						
(Built 5/19/31 -11/31).						
2d RS Rds	1750	5500	9200	18,400	32,200	46,000
4d Lke DC Phae	1650	5300	8800	17,600	30,800	44,000
2d RS Conv	1550	4900	8200	16,400	28,700	41,000
2d RS Cpe	850	2750	4600	9200	16,100	23,000
2d Roy Cpe	850	2650	4400	8800	15,400	22,000
4d Sed	600	1900	3200	6400	11,200	16,000
Imperial, CG, 8-cyl., 125 hp, 145" wb						
(Built July 17, 1930 thru Dec. 1931).						
Standard Line						
4d CC Sed	1600	5050	8400	16,800	29,400	42,000
4d 5P Sed	1000	3250	5400	10,800	18,900	27,000
4d 7P Sed	1000	3250	5400	10,800	18,900	27,000
4d Limo	1150	3600	6000	12,000	21,000	30,000
Custom Line						
2d LeB RS Rds	10,900	34,800	58,000	116,000	203,000	290,000
4d LeB DC Phae	10,700	34,200	57,000	114,000	199,500	285,000
4d LeB Conv Sed	10,500	33,600	56,000	112,000	196,000	280,000
2d LeB RS Cpe	3750	12,000	20,000	40,000	70,000	100,000
2d Wths Conv Vic	9750	31,200	52,000	104,000	182,000	260,000
2d LeB Conv Spds	9400	30,000	50,000	100,000	175,000	250,000

1932

	6	5	4	3	2	1
Second Series, CI, 6-cyl., 116-1/2" wb, 82 hp						
(Begun 1/1/32).						
2d RS Rds	1000	3250	5400	10,800	18,900	27,000
4d Phae	1000	3100	5200	10,400	18,200	26,000
2d RS Conv	950	3000	5000	10,000	17,500	25,000
4d Conv Sed	1000	3100	5200	10,400	18,200	26,000
2d Bus Cpe	650	2050	3400	6800	11,900	17,000
2d RS Cpe	700	2150	3600	7200	12,600	18,000
4d Sed	550	1800	3000	6000	10,500	15,000
Series CP, 8-cyl., 125" wb, 100 hp						
(Began 1/1/32).						
2d RS Conv	1150	3600	6000	12,000	21,000	30,000
4d Conv Sed	1150	3700	6200	12,400	21,700	31,000
2d RS Cpe	900	2900	4800	9600	16,800	24,000
2d Cpe	850	2650	4400	8800	15,400	22,000
4d Sed	600	1900	3200	6400	11,200	16,000
4d LeB T&C	850	2650	4400	8800	15,400	22,000
Imperial Series, CH, 8-cyl., 135" wb, 125 hp						
(Began 1/1/32).						
Standard Line						
4d Conv Sed	7150	22,800	38,000	76,000	133,000	190,000
2d RS Cpe	2350	7450	12,400	24,800	43,400	62,000
4d Sed	1550	4900	8200	16,400	28,700	41,000
Imperial Series, CL, 8-cyl., 146" wb, 125 hp						
(Began 1/1/32).						
Custom Line -LeBaron bodies						
2d RS Conv	10,150	32,400	54,000	108,000	189,000	270,000
4d DC Phae	11,250	36,000	60,000	120,000	210,000	300,000
4d Conv Sed	11,050	35,400	59,000	118,000	206,500	295,000

1933

	6	5	4	3	2	1
Series CO, 6-cyl., 116.5" wb						
2d RS Conv	850	2750	4600	9200	16,100	23,000
4d Conv Sed	1000	3250	5400	10,800	18,900	27,000
2d Bus Cpe	750	2400	4000	8000	14,000	20,000
2d RS Cpe	850	2650	4400	8800	15,400	22,000
2d Brgm	600	1900	3200	6400	11,200	16,000
4d Sed	600	1900	3200	6400	11,200	16,000
Royal Series CT, 8-cyl., 119.5 wb						
2d RS Conv	1150	3600	6000	12,000	21,000	30,000
4d Conv Sed	1150	3700	6200	12,400	21,700	31,000
2d Bus Cpe	850	2650	4400	8800	15,400	22,000
2d RS Cpe	850	2750	4600	9200	16,100	23,000
4d Sed	650	2050	3400	6800	11,900	17,000
4d 7P Sed	700	2150	3600	7200	12,600	18,000
Imperial Series CQ, 8-cyl., 126" wb						
2d RS Conv	1350	4300	7200	14,400	25,200	36,000
4d Conv Sed	1450	4550	7600	15,200	26,600	38,000
2d RS Cpe	950	3000	5000	10,000	17,500	25,000
2d 5P Cpe	900	2900	4800	9600	16,800	24,000
4d Sed	850	2650	4400	8800	15,400	22,000
Imperial Custom, Series CL, 8-cyl., 146" wb						
2d RS Conv	9400	30,000	50,000	100,000	175,000	250,000
4d WS Phae	9750	31,200	52,000	104,000	182,000	260,000
4d CC Sed	2550	8150	13,600	27,200	47,600	68,000

1934

	6	5	4	3	2	1
Series CA, 6-cyl., 117" wb						
2d RS Conv	1300	4100	6800	13,600	23,800	34,000
2d Bus Cpe	800	2500	4200	8400	14,700	21,000
2d RS Cpe	850	2650	4400	8800	15,400	22,000
2d Brgm	600	1900	3200	6400	11,200	16,000
4d Sed	550	1800	3000	6000	10,500	15,000
Series CB, 6-cyl., 121" wb						
4d Conv Sed	1500	4800	8000	16,000	28,000	40,000
4d CC Sed	750	2400	4000	8000	14,000	20,000
Airflow, Series CU, 8-cyl., 123" wb						
2d Cpe	1250	3950	6600	13,200	23,100	33,000
2d Brgm	1150	3600	6000	12,000	21,000	30,000
4d Sed	1050	3350	5600	11,200	19,600	28,000
4d Twn Sed	1100	3500	5800	11,600	20,300	29,000
Imperial Airflow, Series CV, 8-cyl., 128" wb						
2d Cpe	1400	4450	7400	14,800	25,900	37,000
4d Sed	1100	3500	5800	11,600	20,300	29,000
4d Twn Sed	1150	3700	6200	12,400	21,700	31,000
Imperial Custom Airflow, Series CX, 8-cyl., 137.5" wb						
4d Sed	1700	5400	9000	18,000	31,500	45,000
4d Twn Sed	1750	5500	9200	18,400	32,200	46,000
4d Limo	2350	7450	12,400	24,800	43,400	62,000
4d Twn Limo	2500	7900	13,200	26,400	46,200	66,000
Imperial Custom Airflow, Series CW, 8-cyl., 146.5" wb						
4d Sed	4900	15,600	26,000	52,000	91,000	130,000
4d Twn Sed	5100	16,300	27,200	54,400	95,200	136,000
4d Limo	5200	16,550	27,600	55,200	96,600	138,000

1935

	6	5	4	3	2	1
Airstream Series C-6, 6-cyl., 118" wb						
2d RS Conv	1100	3500	5800	11,600	20,300	29,000
2d Bus Cpe	600	1900	3200	6400	11,200	16,000
2d RS Cpe	650	2050	3400	6800	11,900	17,000
4d Tr Brgm	550	1700	2800	5600	9800	14,000
4d Sed	500	1550	2600	5200	9100	13,000
4d Tr Sed	500	1550	2600	5200	9100	13,000
Airstream Series CZ, 8-cyl., 121" wb						
2d Bus Cpe	650	2050	3400	6800	11,900	17,000
2d RS Cpe	700	2150	3600	7200	12,600	18,000
2d Tr Brgm	550	1800	3000	6000	10,500	15,000
4d Sed	550	1700	2800	5600	9800	14,000
4d Tr Sed	550	1700	2800	5600	9800	14,000
Airstream DeLuxe Series CZ, 121" wb						
2d RS Conv	1150	3600	6000	12,000	21,000	30,000
2d Bus Cpe	700	2150	3600	7200	12,600	18,000
2d RS Cpe	700	2300	3800	7600	13,300	19,000
2d Tr Brgm	600	2000	3300	6600	11,600	16,500
4d Sed	550	1750	2900	5800	10,200	14,500
4d Tr Sed	550	1750	2900	5800	10,200	14,500
Airstream DeLuxe, Series CZ, 8-cyl., 133" wb						
4d Trav Sed	600	1850	3100	6200	10,900	15,500
4d 7P Sed	600	1850	3100	6200	10,900	15,500
Airflow Series C-1, 8-cyl., 123" wb						
2d Bus Cpe	1200	3850	6400	12,800	22,400	32,000
2d Cpe	1250	3950	6600	13,200	23,100	33,000
4d Sed	1000	3100	5200	10,400	18,200	26,000
Imperial Airflow Series C-2, 8-cyl., 128" wb						
2d Cpe	1300	4200	7000	14,000	24,500	35,000
4d Sed	1050	3350	5600	11,200	19,600	28,000
Imperial Custom Airflow Series C-3, 8-cyl., 137" wb						
4d Sed	1150	3600	6000	12,000	21,000	30,000
4d Twn Sed	1150	3700	6200	12,400	21,700	31,000
4d Sed Limo	1450	4700	7800	15,600	27,300	39,000
4d Twn Limo	1550	4900	8200	16,400	28,700	41,000
Imperial Custom Airflow Series C-W, 8-cyl., 146.5" wb						
4d Sed	4000	12,700	21,200	42,400	74,200	106,000
4d Sed Limo	4050	12,950	21,600	43,200	75,600	108,000
4d Twn Limo	4150	13,200	22,000	44,000	77,000	110,000

1936

	6	5	4	3	2	1
Airstream Series C-7, 6-cyl., 118" wb						
2d RS Conv	1000	3100	5200	10,400	18,200	26,000
4d Conv Sed	1000	3250	5400	10,800	18,900	27,000
2d Bus Cpe	650	2050	3400	6800	11,900	17,000
2d RS Cpe	700	2150	3600	7200	12,600	18,000
2d Tr Brgm	550	1800	3000	6000	10,500	15,000
4d Tr Sed	600	1900	3200	6400	11,200	16,000
Airstream DeLuxe Series C-8, 8-cyl., 121" wb						
2d RS Conv	1050	3350	5600	11,200	19,600	28,000
4d Conv Sed	1150	3600	6000	12,000	21,000	30,000
2d Bus Cpe	700	2150	3600	7200	12,600	18,000
2d RS Cpe	700	2300	3800	7600	13,300	19,000
2d Tr Brgm	600	1900	3200	6400	11,200	16,000
4d Tr Sed	600	1900	3200	6400	11,200	16,000
Airstream DeLuxe, Series C-8, 8-cyl., 133" wb						
4d Trav Sed	600	2000	3300	6600	11,600	16,500
4d Sed	600	1900	3200	6400	11,200	16,000
4d Sed Limo	650	2050	3400	6800	11,900	17,000
4d LeB Twn Sed	700	2150	3600	7200	12,600	18,000

	6	5	4	3	2	1
Airflow, 8-cyl., 123" wb						
2d Cpe	1150	3600	6000	12,000	21,000	30,000
4d Sed	950	3000	5000	10,000	17,500	25,000
Imperial Airflow, 8-cyl., 128" wb						
2d Cpe	1200	3850	6400	12,800	22,400	32,000
4d Sed	1000	3100	5200	10,400	18,200	26,000
Imperial Custom Airflow, 8-cyl., 137" wb						
4d Sed	1050	3350	5600	11,200	19,600	28,000
4d Sed Limo	1150	3700	6200	12,400	21,700	31,000
Imperial Custom Airflow, 8-cyl., 146.5" wb						
4d 8P Sed	4900	15,600	26,000	52,000	91,000	130,000
4d Sed Limo	5100	16,300	27,200	54,400	95,200	136,000

1937

	6	5	4	3	2	1
Royal, 6-cyl., 116" wb						
2d RS Conv	950	3000	5000	10,000	17,500	25,000
4d Conv Sed	1050	3350	5600	11,200	19,600	28,000
2d Bus Cpe	550	1800	3000	6000	10,500	15,000
2d RS Cpe	600	1900	3200	6400	11,200	16,000
2d Brgm	500	1550	2600	5200	9100	13,000
2d Tr Brgm	550	1700	2800	5600	9800	14,000
4d Sed	450	1500	2500	5000	8800	12,500
4d Tr Sed	500	1550	2600	5200	9100	13,000
Royal, 6-cyl., 133" wb						
4d Sed	550	1700	2800	5600	9800	14,000
4d Sed Limo	550	1800	3000	6000	10,500	15,000
4d Der T&C	850	2650	4400	8800	15,400	22,000
Airflow, 8-cyl., 128" wb						
2d Cpe	1150	3600	6000	12,000	21,000	30,000
4d Sed	1050	3350	5600	11,200	19,600	28,000
Imperial, 8-cyl., 121" wb						
2d RS Conv	1050	3350	5600	11,200	19,600	28,000
4d Conv Sed	1150	3600	6000	12,000	21,000	30,000
2d Bus Cpe	700	2150	3600	7200	12,600	18,000
2d RS Cpe	700	2300	3800	7600	13,300	19,000
2d Tr Brgm	700	2300	3800	7600	13,300	19,000
4d Tr Sed	700	2150	3600	7200	12,600	18,000
Imperial Custom, 8-cyl., 140" wb						
4d 5P Sed	950	3000	5000	10,000	17,500	25,000
4d 7P Sed	1000	3250	5400	10,800	18,900	27,000
4d Sed Limo	1450	4550	7600	15,200	26,600	38,000
4d Twn Limo	1450	4700	7800	15,600	27,300	39,000
Custom Built Models						
4d Der Fml Conv Twn Car	3550	11,300	18,800	37,600	65,800	94,000
4d Der Conv Vic	3400	10,800	18,000	36,000	63,000	90,000
Imperial Custom Airflow, 8-cyl., 146.5" wb						
4d Sed Limo				value inestimable		

1938

	6	5	4	3	2	1
Royal (6-cyl.) 119" wb						
2d RS Conv	850	2750	4600	9200	16,100	23,000
4d Conv Sed	900	2900	4800	9600	16,800	24,000
2d Bus Cpe	600	1900	3200	6400	11,200	16,000
2d RS Cpe	650	2050	3400	6800	11,900	17,000
2d Brgm	500	1550	2600	5200	9100	13,000
2d Tr Brgm	600	1900	3200	6400	11,200	16,000
4d 4d Sed	500	1550	2600	5200	9100	13,000
4d Tr Sed	550	1700	2800	5600	9800	14,000
4d Royal, 6-cyl., 136" wb						
4d 7P Sed	550	1800	3000	6000	10,500	15,000
4d 7P Limo Sed	600	1900	3200	6400	11,200	16,000
Imperial, 8-cyl., 125" wb						
2d RS Conv	1000	3100	5200	10,400	18,200	26,000
4d Conv Sed	1050	3350	5600	11,200	19,600	28,000
2d Bus Cpe	700	2150	3600	7200	12,600	18,000
2d RS Cpe	700	2300	3800	7600	13,300	19,000
4d Tr Brgm	600	1900	3200	6400	11,200	16,000
4d Tr Sed	650	2050	3400	6800	11,900	17,000
New York Special, 8-cyl., 125" wb						
4d Tr Sed	700	2150	3600	7200	12,600	18,000
Imperial Custom, 8-cyl., 144" wb						
4d 5P Sed	900	2900	4800	9600	16,800	24,000
4d Sed	850	2750	4600	9200	16,100	23,000
4d Limo Sed	1000	3250	5400	10,800	18,900	27,000
Derham customs on C-20 chassis						
4d Twn Sed	1150	3700	6200	12,400	21,700	31,000
4d Twn Limo	1350	4300	7200	14,400	25,200	36,000
2d Conv Vic	3250	10,300	17,200	34,400	60,200	86,000
4d Conv Sed	3450	11,050	18,400	36,800	64,400	92,000

1939

	6	5	4	3	2	1
Royal, 6-cyl., 119" wb						
2d Cpe	600	1900	3200	6400	11,200	16,000
2d Vic Cpe	650	2050	3400	6800	11,900	17,000
2d Brgm	500	1550	2600	5200	9100	13,000
4d Sed	550	1700	2800	5600	9800	14,000
Royal, 6-cyl., 136" wb						
4d 7P Sed	550	1800	3000	6000	10,500	15,000
4d Limo	600	1900	3200	6400	11,200	16,000
Royal Windsor, 6-cyl., 119" wb						
2d Cpe	650	2050	3400	6800	11,900	17,000
2d Vic Cpe	700	2150	3600	7200	12,600	18,000
2d Clb Cpe	700	2300	3800	7600	13,300	19,000
4d Sed	500	1550	2600	5200	9100	13,000
Imperial, 8-cyl., 125" wb						
2d Cpe	650	2050	3400	6800	11,900	17,000
2d Vic Cpe	700	2150	3600	7200	12,600	18,000
2d Brgm	500	1550	2600	5200	9100	13,000
4d Sed	550	1800	3000	6000	10,500	15,000
New Yorker, 8-cyl., 125" wb						
2d Cpe	700	2150	3600	7200	12,600	18,000
2d Vic Cpe	700	2300	3800	7600	13,300	19,000
2d Clb Cpe	700	2300	3800	7600	13,300	19,000
4d Sed	550	1800	3000	6000	10,500	15,000
Saratoga, 8-cyl., 125" wb						
2d Clb Cpe	700	2300	3800	7600	13,300	19,000
4d Sed	600	1900	3200	6400	11,200	16,000
Imperial Custom, 8-cyl., 144" wb						
4d 5P Sed	900	2900	4800	9600	16,800	24,000
4d 7P Sed	950	3000	5000	10,000	17,500	25,000
4d Limo	1000	3100	5200	10,400	18,200	26,000
Special Derham customs on C-24 chassis						
4d 7P Tr	1200	3850	6400	12,800	22,400	32,000
4d Conv Sed	2650	8400	14,000	28,000	49,000	70,000
4d Conv T&C	2700	8650	14,400	28,800	50,400	72,000

1940

	6	5	4	3	2	1
Royal, 6-cyl., 122.5" wb						
2d 3P Cpe	550	1800	3000	6000	10,500	15,000
2d 6P Cpe	600	1850	3100	6200	10,900	15,500
2d Vic Sed	500	1600	2650	5300	9300	13,300
4d Sed	500	1550	2600	5200	9100	13,000
Royal, 6-cyl., 139.5" wb						
4d 8P Sed	550	1700	2800	5600	9800	14,000
4d 8P Limo	550	1800	3000	6000	10,500	15,000
Windsor, 6-cyl., 122.5 wb						
2d Conv Cpe	900	2900	4800	9600	16,800	24,000
2d 3P Cpe	600	1900	3200	6400	11,200	16,000
2d 6P Cpe	600	2000	3300	6600	11,600	16,500
2d Vic Sed	500	1600	2650	5300	9300	13,300
4d Sed	500	1600	2700	5400	9500	13,500
Windsor, 6-cyl., 139.5 wb						
4d 8P Sed	550	1700	2800	5600	9800	14,000
4d 8P Limo	550	1800	3000	6000	10,500	15,000
Traveler, 8-cyl., 128" wb						
2d 3P Cpe	650	2050	3400	6800	11,900	17,000
2d 6P Cpe	700	2150	3600	7200	12,600	18,000
2d Vic Sed	550	1700	2850	5700	10,000	14,300
4d Sed	550	1700	2800	5600	9800	14,000
Saratoga, 8-cyl., 128.5" wb						
4d Sed	600	1900	3200	6400	11,200	16,000
4d Fml Sed Div	650	2050	3400	6800	11,900	17,000
4d T&C Der	800	2500	4200	8400	14,700	21,000
New Yorker, 8-cyl., 128.5" wb						
2d Conv Cpe	1000	3250	5400	10,800	18,900	27,000
2d 3P Cpe	700	2300	3800	7600	13,300	19,000
2d 6P Cpe	750	2400	4000	8000	14,000	20,000
2d Vic Sed	550	1850	3050	6100	10,700	15,300
4d Sed	550	1800	3000	6000	10,500	15,000
4d Fml Sed Div	650	2050	3400	6800	11,900	17,000
Crown Imperial, 8-cyl., 145.5" wb						
4d 6P Sed	750	2400	4000	8000	14,000	20,000
4d 6P Twn Limo	850	2750	4600	9200	16,100	23,000
4d 8P Twn Limo	850	2750	4600	9200	16,100	23,000
4d 8P Sed	800	2500	4200	8400	14,700	21,000
4d 8P Sed Limo	850	2750	4600	9200	16,100	23,000
4d 8P Limo	900	2900	4800	9600	16,800	24,000
4d Nwpt Parade Phae	10,300	33,000	55,000	110,000	192,500	275,000
2d Thunderbolt	10,300	33,000	55,000	110,000	192,500	275,000

1941

	6	5	4	3	2	1
Royal, 6-cyl., 121.5" wb						
2d 3P Cpe	550	1750	2900	5800	10,200	14,500
2d 6P Clb Cpe	550	1800	3000	6000	10,500	15,000
2d Brgm	450	1450	2400	4800	8400	12,000
4d Sed	450	1500	2500	5000	8800	12,500
4d Twn Sed	500	1550	2600	5200	9100	13,000
Royal, 6-cyl., 121.5" wb						
4d T&C Wag	1000	3100	5200	10,400	18,200	26,000
Royal, 6-cyl., 139.5" wb						
4d 8P Sed	500	1550	2600	5200	9100	13,000
4d 8P Limo Sed	550	1700	2800	5600	9800	14,000
Windsor, 6-cyl., 121.5" wb						
2d Conv Cpe	950	3000	5000	10,000	17,500	25,000
2d 3P Cpe	650	2050	3400	6800	11,900	17,000
2d 6P Clb Cpe	650	2100	3500	7000	12,300	17,500
2d Brgm	500	1550	2600	5200	9100	13,000
4d Sed	550	1700	2800	5600	9800	14,000
4d Twn Sed	550	1800	3000	6000	10,500	15,000
Windsor, 6-cyl., 139.5" wb						
4d 8P Sed	600	1900	3200	6400	11,200	16,000
4d 8P Sed Limo	650	2050	3400	6800	11,900	17,000
Saratoga, 8-cyl., 127.5" wb						
2d 3P Cpe	700	2150	3600	7200	12,600	18,000
2d 6P Clb Cpe	700	2200	3700	7400	13,000	18,500
2d Brgm	550	1700	2800	5600	9800	14,000
4d Sed	550	1800	3000	6000	10,500	15,000
4d Twn Sed	600	1850	3100	6200	10,900	15,500
New Yorker, 8-cyl., 127.5" wb						
2d Conv Cpe	1050	3350	5600	11,200	19,600	28,000
3P Cpe	750	2400	4000	8000	14,000	20,000
2d 6P Cpe	800	2500	4200	8400	14,700	21,000
2d Brgm	550	1800	3000	6000	10,500	15,000
4d Sed	600	1900	3200	6400	11,200	16,000
4d Twn Sed	600	2000	3300	6600	11,600	16,500
4d 6P Sed	650	2050	3400	6800	11,900	17,000
4d 8P Sed	700	2150	3600	7200	12,600	18,000
4d 8P Sedan Limo	800	2500	4200	8400	14,700	21,000
4d 8P Limo	850	2650	4400	8800	15,400	22,000
4d Laudalet Limo	1000	3250	5400	10,800	18,900	27,000
4d LeB Twn Limo	1100	3500	5800	11,600	20,300	29,000
New Yorker Special/Crown Imperial, 8-cyl., 127.5" wb						
4d Twn Sed	850	2650	4400	8800	15,400	22,000

C-33 series.

1942

	6	5	4	3	2	1
Royal, 6-cyl., 121.5" wb						
2d 3P Cpe	550	1700	2800	5600	9800	14,000
2d 6P Clb Cpe	550	1750	2900	5800	10,200	14,500
2d Brgm	450	1400	2300	4600	8100	11,500
4d Sed	450	1450	2400	4800	8400	12,000
4d Twn Sed	450	1500	2500	5000	8800	12,500
Royal, 6-cyl., 139.5" wb						
4d 8P Sed	450	1500	2450	4900	8600	12,300
4d 8P Limo	500	1550	2550	5100	9000	12,800
Windsor, 6-cyl., 121.5" wb						
2d Conv Cpe	800	2500	4200	8400	14,700	21,000
2d 3P Cpe	600	1850	3100	6200	10,900	15,500
2d 6P Cpe	600	1900	3200	6400	11,200	16,000
2d Brgm	450	1450	2400	4800	8400	12,000
4d Sed	450	1500	2500	5000	8800	12,500
4d Twn Sed	450	1450	2400	4800	8400	12,000
4d 6P T&C Wag	1300	4200	7000	14,000	24,500	35,000
4d 9P T&C Wag	1400	4450	7400	14,800	25,900	37,000
Windsor, 6-cyl., 139.5" wb						
4d 8P Sed	500	1550	2550	5100	9000	12,800
4d 8P Limo	500	1600	2650	5300	9300	13,300
Saratoga, 8-cyl., 127.5" wb						
2d 6P Cpe	650	2100	3500	7000	12,300	17,500
2d 3P Cpe	650	2050	3400	6800	11,900	17,000
2d Brgm	450	1500	2450	4900	8600	12,300

	6	5	4	3	2	1
4d Sed	450	1500	2500	5000	8700	12,400
4d Twn Sed	500	1650	2750	5500	9700	13,800
New Yorker, 8-cyl., 127.5" wb						
2d Conv Cpe	900	2900	4800	9600	16,800	24,000
2d Der Conv Cpe	1250	3950	6600	13,200	23,100	33,000
2d 6P Cpe	700	2200	3700	7400	13,000	18,500
2d 3P Cpe	700	2150	3600	7200	12,600	18,000
2d Brgm	500	1550	2550	5100	9000	12,800
4d Sed	500	1550	2600	5200	9000	12,900
4d Twn Sed	550	1700	2850	5700	10,000	14,300
Crown Imperial, 8-cyl., 145.5" wb						
4d 6P Sed	550	1800	3000	6000	10,500	15,000
4d 8P Sed	600	1900	3200	6400	11,200	16,000
4d 8P Sed Limo	700	2150	3600	7200	12,600	18,000
Derham Customs						
4d Conv Sed	1200	3850	6400	12,800	22,400	32,000
4d T&C	850	2750	4600	9200	16,100	23,000
4d Fml T&C	900	2900	4800	9600	16,800	24,000

1946-1948

	6	5	4	3	2	1
Royal Series, 6-cyl., 121.5" wb						
2d Cpe	550	1800	3000	6000	10,500	15,000
2d Clb Cpe	600	1850	3100	6200	10,900	15,500
2d Sed	450	1450	2400	4800	8400	12,000
4d Sed	450	1450	2400	4800	8400	12,000
Royal Series, 6-cyl., 139.5" wb						
4d Sed	550	1750	2900	5800	10,200	14,500
4d Limo	600	2000	3300	6600	11,600	16,500
Windsor Series, 6-cyl., 121.5" wb						
2d Conv	1000	3100	5200	10,400	18,200	26,000
2d Cpe	600	1900	3200	6400	11,200	16,000
2d Clb Cpe	600	2000	3300	6600	11,600	16,500
2d Sed	450	1450	2400	4800	8400	12,000
4d Sed	450	1450	2450	4900	8500	12,200
4d Trav Sed	450	1500	2500	5000	8700	12,400
Windsor Series, 6-cyl., 139.5" wb						
4d Sed	600	1850	3100	6200	10,900	15,500
4d Limo	650	2050	3400	6800	11,900	17,000
Saratoga Series, 8-cyl., 127.5" wb						
2d 3P Cpe	600	2000	3300	6600	11,600	16,500
2d Clb Cpe	650	2050	3400	6800	11,900	17,000
2d Sed	500	1500	2550	5100	8900	12,700
4d Sed	500	1550	2550	5100	9000	12,800
New Yorker, 8-cyl., 127.5" wb						
2d Conv	1100	3500	5800	11,600	20,300	29,000
2d Cpe	600	1900	3200	6400	11,200	16,000
2d Clb Cpe	600	2000	3300	6600	11,600	16,500
2d Sed	500	1550	2550	5100	9000	12,800
4d Sed	500	1550	2600	5200	9100	13,000
Town & Country						
2d Conv	3400	10,800	18,000	36,000	63,000	90,000
4d Sed	1700	5400	9000	18,000	31,500	45,000
Imperial C-40						
4d Limo	700	2300	3800	7600	13,300	19,000
4d 8P Sed	700	2150	3600	7200	12,600	18,000

1949

First Series 1949 is the same as 1948

	6	5	4	3	2	1
Royal - Second Series, 6-cyl., 125.5" wb						
2d Clb Cpe	550	1700	2800	5600	9800	14,000
4d Sed	450	1500	2500	5000	8800	12,500
4d Sta Wag	900	2900	4800	9600	16,800	24,000
Royal - Second Series, 6-cyl., 139.5" wb						
4d Sed	500	1550	2550	5100	9000	12,800
Windsor - Second Series, 6-cyl., 125.5" wb						
2d Conv	850	2750	4600	9200	16,100	23,000
2d Clb Cpe	550	1750	2900	5800	10,200	14,500
4d Sed	500	1500	2550	5100	8900	12,700
Windsor Second Series, 6-cyl., 139.5" wb						
4d Sed	550	1700	2800	5600	9800	14,000
4d Limo	550	1800	3000	6000	10,500	15,000
Saratoga - Second Series, 8-cyl., 131.5" wb						
2d Clb Cpe	550	1750	2900	5800	10,200	14,500
4d Sed	450	1450	2400	4800	8400	12,000
New Yorker - Second Series, 8-cyl., 131.5" wb						
2d Conv	950	3000	5000	10,000	17,500	25,000
2d Clb Cpe	550	1800	3000	6000	10,500	15,000
4d Sed	500	1550	2600	5200	9100	13,000
Town & Country - Second Series, 8-cyl., 131.5" wb						
2d Conv	2250	7200	12,000	24,000	42,000	60,000
Imperial - Second Series, 8-cyl., 131.5" wb						
4d Sed Der	650	2050	3400	6800	11,900	17,000
Crown Imperial, 8-cyl., 145.5" wb						
4d 8P Sed	700	2150	3600	7200	12,600	18,000
4d Limo	750	2400	4000	8000	14,000	20,000

1950

	6	5	4	3	2	1
Royal Series, 6-cyl., 125.5" wb						
4d Sed	450	1400	2350	4700	8300	11,800
4d Clb Cpe	500	1550	2600	5200	9100	13,000
4d T&C Sta Wag	850	2750	4600	9200	16,100	23,000
4d Sta Wag	950	3000	5000	10,000	17,500	25,000
Royal Series, 6-cyl., 139.5" wb						
4d Sed	500	1550	2600	5200	9100	13,000
Windsor Series, 6-cyl., 125.5" wb						
2d Conv	900	2900	4800	9600	16,800	24,000
2d HT	700	2150	3600	7200	12,600	18,000
2d Clb Cpe	550	1750	2900	5800	10,200	14,500
4d Sed	450	1450	2400	4800	8400	12,000
4d Trav Sed	450	1450	2400	4800	8500	12,100
Windsor Series, 6-cyl., 139.5" wb						
4d Sed	550	1700	2800	5600	9800	14,000
4d Limo	600	1900	3200	6400	11,200	16,000
Saratoga, 8-cyl., 131.5" wb						
2d Clb Cpe	550	1700	2800	5600	9800	14,000
4d Sed	450	1450	2450	4900	8500	12,200
New Yorker, 8-cyl., 131.5" wb						
2d Conv	1050	3350	5600	11,200	19,600	28,000
2d HT	850	2650	4400	8800	15,400	22,000
2d Clb Cpe	550	1700	2800	5600	9800	14,000
4d Sed	500	1550	2600	5200	9100	13,000
Town & Country, 8-cyl., 131.5" wb						
2d HT	1700	5400	9000	18,000	31,500	45,000
Imperial , 8-cyl., 131.5" wb						
4d Sed	550	1800	3000	6000	10,500	15,000
Crown Imperial, 8-cyl., 145.5" wb						
4d Sed	600	1900	3200	6400	11,200	16,000
4d Limo	700	2150	3600	7200	12,600	18,000

1951-1952

	6	5	4	3	2	1
Windsor Series, 6-cyl., 125.5" wb						
2d Clb Cpe	550	1700	2800	5600	9800	14,000
4d Sed	450	1400	2300	4600	8100	11,500
4d T&C Sta Wag	850	2750	4600	9200	16,100	23,000
Windsor Series, 6-cyl., 139.5" wb						
4d Sed	450	1400	2300	4600	8100	11,500
Windsor DeLuxe, 6-cyl., 125.5" wb						
2d Conv	850	2650	4400	8800	15,400	22,000
2d HT	700	2150	3600	7200	12,600	18,000
2d Clb Cpe (1951 only)	550	1700	2800	5600	9800	14,000
4d Sed	450	1400	2300	4600	8100	11,600
4d Trav Sed	450	1450	2400	4800	8400	12,000
Windsor DeLuxe, 6-cyl., 139.5" wb						
4d Sed	450	1500	2500	5000	8800	12,500
4d Limo	500	1550	2600	5200	9100	13,000
Saratoga, 8-cyl., 125.5" wb						
2d Conv (1952 only)	850	2650	4400	8800	15,400	22,000
2d HT Nwpt (1952 only)	700	2300	3800	7600	13,300	19,000
2d Clb Cpe (1951 only)	550	1800	3000	6000	10,500	15,000
4d Sed	500	1600	2700	5400	9500	13,500
4d T&C Sta Wag (1951 only)	900	2900	4800	9600	16,800	24,000
Windsor or Saratoga, 8-cyl., 125.5" wb						
4d Sed	550	1750	2900	5800	10,200	14,500
2d Clb Cpe (1952 only)	550	1750	2900	5800	10,200	14,500
4d T&C Sta Wag (1952 only)	850	2650	4400	8800	15,400	22,000
4d Limo (1951 only)	600	2000	3300	6600	11,600	16,500
New Yorker, 8-cyl., 131.5" wb						
2d Conv	950	3000	5000	10,000	17,500	25,000
2d HT	750	2400	4000	8000	14,000	20,000
2d Clb Cpe (1951 only)	600	2000	3300	6600	11,600	16,500
4d Sed	600	1850	3100	6200	10,900	15,500
4d T&C Sta Wag (1951 only)	900	2900	4800	9600	16,800	24,000
Imperial, 8-cyl., 131.5" wb						
2d Conv (1951 only)	900	2900	4800	9600	16,800	24,000
2d HT	800	2500	4200	8400	14,700	21,000
2d Clb Cpe	650	2050	3400	6800	11,900	17,000
4d Sed	600	2000	3300	6600	11,600	16,500
Crown Imperial, 8-cyl., 145.5" wb						
4d Sed	600	1900	3200	6400	11,200	16,000
4d Limo	700	2300	3800	7600	13,300	19,000

1953

	6	5	4	3	2	1
Windsor Series, 6-cyl., 125.5" wb						
2d Clb Cpe	500	1550	2600	5200	9100	13,000
4d Sed	450	1450	2400	4800	8400	12,000
4d T&C Sta Wag	850	2650	4400	8800	15,400	22,000
Windsor Series, 6-cyl., 139.5" wb						
4d Sed	450	1450	2400	4800	8500	12,100
Windsor DeLuxe Series, 6-cyl., 125.5" wb						
2d Conv	700	2300	3800	7600	13,300	19,000
2d HT	650	2050	3400	6800	11,900	17,000
4d Sed	450	1500	2450	4900	8600	12,300
New Yorker, 8-cyl., 125.5" wb						
2d Clb Cpe	550	1750	2900	5800	10,200	14,500
2d HT	700	2300	3800	7600	13,300	19,000
4d Sed	500	1550	2550	5100	9000	12,800
4d T&C Sta Wag	850	2750	4600	9200	16,100	23,000
New Yorker, 8-cyl., 139.5" wb						
4d Sed	500	1600	2650	5300	9300	13,300
New Yorker Deluxe, 8-cyl., 125.5" wb						
2d Conv	900	2900	4800	9600	16,800	24,000
2d HT	750	2400	4000	8000	14,000	20,000
2d Clb Cpe	550	1800	3000	6000	10,500	15,000
4d Sed	500	1550	2600	5200	9200	13,100
Custom Imperial Series, 8-cyl., 133.5" wb						
4d Sed	550	1800	3000	6000	10,500	15,000
4d Twn Limo	650	2050	3400	6800	11,900	17,000
Custom Imperial, 8-cyl., 131.5" wb						
2d HT	950	3000	5000	10,000	17,500	25,000
Crown Imperial, 8-cyl., 145.5" wb						
4d Sed	600	2000	3300	6600	11,600	16,500
4d Limo	700	2150	3600	7200	12,600	18,000

1954

	6	5	4	3	2	1
Windsor DeLuxe Series, 6-cyl., 125.5" wb						
2d Conv	900	2900	4800	9600	16,800	24,000
2d HT	750	2400	4000	8000	14,000	20,000
2d Clb Cpe	500	1600	2700	5400	9500	13,500
4d Sed	450	1450	2400	4800	8400	12,000
4d T&C Sta Wag	750	2400	4000	8000	14,000	20,000
Windsor DeLuxe Series, 6-cyl., 139.5" wb						
4d Sed	500	1600	2700	5400	9500	13,500
New Yorker Series, 8-cyl., 125.5" wb						
2d HT	850	2650	4400	8800	15,400	22,000
2d Clb Cpe	550	1800	3000	6000	10,500	15,000
4d Sed	500	1600	2700	5400	9500	13,500
4d T&C Sta Wag	800	2500	4200	8400	14,700	21,000
New Yorker Series, 8-cyl., 139.5" wb						
4d Sed	550	1700	2800	5600	9800	14,000
New Yorker DeLuxe Series, 8-cyl., 125.5" wb						
2d Conv	1150	3600	6000	12,000	21,000	30,000
2d HT	850	2750	4600	9200	16,100	23,000
2d Clb Cpe	550	1700	2800	5600	9800	14,000
4d Sed	550	1750	2900	5800	10,200	14,500
Custom Imperial Line, 8-cyl., 133.5" wb						
4d Sed	650	2050	3400	6800	11,900	17,000
4d Limo	700	2300	3800	7600	13,300	19,000
Custom Imperial Line, 8-cyl., 131" wb						
2d HT Newport	950	3000	5000	10,000	17,500	25,000
Crown Imperial Line, 8-cyl., 145.5" wb						
4d Sed	650	2100	3500	7000	12,300	17,500
4d Limo	750	2400	4000	8000	14,000	20,000

1955

	6	5	4	3	2	1
Windsor DeLuxe Series, V-8, 126" wb						
2d Conv	1050	3350	5600	11,200	19,600	28,000
2d HT Newport	800	2500	4200	8400	14,700	21,000

	6	5	4	3	2	1
2d HT Nassau	750	2400	4000	8000	14,000	20,000
4d Sed	500	1550	2600	5200	9100	13,000
4d T&C Sta Wag	700	2150	3600	7200	12,600	18,000
New Yorker Deluxe Series, V-8, 126" wb						
2d Conv	1150	3700	6200	12,400	21,700	31,000
2d HT St Regis	850	2650	4400	8800	15,400	22,000
2d HT Newport	800	2500	4200	8400	14,700	21,000
4d Sed	550	1700	2800	5600	9800	14,000
4d T&C Sta Wag	750	2400	4000	8000	14,000	20,000
300 Series, V-8, 126" wb						
2d Spt Cpe	1350	4300	7200	14,400	25,200	36,000
Imperial Series, V-8						
4d Sed	550	1800	3000	6000	10,500	15,000
2d HT Newport	950	3000	5000	10,000	17,500	25,000
Crown Imperial Series, V-8						
4d 8P Sed	700	2300	3800	7600	13,300	19,000
4d 8P Limo	850	2750	4600	9200	16,100	23,000

1956

	6	5	4	3	2	1
Windsor Series, V-8						
2d Conv	1000	3250	5400	10,800	18,900	27,000
2d HT Newport	850	2650	4400	8800	15,400	22,000
2d HT Nassau	800	2500	4200	8400	14,700	21,000
4d HT	550	1800	3000	6000	10,500	15,000
4d Sed	500	1550	2600	5200	9100	13,000
4d T&C Sta Wag	700	2300	3800	7600	13,300	19,000
New Yorker Series, V-8						
2d Conv	1150	3600	6000	12,000	21,000	30,000
2d HT St Regis	900	2900	4800	9600	16,800	24,000
2d HT Newport	850	2750	4600	9200	16,100	23,000
4d HT	700	2150	3600	7200	12,600	18,000
4d Sed	550	1700	2800	5600	9800	14,000
4d T&C Sta Wag	750	2400	4000	8000	14,000	20,000
300 Letter Series "B", V-8						
2d HT	1350	4300	7200	14,400	25,200	36,000
Imperial Line, V-8						
4d Sed	550	1800	3000	6000	10,500	15,000
4d HT S Hamp	700	2150	3600	7200	12,600	18,000
2d HT S Hamp	950	3000	5000	10,000	17,500	25,000
Crown Imperial Line, V-8						
4d 8P Sed	750	2400	4000	8000	14,000	20,000
4d 8P Limo	850	2650	4400	8800	15,400	22,000

1957

	6	5	4	3	2	1
Windsor Series, V-8						
2d HT	750	2400	4000	8000	14,000	20,000
4d HT	550	1800	3000	6000	10,500	15,000
4d Sed	450	1450	2400	4800	8400	12,000
4d T&C Sta Wag	550	1700	2800	5600	9800	14,000
Saratoga Series, V-8						
2d HT	850	2650	4400	8800	15,400	22,000
4d HT	650	2050	3400	6800	11,900	17,000
4d Sed	450	1500	2500	5000	8800	12,500
New Yorker Series, V-8						
2d Conv	1150	3600	6000	12,000	21,000	30,000
2d HT	950	3000	5000	10,000	17,500	25,000
4d HT	700	2150	3600	7200	12,600	18,000
4d Sed	500	1550	2600	5200	9100	13,000
4d T&C Sta Wag	550	1800	3000	6000	10,500	15,000
300 Letter Series "C", V-8						
2d Conv	1800	5750	9600	19,200	33,600	48,000
2d HT	1450	4700	7800	15,600	27,300	39,000
Imperial Line, V-8						
2d HT S Hamp	850	2750	4600	9200	16,100	23,000
4d HT S Hamp	750	2400	4000	8000	14,000	20,000
4d Sed	700	2150	3600	7200	12,600	18,000
Crown Imperial Line, V-8						
2d Conv	1100	3500	5800	11,600	20,300	29,000
2d HT S Hamp	900	2900	4800	9600	16,800	24,000
4d HT S Hamp	800	2500	4200	8400	14,700	21,000
4d Sed	700	2300	3800	7600	13,300	19,000
Imperial LeBaron Line, V-8						
4d Sed	750	2400	4000	8000	14,000	20,000
4d HT S Hamp	850	2650	4400	8800	15,400	22,000
Crown Imperial Ghia, V-8						
4d 8P Limo	1000	3100	5200	10,400	18,200	26,000

1958

	6	5	4	3	2	1
Windsor Series, V-8						
2d HT	700	2300	3800	7600	13,300	19,000
4d HT	550	1700	2800	5600	9800	14,000
4d Sed	450	1450	2400	4800	8400	12,000
4d T&C Sta Wag	550	1750	2900	5800	10,200	14,500
Saratoga Series, V-8						
2d HT	750	2400	4000	8000	14,000	20,000
4d HT	550	1800	3000	6000	10,500	15,000
4d Sed	500	1550	2600	5200	9100	13,000
New Yorker Series, V-8						
2d Conv	1200	3850	6400	12,800	22,400	32,000
2d HT	850	2650	4400	8800	15,400	22,000
4d HT	600	1900	3200	6400	11,200	16,000
4d Sed	550	1700	2800	5600	9800	14,000
4d 6P T&C Sta Wag	550	1750	2900	5800	10,200	14,500
4d 9P T&C Sta Wag	550	1750	2950	5900	10,300	14,700
300 Letter Series "D"						
2d Conv	1850	5900	9800	19,600	34,300	49,000
2d HT	1500	4800	8000	16,000	28,000	40,000

NOTE: Add 40 percent for EFI.

	6	5	4	3	2	1
Imperial Line, V-8						
2d HT S Hamp	850	2650	4400	8800	15,400	22,000
4d HT S Hamp	700	2300	3800	7600	13,300	19,000
4d Sed	700	2150	3600	7200	12,600	18,000
Crown Imperial Line, V-8						
2d Conv	1050	3350	5600	11,200	19,600	28,000
2d HT S Hamp	900	2900	4800	9600	16,800	24,000
4d HT S Hamp	750	2400	4000	8000	14,000	20,000
4d Sed	700	2300	3800	7600	13,300	19,000
Imperial LeBaron Line, V-8						
4d Sed	750	2400	4000	8000	14,000	20,000
4d HT S Hamp	850	2650	4400	8800	15,400	22,000
Crown Imperial Ghia, V-8						
4d Limo	1000	3100	5200	10,400	18,200	26,000

1959

	6	5	4	3	2	1
Windsor Series, V-8						
2d Conv	850	2650	4400	8800	15,400	22,000
2d HT	650	2050	3400	6800	11,900	17,000
4d HT	500	1550	2600	5200	9100	13,000
4d Sed	400	1300	2200	4400	7700	11,000
Town & Country Series, V-8						
4d 6P Sta Wag	450	1500	2500	5000	8800	12,500
4d 9P Sta Wag	450	1400	2350	4700	8200	11,700
Saratoga Series, V-8						
4d Sed	400	1300	2200	4400	7700	11,000
4d HT	550	1700	2800	5600	9800	14,000
2d HT	700	2150	3600	7200	12,600	18,000
New Yorker Series, V-8						
2d Conv	1150	3600	6000	12,000	21,000	30,000
2d HT	750	2400	4000	8000	14,000	20,000
4d HT	550	1800	3000	6000	10,500	15,000
4d Sed	450	1400	2300	4600	8100	11,500
Town & Country, V-8						
4d 6P Sta Wag	550	1700	2800	5600	9800	14,000
4d 9P Sta Wag	550	1700	2850	5700	9900	14,200
300 Letter Series "E", V-8						
2d Conv	1750	5500	9200	18,400	32,200	46,000
2d HT	1500	4800	8000	16,000	28,000	40,000
Imperial Custom Line, V-8						
4d Sed	550	1700	2800	5600	9800	14,000
4d HT S Hamp	650	2050	3400	6800	11,900	17,000
2d HT S Hamp	850	2650	4400	8800	15,400	22,000
Crown Imperial Line, V-8						
2d Conv	1050	3350	5600	11,200	19,600	28,000
2d HT S Hamp	900	2900	4800	9600	16,800	24,000
4d Sed	550	1800	3000	6000	10,500	15,000
4d HT S Hamp	700	2150	3600	7200	12,600	18,000
Imperial LeBaron Line, V-8						
4d Sed	600	1900	3200	6400	11,200	16,000
4d HT S Hamp	700	2300	3800	7600	13,300	19,000
Crown Imperial Ghia, V-8						
4d Limo	1000	3100	5200	10,400	18,200	26,000

1960

	6	5	4	3	2	1
Windsor Series, V-8						
2d Conv	600	1900	3200	6400	11,200	16,000
2d HT	450	1450	2400	4800	8400	12,000
4d HT	400	1300	2200	4400	7700	11,000
4d Sed	400	1200	2000	4000	7000	10,000
Town & Country Series, V-8						
4d 9P Sta Wag	400	1350	2250	4500	7800	11,200
4d 6P Sta Wag	400	1300	2200	4400	7700	11,000
Saratoga Series, V-8						
2d HT	500	1550	2600	5200	9100	13,000
4d HT	450	1450	2400	4800	8400	12,000
4d Sed	400	1200	2050	4100	7100	10,200
New Yorker Series, V-8						
2d Conv	700	2300	3800	7600	13,300	19,000
2d HT	550	1800	3000	6000	10,500	15,000
4d HT	500	1550	2600	5200	9100	13,000
4d Sed	400	1250	2100	4200	7400	10,500
Town & Country Series, V-8, 126" wb						
4d 9P Sta Wag	450	1450	2450	4900	8500	12,200
4d 6P Sta Wag	450	1450	2400	4800	8400	12,000
300 Letter Series "F", V-8						
2d Conv	2250	7200	12,000	24,000	42,000	60,000
2d HT	1800	5750	9600	19,200	33,600	48,000

NOTE: 300 Letter Series cars containing the Pont-A-Mousson 4-speed transmission, the value is not estimable.

	6	5	4	3	2	1
Custom Imperial Line, V-8						
2d HT S Hamp	550	1800	3000	6000	10,500	15,000
4d HT S Hamp	500	1550	2600	5200	9100	13,000
4d Sed	400	1300	2200	4400	7700	11,000
Crown Imperial Line, V-8						
2d Conv	1050	3350	5600	11,200	19,600	28,000
2d HT S Hamp	850	2650	4400	8800	15,400	22,000
4d HT S Hamp	650	2050	3400	6800	11,900	17,000
4d Sed	550	1700	2800	5600	9800	14,000
Imperial LeBaron Line						
4d Sed	550	1750	2900	5800	10,200	14,500
4d HT S Hamp	650	2100	3500	7000	12,300	17,500
Crown Imperial Ghia, V-8						
4d Limo	1000	3100	5200	10,400	18,200	26,000

1961

	6	5	4	3	2	1
Newport Series, V-8						
2d Conv	550	1700	2800	5600	9800	14,000
2d HT	400	1300	2200	4400	7700	11,000
4d HT	400	1250	2100	4200	7400	10,500
4d Sed	450	1140	1900	3800	6650	9500
4d 6P Sta Wag	400	1200	2000	4000	7000	10,000
4d 9P Sta Wag	400	1200	2000	4000	7100	10,100
Windsor Series, V-8						
2d HT	450	1400	2300	4600	8100	11,500
4d HT	400	1300	2200	4400	7700	11,000
4d Sed	400	1200	2000	4000	7000	10,000
New Yorker Series, V-8						
2d Conv	600	1900	3200	6400	11,200	16,000
2d HT	450	1450	2400	4800	8400	12,000
4d HT	400	1300	2200	4400	7700	11,000
4d Sed	400	1250	2100	4200	7400	10,500
4d 6P Sta Wag	400	1300	2200	4400	7700	11,000
4d 9P Sta Wag	400	1350	2200	4400	7800	11,100
300 Letter Series "G", V-8						
2d Conv	1750	5500	9200	18,400	32,200	46,000
2d HT	1350	4300	7200	14,400	25,200	36,000

NOTE: Add 20 percent for 400HP engine.

	6	5	4	3	2	1
Custom Imperial Line, V-8						
2d HT S Hamp	450	1500	2500	5000	8800	12,500
4d HT S Hamp	400	1300	2200	4400	7700	11,000
Crown Imperial Line, V-8						
2d Conv	750	2400	4000	8000	14,000	20,000
2d HT S Hamp	500	1550	2600	5200	9100	13,000
4d HT S Hamp	450	1400	2300	4600	8100	11,500
Imperial LeBaron Line, V-8						
4d HT S Hamp	450	1450	2400	4800	8400	12,000
Crown Imperial Ghia, V-8						
4d Limo	900	2900	4800	9600	16,800	24,000

1962

	6	5	4	3	2	1
Newport Series, V-8						
4d Sed	450	1150	1900	3850	6700	9600
4d HT	400	1200	2000	4000	7000	10,000
2d Conv	500	1550	2600	5200	9100	13,000
2d HT	450	1400	2300	4600	8100	11,500
4d 6P HT Wag	400	1300	2200	4400	7700	11,000
4d 9P HT Wag	400	1350	2250	4500	7800	11,200
300 Series						
2d Conv	600	1900	3200	6400	11,200	16,000
2d HT	450	1450	2400	4800	8400	12,000
4d HT	400	1300	2200	4400	7700	11,000
300 Letter Series "H", V-8						
2d Conv	1700	5400	9000	18,000	31,500	45,000
2d HT	1300	4200	7000	14,000	24,500	35,000
New Yorker Series, V-8						
4d Sed	450	1080	1800	3600	6300	9000
4d HT	450	1400	2300	4600	8100	11,500
4d 6P HT Wag	450	1450	2400	4800	8400	12,000
4d 9P HT Wag	450	1450	2450	4900	8500	12,200
Custom Imperial Line, V-8						
2d HT S Hamp	500	1550	2600	5200	9100	13,000
4d HT S Hamp	400	1300	2200	4400	7700	11,000
Crown Imperial Line, V-8						
2d Conv	700	2300	3800	7600	13,300	19,000
2d HT S Hamp	450	1450	2400	4800	8400	12,000
4d HT S Hamp	450	1400	2300	4600	8100	11,500
Imperial LeBaron Line, V-8						
4d HT S Hamp	450	1450	2400	4800	8400	12,000

1963

	6	5	4	3	2	1
Newport Series, V-8						
2d Conv	550	1700	2800	5600	9800	14,000
2d HT	450	1400	2300	4600	8100	11,500
4d HT	450	1080	1800	3600	6300	9000
4d Sed	350	1020	1700	3400	5950	8500
4d 6P Sta Wag	400	1300	2200	4400	7700	11,000
4d 9P Sta Wag	400	1350	2250	4500	7800	11,200
300 Series, "383" V-8						
2d Conv	600	1900	3200	6400	11,200	16,000
2d HT	450	1500	2500	5000	8800	12,500
4d HT	400	1250	2100	4200	7400	10,500
300 "Pacesetter" Series, "383" V-8						
2d Conv	600	1900	3200	6400	11,200	16,000
2d HT	450	1450	2400	4800	8400	12,000
300 Letter Series "J", "413" V-8						
2d HT	1000	3100	5200	10,400	18,200	26,000
New Yorker Series, V-8						
4d Sed	450	1080	1800	3600	6300	9000
4d HT	400	1200	2000	4000	7000	10,000
4d HT Salon	400	1200	2050	4100	7100	10,200
4d 6P Sta Wag	450	1400	2350	4700	8200	11,700
4d 9P Sta Wag	450	1400	2350	4700	8200	11,700
Custom Imperial Line, V-8						
2d HT S Hamp	450	1500	2500	5000	8800	12,500
4d HT S Hamp	400	1300	2200	4400	7700	11,000
Crown Imperial Line, V-8						
2d Conv	650	2050	3400	6800	11,900	17,000
2d HT S Hamp	450	1500	2500	5000	8800	12,500
4d HT S Hamp	400	1300	2200	4400	7700	11,000
Imperial LeBaron Line, V-8						
4d HT S Hamp	450	1450	2400	4800	8400	12,000
Crown Imperial Ghia, V-8						
4d 8P Sed	550	1800	3000	6000	10,500	15,000
4d 8P Limo	750	2400	4000	8000	14,000	20,000

1964

	6	5	4	3	2	1
Newport Series, V-8						
2d Conv	500	1550	2600	5200	9100	13,000
2d HT	400	1200	2000	4000	7000	10,000
4d HT	450	1080	1800	3600	6300	9000
4d Sed	350	1020	1700	3400	5950	8500
Town & Country Series, V-8						
4d 9P Sta Wag	450	1140	1900	3800	6650	9500
4d 6P Sta Wag	450	1130	1900	3800	6600	9400
300 Series						
2d Conv	600	1900	3200	6400	11,200	16,000
2d HT	400	1250	2100	4200	7400	10,500
4d HT	450	1140	1900	3800	6650	9500
300 Letter Series "K", V-8						
2d Conv	1200	3850	6400	12,800	22,400	32,000
2d HT	1000	3100	5200	10,400	18,200	26,000

NOTE: Add 10 percent for two 4 barrel carbs.

	6	5	4	3	2	1
New Yorker Series, V-8						
4d Sed	450	1140	1900	3800	6650	9500
4d HT	400	1200	2000	4000	7000	10,000
4d HT Salon	400	1250	2100	4200	7400	10,500
Town & Country Series, V-8						
4d 9P HT Wag	400	1350	2250	4500	7800	11,200
4d 6P HT Wag	400	1300	2200	4400	7700	11,000
Imperial Crown, V-8						
2d Conv	700	2150	3600	7200	12,600	18,000
2d HT	450	1450	2400	4800	8400	12,000
4d HT	450	1400	2300	4600	8100	11,500
Imperial LeBaron, V-8						
4d HT	500	1550	2600	5200	9100	13,000
Crown Imperial Ghia, V-8						
4d Limo	750	2350	3900	7800	13,700	19,500

1965

	6	5	4	3	2	1
Newport Series, V-8						
2d Conv	450	1500	2500	5000	8800	12,500
2d HT	400	1250	2100	4200	7400	10,500
4d HT	450	1140	1900	3800	6650	9500
4d Sed	350	1020	1700	3400	5950	8500
4d 6W Sed	350	1000	1650	3350	5800	8300
Town & Country Series, V-8						
4d 6P Wag	400	1200	2000	4000	7000	10,000
4d 9P Wag	400	1200	2050	4100	7100	10,200
300 Series						
2d Conv	550	1800	3000	6000	10,500	15,000
2d HT	400	1300	2200	4400	7700	11,000
4d HT	450	1140	1900	3800	6650	9500

300 Letter Series "L", V-8	6	5	4	3	2	1
2d Conv	1100	3500	5800	11,600	20,300	29,000
2d HT	950	3000	5000	10,000	17,500	25,000
New Yorker Series, V-8						
2d HT	450	1400	2300	4600	8100	11,500
4d HT	400	1200	2000	4000	7000	10,000
4d 6W Sed	450	1080	1800	3600	6300	9000
Town & Country Series, V-8						
4d 6P Wag	400	1300	2200	4400	7700	11,000
4d 9P Wag	400	1350	2250	4500	7800	11,200
Crown Imperial Line, V-8						
2d Conv	650	2050	3400	6800	11,900	17,000
2d HT	450	1450	2400	4800	8400	12,000
4d HT	400	1300	2200	4400	7700	11,000
Imperial LeBaron Line, V-8						
4d HT	450	1500	2500	5000	8800	12,500
Crown Imperial Ghia, V-8						
4d Limo	750	2400	4000	8000	14,000	20,000

1966

	6	5	4	3	2	1
Newport Series, V-8						
2d Conv	550	1700	2800	5600	9800	14,000
2d HT	400	1300	2200	4400	7700	11,000
4d HT	400	1200	2000	4000	7000	10,000
4d Sed	450	1080	1800	3600	6300	9000
4d 6W Sed	450	1050	1800	3600	6200	8900
Town & Country Series, V-8						
4d 6P Sta Wag	400	1300	2200	4400	7700	11,000
4d 9P Sta Wag	400	1350	2250	4500	7800	11,200
Chrysler 300, V-8						
2d Conv	750	2400	4000	8000	14,000	20,000
2d HT	550	1800	3000	6000	10,500	15,000
4d HT	400	1300	2200	4400	7700	11,000
New Yorker, V-8						
2d HT	450	1400	2300	4600	8100	11,500
4d HT	400	1300	2200	4400	7700	11,000
4d 6W Sed	400	1250	2100	4200	7400	10,500
Imperial, V-8						
2d Conv	700	2150	3600	7200	12,600	18,000
2d HT	500	1550	2600	5200	9100	13,000
4d HT	450	1450	2400	4800	8400	12,000
Imperial LeBaron, V-8						
4d HT	550	1700	2800	5600	9800	14,000

1967

	6	5	4	3	2	1
Newport, V-8, 124" wb						
2d Conv	550	1700	2800	5600	9800	14,000
2d HT	450	1400	2300	4600	8100	11,500
4d HT	400	1250	2100	4200	7400	10,500
4d Sed	450	1090	1800	3650	6400	9100
4d Sta Wag	450	1400	2300	4600	8100	11,500
Newport Custom, V-8, 124" wb						
2d HT	450	1400	2300	4600	8100	11,500
4d HT	400	1250	2100	4200	7400	10,500
4d Sed	950	1100	1850	3700	6450	9200
300, V-8, 124" wb						
2d Conv	700	2150	3600	7200	12,600	18,000
2d HT	450	1500	2500	5000	8800	12,500
4d HT	400	1300	2200	4400	7700	11,000
New Yorker, V-8, 124" wb						
2d HT	450	1450	2400	4800	8400	12,000
4d HT	400	1300	2200	4400	7700	11,000
4d Sed	450	1140	1900	3800	6650	9500
Imperial, V-8, 127" wb						
2d Conv	750	2400	4000	8000	14,000	20,000
4d Sed	450	1500	2500	5000	8800	12,500
Imperial Crown						
4d HT	500	1550	2600	5200	9100	13,000
2d HT	600	1850	3100	6200	10,900	15,500
4d HT	500	1550	2600	5200	9100	13,000
4d HT	500	1600	2700	5400	9500	13,500

1968

	6	5	4	3	2	1
Newport, V-8, 124" wb						
2d Conv	550	1700	2800	5600	9800	14,000
2d HT	450	1450	2400	4800	8400	12,000
4d HT	400	1300	2200	4400	7700	11,000
4d Sed	400	1200	2000	4000	7000	10,000
Newport Custom, V-8, 124" wb						
2d HT	450	1450	2400	4800	8400	12,000
4d HT	400	1250	2100	4200	7400	10,600
4d Sed	450	1160	1950	3900	6800	9700
300, V-8, 124" wb						
2d Conv	700	2150	3600	7200	12,600	18,000
2d HT	450	1500	2500	5000	8800	12,500
4d HT	400	1300	2200	4400	7700	11,000
Town & Country, V-8, 122" wb						
4d Sta Wag	450	1400	2300	4600	8100	11,500
New Yorker, V-8, 124" wb						
2d HT	450	1500	2500	5000	8800	12,500
4d HT	450	1400	2300	4600	8100	11,500
4d Sed	400	1200	2000	4000	7000	10,000
Imperial, V-8, 127" wb						
2d Conv	750	2400	4000	8000	14,000	20,000
2d HT	600	1850	3100	6200	10,900	15,500
4d HT	500	1550	2600	5200	9100	13,000
4d Sed	450	1400	2300	4600	8100	11,500
Imperial LeBaron						
4d HT	550	1750	2900	5800	10,200	14,500

1969

	6	5	4	3	2	1
Newport, V-8, 124" wb						
2d Conv	400	1300	2200	4400	7700	11,000
2d HT	350	840	1400	2800	4900	7000
4d HT	200	685	1150	2300	3990	5700
4d Sed	200	700	1050	2100	3650	5200
Newport Custom, V-8, 124" wb						
2d HT	350	860	1450	2900	5050	7200
4d HT	200	670	1200	2300	4060	5800
4d Sed	200	700	1075	2150	3700	5300
300, V-8, 124" wb						
2d Conv	400	1300	2200	4400	7700	11,000
2d HT	350	975	1600	3200	5600	8000
4d HT	350	780	1300	2600	4550	6500
New Yorker, V-8, 124" wb						
2d HT	350	975	1600	3200	5600	8000

	6	5	4	3	2	1
4d HT	200	720	1200	2400	4200	6000
4d Sed	200	670	1200	2300	4060	5800
Town & Country, V-8, 122" wb						
4d Sta Wag	200	720	1200	2400	4200	6000
Imperial Crown, V-8, 127" wb						
2d HT	350	975	1600	3200	5600	8000
4d HT	350	780	1300	2600	4550	6500
4d Sed	200	720	1200	2400	4200	6000
Imperial LeBaron						
2d HT	350	1020	1700	3400	5950	8500
4d HT	350	780	1300	2600	4550	6500

1970

Newport, V-8, 124" wb

	6	5	4	3	2	1
2d HT	350	900	1500	3000	5250	7500
2d Conv	400	1250	2100	4200	7400	10,500
4d HT	200	720	1200	2400	4200	6000
4d Sed	200	685	1150	2300	3990	5700
Newport Custom						
2d HT	350	840	1400	2800	4900	7000
4d HT	350	800	1350	2700	4700	6700
4d Sed	200	720	1200	2400	4200	6000
300, V-8, 124" wb						
2d Conv	550	1800	3000	6000	10,500	15,000
2d HT Hurst	500	1550	2600	5200	9100	13,000
2d HT	350	975	1600	3200	5600	8000
4d HT	350	900	1500	3000	5250	7500
New Yorker, V-8, 124" wb						
2d HT	350	1020	1700	3400	5950	8500
4d HT	350	840	1400	2800	4900	7000
4d Sed	350	780	1300	2600	4550	6500
Town & Country, V-8, 122" wb						
4d Sta Wag	350	780	1300	2600	4550	6500
Imperial Crown, V-8, 127" wb						
2d HT	450	1080	1800	3600	6300	9000
4d HT	350	900	1500	3000	5250	7500
Imperial LeBaron, V-8, 127" wb						
2d HT	450	1140	1900	3800	6650	9500
4d HT	350	975	1600	3200	5600	8000

1971

Newport Royal, V-8, 124" wb

	6	5	4	3	2	1
2d HT	200	720	1200	2400	4200	6000
4d HT	200	675	1000	1950	3400	4900
4d Sed	150	650	975	1950	3350	4800
Newport, V-8, 124" wb						
2d HT	350	840	1400	2800	4900	7000
4d HT	200	700	1050	2100	3650	5200
4d Sed	200	675	1000	1950	3400	4900
Newport Custom						
2d HT	350	900	1500	3000	5250	7500
4d HT	200	660	1100	2200	3850	5500
4d Sed	200	675	1000	2000	3500	5000
300						
2d HT	350	975	1600	3200	5600	8000
4d HT	200	700	1050	2100	3650	5200
New Yorker						
2d HT	350	975	1600	3200	5600	8000
4d HT	200	720	1200	2400	4200	6000
4d Sed	200	700	1050	2050	3600	5100
Town & Country						
4d Sta Wag	200	660	1100	2200	3850	5500
Imperial LeBaron						
2d HT	350	1020	1700	3400	5950	8500
4d HT	350	780	1300	2600	4550	6500

1972

Newport Royal

	6	5	4	3	2	1
2d HT	350	780	1300	2600	4550	6500
4d HT	200	675	1000	2000	3500	5000
4d Sed	150	575	900	1750	3100	4400
Newport Custom						
2d HT	350	840	1400	2800	4900	7000
4d HT	200	660	1100	2200	3850	5500
4d Sed	150	600	900	1800	3150	4500
New Yorker Brougham						
2d HT	350	900	1500	3000	5250	7500
4d HT	200	720	1200	2400	4200	6000
4d Sed	200	675	1000	2000	3500	5000
Town & Country						
4d Sta Wag	200	660	1100	2200	3850	5500
Imperial LeBaron						
2d HT	350	975	1600	3200	5600	8000
4d HT	350	780	1300	2600	4550	6500

1973

Newport, V-8, 124" wb

	6	5	4	3	2	1
2d HT	200	660	1100	2200	3850	5500
4d HT	150	500	800	1600	2800	4000
4d Sed	150	475	775	1500	2650	3800
Newport Custom V-8						
2d HT	200	685	1150	2300	3990	5700
4d HT	150	550	850	1650	2900	4100
4d Sed	150	500	800	1600	2800	4000
New Yorker Brgm V-8						
2d HT	200	720	1200	2400	4200	6000
4d HT	150	600	900	1800	3150	4500
4d Sed	150	550	850	1650	2900	4100
Town & Country V-8						
4d 3S Sta Wag	150	475	775	1500	2650	3800
Imperial LeBaron V-8						
2d HT	200	745	1250	2500	4340	6200
4d HT	150	650	950	1900	3300	4700

1974

Newport V-8

	6	5	4	3	2	1
2d HT	150	650	975	1950	3350	4800
4d HT	125	450	700	1400	2450	3500
4d Sed	125	400	700	1375	2400	3400
Newport Custom V-8						
2d HT	200	675	1000	2000	3500	5000
4d HT	150	475	750	1475	2600	3700
4d Sed	125	450	750	1450	2500	3600
New Yorker V-8						
4d Sed	150	475	750	1475	2600	3700

	6	5	4	3	2	1
4d HT	150	550	850	1675	2950	4200
New Yorker Brgm V-8						
2d HT	200	700	1050	2100	3650	5200
4d HT	150	500	800	1600	2800	4000
4d Sed	150	500	800	1550	2700	3900
Town & Country V-8						
4d 3S Sta Wag	150	500	800	1550	2700	3900
Imperial LeBaron						
2d HT	200	650	1100	2150	3780	5400
4d HT	150	575	875	1700	3000	4300

NOTE: Add 20 percent for Crown Coupe package (Orig. price $542.).

1975

Cordoba V-8

	6	5	4	3	2	1
2d HT	200	660	1100	2200	3850	5500
Newport V-8						
2d HT	150	600	900	1800	3150	4500
4d HT	125	450	700	1400	2450	3500
4d Sed	125	400	700	1375	2400	3400
Newport Custom V-8						
2d HT	150	600	950	1850	3200	4600
4d HT	125	450	750	1450	2500	3600
4d Sed	125	450	700	1400	2450	3500
New Yorker Brgm V-8						
2d HT	150	650	975	1950	3350	4800
4d HT	150	475	775	1500	2650	3800
4d Sed	125	450	750	1450	2500	3600
Town & Country V-8						
4d 3S Sta Wag	125	450	750	1450	2500	3600
Imperial LeBaron						
2d HT	200	700	1050	2050	3600	5100
4d HT	150	500	800	1600	2800	4000

NOTE: Add 20 percent for Crown Coupe package (Orig. price $569.).

1976

Cordoba, V-8

	6	5	4	3	2	1
2d HT	200	720	1200	2400	4200	6000
Newport, V-8						
2d HT	150	650	950	1900	3300	4700
4d HT	150	500	800	1550	2700	3900
4d Sed	125	450	700	1400	2450	3500
Newport Custom, V-8						
2d HT	200	675	1000	2000	3500	5000
4d HT	150	475	775	1500	2650	3800
4d Sed	125	450	750	1450	2500	3600
Town & Country, V-8						
4d 2S Sta Wag	125	450	750	1450	2500	3600
4d 3S Sta Wag	150	475	750	1475	2600	3700
New Yorker Brougham, V-8						
2d HT	200	700	1050	2100	3650	5200
4d HT	150	475	775	1500	2650	3800

1977

LeBaron, V-8

	6	5	4	3	2	1
2d Cpe	150	500	800	1600	2800	4000
4d Sed	150	475	775	1500	2650	3800
LeBaron Medallion, V-8						
2d Cpe	150	550	850	1675	2950	4200
4d Sed	150	500	800	1600	2800	4000
Cordoba, V-8						
2d HT	200	660	1100	2200	3850	5500
Newport, V-8						
2d HT	150	600	900	1800	3150	4500
4d HT	150	475	775	1500	2650	3800
4d Sed	125	450	750	1450	2500	3600
Town & Country, V-8						
4d 2S Sta Wag	150	475	750	1475	2600	3700
4d 3S Sta Wag	150	475	775	1500	2650	3800
New Yorker Brougham, V-8						
2d HT	150	650	950	1900	3300	4700
4d HT	150	500	800	1550	2700	3900

1978

LeBaron

	6	5	4	3	2	1
2d Cpe	125	450	750	1450	2500	3600
2d 'S' Cpe	125	450	700	1400	2450	3500
4d 'S' Cpe	125	450	700	1400	2450	3500
4d Sed	125	450	700	1400	2450	3500
Town & Country						
4d Sta Wag	125	450	700	1400	2450	3500
LeBaron Medallion						
2d Cpe	150	475	750	1475	2600	3700
4d Sed	125	450	750	1450	2500	3600
Cordoba						
2d Cpe	200	660	1100	2200	3850	5500
Newport						
2d Cpe	150	475	775	1500	2650	3800
4d Sed	150	475	750	1475	2600	3700
New Yorker Brougham						
2d Cpe	150	500	800	1600	2800	4000
4d Sed	150	500	800	1550	2700	3900

1979

LeBaron, V-8

	6	5	4	3	2	1
2d Cpe	125	450	750	1450	2500	3600
4d Sed	125	450	700	1400	2450	3500
LeBaron Salon, V-8						
2d Cpe	150	475	750	1475	2600	3700
4d Sed	125	450	750	1450	2500	3600
LeBaron Medallion, V-8						
2d Cpe	150	500	800	1550	2700	3900
4d Sed	150	475	775	1500	2650	3800
LeBaron Town & Country						
4d Sta Wag	150	475	775	1500	2650	3800

NOTE: Deduct 5 percent for 6-cyl.

Cordoba, V-8

	6	5	4	3	2	1
2d Cpe	200	700	1050	2100	3650	5200

NOTE: Add 20 percent for 300 option.

Newport, V-8

	6	5	4	3	2	1
4d Sed	150	500	800	1550	2700	3900

NOTE: Deduct 7 percent for 6-cyl.

New Yorker, V-8

	6	5	4	3	2	1
4d Sed	150	550	850	1650	2900	4100

	6	5	4	3	2	1
1980						
LeBaron, V-8						
2d Cpe Medallion	150	500	800	1600	2800	4000
4d Sed Medallion	150	500	800	1550	2700	3900
4d Sta Wag T&C	150	500	800	1600	2800	4000
NOTE: Deduct 5 percent for lesser models.						
Cordoba, V-8						
2d Cpe Specialty	200	720	1200	2400	4200	6000
2d Cpe Spl Crown	350	780	1300	2600	4550	6500
2d Cpe Spl LS	200	700	1200	2350	4130	5900
NOTE: Deduct 12 percent for 6-cyl.						
Newport, V-8						
4d Sed	150	575	875	1700	3000	4300
New Yorker, V-8						
4d Sed	150	600	900	1800	3150	4500
1981						
LeBaron, V-8						
2d Cpe Medallion	150	550	850	1650	2900	4100
4d Sed Medallion	150	500	800	1600	2800	4000
4d Sta Wag T&C	150	550	850	1650	2900	4100
NOTE: Deduct 12 percent for 6-cyl. Deduct 5 percent for lesser models.						
Cordoba, V-8						
2d Cpe Specialty LS	200	720	1200	2400	4200	6000
2d Cpe Specialty	200	730	1250	2450	4270	6100
NOTE: Deduct 12 percent for 6-cyl.						
Newport, V-8						
4d Sed	150	575	900	1750	3100	4400
NOTE: Deduct 10 percent for 6-cyl.						
New Yorker, V-8						
4d Sed	150	600	950	1850	3200	4600
Imperial, V-8						
2d Cpe	200	720	1200	2400	4200	6000
1982						
LeBaron, 4-cyl.						
2d Conv	200	720	1200	2400	4200	6000
2d Cpe Specialty	150	500	800	1600	2800	4000
4d Sed Medallion	150	550	850	1650	2900	4100
4d Sed	150	500	800	1600	2800	4000
2d Conv Medallion	200	720	1200	2400	4200	6000
2d Cpe Spec Medallion	150	550	850	1650	2900	4100
4d Sta Wag T&C	150	575	900	1750	3100	4400
Cordoba, V-8						
2d Cpe Specialty LS	200	730	1250	2450	4270	6100
2d Cpe Specialty	200	745	1250	2500	4340	6200
NOTE: Deduct 12 percent for 6-cyl.						
New Yorker, V-8						
4d Sed	200	675	1000	1950	3400	4900
NOTE: Deduct 11 percent for 6-cyl.						
Imperial, V-8						
2d Cpe Luxury	200	720	1200	2400	4200	6000
1983						
LeBaron, 4-cyl.						
2d Conv	200	730	1250	2450	4270	6100
2d Conv T&C Marc Cross	350	790	1350	2650	4620	6600
2d Cpe	150	550	850	1650	2900	4100
4d Sed	150	550	850	1650	2900	4100
4d Sta Wag T&C	150	600	900	1800	3150	4500
4d Limo	200	675	1000	1950	3400	4900
E Class, 4-cyl.						
4d Sed	150	600	900	1800	3150	4500
Cordoba, V-8						
2d Cpe	200	750	1275	2500	4400	6300
NOTE: Deduct 12 percent for 6-cyl.						
New Yorker, 4-cyl.						
4d Sed	150	650	975	1950	3350	4800
New Yorker Fifth Avenue, V-8						
4d Sed	200	675	1000	1950	3400	4900
4 dr Sed Luxury	200	675	1000	2000	3500	5000
NOTE: Deduct 12 percent for 6-cyl.						
Imperial, V-8						
2d Cpe	200	720	1200	2400	4200	6000
1984						
LeBaron, 4-cyl.						
2d Conv	200	745	1250	2500	4340	6200
2d Conv Marc Cross	350	800	1350	2700	4700	6700
2d Conv T&C Marc Cross	350	790	1350	2650	4620	6600
2d Sed	150	550	850	1650	2900	4100
4d Sed	150	550	850	1650	2900	4100
4d Sta Wag T&C	150	550	850	1675	2950	4200
Laser, 4-cyl.						
2d HBk	150	550	850	1675	2950	4200
2d HBk XE	150	575	875	1700	3000	4300
E Class, 4-cyl.						
4d Sed	150	600	900	1800	3150	4500
New Yorker, 4-cyl.						
4d Sed	150	650	975	1950	3350	4800
New Yorker Fifth Avenue, V-8						
4d Sed	200	675	1000	2000	3500	5000
1985						
LeBaron, 4-cyl.						
2d Conv	200	745	1250	2500	4340	6200
2d Conv Marc Cross	350	800	1350	2700	4700	6700
2d Conv T&C Marc Cross	350	820	1400	2700	4760	6800
2d Cpe	150	550	850	1650	2900	4100
4d Sed	150	550	850	1675	2950	4200
4d Sta Wag T&C	150	575	875	1700	3000	4300
Laser, 4-cyl.						
2d HBk	150	575	875	1700	3000	4300
2d HBk XE	150	575	900	1750	3100	4400
LeBaron GTS, 4-cyl.						
4d Spt	150	600	950	1850	3200	4600
4d Spt Premium	150	650	950	1900	3300	4700
New Yorker, 4-cyl.						
4d	200	675	1000	1950	3400	4900
Fifth Avenue, V-8						
4d Sed	200	700	1050	2050	3600	5100
1986						
Laser						
2d HBk	150	575	875	1700	3000	4300
LeBaron						
2d Conv	200	745	1250	2500	4340	6200
2d Mac Cross Conv	350	840	1400	2800	4900	7000
2d Cpe	150	600	950	1850	3200	4600
4d Sed	150	650	950	1900	3300	4700
4d T&C Sta Wag	150	650	975	1950	3350	4800
New Yorker						
4d Sed	200	675	1000	2000	3500	5000
Fifth Avenue						
4d Sed	200	700	1050	2100	3650	5200
Executive						
4d Limo	200	660	1100	2200	3850	5500
NOTES: Add 10 percent for deluxe models. Deduct 5 percent for smaller engines.						
1987						
LeBaron						
2d Conv	350	780	1300	2600	4550	6500
2d Cpe	150	550	850	1675	2950	4200
2d Cpe Premium	150	575	875	1700	3000	4300
4d Sed	150	575	875	1700	3000	4300
4d HBk Spt GTS	150	600	900	1800	3150	4500
4d HBk Spt Prem GTS	150	600	950	1850	3200	4600
4d Sta Wag	150	575	900	1750	3100	4400
NOTE: Add 5 percent for 2.2 Turbo engine.						
Conquest, 4-cyl. Turbo						
2d HBk	150	575	875	1700	3000	4300
New Yorker, 4-cyl.						
4d Sed	200	660	1100	2200	3850	5500
New Yorker, V-6						
4d Sed	150	650	950	1900	3300	4700
4d Sed Lan	200	675	1000	1950	3400	4900
NOTE: Add 5 percent for 2.2 Turbo engine.						
NOTE: Add 10 percent for V-6.						
Fifth Avenue, V-8						
4d Sed	200	720	1200	2400	4200	6000
1988						
LeBaron, 4-cyl.						
2d Conv	350	820	1400	2700	4760	6800
2d Cpe	150	475	775	1500	2650	3800
2d Cpe Prem	150	600	900	1800	3150	4500
4d Sed	125	400	675	1350	2300	3300
4d HBk GTS	125	380	650	1300	2250	3200
4d HBk Prem GTS	125	450	700	1400	2450	3500
4d Sta Wag T&C	150	550	850	1675	2950	4200
Conquest, 4-cyl.						
2d HBk	150	500	800	1600	2800	4000
New Yorker, 4-cyl., Turbo						
4d Sed	150	600	950	1850	3200	4600
New Yorker, V-6						
4d Sed	200	700	1050	2100	3650	5200
4d Sed Landau	200	670	1150	2250	3920	5600
Fifth Avenue,V-8						
4d Sed	350	820	1400	2700	4760	6800
1989						
LeBaron, 4-cyl.						
2d Conv	350	840	1400	2800	4900	7000
2d Conv Prem	350	975	1600	3200	5600	8000
2d Cpe	200	670	1150	2250	3920	5600
2d Prem	200	670	1200	2300	4060	5800
4d HBk	200	660	1100	2200	3850	5500
4d HBk Prem	200	685	1150	2300	3990	5700
2d Conv	350	840	1400	2800	4900	7000
Conquest, 4-cyl.						
2d HBk	200	720	1200	2400	4200	6000
New Yorker, V-6						
4d Sed	350	790	1350	2650	4620	6600
4d Lan Sed	350	820	1400	2700	4760	6800
Fifth Avenue, V-8						
4d Sed	350	860	1450	2900	5050	7200
TC, 4-cyl. Turbo by Maserati						
2d Conv	650	2050	3400	6800	11,900	17,000
1990						
LeBaron						
4-cyl.						
2d Conv	350	780	1300	2600	4550	6500
2d Cpe	200	675	1000	2000	3500	5000
V-6						
2d Conv	350	840	1400	2800	4900	7000
2d Prem Conv	350	900	1500	3000	5250	7500
2d Cpe	200	660	1100	2200	3850	5500
2d Prem Cpe	200	720	1200	2400	4200	6000
4d Sed	200	660	1100	2200	3850	5500
New Yorker, V-6						
4d Sed	350	780	1300	2600	4550	6500
4d Lan Sed	350	840	1400	2800	4900	7000
4d Fifth Ave Sed	350	975	1600	3200	5600	8000
Imperial, V-6						
4d Sed	450	1080	1800	3600	6300	9000
TC, V-6 by Maserati						
2d Conv	550	1800	3000	6000	10,500	15,000
1991						
TC, V-6 by Maserati						
2d Conv	600	1900	3200	6400	11,200	16,000
1991						
LeBaron						
4-cyl.						
2d Conv	350	780	1300	2600	4550	6500
2d Cpe	150	600	900	1800	3150	4500
V-6						
2d LX Conv	350	840	1400	2800	4900	7000
2d LX Cpe	200	675	1000	2000	3500	5000
4d Sed	200	660	1100	2200	3850	5500
New Yorker & Imperial, V-6						
4d Salon Sed	200	745	1250	2500	4340	6200
4d Fifth Ave Sed	350	780	1300	2600	4550	6500
4d Imperial Sed	350	860	1450	2900	5050	7200
1992						
LeBaron, 4-cyl.						
2d Cpe	200	660	1100	2200	3850	5500

	6	5	4	3	2	1
2d Conv	350	840	1400	2800	4900	7000
4d Sed	200	650	1100	2150	3780	5400
4d Lan Sed	200	660	1100	2200	3850	5500
2d LX Cpe	350	900	1500	3000	5250	7500
2d LX Conv	200	720	1200	2400	4200	6000
4d LX Sed	350	780	1300	2600	4550	6500
NOTE: Add 10 percent for V-6 where available.						
New Yorker, V-6						
4d Salom Sed	350	840	1400	2800	4900	7000
4d Fifth Ave Sed	350	900	1500	3000	5250	7500
Imperial, V-6						
4d Sed	350	1020	1700	3400	5950	8500
1993						
LeBaron, 4-cyl.						
4d Sed	200	670	1150	2250	3920	5600
2d Cpe	200	660	1100	2200	3850	5500
2d LE Conv	350	850	1450	2850	4970	7100
LeBaron, V-6						
4d LE Sed	200	685	1150	2300	3990	5700
4d Landau Sed	200	670	1200	2300	4060	5800
2d Cpe	200	670	1200	2300	4060	5800
2d LX Cpe	200	700	1200	2350	4130	5900
2d Conv	350	880	1500	2950	5180	7400
2d LX Conv	350	950	1500	3050	5300	7600
Concorde, V-6						
4d Sed	350	780	1300	2600	4550	6500
New Yorker, V-6						
4d Salom Sed	350	850	1450	2850	4970	7100
4d Fifth Ave Sed	350	900	1500	3000	5250	7500
Imperial, V-6						
4d Sed	350	1040	1700	3450	6000	8600

DESOTO

	6	5	4	3	2	1
1929						
Model K, 6-cyl.						
2d Rds	1050	3350	5600	11,200	19,600	28,000
4d Phae	1100	3500	5800	11,600	20,300	29,000
2d Bus Cpe	500	1600	2700	5400	9500	13,500
2d DeL Cpe	500	1550	2600	5200	9100	13,000
2d Sed	400	1300	2150	4300	7500	10,700
4d Sed	400	1300	2150	4300	7500	10,700
4d DeL Sed	400	1300	2200	4400	7700	11,000
1930						
Model CK, 6-cyl.						
2d Rds	1000	3250	5400	10,800	18,900	27,000
4d Tr	1050	3350	5600	11,200	19,600	28,000
2d Bus Cpe	500	1550	2600	5200	9100	13,000
2d DeL Cpe	500	1600	2700	5400	9500	13,500
2d Sed	400	1200	2000	4000	7000	10,000
4d Sed	400	1250	2100	4200	7400	10,500
Model CF, 8-cyl.						
2d Rds	1050	3350	5600	11,200	19,600	28,000
4d Phae	1100	3500	5800	11,600	20,300	29,000
2d Bus Cpe	500	1600	2700	5400	9500	13,500
2d DeL Cpe	550	1700	2800	5600	9800	14,000
4d Sed	450	1400	2300	4600	8100	11,500
4d DeL Sed	450	1450	2400	4800	8400	12,000
2d Conv	1000	3250	5400	10,800	18,900	27,000
1931						
Model SA, 6-cyl.						
2d Rds	1050	3350	5600	11,200	19,600	28,000
4d Phae	1100	3500	5800	11,600	20,300	29,000
2d 2d Cpe	500	1550	2600	5200	9100	13,000
2d DeL Cpe	550	1750	2900	5800	10,200	14,500
2d Sed	400	1300	2200	4400	7700	11,000
4d Sed	400	1350	2250	4500	7800	11,200
4d DeL Sed	450	1400	2300	4600	8100	11,500
2d Conv	1000	3250	5400	10,800	18,900	27,000
Model CF, 8-cyl.						
2d Rds	1100	3500	5800	11,600	20,300	29,000
2d Bus Cpe	550	1800	3000	6000	10,500	15,000
2d DeL Cpe	600	1850	3100	6200	10,900	15,500
4d Sed	450	1400	2350	4700	8300	11,800
4d DeL Sed	450	1450	2400	4800	8400	12,000
2d Conv	1050	3350	5600	11,200	19,600	28,000
1932						
SA, 6-cyl., 109" wb						
4d Phae	1150	3600	6000	12,000	21,000	30,000
2d Rds	1100	3500	5800	11,600	20,300	29,000
2d Cpe	600	1850	3100	6200	10,900	15,500
2d DeL Cpe	600	1900	3200	6400	11,200	16,000
2d Conv	1050	3350	5600	11,200	19,600	28,000
2d Sed	400	1300	2200	4400	7700	11,000
4d Sed	400	1350	2250	4500	7800	11,200
4d DeL Sed	450	1400	2300	4600	8100	11,500
SC, 6-cyl., 112" wb						
2d Conv Sed	1050	3350	5600	11,200	19,600	28,000
2d Rds	1100	3500	5800	11,600	20,300	29,000
4d Phae	1150	3600	6000	12,000	21,000	30,000
2d Conv	1000	3250	5400	10,800	18,900	27,000
2d Bus Cpe	550	1800	3000	6000	10,500	15,000
2d RS Cpe	600	1850	3100	6200	10,900	15,500
4d Sed	450	1450	2400	4800	8400	12,000
4d DeL Sed	450	1500	2500	5000	8800	12,500
CF, 8-cyl., 114" wb						
2d Rds	1150	3600	6000	12,000	21,000	30,000
2d Bus Cpe	600	1850	3100	6200	10,900	15,500
2d DeL Cpe	600	1900	3200	6400	11,200	16,000
4d Brgm	450	1450	2400	4800	8400	12,000
4d Sed	450	1500	2500	5000	8800	12,500
4d DeL Sed	500	1550	2600	5200	9100	13,000
1933						
SD, 6-cyl.						
2d Conv	1000	3100	5200	10,400	18,200	26,000
2d Conv Sed	1050	3350	5600	11,200	19,600	28,000
2d 2P Cpe	500	1550	2600	5200	9100	13,000
2d RS Cpe	500	1600	2700	5400	9500	13,500
2d DeL Cpe	500	1600	2700	5400	9500	13,500
2d Std Brgm	400	1300	2150	4300	7500	10,700

	6	5	4	3	2	1
4d Cus Brgm	400	1300	2200	4400	7700	11,000
4d Sed	400	1250	2100	4200	7400	10,500
4d Cus Sed	400	1300	2150	4300	7600	10,800
1934						
Airflow SE, 6-cyl.						
2d Cpe	600	2000	3300	6600	11,600	16,500
4d Brgm	600	1850	3100	6200	10,900	15,500
4d Sed	550	1750	2900	5800	10,200	14,500
4d Twn Sed	600	1850	3100	6200	10,900	15,500
1935						
Airstream, 6-cyl.						
2d Bus Cpe	500	1600	2700	5400	9500	13,500
2d Cpe	550	1700	2800	5600	9800	14,000
2d Conv	1000	3100	5200	10,400	18,200	26,000
2d Sed	400	1200	2000	4000	7000	10,000
2d Tr Sed	400	1200	2000	4000	7100	10,100
4d Sed	450	1170	1975	3900	6850	9800
4d Tr Sed	400	1200	2000	4000	7000	10,000
Airflow, 6-cyl.						
2d Bus Cpe	600	1900	3200	6400	11,200	16,000
2d Cpe	650	2050	3400	6800	11,900	17,000
4d Sed	550	1700	2800	5600	9800	14,000
4d Twn Sed	550	1800	3000	6000	10,500	15,000
1936						
DeLuxe Airstream S-1, 6-cyl.						
2d Bus Cpe	500	1600	2700	5400	9500	13,500
4d Tr Brgm	400	1300	2150	4300	7600	10,800
4d Tr Sed	400	1350	2200	4400	7800	11,100
Custom Airstream S-1, 6-cyl.						
2d Bus Cpe	550	1700	2800	5600	9800	14,000
2d Cpe	550	1750	2900	5800	10,200	14,500
2d Conv	1050	3350	5600	11,200	19,600	28,000
4d Tr Brgm	400	1350	2250	4500	7800	11,200
4d Tr Sed	450	1350	2300	4600	8000	11,400
4d Conv Sed	1000	3100	5200	10,400	18,200	26,000
4d Trv Sed	450	1400	2350	4700	8200	11,700
4d 7P Sed	450	1400	2350	4700	8300	11,800
Airflow III S-2, 6-cyl.						
2d Cpe	600	2000	3300	6600	11,600	16,500
4d Sed	500	1600	2700	5400	9500	13,500
1937						
S-3, 6-cyl.						
2d Conv	1050	3350	5600	11,200	19,600	28,000
4d Conv Sed	1100	3500	5800	11,600	20,300	29,000
2d Bus Cpe	500	1550	2600	5200	9100	13,000
2d Cpe	500	1600	2700	5400	9500	13,500
4d Brgm	400	1250	2100	4200	7300	10,400
4d Tr Brgm	400	1250	2100	4200	7400	10,500
4d Sed	400	1250	2100	4200	7400	10,600
4d Tr Sed	400	1300	2150	4300	7500	10,700
4d 7P Sed	400	1300	2150	4300	7600	10,800
4d Limo	450	1450	2400	4800	8400	12,000
1938						
S-5, 6-cyl.						
2d Conv	1050	3350	5600	11,200	19,600	28,000
4d Conv Sed	1100	3500	5800	11,600	20,300	29,000
2d Bus Cpe	500	1550	2600	5200	9100	13,000
2d Cpe	500	1600	2700	5400	9500	13,500
4d Tr Brgm	400	1300	2150	4300	7600	10,800
4d Sed	400	1300	2200	4400	7700	11,000
4d Tr Sed	400	1350	2200	4400	7800	11,100
4d 7P Sed	450	1400	2300	4600	8100	11,600
4d Limo	500	1550	2600	5200	9100	13,000
1939						
S-6 DeLuxe, 6-cyl.						
2d Bus Cpe	500	1600	2700	5400	9500	13,500
2d Cpe	550	1700	2800	5600	9800	14,000
4d Tr Sed	400	1300	2150	4300	7600	10,800
4d Tr Sed	400	1300	2200	4400	7700	11,000
4d Limo	500	1550	2600	5200	9100	13,000
S-6 Custom, 6-cyl.						
2d Cpe	550	1700	2800	5600	9800	14,000
2d Cus Cpe	550	1750	2900	5800	10,200	14,500
2d Cus Clb Cpe	550	1800	3000	6000	10,500	15,000
2d Tr Sed	450	1400	2300	4600	8100	11,500
4d Tr Sed	450	1400	2300	4600	8100	11,600
4d 7P Sed	450	1400	2350	4700	8200	11,700
4d Limo	550	1700	2800	5600	9800	14,000
1940						
S-7 DeLuxe, 6-cyl.						
2d Bus Cpe	550	1700	2800	5600	9800	14,000
2d Cpe	550	1750	2900	5800	10,200	14,500
2d Tr Sed	450	1400	2350	4700	8200	11,700
4d Tr Sed	450	1450	2400	4800	8400	12,000
4d 7P Sed	500	1600	2700	5400	9500	13,500
S-7 Custom, 6-cyl.						
2d Conv	1000	3100	5200	10,400	18,200	26,000
2d 2P Cpe	550	1800	3000	6000	10,500	15,000
2d Clb Cpe	600	1850	3100	6200	10,900	15,500
2d Sed	450	1450	2400	4800	8400	12,000
4d Sed	400	1300	2200	4400	7700	11,000
4d 7P Sed	450	1500	2500	5000	8800	12,500
4d Limo	500	1550	2600	5200	9100	13,000
1941						
S-8 DeLuxe, 6-cyl.						
2d Bus Cpe	550	1700	2800	5600	9800	14,000
2d Cpe	550	1750	2900	5800	10,200	14,500
2d Sed	450	1450	2400	4800	8400	12,000
4d Sed	450	1450	2400	4800	8500	12,100
4d 7P Sed	500	1550	2600	5200	9100	13,000
S-8 Custom, 6-cyl.						
2d Conv	1000	3250	5400	10,800	18,900	27,000
2d Cpe	550	1750	2900	5800	10,200	14,500
2d Clb Cpe	550	1800	3000	6000	10,500	15,000
2d Brgm	450	1500	2450	4900	8600	12,300
4d Sed	450	1500	2500	5000	8700	12,400
4d Twn Sed	450	1500	2500	5000	8800	12,500
4d 7P Sed	500	1600	2700	5400	9500	13,500
4d Limo	550	1700	2800	5600	9800	14,000
1942						
S-10 DeLuxe, 6-cyl.						
2d Bus Cpe	500	1600	2700	5400	9500	13,500

	6	5	4	3	2	1
2d Cpe	550	1700	2800	5600	9800	14,000
2d Sed	450	1450	2400	4800	8500	12,100
4d Sed	450	1450	2450	4900	8500	12,200
4d Twn Sed	450	1500	2450	4900	8600	12,300
4d 7P Sed	500	1650	2700	5400	9500	13,600
2d S-10 Custom, 6-cyl.						
2d Conv	1000	3100	5200	10,400	18,200	26,000
2d Cpe	550	1700	2800	5600	9800	14,000
2d Clb Cpe	600	1850	3100	6200	10,900	15,500
4d Brgm	450	1500	2500	5000	8800	12,500
4d Sed	450	1500	2500	5000	8800	12,600
4d Twn Sed	500	1550	2600	5200	9100	13,000
4d 7P Sed	550	1700	2800	5600	9800	14,000
4d Limo	550	1700	2850	5700	9900	14,200

1946-1948

	6	5	4	3	2	1
S-11 DeLuxe, 6-cyl.						
2d Cpe	450	1500	2500	5000	8800	12,500
2d Clb Cpe	550	1700	2800	5600	9800	14,000
2d Sed	400	1300	2200	4400	7700	11,000
4d Sed	400	1350	2250	4500	7900	11,300
S-11 Custom, 6-cyl.						
2d Conv	950	3000	5000	10,000	17,500	25,000
2d Clb Cpe	550	1750	2900	5800	10,200	14,500
2d Sed	400	1350	2250	4500	7900	11,300
4d Sed	450	1400	2300	4600	8100	11,500
4d 7P Sed	450	1450	2400	4800	8400	12,000
4d Limo	500	1550	2600	5200	9100	13,000
4d Sub	500	1600	2700	5400	9500	13,500

1949

First series values same as 1947-48

	6	5	4	3	2	1
S-13 DeLuxe, 6-cyl.						
2d Clb Cpe	500	1550	2600	5200	9100	13,000
4d Sed	450	1400	2300	4600	8100	11,500
4d C-A Sed	450	1400	2350	4700	8200	11,700
4d Sta Wag	650	2050	3400	6800	11,900	17,000
S-13 Custom, 6-cyl.						
2d Conv	800	2500	4200	8400	14,700	21,000
2d Clb Cpe	500	1600	2700	5400	9500	13,500
4d Sed	450	1450	2400	4800	8400	12,000
4d 8P Sed	450	1500	2500	5000	8800	12,500
4d Sub	550	1800	3000	6000	10,500	15,000

1950

	6	5	4	3	2	1
S-14 DeLuxe, 6-cyl.						
2d Clb Cpe	450	1500	2500	5000	8800	12,500
4d Sed	450	1400	2300	4600	8100	11,500
4d C-A Sed	450	1400	2350	4700	8200	11,700
4d 8P Sed	450	1450	2400	4800	8400	12,000
S-14 Custom, 6-cyl.						
2d Conv	850	2750	4600	9200	16,100	23,000
2d HT Sptman	650	2050	3400	6800	11,900	17,000
2d Clb Cpe	500	1550	2600	5200	9100	13,000
4d Sed	450	1450	2400	4800	8400	12,000
4d 6P Sta Wag	650	2050	3400	6800	11,900	17,000
4d Stl Sta Wag	550	1800	3000	6000	10,500	15,000
4d 8P Sed	500	1550	2550	5100	9000	12,800
4d Sub Sed	450	1500	2500	5000	8800	12,500

1951-1952

	6	5	4	3	2	1
DeLuxe, 6-cyl., 125.5" wb						
4d Sed	400	1350	2250	4500	7900	11,300
2d Clb Cpe	450	1500	2500	5000	8800	12,500
4d C-A Sed	400	1350	2250	4500	7900	11,300
DeLuxe, 6-cyl., 139.5" wb						
4d Sed	450	1350	2300	4600	8000	11,400
Custom, 6-cyl., 125.5" wb						
4d Sed	450	1400	2300	4600	8100	11,500
2d Clb Cpe	500	1550	2600	5200	9100	13,000
2d HT Sptman	700	2300	3800	7600	13,300	19,000
2d Conv	850	2750	4600	9200	16,100	23,000
4d Sta Wag	650	2050	3400	6800	11,900	17,000
Custom, 6-cyl., 139.5" wb						
4d Sed	450	1400	2350	4700	8200	11,700
4d Sub	450	1450	2400	4800	8400	12,000
Firedome, V-8, 125.5" wb (1952 only)						
4d Sed	450	1450	2400	4800	8400	12,000
2d Clb Cpe	550	1800	3000	6000	10,500	15,000
2d HT Sptman	750	2400	4000	8000	14,000	20,000
2d Conv	1000	3100	5200	10,400	18,200	26,000
4d Sta Wag	650	2050	3400	6800	11,900	17,000
Firedome, V-8, 139.5" wb (1952 only)						
4d 8P Sed	450	1500	2500	5000	8800	12,500

1953-1954

	6	5	4	3	2	1
Powermaster Six, 6-cyl., 125.5" wb						
4d Sed	400	1300	2200	4400	7700	11,000
2d Clb Cpe	450	1400	2300	4600	8100	11,500
4d Sta Wag	450	1350	2300	4600	8000	11,400
2d HT Sptman ('53 only)	650	2050	3400	6800	11,900	17,000
Powermaster Six, 6-cyl., 139.5" wb						
4d Sed	400	1300	2150	4300	7600	10,800
Firedome, V-8, 125.5" wb						
4d Sed	450	1400	2300	4600	8100	11,600
2d Clb Cpe	450	1500	2500	5000	8800	12,500
2d HT Sptman	750	2400	4000	8000	14,000	20,000
2d Conv	1000	3100	5200	10,400	18,200	26,000
4d Sta Wag	600	1900	3200	6400	11,200	16,000
Firedome, V-8, 139.5" wb						
4d Sed	400	1350	2250	4500	7900	11,300

1955

	6	5	4	3	2	1
Firedome, V-8						
4d Sed	400	1350	2250	4500	7900	11,300
2d HT	700	2150	3600	7200	12,600	18,000
2d HT Sptman	850	2650	4400	8800	15,400	22,000
2d Conv	1000	3100	5200	10,400	18,200	26,000
4d Sta Wag	800	2500	4200	8400	14,700	21,000
Fireflite, V-8						
4d Sed	450	1400	2350	4700	8300	11,800
2d HT Sptman	850	2750	4600	9200	16,100	23,000
2d Conv	1000	3250	5400	10,800	18,900	27,000

1956

	6	5	4	3	2	1
Firedome, V-8						
4d Sed	400	1250	2100	4200	7400	10,500
4d HT Sev	500	1550	2600	5200	9100	13,000
4d HT Sptman	600	1900	3200	6400	11,200	16,000
2d HT Sev	750	2400	4000	8000	14,000	20,000
2d HT Sptman	850	2650	4400	8800	15,400	22,000
2d Conv	1000	3250	5400	10,800	18,900	27,000
4d Sta Wag	650	2050	3400	6800	11,900	17,000
Fireflite, V-8						
4d Sed	400	1300	2200	4400	7700	11,000
4d HT Sptman	600	1900	3200	6400	11,200	16,000
2d HT Sptman	850	2750	4600	9200	16,100	23,000
2d Conv	1050	3350	5600	11,200	19,600	28,000
2d Conv IPC	1150	3700	6200	12,400	21,700	31,000
Adventurer						
2d HT	900	2900	4800	9600	16,800	24,000

1957

	6	5	4	3	2	1
Firesweep, V 8, 122" wb						
4d Sed	400	1200	2000	4000	7000	10,000
4d HT Sptman	500	1550	2600	5200	9100	13,000
2d HT Sptman	700	2300	3800	7600	13,300	19,000
4d 2S Sta Wag	450	1400	2300	4600	8100	11,500
4d 3S Sta Wag	450	1400	2350	4700	8200	11,700
Firedome, V-8, 126" wb						
4d Sed	450	1080	1800	3600	6300	9000
4d HT Sptman	550	1700	2800	5600	9800	14,000
2d HT Sptman	750	2400	4000	8000	14,000	20,000
2d Conv	1050	3350	5600	11,200	19,600	28,000
Fireflite, V-8, 126" wb						
4d Sed	450	1140	1900	3800	6650	9500
4d HT Sptman	550	1800	3000	6000	10,500	15,000
2d HT Sptman	800	2500	4200	8400	14,700	21,000
2d Conv	1300	4100	6800	13,600	23,800	34,000
4d 2S Sta Wag	450	1450	2400	4800	8400	12,000
4d 3S Sta Wag	450	1450	2450	4900	8500	12,200
Fireflite Adventurer, 126" wb						
2d HT	1050	3350	5600	11,200	19,600	28,000
2d Conv	1600	5050	8400	16,800	29,400	42,000

1958

	6	5	4	3	2	1
Firesweep, V-8						
4d Sed	400	1200	2000	4000	7000	10,000
4d HT Sptman	500	1550	2600	5200	9100	13,000
2d HT Sptman	600	1900	3200	6400	11,200	16,000
2d Conv	1000	3250	5400	10,800	18,900	27,000
4d 2S Sta Wag	400	1300	2200	4400	7700	11,000
4d 3S Sta Wag	400	1350	2250	4500	7800	11,200
Firedome, V-8						
4d Sed	400	1200	2050	4100	7100	10,200
4d HT Sptman	550	1800	3000	6000	10,500	15,000
2d HT Sptman	650	2050	3400	6800	11,900	17,000
2d Conv	1100	3500	5800	11,600	20,300	29,000
Fireflite, V-8						
4d Sed	400	1250	2100	4200	7400	10,500
4d HT Sptman	600	1900	3200	6400	11,200	16,000
2d HT Sptman	700	2300	3800	7600	13,300	19,000
2d Conv	1300	4100	6800	13,600	23,800	34,000
4d 2S Sta Wag	450	1400	2300	4600	8100	11,500
4d 3S Sta Wag	450	1400	2300	4600	8100	11,600
Adventurer, V-8						
2d HT	900	2900	4800	9600	16,800	24,000
2d Conv	1550	4900	8200	16,400	28,700	41,000

1959

	6	5	4	3	2	1
Firesweep, V-8						
4d Sed	450	1080	1800	3600	6300	9000
4d HT Sptman	500	1550	2600	5200	9100	13,000
2d HT Sptman	550	1800	3000	6000	10,500	15,000
2d Conv	850	2650	4400	8800	15,400	22,000
4d 2S Sta Wag	400	1250	2100	4200	7400	10,500
4d 3S Sta Wag	400	1300	2150	4300	7500	10,700
Firedome, V-8						
4d Sed	450	1140	1900	3800	6650	9500
4d HT Sptman	550	1700	2800	5600	9800	14,000
2d HT Sptman	600	1900	3200	6400	11,200	16,000
2d Conv	950	3000	5000	10,000	17,500	25,000
Fireflite, V-8						
4d Sed	400	1200	2000	4000	7000	10,000
4d HT Sptman	550	1800	3000	6000	10,500	15,000
2d HT Sptman	650	2050	3400	6800	11,900	17,000
2d Conv	1050	3350	5600	11,200	19,600	28,000
4d 2S Sta Wag	400	1300	2150	4300	7500	10,700
4d 3S Sta Wag	400	1300	2150	4300	7600	10,800
Adventurer, V-8						
2d HT	700	2150	3600	7200	12,600	18,000
2d Conv	1300	4100	6800	13,600	23,800	34,000

1960

	6	5	4	3	2	1
Fireflite, V-8						
4d Sed	450	1140	1900	3800	6650	9500
4d HT	400	1250	2100	4200	7400	10,500
2d HT	450	1400	2300	4600	8100	11,500
Adventurer, V-8						
4d Sed	400	1200	2000	4000	7000	10,000
4d HT	450	1450	2400	4800	8400	12,000
2d HT	550	1700	2800	5600	9800	14,000

1961

	6	5	4	3	2	1
Fireflite, V-8						
4d HT	450	1500	2500	5000	8800	12,500
2d HT	550	1800	3000	6000	10,500	15,000

DODGE

1914

	6	5	4	3	2	1
4-cyl., 110" wb						
(Serial #1-249)						
4d Tr	700	2300	3800	7600	13,300	19,000

1915

	6	5	4	3	2	1
4-cyl., 110" wb						
2d Rds	700	2150	3600	7200	12,600	18,000
4d Tr	700	2300	3800	7600	13,300	19,000

1916

	6	5	4	3	2	1
4-cyl., 110" wb						
2d Rds	700	2150	3600	7200	12,600	18,000
2d W.T. Rds	700	2300	3800	7600	13,300	19,000

	6	5	4	3	2	1
4d Tr	750	2400	4000	8000	14,000	20,000
4d W.T. Tr	800	2500	4200	8400	14,700	21,000
1917						
4-cyl., 114" wb						
2d Rds	650	2050	3400	6800	11,900	17,000
2d W.T. Rds	700	2150	3600	7200	12,600	18,000
4d Tr	700	2300	3800	7600	13,300	19,000
4d W.T. Tr	750	2400	4000	8000	14,000	20,000
2d Cpe	350	1020	1700	3400	5950	8500
4d C.D. Sed	350	975	1600	3200	5600	8000
1918						
4-cyl., 114" wb						
2d Rds	650	2050	3400	6800	11,900	17,000
2d W.T. Rds	700	2150	3600	7200	12,600	18,000
4d Tr	700	2300	3800	7600	13,300	19,000
4d WT Tr	750	2400	4000	8000	14,000	20,000
2d Cpe	350	975	1600	3200	5600	8000
4d Sed	350	900	1500	3000	5250	7500
1919						
4-cyl., 114" wb						
2d Rds	600	1900	3200	6400	11,200	16,000
4d Tr	650	2050	3400	6800	11,900	17,000
2d Cpe	350	975	1600	3200	5600	8000
2d Rex Cpe	350	1020	1700	3400	5950	8500
4d Rex Sed	350	880	1500	2950	5180	7400
4d Sed	350	900	1500	3000	5250	7500
4d Dep Hk	350	840	1400	2800	4900	7000
2d Sed Dely	350	975	1600	3200	5600	8000
1920						
4-cyl., 114" wb						
2d Rds	550	1800	3000	6000	10,500	15,000
4d Tr	600	1850	3100	6200	10,900	15,500
2d Cpe	200	720	1200	2400	4200	6000
4d Sed	200	660	1100	2200	3850	5500
1921						
4-cyl., 114" wb						
2d Rds	550	1700	2800	5600	9800	14,000
4d Tr	550	1750	2900	5800	10,200	14,500
2d Cpe	200	675	1000	2000	3500	5000
4d Sed	150	600	900	1800	3150	4500
1922						
1st series, 4-cyl., 114" wb, (low hood models)						
2d Rds	550	1700	2800	5600	9800	14,000
4d Tr	550	1750	2900	5800	10,200	14,500
2d Cpe	200	700	1050	2100	3650	5200
4d Sed	200	675	1000	2000	3500	5000
2nd series, 4-cyl., 114" wb, (high hood models)						
2d Rds	500	1600	2700	5400	9500	13,500
4d Tr	550	1700	2800	5600	9800	14,000
2d Bus Cpe	200	660	1100	2200	3850	5500
4d Bus Sed	200	700	1050	2050	3600	5100
4d Sed	200	675	1000	2000	3500	5000
1923						
4-cyl., 114" wb						
2d Rds	450	1450	2400	4800	8400	12,000
4d Tr	450	1500	2500	5000	8800	12,500
2d Bus Cpe	200	700	1075	2150	3700	5300
4d Bus Sed	200	700	1050	2100	3650	5200
4d Sed	200	675	1000	2000	3500	5000
1924						
4-cyl., 116" wb						
2d Rds	500	1550	2600	5200	9100	13,000
4d Tr	500	1600	2700	5400	9500	13,500
2d Bus Cpe	200	720	1200	2400	4200	6000
2d 4P Cpe	200	745	1250	2500	4340	6200
4d Bus Sed	200	720	1200	2400	4200	6000
4d Sed	200	700	1200	2350	4130	5900
Special Series (deluxe equip.-introduced Jan. 1924)						
2d Rds	500	1600	2700	5400	9500	13,500
4d Tr	550	1700	2800	5600	9800	14,000
2d Bus Cpe	200	720	1200	2400	4200	6000
2d 4P Cpe	350	780	1300	2600	4550	6500
4d Bus Sed	200	720	1200	2400	4200	6000
4d Sed	200	730	1250	2450	4270	6100
1925						
4-cyl., 116" wb						
2d Rds	450	1450	2400	4800	8400	12,000
2d Spl Rds	450	1500	2500	5000	8800	12,500
4d Tr	500	1550	2600	5200	9100	13,000
4d Spl Tr	500	1600	2700	5400	9500	13,500
2d Bus Cpe	350	780	1300	2600	4550	6500
2d Spl Bus Cpe	350	800	1350	2700	4700	6700
2d 4P Cpe	350	770	1300	2550	4480	6400
2d Sp Cpe	350	780	1300	2600	4550	6500
4d Bus Sed	200	720	1200	2400	4200	6000
4d Spl Bus Sed	200	730	1250	2450	4270	6100
4d Sed	200	745	1250	2500	4340	6200
4d Spl Sed	200	750	1275	2500	4400	6300
2d Sed	200	720	1200	2400	4200	6000
2d Spl Sed	200	730	1250	2450	4270	6100
1926						
4-cyl., 116" wb						
2d Rds	400	1300	2200	4400	7700	11,000
2d Spl Rds	450	1400	2300	4600	8100	11,500
2d Spt Rds	450	1450	2400	4800	8400	12,000
4d Tr	450	1400	2300	4600	8100	11,500
4d Spl Tr	450	1450	2400	4800	8400	12,000
4d Spt Tr	500	1550	2600	5200	9100	13,000
2d Cpe	200	720	1200	2400	4200	6000
2d Spl Cpe	350	780	1300	2600	4550	6500
2d Sed	200	670	1200	2300	4060	5800
2d Spl Sed	200	720	1200	2400	4200	6000
4d Bus Sed	200	685	1150	2300	3990	5700
4d Spl Bus Sed	200	730	1250	2450	4270	6100
4d Sed	200	670	1200	2300	4060	5800
4d Spl Sed	200	720	1200	2400	4200	6000
4d DeL Sed	200	730	1250	2450	4270	6100
1927-28						
4-cyl., 116" wb						
2d Rds	450	1400	2300	4600	8100	11,500
2d Spl Rds	450	1450	2400	4800	8400	12,000
2d Spt Rds	450	1500	2500	5000	8800	12,500
2d Cabr	400	1300	2200	4400	7700	11,000
4d Tr	400	1300	2200	4400	7700	11,000
4d Spl Tr	450	1400	2300	4600	8100	11,500
4d Spt Tr	450	1450	2400	4800	8400	12,000
2d Cpe	200	730	1250	2450	4270	6100
2d Spl Cpe	350	780	1300	2600	4550	6500
4d Sed	200	720	1200	2400	4200	6000
4d Spl Sed	200	730	1250	2450	4270	6100
4d DeL Sed	200	745	1250	2500	4340	6200
4d A-P Sed	350	780	1300	2600	4550	6500
1928						
'Fast Four', 4-cyl., 108" wb						
2d Cabr	400	1200	2000	4000	7000	10,000
2d Cpe	350	860	1450	2900	5050	7200
4d Sed	350	840	1400	2800	4900	7000
4d DeL Sed	350	850	1450	2850	4970	7100
Standard Series, 6-cyl., 110" wb						
2d Cabr	450	1400	2300	4600	8100	11,500
2d Cpe	350	975	1600	3200	5600	8000
4d Sed	350	900	1500	3000	5250	7500
4d DeL Sed	350	975	1600	3200	5500	7900
Victory Series, 6-cyl., 112" wb						
4d Tr	600	1900	3200	6400	11,200	16,000
2d Cpe	350	1020	1700	3400	5950	8500
2d RS Cpe	450	1080	1800	3600	6300	9000
4d Brgm	350	1020	1700	3400	5950	8500
Series 2249, Standard 6-cyl., 116" wb						
2d Cabr	600	1900	3200	6400	11,200	16,000
4d Brgm	350	1020	1700	3400	5900	8400
4d Sed	350	900	1500	3000	5250	7500
4d DeL Sed	350	975	1600	3200	5600	8000
Series 2251, Senior 6-cyl., 116" wb						
2d Cabr	700	2150	3600	7200	12,600	18,000
2d Spt Cabr	700	2300	3800	7600	13,300	19,000
2d RS Cpe	350	1020	1700	3400	5950	8500
2d Spt Cpe	450	1080	1800	3600	6300	9000
4d Sed	350	975	1600	3200	5600	8000
4d Spt Sed	350	1020	1700	3400	5950	8500
1929						
Standard Series, 6-cyl., 110" wb						
2d Bus Cpe	400	1250	2100	4200	7400	10,500
2d Cpe	400	1300	2200	4400	7700	11,000
4d Sed	450	1140	1900	3800	6650	9500
4d DeL Sed	400	1200	2000	4000	7000	10,000
4d Spt DeL Sed	400	1250	2100	4200	7400	10,500
4d A-P Sed	400	1300	2150	4300	7500	10,700
Victory Series, 6-cyl., 112" wb						
2d Rds	900	2900	4800	9600	16,800	24,000
2d Spt Rds	950	3000	5000	10,000	17,500	25,000
4d Tr	950	3000	5000	10,000	17,500	25,000
4d Spt Tr	1000	3100	5200	10,400	18,200	26,000
2d Cpe	400	1250	2100	4200	7400	10,500
2d DeL Cpe	400	1300	2200	4400	7700	11,000
4d Sed	450	1080	1800	3600	6300	9000
4d Spt Sed	450	1140	1900	3800	6650	9500
Standard Series DA, 6-cyl., 63 hp, 112" wb (Introduced Jan. 1, 1929).						
2d Rds	950	3000	5000	10,000	17,500	25,000
2d Spt Rds	1000	3100	5200	10,400	18,200	26,000
4d Phae	1000	3250	5400	10,800	18,900	27,000
4d Spt Phae	1050	3350	5600	11,200	19,600	28,000
2d Bus Cpe	400	1300	2200	4400	7700	11,000
2d DeL RS Cpe	450	1400	2300	4600	8100	11,500
2d Vic	400	1250	2100	4200	7400	10,500
4d Brgm	450	1080	1800	3600	6300	9000
4d Sed	350	1020	1700	3400	5950	8500
4d DeL Sed	450	1050	1750	3550	6150	8800
4d DeL Spt Sed	450	1080	1800	3600	6300	9000
Senior Series, 6-cyl., 120" wb						
2d Rds	1000	3100	5200	10,400	18,200	26,000
2d 2P Cpe	450	1400	2300	4600	8100	11,500
2d RS Spt Cpe	450	1500	2500	5000	8800	12,500
2d Vic Brgm	450	1400	2300	4600	8100	11,500
4d Sed	400	1250	2100	4200	7400	10,500
4d Spt Sed	400	1300	2200	4400	7700	11,000
4d Lan Sed	450	1400	2300	4600	8100	11,500
4d Spt Lan Sed	450	1450	2400	4800	8300	11,900
1930						
Series DA, 6-cyl., 112" wb						
2d Rds	1050	3350	5600	11,200	19,600	28,000
4d Phae	1100	3500	5800	11,600	20,300	29,000
2d Bus Cpe	400	1200	2000	4000	7000	10,000
2d DeL Cpe	400	1250	2100	4200	7400	10,500
2d Vic	400	1300	2150	4300	7500	10,700
4d Brgm	400	1200	2000	4000	7000	10,000
2d Sed	450	1160	1950	3900	6800	9700
4d Sed	450	1170	1975	3900	6850	9800
4d DeL Sed	400	1200	2000	4000	7000	10,000
2d RS Rds	1100	3500	5800	11,600	20,300	29,000
2d RS Cpe	450	1500	2500	5000	8800	12,500
4d Lan Sed	400	1250	2100	4200	7400	10,500
Series DD, 6-cyl., 109" wb (Introduced Jan. 1, 1930).						
2d RS Rds	1000	3250	5400	10,800	18,900	27,000
4d Phae	1050	3350	5600	11,200	19,600	28,000
2d RS Conv	1050	3350	5600	11,200	19,600	28,000
2d Bus Cpe	500	1550	2600	5200	9100	13,000
2d RS Cpe	550	1700	2800	5600	9800	14,000
4d Sed	450	1140	1900	3800	6650	9500
Series DC, 8-cyl., 114" wb (Introduced Jan. 1, 1930).						
2d Rds	1050	3350	5600	11,200	19,600	28,000
2d RS Conv	1000	3250	5400	10,800	18,900	27,000
4d Phae	1100	3500	5800	11,600	20,300	29,000
2d Bus Cpe	500	1600	2700	5400	9500	13,500
2d RS Cpe	550	1750	2900	5800	10,200	14,500
4d Sed	400	1200	2000	4000	7000	10,000
1931						
Series DH, 6-cyl., 114" wb (Introduced Dec. 1, 1930).						
2d Rds	1100	3500	5800	11,600	20,300	29,000

	6	5	4	3	2	1
2d RS Conv	1050	3350	5600	11,200	19,600	28,000
2d Bus Cpe	500	1550	2600	5200	9100	13,000
2d RS Cpe	550	1700	2800	5600	9800	14,000
4d Sed	350	1020	1700	3400	5950	8500
Series DG, 8-cyl., 118.3" wb						
(Introduced Jan. 1, 1931).						
2d RS Rds	1150	3700	6200	12,400	21,700	31,000
2d RS Conv	1100	3500	5800	11,600	20,300	29,000
4d Phae	1150	3700	6200	12,400	21,700	31,000
2d RS Cpe	550	1800	3000	6000	10,500	15,000
4d Sed	450	1450	2400	4800	8400	12,000
2d 5P Cpe	550	1800	3000	6000	10,500	15,000
1932						
Series DL, 6-cyl., 114.3" wb						
(Introduced Jan. 1, 1932).						
2d RS Conv	1000	3250	5400	10,800	18,900	27,000
2d Bus Cpe	550	1700	2800	5600	9800	14,000
2d RS Cpe	550	1800	3000	6000	10,500	15,000
4d Sed	400	1250	2100	4200	7400	10,500
Series DK, 8-cyl., 122" wb						
(Introduced Jan. 1, 1932).						
2d Conv	1050	3350	5600	11,200	19,600	28,000
4d Conv Sed	1150	3600	6000	12,000	21,000	30,000
2d RS Cpe	600	1850	3100	6200	10,900	15,500
2d 5P Cpe	550	1750	2900	5800	10,200	14,500
4d Sed	400	1300	2200	4400	7700	11,000
1933						
Series DP, 6-cyl., 111.3" wb						
2d RS Conv	1150	3600	6000	12,000	21,000	30,000
2d Bus Cpe	500	1600	2700	5400	9500	13,500
2d RS Cpe	550	1700	2800	5600	9800	14,000
4d Sed	400	1250	2100	4200	7400	10,500
4d Brgm	400	1300	2150	4300	7500	10,700
4d DeL Brgm	400	1300	2200	4400	7700	11,000
NOTE: Second Series DP introduced April 5, 1933 increasing WB from 111" to 115" included in above.						
Series DO, 8-cyl., 122" wb						
2d RS Conv	1250	3950	6600	13,200	23,100	33,000
4d Conv Sed	1250	3950	6600	13,200	23,100	33,000
2d RS Cpe	600	1900	3200	6400	11,200	16,000
2d Cpe	600	1850	3100	6200	10,900	15,500
4d Sed	450	1500	2500	5000	8800	12,500
1934						
DeLuxe Series DR, 6-cyl., 117" wb						
2d RS Conv	1150	3600	6000	12,000	21,000	30,000
2d Bus Cpe	550	1750	2900	5800	10,200	14,500
2d RS Cpe	550	1800	3000	6000	10,500	15,000
2d Sed	400	1250	2100	4200	7400	10,500
4d Sed	400	1200	2050	4100	7100	10,200
Series DS, 6-cyl., 121" wb						
4d Conv Sed	1150	3700	6200	12,400	21,700	31,000
4d Brgm	400	1300	2200	4400	7700	11,000
DeLuxe Series DRXX, 6-cyl., 117" wb						
(Introduced June 2, 1934).						
2d Conv	1100	3500	5800	11,600	20,300	29,000
2d Bus Cpe	550	1800	3000	6000	10,500	15,000
2d Cpe	600	1850	3100	6200	10,900	15,500
2d Sed	400	1200	2000	4000	7100	10,100
4d Sed	400	1200	2000	4000	7000	10,000
1935						
Series DU, 6-cyl., 116" wb - 128" wb, (*)						
2d RS Conv	1000	3250	5400	10,800	18,900	27,000
2d Cpe	500	1600	2700	5400	9500	13,500
2d RS Cpe	550	1700	2800	5600	9800	14,000
2d Sed	400	1250	2100	4200	7400	10,600
2d Tr Sed	400	1300	2150	4300	7500	10,700
4d Sed	400	1300	2150	4300	7600	10,800
4d Tr Sed	400	1300	2200	4400	7700	11,000
4d Car Sed (*)	400	1350	2250	4500	7900	11,300
4d 7P Sed (*)	450	1400	2350	4700	8300	11,800
1936						
Series D2, 6-cyl., 116" wb - 128" wb, (*)						
2d RS Conv	1000	3250	5400	10,800	18,900	27,000
4d Conv Sed	1050	3350	5600	11,200	19,600	28,000
2d 2P Cpe	500	1600	2700	5400	9500	13,500
2d RS Cpe	550	1700	2800	5600	9800	14,000
2d Sed	400	1250	2050	4100	7200	10,300
2d Tr Sed	400	1250	2100	4200	7300	10,400
4d Sed	400	1250	2100	4200	7300	10,400
4d Tr Sed	400	1250	2100	4200	7400	10,500
4d 7P Sed (*)	400	1300	2150	4300	7600	10,800
1937						
Series D5, 6-cyl., 115" wb - 132" wb, (*)						
2d RS Conv	900	2900	4800	9600	16,800	24,000
4d Conv Sed	950	3000	5000	10,000	17,500	25,000
2d Bus Cpe	500	1600	2700	5400	9500	13,500
2d RS Cpe	550	1700	2800	5600	9800	14,000
2d Sed	400	1250	2050	4100	7200	10,300
2d Tr Sed	400	1250	2100	4200	7400	10,600
4d Sed	400	1250	2100	4200	7400	10,600
4d Tr Sed	400	1300	2150	4300	7600	10,800
4d 7P Sed (*)	450	1400	2300	4600	8100	11,500
4d Limo (*)	450	1450	2400	4800	8400	12,000
1938						
Series D8, 6-cyl., 115" wb - 132" wb, (*)						
2d Conv Cpe	950	3000	5000	10,000	17,500	25,000
4d Conv Sed	1000	3100	5200	10,400	18,200	26,000
2d Bus Cpe	500	1550	2600	5200	9100	13,000
2d Cpe 2-4	550	1700	2800	5600	9800	14,000
2d Sed	400	1250	2100	4200	7400	10,500
2d Tr Sed	400	1300	2150	4300	7500	10,700
4d Sed	400	1300	2200	4400	7700	11,000
4d Tr Sed	400	1350	2200	4400	7800	11,100
4d Sta Wag	450	1500	2450	4900	8600	12,300
4d 7P Sed (*)	450	1450	2400	4800	8400	12,000
4d Limo	450	1500	2500	5000	8800	12,600
1939						
Special Series D11S, 6-cyl., 117" wb						
2d Cpe	500	1600	2650	5300	9300	13,300
2d Sed	400	1250	2050	4100	7200	10,300
4d Sed	400	1250	2100	4200	7400	10,500

	6	5	4	3	2	1
DeLuxe Series D11, 6-cyl., 117" wb - 134" wb, (*)						
2d Cpe	550	1700	2800	5600	9800	14,000
2d A/S Cpe	600	1900	3200	6400	11,200	16,000
2d Twn Cpe	550	1800	3000	6000	10,500	15,000
2d Sed	400	1250	2100	4200	7400	10,500
4d Sed	400	1300	2150	4300	7500	10,700
4d Ewb Sed (*)	500	1550	2550	5100	9000	12,800
4d Limo (*)	500	1550	2600	5200	9100	13,000
1940						
Special Series D17, 6-cyl., 119.5" wb						
2d Cpe	500	1600	2700	5400	9500	13,500
2d Sed	400	1300	2200	4400	7700	11,000
4d Sed	400	1350	2250	4500	7800	11,200
DeLuxe Series D14, 6-cyl., 119.5" wb - 139.5" wb, (*)						
2d Conv	1000	3100	5200	10,400	18,200	26,000
2d Cpe	550	1700	2800	5600	9800	14,000
2d 4P Cpe	550	1750	2900	5800	10,200	14,500
2d Sed	450	1400	2300	4600	8100	11,500
4d Sed	450	1400	2350	4700	8300	11,800
4d Ewb Sed (*)	450	1450	2400	4800	8300	11,900
4d Limo (*)	450	1450	2400	4800	8400	12,000
1941						
DeLuxe Series D19, 6-cyl., 119.5" wb						
2d Cpe	500	1550	2600	5200	9100	13,000
2d Sed	400	1350	2250	4500	7900	11,300
4d Sed	450	1400	2300	4600	8100	11,500
Custom Series D19, 6-cyl., 119.5" wb - 137.5" wb, (*)						
2d Conv	1000	3100	5200	10,400	18,200	26,000
2d Clb Cpe	500	1600	2700	5400	9500	13,500
2d Brgm	450	1400	2350	4700	8200	11,700
4d Sed	450	1400	2300	4600	8100	11,600
4d Twn Sed	450	1400	2350	4700	8300	11,800
4d 7P Sed (*)	450	1450	2400	4800	8300	11,900
4d Limo (*)	450	1500	2450	4900	8600	12,300
1942						
DeLuxe Series D22, 6-cyl., 119.5" wb						
2d Cpe	500	1550	2550	5100	9000	12,800
2d Clb Cpe	500	1550	2600	5200	9100	13,000
2d Sed	400	1300	2200	4400	7700	11,000
4d Sed	400	1350	2200	4400	7800	11,100
Custom Series D22, 6-cyl., 119.5" wb - 137.5" wb, (*)						
2d Conv	900	2900	4800	9600	16,800	24,000
2d Clb Cpe	550	1700	2800	5600	9800	14,000
2d Brgm	450	1500	2500	5000	8800	12,500
4d Sed	450	1500	2450	4900	8600	12,300
4d Twn Sed	450	1500	2500	5000	8700	12,400
4d 7P Sed (*)	500	1550	2550	5100	9000	12,800
4d Limo (*)	550	1700	2800	5600	9800	14,000
1946-1948						
DeLuxe Series D24, 6-cyl., 119.5" wb						
2d Cpe	400	1300	2200	4400	7700	11,000
2d Sed	400	1200	2050	4100	7100	10,200
4d Sed	400	1250	2050	4100	7200	10,300
Custom Series D24, 6-cyl., 119.5" wb - 137.5" wb, (*)						
2d Conv	900	2900	4800	9600	16,800	24,000
2d Clb Cpe	450	1400	2300	4600	8100	11,500
4d Sed	400	1250	2100	4200	7400	10,500
4d Twn Sed	400	1250	2100	4200	7400	10,600
4d 7P Sed (*)	400	1300	2150	4300	7500	10,700
1949						
First Series 1949 is the same as 1948						
Series D29 Wayfarer, 6-cyl., 115" wb						
2d Rds	950	3000	5000	10,000	17,500	25,000
2d Bus Cpe	400	1250	2100	4200	7400	10,500
2d Sed	400	1200	2000	4000	7100	10,100
Series D30 Meadowbrook, 6-cyl., 123.5" wb						
4d Sed	400	1200	2000	4000	7000	10,000
Series D30 Coronet, 6-cyl., 123.5" wb - 137.5" wb, (*)						
2d Conv	850	2750	4600	9200	16,100	23,000
2d Clb Cpe	400	1300	2200	4400	7700	11,000
4d Sed	400	1250	2050	4100	7200	10,300
4d Twn Sed	400	1250	2100	4200	7400	10,500
4d Sta Wag	550	1700	2800	5600	9800	14,000
4d 8P Sed (*)	450	1400	2300	4600	8100	11,500
1950						
Series D33 Wayfarer, 6-cyl., 115" wb						
2d Rds	950	3000	5000	10,000	17,500	25,000
2d Cpe	400	1300	2200	4400	7700	11,000
2d Sed	400	1200	2050	4100	7100	10,200
Series D34 Meadowbrook, 6-cyl., 123.5" wb						
4d Sed	400	1200	2000	4000	7000	10,000
Series D34 Coronet, 123.5" wb - 137.5" wb, (*)						
2d Conv	950	3000	5000	10,000	17,500	25,000
2d Clb Cpe	400	1300	2200	4400	7700	11,000
2d HT Dipl	550	1800	3000	6000	10,500	15,000
4d Sed	400	1200	2050	4100	7100	10,200
4d Twn Sed	400	1250	2100	4200	7300	10,400
4d Sta Wag	600	1900	3200	6400	11,200	16,000
4d Mtl Sta Wag	500	1550	2600	5200	9100	13,000
4d 8P Sed (*)	450	1400	2300	4600	8100	11,600
1951-1952						
Wayfarer Series D41, 6-cyl., 115" wb						
2d Rds (1951 only)	850	2750	4600	9200	16,100	23,000
2d Sed	450	1080	1800	3600	6300	9000
2d Cpe	400	1200	2000	4000	7000	10,000
Meadowbrook Series D42, 6-cyl., 123.5" wb						
4d Sed	450	1140	1900	3800	6650	9500
Coronet Series D42, 6-cyl., 123.5" wb						
4d Sed	450	1160	1950	3900	6800	9700
2d Clb Cpe	400	1250	2100	4200	7400	10,600
2d HT Dipl	650	2050	3400	6800	11,900	17,000
2d Conv	850	2750	4600	9200	16,100	23,000
4d Mtl Sta Wag	500	1550	2600	5200	9100	13,000
4d 8P Sed	400	1200	2000	4000	7100	10,100
1953						
Meadowbrook Special, 6-cyl., disc 4/53						
4d Sed	400	1250	2050	4100	7200	10,300
2d Clb Cpe	400	1250	2100	4200	7400	10,500
Series D46 Meadowbrook, 6-cyl., 119" wb						
4d Sed	400	1250	2100	4200	7400	10,500

	6	5	4	3	2	1
2d Clb Cpe	400	1250	2100	4200	7400	10,600
2d Sub	400	1250	2100	4200	7400	10,500
Coronet, 6-cyl., 119" wb						
4d Sed	400	1300	2150	4300	7500	10,700
2d Clb Cpe	400	1300	2150	4300	7600	10,800
Series D44 Coronet, V-8, 119" wb						
4d Sed	400	1300	2200	4400	7700	11,000
2d Clb Cpe	400	1350	2200	4400	7800	11,100
Series D48 Coronet, V-8, 119" wb - 114" wb, (*)						
2d HT Dipl	600	1900	3200	6400	11,200	16,000
2d Conv	850	2750	4600	9200	16,100	23,000
2d Sta Wag (*)	450	1450	2400	4800	8400	12,000
1954						
Series D51-1 Meadowbrook, 6-cyl., 119" wb						
4d Sed	400	1300	2150	4300	7600	10,800
2d Clb Cpe	400	1300	2150	4300	7600	10,800
Series D51-2 Coronet, 6-cyl., 119" wb						
4d Sed	400	1300	2200	4400	7600	10,900
2d Clb Cpe	400	1300	2200	4400	7700	11,000
Series D52 Coronet, 6-cyl., 114" wb						
2d Sub	450	1400	2300	4600	8100	11,500
4d 6P Sta Wag	500	1550	2600	5200	9100	13,000
4d 8P Sta Wag	550	1700	2800	5600	9800	14,000
Series D50-1 Meadowbrook, V-8, 119" wb						
4d Sed	400	1300	2150	4300	7600	10,800
2d Clb Cpe	400	1300	2200	4400	7700	11,000
Series D50-2 Coronet, V-8, 119" wb						
4d Sed	400	1350	2250	4500	7900	11,300
2d Clb Cpe	450	1400	2300	4600	8100	11,500
Series D53-2 Coronet, V-8, 114" wb						
2d Sub	400	1350	2250	4500	7900	11,300
4d 2S Sta Wag	500	1600	2700	5400	9500	13,500
4d 3S Sta Wag	550	1750	2900	5800	10,200	14,500
Series D50-3 Royal, V-8, 119" wb						
4d Sed	500	1550	2600	5200	9100	13,000
2d Clb Cpe	500	1550	2600	5200	9100	13,000
Series D53-3 Royal, V-8, 114" wb						
2D HT	700	2300	3800	7600	13,300	19,000
2d Conv	900	2900	4800	9600	16,800	24,000
2d Pace Car Replica Conv	1000	3250	5400	10,800	18,900	27,000
1955						
Coronet, V-8, 120" wb						
4d Sed	400	1300	2150	4300	7600	10,800
2d Sed	400	1300	2150	4300	7500	10,700
2d HT	700	2300	3800	7600	13,300	19,000
2d Sub Sta Wag	450	1450	2400	4800	8400	12,000
4d 6P Sta Wag	450	1500	2500	5000	8800	12,500
4d 8P Sta Wag	500	1500	2550	5100	8900	12,700
NOTE: Deduct 5 percent for 6-cyl. models.						
Royal, V-8, 120" wb						
4d Sed	400	1300	2150	4300	7600	10,800
2d HT	750	2400	4000	8000	14,000	20,000
4d 6P Sta Wag	500	1550	2600	5200	9100	13,000
4d 8P Sta Wag	500	1600	2700	5400	9500	13,500
Custom Royal, V-8, 120" wb						
4d Sed	450	1450	2400	4800	8400	12,000
4d Lancer	550	1800	3000	6000	10,500	15,000
2d HT	800	2500	4200	8400	14,700	21,000
2d Conv	950	3000	5000	10,000	17,500	25,000
NOTE: Deduct 5 percent for 6-cyl. models. Add 10 percent for La-Femme.						
1956						
Coronet, V-8, 120" wb						
4d Sed	400	1250	2100	4200	7400	10,500
4d HT	450	1450	2400	4800	8400	12,000
2d Clb Sed	400	1300	2200	4400	7700	11,000
2d HT	700	2150	3600	7200	12,600	18,000
2d Conv	1000	3250	5400	10,800	18,900	27,000
2d Sub Sta Wag	450	1450	2400	4800	8400	12,000
4d 6P Sta Wag	450	1450	2450	4900	8500	12,200
4d 8P Sta Wag	450	1500	2500	5000	8800	12,500
NOTE: Deduct 5 percent for 6-cyl. models.						
Royal, V-8, 120" wb						
4d Sed	450	1400	2300	4600	8100	11,600
4d HT	500	1550	2600	5200	9100	13,000
2d HT	750	2400	4000	8000	14,000	20,000
2d Sub Sta Wag	450	1500	2500	5000	8800	12,500
4d 6P Sta Wag	500	1500	2550	5100	8900	12,700
4d 8P Sta Wag	500	1550	2600	5200	9000	12,900
Custom Royal, V-8, 120" wb						
4d Sed	450	1400	2350	4700	8200	11,700
4d HT	550	1800	3000	6000	10,500	15,000
2d HT	850	2650	4400	8800	15,400	22,000
2d Conv	1150	3600	6000	12,000	21,000	30,000
NOTE: Add 30 percent for D500 option. Add 10 percent for Golden Lancer. Add 10 percent for La-Femme or Texan options.						
1957						
Coronet, V-8, 122" wb						
4d Sed	400	1300	2150	4300	7500	10,700
4d HT	450	1400	2300	4600	8100	11,500
2d Sed	400	1300	2150	4300	7600	10,800
2d HT	700	2150	3600	7200	12,600	18,000
NOTE: Deduct 5 percent for 6-cyl. models.						
Coronet Lancer						
2d Conv	1100	3500	5800	11,600	20,300	29,000
Royal, V-8, 122" wb						
4d Sed	400	1300	2200	4400	7600	10,900
4d HT	450	1500	2500	5000	8800	12,500
2d HT	900	2900	4800	9600	16,800	24,000
Royal Lancer						
2d Conv	1250	3950	6600	13,200	23,100	33,000
Custom Royal, V-8, 122" wb						
4d Sed	400	1300	2200	4400	7700	11,000
4d HT	450	1400	2300	4600	8100	11,500
2d HT	950	3000	5000	10,000	17,500	25,000
4d 6P Sta Wag	400	1300	2200	4400	7700	11,000
4d 9P Sta Wag	400	1350	2250	4500	7800	11,200
2d Sub Sta Wag	450	1400	2300	4600	8100	11,500

	6	5	4	3	2	1
Custom Royal Lancer						
2d Conv	1350	4300	7200	14,400	25,200	36,000
NOTE: Add 30 percent for D500 option.						
1958						
Coronet, V-8, 122" wb						
4d Sed	350	1040	1750	3500	6100	8700
4d HT	400	1200	2050	4100	7100	10,200
2d Sed	450	1050	1750	3550	6150	8800
2d HT	650	2050	3400	6800	11,900	17,000
2d Conv	1000	3250	5400	10,800	18,900	27,000
NOTE: Deduct 5 percent for 6-cyl. models.						
Royal						
4d Sed	450	1080	1800	3600	6300	9000
4d HT	400	1250	2100	4200	7400	10,500
2d HT	750	2400	4000	8000	14,000	20,000
Custom Royal						
4d Sed	450	1140	1900	3800	6650	9500
4d HT	400	1300	2200	4400	7700	11,000
2d HT	750	2400	4000	8000	14,000	20,000
2d Conv	1300	4100	6800	13,600	23,800	34,000
4d 6P Sta Wag	400	1200	2000	4000	7000	10,000
4d 9P Sta Wag	400	1200	2050	4100	7100	10,200
4d 6P Cus Wag	400	1250	2100	4200	7400	10,500
4d 9P Cus Wag	400	1300	2150	4300	7500	10,700
2d Sub Sta Wag	400	1250	2050	4100	7200	10,300
NOTE: Add 30 percent for D500 option. Add 50 percent for E.F.I. Super D500. Add 20 percent for Regal Lancer.						
1959						
Eight cylinder models						
Coronet						
4d Sed	350	1000	1650	3300	5750	8200
4d HT	450	1160	1950	3900	6800	9700
2d Sed	350	1000	1650	3350	5800	8300
2d HT	600	1900	3200	6400	11,200	16,000
2d Conv	1000	3250	5400	10,800	18,900	27,000
NOTE: Deduct 10 percent for 6-cyl. models.						
Royal						
4d Sed	350	975	1600	3250	5700	8100
4d HT	450	1090	1800	3650	6400	9100
2d HT	650	2050	3400	6800	11,900	17,000
Custom Royal						
4d Sed	350	1020	1700	3400	5950	8500
4d HT	450	1140	1900	3800	6650	9500
2d HT	700	2150	3600	7200	12,600	18,000
2d Conv	1200	3850	6400	12,800	22,400	32,000
Sierra						
4d 6P Sta Wag	400	1200	2000	4000	7000	10,000
4d 9P Sta Wag	400	1200	2050	4100	7100	10,200
4d 6P Cus Wag	400	1200	2050	4100	7100	10,200
4d 9P Cus Wag	400	1250	2050	4100	7200	10,300
NOTE: Add 30 percent for D500 option.						
1960						
Dart Series						
Seneca, V-8, 118" wb						
4d Sed	350	860	1450	2900	5050	7200
2d Sed	350	850	1450	2850	4970	7100
4d Sta Wag	350	1020	1700	3400	5950	8500
Pioneer, V-8, 118" wb						
4d Sed	350	950	1500	3050	5300	7600
2d Sed	350	950	1550	3100	5400	7700
2d HT	400	1300	2150	4300	7500	10,700
4d 6P Sta Wag	450	1080	1800	3600	6300	9000
4d 9P Sta Wag	950	1100	1850	3700	6450	9200
Phoenix, V-8, 118" wb						
4d Sed	350	1000	1650	3300	5750	8200
4d HT	400	1300	2200	4400	7700	11,000
2d HT	550	1700	2800	5600	9800	14,000
2d Conv	700	2150	3600	7200	12,600	18,000
Dodge Series						
Matador						
4d Sed	350	1000	1650	3350	5800	8300
4d HT	450	1400	2300	4600	8100	11,500
2d HT	550	1800	3000	6000	10,500	15,000
4d 6P Sta Wag	450	1130	1900	3800	6600	9400
4d 9P Sta Wag	450	1150	1900	3850	6700	9600
Polara						
4d Sed	350	1020	1700	3400	5950	8500
4d HT	450	1400	2350	4700	8200	11,700
2d HT	550	1800	3000	6000	10,500	15,000
2d Conv	700	2300	3800	7600	13,300	19,000
4d 6P Sta Wag	450	1150	1900	3850	6700	9600
4d 9P Sta Wag	450	1170	1975	3900	6850	9800
NOTE: Deduct 5 percent for 6-cyl. models. Add 30 percent for D500 option.						
1961						
Lancer, 6-cyl., 106.5" wb						
4d Sed	350	840	1400	2800	4900	7000
2d HT	350	1000	1650	3300	5750	8200
2d Spt Cpe	350	880	1500	2950	5180	7400
Lancer 770						
NOTE: Add 10 percent for Hyper Pak 170-180 hp engine option, and 20 percent for Hyper Pak 225-200 hp.						
4d Sta Wag	350	840	1400	2800	4900	7000
Dart Series						
Seneca, V-8, 118" wb						
4d Sed	350	860	1450	2900	5050	7200
2d Sed	350	850	1450	2850	4970	7100
4d Sta Wag	350	975	1600	3200	5600	8000
Pioneer, V-8, 118" wb						
4d Sed	350	870	1450	2900	5100	7300
2d Sed	350	850	1450	2850	4970	7100
2d HT	350	1020	1700	3400	5950	8500
4d 6P Sta Wag	350	1020	1700	3400	5900	8400
4d 9P Sta Wag	350	1020	1700	3400	5950	8500
Phoenix, V-8, 118" wb						
4d Sed	350	870	1450	2900	5100	7300
4d HT	450	1080	1800	3600	6300	9000
2d HT	400	1200	2000	4000	7000	10,000
2d Conv	550	1800	3000	6000	10,500	15,000
Polara						
4d Sed	350	950	1550	3100	5400	7700
4d HT	450	1140	1900	3800	6650	9500

	6	5	4	3	2	1
2d HT	450	1400	2300	4600	8100	11,500
2d Conv	600	1900	3200	6400	11,200	16,000
4d 6P Sta Wag	350	1020	1700	3400	5950	8500
4d 9P Sta Wag	350	1040	1700	3450	6000	8600

NOTE: Deduct 5 percent for 6-cyl. models. Add 30 percent for D500 option. Add 30 percent for Ram Charger "413".

1962
Lancer, 6-cyl., 106.5" wb

	6	5	4	3	2	1
4d Sed	350	820	1400	2700	4760	6800
2d Sed	350	800	1350	2700	4700	6700
4d Sta Wag	350	840	1400	2800	4900	7000
Lancer 770, 6-cyl., 106.5" wb						
4d Sed	350	830	1400	2950	4830	6900
2d Sed	350	830	1400	2950	4830	6900
4d Sta Wag	350	860	1450	2900	5050	7200
2d GT Cpe	350	975	1600	3200	5600	8000

Dart Series

Dart, V-8, 116" wb

	6	5	4	3	2	1
4d Sed	350	850	1450	2850	4970	7100
2d Sed	350	840	1400	2800	4900	7000
2d HT	350	900	1500	3000	5250	7500
4d 6P Sta Wag	350	975	1600	3200	5500	7900
4d 9P Sta Wag	350	900	1500	3000	5250	7500
Dart 440, V-8, 116" wb						
4d Sed	350	860	1450	2900	5050	7200
4d HT	350	950	1550	3100	5400	7700
2d HT	350	975	1600	3200	5600	8000
2d Conv	400	1300	2200	4400	7700	11,000
4d 6P Sta Wag	350	900	1500	3000	5250	7500
4d 9P Sta Wag	350	950	1500	3050	5300	7600
Polara 500, V-8, 116" wb						
4d HT	350	975	1600	3200	5600	8000
2d HT	350	1020	1700	3400	5950	8500
2d Conv	600	1900	3200	6400	11,200	16,000

NOTE: Add 20 percent for Daytona 500 Pace Car.

Custom 880, V-8, 122" wb

	6	5	4	3	2	1
4d Sed	350	870	1450	2900	5100	7300
4d HT	350	1020	1700	3400	5950	8500
2d HT	450	1080	1800	3600	6300	9000
2d Conv	550	1700	2800	5600	9800	14,000
4d 6P Sta Wag	350	900	1500	3000	5250	7500
4d 9P Sta Wag	350	950	1550	3100	5400	7700

NOTE: Deduct 5 percent for 6-cyl. models. Add 75 percent for Ram Charger "413".

1963
Dart 170, 6-cyl., 111" wb

	6	5	4	3	2	1
4d Sed	200	745	1250	2500	4340	6200
2d Sed	200	730	1250	2450	4270	6100
4d Sta Wag	350	780	1300	2600	4550	6500
Dart 270, 6-cyl., 111" wb						
4d Sed	200	750	1275	2500	4400	6300
2d Sed	200	745	1250	2500	4340	6200
2d Conv	350	1040	1700	3450	6000	8600
4d Sta Wag	350	800	1350	2700	4700	6700
Dart GT						
2d HT	400	1200	2000	4000	7000	10,000
2d Conv	400	1300	2200	4400	7700	11,000
Dodge, 330/440, V-8, 119" wb						
4d Sed	350	790	1350	2650	4620	6600
2d Sed	350	800	1350	2700	4700	6700
2d HT	350	975	1600	3200	5600	8000
4d 6P Sta Wag	350	900	1500	3000	5250	7500
4d 9P Sta Wag	350	950	1500	3050	5300	7600
Polara, 318 CID V-8, 119" wb						
4d Sed	350	830	1400	2950	4830	6900
4d HT	350	880	1500	2950	5180	7400
2d HT	350	1020	1700	3400	5950	8500
2d Conv	450	1080	1800	3600	6300	9000
Polara 500, 383 CID V-8, 119" wb						
2d HT	450	1140	1900	3800	6650	9500
2d Conv	450	1500	2500	5000	8800	12,500
880, V-8, 122" wb						
4d Sed	350	880	1500	2950	5180	7400
4d HT	350	975	1600	3200	5600	8000
2d HT	450	1080	1800	3600	6300	9000
2d Conv	450	1450	2400	4800	8400	12,000
4d 6P Sta Wag	350	950	1500	3050	5300	7600
4d 9P Sta Wag	350	950	1550	3100	5400	7700

NOTE: Deduct 5 percent for 6-cyl. models. Add 75 percent for Ramcharger 426.

1964
Dart 170, 6-cyl., 111" wb

	6	5	4	3	2	1
4d Sed	200	745	1250	2500	4340	6200
2d Sed	200	730	1250	2450	4270	6100
4d Sta Wag	350	780	1300	2600	4550	6500
Dart 270, 6-cyl., 106" wb						
4d Sed	200	750	1275	2500	4400	6300
2d Sed	200	745	1250	2500	4340	6200
2d Conv	500	1550	2600	5200	9100	13,000
4d Sta Wag	350	790	1350	2650	4620	6600
Dart GT						
2d HT	400	1250	2100	4200	7400	10,500
2d Conv	600	1900	3200	6400	11,200	16,000
Dodge, V-8, 119" wb						
4d Sed	350	790	1350	2650	4620	6600
2d Sed	350	800	1350	2700	4700	6700
2d HT	350	975	1600	3200	5600	8000
4d 6P Sta Wag	350	900	1500	3000	5250	7500
4d 9P Sta Wag	350	950	1500	3050	5300	7600
Polara, V-8, 119" wb						
4d Sed	350	975	1600	3200	5500	7900
4d HT	350	880	1500	2950	5180	7400
2d HT	450	1140	1900	3800	6650	9500
2d Conv	550	1700	2800	5600	9800	14,000
880, V-8, 122" wb						
4d Sed	350	850	1450	2850	4970	7100
4d HT	350	950	1500	3050	5300	7600
2d HT	400	1200	2000	4000	7000	10,000
2d Conv	550	1750	2900	5800	10,200	14,500
4d 6P Sta Wag	350	950	1500	3050	5300	7600
4d 9P Sta Wag	350	950	1550	3100	5400	7700

NOTE: Add 50 percent for 426 street wedge.
  Add 75 percent for 426 Ramcharger.
  Add 30 percent for Polara 500 option.
  Deduct 5 percent for 6-cyl. models.

1965
Dart, V8, 106" wb

	6	5	4	3	2	1
4d Sed	200	745	1250	2500	4340	6200
2d Sed	200	730	1250	2450	4270	6100
4d Sta Wag	350	780	1300	2600	4550	6500
Dart 270, V-8, 106" wb						
4d Sed	200	750	1275	2500	4400	6300
2d Sed	200	745	1250	2500	4340	6200
2 Dr HT	350	975	1600	3200	5600	8000
2d Conv	450	1500	2500	5000	8800	12,500
4d Sta Wag	350	790	1350	2650	4620	6600
Dart GT						
2 Dr HT	450	1500	2500	5000	8800	12,500
2d Conv	750	2350	3900	7800	13,700	19,500
Coronet, V-8, 117" wb						
4d Sed	350	770	1300	2550	4480	6400
2d Sed	200	750	1275	2500	4400	6300
Coronet Deluxe, V-8, 117" wb						
4d Sed	350	790	1350	2650	4620	6600
2d Sed	350	780	1300	2600	4550	6500
4d Sta Wag	350	840	1400	2800	4900	7000
Coronet 440, V-8, 117" wb						
4d Sed	350	800	1350	2700	4700	6700
4d HT	400	1200	2000	4000	7000	10,000
2d Conv	600	1850	3100	6200	10,900	15,500
4d 6P Sta Wag	350	900	1500	3000	5250	7500
4d 9P Sta Wag	350	950	1500	3050	5300	7600
Coronet 500, V-8, 117" wb						
2d HT	400	1250	2100	4200	7400	10,500
2d Conv	600	1900	3200	6400	11,200	16,000
Polara, V-8, 121" wb						
4d Sed	350	800	1350	2700	4700	6700
4d HT	350	830	1400	2950	4830	6900
2d HT	350	1020	1700	3400	5950	8500
2d Conv	600	2000	3300	6600	11,600	16,500
4d 6P Sta Wag	350	950	1500	3050	5300	7600
4d 9P Sta Wag	350	950	1550	3100	5400	7700
Custom 880, V-8, 121" wb						
4d Sed	350	820	1400	2700	4760	6800
4d HT	350	780	1300	2600	4550	6500
2d HT	450	1140	1900	3800	6650	9500
2d Conv	650	2050	3400	6800	11,900	17,000
4d 6P Sta Wag	350	950	1550	3100	5400	7700
4d 9P Sta Wag	350	950	1550	3150	5450	7800
Monaco, V-8, 121" wb						
2d HT	450	1080	1800	3600	6300	9000

NOTE: Deduct 5 percent for 6-cyl. models. Autos equipped with 426 Hemi, value inestimable.

1966
Dart, 6-cyl., 111" wb

	6	5	4	3	2	1
4d Sed	200	750	1275	2500	4400	6300
2d Sed	200	745	1250	2500	4340	6200
4d Sta Wag	350	780	1300	2600	4550	6500
Dart 270, V-8, 111" wb						
4d Sed	350	770	1300	2550	4480	6400
2d Sed	200	750	1275	2500	4400	6300
2d HT	350	1040	1700	3450	6000	8600
2d Conv	500	1600	2700	5400	9500	13,500
4d Sta Wag	350	790	1350	2650	4620	6600
Dart GT, V-8, 111" wb						
2d HT	450	1160	1950	3900	6800	9700
2d Conv	500	1600	2700	5400	9500	13,500

NOTE: Add 30 percent for 273 V-8, 275 hp engine option.

Coronet, V-8, 117" wb

	6	5	4	3	2	1
4d Sed	200	720	1200	2400	4200	6000
2d Sed	200	720	1200	2400	4200	6000
Coronet DeLuxe, V-8, 117" wb						
4d Sed	200	745	1250	2500	4340	6200
2d Sed	200	730	1250	2450	4270	6100
4d Sta Wag	350	840	1400	2800	4900	7000
Coronet 440, V-8, 117" wb						
4d Sed	200	750	1275	2500	4400	6300
2d HT	450	1080	1800	3600	6300	9000
2d Conv	450	1400	2300	4600	8100	11,500
4d Sta Wag	350	780	1300	2600	4550	6500
Coronet 500, V-8, 117" wb						
4Dr Sed	200	750	1275	2500	4400	6300
2Dr HT	450	1140	1900	3800	6650	9500
2d Conv	550	1750	2900	5800	10,200	14,500

NOTE: Deduct 5 percent for all Dodge 6-cyl.

Polara, V-8, 121" wb

	6	5	4	3	2	1
4d Sed	350	770	1300	2550	4480	6400
4d HT	350	830	1400	2950	4830	6900
2d HT	350	1020	1700	3400	5950	8500
2d Conv	400	1200	2000	4000	7000	10,000
4d Sta Wag	350	950	1550	3100	5400	7700
Monaco, V-8, 121" wb						

NOTE: Add 10 Percent for Polara 500 Option.

	6	5	4	3	2	1
4d Sed	350	770	1300	2550	4480	6400
4d HT	350	975	1600	3200	5600	8000
2d HT	350	1040	1700	3450	6000	8600
4d Sta Wag	350	950	1550	3150	5450	7800
Monaco 500						
2d HT	450	1090	1800	3650	6400	9100
Charger, 117" wb						
2d HT	550	1750	2900	5800	10,200	14,500

NOTE: Autos equipped with 426 Hemi, value inestimable.

1967
Dart, 6-cyl., 111" wb

	6	5	4	3	2	1
4d Sed	200	745	1250	2500	4340	6200
2d Sed	200	730	1250	2450	4270	6100
Dart 270, 6-cyl., 111" wb						
4d Sed	200	750	1275	2500	4400	6300
2d Ht	350	840	1400	2800	4900	7000
Dart GT, V-8						
2d HT	400	1250	2100	4200	7400	10,500
2d Conv	550	1800	3000	6000	10,500	15,000

Coronet DeLuxe, V-8, 117" wb	6	5	4	3	2	1
4d Sed	200	745	1250	2500	4340	6200
2d Sed	200	730	1250	2450	4270	6100
4d Sta Wag	350	790	1350	2650	4620	6600
Coronet 440, V-8, 117" wb						
4d Sed	200	750	1275	2500	4400	6300
2d HT	450	1080	1800	3600	6300	9000
2d Conv	450	1500	2500	5000	8800	12,500
4d Sta Wag	350	800	1350	2700	4700	6700
Coronet 500, V-8, 117" wb						
4d Sed	350	770	1300	2550	4480	6400
2d HT	400	1200	2000	4000	7000	10,000
2d Conv	450	1450	2400	4800	8400	12,000
Coronet R/T, V-8, 117" wb						
2d HT	600	1900	3200	6400	11,200	16,000
2d Conv	650	2050	3400	6800	11,900	17,000
Charger, V-8, 117" wb						
2d HT	600	2000	3300	6600	11,600	16,500
Polara, V-8, 122" wb						
4d Sed	200	750	1275	2500	4400	6300
4d HT	350	780	1300	2600	4550	6500
2d HT	350	900	1500	3000	5250	7500
2d Conv	450	1400	2300	4600	8100	11,500
4d Sta Wag	350	840	1400	2800	4900	7000
Polara 500, V-8, 122" wb						
2d HT	350	975	1600	3200	5600	8000
2d Conv	450	1450	2400	4800	8400	12,000
Monaco, V-8, 122" wb						
4d Sed	350	840	1400	2800	4900	7000
4d HT	350	850	1450	2850	4970	7100
2d HT	350	1020	1700	3400	5950	8500
4d Sta Wag	350	900	1500	3000	5250	7500
Monaco 500, V-8, 122" wb						
2d HT	450	1140	1900	3800	6650	9500

NOTE: Add 40 percent for 440 Magnum. Autos equipped with 426 Hemi, value inestimable.

1968

Dart, 6-cyl., 111" wb	6	5	4	3	2	1
4d Sed	350	770	1300	2550	4480	6400
2d Sed	200	750	1275	2500	4400	6300
Dart 270, 6-cyl., 111" wb						
2d HT	350	840	1400	2800	4900	7000
4d Sed	350	780	1300	2600	4550	6500
Dart, V-8, 111" wb						
4d Sed	350	780	1300	2600	4550	6500
2d HT	350	975	1600	3250	5700	8100
Dart GT						
2d HT	400	1250	2100	4200	7400	10,500
2d Conv	450	1450	2400	4800	8400	12,000
Dart GT Sport 340, 111" wb						
2d HT	550	1700	2800	5600	9800	14,000
2d Conv	700	2150	3600	7200	12,600	18,000
Dart GT Sport 383, 111" wb						
2d HT	600	1900	3200	6400	11,200	16,000
2d Conv	700	2300	3800	7600	13,300	19,000
Coronet DeLuxe, V-8, 117" wb						
4d Sed	200	750	1275	2500	4400	6300
2d Sed	200	745	1250	2500	4340	6200
4d Sta Wag	350	840	1400	2800	4900	7000
Coronet 440						
2d Sed	350	770	1300	2550	4480	6400
2d HT	400	1250	2100	4200	7400	10,500
4d Sed	350	780	1300	2600	4550	6500
4d Sta Wag	350	870	1450	2900	5100	7300
Coronet 500						
4d Sed	350	780	1300	2600	4550	6500
2d HT	400	1300	2200	4400	7700	11,000
2d Conv	500	1550	2600	5200	9100	13,000
4d Sta Wag	350	900	1500	3000	5250	7500
Coronet Super Bee, V-8, 117" wb						
2d Sed	650	2050	3400	6800	11,900	17,000
Coronet R/T						
2d HT	850	2750	4600	9200	16,100	23,000
2d Conv	1000	3100	5200	10,400	18,200	26,000
Charger						
2d HT	650	2050	3400	6800	11,900	17,000
Charger R/T						
2d HT	750	2400	4000	8000	14,000	20,000
Polara, V-8, 122" wb						
4d Sed	350	770	1300	2550	4480	6400
2d HT	350	975	1600	3250	5700	8100
4d HT	350	950	1500	3050	5300	7600
2d Conv	450	1500	2500	5000	8800	12,500
4d Sta Wag	350	950	1550	3150	5450	7800
Polara 500						
2d HT	350	1020	1700	3400	5950	8500
2d Conv	500	1550	2600	5200	9100	13,000
Monaco						
2d HT	400	1200	2050	4100	7100	10,200
4d HT	350	975	1600	3200	5600	8000
4d Sed	350	840	1400	2800	4900	7000
4d Sta Wag	350	975	1600	3200	5600	8000
Monaco 500						
2d HT	400	1250	2100	4200	7400	10,500

NOTE: Add 40 percent for 440 Magnum. Autos equipped with 426 Hemi, value inestimable.

1969

Dart V-8	6	5	4	3	2	1
2d HT	200	675	1000	2000	3500	5000
4d Sed	200	670	1200	2300	4060	5800
Dart Swinger						
2d HT	350	820	1400	2700	4760	6800
Dart Swinger 340						
2d HT	550	1750	2900	5800	10,200	14,500
Dart Custom, V-8, 111" wb						
4d Sed	200	700	1200	2350	4130	5900
2d HT	350	975	1600	3200	5600	8000
Dart GT						
2d HT	500	1550	2600	5200	9100	13,000
2d Conv	550	1800	3000	6000	10,500	15,000
Dart GT Sport 340						
2d HT	600	1900	3200	6400	11,200	16,000
2d Conv	700	2300	3800	7600	13,300	19,000

Dart GT Sport 383, 111" wb	6	5	4	3	2	1
2d HT (383 HP)	700	2150	3600	7200	12,600	18,000
2d Conv (330 HP)	750	2400	4000	8000	14,000	20,000
Dart GT Sport 440, 111" wb						
2d HT	750	2400	4000	8000	14,000	20,000
Coronet DeLuxe, V-8, 117" wb						
4d Sed	200	685	1150	2300	3990	5700
2d Sed	200	670	1150	2250	3920	5600
4d Sta Wag	200	700	1200	2350	4130	5900
Coronet 440						
2d Sed	200	685	1150	2300	3990	5700
2d HT	400	1250	2100	4200	7400	10,500
4d Sed	200	670	1200	2300	4060	5800
4d Sta Wag	200	700	1200	2350	4130	5900
Coronet 500						
2d HT	400	1300	2200	4400	7700	11,000
2d Conv	500	1550	2600	5200	9100	13,000
4d Sta Wag	200	700	1200	2350	4130	5900
4d Sed	200	720	1200	2400	4200	6000
Coronet Super Bee, V-8						
2d HT	750	2400	4000	8000	14,000	20,000
2d Cpe (base 440/375)	700	2150	3600	7200	12,600	18,000

NOTE: Add 75 percent for Super Bee six pack.

Coronet R/T	6	5	4	3	2	1
2d HT	850	2750	4600	9200	16,100	23,000
2d Conv	1000	3100	5200	10,400	18,200	26,000
Charger						
2d HT	850	2650	4400	8800	15,400	22,000
Charger SE						
2d HT	700	2150	3600	7200	12,600	18,000
Charger 500						
2d HT	1000	3250	5400	10,800	18,900	27,000
Charger R/T						
2d HT	800	2500	4200	8400	14,700	21,000
Charger Daytona						
2d HT	2050	6500	10,800	21,600	37,800	54,000
Polara V-8						
4d Sed	200	700	1050	2100	3650	5200
2d HT	200	730	1250	2450	4270	6100
4d HT	200	650	1100	2150	3780	5400
2d Conv	450	1150	1900	3850	6700	9600
4d Sta Wag	200	660	1100	2200	3850	5500
Polara 500						
2d HT	350	790	1350	2650	4620	6600
2d Conv	400	1200	2000	4000	7100	10,100
Monaco						
2d HT	350	800	1350	2700	4700	6700
4d HT	200	670	1200	2300	4060	5800
4d Sed	200	700	1050	2100	3650	5200
4d Sta Wag	200	700	1050	2100	3600	5100

NOTE: Add 40 percent for 440 Magnum 440/1x4V. Autos equipped with 426 Hemi, value inestimable. Add 20 percent for 383 engine. Add 75 percent for 440/3x2V.

1970

Dart, V-8, 111" wb	6	5	4	3	2	1
4d Sed	150	650	975	1950	3350	4800
2d HT Swinger	200	720	1200	2400	4200	6000
Dart Custom						
4d Sed	200	675	1000	1950	3400	4900
2d HT	350	780	1300	2600	4550	6500
Dart Swinger 340						
2d HT	350	1040	1700	3450	6000	8600
Challenger, V-8, 110" wb						
2d HT	550	1800	3000	6000	10,500	15,000
2d HT Fml	600	1900	3200	6400	11,200	16,000
2d Conv	750	2400	4000	8000	14,000	20,000
Challenger R/T						
2d HT	650	2050	3400	6800	11,900	17,000
2d HT Fml	700	2150	3600	7200	12,600	18,000
2d Conv	850	2650	4400	8800	15,400	22,000
Challenger T/A						
2d Cpe	1150	3600	6000	12,000	21,000	30,000
Coronet, V-8, 117" wb						
4d Sed	150	650	950	1900	3300	4700
2d Sed	150	650	975	1950	3350	4800
4d Sta Wag	150	650	950	1900	3300	4700
Coronet 440						
2d HT	450	1080	1800	3600	6300	9000
4d Sed	200	675	1000	2000	3500	5000
2d Sed	200	700	1050	2050	3600	5100
4d Sta Wag	150	650	975	1950	3350	4800
Coronet 500						
4d Sed	200	660	1100	2200	3850	5500
2d HT	400	1200	2000	4000	7000	10,000
2d Conv	500	1550	2600	5200	9100	13,000
4d Sta Wag	200	675	1000	1950	3400	4900
Coronet Super Bee						
2d HT	700	2300	3800	7600	13,300	19,000
2d Cpe	650	2050	3400	6800	11,900	17,000
Coronet R/T						
2d HT	900	2900	4800	9600	16,800	24,000
2d Conv	1050	3350	5600	11,200	19,600	28,000
Charger						
2d HT	700	2300	3800	7600	13,300	19,000
2d HT 500	850	2650	4400	8800	15,400	22,000
2d HT R/T	1000	3100	5200	10,400	18,200	26,000
Polara, V-8, 122" wb						
2d HT	200	720	1200	2400	4200	6000
4d HT	200	675	1000	2000	3500	5000
2d Conv	450	1080	1800	3600	6300	9000
4d Sed	200	675	1000	1950	3400	4900
Polara Custom						
4d Sed	200	675	1000	2000	3500	5000
2d HT	350	780	1300	2600	4550	6500
4d HT	150	650	950	1900	3300	4700
Monaco						
4d Sed	200	675	1000	1950	3400	4900
2d HT	200	720	1200	2400	4200	6000
4d HT	150	650	950	1850	3200	4600
4d Sta Wag	150	600	900	1800	3150	4500

NOTE: Add 40 percent for 440 Magnum. 440/1x4V Autos equipped with 426 Hemi, value inestimable. Add 20 percent for 383 engine. Add 60 percent for 440/3x2V.

1971

	6	5	4	3	2	1
Demon						
2d Cpe	150	600	900	1800	3150	4500
2d 340 Cpe	200	660	1100	2200	3850	5500
Dart						
4d Cus Sed	150	575	875	1700	3000	4300
Swinger						
2d HT	350	840	1400	2800	4900	7000
Challenger						
2d HT	550	1700	2800	5600	9800	14,000
2d Conv	700	2300	3800	7600	13,300	19,000
2d HT R/T	700	2150	3600	7200	12,600	18,000
Coronet Brougham						
4d Sed	125	450	750	1450	2500	3600
4d Sta Wag	150	475	750	1475	2600	3700
Charger						
2d HT 500	650	2050	3400	6800	11,900	17,000
2d HT	550	1800	3000	6000	10,500	15,000
2d Super Bee HT	700	2150	3600	7200	12,600	18,000
2d HT R/T	750	2400	4000	8000	14,000	20,000
2d HT SE	700	2300	3800	7600	13,300	19,000
Polara Brougham						
4d Sed	150	475	750	1475	2600	3700
2d HT	150	475	775	1500	2650	3800
Monaco						
4d HT	150	475	775	1500	2650	3800
2d HT	150	500	800	1550	2700	3900
4d Sta Wag	150	475	775	1500	2650	3800

NOTE: Add 40 percent for 440 Magnum. Autos equipped with 426 Hemi, value inestimable. Add 50 percent for 440/3x2V.

1972

	6	5	4	3	2	1
Colt						
4d Sed	125	450	700	1400	2450	3500
2d Cpe	125	450	750	1450	2500	3600
2d HT	150	500	800	1550	2700	3900
4d Sta Wag	125	450	700	1400	2450	3500
Dart						
4d Sed	150	575	900	1750	3100	4400
2d Demon 340 Cpe	350	975	1600	3200	5600	8000
Swinger						
2d HT	350	840	1400	2800	4900	7000
Challenger						
2d HT	500	1550	2600	5200	9100	13,000
2d HT Rallye	550	1700	2800	5600	9800	14,000
Coronet						
4d 4d Sed	150	475	750	1475	2600	3700
4d Sta Wag	125	450	750	1450	2500	3600
Charger						
2d Sed	400	1200	2000	4000	7000	10,000
2d HT	400	1200	2000	4000	7000	10,000
2d HT SE	450	1450	2400	4800	8400	12,000

NOTE: Add 20 percent for Rallye.

	6	5	4	3	2	1
Polara V-8						
4d Sed	125	450	700	1400	2450	3500
4d HT	125	450	750	1450	2500	3600
2d HT	150	500	800	1550	2700	3900
4d Sta Wag	150	475	750	1475	2600	3700
Polara Custom						
4d Sed	150	475	750	1475	2600	3700
4d HT	150	475	775	1500	2650	3800
2d HT	150	600	900	1800	3150	4500
4d 2S Sta Wag	150	550	850	1675	2950	4200
4d 3S Sta Wag	150	575	875	1700	3000	4300
Monaco						
4d Sed	150	475	775	1500	2650	3800
4d HT	150	500	800	1550	2700	3900
2d HT	150	650	950	1900	3300	4700
4d 2S Sta Wag	150	575	900	1750	3100	4400
4d 3S Sta Wag	150	600	900	1800	3150	4500

NOTE: Add 60 percent for 440/3x2V

1973

	6	5	4	3	2	1
Colt						
4d Sed	125	450	700	1400	2450	3500
2d Cpe	125	400	700	1375	2400	3400
2d HT	150	475	750	1475	2600	3700
4d Sta Wag	125	450	700	1400	2450	3500
2d HT GT	150	500	800	1600	2800	4000
Dart						
4d Sed	125	450	750	1450	2500	3600
2d Cpe	150	550	850	1650	2900	4100
Dart Sport						
2d Cpe	150	600	950	1850	3200	4600
Dart Sport '340'						
2d Cpe	200	660	1100	2200	3850	5500
Dart Custom						
2d Cpe	150	550	850	1675	2950	4200
Swinger						
2d HT	200	670	1200	2300	4060	5800
2d Spl HT	200	650	1100	2150	3780	5400
Challenger						
2d HT	450	1450	2400	4800	8400	12,000
2d Rallye HT	500	1550	2600	5200	9100	13,000
Coronet						
4d Sed	125	370	650	1250	2200	3100
4d Sta Wag	125	380	650	1300	2250	3200
Coronet Custom						
4d Sed	125	400	700	1375	2400	3400
4d Sta Wag	125	450	700	1400	2450	3500
Crestwood						
4d 6P Sta Wag	125	450	750	1450	2500	3600
4d 9P Sta Wag	150	475	750	1475	2600	3700
Charger						
2d Cpe	350	975	1600	3250	5700	8100
2d HT	450	1080	1800	3600	6300	9000
2d 'SE' HT	950	1100	1850	3700	6450	9200
2d Rallye	450	1140	1900	3800	6650	9500
Polara						
4d Sed	125	380	650	1300	2250	3200
2d HT	125	450	750	1450	2500	3600
4d Sta Wag	125	380	650	1300	2250	3200

	6	5	4	3	2	1
Polara Custom						
4d Sed	125	400	700	1375	2400	3400
2d HT	150	475	775	1500	2650	3800
4d HT Sed	150	475	750	1475	2600	3700
4d 2S Sta Wag	125	400	675	1350	2300	3300
4d 3S Sta Wag	125	400	700	1375	2400	3400
Monaco						
4d Sed	125	450	700	1400	2450	3500
4d HT Sed	150	475	750	1475	2600	3700
2d HT	150	550	850	1650	2900	4100
4d 2S Sta Wag	125	400	675	1350	2300	3300
4d 3S Sta Wag	125	450	700	1400	2450	3500

1974

	6	5	4	3	2	1
Colt						
4d Sed	100	360	600	1200	2100	3000
2d Cpe	100	350	600	1150	2000	2900
2d HT	125	380	650	1300	2250	3200
2d Sta Wag	100	360	600	1200	2100	3000
2d HT GT	125	450	700	1400	2450	3500
4d Sta Wag	100	360	600	1200	2100	3000
Dart						
4d Sed	150	475	750	1475	2600	3700
2d Spe Cpe	150	550	850	1675	2950	4200
Dart Sport '360'						
2d Cpe	150	600	950	1850	3200	4600
Dart Special Edition						
2d HT	150	550	850	1650	2900	4100
4d Sed	150	500	800	1550	2700	3900
Dart Custom						
4d Sed	150	475	775	1500	2650	3800
Swinger						
2d HT	150	500	800	1550	2700	3900
Swinger Special						
2d HT	150	500	800	1600	2800	4000
Challenger						
2d HT	400	1300	2200	4400	7700	11,000
Coronet						
4d Sta Wag	125	450	700	1400	2450	3500
4d Sta Wag	125	400	675	1350	2300	3300
Coronet Custom						
4d Sed	125	400	700	1375	2400	3400
4d Sta Wag	125	400	700	1375	2400	3400
Coronet Crestwood						
4d Sta Wag	125	450	750	1450	2500	3600
Coronet Charger						
2d Cpe	200	670	1150	2250	3920	5600
2d HT	350	780	1300	2600	4550	6500
2d 'SE' HT	350	840	1400	2800	4900	7000
Monaco						
4d Sed	125	400	675	1350	2300	3300
2d HT Cpe	125	450	700	1400	2450	3500
4d Sta Wag	125	400	675	1350	2300	3300
Monaco Custom						
4d Sed	125	450	700	1400	2450	3500
2d HT	150	475	775	1500	2650	3800
4d HT Sed	150	475	750	1475	2600	3700
4d 2S Sta Wag	125	400	700	1375	2400	3400
4d 3S Sta Wag	125	450	700	1400	2450	3500
Monaco Brougham						
2d Sed	125	450	750	1450	2500	3600
2d HT	150	500	800	1550	2700	3900
4d HT Sed	150	475	775	1500	2650	3800
4d 2S Sta Wag	125	450	750	1450	2500	3600
4d 3S Sta Wag	150	475	775	1500	2650	3800

1975

	6	5	4	3	2	1
Dart						
4d Sed	125	380	650	1300	2250	3200
Dart Sport						
2d Cpe	125	450	750	1450	2500	3600
Swinger						
2d HT	150	475	775	1500	2650	3800
2d Spl HT	125	400	675	1350	2300	3300
Dart Custom						
4d Sed	150	475	775	1500	2650	3800
2d '360' Cpe	150	600	950	1850	3200	4600
Dart S.E.						
2d HT	150	550	850	1650	2900	4100
4d Sed	125	450	750	1450	2500	3600
Coronet						
2d HT	150	475	775	1500	2650	3800
4d Sed	125	380	650	1300	2250	3200
4d Sta Wag	125	400	700	1375	2400	3400
Coronet Custom						
2d HT	150	500	800	1600	2800	4000
4d Sed	125	400	675	1350	2300	3300
4d Sta Wag	125	400	700	1375	2400	3400
Coronet Brougham						
2d HT	150	550	850	1650	2900	4100
Crestwood						
4d Sta Wag	125	450	750	1450	2500	3600
Charger S.E.						
2d HT	150	650	975	1950	3350	4800
Monaco						
2d HT	150	550	850	1675	2950	4200
4d Sed	125	400	675	1350	2300	3300
4d Sta Wag	125	400	700	1375	2400	3400
Royal Monaco						
2d HT	150	575	900	1750	3100	4400
4d Sed	125	450	700	1400	2450	3500
4d HT Sed	150	550	850	1650	2900	4100
4d 2S Sta Wag	125	450	700	1400	2450	3500
4d 3S Sta Wag	125	450	750	1450	2500	3600
Royal Monaco Brougham						
2d Cpe	150	600	900	1800	3150	4500
4d Sed	125	450	750	1450	2500	3600
4d HT Sed	150	550	850	1675	2950	4200
4d 2S Sta Wag	150	475	750	1475	2600	3700
4d 3S Sta Wag	150	475	775	1500	2650	3800

1976

	6	5	4	3	2	1
Colt, 4-cyl.						
4d Sed	125	370	650	1250	2200	3100

	6	5	4	3	2	1
2d Cpe	125	380	650	1300	2250	3200
2d HT Carousel	125	450	700	1400	2450	3500
4d Sta Wag	125	380	650	1300	2250	3200
2d HT GT	125	400	700	1375	2400	3400
Dart Sport, 6-cyl.						
2d Spt Cpe	125	400	700	1375	2400	3400
Dart Swinger Special, 6-cyl.						
2d HT	125	450	700	1400	2450	3500
Dart, 6-cyl.						
4d Sed	125	400	675	1350	2300	3300
2d Swinger	125	400	700	1375	2400	3400
2d HT	125	450	750	1450	2500	3600
Aspen, V-8						
4d Sed	125	400	700	1375	2400	3400
2d Spt Cpe	125	450	750	1450	2500	3600
4d Sta Wag	125	450	700	1400	2450	3500
Aspen Custom, V-8						
4d Sed	125	450	700	1400	2450	3500
2d Spt Cpe	150	475	750	1475	2600	3700
Aspen Special Edition, V-8						
4d Sed	125	450	750	1450	2500	3600
2d Spt Cpe	150	475	775	1500	2650	3800
4d Sta Wag	150	475	750	1475	2600	3700
Coronet, V-8						
4d Sed	125	400	700	1375	2400	3400
4d 2S Sta Wag	125	400	675	1350	2300	3300
4d 3S Sta Wag	125	400	700	1375	2400	3400
Coronet Brougham, V-8						
4d Sed	125	450	700	1400	2450	3500
Crestwood, V-8						
4d 2S Sta Wag	125	400	700	1375	2400	3400
4d 3S Sta Wag	125	450	700	1400	2450	3500
Charger, V-8						
2d HT	150	650	950	1900	3300	4700
2d HT Spt	150	650	975	1950	3350	4800
Charger Special Edition, V-8						
2d HT	200	675	1000	1950	3400	4900
Monaco, V-8						
4d Sed	150	500	800	1550	2700	3900
4d Sta Wag	150	475	750	1475	2600	3700
Royal Monaco, V-8						
4d Sed	150	500	800	1600	2800	4000
2d HT	150	550	850	1675	2950	4200
4d 2S Sta Wag	150	500	800	1600	2800	4000
4d 3S Sta Wag	150	550	850	1650	2900	4100
Royal Monaco Brougham, V-8						
4d Sed	125	450	750	1450	2500	3600
2d HT	150	550	850	1675	2950	4200
4d Sta Wag	150	550	850	1650	2900	4100

1977

	6	5	4	3	2	1
Colt, 4-cyl.						
4d Sed	125	380	650	1300	2250	3200
2d Cpe	125	400	675	1350	2300	3300
2d Cus Cpe	125	400	700	1375	2400	3400
2d HT Carousel	125	450	750	1450	2500	3600
4d Sta Wag	125	400	675	1350	2300	3300
2d HT GT	125	450	700	1400	2450	3500
Aspen, V-8						
4d Sed	125	450	700	1400	2450	3500
2d Spt Cpe	150	475	750	1475	2600	3700
4d Sta Wag	125	400	700	1375	2400	3400
Aspen Custom, V-8						
4d Sed	125	450	750	1450	2500	3600
2d Spt Cpe	150	475	775	1500	2650	3800
Aspen Special Edition, V-8						
4d Sed	150	475	750	1475	2600	3700
2d Spt Cpe	150	500	800	1600	2800	4000
4d Sta Wag	150	475	775	1500	2650	3800
Monaco, V-8						
4d Sed	125	450	700	1400	2450	3500
2d HT	150	475	775	1500	2650	3800
4d 2S Sta Wag	125	400	700	1375	2400	3400
4d 3S Sta Wag	125	450	700	1400	2450	3500
Monaco Brougham, V-8						
4d Sed	150	475	750	1475	2600	3700
2d HT	150	500	800	1600	2800	4000
Monaco Crestwood, V-8						
4d 2S Sta Wag	125	400	700	1375	2400	3400
4d 3S Sta Wag	125	450	700	1400	2450	3500
Charger Special Edition, V-8						
2d HT	200	700	1050	2050	3600	5100
Diplomat, V-8						
4d Sed	150	550	850	1675	2950	4200
2d Cpe	150	575	900	1750	3100	4400
Diplomat Medallion, V-8						
4d Sed	150	575	900	1750	3100	4400
2d Cpe	150	600	950	1850	3200	4600
Royal Monaco, V-8						
4d Sed	150	575	875	1700	3000	4300
2d HT	150	600	900	1800	3150	4500
4d Sta Wag	150	575	900	1750	3100	4400
Royal Monaco Brougham, V-8						
4d Sed	150	475	750	1475	2600	3700
2d HT	150	575	875	1700	3000	4300
4d 2S Sta Wag	150	550	850	1650	2900	4100
4d 3S Sta Wag	150	550	850	1675	2950	4200

1978

	6	5	4	3	2	1
Omni						
4d HBk	125	400	675	1350	2300	3300
Colt						
4d Sed	125	380	650	1300	2250	3200
2d Cpe	125	400	675	1350	2300	3300
2d Cus Cpe	125	400	700	1375	2400	3400
4d Sta Wag	125	380	650	1300	2250	3200
Aspen						
4d Sed	125	450	700	1400	2450	3500
2d Cpe	125	450	750	1450	2500	3600
4d Sta Wag	125	450	700	1400	2450	3500
Monaco						
4d Sed	125	450	750	1450	2500	3600
2d	150	475	750	1475	2600	3700

	6	5	4	3	2	1
4d 3S Sta Wag	150	475	750	1475	2600	3700
4d 2S Sta Wag	125	450	750	1450	2500	3600
Monaco Brougham						
4d Sed	150	475	750	1475	2600	3700
2d Cpe	150	475	775	1500	2650	3800
4d 3S Sta Wag	150	475	775	1500	2650	3800
4d 2S Sta Wag	150	475	750	1475	2600	3700
Charger SE						
2d Cpe	200	700	1050	2100	3650	5200
Magnum XE						
2d Cpe	200	700	1075	2150	3700	5300
Challenger						
2d Cpe	200	670	1150	2250	3920	5600
Diplomat						
4d 'S' Sed	150	500	800	1550	2700	3900
2d 'S' Cpe	150	500	800	1600	2800	4000
4d Sed	150	500	800	1600	2800	4000
2d Cpe	150	500	800	1600	2800	4000
4d Sta Wag	150	550	850	1650	2900	4100
Diplomat Medallion						
4d Sed	150	550	850	1650	2900	4100
2d Cpe	150	550	850	1675	2950	4200

1979

	6	5	4	3	2	1
Omni, 4-cyl.						
4d HBk	125	380	650	1300	2250	3200
2d HBk	125	400	675	1350	2300	3300
Colt, 4-cyl.						
2d HBk	125	370	650	1250	2200	3100
2d Cus HBk	125	380	650	1300	2250	3200
2d Cpe	125	400	675	1350	2300	3300
4d Sed	125	380	650	1300	2250	3200
4d Sta Wag	125	400	675	1350	2300	3300
Aspen, V-8						
4d Sed	125	450	750	1450	2500	3600
2d Cpe	150	475	750	1475	2600	3700
4d Sta Wag	125	450	750	1450	2500	3600

NOTE: Deduct 5 percent for 6-cyl.

	6	5	4	3	2	1
Magnum XE, V-8						
2d Cpe	200	660	1100	2200	3850	5500
Challenger, 4-cyl.						
2d Cpe	200	685	1150	2300	3990	5700
Diplomat, V-8						
4d Sed	150	500	800	1550	2700	3900
2d Cpe	150	500	800	1600	2800	4000
Diplomat Salon, V-8						
4d Sed	150	500	800	1600	2800	4000
2d Cpe	150	550	850	1650	2900	4100
4d Sta Wag	150	500	800	1600	2800	4000
Diplomat Medallion, V-8						
4d Sed	150	550	850	1675	2950	4200
2d Cpe	150	575	875	1700	3000	4300

NOTE: Deduct 5 percent for 6-cyl.

	6	5	4	3	2	1
St. Regis, V-8						
4d Sed	150	575	900	1750	3100	4400

NOTE: Deduct 5 percent for 6-cyl.

1980

	6	5	4	3	2	1
Omni, 4-cyl.						
4d HBk	125	450	700	1400	2450	3500
2d HBk 2 plus 2 024	150	500	800	1550	2700	3900
Colt, 4-cyl.						
2d HBk	125	400	700	1375	2400	3400
2d HBk Cus	125	450	700	1400	2450	3500
4d Sta Wag	125	450	750	1450	2500	3600
Aspen, 6-cyl.						
4d Sed Spl	150	475	775	1500	2650	3800
2d Cpe Spl	150	500	800	1550	2700	3900
Aspen, V-8						
4d Sed	150	500	800	1600	2800	4000
2d Cpe	150	550	850	1650	2900	4100
4d Sta Wag	150	550	850	1650	2900	4100

NOTE: Deduct 10 percent for 6-cyl.

	6	5	4	3	2	1
Challenger						
2d Cpe	150	600	950	1850	3200	4600
Diplomat, V-8						
4d Sed Salon	125	450	750	1450	2500	3600
2d Cpe Salon	150	475	750	1475	2600	3700
4d Sta Wag Salon	150	500	800	1550	2700	3900

NOTE: Deduct 5 percent for lesser models.

	6	5	4	3	2	1
4d Sed Medallion	150	475	750	1475	2600	3700
2d Cpe Medallion	150	475	775	1500	2650	3800

NOTE: Deduct 10 percent for 6-cyl.

	6	5	4	3	2	1
Mirada, V-8						
2d Cpe Specialty S	200	700	1200	2350	4130	5900
2d Cpe Specialty	200	730	1250	2450	4270	6100

NOTE: Deduct 12 percent for 6-cyl.

	6	5	4	3	2	1
St. Regis, V-8						
4d Sed	150	550	850	1650	2900	4100

NOTE: Deduct 12 percent for 6-cyl.

1981

	6	5	4	3	2	1
Omni, 4-cyl.						
4d HBk	150	475	775	1500	2650	3800
2d HBk 024	150	550	850	1650	2900	4100

NOTE: Deduct 5 percent for lesser models.

	6	5	4	3	2	1
Colt, 4-cyl.						
2d HBk	125	450	700	1400	2450	3500
2d HBk DeL	125	450	750	1450	2500	3600
2d HBk Cus	150	475	750	1475	2600	3700
Aries, 4-cyl.						
4d Sed SE	150	500	800	1550	2700	3900
2d Sed SE	150	500	800	1600	2800	4000
4d Sta Wag SE	150	550	850	1675	2950	4200

NOTE: Deduct 5 percent for lesser models.

	6	5	4	3	2	1
Challenger, 4-cyl.						
2d Cpe	150	600	900	1800	3150	4500
Diplomat, V-8						
4d Sed Medallion	150	500	800	1550	2700	3900
2d Cpe Medallion	150	500	800	1600	2800	4000
4d Sta Wag	150	550	850	1650	2900	4100

	6	5	4	3	2	1

NOTE: Deduct 5 percent for lesser models.
Deduct 10 percent for 6-cyl.

Mirada, V-8

	6	5	4	3	2	1
2d Cpe	200	720	1200	2400	4200	6000

NOTE: Deduct 12 percent for 6-cyl.

St. Regis, V-8

4d Sed	150	550	850	1675	2950	4200

NOTE: Deduct 12 percent for 6-cyl.

1982

Colt, 4-cyl.

2d HBk Cus	150	500	800	1600	2800	4000
4d HBk Cus	150	500	800	1550	2700	3900

NOTE: Deduct 5 percent for lesser models.

Omni, 4-cyl.

4d HBk Euro	150	575	875	1700	3000	4300
2d HBk 024 Charger	150	600	900	1800	3150	4500

NOTE: Deduct 5 percent for lesser models.

Aries, 4-cyl.

4d Sed SE	150	500	800	1550	2700	3900
2d Cpe SE	150	550	850	1675	2950	4200
4d Sta Wag SE	150	575	900	1750	3100	4400

NOTE: Deduct 5 percent for lesser models.

400, 4-cyl.

2d Cpe Specialty LS	150	550	850	1675	2950	4200
4d Sed LS	150	575	875	1700	3000	4300
2d Conv	200	660	1100	2200	3850	5500

NOTE: Deduct 5 percent for lesser models.

Challenger, 4-cyl.

2d Cpe	150	650	950	1900	3300	4700

Diplomat, V-8

4d Sed	150	550	850	1650	2900	4100
4d Sed Medallion	150	575	875	1700	3000	4300

NOTE: Deduct 10 percent for 6-cyl.

Mirada, V-8

2d Cpe Specialty	200	730	1250	2450	4270	6100

NOTE: Deduct 12 percent for 6-cyl.

1983

Colt, 4-cyl.

4d HBk Cus	150	500	800	1550	2700	3900
2d HBk Cus	150	550	850	1675	2950	4200

NOTE: Deduct 5 percent for lesser models.

Omni, 4-cyl.

4d HBk	150	500	800	1600	2800	4000
4d HBk Cus	150	575	875	1700	3000	4300

Charger, 4-cyl.

2d HBk	150	575	900	1750	3100	4400
2d HBk 2 plus 2	150	600	950	1850	3200	4600
2d HBk Shelby	200	660	1100	2200	3850	5500

Aries, 4-cyl.

4d Sed SE	150	500	800	1600	2800	4000
2d Sed SE	150	500	800	1550	2700	3900
4d Sta Wag SE	150	600	900	1800	3150	4500

NOTE: Deduct 5 percent for lesser models.

Challenger, 4-cyl.

2d Cpe	150	650	975	1950	3350	4800

400, 4-cyl.

4d Sed	150	550	850	1675	2950	4200
2d Cpe	150	550	850	1650	2900	4100
2d Conv	200	685	1150	2300	3990	5700

600, 4-cyl.

4d Sed	150	575	900	1750	3100	4400
4d Sed ES	150	600	950	1850	3200	4600

Diplomat, V-8

4d Sed	150	550	850	1675	2950	4200
4d Sed Medallion	150	575	900	1750	3100	4400

NOTE: Deduct 10 percent for 6-cyl.

Mirada, V-8

2d Cpe Specialty	200	745	1250	2500	4340	6200

NOTE: Deduct 12 percent for 6-cyl.

1984

Colt, 4-cyl.

4d HBk DL	150	550	850	1675	2950	4200
2d HBk DL	150	550	850	1650	2900	4100
4d Sta Wag	150	500	800	1600	2800	4000

NOTE: Deduct 5 percent for lesser models.

Omni, 4-cyl.

4d HBk GLH	150	550	850	1675	2950	4200

NOTE: Deduct 5 percent for lesser models.

Charger, 4-cyl.

2d HBk	150	575	900	1750	3100	4400
2d HBk 2 plus 2	150	600	950	1850	3200	4600
2d HBk Shelby	200	660	1100	2200	3850	5500

Aries, 4-cyl.

4d Sed SE	150	550	850	1650	2900	4100
2d Sed SE	150	550	850	1675	2950	4200
4d Sta Wag SE	150	575	875	1700	3000	4300

NOTE: Deduct 5 percent for lesser models.

Conquest, 4-cyl. Turbo

2d HBk	150	600	900	1800	3150	4500

Daytona, 4-cyl.

2d HBk	150	600	900	1800	3150	4500
2d HBk Turbo	150	650	950	1900	3300	4700
2d HBk Turbo Z	200	675	1000	1950	3400	4900

600, 4-cyl.

4d Sed	150	575	900	1750	3100	4400
2d Sed	150	575	900	1750	3100	4400
4d Sed ES	150	600	900	1800	3150	4500
2d Conv	200	670	1200	2300	4060	5800
2d Conv ES	200	745	1250	2500	4340	6200

Diplomat, V-8

4d Sed	150	575	900	1750	3100	4400
4d Sed SE	150	600	950	1850	3200	4600

1985

Colt, 4-cyl.

4d Sed DL	150	500	800	1550	2700	3900
2d HBk DL	150	500	800	1600	2800	4000
4d Sed Premiere	150	500	800	1600	2800	4000
4d Sta Wag Vista	150	600	900	1800	3150	4500

	6	5	4	3	2	1
4d Sta Wag Vista 4WD	200	660	1100	2200	3850	5500

NOTE: Deduct 5 percent for lesser models.

Omni, 4-cyl.

4d HBk GLH	150	575	875	1700	3000	4300

NOTE: Deduct 5 percent for lesser models.

Charger, 4-cyl.

2d HBk	200	675	1000	1950	3400	4900
2d HBk 2 plus 2	200	700	1050	2050	3600	5100
2d HBk Shelby	200	660	1100	2200	3850	5500

Aries, 4-cyl.

4d Sed LE	150	550	850	1675	2950	4200
2d Sed LE	150	550	850	1675	2950	4200
4d Sta Wag LE	150	575	900	1750	3100	4400

NOTE: Deduct 5 percent for lesser models.

Conquest, 4-cyl.

2d HBk Turbo	150	600	950	1850	3200	4600

Daytona, 4-cyl.

2d HBk	150	600	950	1850	3200	4600
2d HBk Turbo	150	650	975	1950	3350	4800
2d HBk Turbo Z	200	675	1000	2000	3500	5000

600, 4-cyl.

4d Sed SE	150	600	900	1800	3150	4500
2d Sed	150	600	950	1850	3200	4600
Conv	200	670	1200	2300	4060	5800
Conv ES Turbo	200	745	1250	2500	4340	6200

Lancer

4d HBk	150	650	975	1950	3350	4800
4d HBk ES	200	675	1000	1950	3400	4900

Diplomat, V-8

4d Sed	150	600	900	1800	3150	4500
4d Sed SE	150	650	950	1900	3300	4700

1986

Colt

4d E Sed	150	550	850	1650	2900	4100
2d E HBk	150	500	800	1600	2800	4000
4d DL Sed	150	550	850	1675	2950	4200
2d DL HBk	150	550	850	1650	2900	4100
4d Premiere Sed	150	575	875	1700	3000	4300
4d Vista Sta Wag	150	600	950	1850	3200	4600
4d Vista Sta Wag 4WD	200	670	1150	2250	3920	5600

Omni

4d HBk	150	550	850	1675	2950	4200
4d HBk GLH	150	600	900	1800	3150	4500

Charger

2d HBk	200	675	1000	2000	3500	5000
2d Hbk 2 plus 2	200	700	1075	2150	3700	5300
2d Hbk Shelby	200	685	1150	2300	3990	5700
2d Hbk Daytona	200	650	1100	2150	3780	5400
HBk Daytona Turbo	200	670	1150	2250	3920	5600

Aries

2d Sed	150	575	875	1700	3000	4300
4d Sed	150	575	875	1700	3000	4300

Lancer

4d HBk	200	675	1000	1950	3400	4900

600

2d Cpe	150	600	900	1800	3150	4500
2d Conv	200	720	1200	2400	4200	6000
2d ES Conv	350	770	1300	2550	4480	6400
4d Sed	150	600	950	1850	3200	4600

Conquest

2d HBk	200	700	1200	2350	4130	5900

Diplomat

4d Sed	150	650	975	1950	3350	4800

NOTES: Add 10 percent for deluxe models. Deduct 5 percent for smaller engines.

1987

Colt, 4-cyl.

4d E Sed	150	550	850	1675	2950	4200
2d E HBk	150	550	850	1650	2900	4100
4d DL Sed	150	575	875	1700	3000	4300
2d DL HBk	150	550	850	1675	2950	4200
4d Sed Premiere	150	575	900	1750	3100	4400
4d Vista Sta Wag	150	650	950	1900	3300	4700
4d Vista Sta Wag 4WD	200	685	1150	2300	3990	5700

Omni, 4-cyl.

4d HBk America	150	550	850	1675	2950	4200
2d HBk Charger	150	600	900	1800	3150	4500
2d HBk Charger Shelby	200	675	1000	2000	3500	5000

Aries, 4-cyl.

2d Sed	150	550	850	1675	2950	4200
4d Sed	150	575	875	1700	3000	4300
2d LE Sed	150	575	875	1700	3000	4300
4d Sed LE	150	575	900	1750	3100	4400
4d LE Sta Wag	150	575	900	1750	3100	4400

Shadow, 4-cyl.

2d LBk	150	575	875	1700	3000	4300
4d LBk	150	575	900	1750	3100	4400

NOTE: Add 5 percent for 2.2 Turbo.

Daytona, 4-cyl.

2d HBk	150	650	975	1950	3350	4800
2d HBk Pacifica	200	685	1150	2300	3990	5700
2d HBk Shelby 2	200	745	1250	2500	4340	6200

600, 4-cyl.

4d Sed	150	600	900	1800	3150	4500
4d Sed SE	150	600	950	1850	3200	4600

NOTE: Add 5 percent for 2.2 Turbo.

Lancer, 4-cyl.

4d HBk	150	650	950	1900	3300	4700
4d HBk ES	150	650	975	1950	3350	4800

NOTE: Add 5 percent for 2.2 Turbo.

Diplomat, V-8

4d Sed	200	670	1150	2250	3920	5600
4d Sed SE	200	670	1200	2300	4060	5800

1988

Colt, 4-cyl.

3d HBk	100	260	450	900	1540	2200
4d E Sed	100	330	575	1150	1950	2800
3d E HBk	100	320	550	1050	1850	2600
4d DL Sed	100	350	600	1150	2000	2900
3d DL HBk	100	330	575	1150	1950	2800
4d DL Sta Wag	100	360	600	1200	2100	3000

	6	5	4	3	2	1
4d Sed Premiere	125	450	700	1400	2450	3500
4d Vista Sta Wag	150	500	800	1600	2800	4000
4d Vista Sta Wag 4x4	200	675	1000	2000	3500	5000
Omni, 4-cyl.						
4d HBk	100	330	575	1150	1950	2800
Aries, 4-cyl.						
2d Sed	100	330	575	1150	1950	2800
4d Sed	100	330	575	1150	1950	2800
4d Sta Wag	125	400	675	1350	2300	3300
Shadow, 4-cyl.						
2d HBk	125	380	650	1300	2250	3200
4d HBk	125	400	700	1375	2400	3400
Daytona, 4-cyl.						
2d HBk	150	600	900	1800	3150	4500
2d HBk Pacifica	200	670	1150	2250	3920	5600
2d HBk Shelby Z	200	720	1200	2400	4200	6000
600, 4-cyl.						
4d Sed	125	450	700	1400	2450	3500
4d SE Sed	150	500	800	1550	2700	3900
Lancer, 4-Cyl.						
4d Spt HBk	150	550	850	1675	2950	4200
4d Spt ES HBk	200	675	1000	2000	3500	5000
Dynasty						
4d Sed, 4-cyl.	150	500	800	1600	2800	4000
4d Sed Prem, 4-cyl.	150	575	875	1700	3000	4300
4d Sed, V-6	150	600	900	1800	3150	4500
4d Sed Prem, V-6	150	600	950	1850	3200	4600
Diplomat, V-8						
4d Sed Salon	150	475	775	1500	2650	3800
4d Sed	125	400	675	1350	2300	3300
4d SE Sed	150	550	850	1675	2950	4200

1989

	6	5	4	3	2	1
Colt, 4-cyl.						
2d HBk	150	475	775	1500	2650	3800
2d HBk E	150	500	800	1550	2700	3900
2d HBk GT	150	550	850	1650	2900	4100
4d DL Sta Wag	200	675	1000	2000	3500	5000
4d DL Sta Wag 4x4	200	650	1100	2150	3780	5400
4d Vista Sta Wag	200	700	1050	2100	3650	5200
4d Vista Sta Wag 4x4	200	670	1150	2250	3920	5600
Omni, 4-cyl.						
4d HBk	125	450	750	1450	2500	3600
Aries, 4-cyl.						
4d Sed	125	450	700	1400	2450	3500
2d Sed	125	400	700	1375	2400	3400
Shadow, 4-cyl.						
4d HBk	150	550	850	1675	2950	4200
2d HBk	150	550	850	1650	2900	4100
Daytona, 4-cyl.						
2d HBk	150	600	950	1850	3200	4600
2d ES HBk	200	675	1000	2000	3500	5000
2d ES HBk Turbo	200	660	1100	2200	3850	5500
2d HBk Shelby	200	745	1250	2500	4340	6200
Spirit, 4-cyl.						
4d Sed	150	550	850	1675	2950	4200
4d LE Sed	150	600	900	1800	3150	4500
4d ES Sed Turbo	200	700	1050	2050	3600	5100
4d ES Sed V-6	200	700	1050	2050	3600	5100
Lancer, 4-cyl.						
4d Spt HBk	200	700	1050	2050	3600	5100
4d Spt HBk ES	200	700	1075	2150	3700	5300
4d Spt HBk Shelby	350	780	1300	2600	4550	6500
Dynasty						
4-cyl.						
4d Sed	150	600	950	1850	3200	4600
V-6						
4d Sed	150	650	975	1950	3350	4800
4d LE Sed	200	650	1100	2150	3780	5400
Diplomat, V-8						
4d Sed Salon	200	660	1100	2200	3850	5500
4d SE Sed	200	670	1150	2250	3920	5600

1990

	6	5	4	3	2	1
Colt, 4-cyl.						
2d HBk	150	475	775	1500	2650	3800
2d GL HBk	150	500	800	1600	2800	4000
2d GT HBk	150	550	850	1675	2950	4200
4d DL Sta Wag	150	600	950	1850	3200	4600
4d DL Sta Wag, 4x4	200	660	1100	2200	3850	5500
4d Vista	200	700	1050	2100	3650	5200
4d Vista, 4x4	200	745	1250	2500	4340	6200
Omni, 4-cyl.						
4d HBk	125	450	700	1400	2450	3500
Shadow, 4-cyl.						
2d HBk	150	550	850	1650	2900	4100
4d HBk	150	550	850	1675	2950	4200
Daytona, 4-cyl.						
2d HBk	200	675	1000	2000	3500	5000
2d ES HBk	200	660	1100	2200	3850	5500
2d ES HBk Turbo	200	720	1200	2400	4200	6000
2d Shelby HBk	350	780	1300	2600	4550	6500
NOTE: Add 10 percent for V-6 where available.						
Spirit, 4-cyl.						
4d Sed	150	500	800	1600	2800	4000
4d LE Sed	150	600	900	1800	3150	4500
4d ES Sed Turbo	200	675	1000	2000	3500	5000
NOTE: Add 10 percent for V-6 where available.						
Monaco, V-6						
4d LE Sed	150	500	800	1600	2800	4000
4d ES Sed	150	575	900	1750	3100	4400
Dynasty						
4-cyl.						
4d Sed	150	650	975	1950	3350	4800
V-6						
4d Sed	200	660	1100	2200	3850	5500
4d LE Sed	200	720	1200	2400	4200	6000

1991

	6	5	4	3	2	1
Colt, 4-cyl.						
2d HBk	100	360	600	1200	2100	3000
2d GL HBk	125	450	700	1400	2450	3500
4d Vista Sta Wag	150	600	900	1800	3150	4500

	6	5	4	3	2	1
4d Vista Sta Wag, 4x4	200	660	1100	2200	3850	5500
Shadow, 4-cyl.						
2d America HBk	125	450	700	1400	2450	3500
4d America HBk	125	450	700	1400	2450	3500
2d HBk	150	475	750	1475	2600	3700
4d HBk	150	475	750	1475	2600	3700
2d Conv	200	720	1200	2400	4200	6000
2d ES HBk	150	550	850	1675	2950	4200
4d ES HBk	150	550	850	1675	2950	4200
2d ES Conv	350	780	1300	2600	4550	6500
Daytona, 4-cyl.						
2d HBk	150	600	900	1800	3150	4500
2d ES HBk	150	600	950	1850	3200	4600
Daytona, V-6						
2d HBk	200	675	1000	2000	3500	5000
2d ES HBk	200	675	1000	2000	3500	5000
2d IROC HBk	200	720	1200	2400	4200	6000
Sprint, 4-cyl.						
4d Sed	150	500	800	1600	2800	4000
4d ES Sed Turbo	150	575	875	1700	3000	4300
4d R/T Turbo Sed	200	675	1000	2000	3500	5000
Sprint, V-6						
4d Sed	200	700	1050	2100	3650	5200
4d LE Sed	150	575	875	1700	3000	4300
4d ES Sed	150	600	950	1850	3200	4600
Monaco, V-6						
4d LE Sed	150	650	975	1950	3350	4800
4d ES Sed	125	450	700	1400	2450	3500
Dynasty						
4d Sed 4-cyl.	150	500	800	1600	2800	4000
4d Sed V-6	150	600	900	1800	3150	4500
4d LE Sed V-6	200	675	1000	2000	3500	5000
Stealth, V-6						
2d LBk	200	650	1100	2150	3780	5400
2d ES LBk	350	1020	1700	3400	5950	8500
2d R/T LBk	450	1140	1900	3800	6650	9500
2d R/T LBk Turbo, 4x4	500	1550	2600	5200	9100	13,000
	550	1800	3000	6000	10,500	15,000

1992

	6	5	4	3	2	1
Colt, 4-cyl.						
2d HBk	125	450	750	1450	2500	3600
2d GL HBk	150	500	800	1600	2800	4000
Shadow						
4d America HBk	150	500	800	1600	2800	4000
2d America HBk	150	500	800	1600	2800	4000
4d HBk	150	550	850	1675	2950	4200
2d HBk	150	550	850	1675	2950	4200
2d Conv	200	660	1100	2200	3850	5500
4d ES HBk	200	675	1000	2000	3500	5000
2d ES HBk	200	675	1000	2000	3500	5000
2d ES Conv	200	720	1200	2400	4200	6000
Daytona, 4-cyl.						
2d HBk	200	675	1000	2000	3500	5000
2d ES HBk	200	700	1050	2100	3650	5200
2d IROC HBk	200	720	1200	2400	4200	6000
NOTE: Add 10 percent for V-6 where available.						
Spirit, 4-cyl.						
4d Sed	150	600	900	1800	3150	4500
4d LE Sed	150	650	950	1900	3300	4700
4d ES Turbo Sed	200	675	1000	2000	3500	5000
NOTE: Add 10 percent for V-6 where available.						
Monaco, V-6						
4d LE Sed	150	500	800	1600	2800	4000
4d ES Sed	150	600	900	1800	3150	4500
Dynasty, V-6						
4d Sed, 4-cyl.	150	600	900	1800	3150	4500
4d Sed	200	675	1000	2000	3500	5000
4d Sed	200	660	1100	2200	3850	5500
Stealth, V-6						
2d Cpe	350	1020	1700	3400	5950	8500
2d ES Cpe	450	1080	1800	3600	6300	9000
2d R/T Cpe	400	1300	2200	4400	7700	11,000
2d R/T Cpe Turbo 4x4	550	1800	3000	6000	10,500	15,000

1993

	6	5	4	3	2	1
Colt						
2d Cpe	150	475	775	1500	2650	3800
4d Sed	150	500	800	1550	2700	3900
2d Cpe	150	500	800	1550	2700	3900
4d Sed	150	500	800	1600	2800	4000
Shadow						
2d HBk	150	550	850	1650	2900	4100
4d HBk	150	550	850	1675	2950	4200
2d ES HBk	150	550	850	1675	2950	4200
4d ES HBk	150	575	875	1700	3000	4300
2d Conv	200	660	1100	2200	3850	5500
2d ES Conv	200	720	1200	2400	4200	6000
Daytona, 4-cyl.						
2d HBk	200	700	1050	2100	3650	5200
2d ES HBk	200	700	1075	2150	3700	5300
Daytona, V-6						
2d HBk	200	650	1100	2150	3780	5400
2d ES HBk	200	660	1100	2200	3850	5500
2d IROC HBk	200	720	1200	2400	4200	6000
Spirit, 4-cyl.						
4d Sed	150	600	950	1850	3200	4600
4d ES Sed	150	650	950	1900	3300	4700
Spirit, V-6						
4d Sed	150	650	950	1900	3300	4700
4d ES Sed	150	650	975	1950	3350	4800
Dynasty						
4d Sed, 4-cyl.	150	650	975	1950	3350	4800
4d Sed, V-6	200	675	1000	1950	3400	4900
4d LE Sed, V-6	200	675	1000	2000	3500	5000
Intrepid, V-6						
4d Sed	200	700	1050	2100	3650	5200
4d ES Sed	200	650	1100	2150	3780	5400
Stealth, V-6						
2d HBk	350	1040	1700	3450	6000	8600
2d ES HBk	450	1090	1800	3650	6400	9100
2d R/T HBk	750	2350	3900	7800	13,700	19,500
2d R/T HBk Turbo, 4x4	600	1850	3100	6200	10,900	15,500

EAGLE

	6	5	4	3	2	1
1988						
Medallion, 4-cyl.						
4d Sed	100	325	550	1100	1900	2700
4d Sta Wag	100	350	600	1150	2000	2900
4d LX Sed	100	360	600	1200	2100	3000
Premier, V-6						
4d LX Sed	125	450	700	1400	2450	3500
4d ES Sed	150	500	800	1600	2800	4000
Eagle, 6-cyl.						
4d Ltd Sta Wag	200	720	1200	2400	4200	6000
1989						
Jeep/Eagle						
Summit, 4-cyl.						
4d DL Sed	125	450	700	1400	2450	3500
4d LX Sed	150	500	800	1600	2800	4000
4d LX Sed DOHC	150	550	850	1675	2950	4200
Medallion, 4-cyl.						
4d DL Sed	125	370	650	1250	2200	3100
4d DL Sta Wag	125	380	650	1300	2250	3200
4d LX Sed	125	400	675	1350	2300	3300
4d LX Sta Wag	125	400	700	1375	2400	3400
Premier, V-6						
4d LX Sed, 4-cyl.	125	400	700	1375	2400	3400
4d LX Sed	150	475	775	1500	2650	3800
4d ES Sed	150	500	800	1550	2700	3900
4d ES Sed Ltd	150	600	900	1800	3150	4500
1990						
Jeep/Eagle						
Summit, 4-cyl.						
4d Sed	125	450	700	1400	2450	3500
4d DL Sed	150	475	750	1475	2600	3700
4d LX Sed	150	500	800	1600	2800	4000
4d ES Sed	150	550	850	1675	2950	4200
Talon, 4-cyl.						
2d Cpe	350	840	1400	2800	4900	7000
2d Cpe Turbo	350	975	1600	3200	5600	8000
2d Cpe Turbo 4x4	450	1080	1800	3600	6300	9000
Premier, V-6						
4d LX Sed	150	500	800	1600	2800	4000
4d ES Sed	150	600	900	1800	3150	4500
4d ES Sed Ltd	200	675	1000	2000	3500	5000
1991-92						
Summit, 4-cyl.						
2d HBk	125	450	700	1400	2450	3500
2d ES HBk	125	450	750	1450	2500	3600
4d Sed	125	450	750	1450	2500	3600
4d ES Sed	150	475	750	1475	2600	3700
Talon, 4-cyl.						
2d Cpe	200	660	1100	2200	3850	5500
2d TSi Cpe Turbo	350	780	1300	2600	4550	6500
2d TSi Cpe Turbo 4x4	350	900	1500	3000	5250	7500
Premier, V-6						
4d LX Sed	125	450	750	1450	2500	3600
4d ES Sed	150	550	850	1675	2950	4200
4d ES Sed Ltd	150	600	900	1800	3150	4500
1993						
Summit, 4-cyl.						
2d DL Cpe	150	475	775	1500	2650	3800
2d ES Cpe	150	500	800	1550	2700	3900
4d DL Sed	150	500	800	1550	2700	3900
4d ES Sed	150	500	800	1600	2800	4000
2d DL Sta Wag	150	550	850	1650	2900	4100
2d LX Sta Wag	150	550	850	1675	2950	4200
2d Sta Wag 4x4	200	700	1050	2100	3650	5200
Talon, 4-cyl.						
2d DL HBk	150	550	850	1650	2900	4100
2d ES HBk	150	550	850	1675	2950	4200
2d HBk Turbo	200	660	1100	2200	3850	5500
2d HBk Turbo 4x4	350	780	1300	2600	4550	6500
Vision, V-6						
4d ESi Sed	150	550	850	1675	2950	4200
4d TSi Sed	150	575	875	1700	3000	4300

PLYMOUTH

	6	5	4	3	2	1
1928						
Model Q, 4-cyl.						
2d Rds	850	2650	4400	8800	15,400	22,000
4d Tr	800	2500	4200	8400	14,700	21,000
2d Cpe	400	1200	2000	4000	7000	10,000
2d DeL Cpe	400	1250	2100	4200	7400	10,500
2d Sed	350	950	1550	3100	5400	7700
4d Sed	350	975	1600	3200	5600	8000
4d DeL Sed	350	975	1600	3250	5700	8100
1929-30						
Model U, 4-cyl.						
2d Rds	850	2750	4600	9200	16,100	23,000
4d Tr	850	2650	4400	8800	15,400	22,000
2d Cpe	450	1140	1900	3800	6650	9500
2d DeL Cpe	400	1200	2000	4000	7000	10,000
2d Sed	350	1040	1700	3450	6000	8600
4d Sed	350	1020	1700	3400	5950	8500
4d DeL Sed	450	1080	1800	3600	6300	9000

NOTE: Factory prices reduced app. 40 percent for 1930 model year.

	6	5	4	3	2	1
1931						
PA, 4-cyl.						
2d Rds	900	2900	4800	9600	16,800	24,000
4d Tr	850	2750	4600	9200	16,100	23,000
2d Conv	800	2500	4200	8400	14,700	21,000
2d Cpe	400	1200	2000	4000	7000	10,000
2d Sed	350	950	1500	3050	5300	7600
4d Sed	350	1000	1650	3300	5750	8200
4d DeL Sed	450	1080	1800	3600	6300	9000
1932						
Model PA, 4-cyl., 109" wb						
2d Rds	850	2750	4600	9200	16,100	23,000

	6	5	4	3	2	1
2d Conv	900	2900	4800	9600	16,800	24,000
2d Cpe	400	1250	2100	4200	7400	10,500
2d RS Cpe	400	1300	2200	4400	7700	11,000
2d Sed	450	1080	1800	3600	6300	9000
4d Sed	450	1080	1800	3600	6300	9000
4d Phae	850	2750	4600	9200	16,100	23,000
Model PB, 4-cyl., 112" wb						
2d Rds	850	2750	4600	9200	16,100	23,000
2d Conv	900	2900	4800	9600	16,800	24,000
4d Conv Sed	950	3000	5000	10,000	17,500	25,000
2d RS Cpe	450	1400	2300	4600	8100	11,500
2d Sed	450	1140	1900	3800	6650	9500
4d Sed	450	1140	1900	3800	6650	9500
4d DeL Sed	450	1160	1950	3900	6800	9700
1933						
PC, 6-cyl., 108" wb						
2d Conv	950	3000	5000	10,000	17,500	25,000
2d Cpe	400	1300	2200	4400	7700	11,000
2d RS Cpe	450	1400	2300	4600	8100	11,500
2d Sed	400	1200	2000	4000	7100	10,100
4d Sed	400	1200	2000	4000	7000	10,000
PD, 6-cyl.						

NOTE: Deduct 4 percent for PCXX models.

	6	5	4	3	2	1
2d Conv	1000	3100	5200	10,400	18,200	26,000
2d Cpe	450	1400	2300	4600	8100	11,500
2d RS Cpe	450	1450	2400	4800	8400	12,000
2d Sed	400	1250	2100	4200	7400	10,600
4d Sed	400	1250	2100	4200	7300	10,400
1934						
Standard PG, 6-cyl., 108" wb						
2d Bus Cpe	400	1200	2000	4000	7000	10,000
2d Sed	350	900	1500	3000	5250	7500
Standard PF, 6-cyl., 108" wb						
2d Bus Cpe	400	1200	2050	4100	7100	10,200
2d RS Cpe	400	1300	2200	4400	7700	11,000
2d Sed	350	950	1550	3100	5400	7700
4d Sed	350	950	1550	3150	5450	7800
DeLuxe PE, 6-cyl., 114" wb						
2d Conv	950	3000	5000	10,000	17,500	25,000
2d Cpe	400	1250	2100	4200	7400	10,500
2d RS Cpe	450	1400	2300	4600	8100	11,500
2d Sed	350	1020	1700	3400	5950	8500
4d Sed	350	1040	1700	3450	6000	8600
4d Twn Sed	450	1080	1800	3600	6300	9000
1935						
PJ, 6-cyl., 113" wb						
2P Cpe	450	1140	1900	3800	6650	9500
2d Bus Cpe	350	1040	1700	3450	6000	8600
2d Sed	350	950	1550	3150	5450	7800
4d Bus Sed	350	1000	1650	3350	5800	8300
PJ DeLuxe, 6-cyl., 113" wb						
2d Conv	850	2650	4400	8800	15,400	22,000
2d Bus Cpe	400	1200	2000	4000	7000	10,000
2d RS Cpe	400	1250	2100	4200	7400	10,500
2d Sed	350	1000	1650	3350	5800	8300
2d Tr Sed	350	1020	1700	3400	5950	8500
4d Sed	450	1050	1750	3550	6150	8800
4d Tr Sed	450	1120	1875	3750	6500	9300
4d 7P Sed	450	1170	1975	3900	6850	9800
4d Trav Sed	450	1190	2000	3950	6900	9900
1936						
P1 Business Line, 6-cyl., 113" wb						
2d Bus Cpe	450	1140	1900	3800	6650	9500
2d Bus Sed	350	1000	1650	3350	5800	8300
4d Bus Sed	350	1020	1700	3400	5900	8400
4d Sta Wag	500	1600	2700	5400	9500	13,500
P2 DeLuxe, 6-cyl., 113"-125" wb						
2d Conv	950	3000	5000	10,000	17,500	25,000
2d Cpe	400	1200	2000	4000	7000	10,000
2d RS Cpe	400	1250	2050	4100	7200	10,300
2d Sed	450	1050	1750	3550	6150	8800
2d Tr Sed	450	1120	1875	3750	6500	9300
4d Sed	450	1050	1750	3550	6150	8800
4d Tr Sed	450	1120	1875	3750	6500	9300
4d 7P Sed	450	1140	1900	3800	6650	9500
1937						
Roadking, 6-cyl., 112" wb						
2d Cpe	450	1140	1900	3800	6650	9500
2d Sed	350	850	1450	2850	4970	7100
4d Sed	350	870	1450	2900	5100	7300
DeLuxe, 6-cyl., 112"-132" wb						
2d Conv	850	2750	4600	9200	16,100	23,000
2d Cpe	400	1200	2000	4000	7000	10,000
2d RS Cpe	400	1250	2050	4100	7200	10,300
2d Sed	350	975	1600	3200	5600	8000
2d Tr Sed	350	1000	1650	3300	5750	8200
4d Sed	350	975	1600	3200	5500	7900
4d Tr Sed	350	975	1600	3200	5600	8000
4d Limo	450	1170	1975	3900	6850	9800
4d Sub	400	1200	2000	4000	7000	10,000
1938						
Roadking, 6-cyl., 112" wb						
2d Cpe	450	1140	1900	3800	6650	9500
2d Sed	350	850	1450	2850	4970	7100
4d Sed	350	870	1450	2900	5100	7300
2d Tr Sed	350	900	1500	3000	5250	7500
4d Tr Sed	350	770	1300	2550	4480	6400
DeLuxe, 6-cyl., 112"-132" wb						
2d Conv	850	2750	4600	9200	16,100	23,000
2d Cpe	400	1200	2000	4000	7000	10,000
2d RS Cpe	400	1250	2050	4100	7200	10,300
2d Sed	350	975	1600	3200	5600	8000
2d Tr Sed	350	975	1600	3250	5700	8100
4d Sed	350	975	1600	3200	5500	7900
4d Tr Sed	350	975	1600	3200	5600	8000
4d 7P Sed	450	1120	1875	3750	6500	9300
4d Limo	400	1250	2100	4200	7400	10,500
4d Sub	400	1200	2000	4000	7000	10,000
1939						
P7 Roadking, 6-cyl., 114" wb						
2d Cpe	450	1140	1900	3800	6650	9500
2d Sed	350	900	1500	3000	5250	7500

	6	5	4	3	2	1
2d Tr Sed	350	950	1500	3050	5300	7600
4d Sed	350	950	1550	3100	5400	7700
4d Tr Sed	350	950	1550	3150	5450	7800
4d Utl Sed	350	950	1550	3100	5400	7700
P8 DeLuxe, 6-cyl., 114"-134" wb						
2d Conv	800	2500	4200	8400	14,700	21,000
4d Conv Sed	850	2650	4400	8800	15,400	22,000
2P Cpe	400	1200	2000	4000	7000	10,000
2d RS Cpe	400	1250	2100	4200	7400	10,500
2d Sed	350	975	1600	3200	5600	8000
2d Tr Sed	350	975	1600	3250	5700	8100
4d Sed	350	975	1600	3200	5600	8000
4d Tr Sed	350	1000	1650	3300	5750	8200
4d Sta Wag W/C	800	2500	4200	8400	14,700	21,000
4d Sta Wag W/G	850	2650	4400	8800	15,400	22,000
4d 7P Ewb Sed	450	1080	1800	3600	6300	9000
4d Ewb Limo	400	1200	2000	4000	7000	10,000

1940
P9 Roadking, 6-cyl., 117" wb

	6	5	4	3	2	1
2d Cpe	400	1200	2000	4000	7000	10,000
2d Tr Sed	350	1020	1700	3400	5950	8500
4d Tr Sed	350	1020	1700	3400	5900	8400
4d Utl Sed	350	870	1450	2900	5100	7300
P10 DeLuxe, 6-cyl., 137" wb						
2d Conv	850	2750	4600	9200	16,100	23,000
2d DeL Cpe	400	1300	2200	4400	7700	11,000
2d 4P Cpe	450	1400	2300	4600	8100	11,500
2d Sed	350	975	1600	3200	5600	8000
4d Sed	350	975	1600	3200	5500	7900
4d Sta Wag	850	2650	4400	8800	15,400	22,000
4d 7P Sed	450	1050	1750	3550	6150	8800
4d Limo	400	1250	2100	4200	7400	10,500

1941
P11 Standard, 6-cyl., 117" wb

	6	5	4	3	2	1
2d Cpe	400	1250	2100	4200	7400	10,500
2d Sed	350	1020	1700	3400	5950	8500
4d Sed	350	1020	1700	3400	5900	8400
4d Utl Sed	350	900	1500	3000	5250	7500
P11 DeLuxe, 6-cyl., 117" wb						
2d Cpe	400	1300	2150	4300	7500	10,700
2d Sed	350	1040	1750	3500	6100	8700
4d Sed	350	1040	1700	3450	6000	8600
P12 Special DeLuxe, 6 cyl., 117"-137" wb						
2d Conv	850	2650	4400	8800	15,400	22,000
2d DeL Cpe	400	1300	2200	4400	7700	11,000
2d 4P Cpe	450	1400	2300	4600	8100	11,500
2d Sed	350	1020	1700	3400	5950	8500
4d Sed	350	1040	1700	3450	6000	8600
4d Sta Wag	850	2650	4400	8800	15,400	22,000
4d 7P Sed	450	1050	1750	3550	6150	8800
4d Limo	400	1250	2100	4200	7400	10,500

1942
P14S DeLuxe, 6-cyl., 117" wb

	6	5	4	3	2	1
2d Cpe	400	1200	2000	4000	7000	10,000
2d Sed	350	830	1400	2950	4830	6900
4d Utl Sed	350	790	1350	2650	4620	6600
2d Clb Cpe	400	1250	2100	4200	7400	10,500
4d Sed	350	800	1350	2700	4700	6700
P14C Special DeLuxe, 6-cyl., 117" wb						
2d Conv	700	2300	3800	7600	13,300	19,000
2d Cpe	400	1300	2200	4400	7700	11,000
2d Sed	350	850	1450	2850	4970	7100
4d Sed	350	840	1400	2800	4900	7000
4d Twn Sed	350	850	1450	2850	4970	7100
2d Clb Cpe	450	1400	2300	4600	8100	11,500
4d Sta Wag	850	2650	4400	8800	15,400	22,000

1946-1948
P15 DeLuxe, 6-cyl., 117" wb

	6	5	4	3	2	1
2d Cpe	400	1200	2000	4000	7000	10,000
2d Clb Cpe	400	1250	2100	4200	7400	10,500
2d Sed	450	1080	1800	3600	6300	9000
4d 2d Sed	450	1050	1800	3600	6200	8900
P15 Special DeLuxe, 6-cyl., 117" wb						
2d Conv	850	2650	4400	8800	15,400	22,000
2d Cpe	400	1250	2100	4200	7400	10,500
2d Clb Cpe	400	1300	2200	4400	7700	11,000
2d Sed	450	1140	1900	3800	6650	9500
4d Sed	450	1130	1900	3800	6600	9400
4d Sta Wag	850	2750	4600	9200	16,100	23,000

1949
First Series 1949 is the same as 1948

Second Series

DeLuxe, 6-cyl., 111" wb

	6	5	4	3	2	1
2d Cpe	450	1080	1800	3600	6300	9000
2d Sed	350	1020	1700	3400	5950	8500
2d Sta Wag	400	1200	2000	4000	7000	10,000
DeLuxe, 6-cyl., 118.5" wb						
2d Clb Cpe	450	1140	1900	3800	6650	9500
4d Sed	350	1020	1700	3400	5900	8400
Special DeLuxe, 6-cyl., 118.5" wb						
2d Conv	750	2400	4000	8000	14,000	20,000
2d Clb Cpe	450	1160	1950	3900	6800	9700
4d Sed	350	1040	1700	3450	6000	8600
4d Sta Wag	500	1550	2600	5200	9100	13,000

1950
DeLuxe, 6-cyl., 111" wb

	6	5	4	3	2	1
2d Cpe	450	1140	1900	3800	6650	9500
2d Sed	450	1080	1800	3600	6300	9000
2d Sta Wag	400	1200	2000	4000	7000	10,000
DeLuxe, 6-cyl., 118.5" wb						
2d Clb Cpe	450	1150	1900	3850	6700	9600
4d Sed	950	1100	1850	3700	6450	9200
Special DeLuxe, 6-cyl., 118.5" wb						
2d Conv	700	2300	3800	7600	13,300	19,000
2d Clb Cpe	450	1160	1950	3900	6800	9700
4d Sed	450	1140	1900	3800	6650	9500
4d Sta Wag	550	1800	3000	6000	10,500	15,000

NOTE: Add 5 percent for P-19 Special DeLuxe Suburban.

1951-1952
P22 Concord, 6-cyl., 111" wb

	6	5	4	3	2	1
2d Sed	350	975	1600	3200	5600	8000
2d Cpe	350	1020	1700	3400	5950	8500
2d Sta Wag	400	1200	2000	4000	7000	10,000
P23 Cambridge, 6-cyl., 118.5" wb						
4d Sed	350	1000	1650	3300	5750	8200
2d Clb Cpe	450	1080	1800	3600	6300	9000
P23 Cranbrook, 6-cyl., 118.5" wb						
4d Sed	350	1020	1700	3400	5900	8400
2d Clb Cpe	450	1140	1900	3800	6650	9500
2d HT	550	1700	2800	5600	9800	14,000
2d Conv	700	2300	3800	7600	13,300	19,000

1953
P24-1 Cambridge, 6-cyl., 114" wb

	6	5	4	3	2	1
4d Sed	350	950	1550	3100	5400	7700
2d Sed	350	950	1500	3050	5300	7600
2d Bus Sed	350	950	1550	3150	5450	7800
2d Sta Wag	400	1300	2200	4400	7700	11,000
P24-2 Cranbrook, 6-cyl., 114" wb						
4d Sed	350	975	1600	3200	5600	8000
2d Clb Cpe	350	1020	1700	3400	5950	8500
2d HT	550	1800	3000	6000	10,500	15,000
2d Sta Wag	400	1200	2000	4000	7000	10,000
2d Conv	800	2500	4200	8400	14,700	21,000

1954
P25-1 Plaza, 6-cyl., 114" wb

	6	5	4	3	2	1
4d Sed	450	1050	1750	3550	6150	8800
2d Sed	450	1050	1800	3600	6200	8900
2d Bus Cpe	450	1080	1800	3600	6300	9000
2d Sta Wag	450	1400	2300	4600	8100	11,500
P25-2 Savoy, 6-cyl., 114" wb						
4d Sed	450	1080	1800	3600	6300	9000
2d Sed	450	1090	1800	3650	6400	9100
2d Clb Cpe	450	1140	1900	3800	6650	9500
P25-3 Belvedere, 6-cyl., 114" wb						
4d Sed	450	1140	1900	3800	6650	9500
2d HT	650	2050	3400	6800	11,900	17,000
2d Conv	850	2650	4400	8800	15,400	22,000
4d Sta Wag	400	1300	2200	4400	7700	11,000

1955
Plaza, V-8, 115" wb

	6	5	4	3	2	1
4d Sed	350	975	1600	3200	5500	7900
2d Sed	350	975	1600	3200	5600	8000
2d Sta Wag	350	975	1600	3200	5600	8000
4d Sta Wag	450	1080	1800	3600	6300	9000
Savoy, V-8, 115" wb						
4d Sed	350	975	1600	3200	5500	8000
2d Sed	350	975	1600	3250	5700	8100
Belvedere, V-8, 115" wb						
4d Sed	350	1020	1700	3400	5950	8500
2d Sed	350	1020	1700	3400	5900	8400
2d HT	700	2150	3600	7200	12,600	18,000
2d Conv	950	3000	5000	10,000	17,500	25,000
4d Sta Wag	400	1200	2000	4000	7000	10,000

NOTE: Deduct 10 percent for 6-cyl. models.

1956
Plaza, V-8, 115" wb

	6	5	4	3	2	1
4d Sed	350	880	1500	2950	5180	7400
2d Sed	350	900	1500	3000	5250	7500
Bus Cpe	350	860	1450	2900	5050	7200
Savoy, V-8, 115" wb						
4d Sed	350	900	1500	3000	5250	7500
2d Sed	350	950	1500	3050	5300	7600
2d HT	650	2050	3400	6800	11,900	17,000
Belvedere, V-8, 115" wb (conv. avail. as 8 cyl. only)						
4d Sed	350	975	1600	3200	5600	8000
4d HT	400	1200	2000	4000	7000	10,000
2d Sed	350	975	1600	3200	5600	8000
2d HT	800	2500	4200	8400	14,700	21,000
2d Conv	1000	3100	5200	10,400	18,200	26,000
Suburban, V-8, 115" wb						
4d DeL Sta Wag	450	1140	1900	3800	6650	9500
4d Cus Sta Wag	400	1200	2000	4000	7000	10,000
4d Spt Sta Wag	400	1250	2100	4200	7400	10,500
Fury, V-8, (avail. as 8-cyl. only)						
2d HT	900	2900	4800	9600	16,800	24,000

NOTE: Deduct 10 percent for 6-cyl. models.

1957-1958
Plaza, V-8, 118" wb

	6	5	4	3	2	1
4d Sed	200	750	1275	2500	4400	6300
2d Sed	200	745	1250	2500	4340	6200
2d Bus Cpe	200	730	1250	2450	4270	6100
Savoy, V-8						
4d Sed	350	770	1300	2550	4480	6400
4d HT	350	1020	1700	3400	5950	8500
2d Sed	350	880	1500	2950	5180	7400
2d HT	600	1900	3200	6400	11,200	16,000
Belvedere, V-8, 118" wb (conv. avail. as 8-cyl. only)						
4d Sed	350	850	1450	2850	4970	7100
4d Spt HT	450	1140	1900	3800	6650	9500
2d Sed	350	840	1400	2800	4900	7000
2d HT	850	2750	4600	9200	16,100	23,000
2d Conv	1100	3500	5800	11,600	20,300	29,000
Suburban, V-8, 122" wb						
4d Cus Sta Wag	450	1080	1800	3600	6300	9000
2d Cus Sta Wag	450	1140	1900	3800	6650	9500
4d Spt Sta Wag	400	1200	2000	4000	7000	10,000
Fury, V-8, 118" wb (318 cid/290 hp, 1958)						
2d HT	950	3000	5000	10,000	17,500	25,000

NOTE: Deduct 10 percent for 6-cyl. model. Add 20 percent for 350 cid/305 hp V-8. (1957). Add 50 percent for 315 hp Bendix EFI V-8.

1959
Savoy, 6-cyl., 118" wb

	6	5	4	3	2	1
4d Sed	200	730	1250	2450	4270	6100
2d Sed	200	720	1200	2400	4200	6000
Belvedere, V-8, 118" wb						
4d Sed	200	720	1200	2400	4200	6000
4d HT	350	900	1500	3000	5250	7500
2d Sed	200	720	1200	2400	4200	6000
2d HT	550	1800	3000	6000	10,500	15,000
2d Conv	950	3000	5000	10,000	17,500	25,000

Fury, V-8, 118" wb	6	5	4	3	2	1
4d Sed	200	720	1200	2400	4200	6000
4d HT	350	975	1600	3200	5600	8000
2d HT	600	1900	3200	6400	11,200	16,000
Sport Fury, V-8, 118" wb (260 hp - V-8 offered)						
2d HT	650	2050	3400	6800	11,900	17,000
2d Conv	1000	3250	5400	10,800	18,900	27,000
Suburban, V-8, 122" wb						
4d Spt Sta Wag	350	950	1550	3100	5400	7700
2d Cus Sta Wag	350	950	1500	3050	5300	7600
4d Cus Sta Wag	350	900	1500	3000	5250	7500

NOTE: Deduct 10 percent for 6-cyl. models.

1960

	6	5	4	3	2	1
Valiant 100, 6-cyl., 106.5" wb						
4d Sed	200	745	1250	2500	4340	6200
4d HT	200	750	1275	2500	4400	6300
Valiant 200, 6-cyl., 106" wb						
4d Sed	200	750	1275	2500	4400	6300
4d Sta Wag	350	770	1300	2550	4480	6400
Fleet Special, V8, 118" wb						
4d Sed	200	750	1275	2500	4400	6300
2d Sed	200	745	1250	2500	4340	6200
Savoy, V-8, 118" wb						
4d Sed	350	820	1400	2700	4760	6800
2d Sed	350	800	1350	2700	4700	6700
Belvedere, V-8, 118" wb						
4d Sed	350	830	1400	2950	4830	6900
2d Sed	350	800	1400	2700	4760	6800
2d HT	400	1300	2200	4400	7700	11,000
Fury, V-8, 118" wb (conv. avail. as 8-cyl. only)						
4d Sed	350	900	1500	3000	5250	7500
4d HT	450	1080	1800	3600	6300	9000
2d HT	500	1550	2600	5200	9100	13,000
2d Conv	600	1900	3200	6400	11,200	16,000
Suburban, V-8, 122" wb						
4d DeL Sta Wag	350	950	1550	3100	5400	7700
2d DeL Sta Wag	350	950	1500	3050	5300	7600
4d 9P Cus Sta Wag	350	950	1550	3100	5400	7700
4d 9P Spt Sta Wag	350	950	1550	3150	5450	7800

NOTE: Deduct 20 percent for 6-cyl. model except Valiant.

1961

	6	5	4	3	2	1
Valiant 100, 6-cyl., 106.5" wb						
4d Sed	350	830	1400	2950	4830	6900
2d Sed	350	820	1400	2700	4760	6800
4d Sta Wag	350	820	1400	2700	4760	6800
Valiant 200, 6-cyl., 106.5" wb						
4d Sed	350	840	1400	2800	4900	7000
2d HT	450	1080	1800	3600	6300	9000
4d Sta Wag	350	800	1350	2700	4700	6700

NOTE: Add 20 percent for Hyper Pak 170 cid/148 hp and 30 percent for Hyper Pak 225 cid/200 hp engines.

	6	5	4	3	2	1
Fleet Special, V8, 118" wb						
4d Sed	350	800	1350	2700	4700	6700
2d Sed	350	790	1350	2650	4620	6600
Savoy, V-8, 118" wb						
4d Sed	350	820	1400	2700	4760	6800
2d Sed	350	800	1350	2700	4700	6700
Belvedere, V-8, 118" wb						
4d Sed	350	800	1350	2700	4700	6700
2d Clb Sed	350	800	1350	2700	4700	6700
2d HT	350	1020	1700	3400	5950	8500
Fury, V-8, 118" wb						
4d Sed	350	830	1400	2950	4830	6900
4d HT	350	975	1600	3200	5600	8000
2d HT	450	1450	2400	4800	8400	12,000
2d Conv	550	1700	2800	5600	9800	14,000
Suburban, V-8, 122" wb						
4d 6P DeL Sta Wag	350	860	1450	2900	5050	7200
2d 6P DeL Sta Wag	350	850	1450	2850	4970	7100
4d 6P Cus Sta Wag	350	860	1450	2900	5050	7200
4d 9P Spt Sta Wag	350	870	1450	2900	5100	7300

NOTE: Deduct 10 percent for 6-cyl. models.
Add 30 percent for 330, 340, 350, 375 hp engines.

1962

	6	5	4	3	2	1
Valiant 100, 6-cyl., 106.5" wb						
4d Sed	350	800	1350	2700	4700	6700
2d Sed	350	790	1350	2650	4620	6600
4d Sta Wag	350	820	1400	2700	4760	6800
Valiant 200, 6-cyl., 106.5" wb						
4d Sed	350	820	1400	2700	4760	6800
2d Sed	350	800	1350	2700	4700	6700
4d Sta Wag	350	830	1400	2950	4830	6900
Valiant Signet, 6-cyl., 106.5" wb						
2d HT	350	1020	1700	3400	5950	8500

NOTE: Add 20 percent for Hyper Pak 170 cid/148 hp and 30 percent for Hyper Pak 225 cid/200 hp engines.

	6	5	4	3	2	1
Fleet Special, V8, 116" wb						
4d Sed	350	790	1350	2650	4620	6600
2d Sed	350	780	1300	2600	4550	6500
Savoy, V-8, 116" wb						
4d Sed	350	800	1350	2700	4700	6700
2d Sed	350	790	1350	2650	4620	6600
Belvedere, V-8, 116" wb						
4d Sed	350	820	1400	2700	4760	6800
2d Sed	350	800	1350	2700	4700	6700
2d HT	450	1140	1900	3800	6650	9500
Fury, V-8, 116" wb						
4d Sed	350	830	1400	2950	4830	6900
4d HT	350	900	1500	3000	5250	7500
2d HT	400	1300	2200	4400	7700	11,000
2d Conv	550	1700	2800	5600	9800	14,000
Sport Fury, V-8, 116" wb						
2d HT	450	1450	2400	4800	8400	12,000
2d Conv	550	1800	3000	6000	10,500	15,000
Suburban, V-8, 116" wb						
4d 6P Savoy Sta Wag	350	860	1450	2900	5050	7200
4d 6P Belv Sta Wag	350	870	1450	2900	5100	7300
4d 9P Fury Sta Wag	350	880	1500	2950	5180	7400

NOTE: Deduct 10 percent for 6-cyl. models.
Add 30 percent for Golden Commando 361 ci.
Add 50 percent for Golden Commando 383 ci.
Add 75 percent for Super Stock 413, 410 hp.

1963

	6	5	4	3	2	1
Valiant 100, 6-cyl., 106.5" wb						
4d Sed	200	730	1250	2450	4270	6100
2d Sed	200	720	1200	2400	4200	6000
4d Sta Wag	200	730	1250	2450	4270	6100
Valiant 200, 6-cyl., 106.5" wb						
4d Sed	200	745	1250	2500	4340	6200
2d Sed	200	730	1250	2450	4270	6100
2d Conv	400	1250	2100	4200	7400	10,500
4d Sta Wag	200	730	1250	2450	4270	6100
Valiant Signet, 6-cyl., 106.5" wb						
2d HT	400	1250	2100	4200	7400	10,500
2d Conv	450	1400	2300	4600	8100	11,500
Savoy, V-8, 116" wb						
4d Sed	350	780	1300	2600	4550	6500
2d Sed	350	790	1350	2650	4620	6600
4d 6P Sta Wag	350	770	1300	2550	4480	6400
Belvedere, V-8, 116" wb						
4d Sed	350	790	1350	2650	4620	6600
2d Sed	350	790	1350	2650	4620	6600
4d HT	350	860	1450	2900	5050	7200
4d 6P Sta Wag	350	840	1400	2800	4900	7000
Fury, V-8, 116" wb						
4d Sed	350	800	1350	2700	4700	6700
4d HT	350	900	1500	3000	5250	7500
2d HT	450	1400	2300	4600	8100	11,500
2d Conv	500	1550	2600	5200	9100	13,000
4d 9P Sta Wag	350	850	1450	2850	4970	7100
Sport Fury, V-8, 116" wb						
2d HT	450	1500	2500	5000	8800	12,500
2d Conv	500	1600	2700	5400	9500	13,500

NOTES: Deduct 10 percent for 6-cyl. models.
Add 75 percent for Max Wedge II 426 engine.
Add 40 percent for 413.

1964

	6	5	4	3	2	1
Valiant 100, 6-cyl., 106.5" wb						
4d Sed	200	730	1250	2450	4270	6100
2d Sed	200	720	1200	2400	4200	6000
4d Sta Wag	200	730	1250	2450	4270	6100
Valiant 200, 6 or V-8, 106.5" wb						
4d Sed	200	745	1250	2500	4340	6200
2d Sed	200	730	1250	2450	4270	6100
2d Conv	450	1450	2400	4800	8400	12,000
4d Sta Wag	200	730	1250	2450	4270	6100
Valiant Signet, V-8 cyl., 106.5" wb						
2d HT	400	1300	2200	4400	7700	11,000
2d Barracuda	500	1550	2600	5200	9100	13,000
2d Conv	600	1900	3200	6400	11,200	16,000
Savoy, V-8, 116" wb						
4d Sed	350	780	1300	2600	4550	6500
2d Sed	350	790	1350	2650	4620	6600
4d 6P Sta Wag	350	800	1350	2700	4700	6700
Belvedere, V-8, 116" wb						
2d HT	400	1200	2000	4000	7000	10,000
4d Sed	350	790	1350	2650	4620	6600
2d Sed	350	790	1350	2650	4620	6600
4d 6P Sta Wag	350	830	1400	2950	4830	6900
Fury, V-8, 116" wb						
4d Sed	350	800	1350	2700	4700	6700
4d HT	350	850	1450	2850	4970	7100
2d HT	450	1450	2400	4800	8400	12,000
2d Conv	500	1550	2600	5200	9100	13,000
4d 9P Sta Wag	350	850	1450	2850	4970	7100
Sport Fury, V-8, 116" wb						
2d HT	550	1700	2800	5600	9800	14,000
Conv	650	2050	3400	6800	11,900	17,000

NOTES: Deduct 10 percent for 6-cyl. models.
Add 75 percent for 426-415 MW III.
Autos equipped with 426 Hemi value inestimable.

1965

	6	5	4	3	2	1
Valiant 100, V8, 106" wb						
4d Sed	200	730	1250	2450	4270	6100
2d Sed	200	720	1200	2400	4200	6000
4d Sta Wag	200	730	1250	2450	4270	6100
Valiant 200, V-8, 106" wb						
4d Sed	200	745	1250	2500	4340	6200
2d Sed	200	730	1250	2450	4270	6100
2d Conv	450	1450	2400	4800	8400	12,000
4d Sta Wag	200	730	1250	2450	4270	6100
Valiant Signet, V8, 106" wb						
2d HT	500	1550	2600	5200	9100	13,000
2d Conv	650	2050	3400	6800	11,900	17,000
Barracuda, V-8, 106" wb						
2d HT	600	1900	3200	6400	11,200	16,000

NOTE: Add 10 percent for Formula S option.

	6	5	4	3	2	1
Belvedere I, V-8, 116" wb						
4d Sed	200	745	1250	2500	4340	6200
2d Sed	200	730	1250	2450	4270	6100
4d Sta Wag	200	745	1250	2500	4340	6200
Belvedere II, V8, 116" wb						
4d Sed	350	770	1300	2550	4480	6400
2d HT	350	1020	1700	3400	5950	8500
2d Conv	450	1140	1900	3800	6650	9500
4d 9P Sta Wag	350	780	1300	2600	4550	6500
4d 6P Sta Wag	350	770	1300	2550	4480	6400
Satellite, V8, 116" wb						
2d	450	1450	2400	4800	8400	12,000
2d Conv	700	2300	3800	7600	13,300	19,000
Fury, V-8, 119" wb.; 121" Sta. Wag.						
4d Sed	350	790	1350	2650	4620	6600
2d Sed	350	780	1300	2600	4550	6500
4d Sta Wag	350	790	1350	2650	4620	6600
Fury II, V8, 119" wb, Sta Wag 121" wb						
4d Sed	350	800	1350	2700	4700	6700
2d Sed	350	820	1400	2700	4760	6800
4d 9P Sta Wag	350	820	1400	2700	4760	6800
4d 6P Sta Wag	350	800	1350	2700	4700	6700
Fury III, V8, 119" wb, Sta Wag 121" wb						
4d Sed	350	820	1400	2700	4760	6800
4d HT	350	900	1500	3000	5250	7500
2d HT	400	1250	2100	4200	7400	10,500

	6	5	4	3	2	1
2d Conv	600	1900	3200	6400	11,200	16,000
4d 9P Sta Wag	350	830	1400	2950	4830	6900
4d 6P Sta Wag	350	820	1400	2700	4760	6800
Sport Fury, V-8						
2d HT	500	1550	2600	5200	9100	13,000
2d Conv	600	1900	3200	6400	11,200	16,000

NOTES: Deduct 5 percent for 6-cyl. models.
Add 60 percent for 426 Commando engine option.
Add 75 percent for 426 Hemi.

1966

	6	5	4	3	2	1
Valiant 100, V8, 106" wb						
4d Sed	200	745	1250	2500	4340	6200
2d Sed	200	730	1250	2450	4270	6100
4d Sta Wag	350	770	1300	2550	4480	6400
Valiant 200, V8, 106" wb						
4d Sed	200	750	1275	2500	4400	6300
4d Sta Wag	350	780	1300	2600	4550	6500
Valiant Signet, V8, 106" wb						
2d HT	450	1400	2300	4600	8100	11,500
2d Conv	550	1700	2800	5600	9800	14,000
Barracuda, V8, 106" wb						
2d HT	500	1550	2600	5200	9100	13,000

NOTE: Add 10 percent for Formula S.

	6	5	4	3	2	1
Belvedere I, V-8, 116" wb						
4d Sed	200	750	1275	2500	4400	6300
2d Sed	200	745	1250	2500	4340	6200
4d Sta Wag	350	790	1350	2650	4620	6600
Belvedere II, V-8, 116" wb						
4d Sed	350	770	1300	2550	4480	6400
2d HT	400	1250	2100	4200	7400	10,500
2d Conv	450	1450	2400	4800	8400	12,000
4d Sta Wag	350	800	1350	2700	4700	6700
Satellite, V-8, 116" wb						
2d HT	500	1550	2600	5200	9100	13,000
2d Conv	550	1800	3000	6000	10,500	15,000
Fury I, V-8, 119" wb						
4d Sed	350	780	1300	2600	4550	6500
2d Sed	350	770	1300	2550	4480	6400
4d 6P Sta Wag	350	820	1400	2700	4760	6800

NOTE: Deduct 5 percent for 6-cyl. models.

	6	5	4	3	2	1
Fury II, V-8, 119" wb						
4d Sed	350	790	1350	2650	4620	6600
2d Sed	350	780	1300	2600	4550	6500
4d 9P Sta Wag	350	830	1400	2950	4830	6900
Fury III, V8, 119" wb						
4d Sed	350	800	1350	2700	4700	6700
2d HT	450	1400	2300	4600	8100	11,500
4d HT	350	860	1450	2900	5050	7200
2d Conv	550	1800	3000	6000	10,500	15,000
4d 9P Sta Wag	350	840	1400	2800	4900	7000
Sport Fury, V-8, 119" wb						
2d HT	450	1450	2400	4800	8400	12,000
2d Conv	600	1900	3200	6400	11,200	16,000
VIP, V-8, 119" wb						
4d HT	350	1020	1700	3400	5950	8500
2d HT	450	1450	2400	4800	8400	12,000

NOTE: Autos equipped with 426 Street Hemi or Race Hemi, value inestimable.

1967

	6	5	4	3	2	1
Valiant 100, V-8, 108" wb						
4d Sed	200	745	1250	2500	4340	6200
2d Sed	200	730	1250	2450	4270	6100
Valiant Signet, V-8, 108" wb						
4d Sed	200	750	1275	2500	4400	6300
2d Sed	200	745	1250	2500	4340	6200
Barracuda, V-8, 108" wb						
2d HT	450	1450	2400	4800	8400	12,000
2d FBk	500	1550	2600	5200	9100	13,000
2d Conv	550	1800	3000	6000	10,500	15,000

NOTE: Add 10 percent for Formula S and 40 percent for 383 CID.

	6	5	4	3	2	1
Belvedere I, V-8, 116" wb						
4d Sed	200	750	1275	2500	4400	6300
2d Sed	200	745	1250	2500	4340	6200
4d 6P Sta Wag	200	745	1250	2500	4340	6200
Belvedere II, V-8, 116" wb						
4d Sed	350	770	1300	2550	4480	6400
2d HT	400	1250	2100	4200	7400	10,500
2d Conv	500	1550	2600	5200	9100	13,000
4d 9P Sta Wag	350	770	1300	2550	4480	6400
Satellite, V-8, 116" wb						
2d HT	700	2150	3600	7200	12,600	18,000
2d Conv	650	2100	3500	7000	12,300	17,500
GTX, V8, 116" wb						
2d HT	700	2300	3800	7600	13,300	19,000
2d Conv	700	2300	3800	7600	13,300	19,000
Fury I, V8, 122" wb						
4d Sed	350	790	1350	2650	4620	6600
2d Sed	350	780	1300	2600	4550	6500
4d 6P Sta Wag	350	800	1350	2700	4700	6700
Fury II, V8, 122" wb						
4d Sed	350	800	1350	2700	4700	6700
2d Sed	350	790	1350	2650	4620	6600
4d 9P Sta Wag	350	820	1400	2700	4760	6800
Fury III, V8, 122" wb						
4d Sed	350	820	1400	2700	4760	6800
4d HT	350	870	1450	2900	5100	7300
2d HT	400	1250	2100	4200	7400	10,500
2d Conv	500	1550	2600	5200	9100	13,000
4d 9P Sta Wag	350	820	1400	2700	4760	6800
Sport Fury, V-8, 119" wb						
2d HT	400	1200	2000	4000	7000	10,000
2d FBk	400	1250	2100	4200	7400	10,500
2d Conv	500	1550	2600	5200	9100	13,000
VIP, V-8, 119" wb						
4d HT	350	1020	1700	3400	5950	8500
2d HT	400	1250	2100	4200	7400	10,500

NOTE: Add 50 percent for 440 engine. Autos equipped with 426 Hemi, value inestimable.

1968

	6	5	4	3	2	1
Valiant 100, V-8, 108" wb						
4d Sed	200	750	1275	2500	4400	6300
2d Sed	200	745	1250	2500	4340	6200
Valiant Signet, V-8, 108" wb						
4d Sed	350	780	1300	2600	4550	6500
2d Sed	350	770	1300	2550	4480	6400
Barracuda, V-8, 108" wb						
2d HT	500	1550	2600	5200	9100	13,000
2d FBk	550	1700	2800	5600	9800	14,000
2d Conv	650	2050	3400	6800	11,900	17,000

NOTE: Add 20 percent for Barracuda/Formula S' and 40 percent for 383 cid.

	6	5	4	3	2	1
Belvedere, V-8, 116" wb						
4d Sed	350	770	1300	2550	4480	6400
2d Sed	200	750	1275	2500	4400	6300
4d 6P Sta Wag	350	780	1300	2600	4550	6500
Satellite, V-8, 116" wb						
4d Sed	350	780	1300	2600	4550	6500
2d HT	450	1450	2400	4800	8400	12,000
2d Conv	500	1550	2600	5200	9100	13,000
4d Sta Wag	350	790	1350	2650	4620	6600
Sport Satellite, V-8, 116" wb						
2d HT	550	1700	2800	5600	9800	14,000
2d Conv	550	1800	3000	6000	10,500	15,000
4d Sta Wag	350	800	1350	2700	4700	6700
Road Runner, V-8, 116" wb						
2d Cpe	800	2500	4200	8400	14,700	21,000
2d HT	850	2700	4500	9000	15,800	22,500
GTX, V8, 116" wb						
2d HT	850	2650	4400	8800	15,400	22,000
2d Conv	950	3050	5100	10,200	17,900	25,500
Fury I, V-8, 119" & 122" wb						
4d Sed	350	800	1350	2700	4700	6700
2d Sed	350	790	1350	2650	4620	6600
4d 6P Sta Wag	350	820	1400	2700	4760	6800
Fury II, V-8, 119" & 122" wb						
4d Sed	350	820	1400	2700	4760	6800
2d Sed	350	800	1350	2700	4700	6800
4d 6P Sta Wag	350	830	1400	2950	4830	6900
Fury III, V-8, 119" & 122" wb						
4d Sed	350	830	1400	2950	4830	6900
4d HT	350	950	1550	3100	5400	7700
2d HT	400	1300	2200	4400	7700	11,000
2d HT FBk	400	1250	2100	4200	7400	10,500
2d Conv	500	1550	2600	5200	9100	13,000
4d 6P Sta Wag	350	840	1400	2800	4900	7000
Suburban, V-8, 121" wb						
4d 6P Cus Sta Wag	350	800	1350	2700	4700	6700
4d 9P Cus Sta Wag	350	820	1400	2700	4760	6800
4d 6P Spt Sta Wag	350	830	1400	2950	4830	6900
4d 9P Spt Sta Wag	350	840	1400	2800	4900	7000
Sport Fury, V8, 119" wb						
2d HT	400	1300	2200	4400	7700	11,000
2d HT FBk	450	1400	2300	4600	8100	11,500
2d Conv	500	1550	2600	5200	9100	13,000
VIP, V8, 119" wb						
4d HT	450	1140	1900	3800	6650	9500
2d FBk	450	1400	2300	4600	8100	11,500

NOTES: Add 50 percent for 440 engine.
Autos equipped with 426 Hemi value inestimable.

1969

	6	5	4	3	2	1
Valiant 100, V8, 108" wb						
4d Sed	200	700	1200	2350	4130	5900
2d Sed	200	670	1200	2300	4060	5800
Valiant Signet, V-8, 108" wb						
4d Sed	200	720	1200	2400	4200	6000
2d Sed	200	700	1200	2350	4130	5900
Barracuda, V-8, 108" wb						
2d HT	600	1900	3200	6400	11,200	16,000
2d HT FBk	650	2050	3400	6800	11,900	17,000
2d Conv	700	2300	3800	7600	13,300	19,000

NOTE: Add 40 percent for Formula S 383 cid option. Add 50 percent for Barracuda 440.

	6	5	4	3	2	1
Belvedere, V-8, 117" wb						
4d Sed	200	745	1250	2500	4340	6200
2d Sed	200	730	1250	2450	4270	6100
4d 6P Sta Wag	200	745	1250	2500	4340	6200
Satellite, V8, 116" & 117" wb						
4d Sed	200	750	1275	2500	4400	6300
2d HT	450	1450	2400	4800	8400	12,000
2d Conv	550	1700	2800	5600	9800	14,000
4d 6P Sta Wag	350	770	1300	2550	4480	6400
Sport Satellite, V8, 116" & 117" wb						
4d Sed	350	770	1300	2550	4480	6400
2d HT	500	1550	2600	5200	9100	13,000
2d Conv	650	2050	3400	6800	11,900	17,000
4d 9P Sta Wag	350	780	1300	2600	4550	6500
Road Runner, V-8, 116" wb						
2d Sed	750	2400	4000	8000	14,000	20,000
2d HT	850	2750	4600	9200	16,100	23,000
2d Conv	1000	3250	5400	10,800	18,900	27,000
GTX, V8, 116" wb						
2d HT	850	2700	4500	9000	15,800	22,500
2d Conv	1000	3200	5300	10,600	18,600	26,500
Fury I, V-8, 120" & 122" wb						
4d Sed	350	790	1350	2650	4620	6600
2d Sed	350	780	1300	2600	4550	6500
4d 6P Sta Wag	350	800	1350	2700	4700	6700
Fury II, V8, 120" & 122" wb						
4d Sed	350	800	1350	2700	4700	6700
2d Sed	350	790	1350	2650	4620	6600
4d 6P Sta Wag	350	820	1400	2700	4760	6800
Fury III, V8, 120" & 122" wb						
4d Sed	350	820	1400	2700	4760	6800
4d HT	350	870	1450	2900	5100	7300
2d HT	400	1200	2000	4000	7000	10,000
2d Conv	450	1400	2300	4600	8100	11,500
4d 9P Sta Wag	350	830	1400	2950	4830	6900
Sport Fury						
2d HT	400	1250	2100	4200	7400	10,500
2d Conv	450	1450	2400	4800	8400	12,000
VIP						
4d HT	350	900	1500	3000	5250	7500
2d HT	400	1300	2200	4400	7700	11,000

NOTES: Add 75 percent for 440 6 pack.
Autos equipped with 426 Hemi value inestimable.

	6	5	4	3	2	1
Valiant						
4d Sed	200	670	1200	2300	4060	5800
Valiant Duster						
2d Cpe	350	840	1400	2800	4900	7000
Duster '340'						
2d Cpe	450	1140	1900	3800	6650	9500
Barracuda						
2d HT	700	2150	3600	7200	12,600	18,000
2d Conv	700	2300	3800	7600	13,300	19,000
Gran Coupe						
2d HT	850	2650	4400	8800	15,400	22,000
2d Conv	850	2750	4600	9200	16,100	23,000
Cuda						
2d HT	900	2900	4800	9600	16,800	24,000
2d Conv	950	3000	5000	10,000	17,500	25,000
2d Hemi Cuda Conv					value inestimable	
Cuda AAR						
2d HT	1150	3700	6200	12,400	21,700	31,000
Belvedere						
4d Sed	200	745	1250	2500	4340	6200
2d Cpe	200	730	1250	2450	4270	6100
4d Wag	200	750	1275	2500	4400	6300
Road Runner						
2d Cpe	650	2050	3400	6800	11,900	17,000
2d HT	750	2400	4000	8000	14,000	20,000
2d Superbird	2050	6600	11,000	22,000	38,500	55,000
2d Conv	950	3000	5000	10,000	17,500	25,000
Satellite						
4d Sed	200	750	1275	2500	4400	6300
2d HT	450	1450	2400	4800	8400	12,000
2d Conv	500	1550	2600	5200	9100	13,000
4d 6P Wag	350	770	1300	2550	4480	6400
4d 9P Wag	350	780	1300	2600	4550	6500
Sport Satellite						
4d Sed	350	780	1300	2600	4550	6500
2d HT	550	1800	3000	6000	10,500	15,000
4d 6P Wag	350	780	1300	2600	4550	6500
4d 9P Wag	350	790	1350	2650	4620	6600
GTX						
2d HT	750	2400	4000	8000	14,000	20,000
Fury I						
4d Sed	350	790	1350	2650	4620	6600
2d Sed	350	780	1300	2600	4550	6500
Fury II						
4d Sed	350	800	1350	2700	4700	6700
2d Sed	350	790	1350	2650	4620	6600
4d 6P Wag	350	800	1350	2700	4700	6700
4d 9P Wag	350	820	1400	2700	4760	6800
Gran Coupe						
2d Sed	450	1080	1800	3600	6300	9000
Fury III						
4d Sed	350	820	1400	2700	4760	6800
2d HT	350	1020	1700	3400	5950	8500
4d HT	350	870	1450	2900	5100	7300
2d Fml	350	1000	1650	3300	5750	8200
2d Conv	450	1450	2400	4800	8400	12,000
4d 6P Wag	350	820	1400	2700	4760	6800
4d 9P Wag	350	830	1400	2950	4830	6900
Sport Fury						
4d Sed	350	830	1400	2950	4830	6900
2d HT	450	1140	1900	3800	6650	9500
4d HT	350	880	1500	2950	5180	7400
2d Fml	450	1080	1800	3600	6300	9000
4d Wag	350	830	1400	2950	4830	6900
Fury S-23						
2d HT	450	1500	2500	5000	8800	12,500
Fury GT						
2d HT	500	1550	2600	5200	9100	13,000

NOTES: Add 60 percent for 440 6 pack.
Autos equipped with 426 Hemi value inestimable.
Add 10 percent for 'Cuda 340 package.

1971

	6	5	4	3	2	1
Valiant						
4d Sed	200	685	1150	2300	3990	5700
Duster						
2d Cpe	200	720	1200	2400	4200	6000
Duster '340'						
2d Cpe	450	1150	1900	3850	6700	9600
Scamp						
2d HT	350	1020	1700	3400	5950	8500
Barracuda						
2d Cpe	550	1700	2800	5600	9800	14,000
2d HT	600	1900	3200	6400	11,200	16,000
2d Conv	700	2150	3600	7200	12,600	18,000
Gran Coupe						
2d HT	700	2150	3600	7200	12,600	18,000
'Cuda						
2d HT	750	2400	4000	8000	14,000	20,000
2d Conv	850	2650	4400	8800	15,400	22,000
Satellite						
4d Sed	200	670	1200	2300	4060	5800
2d Cpe	350	840	1400	2800	4900	7000
4d Sta Wag	200	685	1150	2300	3990	5700
Satellite Sebring						
2d HT	450	1500	2500	5000	8800	12,500
Satellite Custom						
4d Sed	200	700	1200	2350	4130	5900
4d 6P Sta Wag	200	670	1200	2300	4060	5800
4d 9P Sta Wag	200	700	1200	2350	4130	5900
Road Runner						
2d HT	650	2050	3400	6800	11,900	17,000
Sebring Plus						
2d HT	450	1450	2400	4800	8400	12,000
Satellite Brougham						
4d Sed	200	720	1200	2400	4200	6000
Regent Wagon						
4d 6P Sta Wag	200	720	1200	2400	4200	6000
4d 9P Sta Wag	200	730	1250	2450	4270	6100
GTX						
2d HT	500	1550	2600	5200	9100	13,000

	6	5	4	3	2	1
Fury I						
4d Sed	200	745	1250	2500	4340	6200
2d Sed	200	730	1250	2450	4270	6100
Fury Custom						
4d Sed	200	750	1275	2500	4400	6300
2d Sed	200	745	1250	2500	4340	6200
Fury II						
4d Sed	350	770	1300	2550	4480	6400
2d HT	450	1080	1800	3600	6300	9000
4d 6P Sta Wag	350	770	1300	2550	4480	6400
4d 9P Sta Wag	350	780	1300	2600	4550	6500
Fury III						
4d Sed	350	780	1300	2600	4550	6500
2d HT	450	1140	1900	3800	6650	9500
4d HT	350	840	1400	2800	4900	7000
2d Fml Cpe	450	1170	1975	3900	6850	9800
4d 6P Sta Wag	350	780	1300	2600	4550	6500
4d 9P Sta Wag	350	790	1350	2650	4620	6600
Sport Fury						
4d Sed	350	800	1350	2700	4700	6700
4d HT	350	860	1450	2900	5050	7200
2d Fml Cpe	350	975	1600	3200	5600	8000
2d HT	350	1020	1700	3400	5950	8500
4d 9P Sta Wag	350	820	1400	2700	4760	6800
4d 6P Sta Wag	350	800	1350	2700	4700	6700
Sport Fury 'GT'						
2d HT	450	1400	2300	4600	8100	11,500

NOTES: Add 40 percent for 440 engine.
Add 10 percent for Cuda 340 package.
Add 70 percent for 440 6 pack.
Autos equipped with 426 Hemi value inestimable.

1972

	6	5	4	3	2	1
Valiant						
4d Sed	200	685	1150	2300	3990	5700
Duster						
2d Cpe	350	900	1500	3000	5250	7500
2d '340' Cpe	450	1140	1900	3800	6650	9500
Scamp						
2d HT	450	1140	1900	3800	6650	9500
Barracuda						
2d HT	500	1550	2600	5200	9100	13,000
'Cuda						
2d HT	550	1700	2800	5600	9800	14,000
Satellite						
4d Sed	200	700	1200	2350	4130	5900
2d Cpe	350	900	1500	3000	5250	7500
4d 6P Wag	200	700	1200	2350	4130	5900
Satellite Sebring						
2d HT	450	1400	2300	4600	8100	11,500
Satellite Custom						
4d Sed	200	720	1200	2400	4200	6000
4d 6P Wag	200	750	1275	2500	4400	6300
4d 9P Wag	200	745	1250	2500	4340	6200
Sebring-Plus						
2d HT	450	1450	2400	4800	8400	12,000
Regent						
4d 6P Wag	200	650	1100	2150	3780	5400
4d 9P Wag	200	660	1100	2200	3850	5500
Road Runner						
2d HT	550	1800	3000	6000	10,500	15,000
Fury I						
4d Sed	200	670	1150	2250	3920	5600
Fury II						
4d Sed	200	685	1150	2300	3990	5700
2d HT	350	1020	1700	3400	5950	8500
Fury III						
4d Sed	200	670	1200	2300	4060	5800
4d HT	200	720	1200	2400	4200	6000
2d Fml Cpe	350	1040	1750	3500	6100	8700
2d HT	350	1040	1700	3450	6000	8600
Gran Fury						
4d HT	200	745	1250	2500	4340	6200
2d Fml Cpe	450	1050	1750	3550	6150	8800
Suburban						
4d 6P Sta Wag	200	650	1100	2150	3780	5400
4d 9P Sta Wag	200	660	1100	2200	3850	5500
4d 6P Cus Wag	200	660	1100	2200	3850	5500
4d 9P Cus Wag	200	670	1150	2250	3920	5600
4d 6P Spt Wag	200	685	1150	2300	3990	5700
4d 9P Spt Wag	200	670	1200	2300	4060	5800

NOTE: Add 20 percent for 440 engine where available.

1973

	6	5	4	3	2	1
Valiant, V-8						
4d Sed	200	700	1050	2050	3600	5100
Duster, V-8						
2d Cpe Sport	200	670	1150	2250	3920	5600
2d 340 Cpe Spt	350	840	1400	2800	4900	7000
Scamp, V-8						
2d HT	350	860	1450	2900	5050	7200
Barracuda, V-8						
2d HT	450	1450	2400	4800	8400	12,000
2d 'Cuda HT	500	1550	2600	5200	9100	13,000
Satellite Custom, V-8						
4d Sed	200	700	1200	2350	4130	5900
4d 3S Sta Wag	200	700	1200	2350	4130	5900
4d 3S Sta Wag Regent	200	720	1200	2400	4200	6000
4d Satellite Cpe	200	750	1275	2500	4400	6300
Road Runner, V-8						
2d Cpe	400	1200	2000	4000	7000	10,000
Satellite Plus, V-8						
2d HT	450	1140	1900	3800	6650	9500
Satellite Sebring, V-8						
2d HT	450	1080	1800	3600	6300	9000
Fury, V-8						
4d Sed I	200	720	1200	2400	4200	6000
4d Sed II	200	730	1250	2450	4270	6100
4d Sed III	200	745	1250	2500	4340	6200
4d HT	350	975	1600	3200	5600	8000
4d HT	200	750	1275	2500	4400	6300

Model	6	5	4	3	2	1
Gran Fury, V-8						
2d HT	350	1020	1700	3400	5950	8500
4d HT	200	750	1275	2500	4400	6300
Fury Suburban, V-8						
4d 3S Spt Sta Wag	200	670	1200	2300	4060	5800

NOTE: Add 20 percent for 440 engine where available.

1974

Model	6	5	4	3	2	1
Valiant						
4d Sed	200	675	1000	2000	3500	5000
Duster						
2d Cpe	200	700	1050	2050	3600	5100
Scamp						
2d HT	350	790	1350	2650	4620	6600
Duster '360'						
2d Cpe	200	745	1250	2500	4340	6200
Valiant Brougham						
4d Sed	200	700	1050	2100	3650	5200
2d HT	350	900	1500	3000	5250	7500
Barracuda						
2d Spt Cpe	400	1300	2200	4400	7700	11,000
'Cuda						
2d Spt Cpe	450	1450	2400	4800	8400	12,000
Satellite						
4d Sed	200	700	1050	2050	3600	5100
2d Cpe	200	700	1050	2100	3650	5200
Satellite Custom						
4d Sed	200	700	1075	2150	3700	5300
Sebring						
2d HT	450	1050	1750	3550	6150	8800
Sebring-Plus						
2d HT	450	1090	1800	3650	6400	9100
Road Runner						
2d Cpe	400	1200	2000	4000	7100	10,100
Satellite Wagon						
4d Std Wag	200	650	1100	2150	3780	5400
4d 6P Cus Wag	200	660	1100	2200	3850	5500
4d 9P Cus Wag	200	670	1150	2250	3920	5600
4d 6P Regent	200	660	1100	2200	3850	5500
4d 9P Regent	200	670	1150	2250	3920	5600
Fury I						
4d Sed	200	700	1050	2100	3650	5200
Fury II						
4d Sed	200	700	1075	2150	3700	5300
Fury III						
4d Sed	200	650	1100	2150	3780	5400
2d HT	200	700	1200	2350	4130	5900
4d HT	200	685	1150	2300	3990	5700
Gran Fury						
2d HT	350	780	1300	2600	4550	6500
4d HT	200	670	1200	2300	4060	5800
Suburban						
4d Std Wag	200	700	1050	2050	3600	5100
4d 6P Cus	200	700	1050	2100	3650	5200
4d 9P Cus	200	700	1075	2150	3700	5300
4d 6P Spt	200	700	1075	2150	3700	5300
4d 9P Spt	200	650	1100	2150	3780	5400

1975

Model	6	5	4	3	2	1
Valiant						
4d Sed	150	600	900	1800	3150	4500
4d Cus Sed	125	450	750	1450	2500	3600
Brougham						
4d Sed	150	600	950	1850	3200	4600
2d HT	200	700	1075	2150	3700	5300
Duster						
2d Cpe	150	550	850	1650	2900	4100
2d Cus	150	550	850	1675	2950	4200
2d '360' Cpe	200	675	1000	2000	3500	5000
Scamp						
2d HT	150	600	900	1800	3150	4500
2d Brghm	150	650	950	1900	3300	4700
Fury						
2d HT	150	600	950	1850	3200	4600
2d Cus HT	150	650	950	1900	3300	4700
2d Spt HT	150	650	975	1950	3350	4800
4d Sed	150	650	950	1900	3300	4700
4d Cus Sed	150	650	975	1950	3350	4800
Suburban						
4d Std Wag	150	550	850	1650	2900	4100
4d 6P Cus	150	550	850	1675	2950	4200
4d 9P Cus	150	575	900	1750	3100	4400
4d 6P Spt	150	575	875	1700	3000	4300
4d 9P Spt	150	600	900	1800	3150	4500
Road Runner						
2d HT	150	550	850	1650	2900	4100
Gran Fury						
4d Sed	150	650	950	1900	3300	4700
Gran Fury Custom						
4d Sed	200	675	1000	1950	3400	4900
4d HT	200	650	1100	2150	3780	5400
2d HT	200	670	1200	2300	4060	5800
Gran Fury Brougham						
4d HT	200	660	1100	2200	3850	5500
2d HT	200	700	1200	2350	4130	5900
Suburban						
4d Std	200	675	1000	1950	3400	4900
4d 6P Cus	200	675	1000	2000	3500	5000
4d 9P Cus	200	700	1050	2050	3600	5100
4d 6P Spt	200	700	1050	2050	3600	5100
4d 9P Spt	200	700	1050	2100	3650	5200

1976

Model	6	5	4	3	2	1
Arrow, 4-cyl.						
2d HBk	125	400	675	1350	2300	3300
2d GT HBk	125	400	700	1375	2400	3400
Valiant, 6-cyl.						
2d Duster Spt Cpe	125	400	700	1375	2400	3400
4d Sed Valiant	125	380	650	1300	2250	3200
2d HT Scamp Spec	125	400	675	1350	2300	3300
2d HT Scamp	125	450	700	1400	2450	3500
Volare, V-8						
4d Sed	150	475	750	1475	2600	3700
2d Spt Cpe	150	550	850	1650	2900	4100
4d Sta Wag	150	475	775	1500	2650	3800
Volare Custom, V-8						
4d Sed	150	475	775	1500	2650	3800
2d Spt Cpe	150	550	850	1675	2950	4200
Volare Premier, V-8						
4d Sed	150	500	800	1550	2700	3900
2d Spt Cpe	150	575	900	1750	3100	4400
4d Sta Wag	150	500	800	1600	2800	4000
Fury, V-8						
4d Sed	125	400	675	1350	2300	3300
2d HT	150	550	850	1650	2900	4100
4d Sed Salon	125	400	700	1375	2400	3400
2d HT Spt	150	575	875	1700	3000	4300
4d 2S Suburban	125	400	700	1375	2400	3400
4d 3S Suburban	125	450	700	1400	2450	3500
4d 2S Spt Suburban	125	450	750	1450	2500	3600
4d 3S Spt Suburban	150	475	775	1500	2650	3800
Gran Fury, V-8						
4d Sed	125	400	700	1375	2400	3400
Gran Fury Custom, V-8						
4d Sed	125	450	700	1400	2450	3500
2d HT	150	475	775	1500	2650	3800
Gran Fury Brougham, V-8						
4d Sed	125	450	700	1400	2450	3500
2d HT	150	550	850	1650	2900	4100
4d 2S Gran Fury Sta Wag	150	475	775	1500	2650	3800
4d 3S Gran Fury Sta Wag	150	500	800	1600	2800	4000

1977

Model	6	5	4	3	2	1
Arrow, 4-cyl.						
2d HBk	125	400	675	1350	2300	3300
2d GS HBk	125	400	700	1375	2400	3400
2d GT HBk	125	450	700	1400	2450	3500
Volare, V-8						
4d Sed	125	400	675	1350	2300	3300
2d Spt Cpe	125	450	700	1400	2450	3500
4d Sta Wag	125	400	700	1375	2400	3400
Volare Custom, V-8						
4d Sed	125	400	700	1375	2400	3400
2d Spt Cpe	125	450	750	1450	2500	3600
Volare Premier, V-8						
4d Sed	125	450	700	1400	2450	3500
2d Spt Cpe	150	475	750	1475	2600	3700
4d Sta Wag	125	450	750	1450	2500	3600
Fury, V-8						
4d Spt Sed	125	400	700	1375	2400	3400
2d Spt HT	150	550	850	1675	2950	4200
4d 3S Sub	125	380	650	1300	2250	3200
4d 3S Spt Sub	125	400	675	1350	2300	3300
Gran Fury, V-8						
4d Sed	125	450	700	1400	2450	3500
2d HT	150	500	800	1600	2800	4000
Gran Fury Brougham, V-8						
4d Sed	125	450	750	1450	2500	3600
2d HT	150	550	850	1675	2950	4200
Station Wagons, V-8						
2S Gran Fury	125	400	700	1375	2400	3400
3S Gran Fury Spt	125	450	750	1450	2500	3600

1978

Model	6	5	4	3	2	1
Horizon						
4d HBk	125	400	700	1375	2400	3400
Arrow						
2d HBk	125	450	700	1400	2450	3500
2d GS HBk	125	450	750	1450	2500	3600
2d GT HBk	150	475	750	1475	2600	3700
Volare						
4d Sed	125	450	750	1450	2500	3600
Spt Cpe	150	475	775	1500	2650	3800
Sta Wag	150	475	750	1475	2600	3700
Sapporo						
Cpe	150	475	775	1500	2650	3800
Fury						
4d Sed	125	450	750	1450	2500	3600
2d	150	475	775	1500	2650	3700
4d Salon	150	475	750	1475	2600	3700
2d Spt	150	475	775	1500	2650	3800
Station Wagons						
3S Fury Sub	150	475	750	1475	2600	3700
2S Fury Sub	125	450	750	1450	2500	3600
3S Spt Fury Sub	150	475	775	1500	2650	3800
2S Spt Fury Sub	150	475	750	1475	2600	3700

1979

Model	6	5	4	3	2	1
Champ, 4-cyl.						
2d HBk	125	400	700	1375	2400	3400
2d Cus HBk	125	450	700	1400	2450	3500
Horizon, 4-cyl.						
4d HBk	125	450	700	1400	2450	3500
TC 3 HBk	150	475	750	1475	2600	3700
Fire-Arrow, 4-cyl.						
2d HBk	125	450	750	1450	2500	3600
2d GS HBk	150	475	750	1475	2600	3700
2d GT HBk	150	475	775	1500	2650	3800
Volare, V-8						
Sed	150	475	775	1500	2650	3800
Spt Cpe	150	500	800	1600	2800	4000
Sta Wag	150	500	800	1550	2700	3900
Sapporo, 4-cyl.						
Cpe	150	500	800	1550	2700	3900

1980

Model	6	5	4	3	2	1
Champ, 4-cyl.						
2d HBk	125	400	675	1350	2300	3300
2d Cus HBk	125	400	700	1375	2400	3400
Horizon, 4-cyl.						
4d HBk	125	400	700	1375	2400	3400
2d HBk 2 plus 2 TC3	150	475	775	1500	2650	3800
Arrow, 4-cyl.						
2d HBk	150	600	900	1800	3150	4500
Fire Arrow, 4-cyl.						
2d HBk	150	600	950	1850	3200	4600
Volare, V-8						
4d Sed	125	400	700	1375	2400	3400

	6	5	4	3	2	1
2d Cpe	125	450	700	1400	2450	3500
4d Sta Wag	150	475	750	1475	2600	3700

NOTE: Deduct 10 percent for 6-cyl.

	6	5	4	3	2	1
Sapporo, 4-cyl.						
2d Cpe	150	500	800	1550	2700	3900
Gran Fury, V-8						
4d Sed	150	475	775	1500	2650	3800

NOTE: Deduct 10 percent for 6-cyl.

	6	5	4	3	2	1
Gran Fury Salon, V-8						
4d Sed	150	500	800	1600	2800	4000

NOTE: Deduct 10 percent for 6-cyl.

1981

	6	5	4	3	2	1
Champ, 4-cyl.						
2d HBk	125	400	700	1375	2400	3400
2d DeL HBk	125	450	700	1400	2450	3500
2d Cus HBk	125	450	750	1450	2500	3600
Horizon, 4-cyl.						
4d Miser HBk	125	450	700	1400	2450	3500
4d Miser HBk TC3	150	475	775	1500	2650	3800
4d HBk	150	475	750	1475	2600	3700
2d HBk TC3	150	500	800	1600	2800	4000
Reliant, 4-cyl.						
4d Sed	125	400	700	1375	2400	3400
2d Cpe	125	450	700	1400	2450	3500
Reliant Custom, 4-cyl.						
4d Sed	125	450	700	1400	2450	3500
2d Cpe	125	450	750	1450	2500	3600
4d Sta Wag	150	475	775	1500	2650	3800
Reliant SE, 4-cyl.						
4d Sed	125	450	750	1450	2500	3600
2d Cpe	150	475	750	1475	2600	3700
4d Sta Wag	150	500	800	1550	2700	3900
Sapporo, 4-cyl.						
2d HT	150	500	800	1600	2800	4000
Gran Fury, V-8						
4d Sed	150	550	850	1650	2900	4100

NOTE: Deduct 10 percent for 6-cyl.

1982

	6	5	4	3	2	1
Champ, 4-cyl.						
4d Cus HBk	125	450	750	1450	2500	3600
2d Cus HBk	150	475	750	1475	2600	3700

NOTE: Deduct 5 percent for lesser models.

	6	5	4	3	2	1
Horizon, 4-cyl.						
4d Miser HBk	125	450	750	1450	2500	3600
2d Miser HBk TC3	150	500	800	1550	2700	3900
4d Cus HBk	150	475	750	1475	2600	3700
2d Cus HBk	150	475	775	1500	2650	3800
4d E Type HBk	150	500	800	1550	2700	3900
Turismo, 4-cyl.						
2d HBk TC3	150	600	900	1800	3150	4500
Reliant, 4-cyl.						
4d Sed	125	450	750	1450	2500	3600
2d Cpe	150	475	750	1475	2600	3700
Reliant Custom, 4-cyl.						
4d Sed	150	475	750	1475	2600	3700
2d Cpe	150	475	775	1500	2650	3800
4d Sta Wag	150	500	800	1550	2700	3900
Reliant SE, 4-cyl.						
4d Sed	150	475	775	1500	2650	3800
2d Cpe	150	500	800	1550	2700	3900
4d Sta Wag	150	500	800	1600	2800	4000
Sapporo						
2d HT	150	650	950	1900	3300	4700
Gran Fury, V-8						
4d Sed	150	500	800	1600	2800	4000

NOTE: Deduct 10 percent for 6-cyl.

1983

	6	5	4	3	2	1
Colt, 4-cyl.						
4d Cus HBk	150	500	800	1600	2800	4000
2d Cus HBk	150	550	850	1650	2900	4100

NOTE: Deduct 5 percent for lesser models.

	6	5	4	3	2	1
Horizon, 4-cyl.						
4d HBk	150	475	775	1500	2650	3800
4d Cus HBk	150	500	800	1550	2700	3900
Turismo, 4-cyl.						
2d HBk	150	600	900	1800	3150	4500
2d HBk 2 plus 2	150	650	975	1950	3350	4800
Reliant, 4-cyl.						
4d Sed	150	475	750	1475	2600	3700
2d Cpe	150	475	775	1500	2650	3800
4d Sta Wag	150	500	800	1600	2800	4000
Reliant SE, 4-cyl.						
4d Sed	150	475	775	1500	2650	3800
2d Cpe	150	500	800	1550	2700	3900
4d Sta Wag	150	550	850	1650	2900	4100
Sapporo, 4-cyl.						
2d HT	150	650	975	1950	3350	4800
Gran Fury, V-8						
4d Sed	150	550	850	1650	2900	4100

NOTE: Deduct 10 percent for 6-cyl.

1984

	6	5	4	3	2	1
Colt, 4-cyl.						
4d HBk DL	150	475	750	1475	2600	3700
2d HBk DL	150	475	750	1475	2600	3700
4d Sta Wag Vista	150	475	750	1475	2600	3700

NOTE: Deduct 5 percent for lesser models.

	6	5	4	3	2	1
Horizon, 4-cyl.						
4d HBk	150	475	775	1500	2650	3800
4d HBk SE	150	500	800	1550	2700	3900
Turismo, 4-cyl.						
2d HBk	150	650	950	1900	3300	4700
2d HBk 2 plus 2	150	650	975	1950	3350	4800
Reliant, 4-cyl.						
4d Sed	125	450	750	1450	2500	3600
2d Sed	125	450	750	1450	2500	3600
4d Sta Wag	150	475	750	1475	2600	3700
Conquest, 4-cyl.						
2d HBk	150	600	900	1800	3150	4500
Gran Fury, V-8						
4d Sed	150	550	850	1675	2950	4200

1985

	6	5	4	3	2	1
Colt, 4-cyl.						
4d HBk E	150	475	750	1475	2600	3700
2d HBk E	150	475	750	1475	2600	3700
4d Sed DL	150	475	775	1500	2650	3800
2d HBk DL	150	475	775	1500	2650	3800
4d Sed Premier	150	475	775	1500	2650	3800
4d Sta Wag Vista	150	500	800	1550	2700	3900
4d Sta Wag Vista 4WD	150	650	950	1900	3300	4700
Horizon, 4-cyl.						
4d HBk	150	500	800	1550	2700	3900
4d HBk SE	150	500	800	1600	2800	4000
Turismo, 4-cyl.						
2d HBk	150	650	975	1950	3350	4800
2d HBk 2 plus 2	200	675	1000	1950	3400	4900
Reliant, 4-cyl.						
4d Sed	150	475	750	1475	2600	3700
2d Sed	150	475	750	1475	2600	3700
4d Sed SE	150	475	775	1500	2650	3800
2d Sed SE	150	475	775	1500	2650	3800
4d Sta Wag SE	150	475	775	1500	2650	3800
4d Sed LE	150	500	800	1550	2700	3900
2d Sed LE	150	500	800	1550	2700	3900
4d Sta Wag LE	150	500	800	1550	2700	3900
Conquest, 4-cyl.						
2d HBk Turbo	150	650	950	1900	3300	4700
Caravelle, 4-cyl.						
4d Sed SE	150	550	850	1650	2900	4100

NOTE: Add 10 percent for turbo.

	6	5	4	3	2	1
Grand Fury, V-8						
4d Sed Salon	150	575	875	1700	3000	4300

1986

	6	5	4	3	2	1
Colt						
4d Sed E	150	550	850	1650	2900	4100
2d HBk E	150	500	800	1600	2800	4000
4d Sed DL	150	550	850	1675	2950	4200
2d HBk DL	150	550	850	1650	2900	4100
4d Sed Premier	150	575	875	1700	3000	4300
4d Vista Sta Wag	150	600	950	1850	3200	4600
4d Vista Sta Wag 4WD	200	670	1150	2250	3920	5600
Horizon						
4d HBk	150	500	800	1600	2800	4000
Turismo						
2d HBk	200	675	1000	1950	3400	4900
Reliant						
2d Sed	150	475	775	1500	2650	3800
4d Sed	150	500	800	1550	2700	3900
Caravelle						
4d Sed	150	550	850	1675	2950	4200
Grand Fury						
4d Salon Sed	150	650	950	1900	3300	4700

NOTES: Add 10 percent for deluxe models.
Deduct 5 percent for smaller engines.

1987

	6	5	4	3	2	1
Colt, 4-cyl.						
4d Sed E	150	550	850	1675	2950	4200
2d HBk E	150	550	850	1650	2900	4100
4d Sed DL	150	575	875	1700	3000	4300
2d HBk DL	150	550	850	1675	2950	4200
4d Sed Premier	150	575	900	1750	3100	4400
4d Vista Sta Wag	150	650	950	1900	3300	4700
4d Vista Sta Wag 4WD	200	685	1150	2300	3990	5700
Horizon, 4-cyl.						
4d HBk	150	550	850	1675	2950	4200
Turismo, 4-cyl.						
2d HBk	150	600	900	1800	3150	4500
Sundance, 4-cyl.						
2d LBk	150	575	875	1700	3000	4300
4d LBk	150	575	900	1750	3100	4400

NOTE: Add 5 percent for 2.2 Turbo.

	6	5	4	3	2	1
Reliant, 4-cyl.						
2d Sed	150	550	850	1675	2950	4200
4d Sed	150	575	875	1700	3000	4300
2d Sed LE	150	575	875	1700	3000	4300
4d Sed LE	150	575	900	1750	3100	4400
4d Sta Wag LE	150	575	900	1750	3100	4400
Caravelle, 4-cyl.						
4d Sed	150	600	900	1800	3150	4500
4d Sed SE	150	600	950	1850	3200	4600

NOTE: Add 5 percent for 2.2 Turbo.

	6	5	4	3	2	1
Grand Fury, V-8						
4d Sed	200	660	1100	2200	3850	5500

1988

	6	5	4	3	2	1
Colt, 4-cyl.						
3d HBk	100	260	450	900	1540	2200
4d Sed E	100	330	575	1150	1950	2800
3d HBk E	100	320	550	1050	1850	2600
4d Sed DL	100	350	600	1150	2000	2900
3d HBk DL	100	330	575	1150	1950	2800
4d Sta Wag DL	100	360	600	1200	2100	3000
4d Sed Premier	125	450	700	1400	2450	3500
4d Sta Wag Vista	150	500	800	1600	2800	4000
4d Sta Wag Vista 4x4	200	675	1000	2000	3500	5000
Horizon, 4-cyl.						
4d HBk	100	330	575	1150	1950	2800
Reliant, 4-cyl.						
2d Sed	100	330	575	1150	1950	2800
4d Sed	100	350	600	1150	2000	2900
4d Sta Wag	125	400	675	1350	2300	3300
Sundance, 4-cyl.						
2d HBk	125	380	650	1300	2250	3200
4d HBk	125	400	700	1375	2400	3400
Caravelle, 4-cyl.						
4d Sed	125	450	700	1400	2450	3500
4d Sed SE	150	500	800	1550	2700	3900
Gran Fury, V-8						
4d Salon	150	475	775	1500	2650	3800
4d SE	150	550	850	1675	2950	4200

1989

	6	5	4	3	2	1
Colt, 4-cyl.						
2d HBk	150	475	775	1500	2650	3800
2d HBk E	150	500	800	1550	2700	3900
2d HBk GT	150	550	850	1650	2900	4100
4d Sta Wag DL	200	675	1000	2000	3500	5000
4d Sta Wag DL 4x4	200	650	1100	2150	3780	5400
4d Sta Wag Vista	200	700	1050	2100	3650	5200
4d Sta Wag Vista 4x4	200	670	1150	2250	3920	5600
Horizon, 4-cyl.						
4d HBk	125	450	750	1450	2500	3600
Reliant, 4-cyl.						
4d Sed	125	450	700	1400	2450	3500
2d Sed	125	400	700	1375	2400	3400
Sundance, 4-cyl.						
4d HBk	150	550	850	1675	2950	4200
2d HBk	150	550	850	1650	2900	4100
Acclaim, 4-cyl.						
4d Sed	200	700	1050	2100	3650	5200
4d Sed LE	200	700	1075	2150	3700	5300
Gran Fury, V-8						
4d Sed Salon	200	650	1100	2150	3780	5400

1990

	6	5	4	3	2	1
Colt, 4-cyl.						
2d HBk	150	475	775	1500	2650	3800
2d HBk GL	150	500	800	1600	2800	4000
2d HBk GT	150	550	850	1675	2950	4200
4d Sta Wag DL	150	600	950	1850	3200	4600
4d Sta Wag DL 4x4	200	660	1100	2200	3850	5500
4d Vista	200	700	1050	2100	3650	5200
4d Vista 4x4	200	745	1250	2500	4340	6200
Horizon, 4-cyl.						
4d HBk	125	450	700	1400	2450	3500
Sundance, 4-cyl.						
2d HBk	150	550	850	1675	2950	4200
4d HBk	150	550	850	1650	2900	4100
Laser, 4-cyl.						
2d HBk	200	675	1000	2000	3500	5000
2d HBk RS	200	660	1100	2200	3850	5500
2d HBk Turbo RS	200	720	1200	2400	4200	6000
Acclaim						
4-cyl.						
4d Sed	150	500	800	1600	2800	4000
4d Sed LE	150	600	900	1800	3150	4500
V-6						
4d Sed	150	575	900	1750	3100	4400
4d Sed LE	200	675	1000	2000	3500	5000
4d Sed LX	200	660	1100	2200	3850	5500

1991

	6	5	4	3	2	1
Colt, 4-cyl.						
2d HBk	100	360	600	1200	2100	3000
2d HBk GL	125	450	700	1400	2450	3500
Sundance, 4-cyl.						
2d HBk America	125	450	700	1400	2450	3500
4d HBk America	125	450	700	1400	2450	3500
2d HBk	150	475	750	1475	2600	3700
4d HBk	150	475	750	1475	2600	3700
2d HBk RS	150	550	850	1675	2950	4200

(1991 continued)

	6	5	4	3	2	1
4d HBk RS	150	550	850	1675	2950	4200
Laser, 4-cyl.						
2d HBk	150	600	900	1800	3150	4500
2d HBk RS	150	600	950	1850	3200	4600
2d HBk Turbo RS	150	650	975	1950	3350	4800
Acclaim						
4-cyl.						
4d Sed	150	500	800	1600	2800	4000
4d Sed LE	150	575	875	1700	3000	4300
V-6						
4d Sed	150	575	875	1700	3000	4300
4d Sed LE	150	600	950	1850	3200	4600
4d LX Sed	150	650	975	1950	3350	4800

1992

	6	5	4	3	2	1
Colt, 4-cyl.						
2d HBk	125	450	750	1450	2500	3600
2d GL HBk	150	500	800	1600	2800	4000
3d Sta Wag	150	600	900	1800	3150	4500
3d SE Sta Wag	150	600	950	1850	3200	4600
3d Sta Wag 4x4	200	660	1100	2200	3850	5500
Sundance, 4-cyl. & V-6						
4d HBk America	150	500	800	1600	2800	4000
2d HBk America	150	500	800	1600	2800	4000
4d HBk	150	550	850	1675	2950	4200
2d HBk	150	550	850	1675	2950	4200
4d Duster HBk, V-6	200	675	1000	2000	3500	5000
2d Duster HBk, V-6	200	675	1000	2000	3500	5000
Laser, 4-cyl.						
2d HBk	200	675	1000	2000	3500	5000
2d RS HBk	200	660	1100	2200	3850	5500
2d RS HBk Turbo	200	720	1200	2400	4200	6000
2d RS HBk Turbo 4x4	350	900	1500	3000	5250	7500
Acclaim, 4-cyl. & V-6						
4d Sed	200	675	1000	2000	3500	5000
4d Sed, V-6	200	660	1100	2200	3850	5500

1993

	6	5	4	3	2	1
Colt, 4-cyl.						
2d Sed	150	475	775	1500	2650	3800
2d GL Sed	150	500	800	1550	2700	3900
4d Sed	150	475	775	1500	2650	3800
4d GL Sed	150	500	800	1550	2700	3900
3d Vista	150	600	900	1800	3150	4500
3d SE Vista	150	600	950	1850	3200	4600
3d Vista, 4x4	200	670	1150	2250	3920	5600
Sundance						
2d HBk, 4-cyl	150	500	800	1600	2800	4000
2d Duster HBk, V-6	150	550	850	1650	2900	4100
4d HBk, 4-cyl.	150	500	800	1600	2800	4000
4d Duster HBk, V-6	150	550	850	1650	2900	4100
Laser						
2d HBk	200	675	1000	2000	3500	5000
2d RS HBk	200	700	1050	2050	3600	5100
2d HBk Turbo	200	700	1075	2150	3700	5300
2d HBk 4x4	350	780	1300	2600	4550	6500
Acclaim						
4d Sed, 4-cyl.	200	700	1050	2100	3650	5200
4d Sed, V-6	200	650	1100	2150	3780	5400

PRICE GUIDE ABBREVIATIONS

Alphabetical

A/C . . . . Air Conditioning
Aero . . . . Aerodynamic
Anniv . . . . Anniversary
Auto . . . . . . Automatic Transmission
A/W or A-W . . . . All-Weather
Berl . . . . Berline
Brgm . . . . Brougham
Brn . . . . Brunn
BT . . . . Boattail
Bus. . . . . . Business (as in Bus Cpe)
Cabr . . . . Cabriolet
cc . . . . Close-coupled
cid . . . . . . Cubic Inch Displacement
Clb . . . . . Club (as in Clb Cpe/Clb Cab)
Cpe. Coupe
Coll . . Collapsible (as in Semi-Coll)
Conv . . . . Convertible
Ctry . . . . Country
Cus . . . . Custom
DC . . . . Dual-Cowl
DeL . . . . Deluxe
Der . . . . Derham
DEx . . . . Dual Exhausts
Dly . . Delivery (as in Sed Dly)
Dtrch . . . . Dietrich
DuW . . . . Dual Windshield
DW . . . . Division Window
Edn . . . . Edition
EFI . . . . Electronic Fuel Injection
Encl . . . . Enclosed
Eng . . . . Engine
FBk . . . . Fastback
Fcty . . . . Factory
FHC . . . . Fixed Head Coupe
FI . . . . Fuel Injection
Fml . . . . Formal
FWD . . . . Front-wheel Drive
GT . Gran Turismo (Grand Touring)
HBk . . . . Hatchback
H&E . . . . Hess & Eisenhart
Hemi . . Hemispherical-head engine
HD . . . . Heavy Duty
Hlbrk . . . . Holbrook
hp . . . . Horsepower
HT . . . . Hardtop
Imp . . . . Imperial
Int . . . . Interior
IPC . . Indy (Indianapolis) Pace Car
IROC . . . . International
Race of Champions
Jud . . . . Judkins
KO . . . . Knock-off Wheels
Lan . . . . Landau
Lan'let . . . . Landaulet
LBx . . . Long Box (pickup truck bed)
LeB or Leb . . . . LeBaron
LHD . . . . Left-Hand Drive
Limo . . . . Limousine
Lke . . . . Locke
LWB . . . . Long-Wheelbase
mph . . . . Miles Per Hour
M/R. . . . . Moonroof
nhp . . . . Net Horsepower
O/D . . . . Overdrive
opt . . . . Option(s)
orig . . . . Original
P . . . . . Passenger (as in 3P Cpe)
Phae . . . . Phaeton
PT . . . . . . Power (Convertible) Top
Pwr . . . . Power
Rbt . . . . Runabout
Rds . . . . Roadster
Ret . . . . Retractable
RHD . . . . Right-Hand Drive
Rlstn or Roll . . . . Rollston
R/S . . . . Rumbleseat
R/T . . . . Dodge model
SCCA . . Sports Car Club of America
S/C . . . . Supercharged
SE . . . . Special Edition
Sed . . . . Sedan
SMt or SMts . . . . Sidemount(s)
Spds . . . . Speedster
Spec or Spl . . . . Special
Spt . . . . Sport
S/R . . . . Sunroof
Sta Wag . . . . Station Wagon
Std . . . . Standard
SWB . . . . Short Wheelbase
T&C . . . . Town & Country
T-top . . . . T-top Roof
Trg . . . . Touring Car (not Targa)
Turbo . . . . Equipped with
turbocharger(s)
Twn . . . . Town (as in Twn Sed)
V-4, -6, -8 . . . . V-block engine
Vic . . . . Victoria
W . . . . Window (as in 3W Cpe)
WW . . . . Wire Wheels
W'by . . . . Willoughby
Woodie . . . . partially
wood-bodied vehicle
W.T . . . . WinterTop
Wtrhs . . . . Waterhouse

Numerical

2d . . . . Two-door (also 4d, 6d, etc)
2P . . . . Two-Passenger
(also 3P, 4P, etc)
2S . . . Two-Seat (also 3S, 4S, etc)
3W . . . . Three-Window
(also 4W, 5W, etc)
4-cyl . . . . In-line Engine
(also 5-cyl, 6-, 8-,)
4-Spd . . Four-speed Transmission
(also 3-, 5-, etc)
4V . . . . Four-barrel Carburetor
4x4 . . Four-wheel drive (not FWD)
8/9P . . . Eight- or Nine-Passenger